The Animated
Film Encyclopedia

SECOND EDITION

The Animated Film Encyclopedia

*A Complete Guide to
American Shorts, Features
and Sequences, 1900–1999*

SECOND EDITION

Graham Webb

McFarland & Company, Inc., Publishers
Jefferson, North Carolina, and London

LIBRARY OF CONGRESS CATALOGUING-IN-PUBLICATION DATA

Webb, Graham.
The animated film encyclopedia : a complete guide to American
shorts, features and sequences, 1900–1999 / Graham Webb.— 2nd ed.
p.   cm.
Includes index.

ISBN 978-0-7864-4985-9
softcover : 50# alkaline paper ∞

1. Animated films — United States — Encyclopedias.   I. Title.
NC1766.U5W44   2011   791.43'34097303 — dc22   2011005162

BRITISH LIBRARY CATALOGUING DATA ARE AVAILABLE

On the cover: (left to right) *Gertie the Dinosaur,* 1914; *The Land Before Time,* 1988
(Lucasfilm Ltd./Universal/Photofest); CGI dinosaurs © 2011 by Linda Bucklin
Background photograph by Hal Bergman

Manufactured in the United States of America

*McFarland & Company, Inc., Publishers
Box 611, Jefferson, North Carolina 28640
www.mcfarlandpub.com*

Contents

Acknowledgments

Over the years, many have contributed their services in helping with the preparation of this volume, and deserve recognition for their able assistance: Els Barthen, Howard Beckerman, Lee Boyett, Bob Clampett, Pat Coward, Shamus Culhane, Gene Deitch, Jan Emberton, Al Eugster, June Foray, Friz Freleng, Jere Guldin, Mike Hankin, Jack Hannah, Reg Hartt, Richard Holliss, Cal Howard, Ollie Johnston, Chuck Jones, Laura Kaiser of the USC Film & TV Archives, Jack Kinney, I. Klein, Bob Little, Norm McCabe, Bob McKimson, Jack and Virginia Mercer, Grim Natwick, Neil Pettigrew, Sid Raymond, Virgil Ross, Brian Rust, Markku Salmi, David R. Smith of the Disney Archives, Frank Thomas, Myron Waldman, Edith and Peter Webb, John Wood, David Wyatt, Cy Young and Jack Zander. Those lost in the annals of time I hope will forgive me if I have forgotten to mention them.

In particular, a debt of eternal gratitude should go to loyal companions Mark Kausler, Hames Ware and Keith Scott, without whose valuable assistance this tome would only be half its size.

An overall vote of thanks also goes to David Rider, who was the initial inspiration in getting me to collect cartoon credits.

Introduction

This encyclopedia is an alphabetical listing of every American theatrical cartoon released from 1900 through 1999, many of which are likely to be new to the reader. The first edition of this encyclopedia ended at 1979, before the advent of computerized animation. Much difficult-to-find information has been included, from who worked on the early sound cartoons to various musicians and songwriters involved and who provided many of the anonymous cartoon voices over the years.

This volume is the result of many, many years of research, much of the information coming from viewings of the films, trade magazines and discussions with the artists involved. A large number of animated film works have been discovered that this author could not find in any other published reference work; they have remained essentially unknown for a long time.

Many of the silent cartoons especially are no longer in existence, lost or decomposed, with the trade magazines never deeming them worthy of reviewing. In such cases, as much existing information as can be garnered has been supplied.

By 1980, television cartoons had overtaken the theatrical release and production had halted on most shorts and feature cartoons. Animated cartoons were no longer considered a viable property by the late 1950s, when production costs soared, standards plummeted and the idea of releasing a fresh cartoon short with the studio's main features had long since fallen by the wayside.

Hand-drawn cel animation was the norm for many years; the 1980s heralded the advent of a completely new concept in the animated arts. Computer generated imagery (CGI) had arrived!

This process would eventually not only replace the old school cel animation but also seep into countless live-action epics by not only enhancing special effects but also managing to create dinosaurs, monsters, aliens and making the impossible even more possible. The computer could now even replace human actors and, in some cases, turn the actor into "human cartoons."

Computer graphics began their life by providing sparkling special effects to live-action movies such as *Star Wars* and then rapidly spread its wings to dominate entire feature films, such as *Jurassic Park* and *Toy Story*. Those films, and many others that utilized CGI, even briefly, are covered herein.

Another important change that affected animation came about in the 1980s. Cel animation had become far too expensive to produce in the U.S. Those who still used cel animation found it was now cheaper to farm out animation and production to companies abroad than it was to produce them at home. China, Korea and Europe became popular sources of outsourced animation and, in particular, inking and painting. Many companies farmed out their products all over the world, and even Disney opened up its own animation studios in France and Australia. Don Bluth moved his studio to Ireland and many products were made only partially in the U.S., leaving the bulk to be completed in Japan, China, Poland or elsewhere.

Cartoon features, series, shorts, puppet animation, Cinemascope, 3-D, stop-motion, sequences in live-action films, computer generated imagery, animated titles, and commercials are all included in this volume — in fact, every form of the animated medium that has been made for the American theatrical market from the early days of the motion picture right up to the end of the twentieth century.

An entry consists of a series name if applicable, date of release, screen credits, running time and other specific data, and a short synopsis.

In cases where direct screen credits are not available, a composite list of studio personnel is provided under a company heading. Some of the larger companies, however, such as Disney, the Fleischer Studio or Terry-Toons have had so many employees over so long a period that it is impossible to specify them all.

Other companies, such as Warner or George Pal, often used a rotation system for their credits in the early days. That is to say, of a team of animators who worked with a particular director's unit, only *one* would get screen recognition at a time. This meant that sometimes a person who was not even directly involved with that particular film would get recognition. However, by the 1940s, this system had been ironed out and most of the correct people received their deserved accolades. It is safe to say that the earlier system is around 80 percent accurate.

It is also safe to assume that in the case of the Fleischer Studio, the main credited animator was, in actuality, the "director." Dave Fleischer, the credited director, was chiefly a supervisor or overseer. The reverse is true of Terry-Toons, where the director credited was normally the head animator involved.

Studios were often owned by either individuals or motion picture companies. The individuals such as Walt Disney, Walter Lantz, Stephen Bosustow (UPA) and Paul Terry (Terry-Toons) were known to be actively involved with their products whereas studio heads such as Leon Schlesinger, Fred Quimby and Charles Mintz were not creative enough to contribute any advice other than "Keep it within the budget!"

An appendix gives a full series list of shorts. The series listed here account for the bulk of the contents, but of course features, one-offs, commercials, and the like could not be itemized in such a fashion. An index of artists, directors, producers and others provides reference to those films in which that person served a function.

Abbreviations

Note: The date following the film title in each entry is the official release date of the film.

adapt .... adaptation
addit .... additional
ADR .... Automated Dialogue Replacement
aka .... also known as
anim .... animation
arr .... arrangement
asso .... associate
asst .... assistant
b&w .... black and white
back .... backgrounds
break .... breakdown
cg/cgi .... computer graphics imagery
CAPS .... Computer Animation Production System
Co .... company
col .... color
co-ord .... co-ordinator
© .... copyright
Corp .... Corporation
des .... design
dial .... dialogue
dir .... direction
ed .... film editor
ex prod .... executive producer
fx .... special effects
i&p .... ink and paint
inbet .... inbetweens
l/a .... live-action
lay .... layout
mgr .... manager

min .... minutes
mus .... music
orch .... orchestrations
prod .... production
ph .... photography
p.c. .... production company
rec .... recording
scr .... screenplay
sd .... sound
s/r .... split-reel
sec .... secretary
sep .... sepia
seq .... sequences
sets .... layouts and backgrounds
sil .... silent
snr .... senior
sup .... supervision

Color and Sound Systems

Ciné .... Cinécolor
CS .... Cinemascope
DDS .... Dolby Dynamic Sound
DPC .... DeForest Phonofilm Co
East .... Eastman Color
Pola .... Polacolor
PCP .... Powers Cinephone Process
SDDS .... Sony Dynamic Digital Sound
sep .... sepia
Tech .... Technicolor

3

Tru . . . . Trucolor
Vit . . . . Vitaphone
WE . . . . Western Electric Sound System

Production Companies

A-C . . . . Audio-Cinema
BV . . . . Buena Vista Distribution
BVI . . . . Buena Vista International
Colum . . . . Columbia/Screen Gems
DFE . . . . DePatie-Freleng Enterprises
Educational . . . . Educational Exchange
Ess . . . . Essanay
Famous . . . . Famous Studios
FBO . . . . Film Booking Office
Fox . . . . 20th Century–Fox Film
                 Corporation

IFS . . . . International Features Service
ILM . . . . Industrial Light and Magic
MGM . . . . Metro-Goldwyn-Mayer
M-in-A . . . . . . Made in America
Mono . . . . Monogram
NFB . . . . National Film Board of Canada
Para . . . . Paramount Pictures
Rep . . . . Republic
UA . . . . United Artists
UIP . . . . Universal International Pictures
Univ . . . . Universal/Universal-International
UPA . . . . United Productions of America
Vit . . . . The Vitaphone Corporation
WB . . . . Warner Bros. Pictures Inc.
WB/7A . . . . . . Warner Bros/7 Arts
Winkler . . . . . . Winkler Pictures

THE ENCYCLOPEDIA

1. A Is for Atom 1 June 1953; *p.c.:* John Sutherland Productions for GEC. *prod:* John Sutherland; *dir:* Carl Urbano; *story:* True Boardman; *anim:* Arnold Gillespie, Emery Hawkins; *des:* Tony Rivera; *sets:* Gerald Nevius, Lew Keller; *mus:* Eugene Poddany; *assoc prod:* George Gordon; *col:* Ansco. *sd.* 10 min. • Demonstrating how the shadow of the atomic bomb can change the world.

2. Abdul the Bulbul-Ameer *(MGM cartoon)* 22 Feb. 1941: *p.c.:* MGM; *prod:* Hugh Harman; *dir:* Robert Allen; *voices:* Cliff Nazarro, Harry Stanton, Leon Belasco, Hans Conried; *mus:* Scott Bradley; *song:* Frank Crumit; *col:* Tech. *sd:* WE. 9 min. • A duel to the death between two rival soldiers.

3. Abner the Baseball Nov. 1961; *p.c.:* Para Cartoons. *dir:* Seymour Kneitel; *story/voices:* Eddie Lawrence; *anim:* Jack Ehret, John Gentilella, Irving Dressler, I. Klein; *des:* Irving Spector; *sets:* Robert Owen; *mus:* Bernie Wayne, Winston Sharples; *prod mgr:* Abe Goodman; *col:* Tech. *sd:* RCA. 10 min. • A baseball relates the story of how he finally ended up in baseball's "Hall of Fame."

4. Abominable Mountaineers *(Sad Cat)* 10 Dec. 1968; *p.c.:* TT for Fox; *col:* DeLuxe. *sd:* RCA. 5 min. • Super Ego allows Sad Cat beat his mean brothers to the summit of Mount Everest. • See: *Sad Cat*

5. The Abominable Snow Rabbit *(Looney Tunes)* May 1961; *p.c.:* WB; *dir:* Chuck Jones; *asst dir/lay:* Maurice Noble; *story:* Tedd Pierce; *anim:* Ken Harris, Richard Thompson, Bob Bransford, Tom Ray, David R. Green; *back:* Philip de Guard; *ed:* Treg Brown; *voices:* Mel Blanc; *mus:* Milt Franklyn; *prod mgr:* William Orcutt; *prod:* David H. DePatie; *col:* Tech. *sd:* Vit. 7 min. • Bugs and Daffy find themselves in the Himalayan mountains where they encounter The Abominable Snowman who fancies Bugs as a pet "bunny rabbit."

6. Abou Ben Boogie *(Swing Symphony)* 18 Sept. 1944; *p.c.:* Walter Lantz prods for Univ; *dir:* James Culhane; *story:* Ben Hardaway, Milt Schaffer; *anim:* Paul Smith, Pat Matthews, La Verne Harding, Les Kline, Dick Lundy, Grim Natwick, Don Williams; *lay:* Art Heinemann; *back:* Philip de Guard; *voice:* Patricia Kay; *mus:* Darrell Calker; *song:* Tot Seymour, Vee Lawnhurst; *col:* Tech. *sd:* WE. 7 min. • An Oriental "Don Juan's" advances towards a shapely singer are repeatedly marred by the intrusion of Camellia, the dancing camel.

7. Abusement Park *(Popeye)* 25 Apr. 1947; *p.c.:* Famous for Para; *dir:* I. Sparber; *story:* Joe Stultz, Carl Meyer; *anim:* Dave Tendlar, Tom Golden; *sets:* Anton Loeb; *voices:* Mae Questel, Jackson Beck, Harry F. Welch; *mus:* Winston Sharples; *ph:* Leonard McCormick; *prod mgr:* Sam Buchwald; *col:* Ciné. *sd:* RCA. 7 min. • Bluto disposes of Popeye at the carnival so that he can take Olive on a reckless roller-coaster ride.

8. The Abyss 9 Aug. 1989; *p.c.:* Fox; *Dream Quest Images: visual fx sup:* Hoyt Yeatman; *ILM: visual fx sup:* Dennis Muren; *Pseudopod seq:* ILM; *visual fx prod:* Jim Morris; *cg des:* John Knoll; *cg sup:* A. Jay Riddle; *optical sup:* Stuart Robertson, Bruce Vecchito; *cg anim:* Scott E. Anderson, Mark A. Z. Dippe, Lincoln Hu, Steve Williams; *fx ed:* Bill Kimberlin; *fx ph:* Terry Chostner, Harry V. Walton, Yuri Farrant, Paul Huston, Randy Johnson, Robert Hill; *fx art dir:* Steve Beck; *anim sup:* Wes Takahashi; *modelmaker:* Kendall Nishimine; *fx co-ord:* Roni McKinley; *prod asst:* Camille Cellucci; *HTI beings created by Steve Johnson's X.F.X., Inc.: sup:* Steve Johnson; *prod co-ord:* Kristina Birkmayer; *Spite rising seq: Fantasy II Film Effects, Inc.: fx sup:* Gene Warren Jr.; *asst:* Gregory Orr, Christopher Warren; *prod sup:* Leslie Huntley; *set co-ord:* Jerry Pojawa; *modelmakers:* Gary Rhodeback, Michael Joyce; *ph:* John Huneck, Michael Griffin; *prod asso:* Scott Beverly, Arthur Ruiz; *prod asst:* Heather Pumphrey, Daniel Deschamps; *addit model construction: The Design Setters Corp.: model painter:* Kevin Scott Mack; *modelmakers:* Michael Stuart, Henry R. Darnell, Ray Cavaluzzi, Daniel D. Brown, Thomas van Ottern, Fernando Lau, Jim LeGladice; *col:* DeLuxe. *sd:* Dolby stereo. Panavision. 138 min. *l/a.* • Live-action adventure: A diver encounters alien water creatures while trying to rescue survivors from a stricken submarine. Academy Award winner for its ground-breaking special effects.

9. Academy Award Review of Walt Disney Cartoons 20 May 1937; *p.c.:* Walt Disney prods for UA; *col:* Tech. *sd:* RCA. 40 min. • Selection of five Oscar-winning *Silly Symphony* cartoons with additional linking material. • See: *The Country Cousin; Flowers and Trees; The Three Little Pigs; Three Orphan Kittens; The Tortoise and the Hare*

10. Accidents Will Happen *(Swifty & Shorty)* Sept. 1964; *p.c.:* Para Cartoons; *dir:* Seymour Kneitel; *story:* Bill Ballard; *anim:* Nick Tafuri; *sets:* Robert Little; *voices:* Eddie Lawrence; *mus:* Winston Sharples; *ph:* Leonard McCormick; *prod mgr:* Abe Goodman; *col:* Tech. *sd:* RCA. 6 min. • Swifty tries to sell Shorty an accident policy.

11. Accordian Joe *(Talkartoon)* 13 Dec. 1930; *p.c.:* The Fleischer Studios for Para; *prod:* Max Fleischer; *dir:* Dave Fleischer; *anim:* Ted Sears, Grim Natwick; *mus:* Art Turkisher; *b&w. sd:* WE. 7 min. • Aviator Bimbo crash-lands in Indian territory where he meets a native princess, is captured and escapes from the savages.

12. Ace in the Hole *(Woody Woodpecker)* 22 June 1942; *p.c.:* Walter Lantz prods for Univ; *dir:* Alex Lovy; *story:* Ben Hardaway, Milt Schaffer; *anim:* George Dane; *sets:* Fred Brunish; *voices:* Kent Rogers; *prod mgr:* George E. Morris; *col:* Tech. *sd:* WE. 7 min. • The Sergeant won't let Pvt. Woodpecker fly a plane but upon finding himself in the pilot's seat, Woody takes full advantage of the situation.

13. The Ace of Spades *(Talkartoons)* 17 Jan. 1931; *p.c.:* The Fleischer Studios for Para; *prod:* Max Fleischer; *dir:* Dave Fleischer; *anim:* Al Eugster; *mus:* Art Turkisher; *b&w. sd:* WE. 7 min. • Bimbo is a magician with cards in a pool hall.

14. Aces Up *(Toby the Pup)* 16 May 1931; *p.c.:* Winkler for RKO; *prod:* Charles Mintz; *anim:* Dick Huemor, Sid Marcus; *mus:* Joe de Nat; *prod mgr:* James Bronis. *b&w.: sd:* RCA. 7 min. • No story available.

15. Aches and Snakes *(Blue Racer)* 10 Aug. 1973; *p.c.:* DFE/Mirisch for UA; *dir:* David Deneen; *story:* John W. Dunn; *anim:* Kenny Uset, Phil Normle, Warren Peace Jr., Dick Fitz; *lay:* Harry Case; *back:* Roman Hans; *ed:* Rick Steward; *voices:* Larry D. Mann; *mus:* Doug Goodwin; *ph:* John Burton Jr.; *prod mgr:* Lee Gunther; *col:* DeLuxe. *sd:* RCA. 5 min. • Crazylegs Crane and the Racer pursue the same bee. For no given reason, the animation credits are fictitious.

16. Acrobatty Bunny *(Looney Tunes)* 29 June 1946. *p.c.:* WB; *dir:* Robert McKimson; *story:* Warren Foster; *anim:* Arthur Davis, Cal Dalton, Richard Bickenbach; *lay:* Cornett Wood; *back:* Richard H. Thomas; *ed:* Treg Brown; *voices:* Mel Blanc; *mus:* Carl Stalling; *prod mgr:* John W. Burton; *prod:* Edward Selzer; *col:* Tech. *sd:* Vit. 7 min. • Bugs' home is invaded by a lion when a circus is erected over of his burrow. Animator McKimson's first crack at directing Bugs Bunny.

17. Addams Family 22 Nov. 1991; *p.c.:* Para/Orion Pictures for Colum Tri-Star; *anim fx:* Kevin Kutchaver, Al Mag, Pam Vick; *"Thing" prosthetics & puppets:* David Miller Studio; *anim:* David Miller; *col:* DeLuxe. *sd:* Dolby stereo. 99 min. *l/a.* • Live-action comedy: Cartoonist Charles Addams' macabre family springs from television to the silver screen in a live-action comedy. Stop-motion animation for "Thing," a dismembered hand with a mind of its own.

18. Addams Family Reunion 22 Sept. 1998; *p.c.:* Para; *model maker:* Mark Santora; *3d visual fx anim:* Brian Thomas; *visual fx Rotoscope:* Dan Walker, William Ward; *col. sd:* Dolby stereo. 87 min. *Academy Award.* • Live-action comedy based on the 1960s television series. Upon hearing that Grandpa and Grandma both have a rare disease that will turn them "normal," Gomez and Morticia organize a family reunion in the hopes that somebody knows of a treatment. "Thing," the Addams' dismembered pet hand, helps matters along.

19. Addams Family Values 19 Nov.1993; *p.c.:* Para/Univ; *anim:* Pam Vick, Ingin Kim, Craig Clark; *stop-motion anim:* Don Waller; *col. sd:* Dolby stereo. 94 min. *l/a.* • Live action comedy with television's offbeat family: The Addams hire a nanny for their newborn baby, "Pubert," unaware of her murderous designs. "Thing" assists the proceedings.

20. Admiral Byrd 1931; *p.c.:* The Fleischer Studio; *anim:* Max Fleischer; *b&w. sd. l/a/anim.* • Live-action coverage of Admiral Richard E. Byrd's exploration of Antarctica illustrated by animated charts and maps.

21. Admission Free *(Talkartoons)* 10 June 1932; *p.c.:* The Fleischer Studio for Para; *prod:* Max Fleischer; *sup:* Dave Fleischer; *dir:* James Culhane; *anim:* Thomas Johnson, Rudolph Eggeman, James Culhane; *voices:* Mae Questel; *mus:* Art Turkisher; *b&w. sd:* WE. 6 min. • Betty is in charge of an amusement arcade visited by the populous including Bimbo and Ko-Ko.

22. Advance and Be Mechanized *(Tom & Jerry)* 1967; *p.c.:* MGM; *prod:* Chuck Jones; *dir:* Ben Washam; *story:* Bob Ogle; *anim:* Dick

Thompson, Ben Washam, Don Towsley, Philip Roman; *lay:* Don Morgan; *back:* Philip de Guard; *des:* Maurice Noble; *mus:* Dean Elliott; *prod sup:* Earl Jonas, Nick Iuppa, Les Goldman; *col:* Met. *sd:* WE. 7 min. • Life on a Space Station: Jerry sends a robot mouse to get some cheese guarded by a robot police cat.

23. Adventure by the Sea *(Luno)* July 1964. *p.c.:* TT for Fox; *ex prod:* Bill Weiss; *dir/anim:* Art Bartsch; *story sup:* Tom Morrison; *story:* Bob Ogle, Glan Heisch; *sets:* Robert Owen, John Zago; *voices:* Bob MacFadden; *mus:* Phil Scheib; *ph:* Charles Schettler, Jack MacConnell; *sd:* Elliot Grey; *col:* DeLuxe. *sd:* RCA. 6 min. • Tim and Luno join a cowardly Captain Ahab in pursuit of Moby Dick.

24. Adventures of * 5 July 1957; *p.c.:* Storyboard for the Soloman J. Guggenheim Museum. *dir/des:* John Hubley; *story:* John Hubley, Faith Elliott; *anim:* Emery Hawkins, Ed Smith; *ed:* Faith Elliott; *mus:* Benny Carter, Lionel Hampton; *technical advisor:* James Johnson Sweeney; *col:* East. *sd.* 10 min. • A film about the need by the old of the vision of the young.

25. Adventures of Adenoid *(Aesop's Film Fable)* 25 Apr. 1925; *p.c.:* Fables Pictures for Pathé; *dir:* Paul Terry; *b&w. sil.* 6 min. • A mouse's sweetheart is whisked away in his rival's flivver which ends in the sea. A shark steals the girl but our hero rescues her.

26. The Adventures of Baron Munchausen 1927; *p.c.:* Peroff Pictures; *dir/prod:* Paul Peroff; *story:* R.E. Raspe. *col. sil.* 1 reel. • An egotistical Baron relays an extraordinary anecdote regarding how he once had an encounter with a whale that shot him up to the moon. After an extraterrestrial adventure he returned to earth where a great memorial was erected to his honor. His audience promptly "crowns" the Baron.

27. The Adventures of Buckaroo Banzai Across the 8th Dimension 15 Aug. 1984; *p.c.:* Sherwood Prods for Orion; *dir:* W.D. Richter; *ex prod:* Sidney Beckerman; *prod:* Neil Canton, W.D. Richter; *anim visual fx:* VCE (sup): Peter Kuran, (anim): R. J. Robertson, Rick L. Taylor, James Belohovek, Stephen Burg, Layne Bourgoyne, Chris Cassady; *fx anim/anim (8th Dimension seq):* John Van Vliet; *stop-motion anim:* Rick Heinrichs; *col:* Metrocolor. *sd.* Panavision. 102 min. *l/a.* • Live-action adventure: A Japanese-American genius, Buckaroo Banzai, tests a high-speed jet car and manages to pass through into the eighth dimension while doing so.

28. The Adventures of Ichabod and Mr. Toad 5 Oct. 1949; *p.c.:* Walt Disney prods for RKO; *dir:* Jack Kinney, Clyde Geronimi, James Algar; adapted from "The Ledgend of Sleepy Hollow" by Washington Irving and "The Wind in the Willows" by Kenneth Grahame; *story:* Erdman Penner, Winston Hibler, Joe Rinaldi, Ted Sears, Homer Brightman, Harry Reeves; *anim dir:* Frank Thomas, Ollie Johnston, Wolfgang Reitherman, Milt Kahl, John Lounsbery, Ward Kimball; *"Mr. Toad"; dir:* Jack Kinney, James Algar; *anim:* Hal Ambro, Al Bertino, Marc Davis, Hugh Fraser, Milt Kahl, Ollie Johnston, Bill Justice, Ward Kimball, Hal King, Rudy Larriva, Eric Larson, Murray McClellan, Wolfgang Reitherman, John Sibley, Henry Tanous, Harvey Toombs, Clair Weeks, Judge Whitaker, Bob Youngquist; *fx:* Ed Aardal, Jack Boyd; *lay:* Lance Nolley, Charles Philippi, Al Zinnen; *voices: Narration:* Basil Rathbone; *J. Thaddeus Toad:* Eric Blore; *Cyril Proudbottom:* Pat O'Malley; *Prosecuting Council/misc.:* John Ployardt; *Mole:* Colin Campbell; *Angus MacBadger:* Campbell Grant; *Ratty:* Claud Allister; *Judge/weasel:* Leslie Dennison; *Winky/Jailer/Postman:* Alec Harford; *weasels:* Edmond Stevens, John Ployardt, Jim Bodrero; *Policeman:* Edmond Stevens; "Drinking Song" *sung by* Ken Darby, Charles Bennett, J. Delos Jewkes, Robert Tait, Allan Watson; "Christmas Carol" *sung by* Betty Bruce, Michael Morgan, Mary Moder, Sally Mueller, Colin Sly, Pauline Sly; *Title chorus:* The Rhythmaires; "Ichabod"; *dir:* Clyde Geronimi, James Algar; *anim:* Les Clark, Hugh Fraser, Al Geiss, Volus Jones, Milt Kahl, Hal King, Ward Kimball, Oliver Johnston, Eric Larson, John Lounsbery, Don Lusk, Fred Moore, Wolfgang Reitherman, John Sibley, Frank Thomas; *fx:* George Rowley; *des:* Claude Coats, Don da Gradi, Mary Blair, John Hench; *lay:* Tom Codrick, Thor Putnam, Hugh Hennesy, *back:* Ray Huffine, Merle Cox, Art Riley, Brice Mack, Dick Anthony; *ed:* John O. Young; *Narration:* Bing Crosby; *special processes:* Ub Iwerks; *sd:* C. O. Slyfield, Robert O. Cook. *mus ed:* Al Teeter; *mus:* Oliver Wallace; *Orch:* Joseph S. Dubin; *mus arr:* Ken Darby; *songs:* Don Raye, Gene de Paul; *prod sup:* Ben Sharpsteen; *col:* Tech. *sd:* RCA. 68 min. • Two distinct stories; The first features the reckless Mr. Toad who trades his ancestral home to unscrupulous weasels

in exchange for a stolen motor car. The second concerns an ungainly school teacher who contests for the local beauty with a rival who finally manages to frighten him away from the area. • See: *The Legend of Sleepy Hollow*

29. Adventures of Popeye *(Popeye)* 25 Oct. 1935; *p.c.:* The Fleischer Studio for Para; *prod:* Max Fleischer; *dir:* Dave Fleischer; *voices:* Jack Mercer, Mae Questel, Gus Wickie; *mus:* Sammy Timberg. *b&w. sd:* WE. 7 min. *l/a/anim.* • Seq: *I Eats My Spinach; Popeye the Sailor; Wild Elephinks; Axe Me Another.* Popeye exhumes himself from the confines of a comic book in order to demonstrate to a small boy how spinach helps conquer all bullies.

30. The Adventures of Roving Thomas *(Urban Popular Classics); p.c.:* Kineto Films for Vitagraph. *prod:* Charles Urban • **1922: Roving Thomas in Seeing New York** 17 Sept. **Roving Thomas on an Aeroplane** 22 Oct. **Roving Thomas on a Fishing Trip** 10 Dec. **Roving Thomas in Nova Scotia Roving Thomas in Banff, Canada. Roving Thomas in San Francisco and China Town. Roving Thomas in Mountains of Utah and Colorado. Roving Thomas From Van Couver to Frisco. Roving Thomas in Chicago. Roving Thomas Takes a Trip on a Fishing Trawler.** • *1923:* **Roving Thomas at the Winter Carnival** Feb. • Sight-seeing with animated characters over a live-action scenic; *l/a/anim; b&w; sil.* Also known as *Cat Cartoons.* 1927 reissues by Film Exchange Inc.

31. The Adventures of the American Rabbit 17 Jan. 1986; *p.c.:* Toei Animation for Clubhouse Pictures; *dir:* Fred Wolf, Nobutaka Nishizawa; *prod:* Masaharu Etoh, Masahisa Saeki, John G. Marshall; *story:* Norm Lenzer; based on the characters created by Stewart Moskowitz; *anim:* Shingo Araki, Kenji Yokoyama, Yukiyoshi Hane, Yoshitaka Yashima, Shigeo Matoba, Hirohide Shikishima, Ikuo Fudanoki, Katsuyoshi Nakatsuru, Takashi Nashizawa; *voices: Theo:* Bob Arbogast; *Tini Meeny:* Pat Fraley; *Rob Rabbit/The American Rabbit:* Barry Gordon; *Rodney:* Bob Holt; *Dipl/misc:* Lew Horn; *Bruno:* Norm Lenzer; *Vulture/Buzzard:* Ken Mars; *Too Loose:* John Mayer; *Lady Pig:* Maitzi Morgan; *Fred Red:* Fred Wolf; *Mother:* Russi Taylor; *Ping Pong:* Lorenzo Music; *Bunny O'Hare:* Lauri O'Brien; *Mentor:* Hal Smith; *col. sd:* Mono. 85 min. • A wizard provides mild-mannered Rob Rabbit with superhuman powers, thus turning him into a Super Rabbit.

32. The Adventures of Tom Thumb Jr. *(Cartune)* 4 Mar. 1940; *p.c.:* Walter Lantz prods for Univ; *dir:* Burt Gillett. *story/des/sets:* Willy Pogàny; *voice:* Marjorie Tarlton; *mus:* Frank Marsales; *prod mgr:* George Hall; *col:* Tech. *sd:* WE. 7 min. • Tom and his grasshopper friend arrive at an island where Tom is adopted by a giant woman and the grasshopper wages war against a canned sardine.

33. Aero-Nutics *(Kartune)* 8 May 1953. *dir:* Seymour Kneitel; *story:* Irving Spector; *anim:* Al Eugster, George Germanetti; *sets:* Robert Owen; *voices:* Jackson Beck, Jack Mercer; *mus:* Winston Sharples; *song:* Alfred Bryant, Fred Fisher; *ph:* Leonard McCormick; *prod sup:* Seymour Shultz; *col:* Tech. *sd:* RCA. 7 min. • Spot-gags on air travel from the Wright Brothers to present day.

34. Aesop's Fables Studio (1921–1929) *artists:* Paul Houghton Terry, C.T. "Vet" Anderson, Harry Bailey; *head anim:* George Stallings; *assist anim:* Steve Muffatti, Ed Donnelly, Jim Tyer; *anim:* Frank Chambers, Mannie Davis, Norman Ferguson, John Foster, Bill Hicks, Ferdinand Huszti Horvath, Eddie Link, Hicks Lokey, George MacAvoy, John McManus, Frank Moser, Theodore C. Paton, Frank Sherman, Hugh Shields, Jerry Shields, Vladimir Tytla, Oscar van Brunt, Ted Waldyer, George Williams; *ed:* Charles Wolfe; *gags:* Puzant Thomajan; *orch:* Gene Rodemich; *mus dir:* Winston Sharples.

35. Africa *(Oswald)* 1 Dec. 1930; *p.c.:* Univ; *dir:* Walter Lantz, "Bill" Nolan; *anim:* Clyde Geronimi, Manuel Moreno, Ray Abrams, Fred Avery, Lester Kline; *voice:* Mickey Rooney; *mus:* James Dietrich; *b&w. sd:* WE. 5½ min. • Oswald is depicted as an explorer astride a camel.

36. Africa Before Dark *(Oswald the Lucky Rabbit)* 20 Feb. 1928. *dir:* Walt Disney; *anim:* Ubbe Iwerks; *ph:* Mike Marcus; *b&w. sil.* 7 min. • Oswald's hunting expedition surrounds him with lions. He makes his getaway by converting an elephant into a plane and zooming away.

37. Africa Squawks *(Terry-Toon)* 30 June 1939. *p.c.:* TT for Fox. *dir:* Connie Rasinski. *story:* John Foster. *mus:* Philip A. Scheib. *b&w. sd:* RCA. 7 min. • No story available.

38. Africa Squeaks (*Flip the Frog*) 9 Jan. 1932; *p.c.:* Celebrity prods for MGM; *prod/dir:* Ub Iwerks; b&w. *sd:* PCP. 8 min. • While hunting in Africa, Flip is captured by cannibals and immersed in a cooking pot. He performs magical stunts that scare the natives away and their deserted wives appoint Flip their king.

39. Africa Squeaks (*Looney Tunes*) 27 Jan. 1940; *p.c.:* Leon Schlesinger prods for WB; *dir:* Robert Clampett; *anim:* John Carey, Dave Hoffman; *sets:* Elmer Plummer; *ed:* Treg Brown; *voices:* Mel Blanc, Kay Kyser; *mus:* Carl W. Stalling; *prod sup:* Henry Binder, Raymond G. Katz; b&w. *sd:* Vit. 7 min. • Porky leads an African safari, only succeeding in finding Kay Kyser who leads the jungle animals in a hot swing session.

40. African Diary (*Goofy*) 20 Apr. 1944; *p.c.:* Walt Disney prods for RKO; *dir:* Jack Kinney; *asst dir:* Ted Sebern; *story:* Bill Peed; *anim:* Eric Larson, Marc Davis, Murray McClellan, Milt Kahl; *fx:* Andy Engman, Jack Boyd; *lay:* Lance Nolley; *back:* Ray Huffine; *voices:* Frank Graham, Pinto Colvig, James MacDonald; *mus:* Oliver Wallace *col:* Tech. *sd:* RCA. 7 min. • The Goof leads a safari into the interior with all intents of hunting rhino but beats a hasty retreat when actually confronted by one.

41. African Huntsman (*Aesop's Film Fable*) 11 Dec. 1924; *p.c.:* Fables Pictures Inc for Pathé; *dir:* Paul Terry; b&w. sil. 6 min. • A cat seduces mice to leave their tree-trunk homes and come out into the open where he can bag them.

42. African Jungle Hunt (*Terry-Toon*) Mar. 1957; *p.c.:* TT for Fox; *dir:* Connie Rasinski; *story:* Tom Morrison; *anim:* Jim Tyer; *mus:* Philip A. Scheib; *col:* Tech. *sd:* RCA. 6 min. • Phoney Baloney tells a far-fetched yarn of how he went to the Gold Coast, was captured by pigmies and shrunk down to their size.

43. After the Ball (*Screen Songs*) 8 Nov. 1929; *p.c.:* The Fleischer Studio for Para; *prod:* Max Fleischer; *dir:* Dave Fleischer; *mus:* Art Turkisher; *song:* Charles K. Harris; b&w. *sd:* WE. 6 min. • Caricature of Charles Harris' musical composition.

44. After the Ball (*Woody Woodpecker*) 13 Feb. 1956; *p.c.:* Walter Lantz prods for Univ; *dir:* Paul J. Smith; *story:* Jack Cosgriff; *anim:* Robert Bentley, Gil Turner. Herman R. Cohen; *sets:* Art Landy; *voices:* Daws Butler, Grace Stafford; *mus:* Clarence Wheeler; *col:* Tech. *sd:* RCA. 6 min. • A lumberjack makes Woody's tree-home into a bowling ball.

45. Aged in the Wood (*Aesop's Film Fable*) 29 Sept. 1929; *p.c.:* Fables Pictures Inc for Pathé; *dir:* Paul Terry; b&w. sil. 6 min. • Henry Cat gives some home-brewed "hooch" to a parrot who is instantly knocked out, so he drinks some himself and imagines he is traveling through space.

46. Ah, Sweet Mouse-Story of Life (*Tom & Jerry*) 1965; *p.c.:* MGM; *prod/dir:* Chuck Jones; *asst dir:* Maurice Noble; *story:* Michael Maltese, Chuck Jones; *anim:* Dick Thompson, Ben Washam, Ken Harris, Don Towsley, Tom Ray; *back:* Robert Gribbroek; *voices:* June Foray, Mel Blanc; *mus:* Eugene Poddany; *prod mgr:* Les Goldman; *col:* Met. *sd:* WE. 7 min. • Tom chases his prey around the ledge of a very high building until Jerry wreaks revenge with the aid of a very noisy claxon.

47. A Haunting We Will Go (*Cartune*) 4 Sept. 1939; *p.c.:* Walter Lantz prods for Univ; *dir:* Burt Gillett; *story:* Gil Burton, Kin Platt; *anim:* Fred Kopietz, Lester Kline; *sets:* Edgar Keichle; *voices:* Mel Blanc, Marjorie Tarlton, Candy Candido; *mus:* Frank Marsales; *prod mgr:* George Hall; *col:* Tech. *sd:* WE. 7 min. • A small ghost proves to Eightball that "there *are* such things as ghosts." Lantz's first in three-strip Technicolor.

48. A-Haunting We Will Go (*Looney Tunes*) 16 Apr. 1966; *p.c:* DFE for WB; *dir:* Robert McKimson; *anim:* Manuel Perez, George Grandpré, Warren Batchelder, Bob Matz; *lay:* Dick Ung; *back:* Tom O'Loughlin; *ed:* Al Wahrman; *voices:* Mel Blanc, June Foray; *mus:* Bill Lava; *col:* Tech. *sd:* Vit. 7 min. • Daffy's nephew returns from "Trick-or-Treat" having seen a *real* witch! Investigating, Daffy finds Speedy Gonzales in the form of Witch Hazel (who is on holiday). Re-uses animation from *Broomstick Bunny* and *A Duck Amuck*.

49. A-Haunting We Will Go (*Noveltoon*) 13 May 1949. *p.c.:* Famous for Para; *dir:* Seymour Kneitel; *story:* Larz Bourne; *anim:* Myron Waldman, Irving Dressler; *sets:* Anton Loeb; *voices:* Frank Gallop, Jack Mercer; *mus:* Winston Sharples; *ph:* Leonard McCormick; *prod mgr:* Sam Buchwald; *col:* Tech. *sd:* RCA. 9 min. • Casper thinks he's lost a friend when his duckling companion is shot but the duck returns as a ghost.

50. A-Hunting We Will Go (*Talkartoons*) 29 Apr. 1932; *p.c.:* The Fleischer Studio for Para; *prod:* Max Fleischer; *dir:* Dave Fleischer; *anim:* Alfred Eugster, Rudolph Eggeman; *mus:* Art Turkisher; b&w. *sd:* WE. 7 min. • Ko-Ko and Bimbo overhear Betty singing about wanting a fur coat and set about hunting some animals for their pelts.

51. A-Hunting We Won't Go (*Color Rhapsody*) 23 Aug. 1943; *p.c.:* Colum; *prod:* Dave Fleischer; *dir:* Bob Wickersham; *story:* Jack Cosgriff; *anim:* Howard Swift, Phil Duncan; *sets:* Clark Watson; *ed:* Edward Moore; *voices:* Frank Graham; *mus:* Eddie Kilfeather, Leo Erdody; *prod mgr:* Albert Spar; *col:* Tech. *sd:* RCA. 7 min. • The Fox and Crow hunt each other for a rich reward.

52. Ain't Nature Grand? (*Looney Tunes*) 24 Jan. 1931; *p.c.:* Hugh Harman, Rudolf Ising prods for WB; *anim:* Isadore Freleng, Norman Blackburn; *mus:* Frank Marsales; *prod:* Leon Schlesinger; b&w. *sd:* Vit. 8 min. • Bosko takes pity on his fishing worm and sets it free, whereupon it is chased by the early bird.

53. Ain't She Sweet (*Screen Songs*) 3 Feb. 1933; *p.c.:* The Fleischer Studio for Para; *prod:* Max Fleischer. *dir:* Dave Fleischer; *anim:* Seymour Kneitel, Thomas Johnson; *mus:* Art Turkisher; *song:* Jack Yellen, Milton Ager; *l/a:* Lillian Roth; b&w. *sd:* WE. 9 min. *l/a/anim:* • Cats dance "The Cake Walk."

54. Ain't She Tweet (*Looney Tunes*) 21 June 1952. *p.c.:* WB; *dir:* I. Freleng; *story:* Warren Foster; *anim:* Virgil Ross, Arthur Davis, Manuel Perez, Ken Champin; *lay:* Hawley Pratt; *back:* Irv Wyner; *ed:* Treg Brown; *voices:* Mel Blanc, Bea Benaderet; *mus:* Carl Stalling; *prod mgr:* John W. Burton; *prod:* Edward Selzer; *col:* Tech. *sd:* Vit. 7 min. • Sylvester has to first overcome a yard full of ferocious bulldogs before he can reach his breakfast ... Tweety.

55. Ain't That Ducky (*Looney Tunes*) 19 May 1945; *p.c.:* WB. *dir:* I. Freleng; *story:* Michael Maltese; *anim:* Gerry Chiniquy; *lay:* Hawley Pratt; *back:* Paul Julian; *ed:* Treg Brown; *voices:* Mel Blanc, Victor Moore; *mus:* Carl W. Stalling; *prod mgr:* John W. Burton; *prod:* Edward Selzer; *col:* Tech. *sd:* Vit. 7 min. • Daffy protects an obnoxious ingrate duckling from the hunter.

56. Ain't We Got Fun (*Merrie Melodies*) 1 May 1937; *p.c.:* Leon Schlesinger prods for WB; *dir:* Fred Avery; *story:* Bob Clampett; *anim:* Charles Jones, Bob Clampett; *lay:* Griff Jay; *back:* Arthur Loomer; *ed:* Tregoweth E. Brown; *voices:* Elmore Vincent, Billy Bletcher, Elvia Allman, Bernice Hansel; *mus:* Carl W. Stalling; *song:* Gus Kahn, Raymond B. Egan, Richard A. Whiting; *prod sup:* Henry Binder, Raymond G. Katz; *col:* Tech. *sd:* Vit. 8 min. • Mice cause the cat to be thrown out by his master but the old man soon realizes the rodents are to blame and tries to tempt him back in the house.

57. Air Cooled (*Aesop's Film Fables*) 17 Oct. 1925; *p.c.:* Fables Pictures Inc for Pathé; *dir:* Paul Terry; b&w. sil. 6 min. • The animals join forces to help Farmer Al Falfa's dirigible flight.

58. The Air Express (*Meany Miny Mo*) 20 Sept. 1937; *p.c.:* Univ; *story:* Walt Lantz, Victor McLeod; *anim:* Lester Kline, Fred Kopietz, La Verne Harding; *mus:* James Dietrich. b&w. *sd:* WE. 7 min. • An ostrich wrecks the monkeys' airline.

59. The Air Hostess (*Color Rhapsody*) 22 Oct. 1937; *p.c.:* Charles Mintz prods for Colum; *story:* Sid Marcus; *anim:* Art Davis; *voices:* Elvia Allman, Leone Le Doux, the Rhythmettes; *mus:* Joe de Nat; *prod mgr:* James Bronis; *col:* Tech-2; *sd:* RCA. 8 min. • Pilot Scrappy and air hostess Margie have a tough time trying to get their collapsible plane into the air.

60. Airlift à la Carte (*Chilly Willy*) 1971; *p.c.:* Walter Lantz prods for Univ; *dir:* Paul J. Smith; *story:* Dale Hale; *anim:* Virgil Ross, Al Coe, Tom Byrne, Joe Voght; *sets:* Nino Carbe; *voices:* Daws Butler; *mus:* Walter Greene; *col:* Tech. *sd:* RCA. 6 min. • The Gooney Bird assists Chilly and Maxie in stealing food from Smedley's store.

61. Aladdin 25 Nov. 1992; *p.c.:* The Walt Disney Company for BV; *prod/dir:* John Musker, Ron Clements; *co-prod:* Donald W. Ernst, Amy Pell; *scr:* Ron Clements, John Musker, Ted Elliott, Terry Rossio; *art sup:* (story): Ed Gombert; (Lay): Rasoul Azadani; (back): Kathy Altieri; (clean-up): Vera Lanpher; (visual fx): Don Paul; (cgi): Steve Goldberg; (artistic co-ord): Dan Hansen; (prod mgr): Alice Dewey; *story:* Burny Mattinson, Roger Allers, Daan Jippes, Kevin Harkey, Sue Nichols, Francis Glebas, Darrell Rooney, Larry Leker, James Fujii, Kirk Hanson, Kevin Lima, Rebecca Rees, David S. Smith, Chris Sanders, Brian Pimental, Patrick A. Ventura; *"Aladdin" anim sup:* Glen Keane; *anim:* Alex Kuperschmidt, Michael Cedeno, Anthony De Rosa, David P. Stephan, Michael Surrey, Brad Kuha, Russ Edmonds, Tony Fucile, Ken Hettig, Mike Swofford; *clean-up anim:* Bill Berg, Scott Anderson, Dorothea Baker, Susan Lantz, Tracy M. Lee, Kaaren Lundeen, Brett Newton, Jennifer Oliver, Marshall L. Toomey, Terry Wozniak, Sue Adnopoz, Wes Chun, Lee Dunkman, Karen Hardenbergh, Rick Kohlschmidt, Maria Rosetti, Dan Tanaka, Peggy Tonkonogy; *break:* Carl Hall, Kris Heller, James Y. Jackson, Lee McCaulla, Anthony W. Michaels, David Nethery, Andrew Ramos, Jacqueline M. Sanchez, Bryan M. Sommer, Charles R. Vollmer, Wendy J. Werner; *inbet:* Samantha Lair; *"Genie" anim sup:* Eric Goldberg; *anim:* David Burgess, Raul Garcia, Tom Sito, Joe Haidar, Broose Johnson, Rejean Bourdages, Gilda Palinginis; *clean-up:* Brian Clift, Allison Hollen, Lori M. Noda, Terry Naughton, Dave Suding; *asst anim:* Susan Y. Sugita; *break:* Wendie Fischer, Norma Rivera, Martin Schwartz; *inbet:* Laurey Foulkes, Craig R. Maras; *"Jasmine" anim sup:* Mark Henn; *anim:* Aaron Blaise, Doug Krohn; *clean-up:* Reneè Holt, Merry K. Clingen, Daniel A. Gracey, Emily Jiuliano, Ginny Parmele, Tony Anselmo, Teresa Eidenbock, Christine Lawrence, Steve Lubin, Laura Nichols; *break:* Jang W. Lee, Tamarad D. Lusher, Ron Westlund; *inbet:* Travis Blaise, Monica Murdock, Chang Yei Kim, Richard D. Rocha; *"Jafar" anim sup:* Andreas Deja; *anim:* Ron Husband, Nik Ranieri, Ken Duncan, Lou Dellarosa; *clean-up:* Marty Korth, Kathleen M. Bailey, Sam Ewing, Randy Sanchez, Bruce Strock; *asst anim:* Kent Holaday, Dana M. Reemes; *break:* Lillian A. Chapman, James McArdle, Anthony Cipriano, Mary-Jean Repchuk; *inbet:* Vincent de Frances, Diana Falk, Miriam McDonnell; *"Abu" anim sup:* Duncan Marjoribanks; *anim:* Tim Allen, Michael Show, Ellen Woodbury, Rick Farmiloe, Teresa Martin, Dan M. Wawrzaszek; *"Abu/Narrator" clean-up:* Debra Armstrong, Philip S. Boyd, Margie Daniels, Gail Frank, Bette Holmquist; *asst anim:* Edward R. Gutierrez, Michael Hazy, Brian B. McKim; *break:* Janet Heerhan Bae, Kellie D. Lewis; *inbet:* Maurilio Morales, Gary D. Payne; *"Carpet" anim sup:* Randy Cartwright; *anim:* Tina Price, William Recinos, *"Iago" anim sup:* Will Finn; *anim:* Brian Ferguson, Tony Bancroft, Tom Bancroft; *clean-up:* Nancy Kniep, Marianne Tucker; *asst anim:* Juliet Stroud Duncan; *break:* B. Adams, Marsha W.J. Park-Yum, Bill Thinnes; *"Sultan" anim sup:* David Pruiksma; *anim:* Barry Temple, Larry White, Bob Bryan, Cynthia Overman; *clean-up:* Richard Hoppe, Robert O. Corley, Marcia Dougherty, Stephan Zupkas; *asst anim:* Mike McKinney, Elizabeth Watasin; *break:* Elliot M. Bour, Kevin Smith; *inbet:* Karen Rosenfield; *"Rajah" anim:* Aaron Blaise; *"Jafar as Beggar/Snake" anim:* Kathy Zielinski; *"Jafar as Gaseem/Achmed" anim:* T. Daniel Hofstedt; *"Guards" anim:* Phil Young, Chris Wahl; *fx anim:* Dorse Lanpher, David A. Bossert, Ted C. Kiercey, Scott Santoro, Mark Myer, Mark Dindal, Christine Harding, Eusebio Torres, Allen Blyth, Kelvin Yasuda, Chris Jenkins; *"Rajah/Guards" clean-up:* Alex Topete, Eric Pigors; *break:* Noreen Beasley, Yung Soo Kim, Vincent Siracusano; *inbet:* Will Huneycutt, David Recinos; *asst anim:* Randy Haycock, Mark Kennedy; *rough inbet:* Trey Finney, Grant Hiestand, Paul McDonald, John Ramirez, Pres Romanillos, Henry Sato Jr., Eric Walls, David Zaboski *"Misc. characters" clean-up:* Vera Lanpher, Jesus Cortes, Ray Harris, Natasha Selfridge; *asst anim:* Carl A. Bell, Inna Chon, Johan Klingler; *break:* Cheryl Polakow, Dave Woodman; *inbet:* Jody Kooistra, Jane Misek, Wes Sullivan; *prod des:* R.S. Van der Wende; *art dir:* Bill Perkins; *lay:* Karen Keller, Tom Shannon, Daniel Hu, Jeff Dickson, Mitchell G. Bernal, Fred Craig, Allen C. Tam, Dan St. Pierre; *back:* Allison Belliveau, Justin L. Brandstater, Thomas Cardone, Daniel Cooper, Debbie DuBois, John Emerson, Ian S. Gooding, Dean Gordon, Tia Kratter, Cristy Maltese, Serge Michaels, Philip Phillipson, Donald A. Towns, Kevin Turcotte, Thomas Woodington, Gregory Alexander Droletti, Natalie Franscioni-Karp; *scene plan sup:* Ann Tucker; *check sup:* Janet Bruce; *col model sup:* Karen Comella; *i&p sup:* Gretchen Maschmeyer Albrecht; *check/paint sup:* Hortensia M. Casagran; *Digitizing ph sup:* Robyn Roberts; *asst ed:* Mark A. Hester; *Florida unit sup: lay:* Robert Walker; *back:* Richard Sluiter, Robert E. Stanton; *clean-up:* Ruben Procopio; *visual fx:* Barry Cook, Jeff Dutton; *ed:* Chuck Williams; *prod mgr (Florida):* Baker Bloodworth; *prod mgr (lay unit):* Michael O'Mara, Mac George, Davy Liu, Mark Kalesniko, Doug Walker, Michael Vash, Tim Callahan; *blue sketch:* Madlyn O'Neil; *key fx asst:* Mabel Gesner, Dan Chaika, John Tucker; *asst fx anim:* Cynthia Neill-Knizek, Masa Oshiro, Dan Kuemmel, Mark Barrows, Steve Starr, Tony West; *fx*

break/inbet: Dan Lund, Kristine Brown, Sandra Groeneveld, Peter de Mund, Geoffrey C. Everts, John Eddings; *cgi: mgr:* Dan Philips; *model & anim:* James R.Tooley, Darren Kiner, Rob Bekuhrs, Linda Bel, Gregory Griffith; *lighting & softwear engineering:* Edward Kummer, Don Gworek, Mary Jane Turner, Scott F. Johnson, Tad Gielow, Kiran Bhakta Joshi; *visual development:* Hans Bacher, Francis Glebas, Peter Gullerud; *character des:* Jean Gillmore, Daan Jippes, Eric Goldberg; *pre-prod: story development:* Howard Ashman, Linda Woolverton, Gary Trousdale; *asst ed:* Sharon Smith Holley, Audrey Chang, Barbara Gerety, Jacqueline Kinney, Eric C. Daroca, Beth Collins-Stegmaier; *scene plan:* Annamarie Costa, John Cunningham, Donna Weir; *anim check:* Karen Hepburn, Karen S. Paat, Laurie A. Sacks, Gary Shafer, Mavis Shafer, Barbara Wiles; *col model asst:* Penny Coulter, Ann Sorensen, Leslie Ellery; *prod admin:* Suzanne Vissotzky; *asst prod mgrs: ed:* Chip Washabaugh; *lay:* Dana Axelrod; *anim:* Susan Blanchard; *clean-up:* Brett Hayden; *back/col model/check:* Bruce Grant Williams; *cgi snr prod co-ord:* Rozanne Marie Cazian; *i&p asst mgr:* Chris Hecox; *Florida unit:* Paul Steele; *prod asst:* Lisa M. Smith; *prod secretary:* Grances P. Benham; *Florida prod secretary:* Barbara J. Poirier; *enginerering: mgr:* Dave Inglish, David F. Wolf; *development:* David Coons, James D. Houston, Mark R. Kimball, Marty Prager; *support:* Raul E. Anya, Michael Bolds, Carol J. Choy, Bijan Forutanpour, Randy Fukuda, Bruce Hatakeyama, Marcus W. Hobbs, Shyh-Chyuan Huang, Kevin E. Keech, Blaine Kennison, Brad Lowman, Michael K. Purvis, Carlos Quinonez, Grace Shirado, Michael Sullivan, Mark M. Tokunaga, Paul Yanover; *Pixar:* Thomas Hahn, Peter Nye, Michael A. Shantzis; *prod asst:* Matt Allen, Leelannee Beckner, Kirk Bodyfelt, Kevin L. Briggs, Cliff Freitas, Matthew Garbera, Heather Hutchinson, Francine Luna, Gary Matanky, Karenna Mazur, Joe Morris, Rebecca L. Pahr, Sylvia Sanchez, Christopher Tapia, Manda Vinson, Angelique N. Yen; *character sculptures:* Kent Melton; *title des:* Burke Mattsson; *digitizing mark-up:* Gina Wootten; *asst sup-digitizing ph:* Jo Ann Breuer; *digitizing ph:* Kent Gordon, Tina Baldwin, Karen China, Lynnette Cullen, Gary Fishbaugh, Cindy Garcia; *asst paint sup:* Barbara Lynn Hamane, Rhonda L. Hick; *col mark-up:* Beth Ann McCoy, Debra Y. Siegel; *paint mark-up:* Irma Velez, Micki Zurcher; *paint:* Carmen Sanderson, Joyce Alexander, Phyllis Bird, Russell Blandino, Sherrie Cuzzort, Phyllis Fields, Cindy Finn, Chuck Gefre, Anne Hazard, Janette Hulett, Paulino G. Inigo, David Karp, Angelika Katz, Harlene Mears, Debbie Mihara, Deborah Mooneyham, Karen Nugent, Leyla del C. Pelaez, Bruce Phillipson, Heidi Shellhorn, Fumiko Sommer, Roxanne Taylor, Britt Van der Nagel, Susan Wileman; *final check:* Teri McDonald, Monica Marroquin; *compositing: asst sup:* James "J.R" Russell, Shannon Fallis-Kane, David J. Rowe; *ph mgr:* Joe Jiuliano; *digital film printing & opticals: sup:* Ariel Velasco Shaw, Christine Beck, Christopher Gee, Chuck Warren; *anim ph:* John Aardal, Mary Lescher, Gary W. Smith; *post prod sup:* Sara Duran; *casting:* Albert Tavares; *l/a reference:* Robb Willoughby, Robina Ritchie; *voices: Aladdin:* Scott Weinger; *Aladdin's singing voice:* Brad Kane; *Genie:* Robin Williams; *Jasmine:* Linda Larkin; *Jasmine's singing voice:* Lea Salonga; *Jafar:* Jonathan Freeman; *Iago:* Gilbert Gottfried; *Abu:* Frank Welker; *The Sultan:* Douglas Seale; *Prince Achmed, Merchant, Camel:* Corey Burton; *Guard:* Jim Cummings; *also:* Charlie Adler, Jack Angel, Philip Clarke, Jennifer Darling, Debi Derryberry, Bruce Gooch, Jerry Houser, Vera Lockwood, Sherry Lyn, Mickie McGowan, Patrick Pinney, Phil Proctor; *"Arabian Nights" sung by* Bruce Adler; *"A Whole New World" sung by* Regina Belle, Peabo Bryson; *songs:* Howard Ashman, Alan Menken, Tim Rice; *mus:* Alan Menken; *song arrangement:* Alan Menken, Danny Troob; *orch:* Danny Troob, Michael Starobin; *vocal arrangement/conductor:* David Friedman; *mus ed:* Kathleen Bennett, Segue Music, Bruce Botnick, Michael Farrow; *Orchestral contractors: New York:* Emil Charlap; *Los Angeles:* Ken Watson; *sup copyist:* Dominic Fidelibus; *song prod:* Walter Afanasieff; *arrangers:* Walter Afanasieff, Robbie Buchanan; *sd fx:* Mark Mangini, Weddington Prods Inc.; *sd ed:* Teresa Eckton, Ron Bartlett, Donald Flick, Mary Ruth Smith, Clayton Collins, John Pospisil; *dialogue ed:* Curt Schulkey, Jim Melton; *asst sd ed:* Sonny Pettijohn, Deirdre Mangione; *foley:* John Roesch, Alicia Stevenson; *mix:* Terry Porter, Mel Metcalfe, David J. Hudson; *dialogue rec:* Doc Kane, Denis Blackerby; *PDL:* Judy Nard; *ADR mix:* Bob Baron; *b&w processing:* Joe Parra, John White; *fx graphics:* Bernie Gagliano; *col timer:* Dale Grahn; *l/a co-ord:* Tod Marsden; *video crew:* Al Vasquez, Dan Buchannan; *props:* David Weiss; *choreographer:* Brad Flanagan; *models:* Auroah Allain Drinco, Peter Fitzgerald, Lance McDonald, Mary Oedy, Stefanie Roos, Jamie Torcellini, Kim Wolfe, Leslie Woodies; *projection:*

Don Henry; *post prod admin:* Jeannine Berger; *neg cutters:* Mary Beth Smith, Rick MacKay; *New York casting:* Jennifer M. Shotwell; *digital film recorders by* CELCO; *modeling/motion software:* Alias Research Inc.; *col:* Tech. *sd:* Dolby stereo. 91 min. • Aladdin, a street-wise thief in the fabled city of Agrabah, falls for Princess Jasmine, who wants to escape from her restricted lifestyle. The wicked Vizier, Jafar, needs to get his hands on a magic lamp in order to gain power and tricks Aladdin into getting the lamp from an underground cave. When things go wrong, Aladdin is promoted to "Master of the Lamp" and presented with the wish-granting Genie. The Genie turns Aladdin into a prince to help impress the princess although the pretext fails to impress Jasmine. Jafar pulls out all the stops to defeat Aladdin and get the lamp back for himself but the lad's natural cunning manages to defeat the Vizier's evil designs.

62. Aladdin and the Wonderful Lamp *(ComiColor)* 30 July 1934; *p.c.:* Celebrity prods Inc.; *prod:* Ub Iwerks; *dir:* Jimmie Culhane, Al Eugster; *anim:* Grim Natwick, Berny Wolf; *lay:* Jimmie Culhane; *mus:* Art Turkisher; *col:* Ciné. *sd:* PCP. 8 min. • Aladdin slaves away in the junk business until he polishes a lamp which summons up a genie. He ends with untold riches and marries a princess while his villainous employer gets his just deserts.

63. Aladdin's Lamp *(Mighty Mouse)* 28 Mar. 1947; *p.c.:* TT for Fox; *dir:* Eddie Donnelly; *story:* John Foster; *anim:* Connie Rasinski, Carlo Vinci; *mus:* Philip A. Scheib; *col:* Tech. *sd:* RCA. 7 min. • A villainous cat kidnaps the Sultan's (mouse) daughter but Mighty Mouse is soon on the scene to rescue her.

64. Aladdin's Lamp *(Paul Terry-Toons)* 27 Dec. 1931; *p.c.:* Terry, Moser & Coffman for Educational/Fox; *dir:* Paul Terry, Frank Moser; *mus:* Philip A. Scheib; *b&w. sd:* WE. 9 min. • An apple-seller finds a Magic Lamp. When he wishes for a Harem beauty, she is kidnapped by Arabs and presented to the Sultan. Aladdin to the rescue.

65. Aladdin's Lamp *(Paul Terry-Toons)* 15 Nov. 1935; *p.c.:* Terry, Moser & Coffman for Educational/Fox; *dir:* Paul Terry, Frank Moser; *mus:* Philip A. Scheib; *b&w. sd:* WE. 9 min. • No story available.

66. Aladdin's Lamp *(Terry-Toon)* 22 Oct. 1943; *p.c.:* TT for Fox; *dir:* Eddie Donnelly; *story:* John Foster; *voices:* Arthur Kay, Thomas Morrison; *mus:* Philip A. Scheib; *col:* Tech. *sd:* RCA. 7 min. • Gandy Goose and Sourpuss dream they are in ancient China where they meet Aladdin with his magic lamp.

67. Aladin and His Wonderful Lamp *(Popeye)* rel: 7 Apr. 1939; *p.c.:* The Fleischer Studio for Para; *prod:* Max Fleischer; *dir:* Dave Fleischer; *anim:* David Tendlar, William Sturm, Nicholas Tafuri, Reuben Grossman; *sets:* Shane Miller; *voices:* Jack Mercer, Margie Hines, Arthur Boran; *mus:* Sammy Timberg; *col:* Tech. *sd:* WE. 22 min. • Olive writes a screenplay for "Aladin's Lamp," casting herself as the fair Princess and Popeye as Aladin.

68. Alaska *(Oswald)* 15 Dec. 1930; *p.c.:* Univ; *dir:* Walter Lantz, "Bill" Nolan; *anim:* Clyde Geronimi, Manuel Moreno, Ray Abrams, Fred Avery, Lester Kline, "Pinto" Colvig; *voices:* Mickey Rooney, Pinto Colvig; *mus:* James Dietrich; *b&w. sd:* WE. 7 min. • Gold miner Oswald vies with Pete over his girl in an Alaskan saloon.

69. Alaska or Bust *(Aesop's Film Fables)* 16 Aug. 1928; *p.c.:* Fables Pictures Inc for Pathé; *dir:* Paul Terry; *b&w. sil.* 6 min. • No story available.

70. Alaska Sweepstakes *(Oswald)* 26 Aug. 1936. *p.c.:* Univ; *dir:* Walter Lantz; *story:* Walter Lantz, Victor McLeod; *anim:* Fred Kopietz, Ed Benedict; *mus:* James Dietrich; *b&w. sd:* WE. 7 min. • Oswald enters the Alaska dog race team and, despite many hazards and some cheating by the competitors, manages to come in first.

71. Alaskan Nights *(Krazy Kat)* 23 Apr. 1930; *p.c.:* Winkler for Colum; *anim:* Ben Harrison, Manny Gould; *mus:* Joe de Nat; *prod:* Charles Mintz; *b&w. sd:* WE. 6 min. • In an Alaskan barroom, Krazy falls for a dancing Señorita. A large villain appears and Krazy bursts him, releasing smaller villains.

72. Albert in Blunderland *(Fun and Facts About America)* 26 Aug. 1950; *p.c.:* John Sutherland prods for Harding College/MGM; *prod/dir:* John Sutherland. *col. sd.* 8 min. • No story available.

73. Alexander's Ragtime Band *(Screen Songs)* 9 May 1931; *p.c.:* The Fleischer Studio for Para; *prod:* Max Fleischer; *dir:* Dave Fleischer.

story/dir/anim: Rudy Zamora, Jimmie Culhane; *mus:* Art Turkisher; *song:* Irving Berlin; *b&w. sd:* WE. 6½ min. • A music teacher tries to teach a dog to play the piano. The instruments metamorphose and play themselves.

74. Ali Baba *(ComiColor)* 15 Jan. 1936; *p.c.:* Celebrity prods; *prod/dir:* Ub Iwerks; *mus:* Carl W. Stalling; *col:* Ciné. *sd:* PCP. 8 min. • Ali and his friend follow the thieves into a cave to recover stolen jewels.

75. Ali-Baba Bound *(Looney Tunes)* 10 Feb. 1940; *p.c.:* Leon Schlesinger prods for WB; *dir:* Robert Clampett; *story:* Melvin Millar; *anim/des:* Vive Risto; *ed:* Treg Brown; *voices:* Mel Blanc; *mus:* Carl W. Stalling; *prod sup:* Henry Binder, Raymond G. Katz; *b&w. sd:* Vit. 7 min. • Legionaire Porky is left to defend the fort against Ali Baba and his Dirty Sleeves with help from a baby camel.

76. Ali Baba Bunny *(Merrie Melodies)* 9 Feb. 1957; *p.c.:* WB; *dir:* Chuck Jones; *story:* Michael Maltese; *anim:* Richard Thompson, Ken Harris, Abe Levitow, Ben Washam. *fx:* Harry Love; *lay:* Maurice Noble. *back:* Philip de Guard; *ed:* Treg Brown; *voices:* Mel Blanc; *mus:* Carl Stalling, Milt Franklyn; *prod mgr:* John W. Burton; *prod:* Edward Selzer; *col:* Tech. *sd:* Vit. 7 min. • Bugs and Daffy stumble across Ali Baba's jewel-laden cave. Daffy immediately claims the contents for himself but has first to reckon with Hassan, the treasury guard.

77. Alias St. Nick *(Happy Harmonies)* 16 Nov. 1935; *p.c.:* MGM. *prod/dir:* Hugh Harman, Rudolf Ising; *voices:* Bernice Hansel; *mus:* Scott Bradley; *col:* Tech. *sd:* WE. 9 min. • All the mice are eagerly awaiting Santa's arrival on Christmas Eve when a hungry cat takes advantage of the situation.

78. Alice • *1930:* Alice's Little Parade 1 Sept. Alice's Tin Pony 15 Sept. Alice on the Farm 1 Oct. Alice Gets Stung 15 Oct. Alice the Jail Bird 1 Nov. Alice Wins the Derby 15 Nov. Alice's Egg Plant 1 Dec. Alice's Balloon Race 15 Dec. 1931. Alice in the Jungle 1 Jan. Alice Gets Stage Struck 15 Jan. Alice Chops the Suey 1 Feb. Alice's Orphan 15 Feb. Alice Loses Out 1 Mar. Alice Picks the Champ 15 Mar. Alice Plays Cupid 1 Apr. Alice Solves the Puzzle 15 Apr. Alice Rattled by Rats 1 May. Alice's Mysterious Mystery 15 May. • *b&w. sd:* Brunswick. *film/disc. l/a/anim.* • Sound reissues by Raytone Pictures. Distributed by Syndicate Pictures Corp. See separate items for stories.

79. Alice and the Dog Catcher *(Alice)* 1 July 1924; *p.c.:* Winkler for R-C Pictures; *dir:* Walt Disney; *anim:* Walt Disney, Rollin C. Hamilton; *i&p:* Lillian Bounds, Kathleen Dollard; *ph:* Harry Forbes; *l/a:* Virginia Davis, Leon Holmes, Joe Allen, Tommy Hicks; *b&w. sil.* 9 min. *l/a/anim.* • With the aid of her animal allies, Alice wrecks the dog catcher's wagon and frees the captives.

80. Alice and the Three Bears *(Alice)* 1 Dec. 1924; *p.c.:* Winkler for R-C Pictures; *dir:* Walt Disney; *anim:* Ubbe Iwerks, Rollin C. Hamilton; *i&p:* Lillian Bounds, Kathleen Dollard; *ph:* Mike Marcus; *ed:* George Winkler; *l/a:* Virginia Davis; *b&w. sil.* 9 min. *l/a/anim.* • Alice is captured by the Three Bears to be used as a vital ingredient in their "Hooch"! Julius, her cat, saves her from the sawmill with the aid of every one of his nine lives.

81. Alice at the Carnival *(Alice)* 7 Feb. 1927; *p.c.:* Winkler for R-C Pictures; *dir:* Walt Disney; *anim:* Ubbe Iwerks, Rollin C. Hamilton, Hugh Harman, Rudolf Ising; *i&p:* Irene Hamilton, Walker Harman; *ph:* Rudolf Ising; *l/a:* Margie Gay; *b&w. sil.* 9 min. *l/a/anim.* • Alice and Julius have fun on a scenic railway.

82. Alice Cans the Cannibals *(Alice)* 1 Jan. 1925; *p.c.:* Winkler for R-C Pictures; *dir:* Walt Disney; *anim:* Ubbe Iwerks, Rollin C. Hamilton, Thurston Harper; *i&p:* Lillian Bounds, Kathleen Dollard; *ed:* George Winkler; *ph:* Mike Marcus; *l/a:* Virginia Davis; *b&w. sil.* 9 min. *l/a/anim.* • Alice and Julius land on an island and succeed in fighting off a pack of hungry cannibals.

83. Alice Charms the Fish *(Alice)* 6 Sept. 1926; *p.c.:* Winkler for R-C Pictures. *dir:* Walt Disney. *anim:* Ubbe Iwerks, Rollin C. Hamilton, Hugh Harman, Rudolf Ising. *i&p:* Irene Hamilton, Walker Harman. *ph:* Rudolf Ising. *l/a:* Margie Gay; *b&w. sil.* 9 min. *l/a/anim.* • Alice and Julius try various methods to lure fish from the lake for their fish market. First cartoon be completed at Disney's new Hyperion Avenue studio.

84. Alice Chops the Suey *(Alice)* 17 Aug. 1925; *p.c.:* Winkler for R-C Pictures. *dir:* Walt Disney. *anim:* Ubbe Iwerks, Rollin C. Hamilton,

Hugh Harman, Rudolf Ising, Thurston Harper. *i&p:* Ruth Disney, Irene Hamilton, Hazelle Linston, Walker Harman; *ed:* George Winkler; *ph:* Rudolf Ising, Rees brothers; *l/a:* Margie Gay; b&w. sil. 9 min. *l/a/anim.* • Alice is kidnapped and taken to Chinatown with Julius in hot pursuit, disguised as a Chinaman.

85. Alice Cuts the Ice *(Alice)* 1 Nov. 1926; *p.c.:* Winkler for R-C Pictures; *dir:* Walt Disney; *anim:* Ubbe Iwerks, Rollin C. Hamilton, Hugh Harman, Rudolf Ising; *i&p:* Irene Hamilton, Walker Harman; *ph:* Rudolf Ising; *l/a:* Margie Gay; b&w. sil. 9 min. *l/a/anim.* • Ice-man Julius elopes with Alice's maid. Alice summons a cop and a chase ensues.

86. Alice Foils the Pirates *(Alice)* 24 Jan. 1927; *p.c.:* Winkler for R-C Pictures; *dir:* Walt Disney; *anim:* Ubbe Iwerks, Rollin C. Hamilton, Hugh Harman, Rudolf Ising; *i&p:* Irene Hamilton, Walker Harman; *ph:* Rudolf Ising; *l/a:* Margie Gay; b&w. sil. 9 min. *l/a/anim.* • Alice is held captive on Pete's pirate ship. Julius arrives and has a single-handed fight with captain and crew.

87. Alice Gets in Dutch (at School) *(Alice)* 1 Nov. 1924; *p.c.:* Winkler for R-C Pictures; *dir:* Walt Disney; *anim:* Ubbe Iwerks, Rollin C. Hamilton; *i&p:* Kathleen Dollard, Lillian Bounds; *ed:* George Winkler; *ph:* Harry Forbes, Mike Marcus; *l/a:* Virginia Davis, Walter "Spec" O'Donnell, Leon Holmes, David F. Hollander, Marjorie Sewell, Mrs. Hunt; b&w. sil. 9 min. *l/a/anim.* • While sitting in the classroom, Alice daydreams that her teacher mobilizes the school books to lead as an army against her.

88. Alice Gets Stung *(Alice)* 1 Feb. 1925; *p.c.:* Winkler for R-C Pictures; *dir:* Walt Disney; *anim:* Ubbe Iwerks, Rollin C. Hamilton, Thurston Harper; *i&p:* Lillian Bounds, Kathleen Dollard; *ph:* Mike Marcus, Phil Tannura; *l/a:* Virginia Davis; b&w. sil. 9 min. *l/a/anim.* • Alice and Julius go rabbit hunting. In the course of events Alice accidentally shoots a bear who chases them into a barrel along with a hornets' nest.

89. Alice Helps the Romance *(Alice)* 15 Nov. 1926; *p.c.:* Winkler for R-C Pictures. *dir:* Walt Disney; *anim:* Ubbe Iwerks, Rollin C. Hamilton, Hugh Harman, Rudolf Ising; *i&p:* Irene Hamilton, Walker Harman; *ph:* Rudolf Ising; *l/a:* Margie Gay; b&w. sil. 9 min. *l/a/anim.* • Alice hatches a plan to get Julius' girl back.

90. Alice Hunting in Africa *(Alice)* 15 Nov. 1924; *p.c.:* Winkler for R-C Pictures; *dir:* Walt Disney; *anim:* Ubbe Iwerks, Rollin C. Hamilton, Thurston Harper; *ed:* Margaret Winkler; *ph:* Roy O. Disney; *l/a:* Virginia Davis; b&w. sil. 7 min. *l/a/anim.* • Alice and Julius go on safari and shoot everything in sight from a lion to a mouse.

91. Alice in the Alps *(Alice)* 21 Mar. 1927; *p.c.:* Winkler for R-C Pictures; *dir:* Walt Disney; *anim:* Ubbe Iwerks, Rollin C. Hamilton, Hugh Harman, Rudolf Ising; *i&p:* Irene Hamilton, Walker Harman; *ph:* Rudolf Ising; *l/a:* Margie Gay; b&w. sil. 7 min. *l/a/anim.* • Julius acts as guide in the Swiss Alps.

92. Alice in the Big League *(Alice)* 22 Aug. 1927; *p.c.:* Winkler for R-C Pictures; *dir:* Walt Disney; *anim:* Ubbe Iwerks, Isadore Freleng, Hugh Harman, Rollin C. Hamilton, Ben Clopton, Les Clark, Norman Blackburn; *ph:* Rudolf Ising; *l/a:* Lois Hardwick; b&w. sil. 7 min. *l/a/anim.* • Alice plays umpire to the animals' baseball game.

93. Alice in the Jungle *(Alice)* 15 Dec. 1925; *p.c.:* Winkler for R-C Pictures; *dir:* Walt Disney; *anim:* Ubbe Iwerks, Rollin C. Hamilton, Hugh Harman, Rudolf Ising, Thurston Harper; *i&p:* Ruth Disney, Irene Hamilton, Hazelle Linston, Walker Harman; *ph:* Rudolf Ising; *l/a:* Virginia Davis; b&w. sil. 9 min. *l/a/anim.* • Alice and Julius are on safari until they are chased out of the jungle by lions, making their getaway on a flying pachyderm.

94. Alice in the Klondike *(Alice)* 27 June 1927; *p.c.:* Winkler for R-C Pictures; *dir:* Walt Disney; *anim:* Ubbe Iwerks, Rollin C. Hamilton, Hugh Harman, Rudolf Ising, Ben Clopton, Isadore Freleng, Norman Blackburn; *ph:* Rudolf Ising; *l/a:* Lois Hardwick; b&w. sil. 9 min. *l/a/anim.* • While in the Klondike, Alice and Julius strike gold. Peg-Leg Pete steals the gold but Julius manages to retrieve it.

95. Alice in the Wooly West *(Alice)* 4 Oct. 1926; *p.c.:* Winkler for R-C Pictures; *dir:* Walt Disney; *anim:* Ubbe Iwerks, Rollin C. Hamilton, Hugh Harman, Rudolf Ising; *i&p:* Ruth Disney, Irene Hamilton, Walker Harman; *ph:* Rudolf Ising; *l/a:* Margie Gay; b&w. sil. 9 min. *l/a/anim.* • Bootleg Pete robs the stagecoach and kidnaps Alice. Julius rides to the rescue.

96. Alice in Wonderland 22 Dec. 1933; *p.c.:* Leon Schlesinger Prods for Para; *anim seq:* Hugh Harman, Rudolf Ising. b&w. sd: WE. • Live-action version of Lewis Carroll's classic story: Tweedle Dum and Tweedle Dee (Jack Oakie & Roscoe Karns) meet Alice in the woods. They open a tiny door in a tree, revealing a screen where we see an animated sequence of *the Walrus and the Carpenter.*

97. Alice in Wonderland 28 July 1951; *p.c.:* Walt Disney Productions for RKO; *dir:* Clyde Geronimi, Hamilton Luske, Wilfred Jackson; adapted from "Alice in Wonderland" and "Through the Looking Glass" by Lewis Carroll; *story:* Winston Hibler, Ted Sears, Bill Peet, Erdman Penner, Joe Rinaldi, Milt Banta, Bill Cottrell, Dick Kelsey, Joe Grant, Dick Huemer, Del Connell, Tom Oreb, John Walbridge; *anim dir:* Milt Kahl, Ward Kimball, Frank Thomas, Eric Larson, John Lounsbery, Ollie Johnston, Wolfgang Reitherman, Marc Davis, Les Clark, Norm Ferguson; *anim:* Hal King, Don Lusk, Judge Whitaker, Cliff Nordberg, Hal Ambro, Harvey Toombs, Bill Justice, Fred Moore, Phil Duncan, Marvin Woodward, Bob Carlson, Hugh Fraser, Charles Nichols, Clarke Mallory; *fx:* Josh Meador, George Rowley, Dan MacManus, Blaine Gibson. *des:* Mary Blair, John Hench, Claude Coats, Ken Anderson, Don da Gradi; *lay:* Mac Stewart, Tom Codrick, Charles Philippi, A. Kendall O'Connor, Hugh Hennesy, Don Griffith, Thor Putnam, Lance Nolley; *back:* Ray Huffine, Ralph Hulett, Art Riley, Brice Mack, Dick Anthony, Thelma Witmer; *ed:* Lloyd Richardson; *sd:* C.O. Slyfield, Robert O. Cook, Harold J. Steck; special process: Ub Iwerks; *voices:* The Mad Hatter: Ed Wynn; *The Caterpillar:* Richard Haydn; *The Cheshire Cat:* Sterling Holloway; *The March Hare:* Jerry Colonna; *Alice:* Kathryn Beaumont *The Queen of Hearts:* Verna Felton; *Dum & Dee/Walrus & Carpenter:* Pat O'Malley; *The White Rabbit/Dodo:* Bill Thompson; *Alice's Sister:* Heather Angel; *The Doorknob:* Joseph Kearns; *Bill:* Larry Grey; *Bird in the tree:* Queenie Leonard; *The King of Hearts:* Dink Trout; *The Rose:* Doris Lloyd; *The Dormouse:* James MacDonald; *Card Painters:* The Mello-Men, Larry Grey, Ken Beaumont; *Flowers:* Queenie Leonard, Lucille Bliss; *White Rose:* Norma Zimmer; *Young Pansy voices:* Jimmy & Tommy Luske; *Flamingoes:* Pinto Colvig; *Eaglet:* Erdman Penner; *Chorus:* The Jud Conlon Chorus; *mus:* Oliver Wallace. *songs:* Bob Hilliard, Sammy Fain, Don Raye, Gene de Paul, Mack David, Jerry Livingston, Al Hoffman; *orch:* Joseph Dubin; *mus arr:* Jud Conlon; *mus ed:* Al Teeter; *prod sup:* Ben Sharpsteen. *col:* Tech. *sd:* RCA. 75 min. • Alice follows a white rabbit into a burrow and finds herself in a curious world where she can converse with anything animate or inanimate. She soon tires of this and wants to go home but discovers that leaving isn't quite so easy.

98. Alice in Wonderland 1951; *p.c.:* Punch Films *(New York)*/Union Generale Cinematographie *(Paris)*/Rank *(London)* for Electric Pictures. *prod/dir:* Lou Bunin; *l/a dir:* Dallas Bower; *des:* Ben W. Rubin; *unit mgr:* Sam Fisher; *asso dir (France):* Marcelle Maurette; *ass (France):* Vincent Permane; adapted from *Alice's Adventures in Wonderland* by Lewis Carroll; *story:* Henry Myers, Albert E. Lewin, Edward Eliscu; *ph (France):* Claude Renoir; *anim:* Erwin Broner, William King, Ben Radin, Oscar Fessler; *anim consultant:* Art Babbitt; *lay:* Eugene Fleury; *ed:* Inman (Ted) Hunter, Marity Cleris, Jacqueline Thiebot; *des:* Bernyce Polifka (Fleury); *art dir:* Irving Block; *tech dir:* Benjamin Berg; *fx:* Irving Block, Lloyd Knetchel; models: Jacques Lecoz, Herrmann Silversheer, Lillian Davis; *voices: Knave of Hearts:* Stephen Murray; *Queen of Hearts:* Pamela Brown; *The Cheshire Cat:* Felix Aylmer; *The White Rabbit:* Ernest Milton; *The King of Hearts:* David Read; *The Mad Hatter:* Raymond Bussieres; *The Ugly Duchess:* Joyce Grenfell; *also:* Jack Train, Ivan Staff, Peter Bull, Claude Hulbert; *mus:* Sol Kaplan; performed by the London Symphony Orchestra; *mus dir:* Ernest Irving; *mus ed:* Steve Dalby; *songs:* Henry Myers, Edward Eliscu; *snd ed:* Dennis Gurney; *sd:* Charles Testo, Gordon McCallum, Peter Davies, Bill Matthews, Tabarin; *col:* Ansco. *sd.* 83 min. (cut to 75 min). *l/a/anim.* • A live-action prologue has Stephen Murray as the Reverend Charles Dodgson telling Alice (Carol Marsh) and her sisters the story of how Alice follows a White Rabbit down a rabbit hole and discovers a fantasy world therein. Initiated in December of 1946, the live action and recordings were made in England, the animation was done in France and completed in New York. This combination of live-action and puppet animation was overshadowed by Disney's version of *Alice in Wonderland* on its initial release and was not reissued until 1986.

99. Alice Loses Out *(Alice)* 29 Apr. 1925; *p.c.:* Winkler for R-C Pictures; *dir:* Walt Disney; *anim:* Ubbe Iwerks, Rollin C. Hamilton,

Thurston Harper. *i&p:* Lillian Bounds, Kathleen Dollard; *ed:* George Winkler; *ph:* Mike Marcus; *l/a:* Margie Gay; b&w. *sil.* 9 min. *l/a/anim.* • Alice runs an animal hotel which has Julius doing all the work.

100. Alice on the Farm *(Alice)* 1 Jan. 1926; *p.c.:* Winkler for R-C Pictures; *dir:* Walt Disney; *anim:* Ubbe Iwerks, Rollin C. Hamilton, Hugh Harman, Rudolf Ising, Thurston Harper. *i&p:* Ruth Disney, Irene Hamilton, Hazelle Linston, Walker Harman; *ph:* Rudolf Ising; *l/a:* Margie Gay. b&w. *sil.* 9 min. *l/a/anim.* • Alice is kidnapped by Bootleg Pete and Julius rushes to her aid, armed with a bucket of starch.

101. Alice Picks the Champ *(Alice)* July 1925; *p.c.:* Winkler for R-C Pictures; *dir:* Walt Disney; *anim:* Ubbe Iwerks, Rollin C. Hamilton, Thurston Harper; *i&p:* Lillian Bounds, Kathleen Dollard, Hazelle Linston; *ed:* George Winkler; *ph:* Mike Marcus; *l/a:* Margie Gay; b&w. *sil.* 9 min. *l/a/anim.* • Alice spurs Julius into being Tough Pete's latest sparring partner.

102. Alice Plays Cupid *(Alice)* 15 Oct. 1925; *p.c.:* Winkler for R-C Pictures; *dir:* Walt Disney; *anim:* Ubbe Iwerks, Rollin C. Hamilton, Hugh Harman, Rudolf Ising, Thurston Harper; *i&p:* Ruth Disney, Irene Hamilton, Hazelle Linston, Walker Harman; *ed:* George Winkler; *ph:* Rudolf Ising; *l/a:* Margie Gay; b&w. *sil.* 9 min. *l/a/anim.* • Lifeguard Julius flirts with a girl cat he saves from drowning and they elope in a car driven by Alice.

103. Alice Rattled by Rats *(Alice)* 15 Nov. 1925; *p.c.:* Winkler for R-C Pictures; *dir:* Walt Disney; *anim:* Ubbe Iwerks, Rollin C. Hamilton, Hugh Harman, Rudolf Ising, Thurston Harper; *i&p:* Ruth Disney, Irene Hamilton, Hazelle Linston, Walker Harman; *ph:* Rudolf Ising; *l/a:* Margie Gay; b&w. *sil.* 9 min. *l/a/anim.* • Julius gets drunk while guarding Alice's house and lets the rats run rampant.

104. Alice Solves the Puzzle *(Alice)* 12 July 1925; *p.c.:* Winkler for R-C Pictures; *dir:* Walt Disney; *anim:* Ubbe Iwerks, Rollin C. Hamilton, Thurston Harper; *i&p:* Lillian Bounds, Kathleen Dollard; *ph:* Mike Marcus; *l/a:* Margie Gay; b&w. *sil.* 9 min. *l/a/anim.* • While Alice and Julius are swimming, Bootleg Pete "Collector of Rare Crossword Puzzles" gets drunk and tries to filch Alice's crossword.

105. Alice Stage Struck *(Alice)* 23 June 1925; *p.c.:* Winkler for R-C Pictures; *dir:* Walt Disney; *anim:* Ubbe Iwerks, Rollin C. Hamilton, Thurston Harper; *i&p:* Lillian Bounds; *ed:* George Winkler; *ph:* Mike Marcus; *l/a:* Margie Gay, Leon Holmes, Joe Allen, Marjorie Sewell; b&w. *sil.* 9 min. *l/a/anim.* • While in a production of "Uncle Tom's Cabin," Alice is knocked unconcious and dreams she and Julius are escaping on the ice floes from the villainous Bootleg Pete.

106. Alice the Beach Nut *(Alice)* 8 Aug. 1927; *p.c.:* Winkler for R-C Pictures; *dir:* Walt Disney; *anim:* Ubbe Iwerks, Isadore Freleng, Hugh Harman, Les Clark, Ben Clopton, Norman Blackburn; *ph:* Mike Marcus; *l/a:* Lois Hardwick; b&w. *sil.* 9 min. *l/a/anim.* • Lifeguard Julius saves a drowning female cat.

107. Alice the Collegiate *(Alice)* 7 Mar. 1927; *p.c.:* Winkler for R-C Pictures; *dir:* Walt Disney; *anim:* Ubbe Iwerks, Rollin C. Hamilton, Hugh Harman, Rudolf Ising, Robert Edmunds; *i&p:* Irene Hamilton, Walker Harman; *ph:* Rudolf Ising; *l/a:* Margie Gay; b&w. *sil.* 9 min. *l/a/anim.* • Alice is coach to an all-cartoon football team.

108. Alice the Fire Fighter *(Alice)* 18 Oct. 1926; *p.c.:* Winkler for R-C Pictures; *dir:* Walt Disney; *anim:* Ubbe Iwerks, Rollin C. Hamilton, Hugh Harman, Rudolf Ising; *i&p:* Irene Hamilton, Walker Harman; *ph:* Rudolf Ising; *l/a:* Margie Gay; b&w. *sil.* 9 min. *l/a/anim.* • Alice and her fire brigade rescue animals from a burning building.

109. Alice the Golf Bug *(Alice)* 10 Jan. 1927; *p.c.:* Winkler for R-C Pictures; *dir:* Walt Disney; *anim:* Ubbe Iwerks, Rollin C. Hamilton, Hugh Harman, Rudolf Ising; *i&p:* Irene Hamilton, Walker Harman; *ph:* Rudolf Ising; *l/a:* Margie Gay; b&w. *sil.* 9 min. *l/a/anim.* • Alice and Julius compete in a golf tournament.

110. Alice the Jail Bird *(Alice)* 15 Sept. 1925; *p.c.:* Winkler for R-C Pictures; *dir:* Walt Disney; *anim:* Ubbe Iwerks, Rollin C. Hamilton, Hugh Harman, Rudolf Ising, Thurston Harper; *i&p:* Ruth Disney, Irene Hamilton, Hazelle Linston, Walker Harman; *ed:* George Winkler; *ph:* Rudolf Ising; *l/a:* Margie Gay. b&w. *sil.* 9 min. *l/a/anim.* • Alice and Julius land in a jailyard rock-pile. They escape this penance by means of an ostrich.

111. Alice the Lumberjack *(Alice)* 27 Dec. 1926; *p.c.:* Winkler for R-C Pictures; *dir:* Walt Disney; *anim:* Ubbe Iwerks, Rollin C. Hamilton, Hugh Harman, Rudolf Ising; *i&p:* Irene Hamilton, Walker Harman; *ph:* Rudolf Ising; *l/a:* Margie Gay; b&w. *sil.* 9 min. *l/a/anim.* • While felling trees, Alice is kidnapped by Bootleg Pete and Julius pursues on a homemade sled.

112. Alice the Peacemaker *(Alice)* 1 Aug. 1924; *p.c.:* Winkler for R-C Pictures; *dir:* Walt Disney; *anim:* Ubbe Iwerks, Rollin C. Hamilton; *i&p:* Lillian Bounds, Kathleen Dollard; *ph:* Harry Forbes, Mike Marcus; *l/a:* Virginia Davis, Leon Holmes, Walter "Spec" O'Donnell; b&w. *sil.* 9 min. *l/a/anim.* • Alice relates the tale of a feuding cat and mouse who united when a reward was offered for their capture.

113. Alice the Piper *(Alice)* 15 Dec. 1924; *p.c.:* Winkler for R-C Pictures; *dir:* Walt Disney; *anim:* Ubbe Iwerks, Rollin C. Hamilton, Thurston Harper; *i&p:* Lillian Bounds, Kathleen Dollard; *ph:* Harry Forbes, Mike Marcus; *l/a:* Virginia Davis; b&w. *sil.* 9 min. *l/a/anim.* • Alice and Julius rid the town of Hamelin of their plague of rats by sucking them into a vacuum cleaner.

114. Alice the Toreador *(Alice)* 15 Jan. 1925; *p.c.:* Winkler for R-C Pictures; *dir:* Walt Disney; *anim:* Ubbe Iwerks, Rollin C. Hamilton, Thurston Harper; *i&p:* Lillian Bounds, Kathleen Dollard; *ed:* George Winkler; *ph:* Mike Marcus; *l/a:* Virginia Davis; b&w. *sil.* 9 min. *l/a/anim.* • Julius disguises himself as a bull in order to win a $10,000 bullfighting prize.

115. Alice the Whaler *(Alice)* 25 July 1927; *p.c.:* Winkler for R-C Pictures; *dir:* Walt Disney; *anim:* Ubbe Iwerks, Isadore Freleng, Hugh Harman, Rudolf Ising, Ben Clopton, Les Clark, Norman Blackburn; *ph:* Mike Marcus; *l/a:* Lois Hardwick; b&w. *sil.* 9 min. *l/a/anim.* • When Alice and crew finally harpoon a whale the creature drags them off into the sunset.

116. Alice Wins the Derby *(Alice)* 12 July 1925; *p.c.:* Winkler for R-C Pictures; *dir:* Walt Disney; *anim:* Ubbe Iwerks, Rollin C. Hamilton, Thurston Harper; *i&p:* Lillian Bounds, Kathleen Dollard, Hazelle Linston; *ed:* George Winkler; *ph:* Mike Marcus; *l/a:* Margie Gay; b&w. *sil.* 9 min. *l/a/anim.* • Julius rides a mechanical horse across the winning line in a steeplechase.

117. Alice's Auto Race *(Alice)* 4 Apr. 1927; *p.c.:* Winkler for R-C Pictures; *dir* Walt Disney; *anim:* Ubbe Iwerks, Rollin C. Hamilton, Hugh Harman, Rudolf Ising, Robert Edmunds, Paul J. Smith; *i&p:* Irene Hamilton, Walker Harman; *ph:* Rudolf Ising; *l/a:* Margie Gay; b&w. *sil.* 7 min. *l/a/anim.* • Alice and Julius compete in a road-race against their old adversary, Bootleg Pete.

118. Alice's Balloon Race *(Alice)* 15 Jan. 1926; *p.c.:* Winkler for R-C Pictures; *dir:* Walt Disney; *anim:* Ubbe Iwerks, Rollin C. Hamilton, Hugh Harman, Rudolf Ising, Thurston Harper. *i&p:* Ruth Disney, Irene Hamilton, Hazelle Linston, Walker Harman; *ph:* Rudolf Ising; *l/a:* Margie Gay; b&w. *sil.* 9 min. *l/a/anim.* • Alice and Julius are in a hot-air balloon race up against their arch rival, Bootleg Pete.

119. Alice's Brown Derby *(Alice)* 13 Dec. 1926; *p.c.:* Winkler for R-C Pictures; *dir:* Walt Disney; *anim:* Ubbe Iwerks, Rollin C. Hamilton, Hugh Harman, Rudolf Ising; *i&p:* Irene Hamilton, Walker Harman; *ph:* Rudolf Ising; *l/a:* Margie Gay; b&w. *sil.* 9 min. *l/a/anim.* • Julius rides a mechanical horse alongside Bootleg Pete in the Derby.

120. Alice's Channel Swim *(Alice)* 13 June 1927; *p.c.:* Winkler for R-C Pictures; *dir:* Walt Disney; *anim:* Ubbe Iwerks, Isadore Freleng, Hugh Harman, Rudolf Ising, Ben Clopton, Norman Blackburn, Les Clark; *ph:* Rudolf Ising; *l/a:* Lois Hardwick; b&w. *sil.* 9 min. *l/a/anim.* • Julius and Bootleg Pete compete to swim the English Channel with Alice as referee.

121. Alice's Circus Daze *(Alice)* 18 Apr. 1927; *p.c.:* Winkler for R-C Pictures; *dir:* Walt Disney; *anim:* Ubbe Iwerks, Rollin C. Hamilton, Hugh Harman, Rudolf Ising, Paul J. Smith; *i&p:* Irene Hamilton, Walker Harman; *ph:* Rudolf Ising; *l/a:* Lois Hardwick; b&w. *sil.* 9 min. *l/a/anim.* • Alice and Julius entertain the crowds as high-wire walkers.

122. Alice's Day at Sea *(Alice)* 1 Mar. 1924; *p.c.:* Winkler for R-C Pictures; *dir:* Walt Disney; *anim:* Ubbe Iwerks, Rollin C. Hamilton, Thurston Harper; *i&p:* Lillian Bounds, Kathleen Dollard; *ed:* Margaret Winkler; *ph:* Roy O. Disney; *l/a:* Virginia Davis; b&w. *sil.* 9 min. *l/a/anim.* • Alice daydreams she is involved with a shipwreck, encountering the denizen of the deep.

123. Alice's Egg Plant *(Alice)* 3 Apr. 1925; *p.c.:* Winkler for R-C Pictures; *dir:* Walt Disney; *anim:* Ubbe Iwerks, Rollin C. Hamilton, Thurston Harper; *i&p:* Lillian Bounds, Kathleen Dollard; *ph:* Mike Marcus; *l/a:* Dawn O'Day; b&w. sil. 9 min. *l/a/anim.* • When Alice's chickens go on strike, Julius manages to collect a wagonload of eggs as payment to watch a prize fight! Dawn O'Day continued her acting career under the name of Anne Shirley.

124. Alice's Fishy Story *(Alice)* 1 June 1924; *p.c.:* Winkler for R-C Pictures; *dir:* Walt Disney; *anim:* Walt Disney, Rollin C. Hamilton; *i&p:* Lillian Bounds, Kathleen Dollard; *ed:* Margaret Winkler; *l/a:* Virginia Davis, Leon Holmes, Walt Disney, Tommy Hicks; b&w. sil. 9 min. *l/a/anim.* • Alice abandons her piano lesson to go fishing. She spins a yarn of how she and Julius saved the Eskimos from starving by catching fish in an unorthordox fashion.

125. Alice's Knaughty Knight *(Alice)* 2 May 1927; *p.c.:* Winkler for R-C Pictures; *dir:* Walt Disney; *anim:* Ubbe Iwerks, Rollin C. Hamilton, Hugh Harman, Rudolf Ising, Paul J. Smith, Isadore Freleng; *i&p:* Irene Hamilton, Walker Harman; *ph:* Rudolf Ising; *l/a:* Lois Hardwick; b&w. sil. 9 min. *l/a/anim.* • Alice makes Julius a suit of armor out of junk so that he can fight an armor-clad Pete.

126. Alice's Little Parade *(Alice)* 1 Feb. 1926; *p.c.:* Winkler for R-C Pictures; *dir:* Walt Disney; *anim:* Ubbe Iwerks, Rollin C. Hamilton, Hugh Harman, Rudolf Ising, Thurston Harper; *i&p:* Ruth Disney, Irene Hamilton, Hazelle Linston, Walker Harman; *ph:* Rudolf Ising; *l/a:* Margie Gay; b&w. sil. 9 min. *l/a/anim.* • Julius leads an army of assorted animals in defeating the mice.

127. Alice's Medicine Show *(Alice)* 11 July 1927; *p.c.:* Winkler for R-C Pictures. *dir:* Walt Disney; *anim:* Ubbe Iwerks, Isadore Freleng, Hugh Harman, Rudolf Ising, Ben Clopton, Paul J. Smith, Les Clark, Norman Blackburn; *ph:* Rudolf Ising; *l/a:* Lois Hardwick; b&w. sil. 9 min. *l/a/anim.* • Alice and Julius demonstrate the benefits of their patent medicine then chase two pigs who steal some.

128. Alice's Monkey Business *(Alice)* 20 Sept. 1926; *p.c.:* Winkler for R-C Pictures; *dir:* Walt Disney; *anim:* Ubbe Iwerks, Rollin C. Hamilton, Hugh Harman, Rudolf Ising; *i&p:* Ruth Disney, Irene Hamilton, Walker Harman. *ph:* Rudolf Ising; *l/a:* Margie Gay; b&w. sil. 9 min. *l/a/anim.* • While big game hunting, Alice and Julius are put on trial before a lion judge ... then booted out of the jungle.

129. Alice's Mysterious Mystery *(Alice)* 15 Feb. 1926; *p.c.:* Winkler for R-C Pictures; *dir:* Walt Disney; *anim:* Ubbe Iwerks, Rollin C. Hamilton, Hugh Harman, Rudolf Ising, Thurston Harper; *i&p:* Ruth Disney, Irene Hamilton, Hazelle Linston, Walker Harman; *ph:* Rudolf Ising; *l/a:* Margie Gay; b&w. sil. 9 min. *l/a/anim.* • Alice and Julius track down a number of missing dogs to Bootleg Pete's sausage factory.

130. Alice's Orphan *(Alice)* Jan. 1926; *p.c.:* Winkler for R-C Pictures; *dir:* Walt Disney; *anim:* Ubbe Iwerks, Rollin C. Hamilton, Hugh Harman, Rudolf Ising, Thurston Harper; *i&p:* Ruth Disney, Irene Hamilton, Hazelle Linston, Walker Harman; *ph:* Rudolf Ising; *l/a:* Margie Gay; b&w. sil. 9 min. *l/a/anim.* • Julius finds an abandoned baby. Bathing and feeding the child proves quite a task.

131. Alice's Picnic *(Alice)* 30 May 1927; *p.c.:* Winkler for R-C Pictures; *dir:* Walt Disney; *anim:* Ubbe Iwerks, Rollin C. Hamilton, Hugh Harman, Rudolf Ising, Ben Clopton, Isadore Freleng, Norman Blackburn, Les Clark; *ph:* Rudolf Ising; *l/a:* Lois Hardwick; b&w. sil. 9 min. *l/a/anim.* • Alice's picnic is marred by the invasion of mice who steal their food.

132. Alice's Rodeo *(Alice)* 21 Fan. 1927; *p.c.:* Winkler for R-C Pictures; *dir:* Walt Disney; *anim:* Ubbe Iwerks, Rollin C. Hamilton, Rudolf Ising, Robert Edmunds; *i&p:* Irene Hamilton, Walker Harman; *ph:* Rudolf Ising; *l/a:* Margie Gay; b&w. sil. 9 min. *l/a/anim.* • Bootleg Pete steals Julius' prize money for "bucking bronco" riding. He and Alice pursue the bear and retrieve the cash.

133. Alice's Spanish Guitar *(Alice)* 29 Nov. 1926; *p.c.:* Winkler for R-C Pictures; *dir:* Walt Disney; *anim:* Ubbe Iwerks, Rollin C. Hamilton, Hugh Harman, Rudolf Ising; *i&p:* Irene Hamilton, Walker Harman; *ph:* Rudolf Ising; *l/a:* Margie Gay; b&w. sil. 9 min. *l/a/anim.* • Senorita Alice

is kidnapped by Putrid Pete and Gaucho Julius does his "Douglas Fairbanks" bit.

134. Alice's Spooky Adventure *(Alice)* 1 Apr. 1924; *p.c.:* Winkler for R-C Pictures; *dir:* Walt Disney; *anim:* Walt Disney, Rollin C. Hamilton; *ed:* Margaret Winkler; *ph:* Roy O. Disney; *l/a:* Virginia Davis, Leon Holmes, Walter "Spec" O'Donnell; b&w. sil. 9 min. *l/a/anim.* • As Alice dozes, she dreams she's in "Spooksville" where the ghosts give a concert.

135. Alice's Three Bad Eggs *(Alice)* 16 May 1927; *p.c.:* Winkler for R-C Pictures; *dir:* Walt Disney; *anim:* Ubbe Iwerks, Rollin C. Hamilton, Hugh Harman, Rudolf Ising, Paul J. Smith, Isadore Freleng, Norman Blackburn, Ben Clopton; *ph:* Rudolf Ising; *l/a:* Lois Hardwick; b&w. sil. 9 min. *l/a/anim.* • Pepper repels marauders from attacking the fort Alice is guarding.

136. Alice's Tin Pony *(Alice)* 20 Sept. 1925; *p.c.:* Winkler for R-C Pictures; *dir:* Walt Disney; *anim:* Ubbe Iwerks, Rollin C. Hamilton, Hugh Harman, Rudolf Ising, Thurston Harper; *i&p:* Ruth Disney, Irene Hamilton, Hazelle Linston, Walker Harman; *ed:* George Winkler; *ph:* Rudolf Ising; *l/a:* Margie Gay; b&w. sil. 9 min. *l/a/anim* • Bootleg Pete and his gang's plans to rob a train of its payroll shipment are thwarted by Alice and Julius.

137. Alice's Wild West Show *(Alice)* 1 May 1924; *p.c.:* Winkler for R-C Pictures; *dir:* Walt Disney; *anim:* Walt Disney, Rollin C. Hamilton; *i&p:* Lillian Bounds, Kathleen Dollard; *ed:* Margaret Winkler; *l/a:* Virginia Davis, Leon Holmes, Tommy Hicks; b&w. sil. 9 min. *l/a/anim* • The participants of Alice's show go on strike, so it's up to her to entertain the audience with tales of her harrowing adventures out west.

138. Alien: Resurrection 26 Nov. 1997; *p.c.:* Fox; *visual fx unit: visual fx prod:* Kerry Shea; *asst prod co-ord:* Wendy Grossberg, Theresa Lynch; *prod asst:* Jose Martin del Campo; *ed:* Marty November, Kristine McPherson, Leah Culton; *cg Aliens:* Blue Sky Studios, Inc.: *project creative sup:* Jan Carlée; *digital fx prod:* Christopher Scollard; *digital fx sup:* Mitch Kopelman; *digital fx co-ord:* Leslie Schor; *digital fx prod mgr:* Larry Gradus; *digital fx prod asst:* Christina Reyes; *modellers:* Mike Defeo, Alexander Levinson, Shaun Cusick; *anim:* Nina Bafaro, James Brishahan, Doug Dooley, Jesse Sugarman, Steve Talkowski; *digital fx art:* Rhett Bennatt, David Eshfault, Thame Hawkins; *technical anim:* Michael Eringis; *digital art:* John Siczewicz; David Mei; *digital fx ed:* Fritz Archer; *col:* Tech. *sd:* Dolby digital. Panavision. 93 min. *l/a.* • Live-action science fiction: Two thousand years after her death, Ellen Ripley is revitalized as a powerful human/alien cross-breed replica who continues her war against the aliens. Animated alien monsters, etc.

139. All a Bir-r-r-rd *(Looney Tunes)* 24 June 1950. *p.c.:* WB; *dir:* I. Freleng; *story:* Tedd Pierce; *anim:* Ken Champin, Virgil Ross, Arthur Davis, Emery Hawkins, Gerry Chiniquy; *lay:* Hawley Pratt; *back:* Paul Julian; *ed:* Treg Brown; *voices:* Mel Blanc, Bea Benaderet; *mus:* Carl Stalling; *prod mgr:* John W. Burton; *prod:* Edward Selzer; *col:* Tech. *sd:* Vit. 7 min. • Tweety is set upon by the ever-hungry Sylvester the cat while travelling in the baggage car of a train.

140. All About Dogs *(Terry-Toon)* 12 June 1942; *p.c.:* TT for Fox; *dir:* Connie Rasinski; *story:* John Foster; *mus:* Philip A. Scheib; *col:* Tech. *sd:* RCA. 7 min. • All types of "Man's Best Friend" and their peculiarities are depicted.

141. All Bull and a Yard Wide *(Aesop's Film Fables)* 16 Aug. 1927; *p.c.:* Fables Pictures Inc for Pathé; *dir:* Paul Terry; b&w. sil. 6 min. • No story available.

142. All Dogs Go to Heaven 17 Nov. 1989; *p.c.:* Goldcrest & Sullivan-Bluth Ltd.; *dir:* Don Bluth; *prod:* Don Bluth, Gary Goldman, John Pomeroy; *ex prod:* George A. Walker, Morris F. Sullivan; *co-dir:* Dan Kuenster, Gary Goldman; *story:* Don Bluth, Ken Cromar, Gary Goldman, Larry Leker, Linda Miller, Monica Parker, John Pomeroy, Guy Schulman, David Steinberg, David N. Weiss; *scr:* David N. Weiss; *storyboard:* Don Bluth, Dan Kuenster, Larry Leker, T. Daniel Hofstedt; *prod des:* Don Bluth, Larry Leker; *anim dir:* John Pomeroy, Linda Miller, Ralph Zondag, Dick Zondag, Lorna Pomeroy-Cook, Jeff Etter, Ken Duncan; *anim:* Jeffrey J. Varab, Jean Morel, Cathy Jones, Anne-Marie Bardwell, Silvia Hoefnagels, John Hill, Gary Perkovac, Fernando Moro, Ralf Palmer, Tom Roth, Charlie Bonifacio, Paul Newberry, Alain Costa, David G. Simmons, Michael Gagne, John Power, Enis Tahsin Özgûr, T. Daniel Hofstedt, Dave Brewster, Jose Abel,

Jesse Cosio, Donnachada Daly, Colm Duggan, Manuel Galiana, Kim Hagen-Jensen; Kent Hammerstrom, Dan Harder, Jon Hooper, Michael Kiely, Dave Kupczyk, Jorgen Lerdam, Josè Luis Moro, Wendy Perdue; *fx anim:* Stephen B. Moore, David Tidgwell, Diann Landau, Tom Hush, Joey Mildenberger, Bruce Heller, Peter Matheson, Bob Simmons, Peter Yamasaki, James Mansfield Jr., Kathleen Hodge, Jeff Howard, Brett Hisey, Jeff Topping, Garrett Wren, Arnie Wong, Sari Gennis, Marion Mathieu, Orla Madden, Rolando Mercado, Janette Owens, Conor Thunder, Phil Cummings, Martine Finucane, Debbie Middleton-Kupczyk, Gillian Anderson, Julie Phelan; *lay:* Scott Caple, David Goetz, Amy Berenz, John Byrne, David Gardner, Kevin Gollaher, Eddie Gribbin, Giorgio Mardegan, Fred Reilly, Mark Swan; *back stylist:* Don Moore; *back:* Barry Atkinson, Rick Bentham, Carl Jones, Sunny Apinchapong, David McCamley, Mannix Bennett, Paul M. Kelly; *rough break/inbet:* Tamara Anderson, Hope Devlin, Sandra Ryan, Jane Anderson, Peter Anderson, Leslie Aust, Matthew Bates, Adrienne Bell, Celine Cahill, Marc Christiansen, David Cribbin, Frank Doyle, John Eddings, Robert Fox, Damien Gilligan, David Groome, Martin Hanley, Michael Hansen, Tom Higgins, Paul Houlihan, Roisin Hunt, Noel Kiernan, Fiona Lynch, Jane Leganger, Joe McDonough, Paddy Malone, Maibritt Mortsensen, Randy Sanchez, Andrea Simonti, Michael Stocker, Todd Waterman; *clean-up:* Olivia O'Mahony, Mark Pudleiner, Doug Bennett, Eileen Conway, Bob Cowan, Nollaig Crombie, Alan Fleming, Bill Giggie, Anne Heeney, Silvia Hoefnagels, Paul Kelly, Helen Lawlor, Ashley McGovern, Neil McNeill, Brian McSweeney, Terry Pike, Jens Pindal, Robert Rivard, Wendo van Essen, Richard Vanette, Annette Byrne-Morel, Kris van Alphen, Richard Bazley, Mark Byrne, Michael Carey, Michael Cassidy, Mary Connors, Peter Donnelly, Martin Fagan, Sylvia Fitzpatrick, Conor Flynn, Des Forde, Kevin Fraser, Melissa Freeman, Michael Garry, Gerry Gogan, Catherine Gurry, Tine Karebeck, Barbara Krueger, Ann McCormick, Margaret McKenna, James McLoughlin, Maria Malone, Anne-Marie Mockler, James Moller, Jan Naylor, Anna Neilsen, Dympna O'Halloran, Gary O'Neill, Tara O'Reilly, John A. Power, Miriam Reid, Eileen Ridgeway, Julie Ryan, Paul Shannahan, Melanie Sowell, Hugh Tattan, Barbara Butterworth, Leonard Johnson; *anim check:* Carla Washburn, Lisa Joko, Pam Kleyman, Christine Fluskey, Orla Coughlan, Michele McKenna, Debra Pugh, Helen O'Flynn, Mary Walsh, Mary Boyle, Lucy Melia, Nina Phipps, Aoife Woodlock; *col stylists:* Carmen Oliver, Susan Vanderhorst, Laurie Curran, Donal Freeney, Violet McKenna, Suzanne O'Reilly, Melanie Burke, Majella Burns, Mary Cuthbert, Josephine Mulraney-Hales; *fx paint:* Shirley (Sam) Mapes, Iseult Travers; *ed:* John K. Carr, Lisa Dorney, Fiona Trayler, Gary Keleghan; *voices: Itchy:* Dom de Luise; *Charlie;* Burt Reynolds; *Dog Caster:* Daryl Gilley; *Vera:* Candy Devine; *Killer:* Charles Nelson Reilly; *Carface:* Vic Tayback; *Whippet Angel:* Melba Moore; *Anne-Marie:* Judith Barsi; *Harold:* Rob Fuller; *Kate:* Earleen Carey; *Stella Dallas:* Anna Manahan; *Sir Reginald:* Nigel Pegram; *Flo:* Loni Anderson; *King Gator:* Ken Page; *Terrier:* Godfrey Quigley; *Mastiff:* Jay Stevens; "Love Survives" sung by Irene Cara, Freddie Jackson; *mus:* Ralph Burns; *songs:* Charles Strouse, T.J. Kuenster; *title song:* Al Kasha, Joel Hirschhorn, Michael Lloyd; *mus/post prod ex:* Roy Simpson; *prod:* Michael Lloyd; *ex prod:* David Franco; music performed by The London Symphony Orchestra/The UK Orchestra Ensemble; *arrangers:* Harvey R. Cohen, Richard Bronskill; *mus copyist:* Vic Frazer; *mus rec:* Keith Grant, Jerry O'Riordan; *mus editor:* Michael O'Connor, Simon Cowper; *sd mix:* Gerry Humphreys, Dean Humphreys; *sd ed:* John C. Carr, Kevin Brazier, Joe Gallagher, Anthony Morris; *foley:* Taj Soundworks, Andrew Stears, Kevin Bartnof, Alicia Stevenson, Dan O'Connell, Jim Ashwill, Greg Orloff, Mary Jo Lang, Rody Hassano; *col timer:* John Stanborough; *neg cutter:* Colin Ives; *ph:* Ciavàn Morris, Jim Mann, Aidan Farrell, Gary Hall, Eimear Joyce, Fiona Mackle, Jeanette Maher, John O'Flaherty, Eithne Quinn, Eric Ryan, Paddy Duffy, Freddy McGavin; *asst dial ed:* Jim Fleming; *video ph:* Wayne Farrar, Annette Stone; *scene plan:* Aran O'Reilly, Gerard Carty, Sean Dempsey, John Phelan; *Xerography:* Michael Murray, Daryl Carstensen, Collette O'Brien, Pedar O'Reilly, Emmet Doyle, Mary Boylan, Tommy Brennan, Robert Byrne, William Colgan, Pearse Cullinane, Yvonne McSweeney, Dympna Murray, Anthony O'Brien, Frank Richards, Kieron White; *Xerox check:* John Finnegan, Brendan Harris, Stuart Johnstone, Siobhan O'Brien, Paul Roy, Pauline Walsh, Andy Fitzgerald, Anne-Marie Daly; *mark-up:* Patricia Browne, Maria Farrell, Karl Hayes, Elaine Woods; *ink:* Jacqueline Hooks, Mary Gavin, Maureen Buggy, Madeleine Downes, Claudia Dickerson, Joseph Manifold, Karen Dwyer, Ailish Mullally, Mary

Sheridan, Kenneth Slevin, Karin Stover; *computer anim dir:* Mark Swanson; *asst dir:* Nuala O'Toole, Moya Mackle; *computer anim:* Dave Goetz, Don Pierce, Paul Bolger, Ben Burgess, Denis Deegan, Patrick Gleeson, Edward Goral, Rob Koo, Jerr O'Carroll, Kevin O'Neil, Mark Povey, Russell Stoll, Greg Tiernan, Konrad Winterlich; *blue sketch:* Mary Delaney, Linda Fitzpatrick, Sheila Kelly; *paint:* Deborah Rykoff, Brenda McGuirk, Melanie Strickland, John P. Brennan, Andrew Molloy, Noirin Dunne, Janet O'Carroll, Pauline Morahan, Seamus Grogan; *cel painters:* Ann Brennan, Louise Carroll, Michael Carroll, Yvonne Carthy, Nicholas Connolly, Conor Coughlan, Bryan Doyle, Gloria Dunne, Tom English, Greg Fulton, Philip Garry, Patricia Gordan, Liam Hannan, Karen Hennessy, Liam Hoban, David Hogan, Fiona Hogan, Sandra Keely, Linda Kellagher, Brian Kelly, Pearse Love, Petula Masterson, Ciara McCabe, Caroline McCann, Martina McCarron, Shane McCormick, Colin McGrath, Geraldine McGuinness, Ian McLoughlin, Ann May, Kate Meredith, Majella Milne, Mary B. Mulvihill, Moira Murphy, Ronan Nally, Tracy Nelson, David Nolan, Catherine O'Connor, Hugh O'Connor, Philip O'Connor, Brid Ni Dhonaill, Cathy O'Leary, Barry O'Shea, Gerard J.D. Philips, Antoinette Rafter, Derek Reid, Carlyn Rumgay, June Scannell; *paint check:* Michael Casey, Gerard Coleman, Sinead Murray, Colum Slevin; *cel service:* Sandra Breslin, Kevin Condron; *models:* Barry Atkinson, Mannix Bennett, Rick Bentham; *l/a models:* Kerri-Ellen Lawlor, Cami Pomeroy; *opticals:* Caroline Gaynor, Sullivan-Bluth Studios, Optical Film Effects Ltd.; *service systems engineer:* Karl Bredendieck; *engineering:* Liam Halpin, John Henry. Neil Neaveney; *studio ex:* Andrew Fitzpatrick; *prod D.P.:* Fiona Keating; *prod mgrs:* Gerry Shirren, Thad Weinlein; *prod sup:* Russell Boland, Cathy Carr-Goldman, Olga Craig; *prod asst:* Yvonne Costello, Bernie Keogh, Jane McLoughlin, Anne Murray, Caroline Lynch, Deborah Morgan, Mary O'Halloran, Kerri Swanson, *(USA):* Caralyn Warren, Julie Heinz, Dan Levine, Carol Raikes; *post prod admin:* Tina Jones; *col:* Tech. *sd:* Dolby stereo. 84 min. • Having escaped from the dog pound, Charlie, a German Shepherd, and his pal Itchy return to his gambling casino now run by his business partner, a pitbull named Carface. Unwilling to split the profits, the pitbull orders the demise of his former colleague. Charlie is hit by an automobile and drowns in the bay, resulting in finding himself at the gates of Dog Heaven. As there are no records of any good deeds carried out by Charlie to assure his entrance, he is returned to earth and seeks revenge but not before first stealing a "Heavenly Watch" which will prolong his life on Earth. Charlie and Itchy discover that Carface has been using the talents of an orphan girl who can converse with animals and predict racing winners. They unite with the girl and win on a long shot. Carface snatches the girl back and Charlie rushes to her rescue, sending the villain to a fitting end but, dropping his heavenly watch, is immediately summoned back to Dog Heaven.

143. All Dogs Go to Heaven 2 29 Mar. 1996; *p.c.:* MGM; *dir:* Larry Leker, Paul Sabella; *story:* Mark Young, Kelly Ward; *scr:* Arne Olsen, Kelly Ward, Mark Young; *prod:* Jonathan Dern, Paul Sabella, Kelly Ward, Mark Young; *asso prod:* Helene Blitz; *storyboard:* Dino Athanassiou, John Byrne, John Dorman, Thom Enriquez, David Feiss, Silvia Hoefnagels, Cathy Jones, Andrew Knight, Jørgen Lerdam, Jesper Møller, Larry Scholl, Todd Waterman; *seq dir:* Dino Athanassiou, Paul Schibli; *anim prod:* Gillian Bolger; *anim sup:* Emmanuel Franck, Maurice Giacomini; *anim co-ord:* Bernie Keogh; *dir anim:* Doug Bennett, Eric "Bibo" Bergeron, David Feiss, Manuel Galiana, Julian Harris, Silvia Hoefnagels, Jørgen Lerdam, Daniel Sumich, Todd Waterman, John Williamson; *character anim:* Juan Antonio Torres Garcia, Carmen González Gómez, Michael Helmuth Hansen, Borja Montoro, Jens Pindal, John Power, Ventura Rodriguez, Jesper Møller, Borja Montoro, Tony Tulipano, Jan Van Buyten; *anim:* José Sánchez Alonso, Ian B. Anderson, Meelis Arulepp, Barry Baker, Cécile Bender, Arnaud Berthier, Neil Boyle, Rune Brandt Bennicke, Michael Burgess, Rafael Diaz Canales, Peter Candeland, Farouk Cherfi, Stan Chiu, Paul Chung, Odile Comon, Marcos Aurelio Corrêa, Denis Couchon, Caroline Cruikshank, Ricardo Curtis, Denis Deegan, Rogerio DeGodoy, Nivaldo Delmaschio, Piet De Rycker, Colm Duggan, Luca Fattore, Bruce Ferriz, Chuck Gammage, Bill Giggie, Morgan Ginsberg, David Gosman, Antony Gray, Jurgen Gross, Julian Harris, Lesley Headrick, Krista Heij, Alexandre Hesse, Magnus Hjerpe, Francisco Alaminos Hódar (Paco Alaminos), Miguel Alaminos Hódar (Miguel Alaminos), Steve Horrocks, Jakob Hjort Jensen, Bo Johannesson, Ken Keys, Sean Leaning, Philippe

Le Brun, Williams Le Métayer, Thomas Lock, Anders Neisum Madsen, Martin Madsen, Kevin McDonagh, Sylvia Muller, Khai Nguyen, Karin Nilsson, Jens Pindal, Panagiotis Rappas, Mitch Rose, Marc Sevier, Robert Shedlowich, Maureen Shelleau, Andrew Shortt, John Skibinski, Janus Sorgenfrey, Kevin Spruce, Greg Stainton, Rob Stevenhagen, Ando Tammik, Tony Tulipano, Athanassios Vakalis, Darren Vandenburg, Duncan Varley, Andreas von Andrian, Simon Ward-Horner, Jonathan Webber, Andreas Wessel-Therhorn, Peter Western, Mark Williams; *asst anim:* Paul Baker, Janine Dawson, Hope Devlin Kristiansen, Thomas Fenger, Robin Gott, Gerard Hannigan, Damien Harris, Judy Howieson, Anne-Marie Irlande, Søren Jacobsen, Tinna Jespersen, Tine Karrebæk, Marlene Laugesen, Adam Rapson, Antonella Russo, Valérie Schaefer, Christian "Micro" Seidel, Bruce Simpson, Irene Sparre Hjorthøi, Rigmor Tokerød; *trainee anim:* Des Forde, Leon Gruizinga, Róisin Hunt, Paul Lee, Paddy Malone, Niall Mooney, Niall O'Loughlin; *rough inbet:* Gerard Brady, Mark C. Byrne, Michael Carroll, Sarah Dick, Hilary Gough, Joseph Haugh, Paul Joyce, Matt Kowaliszyn, Ryan McElhinney, Majella Milne, Bernadette Moley, Gavin Murphy, Simon Northwood, Lorraine O'Connell, Andrea Preda, Ray Woods, June Wright; *overseas clean-up sup:* Miriam Reid; *clean-up sup:* Deborah Ahee, Fionnuala Balance, Denise Bradshaw, Alan Dickson, Cathy Jones, Jane McLoughlin, Eileen Ridgeway; *key clean-up:* Melanie Allen, Lillian Andre, Kyung-Hee Baker, Vittoria Bologna, Thomas Brennan, Peter R. Brown, Elsie Chen, Kevin Condron, Mary Connors, Nollaig Crombie, Rowena Cruz, Teresa Cunliffe, Anne Daniels, Michel Dazé, Helga Egilson, Nicola Flynn, Jon Hammond, Craig Hilditch, Weronika Kapelanska, Linda Kellagher, Royce Langford, Namkook Lee, Beverly Lehman, Kurt Lehner, Charlene Logan, Grant Lounsbury, Shane McCormack, Kevin McGibbon, Kevin Mecalfe, Anne Marie Mockler, Bernadette Moley, Sinead Murray, Carol O'Mara, Alan O'Regan, Chris Palimaka, Andy Paraskos, Darren Power, Royston Robinson, Patrick Rowsome, Julie Ryan, Jen Sherman, Cindy Tanner, Davoud Teleghani, Mark Thornton, Jan Tillcock, Lynn Yamazaki, Julie Jie Yuan; *clean-up:* Martyn Jones, Philip Anderson, Eric Athanassiou, Mike Bass, Michael Boylan, Monique Buchens, Paul Clare, John Cooley, Nicola Courtney, Jason Deegan, Chris Drew, Stuart Evans, Tanya Fenton, Nathalie Gavet, Thomas Gravestock, Aidan Heffernan, Natalie Higgs, Hon-sik Kim, Niall Laverty, John Lin, Roger Lougher, Simon Loxton, Gianni Malpeli, Katerina Manolessou, Rowena Marella-Daw, Sarah Marsden, Dave McFall, Janet McKay, Helen Michael, Kamye Miessen, Robert Milne, Karen Narramore, Annie O'Dell, George O'Shea, Terry O'Toole, David Parle, Thomas Payne, J.C. Pearson, Mike Pfeil, Kristina Pindal, Vittoria Quane, Isabel Radage, Kay Sales, Alan Shannon, Donnacha Treacy, Audrey Walsh, John R. Walsh, Alison Wells; *clean-up inbet:* Enzo Avolio, Jee Chan Baylis, Joselito Bien, Ron Chevarie, Jean Deleani, Mike Demur, Sheryl Doland, Gloria Hsu, Karen Kewell, Joel de la Cruz, Brad Lucas, Lynn MacQuarrie, Gus Papoutsis, Oleh Prus, Donna Rutz, Kim Stubbs-Law, Allen Swerling, Paul West, Tim White; *fx anim sup:* Raymond Pang; *fx anim:* Peter R. Brown, Bob Cowan, Mark Cumberton, Trevor Davies, Peter Denomme, Michael Ho, Orla Madden, Kevin McGibbon, Mike McKay, Janette Owens; *fx anim asst:* Michaela Budde, Janet Cable, Marc Ellis, Joanne Gooding; *computer anim:* David Satchwell; *anim check:* Fiona Mackle, Martina McCarron, Moira Murphy; *character des:* Dino Athanassiou, David Feiss, Jon Hammond, Cathy Jones, Neill McNeil, Rob Stevenhagen, Deane Taylor; *art dir:* Deane Taylor; *asst art dir:* Paul M. Kelly, Peter Sheehan, Richard Zaloudek; *col stylist:* Violet McKenna, Sharon Blake, Yvonne Carthy, Karen Hennessy, Linda Keegan, Ann McCormick, Dallas Synnott; *lay:* Edward Gribbin, Amy Louise Berenz, Mark T. Byrne, Des Duggan, Stefan Fjeldmark, Stefanie Gignac, Martin Hanley, Andrew Hickson, Brendan Houghton, Glenn Jeffs, Kevin Klis, Brad Markewitz, Robert McCauley, Panagiotis Rappas, Aaron Ryan, Christopher Scully, Richard Simmons, Mike Tweedle, Sonya Wade, Ron Wilson; *back sup:* Niamh McClean; *back:* Erric Fokkens, Miguel Gil, Charlotte Houwing, Kevin McNamara, Thierry Million, David Nolan, Stephen Robinson, Owen Rohu, Norman Teeling; *ed:* Tony Garber, Michael Bradley, Karen Doulac, Paula Fitzpatrick, Christopher Kroll, Susan Odjakjian; *voices: Carface:* Ernest Borgnine; *Anabelle, the Dog Goddess:* Bebe Neuwirth; *Charles B. "Charlie" Barkin:* Charlie Sheen; *Chihuahua:* Hamilton Camp; *Short Customs Dog:* Steve MacKall; *Tall Customs Dog:* Dan Castellaneta; *Itchy Itchiford:* Dom de Luise; *Reginald:* Tony Jay; *Jingles:* Jim Cummings; *Labrador M.C.:* Wallace Shawn; *Sasha la Fleur:* Sheena Easton; *Red:* George Hearn; *David:* Adam Wylie; *St. Bernard Diliter Andrews:*

Kevin Michael Richardson; *Officer McDowell:* Pat Corley; *Officer Reyes:* Marabina James; *Thom:* Bobby Di Cicco; *Claire:* Annette Helde; *Lost and Found Officer:* Maurice La Marche; *Charlie singing voice:* Jesse Corti; *mus:* Mark Watters, Charles Fernandez; *orch:* Larry Blank, John Given, Ira Hearshen, Larry Kenton, Christopher Klatman, Mark Watters, Rick Wentworth; *score rec:* Niall Acott, Dan Gellert, Steve Price; *mus ed:* Joseph R. Thygesen; *mus copyist:* Tony Stanton; *mus rec engineer:* Rick Winquest; *scene plan:* Carl Keenan, Kieran Cummings, Eimear Clonan, Noelle Quinn; *paint:* Carmel Gavin; *ph:* Joseph Chan, Steve Sanderson; *neg cutter:* Gary Burritt, *col timer:* Jim Passon; *telecine colorist:* Kathy Thomson; *model clean-up:* Soonjin Mooney; *final check:* Sue O'Loughlin; *continuity:* Sinead Price; *dial rec engineer:* Harry Andronis, Kraig Knutson, Tom Maydeck, Jeff Robeff, Jeff Sheridan; *dial ed:* Bonnie Dombrowski; *foley:* Jim Ashwill, John T. Cucci, Linda Lew, Dan O'Connell; *ADR rec:* Dana Johnson-Porter, Robert Deschaine, Roy B. Yokelson; *mix engineer:* Karal Brendendieck; *re-rec mix:* Chris David, Paul Massey; *sd ed:* Elliott Koretz, Gary S. Gerlich, Gregory M. Gerlich, Anne Laing; *sd rec:* Robin Johnson, Matt Patterson; *re-take:* Susan Kapigian; *dts stereo sound consult:* Mark Lewer; *machine room loader:* Brian D. Lucas, Art Schiro; *prod sup:* Pascal Chevé, Michele McKenna-Mahon, Hughie Shevlin; *prod mgr:* Jesse Fawcett, Daniel J. Wiley; *co-prod mgr:* Robert Winthrop; *ex asst:* Deena Doherty; *asst to sup:* Karen Dove; *prod asst:* Jason Boyer, Sandra Breslin, Aaron Daniel, Bernadette Dowling, Lucy McMahon, Siobhan O'Brien, Nina Phipps, Paul Rudyk, Kim Stubbs-Law; *col. sd:* dts. 82 min. • Charlie the German Shepherd is in Dog Heaven when Gabriel's Horn, essential in opening the Pearly Gates, plummets Earthwards. He manages to persuade the Head Angel to let him return to San Francisco to retrieve it. After teaming up with his old buddy Itchy, a canine nightclub entertainer named Sasha and a runaway boy called David, Charlie discovers that Carface, the mobster pitbull, has posession of the horn for use against Dog Heaven.

144. All for a Bride *(Aesop's Film Fables)* 13 Mar. 1927; *p.c.:* Fables Pictures Inc for Pathé; *dir:* Paul Terry; b&w. sil. 6 min. • No story available.

145. All Fowled Up *(Looney Tunes)* 19 Feb. 1955; *p.c.:* WB; *dir:* Robert McKimson; *story:* Charles McKimson, Sid Marcus; *anim:* Phil de Lara, Richard Thompson, Keith Darling; *lay:* Robert Givens; *back:* Richard H. Thomas; *ed:* Treg Brown; *voices:* Mel Blanc; *mus:* Carl Stalling; *prod mgr:* John W. Burton; *prod:* Edward Selzer; *col:* Tech. *sd:* Vit. 7 min. • Foghorn Leghorn's physical excercises are momentarily interrupted by Henry Hawk's persistance in securing a chicken for lunch.

146. All Hams on Deck *(Woody Woodpecker)* 9 Nov. 1970; *p.c.:* Walter Lantz prods for Univ; *dir:* Paul J. Smith; *story:* Sid Marcus; *anim:* Les Kline, Al Coe; *sets:* Nino Carbe; *voices:* Dal McKennon, Grace Stafford; *mus:* Walter Greene; *prod mgr:* William E. Garity; *col:* Tech. *sd:* RCA. 6 min. • Woody deals with Captain Blah, the pirate, who is just about to bury some stolen gold.

147. All in a Nutshell *(Donald Duck)* 2 Sept. 1949; *p.c.:* Walt Disney prods for RKO; *dir:* Jack Hannah; *story:* Bill Berg, Nick George; *anim:* Bill Justice, Judge Whitaker, Bob Carlson, Volus Jones; *fx:* Jack Boyd; *lay:* Yale Gracey; *back:* Thelma Witmer; *voices:* Clarence Nash, Dessie Flynn, James MacDonald; *mus:* Oliver Wallace; *col:* Tech. *sd:* RCA. 7 min. • Donald manages a successful nut-butter factory until the chipmunks show up and eat all his produce.

148. All Out for V *(Terry-Toon)* 7 Aug. 1942; *p.c.:* TT for Fox; *dir:* Mannie Davis; *story:* John Foster; *mus:* Philip A. Scheib; *col:* Tech. *sd:* RCA. 7 min. *Academy Award nomination.* • All the forest animals mobilize for further war production.

149. The All Star Cast *(Aesop's Film Fable)* 9 Mar. 1924; *p.c.:* Fables Pictures Inc for Pathé; *dir:* Paul Terry; b&w. sil. 6 min. • A menagerie of circus acts play to an all-animal audience.

150. All Teed Off *(Sad Cat)* Dec. 1967; *p.c.:* TT for Fox; *col:* DeLuxe. *sd:* RCA. 5 min. • Sad Cat caddies for his mean brothers until his Super Ego turns him into a golf pro. • See: *Sad Cat*

151. All This and Rabbit Stew *(Dingbat)* Aug. 1950; *p.c.:* TT for Fox; *dir:* Connie Rasinski; *story:* Tom Morrison; *anim:* Jim Tyer; *voices:* Dayton Allen, Tom Morrison; *mus:* Philip A. Scheib; *ph:* Douglas Moye; *col:* Tech. *sd:* RCA. 7 min. • Dingbat joins forces with a rabbit against two hungry buzzards.

152. All This and Rabbit Stew (*Merrie Melodies*) 13 Sept. 1941; *p.c.:* Leon Schlesinger for WB; *dir:* Fred Avery; *story:* Dave Monahan, Robert Clampett; *anim:* Virgil Ross; *ed:* Treg Brown; *back:* John Didrik Johnsen; *voices:* Mel Blanc, Darrell R. Payne; *mus:* Carl W. Stalling; *prod sup:* Henry Binder, Raymond G. Katz; *col:* Tech. *sd:* Vit. 7 min. • A colored hunter tries to shoot Bugs who eventually wins all his clothes in a crap game.

153. All Together 13 Jan. 1942; *p.c.:* Walt Disney prods for NFB; *dir:* Ub Iwerks; *asst dir:* Erwin Verity; *anim:* Joshua Meador; *lay:* Robert Cormack; *voice:* Cliff Edwards, Kate Ellen Murtagh; *col:* Tech. *sd:* RCA. 2 min. • Pinocchio, Gepetto, Figaro, Donald and his nephews, Mickey, Goofy, Clarabelle Cow, Horace Horsecollar and the Seven Dwarfs all march past the Canadian Parliament Building. Produced to show the availability and necessity of purchasing Canadian War Bonds.

154. All Wet (*Oswald the Lucky Rabbit*) 31 Oct. 1927; *p.c.:* Winkler for Univ; *dir:* Walt Disney; *story:* Ubbe Iwerks; *anim:* Ubbe Iwerks, Rollin C. Hamilton, Hugh Harman, Isadore Freleng, Ben Clopton, Paul J. Smith, Norman Blackburn; *i&p:* Les Clark; *ph:* Mike Marcus; b&w. sil. 7 min. • Oswald quickly switches from hot-dog vendor to lifeguard when he spies a pretty lady rabbit drowning in the sea.

155. Allegretto 1936; *p.c.:* Oskar Fischinger for Pyramid Films; *prod/dir/anim:* O.W. Fischinger; *mus:* Ralph Rainger; *col:* Gaspar. *sd.* 8 min. • Color designs set to music. Originally commissioned by Paramount for inclusion in *The Big Broadcast of 1937*, then scrapped as being too lengthy. Issued independently at a later date.

156. Allegro 1939; *p.c.:* Norman McLaren for the Guggenheim Museum; *dir/anim:* Norman McLaren; *col. sd.* 2 min. • Designs animated directly on to film.

157. The Alley Cat (*MGM cartoon*) 5 July 1941; *p.c.:* MGM; *prod:* Hugh Harman; *anim:* Preston Blair; *sets:* John Meandor; *back:* Joe Smith; *voices:* Harry E. Lang, Sara Berner; *mus:* Scott Bradley; *prod mgr:* Fred Quimby; *col:* Tech. *sd:* WE. 9 min. • An alley cat invades the mansion of a pedigree kitten, giving the guard dog the run-around.

158. Alley to Bali (*Woody Woodpecker*) 15 Mar. 1954.; *p.c.:* Walter Lantz prods for Univ; *dir:* Don Patterson; *story:* Homer Brightman; *anim:* Herman Cohen. Ray Abrams, Ken Southworth; *sets:* Raymond Jacobs, Art Landy; *voices:* Dallas McKennon, Grace Stafford; *mus:* Clarence Wheeler; *prod mgr:* William E. Garity; *col:* Tech. *sd:* RCA. 6 min. • Woody and Buzz Buzzard are sailors on leave in Tahiti, vying for the attentions of a beautiful Princess. She only needs them as a sacrifice to the local Volcano God.

159. All's Fair at the Fair (*Color Classic*) 26 Aug. 1938; *p.c.:* The Fleischer Studio for Para; *prod:* Max Fleischer; *dir:* Dave Fleischer; *anim:* Myron Waldman, Graham Place, Lillian Friedman; *voices:* Everett Clark; *mus:* Sammy Timberg; *col:* Tech. *sd:* WE. 8 min. • A rural couple travel to the World's Fair and experience various new-fangled robotic apparatus.

160. All's Fair at the Fair (*Popeye*) 19 Dec. 1947; *p.c.:* Famous for Para; *dir:* Seymour Kneitel; *story:* I. Klein, Jack Ward; *anim:* Dave Tendlar, Martin Taras; *sets:* Robert Connavale; *voices:* Jack Mercer, Mae Questel, Jackson Beck, Sid Raymond; *mus:* Winston Sharples; *prod mgr:* Sam Buchwald; *col:* Ciné. *sd:* RCA. 8 min. • Popeye and Olive visit the fair where they encounter a strong-man who makes off with Olive in a hot-air balloon.

161. All's Well (*Gabby*) 17 Jan. 1941; *p.c.:* The Fleischer Studio for Para; *prod:* Max Fleischer; *dir:* Dave Fleischer; *story:* Bob Wickersham; *anim:* David Tendlar, William Nolan; *ed:* Kitty Pfister; *voices:* Pinto Colvig, Margie Hines; *mus:* Sammy Timberg; *prod sup:* Sam Buchwald, I. Sparber; *col:* Tech. *sd:* WE. 7 min. • Gabby attempts to put a diaper on a baby he assumes to be abandoned.

162. All's Well That Ends Well (*Terry-Toon*) 8 Mar. 1940; *p.c.:* TT for Fox; *dir:* Mannie Davis; *story:* John Foster; *mus:* Philip A. Scheib; b&w. *sd:* RCA. 7 min. • Four orphan kittens try to obtain food from under the watchful eye of the watchdog.

163. Aloha Hooey (*Merrie Meldoies*) 31 Jan. 1942; *p.c.:* Leon Schlesinger for WB; *dir:* Fred Avery; *story:* Michael Maltese; *anim:* Virgil Ross; *back:* John Didrik Johnsen; *ed:* Treg Brown; *voices:* Mel Blanc, Pinto Colvig, Sara Berner; *mus:* Carl W. Stalling; *prod sup:* Henry Binder, Raymond G. Katz; *col:* Tech. *sd:* Vit. 7 min. • Sammy Seagull and Cecil Crow visit Hawaii where they contest for the affections for a saronged beauty.

164. Aloha Oe (*Screen Songs*) 17 Mar. 1933; *p.c.:* The Fleischer Studio for Para; *prod:* Max Fleischer; *dir:* Dave Fleischer; *anim:* Bernard Wolf, David Tendlar; *mus:* Art Turkisher; *l/a:* The Royal Samoans; b&w. *sd:* WE. 7 min. *l/a/anim.* • The monkeys stage a jungle wedding.

165. Alona on the Sarong Seas (*Popeye*) 4 Sept. 1942; *p.c.:* Famous for Para; *dir:* I. Sparber; *story:* Jack Ward, Jack Mercer; *anim:* David Tendlar, Abner Kneitel; *voices:* Jack Mercer, Margie Hines; *mus:* Sammy Timberg; *prod mgr:* Sam Buchwald; b&w. *sd:* RCA. 7 min. • While anchored at a South Seas port, Popeye and Bluto both swear off women ... until a sarong-clad Olive passes on a surf board.

166. Along Came a Duck (*Burt Gillett's Toddle Tales*) 10 Aug. 1934; *p.c.:* Van Beuren for RKO; *dir:* Burt Gillett, Steve Muffatti; *mus:* Winston Sharples; *l/a ph:* Harry E. Squires; b&w. *sd:* RCA. 8 min. *l/a/anim.* • A runaway boy and his duck are told by Freddy Frog how he once befriended the whole duck family.

167. Along Came Daffy (*Looney Tunes*) 14 Sept. 1946; *p.c.:* WB; *dir:* I. Freleng; *story:* Tedd Pierce, Michael Maltese; *anim:* Gerry Chiniquy, Virgil Ross, Ken Champin, Manuel Perez; *lay:* Hawley Pratt; *back:* Paul Julian; *ed:* Treg Brown; *voices:* Mel Blanc; *mus:* Carl Stalling; *prod mgr:* John W. Burton; *prod:* Edward Selzer; *col:* Tech. *sd:* Vit. 7 min. • Daffy tries selling a cookbook to two starving trappers.

168. Along Came Fido (*Hot Dog*) 31 Jan. 1927; *p.c.:* Bray prods; *dir:* Walt Lantz, Clyde Geronimi; b&w. sil. 5 min. *l/a/anim.* • Pete disguises as a Harem dancer in order to rescue his sweetheart who has been abducted by a desert Shiek. He finally manages to trap the scoundrel in a motion picture camera.

169. Along Flirtation Walk (*Merrie Melodies*) 6 Apr. 1935; *p.c.:* Leon Schlesinger for WB; *dir:* Isadore Freleng; *anim:* Bob McKimson, Paul Smith, Robert Clampett; *mus:* Norman Spencer; *song:* Allie Wrubel; *prod sup:* Henry Binder, Raymond G. Katz; *col:* Tech-2. *sd:* Vit. 7 min. • The birds have a football match.

170. Alpine Antics (*Looney Tunes*) 4 Jan. 1936; *p.c.:* Leon Schlesinger prods for WB; *dir/lay:* Jack King; *anim:* Riley Thomson, Jack Carr; *voices:* Bernice Hansel, Tommy Bond; *mus:* Norman Spencer; *prod sup:* Henry Binder, Raymond G. Katz; b&w. *sd:* Vit. 7 min. • Beans, Little Kitty and Porky are involved with snow sports, culminating in a ski race.

171. Alpine Antics (*Oswald*) 13 Feb. 1929; *p.c.:* Winkler for Univ; *dir:* Tom Palmer; b&w. *sd.* 5 min. • Oswald answers a cry for help and resourcefully escapes from a wild bear.

172. Alpine Climbers (*Mickey Mouse*) 28 Oct. 1936; *p.c.:* Walt Disney prods for UA; *dir:* David D. Hand; *anim:* Norman Ferguson, Jack Hannah, Dick Huemer, Grim Natwick, William O. Roberts; *voices:* Clarence Nash, V.J. Nelson, Pinto Colvig, Lee Millar; *mus:* Albert Hay Malotte; *col:* Tech. *sd:* RCA. 10 min. • While scaling a mountain, Donald runs into difficulties with a goat, Mickey encounters an angry eagle and Pluto gets drunk.

173. An Alpine Flapper (*Aesop's Film Fables*) 16 May 1926; *p.c.:* Fables Pictures Inc for Pathé; *dir:* Paul Terry; b&w. sil. 5 min. • George Goat is showing off on skates before his best gal when along comes a villain to steal her away. George pursues and wins her back.

174. Alpine for You (*Popeye*) 18 May 1951; *p.c.:* Famous for Para; *dir:* I. Sparber; *story:* Carl Meyer, Jack Mercer; *anim:* Steve Muffatti, George Germanetti; *sets:* Robert Connavale; *voices:* Jack Mercer, Mae Questel, Jackson Beck; *mus:* Winston Sharples; *prod mgr:* Seymour Shultz; *col:* Tech. *sd:* RCA. 7 min. • While mountain climbing, Popeye and Olive run afoul of a mountain guide who proceeds to sabotage their excursion.

175. An Alpine Yodeller (*Paul Terry-Toons*) 21 Feb. 1936; *p.c.:* Moser & Terry Inc for Educational/Fox; *dir:* Paul Terry, Frank Moser; *mus:* Philip A. Scheib; b&w. *sd:* 6 min. • No story available.

176. Alter Egotist (*Honey Halfwitch*) June 1967; *p.c.:* Para; *ex prod:* Shamus Culhane; *dir:* Chuck Harriton; *story:* Howard Post; *anim:* Doug Crane, Irv Dressler, Nick Tafuri; *sets:* Danté Barbetta, Dave Ubinas, Howard Beckerman; *mus:* Winston Sharples; *prod sup:* Harold Robins, Burt Hanft; *col:* Tech. *sd:* RCA. 6 min. • Honey draws herself a playmate who comes to life, causing havoc about the house.

177. Alvin's Solo Flight (*Noveltoon*) Apr. 1961; *p.c.:* Para Cartoons; *dir:* Seymour Kneitel; *story:* Marjorie H. Buell, Bill C. Ershine; *anim:* Nick

Tafuri, I. Klein; *sets:* Robert Little; *voices:* Cecil Roy; *mus:* Winston Sharples; *ph:* Leonard McCormick; *prod mgr:* Abe Goodman; *col:* Tech. *sd:* RCA. 6 min. • Lulu and Alvin visit the beach and Alvin floats away with a helium-filled balloon.

178. Always Kickin' *(Color Classic)* 6 Jan. 1939; *p.c.:* The Fleischer Studio for Para; *prod:* Max Fleischer; *dir:* Dave Fleischer; *anim:* Myron Waldman, Arnold Gillespie, Lillian Friedman; *des:* Myron Waldman; *voices:* Donald Bain; *mus:* Sammy Timberg; *col:* Tech. *sd:* WE. 7 min. • Spunky the donkey wants to emulate the songbirds but they won't let him. When one of the smaller birds is captured he comes to its rescue, ingratiating himself with the others again.

179. A.M. to P.M. *(Aesop's Sound Fables)* 28 July 1933; *p.c.:* Van Beuren for RKO; *dir:* Harry Bailey; *mus:* Gene Rodemich; b&w. *sd:* RCA. 7 min. • Many strange people and occurrences pass Sentinal Louie while on sentry duty outside the palace.

180. Amateur Broadcast *(Oswald)* 26 Aug. 1935; *p.c.:* Univ; *dir:* Walter Lantz; *story:* Walter Lantz, Victor McLeod; *anim:* Cecil Surry, Ray Abrams, Ed Benedict; *mus:* James Dietrich; b&w. *sd:*WE. 6 min. • Oswald plays Major Bowes to the animals' acts.

181. Amateur Night *(Paul Terry-Toon)* 12 July 1935; *p.c.:* Moser & Terry Inc for Educational/Fox; *dir:* Paul Terry, Frank Moser; *mus:* Philip A. Scheib; b&w. *sd:*WE. 6 min. • No story available.

182. Amateur Night on the Ark *(Aesop's Film Fables)* 24 Apr. 1923; *p.c.:* Fables Pictures Inc for Pathé; *dir:* Paul Terry; b&w. *sil.* 6 min. • Noah's Ark inhabitants present amateur turns. Noah, himself, appears in the guise of a performing bear but the animals uncover his disguise and force him to swim for the rest of the journey.

183. Amateur Nite *(Oswald)* 11 Nov. 1929; *p.c.:* Univ; *dir:* Walter Lantz; *anim:* R.C. Hamilton, "Bill" Nolan, Tom Palmer; *mus:* David Broekman; b&w. *sd:* WE. 6½ min. • Oswald conducts an orchestra playing "St Louis Blues," introduces the acts and gets pelted with eggs for his trouble.

184. Amelia Comes Back *(Aesop's Film Fables)* 10 Aug. 1924; *p.c.:* Fables Pictures Inc for Pathé; *dir:* Paul Terry; b&w. *sil.* 6 min. • Farmer Al Falfa's sleep is disturbed by a back-fence feline serenader. He tries to drown the beast but the cat escapes a watery grave and returns to haunt the poor farmer.

185. An American March 1941. *dir/anim:* Oskar Fischinger; *mus:* John Philip Souza's "Stars and Stripes Forever"; *col:* Tech. *sd.* 2 min. • Colorful march featuring the American flag design.

186. The American Picture Book 11 Mar. 1922; *p.c.:* Aywon Film Corp; b&w. *sil.* • A series of decidedly novel animated drawings.

187. American Pop 13 Feb. 1981; *p.c.:* Colum TriStar; *dir:* Ralph Bakshi; *prod:* Ralph Bakshi, Martin Rasohoff; *ex prod:* Richard R. St. Johns, Maggie Abbott; *prod asst:* Lynne Betner, Cathleen Summers, Jeffrey Chernov; *asst dir:* John Sparey; *story:* Ronni Kern; *anim:* Lillian Evans, Carl Bell, Craig Armstrong, Debbie Hayes, Steve Gordon, Brenda Banks, Jesus Cortes, James A. Davis, Robert Laduca, Chrystal Russell, George Scribner, Paul Smith, Tom Tataranowicz, Robert Carr, Xenia (de Mattia), Tim Callahan, Christopher Dent, Davis Doi, Derek Eversfield, Bonnie Fishbon, Richard Hoppe, Martin Korth, Alida Krumina, Kathryn Staats, Michael Svayko, Wesley Takahashi, Scott Tolmie, Ben Trujillo, Craig Zukowski; *anim check:* Dotti Foell; *lay/des:* Louise Zingarelli, Johnnie Vita, Marcia Adams, Barry Jackson; *back:* Jeff Skrimstad, Frank Frezzo, Gary Eggleston, Russ Heath; *painters:* Roxanne Taylor, Mary Yanish; *ed:* David Ramirel, Michael A. Stevenson; *voices:* Tony Bolinski/Pete Bolinski: Ron Thompson; *Franki:* Mary Small; *Toue:* Jerry Holland; *Bella:* Lisa Jane Persky; *Zalmie Bolinski:* Jeffrey Lippa; *Eva Tanguay:* Roz Kelly; *Crisco:* Frank de Kova; *Ben Bolinski:* Richard Singer; *Hannele:* Elsa Raven; *Nicky Palumbo:* Ben Frommer; *Nancy:* Amy Levitt; *Leo Stern:* Leonard Stone; *Little Pete:* Eric Taslitz; *Izzy:* Gene Borkan; *Beat Poet:* Richard Moll; *Prostitute:* Beatrice Colen; *Theatre Owner:* Vincent Schiavelli; *Showgirls:* Hilary Beane, A'leashaia Brevano; *The Blonde:* Linda Wiesmeier; *Dwayne:* Phil Simms; *Little Zalmie:* Marcello Krakoff; *Halley:* Ken Johnson; *Young Zalmie:* Barney Pell; *Space:* Marc Levine; *Club Manager:* Robert Strom; *August:* Gene Woodbury; *Johnny:* Ty Grimes; *Reed:* Peter Glindeman; *Jeffrey:* Auburn Burrell; *Tuba Player:* Elya Baskin; *Prostitute:* M.B. West; *Freddie:* Joey Camen; *Little Benny:* Bert Autore; *Young Benny:* Tony Autore; *Tony's Brother:* Johnny

Brogna; *Tony's Sisters:* Dawn Agrella, Cari Ann Warden; *Stage Hand:* Don Carlson; *Hoboes:* Vance Colvig, Robert Beecher; *Crapshooters:* Tony Fasce, Frank Ciaravino; *Hippy:* Gene Krischner; *Curtis:* David Allen Young; *Punk Rock Group:* Lee James Jude, Timothy J. Leitch, Frederick C. Milner, Philo J. Cramer; *Organ Grinder:* Chester Haze; *Doorkeeper:* Chuck Mitchell; *Piano Player:* Bill Schneider; *Songs performed by:* Bob Dylan, Bob Grant and his orchestra, Helen Morgan, Benny Goodman and his orchestra, Herbie Hancock, The Dave Brubeck Quartet, Fabian, Art Blakey, Sam Cooke, Peter Paul and Mary, The Mamas and The Papas, The Dools, Jimi Hendrix, Big Brother and the Holding Co, Lou Reed, Bob Seeger; *mus:* Lee Holdridge; *songs:* the Rev. Sabine Baring-Gould, P. Benatar, Ben Bernie, Irving Càesar, J. Will Callahan, R. Capps, Kenneth Casey, George M. Cohan, Allen Collins, Tommie Connor, Paul Cook, Sam Cooke, Eddie de Lange, B.G. de Sylva, John Densmore, Paul Desmond, Bob Dylan, Ray Evans, Frank Eyton, Roger Fisher, N. Geraldo, George Gershwin, Ira Gershwin, Michelle Gillian, Jerry Gray, John W. Green, Oscar Hammerstein II, Herbie Hancock, Jimi Hendrix, Edward Heyman, DuBose Heyward, Herman Hupfield, Jimmy Johnson, Steve Jones, Scott Joplin, Wayne Keller, Jerome Kern, Robert Krieger, Ernesto Lecugna, Hans Leip, Jean Lenox, Jay Livingstone, Fred Long, Francia Luban, Barlard MacDonald, Cecil Mack, Raymond Manzarek, Glen Matlock, Jim Morrison, Maureen O'Heron, Carl Perkins, John Phillips, Maceo Pinkard, Jerome "Doc" Pomus, Cole Porter, Louis Prima, Lou Reed, Lee S. Roberts, Richard Rogers, Johnny Rotten, Norbert Schultze, Bob Seeger, Mort Shuman, Phil Silvers, Darby Slick, Robert Sour, William Stevenson, Al Stillman, Paul Stookey, Sir Arthur Sullivan, Harry O. Sutton, Bobby Timmons, Jimmy van Heusen, Ron van Zandt, Jim Webb, Ann Wilson, Nancy Wilson, P.G. Wodehouse, Peter Yarrow; *mus sup:* John Beug, Mark Bakshi; *mus ed:* Jeff Carson, La Da Productions; *col models:* Janet Cummings; *research:* Jackie Herst, Leslie Taubman; *laser fx:* Laserium; *opticals:* The Optical House; *ph:* Frances Grumman, R&B Effects; *mark-up:* Jeff Angel; *cel polisher:* Dean Korth; *cel reproduction:* Steve Gulsvie, Daniel Schneider; *Xerox:* Daryl Carstensen, Karen China, Casey Clayton, Rosemarie S. Cruz, Janet Zoll; *check:* Patricia Capozzi, Betty Brooks, Eleanor Dahlen, Letha Prince, Harriette Rossall; *sd:* John Glasgow, Richard Portman, David Horton; *titles:* MGM; *prod staff:* Roy P. Disney, J. Sidney Kramer, Kenneth Bornstein, Chris Danzo, Paula Berteif, Cathy Rose, Bob Hippard, Dick Davis, Scott Thaler, Michael Winter; *col:* Tech. *sd:* Dolby stereo. 96 min. • The story of four generations of the Bolinski family whose lives revolve around American popular music: Five-year-old Zalmie flees Tsarist Russia with his mother in 1905, settling in New York where he grows up, meets and marries showgirl Bella. Zalmie gets mixed up with the Mafia and spends a period in prison. His son becomes a pianist who marries, sires a son and is killed while serving overseas in the Second World War. His son, Tony, becomes a songwriter with a rock band and, while on tour, discovers that the band boy calling himself "Little Pete" is his own illigitimate son. When Tony disappears from the scene, "Little Pete" becomes a rock superstar. Ralph Bakshi made this by using the Rotoscope system of tracing live-action.

188. An American Tail 21 Nov. 1986; *p.c.:* Sullivan Studios Inc/Amblin for Univ/U-Drive Prods Inc.; *dir:* Don Bluth; *ex prod:* Steven Spielberg, David Kirschner, Kathleen Kennedy, Frank Marshall; *prod:* Don Bluth, John Pomeroy, Tony Geiss; *asst dir:* G. Sue Shakespeare, David Steinberg; *created by* David Kirschner; *story:* David Kirschner, Judy Freudberg, Tony Geiss; *scr:* Judy Freudberg, Tony Geiss; *des/storyboard:* Don Bluth, Larry Leker; *anim dir:* John Pomeroy, Dan Kuenster, Linda Miller; *anim:* Lorna Pomeroy, Gary Perkovac, Jeff Etter, Ralph Zondag, Dave Molina, Heidi Guedel, Anne Marie Bardwell, Skip Jones, Kevin Wurzer, Dave Spafford, Dick Zondag, Jesse Cosio, Ralf Palmer, T. Daniel Hofstedt, Michael Cedeno, David Concepcion, Jorgen Klubien; *fx anim:* Dorse A. Lanpher, Don Paul, Diann Landau, Tom Hush, Kathleen Quaife-Hodge, Jeff Howard, Joey Mildenberger, Michael Casey, David McCamley, David Tidgwell; *special fx:* A&A Special Effects Inc., Special Effects Unlimited Inc.; *character key:* Vera Lanpher, Terry Shakespeare, Emily Juliano, Silvia Hoefnagels, Mark Pudleiner, Jon Hooper, Cathy Jones; *character clean-up:* Jan Naylor, Carlos Tavares, Jean Morel, Tim Allen, Debbie Armstrong, Barbara Butterworth, Kent Butterworth, Mark Christiansen, Eric Daniels, Mike Genz, Todd Hoff, Ross Marshall, Jeff Merghart, Julie Molina, David Nethery, Brendan O'Reilly, Brian Pimental, Sally Voorheis, Todd Waterman; *color styling:* Carmen Oliver, Jill Everett, Susan Vanderhorst, Shirley Mapes;

layout: Larry Leker, Mark Swan, Mark Swanson; *back:* Don Moore, William Lorencz, David Goetz, Barry Atkinson, Richard Bentham; *ed:* Dan Molina, John K. Carr; *voices: Bridget:* Catherianne Blore; *Tiger:* Dom de Luise; *Warren T. Rat:* John Finnegan; *Fievel Mousekewitz:* Philip Glasser; *Tanya Mousekewitz:* Amy Green; *Tony Toponi:* Pat Musick; *Papa Mousekewitz:* Nehemiah Persoff; *Henri:* Christopher Plummer; *Honest John:* Neil Ross; *Didgit:* Will Ryan; *Moe:* Hal Smith; *Mama Mousekewitz;* Erica Yohn; *singers:* Betsy Cathcart, Warren Hayes, James Ingram, Linda Ronstadt; *song prod:* Peter Asher; *casting:* Michael Fenton, Jane Feinberg, Linda Gordon; *rough inbet:* T. Daniel Hofstedt, Tamara Anderson, Mannix Bennett, Don Casey, Nollaig Crombie, Colm Duggan, Patrick Gleeson, Helen Lawlor, Marion Mathieu, Ashley McGovern, John Power, Mary Walsh, Konrad Winterlich; *mus:* James Horner; *orch:* Grieg McRitchie; performed by The London Symphony Orchestra; *mus ed:* Michael Clifford; *mus copyist:* Ernie Locker; *songs:* Cynthia Weil, James Horner, Barry Mann; *rec:* Eric Tomlinson, Ken Berger, Sean Murphy, Bill Rowe, Ray Merrin; *sd ed:* Dan Molina, Christopher Ackland, Andy Stears, Kevin Brazier, Louis L. Edemann; *foley:* TAJ Soundworks, Horta Editorial; *check:* Carla Washburn, Vonnie Batson, Barbara Ritchie, Anna Marie Costa, Saskia Raevouri, Victor Solis, Robin Police; *col mark-up:* Olga Tarin Craig, Diane Albracht, Sarah-Jane King; *paint:* Deborah Rykoff, Violet McKenna, Brenda McGuirk; *ph:* Scott McCartor, David R. Ankney, Joe Jiuliano, Karl Bredendieck, Rocky Solotoff, Ralph Migliori, Stan Miller, Marlyn O'Connor; *ph fx:* Fred Craig; *Xerox:* John Eddings, Terri Eddings, Mike Vest, Karen China, Vernette Griffee, Edgar Gutierrez; *i&p:* Sullivan Studios (*Ireland*) Ltd., Olga Tarin Craig, Laurie Curran (*Ireland*), Diane Albracht (*USA*), Jacqueline Hooks, Kerri Swanson, Deborah Goddard, Anne Duffy Hazard, Karin Stover, Michelle Urbano, Paul Kelly, Leslie Aust, Christopher Wirosko, Jan Stokes, Jill Coughlin, Conor Thunder, Reneè Alcazar, Jane Anderson, Peter Anderson, Charlotte Armstrong, Brian Boylan, Ann Brennan, Annette Byrne, Robert Byrne, Michael Carey, Yvonne Carthy, Gerard Coleman, Nicholas Connolly, Eileen Conway, Aidan Cooney, Lisa Cocoran, Anne-Marie Daly, Donnachada Daly, Paul Daly, Tom Daly, Denis Deegan, Brian Dempsey, Sean Dempsey, Madeleine Downes, Karen Dwyer, Gina Evans, John Fitzgerald, Sylvia Fitzpatrick, Elaine Fox, Donal Freeney, Michael Garry, Philip Garry, Fiona Gavin, Mary Gavin, Peter Gentle, David Groome, Gary Hall, Barbara Hamane, Brendan Harris, Bernard Heriott, Carl Jones, Gary Jones, Eimear Joyce, Conor Kavanagh, Paul Kelly, Geraldine Kieernan, Siobhan Larkie, Fiona Mackle, Moya Mackle, Orla Madden, Thomas Maher, James Mansfield, Ann May, Miriam McDonnell, Michele McKenna, Ian McLoughlin, Brian McSweeney, Deborah Mooneyham, Pauline Morahan, Thomas Nicky Moss, Aileesh Mulligan, John Murray, Sinead Murray, Brendan O'Brian, Colm O'Brien, Philip O'Connor, John O'Neill, Aran O'Reilly, Suzanne O'Reilly, Tara O'Reilly, Paul O'Rourke, Janette Owens, Melanie Pava, Eithne Quinn, Miriam Reid, Denis Riordan, Eric Ryan, Julie Ryan, Sandra Ryan, Gary Shafer, Paul Shanahan, Graham Tiernan, Greg Tiernan, Fiona Trayler, Sandy Ugarte; *title des:* Don Bluth, Larry Leka, Dan Kuenster, Don Moore, David Goetz, Dorse Lanpher; *titles/opticals:* Cinema Research Corp., Apogee Inc., Title House; *miniature model makers:* Dan Kuenster, Patrick Lorencz, David Goetz, Mark Swan, Barry Atkinson, Bill Lorencz, Ralph Palmer; *col timer:* James Schurman, Bob Hagans; *neg cutter:* Donah Bassett, Cathy Carr; *Dolby consultant:* Chris David; *choreog:* Estelle & Alfonso; *prod mgrs:* Fred Craig, Thad Weinlein; *asso prods:* Kate Barher, Deborah Jelin; *prod asst:* John Cawley, Ken Cromar, Cynthia Ankney, Caralyn Warren, Steve Stovall, John Vallone, Jill Schachne, Matthew Reeder, Paul Fletcher, Paul Frost, Jason Carr, Lori Falchi, Vanessa Solis, Linda Strongin, Joe Ryan; *AMBLIN controller:* Bonne Radford; *ex asst* (*Ireland*): Eithne Agnew; *prod asst* (*Ireland*): Ann Costello; *camera stand engineering:* Mechanical Concepts Inc.; *camera computer;* Cinetron Computer Systems Inc.; *graphics:* Studio Graphics; *col:* DeLuxe. *sd:* Dolby stereo. 76 min. • A Russian mouse family flees to America in 1885 to escape Cossack cats. When they arrive in the United States, young Fievel gets separated from the rest of his family and encounters a number of adventures in his search for them.

189. An American Tail: Fievel Goes West 21 Nov. 1991; *p.c.:* Amblin Entertainment, Inc. for Univ; *dir:* Phil Nibbelink, Simon Wells; *prod:* Steven Spielberg, Robert Watts; *ex prod:* Frank Marshall, Kathleen Kennedy, David Kirschner; *created by* David Kirschner; *story:* Charles Swenson; *scr:* Flint Dille; *art dir:* Neil Ross; *character des:* Uli Meyer; *ed:* Nick

Fletcher; *anim:* Nancy Beiman, Kristof Serrand, Rob Stevenhagen, Bibo E. Bergeron, Raul Garcia, Ceu D'elia, Phil Morris, Patrick Mate, Rodolphe Guenoden, Roy Meurin, Greg Manwaring, Daniel Jeannette, Andreas von Andrian, Ute von Munchow-Pohl, Nadia Cozic, Thierry Schiel, Pete Western, Jurgen Richter, Shane Doyle, Eric Bouillette, Janvan Buyten, Denis Couchon, Paul MacDonald, Alain Maindron, Olivier Pont, Georges Abolin, Wolf-Ruediger Bloss, Jean Pilotte, Quentin Miles, Fabio Lignini, Miguel Fuertes, Mark Wolfgang Broecking, Angelos Rouvas, Joe McCaffrey, Claude Aaron, Isabelle Beaudoin, David Berthier, Sylvianne Burnet, Malcolm Clarke, Tony Cope, Connor Flynn, Jody Gannon, Stephen Grant, Gerrard Kenny, Sophie Law, Janet MacKay, Brenda McKie-Chat, Ignacio Meneu, Andrew Moss, Steve Perry, Silvia Pompei, John Powers, William Salazar, Steffan Schaffler, Erik Christian Schmidt, Emil Sergiev, Andrea Simonti, Philip Anderson, Arnaud Berthier, Kevin Brownie, Roland Chat, Shari Cohen, Michael Eames, Stephan Franck, Max Graenitz, Clark Irving, Cathy Kiss, John Lin, John McCartney, Luba Medekova-Klein, Eckhardt Milz, Fernando Pastor, Birgitta Pollaneni, Mark Povey, Rick Richards, Sheryl Sardina, Andrew Schmidt, Kieron Seamons, Emil Simeonov, Vladimir Todorov, Frank Vibert; *inbet:* Cecile Bender, Shaun Blake, Jamie Bolio, Bram Calcoen, Stephen Cavalier, Juan Cecilia, David Clarvis, Denise Dean, Heather Doyle, Gavin Emerson, Stuart Evans, Susan Goldberg, Darren Goodacre, Antony Gray, Nina Haley, Paul Hallewell, Debbie Hamed, Nicholas Harrop, Mark Hessler, Janette Hynes, Lawrence Keogh, Sarah Keogh, Veronique Langdon, Alex Lawrence, Roger Lougher, Michaela Muller, David Navarro, Andy Paraskos, Dawn Pearce, Jane Poole, Maria Jesus Rubio, Kay Sales, Christopher Shaw, Jason Shipley, Marc Smith, Kevin Spruce, John Sweeney, Simon Swift, Matthew Taylor, Lee Taylor, Marco Trandafilov, David Webster, Tim White; *fx:* Scott Santoro, Jon Brooks, Steve Burch, Ed Coffey, Mike Smith, Brice Mallier, Paul van Geyt, Al Holter, Craig Clark, Glenn Chaika, Alexs Stadermann, Hock-Lian Law, Vito Lo Russo, Amanda Talbot, Kristine Humber, Barney Russel, Mick Harper, Pat C. Morton, Phillipe Angeles, Grace Waddington, Stephanie Walker; *fx inbet:* Guner Behich, Michaela Budde, Duncan Henry, John O'Neill, Albert Price, Richard Tang, Stephen McDermott; *lay:* Mark Marren, Brendan Houghton, Armen Melkonian, Panagiotis Rappas, Giorgio Mardegan, Tom Humber, Marco Cinello, Antonio Navarro; *scene planning:* Harold Kraut, Karen Hansen; *back:* Shelley Page, Gary Sycamore, Rachel Stedman, Sean Eckett, Walter Toessler, Darek Gogol, Michael Rose, Ennio Torresan Jr., Daniel Cacouault, Colin Stimpson, David Womersley; *voices: Fievel:* Philip Glasser; *Wylie Burp:* James Stewart; *Mama:* Erica Yohn; *Tanya:* Cathy Cavadini; *Papa:* Nehemiah; *Tiger:* Dom DeLuise; *Miss Kitty:* Amy Irving; *Cat R. Wall:* John Cleese; *Chula:* Jon Lovitz; *also:* Jack Angel, Fausto Bara, Vanna Bonta, Philip Clarke, Jennifer Darling, Annie Holliday, Sherry Linn, Mickie McGowan, Larry Moss, Nigel Pegram, Patrick Pinney, Lisa Raggio, Lawrence Steffan, David Tate, Robert Watts; *Dreams to Dream* performed by Linda Ronstadt; *mus:* James Horner; *songs:* James Horner, Will Jennings, Barry Mann; "Rawhide" by Dimitri Tiomkin & Ned Washington, performed by The Blues Brothers; *mus ed:* Jim Hendrikson; *team leaders:* Sarah Marsden, Brian Holmes, Celine O'Sullivan, Fenella Page, Janice Eason, Lorraine Ward, Sue Woodward, Karen Narramore, Tommy Calligan; *anim check:* Joan Topley, Lucie Belanger, David Allonby, Corine Marcel, Tuula Milz, Jill Yudor, Steve Pegram, Chantal Marsolais, Michelle Povey, Marianne Rousseau, Helen O'Brien; *checking:* Frances Jacob; *Xerox sup:* Sandy Gordon; *model des:* Annie Elvin; *col models:* Alison Flintham, Sarah Fletcher; *Xerox:* Shaun Caton, Sarah McLoughlin, Harry R.C. Elvin, Adam Binham; *mark-up:* Victoria Morrison-Glenys, Nondus Banning-Boddy, Caroline Baxter; *i&p:* Corona Esterhazy, Jane Cotts, Matthew Teevan, Karin Adams; *airbrush art:* Christian Schmidt, Laurent Ben-Mimoun; *ph:* Robert Crawford, Stuart Campbell, Tim Francis, Graham Tiernan, Kevin Wooldridge, Brian Riley, Stuart Holloway, Barry Newan, Russell Tagg, Deirdre Creed, James Williams, Jay Watson; *sd mix:* Daniel Leahy, Thomas Gerard, Charlie Ajar Jr.; *sd fx ed:* Nils C. Jensen, Doug Jackson, Leonard T. Geschke, Gary M. Mundheim, Don Malouf; *ADR ed:* Alan Nineberg, Rod Rogers, Doc Kane; *post prod:* Martin Cohen, Bradley Goodman, Michelle Fandetti; *foley:* TAJ Soundtracks, Kevin Bartnof, Hilda Hodges, James Ashwill, Marilyn Graf; *neg cutter:* Kevin Daley; *prod co-ord:* Colin J. Alexander; *prod ex:* Deborah Newmyer; *asso mgr:* Stephen Hickner; *prod mgr:* Cynthia Woodbyrne; *col.* *sd:* Dolby stereo. 68 min. • A scheming cat persuades the mice to head to a western town and there he tricks them into unwittingly building a giant mousetrap. Fievel Mousekewitz gets separated from his family, learns of this plot and tries to prevent it.

190. Amoozin' But Confoozin' (*Li'l Abner*) 17 Feb. 1944; *p.c.:* Colum; *prod:* Dave Fleischer; *story:* Sid Marcus; *ed:* Edward Moore; *mus:* Eddie Kilfeather; *voice:* Lurene Tuttle; *ph:* Frank Fisher; *prod mgr:* Albert Spar; *col:* Tech. *sd:* RCA. 8 min. • Abner returns from the big city with a bathtub, making himself very unpopular with the local residents.

191. Anastasia 14 Nov. 1997; *p.c.:* Fox; *prod/dir:* Don Bluth, Gary Goldman; *ex prod:* Maureen Donley; based on the play by Marcelle Maurette as adapted by Guy Bolton and the screenplay by Arthur Laurents; *scr:* Susan Gauthier, Bruce Graham, Bob Tzudiker, Noni White; *adapt:* Eric Tuchman; *asst dir:* Jason Ayon; *anim dir:* Len Simon, John Hill, Troy Saliba, Fernando Moro, Sandro Cleuzo, Paul Newberry; *pre-prod: col key styling:* Richard C. Bentham, Kenneth Valentine Slevin; *character lay/des:* Chris Schouten; *prod des:* Mike Peraza; *conceptual artist:* Suzanne Lemieux Wilson; *post prod des:* John Lakey; *storyboard art:* Larry Leker, Joe Orrantia, Chip Pace, Jay Schultz, Ferran Xalabarder; *storyboard assembler:* Jon Kerbaugh; *pre-prod co-ord:* Martha Richter; *anim:* Edison Goncalves, Dave Mac-Dougall, John Power, Kelly Baigent, Robert Sprathoff, Marco Plantilla, Hugo M. Takahashi, Melvin Silao, Manuel Galiana, Paul J. Kelly, Robert Fox, Allan Fernando, Gàbor T. Steisinger, Maximillan Nepomuceno, Glen McIntosh, Joey Paraiso, JoJo Young, Alan Fleming, Celine Kiernan, Cynthia Wells, Sandra R. Keely, Dimitri Tenev, Rafael Diaz Canales, Helio Takahashi, Tobias Schwarz, David Lux, Steve Gordon, Todd Waterman, Ròisìn Hunt, Adam Beck, Jane Anderson, Grant Lounsbury, Steve Cunningham, Joseph Manifold, Renato Dos Anjos, Dana O'Connor, Barry Iremonger, Paul Shanahan, Michael Tweedle; *co-ord sup:* Bernie Keogh; *rough inbet: sup:* Anne Murray-O'Craobhach; *training officer/break artist:* Debbie J. Gold; *rough break/inbet:* Tom Bernardo, Sharon Morgan, Colby Bluth, John L. Morris, Jason Boose, Darren Nicholl, Nancy Cox, Declan O'Connor, Jason Deegan, Vikki Pana, Christopher Elsner, Shannon Penner, John Hoffman, Michael Pennington, Mike Hogue, Stephen Reid, Roberto Islas, John B. Rice, Adrian Kilkenny, Alberto Rodriquez, Michael Lahay, Ed Rooney, Niall Laverty, Jim Seville, Jeff Lujan, Bruce Tinnin, Ryan McElhinney, James Wood, June Wright; *clean-up: sup:* Eileen Conway Newberry; *ass sup:* Peter Donnelly; *key character clean-up:* Rosie Ahern, Stephen Lynes, Cesar Avalos, Ciara McCabe, Mickie Cassidy, Jenni Mc-Cosker, Kevin Condron, James McLoughlin, Teresa Cunliffe, Mark McLoughlin, Martin Fagan, Terry O'Toole Jr., Nicola Flynn, Curt Spurging, Shawn Gibson, Wendo van Essen, John Walsh, Don Arado, Juliet Indonila-Cabral, Sarah Ardo, Jack Joseph, Ochie Atienza Alferez, Patrice Leech, Victoria Belleza, Jhun Licas, Carol David Bocalan, Richard Manginsay, Arnel Cabanela Martin, Jian Cheng Chen, Cesar Mondala, Greg Chin, David O'Brien, Pearse Cullinane, Enrico Paz, Joel Cunanan, Alex Perez, Manny de Guzman, Andrzej Piotrowski, Narz Dela Rosa, Michael Rider, Willie de Leon, Joven Sampang, Scott Douthitt, Raul Sibayan, Jeff Edwards, Richard Simms, Albert Feliciano, Gail Springsteen, Regner Frondozo, Kenna Stevens, Cash Imutan, Imelda Tolledo Mondala, Jojie Calingo Imutan, Jake Yago, Rodrigo Zafe Jr., Siobhàn Larkin, Mick Cassidy; *dpt co-ord:* Courtney Cook; *fx anim: sup:* Peter Matheson; *anim dir:* Julian Hynes, Declan Walsh; *anim:* Leslie Aust, Sonniel Lagonera, Edwin Bocalan, Paul Morris, John Costello, Raquel V. Omana, Marek Kochout, Deirdre Reynolds-Behan, Martine Cunningham, John Bermudes, Karl Hayes, Gorio Vicuna, Noel P. Kiernan, Jane Smethurst, Suzanne d'Arcy, Mark Irvine, Stephen Deane, Tracey Meighan, Paul Fogarty, Angelito Ramos, Stephen Smyth, Rich Contadino, Gary Ham, Adriano S. Mondala Jr.; *inbet:* Greg Ham, Pete Newbauer, Rory Hensley, Amy Newman, Harper Jaten, Sorcha Ni Chuimin, Dean Kawada, Andeè Ott, William A. Kobylka, Tod Price, Chris Kurash, Robert J. Reed, Jon le Mond, Rick Remender, Rob Meyers, Eric Simmons, Lance Nelson, Melanie Walchek; *co-ord sup:* Brenda McGuirk; *dpt co-ord:* Sue Vyvyan; *3-D anim: sup:* Thomas M. Miller; *anim dir:* Mary F. Clarke-Miller; *journeyman anim:* Olun Riley, Chris Kazmier, David Satchwell; *anim:* David Munier, Mark A. Kauffman, Kelly Nelson, John P. Rand, Bill van Ness, Bruce Edwards; *dpt co-ord:* Karri Lindamood, Diane Youngs, Linda Kaul; *lay des: sup:* Philip A. Cruden; *lay art:* Nelson "Rey" Bohol, F.Q. "Jun" Lofamia, Troylan Caro, Juan "Jo" Luna, Daniel Hung Yuan Chiang, Will Makra, Alan Cranny, Fred A. Reilly, Abraham "Abe" de Ocampo, Sinèad Somers, Martin Hanley, Danny Taverna, David J. Hardy, Danny I. Tolentino, Stephen L. Holt, George

Villaflor, Michael Isaak, Vic Villacorta, Noly Zamora; *dpt co-ord:* Caroline Lynch; *back: sup:* Robyn C. Nason; *ass sup:* Dick Heichberger; *back art:* Winston B. Aquino, Derek Holmes, Paul X.X. Cheng, Paul M. Kelly, Jocelyn "Joy" D. Clemente, Henry McGrane, Phaedra Craig, David M. Rabbitte, John Devlin, Pio D. Ravago III, Zoe J. Evamy, Owen Rohu, Micah R. Gosney, Joseph M. Tangonan; *co-ord sup:* Gary Busacca; *continuity: sup:* Cathy Goldman, Cindy Nelson, Jennifer Alton; *ed:* Mark Server, Fiona Trayler, Annette Stone, Danny Mundhenk, Bob Bender, Scott B. Seymann, Tom Wheeler, Jay Chapman; *voices: Anastasia:* Meg Ryan; *Dimitri:* John Cusack; *Vladimir:* Kelsey Grammer; *Rasputin:* Christopher Lloyd; *Bartok:* Hank Azaria; *Sophie:* Bernadette Peters; *Young Anastasia:* Kirsten Dunst; *Dowager Empress Marie:* Angela Lansbury; *Singing voice of Anastasia:* Liz Callaway; *Singing voice of Young Anastasia:* Lacey Chabert; *Singing voice of Rasputin:* Jim Cummings; *Singing voice of Dimitri:* Jonathan Dokuchitz; *Czar Nicholas/Servant/Revolutionary Soldier/Ticket Agent:* Rock Jones; *Phlegmenkoff/Old Woman:* Andrea Martin; *Young Dimitri:* Glenn Walker Harris Jr.; *Actress:* Debra Mooney; *Travelling Man/Major Domo:* Arthur Malet; *Anastasia Impostor:* Charity James; *crowd walla:* The Loop Group; *singers:* Richard Marx, Donna Lewis, Aaliyah, Deana Carter; *ensemble/character vocals:* Brooks Almy, John Jellison, Ellen Bernfeld, Kenny Karen, Judith Blazer, Curtis King Jr., Jeff Blumenkrantz, Joseph Kolinski, Ted Brunetti, Alix Korey, Glen Burtnick, David Lowenstein, Vivian Cherry, Cindy Mizelle, Robin Clark, Bill Nolte, Victoria Clark, Michele Pawk, Madeline Doherty, Billy Porter, Robert du Sold, Patrick Quinn, Gregg Edelman, Karen Silver, Al Fritsch, J.K. Simmons, Kyle Gordon, Frank Simms, Darius de Haas, Emily Skinner, Michael Louis Harvey, Ted Sperling, Jan Horvath, Vaneese Y. Thomas, Lillias White; *Prokofiev: "Cinderella":* London Symphony Orchestra conducted by Andrè Previn; *mus:* David Newman; music performed by Los Angeles and New York AFM Musicians; *songs: (lyrics)* Lynn Ahrens; *(mus)* Stephen Flaherty; *orch:* Douglas Besterman, William D. Brohn; songs conducted by Douglas Besterman, Theodore Sperling, Eric Stern, Lucas Richman; *vocal arrangements:* Stephen Flaherty; *song prod sup:* Andy Hill; *score orch:* Xandy Janko, David Newman, Daniel Hamuy, Douglas Besterman; *scoring consult:* Krystyna Newman; *mus rec/mic:* John Kurlander; *synthesizer programming:* Marty Frasu; *casting:* Brian Chavanne, Mary Hildalgo; *prod sup:* Ciavàn Morris, Gerry Carty; *scene planning:* Vincent Clarke, Derek Nielsen, Kip Goldman, Aran O'Reilly; *digital checking: sup:* Colum Slevin; *asst sup:* Carol Hannan; *anim check:* Linda Fitzpatrick, Lisa Maher, Brian Forsythe, Frances Kumashiro, Joanne Sugrue, Jamie Vallee; *anim col styling: sup:* Carmen Oliver, Donal Freeney; *stylists:* Lyn Mulvany, Berenice Keegan, Noirìn Hanley, Kathy Carter-Costello, Gareth McKinney, Carrie Dahl Marino, Suzanne O'Reilly; *digital scanning: sup:* Frank Richards; *key processor:* Joseph Cop; *scanners/checkers:* Brett Long, Jason Salata, Kenneth Vallee, Brandi Young, Neil Zawicki; *digital paint: sup:* Liam T. Hannan, Kenneth J. Cioe; *shift sup:* James J. Stoyanof; *mark-up painters;* Cindy Dankworth-Kelsey, Brien Manning, Crystal C. Mathews; *i&p:* Sharon Ann Addair, Carrie-Ann Hall, Jennifer Andras-Vallecorsa, Heather Heichberger, Adrienne J. Augustain, Shelly Leigh, Elaine Blea-Starace, Hoyko Lim, Tracy A. Butenko, Jeff J. Marshall, Benjamin Cohen, Danelle Murtaugh, Jerry Crow, Mollie I. Pena, Matthew K. Englehart, Nikki Rivera, Laurie Engler, Volcano Sanders, Valerie J. Gately, David Spencer, Wendy Wilson; *i&p check:* R. Scott Henricks, Alex Mitchell, Clifton L. Wegener; *compositing: sup:* Jeanette Maher, Kenneth Brain; *compositors:* Emmet Doyle, Eric Ryan, John O'Flaherty, Brad Gayo, Christopher Olson; *computer back art:* Gary Cooper; *asst to Don Bluth:* R. Charles "Chaz" Smith; *asst to Gary Goldman:* Fiona Byrne-Morris; *asst to Maureen Donley:* Mark Misch; *prod sec:* Debbie Vercellino; *subcontracting co-ord:* Shareena Carlson; *key copier operator:* Jon Schmitt; *licensing co-ord:* Mary Busacca; *ADR voice casting:* Barbara Harris; *choreog:* Adam M. Shankman; *addit rec:* Danny Wallin; *orch contractors:* Emil Charlap, Sandy de Crescent; *vocal contractors:* Alan Filderman, Bobbi Page; *Russian choral translations:* Lev Volod; *mus preparation:* Larry Abel, Jo Ann Kane Music Services; *Sony scoring crew:* Sue McLean, Greg Dennen, Mark Eshelman, Pat Weber, Richard Dearmas; *International mus co-ord:* Maggie Rodford & Air-Edel Associates Ltd; *computer technology dir:* Mark Weathers; *fx software design:* Giovanni Colombo; *snr network engineer:* Terry Merrill; *software development engineers:* Randy Groom, Ben S. Choi; *software support:* Jody Smaciarz; *graphics:* Sean Hart; *data control mgr:* John R. Brain; *applications specialist:* Marie A. Slevin; *data management:* Howard J. Levenson; *engineering dir:* Scott Hamilton; *audio/video engineering:* Diarmuid

MacAlasdair, Neil Keaveney, Burl L. Doty, Sam Davisson, Jennifer M. Jolls, Jeff A. Snodgrass; *electrician:* Dean Umfress; *post prod: sd ed:* Richard L. Anderson, Brent Brooks, Ken Karmen, Tom Villano, Ralph Stuart, Chris Carpenter, Bill W. Benton, Jim Bolt, Robert Renga, Craig Heath; *dialogue ed:* Avram D. Gold; *special sd des:* Eric Lindemann; *sd fx ed:* John Dunn, Julia Evershade, Ken J. Johnson; *foley:* John B. Roesch, Hilda Hodges, Mary Jo Lang, Rick Mitchell, Jason King, F. Scott Taylor; *post prod co-ord:* Steven D. Parent; *col timer:* Dale Grahn; *neg cutter:* Mo Henry; *prod asst:* John Corsi, Adam Cresswell, Cary Curley, Matt Dougherty, Nikki Hill, Matthew Leivian, Robert Marino, John Piegzik, Nick Quan, Dana Sulceski; *computer hardware:* Silicon Graphics Computer Systems Inc., Ciprico Inc.; *computer software:* Cel Animation — Digital Video S.R.L. Toonz, Uli Meyer Features Ltd., Bardel Animation Ltd., Dynomight Cartoons, Character Builders Inc., Canuck Creations Inc., Averkios Maltezos, Michael Mills Prods Ltd., Monster Prods Ltd., Diann Landau, Little Wolf Entertainment; *Russian research:* Paul Kinsinger, Linda Wetzel, Mary Ann Allin, Evgenia Zimnukhova, Yuri Petrochenkov, Slava Pazhitnov, Sasha Goutman, Irina Yegorova; *col:* Tech. *sd:* Dolby digital. CS. 94 min. • St. Petersberg in 1917, eight-year-old Princess Anastasia is celebrating her birthday when Rasputin, the Mad Monk, gatecrashes the party and puts a curse on the royal family. Not long after, the Russian Revolution commences and, in a desperate escape, Anastasia loses her memory when she has another run-in with Rasputin. Ten years pass and a rich reward is offered to locate the missing princess. Dimitri, a former servant boy to the family devises a scam, auditioning a number of girls to play the part of Anastasia, not realizing that the girl he has chosen is the genuine princess.

192. Anatole Sept. 1962; *p.c.:* Rembrandt for Para; *prod:* William L. Snyder; *dir/story:* Gene Deitch; adapted from the book by Eve Titus, illustrated by Paul Galdone; *anim dir:* Václav Bedřich; *anim:* Zdeněk Smetana, Milan Klikar, Antonín Bureš, Věra Marešová, Mirko Kačena, Bohumil Šiška, Bohumil Šejda, Věra Kudrnová, Jindřich Barta, Zdenka Skřípková, Olga Šišková; *lay:* Gene Deitch; *back:* Bohumil Šiška; *voices:* Carl Reiner, Allen Swift; *mus:* Václav Lidl; col. *sd.* 9 min. • Eve Titus' story of a Parisian mouse who is appointed Vice President of a cheese factory.

193. Anchors Aweigh 1945; *p.c.:* MGM; *dir:* William Hanna, Joseph Barbera; *anim:* Ed Barge, Michael Lah, Kenneth Muse, Ray Patterson, Irven Spence; *technical:* Carmen G. Maxwell; *voices:* Sara Berner; *song:* Ralph Freed, Sammy Fain; *mus:* Georgie Stoll; *l/a:* Gene Kelly; *col:* Tech. *sd:* WE. 7 min. • Seq: *l/a/anim; Academy Award nomination.* Live-action film in which Gene Kelly tells of how he once stumbled across a land where music was forbidden. He goes to see the king (Jerry the mouse) and finds out that the law was passed because he couldn't sing or dance. Kelly shows him how. Mickey Mouse was originally wanted for Kelly's dance routine but when Disney declined, MGM tried closer to home with legendary results.

194. Ancient Fistory (*Popeye*) 30 Jan. 1953; *p.c.:* Famous for Para; *dir:* Seymour Kneitel; *story:* Irving Spector; *anim:* Al Eugster, Wm. B. Pattengill; *sets:* Robert Connavale; *voices:* Jack Mercer, Mae Questel, Jackson Beck; *mus:* Winston Sharples; *ph:* Leonard McCormick; *prod mgr:* Seymour Shultz; *col:* Tech. *sd:* RCA. 7 min. • Re-working of the Cinderella story. A magic can of spinach conjours up Popeye's fairy godfather who sends him to the ball with the prospects of marrying the fair princess Olive.

195. And His Goat Came Back 1909; *p.c.:* Vit Corp; *anim:* James Stuart Blackton; b&w. sil. • No story available.

196. And So Tibet (*Modern Madcap*) Oct. 1964; *p.c.:* Para Cartoons; *dir:* Seymour Kneitel; *story:* Jack Mendelsohn; *anim:* Martin Taras; *sets:* Robert Little; *voices:* Bob MacFadden; *mus:* Winston Sharples; *ph:* Leonard McCormick; *prod mgr:* Abe Goodman; *col:* Tech. *sd:* RCA. 6 min. • The museum curator sends two of his able-bodied assistants to Tibet to capture the Abominable Snowman.

197. And the Green Grass Grew All Around (*Screen Songs*) 30 Apr. 1931; *p.c.:* The Fleischer Studio for Para; *prod:* Max Fleischer; *dir:* Dave Fleischer; *anim:* Al Eugster; *mus:* Art Turkisher; b&w. *sd:* WE. 6 min. • A shotgun wedding ceremony for insects. A little bug attempts to grow a flower which is repeatedly stepped on. In his frustration, the diminutive insect turns into the "bouncing ball" and bounces over the words to the song.

198. And to Think That I Saw It in Mulberry Street (*Puppetoon*) 5 May 1944; *p.c.:* George Pal prods for Para; *prod/dir:* George Pal; *story:* Dr. Seuss; *adapt:* Jack Miller; *mus:* Maurice de Packh; *voice:* Tommy Cook; *the boy:* Gary Gray; *col:* b&w/Tech. *sd:* WE. 8 min. *l/a/anim. Academy Award nomination.* • From a drab horse and wagon, a small boy imagines a grand parade that he might have seen going down the street.

199. Andy Panda: Air Raid Warden (*Cartune*) 21 Dec. 1942; *p.c.:* Walter Lantz prods for Univ; *dir:* Alex Lovy; *story:* Ben Hardaway, Milton Schaffer; *anim:* George Dane; *sets:* Fred Brunish; *voices:* Margaret Hill, Mel Blanc (pre-recorded); *mus:* Darrell Calker; *prod mgr:* George Hall; *col:* Tech. *sd:* WE. 7 min. • A troublesome goat eats Andy's air-raid siren and some traffic lights in the bargain.

200. Andy Panda Goes Fishing (*Andy Panda*) 22 Jan. 1940; *p.c.:* Walter Lantz prods for Univ; *dir:* Burt Gillett; *story:* Victor McLeod, Gil Burton; *anim:* Ray Fahringer, Fred Kopietz; *sets:* Edgar Keichle; *voices:* Sara Berner, Danny Webb; *mus:* Frank Marsales; *prod mgr:* George Hall; *col:* Tech. *sd:* WE. 8 min. • Andy and his turtle friend go fishing and find themselves being hunted by pygmies.

201. Andy Panda's Pop (*Cartune*) 28 July 1941; *p.c.:* Walter Lantz prods for Univ; *story:* Ben Hardaway, Lowell Elliot; *anim:* Alex Lovy, George Dane; *sets:* Fred Brunish; *voice:* Kent Rogers; *mus:* Darrell Calker; *prod mgr:* George Hall; *col:* Tech. *sd:* WE. 7 min. • Pop won't pay to have his roof repaired professionally and decides to mend it himself.

202. Andy Panda's Victory Garden (*Cartune*) 7 Sept. 1942; *p.c.:* Walter Lantz prods for Univ; *dir:* Alex Lovy; *story:* Ben Hardaway, Milt Schaffer; *anim:* Lester Kline; *sets:* Fred Brunish; *voices:* Margaret Hill, Kent Rogers; *mus:* Darrell Calker; *prod mgr:* George Hall; *col:* Tech. *sd:* WE. 7 min. • Andy's gardening runs into a hazard with the arrival of a gopher.

203. Angel Puss (*Looney Tunes*) 3 June 1944; *p.c.:* Leon Schlesinger prods for WB; *dir:* Charles M. Jones; *story:* Lou Lilly; *anim:* Ken Harris; *lay:* Art Heinemann; *ed:* Treg Brown; *voices:* Mel Blanc; *mus:* Carl W. Stalling; *prod sup:* Henry Binder, Raymond G. Katz; *col:* Tech. *sd:* Vit. 7 min. • A little black boy sets out to drown a cat but the feline escapes to haunt him.

204. Angels in the Outfield 15 July 1994; *p.c.:* Walt Disney/Caravan Pictures for BV; *anim:* Steve Braggs, George Bruder, Mike Collery, Aliza Corson, Jamie Dixon, Terry Emmons, Philippe Gluckman, Rex Grignon, Roger Guyett, Betsy Asher Hall, Rebecca Marie, Cleveland Mitchell, Michael Necci, Karen Schneider, Amie Slate, Larry Weiss; *character anim:* Shawn Broes; *motion sup:* Raman Hui; *motion anim prod:* Doug Nichols; *col:* Tech. *sd:* Dolby stereo. 103 min. *l/a.* • Live-action fantasy: Celestial beings help the "Angels" baseball team win the pennant.

205. Anima Drawings (*Cartoonlets*) June 1914. *p.c.:* M.P. Sales; b&w. *sil.* 3 min. • A magic pencil draws comic drawings that come to life.

206. The Animal Cracker Circus (*Color Rhapsody*) 23 Sept. 1938; *p.c.:* Charles Mintz prods for Colum; *dir:* Ben Harrison; *anim:* Manny Gould; *voices:* Leone Le Doux, Dave Weber; *mus:* Joe de Nat; *prod mgr:* James Bronis; *col:* Tech. *sd:* RCA. 7 min. • Scrappy is told that if he eats his soup the animal crackers will come alive and perform ... which they do.

207. The Animal Fair (*Aesop's Sound Fable*) 31 Jan. 1931; *p.c.:* Van Beuren for Pathé; *dir:* Mannie Davis, John Foster; *mus:* Gene Rodemich; b&w. *sd:* RCA. 9 min. • The animals go to the fair and enjoy the sideshows.

208. The Animal Fair (*Noveltoon*) 30 Jan. 1959. *p.c.:* Para Cartoons; *dir:* Seymour Kneitel; *sets:* Robert Little; *mus:* Winston Sharples; *ph:* Leonard McCormick; *prod mgr:* Abe Goodman; *col:* Tech. *sd:* RCA. 6 min. *seq: Fun at the Fair; Philharmaniacs.* • Animals enjoy the fun of the fair, then a mouse who is annoyed by "long haired" music sets out to destroy it.

209. The Animal World 1956; *p.c.:* Windsor for WB; *anim dir:* Willis O'Brien; *anim:* Ray Harryhausen, Pasqual Manuelli, Harold Wilson, Arthur S. Rhoades; *voices:* Theodore Von Eltz, John Storm; *mus:* Paul Sawtell; Tech. *sd.* 82 min. *l/a/anim.* • Live-action documentary by Irwin Allen, depicting the development of animal life on earth starting from prehistoric days. Ray Harryhausen was engaged to animate the dinosaur sequence. Completed in a record six weeks.

210. The Animal's Fair *(Aesop's Film Fables)* 14 Dec. 1923; *p.c.:* Fables Pictures Inc for Pathé; *dir:* Paul Terry; b&w. *sil.* 5 min. • The animals hold a fair and indulge in some unusual and highly improbable stunts.

211. Animalympics 15 May 1980; *p.c.:* Lisberger Studios, Inc.; *dir:* Steven Lisberger; *prod:* Steven Lisberger, Donald Kushner; *story:* Michael Fremer, Steven Lisberger; *character development/story:* Steven Lisberger, Roger Allers, John Norton; *graphic des/anim:* Rich Fernalld; *anim dir:* Bill Kroyer; *anim:* John Norton, Roger Allers, Bill Kroyer, Chuck Harvey, Steve Chorney, Brad Bird, Arnie Wong, Dan Haskett, Bruce Woodside; *underwater seq des:* Arnie Wong; *asst anim:* Darrell Rooney, Dave Stephan, Keath Bambury, Mary Burney, Cynthia Swift, Tom Sito, Sean Joyce, Maria Ramocki, David Virgien, Ron Wong, Beverly Zlozower; *fx anim:* Paul Nevitt, Rich Fernalld; *lay:* Roger Allers, John Norton, Peter Mueller; *back:* Peter Mueller, Richard Blair, K.W. Henderson; *ed:* Matt Cope; *voices: Barbara Warblers/ Brenda Springer/ Cora Lee Perrier/ Tatyana Tushenko/ Dorrie Turnell:* Gilda Radner; *Rugs Turkell:* Billy Crystal; *Keen Hackshaw:* Harry Shearer; *Henry Hummel/René Fromage/ Kit Mambo/ Bolt Jenkins/ Joey Gongolong:* Michael Fremer; *mus:* Graham Gouldman (of *10CC*); *mus sup:* Joel Sill; *addit mus/orchestration:* Jamie Haskell; *mus ed:* Michael Fremer; *mus engineers:* Larry Forkner, Tony Spath; *asst dir:* Michael Fremer; *anim check:* Gino Gallo, Sara Bleick; *i&p:* Susan Allison Bomzer, *(East:)* Gloria Runne, Die Modlin, Kathryn Does, Jayne Tobin, Steven Smith, Jeanne Bosari, Joan Hurley, Stephanie Kaplan, Kathleen McManus, Laura Moroney, Beth Auman, Mary Earley, Margaret Bailey Michael Chandler, Paul Schulenburg, Neva Savath, Linda Mellen, Amy Myers, Carol Dobson, George Tilton, Amy Kock, *(West:)* Auril Thompson-Pebley, Nancy Thompson, Peggy Matz, Margaret Colenne Gonzales, Mary L. Norris, Judi Cassell, Denise Wethington, Wendy Copple, Martha Sigal, Malissa Bourgois, Norma B. Nuwman, Raynell Day, Cathy Crum, Harriette Rossall, Bonny Nardini, Gloria Estrada, Eileen Ridgeway, Sharon Dabek, Robin Draper; *mattes:* Carol Nevitt, Barbara Terezrgoggin, Nancy Wong; *prod asst:* Barry Petersen, Shelley Price, Amanda Julian; *neg cutter:* Bob Lass; *ph:* Paul Nevitt, Ted Bemiller Jr.; *mix:* James R. Cook, Don MacDougall, Robert L. Harman; *Dolby engineer:* Don Digiroland; *asso prod:* Peggy Flook; *prod mgr:* Kris Weber; *col:* Tech. *sd:* Dolby stereo. 79 min. • The first animal Olympics are being held in 1980 at Pawprint Stadium. Z.O.O. Network secures the television rights to broadcast throughout the animal kingdom. The competitors are followed by the cameras and a romance blossoms during the cross-country marathon between René Fromage and Kit Mambo. Originally completed with an independent filmmaker grant from the American Film Institute in conjunction with the National Endowment for the Arts. Initially produced as two thirty-minute specials ("Anamalympics Winter Games" and "Anamalympics Summer Games") with "Winter Games" airing in 1979 on NBC. "Summer Games" never got to air because of the U.S. boycott of the Soviet Union's Olympics, due to its invasion of Afghanistan. The following year the two parts were connected with new linking material and aired on HBO and also got a theatrical release.

212. Animated Cotton Sept. 1909; *p.c.:* Urban Trading Co; *prod:* Charles Urban; *anim:* Walter R. Booth; b&w. *sil.* 3½ min. • Animated needle and cotton.

213. Animated Crosswords 27 Jan. 1925; *p.c.:* Banner prods Inc.; *prod:* C.H. Ferrell; *anim:* Bert Green; b&w. *sil.* • The current trend for crosswords is brought to the screen.

214. The Animated Grouch Chaser ; *p.c.:* Barré Cartoons for Edison; *prod:* Raoul Barré; *anim:* Raoul Barré, Gregory la Cava, Frank Moser; b&w. *sil. s/r: l/a/anim.* • **1915: The Animated Grouch Chaser** 4 Mar. **The Animated Grouch Chaser** 17 Mar. **Cartoons in the Kitchen** 21 Apr. **Cartoons in the Barber Shop** 22 May. **Cartoons in the Parlor** 5 June. **Cartoons in the Hotel** 21 June. **Cartoons in the Laundry** 8 July. **Cartoons on Tour** 6 Aug. **Cartoons on the Beach** 25 Aug. **Cartoons in a Seminary** 9 Sept. **Cartoons in the Country** 15 Oct. **Cartoons on a Yacht** 29 Oct. **Cartoons in a Sanitarium** 12 Nov. **Hicks in Nightmare Land** 4 Dec. • **1916: The Adventures of Tom the Tamer** *and* **Kid Kelly** 19 May. **The Story of Cook vs. Chef** *and* **Hicks in Nightmareland** 25 May. **Love's Labor's Lost** June. • Cartoons featuring "Silas Bumpkin" on split-reel with live-action playlets.

215. Animated Hair Cartoons *p.c.:* Red Seal; *drawn by* Edwin Marcus; b&w. *sil.* 3 min. • **1924:** (AA): 1 Oct.; (BB): 22 Nov. • **1925:** (CC):

2 Feb.; (DD): 2 Mar.; (EE): 2 Apr.; (FF): 9 Apr.; (GG): 16 Apr.; (HH): 25 Apr.; (II): 9 May; (JJ): 17 May; (KK): 24 May; (LL): 30 May; (MM): 6 June; (NN): 13 June; (OO): 20 June; (PP): 27 June; (QQ): 4 July; (RR): 11 July; (SS): 18 July; (TT): 25 July; (UU): 1 Aug.;(VV): 8 Aug.; (WW): 15 Aug.; (XX): 22 Aug.; (YY): 29 Aug.; (ZZ): 5 Sept.; 15 Oct.; 15 Nov.; 15 Dec. • **1926:** 15 Jan.; 15 Feb.; 15 Mar.; 10 Apr.; 1 May; 12 June; 25 June; 17 July; 31 July; 14 Aug.; 28 Aug.; 11 Sept.; 25 Sept.; 16 Oct.; 15 Nov.; 1 Dec.; 15 Dec. • Drawn by "Marcus," the celebrated cartoonist of *The New York Times,* based on the idea of what a difference hair makes in a person's appearance. A typical example has the artist manipulating a London policeman's hair and changing him into Lady Astor. Shakespeare into John Barrymore, Lenin to William Farnum, the British Lion into Lloyd George and so on.

216. The Animated Weekly ; *p.c.:* Univ Film Mfg Co Inc.; *prod:* P.A. Powers; *anim:* Hal Reid; b&w. *sil.* • Animated items in weekly pictorial lasting from 1 Oct. 1912 to 9 Dec. 1914; 20 Dec. 1916 to 28 Nov. 1917

217. The Animated Weekly ; *p.c.:* Univ Film Mfg Co Inc.; *prod:* P.A. Powers; *anim:* Hy Mayer; b&w. *sil.* • Cartoons by the world famous caricaturist Hy Mayer of *Puck.* Animated items in weekly pictorial lasting from 16 Dec. 1914 to 29 Dec. 1915; 21 Nov. 1917 to 18 Dec. 1918. Such was the importance of this series that the Director of Public Information selected one of Hy Mayer's ("The Eagle's Brood") as fitting propaganda to be screened to the allies as "officially authorised action in support of the war."

218. Annie Hall 20 Apr. 1977; *p.c.:* UA/Jack Rollins-Charles H. Joffe; *anim seq:* Chris Ishi; *col:* DeLuxe. *sd:* Mono. Panavision. 20 sec. • Live-action Woody Allen feature with an animated insert illustrating Allen's failure with romance. When he was a kid and saw *Snow White,* he fell for the Wicked Queen.

219. Annie Laurie *(Song Car-Tune)* 1924; *p.c.:* Inkwell Studios for Red Seal; *prod:* Max Fleischer; *dir:* Dave Fleischer; b&w. *sil.* • No story available.

220. Annie Moved Away *(Oswald)* 28 May 1934; *p.c.:* Univ; *anim:* Walter Lantz, "Bill" Nolan; *anim:* Ray Abrams, Fred Avery, Cecil Surry, Jack Carr, Victor McLeod, Merle Gilson; *mus:* James Dietrich; b&w. *sd:* WE. 7 min. • Annie invites Oswald to come over but a villain spirits her away before he arrives. With the aid of a dog, Oswald tracks her down and vanquishes the blackguard.

221. Another Day, Another Doormat *(Terry-Toon)* Mar. 1959; *p.c.:* TT for Fox; *ex prod:* Bill Weiss; *sup dir:* Gene Deitch; *dir:* Al Kouzel; *story:* Tom Morrison; *anim:* Mannie Davis, Hal Shipero, Ed Donnelly, Vinnie Bell; *lay:* Jules Feiffer; *back:* Bill Hilliker; *voices:* Allen Swift; *mus:* Philip Scheib; *prod mgr:* Sparky Schudde; *col:* Tech. *sd:* RCA. 7 min. CS. • Henpecked John Doormat becomes a raging bull when away from his tyrannical wife. He storms to the department store to return a defective pipe but, seeing his wife there, reverts to form.

222. The Ant and the Aardvark *(Ant & Aardvark)* 5 Mar. 1969; *p.c.:* Mirisch/DFE for UA; *dir:* Friz Freleng; *story:* John W. Dunn; *anim:* Manny Perez, Warren Batchelder, Manny Gould, Don Williams; *lay:* Corny Cole; *back:* Tom O'Loughlin; *ed:* Lee Gunther; *voices:* John Byner; *mus:* Doug Goodwin; *featuring:* Pete Candoli, Billy Byers, Jimmy Rowles, Tommy Tedesco, Ray Brown, Shelly Manne; *ph:* John Burton Jr.; *prod sup:* Jim Foss, Harry Love; *col:* DeLuxe. *sd:* RCA. 6 min. • The Aardvark begins his arduous career in pursuit of the elusive Ant, only succeeding in snaring a picnic lunch.

223. The Ant from Uncle *(Ant & Aardvark)* 2 Apr. 1969; *p.c.:* Mirisch/DFE for UA; *dir:* George Gordon; *story:* John W. Dunn; *anim:* Art Leonardi, Warren Batchelder, Don Williams; *lay:* Corny Cole; *back:* Tom O'Loughlin; *ed:* Lee Gunther; *voices:* John Byner. *mus:* Doug Goodwin; *featuring:* Pete Candoli, Billy Byers, Jimmy Rowles, Tommy Tedesco, Ray Brown, Shelly Manne; *ph:* John Burton Jr.; *prod sup:* Jim Foss, Harry Love; *col:* DeLuxe. *sd:* RCA. 6 min. • The Aardvark disguises himself as a social club for ants and when that doesn't work he tunnels underground through a mine-field.

224. Ant Life As It Isn't *(Aesop's Film Fables)* 20 June 1927; *p.c.:* Fables Pictures Inc for Pathé; *dir:* Paul Terry; b&w. *sil.* 6 min. • An ant gallantly rescues his girlfriend from a bird with help from the Bug Fire Department.

225. Ant Pasted *(Looney Tunes)* 9 May 1953; *p.c.:* WB; *dir:* I. Freleng;

story: Warren Foster; *anim:* Virgil Ross, Arthur Davis, Manuel Perez, Ken Champin; *fx:* Harry Love; *lay:* Hawley Pratt; *back:* Irv Wyner; *ed:* Treg Brown; *voices:* Arthur Q. Bryan; *mus:* Carl Stalling; *prod mgr:* John W. Burton; *prod:* Edward Selzer; *col:* Tech. *sd:* Vit. 7 min. • Elmer Fudd upsets a colony of ants with his July 4th celebrations.

226. Anti-Cats *(Mighty Mouse)* Mar. 1950; *p.c.:* TT for Fox; *dir:* Mannie Davis; *story:* John Foster; *anim:* Jim Tyer; *sets:* Art Bartsch; *mus:* Philip A. Scheib; *ph:* Douglas Moye; *col:* Tech. *sd:* RCA. 7 min. • Three mice are turned out of a house into a blizzard by a cruel cat landlord. Mighty Mouse arrives on skis to put matters right.

227. Anti-Fat *(Aesop's Film Fable)* 17 Feb. 1927. *p.c.:* Fables Pictures Inc for Pathé; *dir:* Paul Terry; b&w. sil. 6 min. • A patent medicine salesman peddles "Anti-Fat" and "Anti-Thin" panacea. A pig expires from drinking too much "Anti-Fat," an obese dog also drinks too much and disappears. Farmer Al's dog swaps labels on the bottles and when the salesman drinks what he believes to be "Anti-Fat," he grows to gargantuan proportions and explodes while Al and the dog make off with his valise of money.

228. Antique Antics *(Krazy Kat)* 14 June 1933. *p.c.:* Winkler for Colum; *story:* Ben Harrison, Manny Gould; *anim:* Al Eugster, Preston Blair; *mus:* Joe de Nat; *prod mgr:* James Bronis; b&w. *sd:* WE. 6 min. • No story available.

229. The Ants and the Grasshopper *(Aesop's Film Fables)* 10 July 1921. *p.c.:* Fables Pictures Inc for Pathé; *dir:* Paul Terry; b&w. sil. 6 min. • No story available.

230. Ants in the Pantry *(Ant & Aardvark)* 10 June 1970; *p.c.:* Mirisch/DFE for UA; *dir:* Hawley Pratt; *story:* John W. Dunn; *anim:* Manny Perez, Don Williams; *lay:* Dick Ung; *back:* Richard H. Thomas; *ed:* Lee Gunther; *voices:* John Byner; *mus:* Doug Goodwin; Featuring: Pete Candoli, Billy Byers, Jimmy Rowles, Tommy Tedesco, Ray Brown, Shelly Manne; *prod sup:* Jim Foss, Harry Love; *col:* DeLuxe. *sd:* RCA. 6 min. • The Aardvark overhears an address that's over-run with ants.

231. Ants in the Plants *(Color Classic)* 15 Mar. 1940. *p.c.:* The Fleischer Studio for Para; *prod:* Max Fleischer; *dir:* Dave Fleischer; *story:* George Manuel; *anim:* Myron Waldman, George Moreno; *mus:* Sammy Timberg; *col:* Tech. *sd:* WE. 7 min. • An ant colony deals with a greedy anteater.

232. Ants in Your Pantry *(Terry-Toon)* 16 Feb. 1945; *p.c.:* TT for Fox; *dir:* Mannie Davis; *story:* John Foster; *mus:* Philip A. Scheib; *col:* Tech. *sd:* RCA. 6 min. • The ants build a giant community center for their expectant Queen. As soon as the eggs are hatched, fathers are pushing their respective baby carriages.

233. Antz 2 Oct. 1998. *p.c.:* Dreamworks Pictures/PDI for United International Pictures; *dir:* Eric Darnell, *prod:* Tim Johnson, Brad Lewis, Aron Warner, Patty Wooton; *ex prod:* Penney Finkelman Cox, Sandra Rabins, Carl Rosendahl; *scr:* Todd Alcott, Chris Weitz, Paul Weitz; *story consultant:* Zak Penn; *story head:* Randy Cartwright; *story artists:* Mike Cahuela, Roger Koo, Chris Miller, Anthony F. Stacchi, Conrad Vernon, Catherine Yun, James Fujii, Steve Hickner, Todd Kurosawa, Mike Mitchell, Simon Wells; *prod des:* John Bell; *anim dir:* Denis Couchon, Sean Curran, Donnachada Daly; *anim:* Edip Agi, Chung Min Chan, Tim Chelung, Webster Colcord, Raffaella Filipponi, David Gainey, Enrique Navarrete Gil, Collin Hennen, Anthony Hodgson, Tim Keon, Justin Kohn, Eric Lessard, Noel McGinn Jr., Fred Nilsson, David Rader, Jason A. Reisig, David Spivack, Don Venhaus, Larry Bafia, Kenny Chung, Patricia Hannaway, David House, Ken Keys, Boris Kossmehi. Judy Kriger, Michelle R. Meeker, Rick Richards, Emmanuel Roth, Vanessa Schwartz; *art dir:* Kendal Cronkhite; *seq dir:* Lawrence Guterman; *creative consultants:* Ted Elliott, Terry Rossio; *voices: Z-1948:* Woody Allen; *Chip:* Dan Ackroyd; *Queen:* Anne Bancroft; *Mully:* Jane Curtin; *Barbatus:* Danny Glover; *General Mandible:* Gene Hackman; *Azteca:* Jennifer Lopez; *Drunk Scout:* John Mahoney; *Psychologist:* Paul Mazursky; *Foreman:* Grant Shaud; *Weaver:* Sylvester Stallone; *Princess Bala:* Sharon Stone; *Cutter:* Christopher Walken; *also:* Jim Cummings, Jerry Sroka, April Winchell; *looping:* Charles Bartlett, Jack Blessing, Thomas Brunelle, William Calvert, Richard Casino, Kate Carlin, Jane Christopher, David Coburn, Jennifer Crystal, Alex Daniels, James Dean, Peter Doyle, Murphy Dunne, Chad Einbinder, Jeff Fischer, Robin Florence, Rebecca Forstadt, Val Franco, Anne Liese Goldman, Brian Herskovitz, Bobby Jacoby, Nick Jameson, Laurie Johnson, Holly Kane, Daamen Kraal, Marsha Kramer, Steve Kramer, Anne Lockhart, Anne

Mathias, Katie Leigh, Don Maxwell, David McCharen, Christie Mellor, Jonathan Nichols, Julie Payne, Tony Pope, Michelle Ruff, Gary Schwartz, Steve Staley, Arnold Turner, Ruth Zalduondo; *ed:* Stan Webb; *visual development: character des:* Raman Hui; *conceptual art:* Mary Grandpré, Peter Chan, H.B. (Buck) Lewis, Eric Tiemens; *prod illustrators:* Guill Aume Aretos, Cliff Boulo, Shannon Jeffries; *set des:* Don Weinger; *digital paint:* Michael Collery, Steven Albert, Alan Sonneman, Thomas Esmeralda, Mark Sullivan, Keith Goreham; *production engineering: technical dir:* George Bruder, Mitch Amino, Gregory A. Dismond, Eric Salituro; *systems/network architect:* Mark Kirk; *ld tools programmer:* Kevin Cureton; *prod co-ord:* Michael Garner, Edward Granlund; *character technical dir: sup:* Beth Hofer; *prod sup character ld modeling:* Hael Kobayashi; *facial anim system:* Dick Walsh; *lead character ld/character ld's:* Bart Coughlin, Lucia Modesto, James Rowell, Robert Vogt; *prod co-ord:* Patty Kaku; *modelling: sup:* Konrad Dunton; *modelers:* Jeff Hayes, Lee Lanier, Brian Deans-Rowe, Lioudmila Golynskaia, Nick Walker, Ken Whitaker; *sculptors:* Damon Bard, Cecile Picard; *mold & cast makers:* Christopher Goehe, Victoria Lewis; *lay: sup:* Simon J. Smith; *prod sup:* Denise Nolan Cascino; *lay:* James Buckhouse, Sylvain Doreau, Sean D. Pollack, Bert Ong, Peter Plevritis; *lead seq technical dir:* Todd Heapy, Marty Sixkiller; *seq technical dir:* Brian Danker, Irene Deery, Sue Gleadhill, Melissa Teeng, Bob Whitehill, Steve R.J. Bell, John Braunreuther, Steve Kirchner, Jason Mellein; *prod co-ord:* Heather Freeman; *animation: anim sup:* Rex Grignon, Haman Hui; *prod sup:* Triva von Klark; *prod co-ord:* Jennifer Dahlman; *prod asst:* Alexander J. Ball; *lighting: sup & development leads:* Jean M. Cunningham, Janet Rentel; *sup:* Crag Ring, Paul Wing, Lisa Atkinson, Michael Warch, Lucy T. Gorman; *leads:* Michael Day, Susan Hayden, Sherry Y.S. Hsieh, Stephanie Katritos Sautai, Annmarie Koenig, Jin Liou, Joe Palrang, Frederic Sautai; *lighters:* Ken Ball, Philippe Denis, Dado Feigenblatt, Chad Greene, Thame Edwin Hawkins III, Ed LazorBarbara A. Meyers, Stephanie Mulqueen, Ronman Yu Yan Ng, Thomas Pushpathadam, Milton E. Rodriguez Rios, Pablo Valle, Carlos A. Videl, Nathania Ann Vishnevsky, David Blizzard, Chanda Cummings, Curt Stewart, Allesandro Tento, Chris Trimble, Alan Wolf; *lighting ld:* David de Bry (Gruf), Mark Edwards, Mark Authement, Kitt Hodsden; *3d surfacing:* Edward Deren, David Doepp, Bert T. Poole; *2d painter:* Rachel Falk; *prod cood:* Monty Kimball, Stacy Rentel; *visual efx: sup:* Ken Bielenberg, Philippe Gluckman, John "Jr." Robeck; *leads:* Karen Schneider Brodine, Juan J. Buhler, Jonathan Gibbs, Bill Seneshen, Scott Singer, Apurva Shah; *efx:* Alain de Hoe, Chzecorz Dude, Randall Hammond, Matthew Head, Scott Peterson, Erdeml Taylor, Martin Usiak, Joshua Wachman, Rhett Collier, Kristi Hewek, Jonah Hall, Kryzysztof Rostek, Adam Valdez; *prod co-ord:* Jennifer Freeman; *rendering: wranglers:* Grazia Como Ojeda, Vladmir Kanevsky, Mel Kangleon, Gerald McAleece III, Michael C. Walling, Betsy Brait, Alicia Bissinger, Michael Macias; *editorial:* Steve Bloom, Curtis Frelich, Devon Miller; *avid asst:* Michelle Belforte, David Fent, Lorelei David, Annemarie McCallion, Ingrid Schulz; *ed co-ord:* Carol Norton; *film room:* Tripp Hudson; *ph:* John M. Hannashiro; *sd:* Jeffrey Stephens, Bruce Parker, Alex Zaphiris; *software development: r&d staff:* Ken Pearce, Shawn Neely, Barry Fowler, Drew Olbrich, Daniel Wexler, Lawrence Kesteloot, Rahul C. Thakxer, Nick Foster, Gilles Dezeustre, Joanna Mason, Sumit Das; *production:* Gary Wohlleben, Deanne Koehn; *prod asst:* Gabriel Hvillerrubia, Jeff Tyler, Latifa Quacu, Hannah Harriette Kanew, Katie Fisher Intrieri, Paul Monteiro, Russell Peavey; *Information Technology/Training: IT training:* Jennifer Yu, Yumi Nishiyama, Jennie Posthumus; *technical writers:* Nick Gervas, Nick Thomas, Wendy Vogt; *systems programmers:* Curtis Calloway, Mark Harris, Denise Howard; *systems admin:* Grahame Breeze, Mike Chang, Michael Cutler, Margaret Myers, Mike Thompson, Rob Toy; *sd:* Richard L. Anderson, Elliott L. Koretz, Steve Maslow, Gregg Lanaker; *post production:* Martin Cohen, Erica Frauman, Sven E.M. Fahlgren; *dial ed:* Avram D. Gold; *sd fx:* John Popisil, Julia Evershade, Eric Lindemann, Marvin Walowitz; *sd ed:* Ralph Stuart, Sonny Pettijohn, Steve Lee, Mark Coffey, Bruce Balestier; *foley:* Dan O'Connell, John Cucci; *sd:* Linda Law, Brion Paccassi, Frank Fleming, Carlos Sotolongo; *Russian Hill rec engineer:* Daryn Roven; *sd asst:* Kyle Carbone, Howard Schwartz, Steve Rosen, Fernando Ascani; *choreog:* Adam Shankman, Ann Fletcher; *songs: Give Peace a Chance* by John Lennon; *Guantanamera* by Pete Seeger, Julian Orbon, Jose Fernandez, Diaz & José Marti; *Almost Like Being in Love* by Alan Jay Lerner, Frederick Loewe; *I Can See Clearly Now* by Johnny Nash, performed by Neil Finn; *High Hopes* by Sammy Cahn, James van Heusen, performed by Doris Day; *mus:* mus *prod:* Hans Zimmer; *orch:* Bruce Fowler, Nick Wollage; *mix:* Alan Meyerson; *mus ed:* Brian Richards, Adam Smalley; *mus conducted by* Gavin Greenaway; *model maker:* Facundo Rabaudi; *modelling:* Richard Agren, Bryan Allen, Matt Barlow, Ryan Bird, Jeff Bott, Emil Degrey, Wayne Hammer, Ben Jarvis, Ardie Johnson, Steve Keele, Takao Miyazawa, David Mooy, Tony Morrill, Matthew Paulson, Kent Ringger, Brian Salisbury, Kevin Scheidle; *prod mgr:* Patty Bonfilio, Jane Hartwell, Denise Minter; *prod co-ord:* Andre de Oliveira Araujo, Catherine Dingman, Stacey Vandermeer; *special thanks to:* Yoko Ono, Nina Jacobsen, Susan Amar, Bob Badami, Pat Crane, Wendy Crewson, John Doret, Les Hunter, Michael Kahn, Phil Lazebnik, Larry Lessler, David Lipman, Melody Meisel, Jennifer Nash, Ignacio Navarette, Martin Oppu, Amy Rabins, Rex Ray, Brian Williams, Karen Woods. *col:* Tech. *sd:* Dolby digital/Digital dts/SDDS. 83 min. • A dissatisfied worker ant named Z meets Princess Bala at a dance. She has escaped from her royal life to see how the other half lives but soon has to return. Z swaps places with his soldier ant buddy for a chance to see the Princess again but instead gets sent off to war, returning as the sole survivor and a "hero." The hard-nosed General Mandible has plans on liquidating the whole ant colony and sees Z as an obstacle to be disposed of. Z manages to escape with the princess and they go in search of the utopian land of "Insectopia" but return in time to save the colony from liquidation.

234. The Anvil Chorus Girl *(Popeye)* 26 May 1944; *p.c.:* Famous for Para; *dir:* I. Sparber; *story:* Bill Turner, Jack Ward; *anim:* Dave Tendlar, Morey Reden; *voices:* Jack Mercer, Mae Questel, Jackson Beck; *mus:* Sammy Timberg; *ph:* Leonard McCormick; *prod mgr:* Sam Buchwald; b&w. *sd:* RCA. 7 min.; Tech reissue: 5 Oct. 1951. • Popeye and Bluto help out in Olive's blacksmith shop.

235. Any Bonds Today *p.c.:* Leon Schlesinger prods for U.S. Treasury/National Screen; *dir:* Robert Clampett; *story:* Frank Tashlin; *anim:* Robert McKimson, Rod Scribner, Virgil Ross, Sid Sutherland; *lay:* Thomas McKimson; *back:* Michael Sasanoff; *ed:* Treg Brown; *voices:* Mel Blanc, Arthur Q. Bryan; *mus:* Carl W. Stalling; *song:* Irving Berlin; *col:* Tech. *sd:* Vit. 3 min. • Bugs, Porky and Elmer sing the patriotic title song against a background of "The Spirit of '76," encouraging patrons to buy War Bonds.

236. Any Little Girl That's a Nice Little Girl *(Screen Songs)* 18 Apr. 1931; *p.c.:* The Fleischer Studio for Para; *prod:* Max Fleischer; *dir:* Dave Fleischer; *anim:* Seymour Kneitel; *mus:* Art Turkisher; b&w. *sd:* WE. 6 min. • A popular cat-about-town romances Lulu Belle, a "Flapper" type cat.

237. Any Rags *(Talkartoon)* 2 Jan. 1932; *p.c.:* The Fleischer Studio for Para; *prod:* Max Fleischer; *dir:* Dave Fleischer; *anim:* Willard Bowsky; *mus:* Art Turkisher; b&w. *sd:* WE. 6 min. • Rag and Bone merchant Bimbo goes around the streets collecting while the rags come alive and cut capers. Betty and Ko-Ko also appear.

238. The Apache Kid *(Krazy Kat)* 9 Oct. 1930; *p.c.:* Winkler for Colum; *anim:* Ben Harrison, Manny Gould; *mus:* Joe de Nat; *prod:* Charles Mintz; b&w. *sd:* WE. 6 min. • A professional dancer grabs Krazy's sweetie.

239. Apache on the County Seat *(Hoot Kloot)* 16 June 1973. *p.c.:* Mirisch/DFE for UA; *dir:* Hawley Pratt; *story:* John W. Dunn; *anim:* Bob Richardson, Manny Gould, Warren Batchelder, Don Williams; *lay:* Dick Ung; *back:* Richard H. Thomas; *ed:* Lee Gunther; *voices:* Bob Holt; *mus:* Doug Goodwin; *ph:* Ray Lee, Larry Hogan; *titles:* Art Leonardi; *prod sup:* Stan Paperny, Harry Love; *col:* DeLuxe. *sd:* RCA. 5 min. • Sheriff Kloot sets out to bring in a huge Indian named "The Jolly Red Giant" to court.

240. Ape Suzette *(Inspector)* 24 June 1966. *p.c.:* Mirisch/Geoffrey/DFE for UA; *dir:* Gerry Chiniquy; *story:* John W. Dunn; *anim:* Don Williams, Warren Batchelder, Ted Bonnicksen, George Grandpré; *sets:* T.M. Yakutis; *ed:* Eugene Marks; *voices:* Pat Harrington Jr., Paul Frees; *mus:* Walter Greene; *theme tune:* Henry Mancini; *prod mgr:* Bill Orcutt; *col:* DeLuxe. *sd:* RCA. 6 min. • The Inspector is sent to investigate the disappearance of a cargo of bananas.

241. Apes of Wrath *(Merrie Melodies)* 18 Apr. 1959; *p.c.:* WB; *dir:* Friz Freleng. *story:* Warren Foster; *anim:* Art Davis, Virgil Ross, Gerry Chiniquy; *lay:* Hawley Pratt; *back:* Tom O'Loughlin; *ed:* Treg Brown; *voices:* Mel Blanc, June Foray; *mus:* Milt Franklyn; *prod mgr:* William Orcutt; *col:* Tech. *sd:* Vit. 7 min. • A mother gorilla believes Bugs to be her own baby, but father ape knows better.

242. Apple Andy *(Andy Panda)* 20 May 1946; *p.c.:* Walter Lantz prods for Univ; *dir:* Dick Lundy; *story:* Ben Hardaway, Milt Schaffer; *anim:* La Verne Harding, Emery Hawkins; *sets:* Terry Lind; *voices:* Walter Tetley, Will Wright, Sara Berner, Del Porter; *mus:* Darrell Calker; *song:* Johnny Lange, Hy Heath, Richard Loring; *col:* Tech. *sd:* WE. 7 min. • Andy has a nightmare after eating too many green apples whereupon he's enticed to Hades and forced to overindulge on apples.

243. April Showers *(Aesop's Film Fables)* 14 June 1929; *p.c.:* Fables Pictures Inc for Pathé; *dir:* Paul Terry, John Foster; b&w. *sil.* 6 min. • When a violent rainstorm attacks, Farmer Al loads his wagon with household effects to evacuate. He loses everything but a goldfish bowl when crossing a stream.

244. Aqua Duck *(Merrie Melodies)* Sept. 1963; *p.c.:* WB; *dir:* Robert McKimson; *story:* John Dunn; *anim:* Keith Darling, Ted Bonnicksen, Warren Batchelder, George Grandpré; *sets:* Robert Gribbroek; *ed:* Treg Brown. *voice:* Mel Blanc; *mus:* Bill Lava; *prod mgr:* William Orcutt; *prod:* David H. DePatie; *col:* Tech. *sd:* Vit. 7 min. • Daffy is dying of thirst in the desert when he strikes gold. A pack-rat offers him a glass of water for the nugget.

245. Aquamania 20 Feb. 1961; *p.c.:* Walt Disney prods for BV; *dir:* Wolfgang Reitherman; *asst dir:* Danny Alguire; *story:* Vance Gerry, Ralph Wright; *anim:* John Lounsbery, Art Stevens, John Sibley, Dick Lucas, Cliff Nordberg; *fx:* Dan MacManus; *lay:* Basil Davidovich, Dale Barnhart; *back:* Ralph Hulett; *voices:* John Dehner, Pinto Colvig, Kevin & Brian Corcoran; *mus:* Buddy Baker; *col:* Tech. *sd:* RCA. 8 min. *Academy Award nomination.* • Goofy succumbs to the pleasures of boating and reluctantly gets involved in a water-skiing contest.

246. Aquarela Do Brazil *("Watercolor of Brazil")* 24 June 1955; *p.c.:* Walt Disney prods for BV; *dir:* Wilfred Jackson; *col:* Tech. *sd:* RCA. 8 min. • Donald meets José Carioca and the two of them paint the town red on a tour of South America. • See: *Saludos Amigos*

247. Arabs with Dirty Fezzes *(Cartune)* 31 July 1939; *p.c.:* Walter Lantz prods for Univ; *dir:* Alex Lovy; *story:* James Miele, Victor McLeod; *sets:* Edgar Keichle; *voice:* Bill Thompson, Sara Berner; *mus:* Frank Marsales; *prod mgr:* George Hall; b&w. *sd:* WE. 7 min. • Grandpa Mouse tells Baby Face of when he was in the Foreign Legion and left to defend the fort against marauders.

248. Arctic Antics *(Silly Symphony)* 26 June 1930. *p.c.:* Walter E. Disney for Colum; *dir:* Ub Iwerks; *anim:* Johnny Cannon, Les Clark, Gilles de Tremaudan, Norman Ferguson, David D. Hand, Wilfred Jackson, Jack King, Richard Lundy, Ben Sharpsteen; *asst anim:* Charles Byrne, Chuck Couch, Jack Cutting, George Lane, Tom McKimson, Roy Williams; *mus:* Bert Lewis; *ph:* William Cottrell; b&w. *sd:* PCP. 7 min. • Arctic fantasy with frolicking polar bears, penguins and seals.

249. Arctic Rivals *(Terry-Toon)* May 1954; *p.c.:* TT; for Fox. *dir:* Mannie Davis; *story:* Tom Morrison; *anim:* Jim Tyer; *mus:* Philip A. Scheib; *ph:* Douglas Moye; *col:* Tech. *sd:* RCA. 6 min. • Willie Walrus' girl is enchanted by a muscle-bound rival named Walter. When a dangerous fish attacks her, Walter departs, leaving Willie to save the day.

250. Aries 1967; *p.c.:* Murakami/Wolf Films for Expo '67; *dir/anim:* Fred Wolf; *ed:* Rich Harrison; *col:* East. *sd:* 50 sec. • Made on the theme of "Man and his Universe."

251. The Aristo-Cat *(Merrie Melodies)* 12 June 1943; *p.c.:* Leon Schlesinger prods for WB; *dir:* Charles M. Jones; *story:* Tedd Pierce; *anim:* Rudolph Larriva, Ken Harris, Robert Cannon; *lay:* John McGrew; *back:* Eugene Fleury, Bernice Polifka; *ed:* Treg Brown; *voices:* Mel Blanc, Tedd Pierce, Michael Maltese; *mus:* Carl W. Stalling; *prod sup:* Henry Binder, Raymond G. Katz; *col:* Tech. *sd:* Vit. 7 min. • A pampered cat, left to fend for himself, discovers he's supposed to catch mice. Not knowing what a mouse looks like, he asks the first people he sees ... two mice.

252. The Aristocats 24 Dec. 1970; *p.c.:* Walt Disney prods for BV; *prod:* Wolfgang Reitherman, Winston Hibler; *dir:* Wolfgang Reitherman; *asst dir:* Ed Hansen, Dan Alguire; *story:* Tom McGowan, Tom Rowe; *adapt:* Larry Clemmons, Vance Gerry, Ken Anderson, Frank Thomas, Eric Cleworth, Julius Svendsen, Ralph Wright; *anim dir:* Milt Kahl, Ollie Johnston, Frank Thomas, John Lounsbery; *anim:* Hal King, Eric Larson, Eric Cleworth, Julius Svendsen, Fred Hellmich, Walt Stanchfield, Dave Michener; *fx:* Dan MacManus, Dick Lucas; *des:* Ken Anderson; *lay:* Don Griffith,

Basil Davidovich, Sylvia Roemer; *back:* Al Dempster, Bill Layne, Ralph Hulett; *ed:* Tom Acosta; *voices:* Thomas O'Malley; Phil Harris; *Duchess:* Eva Gabor; *Roquefort:* Sterling Holloway; *Scat Cat:* Sherman "Scatman" Crothers; *Chinese Cat:* Paul Winchell; *English Cat:* Lord Tim Hudson; *Italian Cat:* Vito Scotti; *Russian Cat:* Thurl Ravenscroft; *Berlioz:* Dean Clark; *Marie:* Liz English; *Toulouse:* Gary Dubin; *Frou Frou:* Nancy Kulp/Ruth Buzzi; *Napoleon:* Pat Buttram; *Lafayette:* George Lindsey; *Abigail Gabble:* Monica Evans; *Amelia Gabble:* Carole Shelley; *Georges Hautecourt:* Charles Lane; *Mme Bonfamille:* Hermoine Baddeley; *Edgar/Removal Man:* Roddy Maude-Roxby; *Uncle Waldo:* Bill Thompson; *Milkman/Chef:* Pete Renoudet; *Duchess' singing voice:* Robie Lester; *title singer:* Maurice Chevalier; *songs:* Richard M. Sherman, Robert B. Sherman, Terry Gilkyson, Floyd Huddleston, Al Rinker; *mus:* George Bruns; *orch:* Walter Sheets; *mus ed:* Evelyn Kennedy; *sd:* Robert O. Cook; *prod mgr:* Don Duckwall; *col:* Tech. *sd:* RCA. 78 min. • Edgar the butler learns that Mme. Bonfamille is leaving all her money to her cat, Duchess, and her three kittens. He decides to make them "disappear" and deposits them way out in the country. Duchess and the children soon meet up with an alley cat named O'Malley who takes them on an adventure-filled journey back home to Paris.

253. The Army Mascot (*Pluto*) 22 May 1942; *p.c.:* Walt Disney prods for RKO; *dir:* Clyde Geronimi; *asst dir:* Jack Bruner; *story:* Carl Barks, Jack Hannah; *anim:* George Nicholas, Claude Smith. Norman Tate, Charles A. Nichols; *lay:* Bruce Bushman; *voices:* Chester Cobb; *mus:* Frank E. Churchill; *col:* Tech. *sd:* RCA. 7 min. • Pluto yearns for a decent meal that Gunther the Army mascot goat gets. He outwits the goat and finally replaces him. The name of "Gunther," given to the mascot, was a dig at Disney attorney Gunther R. Lessing.

254. Army of Darkness 19 Feb. 1992; *p.c.:* Renaissance Pictures Introvision International for Guild; *stop-motion sup:* Peter Kleinow; *title anim:* Perpetual motion Pictures; *visual fx sup:* Richard Malzahn; *optical sup:* Robert Habros; *anim:* Sallie McHenry; *i&p:* Heather Davis, Judith Bell, Liz Lord; "Book of the Dead" *anim/des:* Tom Sullivan; *col:* Dolby SR. 81 min. *l/a.* • Live-action fantasy from *The Evil Dead* stables: A supermarket employee is transported into the past where he has to search a graveyard for the *Book of the Dead* which contains a spell to return him to the 20th century. Along the way he comes up against mutants, etc.

255. Around the World (*Paul Terry-Toons*) 4 Oct. 1931; *p.c.:* Terry, Moser & Coffman for Educational/Fox; *dir:* Frank Moser, Paul Terry; *anim:* Arthur Babbitt, George Gordon, Ferdinand Huszti Horvath, Connie Rasinski, Hugh Shields, Vladimir Tytla; *mus:* Philip A. Scheib; b&w. sd. 6 min. • No story available.

256. Around the World in Eighty Days 1956; Shamus Culhane prods for Michael Todd Productions/UA; *dir:* Saul Bass; *anim:* Shamus Culhane; *lay:* Robert E. Balsar; *mus:* Victor Young; *prod mgr:* William T. Hurtz; *col:* Tech. *sd.* (titles): 6 mins. • Animated titles for the live-action feature film, caricaturing the main players.

257. Around the World in Ten Minutes 29 Mar. 1915; *p.c.:* Joker for Univ Film Mfg Co Inc.; b&w. sil. s/r. • No story available.

258. The Arrival 31 May 1996; *p.c.:* Live Film & Mediaworks, Inc. for Entertainment; *alien anim:* Pacific Data Images; *anim dir:* Raman Hui; *anim:* Apurva Shah, Collin Hennen, Fred Nilsson, Dave Rader, Peter Plevritis, Terry Emmons; *Imploder fx anim/compositing:* Available Light Ltd.; *visual fx sup:* John T. van Vliet; *fx prod:* Katherine Kean; *digital sup:* Laurel Klick; *digital anim:* W.I. Arnace, Cynthia Hyland, Larry Stanton, Scott Coulter; *anim ph:* Joseph Thomas; *anim:* Karl Fornander; *col:* Tech. *sd:* dts. 115 min. *l/a. Academy Award* • Live-action science fiction feature: An astronomer recieves extraterrestial radio signals and gets involved in a conspiracy involving NASA and governmental agents.

259. Art for Art's Sake (*Aesop's Fable*) 11 May 1934; *p.c.:* Van Beuren for RKO; *dir:* George Stallings; *anim:* Jim Tyer; *mus:* Gene Rodemich; b&w. *sd:* RCA. 6 min. • The Little King creates havoc when he goes on a tour of an art gallery.

260. The Art Gallery (*MGM cartoon*) 13 May 1939; *p.c.:* MGM; *prod/dir:* Hugh Harman; *voices:* The Rhythmettes; *mus:* Scott Bradley; *col:* Tech. *sd:* WE. 9 min. • When the art gallery is closed at night the statue of Nero delights in setting fire to everything in sight.

261. The Art of Self Defence (*Goofy*) 26 Dec. 1941; *p.c.:* Walt Disney prods for RKO; *dir:* Jack Kinney; *asst dir:* Lou Debney; *story:* Ralph Wright, Rex Cox, Leo Thiele; *anim:* Art Babbitt, Rex Cox, Richard McDermott, James Moore; *fx:* Andy Engman, Jack Boyd, Jack Huber, Joseph Gayek, Reuben Timmens; *lay:* Leo Thiele; *voice:* John McLeish; *mus:* Leigh Harline; *col:* Tech. *sd:* RCA. 8 min. • The Goof demonstrates pugilism throughout the ages before he enters the ring himself.

262. The Art of Skiing (*Goofy*) 14 Nov. 1941; *p.c.:* Walt Disney prods for RKO; *dir:* Jack Kinney; *asst dir:* Lou Debney; *story:* Ralph Wright, Leo Thiele; *anim:* Chester Cobb, Rex Cox, Edwin T. Fourcher, Richard McDermott, Frank Onaitis, Frank Oreb, Wolfgang Reitherman, John Sibley, Louis Terri; *fx:* Jack Boyd, Andy Engman, Joseph Gayek, Jack Huber, Ed Parks, Reuben Timmens. *lay:* Leo Thiele; *voice:* John McLeish, Hannès Schrolle; *mus:* Charles Wolcott; *col:* Tech. *sd:* RCA. 7 min. • Goofy demonstrates the advantages and pitfalls of skiing. Yodeller Hannès Schrolle recorded various yells for Goofy's misadventures that are still being used to this day.

263. The Artist's Dream 7 June 1913; *p.c.:* Pathé/Eclectic; *dir/anim:* John Randolph Bray; b&w. sil. • When the artist retires to bed, his drawn dog creation attempts to steal a sausage. • Reissue: *The Dachshund and the Sausage.*

264. An Artist's Model (*Pen & Ink Vaudeville*) 10 Dec. 1924; *p.c.:* Hurd Productions for Educational; *dir/anim:* Earl Hurd; b&w. sil. 5 min. • A scantily-clad girl steps from a poster and dances to a wild Zulu band. Props cleans out the group with a dice and the black conductor seeks revenge.

265. Arts and Flowers (*Woody Woodpecker*) 19 Nov. 1956; *p.c.:* Walter Lantz prods for Univ; *dir:* Paul J. Smith; *story:* Homer Brightman, Frank J. Goldberg; *anim:* Don Patterson, Robert Bentley, Herman R. Cohen; *sets:* Art Landy, Raymond Jacobs; *voices:* Dal McKennon, Grace Stafford; *mus:* Clarence Wheeler; *prod mgr:* William E. Garity; *col:* Tech. *sd:* RCA. 6 nin. • Woody and an artist battle to paint a rare flower for a rich reward.

266. As the Crow Lies (*Noveltoon*) 1 June 1951; *p.c.:* Famous for Para; *dir:* Seymour Kneitel; *story:* Carl Meyer, Jack Mercer; *anim:* Dave Tendlar, Morey Reden; *sets:* Robert Owen; *voices:* Jackson Beck, Sid Raymond, Jack Mercer; *mus:* Winston Sharples; *ph:* Leonard McCormick; *col:* Tech. *sd:* RCA. 7 min. • Katnip believes the only way to cure his hiccups is to eat a fresh crow.

267. As the Fly Flies (*Phantasy*) 17 Nov. 1944; *p.c.:* Colum; *prod:* Dave Fleischer; *dir:* Howard Swift; *anim:* Grant Simmons; *voices:* John McLeish, Harry E. Lang; *mus:* Eddie Kilfeather; *i&p:* Elizabeth F. McDowell; *ph:* Frank Fisher; *prod mgr:* Albert Spar; b&w. *sd:* RCA. 6 min. • Professor Puzzlewitz demonstrates his fly-catching invention.

268. As the Tumbleweed Turns (*Hoot Kloot*) 8 Apr. 1974; *p.c.:* Mirisch/DFE for UA; *dir:* Gerry Chiniquy; *story:* John W. Dunn; *anim:* Bob Bransford, Norm McCabe, Ken Muse, Bob Bemiller; *lay:* Dick Ung; *back:* Richard Thomas; *ed:* Rick Steward; *voices:* Bob Holt, Hazel Shermet; *mus:* Doug Goodwin; *ph:* John Burton Jr.; *titles:* Arthur Leonardi; *prod mgr:* Lee Gunther; *col:* DeLuxe. *sd:* RCA. 6 min. • Kloot has an encounter with an old lady's guard dog while trying to evict her.

269. Assault and Flattery (*Popeye*) 6 July 1956; *p.c.:* Famous for Para; *dir:* I. Sparber; *story:* I. Klein; *anim:* Al Eugster, Wm. B. Pattengill; *sets:* Joseph Dommerque; *voices:* Jack Mercer, Jackson Beck, Frank Matalone; *mus:* Winston Sharples; *prod mgr:* Seymour Shultz; *col:* Tech. *sd:* RCA. 6 min. • Seq: *The Farmer and the Belle; A Balmy Swami; How Green Is My Spinach.* Bluto takes Popeye to court and lets Judge Wimpy decide whether or not our hero has been too brutal with him.

270. Assault and Peppered (*Merrie Melodies*); rel: 24 Apr. 1965; *p.c.:* DFE for WB; *dir:* Robert McKimson; *story:* John Dunn; *anim:* Manny Perez, Warren Batchelder, Bob Matz, La Verne Harding, Norm McCabe, Don Williams; *lay:* Dick Ung; *back:* Tom O'Loughlin; *ed:* Lee Gunther; *voices:* Mel Blanc; *mus:* Bill Lava; *col:* Tech. *sd:* Vit. 6 min. • Senor Daffy wants Speedy Gonzales off his property, so they wage a firearm battle.

271. Associated Animators (1925–1926) *Mutt and Jeff* created by Harry "Bud" Fisher; *prod:* Burton F. Gillett; *artists:* Richard M. Friel, Manny Gould, Ben Harrison, Dick Huemor, I. Klein, Sid Marcus, George Rufle.

272. The Astroduck (*Looney Tunes*) 1 Jan. 1966; *p.c.:* DFE for WB; *dir:* Robert McKimson; *anim:* Bob Matz, Manny Perez, Warren Batchelder,

Don Williams, George Grandpré, Norm McCabe; *lay:* Dick Ung; *back:* Tom O'Loughlin; *ed:* Lee Gunther; *voices:* Mel Blanc; *mus:* Bill Lava; *col:* Tech. *sd:* Vit. 7 min. • Daffy rents a Mexican hacienda only to find his deadly nemesis, Speedy Gonzales, already in residence.

273. The Astronut (*Deputy Dawg*) Mar. 1963 (© 1961); *p.c.:* TT for Fox; *ex prod:* Bill Weiss; *dir:* Connie Rasinski; *story sup:* Tom Morrison; *story:* Larz Bourne; *anim:* Ed Donnelly, Mannie Davis, Vinnie Bell, Johnny Gent; *sets:* John Zago; *voices:* Dayton Allen; *mus:* Phil Scheib; *prod mgr:* Frank Schudde; *col:* Tech. *sd:* RCA. 5 min. • Deputy Dawg's rural life is interrupted when a visitor from outer space wants to take the Sheriff's car back home to his planet.

274. Astronut Woody (*Woody Woodpecker*) Apr. 1966; *p.c.:* Walter Lantz prods for Univ; *dir:* Paul J. Smith; *story:* Cal Howard; *anim:* Les Kline, Al Coe; *sets:* Ray Huffine; *voices:* Dal McKennon, Grace Stafford; *mus:* Walter Greene; *prod mgr:* William E. Garity; *col:* Tech. *sd:* RCA. 6 min. • Woody mistakes a rocketship for an apartment block and the Colonel attempting to evict him, for the landlord.

275. At the Circus (*Out of the Inkwell*) 1 Mar. 1926; *p.c.:* Inkwell Studios for Red Seal; *prod:* Max Fleischer; *dir:* Dave Fleischer; b&w. sil. 5 min. • Ko-Ko finds himself at the mercy of the circus Giant but manages to turn the tables to overpower the ogre. The Giant then clambers over real-life footage of the Hudson River in his escape from the Clown.

276. At the Zoo (*Aesop's Film Fable*) 28 Mar. 1925; *p.c.:* Fables Pictures Inc for Pathé; *dir:* Paul Terry; b&w. sil. 6 min. • All the animals present themselves at the zoo ending in Farmer Al Falfa getting a royal trouncing by a gorilla.

277. At Your Service (*Oswald*) 8 July 1935. *p.c.:* Univ; *dir:* Walter Lantz; *story/lyrics:* Walter Lantz, Victor McLeod; *anim:* Ray Abrams, Cecil Surry, Sid Sutherland, Virgil Ross; *mus:* James Dietrich; b&w. sd. 6 min. • Fun at Oswald's Service Station.

278. At Your Service, Madame (*Merrie Melodies*) 29 Aug. 1936; *p.c.:* Leon Schlesinger prods for WB; *dir:* I. Freleng; *anim:* Don Williams, Cal Dalton; *sets:* Arthur Loomer; *voices:* Bernice Hansel, Ted Pierce; *mus:* Norman Spencer; *prod sup:* Henry Binder, Raymond G. Katz; *col:* Tech. *sd:* Vit. 7 min. • Mr. Squeals (a W.C. Fieldsian pig) plights his troth with Mrs. Hamhock, a wealthy widow ... much to her kids' disgust.

279. The Athlete (*Pooch the Pup*) 29 Aug. 1932; *p.c.:* Univ; *dir:* Walter Lantz, *anim:* Manuel Moreno, Lester Kline, George Cannata, "Bill" Weber; *mus:* James Dietrich; b&w. sd. 7 min. • No story available.

280. Atlantis, the Lost Continent 1961; *p.c.:* MGM/Galaxy; *prod/dir:* George Pal; *anim:* Projects Unlimited (*Jim Danforth & Associates*); *voice:* Paul Frees; *mus:* Russell Garcia; *col:* Metro; *sd:* WE. 90 min. *l/a/anim.* • Atlantis plans to conquer the world by means of atomic energy. Live-action feature with minor animated special effects.

281. Atom Man vs. Superman 1950. *p.c.:* Colum; *prod:* Sam Katzman; based on *Superman* and *Action* comics and the *Superman* radio program; characters created by Jerome Siegel and Joe Shuster; *special anim fx:* Howard Swift. b&w. *sd:* WE. 20 min each. • Live-action fifteen-episode serial involving animated flying effects for Superman.

282. The A-Tom-inable Snowman (*Tom & Jerry*); *p.c.:* MGM; *prod:* Chuck Jones; *dir:* Abe Levitow; *story:* Bob Ogle; *anim:* Ken Harris, Don Towsley, Tom Ray, Dick Thompson, Ben Washam, Philip Roman; *des:* Maurice Noble; *lay:* Robert Givens; *back:* Robert Inman; *mus:* Dean Elliott; *prod sup:* Earl Jonas, Les Goldman; *col:* Metro. *sd:* WE. 7 min. • An eager Alpine rescue dog plies Tom with brandy, rendering him incapable.

283. Audio-Cinema Studio (1930) *prod:* Paul Terry, Frank Moser; *artists:* Arthur Babbitt, Thomas Bonfiglio, Tom Byrne, Mannie Davis, George Gordon, Ferdinand Huszti Horvath, Jack King, I. Klein, Frank Little, Frank Moser, Pearson, Connie Rasinski, Sarka, Sculia, Frank Sherman, Hugh Shields, John Terry, Paul Terry, Ralph Tiller, Vladimir Tytla; *mus:* Philip A. Scheib; *mus arranger:* Alexander N. Ivanoff.

284. Audrey the Rain Maker (*Noveltoon*) 26 Oct. 1951; *p.c.:* Famous Studio for Para; *dir:* I. Sparber; *story:* I. Klein; *anim:* Steve Muffatti, Bill Hudson; *sets:* Tom Ford; *voices:* Mae Questel, Gwen Davies, Jackson Beck, Jack Mercer; *mus:* Winston Sharples; *ph:* Leonard McCormick; *col:* Tech. *sd:* RCA. 8 min. • Audrey dreams there is a terrible drought and talks the Rain God into making rain again.

285. The Auto Clinic (*Krazy Kat*) 4 Mar. 1938; *p.c.:* Charles Mintz prods for Colum; *story:* Allen Rose; *anim:* Harry Love; *voice:* Dave Weber; *mus:* Joe de Nat; *prod mgr:* James Bronis; b&w. *sd:* RCA. 7 min. • A streamlined robot-powered gas station and the humanized cars that patronize it.

286. The Autograph Hound (*Donald Duck*) 1 Sept. 1939; *p.c.:* Walt Disney prods for RKO; *dir:* Jack King; *asst dir:* Harry Tytle, Bob Newman; *story:* Carl Barks, Jack Hannah; *anim:* Paul Allen, Johnny Cannon, Larry Clemmons, Rex Cox, Nick de Tolly, Ed Dunn, John Elliotte, Osmond Evans, Emery Hawkins, Ward Kimball, Edward Love, Lee Morehouse, Kenneth Muse, Ray Patin, Kenneth Paterson, Dunbar Roman, Claude Smith, Robert Stokes, Judge Whitaker; *fx:* Andy Engman; *des:* T. Hee; *lay:* Bill Herwig, James Carmichael; *voices:* Billy Bletcher, Clarence Nash, Donald Barry, Barbara Jean Wong, Lou Merrill, (Peter) Lind Hayes, Sara Berner, Billy Sheets; *mus:* Oliver Wallace; *col:* Tech. *sd:* RCA. 8 min. • Donald gatecrashes the movie studio and is chased by the studio cop. Caricatures: Henry Armetta, Edward Arnold, Mischa Auer, John Barrymore, Charles Boyer, Eddie Cantor, Irvin S. Cobb, Joan Crawford, Bette Davis, Step'n'Fetchit, Clark Gable, Greta Garbo, Sonja Henie, Katharine Hepburn, Hugh Herbert, Chico & Groucho Marx, Charlie McCarthy, The Lone Ranger, Martha Raye, The Ritz Bros., Slim Summerville, Mickey Rooney, Shirley Temple and Roland Young.

287. The Autograph Hunter (*Krazy Kat*) 5 Jan. 1934; *p.c.:* Charles Mintz prods for Colum; *story:* Harry Love; *anim:* Allen Rose, Preston Blair; *mus:* Joe de Nat; *prod mgr:* James Bronis; b&w. *sd:* RCA. 6 min. • Krazy goes autograph hunting at the Brown Derby and is chased by the doorman. Caricatures of Charlie Chaplin, Greta Garbo, Marie Dressler, Jimmy Durante, Laurel & Hardy, The Marx Bros., John, Lionel and Ethel Barrymore.

288. The Automobile Ride (*Out of the Inkwell*) 12 Mar. 1921; *p.c.:* Bray prods for Goldwyn; *prod/l/a:* Max Fleischer; *dir:* Dave Fleischer; b&w. sil. *l/a/anim.* • Ko-Ko gets jealous when Max takes a girl on an automobile ride and sets out to stop it. • See: *Goldwyn-Bray Pictographs*

289. Autumn (*Silly Symphony*) 15 Feb. 1930; *p.c.:* Walter E. Disney for Colum; *dir:* Ub Iwerks; *anim:* Ub Iwerks, Wilfred Jackson, Les Clark, Floyd Gottfredson; *mus:* Carl W. Stalling; *ph:* William Cottrell; b&w. *sd:* PCP. 7 min. • The animals prepare for the oncoming winter.

290. Aviation Vacation (*Merrie Melodies*) 2 Aug. 1941; *p.c.:* Leon Schlesinger prods for WB; *dir:* Fred Avery; *story:* Dave Monahan, Robert Clampett; *anim:* Sidney Sutherland; *sets:* John Didrik Johnsen; *ed:* Treg Brown; *voices:* Robert C. Bruce, Mel Blanc; *mus:* Carl W. Stalling; *prod sup:* Henry Binder, Raymond G. Katz; *col:* Tech. *sd:* Vit. 7 min. • Embarking on a round-the-world flight.

291. Aw Nurse (*Scrappy*) 9 Mar. 1934; *p.c.:* Winkler for Colum; *prod:* Charles Mintz; *story:* Sid Marcus; *anim:* Art Davis; *mus:* Joe de Nat; *prod mgr:* James Bronis; b&w. *sd:* RCA. 7 min. • Scrappy and Oopy cope with a hoarde of kittens running riot through the hospital.

292. Awful Orphan (*Merrie Melodies*) 29 Jan. 1949; *p.c.:* WB; *dir:* Charles M. Jones; *story:* Michael Maltese; *anim:* Phil Monroe, Ben Washam, Lloyd Vaughan, Ken Harris; *lay:* Robert Gribbroek; *back:* Peter Alvarado; *ed:* Treg Brown; *voices:* Mel Blanc; *mus:* Carl Stalling; *prod mgr:* John W. Burton; *prod:* Edward Selzer; *col:* Tech. *sd:* Vit. 7 min. • Porky orders a canary from the pet shop but is delivered a pet nuisance, Charlie Dog, instead.

293. The Awful Tooth (*Noveltoon*) 2 May 1952; *p.c.:* Famous Studio for Para; *dir:* Seymour Kneitel; *story:* Carl Meyer, Jack Mercer; *anim:* Al Eugster, George Rufle; *sets:* Robert Owen; *voices:* Jackson Beck, Sid Raymond; *mus:* Winston Sharples; *ph:* Leonard McCormick; *prod mgr:* Seymour Shultz; *col:* Tech. *sd:* RCA. 7 min. • Katnip believes the only way to cure his toothache is to eat a crow. Buzzy tries to talk him out of this idea by posing as a dentist.

294. A.W.O.L. (*Hearst-Vitagraph News Pictorial*) 1918; *p.c.:* Barré Studio for U.S. Army Signal Corps./American Motion Picture Corp; *prod:* Raoul Barré; *des:* T.E. Powers; *anim:* Charles Bowers; b&w. sil. 10 min. • A doughboy complains he should have been demobilized at the signing of Armistace. Miss AWOL arrives and takes him for a joy-ride, leaving him penniless! A significant message for the Forces about demobilization. • aka: *All Wrong Old Laddiebuck; Reminiscent of Days "Over There"*

295. Axe Me Another *(Popeye)* 21 Aug. 1934; *p.c.:* The Fleischer Studio for Para; *prod:* Max Fleischer; *dir:* Dave Fleischer; *anim:* Seymour Kneitel, Roland Crandall; *voices:* William A. Costello, Mae Questel, Charles Carver; *mus:* Sammy Timberg; b&w. *sd:* WE. 7 min. • Popeye seeks revenge for lumberjack Bluto having tossed Olive in the river (for serving the men spinach!) and the two of them have a lumberjack contest.

296. Baa Baa Blacksmith *(Modern Madcap)* Feb. 1967; *p.c.:* Para Cartoons; *dir:* Shamus Culhane; *story:* Heyward Kling; *anim:* Nick Tafuri, Al Eugster; *des:* Danté Barbetta, Howard Beckerman, Gil Miret; *sets:* Robert Owen; *voices:* Allen Swift; *mus:* Winston Sharples; *prod sup:* Harold Robins, Burt Hanft; *col:* Tech. *sd:* RCA. 6 min. • Sir Blur, the nearsighted medieval mailman, takes on the local blacksmith's job with disasterous results.

297. Babe 4 Aug. 1995; *p.c.:* Univ; *anim/visual fx:* Rhythm & Hues: *visual fx sup:* Charles Gibson; *visual fx prod:* Liz Ralston; *cg sup:* Harold Buchman, Todd Shifflet, Eileen Jensen, Liz Kupinski; *anim sup:* Sylvia Wong, Nancy Kato; *technical dir:* Ed Batres, George Cano, Charles D'Autremont, Mark Hamilton, Alessandro Jacomini, Rodian Paul, Jay Redd, Jerome Solomon, Andy Sheng, David E. Smith, Hiroyuki Takagai, Michael Tigar, Nicholas Titmarsh; *voices: Babe:* Christine Cavanaugh; *Fly:* Miriam Margolyes; *Ferdinand:* Danny Mann; *Rex:* Hugo Weaving; *Maa:* Miriam Flynn; *Duchess:* Russi Taylor; *Old Ewe:* Evelyn Krape; *horse:* Michael Edward-Stevens; *cow:* Charles Bartlett; *Rooster:* Paul Livingston; *puppies' voices:* Ross Bagley, Gemini Barnett, Rachel Davey, Debi Derryberry, Jazzmine Dillingham, Courtland Mead, Kevin Woods; *sheep voices:* Jane Alden, Kimberly Bailey, Patrika Darbo, Michelle Davison, Julie Forsyth, Maeve Germaine, Rosanna Huffman, Carlyle King, Tina Lifford, Genni Nevinson, Linda Phillips, Paige Pollack, Kerry Walker; *other voices:* Barbara Harris, Jacqueline Breman, Doug Burch, John Erwin, Doris Grau, Tony Hughes, Linda Janssen, Daamen Krall, Charlie MacLean, Justin Monjo, Antonia Murphy, Helen O'Connor, Neil Ross, Scott Vernon; *Narrator:* Roscoe Lee Browne; *col. sd:* dts Stereo. 92 min. • Live-action fantasy: "Babe," a farmyard pig raised by a sheepdog, becomes skilled at herding sheep after helping capture sheep rustlers. Animated mouths and facial expressions allow the animals to voice their own opinions.

298. Babe: Pig in the City 25 Nov. 1998; *p.c.:* Univ; *visual fx/anim:* Rhythm & Hues Visual Effects: *sup:* Bill Westenhofer; *visual fx prod:* Crystal Dowd; *anim sup:* Nancy Kato; *lighting sup:* Eileen Jensen; *pilate prod:* Jill Sheree Bergin; *cgi prod:* Chad Merriam; *cgi sup:* Mary Lynn Machado, Todd Shifflet; *compositing sup:* Betsy Paterson; *visual fx ed:* Michael Backauskas; *technical sup:* Juan Luis Sanchez; *visual fx co-ord:* Rachel Fondiller; *anim leads:* Keith Roberts, Erik de Boer; *anim:* Brian Dowrick, Ian Hulbert, John Goodman, Roberto Smith, Glen Ramos, Kent Yoshida, Melanie Cordan, Lyndon Barrois, Scott O'Brien, David E. Smith; *anim set-up:* Hans Rupkema, Joe Mancewicz, J.J. Blumenkrantz; *3d modelling/anim:* Peter Richards, Rachel Ward, Michael Twigg, Brett Feeney; *cgi art:* Tanya Doskova, Mike Eames, Andy Kind, Dave Lomax, Ivor Middleton, Quentin Miles, Kevin Modeste, Craig Penn, Mike Perry, Chris Shaw, Tim Zaccheo; *addit cgi art:* Rob Allman, John-Paul Harney, Linda Johnson, Charlie Lovette, Carol Ostick, Ben Morris, Ben White; *voices: Babe:* E.G. Daily; *Ferdinand/Tug:* Danny Mann; *Zootie:* Glenne Headly; *Bob:* Steven Wright; *Thelonius:* James Cosmo; *Easy/tough pup:* Nathan Kress, Myles Jeffrey; *the Pitbull/the Doberman:* Stanley Ralph Ross; *the pink Poodle/choir cat:* Russi Taylor; *Flealick:* Adam Goldberg; *Nigel/Alan:* Eddie Barth; *the sniffer dog:* Bill Capizzi; *Fly:* Miriam Margolyes; *Rex:* Hugo Weaving; *kitten:* Katie Leigh; *old ewe/alley cats:* Evelyn Krape; *cow:* Charles Bartlett; *horse:* Michael Edward-Stevens; *feisty fishes:* Al Mancini, Larry Moss; *pelican:* Jim Cummings; *also:* Lisa Baily, Blayn Barbosa, Victor Brandt, Jeannie Elias, Pippa Grandison, J.D. Hall, Mark Hammond, Wendy Kamenoff, Scotty Leavenworth, Julie Oppenheimer, Deborah Packer, Roger Rose, Carly Schroeder, Joseph Sicari, Aaron Spann, Drew Lexi Thomas, Naomi Watts, Barbara Harris, The Looping Group; *singing animals:* Leslie Andrews, Christine Douglas, Jenny Duck-Chong, Daryn Elston-Smith, Michael Halliwell, Gordon Holleman, Tyrone Landau, Catherine Lukin, Susan Reppion-Brooke, Kate Swadling, Vicki Watson, Brett Weymark, Mara Kiek, Jane Birmingham, Stuart Davis, Joanne Maunsell; *narrator:* Roscoe Lee Browne; *col. sd:* Dolby digital/ SDDS/Digital dts. 95½ min. *l/a.* • Live-action fantasy: The farmer's wife accepts an offer for Babe to open a state fair and they set off for the metropolis. Missing a connecting flight, they find themselves stranded in the big city and check

in to the Flealands Hotel — the only hotel that will accept animals. USA/ Australia.

299. Babes at Sea *(Color Rhapsody)* 12 Dec. 1934. *p.c.:* Charles Mintz prods for Colum; *story:* Art Davis; *anim:* Sid Marcus; *voice:* Leone le Doux; *mus:* Joe de Nat; *prod mgr:* James Bronis; *col:* Tech-2. *sd:* RCA. 7 min. • A baby falls down a well and finds himself in a marine fairyland. He torments the creatures and is finally sent back home in disgrace.

300. The Babes in the Woods *(Dinky Doodle)* 16 Aug. 1925; *p.c.:* Bray prods for FBO; *dir/story:* Walt Lantz; *anim:* Clyde Geronimi; b&w. *sil.* 5 min. *l/a/anim.* • Dinky Doodle and his dog steal away from the confines of the drawing board to go skylarking in the woods. They come across an old witch who entices them into her hut with intentions of eating them. They save their hides in their own particular way.

301. Babes in the Woods *(Silly Symphony)* 19 Nov. 1932; *p.c.:* Walt Disney prods for UA; *dir:* Burton F. Gillett; *anim:* Johnny Cannon, Les Clark, Gilles de Tremaudan, Ed Donnelly, Hardie Gramatky, Jack King, Richard Lundy, Ben Sharpsteen. *des:* Albert Hurter; *mus:* Bert Lewis; *col:* Tech. *sd:* RCA. 8 min. • A witch lures two children into her gingerbread house. She turns the boy into a spider but the girl escapes to rescue her brother.

302. Babes in Toyland 14 Dec. 1961 *p.c.:* Walt Disney prods for BV; *screenplay:* Ward Kimball, Joe Rinaldi, Lowell S. Hawley; *Toy seq:* Bill Justice, Joshua Meador, Xavier Atencio; *fx:* Eustace Lycett, Robert A. Mattey; *ed:* Robert Stafford; *mus:* George Bruns; *orch:* Franklyn Marks; *sd:* Robert O. Cook; *mus ed:* Evelyn Kennedy; *l/a dir:* Jack Donohue; *col:* Tech. *sd:* RCA. 7 min. (total 105). *l/a/anim.* • This live-action adaptation of Victor Herbert and Glen McDonough's operetta has Tom Piper (Tommy Sands) shrunk to the size of a toy and fighting off the villain (Ray Bolger) with an animated battalion of toy soldiers.

303. Baby Be Good *(Betty Boop)* 18 Jan. 1935; *p.c.:* The Fleischer Studio for Para; *prod:* Max Fleischer; *dir:* Dave Fleischer; *anim:* Myron Waldman, Edward Nolan, Lillian Friedman; *voice:* Mae Questel; *mus:* Sammy Timberg; b&w. *sd:* WE. 7 min. • Betty has her work cut-out for her when coping with a troublesome baby.

304. Baby Boogie 19 May 1955; *p.c.:* UPA for Colum; *ex prod:* Stephen Bosustow; *dir/sets:* Paul Julian; *story:* Abe Liss, Leo Salkin; *anim:* Fred Grable; *voices:* Ann Whitfield, Gil Herman, Grace Lenard, Lynn Salkin; *mus:* Jack Easton; *prod mgr:* Herbert Klynn; *col:* Tech. *sd:* RCA. 6 min. • Drawn as a child's scribblings, a small girl asks her parents, "Where do babies come from?" They tell her "The Hospital!" and she sets off to collect a baby brother.

305. Baby Bottleneck *(Merrie Melodies)* 16 Mar. 1946. *p.c.:* WB; *dir:* Robert Clampett; *story:* Warren Foster; *anim:* Rod Scribner, Manny Gould, Robert McKimson, J.C. Melendez; *lay:* Thomas McKimson; *back:* Dorcy Howard; *ed:* Treg Brown; *voices:* Mel Blanc, Sara Berner; *mus:* Carl W. Stalling; *prod mgr:* John W. Burton; *prod:* Edward Selzer; *col:* Tech. *sd:* Vit. 7 min. • Daffy and Porky help out the stork's overload of baby deliveries.

306. Baby Buggy Bunny *(Merrie Melodies)* 18 Dec. 1954; *p.c.:* WB; *dir:* Charles M. Jones; *story:* Michael Maltese; *anim:* Abe Levitow, Lloyd Vaughan, Ken Harris, Ben Washam; *lay:* Ernest Nordli; *back:* Philip de Guard; *ed:* Treg Brown; *voices:* Mel Blanc; *mus:* Milt Franklyn; *prod mgr:* John W. Burton; *prod:* Edward Selzer; *col:* Tech. *sd:* Vit. 7 min. • A midget bank robber poses as a baby on Bugs' doorstep in order to avoid the police.

307. Baby Butch *(Tom & Jerry)* 14 Aug. 1954; *p.c.:* MGM; *dir:* William Hanna, Joseph Barbera; *anim:* Irven Spence, Kenneth Muse, Ed Barge; *back:* Vera Ohman; *ed:* Jim Faris; *voice:* Paul Frees; *mus:* Scott Bradley; *ph:* Jack Stevens; *prod:* Fred Quimby; *col:* Tech. *sd:* WE. 7 min. • An alley cat disguises himself as a baby in order to get himself a leg of ham guarded by Tom and Jerry.

308. Baby Checkers *(Gran' Pop)* 1939; *p.c.:* Cartoon Films Ltd for Mono; *prod:* Dave Biederman, Lawson Haris; *dir:* Paul Fennell. *ed:* Almon Teeter. *voices:* Danny Webb; *mus:* Clarence Wheeler. *ph:* Richard M. Ising. *col:* Ciné. *sd:* 7 min. • Gran'Pop and his monkey friends look after the jungle babies.

309. Baby Kittens *(Cartune)* 28 Nov. 1938; *p.c.:* Univ; *prod:* Walter Lantz; *dir:* Alex Lovy; *story:* Victor McLeod; *anim:* Hicks Lokey, Merle

Gilson; *sets:* Edgar Keichle; *mus:* Scott Bradley; *b&w. sd:* WE. 7 min. • A mother cat's kittens wander off and adopt a dog as their mother.

310. Baby Puss *(Tom & Jerry)* 25 Dec. 1943; *p.c.:* MGM; *dir:* William Hanna, Joseph Barbera; *anim:* Kenneth Muse, Ray Patterson, Irven Spence, Pete Burness; *ed:* Fred MacAlpin; *voices:* Jack Mather, Harry E. Lang, The King's Men; *mus:* Scott Bradley; *song:* Jararaca, Vincent Paiva, Al Stillman; *prod:* Fred Quimby; *col:* Tech. *sd:* WE. 8 min. • A child dresses Tom in a baby outfit. Jerry, quick to realise the potential of this situation, summons some alley cats who torment him.

311. The Baby Seal *(Terry-Toon)* 10 Apr. 1941; *p.c.:* TT for Fox; *dir:* Connie Rasinski; *story:* John Foster; *mus:* Philip A. Scheib; *b&w. sd:* RCA. 7 min. • No story available.

312. The Baby Show *(Aesop's Film Fables)* 26 June 1928; *p.c.:* Fables Pictures Inc for Pathé; *dir:* Paul Terry, Mannie Davis; *b&w. sil.* 5 min. • When the animals run a Baby Show, Al Falfa and Henry Cat dress-up Milton Mouse as a baby against his will. The Judge awards him as a prize baby until his family of kids arrive, calling him "Papa." The animals run Al and Henry out of town.

313. The Baby Sitter *(Little Lulu)* 28 Nov. 1947; *p.c.:* Famous for Para; *dir:* Seymour Kneitel; *story:* Bill Turner, Larry Riley; *anim:* Dave Tendlar, Marty Taras, Al Eugster, Tom Golden; *sets:* Robert Little; *voice:* Cecil Roy. *mus:* Winston Sharples; *title song:* Buddy Kaye, Fred Wise, Sammy Timberg; *prod mgr:* Sam Buchwald; *col:* Tech. *sd:* RCA. 7 min. • Lulu babysits Alvin and gets knocked unconcious where she dreams she's in a Stork Club exclusively for babies. Caricatured as babies are Cab Calloway, Bing Crosby, Jerry Colonna, W.C. Fields, Dorothy Lamour, Bob Hope, Harpo Marx and Frank Sinatra.

314. Baby Wants a Battle *(Popeye)* 24 July 1953; *p.c.:* Famous for Para; *dir:* Seymour Kneitel; *story:* Carl Meyer, Jack Mercer; *anim:* Al Eugster, George Germanetti; *sets:* Robert Connavale; *voices:* Jack Mercer, Mae Questel, Jackson Beck; *mus:* Winston Sharples; *ph:* Leonard McCormick; *prod mgr:* Seymour Shultz; *col:* Tech. *sd:* RCA. 6 min. • Popeye explains how he got a black eye in a baby photo. When Pappy took baby Popeye to the park, baby Bluto and dad both pick on them ... Spinach juice puts matters right.

315. Baby Wants a Bottleship *(Popeye)* 3 July 1942; *p.c.:* The Fleischer Studio for Para; *prod:* Max Fleischer; *dir:* Dave Fleischer; *story:* Jack Ward, Jack Mercer; *anim:* Alfred Eugster, Joseph Oriolo; *voices:* Jack Mercer, Margie Hines; *mus:* Sammy Timberg; *ph:* Charles Schettler; *prod sup:* Isadore Sparber; *b&w. sd:* WE. 7 min. • Swee'Pea causes havoc aboard Popeye's battleship, "The Pensyltucky."

316. Baby Wants Spinach *(Popeye)* 29 Sept. 1950; *p.c.:* Famous for Para; *dir:* Seymour Kneitel; *story:* Carl Meyer, Jack Mercer; *anim:* Al Eugster, Wm. B. Pattengill; *sets:* Robert Owen; *voices:* Jack Mercer, Mae Questel; *mus:* Winston Sharples; *ph:* Leonard McCormick; *prod mgr:* Sam Buchwald; *col:* Tech. *sd:* RCA. 6 min. • While babysitting Swee'Pea, the child crawls away into a zoo and Popeye has a hair-raising time rescuing him from the animals.

317. Bacall to Arms *(Merrie Melodies)* 3 Aug. 1946; *p.c.:* WB; *dir:* Robert Clampett, Art Davis; *anim:* Manny Gould, Rod Scribner, Don Williams, I. Ellis; *lay:* Thomas McKimson; *back:* Philip de Guard; *ed:* Treg Brown; *voices:* Robert C. Bruce, Dave Barry, Sara Berner, Mel Blanc; *mus:* Carl Stalling; *prod mgr:* John W. Burton; *prod:* Edward Selzer; *col:* Tech. *sd:* Vit. 7 min. • A wolf visits the movies and goes ape over the appearance of Lauren Bacall ... but first has to get past Humphrey Bogart on screen.

318. Back Alley Oproar *(Merrie Melodies)* 27 Mar. 1948; *p.c.:* WB; *dir:* I. Freleng; *story:* Michael Maltese, Tedd Pierce; *anim:* Manuel Perez, Ken Champin, Virgil Ross, Gerry Chiniquy. *lay:* Hawley Pratt; *back:* Paul Julian; *ed:* Treg Brown; *voices:* Mel Blanc, Arthur Q. Bryan, Gloria Curran, Tudor Williams; *mus:* Carl Stalling; *prod mgr:* John W. Burton; *prod:* Edward Selzer; *col:* Tech. *sd:* Vit. 7 min. • Sylvester's nocturnal singing keeps Elmer awake throughout the night. Technicolor remake of "Notes to You."

319. Back to the Soil *(Terry-Toon)* 14 Nov. 1941; *p.c.:* TT for Fox; *dir:* Eddie Donnelly; *story:* John Foster; *mus:* Philip A. Scheib; *b&w. sd:* RCA. 7 min. • No story available.

320. Back to the Soil *(Aesop's Film Fable)* 3 Mar. 1929; *p.c.:* Fables Pictures Inc for Pathé; *dir:* Paul Terry; *b&w. sil.* 6 min. • Al Falfa goes for a ride in his flivver when an army of dogs hop aboard, raising a riot. He dumps them in a muddy ditch and drives off, laughing at their predicament. He later goes for a ride in a plane that does a loop-the-loop, spilling him out into a mud hole. The dogs sit around, laughing at him.

321. Backwoods Bunny *(Merrie Melodies)* 13 June 1959; *p.c.:* WB; *dir:* Robert McKimson; *story:* Tedd Pierce; *anim:* Warren Batchelder, Tom Ray, George Grandpré, Ted Bonnicksen; *lay:* Robert Gribbroek; *back:* William Butler; *ed:* Treg Brown; *voices:* Mel Blanc, Daws Butler; *mus:* Milt Franklyn; *prod mgr:* William Orcutt; *prod:* David H. DePatie; *col:* Tech. *sd:* Vit. 7 min. • While vacationing in the Ozarks, Bugs falls afoul of B.O. Buzzard and his son who want to eat our hero for supper.

322. The Bad Bandit *(Aesop's Film Fable)* 19 July 1923; *p.c.:* Fables Pictures Inc for Pathé; *dir:* Paul Terry; *b&w. sil.* 5 min. • The mouse robs the Farmer's refrigerator and leads the cat a merry chase over land and sea.

323. Bad Day at Cat Rock *(Tom & Jerry)* 1965; *p.c.:* MGM; *prod/dir/story:* Chuck Jones; *asst dir:* Maurice Noble; *anim:* Ben Washam, Ken Harris, Don Towsley, Dick Thompson. *lay:* Erni Nordli; *back:* Philip de Guard; *voices:* Mel Blanc; *mus:* Eugene Poddany; *prod mgr:* Les Goldman; *col:* Metro. *sd:* WE. 7 min. • High jinks on a skyscraper, culminating in Tom trying to catapult himself up to Jerry by means of a girder and a rock.

324. The Bad Genius *(Scrappy)* 1 Dec. 1932; *p.c.:* Winkler for Colum; *prod:* Charles Mintz; *story:* Dick Huemor; *anim:* Sid Marcus, Art Davis; *mus:* Joe de Nat; *prod mgr:* James Bronis; *b&w. sd:* WE. 6 min. • In a struggle to clean-up "The Progidy" (Scrappy's cello-playing kid brother) in time for tonight's concert, the kid is knocked senseless. The musical genius is presented on stage via puppet strings.

325. Bad Luck Blackie 22 Jan. 1949; *p.c.:* MGM; *dir:* Tex Avery; *story:* Rich Hogan; *anim:* Grant Simmons, Walter Clinton, Preston Blair, Louie Schmitt; *character des:* Louie Schmitt; *sets:* John Didrik Johnsen; *ed:* Fred MacAlpin; *voices:* Patrick J. McGeehan, Tex Avery; *mus:* Scott Bradley; *prod:* Fred Quimby; *col:* Tech. *sd:* WE. 7 min. • A bullied kitten employs a black cat to cause bad luck for his tormentor.

326. Bad Ol' Putty Tat *(Merrie Melodies)* 23 Aug 1949; *p.c.:* WB; *dir:* I. Freleng; *story:* Tedd Pierce; *anim:* Gerry Chiniquy, Manuel Perez, Ken Champin, Virgil Ross; *lay:* Hawley Pratt; *back:* Paul Julian; *ed:* Treg Brown; *voices:* Mel Blanc; *mus:* Carl Stalling; *prod mgr:* John W. Burton; *prod:* Edward Selzer; *col:* Tech. *sd:* Vit. 8 min. • Sylvester employs many devious ploys in pursuit of Tweety, culminating in his being turned into a locomotive by the resourceful bird.

327. The Badge and the Beautiful *(Hoot Kloot)* 17 Apr. 1974; *p.c.:* Mirisch/DFE for UA; *dir:* Bob Balsar; *story:* John W. Dunn; *anim:* Tim Miller, John Ward, Richard Rudler; *lay:* Don Roy; *back:* Richard Thomas; *ed:* Allan R. Potter; *voices:* Bob Holt, Larry Mann, Joan Gerber; *mus:* Doug Goodwin; *ph:* John Burton Jr.; *titles:* Arthur Leonardi; *prod mgr:* Lee Gunther; *col:* DeLuxe. *sd:* RCA. 5 min. • Calamitous Jane arrives in town fixin' to marry-up with Kloot.

328. Baffling Bunnies *(Terry-Toon)* Apr. 1956; *p.c.:* TT for Fox; *dir:* Connie Rasinski; *story:* Tom Morrison; *anim:* Jim Tyer; *back:* Artie Bartsch; *voice/ph:* Douglas Moye; *mus:* Philip A. Scheib; *col:* Tech. *sd:* RCA. 6 min. • Papa Bear and his dog, Pago, go hunting but only succeed in having the rabbits run rings around them both.

329. Baggage Buster *(Goofy)* 18 Apr. 1941; *p.c.:* Walt Disney prods for RKO; *dir:* Jack Kinney; *asst dir:* Lou Debney; *anim:* Art Babbitt, George Cannata, Bob Carlson, Fred Moore, Ken Peterson; *fx:* Jack Boyd, Jerome Brown, Andy Engman, Art Fitzpatrick; *lay:* Leo Thiele; *voice:* George A. Johnson; *mus:* Leigh Harline; *col:* Tech. *sd:* RCA. 7 min. • Station porter Goofy has problems when packing a magician's trunk.

330. Baggin' the Dragon *(Honey Half-witch)* Feb. 1966; *p.c.:* Para Cartoons; *dir:* Howard Post; *story:* Jack Mendelsohn; *anim:* Al Eugster, Wm. B. Pattengill; *sets:* Robert Little; *voices:* Shari Lewis, Bob MacFadden; *mus:* Winston Sharples; *prod mgr:* Abe Goodman; *col:* Tech. *sd:* RCA. 6 min. • Honey upsets a dragon who chases her until Cousin Maggie arrives and turns it into a tiny pet.

331. Bah Wilderness *(MGM cartoon)* 13 Feb. 1943; *p.c.:* MGM; *prod/dir:* Rudolf Ising; *voices:* Harlow Wilcox, Jeanne Dunn; *mus:* Scott

Bradley; *col:* Tech. *sd:* WE. 7 min. • Barney Bear decides to sleep rough in the woods ... but conditions make this difficult for him.

332. Le Ball and Chain Gang *(Inspector)*; 24 July 1968; *p.c.:* Mirisch/Geoffrey/DFE for UA; *dir:* Gerry Chiniquy; *story:* Jim Ryan; *anim:* Don Williams, Manny Gould, Warren Batchelder, Manny Perez; *lay:* Dick Ung; *back:* Tom O'Loughlin; *ed:* Lee Gunther; *voices:* Pat Harrington Jr., June Foray, Hal Smith; *mus:* Walter Green; *theme tune:* Henry Mancini; *ph:* John Burton Jr.; *prod sup:* Jim Foss, Harry Love; *col:* DeLuxe; *sd:* RCA. 6 min. • A bickering couple avoid the inspector, imagining he wants them for some crime they committed, but he only wants them with a "jury duty" summons.

333. The Ball Game *(Aesop's Fable)* 30 July 1932; *p.c.:* Van Beuren for RKO; *dir:* John Foster, George Rufle; *mus:* Gene Rodemich; b&w. *sd:* RCA. 7 min. • The Big Bugs vs. the Little Bugs in an insect baseball game. Babe Ruth caricatured as a bug.

334. The Ball Park *(Aesop's Film Fable)* 4 May 1929; *p.c.:* Fables Pictures Inc for Pathé; *dir:* Paul Terry; b&w. sil. 5 min. • Farmer Al plays umpire in the animals' baseball game. When he declares an ape player "Out," the ape takes offense and punches Al's lights out.

335. Ballet-Oop 11 Feb. 1954; *p.c.:* UPA for Colum; *ex prod:* Stephen Bosustow; *dir:* Robert Cannon; *story:* T. Hee, Robert Cannon; *anim:* Frank Smith, Bill Melendez, Tom McDonald; *lay:* T. Hee; *back:* Jules Engel; *voices:* Marvin Miller, Marian Richman; *mus:* George Bruns; *choreography:* Olga Lunick; *prod mgr:* Herbert Klynn; *col:* Tech. *sd:* RCA. 8 min. • A ballet teacher is alarmed to hear that her inexperienced class is to appear in a "Ballet for Beginners" festival in three weeks' time.

336. Balloon Snatcher *(Terry-Toon)* Sept. 1969 (© 1965); *p.c.:* TT for Fox; *ex prod:* Bill Weiss; *dir/anim:* Art Bartsch, Dave Tendlar, Connie Rasinski, Cosmo Anzilotti, Ralph Bakshi; *story sup:* Tom Morrison; *story:* Larz Bourne, Eli Bauer; *sets:* Bill Focht, John Zago, Bob Owen; *ed:* Jack MacConnell; *voices:* Dayton Allen; *mus:* Jim Timmens; *ph:* Ted Moskowitz, Joe Rasinski, Charles Schettler; *sd:* Elliot Grey; *col:* DeLuxe. *sd:* RCA. 5 min. • Astro loses his Martian powers and is mistaken by a small boy for a balloon.

337. Balloon Tired *(Life Cartoon Comedy)* 5 Dec. 1926; *p.c.:* Sherwood Wadsworth Pictures for Educational; *prod:* John R. McCrory; b&w. sil. 5 min. • An auto race with Mike Monkey in a homemade affair against High-Hat Harold in his high-powered racer. While Mike is away chasing a fugitive tire, Little Nibbens plays with the controls, accidentally piloting Mike's roadster to victory.

338. Balloonland *(ComiColor)* 30 Sept. 1935; *p.c.:* Celebrity prods.; *prod/dir:* Ub Iwerks; *voices:* Billy Bletcher, Leone le Doux; *mus:* Carl Stalling; *col:* Ciné. *sd:* PCP. 7 min. • The Pincushionman holds a reign of terror throughout a land where everyone is made of balloons. Caricatures of Laurel & Hardy and Charlie Chaplin.

339. Balloons *(Ko-Ko)* Oct. 1923; *p.c.:* Inkwell Studios for Rodner; *dir:* Dave Fleischer; *anim/l/a:* Max Fleischer; b&w. sil. 5 min. *l/a./anim.* • Ko-Ko takes a balloon ride to visit his brother. The balloon won't take off, so Max draws lots of them that raise the whole house up.

340. Ballot Box Bunny *(Merrie Melodies)* 6 Oct. 1951; *p.c.:* WB; *dir:* I. Freleng; *story:* Warren Foster; *anim:* Ken Champin, Virgil Ross, Arthur Davis, Manuel Perez; *lay:* Hawley Pratt. *back:* Paul Julian; *ed:* Treg Brown; *voices:* Mel Blanc; *mus:* Carl Stalling; *prod mgr:* John W. Burton; *prod:* Edward Selzer; *col:* Tech. *sd:* Vit. 7 min. • Bugs and Yosemite Sam compete in an election for Mayor.

341. Bally Hooey *(Woody Woodpecker)* 20 Apr. 1960; *p.c.:* Walter Lantz prods for Univ; *dir:* Alex Lovy; *story:* Homer Brightman; *anim:* La Verne Harding, Les Kline, Ray Abrams; *sets:* Raymond Jacobs, Art Landy; *voices:* Paul Frees, Dal McKennon, Grace Stafford; *mus:* Clarence Wheeler; *prod mgr:* William E. Garity; *col:* Tech. *sd:* RCA. 6 min. • Woody attempts to get past a TV station guard in order to submit his answer to a quiz show.

342. A Balmy Knight *(Modern Madcap)* Aug. 1966; *p.c.:* Para Cartoons; *dir:* Shamus Culhane; *story:* Heyward Kling; *anim:* Chuck Harriton, Al Eugster, Nick Tafuri; *des:* Danté Barbetta, Howard Beckerman, Robert Little; *voices:* Allen Swift; *mus:* Winston Sharples; *prod sup:* Harold Robins, Burt Hanft; *col:* Tech. *sd:* RCA. 6 min. • Sir Blur believes it's

"Dragon Day" while an old dragon and his young grandson are picnicking, unaware of the interruption that's about to occur.

343. A Balmy Swami *(Popeye)* 22 July 1949; *p.c.:* Famous for Para; *dir:* I. Sparber; *story:* Carl Meyer, Jack Mercer; *anim:* Tom Johnson, George Rufle; *sets:* Anton Loeb; *voices:* Jack Mercer, Mae Questel, Jackson Beck; *mus:* Winston Sharples; *ph:* Leonard McCormick; *prod mgr:* Sam Buchwald; *col:* Pola. *sd:* RCA. 7 min. • Popeye and Olive visit the theatre where Swami Bluto hypnotizes Olive.

344. Balto 22 Dec. 1995; *p.c.:* Amblin for Univ; *dir:* Simon Wells; *prod:* Steve Hickner; *ex prod:* Steven Spielberg, Kathleen Kennedy, Bonne Radford; *story:* Cliff Ruby, Elana Lesser; *scr:* Cliff Ruby, Elana Lesser, David Steven Cohen, Roger S.H. Schulman; *prod des:* Hans Bacher; *character des:* Carlos Grangel, Nicholas Marlet, Patrick Mate, Luc Desmarchelier, Colin Stimpson; *storyboard:* Daan Jippes, David Bowers, Rudolphe Guenoden, Fabio Lignini, William Salazar, Harold Siepermann, Dick Zondag; *anim:* *(Balto):* Jeffrey J. Varab, Dick Zondag, Paul Jesper, Sean Leaning, Kevin Spruce, Vladimir Todorov, Julia Woolf, Anne Heeney, Thomas Matzeit, Valentina d'Ambrosio, Mick de Falco, Deborah Dryland, Andrew Griffiths, Nick Harrop, Ivelina Nacheva, Tom Newman, Claudio Pacciarella, Stephen Perry, Emil Simeonov, Ronan Spelman, Andy Eracleous, Edmond Hallahan, Craig Hilditch, Samuele Pagliarani, Pol Sigerson, Askel Studsgarth; *inbet:* Marcus Arnull, Cathy Lowdell, Gabriele Pennacchioli; *(Boris):* Kristof Serrand, Arnaud Berthier, Denis Couchon, Emanuela Cozzi, Fabio Lignini, Quentin Miles, Sylviane Burnet, Manuel Almela, Louise Keating, Simon Loxton, Pascal Ludowissy, Tanja Majerus, Jerry Verschoor, Jerome Guillaud, Stephen Palmer, Eric Serre, Xavier Riffault; *inbet:* Darren Kordich; *(Jenna):* Rob Stevenhagen, Maximilian Graenitz, Jurgen Richter, Andreas Wessel-Therhorn, Antony Gray, Janet MacKay, Louise Haley, Sarah Marsden, Tim Window, Jason Sallin, Gerald Gallego, Natalie Higgs; *inbet:* Charles Drew, Lee Huxtable, Tim White, Claudia Sturli; *(Steele):* Sahin Ersoz, Andreas von Andrian, Philippe le Brun, Ken Keys, Andy Schmidt, Claire Bramwell-Pearson, Gerhard Brammer, Rick Richards, Robin White, Tom Lock, Christopher Lourdelet, John McCartney, Kamye Miessen, Philippe Tilikete; *(Steele & Jenna seq):* Rodolphe Guenoden, Jean-Francois Rey, Aurea Terribili, Uriel Mimran, Pascal Alixe, Alexa Goriup, Raffaello Vecchione, Jonathan Wren; *inbet:* Andrea Blasich, Guy Duchet, *(Muk & Luk):* Nicholas Marlet, Steve Horrocks, Mark Williams, Marc Bascougnano, Oliver Coipel, Nicola Courtney, Helen Michael, Paola Lecler; *(Nikki/ Kaltag/Star):* William Salazar, Rune Bennicke, Andrea Simonti, June Poole, Cécile Bender, Julia Bracegirdle, Tony Hamilton-White, Judy Howieson, Jennie Langley, Martin Lanzinger, Robert Milne, Fernando Pastor, Simon Ashford, Lui Jauregus, Pascal Menager, Pedro Ramos; *(Rosy):* David Bowers, Kay Sales, Mariateresa Scarpone; *(Sylvie & Dixie/principal humans):* Patrick Mate, Stuart Evans, Jane Barnet, Tony Cope, Sue Woodward; *inbet:* Cinzia Angelini; *(Grizzly/Wolf unit):* Daniel Jeannette, Erik Schmidt, Dawn Pearce, Karen Narramore, Debbie Forster; *(addit anim):* Cecile Bender, Jan van Buyten, Mike Eames, Luca Fattore, Stefan Fjeldmark, Miguel Fuertes, Antony Gray, Keith Greig, Jurgen Gross, Jakob Hjort Jensen, Jorgen Lerdam, Jane Poole, Andy Schmidt, Oskar Urretabizkaia, Mark Williams, Peter Candeland, Joan Freestone, Bruno Martineau, Brenda McKie-Chat, Colin Pinchbeck, Steffan Schaffler, Ulrich Siemonsen, John Tynan; *inbet:* Marianne Rasmussen, Maiken Rix; *anim fx:* Mike Smith, Jon Brooks, Andrew Brownlow, Steven Burch, Leonard F.W. Green, Hock-Lian Law, Andrew Smith, Paul Smith, Graham Bebbington, Lynette Charters, Earl Hibbert, Steve McDermott; *fx co-ord:* Eddie Bignell; *digital fx:* Mick Harper, Isabelle Beaudoin, Guner Behich, David Navarro, Antonio Palermo, Steven Burch, Hock Lian Law, Doug Ikeler, Dave Morehead; *digital fx co-ord:* Lorea Hoye; *fx asst:* Barry Goff, Albert Price, Mary Sheridan, Amanda Talbot, Martin Buckingham, Shaun McGlinchey, Volker Pajatsch, Lorraine Ward, David Birkenshaw, Sky Bone, Matthew Freeth, Helena Grant, Giulia Mazz Casling, Jem Mirza, Heather Tailby; *lay/back co-ord:* Adam Binham; *lay:* Douglas Kirk, Guillaume Bonamy, Bolhem Bouchiba, Olsen Groiseau, Tass Hesom, Brendan Houghton, Clive Hutchings, Glenn Jeffs, John Koch, Benoit le Pennec, Mark Marren, Marcos Mateu, Philippe Mest, Roy Naisbitt, Damon O'Beirne, Christian Schellewald, Jean-Luc Serrano; *back:* Ray Rankine, Colin Stimpson, Steve Albert, Luc Desmarchelier, Julie Gleeson, Natasha Gross, Stephen Hansen, Michael Hirsh, Walter Kossler, Paul Shardlow, Rachel Stedman, Gary Sycamore, Claire Wright; *ed:* Nick Fletcher, Sim Evan-Jones, Clare de

Chenu, Marcus Taylor, Kieran Evans; *voices: Balto:* Kevin Bacon; *Jenna:* Bridget Fonda; *Muk & Luk:* Phil Collins; *Boris:* Bob Hoskins; *Steele:* Jim Cummings; *Star:* Robbie Rist; *Kaltag:* Danny Mann; *Nikki:* Jack Angel; *Sylvie/Dixie/Rosy's Mother:* Sandra Searles Dickinson; *Rosy:* Juliette Brewer; *Doc:* Donald Sinden; *Rosy's Father:* William Roberts; *Telegraph Operator:* Garrick Hagon; *Butcher:* Bill Bailey; *Town Dog:* Big Al; *also:* Mike McShane, Miriam Margolyes, Austin Tichenor, Reed Martin, Adam Long; *mus:* James Horner; *Reach for the Light: mus:* Barry Mann, James Horner; *lyrics:* Cynthia Weil; performed by Steve Winwood; *line test:* Tim Davies, Christopher Knight, Brian Burgess, Michael O'Neil; *ph:* Graham Tiernan, Stuart Holloway, Craig Simpson, Mark Swaffield, Trevor Withers; *scene plan:* Harold Kraut, Jean Maluta; *check:* Corona Maher-Esterhazy, Frances Jacob, David Allonby, Deborah Campbell, Helen O'Brien, Marianne Rousseau, Joan Topley; *technical:* Margaret Rousseau; *computer:* Doug Cooper, Brandon Lenz; *digital engineer:* Marcus Hutchinson, Dave Morehead, Robert Crawford, James Williams; *systems admin:* Alan Horn, Edwin Thornber, Alex Volovsek, Martin Elvin, Chris Jones; *scan sup:* Stuart Campbell; *back scan operator:* Brian Riley; *digital ph:* Jim Bird, Christopher Knights; *scan operators:* Peter Brady, Karl Dunne, Ross Leslie; *digital check:* Shauna Stevens, Lizzie Bentley, Deirdre Creed, Chantal Marsolais; *col des:* E. Jane Gotts, Janet Cable, Ray Rankine, Annie Elvin; *digital paint:* Geoff Portass, Kevin Prendergast, Jill Tudor, Andrew Awbery, Claire Baker, John Baldwin, Tim Bertani, Frankie Brook, Rob Buck, Adam Coglan, Martin Duncan, Stuart Ellis, Simon Edwards, Lucy Fellows, Harry Elvin, Chanchal Gill, Alex Godsill, Dave Hibberd, Christian Huffman, Timothy King, George Kingsnorth, Niall Murphy, Graeme Nattrass, Rebecca Neville, Chris Ogden, Roy Puddlefoot, Gideon Rigal, Bryan Rogers, Damian Rogers, Fiona Stewart, David Swift, Bramble Twheam, Danny Wells; *Franck & Franck Studios:* Emmanuel Franck, Stephan Franck, Laurent Donnay, Yvonne Jouannot, Sophie Baraduc, Annick Biaudet, Emmanuel Brughera, Isabelle Faivre, Jose-Antonio Garcia Villameriel, Gontran Hoarau, Anne-Marie Irlande, Patrick Lambert, Christine le Coz, Ludovic Maire, Joan-Noel Manthe, Charlotte Mazeran, Nicolas Ruedy, Antonella Russo, Mireille Sarault, Valerie Schaefer; *soft image:* Bill Perkins, Claudio Mattei, Gianmarco Todesco, Vincent Vennarini, Walter Tross; *casting:* Patsy Pollock, Bob Litvak, Ellen Parks, Mary Kate McCormick; *sd:* Matthew Roberts; *paint check:* Javier Gallego, Ron McMinn, Gloria Vassiliou; *asso prod:* Rich Arons; *prod mgr:* Jill Hopper; *technology dir:* Lem Davis; *asst prod mgr:* Mark Swift; *anim prod sup:* Colin J. Alexander; *col prod sup:* Matthew Teevan; *creative ex:* Douglas Wood; *prod asst:* Steve Pegram, Shelley Page, Catherine Foulkes, Sophie Law, Peter Nixon, Caroline Welch; *col:* Eastman/DeLuxe. *sd:* dts Stereo. Panavision. 77 min. *anim/l/a.* • Balto is an Alaskan husky whose moment of glory comes when a serious diptheria epidemic arrives at the same time as a blizzard. It's up to the sled dogs to race 600 miles through the blinding storm to obtain the life-saving medicine.

345. Bambi 13 Aug. 1942; *p.c.:* Walt Disney prods for RKO; *dir sup:* David D. Hand; *story dir:* Perce Pearce; *story adapt:* Larry Morey; *story:* Chuck Couch, Carl Fallberg, Melvin Shaw, George Stallings, Ralph Wright; *seq dir:* James Algar, Sam Armstrong, Graham Heid, Bill Roberts, Paul Satterfield, Norman Wright; *anim sup:* Milton Kahl, Oliver M. Johnston Jr., Eric Larson, Franklyn Thomas; *anim:* Albert Bertino, Preston Blair, John Bradbury, Paul Busch, Fraser Davis, Marc Davis, Ugo d'Orsi, Phil Duncan, Art Elliott, James S. Escalante, Bernard Garbutt, Al Geiss, Morris Gollub, Franklin Grundeen, Harry Hamsel, Kenneth Hultgren, Lynn Karp, Rico le Brun, Fred Madison, Murray McClellan, Lee Morehouse, Dan Noonan, Kenneth O'Brien, Tom Palmer, Willis Pyle, Louis Schmitt, Retta Scott, Don Tobin, Harvey Toombs, Robert W. Youngquist, Richard Wright; *fx:* Edwin Aardal, Joseph Gayek, John McManus, Joshua Meador, Art Palmer, John F. Reed, George Rowley; John Sewall, John Noel Tucker, James Will, Cornett Wood; *atmospheric sketches:* John Arensma, Jules Engel, David Hall, Lew Keller, Harold Miles, Maurice Noble, Glen Scott, Zack Schwartz, Sylvia Moberly Holland, Gustav Tenggren. *lay:* Thomas H. Codrick, Robert C. Cormack, Lloyd Harting, David Hilberman, John Hubley, Dick Kelsey, Glenn Scott, McLaren Stewart, Al Zinnen; *back:* W. Richard Anthony, Merle T. Cox, Ray Huffine, Travis Johnson, Ed Levitt, Robert McIntosh, Art Riley, Stan Spohn, Joe Stahley, Tyrus Wong; *voices: Friend Owl:* Will Wright; *Bambi (infant):* Bobby Stewart; *(child):* Donnie Dunagan; *(adolescent):* Hardy Albright; *(adult):* John Sutherland; *Thumper*

(child): Peter Behn; *(adolescent):* Sam Edwards; *(adult):* Tim Davis; *Faline (child):* Cammie King; *(adolescent);* Ann Gillis; *Flower (child):* Stanley Alexander; *(adolescent)* Sterling Holloway; *Mother Hare:* Marjorie Lee; *Bambi's Mother/pheasant:* Paula Winslowe; *The Prince of the Forest:* Fred Shields; *Aunt Ena/Mrs. Possum/girl skunk/pheasant:* Mary Lansing; *Mrs. Quail/girl bunny/frightened pheasant:* Thelma Boardman; *Bunnies and other children:* Bobette Chapman, Janet Chapman, Jeanne Christy, Dolyn Bramston Cook, Jack Horner, Sandra Lee Richards, Babs Nelson, Joey Pennario, Francesca Santoro, Elouise Wohlwend; *Mole:* Otis Harlan; *Chipmunks:* J. Donald Wilson, Eddie Holden; *Mouse:* Robert Winkler; *Squirrel:* Stuart Erwin; *Bullfrog:* Clarence Nash; *Wind fx:* The Ken Darby Chorus; "Love Is a Song" sung by Donald Novis; "I Bring You a Song": Robert Carroll; "Let's Sing a Gay Little Spring Song" sung by Georgina Clark, Jean MacMurray; *Whistling:* Marion Darlington; "April Showers" sung by Amy Lou Barnes, Betty Bruce, Sally Mueller, Mary Moder, Alice Sizer; *music/songs:* Frank Churchill, Edward Plumb; conducted by Alexander Steinert; *orch:* Charles Wolcott, Paul J. Smith; *choral arrangements:* Charles Henderson; *col:* Tech. *sd:* RCA. 69 min. Photographed in Multiplane. • Falix Salten's enchanting story about a year in the life of a young deer growing up in the forest.

346. Bananas? Si Senor 1955; *p.c.:* John Sutherland prods for United Fruit Co; *prod:* Earl Jonas; *dir:* Carl Urbano; *col:* East. *sd.* 13½ min. *l/a/anim.* • Emphasizing the usefulness of the banana crop to the economy of Middle America featuring Chiquita Banana.

347. The Band Concert *(Mickey Mouse)* 23 Feb. 1935; *p.c.:* Walt Disney prods for UA; *dir:* Wilfred Jackson; *story:* Ted Sears, Pinto Colvig, Hugh Hennesy, Terrell Stapp; *anim:* Johnny Cannon, Les Clark, Ugo d'Orsi, Gilles de Tremaudan, Clyde Geronimi, Jack Hannah, Ferdinand Huszti Horvath, Dick Huemer, Jack Kinney, Wolfgang Reitherman, Archie Robin, Louis Schmitt, Dick Williams, Roy Williams; *fx:* Cy Young; *lay:* Hugh Hennesy, Terrell Stapp; *back:* Ferdinand Huszti Horvath; *voices:* Clarence Nash, Pinto Colvig; *mus:* Leigh Harline; *col:* Tech. *sd:* RCA. 8 min. • Mickey (in his first Technicolor) conducts a park concert that gets heckled first by Donald then by a whirlwind, sweeping them all away.

348. The Bandmaster *(Oswald)* 27 May 1931; *p.c.:* Univ; *dir:* Walter Lantz, "Bill" Nolan; *anim:* Clyde Geronimi, Manuel Moreno, Ray Abrams, Fred Avery, Lester Kline, Chet Karrberg, Pinto Colvig; *mus:* James Dietrich; *b&w. sd:* WE. 6 min. • Oswald leads a street band and entertains a baby hippo.

349. The Bandmaster *(Andy Panda)* 19 Dec. 1947; *p.c.:* Walter Lantz prods for UA; *dir:* Dick Lundy; *story:* Ben Hardaway, Webb Smith; *anim:* (La) Verne Harding, Les Kline, Pat Matthews, Grim Natwick, Hal Mason, S.C. Onaitis; *sets:* Fred Brunish; *ed:* Dave Lurie; *mus:* Darrell Calker; *prod mgr:* William E. Garity; *col:* Tech. *sd:* RCA. 6 min. • Andy conducts *The Overture to Zampa* against a circus environment.

350. The Bandmaster *(Krazy Kat)* 8 Sept 1930; *prod:* Charles Mintz; *story:* Ben Harrison; *anim:* Manny Gould; *mus:* Joe de Nat; *b&w. sd:* WE. 6 min. • Krazy is a band leader in a park concert. He imitates Paul Whiteman, Chaplin, Ted Lewis and Ben Turpin and then plays "Stars and Stripes Forever."

351. The Banker's Daughter *(Oswald the Lucky Rabbit)* 28 Nov. 1927; *p.c.:* Winkler for Univ; *dir:* Walt Disney; *anim:* Ubbe Iwerks, Isadore Freleng; *ph:* Mike Marcus; *b&w. sil.* 5 min. • Chauffeur Oswald is fired by the Banker for flirting with his daughter but regains favor when he foils Peg Leg Pete's attempt to rob the bank.

352. The Banker's Daughter *(Paul Terry-Toon)* 25 June 1933; *p.c.:* Moser & Terry for Educational/Fox; *dir:* Frank Moser, Paul Terry; *mus:* Philip A. Scheib; *b&w. sd:* WE. 6 min. • Performed as an operatic melodrama: Fanny Zilch, the banker's daughter, is abducted by Oil Can Harry. Strongheart arrives in time to save her from being divided by a circular saw.

353. Banquet Busters *(Woody Woodpecker)* 12 Mar. 1948; *p.c.:* Walter Lantz prods for UA; *dir:* Dick Lundy; *story:* Ben Hardaway, Jack Cosgriff; *anim:* (La) Verne Harding, Pat Matthews; *sets:* Fred Brunish; *ed:* Dave Lurie; *mus:* Darrell Calker; *prod mgr:* William E. Garity; *col:* Tech. *sd:* RCA. 7 min. • Starving musicians Woody, Andy and a mouse gatecrash Mrs. van Glutton's banquet.

354. Banty Raids *(Merrie Melodies)* June 1963; *p.c.:* WB; *dir:* Robert McKimson; *story:* Robert McKimson, Nick Bennion; *anim:* George Grandpré, Keith Darling, Ted Bonnicksen, Warren Batchelder; *sets:* Robert Gribbroek; *ed:* Treg Brown; *voices:* Mel Blanc; *mus:* Bill Lava; *prod mgr:* William Orcutt; *prod:* David H. DePatie; *col:* Tech. *sd:* Vit. 6 min. • A beatnik rooster ingratiates himself into Foggy's confidence, then makes a B-line for the hens.

355. Barbary-Coast Bunny *(Looney Tunes)* 21 July 1956; *p.c.:* WB; *dir:* Chuck Jones; *story:* Tedd Pierce; *anim:* Abe Levitow, Richard Thompson, Ken Harris; *lay:* Robert Gribbroek; *back:* Philip de Guard; *ed:* Treg Brown; *voices:* Mel Blanc, Daws Butler; *mus:* Carl Stalling; *prod mgr:* John W. Burton; *prod:* Edward Selzer; *col:* Tech. *sd:* Vit. 7 min. • Bugs is robbed of of a gold rock by an unscrupulous crook named Nasty Canasta. He later arrives at Canasta's crooked gambling den, winning the gold back in a game of chance.

356. Barbecue Brawl *(Tom & Jerry)* 14 Dec. 1956; *p.c.:* MGM; *prod/dir:* William Hanna, Joseph Barbera; *anim:* Irven Spence, Lewis Marshall, Kenneth Muse, Ed Barge; *lay:* Dick Bickenbach; *back:* Robert Gentle; *ed:* Jim Faris; *voice:* Daws Butler; *mus:* Scott Bradley; *ph:* Jack Stevens; *prod mgr:* Hal Elias; *col:* Tech. *sd:* WE. 6 min. CS. • Spike and Tyke's barbecue is marred by Tom's relentless pursuit of Jerry.

357. The Barber of Seville *(Woody Woodpecker)* 10 Apr. 1944; *p.c.:* Walter Lantz prods for Univ; *dir:* James Culhane; *story:* Ben Hardaway, Milt Schaffer; *anim:* (La) Verne Harding, Emery Hawkins, Les Kline, Pat Matthews, Paul J. Smith; *lay:* Art Heinemann; *back:* Philip de Guard; *voices:* Nestor Paiva, Lee Sweetland, Ben Hardaway; *mus:* Darrell Calker; *prod mgr:* George Hall; *col:* Tech. *sd:* WE. 6 min. • Woody takes over in a barber's shop, giving a hapless riveter "the whole works."

358. Barefaced Flatfoot *(Mr. Magoo)* 26 Sept. 1951; *p.c.:* UPA for Colum; *ex prod:* Stephen Bosustow; *dir:* John Hubley; *story:* Phil Eastman, Bill Scott; *anim:* Pat Matthews, Rudy Larriva, Frank Smith, Art Babbitt, Cecil Surry; *sets:* Abe Liss, Jules Engel; *voices:* Jim Backus, Jerry Hausner; *mus:* Del Castillo; *prod sup:* Sherman Glas, Herbert Klynn; *col:* Tech. *sd:* RCA. 7 min. • When Waldo asks for a loan, Magoo is convinced he's involved with the underworld and decides to shadow him.

359. Bargain Counter Attack *(Little Lulu)* 3 May 1946; *p.c.:* Famous for Para; *dir:* I. Sparber; *story:* Bill Turner, Otto Messmer; *anim:* Nick Tafuri, John Walworth, Tom Golden; *sets:* Anton Loeb; *voices:* Cecil Roy, Jackson Beck; *mus:* Winston Sharples; *ph:* Leonard McCormick; *title song:* Buddy Kaye, Fred Wise, Sammy Timberg; *prod mgr:* Sam Buchwald; *col:* Tech. *sd:* RCA. 7 min. • Lulu returns a doll to the department store, causing the floorwalker a good deal of trouble.

360. Bargain Daze *(Heckle & Jeckle)* Aug. 1953; *p.c.:* TT for Fox; *dir:* Mannie Davis; *story:* Tom Morrison; *anim:* Jim Tyer; *voices:* Tom Morrison, Douglas Moye; *mus:* Philip A. Scheib; *ph:* Douglas Moye; *col:* Tech. *sd:* RCA. 6 min. • The Magpies cause havoc in a department store.

361. Barking Dogs *(Aesop's Sound Fable)* 18 May 1933; *p.c.:* Van Beuren for RKO; *dir:* Mannie Davis; *mus:* Gene Rodemich; b&w. *sd:* RCA. 6 min. • No story available.

362. Barking Dogs Don't Fite *(Popeye)* 28 Oct. 1949; *p.c.:* Famous for Para; *dir:* I. Sparber; *story:* Carl Meyer, Jack Mercer; *anim:* Tom Johnson, John Gentilella; *sets:* Tom Ford; *voices:* Jack Mercer, Jackson Beck, Mae Questel; *mus:* Winston Sharples; *ph:* Leonard McCormick; *prod mgr:* Sam Buchwald; *col:* Tech. *sd:* RCA. 6 min. • Popeye is forced to take Olive's French poodle for a walk and runs afoul of Bluto and his bulldog. Remake of *Proteck the Weakerest.*

363. The Barn Dance *(Mickey Mouse)* 15 Nov. 1928; *p.c.:* Walter E. Disney for Colum; *dir:* Walt Disney; *anim:* Ub Iwerks; *mus:* Carl W. Stalling; b&w. *sd:* PCP. 6 min. • Due to his inability to dance, Mickey has problems with Minnie and Pete.

364. Barnacle Bill *(Talkartoon)* 30 Aug. 1930; *p.c.:* The Fleischer Studio for Para; *prod:* Max Fleischer; *dir:* Dave Fleischer; *anim:* Rudy Zamora, Seymour Kneitel; *voice:* Little Ann Little; *mus:* Art Turkisher; b&w. *sd:* WE. 6 min. • Bimbo, a sailor on leave, visits Nancy Lee (Betty) and when he is finally invited in, a group of cats outside discuss the goings-on.

365. Barney Bear and the Uninvited Pest *(MGM cartoon)* 17 July 1943; *p.c.:* MGM; *prod/dir:* Rudolf Ising; *mus:* Scott Bradley; *col:* Tech. *sd:* WE. 7 min. • Barney Bear's slumber is disturbed by a squirrel raiding his cache of walnuts.

366. Barney Bear's Victory Garden *(MGM cartoon)* 26 Dec. 1942; *p.c.:* MGM; *prod/dir:* Rudolf Ising; *voice:* Gayne Whitman; *mus:* Scott Bradley; *col:* Tech. *sd:* WE. 7 min. • Barney tries to grow a "Victory Garden" against all odds ... including a hungry gopher.

367. Barney's Animated Film Commercial 13 May 1953; *p.c.:* Emil Mogul Co; *anim:* Myron Mahler; b&w. *sd.* 20 sec. • No story available.

368. Barney's Hungry Cousin *(Barney Bear)* 31 Jan. 1953; *p.c.:* MGM; *dir:* Dick Lundy; *story:* Heck Allen, Jack Cosgriff; *anim:* Robert Bentley, Michael Lah, Walter Clinton, Grant Simmons, Ray Patterson; *sets:* John Didrik Johnsen; *ed:* Jim Faris; *voice:* Paul Frees; *mus:* Scott Bradley; *ph:* Jack Stevens; *prod:* Fred Quimby; *col:* Tech. *sd:* WE. 7 min. • Barney encounters a hungry bear who wants to steal his picnic.

369. Barnum Was Right *(Life Cartoon Comedy)* 16 Dec. 1926; *p.c.:* Sherwood Wadsworth Pictures Inc for Educational; *prod:* John R. McCrory; b&w. sil. 5 min. • A circus setting has High-Hat Harold inflating an elephant with helium so he can abduct Myrtle and float away. Mike Monkey pursues his trapeze-artist friend, landing Harold in the lion's cage.

370. The Barnyard Actor *(Gandy Goose)* Jan. 1955; *p.c.:* TT for Fox; *dir:* Connie Rasinski; *story:* Tom Morrison; *anim:* Jim Tyer; *voice:* Arthur Kay; *mus:* Philip A. Scheib; *ph:* Douglas Moye; *col:* Tech. *sd:* RCA. 6 min. • Gandy irritates the barnyard personnel with his impersonations of Groucho, Durante and others.

371. Barnyard Amateurs *(Paul Terry-Toon)* 6 Mar. 1936; *p.c.:* Moser & Terry for Educational/Fox; *dir:* Frank Moser, Paul Terry; *mus:* Philip A. Scheib; b&w. *sd:* WE. 6 min. • Farmer Al Falfa plays "Major Bowes."

372. Barnyard Artists *(Aesop's Film Fable)* 8 Apr. 1928; *p.c.:* Fables Pictures Inc for Pathé; *dir:* Paul Terry, Hugh Shields; b&w. sil. 10 min. • Al Falfa and Henry Cat create their own animated cartoon. When "The Pup" is completed, it is shown in a theater and features a conceited pup chasing jungle animals. An elephant in the cartoon falls into a river, causing a tidal wave that floods the whole theater.

373. Barnyard Babies *(Fable)* 14 June 1940; *p.c.:* Colum; *story:* Art Davis; *anim:* Sid Marcus; *back:* Phil Davis; *ed:* George Winkler; *voices:* Robert Winkler, Mel Blanc, Danny Webb; *mus:* Joe de Nat; *ph:* Otto Reimer; *prod mgr:* James Bronis; b&w. *sd:* RCA. 7 min. • One of Mother Hen's chicks wants to be a G-man but lives to regret it.

374. Barnyard Babies *(Happy Harmonies)* 25 May 1935; *p.c.:* MGM; *prod/dir:* Hugh Harman, Rudolf Ising; *mus:* Scott Bradley; *col:* Tech-2. *sd:* WE. 9 min. • Mr. and Mrs. Rooster try to speed-up the hatching process in time for tomorrow's "Better Babies Contest."

375. Barnyard Baseball *(Terry-Toon)* 14 July 1939; *p.c.:* TT for Fox; *dir:* Mannie Davis; *story:* John Foster; *mus:* Philip A. Scheib; *col:* Tech. *sd:* RCA. 6 min. • Gandy Goose is the star baseball player.

376. The Barnyard Battle *(Mickey Mouse)* 2 July 1929; *p.c.:* Walter E. Disney for Colum; *dir:* Walt Disney; *anim:* Ub Iwerks; *mus:* Carl W. Stalling; b&w. *sd:* PCP. 6 min. • A fight between Mickey, some mice and a gang of cats.

377. Barnyard Blackout *(Terry-Toon)* 5 Mar. 1943; *p.c.:* TT for Fox; *dir:* Mannie Davis; *story:* John Foster; *voices:* Arthur Kay, Thomas Morrison; *mus:* Philip A. Scheib; *col:* Tech. *sd:* RCA. 6 min. • A stubborn rooster refuses to take blackout precautions and when the siren finally sounds he has to face the irate Sector Warden.

378. Barnyard Boss *(Paul Terry-Toon)* 24 Dec. 1937; *p.c.:* TT for Educational/Fox; *dir:* Connie Rasinski; *story:* John Foster; *mus:* Philip A. Scheib; b&w. *sd:* WE. 6 min. • The hens aren't laying because they are playing Bingo, so the rooster runs his own Bingo game.

379. The Barnyard Brat *(Color Classic)* 30 June 1939; *p.c.:* The Fleischer Studio for Para; *prod:* Max Fleischer; *dir:* Dave Fleischer; *anim:* Myron Waldman, Anthony Pabian, Lillian Friedman; *character des:* Myron Waldman; *voices:* Pinto Colvig, Everett Clark; *mus:* Sammy Timberg; *col:* Tech. *sd:* WE. 7 min. • Spunky the donkey won't eat his food and annoys all the other animals who soon repay him for his nonsense.

380. The Barnyard Broadcast *(Mickey Mouse)* 30 Sept. 1931; *p.c.:* Walter E. Disney for Colum; *dir:* Burton F. Gillett; *anim:* Les Clark, Chuck

Couch, Joseph d'Igalo, Gilles de Tremaudan, Norman Ferguson, David D. Hand, Frank Kelling, Jack King, Richard Lundy, Hamilton S. Luske, Tom Palmer, Ben Sharpsteen; *asst anim:* Charles Byrne, Jack Cutting, Hardie Gramatky, Andrew Hutchinson, George Lane, Harry Reeves, Cecil Surry; *sets:* Carlos Manriquez; *voices:* Walt Disney, Lee Millar; *mus:* Bert Lewis; b&w. *sd:* PCP. 7 min. • Mickey's radio broadcast is marred by howling cats. A chase wrecks the whole studio, leaving Mickey to sign-off amid the debris.

381. Barnyard Bunk (*Tom & Jerry*) 16 Sept. 1932; *p.c.:* Van Beuren for RKO; *dir:* John Foster, George Rufle; *mus:* Gene Rodemich; b&w. *sd:* RCA. 6 min. • Tom and Jerry arrive at a dilapidated farm and play music to help the struggling farmer's chickens lay and the cow to yield milk. Mice dump the boys in a river at the end.

382. The Barnyard Concert (*Mickey Mouse*) 5 Apr. 1930; *p.c.:* Walter E. Disney for Colum; *dir:* Walt Disney; *mus:* Bert Lewis; *ph:* William Cottrell; b&w. *sd:* PCP. 6 min. • Mickey conducts the barnyard animals' concert.

383. Barnyard Egg-Citement (*Terry-Toon*) 5 May 1939; *p.c.:* TT for Fox; *dir:* Connie Rasinski; *story:* John Foster; *mus:* Philip A. Scheib; *col:* Tech. *sd:* RCA. 6 min. • A baby chick is captured by a hawk and the barnyard animals set out to rescue him.

384. The Barnyard Five (*Oswald*) 20 Apr. 1936; *p.c.:* Univ; *dir:* Walter Lantz; *story:* Walter Lantz, Victor McLeod; *anim:* Manuel Moreno, George Nicholas; *voice:* The Crockett Family; *mus:* James Dietrich; b&w. *sd:* RCA. 6 min. • Oswald invites Mme. Duck's quinducklets over to eat. The outing turns into a food fight.

385. Barnyard Follies (*Aesop's Film Fable*) 5 Sept. 1925; *p.c.:* Fables Pictures Inc for Pathé; *dir:* Paul Terry; b&w. *sil.* 10 min. • A vaudeville show staged by the farm animals.

386. The Barnyard Hamlet (*Sullivan Cartoon Comedy*) 26 Nov. 1917; *p.c.:* Powers for Univ; *dir:* Pat Sullivan; *anim:* W.E. Stark; b&w. *sil.* 4 min. • An actor performs "Mendelssohn's Spring Song" for the farm animals who are less appreciative than he had hoped.

387. Barnyard Lodge No.1 (*Aesop's Film Fable*) 2 Apr. 1928; *p.c.:* Fables Pictures Inc for Pathé; *dir:* Paul Terry, Frank Moser; b&w. *sil.* 10 min. • By knowing the Barnyard Lodge's secret sign, you can get free milk from the cow. When Farmer Al Falfa tries the secret sign, all the animals find various methods of torturing him for the initiation ceremony. He gets knocked unconscious by the mule and fantasizes that he is in the arms of a beautiful girl. He awakes from the dream but knocks himself out again to enjoy the girl's company. Moral: "Give us life, liberty and the pursuit of Flappers."

388. The Barnyard Melody (*Aesop's Sound Fable*) 1 Nov. 1929; *p.c.:* Fables Pictures Inc for Pathé; *dir:* John Foster, Harry Bailey; *mus:* Carl Edouarde; b&w. *sd:* RCA. 7 min. • Farmer Al and Milton Mouse join the dog and pig in a harmony group. They are doing pretty well until Al is kicked by a mule.

389. Barnyard Olympics (*Aesop's Film Fable*) 7 Sept. 1924; *p.c.:* Fables Pictures Inc for Pathé; *dir:* Paul Terry; b&w. *sil.* 5 min. • High-diving pigs and elephants coupled with a kangaroo on the chinning bar and a race between the tortoise and the hare.

390. Barnyard Olympics (*Mickey Mouse*) 13 Apr. 1932; *p.c.:* Walter E. Disney for Colum; *dir:* Wilfred Jackson; *anim:* Johnny Cannon, Les Clark, Gilles de Tremaudan, Clyde Geronimi, Albert Hurter, Jack King, Richard Lundy, Ben Sharpsteen; *voice:* Pinto Colvig; *mus:* Frank E. Churchill; b&w. *sd:* PCP. 7 min. • Burlesque on athletic events with a bicycle race.

391. Barnyard Politics (*Aesop's Film Fable*) 26 Nov. 1928; *p.c.:* Fables Pictures Inc for Pathé; *dir:* Paul Terry, Hugh Shields; b&w. *sil.* 10 min. • No story available.

392. A Barnyard Rodeo (*Aesop's Film Fable*) 29 Sept. 1923; *p.c.:* Fables Pictures Inc for Pathé; *dir:* Paul Terry; b&w. *sil.* 5 min. • The animals stage a rodeo on Al Falfa's farm. A bull-fight between Señor Tomalé and Firporino the "bull" (two cats in a bull costume) is the main event. The real cattle take offence and chase the fakers away.

393. Barnyard Romeo (*Oswald*) 1 Aug. 1938; *p.c.:* Walter Lantz prods for Univ; *dir:* Alex Lovy; *story:* Victor McLeod, James Miele, *anim:* La Verne Harding, George Dane; *sets:* Edgar Keichle; *voices:* Mel Blanc, Sara Berner; *mus:* Frank Marsales; b&w. *sd:* WE. 6 min. • A goose (Fanny Brice) loves a turkey named Clark Gobble who, in turn, loves a peacock (Katharine Hepburn)! Disguised as a Mexican singer, the goose makes her desert Gobble.

394. Barnyard WAAC (*Terry-Toon*) 11 Dec. 1942; *p.c.:* TT for Fox; *dir:* Eddie Donnelly; *story:* John Foster; *mus:* Philip A. Scheib; *col:* Tech. *sd:* RCA. 7 min. • The rooster discovers all the hens have joined the WAACs. Foxes take advantage of the situation and make off with the chicks.

395. Baron Von Go-Go (*James Hound*) Dec. 1967; *p.c.:* TT for Fox; *dir sup:* Ralph Bakshi; *col:* DeLuxe. *sd:* RCA. 6 min. • Selfish art collector, Vincent van Go-Go, steals the art treasures of the world. • See: *James Hound*

396. Barré-Bowers Studio 1918; *prods:* Raoul Barré, Charles R. Bowers; *artists:* J.L. "Vet" Anderson, Dick Boyle, Nat Collier, Mannie Davis, F.M. Follett, Richard McShay Friel, Burton F. Gillett, Milt Gross, Dick Huemor, Albert Hurter, Isadore Klein, Helen Kroll, Lubotsky, Frank & Edith Nankerville, John Renza, Ted Sears, Frank Sherman, George Stallings, Paul Houghton Terry, Vladimir Tytla; *tracing:* Edward J. White; *exposure sheets:* Grace Ashton.

397. Bars and Stripes (*Aesop's Film Fable*) 12 Dec. 1926; *p.c.:* Fables Pictures Inc for Pathé; *dir:* Paul Terry; b&w. *sil.* 10 min. • The cat and mouse are in prison and manage to escape after an encounter with dog guards.

398. Bars and Stripes (*Krazy Kat*) 15 Oct. 1931; *p.c.:* Winkler for Colum; *story:* Manny Gould; *anim:* Allen Rose, Jack Carr; *voice:* Jack Carr; *mus:* Joe de Nat; *prod:* Charles Mintz; b&w. *sd:* WE. 6 min. • Krazy is such a bad violinist that he gets banished by the other instruments.

399. Bars and Stripes Forever (*Merrie Melodies*) 8 Apr. 1939; *p.c.:* Leon Schlesinger prods for WB; *dir:* J.B. Hardaway, Cal Dalton; *story:* Jack Miller; *anim:* Rod Scribner; *lay:* Griff Jay; *back:* Art Loomer; *ed:* Tregoweth E. Brown; *voice:* Mel Blanc, Danny Webb; *mus:* Carl W. Stalling; *prod sup:* Henry Binder, Raymond G. Katz; *col:* Tech. *sd:* Vit. 7 min. • A convict escapes from Alcatrazz Prison but is rapidly recovered.

400. Bartholomew Versus the Wheel (*Merrie Melodies*) 29 Feb. 1964; *p.c.:* WB; *dir:* Robert McKimson; *story:* John Dunn.; *anim:* George Grandpré, Ted Bonnicksen, Warren Batchelder; *lay:* Bob Givens; *back:* Robert Gribbroek; *ed:* Treg Brown; *voices:* Leslie Barringer, Mel Blanc; *mus:* Bill Lava; *prod mgr:* William Orcutt; *prod:* David H. DePatie; *col:* Tech. *sd:* Vit. 6 min. • Bartholomew the dog enjoys chasing wheels. One day he catches the wheel of a jet plane and finds himself in Africa.

401. Base Brawl (*Screen Song*) 23 Jan. 1948; *p.c.:* Famous for Para; *dir:* Seymour Kneitel; *story:* Larz Bourne, Bill Turner; *anim:* David Tendlar, Thomas Golden; *sets:* Robert Connavale; *mus:* Winston Sharples; *ph:* Leonard McCormick; *prod mgr:* Sam Buchwald; *col:* Pola. *sd:* RCA. 8 min. • The Forest All-Stars play the Jungle Jumbos and build up the score 89–0.

402. Baseball Bugs (*Looney Tunes*) 2 Feb. 1946; *p.c.:* WB; *dir:* I. Freleng; *story:* Michael Maltese; *anim:* Manuel Perez, Ken Champin, Virgil Ross, Gerry Chiniquy; *lay:* Hawley Pratt; *back:* Paul Julian; *ed:* Treg Brown; *voices:* Mel Blanc, Frank Graham, Bea Benaderet, The Sportsmen Quartet, Tedd Pierce; *mus:* Carl W. Stalling; *prod mgr:* John W. Burton; *prod:* Edward Selzer; *col:* Tech. *sd:* Vit. 7 min. • Bugs is challenged to play baseball against the brutal team of "Bernie's Gashouse Gorillas."

403. The Bashful Buzzard (*Looney Tunes*) 15 Sept. 1945; *p.c.:* WB; *dir:* Robert Clampett; *story/back:* Michael Sasanoff; *anim:* Robert McKimson, Rod Scribner; *character des/lay:* Tom McKimson; *ed:* Treg Brown; *voices:* Mel Blanc, Kent Rogers, Sara Berner; *prod mgr:* John W. Burton; *prod:* Edward Selzer; *col:* Tech. *sd:* Vit. 7 min. • Mama Buzzard sends her slow-witted offspring to catch food for supper. He surprises all by bagging the biggest catch of the day.

404. Bass, Saul (Title Designs) (*animated and non-animated*) *p.c.:* Saul Bass & Associates. **Carmen Jones** (Fox) 1954. **The Racers** (Fox) 1955. **The Shrike** (Univ) 1955. **The Seven Year Itch** (Para) 1955. **The Big Knife** (UA) 1955. **The Man with the Golden Arm** (UA) 1955. **Storm Centre**

(Colum) 1956. **Attack!** (UA) 1956. **Johnny Concho** (UA) 1956. **Around the World in 80 Days** (UA) 1956. **Edge of the City** (MGM) 1956. **The Man Who Knew Too Much** (Par) 1956. **Trapeze** (UA) 1956. **The Young Stranger** (Univ) 1957. **Saint Joan** (UA) 1957. **The Pride and the Passion** (UA) 1957. **Bonjour Tristesse** (Colum) 1957. **Cowboy** (Colum) 1958. **Vertigo** (Univ) 1958. **The Big Country** (UA) 1958. **North by North-West** (MGM) 1959. **Anatomy of a Murder** (Colum) 1959. **Psycho** (Para) 1960. **Ocean's Eleven** (WB) 1960. **Spartacus** (Univ) 1961. **Exodus** (UA) 1960. **The Facts of Life** (UA) 1960. **West Side Story** (UA) 1961. **Something Wild** (UA) 1961. **Walk on the Wild Side** (Colum) 1962. **Advise and Consent** (Colum) 1962. **Nine Hours to Rama** (Fox) 1962. **It's a Mad, Mad, Mad, Mad World** (UA) 1963. **The Cardinal** (Colum) 1963. **The Victors** (Colum) 1963. **In Harm's Way** (Para) 1963. **Bunny Lake Is Missing** (Colum) 1965. **Seconds** (Para) 1966. **Not with My Wife, You Don't** (WB) 1966. **Grand Prix** (MGM) 1966. **Such Good Friends** (Para) 1971. **Phase IV** (Para) 1973. **Rosebud** (UA) 1974. **That's Entertainment (part II)** (MGM) 1976. **The Human Factor** 1979.

405. Bath Day *(Figaro)* 11 Oct. 1946; *p.c.:* Walt Disney prods for RKO; *dir:* Charles Nichols; *asst dir:* Bob North; *story:* Eric Gurney; *anim:* Marvin Woodward, Murray McClellan, George Nicholas, Jerry Hathcock, Harry Holt, George Kreisl, Ken O'Brien, Robert Youngquist; *fx:* Brad Case, Andy Engman, Ernie Lynch; *lay:* Karl Karpé; *back:* Merle Cox; *voices:* Leone Le Doux, Clarence Nash; *mus:* Oliver Wallace; *col:* Tech. *sd:* RCA. 7 min. • Minnie bathes, perfumes and ribbons Figaro then sends him out in the street where he runs afoul of a gang of alley cats intent on a fight.

406. Bathing Buddies *(Woody Woodpecker)* 1 July 1946; *p.c.:* Walter Lantz prods for Univ; *dir:* Dick Lundy; *story:* Ben Hardaway, Milt Schaffer; *anim:* Paul Smith, Bernard Garbutt, (La) Verne Harding, Emery Hawkins, Les Kline, Grim Natwick, Sydney Pillet; *sets:* Fred Brunish; *voices:* Jack Mather, Ben Hardaway; *mus:* Darrell Calker; *prod mgr:* William E. Garity; *col:* Tech. *sd:* WE. 6 min. • When Woody loses a dime down the drain, his efforts to retrieve it disrupt Wally's bathing.

407. Batman and Robin 20 June 1997; *p.c.:* WB; *visual fx: anim:* Olivier Gilbert, Yves LePeiliet, Oliver Luffin, Geoffrey Niquet, Marie Laure LaFitte, Stéphane Naze, Dominique Vidal, Christophe Depuis, Pasquale Croce, Jérôme Bacquet, David Verbeke, Jean Michael Ponzio, Derick Delatour, Rafael Marque, Stéphane Ceretti; *col:* Tech. *sd:* Dolby Digital/dts/SDDS. 124 min. *l/a.* • Live-action action fantasy feature: The crime-fighting duo pit their wits against Mr. Freeze.

408. Batman: Mask of the Phantasm 25 Dec. 1993; *p.c.:* WB Animation; *dir:* Eric Radomski, Bruce W. Timm; *story/scr:* Alan Burnett; *writers:* Paul Dini, Martin Pasko, Michael Reaves; based on the comic book and characters by Bob Kane; *prod:* Alan Burnett, Benjamin Melniker, Eric Radomski, Bruce W. Timm; *ex prod:* Tom Ruegger, Michael E. Uslan; *storyboard:* Troy Adomitis, Kevin Altieri, Gregg Davidson, Ronaldo Del Carmen, Joe Denton, Curt Geda, Michael Goguen, Boyd Kirkland, Butch Lukic, Doug Murphy, Frank Paur, Brad Rader, Dan Riba, Jeff Snow, Bruce W. Timm, Mark Wallace; *seq dir:* Kevin Altieri, Boyd Kirkland, Frank Paur, Dan Riba; *voices: Bruce Wayne/Batman:* Kevin Conroy; *Andrea "Andi" Beaumont/The Phantasm:* Dana Delany; *City Councilman Arthur Reeves:* Hart Bochner; *Carl Beaumont/The Phantasm:* Stacy Keach; *Salvatore "Sal the Wheezer" Valestra:* Abe Vigoda; *Charles "Chuckie" Sol:* Dick Miller; *"Buzz" Bronski:* John P. Ryan; *Alfred Pennyworth:* Efrem Zimbalist Jr.; *Commissioner Jim Gordon:* Bob Hastings; *Detective Harvey Bullock:* Robert Costanzo; *The Joker:* Mark Hamill; *Veronica Vreeland:* Marilu Henner; *Bambi:* Arleen Sorkin; *also:* Jeff Bennett, Jane Downs, Ed Gilbert, Charles Howerton, Pat Musick, Thom Pinto, Peter Renaday, Neil Ross, Vernee Watson-Johnson; *character des:* Chen-Yi Chang, Michael Diedrich, Craig Kellman, Glen Murakami, Dexter Smith, Jeff Snow, Bruce W. Timm; *vehicle/prop des:* Trish Burgio, Shayne Poindexter; *anim check:* Jan Browning, Brenda Brummet, Jennifer Damiani, Bunty Dranko, Ana Durand, Karl Jacobs, Howard Schwartz; *key back des:* Ted Blackman, Troy Adomitis, Robert Haverland, David S. Karoll, Lawrence Kim, Rae McCarson, Felipe Morell, Rae McCarson, Jeff Starling, Keith Weesner, Todd Winter; *col key stylist:* Kathy Gilmore, Pamela Long; *back stylist:* Eric Radomski; *back:* Steve Butz, John Calmette, Russell G. Chong, Charles Pickens, Lawrence Kim; *mark-up:* Gene DuBois, Lisa Leonard-Knight, Valerie Walker; *back col correction:* Carolyn Guske; *digital anim:* Alan G. Brown, Bo Ferger, Hiroki Itokazu, Vicki Radomski, Eugene Jeong; *mus:* Shirley Walker; *orch:*

Richard Bronskill, Lolita Ritmanis, Peter Tomashek, Michael McCuistion; *synthesizer:* Hans Zimmer; *score:* Robert Fernandez; *mus ed:* Thomas Milano; *ed:* Al Breitenbach; *col timer:* Dale E. Grahn; *timing dir:* Maxwell Becraft, Richard Collado, Tom McLaughlin, James T. Walker; *overseas co-ord:* Clive Nakayashiki; *overseas anim sup:* Ric Machin; *overseas back sup:* Don Schweikert; *i&p:* Bunny Munns, Robin D. Kane, Eric Nordberg; *Dong Yang Animation: anim prod:* Myung-Ok Jeun, Ki-Soo Seo, Jung-Bum Youn, Geum Nam Cho, Hae Ran Ha, Jong Tae Kim, Sook Young Song, Jae Young Son, Mi Sung Kim, Tae Hyoung Kim, Hae Sung Park, Byng Ryong Yu; *anim dir:* Chung Ho Kim, Se-won Kim, Je Dong Lee, Sun Hee Lee, Min Ho Park, Young-Hwan Song; *key anim:* Tae Kun Ahn, Yosio Chatani, Wook Cho, Woo Yong Chung, Kang Ro Lee, Sang Wan Lee, Jung Won Ma, Young-Cho Myung, Bong-ll Park, Sang Kyoun Shin, Jin Sung Woo, Hea Young Yoo, Sung Yul Yoo; *inbet:* Hyun Ju Ahn, Eun Soo An, Young Yoo An, Hee Jeong Back, Jung Ah Bang, Hay Youn Chang, Jeong Jin Choi, Jong Hwa Im, Hea Kyung Jeong, Min Yong Jeong, Sun Mi Kang, Dae Ryoung Kim, Hyea Ju Kim, Hye Soo Kim, Jun Hee Kim, Song Hee Kim, Tae Jun Kim, Chung Wook Koh, Chui Woo Lee, Eun Mi Lee, Gun Sig Lee, Jun Ho Lee, Ki Sup Lee, Sung Sook Lee, He Joung Park, Chung Hwa Se, Mi Jin Shin, Gil Suk Sun, Jae Myeung Woo, Ri Eui Yang, Hong Suk Yeou, Jong Seng Yu; *clean-up:* Chel Woo Ahn, Ok Ra Ban, Byoung In Han, Hye Young Jung, Gwan Woo Lee, Hyoung Lim Son; *back:* Eun Young Choe, Yae Roo Han, Kyoung Koo Jang, Sung Hi Jang, Young Yoon Jang, Aee Lyoung Jun, Hang Sook Jung, Hi Whan Kim, Hyun Soo Kim, Kyoung Ae Kim, Mi-kyung Kim, Yong Sung Kim, Joung Ran Ku, Eun Kyoung Lee, Joung Min Lee, Joung Sook Lim, Hye Kyoung Min, Ung-Hwan Oh, Eun Ah Park, Kyeong Sook Park, Kyoung Sun Park, Sung Sook Park, Hyun Kyoung Seo, Jee Joung Sim; *ph dir:* Sung-ll Choi; *Spectrum Animation Studio: anim prod:* Norio Fukuda, Shinichi Kota, Yukimi Umeda; *asst dir:* Yukio Suzuki, Noboru Takahashi, Shigeru Kimiya; *anim dir:* Yutaka Oka, Yukio Suzuki, Noboru Takahashi; *key anim/lay:* Yosio Chatani, Shingo Kaneko, Masahito Kimura, Yoshishige Kosako, Hidemi Kubo, Hiroshi Kuzuka, Kôji Miura, Yutaka Oka, Masahiro Shigemoto, Nobumasa Shinkawa, Noboru Takahashi, Masaki Tamakoshi, Takeru Yamazaki; *inbet anim check:* Akihiko Mamashita; *sd ed:* Julia Evershade, Oscar Mitt; *foley:* Eric Gotthelf, Rick Partlow; *prod sup:* Joey Franks; *prod mgr:* Haven Alexander; *prod asst:* Christopher Keenan, Steve Walby; *col:* CFI. *sd:* Dolby Digital. 76 min. • Batman is wrongly accused for a number of murders of Mob bosses that were actually carried out by a vigilante assassin. It's up to Batman to clear his name and bring the rightful criminal to justice. Originally made as a "direct-to-video" item but with added scenes received a national big screen release.

409. Baton Bunny *(Looney Tunes)* 10 Jan. 1959; *p.c.:* WB; *dir:* Chuck Jones, Abe Levitow; *story:* Michael Maltese; *anim:* Ken Harris, Richard Thompson, Ben Washam; *lay:* Maurice Noble; *back:* Tom O'Loughlin; *ed:* Treg Brown; *voice:* Mel Blanc; *mus:* Milt Franklyn, The Warner Bros. Symphony Orchestra; *prod:* John W. Burton; *col:* Tech. *sd:* Vit. 6 min. • Bugs conducts Franz von Suppé's *Morning, Noon and Night in Vienna* in the Hollywood Bowl when a troublesome fly bothers him.

410. Bats in the Belfry *(MGM cartoon)* 4 July 1942; *p.c.:* MGM; *prod:* Rudolf Ising; *dir/story:* Jerry Brewer; *voices:* Dick Nelson, Sara Berner; *mus:* Scott Bradley; *col:* Tech. *sd:* WE. 6½ min. • At the stroke of midnight, three jitterbug bats come to life in the belfrey tower.

411. Bats in the Belfry *(Woody Woodpecker)* 16 June 1960; *p.c.:* Walter Lantz prods for Univ; *dir:* Paul J. Smith; *story:* Homer Brightman; *anim:* La Verne Harding, Les Kline, Ray Abrams; *sets:* Art Landy; *voices:* Paul Frees, Grace Stafford; *mus:* Clarence Wheeler; *prod mgr:* William E. Garity; *col:* Tech. *sd:* RCA. 6 min. • Rest is prescribed for the Colonel and it's up to his butler to stop Woody from creating any noise with church bells.

412. *batteries not included 18 Dec. 1987; *p.c.:* Amblin Entertainment for Univ; *rod puppet/stop-motion anim:* ILM; David Allen; *go-motion anim:* Tom St. Amand; *anim:* Nick Stern, Sean Turner, Wes Takahashi, John Hayes, Tim Berglund; *anim ph:* Charlie Mullen; *col:* DeLuxe. *sd:* Dolby stereo. 106 min. *l/a.* • Live-action fantasy about a couple of extra-terrestrials who help the tenants of a crumbling New York apartment building.

413. The Battle *(Out of the Inkwell)* 1 July 1923; *p.c.:* Inkwell Studio for Rodner; *prod/l/a:* Max Fleischer; *dir:* Dave Fleischer; b&w. sil. 6 min. *l/a/anim.* • Max draws his little clown and a colleague draws a "Harlequin."

The artists get into a scrap over using the same inkwell, encouraging the clowns to follow suit. An actual war takes place on paper which spills over into the studio.

414. A Battle for a Bottle (*Phantasy*) 29 May 1942; *p.c.:* Colum; *prod:* Frank Tashlin; *dir:* Alec Geiss; *story:* Jack Cosgriff; *anim:* Ray Patterson; *sets:* Clark Watson; *ed:* Edward Moore; *voice:* Harry E. Lang; *mus:* Paul Worth; *ph:* Frank Fisher; *prod mgr:* Ben Schwalb; b&w. *sd:* RCA. 6 min. • A cat attempts to steal a bottle of milk from under the watchful eye of Butch the Bulldog.

415. Battle of the Barn (*Scrappy*) 31 May 1932; *p.c.:* Winkler for Colum; *prod:* Charles Mintz; *story:* Dick Huemor; *anim:* Sid Marcus, Art Davis; *mus:* Joe de Nat; *prod mgr:* James Bronis; b&w. *sd:* RCA. 6 min. • Scrappy's gang battle with a group of bullies. When little Heidi is splashed with mud, she gives the bullies a sound trouncing.

416. Battle Royal (*Oswald*) 22 June 1936; *p.c.:* Univ; *dir:* Walter Lantz; *story:* Walter Lantz, Victor McLeod; *anim:* Ed Benedict, Fred Kopietz; *mus:* James Dietrich; b&w. *sd:* RCA. 6 min. • Involving a spider and his machinations when boxer Oswald fights Punchy Pig.

417. Battling Bosko (*Looney Tunes*) 6 Feb. 1932; *p.c.:* Hugh Harman, Rudolf Ising prods for WB; *anim:* Isadore Freleng, Paul Smith, Robert Clampett; *voices:* John T. Murray, Mary Moder; *mus:* Frank Marsales; *asso prod:* Leon Schlesinger; b&w. *sd:* Vit. 7 min. • Bosko enters the ring against a mountainous opponent named Gas House Harry.

418. A Battling Duet (*Aesop's Film Fable*) 2 Apr. 1928; *p.c.:* Fables Pictures Inc for Pathé; *dir:* Paul Terry, Harry Bailey; b&w. *sil.* 10 min. • No story available.

419. Batty Baseball 22 Apr. 1944; *p.c.:* MGM; *dir:* Tex Avery; *anim:* Ray Abrams, Preston Blair, Ed Love; *character des:* Claude Smith; *sets:* John Didrik Johnsen; *ed:* Fred MacAlpin; *voices:* John Wald, Jack Mather, Leone le Doux; *mus:* Scott Bradley; *prod:* Fred Quimby; *col:* Tech. *sd:* WE. 6 min. • An unconventional baseball game between The Yankee Doodlers and The Draft Dodgers.

420. B.D.F. Film Co *prods:* Hobart Bosworth, Joseph deFrenes, Paul M. Felton; *dir:* Paul M. Felton; *story:* Paul Barnett; b&w. st. • *1918:* W.S.S. Thriftettes (War Bonds). Old Tire Man Diamond Cartoon Film 13 July. • *1919:* Re-Blazing the '49 Trail in a Motor Car Train 10 Sept. Tire Injury 13 Sept. Paradental Anesthesia 13 Sept. • *1921:* A Movie Trip Through Film Land 17 Dec. • *1922:* For Any Occasion 20 Nov. In Hot Water 20 Nov. • *1923:* The Champion 30 Sept. The Land of the Unborn Children 1 Nov. • *1924:* Some Impressions on the Subject of Thrift. • *1925:* Live and Help Live 22 May. • *1926:* The Carriage Awaits 15 June. Family Album 15 June. What Price Noises 16 June. For Dear Life 30 Dec. • Advertising cartoons.

421. Be Human (*Betty Boop*) 20 Nov. 1936; *p.c.:* The Fleischer Studio for Para; *prod:* Max Fleischer; *dir:* Dave Fleischer; *anim:* Myron Waldman, Lillian Friedman; *voices:* Mae Questel, Everett Clark; *mus:* Sammy Timberg; *ph:* Johnny Burks; b&w. *sd:* WE. 6 min. • Grampy punishes an animal-tormenting farmer by putting him on a treadmill that operates the feeding of animals in his sanctuary.

422. Be Kind to Aminals (*Popeye*) 22 Feb. 1935; *p.c.:* The Fleischer Studio for Para; *prod:* Max Fleischer; *dir:* Dave Fleischer; *anim:* Willard Bowsky, Charles Hastings; *voices:* Mae Questel, Detmar Poppen, Charles Carver; *mus:* Sammy Timberg; b&w. *sd:* WE. 7 min. • Popeye's philosophy of "Be Kind to Animals" is put into practice when he finds Bluto ill-treating a horse.

423. Be Mice to Cats (*Noveltoon*) 5 Feb. 1960; *p.c.:* Para Cartoons; *dir:* Seymour Kneitel; *story:* Carl Meyer, Jack Mercer; *anim:* Nick Tafuri, Wm. B. Pattengill; *sets:* Robert Owen; *voices:* Cecil Roy, Jack Mercer; *mus:* Winston Sharples; *ph:* Leonard McCormick; *prod mgr:* Abe Goodman; *col:* Tech. *sd:* RCA. 6 min. • Skit's "Gramps" arrives from Texas, proving to be a hazard for Skat, the cat, who tries to return him back to where he came from.

424. Be Patient, Patient (*Fox & Crow*) 27 Oct. 1944; *p.c.:* Colum; *dir:* Bob Wickersham; *story:* Dun Roman; *anim:* Chic Otterstrom, Phil Duncan; *sets:* Clark Watson; *i&p:* Elizabeth F. McDowell; *voices:* Frank Graham; *mus:* Eddie Kilfeather; *ph:* Frank Fisher; *prod mgr:* Paul Worth; *col:* Tech. *sd:* WE. 6½ min. • In order to get his hands on his groceries, The Crow convinces The Fox to stick to a strict diet.

425. Be Up to Date (*Betty Boop*) 25 Feb 1938; *p.c.:* The Fleischer Studio for Para; *prod:* Max Fleischer; *dir:* Dave Fleischer; *anim:* Harold Walker, Thomas Johnson; *voice:* Mae Questel; *mus:* Sammy Timberg; *song:* Sammy Lerner, Sammy Timberg; b&w. *sd:* WE. 7 min. • Betty's travelling Department Store arrives in Hillbillyville where she tries to sell goods to the rural inhabitants.

426. Beach Combers (*Oswald*) 5 Oct. 1936; *p.c.:* Univ; *dir:* Walter Lantz; *story:* Walter Lantz, Victor McLeod; *anim:* Manuel Moreno, Lester Kline; *voices:* Shirley Reed, Bernice Hansel; *mus:* James Dietrich; b&w. *sd:* RCA. 6 min. • Oswald leaves his dog guarding his lunch while he fishes. A duck and his pals try to filch it, ending in a battle with an octopus.

427. The Beach Nut (*Woody Woodpecker*) 16 Oct. 1944; *p.c.:* Walter Lantz prods for Univ; *dir:* James Culhane; *story:* Ben Hardaway, Milt Schaffer; *anim:* Dick Lundy, Les Kline, (La)Verne Harding, Emery Hawkins, Paul J. Smith, Don Williams; *lay:* Art Heinemann; *back:* Philip de Guard; *ed:* Dave Lurie; *voices:* Jack Mather, Lee Sweetland, Ben Hardaway; *mus:* Darrell Calker; *prod mgr:* George E. Morris; *col:* Tech. *sd:* WE. 7 min. • Woody wrecks Wally Walrus' relaxation at the beach culminating in a public brawl.

428. The Beach Party (*Mickey Mouse*) 28 Oct. 1931; *p.c.:* Walter E. Disney for Colum; *dir:* Burton F. Gillett; *anim:* Joseph d'Igalo, Gilles de Tremaudan, Norman Ferguson, Clyde Geronimi, David D. Hand, Frank Kelling, Jack King, Richard Lundy, Tom Palmer, Ben Sharpsteen, Cecil Surry, Marvin Woodward; *asst anim:* Chuck Couch, Jack Cutting, Hardie Gramatky, Andrew Hutchinson, Harry Reeves; *voice:* Marcellite Garner; *mus:* Bert Lewis; b&w. *sd:* PCP. 6 min. • Mickey and the gang have fun at the beach.

429. Beach Peach (*Popeye*) 12 May 1950; *p.c.:* Famous for Para; *dir:* Seymour Kneitel; *story:* Larz Bourne, Larry Riley; *anim:* Tom Johnson, Frank Endres, Els Barthen; *sets:* Tom Ford; *voices:* Jack Mercer, Jackson Beck, Mae Questel; *mus:* Winston Sharples; *ph:* Leonard McCormick; *prod mgr:* Sam Buchwald; *col:* Tech. *sd:* RCA. 6 min. • Popeye has problems in dissuading a Life Guard from making amorous advances towards Olive.

430. Beach Picnic (*Donald Duck*) 9 June 1939; *p.c.:* Walt Disney prods for RKO; *dir:* Clyde Geronimi; *anim:* Preston Blair, Lars Calonius, Chester Cobb, James Culhane, Al Eugster, Norman Ferguson, Eric Larson, Fred Moore, Lester Novros, Thomas Oreb, Stan Quackenbush, Paul Satterfield, Milt Schaffer, Claude Smith; *lay:* David Hilberman; *voice:* Clarence Nash; *mus:* Paul J. Smith; *col:* Tech. *sd:* RCA. 8 min. • Donald and Pluto at the seashore. Don tries to ride a rubber horse and then has problems with a colony of ants trying to pilfer his picnic.

431. Beanstalk Bunny (*Merrie Melodies*) 12 Feb. 1955; *p.c.:* WB; *dir:* Charles M. Jones; *story:* Michael Maltese; *anim:* Ken Harris, Richard Thompson, Abe Levitow, Keith Darling; *lay:* Robert Givens; *back:* Richard H. Thomas; *ed:* Treg Brown; *voices:* Mel Blanc, Arthur Q. Bryan; *mus:* Carl Stalling; *prod mgr:* John W. Burton; *prod:* Edward Selzer; *col:* Tech. *sd:* Vit. 7 min. • Bugs and Daffy get embroiled in the "Jack and the Beanstalk" story, with Elmer Fudd substituting for the giant.

432. Beanstalk Jack (*Paul Terry-Toon*) 20 Oct. 1933; *p.c.:* Moser & Terry for Educational/Fox; *dir:* Frank Moser, Paul Terry; *mus:* Philip A. Scheib; b&w. *sd:* WE. 5½ min. • The tale of "Jack and the Beanstalk" becomes mixed with Mother Hubbard's cupboard and a horrific giant.

433. Beanstalk Jack (*Terry-Toon*) 20 Dec. 1946; *p.c.:* TT for Fox; *dir:* Eddie Donnelly; *story:* John Foster; *voice:* Tom Morrison; *mus:* Philip A. Scheib; *col:* Tech. *sd:* RCA. 6 min. • An updated version of "Jack and the Beanstalk" with the magic hen replaced by a Jackpot laying gold coins and swinging a huge mallet in the process of defending the giant.

434. The Bear and the Bean (*Barney Bear*) 31 Jan. 1948; *p.c.:* MGM; *sup:* William Hanna, Joseph Barbera; *dir:* Michael Lah, Preston Blair; *anim:* Ray Abrams, Don Patterson, Gil Turner, Ed Barge; *ed:* Fred MacAlpin; *mus:* Scott Bradley; *prod:* Fred Quimby; *col:* Tech. *sd:* WE. 8 min. • Barney is presented with an energetic Mexican jumping bean.

435. The Bear and the Beavers (*MGM cartoon*) 28 Mar. 1942; *p.c.:* MGM; *prod/dir:* Rudolf Ising; *mus:* Scott Bradley; *col:* Tech. *sd:* WE. 9 min. • Barney Bear finds a labor-saving way of collecting fuel ... by stealing it!

436. The Bear and the Bees (*Aesop's Film Fable*) 26 Jan. 1922; *p.c.:*

Fables Pictures Inc for Pathé; *dir:* Paul Terry; b&w. *sil.* 5 min. • A merry troubadour bear steals the Farmer's cider barrel and, after an exciting chase, disrupts a beehive. Moral: "Evil gain brings pain."

437. Bear and the Bees (*Cartune*) 13 June 1961; *p.c.:* Walter Lantz prods for Univ; *dir:* Jack Hannah; *story:* Dalton Sandifer; *anim:* Roy Jenkins, Al Coe; *sets:* Art Landy, Ray Huffine; *voices:* Dal McKennon, Grace Stafford; *mus:* Eugene Poddany; *prod mgr:* William E. Garity; *col:* Tech. *sd:* RCA. 6 min. • Cupid attempts to bring romance into the life of Fatso the bear.

438. The Bear and the Hare (*Barney Bear*) 26 June 1948; *p.c.:* MGM; *dir:* Michael Lah, Preston Blair; *anim:* Don Patterson, Ray Abrams, Irving Levine, Gil Turner; *ed:* Fred MacAlpin; *mus:* Scott Bradley; *ph:* Jack Stevens; *prod:* Fred Quimby; *col:* Tech. *sd:* WE. 7 min. • Barney sets out to capture a white snow rabbit who appears invisible against a winter setting.

439. Bear De Guerre (*Inspector*) 26 Apr. 1968; *p.c.:* Mirisch/Geoffrey/DFE for UA; *dir:* Gerry Chiniquy; *story:* Jim Ryan; *anim:* Manny Gould, Warren Batchelder, Tom Ray, Manny Perez, Don Williams; *lay:* Dick Ung; *back:* Tom O'Loughlin; *ed:* Lee Gunther; *voice:* Pat Harrington Jr., Marvin Miller; *mus:* Walter Greene; *theme tune:* Henry Mancini; *prod sup:* Harry Love, David DeTiege; *col:* DeLuxe. *sd:* RCA. 6 min. • The Inspector's quail hunting upsets the Park Ranger and a bear.

440. Bear Feat (*Looney Tunes*) 10 Dec. 1949; *p.c.:* WB; *dir:* Charles M. Jones; *story:* Michael Maltese; *anim:* Ben Washam, Lloyd Vaughan, Ken Harris, Phil Monroe; *lay:* Robert Gribbroek; *back:* Peter Alvarado; *ed:* Treg Brown; *voices:* Billy Bletcher, Stan Freberg, Bea Benaderet; *mus:* Carl Stalling; *prod mgr:* John W. Burton; *prod:* Edward Selzer; *col:* Tech. *sd:* Vit. 7 min. • Pa Bear and Junior try to break into show business by practicing vaudeville acts.

441. Bear for Punishment (*Looney Tunes*) 20 Oct. 1951; *p.c.:* WB; *dir:* Charles M. Jones; *story:* Michael Maltese; *anim:* Ken Harris, Phil Monroe, Lloyd Vaughan, Ben Washam; *lay:* Robert Gribbroek; *back:* Philip de Guard; *ed:* Treg Brown; *voice:* Billy Bletcher, Stan Freberg, Bea Benaderet; *mus:* Carl Stalling; *prod mgr:* John W. Burton; *prod:* Edward Selzer; *col:* Tech. *sd:* Vit. 7 min. • Mama and Junior Bear are intent on giving a happy "Father's Day" to a reluctant Pa Bear.

442. Bear Hug (*Loopy de Loop*) Mar. 1964; *p.c.:* Hanna-Barbera for Colum; *prod/dir:* William Hanna, Joseph Barbera; story *dir:* Alex Lovy; *story:* Michael Maltese; anim *dir:* Charles A. Nichols; *anim:* George Nicholas, Bill Keil; *lay:* Bill Perez; *back:* Robert Gentle; *ed:* Warner Leighton; *voices:* Daws Butler, Mel Blanc, Janet Waldo; *mus:* Hoyt Curtin; *titles:* Lawrence Gobel; *prod mgr:* Howard Hanson; *col:* East. *sd:* RCA. 6½ min. • Jealous Braxton Bear employs Loopy to win Emmy-Lou's affection for him. In the meantime, Braxton falls for Emmy-Lou's sister, Jenny Lee and Emmy falls for Loopy.

443. Bear Knuckles (*Loopy de Loop*) Oct. 1964; *p.c.:* Hanna-Barbera for Colum; *prod/dir:* William Hanna, Joseph Barbera; *story dir:* Paul Sommer; *story:* Michael Maltese; *anim dir:* Charles A. Nichols; *anim:* George Nicholas, George Goepper; *lay:* Willie Ito; *back:* Art Lozzi; *ed:* Warner Leighton; *voices:* Daws Butler, Mel Blanc, Janet Waldo; *mus:* Hoyt Curtin; *titles:* Lawrence Gobel; *prod mgr:* Howard Hanson; *col:* East. *sd:* RCA. 6 min. • Braxton Bear disposes of Emmy-Lou's suitor, who employs Loopy to help him win her back.

444. Bear-Raid Warden (*Barney Bear*) 9 Sept. 1944; *p.c.:* MGM; *dir:* George Gordon; *anim:* Arnold Gillespie, Michael Lah, Ed Barge, Jack Carr; *ed:* Fred MacAlpin; *voice:* Kent Rogers; *mus:* Scott Bradley; *prod:* Fred Quimby; *col:* Tech. *sd:* WE. 6 min. • Air Raid Warden Barney has trouble in getting a firefly to douse his light.

445. The Bear That Couldn't Sleep (*MGM cartoon*) 10 June 1939; *p.c.:* MGM; *prod/dir/voice:* Rudolf Ising; *anim:* Carl Urbano; *sets:* Joe Smith; *ed:* Fred MacAlpin; *mus:* Scott Bradley; *col:* Tech. *sd:* WE. 9 min. • Mr. Bear, getting set for a winter's hibernation, is kept awake until Spring.

446. The Bear That Wasn't 31 Dec. 1967; *p.c.:* MGM; *prod:* Chuck Jones, Frank Tashlin; *dir:* Chuck Jones; *asst dir/des:* Maurice Noble; *story:* Frank Tashlin, Irv Spector; *anim sup:* Ben Washam; *anim:* Philip Roman, Don Towsley, Dick Thompson, Tom Ray; *back:* Philip de Guard, Don Morgan; *voice:* Paul Frees; *mus:* Dean Elliott; *prod sup:* Earl Jonas, Les

Goldman; *col:* Metro. *sd:* WE. 10½ min. • A bear awakens from winter hibernation to find a factory has been built around his home. As he emerges, nobody will believe he is a bear.

447. Bear Up (*Loopy de Loop*) Nov. 1963; *p.c.:* Hanna-Barbera for Colum; *prod/dir:* Joseph Barbera, William Hanna; *story dir:* Lew Marshall; *story:* Michael Maltese; *anim dir:* Charles A. Nichols; *anim:* Jerry Hathcock, Kenneth Muse; *lay:* Jack Huber; *back:* F. Montealegre; *ed:* Donald A. Douglas; *voices:* Daws Butler, Don Messick, Jean van der Pyl; *mus:* Hoyt Curtin; *titles:* Lawrence Gobel; *prod mgr:* Howard Hanson; *col:* East. *sd:* RCA. 6½ min. • No story available.

448. Bearly Able (*Loopy de Loop*) 28 June 1962; *p.c.:* Hanna-Barbera for Colum; *prod/dir:* Joseph Barbera, William Hanna; *story dir:* Paul Sommer; *story:* Michael Maltese; *anim dir:* Charles A. Nichols; *anim:* Jack Ozark; *lay:* Walter Clinton; *back:* Art Lozzi; *ed:* Warner Leighton; *voices:* Daws Butler, Don Messick, Jean van der Pyl; *mus:* Hoyt Curtin; *prod mgr:* Howard Hanson; *col:* East. *sd:* RCA. 6 min. • Loopy stands-in as babysitter for the Three Bears' "Baby Bear," which proves to be more trouble than it's worth.

449. Bearly Asleep (*Donald Duck*) 19 Aug. 1955; *p.c.:* Walt Disney prods for BV; *dir:* Jack Hannah; *story:* Al Bertino, Dave DeTiege; *anim:* Bob Carlson Al Coe, Volus Jones, Bill Justice, John Sibley; *fx:* Dan MacManus; *lay:* Yale Gracey; *back:* Ray Huffine; *voices:* Art Gilmore, Clarence Nash, James MacDonald; *mus:* Oliver Wallace; *col:* Tech. *sd:* RCA. 7 min. CS. • Humphrey the bear seeks refuge for the winter months in Ranger Donald's lodge.

450. The Bears and the Bees (*Silly Symphony*) 9 July 1932; *p.c.:* Walt Disney prods for UA; *dir:* Wilfred Jackson; *anim:* Les Clark, Gilles de Tremaudan, Clyde Geronimi, David D. Hand, Albert Hurter, Jack King, Richard Lundy, Ben Sharpsteen; *character des/lay:* Albert Hurter; *back:* Carlos Manriquez; *mus:* Frank E. Churchill; b&w. *sd:* PCP. 7 min • Two cubs are chased away from eating berries by a bigger bear who, in turn, is chased by bees for stealing their honey.

451. The Bear's Tale (*Merrie Melodies*) 13 Apr. 1940; *p.c.:* Leon Schlesinger prods for WB; *dir:* Fred Avery; *story:* J.B. Hardaway; *anim:* Rod Scribner; *sets:* John Didrik Johnsen; *ed:* Treg Brown; *voices:* Robert C. Bruce, Mel Blanc, Margaret Hill, Sara Berner, Fred Avery; *mus:* Carl W. Stalling; *prod sup:* Henry Binder, Raymond G. Katz; *col:* Tech. *sd:* Vit. 7 min. • A distorted version of the "Goldilocks and the Three Bears" story involving Little Red Riding Hood et al.

452. The Beast of Hollow Mountain 1956; *p.c.:* Peliculas Rodriguez for UA; *story/anim:* Willis O'Brien; *prod:* William & Edward Nassour; *col:* DeLuxe. *sd.* 81 min. *l/a/anim.* Regiscope. • Live-action western fantasy with an exciting few minutes of animated monster tacked onto the final reel.

453. Beau and Arrows (*Oswald*) 28 Mar. 1932; *p.c.:* Univ; *dir:* Walter Lantz, "Bill" Nolan; *anim:* Manuel Moreno, Ray Abrams, Fred Avery, Lester Kline, Vet Anderson; *mus:* James Dietrich; b&w. *sd:* WE. 7 min. • Wagon Master Oswald does his best to defend the wagon train against an Indian attack.

454. Beau Best (*Oswald*) 22 May 1933; *p.c.:* Univ; *dir:* Walter Lantz, "Bill" Nolan; *anim:* Ray Abrams, Fred Avery, Cecil Surry, Jack Carr, Don Williams; *mus:* James Dietrich; b&w. *sd:* WE. 6 min. • While in the desert, Oswald engages in combat to rescue a veiled beauty. Once he vanquishes the villain he lifts her veil to realize his mistake.

455. Beau Bosko (*Looney Tunes*) 1 July 1933; *p.c.:* Hugh Harman, Rudolf Ising prods for WB; *dir:* Isadore Freleng; *anim:* Rollin Hamilton, Norm Blackburn, Robert Clampett; *ed:* Dale Pickett; *voices:* John T. Murray, Mary Moder, Ted Pierce; *mus:* Frank Marsales; *asso prod:* Leon Schlesinger; b&w. *sd:* Vit. 6 min. • Legionnaire Bosko is sent on a dangerous mission to rescue Honey from her Arab captor.

456. Beau Ties (*Little Lulu*) 29 Dec. 1944; *p.c.:* Famous for Para; *dir:* Seymour Kneitel; *story:* Carl Meyer, Joe Stultz; *anim:* Orestes Calpini, Reuben Grossman, Otto Feuer, Frank Little; *sets:* Shane Miller; *voices:* Cecil Roy, Arnold Stang; *mus:* Sammy Timberg; *title song:* Buddy Kaye, Fred Wise, Sammy Timberg; *ph:* Leonard McCormick; *prod mgr:* Sam Buchwald; *col:* Tech. *sd:* RCA. 7 min. • Fatso standsup Lulu for a date with a pretty blonde. Lulu knocks him out, giving him a nightmare about being married to Lulu.

457. Beaus Will Be Beaus (*Popeye*) 20 May 1955; *p.c.:* Famous for Para; *dir:* Seymour Kneitel; *story:* I. Klein; *anim:* Tom Johnson, John Gentilella, Els Barthen; *sets:* Robert Little; *voices:* Jack Mercer, Jackson Beck, Mae Questel; *mus:* Winston Sharples; *ph:* Leonard McCormick; *prod mgr:* Seymour Shultz; *col:* Tech. *sd:* RCA. 6 min. • Olive insists that the boys don't fight while at the beach which inspires Popeye to feed Bluto spinach, making him appear the bully he is.

458. Beauty and the Beast (*Merrie Melodies*) 14 Apr. 1934; *p.c.:* Leon Schlesinger prods for WB; *dir:* Isadore Freleng; *anim:* Jack King, Rollin Hamilton, Robert Clampett; *ed:* Dale Pickett; *mus:* Norman Spencer; *song:* Bert Kalmar, Harry Ruby; *col:* Ciné. *sd:* Vit. 6 min. • A small girl overindulges on candy and is transported into a nightmare where she meets storybook characters.

459. Beauty and the Beast 22 Nov.1991; *p.c.:* The Walt Disney Co. for BV/Silver Screen Partners IV; *dir:* Gary Trousdale, Kirk Wise; *prod:* Don Hahn; *ex prod:* Howard Ashman; *scr:* Linda Woolverton; *asso prod:* Sarah McArthur; *art dir:* Brian McEntee; *ed:* John Carnochan; *artistic sup: story:* Roger Allers; *lay:* Ed Ghertner; *back:* Lisa Keene; *cleanup:* Vera Lanpher; *visual fx:* Randy Fullmer; *cgi:* Jim Hillin; *story:* Brenda Chapman, Christopher Sanders, Burny Mattinson, Kevin Harkey, Brian Pimental, Bruce Woodside, Joe Ranft, Tom Ellery, Kelly Asbury, Robert Lence; *character animation: (Belle) sup anim:* James Baxter; *anim:* Michael Cedeno, Randy Cartwright, Lorna Cook, Ken Duncan, Doug Krohn, Mike Nguyen; *Florida sup anim: (Beast) sup anim:* Glen Keane; *anim:* Anthony DeRosa, Aaron Blaise, Geefwee Boedoe, Broose Johnson, Tom Sito, Brad Kuha; *(Gaston) sup anim:* Andreas Deja; *anim:* Joe Heider, Ron Husband, David Burgess, Alexander S. Kuperschmidt, Tim Allen; *(Lumiere) sup anim:* Nik Ranieri; *anim:* David P. Stephan, Rejean Bourdages, Barry Temple; *(Cogsworth) sup anim:* Will Finn; *anim:* Michael Show, Tony Bancroft; *(Mrs. Potts & Chip) sup anim:* David Pruiksma; *anim:* Phil Young, Dan Boulos; *(Maurice) sup anim:* Ruben A. Aquino; *anim:* Mark Kausler, Ellen Woodbury, Cynthia Overman; *(Lefou) sup anim:* Chris Wahl; *anim:* Rick Farmiloe, Lennie Graves; *(Philippe) sup anim:* Russ Edmonds; *(Wolves)* Larry White; *(Wardrobe)* Tony Anselmo; *asst anim:* Tom Bancroft, Arland Barron, Bob Bryan, Brian Ferguson, Michael Gerard, Mark Kennedy, Michael Surrey; *rough inbet:* Kent Culotta, Henry Sato Jr., Eric Walls, David Zaboski; *clean-up anim: (Belle) sup character lead:* Renee Holt; *asst anim:* Dorothea Baker, Merry Kanawyer Clingen, Margie Daniels, Daniel A. Gracey, Lureline Kohler, Christine Lawrence, Kaaren Lundeen, Teresa Martin, Brett Newton, Jennifer Gwynne Oliver, Ginny Parmele, Kent Culotta, Juliet Stroud Duncan, Teresa Eidenbock, Denise Meara Hahn, Karen Hardenbergh, Leticia Lichtwardt, Steve Lubin, Laura Nichols, Natasha Selfridge; *break:* Wendie Fischer, Tamara Lusher, Anthony Wayne Michaels, Bryan M. Sommer; *inbet:* Elliot M. Bour, Ken Kinoshita; *(Beast) sup character lead:* Bill Berg; *asst anim:* Tracy M. Lee, Scott Anderson, Johan Klingler, Rick Kohlschmidt, Susan Lantz, Terry Naughton, Prescillano A. Romanillos, Marshall Toomey; *break:* Kris Heller, James Y. Jackson, Wendy Werner; *inbet:* Travis Blaise, Vincent DeFrances, Paul McDonald, Charles R. Vollmer; *(Gaston) sup character lead:* Marty Korth; *asst anim:* Kathleen M. Bailey, Sam Ewing, Randy Sanchez, Bruce Strock, James Davis, Dana Reemes, Maria Rosetti; *break:* Robert O. Corley, James Fujii; *inbet:* Lillian Chapman, Anthony Cipriano, Laurey Foulkes, Dylan Kohler, Mary-Jean Repchuk; *(Lumiere) sup character lead:* Debra Armstrong; *asst anim:* Matt Novak, Gilda Palinginis, Arland Barron, Trey Finney, Richard Green, Brian McKim; *break:* Hee Rhan Bae, Edward Gutierrez; *inbet:* Maurilio Morales; *(Cogsworth) sup character lead:* Nancy Kniep; *asst anim:* Marianne Tucker, Karen Rosenfield; *break:* Beverly Adams, Bill Thinnes; *inbet:* Marsha Park; *(Mrs. Potts) sup character lead:* Stephan Zupkas; *asst anim:* Dan Tanaka, Mike McKinney, Susan Sugita; *(Maurice) sup character lead:* Richard Hoppe; *asst anim:* Marcia Dougherty, Peggy Tonkonogy; *break:* Norma Rivera, Elizabeth Watasin; *(Lefou) sup character lead:* Emily Jiuliano; *asst anim:* Gail Frank, Sue Adnopoz, Michael Hazy; *(Philippe) sup character lead:* Brian Clift; *break:* Allison Hollen; *inbet:* Jacqueline M. Sanchez; *(Wolves) character lead:* Alex Topete; *asst anim:* Terry Wozniak, Grant Hiestand; *(objects, townspeople, etc.) character lead:* Vera Lanpher, Dave Suding; *asst anim:* Philip S. Boyd, Ken Cope, Lou Dellarosa, Ray Harris, Bette Holmquist, William Recinos, Maureen Trueblood, Carl Bell, Jesus Cortes; *break:* Noreen Beasley, Inna Chon, Kellie Deron Lewis, Cheryl Polakow, Martin Schwartz, Ron Westlund, Dave Woodman; *inbet:* Ken

Hettig, Tom LaBuff, Jane Misek, Kevin Smith, Michael Swofford, Daniel A. Wawrzaszek; *corrections:* Diana Falk, Miriam McDonnell, John Ramirez; *special fx: fx anim:* Dave Bossert, Ted Kierscey, Dorse Lanpher, Mark Myer, Ed Coffey, Christine Harding, Chris Jenkins, Eusebio Torres, Kelvin Yasuda, Allen Blyth, Dan Chaika, Mabel Geener, John Tucker, Mark Barrows, Jeff Dutton, James Mansfield, Steve Starr, Cynthia Neill-Knizek, Allen Stovall; *fx break/inbet:* Kennard Betts, Kristine Brown, Peter DeMund, Paul Lewis, Sandra Groeneveld, Dan Lund, Masa Oshiro, Lisa Ann Reinert, Tony West; *key lay/workbook:* Dan St. Pierre, Larry Laker, Fred Craig, Lorenzo Martinez, Tom Shannon, Tanya Wilson, Thom Enriquez, Rasoul Azadani, Bill Perkins; *lay asst:* Mac George, Jeff Dickson, David Gardner, Mitchell Bernal, Daniel Hu, Allen Tam, Davy Liu, Mark Wallace; *blue sketch:* Madlyn O'Neill; *back:* Doug Bell, Jim Coleman, Donald Towns, Cristy Maltese, Phil Phillipson, Dean Gordon, Robert E. Stanton, Tom Woodington, Tia Kratter, Diana Wakeman, John Emerson, Gregory Alexander Drolette, Debbie DuBois, Natalie Franscioni-Karp, Serge Michaels, William Dely, Bill Kaufmann, Kevin Turcotte; *visual development:* Kelly Asbury, Michael Cedeno, Joe Grant, Jean Gillmore, Kevin Lima, Dave Molina, Sue C. Nichols, Christopher Sanders, Terry Shakespeare; *prod consultants/visual development:* Hans Bacher, Mel Shaw; *pre-production script development:* Jim Cox, Dennis Edwards, Tim Hauser, Rob Minkoff, Rebecca Rees, Darrell Rooney; *ed:* Gregory Perler, Deirdre Hepburn, Jim Melton, Pamela G. Kimber; *Florida editorial staff:* Chuck Williams, Beth Ann Collins; *casting:* Albert Tavares; *prod mgr:* Baker Bloodworth; *scene planning:* Ann Tucker; *anim check:* Janet Bruce; *color models:* Karen Comella, Penny Coulter, Ann Sorensen; *i&p:* Gretchen Maschmeyer Albrecht, Hortensia M. Casagran; *digitizing ph:* Robyn Roberts; *scene plan:* Dave Thomas, Annamarie Costa, Donna Weir; *anim check:* Karen Hepburn, Karen S. Paat, Gary Shafer, Mavis Shafer, Barbara Wiles; *artistic sup (Florida): lay:* Robert Walker; *back:* Richard John Silver; *cleanup:* Ruben Procopio; *visual fx:* Barry Cook; *prod mgr:* Tim O'Donnell, Ron Rocha, Dorothy McKim; *asst ed:* Deborah Tobias; *asst lay:* Patricia Hicks; *asst anim:* Leslie Hough; *fx/computer graphics:* Brett Hayden; *back/color model/checking:* Bruce Grant Williams; *compositing & retakes:* Suzi Vissotzky; *Florida unit:* Paul Steele; *i&p asst mgr:* Chris Hecox; *computer anim:* Linda Bel, Greg Griffith, James R. Tooley, Mary Jane "M.J" Turner, Scott F. Johnson, Edward Kummer; *digital paint:* Thomas Cardone; *snr prod co-ord:* Rozanne Cazian; *cgi mgr:* Dan Philips; *engineering:* Dave Inglish, David F. Wolf, David Coons, Scot Greenidge, James D. Houston, Mark R. Kimball, Marty Prager; *support:* Raul E. Anaya, Michael Bolds, Randy Fukuda, Bruce Hatakeyama, Pradeep Hiremath, Kiran B. Joshi, Brad Lowman, Michael K. Purvis, Carlos Quinonez Shirado, Michael Sullivan, Mark M. Tokunaga, Paul Yanover; *Pixar:* Thomas Hahn, Peter Nye, Michael A. Shantzis; *prod:* Patricia Conklin, Charlie Desrochers, Kevin Wade, Kirk Bodyfelt, Holly E. Bratton, Kevin L. Briggs, Greg Chalekian, Matthew Garbera, Sean Hawkins, Eric Lee, Tod Marsden, Karenna Mazur, Janet McLaurin, Laura Perrotta, Laurie Sacks, Dale A. Smith, Christopher Tapia, Kevin Traxler, Anthony Faust Rocco; *character sculptures:* Ruben Procopio, Kenny Thompkins; *title design:* Saxon/Ross Film design; *stained glass des:* Mac George; *digitizing mark-up:* Gina Wootten; *line repair:* Angelika Katz; *digitizing ph:* Tina Baldwin, Jo Ann Breuer, Karen China, Bob Cohen, Lynnette Cullen, Gary Fishbaugh, Cindy Garcia, Kent Gordon; *color models:* Barbara Lynn Hamane, Rhonda L. Hicks, Leslie Ellery, Beth Ann McCoy, Irma Velez, Micki Zurcher, Carmen Sanderson, Phyllis Bird, Russell Blandino, Sherrie Cuzzort, Phyllis Fields, Paulino Garcia DeMingo, Ann Hazard, David Karp, Harlene Cooper-Mears, Deborah Jane Mooneyham, Karen Nugent, Leyla C. dePelaez, Bruce Phillipson, Heidi Shellhorn, Fumiko Roche Sommer, Britt Van der Nagel, Susan Wileman; *final check:* Teri McDonald, Saskia Raevouri; *compositing:* James "J.R" Russell, David J. Rowe, Shannon Fallis-Kane; *ph:* Joe Jiuliano, John Cunningham, John Aardal, Mary Lescher, Gary W. Smith; *film rec:* Ariel Shaw, Christopher Gee, Chuck Warren, Christine Beck; *voices: Belle:* Paige O'Hara; *the Beast:* Robby Benson; *Lumiere:* Jerry Orbach; *Mrs. Potts:* Angela Lansbury; *Gaston:* Richard White; *Cogsworth/Narrator:* David Ogden Stiers; *Le Fou:* Jesse Corti; *Maurice:* Rex Everhart; *Chip:* Bradley Michael Pierce; *Wardrobe:* Jo Anne Worley; *Featherduster:* Kimmy Robertson; *Bimbettes:* Mary Kay Bergman, Kath Soucie; *Stove:* Brian Cummings; *Bookseller:* Alvin Epstein; *Monsieur D'Arque:* Tony Jay; *Baker:* Alec Murphy; *Philippe:* Hal Smith; *Footstool/vocal fx:* Frank Welker; *also:* Jack Angel, Bruce Adler, Scott Barnes, Vanna Bonta, Maureen Brennan, Liz Callaway, Philip Clarke, Margery

Daley, Jennifer Darling, Albert de Ruiter, George Dvorsky, Bill Farmer, Bruce Fifer, Johnson Flucker, Larry Hansen, Randy Hansen, Mary Ann Hart, Alix Korey, Phyllis Kubey, Hearndon Lackey, Sherry Lyn, Mickie McGowan, Larry Moss, Pancheli Null, Wilbur Pauley, Jennifer Perito, Caroline Peyton, Patrick Pinney, Phil Proctor, Cynthia Richards-Hewes, Stephani Ryan, Gordon Stanley, Stephen Sturk; *songs:* Howard Ashman, Alan Menken; *original score:* Howard Ashman; *arrangement:* Alan Menken, Danny Troob; *orch:* Danny Troob, Michael Starobin; *mus conducted by* David Friedman; *mus ed:* Kathleen Bennett, Segue Music; *orchestra contractors: New York:* Emil Charlap; *Los Angeles:* Ken Watson; *Beauty and the Beast* performed by Celine Dion, Peabo Bryson; *prod:* Walter Afanasieff; *arrangement:* Walter Afanasieff, Robbie Buchanan; *sd fx:* Mark Mangini, Dave Stone, Weddington Prods, Drew Neumann; *sd:* Julia Evershade, Michael Benavents, Jessica Gallavan, J.H. Arrufat, Ron Bartlett, Sonya "Sonny" Pettijohn, Oscar Mitt; *foley:* John Roesch, Catherine Rowe, Vanessa Theme Ament; *rec:* Terry Porter, Mel Metcalfe, David J. Hudson, Denis Blackerby; *PDI:* Judy Nord; *ADR mix:* Doc Kane, Vince Caro; *opticals:* Mark Dornfeld, Peter Montgomery, Allen Gonzales; *graphics:* Joe Parra, John White, Bernie Gagliano, Dale Grahn. *col:* Tech. *sd:* Dolby stereo. 84 min. • When Maurice, Belle's father, stumbles across a sinister castle in the woods, he is held prisoner there. His daughter comes to rescue her father and encounters a Beast with his servants who have all been enchanted into household articles. She agrees to trade places with her father and remains captive in the castle until the Beast learns to "love another and be loved in return" in order to break his enchantment. Belle's egotistical suitor, Gaston, sees the Beast as an adversary for her love and rallies the villagers to storm the castle. Belle races to save the Beast from the mob and, realizing her love for him, breaks the spell, returning him and his servants back to human form.

460. Beauty on the Beach (*Mighty Mouse*) Oct. 1950; *p.c.:* TT for Fox; *dir:* Connie Rasinski; *story:* Tom Morrison; *anim:* Jim Tyer; *voices:* Roy Halee, Tom Morrison; *mus:* Philip A. Scheib; *col:* Tech. *sd:* RCA. 6 min. • Oil Can Harry ties Pearl Pureheart on the tracks of a Coney Island Switchback.

461. The Beauty Parlor (*Aesop's Film Fable*) 6 June 1923; *p.c.:* Fables Pictures Inc for Pathé; *dir:* Paul Terry; b&w. sil. 5 min. • Mary Mouse has her tail permed, Mrs. Hippo has a drastic weight reduction in a steam cabinet and Gertie Greyhound has a crop of hair raised by hair tonic. Moral: "He who laughs last laughs best."

462. Beauty Shoppe (*Gran'Pop*) 1939; *p.c.:* Cartoon Films Ltd for Mono; *prod:* Dave Biedermann, Lawson Haris; *dir:* Paul Fennell; *ed:* Almon Teeter; *voice:* Danny Webb, Bernice Hansel; *mus:* Clarence Wheeler; *ph:* Richard M. Ising; *col:* Ciné. *sd:* RCA. 6 min. • A tough gorilla enters Gran'Pop's beauty parlor, demanding he makes a beauty of his hippo girlfriend before he returns.

463. Beauty Shoppe (*Oswald*) 30 Mar. 1936; *p.c.:* Univ; *dir:* Walter Lantz; *story:* Walter Lantz, Victor McLeod; *anim:* Ray Abrams, Fred Kopietz; *mus:* James Dietrich; b&w. *sd:* WE. 6 min. • Three escaped monkeys wreck Oswald's beauty parlor.

464. Beaver Trouble (*Terry-Toon*) Dec. 1951; *p.c.:* TT for Fox; *dir:* Connie Rasinski; *story/voice:* Tom Morrison; *anim:* Jim Tyer; *mus:* Philip A. Scheib; *ph:* Douglas Moye; *col:* Tech. *sd:* RCA. 6 min. • Two beavers remove wood from Dimwit's dog house to build a dam.

465. Beavis and Butt-Head Do America 20 Dec. 1996. *p.c.:* Geffen Pictures/MTV Networks for Para; *dir/creator:* Mike Judge; *prod:* Abby Terkuhle; *ex prod:* David Gale, Van Toffler; *anim dir:* Yvette Kaplan; *line prod:* Winnie Chaffee; *co-prod:* John Andrews; *scr:* Mike Judge, Joe Stillman; *script consultants:* Kristofor Brown, Larry Doyle; *art dir:* Jeff Buckland; *des:* Sharon Fitzgerald; *technical dir:* Rudy Tomaselli; *technical advisor:* John Conning; *seq dir:* Mike de Seve, Miguel Martinez Joffre, Geoffrey Johnson, Tony Kluck, Ray Kosarin, Carol Millican, Brian Mulroney, Ilya Skorupsky, Paul Sparagano; *storyboard:* Kevin Brownie, Ray de Silva, Tony Eastman, Tony Kluck, Michael le Bash, Guy Moore, Chris Prynoski, John Rice, Dan Shefelman, Ilya Skorupsky, Ted Stearn; *storyboard consultant:* Patrick Worlock; *snr character des:* Michael A. Baez, Elaine Despins, Kaori Hamura, Bill Schwab, Monica Smith; *character des:* Karen Hyden, Martin Polansky; *prop des:* Edward Artinian, Jody Schaeffer; *character/prop des co-ord:* Patrick Intrieri; *des consult:* Michael Breton; *back des:* Miriam Katin, Donald Bruce

Poynter, Ray de Silva, Freya Tanz, Laura Wakefield; *back lay sup:* Maurice Joyce; *back lay art:* Kimson Albert, John D. Allemano, Edward Artinian, Kevin Brownie, Ray de Silva, Isauro de la Rosa, Eric Elder, Willy Hartland, Brian Moyer, Guy Moore, Siobhan Mullen, Wayne Arthur Poynter, Bill Schwab, Dan Shefelman, Natterjack Animation Co., Ltd.; *back key/back lay co-ord:* Meika Rouda; *scene plan:* Janet Benn, Rudy Tomaselli; *ed:* Terry Kelly, Gunter Glinka, Neil Lawrence; *voice sup:* Kristofor Brown; *voices: Beavis/Tom Anderson (old guy with campers)/Van Driessen/hippie teacher/Principal McVicer/Butt-Head:* Mike Judge; *Muddy:* Bruce Willis; *Dallas:* Demi Moore; *Old woman on plane and bus:* Cloris Leachman; *Agent Flemming:* Robert Stack; *Agent Hurly:* Jacqueline Barba; *Flight Attendant/White House Tour Guide:* Pamela Blair; *Ranger at Old Faithful/Press Secretary/Lieutenant at Strategic Air Command:* Eric Bogosian; *Man on plane/2nd man in confession booth/old guy/Jim:* Kristofor Brown; *2nd Motley Crue Roadie/Tourist man:* Tony Darling; *Airplane Captain/White House rep.:* John Dorman; *French Dignitary:* Francis DuMaurier; *Petrified Forest recording:* Jim Flaherty; *Hoover guide/ATF Agent:* Tim Quinee; *1st Motley Crue Roadie:* Earl Hofert; *2nd TV thief/Concierge/Bellboy/Male TV reporter:* Tony Huss; *Limo driver/1st TV thief/1st Man in confession booth/Petrified Forest Ranger:* Sam Johnson; *Tour Bus Driver:* Richard Linklater; *2nd Flight Attendant:* Rosemary McNamara; *Indian Dignitary:* Harsh Nayyar; *Announcer in Capitol:* Karen Phillips; *President Clinton:* Dale Reeves; *Hoover technician/General at Strategic Air Command:* Mike Ruschak; *3rd Flight Attendant/Female TV reporter:* Gail Thomas; *mus:* John Frizzell, Mark Cross; *mus ed:* Abby Treloggen, Jennifer Nash; *mus prod sup:* Graham Walker; *mus co-ord:* Liz Schrek; *score performed by:* London Metropolitan Orchestra; *orch leader:* Jackie Shave; *mus contractor:* Andy Brown; *orch conducted by* Allan Wilson; *orchestration:* Frank Bennett, Emilie A. Bernstein; *mus preparation:* Vic Frazer, Bob Lowdell; "Two Cool Guys" (*theme from "Beavis & Butt-Head do America"*): Isaac Hayes, Mike Judge; *performed by* Isaac Hayes; "White Trash": R. Miller; *performed by* Southern Culture on the Side; "Snakes": Tony Kanal, Gwen Stefani; *performed by* No Doubt; "Pimp'n Ain't EZ": Jerry Lewis, Jakell Brown, Jerome Evans Jr.; *performed by* Madd Head; "Love Rollercoaster": J. Williams, W. Beck; *performed by* Red Hot Chili Peppers; "Blue Sax" *by* and *performed by* Steve Gray; "Gone Shootin'": Malcolm Young & Bon Scott; *performed by* AC/DC; "I Wanna Riot": Armstrong, Freeman & Frederikson; *performed by* Rancid with Stubborn All-Stars; "Ratfinks, Suicide Tanks and Cannibal Girls": Rob Zombin, J. Yuenger, Sean Ysoult, John Tempesta, Charlie Clouser; *performed by* White Zombie; "Walk on Water": Ozzy Osbourne, Jim Vallance; *performed by* Ozzy Osbourne; "Heart and Soul": Frank Loesser, Hoagy Carmichael; "The Lord is a Monkey" *by* and *performed by* Butthole Surfers; "Ain't Nobody": Hawk Wolinski, J.T. Smith; *performed by* I.L. Cool; "Mucha Muchacha" *by* and *performed by* Juan Garcia Esquivel; "Lesbian Seagull": Tom Wilson Weinberg; *performed by* Engelbert Humperdinck; *posing sup:* Carol Milligan, Byron Moore, Paul Sparagano; *key posing art:* Michael A. Baez, Karen Disher, Sue Perrotto; *posing art:* Doug Crane, Nick de Mayo, Gloria de Ponte, Miguel Martinez Joffre, Kevin Lofton, Roger Mejia, Bill Moore, Christopher Palesty, John Paratore, Martin Polansky, Ben Price, Chris Prynoski, Stephen Robertson, Margaret E. Rutherford, Frank Suarez, Eric Wight, Martin Wittig, Nataliya Zurabova, Fourmi Rouge Animation Inc.; *posing dpt mgr:* Bryon Moore; *posing co-ord:* Barbara Jean Kearney; *back col sup:* Michael Rose; *back paint:* Nick Campese, Isauro de la Rosa, Sophie Kittredge, Bill Long, Adrian Newkirk, Michael Zodorozny; *prop/character col sup:* Sally Burden, Monica Smith; *col key art:* Sophie Kittredge, Adrian Newkirk; *cel painters:* Mark Canter, Chris Costan, Donna Evans, Christine Ferrado, Teri Hackett, Pat Ingram-Rich, Lisa Klein, Laura Margulies, Maddy Rosenberg; *col dpt. co-ord:* Jeff Mertz, Tati Nguyen; *overseas anim sup:* Tony Kluck; *overseas back sup:* Michael Rose; *overseas i&p sup:* Sally Burden, Kukhee Lee; *overseas ph sup:* Normand Rompre; *overseas prod co-ord:* David McGrath; *mouth dir:* Mike de Seve, Brian Mulroney, Simie Nallaseth; *track readers:* Don Barrozo, Lee Harting; *animatic ed:* John Holswade, Brian Kates, Nick Litwinko, Brian Russman; *fx sup:* Normand Rompre; *fx art:* Peggy Collen, Robert Scull; *fx matte cutter:* Veronica Soul; *fx co-ord:* Dave Hughes; *retake sup:* Janet Benn; *anim check:* Rhonda Cox, Janet Benn, Nancy Lane, David McGrath; *overseas anim: Plus One Animation Co.;* *sup dir:* Choon Man Lee; *anim dir:* Jae Joong Kim, Jun Nam Park; *art dir:* Kye Jeong An; *prod mgrs:* Ji Byung Kim, Jin Seon Kim; *prod co-ord:* Soo Ryung Sim; *key anim:* Sang Seong An, Eun Sook Baik, Hyung Ook Kim, Hyung Tae Kim, Ji Yeon Kim, Min Seon

Kim, Hyun Ja Lee, Joon Chul Park, Yong Soo Park, Yong Hwa Seo, Eun Sook Song; *drawing check:* Hyun Sook Park; *i&p check sup:* Young Yea Han, Hye Ja Kim, Myung Ae Kim; *back sup:* Jae Boong Kim; *anim check:* Yoo Rae Lee, Jong Bum Park; *ph dir:* Bok Dong Jo; *fx sup:* Yeon Kwan Jeong; *prod translator:* Wun Ae Cha; *anim ed:* Young Ok Kim; *Rough Draft Studios, Inc.: studio dir:* Nikki Vanzo; *overseas head prod:* Byung Chul Yea; *anim dir:* Jong Ho Kim; *technical dir:* Yong Nam Park; *prod liaison:* Hye Joon Yun; *prod mgrs:* Chung Ho Kim, Kyung Bok Lee; *prod co-ord:* Yeon Hwa Jeong, Hye Sun Kim, So Young Park; *asst prod co-ord:* Hyun Sub Kim, Sang Hun Lee, Min Suk Lee; *key anim:* Chan Jo Kim, Suk Woon Rim, Wook Cho, Young Jin Myung, Young Shim Rim, Hyun Nyung Chun; *asst anim sup:* Hong Ran Kim, Mee Suk Park; *anim check sup:* Hong Dae Joo; *Xerox dpt sup:* Sung Hoon Lee; *i&p dpt sup:* Young Ran Lee, Ji Yeon You; *back paint sup:* Young Kil Kim; *final check sup:* Jae Chun Park; *fx sup:* Duk Ho Cho; *retakes sup:* Mee Hwa Ahn, Hye Soo Kim; *ph sup:* Chul Kyu Rim; *ed:* Dong Jae Rim; *3d seq by Rough Draft Studios, Inc.: 3d anim & composite:* Scott Vanzo; *3d anim sup:* Claudia Katz; *digital paint:* Liz Werden; *"Hallucination Sequence"* design based on and including artwork by Rob Zombin; *anim dir:* Chris Prynoski; *storyboard art:* Dan Shefelman; *des:* Brian Moyer, Chris Prynoski, Jody Schaeffer; *prod mgr:* Vicky Smith; *sup key clean-up art:* Donald Bruce Poynter; *mouth dir:* Mike de Seve; *anim:* Kimson Albert, Doug Crane, Nick de Mayo, Karen Disher, Geoffrey Johnson, Richard Krantz, Kevin Lofton, Miguel Martinez Joffre, Sue Perrotto, Ben Price, Eugene Salandra, Ilya Skorupsky, Frank Suarez, Pat Smith; *fx/back anim:* John D. Allemano, Peggy Collen, Chris Palesty; *asst anim:* James Dean Conklin, Eric Elder, Michael le Bash, Brad Mac-Donald, Bill Moore, John Paratore; *clean-up/ink:* Nick Campese, Wayne Arthur Poynter, Martin Polansky, Stephen Robertson, Bill Schwab, Eric Wight, Nataliya Zurabova; *track reader:* Lee Harting; *anim check:* Nancy Lane, Rudy Tomaselli; *avid ed:* Dave Hughes; *computer consultant:* Eric Calderon; *col & compositing:* Tape House; *computer, i&p:* Robert Aleman, Matthew Disefano, Michael Dunn, Jeffrey Gaut, Rob Issen, Kenneth J. Wilson; *anim project mgr:* Jackie Barba; *anim project co-ord:* Todd Roeland; *anim project asso:* Joe Buoyn; *asst ed:* David Reale, Julia Dole, Dennis Newman, Damian van den Burgh; *sd des:* John Benson, John Lynn; *post audio facility:* NY Sync Sound; *sd ed:* Tony Pipitone, John Bowen, Philippe deSloovre; *sd ds:* David Relly; *sd ed:* John Benson, Randy Akerson, Chuck Michaels; *foley ed:* Thomas Small, Scott Curtis, Linda di Franco, Paul O'Bryan; *ADR rec:* Michael Ruschak, Bob Baron; *rec co-ord:* Cole Kazoin; *foley mix:* Randy Singer; *looping/foley rec:* Neil Cedar, David Jaunai, Kenneth R. Dufva, David Lee Fein, Robin Harlan, Sarah Monat, Rick Wessler; *re-rec mix:* Steve Pederson, Anna Behlmer, Tom Perry; *Austin, Tx:* Mike Castord, Eric Friend, Mike Flannioin; *remote audio rec engineer:* Charles Hunt; *anim ph:* Eighth Frame Camera, Ramon Ferro, David Mc-Grath, Rick Rodine; *ph dpt co-ord:* Christopher Barnes; *vocal fx (N.Y):* David Sharpe, Totally Looped Group; *prod services:* FRB Prods, Inc.; *anim studio mgrs:* Rhodri J. Murphy, Sara Duffy; *prod mgr:* Joellyn Marlow; *prod co-ord:* Barbara Jean Kearney, Andrea Wortham; *post prod co-ord:* Amy Jackson, Momita Sengupta; *prod sup:* Machi Tantillo; *prod asst:* Pinar Barut, George Brennan, Lisa Collins, Courtney H. Diener, Philippe Gagnon, Ben Gruber, Matt LeBarge, Nicole Monte, Samson Laub, Brendan McGee, Jennifer Ostrega, Stacey Schmetz, William Soto, Haya Tawato; *col timer:* Jim Passon; *neg cutter:* Theresa Repola Mohammed; *titles & optics:* Pacific Title; *title des:* Deborah Ross Film Design; *spiritual advisor:* David Felton; *mus sup:* Mark Kates, Lewis Largent; *col:* DeLuxe. *sd:* Dolby stereo. 80 min. • When Beavis and Butt-Head go searching for their missing television, their quest takes them to a man who assumes they are the hired assassins he is expecting. Offering $10,000 to "do" his wife who has absconded to Las Vegas, the boys misinterpret the word "do" and take up his offer. They track her down in Vegas, unaware that she has stolen a vial containing a deadly virus and is planning to blackmail the U.S. Government with it. A federal agent trails them as they visit various American landmarks.

466. Bebe's Kids 31 July 1992; *p.c.:* Hudlin Hyperion Studio/Para.; *dir/character des:* Bruce Smith; *prod:* Willard Carroll, Thomas L. Wilhite; *ex prod:* Reginald Hudlin, Warrington Hudlin; *co-prod:* David R. Cobb; based on characters created by Robin Harris; *scr:* Reginald Hudlin; *asso prod/ed:* Lynne Southerland; *prod des:* Fred Cline; *addit character des:* David Mucci Fasset, Richie Chavez, Steve Moore, Patrick Gleeson, Jim

Kammerud, Marlon West; *anim dir:* Lennie Graves, Chris Buck, Frans Vischer, Steven Wahl, James Lopez, Colm Duggan, Thomas E. Decker, Stephen Anderson, Raymond Johnson Jr., Jeff Etter, David Simmons, Patrick Gleeson, Arland M. Barron, Gavin Dell, Ernest Keen; *asst anim sup:* Don Parmele, Terry Wozniak; *lead character keys:* Francesca Allen, Stan Somers; *anim asst:* Juliana Korsborn, Doris Plough, Melissa Freeman, Sheldon Borenstein, John Eddings, Mi Yul Lee, Kent S. Culotta, Andy Tougas, Nelson Recinos, Brad Neave, Michael Alcouloumre, Kevin Davis, Michael Lerman, Ernie Schmidt, Myron Born, Leah Waldron, Tom Rosamond, Leslie Rogers, Mauro Casalese, Sandy Henkin, Sharon Morray, Celeste Marino, Levi Louis, Joe Elliot, William Mims, Gary Scott, Dave Fox, Monica Luciani, Mary Leire, Larry Hall, Danica Bennette, Dan Wagner, Judy Drake, Ron Brown, Scott Bern, William Exter; *inbet:* Jason Katz, Kaan Kaylon; *storyboard art:* Tom Ellery, Dan Fausett, Raymond Johnson Jr., Phil Mendez, Jim Kammerud, D. Edward Bell Jr.; *asst dir:* Michael Sarrian, Russell Marleau; *prod sup:* Leslie Hough, Kara Vallow, Ron Rich, Rick Allen; *art dir:* Doug Walker; *lay:* Dan Fausett, Andrew Austin, Marc Christenson, Ken Mimura, Kevyn Wallace, David Dunnet, Clint Taylor, Tim Callahan, Gary Mouri, David Gardner; *back:* Lucy Tanashian-Gentry, William Bonar, David McCamley, Jane Nussbaum, Marzette Bonar; *scene plan:* David Thomson, Neil Viker; *fx:* Joey Mildenberger, Marlon West, James D. Mansfield, Esther Barr, Cathy Schoch, Bob Bennett, Bill Schwarz, Michael Carmarillo; *color stylist:* Brigitte Strother, Janette Hulett, Melanie Pava; *painters:* Lada Babicka, Betsy Ergenbright; *main titles:* James Lopez, D. Edward Bell Jr.; *London unit: sup:* Christopher O'Hare, Tony Collingwood; *anim:* Simon Ward-Horner, Duncan Varley, Eric Bouilette, Steve Evangelatos, Al Gaivoto, Chuck Gammage, Clive Pallant, Helga Egilson, Jenny McKosker, Martyn Jones, Anne Brockett, Antony Zmak, Derek L'Estrange, Chris Trorey, Anne Daniels; *prod sup:* Sarah Banbery, Paula Dowie; *Ohio unit: character anim:* Martin Fuller, Jim Kammerud, Dan Root, Thomas Riggin, Brian Smith, Jeff Smith; *asst anim:* Catalina Kiss, Mark Mitchell; *inbet:* Janelle C. Bell, Todd Cronin, Jason Piel, Pamela Mathues, Ron Price, Rafael Rosado; *voices: Robin Harris:* Faizon Love; *Jamika:* Vanessa Bell Calloway; *Leon:* Wayne Collins; *Le Shawn:* Jonell Green; *Kahill:* Marques Houston; *Pee Wee:* Tone Loc; *Dorothea:* Myra J.; *Vivian:* Nell Carter; *Card players:* John Witherspoon, Chino "Fats" Williams, Rodney Winfield, George Wallace; *Bartender:* Brad Senders; *Lush:* Reynaldo Rey; *Barfly:* Bebe Drake Massey; *Richie:* Jack Lynch; *Opie:* Philip Glasser; *Security Guards:* Louis Anderson, Tom Everett, Kerrigan Mahan; *Fun World Patrolman:* Kerrigan Mahan; *Ticket lady/Saleswoman/Nuclear Mother/Rodney Rodent:* Susan Silo; *Announcer/President Lincoln/Imperition/Tommy Toad:* Peter Renaday; *President Nixon:* Rich Little; *Titanic Captain:* "David" Robert Cobb; *Nuclear Father/Motorcycle Cop:* Barry Diamond; *also:* Stanley B. Clay, Michelle Davison, Judi Durand, Greg Finley, Mauri France, Jaquita Green, Jamie Gunderson, J.D. Hall, Doris Hess, Barbara Iley, Daamen Krall, John la Fayette, Tina Lifford, John Lindsay, Arvie Lowe Jr., de'Vaughan Nixon, David Randolph, Noreen Reardon, Gary Schwartz, Cheryl Tyre Smith; *mus:* John Barnes; *additional anim services:* Wang Film Prods, Co., Ltd., Character Builders Inc., Tony Collingwood Prods, Ltd., Bardel Animation Ltd.; *anim check:* Orla Coughlan, Julia Orr, Denise Link, Andy Pye, Maureen McCann, Jacqueline Power, Pat Connoly-Sito, Steve MacVittie, Twyla Motkaluk; *i&p:* Pamela Kleibrink Thompson; *paint check:* Leslie Hinton, Mary Jane Hadley, Jill Petrilak, Mark C. Hadley, Lea Stewart, Joan Boodnik Chang, Allen Chang, April Saniga, Cathy O'Leary, Joseph C. Lee, Eleanor Dahlen, Christine Long, Karan Lee Storr; *prod co-ord:* Judy Kriger, Alex Leo, Don Fuller; *prod asst:* Deborah R. Mayo, Pamela Williamson, Jon R. Spradley; *art dpt sup:* John W. Lanza Jr.; *ed:* Armetta Jackson-Hamlett, Angela T. Robinson, Michelle R. Rochester; *sd ed:* Lee Dragu, Sanford Ponder, Christopher Aud, John Reynolds, Harry Cheney, Michael Lawshe, Michael J. Mitchell, Michael Fay O'Corrigan, Greg Jacobs; *foley:* Keith Olson, Alan Holly, Jerry Trent, Audrey Trent; *digital prelay sup:* Barry Snyder; *re-rec mix:* Robert L. Harman, Jerry Clemans, Dan Hiland; *mus score:* Jack Rouban; *mus ed:* George A. Martin; *col timer:* Dennis McNeill; *neg cutter:* Theresa Repola Mohammed; *prod ph:* Animagraphics Inc., Sharpshooters Inc.; *Xerography:* Dean Stanley, John Remmel, Judi Cassell; *computer models:* Mark Swanson; *cgi:* Sidney Wright; *video operator:* Kristine Kirk; *prod asst:* Scott Keough, Andy Sorcini, Ross Mapletoft, Scott Champagne, Kathleen C. Andrews, Mark McGroarty, Tyler Tharpe, Mark Holte, Denise Mitchell, Corey Powell, Sheryl Farber, David J. McClure, Stephen H. Vera; *mus sup:* Bill Stephney, Ken Kushnick, David Passick; *prod mgr:* Igor Khait. *col:* DeLuxe. *sd:* Dolby stereo. 67 min. • Robin meets a new girl and takes her on a date. He is shocked to find she has brought along her son plus three other kids she is minding. They all go to "Fun World" amusement park where the kids run riot and, to make matters worse, Robin's ex-wife also makes an appearance.

467. Bedelia *(Screen Songs)* 4 Jan. 1930; *p.c.:* The Fleischer Studio for Para; *prod:* Max Fleischer; *dir:* Dave Fleischer; *mus:* Art Turkisher; *song:* Jean Schwartz; b&w. *sd:* WE. 6½ min. • A suitor comes to woo his lady love.

468. Bedevilled Rabbit *(Merrie Melodies)* 13 Apr. 1957; *p.c.:* WB; *dir:* Robert McKimson; *story:* Tedd Pierce; *anim:* George Grandpré, Ted Bonnicksen, Keith Darling; *lay:* Robert Gribbroek; *back:* Richard H. Thomas; *ed:* Treg Brown; *voices:* Mel Blanc; *mus:* Milt Franklyn; *prod mgr:* John W. Burton; *prod:* Edward Selzer; *col:* Tech. *sd:* Vit. 6 min. • Bugs finds himself in Tasmania where he runs afoul of the rabbit-eating Tasmanian Devil.

469. Bedknobs and Broomsticks 13 Dec. 1971; *p.c.:* Walt Disney prods for BV; *anim dir:* Ward Kimball; *story:* Ralph Wright, Ted Berman; *anim:* Milt Kahl, Julius Svendsen, Eric Larson, Hal King, Fred Hellmich; *fx:* Jack Boyd, Jack Buckley, Josh Meador, Art Stevens; *anim/l/a des:* McLaren Stewart; *lay:* Don Griffith, Joe Hale; *back:* Al Dempster, Dick Kelsey, Bill Layne, Ralph Hulett; *anim ed:* James W. Swain; *voices: Codfish:* Robert Holt; *Bear:* Dal McKennon; *Lion/Secretary Bird:* Lennie Weinrib; *misc:* James MacDonald; *mus:* Irwin Kostal; *songs:* Richard M. Sherman, Robert B. Sherman; *col:* Tech. *sd:* RCA. rt *(seq):* 21 min. *l/a/anim.* • Live-action feature about an amateur witch (Angela Lansbury) who takes in three evacuees during the Second World War. Together with a bogus Professor (David Tomlinson), they all travel to a magical land where they can solve part of a magic spell. There they have an adventure undersea and the Professor referees an all-animal soccer game.

470. Bedtime *(Out of the Inkwell)* 1 Mar. 1923; *p.c.:* Inkwell Studio for Rodner; *prod/l/a:* Max Fleischer; *dir:* Dave Fleischer; b&w. *sil.* 6 min. *l/a/anim.* • Ko-Ko wreaks his revenge on Max by growing to gigantic proportions and stalking the city in search of the hapless artist.

471. Bedtime Bedlam *(Woody Woodpecker)* 4 July 1955; *p.c.:* Walter Lantz prods for Univ; *dir:* Paul J. Smith; *story:* Homer Brightman; *anim:* Gil Turner, Robert Bentley, Herman R. Cohen; *sets:* Art Landy, Raymond Jacobs; *voices:* Grace Stafford, Daws Butler, June Foray; *mus:* Clarence Wheeler; *prod mgr:* William E. Garity; *col:* Tech. *sd:* RCA. 6 min. • Woody is offered $50 for babysitting with a pet gorilla.

472. Bedtime for Bonzo 9 Jan. 1951; *p.c.:* Univ; Trailer *dir:* Dave Fleischer. b&w. *sd:* WE. 2 min. *l/a/anim.* • Animated/live-action trailer for the comedy featuring Ronald Reagan.

473. Bedtime for Sniffles *(Merrie Melodies)* 23 Nov. 1940; *p.c.:* Leon Schlesinger prods for WB; *dir:* Charles M. Jones; *story:* Rich Hogan, Ted Pierce; *anim:* Robert Cannon; *character des:* Charles Thorson; *lay:* John McGrew; *back:* Paul Julian; *ed:* Treg Brown; *voices:* Margaret Hill, The Sportsmen; *mus:* Carl W. Stalling; *ph:* John W. Burton; *prod sup:* Henry Binder, Raymond G. Katz; *col:* Tech. *sd:* Vit. 8 min. • Sniffles' attempts to keep awake on Christmas Eve in an effort to see Santa Claus.

474. Bee at the Beach *(Donald Duck)* 13 Oct. 1950; *p.c.:* Walt Disney prods for RKO; *dir:* Jack Hannah; *story:* Nick George, Bill Berg; *anim:* Bill Justice, Bob Carlson, Judge Whitaker, Volus Jones; *fx:* Jack Boyd; *lay:* Yale Gracey; *back:* Ralph Hulett; *voices:* Clarence Nash, James MacDonald; *mus:* Joseph S. Dubin; *col:* Tech. *sd:* RCA. 6 min. • Donald's break by the sea shore is ruined by a vengeful bee.

475. Bee Bopped *(Cartune)* June 1959; *p.c.:* Walter Lantz prods for Univ; *dir:* Paul J. Smith; *story:* Homer Brightman; *anim:* Robert Bentley, Don Patterson, Les Kline; *sets:* Ray Jacobs, Art Landy; *voices:* Daws Butler; *mus:* Clarence Wheeler; *prod mgr:* William E. Garity; *col:* Tech. *sd:* RCA. 6 min. • Windy the bear employs many tactics to steal honey from a hive guarded by a wary bee.

476. The Bee-Devilled Bruin *(Merrie Melodies)* 14 May 1949; *p.c.:* WB; *dir:* Charles M. Jones; *story:* Michael Maltese; *anim:* Ken Harris, Phil Monroe, Ben Washam, Lloyd Vaughan; *fx:* A.C. Gamer; *character des:* Art Heinemann; *lay:* Robert Gribbroek; *back:* Peter Alvarado; *ed:* Treg Brown; *voices:* Billy Bletcher, Stan Freberg, Bea Benaderet; *mus:* Carl Stalling; *prod*

mgr: John W. Burton; *prod:* Edward Selzer; *col:* Tech. *sd:* Vit. 7 min. • Pa Bear and Junior set out to get some fresh honey for breakfast from some irate bees.

477. Bee on Guard *(Donald Duck)* 14 Dec. 1951; *p.c.:* Walt Disney prods for RKO; *dir:* Jack Hannah; *story:* Nick George, Bill Berg; *anim:* Bob Carlson, Bill Justice, George Kreisl, Volus Jones; *fx:* Jack Boyd, Blaine Gibson; *lay:* Yale Gracey; *back:* Thelma Witmer; *voices:* Clarence Nash, James MacDonald; *mus:* Oliver Wallace; *col:* Tech. *sd:* RCA. 7 min. • Donald tries to steal the bees' honey by disguising himself as a giant bee.

478. Beef for and After *(Loopy de Loop)* Mar. 1962; *p.c.:* Hanna-Barbera for Colum; *prod/dir:* Joseph Barbera, William Hanna; *story dir:* Art Davis; *story:* Michael Maltese; *anim dir:* Charles A. Nichols; *anim:* Dick Lundy; *lay:* Walter Clinton; *back:* Art Lozzi; *ed:* Greg Watson; *voices:* Daws Butler, Don Messick, Doug Young; *mus:* Hoyt Curtin; *titles:* Lawrence Gobel; *prod mgr:* Howard Hanson; *col:* East. *sd:* RCA. 6½ min. • Loopy tries to prevent his little nephew, Bon-Bon, from cattle rustling.

479. Beep Beep *(Merrie Melodies)* 24 May 1952; *p.c.:* WB; *dir:* Charles M. Jones; *story:* Michael Maltese; *anim:* Ben Washam, Ken Harris, Lloyd Vaughan, Phil Monroe; *lay:* Robert Gribbroek; *back:* Philip de Guard; *ed:* Treg Brown; *voice:* Paul Julian; *mus:* Carl Stalling; *prod mgr:* John W. Burton; *prod:* Edward Selzer; *col:* Tech. *sd:* Vit. 7 min. • We follow the Coyote on another venture after the Road-Runner, this time down an abandoned mine. When this fails he resorts to "Rocket-Powered Skates" … all to no avail.

480. Beep Prepared *(Merrie Melodies)* 11 Nov. 1961; *p.c.:* WB; *dir:* Chuck Jones; *story:* John Dunn, Chuck Jones; *asst dir/lay:* Maurice Noble; *anim:* Bob Bransford, Tom Ray, Ken Harris, Richard Thompson; *fx:* Harry Love; *back:* Philip de Guard; *ed:* Treg Brown; *voice:* Paul Julian; *mus:* Milt Franklyn; *prod mgr:* William Orcutt; *prod:* David H. DePatie; *col:* Tech. *sd:* Vit. 7 min. *Academy Award nomination.* • The Coyote suffers many indignities including falling through a portable hole, being flattened by a segment of highway and being shot into the heavens by a Rocket Sled.

481. The Beer Parade *(Scrappy)* 4 Mar. 1933; *p.c.:* Winkler for Colum; *prod:* Charles Mintz; *story:* Dick Huemor; *anim:* Sid Marcus, Art Davis; *mus:* Joe de Nat; *prod mgr:* James Bronis; b&w. *sd:* RCA. 6 min. • No story available.

482. Beetle Juice 30 Mar. 1988; *p.c.:* The Geffen Film Company for WB; *Snake seq:* Ted Rae; *Sandworm seq:* Doug Beswick; *Barbara/Adam transformation:* Tim Lawrence; *anim:* Jammie Friday, Mark Myer; *col:* Tech. *sd:* Dolby stereo. 92 min. *l/a.* • A newlywed couple's daughter befriends Betelgeuse, a crazed spirit who works as a bio-exorcist, ridding ghosts' houses of infestations of the living. Animated ghosts, etc.

483. Beezy Bear *(Donald Duck)* 1 Apr. 1955; *p.c.:* Walt Disney prods for BV; *dir:* Jack Hannah; *story:* Dave DeTiege, Al Bertino; *anim:* Bill Justice, Volus Jones, Bob Carlson, Al Coe; *fx:* Dan McManus; *lay:* Yale Gracey; *back:* Brice Mack; *voices:* Bill Thompson, Clarence Nash, James MacDonald, Jack Hannah; *mus:* Oliver Wallace; *col:* Tech. *sd:* RCA. 6 min. CS. • Bee farmer Donald is forever being plagued by the honey pilfering of Humphrey, the bear from the National Park next door.

484. Behind the Meat-Ball *(Looney Tunes)* 7 Apr. 1945; *p.c.:* WB; *dir:* Frank Tashlin; *story:* Melvin Millar; *anim:* I. Ellis; *sets:* Richard H. Thomas; *ed:* Treg Brown; *voices:* Mel Blanc, Sara Berner; *mus:* Carl Stalling; *prod mgr:* John W. Burton; *prod:* Edward Selzer; *col:* Tech. *sd:* Vit. 7 min. • A starving dog finds a steak but believing it to be a mirage, leaves it. A smaller dog walks off with it and now he has to retrieve it.

485. Believe It or Else *(Merrie Melodies)* 3 June 1939; *p.c.:* Leon Schlesinger prods for WB; *dir:* Fred Avery; *story:* Dave Monahan, Robert Clampett; *anim:* Virgil Ross; *sets:* John Didrik Johnsen; *ed:* Tregoweth E. Brown; *voices:* Cliff Nazarro, Mel Blanc, Fred Avery; *mus:* Carl W. Stalling; *prod sup:* Henry Binder, Raymond G. Katz; *col:* Tech. *sd:* Vit. 7 min. • Parody of Ripley's "Believe It or Else" involving many outrageous "unusual" facts.

486. A Bell for Philadelphia *(Hector Heathcote)* July 1963; *p.c.:* TT for Fox; *ex prod:* Bill Weiss; *dir:* Bob Kuwahara; *story dir:* Tom Morrison; *story:* Larz Bourne; *anim:* Cosmo Anzilotti; *sets:* Bill Focht, John Zago; *ed:* George McAvoy; *voices:* John Myhers; *mus:* Phil Scheib; *ph:* Joe Rasinski; *col:* DeLuxe. *sd:* RCA. 5½ min. • Heathcote is given a contract to move the famous Liberty Bell but a rival moving firm prevents him from doing so.

487. Bell Hoppy (*Merrie Melodies*) 17 Apr. 1954; *p.c.:* WB; *dir:* Robert McKimson; *story:* Tedd Pierce; *anim:* Charles McKimson, Herman Cohen, Rod Scribner, Phil de Lara; *lay:* Robert Givens; *back:* Richard H. Thomas; *ed:* Treg Brown; *voices:* Mel Blanc, Tedd Pierce; *mus:* Carl Stalling; *prod mgr:* John W. Burton; *prod:* Edward Selzer; *col:* Tech. *sd:* Vit. 7 min. • In order to be admitted to an exclusive club, Sylvester is told to catch a big mouse. Simultaneously, a baby kangaroo happens to be on the loose.

488. Bellboy Donald (*Donald Duck*) 18 Dec. 1942; *p.c.:* Walt Disney prods for RKO; *dir:* Jack King; *story:* Harry Reeves, Carl Barks, Jack Hannah; *anim:* Paul Allen, James Armstrong, Ed Love, Lee Morehouse, Kenneth Muse, Hal King, Ray Patin, Art Scott, Vladimir Tytla, Judge Whitaker; *fx:* George Rowley; *lay:* Bill Herwig; *voices:* Clarence Nash, John F. McLeish, J. Dehner Forkum, Glen Couch; *mus:* Oliver Wallace; *col:* Tech. *sd:* RCA. 7 min. • The hotel manager assigns bellboy Danald to look after Senator Pete and his obnoxious son.

489. Belle Boys (*Woody Woodpecker*) 14 Sept. 1953; *p.c.:* Walter Lantz prods for Univ; *dir:* Don Patterson; *story:* Homer Brightman; *anim:* La Verne Harding, Ray Abrams, Ken Southworth; *sets:* Raymond Jacobs, Art Landy; *voices:* Dal McKennon, Grace Stafford, Gladys Holland; *mus:* Clarence Wheeler; *prod mgr:* William E. Garity; *col:* Tech. *sd:* RCA. 6 min. • Bellboys Buzz Buzzard and Woody fight over the privilege of tending to the famous movie star, Ga-Ga Gazoo.

490. Ben and Me 11 Nov. 1953; *p.c.:* Walt Disney prods for BV; *dir:* Hamilton S. Luske; *asst dir:* Rusty Jones; *story adapt:* Bill Peet, Winston Hibler, Del Connell, Ted Sears, Ernie Colon; *anim:* Wolfgang Reitherman, Ollie Johnston, John Lounsbery, Hal King, Cliff Nordberg, Les Clark, Marvin Woodward, Don Lusk, Hugh Fraser, Jerry Hathcock, Eric Cleworth, Harvey Toombs, Hal Ambro, Merle Gilson, Milt Kahl, Eric Larson, Bob McCrea, Art Stevens; *fx:* George Rowley; *art dir:* Ken Anderson, Claude Coats; *lay:* Hugh Hennesy, Thor Putnam, Al Zinnen; *back:* Dick Anthony, Al Dempster, Thelma Witmer; *voices: Amos Mouse:* Sterling Holloway; *Ben Franklin:* Charlie Ruggles; *Thomas Jefferson:* Hans Conried; *Governor/Guide:* Bill Thompson; *Mouse Guide:* Stan Freberg; *Misc. voices:* Hans Conried, Stan Freberg, James MacDonald, Bill Thompson; *mus:* Oliver Wallace; *col:* Tech. *sd:* RCA. 21 min. *Academy Award nomination.* • Entertaining adaptation of Robert Lawson's story about how a mouse influenced Benjamin Franklin's inventions and the opening words to The Declaration of Independence.

491. Benny the Bear in a Cowboy I Would Be 14 Jan. 1930; *p.c.:* Elias Brucker; *prod/dir:* Elias Brucker; b&w. sd. • No story available.

492. Berry Funny (*Possible Possum*) Mar. 1971; *p.c.:* TT for Fox; *ex prod:* Bill Weiss; *dir/anim:* Cosmo Anzilotti; *col:* DeLuxe. *sd:* RCA. 5½ min. • Poss and his friends try to stop a blue jay from stealing their entire blackberry crop. • See: *Possible Possum*

493. Bert Green's Animated Crossword Puzzles 1925; *p.c.:* Banner Prods, Inc.; *anim:* Bert Green; *prod:* C.H. Ferrell; b&w. *st.* • Using the current craze for crosswords, this series featured "Blotto," a little black boy, and his dog, "Bozo." The producer claims not to give the answers on screen under their novel "protected plan" but to bring the fans back to see it again for help in solving the puzzle.

494. Bertlevyettes *p.c.:* World Film Corp; *prod/story:* Bert Levy; *dir:* Sidney Olcott; b&w. sil. *l/a/anim.* • **1915: Great Americans Past and Present** 4 Jan. **Famous Men of Today** 11 Jan. **Famous Rulers of the World** 18 Jan. **New York and It's People** 25 Jan.

495. Beside a Moonlit Stream (*Screen Songs*) 27 May 1938; *p.c.:* The Fleischer Studio for Para; *prod:* Max Fleischer; *dir:* Dave Fleischer; *anim:* Roland Crandall; *l/a:* Frank Dailey & his Orchestra; b&w. sd: WE. 7 min. *l/a/anim.* • The animals celebrate baby bear's birthday.

496. The Best Man Wins (*Aesop's Film Fable*) 9 Nov. 1923; *p.c.:* Fables Pictures Inc for Pathé; *dir:* Paul Terry; b&w. sil. 5 min. • A mouse defeats the village bully, four times his own size.

497. Better Bait Than Never (*Noveltoon*) 5 June 1953; *p.c.:* Famous for Para; *dir:* Seymour Kneitel; *story:* Irving Spector; *anim:* Dave Tendlar, Martin Taras; *sets:* Jack Henegan; *voices:* Jackson Beck, Sid Raymond; *mus:* Winston Sharples; *ph:* Leonard McCormick; *prod mgr:* Seymour Shultz;

col: Tech. *sd:* RCA. 6 min. • Katnip believes his failing ability to catch fish is due to lack of "Crow Bait." Buzzy fits the bill.

498. Better Late Than Never (*Victor the Volunteer*) Mar. 1950; *p.c.:* TT for Fox; *dir:* Eddie Donnelly; *story:* John Foster; *anim:* Jim Tyer; *mus:* Philip A. Scheib; *ph:* Douglas Moye; *col:* Tech. *sd:* RCA. 6 min. • Fireman Victor spruces himself up and stops to buy a boquet of flowers before rescuing a pretty girl trapped in a burning building.

499. Betty Boop and Grampy (*Betty Boop*) 16 Aug. 1935; *p.c.:* The Fleischer Studio for Para; *prod:* Max Fleischer; *dir:* Dave Fleischer; *story:* William Turner; *anim:* David Tendlar, Charles Hastings, Tex Henson; *voices:* Mae Questel, Everett Clark, Jack Mercer; *mus:* Sammy Timberg; *ph:* Johnny Burks; b&w. *sd:* WE. 7 min. • Betty and the gang go to Professor Grampy's house and enjoy an improvised party.

500. Betty Boop and Little Jimmy (*Betty Boop*) 27 Mar. 1936; *p.c.:* The Fleischer Studio for Para; *prod:* Max Fleischer; *dir:* Dave Fleischer; *anim:* Myron Waldman, Hicks Lokey, Lillian Friedman; *voice:* Mae Questel; *mus:* Sammy Timberg; b&w. *sd:* WE. 6 min. • James Swinnerton's comic strip character joins Betty in an adventure that leaves her trapped on a slimming device. Jimmy goes for an electrician ... but he soon forgets his mission.

501. Betty Boop and the Little King (*Betty Boop*) 31 Jan. 1936; *p.c.:* The Fleischer Studio for Para; *prod:* Max Fleischer; *dir:* Dave Fleischer; *anim:* Myron Waldman, Hicks Lokey, Lillian Friedman; *voice:* Mae Questel; *mus:* Sammy Timberg; *ph:* Johnny Burks; b&w. *sd:* WE. 7 min. • Betty encounters O. Soglow's comic character when, bored by the opera, the King sneaks out to join in with her rodeo routine.

502. Betty Boop for President (*Betty Boop*) 4 Nov. 1932; *p.c.:* The Fleischer Studio for Para; *prod:* Max Fleischer; *dir:* Dave Fleischer; *anim:* Seymour Kneitel, Roland Crandall; *voice:* Mae Questel; *mus:* Art Turkisher; b&w. *sd:* WE. 7 min. • Betty puts forward her benefits for being elected president. Caricature of former governor, Alfred E. Smith.

503. Betty Boop in I Heard (*Betty Boop*) 11 Sept. 1933; *p.c.:* The Fleischer Studio for Para; *prod:* Max Fleischer; *dir:* Dave Fleischer; *anim:* Willard Bowsky, Myron Waldman; *voice:* Mae Questel; *mus:* Don Redman & his Orchestra; b&w. *sd:* WE. 6 min. • Betty serves the miners in her café. When they return to the "Never Mine," they find it inhabited by ghosts playing baseball.

504. The Betty Boop Limited (*Talkartoon*) 1 July 1932; *p.c.:* The Fleischer Studio for Para; *prod:* Max Fleischer; *dir:* Dave Fleischer; *anim:* Willard Bowsky, Thomas Bonfiglio; *voice:* Mae Questel; *mus:* Art Turkisher; b&w. *sd:* WE. 7 min. • Betty, Bimbo and Ko-Ko have a hectic train journey.

505. Betty Boop, M.D. (*Betty Boop*) 2 Sept. 1932; *p.c.:* The Fleischer Studio for Para; *prod:* Max Fleischer; *dir:* Dave Fleischer; *anim:* Willard Bowsky, Thomas Golden; *voices:* William A. Costello; *mus:* Art Turkisher; b&w. *sd:* WE. 7 min. • Betty sells patent medicine to the local yokels until they discover it came from the town pump.

506. Betty Boop with Henry, the Funniest Living American (*Betty Boop*) 22 Nov. 1935; *p.c.:* the Fleischer Studio for Para; *prod:* Max Fleischer; *dir:* Dave Fleischer; *anim:* Myron Waldman, Sam Stimson, Lillian Friedman; *voice:* Mae Questel, Frances Reynolds; *mus:* Sammy Timberg; b&w. *sd:* WE. 7 min. • Carl Anderson's comic strip character Henry is put in charge of Betty's Pet Shop. He causes all the animals to escape ... but they soon return!

507. Betty Boop's Bamboo Isle (*Betty Boop*) 23 Sept. 1932; *p.c.:* The Fleischer Studio for Para; *prod:* Max Fleischer; *sup:* Dave Fleischer; *dir/anim:* James H. Culhane, Alfred Eugster; *add anim:* Seymour Kneitel, Bernard Wolf; *voice:* Mae Questel; *mus:* The Royal Samoans; b&w. *sd:* WE. 8 min. • Betty and Bimbo find themselves stranded on a cannibal isle.

508. Betty Boop's Big Boss (*Betty Boop*) 2 June 1933; *p.c.:* The Fleischer Studio for Para; *prod:* Max Fleischer; *dir:* Dave Fleischer; *anim:* Bernard Wolf, David Tendlar; *mus:* Sammy Timberg; b&w. *sd:* WE. 6 min. • Betty applies for a secretarial job but all the boss wants to do is chase her.

509. Betty Boop's Birthday Party (*Betty Boop*) 21 Apr. 1933; *p.c.:* The Fleischer Studio for Para; *prod:* Max Fleischer; *dir:* Dave Fleischer;

anim: Seymour Kneitel, Myron Waldman; *mus:* Sammy Timberg; b&w. *sd:* WE. 6 min. • Ko-Ko, Bimbo and all Betty's friends arrive to help celebrate her birthday.

510. Betty Boop's Bizzy Bee (*Betty Boop*) 19 Aug. 1932; *p.c.:* The Fleischer Studio for Para; *prod:* Max Fleischer; *dir:* Dave Fleischer; *anim:* Seymour Kneitel, Bernard Wolf; *voice:* Charles Carver; *mus:* Art Turkisher; b&w. *sd:* WE. 6 min. • Betty's Diner does good trade until the effects of her wheatcakes take their toll.

511. Betty Boop's Crazy Inventions (*Betty Boop*) 27 Jan. 1933; *p.c.:* The Fleischer Studio for Para; *prod:* Max Fleischer; *dir:* Dave Fleischer; *anim:* Willard Bowsky, Ugo d'Orsi; *voice:* Mae Questel; *mus:* Sammy Timberg; *song:* Sammy Lerner, Sammy Timberg; b&w. *sd:* WE. 7 min. • Betty, Bimbo and Ko-Ko demonstrate some strange inventions culminating in havoc being caused by a runaway sewing machine.

512. Betty Boop's Hallowe'en Party (*Betty Boop*) 3 Nov. 1933; *p.c.:* The Fleischer Studio for Para; *prod:* Max Fleischer; *dir:* Dave Fleischer; *anim:* Willard Bowsky, Myron Waldman; *mus:* Sammy Timberg; b&w. *sd:* WE. 6 min. • Betty's party is gatecrashed by a Kong-like ape who is quickly put to flight by "evil spirits."

513. Betty Boop's Ker-Choo (*Betty Boop*) 6 Jan. 1933; *p.c.:* The Fleischer Studio for Para; *prod:* Max Fleischer; *dir:* Dave Fleischer; *anim:* Seymour Kneitel, Bernard Wolf; *voice:* Mae Questel; *mus:* Sammy Timberg; b&w. *sd:* WE. 7 min. • Betty, Bimbo and Ko-Ko enter an auto race. Betty has a cold and her sneezing upsets the other drivers, enabling her to win.

514. Betty Boop's Life Guard (*Betty Boop*) 13 July 1934; *p.c.:* The Fleischer Studio for Para; *prod:* Max Fleischer; *dir:* Dave Fleischer; *anim:* Willard Bowsky, David Tendlar; *character des:* Seymour Kneitel; *voice:* Mae Questel; *mus:* Sammy Timberg; b&w. *sd:* WE. 7 min. • When Betty goes swimming, she sinks to the ocean's bed and dreams she's a mermaid.

515. Betty Boop's Little Pal (*Betty Boop*) 21 Sept. 1934; *p.c.:* The Fleischer Studio for Para; *prod:* Max Fleischer; *dir:* Dave Fleischer; *anim:* Myron Waldman, Edward Nolan, Lillian Friedman; *voice:* Mae Questel; *mus:* Sammy Timberg; b&w. *sd:* WE. 7 min. • Betty scolds her pup, Pudgy, who runs away and is caught by the dog-catcher. He escapes, sets the other dogs free, then runs home to Betty.

516. Betty Boop's May Party (*Betty Boop*) 12 May 1933; *p.c.:* The Fleischer Studio for Para; *prod:* Max Fleischer; *dir:* Dave Fleischer; *anim:* David Tendlar, William Henning; *mus:* Sammy Timberg; b&w. *sd:* WE. 6 min. • Betty is crowned "Queen of the May," while a leaky rubber tree coats all with solution.

517. Betty Boop's Museum (*Betty Boop*) 16 Dec. 1932; *p.c.:* The Fleischer Studio for Para; *prod:* Max Fleischer; *dir:* Dave Fleischer; *anim:* William Henning, Reuben Timinsky; *mus:* Art Turkisher; b&w. *sd:* WE. 9 min. • Lost in a museum at midnight, Betty witnesses skeletons coming to life and roaming the corridors.

518. Betty Boop's Penthouse (*Betty Boop*) 10 Mar. 1933; *p.c.:* The Fleischer Studio for Para; *prod:* Max Fleischer; *dir:* Dave Fleischer; *anim:* Willard G. Bowsky; *voice:* Mae Questel; *mus:* Sammy Timberg; b&w. *sd:* WE. 6 min. • Ko-Ko and Bimbo forsake their latest invention to watch Betty sunbathing. Their formula overflows, creating a "Frankenstein"-like monster who stalks Betty.

519. Betty Boop's Prize Show (*Betty Boop*) 19 Oct. 1934; *p.c.:* The Fleischer Studio for Para; *prod:* Max Fleischer; *dir:* Dave Fleischer; *anim:* Myron Waldman, Lillian Friedman; *mus:* Sammy Timberg; *song:* Harold Levey, Cecil Mack; b&w. *sd:* WE. 7 min. • Betty and her pals enact an old fashioned melodrama.

520. Betty Boop's Rise to Fame (*Betty Boop*) 18 May 1934; *p.c.:* The Fleischer Studio for Para; *prod/l/a:* Max Fleischer; *dir:* Dave Fleischer; *anim:* Lillian Friedman; *voice:* Mae Questel; *mus:* Sammy Timberg; b&w. *sd:* WE. 7 min. *l/a/anim.* • For an interview, Max lets Betty recreate famous scenes from her previous cartoons. • Seq: *Stopping the Show; Betty Boop's Bamboo Isle; The Old Man of the Mountains.*

521. Betty Boop's Trial (*Betty Boop*) 15 June 1934; *p.c.:* The Fleischer Studio for Para; *prod:* Max Fleischer; *dir:* Dave Fleischer; *anim:* Myron Waldman, Hicks Lokey, Lillian Friedman; *voices:* Mae Questel, Everett Clark; *mus:* Sammy Timberg; b&w. *sd:* WE. 7 min. • Betty is arrested for speeding and has to face the ordeal of a full trial.

522. Betty Boop's Ups and Downs (*Betty Boop*) 14 Oct. 1932; *p.c.:* The Fleischer Studio for Para; *prod:* Max Fleischer; *dir:* Dave Fleischer; *anim:* Willard Bowsky, Ugo d'Orsi; *voice:* Mae Questel; *mus:* Art Turkisher; b&w. *sd:* WE. 7 min. • The planets auction the Earth. Saturn wins and proceeds to pull gravity from the Earth's center, thus causing chaos.

523. Betty Co-Ed (*Screen Songs*) 1 Aug. 1931; *p.c.:* The Fleischer Studio for Para; *prod:* Max Fleischer; *dir:* Dave Fleischer; *voice:* Mae Questel; *mus:* Art Turkisher; *song:* Carl Fischer; *l/a:* Rudy Vallee & his Connecticut Yankees; b&w. *sd:* WE. 7 min. *l/a/anim.* • Bimbo is prevented from seeing college favorite Betty Boop. After Rudy Vallee's song, he manages to see her and we get an insight into college graduation. Mae Questel's first time as "Betty Boop."

524. Betty in Blunderland (*Betty Boop*) 6 Apr. 1934; *p.c.:* The Fleischer Studio for Para; *prod:* Max Fleischer; *dir:* Dave Fleischer; *anim:* Roland Crandall, Thomas Johnson; *voice:* Mae Questel; *mus:* Sammy Timberg; *song:* Bert Kalmar, Harry Ruby; b&w. *sd:* WE. 7 min. • Betty dreams she is "Alice in Wonderland." Jabberwocky chases her and all the other characters come to her rescue.

525. Beware of Barnacle Bill (*Popeye*) 25 Jan. 1935; *p.c.:* The Fleischer Studio for Para; *prod:* Max Fleischer; *dir:* Dave Fleischer; *anim:* Willard Bowsky, Harold Walker; *voices:* Jack Mercer, Mae Questel, Charles Carver; *mus:* Sammy Timberg; b&w. *sd:* WE. 7 min. • The ballad of "Barnacle Bill" is acted out by Popeye and Olive with Bluto as the rival suitor for the fair maiden's hand.

526. Bewitched Bunny (*Looney Tunes*) 24 July 1954; *p.c.:* WB; *dir:* Charles M. Jones; *story:* Michael Maltese; *anim:* Lloyd Vaughan, Ken Harris, Ben Washam; *lay:* Maurice Noble; *back:* Philip de Guard; *ed:* Treg Brown; *voices:* Mel Blanc, Bea Benaderet; *mus:* Carl Stalling; *prod mgr:* John W. Burton; *prod:* Edward Selzer; *col:* Tech. *sd:* Vit. 7 min. • Bugs rescues Hansel and Gretel from the clutches of Witch Hazel, placing himself in jeopardy.

527. Beyond Civilization to Texas (*Jerky Journeys*) 15 Mar. 1949; *p.c.:* Impossible Pictures for Republic; *ex prod:* David Flexer; *prod, dir, story:* Leonard Lewis Levinson; *des:* Art Heinemann; *back:* Peter Alvarado Jr.; *voice:* Frank Nelson; *col:* Tru. *sd.* 8 min. • Senator Claghorn presents a bill in Congress to move the United States to Texas.

528. A Bicep Built for Two (*Herman & Katnip*) 8 Apr. 1955; *p.c.:* Famous for Para; *dir:* Seymour Kneitel; *story:* Larz Bourne; *anim:* Tom Golden, Morey Reden; *sets:* Robert Connavale; *voices:* Arnold Stang, Sid Raymond, Jackson Beck; *mus:* Winston Sharples; *title song:* Hal David, Leon Carr; *ph:* Leonard McCormick; *prod mgr:* Seymour Shultz; *col:* Tech. *sd:* RCA. 6 min. • Katnip wishes to impress a girl who goes for "He-Men," so Herman helps him train to get some muscle.

529. Big Bad Bobcat (*Possible Possum*) Oct. 1967; *p.c.:* TT for Fox; *dir/anim:* Cosmo Anzilotti; *col:* DeLuxe. *sd:* RCA. 5¹/₂ min. • A bobcat arrives, looking for a Southern mouse to eat. Poss and his pals try to keep him away from Macon Mouse. • See: *Possible Possum.*

530. Big Bad Sindbad (*Popeye*) 12 Dec. 1952; *p.c.:* Famous for Para; *dir:* Seymour Kneitel; *story:* I. Klein; *anim:* Tom Johnson, William Henning; *sets:* Robert Connavale; *voices:* Jack Mercer, Mae Questel, Jackson Beck; *mus:* Winston Sharples; *ph:* Leonard McCormick; *prod mgr:* Seymour Shultz; *col:* Tech. *sd:* RCA. 10 min. • Popeye explains to his nephews how he beat the mighty Sindbad. • Seq: *Popeye the Sailor Meets Sindbad the Sailor.*

531. The Big Bad Wolf (*Silly Symphony*) 14 Apr. 1934; *p.c.:* Walt Disney prods for UA; *dir:* Burton F. Gillett; *anim sup:* Norman Ferguson; *anim:* Les Clark, Clyde Geronimi, Jack Hannah, Richard Lundy, Hamilton S. Luske, Fred Moore, Ben Sharpsteen; *voices:* Billy Bletcher, Pinto Colvig, Alyce Ardell, The Rhythmettes; *mus:* Frank E. Churchill; *col:* Tech. *sd:* RCA. 9 min. • Despite their brother's warnings, the two pigs take Red Riding Hood through the woods where they encounter the Big Bad Wolf.

532. Big Beef at the O.K. Corral (*Hoot Kloot*) 17 Apr. 1974; *p.c.:* Mirisch/DFE for UA; *dir:* Bob Balsar; *story:* John W. Dunn; *anim:* John Ward, Richard Rudler, Tim Miller; *lay:* Don Roy; *back:* Richard Reuben; *ed:* Roger Donley; *voices:* Bob Holt, Larry Mann; *mus:* Doug Goodwin; *titles:* Arthur Leonardi; *ph:* John Burton Jr.; *prod mgr:* Lee Gunther; *col:* DeLuxe. *sd:* RCA. 5 min. • Sheriff Kloot sets out to trap Billy the Kidder who has been stealing cattle.

533. The Big Berg (*Aesop's Film Fable*) 24 Mar. 1929; *p.c.:* Fables Pictures Inc for Pathé; *dir:* Paul Terry; b&w. *sil.* 10 min. • No story available.

534. The Big Birdcast (*Color Rhapsody*) 13 May 1938; *p.c.:* Charles Mintz prods for Colum; *story:* Ben Harrison; *anim:* Manny Gould; *sets:* Phil Davis; *voices:* Dave Weber, Cliff Nazarro; *mus:* Joe de Nat; *prod mgr:* James Bronis; *col:* Tech. *sd:* RCA. 6½ min. • The birds present their own broadcasting service featuring feathered versions of Fred Allen, Jack Benny, Milton Berle, Ben Bernie, Eddie Cantor, Primo Carnera, Bing Crosby, Andy Devine, Wendell Hall, Tommy Mack, Parkyakarkas, Joe Penner, Rudy Vallee, Harry von Zell, Walter Winchell and Ed Wynn.

535. The Big Bite (*Woody Woodpecker*) Apr. 1966; *p.c.:* Walter Lantz prods for Univ; *dir:* Paul J. Smith; *story:* Cal Howard; *anim:* Les Kline, Al Coe; *sets:* Ray Huffine; *voices:* Grace Stafford; *mus:* Walter Greene; *prod mgr:* William E. Garity; *col:* Tech. *sd:* RCA. 6 min. • Woody encounters a small dog with an insatiable appetite.

536. The Big Build Up (*Terry-Toon*) 4 Sept. 1942; *p.c.:* TT for Fox; *dir:* Mannie Davis; *story:* John Foster; *mus:* Philip A. Scheib; b&w. *sd:* RCA. 6 min. • Puddy the Pup's attempts to discipline a mischievous kitten.

537. The Big Cat and the Little Mousie (*Oswald*) 15 Aug. 1938; *p.c.:* Walter Lantz prods for Univ; *dir:* Alex Lovy; *story:* Victor McLeod, James Miele; *anim:* Frank Tipper, George Grandpré; *sets:* Edgar Keichle; *voice:* Bernice Hansel, Dave Weber; *mus:* Frank Marsales; b&w. *sd:* WE. 6½ min. • A cat gets a mouse drunk but can't eat him at the moment. The mouse promises to return.

538. The Big Cheese (*Aesop's Sound Fable*) 26 Oct. 1930; *p.c.:* Van Beuren for Pathé; *dir:* John Foster; *mus:* Gene Rodemich; b&w. *sd:* RCA. 6 min. • Champion dog and cat fighters slog it out in the ring although the fight turns into a dance.

539. Big Chief Ko-Ko (*Out of the Inkwell*) 2 Mar. 1925; *p.c.:* Inkwell Studio for Red Seal; *prod/l/a:* Max Fleischer; *dir:* Dave Fleischer; b&w. *sil.* 6 min. *l/a/anim.* • A real, live Indian chief enters the studio and an Indian is drawn. Ko-Ko gives this pen character the "Razz" and receives a volley of arrows. Reissued in 1930 with added sound-track.

540. Big Chief No Treaty (*Deputy Dawg*) Sept. 1962; *p.c.:* TT for Fox; *ex prod:* Bill Weiss; *dir:* Bob Kuwahara; *story sup:* Tom Morrison; *story:* Larz Bourne; *anim:* Ed Donnelly, Mannie Davis, Vinnie Bell, Johnny Gent, Larry Silverman; *sets:* John Zago; *voices:* Dayton Allen; *mus:* Phil Scheib; *prod mgr:* Frank Schudde; *col:* Tech. *sd:* RCA. 5 min. • A reluctant Indian Chief won't sign a peace treaty, thus getting away with any crime he cares to commit.

541. Big Chief Ugh-Amugh-Ugh (*Popeye*) 15 Apr. 1938; *p.c.:* The Fleischer Studio Inc for Para; *prod:* Max Fleischer; *dir:* Dave Fleischer; *anim:* Willard Bowsky, George Germanetti; *voices:* Jack Mercer, Gus Wickie, Margie Hines; *mus:* Sammy Timberg; b&w. *sd:* WE. 7 min. • Olive is taken by an Indian Chief for his princess and our hero sets out to rescue her.

542. The Big Cleanup (*Hector Heathcote*) Sept. 1963; *p.c.:* TT for Fox; *ex prod:* Bill Weiss; *dir/anim:* Dave Tendlar; *story sup:* Tom Morrison; *story:* Eli Bauer; *sets:* Bill Focht, John Zago; *ed:* George McAvoy; *voices:* John Myhers; *mus:* Phil Scheib; *ph:* Joe Rasinski; *col:* DeLuxe. *sd:* RCA. 6 min. • Heathcote is engaged to clean up Untidy Gulch of a villain named Black Bart Bromide.

543. The Big Drip (*Screen Song*) 25 Nov. 1949; *p.c.:* Famous for Para; *dir:* I. Sparber; *story:* Larz Bourne, Larry Riley; *anim:* Myron Waldman, Nick Tafuri; *sets:* Tom Ford; *voices:* Jack Mercer, Sid Raymond; *mus:* Winston Sharples; *ph:* Leonard McCormick; *prod mgr:* Sam Buchwald; *col:* Tech. *sd:* RCA. 8 min. • The animals construct an ark in anticipation of the big rain.

544. The Big Flame-Up (*Screen Song*) 30 Sept. 1949; *p.c.:* Famous for Para; *dir:* I. Sparber; *story:* I. Klein; *anim:* Dave Tendlar, Martin Taras; *sets:* Tom Ford; *voices:* Jack Mercer; *mus:* Winston Sharples; *song:* Joe Hayden, Theodore Metz; *ph:* Leonard McCormick; *prod mgr:* Sam Buchwald; *col:* Tech. *sd:* RCA. 7 min. • The animals' Fire Brigade put out a fire.

545. The Big Freeze (*Mighty Heroes*) Dec. 1971 (© 1967); *p.c.:* TT for Fox; *ex prod:* Bill Weiss; *dir:* Robert Taylor; *col:* DeLuxe. *sd:* RCA. 6 min.

• The Mighty Heroes prevent "The Super Cooler" from freezing the town of Goodhaven.

546. Big Game (*Aesop's Film Fable*) 2 Oct. 1928; *p.c.:* Fables Pictures Inc for Pathé; *dir:* Paul Terry, Harry Bailey; b&w. *sil.* 10 min. • Farmer Al and his dog are shipwrecked on an island inhabited by an explorer and jungle animals. Al thinks he can make some easy cash by selling animal pelts. He tries unsuccessfully to shoot some creatures and gets pursued by a lion which knocks itself out when chasing Al and his dog into a hollow tree. Al assumes the beast to be dead and rounds up the cubs but the lion recovers and punches Al over the horizon.

547. Big Game (*Aesop's Sound Fable*) 3 Aug. 1931; *p.c.:* Van Beuren for Pathé; *dir:* John Foster; *mus:* Gene Rodemich; b&w. *sd:* RCA. 6 min. • No story available.

548. Big Game Fishing (*Sad Cat*) Aug. 1967; *p.c.:* TT for Fox; *dir/anim:* Art Bartsch; *col:* DeLuxe. *sd:* RCA. 5 min. • Super Ego turns Sad Cat into a champion fisherman when he enters a fishing contest. • See: *Sad Cat*

549. Big Game Haunt (*Merrie Melodies*) 10 Feb. 1968; *p.c.:* WB/7A; *dir:* Alex Lovy; *story:* Cal Howard; *anim:* Ted Bonnicksen, La Verne Harding, Volus Jones, Ed Solomon; *lay:* Bob Givens; *back:* Bob Abrams; *ed:* Hal Geer; *voices:* Larry Storch; *mus:* William Lava; *prod:* Bill L. Hendricks; *col:* Tech. *sd:* Vit. 6 min. • Colonel Rimfire chases Cool Cat into a haunted house.

550. Big Hearted Bosko (*Looney Tunes*) 16 Apr. 1932; *p.c.:* Hugh Harman, Rudolf Ising prods for WB; *anim:* Isadore Freleng, Rollin Hamilton, Carmen Maxwell; *voices:* John T. Murray, Mary Moder; *mus:* Frank Marsales; *prod:* Leon Schlesinger; b&w. *sd:* Vit. 6 min. • Bosko and Bruno find an abandoned baby, take him home and try to stop his crying.

551. The Big Hearted Fish (*Aesop's Film Fable*) 20 Apr. 1926; *p.c.:* Fables Pictures Inc for Pathé; *dir:* Paul Terry; b&w. *sil.* 10 min. • While a couple of mice feed a fish on the river bank, a cat abducts the girl, throwing the boy mouse into the lake. A big fish remembers the kindness of the mice and rescues the boy mouse. He takes him to the villainous cat's cabin where the mouse beats up the cat, saving the girl and the fish gives them a ride back to the lake.

552. Big Heel-Watha (*Screwy Squirrel*) 21 Oct. 1944; *p.c.:* MGM; *dir:* Tex Avery; *story:* Heck Allen; *anim:* Ray Abrams, Preston Blair, Ed Love; *character des/lay:* Claude Smith; *sets:* John Didrik Johnsen; *ed:* Fred MacAlpin; *voices:* Wally Maher, Bill Thompson, Frank Graham, Sara Berner; *mus:* Scott Bradley; *prod:* Fred Quimby; *col:* Tech. *sd:* WE. 7 min. • The first Indian brave to capture food for the cooking pot is promised the hand of the chief's beautiful daughter, Minnie Hot-Cha.

553. A Big House Ain't a Home (*The Dogfather*) 31 Oct. 1974; *p.c.:* Mirisch/DFE for UA; *dir:* Gerry Chiniquy; *story:* David DeTiege; *anim:* Bob Richardson, Nelson Shin, Bob Bransford, John V. Gibbs; *lay:* Dick Ung; *back:* Richard H. Thomas; *voices:* Bob Holt, Daws Butler; *titles:* Arthur Leonardi; *mus:* Dean Elliott; *col:* DeLuxe. *sd:* RCA. 6 min. • Pug and Louie attempt to break a fellow hood out of prison.

554. Big House Blues (*Color Rhapsody*) 6 Mar. 1947; *p.c.:* Colum; *prod:* Raymond Katz, Henry Binder; *dir:* Howard Swift; *story:* Roy Jenkins; *anim:* Grant Simmons, Jay Sarbry; *lay:* Bill Weaver; *back:* Ed Starr; *ed:* Richard S. Jensen; *voice:* Harry E. Lang; *mus:* Eddie Kilfeather; *ph:* Frank Fisher; *col:* Tech. *sd:* WE. 6½ min. • Flippy the canary goes "Stir Crazy," imagining his cage to be a prison and the cat to be a prison warder.

555. Big House Bunny (*Looney Tunes*) 22 Apr. 1950; *p.c.:* WB; *dir:* I. Freleng; *story:* Tedd Pierce; *anim:* Virgil Ross, Arthur Davis, Gerry Chiniquy, Ken Champin; *lay:* Hawley Pratt; *back:* Phil de Guard; *ed:* Treg Brown; *voices:* Mel Blanc; *mus:* Carl Stalling; *prod mgr:* John W. Burton; *prod:* Edward Selzer; *col:* Tech. *sd:* Vit. 7 min. • Bugs tunnels away from the hunters and comes up in Sing Song Prison. There he encounters Warder Sam Schultz.

556. Big Man from the North (*Looney Tunes*) 10 Jan. 1931; *p.c.:* Hugh Harman, Rudolf Ising prods for WB; *anim:* Isadore Freleng, Robert Edmunds; *ed:* Dale Pickett; *voices:* Mary Moder; *mus:* Frank Marsales; b&w. *sd:* Vit. 6 min. • Mountie Bosko pursues a peg-legged desperado through a raging blizzard.

557. Big Mo (*Possible Possum*) July 1971; *p.c.:* TT for Fox; *col:* DeLuxe. *sd:* RCA. 5 min. • Poss and Menken Mouse's fishing is disrupted by the arrival of a giant mosquito. • See: *Possible Possum*

558. The Big Mouse-Take (*Loopy de Loop*) June 1965; *p.c.:* Hanna-Barbera for Colum; *prod/dir:* Joseph Barbera, William Hanna; *story dir:* Alex Lovy; *story:* Michael Maltese; *anim dir:* Charles A. Nichols; *anim:* Carlo Vinci, Hugh Fraser; *lay:* Bill Perez; *back:* Richard H. Thomas; *ed:* Donald A. Douglas; *voices:* Daws Butler, Doug Young, Jean van der Pyl; *mus:* Hoyt Curtin; *titles:* Lawrence Gobel; *prod mgr:* Howard Hanson; *col:* East. *sd:* RCA. 6½ min. • Loopy substitutes for a timid cat who's too afraid to catch a tough little mouse.

559. The Big Race (*Meany Miny Mo*) 3 Mar. 1937; *p.c.:* Univ; *dir:* Walter Lantz; *story:* Walter Lantz, Victor McLeod; *anim:* George Nicholas, Ben Clopton; *mus:* James Dietrich; b&w. *sd:* WE. 7 min. • The monks participate in a sixty-cylinder road race.

560. The Big Retreat (*Aesop's Film Fable*) 6 June 1926; *p.c.:* Fables Pictures Inc for Pathé; *dir:* Paul Terry; b&w. *sil.* 5 min. • Milton Mouse and Thomas Cat are recruited and transported to France, capture a wooden horse and bring it home to Mildred Mouse. While they fight over her, the enemy emerges from the horse and elopes with her.

561. The Big Reward (*Aesop's Film Fable*) 3 June 1927; *p.c.:* Fables Pictures Inc for Pathé; *dir:* Paul Terry; b&w. *sil.* 10 min. • Farmer Al Falfa captures a bandit dog and is rewarded with a bag full of more mice.

562. The Big Scare (*Aesop's Sound Fable*) 15 Aug. 1929; *p.c.:* Van Beuren for Pathé; *dir:* Paul Terry; *anim:* Frank Moser, Hugh Shields; *mus:* Josiah Zuro; *sd:* Maurice Manne; b&w. *sd:* RCA. 10 min. • Farmer Al decides to leave the earth before it leaves him when he is told of "The End of the World." He departs in an airplane and his family of animals hitch a ride.

563. The Big Shot (*Aesop's Film Fable*) 12 Apr. 1929; *p.c.:* Fables Pictures Inc for Pathé; *dir:* Paul Terry; b&w. *sil.* 10 min. • No story available.

564. The Big Snooze (*Chilly Willy*) 21 Oct. 1957; *p.c.:* Walter Lantz prods for Univ; *dir:* Alex Lovy; *story:* Homer Brightman; *anim:* Ray Abrams, La Verne Harding; *sets:* Raymond Jacobs, Art Landy; *voice:* Daws Butler; *mus:* Clarence Wheeler; *prod mgr:* William E. Garity; *col:* Tech. *sd:* RCA. 6 min. • The Grizzly National Park ranger tries to evict Chilly from sleeping with the hibernating bears without waking their slumber.

565. The Big Snooze (*Looney Tunes*) 5 Oct. 1946; *p.c.:* WB; *dir:* Robert Clampett; *anim:* Rod Scribner, I. Ellis, Manny Gould, J.C. Melendez; *lay:* Thomas McKimson; *back:* Philip de Guard; *ed:* Treg Brown; *voices:* Mel Blanc, Arthur Q. Bryan; *mus:* Carl Stalling; *prod mgr:* John W. Burton; *prod:* Edward Selzer *col:* Tech. *sd:* Vit. 7 min. • Tired of being Bugs' stooge, Elmer tears up his contract for a life of fishing. Bugs makes a nightmare of Elmer's tranquil dream.

566. The Big Tent (*Aesop's Film Fable*) 2 Sept. 1927; *p.c.:* Fables Pictures Inc for Pathé; *dir:* Paul Terry; b&w. *sil.* 10 min. • Milton Mouse is in love with Rita, the circus star. Tom Cat enters the scene and kidnaps Rita and, to add to the excitement, a lion breaks loose. Milton finally puts both the villain and the lion out of business.

567. The Big Top (*Paul Terry-Toon*) 12 May 1938; *p.c.:* TT for Educational/Fox; *dir:* Mannie Davis; *story:* John Foster; *mus:* Philip A. Scheib; b&w. *sd:* RCA. 6 min. • Puddy the pup crashes a "No Dogs Allowed" circus and ends up featuring as the "star act."

568. Big Top Bunny (*Merrie Melodies*) 6 Oct. 1951; *p.c.:* WB; *dir:* Robert McKimson; *story:* Tedd Pierce; *anim:* Charles McKimson, Rod Scribner, Phil de Lara, Bob Wickersham; *lay:* Peter Alvarado; *back:* Richard H. Thomas; *ed:* Treg Brown; *voices:* Mel Blanc; *mus:* Carl Stalling; *prod mgr:* John W. Burton; *prod:* Edward Selzer; *col:* Tech. *sd:* Vit. 7 min. • Bugs is brought into a circus act to replace Bruno the performing bear ... and Bruno intends to do something about it!

569. Big Trouble in Little China 2 July 1986; *p.c.:* Fox; *visual fx crew:* Boss Film: *creatures created by* Steve Johnson; *technical anim:* Annick Therrien, Rebecca Petrulli-Heskes, Samuel Recinos; *anim:* Glenn Chaika, Jeff Howard, Mauro Maressa, Peggy Ryan; *asst anim:* Renee Holt, Margaret Craig-Chang, Deborah Ann Gaydos, Eusebio Torres; *prod illustrator:* Brent Boates; *col:* DeLuxe. *sd:* Dolby stereo. Panavision 100 min. *l/a.* • Live-action comedy-fantasy set in San Francisco's Chinatown featuring Eastern mythology and magical martial artistry.

570. Big Wash (*Goofy*) 6 Feb. 1948; *p.c.:* Walt Disney prods for RKO; *dir:* Clyde Geronimi; *asst dir:* Lou Debney, Rusty Jones, Ralph Chadwick; *story:* Bill Berg, Milt Banta; *anim:* John Sibley, Hugh Fraser, Cliff Nordberg, Al Bertino, Phil Duncan; *fx:* George Rowley; *lay:* Al Zinnen; *back:* Merle Cox; *voices:* Pinto Colvig, James MacDonald; *mus:* Oliver Wallace; *col:* Tech. *sd:* RCA. 6 min. • Goofy sets out to wash Dolores, the circus elephant who adopts many guises to avoid having a bath.

571. Bigger and Better Jails (*Aesop's Film Fable*) 19 Jan. 1925; *p.c.:* Fables Pictures Inc for Pathé; *dir:* Paul Terry; b&w. *sil.* 10 min. • A wholesale jail delivery of mice, one elephant and a cat all escape by playing ball with rocks. The cats knock the guards unconcious with their baseball bats.

572. Bill of Hare (*Merrie Melodies*) June 1963; *p.c.:* WB; *dir:* Robert McKimson; *story:* John Dunn; *anim:* Keith Darling, Ted Bonnicksen, Warren Batchelder, George Grandpré; *sets:* Robert Gribbroek; *ed:* Treg Brown; *voices:* Mel Blanc; *mus:* Milt Franklyn; *prod mgr:* William Orcutt; *prod:* David H. DePatie; *col:* Tech. *sd:* Vit. 7 min. • Bugs fixes a meal for the Tazmanian Devil as a substitute for his eating a rabbit dinner.

573. The Bill Poster (*Krazy Kat*) 24 Nov. 1933; *p.c.:* Winkler for Colum; *prod:* Charles Mintz; *story:* Harry Love; *anim:* Allen Rose, Preston Blair; *mus:* Joe de Nat; *prod mgr:* James Bronis; b&w. *sd:* WE. 6 min. • Krazy is a bill poster whose horse is stung by a hornet and he has to chase after it.

574. Billboard Frolics (*Merrie Melodies*) 27 Jan. 1936; *p.c.:* Leon Schlesinger prods for WB; *dir:* I. Freleng; *anim:* Cal Dalton, Sandy Walker, Robert Clampett; *voices:* Billy Bletcher, Cliff Nazarro; *mus:* Bernard Brown; *prod sup:* Henry Binder, Raymond G. Katz; *col:* Tech. *sd:* Vit. 7 min. • Billboard signs come to life. A chick wanders away, is bothered by a cat and rescued by the other billboard characters.

575. Billion Dollar Boner (*Woody Woodpecker*) 5 Jan. 1960; *p.c.:* Walter Lantz prods for Univ; *dir:* Alex Lovy; *story:* Homer Brightman; *anim:* La Verne Harding, Don Patterson, Ray Abrams; *sets:* Raymond Jacobs, Art Landy; *voices:* Dal McKennon, Grace Stafford; *mus:* Eugene Poddany; *prod mgr:* William E. Garity; *col:* Tech. *sd:* RCA. 6 min. • O'Hoolihan stands to inherit one billion dollars providing he doesn't hurt a bird of any description. Woody is quick see the potential of this situation.

576. Billposters (*Donald & Goofy*) 17 May 1940; *p.c.:* Walt Disney prods for RKO; *dir:* Clyde Geronimi; *asst dir:* Errol Gray; *anim:* Larry Clemmons, Rex Cox, Edward Love, Ray Patin, Ken Peterson, Grant Simmons, Eddie Strickland; *fx:* George Rowley; *lay:* Lloyd Harting; *voices:* Clarence Nash, George A. Johnson; *mus:* Oliver Wallace; *col:* Tech. *sd:* RCA. 7 min. • The Goof runs into difficulties while pasting posters on windmill sales and Donald meets his nemesis in a goat.

577. Billy Boy 8 May 1954; *p.c.:* MGM; *dir:* Tex Avery; *story:* Heck Allen; *anim:* Ray Patterson, Robert Bentley, Walter Clinton, Grant Simmons, Michael Lah; *lay:* Ed Benedict *back:* John Didrik Johnsen; *ed:* Jim Faris; *voice:* Daws Butler; *mus:* Scott Bradley; *prod:* Fred Quimby; *col:* Tech. *sd:* WE. 6 min. • A farmer recieves the gift of a baby goat who literally eats him out of house and home.

578. The Billy Goat's Whiskers (*Paul Terry-Toon*) 10 Dec. 1937; *p.c.:* TT for Educational/Fox; *dir:* John Foster; *mus:* Philip A. Scheib; b&w. *sd:* WE. 6 min. • No story available.

579. Billy Mouse's Akwakade (*Terry-Toon*) 11 Aug. 1940; *p.c.:* TT for Fox; *dir:* Eddie Donnelly; *story:* John Foster; *mus:* Philip A. Scheib; *col:* Tech. *sd:* RCA. 6 min. • The mice provide an aquatic show in the bathtub. The cat and dog discover them and use a vacuum cleaner to eradicate them.

580. Bimbo's Express (*Talkartoon*) 22 Aug. 1931; *p.c.:* The Fleischer Studio for Para; *prod:* Max Fleischer; *dir:* Dave Fleischer; *mus:* Art Turkisher; b&w. *sd:* WE. 6 min. • Bimbo helps Betty move her house.

581. Bimbo's Initiation (*Talkartoon*) 24 July 1931; *p.c.:* The Fleischer Studio for Para; *prod:* Max Fleischer; *voice:* Charles Carver; *dir:* Dave Fleischer; *mus:* Art Turkisher; b&w. *sd:* WE. 6 min. • Bimbo is put through a rigorous and scary initiation for a club that he doesn't even wish to join.

582. Bingo Crosbyana (*Merrie Melodies*) 30 May 1936; *p.c.:* Leon Schlesinger prods for WB; *dir:* I. Freleng; *anim:* Cal Dalton, Sandy Walker; *des:* Zack Schwartz; *lay:* Melvin Millar; *ed:* Tregoweth E. Brown; *voices:*

Cliff Nazarro, Billy Bletcher; *mus:* Norman Spencer; *prod sup:* Henry Binder, Raymond G. Katz; *col:* Tech. *sd:* Vit. 7 min. • The local Don Juan fly steals the hearts of all the female flies but is proven yellow when a monstrous spider attacks.

583. The Bird 1965; *p.c.:* Murakami/Wolf Films; *dir/des/anim:* Fred Wolf; *ed:* Rich Harrison; *mus:* Paul Horn; *ph:* Wally Bulloch; *col. sd.* 4 min. • A man attempts to seduce a woman by caring for a bird. Once he's had his wicked way with her, he disposes with them both.

584. Bird-Brain Bird Dog (*Barney Bear*) 31 July 1954; *p.c.:* MGM; *dir:* Dick Lundy; *story:* Heck Allen, Jack Cosgriff; *anim:* Robert Bentley, Walter Clinton, Grant Simmons; *sets:* John Didrik Johnsen; *ed:* Jim Faris; *voice:* Paul Frees; *mus:* Scott Bradley; *ph:* Jack Stevens; *prod:* Fred Quimby; *col:* Tech. *sd:* WE. 6 min. • Barney buys a hunting dog, only to discover that it's a bird lover.

585. The Bird Came C.O.D. (*Merrie Melodies*) 17 Jan. 1942; *p.c.:* Leon Schlesinger prods for WB; *dir:* Charles M. Jones; *story:* E.S. (Ted) Pierce; *anim:* Ken Harris; *lay:* John McGrew; *back:* Eugene Fleury; *ed:* Treg Brown; *voices:* Mel Blanc; *mus:* Carl W. Stalling; *ph:* John W. Burton; *prod sup:* Henry Binder, Raymond G. Katz; *col:* Tech. *sd:* Vit. 7 min. • Goofy Cat has problems when delivering a palm tree to a theater.

586. A Bird in a Bonnet (*Merrie Melodies*) 27 Sept. 1957; *p.c.:* WB; *dir:* Friz Freleng; *story:* Warren Foster; *anim:* Gerry Chiniquy, Art Davis, Virgil Ross; *lay:* Hawley Pratt; *back:* Tom O'Loughlin; *ed:* Treg Brown; *voices:* Mel Blanc, June Foray, Daws Butler; *mus:* John Seeley; *prod:* John W. Burton; *col:* Tech. *sd:* Vit. 6 min. • Tweety takes refuge from the cat by posing as decoration on Granny's new hat.

587. A Bird in a Guilty Cage (*Merrie Melodies*) 30 Aug. 1952; *p.c.:* WB; *dir:* I. Freleng; *story:* Warren Foster; *anim:* Manuel Perez, Ken Champin, Virgil Ross, Arthur Davis; *lay:* Hawley Pratt; *back:* Irv Wyner; *ed:* Treg Brown; *voices:* Mel Blanc; *mus:* Carl Stalling; *prod mgr:* John W. Burton; *prod:* Edward Selzer; *col:* Tech. *sd:* Vit. 7 min. • Sylvester continues his pursuit of Tweety, this time in a Department Store.

588. The Bird Man (*Krazy Kat*) 1 Feb. 1935; *p.c.:* Winkler for Colum; *prod:* Charles Mintz; *story/anim:* Ben Harrison, Manny Gould; *mus:* Charles Rosoff; *prod mgr:* James Bronis; b&w. *sd:* RCA. 6 min. • No story available.

589. The Bird on Nellie's Hat (*Mello-Drama*) 19 June 1939; *p.c.:* Walter Lantz prods for Univ; *dir:* Alex Lovy; *story:* Victor McLeod, James Miele; *anim:* George Grandpré, Hicks Lokey; *sets:* Edgar Keichle; *mus:* Frank Marsales; *prod mgr:* George Hall; b&w. *sd:* WE. 7 min. • Nellie is tied to the railroad tracks by the villain and the bird on her hat flies to warn Dan the blacksmith, who comes to her assistance.

590. Bird Scouts (*Rainbow Parade*) 20 Sept. 1935; *p.c.:* Van Beuren for RKO; *dir:* Burt Gillett, Tom Palmer; *mus:* Winston Sharples; *col:* Ciné. *sd:* RCA. 7 min. • A cat invades the birds' scout camp.

591. The Bird Store (*Silly Symphony*) 5 Jan. 1932; *p.c.:* Walt Disney prods for Colum; *dir:* Wilfred Jackson; *anim:* Johnny Cannon, Les Clark, Gilles de Tremaudan, Norman Ferguson, Clyde Geronimi, David D. Hand, Albert Hurter, Jack King, Richard Lundy, Tom Palmer, Ben Sharpsteen, Rudy Zamora; *asst anim:* Chuck Couch; *voices:* A. Purvis Pullen; *mus:* Frank E. Churchill; b&w. *sd:* PCP. 6½ min. • A feline intruder attempts to catch a baby canary in a pet shop. The other birds attack the cat, forcing him into one of the cages.

592. The Bird Stuffer (*Krazy Kat*) 2 Jan. 1936; *p.c.:* Charles Mintz prods for Colum; *story:* Sid Marcus; *anim:* Art Davis; *mus:* Joe de Nat; *prod mgr:* James Bronis; b&w. *sd:* RCA. 6 min. • Taxidermist Krazy has a nightmare where all his stuffed animals come alive.

593. The Bird Symphony (*Terry-Toon*) July 1955; *p.c.:* TT for Fox; *dir:* Connie Rasinski; *story:* Tom Morrison; *anim:* Jim Tyer; *mus:* Philip A. Scheib; *ph:* Douglas Moye; *col:* Tech. *sd:* RCA. 6 min. • The birds stage a musical gathering in the forest, interrupted by the arrival of two cats.

594. The Bird Tower (*Terry-Toon*) 28 Nov. 1941; *p.c.:* TT for Fox; *dir:* Mannie Davis; *story:* John Foster; *voice:* Thomas Morrison; *mus:* Philip A. Scheib; *col:* Tech. *sd:* RCA. 7 min. • Our feathered friends establish themselves in a special hotel for birds while Storkowski conducts his orchestra.

595. The Bird Who Came to Dinner (*Woody Woodpecker*) 7 Mar. 1961; *p.c.:* Walter Lantz prods for Univ; *dir:* Paul J. Smith; *story:* Homer Brightman; *anim:* La Verne Harding, Les Kline, Ray Abrams; *sets:* Ray Huffine, Art Landy; *voices:* Dal McKennon, Grace Stafford; *mus:* Clarence Wheeler; *prod mgr:* William E. Garity; *col:* Tech. *sd:* RCA. 6 min. • Woody poses as a wind-up toy to gain access to a mansion and a free feed. He unfortunately falls victim to a destructive spoiled brat.

596. Birdland (*Paul Terry-Toon*) 23 Aug . 1935; *p.c.:* Moser & Terry for Educational/Fox; *dir:* Frank Moser, Paul Terry; *mus:* Philip A. Scheib; b&w. *sd:* WE. 5½ min. • Commentary on bird life.

597. Birds Anonymous (*Merrie Melodies*) 10 Aug. 1957; *p.c.:* WB; *dir:* Friz Freleng; *story:* Warren Foster; *anim:* Art Davis, Virgil Ross, Gerry Chiniquy; *lay:* Hawley Pratt; *back:* Boris Gorelick; *ed:* Treg Brown; *voices:* Mel Blanc; *mus:* Milt Franklyn; *prod mgr:* John W. Burton; *prod:* Edward Selzer; *col:* Tech. *sd:* Vit. 7 min. *Academy Award.* • Sylvester joins an organization to help stop him from eating birds.

598. Birds in Love (*Color Rhapsody*) 28 Oct. 1936; *p.c.:* Charles Mintz prods for Colum; *story:* Ben Harrison; *anim:* Manny Gould; *voices:* Elvia Allman, Leone Le Doux; *mus:* Joe de Nat; *prod mgr:* James Bronis; *col:* Tech. *sd:* RCA. 7 min. • The strains of "One Night of Love" puts two lovebirds in a romantic mood.

599. Birds in the Spring (*Silly Symphony*) 11 Mar. 1933; *p.c.:* Walt Disney prods for UA; *dir:* David D. Hand; *anim:* Johnny Cannon, Les Clark, Gilles de Tremaudan, Norman Ferguson, Clyde Geronimi, Jack King, Ben Sharpsteen; *mus:* Bert Lewis, Frank E. Churchill; *col:* Tech. *sd:* RCA. 7 min. • A baby bird wanders away, encounters a snake, upsets a hornets' nest and finally has to be rescued by his father ... then spanked!

600. Birds of a Father (*Looney Tunes*) Apr. 1961; *p.c.:* WB; *dir:* Robert McKimson; *story:* Dave DeTiege; *anim:* Warren Batchelder, George Grandpré, Ted Bonnicksen; *lay:* Robert Gribbroek; *back:* William Butler; *ed:* Treg Brown; *voices:* Mel Blanc; *mus:* Milt Franklyn; *prod mgr:* William Orcutt; *prod:* David H. DePatie; *col:* Tech. *sd:* Vit. 6 min. • Sylvester makes a desperate attempt to teach his bird-loving son how to catch and eat birds.

601. Birds of a Feather (*Silly Symphony*) 23 Jan. 1931; *p.c.:* Walt Disney prods for Colum; *dir:* Burton F. Gillett; *anim:* Johnny Cannon, Les Clark, Jack Cutting, Gilles de Tremaudan, Norman Ferguson, David D. Hand, Jack King, Richard Lundy, Tom Palmer, Ben Sharpsteen; *mus:* Bert Lewis; b&w. *sd:* PCP. 7 min. • A hawk snatches a chick from his brood, the other birds rescue and return him to his mother.

602. Birds of a Feather (*Woody Woodpecker*) Mar. 1965; *p.c.:* Walter Lantz prods for Univ; *dir:* Sid Marcus; *story:* Cal Howard; *anim:* Ray Abrams, Art Davis; *sets:* Ray Huffine, Art Landy; *voices:* Grace Stafford; *mus:* Walter Greene; *prod mgr:* William E. Garity; *col:* Tech. *sd:* RCA. 6 min. • Birdwatcher, Mrs. Meanie concentrates on watching Woody.

603. Birdy and the Beast (*Merrie Melodies*) 19 Aug. 1944; *p.c.:* Leon Schlesinger prods for WB; *dir:* Robert Clampett; *story:* Warren Foster; *anim/lay:* Tom McKimson; *back:* Michael Sasanoff; *ed:* Treg Brown; *voices:* Mel Blanc; *mus:* Carl W. Stalling; *prod mgr:* Henry Binder, Raymond G. Katz; *col:* Tech. *sd:* Vit. 7 min. • Tweety gives the cat who wants to eat him a run for his money.

604. Birth and Adventures of a Fountain Pen 1909; *p.c.:* Vit Corp; *dir:* James Stuart Blackton; b&w. *sil.* • An animated pen magically draws.

605. The Birth of a Flivver 1917; *p.c.:* Conquest Pictures for Thomas A. Edison; *dir:* Willis H. O'Brien; b&w. *sil.* • Two cavemen invent the wheel and try to attach it to an uncooperative dinosaur. Model animation.

606. The Birth of a Notion (*Looney Tunes*) 12 Apr. 1947; *p.c.:* WB; *dir:* Robert McKimson; *story:* Warren Foster, Robert Clampett; *anim:* Rob Scribner, Cal Howard, I. Ellis, Richard Bickenbach, Anatole Krisanoff, Fred Jones; *lay:* Cornett Wood; *back:* Richard H. Thomas; *ed:* Treg Brown; *character des:* Ben Shenkman; *voices:* Mel Blanc, Stan Freberg; *mus:* Carl Stalling; *prod mgr:* John W. Burton; *prod:* Edward Selzer; *col:* Tech. *sd:* Vit. 7 min. • A mad scientist (Peter Lorre) tries to remove Daffy's wishbone for an experiment.

607. Birth of a Toothpick (*Cartune*) 27 Feb. 1939; *p.c.:* Walter Lantz prods for Univ; Burt Gillett; *story:* Vic McLeod, Kin Platt; *anim:* Frank Tipper, La Verne Harding; *sets:* Edgar Keichle; *voices:* Danny Webb, Mel Blanc; *mus:* Frank Marsales; *prod mgr:* George Hall; *col:* Tech-2; *sd:* WE. 7½ min. • Big Dan, guardian of a huge pine tree named "Sylvia," rushes to curtail his beloved tree from being made into toothpicks.

608. The Birth of Jazz (*Krazy Kat*) 13 Apr. 1932; *p.c.:* Winkler for Colum; *prod:* Charles Mintz; *story:* Manny Gould; *anim:* Allen Rose, Jack Carr; *voice:* Jack Carr; *mus:* Joe de Nat; b&w. *sd:* WE. 6 min. • Krazy broadcasts "St Louis Blues" to the world.

609. Birthday (*Out of the Inkwell*) 4 Nov. 1922; *p.c.:* Inkwell Studio for Winkler; *prod:* Max Fleischer; *dir:* Dave Fleischer; b&w. sil. 8 min. • Ko-Ko lets off some celebration fireworks for his birthday and gets covered in wallpaper paste.

610. The Birthday Party (*Mickey Mouse*) 2 Jan. 1931; *p.c.:* Walter E. Disney for Colum; *dir:* Burton F. Gillett; *anim:* Johnny Cannon, Les Clark, Jack Cutting, Gilles de Tremaudan, David D. Hand, Wilfred Jackson, Jack King, Richard Lundy, Tom Palmer, Ben Sharpsteen; *voices:* Marcellite Garner, Walt Disney; *mus:* Bert Lewis; b&w. *sd:* PCP. 9 min. • Minnie stages a surprise party for Mickey. He is presented with a piano and has troubles with a runaway xylophone.

611. The Birthday Party (*Oswald*) 29 Mar. 1937; *p.c.:* Univ; *dir:* Walter Lantz; *story:* Walter Lantz, Victor McLeod; *anim:* Manuel Moreno, Louis Zukor, George Dane; *mus:* James Dietrich; b&w. *sd:* WE. 7 min. • Oswald and Elmer invite duck quintuplets to their birthday party. When they arrive, they proceed to wreck Oswald's happy home.

612. Biting the Dust (*Aesop's Film Fable*) 11 Dec. 1924; *p.c.:* Fables Pictures Inc for Pathé; *dir:* Paul Terry; b&w. sil. 5 min. • An animal football game between the baboons and a bunch of cats led by Farmer Al Falfa.

613. The Black Cauldron 24 July 1985; *p.c.:* The Walt Disney Co. for BV/Silver Screen Partners II; *dir:* Ted Berman, Richard Rich; *prod:* Joe Hale; *ex prod:* Ron Miller; *prod ex:* Edward Hanson; *prod co-ord:* Joseph Morris, Dennis Edwards, Ronald Rocha; *prod mgr:* Don Hahn; *asst dir:* Mark Hester, Terry Noss, Randy Paton; *story:* David Jonas, Vance Gerry, Ted Berman, Richard Rich, Al Wilson, Roy Morita, Peter Young, Art Stevens, Joe Hale, Tony Marino, Steve Hulett, Mel Shaw, Burny Mattinson, John Musker, Ron Clements, Doug Lefler; based on *The Chronicles of Prydain* series by Lloyd Alexander; *addit dial:* Rosemary Anne Sisson, Roy Edward Disney; *col styling:* James Colman; *ph fx:* Philip Meador, Ron Osenbaugh, Bill Kilduff; *key anim:* Walt Stanchfield; *anim:* Andreas Deja, Hendel Butoy, Dale Baer, Ron Husband, Jay Jackson, Barry Temple, Tom Ferriter, Ruben Aquino, Cyndee Whitney, George Scribner, Mark Henn, Terry Harrison, Phil Nibbelink, Steven Gordon, Doug Krohn, Shawn Keller, Mike Gabriel, Philip Young, Jesse Cosio, Ruben Procopio, Viki Anderson, David Block, Charlie Downs, Sandra Borgmeyer, David Pacheco, Kathy Zielinski, Sue Dicicco, Jill Colbert, Richard Hoppe, Kevin Wurzer, David Brain, Sylvia Mattinson, Maurice Hunt, Tony Anselmo, Jane Baer, Dorothea Baker, Philo Barnhart, Bill Berg, Ben Burgess, Reed Cardwell, Brian Clift, Jesus Cortes, Rick Farmiloe, June Fujimoto, Terry Hamada, Ray Harris, Jeffrey Lynch, Mauro Maressa, Michael McKinley, Jim Mitchell, Brett Newton, Gilda Palinginis, Phil Phillipson, David Pruiksma, Natasha Selfridge, Toby Shelton, David Stephan, Russ Stoll, George Sukara, Larry White; *fx:* Don Paul, Mark Dindal, Jeff Howard, Patricia Peraza, Scott Santoro, Glenn Chaika, Barry Cook, Ted Kierscey, Kelvin Yasuda, Bruce Woodside, Kimberley Knowlton, Alex Gonzales, Gail Finkeldei, Tom Hush, Joe Lanzisero, Rolando Mercado, Steve Starr, John Tucker; *back:* Sue Adnopoz, Anthony DeRosa, Barbara DeRosa, Denise Ford, Edward Goral, Tina Grued, Christine Liffers, Elyse Pastel, Kaaren Spooner, Louis Tate, Peggy Tonkonogy, Jane Tucker, Maria Ramocki-Rosett, Stephan Zupkas; *fx:* Ed Coffey, Peter Gullerud, Christine Harding, Vicki Banks, Esther Barr, Dave Bossert, Gary Trousdale; *inbet:* Kelly Asbury, Stephen Hickman, Michael Horowitz, Mona Hosbjor, Eileen Lambert, Robert Minkoff, Alex Topete; *lay:* Mike Hodgson; *styling:* Don Griffith, Guy Vasilovich, Glenn Vilppu, Dan Hansen, William Frake III, David Dunnet, Karen Keller, Greg Martin, Kurt Anderson, Carol Holman Grosvenor, Frank Frezzo; *character des:* Andreas Deja, Mike Ploog, Phil Nibbelink, Al Wilson, David Jonas; *Scene plan:* David Thomas, Don Bourland, Brian Legrady, Bob Mills, Rick Sullivan; *back:* Donald Towns, Brian Sebern, John Emerson, Tia Kratter, Lisa Keene, Andrew Phillipson; *Xerox:* Bill Brazner, Carmen Sanderson, Dede Faber, Jean-Pierre Gagnon, Raffi Koumashian, Robyn Roberts, Bert Wilson; *fx:* Bernie Gagliano; *col models:* Sylvia Roemer, Brigitte Strother, Debbie Jorgensborg, Ann Paeff; *blue sketch:* Roxy Novotny Steven, Cathy Zar; *i&p:* Becky Fallberg, Gretchen Albrecht, Ginni Mack, Penny Campsie, Karen Comella, Dodie Roberts, Betty Stark, Ray Owens; *clean-up:* Retta Davidson, Dave Suding, Chuck Williams, M. Flores Nichols, Martin Korth, Tom Ferriter, Fujiko MillerIsis Thompson, Lureline Weatherly, Wesley Chun; *anim check:* Janet Bruce, Karen Paat, Lisa Poitevint, Jill Stirdivant, Mavis Shafer; *Xerox check:* Margaret Trindade, Darlene Kanagy, Cherie Miller, Tatsuko Deramirez, Maria Fenyvesi, Hortensia Casagran, Wilma Baker, Robin Police; *anim consultant:* Eric Larson; *voices: Narration:* John Huston; *Taran:* Grant Bardsley; *Princess Eilonwy:* Susan Sheridan; *The Horned King:* John Hurt; *Dallben:* Freddie Jones; *Fflewddur:* Nigel Hawthorne; *King Eidilleg:* Arthur Malet; *Gurgi & Doli:* John Byner; *Fairfolk:* Lindsey Rich, Brian Call, Gregory Levinson; *Orddo:* Eda Reise Merin; *Orwen:* Adele Malis-Morey; *Orgoch:* Billie Hayes; *Henchmen:* Peter Renoudet, Wayne Allwine, Steve Hale, James Almanazar, Phil Nibbelink, Phil Fundacaro, Jack Laing; *Creeper:* Phil Fundacaro; *mus:* Elmer Bernstein; *orch:* Peter Bernstein; *mus sup:* Jay Lawton; *mus preperation:* Norman Corey; *mus ed:* Jack Wadsworth, Kathy Durning; *titles:* David Jonas, Ed Garbert; *sd:* Bob Hathaway, Shawn Murphy, Richard Portman, Nick Alphin, Frank C. Regula; *sd fx:* Mike McDonough, James Melton, Jim Koford, Armetta Jackson, Paul Holzborn, Wayne Allwine; *anim ph:* Jim Pickel, Ed Austin, John Aardal, Errol Laubry, Frank Tompkins, Brandy Whittington, James Catania, Paul Wainess, Kieran Mulgrew, Roy Harris, Jere Kepeneck, Neil Viker, Steve Hale, Brian Holechek, Rick Taylor, Dan Bunn; *special ph fx:* Philip Meador, Ron Osenbaugh, Bill Kilduff; *prod co-ord:* Joseph Morris, Dennis Edwards, Ronald Rocha; *prod mgr:* Don Hahn; *col:* Tech. *sd:* Dolby stereo. 80 min. • Taran, a young pig keeper, goes on an adventure to rescue his clairvoyant pig who has been kidnapped by the evil Horned King in expectation of the creature leading him to the mysterious Black Cauldron. Taran and his friends do their best to reach the Cauldron and destroy it before the Horned King can unleash its malevolent powers.

614. The Black Duck (*Aesop's Film Fable*) 17 Mar. 1929; *p.c.:* Fables Pictures Inc for Pathé; *dir:* Paul Terry; b&w. sil. 10 min. • No story available.

615. The Black Hole 20 Dec.1979; *p.c.:* Walt Disney Prods for BV; *dir:* Gary Nelson; *miniature fx:* Peter Ellenshaw; *miniature fx ph:* Art Cruikshank; *fx anim:* Joe Hale, Dorse A. Lanpher, Ted C. Kiercey; *miniature mechanical fx/chief model maker:* Terence Saunders. *col:* Tech. *sd:* RCA. 98 min. *l/a.* Academy Award nomination. • Live-action science fiction fantasy: An exploring spaceship, the U.S.S. *Palomino*, on its return to Earth stumbles across a lost ship drifting near a black hole. The ship is commanded by a captain who intends to turn his former crew into robots and enter the Hole. The *Palomino* is damaged by a storm as they escape and the crew plummets into the abyss. Computer animation used.

616. Black Magic (*Aesop's Film Fable*) 19 Oct. 1924; *p.c.:* Fables Pictures Inc for Pathé; *dir:* Paul Terry; b&w. sil. 5 min. • Friend mouse eludes and annoys the cat by using his knowledge of magical stunts.

617. The Black Scorpion 1957; *p.c.:* WB; *prod:* Frank Melford, Jack Dietz; *fx:* Willis O'Brien, Peter Peterson; b&w. *sd.* 86 min. *l/a/anim.* • Live-action science fiction feature where giant (animated) scorpions rampage Mexico.

618. The Black Sheep (*Aesop's Film Fable*) 9 Jan. 1924; *p.c.:* Fables Pictures Inc for Pathé; *dir:* Paul Terry; b&w. sil. 5 min. • A pup disgraces his family by smoking a pipe and is banished. His chance to atone comes when an eagle snatches the pet gosling and he rescues it by air-plane, becoming a public hero.

619. The Black Sheep (*Paul Terry-Toon*) Oct. 1934; *p.c.:* Moser & Terry for Educational/Fox; *dir:* Frank Moser, Paul Terry; *mus:* Philip A. Scheib; b&w. *sd:* WE. 5 min. • The little black sheep scares the others by shouting "Wolf!" but when a real wolf arrives on the scene they think it's another trick.

620. The Black Sheep (*Scrappy*) 7 Sept. 1932; *p.c.:* Winkler for Colum; *prod:* Charles Mintz; *story:* Dick Huemor; *anim:* Sid Marcus, Art Davis; *mus:* Joe de Nat; *prod mgr:* James Bronis; b&w. *sd:* RCA. 6 min. • Scrappy and his flock won't let the gravel-voiced black sheep sing with them. The lamb has his revenge by trapping them all in a barn and stealing their wool.

621. The Black Spider (*Paul Terry-Toon*) 1 Nov. 1931; *p.c.:* Terry, Moser & Coffman for Educational/Fox; *dir:* Frank Moser, Paul Terry; *mus:* Philip A. Scheib; b&w. *sd:* WE. 6 min. • A villainous spider invades the bugs' castle, imprisons the King and inflicts his wicked designs on the beautiful princess.

622. Blackboard Jumble (*Droopy*) 4 Oct 1957; *p.c.:* MGM; *prod:* William Hanna, Joseph Barbera; *dir:* Michael Lah; *anim:* Herman Cohen, Bill Schipek, Ken Southworth, Irven Spence; *character des/lay:* Ed Benedict; *back:* F. Montealegre; *ed:* Jim Faris; *voices:* Daws Butler; *mus:* Scott Bradley; *ph:* Jack Stevens; *prod mgr:* Hal Elias; *col:* Tech. *sd:* WE. 6 min. CS. • A wolf takes over as teacher to classroom of Droopies in a reworking of *Three Little Pups*.

623. Blackboard Revue (*Color Rhapsody*) 15 Mar. 1940; *p.c.:* Cartoon Films Ltd for Colum; *prod/dir:* Ub Iwerks; *ed:* George Winkler; *voices:* Mel Blanc, The Rhythmettes; *mus:* Eddie Kilfeather, Joe de Nat; *ph:* Otto Reimer; *prod mgr:* James Bronis; *col:* Tech. *sd:* RCA. 6½ min. • Chalk drawings on a schoolroom blackboard come alive at midnight.

624. The Blacksheep Blacksmith • See: *Baa Baa Blacksmith*

625. Blame It on the Samba 1 Apr. 1955; *p.c.:* Walt Disney prods for BV; *dir:* Clyde Geronimi; *col:* Tech. *sd:* RCA. 6 min. *l/a/anim.* • Donald and José Carioca get rid of their "blues" when they dance to Ethel Smith's organ music. • See: *Melody Time*

626. A Blaze of Glory (*Aesop's Film Fable*) 28 Jan. 1928; *p.c.:* Fables Pictures Inc for Pathé; *dir:* Paul Terry, Mannie Davis; b&w. *sil.* 10 min. • Thomas Cat is booted out when he fails to rid the farmhouse of mice. As the farmer sleeps, his house burns and the mice fill a fire extinguisher with benzine, resulting in his property becoming a total loss.

627. Blind Date (*Heckle & Jeckle*) Feb. 1954; *p.c.:* TT for Fox; *dir:* Eddie Donnelly; *story/voices:* Tom Morrison; *anim:* Jim Tyer; *mus:* Philip A. Scheib; *ph:* Douglas Moye; *col:* Tech. *sd:* RCA. 7 min. • A millionaire offers a reward for his long-lost childhood sweetheart. Heckle disguises Jeckle as the girl but obtaining the cash isn't as easy as they had imagined.

628. Blitz Wolf 22 Aug. 1942; *p.c.:* MGM; *dir:* Tex Avery; *story:* Rich Hogan; *anim:* Ray Abrams, Irven Spence, Preston Blair, Ed Love; *sets:* John Didrik Johnsen; *ed:* Fred MacAlpin; *voices:* Bill Thompson, Frank Graham, Sara Berner, Leone Le Doux; *mus:* Scott Bradley; *ph:* Gene Moore; *prod:* Fred Quimby; *col:* Tech. *sd:* WE. 9 min. *Academy Award nomination.* • The story of the Three Little Pigs in a wartime setting featuring the wolf as Hitler.

629. The Blob 8 Aug. 1988; *p.c.:* Palisades California, Inc./Braveworld for TriStar; *creature fx designed and created by* Lyle Conway; *fx:* Dream Quest Images sup: Hoyt Yeatman; *anim sup:* Jeff Burks; *stop-motion anim:* Mark Sullivan; *addit creature fx des/sup:* Stuart Ziff; *miniature construction:* Greg Jein, Inc.; *Rotoscope sup:* James Valentine; *col:* Tech. *sd:* Ultra Stereo. 95 min. *l/a.* • Live-action science fiction remake of the 1958 classic about a fireball that creates a glutinous mass which terrifies a town when it comes alive.

630. Blow Me Down (*Popeye*) 27 Oct. 1933; *p.c.:* The Fleischer Studio for Para; *prod:* Max Fleischer; *dir:* Dave Fleischer; *anim:* Willard Bowsky, William Sturm; *voice:* William A. Costello, Charles Carver; *mus:* Sammy Timberg; b&w. *sd:* WE. 7 min. • Popeye visits a Mexican cantina to see Olive as a dancer. Bandito Bluto arrives and shoots the place up but Popeye and spinach save the day.

631. The Blow-Out (*Looney Tunes*) 4 Apr. 1936; *p.c.:* Leon Schlesinger for WB; *dir:* Fred Avery; *anim:* Charles Jones, Sidney Sutherland; *voices:* Joe Dougherty, Fred Avery; *mus:* Bernard Brown; b&w. *sd:* Vit. 6 min. • Porky tries to gain a gratuity by returning a package containing (unbeknown to him) a bomb to a Mad Bomber.

632. Blue Aces Wild (*Blue Racer*) 16 Mar. 1973; *p.c.:* Mirisch/DFE for UA; *dir:* Gerry Chiniquy; *story:* John W. Dunn; *anim:* Bob Matz, Manny Gould, Don Williams, John Gibbs; *lay:* Dick Ung; *back:* Richard H. Thomas; *ed:* Rick Steward; *voices:* Larry D. Mann, Anthena Lorde, Paul Winchell; *mus:* Doug Goodwin; *ph:* John Burton Jr.; *prod mgr:* Stan Paperny; *col:* DeLuxe. *sd:* RCA. 6 min. • In exchange for some "Snake Sweat," a wizard grants The Racer three wishes.

633. Blue Cat Blues (*Tom & Jerry*) 16 Nov. 1956; *p.c.:* MGM; *prod/dir:* William Hanna, Joseph Barbera; *anim:* Ed Barge, Irven Spence, Lewis Marshall, Kenneth Muse; *lay:* Dick Bickenbach; *back:* Robert Gentle; *ed:* Jim Faris; *voice:* Paul Frees; *mus:* Scott Bradley; *ph:* Jack Stevens; *prod mgr:* Hal Elias; *col:* Tech. *sd:* WE. 6 min. CS. • Jerry relates a tale of unrequited love that has led to Tom's present condition ... sitting on the railroad tracks awaiting the next train.

634. The Blue Danube (*MGM cartoon*) 28 Oct. 1939; *p.c.:* MGM; *prod/dir:* Hugh Harman; *story:* Hugh Harman, Jack Cosgriff, Charles McGirl; *anim:* William Hanna, William Littlejohn; *lay:* John Meandor; *back:* Joe Smith; *ed:* Fred MacAlpin; *mus:* Scott Bradley; *prod mgr:* Fred Quimby; *col:* Tech. *sd:* WE. 7 min. • Set to Johann Strauss' music, the woodland creatures and nymphs gather "Nature's Blue" to make the Danube the right color.

635. Blue Hawaii (*Screen Song*) 13 Jan. 1950; *p.c.:* Famous for Para; *dir:* Seymour Kneitel; *story:* Larz Bourne; *anim:* Al Eugster, Wm. B. Pattengill; *sets:* Lloyd Hallock Jr.; *mus:* Winston Sharples; *song:* Leo Robin, Ralph Rainger; *ph:* Leonard McCormick; *prod mgr:* Sam Buchwald; *col:* Tech. *sd:* RCA. 7 min. • An exposé on Hawaii where pineapples grow already canned and a grass-skirted moon bounces over the singalong. Caricatures of Jimmy Durante, Groucho and Harpo Marx.

636. Blue Monday (*Captain & the Kids*) 5 Feb. 1938; *p.c.:* MGM; *dir:* William Hanna; *voices:* Billy Bletcher, Martha Wentworth; *mus:* Scott Bradley; *prod mgr:* Fred Quimby; *col:* sep. *sd:* WE. 7 min. • Der Captain takes over the housekeeping from Mama with disastrous results.

637. Blue Plate Symphony (*Heckle & Jeckle*) Nov. 1954; *p.c.:* TT for Fox; *dir:* Connie Rasinski; *story/voices:* Tom Morrison; *anim:* Jim Tyer; *mus:* Philip A. Scheib; *ph:* Douglas Moye; *col:* Tech. *sd:* RCA. 6 min. • Some gangsters take over the magpies' Diner. A fight breaks out and they beat off their adversaries with kitchen utensils.

638. Blue Racer Blues (*Blue Racer*) 31 Dec. 1972; *p.c.:* Mirisch/DFE for UA; *dir:* Art Davis; *story:* John W. Dunn; *anim:* Bob Richardson, Jim Davis, Manny Gould, Don Williams; *lay:* Dick Ung; *back:* Richard H. Thomas; *ed:* Allan R. Potter; *voices:* Larry D. Mann, Tom Holland; *mus:* Doug Goodwin; *ph:* John Burton Jr.; *prod sup:* Stan Paperny, Harry Love; *col:* DeLuxe. *sd:* RCA. 6 min. • The Racer ventures to the big city in search of love and affection from humans.

639. Blue Rhythm (*Mickey Mouse*) 7 Aug. 1931; *p.c.:* Walter E. Disney for Colum; *dir:* Burton F. Gillett; *anim:* Ed Benedict, Johnny Cannon, Les Clark, Joseph d'Igalo, Gilles de Tremaudan, Norman Ferguson, Jack King, Richard Lundy, Tom Palmer, Frank Tipper, Rudy Zamora; *asst anim:* Charles Byrne, Jack Cutting, Hardie Gramatky, Harry Reeves, Cecil Surry; *voices:* Marcellite Garner, Walt Disney; *mus:* Bert Lewis; b&w. *sd:* PCP. 6 min. • Mickey leads the orchestra, imitates Ted Lewis and plays W.C. Handy's "St. Louis Blues."

640. Blue Ribbon Hit Parade *p.c.:* WB; *col:* Tech; *sd:* Vit. • **1944: Let It Be Me** 16 Sept. **September in the Rain** 30 Sept. **Sunday Go to Meetin' Time** 28 Oct. **I Love to Singa** 18 Nov. **Plenty of Money and You** 9 Dec. • **1945: The Fella with the Fiddle** 20 Jan. **When I Yoo Hoo** 24 Feb. **I Only Have Eyes for You** 17 Mar. **Ain't We Got Fun** 21 Apr. **I'm a Big Shot Now** 4 Aug. **Speaking of the Weather** 21 Aug. **Old Glory** 25 Aug. **The Busy Bakers** 15 Sept. **A Sunbonnet Blue** 6 Oct. **The Lyin' Mouse** 22 Dec. • **1946: The Good Egg** 5 Jan. **The Trial of Mr. Wolf** 9 Feb. **The Little Lion Hunter** 23 Mar. **Fresh Fish** 6 Apr. **Daffy Duck and Egghead** 20 Apr. **Katnip Kollege** 4 May. **The Night Watchman** 18 May. **Little Brother Rat** 8 Jun. **Johnny Smith & Poka Huntas** 22 Jun. **Robin Hood Makes Good** 6 July. **Little Red Walking Hood** 17 Aug. **Fox Pop** 28 Sept. **The Wacky Worm** 12 Oct. **You're An Education** 26 Oct. **Have You Got Any Castles?** 7 Dec. • **1947: Pigs Is Pigs** 22 Feb. **A Cat's Tale** 29 Mar. **Goofy Groceries** 19 Apr. **Dog Gone Modern** 14 Jun. **The Sneezing Weasel** 26 July. **Rhapsody in Rivets** 16 Aug. **Sniffles Bells the Cat** 20 Sept. **Cagey Canary** 11 Oct. **Now That Summer Is Gone** 22 Nov. **Dangerous Dan McFoo** 20 Dec. • **1948: Hobo Gadget Band** 17 Jan. **Little Pancho Vanilla** 20 Mar. **Don't Look Now** 10 Apr. **The Curious Puppy** 24 Apr. **Circus Today** 22 May. **Little Blabber Mouse** 12 Jun. **The Squawink' Hawk** 10 July. **A Tale of Two Kitties** 31 July. **Pigs in a Polka** 14 Aug. **Greetings Bait** 28 Aug. **Hiss and Make Up** 18 Sept. **Hollywood Steps Out** 2 Oct. **An Itch in Time** 30 Oct. **Fin 'n Catty** 11 Dec. • **1949: Bedtime for Sniffles** 1 Jan. **Presto Change-o** 5 Feb. **The Swooner Crooner** 12 Feb. **Hop, Skip and a Chump** 5 Mar. **He Was Her Man** 2 Apr. **I Wanna Be a Sailor** 30 Apr. **Flop Goes the Weasel** 21 May. **Horton Hatches the Egg** 18 Jun. **The Egg Collector** 16 July. **The Mice Will Play** 6 Aug. **Inki and the Minah Bird** 20 Aug. **Tom Thumb in Trouble** 23 Sept. **Farm Frolics** 14 Oct. **The Hep Cat** 12 Nov. **Toy Trouble** 31 Dec. • **1950: My Favorite Duck** 28 Jan. **The Sheepish Wolf** 4 Mar. **Double**

Chaser 25 Mar. **Fifth Column Mouse** 22 Apr. **Inki and the Lion** 20 May. **Tick Tock Tuckered** 3 Jun. **Booby Hatched** 1 July. **Trap Happy Porky** 5 Aug. **Lost and Foundling** 26 Aug. **Fagin's Freshmen** 16 Sept. **Slightly Daffy** 14 Oct. **The Aristo-Cat** 11 Nov. **The Unbearable Bear** 9 Dec. • *1951:* **Duck Soup to Nuts** 6 Jan. **Flowers for Madame** 3 Feb. **Life with Feathers** 3 Mar. **Peck Up Your Troubles** 24 Mar. **The Odor-Able Kitty** 21 Apr. **Book Revue** 19 May. **Stage Fright** 23 Jun. **Sioux Me** 21 July. **Stupid Cupid** 1 Sept. **Holiday for Shoestrings** 15 Sept. **The Lady in Red** 13 Oct. **Sniffles and the Bookworm** 10 Nov. **Goldilocks & the Jivin' Bears** 1 Dec. • *1952:* **Of Thee I Sting** 12 Jan. **From Hand to Mouse** 9 Feb. **The Brave Little Bat** 15 Mar. **Snow Time for Comedy** 12 Apr. **Hush My Mouse** 3 May. **Baby Bottleneck** 14 June. **The Bug Parade** 12 July. **Merry Old Soul** 2 Aug. **Fresh Airedale** 30 Aug. **A Feud There Was** 13 Sept. **A Day at the Zoo** 8 Nov. **The Early Worm Gets the Bird** 29 Nov. • *1953:* **A Tale of Two Mice** 10 Jan. **The Bashful Buzzard** 7 Feb. **The Country Mouse** 14 Mar. **The Little Dutch Plate** 11 Apr. **Ain't That Ducky** 2 May. **The Mighty Hunters** 13 Jun. **The Fighting 691/2** 11 July. **Sniffles Takes a Trip** 1 Aug. **Wacky Wild Life** 29 Aug. **Old Glory** 12 Sept. **Walky Talky Hawky** 17 Oct. **Birth of a Notion** 7 Nov. **The Eager Beaver** 28 Nov. **Scent-Imental Over You** 26 Dec. • *1954:* **Of Fox and Hounds** 6 Feb. **Roughly Squeeking** 27 Feb. **Hobo Bobo** 27 Mar. **The Gay Anties** 24 Apr. **The Cat Came Back** 5 Jun. **One Meat Brawl** 10 July. **Along Came Daffy** 24 July. **Mouse Menace** 14 Aug. **Rhapsody in Rivets** 11 Sept. **Inki at the Circus** 16 Oct. **The Foxy Duckling** 6 Nov. **The Shell-Shocked Egg** 27 Nov. **The Trial of Mr. Wolf** 26 Dec. • *1955:* **Back Alley Oproar** 5 Feb. **You Were Never Duckier** 26 Feb. **House Hunting Mice** 2 Apr. **Crowing Pains** 23 Apr. **Hop, Look and Listen** 4 Jun. **Tweetie Pie** 25 Jun. **The Goofy Gophers** 23 July. **What's Brewin' Bruin?** 20 Aug. **Dog-gone Cats** 10 Sept. **The Rattled Rooster** 22 Oct. **Fair and Worm-er** 5 Nov. **The Mouse-Merized Cat** 26 Nov. **The Foghorn Leghorn** 24 Dec. • *1956:* **Bone, Sweet Bone** 21 Jan. **I Taw a Putty Tat** 25 Feb. **Two Gophers from Texas** 31 Mar. **Kit for Cat** 21 Apr. **Scaredy Cat** 2 May. **Horse Fly Fleas** 7 July. **Little Orphan Airedale** 4 Aug. **Daffy Dilly** 18 Aug. **Mouse Mazurka** 15 Sept. **Paying the Piper** 20 Oct. **Daffy Duck Hunt** 17 Nov. **Henhouse Henery** 1 Dec. • *1957:* **Swallow the Leader** 19 Jan. **For Scent-Imental Reasons** 2 Feb. **Mouse Wreckers** 9 Mar. **Dough for the Do-Do** 6 Apr. **Fast and Furry-ous** 27 Apr. **Bear Feat** 18 May. **Each Dawn I Crow** 29 Jun. **Bad Ol' Putty Tat** 27 July. • 1957 reissues of 168 Warner Bros. color cartoons with new title cards.

641. Bluebeard's Brother (*Paul Terry–Toon*) 29 May 1932; *p.c.:* Moser & Terry for Educational/Fox; *dir:* Frank Moser, Paul Terry; *mus:* Philip A. Scheib; b&w. *sd:* WE. 6 min. • A crazed spider travels from his castle to capture the circus bareback rider.

642. Bluebird's Baby (*Color Rhapsody*) 21 Jan. 1938; *p.c.:* Charles Mintz prods for Colum *story:* Ben Harrison; *anim:* Manny Gould; *voices:* Dave Weber, Leone Le Doux, The Rhythmettes; *mus:* Joe de Nat; *prod mgr:* James Bronis; *col:* Tech. *sd:* RCA. 7 min. • A mother and father bluebird find an orphan on their doorstep and set out to find his parents.

643. Blues (*Paul Terry-Toons*) 3 Sept. 1931; *p.c.:* Terry, Moser & Coffman for Educational/Fox; *dir:* Frank Moser, Paul Terry; *anim:* Pearson, Vladimir Tytla; *mus:* Philip A. Scheib; b&w. *sd:* WE. 6 min. • Frogs in a mill pond.

644. Blunder Below (*Popeye*) 13 Feb. 1942; *p.c.:* The Fleischer Studio for Para; *prod:* Max Fleischer; *dir:* Dave Fleischer; *story:* Bill Turner, Ted Pierce; *anim:* David Tendlar, Harold Walker; *ed:* Kitty Pfister; *voices:* Jack Mercer, Michael Fitzmaurice; *mus:* Sammy Timberg; *ph:* Charles Schettler. *prod sup:* Sam Buchwald, Isadore Sparber; b&w. *sd:* WE. 6½ min. • Popeye can't comprehend the anti-sub maneuvers he receives but goes into action in his own inimitable way when an enemy sub is sighted.

645. The Boa Friend (*Blue Racer*) 11 Feb. 1973; *p.c.:* Mirisch/DFE for UA; *dir:* Gerry Chiniquy; *story:* John W. Dunn; *anim:* Lloyd Vaughan, Bob Matz, Bob Bransford, Reuben Timmens, Norm McCabe; *lay:* Dick Ung; *back:* Richard H. Thomas; *ed:* Rick Steward; *voices:* Larry D. Mann, Joan Gerber; *mus:* Doug Goodwin; *ph:* John Burton Jr.; *prod sup:* Stan Paperny, Harry Love; *col:* DeLuxe. *sd:* RCA. 6 min. • The Racer attempts to woo his girl away from the attentions of a Boa Constrictor.

646. Boat Builders (*Mickey Mouse*) 25 Feb. 1938; *p.c.:* Walt Disney prods for RKO; *dir:* Ben Sharpsteen; *story:* Jack Kinney; *anim:* Chuck Couch, Jack Hannah, Gilles de Tremaudan, Clyde Geronimi, Ray Patterson, Archie Robin, Paul Satterfield, Eddie Strickland; *voices:* Clarence Nash, Pinto Colvig, Leone Le Doux, Walt Disney; *mus:* Paul J. Smith; *col:* Tech. *sd:* RCA. 7 min. • Mickey, Donald and Goofy join forces in a hapless attempt to assemble a "Do-It-Yourself" boat.

647. Bobby Bumps' Adventures 13 Aug 1915; *p.c.:* Bray prods for Univ; *dir/anim:* Earl Hurd; b&w. *sil.* 5 min. *l/a/anim.* • No story available.

648. Bobby Bumps and Co. (*Pen & Ink Vaudeville*) 4 July 1925; *p.c.:* Hurd prods for Educational; *dir/anim:* Earl Hurd; b&w. *sil.* 5 min. *l/a/anim.* • Earl Hurd sketches a vaudeville house with overture and a regular line of performers.

649. Bobby Bumps in Before and After (*Paramount Cartoons*) 20 Nov. 1918; *p.c.:* Bray prods for Para; *dir/anim:* Earl Hurd; b&w. *sil.* 5 min. • Bobby sells Dad a lotion as "Hair Restorer" then glues feathers to Pa's head as he snoozes.

650. Bobby Bumps Puts a Beanery on the Bum (*Paramount-Bray Pictograph*) 4 Dec. 1918; *p.c.:* Bray prods for Para; *dir/anim:* Earl Hurd; b&w. *sil.* 5 min. *l/a/anim.* • The artist forgets to draw Fido's tail, then Bobby fills-in for the chef in a beanery.

651. Bobolink Pink (*Pink Panther*) 30 Dec. 1975; *p.c.:* Mirisch/Geoffrey/DFE for UA; *dir:* Gerry Chiniquy; *story:* John W. Dunn; *anim:* John Gibbs, Virgil Ross, Don Williams, Nelson Shin; *lay:* Dick Ung; *back:* Richard H. Thomas; *ed:* Rick Steward; *mus:* Walter Greene; *theme tune:* Henry Mancini; *ph:* John Burton Jr.; *prod mgr:* Lee Gunther; *col:* DeLuxe. *sd:* RCA. 6 min. • The Panther teaches a young bird, who's scared of high places, to fly.

652. The Body in the Bag (*Aesop's Film Fable*) 13 July 1924; *p.c.:* Fables Pictures Inc for Pathé; *dir:* Paul Terry; b&w. *sil.* 5 min. • A villain abducts the bride and the groom pursues them over land, sea and air, finally crowning the blackguard with a brick.

653. The Bodyguard (*Tom & Jerry*) 27 July 1944; *p.c.:* MGM; *dir:* William Hanna, Joseph Barbera; *anim:* Kenneth Muse, Pete Burness, Ray Patterson, Irven Spence; *lay:* Harvey Eisenberg; *back:* Robert Gentle; *ed:* Fred MacAlpin; *voice:* Billy Bletcher; *mus:* Scott Bradley; *prod:* Fred Quimby; *col:* Tech. *sd:* WE. 7 min. • Jerry helps a bulldog who, in return, says "Whenever you need me ... Whistle!," all of which gives Tom a rough time.

654. Boilesk (*Screen Songs*) 8 June 1933; *p.c.:* The Fleischer Studio for Para; *prod:* Max Fleischer; *dir:* Dave Fleischer; *anim:* Willard Bowsky, Myron Waldman; *sets:* Myron Waldman; *mus:* Art Turkisher *l/a:* The Watson Sisters; b&w. *sd:* WE. 7 min. • The animals stage a burlesque show and a husband bids his wife goodbye, much to the delight of her hidden suitors.

655. The Bold Eagle (*Possible Possum*) May 1969; *p.c.:* TT for Fox; *col:* DeLuxe. *sd:* RCA. 6 min. • No story available. • See: *Possible Possum*

656. Bold King Cole (*Rainbow Parade*) 22 May 1936; *p.c.:* Van Beuren for RKO; *dir:* Burt Gillett, Tom Palmer; *voice:* Jimmy Donnelly; *mus:* Winston Sharples; *col:* Tech. *sd:* RCA. 7 min. • Felix the Cat meets Old King Cole, a profound windbag whose ghostly ancestors decide to knock the wind out of him.

657. Boliver, the Squawking Ostrich 1930; *p.c.:* Independant Distributing Corp; *dir/voices:* Pinto Colvig; b&w. sd. • Made as an experiment in sound cartoon by Colvig. No story available.

658. Bolo-Mola Land (*New Universal*) 26 May 1939; *p.c.:* Walter Lantz prods for Univ; *dir:* Alex Lovy; *story:* Victor McLeod, James Miele; *anim:* Frank Tipper, Dick Marion; *sets:* Edgar Keichle; *voice:* Knox Manning; *mus:* Frank Marsales; *prod mgr:* George Hall; b&w *sd:* WE. 6 min. • A satire on travelogues featuring Corrigan birds that fly backwards and whispering pines that actually whisper.

659. Bomb Voyage (*Inspector*) 22 May 1967; *p.c.:* Mirisch/Geoffrey/DFE for UA; *dir:* Robert McKimson; *story:* Tony Benedict; *anim:* Manny Perez, Don Williams, Manny Gould, Bob Matz, Ted Bonnicksen, Warren Batchelder; *lay:* Lin Larsen; *back:* Tom O'Loughlin; *ed:* Lee Gunther; *voices:* Pat Harrington Jr., Paul Frees; *mus:* Walter Greene; *theme tune:* Henry Mancini; *prod sup:* Harry Love, Bill Orcutt; *col:* DeLuxe. *sd:* RCA. 6 min. • The Inspector follows in hot pursuit when The Commissioner is abducted by a Martian.

660. Bon Bon Parade (*Color Rhapsody*) 26 Nov. 1935; *p.c.:* Charles Mintz prods for Colum; *story:* Ben Harrison; *anim:* Manny Gould; *sets:* Phil Davis; *ed:* George Winkler; *voices:* The Rhythmettes, Abe Dinevitz, Harry Stanton; *mus:* Joe de Nat; *ph:* Otto Reimer; *prod mgr:* James Bronis; *col:* Tech. *sd:* RCA. 8½ min. • A poor child is transported to Candyland where he can eat his fill and the candy performs a carnival.

661. Bon Voyage, Charlie Brown (and Don't Come Back) 30 May 1980; *p.c.:* Lee Mendelson-Bill Melendez/Par. *dir:* Bill Melendez; *prod:* Lee Mendelson, Bill Melendez; *created and written by* Charles M. Schulz; *co-dir:* Phil Roman; *anim:* Sam Jaimes, Hank Smith, Al Pabian, Joe Roman, Ed Newman, Bill Littlejohn, Bob Carlson, Dale Baer, Spencer Peel, Larry Leichliter, Sergio Bertolli; *des:* Evert Brown, Bernard Gruver, Dean Spille, Lance Nolley; *ed:* Chuck McCann, Roger Donley; *check:* Carole Barnes, Eve Fletcher, Jane Gonzales; *i&p:* Joanne Lansing, Lee Guttman, Julie Maryon, Joan Pabian, Lee Hoffman, Adele Lenart, Valerie Green, Karin Stover, Mickey Kreyman, Chandra Poweris, Roubina Babajanian; *voices: Charlie Brown:* Arrin Skelley; *Peppermint Patty:* Laura Plantino; *Marcia:* Casey Carlson; *Linus:* Daniel Anderson; *Sally:* Anna Lisa Bartolin; *Snoopy:* Bill Melendez; *Waiter/Baron/Tennis Announcer/English voice/American male:* Scott Beads; *also:* Debbie Muller, Releline Rubens, Pascale de Barolet; *mus:* Ed Bogas; *mus ed:* Roger Donlay; *ph:* Nick Vasu Inc.; *neg cutting:* Alice Keillor; *sd:* Producers' Sound Service; *dial:* Music Annex; *prod mgr:* Carole Barnes; *prod asst:* Lora Sackett, Martha Grace, Sandy Claxton Arnold; *col:* Movielab. *sd:* Stereo. 75 min. • Charlie Brown and the gang are exchange students in France.

662. Bonanza Bunny (*Merrie Melodies*) 5 Sept. 1959; *p.c.:* WB; *dir:* Robert McKimson; *story:* Tedd Pierce; *anim:* Tom Ray, George Grandpré, Ted Bonnicksen, Warren Batchelder; *lay:* Robert Gribbroek; *back:* William Butler; *ed:* Treg Brown; *voices:* Mel Blanc, Robert C. Bruce; *mus:* Milt Franklyn; *prod mgr:* William Orcutt; *prod:* David H. DePatie; *col:* Tech. *sd:* Vit. 7 min. • When Bugs arrives at a Klondike saloon sporting a sack of gold nuggets, the villainous Blacq Jacq Shellacq tries to relieve him of it.

663. Bone Bandit (*Pluto*) 30 Apr. 1947; *p.c.:* Walt Disney prods for RKO; *dir:* Charles Nichols; *asst dir:* Chuck Wheeler; *story:* Art Scott, Sterling Sturtevant; *anim:* George Nicholas, George Kreisl, Jerry Hathcock, Marvin Woodward, Bob Youngquist; *fx:* Sandy Strother, Jack Boyd; *lay:* Karl Karpé; *back:* Art Landy; *voice:* James MacDonald; *mus:* Oliver Wallace; *col:* Tech. *sd:* RCA. 6½ min. • A gopher interferes with Pluto's supply of buried bones.

664. Bone Dry (*Hot Dog*) 14 May 1927; *p.c.:* Bray prods; *dir:* Walt Lantz, Clyde Geronimi; b&w. sil. 5 min. *l/a/anim.* • Walter and Pete go fishing in a restricted area. Pooch catches more fish than Walter who gets chased by the local constabulary.

665. A Bone for a Bone (*Looney Tunes*) 7 Apr. 1951; *p.c.:* WB; *dir:* I. Freleng; *story:* J.B. Hardaway; *anim:* Virgil Ross, Arthur Davis, Manny Perez, Ken Champin; *fx:* Harry Love; *lay:* Hawley Pratt; *back:* Paul Julian; *ed:* Treg Brown; *voices:* Mel Blanc, Stan Freberg; *mus:* Carl Stalling; *prod mgr:* John W. Burton; *prod:* Edward Selzer; *col:* Tech. *sd:* Vit. 7 min. • George P. Dog makes the cardinal error of burying a bone in the underground home of the Goofy Gophers, Mack n' Tosh.

666. The Bone Ranger (*Terry-Toon*) Apr. 1957; *p.c.:* TT for Fox; *dir:* Connie Rasinski; *story:* Tom Morrison; anim Jim Tyer; *mus:* Philip A. Scheib; *col:* Tech. *sd:* RCA. 6 min. CS. • Sniffy the dog has a number of uncomfortable adventures in pursuit of a bone.

667. Bone Sweet Bone (*Merrie Melodies*) 22 May 1948; *p.c.:* WB; *dir:* Arthur Davis; *story:* William Scott; *anim:* Don Williams, Emery Hawkins, Basil Davidovich, J.C. Melendez; *lay:* Don Smith; *back:* Philip de Guard; *ed:* Treg Brown; *voice:* Mel Blanc; *mus:* Carl Stalling; *prod mgr:* John W. Burton; *prod:* Edward Selzer; *col:* Ciné. *sd:* Vit. 7 min. • Shep, a dog, has problems in getting a bone away from a bulldog whom he believes has stolen it from a museum.

668. Bone Trouble (*Pluto*) 28 June 1940; *p.c.:* Walt Disney *prods* for RKO; *dir:* Jack Kinney; *asst dir:* Lloyd L. Richardson; *story sup:* Carl Barks; *story:* Earl Hurd; *anim:* Nick de Tolly, Norman Ferguson, Bill Justice, Fred Madison, Bill McIntyre, Lee Morehouse, Charles A. Nichols, Chic F. Otterstrom, Ray Patterson, Kosti Ruomonaa, Grant Simmons, Robert W. Youngquist; *fx:* Jack Boyd, Andrew Engman, Joseph Gayek, Art Fitzpatrick, Jack Huber, Ed Parks, Miles E. Pike, Reuben Timmens,; *lay:* Don Griffith, John Hubley; *voices:* Lee Millar, Hal Rees, Clarence Nash, James MacDonald; *mus:* Frank E. Churchill, Paul J. Smith; *col:* Tech. *sd:* RCA. 9 min. • Having stolen a bulldog's bone, Pluto is chased around a carnival fun house by the bully. Jack Kinney's first crack at directing.

669. The Bonehead Age (*Aesop's Film Fable*) 25 Dec. 1925; *p.c.:* Fables Pictures Inc for Pathé; *dir:* Paul Terry; b&w. sil. 10 min. • Farmer Al Falfa and his girl appear as cavemen.

670. Boneyard Blues (*Pen & Ink Vaudeville*) 31 Aug. 1924; *p.c.:* Hurd prods for Educational; *dir/anim:* Earl Hurd; b&w. sil. 5 min. • "Props" auditions: First a woman and her four children do an interpretive dance, followed by an elephant act and a farmer playing "Boneyard Blues" on a boney horse, squealing pigs and a goat that butts a drum.

671. Bongo 20 Jan. 1971; *p.c.:* Walt Disney prods for BV; *dir:* Jack Kinney; *col:* Tech. *sd:* RCA. 32 min. • Sinclair Lewis' story about a circus bear who escapes to live in the wild. • See: *Fun and Fancy Free*

672. The Bongo Punch (*Cartune*) 30 Dec. 1957; *p.c.:* Walter Lantz prods for Univ; *dir:* Alex Lovy; *story:* Dick Kinney; *anim:* La Verne Harding, Ray Abrams; *sets:* Raymond Jacobs, Art Landy; *voices:* Grace Stafford, June Foray, Hal Smith, "Those Smiths" trio; *mus:* Clarence Wheeler; *song:* Irving Bibo; *prod mgr:* William E. Garity; *col:* Tech. *sd:* RCA. 5 min. • A Latin-American fighting cock wants his son to replace him in the ring but Pepito prefers to play the bongo drums.

673. Boo, Boo, Theme Song (*Screen Songs*) 13 Oct. 1933; *p.c.:* The Fleischer Studio for Para; *prod:* Max Fleischer; *dir:* Dave Fleischer; *anim:* Willard Bowsky, Myron Waldman; *mus:* Art Turkisher; *l/a:* The Funny Boners; b&w. *sd:* WE. 8 min. • Ghosts feature with spiders and a knockout drink.

674. Boo Bop (*Casper*) 11 Nov. 1957; *p.c.:* Para Cartoons; *dir:* Seymour Kneitel; *story:* Carl Meyer; *anim:* Tom Golden, Nick Tafuri; *sets:* John Zago; *voices:* Norma MacMillan, Allen Swift; *mus:* Winston Sharples; *ph:* Leonard McCormick; *col:* Tech. *sd:* RCA. 6 min. • Casper helps the ghost of Franz Schubert complete his Unfinished Symphony.

675. Boo Hoo Baby (*Casper*) 30 Mar. 1951; *p.c.:* Famous for Para; *dir:* Seymour Kneitel; *story:* Larz Bourne; *anim:* Steve Muffatti, George Germanetti; *sets:* Robert Owen; *voices:* Alan Shay, Cecil Roy, Sid Raymond, Jack Mercer; *mus:* Winston Sharples; *title song:* Mack David, Jerry Livingston; *ph:* Leonard McCormick; *prod mgr:* Seymour Shultz; *col:* Tech. *sd:* RCA. 7 min. • Casper finds an abandoned baby and takes him to an orphanage.

676. Boo Kind to Animals (*Casper*) 23 Dec. 1955; *p.c.:* Famous for Para; *dir:* I. Sparber; *story:* Carl Meyer; *anim:* Tom Golden, Bill Hudson; *sets:* Robert Owen; *voices:* Norma MacMillan, Jackson Beck, Sid Raymond, Jack Mercer; *mus:* Winston Sharples; *ph:* Leonard McCormick; *prod mgr:* Seymour Shultz; *col:* Tech. *sd:* RCA. 7 min. • All the jobs Casper gets Spunky the mule fail until he blunders into the Army and rescues the Corporal.

677. Boo Moon (*Casper*) 1 Jan. 1954; *p.c.:* Famous for Para; *dir:* I. Sparber; *story:* I. Klein; *anim:* Myron Waldman, Larry Silverman; *sets:* Robert Little; *voices:* Alan Shay, Jackson Beck, Sid Raymond; *mus:* Winston Sharples; *title song:* Mack David, Jerry Livingston; *ph:* Leonard McCormick; *prod mgr:* Seymour Shultz; *col:* Tech. *sd:* RCA. 8 min. Stereotoon in 3-D. • Casper pays a visit to the Man in the Moon, only to be captured by Moonmen. He saves them from the attacking Tree People and is made a hero.

678. Boo Ribbon Winner (*Casper*) 3 Dec. 1954; *p.c.:* Famous for Para; *dir:* Seymour Kneitel; *story:* I. Klein; *anim:* Myron Waldman, Nick Tafuri; *sets:* Robert Owen; *voices:* Alan Shay, Jack Mercer; *mus:* Winston Sharples; *title song:* Mack David, Jerry Livingston; *ph:* Leonard McCormick; *prod mgr:* Seymour Shultz; *col:* Tech. *sd:* RCA. 6 min. • Casper helps a slow greyhound win the race with the aid of some bees.

679. Boo Scout (*Casper*) 27 July 1951; *p.c.:* Famous for Para; *dir:* I. Sparber; *story:* Larz Bourne; *anim:* Myron Waldman, Nick Tafuri; *sets:* Robert Owen; *voices:* Alan Shay, Gwen Davies, Jackson Beck; *mus:* Winston Sharples; *title song:* Mack David, Jerry Livingston; *ph:* Leonard McCormick; *col:* Tech. *sd:* RCA. 6 min. • A small boy is considered to be too young to become a boy scout. He and Casper help save the troop when a bear attacks.

680. Boobs in the Woods (*Looney Tunes*) 28 Jan. 1950; *p.c.:* WB; *dir:* Robert McKimson; *story:* Warren Foster; *anim:* Phil de Lara, J.C. Melendez, Emery Hawkins, Charles McKimson, Pete Burness; *lay:* Cornett Wood; *back:* Richard H. Thomas; *ed:* Treg Brown; *voices:* Mel Blanc; *mus:* Carl Stalling; *prod mgr:* John W. Burton; *prod:* Edward Selzer; *col:* Tech. *sd:* Vit. 7 min. • Porky retires to the mountains for a rest and encounters Daffy, who disrupts the peaceful atmosphere.

681. Booby Hatched (*Looney Tunes*) 14 Oct. 1944; *p.c.:* Leon Schlesinger prods for WB; *dir:* Frank Tashlin; *story:* Warren Foster; *anim:* I. Ellis; *sets:* Richard H. Thomas; *ed:* Treg Brown; *voices:* Mel Blanc, Sara Berner; *mus:* Carl W. Stalling; *prod sup:* Henry Binder, Raymond G. Katz; *col:* Tech. *sd:* Vit. 7 min. • A half-hatched duckling searches for his mother, keeping one step ahead of a hungry wolf.

682. Booby Socks (*Phantasy*) 12 July 1945; *p.c.:* Colum; *dir:* Howard Swift, Bob Wickersham; *story:* Sid Marcus; *anim:* Chic Otterstrom, Grant Simmons; *sets:* Clark Watson; *ed:* Richard S. Jensen; *voice:* Dave Barry; *mus:* Eddie Kilfeather; *ph:* Frank Fisher; *prod mgr:* Hugh McCollum; *b&w. sd:* WE. 6 min. • A crooning cat attempts to get past a watchdog for a rendezvous with a kitten.

683. Boogie-Doodle 1940; *p.c.:* Guggenheim Museum; *dir/anim:* Norman McLaren; *mus:* (piano) Albert Ammons; (trumpet): Henry "Red" Allen; (trombone): J.C. Higginbotham; *col. sd.* 3½ min. • Jazz accompanying colored images.

684. The Boogie Woogie Bugle Boy of Company B (*Cartune*) 1 Sept. 1941 *p.c.:* Walter Lantz prods for Univ; *story:* Ben Hardaway, Lowell Elliot; *anim:* Alex Lovy, La Verne Harding, Grim Natwick; *sets:* Fred Brunish; *voice:* Danny Webb; *mus:* Darrell Calker; *song:* Don Raye, Hughie Prince; *prod mgr:* George Hall; *col:* Tech. *sd:* WE. 7 min. *Academy Award nomination.* • Hot-Breath Harry, the "Harlem Heatwave," is drafted and soon has the camp rocking with his swing version of reveille.

685. Boogie Woogie Man Will Get You If You Don't Watch Out (*Swing Symphony*) 27 Sept. 1943; *p.c.:* Walter Lantz prods for Univ; *dir:* James Culhane; *story:* Ben Hardaway, Milt Schaffer; *anim:* (La) Verne Harding, Les Kline, Grim Natwick; *back:* Fred Brunish; *voices:* Lou Mel Morgan Trio, Dick Nelson; *mus:* Darrell Calker; *song:* Alberta Nichols, Mann Holiner; *prod sup:* George Hall; *col:* Tech. *sd:* WE. 7 min. • The Ghost Town spooks confront some dark spirits from Harlem who stage a demonstration of modern "Boogie Woogie" music.

686. Boogie Woogie Sioux (*Swing Symphony*) 30 Nov. 1942; *p.c.:* Walter Lantz prods for Univ; *dir:* Alex Lovy; *story:* Ben Hardaway, Milt Schaffer; *anim:* Bob Bentley; *sets:* Fred Brunish; *voice:* Dick Nelson, Del Porter, Carl Grayson; *mus:* Darrell Calker; *prod mgr:* George Hall; *col:* Tech. *sd:* WE. 6 min. • Chief Red Corpuscle gets collegiate, Tommy Hawk and his Five Scalpers to perform jazz to put an end to the draught with a downpour.

687. Book Revue (*Looney Tunes*) 5 Jan. 1946; *p.c.:* WB; *dir:* Robert Clampett; *story:* Warren Foster; *anim:* Rod Scribner, Emanuel Gould, Robert McKimson, J.C. Melendez; *lay:* Thomas McKimson; *back:* Cornett Wood; *ed:* Treg Brown; *voices:* Mel Blanc, Sara Berner, Richard Bickenbach, Robert C. Bruce, The Sportsmen (Maxwell Smith, John Rarig, Gurney Bell, Martin Sperzel); *mus:* Carl W. Stalling; *prod mgr:* John W. Burton; *prod:* Edward Selzer; *col:* Tech. *sd:* Vit. 7 min. • Daffy invades the serenity of a book store where the characters on book covers come to life. Caricatures of Tommy Dorsey, Benny Goodman, Harry James, Gene Krupa and Frank Sinatra.

688. The Bookworm (*MGM cartoon*) 26 Aug. 1939; *p.c.:* MGM; *prod:* Hugh Harman; *dir:* Isadore Freleng; *story:* Hugh Harman, Jack Cosgriff, Charles McGirl; *lay:* John Meandor; *back:* Joe Smith; *voice:* Mel Blanc, Frank Elmquist, Martha Wentworth; *mus:* Scott Bradley; *col:* Tech. *sd:* WE. 9 min. • A witch needs a worm to complete a potion and sends out her raven who catches The Bookworm. Literary characters come to his rescue.

689. The Bookworm Turns (*MGM cartoon*) 20 July 1940; *p.c.:* MGM; *prod:* Hugh Harman; *dir:* Isadore Freleng; *story:* Hugh Harman, Jack Cosgriff, Charles McGirl; *lay:* John Meandor; *back:* Joe Smith; *voices:* Mel Blanc, Frank Elmquist; *mus:* Scott Bradley; *col:* Tech. *sd:* WE. 8 min. • The Raven seeks medical advice from Dr. Jekyll, who transfers the Raven's brain and personality with that of The Bookworm.

690. Boom Boom (*Looney Tunes*) 29 Feb 1936; *p.c.:* Leon Schlesinger prods for WB; *dir:* Jack King; *anim:* Cal Dalton, Sandy Walker; *voices:* Tommy Bond, Joe Dougherty, Billy Bletcher; *mus:* Norman Spencer; *b&w. sd:* Vit. 7 min. • Porky and Beans are Doughboys in The Great War and rescue General Hardtrack from the enemy amidst a vast battle.

691. Boop-Oop-A-Doop (*Betty Boop*) 16 Jan. 1932; *p.c.:* The Fleischer Studio for Para; *prod:* Max Fleischer; *dir:* Dave Fleischer; *anim:* Alfred Eugster; *voices:* Mae Questel, Charles Carver; *mus:* Art Turkisher; *b&w. sd:* WE. 8 min. • The cruel circus ringmaster threatens to take Betty's "Boop-Oop-a-Doop" away if she doesn't comply with his wishes. Ko-Ko rescues her in time, leaving her "Boop-Oop-a-Doop" intact.

692. Boos and Arrows (*Casper*) 15 Oct. 1954; *p.c.:* Famous for Para; *dir:* Seymour Kneitel; *story:* I. Klein; *anim:* Myron Waldman, Gordon Whittier; *sets:* Robert Little; *voices:* Alan Shay, Gwen Davies, Jack Mercer; *mus:* Winston Sharples; *title song:* Mack David, Jerry Livingston; *ph:* Leonard McCormick; *prod mgr:* Seymour Shultz; *col:* Tech. *sd:* RCA. 6 min. • Casper saves an Indian papoose from an attacking eagle.

693. Boos and Saddles (*Casper*) 25 Dec. 1953; *p.c.:* Famous for Para; *dir:* I. Sparber; *story:* Larz Bourne; *anim:* Myron Waldman, Larry Silverman; *sets:* Jack Henegan; *voices:* Alan Shay, Gwen Davies, Sid Raymond, Jack Mercer; *mus:* Winston Sharples; *title song:* Mack David, Jerry Livingston; *ph:* Leonard McCormick; *prod mgr:* Seymour Shultz; *col:* Tech. *sd:* RCA. 6 min. • Casper finds himself in a western town where Billy, a very young cowboy, helps capture a dangerous desperado.

694. Boos in the Nite (*Screen Song*) 22 Sept. 1950; *p.c.:* Famous for Para; *dir:* I. Sparber; *story:* Joe Stultz, Larry Riley; *anim:* Myron Waldman, Nick Tafuri; *sets:* Anton Loeb; *mus:* Winston Sharples; *song:* Felix Powell, Joe Asaf; *ph:* Leonard McCormick; *prod mgr:* Sam Buchwald; *col:* Tech. *sd:* RCA. 6 min. • At a Hallowe'en party, all the ghosts sing "Pack up Your Troubles."

695. Bootle Beetle (*Donald Duck*) 22 Aug. 1947; *p.c.:* Walt Disney prods for RKO; *dir:* Jack Hannah; *asst dir:* Bee Selck; *story:* Bill Berg, Milt Banta; *anim:* Bill Justice, Art Babbitt, Judge Whitaker, Volus Jones, Hal King; *fx:* Andy Engman; *lay:* Yale Gracey; *back:* Thelma Witmer; *voices:* Francis "Dink" Trout, Larry Keating, Clarence Nash; *mus:* Oliver Wallace; *col:* Tech. *sd:* RCA. 6½ min. • The elder Bootle Beetle tells of how, when he was a lad, he ran away from home and was captured by Donald for his bug collection.

696. The Booze Hangs High (*Looney Tunes*) 4 Oct. 1930; *p.c.:* Hugh Harman, Rudolf Ising prods for WB; *anim:* Isadore Freleng, Paul Smith; *voice:* Johnny Murray; *mus:* Frank Marsales; *prod:* Leon Schlesinger; *b&w. sd:* Vit. 7 min. • Bosko gets drunk while working on the farm.

697. Bopin' Hood Aug. 1961; *p.c.:* Para Cartoons; *dir:* Seymour Kneitel; *story:* Carl Meyer, Jack Mercer; *anim:* Irving Spector, Jack Ehret, John Gentilella; *sets:* Robert Owen; *voices:* Jack Mercer, Corinne Orr; *mus:* Winston Sharples; *ph:* Leonard McCormick; *prod mgr:* Abe Goodman; *col:* Tech. *sd:* RCA. 6 min. • A violin-playing King bans all jazz music until a "hip" Robin Hood infiltrates, wins over his daughter and saves his life.

698. The Bored Cuckoo (*Noveltoon*) 9 Apr. 1948; *p.c.:* Famous for Para; *dir:* Bill Tytla; *story:* Bunny Gough, Bill Turner, Larry Riley; *anim:* George Germanetti, Steve Muffatti; *sets:* Robert Connavale; *voices:* Jack Mercer, Sid Raymond; *mus:* Winston Sharples; *ph:* Leonard McCormick; *prod mgr:* Sam Buchwald; *col:* Tech. *sd:* RCA. 8 min. • Cadmus Cuckoo, tired of being a cuckoo in the clock, goes out into the world where he rescues a songbird from a nightclub environment and they live happily ever after.

699. Bored of Education (*Little Lulu*) 26 July 1946; *p.c.:* Famous for Para; *dir:* Bill Tytla; *story:* I. Klein, George Hill; *sets:* Shane Miller; *voices:* Cecil Roy, Arnold Stang, Jackson Beck; *mus:* Winston Sharples; *title song:* Buddy Kaye, Fred Wise, Sammy Timberg; *prod mgr:* Sam Buchwald; *col:* Tech. *sd:* RCA. 7 min. • Lulu is made to sit in the corner at school and daydreams herself into history where she encounters Tubby as Christopher Columbus.

700. Born to Peck (*Woody Woodpecker*) 25 Feb. 1952; *p.c.:* Walter Lantz prods for Univ; *dir:* Walter Lantz; *anim:* Don Patterson, La Verne Harding, Ray Abrams, Paul Smith; *sets:* Fred Brunish; *mus:* Clarence E. Wheeler; *prod mgr:* William E. Garity; *col:* Tech. *sd:* RCA. 6 min. • The life of Woody is depicted from egg to old age. The artist helps out by putting him in "The Fountain of Youth."

701. Bosko and Bruno (*Looney Tunes*) 30 Apr. 1932; *p.c.*: Hugh Harman, Rudolf Ising prods for WB; *anim*: Isadore Freleng, Paul Smith, Robert Clampett; *ed*: Dale Pickett; *voices*: John T. Murray, Mary Moder; *mus*: Frank Marsales; *prod*: Leon Schlesinger; b&w. *sd*: Vit. 7 min. • Bosko and his dog steal eggs, are chased by the Sheriff and make their getaway on a train.

702. Bosko at the Beach (*Looney Tunes*) 23 July 1932; *p.c.*: Hugh Harman, Rudolf Ising prods for WB; *anim*: Isadore Freleng, Rollin Hamilton, Robert Clampett; *ed*: Dale Pickett; *voices*: John T. Murray, Mary Moder; *mus*: Frank Marsales; *prod*: Leon Schlesinger; b&w. *sd*: Vit. 7 min. • Bosko, Honey and Wilber go to the beach. Wilber gets washed out to sea while Bosko stages a rescue.

703. Bosko at the Zoo (*Looney Tunes*) 5 Mar. 1932; *p.c.*: Hugh Harman, Rudolf Ising prods for WB; *anim*: Isadore Freleng, Larry Martin, Robert Clampett; *ed*: Dale Pickett; *voices*: John T. Murray, Mary Moder; *mus*: Frank Marsales; *asso prod*: Leon Schlesinger; b&w. *sd*: Vit. 7 min. • An ostrich swallows Bosko's derby but soon lays an egg so he can retrieve it.

704. Bosko in Dutch (*Looney Tunes*) 25 Mar. 1933; *p.c.*: Hugh Harman, Rudolf Ising prods for WB; *anim*: Isadore Freleng, Thomas McKimson, Robert Clampett; *ed*: Dale Pickett; *voices*: Mary Moder; *mus*: Frank Marsales; *prod*: Leon Schlesinger; b&w. *sd*: Vit. 6 min. • Bosko appears as a Dutch boy who becomes a hero when rescuing a pair of drowning kittens.

705. Bosko in Person (*Looney Tunes*) 10 Apr. 1933; *p.c.*: Hugh Harman, Rudolf Ising prods for WB; *anim*: Rollin Hamilton, Bob McKimson, Robert Clampett; *ed*: Dale Pickett; *voices*: Johnny Murray; *mus*: Frank Marsales; *prod*: Leon Schlesinger; b&w. *sd*: Vit. 7 min. • Bosko entertains with impersonations of Maurice Chevalier, Jimmy Durante, Greta Garbo, Eddie Cantor and Ted Lewis while Honey does Tess Gardella singing "Was That the Human Thing to Do?"

706. Bosko Shipwrecked (*Looney Tunes*) 19 Sept. 1931; *p.c.*: Hugh Harman, Rudolf Ising for WB; *anim*: Rollin Hamilton, Larry Martin, Robert Clampett; *ed*: Dale Pickett; *voice*: Mary Moder; *mus*: Frank Marsales; *prod*: Leon Schlesinger; b&w. *sd*: Vit. 6 min. • Bosko is shipwrecked on a desert isle where he gets chased by a lion and a pack of hungry cannibals.

707. Bosko the Doughboy (*Looney Tunes*) 17 Oct. 1931; *p.c.*: Hugh Harman, Rudolf Ising Prods for WB; *anim*: Rollin Hamilton, Max Maxwell, Robert Clampett; *ed*: Dale Pickett; *voice*: Mary Moder; *mus*: Frank Marsales; *prod*: Leon Schlesinger; b&w. *sd*: Vit. 6 min. • Bosko finds himself in the center of an all-out war.

708. Bosko the Drawback (*Looney Tunes*) 24 Feb. 1933; *p.c.*: Hugh Harman, Rudolf Ising prods for WB; *anim*: Isadore Freleng, Bob McKimson, Robert Clampett; *ed*: Dale Pickett; *voices*: Johnny Murray, Ted Pierce; *mus*: Frank Marsales; *asso prod*: Leon Schlesinger; b&w. *sd*: Vit. 7 min. • Bosko faces a tough opposing football team and outwits them.

709. Bosko the Lumberjack (*Looney Tunes*) 22 Oct. 1932; *p.c.*: Hugh Harman, Rudolf Ising prods for WB; *anim*: Isadore Freleng, Max Maxwell, Robert Clampett; *ed*: Dale Pickett; *voices*: John T. Murray, Mary Moder, *mus*: Frank Marsales; *prod*: Leon Schlesinger; b&w. *sd*: Vit. 7 min. • Lumberjack Bosko has trouble with Pierre, a tough woodsman who abducts Honey.

710. Bosko the Musketeer (*Looney Tunes*) 16 Sept. 1933; *p.c.*: Hugh Harman, Rudolf Ising prods for WB; *anim*: Rollin Hamilton, Robert Stokes, Robert Clampett; *ed*: Dale Pickett; *voices*: John T. Murray, Mary Moder; *mus*: Frank Marsales; *prod*: Leon Schlesinger; b&w. *sd*: Vit. • Musketeer Bosko rescues Honey when she is kidnapped by a villain.

711. Bosko the Sheep-Herder (*Looney Tunes*) 14 June 1933; *p.c.*: Hugh Harman, Rudolf Ising prods for WB; *anim*: Rollin Hamilton, Max Maxwell, Robert Clampett; *ed*: Dale Pickett; *voices*: John T. Murray; *mus*: Frank Marsales; *prod*: Leon Schlesinger; b&w. *sd*: Vit. 8 min. • Bosko and Bruno rescue one of their lambs from the jaws of a wolf.

712. Bosko the Speed King (*Looney Tunes*) 22 Mar. 1933; *p.c.*: Hugh

Harman, Rudolf Ising prods for WB: *anim*: Isadore Freleng, Paul Smith, Robert Clampett; *ed*: Dale Pickett; *voices*: John T. Murray, Mary Moder; *mus*: Frank Marsales; *asso prod*: Leon Schlesinger; b&w. *sd*: Vit. 7 min. • Bosko is up against some mean opposition when he enters a car race.

713. Bosko's Dizzy Date (*Looney Tunes*) 6 Feb. 1933; *p.c.*: Hugh Harman–Rudolf Ising prods for WB; *anim*: Rollin Hamilton, Bob McKimson, Robert Clampett; *ed*: Dale Pickett; *voices*: John T. Murray, Mary Moder; *mus*: Frank Marsales; *prod*: Leon Schlesinger; b&w. *sd*: Vit. 7 min. • Bosko and Bruno find Honey giving Wilber piano lessons and take them both for a picnic.

714. Bosko's Dog Race (*Looney Tunes*) 8 July 1932; *p.c.*: Hugh Harman, Rudolf Ising prods for WB; *anim*: Rollin Hamilton, Norm Blackburn, Robert Clampett; *ed*: Dale Pickett; *voices*: John T. Murray, Mary Moder, Ted Pierce; *mus*: Frank Marsales; *prod*: Leon Schlesinger; b&w. *sd*: Vit. 7 min. • Bosko enters Bruno in a whippet race. A bee swarm spurs him on to winning the race.

715. Bosko's Easter Eggs (*Happy Harmonies*) 20 Mar. 1937; *p.c.*: MGM; *prod/dir*: Hugh Harman, Rudolf Ising; *voices*: Ruby Dandridge, Eugene Jackson; *mus*: Scott Bradley; *col*: Tech. *sd*: WE. 8 min. • Bruno breaks all Bosko's Easter eggs and tries to replace them by taking a hen's eggs.

716. Bosko's Fox Hunt (*Looney Tunes*) 23 Jan. 1932; *p.c.*: Hugh Harman, Rudolf Ising prods for WB; *anim*: Rollin Hamilton, Norm Blackburn, Robert Clampett; *ed*: Dale Pickett; *voice*: Carmen Maxwell; *mus*: Frank Marsales; *prod*: Leon Schlesinger; b&w. *sd*: Vit. 6 min. • Bosko and Bruno go on a fox hunt where the fox comes out befriending them both.

717. Bosko's Holiday (*Looney Tunes*) 9 May 1931; *p.c.*: Hugh Harman, Rudolf Ising prods for WB; *anim*: Isadore Freleng, Paul Smith; *ed*: Dale Pickett; *voices*:Mary Moder, Carmen Maxwell; *mus*: Frank Marsales; *prod*: Leon Schlesinger; b&w. *sd*: Vit. 7 min. • Honey invites Bosko to a picnic.

718. Bosko's Knight-Mare (*Looney Tunes*) 8 June 1933; *p.c.*: Hugh Harman, Rudolf Ising prods for WB; *anim*: Bob McKimson, Robert Stokes, Robert Clampett; *ed*: Dale Pickett; *voices*:Mary Moder; *mus*: Frank Marsales; *prod*: Leon Schlesinger; b&w. *sd*: Vit. 7 min. • Bosko imagines he's a knight of the Round Table along with Jimmy Durante, Mahatma Ghandi, Laurel & Hardy, the four Marx Brothers and Ed Wynn. The Black Knight kidnaps Honey and it's Bosko to the rescue.

719. Bosko's Mechanical Man (*Looney Tunes*) 27 Sept. 1933; *p.c.*: Hugh Harman, Rudolf Ising prods for WB; *anim*: Isadore Freleng, Thomas McKimson, Robert Clampett; *ed*: Dale Pickett; *voices*:Mary Moder, Ted Pierce; *mus*: Frank Marsales; *asso prod*: Leon Schlesinger; b&w. *sd*: Vit. 6 min. • Bosko builds a robot to wash Honey's dishes. It chases them all over the shop until Bosko pacifies it by inserting a record of "Mary Had a Little Lamb."

720. Bosko's Parlor Pranks (*Happy Harmonies*) 24 Nov. 1934; *p.c.*: MGM; *prod/dir*: Hugh Harman, Rudolf Ising; *mus*: Scott Bradley; *col*: Tech-2. *sd*: RCA. 7½ min. • No story available.

721. Bosko's Party (*Looney Tunes*) 7 May 1932; *p.c.*: Hugh Harman, Rudolf Ising prods for WB; *anim*: Isadore Freleng, Larry Martin, Robert Clampett; *ed*: Dale Pickett; *voices*: John T. Murray, Mary Moder; *mus*: Frank Marsales; *prod*: Leon Schlesinger; b&w. *sd*: Vit. 7 min. • Honey's party goes well until Bruno catches his tail in a mouse-trap and lands right in the middle of the birthday cake.

722. Bosko's Picture Show (*Looney Tunes*) 18 Sept. 1933; *p.c.*: Hugh Harman, Rudolf Ising prods for WB; *anim*: Isadore Freleng, Max Maxwell, Robert Clampett; *ed*: Dale Pickett; *voices*: John T. Murray, Mary Moder; *mus*: Frank Marsales; *prod*: Leon Schlesinger; b&w. *sd*: Vit. 7 min. • Bosko's matinee starts with a sing-along, then a newsreel showing Jimmy Durante being chased by Hitler, next a "Haurel and Lardy" short and the main feature stars Bosko and Honey in "He Done Her Dirt." Caricatures also featured are Jack Dempsey and the Marx Bros.

723. Bosko's Soda Fountain (*Looney Tunes*) 21 Nov. 1931; *p.c.*: Hugh Harman, Rudolf Ising prods for WB; *anim*: Isadore Freleng, Rollin Hamilton, Robert Clampett; *ed*: Dale Pickett; *voices*: Mary Moder; *mus*: Frank Marsales; *prod*: Leon Schlesinger; b&w. *sd*: Vit. 7 min. • A fresh kid throws ice cream at soda jerk Bosko, who chases him and gets the worst of it.

724. Bosko's Store (*Looney Tunes*) Sept. 1932; *p.c.:* Hugh Harman, Rudolf Ising prods for WB; *anim:* Isadore Freleng, Bob McKimson; *ed:* Dale Pickett; *voices:* Mary Moder, John T. Murray; *mus:* Frank Marsales; *prod:* Leon Schlesinger; b&w. *sd:* Vit. 7 min. • Bosko performs various antics around his grocery store. Honey enters with Bruno who wreaks havoc.

725. Bosko's Woodland Daze (*Looney Tunes*) 22 Mar. 1933; *p.c.:* Hugh Harman, Rudolf Ising prods for WB; *anim:* Isadore Freleng, Paul Smith; *ed:* Dale Pickett; *voice:* John T. Murray; *mus:* Frank Marsales; *asso prod:* Leon Schlesinger; b&w. *sd:* Vit. 6 min. • Bosko and Bruno play hide and seek in the woods until Bosko falls asleep and dreams he's playing with elves and fairies.

726. The Boss Is Always Right (*Jeepers & Creepers*) 15 Jan. 1960; *p.c.:* Para Cartoons; *dir:* Seymour Kneitel; *story:* Carl Meyer, Jack Mercer; *anim:* Nick Tafuri, Irving Dressler; *sets:* Robert Owen; *voices:* Jack Mercer, Jackson Beck; *mus:* Winston Sharples; *ph:* Leonard McCormick; *prod mgr:* Abe Goodman; *col:* Tech. *sd:* RCA. 6 min. • Jeepers pushes Creepers into asking his boss for a raise.

727. Boston Beanie (*Color Rhapsody*) 4 Dec. 1947; *p.c.:* Colum; *prod:* Raymond Katz, Henry Binder; *dir:* Sid Marcus; *story:* Cal Howard, Dave Monahan; *anim:* Ben Lloyd, Howard Swift, Roy Jenkins; *lay:* Clark Watson; *back:* Al Boggs; *ed:* Richard S. Jensen; *voices:* Harry E. Lang, Dave Barry; *mus:* Darrell Calker; *ph:* Frank Fisher; *creative consultant:* Robert Clampett; *col:* Tech. *sd:* WE. 5 min. • Lavish McTavish, a frugal Scotsman, gives his cat one solitary bean for each mouse he catches. The rodent comes to an arrangement whereupon the cat gets fed without harming him.

728. Boston Quackie (*Looney Tunes*) 22 June 1957; *p.c.:* WB; *dir:* Robert McKimson; *story:* Tedd Pierce; *anim:* George Grandpré, Ted Bonnicksen, Keith Darling, Russ Dyson, David R. Green; *lay:* Robert Gribbroek; *back:* Bob Majors; *ed:* Treg Brown; *voices:* Mel Blanc, June Foray; *mus:* Milt Franklyn; *prod mgr:* John W. Burton; *prod:* Edward Selzer; *col:* Tech. *sd:* Vit. 7 min. • Daffy Duck, in a parody on "Boston Blackie," has to guard a secret formula which gets stolen by an espionage spy in a green hat.

729. Bottles (*Happy Harmonies*) 11 Jan. 1936; *p.c.:* MGM; *prod/dir:* Hugh Harman, Rudolf Ising; *voices:* Elmore Vincent, Martha Wentworth, Bernice Hansel, J. Delos Jewkes, The King's Men, The Rhythmettes, Frank Nelson; *mus:* Scott Bradley; *col:* Tech. *sd:* WE. 8 min. • A Druggist falls asleep while mixing potions and dreams that all his pharmacy bottles come to life.

730. Boulder Wham! (*Merrie Melodies*) 9 Oct. 1965; *p.c.:* DFE for WB; *dir:* Rudy Larriva; *story:* Len Janson; *anim:* Virgil Ross, Bob Bransford, Hank Smith; *lay:* Erni Nordli; *back:* Anthony Rizzo; *ed:* Lee Gunther; *mus:* Bill Lava; *col:* Tech. *sd:* Vit. 6 min. • The Coyote's attempts to entice the Road-Runner from the opposite side of a revine.

731. Boulevardier from the Bronx (*Merrie Melodies*) 10 Oct. 1936; *p.c.:* Leon Schlesinger prods for WB; *dir:* I. Freleng; *anim:* Paul Smith, Cal Dalton; *lay:* Griff Jay; *back:* Arthur Loomer; *ed:* Tregoweth E. Brown; *voices:* Bernice Hansel, Jack Carr, Ted Pierce; *mus:* Carl W. Stalling; *prod sup:* Henry Binder, Raymond G. Katz; *col:* Tech. *sd:* Vit. 7 min. • A boastful cockerel and his team arrive to play a baseball match against the Hickville team. All are surprised when the local rube beats him.

732. Bouncing Benny (*Modern Madcap*) Nov. 1960; *p.c.:* Para Cartoons; *dir:* Seymour Kneitel; *story:* Carl Meyer, Jack Mercer; *anim:* Graham Place, Otto Feuer; *sets:* Robert Little; *voices:* Cecil Roy, Jack Mercer; *mus:* Winston Sharples; *prod mgr:* Abe Goodman; *col:* Tech. *sd:* RCA. 6 min. • Mr. and Mrs. Brown are delivered a bonny bouncing boy in every sense of the word.

733. A Bout with a Trout (*Little Lulu*) 10 Oct. 1947; *p.c.:* Famous for Para; *dir:* I. Sparber; *story:* I. Klein, Jack Ward; *anim:* Myron Waldman, Gordon Whittier, Nick Tafuri, Irving Dressler, Wm. B. Pattengill; *sets:* Anton Loeb; *voices:* Cecil Roy; *mus:* Winston Sharples; *prod mgr:* Sam Buchwald; *col:* Tech. *sd:* RCA. 7 min. • Lulu goes fishing and has a run-in with a trout.

734. Bowery Bimbos (*Oswald*) 18 Mar. 1930; *p.c.:* Univ; *dir:* Walter Lantz; *anim:* Walter Lantz, "Bill" Nolan. Manuel Moreno; *mus:* David Broekman; b&w. *sd:* WE. 7 min. • After a period of song and dance, Oswald becomes lovesick.

735. Bowery Bugs (*Merrie Melodies*) 4 June 1949; *p.c.:* WB; *dir:* Arthur Davis; *story:* Lloyd Turner, William Scott; *anim:* Emery Hawkins, Basil Davidovich, J.C. Melendez, Don Williams; *lay:* Don Smith; *back:* Philip de Guard; *ed:* Treg Brown; *voices:* Mel Blanc, Billy Bletcher; *mus:* Carl Stalling; *prod mgr:* John W. Burton; *prod:* Edward Selzer; *col:* Tech. *sd:* Vit. 7 min. • Bugs tells of Steve Brody, a luckless case, who needs a rabbit's foot as a lucky charm.

736. Bowery Daze (*Krazy Kat*) 30 Mar. 1934; *p.c.:* Charles Mintz prods for Colum; *story:* Harry Love; *anim:* Allen Rose, Preston Blair; *mus:* Joe de Nat; *prod mgr:* James Bronis; b&w. *sd:* RCA. 10 min. • Krazy as a Bowery Copper.

737. The Bowling Alley-Cat (*Tom & Jerry*) 18 July 1942; *p.c.:* MGM; *dir:* William Hanna, Joseph Barbera; *anim:* Wilson D. Burness, Kenneth Muse, Jack Zander; *sets:* Joe Smith; *ed:* Fred MacAlpin; *mus:* Scott Bradley; *ph:* Gene Moore; *prod:* Fred Quimby; *col:* Tech. *sd:* WE. 9 min. • Jerry's rest in a bowling alley receives a rude awakening when Tom the cat arrives.

738. Bows and Errors (*The Dogfather*) 29 Dec. 1974; *p.c.:* Mirisch/DFE for UA; *dir:* Gerry Chiniquy; *story:* John Dunn; *anim:* Nelson Shin, Bob Bransford, Norm McCabe; *ed:* Rick Steward; *lay:* Dick Ung; *back:* Richard H. Thomas; *voices:* Bob Holt, Daws Butler; *mus:* Dean Elliott; *col:*DeLuxe. *sd:*RCA. 6 min. • Pug and Louie try the "Robin Hood" approach by robbing from the rich and giving to the poor.

739. Le Bowser Bagger (*Inspector*) 30 May 1967; *p.c.:* Mirisch/Geoffrey/DFE for UA; *dir:* Gerry Chiniquy; *anim:* Bob Matz; Warren Batchelder, Manny Perez, Don Williams, Manny Gould; *lay:* Dick Ung; *back:* Tom O'Loughlin; *ed:* Lee Gunther; *voices:* Pat Harrington Jr., Marvin Miller; *mus:* Walter Greene; *theme tune:* Henry Mancini; *prod sup:* Harry Love, Basil Cox; *col:* DeLuxe. *sd:* RCA. 6 min. • The Inspector enlists the aid of a Police Dog to help him pursue an arch criminal.

740. The Box 1967; *p.c.:* Murakami-Wolf Films for Brandon; *dir/anim:* Fred Wolf; *ed:* Rich Harrison; *mus:* Shelley Manne; *ph:* Wally Bulloch; *col:* East. *sd:* 7 min. *Academy Award.* • A man arrives in a bar on a stormy night carrying a mysterious box containing a strange creature. A pretty girl appears with a similar box containing the female of the species. They leave together in the rain and take their pets with them onto a huge ark.

741. Box Car Bandit (*Woody Woodpecker*) 8 Apr. 1957; *p.c.:* Walter Lantz prods for Univ; *dir:* Paul J. Smith; *story:* Homer Brightman; *anim:* Les Kline, Robert Bentley; *sets:* Art Landy, Raymond Jacobs; *voices:* Dal McKennon, Grace Stafford; *mus:* Clarence Wheeler; *prod mgr:* William E. Garity; *col:* Tech. *sd:* RCA. 6 min. • Woody guards a train full of gold bullion from a bandit known as Dapper Denver Dooley.

742. Box-Car Bill Falls in Luck (*Sullivan Cartoon Comedy*) 16 July 1917; *p.c.:* Powers for Univ; *dir:* Pat Sullivan; *anim:* Bill Cause; b&w. sil. 5 min. • After being thrown off a train, Bill finds some money and buys "Prune Juice" which gives him hallucinations of snakes and mice.

743. Box Car Blues (*Looney Tunes*) Nov. 1930; *p.c.:* Hugh Harman, Rudolf Ising for WB; *anim:* Rollin Hamilton, Max Maxwell, Robert Clampett; *ed:* Dale Pickett; *voice:* Johnny Murray; *mus:* Frank Marsales; b&w. *sd:* Vit. 6 min. • In a story borrowed from *Mickey's Choo Choo*, Bosko and a hobo pig ride the rails until their car becomes unhitched.

744. Box-Office Bunny (*Looney Tunes*) 11 Feb. 1991; *p.c.:* WB Animation; *dir:* Darrell Van Citters; *prod:* Kathleen Helppie-Shipley; *story:* Charles Carney; *sup:* Chris Buck, Gregg Vanzo, Bob Scott, Tony Fucile; *anim:* Ed Bell, Mark Kausler, Toby Shelton, Lennie Graves; *sup fx anim:* Diane Keener; *key asst:* Harry Sabin; *lead asst anim:* Kathleen Castillo, George Goodchild, Tom Mazzocco, Bronwen Barry, Dori Little-Herrick, Karenia Kaminski, Nancy Avery, Alan Smart, Ken Bruce, Shawn Keller; *character des:* Michael Giaimo; *ed:* Rick Gehr; *lay:* Alan Bodner, Patricia Keppler, Roseann Stire; *scene plan:* Dora Yakutis; *voices:* Jeff Bergman; *mus:* Hummie Mann; *post prod sup:* Jim Champin; *fx ed:* Frank Raciti; *col:* Tech. *sd:* Dolby stereo. 5 min. • A multiplex cinema is erected over Bugs' rabbit hole entrance. He emerges into the theater and starts to watch the movie when the usher, Elmer Fudd, tries to evict him.

745. The Boxing Kangaroo (*Out of the Inkwell*) 2 Feb. 1920; *p.c.:* Bray prods for Goldwyn; *prod/l/a:* Max Fleischer; *dir:* Dave Fleischer; b&w. sil. 5 min. *l/a/anim.* • Max draws Ko-Ko and a boxing kangaroo. He leaves them and returns to find the kangaroo beaten-up by Ko-Ko. • See: *Gold-wyn-Bray Pictographs*

746. A Boy, a Gun and Birds *(Color Rhapsody)* 12 Jan. 1940; *p.c.:* Colum; *dir:* Ben Harrison; *anim:* Manny Gould; *ed:* George Winkler; *voice:* Robert Winkler; *mus:* Joe de Nat; *prod mgr:* James Bronis; *col:* Tech. *sd:* RCA. 7½ min. • A boy injures a bird. The others birds attack him and the wounded bird stops the onslaught, making the boy feel remorse.

747. A Boy and His Dog *(Color Rhapsody)* 23 Dec. 1936; *p.c.:* Charles Mintz prods for Colum; *story:* Sid Marcus; *anim:* Art Davis; *sets:* Phil Davis; *voices:* Leone Le Doux, Billy Bletcher; *mus:* Joe de Nat; *prod mgr:* James Bronis; *col:* Tech. *sd:* RCA. 6½ min. • A boy mistreats his pup and dreams the dog has grown to gigantic proportions and repays his master's mistreating.

748. The Boy and the Dog *(Aesop's Film Fable)* 3 Apr. 1922; *p.c.:* Fables Pictures Inc for Pathé; *dir:* Paul Terry; b&w. *sil.* 5 min. • A small boy creates an award-winning dog from a dog, a cat and a stovepipe. Moral: "Necessity is the mother of invention."

749. The Boy and the Wolf *(MGM Cartoon)* 24 Apr. 1943; *p.c.:* MGM; *dir:* Robert Allen; *mus:* Scott Bradley; *prod mgr:* Fred Quimby; *col:* Tech. *sd:* WE. 7½ min. • A Mexican shepherd boy fools his dog into thinking a wolf is attacking the flock. When the wolf does arrive, the dog thinks it's another trick.

750. The Boy Friend 18 Dec. 1927; *p.c.:* Fables Pictures Inc for Pathé; *dir:* Paul Terry, Harry Bailey; b&w. *sil.* 10 min. • No story available.

751. Boy Meets Dog! 1939; *p.c.:* Walter Lantz prods for Ipana Bristol Mayers Co; *dir:* Burt Gillett; *sets:* Willy Pogàny; *voices:* Billy Bletcher, Danny Webb, Margaret McKay; *mus:* Frank E. Churchill; conducted by Nathaniel Shilkret; *col:* Tech. *sd:* WE. 9 min. • Commercial for Ipana toothpaste featuring Gene Byrnes' *Reg'lar Fellers:* A boy's father won't let him keep a pup. Father is knocked unconcious and dreams he's on trial by gnomes with his son as judge.

752. A Boy Named Charlie Brown 1969; *p.c.:* National General/ Cinema Center for Fox; *prod:* Lee Mendelson, Bill Melendez; *dir:* Bill Melendez; *asst dir:* Bernard Gruver; *story:* Charles M. Schulz; *anim:* Don Lusk, Frank Smith, Rudy Zamora, Bob Carlson, Bill Littlejohn, Ken O'Brien, Bob Matz, Russ von Neida, Barrie Nelson, Ken Champin, Hank Smith, Spencer Peel, Sam Jaimes, Maggie Bowen, Herm Cohen, Lee Irwin, Bror Lansing, Jay Sarbry, Gerry Kane; *art ed:* Ed Levitt; *sets:* Bernard Gruver, Evert Brown, Ruth Kissane, Charles McElmurry, Dean Spille, Ellie Bonnard, Jan Green, Al Shean; *ed:* Robert Gillis, Charles McCann, Steve Melendez; *voices: Charlie Brown:* Peter Robbins; *Lucy:* Pamelyn Ferdin; *Linus:* Glenn Gilger; *Schroeder:* Andy Pforsich; *Patty:* Sally Dryer Barker; *Violet:* Anne Altiere; *Boy #2:* David Carey; *Boy #3:* Guy Pforsich; *Frieda:* Linda Mendelson; *Pig Pen:* Christopher de Faria; *Sally:* Erin Sullivan; *Snoopy:* Bill Melendez; *Title singer:* Rod McKuen; *Singers:* Betty Allen, Loulie Norman, Gloria Wood; *mus score:* Vince Guaraldi, Beethoven; *mus dir:* John Scott Trotter; *Pathétique Sonata* played by Ingult Dahl; *songs: Failure Face, Champion Charlie Brown, I Before E* by Rod McKuen; *Champion Charlie Brown:* John Scott Trotter; *choreography:* Skippy Baxter; *ph:* Nick Vasu; *col:* Tech. *sd: prods sd.* 79 min. • Charles M. Schulz's "Peanuts" characters brought to the big screen. Charlie Brown wins the classroom spelling bee and is chosen to represent his class in the national finals in New York City.

753. Boy Pest *(Muggy-Doo)* Dec. 1963; *p.c.:* Hal Seeger prods for Para; *prod/dir:* Hal Seeger; *anim:* Myron Waldman, Beverly Arnold; *voices:* Larry Best, Bob MacFadden, Beverly Arnold; *mus:* Winston Sharples; *col:* Tech. *sd:* RCA. 6 min. • Muggy-Doo, boy cat, grooms Osh so he can appear on a "Doctor" television show as a patient.

754. Boyhood Daze *(Merrie Melodies)* 20 Apr. 1957; *p.c.:* WB; *dir:* Chuck Jones; *story:* Michael Maltese; *anim:* Abe Levitow, Richard Thompson, Ken Harris; *fx:* Harry Love; *lay:* Maurice Noble; *back:* Philip de Guard; *ed:* Treg Brown; *voices:* Dick Beals, Daws Butler, Marian Richman; *mus:* Milt Franklyn; *prod mgr:* John W. Burton; *prod:* Edward Selzer; *col:* Tech. *sd:* Vit. 7 min. • Ralph Phillips, a small boy, is confined to his room for breaking a window and imagines gaining his parents' respect by his saving their lives.

755. Les Boys *(Swifty & Shorty)* Dec. 1965; *p.c.:* Para Cartoons; *dir/story:*

Howard Post; *anim:* Morey Reden; *sets:* John Zago; *mus:* Winston Sharples; *ph:* Leonard McCormick; *prod mgr:* Abe Goodman; *col:* Tech. *sd:* RCA. 6 min. • Shorty has problems in waking Swifty for an early morning fishing trip. Different from other entries in this series in that both characters are painted solid white against colorful scenery and neither character speaks.

756. The Brave Engineer 3 Mar. 1950; *p.c.:* Walt Disney prods for RKO: *dir:* Jack Kinny; *The Ballad of Casey Jones* by T. Lawrence Siebert, Eddie Newton; *story:* Dick Kinney, Dick Shaw; *anim:* Milt Kahl, Fred Moore, Al Bertino, Ward Kimball, Murray McClellan; *fx:* Andy Engman, Josh Meador; *lay:* Don da Gradi; *back:* Don Griffith, Ray Huffine; *voices:* Jerry Colonna, The King's Men; *mus:* Ken Darby; *col:* Tech. *sd:* RCA. 8 min. • Hilarious account of the troubles that face Casey Jones, the railroad engineer, in getting the mail delivered on time. Enhanced by Jerry Colonna's manic narrative.

757. A Brave Heart *(Aesop's Film Fable)* 17 Sept. 1927; *p.c.:* Fables Pictures Inc for Pathé; *dir:* Paul Terry; b&w. *sil.* 10 min. • "Chisel" Simpson, a villainous cat, finds Milton Mouse has the inside track with pretty Rita Mouse. He marries Rita's grandma to obtain guardianship but errs by tying Granny to a log in a swift stream. Moral: "Don't bet on fights."

758. The Brave Little Bat *(Merrie Melodies)* 27 Sept. 1941; *p.c.:* Leon Schlesinger prods for WB; *dir:* Charles M. Jones; *story:* Rich Hogan; *anim:* Rudolph Larriva; *lay:* John McGrew; *ed:* Treg Brown; *voices:* Margaret Hill, Marjorie Tarlton; *mus:* Carl W. Stalling; *prod sup:* Henry Binder, Raymond G. Katz; *col:* Tech. *sd:* Vit. 7 min. • Sniffles shelters from a storm in a windmill where he meets a bat. He ridicules the bat's wings until they save him from the jaws of a cat.

759. The Brave Little Brave *(Terry-Toon)* 171 Aug. 1956; *p.c.:* TT for Fox; *dir:* Mannie Davis; *story/voice:* Tom Morrison; *anim:* Jim Tyer; *sets:* Art Bartsch; *mus:* Philip A. Scheib; *ph:* Douglas Moye; *col:* Tech. *sd:* RCA. 6 min. CS. • A little Indian brave sets out to hunt moose but when the creature saves him from a fire, he returns empty-handed.

760. The Brave Little Tailor *(Mickey Mouse)* 23 Sept. 1938; *p.c.:* Walt Disney prods for RKO; *dir:* William O. Roberts; *story:* Jack Kinney; *anim:* Jack Campbell, Les Clark, Frank Follmer, Oliver M. Johnston Jr., Richard McDermott, Fred Moore, Arthur W. Palmer, Don Patterson, Archie Robin, Milt Schaffer, Franklin Thomas, Riley Thomson, Noel Tucker, Vladimir Tytla, Roy Williams, Cornett Wood; *fx:* Andrew Engman; *voices:* Eddie Holden, Walt Disney, William E. Sheets; *mus:* Albert Hay Malotte; *col:* Tech. *sd:* RCA. 9 min. *Academy Award nomination.* • Tailor Mickey is sent by the King to dispose of a troublesome giant. Disney veteran Ollie Johnston's first animation job.

761. The Brave Little Toaster 10 July 1987; *p.c.:* Hyperion/Kushner-Locke in asso with Wang Film Prods, Co., Global Communications Corp. for Castle Premiere; *dir:* Jerry Rees; *prod:* Donald Kushner, Thomas L. Wilhite; *ex prod:* Willard Carroll, Peter Locke; based on the novella by Thomas M. Disch; *scr:* Jerry Rees, Joe Ranft; *story:* Jerry Rees, Joe Ranft, Brian McEntee; *storyboard:* Joe Ranft, Jerry Rees, Darrell Rooney, Alex Mann; *anim dir:* Randy Cartwright, Joe Ranft, Rebecca Rees; *developmental anim:* Kevin Lima, Steve Moore, Rebecca Rees, Kirk Wise; *anim:* Kevin Lima, Steve Moore, Ann Telnaes, Chris Wahl, Tanya Wilson; *anim (overseas):* Lilmin, Weng Chunfa; *fx anim consultant:* Mark Dindal; *fx anim (overseas):* Wu Wei-Chang, Chen Hsiahsiang, Lin Mingjier, Ho Yuehlan, Lin Shunfa, Lai Chunying, Hseih Mingylang, Ho Tienyun, Peng Hsinfa, Hsieh Mingchuan, Yen Shunfa, Yang Chichang, Hsiao Shihko, Hu Chengtsung; *asst anim sup:* Rebecca Rees; *character des:* Kevin Lima, Chris Buck, Mike Giaimo, Dan Haskett, Skip Jones, Rob Minkoff, John Norton; *art dir:* Brian McEntee; *col stylist:* A. Kendall O'Connor; *col models:* Brigitte Strother; *lay sup:* Brian McEntee, Darrell Rooney, Chris Wahl; *lay:* James Beihold, Kirk Hanson, Tim Hauser, Alex Mann, John Norton, Kevin Richardson, Darrell Rooney, Ann Telnaes, Chris Wahl, Steve Wahl, Tanya Wilson; *back (overseas):* Yu Manhua, Chen Yungtsung, Wu Shuhui, Hsiao Shihko, Li Kuanghan, Yu Changhsien, Chen Chialiang, Kao Yaote, Kao Chienhua, Li Yungchi, Lu Chunghui, Li Tsungmou; *scene planning:* Glenn Higa, Steve Segal; *scene checkers:* Jo Tihan, Chen Meiliang, Ching Shuyi, Li Chinghua, Huang Yuhui, Chou Paotsu, Yang Yuanfang, Ma Li, Wu Yintsu, Hu Peihui, Lo Yunfang, Fei Wenwan, Hsu Jochien, Tou Yuling, Hsu Yumei, Chien Meihua, Peng Yuchih; *special des:* Eartown Movies, Bob Walter, Rick Johnson, Aseley Otten; *ed:* Donald W. Ernst,

Shelley Hinton (*overseas*) Maio Tsetien, Ho Meiling, Liang Tsungkeh, Chou Taili; *ADR ed:* Eileen Horta; *sd ed:* Sam Horta, Terence Thomas, Kevin Spears, Andrea Horta; *mus ed:* Michael Dittrick, Brian F. Mars; *foley ed:* Randal Scott Thomas; *dialogue rec engineers:* George Thompson, Andrew Morris; *foley:* Mary Louise Rodgers, Michael Anthony Salvetti; *re-rec mix:* John T. Reitz, David E. Campbell, Gregg C. Rudloff; *col timer:* John Nicolard; *voices: Radio:* Jon Lovitz; *Lampy/Zeke:* Tim Stack; *Blanky/ Young Master:* Timothy E. Day; *Kirby:* Thurl Ravenscroft; *Toaster:* Deanna Oliver; *Air Conditioner/Hanging Lamp:* Phil Hartman; *Elmo St. Peters:* Joe Ranft; *Mish-Mash:* Judy Toll; *Rob:* Wayne Kaatz; *Chris:* Colette Savage; *Mother:* Mindy Stern; *Plugsy:* Jim Jackson; *Entertainment Complex:* Randy Cook; *Computer:* Randy Bennett; *Two-Faced Sewing Machine:* Mindy Stern, Judy Tolley; *Black & White TV:* Jonathon Benair; *Spanish Announcer:* Louis Conti; *mus:* David Newman; score performed by New Japan Philharmonic Orchestra; *orchestra rec prod:* Shawn Murphy; *songs:* Van Dyke Parks; "Tutti Frutti" by Lubin Penniman & La Bostrie, performed by Little Richard; "My Mammy" by Walter Donaldson, Sam Lewis & Joe Young, performed by Al Jolson; "April Showers" by Louis Silvers & B.G. DeSylva; *ph sup* (*overseas*): Jackson Wany, Lin Chinyi; *ph* (*overseas*): Liu Hsinguan, Wu Yihsueh, Chen Shiehsiung, Keng Yufang, Chen Mingyi, Shih Paiting, Chao Juchang, Ping Tsungyao, Kud Tunghuang, Sung Shiehming, Lin Chinyi, Tang Jungtsan, Chang Chinnan, Hsu Chengwei, Tang Hsiangyi; *i&p:* Chao Lipin, Wang Shuhua, Fan Chiang Yuhui, Chiang Chinyun, Fang Yuehchin, Lin Chunfeng, Huang Shuyi, Hsiao Chuanyu, Wu Shuching, Chang Hsiumei, Sun Pitsu, Wang Pitsu, Chiu Yueheh, Chen Manling, Liu Fengchiao, Wang Hsiaomei, Peng Meiying, Hsu Shuchen, Chang Liching, Sun Yuehkuei; *airbrush:* Wu Pifeng, Lin Liling, Tsu Ying, Liang Shufeng, Han Pinghui; *translators:* Yeh Shuwen, Wu Mingli, Li Hsiangyun, Ho Wanyu, Chiu Wanling; *asso prod:* James Wang; *co-prod:* Cleve Reinhard; *prod sup:* Charles Leland Richardson; *prod asst* (*overseas*): Tsai Tingting; *col:* DeLuxe. *sd:* Dolby stereo. 90 min. • In an isolated rural cottage, all the household equipment are shocked to find a "For Sale" sign erected outside. They embark on going in search for the house's young Master, encountering many setbacks along the way, landing them all in a junk yard. The Master comes searching for them and is about to rescue them from being crushed when he gets caught in the crusher himself. About to be compressed with the other equipment, all are saved by the little Toaster sacrificing himself into the mechanism of the crusher, bringing it to a grinding halt. Safe, the Master collects all his appliances, repairs the Toaster and takes them to college with him.

762. The Brave Tin Soldier (*ComiColor*) 7 Apr. 1934; *p.c.:* Celebrity prods; *prod:* Ub Iwerks; *dir/anim:* Jimmie Culhane, Al Eugster; *story:* Otto Englander; *lay:* Jimmy Culhane; *mus:* Art Turkisher; *col:* Ciné. *sd:* PCP. 8 min. • The one-legged toy soldier rescues a pretty ballerina from the grasp of the letcherous King who sentences him to execution. Caricatures of Eddie Cantor, Laurel & Hardy, Groucho & Harpo Marx.

763. Bravo, Mr. Strauss (*Puppetoon*) 12 Mar. 1943; *p.c.:* George Pal prods for Para; *prod/dir:* George Pal; *story:* George Pal, Jack Miller, Cecil Beard; *mus:* William Eddison; *col:* Tech. *sd:* WE. 9 min. • The Screwball Army conquers Vienna and tries to re-educate its inhabitants with their own culture but Johann Strauss' statue comes alive and marches them out.

764. Bray, J.R., Studio *prod:* John Randolph Bray; *dir/anim:* C.T. Anderson, Raoul Barré, Leighton Budd, Wallace A. Carlson, James Culhane, Dave Fleischer, Max Fleischer, F.M. Follett, Ving Fuller, Clyde Geronimi, Jean Gic, C. Allen Gilbert, L.M. Glackens, F. Lyle Goldman, H.C. Greening, Milt Gross, David D. Hand, Earl Hurd, Gregory la Cava, Lank Leonard, J.(Jack) F. Leventhal, Ashley Miller, Frank Moser, A.D. Reed, Clarence Rigby, Vernon Stallings, Pat Sullivan, Paul H. Terry; *educational slides for BRAYCO:* Cy Young; *ph:* Harry Squires, Frank Paiker; *dark room:* Dutch Heins, Anton Breuhl; *prod mgr:* H.D. Bailery. • Animation studio consisting chiefly of newspaper cartoonists.

765. Bray Magazine (*Inkraving*); *p.c.:* Bray prods for State Right Release; b&w. sil. 3 min. Interest magazine with occasional cartoon items. • **1922: Strap Hangers**; *anim:* Milt Gross, 16 Dec. Satirising commuters. **Bobby Bumps at School**; *anim:* Earl Hurd, 23 Dec. Bobby's experiences in the classroom. **Taxes**; *anim:* Milt Gross, 30 Dec. The possibility of taxing the air, walking, etc. • **1923: If We Reversed**; *anim:* Milt Gross, Jan. • No story available.

766. Bray Novelty Magazine *p.c.:* Bray prods; *prod:* John R. Bray; b&w. st. • Interest magazine with animated inserts. • **1927:** (1) 15 Jan; () 7 Feb; (3) 15 Mar; (4) 8 Apr; (5) 30 Apr.

767. The Break of Day (*Aesop's Film Fable*) 27 Jan. 1929; *p.c.:* Fables Pictures Inc for Pathé; *dir:* Paul Terry, Mannie Davis; b&w. sil. 10 min. • While Al has an early morning wash in a pelican's bill, the cat beans him with a horseshoe. The cat, mouse and Al Falfa go up in a hot-air balloon but a passing bird bursts it and they plunge into a lake where they are pursued by a fish Cop.

768. Breakfast Pals 1938; *p.c.:* Cartoon Films Ltd for Kellogg; *dir:* Paul Fennell; *anim:* Ed Benedict, Rudy Zamora; *col:* Tech. *sd:* 2 min. • Snap, Crackle and Pop have a battle over the breakfast table.

769. Breaking the Habit 1964; *prod/dir:* Henry Jacobs, John Korty; *des/ph:* John Korty; *voices:* Henry Jacobs, Chuck Levy; *col.* sd. 5 min. • Satirical cartoon about the evils of smoking.

770. Breath 1967; *p.c.:* Murakami-Wolf Films Inc.; *dir/story/anim/des:* Jimmy Murakami; *ed:* Rich Harrison; *col:* East. sd. 4 min. • The various things a man breathes in and out during his lifetime.

771. The Brementown Musicians (*ComiColor*) 17 Feb. 1935; *p.c.:* Celebrity prods; *prod/dir:* Ub Iwerks; *anim:* Al Eugster; *mus:* Carl Stalling; *col:* Ciné. sd: PCP. 7 min. • A rooster, dog, cat and mule are banished by the farmer. After failing as musicians, they foil a robbery at the farm, thus ingratiating themselves with the farmer once more.

772. Bride and Gloom (*Popeye*) 2 July 1954; *p.c.:* Famous for Para; *dir:* I. Sparber; *story:* Larz Bourne; *anim:* Tom Johnson, John Gentilella; *sets:* Robert Connavale; *voices:* Jack Mercer, Mae Questel; *mus:* Winston Sharples; *ph:* Leonard McCormick; *prod mgr:* Seymour Shultz; *col:* Tech. *sd:* RCA. 6 min. • On their wedding eve, Olive has a nightmare about being married to Popeye and calls the wedding off. Remake of *Wimmin Is a Myskery.*

773. Bridge Ahoy! (*Popeye*) 1 May 1936; *p.c.:* The Fleischer Studio for Para; *prod:* Max Fleischer; *dir:* Dave Fleischer; *story:* Elsworth Barthen; *anim:* Seymour Kneitel, Roland Crandall; *voices:* Jack Mercer, Mae Questel, Gus Wickie, Louis Fleischer; *mus:* Sammy Timberg; b&w. *sd:* WE. 7 min. • Bluto's ferry costs too much so Popeye decides to build a bridge across the canal.

774. A Bridge Grows in Brooklyn (*GoGo Toon*) Oct. 1967; *p.c.:* Para Cartoons; *ex prod:* Shamus Culhane; *dir:* Chuck Harriton; *story:* Howard Beckerman; *anim:* Doug Crane, Nick Tafuri; *des:* Danté Barbetta, Gil Miret, Dave Ubinas, Howard Beckerman; *voice:* Joe Silver; *mus:* Winston Sharples; *prod sup:* Harold Robins, Burt Hanft; *col:* Tech. *sd:* RCA. 5½ min. • A seasoned riveter scorns his young assistant for lack of interest in building a bridge. Fred Fallguy, his assistant, prefers flowers ... and they eventually come to his rescue.

775. Bridgework (*Roland & Rattfink*) 26 Aug. 1970; *p.c.:* Mirisch/DFE for UA; *dir:* Art Davis; *story:* Dale Hale; *anim:* Manny Perez, Irv Spence, Robert Taylor, Ken Muse, Warren Batchelder, Don Williams; *lay:* Lin Larsen; *back:* Richard Thomas; *ed:* Lee Gunther; *voices:* Leonard Weinrib; *mus:* Doug Goodwin; *prod sup:* Jim Foss, Harry Love; *col:* DeLuxe. *sd:* RCA. 6 min. • Rattfink gets a job on a bridge-building excavation in order to sabotage the works so his uncle can sell inferior goods to the foreman.

776. Bright Lights (*Oswald the Lucky Rabbit*) 13 Mar. 1928; *p.c.:* Winkler for Univ; *dir:* Walt Disney; *anim:* Hugh Harman, Rollin C. Hamilton; *ph:* Mike Marcus; b&w. sil. 6 min. • Oswald slips backstage at the Follies, eventually emptying the theater when chased by a pack of lions and a tiger.

777. Bring 'Em Back Half-Shot (*Aesop's Sound Fable*) 9 Sept. 1932; *p.c.:* Van Beuren for RKO; *dir:* John Foster, Mannie Davis; *mus:* Gene Rodemich; b&w. *sd:* RCA. 7 min. • Parody of Van Beuren's wildlife series, "Bring 'em Back Alive" featuring Cubby Bear as an intrepid big game hunter finding ferocious animals disporting themselves in a languorous style.

778. Bring Himself Back Alive (*Animated Antics*) 20 Dec. 1940; *p.c.:* The Fleischer Studio for Para; *prod:* Max Fleischer; *dir:* Dave Fleischer; *story:* Cal Howard; *anim:* Tom Johnson, Graham Place, Jack Ozark; *ed:* Kitty Pfister; *mus:* Sammy Timberg; *ph:* Charles Schettler; *prod sup:* Sam Buchwald, Isidore Sparber; b&w. *sd:* WE. 7 min. • Hyde Skinner, unscrupulous jungle trapper, embarks on safari. He manages to trap a lion in its lair and plans to blow the creature up with explosives but in the process finds himself ensnared in his one of his own traps. The lion departs, leaving Hyde with the lighted stick of dynamite. He sends his faithful turtle companion for help but this gesture proves to be too late.

779. Bringing Home the Bacon (*Terry-Toon*) 11 July 1941; *p.c.:* TT for Fox; *dir:* Mannie Davis; *story:* John Foster; *mus:* Philip A. Scheib; b&w. *sd:* RCA. 7 min. • No story available.

780. Bringing Up Mother (*Family Circus*) 14 Jan. 1954; *p.c.:* UPA for Colum; *ex prod:* Stephen Bosustow; *dir:* William T. Hurtz; *story:* Tedd Pierce, William Hurtz; *anim:* Fred Grable, Tom McDonald; *sets:* Robert Dranko; *voices:* Jerry Hausner, Marian Richman; *mus:* Benjamin Lees; *prod mgr:* Herbert Klynn; *col:* Tech. *sd:* RCA. 6 min. • A small boy feels neglected and runs away from home when his mother brings home a new baby brother.

781. Broadcasting (*Pen & Ink Vaudeville*) 14 Jan. 1925; *p.c.:* Hurd prods for Ed; *dir/anim:* Earl Hurd; b&w. *sil.* 5 min. • Props, in a broadcasting station, tries to select artists that please both him and the manager. Fat singers, dancers and numerous others perform to the dissatisfaction of the audience of two.

782. Broadway Bow Wow's (*Cartune*) 2 Aug. 1954; *p.c.:* Walter Lantz prods for Univ; *dir/story:* Grant Simmons, Ray Patterson; *sets:* Raymond Jacobs, Art Landy; *voices:* Dick Nelson, Gladys Holland; *mus:* Clarence Wheeler; *prod mgr:* William E. Garity; *col:* Tech. *sd:* RCA. 6 min. • Canine vaudeville team, John and Mary, have their careers elevated from Petoria to "The Palace." John leaves Mary for another but they are reunited for the finale.

783. Broadway Folly (*Oswald*) 19 Feb. 1930; *p.c.:* Univ; *anim:* Walter Lantz, "Bill" Nolan, Manuel Moreno; *mus:* David Broekman;; b&w. *sd:* WE. 6 min. • No story available.

784. The Broadway Malady (*Krazy Kat*) 18 Apr. 1933; *p.c.:* Winkler for Colum; *story:* Ben Harrison, Manny Gould; *anim:* Al Rose, Harry Love, Al Eugster; *mus:* Joe de Nat; *prod:* Charles Mintz; b&w. *sd:* WE. 6 min. • Each time Krazy tries to enter a subway car he gets trampled underfoot.

785. A Broken Leghorn (*Looney Tunes*) 26 Sept. 1959; *p.c.:* WB; *dir:* Robert McKimson; *story:* Warren Foster; *anim:* Ted Bonnicksen, Warren Batchelder, Tom Ray, George Grandpré; *lay:* Robert Gribbroek; *back:* William Butler; *ed:* Treg Brown; *voices:* Mel Blanc, June Foray; *mus:* Milt Franklyn; *prod mgr:* William Orcutt; *prod:* David H. DePatie; *col:* Tech. *sd:* Vit. 7 min. • Foggy tries to dispose of a young rooster who is intent on taking over his job.

786. Broken Toys (*Silly Symphony*) 14 Dec. 1935; *p.c.:* Walt Disney prods for UA; *dir:* Ben Sharpsteen; *anim:* Arthur Babbitt, Johnny Cannon, George Drake, Dick Huemor, John McManus, Grim Natwick, Wolfgang Reitherman, Leonard Sebring, Vladimir Tytla, Berny Wolf, Marvin Woodward, Bob Wickersham; *asst anim:* James Algar; *fx:* Cy Young; *voices:* Alyce Ardell, Jesus Topete, Tommy Bupp; *mus:* Albert Hay Malotte; *col:* Tech. *sd:* RCA. 8 min. • Discarded toys on the City Dump decide to rejuvenate themselves. Caricatures of Step'n Fetchit, W.C. Fields, ZaSu Pitts and Ned Sparks.

787. Broken Treaties (*This Changing World*) 1 Aug. 1941; *p.c.:* Cartoon Films Ltd for Colum; *dir:* Paul Fennell; *ed:* Almond Teeter; *mus:* Clarence Wheeler; *ph:* Richard M. Ising; *l/a:* Raymond Gram Swing; *prod:* Lawson Haris; *col:* Dunning. *sd:* 8 min. • An animated piece showing Adolph Hitler making a deal with Mussolini (both with crossed fingers). The invasion of Poland is shown and Uncle Sam watching over America.

788. The Bronco Buster (*Aesop's Film Fable*) 1 Jan. 1928; *p.c.:* Fables Pictures Inc for Pathé; *dir:* Paul Terry, Frank Moser; b&w. *sil.* 10 min. • Farmer Al trains for the big rodeo concurrently with mechanical horses. The mechanical horse kicks the farmer and is carried off in glory by his fellow mechanical equines. Moral: "Don't brag; it's not the whistle that pulls the locomotive."

789. Bronco Buster (*Oswald*) 5 Aug. 1935; *p.c.:* Univ; *prod/dir:* Walter Lantz; *story/lyrics:* Walter Lantz, Victor McLeod; *anim:* Fred Kopietz, Lester Kline, Bill Mason, La Verne Harding; *voices:* The Sons of the Pioneers; *mus:* James Dietrich; b&w. *sd:* WE. 7 min. • Travelling salesman Oswald hits a ranch. He feeds a tough bronco Hare Tonic, thus rendering the creature conquerable.

790. Broom-Stick Bunny (*Looney Tunes*) 25 Feb. 1956; *p.c.:* WB; *dir:* Chuck Jones; *story:* Tedd Pierce; *anim:* Ken Harris, Richard Thompson, Ben Washam, Abe Levitow; *lay:* Ernie Nordli; *back:* Philip de Guard; *ed:* Treg Brown; *voices:* Mel Blanc, June Foray; *mus:* Milt Franklyn; *prod mgr:* John W. Burton; *prod:* Edward Selzer; *col:* Tech. *sd:* Vit. 7 min. • Bugs, in a "Trick-or-Treat" costume encounters Witch Hazel who believes him to be another witch that's uglier than she is and has to dispose of him.

791. Brother Bat (*Honey Halfwitch*) June 1967; *p.c.:* Para Cartoons; *ex prod:* Shamus Culhane; *dir:* Chuck Harriton; *story:* Howard Post; *anim:* Doug Crane, Nick Tafuri; *sets:* Danté Barbetta, Dave Ubinas; *voices:* Bob MacFadden; *mus:* Winston Sharples; *prod sup:* Harold Robins, Burt Hanft; *col:* Tech. *sd:* RCA. 6½ min. • Honey turns Fraidy Bat invisible so Cousin Maggie won't know he's in the house.

792. Brother Brat (*Looney Tunes*) 15 July 1944; *p.c.:* Leon Schlesinger prods for WB; *dir:* Frank Tashlin; *story:* Melvin Millar; *anim:* Art Davis; *sets:* Richard H. Thomas; *ed:* Treg Brown; *voices:* Mel Blanc, Bea Benaderet, Paul Regan; *mus:* Carl W. Stalling; *ph:* John W. Burton; *prod sup:* Henry Binder, Raymond G. Katz; *col:* Tech. *sd:* Vit. 7 min. • Porky babysits a shift-worker's brat.

793. Brother from Outer Space (*Terry Toon*) Mar. 1964; *p.c.:* TT for Fox; *ex prod:* Bill Weiss; *dir/anim:* Connie Rasinski; *story sup:* Tom Morrison; *story:* Larz Bourne; *sets:* Bill Focht, John Zago; *ed:* Jack MacConnell; *voices:* Dayton Allen; *mus:* Phil Scheib; *ph:* Charles Schettler, Ted Moskowitz, Joe Rasinski; *sd:* Elliot Grey; *col:* DeLuxe. *sd:* RCA. 5½ min. • Astro arrives from outer space and helps Oscar Mild capture a gang of bank robbers before returning back home.

794. Brotherly Love (*Popeye*) 6 Mar. 1936; *p.c.:* The Fleischer Studio for Para; *prod:* Max Fleischer; *dir:* Dave Fleischer; *anim:* Seymour Kneitel, Roland Crandall; *voices:* Jack Mercer, Mae Questel, Gus Wickie; *mus:* Sammy Timberg; *song:* Bob Rothberg, Sammy Timberg; b&w. *sd:* WE. 7 min. • Popeye tries to encourage Olive's "Brotherly Love" policy but has difficulties in advocating peace during a street brawl.

795. The Brothers Carry-Mouse-Off (*Tom & Jerry*) 1966; *p.c.:* MGM; *prod:* Chuck Jones; *dir:* Jim Pabian; *asst dir:* Maurice Noble; *story:* Chuck Jones, Jim Pabian; *anim:* Tom Ray, Dick Thompson, Ben Washam, Ken Harris, Don Towsley; *back:* Robert Gribbroek; *mus:* Eugene Poddany; *prod sup:* Les Goldman, Earl Jonas; *col:* Metro. *sd:* WE. 7 min. • Tom resorts to dressing as a mouse to lure Jerry into his clutches.

796. Bruce Gentry — Daredevil of the Skies 1949. *p.c.:* Colum; *prod:* Sam Katzman; *special anim fx:* Howard Swift. b&w. *sd:* WE. 20 min each. *l/a.* • Live-action fifteen-episode serial in which Bruce Gentry investigates an (animated) lethal flying disc.

797. Bubble Bee (*Pluto*) 24 June 1949; *p.c.:* Walt Disney prods for RKO; *dir:* Charles Nichols; *story:* Eric Gurney, Milt Schaffer; *anim:* Phil Duncan, Hugh Fraser, George Kreisl, George Nicholas; *fx:* Dan MacManus, Jack Boyd; *lay:* Karl Karpé; *back:* Brice Mack; *voice:* James MacDonald; *mus:* Oliver Wallace; *col:* Tech. *sd:* RCA. 6½ min. • Pluto has a brush with a bee who has a penchant for bubble gum.

798. Bubbles (*Aesop's Film Fable*) 8 Aug. 1925; *p.c.:* Fables Pictures Inc for Pathé; *dir:* Paul Terry; b&w. *sil.* 10 min. • The cat and mice blow bubbles and sail through the air. Farmer Al takes a tumble when he tries it.

799. Bubbles (*Out of the Inkwell*) 20 Apr. 1922; *p.c.:* Inkwell Studio for Winkler; *prod/l/a:* Max Fleischer; *dir:* Dave Fleischer; b&w. *sil.* 5 min. *l/a/anim.* • Ko-Ko sees a child blowing bubbles and bets Max who can blow the largest bubble. The results are weird and wonderful.

800. Bubbles and Troubles (*Aesop's Sound Fable*) 28 Apr. 1933; *p.c.:* Van Beuren for RKO; *dir:* Mannie Davis; *mus:* Gene Rodemich; b&w. *sd:* RCA. 6 min. • Cubby Bear's wash day sees him carried away in a giant bubble.

801. Bubbling Over (*Aesop's Film Fable*) 8 May 1927; *p.c.:* Fables Pictures Inc for Pathé; *dir:* Paul Terry; b&w. *sil.* 10 min. • A villainous cat steals a mouse's sweetheart in an airplane. The resourceful mouse trails them in a huge bubble.

802. Buccaneer Bunny (*Looney Tunes*) 8 May 1948; *p.c.:* WB; *dir:* I. Freleng; *story:* Michael Maltese, Tedd Pierce, Robert Clampett; *anim:* Manuel Perez, Ken Champin, Virgil Ross, Gerry Chiniquy; *lay:* Hawley

Pratt; *back:* Paul Julian; *ed:* Treg Brown; *voices:* Mel Blanc; *mus:* Carl Stalling; *prod mgr:* John W. Burton; *prod:* Edward Selzer; *col:* Tech. *sd:* Vit. 7 min. • Yosemite Sam the pirate buries his loot in Bugs' home. He pursues Bugs to his galleon and there a chase ensues.

803. Buccaneer Woodpecker *(Woody Woodpecker)* 20 Apr. 1953; *p.c.:* Walter Lantz prods for Univ; *dir:* Don Patterson; *story:* Homer Brightman; *anim:* La Verne Harding, Ray Abrams; *sets:* Art Landy; *voices:* Dal McKennon, Grace Stafford; *mus:* Clarence Wheeler; *prod mgr:* William E. Garity; *col:* Tech. *sd:* RCA. 6 min. • Woody tries to capture pirate Buzz Buzzard for a handsome reward.

804. Buck Fever *(Aesop's Film Fable)* 28 Nov. 1926; *p.c.:* Fables Pictures Inc for Pathé; *dir:* Paul Terry; *b&w. sil.* 10 min. • Farmer Al Falfa and his pup go hunting. When a lion knocks the farmer about, the pup chases the beast into a cave, returning with five lions in tow, having licked them all. Moral: "Hunting is like hash; you must have confidence to enjoy it."

805. Buckaroo Bugs *(Looney Tunes)* 26 Aug. 1944; *p.c.:* Leon Schlesinger prods for WB; *dir:* Robert Clampett; *story:* Lou Lilly; *anim:* Manny Gould; *lay:* Thomas McKimson; *back:* Michael Sasanoff; *ed:* Treg Brown; *voices:* Mel Blanc, Robert Cameron Bruce; *mus:* Carl W. Stalling; *prod sup:* Henry Binder, Raymond G. Katz; *col:* Tech. *sd:* Vit. 7 min. • "The Masked Marauder" (Bugs) steals carrots from the townsfolk's Victory gardens and it's up to Red Hot Ryder to put a stop to him doing so.

806. Buddies Thicker Than Water *(Tom & Jerry)* Nov. 1962; *p.c.:* Rembrandt for MGM; *prod:* William L. Snyder; *dir:* Gene Deitch; *story:* Larz Bourne; *mus:* Stepan Konícek; *col:* Metro. *sd:* WE. 8 min. • Jerry takes pity on Tom and brings him up to his penthouse suite. The owner arrives and tries to throw the cat out, so Tom proves himself to be a good mousecatcher by throwing Jerry out. • See: *Tom & Jerry (Rembrandt Studio)*

807. Buddy and Towser *(Looney Tunes)* 24 Feb. 1934; *p.c.:* Leon Schlesinger prods for WB; *dir:* Isadore Freleng; *anim:* Jack King, Bob McKimson, Robert Clampett; *voice:* Jack Carr; *mus:* Norman Spencer; *prod sup:* Henry Binder, Raymond G. Katz; *b&w. sd:* Vit. 7 min. • Buddy and Towser go fox hunting but the crafty beast rolls a giant snowball atop of them.

808. Buddy Bear (series) 1931; *p.c.:* Bromberg Pictures; *prod:* A.J. Bromberg; *b&w. sd.* • Titles and stories untraced.

809. Buddy in Africa *(Looney Tunes)* 6 July 1935; *p.c.:* Leon Schlesinger prods for WB; *dir:* Ben Hardaway; *anim:* Jack Carr, Don Williams, Robert Clampett; *voices:* Jackie Morrow, the Four Blackbirds; *mus:* Norman Spencer; *prod sup:* Henry Binder, Raymond G. Katz; *b&w. sd:* Vit. 7 min. • Buddy takes his traveling store into the jungle to sell his wares to the natives.

810. Buddy of the Apes *(Looney Tunes)* 26 May 1934; *p.c.:* Leon Schlesinger prods for WB; *dir:* Ben Hardaway; *anim:* Paul Smith, Sandy Walker; *voices:* Billy Bletcher, Bernard Brown; *mus:* Bernard Brown; *prod sup:* Henry Binder, Raymond G. Katz; *b&w. sd:* Vit. 7 min. • This burlesque on the recent spate of nature pictures has Buddy and his jungle chums beating up the natives.

811. Buddy of the Legion *(Looney Tunes)* 6 Apr. 1935; *p.c.:* Leon Schlesinger prods for WB; *dir:* Ben Hardaway; *anim:* Bob Clampett, Charles Jones; *voices:* Tommy Bond; *mus:* Bernard Brown; *prod sup:* Henry Binder, Raymond G. Katz; *b&w. sd:* Vit. 7 min. • Buddy dreams he's a Legionaire who has to rescue his troop that's been captured by a tribe of Amazon women.

812. Buddy Steps Out *(Looney Tunes)* 20 July 1935; *p.c.:* Leon Schlesinger prods for WB; *dir:* Jack King; *anim:* Charles Jones, Robert Clampett; *voice:* Tommy Bond; *mus:* Bernard Brown; *prod sup:* Henry Binder, Raymond G. Katz; *b&w. sd:* Vit. 7 min. • Buddy and Cookie step out from their photographic frames to rescue a little bird.

813. Buddy the Dentist *(Looney Tunes)* 5 Mar. 1935; *p.c.:* Leon Schlesinger prods for WB; *dir:* Ben Hardaway; *anim:* Rollin Hamilton, Jack King, Robert Clampett; *voices:* Jackie Morrow, Dorothy Varden; *mus:* Norman Spencer; *prod sup:* Henry Binder, Raymond G. Katz; *b&w. sd:* Vit. 7 min. • Buddy tries to pull Towser's aching tooth.

814. Buddy the Detective *(Looney Tunes)* 5 Mar. 1935; *p.c.:* Leon Schlesinger prods for WB; *dir:* Jack King; *anim:* Paul Smith, Don Williams, Robert Clampett; *voices:* Billy Bletcher, Dorothy Varden, Jackie Morrow;

mus: Bernard Brown; *prod sup:* Henry Binder, Raymond G. Katz; *b&w. sd:* Vit. 7 min. • A mad musician hypnotizes Cookie and gets her to play somber sonatas for him on the piano.

815. Buddy the Gee Man *(Looney Tunes)* 24 Aug. 1935; *p.c.:* Leon Schlesinger prods for WB; *dir:* Jack King; *anim:* Sandy Walker, Cal Dalton; *voices:* Billy Bletcher, Jackie Morrow; *mus:* Norman Spencer; *prod sup:* Henry Binder, Raymond G. Katz; *b&w. sd:* Vit. 7 min. • Buddy is put in charge of Sing Song Prison and turns it into a holiday camp.

816. Buddy the Gob *(Looney Tunes)* 13 Jan. 1935; *p.c.:* Leon Schlesinger prods for WB; *dir:* Isadore Freleng; *anim:* Jack King, Ben Clopton, Robert Clampett; *voices:* Jack Carr; *mus:* Norman Spencer; *prod sup:* Henry Binder, Raymond G. Katz; *b&w. sd:* Vit. 6 min. • Sailor Buddy docks in China where he rescues a girl about to be sacrificed in a ceremony. Caricatures of Marie Dressler and Jimmy Durante.

817. Buddy the Woodsman *(Looney Tunes)* 20 Oct. 1934; *p.c.:* Leon Schlesinger prods for WB; *dir/lay:* Jack King; *anim:* Paul Smith, Don Williams, Robert Clampett; *voices:* Mary Moder, Billy Bletcher, Jack Carr; *mus:* Bernard Brown; *prod sup:* Henry Binder, Raymond G. Katz; *b&w. sd:* Vit. 7 min. • The lumberjacks' lunch is disturbed by the arrival of a bear but Buddy and Cookie in the cookhouse send him packing with some pepper.

818. Buddy's Adventures *(Looney Tunes)* 4 Mar. 1935; *p.c.:* Leon Schlesinger prods for WB; *dir:* Ben Hardaway; *anim:* Bob McKimson, Don Williams, Bob Clampett; *voices:* Billy Bletcher, Elmore Vincent, Bernard B. Brown; *mus:* Bernard B. Brown; *prod sup:* Henry Binder, Raymond G. Katz; *b&w. sd:* Vit. 7 min. • Buddy and Cookie find themselves in "Sour Town" where King Sourpan bans music and dancing. They finally cheer the place up by singing and dancing. Caricatures of Laurel & Hardy, Ned Sparks.

819. Buddy's Bearcats *(Looney Tunes)* 25 June 1934; *p.c.:* Leon Schlesinger prods for WB; *dir:* Jack King; *anim:* Ben Clopton, Bob Clampett; *voices:* Mary Moder, Jack Carr; *mus:* Norman Spencer; *prod sup:* Henry Binder, Raymond G. Katz; *b&w. sd:* Vit. 7 min. • A baseball game between Buddy's Bearcats and the Battling Bruisers with Joe E. Brown as the announcer.

820. Buddy's Beer Garden *(Looney Tunes)* 11 Nov. 1933; *p.c.:* Leon Schlesinger prods for WB; *dir:* Earl Duval; *anim:* Jack King "Tish-Tash" (Frank Tashlin), Bob Clampett; *voices:* Billy Bletcher, Charles Judels, Mary Moder, Jack Carr; *mus:* Norman Spencer; *prod mgr:* Henry Binder, Raymond G. Katz; *b&w. sd:* Vit. 6 min. • Buddy and Cookie entertain in a German Beer Garden where Mae West provides a surprise appearance.

821. Buddy's Bug Hunt *(Looney Tunes)* 22 June 1935; *p.c.:* Leon Schlesinger prods for WB; *dir:* Jack King; *anim:* Bob McKimson, Paul Smith, Bob Clampett; *voices:* Billy Bletcher, Bernice Hansel, Jackie Morrow; *mus:* Norman Spencer; *prod mgr:* Henry Binder, Raymond G. Katz; *b&w. sd:* Vit. 7 min. • Buddy dreams his bug collection comes alive and forces him to take reducing pills so he can be put on trial by the insects.

822. Buddy's Circus *(Looney Tunes)* 8 Nov. 1934; *p.c.:* Leon Schlesinger prods for WB; *dir:* Jack King; *anim:* Bob McKimson, Ben Clopton, Bob Clampett; *voices:* Mary Moder, Jack Carr; *mus:* Norman Spencer; *prod sup:* Henry Binder, Raymond G. Katz; *b&w. sd:* Vit. 7 min. • Buddy has his hands full while running his circus when a baby from the audience gets mixed up with the aerial act.

823. Buddy's Day Out *(Looney Tunes)* 9 Sept. 1933; *p.c.:* Leon Schlesinger prods for WB; *dir:* Tom Palmer; *anim:* Bill Mason, Bob Clampett; *voices:* Mary Moder, Bernard Brown; *mus:* Norman Spencer, Bernard Brown; *prod sup:* Henry Binder, Raymond G. Katz; *b&w. sd:* Vit. 8 min. • Buddy, Cookie, baby Elmer and their dog, Bozo, go on a picnic.

824. Buddy's Garage *(Looney Tunes)* 14 Apr. 1934; *p.c.:* Leon Schlesinger prods for WB; *dir:* Earl Duval; *anim:* Jack King, Sandy Walker, Bob Clampett; *voices:* Bernice Hansel, Bernard Brown; *mus:* Bernard Brown; *prod sup:* Henry Binder, Raymond G. Katz; *b&w. sd:* Vit. 6½ min. • A villain makes off with Cookie with Buddy in hot pursuit in a tow-truck.

825. Buddy's Lost World *(Looney Tunes)* 18 May 1935; *p.c.:* Leon Schlesinger prods for WB; *dir/lay:* Jack King; *story:* Bob Clampett; *anim:*

Rollin Hamilton, Sandy Walker, Bob Clampett; *voice:* Tommy Bond; *mus:* Norman Spencer; *prod sup:* Henry Binder, Raymond G. Katz; b&w. *sd:* Vit. 7 min. • Buddy and Bozo discover a lost civilization where cavemen and dinosaurs still roam the earth. Caricature of The Three Stooges.

826. Buddy's Pony Express *(Looney Tunes)* 9 Mar. 1935; *p.c.:* Leon Schlesinger prods for WB; *dir:* Ben Hardaway; *anim:* Ben Clopton, Cal Dalton; *voices:* Bernice Hansel, Billy Bletcher, Jack Carr; *mus:* Bernard Brown; *prod sup:* Henry Binder, Raymond G. Katz; b&w. *sd:* Vit. 7 min. • Cowboy Buddy gets involved with The Pony Express.

827. Buddy's Showboat *(Looney Tunes)* 9 Dec. 1933; *p.c.:* Leon Schlesinger prods for WB; *dir:* Earl Duval; *anim:* Jack King, James Pabian, Bob Clampett; *voices:* Mary Moder, Jack Carr; *mus:* Bernard Brown; *prod sup:* Henry Binder, Raymond G. Katz; b&w. *sd:* Vit. 6½ min. • Buddy and Cookie do their showboat performance when a villainous deck hand abducts Cookie. He is promptly squelched by a walrus.

828. Buddy's Theatre *(Looney Tunes)* 1 Apr. 1935; *p.c.:* Leon Schlesinger prods for WB; *dir:* Ben Hardaway; *story:* Robert Clampett; *anim:* Don Williams, Sandy Walker, Robert Clampett; *voices:* Bernice Hansel, Jack Carr; *mus:* Norman Spencer; *prod sup:* Henry Binder, Raymond G. Katz; b&w. *sd:* Vit. 7 min. • Buddy runs the "Coming Attraction" starring Cookie, becoming involved with the movie when she's captured by a wild gorilla.

829. Buddy's Trolley Troubles *(Looney Tunes)* 5 May 1934; *p.c.:* Leon Schlesinger prods for WB; *dir:* Isadore Freleng; *anim:* Ben Clopton, Frank Tipper, Robert Clampett; *voices:* Mary Moder, Jack Carr, Ted Pierce; *mus:* Norman Spencer; *prod sup:* Henry Binder, Raymond G. Katz; b&w. *sd:* Vit. 8 min. • An escaped convict makes his getaway on Buddy's trolleybus, taking Cookie as hostage.

830. The Bug Carnival *(Paul Terry-Toon)* 16 Apr. 1937; *p.c.:* TT for Educational/Fox; *dir:* Mannie Davis, George Gordon; *mus:* Philip A. Scheib; b&w. *sd:* RCA. 6 min. • A spider kidnaps a female acrobat bug.

831. The Bug Parade *(Merrie Melodies)* 11 Oct. 1941; *p.c.:* Leon Schlesinger prods for WB; *dir:* Fred Avery; *story:* Dave Monahan, Robert Clampett; *anim:* Rod Scribner, sets: John Didrik Johnsen; *ed:* Treg Brown; *voices:* Robert C. Bruce, Mel Blanc, Billy Bletcher; *mus:* Carl W. Stalling; *ph:* John W. Burton; *prod sup:* Henry Binder, Raymond G. Katz; *col:* Tech. *sd:* Vit. 7 min. • An in-depth look at insect life.

832. Bug Vaudeville *(Dreams of the Rarebit Fiend)* 1921; *p.c.:* Rialto prods for Vit; *dir/anim:* Winsor McCay; b&w. st. • A man eats a hearty meal, sleeps and dreams of performing insects cavorting around him.

833. Bugged By a Bee *(Looney Tunes)* 9 May 1969; *p.c.:* WB/7A; *dir:* Bob McKimson; *story:* Cal Howard; *anim:* Ted Bonnicksen, La Verne Harding, Jim Davis, Ed Solomon; *lay:* Bob Givens, Jaime Diaz; *back:* Bob Abrams; *ed:* Hal Geer, Don Douglas; *voices:* Larry Storch; *mus:* William Lava; *prod:* Bill L. Hendricks; *col:* Tech. *sd:* Vit. 6 min. • A bothersome bee forces Cool Cat to win all the athletic events in the Disco Tech sports.

834. Bugged By a Bug *(James Hound)* June 1967; *p.c.:* TT for Fox; *dir:* Ralph Bakshi; *col:* DeLuxe. *sd:* RCA. 6 min. • An information leak at HQ leads Hound to the hideout of Professor Mad who has put bugging devices in a swarm of insects. • See: *James Hound*

835. Bugged in a Rug *(Beary Family)* May 1965; *p.c.:* Walter Lantz prods for Univ; *dir:* Paul J. Smith; *story:* Cal Howard; *anim:* Les Kline, Al Coe; *sets:* Nino Carbe; *voices:* Paul Frees, Grace Stafford; *mus:* Walter Greene; *prod mgr:* William E. Garity; *col:* Tech. *sd:* RCA. 5½ min. • Charlie tries to fit a new carpet on his own.

836. A Buggy Ride *(Aesop's Film Fable)* 12 Sept. 1926; *p.c.:* Fables Pictures Inc for Pathé; *dir:* Paul Terry; b&w. sil. 10 min. • Benny Beetle dashes to the rescue of June Bug when she's abducted by King Cricket in a swashbuckling melodrama for insects.

837. Bughouse College Days *(Aesop's Sound Fable)* 4 Aug. 1929; *p.c.:* Fables Pictures Inc for Pathé; *dir:* Paul Terry; *mus:* Josiah Zuro; sd fx: Maurice Manne; b&w. *sd:* RCA. 6 min. • A race between a spider and a fly ends with the spider kidnapping the fly's girl and a duel to the death.

838. Bugs and Books *(Aesop's Sound Fable)* 30 Dec. 1932; *p.c.:* Van Beuren for RKO; *dir:* John Foster, Mannie Davis; *voice:* Marjorie Hines; *mus:* Gene Rodemich; b&w. *sd:* RCA. 7 min. • No story available.

839. Bugs and Thugs *(Looney Tunes)* 13 Mar. 1954; *p.c.:* WB; *dir:* I. Freleng; *story:* Warren Foster; *anim:* Manuel Perez, Ken Champin, Virgil Ross, Arthur Davis; *lay:* Hawley Pratt; *back:* Irv Wyner; *ed:* Treg Brown; *voices:* Mel Blanc; *mus:* Milt Franklyn; *prod mgr:* John W. Burton; *prod:* Edward Selzer; *col:* Tech. *sd:* Vit. 7 min. • When Bugs mistakes a getaway car for a taxi, two gangsters take him to their hideout to dispose of him.

840. Bugs Beetle and His Orchestra *(Terry-Toon)* 21 Jan. 1938; *p.c.:* TT for Educational/Fox; *dir:* John Foster; *mus:* Philip A. Scheib; b&w. *sd:* RCA. 6 min. • A spider disrupts the festivities at The Big Apple Nightclub. He then fights a duel with some bugs.

841. Bugs' Bonnets *(Merrie Melodies)* 14 Jan. 1956; *p.c.:* WB; Chuck Jones; *story:* Tedd Pierce; *anim:* Ben Washam, Abe Levitow, Richard Thompson, Ken Harris; *lay:* Robert Givens; *back:* Richard H. Thomas; *ed:* Treg Brown; *voices:* Mel Blanc, Arthur Q. Bryan, Robert C. Bruce; *mus:* Milt Franklyn; *prod mgr:* John W. Burton; *prod:* Edward Selzer; *col:* Tech. *sd:* Vit. 7 min. • The old adage that a person's character changes by the hat he wears is put to the test when a truckload of hats lands in the midst of Elmer's rabbit hunt.

842. Bugs Bunny and the Three Bears *(Merrie Melodies)* 26 June 1944; *p.c.:* Leon Schlesinger prods for WB; *dir:* Charles M. Jones; *story:* Tedd Pierce; *anim:* Robert Cannon; *ed:* Treg Brown; *lay:* Bernice Polifka; *voices:* Mel Blanc, Kent Rogers, Bea Benaderet; *mus:* Carl W. Stalling; *ph:* John W. Burton; *prod sup:* Henry Binder, Raymond G. Katz; *col:* Tech. *sd:* Vit. 7 min. • The Three Bears place carrot soup on the menu in hopes of luring Goldilocks into their clutches ... Bugs Bunny arrives instead.

843. Bugs Bunny Gets the Boid *(Merrie Melodies)* 4 July 1942; *p.c.:* Leon Schlesinger prods for WB; *dir:* Robert Clampett; *story:* Warren Foster; *anim:* Rod Scribner, Robert McKimson; *lay/character des:* Thomas McKimson; *back:* Michael Sasanoff; *ed:* Treg Brown; *voices:* Mel Blanc, Kent Rogers, Sara Berner; *mus:* Carl W. Stalling; *ph:* John W. Burton; *prod sup:* Henry Binder, Raymond G. Katz; *col:* Tech. *sd:* Vit. 7 min. • Beaky Buzzard is sent by Mama to capture a rabbit for dinner. The dim-witted bird tries to ensnare Bugs, never learning by his mistakes.

844. Bugs Bunny Nips the Nips *(Merrie Melodies)* 22 Apr. 1944; *p.c.:* Leon Schlesinger prods for WB; *dir:* I. Freleng; *story:* Tedd Pierce; *anim:* Gerry Chiniquy, Virgil Ross; *lay:* Hawley Pratt; *back:* Paul Julian; *ed:* Treg Brown; *voices:* Mel Blanc, Bea Benaderet; *mus:* Carl W. Stalling; *ph:* John W. Burton; *prod sup:* Henry Binder, Raymond G. Katz; *col:* Tech. *sd:* Vit. 7 min. • Bugs is marooned on a Pacific island during an invasion of Japanese soldiers.

845. Bugs Bunny Rides Again *(Merrie Melodies)* 12 June 1948; *p.c.:* WB; *dir:* I. Freleng; *story:* Tedd Pierce, Michael Maltese; *anim:* Ken Champin, Virgil Ross, Gerry Chiniquy, Manuel Perez; *lay:* Hawley Pratt; *back:* Paul Julian; *ed:* Treg Brown; *voices:* Mel Blanc; *mus:* Carl Stalling; *prod mgr:* John W. Burton; *prod:* Edward Selzer; *col:* Tech. *sd:* Vit. 7 min. • A tough western hombre named "Slingin' Sam" tells Bugs that the town ain't big enough for the two of them and proceeds to try to run Bugs out of town. This isn't as easy as it sounds.

846. Bugs Bunny Superstar 1975; *p.c.:* Hare-Raising Films for UA; *prod/dir:* Larry Jackson; *asso prods:* Terrence Corey, Rob McMicking, Martha Pinson; *prod sup:* Richard Waltzer; *ph:* Gary Graven; *ph asst:* Michael Ferris, Michael Stringer, Jim Gillie, David Donnelly, Brian King; *sd:* Darcy Vebber; *ed:* Brian King; *des:* Candace Clemens; *prod sup:* Sody Clampett, Lyn Radeloff, Dal Lamagna; *voice:* Orson Welles; featuring Bob Clampett, Tex Avery, Friz Freleng; *mus:* Ian Whitcomb; *Special thanks:* Joe Adamson, Joshua Balgley, Mike Barrier, Columbia Pictures, Roger Dollarhide, Greg Ford, Milt Grey, Mark Kausler, Donald Krim, Lonnie Lloyd, Leonard Maltin, Museum of Modern Art Stills Archive, Paul Satterfield, Frank Siteman, Stock Boston Photos, Richard Simonton, David Stone, Kathy Torrence, Joe Trentin; *col:* Tech. *sd.* 65 min. l/a/anim. • Seq: *What's Cookin' Doc?; The Unmentionables; A Wild Hare; A Corny Concerto; I Taw a Putty Tat; Any Bonds Today?; Rhapsody Rabbit; My Favorite Duck; Hair-Raising Hare; Old Grey Hare.* • Compilation feature peppered with "Home movies" shot around the Schlesinger Studio and interviews with Bob Clampett.

847. Bugs in Love *(Silly Symphony)* 1 Oct. 1932; *p.c.:* Walt Disney prods for UA; *dir:* Wilfred Jackson; *anim:* Les Clark, Gilles de Tremaudan, Norman Ferguson, David D. Hand, Jack King, Tom Palmer; *mus:* Frank E.

Churchill; b&w. *sd:* PCP. 7 min. • A girl bug is captured by a crow and the others come to her rescue, imprisoning the crow in an old shoe.

848. A Bug's Life 25 Nov. 1998; *p.c.:* Disney Enterprises, Inc./Pixar Animation Studios for BV; *dir:* John Lasseter; *co-dir:* Andrew Stanton; *prod:* Darla K. Anderson, Kevin Reher; *story:* John Lasseter, Andrew Stanton, Joe Ranft; *scr:* Andrew Stanton, Donald McEnery, Bob Shaw; *story sup:* Joe Ranft; *addit story:* Geefwee Boedoe, Jason Katz, Jorgen Klubien, Robert Lence, David Reynolds; *story team: story mgr:* Susan E. Levin; *story artists:* Maxwell Brace IV, Ash Brannon, Jim Capobianco, Jason Katz, Jorgen Klubien, Robert Lence, Bud Luckey, Bob Peterson, Andrew Stanton, Nathan Stanton; *addit storyboard:* Geefwee Boedoe, Jill Culton, Pete Docter, Davey Crockett Feiten, Harley Jessup, Jeff Pidgeon; *ed sup:* Lee Unkrich; *sup technical dir:* William Reeves, Eben Ostby; *ph dir:* Sharon Calahan; *prod des:* William Cone; *art dirs:* Tia W. Kratter, Bob Pauley; *sup anim:* Glenn McQueen, Rich Quade; *shading sup:* Rick Sayre; *sup lay artist:* Ewan Johnson; *sd des:* Gary Rydstrom; *prod sup: technical:* Graham Walters; *editorial:* Bill Kinder; *story, art & lay:* B.Z. Petroff; *prod asst: script:* Chris Vallance; *story:* Ron Smith; *art: art dpt mgr:* Katherine Sarafian; *shading des:* Tia W. Kratter; *cg paint:* Robin Cooper, Yvonne Herbst, Bryn Imagire, Glenn Kim; *sketch artists:* Mark Cordell Holmes, Glenn Kim, Dan Lee, Bud Luckey, Lawrence Marvit, Nathaniel McLaughlin; *sculptors:* Norm deCarlo, Jerome Ranft; *character des:* Bob Pauley, Dan Lee, Jason Katz, Bud Luckey, Geefwee Boedoe, James Ford Murphy, Sanjay Patel, Tasha Wedeen; *visual development:* Peter Deséve, Dave Gordon, Steve Johnson, Paul Kratter, Lou Fancher, Jean Gillmore, Bruce Zick, Fred Warter, William Joyce, Kevin Donahue, Rick Maki; *art dpt:* Jonas Rivers, Michael Griffin Kelly, Andrea Warren; *lay:* Molly Naughton, Craig Good, Robert Anderson, Kevin Björke, Shawn Brennan, Bill Carson, Wade Childress, Jeremy Kasky, Patrick Lin, Mark Sanford, Adam Schnitzer; *lead set dresser:* Sophie Vincelette; *set dressers:* David Eisenmann, Derek Williams, Mark Adams, Roman Figun, Shalini Govil-Pai, Sonoko Konishi; *lay co-ord:* Trish Carney; *anim mgr:* Kori Rae; *anim:* Michael Berenstein, Dylan Brown, Sandra Christiansen, Scott Clark, Brett Coderre, David Devan, Andrew Gordon, Timothy Hittle, John Kahis, Karen Kiser, Shawn Krause, Bankole Lasekan, Dan Lee, Les Major, Daniel Mason, Billy Merritt, James Ford Murphy, Mark Oftedal, Michael Parks, Sanjay Patel, Bobby Podesta, Jeff Pratt, Roger Rose, Andrew H. Schmidt, Steve Segal, Doug Sheppeck, Alan Sperling, Doug Sweetland, David Tart, J. Warren Trezevant, Mark Walsh, Tasha Wedeen, Kyle Balda, Alan Barillaro, Ben Catmull, Stephen Barnes, Colin Brady, Jennifer Cha, Tim Crawford, Ike Feldman, Stephen Gregory, Jimmy Hayward, Steven Clay Hunter, Angus MacLane, Jon Mead, Karyn Metian, Valerie Mih, Peter Nash, Jan Pinkava, Brett Pulliam, Mike Quinn, Gini Santos, Anthony Scott, Adam Wood, Christina Yim; *asso anim mgr:* Maureen E. Wylie; *fix anim/co-ord:* Bret "Brooke" Parker; *prod asst:* Tomoko Harada Ferguson, Lance Martin; *"crowd" anim sup:* Dale McBeath; *"crowd" anim:* Davey Crockett Feiten, Patty Kihm, Bob Koch, Robert H. Russ, Ross Stevenson, Kureha Yokoo; *editorial: second ed:* David Ian Salter; *asst ed:* Tom Freeman, Torbin Xan Bullock, Ed Fuller, Phyllis Oyama, Lucas Putnam; *ed co-ord:* Hana Yoon; *film co-ord:* Richard Brodsky; *prod asst:* Mark Yeager; *temp mus ed:* David Slusser; *temp sd ed:* Rona Michele, John K. Carr, Rob Bonz, Ada Cochavi, Tara McKinley, Katherine Ringgold, Christine Steele, James M. Webb; *ed:* Jessica Ambinder Rojas, Mildred Iatrou, Jeff Jones, Ellen Keneshea; *modeling team: modeling artists:* Mark Adams, James Bancroft, Loren Carpenter, Wei-Chung Chang, Michael Fong, Lisa Forssell, Deborah R. Fowler, Damir Frkovic, Shalini Govil-Pai, Brian Green, Mark Thomas Henne, Oren Jacob, Jeffrey "JJ" Jay, Rob Jensen, Keith Olenick, Joyce Powell, Brian M. Rosen, Kelly O'Connell, Andrew Schmidt, Don Schreiter, Eliot Smyrl, Galyn Susman, Tien Truong, Bill Wise, Kim White; *shading team: shading artists:* John B. Anderson, David Batte, Lisa Forssell, Keith B.C. Gordon, Brian Green, Ben Jordan, Ken Lao, Daniel McCoy, Keith Olenick, Chris Perry, Bill Polson, Mitch Prater, Brian M. Rosen, Tien Truong, David Valdez, Bill Wise; *modeling & shading co-ord:* Victoria Jaschob, Mark Nielsen; *lighting:* Lindsey Collins, Deborah R. Fowler, Joyce Powell, Stephanie Andrews, Janet Lucroy, Kim White, Dale Ruffalo, Kelly O'Connell, Patrick Wilson, Jean-Claude J. Kalache, Ana G. Lacaze, Jason Bickerstaff, Bill Wise, Lisa Forssell, Sonoko Konishi, Don Schreiter, Reid Gershbein, Lauren Alpert, Eileen O'Neil, Craig McGillivray, Ken Lao, Bill Polson, Kevin Edwards, Ruieta da Silva, Brian Green, Keith B.C. Gordon, Chris Perry, Brad Andalman, Bena Cur-

rin, John Singh Pottebaum, Sudeep Rangaswamy, Wayne Wooten, Cynthia Dueltgen, Stephen W. King, Gary Schultz, John Warren, Kirk Bowers, Jun Han Cho; *lighting co-ord:* Tora Kim; *crowds & fx team: crowd technical sup:* Michael Fong; *fx & crowd mgr:* Nicole Paradis Grindle, Deirdre Warin; *fx technical artists:* James Bancroft, Keith B.C. Gordon, Mark Thomas Henne, Dan Herman, Christian Hoffman, Leo Hourvitz, Jeffrey "JJ" Jay, Quintin King, Chris Perry, Bill Polson, Don Schreiter, Brad Winemiller, Adam Woodbury; *crowd technical artists:* Kirk Bowers, Onny P. Carr, Shalini Govil-Pai, Quintin King, Michael Lorenzen, Cynthia Pettit, Leslie Picardo, Lawrence D. Cutler, Andrea Schultz, Steve Upstill; *crowds & fx co-ord:* Kelly T. Peters; *rendering: render ld:* Danielle Feinberg, Victoria Jaschob, Kirk Bowers, Jun Han Cho, Mark Fontana, Thomas Jordan, Steve Kani, James Rose, Jerome Strach, John Warren, Brad Winemiller; *optimization consultant:* Oren Jacob; *anim software development: dir:* Darwyn Peachey; *Software engineers:* Brad Andalman, Ronen Barzel, Bena Currin, Tony de Rosa, Kurt Fleischer, Lisa Forssell, Thomas Hahn, Mark Thomas Henne, Kitt Hirasaki, Michael B. Johnson, Steve Johnson, Michael Kass, Chris King, Eric Lebel, Peter Nye, Lee Ozer, Bruce Perens, John Singh Pottebaum, Sudeep Rangaswamy, Arun Rad, Drew Rogge, Michael Shantzis, Heidi Stettner, Dirk van Gelder, James W. Williams, Wayne Wooten; *document & support:* Tom Deering, Kay Seirup, Gill Stanfield; *rendering Software development: dir:* Anthony A. Apodaca; *special rendering techniques:* Tom Duff, Larry Gritz, Tien Truong; *prod support:* Craig Kolb, Tom Lokovic; *Software engineers:* Maneesh Agrawala, Dana Batali, Phil Beffrey, Sam "Penguin" Black, Reid Gershbein, David Laur, Dan Lyke, Daniel McCoy, Shaun Oborn, Matt Pharr, Brian M. Rosen, Mark Van der Wettering, Eric Veach; *ph:* James Burgess, David Difrancesco, Louis Rivera; *ph software & engineering:* Hunter Kelly, Matthew Martin, Alec Wong; *ph technicians:* Don Conway, Jeff Wan; *col science engineers:* Arun Rad, Malcolm Blanchard; *dpt admin:* Beth Sullivan; *production: scheduling co-ord:* Sarah Jo Daughters; *information systems: dir:* Greg Brandead; *mgr:* Duncan Keefe, Michael O'Brien; *systems admin & support:* Naftali "El Magnifico" Alvarez, Nathan Ardaiz, George Baglas, Adam Beeman, Bryan Bird, Lars R. Damerow, Erik Forman, Patrick Guenette, Alisa Gilden, Warren Hays, Jason Hendrix, Ling Hsu, Ken Huey, John Hee Soo Lee, Jeff "Heffe" Millhollen, Gregory Yong Paik, Kristina Perez, Anne Pia, May Pon, Josh Qualtieri, Edgar Quinones, Auburn "Aubie" C. Schmidt, M.T. Silvia, Nelson Siu, Edilberto A. Soriano Jr., Alex Stahl, Andy Thomas, Christopher C. Walker, Dallas Wisehaupt; *post prod:* Brian McNulty, Patsy Bougé, Timothy Sorensen; *post prod sd:* Skywalker Sound; *rec mix:* Gary Rydstrom, Gary Summers; *digital dial mix:* Doc Kane; *sd ed:* Tim Holland, Ben Gold; *casting:* Ruth Lambert, Mary Hidalgo; *ADR ed:* Michael Silvers, Jonathan Null, Mickie T. McGowan; *sd fx ed:* Pat Jackson; *foley ed:* Mary Helen Leasman, Marian Wilde; *sd des:* Shannon Mills; *foley artists:* Dennie Thorpe, Jana Vance; *foley rec:* Tony Eckert; *foley rec:* Frank "Pepé" Merel; *asst ed:* J.R. Grubbs; *mix technicians:* Gary A. Rizzo, Tony Sereno; *addit dial rec:* Bob Baron, Vince Caro, John McGleenan, Jackson Schwartz; *voices: Flik:* Dave Foley; *Hopper:* Kevin Spacey; *Princess Atta:* Julia Louis-Dreyfus; *Princess Dot:* Hayden Panettiere; *The Queen:* Phyllis Diller; *Molt:* Richard Kind; *Slim:* David Hyde Pierce; *Heimlich:* Joe Ranft; *Francis:* Dennis Leary; *Manny:* Jonathan Harris; *Gypsy:* Madeline Kahn; *Rosie:* Bonnie Hunt; *Tuck & Roll:* Michael McShane; *P.T. Flea:* John Ratzenberger; *Dim:* Brad Garrett; *Mr. Soil:* Roddy McDowell; *Dr. Flora:* Edie McClurg; *Thorny:* Alex Rocco; *Cornelius:* David Ossman; *also:* Carlos Alazizaqui, Jack Angel, Bob Bergen, Kimberly Brown, Rodger Bumpass, Anthony Burch, Jennifer Darling, Rachel Davey, Debi Derryberry, Paul Eiding, Jessica Evans, Bill Farmer, Sam Gifaldi, Brad Hall, Jess Harnell, Brenden Hickey, Kate Hodges, Denise Johnson, David Lander, John Lasseter, Sherry Lynn, Mickie T. McGowan, Courtland Mead, Christine Milian, Kelsey Mulrooney, Ryan O'Donohue, Jeff Pidgeon, Phil Proctor, Jan Rabson, Jordan Ranft, Brian M. Rosen, Rebecca Schneider, Francesca Smith, Andrew Stanton, Hannah Swanson, Russi Taylor, Travis Tedford, Ashley Tisdale, Lee Unkrich, Jordan Warkol; *"The Time of Your Life" performed by* Randy Newman; *mus/song:* Randy Newman; *ex mus prod:* Chris Montan; *orch:* Jonathan Sacks, Don Davis, Ira Hearshen; *mus rec/mix:* Frank Wolf; *mus ed:* Lori Eschier Frystak, Bruno Coon, Brenda Heins; *mus prod:* Tom McDonald, Sandy de Crescent, Jo Ann Kane Music Service; *mus rec:* Sony Pictures Scoring Stage; *mus mix:* Signet Soundelux Studios; *interactive computer work stations:* Silicon Graphics Inc.; *3d modeling software:* Alias Research Inc.; *2d paint software:* Interactive Effects Inc.; *network equipment:* Cisco Systems; *digital disk rec:*

Sierra Design Labs.; *modeling & animation software:* Marionette; *render:* Renderman; *processing:* Monaco Labs.; *prod mgr:* Susan Tatsuno Hamana; *col:* Tech. *sd:* Dolby Digital. 93 min. • Flik is an ant living in a colony oppressed by a pack of tyrannical grasshoppers. He rebels and sets out to hire "Warrior bugs" to put a stop to this dictatorship. When he comes across a bug circus, he thinks the artists are performing acts of heroism and takes them back to defend the colony. Once the truth is known, Flik sets about making his own trap to thwart the bullying grasshoppers.

849. Bugsy and Mugsy (*Looney Tunes*) 31 Aug. 1957; *p.c.:* WB; *dir:* Friz Freleng; *story:* Warren Foster; *anim:* Virgil Ross, Gerry Chiniquy, Art Davis; *lay:* Hawley Pratt; *back:* Boris Gorelick; *ed:* Treg Brown; *voices:* Mel Blanc; *mus:* Carl Stalling, Milt Franklyn; *prod mgr:* John W. Burton; *prod:* Edward Selzer; *col:* Tech. *sd:* Vit. 7 min. • Two gangsters take refuge in an abandoned house where Bugs is sheltering from the rain. Bugs takes the opportunity of turning one against the other.

850. Bugville Field Day (*Aesop's Film Fable*) 25 July 1925; *p.c.:* Fables Pictures Inc for Pathé; *dir:* Paul Terry; *b&w. sil.* 10 min. • While the various sporting events are taking place, a spider kidnaps a princess fly from her tiny fiancé.

851. A Bugville Romance (*Aesop's Sound Fable*) 8 June 1930; *p.c.:* Van Beuren for Pathé; *dir:* John Foster, Harry Bailey; *mus:* Gene Rodemich; *b&w. sd:* RCA. 6 min. • Transformations and dances with flowers, birds and insects concluding with a wedding.

852. Building a Building (*Mickey Mouse*) 7 Jan. 1933; *p.c.:* Walt Disney prods for UA; *dir:* David D. Hand; *anim:* Johnny Cannon, Les Clark, Gilles de Tremaudan, Clyde Geronimi, Richard Lundy, Tom Palmer, Ben Sharpsteen; *character des/lay:* Albert Hurter; *voices:* Marcellite Garner, Pinto Colvig, Walt Disney; *music/song:* Frank E. Churchill; *b&w. sd:* RCA. 7 min. • While Mickey attends to his Steam Shovel, foreman Peg-Leg Pete abducts Minnie, leading to a hectic chase over scaffolding.

853. Bull-Ero (*Paul Terry-Toons*) 3 Apr. 1932; *p.c.:* Moser & Terry for Educational/Fox; *dir:* Frank Moser, Paul Terry; *mus:* Philip A. Scheib; *b&w. sd:* WE. 6 min. • Two bulls fight it out in the Bull Ring.

854. The Bull Fight (*Paul Terry-Toon*) 8 Feb. 1935; *p.c.:* Moser & Terry for Educational/Fox; *dir:* Frank Moser, Paul Terry; *mus:* Philip A. Scheib; *b&w. sd:* WE. 5½ min. • Burlesque on a Bull Fight.

855. Bull Fright (*Casper*) 15 July 1955; *p.c.:* Famous for Para; *dir:* Seymour Kneitel; *story:* Carl Meyer; *anim:* Myron Waldman, Nick Tafuri; *sets:* Robert Little; *voices:* Norma MacMillan, Jackson Beck, Gwen Davies; *mus:* Winston Sharples; *title song:* Mack David, Jerry Livingston; *ph:* Leonard McCormick; *prod mgr:* Seymour Shultz; *col:* Tech. *sd:* RCA. 6 min. • Casper helps a small bull train for a bull fight.

856. The Bulldog and the Baby (*Fable*) 3 July 1942; *p.c.:* Colum; *prod:* Frank Tashlin; *dir:* Alec Geiss; *story:* Jack Cosgriff; *anim:* Volus Jones; *sets:* Clark Watson; *ed:* Edward Moore; *voice:* Sara Berner; *mus:* Paul Worth; *prod mgr:* Ben Schwalb; *b&w. sd:* RCA. 6 min. • A bulldog, left to babysit, attempts to entertain the youngster but soon has to rescue him from atop a skyscraper scaffolding.

857. Bulldozing the Bull (*Popeye*) 19 Aug. 1938; *p.c.:* The Fleischer Studio for Para; *prod:* Max Fleischer; *dir:* Dave Fleischer; *anim:* Willard Bowsky, George Germanetti; *voices:* Jack Mercer, Margie Hines; *ed:* Kitty Pfister; *mus:* Sammy Timberg; *prod sup:* Sam Buchwald, Isidore Sparber; *b&w. sd:* WE. 7 min. • Popeye is forced to fight a bull although he abhors cruelty to animals ... so he makes peace with the creature.

858. Bulldozing the Bull (*Heckle & Jeckle*) Apr. 1951; *p.c.:* TT for Fox; *dir:* Eddie Donnelly; *story/voices:* Tom Morrison; *mus:* Philip A. Scheib; *ph:* Douglas Moye; *col:* Tech. *sd:* RCA. 6 min. • The magpies sell hot tamales outside the bullfight. They avoid the wrath of the stadium manager by ducking into the arena only to find themselves having to fight the bull!

859. Bulloney (*Flip the Frog*) 30 May 1933; *p.c.:* Celebrity prods for MGM; *prod/dir:* Ub Iwerks; *anim:* Jimmie Culhane; *mus:* Carl W. Stalling; *b&w. sd:* PCP. 8 min. • No story available.

860. Bull-Oney (*Oswald*) 28 Oct. 1928; *p.c.:* Winkler for Univ; *anim:* Walt Lantz, Tom Palmer; *b&w. sil.* 6 min. • No story available.

861. The Bully (*Aesop's Film Fable*) 20 June 1927; *p.c.:* Fables Pictures Inc for Pathé; *dir:* Paul Terry; *b&w. sil.* 10 min. • A brute of a cat forces a

mouse to get him the cuckoo in a clock. The cuckoo enlists help from the Grandfather's clock, the cat gets licked and the mouse turns on him.

862. The Bully (*Flip the Frog*) 8 June 1932; *p.c.:* Celebrity prods for MGM; *prod/dir:* Ub Iwerks; *b&w. sd:* PCP. 7 min. • Flip is challenged to take on a beefy boxing champ in the ring.

863. Bully Beef (*Paul Terry-Toon*) 13 July 1930; *p.c.:* A-C for Educational/Fox; *dir:* Frank Moser, Paul Terry; *mus:* Philip A. Scheib; *b&w. sd:* WE. 9 min. • Parody of *All's Quiet on the Western Front* with animals fighting in the front-line trenches.

864. Bully for Bugs (*Looney Tunes*) 9 Aug. 1953; *p.c.:* WB; *dir:* Charles M. Jones; *story:* Michael Maltese; *anim:* Ben Washam, Lloyd Vaughan, Ken Harris; *lay:* Maurice Noble; *back:* Philip de Guard; *ed:* Treg Brown; *voice:* Mel Blanc; *mus:* Carl Stalling; *prod mgr:* John W. Burton; *prod:* Edward Selzer; *col:* Tech. *sd:* Vit. 7 min. • Bugs finds himself doing battle with a ferocious bull in a Mexican bullring.

865. Bully for Pink (*Pink Panther*) 14 Dec. 1965; *p.c.:* Mirisch/Geoffrey/DFE for UA; *dir:* Hawley Pratt; *story:* John W. Dunn; *anim:* Norm McCabe, Warren Batchelder, Don Williams; *lay:* Dick Ung; *back:* Tom O'Loughlin; *ed:* Lee Gunther; *mus:* William Lava; *theme tune:* Henry Mancini; *prod mgr:* William Orcutt; *col:* DeLuxe. *sd:* RCA. 6 min. • The Panther fights a bullfight using a magician's magic cape.

866. A Bully Frog (*Terry-Toon*) 18 Sept. 1936; *p.c.:* TT for Educational/Fox: *dir:* Mannie Davis, George Gordon; *mus:* Philip A. Scheib; *b&w. sd:* WE. 6 min. • Dissatisfied with his pond life, an assertive frog moves to a bigger pond. The metropolis proves too much and he returns.

867. A Bully Romance (*Gandy Goose*) 16 June 1939; *p.c.:* TT for Fox; *dir:* Eddie Donnelly; *story:* John Foster; *voice:* Arthur Kay; *mus:* Philip A. Scheib. *sd:* RCA. 7 min. • Gandy tells of his romance in Mexico.

868. The Bully's End (*Aesop's Sound Fable*) 16 June 1933; *p.c.:* Van Beuren for RKO; *dir:* Harry Bailey; *mus:* Gene Rodemich; *b&w. sd:* RCA. 6½ min. • Ducks fight a boastful rooster.

869. The Bum Bandit (*Talkartoon*) 4 Apr. 1931; *p.c.:* The Fleischer Studio for Para; *prod:* Max Fleischer; *dir:* Dave Fleischer; *anim:* Willard Bowsky, Al Eugster; *voice:* Little Ann Little; *mus:* Art Turkisher; *b&w. sd:* WE. 7 min. • Dangerous Nan McGrew (Betty Boop) stops Bimbo from robbing a train. She then realises that he is her long-lost husband.

870. A Bum Steer (*Terry-Toon*) Feb. 1957; *p.c.:* TT for Fox; *ex prod:* Bill Weiss; *dir sup:* Gene Deitch; *dir:* Mannie Davis; *story sup/voices:* Tommy Morrison; *story:* Larz Bourne, Bob Kuwahara; *anim:* Jim Tyer, John Gentilella, Ed Donnelly, Larry Silverman, George Bakes, Al Chiarito; *lay:* Art Bartsch; *back:* Bill Hilliker; *mus:* Phil Scheib; *prod mgr:* Frank Schudde; *col:* Tech. *sd:* RCA. 7 min. CS. • The champion bull hangs up his horns from bullfighting and it's up to his son to replace him.

871. A Bumper Crop (*Aesop's Film Fable*) 30 May 1926; *p.c.:* Fables Pictures Inc for Pathé; *dir:* Paul Terry; *b&w. sil.* 10 min. • No story available.

872. Bunco Busters (*Woody Woodpecker*) 21 Nov. 1955; *p.c.:* Walter Lantz prods for Univ; *dir:* Paul J. Smith; *story:* Milt Schaffer; *anim:* Herman R. Cohen, Gil Turner, Robert Bentley; *sets:* Art Landy; *voices:* Dal McKennon, Grace Stafford; *mus:* Clarence Wheeler; *prod mgr:* William E. Garity; *col:* Tech. *sd:* RCA. 6 min. • Buzz Buzzard tricks Woody into buying a fake treasure map then proceeds to con him out of all his money.

873. Bungle in the Jungle (*Jerky Journeys*) 15 May 1949; *p.c.:* Impossible Pictures for Rep; *ex prod:* David Flexer; *prod/dir/story:* Leonard Louis Levinson; *anim:* Art Heinemann; *voice:* Frank Nelson; *col:* Tru. *sd.* 8 min. • An African expedition.

874. Bungle Uncle (*Loopy de Loop*) Jan. 1962; *p.c.:* Hanna-Barbera prods for Colum; *prod/dir:* William Hanna, Joseph Barbera; *story dir:* Alex Lovy; *story:* Michael Maltese; *anim dir:* Charles A. Nichols; *anim:* Jack Ozark; *lay:* Jerry Eisenberg; *back:* Art Lozzi; *ed:* Greg Watson; *voices:* Daws Butler, Don Messick; *mus:* Hoyt Curtin; *titles:* Lawrence Gobel; *prod mgr:* Howard Hanson; *col:* East. *sd:* RCA. 6½ min. • Loopy's nephew, Bon-Bon supplies a live lamb for dinner and Loopy attempts to return the creature to the flock, guarded by an irate watchdog. The lamb, then, befriends Loopy.

875. Bungled Bungalow (*Mr. Magoo*) 28 Dec. 1950; *p.c.:* UPA for

Colum; *ex prod:* Stephen Bosustow; *dir sup:* John Hubley; *dir:* Pete Burness; *story:* Bill Scott, Phil Eastman; *anim:* Rudy Larriva, Grim Natwick, Bill Melendez, Pat Matthews; *lay:* Abe Liss; *back:* Herb Klynn, Jules Engel; *voices:* Jim Backus, Jerry Hausner; *mus:* Hoyt Curtin; *prod mgr:* Adrian Woolery; *col:* Tech. *sd:* RCA. 6½ min. • Hot-House Harry, a notorious house stealer, removes Magoo's house, giving vent for the myopic old gent to think it's infested with termites. He sets off to buy a new home and finds himself viewing his own house.

876. The Bungling Builder *(Beary Family)* 1970; *p.c.:* Walter Lantz prods for Univ; *dir:* Paul J. Smith; *story:* Cal Howard; *anim:* Virgil Ross, Al Coe, Tom Byrne, Joe Voght; *sets:* Nino Carbe; *voices:* Paul Frees, Grace Stafford; *mus:* Walter Greene; *prod mgr:* William E. Garity; *col:* Tech. *sd:* RCA. 5½ min. • Charlie tries to build a home extension.

877. Bunker Hill Bunny *(Merrie Melodies)* 23 Sept. 1950; *p.c.:* WB; *dir:* I. Freleng; *story:* Tedd Pierce; *anim:* Gerry Chiniquy, Ken Champin, Virgil Ross, Arthur Davis; *lay:* Hawley Pratt; *back:* Paul Julian; *ed:* Treg Brown; *voices:* Mel Blanc; *mus:* Carl Stalling; *prod mgr:* John W. Burton; *prod:* Edward Selzer; *col:* Tech. *sd:* Vit. 7 min. • Bugs is soul survivor in a fort battling against Sam von Spam the Hessian.

878. Bunnies Abundant *(Loopy de Loop)* Dec. 1962; *p.c.:* Hanna-Barbera prods for Colum; *prod/dir:* William Hanna, Joseph Barbera; *story dir:* Alex Lovy; *story:* Dalton Sandifer; *anim dir:* Charles A. Nichols; *anim:* George Nicholas; *lay:* Walter Clinton; *back:* Richard H. Thomas; *ed:* Greg Watson; *voices:* Daws Butler, Don Messick, Doug Young; *mus:* Hoyt Curtin; *titles:* Lawrence Gobel; *prod mgr:* Howard Hanson; *col:* East. *sd:* RCA. 6 min. • No story available.

879. Bunnies and Bonnets *(Krazy Kat)* 29 Mar. 1933; *p.c.:* Winkler for Colum; *story:* Ben Harrison, Manny Gould; *anim:* Al Eugster, Preston Blair; *voice:* Ernie Stanton; *mus:* Joe de Nat; *prod:* Charles Mintz; *b&w. sd:* WE. 6 min. • Krazy and Kitty prepare for the Easter Parade but rain spoils it all.

880. Bunny and Claude *(Looney Tunes)* 9 Nov. 1968; *p.c.:* WB/7A; *dir:* Bob McKimson; *story:* Cal Howard; *anim:* Ted Bonnicksen, La Verne Harding, Jim Davis, Ed Solomon; *lay:* Bob Givens; *back:* Bob Abrams; *ed:* Hal Geer; *voices:* Mel Blanc, Pat Woodell; *The Ballad of Bunny and Claude* sung by Billy Strange; *mus:* William Lava; *prod:* Bill L. Hendricks; *col:* Tech. *sd:* Vit. 6 min. • In a parody of *Bonnie and Clyde*, rabbit gangsters rob carrot patches, giving the Sheriff the run-around.

881. Bunny Hugged *(Merrie Melodies)* 10 Mar. 1951; *p.c.:* WB; *dir:* Charles M. Jones; *story:* Michael Maltese; *anim:* Ken Harris, Phil Monroe, Ben Washam, Lloyd Vaughan; *lay:* Peter Alvarado; *back:* Philip de Guard; *ed:* Treg Brown; *voices:* Mel Blanc, John T. Smith; *mus:* Carl Stalling; *prod mgr:* John W. Burton; *prod:* Edward Selzer; *col:* Tech. *sd:* Vit. 7 min. • Mascot Bugs is forced to replace his boss in a wrestling match against "The Crusher."

882. Bunny Mooning *(Color Classic)* 12 Feb. 1937; *p.c.:* The Fleischer Studio for Para; *prod:* Max Fleischer; *dir:* Dave Fleischer; *anim:* Myron Waldman, Edward Nolan, Lillian Friedman; *sets:* Robert Little; *mus:* Sammy Timberg; *col:* Tech-2. *sd:* WE. 7 min. • Jack and Jill rabbit are about to wed and all the other animals prepare for the wedding.

883. The Burglar Alarm *(Aesop's Film Fable)* 6 June 1923; *p.c.:* Fables Pictures Inc for Pathé; *dir:* Paul Terry; *b&w. sil.* 5 min. • A slick salesman sells Farmer Al a burglar alarm which hides a cat and mouse who walk off with the Farmer's house while he goes for the police.

884. Buried Treasure *(Captain & the Kids)* 17 Sept. 1938; *p.c.:* MGM; *dir:* Robert Allen; *voices:* Billy Bletcher, Dave Weber, Robert Winkler; *mus:* Scott Bradley; *prod mgr:* Fred Quimby; *col:* sep. *sd:* WE. 7 min. • The kids fool der Captain with a fake treasure map. John Silver and his cutthroats are also fooled and kidnap the luckless Captain.

885. Burlesque *(Paul Terry-Toon)* 4 Sept. 1932; *p.c.:* Moser & Terry for Educational/Fox; *dir:* Frank Moser, Paul Terry; *mus:* Philip A. Scheib; *b&w. sd:* WE. 6 min. • A couple of prisoners escape and hide out in a vaudeville theatre. They see chorus girls, a magician and a trapeze artist before they are re-captured and returned to jail.

886. Bury the Axis 1943; *prod/dir:* Lou Bunin; *voice:* Danny Webb; *mus:* Arthur Turkisher; *col:* Ciné *sd.* 7 min. • The stork delivers Schickelgruber. He grows up and returns from Russia, whistles for his dog (Mus-solini) and forms The Axis with Hirohito (a snake). They all come to a sticky end in a tank. Propaganda puppet animation.

887. The Bus Way to Travel *(Swifty & Shorty)* Oct. 1964; *p.c.:* Para Cartoons; *dir:* Seymour Kneitel; *story/voices:* Eddie Lawrence; *anim:* Wm. B. Pattengill; *sets:* Robert Little; *mus:* Winston Sharples; *ph:* Leonard McCormick; *prod mgr:* Abe Goodman; *col:* Tech. *sd:* RCA. 6 min. • Shorty gets taken for an unwarranted ride when he boards Swifty's bus.

888. Bushy Hare *(Looney Tunes)* 11 Nov. 1950; *p.c.:* WB; *dir:* Robert McKimson; *story:* Warren Foster; *anim:* Phil de Lara, J.C. Melendez, Charles McKimson, Rod Scribner, John Carey; *lay:* Cornett Wood; *back:* Richard H. Thomas; *ed:* Treg Brown; *voices:* Mel Blanc; *mus:* Carl Stalling; *prod mgr:* John W. Burton; *prod:* Edward Selzer; *col:* Tech. *sd:* Vit. 7 min. • Bugs finds himself in Australia, adopted by a mother kangaroo and hunted by an Aborigine.

889. Busman's Holiday *(Woody Woodpecker)* 25 July 1961; *p.c.:* Walter Lantz prods for Univ; *dir:* Paul J. Smith; *story:* Dalton Sandifer; *anim:* Les Kline, Ray Abrams; *sets:* Art Landy, Ray Huffine; *voices:* Dal McKennon, Grace Stafford; *mus:* Clarence Wheeler; *prod mgr:* William E. Garity; *col:* Tech. *sd:* RCA. 6 min. • Window cleaner Woody causes havoc when travelling on a bus with an extendable ladder.

890. Busted Blossoms *(Paul Terry-Toons)* 10 Aug. 1934; *p.c.:* Moser & Terry for Educational/Fox; *dir:* Frank Moser, Paul Terry; *mus:* Philip A. Scheib; *b&w. sd:* WE. 6 min. • No story available.

891. Buster Bear *(series)* 1930; *p.c.:* McCrory Studios for Vitaphone; *prod/dir:* John R. McCrory; *story:* Howard Moss; *ph:* Frank Shadde; *b&w. sd.* • Series titles and stories untraced.

892. Buster's Last Stand *(Woody Woodpecker)* 1 Oct. 1970; *p.c.:* Walter Lantz prods for Univ; *dir:* Paul J. Smith; *story:* Dale Hale; *anim:* Les Kline, Al Coe; *sets:* Nino Carbe; *voices:* Daws Butler, Grace Stafford; *mus:* Walter Greene; *prod mgr:* William E. Garity; *col:* Tech. *sd:* RCA. 6 min. • To win the hand of an Indian Princess, an Indian Brave needs Woody's feathers for a fancy headdress.

893. Busy Bakers *(Merrie Melodies)* 10 Feb. 1940; *p.c.:* Leon Schlesinger prods for WB; *dir:* Ben Hardaway, Cal Dalton; *story:* Jack Miller; *anim:* Richard Bickenbach; *lay:* Griff Jay; *back:* Arthur Loomer; *ed:* Treg Brown; *voices:* Mel Blanc, The Sportsmen Quartet; *mus:* Carl W. Stalling; *prod sup:* Henry Binder, Raymond G. Katz; *col:* Tech. *sd:* Vit. 7 min. • A Dutch baker feeds a poor man who, in return, brings in a crew of bakers to boost his productivity.

894. The Busy Barber *(Oswald)* 9 Sept. 1932; *p.c.:* Univ; *dir:* Walter Lantz, "Bill" Nolan; *anim:* Ray Abrams, Fred Avery, "Bill" Weber, Jack Carr, Charles Hastings; *mus:* James Dietrich; *b&w. sd:* WE. 7 min. • No story available.

895. The Busy Beavers *(Silly Symphony)* 22 June 1931; *p.c.:* Walt Disney prods for Colum; *dir:* Wilfred Jackson; *anim:* Charles Byrne, Johnny Cannon, Les Clark, Chuck Couch, Jack Cutting, Joseph d'Igalo, Gilles de Tremaudan, Hardie Gramatky, Jack King, George Lane, Richard Lundy, Tom Palmer, Harry Reeves, Ben Sharpsteen, Marvin Woodward, Rudy Zamora; *mus:* Frank E. Churchill; *b&w. sd:* PCP. 7 min. • The beavers' dam is destroyed by a cloudburst but all is saved by a little beaver who cuts down large trees to block the dam.

896. The Busy Bee *(Paul Terry-Toon)* 29 May 1936; *p.c.:* TT for Educational/Fox; *dir:* Mannie Davis, George Gordon; *mus:* Philip A. Scheib; *b&w. sd:* RCA. 6 min. • Hot cakes are the speciality at Mr. and Mrs. Bee's diner, "The Busy Bee." A spider steals some, resulting in a set-to with knives and forks in the lunch wagon.

897. Busy Body Bear *(Barney Bear)* 20 Dec. 1952; *p.c.:* MGM; *dir:* Dick Lundy; *story:* Jack Cosgriff, Heck Allen; *anim:* Grant Simmons, Robert Bentley, Michael Lah, Walter Clinton; *sets:* John Didrik Johnsen; *ed:* Jim Faris; *voice:* Paul Frees; *mus:* Scott Bradley; *ph:* Jack Stevens; *prod:* Fred Quimby; *col:* Tech. *sd:* WE. 6 min. • During "Good Neighbor Week," Barney decides to help Buck Beaver build a dam.

898. Busy Buddies *(Jeepers & Creepers)* June 1960; *p.c.:* Para Cartoons; *dir:* Seymour Kneitel; *story:* Carl Meyer, Jack Mercer; *anim:* Nick Tafuri, Irving Dressler; *sets:* Robert Little; *voices:* Jack Mercer; *mus:* Winston Sharples; *ph:* Leonard McCormick; *prod mgr:* Abe Goodman; *col:* Tech. *sd:* RCA. 6 min. • Creepers needs money to pay his taxes and Jeepers fixes for him to fight Killer McClout for a $25,000 prize. He wins but is heavily taxed on the prize money.

899. Busy Buddies (*Tom & Jerry*) 9 Mar. 1956; *p.c.*: MGM; *prod/dir*: William Hanna, Joseph Barbera; *anim*: Irven Spence, Lewis Marshall, Kenneth Muse, Ed Barge; *lay*: Dick Bickenbach; *back*: Robert Gentle; *ed*: Jim Faris; *voice*: Barbara Eiler; *mus*: Scott Bradley; *ph*: Jack Stevens; *prod mgr*: Hal Elias; *col*: Tech. *sd*: WE. 6 min. CS. • While the babysitter talks on the phone, Tom and Jerry have to retrieve the infant who has wandered off on a jaunt.

900. Busy Bus (*Krazy Kat*) 20 Apr. 1934; *p.c.*: Charles Mintz prods for Colum; *story*: Allen Rose; *anim*: Harry Love, Preston Blair; *mus*: Joe de Nat; *prod mgr*: James Bronis; b&w. *sd*: WE. 5¹/₂ min. • Krazy has a frantic dash in a bus minus it's steering wheel.

901. A Busy Day (*Gran'Pop*) 1939; *p.c.*: Cartoon Films Ltd for Mono; *prod*: Dave Biedermann, Lawson Haris; *dir*: Paul Fennell; *ed*: Almon Teeter; *voice*: Danny Webb; *mus*: Clarence Wheeler; *ph*: Richard M. Ising; *col*: Ciné. *sd*: RCA. 6 min. • Gran'Pop spends a hectic day at the office.

902. The Butcher Boy (*Pooch the Pup*) 26 Sept. 1932; *p.c.*: Univ; *dir*: Walter Lantz, "Bill" Nolan; *anim*: Manuel Moreno, Lester Kline, George Cannata, "Bill" Weber; *voice*: Bernice Hansel; *mus*: James Dietrich; b&w. sd.WE. 7 min. • Pooch delivers a chicken to a customer. A cat tries to steal it and the customer faints. While Pooch revives her, the cat ties a length of rope to him and drags him all over the shop.

903. The Butcher of Seville (*Terry-Toon*) 7 Jan. 1944; *p.c.*: TT for Fox; *dir*: Eddie Donnelly; *story*: John Foster; *voices*: Roy Halee, Tom Morrison; *mus*: Philip A. Scheib; *ph*: Douglas Moye; *col*: Tech. *sd*: RCA. 6 min. • Performed as an operetta, the hero thwarts the butcher and wins the hand of the milkmaid despite a food ration points shortage.

904. Butterscotch and Soda (*Noveltoon*) 4 June 1948; *p.c.*: Famous for Para; *dir*: Seymour Kneitel; *story*: Larz Bourne, Bill Turner; *anim*: Al Eugster, Bill Hudson, Irving Spector; *sets*: Robert Owen; *voices*: Mae Questel, Cecil Roy; *mus*: Winston Sharples; *song*: Buddy Kaye, Winston Sharples; *ph*: Leonard McCormick; *prod mgr*: Sam Buchwald; *col*: Tech. *sd*: RCA. 7 min. • Audrey overindulges on candy and dreams that she's in a land where she can eat as much candy as she wishes, assuming grotesque proportions.

905. Buzzy Boop (*Betty Boop*) 22 July 1938; *p.c.*: The Fleischer Studio for Para; *prod*: Max Fleischer; *dir*: Dave Fleischer; *anim*: David Tendlar, William Sturm; *voice*: Mae Questel; *mus*: Sammy Timberg; b&w. *sd*: WE. 7 min. • Betty is mixed up with the Dead-End Kids.

906. Buzzy Boop at the Concert (*Betty Boop*) 16 Sept. 1938; *p.c.*: The Fleischer Studio for Para; *prod*: Max Fleischer; *dir*: Dave Fleischer; *anim*: Thomas Johnson, Harold Walker; *ed*: Kitty Pfister; *voice*: Margie Hines; *mus*: Sammy Timberg; *prod sup*: Sam Buchwald, Isidore Sparber; b&w. *sd*: WE. 7 min. • Betty and her niece attend a concert. Buzzy stops the contralto by bringing swing music to the proceedings.

907. Bwana Magoo (*Mr. Magoo*) 9 Jan. 1959; *p.c.*: UPA for Colum; *ex prod*: Stephen Bosustow; *dir*: Tom McDonald; *story*: Dick Kinney, Dick Shaw, Pete Burness; *anim*: Ed Friedman, Barney Posner, Fred Grable; *lay*: Robert Dranko; *back*: Jules Engel, Bob McIntosh; *voices*: Jim Backus, Daws Butler; *mus/sd fx*: Joe Siracusa, Earl Bennett, Roger B. Donley; *col*: Tech. *sd*: RCA. 6 min. • Magoo and Waldo are on Safari when Magoo mistakes a lion for Waldo and vice versa.

908. By Hoot or by Crook (*Hoot Kloot*) 17 Apr. 1974; *p.c.*: Mirisch/DFE for UA; *dir*: Bob Balsar; *story*: John W. Dunn; *anim*: Tim Miller, John Ward, Richard Rudler; *lay*: Don Roy; *back*: Richard Reuben; *ed*: Allan R. Potter; *voices*: Bob Holt, Larry Mann; *mus*: Doug Goodwin; *titles*: Arthur Leonardi; *prod mgr*: Lee Gunther; *col*: DeLuxe. *sd*: RCA. 5 min. • A stagecoach driver mistakes Kloot for "The Fox"and hands him his strongbox. Kloot then has to return the box to safety but is hampered by the real "Fox."

909. By Land and Air (*Aesop's Film Fable*) 21 July 1929; *p.c.*: Fables Pictures Inc for Pathé; *dir*: Paul Terry; b&w. sil. 10 min. • Farmer Al Falfa goes for a dizzy ride on his air bike which comes to an abrupt end when a bird yanks at the propeller.

910. By Leaps and Hounds (*Noveltoon*) 14 Dec. 1951; *p.c.*: Famous for Para; *dir*: I. Sparber; *story*: Irving Spector; *anim*: Tom Johnson, John

Gentilella, Howard Beckerman; character *des*: Bill Hudson; *sets*: Robert Connavale; *voices*: Gwen Davies, Frank Matalone; *mus*: Winston Sharples; *ph*: Leonard McCormick; *prod mgr*: Seymour Shultz; *col*: Tech. *sd*: RCA. 6 min. • Herbert, a young fox hound, is left by the pack to fend for himself, eventually catching the fox on his own.

911. By the Beautiful Sea (*Screen Songs*) 24 Jan. 1931; *p.c.*: The Fleischer Studio for Para; *prod*: Max Fleischer; *dir*: Dave Fleischer; *anim*: Willard Bowsky, Reuben Timinsky; *mus*: Art Turkisher; *song*: Harry Carroll, Harold Atteridge; b&w. *sd*: WE. 7 min. • Hot weather prompts Joe to call up his girl and drive her to the seashore.

912. By the Light of the Silvery Moon (*Ko-Ko Song Car-tune*) 21 Aug. 1926; *p.c.*: Inkwell Studio for Red Seal; *prod*: Max Fleischer; *dir*: Dave Fleischer; *song*: Gus Edwards, Edward Madden; b&w. sil. • Ko-Ko cavorts over the words of the song, using the moon as the "bouncing ball."

913. By the Light of the Silvery Moon (*Screen Songs*) 14 Nov. 1931; *p.c.*: The Fleischer Studio for Para; *prod*: Max Fleischer; *sup*: Dave Fleischer; *dir/story/anim*: Jimmie Culhane, Rudy Zamora; *anim*: Seymour Kneitel, Myron Waldman; *mus*: Art Turkisher; *song*: Gus Edwards, Edward Madden; b&w. *sd*: WE. 6¹/₂ min. • The moon encourages young lovers.

914. By the Old Mill Scream (*Casper*) 3 July 1953; *p.c.*: Famous for Para; *dir*: Seymour Kneitel; *story*: Carl Meyer, Jack Mercer; *anim*: Myron Waldman, Nick Tafuri; *sets*: Robert Owen; *voices*: Alan Shay, Cecil Roy, Sid Raymond, Jack Mercer; *mus*: Winston Sharples; *ph*: Leonard McCormick; *prod mgr*: Seymour Shultz; *col*: Tech. *sd*: RCA. 6 min. • Casper helps a little beaver build a dam and scares off Wolfie when he arrives on the scene.

915. By the Sea (*Paul Terry-Toon*) 12 July 1931; *p.c.*: Terry, Moser & Coffman for Educational/Fox; *dir*: Frank Moser, Paul Terry; *anim*: Arthur Babbitt, Vladimir Tytla; *mus*: Philip A. Scheib; b&w. *sd*: WE. 6 min. • The mice have fun at the coast. The hero rescues a maiden from the clutches of a marine monster.

916. By Word of Mouse (*Looney Tunes*) 2 Oct. 1954; *p.c.*: the Sloan Foundation for WB; *dir*: I. Freleng; *story*: Warren Foster; *anim*: Gerry Chiniquy, Arthur Davis, Ben Washam, Ted Bonnicksen; *lay*: Hawley Pratt; *back*: Irv Wyner; *ed*: Treg Brown; *voices*: Mel Blanc, Stan Freberg; *mus*: Milt Franklyn; *prod mgr*: John W. Burton; *prod*: Edward Selzer; *col*: Tech. *sd*: Vit. 7 min. • A Dutch mouse visits The U.S. and learns about mass consumption from his American cousin until Sylvester appears on the scene.

917. Bye, Bye, Blackboard (*Woody Woodpecker*) 1972; *p.c.*: Walter Lantz prods for Univ; *dir*: Paul J. Smith; *story*: Cal Howard; *anim*: Volus Jones, Al Coe, Tom Byrne, Joe Voght; *sets*: Nino Carbe; *voices*: Grace Stafford; *mus*: Walter Greene; *prod mgr*: William E. Garity; *col*: Tech. *sd*: RCA. 5 min. • Woody's dog, Alfie, follows him to school, much to teacher Meany's chagrin.

918. Bye, Bye Bluebeard (*Merrie Melodies*) 21 Oct. 1949; *p.c.*: WB; *dir*: Arthur Davis; *story*: Sid Marcus; *anim*: Basil Davidovich, J.C. Melendez, Don Williams, Emery Hawkins; *lay*: Don Smith; *back*: Philip de Guard; *ed*: Treg Brown; *voices*: Mel Blanc; *mus*: Carl Stalling; *prod mgr*: John W. Burton; *prod*: Edward Selzer; *col*: Tech. *sd*: Vit. 7 min. • An announcement of an escaped murderer frightens Porky, so a mouse takes advantage of the situation and poses as the killer.

919. Caballero Droopy (*Droopy*) 27 Sept. 1952; *p.c.*: MGM; *dir*: Dick Lundy; *story*: Jack Cosgriff, Heck Allen; *anim*: Walter Clinton, Grant Simmons, Michael Lah, Ray Patterson; *ed*: Jim Faris; *voices*: Bill Thompson, Charlie Lung; *mus*: Scott Bradley; *prod*: Fred Quimby; *col*: Tech. *sd*: WE. 6 min. • Droopy and his rival vie for the honor of serenading the beautiful senorita.

920. The Cabaret (*Aesop's Film Fable*) 14 Aug. 1929; *p.c.*: Fables Pictures Inc for Pathé; *dir*: Paul Terry, Frank Moser; b&w. sil. 6 min. • Cats play jazz and imitate a wind-up gramophone. All dance to the music until the "Black Maria" arrives to whisk them off to jail where they sing "Hail! Hail! The Gang's All Here."

921. The Cactus Kid (*Mickey Mouse*) 10 May 1930; *p.c.*: Walter E. Disney for Colum; *dir*: Walt Disney; *voice*: Marcellite Garner; *mus*: Bert Lewis; *ph*: William Cottrell; b&w. *sd*: PCP. 7 min. • Peg-Leg Pedro forces his unwarranted attentions on Minnie and Caballero Mickey pursues the villain on horseback.

922. The Cactus King (*Little King*) 8 June 1934. *p.c.:* Van Beuren for RKO; *dir:* George Stallings; *anim:* Jim Tyer; b&w. *sd:* RCA. 6 min. • Indians kidnap The Little King from The Royal Express. He tames a wild bronco and a chase returns him safely to the train.

923. Cad and Caddy (*Little Lulu*) 18 July 1947; *p.c.:* Famous for Para; *dir:* Seymour Kneitel; *story:* Bill Turner, Larry Riley; *anim:* Myron Waldman, Nick Tafuri, Gordon Whittier, Irving Dressler; *sets:* Robert Connavale; *voices:* Cecil Roy, Jackson Beck; *mus:* Winston Sharples; *title song:* Buddy Kaye, Fred Wise, Sammy Timberg; *ph:* Leonard McCormick; *prod mgr:* Sam Buchwald; *col:* Tech. *sd:* RCA. 8 min. • Caddy Lulu and her pet frog make the golfer sorry he ever picked her to carry his clubs.

924. Cage Fright (*Casper*) 8 Aug. 1952; *p.c.:* Famous for Para; *dir:* Seymour Kneitel; *story:* I. Klein; *anim:* Myron Waldman, Nick Tafuri; *sets:* Robert Owen; *voices:* Alan Shay, Sid Raymond; *mus:* Winston Sharples; *title song:* Mack David, Jerry Livingston; *ph:* Leonard McCormick; *prod mgr:* Seymour Shultz; *col:* Tech. *sd:* RCA. 7 min. • Casper finds a new playmate in Alfred, the zoo's baby elephant.

925. Cagey Bird (*Flippy*) 18 July 1946; *p.c.:* Colum; *dir:* Howard Swift; *story:* Sid Marcus; *anim:* Roy Jenkins; *sets:* Clark Watson; *ed:* Richard S. Jensen; *voices:* Frank Graham, A. Purvis Pullen; *mus:* Eddie Kilfeather; *ph:* Frank Fisher; *prod mgr:* Hugh McCollum; *col:* Tech. *sd:* WE. 7 min. • When Flippy the canary sneezes, his dog friend phones the doctor. The cat intercepts the call and arrives in the guise of a physician.

926. Cagey Business (*Modern Madcap*) Feb. 1965; *p.c.:* Para Cartoons; *dir:* Howard Post; *story/anim:* I. Klein; *sets:* Robert Owen; *voices:* Bob MacFadden; *mus:* Winston Sharples; *ph:* Leonard McCormick. *prod mgr:* Abe Goodman; *col:* Tech. *sd:* RCA. 6 min. • A cage-confined lion is considered too soft, forfeiting his daily ration of rice pudding until he improves. He escapes and goes in search of his favorite dish in the big city.

927. The Cagey Canary (*Merrie Melodies*) 22 Nov. 1941; *p.c.:* Leon Schlesinger prods for WB; *dir:* Fred Avery, Robert Clampett; *story:* Michael Maltese; *anim:* Bob McKimson; *sets:* John Didrik Johnsen; *ed:* Treg Brown; *voices:* Elvia Allman, Mel Blanc; *mus:* Carl W. Stalling; *prod sup:* Henry Binder, Raymond G. Katz; *col:* Tech. *sd:* Vit. 7 min. • The cat's canary-chasing habits keep the old lady awake until he finds a foolproof way the old girl can't hear. Completed by Clampett after Avery departed in mid-production.

928. The Calico Dragon (*Happy Harmonies*) 30 Mar. 1935; *p.c.:* MGM; *prod/dir:* Hugh Harman, Rudolf Ising; *mus:* Scott Bradley; *col:* Tech-2. *sd:* RCA. 8 min. *Academy Award nomination.* • A small girl dreams of her toys travelling to a land of patchwork and quilt to fight the Calico Dragon.

929. Californy 'er Bust (*Goofy*) 13 July 1945; *p.c.:* Walt Disney prods for RKO; *dir:* Jack Kinney; *asst dir:* Ted Sebern; *story:* Bill Peed; *anim:* Al Bertino, John Sibley, Cliff Nordberg, Retta Scott; *fx:* Jack Boyd, Andy Engman; *lay:* Lance Nolley; *back:* Claude Coats; *voice:* Cactus Mack McPeters; *mus:* Paul J. Smith; *col:* Tech. *sd:* RCA. 7 min. • Burlesque on how the settlers moved West in their covered wagons, falling prey to an Indian attack along the way.

930. Call Me a Taxi (*Swifty & Shorty*) July 1964; *p.c.:* Para Cartoons; *dir:* Seymour Kneitel; *story/voices:* Eddie Lawrence; *anim:* Martin Taras; *sets:* Robert Little; *mus:* Winston Sharples; *ph:* Leonard McCormick; *prod mgr:* Abe Goodman; *col:* Tech. *sd:* RCA. 6 min. • Shorty needs a cab during a cloudburst and, when he finally gets one, the driver charges him $10 for a drive around the corner.

931. Calling All Cuckoos (*Woody Woodpecker*) 24 Sept. 1956; *p.c.:* Walter Lantz prods for Univ;. *dir:* Paul J. Smith; *story:* Homer Brightman; *anim:* Les Kline, Robert Bentley; *sets:* Art Landy, Raymond Jacobs; *voices:* Bob Johnson, Grace Stafford; *mus:* Clarence Wheeler; *prod mgr:* William E. Garity; *col:* Tech. *sd:* RCA. 6 min. • Clockmaker, Herr Spring, needs a new cuckoo for his clock and reckons Woody will serve the purpose.

932. Calling Doctor Magoo (*Mr. Magoo*) 24 May 1956; *p.c.:* UPA for Colum; *ex prod:* Stephen Bosustow; *dir:* Pete Burness. *story:* Dick Shaw; *anim:* Rudy Larriva, Cecil Surry, Gil Turner, Barney Posner; *lay:* Robert Dranko; *back:* Bob McIntosh; *voices:* Jim Backus, Jerry Hausner; *mus:* Thomas Cutcomp; *prod mgr:* Herbert Klynn; *col:* Tech. *sd:* RCA. 7 min. CS. • Magoo mistakes a passenger ship in dock for a hospital when visiting a sick friend.

933. Calling Dr. Porky (*Looney Tunes*) 21 Sept. 1940; *p.c.:* Leon Schlesinger prods for WB; *dir:* I. Freleng; *story:* Jack Miller; *anim:* Herman Cohen; *sets:* Robert L. Holdeman; *ed:* Treg Brown; *voices:* Mel Blanc, Sara Berner; *mus:* Carl W. Stalling; *ph:* John Burton; *prod sup:* Henry Binder, Raymond G. Katz; b&w. *sd:* Vit. 7 min. • Porky deals with a patient who has the "D.T.s" and is being followed around by a pack of pink elephants.

934. Calling Dr. Woodpecker (*Woody Woodpecker*) Dec. 1963; *p.c.:* Walter Lantz prods for Univ; *dir:* Paul J. Smith; *story:* Cal Howard; *anim:* Les Kline, Al Coe; *sets:* Art Landy, Ray Huffine; *voices:* Dal McKennon, Grace Stafford; *mus:* Clarence Wheeler; *prod sup:* William E. Garity; *col:* Tech. *sd:* RCA. 6 min. • While delivering flowers to the hospital, Woody falls afoul of Nurse Meany. He disguises himself and is mistaken for a famous surgeon.

935. Calypso Cat (*Tom & Jerry*) June 1962; *p.c.:* Rembrandt for MGM; *prod:* William L. Snyder; *dir:* Gene Deitch; *story:* Larz Bourne; *anim dir:* Vaclav Bedrich; *mus:* Stepan Konícek; *col:* Met. *sd:* WE. 6 min. • While on a Carribean cruise, Jerry louses things up for Tom when he tries to impress a girl kitten. • See: *Tom & Jerry (Rembrandt Studios)*

936. The Camel's Hump (*Unnatural History*) 28 Nov. 1925; *p.c.:* Bray prods for FBO; *dir:* Walter Lantz, Earl Hurd; *l/a:* Walter Lantz, Frankie Evans; *ph:* Joe Rock; b&w. sil. 5 min. l/a/anim. • The camel got his hump through a lump of porous plaster landing on his back and a large bird, thinking it was food, carried it and the camel far away. The skin of the camel was stretched over the plaster, leaving a permanent lump when they landed.

937. Camera Bug (*Blue Racer*) 6 Aug. 1972; *p.c.:* Mirisch/DFE for UA; *dir:* Art Davis; *story:* John W. Dunn; *anim:* Bob Richardson, Manny Gould, Warren Batchelder, Don Williams; *lay:* Dick Ung. *back:* Richard H. Thomas; *ed:* Joe Siracusa; *voices:* Larry D. Mann, Tom Holland; *mus:* Doug Goodwin; *ph:* John Burton Jr.; *prod sup:* Stan Paperny, Harry Love; *col:* DeLuxe *sd:* RCA. 5 min. • A Japanese Beetle, intent on taking photographs, is chased by the Racer.

938. Camera Mysteries *p.c.:* Swartz Pictures; *prod/dir:* George D. Swartz; *anim:* Luis Seel; b&w. sil. l/a/anim. • *1926:* **Finding the Lost World. Rushing the Gold Rush. The Flying Carpet. Safety Not Last. Motoring. Pirate's Bold.** • No further information available.

939. Camouflage (*Terry-Toon*) 27 Aug. 1943; *p.c.:* TT for Fox; *dir:* Eddie Donnelly; *story:* John Foster; *voices:* Arthur Kay, Thomas Morrison; *mus:* Philip A. Scheib; *ph:* Douglas Moye; *col:* Tech. *sd:* RCA. 7 min. • Pvt. Gandy and Sgt. Cat invent a revolutionary camouflage which they try out on the enemy on a Pacific isle.

940. Camp Clobber (*Clint Clobber*) July 1958; *p.c.:* TT for Fox; *ex prod:* Bill Weiss; *dir sup:* Gene Deitch; *dir:* Dave Tendlar; *story:* Larz Bourne, Eli Bauer; *story sup:* Tom Morrison; *anim:* Larry Silverman, Dave Tendlar, Johnny Gent, Bob Kuwahara, Peggy Breese, Vinnie Bell, Al Chiarito, Mannie Davis, Ed Donnelly; *des:* Eli Bauer; *back:* Bill Hilliker; *voices:* Allen Swift; *mus:* Philip A. Scheib; *prod mgr:* Sparky Schudde; *col:* Tech. *sd:* RCA. 7 min. CS. • An Army general keeps the apartment tenants awake with his bugle-blowing.

941. Camp Dog (*Pluto*) 22 Sept. 1950; *p.c.:* Walt Disney prods for RKO; *dir:* Charles Nichols; *story:* Milt Schaffer, Dick Kinney; *anim:* George Kreisl, George Nicholas, Marvin Woodward, Hugh Fraser, Charles Nichols; *fx anim:* Jack Boyd; *lay:* Karl Karpé; *back:* Art Landy; *voice:* James MacDonald; *mus:* Paul J. Smith; *col:* Tech. *sd:* RCA. 7 min. • Two coyotes invade the campers' provisions guarded by Pluto.

942. Camping Out (*Mickey Mouse*) 27 Jan. 1934; *p.c.:* Walt Disney prods for UA; *dir:* David D. Hand; *anim:* Paul Allen, Les Clark, Tom Codrick, Joseph d'Igalo, Ugo d'Orsi, Gilles de Tremaudan, Nick George, Hardie Gramatky, Edward Love, William O. Roberts, Archie Robin, Dick Williams, Marvin Woodward; *voices:* Marcellite Garner, Alyce Ardell; *mus:* Bert Lewis, Frank E. Churchill; b&w. *sd:* RCA. 7 min. • Mickey and the gang go camping. When Horace Horsecollar swats a mosquito, it later returns with reenforcements.

943. Camping Out (*Scrappy*) 10 Aug. 1932; *p.c.:* Winkler for Colum; *prod:* Charles Mintz; *dir:* Dick Huemor; *anim:* Sid Marcus, Art Davis; *mus:* Joe de Nat; *prod mgr:* James Bronis; b&w *sd:* WE. 6 min. • Scrappy and Vontzy take their dog camping. The hound does battle with an irate squirrel, a mosquito and two impudent hares.

944. The Camptown Races (*Screen Song*) 30 July 1948; *p.c.*: Famous for Para; *dir:* Seymour Kneitel; *story:* Bill Turner, Larry Riley; *anim:* Al Eugster, Irving Spector; *sets:* Tom Ford; *voice:* Jack Mercer; *mus:* Winston Sharples; *ph:* Leonard McCormick; *prod mgr:* Sam Buchwald; *col:* Pola. *sd:* RCA. 8 min. • The animals stage an old-time minstrel show.

945. Campus Capers (*Noveltoon*) 1 July 1949; *p.c.*: Famous for Para; *dir:* Bill Tytla; *story:* Carl Meyer, Jack Mercer; *anim:* George Germanetti, Steve Muffatti; *sets:* Robert Connavale; *voices:* Arnold Stang, Sid Raymond; *mus:* Winston Sharples; *prod mgr:* Sam Buchwald; *col:* Tech. *sd:* RCA. 7 min. • A football match between two colleges comes about when the cat overhears Herman and his mouse colleagues boasting at a reunion dinner.

946. Can You Take It? (*Popeye*) 27 Apr. 1934; *p.c.*: The Fleischer Studio for Para; *prod:* Max Fleischer; *dir:* Dave Fleischer; *anim:* Myron Waldman, Thomas Johnson, Lillian Friedman; *voices:* William A. Costello, Charles Carver; *mus:* Sammy Timberg; b&w. *sd:* WE. 6 min. • Nurse Olive inspires Popeye to join "The Bruiser Club" where he is subjected to a rigorous initiation.

947. Canadian Can-Can (*Inspector*) 20 Dec. 1967; *p.c.*: Mirisch/Geoffrey/DFE for UA; *dir:* Gerry Chiniquy; *story:* John W. Dunn; *anim:* Bob Matz, Manny Perez, Don Williams, Manny Gould, Chuck Downs; *lay:* Dick Ung; *back:* Tom O'Loughlin; *ed:* Lee Gunther; *voices:* Pat Harrington Jr., Mark Skor; *mus:* Walter Greene; *theme tune:* Henry Mancini; *ph:* John Burton Jr.; *prod sup:* Harry Love, Basil Cox; *col:* DeLuxe. *sd:* RCA. 6 min. • The Inspector becomes a Mountie in order to track down the notorious Two-Faced Harry.

948. Canadian Capers (*Paul Terry-Toons*) 23 Aug. 1931; *p.c.*: Terry, Moser & Coffman for Educational/Fox; *dir:* Paul Terry, Frank Moser; *anim:* Arthur Babbitt, Frank Moser, Hugh Shields, Vladimir Tytla; *mus:* Philip A. Scheib; b&w. *sd:* WE. 5 min. • A bird makes a nest in Al Falfa's beard. The irascible farmer then goes rabbit hunting and skunks put an end to his exploits.

949. Canary Row (*Merrie Melodies*) 7 Oct. 1950; *p.c.*: WB; *dir:* I. Freleng; *story:* Tedd Pierce; *anim:* Virgil Ross, Arthur Davis, Emery Hawkins, Gerry Chiniquy, Ken Champin; *lay:* Hawley Pratt; *back:* Paul Julian; *ed:* Treg Brown; *voices:* Mel Blanc, Bea Benaderet, Tedd Pierce; *mus:* Carl Stalling; *prod mgr:* John W. Burton; *prod:* Edward Selzer; *col:* Tech. *sd:* Vit. 7 min. • Sylvester tries to get Tweety out from a closely-guarded hotel.

950. The Candid Candidate (*Betty Boop*) 27 Aug. 1937; *p.c.*: The Fleischer Studio for Para; *prod:* Max Fleischer; *dir:* Dave Fleischer; *anim:* Lillian Friedman; *voices:* Mae Questel, Everett Clark; *mus:* Sammy Timberg; b&w. *sd:* WE. 7 min. • Betty campaigns for Grampy. When he is elected he proceeds to right various wrongs to make the people happy.

951. Candy Cabaret (*Noveltoon*) 11 June 1954; *p.c.*: Famous for Para; *dir:* Dave Tendlar; *story:* I. Klein; *anim:* Martin Taras, Thomas Moore; *sets:* Robert Little; *voices:* Jackson Beck, Jack Mercer; *mus:* Winston Sharples; *ph:* Leonard McCormick; *prod mgr:* Seymour Shultz; *col:* Tech. *sd:* RCA. 7 min. • Pieces of candy form a variety show ending with a hearty rendition of "Ain't She Sweet." Caricatures of Hugh Herbert, Humphrey Bogart and Edward G. Robinson are shown.

952. The Candy House (*Oswald*) 15 Jan. 1934; *p.c.*: Univ; *dir:* Walter Lantz, "Bill" Nolan; *anim:* Manuel Moreno, Lester Kline, Fred Kopietz, George Grandpré, Ernest Smythe *mus:* James Dietrich; b&w. *sd:* WE. 9 min. • The story of Hansel and Gretel with Oswald as "Hansel" and his sister, Fanny as "Gretel."

953. Candy Land (*Cartune Classic*) 22 Apr. 1935; *p.c.*: Univ; *story/lyrics:* Walter Lantz, Victor McLeod; *anim:* Manuel Moreno, Lester Kline, Fred Kopietz; *voice:* The Rhythmettes; *mus:* James Dietrich; *col:* Tech-2. *sd:* WE. 8 min. • A small boy and his dog are transported to Candy Land by the Sandman.

954. Cane and Able (*Noveltoon*) Oct. 1961; *p.c.*: Para Cartoons; *dir:* Seymour Kneitel; *story:* Carl Meyer, Jack Mercer; *anim:* Irv Spector, Irving Dressler, Larry Silverman; *sets:* Robert Owen; *voices:* Jackson Beck, Dayton Allen; *mus:* Winston Sharples; *ph:* Leonard McCormick; *prod mgr:* Abe Goodman; *col:* Tech. *sd:* RCA. 6 min. • "The Easterner" arrives in a western town. A tenderfoot, armed with nothing but a cane, but he begins to tame the rowdy inhabitants.

955. Canimated Nooz Pictorial *p.c.*: Essanay Film Mfg Co Inc for General Film; *prod:* P.A. Powers; *dir:* Wallace A. Carlson; b&w. *sil. s/r.* • *1915:* (1) 13 Oct.; (2) 17 Nov.; (3) 22 Dec. • *1916:* (4) 19 Jan.; (5) 22 Feb.; (6) 9 Mar.; (7) 23 Mar.; (8) 4 Apr.; (9) 19 Apr.; (10) 24 May; (11) 7 June; (12) 5 July; (13) 26 July; (14) 16 Aug.; (15) 6 Sept.; (16) 20 Sept.; (17) 11 Oct.; (18) 25 Oct.; (19) 15 Nov.; (20) 13 Dec.; (21) 27 Dec. • *1917:* (22) 10 Jan.; (23) 24 Jan.; (24) 10 Feb.; (25) 3 Mar.; (26) 17 Mar.; (27) 31 Mar.; (28) 28 Apr. • Split-reel (with scenic) featuring Carlson's comic characters, *Joe Boko* and *Dreamy Dud*. • See: *Mile-A-Minute Monty*

956. Canine Caddy (*Mickey Mouse*) 30 May 1941; *p.c.*: Walt Disney prods for RKO; *dir:* Clyde Geronimi; *asst dir:* Donald A. Duckwall; *anim:* Richard Brown, Eric Gurney, Emery Hawkins, Dong Kingman, Volus Jones, Kenneth Muse, George Nicholas, Charles A. Nichols, Chic F. Otterstrom, Morey Reden, Norman Tate; *fx:* Edwin Aardal, Jack Boyd, Brad Case, Andrew Engman, Art Fitzpatrick, Joseph Gayek, Paul B. Kossoff, Jack Huber, Frank Onaitis, Arthur W. Palmer, Ed Parks, John F. Reed, George Rowley, Reuben Timmens; *lay:* Bruce Bushman; *voice:* Walt Disney; *mus:* Paul J. Smith; *col:* Tech. *sd:* RCA. 7 min. • Mickey's caddy, Pluto, has problems with a gopher on the golf course.

957. Canine Capers (*Scrappy*) 16 Sept. 1937; *p.c.*: Charles Mintz prods for Colum; *story:* Allen Rose; *anim:* Harry Love; *voices:* Leone Le Doux; *mus:* Joe de Nat; *prod mgr:* James Bronis; b&w. *sd:* RCA. 7 min. • A Dog-catcher tries to capture Yippy as he helps Scrappy on his paper round.

958. Canine Casanova (*Pluto*) 27 July 1945; *p.c.*: Walt Disney prods for RKO; *dir:* Charles Nichols; *asst dir:* Esther Newell; *story:* Harry Reeves, Jesse Marsh, Rex Cox; *anim:* George Nicholas, Robert Youngquist, Hugh Fraser, Jerry Hathcock, George Kreisl, Art Scott, Marvin Woodward; *fx:* Ed Aardal, Jack Buckley, Andy Engman, John Reed; *lay:* Bruce Bushman, Karl Karpé; *back:* Al Dempster; *voice:* James MacDonald; *mus:* Oliver Wallace; *col:* Tech. *sd:* RCA. 7 min. • Pluto unsuccessfully tries to impress Dinah the Dachshund. When she is captured by the Dog Catcher it's Pluto to the rescue.

959. Canine Commandos (*Andy Panda*) 28 June 1943; *p.c.*: Walter Lantz prods for Univ; *dir/story:* Ben Hardaway, Milt Schaffer; *anim:* (La) Verne Harding; *sets:* Fred Brunish; *voice:* Dick Nelson; *mus:* Darrell Calker; *prod mgr:* George Hall; *col:* Tech. *sd:* WE. 6 min. • Andy has the job of putting canine call-up applicants through an intelligence test.

960. Canine Patrol (*Pluto*) 7 Dec. 1945; *p.c.*: Walt Disney prods for RKO; *dir:* Charles Nichols; *asst dir:* Bob North; *story:* Harry Reeves, Tom Oreb; *anim:* Marvin Woodward, John Lounsbery, Norman Tate, George Kreisl, Jerry Hathcock, George Nicholas, Bob Youngquist; *fx:* Andy Engman, Jack Boyd; *lay:* Karl Karpé; *back:* Nino Carbe; *voice:* James MacDonald; *mus:* Oliver Wallace; *col:* Tech. *sd:* RCA. 7 min. • Coast Guard Pluto tries to stop a baby turtle from swimming in a restricted area.

961. Canned Dog Feud (*Woody Woodpecker*) Apr. 1965; *p.c.*: Walter Lantz prods for Univ; *dir:* Paul J. Smith; *story:* Dalton Sandifer; *anim:* Les Kline, Al Coe; *sets:* Art Landy, Ray Huffine; *voices:* Dal McKennon, Grace Stafford; *mus:* Clarence Wheeler; *prod mgr:* William E. Garity; *col:* Tech. *sd:* RCA. 6 min. • Two feuding hillbillies' dogs vie for the kudos of bringing their respective masters a woodpecker.

962. Canned Feud (*Looney Tunes*) 3 Feb. 1951; *p.c.*: WB; *dir:* I. Freleng; *story:* Warren Foster, Cal Howard; *anim:* Ken Champin, Virgil Ross, Arthur Davis, Manuel Perez, John Carey; *lay:* Hawley Pratt; *back:* Paul Julian; *ed:* Treg Brown; *voices:* Mel Blanc, Marian Richman; *mus:* Carl Stalling; *prod mgr:* John W. Burton; *prod:* Edward Selzer; *col:* Tech. *sd:* Vit. 7 min. • Sylvester is locked in with many cans of food but no can opener. A mouse acquires the opener and taunts the wretched creature with it.

963. Canned Music (*Krazy Kat*) 12 Sept. 1929; *p.c.*: Winkler for Colum; *anim:* Ben Harrison, Manny Gould; *mus:* Rosario Bourdon; *prod:* Charles Mintz; b&w. *sd:* WE. 6 min. • No story available.

964. Cannery Rodent (*Tom & Jerry*) 1967; *p.c.*: MGM; *prod/dir/story:* Chuck Jones; *ass dir:* Maurice Noble; *anim:* Ben Washam, Ken Harris, Don Towsley, Tom Ray, Dick Thompson, O.B. Barkley, Bob Kirk; *back:* Philip de Guard; *mus:* Dean Elliott; *ph:* Buf Nerbovig; *prod sup:* Les Goldman, Earl Jonas, Sam Pal; *col:* Metro. *sd:* WE. 7 min. • Tom chases Jerry around a wharf into a canning factory where a shark gets involved in the whole mêlée.

965. Cannery Woe (*Looney Tunes*) 7 Jan. 1961; *p.c.*: WB; *dir:* Robert

McKimson; *story:* Tedd Pierce; *anim:* George Grandpré, Ted Bonnicksen, Warren Batchelder, Tom Ray; *lay:* Robert Gribbroek; *back:* William Butler; *ed:* Treg Brown; *voices:* Mel Blanc, Tom Holland; *mus:* Milt Franklyn; *prod mgr:* William Orcutt; *col:* Tech. *sd:* Vit. 7 min. • Speedy Gonzales is summoned to save the Cheese Festival by getting some cheese from a factory guarded by Sylvester.

966. Cannibal Capers *(Silly Symphony)* 15 Mar. 1930; *p.c.:* Walter E. Disney for Colum; *dir:* Burt Gillett; *anim:* Norman Ferguson, David D. Hand, Floyd Gottfredson; *mus:* Bert Lewis; *ph:* William Cottrell; b&w. *sd:* PCP. 7 min. • The jungle animals and cannibals are affected by jazz music.

967. Cannonball Run II 29 June 1984; *p.c.:* Golden Harvest/WB for Arcafin BV; *anim seq:* Ralph Bakshi; *col:* Tech. *sd.* 108 min. *l/a.* • Live-action comedy: The king of a Middle Eastern state orders his son to sponsor a Trans-American Cannonball run so that he can win, thus maintaining the honor of their tribe.

968. Canvas-Back Duck *(Donald Duck)* 4 Dec. 1953; *p.c.:* Walt Disney prods for RKO; *dir:* Jack Hannah; *story:* Jack Kinney, Bill Berg; *anim:* George Kreisl, Volus Jones, Bob Carlson, Al Coe; *fx:* Dan MacManus, Ed Aardal; *lay:* Yale Gracey; *back:* Ray Huffine; *voices:* Billy Bletcher, Clarence Nash, Dal McKennon, Bob Jackman, James MacDonald; *mus:* Oliver Wallace; *col:* Tech. *sd:* RCA. 7 min. • Donald is tricked into entering the boxing ring against a champion prizefighter.

969. Cape Kidnaveral *(Noveltoon)* Aug. 1961; *p.c.:* Para Cartoons; *dir:* Seymour Kneitel; *story:* Carl Meyer, Jack Mercer; *anim:* Myron Waldman; *sets:* Robert Little; *voices:* Jack Mercer, Cecil Roy; *mus:* Winston Sharples; *ph:* Leonard McCormick; *prod mgr:* Abe Goodman; *col:* Tech. *sd:* RCA. 6 min. • Specks, a small boy, and his gang create their own astronaut training program.

970. Cap'n Cub Mar. 1945 (made in 1943); *p.c.:* Ted Eshbaugh Studios Inc. for Official Films/Film Classics; *prod/dir:* Ted Eshbaugh; *sup:* Charles B. Hastings; *anim:* Ozzie Evans, A.C. Hutchinson, Jack Tyrrel, Bill Weaver, Winfield Hoskins; *fx:* Harry Hamsel; *sets:* Henri G. Courtais; *mus:* Richard & Florence Dupage; *col:* Tech. *sd.* 10 min. aka: *Cap'n Cub Blasts the Japs.* • A military bear applies himself to the problems of National Emergency. He decrees an increase in plane output. His efforts are unusually successful.

971. Captain Hareblower *(Merrie Melodies)* 16 Feb. 1954; *p.c.:* WB; *dir:* I. Freleng; *story:* Warren Foster; *anim:* Manuel Perez, Ken Champin, Virgil Ross, Arthur Davis; *lay:* Hawley Pratt; *back:* Irv Wyner; *ed:* Treg Brown; *voices:* Mel Blanc; *mus:* Carl Stalling; *prod mgr:* John W. Burton; *prod:* Edward Selzer; *col:* Tech. *sd:* Vit. 7 min. • Yosemite Sam, the pirate, attempts to board a ship that's solely guarded by Bugs Bunny.

972. Captain Kidder *(Aesop's Film Fables)* 24 Feb. 1924; *p.c.:* Fables Pictures Inc for Pathé; *dir:* Paul Terry; b&w. *sil.* 5 min. • The dog, cat and mouse are involved in a quest for buried treasure.

973. The Captain's Christmas *(Captain & the Kids)* 17 Dec. 1938; *p.c.:* MGM; *dir:* Milt Gross; *anim:* Jack Zander; *voices:* Billy Bletcher, Dave Weber, Jeanne Dunn; *Chorus:* Charles Bennett, Robert Tait, Stuart Hall, John Moss; *mus:* Scott Bradley; *col:* Tech. *sd:* WE. 8 min. • Posing as Santa, Pirate John and his crew proceed to wreck the kids' Christmas. Feeling remorse, they sing in the streets to earn money to repay them.

974. Captains Outrageous *(Mr. Magoo)* 25 Dec. 1952; *p.c.:* UPA for Colum; *ex prod:* Stephen Bosustow; *dir:* Pete Burness; *story:* Bill Scott; *anim:* Rudy Larriva, Tom McDonald; *lay:* Ted Parmelee; *back:* Bob McIntosh; *voices:* Jim Backus, Jerry Hausner; *mus:* George Bruns; *prod mgr:* Herbert Klynn; *col:* Tech. *sd:* RCA. 7 min. • Magoo and Waldo set sail to capture "Mighty Moe" the giant marlin.

975. The Captain's Pup *(Captain & the Kids)* 30 Apr. 1938; *p.c.:* MGM; *dir:* Robert Allen; *voices:* Billy Bletcher, Martha Wentworth; *mus:* Scott Bradley; *sep. sd:* WE. 7 min. • The Captain tries to smuggle a pup into the house against Mama's wishes.

976. Car-Azy Drivers *(Popeye)* 22 July 1955; *p.c.:* Famous for Para; *dir:* Seymour Kneitel; *story:* Larz Bourne; *anim:* Tom Johnson, John Gentilella; *sets:* Anton Loeb; *voices:* Jack Mercer, Mae Questel; *mus:* Winston Sharples; *ph:* Leonard McCormick; *prod mgr:* Seymour Shultz; *col:* Tech. *sd:* RCA. 6 min. • Popeye has a disasterous experience when teaching Olive to drive.

977. Car of Tomorrow 22 Sept. 1951; *p.c.:* MGM; *dir:* Tex Avery; *story:* Roy Williams, Rich Hogan; *anim:* Walter Clinton, Grant Simmons, Michael Lah; *sets:* John Didrik Johnsen; *ed:* Jim Faris; *voices:* June Foray; *mus:* Scott Bradley; *prod:* Fred Quimby. *col:* Tech. *sd:* WE. 6 min. • An insight into various improvements for future automobiles.

978. The Care Bears Movie 29 Mar. 1985; *p.c.:* Nelvana/American Greetings Corp./CPG Products Corp. for Miracle; *dir:* Arna Selznick; *prod:* Michael Hirsh, Patrick Loubert, Clive Smith; *ex prod:* Carole MacGillvray, Robert Unkel, Jack Chojnacki, Lou Gioia; *asso prod:* Paul Pressler, John Bohach, Harvey Levin; *prod ex:* Melissa Hoffman; *unit dir:* Bill Parkins, Laura Shepherd; *asst dir:* Dale Schott; *scr:* Peter Sauder; *storyboard:* Alan Bunce, David Thrasher, Sam Dixon, Bill Parkins, Diane Parsons, Ray Jafelice, Dale Schott; *anim dir:* Charles Bonifacio; *anim:* Anne Marie Bardwell, Ralf Palmer, David Brewster, John Collins, Roy Merlin, J. Daniel Smith, Lillian Andre, John De Klein, Ian Freedman, Michelle Houston, Pat Knight, Paul Riley, Lynn Yamazaki, Rejean Bourdages, Chris Delaney, Scott Glynn, Bob Jacques, Beverly Newberg-Lehmann, Dick Zondag, Gian Celestri, Mike Fallows, John Hooper, Trevor Keen, Mark Pudleiner, Cynthia Swift, Ralph Zondag; *quality control:* Brenda Kelly, Betty Oldham, Rob Sadler, Debra Pugh, Lisa Oglesby, Diana Lyle, Susan Albert, Evelyn Baker; *lay:* Ricardo Spinacé, David Thrasher; *(artists):* Jim Craig, Sam Agro, Maria Carter, Wayne Gilbert, Tony Iacobelli, Mark Marren, John Palmer, Brian Poehlman, Rick Allen, Kevin Davies, Ken Hancock, Richard Livingston, Larry MacDougall, Howard Parkins, David Russell, John van Bruggen, Ted Bastien, Sam Dixon, John Howard, Howard Lonn, Tom Nesbitt, Bill Payne, Joseph Sherman; *back:* Peter Moehrle, Louis Krawanga; *(design):* Barry Atkinson, Wayne Gilbert; *paint/color des:* Jan Leitch, Val Fraser, Mary Ecklund, Aggie Krumins; *Xerox:* Paul Hogarth, Stephen Chadwick; *ed:* John Broughton, Rob Kirkpatrick, Jim Erickson, Tom Joerin, Gordon Kidd, Stephen Mitchell, Sheila Murray, Steve Weslak, Michael O'Farrell; *ses:* Charlie Bonifacio, David Brewster, Alan Bunce, John Collins; *fx:* David Marshall, Kate Shepherd, Trevor Davis, Keith Ingham, Willy Ashworth, Kim Cleary, Tony Egizii, Lesley Headrick, Ted Ryan, Jan Steel Moffatt, Peter Yamasaki; *voices: Mr. Cherrywood:* Mickey Rooney; *The Spirit:* Jackie Burroughs; *The Lion:* Harry Dean Stanton; *Jason:* Sunny Besen Thrasher; *Love-a-Lot:* Georgie Engel; *also:* Eva Almos, Bobby Dermer, Gloria Figura, Janet Laine-Green, Dan Hennessey, Maria Lukofsky, Patrice Black, Jayne Eastwood, Cree Summer Francks, Luba Goy, Jim Henshaw, Pauline Rennie, Brent Titcomb, Melleny Brown, Anni Evans, Brian George, Terri Hawkes, Hadley Kay, Billie Mae Richards, Louise Goffin, Sherry Goffin, Robbie Kondor, Levi Larky; *mus:* Patricia Cullen, *(chase sequence)* David Bird, Walt Woodward; *songs:* Carole King; *addit songs by and performed by* John Sebastian, N.R.B.Q., Donna Adams, Terry Adams, Al Anderson, Tom Arpolino, Keith Spring, Joey Spampinato, Roswell Rudd and the Tower of Power, Emilio Castillo, Stephen Kupka, Mike Cichowicz, Marc Russo, Greg Adams; *addit lyrics:* Ken Stephenson; *sung by* David Bird, Becky Goldstein, Susan Kross, Ann Marie Prunty, Christine Seibert; *song seq prepared by* Peter Hudecki; *titles:* Kim Cleary; *sd fx:* Peter Jermyn, Drew King, Michele Moses; *sd ed:* ACES; *foley:* Andy Malcolm, Peter McBurnie; *pro asst:* Nick Campbell, Karyn Booth-Chadwick, Julie Feher, Barbara Fish, Stephen Fitch, Diana Foster-Pease, Brenda Kelly, John Pagan, Garth Roerick; *voice dir:* Rob Kirkpatrick; characters created for *Those Characters From Cleveland* by Linda Edwards, Dave Polter, Murel Fahrion, Tom Schneider, Clark Wiley, Elena Kucharik, Ralph Shaffer; *ph:* David Altman, Jim Christianson, Barbara Sachs; *prod sup:* Lenora Hume; *prod co-ord:* Heather Walker; *prod mgr:* Dale Cox; *unit mgr:* John Cuddy, Richard Pimm; *post prod sup:* John Broughton. *col. sd:* Pathé Sound. 76 min. • Mr. Cherrywood tells some orphans a bedtime story about the Care Bears, who live in the land of Care-a-Lot spreading friendship and good feeling throughout the world. Tender Heart is on his way to help a lonely boy named Nicholas who is an assistant magician. When he opens a book of spells, a demon is unleashed who casts a spell that makes everyone as friendless and cheerless as the boy. The Care Bears set out to return things to normal. USA/Canada

979. Care Bears Movie II: A New Generation 7 Mar. 1986; *p.c.:* Those Characters From Cleveland/Kenner Parker Toys/Nelvana for Colum-EMI-Warner; *dir:* Dale Schott; *sup prod:* Lenora Hume; *ex prod:* John Bohach, Jack Chojnacki, Harvey Levin, Carole MacGillvray, Paul Pressler; *prod:* Michael Hirsh, Patrick Loubert, Clive A. Smith; *prod sup:* Dale Cox;

line prod: Peter Hudecki; *prod mgr:* Karyn Booth Chadwick; *unit mgr:* Richard Pimm; *post prod sup:* Rob Kirkpatrick; *asst dir:* Laura Shepherd; *story:* Peter Sauder; *storyboard:* Sam Agro, Alan Bunce, Roy Meurin, Dale Schott; *des co-ord:* Cathy Parkes; *des:* Charles Bonifacio, Alan Bunce, Ross Campbell, David Quesnelle, Wendy Purdue, Anthony Van Bruggen, Cynthia Swift; *col des:* Jan Leitch, Eileen Middleton, Irene Couloufis, Jackie Allinson, Glen Chadwick, Amanda Robinson; *graphic des:* Kim Cleary; *anim dir:* Charles Bonifacio; *unit anim dir:* Bill Perkins; *anim posing:* Gary Hurst, Roy Meurin, Wendy Purdue, Ken Stephenson, Lynn Yamazaki, Mary Ecklund, Sam Agro, Lillian Andre, Rej Bourdage, Woong Cheon Jang, Ross Campbell, Shane Doyle, Harold Duckett, Tony Egizii, Scott Glynn, Dennis Gonzalez, Mike Girard, Gerry Fournier, Michelle Houston-Jacobs, Bob Jacques, Arnie Lipsey, Pat Knight, Ron Migilore, Dave Quesnelle, Sean Seles, Allen Swerling, Karen Stephenson, Cynthia Swift, Anne-Marie Bardwell, Ralf Palmer; *character development:* Ralph Shaffer, Linda Edwards, Tom Schneider; *character development:* Penne Bender, Robyn Hill, Tom Jacobs, Ingred Koepcke, Elena Kucharik, Esther Narcosny, David Polter, Ernie Ruder, Judi Schuman; *fx anim:* Trevor Davies, Jan Steel Moffatt, David Marshall, Peter Yamasaki, Willy Ashworth, Dawn Lee; *lay sup:* Arna Selznick, John Van Bruggen, Rick Allen, Bob Cowan, Evelyn Baker; *lay co-ord* John Pragan; *lay art:* John Flagg, Anthony Van Bruggen, Peter Blellcki, Sam Dixon, Barb Massey, Bill Payne, Rick Bentham, Dave Pemberton, Paul Bouchard, Brian Poehlman, Charles Bastien, Armen Melkonian, Eric Chu, Brian Lemay, Richard Livingston, Jeff Dickson, Howard Parkins, Brian Lee, Maria Carter, Antonio Iacobelli, Rick Corrigan, Rob Sadler, Scott Bennett, Brian Foster, Faye Hamilton, Roger Jakublec, John Aird, Debra Pugh, Chris Labonte, Lyndon Ruddy, Jim Nakashima; *ed:* Evan Landis; *(pre-prod)* Keith Traver, Brian Feeley, Monica Falton, Peter Branton, Philip Stillman, Jamie Whitney; *art dir:* Wayne Gilbert; *back:* Gabe Csakany, Nancy Eason, Clive Powsey; *voices: Dark Heart/the Boy:* Hadley Kay; *Great Wishing Star:* Chris Wiggins; *Christy:* Cree Summer Francks; *Dawn:* Alyson Court; *John:* Michael Fatini; *Camp Champ:* Sunny Besen Thrasher; *True Heart Bear:* Maxine Miller; *Noble Heart Horse:* Pam Hyatt; *Brave Heart Lion:* Dan Hennessey; *Tender Heart Bear:* Billie Mae Richards; *Friend Bear:* Eva Amos; *Grumpy Bear:* Bob Dormer; *Share & Funshine Bear:* Patrice Black; *Harmony Bear:* Nonnie Griffin; *Bright Heart Raccoon:* Jim Henshaw; *Cheer Bear:* Melleny Brown; *Wish Bear:* Janet-Laine Greene; *Playful Heart Monkey:* Marla Kukofsky; *Bedtime Bear:* Gloria Figura; "I Care for You," "Growing up" performed by Stephen Bishop; "The Fight Song" performed by Debbie Allen; "Our Beginning," "Forever Young" performed by Carol Parks; "Flying My Colors" performed by Dean Parks, Carol Parks, Amanda Parks, Acacia Parks; *mus:* Patricia Cullen; *orch:* Milton Barnes; *mus ed:* Gord Kidd, Stephen Hudecki; *mus prod:* David Greene; *ex mus advisor:* George Massenburg; *songs:* Dean Parks, Carol Parks; *sd fx:* Drew King, Peter Goodale, Greg Holmes, Mac Holyoke, John Baktis, Cindy Romanovitch, Eric Hurlbut, Melody Long, David Altman, Tom Griffin; *sd:* Steve Fraser, Sheila Murray, Richard Bond, Tony van den Akker, Phil Sheridan; *foley ed:* Andy Malcolm, Peter McBurnie, Don White; *prod asst:* Barbara Bjarnson, Paul Hogarth, Steve Chadwick, Nancy Shenton, Garth Roerick. *col. sd:* Pathé Sound. 76 min. • Great Wishing Star rescues a ship full of orphan bear cubs escaping from the evil Dark Heart. The Bears are presented with special powers denoting their new position as guardians of the world of feelings in the Kingdom of Caring. True Heart Bear finds Dawn and John, two children who have run away from Summer Camp and have been separated from their friend, Christy. They are taken to the Kingdom of Caring while Christy has been tempted by Dark Heart, in the guise of a fox, to grant him an unspecified favor in the future in exchange for her becoming Camp Champ. She agrees, only to later find out that the favor is to help kidnap the cubs. USA/Canada

980. The Careless Caretaker *(Woody Woodpecker)* 29 May 1962; *p.c.:* Walter Lantz prods for Univ; *dir:* Paul J. Smith; *story:* Al Bertino, Dick Kinney; *anim:* Les Kline, Roy Jenkins; *sets:* Art Landy, Ray Huffine; *voices:* Daws Butler, Grace Stafford; *mus:* Darrell Calker; *prod mgr:* William E. Garity; *col:* Tech. *sd:* RCA. 6 min. • Smedley appears as a tree surgeon trying to save a tree from Woody's beak.

981. Carmen Get It *(Tom & Jerry)* 1962; *p.c.:* Rembrandt for MGM; *prod:* William L. Snyder; *dir/story:* Gene Deitch; *mus:* Stepan Konícek; *col:* Metro. *sd:* WE. 6 min. • Tom's pursuit of Jerry disrupts a production of Bizet's "Carmen." • See: *Tom & Jerry: (Rembrandt Studios)*

982. Carmen's Veranda *(Terry-Toon)* 28 July 1944; *p.c.:* TT for Fox; *dir:* Mannie Davis; *story:* John Foster; *voices:* Roy Halee, Thomas Morrison; *mus:* Philip A. Scheib; *ph:* Douglas Moye; *col:* Tech. *sd:* RCA. 7 min. • A mock opera starring Gandy Goose as "Tyrone" and Sourpuss as the villain.

983. Carnival Capers *(Oswald)* 12 Oct. 1932; *p.c.:* Univ; *anim:* Walter Lantz, "Bill" Nolan; *anim:* Ray Abrams, Fred Avery, "Bill" Weber, Jack Carr, Charles Hastings; *mus:* James Dietrich; *b&w. sd:* WE. 7 min. • Oswald and his girl are pestered by Putrid Pete at a seaside carnival.

984. Carnival Courage *(Color Rhapsody)* 6 Sept. 1945; *p.c.:* Colum; *dir:* Howard Swift; *story/voice:* John McLeish; *anim:* Grant Simmons, Volus Jones; *ed:* Richard S. Jensen; *mus:* Eddie Kilfeather; *ph:* Frank Fisher; *prod mgr:* Hugh McCollum; *col:* Tech. *sd:* WE. 7 min. • Willoughby Wren buys a cap woven from Samson's hair. As long as he wears it he retains magnificent strength.

985. Carnival Week *(Aesop's Film Fable)* 4 Dec. 1927; *p.c.:* Fables Pictures Inc for Pathé; *dir:* Paul Terry, John Foster; *b&w. sil.* 5 min. • Farmer Al stages a carnival in front of the barn. The festivities end with a race between the elephant and an ostrich. When the intoxicated farmer proclaims a rabbit the winner, the animals are in uproar.

986. The Carpenters *(Color Rhapsody)* 14 Feb. 1941; *p.c.:* Cartoon Films Ltd for Colum; *prod:* Lawson Haris; *dir:* Paul Fennell; *voices:* Mel Blanc; *ed:* Almon Teeter; *mus:* Clarence Wheeler; *ph:* Richard M. Ising; *col:* Tech. *sd:* RCA. 8 min. • Three inept builders with gadget-minded craftmanship try to construct a house. After Ub Iwerks had sold Cartoon Films Ltd, this was made to help fulfil a contract made earlier.

987. Carrotblanca 25 Aug. 1995; *(Looney Tunes) p.c.:* WB Classic Animation; *dir:* Douglas McCarthy; *prod:* Kathleen Helppie-Shipley; *story/prod:* Timothy Cahill, Julie McNally; *asst dir:* Spike Brandt; *anim:* Tony Cervone, Shawn Keller, Harry Sabin, Jeff Siergey, David S. Smith, Bill Snelgrove, Bill Waldman; *asst anim sup:* Nelson Recinos; *key asst:* Frank Moueri, Maureen Trueblood, Chris Waugh; *fx anim:* Phil Cummings, Bill Knoll, Kathleen Mauro; *asst anim:* Doug Bombardier, Ivan Camilli, Ed Gabriel, George Goodchild, David Hancock, Mary Hanley, Sandy Henkin, Myung Kang, Miyul Lee, Myung Miller, Bill Mims, Herb Moore, Myung Nam, Doug Ninneman, David Recinos, Joe Roman, Rodney Tirey, Elyse Whittaker; *art dir:* Alan Bodner, Stephen Lewis; *lay:* Bryan Evans, Ed Haney, Dave Kuhn; *back:* Patricia Keppler, Tim Maloney; *voices: Daffy Duck/Sylvester:* Joe Alaskey; *Tweety:* Bob Bergen; *Bugs Bunny/Pepé le Pew/Foghorn Leghorn:* Greg Burson; *General Pandemonium:* Maurice LaMarche; *Penelope:* Tress MacNeille; *mus:* Richard Stone; *prop des:* Frederick J. Gardner III; *col sup:* Bunny Munns; *ed:* Rick Gehr; *sd fx:* Monterey Post Productions; *i&p:* Howard Schwartz; *scene plan:* Dora Yakutis; *post prod sup:* Jim Champin; *prod mgr:* Steve Donmyer; *col:* Tech. *sd:* Dolby stereo. 7¹/₂ min. • Satire of the movie classic *Casablanca* featuring the Looney Tunes characters.

988. Carte Blanched *(Inspector)* 14 May 1969; *p.c.:* Mirisch/Geoffrey/DFE for UA; *dir:* Gerry Chiniquy; *story:* David DeTiege; *anim:* Don Williams, Manny Perez, Don Towsley; *lay:* Corny Cole; *back:* Tom O'Loughlin; *ed:* Lee Gunther; *voices:* Pat Harrington Jr., Marvin Miller; *mus:* Walter Greene; *theme tune:* Henry Mancini; *ph:* John Burton Jr.; *prod sup:* Harry Love, Jim Foss; *col:* DeLuxe. *sd:* RCA. 6 min. • The Inspector tries to dispose of a trolley he has inadvertently taken from the supermarket.

989. The Cartoon Factory *(Out of the Inkwell)* 21 Feb. 1924; *p.c.:* Out of the Inkwell Studios for Red Seal; *prod:* Max Fleischer. *dir:* Dave Fleischer; *b&w. sil.* 6 min. *l/a/anim.* • Max appears as a life-size toy soldier. Ko-Ko draws a regiment of toy soldiers who come to life and the battle commences.

990. Cartoon Melodies • See: *Sing and Be Happy*

991. A Cartoonist's Nightmare *(Looney Tunes)* 21 Sept. 1935; *p.c.:* Leon Schlesinger prods for WB; *dir:* Jack King; *anim:* Don Williams, Paul Smith, Robert Clampett; *voices:* Billy Bletcher, Tommy Bond; *mus:* Bernard Brown; *prod sup:* Henry Binder, Raymond G. Katz; *b&w. sd:* Vit. 7 min. • The cartoon characters kidnap the artist but Beans is on hand to save the day.

992. Cartoonland *(Out of the Inkwell)* 2 Feb. 1921; *p.c.:* Bray prods for

Goldwyn; *prod/l/a:* Max Fleischer; *dir:* Dave Fleischer; b&w. *sil. l/a/anim.* • Ko-Ko travels to see his father in Cartoonland where he also meets various comic characters such as Mutt and Jeff, The Katzenjammer Kids and Foxy Grandpa. • See: *Goldwyn-Bray Pictographs*

993. Cartoons Ain't Human *(Popeye)* 27 Aug. 1943; *p.c.:* Famous for Para; *dir:* Seymour Kneitel; *story:* Jack Mercer, Jack Ward; *anim:* Orestes Calpini, Otto Feuer; *voices:* Jack Mercer, Margie Hines; *mus:* Sammy Timberg; *ph:* Leonard McCormick; *prod mgr:* Sam Buchwald; b&w. *sd:* WE. 7 min. • Popeye makes his own animated cartoon with himself as the hero and Olive as the damsel in distress.

994. A Car-Tune Portrait *(Color Classic)* 25 June 1937; *p.c.:* Studio for Para; *prod:* Max Fleischer; *dir:* Dave Fleischer; *anim:* David Tendlar, Nicholas Tafuri; *voice:* David Ross; *mus:* King Ross; *col:* Tech. *sd:* WE. 7 min. • An animal orchestra is pestered by a fly.

995. Casanova Cat *(Tom & Jerry)* 16 Jan. 1951; *p.c.:* MGM; *dir:* William Hanna, Joseph Barbera; *anim:* Irven Spence, Ray Patterson, Ed Barge, Kenneth Muse; *ed:* Jim Faris; *voice:* Paul Frees; *mus:* Scott Bradley; *ph:* Jack Stevens; *prod:* Fred Quimby; *col:* Tech. *sd:* WE. 7 min. • Tom's efforts to woo a Park Avenue puss are ruined by Jerry and the arrival of another suitor.

996. The Case of the Cockeyed Canary *(Noveltoon)* 19 Dec. 1952; *p.c.:* Famous for Para; *dir:* Seymour Kneitel; *story:* I. Klein; *anim:* Steve Muffatti, Morey Reden; *sets:* Robert Connavale; *voices:* Mae Questel, Jack Mercer, Gwen Davies; *mus:* Winston Sharples; *ph:* Leonard McCormick; *prod mgr:* Seymour Shultz; *col:* Tech. *sd:* RCA. 7 min. • Private-eye Audrey investigates the case of "Who Killed Cock Robin?" Caricatures of Jimmy Durante, Bob Hope and Harpo Marx.

997. The Case of the Cold Storage Yegg *(Inspector Willoughby)* 18 June 1963; *p.c.:* Walter Lantz prods for Univ; *dir:* Paul J. Smith; *story:* Tedd Pierce, Bill Danch; *anim:* Al Coe, Les Kline; *sets:* Ray Huffine, Art Landy; *voice:* Dal McKennon; *mus:* Darrell Calker; *prod mgr:* William E. Garity; *col:* Tech. *sd:* RCA. 6 min. • A bank robber leads Willoughby half-way around the world to retrieve some stolen money.

998. The Case of the Elephant's Trunk *(Inspector Willoughby)* Jan. 1965; *p.c.:* Walter Lantz prods for Univ; *dir:* Paul J. Smith; *story:* Cal Howard; *anim:* Les Kline, Al Coe; *sets:* Art Landy, Ray Huffine; *voice:* Dal McKennon; *mus:* Walter Greene; *prod mgr:* William E. Garity; *col:* Tech. *sd:* RCA. 6 min. • The Inspector is called upon to track down a Maharajah's stolen elephant.

999. Case of the Lost Sheep *(Oswald)* 9 Dec. 1935; *p.c.:* Univ; *dir:* Walter Lantz; *story:* Walter Lantz, Victor McLeod; *anim:* Manuel Moreno, Lester Kline; *mus:* James Dietrich; b&w. *sd:* WE. 7 min. • Oswald gets involved with Bo Peep.

1000. The Case of the Maltese Chicken *(Inspector Willoughby)* 4 Feb. 1964; *p.c.:* Walter Lantz prods for Univ; *dir:* Paul J. Smith; *story:* Cal Howard; *anim:* Les Kline, Al Coe; *sets:* Art Landy, Ray Huffine; *voice:* Dal McKennon; *mus:* Darrell Calker; *prod mgr:* William E. Garity; *col:* Tech. *sd:* RCA. 6 min. • The Inspector journeys to China in pursuit of Ooo So Fat, who has absconded with the prized Maltese Chicken.

1001. Case of the Missing Hare *(Merrie Melodies)* 12 Dec. 1942; *p.c.:* Leon Schlesinger prods for WB; *dir:* Charles M. Jones; *story:* Tedd Pierce; *anim:* Ken Harris; *lay:* Arthur Heinemann; *back:* Eugene Fleury; *ed:* Treg Brown; *voices:* Mel Blanc; *mus:* Carl W. Stalling; *ph:* John W. Burton; *prod sup:* Henry Binder, Raymond G. Katz; *col:* Tech. *sd:* Vit. 8 min. • A magician lives to rue the day he asked for a volunteer from the audience and Bugs walked up to assist his act.

1002. The Case of the Red-Eyed Ruby *(Inspector Willoughby)* 28 Nov. 1961; *p.c.:* Walter Lantz prods for Univ; *dir:* Paul J. Smith; *story:* Tedd Pierce, Bill Danch; *anim:* Ray Abrams, Les Kline; *sets:* Art Landy, Ray Huffine; *voice:* Dal McKennon; *mus:* Darrell Calker; *prod mgr:* William E. Garity; *col:* Tech. *sd:* RCA. 6 min. • The Inspector's task of returning a ruby to The Green Idol in the heart of the Sahara Desert is further complicated by the presence of an arch criminal intent on stealing it.

1003. The Case of the Screaming Bishop *(Phantasy)* 4 Aug. 1944; *p.c.:* Colum; *dir:* Howard Swift; *story:* John McLeish; *anim:* Jim Armstrong, Grant Simmons; *sets:* Clark Watson; *ed:* Richard S. Jensen; *voices:* John McLeish, Harry E. Lang; *mus:* Eddie Kilfeather; *ph:* Frank Fisher; *prod*

mgr: Albert Spar; *col:* Tech. *sd:* WE. 7 min. • Hairlock Combs and Dr. Got-some trail the mysterious "X" who's stolen a dinosaur's skeleton from the Museum of Unusual History.

1004. The Case of the Stuttering Pig *(Looney Tunes)* 30 Oct. 1937; *p.c.:* Leon Schlesinger prods for WB; *dir:* Frank Tashlin; *story:* Melvin Millar; *anim:* Volney White; *lay:* Griff Jay; *ed:* Tregoweth E. Brown; *voices:* Mel Blanc, Billy Bletcher, Shirley Reed; *mus:* Carl W. Stalling; *ph:* John W. Burton; *prod mgr:* Henry Binder, Raymond G. Katz; b&w. *sd:* Vit. 7 min. Award: *Exhibitor's Cartoon of the Year.* • Porky and his relatives stand to inherit a fortune. Kindly Lawyer Goodwill will inherit if anything happens to them, so he drinks a concoction that turns him into a raging monster.

1005. Casey at the Bat *(Marquee Musical)* 16 July 1954; *p.c.:* Walt Disney prods for BV; *dir:* Clyde Geronimi; *col:* Tech. *sd:* RCA. 7 min. • Baseball hero, Casey, finally strikes out. • See: *Make Mine Music*

1006. Casey Bats Again 18 June 1954; *p.c.:* Walt Disney prods for RKO; *dir:* Jack Kinney; *story:* Dick Kinney, Brice Mack; *anim:* John Sibley, Fred Moore, George Nicholas, Ken O'Brien; *fx:* Blaine Gibson, Ed Aardal, Dan MacManus; *lay:* Bruce Bushman; *back:* Al Dempster; *voice:* William Woodson; *mus:* Oliver Wallace; *col:* Tech. *sd:* RCA. 8 min. • One-time baseball great, Casey, decides to utilize his many daughters by forming an all-girl baseball team.

1007. Casper 28 July 1995; *p.c.:* Amblin Entertainment/Univ; *anim dir:* Eric Armstrong, Phil Nibbelink; *ex prod:* Steven Spielberg, Gerald R. Molen, Jeffrey A. Montgomery; *prod:* Colin Wilson; *sup character anim:* Mark Anthony Austin, Tom "Two Hands" Bertino, Miguel A. Fuertes, Jeffrey B. Light, Doug Smith, James R. Tooley; *character anim:* Philip Arone, Linda Bel, David Byers Brown, Susan Campbell, Jerry Yu Ching, Bruce Dahl, Lou Dellarosa, Bill Farmer, Paul J. Griffin, Steve "Fireplug" Hunter, Daniel Jeannette, Ken Satchel King, Peter Lepeniotis, Fabio Lignini, Maryann Malcomb, Phil Robinson, Erik Chr. Schmidt, Trish Schultz, Andrea Simonti, Oskar Urretabizkaia, Jeffrey J. Varab, Colin White; *character des:* David Carson; *voices: Casper:* Malachi Pearson; *Stretch:* Joe Nipote; *Stinkie:* Joe Alaskey; *Fatso:* Brad Garrett; *Arnold:* Jess Harnell; *the Crypt Keeper:* John Kassir; *song:* Mack David, Jerry Livingston; *performed by* Little Richard; *mus prod:* Richie Zito, Little Richard; *col:* DeLuxe. *sd:* THX/dts Stereo. Panavision. 100 min. *l/a.* • Carrigan Crittenden inherits a mansion that she believes has buried treasure somewhere within the building and doesn't intend to let the threat of a poltergeist prevent her from finding it. A ghost therapist is brought in and Casper, a friendly ghost, befriends her daughter. Animated ghosts, etc.

1008. Casper Comes to Clown *(Casper)* 10 Aug. 1951; *p.c.:* Famous for Para; *dir:* I. Sparber; *story:* I. Klein; *anim:* Myron Waldman, Gordon Whittier; *sets:* Anton Loeb; *voices:* Alan Shay, Sid Raymond, Jack Mercer; *mus:* Winston Sharples; *title song:* Mack David, Jerry Livingston; *ph:* Leonard McCormick; *prod mgr:* Seymour Shultz; *col:* Tech. *sd:* RCA. 7 min. • Casper's friend, a trick bear, is captured for the star attraction at the circus.

1009. Casper Genie *(Casper)* 28 May 1954; *p.c.:* Famous for Para; *dir:* I. Sparber; *story:* I. Klein; *anim:* Tom Golden, Bill Hudson; *sets:* Anton Loeb; *voices:* Alan Shay, Gwen Davies, Sid Raymond; *mus:* Winston Sharples; *title song:* Mack David, Jerry Livingston; *ph:* Leonard McCormick; *prod mgr:* Seymour Shultz; *col:* Tech. *sd:* RCA. 7 min. • Casper pretends to be a genie for a small boy.

1010. Casper Takes a Bow Wow *(Casper)* 7 Dec. 1951; *p.c.* Famous for Para; *dir:* I. Sparber; *story:* Larz Bourne; *anim:* Myron Waldman, Larry Silverman; *sets:* Anton Loeb. *voices:* Alan Shay, Jack Mercer; *mus:* Winston Sharples; *title song:* Mack David, Jerry Livingston; *ph:* Leonard McCormick; *prod mgr:* Seymour Shultz; *col:* Tech. *sd:* RCA. 7 min. • Casper befriends a puppy whom he later rescues from the Dog-catcher.

1011. Casper's Birthday *(Casper)* 31 July 1959; *p.c.:* Para; Cartoons. *dir:* Seymour Kneitel; *anim:* Nick Tafuri, Wm. B. Pattengill; *sets:* Robert Owen; *voices:* Cecil Roy, Jack Mercer; *mus:* Winston Sharples; *ph:* Leonard McCormick; *prod mgr:* Abe Goodman; *col:* Tech. *sd:* RCA. 6 min. • Casper tries to find some friends to invite to his birthday party. Clips are used from many Casper cartoons along the way.

1012. Casper's Spree Under the Sea *(Casper)* 27 Oct. 1950; *p.c.:* Famous for Para; *dir:* Bill Tytla; *story:* I. Klein; *anim:* George Germanetti,

Steve Muffatti; *sets:* Robert Little; *voices:* Alan Shay, Sid Raymond, Cecil Roy, Jack Mercer; *mus:* Winston Sharples; *title song:* Mack David, Jerry Livingston; *ph:* Leonard McCormick; *prod mgr:* Sam Buchwald; *col:* Tech. *sd:* RCA. 8 min. • Casper befriends a goldfish who takes him to the Fish Fair where he saves the denizens of the deep from the fisherman's net. First Casper in the bona fide series.

1013. The Castaway *(Mickey Mouse)* 27 Mar. 1931; *p.c.:* Walter E. Disney for Colum; *dir:* Wilfred Jackson; *anim:* Johnny Cannon, Les Clark, Jack Cutting, Gilles de Tremaudan, David D. Hand, Wilfred Jackson, Richard Lundy, Charles Philippi, Cecil Surry, Rudy Zamora; *voice:* Walt Disney; *mus:* Frank E. Churchill; b&w. *sd:* PCP. 7 min. • Adrift on a raft, Mickey reaches an island, is pursued by a lion, a crocodile, then makes his departure, and atop a turtle's back.

1014. A Cat, a Mouse and a Bell *(Color Rhapsody)* 10 May 1935; *p.c.:* Charles Mintz prods for Colum; *story:* Art Davis; *anim:* Sid Marcus; *mus:* Joe de Nat; *prod mgr:* George Winkler; *col:* Tech. *sd:* RCA. 7 min. • A mouse tries to put a bell around the cat's neck.

1015. The Cat Above and the Mouse Below *(Tom & Jerry)* 1964; *p.c.:* SIB Tower 12 for MGM; *prod/dir:* Chuck Jones; *co-dir:* Maurice Noble; *story:* Michael Maltese, Chuck Jones; *anim:* Tom Ray, Dick Thompson, Ben Washam, Ken Harris, Don Towsley; *back:* Philip de Guard; *voice:* Terence Monck; *mus:* Eugene Poddany; *prod mgr:* Les Goldman; *col:* Metro. *sd:* WE. 7 min. • Signor Thomasino Catti-Cazzaza attempts an operatic solo while Jerry tries to abort the mission.

1016. Cat Alarm *(Mighty Mouse)* Jan. 1961; *p.c.:* TT for Fox; *ex prod:* Bill Weiss. *dir:* Connie Rasinski. *story sup/voices:* Tom Morrison; *story:* Larz Bourne; *anim:* Cosmo Anzilotti, Juan Guidi, Larry Silverman, Art Bartsch; *lay:* Martin Strudler; *back:* Bill Focht; *mus:* Phil Scheib; *prod mgr:* Frank Schudde; *col:* DeLuxe. *sd:* RCA. 6 min. • Mighty Mouse is lured into the grasp of hungry cats who plan to invade Mouseville.

1017. Cat and Dupli-Cat *(Tom & Jerry)* 1967; *p.c.:* MGM. *prod/dir:* Chuck Jones; *co-dir:* Maurice Noble; *story:* Chuck Jones, Michael Maltese; *anim:* Dick Thompson, Ben Washam, Ken Harris, Don Towsley, Tom Ray; *back:* Philip de Guard; *voices:* Mel Blanc, Dal McKennon, Terence Monck; *mus:* Eugene Poddany; *prod sup:* Earl Jonas, Les Goldman; *col:* Metro. *sd:* WE. 7 min. • Tom meets a rival who also wants to eat Jerry.

1018. The Cat and the Bell *(Cartune)* 27 Sept. 1938; *p.c.:* Walter Lantz prods for Univ; *dir:* Alex Lovy; *story:* Victor McLeod, Hicks Lokey; *anim:* Ray Fahringer, La Verne Harding; *sets:* Edgar Keichle; *mus:* Frank Marsales; *col:* Tech. *sd:* WE. 7 min. • Babyface Mouse is detailed to attach a bell to the cat. The cat chases him, eventually swallowing the bell.

1019. The Cat and the Canary *(Aesop's Film Fable)* 7 Aug. 1921; *p.c.:* Fables Pictures Inc for Pathé; *dir:* Paul Terry; b&w. *sil.* 5 min. • The cat sheds bitter tear when his friend, the canary, leaves to get married. The canary's new husband starts a drunken row and the injured bride flys to tell the cat all about it. The furious cat devours the bird and likes the tase so much that he eats the canary. Moral: "Evil wishes come home to roost."

1020. The Cat and the Magnet *(Aesop's Film Fable)* 20 Oct. 1924; *p.c.:* Fables Pictures Inc for Pathé; *dir:* Paul Terry; b&w. *sil.* 5 min. • The cat's magnet attracts the mice in their roadsters. He then proceeds to sell their respective automobiles.

1021. The Cat and the Mermouse *(Tom & Jerry)* 3 Sept. 1949; *p.c.:* MGM; *dir:* William Hanna, Joseph Barbera; *anim:* Kenneth Muse, Ed Barge, Ray Patterson, Irven Spence, Al Grandmain; *lay:* Dick Bickenbach; *back:* Robert Gentle; *ed:* Fred MacAlpin; *mus:* Scott Bradley; *prod:* Fred Quimby; *col:* Tech. *sd:* WE. 8 min. • Tom nearly drowns in the sea and dreams he sees Jerry as a mermaid.

1022. The Cat and the Mice *(Aesop's Film Fable)* 1 Jan. 1922; *p.c.:* Fables Pictures Inc for Pathé; *dir:* Paul Terry; b&w. *sil.* 5 min. • The mouse family are terrorized by the cat and seek refuge in an old boot. One brave mouse manages to run out and get a ball of catnip which they use to lure lure the cat into the boot from which he can't escape. Moral: "Victory comes not always to the strong."

1023. The Cat and the Monkey *(Aesop's Film Fable)* 30 Oct. 1921; *p.c.:* Fables Pictures Inc for Pathé; *dir:* Paul Terry; b&w. *sil.* 5 min. • A scheming cat induces a monkey to do his bidding. Moral: "Don't be a cat's paw."

1024. The Cat and the Pig *(Aesop's Film Fable)* 17 May 1922; *p.c.:* Fables Pictures Inc for Pathé; *dir:* Paul Terry; b&w. *sil.* 5 min. • A hard-done-by employee saves his boss's child from a swordfish. Moral: "Some folks are never satisfied."

1025. The Cat and the Pinkstalk *(Pink Panther)* 1968; *p.c.:* Mirisch/Geoffrey/DFE for UA; *dir:* Dave DeTiege; *story:* Tony Benedict; *anim:* Nelson Shin, Bob Bemiller, Walter Kubiak; *lay:* Martin Strudler; *back:* Richard H. Thomas; *ed:* Richard Corwin; *theme tune:* Henry Mancini; *ph:* Bob Mills; *prod mgr:* Lee Gunther; *col:* DeLuxe. *sd:* RCA. 6 min. • The Panther takes on the role of "Jack and the Beanstalk."

1026. The Cat and the Swordfish *(Aesop's Film Fable)* 26 Jan. 1922; *p.c.:* Fables Pictures Inc for Pathé; *dir:* Paul Terry; b&w. *sil.* 5 min. • A cat saves a swordfish's life from the fisherman. Years later, the fisherman catches the cat and, tying him in a bag, throws him into the sea. The fish returns the favor by cutting open the bag and returning him to dry land. Moral: "One good turn deserves another."

1027. The Cat Came Back *(Aesop's Film Fable)* 16 Nov. 1923; *p.c.:* Fables Pictures Inc for Pathé; *dir:* Paul Terry; b&w. *sil.* 5 min. • The cat dreams of going on a hunt in the Arctic and is chased by mama and papa bear.

1028. The Cat Came Back *(Merrie Melodies)* 8 Feb. 1936; *p.c.:* Leon Schlesinger prods for WB; *dir:* I. Freleng; *anim:* Bob McKimson, Ben Clopton; *lay:* Griff Jay; *back:* Arthur Loomer; *voice:* Bernice Hansel; *mus:* Bernard Brown; *prod sup:* Henry Binder, Raymond G. Katz; *col:* Tech. *sd:* Vit. 7 min. • Mrs. Cat and Mrs. Mouse's respective offsprings are caught fraternizing. When Junior cat falls into a sewer and Junior mouse saves him from drowning, the two families are united.

1029. The Cat Came Back *(Terry-Toon)* 18 Aug. 1944; *p.c.:* TT for Fox; *dir:* Connie Rasinski; *story:* John Foster; *mus:* Philip A. Scheib; *col:* Tech. *sd:* RCA. 6 min. • Farmer Al Falfa and his dog try to rid themselves of a troublesome cat who keeps returning to taunt them.

1030. Cat Carson Rides Again *(Noveltoon)* 4 Apr. 1952; *p.c.:* Famous for Para; *dir:* Seymour Kneitel; *story:* Carl Meyer, Jack Mercer; *anim:* Dave Tendlar, Martin Taras; *sets:* Anton Loeb; *voices:* Arnold Stang, Sid Raymond, Jack Mercer; *mus:* Winston Sharples; *ph:* Leonard McCormick; *prod mgr:* Seymour Shultz; *col:* Tech. *sd:* RCA. 7 min. • The rodent inhabitants of a western town are disrupted by the arrival of Katnip in the guise of a cowboy gunslinger.

1031. Cat Cartoons • See: *The Adventures of Roving Thomas*

1032. Cat-Choo *(Noveltoon)* 12 Oct. 1951; *p.c.:* Famous Studio for Para; *dir:* Seymour Kneitel; *story:* Carl Meyer, Jack Mercer; *anim:* Dave Tendlar, Martin Taras; *sets:* Tom Ford; *voices:* Jackson Beck, Sid Raymond; *mus:* Winston Sharples; *ph:* Leonard McCormick; *prod mgr:* Seymour Shultz; *col:* Tech. *sd:* RCA. 7 min. • Buzzy the crow disguises himself as a doctor to tend to Katnip's cold.

1033. The Cat Concerto *(Tom & Jerry)* 26 Apr. 1947; *p.c.:* MGM; *dir:* William Hanna, Joseph Barbera; *anim:* Kenneth Muse, Ed Barge, Irven Spence. *sets:* Robert Gentle; *ed:* Fred MacAlpin; *mus:* Scott Bradley; *piano:* Jakob Gimpel; *prod:* Fred Quimby; *col:* Tech. *sd:* WE. 7 min. *Academy Award.* • Tom's piano recital is seriously marred by Jerry, who happens to be sleeping in the piano.

1034. Cat Feud *(Merrie Melodies)*; rel 20 Dec. 1958; *p.c.:* WB; *dir:* Chuck Jones; *story:* Michael Maltese; *anim:* Ken Harris, Ben Washam, Abe Levitow, Richard Thompson; *lay:* Maurice Noble; *back:* Philip de Guard; *ed:* Treg Brown; *voices:* Mel Blanc; *mus:* Milt Franklyn; *col:* Tech. *sd:* Vit. 7 min. • A building site watchdog presents a wayward kitten with a salami. A mangy alley cat steals it and the bulldog sets out to retrieve it.

1035. A Cat-Fish Romance *(Aesop's Sound Fable)* 7 Oct. 1932; *p.c.:* Van Beuren for RKO; *dir:* John Foster, Mannie Davis; *mus:* Gene Rodemich; b&w. *sd:* RCA. 7 min. • No story available.

1036. Cat Fishin' *(Tom & Jerry)* 15 Mar. 1947; *p.c.:* MGM; *dir:* William Hanna, Joseph Barbera; *anim:* Kenneth Muse, Ed Barge, Michael Lah; *ed:* Fred MacAlpin; *mus:* Scott Bradley; *prod:* Fred Quimby; *col:* Tech. *sd:* WE. 7 min. • Tom goes fishing using Jerry as bait. None too happy with this arrangement, Jerry fixes the fishing line to the collar of a fierce watchdog.

1037. Cat Happy *(Little Roquefort)* Sept. 1950; *p.c.:* TT for Fox; *dir:*

Connie Rasinski; *story/voice:* Tom Morrison; *mus:* Philip A. Scheib; *sets:* Art Bartsch; *ph:* Douglas Moye; *col:* Tech. *sd:* RCA. 6 min. • Percy the cat gets high on catnip and befriends Roquefort only to revert to form with a knock on the head.

1038. Cat in the Act *(Herman & Katnip)* 22 Feb. 1957; *p.c.:* Famous for Para; *dir:* Dave Tendlar; *story:* Jack Mercer; *anim:* Morey Reden; *sets:* Robert Little; *voices:* Arnold Stang, Sid Raymond, Gwen Davies, Jack Mercer; *mus:* Winston Sharples; *ph:* Leonard McCormick; *prod mgr:* Seymour Shultz; *col:* Tech. *sd:* RCA. 6 min. • Herman and his nephew visit the Paramount Studios where they arouse Katnip. Some quick thinking convinces the cat that he should be in pictures.

1039. Cat Meets Mouse *(Terry-Toon)* 20 Feb. 1942; *p.c.:* TT for Fox; *dir:* Mannie Davis; *story:* John Foster; *mus:* Philip A. Scheib; *col:* Tech. *sd:* RCA. 7 min. • The cat imprisons the mice in a concentration camp.

1040. Cat Nap Pluto *(Pluto)* 13 Aug. 1948; *p.c.:* Walt Disney prods for RKO; *dir:* Charles Nichols; *story:* Eric Gurney; *anim:* Phil Duncan, Jerry Hathcock, George Nicholas, George Kreisl; *fx:* Jack Boyd; *lay:* Karl Karpé; *back:* Claude Coats; *voices:* James MacDonald, Clarence Nash; *mus:* Oliver Wallace; *col:* Tech. *sd:* RCA. 7 min. • Pluto's night on the tiles requires a lot of sleep but Figaro wants to play. Finally they are both put out by their respective Sandmen.

1041. Cat Napping *(Tom & Jerry)* 8 Dec. 1951; *p.c.:* MGM; *dir:* William Hanna, Joseph Barbera; *anim:* Irven Spence, Ray Patterson, Ed Barge, Kenneth Muse; *lay:* Dick Bickenbach; *back:* Robert Gentle; *ed:* Fred MacAlpin; *mus:* Scott Bradley; *prod:* Fred Quimby; *col:* Tech. *sd:* WE. 7 min. • Tom and Jerry fight it out for posession of a comfortable hammock.

1042. Cat Nipped *(Oswald)* 20 May 1932; *p.c.:* Univ; *anim:* Walter Lantz, "Bill" Nolan; *anim:* Manuel Moreno, Ray Abrams, Fred Avery, "Bill" Weber, Vet Anderson, Lester Kline, Bunny Ellison; *mus:* James Dietrich; *b&w. sd:* WE. 7 min. • Oswald gets tormented by mice. He vanquishes them with the assistance of a large cat.

1043. Cat O' Nine Ails *(Noveltoon)* 9 Jan. 1948; *p.c.:* Famous for Para; *dir:* Seymour Kneitel; *story:* Carl Meyer, Jack Mercer; *voices:* Jackson Beck; *mus:* Winston Sharples; *ph:* Leonard McCormick; *prod mgr:* Sam Buchwald; *col:* Tech. *sd:* RCA. 7 min. • Sam, the hypochondriac cat, is pursuaded that he has all number of diseases when Buzzy the crow poses as a doctor.

1044. Cat Tails for Two *(Merrie Melodies)* 29 Aug. 1953; *p.c.:* WB; *dir:* Robert McKimson; *story:* Tedd Pierce; *anim:* Rod Scribner, Phil de Lara, Charles McKimson, Herman Cohen; *lay:* Robert Givens; *back:* Richard H. Thomas; *ed:* Treg Brown; *voices:* Mel Blanc, Stan Freberg; *mus:* Carl Stalling; *prod mgr:* John W. Burton; *prod:* Edward Selzer; *col:* Tech. *sd:* Vit. 7 min. • Two cats, George and Benny, attempt to capture the fastest mouse in all Mexico. Initial appearance of Speedy Gonzales.

1045. Cat Tamale *(Noveltoon)* 9 Nov. 1951; *p.c.:* Famous for Para; *dir:* Seymour Kneitel; *story:* I. Klein; *anim:* Dave Tendlar, Tom Golden; *sets:* Robert Little; *voices:* Arnold Stang, Sid Raymond, Jack Mercer; *mus:* Winston Sharples; *ph:* Leonard McCormick; *prod mgr:* Seymour Shultz; *col:* Tech. *sd:* RCA. 7 min. • Herman and Katnip stage a bullfight.

1046. Cat-Tastrophy *(Phantasy)* 30 June 1949; *p.c.:* Colum; *prod:* Raymond Katz, Henry Binder; *dir:* Sid Marcus; *story:* Cal Howard, Dave Monahan; *anim:* Ben Lloyd, Howard Swift, Roy Jenkins; *lay:* Clark Watson; *back:* Al Boggs; *ed:* Richard S. Jensen; *voice:* Dave Barry; *mus:* Darrell Calker; *ph:* Frank Fisher; *creative consultant:* Robert Clampett; *col:* Tech. *sd:* WE. 6 min. • A cat envisions what life would be like when the puppy he lives with grows up.

1047. The Cat That Failed *(Aesop's Film Fable)* 7 Aug. 1923; *p.c.:* Fables Pictures Inc for Pathé; *dir:* Paul Terry; *b&w. sil.* 5 min. • The cat holds a young mouse for ransom. A dog detective tracks him down and returns the child to his mother.

1048. The Cat That Hated People 20 Nov. 1948; *p.c.:* MGM; *dir:* Tex Avery. *story:* Heck Allen. *anim:* Walter Clinton, Louis Schmitt, William Shull, Grant Simmons; *sets:* John Didrik Johnsen; *ed:* Fred MacAlpin; *character des:* Louis Schmitt; *voices:* Harry E. Lang; *mus:* Scott Bradley; *prod:* Fred Quimby; *col:* Tech. *sd:* WE. 7 min. • A humanity-hating cat takes a rocket trip to the moon where he finds things are a lot worse than on earth.

1049. Cat Trouble *(Heckle & Jeckle)* 11 Apr. 1947; *p.c.:* TT for Fox; *dir:* Connie Rasinski; *story:* John Foster; *voices:* Thomas Morrison; *mus:*

Philip A. Scheib; *ph:* Douglas Moye; *col:* Tech. *sd:* RCA. 7 min. • The magpies are appointed guardians of a small bird. Trouble arrives in the shape of a hungry cat.

1050. Catch as Cats Can *(Merrie Melodies)* 6 Dec. 1947; *p.c.:* WB; *dir:* Arthur Davis; *story:* Dave Monahan; *anim:* Basil Davidovich, J.C. Melendez, Don Williams, Herman Cohen; *fx:* A.C. Gamer; *lay:* Don Smith; *back:* Philip de Guard; *ed:* Treg Brown; *voices:* Mel Blanc, Dave Barry; *mus:* Carl Stalling; *prod mgr:* John W. Burton. *prod:* Edward Selzer. *col:* Tech. *sd:* Vit. 7 min. • A scheming Bing Crosby parrot employs a cat to rid him of his nemesis, a crooning Frank Sinatra canary.

1051. Catch Meow *(Loopy de Loop)* Nov. 1961; *p.c.:* Hanna-Barbera for Columbia. *prod/dir:* Joseph Barbera, William Hanna; *story dir:* Alex Lovy *story:* Tony Benedict; *anim dir:* Charles A. Nichols; *anim:* George Nicholas; *lay:* Dan Noonan; *back:* Richard H. Thomas; *ed:* Greg Watson; *voices:* Daws Butler, Don Messick; *mus:* Hoyt Curtin; *titles:* Lawrence Gobel; *prod mgr:* Howard Hanson; *col:* East. *sd:* RCA. 6½ min. • Loopy stands in for a timid cat.

1052. Catnip Capers *(Terry-Toon)* 31 May 1940; *p.c.:* TT for Fox; *dir:* Mannie Davis; *story:* John Foster; *mus:* Philip A. Scheib; *col:* Tech. *sd:* RCA. 7 min. • A cat samples catnip and hallucinates that a pink elephant takes him to Bagdad where giant mice torment him.

1053. The Catnip Gang *(Mighty Mouse)* June 1949; *p.c.:* TT for Fox; *dir:* Eddie Donnelly; *story:* John Foster; *anim:* Jim Tyer; *mus:* Philip A. Scheib; *col:* Tech. *sd:* RCA. 7 min. • Three villainous cats escape from prison, steal a car and kidnap some mice. Mighty Mouse soon settles the score.

1054. Catnipped *(Flippy)* 22 Feb. 1946; *p.c.:* Colum; *dir:* Bob Wickersham; *story:* Grant Simmons, Roy Jenkins; *anim:* Paul Sommer, Chic Otterstrom; *sets:* Clark Watson; *ed:* Richard S. Jensen; *voice:* Harry E. Lang; *mus:* Eddie Kilfeather; *i&p:* Elizabeth F. McDowell; *ph:* Frank Fisher; *prod mgr:* Hugh McCollum; *col:* Tech. *sd:* WE. 8 min. • Flippy the canary proves more than a match for the cat and dog.

1055. Cats A-Weigh *(Merrie Melodies)* 28 Nov. 1953; *p.c.:* WB; *dir:* Robert McKimson; *story:* Tedd Pierce; *anim:* Phil de Lara, Charles McKimson, Herman Cohen, Rod Scribner; *lay:* Robert Givens; *back:* Richard H. Thomas; *ed:* Treg Brown; *voices:* Mel Blanc; *mus:* Carl Stalling; *prod mgr:* John W. Burton; *prod:* Edward Selzer; *col:* Tech. *sd:* Vit. 7 min. • Sylvester and his son enroll as "Ship's Cats" aboard an ocean liner. Father meets his match when he is forced into capturing an escaped kangaroo which he believes to be a giant mouse.

1056. Cats and Bruises *(Merrie Melodies)* 30 Jan. 1965; *p.c.:* DFE for WB; *dir:* Friz Freleng; *co-dir:* Hawley Pratt; *story:* John Dunn; *anim:* Bob Matz, Norm McCabe, Don Williams, Manny Perez, Warren Batchelder, Lee Halpern; *lay:* Dick Ung; *back:* Tom O'Loughlin; *ed:* Lee Gunther; *voices:* Mel Blanc; *mus:* Bill Lava; *col:* Tech. *sd:* Vit. 6 min. • Sylvester continues his pursuit of Speedy Gonzales.

1057. Cats and Dogs *(Pooch the Pup)* 5 Dec. 1932; *p.c.:* Univ; *dir:* Walter Lantz; *anim:* Manuel Moreno, Lester Kline, George Cannata, "Bill" Weber; *mus:* James Dietrich; *b&w. sd:* WE. 7 min. • No story available.

1058. Cats at Law *(Aesop's Film Fable)* 17 July 1921; *p.c.:* Fables Pictures Inc for Pathé; *dir:* Paul Terry; *b&w. sil.* 5 min. • Two mouse burglars break into an apartment and raid the ice box of cheese. When they are caught and brought to court, the feline Judge decides that the cheese should be divided equally and shared amongst all.

1059. The Cat's Bah *(Looney Tunes)* 20 Mar. 1954; *p.c.:* WB; *dir:* Charles M. Jones; *story:* Michael Maltese; *anim:* Ben Washam, Lloyd Vaughan; *lay:* Maurice Noble; *back:* Phil de Guard; *ed:* Treg Brown; *voices:* Mel Blanc, Bea Benaderet; *mus:* Carl Stalling; *prod mgr:* John W. Burton; *prod:* Edward Selzer; *col:* Tech. *sd:* Vit. 7 min. • While visiting the Casbah, a black cat gets a streak of white painted down her back and is pursued by Pepé le Pew, the amorous skunk.

1060. The Cat's Canary *(Aesop's Sound Fable)* 26 Mar. 1932; *p.c.:* Van Beuren for RKO; *dir:* John Foster, Mannie Davis; *mus:* Gene Rodemich; *b&w. sd:* RCA. 5 min. • A cat swallows a singing canary and becomes musically inclined.

1061. The Cat's Me-ouch *(Tom & Jerry)* 1965; *p.c.:* MGM; *prod/dir:* Chuck Jones; *asst dir:* Maurice Noble; *story:* Michael Maltese, Chuck Jones;

anim: Don Towsley, Dick Thompson, Ben Washam, Ken Harris; *back:* Philip De Guard; *voices:* June Foray, Mel Blanc; *mus:* Eugene Poddany; *prod mgr:* Les Goldman; *col:* Metro. *sd:* WE. 7 min. • Jerry enlists the help of a small bulldog in his battle against Tom.

1062. Cat's Meow 25 Jan. 1957; *p.c.:* MGM; *prod:* William Hanna, Joseph Barbera; *dir:* Tex Avery; *back:* Don Driscoll; *ed:* Jim Faris; *ph:* Jack Stevens; *prod mgr:* Hal Elias; *col:* Tech. *sd:* WE. 7 min. CS. • CS reissue of *The Ventriloquist Cat.*

1063. The Cat's Nine Lives (*Unnatural History*) 15 Jan. 1927; *p.c.:* Bray prods for FBO; *dir/anim/titles:* Walter Lantz, Dave Hand, Clyde Geronimi; *l/a ph:* Joe Rock; b&w. *sil.* 5 min. *l/a/anim.* • No story available.

1064. The Cat's Out (*Silly Symphony*) 20 July 1931; *p.c.:* Walt Disney prods for Colum; *dir:* Wilfred Jackson; *anim:* Charles Byrne, Johnny Cannon, Chuck Couch, Joseph d'Igalo, Gilles de Tremaudan, Hardie Gramatky, George Grandpré, David D. Hand, Albert Hurter, Wilfred Jackson, George Lane, Bill Mason, Harry Reeves, Ben Sharpsteen, Marvin Woodward, Rudy Zamora; *lay:* Albert Hurter; *mus:* Frank E. Churchill; b&w. *sd:* PCP. 7 min. • While chasing a bird, a cat is knocked unconcious by a Weather Vane and dreams he's on trial by the birds.

1065. Cat's Paw (*Looney Tunes*) 15 Aug. 1959; *p.c.:* WB; *dir:* Robert McKimson; *story:* Tedd Pierce; *anim:* George Grandpré, Ted Bonnicksen, Warren Batchelder, Tom Ray, David R. Green; *lay:* Robert Gribbroek; *back:* William Butler; *ed:* Treg Brown; *voices:* Mel Blanc; *mus:* Milt Franklyn; *prod mgr:* William Orcutt; *prod:* David H. DePatie; *col:* Tech. *sd:* Vit. 7 min. • Sylvester and Son go mountain-climbing in the hopes of securing a small bird. The smallest they find happens to be the toughest one around.

1066. The Cat's Revenge (*Aesop's Film Fable*) 11 Aug. 1923; *p.c.:* Fables Pictures Inc for Pathé; *dir:* Paul Terry; b&w. *sil.* 5 min. • Farmer Al Falfa finds the cat a competitor when it comes to fishing and disposes of him. The cat gets even by using a vacuum cleaner to rid the lake of its fish ... and the hapless farmer.

1067. The Cat's Revenge (*Little Roquefort*) Aug. 1954; *p.c.:* TT for Fox; *dir:* Mannie Davis; *story/voice:* Tom Morrison; *anim:* Jim Tyer; *mus:* Philip A. Scheib; *ph:* Douglas Moye; *col:* Tech. *sd:* RCA. 7 min. • Percy the Puss is about to blow Roquefort to kingdom come when his conscience reminds him of all the good times they've had together.

1068. The Cat's Tale (*Merrie Melodies*) 1 Mar. 1941; *p.c.:* Leon Schlesinger prods for WB; *dir:* I. Freleng; *story:* Michael Maltese; *anim:* Herman Cohen; *lay:* Owen Fitzgerald; *back:* Lenard Kester; *ed:* Treg Brown; *voices:* Mel Blanc; *mus:* Carl W. Stalling; *col:* Tech. *sd:* Vit. 7 min. • Tired of being chased all the time, a mouse instructs the cat to strike a bargain with the dog so that nobody chases anybody again.

1069. A Cat's Tale (*Mighty Mouse*) Nov. 1951; *p.c.:* TT; for Fox; *dir:* Mannie Davis; *story/voices:* Tom Morrison; *anim:* Jim Tyer; *mus:* Philip A. Scheib; *ph:* Douglas Moye; *col:* Tech. *sd:* RCA. 7 min. • A cat tells the story of how Mighty Mouse came to be.

1070. The Cat's Whiskers (*Aesop's Film Fable*) 1 Sept. 1923; *p.c.:* Fables Pictures Inc for Pathé; *dir:* Paul Terry; b&w. *sil.* 5 min. • A tom cat wins back his sweetheart with help from some mischievous kittens.

1071. The Cat's Whiskers (*Unnatural History*) 20 June 1926; *p.c.:* Bray prods for FBO; *dir:* Walter Lantz; *anim:* Clyde Geronimi; *l/a ph:* Joe Rock; b&w. *sil.* 5 min. *l/a/anim.* • A bewhiskered grandpa tells a small girl of how once clean-faced cats couldn't attract the female of the species, so one used hair-grower on his face and it worked like a charm.

1072. Cattle Battle (*Roland & Rattfink*) 4 Aug. 1971; *p.c.:* Mirisch/DFE for UA; *dir:* Art Davis; *story:* John W. Dunn; *anim:* Don Williams, Warren Batchelder, Manny Perez, Bob Richardson, Robert Taylor; *lay:* Robert Givens; *back:* Richard H. Thomas; *ed:* Joe Siracusa; *voices:* Leonard Weinrib; *mus:* Doug Goodwin; *prod sup:* Jim Foss, Harry Love; *col:* DeLuxe. *sd:* RCA. 6 min. • Rattfink tries to steal some cows from under the watchful eye of the bull and a not-too-alert cowboy.

1073. Catty Cornered (*Merrie Melodies*) 1 Nov. 1953; *p.c.:* WB; *dir:* I. Freleng; *story:* Warren Foster; *anim:* Arthur Davis, Manuel Perez, Ken Champin, Virgil Ross; *lay:* Hawley Pratt; *back:* Irv Wyner; *ed:* Treg Brown; *voices:* Mel Blanc; *mus:* Carl Stalling; *prod mgr:* John W. Burton; *prod:* Ed-

ward Selzer; *col:* Tech. *sd:* Vit. 7 min. • Tweety is held to ransom by Rocky and his gang. Sylvester spies the bird and tries to bag him for himself but is thwarted by the gangsters each time.

1074. Catty Cornered (*Tom & Jerry*) 1966; *p.c.:* MGM; *prod:* Chuck Jones; *dir:* Abe Levitow; *story:* John Dunn; *anim:* Tom Ray, Richard Thompson, Ben Washam, Ken Harris, Don Towsley; *lay:* Don Morgan; *back:* Hal Ashmead; *des:* Maurice Noble; *voices:* Mel Blanc, June Foray; *mus:* Carl Brandt; *prod sup:* Les Goldman, Earl Jonas; *col:* Metro. *sd:* WE. 7 min. • Tom unwittingly does battle with the cat next door when Jerry opens adjacent doors in his mousehole.

1075. The Cave Man (*Willie Whopper*) 6 July 1934; *p.c.:* Celebrity prods for MGM; *prod/dir:* Ub Iwerks; *anim:* Grim Natwick, Berny Wolf; *mus:* Art Turkisher; b&w. *sd:* PCP. 6 min. • Willie spins a tale of how he was once a caveman who saves a girl from a dinosaur.

1076. Caveman Inki (*Looney Tunes*) 25 Nov. 1950; *p.c.:* WB; *dir:* Charles M. Jones; *story:* Michael Maltese; *anim:* Lloyd Vaughan, Ken Harris, Phil Monroe, Ben Washam; *lay:* Robert Gribbroek; *back:* Philip de Guard; *ed:* Treg Brown; *mus:* Carl Stalling, Milt Franklyn; *prod mgr:* John W. Burton; *prod:* Edward Selzer; *col:* Tech. *sd:* Vit. 7 min. • Inki is saved from a sabre-toothed lion by the Minah Bird.

1077. Caviar (*Paul Terry-Toon*) 24 Mar. 1930; *p.c.:* A-C Inc for Educational; *dir:* Paul Terry, Frank Moser; *mus:* Philip A. Scheib; b&w. *sd:* WE. 6 min. • The cruel Russian taskmaster cat chases one of his subordinates on a fish. They are both, in turn, chased by wolves.

1078. Ceiling Hero (*Merrie Melodies*) 28 Aug. 1940; *p.c.:* Leon Schlesinger prods for WB; *dir:* Fred Avery; *story:* Dave Monahan, Robert Clampett; *anim:* Rod Scribner, Robert McKimson; *sets:* John Didrik Johnsen; *ed:* Treg Brown; *voices:* Robert C. Bruce, Mel Blanc; *mus:* Carl W. Stalling; *prod sup:* Henry Binder, Raymond G. Katz; *col:* Tech. *sd:* Vit. 7 min. • Spot-gags on aviation.

1079. Celebrity Productions (*1930–1938*); *prod/dir/anim:* Ub Iwerks; *vice president:* P.A. Powers; *anim dir:* Jimmie Culhane, Al Eugster, Grim Natwick, Berny Wolf; *story:* Otto Englander, Ben Hardaway, Cal Howard, Earl Hurd; *anim:* Richard Bickenbach, Godfrey Bjork, Norman Blackburn, Stephen Bosustow, Charlie Connors, Ben Clopton, George Dane, Ted Dubois, I. Ellis, Ray Fahringer, Ed Friedman, Merle Gilson, Al Gould, Murray Griffen, Dick Hall, John Frank Liggre, Ed Love, Lee MacKey, George Manuel, Tom McNamara, James Pabian, Irven Spence, Robert Stokes, Ralph Somerville, Frank Tashlin, William Wheeler, Robert Wickesham, Lou Zukor; *sets:* Robert Holdeman; *mus:* Gene Denny, Carl W. Stalling, Art Turkisher; *i&p:* Peggy Jones, Gladys McArthur, Mary Tebb, Dorothy Webster; *prod mgr:* Emile Offeman. • Ub Iwerks eventually sold out his business (by 1938 known as Cartoon Films Ltd.) to Dave Biedermann who produced chiefly commercials.

1080. Cellbound 25 Nov. 1955; *p.c.:* MGM; *dir:* Tex Avery, Michael Lah; *story:* Heck Allen; *anim:* Kenneth Muse, Ed Barge, Irven Spence, Michael Lah; *lay/des:* Ed Benedict; *back:* Vera Ohman; *ed:* Jim Faris; *voices:* Paul Frees, Tex Avery; *mus:* Scott Bradley; *harmonica:* Gus Bivona; *ph:* Jack Stevens; *prod mgr:* Hal Elias; *prod:* Fred Quimby; *col:* Tech. *sd:* WE. 6 min. • A convict tunnels his way out of prison only to come up inside the warden's television set.

1081. The Centaurs 1921; *p.c.:* Rialto prods for Vit; *dir/anim:* Winsor McCay; b&w. *st.* • Two young centaur lovers have to cope with a matriarchal chaperon. McCay's fifth film drawn on celluloid.

1082. The Chain Gang (*Mickey Mouse*) 18 Aug. 1930; *p.c.:* Walter E. Disney for Colum; *dir:* Burton F. Gillett; *anim:* Charles Byrne, Johnny Cannon, Les Clark, Jack Cutting, Norman Ferguson, David D. Hand, Wilfred Jackson, Jack King, Richard Lundy, Tom Palmer, Ben Sharpsteen; *voice:* Lee Millar; *mus:* Bert Lewis; *ph:* William Cottrell; b&w. *sd:* PCP. 7 min. • Chain-gang prisoner Mickey escapes during a riot, endures a wild horse ride and is thrown right back into his own prison cell.

1083. Chain Letters (*Paul Terry-Toon*) 9 Aug. 1935; *p.c.:* Moser & Terry Inc for Educational/Fox; *dir:* Paul Terry, Frank Moser; *mus:* Philip A. Scheib; b&w. *sd:* WE. 5 min. • The "Chain Letter" writing fad hits the Farmer who churns out many. When the mailman brings his expected response ... it's just a large sack of mice.

1084. The Challenge (*Out of the Inkwell*) 29 Aug. 1922; *p.c.:* Inkwell

Films for Winkler; *prod/l/a:* Max Fleischer; *dir:* Dave Fleischer; b&w. *sil.* 6 min. *l/a/anim.* • Ko-Ko is kept awake by Max's snoring. He wakes Max who draws himself the same size as Ko-Ko and the two have a boxing match. Ko-Ko is just about to deck Max when a tough character from next door who has also been kept awake comes in and floors Max.

1085. The Champ *(Paul Terry-Toon)* 20 Sept. 1931; *p.c.:* Terry, Moser & Coffman for Educational/Fox; *dir:* Paul Terry, Frank Moser; *anim:* Arthur Babbitt, Vladimir Tytla; *mus:* Philip A. Scheib; b&w. *sd:* WE. 6 min. • A cat and mouse in a boxing match. The cat absconds with the cash prize, closely pursued by a mouse mob. He takes refuge in Al Falfa's house and the mice overrun the place.

1086. The Champion *(Aesop's Film Fable)* 30 Mar. 1924; *p.c.:* Fables Pictures Inc for Pathé; *dir:* Paul Terry; b&w. *sil.* 5 min. • A duck and a hen are training for an egg-laying contest.

1087. Champion Chump *(Martian Moochers)* Apr. 1966; *p.c.:* TT for Fox; *ex prod:* Bill Weiss; *dir/anim:* Art Bartsch, Connie Rasinski; *story sup:* Tom Morrison; *story:* Larz Bourne; *back:* Bill Focht; *ed:* Jack McConnell; *voice:* Lionel Wilson; *mus:* Jim Timmens; *ph:* Ted Moskowitz, Joe Rasinski; *sd:* Elliott Grey; *col:* DeLuxe. *sd:* RCA. 5 min. • A prize-winning cat shows off to a hero-worshipping kitten until the Moochers arrive and put him in his place.

1088. The Champion of Justice *(Super Mouse)* 17 Mar. 1944; *p.c.:* TT for Fox; *dir:* Mannie Davis; *story:* John Foster; *voice:* Thomas Morrison; *mus:* Philip A. Scheib; *col:* Tech. *sd:* RCA. 7 min. • Mr. and Mrs. Plushbottom leave everything to their pet mice when they pass away. Willie the spendthrift nephew tries to do away with the rodents and keep the wealth for himself.

1089. Chariots of Fur 21 Dec. 1994; *(Looney Tunes) p.c.:* Chuck Jones Prods./WB; *dir/story:* Chuck Jones, Linda Jones Clough; *story ed:* Don Arioli; *asso prod:* Stephen A. Fossati; *anim:* Claude Raynes, Duane Gretsky, Ralph E. Newman, Bill Snelgrove, Margaret Trudeaux, Irene Arkin, Mike Polvani, Gavin Dell; *asst anim:* Susan Goldberg, M.E. Perez, Tom Mozzacco, Jamison Jones, Miriam Studebaker; *fx:* Joe Studebaker; *art dir:* Maurice Noble; *back:* Jill Petrilak; *mus:* George Daugherty, Cameron Patrick; *sd:* Robb Wenner; *ph:* Ted Bemiller; *col:* Tech. *sd.* 6½ min. • The Coyote *(Dogius Ignoramii)* continues his relentless pursuit of the Road Runner *(Boulevardious-Burnupius)* by using a giant mousetrap, "Instant Road," a cactus costume and Acme Lightning Bolts ... all of which prove ineffective.

1090. The Charleston Queen *(Aesop's Film Fable)* 19 Sept. 1926; *p.c.:* Fables Pictures Inc for Pathé; *dir:* Paul Terry; b&w. *sil.* 5 min. • No story available.

1091. Charlie *p.c.:* Movca Film Service for Herald Film Corp; *prod:* S.J. Sangretti; *dir/anim:* John Colman Terry, G.A. Bronstrup, Hugh M. Shields. b&w. *st.* • **1916: Charlie in Carmen** 15 May. **Charlie and the Windmill** 19 June. **Charlie's White Elephant. Charlie Has Some Wonderful Adventures in India. Charlie in Cuckoo Land. Charlie the Blacksmith. Charlie's Busted Romance. Charlie Across the Rio Grande. The Rooster's Nightmare. Charlie's Barnyard Pets. Charlie Throws the Bull** • Animated version of Charlie Chaplin. • No stories available.

1092. Charlie 1918–1919; *p.c.:* Keen Cartoon Corp for Univ; *prod:* Pat Sullivan; *dir/anim:* Otto Messmer. • **1918: How Charlie Captured the Kaiser** 3 Sept. **Over the Rhine with Charlie** 21 Dec. • **1919: Charlie in Turkey** 29 Jan. **Charlie Treats 'Em Rough** 24 Mar. **Charlie's African Quest** b&w. *sil.* 6 min. • Animated version of Charlie Chaplin (made with Charlie's blessing). Thirteen entries in entire series, other *titles* and stories unavailable except for *How Charlie Captured the Kaiser* in which Charlie sets forth across the sea in a tub to single-handedly wipe out the German Front, capturing Wilhelm II along the way and *Charlie's African Quest* which has Charlie setting out to capture the plumage of the rare Goofus bird for a reward.

1093. Charlie Cuckoo *(Car-Tune Comedy)* 24 Apr. 1939; *p.c.:* Walter Lantz prods for Univ; *dir:* Elmer Perkins; *story:* Elviry Perkins; *anim:* Hank Perkins, Si Perkins; *voices:* Candy Candido; *mus:* Zeke Perkins; b&w. *sd:* WE. 7 min. • Reading about the new 49-hour week that's just been passed, a clock cuckoo sets off to enjoy life to the fullest.

1094. Charlie in Hot Water *(Beary Family)* 1970; *p.c.:* Walter Lantz prods for Univ; *dir:* Paul J. Smith; *story:* Cal Howard; *anim:* Les Kline, Al Coe; *sets:* Nino Carbe; *voices:* Paul Frees, Grace Stafford; *mus:* Walter Greene; *col:* Tech. *sd:* RCA. 6 min. • Charlie tries to fit a hot-water boiler on his own, causing disastrous results.

1095. Charlie the Rainmaker *(Beary Family)* 1971; *p.c.:* Walter Lantz prods for Univ; *dir:* Paul J. Smith; *story:* Cal Howard; *anim:* Les Kline, Al Coe, Tom Byrne, Joe Voght; *sets:* Nino Carbe; *voices:* Paul Frees, Grace Stafford; *mus:* Walter Greene; *prod mgr:* William E. Garity; *col:* Tech. *sd:* RCA. 5 min. • Charlie lays a lawn sprinkling pipeline ... with complications.

1096. Charlie's Campout *(Beary Family)* 1969; *p.c.:* Walter Lantz prods for Univ; *dir:* Paul J. Smith; *story:* Cal Howard; *anim:* Les Kline, Al Coe; *sets:* Nino Carbe; *voices:* Paul Frees, Grace Stafford; *mus:* Walter Greene; *col:* Tech. *sd:* RCA. 6 min. • Charlie goes camping.

1097. Charlie's Golf Classic *(Beary Family)* 1970; *p.c.:* Walter Lantz prods for Univ; *dir:* Paul J. Smith; *story:* Cal Howard; *anim:* Les Kline, Al Coe; *sets:* Nino Carbe; *voices:* Paul Frees, Grace Stafford; *mus:* Walter Greene; *col:* Tech. *sd:* RCA. 5 min. • Charlie teaches Bessie to play golf.

1098. Charlie's Mother-in-Law *(Beary Family)* 16 Apr. 1963; *p.c.:* Walter Lantz prods for Univ; *dir:* Paul J. Smith; *story:* Al Bertino, Dick Kinney; *anim:* Les Kline, Al Coe, Art Davis; *sets:* Art Landy, Ray Huffine; *voices:* Paul Frees, Grace Stafford; *mus:* Darrell Calker; *prod mgr:* William E. Garity; *col:* Tech. *sd:* RCA. 6 min. • The appearance of Mother-in-Law threatens to keep Charlie from a fishing expedition.

1099. Charlotte's Web 1973; *p.c.:* Hanna-Barbera/Sagittarius for Para/Scotia-Barber; *ex prod:* Edgar Bronfman; *prod:* Joseph Barbera, William Hanna; *dir:* Charles Nichols, Iwao Takamoto; story by E.B. White; *story adapt:* Earl Hamner Jr.; *story ed:* Lew Marshall; *story sketch:* Jan Strejan; *anim co-ord:* Jerry Hathcock, Bill Keil; *key anim:* Hal Ambro, Ed Barge, Lars Calonius, Dick Lundy, Irv Spence. *anim:* Ed Aardal, Lee Dyer, Bob Goe, George Kreisl, Don Patterson, Carlo Vinci, O.E. Callahan, Hugh Fraser, Volus Jones, Ed Parks, Ray Patterson, Xenia (De Mattia); *asst anim:* Pat Combs, Bob Hathcock, Rae McSpadden, Joan Orbison, Lillian Evans, Charlotte Huffine, Margaret Nichols, Jay Sarbry; *art dir:* Bob Singer, Ray Aragon, Paul Julian; *lay:* Mo Gollub, Jerry Eisenberg, John Ahern, Jack Huber, Gary Hoffman, Alex Ignatiev, David High, Mike Arens, Don Morgan, Lew Ott, Ric Gonzales, George Wheeler, Leo Swenson; *back sup:* F. Montealegre; *back:* Lorraine Andrina, Fernando Arce, Lyle Beddes, Venetia Epler, Ronald Erickson, Martin Forte, Bob Gentle, Al Gmuer, Joseph Griffith Jr., Gino Guidice, Richard Khim, Tom Knowles, Gary Niblett, Rolando Oliva, Eric Semones, Jeanette Toews, Peter van Elk; *ed:* Larry Cowan, Pat Foley; *fx eds:* Earl Bennett, Richard C. Allen, Joe Sandusky; *neg consult:* William E. de Boer; *voices: Charlotte:* Debbie Reynolds; *Templeton:* Paul Lynde; *Wilbur:* Henry Gibson; *Narrator:* Rex Allen; *Avery:* Danny Bonaduce; *Fern:* Pamelyn Ferdin; *Mrs. Fussy/Mrs. Zuckerman:* Joan Gerber; *Mr. Zuckerman:* Robert Holt; *The Old Sheep:* Dave Madden; *Geoffrey:* Don Messick; *Goose:* Agnes Moorehead; *Mrs. Arable:* Martha Scott; *Mr. Arable:* John Stephenson; *Lurvy/Uncle:* Herb Vigran; *Henry Fussy:* William B. White. *singers:* Jasmin Alberts, Dick Bethi, Fred Frank, Susie McCune, Jay Meyer, Bob Tebov, Jackie Allen, Paul de Korte, Bill Lee, Gene Merlino, Paul Sandberg, Jackie Ward; *songs:* Richard M. Sherman, Robert B. Sherman; *mus sup:* Irwin Kostal; *song dir:* Bill Perez, Takashi Nakagawa; *dialogue dir:* Alex Lovy; *mus coord:* Paul de Korte; *sd dir:* Dick Olsen, Bill Getty, Joe Citarilla; *post prod:* Joed Eaton; *prod mgr:* Victor O. Schipek; *technical :* Frank Paiker; *i&p:* Jayne Barbera; *Xerography:* Robert "Tiger" West; *titles:* Robert Schaefer; *ph:* Roy Wade, Dick Blundell, George Epperson, Ralph Migliori, Dennis Weaver; *col:* East. *sd:* RCA. 96 min. • E.B. White's classic tale of a spider who helps prevent a pig from being slaughtered.

1100. Charm Bracelet *(Phantasy)* 1 Sept. 1939; *p.c.:* Colum; *story:* Harry Love; *anim:* Allen Rose; *ed:* George Winkler; *voice:* Robert Winkler, The King's Men; *mus:* Joe de Nat; *ph:* Otto Reimer; *prod mgr:* James Bronis; b&w. *sd:* RCA. 6 min. • Margie receives a charm bracelet from Scrappy and dreams that all the characters on it come to life.

1101. Chaser on the Rocks *(Merrie Melodies)* 25 Dec. 1965; *p.c.:* DFE for WB; *dir:* Rudy Larriva; *story:* Tom Dagenais; *anim:* Hank Smith, Virgil Ross, Bob Bransford; *lay:* Don Sheppard; *back:* Anthony Rizzo; *ed:* Joe Siracusa; *mus:* Bill Lava; *col:* Tech. *sd:* Vit. 6 min. • The Coyote tries to secure the Road-Runner with the lure of water during a drought.

1102. Chasing Rainbows (*Aesop's Fable*) 16 Jan. 1927; *p.c.*: Fables Pictures Inc for Pathé; *dir*: Paul Terry; *b&w. sil.* 5 min. • Al Falfa's cat and dog set out to find the pot of gold at the rainbow's end. They dig and eventually find themselves at the bottom of the farmer's well. It was only a dream!

1103. Cheese Burglar (*Noveltoon*) 17 May 1946; *p.c.*: Famous for Para; *dir*: I. Sparber; *story*: Carl Meyer, Joe Stultz; *anim*: Jim Tyer, Ben Solomon, William Henning; *sets*: Robert Little; *voices*: Arnold Stang, Jackson Beck, Jack Mercer; *mus*: Winston Sharples; *ph*: Leonard McCormick; *col*: Tech. *sd*: RCA. 7 min. • The dog and cat join forces to stop Herman from getting the food. The mouse manages to convince them that they are trying to assassinate each other.

1104. Cheese Chasers (*Merrie Melodies*) 25 Aug. 1951; *p.c.*: WB; *dir*: Charles M. Jones; *story*: Michael Maltese; *anim*: Ben Washam, Lloyd Vaughan, Phil Monroe, Ken Harris; *lay*: Robert Gribbroek; *back*: Philip de Guard; *ed*: Treg Brown; *voices*: Mel Blanc, Stan Freberg; *mus*: Carl Stalling; *prod mgr*: John W. Burton; *prod*: Edward Selzer; *col*: Tech. *sd*: Vit. 7 min. • Having overeaten at the cheese factory, Hubie and Bertie, the two mice, decide to end it all by throwing themselves at the mercy of a very skeptical Claude Cat.

1105. Cheese It, the Cat! (*Looney Tunes*) 4 May 1957; *dir*: Robert McKimson; *story*: Tedd Pierce; *anim*: Ted Bonnicksen, Keith Darling, George Grandpré; *lay*: Robert Gribbroek; *back*: Bob Majors; *ed*: Treg Brown; *voices*: Daws Butler, June Foray; *mus*: Carl Stalling, Milt Franklyn; *prod mgr*: John W. Burton; *prod*: Edward Selzer. *col*: Tech. *sd*: Vit. 7 min. • All Ralph Crumbden needs for Alice's surprise party is food. He sends Ned Morton out under the watchful eye of the cat to secure some from the refrigerator.

1106. Cheese Nappers (*Cartune*) 16 June 1938; *p.c.*: Univ; *dir*: Alex Lovy; *story*: Victor McLeod, James Miele; *anim*: Ray Fahringer, George Grandpré; *sets*: Edgar Keichle; *voices*: Bernice Hansel, Dave Weber; *mus*: Frank Churchill; *col*: Tech. *sd*: WE. 7 min. • Baby Face Mouse is encouraged by "Public Rat #1 to steal some cheese. He is caught and takes the blame while the villain goes free.

1107. Chef Donald (*Donald Duck*) 5 Dec. 1941; *p.c.*: Walt Disney prods for RKO; *dir*: Jack King; *asst dir*: Bob Newman; *story*: Carl Barks, Jack Hannah. *anim*: Paul Allen, James Armstrong, Walter Clinton, Edward Love, Lee Morehouse, Judge Whitaker; *lay*: Bill Herwig; *voices*: Sarah Selby, Clarence Nash; *mus*: Charles Wolcott; *col*: Tech. *sd*: RCA. 8 min. • Donald accidentally gets rubber cement in the batter when making waffles.

1108. Chemical Ko-Ko (*Inkwell Imps*) 26 July 1929; *p.c.*: Inkwell Studio for Para; *prod/l/a*: Max Fleischer; *dir*: Dave Fleischer; *b&w. st*: 6 min. *l/a/anim*. • Ko-Ko mixes a potion that can change the structure of various animals. He makes thin animals fat and changes a baby hippo into a giraffe, etc.

1109. Cherche Le Phantom (*Inspector*) 13 June 1968; *p.c.*: Mirisch/Geoffrey/DFE for UA; *dir*: Gerry Chiniquy. *story*: Tony Benedict; *anim*: Manny Perez, Don Williams, Manny Gould, Warren Batchelder, Tom Ray; *lay*: Dick Ung; *back*: Tom O'Loughlin; *ed*: Lee Gunther; *voices*: Pat Harrington Jr., Marvin Miller; *mus*: Walter Greene; *theme tune*: Henry Mancini; *ph*: John Burton Jr.; *prod sup*: Harry Love, David DeTiege; *col*: DeLuxe. *sd*: RCA. 6 min. • The Inspector is called upon to arrest "The Phantom of the Opera" who turns out to be a gorilla.

1110. Cherry Blossom Festival (*Hashimoto*) July 1963; *p.c.*: TT for Fox; *ex prod*: Bill Weiss; *dir*: Bob Kuwahara; *voices*: John Myhers; *mus*: Phil Scheib; *prod mgr*: Frank Schudde; *col*: DeLuxe. *sd*: RCA. 6 min. CS. • No story available.

1111. Chess-Nuts (*Talkartoons*) 13 May 1932; *p.c.*: The Fleischer Studio for Para; *prod*: Max Fleischer; *dir*: Dave Fleischer; *dir/story/anim*: James Culhane, Rudy Zamora; *add anim*: William Henning; *mus*: Art Turkisher; *b&w. sd*: WE. 7 min. *l/a/anim*. • A live-action chess game is turned into a fantasy with the arrival of Betty Boop, who is captured by an old man and rescued by Bimbo. The old man in this is a caricature of the studio janitor.

1112. Chew Chew Baby (*Noveltoon*) 15 Aug. 1958; *p.c.*: Para Cartoons; *dir*: I. Sparber; *story*: Irving Spector; *anim*: Tom Johnson, Frank Endres, Al Eugster; *sets*: Robert Owen; *voices*: Jackson Beck, Jack Mercer; *mus*: Winston Sharples; *ph*: Leonard McCormick; *prod mgr*: Abe Goodman; *col*: Tech. *sd*: RCA. 6 min. • An explorer tells a Pygmy cannibal, "If you're ever in Cincinatti, look me up!" ... which he unfortunately does.

1113. Chew-Chew Baby (*Woody Woodpecker*) 5 Feb. 1945; *p.c.*: Walter Lantz prods for Univ; *dir*: James Culhane; *story*: Ben Hardaway, Milt Schaffer; *anim*: Paul Smith, Grim Natwick; *lay*: Art Heinemann; *back*: Philip de Guard; *voices*: Jack Mather, Lee Sweetland, Ben Hardaway; *mus*: Darrell Calker; *col*: Tech. *sd*: WE. 7 min. • Woody is evicted from Wally Walrus' lodging house but returns in the guise of "Clementine" to woo him and steal his groceries in the bargain.

1114. The Chewin' Bruin (*Looney Tunes*) 8 June 1940; *p.c.*: Leon Schlesinger prods for WB; *dir*: Robert Clampett; *anim*: Norman McCabe, Vive Risto; *sets*: Elmer Plummer; *ed*: Treg Brown; *voices*: Robert C. Bruce, Mel Blanc; *mus*: Carl W. Stalling; *prod sup*: Henry Binder, Raymond G. Katz; *b&w. sd*: Vit. 6 min. • An old trapper tells Porky how he once encountered a bear with a partiality for chewing 'baccy.

1115. Chicago Tribune Animated Weekly *prod*: Watterson Rothacker; *anim*: Sidney Smith; *b&w. st*. • *1915:* (13) **Doc in the Ring** 18 Sept. (18) **Doc the Ham Actor** 16 Oct. • Animated items in newsreel featuring Sidney Smith's newspaper creation "Old Doc Yak." No further entries have been traced.

1116. Chick and Double Chick (*Little Lulu*); 16 Aug. 1946; *p.c.*: Famous for Para; *dir*: Seymour Kneitel; *story*: Carl Meyer, Jack Mercer; *anim*: Graham Place, Martin Taras, Lou Zukor; *sets*: Robert Little; *voices*: Cecil Roy, Carl Meyer; *mus*: Winston Sharples; *title song*: Buddy Kaye, Fred Wise, Sammy Timberg; *prod mgr*: Sam Buchwald; *col*: Tech. *sd*: RCA. 6 min. • Lulu trains her dog to guard the hen house against the dog next door.

1117. Chicken B La King (*Color Classic*) 16 Apr. 1937; *p.c.*: The Fleischer Studio for Para; *prod*: Max Fleischer; *dir*: Dave Fleischer; *anim*: David Tendlar, Nicholas Tafuri; *voices*: Everett Clark; *mus*: Sammy Timberg, Bob Rothberg; *col*: Tech. *sd*: WE. 7 min. • A rooster sultan's harem is disrupted by a visit from a Mae West–type vamp named "Ducky Wucky." A Douglas Fairbanks–type chicken arrives to have a duel with the Sultan, turning his harem of pullets against him.

1118. Chicken Dressing (*Mastodon Cartoons*) 24 Feb. 1923; *p.c.*: Earl Hurd prods for Motion Picture Arts Inc./Educational; *dir*: Earl Hurd Jr.; *prod*: C.C. Burr; *b&w. sil.* 5 min. *l/a/anim*. • Live chickens and a live cat serve as sufficient aids for Bobby Bumps and his cartoon dog.

1119. Chicken Fracas-See (*Loopy de Loop*) Mar. 1963; *p.c.*: Hanna-Barbera for Colum; *prod/dir*: Joseph Barbera, William Hanna; *story dir*: Paul Sommer; *story*: Dalton Sandifer; *anim dir*: Charles A. Nichols; *anim*: Carlo Vinci; *lay*: Jack Huber; *back*: Montealegre; *ed*: Greg Watson; *voices*: Daws Butler, Don Messick, Doug Young; *mus*: Hoyt Curtin; *titles*: Lawrence Gobel; *prod sup*: Howard Hansen; *col*: East. *sd*: RCA. 6 min. • Loopy is given an egg that hatches into a chick who believes him to be its mother.

1120. Chicken in the Rough (*Chip 'n' Dale*) 19 Jan. 1951; *p.c.*: Walt Disney prods for RKO; *dir*: Jack Hannah; *story*: Nick George, Bill Berg; *anim*: Bill Justice, Bob Carlson, Judge Whitaker, Volus Jones; *fx*: George Rowley; *lay*: Yale Gracey; *back*: Ray Huffine; *voices*: James MacDonald, Dessie Flynn, Dorothy Lloyd, Clarence Nash; *mus*: Joseph S. Dubin; *col*: Tech. *sd*: RCA. 7 min. • Dale is caught taking an egg (believed to be a large acorn) by the rooster, forcing him to pose as a newly-hatched chick.

1121. Chicken Jitters (*Looney Tunes*) 22 Apr. 1939; *p.c.*: Leon Schlesinger prods for WB; *dir*: Robert Clampett; *anim*: Robert Cannon, Vive Risto; *sets*: Elmer Plummer; *ed*: Tregoweth E. Brown; *voices*: Mel Blanc, Danny Webb; *mus*: Carl W. Stalling; *prod sup*: Henry Binder, Raymond G. Katz; *b&w. sd*: Vit. 7 min. • The fox kidnaps one of Porky's ducks from his chicken ranch. The farm fowl join forces to rescue him.

1122. Chicken Little 17 Dec. 1943; *p.c.*: Walt Disney prods for RKO; *dir*: Clyde Geronimi; *asst dir*: Rusty Jones; *story*: Ralph Wright; *anim*: John Lounsbery, Oliver Johnston, Milt Kahl, Ward Kimball, Norman Tate; *fx*: Edwin Aardal, Andy Engman, George Rowley; *lay*: Charles Philippi; *voices*: Frank Graham, Dorothy Lloyd, Florence Gill, Clarence Nash; *mus*: Oliver Wallace; *col*: Tech. *sd*: RCA. 9 min. • Foxy Loxy fools the chickens by letting weak-minded Chicken Little lead them to "safety" ... straight into the fox's lair. Made under Disney's contract with the Coordinator of Inter-American Affairs as a "Don't Believe Everything You Read" warning.

1123. Chicken Reel (*Oswald*) 1 Jan. 1934; *p.c.:* Univ; *anim:* Walter Lantz, "Bill" Nolan; *anim:* Manuel Moreno, Lester Kline, Fred Kopietz, George Grandpré, Ernest Smythe; *mus:* James Dietrich; b&w. *sd:* WE. 9 min. • No story available.

1124. Chief Charlie Horse (*Woody Woodpecker*) 7 May 1956; *p.c.*; Walter Lantz prods for Univ; *dir:* Paul J. Smith; *story:* Jack Cosgriff; *anim:* Robert Bentley, Herman R. Cohen, Ray Abrams; *sets:* Art Landy; *voices:* Dal McKennon, Grace Stafford; *mus:* Clarence Wheeler; *prod mgr:* William E. Garity; *col:* Tech. *sd:* RCA. 6 min. • On the run from the sheriff, Chief Charlie Horse poses as a wooden Indian in Woody's shop.

1125. Child Psykolojiky (*Popeye*) 11 July 1941; *p.c.:* The Fleischer for Para; *prod:* Max Fleischer; *dir:* Dave Fleischer; *story:* George Manuell; *anim:* Bill Nolan, Joe Oriolo; *ed:* Kitty Pfister; *voices:* Jack Mercer, Margie Hines; *mus:* Sammy Timberg; *ph:* Charles Schettler; *prod sup:* Sam Buchwald, Isidore Sparber; b&w. *sd:* WE. 7 min. • Pappy and Popeye have conflicting views on how Swee'Pea should be raised.

1126. Child Sock-Cology (*Loopy de Loop*) Nov. 1961; *p.c.:* Hanna-Barbera for Colum; *prod/dir:* Joseph Barbera, William Hanna; story *dir:* Alex Lovy; *story:* Tony Benedict; *anim dir:* Charles A. Nichols; *anim:* Dick Lundy; *lay:* Walt Clinton; *back:* Richard H. Thomas; *ed:* Greg Watson; *voices:* Daws Butler, Don Messick; *mus:* Hoyt Curtin; *titles:* Lawrence Gobel. *prod sup:* Howard Hanson; *col:* East. *sd:* RCA. 6 min. • Loopy looks after a baby gorilla.

1127. Child Sockology (*Popeye*) 27 Mar. 1953; *p.c.:* Famous for Para; *dir:* I. Sparber; *story:* Carl Meyer, Jack Mercer; *anim:* Tom Johnson, Frank Endres, Els Barthen; *sets:* Robert Little; *voices:* Jack Mercer, Mae Questel, Jackson Beck; *mus:* Winston Sharples; *ph:* Leonard McCormick; *prod mgr:* Seymour Shultz; *col:* Tech. *sd:* RCA. 6 min. • While Popeye and Bluto argue over who will babysit Swee'pea, the youngster crawls off onto a building site with precarious consequences.

1128. Children of the Sun 1960; *p.c.:* Storyboard prods for UNICEF; *prod/story:* John and Faith Hubley; *dir/des:* John Hubley; *anim:* Robert Cannon, Gary Mooney; *voices:* Georgina, Emily, Hampy and Mark Hubley; *mus:* Pablo Casals and the Budapest String Quartet with Walter Trampler; col. *snd.* 10 min. • Award-winning cartoon for UNICEF, showing the conditions of a child growing up in the west compared to one growing up in the third world where three quarters of the population are starving.

1129. Chilé Con Carmen (*Oswald*) 15 Jan. 1930; *p.c.:* Univ; *anim:* R.C. Hamilton, "Bill" Nolan, Tom Palmer; *mus:* David Broekman; b&w. *sd:* WE. 7 min. • Oswald has a set-to in a boxing ring with a bull.

1130. Chili Con Corny (*Woody Woodpecker*) 1972; *p.c.:* Walter Lantz prods for Univ; *dir:* Paul J. Smith; *story:* Cal Howard; *anim:* Volus Jones, Al Coe, Tom Byrne, Joe Voght; *sets:* Nino Carbe; *voices:* Grace Stafford; *mus:* Walter Greene; *prod mgr:* William E. Garity; *col:* Tech. *sd:* RCA. 5 min. • Woody orders a meal he can't pay for in Mrs. Meanie's eating house.

1131. Chili Corn Corny (*Looney Tunes*) 23 Oct. 1965; *p.c.:* DFE for WB; *dir:* Robert McKimson; *story:* David DeTiege; *anim:* Manny Perez, Warren Batchelder, Bob Matz; *lay:* Dick Ung; *back:* Tom O'Loughlin; *ed:* Lee Gunther; *voices:* Mel Blanc, (Pedro) Gonzalez-Gonzales; *mus:* Bill Lava; *col:* Tech. *sd:* Vit. 6 min. • Speedy Gonzales helps his crow friend get some corn from under the watchful eye of the cornfield's owner ... Daffy Duck.

1132. Chili Weather (*Merrie Melodies*) 17 Aug. 1963; *p.c.:* WB; *dir:* Friz Freleng; *story:* John Dunn; *anim:* Gerry Chiniquy, Virgil Ross, Bob Matz, Lee Halpern, Art Leonardi; *lay:* Hawley Pratt; *back:* Tom O'Loughlin; *ed:* Lee Gunther; *voices:* Mel Blanc; *mus:* Bill Lava; *prod mgr:* William Orcutt; *prod:* David H. DePatie; *col:* Tech. *sd:* Vit. 7 min. • Speedy defies Sylvester's authority by stealing cheese from a food processing plant.

1133. Chiller Dillers (*Chilly Willy*) June 1968; *p.c.:* Walter Lantz prods for Univ; *dir:* Paul J. Smith; *story:* Homer Brightman; *anim:* Les Kline, Al Coe; *sets:* Ray Huffine; *voices:* Daws Butler, Bob Johnson; *mus:* Walter Greene; *prod mgr:* William E. Garity; *col:* Tech. *sd:* RCA. 6 min. • A Captain wants to capture Chilly's singing bear pal and take him to Hollywood.

1134. Chilly and the Looney Gooney (*Chilly Willy*) 1969; *p.c.:* Walter Lantz prods for Univ; *dir:* Paul J. Smith; *story:* Homer Brightman; *anim:* Les Kline, Al Coe; *sets:* Nino Carbe; *voices:* Daws Butler; *mus:* Walter Greene; *prod mgr:* William E. Garity; *col:* Tech. *sd:* RCA. 6 min. • Chilly protects his albatross chum from the clutches of Colonel Potshot.

1135. Chilly and the Woodchopper (*Chilly Willy*) May 1967; *p.c.:* Walter Lantz prods for Univ; *dir:* Paul J. Smith; *story:* Sid Marcus; *anim:* Al Coe, Les Kline; *sets:* Ray Huffine; *voices:* Daws Butler; *mus:* Walter Greene; *prod mgr:* William E. Garity; *col:* Tech. *sd:* RCA. 6 min. • A tough lumberjack arrives at Smedley's lodge suffering from nervous exhaustion. Chilly upsets him and puts the blame on Smedley.

1136. Chilly Chums (*Chilly Willy*) June 1967; *p.c.:* Walter Lantz prods for Univ; *dir:* Paul J. Smith; *story:* Homer Brightman; *anim:* Les Kline, Al Coe; *sets:* Ray Huffine; *voices:* Daws Butler, Grace Stafford. *mus:* Walter Greene; *prod mgr:* William E. Garity; *col:* Tech. *sd:* RCA. 6 min. • Chilly saves his polar bear friend from a fur trapper named "Bring-em-Back-Alive" Clive.

1137. A Chilly Reception (*Chilly Willy*) 11 Aug. 1958; *p.c.:* Walter Lantz prods for Univ; *dir:* Alex Lovy; *story:* Homer Brightman; *anim:* Ray Abrams, La Verne Harding, Don Patterson *sets:* Raymond Jacobs; *voice:* Daws Butler; *mus:* Clarence Wheeler; *prod mgr:* William E. Garity; *col:* Tech. *sd:* RCA. 6 min. • Chilly is adopted as the ship's mascot, putting the former mascot's (Smedley) nose out of joint, forcing him to dispose of the intruder.

1138. Chilly Willy 21 Dec. 1953; *p.c.:* Walter Lantz prods for Univ; *dir:* Paul J. Smith; *story:* Homer Brightman; *anim:* Gil Turner, La Verne Harding, Robert Bentley; *sets:* Raymond Jacobs, Art Landy; *voice:* Dal McKennon; *mus:* Clarence Wheeler; *title song* by Mary Jo Rush; sung by Sara Berner; *prod mgr:* William E. Garity; *col:* Tech. *sd:* RCA. 6 min. • A cold penguin sneaks aboard a ship to get warm and the watchdog has to evict him before the Captain returns. Initial cartoon featuring the mute penguin.

1139. Chilly's Cold War (*Chilly Willy*) 1970; *p.c.:* Walter Lantz prods for Univ; *dir:* Paul J. Smith; *story:* Sid Marcus; *anim:* Les Kline, Al Coe; *sets:* Nino Carbe; *voices:* Daws Butler; *mus:* Walter Greene; *prod mgr:* William E. Garity; *col:* Tech. *sd:* RCA. 5 min. • Caretaker Smedley has to evict Chilly from Colonel Potshot's cabin.

1140. Chilly's Hide-A-Way (*Chilly Willy*) 1971; *p.c.:* Walter Lantz prods for Univ; *dir:* Paul J. Smith; *story:* Sid Marcus; *anim:* Virgil Ross, Al Coe, Tom Byrne, Joe Voght; *sets:* Nino Carbe; *voice:* Daws Butler; *mus:* Walter Greene; *prod mgr:* William E. Garity; *col:* Tech. *sd:* RCA. 5 min. • Chilly, again, intrudes into Colonel Potshot's winter cabin and Smedley has the task of evicting him without the Colonel finding out.

1141. Chilly's Ice Folly (*Chilly Willy*) 1970; *p.c.:* Walter Lantz prods for Univ; *dir:* Paul J. Smith; *story:* Dale Hale; *anim:* Les Kline, Al Coe; *sets:* Nino Carbe; *voice:* Daws Butler; *mus:* Walter Greene; *prod mgr:* William E. Garity; *col:* Tech. *sd:* RCA. 5 min. • Chilly and Maxie's fire thaws out a baby wooly mammoth and they have to look after it.

1142. Chimp & Zee (*Merrie Melodies*) 12 Oct. 1968; *p.c.:* W/7A; *prod:* William L. Hendricks; *dir:* Alex Lovy; *story:* Don Jurwich; *anim:* Ted Bonnicksen, La Verne Harding, Volus Jones, Ed Solomon; *lay:* Bob Givens; *back:* Bob Abrams; *ed:* Hal Geer; *voices:* Mel Blanc; *mus:* William Lava; *col:* Tech. *sd:* Vit. 5 min. • A Professor pursues a rare Blue-Tailed Simean ... only to discover that they are not all that rare.

1143. China (*Oswald*) 12 Jan. 1931; *p.c.:* Univ; *dir:* Walter Lantz, "Bill"Nolan; *anim:* Clyde Geronimi, Manuel Moreno, Ray Abrams, Fred Avery, Lester Kline, "Pinto" Colvig; *mus:* James Dietrich; b&w. *sd:* WE. 6 min. • Oswald works in a Chinese laundry. The owner arrives to see him cavorting with the clothes and a chase ensues.

1144. China (*Paul Terry-Toon*) 13 Nov. 1931; *p.c.:* Terry, Moser & Coffman for Educational/Fox; *dir:* Paul Terry, Frank Moser; *mus:* Philip A. Scheib; b&w. *sd:* WE. 6 min. • A mouse's adventures in the land of pigtails.

1145. China Jones (*Looney Tunes*) 14 Feb. 1959; *p.c.:* WB; *dir:* Robert McKimson; *story:* Tedd Pierce; *anim:* Tom Ray, George Grandpré, Ted Bonnicksen, Warren Batchelder; *lay:* Robert Gribbroek; *back:* William Butler; *ed:* Treg Brown; *voices:* Mel Blanc, Julie Bennett; *mus:* Milt Franklyn; *col:* Tech. *sd:* Vit. 7 min. • A parody of the TV show "China Smith"in which Daffy plays the soldier of fortune who finds a message in a fortune cookie, setting him off on a trail looking for a prisoner in a Chinese laundry.

1146. The China Plate *(Silly Symphony)* 16 May 1931; *p.c.:* Walt Disney prods for Colum; *dir:* Wilfred Jackson; *anim:* Johnny Cannon, Jack Cutting, Joseph d'Igalo, Gilles de Tremaudan, Hardie Gramatky, Richard Lundy, Frank Powers, Ben Sharpsteen, Rudy Zamora; *asst anim:* George Lane, Jack Kinney; *voice:* Marcellite Garner; *mus:* Frank E. Churchill; b&w. *sd:* PCP. 8 min. • Characters on a china plate come alive. A Chinese boy and girl are chased by a Mandarin whom they incarcerate inside a dragon's mouth.

1147. The China Shop *(Silly Symphony)* 15 Jan. 1934; *p.c.:* Walt Disney prods for UA; *dir:* Wilfred Jackson; *storyboard/character design:* Al Hurter; *anim:* Arthur Babbitt, Gilles de Tremaudan, Jack Hannah, Dick Huemor, Jack Kinney, Richard Lundy, Louis Schmitt, Leonard Sebring, Ben Sharpsteen, Roy Williams; *fx:* Cy Young; *mus:* Leigh Harline; *col:* Tech. *sd:* RCA. 10 min. • When the China Shop closes at night, all the objects in it come alive. A villainous Satyr kidnaps a girl ornament and her boy partner comes to her rescue.

1148. A Chinaman's Chance *(Flip the Frog)* 27 June 1933; *p.c.:* Celebrity prods for MGM; *prod/dir:* Ub Iwerks; *anim:* Jimmie Culhane; b&w. *sd:* PCP. 6 min. • Constable Flip is sent to recapture an oriental crook from his Chinese laundry hideout.

1149. Chinatown, My Chinatown *(Screen Songs)* 29 Aug. 1929; *p.c.:* The Fleischer Studio for Para; *prod:* Max Fleischer; *dir:* Dave Fleischer; b&w. *sd:* WE. 6 min. • Incidents in a Chinese laundry when one character inadvertently eats a shirt.

1150. Chinatown Mystery *(Scrappy)* 4 Jan. 1932; *p.c.:* Winkler for Colum; *prod:* Charles Mintz; *story:* Dick Huemor; *anim:* Sid Marcus, Art Davis; *mus:* Joe de Nat; *prod mgr:* James Bronis; b&w. *sd:* WE. 6 min. • Scrappy has a thrilling adventure against an oriental setting.

1151. Chinese Jinks *(Aesop's Sound Fable)* 23 July 1932; *p.c.:* Van Beuren for RKO; *dir:* John Foster, Harry Bailey; *mus:* Gene Rodemich; b&w. *sd:* RCA. 5 min. • No story available.

1152. The Chinese Nightingale *(Happy Harmonies)* 27 Apr. 1935; *p.c.:* MGM; *prod/dir:* Hugh Harman, Rudolf Ising; *voice:* Charlie Lung, The Rhythmettes; *mus:* Scott Bradley; *col:* Tech-2. *sd:* RCA. 9 min. • The Emperor replaces his singing nightingale with a clockwork toy. The bird feels neglected and departs and, when the toy gets broken, the Emperor pines for his musical friend.

1153. Chip 'an' Dale *(Donald Duck)* 28 Nov. 1947; *p.c.:* Walt Disney prods for RKO; *dir:* Jack Hannah; *asst dir:* Bee Selck; *story:* Dick Kinney, Bob North; *anim:* Bill Justice, Volus Jones, Murray McClellan, Ted Bonnicksen, Bob Carlson; *fx:* Jack Boyd, Andy Engman; *lay:* Yale Gracey; *back:* Ralph Hulett; *voices:* Clarence Nash, James MacDonald, Dessie Flynn; *mus:* Oliver Wallace; *col:* Tech. *sd:* RCA. 7 min. *Academy Award nomination.* • Donald chops down the chipmunks' tree-home for firewood. They follow him home to retrieve their property.

1154. The Chipmunk Adventure 22 May 1987; *p.c.:* Bagdasarian Prods.; *dir:* Janice Karman; *prod:* Ross Bagdasarian Jr.; *asso prod:* Gwendolyn Sue Shakespeare; *story:* Ross Bagdasarian Jr., Janice Karman; *storyboard:* Andrew Gaskill, Dan Halkell, Glen Keane, John Norton, Michael Peraza Jr., Roy Allen Smith, Leonard Robinson; *character key sup:* Lureline Kohler, Sandra Berez; *anim dir:* Becky Bristow, Andrew Gaskill, Skip Jones, Mitch Rochon, Don Spencer; *anim:* Viki Anderson, Norman Drew, David Feiss, Raul Garcia, Chuck Harvey, Dan Haskell, Glen Keane, John Norton, David Pruiksma, Paul Riley, Louise Zingarelli; *anim asst:* Beverly Adams, Danny Antonucci, Debra Armstrong, Vicki Banks, Judy Barnes, Dorris Bergstrom, Jim Bird, Susan I. Craig, Kent Culotta, Eileen Dunn, Craig Evans, June Fujimoto, Heidi Guedel, Karen Hardenbergh, Ray Harris, Al Holter, Joe Horne, Michael Horowitz, Mona Hosbjor, William Houchins, Emily Jiuliano, J.K. Kim, Cal Le Duc, Jin-Woo Lee, Mike Lessa, Leticia Lichtwardt, Brian McKim, Sharon Murray, Terry Naughton, Jan Naylor, Frank Rocco, Natasha Selfridge, Terry Shakespeare, Patty Shinagawa, Alan Smart, Ann Telnaes, Bill Thinnes, Alex Topete, Jane Tucker, John Williamson, Nyoung-koo Won, Margie Wright-Stansbery, Susan M. Zytka; *addit anim:* Tim Allen, Ken Boyer, Corny Cole, Jesse Cosio, Tim Hauser, Sue Kroyer, David Molina, Rebecca Rees, Tanya T.

Wilson, Will Finn; *fx anim:* Kathleen Quaife-Hodge, Rob Bekuhrs, Sari Gennis, January Nordman, Don Paul; *optical fx:* Rocky Solotoff; *ed:* Greg Griffin; *voices: David Sevillel/Alvin/ Simon:* Ross Bagdasarian Jr.; *Theodore/ Brittany Miller/Jeanette Miller/ Eleanor Miller:* Janice Karman; *Miss Rebecca Miller:* Dody Goodman; *Klaus Furschtien:* Anthony De Longis; *Claudia Furschtien:* Susan Tyrrell; *Sophie:* Frank Welker; *Arabian Prince:* Nancy Cartwright; *also:* Charles Adler, Philip L. Clarke, George Poulos, Patrick Pinney, Ken Sansom, Frank Welker; *mus:* Randy Edelman; *orch:* Ralph Ferraro; *mus sup:* Rob Matheny, Rick Riccobono; *song arranger:* Howard Pfeifer; *song engineer:* Randy Tominaga; *mus co-ord:* Ralph Velasco; *anim posing art:* Cynthia Ward; *character des:* Sandra Berez, Louise Zingarelli; *prod des:* Carol Holman Grosvenor; *col key:* Ron Dias, Janice Karman, Bunny Munns; *col models:* Renee Ilsa Alcazar, Kevin Anderson, Mary Grant, Mi Kyung Kwon, Beth Ann McCoy, Deborah Mooneyham, Jaki Sommerich; *lay:* Andrew Austin, Dan Fausett, Gary Graham, Mike Hodgson, Jim Schlenker, Roy Allen Smith, J. Michael Spooner, Tapani Knuutila; *back:* Ron Dias, Han Hyung Hak, Byung-Seon Kwak, Jong Hee Lee, William Lorencz, Kwan-sic Park, Donald Towns, Thomas Woodington; *title des:* Andrew Gaskill; *title lay:* Carol Holman Grosvenor, Mike Hodgson; *col mark-up:* Diane Albracht, Sarah-Jane King, Victor Solis, Michelle Urbano, Chris Wirosko; *anim check:* Vonnie Batson, Patty Burns, Annamarie Costa, Sandra Kumashiro, Jan Naylor, Yong Nam Park, Robin Police, Katherine Victor, Thomas Ling Yen; *clean-up:* Raul Garcia, Richard Hoppe, Renee Holt, Rejean Bourdages, Rasoul Azadani, Marc Christenson, Marlene Robinson May, Ron Migilore, Soon Jin Mooney; *scene plan:* Glenn M. Higa, John Sparey; *ed:* Tony Mizgalski, Greg Griffin; *i&p:* Jin-Sook Bae, Park Eunmi, Soon Rae Hwang, Eun-Jung Kim, Tae Jung Lee, Younghyn Park, Chung Yeon-Kwan; *mus ed:* Douglas M. Lackey; *sd ed:* Donald W. Ernst, Cecil Broughton, Sam Horta, Scott D. Jackson, Gary Krivacek; *voice rec:* Greg P. Russell, Jackson Schwartz; *mus rec:* Bob Mallet; *sd re-rec:* Jeffrey J. Haboush, Greg P. Russell; *foley:* Eileen Horta, Mary Louise Rodgers; *foley ed:* Russ Hill, Stephen Janisz, Leonard Wolf Jr., Richard Newman; *track reader:* Shelley Rae Hinton; *ADR ed:* Kevin Spears; *Xerox:* Seon-Ok Park; *ph:* Hyung Hee Kim, Chul-kyu Lim; *back photographer:* John Siskin; *prod ex:* Hope London; *prod sup:* Rocky Solotoff; *prod mgr:* Michael Wolf; *prod asst:* Lourdes Arango, R.A. Brodhead, Greg Hinde, Charlie May, Veronica Wirth; *prod co-ord:* Patty Burns, Roxy Novotny Steven, Choi Young-Chan; *prod controller:* F. James Barry; *special thanks:* Oliver Johnston, Frank Thomas; *col. sd:* Dolby Digital. 77 min. *Academy Award nomination.* • Alvin and the Chipmunks take part in an around-the-world hot-air balloon race.

1155. The Chipper Chipmunk *(Gandy Goose)* 12 May 1948; *p.c.:* TT for Fox; *dir:* Mannie Davis; *story:* John Foster; *mus:* Philip A. Scheib; *col:* Tech. *sd:* RCA. 6 min. • A chipmunk ruins Gandy and Sourpuss' picnic.

1156. Chips Ahoy *(Donald Duck)* 21 May 1955; *p.c.:* Walt Disney prods for BV; *dir:* Jack Kinney; *story:* Dick Kinney, Milt Schaffer; *anim:* Harry Holt, Ed Aardal, John Sibley; *fx:* Dan MacManus; *lay:* Bill Bosché; *back:* Thelma Witmer; *voices:* Clarence Nash, Dessie Miller, Norma Swank; *mus:* Oliver Wallace; *col:* Tech. *sd:* RCA. 7 min. CS. • Donald's model yacht is commandeered by the chipmunks.

1157. Chips Off the Old Block *(MGM cartoon)* 12 Sept. 1942; *p.c.:* MGM; *prod:* Rudolf Ising; *dir:* Robert Allen; *anim:* Carl Urbano, Al Grandmain; *sets:* Don Shaffer; *ed:* Fred MacAlpin; *voices:* Harry E. Lang; *mus:* Scott Bradley; *ph:* Gene Moore; *prod mgr:* Fred Quimby; *col:* Tech. *sd:* WE. 9 min. • Butch, a tomcat, is plagued by the arrival of a group of orphan kittens discovered on his doorstep.

1158. Chiquita Banana Minute Movie Playlets *p.c.:* John Sutherland prods for United Fruit Co; *prod/dir:* John Sutherland; *des:* Dick Brown; *storyboards:* Chester W. Kuleza, James S. Campbell, Thomas A. Wright, Patrick J. White of the BBDO staff; *song: (lyrics)* Garth Montgomery; *(music)* Ken MacKenzie; *voice:* Monica Lewis; *col:* Ansco. *sd.* 3 min. *la/anim.* • **1947: Chiquita Banana's Reception** 9 Aug. **Chiquita Banana on the Air** 2 Oct. **Chiquita Banana Goes North** 27 Oct. **Chiquita Banana** 27 Oct. **Chiquita Banana Helps the Pieman** 27 Oct. **Chiquita Banana's Fan** 27 Oct. **Chiquita Banana Convinces the Cannibals** 27 Oct. **Chiquita Banana's Star Attraction** 27 Oct. • **1948: Chiquita Banana's Magic** 17 Jan. **Chiquita Banana's School for Brides** 2 Oct 1947. **Chiquita Banana's Beauty Treatment** 17 Jan. **Chiquita Banana Tells a**

Fortune 17 Jan. **Chiquita Banana Wins a Medal** 17 Jan. **Chiquita Banana Makes a Better Breakfast** 2 Oct. 1947 • Instructions from a Carmen Miranda–type banana in how to cook with bananas. The character of Chiquita Banana later carried on into TV commercials.

1159. Cholly Polly (*Phantasy*) 18 Dec. 1942; *p.c.:* Colum; *prod:* Dave Fleischer. *dir:* Alec Geiss; *story:* Jack Cosgriff; *anim:* Chic Otterstrom; *ed:* Edward Moore; *i&p:* Elizabeth F. McDowell; *mus:* Paul Worth; *ph:* Frank Fisher; *prod mgr:* Albert Spar; b&w. *sd:* RCA. 6 min. • The parrot is inspired to break up the dog and cat's friendship after reading "Mein Kramp"!

1160. Choo Choo Amigo (*Daffy Ditty*) 5 July 1946; *p.c.:* Plastic prods for UA; *prod:* John Sutherland, Larry Morey; *dir/story:* Frank Tashlin; *col:* Tech. *sd:* 8 min. • The old railroad locomotive is replaced by a modern streamliner that goes at such a pace that it wrecks everything in sight. The Mexican townsfolk fight for the return of the old locomotive. Model animation.

1161. Choose Your Weppins (*Popeye*) 31 May 1935; *p.c.:* The Fleischer Studio for Para; *prod:* Max Fleischer; *dir:* Dave Fleischer; *anim:* David Tendlar, George Germanetti; *voices:* Jack Mercer, Gus Wickie, Mae Questel; *mus:* Sammy Timberg; b&w. *sd:* WE. 7 min. • A felon enters Olive's pawn shop insisting on a good price for some stolen knives. Popeye intervenes and a fight breaks out.

1162. Chop Suey (*Paul Terry-Toons*) 24 Aug. 1930; *p.c.:* A-C for Educational/Fox; *dir:* Frank Moser, Paul Terry; *anim:* Arthur Babbitt; *mus:* Philip A. Scheib; b&w. *sd:* WE. 6 min. • The goings-on in a Chinese laundry. A girl mouse is kidnapped, leading to a chase across the rooftops by the hero.

1163. Chop Suey and Noodles (*Aesop's Film Fable*) 11 July 1926; *p.c.:* Fables Pictures Inc for Pathé; *dir:* Paul Terry; b&w. *sil.* 5 min. • Oriental cats and mice have a Tong war in a Chinatown laundry when the wicked laundry boss kidnaps his worker's girlfriend.

1164. Chow Hound (*Looney Tunes*) 16 June 1951; *p.c.:* WB; *dir:* Charles M. Jones; *story:* Michael Maltese; *anim:* Phil Monroe, Ben Washam, Lloyd Vaughan, Ken Harris; *lay:* Robert Gribbroek; *back:* Philip de Guard; *ed:* Treg Brown; *voices:* Mel Blanc, John T. Smith, Bea Benaderet; *mus:* Carl Stalling; *prod mgr:* John W. Burton; *prod:* Edward Selzer; *col:* Tech. *sd:* Vit. 7 min. • A bullying dog forces a hapless cat to steal food for him.

1165. Chris Columbo (*Terry-Toon*) 12 Aug. 1938; *p.c.:* TT for Fox; *dir:* Ed Donnelly; *mus:* Philip A. Scheib; b&w. *sd:* WE. 7 min. • Chris shoots dice for a loan from Queen Isabella and when he finally reaches America, the Indians take him over.

1166. Chris Columbus Jr. (*Oswald*) 25 June 1934; *p.c.:* Univ; *dir:* Walter Lantz; *story:* Victor McLeod; *anim:* Fred Avery, Jack Carr, Ray Abrams, Joe d'Igalo, Ernest Smythe; Virgil Ross; *mus:* James Dietrich; b&w. *sd:* WE. 9 min. • Manned with a crew of jailbirds, young Chris sails around the world. However, mutiny is afoot and, while the whole crew battles, land is discovered.

1167. Christmas Cheer (*Aesop's Film Fable*) 12 Dec. 1927; *p.c.:* Fables Pictures Inc for Pathé; *dir:* Paul Terry, John Foster; b&w. *sil.* 5 min. • No story available.

1168. Christmas Comes but Once a Year (*Color Classic*) 4 Dec. 1936; *p.c.:* The Fleischer Studio for Para; *prod:* Max Fleischer; *dir:* Dave Fleischer; *anim:* Seymour Kneitel, William Henning; *voices:* Everett Clark; *mus/songs:* Tot Seymour, Sammy Timberg, Bob Rothberg; *col:* Tech. *sd:* WE. 8 min. • Grampy arrives at the orphanage to create some novel toys for the waifs at Christmas.

1169. Christmas Seals *dir/anim:* Harry Bailey; b&w. *st.* • Christmas advertising film. No further information available.

1170. Christopher Crumpet 25 June 1953; *p.c.:* UPA for Colum; *ex prod:* Stephen Bosustow; *dir:* Robert Cannon; *story:* T. Hee, Robert Cannon; *anim:* Bill Melendez, Frank Smith, Tom McDonald; *lay:* T. Hee; *back:* Jules Engel; *voices:* Marvin Miller, Marian Richman; *mus:* George Bruns; *prod mgr:* Herbert Klynn; *col:* Tech. *sd:* RCA. 7 min. *Academy Award nomination.* • A small boy becomes a chicken when he can't get his own way. He wants a rocket ship and when his father isn't able to get him one, he resorts to the chicken.

1171. Christopher Crumpet's Playmate 8 Sept. 1955; *p.c.:* UPA for Colum; *ex prod:* Stephen Bosustow; *dir:* Robert Cannon; *story:* T. Hee, Robt. Cannon; *anim:* Frank Smith, Alan Zaslove, Barney Posner; *lay:* T. Hee; *back:* Jules Engel; *voices:* Marvin Miller, Marian Richman; *mus:* Dennis Farnon; *prod mgr:* Herbert Klynn; *col:* Tech. *sd:* RCA. 6 min. • Christopher's imaginary playmate is an elephant named Webster. When Mr. Crumpet's rival for his job hears of this, he tries to convince the boss that the whole family is unstable.

1172. The Chump Champ (*Droopy*) 4 Nov. 1950; *p.c.:* MGM; *dir:* Tex Avery; *story:* Rich Hogan; *anim:* Grant Simmons, Walter Clinton, Michael Lah; *sets:* John Didrik Johnsen; *ed:* Fred MacAlpin; *voices:* Daws Butler, Paul Frees; *mus:* Scott Bradley; *prod:* Fred Quimby; *col:* Tech. *sd:* WE. 6 min. • Droopy and Spike compete in the Olympic Games.

1173. Cilly Goose (*Noveltoon*) 23 Apr. 1944; *p.c.:* Famous for Para; *dir:* Seymour Kneitel; *story:* Joe Stultz; *anim:* Graham Place, Abner Kneitel, Otto Feuer; *mus:* Winston Sharples; *prod mgr:* Sam Buchwald; *col:* Tech. *sd:* RCA. 8 min. • A goose wants to impress the others, so she paints her egg gold and becomes a "Wonderbird," not realizing the consequences.

1174. Cinder Alley (*Krazy Kat*) 12 Mar. 1934; *p.c.:* Winkler for Colum; *prod:* Charles Mintz; *story:* Harry Love; *anim:* Allen Rose, Preston Blair; *mus:* Joe de Nat; *prod mgr:* James Bronis; b&w. *sd:* WE. 6 min. • No story available.

1175. Cinderella (*Krazy Kat*) 14 Aug. 1930; *p.c.:* Winkler for Colum; *anim:* Ben Harrison, Manny Gould; *mus:* Joe de Nat; *prod:* George Winkler; b&w. *sd:* WE. 6 min. • Krazy is involved in a diverting extravaganza on the popular fairy tale.

1176. Cinderella (*Paul Terry-Toons*) 28 May 1933; *p.c.:* Moser & Terry for Educational/Fox; *dir:* Paul Terry, Frank Moser; *mus:* Philip A. Scheib; b&w. *sd:* WE. 6 min. • A caricature of the timeless story with the ugly sisters and the King with a domineering wife.

1177. Cinderella 4 Mar. 1950; *p.c.:* Walt Disney prods for RKO; *dir:* Wilfred Jackson, Hamilton Luske, Clyde Geronimi; story from original by Charles Perrault; *story adapt:* William Peed, Erdman Penner, Ted Sears, Winston Hibler, Homer Brightman, Harry Reeves, Kenneth Anderson, Joe Rinaldi; *anim:* Eric Larson, Ward Kimball, Milt Kahl, Ollie Johnston, Frank Thomas, Marc Davis, John Lounsbery, Les Clark, Wolfgang Reitherman, Norm Ferguson; *anim:* Don Lusk, Phil Duncan, Hugh Fraser, Hal King, Fred Moore, Harvey Toombs, Judge Whitaker, Cliff Nordberg, Marvin Woodward, Hal Ambro, George Nicholas, Ken O'Brien; *fx:* George Rowley, Josh Meador, Jack Boyd; *des:* Mary Blair, John Hench, Claude Coats, Don da Gradi; *lay:* McLaren Stewart, A. Kendall O'Connor, Tom Codrick, Hugh Hennesy, Lance Nolley, Charles Philippi, Don Griffith, Thor Putnam; *back:* Brice Mack, Art Riley, Merle Cox, Ralph Hulett, Ray Huffine, Dick Anthony, Thelma Witmer; *ed:* Donald Halliday; *voices: Cinderella:* Ilene Woods; *The Stepmother:* Eleanor Audley; *The Fairy Godmother:* Verna Felton; *The King/Grand Duke:* Luis van Rooten *The Prince:* William Phipps; *Drizzella:* Rhoda Elaine Williams; *Anastasia:* Lucille Bliss; *Narration:* Betty Lou Gerson; *Jacq/Gus:* James MacDonald; *The Prince (singing voice):* Mike Douglas; *Footman:* Larry Gray; *Lucifer:* June Foray; *Bruno:* Earl Edward Keen; *Bird whistles:* Marion Darlington, Clarence Nash; *Mice:* Clint MacCauley, Helen Seibert, June Sullivan, Lucille Williams, Thurl Ravenscroft, John Woodbury; *also:* John Fontaine; *Chorus:* The Jud Conlon Chorus; *mus:* Oliver Wallace, Paul Smith; *orch:* Joseph Dubin; *songs:* Mack David, Jerry Livingston, Al Hoffman; *special process:* Ub Iwerks; *sd rec:* C.O. Slyfield, Harold J. Steck, Robert O. Cook; *mus ed:* Al Teeter; *col:* Tech. *sd:* RCA. 74 min. • Classic fairy tale of a badly treated scullery maid who, with help from her Fairy Godmother, is able to go to the Royal Ball and meet her Prince Charming.

1178. Cinderella Blues (*Aesop's Sound Fable*) 12 Apr. 1931; *p.c.:* Van Beuren for RKO/Pathé; *dir:* John Foster, Harry Bailey; *mus:* Gene Rodemich; b&w. *sd:* RCA. 7 min. • The "Cinderella" story with an all-animal cast. The Prince follows Cinderella in his private airplane.

1179. Cinderella Goes to a Party (*Color Rhapsody*) 3 May 1942; *p.c.:* Colum; *prod:* Frank Tashlin; *dir:* Alec Geiss; *story:* Jack Cosgriff; *anim:* William Shull; *sets:* Clark Watson; *ed:* Edward Moore; *voices:* Sara Berner, Ira "Buck" Woods; *mus:* Paul Worth; *ph:* Frank Fisher; *prod mgr:* Ben Schwalb; *col:* Tech. *sd:* RCA. 7 min. • Lockheed riveter Cindy is whisked away in a B19 (made from pots and pans) to a USO ball.

1180. Cinderella Meets Fella (*Merrie Melodies*) 23 July 1938; *p.c.:* Leon Schlesinger prods for WB; *dir:* Fred Avery; *story:* Ted Pierce, Robert Clampett; *anim:* Virgil Ross; *sets:* John Didrik Johnsen; *ed:* Tregoweth E. Brown; *voices:* Dave Weber, Elvia Allman, Bernice Hansel, Fred Avery, Paul Taylor Chorus; *mus:* Carl W. Stalling; *prod sup:* Henry Binder, Raymond G. Katz; *col:* Tech. *sd:* Vit. 7 min. • Cinderella arrives at the ball in a stagecoach where she meets Prince Chowmein (played by Egghead). She departs at midnight and when the Prince comes to search for her, he finds she has grown tired of waiting and is now sitting in the audience watching the cartoon.

1181. The Circus (*Aesop's Film Fable*) 29 Sept. 1923; *p.c.:* Fables Pictures Inc for Pathé; *dir:* Paul Terry. b&w. *sil.* 5 min. • The farm animals go to the circus. Mothers Hen and Cat adopt ingenious ruses to get their respective broods in for free.

1182. Circus (*Flip the Frog*) 27 Aug. 1932; *p.c.:* Celebrity prods for MGM; *prod/dir:* Ub Iwerks; b&w. *sd:* PCP. 6 min. • Hot-Dog seller, Flip, chases a pickpocket.

1183. Circus Capers (*Aesop's Sound Fable*) 28 Sept. 1930; *p.c.:* Van Beuren for Pathé; *dir:* John Foster, Harry Bailey; *mus:* Gene Rodemich; b&w. *sd:* RCA. 10 min. • A circus clown's unrequited love for the bareback rider finds her in the arms of another after being shot from a cannon.

1184. The Circus Comes to Clown (*Screen Song*) 26 Dec. 1947; *p.c.:* Famous for Para; *dir:* I. Sparber; *story:* Bill Turner, Larz Bourne; *anim:* Tom Johnson, Frank Endres; *sets:* Anton Loeb; *voices:* Jack Mercer, Jackson Beck; *mus:* Winston Sharples; *song:* George Leybourne, Alfred Lee; *prod mgr:* Sam Buchwald; *col:* Pola. *sd:* RCA. 7 min. • A circus theme with a spectacular finale involving a pig diving through a blazing hoop.

1185. Circus Days (*Paul Terry-Toon*) 6 Sept. 1935; *p.c.:* Moser & Terry for Educational/Fox; *dir:* Paul Terry, Frank Moser; *mus:* Philip A. Scheib; b&w. *sd:* WE. 6 min. • The circus comes to town with some unusual "turns."

1186. Circus Daze 16 Jan. 1937; *p.c.:* MGM; *prod/dir:* Hugh Harman, Rudolf Ising; *voices:* Eugene Jackson; *mus:* Scott Bradley; *col:* Tech. *sd:* WE. 9 min. • Bosko, Honey and Bruno visit the circus. Bruno explores and runs afoul of a flea circus.

1187. A Circus Romance (*Aesop's Sound Fable*) 25 June 1932; *p.c.:* Van Beuren for RKO; *dir:* John Foster, Harry Bailey; *mus:* Gene Rodemich; b&w. *sd:* RCA. 6 min. • No story available.

1188. Circus Time (*Toby the Pup*) 25 Jan. 1931; *p.c.:* Winkler for RKO; *prod:* Charles Mintz; *dir:* Dick Huemor, Sid Marcus; *mus:* Joe de Nat; b&w. *sd:* 8 min. • The animals stage a circus.

1189. Circus Today (*Merrie Melodies*) 22 June 1940; *p.c.:* Leon Schlesinger prods for WB; *dir:* Fred Avery; *story:* Jack Miller, Robert Clampett, Melvin Millar; *sets:* Sid Sutherland; *ed:* Treg Brown. *voices:* Edward I. Marr, Mel Blanc; *mus:* Carl W. Stalling; *prod sup:* Henry Binder, Raymond G. Katz; *col:* Tech. *sd:* Vit. 8 min. • A look at various circus acts at Jingaling Bros Circus.

1190. Cirrhosis of the Louvre (*Inspector*) 9 Mar. 1966; *p.c.:* Mirisch/Geoffrey/DFE for UA; *dir:* Gerry Chiniquy; *story:* John W. Dunn; *anim:* Bob Matz, Warren Batchelder, Norm McCabe, George Grandpré, Manny Perez, Don Williams; *sets:* T.M. Yakutis; *ed:* Lee Gunther; *voices:* Pat Harrington Jr., Paul Frees; *mus:* William Lava; *theme tune:* Henry Mancini; *prod sup:* Bill Orcutt; *col:* DeLuxe. *sd:* RCA. 6 min. • The Inspector and Doux-Doux guard The Louvre against a notorious art thief known as "The Blotch."

1191. City Kitty (*Noveltoon*) 18 July 1952; *p.c.:* Famous for Para; *dir:* I. Sparber; *story:* I. Klein; *anim:* Al Eugster, George Germanetti; *sets:* Anton Loeb; *voices:* Sid Raymond, Jack Mercer; *mus:* Winston Sharples; *ph:* Leonard McCormick; *prod mgr:* Seymour Shultz; *col:* Tech. *sd:* RCA. 7 min. • Katnip takes a much-needed vacation but after problems with ants, fishing and a mosquito, he beats a hasty retreat to the city.

1192. City Slicker (*Little Roquefort*) Mar. 1952; *p.c.:* TT for Fox; *dir:* Mannie Davis; *story:* Tom Morrison; *anim:* Jim Tyer; *back:* Art Bartsch; *mus:* Philip A. Scheib; *ph:* Douglas Moye; *col:* Tech. *sd:* RCA. 6 min. • Roquefort visits his cousin in the country but finds rural life more hazardous than in the city.

1193. The City Slicker (*Scrappy*) 8 July 1938; *p.c.:* Charles Mintz prods for Colum; *story:* Allen Rose; *anim:* Harry Love, Louie Lilly; *voice:* Robert Winkler; *mus:* Joe de Nat; *prod mgr:* James Bronis; b&w. *sd:* RCA. 6 min. • Scrappy plays practical jokes on his country cousin. The cousin eventually sends him packing by faking the measles.

1194. City Slickers (*Aesop's Film Fable*) 12 June 1928; *p.c.:* Fables Pictures Inc for Pathé; *dir:* Paul Terry, Harry Bailey; b&w. *sil.* 5 min. • A farm yokel travels to the wicked city.

1195. City Slickers 18 Oct. 1991; *p.c.:* Castle Rock Entertainment for Colum; *title des:* Wayne Fitzgerald; *anim:* Kurtz and Friends; *col:* CFI. *sd:* Dolby stereo. 2¹/₂ min. Panavision. • The animated credits for this live-action comedy about a group of "tenderfeet" on a wild west round-up portray a cowboy struggling with rope tricks.

1196. City Slickers II: The Legend of Curly's Gold 23 Sept. 1994; *p.c.:* Castle Rock Entertainment for Colum; *title anim:* Bob Kurtz; *anim:* Kurtz & Friends; *titles:* Pittard-Sullivan-Fitzgerald; *mus:* Marc Shaiman; *col:* Tech. *sd:* Dolby stereo. 3 min. Panavision. • Live-action comedy concerning a treasure hunt. The animated credits involve a cowboy being haunted by a ghost.

1197. Clash and Carry (*Chilly Willy*) 25 Apr. 1961; *p.c.:* Walter Lantz prods for Univ; *dir:* Jack Hannah; *story:* Homer Brightman; *anim:* Roy Jenkins, Al Coe; *sets:* Ray Huffine, Art Landy; *voice:* Paul Frees; *mus:* Eugene Poddany; *prod mgr:* William E. Garity; *col:* Tech. *sd:* RCA. 6 min. • Chilly adopts many ways to steal fish from Wally Walrus' fish market.

1198. Claws for Alarm (*Merrie Melodies*) 22 May 1954; *p.c.:* WB; *dir:* Charles M. Jones; *story:* Michael Maltese; *anim:* Lloyd Vaughan, Ken Harris, Ben Washam, Abe Levitow, Richard Thompson; *lay:* Maurice Noble; *back:* Philip de Guard; *ed:* Treg Brown; *voices:* Mel Blanc; *mus:* Carl Stalling; *prod mgr:* John W. Burton; *prod:* Edward Selzer; *col:* Tech. *sd:* Vit. 7 min. • Porky and Sylvester spend a terrifying night in a hotel infested with homicidal mice.

1199. Claws in the Lease (*Merrie Melodies*) 9 Nov. 1963; *p.c.:* WB; *dir:* Robert McKimson; *story:* John Dunn; *anim:* Warren Batchelder, George Grandpré, Ted Bonnicksen; *lay:* Robert Gribbroek; *back:* Richard H. Thomas; *ed:* Treg Brown; *voices:* Mel Blanc, Nancy Wible; *mus:* Bill Lava; *prod mgr:* William Orcutt. *prod:* David H. DePatie. *col:* Tech. *sd:* Vit. 7 min. • Sylvester Junior is adopted by a lady who wants to give him a decent home but when father arrives on her doorstep it's a different story.

1200. Clay (or The Origin of the Species) July 1965; *p.c.:* Harvard University for Pathé Contemporary; *dir/anim:* Elliott Noyes Jr.; *mus:* Sammy Saltonstall; b&w. *snd.* 8 min. *Academy Award nomination.* • Clay animation tracing our beginnings. Originally made as an excercise at college and ending in being nominated for an Oscar.

1201. Clean Pastures (*Merrie Melodies*) 22 May 1937; *p.c.:* Leon Schlesinger prods for WB; *dir:* I. Freleng; *story/des:* T. Hee; *anim:* Paul Smith, Phil Monroe; *lay:* Griff Jay; *back:* Arthur Loomer; *ed:* Tregoweth E. Brown; *voices:* (Peter) Lind Hayes, The Basin Street Boys, Dave Weber, The Sportsmen Quartet; *mus:* Carl W. Stalling; *prod sup:* Henry Binder, Raymond G. Katz; *col:* Tech. *sd:* Vit. 7 min. • St. Peter sends angels to lead the Harlem jazz enthusiasts on a straight path to Heaven away from a seedy nightclub. Caricatures of Step'n Fetchit, Fats Waller, Bill Robinson, Cab Calloway, Al Jolson, Louis Armstrong and the Mills Brothers.

1202. A Clean Shaven Man (*Popeye*) 7 Feb. 1936; *p.c.:* The Fleischer Studio for Para; *prod:* Max Fleischer; *dir:* Dave Fleischer; *anim:* Seymour Kneitel, Roland Crandall; *voices:* Jack Mercer, Mae Questel, Gus Wickie; *mus:* Sammy Timberg; b&w. *sd:* WE. 7 min. • Olive sings about wanting "A Clean Shaven Man," so Popeye and Bluto go about smartening themselves up.

1203. Clean Sweep (*Honey Halfwitch*) June 1967; *p.c.:* Para Cartoons. *ex prod:* Shamus Culhane; *dir:* Chuck Harriton; *story:* Howard Post; *anim:* Doug Crane, Irv Dressler, Nick Tafuri; *sets:* Danté Barbetta, Dave Ubinas; *voices:* Bob MacFadden; *mus:* Winston Sharples; *prod sup:* Harold Robins, Burt Hanft; *col:* Tech. *sd:* RCA. 6¹/₂ min. • Cousin Maggie and Honey go forth into the outside world to get their magic broomstick repaired.

1204. Clean Up Week (*Aesop's Film Fable*) 28 Feb. 1925; *p.c.:* Fables Pictures Inc for Pathé; *dir:* Paul Terry; b&w. *sil.* 5 min. • The Farmer's cat does a "Mary Pickford" skating act with scrubbing brushes with the mice putting every hazard in his way.

1205. Cleaning House *(Captain & the Kids)* 19 Feb. 1938; *p.c.:* MGM; *dir:* Robert Allen; *voice:* Billy Bletcher, Martha Wentworth, Jeanne Dunne; *mus:* Scott Bradley; *prod mgr:* Fred Quimby; *col:* sep. *sd:* WE. 7 min. • Der Captain feigns illness to avoid doing the chores. Hans and Fritz pose as a doctor who gives him "the works."

1206. Cleaning Up!!? Kansas 1920; *p.c.:* Walt Disney for Kansas City; *dir:* Walt. Disney; b&w. *sil.* 1 min. • A crook is told to "Get out and stay out" of Kansas City and ladies' stockings are depicted as being "Rolled" this year. In connection with a big Kansas City clean-up campaign.

1207. Clint Clobber's Cat *(Clint Clobber)* July 1957; *p.c.:* TT for Fox; *ex prod:* Bill Weiss. *sup:* Gene Deitch; *dir:* Connie Rasinski; *story/sd sup:* Tommy Morrison; *story:* Larz Bourne, Bob Kuwahara; *anim:* Ed Donnelly, Larry Silverman, Mannie Davis, Johnny Gent, Jim Tyer, Al Chiarito; *des:* Al Kouzel; *lay:* Art Bartsch; *back:* Bill Hilliker; *voices:* Doug Moye, Lionel Wilson; *mus:* Phil Scheib; *ph:* Doug Moye; *prod mgr:* Frank Schudde; *col:* Tech. *sd:* RCA. 7 min. CS. • Clobber's "No Pets Allowed" policy is quickly put into practice when a nearsighted tenant adopts a stray dog in the belief it's a cat.

1208. Clippety Clobbered *(Looney Tunes)* 12 Mar. 1966; *p.c.:* DFE for WB; *dir:* Rudy Larriva; *story:* Tom Dagenais; *anim:* Bob Bransford, Hank Smith, Virgil Ross; *lay:* Don Shepard; *back:* Anthony Rizzo; *ed:* Al Wahrman; *mus:* Bill Lava; *col:* Tech. *sd:* Vit. 6 min. • The Coyote's quest of the Road-Runner includes using invisible paint, covering himself in extra strong rubber and using a high-powered spray to propel himself.

1209. Cloak and Stagger *(Terry-Toon)* Aug. 1956; *p.c.:* TT for Fox; *dir:* Connie Rasinski; *story:* Tom Morrison; *anim:* Jim Tyer; *mus:* Philip A. Scheib; *ph:* Douglas Moye; *col:* Tech. *sd:* RCA. 6 min. CS. • Good Deed Daly pursues a villain in order to return a bomb to him.

1210. Clobber's Ballet Ache *(Clint Clobber)* Jan. 1959; *p.c.:* TT for Fox; *ex prod:* Bill Weiss; *sup:* Gene Deitch; *dir:* Connie Rasinski; *story:* Larz Bourne, Eli Bauer; *story dir:* Tom Morrison; *anim:* Larry Silverman, Bob Kuwahara, Johnny Gent, Jim Tyer, Ed Donnelly, Vinnie Bell; *des:* Eli Bauer; *back:* Bill Hilliker; *voices:* Allen Swift; *mus:* Phil Scheib; *prod mgr:* Sparky Schudde; *col:* Tech. *sd:* RCA. 7 min. CS. • Clobber offers "The Champ" his attic to work-out in but first has to evict a ballet dancing tenant from there.

1211. Clock Cleaners *(Mickey Mouse)* 15 Oct. 1937; *p.c.:* Walt Disney prods for RKO; *dir:* Ben Sharpsteen; *asst dir:* Lou Debney; *story dir:* Webb Smith, Otto Englander; *story:* Otto Englander, Jack Kinney, Jack Hannah; *anim:* Chuck Couch, Gilles de Tremaudan, Alfred Eugster, Wolfgang Reitherman, William O. Roberts; *character des:* Ferdinand Huszti Horvath; *lay:* A. Kendall O'Connor; *back:* R.C. Clark; *voices:* Clarence Nash, Pinto Colvig, Walt Disney; *mus:* Paul J. Smith, Oliver Wallace; *col:* Tech. *sd:* RCA. 8 min. • Mickey, Donald and Goofy clean out the clock tower. Each have their problems culminating in the Goof precariously staggering around the outside ledges in a semi-concious state.

1212. The Clock Goes Round and Round *(Scrappy)* 16 Oct. 1937; *p.c.:* Charles Mintz prods for Colum; *story:* Art Davis; *anim:* Sid Marcus; *mus:* Joe de Nat; *prod mgr:* James Bronis; b&w. *sd:* RCA. 6 min. • To avoid school, Scrappy sets all his clocks so they stop, then dreams that the world and all its clocks are in a state of immobility.

1213. The Clock Maker's Dog *(Terry-Toon)* Jan. 1956; *p.c.:* TT for Fox; *dir:* Connie Rasinski; *story:* Tom Morrison; *anim:* Jim Tyer; *mus:* Philip A. Scheib; *ph:* Douglas Moye; *col:* Tech. *sd:* RCA. 7 min. • A dog yearns to be a part of the famous St. Bernard rescue team in the Alps but can't quite make the grade.

1214. The Clock Store *(Silly Symphony)* 16 Sept. 1931; *p.c.:* Walt Disney prods for Colum; *dir:* Wilfred Jackson; *anim:* Charles Byrne, Johnny Cannon, Chuck Couch, Joseph d'Igalo, Gilles de Tremaudan, Hardie Gramatky, Albert Hurter, Jack King, Harry Reeves, Ben Sharpsteen, Cecil Surry, Rudy Zamora; *mus:* Frank E. Churchill; b&w. *sd:* PCP. 7 min. • Timepieces in a clock store come to life.

1215. The Clock Watcher *(Donald Duck)* 26 Jan. 1945; *p.c.:* Walt Disney prods for RKO; *dir:* Jack King; *ass dir:* Joel Greenhalgh; *story:* Harry Reeves, Rex Cox; *anim:* Don Towsley, Bill Justice, Judge Whitaker, Paul Allen, Al Coe, Tom Massey, Murray McClellan, Lee Morehouse; *fx:* Josh Meador, Ed Aardal; *lay:* Ernest Nordli; *back:* Howard Dunn; *voices:* Dehner Forkum, Clarence Nash; *mus:* Oliver Wallace; *col:* Tech. *sd:* RCA. 7 min. • Donald is made to work overtime in the gift-wrapping section of a department store.

1216. A Close Call *(Aesop's Sound Fable)* 1 Dec. 1929; *p.c.:* Van Beuren for Pathé; *dir:* John Foster, Harry Bailey; *mus:* Carl Edouarde; b&w. *sd:* RCA. 5 min. • Melodrama spoof with a villainous cat tying the mouse heroine to the sawmill. The Mounted Police arrive in time to save her.

1217. A Close Shave *(Terry-Toons)* 1 Oct. 1937; *p.c.:* TT for Educational/Fox; *dir:* Mannie Davis; *mus:* Philip A. Scheib; b&w. *sd:* WE. 6 min. • The Farmer gets a "Mad Russian" in his barber shop. Ozzie Ostrich interferes, causing the Russian to get really mad.

1218. Closed Mondays 1974; *p.c.:* Lighthouse prods; *dir/anim:* Will Vinton, Bob Gardiner; *voices:* Todd Oleson, Holly Johnson; *mus:* Bill Scream; *col.* *sd.* 7 min. • A drunk staggers into a closed art museum imagining the exhibits come to life. Clay animation.

1219. Closer Than a Brother *(Aesop's Film Fables)* 24 Oct. 1925; *p.c.:* Fables Pictures Inc for Pathé; *dir:* Paul Terry; b&w. *sil.* 6 min. • When Farmer Al tries to get rid of his faithful cat by throwing her into the ocean, a shark appears and the cat and her kittens emerge from its mouth. The shark, cat and kittens all chase Al over the horizon.

1220. The Clown *(Oswald)* 21 Dec. 1931; *p.c.:* Univ; *dir:* Walter Lantz, "Bill" Nolan; *anim:* Manuel Moreno, Ray Abrams, Fred Avery, Lester Kline, Vet Anderson; *mus:* James Dietrich; b&w. *sd:* WE. 7 min. • Clown Oswald rescues the pretty bareback rider from the evil Circus boss.

1221. Clown of the Jungle *(Donald Duck)* 20 June 1947; *p.c.:* Walt Disney prods for RKO; *dir:* Jack Hannah; *asst dir:* Bee Selck; *story:* Ray Patin, Payne Thebault; *anim:* Volus Jones, Bob Carlson, Hal Ambro, Al Coe, Bill Justice, Hal King, Judge Whitaker; *fx:* Andy Engman, Josh Meador; *lay:* Yale Gracey; *back:* Thelma Witmer; *voices:* Larry Keating, Clarence Nash, José Oliveira, Faith Kruger, Betty Stevens, Betty Ward; *mus:* Oliver Wallace; *col:* Tech. *sd:* RCA. 6 min. • The Aracuran Bird delights in ruining every wildlife photo Donald tries to take.

1222. Clown on the Farm *(Noveltoon)* 22 Aug. 1952; *p.c.:* Famous Studio for Para; *dir:* Seymour Kneitel; *story:* Carl Meyer, Jack Mercer; *anim:* Dave Tendlar, Martin Taras; *sets:* Robert Connavale; *voices:* Sid Raymond, Jackson Beck, Cecil Roy, Jack Mercer; *mus:* Winston Sharples; *ph:* Leonard McCormick; *prod mgr:* Seymour Shultz; *col:* Tech. *sd:* RCA. 7 min. • Huey wants to join the circus and the fox is on hand to teach him all he wants to know.

1223. Clowning *(Paul Terry-Toons)* 5 Apr. 1931; *p.c.:* Terry, Moser & Coffman for Educational/Fox; *dir:* Paul Terry, Frank Moser; *anim:* Connie Rasinski, Vladimir Tytla; *mus:* Philip A. Scheib; b&w. *sd:* WE. 6 min. • The mice stage a circus. The villain kidnaps the girl and the clown traps him in a castle dungeon.

1224. The Clown's Little Brother *(Out of the Inkwell)* 6 July 1920; *p.c.:* Bray prods for Goldwyn; *prod/lla:* Max Fleischer; *dir:* Dave Fleischer; b&w. *sil.* *l/a/anim.* • A kid clown arrives by post and Ko-Ko plays with a real life kitten. • See: *Goldwyn-Bray Pictograph*

1225. The Clown's Pup *(Out of the Inkwell)* 30 Aug. 1919; *p.c.:* Bray prods for Goldwyn *prod/lla:* Max Fleischer; *dir:* Dave Fleischer; b&w. *sil.* *l/a/anim.* • Ko-Ko draws a dog ... so does Max and the two dogs fight. • See: *Goldwyn-Bary Pictographs*

1226. Club Life in the Stone Age *(Terry-Toon)* 23 Aug. 1940; *p.c.:* TT for Fox; *dir:* Mannie Davis; *story:* John Foster; *mus:* Philip A. Scheib; b&w. *sd:* RCA. 6 min. • The Cave-woman gets her man.

1227. Club Sandwich *(Paul Terry-Toons)* 25 Jan. 1931; *p.c.:* A-C for Educational/Fox; *dir:* Paul Terry, Frank Moser; *mus:* Philip A. Scheib; b&w. *sd:* WE. 9 min. • Farmer Al Falfa encounters dancing mice in a rodent nightclub.

1228. A Coach for Cinderella 1936; *p.c.:* The Jamison Handy Organization for Chevrolet; *dir:* Jam Handy; *anim:* Jim Tyer; *col:* Tech. *sd:* WE. 9 min. • The elves help build Cinderella the latest model Chevrolet to take her to the ball.

1229. Coal Black and De Sebben Dwarfs *(Merrie Melodies)* 26

Dec. 1942; *p.c.:* Leon Schlesinger prods for WB; *dir:* Robert Clampett; *story:* Warren Foster; *anim:* Rod Scribner, Robert McKimson, Virgil Ross, Sid Sutherland; *des:* Gene Hazelton; *sets:* Michael Sasanoff; *ed:* Treg Brown; *voices:* Vivian Dandridge, Zoot Watson, Eddie Beal, Ruby Dandridge, Mel Blanc, Danny Webb; *mus:* Carl W. Stalling, Eddie Beal Trio; *prod sup:* Henry Binder, Raymond G. Katz; *col:* Tech. *sd:* RCA. 7 min. • "Snow White" in blackface! The wicked Queen sends for "Murder Inc" to dump So White in the woods where she comes across an Army encampment housing seven black GIs.

1230. Coast to Coast (*Aesop's Film Fable*) 18 Apr. 1928; *p.c.:* Fable Pictures Inc for Pathé; *dir:* Paul Terry, Frank Moser; b&w. *st:* 5 min. • Farmer Al Falfa and his cat enter a "coast to coast" auto race. All sorts of things happen to the cars along the way.

1231. Cobs and Robbers (*Barney Bear*) 14 Mar. 1953; *p.c.:* MGM; *dir:* Dick Lundy; *story:* Jack Cosgriff, Heck Allen; *anim:* Michael Lah, Walter Clinton, Grant Simmons, Robert Bentley, Al Grandmain; *ed:* Jim Faris; *sets:* John Didrik Johnsen; *voices:* Paul Frees; *mus:* Scott Bradley; *ph:* Jack Stevens; *prod:* Fred Quimby; *col:* Tech. *sd:* WE. 7 min. • Two crows disguise themselves as a scarecrow in order to raid Barney's cornfield.

1232. The Cobweb Hotel (*Color Classic*) 15 May 1936; *p.c.:* The Fleischer Studio for Para; *prod:* Max Fleischer; *dir:* Dave Fleischer; *anim:* David Tendlar, William Sturm, Joseph Oriolo; *voice:* Jack Mercer; *song:* Sammy Timberg, Bob Rothberg; *ph:* Johnny Burks; *col:* Tech-2. *sd:* WE. 8 min. • An evil spider entices newlywed flys into his flytrap Honeymoon Hotel.

1233. Coca-Cola Commercials 1948; *p.c.:* Walter Lantz prods for the Coca-Cola Co. *dir:* Dick Lundy; *voice:* Pat Bishop; *mus:* Darrell Calker; *col:* Tech. *sd:* RCA. 3 min. • **Mountain Flower, Fisherman's Luck, Three Pigs, Aladdin's Lamp, Pancho's Rainbow, The Wise Little Woodchopper, Pirate Treasure, Jack and the Beanstalk, Woodland Symphony, Gallant Tailor, The Old Lady in the Shoe, The Town and Country Mouse**

1234. Cock-A-Doodle Deux Deux (*Inspector*) 15 June 1966; *p.c.:* Mirisch/Geoffrey/DFE for UA; *dir:* Robert McKimson; *story:* Michael O'Connor; *anim:* Manny Perez, Don Williams, Warren Batchelder, Ted Bonnicksen, Bob Matz, George Grandpré, Norm McCabe; *sets:* T.M. Yakutis; *ed:* Lee Gunther; *voices:* Pat Harrington Jr., Paul Frees, Helen Gerard; *mus:* William Lava; *theme tune:* Henry Mancini; *prod sup:* Bill Orcutt; *col:* DeLuxe. *sd:* RCA. 6min • The Inspector questions some chickens about a stolen diamond.

1235. Cock-A-Doodle Dino (*Noveltoon*) 6 Dec. 1957; *p.c.:* Para Cartoons; *dir:* I. Sparber; *story:* Larz Bourne; *anim:* Tom Golden; *sets:* Robert Owen; *voices:* Gwen Davies; *mus:* Winston Sharples; *ph:* Leonard McCormick; *prod mgr:* Seymour Shultz; *col:* Tech. *sd:* RCA. 6 min. • A dinosaur egg is hatched out by a hen who takes the creature as her own.

1236. Cock-a-Doodle Dog 10 Feb. 1951; *p.c.:* MGM; *dir/voice:* Tex Avery; *story:* Rich Hogan; *anim:* Michael Lah, Grant Simmons, Walter Clinton; *lay/des:* Ed Benedict; *back:* John Didrik Johnsen; *ed:* Jim Faris; *mus:* Scott Bradley; *prod:* Fred Quimby; *col:* Tech. *sd:* WE. 7 min. • A tired bulldog attempts to stop a rooster from crowing.

1237. Cock O' the Walk (*Silly Symphony*) 30 Nov. 1935; *p.c.:* Walt Disney prods for UA; *dir:* Ben Sharpsteen; *anim:* Clyde Geronimi, Hardie Gramatky, Jack Hannah, Eric Larson, John McManus, Wolfgang Reitherman, Leonard Sebring, Jim Tyer, Vladimir Tytla; *mus:* Frank E. Churchill, Albert Hay Malotte; *col:* Tech. *sd:* RCA. 8 min. • Barnyard battle between a hick rooster and a boxing bantam. Brilliantly realized pastiche of Busby Berkeley choreography.

1238. Cockaboody 1973; *p.c.:* The Hubley Studio for Howard Sayre Weaver; *prod/des/dir:* John Hubley, Faith Hubley; *anim:* Tissa David; *sets:* John Hubley; *voices:* Emily & Georgia Hubley; *i&p:* Faith Hubley, Genevieve Hirsch; *checking:* Sydel Solomon; *sd:* Media Sound Inc.; *ph:* I.F. Studios Inc.; *prod sup:* Robin Johnson, Maggie Glass; *col:* Tech. *snd.* 8 min. • Two children are left alone to explore their parents' bedroom. Award-winning film made in association with the animation class, Yale University School of Art with Robert Abramovitz and Katherine R. Lustman of the Yale Child Study Center as *consultant*s.

1239. Cockatoos for Two (*Color Rhapsody*) 13 Feb. 1947; *p.c.:* Colum; *prod:* Raymond Katz, Henry Binder; *dir:* Bob Wickersham; *story:* Michael

Maltese, Tedd Pierce; *anim:* Chic Otterstrom, Ben Lloyd; *lay:* Clark Watson; *back:* Al Boggs; *ed:* Richard S. Jensen; *voices:* Stan Freberg, Cal Howard; *mus:* Eddie Kilfeather; *creative consultant:* Bob Clampett; *ph:* Frank Fisher; *col:* Tech. *sd:* WE. 6 min. • A starving pigeon swaps places with a rare cockatoo about to be delivered to gourmet Peter Lorre who craves cockatoo as a "new eating sensation."

1240. The Cocky Bantam (*Phantasy*) 12 Nov. 1943; *p.c.:* Colum; *prod:* Dave Fleischer. *dir:* Paul Sommer; *story:* Sam Cobean; *anim:* Volus Jones, Basil Davidovich; *voice:* Harry E. Lang; *mus:* Eddie Kilfeather; *ph:* Frank Fisher; *prod mgr:* Albert Spar; b&w. *sd:* RCA. 6 min. • A falcon buys a Black Market chicken only to have the bird turn out to be an FBI agent.

1241. Cocky Cockroach (*Paul Terry-Toons*) 10 July 1932. *p.c.:* Moser & Terry for Educational/Fox; *dir:* Paul Terry, Frank Moser; *mus:* Philip A. Scheib; b&w. *sd:* WE. 6 min. • Performed as Grand Opera, the hero saves his girl from a villainous spider.

1242. Codfish Balls (*Paul Terry-Toons*) 15 June 1930; *p.c.:* A-C for Educational/Fox; *dir:* Paul Terry, Frank Moser; *anim:* Arthur Babbitt, Frank Moser; *mus:* Philip A. Scheib; b&w. *sd:* WE. 6 min. • A fish chases the cat.

1243. Cohl, Emile b&w. st. • **1913:** Universal Trade Mark Mar. Eclair Trade Mark Mar. W.T. & M.W. Trade Mark May. Diana Film and Co. Trade Mark Sept. Thaw & l'Araignes Sept. • Animated trade symbols made by the celebrated French animator for American distribution. • See: *Eclair Journal*; *The Newlyweds*

1244. Cold Feet (*Oswald*) 13 Aug. 1930; *p.c.:* Univ; *dir:* Walter Lantz; *anim:* "Bill" Nolan, Ray Abrams, Manuel Moreno, Clyde Geronimi, "Pinto" Colvig; *mus:* James Dietrich; b&w. *sd:* WE. 6 min. • No story available.

1245. A Cold Romance (*Mighty Mouse*) Apr. 1949; *p.c.:* TT for Fox; *dir:* Mannie Davis; *story:* John Foster; *anim:* Jim Tyer; *voices:* Roy Halee, Tom Morrison; *mus:* Philip A. Scheib; *ph:* Douglas Moye; *col:* Tech. *sd:* RCA. 7 min. • While in the Yukon, Oil Can Harry captures Nell, who is fishing for furs. Mighty Mouse soon arrives to sort matters out.

1246. Cold Steel (*Aesop's Film Fable*) 23 June 1929; *p.c.:* Fables Pictures Inc for Pathé; *dir:* Paul Terry; b&w. *sil.* 5 min. • The boy and girl's romantic dream is punctured by the outbreak of war. The boy mouse joins the Army who fire catnip shells at the cats, drugging them. The cats retaliate by building a giant Trojan mechanical horse to hide in for a surprise attack. The mechanical horse drinks a ton of water and floods the cats out, leaving the mice to ride the Trojan horse to victory.

1247. Cold Storage (*Pluto*) 9 Feb. 1951; *p.c.:* Walt Disney prods for RKO; *dir:* Jack Kinney; *story:* Dick Kinney, Milt Schaffer; *anim:* George Nicholas, George Kreisl, Charles Nichols, Ed Aardal; *fx:* George Rowley, Jack Boyd; *lay:* Al Zinnen; *back:* Art Landy; *voices:* James MacDonald; *mus:* Joseph S. Dubin; *col:* Tech. *sd:* RCA. 7 min. • Pluto and a stork battle for occupancy of Pluto's kennel.

1248. Cold Turkey (*Oswald*) 14 Oct. 1929; *p.c.:* Univ; *anim:* Walter Lantz, "Bill" Nolan, Tom Palmer; *mus:* Bert Fiske; b&w. *sd:* WE. 6 min. • Oswald's brutal treatment towards a turkey in capturing him for luncheon.

1249. Cold Turkey (*Pluto*) 21 Sept. 1951; *p.c.:* Walt Disney prods for RKO; *dir:* Charles Nichols; *story:* Leo Salkin, Al Bertino; *anim:* Norman Ferguson, Marvin Woodward, Bob Carlson, Charles Nichols; *lay:* Lance Nolley; *back:* Thelma Witmer; *voices:* Dick Lane, Helen Seibert, Lucille Williams, James MacDonald; *mus:* Paul Smith; *col:* Tech. *sd:* RCA. 7 min. • Inspired by a TV commercial, Pluto and Milton the cat fight over a frozen turkey.

1250. Cold War (*Goofy*) 27 Apr. 1941; *p.c.:* Walt Disney prods for RKO; *dir:* Jack Kinney; *story:* Dick Kinney, Milt Schaffer; *anim:* Hugh Fraser, Ed Aardal, Wolfgang Reitherman, John Sibley; *fx:* Jack Boyd; *lay:* Al Zinnen; *back:* Art Riley; *voices:* Jack Rourke, Bob Jackman, Helen Parrish, Bill Anderson, James MacDonald; *mus:* Joseph S. Dubin; *col:* Tech. *sd:* RCA. 7 min. • Geef tries a selection of remedies to rid himself of a cold.

1251. College (*Oswald*) 26 Jan. 1931; *p.c.:* Univ; *dir:* Walter Lantz, "Bill" Nolan; *anim:* Clyde Geronimi, Manuel Moreno, Ray Abrams, Fred Avery, Lester Kline, "Pinto" Colvig; *voice:* Mickey Rooney; *mus:* James Dietrich; b&w. *sd:* WE. 7 min. • Soda Jerk Oswald enters the college cross country run against Putrid Pete.

1252. College Capers *(Aesop's Sound Fable)* 15 Mar. 1931; *p.c.:* Van Beuren for Pathé; *dir:* John Foster, Harry Bailey; *mus:* Gene Rodemich; b&w. *sd:* RCA. 6 min. • A football game featuring hippos, apes, etc..

1253. College Spirit *(Paul Terry-Toons)* 16 Oct. 1932; *p.c.:* Moser & Terry for Educational/Fox; *dir:* Paul Terry, Frank Moser; *mus:* Philip A. Scheib; b&w. *sd:* WE. 6 min. • A cat and mouse are rivals for the Campus cutie and fight out their differences in a football game.

1254. Colonel Heeza Liar *(series); p.c.:* Bray prods for Pathé; *prod:* John R. Bray. b&w. *sil. l/a/anim.* • **1913: Col. Heeza Liar in Africa** 29 Nov. • **1914: Col. Heeza Liar's African Hunt** 10 Jan. **Col. Heeza Liar, Shipwrecked** 14 Mar. **Col. Heeza Liar in Mexico** 18 Apr. **Col. Heeza Liar, Farmer** 18 May. **Col. Heeza Liar, Explorer** 15 Aug. **Col. Heeza Liar in the Wilderness** 26 Sept. **Col. Heeza Liar, Naturalist** 24 Oct. • **1916: Col. Heeza Liar on Strike** 17 Aug. **Col. Heeza Liar at the Vaudeville Show** 21 Dec. • The series continued as part of *Paramount-Bray Pictographs*, then reappeared with a new distributor; W.W. Hodkinson Corp and Vernon Stallings supervising direction and story. Walter Lantz is known to have animated, directed and appeared live in the series with Harry Squires handling the live-action camerawork. • **1922: Col. Heeza Liar's Treasure Island** 17 Dec. • **1923: Col. Heeza Liar and the Ghost** 14 Jan. **Col. Heeza Liar, Detective** 11 Feb. **Col. Heeza Liar and the Burglar** 11 Mar. **Col. Heeza Liar in the African Jungles** 3 June. **Col. Heeza Liar in Uncle Tom's Cabin** 8 June. **Col. Heeza Liar's Vacation** 5 Aug. **Col. Heeza Liar's Forbidden Fruit** 1 Nov. **Col. Heeza Liar, Strikebreaker** 1 Dec. • A subsequent series in 1924 was distributed by *Standard Cinema Corp* with Vernon Stallings still taking care of production. • **1924: Col. Heeza Liar, Nature Faker** 1 Jan. **Col. Heeza Liar's Mysterious Case** 1 Feb. **Col. Heeza Liar's Ancestors** 1 Mar. **Col. Heeza Liar's Knighthood** 1 Apr. **Col. Heeza Liar, Sky Pilot** 1 May. **Col. Heeza Liar, Daredevil** 1 June. **Col. Heeza Liar's Horseplay** 1 July. **Col. Heeza Liar, Cave Man** 1 Aug. **Col. Heeza Liar, Bull Thrower** 1 Sept. **Col. Heeza Liar the Lyin' Tamer** 1 Oct. **Col. Heeza Liar's Romance** 1 Nov. • Adventures of a braggadocio hunter patterned after Teddy Roosevelt. Most of these are lost in the annals of time but a few have been reviewed: **Col. Heeza Liar and the Burglar** The Colonel delves into the pages of a magazine and has an experience with the burglar he has been reading about. **Col. Heeza Liar and the Ghost** By means of a balloon and a shroud, the Colonel gets revenge on the artist by posing as a ghost. **Col. Heeza Liar, Detective** The Colonel goes in search of a stolen prize rooster for a $10,000 reward. **Col. Heeza Liar, Ghostbreaker** To prove ghosts are only mice and rats, the Colonel wagers to spend a week in a haunted house. The first night a ghost appears. **Col. Heeza Liar in Africa** The Colonel has many exploits with the African jungle animals, trying to better Teddy Roosevelt's record. **Col. Heeza Liar in the African Jungles** The Colonel has all manner of adventures up against some live-action animals. **Col. Heeza Liar in the Trenches** Heeza Liar is war correspondent for the "Daily Bluff." **Col. Heeza Liar, Nature Faker** Our hero treks across the desert and encounters a bear, a monkey and a kangaroo. **Col. Heeza Liar's Treasure Island** Upon hearing of the location of a treasure, the Colonel transports himself via radio to a desert isle and meets with some cannibals. **Col. Heeza Liar, Strikebreaker** The Colonel helps egg producton with some real-life chickens. **Col. Heeza Liar's Vacation** The Colonel meets with many adventures on a dairy farm. **Col. Heeza Liar, Shipwrecked** The Colonel sets sail for Mexico, is shipwrecked and suffers as only a liar can. **Col. Heeza Liar's Mysterious Case** Posing as notorious crook, "Klaxon Horn," the Colonel helps out two friends who owe rent by collecting money from passing motorists. One hands him a case full of bottles that turn out to be hair oil instead of Hooch. **Col. Heeza Liar, War Dog** While aboard his yacht, Heeza Liar has an encounter with a submarine. **Col. Heeza Liar Wins the Pennant** After reading a war article, the Colonel returns to No Man's Land to beat the Hun at their own game. • See: *Paramount-Bray Pictographs; Pathé News*

1255. Colonel Pepper's Mobilized Farm *(Sullivan Cartoon Comedy)* 20 Aug. 1917; *p.c.:* Powers for Univ; *prod/dir:* Pat Sullivan; b&w. *sil.* 4 min. • The hens on the farm are busy laying "Hen-Shells" for the war effort and the other farmyard critters are receiving training to be able to use the home-grown munitions.

1256. Color Rhythm *(Radio Dynamics)* 1942; *dir/anim:* Oskar Fischinger; col. sd. • Fischinger's unique use of color and music drawn directly onto film.

1257. Colored Cartoon Comics *(series of 26)* 1925; *p.c.:* Charles Bowers Cartoons for Short Film Syndicate; *prod/dir:* Charles Bowers; col. st. • Series untraced.

1258. Columbia Favorites *p.c.:* Colum; *col:* Tech. *sd:* RCA • **1947: Dreams on Ice** 30 Oct. **The Novelty Shop** 20 Nov. **Dr. Bluebird** 18 Dec. • **1948: In My Gondola** 22 Jan. **Animal Cracker Circus** 19 Feb. **Bon-Bon Parade** 8 Apr. **The House That Jack Built** 6 May. **The Untrained Seal** 15 July. **The Stork Takes a Holiday** 9 Sept. **Swing, Monkeys, Swing** 14 Oct. **The Little Match Girl** 25 Nov. **Glee Worms** 16 Dec. • **1949: A Boy and His Dog** 6 Jan. **Spring Festival** 17 Mar. **Indian Serenade** 5 May. **Two Lazy Crows** 13 July. **The Foxy Pup** 1 Sept. **Window Shopping** 6 Oct. **The Happy Tots** 3 Nov. **Hollywood Sweepstakes** 1 Dec. **Poor Elmer** 29 Dec. • **1950: Ye Olde Swap Shop** 19 Jan. **The Kangaroo Kid** 2 Feb. **Tom Thumb's Brother** 23 Mar. **The Wise Owl** 4 May. **Little Moth's Big Flame** 1 June. **The Timid Pup** 6 July. **The Gorilla Hunt** 3 Aug. **The Happy Tots' Expedition** 7 Sept. **Land of Fun** 5 Oct. **Peaceful Neighbors** 6 Nov. **The Foolish Bunny** 7 Dec. • **1951: Midnight Frolics** 11 Jan. **The Carpenters** 8 Feb. **Poor Little Butterfly** 15 Mar. **Jitterbug Knights** 15 Apr. **Birds in Love** 17 May. **The Air Hostess** 21 June. **The Egg Hunt** 28 July. **Merry Manikins** 23 Aug. **Horse on a Merry-Go-Round** 13 Sept. **The Shoemaker and the Elves** 18 Oct. **Lucky Pigs** 8 Nov. **Holiday Land** 13 Dec. • **1952: Snow Time** 17 Jan. **Bluebird's Baby** 14 Feb. **Monkey Love** 13 Mar. **Babes at Sea** 10 Apr. **Let's Go** 8 May. **Crop Chasers** 12 June. **The Mountain Ears** 10 July. **The Frog Pond** 14 Aug. **The Fox and the Grapes** 4 Sept. **Wacky Wigwams** 2 Oct. **Tollbridge Trouble** 6 Nov. **The Cuckoo I.Q.** 27 Nov. **Cinderella Goes to a Party** 11 Dec. • **1953: Plenty Below Zero** 8 Jan. **Tito's Guitar** 5 Feb. **Professor Small and Mr. Tall** 26 Feb. **Make Believe Revue** 12 Mar. **A Helping Paw** 7 May. **King Midas Jr.** 7 May. **The Mad Hatter** 28 May. **Mother Hen's Holiday** 18 June. **The Dream Kids** 9 July. **The Rocky Road to Ruin** 6 Aug. **Carnival Courage** 3 Sept. **Fiesta Time** 8 Oct. **Room and Bored** 5 Nov. **A Boy, a Gun and Birds** 26 Nov. **Skeleton Frolics** 17 Dec. • **1954: Tree for Two** 7 Jan. **Way Down Yonder in the Corn** 28 Jan. **Dog, Cat and Canary** 28 Feb. **The Egg Yegg** 31 Mar. **The Way of All Pests** 15 Apr. **Amoozin' but Confoozin'** 29 Apr. **A Cat, a Mouse and a Bell** 13 May. **The Disillusioned Bluebird** 27 May. **Mr. Moocher** 8 July. **The Herring Murder Mystery** 22 July. **Imagination** 2 Sept. **Red Riding Hood Rides Again** 7 Oct. **A-Hunting We Won't Go** 4 Nov. **Gifts from the Air** 25 Nov. **Mysto Fox** 9 Dec. • **1955: Polar Playmates** 6 Jan. **Catnipped** 3 Feb. **Unsure Runts** 7 Feb. **River Ribber** 10 Mar. **Treasure Jest** 7 Apr. **Picnic Panic** 12 May. **Mother Hubba Hubba Hubbard** 12 May. **Ku Ku Nuts** 2 June. **Scary Crows** 23 June. **Little Rover** 14 July. **Tooth Or Consequences** 1 Sept. **Up 'n' Atom** 6 Oct. **Hot Footlights** 3 Nov. **Rippling Romance** 24 Nov. **Foxy Flatfoots** 8 Dec. • **1956: Cagey Bird** 12 Jan. **Boston Beanie** 2 Feb. **Swiss Tease** 23 Feb. **A Pee-Kool-Yar Sit-Chee-Ay-Shun** 15 Mar. **Phoney Baloney** 5 Apr. **Pickled Puss** 19 Apr. **The Uncultured Vulture** 10 May. **Be Patient, Patient** 7 June. **Loco Lobo** 21 June. **Woodman, Spare That Tree** 12 July. **Leave Us Chase It** 4 Oct. **Topsy Turkey** 4 Oct. **Silent Tweetment** 1 Nov. **The Coo-Coo Bird Dog** 15 Nov. **Concerto in B-Flat** 13 Dec. • **1957: Robin Hoodlum** 17 Jan. **Fowl Brawl** 7 Feb. **The Magic Fluke** 21 Feb. **Cat-Tastrophy** 14 Mar. **Punchy De Leon** 2 May. **Wacky Quacky** 23 May. **Grape Nutty** 6 June. **Swing, Monkeys, Swing** 20 June. **Two Lazy Crows** 4 July. **Indian Serenade** 18 July. **The Miner's Daughter** 12 Sept. **Big House Blues** 10 Oct. **Giddyap** 7 Nov. **Snowtime** 21 Nov. **Let's Go** 12 Dec. • **1958: Family Circus** 16 Jan. **The Foxy Pup** 6 Feb. **The Popcorn Story** 20 Feb. **Dr. Bluebird** 30 Mar. **Georgie and the Dragon** 3 Apr. **The Wonder Gloves** 24 Apr. **A Boy and His Dog** 22 May. **The Happy Tots** 5 June. **The Oompahs** 19 June. **The Air Hostess** 7 July. • Reissue of every *Color Rhapsody* with opening credits replaced by a stock title. Including a selection of UPA cartoons. For credits and stories see under individual items.

1259. Come On In! The Water's Pink *(Pink Panther)* 10 Apr. 1968; *p.c.:* Mirisch/Geoffrey/DFE for UA; *dir:* Hawley Pratt; *story:* Jim Ryan; *anim:* Manny Perez, Warren Batchelder, Don Williams, Tom Ray, Manny Gould; *lay:* Dick Ung; *back:* Tom O'Loughlin; *ed:* Allan Potter; *mus:* Walter Greene; *theme tune:* Henry Mancini; *ph:* John Burton Jr.; *prod sup:* Harry Love, Dave DeTiege; *col:* DeLuxe. *sd:* RCA. 7 min. • Down at Bicep Beach the Panther is enjoying himself with inflatable gear until a muscle-bound bully interferes.

1260. Come Take a Trip in My Airship (*Screen Songs*) 24 May 1930; *p.c.:* The Fleischer Studio for Para; *prod:* Max Fleischer; *dir:* Dave Fleischer; *anim:* Seymour Kneitel; *song:* Charles K. Harris; *mus:* Art Turkisher; b&w. *sil.* 6½ min. • A piano is hoisted to the top floor of a skyscraper where a girl cat plays a tune and then goes off with her boyfriend in a dirigible. Live-action footage of an aerial view of New York.

1261. Come Take a Trip in My Airship (*Song Car-Tune*) 1925; *p.c.:* Inkwell Studio for Red Seal; *prod:* Max Fleischer; *dir:* Dave Fleischer; b&w. *sil.* 5 min. • No story available.

1262. Comic Book Land (*Terry-Toon*) Jan. 1950; *p.c.:* TT for Fox; *dir:* Mannie Davis; *story:* John Foster; *voices:* Arthur Kay, Roy Halee, Thomas Morrison; *mus:* Philip A. Scheib; *col:* Tech. *sd:* RCA. 6 min. • Gandy and Sourpuss have simultaneous dreams about visiting Comic Book Land. An ogre appears and makes off with the characters and Mighty Mouse comes to the rescue.

1263. Comin' Round the Mountain (*Screen Song*) 11 Mar. 1949; *p.c.:* Famous for Para; *dir:* I. Sparber; *story:* Bill Turner; *anim:* Tom Johnson, Frank Endres, Els Barthen; *sets:* Anton Loeb; *voices:* Jack Mercer; *mus:* Winston Sharples; *prod mgr:* Sam Buchwald; *col:* Tech. *sd:* RCA. 7 min. • A feud between The Catfields and the McHounds is put on hold with the arrival of the new school ma'rm ... a skunk!

1264. Comin' Thru the Rye (*Song Car-Tune*) 1 June 1926; *p.c.:* Inkwell Studio for Red Seal; *prod:* Max Fleischer; *dir:* Dave Fleischer; b&w. *sil.* 5 min. • No story available.

1265. Coming Out Party (*Inspector Willoughby*) Feb. 1963; *p.c.:* Walter Lantz prods for Univ; *dir:* Paul J. Smith; *story:* Dave DeTiege; *anim:* Les Kline, Al Coe, Art Davis; *sets:* Art Landy, Ray Huffine; *voice:* Dal McKennon; *mus:* Walter Greene; *prod mgr:* William E. Garity; *col:* Tech. *sd:* RCA. 6 min. • Inspector Willoughby tries to prevent a prison breakout.

1266. Commander Great Guy (*Sad Cat*) Nov. 1967; *p.c.:* TT for Fox; *dir/anim:* Art Bartsch; *col:* DeLuxe. *sd:* RCA. 6 min. • Latimore and Fenimore try their hands at being a TV super hero but Sad Cat puts them in their place. • See: *Sad Cat*

1267. Commando Duck (*Donald Duck*) 2 June 1944; *p.c.:* Walt Disney prods for RKO; *dir:* Jack King; *story:* Jack Hannah. *anim:* Paul Allen, Bill Justice, Hal King, Dick Lundy, Harvey Toombs, Don Towsley, Judge Whitaker; *fx:* Ed Aardal; *voices:* Dehner Forkum, Eddie Holden, Clarence Nash; *mus:* Oliver Wallace; *col:* Tech. *sd:* RCA. 7 min. • Pvt. Duck is dropped behind enemy lines. He journeys downstream in a rubber raft that inflates with water until it explodes, washing out a Jap airfield.

1268. Common Scents (*Loopy de Loop*) May 1962; *p.c.:* Hanna-Barbera for Colum; *prod/dir:* Joseph Barbera, William Hanna; *story dir:* Alex Lovy; *story:* Tony Benedict; *anim dir:* Charles A. Nichols; *anim:* Dick Lundy; *lay:* Lance Nolley; *back:* F. Montealegre; *ed:* Hank Gotzenberg; *voices:* Daws Butler, Don Messick, Julie Bennett; *mus:* Hoyt Curtin; *titles:* Lawrence Gobel; *prod sup:* Howard Hanson; *col:* East. *sd:* RCA. 6 min. • Loopy tries to convince a suicidal skunk that somebody must love him!

1269. Compressed Hare (*Merrie Melodies*) Aug. 1961; *p.c.:* WB; *dir:* Chuck Jones; *asst dir:* Maurice Noble; *story:* Dave DeTiege; *anim:* Ken Harris, Richard Thompson, Bob Bransford, Tom Ray; *fx:* Harry Love; *lay:* Corny Cole; *back:* Philip de Guard, William Butler; *ed:* Treg Brown; *voices:* Mel Blanc; *mus:* Milt Franklyn; *prod mgr:* William Orcutt; *prod:* David H. DePatie; *col:* Tech. *sd:* RCA. 7 min. • Wile E. Coyote tries to tempt Bugs to dinner at his place, finally resorting to using a giant electro-magnet that attracts all and sundry except our hero.

1270. The Conceited Donkey (*Aesop's Film Fable*) 11 Dec. 1921; *p.c.:* Fables Pictures Inc for Pathé; *dir:* Paul Terry; b&w. *sil.* 5 min. • The Farmer loads his donkey with a prize watermelon and heads for the fair. The donkey takes the spectator's praise for himself, bows and loses the melon.

1271. Concentrate (*Aesop's Sound Fable*) 4 May 1929; *p.c.:* Fables Pictures Inc for Pathé; *dir:* Paul Terry; *mus:* Josiah Zuro; *sd:* Maurice Manne; b&w. *sd:* RCA. 5 min. • Farmer Al Falfa reads that all sorts of feats can be achieved by concentration and gives it a try. He uses it to increase the hens'

laying power. The trouble starts when the animals get hold of the book on concentration and start abusing the powers.

1272. The Concert Kid (*Scrappy*) 2 Nov. 1934; *p.c.:* Winkler for Colum; *prod:* Charles Mintz; *story:* Sid Marcus; *anim:* Art Davis; *mus:* Joe de Nat; *prod mgr:* James Bronis; b&w. *sd:* RCA. 7 min. • Scrappy gives Oopy gum before performing his violin act and before they know it they all get entangled in the gooey substance.

1273. Concerto in B Flat Minor (*Color Rhapsody*) 20 Mar. 1942; *p.c.:* Colum; *prod:* Frank Tashlin; *dir:* Bob Wickersham; *story:* Leo Salkin, John Hubley; *anim:* William N. Shull, James Armstrong; *sets:* Clark Watson; *ed:* Edward Moore; *mus:* Edward Kilfeather; *ph:* Frank Fisher; *prod mgr:* Ben Schwalb; *col:* Tech. *sd:* RCA. 8 min. • An eccentric symphony conductor has trouble with his musicians while conducting Tchaikovsky's concerto.

1274. Condorman 7 Aug. 1981; *p.c.:* Walt Disney Prods., for BV; *title anim:* Michael Cedeno; *anim fx:* Jack Boyd; *mus:* Henry Mancini. *col:* Tech. *sd:* RCA/Dolby stereo. Panavision. 3 min. • Live-action comedy about a superhero. The animated titles show Condorman flying through the streets of Paris.

1275. Confederate Honey (*Merrie Melodies*) 30 Mar. 1940; *p.c.:* Leon Schlesinger prods for WB; *dir:* I. Freleng; *story:* Ben Hardaway; *anim:* Cal Dalton; *sets:* Robert L. Holdeman; *ed:* Treg Brown; *voices:* Jim Bannon, Arthur Q. Bryan, Sara Berner, Mel Blanc, The Sportsmen Quartet; *mus:* Carl W. Stalling; *prod sup:* Henry Binder, Raymond G. Katz; *col:* Tech. *sd:* Vit. 7 min. • Parody of *Gone with the Wind* starring Elmer Fudd as Cpt. Nett Cutler pursuing the beautiful Crimson O'Hairoil.

1276. Confidence (*Oswald*) 28 July 1933; *p.c.:* Univ; *dir:* Walter Lantz, "Bill" Nolan; *anim:* Ray Abrams, Fred Avery, Cecil Surry, Jack Carr, Ernest Smythe; *mus:* James Dietrich; b&w. *sd:* WE. 7 min. • Depression covers the country and Farmer Oswald flies to Washington to meet FDR! Loaded with confidence, he returns to inject his stock and the populous with it.

1277. Confusions of a Nutzi Spy (*Looney Tunes*) 26 Dec. 1942; *p.c.:* Leon Schlesinger prods for WB; *dir/lay:* Norman McCabe; *story:* Don Christensen; *anim:* I. Ellis, John Carey, Cal Dalton, Arthur Davis, David Hoffman, Vive Risto; *des:* Melvin Millar; *sets:* Richard H. Thomas; *ed:* Tregoweth E. Brown; *voices:* Mel Blanc; *mus:* Carl W. Stalling; *prod sup:* Henry Binder, Raymond Katz; b&w. *sd:* Vit. 7 min. • Porky and his bloodhound Eggbert track down the notorious Nazi spy, "Missing Lynx."

1278. Congo Jazz (*Looney Tunes*) 19 Mar. 1931; *p.c.:* Hugh Harman–Rudolf Ising prods for WB; *prod:* Leon Schlesinger; *anim:* Max Maxwell, Paul Smith; *ed:* Dale Pickett; *voice:* Rochelle Hudson; *mus:* Frank Marsales; b&w. *sd:* Vit. 6 min. • Bosko sweetens the jungle animals with music.

1279. Congratulations, It's Pink (*Pink Panther*) 27 Oct. 1967; *p.c.:* Mirisch/Geoffrey/DFE for UA; *dir:* Hawley Pratt; *story:* John W. Dunn; *anim:* Manny Gould, Bob Matz, Manny Perez, Warren Batchelder, Chuck Downs, Don Williams; *lay:* Dick Ung; *back:* Tom O'Loughlin; *ed:* Lee Gunther; *voice:* June Foray; *mus:* Walter Greene; *theme tune:* Henry Mancini; *prod sup:* Harry Love, Basil Cox; *col:* DeLuxe. *sd:* RCA. 6 min. • The Panther finds a baby in a picnic hamper and tends to the infant until the parents return.

1280. Conrad the Sailor (*Merrie Melodies*) 14 Feb. 1942; *p.c.:* Leon Schlesinger prods for WB; *dir:* Charles M. Jones; *story:* Dave Monahan; *anim:* Ben Washam; *lay:* John McGrew; *back:* Eugene Fleury; *ed:* Treg Brown; *voices:* Mel Blanc, Pinto Colvig, The Sportsmen Quartet; *mus:* Carl W. Stalling; *song:* Harry Warren, Al Dubin; *ph:* John W. Burton; *prod sup:* Henry Binder, Raymond G. Katz; *col:* Tech. *sd:* Vit. 7 min. • Daffy disrupts Conrad's ship-cleaning activities. The character "Conrad" was originally christened "Goofy Cat."

1281. The Constable (*Gabby*) 15 Nov. 1940; *p.c.:* The Fleischer Studio for Para; *prod:* Max Fleischer; *dir:* Dave Fleischer; *story:* Dan Gordon; *anim:* Bill Nolan, George Germanetti; *ed:* Kitty Pfister; *voices:* Pinto Colvig; *mus:* Sammy Timberg; *prod sup:* Isidore Sparber, Sam Buchwald; *col:* Tech. *sd:* WE. 7 min. • Disguised as a hog, Constable Gabby attempts to discover who's been stealing the Royal pigs.

1282. Contact 11 July 1997; *p.c.:* Southside Amusement Company for WB; *3d fx anim:* Geoff Harvey, Spencer Knapp, John Lee, Dylan Robinson; *anim:* Kevin Hudson, Kelvin Lee, David Vallone; *col:* Tech. *sd:* dts 149 min. *l/a.* • A woman who can communicate with distant planets is chosen to fly to the dwarf star of Vega. She encounters an alien who takes its shape from her memories.

1283. The Contest *(Out of the Inkwell)* 1923; *p.c.:* Inkwell Studio for Rodner. *prod:* Max Fleischer; *dir:* Dave Fleischer; b&w. *sil.* 6 min. *l/a/anim.* • $100 is offered to anyone who can stay on Ko-Ko's mechanical mule, "Dynamite." The trick is discovered and the clown chased back into the inkwell.

1284. Contrary Condor *(Donald Duck)* 21 Apr. 1944; *p.c.:* Walt Disney prods for RKO; *dir:* Jack King; *asst dir:* Joel Greenhalgh; *anim:* Paul Allen, Hal King, Jim McManus, George Nicholas, Charles A. Nichols, Don Towsley, Judge Whitaker, Marvin Woodward; *lay:* Ernest Nordli; *voices:* Dehner Forkum, Clarence Nash, Dorothy Lloyd; *mus:* Paul J. Smith; *col:* Tech. *sd:* Vit. 7 min. • While mountain climbing in the Andes, Donald is about to steal a condor's egg when Mama returns, taking him for a newly-hatched chick.

1285. Contrasts in Rhythm 11 Mar. 1955; *p.c.:* Walt Disney prods for BV; "Trees": poem by Joyce Kilmer; *dir:* Hamilton S. Luske; "Bumble Boogie": *dir:* Jack Kinney; *col:* Tech. *sd:* RCA. 8 min. • An assortment of trees are shown to Joyce Kilmer's poem and a bee gets entangled with jazz instruments. • See: *Melody Time*

1286. Convict Concerto *(Woody Woodpecker)* 20 Nov. 1954; *p.c.:* Walter Lantz prods for Univ; *dir:* Don Patterson; *story:* Hugh Harman; *anim:* Ray Abrams, Don Patterson, Herman Cohen; *sets:* Raymond Jacobs, Art Landy; *voices:* Daws Butler, Grace Stafford; *mus:* Clarence Wheeler; *piano:* Raymond Turner; *prod mgr:* William E. Garity; *col:* Tech. *sd:* RCA. 6 min. • Piano tuner Woody is held captive by a bank robber hiding-out in the piano.

1287. The Coo Coo Bird *(Woody Woodpecker)*; rel; 9 June 1947; *p.c.:* Walter Lantz prods for Univ; *dir:* Dick Lundy; *story:* Ben Hardaway, Milt Schaffer; *anim:* (La)Verne Harding, Les Kline, Hal Mason, Grim Natwick, S.C. Onaitis, Sid Pillet; *sets:* Fred Brunish; *voice:* Lee Sweetland, Ben Hardaway; *mus:* Darrell Calker; *prod mgr:* William E. Garity; *col:* Tech. *sd:* RCA. 7 min. • Woody tries to get some sleep before quail hunting season begins.

1288. The Coo Coo Bird Dog *(Phantasy)* 3 Feb. 1949; *p.c.:* Colum; *prod:* Raymond Katz, Henry Binder; *dir:* Sid Marcus; *story:* Cal Howard, Dave Monahan; *anim:* Howard Swift. Roy Jenkins, Ben Lloyd; *lay:* Clark Watson; *back:* Al Boggs; *ed:* Richard S. Jensen; *voices:* Dick Nelson; *mus:* Darrell Calker; *ph:* Frank Fisher; *creative consultant:* Robert Clampett; *col:* Tech. *sd:* WE. 6 min. • A parrot tries to retrieve a cuckoo clock swallowed by his dog friend.

1289. The Coo Coo Nut Grove *(Merrie Melodies)* 28 Nov. 1936; *p.c.:* Leon Schlesinger prods for WB; *dir:* I. Freleng; *story:* T. Hee, Robert Clampett; *anim:* Bob McKimson, Sandy Walker; *des:* T. Hee; *voices:* Lind Hayes, The Rhythmettes, Ted Pierce, Berna Deane, Bernice Hansel; *mus:* Carl W. Stalling; *song:* Harry Warren; *prod sup:* Henry Binder, Raymond G. Katz; *col:* Tech. *sd:* Vit. 7 min. • Ben Birdie invites all to dine and dance with the stars. Caricatures of George Arliss, John & Lionel Barrymore, Wallace Beery, Ben Bernie, Joe E. Brown, Gary Cooper, the Dionne Quins, Bette Davis, W.C. Fields, Clark Gable, Katharine Hepburn, Hugh Herbert, Hildegarde, Charles Laughton, Laurel & Hardy, Edna May Oliver, Groucho & Harpo Marx, Helen Morgan, George Raft, Edward G. Robinson, Ned Sparks, Lupé Velez, Johnny Weissmuller, Mae West and Walter Winchell.

1290. Coo Coo the Magician *(Flip the Frog)* 21 Jan. 1933; *p.c.:* Celebrity prods for MGM; *prod/dir:* Ub Iwerks; *anim:* Jimmie Culhane; *mus:* Gene Denny; b&w. *sd:* PCP. 7 min. • Flip and his girlfriend are in an Arabian nightclub. He annoys a magician who kidnaps Flip's girl and sells her into slavery. Flip manages to rescue her along with the other prisoners.

1291. CooCoo Nuts *(Woody Woodpecker)* 1 July 1970; *p.c.:* Walter Lantz prods for Univ; *dir:* Paul J. Smith; *story:* Sid Marcus; *anim:* Les Kline, Al Coe; *sets:* Nino Carbe; *voices:* Daws Butler, Grace Stafford; *mus:* Walter Greene; *prod mgr:* William E. Garity; *col:* Tech. *sd:* RCA. 6 min. • Woody is shipwrecked on an island with Robinson Crusoe who, tired of eating coconuts, sets his sights on fresh woodpecker for dinner.

1292. The Cookie Carnival *(Silly Symphoney)* 25 May 1935; *p.c.:* Walt Disney prods for UA; *dir:* Ben Sharpsteen; *anim:* Johnny Cannon, Nick George, Jack Hannah, Paul Hopkins, Ferdinand Huszti Horvath, Milton Kahl, Jack Kinney, John McManus, Grim Natwick, Milt Schaffer, Leonard Sebring, Fred Spencer, Eddie Strickland, Don Towsley, Vladimir Tytla; *lay:* Albert Hurter; *character des/back:* Ferdinand Huszti Horvath; *voices:* Pinto Colvig, Marcellite Garner, Harry Stanton; *mus:* Leigh Harline; *col:* Tech. *sd:* RCA. 8 min. • Cookie Boy helps Cookie girl win the beauty pageant.

1293. Cookin' with Gags *(Popeye)* 12 Jan. 1955; *p.c.:* Famous for Para; *dir:* I. Sparber; *story:* Carl Meyer; *anim:* Thomas Johnson, William Henning, Els Barthen; *sets:* Anton Loeb; *voices:* Jack Mercer, Mae Questel, Jackson Beck; *mus:* Winston Sharples; *ph:* Leonard McCormick; *prod mgr:* Seymour Shultz; *col:* Tech. *sd:* RCA. 6 min. • Bluto's "April Fool" gags get Popeye's goat but the mighty mariner has the last laugh.

1294. Cool Cat *(Looney Tunes)* Oct. 1967; *p.c.:* W/7A; *prod:* William L. Hendricks; *dir:* Alex Lovy; *story:* Bob Kurtz; *anim:* Ted Bonnicksen, La Verne Harding, Volus Jones, Ed Solomon; *sets:* David Hanan; *ed:* Hal Geer; *voices:* Larry Storch, The Clingers; *mus:* William Lava; *col:* Tech. *sd:* Vit. 5 min. • Colonel Rimfire tracks down Cool Cat, the tiger, inside a mechanical elephant.

1295. Cool Cat Blues *(The Cat)* Jan. 1961; *p.c.:* Para Cartoons; *dir:* Seymour Kneitel; *story:* Irving Spector; *anim:* Irving Spector, Jerry Dvorak, Jack Ehret, Wm. B. Pattengill; *sets:* Robert Owen; *voices:* Bob MacFadden; *mus:* Winston Sharples; *ph:* Leonard McCormick; *prod mgr:* Abe Goodman; *col:* Tech. *sd:* RCA. 6 min. • A private-eye cat is called in to guard TV's hottest property, Ed Solvent, from being kidnapped by a rival TV network.

1296. Cool It, Charlie *(Beary Family)* 1969; *p.c.:* Walter Lantz prods for Univ; *dir:* Paul J. Smith; *story:* Cal Howard; *anim:* Les Kline, Al Coe; *sets:* Nino Carbe; *voices:* Paul Frees, Grace Stafford; *mus:* Walter Greene; *prod mgr:* William E. Garity; *col:* Tech. *sd:* RCA. 5 min. • Charlie tries to save money by installing his own air conditioner.

1297. Cool World 18 Dec. 1992; *p.c.:* Par/Blue Dolphin; *dir:* Ralph Bakshi; *prod:* Frank Mancuso Jr.; *story:* Michael Grais, Mark Victor; *ass dir:* Marty Eli Schwartz, Richard Coad; *anim sup:* Bruce Woodside; *character lay/des:* Louise Zingarelli; *character lay/des:* Thomas McGrath, Evan Gwynne; *lay anim:* Greg Hill, David Watson; *back character:* Milton Knight, Mark S. O'Hare; *anim:* George Bakes, Anne Marie Bardwell, Paul Bolger, James Davis, Michael R. Gerard, Steve Gordon, Ronald P. Hughart, Mike Kazaleh, Gregory S. Manwaring, Julie Marino, Bill Melendez, Roy Meurin, James Murphy, Samuel W. Nicholson, Dana O'Connor, Alan Sperling, Greg Tiernan, Kenneth D. Walker; *asst anim:* Ron Brown, Roy Burdine, Darryl Gordon, Joe Hawkins, Will Huneycutt, Sam Jones, Donald Judge, Elena Kravitz, Daniel Lim, Buddy James McArdle, Ken McDonald, Frank Moyeri, Celeste Moreno, Uoon Nan, David Preston, Andrew Ramos, David Recinos, Lucinda Sanderson, Vincent Siracusano, Theresa Smythe; *fx:* Lee Crowe, Ellen Greenblatt, Craig Clark, Pat Clark, Phil Cummings, Michael D'isa, Al Holter, Joey Mildenberger, Juli Murphy, Conrad Vervon, Dan Wanket, Kristine Brown; *asst anim:* Daniel Eblen, Hae Sook H. Wang, David M. Kcenich, Kang Tae Kim, Chang Yei Kim, David Kracov, Nate Pacheco, Tom Pope; *anim consult:* Silvia Pompei, Robert Gibbs, Klay R. Hall, Cristi Lyon; *clean-up:* Eric Abjornson, Scott Bern, David Bombardier, Daniel L. Bond, Irene Couloufis, Sandy Henkin, Lureline Kohler, Boowon Lee, Leticia Lichtwardt, Chris Miller, Judith M. Niver, Edward Rivers, Sandra Ryan, Maureen Trueblood; *back:* Patricia Doktor, Brad Hicks, Ian Miller, Charles Pickins; *back co-ord:* Lisa O'Loughlin; *articulate mattes:* Angela Diamos, Ko Hashiguchi, Craig Littel Herrick, John Shourt; *scene tracker:* Don Shump; *ed:* Steve Mirkovich, Annamarie Szanto, Brett Marnell, Timothy Alverson, Fred Wardell; *music ed:* Christopher Kennedy, Scott Grusin; *visual fx ed:* Kelly G. Crawford; *l/a: Holli Would:* Kim Basinger; *Jack Deebs:* Gabriel Byrne; *Detective Frank Harris:* Brad Pitt; *voices: Jennifer Malley:* Michele Abrams; *Isabelle Malley:* Deirdre O'Connell; *Mom Harris:* Janni Brenn-Lowen; *Cops:* William Frankfather, Greg Collins; *voices: Interrogator/Doc Whiskers/Mash/Drunk Bar Patron/Super Jack:* Maurice La Marche; *Sparks:* Michael David Lally; *Comic Bookstore Cashier:* Carrie Hamilton; *Store Patrons:* Stephen Worth, Murray Podwal; *Crops Bunny:* Jenine Jennings; *Interrogator/Slash/Holli's Door:* Joey Camen; *Bash:* Gregory Snegoff; *Bob/Lonette:* Candi Milo; *Nails:* Charles Adler; *Bouncer:*

Patrick Pinney; *Himself:* Frank Sinatra Jnr; *Lucky's Bouncer:* Lamont Jackson; *Valet:* Paul Benvictor; *Plaza Bouncer:* Big Yank; *mus:* Mark Isham, John Dickson; *mus conductor:* Gaylon J. Horton, Susan K. Mann; *mus prod co-ord:* Graham Walker, Jane Bridgeman; *mus performed by* The Munich Symphony Orchestra *conducted by* Allan Wilson; *instrumentalists:* Ray Babbington, Terry Hartley, Nigel Hitchcock, Greg Knowles; *orch mgr:* Paula Talkington; *songs:* "Play With Me" by/performed by Thompson Twins; "My Ideal" by Leo Robin, Richard A. Whiting & Newell Chose; "N.W.O." by/performed by Ministry; "Under" by/performed by Brian Eno; "The Devil Does Drugs/Sex on Wheels" by Buzz McCoy, Groovie Mann performed by My Life with the Thrill Kill Kult; "Ah-Ah/Next is the E" by Richard M. Hall performed by Moby; "Holli's Groove/Her Sassy Kiss/Seduce" by Buzz McCoy performed by My Life with the Thrill Kill Kult; "The Witch" by Ian Astbury & Billy Duffy performed by The Cult; "Do That Thang" by Yuri Dektor performed by Da Juke; "Papua New Guinea" by Brian Douglas, Gerry Cockburn performed by The Future Sound of London; "That Old Black Magic" by Harold Arlen & Johnny Mercer performed by Frank Sinatra Jr.; "Industry and Seduction" by/performed by Tom Bailey; "Mindless" by/performed by Mindless; "Let's Make Love" by Sammy Cahn, James van Heusen performed by Kim Basinger, Frank Sinatra Jr.; "Disappointed" by Johnny Marr, Bernard Sumner, Neil Tennant performed by Electronic; "Reel Cool World" by/performed by David Bowie; *mus copyist:* Vic Fraser; *mus co-ord/choreog:* Jenine Jennings; *anim check:* Stephanie Myers, Letha Prince, Renee Alcazar, Eleanor Dahlen, Charles Gefre, Beverly Randall, Myoung Smith; *fx:* Leonore M. Wood, Joe Quinlivan; *anim prod co-ord:* Gina Shay; *main title des:* Dan Curry; *i&p:* Tania M. Burton, Jon Terada, Joyce Alexander, Mimi Clayton, Casey Clayton, Shigeko Doyle, Deborah Goddard, Kathy Wilbur, Catherine Bazzano, Estelle Beck, Joan Boonick, Stuart Brooks, Carmen Brooks, Diana Dixon, Andrew Haggin, Veronica Halmos, Kit Harper, Stephanie Hirsch, Mi Kyung Kwon, Renate Leff, Florence Luboutry, Christina M. Long, Jackie Stewart-Mache, Kim Manley, Randy McFerren, Catherine Parotino, Cathy Peterson, Bruce Phillipson, Marilyn Pierson, Dorothy Roberts, Dirk van Besser, Debbie Weilhart, Roger Wilbur, Yi So Young; *paint check:* Wilma Baker, Peter Gentile, Melody Hughes, Debbie Mihara, Delmy Navas, Sheryl Smith, Roxanne M. Taylor, Helga van den Berge; *paint lab:* Ann Sullivan; *col model:* Clayton Stang, Anthony Ostyn; *overseas co-ord:* Won Chul Shin; *mark-up:* Gale Raleigh, Bonnie Ramsey, Irma Velez, Michele Zurcher; *Xerox:* Karen N. China, Lillian Fitts, Deanna Spears, Lea Stewart; *repairs:* Kristin Lande; *pencil test:* Lajos Kandra; *neg cutter:* Theresa Repola Mohammed; *ph:* John A. Alonzo, Matthew F. Leonetti, Chris Schwiebert, José Sanchez, Gregory Smith, Michael Sofronski; *film loaders:* Christopher Blayvelt, Jeffrey A. Sklar; *stills:* Merrick Morton; *anim format ph:* Michael Middleton; *spacecam:* Ron Goodman, Steven A. Sass; *sd:* James Thornton, David Halbert, Steven Klinghoffer; *sd des:* Skip Lievsay, Eugene Gearty, Hamilton Sterling; *sd fx ed:* Bill Koepnik, John Joseph Thomas, Catherine Calleson, David Finkelstein, Craig Weintraub; *re-rec mix:* David O. Mitchell, Rick Hart, Frank Montano; *adr:* Renèe Tondelli, James Bogardt, Chris Jargo; *foley:* Bruce Pross, Frank Kern, Eliza Paley, Steve Visscher; *dial ed:* Duncan Burns, Bob Newlan, Hugo Weng; *dial sup:* Harry B. Miller III; *prod des:* Michael Corenblith; *costume:* Malissa Deniel; *Cool World conceptual des:* Barry Jackson; *art dir:* David James Bomba; *set dir:* Merideth Boswell; *sets:* Lori Rowbotham, Mitchell Lee Simmons; *lead person:* Brett Smith; *property persons:* Jonathan Bobbitt, Stacy Doran, Kristin Jones, Edward J. Protiva; *props des painter:* Spain Rodriguez, David T. Cannon, David A. Weinmann, Matt Martin, Jim Ricker, Rick Rose; *paint:* Felise Finn, Scott Dietz, Leeza Ingalls; *asso prod:* Vikki Williams; *prod mgr:* Scott White, Christine M. Johnson, Fernando A. Castroman; *DGA trainee:* Nunzio Fazio; *lighting:* Reginald F. Lake, Robert S. Neville; *prod asst:* Chris D. Brewster, Amber Cordero, Patrick Gaynes, Aimes Johnson, Michael Larsen, William Leahy, William R. Leavitt, Gregory McKnight, Joey Mullen, Maura Reyes, Richard Smith, Kane Wickham; *col timer:* Bob Putynkowski; *col:* Tech. *sd:* Dolby stereo. Panavision. 102 min. *anim/l/a.* • In 1945 the recently demobbed Frank Harris gets sucked into a cartoon existance ("Cool World") by a spike gun. The sensual cartoon character Holli Would, trapped in this world for forty-seven years, tells Frank, now a CWPD detective, that she wishes to have sex with an ex-con she has seen in the human world. The former convict is spirited into the cartoon sphere where he is informed by Frank that anything goes in Cool World except sex between humans and "doodles," which

would annihilate both worlds. Holli seduces him and they both materialize back in the human world, followed by Frank, who tries to find the spike gun before Holli does.

1298. Coonskin Aug. 1975; *p.c.:* Albert S. Ruddy prods Inc/Bakshi prods Inc for Bryanston/Para; *prod:* Albert S. Ruddy; *dir/story:* Ralph Bakshi; *asst dir:* James Roden; *anim seq:* Irven Spence, Charlie Downs, Ambrozi Paliwoda, John E. Walker, Xenia (De Mattia); *anim:* Thomas A. Ray, Edward J. Barge, Fred C. Hellmich, Bob Carlson, John Sparey, Lars Calonius, Raymond Patterson; *asst anim:* Carol Beers, Jean Blanchard, Johnny Bond, Zeon Davush, Joan Drake, Mabel Gesner, René Garcia, Milton Gray, George Herbert, Randy Hollar, Larry Huber, Charlotte Huffine, Louie Kachivas, Mark Kausler, Jack Kerns, Chris Lane, Sammy Lanham, Fred McManus, Anna L. Ray, Tom Roth, Ron Scholefield, Don Selders, Ben Shenkman, Grace Stanzell, Emily Steele, Joan Swanson, James T. Walker, Gwen Wetzler, Art Vitello; *lay/des:* Don Morgan, John Sparey, Charlie Downs; *stills:* Ralph Bakshi, Johnnie Vita; *back:* Ira Turek, René Garcia; *models:* Susan Carey, Janet Cummings; *fx:* Dutch Van Der Byle; *ed:* Donald W. Ernst, Jack Hooper; *voices: Brother Bear:* Barry White; *Brother Fox:* Charles Gordone; *Old Man Bone:* Scatman Crothers; *Brother Rabbit:* Philip Thomas; *Clown:* Danny Rees; *Also:* Buddy Douglas, Jim Moore; *mus:* Chico Hamilton; *songs:* Ralph Bakshi, Scatman Crothers, Grover Washington, Charlie Brown; *mus prod:* Forrest Hamilton, Stu Gardner; *mus ed:* Milton Lustig; *checkers:* Janis Cornell, Dorothy Foell, Robert Revell-Cornell, Mary J. Adams, Eve Fletcher, Nelda Ridley, Beverly Robbins, Eleanor Warren; *i&p:* Vickie Caplan, Rich Chidlaw, Peggy Gregory, Paulette Marcus, Lynda Nardone, Michael Sheeler, Charlene Singleton; *titles:* Howard Miller; *ph:* Ted C. Bemiller; *sd fx:* Sam Shaw; *prod sup:* Juanita McClurg, Leah Bernstein, Don Selders; *l/a: prod:* Alan P. Horowitz; *dir:* William H. Fraker; *col:* Tech. *sd:* 82 min. *l/a/anim.* • Live-action/animated updated retelling of the Br'er Rabbit stories with distinctive sexual overtones and an all-black cast. Quickly hidden away by the distributors after a limited release.

1299. Le Cop on the Rocks *(Inspector)* 30 May 1967; *p.c.:* Mirisch/Geoffrey/DFE for UA; *dir:* George Singer; *story:* Jim Ryan; *anim:* Manny Perez, Don Williams; *lay:* Dick Ung; *back:* Tom O'Loughlin; *ed:* Lee Gunther; *voices:* Path Harrington Jr., Marvin Miller; *mus:* Walter Greene; *theme tune:* Henry Mancini; *prod sup:* Harry Love, Basil Cox; *col:* DeLuxe. *sd:* RCA. 6 min. • Due to mistaken identity, the Inspector is given a life sentence in prison.

1300. The Cop's Bride *(Aesop's Film Fable)* 17 Mar. 1923; *p.c.:* Fables Pictures Inc for Pathé; *dir:* Paul Terry; b&w. sil. 5 min. • Motorcycle cop Waffles Cat's bride, Little Kitty, is abducted by a top-hatted gangster cat. The villain of the piece takes her to the "Cat-acombs" under Al Falfa's house where the cop tracks them down. A showdown takes place in Al's cellar, ending in the whole house blowing-up. Moral: "Autos may be making the legs of men weak, but there are still long runs in women's stockings."

1301. Cops Is Always Right *(Popeye)* 29 Dec. 1938; *p.c.:* The Fleischer Studio for Para; *prod:* Max Fleischer; *dir:* Dave Fleischer; *anim:* Seymour Kneitel, William Henning; *voices:* Jack Mercer, Margie Hines; *mus:* Sammy Timberg; b&w. *sd:* WE. 7 min. • While assisting Olive with spring cleaning, our law-abiding hero becomes embroiled with a traffic officer.

1302. Cops Is Tops *(Popeye)* 4 Nov. 1955; *p.c.:* Famous for Para; *dir:* I. Sparber; *story:* Carl Meyer; *anim:* Tom Johnson, Frank Endres; *sets:* Anton Loeb; *voices:* Jack Mercer, Mae Questel, Jackson Beck, Gwen Davies; *mus:* Winston Sharples; *ph:* Leonard McCormick; *prod mgr:* Seymour Shultz; *col:* Tech. *sd:* RCA. 6 min. • Popeye helps out Policewoman Olive when she's out on her beat.

1303. Copy Cat *(Animated Antics)* 18 July 1941; *p.c.:* The Fleischer Studio for Para; *prod:* Max Fleischer; *dir:* Dave Fleischer; *story:* Bob Wickersham; *mus:* Sammy Timberg; *col:* Tech. *sd:* WE. 7 min. • A dumb cat tries to catch an artful mouse.

1304. Corn Chips *(Donald Duck)* 6 Apr. 1951; *p.c.:* Walt Disney prods for RKO; *dir:* Jack Hannah; *story:* Bill Berg, Nick George; *anim:* Volus Jones, Bill Justice, Bob Carlson, Judge Whitaker; *fx:* George Rowley, Jack Boyd; *lay:* Yale Gracey; *back:* Thelma Witmer; *voices:* Clarence Nash, Dessie Miller, James MacDonald; *mus:* Oliver Wallace, Joseph S. Dubin; *col:* Tech.

sd: RCA. 7 min. • Donald tricks the chipmunks into clearing the snow from his path. The chips take their revenge by swiping all his popcorn.

1305. Corn on the Cop *(Looney Tunes)* 24 July 1965; *p.c.:* DFE for WB; *dir:* Irv Spector; *story:* Friz Freleng; *anim:* Manny Perez. Warren Batchelder, Bob Matz; *lay:* Dick Ung; *back:* Tom O'Loughlin; *ed:* Lee Gunther; *voices:* Mel Blanc, Joanie Gerber; *mus:* Bill Lava; *col:* Tech. *sd:* Vit. 6 min. • Daffy and Porky are policemen assigned to bring in a bandit dressed as a little old lady.

1306. Corn Plastered *(Merrie Melodies)* 3 Mar. 1951; *p.c.:* WB; *dir:* Robert McKimson; *story:* Warren Foster; *anim:* Charles McKimson, Rod Scribner, Phil de Lara, J.C. Melendez, John Carey; *lay:* Cornett Wood; *back:* Richard H. Thomas; *ed:* Treg Brown; *voices:* Mel Blanc, Stan Freberg; *mus:* Carl Stalling; *prod mgr:* John W. Burton; *prod:* Edward Selzer; *col:* Tech. *sd:* Vit. 7 min. • A crazy crow gives a farmer the run-around.

1307. A Corny Concerto *(Merrie Melodies)* 21 Aug. 1943; *p.c.:* Leon Schlesinger prods for WB; *dir:* Robert Clampett; *story:* Frank Tashlin; *anim:* Robert McKimson; *lay:* Thomas McKimson; *back:* Michael Sasanoff; *ed:* Treg Brown; *voices:* Arthur Q. Bryan, Robert Clampett; *mus:* Carl W. Stalling; *prod sup:* Henry Binder, Raymond G. Katz; *col:* Tech. *sd:* Vit. 8 min. • Parody of Disney's *Fantasia* starring Elmer Fudd in the Deems Taylor role. "Tales of the Vienna Woods" has Porky hunting Bugs Bunny and "The Blue Danube" unfolds the tale of a black duck who wants to join a group of snobbish swans.

1308. Corny Concerto 30 Oct. 1962; *p.c.:* Walter Lantz prods for Univ; *dir:* Jack Hannah; *story:* Dave DeTiege; *anim:* Roy Jenkins, Art Davis; *sets:* Ray Huffine, Art Landy; *voices:* Paul Frees, Dal McKennon; *mus:* Darrell Calker; *prod mgr:* William E. Garity; *col:* Tech. *sd:* RCA. 6 min. • Champ has a hammer dropped on his foot, causing him to dance in pain. A Beatnick cat sees this and encourages Doc to make him appear at the coffee bar with his new "dance."

1309. Count-Down Clown *(Loopy de Loop)* Jan. 1961; *p.c.:* Hanna-Barbera for Colum; *prod/dir:* Joseph Barbera, William Hanna; *story dir:* Alex Lovy; *story:* Warren Foster; *anim dir:* Charles A. Nichols; *anim:* Dick Lundy; *lay:* Walter Clinton; *back:* Art Lozzi; *ed:* Warner Leighton; *voices:* Daws Butler, Hal Smith; *mus:* Hoyt Curtin; *titles:* Lawrence Gobel; *prod mgr:* Howard Hanson; *col:* East. *sd:* RCA. 6 min. • Loopy is selected to be shot to the moon but doesn't get further than the local beach.

1310. Count Me Out *(Merrie Melodies)*; *rel;* 17 Dec. 1938; *p.c.:* Leon Schlesinger prods for WB; *dir:* Ben Hardaway, Cal Dalton; *story:* Melvin Millar; *anim:* Herman Cohen; *lay:* Griff Jay; *back:* Arthur Loomer; *ed:* Tregoweth E. Brown; *voices:* Dave Weber, Mel Blanc, Fred Avery; *mus:* Carl W. Stalling; *prod sup:* Henry Binder, Raymond G. Katz; *col:* Tech. *sd:* Vit. 7 min. • Egghead takes a mail-order course in boxing and assumes he's ready to fight the champ.

1311. Counter Attack *(Noveltoon)* June 1960; *p.c.:* Para Cartoons. *dir:* Seymour Kneitel; *story:* Carl Meyer, Jack Mercer; *anim:* Wm. B. Pattengill, Jack Ehret; *sets:* Robert Owen; *voices:* Jack Mercer; *mus:* Winston Sharples; *ph:* Leonard McCormick; *prod mgr:* Abe Goodman; *col:* Tech. *sd:* RCA. 6 min. • Skat the cat chases Skit the mouse into a novelty shop.

1312. Counterfeit Cat 24 Dec. 1949; *p.c.:* MGM; *dir:* Tex Avery; *story:* Rich Hogan; *anim:* Michael Lah, Grant Simmons, Walter Clinton; *character des:* Louis Schmitt; *sets:* John Didrik Johnsen; *ed:* Fred MacAlpin; *voices:* Daws Butler, Colleen Collins; *mus:* Scott Bradley; *prod:* Fred Quimby; *col:* Tech. *sd:* WE. 7 min. • In order to get past the watchdog to the canary, a cat disguises himself as the next-door dog.

1313. A Country Boy *(Merrie Melodies)* 18 Feb. 1935; *p.c.:* Leon Schlesinger prods for WB; *dir:* Isadore Freleng; *anim:* Bob McKimson, Paul Smith, Robert Clampett; *voice:* Bernice Hansel; *mus:* Norman Spencer; *prod sup:* Henry Binder, Raymond G. Katz; *col:* Tech-2. *sd:* Vit. 7 min. • A rebellious rabbit attempts to break into the farmer's garden but is soon chased home.

1314. The Country Cousin *(Silly Symphony)* 31 Oct. 1936; *p.c.:* Walt Disney prods for UA; *dir:* David D. Hand; *story dir:* Carl Fallberg; *story:* Dick Rickard. *anim:* Paul Allen, Arthur Babbitt, Johnny Cannon, Les Clark, Jack Hannah, Armin Shafer, Marvin Woodward; *fx:* Cy Young; *atmospheric sketches:* Maurice Noble; *voice:* Clarence Nash; *mus:* Leigh Harline; *ph:* Earl Colgrove; *col:* Tech. *sd:* RCA. 10 min. *Academy Award.* •

Abner, a country mouse, visits his town cousin, gets drunk on champagne and is chased back home by a cat.

1315. The Country Mouse 1914; *p.c.:* Bosworth Inc.; *dir:* Hobart Bosworth; b&w. sil. • No story available.

1316. Country Mouse *(Merrie Melodies)* 9 Oct. 1935; *p.c.:* Leon Schlesinger prods for WB; *dir:* Isadore Freleng; *anim:* Don Williams, Jack Carr, Robert Clampett; *voices:* Bernice Hansel, Ted Pierce; *mus:* Bernard Brown; *prod sup:* Henry Binder, Raymond G. Katz; *col:* Tech-2. *sd:* Vit. 7 min. • Elmer, a hick mouse, leaves home to go to the big city to fight the champ but Granny soon brings him down to earth.

1317. Country Mouse and City Mouse *(Aesop's Film Fable)* 31 July 1921; *p.c.:* Fables Pictures Inc for Pathé; *dir:* Paul Terry; b&w. sil. 5 min. • The city mouse drives to the country in his flivver and has to stop at a farm for water. He thanks the farmer for his hospitality and invites him to visit when in the city. This the farmer does but finds city life too strenuous and returns to rural life. Moral: "Contentment is greater than riches."

1318. The Country Mouse and the City Cat *(Aesop's Film Fable)* 26 June. 1922; *p.c.:* Fables Pictures Inc for Pathé; *dir:* Paul Terry; b&w. sil. 5 min. • No story available.

1319. Country School *(Oswald)* 6 Apr. 1931; *p.c.:* Univ; *dir:* Walter Lantz, "Bill" Nolan; *anim:* Clyde Geronimi, Manuel Moreno, Ray Abrams, Fred Avery, Lester Kline, Chet Karrberg, "Pinto" Colvig; *mus:* James Dietrich; b&w. *sd:* WE. 6 min. • Oswald rushes to school and meets Mary with her lamb. Teacher plays the piano and a hippo gets Oswald in bad with her.

1320. The Country Store *(Meany Miny Mo)* 5 July 1937; *p.c.:* Walter Lantz prods for Univ;. *dir:* Walter Lantz; *story:* Walt Lantz, Victor McLeod; *anim:* La Verne Harding, Jack Dunham, Leo Salkin; *mus:* George Lessner; b&w. *sd:* WE. 7 min. • The monks own a store and jump to it when Mrs. Hen phones through an order. One goes off in search of lamb chops by stealing a lamb from nearby. A ram sees this and wrecks their store.

1321. The County Fair *(Aesop's Film Fable)* 28 Jan. 1928; *p.c.:* Fables Pictures Inc for Pathé; *dir:* Paul Terry, Harry Bailey; b&w. sil. 5 min. • Farmer Al and his cat prepare for the big County Fair. The dog and cat feed the hen yeast that inflates her like a balloon. The hen floats away, taking Al with her, depositing him at the judges stand. He wins the prize but the dog and cat have substituted a beehive for the money bag and the bees chase Al and the judge away.

1322. The County Fair *(Oswald)* 5 Feb. 1934; *p.c.:* Univ; *dir:* Walter Lantz, "Bill" Nolan; *anim:* Ray Abrams, Fred Avery, Cecil Surry, Jack Carr, Ernest Smythe, Merle Gilson; *mus:* James Dietrich; b&w. *sd:* WE. 8 min. • No story available.

1323. The Covered Pushcart *(Aesop's Film Fable)* 6 June 1923; *p.c.:* Fables Pictures Inc for Pathé; *dir:* Paul Terry; b&w. sil. 5 min. • A wagon train rolls past Al Falfa's farmhouse and a man deposits his girl cat with Al. The boy cat romances the girl, disturbing Al's sleep, prompting him to boot the cat away. The cat returns with his gang to pelt Al's house with rocks. Al escapes the onslaught with the girl cat in his own covered wagon with the boy cat in hot pursuit, driving Al's wagon over a cliff. The two cats are reunited and kiss.

1324. The Covered Pushcart *(Sourpuss)* Sept. 1949; *p.c.:* TT for Fox; *dir:* Mannie Davis; *story:* John Foster; *back:* Art Bartsch; *voices:* Arthur Kay, Tom Morrison; *mus:* Philip A. Scheib; *ph:* Douglas Moye; *col:* Tech. *sd:* RCA. 7 min. • An Indian attacks Gandy and Sourpuss in their ultra-modern trailer and gets entangled in the machinery.

1325. Cow Cow Boogie *(Swing Symphony)* 4 Jan. 1943; *p.c.:* Walter Lantz prods for Univ; *dir:* Alex Lovy; *story:* Ben Hardaway, Milt Schaffer; *anim:* Hal Mason; *voice:* Meade Lux Lewis, King Jackson, Jack Mather; *mus:* Darrell Calker; *song:* Don Raye, Gene de Paul; *piano:* Meade Lux Lewis; *col:* Tech. *sd:* WE. 7 min. • A ranch foreman has a tough job keeping his ranch hands and the cattle moving until a colored boy arrives singing the *title song*.

1326. The Cowardly Watchdog *(Terry-Toon)* Aug. 1966; *p.c.:* TT for Fox; *ex prod:* Bill Weiss; *dir/anim:* Dave Tendlar; *story sup:* Tom Morrison *story:* Larz Bourne; *sets:* Bill Focht; *ed:* Jack MacConnell; *mus:* Jim Timmens; *ph:* Ted Moskowitz, Joe Rasinski; *sd:* Elliott Grey; *col:* DeLuxe. *sd:* RCA. 6 min. • The Martian Moochers help a timid dog who is being bullied by a cat.

1327. Cowboy Blues (*Aesop's Sound Fable*) 15 Feb. 1931; *p.c.:* Van Beuren for Pathé; *dir:* John Foster, Harry Bailey; *mus:* Gene Rodemich; b&w. *sd:* RCA. 8 min. • Milton Mouse with his sweetie, Kitty Kat, find themselves involved with a villain known as Bad-Egg Cat who, disguised as a woman, robs the safe at The Red Dog Café.

1328. Cowboy Cabaret (*Aesop's Sound Fable*) 26 Oct. 1931; *p.c.:* Van Beuren for RKO; *dir:* John Foster, Mannie Davis; *mus:* Gene Rodemich; b&w. *sd:* RCA. 7 min. • A western bandit stages a hold-up but the gang outwits him.

1329. A Cowboy Needs a Horse 6 Nov. 1956; *p.c.:* Walt Disney prods for BV; *dir:* Bill Justice; *asst dir:* George Probert; *story:* Dick Kinney, Roy Williams; *anim:* Cliff Nordberg, Al Coe, Jack Parr, Fred Hellmich, Xavier Atencio, Jerry Hathcock, Bill Justice; *lay/des:* Xavier Atencio; *back:* Ralph Hulett, Al Dempster; *voices:* The Jud Conlon Chorus; *mus:* George Bruns; *song:* Paul Mason Howard, Billy Mills; *col:* Tech. *sd:* RCA. 7 min. CS. • A small boy dreams of becoming a cowboy.

1330. The Cow's Husband (*Talkartoon*) 14 Mar. 1931; *p.c.:* The Fleischer Studio for Para; *prod:* Max Fleischer; *dir:* Dave Fleischer; *mus:* Art Turkisher; b&w. *sd:* WE. 6 min. • The Matador and bull perform a ballet.

1331. A Coy Decoy (*Looney Tunes*) 7 June 1941; *p.c.:* Leon Schlesinger prods for WB; *dir:* Robert Clampett; *story:* Melvin Millar; *anim:* Norman McCabe; *ed:* Treg Brown; *voices:* Mel Blanc; *mus:* Carl W. Stalling; *prod sup:* Henry Binder, Raymond G. Katz; b&w. *sd:* Vit. 7 min. • Daffy, pursued by a hungry wolf is lured into his clutches by a female decoy duck.

1332. Coy Decoy (*Woody Woodpecker*) 9 July 1963; *p.c.:* Walter Lantz prods for Univ; *dir:* Sid Marcus; *story:* Dalton Sandifer; *anim:* Ray Abrams, Art Davis; *sets:* Ray Huffine, Art Landy; *voices:* Daws Butler, Grace Stafford; *mus:* Clarence Wheeler; *prod mgr:* William E. Garity; *col:* Tech. *sd:* RCA. 6 min. • Woody leads a duck hunter and his dopey dog a merry chase when he poses as a duck.

1333. Cracked Ice (*Aesop's Film Fable*) 27 Feb. 1927; *p.c.:* Fables Pictures Inc for Pathé; *dir:* Paul Terry; b&w. *sil.* 5 min. • Al Falfa goes skating and falls through the ice, then falls prey to the mischievous mice and a gang of cats who pelt him with snowballs.

1334. Cracked Ice (*Funny Face Comedies*) 26 June 1924; *p.c.:* Red Seal; *prod:* Edwin Miles Fadman; b&w. *sil.* 4 min. • Puppet film: Mugsy, a cheap doll, watches two dolls skating. He bores a hole in the ice pond and drains the water, sending his two rivals crashing through the ice.

1335. Cracked Ice (*Merrie Melodies*) 10 Sept. 1938; *p.c.:* Leon Schlesinger prods for WB; *dir:* Frank Tashlin; *story:* Jack Miller; *anim:* Bob McKimson; *lay:* Griff Jay; *back:* Arthur Loomer; *ed:* Tregoweth E. Brown; *voices:* Dave Weber, Ted Pierce, Mel Blanc; *mus:* Carl W. Stalling; *prod sup:* Henry Binder, Raymond G. Katz; *col:* Tech. 7 min. • W.C. Squeals, an alcoholic pig, attempts to get a barrel of brandy away from a St. Bernard.

1336. Cracked Ice (*Motoy Films*) 1917; *p.c.:* Toyland Films (*Chicago*) for Peter Pan Films; *dir:* Howard S. Moss; b&w. *st.* • Ben Turpin stars in this puppet film.

1337. Cracked Quack (*Merrie Melodies*) 5 July 1952; *p.c.:* WB; *dir:* I. Freleng; *story:* Warren Foster; *anim:* Arthur Davis, Manuel Perez, Ken Champin, Virgil Ross; *lay:* Hawley Pratt; *back:* Irv Wyner; *ed:* Treg Brown; *voices:* Mel Blanc; *mus:* Carl Stalling; *prod mgr:* John W. Burton; *prod:* Edward Selzer; *col:* Tech. *sd:* Vit. 7 min. • Daffy replaces an ornamental stuffed duck in order to stay in Porky's house during the winter.

1338. Crackpot Cruise (*Car-Tune Comedy*) 9 Jan. 1939; *p.c.:* Walter Lantz prods for Univ; *dir:* Alex Lovy; *story:* Cal Howard; *anim:* Frank Tipper, George Grandpré; *sets:* Edgar Keichle; *voices:* Knox Manning, Harry E. Lang; *mus:* Frank Marsales; b&w. *sd:* WE. 6 min. • Spot-gags on a world cruise.

1339. The Crackpot King (*Mighty Mouse*) 15 Nov. 1946; *p.c.:* TT for Fox; *dir:* Eddie Donnelly; *story:* John Foster; *voices:* Thomas Morrison, Dayton Allen; *mus:* Philip A. Scheib; *col:* Tech. *sd:* RCA. 6 min. • Sweet Suzette is opposed to marrying the King. Mighty Mouse arrives in time to halt the wedding.

1340. The Crackpot Quail (*Merrie Melodies*) 15 Feb. 1941; *p.c.:* Leon Schlesinger prods for WB; *dir:* Fred Avery; *story:* Rich Hogan, Robert Clampett; *anim/des:* Robert McKimson; *sets:* John Didrik Johnsen; *ed:* Treg Brown; *voices:* Mel Blanc; *mus:* Carl W. Stalling; *prod sup:* Henry Binder, Raymond G. Katz; *col:* Tech. *sd:* Vit. 7 min. • Willoughby the hunting dog comes into contact with a good number of trees when out hunting a crazy quail.

1341. The Crawl Stroke Kid (*Aesop's Film Fable*) 13 Feb. 1927; *p.c.:* Fables Pictures Inc for Pathé; *dir:* Paul Terry; b&w. *sil.* 5 min. • The cat trains the mouse for the English Channel swim.

1342. Crazy Cruise (*Merrie Melodies*) 28 Feb. 1942; *p.c.:* Leon Schlesinger prods for WB; *dir:* Fred Avery, Robert Clampett; *story:* Michael Maltese; *anim:* Rod Scribner; *sets:* John Didrik Johnsen; *ed:* Treg Brown; *voices:* Robert Cameron Bruce, Mel Blanc; *mus:* Carl W. Stalling; *ph:* John W. Burton *prod sup:* Henry Binder, Raymond G. Katz; *col:* Tech. *sd:* Vit. 6 min. • A lightning world cruise taking in everything from the Pyramids to the Alps with a guest appearance of Bugs Bunny for good measure. Completed by Clampett after Avery left the studio.

1343. Crazy House (*Andy Panda*) 23 Sept. 1940; *p.c.:* Walter Lantz prods for Univ; *dir:* Walter Lantz; *anim:* Alex Lovy, La Verne Harding; *sets:* Fred Brunish; *voices:* Danny Webb, Sara Berner; *mus:* Frank Marsales; *prod mgr:* George Hall; *col:* Tech. *sd:* WE. 8 min. • Andy and Pop seek refuge from a storm in an old house that turns out to be a fairground crazy house.

1344. Crazy Mixed-Up Pup (*Cartune*) 14 Feb. 1955; *p.c.:* Walter Lantz prods for Univ; *dir/story:* Tex Avery; *anim:* La Verne Harding, Don Patterson, Ray Abrams; *sets:* Raymond Jacobs; *voices:* Daws Butler, Grace Stafford; *mus:* Clarence Wheeler; *prod mgr:* William E. Garity; *col:* Tech. *sd:* RCA. 6 min. *Academy Award nomination.* • Sam and his dog are given blood transfusions which get mixed-up, causing Sam to act like a dog and Rover to behave as a human.

1345. Crazy Over Daisy (*Donald Duck*) 24 Mar. 1950; *p.c.:* Walt Disney prods for RKO; *dir:* Jack Hannah; *story:* Roy Williams, Milt Banta; *anim:* Volus Jones, Bill Justice, Judge Whitaker, Bob Carlson; *fx:* Jack Boyd; *lay:* Yale Gracey; *back:* Thelma Witmer; *voices:* The Ken Darby Chorus: (Charles Goodman, Betty Holland, Ross Mendell, Wayne Warren Tipple, John Woodbury), Clarence Nash, Gloria Blondell, James MacDonald, Dessie Flynn; *mus/song:* Oliver Wallace; *col:* Tech. *sd:* RCA. 6 min. • Donald rides his Penny-Farthing to meet Daisy when he encounters the chipmunks who do all in their power to stop him.

1346. Crazy Town (*Noveltoon*) 12 Feb. 1954; *p.c.:* Famous for Para; *dir:* I. Sparber; *story:* I. Klein; *anim:* Al Eugster, Wm. B. Pattengill; *sets:* Robert Little; *voices:* Jack Mercer, Mae Questel; *mus:* Winston Sharples; *ph:* Leonard McCormick; *prod mgr:* Seymour Shultz; *col:* Tech. *sd:* RCA. 6 min. • Spot-gags on a town where everything is topsy-turvy. A re-working of the Betty Boop cartoon.

1347. Crazy-Town (*Talkartoons*) 25 Mar. 1932; *p.c.:* The Fleischer Studio for Para; *prod:* Max Fleischer; *sup:* Dave Fleischer; *dir:* James H. Culhane; *anim:* James H. Culhane, David Tendlar; *mus:* Art Turkisher; b&w. *sd:* WE. 6 min. • Betty and Bimbo encounter a town where everything is either back-to-front or upside-down. Fish fly in the air and the railway platform leaves a stationary train.

1348. Crazy with the Heat (*Donald & Goofy*) 1 Aug. 1947; *p.c.:* Walt Disney prods for RKO; *dir:* Bob Carlson; *story:* Ralph Wright, Bill Berg; *anim:* Ed Aardal, Fred Kopietz, Don Towsley, Fred Jones, Paul Allen, Bob Carlson, Jerry Hathcock, George Kreisl, Frank Mc Savage, George Nicholas, Sandy Strother; *fx:* Jack Boyd, Andy Engman; *lay:* Philip Barber, Karl Karpé; *back:* Ray Huffine; *voices:* Pinto Colvig, Clarence Nash, Fred Shields; *mus:* Oliver Wallace; *col:* Tech. *sd:* RCA. 6 min. • Whilst stranded in the desert. Donald envisions an iceberg mirage while Goofy envisions a soda fountain.

1349. Creepshow 2 1 May 1987; *p.c.:* Laurel for New World Pictures; *anim des/sup:* Rick Catizone; *anim:* Rick Catizone, Gary Hartle, Phil Wilson; *back:* Phil Wilson; *i&p:* Lori Chontos; *comic pages:* Ron Frenz; *voices: the Creep:* Joe Silver; *also:* Gordon Connell, Jason Late, Brian Noodt, Marc Stephen Delgatto, P.J. Morrison, Clark Utterback; *sd reader:* Jim Allen; *col:* Tech. *sd:* Mono. 90 min. *l/a.* • Horror film based on the short stories of Stephen King, one of which involves comic book characters coming to life.

1350. Creepy-Time Pal (*Loopy de Loop*) 19 May 1960; *p.c.:* Hanna-

Barbera for Columbia; *prod/dir:* William Hanna, Joseph Barbera; *story dir:* Alex Lovy; *story:* Warren Foster; *anim dir:* Charles A. Nichols; *anim:* Carlo Vinci; *lay:* Walter Clinton; *back:* Robert Gentle; *ed:* Joseph Ruby; *voices:* Daws Butler, Don Messick, Jean van der Pyl; *mus:* Hoyt Curtin; *titles:* Lawrence Gobel; *prod mgr:* Howard Hansen; *col:* East. *sd:* RCA. 6 min. • Loopy intrudes into the Hansel and Gretel story.

1351. Crime in the Big City *(Aesop's Film Fable)* 29 May 1922; *p.c.:* Fables Pictures Inc for Pathé; *dir:* Paul Terry; b&w. *sil.* 5 min. • Farmer Al Falfa goes to the city with his dog who manages to save him from a flapper who pockets his money along with a crooked card game. Moral: "Those who lay traps for others often get caught by their own bait."

1352. The Critic 1963; *p.c.:* Pintoff/Crossbow prods for Colum; *prod/dir:* Ernest Pintoff; created by Mel Brooks; *des/anim:* Bob Heath; *ed:* Harry Chang; *voices:* Mel Brooks, Carl Reiner; *mus:* J.S. Bach; *asso prod:* Arnold Stone; *col:* East. *sd.* 5 min. *Academy Award.* • A disembodied voice from the audience passes comment on an abstract cartoon on screen. Brooks uses his "2000 Year Old Man" character for the world-weary patron.

1353. Croakus Pocus *(Tijuana Toads)* 26 Dec. 1971; *p.c.:* Mirisch/DFE for UA; *dir:* Art Davis; *story:* John W. Dunn; *anim:* Warren Batchelder, Don Williams, Bob Richardson, Manny Gould; *lay:* Dick Ung; *back:* Richard H. Thomas; *ed:* Lee Gunther; *voices:* Don Diamond, Tom Holland, Athena Lorde; *mus:* Doug Goodwin; *ph:* John Burton Jr.; *prod sup:* Jim Foss, Harry Love; *col:* DeLuxe. *sd:* RCA. 5 min. • The Toads have a run-in with a witch.

1354. Crockett-Doodle-Do *(Merrie Melodies)* 25 June 1960; *p.c.:* WB; *dir:* Robert McKimson; *story:* Tedd Pierce; *anim:* Warren Batchelder, Tom Ray, George Grandpré, Ted Bonnicksen, David R. Green; *fx:* Harry Love; *lay:* Robert Givens. *back:* Bob Singer; *ed:* Treg Brown; *voices:* Mel Blanc; *mus:* Milt Franklyn; *prod mgr:* William Orcutt. *prod:* David H. De-Patie. *col:* Tech. *sd:* Vit. 7 min. • Foggy tries to teach Egghead Jr to fend for himself in the wild outdoors.

1355. The Crook Who Cried Wolf *(Loopy de Loop)* Dec. 1963; *p.c.:* Hanna-Barbera for Colum; *prod/dir:* Joseph Barbera, William Hanna; *story dir:* Lew Marshall. *story:* Dalton Sandifer; *anim dir:* Charles A. Nichols; *anim:* Don Patterson; *lay:* Jack Huber, Willie Ito; *back:* Lee Branscombe; *ed:* Donald A. Douglas; *voices:* Daws Butler, Don Messick, Doug Young; *mus:* Hoyt Curtin; *titles:* Lawrence Gobel; *prod sup:* Howard Hanson; *col:* East. *sd:* RCA. 5 min. • Loopy gets mistaken for a gangster disguised as a wolf.

1356. Croon Crazy *(Aesop's Fable)* 29 Dec. 1933; *p.c.:* Van Beuren for RKO; *dir:* Steve Muffatti; *mus:* Gene Rodemich; b&w. *sd:* RCA. 7 min. • Cubby Bear has to give impersonations of the stars (Kate Smith, Al Jolson and Mae West) when they fail to show up for his radio broadcast.

1357. Crop Chasers *(Color Rhapsody)* 22 Sept. 1939; *p.c.:* Cartoon Films Ltd/Charles Mintz prods for Colum; *prod/dir:* Ub Iwerks; *ed:* George Winkler; *voices:* Mel Blanc, Danny Webb; *mus:* Eddie Kilfeather, Joe de Nat; *ph:* Otto Reimer; *prod mgr:* James Bronis; *col:* Tech. *sd:* RCA. 7 min • The farmer employs two scarecrows to put a stop to the protection racket the crows inflict on him.

1358. Crosby, Columbo and Vallee *(Merrie Melodies)* 9 Apr. 1932; *p.c.:* WB; *prod:* Leon Schlesinger; *dir:* Hugh Harman, Rudolf Ising; *anim:* Rollin Hamilton, Max Maxwell, Robert Clampett; *voice:* Mary Moder; *mus:* Frank Marsales; b&w. *sd:* Vit. 7 min. • An Indian woos his girl by playing the radio to her.

1359. Cross-Country Detours *(Merrie Melodies)* 16 Mar. 1940; *p.c.:* Leon Schlesinger prods for WB; *dir:* Fred Avery; *story:* Rich Hogan, Robert Clampett; *anim:* Paul Smith; *sets:* John Didrik Johnsen; *ed:* Treg Brown; *voices:* Carlton KaDell, Mel Blanc, Sara Berner; *mus:* Carl W. Stalling; *prod sup:* Henry Binder, Raymond G. Katz; *col:* Tech. *sd:* Vit. 7 min. • Travelogue with insights into a frog croaking, forest fire hazards and how a lizard sheds its skin.

1360. A Cross-Country Run *(Aesop's Film Fable)* 26 July 1928; *p.c.:* Fables Pictures Inc for Pathé; *dir:* Paul Terry, Harry Bailey; b&w. *sil.* 5 min. • The menagerie cuts loose for a cross-country run. Farmer Al is the winner when a disgruntled mule kicks him over the finish line.

1361. The Cross Eyed Bull *(Daffy Ditty)* 4 Oct. 1944; *p.c.:* Plastic Cartoons Inc for UA; *prod:* Larry Morey, John Sutherland; *dir:* Robert Newman; *anim:* Bill Nolan; *sets:* Harold Miles, Tim Barr; *ph:* Paul Sprunk; *prod mgr:* Miles E. Pike; *col:* Tech. *snd.* 9 min. • The bull in question can't fight in the ring because he sees two toreadors but finally gets the opportunity to smash the most prominent bull fighter.

1362. Crossing the Delaware *(Terry-Toon)* June 1961; *p.c.:* TT for Fox; *ex prod:* Bill Weiss; *dir:* Art Bartsch; *story sup:* Tom Morrison; *voice:* John Myhers; *mus:* Philip Scheib; *col:* DeLuxe. *sd:* RCA. 5 min. • Hector Heathcote had a hand in building the very boat that carried George Washington and his troops across the Delaware.

1363. Crow Crazy *(Andy Panda)* 28 May 1945; *p.c.:* Walter Lantz prods for Univ; *dir:* Dick Lundy; *story:* Ben Hardaway, Milt Schaffer; *anim:* Les Kline, Paul Smith; *sets:* Fred Brunish; *voices:* Walter Tetley, Bill Shaw; *mus:* Darrell Calker; *prod mgr:* William E. Garity; *col:* Tech. *sd:* RCA. 7 min. • Andy's cornfield is besieged by crows, so he sends his dog, Milo, to scare them away.

1364. Crow De Guerre *(Inspector)* 16 Aug. 1967; *p.c.:* Mirisch/Geoffrey/DFE for UA; *dir:* Gerry Chiniquy; *story:* John W. Dunn; *anim:* Don Williams, Chuck Downs, Warren Batchelder, John Gibbs, Manny Perez, Bob Matz; *lay:* Dick Ung; *back:* Tom O'Loughlin; *ed:* Lee Gunther; *voices:* Pat Harrington Jr., Marvin Miller; *mus:* Walter Greene; *theme tune:* Henry Mancini; *prod sup:* Harry Love, Basil Cox; *col:* DeLuxe. *sd:* RCA. 6 min. • The Inspector chases a ruby-stealing crow through the streets of Paris.

1365. The Crowd Snores *(Pooch the Pup)* 24 Oct. 1932; *p.c.:* Univ; *dir:* Walter Lantz; *anim:* Manuel Moreno, Lester Kline, George Cannata, "Bill" Weber; *mus:* James Dietrich; b&w. *sd:* WE. 6 min. • Pooch enters an auto race.

1366. Crowin' Pains *(Woody Woodpecker)* 25 Sept. 1962; *p.c.:* Walter Lantz prods for Univ; *dir:* Paul J. Smith; *story:* Tedd Pierce, Bill Danch; *anim:* Ray Abrams, Les Kline, Art Davis; *sets:* Art Landy, Ray Huffine; *voices:* Daws Butler, Grace Stafford; *mus:* Clarence Wheeler; *prod mgr:* William E. Garity; *col:* Tech. *sd:* RCA. 6 min. • Woody replaces the farmer's dancing crow in order to get some food.

1367. Crowing Pains *(Looney Tunes)* 12 July 1947; *p.c.:* WB; *dir:* Robert McKimson; *story:* Warren Foster; *anim:* John Carey, I. Ellis, Charles McKimson, Manny Gould; *lay:* Cornett Wood; *back:* Richard H. Thomas; *voice:* Mel Blanc, Tedd Pierce; *ed:* Treg Brown; *mus:* Carl Stalling; *prod mgr:* John W. Burton; *prod:* Edward Selzer; *col:* Tech. *sd:* Vit. 7 min. • Foghorn Leghorn informs Henery Hawk that Sylvester the cat is a chicken ... and thereby hangs a tale.

1368. Crows' Feet *(Merrie Melodies)* 21 Apr. 1962; *p.c.:* WB; *dir:* Friz Freleng; *asst dir/lay:* Hawley Pratt; *story:* John Dunn; *anim:* Gerry Chiniquy, Virgil Ross, Bob Matz, Lee Halpern, Art Leonardi; *back:* Tom O'Loughlin; *voices:* Mel Blanc, Tom Holland; *mus:* Milt Franklyn; *prod mgr:* William Orcutt; *prod:* David H. DePatie; *col:* Tech. *sd:* Vit. 6 min. • Manuel and José, the crows, attempt to steal corn from farmer Fudd's cornfield.

1369. Crow's Feet *(Loopy de Loop)* Apr. 1965; *p.c.:* Hanna-Barbera for Colum; *prod/dir:* Joseph Barbera, William Hanna; *story dir:* Paul Sommer; *story:* Dalton Sandifer; *anim dir:* Charles A. Nichols; *anim:* Ed Aardal, Chuck Harriton; *lay:* Dick Bickenbach; *back:* Art Lozzi; *ed:* Warner Leighton; *voices:* Daws Butler, Mel Blanc; *mus:* Hoyt Curtin; *titles:* Lawrence Gobel; *prod mgr:* Howard Hanson; *col:* East. *sd:* RCA. 6 min. • Loopy substitutes for a scarecrow.

1370. Cruise Cat *(Tom & Jerry)* 18 Oct. 1952; *p.c.:* MGM; *dir:* William Hanna, Joseph Barbera; *anim:* Irven Spence, Ray Patterson, Ed Barge, Kenneth Muse; *ed:* Jim Faris; *sets:* Robert Gentle; *voice:* Paul Frees; *mus:* Scott Bradley; *ph:* Jack Stevens; *prod:* Fred Quimby; *col:* Tech. *sd:* WE. 7 min. • Ship's mascot, Tom, is assigned to keep the vessel free of mice. Jerry arrives, all set for a cruise, and finds a hostile asmosphere aboard.

1371. Crumley Cogwheel *(Modern Madcap)* Jan. 1961; *p.c.:* Para Cartoons; *dir:* Seymour Kneitel; *story:* Irving Spector; *anim:* Irving Spector, Jack Ehret, Larry Silverman; *sets:* Robert Little; *voices:* Eddie Lawrence, Corinne Orr; *mus:* Winston Sharples; *ph:* Leonard McCormick; *col:* Tech. *sd:* RCA. 6 min. • A servile accountant has the ultimatum of finding the courage to ask the boss for a raise or being fired.

1372. The Crunch Bird 1971; *p.c.:* Maxwell-Petok Petrovich for Regency; *prod/dir/story:* Ted Petok; *des:* Karl Fischer; *voices:* Len Maxwell; *col. sd.* 2 min. *Academy Award.* • A wife buys a pet bird for her husband who has a negative attitude about everything.

1373. Crying Wolf *(Mighty Mouse)* 10 Jan. 1947; *p.c.:* TT for Fox; *dir:* Connie Rasinski; *story:* John Foster; *voice:* Tom Morrison; *mus:* Philip A. Scheib; *col:* Tech. *sd:* RCA. 6 min. • A bored sheep cries "Wolf" once too often but when a real wolf arrives, Mighty Mouse has to save the flock and sheepdog from him.

1374. The Crystal Brawl *(Popeye)* 5 Apr. 1957; *p.c.:* Para Cartoons; *dir:* Seymour Kneitel; *story:* Carl Meyer; *anim:* Al Eugster, Wm. B. Pattengill; *sets:* Joe Dommerque; *voices:* Jack Mercer, Mae Questel, Jackson Beck; *mus:* Winston Sharples; *ph:* Leonard McCormick; *prod mgr:* Seymour Shultz; *col:* Tech. *sd:* RCA. 6 min. Seq: *Alpine for You; Quick on the Vigor.* • Bluto disposes with our hero and takes Olive to the fair. There they visit a fortune teller who turns out to be Popeye in disguise.

1375. The Crystal Gazebo *(Krazy Kat)* 7 Nov. 1932; *p.c.:* Winkler for Colum; *dir:* Ben Harrison, Manny Gould; *anim:* Al Rose, Harry Love, Al Eugster; *mus:* Joe de Nat; *prod:* George Winkler; b&w. *sd:* WE. 6 min. • Krazy hops a camel and pursues his lady love who has been kidnapped by No-Can-Do the Magician.

1376. The Crystal Gazer *(Phantasy)* 8 Aug. 1941; *p.c.:* Colum; *dir:* Sid Marcus; *sets:* Clark Watson; *ed:* Edward Moore; *voices:* Mel Blanc, Sara Berner; *mus:* Eddie Kilfeather; *prod mgr:* George Winkler; b&w. *sd:* RCA. 6 min. • Zaza Raja, renown mystic, journeys to the Pharaohs' tomb in order to answer a question.

1377. Cubby's Picnic *(Aesop's Sound Fable)* 6 Oct. 1933; *p.c.:* Van Beuren for RKO; *dir:* Steve Muffatti, Ed Donnelly; *mus:* Gene Rodemich; b&w. *sd:* RCA. 6 min. • Cubby and his lady friend have a hectic day in the country.

1378. Cubby's Stratosphere Flight *(Aesop's Fables)* 20 Apr. 1934; *p.c.:* Van Beuren for RKO; *dir:* George Stallings; *anim:* Steve Muffatti; *mus:* Gene Rodemich; b&w. *sd:* RCA. 6 min. • No story available.

1379. Cubby's World Flight *(Aesop's Sound Fable)* 25 Aug. 1933; *p.c.:* Van Beuren for RKO; *dir:* Hugh Harman, Rudolf Ising; *mus:* Gene Rodemich; b&w. *sd:* RCA. 7 min. • No story available.

1380. The Cuckoo Bird *(Terry-Toon)* 7 Apr. 1939; *p.c.:* TT for Fox; *dir:* Mannie Davis; *story:* John Foster; *mus:* Philip A. Scheib; *col:* Tech. *sd:* RCA. 7 min. • No story available.

1381. The Cuckoo Clock 10 June 1950; *p.c.:* MGM; *dir:* Tex Avery; *story:* Rich Hogan; *anim:* Grant Simmons, Walter Clinton, Michael Lah; *lay/des:* Louis Schmitt; *back:* John Didrik Johnsen; *ed:* Jim Faris; *voice:* Daws Butler; *mus:* Scott Bradley; *ph:* Jack Stevens; *col:* Tech. *sd:* WE. 8 min. • A cat is driven insane by a cuckoo clock's cuckoo and decides to dispose of it.

1382. The Cuckoo I.Q. *(Color Rhapsody)* 3 July 1941; *p.c.:* Colum; *dir:* Sid Marcus; *anim:* Art Davis; *sets:* Clark Watson; *ed:* Ed Moore; *voices:* Mel Blanc; *mus:* Paul Worth; *ph:* Otto Reimer; *prod mgr:* George Winkler; *col:* Tech. *sd:* RCA. 7 min. • A burlesque on radio quiz shows.

1383. The Cuckoo Murder Case *(Flip the Frog)* 18 Oct. 1930; *p.c.:* Celebrity prods for MGM; *prod/dir:* Ub Iwerks; *mus:* Carl Stalling; b&w. *sd:* PCP. 8 min. • Sherlock Flip is called to investigate when a cuckoo clock is shot by a mysterious stranger. Flip narrowly escapes "The Grim Reaper."

1384. Cue Ball Cat *(Tom & Jerry)* 25 Nov. 1950; *p.c.:* MGM; *dir:* William Hanna, Joseph Barbera; *anim:* Kenneth Muse, Irven Spence, Ray Patterson, Ed Barge; *sets:* Robert Gentle; *ed:* Jim Faris; *mus:* Scott Bradley; *ph:* Jack Stevens; *prod:* Fred Quimby; *col:* Tech. *sd:* WE. 7 min. • Tom disrupts Jerry's slumber in a pool hall.

1385. Cupid Gets His Man *(Rainbow Parade)* 24 July 1934; *p.c.:* Van Beuren for RKO; *dir:* Tom Palmer; *voices:* Jimmy Donnelly; *mus:* Winston Sharples; *col:* Tech-2. *sd:* RCA. 7 min. • Ulysses D. Cupid poses as a mountie in order to unite feuding neighbors, Edna May Oliver and W.C. Fields.

1386. Cupid Gets Some New Dope *(Sullivan Cartoon Comedy)* 17 Sept. 1917; *p.c.:* Powers for Univ; *prod/dir:* Pat Sullivan; b&w. sil. 4 min. • Cupid puts a new love potion and sprays it over a black mammy doing her washing and a policeman on the beat ... with devastating results.

1387. The Cure *(Out of the Inkwell)* 13 Dec. 1924. *p.c.:* Inkwell Studios for Red Seal; *prod:* Max Fleischer; *dir:* Dave Fleischer; b&w. sil. 6 min. *l/a/anim.* • The little clown helps pull Max's aching tooth with help from a rabbit and a dose of laughing gas.

1388. Cure or Kill *(Aesop's Film Fable)* 20 Sept. 1928; *p.c.:* Fables Pictures Inc for Pathé; *dir:* Paul Terry, Hugh Shields; b&w. sil. 5 min. • Al Falfa is a snake oil salesman with the cat as a shill for his medicine show. A monkey and elephant throw their crutches away after a swig from his elixir and a monkey grows hair on his bald head. Later, the grandson of the bald monkey beats Al up for giving his Grandpa too much hair restorer. Al and the cat make a hasty exit in a donkey cart after feeding the donkey a good dose of the elixir.

1389. Cured Duck *(Donald Duck)* 26 Oct. 1945; *p.c.:* Walt Disney prods for RKO; *dir:* Jack King; *asst dir:* Joel Greenhalgh; *story:* Roy Williams; *anim:* Don Towsley, Bill Justice, Fred Kopietz, Sandy Strother, Paul Allen, Ed Aardal, Art Scott. Tom Massey, Lee Morehouse; *fx:* Josh Meador, John McManus; *lay:* Ernest Nordli; *back:* Merle Cox; *voices:* Wendell Niles, Clarence Nash, Gloria Blondell, J. Dehner Forkum; *mus:* Oliver Wallace; *col:* Tech. *sd:* RCA. 7 min. • Donald takes a crash course to cure his temper.

1390. The Curio Shop *(Krazy Kat)*; rel; 15 Dec. 1933; *p.c.:* Winkler for Colum; *prod:* Charles Mintz; *story:* Harry Love; *anim:* Allen Rose, Preston Blair; *mus:* Joe de Nat; *prod mgr:* James Bronis; b&w. *sd:* WE. 6 min. • Krazy and Kitty witness all the characters on a Chinese tapestry come alive and act out the story of a girl who's father wants her to marry a decrepit mandarin.

1391. The Curious Puppy *(Merrie Melodies)* 30 Dec. 1939; *p.c.:* Leon Schlesinger prods for WB; *dir:* Charles Jones; *story/lay:* Robert Givens; *anim:* Philip Monroe; *back:* Paul Julian; *ed:* Tregoweth E. Brown; *voices:* Mel Blanc; *mus:* Carl W. Stalling; *prod sup:* Henry Binder, Raymond G. Katz; *col:* Tech. *sd:* Vit. 7 min. • A puppy is chased into an amusement park after closure and accidentally sets it all in motion.

1392. Current Events 1981; *p.c.:* Stan Phillips & Associates for Southern California Edison Co.; *dir:* Bruce Woodside; *prod:* Stan Phillips; *des:* Paul Coker Jr.; *story:* Bruce Woodside, Stan Phillips; *anim:* Pam Cootes, Tom Hush, Margaret Parker, Mike Sanger, Mark R. Hubley, James Wahlberg; *back:* Nancy Avery; *graphic prod:* Jan Avery, Christopher Boyer, Eileen Giaffy, John Dawson, D.T. Lavercoombe, Matt Musial, Angelina Onofrio, Chuck Onofrio, Tony Pezone, Elizabeth Roberts; *mus:* Paul Conly, Jeff Jurich; *ph:* Richard Estrada; *col. sd.* • Presented as a public service for SCE with the slogan "Make Every Kilowatt Count." Blackout gags on the use of electricity: A man turns up his air-conditioner so that his house becomes arctic and a woman turns up her heat so that her house melts.

1393. Curse of the Pink Panther 12 Aug. 1983; *p.c.:* Titan Prods./Jewel Prods. for UA; *title anim:* Marvel Prods., Ltd. based on characters created by DePatie-Freleng; *anim dir/story:* Arthur Leonardi; *mus:* Henry Mancini; *col:* Tech. *sd:* Stereo. Panavision. 5 min. • Live-action comedy concerning a hunt for the missing Inspector Clouseau. The title animation involves the Panther creating the Inspector with a computer.

1394. Curtain Razor *(Looney Tunes)* 21 May 1949; *p.c.:* WB; *dir:* I. Freleng; *story:* Tedd Pierce; *anim:* Manuel Perez, Ken Champin, Virgil Ross, Pete Burness; *lay:* Hawley Pratt; *back:* Paul Julian; *ed:* Treg Brown; *voices:* Mel Blanc, Dave Barry, Cliff Nazarro; *mus:* Carl Stalling; *prod mgr:* John W. Burton; *prod:* Edward Selzer; *col:* Tech. *sd:* Vit. 7 min. • Theatrical agent Porky auditions some curious acts.

1395. Custard Pies *(Aesop's Sound Fable)* 9 May 1929; *p.c.:* Fables Pictures Inc for Pathé; *dir:* Paul Terry; *mus:* Josiah Zuro; *sd fx:* Maurice Manne; b&w. *sd:* RCA. 6 min. • No story available.

1396. Customers Wanted *(Popeye)* 27 Jan. 1939; *p.c.:* The Fleischer Studio for Para; *prod:* Max Fleischer; *dir:* Dave Fleischer; *anim:* Seymour Kneitel, William Henning; *voices:* Jack Mercer, William Pennell, Lou Fleischer, Margie Hines; *mus:* Sammy Timberg; *ph:* Charles Schettler; *prod sup:* Sam Buchwald, Isidore Sparber; b&w. *sd:* WE. 7 min. Seq: *Let's Get Movin'; The Twisker Pitcher.* • Popeye and Bluto run rival penny arcades and vie for Wimpy's custom.

1397. Cut Price Glory *(Life Cartoon Comedy)* 10 Oct. 1926; *p.c.:* Sherwood Wadsworth Pictures Inc for Educational; *prod/dir:* John R. McCrory; b&w. sil. 6 min. • Mike Monkey and High-Hat Harold in a travesty of war-play.

1398. The Cute Recruit *(Phantasy)* 2 May 1941; *p.c.:* Colum; *story:* Art Davis; *anim:* Sid Marcus; *lay:* Clark Watson; *back:* Phil Davis; *voice:*

Mel Blanc, Sara Berner; *mus:* Eddie Kilfeather; b&w. *sd:* RCA. 6 min. • Scrappy imagines himself in the armed forces.

1399. Cutting a Melon (*Aesop's Film Fable*) 22 July 1927; *p.c.:* Fables Pictures Inc for Pathé; *dir:* Paul Terry; b&w. *sil.* 5 min. • Farmer Al tries to market some melons, only to be thwarted by some mutts who steal the fruit and his wagon. Moral: "The coat and pants do all the work, but the vest gets all the gravy."

1400. The Dachshund and the Sausage • See: *The Artist's Dream*

1401. Dad, Can I Borrow the Car? 30 Sept. 1970; *p.c.:* Walt Disney prods for BV; *prod/dir:* Ward Kimball; *story:* Ted Berman; *anim:* Art Stevens; *lay:* Joe Hale; *des:* John Emerson, Ed Gombert; *ed:* Lloyd L. Richardson, Robert O. Cook; *voice:* Kurt Russell; *mus:* George Bruns; *col:* Tech. *sd:* RCA. 22 min. *l/a/anim.* • A young man's interest in cars from child to adulthood.

1402. Daddy Duck (*Donald Duck*) 16 Apr. 1948; *p.c.:* Walt Disney prods for RKO. *dir:* Jack Hannah; *asst dir:* Bee Selck; *story:* Jack Cosgriff, Bob McCormick; *anim:* Phil Duncan, Bob Carlson, Tom Massey, Hal Ambro, Murray McClellan, Ken O'Brien; *fx:* Jack Boyd; *lay:* Ernie Nordli; *back:* Thelma Witmer; *voices:* Gloria Blondell, Clarence Nash; *mus:* Oliver Wallace; *col:* Tech. *sd:* RCA. 7 min. • Donald plays foster parent to a baby kangaroo.

1403. Daddy's Little Darling (*Terry-Toon*) Apr. 1957; *p.c.:* TT for Fox; *dir:* Connie Rasinski; *story:* Tom Morrison; *anim:* Jim Tyer; *mus:* Philip A. Scheib; *col:* Tech. *sd:* RCA. 6 min. • Father dog takes a hand in raising his ferocious offspring, especially when trying to bathe the child.

1404. Daffy Dilly (*Merrie Melodies*) 30 Oct. 1948; *p.c.:* WB. *dir:* Charles M. Jones; *story:* Michael Maltese; *anim:* Ben Washam, Lloyd Vaughan, Ken Harris, Phil Monroe; *lay:* Robert Gribbroek; *back:* Peter Alvarado; *ed:* Treg Brown; *voices:* Mel Blanc; *mus:* Carl Stalling; *prod mgr:* John W. Burton; *prod:* Edward Selzer; *col:* Ciné. *sd:* Vit. 7 min. • Daffy attempts to make a millionaire laugh for a rich reward.

1405. The Daffy Doc (*Looney Tunes*) 26 Nov. 1938; *p.c.:* Leon Schlesinger prods for WB; *dir:* Robert Clampett; *anim:* John Carey, Vive Risto; *sets:* Elmer Plummer; *ed:* Tregoweth E. Brown; *voices:* Mel Blanc, Sara Berner; *mus:* Carl W. Stalling; *ph:* John W. Burton; *prod sup:* Henry Binder, Raymond G. Katz; b&w. *sd:* Vit. 7 min. • Dr. Daffy needs a patient to operate on and picks on Porky who just happens to be passing the hospital at the time.

1406. Daffy Doodles (*Looney Tunes*) 8 Apr. 1946; *p.c.:* WB; *dir:* Robert McKimson; *story:* Warren Foster; *anim:* Cal Dalton, Don Williams, Richard Bickenbach; *lay:* Cornett Wood; *back:* Richard H. Thomas; *character des:* Jean Blanchard; *ed:* Treg Brown; *voices:* Mel Blanc, Robert C. Bruce; *mus:* Carl Stalling; *prod mgr:* John W. Burton; *prod:* Edward Selzer; *col:* Tech. *sd:* Vit. 7 min. • Patrolman Porky is after a fiend (Daffy Duck) who draws moustaches on all billboards. • Animator McKimson's first solo directorial.

1407. Daffy Duck and Egghead (*Merrie Melodies*) 1 Jan. 1938; *p.c.:* Leon Schlesinger prods. for WB; *dir:* Fred Avery; *story:* J.B. Hardaway, Robert Clampett; *anim:* Virgil Ross; *sets:* John Didrik Johnsen; *ed:* Tregoweth E. Brown; *voices:* Mel Blanc, Dave Weber; *mus:* Carl W. Stalling; *song:* Cliff Friend, Dave Franklin; *prod sup:* Henry Binder, Raymond G. Katz; *col:* Tech. *sd:* Vit. 7 min. • Egghead goes hunting Daffy Duck but is beaten to capturing him by the ambulance drivers taking him back to the asylum. Daffy sings the "Merrie Melodies" theme song, *The Merry-Go-Round Broke Down.*

1408. Daffy Duck and the Dinosaur (*Merrie Melodies*) 22 Apr. 1939; *p.c.:* Leon Schlesinger prods for WB; *dir:* Charles M. Jones; *story:* Dave Monahan; *anim:* A.C. Gamer; *character des:* Charles Thorson; *lay:* Robert Givens; *back:* Paul Julian; *ed:* Tregoweth E. Brown; *voices:* Mel Blanc, Jack Lescoulie; *mus:* Carl W. Stalling; *prod mgr:* Henry Binder, Raymond G. Katz; *col:* Tech. *sd:* Vit. 7 min. • Casper Caveman and his dinosaur, Fido, go hunting for prehistoric duck for breakfast.

1409. Daffy Duck Hunt (*Looney Tunes*) 20 Mar. 1949; *p.c.:* WB; *dir:* Robert McKimson; *story:* Warren Foster; *anim:* John Carey, Charles McKimson, Phil de Lara, Manny Gould; *lay:* Cornett Wood; *back:* Richard H. Thomas; character *des:* Jean Blanchard; *ed:* Treg Brown; *voice:* Mel Blanc; *mus:* Carl Stalling; *prod mgr:* John W. Burton; *prod:* Edward Selzer;

col: Tech. *sd:* Vit. 7 min. • Porky believes he has successfully bagged Daffy and puts him in the freezer. Needless to say, Daffy is anything but "bagged."

1410. Daffy Duck in Hollywood (*Merrie Melodies*) 12 Dec. 1938; *p.c.:* Leon Schlesinger prods for WB; *dir:* Fred Avery; *story:* Dave Monahan, Robert Clampett; *anim:* Virgil Ross; *sets:* John Didrik Johnsen; *ed:* Tregoweth E. Brown; *voices:* Mel Blanc, Rolfe Sedan, Dave Weber, Jim Bannon; *mus:* Carl W. Stalling; *prod sup:* Henry Binder, Raymond G. Katz; *col:* Tech. *sd:* Vit. 7 min. • Daffy pesters a Hollywood film director to let him make a movie. When he refuses, Daffy proceeds to wreck the film the director is making.

1411. Daffy Duck Slept Here (*Merrie Melodies*) 6 Mar. 1948; *p.c.:* WB; *dir:* Robert McKimson; *story:* Warren Foster; *anim:* Manny Gould, Charles McKimson, I. Ellis; *lay:* Cornett Wood; *back:* Richard H. Thomas; *ed:* Treg Brown; *voices:* Mel Blanc; *mus:* Carl Stalling; *prod mgr:* John W. Burton; *prod:* Edward Selzer; *col:* Tech. *sd:* Vit. 7 min. • Porky's roommate, Daffy, keeps him awake all night with his antics.

1412. The Daffy Duckaroo (*Looney Tunes*) 24 Oct. 1942; *p.c.:* Leon Schlesinger prods for WB; *dir/lay:* Norman McCabe; *story:* Melvin Millar; *anim:* John Carey, Cal Dalton, Arthur Davis, David Hoffman, Vive Risto; *sets:* Richard H. Thomas; *ed:* Treg Brown; *voices:* Mel Blanc, Sara Berner, Mina Farragut; *mus:* Carl W. Stalling. *song:* Mort Dixon, Fred Rose, Harry Warren; *ph:* John W. Burton; *prod mgr:* Henry Binder, Raymond G. Katz; b&w. *sd:* Vit. 8 min. • Radio crooner Daffy travels west and finds romance with an Indian girl duck but has a rival in her elephantine boyfriend, Little Beaver.

1413. Daffy Rents (*Looney Tunes*) 26 Mar. 1966; *p.c.:* DFE for WB; *dir:* Robert McKimson; *story:* Michael O'Connor; *anim:* Bob Matz, Manny Perez, George Grandpré, Norm McCabe; *lay:* Dick Ung; *back:* Tom O'Loughlin; *ed:* Al Wahrman; *voices:* Mel Blanc, Gonzalez-Gonzales; *mus:* Irving Gertz; *col:* Tech. *sd:* Vit. 6 min. • The manager of a rest home for neurotic cats calls in Daffy to dispose of Speedy Gonzales.

1414. Daffy — The Commando (*Looney Tunes*) 20 Nov. 1943; *p.c.:* Leon Schlesinger prods for WB; *dir:* I. Freleng; *story:* Michael Maltese; *anim:* Ken Champin; *lay:* Owen Fitzgerald; *back:* Lenard Kester; *ed:* Treg Brown; *voices:* Mel Blanc. *mus:* Carl W. Stalling; *ph:* John W. Burton; *prod sup:* Henry Binder, Raymond Katz; *col:* Tech. *sd:* Vit. 7 min. • Daffy parachutes into "No-Man's Land" and comes face-to-face with the notorious German, General Von Vulture! Caricature of Adolf Hitler.

1415. Daffydilly Daddy (*Little Lulu*) 25 May 1945; *p.c.:* Famous for Para; *dir:* Seymour Kneitel; *story:* Joe Stultz, Carl Meyer; *anim:* Orestes Calpini, Reuben Grossman, Otto Feuer, Frank Little; *sets:* Anton Loeb; *voice:* Cecil Roy; *mus:* Winston Sharples; *title song:* Buddy Kaye, Fred Wise, Sammy Timberg; *prod mgr:* Sam Buchwald; *col:* Tech. *sd:* RCA. 8 min. • Lulu puts a posy for the Flower Show in a barrel of "Vigro." It bursts in bloom but she loses it and a bulldog prevents her from retrieving it.

1416. Daffy's Diner (*Merrie Melodies*) 21 Jan. 1967; *p.c.:* DFE for WB; *dir:* Robert McKimson; *story:* Michael O'Connor; *anim:* Manny Perez, Warren Batchelder, Ted Bonnicksen, Art Leonardi, Don Williams, Bob Matz, Norm McCabe; *lay:* Dick Ung; *back:* Tom O'Loughlin; *ed:* Lee Gunther; *voices:* Mel Blanc; *mus:* Walter Greene; *col:* Tech. *sd:* Vit. 6 min. • Daffy's roadside eating establishment's speciality is "mouseburgers" for hungry cats.

1417. Daffy's Inn Trouble (*Looney Tunes*) 23 Sept. 1961; *p.c.:* WB; *dir:* Robert McKimson; *story:* Dave DeTiege; *anim:* Ted Bonnicksen, Warren Batchelder, George Grandpré; *lay:* Robert Gribbroek; *back:* William Butler; *ed:* Treg Brown; *voices:* Mel Blanc; *mus:* Milt Franklyn; *prod mgr:* William Orcutt; *prod:* David H. DePatie; *col:* Tech. *sd:* Vit. 7 min. • Weary of being a hotel janitor, Daffy opens a western hotel in opposition to Porky's.

1418. Daffy's Southern Exposure (*Looney Tunes*) 2 May 1942; *p.c.:* Leon Schlesinger prods for WB; *dir/lay:* Norm McCabe; *story:* Don Christensen; *anim:* John Carey, Cal Dalton, Arthur Davis, David Hoffman, Vive Risto; *sets:* Richard H. Thomas; *ed:* Treg Brown; *voices:* Mel Blanc, Stella Friend; *mus:* Carl W. Stalling; *song:* Harry Warren; *ph:* John W. Burton; *prod sup:* Henry Binder, Raymond G. Katz; b&w. *sd:* Vit. 7 min. • Daffy stays home for the winter until a fox and weasel, disguised as two old maids, take him in and the try to cook him.

1419. Daisy Bell (*Ko-Ko Song Car-Tune*) 30 May 1925; *p.c.:* Inkwell Studio for Red Seal; *prod/story:* Max Fleischer; *dir:* Dave Fleischer; *song:* Harry Dacre; b&w. *sil.* 5 min. • Ko-Ko leads a quartette singing "A Bicycle Built for Two." When the chorus is reached, the bouncing ball becomes a man who makes off with his bride ... followed by a troop of kids on bicycles. Reissued with sound 31 May 1929.

1420. The Dance Contest (*Popeye*) 23 Nov. 1934; *p.c.:* The Fleischer Studio for Para; *prod:* Max Fleischer; *dir:* Dave Fleischer; *anim:* Willard Bowsky, Dave Tendlar; *voices:* William A. Costello, Charles Carver; Louis Fleischer; *mus:* Sammy Timberg; b&w. *sd:* WE. 7 min. • Popeye and Olive enter a dance contest but Bluto soon takes over and ousts our hero. A bowl of spinach enables Popeye to win the contest ... and his girl.

1421. Dance of the Weed (*MGM cartoon*) 7 June 1941; *p.c.:* MGM. *prod:* Rudolf Ising; *dir:* Jerry Brewer; *mus:* Scott Bradley; *prod mgr:* Fred Quimby; *col:* Tech. *sd:* WE. 9 min. • A garden weed finds romance with a ballerina flower. They have an adventure together where they are chased by a three-headed snap-dragon.

1422. The Dancing Bear (*Terry-Toon*) 15 Oct. 1937; *p.c.:* TT for Educational/Fox; *mus:* Philip A. Scheib; b&w. *sd:* WE. 6 min. • Farmer Al Falfa meets a dancing bear that has escaped from a group of gypsies. He gets covered in a bearskin rug and is captured in mistake of the real thing.

1423. The Dancing Fool (*Talkartoons*) 8 Apr. 1932; *p.c.:* The Fleischer Studio for Para; *prod:* Max Fleischer; *dir:* Dave Fleischer; *anim:* Seymour Kneitel, Bernard Wolf; *mus:* Art Turkisher; b&w. *sd:* WE. 6 min. • Betty Boop's dancing school.

1424. Dancing on the Moon (*Color Classic*) 12 July 1935; *p.c.:* The Fleischer Studio for Para; *prod:* Max Fleischer; *dir:* Dave Fleischer; *anim:* Seymour Kneitel, Roland Crandall; *voice:* Mae Questel; *mus:* Sammy Timberg; *song:* Charles Tobias, Murray Mencher; *col:* Tech-2. *sd:* WE. 7 min. • The newlywed animals take a rockship to a Honeymoon planet.

1425. The Dancing Pirate 1936; *p.c.:* Pioneer Pictures for RKO. *prod:* John Speaks; *fx:* Willis O'Brien; *col:* Tech. *sd:* RCA. • Live-action story about a dancing master shanghaied by pirates. O'Brien animated a galleon lying at anchor painted onto glass.

1426. Dancing Shoes (*Heckle & Jeckle*) Nov. 1949; *p.c.:* TT for Fox; *dir:* Mannie Davis; *story:* John Foster; *voices:* Thomas Morrison; *mus:* Philip A. Scheib; *ph:* Douglas Moye; *col:* Tech. *sd:* RCA. 7 min. • The magpies set up their mechanical shoe business in a hotel lobby. The Hotel detective tries to evict them without much luck.

1427. The Dandy Lion (*Animated Antics*) 20 Sept. 1940; *p.c.:* The Fleischer Studio for Para; *prod:* Max Fleischer; *dir:* Dave Fleischer; *story:* Dan Gordon; *anim:* James Culhane, Alfred Eugster; *voices:* Margie Hines, Jack Mercer *mus:* Sammy Timberg; *i&p:* Kitty Pfister; *prod sup:* Sam Buchwald, Isidore Sparber; b&w. *sd:* WE. 7 min. • A small Indian girl brings into the encampment a lion disguised as a pet dog.

1428. Dangerous Dan McFoo (*Merrie Melodies*) 15 July 1939; *p.c.:* Leon Schlesinger prods for WB; *dir:* Fred Avery; *story:* Rich Hogan, Robert Clampett; *anim:* Paul Smith; *sets:* John Didrik Johnsen; *ed:* Tregoweth E. Brown; *voices:* Robert Cameron Bruce, Arthur Q. Bryan, Mel Blanc, Sara Berner, The Sportsmen Quartet; *mus:* Carl W. Stalling; *prod sup:* Henry Binder, Raymond G. Katz; *col:* Tech. *sd:* Vit. 7 min. • Dan McFoo battles to the death with a wolf over the hand of his girl.

1429. Dangerous When Wet 1953; *p.c.:* MGM; *seq dir (cartoon):* William Hanna, Joseph Barbera; *anim:* Irven Spence; *mus:* Scott Bradley; *prod:* Fred Quimby; *col:* Tech. *sd:* WE. 7 min. *l/a/anim.* • Live-action film about Esther Williams swimming the English Channel. A dream sequence has Tom and Jerry helping Esther swim to Dover despite many distractions.

1430. Daniel Boone Jr. (*Terry-Toon*) Dec. 1960; *p.c.:* TT for Fox; *ex prod:* Bill Weiss; *dir:* Dave Tendlar; *story sup:* Tom Morrison; *story:* Eli Bauer; *anim:* Ed Donnelly, Armand Guidi, Cosmo Anzilotti, Dick Hall, John Guidi; *des:* Martin Strudler; *back:* John Zago; *voices:* John Myhers; *mus:* Phil Scheib; *prod mgr:* Frank Shudde; *col:* DeLuxe. *sd:* RCA. 6 min. • Hector Heathcote joins Daniel Boone but the outdoor life proves too much for him.

1431. Danté Dreamer (*Noveltoon*) 3 Jan. 1958; *p.c.:* Para Cartoons. *dir:* I. Sparber; *story:* Jack Mercer; *anim:* Al Eugster, Danté Barbetta; *sets:* John Zago; *mus:* Winston Sharples; *ph:* Leonard McCormick; *prod mgr:* Abe Goodman; *col:* Tech. *sd:* RCA. 6 min. • A boy daydreams that he's a knight slaying a dragon.

1432. Dare-Devil Droopy (*Droopy*) 31 Mar. 1951; *p.c.:* MGM; *dir:* Tex Avery; *story:* Rich Hogan; *anim:* Grant Simmons, Walter Clinton, Michael Lah; *lay/des:* Ed Benedict; *back:* John Didrik Johnsen; *ed:* Jim Faris; *voices:* Bill Thompson, Stan Freberg; *mus:* Scott Bradley; *ph:* Jack Stevens; *prod:* Fred Quimby; *col:* Tech. *sd:* RCA. 6 min. • Droopy and Butch vie for the job of a circus daredevil.

1433. A Dark Horse (*Aesop's Film Fable*) 23 Nov. 1923; *p.c.:* Fables Pictures Inc for Pathé; *dir:* Paul Terry; b&w. *sil.* 5 min. • Al Falfa's mule gets drunk on cider and wins the Derby. It turns out to be a dream.

1434. Darkest Africa (*Aesop's Film Fable*) 4 May 1925; *p.c.:* Fables Pictures Inc for Pathé; *dir:* Paul Terry; b&w. *sil.* 7 min. • A monkey manufactures a metal elephant and rides around the jungle in it.

1435. Darn Barn (*Possible Possum*) June 1965; *p.c.:* TT for Fox; *dir/anim:* Connie Rasinski; *col:* DeLuxe. *sd:* RCA. 5 min. • Poss and his friends rebuild the General's barn with opposition from the local builder. • See: *Possible Possum*

1436. Darwin's Theory of Evolution 1923; *p.c.:* Inkwell Studio for the Museum of Natural History; *prod:* Max Fleischer; *dir:* Dave Fleischer; b&w. *sil.* • A straightforward telling of the evolution of man.

1437. A Date for Dinner (*Mighty Mouse*) 29 Aug. 1947; *p.c.:* TT for Fox; *dir:* Eddie Donnelly; *story:* John Foster; *mus:* Philip A. Scheib; *col:* Tech. *sd:* RCA. 7 min. • When the mice tease the cat, it's up to Mighty Mouse to save them.

1438. A Date to Skate (*Popeye*) 18 Nov. 1938; *p.c.:* The Fleischer Studio for Para; *prod:* Max Fleischer; *dir:* Dave Fleischer; *anim:* Willard Bowsky, Orestes Calpini; *voices:* Jack Mercer, Mae Questel; *mus:* Sammy Timberg; *prod sup:* Sam Buchwald, Isidore Sparber; b&w. *sd:* WE. 7 min. • Popeye and Olive visit a roller-skating rink and Olive is trapped on a pair of runaway rollers.

1439. A Date with Duke (*Puppetoon*) 31 Oct. 1947; *p.c.:* George Pal prods for Para; *prod/dir:* George Pal; *story:* Jack Miller; *anim:* Gene Warren; *models:* John S. Abbott; *voices:* Duke Ellington, Walter Tetley; *mus:* Duke Ellington & His Orchestra; *ph:* William Snyder ASC; *col:* Tech. *sd:* WE. 8 min. *l/a/anim.* • Perfume bottles all fall easily into the music but one has to be coaxed with extracts from *The Perfume Suite*.

1440. Davey Cricket (*Beary Family*) May 1965; *p.c.:* Walter Lantz prods for Univ; *dir:* Paul J. Smith; *story:* Cal Howard; *anim:* Les Kline, Al Coe; *sets:* Art Landy, Ray Huffine; *voices:* Paul Frees, Grace Stafford; *mus:* Walter Greene; *prod mgr:* William E. Garity; *col:* Tech. *sd:* RCA. 6 min. • Charlie tries to find the source of an irritating squeak in the house implements.

1441. Davy 1970; *p.c.:* Murakami/Wolf. *dir/anim:* Fred Wolf; *col. sd.* • No story available.

1442. Davy Jones' Locker (*Willie Whopper*) 9 Dec. 1933; *p.c.:* Celebrity prods for MGM; *prod/dir:* Ub Iwerks; *anim:* Grim Natwick, Berny Wolf, Al Eugster; *voice:* Jane Withers; *mus:* Art Turkisher; *col:* Ciné. *sd:* PCP. 9 min. • Willie and his girl are dragged down to the bottom of the ocean and have adventures avoiding Davy Jones' clutches. One of three *Willie Whopper* cartoons to be made in color.

1443. Dawg Gawn (*Noveltoon*) 12 Dec. 1958; *p.c.:* Para Cartoons; *dir:* Seymour Kneitel; *story:* Carl Meyer; *anim:* Tom Johnson, Nick Tafuri; *sets:* Robert Owen; *voices:* Mae Questel, Jackson Beck; *mus:* Winston Sharples; *ph:* Leonard McCormick; *prod mgr:* Abe Goodman; *col:* Tech. *sd:* RCA. 6 min. • Audrey has a job keeping her pup, Pal, from the clutches of the dog catcher.

1444. A Day at the Beach (*Captain & the Kids*) 25 June 1938; *p.c.:* MGM; *dir:* Isadore Freleng; *voices:* Billy Bletcher, Jeanne Dunne, Bobbie Winkler; *mus:* Scott Bradley; *prod mgr:* Fred Quimby; *sep. sd:* WE. 8 min. • Der Captain's family visit the seaside. Mama has a futile attempt to bathe, the Inspector tries to build a sandcastle and Der Captain is plagued with lack of shade.

1445. A Day at the Zoo (*Merrie Melodies*) 11 Mar. 1939; *p.c.:* Leon Schlesinger prods for WB; *dir:* Fred Avery; *story:* Melvin Millar, Robert

Clampett; *anim:* Rollin Hamilton; *sets:* John Didrik Johnsen; *ed:* Tregoweth E. Brown; *voices:* Gil Warren, Mel Blanc, Danny Webb; *mus:* Carl W. Stalling; *prod sup:* Henry Binder, Raymond G. Katz; *col:* Tech. *sd:* Vit. 7 min. • A tour of the local zoo where Egghead keeps annoying the lion with dire consequences.

1446. The Day Dreamer 1966; *p.c.:* Videocraft for Avco/Embassy; *ex prod:* Joseph E. Levine; *prod/story:* Arthur Rankin Jr.; *dir:* Jules Bass; *seq dir:* Don Duga; *asst dir:* Kizo Nagashima; *dialogue:* Romeo Muller; *art dir:* Maurice Gordon; *fx:* Coastal Films Inc.; *voices: The Sandman:* Cyril Ritchard; *The Little Mermaid:* Hayley Mills; *Father Neptune:* Burl Ives; *The Sea Witch:* Tallulah Bankhead; *Tailors:* Terry-Thomas, Victor Borge; *The Emperor:* Ed Wynn; *Thumbelina:* Patty Duke; *The Rat:* Boris Karloff; *The Mole:* Sessue Hayakawa; *Title Singer:* Robert Goulet; *additional voices:* Larry Mann, Billie Richards, James Dougherty, William Marine; *mus:* Maury Laws; *songs:* Maury Laws, Jules Bass; *orch:* Don Costa; *anim ph:* Tad Mochinga; *l/a dir:* Ezra Stone; *l/a cast: Chris:* Paul O'Keefe; *Papa Anderson:* Jack Gilford; *The Pieman:* Ray Bolger; *Mrs. Klopplebopper:* Margaret Hamilton; *Big Claus:* Robert Harter; *l/a ph:* Daniel Cavelli; *choreography:* Tony Mordente; *sd:* Alan Mirchin, Eric Tomlinson, Peter Page, Richard Gramaglia; *rec sup:* Bernard Cowan; *Emperor's clothes des:* Oleg Cassini; *mobility fx:* John Hoppe; *optical fx:* Coastal Films Inc.; *make-up:* Phyllis Grens; *title des:* Al Hirschfeld; *prod mgr:* Sal Scoppa; *asso prod:* Larry Roemer; *col:* Pathé. *sd.* 101 min. *l/a/anim.* • A sequential adaptation of Hans Christian Andersen's stories: *The Little Mermaid, The Emperor's New Clothes* and *The Garden of Paradise* using puppet animation.

1447. A Day in June *(Terry-Toon)* 3 Mar. 1944; *p.c.:* TT for Fox; *dir:* Eddie Donnelly; *story:* John Foster; *mus:* Philip A. Scheib; *col:* Tech. *sd:* RCA. 6 min. • James Russell Lowell's famous poem is pictured with insects spending a summer's day by the river.

1448. Day Nurse *(Oswald)* 10 July 1932. *p.c.:* Univ; *dir:* Walter Lantz, "Bill" Nolan; *anim:* Ray Abrams, Fred Avery, "Bill" Weber, Jack Carr, Charles Hastings; *mus:* James Dietrich; b&w. *sd.* 6 min. • No story available.

1449. A Day Off *(Aesop's Film Fable)* 24 Nov. 1928; *p.c.:* Fables Pictures Inc for Pathé; *dir:* Paul Terry, John Foster; b&w. *sil.* 5 min. • No story available.

1450. A Day to Live *(Paul Terry-Toons)* 31 May 1931; *p.c.:* Terry, Moser & Coffman for Educational/Fox; *dir:* Paul Terry, Frank Moser; *anim:* Arthur Babbitt, Frank Moser, Vladimir Tytla; *mus:* Philip A. Scheib; b&w. *sd:* WE. 6 min. • Farmer Al Falfa's dream to disprove his doctor's prediction.

1451. A Day's Outing *(Aesop's Film Fable)* 28 Nov. 1925; *p.c.:* Fables Pictures Inc for Pathé; *dir:* Paul Terry; b&w. *sil.* 7 min. • The Farmer takes the animals to a circus. When a lion escapes he insists on licking Al Falfa's face.

1452. The Dead End Cats *(Mighty Mouse)* 14 Feb. 1947; *p.c.:* TT for Fox; *dir:* Eddie Donnelly; *story:* John Foster; *mus:* Philip A. Scheib; *col:* Tech. *sd:* RCA. 6 min. • Mighty Mouse's life is threatened by Black-Marketeering cats.

1453. The Deadwood Thunderball *(Roland & Rattfink)* 6 June 1969; *p.c.:* Mirisch/DFE for UA; *dir:* Hawley Pratt; *story:* John W. Dunn; *anim:* Manny Gould, Manny Perez, Art Leonardi, Warren Batchelder, Don Williams; *lay:* Dick Ung; *back:* Tom O'Loughlin; *ed:* Lee Gunther; *voices:* John Byner, Dave Barry; *mus:* Doug Goodwin; *ph:* John Burton Jr.; *prod sup:* Harry Love, Jim Foss; *col:* DeLuxe. *sd:* RCA. 6 min. • A crooked stage-coach company engages Rattfink to stop a new railroad getting through.

1454. Dear Mr. President 1972; *p.c.:* Hanna-Barbera prods; *prod:* William Hanna, Joseph Barbera. *dir:* Carl Urbano; *story:* Dean Elliot; *anim:* Ed Barge, Oliver E. Callahan, Bob Goe; *des:* John de Marco, Roy Morita; *back:* Walt Peregoy, Cathy Clark; *Xerography:* Robert "Tiger" West; *ph:* Frank Paiker; *sd:* Richard Olsen, Bill Getty; col. *sd.* • No story available.

1455. Dear Old Pals *(Song Car-Tune)* 1924; *p.c.:* Inkwell Studio for Red Seal; *prod:* Max Fleischer; *dir:* Dave Fleischer; b&w. *sil.* • No story available.

1456. Dear Old Switzerland *(Terry-Toons)* 22 Dec. 1944; *p.c.:* TT for Fox; *dir:* Eddie Donnelly; *story:* John Foster; *mus:* Philip A. Scheib; *ph:* Douglas Moye; *col:* Tech. *sd:* RCA. 7 min. • When an Alpine skiier is lost in the Alps, a St. Bernard sets out to rescue him.

1457. Dear Uncle *(Fun and Facts About America)* 1953; *p.c.:* John Sutherland prods for Harding College/MGM; *asso prod:* George Gordon; *dir:* Carl Urbano; *anim:* Arnold Gillespie, Henry Hoffman, Phil Monroe; *sets:* Gerald Nevius, Edgar Starr; *voices:* Frank Nelson, Herburt Vigran; *mus:* Eugene Poddany; *col:* Tech. *sd:* RCA. 10 min. • Uncle Sam explains to a businessman and a worker about why we should have to pay taxes.

1458. Death Becomes Her 31 July 1992; *p.c.:* UIP; *anim:* Gordon Baker, Scott Bonnenfant; *Rotoscope:* Tom Bertino, Jack Mongovan, Terry Molatore, Joanne Hafner, Lisa Drostova, Leslie Arvio, Debra Bainum; *cgi prod sup:* Judith Weaver; *artists:* Barbara Brennan, Geoff Campbell, Richard L. Cohen, Rachel Falk, Carl N. Frederick, John Horn, Sandy Houston, Sandra Ford Karpman, Laurel Klick, Jeffrey B. Light, Greg Maloney, Jim Mitchell, Ron Moreland, George Murphy, Patrick T. Myers, Joseph Pasquale, Carolyn Ensle Rendu, Stuart Robertson, Stephen Rosenbaum, John Schlag, Andrew H. Schmidt, Alex Seiden, Thomas J. Smith, Robert Weaver; *col. sd:* Dolby SR. 104 min. *l/a.* • Live-action comedy: A playwright plots the demise of an actress who has stolen her husband. She drinks an "elixir of life," rendering her indestructable. When it is discovered her nemisis has also drunk the elixir, they both try to kill each other ... but to no avail. Animation adds to the comic fun of the rivals' bodies distorting with each attack getting more extreme than the last.

1459. Deduce, You Say *(Looney Tunes)* 29 Sept. 1956; *p.c.:* WB; *dir:* Chuck Jones; *story:* Michael Maltese; *anim:* Abe Levitow, Richard Thompson, Ken Harris, Ben Washam; *lay:* Maurice Noble; *back:* Philip de Guard; *ed:* Treg Brown; *voices:* Mel Blanc, June Foray; *mus:* Milt Franklyn; *prod mgr:* John W. Burton; *prod:* Edward Selzer; *col:* Tech. *sd:* Vit. 7 min. • Daffy and Porky take on the identity of Holmes and Watson to track down "The Shropshire Slasher."

1460. The Deep Boo Sea *(Casper)* 15 Feb. 1952; *p.c.:* Famous for Para; *dir:* Seymour Kneitel; *story:* Larz Bourne; *anim:* Myron Waldman, Nick Tafuri; *sets:* Anton Loeb; *voices:* Alan Shay, Cecil Roy, Jack Mercer, Jackson Beck; *mus:* Winston Sharples; *ph:* Leonard McCormick; *prod mgr:* Seymour Shultz; *col:* Tech. *sd:* RCA. 7 min. • Casper plays "pirates" with Billy, a small boy who later has to be rescued from the jaws of a whale.

1461. Deep Freeze Squeeze *(Chilly Willy)* 1 Mar. 1964; *p.c.:* Walter Lantz prods for Univ; *dir:* Sid Marcus; *anim:* Ray Abrams, Art Davis; *sets:* Art Landy, Ray Huffine; *voices:* Daws Butler; *mus:* Walter Greene; *prod mgr:* William E. Garity; *col:* Tech. *sd:* RCA. 6 min. • Chilly gets fired from his job as a waiter in Smedley's cafe and seeks revenge.

1462. Deep Rising 30 Jan. 1998; *p.c.:* Hollywood Pictures Company; *addit creature anim/special visual fx:* ILM visual fx sup: John Berton; *anim sup:* Dan Taylor; *anim visual fx prod:* Tom Kennedy; *cg sup:* Michael Bauer, Scott Frankel; *cg anim:* Paul Kavanagh, Julie Nelson, Steve Nichols, Tom St. Amand, Glenn Sylvester, William R. Wright; "Half-digested Billy": *Blur Studio: cg sup:* David Stinnett; *prod:* Ryan Berg; *anim:* Greg Tsadilas, Tim Montijo, Jennifer Rama; *systems admin:* Duane Powell; *col:* Tech. *sd:* SDDS/Dolby Digital/dts sound. Panavision. 106 min. *l/a.* • Live-action adventure: A hire boat transporting a band of mercinaries across the China Sea is attacked by a sea monster.

1463. Deep Sea Doodle *(Heckle & Jeckle)* Oct. 1960; *p.c.:* TT for Fox; *ex prod:* Bill Weiss; *dir:* Dave Tendlar; *story sup:* Tom Morrison; *story:* Eli Bauer; *anim:* Ed Donnelly, Cosmo Anzilotti, Mannie Davis; *des:* John Zago; *back:* Frank Endres; *voices:* Roy Halee; *mus:* Phil Scheib; *prod mgr:* Frank Schudde; *col:* DeLuxe. *sd:* RCA. 6 min. • The magpies take Dimwit on a fishing excursion.

1464. Deep Stuff *(Aesop's Film Fable)* 25 Apr. 1925; *p.c.:* Fables Pictures Inc for Pathé; *dir:* Paul Terry; b&w. *sil.* 9 min. • The Farmer and his cat go fishing. Family life of the denizen of the deep is depicted.

1465. The Defiant Giant *(Honey Halfwitch)*; June 1966; *p.c.:* Para Cartoons; *dir:* Shamus Culhane; *story:* Heyward Kling, Howard Post; *anim:* Al Eugster, Wm. B. Pattengill, Nick Tafuri, Martin Taras; *sets:* Robert Little; *voices:* Shari Lewis, Bob MacFadden; *mus:* Winston Sharples; *col:* Tech. *sd:* RCA. 6 min. • George the Giant wants Honey to shrink a bully who keeps picking on him.

1466. The Delivery Boy *(Mickey Mouse)* 6 June 1931; *p.c.:* Walter E. Disney for Colum; *dir:* Burton F. Gillett; *anim:* Charles Byrne, Johnny Cannon, Les Clark, Chuck Couch, Jack Cutting, Gilles de Tremaudan,

Norman Ferguson, Hardie Gramatky, David D. Hand, Jack King, George Lane, Richard Lundy, Bill Mason, Tom Palmer, Harry Reeves, Frank Tipper, Rudy Zamora; *voices:* Marcellite Garner, Walt Disney; *mus:* Bert Lewis; b&w. *sd:* PCP. 7 min. • Delivery boy Mickey upsets a case of musical instruments into the barnyard and the animals get to them.

1467. DePatie-Freleng Film • *Titles (animated and non-animated):* **The Pink Panther** 1963, **A Shot in the Dark** *(animated by TVC)* 1964, **Dead Ringer** 1964, **How to Murder Your Wife** 1964, **The Best Man** 1964, **Sex and the Single Girl** 1964, **Love Has Many Faces** 1964, **The Art of Love** 1965, **Do Not Disturb** 1965, **The Great Race** 1965, **The Hallelujah Trail** *(animated maps)* 1965, **The Satan Bug** 1965, **The Trouble with Angels** 1966, **The President's Analyst** 1967, **Inspector Clouseau** *(animated by TVC)* 1968, **With Six You Get Egg Roll** 1968, **Star Wars** *(photographic fx)* 1977, **The Revenge of the Pink Panther** 1978

1468. Deputy Droopy *(Droopy)* 28 Oct. 1955; *p.c.:* MGM; *dir:* Tex Avery, Michael Lah; *story:* Heck Allen; *anim:* Ed Barge, Irven Spence, Kenneth Muse, Lewis Marshall, Walter Clinton, Ray Patterson; *lay/des:* Ed Benedict; *back:* Vera Ohman; *ed:* Jim Faris; *voices:* Daws Butler; *mus:* Scott Bradley; *ph:* Jack Stevens; *col:* Tech. *sd:* WE. 7 min. • Two bandits try to rob the Sheriff's safe, guarded by Deputy Droopy.

1469. Der Fuehrer's Face *(Donald Duck)* 1 Jan. 1943; *p.c.:* Walt Disney prods for RKO; *dir:* Jack Kinney; *asst dir:* Bee Selck; *story sup:* Joe Grant, Dick Huemer; *anim:* Bob Carlson, Les Clark, Hugh Fraser, Bill Justice, Milt Neil, George Nicholas, John Sibley; *fx:* Andy Engman; *lay:* Don da Gradi; *voices:* Charles Judels, Clarence Nash; *mus/song:* Oliver Wallace; *col:* Tech. *sd:* RCA. 7 min. *Academy Award.* • Donald dreams he's living in a Nazi-governed land of bayonet discipline, starvation and hard work. Excellent example of war-time propaganda with the theme tune becoming a popular hit of the time and Hitler's face becoming the target for a well-aimed tomato!

1470. Derby Day *(Aesop's Film Fable)* 1 Sept. 1923; *p.c.:* Fables Pictures Inc for Pathé; *dir:* Paul Terry; b&w. sil. 5 min. • A "Dark Horse" is fed a tonic which makes him sail over the heads of the other Derby entries. He lands at the winning post, only to expire. Moral: "The straight way is the best way."

1471. A Desert Dilemma (4) 1930; *p.c.:* A-C/Aetna Insurance Co. b&w. *sd:* WE. 5 min. • The family set out to cross the continent in a flivver. When they collide with another car in the desert, the journey can't continue until Father remembers that he is insured with Aetna.

1472. Desert Sunk *(Krazy Kat)* 27 Mar. 1930; *p.c.:* Winkler for Colum; *prod:* Charles Mintz; *anim:* Ben Harrison, Manny Gould; *mus:* Joe de Nat; b&w. *sd:* RCA. 6 min. • No story available.

1473. Deserted Sheiks *(Aesop's Film Fable)* 31 July 1924; *p.c.:* Fables Pictures Inc for Pathé; *dir:* Paul Terry; b&w. sil. 5 min. • The larger beasts of the jungle visit Monsieur Rat's Beauty Parlor to lessen their weight.

1474. Design for Leaving *(Merrie Melodies)* 27 Mar. 1954; *p.c.:* WB; *dir:* Robert McKimson; *story:* Tedd Pierce; *anim:* Phil de Lara, Charles McKimson, Herman Cohen, Rod Scribner; *lay:* Robert Givens; *back:* Richard H. Thomas; *ed:* Treg Brown; *voices:* Mel Blanc, Arthur Q. Bryan; *mus:* Carl Stalling; *prod mgr:* John W. Burton; *prod:* Edward Selzer; *col:* Tech. *sd:* Vit. 7 min. • Daffy equips Elmer's house with unwanted futuristic gadgets.

1475. Designs on Jerry *(Tom & Jerry)* 2 Sept. 1955; *p.c.:* MGM; *dir:* William Hanna, Joseph Barbera; *anim:* Irven Spence, Kenneth Muse, Ed Barge; *back:* John Didrik Johnsen; *mus:* Scott Bradley; *prod:* Fred Quimby; *col:* Tech. *sd:* WE. 7 min. • While Tom sleeps, Jerry alters his blueprint for "The Perfect Mousetrap."

1476. A Desperate Love 1918; *p.c.:* Hy Mayer for Univ; *prod:* P.A. Powers; *dir/anim:* Hy Mayer; b&w. sil. • No story available.

1477. Desperately Seeking Susan 29 May 1985; *p.c.:* Orion for Rank; *title des:* Michael Sporn Animation; *col:* DeLuxe. *sd:* Stereo. • Live-action comedy about a bored housewife seeking escape through newspaper columns. Animated titles.

1478. Destination Magoo *(Mr. Magoo)* 16 Dec. 1954; *p.c.:* UPA for Colum; *ex prod:* Stephen Bosustow; *dir:* Pete Burness; *story/voices:* Jim Backus, Jerry Hausner; *story treatment:* Tedd Pierce; *anim:* Rudy Larriva, Cecil Surry, Tom McDonald; *lay:* Sterling Sturtevant; *back:* Bob McIntosh;

mus: Lou Maury; *prod mgr:* Herbert Klynn; *col:* Tech. *sd:* RCA. 7 min. • Magoo accidentally ignites a rocket ship and blasts off ... falling to earth in Coney Island.

1479. Destination Meatball *(Woody Woodpecker)* 24 Dec. 1951; *p.c.:* Walter Lantz prods for Univ; *dir:* Walter Lantz; *anim:* Don Patterson, Ray Abrams, La Verne Harding, Paul Smith; *sets:* Fred Brunish; *mus:* Clarence E. Wheeler; *prod mgr:* William E. Garity; *col:* Tech. *sd:* RCA. 6 min. • Supermarket manager, Buzz Buzzard, ups his prices as soon as Woody enters, eliminating "hidden taxes" with invisible ink. The ink turns Woody invisible and he seeks his revenge.

1480. Destination Moon 1950; *p.c.:* Eagle-Lion for Univ; *prod:* George Pal; *anim fx:* John S. Abbott, Fred Madison; *seq dir:* Walter Lantz, Irving Pichel; *anim:* Don Patterson, Ray Abrams, La Verne Harding; *sets:* Fred Brunish; *voices:* Michael Miller, Grace Stafford; *col:* Tech. *sd:* WE. (seq) 4 min • Live-action science fiction feature. The astronaut crew watches a light hearted instructional about the problems of space travel featuring Woody Woodpecker. • See: *Lantz, Walter, Productions (Titles and Sequences)*

1481. The Detective *(Oswald)* 22 Sept. 1930; *p.c.:* Univ; *dir:* Walter Lantz, "Bill" Nolan; *anim:* Clyde Geronimi, Manuel Moreno, Ray Abrams, Fred Avery, Lester Kline, "Pinto" Colvig; *mus:* James Dietrich; b&w. *sd:* WE. 6 min. • Father worm shoots Cock Robin for trying to eat his son. Oswald gets the blame and goes on trial.

1482. Detouring America *(Merrie Melodies)* 26 Aug. 1939; *p.c.:* Leon Schlesinger prods for WB; *dir:* Fred Avery; *story:* Jack Miller, Robert Clampett; *anim:* Rollin Hamilton; *sets:* John Didrik Johnsen; *ed:* Tregoweth E. Brown; *voices:* Robert C. Bruce, Mel Blanc; *mus:* Carl W. Stalling; *prod sup:* Henry Binder, Raymond G. Katz; *col:* Tech. *sd:* Vit. 9 min. • Spot-gags on and about America, featuring an on-going story of a "Human Fly" climbing the Empire State Building.

1483. Detouring Through Maine *(Screen Song)* 10 Feb. 1950; *p.c.:* Famous for Para; *dir:* Seymour Kneitel; *story:* Larz Bourne; *anim:* Al Eugster, Bill Hudson; *sets:* Robert Connavale, mus: Winston Sharples; *song:* Lincoln Colcord, E.A. Fenstad; *prod mgr:* Sam Buchwald; *col:* Tech. *sd:* RCA. 7 min. • The rockbound coast of Maine is the subject, looking at hatcheries, lumberjacks and lobster catching, culminating in *The Maine Stein Song.*

1484. Devil May Hare *(Looney Tunes)* 19 June 1954; *p.c.:* WB; *dir:* Robert McKimson; *story:* Sid Marcus; *anim:* Herman Cohen, Rod Scribner, Phil de Lara, Charles McKimson; *lay:* Robert Givens; *back:* Richard H. Thomas; *ed:* Treg Brown; *voices:* Mel Blanc; *mus:* Carl Stalling; *prod mgr:* John W. Burton; *prod:* Edward Selzer; *col:* Tech. *sd:* Vit. 7 min. • Bugs encounters the Tasmanian Devil for the first time — A beast that will eat anything ... especially rabbit!

1485. Devil of the Deep *(Paul Terry-Toon)* 24 May 1938; *p.c.:* TT for Educational/Fox; *dir:* John Foster; *mus:* Philip A. Scheib; b&w. *sd:* WE. 6 min. • A "Captain Bob Bartlett" type describes how he captured a huge fish.

1486. Devilled Yeggs *(The Dogfather)* 29 Dec. 1974; *p.c.:* DFE for UA; *dir:* Gerry Chiniquy; *story:* John Dunn; *anim:* Bob Richardson, Nelson Shin, Bob Bransford, Norm McCabe; *ed:* Rick Steward; *lay:* Dick Ung; *back:* Richard H. Thomas; *voices:* Bob Holt, Frank Welker; *mus:* Dean Elliott; *col:* DeLuxe. *sd:* RCA. 6 min. • Croaker McClaw, a feline gangster, is assigned to eliminate Charlie the Singer ... a bird.

1487. Devil's Feud Cake *(Merrie Melodies)* Feb. 1963; *p.c.:* WB; *dir:* Friz Freleng; *story:* Friz Freleng, Warren Foster; *anim:* Gerry Chiniquy, Virgil Ross, Bob Matz, Art Leonardi, Lee Halpern; *lay:* Hawley Pratt; *back:* Tom O'Loughlin, Irv Wyner; *ed:* Treg Brown; *voices:* Mel Blanc; *mus:* Bill Lava; *prod mgr:* Bill Orcutt; *prod:* David H. DePatie; *col:* Tech. *sd:* Vit. 6 min. *Seq: Hare Lift; Roman Legion Hare; Sahara Hare.* • Yosemite Sam finds himself in Hades and is given the ultimatum of luring Bugs down or staying himself.

1488. D'Fightin' Ones *(Merrie Melodies)* 22 Apr. 1961; *p.c.:* WB; *dir:* Friz Freleng; *anim:* Gerry Chiniquy, Virgil Ross, Art Davis; *lay:* Hawley Pratt; *back:* Tom O'Loughlin; *ed:* Treg Brown; *voices:* Mel Blanc; *mus:* Milt Franklyn; *prod mgr:* William Orcutt; *prod:* David H. DePatie; *col:* Tech. *sd:* Vit. 7 min. • Sylvester finds himself handcuffed to a dog and on the run from the city pound in this witty parody of *The Defiant Ones.*

1489. Dial P for Pink (*Pink Panther*) 17 Mar. 1965; *p.c.*: Mirisch/Geoffrey/DFE for UA; *dir*: Friz Freleng, Hawley Pratt; *story*: Bob Kurz; *anim*: La Verne Harding, Don Williams, Manny Perez, Warren Batchelder, Bob Matz, Norm McCabe; *back*: Tom O'Loughlin; *ed*: Lee Gunther; *mus*: Bill Lava; *theme tune*: Henry Mancini; *prod mgr*: Bill Orcutt; *col*: DeLuxe. *sd*: RCA. 8 min. • A burglar attempts to crack a safe, unaware the Panther is asleep inside.

1490. Dick Whittington's Cat (*ComiColor*) 30 May 1936; *p.c.*: Celebrity prods; *prod/dir*: Ub Iwerks; *anim*: Irven Spence; *mus*: Carl Stalling; *col*: Ciné. *sd*: PCP. 7 min. • Dick's cat rids an oriental potentate's palace of mice and wins his master a chest of gold.

1491. Dickey Moe (*Tom & Jerry*) 1960 *p.c.*: Rembrandt for MGM; *prod*: William L. Snyder; *dir*: Gene Deitch; *story*: Eli Bauer, Gene Deitch; *anim*: Vaclav Bedrich; *voice*: Allen Swift; *mus*: Stepan Koníchek; *col*: Metro. *sd*: WE. 8 min. • Tom is shanghaied aboard Cpt. Ahab's ship to search for Dickey Moe, the great white whale. • See: *Tom and Jerry (Rembrandt Studio)*

1492. Died in the Wool (*Aesop's Film Fable*) 19 June 1927; *p.c.*: Fables Pictures Inc for Pathé; *dir*: Paul Terry; b&w. sil. 6 min. • Shepherd Milt Mouse is spotted by Tom Cat with his sweetie, Rita. Tom makes a bargain with a wolf, forcing his dupe to don female garb to vamp Milt.

1493. Dietetic Pink (*Pink Panther*) 1978; *p.c.*: Mirisch/Geoffrey/DFE for UA; *dir*: Sid Marcus; *story*: Cliff Roberts; *anim*: Don Williams, Lee Halpern, Bernard Posner, Joan Case; *lay*: Martin Strudler; *back*: Richard H. Thomas; *ed*: Ray Lee; *mus*: Doug Goodwin; *theme tune*: Henry Mancini; *ph*: John Burton Jr.; *prod mgr*: Lee Gunther; *col*: DeLuxe. *sd*: RCA. 6 min • The Panther imagines himself overweight and tries a drastic diet.

1494. Dig That Dog 12 Apr. 1954; *p.c.*: Walter Lantz prods for Univ; *dir/story/anim*: Ray Patterson, Grant Simmons; *sets*: Raymond Jacobs, Art Landy; *voices*: Frank Nelson, Dal McKennon, Grace Stafford; *mus*: Clarence Wheeler; *prod mgr*: William E. Garity; *col*: Tech. *sd*: RCA. 6 min. • Cuddles, a Great Dane, has a nasty habit of burying everything he can lay his paws on.

1495. Digging for Gold (*Aesop's Film Fable*) 29 May 1927; *p.c.*: Fables Pictures Inc for Pathé; *dir*: Paul Terry; b&w. sil. 8 min. • Burlesque on the gold strike at Weepah. Farmer Al strikes gold but a bear chases him away while his cat and dog abscond with the takings to a bar.

1496. Dime to Retire (*Looney Tunes*) 27 Mar. 1954; *p.c.*: WB; *dir*: Robert McKimson; *story*: Sid Marcus; *anim*: Robert McKimson, Keith Darling; *lay*: Robert Givens; *back*: Richard H. Thomas; *ed*: Treg Brown; *voices*: Mel Blanc; *mus*: Milt Franklyn; *prod mgr*: John W. Burton; *prod*: Edward Selzer; *col*: Tech. *sd*: Vit. 7 min. • Porky finds a cheap hotel run by Daffy but costs spiral when the need for various pests removed from his room occurs.

1497. Dinah (*Screen Songs*) 12 Jan. 1933; *p.c.*: The Fleischer Studio for Para; *prod*: Max Fleischer; *dir*: Dave Fleischer; *anim*: David Tendlar, William Henning; *song*: Harry Akst, Sam Lewis, Joe Young; *l/a*: The Mills Brothers; b&w. *sd*: WE. 7½ min. *l/a/anim.* • While the animals load the steam ship *Dinah*, three sailors emerge from the porthole to perform to the Mills Brothers' music.

1498. Ding Dog Daddy (*Merrie Melodies*) 28 Nov. 1942; *p.c.*: Leon Schlesinger prods for WB; *dir*: I. Freleng; *story*: Ted Pierce; *anim*: Gerry Chiniquy; *lay*: Owen Fitzgerald; *back*: Lenard Kester; *ed*: Treg Brown; *voices*: Pinto Colvig, Sara Berner, Ted Pierce; *mus*: Carl W. Stalling; *prod sup*: Henry Binder, Raymond G. Katz; *col*: Tech. *sd*: Vit. 7 min. • A dopey dog falls in love with a statue of a greyhound and follows her to the factory where it gets melted for ammunition.

1499. Ding Dong Doggie (*Betty Boop*) 23 July 1937; *p.c.*: The Fleischer Studio for Para; *prod*: Max Fleischer; *dir*: Dave Fleischer; *anim*: Thomas Johnson, Frank Endres; *voices*: Mae Questel, Frances Reynolds; *mus*: Sammy Timberg; b&w. *sd*: WE. 7 min. • Pudgy longs to be a fire dog but a fire in the general store puts him off the whole idea.

1500. Dingbat Land (*Terry-Toon*) Mar. 1949; *p.c.*: TT for Fox; *dir*: Connie Rasinski; *story*: John Foster; *anim*: Jim Tyer; *voices*: Arthur Kay, Thomas Morrison; *mus*: Philip A. Scheib; *ph*: Douglas Moye; *col*: Tech. *sd*: RCA. 6 min. • Gandy and Sourpuss fall asleep and dream they are in a crazy land hunting a lunatic bird known as a Dingbat.

1501. Dinky Doodle and the Bad Man 20 Sept. 1925; *p.c.*: Bray prods for FBO; *dir/story*: Walter Lantz. *anim*: Clyde Geronimi; b&w. sil. 6 min. *l/a/anim.* • Dinky and Walter have a thrilling experience in lassoing a desperado, Dynamite Dan for a $1,000 reward.

1502. Dinky Doodle and the Little Orphan 4 July 1926; *p.c.*: Bray prods for FBO; *dir/story*: Walter Lantz, Clyde Geronimi; b&w sil. 6 min. *l/a/anim.* • Walter finds a baby and seeks to amuse it. The baby's cries force him to draw a stork to deposit it at another address.

1503. Dinky Doodle in Egypt 8 Apr. 1926; *p.c.*: Bray prods; *dir/story*: Walter Lantz. *anim*: Clyde Geronimi; b&w. sil. 6 min. *l/a/anim.* • Walter dresses as an Egyptian to go to a party leaving Dinky and Weakheart at home. They dream they are in Egypt where Dinky has a chariot race with a mummy.

1504. Dinky Doodle in Lost and Found 19 Feb. 1926; *p.c.*: Bray prods for FBO; *dir/story*: Walter Lantz. *anim*: Clyde Geronimi; b&w. sil. 6 min. *l/a/anim.* • Dinky and Weakheart read about a kidnapper and apprehend him via a painting of Apache dancing duo.

1505. Dinky Doodle in the Arctic 21 Mar. 1926; *p.c.*: Bray prods for FBO; *dir/story*: Walter Lantz; *anim*: Clyde Geronimi; b&w. sil. 6 min. *l/a/anim.* • Dinky Doodle and Weakheart go skiing.

1506. Dinky Doodle in the Army 29 Aug. 1926; *p.c.*: Bray prods for FBO; *dir/story*: Walter Lantz; *anim*: Clyde Geronimi; b&w. sil. 6 min. *l/a/anim.* • Walter is a General. Dinky and his pup, Weakheart, are put through various military experiences in the cartoon section.

1507. Dinky Doodle in the Circus 29 Nov. 1925; *p.c.*: Bray prods for FBO; *dir/story*: Walter Lantz; *anim*: Clyde Geronimi; b&w. sil. 6 min. *l/a/anim.* • No story available.

1508. Dinky Doodle in the Hunt 1 Nov. 1925; *p.c.*: Bray prods for FBO; *dir/story*: Walter Lantz; *anim*: Clyde Geronimi; b&w. sil. 6 min. *l/a/anim.* • Walter and Dinky go hunting. A woodpecker eats the bullet from Walt's gun and they get chased by a bear.

1509. Dinky Doodle in the Restaurant rel; 27 Dec. 1925; *p.c.*: Bray prods for FBO; *dir/story*: Walter Lantz; *anim*: Clyde Geronimi; b&w. sil. 6 min. *l/a/anim.* • Dinky gives a child's flapjack balancers some interesting instructions.

1510. Dinky Doodle in the Wild West 12 May 1926; *p.c.*: Bray prods for FBO; *dir/story*: Walter Lantz; *anim*: Clyde Geronimi; b&w. sil. 6 min. *l/a/anim.* • Walter's pen has Dinky and Weakheart encounter a swarm of Indians who invade the stagecoach. The savages chase the pair of them back to the Lantz studio where they grab the opportunity of scalping the one lone hair from Walt's bald pate.

1511. Dinky Doodle in Uncle Tom's Cabin 21 Feb. 1926; *p.c.*: Bray prods for FBO; *dir/story*: Walter Lantz; *anim*: Clyde Geronimi; b&w. sil. 6 min. *l/a/anim.* • Dinky stages his version of the famous story.

1512. Dinky Doodle's Bedtime Story 6 June 1926; *p.c.*: Bray prods for FBO; *dir/story*: Walter Lantz; *anim*: Clyde Geronimi; b&w. sil. 6 min. *l/a/anim.* • Walter tunes in the radio to "Fairyland," encouraging all the Mother Goose characters to emerge from the speaker and cause havoc in the studio.

1513. Dinky Finds a Home (*Dinky Duck*) 7 July 1946; *p.c.*: TT for Fox; *dir*: Eddie Donnelly; *story*: John Foster; *mus*: Philip A. Scheib; *col*: Tech. *sd*: RCA. 7 min. • Dinky leaves home and, after a precarious number of run-ins with a rooster, returns home to his parents.

1514. Dinky in the Beauty Shop (*Dinky Duck*) 28 Apr. 1950; *p.c.*: TT for Fox; *dir*: Eddie Donnelly; *story*: Tom Morrison; *anim*: Jim Tyer; *mus*: Philip A. Scheib; *col*: Tech. *sd*: RCA. 7 min. • A buzzard converts his trailer into a beauty salon in order to lure the farmyard fowl into his clutches.

1515. Dinner Time (*Aesop's Sound Fable*) 17 Dec. 1928; *p.c.*: Fables Pictures Inc for Pathé *dir*: Paul Terry, John Foster; *mus*: Josiah Zuro; *sd fx*: Maurice H. Manne; b&w. *sd*: RCA (disc). 6 min. • Farmer Al Falfa is running a butcher shop which all the dogs invade when his back is turned. He calls the Public Dog Pound but they aren't much help. • Fables' first sound release.

1516. The Dinosaur and the Missing Link 24 Mar. 1917 (made in 1915); *p.c.*: Conquest Pictures for Thomas A. Edison Inc. *prod*: Herman

Wobber; *dir/anim:* Willis H. O'Brien; b&w. *sil.* 7 min. • Two stoneage suitors set out to capture food for the girl they both love. Stonejaw Steve encounters a battle between a dinosaur and Wild Willie (a King Kong prototype), goes to view Willie's corpse and is mistaken for the victor of the fight. Model animation. Reissued as *The Dinosaur and the Baboon*.

1517. Dinosaur Cartoon 1910; *dir/anim:* John R. Bray; *story:* Frederick Melville; b&w. *sil.* • Often mistaken for Winsor McCay's *Gertie the Dinosaur*, this film follows the travels of a prehistoric creature responding to a live off-screen commentator and boasts having used 12000 drawings in the making of it.

1518. Dinosaurus 1960; *p.c.:* Univ/Fairview/Jack Harris; *prod/dir:* Irvin S. Yeaworth Jr.; *anim/fx:* Tim Barr, Wah Chang, Tom Holland, Don Stahlin, Gene Warren; *model maker:* Marcel Delgado; *col:* DeLuxe. *sd:* WE 85 min. *l/a/anim.* • Lightning revives a Neanderthal man and a Tyranasaurus rex who both wreak havoc on the populace. Live-action film with animated dinosaur.

1519. The Dippy Diplomat (*Woody Woodpecker*) 27 Aug. 1945; *p.c.:* Walter Lantz prods for Univ; *dir:* James Culhane; *story:* Ben Hardaway, Milt Schaffer; *anim:* Pat Matthews, Grim Natwick; *lay/des:* Art Heinemann; *voices:* Jack Mather, Lee Sweetland, Ben Hardaway; *mus:* Darrell Calker; *col:* Tech. *sd:* WE. 7 min. • Wally Walrus prepares a banquet for a visiting dignitary which attracts Woody. He poses as the guest and divests Wally of all his food.

1520. Dipsy Gypsy (*Madcap Model*) 4 Apr. 1941; *p.c.:* George Pal prods for Para; *prod/dir:* George Pal; *anim:* Ray Harryhausen; *voice:* Pat McGeehan; *mus:* David Raksin; *conductor:* André Kostelanetz; *col:* Tech. *sd:* WE. 9 min. • Jim Dandy woos and wins Nina, a pretty gypsy girl.

1521. Dirty Duck Sept. 1978; *p.c.:* Murakami-Wolf prods for New World; *prod:* Jerry Good; *dir/story/anim/des:* Charles Swenson; *voices:* Mark Volman, Robert Ridgeley, Walker Edmiston, Cynthia Adler, Janet Lee, Lurene Tuttle, Jerry Good, Howard Kaylan; *songs:* Mark Volman, Howard Kaylan, Flo and Eddie; *ph:* Nick Vasu; col. *sd.* 75 min. • Willard Eisenbaum, a shy insurance salesman is shown a lifestyle he never dreamed of by a large sailor duck. X-rated adaptation of the underground comic characters.

1522. Disarmament Conference (*Krazy Kat*) 27 Apr. 1931; *p.c.:* Winkler for Colum; *prod:* Charles Mintz; *anim:* Ben Harrison, Manny Gould; *mus:* Joe de Nat; b&w. *sd:* WE. 6 min. • Krazy initiates a peace proclamation between warring jungle animals.

1523. The Discontented Canary (*Happy Harmonies*) 1 Sept. 1934; *p.c.:* MGM; *prod/dir:* Hugh Harman, Rudolf Ising; *chorus:* The Three Harmonettes; *mus:* Scott Bradley; *col:* Tech-2. *sd:* WE. 9 min. • A canary finally escapes from his cage, finds the outside world a terrible place and beats a hasty retreat home.

1524. Disguise the Limit (*Modern Madcap*) Sept. 1960; *p.c.:* Para Cartoons; *dir:* Seymour Kneitel; *story:* Carl Meyer, Jack Mercer; *anim:* Tom Johnson, Morey Reden; *sets:* Robert Little; *voices:* Jack Mercer, Cecil Roy, Eddie Lawrence; *mus:* Winston Sharples; *ph:* Leonard McCormick; *prod mgr:* Abe Goodman; *col:* Tech. *sd:* RCA. 6 min. • Mike the Masquerader tries to steal the diamond collar belonging to Mrs. Van Gotrocks's poodle, Fifi.

1525. The Dish Ran Away with the Spoon (*Merrie Melodies*) 24 Sept. 1933; *p.c.:* Hugh Harman, Rudolf Ising prods for WB; *prod:* Leon Schlesinger; *story:* Robert Clampett; *anim:* Rollin Hamilton, Bob McKimson, Robert Clampett; *voices:* Mary Moder, Rudolf Ising; *mus:* Frank Marsales; b&w. *sd:* Vit. 9 min. • Mr. Spoon rescues Miss Dish from the clutches of the villainous Yeast Beast.

1526. The Disillusioned Bluebird (*Color Rhapsody*) 26 May 1944; *p.c.:* Colum; *prod:* Dave Fleischer; *dir:* Howard Swift; *story:* Edmund Seward; *anim:* Jim Armstrong, Grant Simmons; *sets:* Clark Watson; *ed:* Edward Moore; *voices:* Sir Lancelot, Harry E. Lang; *mus:* Eddie Kilfeather; *col:* Tech. *sd:* RCA. 7 min. • A bluebird, caught in an air raid, is blown away to a Carribean setting.

1527. The Disobedient Mouse (*Cartune Comedy*) 28 Nov. 1938; *p.c.:* Walter Lantz prods for Univ; *dir:* Lester Kline; *story:* Victor McLeod; *anim:* George Dane, Ralph Somerville; *voices:* Dave Weber, Margaret Hill; *mus:* Frank Marsales; *col:* Tech-2. *sd:* WE. 7 min. • Baby-Face Mouse joins Prof. Ratface's crime school against his will and is taught to pick pockets along with stealing milk.

1528. The Dissatisfied Cobbler (*Aesop's Film Fable*) 8 Feb. 1922; *p.c.:* Fables Pictures Inc for Pathé; *dir:* Paul Terry; b&w. *sil.* 5 min. • Dissatisfied with his lot, a cobbler tries his hand at various other jobs before becoming a blacksmith. His first attempt to shoe an obstinate mule gets him kicked right back to his shoe shop. Moral: "Shoemaker, stick to your last."

1529. Dixie (*Ko-Ko Song Car-Tune*) 15 Dec. 1925; *p.c.:* Inkwell Studio for Red Seal; *prod:* Max Fleischer; *dir:* Dave Fleischer; b&w. *sil.* 5 min. *l/a/anim.* • No story available.

1530. Dixie (*Screen Songs*) 17 Aug. 1929; *p.c.:* The Fleischer Studio for Para; *prod:* Max Fleischer; *dir:* Dave Fleischer; b&w. *sd:* WE. 5 min. • A wedding ceremony is terminated by the bridegroom declining to wed.

1531. Dixie Days (*Aesop's Sound Fable*) 8 Apr. 1930; *p.c.:* Van Beuren for Pathé; *dir:* John Foster, Mannie Davis; *mus:* Gene Rodemich; b&w. *sd:* RCA. 5 min. • Simon Legree wants to auction Liza but she escapes over the ice floes with Legree in hot pursuit.

1532. The Dixie Fryer (*Merrie Melodies*) 24 Sept. 1960; *p.c.:* WB; *dir:* Robert McKimson; *story:* Tedd Pierce; *anim:* Ted Bonnicksen, Warren Batchelder, Tom Ray, George Grandpré; *lay:* Robert Givens; *back:* Bill Butler; *ed:* Treg Brown; *voices:* Mel Blanc, Daws Butler; *mus:* Milt Franklyn; *prod mgr:* William Orcutt; *prod:* David H. DePatie; *col:* Tech. *sd:* Vit. 7 min. • Foggy flies South and is envisioned as a Southern fried chicken dinner by B.O. Buzzard and son, Elvis.

1533. Dixieland Droopy (*Droopy*) 4 Dec. 1955. *p.c.:* MGM; *dir:* Tex Avery; *story:* Heck Allen; *anim:* Michael Lah, Grant Simmons, Walter Clinton; *lay/character des:* Ed Benedict; *back:* Joe Montell; *ed:* Jim Faris; *voices:* John H. Brown, Bill Thompson; *mus:* Scott Bradley; *ph:* Jack Stevens; *prod:* Fred Quimby; *col:* Tech. *sd:* WE. 8 min. • John Pettybone, a Dixieland-loving dog, is fortunate enough to adopt a group of jazz-playing fleas.

1534. The Dizzy Acrobat (*Woody Woodpecker*) 31 May 1943; *p.c.:* Walter Lantz prods for Univ; *dir:* Alex Lovy; *story:* Ben Hardaway, Milt Schaffer; *anim:* Emery Hawkins; *sets:* Fred Brunish; *voice:* Kent Rogers; *mus:* Darrell Calker; *prod mgr:* George Hall; *col:* Tech. *sd:* WE. 7 min. • Woody is chased by an irate guard for trying to sneak into the circus.

1535. A Dizzy Day (*Aesop's Sound Fable*) 5 May 1933; *p.c.:* Van Beuren for RKO; *dir:* Harry Bailey; *mus:* Gene Rodemich; b&w. *sd:* RCA. 6 min. • A day in the life of Sentinal Louie and all the things that pass by while he is on sentry duty.

1536. Dizzy Dinosaurs (*Kartune*) 8 Aug. 1952; *p.c.:* Famous for Para; *dir:* Seymour Kneitel; *story:* I. Klein; *anim:* Myron Waldman, Gordon Whittier; *sets:* Robert Little; *voices:* Jackson Beck, Sid Raymond; *mus:* Winston Sharples; *prod mgr:* Seymour Shultz; *col:* Tech. *sd:* RCA. 7 min. • The life of a caveman is depicted as having all "modern conveniences."

1537. Dizzy Dishes (*Noveltoon*) 4 Feb. 1955; *p.c.:* Famous for Para; *dir:* I. Sparber; *story:* I. Klein; *anim:* Tom Golden, Bill Hudson; *sets:* Anton Loeb; *voices:* Mae Questel, Cecil Roy, Jack Mercer; *mus:* Winston Sharples; *ph:* Leonard McCormick; *prod mgr:* Seymour Shultz; *col:* Tech. *sd:* RCA. 6 min. • Audrey reads her comic while the dishes are washing and dreams that flying saucers are attacking the earth.

1538. Dizzy Dishes (*Talkartoons*) 9 Aug. 1930; *p.c.:* The Fleischer Studio for Para; *prod:* Max Fleischer; *dir:* Dave Fleischer; *story:* Ted Sears; *anim:* Grim Natwick, Alfred Eugster, Ted Sears; *voices:* Little Ann Little; *mus:* Art Turkisher; b&w. *sd:* WE. 7 min. • Bimbo is a harried waiter in a restaurant. Grim Natwick's creation, Betty Boop, makes her maiden appearance as a cabaret singer.

1539. Dizzy Divers (*Popeye*) 26 July 1935; *p.c.:* The Fleischer Studio for Para; *prod:* Max Fleischer; *dir:* Dave Fleischer; *anim:* Willard Bowsky, Harold Walker; *voices:* Jack Mercer, Gus Wickie; *mus:* Sammy Timberg; b&w. *sd:* WE. 7 min. • Popeye and Bluto are deep sea divers whose 50-50 partnership dissolves when Bluto finds a treasure map.

1540. Dizzy Ducks (*Scrappy*) 28 Nov. 1936; *p.c.:* Charles Mintz prods for Colum; *story:* Art Davis; *anim:* Sid Marcus; *mus:* Joe de Nat; *prod mgr:* James Bronis; b&w. *sd:* RCA. 6 min. • Scrappy and Oopy go duck hunting and hit all but the ducks. To make matters worse, an ostrich swallows their ammunition and spits bullets back at them.

1541. The Dizzy Dwarf (*Oswald*) 6 Aug. 1934; *p.c.:* Univ; *dir:* "Bill"

Nolan; *story:* Victor McLeod; *anim:* Cecil Surry, Ed Benedict, Ernest Smythe; *mus:* James Dietrich; b&w. *sd:* WE. 9 min. • Oswald's girl tells the King that she can spin straw into gold with help from a dwarf, providing she can guess his name within a given time.

1542. Dizzy Kitty (*Cartune*) 26 May 1941; *p.c.:* Walter Lantz prods for Univ; *story:* Ben Hardaway; *anim:* Alex Lovy, Harold Mason; *sets:* Fred Brunish; *voices:* Kent Rogers, Sara Berner; *mus:* Darrell Calker; *col:* Tech. *sd:* WE. 7 min. • Andy Panda and Pop try to give their reluctant cat a bath for the cat show.

1543. Dizzy Newsreel (*Phantasy*) 27 Aug. 1943; *p.c.:* Colum; *prod:* Dave Fleischer; *dir:* Al Geiss; *story:* Sam Cobean; *anim:* Chic Otterstrom, Grant Simmons; *sets:* Clark Watson; *voices:* Patrick J. McGeehan; *mus:* Paul Worth; *ph:* Frank Fisher; *prod mgr:* Albert Spar; b&w. *sd:* RCA. 6 min. • Newsreel spot-gags: The groundhog emerges for his moment of glory; "The Filet Mignon Stakes" are run; and a hog-calling contest gives the hogs a break.

1544. Dizzy Red Riding-Hood (*Talkartoons*) 12 Dec. 31; *p.c.:* The Fleischer Studio for Para; *prod:* Max Fleischer; *dir:* Dave Fleischer; *voice:* Edwin Jerome, Charles Carver; *mus:* Art Turkisher; b&w. *sd:* WE. 7 min. • The wolf follows Betty to Grandma's house. Bimbo disposes of him and dons the wolf's skin to chase Betty himself.

1545. Do a Good Deed (*Oswald*) 25 Mar. 1935; *p.c.:* Univ; *dir:* Walter Lantz; *story:* Victor McLeod; *anim:* Manuel Moreno, George Grandpré, Lester Kline, Fred Kopietz; *mus:* James Dietrich; b&w. *sd:* WE. 9 min. • Oswald's scout troop do good deeds for a bird, some bees and a woodpecker, all who come to their rescue when they are troubled by a bear.

1546. The Do Good Wolf (*Loopy De Loop*) July 1960; *p.c.* Hanna-Barbera for Colum; *prod/dir:* Joseph Barbera, William Hanna; *story dir:* Alex Lovy; *story:* Warren Foster; *anim dir:* Charles A. Nichols; *anim:* Kenneth Muse; *lay:* Dick Bickenbach; *back:* Montealegre; *ed:* Warner Leighton; *voices:* Daws Butler, Don Messic, Jean Van der Pyl; *mus:* Hoyt Curtin; *titles:* Lawrence Gobel; *prod mgr:* Howard Hanson; *col:* East. *sd:* RCA. 6 min. • Loopy attempts to rescue Snow White from the evil Queen, only to have the Seven Dwarfs rescue Snow White from him!

1547. Do or Diet (*Casper*) 16 Oct. 1953; *p.c.:* Famous for Para; *dir:* I. Sparber; *story:* I. Klein; *anim:* Myron Waldman, Nick Tafuri; *sets:* Robert Owen; *voices:* Alan Shay, Sid Raymond, Jack Mercer; *mus:* Winston Sharples; *title song:* Mack David, Jerry Livingston; *ph:* Leonard McCormick; *prod mgr:* Seymour Shultz; *col:* Tech. *sd:* RCA. 7 min. • Casper helps Timothy Turkey on Thanksgiving Day to keep from being the main course on the farmer's table.

1548. Do Women Pay? (*Aesop's Film Fable*) 9 Nov. 1923; *p.c.:* Fables Pictures Inc for Pathé; *dir:* Paul Terry; b&w. *sil.* 5 min. • A mouse melodrama with the heroine kidnapped by the villain and the hero dashing to the rescue in an airplane.

1549. Doc's Last Stand (*Cartune*) 19 Dec. 1961; *p.c.:* Walter Lantz prods for Univ; *dir:* Jack Hannah; *story:* Al Bertino, Dick Kinney; *anim:* Roy Jenkins, Al Coe; *sets:* Ray Huffine, Art Landy; *voices:* Dal McKennon, Paul Frees; *mus:* Eugene Poddany; *prod mgr:* William E. Garity; *col:* Tech. *sd:* RCA. 6 min. • Doc and Champ meet an oil-rich Indian who will pay greatly for a squaw! So Doc dresses Champ as his suitor.

1550. Doctor Bluebird (*Color Rhapsody*) 5 Feb. 1936; *p.c.:* Charles Mintz prods for Colum; *story:* Ben Harrison; *anim:* Manny Gould; *voice:* The Rhythmettes; *mus:* Joe de Nat; *prod mgr:* James Bronis; *col:* Tech. *sd:* RCA. 8½ min. • A bedridden Scrappy is entertained by a cheerful bluebird and his friends. Feathered caricatures of Laurel & Hardy, The Marx Brothers, Charlie Chaplin and Mae West.

1551. Dr. Devil and Mr. Hare (*Merrie Melodies*) 28 Mar. 1964; *p.c.:* WB; *dir:* Robert McKimson; *story:* John Dunn; *anim:* Ted Bonnicksen, Warren Batchelder, George Grandpré; *sets:* Robert Gribbroek; *ed:* Treg Brown; *voices:* Mel Blanc; *mus:* Bill Lava; *prod mgr:* William Orcutt; *prod:* David H. DePatie; *col:* Tech. *sd:* Vit. 7 min. • Bugs sets himself up as a doctor to confuse the Tasmanian Devil.

1552. Dr. Dolittle 26 June 1998; *p.c.:* Davis Entertainment Co./Joseph M. Singer Entertainment for Fox; *digital visual fx: Visionart sup:* Joshua D. Rose; *prod:* Robert D. Crotty; *2d anim sup:* Ted Fay; *3d anim sup:* R. Stirling Duguid; *cg art:* Jon-Marc Kortsch, Mike Bray, Daniel Naulin,

Chris Greenberg, Jimmy Squires, Daniel Kramer, Todd Boyce, Vinh Lee, Barry Safley, Jim "Big Dog" McLean, Jimmy Jewell; *2d art:* Shellaine Corwell, John Peel, Christina Drahos, Jeremy Nelligan; *2d paint art:* Hillary Covey; *compositing sup:* Doreen Haver; *compositors:* Chad Carlberg, John LaFauce Jr.; *visual fx: C.O.R.E. Digital Pictures anim sup:* Bob Munroe, John Mariella; *anim:* Paul Anderson, Terry Bradley, Howard P. Cassidy, Frank Faita, Frank Falcone, Nick Hsieh, Warren J.W. Leathem, Aaron Linton, Luis Lopez, Moris Molino, Brian A. Smeets, Alexander L. Stephan, Claude Theriault, Tracey Vaz, Michael Wile, David Willows; *col:* DeLuxe. *sd:* Dolby digital. Panavision. 85 min. *l/a.* • Live-action comedy: A doctor realizes that he can converse with animals when he accidentally runs over a dog and the creature expresses its opinions. • Animals' reactions and mouth movements are enhanced by computer generated animation.

1553. Doctor Ha-Ha (*James Hound*) Feb. 1966; *p.c.:* TT for Fox; *dir/anim:* Ralph Bakshi; *col:* DeLuxe. *sd:* RCA. 6 min. • A villain uses laughing gas to get what he wants. • See: *James Hound*

1554. Dr. Jekyll and Mr. Mouse (*Tom & Jerry*) 14 June 1947; *p.c.:* MGM; *dir:* William Hanna, Joseph Barbera; *anim:* Ed Barge, Michael Lah, Kenneth Muse, Al Grandmain; *sets:* Robert Gentle; *ed:* Fred MacAlpin; *mus:* Scott Bradley; *prod:* Fred Quimby; *col:* Tech. *sd:* WE. 8 min. *Academy Award nomination.* • Irritated by Jerry stealing his milk, Tom mixes a concoction to lace the milk. Instead it turns the rodent into a super strong monster.

1555. Dr. Jerkyl's Hide (*Looney Tunes*) 8 May 1954; *p.c.:* WB; *dir:* I. Freleng; *story:* Warren Foster; *anim:* Arthur Davis, Manuel Perez, Ken Champin, Virgil Ross; *lay:* Hawley Pratt; *back:* Irv Wyner; *ed:* Treg Brown; *voices:* Mel Blanc, Stan Freberg; *mus:* Carl Stalling; *prod mgr:* John W. Burton; *prod:* Edward Selzer; *col:* Tech. *sd:* Vit. 7 min. • Two dogs chase Sylvester into Dr. Jerkyl's surgery, where he drinks a potion that turns him into a raging monster.

1556. Doctor Monko 29 May 1915; *p.c.:* M-in-A Films; *prod:* David S. Horsley; *anim:* Harry Palmer; b&w. *sil.* • No story available.

1557. Doctor Oswald (*Oswald*) 30 Dec. 1935; *p.c.:* Univ; *prod/dir:* Walter Lantz; *story:* Walter Lantz, Victor McLeod; *anim:* Ray Abrams, Fred Kopietz; *mus:* James Dietrich; b&w. *sd:* WE. 6 min. • When Elmer, Oswald's dog, catches a cold, Oswald accidentally discovers the perfect cure when Elmer swallows rifle bullets.

1558. Doctor Pink (*Pink Panther*) 1978; *p.c.:* Mirisch/Geoffrey/DFE for UA; *dir:* Sid Marcus; *story:* Dave DeTiege; *anim:* Bob Matz, John Gibbs, Tiger West, Tony Love; *lay:* Martin Strudler; *back:* Richard H. Thomas; *ed:* Bob Gillis; *theme tune:* Henry Mancini; *ph:* Steve Wilzback; *prod mgr:* Lee Gunther; *col:* DeLuxe. *sd:* RCA. 6 min. • Hospital janitor Panther is mistaken for a doctor when he dons a white coat.

1559. Dr. Rhinestone's Theory (*James Hound*) Oct. 1967; *p.c.:* TT for Fox; *dir sup:* Ralph Bakshi; *col:* DeLuxe. *sd:* RCA. 6 min. • Hound enrolls in Dr. Rhinestone's mathematics class to investigate a missing agent.

1560. The Dog and the Bone (*Aesop's Film Fable*) 15 Oct. 1921; *p.c.:* Fables Pictures Inc for Pathé; *dir:* Paul Terry; b&w. *sil.* 5 min. • When the dog brings home a bone in his mouth, he sees his mirror image in a brook and, thinking there's a better bone, drops his bone in the water to collect the reflection. Moral: "A bone in the mouth is worth two in the brook."

1561. The Dog and the Bone (*Terry-Toon*) 12 Nov. 1937; *p.c.:* TT for Educational/Fox; *dir:* George Gordon; *story:* Thomas Morrison; *mus:* Philip A. Scheib; b&w. *sd:* WE. 6 min. • Puddy the pup loses his bone, upsets an Italian restauranteur ... then finds another.

1562. The Dog and the Flea (*Aesop's Film Fables*) 31 Dec. 1921; *p.c.:* Fables Pictures Inc for Pathé; *dir:* Paul Terry; b&w. *sil.* 5 min. • A flea alights on a little dog and the scratching begins. The dog finally rids himself of the pest by diving into a river. Moral: "Don't waste your pity on a scamp."

1563. The Dog and the Mosquito (*Aesop's Film Fable*) 12 Aug. 1922; *p.c.:* Fables Pictures Inc for Pathé; *dir:* Paul Terry; b&w. *st:* 5 min. • No story available.

1564. The Dog and the Thief (*Aesop's Film Fable*) 26 Jan. 1922; *p.c.:* Fables Pictures Inc for Pathé; *dir:* Paul Terry; b&w. *sil.* 5 min. • The fox has his eye on a duck in the barnyard that is guarded by a dog. He tries to bribe the dog with a bone but the dog refuses it and proceeds to beat up Mr. Fox anyway. Moral: "Beware of strangers bearing gifts."

1565. The Dog and the Wolves (*Aesop's Film Fable*) 27 Apr. 1922; *p.c.:* Fables Pictures Inc for Pathé; *dir:* Paul Terry; b&w. *sil.* 5 min. • A pup is captured by pirates. He escapes by drilling a hole in the bottom of the boat and is returned to dry land in his baby carriage by a friendly stork. Moral: "Providence protects the innocent."

1566. Dog, Cat and Canary (*Color Rhapsody*) 5 Jan. 1945; *p.c.:* Colum; *dir:* Howard Swift; *story:* Grant Simmons; *anim:* Jim Armstrong, Volus Jones; *sets:* Clark Watson; *ed:* Edward Moore; *voice:* Harry E. Lang; *mus:* Eddie Kilfeather; *i&p:* Elizabeth F. McDowell; *ph:* Frank Fisher; *prod mgr:* Hugh McCollum; *col:* Tech. *sd:* WE. 7 min. *Academy Award nomination.* • The cat ties-up the guard dog and chases the canary but the dog gets free and chases the cat.

1567. Dog Collared (*Merrie Melodies*) 2 Dec. 1950; *p.c.:* WB; *dir:* Robert McKimson; *story:* Warren Foster; *anim:* Charles McKimson, Rod Scribner, Phil de Lara, Manuel Perez, J.C. Melendez; *lay:* Cornett Wood; *back:* Richard H. Thomas; *ed:* Treg Brown; *voices:* Mel Blanc; *mus:* Carl Stalling; *prod mgr:* John W. Burton; *prod:* Edward Selzer; *col:* Tech. *sd:* Vit. 7 min. • A huge dog befriends Porky, forcing him to try to escape the mutt's affections.

1568. Dog Daze (*Merrie Melodies*) 18 Dec. 1937; *p.c.:* Leon Schlesinger prods for WB; *dir:* I. Freleng; *anim:* Bob McKimson, A.C. Gamer; *lay:* Griff Jay; *back:* Arthur Loomer; *ed:* Tregoweth E. Brown; *voices:* Bernice Hansel, Billy Bletcher, Mel Blanc, The Sons of the Pioneers; *mus:* Carl W. Stalling; *prod sup:* Henry Binder, Raymond G. Katz; *col:* Tech. *sd:* Vit. 7 min. • Spot-gags with dogs. Caricatures of Irvin S. Cobb, William Powell, Kate Smith.

1569. Dog Gone Cats (*Merrie Melodies*) 25 Oct. 1947; *p.c.:* WB; *dir:* Arthur Davis; *story:* Lloyd Turner, William Scott; *anim:* Basil Davidovich, J.C. Melendez, Don Williams, Emery Hawkins; *lay:* Don Smith; *back:* Phil de Guard; *ed:* Treg Brown; *voices:* Mel Blanc, Bea Benaderet; *mus:* Carl Stalling; *prod mgr:* John W. Burton; *prod:* Edward Selzer; *col:* Ciné. *sd:* Vit. 7 min. • Two cats that a dog has been tormenting get their revenge when he's asked to deliver a package across town.

1570. Dog Gone It (*Hot Dog*) 4 Jan. 1927; *p.c.:* Bray prods; *dir:* Walter Lantz, Clyde Geronimi; b&w. *sil.* 6 min. *l/a/anim.* • Pete tells Walter that the Channel is too crowded and he will swim the Atlantic.

1571. Dog Gone Modern (*Merrie Melodies*) 14 Jan. 1938; *p.c.:* Leon Schlesinger prods for WB; *dir:* Charles M. Jones; *story:* Rich Hogan; *anim:* Phil Monroe; *lay:* Robert Givens; *back:* Paul Julian; *ed:* Tregoweth E. Brown; *voices:* Mel Blanc, The Sportsmen Quartet; *mus:* Carl W. Stalling; *prod sup:* Henry Binder, Raymond G. Katz; *col:* Tech. *sd:* Vit. 7 min. • Two curious pups explore an automated house.

1572. Dog Gone South (*Merrie Melodies*) 26 Aug. 1950; *p.c.:* WB; *dir:* Charles M. Jones; *story:* Michael Maltese; *anim:* Ben Washam, Lloyd Vaughan, Ken Harris, Phil Monroe, Emery Hawkins; *lay:* Robert Gribbroek; *back:* Phil de Guard; *ed:* Treg Brown; *voices:* Mel Blanc; *mus:* Carl Stalling; *prod mgr:* John W. Burton; *prod:* Edward Selzer; *col:* Tech. *sd:* Vit. 7 min. • Charlie Dog tries to ingratiate himself with a Southern Colonel. The only thing that stands in his path is the Colonel's bulldog, Belvedere.

1573. The Dog House (*Tom & Jerry*) 29 Nov. 1952; *p.c.:* MGM; *dir:* William Hanna, Joseph Barbera; *anim:* Kenneth Muse, Irven Spence, Ray Patterson, Ed Barge; *sets:* John Didrik Johnsen; *ed:* Jim Faris; *voice:* Daws Butler; *mus:* Scott Bradley; *ph:* Jack Stevens; *prod:* Fred Quimby; *col:* Tech. *sd:* WE. 6 min. • Spike endeavors to build himself a dream dog house although his efforts are persistantly ruined by Tom.

1574. A Dog in a Mansion (*Terry-Toon*) 12 Jan. 1940; *p.c.:* TT for Fox; *dir:* Eddie Donnelly; *story:* John Foster; *mus:* Philip A. Scheib; b&w. *sd:* RCA. 7 min. • No story available.

1575. Dog Meets Dog (*Phantasy*) 27 Mar. 1942; *p.c.:* Colum; *prod:* Frank Tashlin; *dir:* Alec Geiss; *story:* Jack Cosgriff; *anim:* Chic Otterstrom; *sets:* Clark Watson; *voices:* Billy Bletcher, Harry E. Lang, Joey Pennario; *mus:* Eddie Kilfeather; *ph:* Frank Fisher; *prod mgr:* Ben Schwalb; b&w. *sd:* RCA. 8 min. • Butch the bulldog steals a spaniel's license, causing him to land in the pound. Feeling remorse, Butch goes to turn himself in but, finding the pound on fire, rescues the spaniel as well as the dog catcher.

1576. Dog Pounded (*Looney Tunes*) 2 Jan 1954; *p.c.:* WB; *dir:* I. Freleng; *story:* Warren Foster; *anim:* Manuel Perez, Ken Champin, Virgil Ross, Arthur Davis; *lay:* Hawley Pratt; *back:* Irv Wyner; *ed:* Treg Brown; *voice:* Mel Blanc; *mus:* Carl Stalling; *prod mgr:* John Burton; *prod:* Edward Selzer; *col:* Tech. *sd:* Vit. 7 min. • Sylvester has to get to Tweety who's atop a telephone pole in the middle of a dog pound.

1577. The Dog Show (*Paul Terry-Toons*) 28 Dec. 1934; *p.c.:* Moser & Terry Inc for Educational/Fox; *dir:* Paul Terry, Frank Moser; *mus:* Philip A. Scheib; b&w. *sd:* WE. 6 min. • All the local canines (including hot dogs) head for the local dog show. The whole proceedings is marred by the arrival of the dog catcher who is looking for an escaped pup.

1578. Dog Show (*Terry-Toon*) Aug. 1950; *p.c.:* TT for Fox; *dir:* Eddie Donnelly; *story:* John Foster; *anim:* Jim Tyer; *mus:* Philip A. Scheib; *col:* Tech. *sd:* RCA. 7 min. • Two mutts sneak into a pedigree dog show and abscond with the prize.

1579. The Dog Show-Off (*Little Lulu*) 30 Jan. 1948; *p.c.:* Famous for Para; *dir:* Seymour Kneitel; *story:* I. Klein, Jack Mercer; *anim:* Myron Waldman, Gordon Whittier, Nick Tafuri, Irving Dressler, Wm. B. Pattengill; *sets:* Lloyd Hallock Jr.; *voices:* Cecil Roy, Jackson Beck; *mus:* Winston Sharples; *title song:* Buddy Kaye, Fred Wise, Sammy Timberg; *ph:* Leonard McCormick; *prod mgr:* Sam Buchwald; *col:* Tech. *sd:* RCA. 7 min • Lulu and Tubby dress their dog as a fox, making all the other dogs in the dog show chase after him. Once he returns they walk away with the prize.

1580. The Dog Snatcher (*Mr. Magoo*) 29 May 1952; *p.c.:* UPA for Colum; *ex prod:* Stephen Bosustow; *prod/dir:* Pete Burness; *story:* Bill Scott, Paul Schneider; *anim:* Rudy Larriva, Cecil Surry; *lay:* Abe Liss; *back:* Bob McIntosh, Bob Dranko; *voices:* Jim Backus, Barney Phillips, Jerry Hausner; *mus:* William Lava; *prod mgr:* Herbert Klynn; *col:* Tech. *sd:* RCA. 7 min. • Magoo takes an escaped panther, which he believes to be his dog "Cuddles," down town to get him a licence.

1581. The Dog Snatcher (*Scrappy*) 15 Oct. 1931; *p.c.:* Winkler for Colum; *prod:* Charles Mintz; *story:* Dick Huemor; *anim:* Sid Marcus; *mus:* Joe de Nat; *prod mgr:* James Bronis; b&w. *sd:* WE. 6 min. • Scrappy tries to break his dog, Yippy, out of the pound.

1582. Dog Tales (*Looney Tunes*) 26 July 1958; *p.c.:* WB; *dir:* Robert McKimson; *story:* Tedd Pierce; *anim:* George Grandpré, Ted Bonnicksen, Warren Batchelder, Tom Ray; *lay:* Robert Gribbroek; *back:* Richard H. Thomas; *ed:* Treg Brown; *voices:* Robert C. Bruce, Mel Blanc, Julie Bennett; *mus:* Milt Franklyn; *col:* Tech. *sd:* Vit. 7 min. • A look at all breeds of dog from a Society Dog Show to a canine who travels clear across America to retrieve a buried bone.

1583. Dog Tax Dodgers (*Andy Panda*) 26 Nov. 1948; *p.c.:* Walter Lantz prods for UA; *dir:* Dick Lundy; *story:* Ben Hardaway, Heck Allen; *anim:* (La) Verne Harding, Pat Matthews; *sets:* Fred Brunish; *ed:* Dave Lurie; *voices:* Walter Tetley, Jack Mather; *mus:* Darrell Calker; *prod mgr:* William E. Garity; *col:* Tech. *sd:* RCA 7 min. • To avoid paying a $3 dog license fee, Andy hides his dog from tax collector Wally.

1584. The Dog That Cried Wolf (*Cartune*) 23 Mar. 1953; *p.c.:* Walter Lantz prods for Univ; *dir:* Paul J. Smith; *anim:* Gil Turner, Cecil Surry, Robert Bentley; *sets:* Raymond Jacobs; *voices:* John T. Smith; *mus:* Clarence Wheeler; *prod mgr:* William E. Garity; *col:* Tech. *sd:* RCA. 6 min. • A watchdog keeps sounding the "Wolf Alarm" while guarding the sheep. When a real wolf arrives, the farmer takes no notice of the alarm. Animator Paul Smith's first directorial.

1585. Dog Tired (*Merrie Melodies*) 25 Apr. 1942; *p.c.:* Leon Schlesinger prods for WB; *dir:* Charles M. Jones; *anim:* Phil Monroe; *lay:* Robert Givens; *back:* Eugene Fleury; *ed:* Treg Brown; *voices:* Mel Blanc; *mus:* Carl W. Stalling; *prod sup:* Henry Binder, Raymond G. Katz; *col:* Tech. *sd:* Vit. 8 min. • Two curious pups' have an encounter in a zoo.

1586. Dog Trouble (*MGM cartoon*) 18 Apr. 1942; *p.c.:* MGM; *dir:* William Hanna, Joseph Barbera; *anim:* Wilson D. Burness, Kenneth Muse, Jack Zander; *voice:* Lillian Randolph; *mus:* Scott Bradley; *prod:* Fred Quimby; *col:* Tech. *sd:* WE. 9 min. • Tom and Jerry join forces to rid the house of a troublesome bulldog.

1587. Dog Watch (*Pluto*) 16 Mar. 1945; *p.c.:* Walt Disney prods for RKO; *dir:* Charles Nichols; *asst dir:* Esther Newell; *story:* Eric Gurney; *anim:* George Nicholas, Norman Tate, Marvin Woodward, Jerry Hathcock, Ed Aardal, Andy Engman, John McManus, Sandy Strother, Robert W.

Youngquist; *lay:* Bruce Bushman; *back:* Claude Coats; *voices:* Dehner Forkum, James MacDonald; *mus:* Oliver Wallace; *col:* Tech. *sd:* RCA. 7 min. • Ship's mascot Pluto is put in charge of guarding the ship from a hungry sea rat.

1588. The Dogfather *(The Dogfather)* 27 June 1974; *p.c.:* Mirisch/DFE for UA; *dir:* Hawley Pratt; *story:* Bob Ogle; *anim:* Bob Richardson, John V. Gibbs, Bob Matz, Norm McCabe; *lay:* Dick Ung; *back:* Richard H. Thomas; *voices:* Bob Holt, Daws Butler, Frank Welker; *titles:* Arthur Leonardi; *mus:* Dean Elliott; *lyrics:* John Bradford; *col:* DeLuxe. *sd:* RCA. 6 min. • The Dogfather puts out a contract on an alley cat at the same time as a fugitive wildcat appears on the scene.

1589. Doggone People *(Merrie Melodies)* 12 Nov. 1960; *p.c.:* WB; *dir:* Robert McKimson; *story:* Tedd Pierce; *anim:* Warren Batchelder, George Grandpré, Ted Bonnicksen, Tom Ray; *lay:* Robert Gribbroek; *back:* William Butler; *ed:* Treg Brown; *voices:* Hal Smith, Mel Blanc; *mus:* Milt Franklyn; *prod mgr:* William Orcutt; *prod:* David H. DePatie; *col:* Tech. *sd:* Vit. 7 min. • Elmer Fudd looks after his boss' dog and has to treat him as "People."

1590. Doggone Tired 30 July 1949 *p.c.:* MGM; *dir:* Tex Avery; *story:* Rich Hogan, Jack Cosgriff; *anim:* Bob Cannon, Michael Lah, Grant Simmons, Walter Clinton; *character des:* Louie Schmitt; *sets:* John Didrik Johnsen; *ed:* Fred MacAlpin; *voice:* Patrick J. McGeehan; *mus:* Scott Bradley; *prod:* Fred Quimby; *col:* Tech. *sd:* WE. 8 min. • A rabbit keeps a hunting dog from sleeping so he'll be in no fit state to hunt rabbit in the morning.

1591. The Dognapper *(Mickey Mouse)* 17 Nov. 1934; *p.c.:* Walt Disney prods for UA; *dir:* David D. Hand; *anim:* Johnny Cannon, Clyde Geronimi, Hardie Gramatky, Bill Justice, Richard Lundy, William O. Roberts, Bob Wickersham, Marvin Woodward; *voices:* Marcellite Garner, Pinto Colvig, Clarence Nash, Walt Disney; *mus:* Bert Lewis, Frank E. Churchill; b&w. *sd:* RCA. 8 min. • Minnie's Pekinese dog is kidnapped by Peg-Leg Pete. Officers Mickey and Donald track them down to a sawmill.

1592. A Dog's Day *(Aesop's Film Fable)* 5 June 1927; *p.c.:* Fables Pictures Inc for Pathé; *dir:* Paul Terry; b&w. sil. 5 min. • Farmer Al's dog runs amuck, chasing ducks, smoking a pipe and getting sick. Al goes hunting a lion but does nothing but upset a crabby bear. The bear chases him over the falls where he encounters a family of apes. The dog shoots at the apes but they all recover and chase Al and the dog over the horizon.

1593. A Dog's Dream *(Terry-Toon)* 2 May 1941; *p.c.:* TT for Fox; *dir:* Eddie Donnelly; *story:* John Foster; *mus:* Philip A. Scheib; b&w. *sd:* RCA. 7 min. • No story available.

1594. Doing His Bit *(Sullivan Cartoon Comedy)* 9 Aug. 1917; *p.c.:* Sullivan Studio for Univ; *dir:* Pat Sullivan; b&w. sil. 4 min. s/r. • No story available.

1595. Doing Impossikible Stunts *(Popeye)* 2 Aug. 1940; *p.c.:* The Fleischer Studio for Para; *prod:* Max Fleischer; *dir:* Dave Fleischer; *story:* Jack Ward; *anim:* Tom Johnson, Frank Endres; *sets:* Louie Sylvester; *voices:* Jack Mercer, Pinto Colvig, Margie Hines; *mus:* Sammy Timberg; *ph:* Charles Schettler; *prod sup:* Sam Buchwald, Isidore Sparber; b&w. *sd:* WE. 7 min. Seq: *I Never Changes My Altitude; Bridge Ahoy; I Wanna Be a Lifeguard; Lost and Foundry.* • Popeye impresses a casting director by showing him films of his death-defying stunts. Swee'Pea changes a reel for one of his own.

1596. Doing Their Bit *(Nancy)* 30 Oct. 1942; *p.c.:* TT for Fox; *dir:* Connie Rasinski; *story:* John Foster; *anim:* I. Klein; *mus:* Philip A. Scheib; *col:* Tech. *sd:* RCA. 6 min. • Nancy and Sluggo are inspired to start their own USO Defense Guard after reading the comics.

1597. Doing What's Fright *(Casper)* 16 Jan. 1959; *p.c.:* Para Cartoons; *dir:* Seymour Kneitel; *story:* Carl Meyer; *anim:* Tom Johnson, Frank Endres, Els Barthen; *sets:* Robert Little; *voices:* Cecil Roy, Jack Mercer, Sid Raymond; *mus:* Winston Sharples; *ph:* Leonard McCormick; *prod mgr:* Abe Goodman; *col:* Tech. *sd:* RCA. 6 min. • Casper finds a way to cure Spooky of playing "April Fool" gags on everybody.

1598. The Dollies of 1917 *(Motoy Comedy)* Aug. 1917; *p.c.:* Toyland Films for Peter Pan Corp; *dir:* Howard S. Moss; b&w. sil. • Animated dolls do their bit for the war effort.

1599. Dolly Gray *(Ko-Ko Song Car-Tune)* 6 Feb. 1926; *p.c.:* Inkwell Studios for Red Seal. *prod:* Max Fleischer; *dir:* Dave Fleischer; b&w. sil. 5 min. • A soldier boy is shown fighting the enemy at the front, racing back and shooting the words away to "Dolly Gray."

1600. Don Donald *(Mickey Mouse)* 9 Jan. 1937; *p.c.:* Walt Disney prods for UA; *dir:* Ben Sharpsteen; *story:* Webb Smith, Jack Hannah; *anim:* Johnny Cannon, Ugo d'Orsi, Alfred Eugster, Jack Hannah, Dick Huemer, Milt Schaffer, Fred Spencer; *voices:* Clarence Nash, Lee Millar; *mus:* Paul J. Smith; *col:* Tech. *sd:* RCA. 7 min. • Troubador Donald tries to win the affections of Senõrita Donna Duck, despite the intervention of a troublesome donkey. Donald Duck's first appearance on his own.

1601. Don Quixote *(ComiColor)* 26 Nov. 1934; *p.c.:* Celebrity prods: *prod/dir:* Ub Iwerks; *anim:* Al Eugster; *mus:* Carl Stalling; *col:* Ciné. *sd:* PCP. 8 min. • An escapee from "Ye Olde Bughouse," imagining the modern times around him to be medieval, seeks a maiden in need of rescuing.

1602. Donald and Pluto *(Mickey Mouse)* 12 Dec. 1936; *p.c.:* Walt Disney prods for UA; *dir:* Ben Sharpsteen; *story:* Jack Kinney, Roy Williams; *anim:* James H. Culhane, Alfred Eugster, Norman Ferguson, Jack Hannah, William O. Roberts, Fred Spencer; *voices:* Clarence Nash; *mus:* Paul J. Smith; *col:* Tech. *sd:* RCA. 9 min. • Pluto accidentally swallows a magnet when Donald attempts some home-plumbing.

1603. Donald and the Wheel 21 June 1961; *p.c.:* Walt Disney prods for BV; *dir:* Hamilton S. Luske; *asst dir:* Jim Swain; *story:* Bill Berg; *anim:* Hal King, Les Clark, Fred Kopietz; *fx:* Joshua Meador, Eustace Lycett, Jack Boyd; *lay:* Don Griffith, McLaren Stewart, Joe Hale; *back:* Art Riley; *voices:* The MelloMen, Paul Frees, Thurl Ravenscroft, Clarence Nash; *mus:* Buddy Baker; *songs:* Mel Leven; *col:* Tech. *sd:* RCA. 18 min. *l/a/anim.* • "The Spirit of Progress" explains the creation and history of the wheel with the help of Donald Duck.

1604. Donald Applecore *(Donald Duck)* 18 Jan. 1952; *p.c.:* Walt Disney prods for RKO; *dir:* Jack Hannah; *story:* Bill Berg, Nick George; *anim:* Volus Jones, Bob Carlson, George Kreisl, Bill Justice; *fx:* Blaine Gibson, Jack Boyd, Dan MacManus; *lay:* Yale Gracey; *back:* Thelma Witmer; *voices:* Clarence Nash, Dessie Miller, James MacDonald; *mus:* Joseph S. Dubin; *col:* Tech. *sd:* RCA. 7 min. • Donald discovers the chipmunks raiding his orchard of apples and tries to evict them.

1605. Donald Duck and the Gorilla *(Donald Duck)* 31 Mar. 1944; *p.c.:* Walt Disney prods for RKO; *dir:* Jack King; *asst dir:* Esther Newell; *anim:* Paul Allen, Jack King, George Nicholas, Charles A. Nichols, Judge Whitaker, Marvin Woodward; *fx:* Joshua Meador; *lay:* Bill Herwig; *voices:* Clarence Nash; *mus:* Oliver Wallace; *col:* Tech. *sd:* RCA. 7 min. • Donald's nephews give him a fright when they dress as a gorilla. In the meantime a real gorilla arrives and the fun begins.

1606. The Donald Duck March of Dimes 13 Oct. 1954; *p.c.:* Walt Disney prods for March of Dimes; *dir:* C. August Nichols; *anim:* Julius Svendsen, Art Stevens; *lay:* A. Kendall O'Connor; *voice:* Clarence Nash; *mus:* Oliver Wallace; b&w. *sd:* RCA. 10 min. *l/a/anim.* • Donald pays his nephews for cleaning the yard and makes them put it in their piggy-bank. They are discovered at the soda fountain where they explain to Donald how they joined The March of Dimes. Don follows suit, encouraging the audience to do the same.

1607. Donald Gets Drafted *(Donald Duck)* 1 May 1942; *p.c.:* Walt Disney prods for RKO; *dir:* Jack King; *asst dir:* Bob Newman, Ralph Chadwick; *story:* Harry Reeves, Carl Barks, Jack Hannah; *anim:* Paul Allen, James Armstrong, Hal King, Edward Love, Ray Patin, Retta Scott, Judge Whitaker; *lay:* Bill Herwig; *voices:* Billy Bletcher, Clarence Nash, John McLeish, The King's Men (Ken Darby, Jon Dodson, Bud Linn, Rad Robinson); *mus:* Paul J. Smith; *song:* Leigh Harline; *col:* Tech. *sd:* RCA. 9 min. • Donald joins the Army and finds life tough with the bullying Sergeant. He goes berserk with a rifle and ends in the guardhouse.

1608. Donald in Mathmagic Land 26 June 1959; *p.c.:* Walt Disney prods for BV; *dir:* Hamilton S. Luske; *asst dir:* Vincent McEveety, Danny Alguire, Jim Swain; *seq dir:* Wolfgang Reitherman, Les Clark, Joshua Meador; *story:* Milt Banta, Bill Berg, Dr. Heinz Haber; *anim:* Jerry Hathcock, John Sibley, Bob Carlson, Eric Cleworth, Cliff Nordberg, Harvey Toombs, Bob McCrea, Ted Berman, Dwight Carlisle, Jane Fowler Boyd, Roy Jenkins, Hal King, Fred Kopietz, George Nicholas, Ken O'Brien, Al

Severns, Bob Youngquist; *fx:* Jack Boyd, Ed Parks; *styling:* John Hench, Art Riley; *lay:* McLaren Stewart, Al Zinnen, Basil Davidovich, Vance Gerry, Dale Barnhart, Jack Huber, Lance Nolley; *back:* Richard H. Thomas, Thelma Witmer, Jimi Trout, Colin Campbell; *ed:* Lloyd L. Richardson; *voices:* Paul Frees, Clarence Nash, Jane Fowler Boyd; *mus:* Buddy Baker. *ph:* Edward Colman; *art dir:* Stan Jolley; *special processes:* Eustace Lycett; *sd:* Robert O. Cook; *col:* Tech. *sd:* RCA. 28 min. *Academy Award nomination.* • Donald visits a mathmagical land and learns how importantly numbers figure in everyday life.

1609. Donald's Better Self *(Donald Duck)* 11 Mar. 1938; *p.c.:* Walt Disney prods for RKO; *dir:* Jack King; *story:* Samuel Armstrong, Harry Reeves, Carl Barks; *anim:* Paul Allen, Chuck Couch, Jack Hannah, Edward Love, Don Towsley, Bernard Wolf; *lay:* James Carmichael, Charles Payzant; *voices:* Don Brodie, Thelma Boardman, Clarence Nash; *mus:* Oliver Wallace; col; Tech. *sd:* RCA. 8 min. • Donald is pursuaded by his "evil" self to go fishing instead of school. His "better self" finds out and battles with the Devil.

1610. Donald's Camera *(Donald Duck)* 24 Oct. 1941; *p.c.:* Walt Disney prods for RKO; *dir:* Richard Lundy; *asst dir:* Ted Baker; *anim:* Theodore Bonnicksen, Robert W. Carlson Jr., Walter Clinton, John Elliotte, Volus Jones, Fred Madison, Frank Onaitis, Ray Patterson, William N. Shull, Bernard Wolf; *fx:* Jack Boyd, Andy Engman, Jack Huber, Ed Parks; *lay:* Thor Putnam; *voices:* Clarence Nash, James MacDonald; *mus:* Leigh Harline; *col:* Tech. *sd:* RCA. 7 min. • Donald's attempts to photograph a woodpecker force him to swap his camera for a gun.

1611. Donald's Cousin Gus *(Donald Duck)* 19 May 1939; *p.c.:* Walt Disney prods for RKO; *dir:* Jack King; *asst dir:* Jim Handley, Harry Tytle; *story:* Carl Barks, Jack Hannah; *anim:* Paul Allen, Johnny Cannon, James H. Culhane, Lee Morehouse, Kenneth Patterson, Wolfgang Reitherman, Don Towsley, Berny Wolf; *fx:* George Rowley, Reuben Timmens; *lay:* Bill Herwig; *voices:* Clarence Nash, Lee Millar; *mus:* Oliver Wallace; *col:* Tech. *sd:* RCA. 8 min. • Greedy Gus Goose arrives at Don's house and proceeds to eat him out of house and home.

1612. Donald's Crime *(Donald Duck)* 29 June 1945: *p.c.:* Walt Disney prods for RKO; *dir:* Jack King; *asst dir:* Joel Greenhalgh; *story:* Ralph Wright, Bill Peed; *anim:* Paul Allen, Don Towsley, Harvey Toombs, Bill Justice, Tom Massey, Lee Morehouse; *fx:* Josh Meador, Edwin Aardal; *lay:* Ernest Nordli; *back:* Merle Cox; *voices:* Harry E. Lang, Ruth Clifford, Clarence Nash; *mus:* Edward Plumb, Paul J. Smith; *col:* Tech. *sd:* RCA. 7 min. *Academy Award nomination.* • Donald robs the kids' piggy-bank to take Daisy on the town, then suffers a monumental guilt complex.

1613. Donald's Decision 11 Jan. 1942; *p.c.:* Walt Disney prods for NFB; *dir:* Ford Beebe; *voices:* Clarence Nash, Dehner Forkum; *col:* Tech. *sd:* RCA. 3 min. • Donald is pursuaded by his better self to buy War Bonds in opposition to a Nazi "Devil"! Footage used from *Donald's Better Self.*

1614. Donald's Diary *(Donald Duck)* 5 Feb. 1953; *p.c.:* Walt Disney prods for RKO; *dir:* Jack Kinney; *story:* Brice Mack, Dick Kinney; *anim:* John Sibley, Ken O'Brien, Harry Holt, Charles A. Nichols, Ed Aardal; *fx:* Dan MacManus; *lay:* Bruce Bushman; *back:* Ralph Hulett; *voices:* Leslie Dennison, Vivi Janiss, Clarence Nash; *mus:* Edward Plumb; *col:* Tech. *sd:* RCA. 7 min. • The story of how Donald met Daisy and had a nightmare in which he marries her ... forcing him to join the Foreign Legion.

1615. Donald's Dilemma *(Donald Duck)* 11 July 1947; *p.c.:* Walt Disney prods for RKO; *dir:* Jack King; *asst dir:* Joel Greenhalgh; *story:* Roy Williams; *anim:* Don Towsley, Ed Aardal, Emery Hawkins, Sandy Strother, Paul Allen, Jack Campbell, Bob Carlson, Fred Kopietz, Tom Massey, Frank McSavage, George Rowley; *lay:* Don Griffith; *back:* Maurice Greenberg; *voices:* Gloria Blondell, Ken Darby, Clarence Nash; *mus:* Oliver Wallace; *col:* Tech. *sd:* RCA. 7 min. • Daisy tells a psychiatrist of how Donald became a crooning sensation after receiving a blow on the head.

1616. Donald's Dog Laundry *(Donald Duck)* 5 Apr. 1940; *p.c.:* Walt Disney prods for RKO; *dir:* Jack King; *asst dir:* Bob Newman; *anim:* Paul Allen, Lee Blair, Johnny Cannon, Nick de Tolly, Nick George, Emery Hawkins, John Lounsbery, Lee Morehouse, Kenneth Muse, Grant Simmons, Claude Smith, Norman Tate, Judge Whitaker; *lay:* Bill Herwig; *voices:* Clarence Nash, Pinto Colvig; *mus:* Oliver Wallace; *col:* Tech. *sd:* RCA. 7 min • Donald tries to entice Pluto into his mechanical dog-washing device.

1617. Donald's Double Trouble *(Donald Duck)* 28 June 1946; *p.c.:* Walt Disney prods for RKO; *dir:* Jack King; *asst dir:* Joel Greenhalgh; *story:* Roy Williams; *anim:* Don Towsley, Fred Kopietz, Tom Massey, Sandy Strother, Paul Allen, Lee Morehouse; *fx:* Ed Aardal, Joshua Meador; *lay:* Ernest Nordli; *back:* Howard Dunn; *voices:* Leslie Dennison, Ruth Clifford, Clarence Nash; *mus:* Oliver Wallace; *col:* Tech. *sd:* RCA. 7 min. • Donald meets his suave identical twin after a row with Daisy and pursuades him to help win back her favor.

1618. Donald's Dream Voice *(Donald Duck)* 21 May 1948; *p.c.:* Walt Disney prods for RKO; *dir:* Jack King; *asst dir:* Joel Greenhalgh; *story:* Roy Williams, Carl Barks; *anim:* Ed Aardal, Paul Allen, Emery Hawkins, Frank McSavage, Ted Bonnicksen, Fred Kopietz, Don Towsley; *lay:* Don Griffith; *back:* Merle Cox; *voices:* Leslie Dennison, Ruth Clifford, Jack Mather, Clarence Nash; *mus:* Oliver Wallace; *col:* Tech. *sd:* RCA. 6 min. • Discouraged as a brush salesman, Donald buys a box of Ajax Voice Pills for development of his larynx. Storyman Roy Williams is caricatured (by T. Hee) as a workman.

1619. Donald's Garden *(Donald Duck)* 21 Jan. 1942; *p.c.:* Walt Disney prods for RKO; *dir:* Richard Lundy; *asst dir:* Ted Baker; *story:* Ralph Wright; *anim:* Theodore Bonnicksen, Robert W. Carlson Jr., Walter Clinton, Jack Hannah, Volus Jones, Kenneth Muse, Don Patterson; *fx:* Jack Boyd, Andy Engman, Reuben Timmens; *lay:* Thor Putnam; *voices:* Clarence Nash, Harriet Reagh; *mus:* Oliver Wallace; *col:* Tech. *sd:* RCA. 7 min. • Farmer Don has problems with his watering-can, a pump and a gopher eating his watermelons.

1620. Donald's Gold Mine *(Donald Duck)* 24 July 1942; *p.c.:* Walt Disney prods for RKO; *dir:* Richard Lundy; *asst dir:* Norman Wright; *story:* Harry Reeves, Carl Barks; *anim:* Robert W. Carlson Jr., Theodore Bonnicksen, Walter Clinton, Volus Jones, Richard Lundy, Ray Patterson; *fx:* Andy Engman, Ed Parks; *lay:* McLaren Stewart; *voices:* Clarence Nash, Bill Reinelie; *mus:* Oliver Wallace; *col:* Tech. *sd:* RCA. 7 min. • Don has problems with his pick-axe and a mule while digging for gold.

1621. Donald's Golf Game *(Donald Duck)* 4 Nov. 1938; *p.c.:* Walt Disney prods for RKO; *dir:* Jack King; *asst dir:* James Handley; *story:* Carl Barks, Jack Hannah; *anim:* Lars Calonius, Johnny Cannon, Alfred Eugster, Jack Hannah, Fred Spencer, Don Towsley, Bob Wickersham. *fx:* Reuben Timmins; *lay:* Bill Herwig; *back:* Eugene Fleurey; *voice:* Clarence Nash; *mus:* Oliver Wallace; *col:* Tech. *sd:* RCA. 8 min. • Donald's questionable golfing abilities are sabotaged by his three nephews.

1622. Donald's Happy Birthday *(Donald Duck)* 11 Feb. 1949; *p.c.:* Walt Disney prods for RKO; *dir:* Jack Hannah; *story:* Nick George, Bill Berg; *anim:* Bob Carlson, Volus Jones, Bill Justice, Judge Whitaker; *fx:* Jack Boyd; *lay:* Yale Gracey; *back:* Ralph Hulett; *voices:* Clarence Nash; *mus:* Oliver Wallace; *col:* Tech. *sd:* RCA. 7 min. • Donald believes his nephews to have bought cigars for themselves. Outraged, he forces them to smoke every one but discovers too late that they are a present for his birthday.

1623. Donald's Lucky Day *(Donald Duck)* 13 Jan. 1939; *p.c.:* Walt Disney prods for RKO; *dir:* Jack King; *story:* Carl Barks; *anim:* Paul Allen, Johnny Cannon, Alfred Eugster, Jack Hannah, Edward Love, Richard Lundy, James McManus, Kenneth Peterson, Sandy Strother, Don Towsley, Cornett Wood; *voices:* David Kerman, Paul Norby, Dorothy Lloyd, Clarence Nash; *mus:* Oliver Wallace; *col:* Tech. *sd:* RCA. 8 min. • Messenger-boy Donald has a tough time delivering a mysterious package on Friday 13th.

1624. Donald's Nephews *(Donald Duck)* 15 Apr. 1938; *p.c.:* Walt Disney prods for RKO; *dir:* Jack King; *asst dir:* James Handley; *story:* Harry Reeves, Carl Barks, Jack Hannah; *anim:* Paul Allen, Johnny Cannon, Chuck Couch, Andy Engman, Jack Hannah, Edward Love, Stan Quackenbush, Don Towsley, Bernard Wolf, Cornett Wood; *lay:* James Carmichael, Charles Payzant; *voices:* Clarence Nash; *mus:* Oliver Wallace; *col:* Tech. *sd:* RCA. 8 min. • Donald practices child psychology on his visiting three nephews.

1625. Donald's Off Day *(Donald Duck)* 8 Dec. 1944; *p.c.:* Walt Disney prods for RKO; *dir:* Jack Hannah; *asst dir:* Toby Tobelman; *story:* Bill Berg, Dick Shaw; *anim:* Judge Whitaker, Harvey Toombs, Art Scott, Bill Justice, Don Patterson, Don Towsley; *fx:* John Reed; *lay:* Yale Gracey; *back:* Thelma Witmer; *voices:* Dehner Forkum, Clarence Nash, Z. Retzloff; *mus:* Paul J. Smith; *col:* Tech. *sd:* RCA. 7 min. • The nephews make Donald believe he's a dying duck.

1626. Donald's Ostrich (*Donald Duck*) 10 Dec. 1937; *p.c.:* Walt Disney prods for RKO; *dir:* Jack King; *story:* Samuel Armstrong, Carl Barks; *anim:* Paul Allen, Johnny Cannon, Jack Hannah, I. Klein, John McManus, Milt Schaffer, Don Towsley, Roy Williams, Bernard Wolf; *voices:* Elvia Allman, Zena Baer, Billy Bletcher, Don Brodie, Jack Clifford, Pinto Colvig, Jean Murtagh, Clarence Nash; *mus:* Oliver Wallace; *col:* Tech. *sd:* RCA. 9 min. • Station Master Donald has his hands full when he's delivered an ostrich that swallows everything in sight.

1627. Donald's Penguin (*Donald Duck*) 11 Aug. 1939; *p.c.:* Walt Disney prods for RKO; *dir:* Jack King; *asst dir:* James Handley; *story:* Carl Barks, Harry Reeves; *anim:* Paul Allen, Johnny Cannon, Alfred Eugster, Jack Hannah, James McManus, Lee Morehouse, Fred Spencer, Don Towsley; *lay:* Bill Herwig; *voices:* Clarence Nash, Louis Manly; *mus:* Oliver Wallace; *col:* Tech. *sd:* RCA. 8 min. • Donald acquires a baby penguin and has many problems in trying to stop him from eating the goldfish.

1628. Donald's Snow Fight (*Donald Duck*) 15 Jan. 1942; *p.c.:* Walt Disney prods for RKO; *dir:* Jack King; *asst dir:* Bob Newman, Ralph Chadwick; *story:* Harry Reeves, Carl Barks; *anim:* Lee J. Ames, James Armstrong, Walter Clinton, Jack Hannah, Hal King, Edward Love, Lee Morehouse, Ray Patin, Retta Scott, Don Towsley, Judge Whitaker; *fx:* Jack Boyd, Andy Engman, Joseph Gayek, Jack Manning, Ed Parks, Reuben Timmens, Don Tobin; *lay:* Bill Herwig; *voice:* Clarence Nash; *mus:* Oliver Wallace; *col:* Tech. *sd:* RCA. 8 min. • Donald has a snow fight with his unruly nephews.

1629. Donald's Tire Trouble (*Donald Duck*) 29 Jan. 1943; *p.c.:* Walt Disney prods for RKO; *dir:* Richard Lundy; *story:* Harry Reeves, Carl Barks; *anim:* Robert W. Carlson Jr., Arthur W. Palmer, Ray Patterson, Don Towsley; *lay:* A. Kendall O'Connor; *voice:* Clarence Nash; *mus:* Oliver Wallace; *col:* Tech. *sd:* RCA. 7 min. • In an attempt to change a flat tire, Donald manages to break the jack and make the radiator on his car explode.

1630. Donald's Vacation (*Donald Duck*) 9 Aug. 1940; *p.c.:* Walt Disney prods for RKO; *dir:* Jack King; *story:* Frank Tashlin, Carl Barks, Jack Hannah; *anim:* Paul Allen, Larry Clemmons, Emery Hawkins, Jack Hannah, Harry Holt, Volus Jones, Lynn Karp, Hal King, Edward Love, Fred Madison, Murray McClellan, Lee Morehouse, Ray Patin, Ken Peterson, Joseph Starbuck, Gus Tanaka, Judge Whitaker; *voices:* Clarence Nash, James MacDonald; *mus:* Oliver Wallace; *col:* Tech. *sd:* RCA. 7 min. • Donald has problems while camping in the woods.

1631. Donkey in the Lion's Skin (*Aesop's Film Fable*) 21 Aug. 1921; *p.c.:* Fables Pictures Inc for Pathé; *dir:* Paul Terry; b&w. sil. 5 min. • A donkey rebels against mistreatment from his black master. He finds a lion skin in the barn and leads all to believe he's "King of the Beasts." Unfortunately his bray gives him away. Moral: "Fools lose their best opportunity by talking too much."

1632. Don's Fountain of Youth (*Donald Duck*) 30 May 1953; *p.c.:* Walt Disney prods for RKO; *dir:* Jack Hannah; *story:* Ralph Wright; *anim:* Volus Jones, George Kreisl, Bill Justice; *fx:* George Rowley; *lay:* Yale Gracey; *back:* Art Riley; *voices:* Clarence Nash, James MacDonald; *mus:* Joseph S. Dubin; *col:* Tech. *sd:* RCA. 6 min. • While vacationing in Florida, Don teaches his nephews a lesson by pretending to be a baby after falling in "the Fountain of Youth."

1633. Don't Axe Me (*Merrie Melodies*) 4 Jan. 1958; *p.c.:* WB; *dir:* Robert McKimson; *story:* Tedd Pierce; *anim:* Ted Bonnicksen, George Grandpré, Tom Ray; *lay:* Robert Gribbroek; *back:* William Butler; *ed:* Treg Brown; *voices:* Mel Blanc, Arthur Q. Bryan, June Foray; *mus:* Milt Franklyn; *prod:* John W. Burton; *col:* Tech. *sd:* Vit. 7 min. • Farmer Fudd is instructed to slaughter a duck for dinner and Daffy does his best to try to talk him out of the whole idea.

1634. Don't Give Up the Sheep (*Looney Tunes*) 3 Jan. 1953; *p.c.:* WB; *dir:* Chuck Jones; *story:* Michael Maltese; *anim:* Ken Harris, Ben Washam, Lloyd Vaughan; *lay:* Robert Gribbroek; *back:* Carlos Manriquez; *ed:* Treg Brown; *voices:* Mel Blanc; *mus:* Carl Stalling; *prod mgr:* John W. Burton; *prod:* Edward Selzer; *col:* Tech. *sd:* Vit. 7 min. • Ralph Wolf disguises as some shrubbery, then as "Pan," then sets a wildcat on the sheepdog who vigilantly protects the sheep.

1635. Don't Hustle an Ant with Muscle (*Ant & Aardvark*) 27 Dec. 1971; *p.c.:* Mirisch/DFE for UA; *dir:* Art Davis; *story:* Dale Hale; *anim:* Bob Bentley, Manny Gould, Ken Muse, Phil Roman, Warren Batchelder, Manny Perez; *lay:* Dick Ung; *back:* Richard H. Thomas; *ed:* Lee Gunther; *voices:* John Byner; *mus:* Doug Goodwin, Ray Brown, Billy Byers, Pete Candoli, Shelly Manne, Jimmy Rowles, Tommy Tedesco; *prod sup:* Jim Foss, Harry Love; *col:* DeLuxe. *sd:* RCA. 6 min. • The Ant retaliates by taking vitamins to build him up and defeat his nemesis.

1636. Don't Look Now (*Merrie Melodies*) 7 Nov. 1936; *p.c.:* Leon Schlesinger prods for WB; *dir:* Fred Avery; *story:* Robert Clampett; *anim:* Robert Clampett, Joe d'Igalo; *ed:* Tregoweth E. Brown; *voices:* Tommy Bond, Bernice Hansel, Fred Avery; *mus:* Carl W. Stalling; *prod sup:* Henry Binder, Raymond G. Katz; *col:* Tech. *sd:* Vit. 7 min. • A duel between Dan Cupid and a little Devil on St. Valentine's Day.

1637. Don't Spill the Beans (*Terry-Toon*) Apr. 1965; *p.c.:* TT for Fox; *ex prod:* Bill Weiss; *dir/anim:* Ralph Bakshi; *story sup:* Tom Morrison; *story:* Eli Bauer; *sets:* Bill Focht; *ed:* Jack McConnell; *voices:* Bob MacFadden; *mus:* Jim Timmens; *ph:* Ted Moskowitz; *sd:* Elliot Grey; *col:* DeLuxe. *sd:* RCA. 6 min. • To ensure "A Happy Ending," the Apprentice Good Fairy issues Sad Cat with magic beans which burrow into the ground and strike oil.

1638. The Door (*Merrie Melodies*) 1 June 1968; *p.c.:* Silver/Campbell/Cosby for WB/7; *prod/dir:* Ken Mundie; *asso prod:* Les Goldman; *mus:* Clark "Mumbles" Terry; *col:* Tech. *sd:* Vit. 6 min. *l/a/anim.* • An Indian discovers a door, behind which lurks live-action images of future wars and depravity. This social message was produced independantly but issued inexplicably as part of Warners' *Merrie Melodies* series.

1639. Dopey Dick the Pink Whale (*Woody Woodpecker*) 18 Nov. 1957; *p.c.:* Walter Lantz prods for Univ; *dir:* Paul J. Smith; *story:* Homer Brightman; *anim:* Les Kline, Robert Bentley; *sets:* Art Landy; *voices:* Dal Mc Kennon, Grace Stafford; *mus:* Clarence Wheeler; *prod mgr:* William E. Garity; *col:* Tech. *sd:* RCA. 6 min. • Woody is shanghaied by a manic Captain who demands revenge against a pink whale.

1640. A Dopey Hacienda (*Tijuana Toads*) 6 Dec. 1970; *p.c.:* Mirisch/DFE for UA; *dir:* Hawley Pratt; *story:* John W. Dunn; *anim:* Irv Spence, Ken Muse, Manny Gould, Don Williams, Bob Bentley; *lay:* Dick Ung; *back:* Richard Thomas; *ed:* Lee Gunther; *voices:* Don Diamond, Tom Holland, Athena Lorde; *mus:* Doug Goodwin; *ph:* John Burton Jr.; *prod sup:* Jim Foss, Harry Love; *col:* DeLuxe. *sd:* RCA. 5 min. • The Toads try to gain access to a house guarded by a ferocious cat.

1641. The Dot and the Line 1964; *p.c.:* SIB/Tower 12 for MGM; *prod:* Chuck Jones, Les Goldman; *dir:* Chuck Jones; *asst dir/des:* Maurice Noble; *story:* Norton Juster; *anim sup:* Don Towsley; *anim:* Ken Harris, Ben Washam, Dick Thompson, Tom Ray, Philip Roman; *lay:* Don Morgan, Don Foster; *back:* Philip de Guard; *voice:* Robert Morley; *mus:* Eugene Poddany; *ph:* Buff Nerbovig; *col:* Metro. *sd:* WE. 7 min. *Academy Award* • A line loves a dot who, in turn, is fascinated by a squiggle. The line practices mathmatical shapes to impress and win over the dot.

1642. Double Chaser (*Merrie Melodies*) 20 June 1942; *p.c.:* Leon Schlesinger prods for WB; *dir:* I. Freleng; *story:* Michael Maltese; *anim:* Gerry Chiniquy; *lay:* Owen Fitzgerald; *back:* Lenard Kester; *ed:* Treg Brown; *mus:* Carl W. Stalling; *prod sup:* Henry Binder, Raymond G. Katz; *col:* Tech. *sd:* Vit. 7 min. • A cat chases a mouse and is, in turn, chased by a dog. Given time, both the cat and dog unite against the mouse.

1643. Double-Cross-Country Race (*Popeye*) 15 May 1951; *p.c.:* Famous for Para: *dir:* Seymour Kneitel; *story:* Larz Bourne; *anim:* Tom Johnson, Bill Hudson; *sets:* Anton Loeb; *voices:* Jack Mercer, Jackson Beck; *mus:* Winston Sharples; *ph:* Leonard McCormick; *prod mgr:* Seymour Shultz; *col:* Tech. *sd:* RCA. 7 min. • Popeye enters a cross-country motor race against the unscrupulous Count Noah Count.

1644. Double Dribble (*Goofy*) 20 Dec. 1946; *p.c.:* Walt Disney prods for RKO; *dir:* Jack Hannah; *asst dir:* Toby Tobelman; *story:* Bill Berg, Milt Banta; *anim:* Bill Justice, Hugh Fraser, John Sibley, Al Bertino, Cliff Nordberg; *fx:* Andy Engman, John F. Reed; *lay:* Yale Gracey; *back:* Maurice Greenberg; *voice:* Frank Bull; *mus:* Oliver Wallace; *col:* Tech. *sd:* RCA. 7 min. • Goofy participates in a raucous basketball game.

1645. Double or Mutton (*Looney Tunes*) 23 July 1955; *p.c.:* WB; *dir:* Charles M. Jones; *story:* Michael Maltese; *anim:* Richard Thompson, Abe Levitow, Keith Darling, Ken Harris; *sets:* Philip de Guard; *ed:* Treg Brown;

voices: Mel Blanc; *mus:* Milt Franklyn; *prod mgr:* John W. Burton; *prod:* Edward Selzer; *col:* Tech. *sd:* Vit. 7 min. • Ralph Wolf employs a tightrope, a "Little Bo Peep" costume and even goes to the extremes of using hair grower to dim the view of the ever-resilient watchdog.

1646. Dough Boys (*Aesop's Film Fable*) 8 Aug. 1926; *p.c.:* Fables Pictures Inc for Pathé; *dir:* Paul Terry; b&w. *sil.* 5 min. • Farmer Al, the cat and mice together run a lunch room. Exploding dough gives cause for a dough-fight involving Officer Oscar.

1647. Dough for the Do-Do (*Merrie Melodies*) 2 Sept. 1949; *p.c.:* WB; *sup:* Art Davis; *prod mgr:* John W. Burton; *prod:* Edward Selzer; *col:* Tech. *sd:* Vit. 7 min. Tech reissue of *Porky in Wacky Land.* • Porky tries to capture a crazy Do-Do bird for a rich reward.

1648. Dough Nuts (*Tom & Jerry*) 10 July 1933; *p.c.:* Van Beuren for RKO; *dir:* Frank Sherman, George Rufle; *mus:* Gene Rodemich; b&w. *sd:* RCA. 7 min. • Tom and Jerry attend a "Baker's Convention" with a drunken peg-legged sailor making the holes in their doughnuts. A group of singers get the whole show swinging.

1649. Dough Ray Me-Ow (*Merrie Melodies*) 14 Aug. 1948; *p.c.:* WB; *dir:* Arthur Davis; *story:* Lloyd Turner; *anim:* Basil Davidovich, J.C. Melendez, Don Williams, Emery Hawkins; *lay:* Don Smith; *back:* Philip de Guard; *ed:* Treg Brown; *voices:* Mel Blanc; *mus:* Carl Stalling; *prod mgr:* John W. Burton; *prod:* Edward Selzer; *col:* Tech. *sd:* Vit. 7 min. • Heathcliff, a dumb cat, stands to inherit a fortune providing he survives Louie the parrot. Louie discovers this and tries to eliminate him.

1650. Doug's 1st Movie 26 Mar. 1999; *p.c.:* Jumbo Pictures, Inc./Walt Disney Pictures for BV; *dir:* Maurice Joyce; *prod:* Jim Jinkins, David Campbell, Jack Spillum, Melanie Grisanti; *created by* Jim Jinkins; *story:* Ken Scarborough; *script co-ord:* Jim Rubin; *storyboard:* Siobhan Mullen, Deidre Stammers; *digital fx:* Buena Vista Imaging, Frank Drucker; *technical sup:* Rudy Tomaselli; *animatic co-ord:* Charlene McBride; *anim prod: Plus One Animation, Inc.: sup dir:* Lee Choon Man; *overseas sup:* Kent Laursen, Ric Machin, Glenn McDonald; *lay:* Lee Kwang-Seok, Jeong Baik-Ma; *anim dir:* Oh Han-Gil, Ma Hyeon-Deok, Shin Soeng-Cheon, Kim Joon-Bok; *anim:* Nam Beom-Woo, Ko Kyung-Nam, Kim Jeong-Taek, You Choon-Yong, Cho Sang-Hyun, Jeong Seung-Tae, Kang Dae-Il, Song Keun-Sik, Lee Jin-Taek, Lee Jang-Pil, Ham Chee-Heon, Lee Kee-Do, Lee Chan-Seop, Park Kyung-Hee, Son Jeong-Seon, Jeong Young-Mee, Choi Jong-Seok, Kim Hyung-Jun, Kim Mee-Young, Shim Seon-Ho, Kim Kee-Ryang, Kim Kyung-Sook, Son Myung-Hee, Jang Joon-Kyung, Choi Deuk-Kwon; *i&p:* Park Soo-Kyung, Kwon In-Sook, Jang Mee-Yeon, Kwon Tae-Seon, Jeong Jae-Hun, Lee Hye-Kyung, Kang Hyun-Joo, Lee Young-Mee, Kim Joo-Young, Kim Hye-Jee, Lee Hee-Sook, Sea Youn-Hee, Jeong In-Young, Lee Eun-Joo, Kim Mee-Jeong, Kim Jong-Sook, Kim Joung-Eun, Kim Eun-Kyung, Kim Un-Ah, Noh Young-Mee, Park Kyung-Hee, Jeon Hye-Sook, Lee Jae-Sook; *model check: sup:* Park Hyeon-Sook; *anim check: sup:* Kim Jeong-Ja; *i&p sup:* Lee Tae-Jeong; *color mark-up:* Park Hae-Won; *i&p check:* Kim Hae-Kyeona, Kim Myeong-Ae, Han Yeong-Yea; *fx:* Jeong Yeon-Kwan, Lee Kyeong-Yong; *back:* Ahn Kye-Jeong; *New York addit anim:* Mike Foran, Ray de Silva, Irene Wu, Chris Dechert; *back:* Freya Tanz, Michael Rose, Sophie Kittredge, Miriam Katin, Andrei Poteryaylo; *col key sup:* Marina Dominis Dunnigan, Doris Santos; *col stylists:* John Brandon, Jason McDonald; *back des:* Nash Dunnigan, Ray Feldman, Miriam Katin, Kim Miskoe, Don Poynter, Ray da Sylva, Meryl Rosner; *character/prop des:* Dick Condor, Moss Freedman, Miguel Martinez Joffre, Tim Chi Ly, Christopher Palesty, Irene Wu; *back col sup:* Michael Zodorozny; *back painters:* Tony Curanaj, Sophie Kittredge, Adrian Newkirk, Michael Rose; *pre-prod ed:* Meredith Watson Jeffrey; *des co-ord:* Marcus Pauls; *storyboard artists:* Liz Rathke, *Barking Bullfrog Cartoon Company,* Jean Charles Finck, Victor Glasko, Tapani Knuutila, Jean Lajeunesse; *storyboard revision artists:* Otis L. Brayboy II, David Concepcion, Christopher McCulloch, Nate Kanfer, Maurice Fontenot, Prentis Rollins, Willy Hartland; *Storyboard slugging/sheet timers:* Gary Blatchford, My Bushman, Kieran Dowling, Anthony Power; *des sup:* Freya Tanz, Pete List, Eugene Salandra; *character development:* Jim Jinkins, Joe Aaron; *ed:* Alysha Nadine Cohen, Christopher W. Gee; *voices: Doug Funnie/Lincoln:* Thomas McHugh; *Skeeter/Mr. Dink/Porkchop/Ned:* Fred Newman; *Roger Klotz/Bloomer/Larry/Mr. Chiminy:* Chris Phillips; *Patti Mayonnaise:* Constance Shulman; *Herman Melville:* Frank Welker; *Mr. Funnie/Mr. Bluff/Willie/Chalky/Bluff Agent 1:* Doug Preis; *Guy Graham:* Guy Hadley; *Beebe Bluff/Elmo:* Alice Playten; *Al Sleech/Moo Sleech/Robocrusher:* Eddie Korbich; *Quailman/stentorian announcer:* David O'Brien; *Mayor Tippi Dink:* Doris Belack; *Judy Funnie/Mrs. Funnie/Connie:* Becca Lish; *Principal White:* Greg Lee; *Bluff Asst:* Bob Bottone; *Mr. Swirley/Bruce Bayley Johnson/Mrs. Perigrew:* Fran Brill; *Briar Langolier:* Melissa Greenspan; *also:* Rodger Bumpass, Paul Eiding, Jackie Gonneau, Sherry Lynn, Mickie McGowan, Phil Proctor, Brianne Siddall, Claudette Wells; *mus:* Mark Watters; *orch:* Harvey Cohen, John Bisharat, John Given, Ira Hearshen, Christopher Klatman, Alan Steinberger; *mus ed:* Dominick Certo; *mix:* John Richards; *songs:* "Mona Mo" written/performed by Dan Sawyer, Fred Newman; "Deep, Deep Water" written/performed by Dan Sawyer & Kristyn Osborn, Linda Garvey; *title version* performed by Shedaisy; "Someone Like Me" written by William Squire & Jeffrey Lodin, performed by Michael Africk; *original theme for "Disney's Doug":* Dan Sawyer; *addit vocals:* Fred Newman; *voice dir:* Jim Jinkins, David Campbell, Kent W. Meredith; *mouth dir:* Simie Nallaseth; *title des:* Susan Bradley; *title anim:* Kieran Dowling; *inbet:* Trevor Murphy, Aveen O'Reilly, Ciaran Bonass; *fx anim:* Robert Byrne; *prod mgr:* Jason Edward; *technical sup:* Rudy Tomaselli; *digital paint/compositing:* Tape House Toons; *digital cinematography:* Tape House Digital Film; *graphic des:* Alisa Klayman; *asso prod:* Bruce Knapp; *prod mgr:* Masako Kanayama; *post prod sup:* Stephen Swofford; *sd des:* Pomann Sound, Inc.; *pre-prod sd co-ord:* Darryl Jefferson; *dial rec:* Juan Dieguez, Jerome Hyman; *rec:* Neal Porter; *mix:* Andy D'Addario, Tom Dahl; *sd ed:* Ron Eng, Louis L. Edemann, Rick Franklin, Leonard T. Geschke, Chuck Neely, Jeff Clark, Scott G.G. Haller, Cail Clark Burch, Howard S.M. Neiman; *dial ed:* Joe Gauci, Dave Chmela; *ADR: rec/ed:* Marc Bazerman, Aria Boediman; *foley:* "Walkers": Ken Dufva, Joan Rowe; *mix:* Lee Pinkham; *ph:* Jo Bok-Dong; *prod mgr:* Kim Ji-Byung, Han Jang-Ho, Kim Jean-Seon; *retake dpt:* Kim Nok-Hoon; *overseas co-ord:* Shim Young-Jeong, Yoon Kyung-Mi, Yang Hae-Won; 77¼ min. *col:* Tech. *sd:* SDDS/Dolby digital/Digital dts sound. • Feature-length version of the television show: Doug and Skeeter discover an affable mutant monster living in Lucky Duck Lake. They take the mutant home and discover it has been caused by local industrialist, Mr. Bluff, dumping pollution in the lake. Bluff learns of the monster and tries to protect his own reputation by killing it but Doug and his friends manage to smuggle it to an unpolluted lake to set it free.

1651. The Dove of Peace 6 Mar. 1915; *p.c.:* M-in-A Films; *prod:* David S. Horsley; *anim:* Harry Palmer; b&w. *sil.* • No story available.

1652. The Dover Boys at Pimento University (or) The Rivals of Roquefort Hall (*Merrie Melodies*) 19 Sept. 1942; *p.c.:* Leon Schlesinger prods for WB; *dir:* Charles M. Jones; *story:* Ted Pierce; *anim:* Robert Cannon; *lay:* John McGrew; *back:* Eugene Fleury; *ed:* Treg Brown; *voices:* John McLeish, Mel Blanc, Marjorie Tarlton, Ted Pierce, Paul Taylor Chorus; *mus:* Carl W. Stalling; *ph:* John W. Burton; *prod sup:* Henry Binder, Raymond G. Katz; *col:* Tech. *sd:* Vit. 7 min. • Tom, Dick and Larry are upstanding collegians who rush to the rescue of a lady when evil Dan Backslide abducts her.

1653. Down Among the Sugar Cane (*Screen Songs*) 26 Aug. 1932; *p.c.:* The Fleischer Studio for Para; *prod:* Max Fleischer; *sup:* Dave Fleischer; *dir/story:* James H. Culhane, Rudy Zamora; *anim:* James H. Culhane, William Henning, Rudy Zamora; *mus:* Art Turkisher; *l/a:* Lillian Roth; b&w. *sd:* WE. 7 min. *l/a/anim.* • Featuring a farmer, a beaver and some bees.

1654. Down and Outing (*Tom & Jerry*) 26 Oct. 1961; *p.c.:* Rembrandt Studio for MGM; *prod:* William L. Snyder; *dir:* Gene Deitch; *story:* Larz Bourne; *voices:* Allen Swift; *sd fx:* Tod Dockstader; *col:* Metro. *sd:* WE. 6 min. • Jerry gets Tom in bad with his master on a fishing trip. • See: *Tom and Jerry (Rembrandt Studio)*

1655. Down by the Old Mill Stream (*Screen Songs*) 21 July 1933; *p.c.:* The Fleischer Studio for Para; *prod:* Max Fleischer; *dir:* Dave Fleischer; *anim:* Willard Bowsky, William Sturm; *mus:* Art Turkisher; *l/a:* The Eton Boys; b&w. *sd:* WE. 8 min. *l/a/anim.* • Harvest time with the apples which turn the mill stream to cider.

1656. Down in Dixie (*Aesop's Sound Fable*) 16 Aug. 1932; *p.c.:* Van Beuren for RKO; *dir:* John Foster, Harry Bailey; *mus:* Gene Rodemich; b&w. *sd:* RCA. 7 min. • No story available.

1657. Down in Jungle Town 1929; *p.c.:* Red Seal; *prod:* Alfred Weiss;

mus: Carl Edouarde; b&w. *sd.* • Pinkie the Pup has adventures in the jungle with monkeys and gets them all singing "Down in Jungle Town."

1658. Down on the Farm *(Aesop's Film Fable)* 3 Dec. 1924; *p.c.:* Fables Pictures Inc for Pathé; *dir:* Paul Terry; b&w. *sil.* 5 min. • Mrs. Duck uses an umbrella as a swimming pool for her brood, the cat's auto uses a mouse's tail for a windshield wiper and the pig's tail serves as a swing for the mice.

1659. Down on the Levee *(Paul Terry-Toon)* 5 Mar. 1933; *p.c.:* Moser & Terry for Educational/Fox; *dir:* Frank Moser, Paul Terry; *mus:* Philip A. Scheib; b&w. *sil.* WE 6 min. • The showboat stages a musical where the villain steals Little Eva's jewels. The hero chases him and recovers her necklace.

1660. Down on the Phoney Farm 16 Oct. 1915; *p.c.:* Thanhouser Film Corp; *dir:* Paul H. Terry; b&w. *sil.* • No story available.

1661. Down to Mirth *(Casper)* 20 Aug. 1958; *p.c.:* Para Cartoons; *dir:* Seymour Kneitel; *story:* Carl Meyer, Jack Mercer; *anim:* Nick Tafuri, Wm. B. Pattengill; *sets:* Robert Owen; *voices:* Cecil Roy, Allen Swift, Jackson Beck; *mus:* Winston Sharples; *ph:* Leonard Mc Cormick; *prod mgr:* Abe Goodman; *col:* Tech. *sd:* RCA. 6 min. • A mad scientist lets loose an anti-gravity ray on the city and Casper puts a stop to it.

1662. Down with Cats *(Terry-Toon)* 7 Oct. 1943; *p.c.:* TT for Fox; *dir:* Connie Rasinski; *story:* John Foster; *sets:* Art Bartsch; *mus:* Philip A. Scheib; *col:* Tech. *sd:* RCA. 7 min. • Hungry cats invade the mices' skating frolics but Super Mouse arrives in time to save them.

1663. Downbeat Bear *(Tom & Jerry)* 12 Oct. 1956; *p.c.:* MGM; *prod/dir:* William Hanna, Joseph Barbera; *anim:* Kenneth Muse, Ed Barge, Irven Spence, Lewis Marshall; *lay:* Dick Bickenbach; *back:* Robert Gentle; *ed:* Jim Faris; *voices:* Paul Frees, Daws Butler; *mus:* Scott Bradley; *ph:* Jack Stevens; *prod mgr:* Hal Elias; *col:* Tech. *Sd:* WE. 6 min. • Jerry fouls Tom's attempts to capture an escaped dancing bear.

1664. Downhearted Duckling *(Tom & Jerry)* 13 Nov. 1954; *p.c.:* MGM; *dir:* William Hanna, Joseph Barbera; *anim:* Irven Spence, Ray Patterson, Kenneth Muse, Ed Barge; *lay:* Dick Bickenbach; *back:* Robert Gentle; *ed:* Jim Faris; *voice:* Red Coffee; *mus:* Scott Bradley; *ph:* Jack Stevens; *prod:* Fred Quimby; *col:* Tech. *sd:* WE. 7 min. • Jerry helps a duck, intent on ending it all because he believes he's ugly.

1665. Dra-Ko Film Company (1916) *anim:* Frank A. Nankievel; b&w. *sil.* • Company producing advertising films.

1666. The Draft Horse *(Merrie Melodies)* 9 May 1942; *p.c.:* Leon Schlesinger prods for WB; *dir:* Charles M. Jones; *story:* Ted Pierce; *anim:* Robert Cannon, Ken Harris, A.C. Gamer; *character des/lay:* Robert Givens; *back:* Eugene Fleury; *ed:* Treg Brown; *voices:* Mel Blanc; *mus:* Carl W. Stalling; *ph:* John W. Burton; *prod sup:* Henry Binder, Raymond G. Katz; *col:* Tech. *sd:* Vit. 7 min. • A plough horse is rejected from the Army when he wants to do his bit for the war effort. A sham battle sends him packing.

1667. Draftee Daffy *(Looney Tunes)* 27 Jan. 1945; *p.c.:* WB; *dir:* Robert Clampett; *story:* Lou Lilly; *anim:* Rod Scribner; *lay:* Thomas McKimson; *back:* Michael Sasanoff; *ed:* Treg Brown; *voices:* Mel Blanc; *mus:* Carl W. Stalling; *prod mgr:* John W. Burton; *prod:* Edward Selzer; *col:* Tech. *sd:* Vit. 7 min. • Daffy dodges his call-up by evading "The little man from the Draft Board."

1668. Drag-A-Long Droopy *(Droopy)* 20 Feb. 1954; *p.c.:* MGM; *dir:* Tex Avery; *story:* Heck Allen; *anim:* Grant Simmons, Michael Lah, Ray Patterson, Robert Bentley, Walter Clinton; *lay/character des:* Ed Benedict; *back:* John Didrik Johnsen; *ed:* Jim Faris; *voices:* Bill Thompson, Tex Avery; *mus:* Scott Bradley; *ph:* Jack Stevens; *prod:* Fred Quimby; *col:* Tech. *sd:* WE. 8 min. • Sheepherder Droopy stages a shootout at dawn with a ruthless cattle baron.

1669. Dragon Around *(Donald Duck)* 16 July 1954; *p.c.:* Walt Disney prods for RKO; *dir:* Jack Hannah; *story:* Nick George, Roy Williams; *anim:* Bill Justice, Volus Jones, Bob Carlson, George Kreisl; *fx:* Dan MacManus; *lay:* Yale Gracey; *back:* Ray Huffine; *voices:* Clarence Nash, James Mac-Donald, Dessie Flynn, Norma Swank; *mus:* Oliver Wallace; *col:* Tech. *sd:* RCA. 7 min. • The chipmunks mistake Donald's excavation machine for a dragon and set about destroying it.

1670. Dragonheart 31 May 1996; *p.c.:* Univ City for UIP; *special visual fx anim:* ILM; *pre-prod co-sup:* Alex Seiden; *sup digital fx art:* Barry Armour; *sup character anim:* Rob Coleman, Douglas Smith; *character anim:* Chris Armstrong, Linda Bel, Patrick Bonneau, David Byers Brown, Sue Campbell, Lou Dellarosa, Michael Eames, Jenn Emberly, Miguel Fuertes, Paul Hunt, Daniel Jeannette, Ken King, Julija Leary, Robert Marinic, Julie Nelson, Steve Nichols, Magali Rigaudias, Trish Schutz, Dan Taylor, James Tooley, Dennis Turner, Tim Waddy, Colin White, William R. Wright; *anim software development:* Carey Phillips; *character anim sup:* James Straus; *Dragon animatics: Tippett Studio: prod:* Jules Roman; *art dir:* Craig Hayes; *character des sculptor:* Peter König; *Dragon sculptor:* Ron Holthuysen; *anim:* Adam Valdez, Blair Clark, *technical sup:* Steve Reding, David Valdez; *voice of "Draco":* Sean Connery; *col:* DeLuxe. *sd:* dts. 103 min. *l/a.* • Live-action sword and sorcery fantasy: Bowen, a 10th century knight, does a deal with "Draco" (the final dragon left on earth) for the dragon to fake attacks on villages. The knight will then offer to drive the creature away for a fee. Animated dragon.

1671. The Dream Kids *(Fox & Crow)* 28 Apr. 1944; *p.c.:* Colum; *prod:* Dave Fleischer; *dir:* Bob Wickersham; *story:* Sam Cobean; *anim:* Phil Duncan, Chic Otterstrom; *lay:* Clark Watson; *ed:* Edward Moore; *voices:* Frank Graham, Sara Berner; *mus:* Eddie Kilfeathher; *prod mgr:* Albert Spar; *col:* Tech. *sd:* RCA. 7 min. • The Crow tries to oust the Fox from his warm bed by inducing dreams into his head.

1672. The Dream of the Rarebit Fiend 1916; *dir:* Winsor McCay; *anim:* Robert Winsor McCay; b&w. *sil.* 13 min. • No story available.

1673. Dream Walking *(Gandy Goose)* May 1950; *p.c.:* TT for Fox; *dir:* Connie Rasinski; *story:* Tom Morrison; *sets:* Art Bartsch; *voices:* Arthur Kay, Tom Morrison; *mus:* Philip A. Scheib; *ph:* Douglas Moye; *col:* Tech. *sd:* RCA. 7 min. • Gandy's sleepwalking keeps Sourpuss busy while saving him from the dangers of a zoo.

1674. A Dream Walking *(Popeye)* 26 Sept. 1934; *p.c.:* The Fleischer Studio for Para; *prod:* Max Fleischer; *dir:* Dave Fleischer; *anim:* Seymour Kneitel, Roland Crandall; *voices:* William A. Costello, Mae Questel, Charles Carver, Lou Fleischer; *mus:* Sammy Timberg; *song:* Harry Revel, Mack Gordon; b&w. *sd:* WE. 7 min. • Popeye and Bluto vie for the honor of rescuing a sleepwalking Olive Oyl from atop a precarious scaffolding.

1675. Dreamboat 1952; *p.c.:* UPA for Fox; *prod:* Sol C. Siegel; *UPA prod:* Stephen Bosustow; b&w. *sd:* WE. 2 min. *l/a/anim.* • Live-action film with Clifton Webb demonstrating the banality of television to the court via an animated hair tonic commercial.

1676. Dreamnapping *(James Hound)* Nov. 1966; *p.c.:* TT for Fox; *dir/anim:* Ralph Bakshi; *col:* DeLuxe. *sd:* RCA. 6 min. • Prof. Sigmund Fryed causes international chaos by giving everybody nightmares. • See: *James Hound*

1677. Dreams on Ice *(Color Rhapsody)* 3 Nov. 1939; *p.c.:* Charles Mintz prods for Colum; *story:* Sid Marcus; *anim:* Art Davis, Herb Rothwill; *voices:* Leone Le Doux, Mel Blanc, The Rhythmettes; *mus:* Joe de Nat; *prod mgr:* James Bronis; *col:* Tech. *sd:* RCA. 6 min. • Scrappy converts his room into a skating rink and dreams his toys perform a gala.

1678. Dreamy Dud *p.c.:* Wallace A. Carlson Cartoons/International Features Syndicate for Essanay Film Mfg Co; *dir/anim:* Wallace A. Carlson; b&w. *sil. s/r.* (with scenic) • **1915: A Visit to the Zoo** 15 May. **An Alley Romance** 15 May. **Dreamy Dud** 26 May. **Dreamy Dud Lost in the Jungle** 1 June. **Dreamy Dud in the Swim** 7 June. **Dreamy Dud Resolves Not to Smoke** 22 June. **Dreamy Dud in King Koo Koo's Kingdom** 30 June. **Dreamy Dud Goes Bear Hunting** 17 July. **A Visit to Uncle Dudley's Farm** 26 July. **Dreamy Dud Sees Charlie Chaplin** 9 Aug. **Dreamy Dud, Cowboy** 31 Aug. **Dreamy Dud at the Ole Swimmin' Hole** 29 Sept. **Dreamy Dud, Up in the Air** 27 Oct. **Dreamy Dud in Love** 8 Nov. • **1916: Dreamy Dud, Lost at Sea** 22 Jan. **Dreamy Dud Has a Laugh on the Boss** 20 Sept. **Dreamy Dud in the African War Zone** 30 Oct. **Dreamy Dud Joy Riding with Princess Zlim** 21 Nov. • Carlson's comic character is a lad whose daydreaming gets him into many scrapes. • See: *Canimated Nooz Pictorial*

1679. The Dresden Doll *(Out of the Inkwell)* 7 Jan. 1922; *p.c.:* Inkwell Studio for WB; *dir/l/a:* Dave Fleischer; *anim/l/a:* Max Fleischer; b&w. *sil.* 5 min. *l/a/anim.* • Ko-Ko draws a doll and falls in love with it. • aka: *The Dancing Doll*; *Mechanical Doll*.

1680. Dress Reversal *(Terry-Toon)* July 1965; *p.c.:* TT for Fox;

dir/anim: Ralph Bakshi; *story sup:* Tom Morrison; *story:* Eli Bauer; *sets:* Bill Focht; *ed:* Jack McConnell; *voices:* Bob MacFadden; *mus:* Jim Timmens; *ph:* Ted Moskowitz; *sd:* Elliot Grey; *col:* DeLuxe. *sd:* RCA. 6 min. • Apprentice 6075 of The Good Fairy Service enters Sad Cat in "The Best Dressed Cat in the Kingdom" with help from a magic mirror.

1681. Dribble Drabble *(Sad Cat)* July 1967; *p.c.:* TT for Fox; *dir:* Artie Bartsch; *col:* DeLuxe. *sd:* RCA. 6 min. • Super Ego turns Sad Cat into an Ace basketball champ. • See: *Sad Cat*

1682. The Drifter *(Mighty Heroes)* Aug. 1970 (© 1966); *p.c.:* TT for Fox; *dir/anim:* Ralph Bakshi; *voices:* Lionel Wilson, Herschel Bernardi; *mus:* Jim Timmens; *col:* DeLuxe. *sd:* RCA. 5 min. • "The Drifter" levitates the town of Peace Haven and will bring it down for a price.

1683. Drinks on the Mouse *(Herman & Katnip)* 28 Aug. 1953; *p.c.:* Famous for Para: *dir:* Dave Tendlar; *story:* James Miele; *anim:* Martin Taras, Thomas Moore; *sets:* Robert Owen; *voices:* Arnold Stang, Sid Raymond, Jack Mercer; *mus:* Winston Sharples; *title song:* Hal David, Leon Carr; *prod mgr:* Seymour Shultz; *col:* Tech. *sd:* RCA. 7 min. • Herman saves the starving mice in a drug store where the food is guarded by the cat.

1684. Drip Along Daffy *(Merrie Melodies)* 17 Nov. 1951; *p.c.:* WB; *dir:* Charles M. Jones; *story:* Michael Maltese; *anim:* Phil Monroe, Lloyd Vaughan, Ben Washam, Ken Harris; *lay:* Robert Gribbroek; *back:* Philip de Guard; *ed:* Treg Brown; *voices:* Mel Blanc; *mus:* Carl Stalling; *prod mgr:* John W. Burton; *prod:* Edward Selzer; *col:* Tech. *sd:* Vit. 7.min. • "The Masked Avenger" (Daffy) arrives in a lawless western town to arrest the notorious villain, Nasty Canasta.

1685. Drip Dippy Donald *(Donald Duck)* 5 Mar. 1947; *p.c.:* Walt Disney prods for RKO; *dir:* Jack King; *asst dir:* Joel Greenhalgh; *story:* Nick George; *anim:* Don Towsley, Paul Allen, Sandy Strother, Emery Hawkins, Fred Kopietz, Frank McSavage; *fx:* Ed Aardal; *lay:* Don Griffith; *back:* Howard Dunn; *voices:* Clarence Nash; *mus:* Oliver Wallace; *col:* Tech. *sd:* RCA. 7 min. • Donald's sleep is disturbed by a dripping tap. Production cost $8,250, using novachord and little music. Also first to use the Donald Duck theme song, "Who's Got the Sweetest Disposition?" written by Oliver Wallace.

1686. Drippy Mississippi *(Screen Song)* 13 Apr. 1951; *p.c.:* Famous Studio for Para; *dir:* Seymour Kneitel; *story:* Larz Bourne; *anim:* Myron Waldman, Gordon Whittier; *sets:* Anton Loeb, Robert Little; *voices:* Michael Fitzmaurice, Sid Raymond, Jack Mercer; *mus:* Winston Sharples; *song:* Bert Manlow; *prod mgr:* Sam Buchwald; *col:* Tech. *sd:* RCA. 7 min. • A guided tour of the mighty river leads neatly into a chorus of "Mis-sis-si-pp-i."

1687. Drive On, Nudnik *(Nudnik)* Nov. 1965; *p.c.:* Rembrandt for Para; *prod:* William L. Snyder; *dir:* Gene Deitch; *col. sd.* 6 min. *Academy Award nomination.* • The luckless Nudnik comes into possession of a stolen car, goes for a ride and gets arrested. • See: *Nudnik*

1688. Driven to Extraction *(Sidney)* Aug. 1963; *p.c.:* TT for Fox; *ex prod:* Bill Weiss; *dir/anim:* Art Bartsch; *story sup:* Tom Morrison; *story:* Larz Bourne; *sets:* Bill Focht, John Zago; *ed:* George McAvoy; *voices:* Dayton Allen, Lionel Wilson; *mus:* Phil Scheib; *ph:* Ted Moskowitz, Joe Rasinski; *col:* DeLuxe. *sd:* RCA. 6 min. • Sidney tries to rid a rhino of his troublesome horn.

1689. Drooler's Delight *(Woody Woodpecker)* 25 Mar. 1949; *p.c.:* Walter Lantz prods for UA; *dir:* Dick Lundy; *story:* Ben Hardaway, Heck Allen; *anim:* Ed Love; *sets:* Fred Brunish; *ed:* Dave Lurie; *voices:* Lionel Stander, Walter Craig, Ben Hardaway; *mus:* Darrell Calker; *prod mgr:* William E. Garity; *col:* Tech. *sd:* RCA. 6 min. • Buzz Buzzard steals Woody's last quarter to buy an ice cream soda.

1690. A Droopy Leprechaun *(Droopy)* 4 July 1958; *p.c.:* MGM; *prod:* William Hanna, Joseph Barbera; *dir:* Michael Lah; *anim:* Bill Schipek, Dick Bickenbach, James Escalante, Carlo Vinci, Ken Southworth, Lewis Marshall; *character des:* Ed Benedict; *lay:* Dick Bickenbach, Ed Benedict; *back:* F. Montealegre; *ed:* Jim Faris; *voices:* Bill Thompson, Lucille Bliss; *mus:* Scott Bradley; *ph:* Jack Stevens; *prod mgr:* Hal Elias; *col:* Tech. *sd:* WE. 6 min. CS. • While vacationing in Ireland, Droopy is mistaken by Spike for a leprechaun.

1691. Droopy's Double Trouble *(Droopy)* 17 Nov. 1951; *p.c.:* MGM; *dir:* Tex Avery; *story:* Rich Hogan; *anim:* Michael Lah, Walter Clinton, Grant Simmons; *sets:* John Didrik Johnsen; *ed:* Jim Faris; *voices:* Bill Thompson, Daws Butler; *mus:* Scott Bradley; *ph:* Jack Stevens; *prod:* Fred Quimby; *col:* Tech. *sd:* WE. 7 min. • A freeloading dog arrives at the mansion where "soft touch" Droopy is butler. He finds, instead, Droopy's muscle-bound twin brother.

1692. Droopy's Good Deed *(Droopy)* 5 May 1951; *p.c.:* MGM; *dir:* Tex Avery; *story:* Rich Hogan; *anim:* Walter Clinton, Michael Lah, Grant Simmons; *character des/lay:* Ed Benedict; *back:* John Didrik Johnsen; *ed:* Jim Faris; *voices:* Bill Thompson, Stan Freberg; *mus:* Scott Bradley; *ph:* Jack Stevens; *prod:* Fred Quimby; *col:* Tech. *sd:* WE. 7 min. • Butch discovers that "the best scout" will receive a reward, so he dons a scout's outfit and proceeds to rid himself of any opposition.

1693. Drop Dead Fred 19 April 1991; *p.c.:* Working Title Films (USA) for Polygram/Rank; *stop-motion anim:* Doug Beswick; *anim ph:* Pam Vick; *title des:* Joe Ranft; *anim:* Steven Segal; *col. sd:* Dolby Stereo. 103 min. *l/a.* • A woman's "Imaginary Friend" becomes real and takes over.

1694. Drum Roll *(Terry-Toon)* Mar. 1961; *p.c.:* TT for Fox; *ex prod:* Bill Weiss; *dir:* Dave Tendlar; *story sup:* Tom Morrison; *story:* Eli Bauer; *anim:* Ed Donnelly, Juan Guidi, Larry Silverman; *lay:* John Zago, Martin Strudler; *back:* Bill Focht; *voices:* John Myhers; *mus:* Phil Scheib; *prod mgr:* Frank Schudde; *col:* DeLuxe. *sd:* RCA. 6 min. • Drummer boy, Heathcote, infiltrates the British enemy fort by hiding in his drum.

1695. Drum Sticked *(Loopy de Loop)* Oct. 1963; *p.c.:* Hanna-Barbera for Colum; *prod/dir:* William Hanna, Joseph Barbera; *story dir:* Walter Clinton; *story:* Michael Maltese; *anim dir:* Charles A. Nichols; *anim:* Alex Ignatiev; *lay:* Jack Ozark; *back:* Art Lozzi; *ed:* Greg Watson; *voices:* Daws Butler, Don Messick, Doug Young; *mus:* Hoyt Curtin; *titles:* Lawrence Gobel; *prod mgr:* Howard Hanson; *col:* East. *sd:* RCA. 6 min. • Loopy protects a turkey from becoming Thanksgiving dinner.

1696. Drum Up a Tenant *(Modern Madcap)* Feb. 1963; *p.c.:* Para Cartoons; *dir:* Seymour Kneitel; *story:* Irving Dressler; *anim:* Morey Reden, George Germanetti, Larry Silverman; *sets:* Robert Owen; *voices:* Bob MacFadden; *mus:* Winston Sharples; *ph:* Leonard McCormick; *prod mgr:* Abe Goodman; *col:* Tech. *sd:* RCA. 6 min. • A beatnik's bongo playing seriously disrupts Luigi's glasswear shop.

1697. A Duck Amuck *(Merrie Melodies)* 28 Feb. 1953; *p.c.:* WB; *dir:* Charles M. Jones; *story:* Michael Maltese; *anim:* Ken Harris, Ben Washam, Lloyd Vaughan; *lay:* Maurice Noble; *back:* Philip de Guard; *ed:* Treg Brown; *voices:* Mel Blanc; *mus:* Carl Stalling; *prod mgr:* John W. Burton; *prod:* Edward Selzer; *col:* Tech. *sd:* Vit. 7 min. • An anonymous artist prevents Daffy from surviving the cartoon in one piece.

1698. The Duck Doctor *(Tom & Jerry)* 16 Feb. 1952; *p.c.:* MGM; *dir:* William Hanna, Joseph Barbera; *anim:* Irven Spence, Ray Patterson, Ed Barge, Kenneth Muse; *lay:* Dick Bickenbach; *back:* Robert Gentle; *ed:* Jim Faris; *voice:* Red Coffee; *mus:* Scott Bradley; *ph:* Jack Stevens; *prod:* Fred Quimby; *col:* Tech. *sd:* WE. 7 min. • Jerry attends to a small duck who has been wounded by Tom.

1699. Duck Dodgers in the 24½th Century *(Merrie Melodies)* 25 July 1953; *p.c.:* WB; *dir:* Charles M. Jones; *story:* Michael Maltese; *anim:* Lloyd Vaughan, Ken Harris, Ben Washam; *lay:* Maurice Noble; *back:* Philip de Guard; *ed:* Treg Brown; *voices:* Mel Blanc; *mus:* Carl Stalling; *prod mgr:* John W. Burton; *prod:* Edward Selzer; *col:* Tech. *sd:* Vit. 7 min. • Space Ranger Daffy is assigned to retrieve a secret formula from a Martian.

1700. Duck Fever *(Terry Bears)* Feb. 1955; *p.c.:* TT for Fox; *dir:* Connie Rasinski; *story:* Tom Morrison; *sets:* Art Bartsch; *voices:* Douglas Moye, Tom Morrison, Philip A. Scheib; *mus:* Philip A. Scheib; *ph:* Douglas Moye; *col:* Tech. *sd:* RCA. 7 min. • Papa and the kids go duck hunting with their St. Bernard, Pago, acting as a pointer.

1701. The Duck Hunt *(Mickey Mouse)* 21 Jan. 1932; *p.c.:* Walter E. Disney for Colum; *dir:* Burton F. Gillett; *anim:* Johnny Cannon, Gilles de Tremaudan, Norman Ferguson, Clyde Geronimi, David D. Hand, Jack King, Richard Lundy, Ben Sharpsteen, Rudy Zamora; *asst anim:* Chuck Couch, Andrew Hutchinson, Harry Reeves; *mus:* Bert Lewis; *b&w. sd:* PCP. 7 min. • Mickey and Pluto have no luck at duck hunting. Finally the ducks pick the two of them up and deposit them out of harm's way.

1702. Duck Hunt *(Oswald)* 8 Mar. 1937; *prod/dir:* Walter Lantz; *story:* Walter Lantz, Victor McLeod; *anim:* La Verne Harding, Dick Bickenbach, Jack Dunham; *voice:* Shirley Reed; *mus:* Irving Actman; *b&w. sd:* WE. 7½ min. • Oswald and Elmer go duck hunting. The ducks attack Oswald while Elmer's motor boat runs amuck.

1703. Duck Pimples *(Donald Duck)* 16 Feb. 1945; *p.c.:* Walt Disney prods for RKO; *dir:* Jack Kinney; *asst dir:* Bee Selck; *story:* Virgil Partch, Dick Shaw; *anim:* Hal King, John Sibley, Milt Kahl, Al Bertino, Marc Davis, Fred Moore; *fx:* Andy Engman; *lay:* Don da Gradi; *back:* Nino Carbe; *voices:* Harry E. Lang, Billy Bletcher, Jack Mather, Doodles Weaver, Clarence Nash, Mary Lenahan; *mus:* Oliver Wallace; *col:* Tech. *sd:* RCA. 8 min. • The characters emerge from Donald's crime novel and re-enact the crime in front of him.

1704. Duck! Rabbit, Duck! *(Merrie Melodies)* 3 Oct. 1953; *p.c.:* WB; *dir:* Charles M. Jones; *story:* Michael Maltese; *anim:* Ken Harris, Ben Washam, Lloyd Vaughan, Richard Thompson, Abe Levitow; *lay:* Maurice Noble; *back:* Philip de Guard; *ed:* Treg Brown; *voices:* Mel Blanc, Arthur Q. Bryan; *mus:* Carl Stalling; *prod mgr:* John W. Burton; *prod:* Edward Selzer; *col:* Tech. *sd:* Vit. 7 min. • For a spot of winter fun, Daffy removes all the "Duck Hunting Season" signs and tells hunter Elmer Fudd that it's Rabbit Season!

1705. Duck Soup to Nuts *(Looney Tunes)* 27 May 1944; *p.c.:* Leon Schlesinger prods for WB; *dir:* I. Freleng; *story:* Tedd Pierce; *anim:* Richard Bickenbach; *lay:* Hawley Pratt; *back:* Paul Julian; *ed:* Treg Brown; *voices:* Mel Blanc; *mus:* Carl W. Stalling; *prod sup:* Henry Binder, Raymond G. Katz; *col:* Tech. *sd:* Vit. 7 min. • Porky goes duck hunting and Daffy manages to convince him that, if he's shot, he'll be leaving behind a widow and orphans.

1706. Duck Tales the Movie: Treasure of the Lost Lamp 3 Aug. 1990; *p.c.:* Walt Disney Animation (France SA); *dir/prod:* Bob Hathcock; *co-prod:* Jean-Pierre Quenet, Robert Taylor; *asso prod:* Liza Ann Warren; *scr:* Alan Burnett; *addit dial:* Ken Koonce, David Wiemers; *seq dir:* Paul Brizzi, Gaëtan Brizzi, Clive Pallant, Mattias Marcus Rodic, Vincent Woodcock; *slogging/timing dir:* Robert Alvarez, Dave Brain, Terence Harrison, Marsh Lamore, Mircea Manta, Mitch Rochon, Bob Shellhorn, Robert Taylor, James Walker, Jamie Mitchell, Ernie Schmidt, Mike Syayko, Richard Trueblood, Neal Warner; *storyboard des:* Kurt Anderson, Viki Anderson, Rich Chidlaw, Warner Greenwood, Bob Kline, Larry Latham, Jim Mitchell, David E. Smith, Robert Taylor, Hank Tucker, Wendell Washer; *anim:* Gary Andrews, James Baker, Javier Gutierrez Blas, Eric Bouilette, Sylvain de Boissy, Joe Ekers, Marc Eoche-Duval, Pierre Fassel, Al Gavioto, Manuel Galiana, Arnold Gransac, Teddy Hall, Peter Hausner, Francesco Alaminos Hodar, Daniel Jeannette, Nicholas Marlet, Bob McKnight, Ramon Modiano, Sean Newton, Brent Odell, Catherine Poulain, Jean-Christophe Roger, Pascal Ropers, Stéphane Sainte-Foi, Albert Conejo Sanz, Anna Saunders, Ventura R. Valleio, Jan van Buyten, Duncan Varley, Simon Ward-Horner, Johnny Zeuten, Laurence Adam, José Sanchez Alonso, Luis Amor, Philipe Balmossiere, Philippe Beziat, Carlos Blanco, Bolhem Bouchiba, Claire Bovirdin, Valerie Braun-Paricio, Patricia Brizzi, Juan José Bravo, Rafael Diaz Canales, Didier Cassegrain, Thierry Chaffoin, Jon Collier, Patrick de Lage, Gwen-Delande Roche, René Dieu, Helga Egilson, James Earrington, Sylvia Fitzpatrick, Jerry Forder, Pierre Girault, Maria del Carmen Gonzales Gonzalez, Charo Morghta Gonzalez, Manuel Sirgo Gonzalez, Miguel Angel Alaminos Hódar, Martyn Jones, Isabelle Lelubre, Javier Pozo Luchena, Gizella Maros, Dominique Monfery, Florence-Montceau, Rosario Moronita, Belinda Murphy, Rob Newman, Tom Newman, Gilles Noll, Andrew Painter, Sylvie Penege, Coile Perrin, Manuel Javier, Garcia Pozo, Isabel Radage, Sophie Rivere, Steve Roberts, Marivi Rodriguez Serrano, Jeffrey Short, Christian Simon, Karen Stephenson, Pierre Sucaud, Juan Antonio Torres, Christophe Villez, Bob Wilk, Karel Zilliacus; *inbet:* Javier Espinosa Banuelos, Sabina Suarez Basant, Isabelle Bourelly, Corinne Bretel, Monica Brown, Marie Cabo, Veerle Calcoen, Carmen Nunez Calogne, Antonia Campolio, Miguel Canoza, Martin Chatfield, Paul Chorley, Mary Coombes, Tony Cope, Anne Daniels, Jean-Pierre Delisse, Helen Domiguez, Michael Douand, Maria Angela Iturriza Freire, Morton Fullerton, Jody Gannon, Jean Antonio Torres Garcia, Bernard Georges, Maximo Diaz Gerveno, Thierry Goulard, Arturo Lopez Iriarte, Ana Carmona Jimenez, Ivan Kassabov, Pierre Leconte, Bill Lee, Marie-Ange Lelong, Ludovic LeTrun, Pierre Lyphoudt, John McCartney, Jenni McCosker, Dave McFall, Colas Mermet, Christopherio Morley, Jean Francois Panavotopoulos, Steve Perry, Vittorio Pirjno, Maria Soledad, Garcia Pozo, Alain Remy, Wolf-Ruediger-Bloss, Daniela Tigano, Emma Tornero, Juan de Dios, Poziblo Valverde, Xavier Villez, Denis Viougeas, Stephanie Walker; *fx anim:* Andrew Brownlow, Glenn Chaika, Hock-Lian Law, Henry Neville, Sean Leaning, Fraser MacLean, Antonio Palermo, Dave Pritchard, Antonio Vrombaut; *fx inbet:* Norma Greenaway, Simon Swales; *lay:* Joe Pearson, Carol Kieffer Police, Douglas Kirk, Jean-Christophe Poulain, Jean Duval, Dave Elvin, Pierre Fassal, Neil Graham, Clive Hutchings, Simon O'Leary, Das Petrou, Pascal Pinon, Zoltan Maros, Vincent Massey, Sean Newton, Andrew Awbery; *back:* Fred Warter, Olivier Adam, Errol Bryant, Nicholas de Crecy-Thierry, Helene Godefroy, Mike Hirsh, Walter Kossler, Pierre Pavloff, Michael Pisson, Andrew McNab, Brigette Reboux, Colin Stimpson, Jane Cooper, Richard Lovett, Richard Nye; *prod des:* Skip Morgan; *prop des:* Terry Hudson; *col key stylists:* Robin Draper, Marta Skwara; *art co-ord:* Karen Silva; *ed:* Charles King, Louis L. Edemann, Howard Newman; *sd ed:* Leonard Geschke, Nils C. Jensen, Colin C. Movat, Chuck Neely, Bob O'Brien, Dave Pettijohn, Samuel F. Kafity, David Lynch, Craig Paulsen, Thomas Needell; *London film ed:* Keith Holden; *dial ed:* Rick Hinson, Peter Harrison; *voices: Scrooge:* Alan Young; *Launchpad:* Terence McGovern; *Huey, Dewey & Louie:* Russi Taylor; *Djion:* Richard Libertini; *Merlock:* Christopher Lloyd; *Mrs. Featherby:* June Foray; *Duckworth:* Chuck McCann; *Mrs. Beakly:* Joan Gerber; *The Genie:* Rip Taylor; *also:* Charlie Adler, Jack Angel, Steve Bulen, Sherry Lynn, Mickie T. McGowan, Patrick Pinney, Frank Welker; *mus:* David Newman; *mus ed:* Craig Pettigrew, Segue Music; *mus score mix:* Tim Boyle; "Duck Tales" theme composed by Mark Mueller, performed by Jeff Pescetto; *2nd asst dir:* Evariste Ferreira, Dominique Helier; *checking:* Onna Caquissine, Nathalie Nicholas, Raphael Vincente, Russel Murch, Janine Arthy, Andrew Ryder; *i&p:* Carol Agaesse, Roslind Allen, Donovan Bechford, Catherine Cowan, Denise Hambry, Matthew Kernan, Priscella Rhodes, Steve Rodger, Dawn White, Andy Wyatt; *ph:* Serge Conchonnet, Nic Jayne, Peter Wood, Filfex Services; King Camera Services: Richard Wolff, Quantum Studios; *computer anim:* Kelly Day, Mike Peraza, Patricia Peraza; *prod co-ords.:* Stephanie Elliott, Noel Matheson; *script co-ord:* Marie Sager; *line test operators:* Francois Desnus, Peter Jassett, Pierre Mialaret, Tania Viskitch, Juana Martos Sevilla; *prod asst:* Sylvie Fauque, Steve Hollowell, Michelle Lazar, Etienne Longa, Scott Wolf; *prod sup:* Marlene Robinson May, Dale Case; *re-rec:* Rick Ash, Nick Alphin, Dean A. Zupancic; *art ed:* Christopher Jargo; *post prod mgr:* Sara Duran; *processed fx:* Mel Nieman, Alan Howarth; *ADR mix:* Doc Kane; *ADR:* Larry Singer, Alan Nineberg, Stephane Dawn Singer, Rod Rogers; *prod des mix:* Jackson Schwartz, Warren Kleiman; *prod des ed:* Steve van Meter, Medi Berger, Dave van Meyer; *foley mix:* Dean Drabin, Dan O'Connell; *foley art:* Ellen Heuer, Dan O'Connell, John Roesch, Catherine Rowe, Joan Rowe, Alicia Stephenson; *sd reader:* Skip Craig; *neg cutter:* D. Bassett, Theresa Repola; *col timer:* Dale Grahn; *col:* Tech. *sd:* Dolby stereo. 74 min. • Scrooge McDuck sets out with Launchpad, Huey, Dewey and Louie and Webby in search of the buried treasure of Collie Baba. An enigmatic madman named Merlock tries to prevent them from finding anything and they return home with nothing other than an old lamp. The kids discover the lamp is a magic lamp and contains a genie who can grant their every wish.

1707. Ducking the Devil *(Merrie Melodies)* 17 Aug. 1957; *p.c.:* WB; *dir:* Robert McKimson; *story:* Tedd Pierce; *anim:* George Grandpré, Ted Bonnicksen; *lay:* Robert Gribbroek; *back:* Bill Butler; *ed:* Treg Brown; *voices:* Mel Blanc; *mus:* Milt Franklyn; *prod:* John W. Burton; *col:* Tech. *sd:* Vit. 7 min. • Daffy sets out to capture the music-loving Tasmanian Devil for a handsome reward.

1708. The Ducksters *(Merrie Melodies)* 2 Sept. 1950; *p.c.:* WB; *dir:* Charles M. Jones; *story:* Michael Maltese; *anim:* Lloyd Vaughan, Ken Harris, Phil Monroe, Ben Washam; *lay:* Robert Gribbroek; *back:* Peter Alvarado; *ed:* Treg Brown; *voices:* Mel Blanc, Tedd Pierce; *mus:* Carl Stalling; *prod mgr:* John W. Burton; *prod:* Edward Selzer; *col:* Tech. *sd:* Vit. 7 min. • Porky is the luckless contestant on a radio quiz game run by Daffy Duck.

1709. The Ducktators *(Looney Tunes)* 1 Aug. 1942; *p.c.:* Leon Schlesinger prods for WB; *dir/lay:* Norman McCabe; *story:* Melvin Millar; *anim:* John Carey, Cal Dalton, Arthur Davis, David Hoffman, Vive Risto; *character des:* John Carey; *sets:* Richard H. Thomas; *ed:* Treg Brown; *voices:* John McLeish, Mel Blanc, Michael Maltese; *mus:* Carl W. Stalling; *ph:* John W. Burton; *prod sup:* Henry Binder, Raymond G. Katz; *b&w. sd:* Vit. 7 min. • The Dove of Peace attempts to make a peace treaty with feathered versions of Hitler, Mussolini and Hirohito.

1710. Dude Duck *(Donald Duck)* 2 Mar. 1950; *p.c.:* Walt Disney prods for RKO; *dir:* Jack Hannah; *story:* Ralph Wright, Riley Thomson; *anim:* Al Bertino, Volus Jones, Bob Carlson, Bill Justice, Jerry Hathcock, John Sibley; *fx:* Jack Boyd; *lay:* Yale Gracey; *back:* Art Riley; *voices:* Clarence Nash, James MacDonald; *mus:* Paul Smith; *col:* Tech. *sd:* RCA. 7 min. • Donald is saddled with a reluctant horse while vacationing at a dude ranch.

1711. Duel Personality *(Tom & Jerry)* 1966; *p.c.:* MGM; *prod/dir:* Chuck Jones; *asst dir:* Maurice Noble; *story:* Chuck Jones, Michael Maltese; *anim:* Don Towsley, Tom Ray, Dick Thompson, Ben Washam, Ken Harris; *sets:* Phil de Guard; *voice:* June Foray; *mus:* Dean Elliot; *prod sup:* Earl Jonas, Les Goldman; *col:* Metro. *sd:* WE. 6 min. • Jerry challenges Tom to a duel at dawn.

1712. Duke Doolittle's Jungle Fizzle *(Sullivan Cartoon Comedy)* 18 June 1917; *p.c.:* Sullivan Studio for Univ; *dir:* Pat Sullivan; *anim:* Charles Saxon; b&w. *sil.* 4 min. • A big game hunter tells a reporter how, while hunting in The Bambazoo, he shot the spots off a leopard. When asked "What happened?" he replies, "It's a serial that won't be finished for another four years!"

1713. Dumb Cluck *(Oswald)* 20 Oct. 1937; *p.c.:* Univ; *prod/dir:* Walter Lantz; *story:* Charles Bowers; *anim:* Jack Dunham, Dick Marion, Ed Benedict; *mus:* George Lessner; b&w. *sd:* WE. 6 min. • Dumb Cluck makes use of the fire department's elephant when trying to save a burning fairground.

1714. The Dumb Conscious Mind *(Phantasy)* 23 Oct. 1942; *p.c.:* Colum; *prod:* Dave Fleischer; *dir:* Paul Sommer, John Hubley; *story:* Jack Cosgriff; *anim:* Grant Simmons; *sets:* Clark Watson; *ed:* Edward Moore; *voices:* Frank Graham, Joey Pennario; *mus:* Paul Worth; *ph:* Frank Fisher; *prod mgr:* Albert Spar; b&w. *sd:* RCA. 6 min. • Butch Bulldog sees an innocent little spaniel as a threat to his happy home. His "better self" wins over when the creature is in danger. Initiated by Frank Tashlin.

1715. Dumb Like a Fox *(Fable)* 18 July 1941; *p.c.:* Colum; *story:* Allen Rose; *anim:* Louie H. Lilly; *sets:* Clark Watson; *ed:* Edward Moore; *voices:* Mel Blanc; *mus:* Eddie Kilfeather; *ph:* Otto Reimer; *prod mgr:* George Winkler; b&w. *sd:* RCA. 6 min. • A sly fox cons a young hunting dog into believing that a skunk is the fox he's after.

1716. Dumb Like a Fox *(Woody Woodpecker)* 7 Jan. 1964; *p.c.:* Walter Lantz prods for Univ; *dir:* Sid Marcus; *story:* Homer Brightman; *anim:* Ray Abrams, Art Davis; *sets:* Ray Huffine, Art Landy; *voices:* Daws Butler, Grace Stafford; *mus:* Walter Greene; *prod mgr:* William E. Garity; *col:* Tech. *sd:* RCA. 6 min. • Just as Fink Fox and Woody dissolve their partnership, the fox discovers a museum that will pay handsomely for a woodpecker.

1717. The Dumb Patrol *(Looney Tunes)* 19 Mar. 1931; *p.c.:* Hugh Harman–Rudolf Ising *prods* for WB; *anim:* Isadore Freleng, Max Maxwell; *ed:* Dale Pickett; *voices:* Johnny Murray, Mary Moder; *mus:* Frank Marsales; *asso prod:* Leon Schlesinger; b&w. *sd:* Vit. 7 min. • Bosko flies to the "Front Line," is shot down by a German Air Ace and lands in the home of a captivating French damsel.

1718. Dumb Patrol *(Looney Tunes)* Jan. 1964; *p.c.:* WB; *dir:* Gerry Chiniquy; *story:* John Dunn; *anim:* Virgil Ross, Bob Matz, Lee Halpern, Art Leonardi; *lay:* Bob Givens; *back:* Tom O'Loughlin; *ed:* Treg Brown; *voices:* Mel Blanc; *mus:* Bill Lava; *prod mgr:* William Orcutt; *prod:* David H. DePatie; *col:* Tech. *sd:* Vit. 6 min. • World War Ace Bugs stages a raging dogfight with "The Red Baron" (Yosemite Sam).

1719. Dumbell of the Yukon *(Donald Duck)* 30 Aug. 1946; *p.c.:* Walt Disney prods for RKO; *dir:* Jack King; *asst dir:* Joel Greenhalgh; *story:* Harry Reeves, Homer Brightman; *anim:* Don Towsley, Fred Kopietz, Sandy Strother, Paul Allen, Tom Massey, Frank McSavage; *fx:* Ed Aardal; *sets:* Ernest Nordli; *voices:* Clarence Nash, James MacDonald; *mus:* Oliver Wallace; *col:* Tech. *sd:* RCA. 7 min. • Donald sets out to trap a fur coat for Daisy. He takes a bear cub from its mother and is soon running for his life.

1720. Dumbhounded 20 Mar. 1943; *p.c.:* MGM; *dir:* Tex Avery; *story:* Rich Hogan; *anim:* Ed Love, Preston Blair, Ray Abrams, Irven Spence; *character des:* Claude Smith; *sets:* John Didrik Johnsen; *ed:* Fred MacAlpin; *voices:* Bill Thompson, Frank Graham; *mus:* Scott Bradley; *prod:* Fred Quimby; *col:* Tech. *sd:* WE. 8 min. • A bloodhound sets out to bring in an escaped convict. • Introducing a lugubrious pooch tentatively titled "Happy Bloodhound" who later became better known as "Droopy."

1721. Dumbo 31 Oct. 1941; *p.c.:* Walt Disney prods for RKO; *dir sup:* Ben Sharpsteen; *seq dir:* Norman Ferguson, Wilfred Jackson, Bill Roberts, Jack Kinney, Sam Armstrong; *story:* Helen Aberson and Harold Pearl; *adapt:* Joe Grant, Dick Huemer; *story dir:* Otto Englander; *story development:* Bill Peet, Aurie Battaglia, Joe Rinaldi, George Stallings, Webb Smith; *anim dir:* Vladimir Tytla, Fred Moore, Ward Kimball, John Lounsbery, Art Babbitt, Woolie Reitherman; *character des:* John P. Miller, Martin Provensen, John Walbridge, James Bodrero, Maurice Noble, Elmer Plummer; *anim:* Hugh Fraser, Harvey Toombs, Milt Neil, Hicks Lokey, Howard Swift, Don Towsley, Les Clark, Claude Smith, Berny Wolf, Jack Campbell, Walt Kelly, Don Patterson, Ray Patterson, Grant Simmons, Bill Shull, Karl van Leuven, Miles Pike, Tony Strobl, Don Tobin, Cornett Wood; *fx:* Ed Aardal, Dan MacManus, Josh Meador, Art Palmer, John F. Reed, George Rowley, Cy Young; *lay:* Herb Ryman, Terrell Stapp, Al Zinnen, Dick Kelsey, Ken O'Connor, Don da Gradi, Ernest Nordli, Charles Payzant; *back:* Claude Coats, Al Dempster, John Hench, Gerald Nevius, Ray Lockrem, Joe Stahley; *voices: Timothy Q. Mouse:* Edward S. Brophy; *Mr. Stork:* Sterling Holloway; *The Ringmaster:* Herman Bing; *Jim Crow:* Cliff Edwards; *Matriarch Elephant:* Verna Felton; *Prissy Elephant:* Sarah Selby; *Giddy Elephant:* Dorothy Scott; *Fidgity Elephant:* Noreen Gammill; *Clowns/Barkers:* Eddie Holden, Earl Hodgins, Billy Bletcher, William E. Sheets; *Skinny:* Malcolm Hutton; *Boys:* Harold Manley, Tony Neil, Charles Stubbs; *Deep-voiced Crow:* Jim Carmichael; *Crow:* James MacDonald; *Narrator:* John McLeish; *Joe the elephant trainer:* William E. Sheets; *Casey Jr (Sonovox):* Margaret Wright; "When I See an Elephant Fly" sung by The Hall Johnson Choir; "It's Circus Day"/"Song of the Roustabouts" sung by Jester Hairston, Elijah Hodges, Chester Jones, Ed Short, Chancey Reynolds; "Look Out for Mr. Stork"/"Pink Elephants on Parade" sung by The King's Men (Ken Darby, Rad Robinson, Bud Linn, Harry Stanton); "Baby Mine" sung by Barbara van Brunt, Elva Kellogg, Nancy Kellogg, Betty Noyes, Barbara Whitson; *mus:* Oliver Wallace, Frank Churchill; *songs:* Ned Washington; *orch:* Edward Plumb; *col:* Tech. *sd:* RCA. 66 min. • A baby circus elephant with over-large ears is shunned by all but his mother and a friendly mouse. He learns to use his oversized appendages for flying and becomes the hit of the circus. This Disney classic was originally intended to be a short but expanded into an hour of pure magic.

1722. Dune Bug *(Ant & Aardvark)* 29 Oct. 1969; *p.c.:* Mirisch/DFE for UA; *dir:* Art Davis; *story:* John W. Dunn; *anim:* Manny Gould, Bob Goe, Tom Ray, Lloyd Vaughan; *lay:* Dick Ung; *back:* Richard H. Thomas; *ed:* Lee Gunther; *voices:* John Byner; *mus:* Doug Goodwin, Pete Candoli, Billy Byers, Jimmy Rowles, Tommy Tedesco, Ray Brown, Shelly Manne; *prod sup:* Jim Foss, Harry Love; *col:* DeLuxe. *sd:* RCA. 6 min. • The Aardvark is evicted from the beach by a Life Guard who believes him to be a dog.

1723. The Dungeonmaster Feb. 1984; *p.c.:* Ragewar Prods. for Empire Pictures; *anim: Rotoscoping fx:* Tony Alderson, Frank H. Isaacs; *visual fx des:* David Allen; *Dragon:* Walt Disney Pictures Special Photographic Dpt., Allen Gonzales; *col:* CFI. *sd:* Glen Glenn Sound. 77 min. *l/a.* • Live-action fantasy concerning a young man and his girlfriend who are conveyed to an infernal region where he is compelled to accept seven challenges. One of the challenges involves a dragon. Also known as *Ragewar*.

1724. Dustcap Doormat *(Terry-Toon)* June 1958; *p.c.:* TT for Fox; *ex prod:* Bill Weiss; *dir sup:* Gene Deitch; *dir:* Al Kouzel; *story dir:* Tom Morrison; *anim:* Jim Tyer *voices:* Allen Swift; *mus:* Phil Scheib; *prod mgr:* Sparky Schudde; *col:* Tech. *sd:* RCA. 7 min. • John Doormat has a fantasy romance.

1725. The Dusters *(Mighty Heroes)* Aug. 1971 (© 1967); *p.c.:* TT for Fox; *dir:* Robert Taylor; *voices:* Lionel Wilson, Herschel Bernardi; *mus:* Jim Timmens; *col:* DeLuxe. *sd:* RCA. 5 min. • "The Shrinker" invents "Happy" and "Sleepy" dust for every criminal occasion.

1726. Dutch Treat *(Casper)* 20 Apr. 1956; *p.c.:* Famous for Para; *dir:* I. Sparber; *story:* I. Klein; *anim:* Myron Waldman, Nick Tafuri; *sets:* Robert Little; *voices:* Norma MacMillan, Gwen Davies, Jack Mercer; *mus:* Winston Sharples; *ph:* Leonard McCor-mick; *prod mgr:* Seymour Shultz; *col:* Tech. *sd:* RCA. 6 min. • Casper helps a Dutch boy do his chores. On their way to market they discover a leak in the dyke ... the rest is history.

1727. Dutch Treat *(Paul Terry-Toon)* 12 Sept. 1930; *p.c.:* A-C for Educational/Fox; *dir:* Frank Moser, Paul Terry; *anim:* Arthur Babbitt, Thomas Bonfiglio, Tom Byrne, Ferdinand Huszti Horvarth, Sarka, Hugh Shields; *mus:* Philip A. Scheib; b&w. *sd:* WE. 6 min. • The Stork delivers a pup to a Dutch dog who chases the kid away. The pup later later rescues a girl when the Dyke breaks and is suitably rewarded.

1728. Duty and the Beast (*Phantasy*) 28 May 1943; *p.c.:* Colum; *prod:* Dave Fleischer; *dir:* Alec Geiss; *anim:* Grant Simmons; *voices:* Frank Graham, John McLeish; *mus:* Paul Worth; *prod mgr:* Albert Spar; b&w. *sd:* RCA. 6 min. • The carefully trained hunting dog's first instincts are to protect the animals from the hunter.

1729. Each Dawn I Crow (*Merrie Melodies*) 23 Sept. 1949; *p.c.:* WB; *dir:* I. Freleng; *story:* Tedd Pierce; *anim:* Virgil Ross, Gerry Chiniquy, Manuel Perez, Ken Champin; *lay:* Hawley Pratt; *back:* Paul Julian; *ed:* Treg Brown; *voices:* Frank Graham, Arthur Q. Bryan, Mel Blanc; *mus:* Carl Stalling; *prod mgr:* John W. Burton; *prod:* Edward Selzer; *col:* Tech. *sd:* Vit. 7 min. • The rooster comes to the conclusion that with Farmer Fudd it's either "Kill or be killed!"

1730. The Eager Beaver (*Merrie Melodies*) 13 July 1945; *p.c.:* WB; *dir:* Charles M. Jones; *story:* Tedd Pierce; *anim:* Ken Harris, Basil Davidovich, Lloyd Vaughan, Ben Washam; *lay:* Robert Gribbroek; *back:* Earl Klein; *ed:* Treg Brown; *voices:* Mel Blanc, Frank Graham; *mus:* Carl Stalling; *prod mgr:* John W. Burton; *prod:* Edward Selzer; *col:* Tech. *sd:* Vit. 7 min. • A beaver is told by the others to cut down a large tree on a hill and in doing so, he saves the colony from disaster.

1731. Eagle's Beagles (*The Dogfather*) 5 May 1975; *p.c.:* DFE for UA; *dir:* Gerry Chiniquy; *story:* John Dunn; *anim:* Bob Richardson, Warren Batchelder, Don Williams, Nelson Shin, Bob Bransford; *ed:* Rick Steward; *lay:* Dick Ung; *back:* Richard H. Thomas; *voices:* Bob Holt; *mus:* Dean Elliott; *col:* DeLuxe. *sd:* RCA. 6 min. • The Dogfather and Pug make their getaway from a robbery in an airplane that neither can fly.

1732. The Eagle's Blood (*Universal Current Events*) 1918; *p.c.:* Univ; *anim:* Hy Mayer. b&w. sil. • No story available. Selected to be shown overseas by the Allies as a work of propaganda.

1733. The Early Bird (*Aesop's Film Fable*) 24 June 1928; *p.c.:* Fables Pictures Inc for Pathé; *dir:* Paul Terry, John Foster; b&w. sil. 5 min. • Willie Bird gets up early to snag a worm which he sells to a fisherman. He then proposes to his girl who is kidnapped by Henry Cat. A chase ensues.

1734. The Early Bird (*Scrappy*) 16 Sept. 1938; *p.c.:* Charles Mintz prods for Colum; *story:* Art Davis; *anim:* Sid Marcus, Robert Winkler, Dave Weber; *mus:* Joe de Nat; *prod mgr:* James Bronis; b&w. *sd:* RCA. 6 min. • Scrappy reads aloud about the early bird catching the worm. A bird overhears this and sets out to capture a tough Brooklynese worm.

1735. The Early Bird and the Worm (*Happy Harmonies*) 8 Feb. 1936; *p.c.:* MGM; *prod/dir:* Hugh Harman, Rudolf Ising; *voices:* Bernice Hansel, The Rhythmettes; *mus:* Scott Bradley; *col:* Tech. *sd:* RCA. 9 min. • An early bird and an even earlier worm are pursued by a snake and two crows.

1736. The Early Bird Dood It! 29 Aug. 1942; *p.c.:* MGM; *dir:* Tex Avery; *story:* Rich Hogan; *anim:* Irven Spence, Preston Blair, Ed Love, Ray Abrams; *character des/lay:* Berny Wolfe; *sets:* John Didrik Johnsen; *ed:* Fred MacAlpin; *voices:* Frank Graham, Kent Rogers; *mus:* Scott Bradley; *prod:* Fred Quimby; *col:* Tech. *sd:* WE. 7 min. • A worm interests a cat in chasing the bird that's been making his life a misery.

1737. Early to Bed (*Donald Duck*) 11 July 1941; *p.c.:* Walt Disney prods for RKO; *dir:* Jack King; *asst dir:* Ralph Chadwick, Bob Newman; *story:* Harry Reeves, Carl Barks, Jack Hannah; *anim:* Paul Allen, James Armstrong, Hal King, Edward Love, Lee Morehouse, Ray Patin, Judge Whitaker; *lay:* Bill Herwig; *voice:* Clarence Nash; *mus:* Oliver Wallace; *col:* Tech. *sd:* RCA. 8 min. • A noisy alarm clock keeps Donald awake.

1738. Early to Bet (*Merrie Melodies*) 5 May 1951; *p.c.:* WB; *dir:* Robert McKimson; *story:* Warren Foster; *anim:* Phil de Lara, Emery Hawkins, Charles McKimson, Rod Scribner; *lay:* Cornett Wood; *back:* Richard H. Thomas; *ed:* Treg Brown; *voices:* Mel Blanc, Stan Freberg; *mus:* Carl Stalling; *prod mgr:* John W. Burton; *prod:* Edward Selzer; *col:* Tech. *sd:* Vit. 7 min. • The Gambling Bug can't resist putting the gambling spirit into a luckless cat.

1739. The Early Worm "Gets the Bird" (*Merrie Melodies*) 13 Jan. 1940; *p.c.:* Leon Schlesinger prods for WB; *dir:* Fred Avery; *story:* Jack Miller; *anim:* Robert Cannon; *sets:* John Didrik Johnsen; *ed:* Treg Brown; *voices:* Mel Blanc, Bernice Hansel; *mus:* Carl W. Stalling; *prod sup:* Henry Binder, Raymond G. Katz; *col:* Tech. *sd:* Vit. 7 min. • Butchie, a baby bird, is warned about the early rising habits of foxes. Eventually he relies on his arch enemy for his protection.

1740. Earth Girls Are Easy 12 May 1989; *p.c.:* Kestrel Films for Braveworld/Fox; *main title anim seq:* Lee Film Design; *anim sup:* Dorne Huebler; *anim des:* Jim Shaw; *anim ph:* James Balsam; *col:* DeLuxe. *sd:* Dolby stereo. • Live-action comedy about three aliens who crash-land on Earth and are given a "makeover" by a manicurist. Animated titles.

1741. East Side, West Side (*Song Car-Tune*) 1927; *p.c.:* Inkwell Studio for Red Seal; *prod:* Max Fleischer; *dir:* Dave Fleischer; b&w. sil. 6 min. • No story available.

1742. Easter Yeggs (*Looney Tunes*) 28 June. 1947; *p.c.:* WB; *dir:* Robert McKimson; *story:* Warren Foster; *anim:* Charles McKimson, Richard Bickenbach, I. Ellis; *lay:* Cornett Wood; *back:* Richard H. Thomas; *ed:* Treg Brown; *voices:* Mel Blanc, Arthur Q. Bryan; *mus:* Carl Stalling; *prod mgr:* John W. Burton; *prod:* Edward Selzer; *col:* Tech. *sd:* Vit. 7 min. • Bugs substitutes for the Easter Bunny delivering eggs but finds this task more trouble than it's worth.

1743. Easy Peckin's (*Merrie Melodies*) 17 Oct. 1953; *p.c.:* WB; *dir:* Robert McKimson; *story:* Tedd Pierce; *anim:* Charles McKimson, Herman Cohen, Rod Scribner, Phil de Lara; *lay:* Robert Givens; *back:* Richard H. Thomas; *ed:* Treg Brown; *voices:* Mel Blanc, Bea Benaderet; *mus:* Carl Stalling; *prod mgr:* John W. Burton; *prod:* Edward Selzer; *col:* Tech. *sd:* Vit. 7 min. • A cunning fox tries to raid the J. Henny Poultry Farm, not reckoning on the ingenuity of the muscular rooster guarding it.

1744. Eat Me Kitty Eight to the Bar (*Terry-Toon*) 6 Mar. 1942; TT for Fox; *dir:* Mannie Davis; *story:* John Foster; *mus:* Philip A. Scheib; *col:* Tech. *sd:* RCA. 6 min. • When the dog sees that the cat is friends with the mice he tries to befriend a goat.

1745. Eatin' on the Cuff (*Looney Tunes*) 22 Aug. 1942; *p.c.:* Leon Schlesinger prods for WB; *dir:* Robert Clampett; *story:* Warren Foster; *anim:* Virgil Ross, Rod Scribner; *sets:* Michael Sasanoff; *ed:* Treg Brown; *voices:* Mel Blanc, Sara Berner; *mus:* Carl W. Stalling; *ph:* John W. Burton; *l/a:* Leo White; *pianist:* David Klatzkin; *song:* Mickey Ford; *prod sup:* Henry Binder, Raymond G. Katz; b&w. *sd:* Vit. 7 min. *anim/l/a.* • A live-action pianist relates the story of a moth, about to be married, who's pursued by a black widow spider.

1746. Ebenezer Ebony *p.c.:* Sering D. Wilson Inc. *dir:* Sering D. Wilson; *titles:* Randolph Bartlett. *col:* Kelly. sil. 6 min. • **1925:** **The Flying Elephant** 22 Apr. **An Ice Boy** 22 May. **Gypping the Gypsies** 22 Jun. **Fire in a Brimstone** 1 July. **High Moon** 1 Aug. **Love, Honor and Oh Boy** 1 Sept. **Foam, Sweet Foam** 1 Oct. **Fisherman's Luck** 31 Oct. • No stories available.

1747. Echo (*Novograph*) 1924; *p.c.:* Ink-well Studio for Red Seal; *prod:* Max Fleischer; *dir:* Dave Fleischer; b&w. sil. 7 min. • No story available.

1748. Echoes from the Alps (*Aesop's Film Fable*) 23 May 1925; *p.c.:* Fables Pictures Inc for Pathé; *dir:* Paul Terry; b&w. sil. 5 min. • Farmer Al Falfa and the animals try winter sports in the Alps.

1749. Eclair Journal *p.c.:* Eclair Co; *anim:* Emile Cohl; b&w. sil. s/r • **1913:** **War in Turkey** 13 Jan. **Castro in New York** 13 Jan. **The Bewitched Matches** 13 Jan. **Rockfeller** 13 Jan. **Confidence** 13 Jan. **Milk** 13 Feb. **Coal** 13 Feb. **The Subway** 13 Feb. **Graft** 13 Feb. **The Two Presidents** 13 Mar. **The Auto** 13 Mar. **Wilson and the Broom** 13 Mar. **The Police Women** 13 Mar. **Wilson and the Hats** 13 Mar. **Poker #2** 13 Mar. **Gaynor and the Night Club** 13 Mar. **Wilson and the Tariffs** 13 Apr. **The Masquerade** 13 Apr. **The Brigand of California** 13 Apr. **The Safety Pin** 13 May. **The Two Suffragettes** 13 May. **The Mosquito** 13 May. **The Red Balloons** 13 May. **The Cubists** 13 June. **Uncle Sam and His Suit** 13 June. **The Polo Boat** 13 June. **The Artist** 13 June. **Clara's Toys** 13 July. **The Vegetables** 13 July. **Wilson's Row-Row** 13 July. **The Hat** 13 Aug. **Thaw and the Lasso** 13 Aug. **Bryant and the Speeches** 13 Aug. **Thaw and the Spider** 13 Sept. **Metamorphoses** 13 Sept. **Exhibition of Caricatures** 13 Nov. **Pick-Me-Up Is a Sportsman** 13 Dec. • **1914:** **The Bath** 13 Jan. **The Future Revealed**

by the Lines of the Feet 13 Jan. **The American Map** 13 Feb. **The Social Group** 13 Nov. **The Greedy Neighbor. What They Eat. The Anti-Neurasthenic Trumpet. His Ancestors. Serbia's Card. The Terrible Scrap of Paper.** • Series of cartoon items by the celebrated French animator, Emile Cohl, made for a weekly newsreel.

1750. Edgar Runs Again *(Terry-Toon)* 26 Jan. 1940; *p.c.:* TT for Fox; *dir:* Mannie Davis; *story:* John Foster; *mus:* Philip A. Scheib; b&w. *sd:* RCA. 7 min. • A once-famous racehorse is now on the run from the glue factory. A junk dealer puts him to work but the sound of a race-track bugle puts him back into action.

1751. Educated Fish *(Color Classic)* 29 Oct. 1937; *p.c.:* The Fleischer Studio for Para; *prod:* Max Fleischer; *dir:* Dave Fleischer. *anim:* Myron Waldman, Hicks Lokey, Lillian Friedman; *mus:* Sammy Timberg; *col:* Tech. *sd:* WE. 7 min. *Academy Award nomination.* • The fish go to school and are taught a lesson from their teacher.

1752. Education for Death 15 Jan. 1943; *p.c.:* Walt Disney prods for RKO; *dir:* Clyde Geronimi; *asst dir:* Ralph Chadwick; *story adapt:* Joe Grant, Dick Huemer; *anim:* Milt Kahl, Ward Kimball, John Lounsbery, Norman Tate, Frank Thomas, Vladimir Tytla; *fx:* Dan MacManus, George Rowley; *lay:* A. Kendall O'Connor, Charles Philippi, Herbert Ryman; *voices:* Art Baker, Aileen Carlisle, Robert Davis, Charles Judels, Lisa Golm, Don Lauria, Harold Manley, Norbert and Steven Muller, John Pinner, Walter O. Stahl; *mus:* Oliver Wallace; *col:* Tech. *sd:* RCA. 9 min. • Powerful adaptation of Gregor Ziemer's book about how Nazi Germany would affect society if it ever gained power.

1753. The Egg and Ay-Yi-Yi! *(Tijuana Toads)* 6 June 1971; *p.c.:* Mirisch/DFE for UA; *dir:* Gerry Chiniquy; *story:* Dale Hale; *anim:* Don Williams, Manny Gould, Robert Taylor, Manny Perez; *lay:* Robert Givens; *back:* Richard Thomas; *ed:* Lee Gunther; *voices:* Don Diamond, Tom Holland, Larry D. Mann; *mus:* Doug Goodwin; *ph:* John Burton Jr.; *prod sup:* Jim Foss, Harry Love; *col:* DeLuxe. *sd:* RCA. 5 min. • The Toads hatch an egg that turns out to be a toad-hungry crane.

1754. The Egg and I 1947; *p.c.:* Walter Lantz prods for Univ; *dir:* Dick Lundy; *col:* Tech. *sd:* RCA. 3 min. • Fully animated trailer for the live-action feature. The first of its kind and featuring Charlie Chicken, a character frequently used in Lantz's "New Funnies" comics.

1755. The Egg and Jerry *(Tom & Jerry)* 23 Mar. 1956; *p.c.:* MGM; *prod/dir:* William Hanna, Joseph Barbera; *lay:* Dick Bickenbach; *back:* Don Driscoll; *ph:* Jack Stevens; *prod mgr:* Hal Elias; *col:* Tech. *sd:* WE. 8 min. CS. CS reissue of *Hatch Up Your Troubles.* • A baby woodpecker thinks Jerry is his mother.

1756. The Egg Collector *(Merrie Melodies)* 20 June 1940; *p.c.:* Leon Schlesinger prods for WB; *dir:* Charles M. Jones; *story/character des:* Robert Givens; *anim:* Rudolph Larriva; *lay:* Paul Julian; *ed:* Treg Brown; *voices:* Margaret Hill, Mel Blanc; *mus:* Carl W. Stalling; *ph:* John W. Burton; *prod sup:* Henry Binder, Raymond G. Katz; *col:* Tech. *sd:* Vit. 7 min. • Sniffles and the Bookworm try to steal an owl's egg but are chased away by mother owl.

1757. The Egg-Cracker Suite *(Swing Symphony)* 10 Mar. 1943; *p.c.:* Walter Lantz prods for Univ; *dir:* Ben Hardaway, Emery Hawkins; *story:* Milt Schaffer; *anim:* Lester Kline; *sets:* Fred Brunish; *voice:* June Foray; *mus:* Darrell Calker; *col:* Tech. *sd:* RCA. 7 min. • Oswald and the other bunnies prepare Easter eggs for world distribution.

1758. The Egg Hunt *(Color Rhapsody)* 31 May 1940; *p.c.:* Cartoon Films Ltd for Colum; *dir:* Ub Iwerks; *ed:* George Winkler; *voices:* Mel Blanc, Elvia Allman; *mus:* Eddie Kilfeather, Joe de Nat; *ph:* Otto Reimer; *col:* Tech. *sd:* RCA. 8 min. • Professor Crackpot's account of his hunt for a rare dinosaur egg in the Gobi Desert.

1759. An Egg Scramble *(Merrie Melodies)* 27 May 1950; *p.c.:* WB; *dir:* Robert McKimson; *story:* Warren Foster; *anim:* Phil de Lara, Rod Scribner, J.C. Melendez, Emery Hawkins, Charles McKimson; *lay:* Cornett Wood; *back:* Richard H. Thomas; *ed:* Treg Brown; *voices:* Mel Blanc, Bea Benaderet; *mus:* Carl Stalling; *prod mgr:* John W. Burton; *prod:* Edward Selzer; *col:* Tech. *sd:* Vit. 7 min. • Prissy sets out to recover an egg she believes she's hatched.

1760. The Egg Yegg *(Fox & Crow)* 19 Jan. 1945; *p.c.:* Colum; *dir:* Bob Wickersham; *story:* Sam Cobean; *anim:* Ben Lloyd, Volus Jones; *sets:* Clark Watson; *ed:* Richard S. Jensen; *voices:* Frank Graham, John McLeish; *mus:* Eddie Kilfeather; *song:* Robert Hargreaves; *i&p:* Elizabeth F. McDowell; *ph:* Frank Fisher; *prod mgr:* Hugh McCollum; *col:* Tech. *sd:* WE. 7 min. • The Fox and Crow fight over posession of a rare egg.

1761. The Eggcited Rooster *(Merrie Melodies)* 4 Oct. 1952; *p.c.:* WB; *dir:* Robert McKimson; *story:* Tedd Pierce; *anim:* Rod Scribner, Phil de Lara, Charles McKimson, Herman Cohen, Keith Darling; *lay:* Robert Givens; *back:* Richard H. Thomas; *ed:* Treg Brown; *voices:* Mel Blanc, Bea Benaderet; *mus:* Carl Stalling; *prod mgr:* John W. Burton; *prod:* Edward Selzer; *col:* Tech. *sd:* Vit. 7 min. • Mrs. Leghorn makes Foggy babysit her egg while she attends a hen party. Henery Hawk arrives on the scene and the dog seizes an opportunity to get revenge on the rooster.

1762. Egged on *(Whirlwind Comedy)* 30 May 1926; *p.c.:* FBO; *dir/ll/a:* Charles R. Bowers; *story:* Charles R. Bowers, H.L. Muller, Ted Sears; *ph:* H.L. Muller; b&w. sil. 24 min. *l/a/anim.* • An inventor designs a machine to make an unbreakable egg. He keeps a basket of eggs under the hood of his car which hatch into a brood of miniature cars. • Live-action comedy with model animation.

1763. Egghead Rides Again *(Merrie Melodies)* 17 July 1937; *p.c.:* Leon Schlesinger prods for WB; *dir:* Fred Avery; *anim:* Paul Smith, Irven Spence; *lay:* Griff Jay; *back:* Arthur Loomer; *ed:* Tregoweth E. Brown; *voices:* Mel Blanc, Billy Bletcher, Fred Avery, The Sons of the Pioneers; *mus:* Carl W. Stalling; *prod sup:* Henry Binder, Raymond G. Katz; *col:* Tech. *sd:* Vit. 8 min. • Egghead goes West to become a cowboy but the tests prove too much for him.

1764. Eggnapper *(Cartune)* 14 Feb. 1961; *p.c.:* Walter Lantz prods for Univ; *dir:* Jack Hannah; *story:* Homer Brightman; *anim:* La Verne Harding, Al Coe, Roy Jenkins; *sets:* Art Landy, Ray Huffine; *voice:* Dal McKennon; *mus:* Eugene Poddany; *prod mgr:* William E. Garity; *col:* Tech. *sd:* RCA. 6 min. • Fatso the bear attempts to steal eggs from the henhouse under the eye of the rooster.

1765. Eggs Don't Bounce *(Little Lulu)* 31 Dec. 1943; *p.c.:* Famous for Para; *dir:* I. Sparber; *story:* Carl Meyer, Jack Mercer, Jack Ward; *anim:* Nick Tafuri, Joe Oriolo, Tom Golden, John Walworth; *voices:* Cecil Roy, Jack Mercer; *mus:* Sammy Timberg; *title song:* Buddy Kaye, Fred Wise, Sammy Timberg; *prod mgr:* Sam Buchwald; *col:* Tech. *sd:* WE. 9 min. • Lulu stumbles and breaks the eggs, then has a fearful nightmare about the incident.

1766. Egyptian Melodies *(Silly Symphony)* 19 Aug. 1931; *p.c.:* Walt Disney prods for Colum; *dir:* Wilfred Jackson; *anim:* Charles Byrne, Johnny Cannon, Chuck Couch, Joseph d'Igalo, Gilles de Tremaudan, David D. Hand, Albert Hurter, Harry Reeves, Ben Sharpsteen, Cecil Surry, Rudy Zamora; *mus:* Frank E. Churchill; b&w. *sd:* PCP. 7 min. • A spider has some adventures in a sphinx and is frightened away when the mummies come to life.

1767. 8 Ball Bunny *(Looney Tunes)* 8 July 1950; *p.c.:* WB; *dir:* Charles M. Jones; *story:* Michael Maltese; *anim:* Phil Monroe, Ben Washam, Lloyd Vaughan, Ken Harris, Emery Hawkins; *sets:* Peter Alvarado; *ed:* Treg Brown; *voices:* Mel Blanc, Dave Barry; *mus:* Carl Stalling; *prod mgr:* John W. Burton; *prod:* Edward Selzer; *col:* Tech. *sd:* Vit. 7 min. • Bugs offers to return a penguin to where he believes is home ... the South Pole. • Caricature of Humphrey Bogart.

1768. The Einstein Theory of Relativity rel: 8 Feb. 1923; *p.c.:* Premier prods Inc for Red Seal; *prod:* Edwin Miles Fadman; *sup:* Prof. S. F. Nicolai, Prof. H. W. Kornblum, Prof. C. Bueck; arranged by Max Fleischer; *ed:* Prof. Garrett P. Serviss; b&w. sil. 4 reels. *l/a/anim.* • Animated explanation to help make Professor Albert Einstein's theory generally understandable.

1769. El Gaucho Goofy *(Goofy)* 10 June 1955; *p.c.:* Walt Disney prods for BV; *dir:* Jack Kinney; *col:* Tech. *sd:* RCA. 8 min. • Goofy demonstrates the art of being a perfect gaucho. • See: *Saludos Amigos*

1770. El Terrible Toreador *(Silly Symphony)* 7 Sept. 1929; *p.c.:* Walter E. Disney for Colum; *dir:* Walt Disney; *anim:* Ub Iwerks; *mus:* Carl W. Stalling; b&w. *sd:* PCP. 7 min. • A burlesque on bull fighting.

1771. The Electronic Mouse Trap *(Mighty Mouse)* 6 Sept. 1946; *p.c.:* TT for Fox; *dir:* Mannie Davis; *story:* John Foster; *mus:* Philip A. Scheib; *col:* Tech. *sd:* RCA. 6 min. • An evil cat scientist invents an electronically operated mousetrap to catch hundreds of mice. Mighty Mouse comes to the rescue once again.

1772. Electronica (*Modern Madcap*) July 1960; *p.c.:* Para; Cartoons; *dir:* Seymour Kneitel; *story:* Irving Dressler; *anim:* Nick Tafuri, Morey Reden; *sets:* Robert Owen; *voices:* Bob MacFadden, Corinne Orr; *mus:* Winston Sharples; *prod mgr:* Abe Goodman; *col:* Tech. *sd:* RCA. 6 min. • A henpecked husband gets a robot to do his housework for him. It will only obey his voice and when he leaves, it destroys the house.

1773. The Elephant Mouse (*Terry-Toon*) June 1951; *p.c.:* TT for Fox; *dir:* Mannie Davis; *story:* John Foster; *anim:* Jim Tyer; *sets:* Art Bartsch; *voices:* Arthur Kay; *mus:* Philip A. Scheib; *ph:* Douglas Moye; *col:* Tech. *sd:* RCA. 6 min. • Half-Pint, a baby elephant, is mistaken for a mouse by a champion mouse-catching cat.

1774. An Elephant Never Forgets (*Color Classic*) 28 Dec. 1934; *p.c.:* The Fleischer Studio for Para; *prod:* Max Fleischer; *dir:* Dave Fleischer; *anim:* Seymour Kneitel, Roland Crandall; *voice:* Everett Clark; *mus:* Sammy Timberg; *song:* Sammy Timberg, Jack Scholl; *col:* Ciné. *sd:* WE. 7 min. • The jungle kids go to school where the elephant is bullied by the gorilla. He repays him later, quoting, "An elephant never forgets."

1775. Elephantastic (*Loopy de Loop*) Feb. 1964; *p.c.:* Hanna-Barbera for Colum; *prod/dir:* William Hanna, Joseph Barbera; *story dir:* Paul Sommer; *story:* Michael Maltese; *anim dir:* Charles A. Nichols; *anim:* Ed Parks, Chuck Harriton; *lay:* Lance Nolley; *back:* Art Lozzi; *ed:* Warner Leighton; *voices:* Daws Butler, Don Messick, Doug Young; *mus:* Hoyt Curtin; *prod mgr:* Howard Hanson; *col:* East. *sd:* RCA. 6 min. • Loopy helps load an elephant onto a ship that houses a tough mouse named Biggelow.

1776. Eliza on the Ice (*Terry-Toons*) 6 June 1944; *p.c.:* TT for Fox; *dir:* Connie Rasinski; *story:* John Foster; *mus:* Philip A. Scheib; *col:* Tech. *sd:* RCA. 6 min. • Eliza flees from Simon Legree and his bloodhounds over the ice when the spirit of Little Eva summons-up Mighty Mouse.

1777. Eliza Runs Again (*Paul Terry-Toon*) 29 July 1938; *p.c.:* TT for Educational/Fox; *dir:* Connie Rasinski; *mus:* Philip A. Scheib; b&w. *sd:* RCA. 6 min. • The famous chase leaves Simon Legree and the spectators all losing to Eliza.

1778. Elmer Elephant (*Silly Symphony*) 28 Mar. 1936; *p.c.:* Walt Disney prods for UA; *dir:* Wilfred Jackson; *story:* George Stallings, Earl Hurd, Bianca Majolie; *anim:* Alfred Eugster, Clyde Geronimi, Jack Hannah, Paul Hopkins, Milton Kahl, Hamilton S. Luske, Wolfgang Reitherman, Robert Wickersham; *asst anim:* Eddie Donnelly, Milt Schaffer; *atmospheric sketches:* Maurice Noble; *voices:* Alyce Ardell, Pinto Colvig, William E. Sheets; *mus:* Leigh Harline; *col:* Tech. *sd:* RCA. 9 min. • Elmer is chided because of his trunk but it comes in useful to douse the flames when Tilly Tiger's house catches fire.

1779. Elmer the Great Dane (*Oswald*) 22 Apr. 1935; *p.c.:* Univ; *prod/dir:* Walter Lantz; *story/lyrics:* Walter Lantz, Victor McLeod; *anim:* Fred Avery, Ray Abrams, Cecil Surry, Virgil Ross; *mus:* James Dietrich; b&w. *sd:* WE. 8 min. • No story available. The title is a parody of Joe E. Brown's 1933 feature, *Elmer the Great*.

1780. Elmer's Candid Camera (*Merrie Melodies*) 2 Mar. 1940; *p.c.:* Leon Schlesinger prods for WB; *dir:* Charles M. Jones; *story:* Rich Hogan, Ted Pierce; *anim:* Bob McKimson; *lay:* Robert Givens; *back:* Paul Julian; *ed:* Treg Brown; *voices:* Mel Blanc, Arthur Q. Bryan; *mus:* Carl W. Stalling; *ph:* John W. Burton; *prod sup:* Henry Binder, Raymond G. Katz; *col:* Tech. *sd:* Vit. 7 min. • Elmer Fudd tries taking some wildlife photographs but doesn't reckon on pitting his wits against a screwball rabbit. Featuring an early Elmer up against a prototype Bugs Bunny.

1781. Elmer's Pet Rabbit (*Merrie Melodies*) 4 Jan. 1941; *p.c.:* Leon Schlesinger prods for WB; *dir:* Charles M. Jones; *story:* Rich Hogan; *anim:* Rudolph Larriva; *character design:* Charles Thorson; *lay:* Robert Givens; *back:* Paul Julian; *ed:* Treg Brown; *voices:* Mel Blanc, Arthur Q. Bryan; *mus:* Carl W. Stalling; *ph:* John W. Burton; *prod sup:* Henry Binder, Raymond G. Katz; *col:* Tech. *sd:* Vit. 7 min. • Elmer buys a rabbit and discovers that the creature, not satisfied with a rabbit pen, wants to move into Elmer's house.

1782. The Emerald Isle (*Screen Song*) 25 Feb. 1949; *p.c.:* Famous for Para; *dir:* Seymour Kneitel; *story:* I. Klein; *anim:* Al Eugster, Bill Hudson; *sets:* Tom Ford, Robert Owen; *mus:* Winston Sharples; *song:* Shamus

O'Connor, John J. Stamford, Dwight "Red" Latham, Wamp Carlton, Guy Bonhan; *prod mgr:* Sam Buchwald; *col:* Tech. *sd:* RCA. 7 min. • A musical travelogue of Ireland leading up to a sing-along of *MacNamara's Band*.

1783. The Emperor's New Clothes rel: 30 Apr. 1953; *p.c.:* UPA for Colum; *ex prod:* Stephen Bosustow; *dir:* Ted Parmelee; *story:* Robinson MacLean; *anim:* Phil Monroe, Pat Matthews, Fred Grable; *sets:* Paul Julian; *voices:* Hans Conried, Gladys Holland, Jerry Hausner; *mus:* Benjamin Lees; *prod mgr:* Herbert Klynn; *col:* Tech. *sd:* RCA. 6 min. • Adapted from Hans Christian Andersen's story: Two confidence tricksters sell the Emperor an invisible suit of clothes convincing him that only a fool would not see it's magnificence.

1784. The Empire Strikes Back • See: *Star Wars V: The Empire Strikes Back*

1785. Empty Socks (*Oswald the Lucky Rabbit*) 12 Dec. 1927; *p.c.:* Winkler for Univ; *dir:* Walter Disney; *anim:* Ubbe Iwerks, Hugh Harman, Rollin C. Hamilton; *ph:* Mike Marcus; b&w. sil. 6 min. • Oswald poses as Santa for some orphans and, again, as a fireman when the orphanage goes up in flames.

1786. The Enchanted Drawing rel: 16 Nov. 1900; *p.c.:* Edison; *anim:* James Stuart Blackton; b&w. sil. 1 min. *l/a/anim.* • J. Stuart Blackton draws on a large pad a man's face with a bottle and glass above it. He removes the receptacles and pours himself a drink while the face looks on in disapproval. • Lightning sketch artist Blackton appeared live on film and used a "stop-motion" camera to achieve his animated tricks.

1787. The Enchanted Flute (*Aesop's Film Fable*) 29 July 1929; *p.c.:* Fables Pictures Inc for Pathé; *dir:* Paul Terry, Frank Moser; b&w. sil. 5 min. • Milton Mouse and Rita are captured by a pack of hungry cannibals. His flute-playing has them all dancing.

1788. The Enchanted Square (*Noveltoon*) 9 May 1947; *p.c.:* Famous for Para; *dir:* Seymour Kneitel; *story:* Shane Miller, Orestes Calpini; *anim:* Orestes Calpini, Al Eugster; *sets:* Shane Miller; *voices:* Joy Terry, Jackson Beck, Cecil Roy, Gwen Davies, Jack Mercer; *mus:* Winston Sharples; *ph:* Leonard McCormick; *prod mgr:* Sam Buchwald; *col:* Tech. *sd:* RCA. 9 min. • A blind girl imagines her Raggedy Ann doll comes alive and transforms Shabby Square, where she lives, into a fairyland.

1789. The End rel: 1970; *p.c.:* Murakami-Wolf prods; *dir/anim:* Fred Wolf; *col.* *sd.* 1 min. • No story available.

1790. The End of the World (*Aesop's Film Fable*) 16 June 1925; *p.c.:* Fables Pictures Inc for Pathé; *dir:* Paul Terry; b&w. sil. 5 min. • No story available.

1791. Enemy Mine 20 Dec. 1985; *p.c.:* Kings Road Entertainment for Fox; *space dogfight seq:* ILM; *cgi:* Jan Christian Martens, Christopher Gurland; *anim:* Bruce Walters, Ellen Lichtwardt, A.J. Riddle, Chuck Eyler, Ellen Ferguson, Joanne Hafner; *mus:* Maurice Jarre; *col:* DeLuxe. *sd:* Dolby Stereo. 93 min. *l/a.* • Live-action science fiction saga: During an outer space battle, an Earthman and an inhabitant of the planet Dracon get shot down, finding themselves marooned on the inhospitable planet Fyrine IV.

1792. The English Channel Swim (*Aesop's Film Fable*) 19 Dec. 1925; *p.c.:* Fables Pictures Inc for Pathé; *dir:* Paul Terry; b&w. sil. 5 min. • No story available.

1793. The Enlarger (*Mighty Heroes*) Apr. 1971 (© 1967); *p.c.:* TT for Fox; *ex prod:* Bill Weiss; *dir/anim:* Robert Taylor; *voices:* Lionel Wilson, Herschel Bernardi; *mus:* Jim Timmens; *col:* DeLuxe. *sd:* RCA. 5 min. • The Mighty Heroes deal with a plague of enlarged bugs.

1794. Eraser 21 June 1995; *p.c.:* WB; *special visual fx:* ILM; *crocodile anim/visual fx sup:* Steve Williams; *cg anim:* Philip Edward Alexy, Tim Harrington, Brenton Fletcher; *col:* Tech. *sd:* Dolby stereo. 114 min. *l/a.* • Live-action adventure. A Federal Witness Protection Program agent helps safeguard a corporation employee who is willing to testify against her employers. Computer animation contributes to a skirmish with crocodiles.

1795. Le Escape Goat (*Inspector*) 29 June 1967; *p.c.:* Mirisch/Geoffrey/DFE for UA; *dir:* Gerry Chiniquy; *story:* Jim Ryan; *anim:* Don Williams, Manny Gould, Bob Matz, Manny Perez, Warren Batcheller; *lay:* Dick Ung; *back:* Tom O'Loughlin; *ed:* Lee Gunther; *voices:* Pat Harrington, Jr., Paul Frees; *mus:* Walter Greene; *theme tune:* Henry Mancini; *prod sup:* Harry Love, Bill Orcutt; *col:* DeLuxe. *sd:* RCA. 6 min.

1796. Eshbaugh, Ted (*Commercials*) rel: 1938–1939; *p.c.:* Ted Eshbaugh Studios Inc.; *prod/dir:* Ted Eshbaugh. • **Borden's Milk** *col:* Tech., **Blue Ribbon Cake Co.** *col:* Tech., **Planter's Nut and Chocolate Co.** *col:* Tech., **National Carbon Co.** (3 items), **Tootsie Rolls, Sweets Co.** 2 min., **Pepsi Cola** *col:* Tech. 1 min., **The March of Time** (3 items); *col:* Tech., **Pathé News** (3 items); *col:* Tech., **Gum, Inc.** (2 items); 1 min., **Birdseye Frozen Foods, American Tobacco (Lucky Strike), Kukan, Ex-Lax (Jests), Shell Oil Co.** 1 min. • These commercials plus other informational films for various companies are a sample of Eshbaugh's indepentent company over the first two years of its existence. Later forming a partnership with Burt Gillett, the company went on for nearly thirty years producing commercials and sponsored films.

1797. Et Tu Otto (*Comic King*) Sept. 1962; *p.c.:* Para Cartoons; *dir:* Seymour Kneitel; *story:* Willy Shawn; *anim:* Nick Tafuri, Wm. B. Pattengill, Larry Silverman; *sets:* Anton Loeb; *voices:* Howard Morris, Allen Melvin; *mus:* Winston Sharples; *prod mgr:* Abe Goodman; *ex prod:* Al Brodax; *col:* Tech. *sd:* RCA. 5 min. • Sgt. Snorkle visits the psychiatrist because nobody loves him. Even Otto, his bulldog, deserts him for a French Poodle. Made as part of a TV series featuring Mort Walker's comic strip character Beetle Bailey.

1798. The Eternal Triangle (*Aesop's Film Fable*) 3 Apr. 1922; *p.c.:* Fables Pictures Inc for Pathé; *dir:* Paul Terry; b&w. *sil.* 5 min. • A shoeshine boy and his customer both contend for the same girl.

1799. The Eternal Triangle Dec. 1934; *p.c.:* Champion prods for MGM; b&w. *snd.* 5 min. • Love triangle between snooker balls. Stop-motion animation.

1800. Everglade Raid (*Woody Woodpecker*) 14 July 1958; *p.c.:* Walter Lantz prods for Univ; *dir:* Paul J. Smith; *story:* Homer Brightman; *anim:* Robert Bentley, Les Kline, Don Patterson; *sets:* Art Landy, Raymond Jacobs; *voices:* Daws Butler, Grace Stafford; *mus:* Clarence Wheeler; *prod mgr:* William E. Garity; *col:* Tech. *sd:* RCA. 6 min. • Woody tries to bag some alligator-skin luggage in the everglades.

1801. Everybody Sing (*Oswald*) 22 Feb. 1937; *p.c.:* Univ; *prod/dir:* Walter Lantz; *story:* Walter Lantz, Victor McLeod; *anim:* Ray Abrams, Bill Mason; *mus:* Irving Actman, Frank Loesser; b&w. *sd:* WE. 6 min. • Three crows terrorize the populace in the Birdville Night Club and Oswald dresses as a scarecrow to rout them.

1802. Everybody's Flying (*Aesop's Film Fable*) 17 Jan. 1928; *p.c.:* Fables Pictures Inc for Pathé; *dir:* Paul Terry; b&w. *sil.* 5 min. • Farmer Al and his livestock join in with the current flying craze.

1803. Evolution 25 July 1925; *p.c.:* Kineto-Urban for Red Seal; *ed:* Max Fleischer; b&w/hand-colored. *sil.* 4,200 ft. *l/a/anim.* • Straightforward depiction of the creation of Earth and origins of early life. Live-action sequences were shot in Germany.

1804. Exercise *dir, des, story:* R.O. Blechman; *anim:* Ed Smith; *mus:* Arnold Black; *col. sd.* 1 min. • A rock rolls itself up some steps becoming a human figure along the way. Finally he falls from the top, reverting back to it's original form.

1805. The Explorer (*Paul Terry-Toon*) 22 Mar. 1931; *p.c.:* Terry, Moser & Coffman for Educational/Fox; *dir:* Paul Terry, Frank Moser; *anim:* Arthur Babbitt, George Gordon, Jack King, I. Klein, Frank Moser, Sarka, Hugh Shields, Vladimir Tytla; *mus:* Philip A. Scheib; b&w. *sd:* WE. 6 min. • Farmer Al Falfa in the Frozen North.

1806. Explorers 12 July 1985; *p.c.:* Para for Blue Dolphin; *Computer graphic dream simulations/visual displays:* J.C. Pennie, Art Durinski, Michiko Suzuki, Doug MacMillan, John S. Howard, Harold Buchman, Michael Kort *Omnibus Computer Graphics Center: anim sup:* Bruce Walters (*ILM*); *visual fx anim:* Ellen Lichtwardt, Barbara Brennan, Jack Mongovan, Jay Riddle, Peggy Regan; *col:* Tech. *sd:* Dolby stereo. 109 min. *l/a.* • Live-action fantasy about a group of schoolboys who build a craft that can travel at high speed via the computer. They have many adventures when devoured by an alien spaceship.

1807. The Explosive Mr. Magoo (*Mr. Magoo*) 8 May 1958; *p.c.:* UPA for Colum; *ex prod:* Stephen Bosustow; *prod/dir:* Pete Burness. *story:* Dick Shaw, Fred Grable; *anim:* Tom McDonald, Fred Grable, Ed Friedman, Barney Posner; *sets:* Robert Dranko; *voices:* Jim Backus, Daws Butler, June Foray; *mus:* Stanley J. Wilson; *prod mgr:* Herbert Klynn; *col:* Tech. *sd:* RCA. 6 min. • Enraged by what he believes to be a liquor ad using his photo, Magoo sets off to complain to the newspaper editor. En route he buys a clockwork toy that the editor mistakes for a bomb.

1808. The Exterminator (*Gandy Goose*) 23 Nov. 1945; *p.c.* TT for Fox; *dir:* Eddie Donnelly; *story:* John Foster; *voices:* Thomas Morrison, Arthur Kay; *mus:* Philip A. Scheib; *col:* Tech. *sd:* RCA. 6 min. • Gandy tries to rid Sourpuss' house of mice.

1809. Extinct Pink (*Pink Panther*) 20 Sept. 1969; *p.c.:* Mirisch/Geoffrey/DFE for UA; *dir:* Hawley Pratt; *story:* John W. Dunn; *anim:* Manny Gould, Manny Perez, Warren Batchelder, Don Williams; *lay:* Dick Ung; *back:* Tom O'Loughlin; *ed:* Lee Gunther; *mus:* Doug Goodwin; *theme tune:* Henry Mancini; *ph:* John Burton Jr.; *prod sup:* Jim Foss, Harry Love; *col:* DeLuxe. *sd:* RCA. 6 min. • Prehistoric Panther has a job surviving when a dinosaur and rival caveman are out to steal his food.

1810. The Extraordinary Adventures of the Mouse and His Child 1977; *p.c.:* Walt de Faria prods/Charles M. Schulz Creative Asso/Sanrio prods/Murakami-Wolf prods; *ex prod:* Warren Lockhart, Shintaro Tsuji, Ronald Benson Wong, Alice Wright, Joyse Yuen, Michele Zurcher; *asso prod:* Alex Lucas; *anim prod:* Murakami-Wolf prods; *dir:* Fred Wolf, Charles Swenson; *novel by* Russell Hoban; *story:* Carol Monpere; *anim:* Irv Anderson, Dave Brain, Bob Bransford, Brad Case, Corny Cole, Vincent Davis, Malcolm Draper, Jim Duffy, John Gibbs, Milt Gray, Lu Guarnier, Bud Luckey, Gary Mooney, Russell Mooney, Willis Pyle, Gerry Ray, Mike Sanger, Joan Swanson, Charles Swenson, Bob Taylor, Rich Trueblood, Tim Walker, Bill Wolf, Fred Wolf, Duane Crowther, Bob Zamboni; *graphics:* Bonnie Blough, Maria Alvarez, Christina Cartusciello, Judy Champin, Laura Craig, Mari Daugherty, Marsha Hunt, Eshnaur Etsuko Fujioka, Kassiani Galinos, Paulino Garcia Noriko, Horiuchi Hawks, Jacqueline Hooks, Pico Hozumi, Corry Kingsbury, Peggy Lynn, Nakaguchi, Linda Navroth, Diana Proud, Pamela Randles, June Rose Ross, Deborah Rykoff, Olaya Stephenson, Karan Storr, Ann Sutherland, Giselle Van Bark, Robin Belle Wagner, Denise Wethington, Jeanette Whiteaker, Tasia Williams, Patty Wolf; *back sup:* Lorraine Andrina; *back:* Richard Blair, Sam Clayberger, Paro Hozumi, Lynn Lascaro, Bob Schaefer; *character des:* Vincent Davis, Joanne McPherson. *col sup:* Wilma Guenot. *ed:* Rich Harrison; *i&p:* Elizabeth Wright; *Xerography:* Celine Miles, Fred Craig; *prod des:* Vincent Davis, Sam Kirson, Bob Mitchell, Al Shean; *art dir:* David McMacken; *voices: Manny the Rat:* Peter Ustinov; *Iggy:* Neville Brand; *Frog:* Andy Devine; *Seal:* Sally Kellerman; *Euterpe:* Cloris Leachman; *Elephant:* Joan Gerber; *Mouse:* Alan Barzman; *Mouse Child:* Marcy Swenson; *Clock:* Regis Cordic; *Muskrat:* Bob Holt; *Ralphie:* Mel Leven; *Teller/Starling:* Maitzi Morgan; *Crows:* Frank Nelson, Cliff Norton. *Serpentina:* Cliff Osmond; *Paper People/Starling:* Iris Rainer; *Jack-in-the-Box:* Bob Ridgley; *Blue Jay/Paper People:* Charles Woolf; *Tramp:* John Carradine; "Scat Rat" sung by Roger Kellaway; "Much in Little" sung by Robin Reed; "Tell Me My Name" sung by Colin Christian Kellaway; *songs:* Roger Kellaway, Gene Lees; *mus sup:* Jules Chaikin; *sd rec (DIAL):* The Recording Place; *ph:* Wally Bulloch; *prod sup:* Donna Evans, Amy Kennedy, Don Coorough, Mike Kubina; *col:* DeLuxe. 83 min. • A mechanical toy mouse and his son have one ambition in life ... to be self-winding.

1811. The Eyes Have It (*Donald Duck*) 30 Mar. 1945; *p.c.:* Walt Disney prods for RKO; *dir:* Jack Hannah; *asst dir:* Toby Tobelman; *story:* Bill Berg, Ralph Wright; *anim:* Bob Carlson, Hugh Fraser, Don Patterson, Al Coe, Jerry Hathcock, Milt Neil, Art Scott, Judge Whitaker; *fx:* John Reed; *lay:* Yale Gracey. *back:* Thelma Witmer; *voices:* Clarence Nash, Dorothy Lloyd, James MacDonald; *mus:* Paul J. Smith; *col:* Tech. *sd:* RCA. 7 min. • Donald has a spot of fun hypnotising Pluto.

1812. Eyes Into Outer Space rel: 1959; *p.c.:* Walt Disney prods for BV; *prod/dir:* Ward Kimball; *story:* William Bosché, Ward Kimball; *art dir:* Carroll Clark; *ed:* Lloyd L. Richardson, Robert O. Cook; *voice:* Paul Frees. *mus:* George Bruns; *ph:* Walter H. Castle, John Frederic Stanton; *col:* Tech. *sd:* RCA. 26 min. • Examination of adverse weather conditions. Award: 1960 Thomas Edison Foundation.

1813. The Fable About the Troubles in the Ark (*Aesop's Film Fable*) 17 Feb. 1923; *p.c.:* Fables Pictures Inc for Pathé; *dir:* Paul Terry; b&w. *sil.* 5 min. • Noah finds himself in a predicament due to a sharp increase of animals in his Ark.

1814. The Fable of a Fish Story (*Aesop's Film Fable*) 27 Apr. 1923; *p.c.:* Fables Pictures Inc for Pathé; *dir:* Paul Terry; b&w. *sil.* 5 min. • Farmer

Al spins a yarn of how, while fishing, he was swallowed by a whale, then made his escape, but not before turning the creature inside out.

1815. The Fable of a Fisherman's Jinx (*Aesop's Film Fable*) 17 Feb. 1923; *p.c.:* Fables Pictures Inc for Pathé; *dir:* Paul Terry; b&w. *sil.* 5 min. • Farmer Al Falfa has no luck while fishing, yet his cat catches great quantities of fish.

1816. The Fable of a Raisin and a Cake of Yeast (*Aesop's Film Fable*) 17 Feb. 1923; *p.c.:* Fables Pictures Inc for Pathé; *dir:* Paul Terry; b&w. *sil.* 5 min. • Farmer Al feeds his home brew to a rabbit who effectively deals with the pursuing hounds. He feeds some to the rooster who gets his feathers blown off, then takes some himself and is transported amongst the stars. Moral: "There is nothing like travel to broaden one."

1817. The Fable of a Stoneage Romeo (*Aesop's Film Fable*) 14 Dec. 1922; *p.c.:* Fables Pictures Inc for Pathé; *dir:* Paul Terry; b&w. *sil.* 5 min. • No story available.

1818. The Fable of Brewing Trouble (*Aesop's Film Fable*) 22 June 1922; *p.c.:* Fables Pictures Inc for Pathé; *dir:* Paul Terry; b&w. *sil.* 5 min. • Farmer Al brews some "Hooch."

1819. The Fable of Cheating the Cheaters (*Aesop's Film Fable*) 14 Dec. 1922; *p.c.:* Fables Pictures Inc for Pathé; *dir:* Paul Terry; b&w. *sil.* 5 min. • Together the dog, cat and mouse steal some sausages and take the spoils back to the farm. The Farmer's motto is "Honesty is the best policy" but is exposed for his watered-down "Pure Milk" policy.

1820. The Fable of Day by Day in Every Way (*Aesop's Film Fable*) 22 Mar. 1923; *p.c.:* Fables Pictures Inc for Pathé; *dir:* Paul Terry; b&w. *sil.* 5 min. • French pharmacist Emile Coue's mantra is "day by day in every way, I'm getting better and better." A mouse's concentration makes a tree sprout bananas, clocks, beer and dressed hogs. The cat heals a lame monkey by hypnosis and then wallops Farmer Al Falfa, who has a dream of being stranded in the ocean on a rock and being hugged by a mermaid. Moral: "No one is mighty but he who conquers himself."

1821. The Fable of Farmer Al Falfa's Bride (*Aesop's Film Fable*) 23 Feb. 1923; *p.c.:* Fables Pictures Inc for Pathé; *dir:* Paul Terry; b&w. *sil.* 5 min. • When rejected, the Farmer takes a lesson from his cat's love affair and threatens to marry another to his hesitating Miss. This does the trick. Moral: "Many a maiden says *No* when she means *Yes.*"

1822. The Fable of Fearless Fido (*Aesop's Film Fable*) 20 July 1922; *p.c.:* Fables Pictures Inc for Pathé; *dir:* Paul Terry; b&w. *sil.* 5 min. • Farmer Al Falfa puts out a "Wanted" poster for a bear who threw a beehive at him. A boy and his dog, Fido, go after the bear with Fido disguising himself as a beehive. The boy shoots the bear and collects a reward.

1823. The Fable of Friday the 13th (*Aesop's Film Fable*) 11 Nov. 1922; *p.c.:* Fables Pictures Inc for Pathé; *dir:* Paul Terry; b&w. *sil.* 5 min. • When the Farmer ignores every sign of superstition all manner of disasters befall him.

1824. The Fable of Henpecked Harry (*Aesop's Film Fable*) 28 Oct. 1922; *p.c.:* Fables Pictures Inc for Pathé; *dir:* Paul Terry; b&w. *sil.* 5 min. • A dog joins the Police Force and overcomes a notorious criminal, only to be ignominiously defeated by his wife when he returns home.

1825. The Fable of Henry's Busted Romance (*Aesop's Film Fable*) 11 Nov. 1922; *p.c.:* Fables Pictures Inc for Pathé; *dir:* Paul Terry; b&w. *sil.* 5 min. • Dealing with a sadder, wiser and better husband after a series of dalliances.

1826. The Fable of One Hard Pull (*Aesop's Film Fable*) 22 Mar. 1923; *p.c.:* Fables Pictures Inc for Pathé; *dir:* Paul Terry; b&w. *sil.* 5 min. • The cat tries to cure Al Falfa's aching tooth.

1827. The Fable of Spooks (*Aesop's Film Fable*) 27 Apr. 1923; *p.c.:* Fables Pictures Inc for Pathé; *dir:* Paul Terry; b&w. *sil.* 5 min. • Henry Cat holds a séance for Farmer Al to go to the spirit world to collect an unpaid debt. Henry hits him on the head and he dreams a weird experience in Heaven where spirits hold a mass meeting.

1828. The Fable of the Alley Cat (*Aesop's Film Fable*) 17 Feb. 1923; *p.c.:* Fables Pictures Inc for Pathé; *dir:* Paul Terry; b&w. *sil.* 5 min. • The Farmer drowns a feline nocturnal serenader and experiences a nightmare in which he's put before a tribunal of Ku Klux Klan cats, then sentenced and beheaded. Moral: "What can't be cured must be endured."

1829. The Fable of the Big Flood (*Aesop's Film Fable*) 27 Sept. 1922; *p.c.:* Fables Pictures Inc from Pathé; *dir:* Paul Terry; b&w. *sil.* 5 min. • Noah prepares his Ark for the flood. Moral: "It's an ill wind that blows no one good."

1830. The Fable of the Boastful Cat (*Aesop's Film Fable*) 26 Aug. 1922; *p.c.:* Fables Pictures Inc for Pathé; *dir:* Paul Terry; b&w. *sil.* 5 min. • A cat fancies himself a great boxer that can lick the world ... until he's teamed against a bulldog! Moral: "It is never wise to be too boastful."

1831. The Fable of the Boy and the Bear (*Aesop's Film Fable*) 9 Aug. 1922; *p.c.:* Fables Pictures Inc for Pathé; *dir:* Paul Terry; b&w. *sil.* 5 min. • A boy, his dog and a bear cub travel home via radio airwaves.

1832. The Fable of the Dog and the Fish (*Aesop's Film Fable*) 22 June 1922; *p.c.:* Fables Pictures Inc for Pathé; *dir:* Paul Terry; b&w. *sil.* 5 min. • A dog goes fishing and catches a minnow which he returns to the water. He falls asleep and dreams the little fish saves him from a difficult situation. Moral: "He who dreams catches no fish."

1833. The Fable of the Dog's Paradise (*Aesop's Film Fable*) 1 Dec. 1922; *p.c.:* Fables Pictures Inc for Pathé; *dir:* Paul Terry; b&w. *sil.* 5 min. • A group of dogs take posession of a butcher's shop.

1834. The Fable of the Elephant's Trunk (*Aesop's Film Fable*) 4 Nov. 1922; *p.c.:* Fables Pictures Inc for Pathé; *dir:* Paul Terry; b&w. *sil.* 5 min. • Two frolicking elephants' fun is disrupted by the arrival of Fido and his master on an elephant hunt. One runs and hides while the other hides in his trunk. Fido conspires with three mice who crawl in and drag him out by the tail.

1835. The Fable of the Enchanted Fiddle (*Aesop's Film Fable*) 18 Nov. 1922; *p.c.:* Fables Pictures Inc for Pathé; *dir:* Paul Terry; b&w. *sil.* 5 min. • The Farmer tries to regain his lost mule and pigs by playing fiddle music. The mule repays the favor with a kick.

1836. The Fable of the Farmer and the Mice (*Aesop's Film Fable*) 26 June 1922; *p.c.:* Fables Pictures Inc for Pathé; *dir:* Paul Terry. b&w. *sil.* 5 min. • The Farmer and his wife bodily move house to escape an invasion of mice.

1837. The Fable of the Fortune Hunters (*Aesop's Film Fable*) 11 Nov. 1922; *p.c.:* Fables Pictures Inc for Pathé; *dir:* Paul Terry; b&w. *sil.* 5 min. • Henry Cat and Milton Mouse break out of prison in pursuit of a legacy left them by their uncle. After many trials and tribulations, they find out that the "pile" they have been left is a rock pile.

1838. The Fable of the Fox and the Crow (*Aesop's Film Fable*) 14 Aug. 1921; *p.c.:* Fables Pictures Inc for Pathé; *dir:* Paul Terry; b&w. *sil.* 5 min. • When a crow presents his lady fair with a piece of cheese stolen from the farmer's wife, the lady crow sends him out for some crackers. The fox then arrives and compliments "Mistress Crow" on her wonderful singing voice. When she opens her bill to sing, she drops the cheese and the fox grabs it.

1839. The Fable of the Frog and the Catfish (*Aesop's Film Fable*) 1 Dec. 1922; *p.c.:* Fables Pictures Inc for Pathé; *dir:* Paul Terry; b&w. *sil.* 5 min. • Depicting the troubles of Freddie Frog whose lady love is carried away by a terrible catfish.

1840. The Fable of the Gamblers (*Aesop's Film Fable*) 22 Mar. 1923; *p.c.:* Fables Pictures Inc for Pathé; *dir:* Paul Terry; b&w. *sil.* 5 min. • The animals soon succumb to Henry Cat's dice-throwing. Farmer Al Falfa steals his dice and Henry plots to get even. Moral: "Never gamble in a hen house."

1841. The Fable of the Gliders (*Aesop's Film Fable*) 17 Mar. 1923; *p.c.:* Fables Pictures Inc for Pathé; *dir:* Paul Terry; b&w. *sil.* 5 min. • Farmer Al Falfa's attempts to emulate his gliding animals gives him a blow to the head that sends him on a trip to the stars.

1842. The Fable of the Hated Rivals (*Aesop's Film Fable*) 27 Sept. 1922; *p.c.:* Fables Pictures Inc for Pathé; *dir:* Paul Terry; b&w. *sil.* 5 min. • Jack's Jill is stolen from him by another suitor who proves too cowardly to protect her from an escaped lion. Moral: "None but the brave deserve the fair."

1843. The Fable of the Jolly Rounders (*Aesop's Film Fable*) 22 Mar. 1923; *p.c.:* Fables Pictures Inc for Pathé; *dir:* Paul Terry; b&w. *sil.* 5 min. • A hippo's rebellion against his wifely rule.

1844. The Fable of the Lion and the Mouse (*Aesop's Film Fable*)

21 Feb. 1922; *p.c.:* Fables Pictures Inc for Pathé; *dir:* Paul Terry; b&w. *sil.* 5 min. • When the animals play baseball, the mouse uses a motorcycle to catch fly balls and runs into a lion. The lion is amused and lets the mouse go on his way. When hunter Al Falfa captures the lion, the mouse sets him free. Moral: "In time of need the weak may help the strong."

1845. The Fable of the Man Who Laughs *(Aesop's Film Fable)* 11 Nov. 1922; *p.c.:* Fables Pictures Inc for Pathé; *dir:* Paul Terry; b&w. *sil.* 5 min. • Farmer Al takes his physician's advice to take life's "bumps" with a smile. Armed with this guidance, the Farmer shouts "Hoo Ray!" whenever things go wrong which leads to trouble with his wife. A mule he is riding becomes spooked and runs wildly, winning a horse race in the bargain.

1846. The Fable of the Mechanical Horse *(Aesop's Film Fable)* 9 Aug. 1922; *p.c.:* Fables Pictures Inc for Pathé; *dir:* Paul Terry; b&w. *sil.* 5 min. • A mechanical horse is entered in a race but the mechanism goes awry.

1847. The Fable of the Mischievious Cat *(Aesop's Film Fable)* 22 June 1922; *p.c.:* Fables Pictures Inc for Pathé; *dir:* Paul Terry; b&w. *sil.* 5 min. • A cat is involved in a bullfight.

1848. The Fable of the Mouse Catcher *(Aesop's Film Fable)* 27 Apr. 1923; *p.c.:* Fables Pictures Inc for Pathé; *dir:* Paul Terry; b&w. *sil.* 5 min. • The cat uses a vacuum cleaner to rid the house of mice. It sucks up everything including the Farmer.

1849. The Fable of the Mysterious Hat *(Aesop's Film Fable)* 17 Feb. 1923; *p.c.:* Fables Pictures Inc for Pathé; *dir:* Paul Terry; b&w. *sil.* 5 min. • A duck takes away a sharpshooting cat's glory by doing magical tricks with a hat.

1850. The Fable of the Pharaoh's Tomb *(Aesop's Film Fable)* 27 Apr. 1923; *p.c.:* Fables Pictures Inc for Pathé; *dir:* Paul Terry; b&w. *sil.* 5 min. • The Farmer drinks some powerful "hooch" and imagines he's on a trip to Egypt and visits the tomb of King Toot-and-come-in.

1851. The Fable of the Rolling Stone *(Aesop's Film Fable)* 18 Nov. 1922; *p.c.:* Fables Pictures Inc for Pathé; *dir:* Paul Terry; b&w. *sil.* 5 min. • A railway passenger dog, in an effort to escape the engineer, is sidetracked into locating some flapjacks.

1852. The Fable of the Romantic Mouse *(Aesop's Film Fable)* 27 Sept. 1922; *p.c.:* Fables Pictures Inc for Pathé; *dir:* Paul Terry; b&w. *sil.* 5 min. • Roller-skating champion, Thomas Cat, proves a desperate rival for Milton Mouse in his wooing of Lizzie Mouse. Jilted by his lady-love, Milton tries a succession of suicide attempts before finally winning over his love by saving her life.

1853. The Fable of the Rooster and the Eagle *(Aesop's Film Fable)* 3 June 1921; *p.c.:* Fables Pictures Inc for Pathé; *dir:* Paul Terry; b&w. *sil.* 5 min. • Petaluma Pete the Rooster beats "Kid Webfoot" the Duck in a boxing match and thinks himself "Cock-of-the-Walk" until an eagle swoops down, carrying him away. Moral: "Braggarts beware; there's always a day of reckoning." And today — a bragging politician is knocked out by a suffragette bearing a mallet labeled: "Women's Votes."

1854. The Fable of the Sheik *(Aesop's Film Fable)* 17 Feb. 1923; *p.c.:* Fables Pictures Inc for Pathé. *dir:* Paul Terry. b&w. *sil.* 5 min. • Little Jack sees a movie about a conquering Sheik after his Jill has been carried off by a rival and determines to follow the example.

1855. The Fable of the Spider and the Fly *(Aesop's Film Fable)* 17 Feb. 1923; *p.c.:* Fables Pictures Inc for Pathé; *dir:* Paul Terry; b&w. *sil.* 5 min. • The tale of an artful spider and an innocent fly.

1856. The Fable of the Traveling Salesman *(Aesop's Film Fable)* 17 Feb. 1923; *p.c.:* Fables Pictures Inc for Pathé; *dir:* Paul Terry; b&w. *sil.* 5 min. • Farmer Al Falfa falls victim to a traveling salesman's remedy.

1857. The Fable of the Two Explorers *(Aesop's Film Fable)* 12 Aug. 1922; *p.c.:* Fables Pictures Inc for Pathé; *dir:* Paul Terry; b&w *sil.* 5 min. • Tom Cat and Jerry Mouse journey forth in a hot-air balloon. Finding a filling station in the ether, they are felled by lightning and fall to earth at the North Pole. Chased by an Eskimo with a spear, Tom jumps in the balloon and departs, leaving the mouse to fend for himself. Upon arriving home, Tom is startled to see Jerry sailing up the river on an ice floe with a group of kangaroos. Moral: "Trouble and adversity are true tests of greatness."

1858. The Fable of the Worm That Turned *(Aesop's Film Fable)* 22 June 1922; *p.c.:* Fables Pictures Inc for Pathé; *dir:* Paul Terry; b&w. *sil.* 5 min. • Henpecked Harry Hippo sees a Paul Terry "Fable" cartoon about a worm who turns on his pursuer. He then goes home and tries the same on his wife with disastrous results. Moral: "Theory and practice are two different things."

1859. The Fable of Two of a Trade *(Aesop's Film Fable)* 14 Oct. 1922; *p.c.:* Fables Pictures Inc for Pathé; *dir:* Paul Terry; b&w. *sil.* 5 min. • Tom Cat steals Dickie Bird's fishing worms. In turn, Farmer Al Falfa does the same and Tom swims after his boat and puts a bottle of hooch in his line. The Farmer drinks it and the fun begins.

1860. The Fabulous Fireworks Family *(Terry-Toon)* Aug. 1959; *p.c.:* TT for Fox; *ex prod:* Bill Weiss; *sup dir:* Gene Deitch; *dir:* Al Kouzel; *story sup:* Tom Morrison; *story:* James Flora; *anim:* Johnny Gent, Vinnie Bell; *sets:* Bill Focht; *voices:* Graciela Chavez, Allen Swift; *mus:* Philip Scheib; *prod mgr:* Frank Schudde; *col:* Tech. *sd:* RCA. 7 min. CS. • A Mexican family make fireworks but nobody else can light the big firework except little Pepito.

1861. The Fade Away *(Out of the Inkwell)* 11 Sept. 1926; *p.c.:* Inkwell Studio for Red Seal; *prod/ll/a:* Max Fleischer; *dir:* Dave Fleischer; b&w. *sil.* 6 min. *l/a/anim.* • Max puts "Fadeaway powder" in the inkwell resulting in everything fading away. Ko-Ko retaliates by getting hold of the powder and causing everything in the real world, even Max's clothing, to disappear.

1862. Fagin's Freshman *(Merrie Melodies)* 18 Nov. 1939; *p.c.:* Leon Schlesinger prods for WB; *dir:* Ben Hardaway, Cal Dalton; *story:* Jack Miller; *anim:* Rod Scribner; *lay:* Griff Jay; *back:* Arthur Loomer; *ed:* Tregoweth E. Brown; *voices:* Lionel Stander, Bobbie Winkler, Mel Blanc, Margaret Hill, The Sportsmen Quartet; *mus:* Carl W. Stalling; *song:* Johnny Mercer, Richard Whiting; *prod sup:* Henry Binder, Raymond G. Katz; *col:* Tech. *sd:* Vit. 7 min. • Blackie, a tough little kitten, dreams he runs away from home and falls afoul of Fagin and his school of gangsters.

1863. Fair and Worm-er *(Looney Tunes)* 28 Sept. 1946; *p.c.:* WB; *dir:* Charles M. Jones; *story:* Tedd Pierce, Michael Maltese; *anim:* Ben Washam, Ken Harris, Basil Davidovich, Lloyd Vaughan; *lay:* Peter Brown; *back:* Richard Morley; *ed:* Treg Brown; *voices:* Robert C. Bruce, Mel Blanc, Bea Benaderet, Tedd Pierce; *mus:* Carl Stalling; *prod mgr:* John W. Burton; *prod:* Edward Selzer; *col:* Tech. *sd:* Vit. 7 min. • A worm is pursued by a hungry bird who, in turn, is chased by a cat. Close behind is a dog who has the dog catcher on his tail and he is closely followed by his nagging wife.

1864. A Fair Exchange *(Aesop's Film Fable)* 1 May 1927; *p.c.:* Fables Pictures Inc for Pathé; *dir:* Paul Terry; b&w. *sil.* 5 min. • Al Falfa trades his old jalopy to a farmer for his farm but the place is haunted. Ghosts and skeletons bedevil Al as the farmer has his troubles with Al's car. The mule kicks Al back into the jalopy again, and he and the farmer shake hands.

1865. The Fair Haired Hare *(Looney Tunes)* Apr. 1951; *p.c.:* WB; *dir:* I. Freleng; *story:* Warren Foster; *anim:* Ken Champin, Virgil Ross, Arthur Davis, Manuel Perez, John Carey; *lay:* Hawley Pratt; *back:* Paul Julian; *ed:* Treg Brown; *voices:* Mel Blanc; *mus:* Carl Stalling; *prod mgr:* John W. Burton; *prod:* Edward Selzer; *col:* Tech. *sd:* Vit. 7 min. • Sam builds his house over Bugs' burrow. The case goes to court and they settle for sharing the house until one of them expires.

1866. Fair Today *(Cartune)* 24 Feb. 1941; *p.c.:* Walter Lantz prods for Univ; *story:* Ben Hardaway; *anim:* Alex Lovy, Ralph Somerville; *sets:* Fred Brunish; *voices:* Robert C. Bruce, Mel Blanc, Grace Stafford; *mus:* Darrell Calker; *prod mgr:* George Hall; *col:* Tech. *sd:* WE. 7 min. • The county fair is in full-swing with blackout gags on the various attractions.

1867. Fair Weather Fiends *(Woody Woodpecker)* 18 Nov. 1946; *p.c.:* Walter Lantz prods for Univ; *dir:* James Culhane; *story:* Ben Hardaway, Milt Schaffer; *anim:* La Verne Harding, Sidney Pillet; *sets:* Terry Lind; *voices:* Will Wright, Ben Hardaway; *mus:* Darrell Calker; *prod mgr:* William E. Garity; *col:* Tech. *sd:* WE. 7 min. • Woody and a wolf are the best of pals until they are shipwrecked, then it's "survival of the fittest."

1868. Fairyland Follies *(Aesop's Sound Fable)* 28 Sept. 1931; *p.c.:* Van Beuren for RKO/Pathé; *dir:* John Foster, Harry Bailey; *mus:* Gene Rodemich; b&w. *sd:* RCA. 8 min. • Mother Goose attempts to quash the jazz element in her classroom but it overcomes her and she demonstrates how to "Step on it."

1869. The Faithful Pup (*Aesop's Sound Fable*) 12 May 1929; *p.c.*: Fables Pictures Inc for Pathé; *dir*: Paul Terry, Harry Bailey; *mus*: Josiah Zuro; *sd fx*: Maurice Manne; b&w. sd: RCA. 7 min. • The pup gains back favor from the Farmer when he saves him from a bear.

1870. Fall Out Fall In (*Donald Duck*) 23 Apr. 1943; *p.c.*: Walt Disney prods for RKO; *dir*: Jack King; *asst dir*: Jack Atwood; *story dir*: Jack Hannah; *anim*: Paul Allen, Hal King, John McManus, Milt Neil, Ray Patterson, Judge Whitaker; *lay*: Bill Herwig; *voices*: Clarence Nash, Henry Ketcham; *mus*: Paul J. Smith; *song*: Tony Strobl; *col*: Tech. *sd*: RCA. 7 min. • Pvt. Duck's Army career consists mainly of marching. When he stops, he can't pitch his tent and when he finally gets to sleep it's time to march again.

1871. A Fallible Fable (*Loopy de Loop*) May 1963; *p.c.*: Hanna-Barbera for Colum; *prod/dir*: Joseph Barbera, William Hanna; *story dir*: Walt Clinton; *story*: Dalton Sandifer; *anim dir*: Charles A. Nichols; *anim*: Robert Bentley; *lay*: Jack Ozark; *back*: Art Lozzi; *ed*: Greg Watson; *voices*: Daws Butler, Don Messick, Jean van der Pyl; *mus*: Hoyt Curtin; *titles*: Lawrence Gobel; *prod mgr*: Howard Hanson; *col*: East. *sd*: RCA. 6 min. • Loopy takes over as the wolf in the Red Riding Hood story when the present incumbent resigns.

1872. Falling Hare (*Merrie Melodies*) 23 Oct. 1943; *p.c.*: Leon Schlesinger prods for WB; *dir*: Robert Clampett; *story*: Warren Foster; *anim*: Rod Scribner; *lay*: Thomas McKimson; *back*: Michael Sasanoff; *ed*: Treg Brown; *voices*: Mel Blanc, Robert Clampett; *mus*: Carl W. Stalling; *ph*: John W. Burton; *prod sup*: Henry Binder, Raymond G. Katz; *col*: Tech. *sd*: Vit. 7 min. • Bugs finds himself flying a bomber plane with a destructive Gremlin as a passenger.

1873. The False Alarm (*Out of the Inkwell*) 1 Aug. 1923; *p.c.*: Inkwell Studio for Rodner; *prod/l/a*: Max Fleischer; *dir*: Dave Fleischer; b&w. sil. 6 min. • The little clown plays fireman. He goes to put out a fire in a prison, breaking a window, thus allowing all the inmates to escape. He soon discovers that the smoke was caused by a convict's pipe.

1874. False Alarm (*Scrappy*) 22 Apr. 1933; *p.c.*: Winkler for Colum; *prod*: Charles Mintz; *story*: Dick Huemor; *anim*: Sid Marcus, Art Davis; *mus*: Joe de Nat; *prod mgr*: James Bronis; b&w. sd: RCA. 6 min. • Scrappy and Oopie are firemen who always arrive too late. The only occasion they are on time is for a false alarm ... then they return to bed.

1875. False Hare (*Looney Tunes*) July 1964; *p.c.*: WB; *dir*: Robert McKimson; *story*: John Dunn; *anim*: Warren Batchelder, George Grandpré, Ted Bonnicksen; *lay*: Robert Givens; *back*: Robert Gribbroek; *ed*: Treg Brown; *voices*: Mel Blanc; *mus*: Bill Lava; *prod mgr*: William Orcutt; *prod*: David H. DePatie; *col*: Tech. *sd*: Vit. 6 min. • In a ruse to get Bugs into the cooking pot, B.B. Wolf creates a bizarre initiation ceremony to gain him admittance to the newly-formed Club del Conejo.

1876. The Family Album 1932; *p.c.*: A-C/WE; *dir*: Paul Terry, Frank Moser; *story/dial*: Charles W. Barrell; *mus*: Philip A. Scheib. b&w. sd: WE. 10 min. • Reporters interview Tel E. Phone, who introduces his family: The radio twins, "Mike and Loudspeaker," Public Address System, Electrical Stethoscope and "Talkie." Promotional cartoon for Western Electric Sound System.

1877. Family Circus (*Jolly Frolics*) 25 Jan. 1951; *p.c.*: UPA for Colum; *ex prod*: Stephen Bosustow; *dir sup*: John Hubley; *dir*: Art Babbitt; *story*: Phil Eastman, Bill Scott; *anim*: Art Babbitt, Cecil Surry; *lay*: Abe Liss; *back*: Paul Julian; *voices*: Jerry Hausner; *mus*: Ernest Gold; *prod mgr*: Adrian Woolery; *col*: Tech. *sd*: RCA. 6 min. • Five-year-old Patsy feels neglected and battles for her daddy's attention from her baby brother. Surreal dream sequence done with childrens' drawings.

1878. The Family Shoe (*Aesop's Sound Fables*) 14 Sept. 1931; *p.c.*: Van Beuren for RKO/Pathé; *dir*: John Foster, Mannie Davis; *mus*: Gene Rodemich; b&w. sd: RCA. 7 min. • Jack lives with his mother in an old shoe. He plants some beans, a beanstalk grows that he climbs and brings home a golden egg-laying goose.

1879. The Family's Night Out (3) 1930. *p.c.*: A-C/Aetna Insurance Co.; b&w. sd: WE. 5 min. • The house gets burgled while the family is out. Thankfully, Father is insured with Aetna.

1880. The Famous Ride (*Terry-Toon*) Apr. 1960; *p.c*: TT for Fox; *ex prod*: Bill Weiss; *dir*: Connie Rasinski; *story sup*: Tom Morrison; *story*: Eli Bauer; *anim*: Eddie Donnelly, Mannie Davis, Vinnie Bell; *des*: John Zago; *back*: Bill Focht; *voices*: John Myhers; *mus*: Phil Scheib; *prod mgr*: Frank Schudde; *col*: DeLuxe. sd: RCA. 5 min. CS. • Stable Boy Heathcote has a tough time grooming Paul Revere's horse for the "Midnight Ride."

1881. Fancy Plants (*James Hound*) July 1967; *p.c.*: TT for Fox; *dir*: Ralph Bakshi; *col*: DeLuxe. sd: RCA. 6 min. • Dr. Noxious installs plants over the city that attack the inhabitants. • See: *James Hound*

1882. Fanny Fidget 21 Dec. 1935; *p.c.*: Ernest Andersson; *dir/anim*: Bill Nolan; b&w. sd. • No story available.

1883. Fanny in the Lion's Den (*Paul Terry-Toon*) 23 July 1933; *p.c.*: Moser & Terry for Educational/Fox; *dir*: Paul Terry, Frank Moser; *mus*: Philip A. Scheib; b&w. sd: WE 6 min. • Performed as an operetta, Fanny Zilch is abducted during a storm by Oil Can Harry and thrown into the lion's den. When the sun comes out, our hero dashes to the rescue.

1884. Fanny's Wedding Day (*Paul Terry-Toon*) 22 Sept. 1933; *p.c.*: Moser & Terry for Educational/Fox; *dir*: Paul Terry, Frank Moser; *mus*: Philip A. Scheib; b&w. *sd*: WE. 6 min. • Villainous Oil Can Harry attempts to stop Fanny Zilch from marrying.

1885. Fantasia premiere: 13 Nov. 1940; *p.c.*: Walt Disney prods for RKO; *featuring*: Leopold Stokowski and music played by the Philadelphia Orchestra; *introductions (l/a)*: Deems Taylor; *prod sup*: Ben Sharpsteen; *story dir*: Joe Grant, Dick Huemer; *mus dir*: Edward H. Plumb; *mus ed*: Stephen Csillag; *sd*: William E. Garity, C.O. Slyfield, J.N.A. Hawkins; *special processes*: Herman Schultheis; *l/a jazz flute*: Art Smith. • *Toccata and Fugue; dir*: Samuel Armstrong; *story*: Lee Blair, Elmer Plummer, Phil Dike; *anim*: Cy Young, Art Palmer, Daniel MacManus, George Rowley, Edwin Aardal, Joshua Meador, Cornett Wood; *lay*: Robert Cormack; *back*: Joe Stahley, John Hench, Nino Carbe. • *The Nutcracker Suite; dir*: Samuel Armstrong; *story*: Sylvia Moberly-Holland, Norman Wright, Albert Heath, Bianca Majolie, Graham Heid; *anim*: Art Babbitt, Les Clark, Don Lusk, Cy Young, Robert Stokes; *character des*: John Walbridge, Elmer Plummer, Ethel Kulsar; *lay*: Robert Cormack, Al Zinnen, Curtiss D. Perkins, Arthur Byram, Bruce Bushman; *back*: John Hench, Ethel Kulsar, Nino Carbe. • *The Sorcerer's Apprentice; dir*: James Algar; *story*: Perce Pearce, Carl Fallberg; *anim sup*: Fred Moore, Vladimir Tytla; *anim*: Les Clark, Riley Thomson, Marvin Woodward, Preston Blair, Edward Love, Ugo d'Orsi, George Rowley, Cornett Wood; *lay*: Tom Codrick, Charles Philippi, Zack Schwartz; *back*: Claude Coats, Stan Spohn, Albert Dempster, Eric Hansen. • *Rite of Spring; dir*: Bill Roberts, Paul Satterfield; *story development/research*: William Martin, Leo Thiele, Robert Sterner, John Fraser McLeish; *anim sup*: Wolfgang Reitherman, Joshua Meador; *anim*: Philip Duncan, John McManus, Paul Busch, Art Palmer, Don Tobin, Edwin Aardal, Paul B. Kossoff; *lay*: McLaren Stewart, Dick Kelsey, John Hubley; *back*: Ed Starr, Brice Mack, Edward Levitt; *ph fx*: Gail Papineau, Leonard Pickley. • *Sound-Track; dir*: Samuel Armstrong; *fx*: Joshua Meador, Art Palmer, Harry Hamsel, George Rowley; *lay*: Lee Blair, Elmer Plummer; *mus: flute/bassoon*: Art Smith. • *The Pastoral Symphony; dir*: Hamilton Luske, Jim Handley, Ford Beebe; *story*: Otto Englander, Webb Smith, Erdman Penner, Joseph Sabo, Bill Peed, George Stallings; *anim sup*: Fred Moore, Ward Kimball, Eric Larson, Art Babbitt, Oliver M. Johnston Jr., Don Towsley; *anim*: Berny Wolf, Jack Campbell, Jack Bradbury, James Moore, Milt Neil, Bill Justice, John Elliotte, Walt Kelly, Don Lusk, Lynn Karp, Murray McClellan, Robert W. Youngquist, Harry Hamsel; *character des*: James Bodrero, John P. Miller, Lorna S. Soderstrom; *lay*: Hugh Hennesy, Kenneth Anderson, J. Gordon Legg, Herbert Ryman, Yale Gracey, Lance Nolley; *back*: Claude Coats, Ray Huffine, W. Richard Anthony, Arthur Riley, Gerald Nevius, Roy Forkum. • *Dance of the Hours; dir*: T. Hee, Norm Ferguson. *anim sup*: Norm Ferguson; *anim*: John Lounsbery, Howard Swift, Preston Blair, Hugh Fraser, Harvey Toombs, Norman Tate, Hicks Lokey, Art Elliott, Grant Simmons, Ray Patterson, Franklin Grundeen; *character des*: Martin Provensen, James Bodrero, Duke Russell, Earl Hurd; *lay*: A. Kendall O'Connor, Harold Doughty, Ernest Nordli; *back*: Albert Dempster, Charles Conner. • *Night on Bald Mountain* and *Ave Maria; dir*: Wilfred Jackson; *story*: Campbell Grant, Arthur Heinemann, Phil Dike; *anim sup*: Vladimir Tytla; *anim*: John McManus, William N. Shull, Robert W. Carlson Jr., Lester Novros, Don Patterson, Robert de Grasse; *inbetweener*:

Bob McCrea; *fx:* Joshua Meador, Miles E. Pike, John F. Reed, Daniel Mac-Manus; *lay:* Kay Nielsen, Terrell Stapp, Charles Payzant, Thor Putnam, Bill Wallett; *back:* Merle Cox, Ray Lockrem, Robert Storms, W. Richard Anthony. *Ave Maria chorus dir:* Charles Henderson; *soloist:* Julietta Novis; *chorus:* the Westminster Choir; *ph fx:* Gail Papineau, Leonard Pickley; *col:* Tech. *sd:* Fantasound/RCA. 120 min. • Visual interpretation of the music of Johann Sebastian Bach, Peter Ilich Tchaikovsky, Paul Dukas, Igor Stravinsky, Ludwig van Beethoven, Amilcare Ponchielli, Modest Mussorgsky and Franz Schubert. Originally intended as a short (Mickey Mouse in *The Sorcerer's Apprentice*) but a meeting with conductor Stokowski pursuaded Walt Disney to expand his idea to a feature. Although initially harshly criticized, *Fantasia* is now rightly considered as one of the all-time classics of the animated cinema.

1886. Fantasia 1982; *p.c.:* Walt Disney for BV. *Narrative introductions:* Hugh Douglas; *mus conductor:* Irwin Kostal; *voices:* Leopold Stokowski: Larry Moss; *Mickey Mouse:* Wayne Allwine; "Avé Maria" *soloist:* Victoria Cutler; *col:* Tech. *sd:* Dolby stereo. • Current sophisticated sound systems could not cope with a reissue of the 1940 film, so a completely new soundtrack in digital stereo was created to replace the original. Deems Taylor's introductions were also replaced.

1887. Fantasia 2000 15 Dec. 1999; *p.c.:* Disney Enterprises for BV; *ex prod:* Roy Edward Disney; *prod:* Donald W. Ernst; *conductor:* James Levine; *performed by* The Chicago Symphony Orchestra; *sup anim dir:* Hendel Butoy; *asso prod:* Lisa C. Cook; *artistic sup: artistic co-ord/visual fx:* David A. Bossert; *lay:* Mitchell Guintu Bernal; *back:* Dean Gordon; *clean-up:* Alex Topete; *cgi:* Steve Goldberg, Shyh-Chyuan Huang, Susan Thayer, Mary Jane "M.J." Turner; *prod mgr:* Angelique N. Yen; *co-asso prod:* David Lovegren; *mus prod:* Peter Gelb, Jay David Saks; *ed:* Jessica Ambinder Rojas, Lois Freeman-Fox; "Symphony No.5" composed by Ludwig van Beethoven; *dir/art dir:* Pixote Hunt; *story development:* Kelvin Yasuda; *anim:* Wayne Carlisi, Raul Garcia; "Pines of Rome"composed by Ottorino Respighi; *dir:* Hendel Butoy; *story development:* James Fujii, Francis Glebas; *original concept:* Brenda Chapman, Christopher Sanders; *art dir:* Dean Gordon, William Perkins; *anim:* Linda Bel, Darrin Butts, Darko Cesar, Sasha Dorogov, Serguei Kouchnerov, Andrea Losch, Teresa Martin, Branko Mihanovic, William Recinos, William Wright; *visual development:* Frances Glebas, Kelvin Yasuda; *character des:* Tina Price, Rick Maki; "Rhapsody in Blue" composed by George Gershwin; *conducted by* Bruce Broughton; *piano:* Ralph Grierson; *dir/story:* Eric Goldberg; *art dir:* Susan McKinsey Goldberg; *prod des:* Al Hirschfeld; *co-prod:* Patricia Hicks; *anim:* Tim Allen, James Baker, Jared Beckstrand, Nancy Beiman, Jerry Yu Ching, Andreas Dejá, Robert Espanto Domingo, Brian Ferguson, Douglas Frankel, Thomas Gately, David Hancock, Sang-Jin Kim, Bert Klein, Joe Oh, Jamie Oliff, Mark Pudleiner, Michael Show, Marc Smith, Chad Stewart, Michael Stocker, Andreas Wessel-Therhorn, Theresa Wiseman, Anthony Ho Wong, Ellen Woodbury, Phil Young; *fx anim:* Marlon West, Colbert Fennelly, Michael Cadwallader Jones, Dorse A. Lanpher, Dan Lund, David J. Mildenberger, Mabel Gesner, Joseph Christopher Pepé, Steven Starr, John Tucker, Dennis Spicer; *break:* Nicole A. Zamora, Jay Baker, Melinda Wang; *inbet:* Philip Pignotti; *lay:* Rasoul Azadani; *back:* Natalie Franscioni-Karp; *journeymen:* Gregory C. Miller, Tom Woodington, John Piampiano; *artistic consult:* Dan Hansen, David Blum; *journeymen:* Douglas Walker, Antonio Navarro, Jeffrey Purves; *asst:* Mark Koerner, Patricia Coveney-Rees, Donivan Howard, Kevyn Lee Wallace, Chung Sup Yoon; *blue sketch:* Bill Davis; *visual fx:* Mauro Maressa; *clean-up:* Emily Jiuliano, Vera Lanpher-Pacheco; *anim check:* Barbara Wiles; *2d anim processing:* Robyn L. Roberts; *col models:* Karen Comella; *paint/final check:* Hortensia M. Casagran; *compositing:* James L. Russell; *visual fx:* Steve Moore, Ted C. Kierscey, John Allen Armstrong, Bruce Heller, Jeff Howard, Tom Hush, Gordon Baker, Graham Bebbington, Joan Doyle, James Menehune Goss, Paul Lewis, Brice Mallier, Madoka Yasue, Sari Gennis; *3d fx anim:* Michael Kaschalk, Roberta Kirkpatrick, Tonya Ramsey, Amie Slate; *fx airbrush artist:* John Emerson, David J. Zywicki; *asst anim:* Ty Elliott, Elizabeth Holmes, Ray Hofstedt, Sean Applegate, Geoffrey C. Everts, Angela Anastasia Diamos, Peter Francis Pepe Jr., Kimberly Burk, John Huey, David M. Kcenich, Tom Pope, Lisa A. Reinert, Van Shirvanian; *break:* Virgilio John Aquino, Eduardo Brieño, Steven "Speedo" Filatro, John E. Hailey, Jeffrey Lawrence van Tuyl; *inbet:* Kevin Sirois, Ernesto Brieño, Carl Canga, John Fargnoli III; *asst technical dir:* Pamela J. Choy; *data entry:* Jamal M.

Davis, Gary Stubblefield; *mus ed:* Patricia Carlin; *musician/orchestra contractor:* Ken Watson; *prod mgr:* Loni Beckner-Black, Theresa Bentz, Patricia Faye Feldstein, Lynn Gephart, Christine A. Griego, Fred Herrman, Joyce Ikemiyashiro, Wendy McNeny, Randy Parker, Erin Riordan, Lorry Ann Shea, Bethann Sherwood, Connie Nartonis Thompson, Tone Thyne, Diana Blazer, Holly E. Bratton, Kim Gray, Doeri Welch Greiner, Suzanne Henderson Holmes, Katherine A. Irwin, Monica Lago-Kaytis, Cathy Leahy, Etienne Longa, Brenda McGirl; "Piano Concerto No. 2, Allegro, Opus 102" based on "The Steadfast Tin Soldier" composed by Dimitri Shostakovich; *piano:* Yefim Bronfman; *dir:* Hendel Butoy; *story development:* James Capobianco, Roy Meurin; *art dir:* Michael Humphries; *anim:* Tim Allen, Doug Bennett, Eamonn Butler, Darrin Butts, Sandro Cleuzo, Steve Hunter, Ron Husband, Mark Kausler, Sang-Jin Kim, David Kuhn, Roy Meurin, Gregory G. Miller, Neil Richmond, Jason Ryan, Henry Sato Jr.; *visual development:* Hans Bacher, Guy Deel, Caroline Hu; *character des:* Sergei Koushnerov, Gary J. Perkovac, Nik Ranieri; *choreog:* Kendra McCool; "Carnival of the Animals (le Carnaval des Animaux), Finale" composed by Camille Saint-Saëns; *dir/anim/story:* Eric Goldberg; *art dir:* Susan McKinsey Goldberg; *original concept:* Joe Grant; *conceptual storyboard:* Vance Gerry, David Cutler; *water colorists:* Jill A. Petrilak, Emily Juliano, Fara Rose, Mary Jo Ayers, Christina Stocks, Jennifer Phillips; *CAPS sup: scene plan:* Annamarie Costa; *anim check:* Karen Somerville, Janet Bruce; *2d anim processing:* Gareth P. Fishbaugh; *col models:* Ann Marie Sorensen; *paint/check:* Carmen Regina Alvarez; *compositing:* Shannon M. Fallis-Kane; *digital film print:* Christopher W. Gee; *technical co-ord:* Ann Tucker; "The Sorcerer's Apprentice" composed by Paul Dukas; *dir:* James Algar; *story development:* Joe Grant, Dick Huemer; *art dir:* Tom Codrick, Charles Philippi, Zack Schwartz; *story development:* Perce Pearce, Carl Fallberg; *anim sup:* Fred Moore, Vladimir Tytla; *anim:* Les Clark, Riley Thomson, Marvin Woodward, Preston Blair, Edward Love, Ugo D'Orsi, George Rowley, Cornett Wood; *back:* Claude Coats, Stan Spohn, Albert Dempster, Eric Hansen; *symphonic transcriptions:* Leopold Stokowski; *mus ed:* Edward H. Plumb; *mus ed:* Stephen Csillag; *rec:* William E. Garity, C.O. Slyfield, J.N.A. Hawkins; *prod sup:* Ben Sharpsteen; "Pomp and Circumstance—Marches 1, 2, 3 and 4" composed by Sir Edward Elgar; *dir:* Francis Glebas; *story development:* Robert Gibbs, Todd Kurosawa, Don Dougherty, Terry Naughton, Patrick Ventura, Stevie Wermers; *art dir:* Daniel Cooper; *lead character anim (Donald & Daisy):* Tim Allen; *anim:* Doug Bennett, Tim George, Mark Kausler, Sang-Jin Kim, Roy Meurin, Gregory G. Miller; *visual development:* William Frake III, Darek Gogol; *character des:* Jeffrey R. Ranjo, Peter Clarke; *choral performance:* The Chicago Symphony Chorus; *soprano:* Kathleen Battle; *mus arranger:* Peter Schickele; *mus rec:* Shawn Murphy, Joseph Magee; *mus prod:* Tod Cooper, Andrew Page, Tom MacDougall, Deniece La Rocca; *mus ed:* Kenneth Hahn, Kathleen Bennett, Mark Green, Earl Ghaffari; *track reader:* Kent Holaday; "Firebird Suite—1919 version" composed by Igor Stravinsky; *dir/des/story:* Gaëtan Brizzi, Paul Brizzi; *art dir:* Carl Jones; *lead character anim (Sprite):* Anthony DeRosa; *lead character anim (Elk):* Ron Husband; *lead character anim (Firebird):* John Pomeroy; *anim:* Tim Allen, Sandro Cleuzo, David Hancock, Sang-Jin Kim, Gregory G. Miller, Joe Oh, David Zaboski; *anim asst:* Mike Disa, Chadd Ferron, Chris Hurtt, Clay Kaytis, Peter Lepeniotis, Mark Alan Mitchell, Oliver Thomas, Alex Tysowsky; *rough inbet:* Casey Coffey, Wendie Lynn Fischer, Neal Stanley Goldstein, Benjamin Gonzalez, Grant Hiestand, Joseph Mateo, Bob Persichetti, Kevin M. Smith, Wes Sullivan, Larry R. Flores, Christopher Hubbard, George A. Benavides, Chris Sonnenburg, Aliki Theofilopoulos, Edmund Gabriel; *back:* Barry Atkinson, Allison Belliveau-Proulx, Mannix Bennett, Miguel Gil, Carl Jones, Michael Kurinsky, Dan Read, Maryann Thomas, Christophe Vacher, Daniel Cooper, Kelvin Yasuda; *visual development:* Kelvin Yasuda; *"Host Sequences":* *dir:* Don Hahn; *written by* Don Hahn, Irene Mecchi, David Reynolds; *story development:* Kirk Hanson; *des:* Pixote Hunt; *anim (Mickey):* Andreas Dejá; *journeymen: lay:* Mac George, Kevin Nelson, Jeff Beazley, James Beihold, Allen C. Tam, Kevin R. Adams, Billy George, Scott Caple, Karen A. Keller, Daniel Hu; *asst:* Gang Pang, Michael Bond O'Mara, Yong-Hong Zhong, Shawn Colbeck, David Krentz, Michael Tracy, Cynthia Ignacio, Scott Uehara, Michael Bagley; *blue sketch:* Madlyn Zusmer O'Neill, Cyndee LaRae Novitch, Noel C. Johnson, Monica Albracht Marroquin; *visual fx sup:* Richard Hollander; *digital sup:* Eric Hansen; *casting:* Ruth Lambert, Mary Hidalgo; *Hosts:* James Earl Jones, Quincy Jones, Angela Lansbury, James Levine, Steve Martin, Bette Midler, Penn & Teller, Itzhak Perlman;

cgi: digital prod mgrs: Toni Pace Carstensen, Jinko Gotoh, Doug Nichols; *lighting:* Michelle Lee Robinson, Yuriko Senoo; *technical dir:* Robert Rosenblum, L. Cliff Brett, Umakanth Thumrugoti, Tal Lancaster, Peter Palombi, Neil Eskuri, Mark Hall, Jason Herschaft, Craig L. Hoffman, Jim Houston, Darren Kiner, Christine C. Lau, Stanley Lippman, Andrea Losch, Mira Nikolic, Chiara Perin-Colajacomo, Tina Price, Ruth Ramos, Francine "Freddi" Rokaw, Sergi Sagas-Rica, Kevin Sheedy, Michael Takayama, Timothy Tompkins, James Tooley, Carolyn Wiegley, Darlene E. Hadrika, Heather Pritchett, Mary Ann Pigora; *modelers:* Kevin Geiger, Paul Giacoppo, David Mullins, Brian Wesley Green; *scene set-up:* Leland J. Hepler, Tina Lee; *render I/0 admin:* James C. Bette; *clean-up anim:* Merry Kanawyer Clingen, Steve Lubin, Vincent Siracusano, Trevor Tamboline, Susan Adnopoz, Scott Anderson, Tony Anselmo, Debbie Armstrong, Kathleen M. Bailey, Bill Berg, Philippe Briones, Serge Bussone, Christophe Charbonnel, Farouk Cherfi, Inna Chon, Marcia Kimura Dougherty, Lee Dunkman, Javier Espinosa, Sean Gallimore, Akemi Gutierrez, Ed Gutierrez, Carl Philip Hall, Karen Hardenbergh, Mike Hazy, Allison Hollen, Renee Holt, Myung Kang, Yung Soo Kim, Nancy E. Kniep, Calvin Le Duc, Leticia Lichtwardt, Kaaren Lundeen, Mike McKinney, Lieve Miessen, Wendy Muir, Terry Naughton, Ginny Parmele, Eric Pigors, Dana Reemes, Richard D. Rocha, Jacqueline Sanchez, Natasha Dukelski Selfridge, Dan Tanaka, Peggy Tonkonogy, Elizabeth Watasin, Eunice (Eun Ok) Yu, Stephan Zupkas; *asst anim:* Todd H. Ammons, Daniel Bowman, Michael Lester, Donnie Long, Mary-Jean Repchuk, Wm. John Thinnes, Mary Jo Ayers, Laurence Adam-Bessière, Dan Bond, Claire Bourdin, Jeroen Dejonckheere, Teresa Eidenbock, Brigitte Franzka-Fritz, Cynthia French, Pierre Girault, Kevin M. Grow, Angela Iturriza, Janet Heerhan Kwon, Christine Landes-Tigano, Ludovic Letrun, Kellie Lewis, Daniel Lim, Brian Mainolfi, Gizella Maros, Benoit Meurzec, Bernadette Moley, Annette Moral, Yoon Sook Nam, Jan Naylor, Christine Chatal Poli, Pierre Seurin, Bryan M. Sommer, Phirum Sou, Susan Sugita, George Sukara, Sylvaine Terriou, Marc Tosolini, Xavier Villez, Jung Chan Woo; *break:* Patricia Ann Billings, Ron Cohee, Regina Conroy, Arturo Alejandro Herández, Sam Levine, Gary Myers, Al Salgado, Michael W. Wiesmeier, Chang Yei Cho, Nicole de Bellefroid, Frank Dietz, Nikolas M. Frangos, Dietz Toshio Ichishita, Steve Lenze, Ely Lester, Philippe Malka, Jim Snider, Chun Yin Joey So, Hugo Soriano, Steven K. Thompson, Kathleen Thorson, Justin "Dusty" Wakefield, Ronald Westlund; *inbet:* Cyndy Bohonovsky, Mike Greenholt, Phil Langone, Tao Nguyen, Robb Pratt, John Webber, Raul Aguirre Jr., Bernard Dourdent, Steven Pierre Gordon, Matthew Haber, James A. Marquez, Kim Moriki, Flora Sung Sook Park, Eddie Pittman; *mus consultant:* Chris Montan; *mus arrangements:* Bruce Coughlin; *prod mgr-CAPS:* Gretchen Maschmeyer Albrecht; *scene plan/ph:* Joe Jiuliano; *anim disk space/retakes:* Shawne Zarubica; *pro co-ord:* Jennifer Booth, Kirsten A. Bulmer, Camille Cavalin-Fay, Stephanie L. Clifford, Wish Foley-Cohen, Jeanne Leone-Sterwerf, Jeffrey Moznett, Victoria Jeela Stevenson; *scene plan:* Scott McCarter, Thomas Baker, S.J. Bleick, John R. Cunningham, Cynthia Goode, Mark Henley, Ronald J. Jackson, Mary Lescher; *data entry:* April Brennan, Donna Weir, Michael Wells, Laura L. Jaime, Sherri H. Villarete; *anim check:* Nicolette Bonnell, Kathleen O'Mara-Svetlik, Karen S. Paat, Mavis Shafer, Denise M. Mitchell, Gary Shafer, Janette Hulett, Helen O'Flynn, Jan Adams; *2d anim processing: digital mark-up:* Corey Dean Fredrickson, Lynnette E. Cullen, Gina Wootten; *2d anim processors:* David Braden, Jo Ann Breuer, Val D'Arcy, Kent Gordon, Michael Alan McFerren, Richard J. McFerren, Robert Lizardo, Stacie K. Reece, David J. Rowe; *asstant sup—"Rhapsody in Blue":* Karen N. China; *col models: col stylists:* Heidi Lin Loring, Fergus J. Hernandez, Maria Gonzalez; *painting: asst sup/paint mark-up:* Vernette Griffee; *asst sup "Rhapsody in Blue":* Irma Velez, Russell Blandino, Phyllis Estelle Fields; *col model mark-up:* Cindy Finn, Christine Ng Wong, Grace H. Shirado, Debra Y. Siegel, Sherrie Cuzzort, Beth Ann McCoy-Gee, Bill Andres; *registration:* Karan Lee-Storr, Leyla C. Amaro-Pelaez; *paint mark-up:* Roberta Lee Borchardt, Myrian Ferron Tello, Bonnie A. Ramsey, Barbara Newby, Patricia L. Gold, Cathy Walters; *painters:* Patrick Sekino, Casey Clayton, Michael Foley, Debbie Green, Phyllis Bird, Joey Calderon, Ofra Afuta Calderon, Sybil Elaine Cuzzort, Florida D'Ambrosio, Robert Edward Dettloff, Stevie Hirsch, Angelika R. Katz, Karen Lynne Nugent, Bruce Gordon Phillipson, Carmen Sanderson, Fumiko Roche Sommer, S. Ann Sullivan, Roxanne M. Taylor, Tami Terusa, Britt-Marie Van der Nagel, Paulino Garcia, Heidi Shellhorn, David Karp, Joyce Davidson Alexander, Deborah Mooneyam

Hughes; *final check:* Saskia Raevouri, Misoon Kim, Sally-Anne King; *compositing:* Timothy B. Gales, Dolores Pope, Michelle A.Sammartino; *digital film services:* Joseph Pfening; *digital film printing & opticals: ph:* William Aylsworth, Bill Fadness, Michael F. Lehman, Stanley E. Miller, Brandy Hill, John Derderian, Johnny D. Aardal, David J. Link, Jennie Kepenek Mouzis, Tony Poriazis, Bruce Tauscher, Chuck Warren, Christine Beck; *ed:* Ellen Keneshea, John Carnochan, Curtis Freilich, Greg Plotts, Craig Paulsen, Julia Gray, James D. Kirkpatrick, Lisa Davis, Carol Folgate; *prod support:* Derek M.C. Billings, Mike Brassell, Brett Drogmund, Andy Lee Johnson, Kevin Larkin, Nanette Leiva, Michael J. Miller, Michelle Orr, Sylvia Sanchez, Melissa K. Schilder, Nancy Smith, Tara Joan Brown, Rodolfo Cárdenas-Ríos, Philip M. Cohen, Renato Lattanzi, Allyson Mitchell, Tina M. Pedigo, Jason I. Strahs, Julie Vieillemaringe, Sabrina Waterman; *asst:* Andrea A. Lamm, Barbara Wilcox, Rhiannon J. Pollock, Susan M. Coffer, Lia Abbate, Rikki Chobanian, Patti Conklin, Chris Hecox, Shari K. Judson, Kathleen Mix, Pauli Moss, Erik K. Smith, Pamela J. Wilson, Suzy Zeffren; *technology:* Graham S. Allen, Richard M. Barnes, Michael S. Blum, Michael C. Bolds, Brad Brooks, Letha L. Burchard, Mark Roy Carlson, Loren Chun, Lawrence Chai, Peter L. Chun, Ben Croy, Elena Driskill, Norbert Faerstain, Robert Falco, Scott Garrett, Mark W. Gilicinski, John D. Hoffman, Kevin John Hussey, Le Hua, Bill James, Michael Jedlicka, Maria Gomez de Lizardo, Mark Jankins, Kevin E. Keech, Mark R. Kimball, Li-Ming Lawrence Lee, Brad Lowman, MaryAnn McLeod, Thomas Moore Jr., Robert A. Mortensen, Jack Muleady, Troy R. Norin, Alan A. Patel, Carlos Quinonez, Todd Scopio, James J. Sepe, Jeffrey L. Sickler, John Stimson, Charles Stoner, Joe Suzow, Scott S. Turek, Laurie Tracy, Mark M. Tokunaga, Derek Elliot Wilson; *l/al visual fx:* Rhythm & Hues; *ex prod:* Lee Berger; *visual fx prod:* Joyce Weisiger; *line prod:* Gary Nolin; *ph:* Tim Suhrstedt; *asst dir:* Bill Hoyt, Steve Fernandez; *chief technologist:* Mark A. Brown; *physical technology dir:* Paul Johnson; *lighting:* George Ball; *digital sup:* Mark Rodahl; *VFX prod mgr:* Daphne Dentz; *VFX prod co-ords:* Carey Smith, Carla Donah; *digital prod mgr:* Gene Kozicki; *tracking sup:* Joel Merritt; *3d artists:* Art Jeppe, Mike Roby, Matt Hausman, Geoff Harvey, Raymond Liu, Mike La Fave, Stu Mintz, Chris Romano, Tsz "Gee" Yeung; *art dir:* Alison Yerxa; *2d sup:* Uel Hormann; *technical support:* Douglas Harshch, Robert Mercier, Fred Simon; *2d artists:* Kenneth Au, Lisa Pollaro, Garret Lam; *anim:* Kevin Bertazzon, Thomas Rosenfeldt, Todd Wilbur; *matte painting:* Marta Recio; *tracking:* Andy Gauvreau, David Santiago, David Gutman; *addit ph:* James Weisiger; *post prod sup:* Patsy L. Bougé; *co-ord:* Lori Korngiebel; *video co-ord:* Robert Bagley; *admin:* Heather Jane Smith; *sd:* Gregory King, Terry Porter, Shawn Murphy, Mel Metcalfe, Yann Delpuech; *sd ed:* Meg Taylor; *dial/ADR sup:* Darren King; *foley:* Warner Hollywood Studios, John Roesch, Hilda Hodges; *post prod engineer:* Michael Kenji Tomizawa; *b&w processing:* John White; *col timer:* Dale Grahn; *neg cutter:* Mary Beth Smith, Rick MacKay; *title des:* Brian King; *projection:* Brian Henry, Don Henry, Ken Moore, Deem Rahall; *music restoration: Sony Music Studios, New York: prod:* Louise de la Fuente; *ex prod:* Laura Mitgang; *mix engineer:* Rob Rapley, Jen Wyler; *restoration engineer:* Darcy Proper; *audio consult:* David Smith; *Richard Purdom Prods:* Dick Purdom, Jill Thomas; *additional artists: story:* Oliver Thomas, Joe Ranft, Tom Sito; *concept for "Death and Re-Birth of the Forest":* Elena Driskill; *anim:* Tony Anselmo, Ruben A. Aquino, Roberto Casale, Alain Costa, Dave Kupczyk, Wm. John Thinnes; *lay:* Marek Buchwald, Ray Chen; *visual development:* Jean Gillmore, Fara Rose, Sherri Vandoli, Tanya T. Wilson, Bruce Zick; *character sculptures:* Bruce Lau; *back:* Sunny Apinchapong, John Watkiss; *visual fx:* Kristine Brown, Kristin Fong-Lukavsky, Joey Mildenberger, Ron Pence, Phil Vigil, Daniel E. Wanket; *cgi:* Roger L. Gould, Thomas C. Meyer, Nathan Warner, Tod Worden; *clean-up:* Jamie Kezlarian Bolio, Wes Chun, Diana Coco, Gail Frank, Cliff Freitas, Jill Friemark, Kris Heller, Celinda S. Kennedy, Marty Korth, Cynthia Landeros, Susan Lantz, Miriam McDonnell, Brian B. McKim, Mary Measures, Lori Benson-Noda, Marsha Park, Doug Post, Bobby Rubio, Marty Schwartz; *addit mus:* "Destino" written by Armando Dominguez; *col:* Tech. *sd:* Dolby Digital. 71 min. *anim/l/a.* • (1) An abstract interpretation of Beethoven's "Symphony No.5." (2) Steve Martin and Itzhak Perlman introduce "Pines of Rome," involving a family of whales. (3) Quincy Jones offers an interpretation of George Gershwin's "Rhapsody in Blue." Featuring a day in the lives of a New York construction worker, an unemployed man, a henpecked husband and a little girl ... all dissatisfied with their lot in life. (4) Bette Midler presents "The Steadfast Tin Soldier,"

Hans Christian Anderson's story about a one-legged toy soldier who is in love with a little toy ballerina. (5) "Carnival of the Animals": James Earl Jones discusses with animator Eric Goldberg the possibilities of what might happen if you presented a yo-yo to a flamingo. (6) Magicians, Penn (Jillette) and Teller retell the story of Mickey Mouse as "The Sorcerer's Apprentice." (7) James Levine introduces "Pomp and Circumstance," which tells the story of Donald Duck stocking the Ark with animals for Noah. In his rush to get all the creatures aboard, his loses Daisy, his own partner. (8) Angela Lansbury helps recount the story of "The Firebird," concerning the coming of Spring being prevented by the eruption of a volcano which kills off all plant life. Spring soon retaliates by regenerating all trees and flowers.

1888. Fare Play *(Scrappy)* 2 July 1932; *p.c.:* Winkler for Colum; *prod:* Charles Mintz; *story:* Dick Huemor; *anim:* Sid Marcus, Art Davis; *mus:* Joe de Nat; *prod mgr:* James Bronis; b&w. *sd:* RCA. 5 min. • No story available.

1889. Farm Foolery *(Aesop's Sound Fable)* 14 Sept. 1930; *p.c.:* Van Beuren for Pathé; *dir:* John Foster; *mus:* Gene Rodemich; b&w. *sd:* RCA. 7 min. • The farmyard animals improvise music and hold a barn dance to the music of "Ain't She Sweet."

1890. Farm Foolery *(Screen Song)* 5 Aug. 1949; *p.c.:* Famous for Para; *dir:* Seymour Kneitel; *story:* Larz Bourne; *anim:* Al Eugster, Bill Hudson; *sets:* Tom Ford; *voices:* Jackson Beck, Jack Mercer; *mus:* Winston Sharples; *song:* Nora Bayes, Jack Norworth; *ph:* Leonard McCormick; *prod sup:* Sam Buchwald; *col:* Tech. *sd:* RCA. 8 min. • The farm animals all do their turn at harvest time, then sing "Shine On Harvest Moon."

1891. Farm Frolics *(Merrie Melodies)* 10 May 1941; *p.c.:* Leon Schlesinger prods for WB; *dir:* Robert Clampett; *anim:* Rod Scribner; *lay:* Thomas McKimson; *back:* Michael Sasanoff; *ed:* Treg Brown; *voices:* Robert C. Bruce, Mel Blanc, Sara Berner, Cliff Nazarro; *mus:* Carl W. Stalling; *prod sup:* Henry Binder, Raymond G. Katz; *col:* Tech. *sd:* Vit. 7 min. • A tour of the farmyard and its animals.

1892. The Farm Hand *(Hot Dog)* 27 May 1927; *p.c.:* Bray prods; *dir:* Walt Lantz, Clyde Geronimi; b&w. *sil. l/a/anim.* • Walt finds employment at a farm and makes Pete do all the work.

1893. Farm Hands *(Aesop's Film Fable)* 2 May 1926; *p.c.:* Fables Pictures Inc for Pathé; *dir:* Paul Terry; b&w. *sil.* 5 min. • Farmer Al, Ignatz Mouse and the gang help on the farm with the mule in tow.

1894. The Farm of Tomorrow 18 Sept. 1954; *p.c.:* MGM; *dir:* Tex Avery; *story:* Heck Allen; *anim:* Walter Clinton, Grant Simmons, Michael Lah, Robert Bentley; *back:* Joe Montell; *ed:* Jim Faris; *voices:* Paul Frees, June Foray; *mus:* Scott Bradley; *ph:* Jack Stevens; *prod:* Fred Quimby; *col:* Tech. *sd:* WE. 7 min. • An insight into tomorrow's farming, featuring many animal-crossing gags, etc.

1895. Farm Relief *(Krazy Kat)* 30 Dec. 1929; *p.c.:* Winkler for Colum; *prod:* Charles Mintz; *anim:* Ben Harrison, Manny Gould; *mus:* Joe de Nat; b&w. *sd:* WE. 6 min. • A mysterious character appears in the farmyard and gets the animals drunk on illegal hooch.

1896. The Farmer *(Oswald)* 23 Feb. 1931; *p.c.:* Univ; *dir:* Walter Lantz, "Bill" Nolan; *anim:* Clyde Geronimi, Manuel Moreno, Ray Abrams, Fred Avery, Lester Kline, "Pinto" Colvig; *voice:* Mickey Rooney; *mus:* James Dietrich; b&w. *sd:* WE. 6 min. • Oswald and Putrid Pete vie for the attentions of a pretty dairy maid at the local barn dance.

1897. Farmer Al Falfa and the Runt *(Terry-Toon)* 15 May 1936; *p.c.:* TT for Educational/Fox; *dir:* George Gordon, Mannie Davis; *mus:* Philip A. Scheib; b&w. *sd:* WE. 6 min. • The Littlest pig saves his family from the butcher.

1898. Farmer Al Falfa in Bedtime Story *(Paul Terry-Toon)* 12 June 1932; *p.c.:* Moser & Terry for Educational/Fox; *dir:* Frank Moser, Paul Terry; *mus:* Philip A. Scheib; b&w. *sd:* WE. 6 min. • As the Farmer retires to his bed, the mice stage a party in the cellar.

1899. Farmer Al Falfa in Flying South *(Terry-Toon)* 19 Mar. 1937; *p.c.:* TT for Educational/Fox; *dir:* George Gordon, Mannie Davis; *mus:* Philip A. Scheib; b&w. *sd:* WE. 6 min. • Farmer Al vents his wrath over the ducks flying through his farm who turn the tables on him.

1900. Farmer Al Falfa in the Big Game Hunt *(Terry-Toon)* 19 Feb. 1937; *p.c.:* TT for Educational/Fox; *dir:* George Gordon, Mannie

Davis; *mus:* Philip A. Scheib; b&w. *sd:* WE. 6 min. • Farmer Al goes on safari riding on an elephant. After escaping the cannibal cooking pot he is chased by a lion.

1901. Farmer Al Falfa in the Health Farm *(Terry-Toon)* 4 Sept. 1936; *p.c.:* TT for Educational/Fox; *dir:* George Gordon, Mannie Davis; *mus:* Philip A. Scheib; b&w. *sd:* WE. 6 min. • A burglar poses as a patient in the health farm and the Farmer gets a $1000 reward for capturing him.

1902. Farmer Al Falfa in the Hot Spell *(Terry-Toon)* 10 July 1936; *p.c.:* TT for Educational/Fox; *dir:* George Gordon, Mannie Davis; *mus:* Philip A. Scheib; b&w. *sd:* WE. 6 min. • During a drought, the Farmer tries his hand at "Rain Making," which irks Jupiter Pluvius.

1903. Farmer Al Falfa in the Tin Can Tourist *(Terry-Toon)* 22 Jan. 1937; *p.c.:* TT for Educational/Fox; *dir:* George Gordon, Mannie Davis; *mus:* Philip A. Scheib; b&w. *sd:* WE. 6 min. • Comic gadgets are displayed for the caravan traveller who is chased away by bees.

1904. Farmer Al Falfa's Ape Girl *(Paul Terry-Toon)* 7 Aug. 1932; *p.c.:* Moser & Terry for Educational/Fox; *dir:* Frank Moser, Paul Terry; *mus:* Philip A. Scheib; b&w. *sd:* WE. 6 min. • Al Falfa is captured by a jungle girl and they raise a family together.

1905. Farmer Al Falfa's Birthday Party *(Paul Terry-Toon)* 2 Oct. 1932; *p.c.:* Moser & Terry for Educational/Fox; *dir:* Frank Moser, Paul Terry; *mus:* Philip A. Scheib; b&w. *sd:* WE. 6 min. • The undaunted Farmer invites his animal friends to his party but things don't go as smoothly as anticipated when the animals bake an explosive birthday cake.

1906. Farmer Al Falfa's Pet Cat *(Aesop's Film Fable)* 9 Nov. 1923; *p.c.:* Fables Pictures Inc for Pathé; *dir:* Paul Terry; b&w. *sil.* 5 min. • While the cat is on his honeymoon, the mice run rampant. The two cats return and the rodents beat a hasty retreat.

1907. Farmer Al Falfa's Prize Package *(Terry-Toon)* 31 July 1936; *p.c.:* TT for Educational/Fox; *dir:* George Gordon, Mannie Davis; *mus:* Philip A. Scheib; b&w. *sd:* WE. 6 min. • Al Falfa receives a present of Kiko the Kangaroo. When the cops try to arrest the farmer, Kiko steps in and saves the day.

1908. Farmer Al Falfa's 20th Anniversary *(Terry-Toon)* 27 Nov. 1936; *p.c.:* TT for Educational/Fox; *dir:* George Gordon, Mannie Davis; *mus:* Philip A. Scheib; b&w. *sd:* WE. 6 min. • A skunk breaks up the animals' surprise anniversary party for the Farmer.

1909. Farmer Al Falfa's Wayward Pup 21 July 1917; *p.c.:* Conquest Pictures for Thomas A. Edison; *dir:* Paul Terry; b&w. *sil.* 4 min. *s/r.* • The pup chases a duck, then the Farmer and finally gets into a scrap with a prize cockerel.

1910. The Farmer and His Cat *(Aesop's Film Fable)* 17 May 1922; *p.c.:* Fables Pictures Inc for Pathé; *dir:* Paul Terry; b&w. *sil.* 5 min. • The Farmer has an awful time trying to rid himself of an undesirable cat.

1911. The Farmer and the Belle *(Popeye)* 1 Dec. 1950; *p.c.:* Famous for Para; *dir:* Seymour Kneitel; *story:* Joe Stultz; *anim:* Tom Johnson, Frank Endres; *sets:* Robert Little; *voices:* Jack Mercer, Jackson Beck, Mae Questel; *mus:* Winston Sharples; *ph:* Leonard McCormick; *prod mgr:* Sam Buchwald; *col:* Tech. *sd:* RCA. 7 min. • Popeye and Bluto vie for a job on Olive's farm.

1912. The Farmer and the Ostrich *(Aesop's Film Fable)* 26 Jan. 1922; *p.c.:* Fables Pictures Inc for Pathé; *dir:* Paul Terry; b&w. *sil.* 5 min. • Al Falfa brings Leary Ostrich into his home and the creature takes over, not only eating all in sight but also the farmer's home brew as well as the whole still. Moral: "Hospitality is a virtue which should be exercised wisely."

1913. Farmer Tom Thumb *(Fable)* 27 Sept. 1940; *p.c.:* Colum; *story:* Allen Rose; *anim:* Harry Love, Louie Lilly; *ed:* George Winkler; *voices:* Brooke Temple, Mel Blanc, Sara Berner; *mus:* Joe de Nat; *ph:* Otto Reimer; *prod mgr:* James Bronis; b&w. *sd:* RCA. 6 min. • Little Tom helps his father's ailing farm by feeding the plants with vitamins.

1914. Farmerette *(Aesop's Fable)* 28 June 1932; *p.c.:* Van Beuren for RKO; *dir:* John Foster, George Rufle; *voice:* Marjorie Hines; *mus:* Gene Rodemich; b&w. *sd:* RCA. 6 min. • No story available.

1915. The Farmer's Goat *(Aesop's Film Fable)* 29 June 1929; *p.c.:* Fables Pictures Inc for Pathé; *dir:* Paul Terry, John Foster; b&w. *sil.* 5 min. • Farmer Al tries to build a brick house but the goat keeps interfering. When he takes a rest, the cats dump a pile of sand on him, annoying him so much that he awakens the goat, who butts the luckless Farmer into the sand truck.

1916. Farming Fools *(Oswald)* 25 May 1936; *p.c.:* Univ; *dir:* Walter Lantz; *story:* Walter Lantz, Victor McLeod; *anim:* Manuel Moreno, Lester Kline; *mus:* James Dietrich; b&w. *sd:* RCA. 6 min. • Three monkeys wreck Oswald's farm.

1917. Farmyard Fables *(Oswald)* 1928; *p.c.:* Winkler for Univ; *anim:* Walter Lantz. b&w. *sil.* 6 min. • No story available.

1918. Farmyard Follies *(Oswald)* 14 Nov. 1928; *p.c.:* Winkler for Univ; *dir:* Walt Lantz, R.C. Hamilton. b&w. *sil.* 6 min. • Oswald's farm chores are hampered by a sassy chicken.

1919. The Farmyard Symphony *(Silly Symphony)* 14 Oct. 1938; *p.c.:* Walt Disney prods for RKO; *dir:* Jack Cutting; *assist dir:* Ray deValley; *anim:* John Bradbury, Paul Busch, Bernard Garbutt, Ken Hultgren, Milton Kahl, Lynn Karp, Eric Larson, Don Lusk, Fred Madison, Paul Satterfield, John Sewall; *lay:* David Hilberman; *voices:* Billy Bletcher, Melvin J. Gibby, Beatrice Hagen, Dorothy Lloyd, Lee Millar, Victor Rodman, Lee Sweetland, Max Turhune; *mus:* Leigh Harline; *col:* Tech. *sd:* RCA. 8 min. • Operatic farmyard animals prevent a piglet from getting his breakfast.

1920. The Fashionable Fox *(Aesop's Film Fable)* 11 Sept. 1921; *p.c.:* Fables Pictures Inc for Pathé; *dir:* Paul Terry; b&w. *sil.* 5 min. • No story available.

1921. Fast and Furry-ous *(Looney Tunes)* 16 Sept. 1949; *p.c.:* WB; *dir:* Charles M. Jones; *story:* Michael Maltese; *anim:* Ken Harris, Phil Monroe, Ben Washam, Lloyd Vaughan; *fx:* A.C. Gamer; *lay:* Robert Gribbroek; *back:* Peter Alvarado; *ed:* Treg Brown; *voice:* Paul Julian; *mus:* Carl Stalling; *prod mgr:* John W. Burton; *prod:* Edward Selzer; *col:* Tech. *sd:* Vit. 7 min. • This initial Road-Runner cartoon has the Coyote trying to snare the evasive bird using many apparatus, finally resorting to Acme Jet-Propelled Tennis Shoes in an attempt to run as fast as the speed demon himself.

1922. Fast Buck Duck *(Merrie Melodies)* Mar. 1963; *p.c.:* WB; *dir:* Robert McKimson, Ted Bonnicksen; *story:* John Dunn; *anim:* Keith Darling, Ted Bonnicksen, Warren Batchelder, George Grandpré; *sets:* Robert Gribbroek; *ed:* Treg Brown; *voices:* Mel Blanc; *mus:* Bill Lava; *prod mgr:* Bill Orcutt; *prod:* David H. DePatie; *col:* Tech. *sd:* Vit. 7 min. • Daffy answers an ad for a personal companion to a millionaire. He has many attempts to get into the grounds but is stopped each time by a persistant guard dog.

1923. A Fast Worker *(Aesop's Film Fable)* 16 May 1925; *p.c.:* Fables Pictures Inc for Pathé; *dir:* Paul Terry; b&w. *sil.* 5 min. • A cat burglar meets a dog cop and changes himself into a shapely canine charmer. The master of disguise later assumes the lines of an auto and, when nabbed robbing a bank, turns himself into bologna.

1924. The Fastest Tongue in the West *(Tijuana Toads)* 20 June 1971; *p.c.:* Mirisch/DFE for UA; *dir:* Gerry Chiniquy; *story:* Larz Bourne; *anim:* Don Williams, Manny Gould, Manny Perez, Robert Taylor, Warren Batchelder; *lay:* Robert Givens; *back:* Richard H. Thomas; *ed:* Lee Gunther; *voices:* Don Diamond, Tom Holland, Larry D. Mann; *mus:* Doug Goodwin; *ph:* John Burton Jr.; *prod sup:* Jim Foss, Harry Love; *col:* DeLuxe. *sd:* RCA. 5 min. • Pancho boasts to be "The Fastest Tongue in the West" until he meets his match in a bandit frog named The Cactus Kid.

1925. Fastest with the Mostest *(Looney Tunes)* 9 Jan. 1960; *p.c.:* WB; *dir:* Chuck Jones; *anim:* Ken Harris, Richard Thompson, Ben Washam, Keith Darling; *sets:* Philip de Guard; *ed:* Treg Brown; *voices:* Paul Julian, Mel Blanc; *mus:* Milt Franklyn; *prod mgr:* William Orcutt; *prod:* David H. DePatie; *col:* Tech. *sd:* Vit. 7 min. • The Coyote is seen trying to drop a bomb on his prey from a hot-air balloon. His final indignity comes from being swept over a waterfall through a number of water outlets.

1926. The Fat Boy 1970; *p.c.:* Murakami-Wolf prods; *dir/anim:* Fred Wolf; *col. sd.* • No story available.

1927. Fat in the Saddle *(Woody Woodpecker)* Feb. 1968; *p.c.:* Walter Lantz prods for Univ; *dir:* Paul J. Smith; *story:* Cal Howard; *anim:* Al Coe, Les Kline; *sets:* Ray Huffine. *voices:* Dal McKennon, Grace Stafford; *mus:* Walter Greene; *prod mgr:* William E. Garity; *col:* Tech. *sd:* RCA. 6 min. • Pony Express rider Woody is hampered by an Indian while delivering a post card.

1928. Fatal Foostseps *(Whirlwind Comedy)* 1926; *p.c.:* FBO; *dir/l/a:* Charles R. Bowers; *story:* Charles R. Bowers, H.L. Muller, Ted Sears; *ph:* H.L. Muller; b&w. *sil.* 22½ min. *la/anim.* • Charley enters a dancing contest with mechanical dancing shoes. Live-action with model animation.

1929. The Fatal Kiss *(Daffy Ditty)* 28 Aug. 1947; *p.c.:* Plastic prods for UA; *prod:* Larry Morey, John Sutherland; *dir:* George Gordon; *anim:* Pete Burness, Irven Spence; *prod mgr:* Tim Barr; *col:* Tech. *sd.* 7 min. • An innocent girl is thrown out of her home after being kissed by a cad. He feels remorse and rescues her as she is about to throw herself from the Eiffel Tower. They marry!

1930. The Fatal Note *(Little King)* 29 Sept. 1933; *p.c.:* Van Beuren for RKO; *dir:* George Stallings; *anim:* Jim Tyer; *mus:* Gene Rodemich; b&w. *sd:* RCA. 6 min. • An anarchist affixes a bomb to the King's piano, arranging it to explode upon playing a certain note.

1931. The Fatal Pie *(Rube Goldberg cartoon)* 5 June 1916; *p.c.:* Barré Studio for Pathé; *prod:* Raoul Barré; *anim:* George Stallings, Raoul Barré, William C. Nolan, Gregory La Cava; b&w. *sil.* 5 min. • No story available.

1932. Father Noah's Ark *(Silly Symphony)* 8 Apr. 1933; *p.c.:* Walt Disney prods for UA; *dir:* Wilfred Jackson; *anim:* Chuck Couch, Joseph d'Igalo, Paul Fennell, Norman Ferguson, Clyde Geronimi, Nick George, Hardie Gramatky, Edward Love, Richard Lundy, Hamilton S. Luske, Harry Reeves, William O. Roberts, Louis Schmitt, Ben Sharpsteen, Roy Williams, Marvin Woodward, Cy Young; *asst anim:* Tom Byrne, Jack Danbry, Richard Williams; *character des:* Ferdinand Huszti Horvath; *voice:* J. Delos Jewkes; *mus:* Leigh Harline; *col:* Tech. *sd:* RCA. 8 min. • Father Noah's family and animals help build an ark in time for the great flood.

1933. Fathers Are People *(Goofy)* 12 Oct. 1951; *p.c.:* Walt Disney prods for RKO; *dir:* Jack Kinney; *story:* Dick Kinney, Milt Schaffer; *anim:* Fred Moore, Ed Aardal, John Sibley, George Nicholas; *fx:* Dan MacManus; *lay:* Al Zinnen; *back:* Ray Huffine; *voices:* Jack Rourke, Bob Jackman, Helen Parrish, Bobby Driscoll, Johnny Young, John Sibley, Dick Kinney, Milt Schaffer; *mus:* Paul Smith; *col:* Tech. *sd:* RCA. 7 min. • The trials and tribulations of being a first-time father.

1934. Father's Day at Home (2) 1930. *p.c.:* A-C/Aetna Insurance Co.; b&w. *sd:* WE. 5 min. • No story available.

1935. Father's Day Off *(Goofy)* 28 Mar. 1953; *p.c.:* Walt Disney prods for RKO; *dir:* Jack Kinney; *story:* Brice Mack, Dick Kinney; *anim:* John Sibley, Ed Aardal, Hugh Fraser, George Nicholas; *fx:* Dan MacManus; *lay:* Al Zinnen; *back:* Ed Starr; *voices:* Pinto Colvig, June Foray, Clint MacCauley, Lucille Williams, Dan MacManus, Xavier Atencio, Bea Tamargo, Joe Nunez, John Sibley, Helen Seibert, Clarke Mallory, Lance Nolley, Al Bertino; *mus:* Paul Smith; *col:* Tech. *sd:* RCA. 7 min. • Geef looks after the housework while the little woman is away for the day.

1936. Father's Lion *(Goofy)* 4 Jan. 1951; *p.c.:* Walt Disney prods for RKO; *dir:* Jack Kinney; *story:* Dick Kinney, Milt Schaffer; *anim:* John Sibley, Ed Aardal, George Nicholas, Hugh Fraser, Fred Moore; *fx:* Dan MacManus, Jack Boyd, Ed Parks; *lay:* Al Zinnen; *back:* Ralph Hulett; *voices:* Jack Rourke, Pinto Colvig, Bobby Driscoll, James MacDonald. *mus:* Joseph S. Dubin; *col:* Tech. *sd:* RCA. 7 min. • Goofy takes his son camping and upsets an irate mountain lion.

1937. Father's Week-End *(Goofy)* 20 June 1953; *p.c.:* Walt Disney prods for RKO; *dir:* Jack Kinney; *story:* Dick Kinney, Brice Mack; *anim:* Hugh Fraser, George Nicholas, John Sibley, Ed Aardal; *fx:* George Rowley, Dan MacManus. *lay:* Al Zinnen; *back:* Al Dempster; *voices:* Art Gilmore, Pinto Colvig, June Foray, Jack Rourke, Dick Kinney, Lance Nolley, John Sibley, Brice Mack, Mary Kinney, James MacDonald; *mus:* Joseph S. Dubin; *col:* Tech. *sd:* RCA. 7 min. • Geef wants a quiet week-end but has to take Junior to the beach and fun fair instead.

1938. Feast and Furious *(Noveltoon)* 26 Dec. 1952; *p.c.:* Famous for Para; *dir:* I. Sparber; *story:* Larz Bourne; *anim:* Myron Waldman, Gordon Whittier; *sets:* Robert Owen; *voices:* Sid Raymond, Jack Mercer; *mus:* Winston Sharples; *ph:* Leonard McCormick; *col:* Tech. *sd:* RCA. 6 min. • Katnip makes many futile attempts to extricate Finny the goldfish from his bowl.

1939. Feather Bluster *(Merrie Melodies)* 10 May 1958; *p.c.:* WB; *dir:* Robert McKimson; *story:* Tedd Pierce; *anim:* Ted Bonnicksen, Tom Ray,

George Grandpré, Warren Batchelder; *lay:* Robert Gribbroek; *back:* Bill Butler; *ed:* Treg Brown; *voices:* Mel Blanc; *mus:* Milt Franklyn, Carl Stalling; *prod mgr:* John W. Burton; *prod:* Edward Selzer; *col:* Tech. *sd:* Vit. 7 min. Seq: *Henhouse Henry, The High & the Flighty* • Foggy and his dog adversary, now old and decrepit, discuss the feud that took up most of their early years.

1940. Feather Dusted (*Merrie Melodies*) 15 Jan. 1955; *p.c.:* WB; *dir:* Robert McKimson; *story:* Tedd Pierce; *anim:* Rod Scribner, Phil de Lara, Charles McKimson, Herman Cohen; *lay:* Robert Givens; *back:* Richard H. Thomas; *ed:* Treg Brown; *voices:* Mel Blanc, Bea Benaderet; *mus:* Milt Franklyn; *prod mgr:* John W. Burton; *prod:* Edward Selzer; *col:* Tech. *sd:* Vit. 7 min. • Foggy decides Egghead Jr should be playing instead of reading all the time ... and wishes he had left well enough alone.

1941. Feather Finger (*Merrie Melodies*) 20 Aug. 1966; *p.c.:* DFE for WB; *dir:* Robert McKimson; *story:* Michael O'Connor; *anim:* Manuel Perez, Norm McCabe, George Grandpré, Ted Bonnicksen, Bob Matz, Don Williams; *lay:* Dick Ung; *back:* Tom O'Loughlin; *ed:* Eugene Marks; *voices:* Mel Blanc; *mus:* Walter Greene; *col:* Tech. *sd:* Vit. 6 min. • "Featherfinger" (Daffy) is hired by Mayor Phur E. Katt to rid his western town of Speedy Gonzalez.

1942. A Feather in His Collar 7 Aug. 1946; *p.c.:* Walt Disney prods for the Community Chest; *dir:* Charles Nichols; *asst dir:* Jack Bruner; *anim:* Jerry Hathcock, George Kreisl, George Nicholas, Robert Youngquist; *mus:* Oliver Wallace; *col:* Tech. *sd:* RCA. 2 min • Pluto sees a "Red Feather" poster being put up heralding the Community Chest. He contributes a wealth of bones and is awarded a feather for his collar.

1943. A Feather in His Hare (*Looney Tunes*) 7 Feb. 1948; *p.c.:* WB; *dir:* Charles M. Jones; *story:* Michael Maltese, Tedd Pierce; *anim:* Ken Harris, Phil Monroe, Ben Washam, Lloyd Vaughan; *lay:* Robert Gribbroek; *back:* Peter Alvarado; *ed:* Treg Brown; *voices:* Mel Blanc, Tedd Pierce; *mus:* Carl Stalling; *prod mgr:* John W. Burton; *prod:* Edward Selzer; *col:* Tech. *sd:* Vit. 8 min. • The Last Mohican attempts to capture Bugs.

1944. Feathered Follies (*Aesop's Sound Fables*) 21 Oct. 1932; *p.c.:* Van Beuren for RKO; *dir:* John Foster; *mus:* Gene Rodemich; b&w. *sd:* RCA. 7 min. • The forest birds do their song and dance act until the arrival of a black cat.

1945. Featherweight Champ (*Dinky Duck*) Apr. 1953; *p.c.:* TT for Fox; *dir:* Eddie Donnelly; *story/voices:* Tom Morrison; *anim:* Jim Tyer; *mus:* Philip A. Scheib; *col:* Tech. *sd:* RCA. 7 min. • The farmyard animals ridicule Dinky for his small stature but when a fox arrives to organize a beauty contest, he comes to their rescue.

1946. Fee Fie Foes (*Loopy de Loop*) 9 June 1961; *p.c.:* Hanna-Barbera for Colum; *prod/dir:* Joseph Barbera, William Hanna; *story:* Michael Maltese; *anim dir:* Charles A. Nichols; *anim:* Robert Bentley; *lay:* Paul Sommer; *back:* Vera Ohman; *ed:* Joseph Ruby; *voices:* Daws Butler, Don Messick, Jean van der Pyl; *mus:* Hoyt Curtin; *titles:* Lawrence Gobel *prod mgr:* Howard Hanson; *col:* East. *sd:* RCA. 6 min. • Loopy gets involved in the "Jack and the Beanstalk" story.

1947. Feed the Kitty (*Oswald*) 14 Mar. 1938; *p.c.:* Walter Lantz prods for Univ; *story:* Victor McLeod, James Miele; *anim:* Lester Kline, George Nicholas; *sets:* Edgar Keichle; *voices:* Mel Blanc, Shirley Reed; *mus:* Frank Churchill; b&w. *sd:* WE. 7 min. • Elmer the great dane almost kills mother cat and, feeling remorse, tends to her kittens.

1948. Feed the Kitty (*Merrie Melodies*) 2 Feb. 1952; *p.c.:* WB; *dir:* Charles M. Jones; *story:* Michael Maltese; *anim:* Ken Harris, Phil Monroe, Lloyd Vaughan, Ben Washam; *lay:* Robert Gribbroek; *back:* Philip de Guard *ed:* Treg Brown; *voices:* Bea Benaderet, Mel Blanc; *mus:* Carl Stalling; *prod mgr:* John W. Burton; *prod:* Edward Selzer; *col:* Tech. *sd:* Vit. 7 min. • Marc Anthony, a bulldog, adopts a kitten and tries to hide it from his owner. He nearly has a seizure when he believes the kitten to have been baked into a cookie.

1949. Feedin' the Kiddie (*Tom & Jerry*) 7 June 1957; *p.c.:* MGM; *prod/dir:* William Hanna, Joseph Barbera; *lay:* Dick Bickenbach; *back:* Don Driscoll; *ph:* Jack Stevens. *prod mgr:* Hal Elias; *col:* Tech. *sd:* WE. 8 min. CS. • Jerry is put in charge of a hungry orphan mouse at Thanksgiving. CS reissue of *Little Orphan*.

1950. La Feet's Defeat (*Inspector*) 24 July 1968; *p.c.:* Mirisch/Geof-

frey/DFE for UA; *dir:* Gerry Chiniquy; *story:* Jim Ryan; *anim:* Manny Gould, Warren Batchelder, Tom Ray, Manny Perez, Don Williams; *lay:* Dick Ung; *back:* Tom O'Loughlin; *ed:* Lee Gunther; *voices:* Pat Harrington Jr., Marvin Miller, Don Messick; *mus:* Walter Greene; *theme tune:* Henry Mancini; *ph:* John Burton Jr.; *prod sup:* Harry Love, David DeTiege; *col:* DeLuxe. *sd:* RCA. 6 min. • The Inspector lets his assistant, Deux-Deux do the dangerous parts in tracking down the escaped criminal, Muddy La Feet.

1951. Feline Follies (*Paramount Magazine*) 18 July 1920; *p.c.:* Sullivan Studio for Para; *prod:* P.A. Powers; *dir:* Pat Sullivan; *anim:* Otto Messmer; b&w. sil. 5 min. • While Master Tom is courting Miss Kitty on the backyard fence, the house is overrun with mice who steal all the food.

1952. Feline Frame-Up (*Looney Tunes*) 13 Feb. 1954; *p.c.:* WB; *dir:* Charles M. Jones; *story:* Michael Maltese; *anim:* Richard Thompson, Abe Levitow; *lay:* Maurice Noble; *back:* Phil de Guard; *ed:* Treg Brown; *voices:* Robert C. Bruce, Mel Blanc; *mus:* Carl Stalling; *prod mgr:* John W. Burton; *prod:* Edward Selzer; *col:* Tech. *sd:* Vit. 7 min. • Jealous Claude cat bullies the kitten, forcing Marc Anthony, the bulldog, to take drastic action.

1953. Felineous Assault (*Herman & Katnip*) 20 Feb. 1959; *p.c.:* Para Cartoons; *dir:* Seymour Kneitel; *story:* Carl Meyer; *anim:* Tom Johnson, Frank Endres; *sets:* Robert Little; *voices:* Sid Raymond, Gwen Davies. *mus:* Winston Sharples; *ph:* Leonard McCormick; *prod mgr:* Abe Goodman; *col:* Tech. *sd:* RCA. 6 min. • Katnip teaches his offspring, Kitnip, to catch mice but the kitten befriends Herman the mouse instead.

1954. Felix "Hyps" the Hippo (*Pat Sullivan Cartoon*) 1 Feb. 1924; *p.c.:* Sullivan Studio for M.J. Winkler; b&w. sil. 6 min. • Hypnotist Adam Sapp hypnotizes a mouse to beat up Felix. Our hero learns hypnosis for himself and uses it to seccure a hippo for the circus and a $1000 reward.

1955. Felix All at Sea (*Pat Sullivan Comic*) Apr. 1922; *p.c.:* Sullivan Studio for M.J. Winkler; b&w. sil. 6 min. • A large tuna snags Felix's fishing line and drags him out to sea. He breaks loose and is picked-up by a rum-runner. Felix creates a raft and sails off loaded with booze, landing to encounter a revenue officer ... who's waiting for a drink!

1956. Felix All Puzzled (*Pat Sullivan Comic*) 15 Jan. 1925; *p.c.:* Sullivan Studio for M.J. Winkler; b&w. sil. 6 min. • In order to get fed, Felix has to visit Russia and find the solution to a crossword clue. He is mistaken for a spy and finally solves the puzzle.

1957. Felix at the Fair (*Pat Sullivan Comic*) 1 Mar. 1922; *p.c.:* Sullivan Studio for M.J. Winkler; b&w. sil. 6 min. • While at the fair, Felix is taken with a pretty dancing cat. He annoys the snake charmer, finally persuading the girl cat to go away with him.

1958. Felix Baffled by Banjos (*Pat Sullivan Comic*) 15 June 1924; *p.c.:* Sullivan Studio for M.J. Winkler; b&w. sil. 6 min. • To avoid his neighbor's ukelele strumming, Felix goes to the South Sea Islands. There he finds the natives strumming and dives to the ocean bed to escape, only to find the fish doing likewise. In desperation he inhales gas and reaches Paradise ... only to find harp-strumming angels.

1959. Felix Brings Home the Bacon (*Pat Sullivan Comic*) 15 Nov. 1924; *p.c.:* Sullivan Studio for M.J. Winkler; b&w. sil. 6 min. • Felix helps Old Mother Hubbard by disguising as Red Riding Hood's Grandma. The Wolf chases him into the sea, then turns into a fish, which Felix brings home to eat.

1960. Felix Comes Back (*Pat Sullivan Comic*) 1924; *p.c.:* Sullivan Studio for M.J. Winkler; b&w. sil. 6 min. • Felix hides from an irate butcher in a fish. The fish goes to Iceland and when caught by an Eskimo, out jumps our hero. He's chased by a polar bear, then set adrift on an iceberg, which Felix sells as an ice block to the butcher on his return.

1961. Felix Crosses the Crooks (*Pat Sullivan Comic*) 15 Feb. 1924; *p.c.:* Sullivan Studio for M.J. Winkler; b&w. sil. 6 min. • Felix assists the police in capturing a bank robber, then spots another robber shoplifting sponges from a store. He enlists the help of an elephant who douses the crook in water, causing the sponges to inflate.

1962. Felix Dines and Pines (*Felix the Cat*) 22 Jan. 1927; *p.c.:* Bijou Film Inc for Educational; b&w. sil. 6 min. • Ever resourceful Felix sets his sights on a menu of soup, spaghetti and mice. Having lost out on all counts, he eats some garbage and suffers a dreadful nightmare.

1963. Felix Doubles for Darwin (*Pat Sullivan Comic*) 1924; *p.c.*: Sullivan Studio for M.J. Winkler; b&w. *sil.* 6 min. • The Evolution Society offers a large reward for proof that man comes after monkeys, so Felix goes to Ape Town to find out which came first.

1964. Felix Fans the Flames (*Felix the Cat*) 21 Feb. 1926; *p.c.*: Bijou Films Inc for Educational; b&w. *sil.* 6 min. • Felix naps beside a hot stove and dreams he's in Hades being chased by the Devil.

1965. Felix Fills a Shortage (*Pat Sullivan Comic*) 15 Nov. 1923; *p.c.*: Sullivan Studio for M.J. Winkler; b&w. *sil.* 6 min. • Hit by a deficit of bananas, Felix reckons his fortune will be made if he goes to Banana Island and brings a stack home. Once on the island, he is chased by cannibals.

1966. Felix Finds a Way (*Pat Sullivan Comic*) 1 Aug. 1922; *p.c.*: Sullivan Studio for M.J. Winkler; b&w. *sil.* 6 min. • Felix helps a farmer run his dilapidated farm. He manages to put an end to some crows in the cornfield by feeding them whiskey.

1967. Felix Finds 'em Fickle (*Pat Sullivan Comic*) 1924; *p.c.*: Sullivan Studio for M.J. Winkler; b&w. *sil.* 6 min. • Felix's girl makes him go through torture to scale a mountain for a flower only to inform him upon his return that he picked the wrong one.

1968. Felix Finds Out (*Pat Sullivan Comic*) 1924; *p.c.*: Sullivan Studio for M.J. Winkler; b&w. *sil.* 6 min. • Felix tries to lure a boy away from his studies, then investigates the origins of "Moonshine."

1969. Felix Finishes First (*Pat Sullivan Comic*) 1 Dec. 1924; *p.c.*: Sullivan Studio for M.J. Winkler; b&w. *sil.* 6 min. • No story available.

1970. Felix Flirts with Fate (*Felix the Cat*) 24 Jan. 1926; *p.c.*: Bijou Films Inc for Educational; b&w. *sil.* 6 min. • Felix is hit by "Spring Fever" and spies a suitable girl up on Mars. Arriving on the planet, he livens up the proceedings by getting everything to dance "The Charleston."

1971. Felix Follows the Swallows (*Pat Sullivan Comic*) 1 Feb. 1925; *p.c.*: Sullivan Studio for M.J. Winkler; b&w. *sil.* 6 min. • Felix dons some wings and flies south for the winter, only to find himself in a cannibal pot.

1972. Felix Foozled (*Pat Sullivan Comic*) 1924; *p.c.*: Sullivan Studio for M.J. Winkler; b&w. *sil.* 6 min. • No story available.

1973. Felix Full O' Fight (*Pat Sullivan Comic*) 13 Apr. 1925; *p.c.*: Sullivan Studio for M.J. Winkler; b&w. *sil.* 6 min. • Felix's suicide plans are aborted when he finds a treasure map, follows it and unearths the "treasure." This turns out to be pre-war prune juice which gives him hallucinations. On return he finds his girl in the arms of another and beats him to a pulp.

1974. Felix Gets Broadcasted (*Pat Sullivan Comic*) 1 July 1923; *p.c.*: Sullivan Studio for M.J. Winkler; b&w. *sil.* 6 min. • Felix annoys a fisherman who broadcasts him to Egypt where he gets chased by a slave.

1975. Felix Gets His Fill (*Pat Sullivan Comic*) 1 Mar. 1925; *p.c.*: Sullivan Studio for M.J. Winkler; b&w. *sil.* 6 min. • Inspired to head south for "Chicken Waffles," Felix gets a job picking cotton. He pinches Uncle Tom's white whiskers and is chased, finally saving him from the jaws of a crocodile.

1976. Felix Gets Left (*Pat Sullivan Comic*) 1 Dec. 1922; *p.c.*: Sullivan Studio for M.J. Winkler; b&w. *sil.* 6 min. • Felix has little luck in finding any food. He chases a mouse who tricks the luckless feline out of being his supper.

1977. Felix Gets Revenge (*Pat Sullivan Comic*) 1 Sept. 1922; *p.c.*: Sullivan Studio for M.J. Winkler; b&w. *sil.* 6 min. • After saving a boy from a dog, Felix is adopted against father's wishes. Dad throws the cat out, but he re-enters the house through the telephone line. Felix and the kid have fun until the boy is inflated with helium from a balloon.

1978. Felix Gets the Can (*Pat Sullivan Comic*) 8 June 1925; *p.c.*: Sullivan Studio for M.J. Winkler; b&w. *sil.* 6 min. • Felix goes to Alaska for better fishing and ends up being "canned" as salmon.

1979. Felix Goes A-Hunting (*Pat Sullivan Comic*) 15 Dec. 1923; *p.c.*: Sullivan Studio for M.J. Winkler; b&w. *sil.* 6 min. • A man offers Felix $1,000 if he can get a fur coat for his wife. The feline sets out, ready to shoot a bear, and has one chase him into the man's house, where the wife proceeds to beat it up and remove the bear's coat for herself.

1980. Felix Goes Hungry (*Pat Sullivan Comic*) 15 Dec. 1924; *p.c.*: Sullivan Studio for M.J. Winkler; b&w. *sil.* 6 min. • After missing out on a dog's bone and fresh lobster, Felix goes after a mouse in a lingerie shop by disguising himself as a ladies' hat.

1981. Felix Grabs His Grub (*Pat Sullivan Comic*) 1924; *p.c.*: Sullivan Studio for M.J. Winkler; b&w. *sil.* 6 min. • Felix journeys to the river in search of breakfast. He battles with an octopus, lobster and shark before pinching a fisherman's catch.

1982. Felix in Blunderland (*Felix the Cat*) 7 Feb. 1926; *p.c.*: Bijou Films Inc for Educational; b&w. *sil.* 6 min. • After reading *Alice in Wonderland*, Felix dreams he's in "Blunderland." He annoys Old King Cole by eating his porridge, escapes a dinosaur, climbs Jack's beanstalk, meets a giant and returns to earth.

1983. Felix in Fairyland (*Pat Sullivan Comic*) 15 Oct. 1923; *p.c.*: Sullivan Studio for M.J. Winkler; b&w. *sil.* 6 min. • A fairy rewards Felix with a trip to Fairyland. There he tangles with an ogre, providing the Old Woman-in-the-Shoe's kids with a home in the giant's shoe.

1984. Felix in Hollywood (*Pat Sullivan Comic*) 1 Oct. 1923; *p.c.*: Sullivan Studio for M.J. Winkler; b&w. *sil.* 8 min. • Intent on becoming an actor, Felix stows away to Hollywood and meets Ben Turpin, Cecil B. De Mille, Charlie Chaplin, William S. Hart, Gloria Swanson and Douglas Fairbanks.

1985. Felix in Love (*Pat Sullivan Comic*) May 1922; *p.c.*: Sullivan Studio for M.J. Winkler; b&w. *sil.* 6 min. • Felix believes his girl would miss him if he were in Africa. He rubs a magic lamp and a genie transports him there.

1986. Felix in the Swim (*Pat Sullivan Comic*) 1 July 1922; *p.c.*: Sullivan Studio for M.J. Winkler; b&w. *sil.* 6 min. • Felix gets mice to prance on the piano keyboard so Willie's mother will think he's still practicing instead of being off swimming with Felix.

1987. Felix Laughs It Off (*Felix the Cat*) 7 Mar. 1926; *p.c.*: Bijou Films Inc for Educational b&w. *sil.* 6 min. • When Felix worries he grows thin. He discovers a book entitled "Laugh and Grow Fat" and gains his former weight by avocating this method.

1988. Felix Laughs Last (*Pat Sullivan Comic*) 1 Nov. 1923; *p.c.*: Sullivan Studio for M.J. Winkler; b&w. *sil.* 6 min. • The pesty mice torment Felix and his owner until Felix gets revenge by luring the rodents into a trap with the expectation of a cheese delivery.

1989. Felix Lends a Hand (*Pat Sullivan Comic*) 15 Nov. 1922; *p.c.*: Sullivan Studio for M.J. Winkler; b&w. *sil.* 6 min. • Abdul's fiancée, Fatima, is kidnapped by a sheikh and Felix rushes to her rescue with the aid of a magic carpet.

1990. Felix Loses Out (*Pat Sullivan Comic*) 15 Jan. 1924; *p.c.*: Sullivan Studio for M.J. Winkler b&w. *sil.* 6 min. • Felix can't compete with his rival for the fair lady. He rigs up a tin lizzie to compete with the other cat's homemade wagon.

1991. Felix Makes a Movie (*Pat Sullivan Comic*) 1924; *p.c.*: Sullivan Studio for M.J. Winkler; b&w. *sil.* 6 min. • No story available.

1992. Felix Makes Good (*Pat Sullivan Comic*) 1 Apr. 1922; *p.c.*: Sullivan Studio for M.J. Winkler; b&w. *sil.* 6 min. • Felix gets the blame and is kicked out of the house when mice steal his Mistress' bottle of milk. He soon gets his revenge.

1993. Felix Minds the Kid (*Pat Sullivan Comic*) 1 Oct. 1922; *p.c.*: Sullivan Studio for M.J. Winkler; b&w. *sil.* 6 min. • When Felix babysits, the kid breaks out to enroll with a Day Nursery. A problem arises with Felix finding the right infant among all the others, finally luring him away with candy.

1994. Felix on the Trail (*Pat Sullivan Comic*) 1 Nov. 1922; *p.c.*: Sullivan Studio for M.J. Winkler; b&w. *sil.* 6 min. • Felix goes in search of Kentucky bootleggers.

1995. Felix Out of Luck (*Pat Sullivan Comic*) 1 Jan. 1924; *p.c.*: Sullivan Studio for M.J. Winkler; b&w. *sil.* 6 min. • Felix goes through a lot to find some food. On returning he finds his master has cooked him a chicken. This gives Felix a seizure and he buries himself.

1996. Felix Pinches the Pole (*Pat Sullivan Comic*) 1 May 1924; *p.c.*: Sullivan Studio for M.J. Winkler; b&w. *sil.* 6 min. • A kid steals a barber's pole as a stick of candy and Felix goes to the North Pole to replace it. Reissued tinted and with sound in 1930 by Copley Pictures Corp.

1997. Felix Puts It Over (*Pat Sullivan Comic*) 15 May 1924; *p.c.:* Sullivan Studio for M.J. Winkler; b&w. *sil.* 6 min. • Felix, the gang leader, flirts with Kitty but is beaten at his own game by the leader of a rival gang.

1998. Felix Revolts (*Pat Sullivan Comic*) 1 May 1923; *p.c.:* Sullivan Studios for M.J. Winkler; b&w. *sil.* 6 min. • The townsfolk get rid of every cat. Felix makes life so miserable for them that they have to call all the cats back.

1999. Felix Saves the Day (*Pat Sullivan Comic*) 1 Mar. 1922; *p.c.:* Sullivan Studio for M.J. Winkler; b&w. *sil.* 8 min. *l/a/anim.* • Felix's ball game is halted by a cop arresting the star player. He saves the day when stepping up to bat at Yankee Stadium. A particularly vicious swipe at the ball angers the gods, who wreak their vengeance on the game and it is rained out. Intercut live-action scenes at Yankee Stadium.

2000. Felix Strikes It Rich (*Pat Sullivan Comic*) 1 July 1923; *p.c.:* Sullivan Studio for M.J. Winkler; b&w. *sil.* 6 min. • "Jazz Baby" Felix blows a mean saxophone, making the local chickens forego egg-laying for dancing. He is then forced to dig his own grave and strikes oil in doing so.

2001. Felix the Cat b&w. *sil.* • See: *Paramount Cartoons; Paramount Magazine; Sullivan, Pat, Studio*

2002. Felix the Cat, a Friend in Need (*Pat Sullivan Comic*) 15 Oct. 1924; *p.c.:* Sullivan Studio for M.J. Winkler; b&w. *sil.* 6 min. • No story available.

2003. Felix the Cat and the Goose That Laid the Golden Egg (*Rainbow Parade*) 7 Feb. 1936; *p.c.:* Van Beuren for RKO; *dir:* Burt Gillett, Tom Palmer; *sets:* Art Bartsch, Eddi Bowlds; *voices:* Jimmy Donnelly; *mus:* Winston Sharples; *col:* Tech. *sd:* RCA. 7 min. • A pirate steals Felix's goose and the ever resourceful feline follows him back to his galleon to retrieve her.

2004. Felix the Cat as Roameo (*Felix the Cat*) 16 May 1927; *p.c.:* Bijou Films Inc for Educational; b&w. *sil.* 6 min. • Felix romances a hometown girl, then hops over to Spain where he wins over a Señorita. Her tempestuous love-making sends him to the North Pole where he flirts with an Eskimo cat, then a Hula girl in Hawaii. He returns home, where he thinks he's safe, but all his affairs turn up on his doorstep.

2005. Felix the Cat at the Rainbow's End (*Felix the Cat*) 13 Dec. 1925; *p.c.:* Bijou Films Inc for Educational; b&w. *sil.* 6 min. • Felix finds himself in Nursery-Rhyme Land with a pot of gold stolen by a witch. He is chased by a giant whom he vanquishes with gum and uses the ogre's shoe to house the Old Woman-in-the-Shoe's children. For this act of kindness, the Good Fairy returns his gold.

2006. Felix the Cat Behind in Front (*Felix the Cat*) 25 Dec. 1927; *p.c.:* Bijou Films Inc for Educational; b&w. *sil.* 6 min. • Felix is transported to the "Front Line" trenches where he uses sausages in the machine-gun to rout the enemy ... then raids their food supply.

2007. Felix the Cat Braves the Briny (*Felix the Cat*) 3 May 1926; *p.c.:* Bijou Films Inc for Educational; b&w. *sil.* 6 min. • Felix hears of buried treasure and builds a home-made submarine to look for it. He battles with denizen of the deep before finding a "treasure" of fish.

2008. Felix the Cat Busts a Bubble (*Felix the Cat*) 17 Oct. 1926; *p.c.:* Bijou Films Inc for Educational; b&w. *sil.* 6 min. • Felix has visions of not being fed by his mistress when she gets "movie struck." He journeys to Hollywood to ruin her screen test.

2009. Felix the Cat Busts Into Business (*Felix the Cat*) 6 Sept. 1925; *p.c.:* Bijou Films Inc for Educational; b&w. *sil.* 6 min. • Felix cures a hippo's toothache and an ostrich's tummy-ache.

2010. Felix the Cat Calms His Conscience (*Pat Sullivan Comic*) 15 May 1923; *p.c.:* Sullivan Studio for M.J. Winkler; b&w. *sil.* 6 min. • Felix's rival takes the form of a tough little Bowery cat. When he has the oportunity to toss his troublesome opponent in the canal, his conscience gets the better of him.

2011. Felix the Cat Collars the Button (*Felix the Cat*) 12 Dec. 1926; *p.c.:* Bijou Films Inc for Educational; b&w. *sil.* 6 min. • Felix pursues a rolling collar-stud that finally comes to rest in a bakery where it's baked into a doughnut.

2012. Felix the Cat Cops the Prize (*Pat Sullivan Comic*) 25 May 1925; *p.c.:* Sullivan Studio for M.J. Winkler; b&w. *sil.* 6 min. • No story available.

2013. Felix the Cat Dopes It Out (*Felix the Cat*) July 1925; *p.c.:* Bijou Films Inc for Educational; b&w. *sil.* 6 min. • Felix encounters an alcoholic tramp.

2014. Felix the Cat Ducks His Duty (*Felix the Cat*) 29 May 1927; *p.c.:* Bijou Films Inc for Educational; b&w. *sil.* 6 min. • When mice declare war on cats, Felix avoids being called-up by getting married. His wife is such a harridan that he finds life quieter "at the Front."

2015. Felix the Cat Hits the Deck (*Felix the Cat*) 11 Dec. 1927; *p.c.:* Bijou Films Inc for Educational; b&w. *sil.* 6 min. • Felix is set upon by a deck of cards.

2016. Felix the Cat Hunts the Hunter (*Felix the Cat*) 3 Oct. 1926; *p.c.:* Bijou Films Inc for Educational; b&w. *sil.* 6 min. • Felix helps a big game hunter who is being held hostage by the jungle animals.

2017. Felix the Cat in a "Loco" Motive (*Felix the Cat*) 26 June 1927; *p.c.:* Bijou Films Inc for Educational; b&w. *sil.* 6 min. • Felix braves the elements when crossing the Atlantic in an airship. An encounter with a storm deposits him in Germany.

2018. Felix the Cat in a Tale of Two Kitties (*Felix the Cat*) 16 May 1926; *p.c.:*; Bijou Films Inc for Educational; b&w. *sil.* 6 min. • Felix has a fling with gilded palaces and jazz butterflies but returns home, disillusioned.

2019. Felix the Cat in April Maze (*Felix the Cat*) 1930; *p.c.:* Bijou Films Inc for Copley Pictures Corp; *prod:* Jacques Kopfstein, Pat Sullivan; *anim:* Otto Messmer; *mus:* Bernard Altshuler; *sd fx:* Harry Edison; b&w. *sd.* 6 min. • Felix takes the kids on a picnic but their fun is ruined by persistent rain and a thieving snake.

2020. Felix the Cat in Arabiantics (*Felix the Cat*) 13 May 1928; *p.c.:* Bijou Films Inc for Educational; b&w. *sil.* 6 min. • Felix rides a magic carpet to Arabia to retrieve a necklace stolen from his lady love. The Forty Thieves spy the necklace and set out to steal it. Reissued tinted and with sound in 1930 by Copley Pictures Corp.

2021. Felix the Cat in Art for Heart's Sake (*Felix the Cat*) 10 July 1927; *p.c.:* Bijou Films Inc for Educational; b&w. *sil.* 6 min. • Felix loses his girl to an aviator rival. Turning to art, he carves a statue of her, hoping it will come to life.

2022. Felix the Cat in Astronomeows (*Felix the Cat*) 8 July 1928; *p.c.:* Bijou Films Inc for Educational; b&w. *sil.* 6 min. • Tired of cats leading a "dog's life" on earth, a group of "Dem-o-Cats" votes to live on Mars. Felix is elected to make a tour of inspection first. • He likes the planet so much that he invites all the earth cats up. The King of Mars is none too pleased about this.

2023. Felix the Cat in Balloonatics (*Felix the Cat*) 1928; *p.c.:* Bijou Films Inc for Educational; b&w. *sil.* 6 min. • Felix has an adventure in a dirigible.

2024. Felix the Cat in Barn Yarns (*Felix the Cat*) 20 Mar. 1927; *p.c.:* Bijou Films Inc for Educational; b&w. *sil.* 6 min. • A duck saves Felix from drowning; then he, in turn, saves the duck from becoming the farmer's dinner. He then helps some fish avoid the farmer's fishhook.

2025. Felix the Cat in Comicalities (*Felix the Cat*) 1 Apr. 1928; *p.c.:* Bijou Films Inc for Educational; b&w. *sil.* 6 min. • Felix searches for a girl to star in the movies and comes across just the one he wants. He changes her facial expression, risks his life to bring her a pearl necklace and a fur coat. Then, when she gives him the cold shoulder, he tears her up, saying "She's only paper after all!"

2026. Felix the Cat in Daze and Knights (*Felix the Cat*) 30 Oct. 1927; *p.c.:* Bijou Films Inc for Educational; b&w. *sil.* 6 min. • Upon entering a castle in search of food, Felix encounters various animals dressed in armor. After saving the castle from marauders, Felix is rewarded by the King. Reissued tinted and with sound in 1930 by Copley Pictures Corp.

2027. Felix the Cat in Dough Nutty (*Felix the Cat*) 12 June 1927; *p.c.:* Bijou Films Inc for Educational; b&w. *sil.* 6 min. • Felix gets involved with an inventor who is looking for a new shape for the doughnut.

2028. Felix the Cat in Draggin' th' Dragon (*Felix the Cat*) 22 Jan. 1928; *p.c.:* Bijou Films Inc for Educational; b&w. *sil.* 6 min. • Felix steals a chop suey recipe and is pursued to China by an angry Chinaman. Here the Army, Secret Police and all the machinery of the law are called upon to capture him.

2029. Felix the Cat in Eats Are West (*Felix the Cat*) 15 Nov. 1925; *p.c.:* Bijou Films Inc for Educational; b&w. *sil.* 6 min. • Felix travels west in search of food, gets entangled in a cowboy shoot-out and is almost cooked.

2030. Felix the Cat in Eskimotive (*Felix the Cat*) 29 Apr. 1928; *p.c.:* Bijou Films Inc for Educational; b&w. *sil.* 6 min. • Felix Junior floats to Eskimoland, trapped inside a bubble with our hero in hot pursuit. After encountering a polar bear they return with a pile of seal skins to sell to the furrier. Reissued tinted and with sound in 1930 by Copley Pictures Corp.

2031. Felix the Cat in Eye Jinks (*Felix the Cat*) 1 May 1927; *p.c.:* Bijou Films Inc for Educational; b&w. *sil.* 6 min. • While Felix dozes in an optician's the mice fit him with magnified spectacles.

2032. Felix the Cat in False Vases (*Felix the Cat*) 1929; *p.c.:* Bijou Films Inc for Copley Pictures Corp; *prod:* Jacques Kopfstein, Pat Sullivan; *anim:* Otto Messmer; *mus:* Bernard Altshuler; *sd fx:* Harry Edison; b&w. *sd.* 6 min. • Felix burrows to China to replace a broken vase.

2033. Felix the Cat in Fifty-Fifty (*Pat Sullivan Comic*) 21 Oct. 1922; *p.c.:* Sullivan Studio for M.J. Winkler; *prod/dir:* Pat Sullivan; *anim:* Otto Messmer; b&w. *sil.* 6 min. • Felix and a hobo agree to split everything fifty-fifty. When he sees his partner devouring all the food without sharing, Felix has the tramp arrested and sentenced to fifty days while Felix gets a $50 reward.

2034. Felix the Cat in Flim Flam Films (*Felix the Cat*) 18 Sept. 1927; *p.c.:* Bijou Films Inc for Educational; b&w. *sil.* 6 min. • Felix and family are thrown out of the local picture house and decide to make their own movies.

2035. Felix the Cat in Forty Winks (*Felix the Cat*) 1930; *p.c.:* Bijou Films Inc for Copley Pictures Corp; *prod:* Jacques Kopfstein, Pat Sullivan; *anim:* Otto Messmer; *mus:* Bernard Altshuler; *sd fx:* Harry Edison; b&w *sd.* 6 min. • Felix's midnight caterwaulling keeps a man from sleeping.

2036. Felix the Cat in Futuritzy (*Felix the Cat*) 24 June 1928; *p.c.*; Bijou Films Inc for Copley Pictures Corp; *prod:* Jacques Kopfstein, Pat Sullivan; b&w. *sil.* 6 min. • Before he can ask Kitty's dad for her hand, Felix asks a fortune teller to see what the future holds for him. The gypsy sees nothing but grief for the cat. He then goes to an astronomer for a second opinion. The outlook seems much better but as soon as he sets foot outside the door, all tough luck befalls him.

2037. Felix the Cat in Germ Mania (*Felix the Cat*) 3 Apr. 1927; *p.c.:* Bijou Films Inc for Educational; b&w. *sil.* 6 min. • A chemist experiments on Felix, using reducing fluid on him and an enlarging fluid on a "love bug" who turns the tables on Felix.

2038. Felix the Cat in Gym Gems (*Felix the Cat*) 8 Aug. 1926; *p.c.:* Bijou Films Inc for Educational; b&w. *sil.* 6 min. • Felix invades a lazy pugilist's training camp where he gets the pug to do lively work by punching a hornets' nest, finally knocking him out with a kick from a mule.

2039. Felix the Cat in Icy Eyes (*Felix the Cat*) 6 Feb. 1927; *p.c.:* Bijou Films Inc for Educational; b&w. *sil.* 6 min. • Felix is given an "icy stare" by Kitty, then is rewarded for capturing a burglar. When his former love hears of his new wealth, she sends for Felix who now gives her the cold shoulder!

2040. Felix the Cat in In and Out Laws (*Felix the Cat*) 27 May 1928; *p.c.:* Bijou Films Inc for Copley Pictures Corp; *prod:* Jacques Kopfstein, Pat Sullivan; b&w. *sil.* 6 min. • Felix crosses the border into Mexico to put his rooster into a fight.

2041. Felix the Cat in Jack from All Trades (*Felix the Cat*) 2 Aug. 1927; *p.c.:* Bijou Films Inc for Educational; b&w. *sil.* 6 min. • In a desperate attempt to make some money, Felix tries several trades: He barbers a mop and broom, repairs a decrepit rake and hitches a tire-pump to a saxophone to make jazz. The result being that the whole neighborhood showers him with coins.

2042. Felix the Cat in Japanicky (*Felix the Cat*) 4 Mar. 1928; *p.c.:* Bijou Films Inc for Educational; b&w. *sil.* 6 min. • Felix demonstrates the art of Jiu Jitsu on lampposts and is chased by a cop for his trouble. He is butted by a goat to Japan, where he gets involved with a geisha girl. Reissued tinted and with sound in 1930 by Copley Pictures Corp.

2043. Felix the Cat in Jungle Bungles (*Felix the Cat*) 22 July 1928; *p.c.:* Bijou Films Inc for Educational; b&w. *sil.* 6 min. • Felix as a wild life cameraman.

2044. Felix the Cat in Land O' Fancy (*Felix the Cat*) 31 Oct. 1926; *p.c.:* Bijou Films Inc for Educational; b&w. *sil.* 6 min. • Felix floats on smoke rings to a fabled land where he is chased by a giant for swiping his milk. He manages to slide down to safety on a wisp of smoke.

2045. Felix the Cat in No Fuelin' (*Felix the Cat*) 16 Oct. 1927; *p.c.:* Bijou Films Inc for Educational; b&w. *sil.* 6 min. • Felix's endeavors to provide wood for the family fire end with him returning home carrying a bag full of bowling pins. Upon opening the bag, out flies a well-fed woodpecker. Reissued tinted and with sound in 1930 by Copley Pictures Corp.

2046. Felix the Cat in Oceantics (*Felix the Cat*) 1930; *p.c.:* Bijou Films Inc for Copley Pictures Corp; *prod:* Jacques Kopfstein, Pat Sullivan; *anim:* Otto Messmer; *mus:* Bernard Altshuler; *sd fx:* Harry Edison; b&w. *sd.* 6 min. • Felix is butted aboard ship by an unfriendly goat.

2047. Felix the Cat in Ohm, Sweet Ohm (*Felix the Cat*) 19 Feb. 1928; *p.c.:* Bijou Films Inc for Educational; b&w. *sil.* 6 min. • Felix makes good use of a thunderstorm by bottling lightning bolts. He replaces a Cabby's old nag with lightning, then harnesses some to a housewife's broom which sweeps him away.

2048. Felix the Cat in One Good Turn (*Felix the Cat*) 22 Feb. 1930; *p.c.:* Bijou Films Inc for Copley Pictures Inc.; *prod:* Jacques Kopfstein, Pat Sullivan; *anim:* Otto Messmer; *mus:* Bernard Altshuler; *sd fx:* Harry Edison; b&w. *sd.* 6 min. • A fox rescues Felix from a bear then Felix returns the favour by putting the Hunt on the wrong scent.

2049. Felix the Cat in Outdoor Indore (*Felix the Cat*) 10 June 1928; *p.c.:* Bijou Films Inc for Educational; b&w. *sil.* 6 min. • Felix travels to India to bring back an elephant for the circus. Reissued tinted and with sound in 1930 by Copley Pictures Corp.

2050. Felix the Cat in Pedigreedy (*Felix the Cat*) 13 Jan. 1927; *p.c.:* Bijou Films Inc for Educational; b&w. *sil.* 6 min. • To gain entrance to the 400 Club, Felix invents a pedigree and tells of how his ancestors saved Noah from drowning, taught the Pharoahs to Charleston and proved to Columbus how the world is round.

2051. Felix the Cat in Polly-Tics (*Felix the Cat*) 18 Mar. 1928; *p.c.:* Bijou Films Inc for Educational; b&w. *sil.* 6 min. • Polly the parrot revolts when the master introduces Felix to the house and enlists the mice and a canary to dispose of him.

2052. Felix the Cat in Reverse English (*Felix the Cat*) 14 Nov. 1926; *p.c.:* Bijou Films Inc for Educational; b&w. *sil.* 6 min. • After being physically evicted by his master, Felix dreams their sizes and roles are reversed. Felix now orders his master around and kicks him out.

2053. Felix the Cat in Romeeow (*Felix the Cat*) 1930; *p.c.:* Bijou Films Inc for Copley Pictures Corp; *prod:* Jacques Kopfstein, Pat Sullivan; *anim:* Otto Messmer; *mus:* Bernard Altshuler; *sd fx:* Harry Edison; b&w. *sd.* 6 min. • Felix woos his lady love.

2054. Felix the Cat in Sax Appeal (*Felix the Cat*) 17 Apr. 1927; *p.c.:* Bijou Films Inc for Educational; b&w. *sil.* 6 min. • Felix's sleep is disturbed by his owner's saxophone playing. When he buries the offending instrument in the garden, a mole unearths it and starts playing.

2055. Felix the Cat in School Daze (*Felix the Cat*) 27 June 1926; *p.c.:* Bijou Films Inc for Educational; b&w. *sil.* 6 min. • Mary is asked in school to name the hottest place, so Felix visits the Equator, then the North Pole. Meeting with various adventures, he returns to announce that it was hottest for him at the North Pole.

2056. Felix the Cat in Scrambled Yeggs (*Felix the Cat*) 5 Sept. 1926; *p.c.:* Bijou Films Inc for Educational; b&w. *sil.* 6 min. • Felix takes a nap in a baby carriage and is used by two burglars to help rob a museum.

2057. Felix the Cat in Sculls and Skulls (*Felix the Cat*) 1930; *p.c.:* Bijou Films Inc for Copley Pictures Corp; *prod:* Jacques Kopfstein, Pat Sullivan; *anim:* Otto Messmer; *mus:* Bernard Altshuler; *sd fx:* Harry Edison; b&w. *sd.* 6 min. • Felix is put through a rigorous college initiation when he helps out on the rowing team.

2058. Felix the Cat in Sure-Locked Homes (*Felix the Cat*) 15 Apr. 1928; *p.c.:* Bijou Films Inc for Educational; b&w. *sil.* 6 min. • Felix turns detective when he seeks refuge in a spooky house where shadow monsters chase him. He employs a spider to weave a web to ensnare the villains.

2059. Felix the Cat in Tee Time *(Felix the Cat)* 1930; *p.c.:* Bijou Films Inc for Copley Pictures Corp; *prod:* Jacques Kopfstein, Pat Sullivan; *anim:* Otto Messmer; *mus:* Bernard Altshuler; *sd fx:* Harry Edison; b&w. *sd.* 6 min. • After playing a round of golf, Felix is transported to Africa.

2060. Felix the Cat in the Bone Age *(Pat Sullivan Comic)* 1 Mar. 1923; *p.c.:* Sullivan Studio for M.J. Winkler; b&w. *sil.* 6 min. • Felix dreams he's in prehistoric times, escaping from a caveman who wants his pelt.

2061. Felix the Cat in the Cold Rush *(Felix the Cat)* 7 Nov. 1925; *p.c.:* Bijou Films Inc for Education; b&w. *sil.* 6 min. • Felix seeks refuge in the refrigerator and dreams about being in iceland where he uses a walrus' tusks as skis and when the fridge door is opened, he is in a block of ice.

2062. Felix the Cat in the Ghost Breaker *(Pat Sullivan Comic)* 1 Apr. 1923; *p.c.:* Sullivan Studio for M.J. Winkler; *col:* tinted. *sil.* 6 min. • Felix's slumber in a graveyard is disturbed by a ghost. He follows it and uncovers a plot to swindle the farmer out of his land.

2063. Felix the Cat in the Last Life *(Felix the Cat)* 5 Aug. 1928; *p.c.:* Bijou Films for Educational; b&w *sil.* 6 min. • When his girl turns her nose up at auto travel, Felix takes up aviation to help impress her. He tries to master the new device and fortunately has insured his life. He collects for eight of his nine lives while performing a parachute jump.

2064. Felix the Cat in the Non-Stop Fright *(Felix the Cat)* 21 Aug. 1927; *p.c.:* Bijou Films Inc for Educational; b&w. *sil.* 6 min. • Felix builds his own trans–Atlantic airplane and meets with a series of adventures during his flight over and under sea.

2065. Felix the Cat in the Oily Bird *(Felix the Cat)* 5 Feb. 1928; *p.c.:* Bijou Films Inc for Educational; b&w. *sil.* 6 min. • Accused of stealing jewels, Felix sets out to find the real culprit ... a wise old hen. Reissued tinted and with sound in 1930 by Copley Pictures Corp.

2066. Felix the Cat in the Smoke-Scream *(Felix the Cat)* 8 Jan. 1928; *p.c.:* Bijou Films Inc for Educational; b&w. *sil.* 6 min. • Felix helps his boss smuggle "smokes" past his wife. When the boss's whiskers catch fire, Felix organizes himself into a Fire Department, saves all from the smoke and is elected a hero. Reissued tinted and with sound in 1930 by Copley Pictures Corp.

2067. Felix the Cat in the Travel-Hog *(Felix the Cat)* 24 July 1928; *p.c.:* Bijou Films Inc for Educational; b&w. *sil.* 6 min. • A mule kicks Felix into a tornado that blows him to the Arctic where seals juggle him to Holland. Windmills propel him into a large horn that blows him to the moon, where he drops to Italy's boot, is toward to Egypt and a volcano transports him back home.

2068. Felix the Cat in Two-Lip Time *(Felix the Cat)* 22 Aug. 1926; *p.c.:* Bijou Films Inc for Educational; b&w. *sil.* 6 min. • Felix finds himself in Holland and gets in "dutch" by flirting with a girl and watering tulips with gin. He is chased around windmills that finally blow his tormentor away.

2069. Felix the Cat in Uncle Tom's Crabbin' *(Felix the Cat)* 13 Nov. 1927; *p.c.:* Bijou Films Inc for Educational; b&w. *sil.* 6 min. • Uncle Tom's banjo playing disturbs Simon Legree. When Felix constructs a new banjo from pancakes, Legree gives chase through an ice wagon. Reissued tinted and with sound in 1930 by Copley Pictures Corp.

2070. Felix the Cat in Why and Other Whys *(Felix the Cat)* 27 Nov. 1927; *p.c.:* Bijou Films Inc for Educational; b&w. *sil.* 6 min. • When Felix arrives home at four A.M., his wife asks "Why?" and he enacts his experiences, explaining that he spent his pay on a fur coat for her and candy for the kids.

2071. Felix the Cat in Wise Guise *(Felix the Cat)* 4 Sept. 1927; *p.c.:* Bijou Films Inc for Educational; b&w. *sil.* 6 min. • Felix impresses Kitty by winning a swimming race (with help from a fish) only to find that his own shadow is his rival for her.

2072. Felix the Cat in Zoo Logic *(Felix the Cat)* 26 Dec. 1926; *p.c.:* Bijou Films Inc for Educational; b&w. *sil.* 6 min. • Felix releases the zoo animals and they run riot around the town, finally realizing that life was happier behind bars.

2073. Felix the Cat Kept on Walking *(Felix the Cat)* 27 Dec. 1925;

p.c.: Bijou Films Inc for Educational; b&w. *sil.* 6 min. • Felix meets a poet who informs him, "Beyond the horizon lie riches." He starts walking toward the horizon but is astonished to find that the more he walks the farther away it seems. Eventually he has traveled the globe.

2074. Felix the Cat Misses His Swiss *(Felix the Cat)* 25 July 1926; *p.c.:* Bijou Film Inc for Educational; b&w. *sil.* 6 min. • Felix pursues mouse marauders all the way to Switzerland where they go for Swiss cheese.

2075. Felix the Cat Misses the Cue *(Felix the Cat)* 18 Apr. 1926; *p.c.:* Bijou Films Inc for Educational; b&w. *sil.* 6 min. • Felix gets mixed in with the family wash and finds himself in a Chinese laundry. He escapes by burrowing down through the earth, arriving in China. After a number of encounters he escapes, pursued by angry Chinamen, finally arriving at Ellis Island where the Immigration Officer holds up a sign saying "Quota from China filled."

2076. Felix the Cat Monkeys with Magic *(Pat Sullivan Comic)* 8 May 1925; *p.c.:* Sullivan Studio for M.J. Winkler; b&w. *sil.* 6 min. • Felix steals a magician's magic book. He makes a lion's picture come alive and it chases him.

2077. Felix the Cat on the Farm *(Felix the Cat)* 4 Oct. 1925; *p.c.:* Sullivan Studio for M.J. Winkler; b&w. *sil.* 6 min. • Felix is booted by the farmer and lands in a swamp. He's chased by a swarm of mosquitoes, landing in a cider keg where they imbibe, attacking Felix and the farmer and causing drunkenness all 'round.

2078. Felix the Cat on the Job *(Felix the Cat)* 18 Oct. 1925; *p.c.:* Sullivan Studio for M. J. Winkler; b&w. *sil.* 6 min. • Stowaway Felix is made to work his passage scrubbing decks. Upon reaching a lighthouse, he gets his revenge by ingeniously diverting hordes from the lighthouse to the ship.

2079. Felix the Cat Outwits Cupid *(Pat Sullivan Comic)* 27 Apr. 1925; *p.c.:* Sullivan Studio for M.J. Winkler; b&w. *sil.* 6 min. • No story available.

2080. Felix the Cat Rests in Peace *(Pat Sullivan Comic)* 15 Feb. 1925; *p.c.:* Sullivan Studio for M.J. Winkler; b&w. *sil.* 6 min. • No story available.

2081. Felix the Cat Rings the Ringer *(Felix the Cat)* 13 June 1926; *p.c.:* Bijou Films Inc for Educational; b&w. *sil.* 6 min. • Felix's search for food finds him at the circus. He pilfers a hot dog and is chased into the Big Top; there he accidentally amuses the audience, earning himself a contract for "plenty of eats" from the manager.

2082. Felix the Cat Scoots Thru Scotland *(Felix the Cat)* 30 May 1926; *p.c.:* Bijou Films Inc for Educational; b&w. *sil.* 6 min. • Felix stows away in a package for Scotland. When golfer Sandy Hook discovers the stowaway, he uses Felix to play in a golf tournament by using his tail as a club and nose as the ball. When the cat proves too much for another Scot, he puts him in a bag and tries to drown the feline. Felix manages to escape this watery grave and runs for his life, still in the bag with the Scotsman in hot pursuit. They enter a hall where a bagpipe contest is in process and, when the Scotsman grabs the bag, Felix squeals and they win the bagpipe championship.

2083. Felix the Cat Seeks Solitude *(Felix the Cat)* 11 July 1926; *p.c.:* Bijou Films Inc for Educational; b&w. *sil.* 6 min. • Felix steals a fish and seeks solitude from prying eyes on the ocean bed. Relatives of the fish threaten him until he returns it.

2084. Felix the Cat Sees 'em in Season *(Felix the Cat)* 6 Mar. 1927; *p.c.:* Bijou Films Inc for Educational; b&w. *sil.* 6 min. • Felix and the mice fall victim to "Spring Fever."

2085. Felix the Cat Shatters the Sheik *(Felix the Cat)* 19 Sept. 1926; *p.c.:* Bijou Films Inc for Educational; b&w. *sil.* 6 min. • Felix helps out an umbrella salesman in the desert by attracting thousands of birds and making them cry (with onions) over a convention of Sheiks.

2086. Felix the Cat Spots the Spook *(Felix the Cat)* 10 Jan. 1926; *p.c.:* Bijou Films Inc for Educational; b&w. *sil.* 6 min. Felix finds solace in a house. The mice disguise themselves as a ghost to evict him. He unmasks them and earns himself a comfortable home and gratitude of the owner.

2087. Felix the Cat Stars in Stripes *(Felix the Cat)* 20 Feb. 1927;

p.c.: Bijou Films Inc for Educational; b&w. *sil.* 6 min. • Felix finds himself in jail, burrows out under a lake, causing the prison yard to flood.

2088. Felix the Cat Switches Witches (*Felix the Cat*) 2 Oct. 1927; *p.c.:* Bijou Films Inc for Educational; b&w. *sil.* 6 min. • An owl fortune-teller tells Felix he's going to find romance. He runs afoul of a witch who chases him but turns out to be a pretty kitty cat. Reissued tinted and with sound in 1930 by Copley Pictures Corp.

2089. Felix the Cat: The Movie 1988; *p.c.:* Felix the Cat Creations, Inc./Productions, Inc. for Transatlantic; *dir:* Tibor Hernádi; *prod:* Don Oriolo, Christian Schneider, Janos Schenk; *ex prod (Hungary):* Jozsef Bujár; *line prod:* István Butala; *asso prods:* Reneé Daalder, Michael Gladishev; *prod mgr:* Lászlo Kun, Gábor Morvay, Péter Kardos, Halinka Swigón; *scr:* Don Oriolo, Pete Brown; *original story:* Don Oriolo; *storyboard/prod des:* Tibor A. Belay, Tibor Hernádi; *addit dial:* Michael Fremer; *video: ed:* Woody Wilson, Julia Moye; *anim dir:* Tibor A. Belay, Grzegorz Handzlik, Roman Klys, Edit Hernádi, Ryszard Lepiure, Tibor Hernádi, Péter Tenkei; *anim:* Ferenc Dékány, Emmi Foky, Julia Glück, Edit Hernádi, Nóra Javorniczky, Ilona Kiss, Casbàné Major, Beáta Olajos, András Paulovics, Gábor Pichler, Yvette Sostarics, Péter Tenkei, Hajnal Eszes, Rita Fülöp, János Hangya, Oszkár Hernádi, Iván Jonkovszky, Imre Kukánvi, Magdolna Bozsóki Nagyne, Hermann Pasitkai, Katalin Kiss Pólfine, József Schibik, Csaba Szóràdy, Janos Uzsàk, Ervinné Zágonyi, Malina Docseva, Janko Trajanov, Deszpina Zseliázova, Atanasz Vasziliev, Rumen Georgiev, Evgebi Linkov, Ivan Hadzsitonev, Anton Trajanov, Szonja Alekszieva, Nasztimir Toacsev, T. Rakowska-klis, P. Byrski, I. Cholerek, J. Radon, St. Swider, M. Kaczmar, O. Sadkowska, L. Habrzyk, K. Lawson, E. Kurysia, J. Matusik, Z. Benkowska, A. Czaderna, M. Grabysa, A. Bylica, M. Kruezah, E. Burek, A. Kuszlsa, A. Duda, A. Flettner, M. Hurda, Z. Kaptocz, J. Klimas; *original Felix character des:* Don Oriolo; *lay:* Tibor Hernádi, Tibor A. Belay, Edit Hernádi, Arpád Szabo, Nándor Marko, Oszkár Hernádi, Julia Glück; *back:* Károly Kismányoki, Andrós Bodó, Sándor Snepp, István Orosz, Gyözo Vida, Kálmán Szijártó, István Fillenz, Zoltán Tardos, Ferenc Cakó, Vladimir Spásojevic; *ed:* Valeria Schenk; *creative des:* Brad Degraf, Michael Wahrman; *puppeteer:* Eren Ozker; *modelling:* Steve Segal; *programming:* John Adamczyk; *voices:* Chris Phillips, Maureen O'Connell, Peter Neuman, Alice Playton, Susan Montanaro, Don Oriolo, Christian Schneider, David Kolin; *mus:* Christopher L. Stone; *mus consult:* Jürgen Korduletsch; *addit mus:* Bernd Schonofen, Don Oriolo, Christian Schneider; *songs:* Don Oriolo, Pete Brown, Christian Schneider; *title des:* Pierluca de Carlo; *opticals:* Greg van der Veer, Pat O'Neill; *i&p sup:* Betti Rozsahegyi, Katalin Bánfalvi, Böbe Melczer; *i&p:* Katalin Abrahám, Judit Bagó, Andrea Bagi, Belinda Bajsz, Gábor Balla, Andrea Balogh, Ilona Balogh, István Bandzsók, Béata Barna, Katalin Bánfalvi, Bea Bányász, Gyula Berki, Erna Bird, Andrea Borbély, Tünde Böezörmónyi, Mónika Bujáki, Zsuzsa Bujáki, Eszter Csáki, Agnes Czáfa, Krisztina Dávid, Julia Demosák, Andrea Demeter, Zsuzsa Déri, Eva Dikász, Gábor Farádi, Krisztina Fehér, Gábor Flór, Noémi Flór, Zsuzsanna Garamszegi, Annamária Gyebnár, Eszter György, Éva Haraszti, Péter Herozeg, Andrea Holczinger, Magdolna Jehoda, Csilla Kabai, Enikó Kaloosai, Lászlóné Kaposi, Geherozodo Kasim, Tiborné Kaszás, Ferenoné Kerekes, Erika Kiss, Bernadett Elcöd Klauszné, Erika Kocsis, Lászloné Kocsis, Lászlo Konoz, Gabriella Gyórössy Kovács, Gabriella Körmöczi, Judit Körmöczi, Edit Kövér, Éva Kurilla, Erzsébet Kurucz, Zsuzsanna Kustra, Katalin Láng, Ella Magyari, Mária Maráczy, Ingrid Martinek, Mária Máté, Levente Mátrai, Éva Óvári Mátrainé, Gézáné Melczer, Tiborne Meleghegyi, Katalin Messing, Tamásné Mirk, Ildikó Magda Molnárné, Kálmánré Nagy, Zsuzsanna Nagy, Eva Keleman Nagyné, Eta Nánási, Bea Nemes, Edit Pansák, Miklós Papp, Raymuncné Pataky, Lászlóné Páhi, István Palfi, Jánosné Páni, Márta Pásztor, Mária Pénzár, Jánosné Pócs, Mónika Polaschek, Klára Polecsak, Borbála, Agnes Remenyi, Lászlóné Remeczky, Eva Románcz, Edit Sárkány, Anna Sasvari, Andrea Siba, Maria Simon, Gabriella Szabo, István Szabó, Mariann Szili, Eniko Szombati, Gizi Gonda Szorádiné, Györgyne Szúcs, Csaba Tóth, Endre Tóth, Klára Tuza, Erzsébet Udvarnoki, Eva Szabo Vágine, Eszter Vágó, Emóké Vata, Attila Vona, Dóra Votin, Ágnes Völler, Mariann Németh Párizné, Mariann Nyakó, Kovácsné Vágasi; *ph:* Laszlo Radocsay, Erzsébet Nemes, Lilla Hambalko, Erzsébet Balàzs; *ph fx:* Làszlo Radocsay; *sd re-rec:* Sherry Kheim, Greg Hodge, Tim Garrity; *sd ed/dial ed:* Gerry Lentz, Sherry Kheim; *Synclavier sd fx:* Jeff Vaughan, Ann Scibelli, Rusty Smith, Harvey Cohen; *foley:* Terry O'Brite, Keith Kresge; *col. sd.*

82 min. • When her kingdom is attacked by the Duke of Zill, Princess Oriana sends for help. The message reaches Felix the Cat who travels through another dimension to reach the Kingdom of Oriana. Along the way he is captured by a reptilian circus owner and put on show where he encounters the imprisoned Princess. With help from his magic bag, Felix spirits her away from the circus to Oriana's castle where they are seized by the Duke's war machines. The Duke threatens to kill his captives unless they hand over *The Book of Ultimate Power*. The Princess gives him the book but its ultimate message about the effectiveness of Truth, Love and Wisdom breaks the Duke and he loses control over Oriana. USA/Hungary.

2090. Felix the Cat Tries for Treasure (*Pat Sullivan Comic*) 15 Apr. 1923; *p.c.:* Sullivan Studio for M.J. Winkler; b&w. *sil.* 6 min. • Felix and Sammy run out of fuel in a submarine while searching for pearls. A "loan Shark" then trades gas for the pearls.

2091. Felix the Cat Tries the Trades (*Felix the Cat*) 5 Dec. 1925; *p.c.:* Bijou Films Inc for Educational; b&w. *sil.* 6 min. • Construction worker Felix causes the other workers to strike when the boss asks for nine workmen and he produces all his "nine lives."

2092. Felix the Cat Trifles with Time (*Felix the Cat*) 23 Aug. 1925; *p.c.:* Bijou Films Inc for Educational; b&w. *sil.* 6 min. • When Felix implores Father Time to send him back to a better age, he does, ending Felix up in prehistoric times.

2093. Felix the Cat Trips Through Toyland (*Felix the Cat*) 20 Sept. 1925; *p.c.:* Bijou Films Inc for Educational; b&w. *sil.* 6 min. • Felix visits Toyland where a clown steals his pretty escort ... but he manages to rescue her.

2094. Felix the Cat Trumps the Ace (*Felix the Cat*) 28 Nov. 1926; *p.c.:* Bijou Films Inc for Educational; b&w. *sil.* 6 min. • Felix encounters "The Ace of Clowns" in a circus who kids him, causing a chase over high-wires and roller-coasters.

2095. Felix the Cat Uses His Head (*Felix the Cat*) 4 Apr. 1926; *p.c.:* Bijou Films Inc for Educational; b&w. *sil.* 6 min. • After our hero drops a broiled chicken into a pond, a hen mistakes his tail for a worm and stretches it to a length that he can lasso the chicken from the pond with it.

2096. Felix the Cat Woos Whoopee (*Felix the Cat*) 1930; *p.c.:* Bijou Films Inc for Copley Pictures Corp; *prod:* Jacques Kopfstein, Pat Sullivan; *anim:* Otto Messmer; *mus:* Bernard Altshuler; *sd fx:* Harry Edison; b&w. *sd.* 6 min. • Homeward bound, an inebriated Felix hallucinates monsters chasing him.

2097. Felix the Fox (*Terry-Toon*) 10 Mar. 1948; *p.c.:* TT for Fox; *dir:* Mannie Davis; *story:* John Foster; *anim:* Jim Tyer; *mus:* Philip A. Scheib; *col:* Tech. *sd:* RCA. 7 min. • Dimwit chases a clever fox who turns out to be a skunk.

2098. Felix the Globe Trotter (*Pat Sullivan Comic*) 1 June 1923; *p.c.:* Sullivan Studios for M.J. Winkler; b&w. *sil.* 6 min. • A fairground boxing kangaroo's owner strikes a deal with Felix to go and bring another one back from Australia when his own one departs this life.

2099. Felix the Goat-Getter (*Pat Sullivan Comic*) 1 Dec. 1923; *p.c.:* Sullivan Studio for M.J. Winkler; b&w. *sil.* 6 min. • Felix helps a kid do his chores by getting a goat to beat a carpet via head-butting.

2100. Felix Tries to Rest (*Pat Sullivan Comic*) 1 Apr. 1924; *p.c.:* Sullivan Studio for M.J. Winkler; b&w. *sil.* 6 min. • Felix catches a snooze in a dog's kennel while the dog is busy chasing a hobo. He is later set upon by the hobo, a donkey, a bird and a pig.

2101. Felix Turns the Tide (*Pat Sullivan Comic*) 1 Jan. 1923; *p.c.:* Sullivan Studios for M.J. Winkler; b&w. *sil.* 6 min. • The rats declare war on cats and Felix joins the Army. After a battle he contacts a butcher who sends an army of sausages which march on the rats and win the war.

2102. Felix Wakes Up (*Pat Sullivan Comic*) 15 Sept. 1922; *p.c.:* Sullivan Studio for M.J. Winkler; b&w. *sil.* 6 min. • Felix's curbside sleep is awakened by a scientist who's discovered the elixir of youth. He feeds it to our hero who returns to kittenhood.

2103. Felix Weathers the Weather (*Felix the Cat*) 21 Mar. 1926; *p.c.:* Bijou Films Inc for Educational; b&w. *sil.* 6 min. • The Felix family repeatedly try to picnic but are foiled by bad weather. He seeks revenge on the weatherman by manipulating the weather control levers.

2104. Felix Wins and Loses *(Pat Sullivan Comic)* 1 Jan. 1925; *p.c.:* Sullivan Studio for M.J. Winkler; b&w. *sil.* 6 min. • While eluding the law for stealing sausages, Felix captures an escaped bear and returns it for a rich reward.

2105. Felix Wins Out *(Pat Sullivan Comic)* 15 Jan. 1923; *p.c.:* Sullivan Studio for M.J. Winkler; b&w. *sil.* 6 min. • Felix makes the circus fat lady thin enough to marry the "Human Skeleton." He gets thrown out by the proprietor and wreaks his revenge by putting fleas on all the animals.

2106. The Fella with the Fiddle *(Merrie Melodies)* 27 Mar. 1937; *p.c.:* Leon Schlesinger prods for WB; *dir:* I. Freleng; *anim:* Cal Dalton, Ken Harris; *lay:* Griff Jay; *back:* Arthur Loomer; *ed:* Tregoweth E. Brown; *voices:* Billy Bletcher, Bernice Hansel, Mel Blanc; *mus:* Carl W. Stalling; *prod sup:* Henry Binder, Raymond G. Katz; *col:* Tech. *sd:* Vit. 7 min. • A mouse tells a cautionary tale of a greedy rodent who hid his vast wealth from the tax assessor and landed in the jaws of the cat.

2107. Females Is Fickle *(Popeye)* 8 Mar. 1940; *p.c.:* The Fleischer Studio for Para; *prod:* Max Fleischer; *dir:* Dave Fleischer; *story:* Joseph E. Stultz; *anim:* David Tendlar, William Sturm; *ed:* Kitty Pfister; *voices:* Jack Mercer, Margie Hines, Pinto Colvig; *mus:* Sammy Timberg; *ph:* Charles Schettler; *prod mgr:* Sam Buchwald; b&w. *sd:* WE. 7 min. • Olive's pet goldfish falls in the sea and she sends Popeye to rescue him.

2108. Ferdinand the Bull 25 Nov. 1938; *p.c.:* Walt Disney prods for RKO; *dir:* Dick Rickard; *story:* Munro Leaf, Robert Lawson; *adapt:* Larry Morey; *anim:* John Bradbury, Johnny Campbell, Bernard Garbutt, Milton Kahl, Ward Kimball, I. Klein, Don Lusk, Hamilton S. Luske, Osmond Evans, Robert Stokes, Stan Quackenbush; *char des:* T. Hee; *back:* Kenneth Anderson, Claude Coats; *voices:* Don Wilson, Milton Kahl; *mus:* Albert Hay Malotte; *col:* Tech. *sd:* RCA. 8 min. *Academy Award.* • Mistaken for a ferocious bull, peace-loving Ferdinand is taken to the bull ring. Bill Tytla, Fred Moore, Art Babbitt, Ham Luske, Johnny Campbell, Ward Kimball and Walt Disney are caricatured as matadors and picadors.

2109. FernGully the Last Rain Forest 10 Apr. 1992; *p.c.:* FAI Film Pty Ltd. for Fox; *dir:* Bill Kroyer; *prod:* Wayne Young, Peter Faiman; *co-prod:* Jim Cox, Brian Rosen, Richard Harper; *ex prod:* Ted Field, Robert W. Cort; *co-ex prod:* Jeff Dowd, William F. Willett; *scr:* Jim Cox; based on the stories of "Ferngully" by Diana Young; *line prod:* Tom Klein; *creative consultant:* Matthew Perry; *art dir:* Susan Kroyer; *anim prod consultant:* Charles Leland Richardson; *ed:* Gillian Hutshing; *mus:* Alan Silvestri; *mus sup:* Tim Sexton, Becky Mancuso; *anim prod:* Kroyer Films, Inc.; *art dir/col styling:* Ralph Eggleston; *lay:* Victoria Jenson; *anim dir:* Tony Fucile; *fx dir:* Sari Gennis; *seq dir:* Bret Hasland, Tim Hauser, Dan Jeup, Susan Kroyer; *artistic sup: storyboard:* Tom Mazzocco; *lay:* Dan McHugh; *anim:* Tim Hauser, Dori Littell Herrick; *computer anim:* Mark Pompian; *back:* Dennis Venizelos; *scene planning:* Geoffrey Schroeder; *check:* Kitty Schoentag, Pat Sito; *character des:* Tony Fucile, Dan Jeup, Kathy Zielinski, Susan Kroyer, Phil Mendez, Mike Giaimo; *leveller des:* Graham (Grace) Walker, Mike Cachuela, Michael Scheffe; *conceptual artist pre-prod:* Jean Perramon; *storyboard:* Craig Armstrong, Ken Bruce, Mike Sosnowski, Victoria Jenson, Doug Lefler, Dan Jeup, Sherilan Weinhart, Mike Cachuela, Ralph Eggleston, Bret Haaland, Doug Frankel, Dave Brewster, Stefan Fjeldmark; *leading character anim: Crysta:* Doug Frankel, David Brewster; *Zak:* Chrystal Klabunde; *Magi Lane:* Jeffrey James Varab; *Hexxus:* Kathy Zielinski, John Allan Armstrong; *Batty Koda:* Dan Kuenster; *Tony/Ralph:* Chuck Gammage; *The Gosama/Pips:* Stefan Fjeldmark; *anim:* Jesse Cosio, Wendy Purdue, Mike Cahuela, Ken Bruce, Tony Fucile, Susan Kroyer, Greg Manwaring, Dan Jeup, Mike Genz, Roy Meurin, Chris Sauve, Susan M. Zytka, Ralph Eggleston, Marc Sevier, Greg Hill, John Collins, Hanna Kukal, Jamie Oliff, Bob Scott, John Eddings, Roger Chiasson, Charlie Bonafacio, Doug Bennett, Bibo Bergeron, Ulrich W. Meyer, Glenn Sylvester, David Bowers, Steve Markowski; *A-Film—Copenhagen:* Asts Sigurdardottir, Karsten Kiilerich, Hans Perk, Kim Hagen Jensen, Jesper Moller, Michael Helmuth Hansen, Jorgen Lerdam, Nancy Carrig, Sahin Ersoz, Anna Gellert Nielsen, Meelis Arulepp; *voices: Crysta:* Samantha Mathis; *Zak:* Jonathan Ward; *Pips:* Christian Slater; *Magi Lune:* Grace Zabriskie; *Batty Koda:* Robin Williams; *Hexxus:* Tim Curry; *Ralph:* Geoffrey Blake; *Tony:* Robert Pastorelli; *Stump:* Cheech Marin; *Root:* Tommy Chong; *Knotty:* Townsend Coleman; *Ock:* Brian Cummings; *Elder 1:* Kathleen Freeman; *Fairy 1:* Janet Gilmore; *Elder 2:* Naomi Lewis; *Ash, Voice of Dispatch:* Danny Mann; *Elder 3:* Neil Ross; *Fairy 2:* Pamela Segall; *Rock:* Anderson Wong; *also:* Lauri Hendler, Rosanna Huffman, Harvey Jason, Dave Mallow, Paige Nan Pollack, Holly Ryan, Gary Schwartz; *songs:* "Life Is a Magical Thing" by Thomas Dolby, performed by Johnny Clegg; "A Dream Is Worth Keeping" by Jimmy Webb & Alan Silvestri, performed by Sheena Easton; "Batty Rap" by Thomas Dalby, Stuart Young & Nic Young, performed by Robin Williams; "Lithuanian Lullaby (traditional)" performed by Veronika Povilionicac; "If I'm Gonna Eat Somebody (It Might as Well be You)" by Jimmy Buffett & Michael Otley, performed by Tone-Loc; "Toxic Love" by Thomas Dolby, performed by Tim Curry; "Spis, Li Milke Le" by Gurorgai Minichev, performed by Le Mysterie des Voix Balgares; "Raining Like Magic" by/performed by Raffi; "Bamnqobile" by Joseph Shibilala, performed by Ladysmith Black Mambazo; "Land of a Thousand Dances" by Chris Kramer, performed by Guy; "Tri Jetrve (traditional)" performed by Zbor Ierkestar; "Some Other World" by Bruce Roberts, Elton John, performed by Elton John; *sd rec:* Thomas Dolby, Mick Guzauski, Chris Porter, Dave Reitzas, Al Schmitt, Brian Shueble, Bobby Summerfield, Dave Way, John Chamberland, Bruce Keen, Ken Keroshetz, Gil Morales, Charles Paakkari, Robert Reed, Phil Reynolds, Chris Rich, Sandy Solomon; *main title des:* Sari Gennis; *titles:* Howard A. Anderson Co.; *enviroment consultant:* Thomas E. Lovejoy; *col:* DeLuxe. *sd:* Dolby stereo. 76 min. • Crysta, a spirit of FernGully, flies beyond the edge of the rainforest and witnesses a logging operation that is destroying her home. She saves the life of one of the logging crew, Zak, but in doing so, shrinks him to the size of a sprite. The two of them return to FernGully and rally to stop their forest from being devastated.

2110. The Feud *(Paul Terry-Toon)* 10 Jan. 1936; *p.c.:* Moser & Terry for Educational/Fox; *dir:* Paul Terry, Frank Moser; *mus:* Philip A. Scheib; b&w. *sd:* WE. 6 min. • Hillbillies feuding as the theme.

2111. A Feud There Was *(Merrie Melodies)* 24 Sept. 1938; *p.c.:* Leon Schlesinger prods for WB; *dir:* Fred Avery; *story:* Melvin Millar, Robert Clampett; *anim:* Sid Sutherland; *sets:* John Didrik Johnsen; *ed:* Tregoweth E. Brown; *voices:* Mel Blanc, The Sons of the Pioneers, Dave Weber, Fred Avery; *mus:* Carl W. Stalling; *prod sup:* Henry Binder, Raymond G. Katz; *col:* Tech. *sd:* Vit. 7 min. • When a peacemaker arrives in the center of a hillbilly feud, both clans agree on one thing ... eliminate the peacemaker!

2112. Feud with a Dude *(Merrie Melodies)* 4 May 1968; *p.c.:* WB; *dir:* Alex Lovy; *story:* Cal Howard; *anim:* Ted Bonnicksen, La Verne Harding, Volus Jones, Ed Solomon; *lay:* Bob Givens; *back:* Bob Abrams; *ed:* Hal Geer; *voices:* Larry Storch; *mus:* William Lava; *prod:* Bill L. Hendricks; *col:* Tech. *sd:* Vit. 6 min. *anim/l/a.* • Merlin the Magic Mouse and Second Banana are caught in the center of a hillbilly feud.

2113. Feudin', Fightin' 'n' Fussin' *(Woody Woodpecker)* Mar. 1968; *p.c.:* Walter Lantz prods for Univ; *dir:* Paul J. Smith; *story:* Cal Howard; *anim:* Les Kline, Al Coe; *sets:* Ray Huffine; *voices:* Dal McKennon, Grace Stafford; *mus:* Walter Greene; *prod mgr:* William E. Garity; *col:* Tech. *sd:* RCA. 6 min. • Paw eats all the food, so Maw tells him to go and get some more food. Armed with his shotgun, Paw sets out to shoot a woodpecker.

2114. The Feudin' Hillbillies *(Mighty Mouse)* Apr. 1948; *p.c.:* TT for Fox; *dir:* Connie Rasinski; *story:* John Foster; *voice:* Tom Morrison; *mus:* Philip A. Scheib; *ph:* Douglas Moye; *col:* Tech. *sd:* RCA. 7 min. • Mighty Mouse acts as arbitrator between two families of feuding hillbillies.

2115. Fiddle-Faddle *(Modern Madcap)* 26 Feb. 1960; *p.c.:* Para Cartoons; *dir:* Seymour Kneitel; *story:* Carl Meyer, Jack Mercer; *anim:* Tom Johnson, Irving Dressler; *sets:* Robert Owen. *voices:* Bob MacFadden; *mus:* Winston Sharples; *prod mgr:* Abe Goodman; *col:* Tech. *sd:* RCA. 6 min. • Professor Schmaltz demonstrates how "music soothes the savage beast."

2116. Fiddlesticks *(Flip the Frog)* Aug. 1930; *p.c.:* Celebrity prods for MGM; *prod/dir:* Ub Iwerks; *anim:* Fred Kopietz, Tony Pabian; *col:* Tech-2. *sd:* PCP. 7 min. • Flip's musical entertainment consists of him dancing a "hornpipe" and battling with an over-active piano.

2117. Fiddlin' Around *(Noveltoon)* Dec. 1962; *p.c.:* Para Cartoons; *dir:* Seymour Kneitel. *story:* I. Klein; *anim:* Nick Tafuri, John Gentilella, I. Klein; *sets:* Anton Loeb; *voices:* Bob MacFadden; *mus:* Winston Sharples; *ph:* Leonard McCormick; *prod mgr:* Abe Goodman; *col:* Tech. *sd:* RCA. 6 min. • When a famous violinist insures his violin for $1 million, the insurance company insists a bodyguard accompanies him on a world tour.

2118. Fiddlin' Fun (*Cubby Bear*) 15 June 1934; *p.c.:* Van Beuren for RKO; *dir:* George Stallings; *anim:* Steve Muffatti; *mus:* Winston Sharples; b&w. *sd:* RCA. 7 min. • Cubby enters a Roman chariot race up against a cheating rival.

2119. Fido Beta Kappa (*Noveltoon*) 29 Oct. 1954; *p.c.:* Famous for Para; *dir:* I. Sparber; *story:* Irving Spector; *anim:* Al Eugster, George Germanetti; *sets:* Robert Little; *voices:* Frank Matalone, Jackson Beck; *mus:* Winston Sharples; *ph:* Leonard McCormick; *prod mgr:* Seymour Shultz; *col:* Tech. *sd:* RCA. 6 min. • A dumb dog is sent to get an education and returns a good deal smarter than his owner.

2120. Field and Scream 30 Apr. 1955; *p.c.:* MGM; *dir:* Tex Avery; *story:* Heck Allen; *anim:* Grant Simmons, Walter Clinton, Michael Lah; *lay/char des:* Ed Benedict; *back:* John Didrik Johnsen; *ed:* Jim Faris; *mus:* Scott Bradley; *ph:* Jack Stevens; *prod:* Fred Quimby; *col:* Tech. *sd:* WE. 7 min. • Spot-gags on the latest hunting and fishing equipment.

2121. The Field Mouse (*MGM Cartoon*) 27 Dec. 1941; *p.c.:* MGM; *prod/dir:* Hugh Harman; *story:* Hugh Harman, Jack Cosgriff, Charles McGirl; *anim:* Robert Allen, Preston Blair, William Littlejohn; *char des:* Robert Allen. *lay:* John Meandor; *back:* Joe Smith; *voices:* Mel Blanc; *mus:* Scott Bradley; *prod mgr:* Fred Quimby; *col:* Tech. *sd:* WE. 9 min. • A lazy little field mouse tries to rescue his Grandpa when the community is threatened by a combined harvester.

2122. The Fiery Fireman (*Oswald the Lucky Rabbit*) 27 Sept. 1928; *p.c.:* Winkler for Univ; *anim:* Isadore Freleng, Rudolf Ising; b&w. *sil.* 6 min. • Oswald and his partner deal in various enterprising ways in extinguishing a fire.

2123. Fiesta Fiasco (*Looney Tunes*) 9 Dec. 1967; *p.c.:* WB/7A; *dir:* Alex Lovy; *story:* Cal Howard; *anim:* Ted Bonnicksen, La Verne Harding, Volus Jones, Ed Solomon; *lay:* Jaime R. Diaz, Bob Givens, David Hanan; *back:* Bob Abrams; *ed:* Hal Geer; *voices:* Mel Blanc; *mus:* William Lava; *prod:* William L. Hendricks; *col:* Tech. *sd:* Vit. 6 min. • Daffy isn't invited to Speedy's party and decides to ruin it for the mice.

2124. Fiesta Time (*Color Rhapsody*) 12 July 1945; *p.c.:* Colum; *dir/story:* Bob Wickersham; *anim:* Paul Sommer, Chic Otterstrom; *sets:* Clark Watson; *ed:* Richard S. Jensen; *voices:* Robert Winkler, Harry E. Lang; *mus:* Eddie Kilfeather; *prod mgr:* Hugh McCollum; *col:* Tech. *sd:* WE. 8 min. • Burro helps sneak Tito's girl out of the hacienda under the disapproving eyes of her father.

2125. Fiesta Time (*Screen Song*) 17 Nov. 1950; *p.c.:* Famous for Para; *dir:* Seymour Kneitel; *story:* I. Klein; *anim:* Myron Waldman, Larry Silverman; *sets:* Anton Loeb; *voices:* Jackson Beck, Sid Raymond; *mus:* Winston Sharples; *ph:* Leonard McCormick; *prod mgr:* Sam Buchwald; *col:* Tech. *sd:* RCA. 7 min. • A trip to Mexico ends with a sing-along — "En El Rancho Grande," using a Mexican jumping bean replacing the bouncing ball.

2126. Fifth Column Mouse (*Merrie Melodies*) 6 Mar. 1943; *p.c.:* Leon Schlesinger prods for WB; *dir:* I. Freleng; *story:* Ted Pierce; *lay:* Owen Fitzgerald; *back:* Lenard Kester; *ed:* Treg Brown; *voices:* Mel Blanc, Ted Pierce; *group:* Sherry Allen, Archie Berhal, Larry Burch, Robert Remington; *mus:* Carl W. Stalling; *ph:* John W. Burton; *prod sup:* Henry Binder, Raymond G. Katz; *col:* Tech. *sd:* Vit. *srt:* 7 min. • A traitor mouse is bribed by the cat to enlist the services of his fellow mice but when the cat desires a diet of mouse meat, the mice rebel.

2127. Figaro and Cleo 15 Oct. 1943 *p.c.:* Walt Disney prods for RKO; *dir:* Jack Kinney; *asst dir:* Lou Debney; *story:* Ralph Wright, Jack Kinney; *anim:* Les Clark, Don Lusk, Hamilton S. Luske, Marvin Woodward; *lay:* Don da Gradi; *voices:* Lillian Randolph, Clarence Nash; *singer:* Kate-Ellen Murtagh; *mus:* Paul J. Smith; *col:* Tech. *sd:* RCA. 8 min. • Figaro's mischief makes Aunt Delilah deprive him of his cream ration. Hunger gets the better of him, so he pursues Cleo the goldfish. • Rescued from an unused segment of *Pinocchio*, substituting the black maid for Gepetto.

2128. Figaro and Frankie (*Figaro*) 30 May 1946; *p.c.:* Walt Disney prods for RKO; *dir:* Charles Nichols; *asst dir:* Jack Bruner; *story:* Eric Gurney, Bill de la Torre; *anim:* Marvin Woodward, George Nicholas, Robert Youngquist, Jerry Hathcock, George Kreisl; *fx:* Blaine Gibson, Harry Holt; *lay:* Karl Karpé; *back:* Art Landy; *voices:* Leone Le Doux, Gloria Blondell, Clarence Nash, James MacDonald; *mus:* Oliver Wallace; *col:* Tech. *sd:* RCA.

7 min. • Minnie warns Figaro about tormenting the canary but they unite in defeating a bulldog.

2129. The Fight Game (*Aesop's Film Fable*) 26 Apr. 1929; *p.c.:* Fables Pictures Inc for Pathé; *dir:* Paul Terry; b&w. *sil.* 6 min. • Farmer Al trains the animals for Exhibition Bouts in the boxing ring. A mouse battles a hot dog, then a rooster. An ape gets in the ring to fight the rooster and Farmer Al is caught in the mêlée.

2130. A Fight to the Finish (*Mighty Mouse*) 14 Nov. 1947; *p.c.:* TT for Fox; *dir:* Connie Rasinski; *story:* John Foster; *voice:* Roy Halee; *mus:* Philip A. Scheib; *ph:* Douglas Moye; *col:* Tech. *sd:* RCA. 7 min. • Melodrama in which Mighty Mouse rescues Pearl Pureheart from the villain and finds himself tied to the railroad tracks.

2131. Fightin' Pals (*Popeye*) 12 July 1940; *p.c.:* The Fleischer Studio for Para; *prod:* Max Fleischer; *dir:* Dave Fleischer; *story:* Joseph E. Stultz; *anim:* Willard Bowsky, Robert Bentley; *ed:* Kitty Pfister; *voices:* Jack Mercer, Pinto Colvig; *mus:* Sammy Timberg; *prod sup:* Sam Buchwald, Isidore Sparber; b&w. *sd:* WE. 7 min. • Popeye heads for darkest Africa in search of his old pal, Dr. Bluto, who's been lost during an expedition.

2132. The Fighting 69¹/₂th (*Merrie Melodies*) 18 Jan. 1941; *p.c.:* Leon Schlesinger prods for WB; *dir:* I. Freleng; *story:* Jack Miller; *anim:* Gil Turner; *lay:* Owen Fitzgerald; *back:* Lenard Kester; *ed:* Treg Brown; *voices:* Mel Blanc, The Sportsmen Quartet; *mus:* Carl W. Stalling; *prod sup:* Henry Binder, Raymond G. Katz; *col:* Tech. *sd:* Vit. 7 min. • Red and black ants battle over food left by picnickers.

2133. Filet Meow (*Tom & Jerry*) 1966; *p.c.:* MGM; *prod:* Chuck Jones; *dir:* Abe Levitow; *story:* Bob Ogle; *anim:* Don Towsley, Tom Ray, Dick Thompson, Ben Washam, Ken Harris; *des:* Maurice Noble; *lay:* Don Morgan, Robert Givens; *back:* Philip de Guard; *mus:* Dean Elliot; *prod mgr:* Les Goldman; *col:* Met. *sd:* WE. 6 min. • Jerry helps protect a goldfish against Tom's ravenous advances.

2134. Film Facts 30 Jan. 1926; *p.c.:* Inkwell Studios for Red Seal; *prod:* Max Fleischer; *dir:* Dave Fleischer; b&w. *sil.* 10 min. *l/a/anim.* • Magazine with animated ending showing how times have changed with an armoured knight on a charger turning into a wimp, grabbing at rings on a Merry-go-Round.

2135. The Film Fan (*Looney Tunes*) 16 Dec. 1939; *p.c.:* Leon Schlesinger prods for WB; *dir:* Robert Clampett; *anim:* Norman McCabe, Vive Risto; *ed:* Tregoweth E. Brown; *voices:* Mel Blanc, Robert C. Bruce, Billy Bletcher; *mus:* Carl W. Stalling; *prod sup:* Henry Binder, Raymond G. Katz; b&w. *sd:* Vit. 7 min. • Porky is sidetracked from running an errand by a special "free" movie show.

2136. Fin 'n' Catty (*Merrie Melodies*) 28 Aug. 1943; *p.c.:* Leon Schlesinger prods for WB; *dir:* Charles M. Jones; *story:* Michael Maltese; *anim:* Ben Washam; *lay:* John McGrew; *back:* Eugene Fleury; *ed:* Treg Brown; *voice:* Robert C. Bruce; *mus:* Carl W. Stalling; *prod sup:* Henry Binder, Raymond G. Katz; *col:* Tech. *sd:* Vit. 7 min. • A goldfish makes use of a cat's fear of water.

2137. Finding His Voice 21 June 1929 *p.c.:* Inkwell Studios for Western Electric Co Inc.; *prod:* W.E. Erpi (pseudonym for Charles Wisner Barrell); *dir:* F. Lyle Goldman, Max Fleischer; b&w. *sd:* WE. 10 min. • A roll of sound film meets a gagged roll of silent film and takes him to see Mr. Western who explains how sound films are made. The silent film is soon fitted with a soundtrack and singing with his vocal companion! Produced to explain the process of sound to movie audiences.

2138. Fine Feathered Fiend (*Noveltoon*) Aug. 1960; *p.c.:* Para Cartoons; *dir:* Seymour Kneitel; *story:* Carl Meyer, Jack Mercer; *anim:* Tom Johnson, Wm. B. Pattengill; *sets:* Robert Owen; *voices:* Cecil Roy, Jack Mercer; *mus:* Winston Sharples. *ph:* Leonard McCormick; *prod mgr:* Abe Goodman; *col:* Tech. *sd:* RCA. 6 min. • A papoose needs an eagle's feather to become a Brave ... but the eagle isn't too willing to give it up.

2139. A Fine Feathered Frenzy (*Woody Woodpecker*) 25 Oct. 1954; *p.c.:* Walter Lantz prods for Univ; *dir:* Don Patterson; *story:* Homer Brightman; *anim:* Herman R. Cohen, Ray Abrams, Don Patterson; *sets:* Raymond Jacobs, Art Landy; *voices:* Grace Stafford; *mus:* Clarence Wheeler; *prod mgr:* William E. Garity; *col:* Tech. *sd:* RCA. 6 min. • Woody encounters a wealthy husband-seeking female.

2140. Fine Feathered Friend (*Tom & Jerry*) 10 Oct. 1942; *p.c.:* MGM; *dir:* William Hanna, Joseph Barbera; *anim:* Kenneth Muse, Peter Burness, George Gordon, Jack Zander, William Littlejohn; *ed:* Fred MacAlpin; *mus:* Scott Bradley; *prod:* Fred Quimby; *col:* Tech. *sd:* WE. 7 min. • Tom falls foul of a mother hen when Jerry takes to hiding in her nest.

2141. A Fink in the Rink (*Roland & Rattfink*) 4 June 1971; *p.c.:* Mirisch/DFE for UA; *dir:* Art Davis; *story:* John W. Dunn; *anim:* Don Williams, Manny Gould, Manny Perez, Robert Taylor, Warren Batchelder; *lay:* Dick Ung; *back:* Richard H. Thomas; *ed:* Lee Gunther; *voices:* Leonard Weinrib; *mus:* Doug Goodwin; *ph:* John Burton Jr.; *prod sup:* Jim Foss, Harry Love; *col:* DeLuxe. *sd:* RCA. 6 min. • Roland vies with Rattfink in a skating rink.

2142. Finnegan's Flea (*Noveltoon*) 4 Apr. 1958; *p.c.:* Para Cartoons; *dir:* I. Sparber; *story:* Irving Spector; *anim:* Tom Johnson, Wm. B. Pattengill; *sets:* John Zago; *voices:* Allen Swift, Jackson Beck; *mus:* Winston Sharples; *ph:* Leonard McCormick; *prod mgr:* Abe Goodman; *col:* Tech. *sd:* RCA. 6 min. • A bartender narrates the tragic tale of a prisoner who befriends a singing flea.

2143. The Fire Alarm (*Looney Tunes*) 9 Mar. 1936; *p.c.:* Leon Schlesinger prods for WB; *dir:* Jack King; *anim:* Bob McKimson, Ben Clopton; *voice:* Bernice Hansel; *mus:* Norman Spencer; *prod sup:* Henry Binder, Raymond G. Katz; *b&w. sd:* Vit. 6 min. • Ham and Ex visit Beans at the Fire House and help him fight a fire.

2144. Fire and Ice 26 Aug. 1982; *p.c.:* Ralph Bakshi-Frank Frazetta Prods. for Polyc International; *dir:* Ralph Bakshi; *prod:* Ralph Bakshi, Frank Frazetta; *ex prod:* John W. Hyde, Richard R. St. Johns; *story:* Roy Thomas, Gerry Conway; based on characters created by Ralph Bakshi, Frank Frazetta; *anim:* Brenda Banks, Carl A. Bell, Bryan Berry, Lillian Evans, Steve Gordon, Debbie Hoover, Charles Howell, Adam Kuhlman, Mauro Maressa, Russell Mooney, Jack Ozark, William Recinos, Mitch Rochon, Tom Tataranowicz, Bruce Woodside; *ed:* A. David Marshall, Alan Balsam; *lay:* John Sparey, Michael Svayko; *back:* Tim Callahan, James Gurney, Thomas Kincade; *painters:* Gina Evans, Ann Marie Sorensen, Christina Stocks; *col model:* Janet Cummings; *voices: Larn:* Randy Norton; *Princess Teegra:* Cynthia Leake; *Darkwolf:* Steve Sandor; *Lord Nekron:* Sean Hannon; *King Jarol:* Leo Gordon; *Prince Taro:* William Ostrander; *Queen Juliana:* Eileen O'Neill; *Roleil:* Elizabeth Lloyd Shaw; *Otwa:* Mickey Morton; *Tutor:* Tamarah Park; *Monga:* Big Yank; *Pako:* Greg Elam; *Subhumans:* Shane Callan, James Bridges, Archie Hamilton, Michael Kellogg, Dale Park, Douglas Payton; *Subhuman Priestess:* Holly Frazetta; *Juliana:* Susan Tyrrell; *Teegra:* Maggie Roswell; *mus dir:* William Kraft; *orch:* Angela Morley; *mus ed:* The Music Design Group, Curtis Roush, Roy Pendergast, Dan Wallin; *costume des:* Lee Dawson, *sup:* Barbara Whitaker; *titles/optical fx:* The Optical House; *cel reproduction:* Edgar Gutierrez; *anim check:* Dotti Foell, Letha Prince, Robert Revell; *Xerox check:* Julie Maryon, Sheryl Staley, Sally Reymond, Frances Kumashiro, Jennifer Couzzi; *ph:* Frances Grumman, (*anim*) R&B Effects; *sd ed:* Echo Film Service, Christopher T. Welch, Peter Harrison, David Elliott, Bill Wistrom, Michael Hilkene; *sd rec:* Bill Varney, Steve Maslow, Gregg Landaker, Moe Harris; *asso prod:* Lynne Betner; *prod sup:* Scott Ira Thaler, (*studio*) Patricia Capozzi, (*anim*) Michael Svayko; *col. sd:* Dolby Stereo. 82 min. • Evil Lord Nekron uses his psychic powers to set a gigantic glacier to create an Ice Kingdom, his goal being the castle Fire Keep and the submission of its ruler, King Jarol, who has vowed to fight Nekron to the death. His daughter, Princess Teegra, is kidnapped by the Subhumans, Nekron's slavish subjects. Prince Taro sets out to rescue her with help from huge flying reptiles known as Dragonhawks. Princess Teegra escapes and hides in the forest with Larn, a warrior from one of the villages that Nekron has devastated. The two are separated and Larn is now joined by a mysterious warrior named Darkwolf. They set out to find the Princess who has been recaptured by the Subhumans and, in the course of events, a mighty battle ensues of axe against psychic weaponry, ending with King Jarol releasing a floe of lava from Fire Keep to destroy the ice kingdom.

2145. Fire Bugs (*Talkartoons*) 10 May 1930; *p.c.:* Inkwell Studio for Para; *prod:* Max Fleischer; *dir:* Dave Fleischer; *anim:* Al Eugster; *mus:* Art Turkisher; *b&w. sd:* WE. 7 min. • No story available.

2146. Fire Cheese (*Gabby*) 20 June 1941; *p.c.:* The Fleischer Studio for Para; *prod:* Max Fleischer; *dir:* Dave Fleischer; *story:* Jack Ward; *anim:* Steve Muffatti, Joe Oriolo; *sets:* Shane Miller; *voices:* Pinto Colvig, Jack Mercer; *mus:* Sammy Timberg; *prod mgr:* Isidore Sparber; *col:* Tech. *sd:* WE. 7 min. • Gabby takes on the role of Fire Chief. His bluff is called when he is called upon to extinguish a real fire.

2147. Fire Chief (*Donald Duck*) 13 Dec. 1940; *p.c.:* Walt Disney prods for RKO; *dir:* Jack King; *asst dir:* Bob Newman, Ralph Chadwick; *story:* Carl Barks, Homer Brightman, Gilles de Tremaudan, Jack Hannah, Harry Reeves; *anim:* Paul Allen, Ted Bonnicksen, Emery Hawkins, Hal Kay, Edward Love, Richard Lundy, Lee Morehouse, Ray Patin, Judge Whitaker; *lay:* Bill Herwig; *back:* Mique Nelson, Eric Hansen, Hubert Rickert; *voices:* Clarence Nash; *mus:* Paul J. Smith; *prod mgr:* Harry Tytle; *col:* Tech. *sd:* RCA. 7 min. • Fire Chief Donald has to put out his own Fire House that his nephews have set ablaze.

2148. The Fire Fighters (*Aesop's Film Fable*) 6 Mar. 1926; *p.c.:* Fables Pictures Inc for Pathé; *dir:* Paul Terry; *b&w. sil.* 6 min. • The workings of the farm animals' own fire department.

2149. The Fire Fighters (*Mickey Mouse*) 20 June 1930; *p.c.:* Walter E. Disney for Colum; *dir:* Burton F. Gillett; *anim:* Johnny Cannon, Les Clark, Norman Ferguson, David D. Hand, Wilfred Jackson, Jack King, Tom Palmer, Ben Sharpsteen; *mus:* Bert Lewis; *ph:* William Cottrell; *b&w. sd:* PCP. 7 min. • Fire Chief Mickey saves Minnie from a burning building.

2150. Fire! Fire! (*Flip the Frog*) 3 May 1932; *p.c.:* Celebrity prods for MGM; *prod/dir:* Ub Iwerks; *mus:* Carl Stalling; *b&w. sd:* PCP. 6 min. • Fireman Flip attempts to rescue a girl trapped in a burning building.

2151. The Fire Plug (*Scrappy*) 16 Oct. 1937; *p.c.:* Charles Mintz prods for Colum; *story:* Allen Rose. *anim:* Harry Love; *voices:* Dave Weber; *mus:* Joe de Nat; *prod mgr:* James Bronis; *b&w. sd:* RCA. 6 min. • The Hickville Fire Department's horse is made redundant but Scrappy rides him to the rescue when a Vaudeville theatre catches fire.

2152. Fire Prevention Week 1951. *p.c.:* National Board of Fire Underwriters; *dir:* Dave Fleischer; *b&w. sd.* 1 min. • Made for Fire Prevention Week 7–13 Oct. 1951, dramatizing fire safety in the home.

2153. The Fireman (*Oswald*) 9 Mar. 1931; *p.c.:* Univ; *dir:* Walter Lantz, "Bill" Nolan; *anim:* Clyde Geronimi, Manuel Moreno, Ray Abrams, Fred Avery, Lester Kline, Chet Karrberg, Charles Hastings, Pinto Colvig; *voice:* Mickey Rooney; *mus:* James Dietrich; *b&w. sd:* WE. 7 min. • Kitty's kid brother tags along and makes a nuisance of himself at Oswald's Fireman's Picnic.

2154. Fireman, Save My Child (*Paul Terry-Toon*) 22 Feb. 1935; *p.c.:* Moser & Terry for Educational/Fox; *dir:* Paul Terry, Frank Moser; *mus:* Philip A. Scheib; *b&w. sd:* WE. 6 min. • No story available.

2155. The Fireman's Bride (*Paul Terry-Toons*) 3 Mar. 1931; *p.c.:* Terry, Moser & Coffman for Educational/Fox; *dir:* Paul Terry, Frank Moser; *anim:* Vladimir Tytla; *mus:* Philip A. Scheib; *b&w. sd:* WE. 6 min. • A little fireman in a sensational rescue from a burning skyscraper.

2156. Firemen's Brawl (*Popeye*) 21 Aug. 1953; *p.c.:* Famous for Para; *dir:* I. Sparber; *story:* Jack Mercer, Carl Meyer; *anim:* Tom Johnson, Frank Endres; *sets:* Robert Connavale; *voices:* Jack Mercer, Jackson Beck, Mae Questel; *mus:* Winston Sharples; *ph:* Leonard McCormick; *prod mgr:* Seymour Shultz; *col:* Tech. *sd:* RCA. 6 min. • Firemen Popeye and Bluto vie for the opportunity of saving Olive from a burning building.

2157. A Firemen's Picnic (*Meany Miny Mo*) 16 Aug. 1937; *p.c.:* Univ; *dir:* Walter Lantz; *story:* Walt Lantz, Victor McLeod; *anim:* Ray Abrams, Ed Benedict, Bill Mason; *mus:* George Lessner; *b&w. sd:* WE. 7 min. • The Firemen monks are out on a picnic when a fire breaks out in their own Firehouse.

2158. First Aiders (*Pluto*) 22 Sept. 1944; *p.c.:* Walt Disney prods for RKO; *dir:* Charles Nichols; *asst dir:* Esther Newell; *story:* Harry Reeves, Rex Cox; *anim:* Norman Tate, George Nicholas, Marvin Woodward, John McManus, Charles Nichols, Bob Youngquist; *fx:* Andy Engman, Ed Aardal; *lay:* Bruce Bushman; *back:* Lenard Kester; *voices:* Leone Le Doux, Clarence Nash; *mus:* Oliver Wallace; *col:* Tech. *sd:* RCA. 7 min. • Minnie practices first-aid on Pluto who gets heckled by Figaro.

2159. The First Bad Man 30 Sept. 1955; *p.c.:* MGM; *dir:* Tex Avery; *story:* Heck Allen; *anim:* Walter Clinton Michael Lah, Ray Patterson, Grant Simmons; *char des:/lay:* Ed Benedict; *back:* John Didrik Johnsen; *ed:* Jim

Faris; *voices:* Tex Ritter, June Foray; *mus:* Scott Bradley; *ph:* Jack Stevens; *prod:* Fred Quimby; *col:* Tech. *sd:* WE. 7 min. • A Stone Age saga of when Texas was in its infancy and how the very first jail was built to hold a western bandit named Dinosaur Dan.

2160. The First Fast Mail (*Hector Heathcote*) May 1961; *p.c.:* TT for Fox; *ex prod:* Bill Weiss; *dir:* Dave Tendlar; *story sup:* Tom Morrison; *story:* Larz Bourne; *anim:* Cosmo Anzilotti, Ed Donnelly; *lay:* Martin Strudler; *back:* Bill Focht; *voices:* John Myhers; *mus:* Phil Scheib; *prod mgr:* Frank Schudde; *col:* DeLuxe. *sd:* RCA. 6 min. • Heathcote unwittingly carries a bomb when he tries to return a Pony Express sack to the rider after it has been dropped.

2161. First Flight Up (*Hector Heathcote*) Oct. 1962; *p.c.:* TT for Fox; *ex prod:* Bill Weiss; *dir/anim:* Bill Tytla; *story sup:* Tom Morrison; *story:* Al Bertino, Dick Kinney; *sets:* Bill Focht, John Zago; *ed:* George McAvoy; *voices:* John Myhers; *mus:* Phil Scheib; *ph:* Ted Moskowitz; *col:* DeLuxe. *sd:* RCA. 6 min. • Heathcote assists Blanchard in his famous balloon flight from the U.S. to France.

2162. The First Flying Fish (*Aesop's Fable*) Mar. 1955; *p.c.:* TT for Fox; *dir:* Connie Rasinski; *story:* Tom Morrison; *anim:* Jim Tyer; *voices:* Roy Halee, Tom Morrison; *mus:* Philip A. Scheib; *ph:* Douglas Moye; *col:* Tech. *sd:* RCA. 7 min. • Philip chooses to be a flying fish and saves the others from a hungry pelican.

2163. The First Robin (*Terry-Toon*) 29 Dec. 1939; *p.c.:* TT for Fox; *dir:* Connie Rasinski; *story:* John Foster; *mus:* Philip A. Scheib; *col:* Tech. *sd:* RCA. 7 min. • The trials and tribulations of mother and father robin teaching their young to fly.

2164. The First Snow (*Mighty Mouse*); rel; 10 Oct. 1947; *p.c.:* TT for Fox; *dir:* Mannie Davis; *story:* John Foster; *voice:* Roy Halee; *mus:* Philip A. Scheib; *ph:* Douglas Moye; *col:* Tech. *sd:* RCA. 6 min. • Wolves disrupt the rabbits' ice skating.

2165. The First Snow (*Paul Terry-Toons*) 11 Jan. 1935; *p.c.:* Moser & Terry for Educational/Fox; *dir:* Paul Terry, Frank Moser; *mus:* Philip A. Scheib; *b&w. sd:* WE. 6 min. • Pups live in a shoe, come out to play in the snow and rescue a pig from an ice floe.

2166. The First Swallow (*MGM Cartoon*) 14 Mar. 1942; *p.c.:* MGM. *prod:* Rudolf Ising; *dir/story:* Jerry Brewer; *voice:* Pedro de Cordoba; *mus:* Scott Bradley; *col:* Tech. *sd:* WE. 9 min. • Padré Victorio relates the tale of why the swallows migrate to Capistrano each year.

2167. Fish and Chips (*Chilly Willy*) 8 Jan. 1963; *p.c.:* Walter Lantz prods for Univ; *dir:* Jack Hannah; *story:* Dalton Sandifer; *anim:* Roy Jenkins, Al Coe, Art Davis; *sets:* Ray Huffine, Art Landy; *voices:* Daws Butler; *mus:* Darrell Calker; *prod mgr:* William E. Garity; *col:* Tech. *sd:* RCA. 6 min. • Smedley tries to prevent Chilly from devouring the Colonel's stuffed barracuda.

2168. Fish and Slips (*Looney Tunes*) Mar. 1962; *p.c.:* WB; *dir:* Robert McKimson; *story:* Dave DeTiege; *anim:* Warren Batchelder, George Grandpré, Ted Bonnicksen; *sets:* Robert Gribbroek; *ed:* Treg Brown; *voices:* Mel Blanc; *mus:* Milt Franklyn; *prod mgr:* William Orcutt; *prod:* David H. De-Patie; *col:* Tech. *sd:* Vit. 6 min. • Sylvester teaches Junior to catch fish the easy way ... in an aquarium.

2169. Fish Day (*Aesop's Film Fable*) 8 May 1929; *p.c.:* Fables Pictures Inc for Pathé; *dir:* Paul Terry; *b&w. sil.* 5 min. • No story available.

2170. Fish Follies (*Phantasy*) 10 May 1940; *p.c.:* Colum; *story:* Allen Rose; *anim:* Harry Love; *ed:* George Winkler; *voices:* Mel Blanc, Robert Winkler; *mus:* Joe de Nat; *ph:* Otto Reimer; *prod mgr:* James Bronis; *b&w. sd:* RCA. 6 min. • A guide gives a small boy an insight into the world of fish.

2171. Fish Fry (*Andy Panda*) 12 June 1944; *p.c.:* Walter Lantz prods for Univ; *dir:* James Culhane; *story:* Ben Hardaway, Milt Schaffer; *anim:* (La) Verne Harding, Emery Hawkins, Les Kline, Dick Lundy, Pat Matthews, Milt Schaffer, Paul J. Smith, Don Williams; *lay:* Art Heinemann; *back:* Philip de Guard; *voices:* Lionel Stander, Grace Stafford; *mus:* Darrell Calker; *col:* Tech. *sd:* WE. 7 min. • A hungry cat eyes the goldfish that Andy brings home from the pet shop.

2172. Fish Hooked (*Chilly Willy*) 10 Aug. 1960; *p.c.:* Walter Lantz prods for Univ; *dir:* Paul J. Smith; *story:* Homer Brightman; *anim:* La Verne

Harding, Les Kline; *sets:* Art Landy, Ray Huffine; *voice:* Daws Butler; *mus:* Eugene Poddany; *prod mgr:* William E. Garity; *col:* Tech. *sd:* RCA. 6 min. • Smedley tries to stop Chilly from fishing in his aquarium tank.

2173. A Fish Story (*Beary Family*) 1972; Walter Lantz prods for Univ; *dir:* Paul J. Smith; *story:* Cal Howard; *anim:* Volus Jones, Al Coe, Tom Byrne, Joe Voght; *sets:* Nino Carbe; *voices:* Paul Frees, Grace Stafford; *mus:* Walter Greene; *prod mgr:* William E. Garity; *col:* Tech. *sd:* RCA. 5 min. • Charlie's doctor tells him that keeping tropical fish will soothe his nerves. Transporting the fish tank makes him more uptight than ever.

2174. Fish Tales (*Looney Tunes*) 23 May 1936; *p.c.:* Leon Schlesinger prods for WB; *dir:* Jack King; *anim:* Bob McKimson, Don Williams; *voices:* Joe Dougherty, Bernice Hansel; *mus:* Norman Spencer; *prod sup:* Henry Binder, Raymond G. Katz; *b&w. sd:* Vit. 7 min. • Porky snoozes while fishing and dreams he is caught for a fish's dinner.

2175. The Fisherman (*Oswald*) 8 Dec. 1931; *p.c.:* Univ; *dir:* Walter Lantz, "Bill" Nolan; *anim:* Manuel Moreno, Ray Abrams, Fred Avery, Lester Kline, Vet Anderson; *voice:* Mickey Rooney; *mus:* James Dietrich; *b&w. sd:* WE. 6 min. • Oswald saves his sweetie from a gang of cut-throats and rewards her with a diamond necklace from the pirates' loot.

2176. Fisherman's Luck (*Aesop's Film Fable*) 19 Jan. 1925; *p.c.:* Fables Pictures Inc for Pathé; *dir:* Paul Terry; *b&w. sil.* 5 min. • Al Falfa and the cat go fishing. The mouse dons a diver's helmet to submerge and lure the fish onto the cat's hook.

2177. Fisherman's Luck (*Aesop's Sound Fable*) 13 June 1931; *p.c.:* Van Beuren for RKO/Pathé; *dir:* John Foster, Harry Bailey; *mus:* Gene Rodemich; *b&w. sd:* RCA. 8 min. • A fisherman has no luck on the land, so he dives in and cavorts with the fishes.

2178. Fisherman's Luck (*Terry-Toon*) 30 Mar. 1945; *p.c.:* TT for Fox; *dir:* Eddie Donnelly; *story:* John Foster; *voices:* Arthur Kay, Thomas Morrison; *mus:* Philip A. Scheib; *ph:* Douglas Moye; *col:* Tech. *sd:* RCA. 7 min. • Gandy and Sourpuss go fishing and have a problem with a "Devil Fish."

2179. Fishin' Around (*Mickey Mouse*) 1 Sept. 1931; *p.c.:* Walter E. Disney for Colum; *dir:* Burton F. Gillett; *anim:* Johnny Cannon, Les Clark, Norman Ferguson, David D. Hand, Jack King, Richard Lundy, Tom Palmer, Ben Sharpsteen; *asst anim:* Charles Byrne, Jack Cutting, Hardie Gramatky; *mus:* Bert Lewis; *b&w. sd:* PCP. 7 min. • The Sheriff tries to arrest Mickey for fishing in a "No Fishing" area.

2180. Fishing (*Out of the Inkwell*) 21 Nov. 21; *p.c.:* Inkwell Studio for WB; *prod:* Max Fleischer; *dir:* Dave Fleischer; *b&w. sil.* 6 min. *l/a/anim.* • Ko-Ko wants to go fishing with Max and Roland Crandall, so Max draws him a pond to fish in. Not satisfied, the clown follows them and leaves them stranded on a rock in the lake. • aka: *The Fish.*

2181. The Fishing Bear (*MGM Cartoon*) 20 Jan. 1940; *p.c.:* MGM; *prod/dir/voice:* Rudolf Ising; *mus:* Scott Bradley; *prod mgr:* Fred Quimby; *col:* Tech. *sd:* WE. 8 min. • Barney Bear's fishing is disturbed by a persistent duck and an electric eel.

2182. Fishing by the Sea (*Heckle & Jeckle*) 19 Sept. 1947; *p.c.:* TT for Fox; *dir:* Connie Rasinski; *story:* John Foster; *voice:* Sid Raymond; *mus:* Philip Scheib; *ph:* Douglas Moye; *col:* Tech. *sd:* RCA. 6 min. • The magpies annoy a fisherman.

2183. The Fishing Fool (*Aesop's Film Fable*) 2 Dec.1928; *p.c.:* Fables Pictures Inc., for Pathé; *dir:* Paul Terry; *b&w. sil.* 5 min. • Farmer Al and Waffles the Cat go on a fishing trip. The cat snags all the fish while the farmer gets all manner of things on his line from a turtle to a mermaid and a walrus. Finally a monster fish repremands Al for violating the rules of fishing by using a mousetrap on his hook.

2184. The Fishing Fool (*Oswald*) 29 Mar. 1929; *p.c.:* Winkler for Univ; *anim:* R.C. Hamilton; *mus:* The Universal Jazz Band; *b&w. sd:* WE. 6 min. • Oswald falls asleep while fishing and has a "fishy" dream. When he does catch a fish, it gets stolen by a thief.

2185. Fishing Made Easy (*Terry-Toon*) 21 Feb. 1941; *p.c.:* TT for Fox; *dir:* Eddie Donnelly; *story:* John Foster; *mus:* Philip A. Scheib; *col:* Tech. *sd:* RCA. 7 min. • A pig succeeds in catching fish while Sourpuss tries the same methods and loses each time.

2186. Fishing Tackler (*Noveltoon*) 29 Mar. 1957; *p.c.:* Para Cartoons; *dir:* I. Sparber; *story:* I. Klein; *anim:* Tom Golden, Bill Hudson; *sets:* John

Zago; *voices:* Mae Questel, Sid Raymond; *mus:* Winston Sharples; *ph:* Leonard McCormick; *prod mgr:* Seymour Shultz; *col:* Tech. *sd:* RCA. 6 min. • The truant officer spies Audrey fishing and suspects her of playing hookey.

2187. Fistic Mystic *(Looney Tunes)* 22 Feb. 1969; *p.c.:* W/7A; *dir:* Bob McKimson; *story:* Cal Howard; *anim:* Ted Bonnicksen, La Verne Harding, Jim Davis, Ed Solomon, Norm McCabe; *lay:* Jaime Diaz; *back:* Bob Abrams; *ed:* Hal Geer; *voices:* Larry Storch; *mus:* William Lava; *prod:* Bill L. Hendricks; *col:* Tech. *sd:* Vit. 6 min. • Merlin the Magic Mouse enters Second Banana in a boxing match with magic gloves.

2188. The Fistic Mystic *(Popeye)* 29 Nov. 1946; *p.c.:* Famous for Para; *dir:* Seymour Kneitel; *story:* I. Klein, Jack Ward; *anim:* Graham Place, Nick Tafuri; *sets:* Robert Little; *voices:* Jackson Beck, Mae Questel, Harry F. Welch, Jack Mercer, Carl Meyer; *mus:* Winston Sharples; *ph:* Leonard McCormick; *prod mgr:* Sam Buchwald; *col:* Tech. *sd:* RCA. 6 min. • While in the Far East, Popeye and Olive fall afoul of a mystic who kidnaps Olive.

2189. Fit to Be Tied *(Tom & Jerry)* 26 July 1952; *p.c.:* MGM; *dir:* William Hanna, Joseph Barbera; *anim:* Kenneth Muse, Irven Spence, Ray Patterson, Ed Barge; *ed:* Jim Faris. *lay:* Dick Bickenbach; *back:* Robert Gentle; *voice:* Daws Butler; *mus:* Scott Bradley; *ph:* Jack Stevens; *col:* Tech. *sd:* WE. 6 min. • A new "All Dogs Must be Kept on a Leash" law puts Tom on a level above Spike the bulldog.

2190. Fit to Be Toyed *(Modern Madcap)* 6 Feb. 1959; *p.c.:* Para Cartoons; *dir:* Seymour Kneitel; *story:* Tom Johnson, Wm. B. Pattengill; *sets:* Robert Owen; *voices:* Jackson Beck, Allen Swift, Jack Mercer, Cecil Roy; *mus:* Winston Sharples; *ph:* Leonard McCormick; *prod mgr:* Abe Goodman; *col:* Tech. *sd:* RCA. 6 min. • The president of a big corporation has flipped and a psychiatrist takes him back to his childhood for the root of his problems.

2191. Five and Dime *(Oswald)* 21 Sept. 1933; *p.c.:* Univ; *dir:* Walter Lantz, "Bill" Nolan; *anim:*Ray Abrams, Fred Avery, Cecil Surry, Jack Carr, Ernest Smythe; *mus:* James Dietrich; *b&w. sd:* WE. 8 min. • A storm drives Oswald into a five-and-dime store where he plays the piano. Caricatures of Jimmy Durante, Charlie Chaplin, Baby Snooks, Laurel & Hardy.

2192. The Five Fifteen *(Aesop's Film Fable)* 9 Nov. 1923; *p.c.:* Fables Pictures Inc for Pathé; *dir:* Paul Terry; *b&w. sil.* 5 min. • A gang of cats hold up the five-fifteen locomotive and scare it into many sections. The compartment containing a bottle of "Old Stuff," however, is saved.

2193. The 500 Hats of Bartholomew Cubbins *(Puppetoon)* 30 Apr. 1943; *p.c.:* George Pal prods for Para; *prod/dir:* George Pal; *story:* Dr. Seuss; *mus:* William Eddison; *col:* Tech. *sd:* WE. 9 min. *Academy Award nomination.* • When a boy is made to doff his hat in the presence of the King, another hat appears in its place each time, impressing the King enough to exchange the hat for his own crown.

2194. Five Orphans of the Storm *(Aesop's Film Fable)* 9 Jan. 1924; *p.c.:* Fables Pictures Inc for Pathé; *dir:* Paul Terry; *b&w. sil.* 5 min. • Santa deposits five pups at the orphanage, one of whom wins them all a home by rescuing a little girl from an ice floe.

2195. Five Puplets *(Paul Terry-Toons)* 17 May 1935; *p.c.:* Moser & Terry for Educational/Fox. *dir:* Paul Terry, Frank Moser; *mus:* Philip A. Scheib; *b&w. sd:* WE. 5 min. • Satire on the Dionne Quintuplets.

2196. Fix That Clock *(Swifty & Shorty)* May 1964; *p.c.:* Para Cartoons; *dir:* Seymour Kneitel; *story/voices:* Eddie Lawrence; *anim:* I. Klein; *sets:* Robert Little; *mus:* Winston Sharples; *ph:* Leonard McCormick; *prod mgr:* Abe Goodman; *col:* Tech. *sd:* RCA. 6 min. • The boys are given the task of mending the town clock.

2197. Fizzicle Fizzle *(Swifty & Shorty)* Apr. 1964; *p.c.:* Para Cartoons; *dir:* Seymour Kneitel; *story:* Bill Ballard; *anim:* I. Klein. *sets:* Robert Little; *voices:* Eddie Lawrence; *mus:* Winston Sharples; *ph:* Leonard McCormick; *prod mgr:* Abe Goodman; *col:* Tech. *sd:* RCA. 6 min. • Swifty gets Shorty excercising.

2198. The Flamboyant Arms *(Clint Clobber)* 28 Apr. 1959; *p.c.:* TT for Fox; *ex prod:* Bill Weiss; *dir sup:* Gene Deitch; *dir:* Connie Rasinski; *story dir:* Tom Morrison; *story:* Larz Bourne, Eli Bauer; *anim:* Johnny Gent, Al Chiarito, Larry Silverman, Don Caulfield, Mannie Davis, Jim Tyer, Dave Fern; *lay:* Eli Bauer; *back:* Bill Hilliker; *voice:* Allen Swift; *mus:* Phil Scheib; *prod mgr:* Sparky Schudde; *col:* Tech. *sd:* RCA. 7 min. CS. • Su-

perintendant Clobber is about to resign when he realizes the tenement "needs" him.

2199. Flaming Ice *(Life Cartoon Comedy)* 25 Sept. 1926; *p.c.:* Sherwood Wadsworth Pictures Inc for Educational; *prod/dir:* John R. McCrory; *b&w. sil.* 10 min. • Percy Cutthroat runs a lumber mill that specialises in portable bungalows. Home-loving Mary orders one which is delivered by aircraft. When Mike calls on her, Percy also arrives to collect the rent and a battle ensues ending in a chase over the ice floes.

2200. Flatfoot Fledgeling *(Dinky Duck)* Apr. 1952; *p.c.:* TT for Fox; *dir:* Mannie Davis. *story:* Tom Morrison; *anim:* Jim Tyer; *mus:* Philip A. Scheib; *ph:* Douglas Moye; *col:* Tech. *sd:* RCA. 7 min. • Wilbur Weasel lures Dinky into his den under the pretext that he can teach him to fly.

2201. The Flea Circus 6 Nov. 1954; *p.c.:* MGM; *dir:* Tex Avery; *story:* Heck Allen; *anim:* Grant Simmons, Michael Lah, Robert Bentley, Walter Clinton; *ed:* Jim Faris; *lay:* Ed Benedict; *back:* Joe Montell; *voices:* Bill Thompson, Stan Freberg, Fleurette Zama; *mus:* Scott Bradley; *ph:* Jack Stevens; *prod:* Fred Quimby; *col:* Tech. *sd:* WE. 7 min. • François, a clown in Pepito's Flea Circus, loves the pretty star attraction. She shows no interest until he rescues her from drowning. They marry and raise their own flea circus.

2202. Flea for Two *(Cartune)* 20 July 1955; *p.c.:* Walter Lantz prods for Univ; *dir:* Don Patterson; *story:* Michael Maltese; *anim:* Ray Abrams, Don Patterson, Herman R. Cohen; *sets:* Raymond Jacobs, Art Landy; *voices:* Dal McKennon, Grace Stafford; *mus:* Clarence Wheeler; *prod mgr:* William E. Garity; *col:* Tech. *sd:* RCA. 6 min. • Fleawee's rural romance is disrupted by villainous François Flea who sweeps his lady love away to the big city.

2203. Flebus Aug. 1957; *p.c.:* TT for Fox; *ex prod:* Bill Weiss; *dir sup:* Gene Deitch; *dir/story/des:* Ernest Pintoff; *anim:* Jim Tyer; *voices:* Allen Swift; *mus:* Phil Scheib; *prod mgr:* Sparky Schudde; *col:* Tech. *sd:* RCA. 6 min. CS. • A little man wishes to be loved by everybody until he meets Rudolf, who hates him.

2204. Fleets of Stren'th *(Popeye)* 13 Mar. 1942; *p.c.:* The Fleischer Studio for Para; *prod:* Max Fleischer; *dir:* Dave Fleischer; *story:* Dan Gordon, Jack Mercer; *anim:* Al Eugster, Tom Golden; *voices:* Jack Mercer, Ted Pierce; *mus:* Sammy Timberg; *prod sup:* Sam Buchwald, Isidore Sparber; *b&w. sd:* WE. 7 min. • The Captain puts Popeye in charge of a highly explosive missile just as enemy aircraft start attacking.

2205. The Fleet's Out *(Silly Sidney)* Oct. 1962; *p.c.:* TT for Fox; *ex prod:* Bill Weiss; *dir/anim:* Connie Rasinski; *story sup:* Tom Morrison; *story:* Larz Bourne; *sets:* Bill Focht, John Zago; *ed:* George McAvoy; *voice:* Dayton Allen; *mus:* Phil Scheib; *ph:* Joe Rasinski; *col:* Tech. *sd:* RCA. 6 min. • Sidney defends his island home against his captors landing there.

2206. The Fleischer Studio (1930–1932); *prod:* Max Fleischer; *dir:* Dave Fleischer; *story:* Ted Sears, Joseph E. Stultz, William Turner; *anim:* "Vet" Anderson, Thomas Bonfiglio, Willard Bowsky, Tom Byrne, George Cannata, Herman Cohen, Roland Crandall, James H. Culhane, Arnold Davis, Arthur Davis, Ugo d'Orsi, Harvey Eisenberg, Andrew Engman, Alfred Eugster, Sidney Garber, William Henning, David Hoffman, Dick Huemor, Thomas Johnson, Sam Kahn, Al Kaplan, Rudolph L. Eggeman, Sidney Marcus, Grim Natwick, Frank Paiker, Edwin Rehberg, Lod Rossner, Ben Shenkman, Ralph Somerville, Sam Stimson, Nick Tafuri, Reuben Timinsky, Myron Waldman, Bernard Wolf, Rudy Zamora; *asst anim:* Charles Biro, Don Figlozzi, Carl O. Wessler; *sets:* Al Geiss; *mus:* Louis Fleischer, Art Turkisher; *ed:* Kitty Pfister; *timing:* Nelly Sanborn, Alice Morgan; *i&pl checking:* Mariana Butts, Ruth Fleischer, Edythe Vernick; *ph/technical:* Mike Balukas, Joe Fleischer, Leonard McCormick, Harry Rytterband, Charles Schettler, William Turner; *misc. contributors:* Frank Carino, H. Cheeseman, Alan Cox, Lucille Cramer, Jenny Falkenberg, Leon A. Flax, Sidney Frankel, Sadie Friedlander, Sidney Friedman, Anne Horowitz, Arthur Hubbard, Elizabeth Hursch, Mary Jones, Sonia Katz, John Lasher, Fred Lewis, Nat Messik, Mary Patrick, Milt Platkin, R. Price, Lilian Richter, Manny Skoultchi, Isidore Sparber, Florence Schlechter, Sydney Wallick, Nathan Welling, Al Windley, Nat Zamoff; *prod mgr:* William A. Gilmartin.

2207. Flesh Gordon 1974; *p.c.:* Graffitti Prod Corp for Variety; *fx des & dir:* Howard Ziehm, Lynn Rogers, Walter R. Cichy; *fx created by* David Allen, Mij Htrofnad; *construction:* Greg Jein; *model anim:* Jim Danforth,

David Allen, Dennis Muren; *titles:* Corny Cole (Corny Films); *voice:* Craig T. Nelson; *mus:* Ralph Ferraro; *prod:* Howard Ziehm, William Osco; *col:* Deluxe. *sd.* 88 min. (complete) • Soft core porn send-up of *Flash Gordon*. On his intergalactic adventures, Flesh encounters the metallic "Beetleman," a ravenous "Penisaur" and a monster who scales a building in search of Dale Ardor, the chesty love interest. Stop-motion model animation.

2208. Fletch Lives 17 Mar. 1989; *p.c.:* Univ; *anim seq:* Dale Baer Animation Co., Inc.; *col:* DeLuxe. *sd:* Dolby stereo. Panavision. *l/a.* • Live-action comedy with Fletch inheriting a residence in the deep South. He dreams that he's inherited a huge Southern mansion, surrounded with animated birds and a dog.

2209. Flies (*Out of the Inkwell*) 16 Sept. 1922; *p.c.:* Inkwell Studio for Rodner; *prod:* Max Fleischer; *dir:* Dave Fleischer; *b&w. sil.* 6 min. *l/a/anim.* • Flies prove a torture for Max and the little clown. Even flypaper is useless when they follow Ko-Ko into his inkwell home.

2210. Flies Ain't Human (*Popeye*) 4 Apr. 1941; *p.c.:* The Fleischer Studio for Paramount; *prod:* Max Fleischer; *dir:* Dave Fleischer; *story:* Eric St Clair; *anim:* Tom Johnson, George Germanetti; *voices:* Jack Mercer, Margie Hines; *mus:* Sammy Timberg; *ph:* Charles Schettler; *prod sup:* Sam Buchwald, Isidore Sparber; *b&w. sd:* WE. 6 min. • Popeye has problems with a solitary fly that just won't let him sleep.

2211. The Flight That Failed (*Aesop's Film Fable*) 7 May 1928; *p.c.:* Fables Pictures Inc for Pathé; *dir:* Paul Terry, Hugh Shields; *b&w. sil.* 5 min. • No story available.

2212. Flight to the Finish (*Hector Heathcote*) 1962; *p.c.:* TT for Fox; *ex prod:* Bill Weiss; *dir/anim:* Dave Tendlar; *story sup:* Tom Morrison; *story:* Larz Bourne; *sets:* Bill Focht, John Zago; *ed:* George McAvoy; *voices:* John Myhers; *mus:* Phil Scheib; *ph:* Ted Moskowitz; *col:* DeLuxe. *sd:* RCA. 6 min. • Heathcote attempts to build a "Flying Machine" but invents a harvester instead.

2213. Flight to the Finish (*Tijuana Toads*) 30 Apr. 1972; *p.c.:* Mirisch/DFE for UA; *dir:* Art Davis; *story:* John W. Dunn; *anim:* Bob Richardson, Don Williams, John Gibbs, Manny Gould; *lay:* Dick Ung; *back:* Richard H. Thomas; *ed:* Rick Steward; *voices:* Don Diamond, Tom Holland, Bob Holt; *mus:* Doug Goodwin; *prod sup:* Stan Paperny, Harry Love; *col:* DeLuxe. *sd:* RCA. 5 min. • Crazylegs Crane pursues the toads for his breakfast.

2214. Flim Flam Fountain (*Woody Woodpecker*) 5 Jan. 1971; *p.c.:* Walter Lantz prods for Univ; *dir:* Paul J. Smith; *story:* Don Christensen; *anim:* Les Kline, Al Coe, Tom Byrne, Joe Voght; *sets:* Nino Carbe; *voices:* Dal McKennon, Grace Stafford; *mus:* Walter Greene; *prod mgr:* William E. Garity; *col:* Tech. *sd:* RCA. 5 min. • Buzz Buzzard cons Woody into bathing in a fake "Fountain of Youth."

2215. The Flintstones 23 May 1994; *p.c.:* Univ City Studios/Amblin Entertainment/Hanna-Barbera; *special visual fx: cgi anim:* Dave Andrews, Geoff Campbell, Kyle Balda, Steve Price. *col:* DeLuxe. *sd:* Dolby stereo. 93 min. *l/a.* • Live-action version of the popular television cartoon series: When Fred gets promoted, he becomes involved in an embezzlement scam. Animated comic dinosaurs, etc.

2216. Flip Animation on Theatre Tickets *dir/anim:* Robert Cannon, Martha Cannon. • No further information available.

2217. Flip Flap (*Noveltoon*) 27 Feb. 1948; *p.c.:* Famous for Para; *dir:* I. Sparber; *story:* Bee Lewi, Mickey Klar Marks, Joe Stultz, Larry Riley; *anim:* Myron Waldman, Wm. B. Pattengill; *sets:* Robert Little; *voices:* Cecil Roy, Jackson Beck; *mus:* Winston Sharples; *prod mgr:* Sam Buchwald; *col:* Tech. *sd:* RCA. 7 min. • A seal is unhappy in the confines of a zoo and heads for the North Pole. There he meets a girl seal who gets captured and ends up in the same zoo Flip Flap has just escaped from.

2218. Flipper Frolics (*Terry-Toons*) June 1952; *p.c.:* TT for Fox; *dir:* Connie Rasinski; *story:* Tom Morrison; *mus:* Philip A. Scheib; *ph:* Douglas Moye; *col:* Tech. *sd:* RCA. 7 min. • Two dogs and a seal have fun on the beach until the dogs are menaced by a goat.

2219. Flip's Circus 1921; *p.c.:* Rialto prods for Vit; *dir/anim:* Winsor McCay; *b&w. sil.* • Flip's attempts to train a Top-Hatted dinosaur who eats his car. McCay's sixth film. Drawn on celluloid.

2220. Flip's Lunch Room (*Flip the Frog*) 3 Apr. 1933; *p.c.:* Celebrity prods for MGM; *prod/dir:* Ub Iwerks; *anim:* Jimmie Culhane; *mus:* Carl W. Stalling; *b&w. sd:* PCP. 6 min. • Flip throws a dog out of his Lunch Room kitchen for stealing food. The cur later comes into his own when an angry customer decides to rob the cash till.

2221. Flirty Birdy (*Tom & Jerry*) 22 Sept. 1945; *p.c.:* MGM; *dir:* William Hanna, Joseph Barbera; *anim:* Irven Spence, Kenneth Muse, Ray Patterson; *ed:* Fred MacAlpin; *voice:* Harry E. Lang; *mus:* Scott Bradley; *prod:* Fred Quimby; *col:* Tech. *sd:* WE. 7 min. • Tom's rival is a hawk who also wants to eat Jerry, so he disguises himself as a female hawk in order to retrieve his property.

2222. The Floor Flusher (*Popeye*) 1 Jan. 1954; *p.c.:* Famous for Para; *dir:* I. Sparber; *story:* Carl Meyer, Jack Mercer; *anim:* Tom Golden, Bill Hudson; *sets:* Robert Owen; *voices:* Jack Mercer, Mae Questel, Jackson Beck; *mus:* Winston Sharples; *ph:* Leonard McCormick; *prod mgr:* Seymour Shultz; *col:* Tech. *sd:* RCA. 6 min. • Bluto takes umbrage when Popeye mends a leak in Olive's house and sets about to cause more leaks for the mighty mariner to fix.

2223. Flop Goes the Weasel (*Merrie Melodies*) 20 Mar. 1943; *p.c.:* Leon Schlesinger prods for WB; *dir:* Charles M. Jones; *story:* Michael Maltese; *lay:* John McGrew; *back:* Eugene Fleury; *ed:* Treg Brown; *voices:* Mel Blanc, Vivian Dandridge, Edward Beal, Darrell R. Payne; *mus:* Carl W. Stalling; *prod sup:* Henry Binder, Raymond G. Katz; *col:* Tech. *sd:* Vit. 8 min. • A weasel snatches an egg from a mother hen only to have a black chick hatch out and think he's it's mother.

2224. The Flop House (*Scrappy*) 9 Nov. 1932; *p.c.:* Winkler for Colum; *prod:* Charles Mintz; *story:* Dick Huemor; *anim:* Sid Marcus, Art Davis; *mus:* Joe de Nat; *prod mgr:* James Bronis; *b&w. sd:* RCA. 6 min. • The arrival of Vontzy in Scrappy's "Flop House" has them both running around spraying all and sundry with DDT.

2225. Flop Secret (*Little Roquefort*) Dec. 1952; *p.c.:* TT for Fox; *dir:* Eddie Donnelly; *story/voice:* Tom Morrison; *mus:* Philip A. Scheib; *ph:* Douglas Moye; *col:* Tech. *sd:* RCA. 6 min. • Percy the puss has a nightmare about a mad scientist who wants to experiment on him and Roquefort.

2226. Flora (*Color Rhapsody*) 18 Mar. 1948; *p.c.:* Colum; *dir:* Alex Lovy; *story:* Cal Howard, Dave Monahan; *anim:* Grant Simmons, Paul Sommer, Chic Otterstrom, Jay Sarbry; *lay:* Jim Carmichael; *back:* Al Boggs; *ed:* Richard S. Jensen; *voice:* Gerald Mohr; *mus:* Darrell Calker; *ph:* Frank Fisher; *creative consultant:* Robert Clampett; *prod:* Raymond Katz, Henry Binder; *col:* Tech. *sd:* WE. 7 min. • A dog falls for Flora, a cat, whose heartbreaking ways almost drive him to suicide.

2227. Flowers and Trees (*Silly Symphony*) 30 July 1932; *p.c.:* Walt Disney prods for UA; *dir:* Burton F. Gillett; *anim:* Les Clark, Norman Ferguson, David D. Hand, Jack King, Richard Lundy, Tom Palmer; *character des/lay:* Albert Hurter; *mus:* Frank E. Churchill; *ph:* William Cottrell; *col:* Tech. *sd:* PCP. 7 min. *Academy Award.* • A love affair between two young trees is affected when a villainous tree stump intervenes. The first use of three-strip Technicolor in a cartoon plus the first cartoon to ever win an Academy Award.

2228. Flowers for Madame (*Merrie Melodies*) 6 Apr. 1936; *p.c.:* Leon Schlesinger prods for WB; *dir:* I. Freleng; *anim:* Paul Smith, Don Williams, Robert Clampett; *voices:* Elmore Vincent, Bernice Hansel; *mus:* Norman Spencer; *prod sup:* Henry Binder, Raymond G. Katz; *col:* Tech. *sd:* Vit. 7 min. • The world's flowers stage their own flower show. A grass fire threatens to ruin the pageant but the cactus puts it out.

2229. Flubber 26 Nov. 1997; *p.c.:* Walt Disney Pictures; *special visual fx/anim:* ILM *Flubber character: anim sup:* Tom Bertino; *visual fx prod:* Roni McKinley; *visual fx co-sup:* Sandra Ford Karpman; *cg sup:* Steve Braggs; *lead technical anim:* Philip Edward Alexy; *visual fx art dir:* Scott Lebrecht; *digital fx art:* Felix Balbas, Jeffrey Benedict, Barbara Brennan, Marc Cooper, Natasha Devaud, Raúl Essig, Howard Gersh, John Helms, Peg Hunter, Hayden Landis, Tia Marshall, Hiromi Ono, Ricardo Ramos, Linda Siegel, Dan Shumaker, Doug Sutton, Chris Townsend; *digital fx anim:* Chris Armstrong, David Byers Brown, Andrew Doucette, Tony Hudson, Paul Kavanagh, David Latour, Steve Lee, Neil Michka, Magali Rigaudias, Glenn Sylvester, Kim Thompson, Tim Waddy, Andy Wong; *addit visual fx: 3d anim:* Chris Cushley, Dale Mayeda, Ron Arrendondo, David Rand; *cg geese:* C.O.R.E. Digital Pictures *anim sup:* John Mariella;

anim: Brian A. Smeets; *prod mgr:* Sara Fillmore; *prod:* Stephen Price; *addit Flubber anim:* Hammerhead Prods., Inc.: *visual fx sup:* Jamie Dixon; *visual fx prod:* Daniel Chuba; *software des:* Thad Beier; *lighting consultant:* Rebecca Marie; *anim sup:* Howard E. Baker; *lead character anim:* Sean Dever; *character anim:* Joshua I. Kolden, Curtis A.J. Edwards, Constance Bracewell; *Mobility, Inc. Digital Effects: sup:* David Ebner; *lead anim:* Oliver Hotz; *compositing:* Kama Moiha; *anim:* Bryant Reif, Mike Bozulich; *prod:* Vicki Weimer; *Flying ball anim:* X.O. Digital Arts digital fx sup: Bruce Walters; *digital fx prod:* Ginny Walters; *digital fx anim:* Todd Staples; *voices: Flubber:* Scott Martin Gershin; *Weebo:* Jodi Benson; *Weebette:* Julie Morrison; *col:* Tech. *sd:* Dolby digital/DTS sound/SDDS. Panavision. 93 min. *l/a.* • Re-make of the 1961 live-action comedy *The Absent Minded Professor:* A college professor invents "Flubber," a gelatinous high-energy material that bounces.

2230. The Fly and the Ants *(Aesop's Film Fable)* 3 Dec. 1921; *p.c.:* Fables Pictures Inc for Pathé; *dir:* Paul Terry; b&w. sil. 5 min. • A fly scorns the ants for working ... then gets swatted while eating pie.

2231. Fly Frolic *(Aesop's Fable)* 5 Mar. 1932; *p.c.:* Van Beuren for RKO/Pathé; *dir:* John Foster, Harry Bailey; *mus:* Gene Rodemich; b&w. *sd:* RCA. 7 min. • A villainous spider captures a girl fly and takes her to his underground lair where he drinks a potion turning him into a suave sophisticate. An army of flies come to her aid.

2232. The Fly Guy *(Aesop's Sound Fable)* 10 May 1931; *p.c.:* Van Beuren for RKO/Pathé; *dir:* John Foster, Harry Bailey; *mus:* Gene Rodemich; b&w. *sd:* RCA. 7 min. • A cabaret for insects, held in a bottle, is subjected to the villainies of a hungry toad.

2233. Fly Hi *(Aesop's Sound Fable)* 31 Aug. 1931; *p.c.:* Van Beuren for RKO/Pathé; *dir:* John Foster, Harry Bailey; *mus:* Gene Rodemich; b&w. *sd:* RCA. 8 min. • A spider plays a piano finale to entice a boy and girl fly into his parlor. They escape and the spider ends up entangled in flypaper.

2234. The Fly in the Ointment *(Phantasy)* 23 July 1943; *p.c.:* Colum; *prod:* Dave Fleischer; *dir:* Paul Sommer; *story:* Dun Roman; *anim:* Jim Armstrong, Volus Jones; *ed:* Richard S. Jensen; *voices:* Hanley Stafford, Harry E. Lang; *mus:* Paul Worth, Maurice de Packh; *prod mgr:* Albert Spar; b&w. *sd:* RCA. 6 min. • A spider has many unsuccessful attempts to lure a fly into his web for supper.

2235. A Fly in the Pink *(Pink Panther)* 23 June 1971; *p.c.:* Mirisch/Geoffrey/DFE for UA; *dir:* Hawley Pratt; *anim:* Manny Gould, Manny Perez, Warren Batchelder, Bob Richardson, Don Williams; *lay:* Dick Ung; *back:* Richard H. Thomas; *ed/voice:* Joe Siracusa; *mus:* Walter Greene; *theme tune:* Henry Mancini; *ph:* John Burton Jr.; *prod sup:* Harry Love, Jim Foss; *col:* DeLuxe. *sd:* RCA. 6 min. • The Panther's orchard is in jeopardy when a fruit fly arrives on the scene.

2236. Fly Time *(Aesop's Film Fable)* 6 Mar. 1926; *p.c.:* Fables Pictures Inc for Pathé; *dir:* Paul Terry; b&w. sil. 5 min. • A villainous spider invades an insect cabaret and abducts the lady fly. Her swain comes to the rescue.

2237. The Fly II 10 Feb. 1989; *p.c.:* Brooksfilms for Fox; *fx anim:* Available Light Ltd.; *anim:* John T. Van Vliet, Katherine Kean, January R. Nordman, Joseph Thomas; *col:* DeLuxe. *sd:* Dolby stereo. Panavision. 104 min. *l/a.* • Live-action horror sequel relaying the story of the scientist who is accidentally turned into a fly. His son is born with as many problems.

2238. The Flying Age *(Aesop's Film Fable)* 30 Apr. 1928; *p.c.:* Fables Pictures Inc for Pathé; *dir:* Paul Terry, John Foster; b&w. sil. 5 min. • Captain Blitz, the feline aviator attempts to impress the farmyard animals but Farmer Al is sceptical. When a cat plants some birdseed and a tree grows from it, producing a flock of birds. Al sees gigantic trains and boats flying through the air and finally gets the flying bug. The animals wind-up his legs like an airplane propeller and he takes off into the sky.

2239. The Flying Bear *(MGM Cartoon)* 1 Nov. 1941; *p.c.:* MGM. *prod:* Rudolf Ising; *dir:* Robert Allen; *anim:* William Littlejohn; *back:* Joe Smith; *mus:* Scott Bradley; *prod mgr:* Fred Quimby; *col:* Tech. *sd:* WE. 9 min. • Pilot Barney Bear takes his airplane out for a spin, gets entangled with a jet and both he and his plane end up in hospital.

2240. Flying Carpet *(Aesop's Film Fable)* 7 June 1924; *p.c.:* Fables Pictures Inc for Pathé; *dir:* Paul Terry; b&w. sil. 5 min. • The Farmer and his cat dream they visit the Orient on a flying carpet.

2241. The Flying Cat *(Tom & Jerry)* 12 Jan. 1952; *p.c.:* MGM; *dir:* William Hanna, Joseph Barbera; *anim:* Kenneth Muse, Irven Spence, Ed Barge, Ray Patterson; *lay:* Dick Bickenbach; *back:* Robert Gentle; *ed:* Jim Faris; *mus:* Scott Bradley; *ph:* Jack Stevens; *prod:* Fred Quimby; *col:* Tech. *sd:* WE. 7 min. • Tom makes himself some wings so he can catch an elusive canary.

2242. Flying Circus *(Looney Tunes)* 14 Sept. 1967; *p.c.:* W/7A; *dir:* Alex Lovy; *story:* Cal Howard; *anim:* Ted Bonnicksen, La Verne Harding, Volus Jones, Ed Solomon; *lay:* Bob Givens; *back:* Bob Abrams; *ed:* Hal Geer; *voices:* Larry Storch; *mus:* William Lava; *prod:* Bill L. Hendricks; *col:* Tech. *sd:* Vit. 6 min. • A War Ace lands his plane in Germany by mistake and encounters the Red Baron face to face.

2243. Flying Cups and Saucers *(Terry-Toon)* Nov. 1949; *p.c.:* TT for Fox; *dir:* Connie Rasinski; *story:* John Foster; *mus:* Philip A. Scheib; *ph:* Douglas Moye; *col:* Tech. *sd:* RCA. 7 min. • Martian cats arrive on Earth in search of mice.

2244. Flying Elephants 2 Sept. 1927; *p.c.:* Hal Roach Studio for Pathé; *dir:* Frank Butler; *anim:* Walter Lantz, Roy Seawright; b&w. sil. *l/a/anim.* • Live-action Laurel and Hardy comedy with the boys as cavemen in search of a wife. When the time is right, they look to the skies and see (animated) flying pachyderms.

2245. Flying Feet *(Roland & Rattfink)* 16 Apr. 1969; *p.c.:* Mirisch/DFE for UA; *dir:* Gerry Chiniquy; *story:* Irv Spector; *anim:* Warren Batchelder, Don Williams, Manny Gould, Manny Perez, Bob Richardson; *lay:* Jack Miller; *back:* Tom O'Loughlin; *ed:* Lee Gunther; *voices:* Leonard Weinrib, June Foray. *mus:* Doug Goodwin; *ph:* John Burton Jr.; *prod sup:* Jim Foss, Harry Love; *col:* DeLuxe. *sd.* RCA. 5 min. • Collegiates Roland and Rattfink compete in a cross-country run.

2246. Flying Fever *(Aesop's Film Fable)* 3 Aug. 1924; *p.c.:* Fables Pictures Inc for Pathé; *dir:* Paul Terry; b&w. sil. 5 min. • Al Falfa's animals take to the air in a "Round-the-World" flying contest. Moral: "Keep your feet on the ground."

2247. Flying Fever *(Terry-Toon)* 26 Dec. 1941; *p.c.:* TT for Fox; *dir:* Mannie Davis; *story:* John Foster; *voice:* Arthur Kay; *mus:* Philip A. Scheib; b&w. *sd:* RCA. 7 min. • Gandy Goose trains as an Army pilot. His first solo flight sees him bailing out in a storm and landing in China.

2248. Flying Fishers *(Aesop's Film Fable)* 26 Oct. 1927; *p.c.:* Fables Pictures Inc for Pathé; *dir:* Paul Terry; b&w. sil. 5 min. • No story available.

2249. Flying Fists *(Flip the Frog)* 6 Sept. 1930; *p.c.:* Celebrity prods for MGM; *prod/dir:* Ub Iwerks; b&w. *sd:* PCP. 7 min. • In Flip's training camp, he trains for a boxing match with a turtle.

2250. The Flying Gauchito 22 July 1955; *p.c.:* Walt Disney prods for BV; *dir:* Norman Ferguson, Eric Larson; *col:* Tech. *sd:* RCA. 8 min. • A young gaucho enters a flying donkey in the big race. • See: *The Three Caballeros*

2251. Flying Hoofs *(Aesop's Film Fable)* 3 Dec. 1928; *p.c.:* Fables Pictures Inc for Pathé; *dir:* Paul Terry, Harry Bailey; b&w. sil. 5 min. • No story available.

2252. The Flying House *(Dreams of the Rarebit Fiend)* 1921; *p.c.:* Rialto prods for Vit; *dir/anim:* Robert Winsor McCay; b&w. sil. • A man dreams his house converts into an airplane and flies above the earth to explore the other planets; McCay's tenth and final film.

2253. The Flying Jalopy *(Donald Duck)* 12 Mar. 1943; *p.c.:* Walt Disney prods for RKO; *dir:* Richard Lundy; *anim:* Bob Carlson, Art Babbitt, Richard Lundy, Don Patterson, Marvin Woodward; *fx:* Andy Engman, John F. Reed; *lay:* A. Kendall O'Connor; *back:* Merle Cox; *voices:* Nestor Paiva, Clarence Nash; *mus:* Paul J. Smith; *col:* Tech. *sd:* RCA. 7 min. • Donald buys a rattletrap airplane from Ben Buzzard who makes Don's insurance in favor of himself.

2254. The Flying Jeep *(Daffy Ditty)* 20 Aug. 1945; *p.c.:* Plastic prods for UA; *prod:* John Sutherland, Larry Morey; *dir/anim:* Bill Nolan; *models:* Wah Chang, Frank Irwin; *sets:* Charles A. King, Charles Mattox, Carl Ryan; *mus:* Paul J. Smith; *prod mgr:* Miles E. Pike; *col:* Tech. *sd.* 9 min. • A small Jeep wants to fly like the combat planes. Armed with an umbrella, he tries out his wings and finally brings down a Japanese Zero.

2255. The Flying Mouse (*Silly Symphony*) 14 July 1934; *p.c.:* Walt Disney prods for UA; *dir:* David D. Hand; *story:* Larry Morey, Bob Kuwahara; *anim:* Jack Bailey, George Drake, Nick George, Hardie Gramatky, Hamilton S. Luske, Fred Moore, Charles A. Nichols, Leonard Sebring, Ben Sharpsteen, Bob Wickersham, Marvin Woodward; *fx:* Cy Young; *voices:* The Rhythmettes, William E. Sheets; *mus:* Bert Lewis, Frank E. Churchill; *song:* Larry Morey, Frank E. Churchill; *col:* Tech. *sd:* RCA. 9 min. • A mouse is granted his wish of having wings. When he flies, all his family and friends flee in terror, thinking he's a bat.

2256. Flying Oil (*Paul Terry-Toon*) 5 Apr. 1935; *p.c.:* Moser & Terry for Educational/Fox; *dir:* Paul Terry, Frank Moser; *mus:* Philip A. Scheib; b&w. *sd:* WE. 5 min. • A medicine man sells Al Falfa "Magic Flying Oil." When rubbed on the animals, they soar about the farmyard alongside the farmer.

2257. The Flying Sorceress (*Tom & Jerry*) 21 Jan. 1956; *p.c.:* MGM; *prod/dir:* William Hanna, Joseph Barbera; *anim:* Ed Barge, Irven Spence, Lewis Marshall, Kenneth Muse; *lay:* Dick Bickenbach; *back:* Robert Gentle; *ed:* Jim Faris; *voice:* June Foray; *mus:* Scott Bradley; *ph:* Jack Stevenson; *prod mgr:* Hal Elias; *col:* Tech. *sd:* WE. 7 min. CS. • Tom has a nasty experience when he applies for the job of a witch's cat.

2258. Flying South (*Heckle & Jeckle*) 15 Aug. 1947; *p.c.:* TT for Fox; *dir:* Mannie Davis; *story:* John Foster; *voices:* Thomas Morrison; *mus:* Philip A. Scheib; *ph:* Douglas Moye; *col:* Tech. *sd:* RCA. 6 min. • The magpies try freeloading off an old granny who turns out to be a wolf in disguise.

2259. The Flying Squirrel (*Donald Duck*) 12 Nov. 1954; *p.c.:* Walt Disney prods for BV; *dir:* Jack Hannah; *story:* Nick George, Roy Williams; *anim:* Bob Carlson, Bill Justice, Al Coe, Volus Jones; *fx:* Dan MacManus; *lay:* Yale Gracey; *back:* Ray Huffine; *voice:* Clarence Nash; *mus:* Oliver Wallace; *col:* Tech. *sd:* RCA. 7 min. • A flying squirrel steals a peanut from Donald's thriving peanut stand ... and Don isn't one to let him get away with that. First short to be released under Disney's own distribution company, Buena Vista.

2260. The Flying Turtle (*Foolish Fable*) 29 June 1953; *p.c.:* Walter Lantz prods for Univ; *dir:* Paul J. Smith; *anim:* Gil Turner, Cecil Surry, Robert Bentley; *sets:* Raymond Jacobs, Art Landy; *voices:* Dal McKennon, Grace Stafford; *mus:* Clarence Wheeler; *prod mgr:* William E. Garity; *col:* Tech. *sd:* RCA. 6 min. • Herman, a turtle, wants to fly so he bribes an eagle to take him up high and let him go.

2261. The Fly's Bride (*Aesop's Sound Fable*) 21 Sept. 1929; *p.c.:* Van Beuren for Pathé; *dir:* John Foster; *mus:* Carl Edouarde; b&w. *sd:* RCA. 7 min. • Fly's inebriation makes him more courageous than normal in saving his lady love from the clutches of a spider.

2262. The Fly's Last Flight (*Popeye*) 23 Dec. 1949; *p.c.:* Famous for Para; *dir:* Seymour Kneitel; *story:* Larz Bourne; *anim:* Tom Johnson, Frank Endres; *sets:* Tom Ford; *voices:* Jack Mercer; *mus:* Winston Sharples; *ph:* Leonard McCormick; *prod mgr:* Sam Buchwald; *col:* Tech. *sd:* RCA. 6 min. • Popeye's rest is disturbed by a pesty fly in this Tech remake of *Flys Ain't Human.*

2263. Fodder and Son (*Woody Woodpecker*) 4 Nov. 1957; *p.c.:* Walter Lantz prods for Univ; *dir:* Paul J. Smith; *story:* Homer Brightman; *anim:* Les Kline, Robert Bentley; *sets:* Art Landy; *voices:* Daws Butler, Grace Stafford; *mus:* Clarence Wheeler; *prod sup:* William E. Garity; *col:* Tech. *sd:* RCA. 6 min. • Woody encounters a freeloading bear and his offspring in a National Park.

2264. The Foghorn Leghorn (*Merrie Melodies*) 9 Oct. 1948; *p.c.:* WB; *dir/char des:* Robert McKimson; *story:* Warren Foster; *anim:* Charles McKimson, Manny Gould, Phil de Lara, John Carey, Pete Burness; *lay:* Cornett Wood; *back:* Richard H. Thomas; *ed:* Treg Brown; *voices:* Mel Blanc; *mus:* Carl Stalling; *prod mgr:* John W. Burton; *prod:* Edward Selzer; *col:* Tech. *sd:* Vit. 7 min. • Henery Hawk sets out to capture a chicken but gets confused when the dog refers to Foghorn Leghorn as a "Schnook."

2265. Foiled Again (*Paul Terry-Toon*) 4 Oct. 1935; *p.c.:* Moser & Terry for Educational/Fox; *dir:* Paul Terry, Frank Moser; *mus:* Philip A. Scheib; b&w. *sd:* WE. 6 min. • Another operatic melodrama featuring Fanny Zilch. Oil Can Harry ties Fanny to a saw mill and T. Leffingwell Strongheart arrives just in time.

2266. Foiling the Fox (*Aesop's Fable*) Apr. 1950; *p.c.:* TT for Fox; *dir:* Connie Rasinski; *story:* John Foster; *anim:* Jim Tyer; *mus:* Philip A. Scheib; *ph:* Douglas Moye; *col:* Tech. *sd:* RCA. 6 min. • Dingbat's antics prevent the fox from catching a lamb.

2267. Foney Fables (*Merrie Melodies*) 18 July 1942; *p.c.:* Leon Schlesinger prods for WB; *dir:* I. Freleng; *story:* Michael Maltese, Robert Clampett; *anim:* Richard Bickenbach; *lay:* Owen Fitzgerald; *back:* Lenard Kester; *ed:* Treg Brown; *voices:* Frank Graham, Mel Blanc, Sara Berner; *mus:* Carl W. Stalling; *prod sup:* Henry Binder, Raymond G. Katz; *col:* Tech. *sd:* Vit. 7 min. • Blackouts on nursery rhymes with a distinct wartime flavor.

2268. Food for Feudin' (*Pluto*) 11 Aug. 1950; *p.c.:* Walt Disney prods for RKO; *dir:* Charles Nichols; *story:* Milt Schaffer, Dick Kinney; *anim:* Phil Duncan, George Kreisl, George Nicholas, Judge Whitaker; *fx:* Jack Boyd; *lay:* Karl Karpé; *back:* Merle Cox; *voices:* James MacDonald, Dessie Flynn; *mus:* Paul Smith; *col:* Tech. *sd:* RCA. 7 min. • Pluto disrupts Chip 'n' Dale's activities by stowing a bone in the same tree as their winter storage of nuts.

2269. Food Will Win the War 21 July 1942; *p.c.:* Walt Disney prods for U.S. Dpt. of Agriculture; *dir:* Ben Sharpsteen; *asst dir:* Ed Gershman; *anim:* Josh Meador, Ray Patterson; *lay:* A. Kendall O'Connor; *voice:* Fred Shields; *col:* Tech. *sd:* RCA. 5½ min. • Interesting comparisons proving food resources of the United States. The Three Pigs appear as "The Spirit of '76."

2270. Foofle's Picnic (*Terry-Toon*) Mar. 1960; *p.c.:* TT for Fox; *ex prod:* Bill Weiss; *dir:* Dave Tendlar; *story sup:* Tom Morrison; *story:* Larz Bourne, Eli Bauer; *anim:* Ed Donnelly, Larry Silverman, Vinnie Bell, Mannie Davis, Johnny Gent; *sets:* Bill Focht, John Zago; *mus:* Phil Scheib; *prod mgr:* Frank Schudde; *col:* Tech. *sd:* RCA. 6 min. CS. • Foofle plans a picnic with his girl ... but she never shows up.

2271. Foofle's Train Ride (*Terry-Toons*) 24 May 1959; *p.c.:* TT for Fox; *ex prod:* Bill Weiss; *dir sup:* Gene Deitch; *dir:* Dave Tendlar; *story sup:* Tom Morrison; *story:* Larz Bourne, Eli Bauer; *anim:* Bob Kuwahara, Jim Tyer, Mannie Davis, Ed Donnelly; *des:* Jules Feiffer; *back:* Bill Focht; *voices:* Bern Bennett; *mus:* Philip Scheib; *prod mgr:* Sparky Schudde; *col:* Tech. *sd:* RCA. 6 min. • Foofle takes a scenic train excursion.

2272. Fool Coverage (*Merrie Melodies*) 13 Dec. 1952; *p.c.:* WB; *dir:* Robert McKimson; *story:* Tedd Pierce; *anim:* Phil de Lara, Charles McKimson, Herman Cohen, Rod Scribner; *lay:* Robert Givens; *back:* Carlos Manriquez; *ed:* Treg Brown; *voices:* Mel Blanc; *mus:* Carl Stalling; *prod mgr:* John W. Burton; *prod:* Edward Selzer; *col:* Tech. *sd:* Vit. 7 min. • Daffy tries to convince Porky to buy an insurance policy.

2273. The Foolish Bunny (*Color Rhapsody*) 11 May 1938; *p.c.:* Charles Mintz prods for Colum; *story:* Sid Marcus; *anim:* Art Davis; *sets:* Phil Davis; *voices:* Robert Winkler, Dave Weber; *mus:* Joe de Nat; *i&p:* Christine Phiederman; *prod mgr:* James Bronis; *col:* Tech. *sd:* RCA. 8 min. • A rabbit devotes his early years at school to upsetting the others, now he has to make up for lost time.

2274. The Foolish Duckling (*Dinky Duck*) July 1952; *p.c.:* TT for Fox; *dir:* Mannie Davis; *story/voices:* Tom Morrison; *anim:* Jim Tyer; *sets:* Art Bartsch; *mus:* Philip A. Scheib; *ph:* Douglas Moye; *col:* Tech. *sd:* RCA. 7 min. • Dinky prefers writing poetry to learning to fly. When time comes to fly south, he wins an airplane trip in a poetry competition.

2275. Foolish Follies (*Aesop's Sound Fables*) 16 Mar. 1930; *p.c.:* Van Beuren for Pathé; *dir:* John Foster, Harry Bailey; *anim:* Hugh Shields; b&w. *sd:* RCA. 6 min. • Animal acts in a jungle casino night club.

2276. Foot Ball (*Paul Terry-Toon*) 18 Oct. 1935; *p.c.:* Moser & Terry for Educational/Fox; *dir:* Paul Terry, Frank Moser; *mus:* Philip A. Scheib; b&w. *sd:* WE. 5 min. • A football game between the cats and the mice. The Cats steamroller the opposing team who retaliate with catapults.

2277. Foot Brawl (*Beary Family*) Jan. 1966; *p.c.:* Walter Lantz prods for Univ; *dir:* Paul J. Smith; *story:* Cal Howard; *anim:* Les Kline, Al Coe; *sets:* Art Landy, Ray Huffine; *voices:* Paul Frees, Grace Stafford; *mus:* Walter Greene; *prod mgr:* William E. Garity; *col:* Tech. *sd:* RCA. 6 min. • Charlie teaches Junior the art of football.

2278. Football Bugs (*Color Rhapsody*) 29 Aug. 1936; *p.c.:* Charles Mintz prods for Colum; *story:* Art Davis; *anim:* Sid Marcus; *sets:* Phil Davis; *voices:* Dave Weber; *mus:* Joe de Nat; *prod mgr:* James Bronis; *col:* Tech.

sd: RCA. *sd:* 7 min. • Alcohol is put in the water to liven the bugs' football game up.

2279. Football Fever *(Oswald)* 15 Nov. 1937; *p.c.:* Univ; *prod/dir:* Walter Lantz; *story:* Walter Lantz, Victor McLeod; *voice:* Shirley Reed; *mus:* James Dietrich; b&w. *sd:* WE. 7 min. • Oswald and his "All Stars" play "The Ruffians," a bunch of apes, in a football game.

2280. Football Now and Then 2 Oct. 1953; *p.c.:* Walt Disney prods for RKO; *dir:* Jack Kinney; *story:* Lance Nolley; *anim:* John Sibley, George Nicholas, Fred Moore; *fx:* Dan MacManus, Ed Aardal; *lay:* Bruce Bushman; *back:* Dick Anthony; *voices:* Bill Walsh, Dal McKennon, John Rovick, Jackson Wheeler; *mus:* Edward Plumb, Paul J. Smith; *col:* Tech. *sd:* RCA. 7 min. • A boy and his grandfather widen the generation gap when they watch a TV football game between Bygone U and Present State.

2281. The Football Toucher-Downer *(Popeye)* 15 Oct. 1937; *p.c.:* The Fleischer Studio for Para; *prod:* Max Fleischer; *dir:* Dave Fleischer; *anim:* Seymour Kneitel, Graham Place; *voices:* Jack Mercer, Mae Questel; *mus:* Sammy Timberg; *prod sup:* Sam Buchwald, Isidore Sparber; b&w. *sd:* WE. 7 min. • Popeye encourages Swee'Pea to eat his spinach by telling of when he was a kid on the football team.

2282. For Better or Nurse *(Popeye)* 8 June 1945; *p.c.:* Famous for Para; *dir:* I. Sparber; *story:* Joe Stultz, Irving Dressler; *anim:* Dave Tendlar, John Gentilella; *sets:* Shane Miller; *voices:* Jackson Beck, Mae Questel; *mus:* Sammy Timberg; *prod mgr:* Sam Buchwald; b&w. *sd:* RCA. 8 min. Tech. Reissue: 5 Oct. 1951. • Popeye and Bluto try to injure themselves so that they can be tended by nurse Olive.

2283. For Better or Worser *(Popeye)* 28 June 1935; *p.c.:* The Fleischer Studio for Para; *prod:* Max Fleischer; *dir:* Dave Fleischer; *anim:* Seymour Kneitel, Roland Crandall; *voices:* William A. Costello, Mae Questel, Gus Wickie, Louis Fleischer; *mus:* Sammy Timberg; b&w. *sd:* WE. 7 min. • Wimpy's Matrimony Agency offers both Popeye and Bluto a photo of Olive and they fight over her.

2284. For Scent-imental Reasons *(Looney Tunes)* 12 Nov. 1949; *p.c.:* WB; *dir:* Charles M. Jones; *story:* Michael Maltese; *anim:* Ben Washam, Lloyd Vaughan, Ken Harris, Phil Monroe; *lay:* Robert Gribbroek; *back:* Peter Alvarado; *ed:* Treg Brown; *voices:* Mel Blanc; *mus:* Carl Stalling; *prod mgr:* John W. Burton; *prod:* Edward Selzer; *col:* Tech. *sd:* Vit. 7 min. *Academy Award* • A cat is sent into a Paris perfumery to rid the place of a skunk but she is mistaken by the creature as one of it's own kind.

2285. For the Love O' Pete *(Hot Dog)* 2 Oct. 1926; *p.c.:* Bray prods; *dir:* Walt Lantz, Clyde Geronimi; b&w. *sil.* 6 min. *l/a/anim.* • When a tramp steals Walter's pants, Pete gets a replacement from a scarecrow which, unfortunately, houses an angry bee.

2286. For the Love of a Gal *(Aesop's Film Fable)* 18 July 1925; *p.c.:* Fables Pictures Inc for Pathé; *dir:* Paul Terry; b&w. *sil.* 5 min. • A mouse's sweetheart is abducted by pirate cats. The hero is shot aboard their ship by cannon and rescues the girl.

2287. For the Love of Pizza *(Woody Woodpecker)* 1972; *p.c.:* Walter Lantz prods for Univ; *dir:* Paul J. Smith; *story:* Cal Howard; *anim:* Volus Jones, Al Coe, Tom Byrne, Joe Voght; *sets:* Nino Carbe; *voice:* Grace Stafford; *mus:* Walter Greene; *prod mgr:* William E. Garity; *col:* Tech. *sd:* RCA. 5 min. • A starving Woody replaces Granny when he discovers Mrs. Meanie is taking her a pizza.

2288. For Whom the Bulls Toil *(Goofy)* 9 May 1953; *p.c.:* Walt Disney prods for RKO; *dir:* Jack Kinney; *story:* Brice Mack, Dick Kinney; *anim:* John Sibley, Ed Aardal, George Nicholas; *fx:* Blaine Gibson, Dan MacManus; *lay:* Bruce Bushman; *back:* Eyvind Earle; *voices:* Joaquin Garay, Pinto Colvig, James MacDonald, Xavier Atencio, Dan MacManus, Al Bertino, Bud Partch, Dick Shaw, Brice Mack, Bruce Bushman, Bea Tamargo, Joe Nunez, Xenia De Mattia, Mario Marion, Toni Varescu; *mus:* Joseph S. Dubin; *trumpet solo:* Rafael Mendez; *col:* Tech. *sd:* RCA. 7 min. • Goofy is taken for a famous matador and given the rare opportunity of fighting a ferocious bull.

2289. The Forbidden Planet 1956; *p.c.:* MGM; *prod:* Nicholas Nayfack; *dir:* Fred M. Wilcox; *col:* East. *sd:* WE. 98 min. CS. *l/a.* • A space ship from earth lands on the planet Altair-4 in the year 2200 where the astronauts meet a father and daughter who know no other life. Cult sci-fi film with some superior special effects contributed by Joshua Meador of the Walt Disney Studios.

2290. Ford Films *p.c.:* UPA for Ford/J.W. Thompson; *ex prod:* Stephen Bosustow; *dir:* Ted Geisel (Dr. Seuss); *col:* Tech. *sd:* RCA. 5 min. • (1) 1 Apr. 1949; (2) 1 Dec. 1949. • Series of five cartoon commercials released to both television and theatres. Three untraced.

2291. Forest Fantasy *(Kartune)* 14 Nov. 1952; *p.c.:* Famous for Para; *dir:* Seymour Kneitel. *story:* I. Klein; *anim:* Myron Waldman, Larry Silverman; *sets:* Anton Loeb; *voices:* Gwen Davies, Jack Mercer; *mus:* Winston Sharples; *ph:* Leonard McCormick; *prod mgr:* Seymour Shultz; *col:* Tech. *sd:* RCA. 7 min. • An insight into the lives of forest animals.

2292. Forget Me Nuts *(MerryMaker)* July 1967; *p.c.:* Para Cartoons; *ex prod:* Shamus Culhane; *dir:* Chuck Harriton; *story:* Joseph Szabo; *anim:* Howard Beckerman; *sets:* Danté Barbetta, Gil Miret, Hal Silvermintz; *mus:* Winston Sharples; *prod sup:* Harold Robins, Burt Hanft; *col:* Tech. *sd:* RCA. 8 min. • Bosko the elephant gets a job as a computer. A mouse causes him to lose his memory and friend, Buddy, helps him regain it.

2293. Fortune Hunters *(Gandy Goose)* 8 Feb. 1946; *p.c.:* TT for Fox; *dir:* Connie Rasinski; *story:* John Foster; *voices:* Arthur Kay, Tom Morrison; *mus:* Philip A. Scheib; *ph:* Douglas Moye; *col:* Tech. *sd:* RCA. 7 min. • Pvt. Gandy dreams he's inherited a country estate but when he visits it with Sgt. Sourpuss he finds it overrun with ghosts. Much reused footage from *Lights Out.*

2294. The Fortune Teller *(Out of the Inkwell)* 1923; *p.c.:* Inkwell Studios for Rodner; *prod:* Max Fleischer; *dir:* Dave Fleischer; b&w. *sil.* 5 min. *l/a/anim.* • A gypsy foretells Max and Ko-Ko they are both to be haunted by evil spirits. The clown spooks the gypsy who puts a curse on him.

2295. Forty Pink Winks *(Pink Panther)* 8 Aug. 1975; *p.c.:* Mirisch/Geoffrey/DFE for UA; *dir:* Gerry Chiniquy; *story:* John W. Dunn; *anim:* Bob Richardson, Don Williams, Bob Matz, Norm McCabe; *lay:* Tony Rivera; *back:* Richard H. Thomas; *ed:* Rick Steward; *mus:* Walter Greene; *theme tune:* Henry Mancini; *ph:* John Burton Jr.; *prod mgr:* Lee Gunther; *col:* DeLuxe. *sd:* RCA. 6 min. • The Panther seeks a respite in the Ritz Plaza but is pursued by the house detective.

2296. The Forty Thieves *(Paul Terry-Toons)* 13 Nov. 1932; *p.c.:* Moser & Terry for Educational/Fox; *dir:* Paul Terry, Frank Moser; *mus:* Philip A. Scheib; b&w. *sd:* WE. 6 min. • Performed as an opera: Thieves spot Ali Baba on a flying carpet and send vultures to bring him down. They capture a dancing girl and our hero rescues her.

2297. Forward March Hare *(Looney Tunes)* 14 Feb. 1953; *p.c.:* WB; *dir:* Charles M. Jones; *story:* Michael Maltese; *anim:* Ben Washam, Lloyd Vaughan, Ken Harris; *lay:* Maurice Noble; *back:* Philip de Guard; *ed:* Treg Brown; *voices:* Mel Blanc, John T. Smith; *mus:* Carl Stalling; *prod mgr:* John W. Burton; *prod:* Edward Selzer; *col:* Tech. *sd:* Vit. 7 min. • Bugs is drafted into the Army by mistake but decides to make the best of it.

2298. The Foul Ball Player *(Stoneage)* 24 May 1940; *p.c.:* The Fleischer Studio for Para; *prod:* Max Fleischer; *dir:* Dave Fleischer; *story:* Jack Ward; *anim:* Bill Nolan, Ralph Somerville; *ed:* Kitty Pfister; *character des:* Charles Thorson; *mus:* Sammy Timberg; *prod sup:* Sam Buchwald, Isidore Sparber; b&w. *sd:* WE. 6 min. • Hay fever upsets the cavemen's baseball game.

2299. Foul Hunting *(Goofy)* 31 Oct. 1947; *p.c.:* Walt Disney prods for RKO; *dir:* Jack Hannah; *asst dir:* Bee Selck; *story:* Dick Kinney, Bob North; *anim:* Art Babbitt, Al Bertino, Volus Jones, Bill Justice, John Sibley, Ken Walker; *fx:* Jack Boyd, Andy Engman; *lay:* Yale Gracey; *back:* Ralph Hulett; *voice:* Pinto Colvig; *mus:* Oliver Wallace; *col:* Tech. *sd:* RCA. 6 min. • The Goof goes duck hunting and ends up having to eat his own decoy.

2300. The Foul Kin *(Roland & Rattfink)* 5 Aug. 1970; *p.c.:* Mirisch/DFE for UA; *dir:* Grant Simmons; *story:* Sid Marcus; *anim:* Ken Muse, Warren Batchelder, Robert Taylor; *lay:* Martin Strudler; *back:* Richard Thomas; *ed:* Lee Gunther; *voices:* Leonard Weinrib; *mus:* Doug Goodwin; *ph:* John Burton Jr.; *prod sup:* Jim Foss, Harry Love; *col:* DeLuxe. *sd:* RCA. 5 min. • Rattfink tries to butter up his hundred-year-old uncle in the hopes of a mention in his will.

2301. The Four Musicians of Bremen *(Laugh-O-Gram)* Apr./May 1922; *p.c.:* Laugh-O-Gram Films for Newman Theater; *dir:* Walt. Disney; *anim:* Walt. Disney, Hugh Harman, Rudolf Ising, Ub Iwerks; b&w. *sil.* 5 min. • A band of animal musicians are run out of town. They find themselves in a cabin full of masked brigands and a fight ensues. Reissued with sound as *The Four Jazz Boys.* • See: *Whoopee Sketches*

2302. Four Wheels No Brakes (*Pete Hothead*) 24 Mar. 1955; *p.c.:* UPA for Colum; *ex prod:* Stephen Bosustow; *dir:* Ted Parmelee; *story:* Ted Pierce, Fred Grable, Jerry Schnitzer; *anim:* Cecil Surry, Ken Hultgren; *lay:* Ted Parmelee, Sam Clayberger; *back:* Robert Dranko; *voices:* Jerry Hausner, Mary Jane Croft; *mus:* Dennis Farnon; *prod mgr:* Herbert Klynn; *col:* Tech. *sd:* RCA. 7 min. • Pete buys a new car but his wife also wins the same model. When her prize is delivered Pete assumes it's what he ordered only the wrong color, so he storms back to the shop to give them a piece of his mind.

2303. The Fourposter 1952; *p.c.:* UPA for Colum; *ex prod:* Stephen Bosustow; *seq dir:* John Hubley, Paul Julian; *des:* Lew Keller; *anim:* Art Babbitt; *col:* Tech. *sd:* RCA. 103 min (complete film) • Live-action adaptation of Jan de Hartog's play suitably enhanced by animated interludes.

2304. 14-Carrot Rabbit (*Looney Tunes*) 15 Mar. 1952; *p.c.:* WB; *dir:* I. Freleng; *story:* Warren Foster; *anim:* Manuel Perez, Ken Champin, Virgil Ross, Arthur Davis; *lay:* Hawley Pratt; *back:* Irv Wyner; *ed:* Treg Brown; *voices:* Mel Blanc; *mus:* Carl Stalling; *prod mgr:* John W. Burton; *prod:* Edward Selzer; *col:* Tech. *sd:* Vit. 7 min. • Sam uses Bugs' "Lucky Feeling" to help him find gold in the Klondike.

2305. The Fowl Ball (*Oswald*) 13 Oct. 1930; *p.c.:* Univ; *dir:* Walter Lantz, Bill Nolan; *anim:* Clyde Geronimi, Manuel Moreno, Ray Abrams, Fred Avery, Lester Kline, "Pinto" Colvig; *mus:* James Dietrich; b&w. *sd.* 6 min. • Oswald conducts a frog orchestra, each member of which finds himself victim of a pelican.

2306. Fowl Brawl (*Phantasy*) 9 Jan. 1947; *p.c.:* Colum; *dir:* Howard Swift; *story:* Cal Howard; *anim:* Grant Simmons, Paul Sommer; *lay:* Bill Weaver; *back:* Ed Starr; *ed:* Richard S. Jensen; *mus:* Eddie Kilfeather; *ph:* Frank Fisher; *creative consultant:* Bob Clampett; *prod:* Raymond Katz, Henry Binder; *col:* Tech. *sd:* WE. 6 min. • The fox dons many disguises to get past the watchdog outside the chicken coop.

2307. Fowl Play (*Blue Racer*) 1 June 1973; *p.c.:* Mirisch/DFE for UA; *dir:* Bob McKimson; *story:* John W. Dunn; *anim:* Don Williams, Ken Muse, John Freeman; *lay:* Owen Fitzgerald; *back:* Richard H. Thomas; *ed:* Roger Donley; *voices:* Larry D. Mann; *mus:* Doug Goodwin; *prod sup:* Stan Paperney; *col:* DeLuxe. *sd:* RCA. 5 min. • A Chick mistakes The Racer for a worm.

2308. Fowl Play (*Popeye*) 17 Dec. 1937; *p.c.:* The Fleischer Studio for Para; *prod:* Max Fleischer; *dir:* Dave Fleischer; *anim:* David Tendlar, William Sturm; *voices:* Jack Mercer, Mae Questel, Gus Wickie; *mus:* Sammy Timberg; *prod sup:* Sam Buchwald, Isidore Sparber; b&w. *sd:* WE. 7 min. • Bluto sees Popeye's "going away" gift to Olive (a parrot) as a potential enemy and decides to dispose of it.

2309. Fowl Weather (*Merrie Melodies*) 4 Apr. 1953; *p.c.:* WB; *dir:* I. Freleng; *story:* Warren Foster; *anim:* Ken Champin, Virgil Ross, Arthur Davis, Manuel Perez; *lay:* Hawley Pratt; *back:* Irv Wyner; *ed:* Treg Brown; *voices:* Mel Blanc, Bea Benaderet; *mus:* Carl Stalling; *prod mgr:* John W. Burton; *prod:* Edward Selzer; *col:* Tech. *sd:* Vit. 7 min. • Sylvester chases Tweety in the hen house and has to disguise himself as a pullet to get past the rooster guarding it.

2310. Fowled-Up Birthday (*Cartune*) 27 Mar. 1962; *p.c.:* Walter Lantz prods for Univ; *dir:* Jack Hannah; *story:* Al Bertino, Dick Kinney; *anim:* Roy Jenkins, Don Lusk; *sets:* Ray Huffine, Art Landy; *voices:* Grace Stafford, Paul Frees, Nancy Wible; *mus:* Darrell Calker; *prod mgr:* William E. Garity; *col:* Tech. *sd:* RCA. 6 min. • Charlie Beary is pursuaded to buy a live goose for Susie's birthday dinner which she takes for a pet.

2311. Fowled-Up Falcon (*Woody Woodpecker*) 20 Dec. 1960; *p.c.:* Walter Lantz prods for Univ; *dir:* Paul J. Smith; *story:* Homer Brightman; *anim:* La Verne Harding, Les Kline; *sets:* Ray Huffine, Art Landy; *voices:* Paul Frees, Grace Stafford; *mus:* Clarence Wheeler; *prod mgr:* William E. Garity; *col:* Tech. *sd:* RCA. 6 min. • Woody has a run-in with a falcon who's trying to deliver him to his Germanic master.

2312. Fowled-Up Party (*Cartune*) 14 Jan. 1957; *p.c.:* Walter Lantz prods for Univ; *dir:* Alex Lovy; *story:* Homer Brightman; *anim:* Ray Abrams, La Verne Harding; *sets:* Raymond Jacobs, Art Landy; *voices:* Daws Butler, Grace Stafford; *mus:* Clarence Wheeler; *prod mgr:* William E. Garity; *col:* Tech. *sd:* RCA. 6 min. • En route to a fancy dress party, Maggie and Sam's car runs out of fuel. Dressed as a chicken, Sam is taken for a real hen by a ravenous farm dog.

2313. The Fox and the Duck (*Terry-Toon*) 24 Aug. 1945; *p.c.:* TT for Fox; *dir:* Mannie Davis; *story:* John Foster; *voice:* Thomas Morrison; *mus:* Philip A. Scheib; *col:* Tech. *sd:* RCA. 6 min. • A fox tries to steal the prize laying hens. It's up to a duck to stop him as the dog, fish and pig won't help.

2314. The Fox and the Goat (*Aesop's Film Fable*) 6 Nov. 1921; *p.c.:* Fables Pictures Inc for Pathé. *dir:* Paul Terry. b&w. sil. 5 min. • A fox finds himself at the bottom of a well. He manages to extricate himself by getting a goat to jump in so that he can stand on its back to get out. Moral: "Look before you leap."

2315. The Fox and the Grapes (*Aesop's Film Fable*) 26 Jan. 1922; *p.c.:* Fables Pictures Inc for Pathé; *dir:* Paul Terry; b&w. sil. 5 min. • A fox wants the grapes that are out of his reach. He retreats, claiming they were sour.

2316. The Fox and the Grapes (*Color Rhapsody*) 5 Nov. 1941; *p.c.:* Colum; *story/dir:* Frank Tashlin; *anim:* Bob Wickersham; *sets:* Clark Watson; *ed:* Edward Moore; *voices:* Mel Blanc; *mus:* Eddie Kilfeather; *ph:* Frank Fisher; *prod mgr:* Ben Schwalb; *col:* Tech. *sd:* RCA. 8 min. • The Crow offers a straight swap of a bunch of grapes for the Fox's picnic. Foxy decides he can get the grapes himself from atop a high tree. An excellent opener to a much underrated series starring the Fox and the Crow.

2317. The Fox and the Hound 10 July 1981; *p.c.:* Walt Disney Prods., for BV; *dir:* Art Stevens, Ted Berman, Richard Rich; *prod:* Wolfgang Reitherman, Art Stevens; *ex prod:* Ron Miller; *asst dir:* Don Hahn, Mark A. Hester, Terry L. Noss; *based on the novel by* Daniel P. Mannix; *story adapt:* Ted Berman, Larry Clemmons, Vance Gerry, Steve Hulett, Burny Mattinson, David Michener; *anim sup:* Randy Cartwright, Cliff Nordberg, Frank Thomas, Glen Keane, Ron Clements, Ollie Johnston; *anim:* Ed Gombert, Dale Oliver, Ron Husband, David Block, Chris Buck, Hendel S. Butoy, Darrell van Citters, Philip Young, John Musker, Jerry Rees, Dick N. Lucas, Jeffrey J. Varab, Chuck Harvey, Phil Nibbelink, Michael Cedeno; *fx anim:* Ted Kierscey, Jack Boyd, Don C. Paul; *anim co-ord:* Walt Stanchfield, Dave Suding, LeRoy Cross, Chuck Williams; *key asst:* Tom Ferriter, Sylvia Mattinson; *ed:* James Melton, Jim Koford; *art dir:* Don Griffith; *lay:* Dan Hansen, Sylvia Roemer, Michael Peraza Jnr., Glenn V. Vilppu, Guy Vasilovich, Joe Hale; *col styling:* Jim Coleman; *back:* Daniela Bielecka, Brian Sebern, Kathleen Swain; *voices:* Tod: Mickey Rooney; Copper: Kurt Russell; Big Mama: Pearl Bailey; Amos Slade: Jack Albertson; Vixey: Sandy Duncan; Widow Tweed: Jeanette Nolan; Chief: Pat Buttram; Porcupine: John Fiedler; Badger: John McIntyre; Dinky: Dick Bakalyan; Boomer: Paul Winchell; Young Tod: Keith Mitchell; Young Copper: Corey Feldman; Squeeks (caterpillar): John Stephenson; *mus:* Buddy Baker; *orch:* Walter Sheets; *mus ed:* Evelyn Kennedy, Jack Wadsworth; *songs:* Best of Friends by Richard O. Johnston, Stan Fidel; Lack of Education/Huntin' Man/Appreciate the Lady by Jim Stafford; Goodbye May Seem for Ever by Richard Rich, Jeffrey Patch; *sd:* Herb Taylor; *creative asst:* Melvin Shaw; *prod mgr:* Edward Hansen, Don A. Duckwall; *col:* Tech. *sd:* RCA. 83 min. • An orphaned baby fox befriends a young hunting pup. As time goes by, Copper, the dog, is trained to hunt foxes and so his friend has to be taken to a game preserve. The showdown comes when Copper is taken hunting and comes up against his old comrade.

2318. The Fox and the Rabbit (*Cartune Classic*) 30 Sept. 1935; *p.c.:* Univ; *prod:* Walter Lantz; *dir:* Walter Lantz; *story/lyrics:* Walter Lantz, Victor McLeod; *anim:* Manuel Moreno, Lester Kline, Fred Kopietz; *voice:* Mary Moder; *mus:* James Dietrich; *col:* Tech-2. *sd:* WE. 8 min. • A bunny feigns measles to play truant and visit the carrot patch which turns out to be a ruse to catch him by the fox. The "measles" puts him off the whole idea.

2319. The Fox Chase (*Oswald the Lucky Rabbit*) 25 June 1928; *p.c.:* Winkler for Univ; *dir:* Walt Disney; *anim:* Hugh Harman, Rollin C. Hamilton; *ph:* Mike Marcus; b&w. sil. 5 min. • Huntsman Oswald corners the fox in a hollow log then brings out a skunk. The entire hunt flees the scene, leaving the fox to remove his "skunk" disguise.

2320. The Fox Hunt (*Aesop's Film Fable*) 20 Nov. 1927; *p.c.:* Fables Pictures Inc for Pathé; *dir:* Paul Terry; b&w. sil. 5 min. • Reynard serenades Fanny Fox but is seen off by the Farmer who enlists six hounds. He returns to let loose a skunk and elope with Fanny.

2321. The Fox Hunt (*Donald & Goofy*) 29 July 1938; *p.c.:* Walt Disney prods for RKO; *dir:* Ben Sharpsteen; *story:* Otto Englander; *anim:* Norman

Ferguson, Clyde Geronimi, John McManus, Milt Schaffer, Fred Spencer; *lay:* Don Peterson; *voices:* Pinto Colvig, Clarence Nash; Richard Edwards; *mus:* Paul J. Smith; *col:* Tech. *sd:* RCA. 8 min. • Goofy has problems with a stubborn horse and Donald can't control his pack of hounds.

2322. The Fox Hunt (*Heckle & Jeckle*) 7 Feb. 1950; *p.c.:* TT for Fox; *dir:* Connie Rasinski; *story:* John Foster; *voices:* Thomas Morrison; *mus:* Philip A. Scheib; *ph:* Douglas Moye; *col:* Tech. *sd:* RCA. 7 min. • The magpies are watching a fox hunt on TV when the fox escapes through the screen followed by a pack of hounds.

2323. The Fox Hunt (*Silly Symphony*) 10 Nov. 1931; *p.c.:* Walt Disney prods for Colum; *dir:* Wilfred Jackson; *anim:* Johnny Cannon, Les Clark, Gilles de Tremaudan, David D. Hand, Jack King, Richard Lundy, Ben Sharpsteen, Rudy Zamora; *asst anim:* Chuck Couch, Jack Cutting, Joe d'Igalo, Hardie Gramatky, Albert Hurter, Andrew Hutchinson, Harry Reeves, Frank Tipper, Cecil Surry, Roy Williams, Marvin Woodward; *mus:* Frank E. Churchill; b&w. *sd:* PCP. 6 min. • The fox hunters only succeed in capturing a skunk.

2324. A Fox in a Fix (*Merrie Melodies*) 21 Jan. 1951; *p.c.:* WB; *dir:* Robert McKimson; *story:* Warren Foster; *anim:* Rod Scribner, Charles McKimson, John Carey, Phil de Lara, J.C. Melendez; *lay:* Cornett Wood; *back:* Richard H. Thomas; *ed:* Treg Brown; *voices:* Mel Blanc; *mus:* Carl Stalling; *prod mgr:* John W. Burton; *prod:* Edward Selzer; *col:* Tech. *sd:* Vit. 7 min. • A fox disguises himself as a dog in order to get past the guard dog into the chicken coop.

2325. Fox Pop (*Merrie Melodies*) 5 Sept. 1942; *p.c.:* Leon Schlesinger prods for WB; *dir:* Charles M. Jones; *story:* Ted Pierce; *lay:* John McGrew; *back:* Eugene Fleury; *ed:* Treg Brown; *voices:* Mel Blanc, Robert C. Bruce, Ted Pierce; *mus:* Carl W. Stalling; *ph:* John W. Burton; *prod sup:* Henry Binder, Raymond G. Katz; *col:* Tech. *sd:* Vit. 7 min. • A red fox believes a life of luxury lies in a Silver Fox Farm, so he paints himself silver, unaware that only his pelt is wanted.

2326. Fox-Terror (*Merrie Melodies*) 11 May 1957; *p.c.:* WB; *dir:* Robert McKimson; *story:* Michael Maltese; *anim:* Keith Darling, George Grandpré, Ted Bonnicksen, David R. Green; *lay:* Robert Gribbroek; *back:* Bob Majors; *ed:* Treg Brown; *voices:* Mel Blanc. *mus:* Carl Stalling, Milt Franklyn; *col:* Tech. *sd:* Vit. 7 min. • A fox attempts to oust Foggy from the chicken coop.

2327. Foxed by a Fox (*Terry-Toon*) Aug. 1955; *p.c.:* TT for Fox; *dir:* Connie Rasinski; *anim:* Jim Tyer; *story:* Tom Morrison; *mus:* Philip A. Scheib; *ph:* Douglas Moye; *col:* Tech. *sd:* RCA. 7 min. • During a fox hunt, the fox calls a halt to the film and proceeds to run the movie his own way with the aid of a pencil and eraser.

2328. Foxy by Proxy (*Merrie Melodies*) 23 Feb. 1952; *p.c.:* WB; *dir:* I. Freleng; *story:* Warren Foster; *anim:* Virgil Ross, Arthur Davis, Manuel Perez, Ken Champin; *lay:* Hawley Pratt; *back:* Irv Wyner; *ed:* Treg Brown; *voices:* Mel Blanc, Stan Freberg; *mus:* Carl Stalling; *prod mgr:* John W. Burton; *prod:* Edward Selzer; *col:* Tech. *sd:* Vit. 7 min. • Bugs fools a dumb hunting dog by disguising himself as a fox.

2329. The Foxy Duckling (*Merrie Melodies*) 23 Aug. 1947; *p.c.:* WB; *dir:* Arthur Davis; *anim:* J.C. Melendez, Manny Gould, Don Williams; *lay/char des:* Thomas McKimson; *back:* Phil de Guard; *ed:* Treg Brown; *mus:* Carl Stalling; *prod mgr:* John W. Burton; *prod:* Edward Selzer; *col:* Tech. *sd:* Vit. 7 min. • An insomniac fox tries to ensnare a duck for a down-filled pillow.

2330. Foxy Flatfoots (*Fox & Crow*) 11 Apr. 1946; *p.c.:* Colum; *dir:* Bob Wickersham; *story:* Webb Smith; *anim:* Paul Sommer, Volus Jones; *sets:* Clark Watson; *ed:* Richard S. Jensen; *voices:* Frank Graham; *mus:* Eddie Kilfeather; *ph:* Frank Fisher; *prod mgr:* Hugh McCollum; *col:* Tech. *sd:* WE. 6 min. • The Fox and Crow go hunting in a haunted house.

2331. The Foxy Fox (*Paul Terry-Toons*) Moser & Terry for Educational/Fox; *dir:* Paul Terry, Frank Moser; *mus:* Philip A. Scheib; b&w. *sd:* WE. 6 min. • A cunning fox outwits his pursuers, finally crossing the winning post miles ahead.

2332. The Foxy Hunter (*Betty Boop*) 26 Nov. 1937; *p.c.:* The Fleischer Studio for Para; *prod:* Max Fleischer; *dir:* Dave Fleischer; *anim:* Thomas Johnson, Hal Walker; *voices:* Mae Questel, Frances Reynolds; *mus:* Sammy Timberg; b&w. *sd:* WE. 6 min. • Junior and Pudgy go hunting and get taught a lesson by an outraged mother duck.

2333. The Foxy Pups (*Color Rhapsody*) 21 May 1937; *p.c.:* Cartoon Films Ltd/Charles Mintz prods for Colum; *prod/dir:* Ub Iwerks; *voices:* Mel Blanc, Robert Winkler; *mus:* Eddie Kilfeather, Joe de Nat; *col:* Tech. *sd:* RCA. 6½ min. • Father hound unsuccessfully tries to teach the kids how to catch a fox.

2334. The Foxy Terrier (*Rainbow Parade*) 31 May 1935; *p.c.:* Van Beuren for RKO; *dir:* Burt Gillett, Jim Culhane; *story:* Ray Kelly, Jim Culhane; *sets:* Art Bartsch, Eddi Bowlds; *mus:* Winston Sharples; *col:* Tech. *sd:* RCA. 7 min. • No story available.

2335. Fractured Friendship (*Chilly Willy*) Feb. 1965; *p.c.:* Walter Lantz prods for Univ; *dir:* Sid Marcus; *anim:* Ray Abrams, Art Davis; *sets:* Ray Huffine, Art Landy; *voice:* Daws Butler; *mus:* Walter Greene; *prod mgr:* William E. Garity; *col:* Tech. *sd:* RCA. 6 min. • Chilly tries to prevent his pal, Smedley, from leaving the north for sunnier climes.

2336. A Fractured Leghorn (*Merrie Melodies*) 16 Sept. 1950; *p.c.:* WB; *dir:* Robert McKimson; *story:* Warren Foster; *anim:* Rod Scribner, Phil de Lara, J.C. Melendez, Charles McKimson; *lay:* Cornett Wood; *back:* Phil de Guard; *ed:* Treg Brown; *voices:* Mel Blanc; *mus:* Carl Stalling; *prod mgr:* John W. Burton; *prod:* Edward Selzer; *col:* Tech. *sd:* Vit. 7 min. • Foghorn Leghorn and a cat are both in pursuit of the same worm.

2337. Fraidy Cat (*Tom & Jerry*) 17 Mar. 1942; *p.c.:* MGM; *dir:* William Hanna, Joseph Barbera; *anim:* Wilson D. Burness, Kenneth Muse, Jack Zander; *lay:* Harvey Eisenberg; *back:* Joe Smith; *ed:* Fred MacAlpin; *voices:* Lillian Randolph, Noreen Gammill; *mus:* Scott Bradley; *prod:* Fred Quimby; *col:* Tech. *sd:* WE. 9 min. • Jerry attempts to frighten Tom by posing as a ghost.

2338. The Framed Cat (*Tom & Jerry*) 21 Oct. 1950; *p.c.:* MGM; *dir:* William Hanna, Joseph Barbera; *anim:* Ed Barge, Kenneth Muse, Irven Spence, Ray Patterson; *lay:* Dick Bickenbach; *back:* Robert Gentle; *ed:* Jim Faris; *voices:* Lillian Randolph, Paul Frees; *mus:* Scott Bradley; *ph:* Jack Stevens; *prod:* Fred Quimby; *col:* Tech. *sd:* WE. 7 min. • Tom steals a chicken leg, putting the blame on Jerry. The mouse has his revenge by repeatedly stealing Spike's bone and framing Tom.

2339. Frank Duck Brings 'em Back Alive (*Donald & Goofy*) 1 Nov. 1946; *p.c.:* Walt Disney prods for RKO; *dir:* Jack Hannah; *asst dir:* Toby Tobelman; *story:* Dick Kinney; *anim:* Hugh Fraser, Jim Moore, Al Coe, Bob Carlson, Lee Morehouse, John Sibley, Judge Whitaker; *fx:* Andy Engman, John Reed; *lay:* Yale Gracey; *back:* Thelma Witmer; *voices:* Clarence Nash, Pinto Colvig; *mus:* Oliver Wallace; *col:* Tech. *sd:* RCA. 7 min. • Don sets out to capture "The Wild Man of the Jungle" (Goofy) but they are both chased off by a hungry lion.

2340. Franken-Stymied (*Woody Woodpecker*) 4 July 1961; *p.c.:* Walter Lantz prods for Univ; *dir:* Jack Hannah; *story:* Homer Brightman; *anim:* Don Lusk, Roy Jenkins, Ray Abrams, Al Coe; *sets:* Ray Huffine, Art Landy; *voices:* Daws Butler, Grace Stafford; *mus:* Clarence Wheeler; *prod mgr:* William E. Garity; *col:* Tech. *sd:* RCA. 6 min. • Woody finds himself at the mercy of a mad scientist and his chicken-plucking monster.

2341. Frankenstein's Cat (*Super Mouse*) 27 Nov. 1942; *p.c.:* TT for Fox; *dir:* Mannie Davis; *story:* John Foster; *mus:* Philip A. Scheib; *col:* Tech. *sd:* RCA. 7 min. • A robot cat captures a small bird and takes it to Dr. Frankenstein's castle. The townsfolk storm the gates but it takes Super Mouse to realize the true danger of the situation.

2342. Freaky Friday 17 Dec. 1976; *p.c.:* Walt Disney prods for BV; *titles:* John Jensen, Art Stevens; *mus:* Johnny Mandel; *song:* Al Kasha, Joel Hirschhorn; *col:* Tech. *sd:* RCA. (*titles*) 3 min. • The titles to this live-action film about a teenager who trades places with her mother show the (animated) girl and her mother skateboarding around her diary where entries are the film's credits.

2343. Freddy the Freshman (*Merrie Melodies*) 12 Mar. 1932; *p.c.:* Hugh Harman–Rudolf Ising prods for WB; *prod:* Leon Schlesinger; *anim:* Isadore Freleng, Paul Smith, Robert Clampett; *voices:* Mary Moder, Carmen Maxwell; *mus:* Frank Marsales; *song:* Cliff Friend, Dave Oppenheim; b&w. *sd:* Vit. 7 min. • Collegiate dormitory pranks followed by a travesty of a football game.

2344. Free 1972; *p.c.:* The Haboush Co; *prod:* Robert Mitchell; *dir/anim:* Robert Mitchell, John Kimball; *artists:* Harry Morrow, Dave Brain, Madeline Finger; *voice/song:* Jesse Fuller; *i&p:* Yvonne Palmer; *ph:* Wally Bulloch;

col. *sd.* 3 min. • A bigoted cop jails a young black kid for ninety-nine years for walking on the grass.

2345. Free Enterprise *(Heckle & Jeckle)* 23 Nov. 1948; *p.c.:* TT for Fox; *dir:* Mannie Davis; *story:* John Foster; *anim:* Jim Tyer; *voices:* Thomas Morrison; *mus:* Philip A. Scheib; *ph:* Douglas Moye; *col:* Tech. *sd:* RCA. 6 min. • The magpies sell electric drills to the prison inmates and get imprisoned for their efforts.

2346. Freedom River 1971; *p.c.:* Stephen Bosustow Prods/Louis Roth Clothes; *dir:* Sam Weiss; *prod:* Nick Bosustow; *story:* Warren H. Schmidt, Phd; *scr:* Joseph Cavella; *des:* Bernie Gruver; *anim:* Vincent Bassols; *continuity:* Sam Cornell; *back:* Tom Roth; *ed:* Tee Bosustow; *voice:* Orson Welles; *mus:* Ken Heller; *ph:* Tony Rivetti, Luis Melendez Jr.; *col. sd.* 6³/₄ min. • A parable of modern times involving a land where freedom flows. If the waters cease to flow, the land will die. There comes a time when people seen as "different" get banned from entering, turning the waters cloudy and destroying the land. Once the inhabitants realize that they are killing the land, things are returned to normal.

2347. Freeloading Feline *(Cartune)* 7 Sept. 1960; *p.c.:* Walter Lantz prods for Univ; *dir:* Jack Hannah; *story:* Jack Hannah, Milt Banta; *anim:* La Verne Harding, Al Coe; *sets:* Raymond Jacobs, Ray Huffine; *voices:* Paul Frees, Dal McKennon, Grace Stafford; *mus:* Eugene Poddany; *prod mgr:* William E. Garity; *col:* Tech. *sd:* RCA. 6 min. • Doc gets Champ a job as a bouncer at a swank dinner party in order to get a free feed.

2348. Freeway Fracas *(Woody Woodpecker)* 9 June 1964; *p.c.:* Walter Lantz prods for Univ; *dir:* Paul J. Smith; *story:* Homer Brightman; *anim:* Les Kline, Al Coe; *sets:* Art Landy, Ray Huffine; *voices:* Daws Butler, Grace Stafford; *mus:* Clarence Wheeler; *prod mgr:* William E. Garity; *col:* Tech. *sd:* RCA. 6 min. • Woody prevents a freeway from being constructed through the middle of his home.

2349. Freewayphobia 13 Feb. 1965. *p.c.:* Walt Disney prods for BV; *dir:* Les Clark; *asst dir:* Jim Swain; *story:* William R. Boché; *anim:* Cliff Nordberg, Bob Youngquist, Bob McCrea, Les Clark; *fx:* Jack Boyd; *lay:* A. Kendall O'Connor, Ray Aragon; *back:* Frank Armitage; *voices:* Paul Frees, Pinto Colvig; *mus:* George Bruns; *asso prod:* Ken Peterson; *col:* Tech. *sd:* RCA. 16 min. *l/a/anim.* • Instructions in common sense on the freeway plus the able assistance of Goofy.

2350. Freeze a Jolly Good Fellow *(Blue Racer)* 1 June 1973; *p.c.:* Mirisch/DFE for UA; *dir:* Sid Marcus; *story:* John W. Dunn; *anim:* Fred Madison, Bob Richardson, Bob Bransford, Ken Muse; *lay:* Owen Fitzgerald; *back:* Richard H. Thomas; *ed:* Joe Siracusa; *voices:* Larry D. Mann; *mus:* Doug Goodwin; *ph:* John Burton Jr.; *prod mgr:* Stan Paperny; *col:* Deluxe *sd:* RCA. 6 min. • The Racer and a W.C. Fieldsian bear battle for posession of a winter cabin.

2351. Freight Fright *(Possible Possum)* Mar. 1965; *p.c.:* TT for Fox; *dir/anim:* Connie Rasinski; *col:* DeLuxe. *sd:* RCA. 5 min. • Poss and the gang are offered a reward of pickles if they will transport a shipment of goods from the station. • See: *Possible Possum*

2352. French Freud *(Inspector)* 22 Jan. 1969; *p.c.:* Mirisch/Geoffrey/DFE for UA; *dir:* Gerry Chiniquy. *story:* Jack Miller; *anim:* Manny Perez, Ed Love, Don Williams, Ed de Mattia; *lay:* Corny Cole; *back:* Tom O'Loughlin; *ed:* Lee Gunther; *voices:* Pat Harrington Jr., Marvin Miller, June Foray; *mus:* Walter Greene; *theme tune:* Henry Mancini; *ph:* John Burton Jr.; *prod sup:* Harry Love, Jim Foss; *col:* DeLuxe. *sd:* RCA. 6 min. • A movie star and her accomplice plan to relieve the Inspector of a rare diamond he is guarding.

2353. French Fried *(Paul Terry Toon)* 7 Sept. 1930. *p.c.:* A-C for Educational/Fox; *dir:* Paul Terry, Frank Moser; *anim:* Arthur Babbitt; *mus:* Philip A. Scheib; *b&w. sd:* WE. 6 min. • Farmer Al Falfa has a hectic time in Paris.

2354. French Rarebit *(Merrie Melodies)* 30 June 1951; *p.c.:* WB; *dir:* Robert McKimson; *story:* Tedd Pierce; *anim:* Rod Scribner, Phil de Lara, Charles McKimson, Emery Hawkins; *lay:* Cornett Wood; *back:* Richard H. Thomas; *ed:* Treg Brown; *voices:* Mel Blanc, Tedd Pierce; *mus:* Eugene Poddany, Milt Franklyn; *prod mgr:* John W. Burton; *prod:* Edward Selzer; *col:* Tech. *sd:* Vit. 7 min. • Two French chefs battle over Bugs as the main course in their respective restaurants.

2355. Fresh Air *(Mastodon Cartoons)* 1923; *p.c.* Earlhurd prods for Motion Picture Arts Inc./Eduational; *dir/anim:* Earl Hurd; *b&w. sil.* 5 min. *l/a/anim.* • Bobby Bumps and his dog, Fido, go fishing and have a great deal of effort trying to catch the reluctant fish.

2356. Fresh Airedale *(Merrie Melodies)* 25 Aug. 1945; *p.c.:* WB; *dir:* Charles M. Jones. *story:* Michael Maltese; *anim:* Ben Washam; *lay:* Robert Gribbroek; *back:* Earl Klein; *ed:* Treg Brown; *voices:* Frank Graham, Mel Blanc; *mus:* Carl W. Stalling; *prod mgr:* John W. Burton; *prod:* Edward Selzer; *col:* Tech. *sd:* Vit. 7 min. • A lazy, greedy dog takes credit from the cat for rousting a burglar. He then reads of a "#1 Dog," sees him as opposition and tries to dispose of him. • The #1 dog referred to was to have been FDR's companion, "Fala," but unfortunately the president passed away just prior to release (12 April 1945) and a hasty replacement was made.

2357. Fresh Fish *(Mastodon Cartoons)* 26 Aug. 1922; *p.c.:* Earl Hurd prods for Motion Picture Arts Inc/Educational; *dir/anim:* Earl Hurd; *prod:* C.C. Burr; *b&w. sil.* 5 min. *l/a/anim.* • Bobby Bumps and his pals attempt to make a movie and the actors nearly drown when they can't distinguish between real scenery and make-believe.

2358. Fresh Fish *(Merrie Melodies)* 4 Nov. 1939; *p.c.:* Leon Schlesinger prods for WB; *dir:* Fred Avery; *story:* Jack Miller, Robert Clampett; *anim:* Sid Sutherland; *sets:* John Didrik Johnsen; *ed:* Tregoweth E. Brown; *voices:* Robert C. Bruce, Mel Blanc, Danny Webb, Sara Berner; *mus:* Carl W. Stalling; *prod sup.* Henry Binder, Raymond G. Katz; *col:* Tech. *sd:* Vit. 7 min. • A marine biologist explores the ocean bed in search of the rare Whim-Wham whistling fish.

2359. Fresh Ham *(Aesop's Film Fable)* 12 July 1933; *p.c.:* Van Beuren for RKO; *mus:* Gene Rodemich; *b&w. sd:* RCA. 7 min. • Cubby Bear runs a vaudeville agency and is persistently bothered by a Shakespearean duck actor.

2360. Fresh Hare *(Merrie Melodies)* 22 Aug. 1942; *p.c.:* Leon Schlesinger prods for WB; *dir:* I. Freleng; *story:* Michael Maltese; *anim:* Manuel Perez; *lay:* Owen Fitzgerald; *back:* Lenard Kester; *ed:* Treg Brown; *voices:* Mel Blanc, Arthur Q. Bryan, the Sportsmen (Maxwell Smith, William Days, Thurl Ravenscroft, Paul Taylor); *mus:* Carl W. Stalling; *ph:* John W. Burton; *prod sup:* Henry Binder, Raymond G. Katz; *col:* Tech. *sd:* Vit. 7 min. • Mountie Elmer Fudd sets out to capture Bugs against a snow-filled setting.

2361. Fresh Laid Plans *(Fun and Facts About America)* 27 Jan. 1951; *p.c.:* Harding College for MGM; *prod/dir:* John Sutherland; *col:* Tech. *snd.* 9 min. • No story available.

2362. The Fresh Vegetable Mystery *(Color Classic)* 29 Sept. 1939; *p.c.:* The Fleischer Studio for Para; *prod:* Max Fleischer; *dir:* Dave Fleischer; *story:* William Turner, Jack Ward; *anim:* David Tendlar, William Sturm, Robert Bemiller, Robert Bentley, Eli Brucker, Nelson Demorest, Thomas Golden, Irv Spector, Edythe Vernick, John Walworth; *voices:* Pinto Colvig, Jack Mercer, Ted Pierce; *mus:* Sammy Timberg; *col:* Tech. *sd:* WE. 7 min. • The baby carrots are kidnapped and Officer Spud is soon on the trail with his entire potato police force.

2363. Fresh Yeggs *(Screen Song)* 17 Nov. 1950; *p.c.:* Famous for Para; *dir:* Seymour Kneitel; *story:* Larz Bourne; *anim:* Myron Waldman, Nick Tafuri; *sets:* Robert Owen; *voices:* Jackson Beck; *mus:* Winston Sharples; *song:* George M. Cohan; *ph:* Leonard McCormick; *prod mgr:* Sam Buchwald; *col:* Tech. *sd:* RCA. 7 min. • Wolfie tries to break out of prison.

2364. Freudy Cat *(Looney Tunes)* 14 Mar. 1964; *p.c.:* WB; *dir:* Robert McKimson; *story:* Tedd Pierce; *anim:* Ted Bonnicksen, George Grandpré, Warren Batchelder; *sets:* Robert Gribbroek; *ed:* Treg Brown; *voices:* Mel Blanc; *mus:* Bill Lava; *prod mgr:* William Orcutt; *prod:* David H. DePatie; *col:* Tech. *sd:* Vit. 6 min. • Sylvester goes to a psychiatrist to find out why he keeps seeing "giant mice." Seq: *Cats Aweigh; Slap-Happy Mouse; Who's Kitten Who?*

2365. Friday the 13th *(Little Roquefort)* July 1953; *p.c.:* TT for Fox; *dir:* Mannie Davis; *story/voice:* Tom Morrison; *anim:* Jim Tyer; *mus:* Philip A. Scheib; *ph:* Douglas Moye; *col:* Tech. *sd:* RCA. 6 min. • Percy the puss proves to Roquefort that Friday the 13th presages a great deal of bad luck for him. The mouse soon turns the tables on him.

2366. Fried Chicken *(Paul Terry-Toons)* 19 Oct. 1930; *p.c.:* A-C for Educational/Fox; *dir:* Paul Terry, Frank Moser; *mus:* Philip A. Scheib; *b&w. sd:* WE. 7 min. • A Southern setting.

2367. A Friend in Tweed (*Swifty & Shorty*) May 1964; *p.c.:* Para Cartoons; *dir:* Seymour Kneitel; *story/voices:* Eddie Lawrence; *anim:* Irving Dressler; *sets:* Robert Little; *mus:* Winston Sharples. *ph:* Leonard Mc-Cormick; *prod mgr:* Abe Goodman; *col:* Tech. *sd:* RCA. 6 min. • Swifty's career as a suit salesman lies in jeopardy if he isn't more courteous. When Shorty enters, he is envisioned as a "troublemaker."

2368. Friend or Phoney (*Popeye*) 20 June 1952; *p.c.:* Famous for Para; *dir:* I. Sparber; *story:* Irving Spector; *anim:* Al Eugster, George Germanetti; *sets:* Robert Owen; *voices:* Jack Mercer, Jackson Beck; *mus:* Winston Sharples; *prod mgr:* Seymour Shultz; *col:* Tech. *sd:* RCA. 6 min. Seq: *Tar with a Star, I'll Be Skiing Ya* • Bluto gets Popeye to throw away his spinach, claiming it helped put him where he is today ... in hospital!

2369. The Friendly Ghost (*Noveltoon*) 16 Nov. 1945; *p.c.:* Famous for Para; *dir:* I. Sparber; *story:* Seymour Reit; *story adapt.* Bill Turner, Otto Messmer; *anim:* Nick Tafuri, John Walworth, Tom Golden; *character des:* John Walworth; *sets:* Shane Miller, Lloyd Hallock Jr.; *voices:* Frank Gallop, Cecil Roy; *mus:* Winston Sharples; *prod mgr:* Sam Buchwald; *col:* Tech. *sd:* RCA. 9 min. • Everyone is afraid of Casper the ghost except two children who befriend him. Their mother accepts him after he scares the landlord away. The initial Casper cartoon.

2370. Fright from Wrong (*Casper*) 2 Nov. 1956; *p.c.:* Famous for Para; *dir:* Seymour Kneitel; *story:* Larz Bourne; *anim:* Tom Golden, Nick Tafuri; *sets:* Robert Owen; *voices:* Norma MacMillan, Jackson Beck, Jack Mercer, Sid Raymond; *mus:* Winston Sharples; *ph:* Leonard McCormick; *prod mgr:* Seymour Shultz; *col:* Tech. *sd:* RCA. 6 min. • The other ghosts feed Casper pills that make him as evil as they are.

2371. Fright Night Part 2 19 May 1989; *p.c.:* Vista for Colum Tri-Star; *visual fx:* Gene Warren Jr.; *Fantasy II Film Effects: prod sup:* Leslie Huntley; *model shop sup:* Michael Joyce; *model makers:* Gary Rhodeback, Mark Joyce, Dennis Schultz; *Stop-motion anim:* Justin Kohn; *col:* DeLuxe. *sd:* Ultra Stereo. Panavision. 104 min. *l/a.* • Live-action vampire horror film with animated special effects.

2372. Fright to the Finish (*Popeye*) 27 Aug. 1954; *p.c.:* Famous for Para; *dir:* Seymour Kneitel; *story:* Jack Mercer; *anim:* Al Eugster, Wm. B. Pattengill; *sets:* Robert Connavale; *voices:* Jack Mercer, Mae Questel, Jackson Beck; *mus:* Winston Sharples; *ph:* Leonard McCormick; *prod mgr:* Seymour Shultz; *col:* Tech. *sd:* RCA. 6 min. • Bluto takes full advantage of Olive's fear of ghosts to make Popeye fall into disfavor.

2373. Frightday the 13th (*Casper*) 13 Feb. 1953; *p.c.:* Famous for Para; *dir:* I. Sparber; *story:* Carl Meyer, Jack Mercer. *anim:* Myron Waldman, Larry Silverman; *sets:* Anton Loeb; *voices:* Alan Shay, Jack Mercer; *mus:* Winston Sharples; *title song:* Mack David, Jerry Livingston; *ph:* Leonard McCormick; *prod mgr:* Seymour Shultz; *col:* Tech. *sd:* RCA. 7 min. • Casper tries to convince a black kitten that he's "good luck" instead of bad.

2374. Frighty Cat (*Herman & Katnip*) 14 Mar. 1958; *p.c.:* Para Cartoons; *dir:* I. Sparber; *story:* Larz Bourne; *anim:* Tom Johnson, Frank Endres, Wm. B. Pattengill; *sets:* Robert Owen; *voices:* Sid Raymond, Jack Mercer; *mus:* Winston Sharples. *ph:* Leonard McCormick; *prod mgr:* Abe Goodman; *col:* Tech. *sd:* RCA. 6 min. • Katnip reads a scary book and Herman takes advantage of the situation.

2375. Frigid Hare (*Merrie Melodies*) 7 Oct. 1949; *p.c.:* WB; *dir:* Charles M. Jones; *story:* Michael Maltese; *anim:* Phil Monroe, Ben Washam, Lloyd Vaughan, Ken Harris; *lay:* Robert Gribbroek; *back:* Peter Alvarado; *ed:* Treg Brown; *voices:* Mel Blanc; *mus:* Carl Stalling; *prod mgr:* John W. Burton; *prod:* Edward Selzer. *col:* Tech. *sd:* Vit. 7 min. • Bugs finds himself at the North Pole protecting a penguin from a hungry eskimo.

2376. Fritz the Cat Apr. 1972; *p.c.:* Fritz prods/Aurica Finance Cinema Industries for Black Ink Films; *prod:* Steve Krantz; *story/dir:* Ralph Bakshi; based on the comics by Robert Crumb; *anim:* John Gentilella, Martin Taras, Lawrence Riley, Clifford Augustine, Norman McCabe, John Sparey, Manuel Perez, Cosmo Anzilotti, Virgil Ross, Milton Gray, Richard Lundy, John Walker, Edwin Aardal, James Davis, Theodore Bonnicksen, Roderick Scribner, James Tyer, Robert Maxfield, Nicholas Tafuri; *lay:* Cosmo Anzilotti, John Sparey, James Davis; *back:* John Vita, Ira Turek; *ed:* Renn Reynolds; *voices:* Fritz: Skip Hinnant; *Pig Policemen:* Phil Seuling, Ralph Bakshi; *also:* Rosetta le Noire, John McCurry, Judy Engles; "It's Wonderful" sung by Billie Holiday; *mus:* Ed Bogas, Ray Shanklyn, B.B. King; *mus dir:*

Ed Bogas; *ph:* Gene Borghi, Ted Bemiller; *titles:* Perri & Smith; *prod mgr:* Bob Revell; *col:* DeLuxe. *sd:* Glenn Glenn. 78 min. • Fritz lives a life of sordid squalor, sex, violence and drug abuse. He finally abstains from all but sex! Noted as the first cartoon to recieve an "X" rating.

2377. The Frog (*Mighty Heroes*) Oct. 1969; *p.c.:* TT for Fox; *ex prod:* Bill Weiss; *dir/anim:* Ralph Bakshi; *voices:* Lionel Wilson, Herschel Bernardi; *mus:* Jim Timmens; *col:* DeLuxe. *sd:* RCA. 5 min. • When "The Swamp Lifter" drains money and jewels from the Peacehaven banks, The Mighty Heroes are called in.

2378. The Frog and the Ox (*Aesop's Film Fable*) 16 Oct. 1921; *p.c.:* Fables Pictures Inc for Pathé; *dir:* Paul Terry; *b&w. sil.* 5 min. • The Frog Emperor, goaded by his own conceit, tries to swell to the size of an ox. Moral: "Conceit begets disaster."

2379. The Frog and the Princess (*Terry-Toon*) 7 Apr. 1944; *p.c.:* TT for Fox; *dir:* Eddie Donnelly; *story:* John Foster; *voice:* Thomas Morrison; *mus:* Philip A. Scheib; *col:* Tech. *sd:* RCA. 7 min. • A frog will retrieve Princess Twinkletoes' ball from the pond if she will love him for the rest of her life. She declines but later finds out he's turned into a handsome prince.

2380. Frog Jog (*Tijuana Toads*) 23 Apr. 1972; *p.c.:* Mirisch/DFE for UA; *dir:* Gerry Chiniquy; *story:* John W. Dunn; *anim:* John Gibbs, Bob Matz, Don Williams; *lay:* Art Leonardi; *back:* Richard H. Thomas; *ed:* Lee Gunther; *voices:* Don Diamond, Tom Holland, Julie Bennett; *mus:* Doug Goodwin; *ph:* John Burton Jr.; *prod sup:* Jim Foss, Harry Love; *col:* DeLuxe. *sd:* RCA. 5 min. • Pancho suggests El Toro should excercise to retain his prowess with the ladies.

2381. The Frog Pond (*Color Rhapsody*) 12 Aug. 1938; *p.c.:* Cartoon Films Ltd/Charles Mintz prods for Colum; *prod/dir:* Ub Iwerks; *voices:* Billy Bletcher, Elmore Vincent, Mel Blanc; *mus:* Eddie Kilfeather, Joe de Nat; *prod mgr:* George Winkler; *col:* Tech. *sd:* RCA. 7 min. • The peaceful life in Frogville is disrupted when a bully frog arrives and forces the inhabitants to build him a home there.

2382. The Froggy, Froggy Duo (*Tijuana Toads*) 15 Mar. 1970; *p.c.:* Mirisch/DFE for UA; *dir:* Hawley Pratt; *story:* John W. Dunn; *anim:* Warren Batchelder, Don Williams, Bob Taylor, Manny Perez, Manny Gould; *lay:* Dick Ung; *back:* Richard H. Thomas; *ed:* Lee Gunther; *voices:* Don Diamond, Tom Holland, Marvin Miller; *mus:* Doug Goodwin; *ph:* John Burton Jr.; *prod sup.* Jim Foss, Harry Love; *col:* DeLuxe. *sd:* RCA. 5 min. • The Toads arrive at a hotel kitchen at the moment the French ambassador desires "frogs legs."

2383. Frogs Legs (*Comic King*) Apr. 1962; *p.c.:* Para Cartoons; *dir:* Seymour Kneitel; *story:* William C. Ershine, Marjorie H. Buell; *anim:* Nick Tafuri, Jack Ehret, Wm. B. Pattengill; *sets:* Robert Little; *voices:* Cecil Roy, Jack Mercer; *mus:* Winston Sharples; *ph:* Leonard McCormick; *prod mgr:* Abe Goodman; *col:* Tech. *sd:* RCA. 6 min. • Lulu and Tubby collect frogs from the pond to sell to an elite restaurant for their legs.

2384. The Frogs That Wanted a King (*Aesop's Film Fable*) 27 Nov. 1921; *p.c.:* Fables Pictures Inc for Pathé; *dir:* Paul Terry; *b&w. sil.* 5 min. • The frogs appoint a stork "King of the Frogs." He then proceeds to eat his subjects. Moral: "Let well enough alone."

2385. Frolicking Fish (*Silly Symphony*) 23 May 1930; *p.c.:* Walter E. Disney for Colum; *dir:* Burton F. Gillett; *anim:* Johnny Cannon, Les Clark, Norman Ferguson, Merle Gilson, David D. Hand, Wilfred Jackson, Jack King, Tom Palmer, Ben Sharpsteen; *asst anim:* Jack Cutting, Gilles de Tremaudan, Richard Lundy, Thomas McKimson, Cecil Surry; *mus:* Bert Lewis; *ph:* William Cottrell; *col:* tinted. *sd:* PCP. 7 min. • Undersea fantasy culminating in a villainous octopus capturing a bubble-dancing fish.

2386. From A to Z-z-z (*Looney Tunes*) 16 Oct. 1954; *p.c.:* WB. *dir:* Charles M. Jones; *story:* Michael Maltese; *anim:* Ken Harris, Ben Washam, Lloyd Vaughan; *lay:* Maurice Noble; *back:* Philip de Guard; *ed:* Treg Brown; *voices:* Dick Beals, Marian Richman, Norman Nesbitt, Mel Blanc; *mus:* Carl Stalling; *prod mgr:* John W. Burton; *prod:* Edward Selzer; *col:* Tech. *sd:* Vit. 7 min. *Academy Award nomination.* • Ralph Phillips, a daydreaming schoolboy, imagines himself in many adventurous situations instead of studying.

2387. From Bed to Worse (*Ant & Aardvark*) 16 May 1971; *p.c.:* Mirisch/DFE for UA; *dir:* Art Davis; *story:* John W. Dunn; *anim:* Robert Taylor, Ken Muse, Manny Gould, Don Williams, Warren Batchelder,

Manny Perez; *lay:* Dick Ung; *back:* Richard Thomas; *ed:* Lee Gunther; *voices:* John Byner, Athena Lorde; *mus:* Doug Goodwin; *Featuring:* Pete Candoli, Shelly Manne, Jimmy Rowles, Tommy Tedesco, Ray Brown, Billy Byers; *ph:* John Burton Jr.; *prod sup:* Jim Foss, Harry Love; *col:* DeLuxe. *sd:* RCA. 6 min. • Both the Ant and Aardvark end up in the same hospital ward. Aardvark tries to eat the Ant but is intercepted by a dog.

2388. From Dime to Dime (*Modern Madcap*) 25 Mar. 1960; *p.c.:* Para Cartoons; *dir:* Seymour Kneitel; *anim:* Nick Tafuri; *sets:* Robert Owen; *voices:* Sid Raymond, Jack Mercer, Jackson Beck; *mus:* Winston Sharples; *ph:* Leonard McCormick; *prod mgr:* Abe Goodman; *col:* Tech. *sd:* RCA. 6 min. • Jonah finds a dime and is persuaded to gamble with it. He eventually wins and loses a huge fortune.

2389. From Hand to Mouse (*Looney Tunes*) 5 Aug. 1944; *p.c.:* Leon Schlesinger prods for WB; *dir:* Charles M. Jones; *story:* Michael Maltese; *anim:* Robert Cannon; *lay:* Art Heinemann; *voice:* Mel Blanc; *mus:* Carl W. Stalling; *prod sup:* Henry Binder, Raymond G. Katz; *col:* Tech. *sd:* Vit. 7 min. • A mouse persuades a lion to release him. As soon as he does, the rodent yells "Sucker!"

2390. From Hare to Heir (*Merrie Melodies*) 3 Sept. 1960; *p.c.:* WB. *dir/story:* Friz Freleng; *anim:* Art Davis, Gerry Chiniquy, Virgil Ross; *lay:* Hawley Pratt; *back:* Tom O'Loughlin; *ed:* Treg Brown; *voices:* Mel Blanc; *mus:* Milt Franklyn; *prod mgr:* William Orcutt; *prod:* David H. DePatie; *col:* Tech. *sd:* Vit. 7 min. • Bugs is the purveyor of the news that Sam stands to inherit a fortune. The only condition is that if he loses his temper ... he loses some cash!

2391. From Mad to Worse (*Herman & Katnip*) 1 Aug. 1957; *p.c.:* Para Cartoons; *dir:* Seymour Kneitel; *story:* Larz Bourne; *anim:* Tom Johnson, Frank Endres, Wm. B. Pattengill; *sets:* Robert Owen; *voices:* Arnold Stang, Sid Raymond, Cecil Roy, Jack Mercer; *mus:* Winston Sharples; *ph:* Leonard McCormick; *prod mgr:* Abe Goodman; *col:* Tech. *sd:* RCA. 6 min. • The mice invade a toy store and play on the toy railway until night watchman, Katnip, discovers them.

2392. From Nags to Riches (*The Dogfather*) 5 May 1975; *p.c.:* Mirisch/DFE for UA; *dir:* Gerry Chiniquy; *story:* John Dunn; *anim:* Bob Richardson, Don Williams, Nelson Shin, Norm McCabe, Warren Batchelder; *ed:* Rick Steward; *lay:* Dick Ung; *back:* Richard H. Thomas; *voices:* Bob Holt, Daws Butler; *mus:* Dean Elliott; *col:* DeLuxe. *sd:* RCA. 5 min. • The Dogfather acquires a race horse ... but has to catch it first.

2393. From Nags to Witches (*Honey Halfwitch*) Feb. 1966; *p.c.:* Para Cartoons; *dir:* Howard Post. *story:* Irving Dressler; *anim:* Nick Tafuri, Wm. B. Pattengill; *sets:* Robert Little; *voices:* Shari Lewis, Bob MacFadden; *mus:* Winston Sharples; *ph:* Leonard McCormick; *prod mgr:* Abe Goodman; *col:* Tech. *sd:* RCA. 6 min. • Honey and Stanley the Sorcerer assist an old horse by helping him win the Derby.

2394. From Orbit to Orbit (*Merry-Maker*) June 1967; *p.c.:* Para Cartoons; *ex prod/dir:* Shamus Culhane; *des:* Danté Barbetta, Gil Miret, Hal Silvermintz; *mus:* Winston Sharples; *prod sup:* Harold Robins, Burt Hanft; *col:* Tech. *sd:* RCA. 6 min. • No story available.

2395. From Rags to Riches and Back Again (*Aesop's Film Fable*) 23 Mar. 1924; *p.c.:* Fables Pictures Inc for Pathé; *dir:* Paul Terry; b&w. sil. 5 min. • A fat cat plays golf by being carried over the links in a vehicle maneuvered by two mice.

2396. The Froze Nose Knows (*Ant & Aardvark*) 18 Nov. 1970; *p.c.:* Mirisch/DFE for UA; *dir:* Gerry Chiniquy; *story:* Dale Hale; *anim:* Manny Perez, Robert Taylor, Bob Bentley, Ken Muse, Manny Gould; *lay:* Dick Ung; *back:* Richard H. Thomas; *ed:* Lee Gunther; *voices:* John Byner; *mus:* Doug Goodwin; *featuring:* Pete Candoli, Billy Byers, Jimmy Rowles, Tommy Tedesco, Ray Brown, Shelly Manne; *ph:* John Burton Jr.; *prod sup:* Jim Foss, Harry Love; *col:* DeLuxe. *sd:* RCA. 6 min. • The Aardvark tries to catch the Ant against a winter setting.

2397. Frozen Feet (*Terry-Toon*) 24 Feb. 1939; *p.c.:* TT for Fox; *dir:* Connie Rasinski; *story:* John Foster; *mus:* Philip A. Scheib; b&w. *sd:* RCA. 6 min. • An Arctic hunter is put on trial by the polar creatures.

2398. Frozen Frolics (*Aesop's Sound Fable*) 31 Aug. 1930; *p.c.:* Van Beuren for Pathé; *dir:* John Foster, Harry Bailey; *mus:* Gene Rodemich; b&w. *sd:* RCA (on film and disk). 6 min. • A cat and dog visit the North Pole. The pole itself is a barber's pole and a polar bear beats the duo up. The cat falls through the ice and is rescued by a brandy-toting St. Bernard.

2399. The Frozen North (*Terry-Toon*) 17 Oct. 1941; *p.c.:* TT for Fox; *dir:* Connie Rasinski; *story:* John Foster; *mus:* Philip A. Scheib; b&w. *sd:* RCA. 6 min. • No story available.

2400. Frozen Sparklers (*James Hound*) Nov. 1967; *p.c.:* TT for Fox; *dir sup:* Ralph Bakshi; *col:* DeLuxe. *sd:* RCA. 6 min. • Diamond Jill manages to con jewellers with her diamonds made of ice. • See: *James Hound*

2401. The Fruitful Farm (*Aesop's Film Fable*) 22 Aug. 1929; *p.c.:* Fables Studio Inc for Pathé; *dir:* John Foster; b&w. sil. 5 min. • When a new crop of animals arrive on Al's farm, he starts studying on birth control. The situation grows worse and so he blames the doctor and chases him off.

2402. Fuddy Duddy Buddy (*Mr. Magoo*) 18 Oct. 1951; *p.c.:* UPA for Colum; *ex prod:* Stephen Bosustow; *prod/dir:* John Hubley; *story:* Bill Scott, Phil Eastman; *anim:* Art Babbitt, Rudy Larriva, Cecil Surry, Pat Matthews; *sets:* Paul Julian; *voices:* Jim Backus, Barney Phillips, Jerry Hausner; *mus:* William Lava; *prod sup:* Sherman Glas, Herbert Klynn; *col:* Tech. *sd:* RCA. 7 min. • Magoo plays an unorthodox game of tennis with a walrus.

2403. Fudget's Budget 17 June 1954; *p.c.:* UPA for Colum; *ex prod:* Stephen Bosustow; *dir:* Robert Cannon; *story:* Tedd Pierce, T. Hee, Robt. Cannon; *anim:* Frank Smith, Alan Zaslove, Gerald Ralf; *lay:* T. Hee; *back:* Jules Engel; *voice:* Marvin Miller, Knox Manning; *mus:* George Bruns; *piano:* Marvin Ash; *prod mgr:* Herbert Klynn; *col:* Tech. *sd:* RCA. 6 min. • Fudget has to make ends meet to live within his family budget.

2404. The Fulla Bluff Man (*Stoneage*) 9 Aug. 1940; *p.c.:* The Fleischer Studio for Para; *prod:* Max Fleischer; *dir:* Dave Fleischer; *story:* Ted Pierce; *anim:* Grim Natwick, Roland Crandal; *ed:* Kitty Pfister; *mus:* Sammy Timberg; *ph:* Charles Schettler; *prod sup:* Sam Buchwald, Isidore Sparber; b&w. *sd:* WE. 7 min. • A prehistoric salesman fails at selling carpet sweepers. He incites a street brawl, then sells clubs to the brawlers.

2405. Fun and Fancy Free 27 Sept. 1947; *p.c.:* Walt Disney prods for RKO; *prod sup:* Ben Sharpsteen; *ed:* Jack Bachom; "Bongo" from a story by Sinclair Lewis narrated by Dinah Shore; *dir:* Jack Kinney; *asst dir:* Ted Sebern, Jane Sinclair; *story adapt:* Lance Nolley, Tom Oreb, John Lagan, Dick Kinney; *anim dir:* Ward Kimball, Les Clark, Fred Moore; *anim:* Hal Ambro, Art Babbitt, Ted Berman, Al Bertino, Al Coe, Marc Davis, Phil Duncan, Hugh Fraser, George Goepper, Harry Holt, Milt Kahl, Hal King, Tom Massey, Ken O'Brien, Henry Tanous, Harvey Toombs, Judge Whitaker; *fx:* Jack Boyd, Blaine Gibson, Sandy Strother; *lay:* Don da Gradi, Glenn Scott, John Niendorff; *back:* Ray Huffine, Ed Starr, Art Riley; *ed:* Ted Sebern; *mus:* Buddy Baker, Eliot Daniel, Oliver Wallace; *songs:* Eliot Daniel, Buddy Kaye, Bobby Worth; "Mickey and the Beanstalk" *dir:* William O. Roberts, Hamilton S. Luske; *story:* Homer Brightman, Harry Reeves, Ted Sears, Eldon Dedini, Jack Hannah, Frank Tashlin; *anim dir:* Les Clark, Ward Kimball, John Lounsbery, Fred Moore, Wolfgang Reitherman; *anim:* Jack Campbell, Phil Duncan, Hugh Fraser, Ferdinand Huszti Horvath, Hal King, John McManus, John Sibley, Harvey Toombs, Judge Whitaker; *fx:* Josh Meador, George Rowley; *lay:* Ken Anderson, John Hench, Hugh Hennesy, A. Kendall O'Connor, Al Zinnen; *back:* Claude Coats, Ralph Hulett, Brice Mack, Art Riley; *voices: The Singing Harp:* Anita Gordon; *Jiminy Cricket:* Cliff Edwards; *Willie the Giant;* Billy Gilbert; *Donald Duck:* Clarence Nash; *Mickey Mouse:* James MacDonald; *Goofy:* Pinto Colvig; *Title song:* The Starlighters; "Lazy Countryside": The Dinning Sisters (Lou, Jean, Ginger); "My What a Happy Day", "Say it with a Slap": The King's Men; *mus dir:* Charles Wolcott; *score:* Paul Smith, Oliver Wallace, Eliot Daniel; *songs:* Ray Noble, William Walsh, Buddy Kaye, Bobby Worth, Bennie Benjamin, George Weiss, Arthur Quenzer; *sd:* C.O. Slyfield, Harold J. Steck, Robert Cook; *l/a dir:* William Morgan; *l/a ph:* Charles P. Boyle ASC; *process fx:* Ub Iwerks; *Tech dir:* Natalie Kalmus, Morgan Padelford; *l/a cast:* Edgar Bergen, Luana Patten; *col:* Tech. *sd:* RCA. 73 min. *l/a/anim.* • Jiminy Cricket plays a record relating the story of a trick bear who escapes the confines of the circus and battles with the elements in the open country. Jiminy then gatecrashes a party where Edgar Bergen tells Luana Patten the story of "Jack and the Beanstalk" with interruptions from Charlie McCarthy and Mortimer Snerd. • See: *Bongo*

2406. Fun at the Fair (*Kartune*) 9 May 1952; *p.c.:* Famous for Para; *dir:* I. Sparber; *story:* Larz Bourne; *anim:* Al Eugster, Wm. B. Pattengill;

sets: Robert Owen; *voices:* Jack Mercer, Sid Raymond; *mus:* Winston Sharples; *ph:* Leonard McCormick; *prod mgr:* Seymour Shultz; *col:* Tech. *sd:* RCA. 8 min. • Mortimer Mouse and Nellie Hippo round off a day at the fair with their trapeze act and everybody sings "Wait Till the Sun Shines Nellie."

2407. Fun from the Press 20 Apr. 1923; *p.c.:* Funk & Wagnalls Co for Hodkinson; *prod:* George A. Dame; *anim:* Max Fleischer; b&w. *sil. l/alanim.* • Series of three cartoon films as inserts in shorts adapted from *The Literary Digest.*

2408. Fun House (*Oswald*) 4 May 1936; *p.c.:* Univ; *dir:* Walter Lantz; *story:* Walter Lantz, Victor McLeod; *anim:* Ray Abrams, Leo Salkin, Jack Dunham; *mus:* James Dietrich; b&w. *sd:* RCA. 6 min. • Oswald and Sissie Rabbit enjoy themselves on roller-skates at the fun fair. Elmer the hound finds his four paws difficult to manage on rollers.

2409. Fun on Furlough (*Herman & Katnip*) 3 Apr. 1959; *p.c.:* Para Cartoons; *dir:* Seymour Kneitel; *story:* Larz Bourne; *anim:* Frank Endres, Wm. B. Pattengill; *sets:* Robert Owen; *voices:* Arnold Stang, Jack Mercer, Gwen Davies; *mus:* Winston Sharples; *ph:* Leonard McCormick; *prod mgr:* Abe Goodman; *col:* Tech. *sd:* RCA. 6 min. • Sgt. Herman Mouse arrives home on leave and treats the cat as if he were still a PFC in the Army.

2410. Fun on the Ice (*Aesop's Sound Fable*) 19 July 1931; *p.c.:* Van Beuren for RKO/Pathé; *dir:* John Foster, Mannie Davis; *mus:* Gene Rodemich; b&w. *sd:* RCA. 8 min. • The animals enjoy skating and playing hockey.

2411. The Fun Shop *p.c.:* Educational; *anim:* Max Fleischer; b&w. *sil.* 10 min. *l/alanim.* • A series containing jokes, witty sayings and epigrams ending with a humorous cartoon. • **A Modern Mother Goose** 26 Apr. 1924 • **Mary and Her Lamb** May 1924. Presents a "Johnnie" who chases a stage beauty and finds she has a spouse and several children.

2412. Funderful Suburbia (*Modern Madcap*) Mar. 1962; *p.c.:* Para Cartoons; *dir:* Seymour Kneitel; *story:* Burton Goodman, Jack Mercer; *anim:* Nick Tafuri, Wm. B. Pattengill; *sets:* Anton Loeb; *mus:* Winston Sharples; *prod mgr:* Abe Goodman. *col:* Tech. *sd:* RCA. 6 min. • A city dweller moves to suburbia, experiencing the trials and tribulations that go with it.

2413. Funny Bunny Business (*Terry-Toon*) 6 Feb. 1942; *p.c.:* TT for Fox; *dir:* Eddie Donnelly; *story:* John Foster; *mus:* Philip A. Scheib; *col:* Tech. *sd:* RCA. 7 min. • A hunter and his dog are given a rough time by the rabbits they are hunting.

2414. Funny Face (*Flip the Frog*) 24 Dec. 1932; *p.c.:* Celebrity for MGM; *prod/dir:* Ub Iwerks; *anim:* Jimmie Culhane; *mus:* Carl W. Stalling; b&w. *sd:* PCP. 8 min. • Flip has plastic surgery on his face to impress his girl. He sees a bully assaulting her, intervenes and gets his new face shattered in the process.

2415. Funny Face Comedies *p.c.:* Red Seal; *prod:* Edwin Miles Fadman. • *1924:* **All Balled up** 24 July. **Holy Smoke** 10 July. **Soldiers of Fortune** 7 Aug. **Their Jonah Day** 24 Aug. **Up and Down** 12 June. **Up to Mischief** 15 May. **Vermin the Great** 1 May. • b&w. *sil.* 4 min. • Puppet animation films.

2416. Funny Is Funny (*Brutus & Brownie*) circa 1960s; *prod/dir:* Ed Graham Jr.; *story/voices:* Ed Graham Jr., Carl Reiner; *anim dir:* Clyde Geronimi; *anim:* Amby Paliwoda, Manny Gould, Ed Friedman, Ed Solomon; *character des:* George Cannata Jr.; *sets:* Rosemary O'Connor; *mus:* George Shearing; *sd:* George Mahana; *also:* Armand Shaw, Lou Owen, Ruth Kennedy; col. *snd.* 5 min. • Brutus demonstrates to Brownie just what makes him laugh.

2417. Funny Little Bunnies (*Silly Symphony*) 24 Feb. 1934; *p.c.:* Walt Disney prods for UA; *dir:* Wilfred Jackson; *story:* Larry Morey; *anim:* Arthur Babbitt, Joe d'Igalo, Ugo d'Orsi, Jack Hannah, Dick Huemer, Hamilton Luske, Richard Lundy, Wolfgang Reitherman, Archie Robin, Louis Schmitt, Leonard Sebring, Ben Sharpsteen, Ed Smith; *fx:* Cy Young; *voices:* The Rhythmettes, Florence Gill; *mus:* Frank E. Churchill, Leigh Harline; *song:* Larry Morey, Frank E. Churchill; *col:* Tech. *sd:* RCA. 9 min. • At the rainbow's end, the bunnies are making Easter Eggs for world distribution. Veteran animator Wolfgang Reitherman's first piece of animation was of the bunnies pushing wheel-barrows.

2418. The Funshine State (*Screen Song*) 7 Jan. 1949; *p.c.:* Famous for Para; *dir:* Seymour Kneitel; *story:* Larz Bourne; *anim:* Dave Tendlar, Morey Reden; *sets:* Shane Miller; *voices:* Charles Irving, Jackson Beck, Jack Mercer; *mus:* Winston Sharples; *ph:* Leonard McCormick; *prod mgr:* Sam Buchwald; *col:* Pola. *sd:* RCA. 7 min. • A musical trip around Florida ending with a sing-along to the song "Tallahassee."

2419. The Further Adventures of Uncle Sam 1971; *p.c.:* The Haboush Co for Goldstone Films; *prod/dir/story/anim:* Robert Mitchell, Dale Case; *ed:* Sam Horta; *ph:* Wally Bulloch; *col. sd.* 13 min. • Uncle Sam and his friend, the bald eagle, foil the moneybag-headed villains who have kidnapped Miss Liberty.

2420. Fuss and Feathers (*Terry-Toon*) 1953; *p.c.:* TT for Fox; *story:* Tom Morrison; *mus:* Philip A. Scheib; *ph:* Douglas Moye; *col:* Tech. *sd:* RCA. 6 min. • A robin wings his way north to find a house for his family. A cat moves in, captures the birds and a battle ensues.

2421. The Fuz (*Fractured Fable*) Dec. 1967; *p.c.:* Para Cartoons; *ex prod/dir:* Ralph Bakshi; *story:* Eli Bauer; *anim:* Doug Crane, Al Eugster, Nick Tafuri; *lay:* Cosmo Anzilotti; *back:* John Zago, James Simon; *voices:* Bob MacFadden; *mus:* Winston Sharples; *col:* Tech. *sd:* RCA. 7 min. • "Super Basher," a super hero with his trusty assistant "Bop," set out to avenge the city of the hairy "Fuzz" who pesters the townswomen.

2422. Gabby Goes Fishing (*Gabby*) 18 July 1941; *p.c.:* The Fleischer Studio for Para; *prod:* Max Fleischer; *dir:* Dave Fleischer; *story:* Carl Meyer; *anim:* Orestes Calpini, Otto Feuer, Al Eugster; *ed:* Kitty Pfister; *voices:* Pinto Colvig; *mus:* Sammy Timberg; *prod sup.* Sam Buchwald, Isidore Sparber; *col:* Tech. *sd:* WE. 8 min. • Gabby teaches a small boy to fish and is given a tough time by an obstreperous fish.

2423. Gabby's Diner (*Woody Woodpecker*) 28 Mar. 1961; *p.c.:* Walter Lantz prods for Univ; *dir:* Jack Hannah; *story:* Homer Brightman; *anim:* La Verne Harding, Al Coe, Roy Jenkins; *Sets:* Ray Huffine, Art Landy; *voices:* Daws Butler, Grace Stafford; *mus:* Eugene Poddany; *prod mgr:* William E. Garity; *col:* Tech. *sd:* RCA. 6 min. • Starving Gabby Gator tricks Woody into believing his oven is a private suite in a hotel.

2424. Gabby's Swing Cleaning (*Gabby*) 21 Mar. 1941; *p.c.:* The Fleischer Studio for Para; *prod:* Max Fleischer; *dir:* Dave Fleischer; *story:* Bob Wickersham; *anim:* Willard Bowsky, Arnold Gillespie; *ed:* Kitty Pfister; *voices:* Pinto Colvig, Jack Mercer; *mus:* Sammy Timberg; *prod sup:* Sam Buchwald, Isidore Sparber; *col:* Tech. *sd:* RCA. 7 min. • Gabby cleans up the palace.

2425. Gabriel Church Kitten (*Noveltoon*) 15 Dec. 1944; *p.c.:* Famous for Para;. *dir:* Seymour Kneitel; *story:* Margot Austin; *anim:* Graham Place, Lou Zukor, George Cannata, Joe Oriolo; *Sets:* Robert Little; *voices:* Jack Mercer; *mus:* Winston Sharples; *prod sup:* Sam Buchwald; *col:* Tech. *sd:* RCA. 9 min. • Gabriel and Peter Church Mouse are nightly left food by a kindly Parson who, unfortunately, sleepwalks and eats it.

2426. Gadmouse, the Apprentice Good Fairy (*Terry-Toon*) Jan. 1965; *p.c.:* TT for Fox; *ex prod:* Bill Weiss; *dir/anim:* Ralph Bakshi; *story sup:* Tom Morrison; *story:* Eli Bauer; *Sets:* Bill Focht; *voices:* Bob MacFadden; *mus:* Jim Timmens; *ph:* Ted Moskowitz; *sd:* Elliot Grey; *col:* DeLuxe. *sd:* RCA. 7 min. • Gadmouse searches for someone to give a "Happy Ending" to and finds it in pathetic Sad Cat who is oppressed by his mean brothers.

2427. Gag and Baggage (*Kartune*) 8 Aug. 1952; *p.c.:* Famous for Para; *dir:* I. Sparber; *story:* Larz Bourne; *anim:* Dave Tendlar, Tom Golden; *Sets:* Robert Little; *voices:* Jackson Beck, Jack Mercer; *mus:* Winston Sharples; *ph:* Leonard McCormick; *prod mgr:* Seymour Shultz; *col:* Tech. *sd:* RCA. 7 min. • A railway journey that begins at the booking office and ends with a chorus of "I've Been Workin' on the Railroad."

2428. Gag Buster (*Terry-Toon*) Feb. 1957; *p.c.:* TT for Fox; *dir:* Connie Rasinski; *story:* Tom Morrison; *anim:* Jim Tyer; *voice:* Bern Bennett; *mus:* Philip A. Scheib; *col:* Tech. *sd:* RCA. 7 min. CS. • A fox tries to capture a Western bandit by means of the cartoon medium.

2429. Galaxia (*Modern Madcap*) Oct. 1960; *p.c.:* Para Cartoons; *dir:* Seymour Kneitel; *story:* Irving Spector; *anim:* Irving Spector, Wm. B. Pattengill, Morey Reden; *Sets:* Robert Owen; *voices:* Bob MacFadden, Corinne Orr; *mus:* Winston Sharples; *ph:* Leonard McCormack; *prod mgr:* Abe Goodman; *col:* Tech. *sd:* RCA. 6 min. • The Matchmaker fixes an outer space visitor up with an old maid he's been trying to pair off for years.

2430. Galaxy Quest 25 Dec. 1999; *p.c.:* Dream Works LLC; *anim lead:* Linda Bel; *anim:* Scott Benza, Andrew Doucette, Andrew Grant, Mark Powers, David Sidley, Victoria Livingstone, Ken King, Tom St. Amand, Kim Thompson; *lead viewpoint art:* Ron Woodall; *digital modeller:* Andrew Cawrse; *animatic art:* James Smentowski, Christopher Stillman; *Rock Monster Character des unit: ILM Digital Model Creature sup:* Geoff Campbell; *technical anim sup:* James Tooley; *anim lead:* Scott Wirtz; *cg seq lead:* Ed Kramer; *cg modeller:* Li-Hsien Wei; *anim sup:* Chris Armstrong; *col:* Tech. *sd:* Dolby digital/Digital dts sound. 102 min. Panavision *l/a.* • Sci-fi spoof: *Star Trek*–type television stars are mistaken for real heroes by aliens, who take the actors to their space ship to help defend them against an attack from their enemy. Animated alien creatures and a being comprised entirely from rocks are some of the high spots.

2431. Gallopin' Fanny (*Aesop's Fable*) 1 Dec. 1933; *p.c.:* Van Beuren for RKO; *anim:* Steve Muffatti, Ed Donnelly; *mus:* Gene Rodemich; b&w. *sd:* RCA. 6 min. • Cubby Bear wins a horse race in a thrilling fashion.

2432. Gallopin' Gals (*MGM Cartoon*) 26 Oct. 1940; *p.c.:* MGM; *dir:* William Hanna, Joseph Barbera; *voices:* Truman Bradley, Elvia Allman, Sara Berner; *mus:* Scott Bradley; *prod:* Fred Quimby; *col:* Tech. *sd:* WE. 7 min. • An outsider wins the race due to the other horses' vanity.

2433. The Gallopin' Gaucho (*Mickey Mouse*) 30 Dec. 1928; *p.c.:* Walter E. Disney for Colum; *dir:* Ub Iwerks; *anim:* Ub Iwerks, Johnny Cannon, Wilfred Jackson; *asst anim:* Les Clark; *mus:* Carl W. Stalling; b&w. *sd:* PCP. 6 min. • Mickey rescues Minnie from Peg-Leg Pete in a South American locale. • Originally made silent (rel: 2 Aug. 1928) then sound added after the success of *Steamboat Willie.*

2434. A Gander at Mother Goose (*Merrie Melodies*) 24 May 1940; *p.c.:* Leon Schlesinger prods for WB; *dir:* Fred Avery; *story:* Dave Monahan, Robert Clampett; *anim:* Charles McKimson; *Sets:* John Didrik Johnsen; *ed:* Treg Brown; *voices:* Robert C. Bruce, Mel Blanc, Sara Berner; *mus:* Carl W. Stalling; *col:* Tech. *sd:* Vit. 7 min. • Spot-gags destroying nursery rhymes.

2435. Gandy Goose in Doomsday (*Terry-Toon*) 16 Dec. 1938; *p.c.:* TT for Fox; *dir:* Connie Rasinski; *story:* John Foster; *voices:* Arthur Kay, Thomas Morrison; *mus:* Philip A. Scheib; *col:* Tech. *sd:* RCA. 7 min. • Gandy tries to tell the King that the end of the world is about to occur and gets slung into prison for his trouble.

2436. Gandy Goose in G-Man Jitters (*Terry-Toon*) 10 Mar. 1939; *p.c.:* TT for Fox; *dir:* Eddie Donnelly; *story:* John Foster; *voices:* Arthur Kay; *mus:* Philip A. Scheib; b&w. *sd:* RCA. 7 min. • Gandy imagines he's Sherlock Holmes.

2437. Gandy Goose in the Frame Up (*Terry-Toon*) 30 Dec. 1938; *p.c.:* TT for Fox; *dir:* Connie Rasinski; *story:* John Foster; *voice:* Arthur Kay; *mus:* Philip A. Scheib; b&w. *sd:* RCA. 6 min. • No story available.

2438. Gandy the Goose (*Terry-Toon*) 4 Mar. 1938; *p.c.:* TT for Educational/Fox; *dir:* John Foster; *voice:* Arthur Kay; *mus:* Philip A. Scheib; b&w. *sd:* RCA. 6 min. • Gandy runs away from home and almost becomes "Duck Soup" at the hands of a wolf.

2439. Gandy's Dream Girl (*Gandy Goose*) 8 Dec. 1944; *p.c.:* TT for Fox; *dir:* Mannie Davis; *story:* John Foster; *voices:* Thomas Morrison, Arthur Kay; *mus:* Philip A. Scheib; *col:* Tech. *sd:* RCA. 7 min. • Gandy dreams he's being caressed by a beautiful girl. This makes Sourpuss so jealous that he invades Gandy's dream.

2440. Garden Gaieties (*Krazy Kat*) 1 Aug. 1935; *p.c.:* Winkler for Colum; *prod:* Charles Mintz; *story:* Ben Harrison; *anim:* Manny Gould, Harry Love, Al Rose; *mus:* Joe de Nat; *prod mgr:* James Bronis; b&w. *sd:* RCA. 6 min. • No story available.

2441. Garden Gopher 30 Sept. 1950; *p.c.:* MGM; *dir:* Tex Avery; *story:* Rich Hogan; *anim:* Michael Lah, Grant Simmons, Walter Clinton; *character des/lay:* Louis Schmitt; *back:* John Didrik Johnsen; *mus:* Scott Bradley; *prod:* Fred Quimby; *col:* Tech. *sd:* WE. 6 min. • A bulldog tries to roust a wily gopher from his garden.

2442. Gaston Go Home (*Gaston Le Crayon*) May 1958; *p.c.:* TT for Fox; *ex prod:* Bill Weiss; *dir sup:* Gene Deitch. *dir:* Connie Rasinski; *story dir:* Tom Morrison; *story:* Larz Bourne, Bob Kuwahara; *anim:* Larry Silverman, Ed Donnelly, Peggy Breese, Mannie Davis, Bob Kuwahara; *sets:* Al Kouzel; *voices:* Allen Swift; *mus:* Phil Scheib; *prod mgr:* Sparky Schudde;

col: Tech. *sd:* RCA. 7 min. CS. • Gaston stows away on a ship bound for Paris but annoys the Captain and is sent packing.

2443. Gaston Is Here (*Gaston Le Crayon*) Apr. 1957; *p.c.:* TT for Fox; *ex prod:* Bill Weiss; *dir sup:* Gene Deitch; *dir:* Connie Rasinski; *story:* Tommy Morrison, Larz Bourne, Bob Kuwahara; *anim:* Larry Silverman, Mannie Davis, George Bakes, Jim Tyer, Al Chiarito, Ed Donnelly; *lay:* Al Kouzel, Art Bartsch; *back:* Bill Hilliker; *voices:* Allen Swift; *mus:* Phil Scheib; *prod mgr:* Frank Schudde; *col:* Tech. *sd:* RCA. 7 min. CS. • Gaston invades an Alfred Hitchcock movie set.

2444. Gaston's Baby (*Gaston Le Crayon*) Mar. 1958; *p.c.:* TT for Fox; *ex prod:* Bill Weiss; *dir sup:* Gene Deitch; *dir:* Connie Rasinski; *story dir:* Tommy Morrison; *story:* Larz Bourne, Bob Kuwahara; *anim:* Ed Donnelly, Larry Silverman, Dave Tendlar, George Bakes, Jim Tyer, Al Chiarito; *lay:* Al Kouzel; *back:* Bill Hilliker; *voices:* Allen Swift, Lionel Wilson; *mus:* Phil Scheib; *prod mgr:* Frank Schudde; *col:* Tech. *sd:* RCA. 7 min. • A couple hire Gaston to babysit while they go to a fancy dress party. The husband is dressed as a baby and here's where the confusion starts.

2445. Gaston's Easel Life (*Gaston Le Crayon*) Oct. 1958; *p.c.:* TT for Fox; *ex prod:* Bill Weiss; *dir sup:* Gene Deitch; *dir:* Dave Tendlar; *story dir:* Tom Morrison; *story:* Larz Bourne, Eli Bauer, Phil Eastman; *anim:* Ed Donnelly, Jim Tyer, Bob Kuwahara, Mannie Davis, Johnny Gent, Vinnie Bell; *lay:* Eli Bauer; *back:* Bill Hilliker; *voices:* Allen Swift; *mus:* Phil Scheib; *prod mgr:* Frank Schudde; *col:* Tech. *sd:* RCA. 7 min. CS. • A wealthy dowager hires Gaston to paint her husband's portrait. Hubby isn't too keen on the idea.

2446. Gaston's Mama Lisa (*Gaston Le Crayon*) June 1959; *p.c.:* TT for Fox; *ex prod:* Bill Weiss; *dir sup:* Gene Deitch; *dir:* Connie Rasinski; *story dir:* Tom Morrison; *story:* Larz Bourne, Eli Bauer, Bob Kuwahara; *anim:* Jim Tyer, Larry Silverman, Bob Kuwahara, Eddie Donnelly, Vinnie Bell, Mannie Davis, Johnny Gent; *back:* Bill Hilliker; *voices:* Allen Swift; *mus:* Phil Scheib; *prod mgr:* Frank Schudde; *col:* Tech. *sd:* RCA. 7 min. • Two art thieves hide a stolen painting amongst Gaston's artwork.

2447. Gaumont Kartoon Komics *p.c.:* Gaumont Co for Mutual Pictures; *anim:* Harry S. Palmer; b&w. sil. s/r. On same reel as See America First. • *1916:* Our National Vaudeville 4 Mar. The Trials of Thoughtless Thaddeus 12 Mar. (*title unknown*) 19 Mar. Signs of Spring 26 Mar. Nosey Ned 2 Apr. The Greatest Show on Earth 5 Apr. Watchful Waiting 12 Apr. (*title unknown*) 19 Apr. Nosey Ned 26 Apr. Estelle and the Movie Hero 3 May. The Escapades of Estelle 10 May. As an Umpire, Nosey Ned Is an Onion 17 May. Nosey Ned and His New Straw Lid 24 May. The Gnat Gets Estelle's Goat 31 May. The Escapades of Estelle 7 June. Johnny's Stepmother and the Cat 14 June. (*title unknown*) 21 June. Johnny's Romeo 28 June. Scrambled Events 5 July. Weary's Dog Dream 12 July. (*title unknown*) 19 July. Old Pfool Pfancy at the Beach 26 July. Music as a Hair Restorer 2 Aug. (*title unknown*) 9 Aug. Kuring Korpulent Karrie 16 Aug. Mr. Jocko from Jungletown 23 Aug. (*title unknown*) 30 Aug. The Tale of a Whale 6 Sept. Nosey Ned Commandeers an Army Mule 13 Sept. Pigs 20 Sept. Golf 27 Sept. Abraham and the Opossum 4 Oct. Babbling Bess 11 Oct. Inspiration 18 Oct. I'm Insured 25 Oct. (*title unknown*) 1 Nov. Babbling Bess 8 Nov. Haystack Horace 15 Nov. What's Home Without a Dog 22 Nov. Diary of a Murderer 29 Nov. Our Forefathers 6 Dec. Curfew Shall Not Ring 13 Dec. 'Twas Ever Thus 20 Dec. Mr. Bonehead Gets Wrecked 27 Dec. • *1917:* Miss Catnip Goes to the Movies 3 Jan. The Gourmand 10 Jan. Mr. Common Peepul Investigates 17 Jan. Absent Minded Willie 24 Jan. Never Again 31 Jan. The Old Roue Visualizes 7 Feb. Taming Tony 14 Feb. Polly's Day at Home 21 Feb. The Elusive Idea 28 Feb. Rastus Runs Amuck 7 Mar. They Say Pigs Is Pigs 14 July.

2448. Gaumont Reel Life *p.c.:* Gaumont Co; b&w. sil. • *1917:* A One Man Submarine 5 Apr. A Flying Torpedo 12 Apr. Cargo Boats of Tomorrow 24 Apr. The Liberty Loan 7 June

2449. The Gaumont Weekly *p.c.:* Gaumont Co; b&w. sil. • *1912:* Waiting for the Robert E. Lee 13 Nov. The War News in Constantinople 27 Nov. The Struggle Between Producer and Consumer 4 Dec. The Fate of the Foxes 18 Dec. What a Fall, Oh My Countrymen 15 Jan. • Technical cartoons.

2450. The Gay Anties (*Merrie Melodies*) 15 Feb. 1947; *p.c.:* WB; *dir:* I. Freleng; *story:* Tedd Pierce, Michael Maltese; *anim:* Virgil Ross, Gerry

Chiniquy, Manuel Perez, Ken Champin; *lay:* Hawley Pratt; *back:* Paul Julian; *ed:* Treg Brown; *mus:* Carl Stalling; *prod mgr:* John W. Burton; *prod:* Edward Selzer; *col:* Tech. *sd:* Vit. 7 min. • A couple having a picnic are plagued by a colony of ants.

2451. The Gay Gaucho (*Aesop's Sound Fable*) 3 Nov. 1933; *p.c.:* Van Beuren for RKO; *dir:* Hugh Harman, Rudolf Ising; *anim:* Rollin Hamilton, Thomas McKimson; *mus:* Gene Rodemich; b&w. *sd:* RCA. 7 min. • Gaucho Cubby rides the Mexican desert to rescue his girl from the clutches of Pedro the Bandit.

2452. The Gay Knighties (*Madcap Models*) 25 July 1941; *p.c.:* George Pal prods for Para; *dir/prod:* George Pal; *story:* Jack Miller; *anim:* George Pal, Ray Harryhausen; *col:* Tech. *sd:* WE. 9 min. • Jim Dandy dreams he's a knight fighting an ogre for the fair princess.

2453. Gay Purr-ee Nov. 1962; *p.c.:* UPA for WB; *ex prod:* Henry G. Saperstein; *dir:* Abe Levitow; *seq dir:* Steve Clark; *story:* Dorothy and Chuck Jones; *dialogue:* Ralph Wright; *anim:* Ben Washam, Phil Duncan, Hal Ambro, Ray Patterson, Grant Simmons, Irv Spence, Don Lusk, Hank Smith, Harvey Toombs, Volus Jones, Ken Harris, Art Davis, Fred Madison; *art dir:* Victor Haboush; *lay:* Robert Singer, Richard Ung, "Corny" Cole, Ray Aragon, Edward Levitt, Ernest Nordli; *back:* Philip de Guard, Richard H. Thomas, Eyvind Earl; *des:* Don Peters, Gloria Wood, Robert Inman, Phill Norman, Richmond Kelsey; *ed:* Ted Baker, Sam Horta, Earl Bennett; *voices:* Mewsette: Judy Garland; *Juan Tom:* Robert Goulet; *Robespierre:* Red Buttons; *Meowrice/Railway Cat:* Paul Frees; *Mme Rubens-Chatte:* Hermione Gingold; *Narrator/Mariner:* Morey Amsterdam *Bartender/Bulldog:* Mel Blanc; *Jeanette:* Joan Gardner; *Marie:* Julie Bennett; *mus:* Mort Lindsey; *songs:* Harold Arlen, E.Y. Harburg; *vocal arranger:* Joseph J. Lilley; *mus ed:* George Probert, Wayne Hughes; *ph:* Roy Hutchcroft, Dan Miller, Jack Stevens, Duane Keegan; *titles:* John Hitesman; *i&p:* Grace McCurdy; *prod sup:* Lee Orsell, Earl Jonas; *col:* Tech. *sd:* RCA. 86 min. • Mewsette, a pretty French farm cat goes to Paris in search of *la joie de vivre.* Once she arrives, she falls into the clutches of a suave sophisticate who wants to groom her. In the meantime, her boyfriend arrives searching for her and is shanghaied aboard a ship travelling to the frozen north. He returns to Paris in time to stop Mewsette from being married-off to the highest bidder and the lovers are reunited.

2454. Gee Whiz-z-z-z-z-z (*Looney Tunes*) 5 May 1956; *p.c.:* WB. *dir:* Charles M. Jones; *story:* Michael Maltese; *anim:* Ben Washam, Abe Levitow, Richard Thompson, Ken Harris; *lay:* Ernie Nordli;. *back:* Philip de Guard; *ed:* Treg Brown; *voice:* Paul Julian. *mus:* Milt Franklyn. *prod mgr:* John W. Burton; *prod:* Edward Selzer; *col:* Tech. *sd:* Vit. 7 min. • In a further attempt to snare the elusive Road-Runner, the luckless coyote uses a re-enforced steel plate, a Super Hero outfit and an Acme Jet Motor ... all to little avail.

2455. Gem Dandy (*Roland & Rattfink*) 25 Oct. 1970; *p.c.:* Mirisch/DFE for UA; *dir:* Gerry Chiniquy; *story:* Dale Hale; *anim:* Ken Muse, Warren Batchelder, Manny Perez, Robert Taylor; *lay:* Martin Strudler; *back:* Richard Thomas; *ed:* Lee Gunther; *voices:* Leonard Weinrib; *mus:* Doug Goodwin; *prod sup:* Jim Foss, Harry Love; *col:* DeLuxe. *sd:* RCA. 6 min. • Roland guards a precious diamond from the thieving fingers of Rattfink.

2456. Gems from Gemini (*Astronut*) Jan. 1966; *p.c.:* TT for Fox; *ex prod:* Bill Weiss; *dir/anim:* Dave Tendlar; *story sup:* Tom Morrison; *story:* Larz Bourne; *Sets:* John Zago; *ed:* Jack MacConnell; *voices:* Dayton Allen; *mus:* Jim Timmens; *ph:* Ted Moskowitz; *col:* DeLuxe. *sd:* RCA. 5 min. • No story available.

2457. The General's Little Helper's (*Possible Possum*) 2 June 1969; *p.c.:* TT for Fox; *col:* DeLuxe. *sd:* RCA. 5 min. • Poss and his pals help out in the general store while Mr. General rests his sore back. • See: *Possible Possum*

2458. Genie with the Light Pink Fur (*Pink Panther*) 14 Sept. 1966; *p.c.:* Mirisch/Geoffrey/DFE for UA. *dir:* Hawley Pratt; *story:* John W. Dunn; *anim:* Dale Case, La Verne Harding, George Grandpré, Don Williams, Virgil Ross; *lay:* Dick Ung; *back:* Tom O'Loughlin; *ed:* Lee Gunther; *voice:* Ralph James; *mus:* Walter Greene; *theme tune:* Henry Mancini; *prod mgr:* Bill Orcutt; *col:* DeLuxe. *sd:* RCA. 6 min. • The Panther replaces the genie in a magic lamp.

2459. The Genie with the Light Touch (*Woody Woodpecker*) 1972; *p.c.:* Walter Lantz prods for Univ; *dir:* Paul J. Smith; *story:* Cal Howard; *anim:* Volus Jones, Al Coe, Tom Byrne, Joe Voght; *sets:* Nino Carbe; *voices:* Dal McKennon, Grace Stafford; *mus:* Walter Greene; *prod mgr:* William E. Garity; *col:* Tech. *sd:* RCA. 5 min. • After Buzz Buzzard sells Woody a fake Magic Lamp, our hero and a mouse "Genie" set out to retrieve their money.

2460. A Gentleman's Gentleman (*Mickey Mouse*) 28 Mar. 1941; *p.c.:* Walt Disney prods for RKO; *dir:* Clyde Geronimi; *asst dir:* Donald A. Duckwall; *anim:* Basil Davidovich, Nick de Tolly, Eric Gurney, Emery Hawkins, Volus Jones, Kenneth Muse, George Nicholas, Chic F. Otterstrom, Norman Tate, Bernard Wolf; *fx:* Edwin Aardal, Russ Dyson, Andy Engman, Art Fitzpatrick, Joe Harbaugh, Jack Huber, Paul B. Kossoff, Ernie Lynch, Frank Onaitis, Ed Parks, Reuben Timmens, Noel Tucker, Vern Witt, Cornett Wood; *lay:* Bruce Bushman; *voice:* Walt Disney; *mus:* Paul J. Smith; *col:* Tech. *sd:* RCA. 7 min. • Pluto suffers many hazards while getting Mickey's morning paper.

2461. George of the Jungle 16 July 1997; *p.c.:* Walt Disney Pictures for Buena Vista; *visual fx:* Dream Quest Images: *visual fx prod:* David McCullough; *ex prod:* Keith Shartle; *visual fx co-ord:* Deborah A. Nikkel; *3d anim sup:* Paul Jordan; *3d character anim:* Steward Burris, Spencer Levy, Bruce Wright; *3d anim:* R. Christopher Biggs; *3d fx art:* Muqueem Khan, Michael A. Ramirez; *2d compositing sup:* David Laur; *digital compositors:* John Huikku, Frank Maurer, Tony Noel, Tim Sassoon; *cartoonists:* Sergio Aragones, Jack White; *anim:* Kurtz & Friends; *opening title des:* Bob Kurtz; *addit title des:* Brian King; *voices:* an ape named "Ape": John Cleese; *narrator:* Keith Scott; *col. sd:* Dolby Digital/SDDS/Digital Sound/dts. 91 min. *l/a.* • Live-action rendition of Jay Ward's popular television cartoon series satirizing *Tarzan:* Lost in the jungle, beautiful heiress Ursula is rescued from a lion attack by George, an ape-man, who lives in the forest with a talking gorilla and an elephant who behaves like a dog.

2462. Georgie and the Dragon (*Jolly Frolics*) 27 Sept. 1951; *p.c.:* UPA for Colum; *ex prod:* Stephen Bosustow; *dir:* Robert Cannon; *story:* John Hubley, Bill Scott, Phil Eastman; *anim:* Rudy Larriva, Bill Melendez, Grim Natwick, Frank Smith; *lay:* Bill Hurtz; *back:* Paul Julian, Jules Engel; *voices:* Walter Tetley, Marvin Miller, Marian Richman; *mus:* Ernest Gold; *prod mgr:* A.D. Woolery; *col:* Tech. *sd:* RCA. 7 min. • A young Scot lad adopts a small dragon that grows to outlandish proportions.

2463. Gerald McBoing Boing (*Jolly Frolics*) 25 Jan. 1951; *p.c.:* UPA for Colum; *ex prod:* Stephen Bosustow; *dir sup:* John Hubley; *dir:* Robert Cannon; *story:* Dr. Seuss (Theodor Seuss Geisel); *story adapt:* Bill Scott, Phil Eastman; *anim:* Bill Melendez, Rudy Larriva, Pat Matthews, Willis Pyle, Frank Smith, Grim Natwick; *lay:* Bill Hurtz; *back:* Herb Klynn, Jules Engel; *voice:* Marvin Miller; *mus:* Gail Kubik; *prod mgr:* Adrian Woolery; *col:* Tech. *sd:* RCA. 9 min; *Academy Award.* • Young Gerald is a social outcast, making noises instead of talking. He finally wins through when he's asked to supply the sound effects for a radio station.

2464. Gerald McBoing! Boing! on Planet Moo 9 Feb. 1956; *p.c.:* UPA for Colum; *ex prod:* Stephen Bosustow; *dir:* Robert Cannon; *story:* T. Hee, Bobe Cannon; *anim:* Frank Smith, Alan Zaslove; *lay:* Lew Keller; *back:* Jules Engel; *voices:* Marvin Miller, Marian Richman; *mus:* Ernest Gold; *prod mgr:* Herbert Klynn; *col:* Tech. *sd:* RCA. 7 min. CS; *Academy Award nomination.* • Gerald is taken to another planet in mistake for a typical earth specimen so their king can learn our language to converse with earth folk.

2465. Gerald McBoing Boing's Symphony 15 July 1953; *p.c.:* UPA for Colum; *ex prod:* Stephen Bosustow; *dir:* Robert Cannon; *story/des:* T. Hee; *anim:* Bill Melendez, Frank Smith; *sets:* Jules Engel, Michi Kataoka; *voices:* Marvin Miller; *mus:* Ernest Gold; *prod mgr:* Herbert Klynn; *col:* Tech. *sd:* RCA. 7 min. • Gerald stands in for a defaulting symphony orchestra but the music sheets get mixed with the sound effects script for a radio melodrama.

2466. Geri's Game 25 Nov. 1997; *p.c.:* Pixar Animation Studios; *dir/story:* Jan Pinkaya; *prod:* Karen Dufilho; *ex prod:* John Lasseter, Edwin Catmull; *technical dir:* David R. Haumann, Leo Hourvitz; *Human Characters/Studio Tools: cloth dynamics:* Michael Kass; *surface modeling:* Tony de Rosa; *prod mgr:* Holly Lloyd; *Technical dir: main & macks:* Quintin King; *facial articulation:* Paul Alchele; *lighting:* Jean-Claude Kalache, Jason Bickerstaff, Ana Lacaze, Ken Lao; *modeling:* Jason Bickerstaff; *shader:* Daniel McCoy; *render wrangler:* Steve Kani; *addit modeling:* Michael Lorenzen, Mark Sanford; *anim:* Bankole Lasekan, Jan Pinkava, Sandy Christensen, Karen Prell, Ross Stevenson, Stephen Barnes, Michelle Meeker, Michael Berenstein, Ben Catmull, Pete Docter, Jeff Pratt, Michael Parke, Valerie Mih, Steve Segal, Doug Sheppeck, Scott Clark, Angus MacLane, Karyn Metian, Adam Wood; *prod artist:* David S. Kelly; *digital painter:* David Valdez; *sculptor:* Jerome Ranft; *anim co-ord:* Tony Sutton; *post prod sup:* Julie McDonald; *film output:* Louis Rivers, Hunter Kelly, Matthew Martin; *sd des:* Tom Myers: Skywalker Sound; *voice of Geri:* Bob Patterson; *mus:* Gus Viseur et son Orchestra; *dial ed:* Dennis Leonard, Joe Wenkoff; *story reel ed:* Tom Freeman; *foley ed:* Sandina Bailo-Lapo, Steven Liu; *mus ed:* Alex Stahl; *film ed:* Jim Kallett, Christina Hills; *anim software:* Darwyn Peachey, Arun Rao, James W. Williams, Dirk van Gelder, Kitt Hirasaki; *renderman software:* Larry Gritz, Tien Truong, Mark Vande Wettering, the Pencchman team; *asst:* Sharon Calahan, Tom Hahn, Galyn Susman, Damir Frkovic, Brad West, Robin Cooper, Ewan Johnson, Ninon Pallavicini, Rick Sayre, Luke Putnam, Rachel Hannah, Jeff Pidgeon, Bert Jordan, Mitch Prater, Michael Fong, James Burgess, Tony Apodaca; *col. sd:* Dolby stereo. 4¹/₂ min. *Academy Award.* • An old man plays a game of chess against himself.

2467. Geronimo & Son (*Noveltoon*) Dec. 1965; *p.c.:* Para Cartoons; *dir:* Shamus Culhane; *story:* Howard Beckerman; *anim:* Chuck Harriton, Nick Tafuri; *sets:* Howard Beckerman, Gil Miret; *mus:* Winston Sharples; *col:* Tech. *sd:* RCA. 6 min. • Geronimo is chosen to shoot in an archery contest. His knowledge is limited and so his son gets Wighead, the bald eagle, to assist with his shooting.

2468. Gertie on Tour 1921; *p.c.:* Vit; *dir/anim:* Winsor McCay; b&w. sil. l/a/anim. • A noted group of comic artists (including George McManus and Roy McCardell) wager Winsor McCay he can't make an animated cartoon. He wins the bet with more antics from Gertie the Dinosaur. McCay's seventh film. Drawn on celluloid.

2469. Gertie the Dinosaur 26 Dec. 1914; *p.c.:* Winsor McCay for the Box Office Attraction Co; *dir/anim:* Winsor McCay; *asst anim:* John A. Fitzsimmons; b&w. sil. 4 min. • aka: *Gertie the Trained Dinosaur.* • Made as part of McCay's stage act. He would stand on stage alongside the screen and appear to put Gertie through her paces. McCay's third film.

2470. Get Lost (*Woody Woodpecker*) 12 Mar. 1956; *p.c.:* Walter Lantz prods for Univ; *dir:* Paul J. Smith; *story:* Jack Cosgriff; *anim:* Herman R. Cohen, Gil Turner, Robert Bentley; *sets:* Art Landy; *voices:* Dal McKennon, June Foray, Grace Stafford; *mus:* Clarence Wheeler; *prod mgr:* William E. Garity; *col:* Tech. *sd:* RCA. 6 min. • Woody's nephews create their own version of Hansel and Gretel when they wander into the woods and meet a hungry cat.

2471. Get Lost! Little Doggy (*Woody Woodpecker*) 27 Oct. 1964; *p.c.:* Walter Lantz prods for Univ; *dir:* Sid Marcus; *story:* Cal Howard; *anim:* Ray Abrams, Art Davis; *sets:* Ray Huffine, Art Landy; *voices:* Grace Stafford, Walter Lantz, Dal McKennon; *mus:* Clarence Wheeler; *prod mgr:* William E. Garity; *col:* Tech. *sd:* RCA. 6 min. • Woody tries to smuggle a puppy into Meany's "No Dogs Allowed" boarding house.

2472. Get Rich Quick (*Goofy*) 31 Aug. 1951; *p.c.:* Walt Disney prods for RKO; *dir:* Jack Kinney; *story:* Milt Schaffer, Dick Kinney; *anim:* John Sibley, Hugh Fraser, Ed Aardal, George Nicholas; *fx:* Jack Boyd; *lay:* Al Zinnen; *back:* Ray Huffine; *voices:* Jack Rourke, Bob Jackman, Helen Parrish, James MacDonald; *mus:* Paul Smith; *col:* Tech. *sd:* RCA. 6 min. • A compulsive gambler demonstrates various methods of winning ... and losing money.

2473. Get Rich Quick Porky (*Looney Tunes*) 28 Aug. 1937; *p.c.:* Leon Schlesinger prods for WB; *dir/story:* Robert Clampett; *anim:* Charles Jones; *lay:* Griff Jay; *back:* Elmer Plummer; *ed:* Tregoweth E. Brown; *voices:* Mel Blanc, Earl Hodgins, Cal Howard; *mus:* Carl W. Stalling; *prod sup:* Henry Binder, Raymond G. Katz; b&w. *sd:* Vit. 7 min. • Porky and Gabby Goat are tricked into buying a worthless plot of land. When a dog tries to bury a bone in it, he uproots an oil gusher.

2474. Getting Ahead (*Swifty & Shorty*) Dec. 1965; *p.c.:* Para Cartoons; *dir:* Howard Post; *story:* Eli Bauer; *anim:* Wm. B. Pattengill; *sets:* Robert Little; *voices:* Eddie Lawrence, Bob MacFadden; *mus:* Winston Sharples; *ph:* Leonard McCormick; *prod mgr:* Abe Goodman; *col:* Tech. *sd:* RCA. 6

min. • The boys answer an advertisement for assistants in an experiment. The job turns out to be working for a mad scientist who wants to use their brains.

2475. Getting Together Feb. 1933; *p.c.:* A-C for American Telephone & Telegraph Co; *prod:* W.P. Bach; *dir:* F. Lyle Goldman; *anim:* Seymour Kneitel; *col:* Tech-2. *sd:* WE. 9 min. • Illustrating in a humorous fashion how the component parts of a telephone fit together.

2476. Ghosks Is the Bunk (*Popeye*) 14 June 1939; *p.c.:* The Fleischer Studio for Para; *prod:* Max Fleischer; *dir:* Dave Fleischer; *anim:* William Henning, Abner Matthews; *sets:* Anton Loeb; *ed:* Kitty Pfister; *voices:* Jack Mercer, Margie Hines, William Pennell; *mus:* Sammy Timberg; *ph:* Charles Schettler; *prod sup:* Sam Buchwald, Isidore Sparber; b&w. *sd:* WE. 7 min. • Bluto gets Popeye and Olive to a deserted hotel to throw a scare into them. Popeye discovers the trick and repays him with help from some invisible paint.

2477. Ghost 13 July 1990; *p.c.:* Dreamworks for Para.; *anim co-ord:* Judith Weaver; *anim:* Sean Turner, Gordon Baker, Peter Crosman, Loring Doyle, Anthony Stacchi; *fx ph:* Charlie Canfield, Eric Swenson; *Rotoscope art:* Kathleen Beeler, Barbara Brennan, Joanne Hafner, Sandy Houston, Terry Molatore, Jack Mongovan, Ellen Mueller, Rebecca Petrulli, Carolyn Rendu; *Dark Ghosts:* W. Larance, Mike Jittlov; *anim:* Jeff Howard, Candy Lewis, Martine Tomczyk; *col:* Tech. *sd:* Dolby Sound. 127 min. l/a. • Live-action fantasy involving a young banker who is killed by a mugger and reappears as a ghost to help warn his girlfriend. Animated ghosts and spirits.

2478. The Ghost Monster (*Mighty Heroes*) Apr. 1970 (© 1966); *p.c.:* TT for Fox; *ex prod:* Bill Weiss; *dir/anim:* Ralph Bakshi; *col:* DeLuxe. *sd:* RCA. 5 min. • Once every hundred years, The Ghost Monster terrorizes the citizens of Goodhaven.

2479. Ghost of Honor (*Casper*) 19 July 1957; *p.c.:* Para Cartoons; *dir:* I. Sparber; *story:* I. Klein; *anim:* Myron Waldman, Nick Tafuri; *sets:* Robert Owen; *voices:* Norma MacMillan, Gwen Davies, Jackson Beck, Jack Mercer, Sid Raymond; *mus:* Winston Sharples; *ph:* Leonard McCormick; *prod mgr:* Abe Goodman; *col:* Tech. *sd:* RCA. 6 min. • At the premiere of his latest film, Casper explains his rise to fame by first visiting Paramount Cartoon Studios. The luxurious studio depicted here is a far cry from their actual studio on New York's West 45th Street.

2480. The Ghost of Slumber Mountain 1919; *p.c.:* World Film Corp; *prod:* Herbert M. Dawley; *fx:* Willis H. O'Brien; b&w. sil. l/a/anim. • A mountain climber dreams he meets the ghost of a hermit who lets him view through a mystic telescope how life was in prehistoric times. Model animation of dinosaurs.

2481. Ghost of the Town (*Casper*) 11 Apr. 1952; *p.c.:* Famous for Para; *dir:* I. Sparber; *story:* I. Klein; *anim:* Steve Muffatti, Morey Reden; *sets:* Anton Loeb; *voices:* Alan Shay, Cecil Roy, Jackson Beck, Sid Raymond; *mus:* Winston Sharples; *title song:* Mack David, Jerry Livingston; *ph:* Leonard McCormick; *prod mgr:* Seymour Shultz; *col:* Tech. *sd:* RCA. 7 min. • Casper saves a baby from a burning building and is awarded the (skeleton) key to the city.

2482. The Ghost Town (*Gandy Goose*) 22 Sept. 1944; *p.c.:* TT for Fox; *dir:* Mannie Davis; *story:* John Foster; *voices:* Arthur Kay, Thomas Morrison; *mus:* Philip A. Scheib; *col:* Tech. *sd:* RCA. 7 min. • Playful ghosts have fun with two gold prospectors.

2483. Ghost Town Frolics (*New Universal cartoon*) 7 Sept. 1938; *p.c.:* Walter Lantz prods for Univ; *dir:* Lester Kline; *story:* Victor McLeod; *anim:* Dick Marion, Ralph Somerville; *sets:* Edgar Keichle; *mus:* Frank Marsales; *col:* Tech-2. *sd:* WE. 7 min. • Jock and Jill, "the simple simeons," wander into a haunted town and ghosts give them the works.

2484. Ghost Wanted (*Merrie Melodies*) 10 Aug. 1940; *p.c.:* Leon Schlesinger prods for WB; *dir:* Charles M. Jones; *story:* Dave Monahan, Ted Pierce; *anim:* Bob McKimson; *lay/char des:* Robert Givens; *back:* Paul Julian; *ed:* Treg Brown; *voice:* Fred Avery; *mus:* Carl W. Stalling; *prod sup:* Henry Binder, Raymond G. Katz; *col:* Tech. *sd:* Vit. 7 min. • A young ghost answers a newspaper ad to haunt a house but finds it occupied by another ghost who just wants someone to scare.

2485. Ghost Writers (*Casper*) 24 Apr. 1958; *p.c.:* Para Cartoons; *dir:* Seymour Kneitel; *story:* Jack Mercer; *anim:* Tom Johnson, Frank Endres;

sets: Robert Owen; *voices:* Cecil Roy, Jackson Beck, Jack Mercer; *mus:* Winston Sharples; *ph:* Leonard McCormick; *prod mgr:* Abe Goodman; *col:* Tech; *sd:* RCA. 6 min. Seq: *To Boo or Not to Boo; Casper's Spree Under the Sea; Once Upon a Rhyme.* • The Paramount Cartoon Studio storymen are creating a new story featuring Casper.

2486. Ghostbusters 7 June 1984; *p.c.:* Delphi for Colum/EMI/WB; *dir:* Ivan Reitman; *anim: (sup):* Garry Waller, Terry Windell; *art dir:* John de Cuir; *visual fx:* Richard Edlund, Entertainment Effects Group; *visual fx sup:* John Bruno; *Chief Matte art:* Matt Vuricich; *mus:* Elmer Bernstein; *ph:* Jim Aupperle, John Lambert; *dimensional anim:* Randall William Cook; *technical:* Annick Therrien, Peggy Regan, Sam Recinos, Pete Langdon, Les Bernstein, Wendie Fischer, Sean Newton, William Recinos, Bruce Woodside, Richard Coleman; *(addit): Available Light, Ltd.; Ghost Shop advisor:* John Berg; *armatures:* Doug Beswick; *col:* Metrocolor. *sd:* Dolby stereo. Panavision. 105 min. *l/a.* • Live-action comedy: A group of academic parapsychologist set up a ghost-expelling business. Among the things to deal with is "Slimer," a slime-producing poltergeist and a giant "Stay Puft Marshmallow Man" who flattens the city.

2487. Ghostbusters II 16 June 1989; *p.c.:* Tri-Star for Colum; *dir:* Ivan Reitman; *optical fx:* Beverly Bernacki, Spencer Gill, Sarah Pasanen, *(anim):* Jammie Friday; *addit anim:* Available Light, Ltd.; *col:* DeLuxe. *sd:* Dolby stereo. Panavision. 108 min. *l/a.* • "The Ghostbusters" get back in the saddle to investigate the possibility of a psychic disturbance at a friend's apartment. Animated ghosts, etc.

2488. G.I. Pink *(Pink Panther)* 1 May 1964; *p.c.:* Mirisch/Geoffrey/DFE; *dir:* Hawley Pratt; *story:* John Dunn; *anim:* Warren Batchelder, Don Williams, Tom Ray, Manny Gould; *lay:* Dick Ung; *back:* Tom O'Loughlin; *ed:* Allan R. Potter; *mus:* Walter Greene; *theme tune:* Henry Mancini; *ph:* John Burton Jr.; *prod sup:* Harry Love, David DeTiege; *col:* DeLuxe. *sd:* RCA. 6 min. • The Panther joins the Army, making life tough for the Sergeant.

2489. The Giant Killer *(Dinky Doodle)* 15 Oct. 1924; *p.c.:* Bray prods for FBO; *dir/story:* Walt Lantz; *anim:* Clyde Geronimi; b&w. sil. 5 min. *l/a.anim.* • Walter feeds his creations on beans. One escapes and grows into a beanstalk which they willingly climb to find a giant.

2490. Giantland *(Mickey Mouse)* 15 Nov. 1933; *p.c.:* Walt Disney prods for UA; *dir:* Burton F. Gillett; *anim:* Johnny Cannon, Les Clark, Ugo d'Orsi, Gilles de Tremaudan, Clyde Geronimi, Dick Huemer, Hamilton S. Luske, Fred Moore, William O. Roberts, Ben Sharpsteen, Dick Williams, Cy Young; *voices:* Walt Disney, Pinto Colvig, Harry Stanton; *mus:* Frank E. Churchill; b&w. *sd:* RCA. 7 min. • Mickey spins a yarn, casting himself in the role of "Jack and the Beanstalk" where he does battle with an ogre.

2491. Giants 1969; *p.c.:* Sim prods/Kratky Film; *prod:* William L. Snyder; *dir/story/sd:* Gene Deitch; *anim:* Milan Klikar; *voices:* Allen Swift; *col. sd.* 9 min. • Parable for the world situation. Two small men keep two giants as bodyguards.

2492. Giddy Gadgets *(Modern Madcap)* Mar. 1962; *p.c.:* Para Cartoons; *dir:* Seymour Kneitel; *story:* Carl Meyer, Jack Mercer; *anim:* Nick Tafuri, Jack Ehret, Larry Silverman; *Sets:* Robert Little; *voices:* Jack Mercer; *mus:* Winston Sharples; *prod mgr:* Abe Goodman; *col:* Tech. *sd:* RCA. 6 min. • Prof. Schmaltz helps his wife out with the housework with his labor-saving inventions.

2493. Giddy Up Woe *(Hoot Kloot)* 9 Jan. 1974; *p.c.:* Mirisch/DFE for UA; *dir:* Sid Marcus; *story:* John W. Dunn; *anim:* Bob Bemiller, Ken Muse, Norm McCabe, Don Williams, Bob Bransford; *lay:* Rick Gonzales. *back:* Richard Thomas; *ed:* Rick Steward; *voices:* Bob Holt; *mus:* Doug Goodwin; *titles:* Arthur Leonardi; *ph:* John Burton Jr.; *prod mgr:* Lee Gunther; *col:* DeLuxe. *sd:* RCA. 6 min. • Kloot trades Fester, his faithful old horse, for a younger, faster model.

2494. Giddy-Yapping *(Phantasy)* 7 Apr. 1944; *p.c.:* Colum; *prod:* Dave Fleischer; *dir:* Howard Swift; *story:* John McLeish; *anim:* Jim Armstrong, Grant Simmons; *voices:* John McLeish, Harry E. Lang; *mus:* Eddie Kilfeather; *ph:* Frank Fisher; *prod mgr:* Albert Spar; b&w. *sd:* RCA. 6 min. • A window-washer's horse has to wash windows before he can be fed.

2495. Giddyap *(Jolly Frolics)* 27 July 1950; *p.c.:* UPA for Colum; *ex prod:* Stephen Bosustow; *dir sup:* John Hubley; *dir:* Art Babbitt; *story:* Bob Russell, Phil Eastman, Bill Scott; *anim:* Bill Melendez, Pat Matthews,

Willis Pyle, Rudy Larriva, Paul Smith; *lay:* Bill Hurtz; *back:* Herb Klynn, Jules Engel; *voices:* Stan Freberg; *mus:* Dave Raksin; *prod mgr:* Adrian Woolery; *col:* Tech. *sd:* RCA. 7 min. • The Iceman's horse is threatened with being replaced by motorization ... until he tells of his show-biz career.

2496. Gift of Gag *(Popeye)* 27 May 1955; *p.c.:* Famous for Para; *dir:* Seymour Kneitel; *story:* I. Klein; *anim:* Tom Johnson, Frank Endres; *sets:* Robert Connavale; *voices:* Jack Mercer; *mus:* Winston Sharples; *ph:* Leonard McCormick; *col:* Tech. *sd:* RCA. 6 min. • Popeye's curiosity gets the better of him when he sees his nephews trying to conceal a large box.

2497. Gift Wrapped *(Looney Tunes)* 16 Feb. 1952; *p.c.:* WB; *dir:* I. Freleng; *story:* Warren Foster; *anim:* Arthur Davis, Manuel Perez, Ken Champin, Virgil Ross; *lay:* Hawley Pratt; *back:* Irv Wyner; *ed:* Treg Brown; *voices:* Mel Blanc, Bea Benaderet, Daws Butler; *mus:* Carl Stalling; *prod mgr:* John W. Burton; *prod:* Edward Selzer; *col:* Tech. *sd:* Vit. 7 min. • Christmas sees the arrival of a Tweety bird for Granny. Sylvester grabs the bird for himself and thereby hangs a tale.

2498. Gifts from the Air *(Color Rhapsody)* 1 Jan. 1937; *p.c.:* Charles Mintz prods for Colum; *story:* Ben Harrison; *anim:* Manny Gould; *voices:* The Radio Rogues (Jimmy Hollywood, Ed Bartell, Henry Taylor), The Rhythmettes; *mus:* Joe de Nat; *prod mgr:* James Bronis; *col:* Tech. *sd:* RCA. 8 min. • A poor boy's Christmas prayers are answered with a shower of toys. Radio characters come to life: Ben Bernie, Eddie Cantor, Bing Crosby, Joe Penner, "The Mad Russian," Kate Smith, Paul Whiteman and Ed Wynn.

2499. The Ginger Bread Boy *(Oswald)* 16 Apr. 1934; *p.c.:* Univ; *dir:* Walter Lantz, "Bill" Nolan; *story:* Victor McLeod; *anim:* Fred Avery, Ray Abrams, Cecil Surry, Jack Carr, Merle Gilson; *mus:* James Dietrich; b&w. *sd:* WE. 5 min. • Oswald and his friend listen to the story of the Gingerbread Boy who came to life over the radio. They are disturbed by a baby and the whole thing ends in a gingerbread batter fight.

2500. The Girl at the Ironing Board *(Merrie Melodies)* 23 Aug. 1934; *p.c.:* Leon Schlesinger prods for WB; *dir:* Isadore Freleng; *anim:* Frank Tipper, Sandy Walker, Robert Clampett; *mus:* Bernard Brown; *song:* Harry Warren, Al Dubin; b&w. *sd:* Vit. 7 min. • After the laundry is closed, the clothes act out a melodrama.

2501. The Girl Next Door 1953; *p.c.:* UPA for Fox. *seq dir:* Robert Cannon; *col:* Tech. *sd:* WE. rt (seq): 4 min/1 min. • Live-action feature about a strip cartoonist (Dan Dailey) who falls for a dancer (June Haver) much to the chagrin of his son. The son (Billy Gray) has an animated dream about going on a fishing trip with dad that's interrupted by the girlfriend, depicted as a witch. The second sequence involves a child's drawings of the animals entering Noah's Ark.

2502. Git Along Li'l Duckie *(Noveltoon)* 25 Mar. 1955; *p.c.:* Famous for Para; *dir:* Dave Tendlar; *story:* Larz Bourne; *anim:* Martin Taras, Thomas Moore; *Sets:* Robert Connavale; *voices:* Sid Raymond, Jackson Beck, Jack Mercer; *mus:* Winston Sharples; *ph:* Leonard McCormack; *col:* Tech. *sd:* RCA. 6 min. • Huey wants to play "cowboy" and the Fox pretends to be one in order to get his hands on the oversized duckling.

2503. Git That Guitar *(Possible Possum)* Sept. 1965; *p.c.:* TT for Fox; *dir/anim:* Artie Bartsch; *col:* DeLuxe. *sd:* RCA. 5 min. • An antiques dealer wants Poss's guitar. • See: *Possible Possum*

2504. Give and Tyke *(Spike & Tyke)* 29 Mar. 1957; *p.c.:* MGM. *prod/dir:* Joseph Barbera, William Hanna; *story:* Homer Brightman; *anim:* Bill Schipek, Lewis Marshall, Herman Cohen, Kenneth Muse, Carlo Vinci; *lay:* Dick Bickenbach; *back:* Don Driscoll; *ed:* Jim Faris; *voices:* Daws Butler; *mus:* Scott Bradley; *ph:* Jack Stevens; *prod mgr:* Hal Elias; *col:* Tech. *sd:* WE. 6 min. CS. • A mutt steals Tyke's collar to keep himself out of the Pound.

2505. Give Me Liberty *(James Hound)* Aug. 1967; *p.c.:* TT for Fox; *dir/anim:* Ralph Bakshi; *col:* DeLuxe. *sd:* RCA. 6 min. • A villain steals The Statue of Liberty in order to lure Secret Agent Hound to his hideout. • See: *James Hound*

2506. The Glass Slipper *(Terry-Toon)* 7 Oct. 1938; *p.c.:* TT for Fox; *dir:* Mannie Davis; *mus:* Philip A. Scheib; *col:* Tech. *sd:* RCA. 7 min. • A Brooklynite tells her girlfriend how her Fairy Godmother (Mae West) transformed her so that she could attend a Grand Ball and meet the Prince (Harpo Marx).

2507. Glee Worms (*Color Rhapsody*) 24 June 1936; *p.c.:* Charles Mintz prods for Colum; *story:* Ben Harrison; *anim:* Manny Gould, I. Klein; *voice:* Leone Le Doux; *mus:* Joe de Nat; *song:* Lilla Cayley Robinson, Paul Lincke; *prod mgr:* James Bronis; *col:* Tech. *sd:* RCA. 8 min. • The fireflies' fun is interrupted by the arrival of a spider who kidnaps a girl. The boy goes in search ... ending with a climactic sword fight.

2508. The Gloom Chasers (*Scrappy*) 18 Jan. 1935; *p.c.:* Charles Mintz prods for Colum; *story:* Art Davis; *anim:* Sid Marcus. *mus:* Joe de Nat; *prod mgr:* James Bronis. b&w. *sd:* RCA. 6 min. • Scrappy and Oopy's music encourages rain in a drought area.

2509. The Glow Worm (*Screen Songs*) 23 Aug. 1930; *p.c.:* The Fleischer Studio for Para; *prod:* Max Fleischer; *dir:* Dave Fleischer; *anim:* Dick Huemor, Rudy Zamora; *mus:* Art Turkisher; *song:* Lilla Cayley Robinson, Paul Lincke; b&w. *sd:* WE. 6 min. • A sick Glow Worm consults a doctor.

2510. Go Away Stowaway (*Merrie Melodies*) Sept. 1967; *p.c.:* WB-7A; *dir:* Alex Lovy; *story:* Cal Howard; *anim:* Volus Jones, La Verne Harding, Ted Bonnicksen, Ed Solomon; *lay:* David Hanan, Lin Larsen; *back:* Bob Abrams; *ed:* Hal Geer; *voices:* Mel Blanc; *mus:* William Lava; *col:* Tech. *sd:* Vit. 6 min. • Speedy joins Daffy on his holiday cruise.

2511. Go Fly a Kit (*Looney Tunes*) 16 Feb. 1957; *p.c.:* WB; *dir:* Chuck Jones; *story:* Michael Maltese; *anim:* Ken Harris, Abe Levitow, Richard Thompson; *lay:* Maurice Noble; *back:* Philip de Guard; *voices:* Daws Butler, Mel Blanc; *mus:* Milt Franklyn; *prod mgr:* John W. Burton; *prod:* Edward Selzer; *col:* Tech. *sd:* Vit. 7 min. • A kitten, reared by a mother eagle, is taught to fly by means of propelling his tail.

2512. Go for Croak (*Tijuana Toads*) 25 Dec. 1969; *p.c.:* Mirisch/DFE for UA; *dir:* Hawley Pratt; *story:* John W. Dunn; *anim:* Manny Perez, Manny Gould, Warren Batchelder, Don Williams; *lay:* Dick Ung; *back:* Dick Thomas; *ed:* Lee Gunther; *voices:* Don Diamond, Tom Holland, Larry D. Mann; *mus:* Doug Goodwin; *prod sup:* Jim Foss, Harry Love; *col:* DeLuxe. *sd:* RCA. 6 min. • The Toads convince Crazylegs Crane that one of them has swallowed explosives and force him to fly them to Havana.

2513. Go Go Amigo (*Merrie Melodies*) 20 Nov. 1965; *p.c.:* DFE for WB; *dir:* Robert McKimson; *story:* Dave DeTiege; *anim:* Warren Batchelder, Bob Matz, Manny Perez; *lay:* Dick Ung; *back:* George de Lado; *ed:* Lee Gunther; *voices:* Mel Blanc, (Pedro) Gonzalez-Gonzales; *mus:* Bill Lava; *col:* Tech. *sd:* Vit. 7 min. • Daffy resents the mice using his records for their party music and tries to stop them.

2514. Go West, Big Boy (*Paul Terry-Toon*) 22 Feb. 1931; *p.c.:* Terry, Moser & Coffman for Educational/Fox; *dir:* Frank Moser, Paul Terry; *anim:* Arthur Babbitt, Jack King, Frank Little, Sarka, Hugh Shields; *mus:* Philip A. Scheib; b&w. *sd:* WE. 6 min. • A mouse finds himself in a desert pursued by vultures, one of which makes off with a shepherdess' sheep. He enlists a mule as a bombing plane and shoots it down.

2515. The Goal Rush (*Flip the Frog*) 3 Oct. 1932; *p.c.:* Celebrity for MGM; *prod/dir:* Ub Iwerks; b&w. *sd:* PCP. 6 min. • Burp U vs. Flip's Nertz U in a raucous football game.

2516. The Goal Rush (*Noveltoon*) 27 Sept. 1946; *p.c.:* Famous for Para; *dir:* I. Sparber; *story adapt:* I. Klein, Jack Ward; *anim:* Dave Tendlar, George Germanetti; *voice:* Ward Wilson; *mus:* Winston Sharples; *ph:* Leonard McCormick; *prod mgr:* Sam Buchwald; *col:* Tech. *sd:* RCA. 6 min. • Canine College vs. Alley Cat College have a football game in the Milk Bowl.

2517. The Goat's Whiskers (*Unnatural History*) 10 Feb. 1926; *p.c.:* Bray prods for FBO; *dir:* Walter Lantz, Earl Hurd; *anim:* Clyde Geronimi; *l/a ph:* Joe Rock; b&w. sil. 5 min. *l/a/anim.* • No story available.

2518. GoBots: Battle of the Rock Lords 21 Mar. 1986; *p.c.:* Hanna-Barbera Prods./Tonka Corp./Cuckoos Nest Studio/Wang Film Prods.; *dir:* Don Lusk, Ray Patterson, Alan Zaslove; *ex prod:* William Hanna, Joseph Barbera; *co-ex prod:* Joe Taritero; *prod:* Kay Wright; *asso prod:* Lynn Hoag; *prod ex:* Jayne Barbera, Jean MacCurdy; *prod sup:* Bob Marples; *post prod sup:* Joed Eaton; *asst dir:* Bob Goe, Don Patterson; *story:* Jeff Segal; *story consult:* Kelly Ward; *graphics:* Iraj Paran, Tom Wogatzke; *anim: sup dir:* Paul Sabella; *sup:* Janine Dawson; *des sup:* Davis Doi; *storyboard:* Rich Chidlaw, Ric Estrada, Tony Sgroi, Bob Taylor; *character des:* Michael McHugh, Rich Chidlaw, John Guerin, Ronald L. Evans, Alfred Gimeno, Tony Sgroi, Bwana Takamoto, Charles Payne, Salene Gerbasi, Terry Keil; *lay sup:* Charles Grosvenor; *back sup:* Al Gmuer; *back col key:* Bill Proctor, Michael Humphries, Fernando Arce, Jeff Richie, Bonnie Goodknight, Martin Forte; *character col key seperation:* Alison Leopold; *col key:* Lisa Brakefield; *mus:* Hoyt Curtin; *mus co-ord:* Joanne Miller; *mus ed:* Cecil Broughton, Terry Moore, Daniels McLean, Joe Sandusky; *ed:* Larry C. Cowan, Gil Iverson; *voices: Solitaire:* Margot Kidder; *Nuggit:* Roddy McDowell; *Boulder:* Michael Nouri; *Magmar:* Telly Savalas; *Nick:* Ike Eisenmann; *Cy-Kill:* Bernard Erhard; *Crasher:* Marilyn Lightstone; *Matt:* Morgan Paull; *Leader-1:* Lou Richards; *A.J.:* Leslie Speights; *Scooter/ Zeemon/ Rest-Q/ Pulver-Eyes/ Sticks/ Narliphant:* Frank Welker; *Slime Stone/ Granite/ Narligator:* Michael Bell; *Stone Heart/ Fossil Lord:* Foster Brooks; *Turbo/ Cop-Tur/ Talc:* Arthur Burghardt; *Vanguard:* Ken Campbell; *Herr Fiend/ Crackpot/ Tork:* Philip Lewis Clarke; *Pincher/ Tombstone/ Stone:* Peter Cullen; *Brimstone/ Klaws/ Rock Narlie:* Dick Gautier; *Marbles/ Hornet:* Darryl Hickman; *Small Foot:* B.J. Ward; *Fitor:* Kelly Ward; *Heat Seeker:* Kirby Ward; *Xerox sup:* Star Wirth, Daniel J. Conti, Martin Crossley, Gene DuBois, Richard Wilson; *titles:* Iraj Paran, Tom Wogatzke; *sd:* Alvy Dorman, Phil Flad, Gordon Hunt, Pat Foley; *sd fx:* Michael Bradley, Mary Gleason, Catherine MacKenzie, Tim Iverson, Carol Lewis, Jerry Winicki, David Cowan, Michelle Iverson; *Tonka: ex prod:* Stephen G. Shank; *prod:* Patrick S. Feely; *co-prod:* Raymond E. McDonald; *asso prod:* Mark W. Ludke; *prod asst:* Sue L. Hamilton, Robert L. Akey; *col. sd.* 75 min. • Solitaire, the Gem Queen of a planet where living rocks dominate, asks for help from the superhero GoBots when her planet is taken over by a rock lord named Magmar.

2519. Gobs of Fun (*Screen Song*) 28 July 1950; *p.c.:* Famous for Para; *dir:* I. Sparber; *story:* Larry Riley, Joe Stultz; *anim:* Al Eugster, Irv Spector; *sets:* Robert Owen; *voices:* Jackson Beck, Jack Mercer; *mus:* Winston Sharples; *col:* Tech. *sd:* RCA. 7 min. • The burly sailors gape at the promise of Nightclub entertainment with "Fifty Beautiful Girls."

2520. The Goddess of Spring (*Silly Symphony*) 3 Nov. 1934; *p.c.:* Walt Disney prods for UA; *dir:* Wilfred Jackson; *anim:* Arthur Babbitt, Baum, Les Clark, Ugo d'Orsi, Gilles de Tremaudan, Clyde Geronimi, Dick Huemer, Hamilton S. Luske, Wolfgang Reitherman, Louis Schmitt, Leonard Sebring; *fx:* Cy Young; *character des:* Albert Hurter; *lay:* Ken Anderson; *voice:* Kenneth Baker; *mus:* Leigh Harline; *col:* Tech. *sd:* RCA. 10 min. • The Devil makes a deal with beautiful Persephone to become his bride and regain her kingdom on Earth by spending half the year in Hades.

2521. Godzilla 20 May 1998; *p.c.:* TriStar; *digital creature anim: Centropolis Effects cgi sup:* Carolin Quis, Steffen M. Wild; *anim sup:* Andy Jones; *fx sup:* Sean Cunningham; *lead anim:* Matthew T. Hackett; *character anim:* Benjamin Cinelli, Michael Ford, Jordan Harris, Michael Zack Huber, Alice V. Kaiserian, Benedikt Niemann, Jay Randall, Eric M. Weiss; *fx anim:* John Michael Courte, Sean Andrew Faden, Michael Edland, Morris May, Rocco Passionino; *lead lighting art:* Frédéric Soumagnas; *lead texture art:* Robin Higgin-Foley; *digital fx: anim sup:* Daniel Kramer, Carl Hooper; *compositing sup:* Doreen Haver; *character development:* Pete Shinners; *lead texture art:* Bethany Berndt-Shackelford; *digital fx co-ord:* Nicholas Devore, Matt D; *cg art/character anim:* Barry Safley, Jim McLean, Ken Bailey, Odeh Kassiner, Todd Boyce, D. Erich Turner, Toan-Vinh Le, Jimmy Jewell, John Peel, Jeremy S. Nelligan, James Peterson, Jon-Marc Kortsch, Mike Bray; *lead flocking anim:* Brian Hall; *compositors:* John LeFauce Jr., Chad Carlberg, Alette Vernon; *digital fx: snr anim:* Kiki Candela, Andrew Titcomb; *digital character anim:* Bill Diaz, David Schaub, Alex Sokoloff; *digital art:* Bill Houston Ball, Kenneth F. Kurras, Douglas Yoshida; *Godzilla des sup:* Patrick Tatopoulos; *creature vocals:* Gary Hecker, Frank Welker; *col:* Tech. *sd:* Dolby/SDDS/dts. 138½ min. *l/a.* • Live-action science-fiction remake of the Japanese cult classic: A giant mutant lizard-like beast terrorizes the city of New York.

2522. Goggle Fishin' Bear (*Barney Bear*) 15 Jan. 1949; *p.c.:* MGM; *dir:* Michael Lah, Preston Blair; *anim:* Ray Abrams, Gil Turner, Don Patterson; *ed:* Fred MacAlpin; *mus:* Scott Bradley; *ph:* Jack Stevens; *prod:* Fred Quimby; *col:* Tech. *sd:* WE. 7 min. • Barney goes deep-sea fishing and is pestered by a friendly seal.

2523. Goin' to Heaven on a Mule (*Merrie Melodies*) 19 May 1934; *p.c.:* Leon Schlesinger prods for WB; *dir:* Isadore Freleng; *anim:* Rollin Hamilton, Bob McKimson, Robert Clampett; *voices:* The King's Men;

mus: Norman Spencer; *song:* Harry Warren, Al Dubin; *prod sup:* Henry Binder, Raymond G. Katz; b&w. *sd:* Vit. 7 min. • A black boy's drinking subjects him to a nightmare where he is taken to a swinging negro heaven.

2524. Going Ape *(Astronut)* Jan. 1970 (© 1965); *p.c.:* TT for Fox; *ex prod:* Bill Weiss; *dir/anim:* Connie Rasinski; *story sup:* Tom Morrison; *story:* Larz Bourne; *sets:* Bill Focht; *ed:* Jack MacConnell; *voices:* Dayton Allen; *mus:* Jim Timmens; *ph:* Ted Moskowitz; *sd:* Elliot Grey; *col:* DeLuxe. *sd:* RCA. 5 min. • When Astro teaches Oscar to talk to the animals, he converses with a gorilla who follows him home.

2525. Going! Going! Gosh! *(Merrie Melodies)* 23 Aug. 1952; *p.c.:* WB; *dir:* Charles M. Jones; *story:* Michael Maltese; *anim:* Lloyd Vaughan, Ben Washam, Ken Harris; *lay:* Robert Gribbroek; *back:* Philip de Guard; *ed:* Treg Brown; *voice:* Paul Julian; *mus:* Carl Stalling, Milt Franklyn; *prod mgr:* John W. Burton; *prod:* Edward Selzer; *col:* Tech. *sd:* Vit. 7 min. • In his quest for the elusive bird, the Coyote now sinks to the depths of disguising himself as a female Road-Runner.

2526. Going Places *(Fun and Facts About America)* 23 Oct. 1948; *p.c.:* Harding College for MGM; *prod/dir:* John Sutherland; *anim:* La Verne Harding; *col:* Tech. *sd:* WE. 9 min. • Freddie Fudsie, a soap marketeer, succumbs to temptation of monopoly, eventually reaching reality by economic law operations.

2527. Going to Blazes *(Oswald)* 6 Apr. 1933; *p.c.:* Univ; *dir:* Walter Lantz, "Bill" Nolan; *anim:* Ray Abrams, Fred Avery, Cecil Surry, Jack Carr, Don Williams; *mus:* James Dietrich; b&w. *sd:* WE. 6 min. • Fire Chief Ozzie and a very effete fireman try to quench the brutal flames of a burning house.

2528. Gold Diggin' Woodpecker *(Woody Woodpecker)* 1972; *p.c.:* Walter Lantz prods for Univ; *dir:* Paul J. Smith; *story:* Tony Benedict; *anim:* Volus Jones, Al Coe, Tom Byrne, Joe Voght; *sets:* Nino Carbe; *voices:* Dal McKennon, Grace Stafford; *mus:* Walter Greene; *col:* Tech. *sd:* RCA. 5 min. • Woody claims gold he finds in an abandoned mine. Another prospector arrives and claims it for himself and a battle ensues.

2529. The Gold Dust Bandit *(Luno)* Oct. 1964; *p.c.:* TT for Fox; *ex prod:* Bill Weiss; *dir/anim:* Art Bartsch; *story sup:* Tom Morrison; *story:* Bob Ogle, Glan Heisch; *sets:* Bill Focht, Robert Owen; *ed:* Jack MacConnell; *voices:* Bob MacFadden; *mus:* Jim Timmens; *ph:* Joe Rasinski; *sd:* Elliot Grey; *col:* DeLuxe. *sd:* RCA. 5 min. • Luno and Tim help a cowardly sheriff capture "The Gold Dust Bandit."

2530. The Gold Getters *(Scrappy)* 1 Mar. 1935; *p.c.:* Charles Mintz prods for Colum; *story:* Sid Marcus; *anim:* Art Davis; *mus:* Joe de Nat; *prod mgr:* James Bronis; b&w. *sd:* RCA. 6 min. • Scrappy pans for gold and gets a wheelbarrow full of nuggets. He arrives at Ye Olde Saloon where he prevents a bandit from robbing the place. It all turns out to be a dream.

2531. Gold Medal Reissues • Reissues of no less than 34 MGM cartoons from 22 Feb. 1947 to 5 Dec. 1952.

2532. The Gold Push *(Aesop's Film Fable)* 9 Jan. 1926; *p.c.:* Fables Pictures Inc for Pathé; *dir:* Paul Terry; b&w. *sil.* 10 min. • Out in the Klondike, a bold, bad cat miner runs off with an unsophisticated girl mouse. Her Mountie boyfriend rushes to the rescue.

2533. Gold Rush Daze *(Merrie Meodies)* 25 Feb. 1939; *p.c.:* Leon Schlesinger prods for WB; *dir:* Ben Hardaway, Cal Dalton; *story:* Melvin Millar; *anim:* Gil Turner; *lay:* Griff Jay; *back:* Arthur Loomer; *ed:* Tregoweth E. Brown; *voices:* Joe Twerp, Mel Blanc, The Sportsmen Quartet; *mus:* Carl W. Stalling; *prod sup:* Henry Binder, Raymond G. Katz; *col:* Tech. *sd:* Vit. 7 min. • An old prospector tells of how he has spent a lifetime searching for gold ... but never found any.

2534. Gold Struck *(Hoot Kloot)* 19 Jan. 1974; *p.c.:* Mirisch/DFE for UA; *dir/lay:* Roy Morita; *story:* John W. Dunn; *anim:* Bob Bransford, Don Williams, Norm McCabe, Ken Muse, John Freeman; *back:* Richard Thomas; *ed:* Joe Siracusa; *voices:* Bob Holt, Larry Mann; *mus:* Doug Goodwin; *titles:* Arthur Leonardi; *ph:* John Burton Jr.; *prod mgr:* Lee Gunther; *col:* DeLuxe. *sd:* RCA. 5 min. • Kloot stops off at a haunted house while transporting a gold shipment to Virginia City.

2535. Golddiggers of '49 *(Looney Tunes)* 6 Jan. 1936; *p.c.:* Leon Schlesinger prods for WB; *dir:* Fred Avery; *story:* Bob Clampett; *anim:* Bob Clampett, Charles Jones, Virgil Ross; *voices:* Joe Dougherty, Bernice Hansel, Tommy Bond, Fred Avery; *mus:* Bernard Brown; b&w. *sd:* Vit.

7 min. • Porky digs up some gold and sends Beans to town to stake a claim.

2536. The Golden Child 12 Dec. 1986; *p.c.:* Para for UIP; *Go-motion anim:* Harry Walton, Tom St. Amand; *anim:* Ellen Lichtwardt, John Armstrong, Gordon Baker, Nick Stern, Sean Turner; *addit anim:* Available Light, Ltd.; *Rotoscope art:* Jack Mongovan, Barbara Brennan, Joanne Hafner; *voices: Kala:* Marilyn Schreffler; *The Thing:* Frank Welker; *anim ph:* Rob Burton, John Knoll; *col. sd.* 94 min. *l/a.* • Live-action fantasy set in Tibet concerning a magical child.

2537. Golden Egg Goosie *(Aesop's Fable)* Aug. 1951; *p.c.:* TT for Fox; *dir:* Eddie Donnelly; *story:* Tom Morrison; *mus:* Philip A. Scheib; *col:* Tech. *sd:* RCA. 7 min. • Two wolves are after a silly goose who has painted his eggs with gold paint, thinking he's the goose who lays golden eggs.

2538. Golden Eggs *(Donald Duck)* 7 Mar. 1941; *p.c.:* Walt Disney prods for RKO; *dir:* Wilfred Jackson; *asst dir:* Jacques Roberts; *story sup:* Harry Reeves, Carl Barks; *anim:* Robert W. Carlson, George de Beeson, Ray Patterson, William N. Shull, Don Tobin, Vladimir Tytla, Bernard Wolf; *fx:* Edwin Aardal, Jack Boyd, Jerome Brown, Russ Dyson, Andrew Engman, Art Fitzpatrick, Joe Harbaugh, Jack Huber, Paul B. Kossoff, Ed Parks, Reuben Timmens; *lay:* Ernie Terrell, Thor Putnam; *voices:* Clarence Nash, Florence Gill; *mus:* Leigh Harline; *col:* Tech. *sd:* RCA. 7 min. • Donald dresses as a chicken to get past the rooster so he can clean-up on the "egg market."

2539. The Golden Hen *(Gandy Goose)* 26 July 1946; *p.c.:* TT for Fox; *dir:* Mannie Davis; *story:* John Foster; *back:* Art Bartsch; *voices:* Arthur Kay, Thomas Morrison; *mus:* Philip A. Scheib; *ph:* Douglas Moye; *col:* Tech. *sd:* RCA. 7 min. • Gandy dreams he has created a mechanical hen that lays an egg large enough to have him and Sourpuss enter and explore it.

2540. Golden Spoon Mary *(Terry Feature Burlesque)* 30 Apr. 1917; *p.c.:* The A Kay Co; *dir:* Paul H. Terry; b&w. *sil.* 5 min. • Literal translation featuring a girl born with a gold spoon in her mouth.

2541. The Golden State *(Screen Song)* 12 Mar. 1948; *p.c.:* Famous for Para; *dir:* Seymour Kneitel; *story:* Larz Bourne, Larry Riley; *anim:* Dave Tendlar, Bill Hudson; *sets:* Robert Little; *voices:* Charles Irving, Sid Raymond; *mus:* Winston Sharples; *song:* Buddy De Sylva, Joseph Meyer, Al Jolson; *ph:* Leonard McCormick; *prod mgr:* Sam Buchwald; *col:* Tec. *sd:* RCA. 8 min. • A humorous tour from the scenic wonders of California to the Hollywood stars, ending with a rousing chorus of "California Here I Come."

2542. The Golden Touch *(Silly Symphony)* 22 Mar. 1935; *p.c.:* Walt Disney prods for UA; *dir:* Walt Disney; *anim:* Norman Ferguson, Fred Moore; *sets:* Ferdinand Huszti Horvath; *voices:* Billy Bletcher, Alyce Ardell; *mus:* Frank E. Churchill; *col:* Tech. *sd:* RCA. 9 min. • King Midas is granted the power of everything he touches turns to gold. He soon discovers this gift is not as desirable as it first appears. • Walt Disney returned to direction after a considerable gap to demonstrate how he thought it should be done. He never directed another and forbade this one to be even mentioned in the studio. In actuality, it's nowhere near as bad as Walt would have us believe.

2543. The Golden West *(Terry-Toon)* 25 Aug. 1939; *p.c.:* TT for Fox; *dir:* Mannie Davis; *story:* John Foster; *mus:* Philip A. Scheib; b&w. *sd:* RCA. 7 min. • A Mountie saves the heroine from the clutches of Oil Can Harry.

2544. Golden Yeggs *(Merrie Melodies)* 5 Aug. 1950; *p.c.:* WB; *dir:* I. Freleng; *story:* Tedd Pierce; *anim:* Arthur Davis, Gerry Chiniquy, Ken Champin, Virgil Ross, Emery Hawkins; *lay:* Hawley Pratt; *back:* Paul Julian; *ed:* Treg Brown; *voices:* Mel Blanc, Stan Freberg; *mus:* Carl Stalling; *prod mgr:* John W. Burton; *prod:* Edward Selzer; *col:* Tech. *sd:* Vit. 7 min. • Daffy is abducted by gangsters who mistake him for the goose that laid the golden egg. He is given the ultimatum of either laying a gold egg or being permanently laid out.

2545. Goldielocks and the Three Bears *(Oswald)* 14 May 1934; *p.c.:* Univ; *dir:* Walter Lantz; *story:* Victor McLeod; *anim:* Manuel Moreno, George Grandpré, Lester Kline, (La)Verne Harding, Fred Kopietz; *mus:* James Dietrich; b&w. *sd:* WE. 8 min. • Goldie arrives at the bears' home when they are away, samples their porridge and retires to bed. The bears come home and chase her to the safety of the arms of Oswald.

2546. Goldilocks and the Jivin' Bears (*Merrie Melodies*) 24 Sept. 1944; *p.c.:* WB; *dir:* I. Freleng; *story:* Tedd Pierce; *anim:* Ken Champin; *lay:* Hawley Pratt; *back:* Paul Julian; *ed:* Treg Brown; *voices:* Ernest Whitman, Mel Blanc, Eddie Beal, Lillian Randolph, Sara Berner, Charlie Evans, J.E. Buckner, Eugene Phillips, Ellis D. Robinson; *mus:* Carl Stalling; *prod mgr:* John W. Burton; *prod:* Edward Selzer; *col:* Tech. *sd:* Vit. 7 min. • The Wolf and Red Riding Hood join the Three Bears in a hot "jam session."

2547. Goldilocks and the Three Bears (*Bear Family*) 15 July 1939; *p.c.:* MGM; *prod/dir:* Hugh Harman; *story:* Jack Cosgriff, Hugh Harman, Charles McGirl; *sets:* John Meandor; *voices:* Martha Wentworth, Rudolf Ising; *mus:* Scott Bradley; *col:* Tech. *sd:* WE. 11 min. • A new twist in the Goldilocks story. Papa Bear is more afraid of Goldie than she is of him.

2548. Goldilox and the Three Hoods (*The Dogfather*) 28 Aug. 1975; *p.c.:* Mirisch/DFE for UA; *dir:* Gerry Chiniquy; *story:* John Dunn; *anim:* Bob Richardson, Don Williams, Norm McCabe, Nelson Shin; *ed:* Rick Steward; *lay:* Dick Ung; *back:* Richard H. Thomas; *voices:* Bob Holt, Daws Butler, Joan Gerber; *mus:* Dean Elliott; *col:* DeLuxe. *sd:* RCA. 5 min. • The Dogfather tells his nephew a bedtime story about three mobsters trying to capture a gangster's moll for a rich reward.

2549. Goldimouse and the Three Cats (*Looney Tunes*) 19 Mar. 1960; *p.c.:* WB; *dir:* Friz Freleng; *story:* Warren Foster; *anim:* Virgil Ross, Art Davis, Gerry Chiniquy; *lay:* Hawley Pratt; *back:* Tom O'Loughlin; *ed:* Treg Brown; *voices:* Mel Blanc, June Foray; *mus:* Milt Franklyn; *prod mgr:* William Orcutt; *prod:* David H. DePatie; *col:* Tech. *sd:* Vit. 7 min. • While Sylvester and family are out, a girl mouse arrives at their house, eats their porridge and sleeps on their beds. When they return, Junior wants Father to catch the mouse for him ... and thereby hangs a tale.

2550. Goldwyn-Bray Comic *p.c.:* Bray prods/IFS for Goldwyn; *prod:* John R. Bray; b&w. sil. *s/r.* • *1920:* **The Great Umbrella Mystery** 17 Apr. *dir:* Gregory la Cava. **Knock on the Window, the Door Is in a Jamb** 17 Apr. **Shimmie Shivers** 21 Apr. **The First Man to the Moon** 21 Apr. *dir:* Max Fleischer. **A Fitting Gift** 7 May. **His Last Legs** 25 May. **Turn to the Right Leg** 2 June. **Smokey Smokes** 6 June. **One Good Turn Deserves Another** 17 June. **All for the Love of a Girl** 18 June. **Doctors Should Have Patience** 19 June. **Lampoons/The Dummy** 27 June. **Lampoons/His Country Cousin** 3 July. **Lampoons/A Fish Story** 3 July. **Lampoons** 10 July. *dir:* Burton F. Gillett. **Lampoons/The Last Rose of Summer** 17 July. **Lampoons/The Rotisserie Brothers** 24 July. *dir:* Grim Natwick. **Lampoons/The Fly Guy** 26 Aug. **Shedding the Profiteer** 5 Sept. **Cupid's Advice** 11 Sept. **Happy Hooldini** 11 Sept. **Lampoons/Apollo** 18 Sept. **Lampoons/The Sponge Man** 22 Sept. **The Prize Dance** 3 Oct. **Lampoons/Hunting Big Game** 9 Oct. *dir:* Burton F. Gillett • Cartoons attached to magazine featuring *Happy Hooligan*, *Judge Rummy* and *The Shenanigan Kids*.

2551. Goldwyn-Bray Pictographs *p.c.:* Bray prods/IFS for Goldwyn; *prod:* John R. Bray; b&w. sil. • *1919:* **The Clown's Pup** 30 Aug. *dir:* Max Fleischer. **How Animated Cartoons Are Made** 6 Sept. *dir:* John R. Bray. **Where Has My Little Coal Bin** 6 Sept. *dir:* Gregory la Cava. **The High Cost of Living** 13 Sept. *dir:* Raoul Barré. **Dud's Home Run** 23 Sept. *dir:* Wallace A. Carlson. **Getting a Story or the Origin of the Shimmie** 27 Sept. *dir:* Pat Sullivan. **Useless Hints by Fuller Prunes** 4 Oct. *dir/story:* Milt Gross. **The Tantalizing Fly** 4 Oct. *dir:* Max Fleischer. **Dud Leaves Home** 9 Oct. *dir:* Wallace A. Carlson. **My How Times Have Changed** 25 Oct. *dir:* Leighton Budd. **We'll Say They Do** 7 Nov. *dir/story:* Milt Gross. **Pigs in Clover** 10 Nov. *dir:* Gregory la Cava. **Dud's Geography Lesson** 17 Nov. *dir:* Wallace A. Carlson. **How Could William Tell?** 26 Nov. *dir:* Gregory la Cava. **Slides** 3 Dec. *dir:* Max Fleischer. **Sauce for the Goose** 9 Dec. *dir:* Vernon Stallings. **Tumult in Toy Town** 16 Dec. *dir/story:* Milt Gross. **Sufficiency** 23 Dec. *dir:* Vernon Stallings. **A Chip Off the Old Block** 31 Dec. *dir:* Wallace A. Carlson. • *1920:* **The Chinese Question** 6 Jan. *dir:* Vernon Stallings. **The Great Cheese Robbery** 16 Jan. *dir:* Vernon Stallings. **Behind the Signs on Broadway** 16 Jan. *dir:* J.D. Leventhal. **The Debut of Thomas Katt** 26 Jan. *dir:* John R. Bray (made in Brewster Color). **Love's Labor Lost** 30 Jan. *dir:* Vernon Stallings. **The Boxing Kangaroo** 2 Feb. *dir:* Max Fleischer. **How You See** 6 Feb. *dir:* J.D. Leventhal. **A Warm Reception** 10 Feb. *dir:* unknown. **All Aboard for a Trip to the Moon** 10 Feb. *dir:* Max Fleischer. **Dud's Haircut** 16 Feb. *dir:* Wallace A. Carlson. **The Wrong Track** 27 Feb. *dir:* unknown. **Wireless Telephony** 27 Feb. *dir:* F. Lyle Goldman. **The Best Mouse Loses** 3 Mar. *dir:* Vernon Stallings. **Hello Mars** 3 Mar. *dir:* Max Fleischer. **The Tale of a Wag** 9 Mar. *dir:* unknown. **Professor B-Flat** 9 Mar. *dir:* J.D. Leventhal; *anim:* Roland C. Crandall. **The Chinaman** 19 Mar. *dir:* Max Fleischer. **A Very Busy Day** 23 Mar. *dir:* Gregory la Cava. **Frenchy Discovers America** 3 Apr. *dir/story:* Milt Gross. **A Tax from the Rear** 14 Apr. *dir:* Vernon Stallings. **The Ear** 14 Apr. *dir:* F. Lyle Goldman. **Spring Fever** 21 Apr. *dir:* Gregory la Cava. **Ginger Snaps** 30 Apr. *dir/story:* Milt Gross. **The Circus** 6 May. *dir:* Max Fleischer. **Swinging His Vacation** 14 May. *dir:* Gregory la Cava. **Here's Your Eyesight** 14 May. *dir:* J.D. Leventhal. **Yes, Times Have Changed** 19 May. *dir:* L.M. Glackens. **The Mysterious Vamp** 29 May. *dir:* Gregory la Cava. **Katz Is Katz** 4 June. *dir:* Vernon Stallings. **The Ouija Board** 4 June. *dir:* Max Fleischer. **A Punk Piper** 12 June. *dir:* Vernon Stallings. **Breathing** 12 June. *dir:* J.D. Leventhal. **How My Vacation Spent Me** 19 June. *dir/story:* Milt Gross. **Quick Chamge** 26 June. *dir:* Vernon Stallings. **The Chinese Honeymoon** 3 July. *dir:* Vernon Stallings. **The Clown's Little Brother** 6 July. *dir:* Max Fleischer. **The Rhyme That Went Wrong** 16 July. *dir:* Vernon Stallings. **The Trained Horse** 27 July. *dir:* Vernon Stallings. **Dots and Dashes** 26 Aug. *dir:* Vernon Stallings. **The Train Robber** 26 Aug. *dir:* Vernon Stallings. **If You Could Shrink** 26 Aug. *dir:* Dave Fleischer. **Dud the Lion Tamer** 4 Sept. *dir:* Wallace A. Carlson. **Water, Water Everywhere** 11 Sept. *dir:* Vernon Stallings. **Ze American Girl** 18 Sept. *dir/story:* Jean Gic. **Ginger Snaps** 25 Sept. *dir/story:* Milt Gross. **If We Went to the Moon** 25 Sept. *dir:* J.D. Leventhal. **Poker** 2 Oct. *dir:* Dave Fleischer. **Jerry and the Five-Fifteen Train** 2 Oct. *dir:* Vernon Stallings. **Lightning** 2 Oct. *dir:* J.D. Leventhal. **Perpetual Motion** 2 Oct. *dir:* Dave Fleischer. **Beaten By a Hare** 7 Oct. *dir:* Vernon Stallings. **A Tough Pull** 7 Oct. *dir:* Vernon Stallings. **Stories in Lines** 21 Oct. *dir/story:* Jean Gic. **A Family Affair** 25 Oct. *dir:* Vernon Stallings. **A Continuous Line of Thought** 4 Nov. *dir/story:* Jean Gic. **The Bomb Idea** 6 Nov. *dir:* Vernon Stallings. **The Restaurant** 16 Nov. *dir:* Dave Fleischer. **A Thrilling Drill** 14 Dec. *dir:* Vernon Stallings. • *1921:* **The Hinges on the Bar-Room Door** 8 Jan. *dir:* Vernon Stallings. **Without Coal** 8 Jan. *dir:* Vernon Stallings. **The Automatic Riveter** 8 Jan. *dir:* J.D. Leventhal. **A Tragedy in One Line** 15 Jan. *dir/story:* Jean Gic. **The Awful Spook** 21 Jan. *dir:* Vernon Stallings. **How I Became Krazy** 26 Jan. *dir:* Vernon Stallings. **Scrambled Eagles** 28 Jan. *dir:* Vernon Stallings. **Cartoonland** 2 Feb. *dir:* Dave Fleischer. **The Automobile Ride** 12 Feb. *dir:* Dave Fleischer. **Izzy Able the Detective** 16 Feb. *dir/story:* Milt Gross. **The Wireless Wire Walkers** 26 Feb. *dir:* Vernon Stallings. **Othello Sapp's Wonderful Invention** 19 Mar. *dir/story:* Milt Gross • Cartoons attached to magazine featuring *Ginger Snaps*; *Jerry on the Job*; *Ko-Ko the Clown*; *Krazy Kat* and *Us Fellers*. • See: *Hearst International Features Service*; *Paramount-Bray Pictographs*

2552. Goldwyn-International Comics *p.c.:* IFS for Goldwyn; *prod:* Gregory la Cava; b&w. sil. • Hearst Newspapers comics featuring Thomas "Tad" Dorgan's comic character *Judge Rummy* and Frederick Burr Opper's *Happy Hooligan*. • *1920:* **A Doity Deed** 25 Oct. *dir:* William C. Nolan. **Hypnotic Hooch** 26 Oct. *dir/anim:* Grim Natwick. **The Village Blacksmith** 27 Oct. **The Hooch Ball** 3 Nov. **Kiss Me** 3 Nov. *dir/anim:* Jack King. **A Romance of '76** 22 Nov. **Snap Judgement** 22 Nov. *dir/anim:* Burton F. Gillett. **Why Change Your Husband** 22 Nov. *dir/anim:* Jack King. **Dr. Jekyll and Mr. Zip** 8 Dec. **Bear Facts** 10 Dec. *dir/anim:* Gregory la Cava. **Yes Dear** 12 Dec. **Happy Hooligan in Oil** 23 Dec. *dir:* William C. Nolan. • *1921:* **Fatherly Love** 3 Jan. *dir:* William C. Nolan. **Roll Your Own** 3 Jan. **Too Much Pep** 4 Jan. *dir/anim:* Jack King. **The Chicken Thief** 17 Jan. *dir/anim:* Grim Natwick. **The Skating Fool** 13 Mar. **A Close Shave** 29 Apr. • See: *Hearst International Features Service*

2553. Golf Chumps (*Krazy Kat*) 6 Apr. 1939; *p.c.:* Chrarles Mintz prods for Colum; *story:* Allen Rose; *anim:* Harry Love, Louie Lilly; *voices:* Dave Weber, Mel Blanc; *mus:* Joe de Nat; b&w. *sd:* RCA. 6 min. • Krazy and Kitty get golf tuition from the narrator.

2554. Golf Nuts (*Paul Terry-Toons*) 14 Dec. 1930; *p.c.:* A-C for Educational/Fox; *dir:* Paul Terry, Frank Moser; *mus:* Philip A. Scheib; b&w. *sd:* WE. 6 min. • No story available.

2555. The Golfers (*Meany Miny Mo*) 11 Jan. 1937; *p.c.:* Univ; *dir:* Walter Lantz; *story:* Walter Lantz, Victor McLeod; *anim:* La Verne Harding, Ed Benedict, Leo Salkin; *mus:* Irving Actman, Frank Loesser; b&w. *sd:*

WE. 6 min. • The monks play golf with a robot who objects to having a spanner thrown in his works.

2556. Goliath II 21 Jan. 1959; *p.c.:* Walt Disney prods for BV; *dir:* Wolfgang Reitherman; *asst dir:* Danny Alguire; *story:* Bill Peet; *anim dir:* John Lounsbery; *anim:* Hal King, Blaine Gibson, John Sibley, Amby Paliwoda, Eric Cleworth, Cliff Nordberg, Bill Keil, Dick Lucas, Ted Berman; *fx:* Dan MacManus; *des:* Ralph Hulett; *lay:* Basil Davidovich, Vance Gerry, Colin Campbell; *back:* Thelma Witmer, Richard H. Thomas, Gordon Legg; *voices: Narrator:* Sterling Holloway; *Mouse:* Paul Frees; *Mother:* Barbara Jo Allen; *Goliath:* Kevin Corcoran; *Elephant:* Rita Shaw; *Also:* James MacDonald; *mus:* George Bruns; *col:* Tech. *sd:* RCA. 15 min. *Academy Award nomination.* • Goliath is by far the smallest of the elephant herd but he earns their respect when he saves the pack from a mouse.

2557. Gone Batty (*Merrie Melodies*) 4 Sept. 1954; *p.c.:* WB; *dir:* Robert McKimson; *story:* Sid Marcus, Ben Washam; *anim:* Charles McKimson, Herman Cohen, Rod Scribner, Phil de Lara; *lay:* Robert Givens; *back:* Richard H. Thomas; *ed:* Treg Brown; *voices:* Robert C. Bruce, Mel Blanc; *mus:* Carl Stalling; *prod mgr:* John W. Burton; *prod:* Edward Selzer; *col:* Tech. *sd:* Vit. 7 min. • A baseball team's elephant mascot takes a stand on the diamond and wins for the entire team.

2558. Gong with the Pink (*Pink Panther*) 20 Oct. 1971; *p.c.:* Mirisch/Geoffrey/DFE for UA; *dir:* Hawley Pratt; *story:* Irv Spector; *anim:* Manny Gould, Bob Richardson, Don Williams; *lay:* Dick Ung; *back:* Richard H. Thomas; *ed:* Joe Siracusa; *mus:* Walter Greene; *theme tune:* Henry Mancini; *ph:* John Burton Jr.; *prod sup:* Jim Foss, Harry Love; *col:* DeLuxe. *sd:* RCA. 6 min. • The Panther works in a Chinese restaurant whose principal is banging a huge gong for service. This proves a constant headache for the man who owns the antique china shop upstairs.

2559. Gonzales' Tamales (*Looney Tunes*) 30 Nov. 1957; *p.c.:* WB; *dir:* Friz Freleng; *story:* Warren Foster; *anim:* Art Davis, Virgil Ross, Gerry Chiniquy; *lay:* Hawley Pratt; *back:* Boris Gorelick; *ed:* Treg Brown; *voices:* Mel Blanc, Jack Edwards; *mus:* Carl Stalling, Milt Franklyn; *prod mgr:* John W. Burton; *prod:* Edward Selzer; *col:* Tech. *sd:* Vit. 7 min. • The mice are tired of Speedy forever entrancing their girls and stir-up ill feeling between Speedy and Sylvester.

2560. Goo Goo Goliath (*Merrie Melodies*) 18 Sept. 1954; *p.c.:* WB; *dir:* I. Freleng; *story:* Warren Foster; *anim:* Arthur Davis, Manuel Perez, Ken Champin, Virgil Ross; *lay:* Hawley Pratt; *back:* Irv Wyner; *ed:* Treg Brown; *voices:* Norman Nesbitt, Mel Blanc, Marian Richman; *mus:* Carl Stalling; *prod mgr:* John W. Burton; *prod:* Edward Selzer; *col:* Tech. *sd:* Vit. 7 min. • An inebriated stork delivers a Giant's offspring to a suburban couple who have to cope with tending to his every need.

2561. Good and Guilty (*Noveltoon*) Feb. 1962; *p.c.:* Para Cartoons; *dir:* Seymour Kneitel; *story:* I. Klein; *anim:* Morey Reden, George Germanetti, Wm. B. Pattengill; *sets:* Robert Owen; *voices:* Eddie Lawrence; *mus:* Winston Sharples; *ph:* Leonard McCormick; *prod mgr:* Abe Goodman; *col:* Tech. *sd:* RCA. 6 min. • Goodie is on trial for "Conduct Unbecoming a Gremlin" by helping to create history.

2562. The Good Bye Kiss 6 June 1928; *p.c.:* Mack Sennett Studios for First National; *dir:* Mack Sennett; *anim:* Walter Lantz; b&w. sil. 9 reels. *l/a* • Live-Action Sally Eilers comedy where an animated "Cootie" is shown marching over the landscape.

2563. Good-Bye Mr. Moth (*Andy Panda*) 11 May 1942; *p.c.:* Walter Lantz prods for Univ; *dir:* Walter Lantz; *story:* Ben Hardaway, "Chuck" Couch; *anim:* Alex Lovy, (La) Verne Harding; *sets:* Fred Brunish; *voices:* Sara Berner, Mel Blanc; *mus:* Darrell Calker; *prod mgr:* George Hall; *col:* Tech. *sd:* WE. 7 min. • A hungry moth eats everything in sight in Andy's tailor shop, including the cuckoo clock.

2564. Good-Bye, My Lady Love (*Screen Songs*) 31 Aug. 1929; *p.c.:* The Fleischer Studio for Para; *prod:* Max Fleischer; *dir:* Dave Fleischer; b&w. *sd:* WE. 6 min. • No story available.

2565. Good Deed Daly (*Terry-Toon*) June 1955; *p.c.:* TT for Fox; *dir:* Connie Rasinski; *story:* Tom Morrison; *anim:* Jim Tyer; *voice/ph:* Douglas Moye; *mus:* Philip A. Scheib. *col:* Tech. *sd:* RCA. 6 min. CS. • Boy Scout Daly is eager to do a good deed when he discovers Desperate Dumkopf in the act of robbing a bank.

2566. The Good Egg (*Merrie Melodies*) 21 Oct. 1939; *p.c.:* Leon

Schlesinger prods for WB; *dir:* Charles M. Jones; *story:* Dave Monahan; *anim:* Ken Harris; *lay:* Robert Givens; *back:* Paul Julian; *ed:* Tregoweth E. Brown; *voices:* Bernice Hansel; *mus:* Carl W. Stalling; *prod sup:* Henry Binder, Raymond G. Katz; *col:* Tech. *sd:* Vit. 7 min. • An old hen hatches a turtle egg. The baby turtle has a tough time amongst the other chicks.

2567. The Good Friend 1969; *p.c.:* Murakami/Wolf for The American Film Institute; *dir/anim:* Jimmy Murakami; *ed:* Rich Harrison; *voices:* Paul Frees, Pat Carroll; *mus:* Krach Yacoubian; *ph:* Mike Gershman; *col. sd.* 8 min. • A man's girlfriend feels pity for a poor wretch who has no eyes, nose or mouth. She persuades her boyfriend to donate what he has to the man. When he finally does, she goes off with the other fellow.

2568. A Good Liar (*Sullivan Cartoon Comedy*) 30 July 1917; *p.c.:* Sullivan Studio for Univ; *dir:* Pat Sullivan; *anim:* Otz Messmer; b&w. sil. 4 min. • A soldier spins a yarn to some kids as to how he got his medal by infiltrating enemy HQ and stole the hun's entire food supply which he transmitted by radio to his own headquarters.

2569. Good Little Monkeys (*Happy Harmonies*) 13 Apr. 1935; *p.c.:* MGM; *prod/dir:* Hugh Harman, Rudolf Ising; *voices:* the Rhythmettes; *mus:* Scott Bradley; *col:* Tech-2. *sd:* WE. 8 min. • In a library, Satan appears from "Dante's Inferno" and tries to entice the Three Good Monkeys into Hades. Other storybook characters emerge to their rescue.

2570. Good Mousekeeping (*Little Roquefort*) Sept. 1952; *p.c.:* TT for Fox; *dir:* Mannie Davis; *story:* Tom Morrison; *anim:* Jim Tyer; *voices:* Tom Morrison; *mus:* Philip A. Scheib. *col:* Tech. *sd:* RCA. 6 min. • Roquefort redecorates his home with paint that's guarded by Percy the Puss.

2571. Good Neighbor Nudnik Oct. 1966; *p.c.:* Rembrant Films for Para; *prod:* William L. Snyder; *dir:* Gene Deitch; *col. sd.* 6 min. • Nudnik offers himself as an odd-job man to a concert pianist. • See: *Nudnik*

2572. Good Night Elmer (*Merrie Melodies*) 26 Oct. 1940; *p.c.:* Leon Schlesinger prods for WB; *dir:* Charles M. Jones; *story:* Rich Hogan; *anim:* Philip Monroe; *character des:* Charles Thorson; *lay:* Robert Givens; *back:* Paul Julian; *ed:* Treg Brown; *voice:* Mel Blanc; *mus:* Carl W. Stalling; *prod sup:* Henry Binder, Raymond G. Katz; *col:* Tech. *sd:* Vit. 7 min. • Elmer Fudd prepares for a night's repose.

2573. Good Night Rusty (*Madcap Models*) 3 Dec. 1943; *p.c.:* George Pal prods for Para; *prod/dir:* George Pal; *anim:* Felix Zelenka; *col:* Tech. *sd:* WE. 8 min. • Rusty conjours up visions while smoking his first cigar.

2574. Good Noose (*Looney Tunes*) Nov. 1962; *p.c.:* WB; *dir:* Robert McKimson; *story:* Dave DeTiege; *anim:* Warren Batchelder, George Grandpré, Keith Darling, Ted Bonnicksen; *fx:* Harry Love; *sets:* Robert Gribbroek; *ed:* Treg Brown; *voices:* Mel Blanc; *mus:* William Lava; *prod mgr:* William Orcutt; *prod:* David H. DePatie; *col:* Tech. *sd:* Vit. 7 min. • Daffy tries to talk his way out of being evicted from a ship by performing magic tricks.

2575. Good Old Circus Days (*Aesop's Film Fable*) 3 Dec. 1924; *p.c.:* Fables Pictures Inc for Pathé; *dir:* Paul Terry; b&w. sil. 5 min • The animals arriving at the circus and some of the acrobatic stunts they witness under the Big Top.

2576. Good Old College Days (*Aesop's Film Fable*) 10 Feb. 1924; *p.c.:* Fables Pictures Inc for Pathé; *dir:* Paul Terry; b&w. sil. 5 min. • A football match between a jungle team and mice known as "The Cheese Grabbers."

2577. The Good Old Days (*Aesop's Film Fable*) 24 Dec. 1923; *p.c.:* Fables Pictures Inc for Pathé; *dir:* Paul Terry; b&w. sil. 5 min • Ancient and modern courtship methods are contrasted from the fig leaf to the present day.

2578. Good Old Irish Tunes (*Terry-Toon*) 27 June 1941; *dir:* Connie Rasinski; *story:* John Foster; *mus:* Philip A. Scheib; b&w. *sd:* RCA. 7 min. • Story not available.

2579. Good Old School Days (*Aesop's Sound Fable*) 7 Mar. 1930; *p.c.:* Van Beuren for Pathé; *dir:* John Foster, Mannie Davis; *mus:* Gene Rodenmich; b&w. sil. 5 min. • All the zoo animals go to school including Mary Mouse and her little lamb.

2580. The Good Scout (*Willie Whopper*) 1 Sept. 1934; *p.c.:* Celebrity prods for MGM; *prod/dir:* Ub Iwerks; *anim:* Robert G. Stokes, Norm Blackburn; *voice:* Jane Withers; *mus:* Jellyroll Morton (pre-recorded), Art

Turkisher; *b&w. sd:* PCP. 6 min. • Willie relates his day's good deeds including assisting an old lady across a puddle, rescuing a kid from a bully and saving a flapper from being abducted.

2581. Good Scouts (*Donald Duck*) 8 July 1938; *p.c.:* Walt Disney prods for RKO; *dir:* Jack King; *story dir:* Harry Reeves, Carl Barks; *anim:* Edwin Aardal, Paul Allen, Johnny Cannon, Alfred Eugster, Frank Follmer, Jack Hannah, Edward Love, Sandy Strother, Don Towsley, Bernard Wolf. *fx:* Andrew Engman, Joshua Meador, George Rowley; *voices:* Clarence Nash; *mus:* Oliver Wallace; *col:* Tech. *sd:* RCA. 7 min. *Academy Award nomination.* • Scoutmaster Donald takes his nephews on a camping trip and upsets a huge, hungry bear.

2582. Good Scream Fun (*Casper*) 1 Oct. 1958; *p.c.:* Para Cartoons; *dir:* Seymour Kneitel; *story:* Jack Mercer; *anim:* Wm. B. Pattengill, Nick Tafuri; *Sets:* Robert Owen; *voices:* Cecil Roy, Jack Mercer; *mus:* Winston Sharples; *ph:* Leonard McCormick; *prod mgr:* Abe Goodman; *col:* Tech. *sd:* RCA. 6 min. • Casper saves an ostrich from the fate that will befall him at the hands of a taxidermist.

2583. The Good Ship Nellie (*Aesop's Film Fable*) 6 Jan. 1928; *p.c.:* Fables Pictures Inc for Pathé; *dir:* Frank Moser, Paul Terry; *b&w. sil.* 5 min. • Pirates attack a ship mastered by Milton Mouse and his girl.

2584. Good Snooze Tonight (*Noveltoon*) Feb. 1963; *p.c.:* Para Cartoons; *dir:* Seymour Kneitel; *story:* Irving Dressler; *anim:* Martin Taras, John Gentilella, Jim Logan; *sets:* Robert Little; *voices:* Bob MacFadden; *mus:* Winston Sharples; *ph:* Leonard McCormick; *prod mgr:* Abe Goodman; *col:* Tech. *sd:* RCA. 6 min. • A wolf tries to encourage a sheepdog to go to sleep so he can steal the sheep.

2585. A Good Story About a Bad Egg (*Sullivan Cartoon Comedy*) 12 Apr. 1917; *p.c.:* Sullivan Studio for Univ; *dir:* Pat Sullivan; *b&w. sil.* 5 min. • An unhatched egg has many adventures, finally arriving at a cheese factory where the proprietor locks it in a safe and the mice steal it for a football game.

2586. The Good Things of Life 1 Feb. 1922; *p.c.:* Key Holding Corp; *prod/dir:* Ashley Miller; *b&w. sil. l/a/anim.* • Series featuring live-action, cartoons, model and clay animation.

2587. A Good Time for a Dime (*Donald Duck*) 9 May 1941; *p.c.:* Walt Disney prods for RKO; *dir:* Richard Lundy; *asst dir:* Ted Baker; *anim:* Theodore Bonnicksen, Robert W. Carlson, Walter Clinton, John Elliotte, Volus Jones, Paul B. Kossoff, Jack Manning, Ray Patterson, Kosti Ruomonaa, William N. Shull; *fx:* Jack Boyd, Jerome Brown, Andrew Engman, Art Fitzpatrick, Joseph Gayek, Jack Huber, John F. Reed, George Rowley, Reuben Timmens, Cornett Wood, Frank Onaitis; *lay:* Thor Putnam; *voices:* Dehner Forkum, Clarence Nash; *mus:* Leigh Harline; *col:* Tech. *sd:* RCA. 8 min. • Donald visits a penny arcade and takes a disastrous free airplane ride.

2588. Good Will to Men (*MGM Cartoon*) 26 Oct. 1955; *p.c.:* MGM; *prod/dir:* William Hanna, Joseph Barbera; *anim:* Lewis Marshall, Kenneth Muse, Ed Barge, Irven Spence, Reuben Timmens; *lay:* Dick Bickenbach; *back:* Robert Gentle, Don Driscoll; *ed:* Jim Faris; *voices:* Elmore Vincent, Robert Mitchell Boys' Choir; *mus:* Scott Bradley; *ph:* Jack Stevens; *prod mgr:* Hal Elias; *prod:* Fred Quimby; *col:* Tech. *sd:* WE. 8 min. CS. *Academy Award nomination.* • Choirmaster Mouse tells the children of how the human race wiped itself out through wars and, ultimately, the Atom Bomb. An updated remake of *Peace on Earth*.

2589. Goodbye My Lady Love (*Song Car-Tune*) 22 May 1926; *p.c.:* Inkwell Studio for Red Seal; *prod:* Max Fleischer; *dir:* Dave Fleischer; *b&w. sil.* 5 min. • No story available.

2590. Goode Knight (*Aesop's Fable*) 23 Feb. 1934; *p.c.:* Van Beuren for RKO; *dir:* George Stallings; *anim:* Steve Muffatti; *mus:* Gene Rodemich; *b&w. sd:* RCA. 7 min. • Burlesque on Robin Hood.

2591. Goodie the Gremlin (*Noveltoon*) Apr. 1961; *p.c.:* Para Cartoons; *dir:* Seymour Kneitel; *story:* Irving Dressler; *anim:* Martin Taras, Jim Logan; *sets:* Robert Little, Robert Owen; *mus:* Winston Sharples; *ph:* Leonard McCormick; *prod mgr:* Abe Goodman; *col:* Tech. *sd:* RCA. 6 min. • Goodie's stems a feud between two neighbors by getting them drunk.

2592. Goodie's Good Deed (*Modern Madcap*) Nov. 1963; *p.c.:* Para Cartoons; *dir:* Seymour Kneitel; *story:* Jack Mercer, Irv Dressler; *anim:* Wm. B. Pattengill; *sets:* Robert Little; *voice:* Allen Swift; *mus:* Winston

Sharples; *ph:* Leonard McCormick; *prod mgr:* Abe Goodman; *col:* Tech. *sd:* RCA. 6 min. • Gremlin Goodie assists a (bear) "Cub" Scout perform a "Good Deed." Meany and Nasty, two mean Gremlins, sabotage all his good work but Goodie finally manages to turn the tables on them.

2593. Goofy and Wilbur (*Mickey Mouse*) 17 Mar. 1939; *p.c.:* Walt Disney prods for RKO; *dir:* Dick Huemer; *story:* Otto Englander; *anim:* Arthur Babbitt, I. Klein, Edward Love, Wolfgang Reitherman, Berny Wolf; *fx:* Joshua Meador; *voices:* Pinto Colvig; *talking violin:* Olcott Vail; *mus:* Paul J. Smith; *col:* Tech. *sd:* RCA. 8 min. • Goofy goes fishing with his grasshopper friend as bait. A stork swallows him and the Goof pursues. The first cartoon featuring Goofy on his own.

2594. Goofy Birds 12 Aug. 1928. (*Educational-Bowers Comedy*) *p.c.:* Bowers Comedy Corp. for Educational; *prod:* Charley Bowers; *dir:* H.L. Muller; *l/a:* Charley Bowers, Buster Brodie; *b&w. sil.* 2 reels. *l/a/anim.* • Charley and Buster go hunting in Africa for the only known specimen of the Umbrella bird. They set a trained worm to lure the bird into the cage.

2595. The Goofy Gardener (*Hercules*) 26 Aug. 1957; *p.c.:* Walter Lantz prods for Univ; *dir:* Alex Lovy; *story:* Dick Kinney; *anim:* Ray Abrams, La Verne Harding; *Sets:* Raymond Jacobs; *voice:* Dal McKennon; *mus:* Eugene Poddany; *prod mgr:* William E. Garity; *col:* Tech. *sd:* RCA. 6 min. • The outdoor event of the social calendar is almost destroyed with the arrival of a gardener.

2596. Goofy Goat Antics 6 July 1931; *p.c.:* Ted Eshbaugh Studio for Van Beuren; *prod/dir:* Ted Eshbaugh; *anim:* Wilson (Pete) Burness, Cal Dalton, Tex Hastings, Andrew Hutchinson, Jack Zander; *mus:* Carl W. Stalling; *col:* Cine. *sd:* 7 min. • Goofy Goat's drive to the "Glee Club" is marred by being stuck behind a slow driver. When he finally arrives, he participates in a variety show with several other animals. Although a series of twelve cartoons were announced, only this and *Getting His Nanny* have been traced.

2597. Goofy Gondolas (*Krazy Kat*) 21 Dec 1934; *p.c.:* Charles Mintz prods for Colum; *story:* Ben Harrison; *anim:* Harry Love, Preston Blair; *mus:* Joe de Nat; *prod mgr:* James Bronis; *b&w. sd:* RCA. 6 min. • No story available.

2598. Goofy, Goofy Gander (*Noveltoon*) 18 Aug. 1950; *p.c.:* Famous for Para; *dir:* Bill Tytla; *story:* I. Klein; *anim:* George Germanetti, Steve Muffatti; *sets:* Anton Loeb; *voices:* Mae Questel, Jack Mercer, Sid Raymond, Gwen Davies; *mus:* Winston Sharples; *ph:* Leonard McCormick; *prod mgr:* Sam Buchwald; *col:* Tech. *sd:* RCA. 7 min. • Audrey dreams she's in Comic Book Land where two villains steal the golden eggs from Mother Goose's goose.

2599. The Goofy Gophers (*Looney Tunes*) 25 Jan. 1947; *p.c.:* WB; *dir:* Arthur Davis; *story:* Lloyd Turner, William Scott, Robert Clampett; *anim:* Don Williams, Manny Gould, J.C. Melendez, Cal Dalton; *lay:* Don Smith; *back:* Philip de Guard; *ed:* Treg Brown; *voices:* Mel Blanc, Stan Freberg; *mus:* Carl Stalling; *prod mgr:* John W. Burton; *prod:* Edward Selzer; *col:* Ciné. *sd:* Vit. 7 min. • Two Gophers (based on radio's *Gus & Alphonse*) raid a vegetable garden from under the very nose of the watchdog.

2600. Goofy Groceries (*Merrie Melodies*) 29 Mar. 1941; *p.c.:* Leon Schlesinger prods for WB; *dir:* Robert Clampett; *story:* Melvin Millar; *anim:* Vive Risto; *Sets:* Michael Sasanoff; *ed:* Treg Brown; *voices:* Mel Blanc, Jack Lescoulie, Sara Berner, Kent Rogers; *mus:* Carl W. Stalling; *prod sup:* Henry Binder, Raymond G. Katz; *col:* Tech. *sd:* Vit. 7 min. • The goods in a grocery shop have their singing and dancing interrupted with the arrival of a gorilla.

2601. Goofy Gymnastics (*Goofy*) 7 Oct. 1948; *p.c.:* Walt Disney prods for RKO; *dir:* Jack Kinney; *story:* Dick Kinney; *anim:* John Sibley, George Nicholas, Wolfgang Reitherman; *fx:* Dan MacManus, Ed Aardal, Jack Boyd; *lay:* Al Zinnen; *back:* Merle Cox; *voices:* Dehner Forkum, Pinto Colvig; *mus:* Oliver Wallace; *col:* Tech. *sd:* RCA. 7 min. • Goofy attempts to build up his physique with an indoor excercise kit.

2602. A Goofy Movie 7 April 1995; *p.c.:* The Walt Disney Company for BV; *dir:* Kevin Lima; *prod:* Dan Rounds; *asso prod:* Patrick Reagan; *prod co-ord:* Marc DeGagne; *dir of operations (Paris):* Jean-Pierre Quenet; *prod mgr:* (Sydney) Terry Smith; (Toronto) Doug Allen; *asso:* Sylvie Bennett-Fauqué, Jean-Luc Florinda, Etienne Longa; *post prod mgr:* Cheryl Murphy; *scr:* Jymm Magon, Chris Matheson, Brian Pimental; *based on a story by Jymm Magon; *addit written material:* Curtis Armstrong, John Doolittle; *story sup:* Brian Pimental; *optical sup:* Mark Dornfeld; *character des:* Carole Holliday, William Finn, Alex Mann, Bob Scott, Bruce Scott; *character model clean-up:* Francesca Allen, David Hancock, Kent Culotta; *Disney Animation—Paris:* Paul Brizzi, Gaëtan Brizzi; *anim sup:* Nancy Beiman, Matias Marcos, Stéphane Sainte Foi, Dominique Monfery; *anim:* Jean-Luc Ballester, Michael Benet, Eric Bergeron, Arnaud Berthier, David Berthier, Wolf-Ruediger Bloss, Bolhem Bouchiba, Sylvain Deboissy, Patrick Delage, Eric Delbecq, Marc Eoche-Duval, Bruce Ferriz, Thierry Goulard, Carole Holliday, Holger Leihe, Philippe Le Brun, Sergio Pablos, Catherine Poulain, Jean-François Rey, Ventura Rodriguez, Yoshimichi Tamura, Andreas Wessel; *clean-up sup:* Claire Bourdin; *inbet sup:* Pierre Girault; *anim fx:* Jean-Christopher Poulain, Thierry Chaffoin, Rosanna Lyons, Jeff Topping; *lay:* J. Michael Spooner, Olivier Adam, Juan José Guarnido Ariza, Susan Butterworth, Mary Margaret Hawley, David Kenyon, Zoltan Maros, Vincent Massy, Dassos Petrou, Neal Petty, Stephane Roux, Bob St. Pierre; *back:* Christophe Vacher, Pierre Pavloff, Olivier Besson, John Boyer, Isabelle Clevenot, Jean-Paul Fernandez, Susan Hackett Dalipagic, Dominique Louis, Patricia Millereau, Joacquim Royo Morales; *3d anim:* Ex Machina, Xavier Duval, Jerome Gordon, Philippe Billon, Patrick Pestel; *scene plan:* Raphael Vicente; *Disney Anim—Sydney:* *seq dir:* Steve Moore; *anim:* Georges Abolin, Andrew Collins, Chris Derochie, Lianne Hughes, Don MacKinnon, Oscar Perez, Troy Saliba, Steven Taylor; *clean-up sup:* Janey Dunn; *inbet sup:* Mickie Cassidy; *anim fx:* Alexs Stadermann, Marek Kouchout, Dave MacDougall, Nilo Santillan; *back:* Beverley McNamara, Jerry Liew; *scene plan:* Daniel Forster; *Disney Anim—Burbank:* *clean-up:* Brett Newton, Scott Anderson, Debra Armstrong Holmes, Dorothea Baker Paul, Margie Daniels, Mike McKinney, Ginny Parmele, Terry Wozniak; *Phoenix Anim—Toronto:* *clean-up:* James McCrimmon; *inbet:* Peter Brown; *fx anim:* John Collins, Dan Brooks, Peter Brown, James Dawkins, Ian Mah, Raymond Pang, Paul Teolis, Darren Vandenberg, Steve Wood; *scanning sup:* Francois Desnus; *checking sup:* Bernard Dourdent; *col model cel painting:* Marie Boughamer, Yolanda Rearick; *digital col models:* Sophie Gauthier, Susan Hackett Dalipagic; *digital compositing/wedging:* Philippe Balmossiere, Nadine Baranton, Didier Bonifay, Pascal Jardin, Ivan Kassabov, Didier Levy, Miroslav Randjelovic, Claire Xavier; *Pixiebox Digital i&p: check:* Dominique Chazy, Frédéric Mauxion; *i&p:* Sylvie Attorresi, Anne Bozzi, Vincent Haqueberge Prod.; *management:* Nicile Guincêtre, Vincent Laporte, Margaux Murray, Jacques Pepiot; *lay:* David Gardner, David Dunnet, Paul Felix, Carol Police, Mark Swan; *back:* Barry Atkinson, Dennis Venizelos; *ed:* Gregory Perler; *(Paris)* Catherine Rascon; *prod des:* Fred Warter; *art dir:* Wendell Luebbe, Lawrence Leker; *storyboards:* Chris Ure, Steve Moore, John Norton, Viki Anderson, Andy Gaskill, Jim Kammerud, Enrique May, Carole Holliday, Darrell Rooney, Hank Tucker, Frans Vischer; *title des:* Deborah Ross Film design; *title anim:* Michael Curtis; *titles/opticals:* Buena Vista Visual Effects; *voices: Goofy:* Bill Farmer; *Max:* Jason Marsden; *Max's singing voice:* Aaron Lohr; *Roxanne:* Kellie Martin; *Stacey:* Jenna von Oy; *Pete:* Jim Cummings; *P.J.:* Rob Paulsen; *Principal Mazur:* Wallace Shawn; *Chad:* Joey Lawrence; *Lisa:* Julie Brown; *Big Foot:* Frank Welker; *Lester:* Kevin Lima; *Waitress:* Florence Stanley; *Miss Maples:* Jo Anne Worley; *Photo Studio Girl:* Brittany Alyse Smith; *Lester's Grinning Girl:* Robyn Richards; *Tourist Kid:* Klée Bragger; *Possum Park Emcee:* Pat Buttram; *Mickey Mouse:* Wayne Allwine; *Security Guard:* Herschel Sparber; *also:* Dante Basco, Sheryl Bernstein, Corey Burton, Pat Carroll, E.G. Daily, Carole Holliday, Steve Moore, Brian Pimental, Jason Willinger; *background vocals:* Danice Axelson, Nathan Carlson, Randy Crenshaw, Donna Davidson, Gary Falcone, Rosie Gaines, Scott Harlan, Linda Harmon, Scottie Haskell, Reece Holland, Luana Jackman, Nick Jameson, Robert Joyce, Michael Lanning, Rick Logan, Susan Logan, Susan McBride, Megan McGinnis, Bobbi Page, Jonathan Redford, Chad Reisser, Carmen Twillie, Julia Waters Tillman, Maxine Waters-Willard, Luther Waters, Oren Waters, Josh Weiner, Jimmie Wood; "Stand Out"/"121" performed by Tevin Campbell; "Lester's Possum Park" performed by Kevin Quinn; "High Hopes" performed by Rick Logan; *mus:* Carter Burwell; *score/orch:* Don Davis, Shirley Walker, Lolita Ritmanis, Bruce Fowler; *songs:* Tom Snow, Jack Feldman, Patrick DeRemer, Roy Freeland, Kevin Quinn; *mus asso prod:* Bambi Moé; *mix:* Michael Farrow, Armin Steiner; *mus ed:* Tom Carlson, Adam Smalley; *sd:* Mike Boudry, Wayne Heitman, Tom E. Dahl, Mel Metcalfe, David Stone; *sd fx:* Rick Freeman, Geoff Rubay, Steve Lee, Doc Kane, Gary Littell; *digital ADR:* Richard "Goofus" Corwin; *foley:* Joan Rowe, Dana Porter, Robert De-

schaine, Vanessa Theme Ament, Solange S. Schwalbe; *choreog:* Anthony Thomas; *col:* Tech. *sd:* Dolby digital stereo. 78 min. • Goofy tries to bridge the generation gap by taking his son, Max, on a fishing trip. Max would rather be with his girlfriend and makes excuses to get out of the trip. This causes many obstacles.

2603. Goofy News Views *(Phantasy)* 27 Apr. 1945; *p.c.:* Colum; *dir/story:* Sid Marcus; *anim:* Paul Sommer; *ed:* Richard S. Jensen; *lay:* Bill Weaver; *back:* Al Boggs; *voices:* Dave Barry; *mus:* Eddie Kilfeather; *ph:* Frank Fisher; *prod mgr:* Hugh McCollum; b&w. *sd:* WE. 6 min. • Parody on newsreels: From the launching of a ship to how to handle a card sharp.

2604. Goofy's Freeway Troubles 22 Sept. 1965; *p.c.:* Walt Disney prods for BV; *dir:* Les Clark; *asst dir:* Jim Swain; *story:* William R. Bosché; *anim:* Cliff Nordberg, Bob Youngquist, Bob McCrea, Les Clark; *fx:* Jack Boyd; *art dir:* A. Kendall O'Connor; *lay:* Ray Aragon; *back:* Walt Peregoy, Bill Layne; *voices:* Paul Frees, Pinto Colvig; *mus:* George Bruns; *asso prod:* Ken Peterson; *col:* Tech. *sd:* RCA. 14 min. aka: *Freeway-Phobia #2.* • With the able assistance of Goofy, we are instructed in freeway common sense.

2605. Goofy's Glider *(Goofy)* 22 Nov. 1940 *p.c.:* Walt Disney prods for RKO; *dir:* Jack Kinney; *asst dir:* Lou Debney; *story dir:* Ralph Wright, Jack Kinney; *anim:* Arthur Babbitt, George de Beeson, Richard McDermot, Frank Onaitis, Wolfgang Reitherman; *fx:* Jack Boyd, Andrew Engman, Jack Huber, Ed Parks, Reuben Timmens; *lay:* Leo Thiele; *voices:* John McLeish, George A. Johnson; *mus:* Charles Wolcott; *col:* Tech. *sd:* Vit. 7 min. • Goofy demonstrates how to fly a glider.

2606. Gooney Golfers *(Heckle & Jeckle)* 1 Dec. 1948; *p.c.:* TT for Fox; *dir:* Connie Rasinski; *story:* John Foster; *anim:* Jim Tyer; *voices:* Thomas Morrison; *mus:* Philip A. Scheib; *ph:* Douglas Moye; *col:* Tech. *sd:* RCA. 6 min • The magpies' home next to the golf course isn't as safe as they imagined, so they sabotage the golfer's game.

2607. A Gooney Is Born *(Chilly Willy)* 1971; *p.c.:* Walter Lantz prods for Univ; *dir:* Paul J. Smith; *anim:* Les Kline, Al Coe; *sets:* Nino Carbe; *voices:* Daws Butler; *mus:* Walter Greene; *prod mgr:* William E. Garity; *col:* Tech. *sd:* RCA. 5 min. • Chilly is left an orphan egg that hatches into the Gooney Bird. He then has to keep him from troubleshooter Colonel Potshot.

2608. Gooney's Goofy Landings *(Chilly Willy)* 2 Mar. 1970; *p.c.:* Walter Lantz prods for Univ; *dir:* Paul J. Smith; *story:* Dale Hale; *anim:* Les Kline, Al Coe; *Sets:* Nino Carbe; *voices:* Daws Butler; *mus:* Walter Greene; *prod mgr:* William E. Garity; *col:* Tech. *sd:* RCA. 5 min. • Chilly and Maxie teach the Looney Gooney Bird how to make a proper landing.

2609. Goonland *(Popeye)* 21 Oct. 1938 *p.c.:* The Fleischer Studio for Para; *prod:* Max Fleischer; *dir:* Dave Fleischer; *anim:* Seymour Kneitel, Abner Matthews; *voices:* Jack Mercer; *mus:* Sammy Timberg; b&w. *sd:* WE. 7 min. • Popeye sails to Goonland in search of his Pappy who is being held captive by it's strange inhabitants.

2610. Goons from the Moon *(Mighty Mouse)* May 1951; *p.c.:* TT for Fox; *dir:* Connie Rasinski; *story:* Tom Morrison; *anim:* Jim Tyer; *voices:* Roy Halee, Tom Morrison; *mus:* Philip A. Scheib; *ph:* Douglas Moye; *col:* Tech. *sd:* RCA. 7 min. • The artist draws Mighty Mouse just in time to save the Earth from outer-space invaders.

2611. Goopy Geer *(Merrie Melodies)* 30 Apr. 1932; *p.c.:* Hugh Harman, Rudolf Ising prods for WB; *prod:* Leon Schlesinger; *anim:* Isadore Freleng, Rollin Hamilton, Robert Clampett; *voices:* Johnny Murray, Mary Moder; *mus:* Frank Marsales; b&w. *sd:* Vit. 6 min. • The animal customers at a night club get the "D.T.'s" and envision fire-breathing dragons.

2612. The Goose Flies High *(Terry-Toon)* 9 Sept. 1938; *p.c.:* TT for Fox; *dir:* John Foster; *mus:* Philip A. Scheib; b&w. *sd:* RCA. 6 min. • Gandy Goose models himself on Charles Lindburgh and, encouraged by two George Givot and Bert Lahr types, takes to the air.

2613. The Goose Goes South *(MGM Cartoon)* 26 Apr. 1941; *p.c.:* MGM; *dir:* William Hanna, Joseph Barbera; *voices:* Truman Bradley, Cliff Nazarro, Mel Blanc, Sara Berner, Harry E. Lang; *mus:* Scott Bradley; *prod:* Fred Quimby; *col:* Tech. *sd:* WE. 9 min. • A small goose hitchhikes south.

2614. Goose in the Rough *(Beary Family)* 30 July 1963; *p.c.:* Walter Lantz prods for Univ; *dir:* Paul J. Smith; *story:* Al Bertino, Dick Kinney; *anim:* Les Kline, Al Coe; *sets:* Art Landy, Ray Huffine; *voices:* Paul Frees; *mus:* Darrell Calker; *prod mgr:* William E. Garity; *col:* Tech. *sd:* RCA. 6

min. • Goose Beary tries to hatch some golf balls, preventing Charlie from playing a round of golf.

2615. Goose Is Wild (*Beary Family*) Oct. 1963; *p.c.:* Walter Lantz prods for Univ; *dir:* Paul J. Smith; *story:* Al Bertino, Dick Kinney; *anim:* Les Kline, Al Coe; *Sets:* Art Landy, Ray Huffine; *voices:* Paul Frees, Grace Stafford; *mus:* Darrell Calker; *prod mgr:* William E. Garity; *col:* Tech. *sd:* RCA. 6 min. • Charlie's first victim for an economy drive is the family goose. To save his skin, Goose Beary convinces Charlie that he can lay golden eggs.

2616. The Goose That Laid a Golden Egg (*The Dogfather*) 4 Oct. 1974; *p.c.:* Mirisch/DFE for UA; *dir:* Hawley Pratt; *story:* Friz Freleng; *anim:* Bob Richardson, John V. Gibbs, Nelson Shin, Bob Bransford; *ed:* Rick Steward; *lay:* Dick Ung; *back:* Richard H. Thomas; *titles:* Arthur Leonardi; *voices:* Bob Holt, Daws Butler, Hazel Shermet; *mus:* Dean Elliott; *col:* DeLuxe. *sd:* RCA. 6 min. • The mob captures a chicken in the expectation of it laying a golden egg.

2617. The Goose That Laid the Golden Egg (*Aesop's Film Fable*) 19 June 1921; *p.c.:* Fables Pictures Inc for Pathé; *dir:* Paul Terry; b&w. *sil.* 5 min. • The farmer and his wife kill a goose that laid an 18-karat egg. The parallel drawn represents Labor and Capital killing the goose that lays the profits.

2618. Gopher Broke (*Beary Family*) 1969; *p.c.:* Walter Lantz prods for Univ; *dir:* Paul J. Smith; *story:* Cal Howard; *anim:* Les Kline, Al Coe; *sets:* Nino Carbe; *voices:* Paul Frees, Grace Stafford; *mus:* Walter Greene; *prod mgr:* William E. Garity; *col:* Tech. *sd:* RCA. 5 min. • Charlie attempts to rid his garden of a gopher.

2619. Gopher Broke (*Looney Tunes*) 15 Nov. 1958; *p.c.:* WB; *dir:* Robert McKimson; *story:* Tedd Pierce; *anim:* Warren Batchelder, Tom Ray, George Grandpré, Ted Bonnicksen; *lay:* Robert Gribbroek; *back:* William Butler; *ed:* Treg Brown; *voices:* Mel Blanc, Stan Freberg; *mus:* John Seely; *prod:* John W. Burton; *col:* Tech. *sd:* Vit. 7 min. • The Goofy Gophers have to get the watchdog out of the way while they raid the barn.

2620. Gopher Goofy (*Looney Tunes*) 20 June 1942; *p.c.:* Leon Schlesinger prods for WB; *dir/lay:* Norman McCabe; *story:* Don Christensen; *anim:* I. Ellis; John Carey, Cal Dalton, Arthur Davis, David Hoffman, Vive Risto; *sets:* Richard H. Thomas; *ed:* Treg Brown; *voices:* Mel Blanc; *mus:* Carl W. Stalling; *ph:* John W. Burton; *prod sup:* Henry Binder, Raymond G. Katz; b&w. *sd:* Vit. 6 min. • A farmer tries to rid his garden of a pair of crazy gophers, succeeding only in wrecking his lawn and his sanity.

2621. Gopher Spinach (*Popeye*) 10 Dec. 1954; *p.c.:* Famous for Para; *dir:* Seymour Kneitel; *story:* Carl Meyer; *anim:* Thomas Johnson, John Gentilella; *Sets:* Robert Connavale; *voice:* Jack Mercer; *mus:* Winston Sharples; *ph:* Leonard McCormick; *prod mgr:* Seymour Shultz; *col:* Tech. *sd:* RCA. 6 min. • A gopher ruins Popeye's spinach patch.

2622. Gopher Trouble (*Oswald*) 30 Nov. 1936; *p.c.:* Univ; *dir:* Walter Lantz; *story:* Walter Lantz, Victor McLeod; *anim:* Manuel Moreno, Fred Kopietz, George Nicholas; *mus:* James Dietrich; b&w. *sd:* WE. 6 min. • Oswald and Elmer help Henrietta Hen exterminate a pesty gopher. They succeed in wrecking the place with dynamite.

2623. The Gorilla Hunt (*Color Rhapsody*) 24 Feb. 1939; *p.c.:* Chaarles Mintz prods for Colum; *dir:* Ub Iwerks; *ed:* George Winkler; *voices:* Mel Blanc; *mus:* Eddie Kilfeather, Joe de Nat; *col:* Tech. *sd:* RCA. 8 min. • A big game hunt for a prize gorilla.

2624. Gorilla My Dreams (*Looney Tunes*) 3 Jan. 1948; *p.c.:* WB; *dir:* Robert McKimson; *story:* Warren Foster; *anim:* Charles McKimson, Manny Gould, John Carey; *lay:* Cornett Wood; *back:* Richard H. Thomas; *ed:* Treg Brown; *character des:* Jean Blanchard; *voices:* Mel Blanc; *mus:* Carl Stalling; *prod mgr:* John W. Burton; *prod:* Edward Selzer; *col:* Tech. *sd:* Vit. 7 min. • Shipwrecked on "The Land of Ferocious Apes," Bugs is adopted by a mother gorilla. Father ape has different ideas.

2625. The Gorilla Mystery (*Mickey Mouse*) 22 Sept. 1930; *p.c.:* Walter E. Disney for Colum; *dir:* Burton F. Gillett; *anim:* Charles Byrne, Johnny Cannon, Les Clark, Norman Ferguson, Burton F. Gillett, David D. Hand, Wilfred Jackson, Jack King, Richard Lundy, Tom Palmer, Ben Sharpsteen; *voices:* Marcellite Garner, Walt Disney; *mus:* Bert Lewis; *ph:* William Cottrell; b&w. *sd:* PCP. 7 min. • Mickey rushes to the rescue of Minnie who's been captured by an escaped gorilla.

2626. Graduation Day in Bugland 18 Feb. 1931; *p.c.:* Leon Schlesinger Prods. for Listerine; *prod:* Leon Schlesinger; b&w. *sd:* WE. • A little girl has a nightmare of hordes of germs filling the air. She awakens and her mother brings her Listerine to gargle with.

2627. Graduation Excercises (*Scrappy*); *p.c.:* Charles Mintz prods for Colum; *story:* Ben Harrison; *anim:* Manny Gould, Harry Love; *mus:* Joe de Nat; *prod mgr:* James Bronis; b&w. *sd:* RCA. 6 min. • Scrappy and Oopy pose as a bearded board member to get into school for their graduation exercises.

2628. Gramps to the Rescue (*Noveltoon*) Sept. 1963; *p.c.:* Para Cartoons; *dir:* Seymour Kneitel; *story:* Jack Mercer, I. Klein; *anim:* Morey Reden; *sets:* Robert Little; *voices:* Jack Mercer; *mus:* Winston Sharples; *ph:* Leonard McCormick; *prod mgr:* Abe Goodman; *col:* Tech. *sd:* RCA. 6 min. • Gramps the mouse arrives in New York from the Deep South and is shown around a Civil War Museum by Skit. Skat the cat follows them dressed as a Civil War soldier.

2629. Grampy's Indoor Outing (*Betty Boop*) 16 Oct. 1936; *p.c.:* The Fleischer Studio for Para; *prod:* Max Fleischer; *dir:* Dave Fleischer; *anim:* David Tendlar, William Sturm; *voices:* Mae Questel, Everett Clark; *mus:* Sammy Timberg; b&w. *sd:* WE. 7 min. • Betty and Junior can't go the carnival in the rain, so Grampy fixes up an indoor carnival.

2630. Grand Canyonscope (*Donald Duck*) 23 Oct. 1954; *p.c.:* Walt Disney prods for BV; *dir:* C. August Nichols; *story:* Milt Schaffer, Nick George; *anim:* John Sibley, Jerry Hathcock, Julius Svendsen, Ed Aardal, Charles A. Nichols; *fx:* Dan MacManus; *lay:* Lance Nolley; *back:* Eyvind Earle; *voices:* Bill Thompson, Clarence Nash; *mus:* Oliver Wallace; *col:* Tech. *sd:* RCA. 7 min. CS. • Donald causes havoc on a sightseeing tour of the Grand Canyon.

2631. Grand Prix Winner (*Sad Cat*) Sept. 1967; *p.c.:* TT for Fox; *dir:* Artie Bartsch; *col:* DeLuxe. *sd:* RCA. 5 min. • Sad Cat participates in a road race. • See: *Sad Cat*

2632. The Grand Uproar (*Talkartoons*) 4 Oct. 1930; *p.c.:* The Fleischer Studio for Para; *prod:* Max Fleischer; *dir:* Dave Fleischer; *anim:* Al Eugster; *mus:* Art Turkisher; b&w. *sd:* WE. 7 min. • A musical performance in an opera house that literally raises the roof.

2633. The Grand Uproar (*Paul Terry-Toons*) 25 Aug. 1933; *p.c.:* Moser & Terry for Educational/Fox; *dir:* Frank Moser, Paul Terry; *mus:* Philip A. Scheib; b&w. *sd:* WE. 6 min. • An all cat orchestra accompanies the mice's interpretation of "Romeo and Juliet" opera. A cat who tries to interfere gets pelted with fruit.

2634. Grandfather's Clock (*Burt Gillett's Toddle Tales*) 29 June 1934; *p.c.:* Van Beuren for RKO; *dir:* Burt Gillett, James Tyer; *anim:* I. Klein, Frank Little, William Littlejohn; *mus:* Winston Sharples; *l/a ph:* Harry E. Squires; b&w. *sd:* RCA. 10 min. *l/a/anim.* • Two children are about to mutilate a timepiece when the Grandfather's Clock says that if they leave it alone, he will tell them about Clock Village.

2635. Grandma's House (*Aesop's Film Fable*) 24 Feb. 1929; *p.c.:* Fables Pictures Inc for Pathé; *dir:* Paul Terry; b&w. *sil.* 5 min. • Little Rita Mouse substitutes for Red Riding Hood and the cat for the wolf. Rita is rescued from the cat's grasps by the arrival of her sweetie, Milton Mouse.

2636. Grandma's Pet (*Oswald*) 12 Jan. 1932; *p.c.:* Univ; *dir:* Walter Lantz, "Bill" Nolan; *anim:* Manuel Moreno, Ray Abrams, Fred Avery, Lester Kline, Vet Anderson; *mus:* James Dietrich; b&w. *sd:* WE. 8 min. • Oswald finds himself in the "Little Red Riding Hood" story but it turns out only to be a dream.

2637. Granite Hotel (*Stoneage*) 26 Apr. 1940; *p.c.:* The Fleischer Studio for Para; *prod:* Max Fleischer; *dir:* Dave Fleischer; *story:* George Manuel; *anim:* Thomas Johnson, Graham Place; *ed:* Kitty Pfister; *character des:* Charles Thorson; *voices:* Jack Mercer, Margie Hines; *mus:* Sammy Timberg; *ph:* Charles Schettler; b&w. *sd:* WE. 7 min. • The telephone operator insists, "Nothing ever happens at the Granite!" in the midst of all the chaos.

2638. Grape Nutty (*Phantasy*) 14 Apr. 1949; *p.c.:* Colum; *prod:* Raymond Katz, Henry Binder; *dir:* Alex Lovy; *story:* Cal Howard, Dave Monahan; *anim:* Chic Otterstrom, Paul Sommer, Jay Sarbry; *lay:* Jim Carmichael; *back:* Al Boggs; *ed:* Richard S. Jensen; *voice:* Patrick J. McGeehan; *mus:* Darrell Calker; *col:* Tech. *sd:* WE. 6 min. • The Fox and Crow come to blows over one solitary grape.

2639. The Graphic *(Sketchographs)*; *p.c.:* Kinograms Publishing Co for Educational; *anim:* Julian Ollendorff; *ph:* Herbert M. Dawley; b&w. *sil.* • Artist Ollendorff draws scenes which fade into items for the live-action magazine. • *1921:* **Just for Fun** 16 Sept. • *1922:* **Famous Men** 21 Oct. **Athletics and Women** 28 Oct. **Champions** 4 Nov. **Animals and Husbands** 11 Nov. **Mackerel Fishing** 2 Dec. **The Coastguard** 16 Dec. • *1923:* **Family Album** 8 Jan. (Further eleven titles in this series untraced). • *1926:* distributed by Cranfield and Clarke. **Beauty and the Beach** 1 Sept. **Everybody Rides** 15 Sept. **Fair Weather** 1 Oct. **The Big Show** 15 Oct. **Watch Your Step** 1 Nov. **Revolution of the Sexes** 15 Nov. **Tin Pan Alley** 1 Dec. (Further five *titles* in this series untraced)

2640. The Grasshopper and the Ants *(Silly Symphony)* 10 Feb. 1934; *p.c.:* Walt Disney prods for UA; *dir:* Wilfred Jackson; *story:* William Cottrell, Larry Morey, Joe Grant; *anim:* Arthur Babbitt, Gilles de Tremaudan, Jack Hannah, Dick Huemer, Richard Lundy, Hamilton S. Luske, William O. Roberts, Louis Schmitt, Leonard Sebring, Ed Smith. *fx:* Cy Young; *lay/des:* Albert Hurter; *back:* Emil Flohri; *voice:* Pinto Colvig; *mus:* Leigh Harline; *lyrics:* Larry Morey; *col:* Tech. *sd:* RCA. 8 min. • The industrious ants garner food for the Winter while the Grasshopper plays his fiddle. When Winter comes, he seeks succor with the ants who will only let him in if he earns shelter by playing his fiddle.

2641. Grateful Gus *(Noveltoon)* 7 Mar. 1958; *p.c.:* Para Cartoons; *dir:* Dave Tendlar; *story:* Irving Spector; *anim:* Charles Harriton, Nick Tafuri; *Sets:* Robert Little; *voices:* Maurice Gosfield, Jackson Beck; *mus:* Winston Sharples; *prod mgr:* Abe Goodman; *col:* Tech. *sd:* RCA. 6 min. • A bank teller steals a case of money and over-tips a panhandler who follows him to the ends of the earth in gratitude.

2642. Grease 13 June 1978; *p.c.:* Para; *main title anim:* John Wilson; *end title des:* Wayne Fitzgerald; *col:* Tech. *sd:* Dolby sound. 2³/₄ min. Panavision. • Animated credits for the high school musical. The credits show caricatures of the featured players driving past billboards containing relevant film credits.

2643. Grease II 11 June 1982; *p.c.:* United International Pictures for Para; *title des:* Wayne Fitzgerald; *col:* Metrocolor. *sd:* Dolby sound. Panavision. • Animated credits for the high school musical.

2644. The Great American Chase 30 Sept. 1979; *p.c.:* Chuck Jones for WB; *prod/dir:* Chuck Jones; *story:* Michael Maltese, Chuck Jones; *anim:* Phil Monroe, Ben Washam, Ken Harris, Abe Levitow, Dick Thompson, Lloyd Vaughan, Tom Ray; *prod des:* Maurice Noble; *back:* Phil de Guard, Bob Gribbroek; *ed:* Treg Brown; *graphics:* Don Foster; *voices:* Mel Blanc, June Foray; *mus:* Carl Stalling, Milt Franklyn; *Bugs at Home;* *co-dir:* Phil Monroe; *sup:* Lloyd Vaughan; *anim:* Virgil Ross, Lloyd Vaughan, Phil Monroe, Manny Perez, Irv Anderson; *lay:* Ray Aragon; *back:* Irv Wyner; *ed:* Horta Editorial; *mus:* Dean Elliott; *prod sup:* Marion Dern, Mary Roscoe; *col:* Tech. *sd:* Vit. 97 min. • Seq: *Hareway to the Stars; Duck Dodgers in the 24¹/₂th Century; Robin Hood Daffy; A Duck Amuck; Bully for Bugs; Ali Baba Bunny; Rabbit Fire; For Scent-imental Reasons; Longhaired Hare; What's Opera Doc?; Operation: Rabbit.* • Bugs shows the audience around his mansion and tells us about his career, illustrated with some of his best loved films. In addition a collection of Road-Runner gags are also shown. • aka: *The Bugs Bunny/Road-Runner Movie.*

2645. A Great Big Bunch of You *(Merrie Melodies)* 9 Jan. 1933; *p.c.:* Hugh Harman, Rudolf Ising prods for WB; *prod:* Leon Schlesinger; *anim:* Rollin Hamilton, Thomas McKimson, Robert Clampett; *voices:* John T. Murray, The Rhythmettes; *mus:* Frank Marsales; *song:* Harry Warren; b&w. *sd:* Vit. 7 min. • A disregarded dummy on a city dump livens up the place with his imitations and piano playing, bringing other items to life.

2646. The Great Bird Mystery *(Scrappy)* 20 Oct. 1932; *p.c.:* Winkler for Colum; *prod:* Charles Mintz; *story:* Dick Huemor; *anim:* Sid Marcus, Art Davis; *mus:* Joe de Nat; *prod mgr:* James Bronis; b&w. *sd:* RCA. 6 min. • Scrappy takes care of a bird who has been framed by Cock Robin. The jury finds Cock Robin to be alive and the case is dismissed.

2647. The Great Carrot Train Robbery *(Merrie Melodies)* 25 Jan. 1969; *p.c.:* WB; *dir:* Bob McKimson; *story:* Cal Howard; *anim:* Ted Bonnicksen, La Verne Harding, Jim Davis, Ed Solomon; *lay:* Bob Givens; *back:* Bob Abrams; *ed:* Hal Geer; *voices:* Mel Blanc, Pat Woodell, Billy Strange; *mus:* William Lava; *prod:* William L. Hendricks; *col:* Tech. *sd:* Vit. 6 min. • Bunny and Claude rob a train of its contents of carrots and when the Sheriff finally catches them, his horse eats the evidence.

2648. The Great Cheese Mystery *(Fable)* 27 Oct. 1941; *p.c.:* Colum; *dir/anim:* Art Davis; *prod/story:* Tish-Tash (Frank Tashlin); *sets:* Clark Watson; *ed:* Edward Moore; *voices:* Mel Blanc; *mus:* Paul Worth; *ph:* Frank Fisher; *prod mgr:* Ben Schwalb; b&w. *sd:* RCA. 6 min. • Two mice devise a way to raid the refrigerator from under the watchful eye of the cat.

2649. Le Great Dane Robbery *(Inspector)* 1968; *p.c.:* Mirisch/Geoffrey/DFE for UA; *dir:* Gerry Chiniquy; *story:* Jim Ryan; *anim:* Manny Gould, Chuck Downs, Bob Matz, Manny Perez, Don Williams; *lay:* Dick Ung; *back:* Tom O'Loughlin; *ed:* Lee Gunther; *voices:* Pat Harrington Jr., Marvin Miller; *mus:* Walter Greene; *theme tune:* Henry Mancini; *ph:* John Burton Jr.; *prod sup:* Harry Love, David De Tiege; *col:* DeLuxe. *sd:* Vit. 6 min. • The Inspector's attempts to retrieve a code book from a foreign embassy guarded by a ferocious watchdog.

2650. The Great De Gaulle Stone Robbery *(Inspector)* 21 Dec. 1965; *p.c.:* Mirisch-Geoffrey/DFE for UA; *dir:* Gerry Chiniquy; *story:* John W. Dunn; *anim:* Manny Perez, Don Williams, Bob Matz, Warren Batchelder, Norm McCabe, George Grandpré; *sets:* T.M. Yakutis; *ed:* Lee Gunther; *voices:* Pat Harrington Jr., Paul Frees, Larry Storch; *mus:* William Lava; *theme tune:* Henry Mancini; *prod mgr:* Bill Orcutt; *col:* DeLuxe. *sd:* RCA. 6 min. • The Inspector guards a precious diamond that gets stolen by a three-headed villain.

2651. The Great Experiment *(Scrappy)* 25 July 1934; *p.c.:* Winkler for Colum; *prod:* Charles Mintz; *story:* Sid Marcus; *anim:* Art Davis; *mus:* Joe de Nat; *prod mgr:* James Bronis; b&w. *sd:* RCA. 7 min. • A mad scientist injects Scrappy and Oopy with a serum of perpetual youth. They arrive in the future where they rescue Marjie from a monster. They awake to find it was all a dream.

2652. The Great Explorers *(Aesop's Film Fable)* 19 July 1923; *p.c.:* Fables Pictures Inc for Pathé; *dir:* Paul Terry; b&w. *sil.* 5 min. • After a hunting expedition, the cat returns with an elephant's tusk but the mouse has a full boatload of animals.

2653. Great Guns *(Oswald the Lucky Rabbit)* 17 Oct. 1927; *p.c.:* Winkler for Univ; *dir:* Walt Disney; *anim:* Walt Disney, Rollin Hamilton, Norman Blackburn, Hugh Harman, Paul J. Smith, Isadore Freleng, Ben Clopton; *i&p:* Les Clark; *ph:* Mike Marcus; b&w. *sil.* 4 min. *sd reissue:* 29 Feb. 1932. • Our hero sees action in the trenches.

2654. Great Moments in Football 1928. *prod:* "Chick" Meehan; *anim seq:* George V. Stallings; *ed:* W.B. Hanna. b&w. *sil.* 1 reel each. • Describing four football games of the past season with animated game plays: (1) **Nebraska vs. NYU;** (2) **Yale vs. Princeton;** (3) **Georgia Tech. vs. Georgia;** (4) **Notre Dame vs. Southern Cal.**

2655. The Great Mouse Detective 2 July 1986; *p.c.:* Walt Disney Prods. for Silver Screen Partners II; *dir:* John Musker, Ron Clements, Dave Michener, Burny Mattinson; *prod:* Burny Mattinson; based on the book *Basil of Baker Street* by Eve Titus; *asst dir:* Timothy O'Donnell, Mark A. Hester; *scr:* Pete Young, Steve Hulett, John Musker, Matthew O'Callaghan, Dave Michener, Vance Gerry, Ron Clements, Bruce M. Morris, Burny Mattinson, Melvin Shaw; *anim sup:* Mark Henn, Glen Keane, Robert Minkoff, Hendel Butoy; *anim consultant:* Eric Larson; *col style:* Jim Coleman; *anim:* Matthew O'Callaghan, Ruben A. Aquino, Kathy Zielinski, Phil Nibbelink, Phil Young, Ron Husband, Rick Farmiloe, Sandra Borgmeyer, Barry Temple, Ed Gombert, Mike Gabriel, Jay Jackson, Doug Krohn, Andreas Deja, Shawn Keller, Joseph Lanzisero, David Pruiksma, Cyndee Whitney, David Block, Steven P. Gordon, Tony Anselmo, Reed Cardwell, Wesley Chun, Brian Clift, Jesus Cortes, Retta Davidson, Anthony DeRosa, Barbara W. DeRosa, Stephen Hickner, Richard Hoppe, Martin Korth, Jeffrey Lynch, Michael G. McKinney, David Pacheco, Tina Price, Ruben Procopio, Natasha D. Selfridge, David Stephan, Jane Tucker, Lureline Weatherly, Stephan Zupkas, Denise Ford, Gail Frank, June M. Fujimoto, Terry Hamada, Ray Harris, Gilda Palinginis, Maria Rosetti, Toby Shelton, Kaaren Spooner, Rusty Stoll, Peggy Tonkondgy, Kirk Wise, Ellen Woodbury; *anim fx:* Ted C. Kierscey, Dave Bossert, Kelvin Yasuda, Patricia Peraza, Mark Dindal, Rolando B. Mercado, Steve Starr, John Tucker; *co-ord:* Tom Ferriter, Chuck Williams, Dave Suding, Walt Stanchfield, Bill Berg; *art dir:* Guy Vasilovich; *lay:* Dan Hensen, Karen A. Keller, Michael A. Peraza Jr., David A. Dunnet, Gil Dicicco, Edward L. Ghertner, Rasoul Azadani, Mark G. Kalesniko, Dan McHugh, Elyse Pastel, Jennifer Yuan; *back:* Donald A. Towns, John Emerson, Michael Humphries, Andrew

Phillipson, Lisa L. Keene, Brian Sebern, Tia Kratter, Philip Phillipson; *ed:* Roy M. Brewer Jr., James Melton; *break/inbet:* Scott Anderson, Judith Barnes, Edward B. Goral, Peter A. Gullerud, Christine Harding, Michael Horowitz, Marcia Y. Kimura, Mona Koth, Christine Liffers, Stephen L. Lubin, David P. Martin, Brian McKim, Edward Murrieta, Terry Naughton, Lori M. Noda, Dan Tanaka, Alex Topete, Cathy Zar; *i&p:* Gretchen L. Albrecht, Bill Brazner, Janet Bruce, Hortensia M. Casagran, Carmen Sanderson, Betty Shark, Penny Campsie, Ginni Mack, *col models:* Cindy Finn, Debbie Jorgensborg, Sylvia Roemer, Brigitte Strother; *voices: Professor Ratigan:* Vincent Price; *Basil/Bartholomew:* Barrie Ingham; *Dr. David Q. Dawson:* Val Bettin; *Olivia Flaversham:* Susan Pollatschek; *Fidget:* Candy Candido; *Mrs. Judson:* Diana Chesney; *The Mouse Queen:* Eve Brenner; *Flaversham:* Alan Young; *Sherlock Holmes:* Basil Rathbone; *Dr. Watson:* Laurie Main; *Lady Mouse:* Shani Wallis; *Barmaid:* Ellen Fitzhugh; *Citizen:* Walker Edmiston; *Thug Guards:* Wayne Allwine, Val Bettin, Tony Anselmo, Walker Edmiston; *Leslie:* Wayne Allwine; *mus:* Henry Mancini; *mus ed:* Jack Wadsworth; *songs:* "The World's Greatest Criminal Mind" by Henry Mancini, Larry Grossman, Ellen Fitzhugh; "Let Me Be Good to You" by/performed by Melissa Manchester; *scene plan:* Glenn Higa, Richard T. Sullivan; *ph:* Ed Austin; *cgi:* Tad A. Gielow; *col:* DeLuxe. *sd:* Todd-AO/Glen Glenn Sound/Dolby stereo. 74 min. • Basil, a mouse contemporary of Sherlock Holmes, searches for young Olivia's toymaker father who has been kidnapped by Basil's archenemy, Professor Ratigan. Flaversham, the toymaker, is being forced to create a robot replica of the Mouse Queen to help the evil Ratigan dominate the mouse world. Some computer animation.

2656. The Great Open Spaces (*Aesop's Film Fable*) 21 Nov. 1925; *p.c.:* Fables Pictures Inc for Pathé; *dir:* Paul Terry; b&w. sil. 10 min. • A western parody involving the hero and villain fight it out on a clifftop. Moral: "A young man should not have a girl on his lap unless he can support her."

2657. The Great Overland Cross-Country Race (*Roland & Rattfink*) 23 May 1971; *p.c.:* Mirisch/DFE for UA; *dir:* Art Davis; *story:* John W. Dunn; *anim:* Robert Taylor, Don Williams, Warren Batchelder, Manny Gould, Bob Richardson, Manny Perez; *lay:* Dick Ung; *back:* Richard H. Thomas; *ed:* Lee Gunther; *voices:* Leonard Weinrib; *mus:* Doug Goodwin; *prod sup:* Jim Foss, Harry Love; *col:* DeLuxe. *sd:* RCA. 5 min. • Roland and Rattfink compete in a road race.

2658. The Great Piggy Bank Robbery (*Looney Tunes*) 27 July 1946; *p.c.:* WB; *dir:* Robert Clampett; *asst dir/back:* Michael Sasanoff; *story:* Warren Foster, Hubie Karp; *anim:* Rod Scribner, Manny Gould, J.C. Melendez, I. Ellis; *lay:* Thomas McKimson; *ed:* Treg Brown; *voices:* Mel Blanc; *mus:* Carl W. Stalling; *prod mgr:* John W. Burton; *prod:* Edward Selzer; *col:* Tech. *sd:* Vit. 7 min. • Avid Dick Tracy fan Daffy assumes the role of "Duck Twacy" and goes on the trail of a piggy bank thief. Bizarre Chester Gould–style villains try to erase our hero.

2659. The Great Rupert 1949; *p.c.:* George Pal prods for Eagle-Lion; *prod/dir:* George Pal; *anim:* John S. Abbott, Fred Madison; *l/a dir:* Irving Pichel; b&w. *sd:* 87 min. *l/a/anim.* • Jimmy Durante comedy about a squirrel (stop-motion animation) who finds some hidden money.

2660. The Great Who-Dood-It (*Woody Woodpecker*) 20 Oct. 1952; *p.c.:* Walter Lantz prods for Univ; *dir:* Don Patterson; *story:* Homer Brightman; *anim:* La Verne Harding, Paul Smith, Ray Abrams; *Sets:* Fred Brunish; *voices:* Dallas McKennon, Grace Stafford; *mus:* Clarence Wheeler; *prod mgr:* William E. Garity; *col:* Tech. *sd:* RCA. 6 min. • Woody upsets Buzz Buzzard's patent medicine act and flees for his life through a fairground, posing as a magician en route.

2661. The Greatest Man in Siam (*Swing Symphony*) 27 Mar. 1944; *p.c.:* Walter Lantz prods for Univ; *dir:* James Culhane; *story:* Ben Hardaway, Milt Schaffer; *anim:* Pat Matthews, Emery Hawkins; *lay:* Art Heinemann; *back:* Phil de Guard; *voices:* Harry E. Lang; *mus:* Darrell Calker; *song:* Delmar Porter; *prod mgr:* George Hall; *col:* Tech. *sd:* WE. 7 min. • A wealthy potentate offers his daughter's hand to "The Greatest Man" who turns out to be a jazz trumpeter.

2662. Greedy for Tweety (*Looney Tunes*) 28 Sept. 1957; *p.c.:* WB; *dir:* Friz Freleng; *story:* Warren Foster; *anim:* Gerry Chiniquy, Art Davis, Virgil Ross; *lay:* Hawley Pratt; *back:* Boris Gorelick; *ed:* Treg Brown; *voices:* Mel Blanc, June Foray; *mus:* Milt Franklyn; *prod:* John W. Burton; *col:* Tech. *sd:* Vit. 7 min. • Sylvester, Tweety and a bulldog are all patients in an animal hospital. Sylvester still pursues Tweety even though his leg is in a cast.

2663. Greedy Gabby Gator (*Woody Woodpecker*) Jan. 1963; *p.c.:* Walter Lantz prods for Univ; *dir:* Sid Marcus; *story:* Milt Schaffer; *anim:* Ray Jacobs, Roy Jenkins, Art Davis; *sets:* Art Landy, Ray Huffine; *voices:* Daws Butler, Grace Stafford; *mus:* Walter Greene; *prod mgr:* William E. Garity; *col:* Tech. *sd:* RCA. 6 min. • Gabby Gator convinces Woody that he needs a holiday at Gabby's Health Resort, where all the activities are geared to cook our hero.

2664. Greedy Humpty Dumpty (*Color Classic*) 10 July 1936; *p.c.:* The Fleischer Studio for Para; *prod:* Max Fleischer; *dir:* Dave Fleischer; *anim:* David Tendlar, William Sturm; *voice:* Mae Questel; *mus:* Sammy Timberg; *song:* Sammy Timberg, Bob Rothberg; *col:* Tech-2. *sd:* WE. 8 min. • The greedy ruler of Mother Goose Land believes there to be gold secreted in the sun and forces his citizens to build a wall high enough to reach it. They do and he has a monumental downfall.

2665. Greek Mirthology (*Popeye*) 13 Aug. 1954; *p.c.:* Famous for Para; *dir:* Seymour Kneitel; *story:* I. Klein; *anim:* Tom Golden, George Germanetti; *sets:* Anton Loeb; *voices:* Jack Mercer, Jackson Beck; *mus:* Winston Sharples; *ph:* Leonard McCormick; *prod mgr:* Seymour Shultz; *col:* Tech. *sd:* RCA. 7 min. • In order to get his nephews to eat their spinach, Popeye tells of how his ancestor beat the mighty Hercules by eating the vegetable.

2666. The Green Line (*Mighty Mouse*) 7 July 1944; *p.c.:* TT for Fox; *dir:* Eddie Donnelly; *story:* John Foster; *anim:* Vladimir Tytla; *voice:* Thomas Morrison; *mus:* Philip A. Scheib; *col:* Tech. *sd:* RCA. 7 min. • A broad green line divides The Village of Nowhere between the cats and the mice.

2667. The Greener Yard (*Donald Duck*) 28 Oct. 1948; *p.c.:* Walt Disney prods for RKO; *dir:* Jack Hannah; *story:* Bill Berg, Milt Banta; *anim:* Volus Jones, Judge Whitaker, Bill Justice, Bob Carlson; *fx:* Dan MacManus, Jack Boyd; *lay:* Yale Gracey; *back:* Ralph Hulett; *voices:* Francis "Dink" Trout, Clarence Nash; *mus:* Oliver Wallace; *col:* Tech. *sd:* RCA. 7 min. • Grandpa Bootle Beetle tells a younger one how he once strayed into Donald Duck's back yard in search of adventure.

2668. Greetings Bait (*Merrie Melodies*) 15 May 1943; *p.c.:* Leon Schlesinger prods for WB; *dir:* I. Freleng; *story:* Ted Pierce; *anim:* Manuel Perez; *lay:* Owen Fitzgerald; *back:* Lenard Kester; *ed:* Treg Brown; *voices:* Mel Blanc; *mus:* Carl W. Stalling; *ph:* John W. Burton; *prod sup:* Henry Binder, Raymond G. Katz; *col:* Tech. *sd:* Vit. 7 min. *Academy Award nomination.* • A Jerry Colonna–like worm finds employment by being bait on a fisherman's line.

2669. Gremlins 2: The New Batch 15 June 1990; *p.c.:* Amblin Entertainment for WB; *Bugs Bunny & Daffy Duck anim:* Chuck Jones; *stop-motion anim:* Doug Beswick Prods.; *voices: Mohawk:* Frank Welker; *Gremlins:* Kirk Thatcher, Mark Dodson; *Announcer:* Neil Ross; *Bugs Bunny/Daffy Duck:* Jeff Bergman; *Gizmo:* Howie Mandel; *"Brain" Gremlin:* Tony Randall; *original cartoon mus:* Fred Steiner; *col:* Tech. *sd:* Dolby stereo. 106 min. *l/a.* • Live-action fantasy sequel: The strange Mogwai creatures help to foil a plan to erect a futuristic complex in Chinatown.

2670. The Greyhound and the Rabbit (*Color Rhapsody*) 19 Apr. 1940; *p.c.:* Colum; *story:* Sid Marcus; *anim:* Art Davis, Herb Rothwill; *sets:* Phil Davis; *ed:* George Winkler; *voices:* Gil Warren; *mus:* Joe de Nat; *ph:* Otto Reimer; *prod mgr:* James Bronis; *col:* Tech. 8 min. • An insight into greyhound racing.

2671. The Greyhounded Hare (*Merrie Melodies*) 6 Aug. 1949; *p.c.:* WB; *dir:* Robert McKimson; *story:* Warren Foster; *anim:* John Carey, Charles McKimson, Phil de Lara, Manny Gould; *lay:* Cornett Wood; *back:* Richard H. Thomas; *character des:* Jean Blanchard; *ed:* Treg Brown; *voices:* Mel Blanc; *mus:* Carl Stalling; *prod mgr:* John W. Burton; *prod:* Edward Selzer; *col:* Tech. *sd:* Vit. 7 min. • Bugs tries to make amorous advances to the electric rabbit at the greyhound race track.

2672. Gridiron Demons (*Aesop's Film Fable*) 4 Oct. 1928; *p.c.:* Fables Pictures Inc for Pathé; *dir:* Frank Moser, Paul Terry; b&w. sil. 10 min. • An Army–Navy ball game with the mice representing the Navy and Al Falfa's cohorts on behalf of the Army in the lineup. The goat scores a touchdown.

2673. Grin and Bear It (*Donald Duck*) 9 Apr. 1954; *p.c.:* Walt Disney prods for RKO; *dir:* Jack Hannah; *story:* Dave DeTiege, Al Bertino; *anim:* Bob Carlson, Al Coe, Bill Justice, Volus Jones; *fx:* Dan MacManus; *lay:* Yale Gracey; *back:* Ray Huffine; *voices:* Bill Thompson, Clarence Nash, Dal McKennon; *mus:* Oliver Wallace; *col:* Tech. *sd:* RCA. 7 min. • The Brownstone National Park bears are warned by the Ranger not to steal picnic food ... however, one bear can't resist the urge.

2674. Grin and Share It (*Droopy*) 17 May 1957; *p.c.:* MGM; *prod:* William Hanna, Joseph Barbera; *dir:* Michael Lah; *anim:* Irven Spence, Herman Cohen, Bill Schipek, Ken Southworth; *lay/character des:* Ed Benedict; *back:* F. Montealegre; *ed:* Jim Faris; *voices:* Bill Thompson; *mus:* Scott Bradley; *ph:* Jack Stevenson; *prod mgr:* Hal Elias; *col:* Tech. *sd:* WE. 6 min. CS. • Droopy and Butch are 50-50 partners in a mine but when gold is discovered, Butch tries to dissolve the partnership by eliminating his partner.

2675. Grizzly Golfer (*Mr. Magoo*) 20 Dec. 1951; *p.c.:* UPA for Colum; *ex prod:* Stephen Bosustow; *prod:* John Hubley; *dir:* Pete Burness; *story:* Bill Scott, Bill Danch; *anim:* Rudy Larriva, Art Babbitt, Cecil Surry; *lay:* Abe Liss; *back:* Paul Julian; *voices:* Jim Backus, Jerry Hausner; *mus:* Hoyt Curtin; *prod mgr:* Herb Klynn; *col:* Tech. *sd:* RCA. 7 min. • Magoo arrives in the Ozarks for a game of golf where he mistakes a bear for Waldo. The game is terminated by feuding hillbillies.

2676. The Grocery Boy (*Mickey Mouse*); 8 Feb. 1932; *p.c.:* Walter E. Disney for Colum; *dir:* Wilfred Jackson; *anim:* Johnny Cannon, Les Clark, Gilles de Tremaudan, Clyde Geronimi, David D. Hand, Albert Hurter, Jack King, Richard Lundy, Tom Palmer, Ben Sharpsteen, Rudy Zamora; *asst anim:* Andrew Hutchinson, Harry Reeves; *voices:* Marcellite Garner, Walt Disney; *mus:* Frank E. Churchill; b&w. *sd:* PCP. 7 min. • Mickey delivers Minnie's groceries and Pluto grabs the turkey.

2677. Ground Hog Play (*Casper*) 10 Feb. 1956; *p.c.:* Famous for Para; *dir:* Seymour Kneitel; *story:* Larz Bourne; *anim:* Tom Golden, Bill Hudson; *Sets:* Robert Connavale; *voices:* Norma MacMillan, Gwen Davies; *mus:* Winston Sharples; *ph:* Leonard McCormick; *prod mgr:* Seymour Shultz; *col:* Tech. *sd:* RCA. 6 min. • Presented in comic strip form, Casper poses as Hillary Groundhog's shadow.

2678. Growing Pains (*Terry Bears*) Dec. 1953; *p.c.:* TT for Fox; *dir:* Eddie Donnelly; *story:* Tom Morrison; *anim:* Jim Tyer; *voices:* Douglas Moye, Tom Morrison, Philip A. Scheib; *mus:* Philip A. Scheib; *ph:* Douglas Moye; *col:* Tech. *sd:* RCA. 6 min. • Papa and the kids have a problem in keeping rabbits and weeds out of their garden.

2679. A Gruesome Twosome (*Merrie Melodies*) 26 May 1945; *p.c.:* WB; *dir:* Robert Clampett; *story:* Warren Foster; *anim:* Bob McKimson, Manny Gould, Rod Scribner, Basil Davidovich; *fx:* A.C. Gamer; *lay/character des:* Thomas McKimson; *back:* Michael Sasanoff; *ed:* Treg Brown; *voices:* Mel Blanc, Sara Berner; *mus:* Carl W. Stalling; *prod mgr:* John W. Burton; *prod:* Edward Selzer; *col:* Tech. *sd:* Vit. 7 min. • Two cats fight over capturing Tweety for the affections of a pretty girl cat.

2680. Guest Who (*Beary Family*) Mar. 1965; *p.c.:* Walter Lantz prods for Univ; *dir:* Paul J. Smith; *story:* Cal Howard; *anim:* Les Kline, Al Coe; *sets:* Art Landy, Ray Huffine; *voices:* Paul Frees, Grace Stafford; *mus:* Walter Greene; *prod mgr:* William E. Garity; *col:* Tech. *sd:* RCA. 6 min. • Junior wins a pet monkey in a dance contest and has to keep it out of Charlie's way when he returns home.

2681. A Guide for the Married Man 1967; *p.c.:* Fox; *col:* DeLuxe. *sd:* WE. • Live-action feature about infidelities between married couples. The animated opening depicts men cheating on their wives over the centuries.

2682. Guided Mouse-ille (*Tom & Jerry*) 1966; *p.c.:* MGM; *prod:* Chuck Jones; *dir:* Abe Levitow; *story:* John Dunn; *anim:* Don Towsley, Tom Ray, Dick Thompson, Ben Washam, Philip Roman; *des:* Maurice Noble; *lay:* Don Morgan; *back:* Thelma Witmer; *mus:* Eugene Poddany; *prod mgr:* Les Goldman; *col:* Metro. *sd:* WE. 7 min. • A space-age Tom and Jerry exercise their feuding through cat and mouse robots.

2683. Guided Muscle (*Looney Tunes*) 10 Dec. 1955; *p.c.:* WB; *dir:* Chuck Jones; *story:* Michael Maltese; *anim:* Richard Thompson, Ken Harris, Ben Washam, Abe Levitow; *lay:* Philip de Guard; *back:* Richard H. Thomas; *ed:* Treg Brown; *voice:* Paul Julian; *mus:* Carl Stalling; *prod mgr:* John W. Burton; *prod:* Edward Selzer; *col:* Tech. *sd:* Vit. 7 min. • The Coyote's attempts to improve his speed to capture the Road-Runner consist of an arrow head attached to the nose, liberally-spread Acme Axel Grease on his feet, finally resorting to a book, "How to Tar and Feather a Road-Runner" ... without too much luck.

2684. The Gullible Canary (*Phantasy*) 18 Sept. 1942; *p.c.:* Colum; *prod:* Dave Fleischer; *dir:* Alec Geiss; *story:* Frank Tashlin; *anim:* Chic Otterstrom; *voices:* Harry E. Lang, Dick Nelson, Sara Berner; *mus:* Eddie Kilfeather; *prod mgr:* Albert Spar; b&w. *sd:* RCA. 6 min. • A swallow pursuades a canary to vacate his cage and fly south for the winter. He soon returns for his home comforts with a southern belle for a wife.

2685. Gulliver Mickey (*Mickey Mouse*) 19 May 1934; *p.c.:* Walt Disney prods for UA; *dir:* Burton F. Gillett; *anim:* Arthur Babbitt, Johnny Cannon, Les Clark, Joseph d'Igalo, Ugo d'Orsi, Norman Ferguson, Jack Hannah, Richard Lundy, Hamilton S. Luske, William O. Roberts, Ben Sharpsteen; *fx:* Cy Young; *voices:* Marcellite Garner, Walt Disney, William E. Sheets; *mus:* Frank E. Churchill; b&w. *sd:* RCA. 7 min. • Mickey spins a yarn to his nephews of when he was shipwrecked and captured by tiny people. He breaks free and does battle with a giant spider.

2686. Gulliver's Travels 22 Dec. 1939; *p.c.:* The Fleischer Studio for Para; *prod:* Max Fleischer; *dir:* Dave Fleischer; *story adapt:* Edmund Seward, Dan Gordon, Cal Howard, Ted Pierce, I. Sparber; *anim dir:* Seymour Kneitel, Willard Bowsky, Tom Palmer, Grim Natwick, William Henning, Roland Crandall, Tom Johnson, Robert Leffingwell, Frank Kelling, Winfield Hoskins, Orestes Calpini; *anim:* Els Barthen, Robert Bentley, Ben Clopton, James Culhane, James Davis, Nelson Demorest, Joseph d'Igalo, Ted Dubois, Frank Endres, Alfred Eugster, Vince Fago, Otto Feuer, George Germanetti, Arnold Gillespie, Reuben Grossman, Thurston Harper, Abner Kneitel, Joe Miller, George Moreno, Stephen Muffatti, Bill Nolan, Joseph Oriolo, Tony Pabian, Graham Place, Stan Quackenbush, Edwin Rehberg, Lod Rossner, Gordon Sheehan, Edward Smith, Frank Smith, Irving Spector, Sam Stimson, William Sturm, Nicholas Tafuri, Harold Walker; Lou Zukor; *sets:* Louis Jambor, Robert Little, Anton Loeb, Shane Miller, Erich Schenk, Marjorie Young; *col planning:* John Cuddy; *voices: Princess Glory:* Jessica Dragonette; *Prince David:* Lanny Ross; *King Little of Lilliput/Chef/Prince David (speaking):* Jack Mercer; *Gabby:* Pinto Colvig; *King Bombo of Blefuscu:* Ted Pierce; *Lemuel Gulliver:* Sam Parker; *Sneak, Snoop & Snitch:* Jack Mercer, Pinto Colvig; *Italian Barber:* Joseph Oriolo; *mus:* Victor Young; *songs:* Ralph Rainger, Leo Robin; "It's a Hap-Hap-Happy Day" by Sammy Timberg, Al J. Neiburg, Winston Sharples; *Tech advisor:* Johnny Burks; *ph:* Charles Schettler; *col:* Tech. *sd:* WE. 74 min. • Lemuel Gulliver is shipwrecked on the island of Lilliput which is inhabited by tiny people. Having befriended them, he sets out to amend the war between Lilliput and the island Blefuscu. This adaptation of Jonathan Swift's classic tale was made in a record eighteen months in Fleischer's new Miami studio. *Gulliver's Travels* was intended to be the answer to Disney's *Snow White* as well as putting Florida on the map as the movie capital opposing to Hollywood.

2687. Gumby: The Movie 1 Dec. 1986; *p.c.:* Arrow; *dir:* Art Clokey; *prod:* Art Clokey, Kevin Reher; *story:* Art Clokey, Gloria Clokey; *ed:* Marilyn McCoppen, Lynn Stevenson; *voices: Gumby/Claybert/Fatbuckle:* Charles Farrington; *Pokey/Prickle/Gumbo:* Art Clokey; *Goo:* Gloria Clokey; *Thinbuckle:* Manny La Carruba; *Ginger:* Alice Young; *Gumba:* Janet McDuff; *Tara:* Patti Morse; *Lowbelly/Farm Lady:* Bonnie Rudolph; *Radio Announcer:* David Ozzie Ahlers; *also:* David Archer, Lillian Nicol, Rick Warren; *mus:* David Ozzie Ahlers; *ph:* Art Clokey; *col. sd:* Dolby stereo. 90 min. • Feature film of the popular 1950s television show. Gumby and his band, "The Clayboys," stage a benefit for the local farmers who are having their farms threatened by The Blockheads' E-Z Loan Company. The Blockheads kidnap Gumby's dog, Lowbelly, when they discover he weeps pearls when he hears The Clayboys perform. When he doesn't cry for them, they kidnap Gumby and the Clayboys and create robot clones. Pokey, Prickle and Goo along with fans Tara and Ginger all take on the robot clones. Stop-motion plasticine animation.

2688. The Gumps *p.c.:* Wallace Carlson Studio (Chicago) for Celebrated Players Film Corp/State Right Releases; *dir:* Wallace A. Carlson; *anim:* David D. Hand, William O. Roberts, Paul Satterfield; b&w. *sil.* 5 min. • *1920: Andy's Dancing Lesson* 5 June. **Flat Hunting** 5 June. **Andy**

Visits His Mama-in-Law 5 June. **Andy Spends a Quiet Day at Home** 26 June. **Andy Plays Golf** 26 June. **Andy's Wash Day** 26 June. **Andy on Skates** 26 June. **Andy's Mother-in-Law Pays Him a Visit** 26 June. **Andy on a Diet** 3 July. **Andy's Night Out** 3 July. **Andy and Min at the Theatre** 14 Aug. **Andy Visits the Osteopath** 14 Aug. **Andy's Inter-Ruben Guest** Sept. **Andy Redecorates His Flat** Sept. **Andy the Model** 23 Oct. **Accidents Will Happen** 23 Oct. **Andy Fights the High Cost of Living** 23 Oct. **Militant Min** 23 Oct. **Ice Box Episodes** 23 Oct. **Wim and Wigor** 23 Oct. **Equestrian Andy** 23 Oct. **Andy the Hero** 23 Oct. **Andy's Picnic** 23 Oct. **Andy the Chicken Farmer** 23 Oct. **Andy the Actor** 23 Oct. **Andy at Shady Rest** 23 Oct. **Andy at the Beach** 23 Oct. **Andy on Pleasure Bent** 23 Oct. **Howdy Partner** 23 Oct. **There's a Raisin** 27 Nov. **Ship Ahoy** 27 Nov. **The To-Re-A-Door** 27 Nov. **The Broilers** 27 Nov. **Flicker, Flicker Little Star** 27 Nov. **Mixing Business with Pleasure** 27 Nov. **Up She Goes** 27 Nov. **Westward Ho** 27 Nov. **A-Hunting We Will Go** 27 Nov. **Get to Work** 27 Nov. • *1921:* **The Best of Luck** 12 Feb. **The Promoters** 12 Feb. **The Masked Ball** 12 Feb. **Give 'er the Gas** 12 Feb. **Chester's Cat** 12 Feb. **Rolling Around** 12 Feb. **Andy's Holiday** 12 Feb. **Andy and Min Have a Caller** 12 Feb. **Il Cuspidoree** 12 Feb. **Andy's Cow** 26 Feb. **Jilted and Jolted** 19 Mar. **A Terrible Time** 19 Mar. **A Quiet Little Game** 14 May. **Andy's Dog Day** 14 May. **Love Thy Neighbor. Midnight Madness** • Animated series featuring Sidney Smith's celebrated comic strip family headed by Andy Gump. The following items were reviewed upon re-release in the 1929–1930 era. No indication has been given as to whether these were reissued with an added soundtrack, which was the current practice: **A-Hunting We Will Go** Andy goes hunting. **Andy and Min Have a Caller** An energetic mouse invades Andy's house. **The Broilers** Andy looks for gold in Alaska and finds a fascinating damsel in a saloon. **Howdy Partner** Andy's attempts to amuse Min's nephew. **Love Thy Neighbor** Andy takes boxing lessons. **Midnight Madness** The matrimonial amenities of the Gump family. **There's a Raisin** Andy and the Minister sample the disastrous effects of Prohibition. **Westward Ho!** The Gumps have an interlude with some Indians.

2689.   Gumshoe Magoo (*Mr. Magoo*) Nov. 1958; *p.c.:* UPA for Colum; *ex prod:* Stephen Bosustow; *dir:* Gil Turner; *story:* Dick Kinney, Dick Shaw, Pete Burness; *anim:* Ed Friedman, Barney Posner, Maurie Fagin; *lay:* Robert Dranko; *back:* Bob McIntosh; *voices:* Jim Backus, Jerry Hausner; *mus:* Frederick Hollander; *col:* Tech. *sd:* RCA. 6 min. • Magoo unwittingly foils a bank robber's attempt to rob a supermarket.

2690.   Gun Shy (*Aesop's Film Fable*) 24 Oct. 1926; *p.c.:* Fables Pictures Inc for Pathé; *dir:* Paul Terry; b&w. *sil.* 10 min. • Farmer Al Falfa goes bear hunting and is robbed by Henry Cat disguised as a bear. Moral: "It doesn't always take a manicurist to trim a Bozo."

2691.   Gym Jam (*Popeye*) 17 Mar. 1950; *p.c.:* Famous for Para; *dir:* I. Sparber; *story:* Carl Meyer, Jack Mercer; *anim:* Tom Johnson, John Gentilella; *sets:* Anton Loeb; *voices:* Jack Mercer, Mae Questel, Jackson Beck; *mus:* Winston Sharples; *ph:* Leonard McCormick; *prod mgr:* Sam Buchwald; *col:* Tech. *sd:* RCA. 6 min. • Bluto disguises himself as a woman in order to gain access to Popeye's "Ladies Only" Gym. Remake of *Vim, Vigor and Vitaliky.*

2692.   Gym Jams (*Krazy Kat*) 2 Sept. 1938; *p.c.:* Charles Mintz prods for Colum; *story:* Allen Rose; *anim:* Harry Love, Louie Lilly; *voices:* Mel Blanc; *mus:* Joe de Nat; b&w. *sd:* RCA. 6 min. • Fun at Krazy's health resort.

2693.   Gypped in Egypt (*Aesop's Sound Fable*) 9 Nov. 1930; *p.c.:* Van Beuren for Pathé; *dir:* John Foster, Mannie Davis; *mus:* Gene Rodemich; b&w. *sd:* RCA. 6 min. • Tom and Jerry experience a nightmare in a pyramid where they are chased by skeletons, sphinxes and ferocious camels.

2694.   A Gypsy Fiddler (*Paul Terry-Toon*) 6 Oct. 1933; *p.c.:* Moser & Terry for Educational/Fox; *dir:* Paul Terry, Frank Moser; *mus:* Philip A. Scheib; b&w. *sd:* WE. 6 min. • No story available.

2695.   Ha! Ha! Ha! (*Betty Boop*) 2 Mar. 1934; *p.c.:* The Fleischer Studio for Para; *prod:* Max Fleischer; *dir:* Dave Fleischer; *anim:* Seymour Kneitel, Roland Crandall; *voice:* Mae Questel; *mus:* Sammy Timberg; b&w. *sd:* WE. 7 min. Remake of *The Cure.* • Betty's attempts to pull Ko-Ko's aching tooth by using laughing gas affects everybody.

2696.   Habit Rabbit (*Loopy de Loop*) Nov. 1964; *p.c.:* Hanna-Barbera for Colum; *prod/dir:* Joseph Barbera, William Hanna; *story dir:* Lew Mar-

shall; *story:* Michael Maltese; *anim dir:* Charles A. Nichols; *anim:* Bill Keil, George Goepper; *lay:* Bill Perez; *back:* Robert Gentle; *ed:* Donald A. Douglas; *voices:* Daws Butler, Howard Morris, Janet Waldo; *mus:* Hoyt Curtin; *titles:* Lawrence Gobel; *prod mgr:* Howard Hanson; *col:* East. *sd:* RCA. 6 min. • Loopy helps a family of rabbits who's father is a chronic "Carrotholic."

2697.   Hair Cut-Ups (*Heckle & Jeckle*) Feb. 1953; *p.c.:* TT for Fox; *dir:* Eddie Donnelly; *story/voices:* Tom Morrison; *mus:* Philip A. Scheib; *ph:* Douglas Moye; *col:* Tech. *sd:* RCA. 6 min. • The Magpies give Dangerous Dan a run for his money when he enters their barber shop.

2698.   Hair-Raising Hare (*Merrie Melodies*) 25 May 1946; *p.c.:* WB; *dir:* Charles M. Jones; *story:* Tedd Pierce; *anim:* Ben Washam, Ken Harris, Basil Davidovich, Lloyd Vaughan; *lay:* Robert Gribbroek; *back:* Earl Klein; *ed:* Treg Brown; *voices:* Mel Blanc; *mus:* Carl W. Stalling; *prod mgr:* John W. Burton; *prod:* Edward Selzer; *col:* Tech. *sd:* Vit. 7 min. • A mad scientist wants to experiment on Bugs with help from his monstrous assistant.

2699.   A Hair-Raising Tale (*Noveltoon*) Jan. 1965; *p.c.:* Para Cartoons; *dir:* Howard Post; *story:* Jack Mendelsohn; *anim:* Morey Reden; *sets:* Robert Little; *voices:* Eddie Lawrence; *mus:* Winston Sharples; *ph:* Leonard McCormick; *prod mgr:* Abe Goodman; *col:* Tech. *sd:* RCA. 6 min. • Boy scientist, Tinker, invents a hair-growing tonic and tries to sell it to a skeptical patents agent.

2700.   Hair Today Gone Tomorrow (*Noveltoon*) 16 Apr. 1954; *p.c.:* Famous for Para; *dir:* Seymour Kneitel; *story:* Irving Spector; *anim:* Dave Tendlar, Martin Taras; *sets:* Joseph Dommerque; *voices:* Jackson Beck, Sid Raymond, Gwen Davies; *mus:* Winston Sharples; *ph:* Leonard McCormick; *prod mgr:* Seymour Shultz; *col:* Tech. *sd:* RCA. 7 min. • Buzzy the Crow manages to talk Katnip into trying some of his patent hair-growing cures.

2701.   Hairried and Hurried (*Merrie Melodies*) 13 Nov. 1965; *p.c.:* DFE for WB; *dir:* Rudy Larriva; *story:* Nick Bennion; *anim:* Hank Smith, Virgil Ross, Bob Bransford; *lay:* Roy Morita, Shirley Silvey; *back:* Anthony Rizzo; *ed:* Lee Gunther; *mus:* Bill Lava; *col:* Tech. *sd:* Vit. 6 min. • The Coyote braves some more attempts to catch the Road-Runner by using snow chains, a bomb attached to a kite, sky-diving and karate.

2702.   Hairless Hector (*Terry-Toon*) 24 Jan. 1941; *p.c.:* TT for Fox; *dir:* Volney White; *story:* John Foster; *mus:* Philip A. Scheib; b&w. *sd:* RCA. 7 min. • The butler and parrot in a mansion are not partial to Hector the dog's demands and shave his mane of hair ... but Hector has his revenge.

2703.   Half-Baked Alaska (*Chilly Willy*) Apr. 1965; *p.c.:* Walter Lantz prods for Univ; *dir:* Sid Marcus; *story:* Cal Howard; *anim:* Ray Abrams, Art Davis; *sets:* Art Landy, Ray Huffine; *voices:* Daws Butler; *mus:* Walter Greene; *prod mgr:* William E. Garity; *col:* Tech. *sd:* RCA. 6 min. • Chilly can't afford hot cakes in Smedley's restaurant, so he filchs them off the plate of a tough customer who vents his wrath on Smedley.

2704.   Half Empty Saddles (*Woody Woodpecker*) 15 June 1958; *p.c.:* Walter Lantz prods for Univ; *dir:* Paul J. Smith; *story:* Dalton Sandifer; *anim:* Les Kline, Robert Bentley; *sets:* Art Landy, Ray Abrams; *voices:* Dal McKennon, Grace Stafford; *mus:* Clarence Wheeler; *prod mgr:* William E. Garity; *col:* Tech. *sd:* RCA. 6 min. • Dooley tries to steal Woody's treasure map.

2705.   Half-Fare Hare (*Merrie Melodies*) 18 Aug. 1956; *p.c.:* WB; *dir:* Robert McKimson; *story:* Tedd Pierce; *anim:* George Grandpré, Russ Dyson, Keith Darling, Ted Bonnicksen; *lay:* Robert Gribbroek; *back:* Richard H. Thomas; *ed:* Treg Brown; *voices:* Mel Blanc, Daws Butler; *mus:* Carl Stalling; *prod mgr:* John W. Burton; *prod:* Edward Selzer; *col:* Tech. *sd:* Vit. 7 min. • Bugs is trapped in a box-car with two hungry hoboes resembling *The Honeymooners* characters, Ralph Cramden and Ed Norton.

2706.   Half-Pint Palomino (*Barney Bear*) 26 Sept. 1953; *p.c.:* MGM; *dir:* Dick Lundy; *story:* Heck Allen, Jack Cosgriff; *anim:* Walter Clinton, Grant Simmons, Robert Bentley, Michael Lah; *sets:* John Didrik Johnsen; *ed:* Jim Faris; *voices:* Paul Frees; *mus:* Scott Bradley; *ph:* Jack Stevens; *prod:* Fred Quimby; *col:* Tech. *sd:* WE. 7 min. • Barney and Benny Burro set out to capture the smallest horse in the world.

2707.   Half-Pint Pygmy rel: 7 Aug. 1948; *p.c.:* MGM; *dir:* Tex Avery; *story:* Heck Allen; *anim:* Grant Simmons, Walter Clinton, Louis Schmitt, William Schull; *character des:* Louis Schmitt; *sets:* John Didrik Johnsen;

voice: Patrick J. McGeehan; *ed:* Fred MacAlpin; *mus:* Scott Bradley; *prod:* Fred Quimby; *col:* Tech. *sd:* WE. 7 min. • George and Junior embark on capturing the world's smallest pygmy.

2708. Halloween *(Toby the Pup)* 1 May 1931; *p.c.:* Winkler for RKO; *prod:* Charles B. Mintz; *anim:* Dick Huemor, Sid Marcus; *mus:* Joe de Nat; *prod mgr:* Nat L. Mintz; b&w. *sd:* RCA. 6 min. • No story available.

2709. Halt! Who Grows There? *(Merry Maker)* Oct. 1966; *p.c.:* Para Cartoons; *ex prod/dir:* Shamus Culhane; *story:* Shamus Culhane, Joseph Szabo; *anim:* Danté Barbetta, Gil Miret, Hal Silvermintz, Dave Ubinas; *des:* Gil Miret; *voices:* Lionel Wilson; *mus:* Winston Sharples; *prod sup:* Harold Robins, Burt Hanft; *col:* Tech. *sd:* WE. 6 min. • No story available.

2710. Ham and Eggs *(Oswald)* 28 July 1933; *p.c.:* Univ; *dir:* Walter Lantz, "Bill" Nolan; *anim:* Ray Abrams, Fred Avery, Cecil Surry, Jack Carr, Don Williams; *mus:* James Dietrich; b&w. *sd:* WE. 6 min. • Oswald and his girl run an active lunch room where, when customers leave without paying, the cash register empties their pockets.

2711. Ham and Hattie *(series);* *p.c.:* UPA for Colum; *ex prod:* Stephen Bosustow; *title anim:* Rod Scribner; *col:* Tech. *sd:* RCA. 7 min. • Two items in each program featuring the adventures of Hattie, a small girl, and Hamilton Ham, a storyteller. "Trees" rel: 30 Jan. 1958; *dir:* Lew Keller; *anim:* Fred Crippen; *sets:* Jules Engel, Ervin L. Kaplan; *voice:* Paul Frees; *song:* Mel Leven. "Jamaica Daddy" *dir/anim:* Fred Crippen; *lay:* Jim Murakami; *back:* Jules Engel, Ervin L. Kaplan; *voice:* Paul Frees; *song:* Mel Leven. Hattie discovers the wonders of the woodlands and the story of a young man urged by society to "Perpetuate de Family Tree" is unfolded. "Sailing" rel: 27 Feb. 1958; *dir:* Lew Keller; *anim:* Fred Crippen; *sets:* Jules Engel, Ervin L. Kaplan; *voice:* Mel Leven. "Village Band" *dir/anim:* Fred Crippen; *lay:* Jim Murakami; *back:* Jules Engel, Jack Heiter; *voice:* Peter Gordon; *song:* Mel Leven, Tak Shindo. Hattie learns the joys of sailing a toy boat on the park fountain. Edmond Dog and Roscoe Cat form a band with George the parrot. "Picnics Are Fun" rel: 16 Jan. 1959; *dir:* Lew Keller; *anim:* Fred Crippen; *sets:* Jules Engel, Ervin L. Kaplan; *voice:* Paul Frees; *song:* Mel Leven. "Dino's Serenade" *dir/anim:* Fred Crippen; *story:* John Urie; *lay:* Jim Murakami; *back:* Jules Engel, Ervin L. Kaplan; *voice:* Hal Peary; *song:* John Elliotte, Jack Meighan. Hattie takes her dolls for a rooftop picnic and Dino, a strolling musician, has his girl stolen. "Spring" rel: 16 Oct. 1958; *dir:* Lew Keller; *anim:* Fred Crippen; *sets:* Jules Engel, Ervin L. Kaplan; *voice:* Paul Frees; *song:* Mel Leven. "Saganaki" *dir/anim:* Fred Crippen; *story:* Jim Murakami, Mel Leven; *sets:* Jules Engel, Ervin L. Kaplan; *voice:* Hal Peary; *song:* John Elliotte, Jack Meighan. Hattie greets the coming of spring and a Japanese woodcutter wants to be an Imperial soldier.

2712. Ham Berger and His Horse "Radish" *(Daffyland);* 1930; *p.c.:* unknown; *col. snd.* 7 min. • Burlesque of western dramas.

2713. A Ham in a Role *(Merrie Melodies)* 31 Dec. 1949; *p.c.:* WB; *dir:* Robert McKimson; *story:* Sid Marcus; *anim:* Charles McKimson, Phil de Lara, J.C. Melendez, Emery Hawkins; *lay:* Cornett Wood; *back:* Richard H. Thomas; *ed:* Treg Brown; *voices:* Mel Blanc, Stan Freberg; *mus:* Carl Stalling; *prod mgr:* John W. Burton; *prod:* Edward Selzer; *col:* Tech. *sd:* Vit. 7 min. • A canine actor, retreats to his country home to rehearse Shakespeare. He evicts two gophers from his home who wreak their revenge.

2714. Ham-Ateur Night *(Merrie Melodies)* 28 Jan. 1939; *p.c.:* Leon Schlesinger prods for WB; *dir:* Fred Avery; *story:* Jack Miller, Robert Clampett; *anim:* Paul Smith; *sets:* John Didrik Johnsen; *ed:* Tregoweth E. Brown; *voices:* Phil Kramer, Mel Blanc, Elvia Allman, Fred Avery; *mus:* Carl W. Stalling; *prod sup:* Henry Binder, Raymond G. Katz; *col:* Tech. *sd:* Vit. 7 min. • Amateur night at the local theatre presents some dreadful talents. Egghead is the hit of the show only because the audience is overflowing with his relatives.

2715. The Hams That Couldn't Be Cured *(Swing Symphony)* 2 Mar. 1942; *p.c.:* Walter Lantz prods for Univ; *story:* Ben Hardaway, L.E. Elliot; *anim:* Alex Lovy, R. Somerville; *sets:* Fred Brunish; *voices:* Kent Rogers; *mus:* Darrell Calker; *prod mgr:* George Hall; *col:* Tech. *sd:* WE. 7 min. • The Wolf is about to be hung for blowing down the pigs' houses. His defense is that he, a classical music teacher, was set upon by the pigs starting a jam session that destroyed his house.

2716. The Hand Is Pinker Than the Eye *(Pink Panther)* 20 Dec. 1967; *p.c.:* Mirisch/Geoffrey/DFE for UA; *dir:* Hawley Pratt; *story:* Jim Ryan; *anim:* Bob Matz, Warren Batchelder, Chuck Downs, Don Williams, Manny Gould; *lay:* Dick Ung; *back:* Tom O'Loughlin; *ed:* Lee Gunther; *mus:* Walter Greene; *theme tune:* Henry Mancini; *prod sup:* Harry Love, Basil Cox; *col:* DeLuxe. *sd:* RCA. 6 min. • The Panther has a harrowing time when let loose in a magician's house.

2717. The Hangman 1964; *p.c.:* Melrose prods for Contemporary; *prod:* Les Goldman; *dir:* Paul Julian, Les Goldman; *poem:* Maurice Ogden; *anim:* Margaret Julian; *des:* Paul Julian; *ed:* Sidney Levin; *voice:* Herschel Bernardi; *mus:* Serge Hovey, Tom Pedrini; *ph:* Ray Bloss; *col:* East. *sd:* 11 min. • A mysterious black-coated stranger sets up a gallows outside the court house. The townsfolk watch on in terror as each are picked as victims.

2718. Hansel and Gretel *(Mighty Mouse)* June 1952; *p.c.:* TT for Fox; *dir:* Connie Rasinski; *story/voice:* Tom Morrison; *anim:* Jim Tyer; *mus:* Philip A. Scheib; *ph:* Douglas Moye; *col:* Tech. *sd:* RCA. 7 min. • Hansel and Gretel encounter The Old Witch of the Woods ... but Mighty Mouse soon comes to their aid.

2719. Hansel and Gretel *(Paul Terry-Toons)* 5 Feb. 1933; *p.c.:* Moser & Terry for Educational/Fox; *dir:* Frank Moser, Paul Terry; *mus:* Philip A. Scheib; b&w. *sd:* WE. 6 min. • A homeless pup meets another and they wander into the woods. A Witch tries to capture them but the pup sees her off and the two of them share her wealth.

2720. Hansel and Gretel rel: 1954; *p.c.:* Michael Myerberg prods for RKO; *dir:* John Paul; *story adapt:* Adelheid Wette, Padraic Colum; *anim:* Joseph Horstmann, Inez Anderson, Daniel Diamond, Ralph Emory, Hobart Rosen, Don Sahlin, Teddy Shapard, Nathalie Schulz; *character des:* Daieves Kis, James Summers; *fx:* Herbert Schaffer; *sets:* Evalds Dajevskis; *ed:* James F. Barclay, Roger Caras; *voices: Rosina Rubylips the witch:* Anna Russell; *Mother:* Mildred Dunnock; *Father:* Frank Rogier; *Sandman:* Delbert Anderson; *Dew Fairy:* Helene Boatright; *Hansel & Gretel:* Constance Brigham; *also:* Appollo Boys' Choir; *mus:* Engelbert Humperdinck, Franz Allers; *technicians; engineer:* Pete Inuzzi, Harry Eisman, Joseph Eisman, Bernard Enke, George Rees, Edward Ruks, Natan Zinri, Albert Abramows, Rudolph Gasio, Lars Johanasson, Charles Nissen, Isador Rosenbear, Meyer Silver, Louis Barlia, Barbara Winters; *ph/lighting:* Martin Munkasci; *costumes:* Ida Vendicktow; *wigs:* F. Bernner; *sd:* Fred Plaut, John McClure; *prod mgr:* William F. Rogers; *col:* Tech. *sd:* Reeves Studio. 74 min. • Puppet version of Humperdinck's opera. The poor woodcutter's children are sent to gather strawberries in the woods. They meet a wicked witch who lives in a gingerbread house. • Entrepreneur Michael Myerberg filmed this in a New York church hall. Puppets were positioned by electromagnets with the animators fixing positions through trap doors in the floor.

2721. Happy and Lucky *(Puddy the Pup)* 18 Mar. 1938; *p.c.:* TT for Educational/Fox; *dir:* Connie Rasinski; *mus:* Philip A. Scheib; b&w. *sd:* RCA. 6 min. • A little girl who has lost her dog sees that Puddy has fleas so she bathes him. When her dog returns ... so do Puddy's fleas.

2722. Happy Birthday *(Scrappy)* 7 Oct. 1938; *p.c.:* Charles Mintz prods for Colum; *story:* Allen Rose; *anim:* Harry Love, Louie Lilly; *voices:* Robert Winkler, Leone Le Doux; *mus:* Joe de Nat; *prod mgr:* James Bronis; b&w. *sd:* RCA. 6 min. • An insufferable brat gate-crashes Scrappy's birthday party and the gang try to throw her out

2723. Happy Birthdaze *(Popeye)* 16 July 1943; *p.c.:* Famous for Para; *dir:* Dan Gordon; *story:* Carl Meyer; *anim:* Graham Place, Abner Kneitel; *voices:* Jack Mercer; *mus:* Sammy Timberg; *ph:* Leonard McCormick; *prod mgr:* Sam Buchwald. b&w. *sd:* WE. 8 min. • Popeye rues the day he invited Shorty to help Olive prepare his birthday party.

2724. The Happy Butterfly *(Scrappy)* 20 Dec. 1934; *p.c.:* Winkler for Colum; *prod:* Charles Mintz; *story:* Sid Marcus; *anim:* Art Davis; *mus:* Joe de Nat; *prod mgr:* James Bronis; b&w. *sd:* RCA. 6 min. • A magical butterfly presents Scrappy and Oopy with a "Wishing Ring." Oopy wishes to become a butterfly but soon regrets this when bugs, squirrels and a hungry bird taunt him.

2725. Happy Circus Days *(Terry-Toon)* 23 Jan. 1942; *p.c.:* TT for Fox; *dir:* Connie Rasinski; *story:* John Foster; *mus:* Philip A. Scheib; *col:* Tech. *sd:* RCA. 7 min. • A boy and his dog are tempted to go to the circus by the images conjured up by the barker.

2726. The Happy Cobblers (*Terry-Toon*) May 1952; *p.c.*: TT for Fox; *dir*: Eddie Donnelly; *story/voice*: Tom Morrison; *anim*: Jim Tyer; *mus*: Philip A. Scheib; *ph*: Douglas Moye; *col*: Tech. *sd*: RCA. 6 min. • A group of elves help make a pair of shoes for the cobbler. He thinks his dog made them and, when word gets around, the king commissions the dog to make five hundred pairs.

2727. Happy Days (*Aesop's Film Fable*) 9 May 1928; *p.c.*: Fables Pictures Inc for Pathé; *dir*: Paul Terry, John Foster; b&w. *sil*. 5 min. • After a chain of calamities instigated by the farm animals, Farmer Al Falfa is prompted to put a "sold" sign on the farmhouse. Moral: "A tombstone has a good word for a man when he's down."

2728. Happy Days (*ComiColor*) 30 Sept. 1936; *p.c.*: Celebrity prods; *prod/dir*: Ub Iwerks; *voice*: Tommy Bupp; *mus*: Carl Stalling; *col*: Ciné. *sd*: PCP. 9 min. • Gene Byrnes' characters "Reg'lar Fellers" buy a wreck of a car which expires on them. Pinhead inflates the tires and the auto floats away.

2729. A Happy Family (*Krazy Kat*) 26 Sept. 1935; *p.c.*: Winkler for Colum; *prod*: Charles Mintz; *story*: Ben Harrison; *anim*: Manny Gould, Harry Love, Al Rose; *mus*: Joe de Nat; *prod mgr*: James Bronis; b&w. *sd*: RCA. 6 min. • Uncle Egbert and family come to visit Krazy and the kids demolish his house.

2730. Happy Go Ducky (*Tom & Jerry*) 3 Jan. 1958; *p.c.*: MGM; *prod/dir*: William Barbera, Joseph Barbera; *anim*: Kenneth Muse, Bill Schipek, Ken Southworth, Herman Cohen, Lewis Marshall, James Escalante; *lay*: Dick Bickenbach; *back*: Robert Gentle; *ed*: Jim Faris; *voice*: Red Coffee; *mus*: Scott Bradley; *ph*: Jack Stevens; *prod mgr*: Hal Elias; *col*: Tech. *sd*: WE. 6 min. CS. • The Easter Bunny brings Tom and Jerry an egg containing a duck who enjoys swimming.

2731. Happy Go Loopy (*Loopy de Loop*) 2 Mar. 1961; *p.c.*: Hanna-Barbera for Colum; *prod/dir*: Joseph Barbera, William Hanna; *story dir*: Alex Lovy; *story*: Warren Foster; *anim dir*: Charles A. Nichols; *anim*: Ed Love; *lay*: Dick Bickenbach; *back*: F. Montealegre; *ed*: Donald A. Douglas; *voices*: Daws Butler, Hal Smith; *mus*: Hoyt Curtin; *titles*: Lawrence Gobel; *prod mgr*: Howard Hanson; *col*: East. *sd*: RCA. 6 min. • Loopy is mistaken for a guest at a fancy dress party.

2732. Happy Go Luckies (*Aesop's Film Fable*) 9 Nov. 1923; *p.c.*: Fables Pictures Inc for Pathé; *dir*: Paul Terry; b&w. *sil*. 5 min. • A dog show with "freak" animals.

2733. Happy Go Lucky (*Heckle & Jeckle*) 28 Feb. 1947; *p.c.*: TT for Fox; *dir*: Connie Rasinski; *story*: John Foster; *voices*: Sid Raymond; *mus*: Philip A. Scheib; *ph*: Douglas Moye; *col*: Tech. *sd*: RCA. 6 min. • Heckle and Jeckle invade an orchard and run afoul of the watchdog.

2734. Happy Go Nutty (*Screwy Squirrel*) 24 June 1944; *p.c.*: MGM; *dir*: Tex Avery; *story*: Heck Allen; *anim*: Ed Love, Ray Abrams, Preston Blair; *character des*: Claude Smith; *sets*: John Didrik Johnsen; *ed*: Fred MacAlpin; *voices*: Wally Maher; *mus*: Scott Bradley; *prod*: Fred Quimby; *col*: Tech. *sd*: WE. 7 min. • Screwy escapes from the local nut house and it's up to the guard dog to return him.

2735. Happy Haunting Grounds (*Terry-Toon*) 18 Oct. 1940; *p.c.*: TT for Fox; *dir*: Mannie Davis; *story*: John Foster; *mus*: Philip A. Scheib; b&w. *sd*: RCA. 6 min. • Herman Pig redecorates a haunted house. Remade in color as *Seeing Ghosts*.

2736. Happy Hoboes (*Tom & Jerry*) 3 Mar. 1933; *p.c.*: Van Beuren for RKO; *dir*: George Stallings, George Rufle; *mus*: Gene Rodemich; b&w. *sd*: RCA. 6 min. • No story available.

2737. Happy Holidays (*Phantasy*) 25 Oct. 1940; *p.c.*: Colum; *story*: Harry Love; *anim*: Allen Rose; *ed*: George Winkler; *voices*: Mel Blanc, Leone Le Doux; *mus*: Joe de Nat; *ph*: Otto Reimer; *prod mgr*: James Bronis; b&w. *sd*: RCA. 6 min. • Snooks rebels against going to school.

2738. Happy Holland (*Mighty Mouse*) Oct. 1952; *p.c.*: TT for Fox; *dir*: Eddie Donnelly; *story*: Tom Morrison; *anim*: Jim Tyer; *sets*: Art Bartsch; *voices*: Roy Halee; *mus*: Philip A. Scheib; *col*: Tech. *sd*: RCA. 6 min. • Oil-Can Harry is once again in pursuit of Pearl Pureheart against a setting of windmills.

2739. Happy Hooligan *p.c.*: International Film Service; *prod/dir*: Gregory la Cava; b&w. *sil*. 4 min. • Based on Frederick Burr Opper's famous comic strip character. • *1919: The Tale of a Shirt* 22 June. **A Wee**

Bit O' Scotch 29 June. **Transatlantic Flight** 20 July. **The Great Handicap** 24 Aug. **Jungle Jumble** 7 Sept. **After the Ball** 28 Sept. **Business Is Business** 23 Nov. • See: *Goldwyn-International Comics*

2740. Happy Landing (*Heckle & Jeckle*) June 1949; *p.c.*: TT for Fox; *dir*: Mannie Davis; *story*: John Foster; *anim*: Jim Tyer; *sets*: Art Bartsch; *voices*: Sid Raymond, Tom Morrison; *mus*: Philip A. Scheib; *ph*: Douglas Moye; *col*: Tech. *sd*: RCA. 6 min. • The magpies sell a timid garage attendant a "lucky tie." When an ill-tempered customer arrives with an autogyro, they lock the attendant in the fuselage.

2741. Happy Polo (*Aesop's Sound Fables*) 14 May 1932; *p.c.*: Van Beuren for RKO; *dir*: John Foster; *mus*: Gene Rodemich; b&w. *sd*: RCA. 6 min. • No story available.

2742. Happy Scouts (*Oswald*) 20 Sept. 1938; *p.c.*: Univ; *dir*: Fred Kopietz; *story*: Victor McLeod, James Miele; *anim*: Merle Gilson, Dick Marion; *sets*: Edgar Keichle; *voice*: Bernice Hansel; *mus*: Frank Churchill; b&w. *sd*: WE. 7 min. • Oswald takes "Duck Troop 13" for a hike and has to rescue a small member from the jaws of an alligator.

2743. The Happy Tots (*Color Rhapsody*) 31 Mar. 1939; *p.c.*: Charles Mintz prods for Colum; *dir*: Ben Harrison; *anim*: Manny Gould; *sets*: Phil Davis; *voices*: The King's Men, The Rhythmettes; *mus*: Joe de Nat; *prod mgr*: James Bronis; *col*: Tech. *sd*: RCA. 8 min. • Harrison Cady's "Happy Tots" celebrate a festive day at the king's palace.

2744. The Happy Tots' Expedition (*Color Rhapsody*) 9 Feb. 1940; *p.c.*: Charles Mintz prods for Colum; *dir*: Ben Harrison; *anim*: Manny Gould; *sets*: Phil Davis; *voices*: Mel Blanc, The King's Men; *mus*: Joe de Nat; *prod mgr*: James Bronis; *col*: Tech. *sd*: RCA. 7 min. • Harrison Cady's "Happy Tots" set out on a rocket ship trip to explore "The Lost Planet."

2745. Happy Valley (*Aesop's Fable*) Sept. 1952; *p.c.*: TT for Fox; *dir*: Eddie Donnelly; *story*: Tom Morrison; *anim*: Jim Tyer; *mus*: Philip A. Scheib; *col*: Tech. *sd*: RCA. 7 min. • No story available.

2746. Happy You and Merry Me (*Betty Boop*) 21 Aug. 1936; *p.c.*: The Fleischer Studio for Para; *prod*: Max Fleischer; *dir*: Dave Fleischer; *anim*: Willard Bowsky, George Germanetti; *voice*: Mae Questel; *mus*: Sammy Timberg; b&w. *sd*: WE. 6 min. • When a kitten overeats and gets a tummy-ache, Betty sends Pudgy to the drug store for catnip.

2747. The Hard Boiled Egg (*Terry-Toon*) 29 Sept. 1948; *p.c.*: TT for Fox; *dir*: Connie Rasinski; *story*: John Foster; *anim*: Jim Tyer *mus*: Philip A. Scheib; *col*: Tech. *sd*: RCA. 7 min. • A hungry fox lives to regret ever deciding on having Dingbat for his breakfast.

2748. Hard Cider (*Aesop's Film Fable*) 12 June 1927; *p.c.*: Fables Pictures Inc for Pathé; *dir*: Paul Terry; b&w. *sil*. 10 min. • Generous quantities of cider cause Al Falfa and Thomas Cat to hallucinate they are floating on clouds and chasing beautiful girls.

2749. The Hardship of Miles Standish (*Merrie Melodies*) 13 Apr. 1940; *p.c.*: Leon Schlesinger prods for WB; *dir*: I. Freleng; *story*: Jack Miller; *anim*: Gil Turner; *sets*: Robert L. Holdeman; *ed*: Treg Brown; *voices*: Robert C. Bruce, Arthur Q. Bryan, Mel Blanc, Sara Berner; *mus*: Carl W. Stalling; *prod mgr*: Henry Binder, Raymond G. Katz; *col*: Tech. *sd*: Vit. 7 min. • A distorted view of the story of Miles Standish's love for Priscilla. Starring Elmer Fudd as John Alden and Edna Mae Oliver as Priscilla.

2750. Hare-Abian Nights (*Merrie Melodies*) 28 Feb. 1959; *p.c.*: WB; *dir*: Ken Harris, Michael Maltese; *story*: Michael Maltese; *anim*: Ben Washam, Ken Harris; *lay*: Samuel Armstrong; *back*: Philip de Guard; *ed*: Treg Brown; *voices*: Mel Blanc; *mus*: Milt Franklyn; *prod*: John W. Burton; *col*: Tech. *sd*: Vit. 7 min.; *seq*: *Bully for Bugs*; *Water Water Every Hare*; *Sahara Hare*. • Bugs finds himself in a Sultan's palace where he's forced to tell stories to the Sultan.

2751. The Hare and the Frog (*Aesop's Film Fable*) 28 Aug. 1921; *p.c.*: Fables Pictures Inc for Pathé; *dir*: Paul Terry; b&w. *sil*. 5 min. • The poor hares are tormented by the other animals. Unable to take this, three of them decide to end it all by jumping in a pond. Their jump frightens the frogs. This gives the hares confidence to go back and confront their enemies. The lesson is, "Your problems are best overcome by meeting them."

2752. The Hare and the Hounds (*Terry-Toon*) 23 Feb. 1940; *p.c.*: TT for Fox; *dir*: Eddie Donnelly; *story*: John Foster; *mus*: Philip A. Scheib; b&w. *sd*: RCA. 7 min. • No story available.

2753. The Hare and the Tortoise (*Aesop's Film Fable*) 25 Sept. 1921; *p.c.:* Fables Pictures Inc for Pathé; *dir:* Paul Terry; b&w. *sil.* 5 min. • While ahead in the race, the hare visits a roadhouse, drinks to excess and impresses the girls with modern jazz dancing, then tries to finish the race while still intoxicated.

2754. The Hare-Brained Hypnotist (*Merrie Melodies*) 31 Oct. 1942; *p.c.:* Leon Schlesinger prods for WB; *dir:* I. Freleng; *story:* Michael Maltese; *anim:* Philip Monroe; *sets:* Robert L. Holdeman; *ed:* Treg Brown; *voices:* Mel Blanc, Arthur Q. Bryan; *mus:* Carl W. Stalling; *prod sup:* Henry Binder, Raymond G. Katz; *col:* Tech. *sd:* Vit. 7 min. • Elmer Fudd tries to hypnotize Bugs.

2755. A Hare-Breadth Finish (*Terry-Toon*) Feb. 1957; *p.c.:* TT for Fox; *dir:* Connie Rasinski; *story:* Tom Morrison; *anim:* Jim Tyer; *mus:* Philip A. Scheib; *ph:* Douglas Moye; *col:* Tech. *sd:* RCA. 7 min. • The Hare trains for a re-match with the Tortoise and then is arrested for speeding when he's about to win the race.

2756. Hare-Breadth Hurry (*Looney Tunes*) June 1963; *p.c.:* WB; *dir:* Chuck Jones, Maurice Noble; *story:* John Dunn; *anim:* Tom Ray, Ken Harris, Richard Thompson, Bob Brabsford; *fx:* Harry Love; *sets:* William Butler; *ed:* Treg Brown; *voices:* Mel Blanc; *mus:* Bill Lava; *prod mgr:* William Orcutt; *prod:* David H. DePatie; *col:* Tech. *sd:* Vit. 7 min. • Bugs replaces the Road-Runner while being pursued by the ever-hungry Coyote.

2757. Hare Brush (*Merrie Melodies*) 7 May 1955; *p.c.:* WB; *dir:* I. Freleng; *story:* Warren Foster; *anim:* Ted Bonnicksen, Arthur Davis, Gerry Chiniquy; *lay:* Hawley Pratt; *back:* Irv Wyner; *ed:* Treg Brown; *voices:* Mel Blanc, Arthur Q. Bryan; *mus:* Milt Franklyn; *prod mgr:* John W. Burton; *prod:* Edward Selzer; *col:* Tech. *sd:* Vit. 7 min. • Millionaire Elmer J. Fudd suffers a breakdown and imagines he's a rabbit.

2758. Hare Conditioned (*Looney Tunes*) 11 Aug. 1945; *p.c.:* WB; *dir:* Charles M. Jones; *story:* Tedd Pierce; *anim:* Ken Harris, Ben Washam, Basil Davidovich, Lloyd Vaughan; *lay:* Robert Gribbroek; *back:* Earl Klein; *ed:* Treg Brown; *voices:* Mel Blanc, Dave Barry, Tedd Pierce; *mus:* Carl W. Stalling; *prod mgr:* John W. Burton; *prod:* Edward Selzer; *col:* Tech. *sd:* Vit. 7 min. • A department store manager wants to stuff Bugs.

2759. Hare-Devil Hare (*Looney Tunes*) 24 July 1948; *p.c.:* WB; *dir:* Charles M. Jones; *story:* Michael Maltese; *anim:* Ben Washam, Lloyd Vaughan, Ken Harris, Phil Monroe; *fx:* Harry Love; *lay:* Robert Gribbroek; *back:* Peter Alvarado; *ed:* Treg Brown; *voices:* Mel Blanc, Stan Freberg; *mus:* Carl Stalling; *prod mgr:* John W. Burton; *prod:* Edward Selzer; *col:* Tech. *sd:* Vit. 7 min. • Bugs is selected to be the first passenger to the moon. Once there he encounters a Martian, bent of destroying the Earth.

2760. Hare Do (*Merrie Melodies*) 15 Jan. 1949; *p.c.:* WB; *dir:* I. Freleng; *story:* Tedd Pierce; *anim:* Ken Champin, Virgil Ross, Gerry Chiniquy, Manuel Perez; *lay:* Hawley Pratt; *back:* Paul Julian; *ed:* Treg Brown; *voices:* Mel Blanc, Arthur Q. Bryan; *mus:* Carl Stalling; *prod mgr:* John W. Burton; *prod:* Edward Selzer; *col:* Tech; *sd:* Vit. 7 min. • Elmer pursues Bugs into a movie theatre.

2761. Hare Force (*Merrie Melodies*) 22 July 1944; *p.c.:* Leon Schlesinger prods for WB; *dir:* I. Freleng; *story:* Tedd Pierce, Robert Clampett; *anim:* Manuel Perez; *lay:* Hawley Pratt; *back:* Paul Julian; *ed:* Treg Brown; *voices:* Mel Blanc, Bea Benaderet, Tedd Pierce; *mus:* Carl W. Stalling; *prod sup:* Henry Binder, Raymond G. Katz; *col:* Tech. *sd:* Vit. 7 min. • Bugs and a dog battle for a warm place by the fire and the affections of an old maid.

2762. A Hare Grows in Manhattan (*Merrie Melodies*) 23 Mar. 1947; *p.c.:* WB; *dir:* I. Freleng; *story:* Michael Maltese, Tedd Pierce; *anim:* Virgil Ross, Gerry Chiniquy, Manuel Perez, Ken Champin; *lay:* Hawley Pratt; *back:* Philip de Guard; *ed:* Treg Brown; *voices:* Mel Blanc, Frances Baruch, Tedd Pierce, Michael Maltese; *mus:* Carl Stalling; *prod mgr:* John W. Burton; *prod:* Edward Selzer; *col:* Tech. *sd:* Vit. 7 min. • Bugs tells the story of how he grew up on the lower East Side of the Bronx and conquered a group of bullying dogs.

2763. Hare-Less Wolf (*Merrie Melodies*) 1 Feb. 1958; *p.c.:* WB; *dir:* Friz Freleng; *story:* Warren Foster; *anim:* Gerry Chiniquy, Art Davis, Virgil Ross; *lay:* Hawley Pratt; *back:* Boris Gorelick; *ed:* Treg Brown; *voices:* Mel Blanc, June Foray; *mus:* Milt Franklyn; *prod:* John W. Burton; *col:* Tech. *sd:* Vit. 7 min. • Charles M. Wolf is sent by his carping wife to catch a rabbit for supper. He soon finds Bugs but forgets the reason why he wanted him.

2764. Hare Lift (*Looney Tunes*) 20 Dec. 1952; *p.c.:* WB; *dir:* I. Freleng; *story:* Warren Foster; *anim:* Manuel Perez, Ken Champin, Virgil Ross, Arthur Davis; *lay:* Hawley Pratt; *back:* Irv Wyner; *ed:* Treg Brown; *voices:* Mel Blanc; *mus:* Carl Stalling; *prod mgr:* John W. Burton; *prod:* Edward Selzer; *col:* Tech. *sd:* Vit. 7 min. • Bank robber Sam forces Bugs to pilot his getaway plane.

2765. The Hare Mail (*Oswald*) 20 Nov. 1931; *p.c.:* Univ; *dir:* Walter Lantz, "Bill" Nolan; *anim:* Manuel Moreno, Ray Abrams, Fred Avery, Lester Kline, Vet Anderson; *voice:* Mickey Rooney; *mus:* James Dietrich; b&w. *sd:* WE. 6 min. • Oswald races to the rescue of a pretty girl being threatened by a villain and a battle takes place, culminating in an airplane chase.

2766. Hare Remover (*Merrie Melodies*) 23 Mar. 1946; *p.c.:* WB; *dir:* Frank Tashlin; *story:* Warren Foster; *anim:* Richard Bickenbach, Art Davis, Cal Dalton, I. Ellis; *fx:* A.C. Gamer; *sets:* Richard H. Thomas; *ed:* Treg Brown; *voices:* Mel Blanc, Arthur Q. Bryan; *mus:* Carl W. Stalling; *prod mgr:* John W. Burton; *prod:* Edward Selzer; *col:* Tech. *sd:* Vit. 7 min. • Elmer invents a potion to experiment on Bugs

2767. Hare Ribbin' (*Merrie Melodies*) 24 June 1944; *p.c.:* Leon Schlesinger prods for WB; *dir:* Robert Clampett; *story:* Lou Lilly; *anim:* Bob McKimson, Rod Scribner; *lay:* Thomas McKimson; *back:* Michael Sasanoff; *ed:* Treg Brown; *voices:* Mel Blanc, Sammy Wolfe; *mus:* Carl Stalling; *prod sup:* Henry Binder, Raymond G. Katz; *col:* Tech. *sd:* Vit. 7 min. • A persistent dog pursues Bugs under water. • Only a small segment was supposed to take place in a lake but Clampett liked the effect so much that he submerged all the action.

2768. Hare Splitter (*Merrie Melodies*) 25 Sept. 1948; *p.c.:* WB; *dir:* I. Freleng; *story:* Tedd Pierce; *anim:* Gerry Chiniquy, Manuel Perez, Ken Champin, Virgil Ross; *lay:* Hawley Pratt; *back:* Paul Julian; *ed:* Treg Brown; *voices:* Mel Blanc, Bea Benaderet; *mus:* Carl Stalling; *prod mgr:* John W. Burton; *prod:* Edward Selzer; *col:* Tech. *sd:* Vit. 7 min. • Bugs battles with Caspar, a rival suitor, for the affections of his girl by posing as her to fool him.

2769. Hare Tonic (*Looney Tunes*) 6 Oct. 1945; *p.c.:* WB; *dir:* Charles M. Jones; *story:* Tedd Pierce; *anim:* Ken Harris, Lloyd Vaughan, Ben Washam, Basil Davidovich; *lay:* Robert Gribbroek; *back:* Earl Klein; *ed:* Treg Brown; *voice:* Mel Blanc, Arthur Q. Bryan; *mus:* Carl W. Stalling; *prod mgr:* John W. Burton; *prod:* Edward Selzer; *col:* Tech. *sd:* Vit. 7 min. • Bugs convinces Elmer that he's caught rabbititus and is turning into a rabbit.

2770. Hare Trigger (*Merrie Melodies*) 5 May 1945; *p.c.:* WB; *dir:* I. Freleng; *story:* Michael Maltese, Robert Clampett; *anim:* Manuel Perez, Ken Champin, Virgil Ross, Gerry Chiniquy; *lay:* Hawley Pratt; *back:* Paul Julian; *ed:* Treg Brown; *voices:* Mel Blanc; *mus:* Carl W. Stalling; *prod mgr:* John W. Burton; *prod:* Edward Selzer; *col:* Tech. *sd:* Vit. 7 min. • Yosemite Sam the bandit tries to rob a train that Bugs is travelling on ... he doesn't succeed.

2771. Hare Trimmed (*Merrie Melodies*) 20 June 1953; *p.c.:* WB; *dir:* I. Freleng; *story:* Warren Foster; *anim:* Manuel Perez, Ken Champin, Virgil Ross, Arthur Davis; *lay:* Hawley Pratt; *back:* Irv Wyner; *ed:* Treg Brown; *voices:* Mel Blanc, Bea Benaderet; *mus:* Carl Stalling; *prod mgr:* John W. Burton; *prod:* Edward Selzer; *col:* Tech. *sd:* Vit. 7 min. • Bugs prevents Sam from marrying a widow who has recently inherited a fortune.

2772. Hare-Way to the Stars (*Looney Tunes*) 29 Mar. 1958; *p.c.:* WB; *dir:* Chuck Jones; *story:* Michael Maltese; *anim:* Richard Thompson, Ken Harris, Abe Levitow; *fx:* Harry Love; *lay:* Maurice Noble; *back:* Philip de Guard; *ed:* Treg Brown; *voices:* Mel Blanc; *mus:* Milt Franklyn; *prod:* John W. Burton; *col:* Tech. *sd:* Vit. 7 min. • Bugs is unwittingly shot off to another planet where he foils a Martian's attempt to blow up the Earth.

2773. Hare We Go (*Merrie Melodies*) 6 Jan. 1951; *p.c.:* WB; *dir:* Robert McKimson; *story:* Warren Foster; *anim:* Phil de Lara, Charles McKimson, John Carey, Rod Scribner, J.C. Melendez; *lay:* Cornett Wood; *back:* Richard H. Thomas; *ed:* Treg Brown; *voices:* Mel Blanc, Bea Benaderet; *mus:* Carl Stalling; *prod mgr:* John W. Burton; *prod:* Edward Selzer; *col:* Tech. *sd:* Vit. 7 min. • Bugs assists Christopher Columbus in the discovery of America.

2774. Harem Scarem (*Oswald the Lucky Rabbit*) 5 Dec. 1927; *p.c.:*

Winkler for Univ; *dir:* Walt Disney; *anim:* Hugh Harman, Rollin C. Hamilton; *ph:* Mike Marcus; b&w. *sil.* 6 min. • Oswald's visit to Morocco ends with him having to rescue an Arab dancing girl from the clutches of Peg-Leg Pete the Sheik.

2775. Harem Scarem rel: 12 Sept. 1931; *anim:* B.M. Powell; b&w. *sd. l/a/anim.* • No story available.

2776. Hare-Um Scare-Um (*Merrie Melodies*) 12 Aug. 1939; *p.c.:* Leon Schlesinger prods for WB; *dir:* Ben Hardaway, Cal Dalton; *story:* Melvin Millar; *lay:* Griff Jay; *back:* Arthur Loomer; *character des:* Charles Thorson; *ed:* Tregoweth E. Brown; *voices:* Mel Blanc; *mus:* Carl W. Stalling; *prod sup:* Henry Binder, Raymond G. Katz; *col:* Tech. *sd:* Vit. 7 min. • Due to a meat shortage, a hunter and his dog set out to hunt rabbit but he doesn't reckon on the wiles of the crazy one he finds. Featuring the prototype of Bugs Bunny.

2777. Harlem Wednesday rel: 1957; *p.c.:* Storyboard prods for Edward Harrison; *dir/ed:* John Hubley, Faith Elliott (Hubley); *mus:* Benny Carter; *ph:* George Jacobson; *col. sd.* 11 min. • A day in the community of Harlem, told by the paintings of Gregorio Prestopino.

2778. Harman–Ising Studio (1934–1938) *prod/dir:* Hugh Harman, Rudolf Ising; *seq dir:* Maurice "Jake" Day; *story:* Jerry Brewer, Jonathan T. "Moe" Caldwell, Jack Cosgriff, William Hanna, Walker Harman, Richard Kinney, Charles McGirl, Melvin Schwartzman; *anim:* Tom Armstrong, Gerald Baldwin, Thomas Barnes, Albert Bertino, Norm Blackburn, Peter Burness, Tom Byrne, Al Coe, Jim Davis, Paul Fennell, Edwin T.Fourcher, Arnold Gillespie, Merle Gilson, George Grandpré, Rollin C. Hamilton, William Hanna, Thurston Harper, Michael Lah, Ernest Lynch, Richard Marion, Thomas J. McKimson, Manuel Mario Moreno, Paul Murphy, S. Casey Onaitis, Albert Pabian, Anthony Pabian, James Pabian, Ray Patin, Francis Smith, Frank Tipper, Carl Urbano; *checking:* Alexander Walker; *color:* Lee Blair; *lay:* Peter Alvarado, James Hezell, Jack Miller, Martin Provensen, Don Smith; *back:* Robert Gentle, John Niendorff, Arthur Riley, Don Schaffer; *ed:* Paul Sprunk; *mus:* Scott Bradley, Clarence E. Wheeler; *music exposure sheet:* Barbara Wirth; *ph:* Jack Stevenson, Howard Hanson, Sid Ising, Bill Tracy, *sd:* Walter Elliott; *prod mgr:* Carmen G. Maxwell; *also:* Alden Bicheno, James Cook, George Miller, F.S. Patterson, A.H. Pickett, W. Earl Schafer, Frank Scheidenberger, Pepé Ruiz, Gwendolyn Wells.

2779. Harry Happy (*Modern Madcap*) Sept. 1963; *p.c.:* Para Cartoons; *dir:* Seymour Kneitel; *story:* Albert Pross, I. Klein; *anim:* Martin Taras, John Gentilella, Wm. B. Pattengill; *sets:* Anton Loeb; *voices:* Bob MacFadden, Corinne Orr; *mus:* Winston Sharples; *prod mgr:* Abe Goodman; *col:* Tech. *sd:* RCA. 6 min. • A "Jekyll and Hyde" character visits a marriage counsellor who pursuades him to switch personalities to become nicer to his wife.

2780. Harryhausen, Ray • Special technical effects created for live-action adventures by the ledgendary model-animator. • *1953:* The Beast from 20,000 Fathoms (WB) • *1955:* It Came from Beneath the Sea (Col) • *1956:* Earth Vs. the Flying Saucers (Col). The Animal World (WB) • Further notable works of Harryhausen, such as *The Mysterious Island, Jason and the Argonauts* and *The Valley of Gwangi*, etc., were all produced outside the United States.

2781. Harvest Time (*Terry-Toon*) 9 Feb. 1940; *p.c.:* TT for Fox; *dir:* Connie Rasinski; *story:* John Foster; *mus:* Philip A. Scheib; *col:* Tech. *sd:* RCA. 6 min. • A grasshopper rescues a helpless butterfly from the clutches of a villainous spider.

2782. Has Anybody Here Seen Kelly? (*Ko-Ko Song Car-Tune*) 21 Feb. 1926; *p.c.:* Inkwell Studio for Red Seal; *prod:* Max Fleischer; *dir:* Dave Fleischer; *vocals:* Metropolitan Quartet; *mus:* Lee Brodye at the recording organ console; hand-colored by Gustave Brock. *sd:* DFP. 7 min. • A leprechaun does his stunts over the words of the song about Michael Kelly who loses his girl at a St. Patrick's Day parade.

2783. Hash-House Blues (*Krazy Kat*) 2 Nov. 1931; *p.c.:* Winkler for Colum; *story:* Manny Gould; *anim/voice:* Jack Carr; *mus:* Joe de Nat; *prod:* George Winkler; b&w. *sd:* WE. 6 min. • Krazy appears as a dancing waiter who pulls a piano's ailing tooth.

2784. Hash Shop (*Oswald*) 12 Apr. 1930; *p.c.:* Univ; *anim:* Walter Lantz, "Bill" Nolan, Manuel Moreno; *mus:* David Broekman; b&w. *sd.* WE. 6 min. • A tough customer becomes violent when waiter Oswald is too slow.

2785. Hashimoto-San (*Terry-Toon*) Oct. 1959; *p.c.:* TT for Fox; *ex prod:* Bill Weiss; *dir:* Bob Kuwahara, Dave Tendlar; *story sup:* Tom Morrison; *story/lay:* Bob Kuwahara; *anim:* Ed Donnelly, Larry Silverman, Johnny Gent, Vinnie Bell; *back:* Bill Hilliker; *voices:* John Myhers; *mus:* Phil Scheib; *prod mgr:* Frank Schudde; *col:* DeLuxe; *sd:* RCA. 7 min. CS. • Hashimoto, the Japanese mouse, demonstrates to his American friend, Joey-San, how to use Ju-Jitsu on a troublesome cat.

2786. Hassle in a Castle (*Woody Woodpecker*) Mar. 1966; *p.c.:* Walter Lantz prods for Univ; *dir:* Paul J. Smith; *story:* Cal Howard; *anim:* Les Kline, Al Coe; *sets:* Art Landy, Ray Huffine; *voices:* Daws Butler, Grace Stafford; *mus:* Clarence Wheeler; *prod mgr:* William E. Garity; *col:* Tech. *sd:* RCA. 6 min. • A dim-witted woodsman sets out to capture a singing bird to win the hand of the king's daughter but catches Woody instead.

2787. Hasty but Tasty (*Ant & Aardvark*) 6 Mar. 1970; *p.c.:* Mirisch-DFE for UA; *dir:* Gerry Chiniquy; *story:* John W. Dunn; *anim:* Don Williams, Bob Taylor, Manny Gould, Manny Perez; *lay:* Dick Ung; *back:* Richard H. Thomas; *ed:* Lee Gunther; *voices:* John Byner; *mus:* Doug Goodwin, Pete Candoli, Billy Byers, Jimmy Rowles, Tommy Tedesco, Ray Brown, Shelly Manne; *prod sup:* Jim Foss, Harry Love; *col:* DeLuxe. *sd:* RCA. 6 min. • The Aardvark uses a portable hole to help capture the Ant.

2788. The Hasty Hare (*Looney Tunes*) 7 June 1952; *p.c.:* WB; *dir:* Charles M. Jones; *story:* Michael Maltese; *anim:* Ken Harris, Lloyd Vaughan, Ben Washam; *lay:* Robert Gribbroek; *back:* Philip de Guard; *ed:* Treg Brown; *voices:* Mel Blanc; *mus:* Carl Stalling; *prod mgr:* John W. Burton; *prod:* Edward Selzer; *col:* Tech. *sd:* Vit. 7 min. • Bugs is kidnapped by a Martian as a "Typical Earth Specimen" to return to Mars.

2789. The Hat (*Comic King*) June 1962; *p.c.:* Para Cartoons; *dir:* Seymour Kneitel; *story:* Michael Ross, Bruce Howard; *anim:* Martin Taras, Irving Dressler, George Germanetti, Wm. B. Pattengill; *sets:* Anton Loeb; *voices:* Paul Frees, Penny Phillips; *mus:* Winston Sharples; *prod mgr:* Abe Goodman; *col:* Tech. *sd:* RCA. 5 min. • Snuffy Smith is tricked into becoming an accomplice in a bank robbery, the only clue being a photograph of Snuffy's hat.

2790. The Hat 1964; *p.c.:* Storyboard prods for World Law Fund/Contempory Films; *dir:* John and Faith Hubley; *anim:* Shamus Culhane, William Littlejohn, Gary Mooney, The Tower 12 Group; *voices/mus:* Dizzy Gillespie, Dudley Moore; *i&p:* Patricia Byron, Nina di Gangi, Irene Rutenberg, Dorothy Tesser; *col. sd.* 18 min. *Academy Award.* • Two sentries, black and white, guard a dividing line. Black's hat falls over the line, causing the two to discuss the world's attention to the line and politics.

2791. Hatch Up Your Troubles (*Tom & Jerry*) 14 May 1949; *p.c.:* MGM; *dir:* William Hanna, Joseph Barbera; *anim:* Ed Barge, Ray Patterson, Irven Spence, Kenneth Muse; *ed:* Fred MacAlpin; *mus:* Scott Bradley; *prod:* Fred Quimby; *col:* Tech. *sd:* WE. 8 min. *Academy Award nomination.* • A baby woodpecker takes Jerry for his mother • See: *The Egg and Jerry*

2792. A Hatful of Dreams (*Puppetoon*) 28 Apr. 1945; *p.c.:* George Pal prods for Para; *prod/dir:* George Pal; *col:* Tech. *sd:* WE. 9 min. • Punchy finds a magic hat that transforms him into a superman. He uses these resources to win the heart of Judy.

2793. A Haul in One (*Popeye*) 14 Dec. 1956; *p.c.:* Famous for Para; *dir:* I. Sparber; *story:* Larz Bourne; *anim:* Al Eugster, Wm. B. Pattengill; *sets:* Robert Owen; *voices:* Jack Mercer, Mae Questel, Jackson Beck; *mus:* Winston Sharples; *ph:* Leonard McCormick; *prod mgr:* Seymour Shultz; *col:* Tech. *sd:* RCA. 6 min. • Popeye and Bluto fight over the honor of moving house for Olive.

2794. The Haunted Cat (*Little Roquefort*) Dec. 1951; *p.c.:* TT for Fox; *dir:* Eddie Donnelly; *story/voice:* Tom Morrison; *anim:* Jim Tyer; *sets:* Art Bartsch; *mus:* Philip A. Scheib; *col:* Tech. *sd:* RCA. 6 min. • Percy the puss believes he's killed Roquefort but the mouse recovers and proceeds to haunt him.

2795. The Haunted Hotel 1907; *dir/anim:* James Stuart Blackton; b&w. *sil.* • Furniture moves about seemingly on its own. Blackton manipulated the furniture by means of stop-motion photography.

2796. The Haunted House (*Aesop's Film Fable*) 13 Dec. 1925; *p.c.:* Fables Pictures Inc for Pathé. *dir:* Paul Terry; b&w. *sil.* 10 min. • No story available.

2797. The Haunted House (*Mickey Mouse*) 2 Dec. 1929; *p.c.:* Walter E. Disney for Colum; *dir:* Walt Disney; *anim:* Ub Iwerks; *mus:* Carl W. Stalling. *sd:* PCP. 7 min. • Mickey plays the organ as the skeletons dance to the music.

2798. Haunted House Cleaning (*Astronut*) May 1966; *p.c.:* TT for Fox; *ex prod:* Bill Weiss; *dir/anim:* Connie Rasinski; *story sup:* Tom Morrison; *sets:* Bill Focht, John Zago, Bob Owen; *ed:* Jack MacConnell; *voices:* Dayton Allen; *mus:* Jim Timmens; *ph:* Ted Moskowitz, Joe Rasinski, Charles Schettler; *sd:* Elliot Grey; *col:* DeLuxe. *sd:* RCA. 5 min. • No story available.

2799. The Haunted Mouse (*Merrie Melodies*) 15 Feb. 1941; *p.c.:* Leon Schlesinger prods for WB; *dir:* Fred Avery; *story:* Michael Maltese; *anim:* Sid Sutherland; *sets:* John Didrik Johnsen; *ed:* Treg Brown; *voices:* Walter Tetley, Mel Blanc; *mus:* Carl W. Stalling; *prod sup:* Henry Binder, Raymond G. Katz; *col:* Tech. *sd:* Vit. 7 min. • The ghost of a mouse comes back to haunt the cat that killed him.

2800. Haunted Mouse (*Tom & Jerry*) 1965; *p.c.:* MGM; *prod/dir:* Chuck Jones; *co-dir:* Maurice Noble; *story:* Jim Pabian, Chuck Jones; *anim:* Ben Washam, Ken Harris, Dick Thompson, Tom Ray, Don Towsley; *back:* Philip de Guard; *voice:* Mel Blanc; *mus:* Eugene Poddany; *prod mgr:* Les Goldman; *col:* Metro. *sd:* WE. 7 min. • Tom encounters a magical mouse with hypnotic powers.

2801. The Haunted Ship (*Aesop's Sound Fable*) 27 Apr. 1930; *p.c.:* Van Beuren for Pathé. *dir:* John Foster, Mannie Davis; *mus:* Gene Rodemich; b&w. *sd:* RCA. 6 min. • A submarine explores a sunken wreck populated by skeletons, etc.

2802. The Haunting 23 July 1999; *p.c.:* Dreamworks; based on *The Haunting of Hill House* by Shirley Jackson; *visual fx sup:* Phil Tippett, Craig Hayes; *fx/anim:* Tippett Studio Visual Effects: *prod:* Jules Roman; *anim sup:* Blair Clark; *art dir:* Paula Lucchesi; *lead anim:* Petey König; *anim:* Simon Allen, Joe Henke, Eric Ingerson, Todd LaBonte, Randy Link, Matt Logue, Virginie Michel, D'Annoville, Eric C. Reynolds, Thomas Schelesny, P. Kevin Scott, Robert Skiena, Jesse Sugarman, Robin Watts; *anim set-up:* Aaron Holly, Kelly Lepkowsky, Jeff Raymond; *fx anim sup:* Eric Leven; *fx anim:* Matt Baer, Matt Hightower, Michael A. Miller, Stephanie Modestowicz, Mike Perry, Tim Teramoto; *anim mgr:* Eve Sakellariou; *anim:* Marc Chu, David Latour; *cg art:* Cathy Burton, Mario Capellari, Kathy Davidson, Dean Foster, Andrew Hardman, David Hisanaga, Keith Johnson, Brian LaFrance, Hohen Leo, David Manos Morris, Ken McGaugh, Sandy Ritts, Hans Uhlig; *addit visual fx/anim:* ILM; *childrens' voices:* David Latour, Debi Derryberry, Jessica Evans, Sherry Lynn, Miles Marsico, Courtland Mead, Kelsey Mulrooney, Kyle McDougie, Hannah Swanson; *col:* Tech. *sd:* Dolby digital surround–EX/Digital dts sound/SDDS. Panavision. 112³/₄ min. *l/a.* • Live-action horror: A psychiatrist investigating "fear" assembles a group of adults to spend a week in an allegedly haunted mansion. Animated ghosts, gargoyles, etc.

2803. Haunting Dog (*The Dogfather*) 2 May 1975; *p.c.:* Mirisch-DFE for UA; *dir:* Gerry Chiniquy; *story:* John Dunn; *anim:* Bob Richardson, Don Williams, Nelson Shin; *ed:* Rick Steward; *lay:* Dick Ung; *back:* Richard H. Thomas; *voices:* Bob Holt; *mus:* Dean Elliott; *col:* DeLuxe. *sd:* RCA. 5 min. • The Dogfather rubs-out a rival gangster who leaves him his getaway car, the ghost of the former owner returns to haunt them.

2804. Have Gun, Can't Travel (*Woody Woodpecker*) Feb. 1967; *p.c.:* Walter Lantz prods for Univ; *dir:* Paul J. Smith; *story:* Cal Howard; *anim:* Les Kline, Al Coe; *sets:* Ray Huffine; *voices:* Dal McKennon, Grace Stafford; *mus:* Clarence Wheeler; *prod mgr:* William E. Garity; *col:* Tech. *sd:* RCA. 6 min. • Sheriff Woody attempts to capture Dirty McNasty with help from McNasty's horse.

2805. Have You Got Any Castles (*Merrie Melodies*) 25 June 1938; *p.c.:* Leon Schlesinger prods for WB; *dir:* Frank Tashlin; *story:* Jack Miller, Robert Clampett; *anim:* Ken Harris; *ed:* Tregoweth E. Brown; *voices:* Mel Blanc, The Basin Street Boys, Tedd Pierce; *mus:* Carl W. Stalling; *song:* Johnny Mercer, Richard A. Whiting; *prod sup:* Henry Binder, Raymond G. Katz; *col:* Tech. *sd:* Vit. 7 min. • Characters on book covers come to life. Caricatures of Cab Calloway, Clark Gable, Step'n Fetchit, W.C. Fields, The Inkspots, Charles Laughton, Victor McLaughlin, Paul Muni, William Powell, Bill Robinson, Shirley Temple, Fats Waller and Paul Whiteman.

2806. Hawaiian Aye-Aye (*Merrie Melodies*) 27 June 1964; *p.c.:* WB; *dir:* Gerry Chiniquy; *story:* Tedd Pierce, Bill Danch; *anim:* Virgil Ross, Bob Matz, Art Leonardi, Lee Halpern; *lay:* Robert Gribbroek; *back:* Tom O'Loughlin; *ed:* Treg Brown; *voices:* Mel Blanc, June Foray; *mus:* Bill Lava; *prod mgr:* William Orcutt; *prod:* David H. DePatie; *col:* Tech. *sd:* Vit. 7 min. • Sylvester tries to reach Tweety on an island surrounded by water and a shark.

2807. Hawaiian Birds (*Color Classic*) 28 Aug. 1936; *p.c.:* The Fleischer Studio for Para; *prod:* Max Fleischer; *dir:* Dave Fleischer; *anim:* Myron Waldman, Sam Stimson, Lillian Friedman; *character des:* Myron Waldman; *sets:* Robert Little; *mus:* Sammy Timberg; *ph:* Johnny Burks; *col:* Tech; *sd:* WE. 9 min. • A boy lovebird tracks down his girl when she departs for the big city. He finds her abandoned and near to suicide and takes her back to Hawaii.

2808. Hawaiian Holiday (*Mickey Mouse*) 24 Sept. 1937; *p.c.:* Walt Disney prods for RKO; *dir:* Ben Sharpsteen; *story:* Otto Englander; *anim:* James H. Culhane, Nick de Tolly, Gilles de Tremaudan, Alfred Eugster, Nick George, Jack Hannah, Wolfgang Reitherman; *lay:* Robert Dranko; *voices:* Clarence Nash, Leone Le Doux, Pinto Colvig; *trio:* Millie Walters, Sally Noble, Mary Rosetti; *mus:* Leigh Harline, Paul J. Smith; *Hawaiian guitar:* Sol Hoopi; *col:* Tech. *sd:* RCA. 7 min. • While Goofy tries to master the surfboard, Pluto battles with a crab and Donald catches his tail on fire while the gang picnic on the beach.

2809. Hawaiian Pineapples (*Paul-Terry Toon*) 18 May 1930; *p.c.:* A-C for Educational; *dir:* Frank Moser, Paul Terry; *mus:* Philip A. Scheib; b&w. *sd:* WE. 7 min. • A mouse arrives by airplane in time to put out a grass-skirted lovely's burning hut.

2810. Hawks and Doves (*Roland & Rattfink*) 18 Dec. 1968; *p.c.:* Mirisch-DFE for UA; *dir:* Hawley Pratt; *story:* John W. Dunn; *anim:* Don Williams, Manny Perez, Art Leonardi, Warren Batchelder, Ed de Mattia; *lay:* Dick Ung; *back:* Tom O'Loughlin; *ed:* Lee Gunther; *voices:* Leonard Weinrib, June Foray; *mus:* Doug Goodwin, Ray Brown, Pete Candoli, Jimmy Rowles, Billy Byers, Shelly Manne, Tommy Tedesco; *prod sup:* Jim Foss, Harry Love; *col:* DeLuxe. *sd:* RCA. 6 min. • Over in Hawkland, Ratfink declares war on Doveland and its ambassador for peace.

2811. Hawks of the Sea (*Aesop's Film Fable*) 28 Sept. 1924; *p.c.:* Fables Pictures Inc for Pathé; *dir:* Paul Terry; b&w. sil. 5 min. • The mouse captain of a pirate ship repels cat marauders but awakes to find it was all a dream.

2812. Hay Rube (*Cartune*) 7 June 1954; *p.c.:* Walter Lantz prods for Univ; *dir:* Paul J. Smith; *story:* Michael Maltese; *anim:* Gil Turner, La Verne Harding, Robert Bentley; *sets:* Raymond Jacobs, Art Landy; *voices:* Dallas McKennon; *mus:* Clarence Wheeler; *prod mgr:* William E. Garity; *col:* Tech. *sd:* RCA. 6 min. • Sugarfoot, a plough horse, falls for a performing mare named Starbright and sneaks off to rescue her from a cruel circus boss.

2813. He Auto Know Better (1) 1930. *p.c.:* A-C/Aetna Insurance Co. • The family, out for a ride, crash into another car. When in court, father is ordered to pay heavy damages ... but then remembers his insurance card. b&w. *sd:* WE. 5 min.

2814. He Can't Make It Stick (*Color Rhapsody*) 23 July 1943; *p.c.:* Colum; *prod:* Dave Fleischer; *dir:* Paul Sommer, John Hubley; *story:* Milt Gross, Stephen Longstreet; *anim:* Volus Jones, Jim Armstrong; *ed:* Edward Moore; *sets:* Clark Watson; *voice:* John McLeish; *mus:* Eddie Kilfeather; *ph:* Frank Fisher; *prod mgr:* Albert Spar; *col:* Tech. *sd:* RCA. 7 min. • An Austrian paper-hanger named Shicklegruber designs Swastika-covered wallpaper and has an uncontrollable desire to see his handiwork plastered all over the world. His attempts to make it stay up soon become a public joke. Caricature of Adolf Hitler.

2815. He Done His Best (*Whirlwind Comedy*) 4 Oct. 1926; *p.c.:* R-C Pictures for FBO; *dir:* Charles R. Bowers, Harold L. Muller; *story:* Charles R. Bowers, H.L. Muller, Ted Sears; *l/a:* Charley Bowers; *ph:* H.L. Muller; b&w. sil. 23¹/₂ min. *l/a/anim.* • When Charley manages to destroy his prospective father-in-law's restaurant, he rebuilds one with a fully-automated kitchen.

2816. He Dood It Again (*Super Mouse*) 5 Feb. 1943; *p.c.:* TT for Fox; *dir:* Eddie Donnelly; *story:* John Foster; *voice:* Thomas Morrison; *mus:* Philip A. Scheib; *ph:* Douglas Moye; *col:* Tech. *sd:* RCA. 6 min. • The mice are having fun at Sol's Diner until the cats break things up. Super Mouse eats "super cheese" and tosses the cats out.

2817. He-Man Seaman (*Hector Heathcote*) Mar. 1962; *p.c.:* TT for Fox; *ex prod:* Bill Weiss; *dir:* Art Bartsch; *story sup:* Tom Morrison; *lay:* John Zago; *back:* Bill Focht; *voices:* John Myhers; *mus:* Phil Scheib; *prod mgr:* Frank Schudde; *col:* DeLuxe. *sd:* RCA. 5 min. • No story available.

2818. He Was Her Man (*Merrie Melodies*) 2 Mar. 1937; *p.c.:* Leon Schlesinger prods for WB; *dir:* I. Freleng; *anim:* Paul Smith, Cal Dalton; *lay:* Griff Jay; *back:* Arthur Loomer; *voices:* Bernice Hansel, Dave Weber, Berna Deane; *mus:* Carl W. Stalling; *song:* Mort Dixon, Allie Wrubel; *prod sup:* Henry Binder, Raymond G. Katz; *col:* Tech. *sd:* Vit. 7 min. • Frankie Mouse sells apples to support her man but when she finds he's spent her hard-earned cash on another female, she goes over to the pool hall and beats him up.

2819. He Who Gets Socked (*Pen & Ink Vaudeville*) 9 Feb. 1925; *p.c.:* Hurd prods for Educational; *prod/dir:* Earl Hurd; *b&w. sil.* 6 min. • "Props" is called on to look after a mischievious infant. The child is captured by a stork and "Props" follows in an airplane. He runs into a flock of storks carrying babies selecting a pickaninny, a Hebrew and a Chinese baby before he finds the right one. He wakens to find it was only a dream.

2820. The Headless Horseman (*ComiColor*) 1 Oct. 1934; *p.c.:* Celebrity prods; *prod/dir:* Ub Iwerks; *anim:* Jimmie Culhane, Al Eugster, Grim Natwick, Berny Wolf; *mus:* Carl Stalling; *col:* Ciné. *sd:* PCP. 9 min. • Schoolmaster Ichabod Crane and Brom Bones are rivals for the fair Katrina. Brom scares off Ichabod by posing as a "Headless Horseman."

2821. Heap Big Hepcat (*Woody Woodpecker*) 30 Mar. 1960; *p.c.:* Walter Lantz prods for Univ; *dir:* Paul J. Smith; *story:* Dalton Sandifer; *anim:* Robert Bentley, Les Kline, Don Patterson; *sets:* Art Landy, Raymond Jacobs; *voices:* Dal McKennon, Grace Stafford; *mus:* Eugene Poddany; *prod mgr:* William E. Garity; *col:* Tech. *sd:* RCA. 6 min. • To win the hand of his sweetheart, Mooseface is told by her Indian chief father to capture something to eat … which is where Woody steps into the picture.

2822. Heap Hep Injuns (*Screen Song*) 30 June 1950; *p.c.:* Famous for Para; *dir:* I. Sparber; *story:* Larz Bourne; *anim:* Tom Johnson, George Rufle; *sets:* Anton Loeb; *mus:* Winston Sharples; *ph:* Leonard McCormick; *prod mgr:* Sam Buchwald; *col:* Tech. *sd:* RCA. 6 min. • Various Indian tribes are depicted including the romance between an Indian boy and girl.

2823. Hearst International Features Service *Artists:* John Foster, Burton F. Gillett, Bert Green, Albert Hurter, Jack King, Isidore Klein, Gregory la Cava, Walter Lantz, Frank Moser, N.M. Natwick, William C. Nolan, Leon Searl, Frank Sherman, George Stallings, John C. Terry.

2824. Hearst-International News Pictorial *p.c.:* International Film Service; *b&w. sil.* Animated inserts as part of a newsreel item by the celebrated cartoonist Tom Powers. • *1916:* **Tom Powers Cartoon** 13 June. **Stripes and Patches** 4 Aug. **On Again — Off Again** 21 July

2825. Hearst-Pathé News *p.c.:* International Film Service for Pathé; *b&w. sil.* Amalgamation of Pathé News and Hearst International News Pictorial with animated items tagged onto a newsreel. • *1917:* **Help Wanted** 3 Jan. *anim:* F.M. Follett. **A Hard Cold Winter** 10 Jan. **Oh Girls What Next?** 13 Jan. *anim:* Leighton Budd. **The Mexican Crisis** 20 Jan. *anim:* F.M. Follett. **Billy Sunday's Tabernacle** 27 Jan. *anim:* F.M. Follett. **Up a Stump** 14 Feb. **Freedom of the Seas** 10 Mar. **The Adventures of Mr. Common Peepul** 21 Mar. **Solid Comfort** 24 Mar. **Mr. Common Peepul's Busy Day** 28 Mar. **Peace Insurance** 31 Mar. *cartoon* 11 Apr. **Heroes of the Past** 21 Apr. **The Great Offensive** 28 Apr. **Mr. Slacker** 2 May. **Potato Is King** 5 May. **Her Crowning Achievement** 16 May. **Have You Bought Your Liberty Bond?** 23 May. **Both Good Soldiers** 26 May. **When Will He Throw Off This Burden?** 30 May. **In the Garden Trenches** 2 June. **Ten Million Men from Uncle Sam** 9 June. **Liberty Loan of 1917** 13 June. **A Regular Man** 4 July. **The Awakening** 14 July. *anim:* Hal Coffman. **America Does Not Forget** 18 July. **They All Look Alike to Me** 4 Aug. **Growing Fast** 15 Aug. **Hoch the Kaiser** 5 Sept. **Fall Styles for Men** 12 Sept. **Buy a Liberty Bond** 13 Oct. **It Has Come At Last** 4 Nov. **Which?** 28 Nov. **The Handwriting in the Sky** 1 Dec. • *1918:* **Dropping the Mask** 19 Jan. **Every Little Bit Helps** 30 Jan. **A New Shadow Haunts Autocracy** 9 Feb. **Progress** 12 Feb. **The Heritage** 15 Feb. **The Threatening Storm** 20 Feb. **The Glutton** 23 Feb. *cartoon* 2 Mar. **Making An Example of Him**

13 Mar. **Join the Land Army** 6 Apr. *cartoon* 13 Apr. **Give Him a Helping Hand** 20 Apr.

2826. Hearst-Vitagraph News Pictorial *p.c.:* Barré Studio for International Film Service/Vitagraph; *b&w. sil.* Animated items in a newsreel featuring George Herriman's *Krazy Kat*, Tom E. Powers' *Joys and Glooms*, Frederick Burr Opper's *Happy Hooligan*, R. Dirks' *The Katzenjammer Kids*, "Tad" Dorgan's *Judge Rummy*, Harry Hershfield's *Abie the Agent* and Walter C. Hoban's *Jerry on the Job*. • *1915:* **The Phable of Sam and Bill** 17 Dec. *anim:* Raoul Barré. **The Phable of a Busted Romance** 24 Dec. *anim:* Raoul Barré. **Feet Is Feet** 31 Dec. *anim:* Raoul Barré. • *1916:* **A Newlywed Phable** 7 Jan. *anim:* Raoul Barré. **The Phable of a Phat Woman** 14 Jan. *anim:* Raoul Barré. **Who Said They Never Come Back?** 18 Jan. *anim:* Raoul Barré. **The Story of Cooks Against Chefs** 21 Jan. *anim:* Raoul Barré. **Twas but a Dream** 28 Jan. *anim:* Raoul Barré. **Mr. Nobody Holme, He Buys a Jitney** 31 Jan. *anim:* Leon Searl. **Poor Si Keeler** 4 Feb. **Never Again: The Story of a Speeder Cop** 4 Feb. *anim:* Raoul Barré. **Parcel Post Pete's Nightmare** 7 Feb. *anim:* Frank Moser. **Old Doc Gloom** 11 Feb. *anim:* Frank Moser. **Parcel Post Pete: All His Troubles Are Little Ones** 14 Feb. *anim:* Frank Moser. **Introducing Krazy Kat and Ignatz Mouse** 18 Feb. *anim:* Frank Moser. **Ignatz Believes in $ Signs** 22 Feb. *anim:* Leon Searl. **Krazy Kat and Ignatz Mouse Discuss the Letter G** 25 Feb. *anim:* Frank Moser. **Krazy Kat Goes A-Wooing** 29 Feb. *anim:* Leon Searl. **A Duet: He Made Me Love Him** 3 Mar. *anim:* Raoul Barré. **Krazy Kat and Ignatz Mouse in Their One Act Tragedy** 7 Mar. *anim:* Leon Searl. **The Joys Elope** 10 Mar. *anim:* Raoul Barré. **Krazy Kat — Bugologist** 13 Mar. *anim:* Frank Moser. **Krazy Kat & Ignatz Mouse at the Circus** 17 Mar. *anim:* Leon Searl. **Krazy Kat: Demi-Tasse** 20 Mar. *anim:* Frank Moser. **Krazy Kat to the Rescue** 24 Mar. *anim:* William C. Nolan. **Krazy Kat: Invalid** 28 Mar. *anim:* Leon Searl. **Do You Know This Man?** 31 Mar. *anim:* Raoul Barré. **Krazy Kat at the Switchboard** 3 Apr. **Krazy Kat the Hero** 7 Apr. **A Tale That Is Knot** 14 Apr. *anim:* Bert Green. **A Quiet Day in the Country** 5 June. **Krazy Kat at Looney Park** 17 June. **Maud the Educated Mule** 3 July. **A Tempest in a Paint Pot** 3 July. **A Gridiron Hero** 6 Oct. **He Tries Movies Again** 9 Oct. **Father Gets into the Movies** 21 Nov. *story:* Louis de Lorme; *anim:* Frank Moser. **The Missing One** 27 Nov. *anim:* Leon Searl. **Der Captain Goes A-Swimming** 11 Dec. *anim:* Gregory la Cava. **Just Like a Woman** 14 Dec. *anim:* Bert Green. **On the Cannibal Isle** 18 Dec. *anim:* Will Powers. **Krazy Kat Takes Little Katrina for an Airing** 19 Dec. *anim:* Edward Grinham. • *1917:* **Ananias Has Nothing on Hooligan** 20 Jan. *anim:* Frank Moser. **Der Great Bear Hunt** 8 Jan. *anim:* George Stallings. **A Tankless Job** 15 Jan. *anim:* Will Powers. **Throwing the Bull** 4 Feb. *story:* H.E. Hancock. **Happy Hooligan** 11 Feb. **Der Captain Is Examined for Insurance** 11 Feb. *anim:* Gregory la Cava. **Roses and Thorns** 11 Mar. **Happy Hooligan: Double-Crossed Nurse** 25 Mar. **Robbers and Thieves** 12 Apr. **The Great Hansom Cab Mystery** 26 Apr. **A Hot Time in the Gym** 26 Apr. **Ananias Has Nothing on Him** 26 Apr. **Der Captain Goes A-Flivvering** 26 Apr. **Sharks Is Sharks** 26 Apr. **The New Recruit** 26 Apr. **Three Strikes, You're Out** 26 Apr. **The Cook** 29 Apr. **Moving Day** 27 May. **Music Hath Charms** 7 June. **Around the World in Half-an-Hour** 9 June. **Down Where the Linburger Blows** 9 June. **The Hansom Cab Mystery** 9 June. **20,000 Legs Under the Sea** 9 June. **Quinine** 9 June. **All Is Not Gold That Glitters** 24 June. **The Great Offensive** 1 July. **The White Hope** 19 July. **A Krazy Katastrophe** 5 Aug. **Iska Worreh** 5 Aug. **Der Captain Discovers the North Pole** 8 Aug. **He Tries His Hand at Hypnotism** 8 Aug. **Der Captain's Valet** 25 Aug. **Happy Hooligan Gets the Razoo** 2 Sept. **Happy Hooligan in the Zoo** 9 Sept. **Abie Kabibble Outwitting His Rival** 23 Sept. **Happy Hooligan in the Tank** 28 Sept. **Happy Hooligan in Soft** 7 Oct. **Der End of der Limit** 14 Oct. **Happy Hooligan at the Picnic** 16 Oct. **By the Sad Sea Waves** 16 Oct. **The Tale of the Fish** 16 Oct. **The Tale of a Monkey** 25 Nov. **Der Last Straw** 8 Dec. **The Mysterious Yarn** 8 Dec. **A Tempest in a Paint Pot** 8 Dec. **Bullets and Bull** 16 Dec. **Happy Hooligan at the Circus** 19 Dec. **Fat and Furious** 23 Dec. **Peace and Quiet** 30 Dec. • *1918:* **Der Captain's Birthday** 6 Jan. **Hearts and Horses** 13 Jan. **Rheumatics** 27 Jan. **All for the Ladies** 10 Feb. **Burglars** 24 Feb. **Too Many Cooks** 3 Mar. **Spirits** 10 Mar. **Vanity and Vengeance** 22 Apr. **Doing His Bit** 29 Apr. **Der Two Twins** 6 May. **His Last Will** 13 May. **Der Black Mitt** 20 May. **Fisherman's Luck** 27 May. **Up in the Air** 3 June. **Swat the Fly** 10 June. **Throwing the Bull** 17 June. **The Best Man Loses** 24 June. **A Heathen Benefit** 15 July.

Mopping Up a Million 22 July. Pep 29 July. His Dark Past 5 Aug. Tramp! Tramp! Tramp! 12 Aug. Judge Rummy's Day Off 19 Aug. Hash and Hypnotism 19 Aug. On the Border 19 Aug. Twinkle Twinkle Dec. • *1919:* Snappy Cheese 22 Mar. Judge Rummy's Miscue Sept. Rubbing It In Oct. A Sweet Pickle Nov. Where Has My Little Coal Bin? 6 Sept. A Bold Bad Man Sept. The Latest in Underwear Sept. Rub-A-Dud-Dud 20 Sept. Where Are the Papers? Oct. A Picnic for Two Oct. Pigs in Clover 10 Nov. Der Wash on der Line Nov. Knocking the "H" Out of Hainie Nov. How Could William Tell? 26 Nov. That Reminds Me Dec. A Smash-Up in China Dec.

2827. Hearts and Glowers (*Terry-Toon*) June 1960; *p.c.:* TT for Fox; *ex prod:* Bill Weiss; *dir:* Martin Taras; *story sup:* Tom Morrison; *story:* Larz Bourne, Eli Bauer; *anim:* Ed Donnelly, Mannie Davis; *lay:* John Zago; *back:* Bill Focht; *voice:* Douglas Moye; *mus:* Phil Scheib; *prod mgr:* Frank Schudde; *col:* Tech. *sd:* RCA. 6 min. CS. • Clobber mistakes a female tenant's suitor for a prospective boarder and tries to get her married to another tenant so he can have a free room to let! Clint Clobber is drawn as a bear.

2828. Hearts and Showers (*Aesop's Film Fable*) 20 Apr. 1926; *p.c.:* Fables Pictures Inc for Pathé; *dir:* Paul Terry; b&w. *sil.* 10. • Farmer Al Falfa depends on his cat, Esmeralda, to keep the mice at bay. When she falls in love, she forgets her duties and the house is soon overrun with mice. When Al can't separate them, he chases them into the country. On return, he discovers Esmeralda with her new husband and a dozen kittens.

2829. The Heat's Off (*James Hound*) Apr. 1967; *p.c.:* TT for Fox; *dir/anim:* Ralph Bakshi; *col:* DeLuxe. *sd:* RCA. 6 min. • Having distorted the world's weather, Professor Mad asks a ransom of one billion dollars to return it to normal. • See: *James Hound*

2830. Heaven and Earth Magic made between 1943 and 1958; *dir:* Harry Smith; b&w. *sd.* 60 min. • Chance and an unequalled imagination determine the contents of this remarkable film.

2831. Heaven Scent (*Merrie Melodies*) 31 Mar. 1956; *p.c.:* WB; *dir/story:* Chuck Jones; *anim:* Abe Levitow, Richard Thompson, Ken Harris, Ben Washam; *lay:* Erni Nordli; *back:* Philip de Guard; *voices:* Mel Blanc; *mus:* Milt Franklyn; *prod mgr:* John W. Burton; *prod:* Edward Selzer; *col:* Tech. *sd:* Vit. 6 min. • A black cat paints a white stripe down her back to warn off some attacking dogs, then has to deal with the amorous advances of Pepé le Pew, the French skunk.

2832. Heavenly Puss (*Tom & Jerry*) 9 July 1949; *p.c.:* MGM; *dir:* William Hanna, Joseph Barbera; *anim:* Ray Patterson, Irven Spence, Kenneth Muse, Ed Barge; *sets:* Robert Gentle; *ed:* Fred MacAlpin; *voice:* Luis van Rooten; *mus:* Scott Bradley; *ph:* Jack Stevens; *prod:* Fred Quimby; *col:* Tech. *sd:* WE. 8 min. • Having used up all his nine lives, Tom arrives at Heaven's Gate and learns he won't be let in until he gets a signed release from Jerry.

2833. The Heavy Date (*Life Cartoon Comedy*) 13 Feb. 1927; *p.c.:* Sherwood Wadsworth Pictures Inc for Educational; *prod/dir:* John R. McCrory; b&w. *sil.* 6 min. • Mike Monkey tries to keep a date with Myrtle while little Nibbins tags along with a bunch of kittens.

2834. Heavy Metal 7 Aug. 1981; *p.c.:* Colum-EMI-Warner; *dir:* Gerald Potterton; *ex prod:* Leonard Mogel; *prod:* Ivan Reitman; *asso prod:* Michael Gross, Peter Lebensold, Lawrence Nesis; *scr:* Dan Goldberg, Len Blum; based on original art and stories by Richard Corben, Angus McKie, Dan O'Bannon, Thomas Warkentin, Berni Wrightson; *ed:* Janice Brown, Eva Ruggiero, Jeff Bushelman; *prod des:* Michael Gross; *fx anim:* John Bruno; *mus dir:* Elmer Bernstein; *mus performed by* the Royal Philharmonic Orchestra; *with* London Voices and Jeanne Loriod and the Ondes Martinot; *orch:* Christopher Palmer, David Spear, Peter Bernstein; *mus ed:* Jeff Carson; *title des:* Burke Mattsson, MGM Title; *main title des:* Jay Teitzell, John le Prevost, Dale Herigstad; *sd ed:* Peter Thillaye; *dial ed:* Tony Reed; *sd re-rec:* Joe Grimaldi, Austin Grimaldi; *sd fx ed:* Rod Crawley, Marc Chiasson, Gordon Thompson, Joanne Hovey, Peter Jermyn, Andy Malcolm, Peter McBurnie; *prod sup:* Christine Larocque; *prod co-ord:* Joe Medjuck; *post prod sup:* Dan Goldberg; *seq prod:* John Coates (TV Cartoons); *prod co-ord:* Dominic Anciano; *seq dir:* Jimmy T. Murakami; *original story:* Dan O'Bannon; *original art:* Thomas Warkentin; *anim ph:* Peter Turner; *anim:* Joanna Fryer, Hilary Audus; *back:* Sam Kirson; *art brush artists:* Mick Crane, Rudolfo Azaro; *ed:* Mick Manning; *fx:* Camera Effects; *models:* Clearwater Productions; *song:* "Radar Rider": Jerry Riggs, Marc Jordan;

performed by Riggs; *"Grimaldi": seq prod:* John Halas; *prod mgr:* Jack King, Philip Lynch; *seq dir/anim dir:* Harold Whitaker; *ph:* Peter Petronio; *model ph:* Arthur Provis; *anim:* Harold Whitaker, Roger Mainwood, John Perkins, Euen Frizzell; *lay:* Lonnie Lloyd, Terry Windell, Lorenzo Martinez; *back:* Ted Pettingell; *model maker:* Brian Borthwick; *i&p:* Alexandra Bex; *fx:* Peter Petronio; *voices: Grimaldi:* Don Francks; *girl:* Caroline Semple; *"Harry Canyon": seq prod:* Vic Atkinson, W.H. Stevenson Jr., Atkinson Film-Arts; *prod mgr:* Bob Yuile; *seq dir:* Pino van Lamsweerde; *asst dir:* Yuile-Omg; *story:* Dan Goldberg, Len Blum; *anim ph:* Haines-Camron; *anim:* Doug Crane, Ray de Silva, Peter Miller, Fabio Pacifico, Greg Reyna, Norm Roen, Chris Schouten, Sebastian, Ken Stephenson, Stephen Weston; *lay:* Sue Butterworth; *back:* Michael Guerin; *Xerox/i&p:* Florence Bach, Robyn Milks, Weldon Poapst; *ed:* Gerald Tripp; *Storyboard/des:* Juan Gimenez; *fx:* Gordon Coulthart; *song:* "Veteran of the Psychic Wars" by Eric Bloom, Michael Moorcock; *performed by* Blue Oyster Cult; "True Companion" by/performed by Donald Fagen; "Heartbeat" by/performed by Jerry Riggs; "Blue Lamp" by/performed by Stevie Nicks; "Open Arms" by Steve Perry, Jonathan Cain; *performed by* Journey; *prod asst:* Nick Roberts; *voices: Harry Canyon:* Richard Romanus; *girl/Satellite:* Susan Roman; *Rudnick:* Al Waxman; *Alien/Henchman:* Harvey Atkin; *Desk Sergeant:* John Candy; *Whores:* Glenis Wootton Gross, Marilyn Lightstone; *"Den": seq prod:* John Coates, Jerry Hibbert; *co-ord:* Clennell Rawson; *seq dir:* Richard Corben; *ph:* Peter Jones, Graham Orrin, Peter Turner, Peter Wolff; *anim:* Hilary Audus, Bobbie Clennel, Rich Cox, Douglas Crane, Michael Dudok deWit, Richard Fawdry, Joanne Frye, Jerry Hibbert, Dick Horn, Dave Livesy, Reg Lodge, Alastair McIlwain, Edrich Raddage, John Perkins, Jack Stokes, Mike Williams; *lay:* David Elvin, Ted Pettingell, Paul Shardlow; *back:* Alan Best, Errol Bryant, Vanessa Clegg, Ian Craig, Michael Hirsch, Bert Kitchen, Richard Ollive, Paul Shardlow, Wyn Thomas; *i&p:* Mike Rayes; *ed:* Ian Llande; *art dir:* Pat Gavin; *fx:* Rex Neville; *voices: Dan/Den:* John Candy; *Queen:* Marilyn Lightstone; *Kathrine Wells:* Jackie Burroughs; *Ard:* Martin Lavut; *Norl:* August Schellenberg; *"Captain Sternn": seq prod:* Boxcar Animation Studios; *prod mgr:* Susan Kapigian; *seq dir:* Paul Sabella, Julian Szuchopa; *original story & art:* Berni Wrightson; *ph:* Claude Lapierre; *anim:* Shivan Ramsaran, Paul Sabella, Julian Szuchoppa; *lay:* Michael Breton, Terry Windell; *back:* Michael Breton; *i&p:* Susan Kapigian; *songs:* "Reach Out" by Robert James, Pete Comita; *performed by* Cheap Trick; *voices: Prosecutor:* John Vernon; *Cpt. Lincoln P. Sternn:* Eugene Levy; *Lawyer Charlie:* Joe Flaherty; *Hanover Fiste:* Rodger Bumpass; *Regolian:* Douglas Kennedy; *"B-17": seq sup:* Vic Atkinson, W.H. Stevenson Jr., Atkinson Film Arts; *prod mgr:* Bob Yuile; *anim seq dir:* Barrie Nelson; *storyboard:* Lee Mishkin; *asst dir:* Bob Yuile; *original story:* Dan O'Bannon; *anim ph:* Hawes-Camron; *stop-motion ph:* Precision Film Group; *anim:* Vic Atkinson, Jeff Hale, Fred Hellmich, Ruth Kissane, Bill Littlejohn, Spencer Peel, Norm Roen, Sebastian, Bill Perkins; *lay:* Fred Hellmich, Blake James, Don Wong; *back:* Barry Atkinson, Art Nelles; *Xerox/i&p:* Robyn Milks, Weldon Poapst, Pierre Tremblay; *des:* Mike Ploog, Blake James; *fx:* Barry Atkinson, Lee Atkinson; *songs:* "Takin' a Ride (on Heavy Metal)" by/performed by Don Felder; *prod asst:* Nick Roberts; *voices: Pilot:* George Touliatos; *co-pilot:* Don Francks; *Navigator:* Zalyanovsky; *"So Beautiful and So Dangerous": prod seq:* Halas & Batchelor Animation; *prod mgr:* Philip Lynch; *seq dir:* John Halas; *anim dir:* Brian Larkin; *original story & art:* Angus McKie; *ph:* Peter Petroni; *anim:* Brian Larkin, Harold Whitaker, Roger Mainwood, John Cousen, Børge Ring; *computer anim:* Systems Simulating; *storyboard/lay:* Brian Larkin, Harold Whitaker; *back:* Angus McKie, Dennis Ryan, Janos Kass; *technical art:* Brian Borthwick; *i&p:* Alexandra Bex, Roland Carter; *des:* Angus McKie, Neal Adams; *fx:* Peter Petronio; *songs:* "Queen Bee": Mark Farner; *performed by* Grand Funk Railroad; "I Must Be Dreamin'" by Rick Nelson; *performed by* Cheap Trick; "Crazy (a Suitable Case for Treatment)" by D. McCafferty, P. Agnew, M. Charlton, D. Sweet; *performed by* Nazareth; "All of You" *by/performed by* Don Felder; "Heavy Metal" by Sammy Hagar, Jim Peterik; *performed by* Sammy Hagar; "Prefabrication" by Bernard Bobvoisin, Norbert Krief; *English version:* Jimmy Pursey; *performed by* Trust; *voices: Woman Reporter:* Patty Dworkin; *Male Reporter:* Eugene Levy; *Senator:* Warren Munson; *General:* Joe Flaherty; *Dr. Anrak:* Rodger Bumpass; *Gloria:* Alice Playten; *Robot:* John Candy; *Zeke:* Harold Ramis; *"Taarna": prod mgr:* Christine Larocque, Valerie Gifford; *l/a:* Frances Gallagher; *unit mgr (l/a):* Andrew Gryn; *seq dir:* John Bruno; *original story:* Dan Goldberg, Len Blum; *ph:* Peter Bromley, Jean Robillard, Claude LaPierre, Serge Langloi, Pierre

Provost; *l/a:* Paul van der Linden; *video ph:* Richard Potterton; *ph fx:* Wayne Kimball, Harry J. Moneau; *anim fx:* Lee Dyer; *anim:* Jose Abel, Gary Mooney, Ernesto Lopez, Sean Newton, Milt Gray, Zdenko Gasparovic, Dan Thompson, Mitch Rochon, Charlie Downs, William Recinos, George Ungar, George Scribner, Mauro Maressa, Russ Mooney, Malcolm Draper, Arnie Wong, Trell W. Yokum, Michael Stribling, Norton Virgien, Spencer Peel, Ruth Kissane, Norm Drew, Alvaro Gaivoto, Colin Baker, Michael Bannon, Roger Chiasson, David Feiss, Mike Longden, Daniel Decelles; *lay:* Kurt Conner, Lonnie Lloyd, Bernie Denk, Richard Hoover, Lorenzo Martinez, Terry Windell, George Ungar, John Dorman; *back:* Danielle Marieau, Brent Boates, Christian Bernard, Raymond LeBrun, Daniel de Niger, Alain Masicotte, Brenda Martin, Carlos Lillo Baeza, Johanne Storch, Pierre Houde, Anne Beauregard, Jean Bello, Bernie Denk, Terry Windell, Lorenzo Martinez; *i&p:* Joan Churchill; *Multiplane:* Wally Bullock, Anicam, Maxwell Morgan, Gregory Schafer; *des:* Mike Ploog, Howard Chaykin, Chris Achilleos, Charles White III, Alex Tavoularis, Philip Norwood, J.S. Goert, Ira Turek, Brent Boates, Christian Bernard, George Ungar; *storyboard:* Kurt Connor, John Dorman, Sherman Labby, Hank Tucker, Jeffrey Gatrall; *fx:* Travelling Shots, Precision Film Company, Alex Funke, Don Admundson; *model makers:* Jerry L. Allen, Judy Allen, Vance Frederick, Scott Sinclair, Tom Tondreault, Terry Allen; *songs:* "The Mob Rules" by Butler, Dio & Iommi; *performed by* Black Sabbath; "Through Being Cool" by M. Mothersbaugh, G.V. Casale, R. Mothersbaugh; *performed by* Devo; "Lookin' in a Coalmine" by Allen Toussaint; *performed by* Devo; *technical advisor (l/a):* David B. Simpson; *prod asst (l/a):* Richard Potterton, Gerald Brunet Michele, Michael Larocque, Irene Rappaport; *voices: Leader:* Vlastra Vrana; *Elder:* Mavor Moore; *Boy:* Thor Bishopric; *Taarak:* August Schellenberg; *Barbarians:* Don Francks, Zal Yanovsky, George Touliatos, Len Doncheff; *Bartender:* Cedric Smith; *Council men:* Joseph Gollard, Charles Joliffe, Ned Conlon; *col:* Metrocolor. *sd:* Dolby Stereo. 90 min. • Sequential science fiction work about various people who acquire a green jewel known as the *Loch-nar*, "the sum of all evil," in their possession: An astronaut gives the precious stone to his little daughter and he is eventually melted by its presence. A Manhattan cab driver is tricked into recovering the stone for a seductress whose late father lost it to a crooked businessman. A teenage boy is transformed into a muscleman by the gem. A submissive prosecution witness for a murder trial is transformed into a raging beast by the gem, allowing the accused to escape. A B-17 bomber is caused to crash. A Pentagon secretary and her boss are sucked into a spaceship and the Taarakian citizens summon help from Taarna, the beautiful defender of their peoples, when they are attacked by a barbarian horde. USA/GB.

2835. Heavy Traffic 1973; *p.c.:* Black Ink Films; *dir/story:* Ralph Bakshi; *anim:* Bob Bransford, Ed de Mattia, Milt Gray, Volus Jones, Bob Maxfield, Manny Perez, Tom Ray, Lloyd Vaughan, Carlo Vinci, John E. Walker snr, Bob Bemiller, Irv Spence, Manny Gould, Barney Posner, Fred Hellmich, Nick Tafuri, Martin Taras, Dave Tendlar, Alex Ignatiev; *fantasy anim:* Mark Kausler; *fx:* Sue Carey; *visual fx:* Modern Film Effects; *titles/lay:* Valleycam; *sets:* John Vita, Bill Butler; *back:* Ira Turek; *col models:* Ellie Abranz; *ed:* Donald W. Ernst; *voices: Michael:* Joseph Kaufmann; *Carole:* Beverly Hope Atkinson; *Angie:* Frank de Kova; *Ida:* Terri Haven; *Molly:* Mary Dean Lauria; *Rosalyn:* Jacqueline Mills; *Rosa:* Lillian Adams; *also:* Jim Bates, Jamie Farr, Robert Easton, Charles Gordone, Morton Lewis, Bill Striglos, Jay Lawrence, Lee Weaver, Phyllis Thompson, Kim Hamilton, Carol Graham, Candy Candido, Helen Winston, William Keene, Peter Hobbs, John Bleifer; *mus:* Ray Shanklyn, Ed Bogas; "Scarborough Fair" by Paul Simon, Art Garfunkel; *performed by* Sergio Mendez and Brazil '77; "Maybelline" by Chuck Berry; "Take Five" by Paul Desmond; *performed by* The Dave Brubeck Quartet; "Twist and Shout" by Phil Medley, Bert Russell: *performed by* The Isley Brothers; *l/a seq:* Oaktree prods; *film creations:* Steve Krantz Animation; *ph:* Ted C. Bemiller, Gregg Heschong; *back ph:* John Vita, Ralph Bakshi; *prod mgr:* Harry Love; *prod:* Steve Krantz; *col:* DeLuxe. *sd.* 76 min. • X-rated story of a depressed New Yorker finding solace from the environment at the drawing board.

2836. The Heckling Hare (*Merrie Melodies*) 5 July 1941; *p.c.:* Leon Schlesinger prods for WB; *dir:* Fred Avery; *story:* Michael Maltese, Robert Clampett; *anim:* Bob McKimson, Rod Scribner; *sets:* John Didrik Johnsen; *ed:* Treg Brown; *voices:* Mel Blanc, Kent Rogers; *mus:* Carl W. Stalling; *prod sup:* Henry Binder, Raymond G. Katz; *col:* Tech. *sd:* Vit. 6 min. •

Willoughby the hunting dog tracks down Bugs, who gives him a run for his money culminating in the both of them falling off a seemingly endless precipice.

2837. Hector the Pup 1935; *p.c.:* Screen Attractions Corp; *dir/anim:* John W. Burton; *story:* Joseph d'Amico; *mus:* Arch B. Fritz; b&w. snd. 6 min. • Sheriff Hector tracks Wooly the Wolf ("Wanted for Everything ... and how!") to a cabin where he has taken Hector's kidnapped bride and they have a shootout. Stop-frame puppet animation.

2838. Hector's Hectic Life (*Noveltoon*) 19 Nov. 1948; *p.c.:* Famous for Para; *dir:* Bill Tytla; *story:* Joe Stultz, Larry Riley; *anim:* George Germanetti, Steve Muffatti; *sets:* Robert Connavale; *voices:* Cecil Roy, Jack Mercer; *mus:* Winston Sharples; *ph:* Leonard McCormick; *prod mgr:* Sam Buchwald; *col:* Tech. *sd:* RCA. 6 min. • The mistress of the house threatens to throw Hector the hound out if he doesn't behave. He then discovers three pups in his own image on the doorstep.

2839. Heidi's Song 19 Nov. 1982; *p.c.:* Hanna-Barbera Prods for Para; *dir:* Robert Taylor; *prod:* Joseph Barbera, William Hanna; *asso prod:* Iwao Takamoto; *prod sup:* Jayne Barbera; *post prod mgr:* Joed Eaton; *story:* Joseph Barbera, Jameson Brewer, Robert Taylor; *based on the novel Heidi by* Johanna Spyri; *anim sup:* Hal Ambro, Charles Downs, Marilyn Taylor; *character des:* Iwao Takamoto; *anim:* Bob Bachman, Ed Barge, Jesse Cosio, John Freeman, Ernesto Lopez, Duncan Marjoribanks, Mauro Maressa, Sean Newton, Margaret Nichols, Spencer Peel, Manny Perez, Mitch Rochon, George Scribner, Irv Spence, Robert Taylor, John Walker, Ken Walker, Ed Aardal, Roger Chiasson, Gail Finkeldei, Al Gaivoto, Terence Harrison, Harry Holt, John Kimball, Marlene Robinson May, Glenn C. Schmitz, Marty Taras, Don Williams, Xenia (deMattia); *art dir:* Paul Julian; *character col:* Billie Kerns; *lay:* Mo Gollub, Tony Sgroi, Marty Strudler, Dick Ung, Sandra Berez, Tom Bird, Marija M. Dail, Bob Dranko, Jack Huber, Homer Jonas, Ron Maidenberg, Lew Ott, R.A. Smith, Pat Wong; *back:* Al Gmuer, Lorraine Andrina, Fernando Arce, Dario Campanile, Gil di Cicco, Dennis Durrell, Flamarion Ferreira, Martin Forte, James Hegedus, Eric Heschong, Jim Hickey, Mike Humphries, Paro Hozumi, Phil Lewis, Bob Gentle, Michelle Moen, Bill Proctor, Andy Phillipson, Phil Phillipson, Jeff Richards, Jeff Richie, Dennis Venizelos, Ron Roesch; *scene planning:* Evelyn White; *ed:* Larry C. Cowan, Pat Foley, Gregory V. Watson Jr.; *fx:* Avril Pebley, Colene Riffo; *voices: Grandfather:* Lorne Greene; *Head Ratte:* Sammy Davis Jr.; *Heidi:* Margery Gray; *Willie:* Michael Bell; *Gruffle:* Peter Cullen; *Peter:* Roger DeWitt; *Herr Sessman:* Richard Erdman; *Sebastian:* Fritz Feld; *Klara:* Pamelyn Ferdin; *Fraulein Rottenmier:* Joan Gerber; *Aunt Dete:* Virginia Gregg; *Tinette:* Janet Waldo; *Schnoodle/Hootie:* Frank Welker; *The Mountain:* Mike Winslow; *Organ Grinder:* Henry Corden; *chorus:* Sue Allen, Betty Jane Baker, John Richard Bolks, Evangeline Carmichael, William R. Cole, Paul de Korte, Sandie Hall, Walter S. Harrah, Ronald Harris, Darlene Lawrence, Douglas Lawrence, Shara Lee Lucas, Ida Sue McCune, Gene J. Merlino, Loulie Jean Norman, Marilyn Powell, Paul Sandberg, Robert Tebow; *mus:* Hoyt Curtin; *orch:* Jack Steps, Tom Worrall; *mus sup:* Paul de Korte; *mus ed:* Joe Sandusky; *songs:* Sammy Cahn, Burton Lane; *titles:* Westheimer Company; *title des:* Iraj Parin, Tom Wogatzke; *i&p:* Alison Victory; *Xerox:* Star Wirth; *ph:* Jerry Mills, Allen Childs, Canadace Edwards, Curt Hall, Raymond Lee, Ralph Migliori, Joe Ponticelle, Neil Viker, Roy Wade, Brandy Whittington, Jerry Whittington; *sd:* Richard Olsen, James Coons, Don MacDougall, Chris Jenkins; *sd fx:* Sam Horta, Terry Moore, Sue Brown, Kerry Williams; *col:* Tech. *sd:* Dolby stereo. 94 min. • Based on the classic tale of a young Swiss girl who is sent by her aunt to live with her grandfather in the mountains. Her sunny disposition eventually warms Grandfather's heart just at a time when her aunt sends her to the big city to stay with a rich family. She gradually manages to spread her personal warmth and magic to all living things.

2840. Heir Bear (*Barney Bear*) 30 June 1953; *p.c.:* MGM; *dir:* Dick Lundy; *story:* Heck Allen, Jack Cosgriff; *anim:* Walter Clinton, Grant Simmons, Robert Bentley, Michael Lah; *sets:* John Didrik Johnsen; *ed:* Jim Faris; *voices:* Paul Frees; *mus:* Scott Bradley; *ph:* Jack Stevens; *prod:* Fred Quimby; *col:* Tech. *sd:* WE. 6 min. • Barney's treasure-digging activities are hampered by a troublesome gopher.

2841. Heir Conditioned (*Looney Tunes*) 26 Nov. 1955; *p.c.:* WB; *dir:* Friz Freleng; *story:* Warren Foster; *anim:* Arthur Davis, Gerry Chiniquy, Virgil Ross; *lay:* Hawley Pratt; *back:* Irv Wyner; *ed:* Treg Brown; *voices:*

Mel Blanc, Arthur Q. Bryan, Stan Freberg, Daws Butler; *mus:* Milt Franklyn; *prod mgr:* John W. Burton; *prod:* Edward Selzer; *col:* Tech. *sd:* Vit. 7 min. • Sylvester inherits a fortune and lawyer Fudd insists he invest the money. Meanwhile Sylvester's cat cronies attempt to relieve Fudd of the cash.

2842. Heir Restorer (*Casper*) 24 Jan. 1958; *p.c.:* Para Cartoons; *dir:* I. Sparber; *story:* Larz Bourne; *anim:* Myron Waldman, Wm. B. Pattengill; *sets:* Robert Little; *voices:* Frank Matalone, Norma MacMillan; *mus:* Winston Sharples; *ph:* Leonard McCormick; *prod mgr:* Seymour Shultz; *col:* Tech. *sd:* RCA. 6 min. • An English ghost has to haunt a castle until it's occupied by a Montague again. Casper helps by searching for someone with that name to take up residency.

2843. Heist and Seek (*The Dogfather*) 4 Oct. 1974; *p.c.:* Mirisch-DFE for UA; *dir:* Gerry Chiniquy; *story:* Don Christensen; *anim:* Bob Bransford, John V. Gibbs, Bob Matz, Nelson Shin; *ed:* Rick Steward; *lay:* Dick Ung; *back:* Richard H. Thomas; *titles:* Art Leonardi; *voices:* Bob Holt, Daws Butler; *mus:* Dean Elliott; *col:* Deluxe. *sd:* RCA. 6 min. • Rocky and Pug hide out in an old house from persistent Sam Spaniel, private eye.

2844. The Helicopter (*Terry-Toon*) 21 Jan. 1944; *p.c.:* TT for Fox; *dir:* Eddie Donnelly; *story:* John Foster; *mus:* Philip A. Scheib; *col:* Tech. *sd:* RCA. 6 min. • A toy helicopter, rejected by the mice, wins their respect when he rescues them from the cat.

2845. Hell-Bent for Election 11 July 1944; *p.c.:* International Education Dpt/Industrial Films for Brandon Films Inc.; *ex prod:* Stephen Bosustow; *dir:* Charles M. Jones; *story:* Robert Lees; *storyboard:* John Hubley, Phil Eastman, William T. Hurtz; *des:* Zack Schwartz; *voices:* Frank Graham, The Sportsmen Quartet; *mus:* Earl Robinson; *lyrics:* E.Y. Harburg, Karen Morley; *prod sup:* Adrian Woolery, Ed Gershman; *United Automobile Workers (CIO): president:* R.J. Thomas; *secretary/treasurer:* George F. Addes; *vice presidents:* Richard T. Frankenstein, Walter P. Reuther; *col:* Tech. *snd.* 5 min. • An evil infiltrator tries to prevent "The Roosevelt Express" from getting through but thanks to railroad worker Joe keeping alert, the train gets through and wins the war. Made for the 1944 presidential campaign by many artists outside working hours with an overall charge of $25 a viewing for union groups.

2846. Hello 1975; *p.c.:* The Hubley Studio; *dir/des/sets:* Faith Hubley; *anim:* William Littlejohn, Emily Hubley, Fred Burns; *voices:* Georgia, Emily, Ray & Mark Hubley; *mus:* William Russo; *soloists:* Dizzy Gillespie, Toots Thielemans; *i&p:* Janet Benn, Elizabeth Sackler Berner; *ph:* Nick Vasu; *prod sup:* Janet Benn, Marie Plagianos; *lab:* CFI. col. sd. 10 min. *Seq: Cockaboody; Moonbird.* • Three outer-space visitors observe the curious goings-on on planet Earth.

2847. Hello Aloha (*Goofy*) 8 Feb. 1952; *p.c.:* Walt Disney prods for RKO; *dir:* Jack Kinney; *story:* Dick Kinney, Milt Schaffer; *anim:* George Nicholas, Ed Aardal, Hugh Fraser, John Sibley; *fx:* Dan MacManus; *lay:* Al Zinnen; *back:* Art Riley; *voices:* Harry Owens, Pinto Colvig, James MacDonald; *mus:* Joseph S. Dubin, Harry Owens & his Royal Hawaiian Orchestra; *col:* Tech. *sd:* RCA. 6 min. • Determined to get away from the pressures of modern day life, Geef escapes to a Hawaiian island where time stands still.

2848. Hello, How Am I? (*Popeye*) 14 July 1939; *p.c.:* The Fleischer Studio for Para; *prod:* Max Fleischer; *dir:* Dave Fleischer; *anim:* William Henning, Abner Matthews; *ed:* Kitty Pfister; *voices:* Jack Mercer, Margie Hines, Lou Fleischer; *mus:* Sammy Timberg; *prod sup:* Sam Buchwald, Isidore Sparber; b&w. *sd:* WE. 8 min. • Popeye meets his double when Wimpy disguises himself in order to get some free hamburgers.

2849. Hell's Bells (*Silly Symphony*) 11 Nov. 1929; *p.c.:* Walter E. Disney for Colum; *dir:* Walt Disney; *anim:* Ub Iwerks; *mus:* Carl W. Stalling; b&w. *sd:* PCP. 6 min. • Burlesque on the Satanic underworld.

2850. Hell's Fire (*Famous Fairytale*) 6 Jan. 1934; *p.c.:* Celebrity prods; *prod/dir:* Ub Iwerks; *anim:* Grim Natwick, Berny Wolf; *voice:* Jane Withers; *mus:* Art Turkisher; *col:* Ciné. *sd:* PCP. 9 min. • Willie Whopper scales a volcano and falls to Hades where he encounters many wicked characters from history and literature.

2851. Hells Heels (*Oswald*) 3 June 1930; *p.c.:* Univ; *dir:* Walter Lantz; *anim:* "Bill" Nolan, Ray Abrams, Manuel Moreno; *voice:* Mickey Rooney; *mus:* James Dietrich; b&w. *sd:* WE. 6½ min. • Oswald and Putrid Pete

arrive in a western town where Pete gets Ozzie to rob the bank. Our hero escapes and discovers an orphan in the desert who turns out to be the sheriff's son.

2852. The Helpful Geni (*Terry-Toon*) Oct. 1951; *p.c.:* TT for Fox; *dir:* Connie Rasinski; *story:* Tom Morrison; *anim:* Jim Tyer; *sets:* Art Bartsch; *voices:* Dayton Allen; *mus:* Philip A. Scheib; *ph:* Douglas Moye; *col:* Tech. *sd:* RCA. 6 min. • A bullied cat enlists the help of a goofy geni to wreak his revenge on the bulldog.

2853. A Helping Paw (*Color Rhapsody*) 7 Jan. 1941; *p.c.:* Colum; *dir:* Sid Marcus; *anim:* Art Davis; *sets:* Clark Watson; *ed:* Edward Moore; *voices:* Mel Blanc; *mus:* Joe de Nat; *prod mgr:* George Winkler; *col:* Tech. *sd:* RCA. 6 min. • Chester is fitted with strong glasses while Tobias, the doctor's inebriated dog, has to guide him home.

2854. Helpless Hippo (*Mighty Mouse*) Mar. 1954; *p.c.:* TT for Fox; *dir:* Connie Rasinski; *story/voice:* Tom Morrison; *anim:* Jim Tyer; *sets:* Art Bartsch; *mus:* Philip A. Scheib; *ph:* Douglas Moye; *col:* Tech. *sd:* RCA. 7 min. • Mighty Mouse babysits with a baby hippo.

2855. Helter Shelter (*Woody Woodpecker*) 17 Jan. 1955; *p.c.:* Walter Lantz prods for Univ; *dir:* Paul J. Smith; *story:* Michael Maltese; *anim:* La Verne Harding, Robert Bentley, Herman Cohen, Gil Turner; *sets:* Art Landy; *voices:* Daws Butler, Grace Stafford; *mus:* Clarence Wheeler; *prod mgr:* William E. Garity; *col:* Tech. *sd:* RCA. 6 min. • An old lady takes pity on Woody and gives him shelter from the storm but her husband and his dog aren't so keen on the idea.

2856. Helter Swelter (*Screen Song*) 25 Aug. 1950; *p.c.:* Famous for Para; *dir:* Seymour Kneitel; *anim:* Al Eugster, Wm. B. Pattengill; *mus:* Winston Sharples; *ph:* Leonard McCormick; *prod mgr:* Sam Buchwald; *col:* Tech. *sd:* RCA. 7 min. • The first day of summer proves too hot even for the sun.

2857. Hen Fruit (*Oswald*) 8 Jan. 1929; *p.c.:* Winkler for Univ; *prod:* Charles B. Mintz; *anim:* Isadore Freleng; b&w. sil. 5 min. • Oswald eventually succeeds in getting a hen to lay eggs.

2858. The Hen Pecked Rooster (*Noveltoon*) 18 Feb. 1944; *p.c.:* Famous for Para; *dir:* Seymour Kneitel; *story:* Jack Mercer, Jack Ward; *anim:* Bill Hudson; *mus:* Sammy Timberg; *prod mgr:* Sam Buchwald; *col:* Tech. *sd:* RCA. 8 min. • Henry Rooster uses a mouse to help keep his domineering wife in her place.

2859. Henhouse Henery (*Looney Tunes*) 2 July 1949; *p.c.:* WB; *dir:* Robert McKimson; *story:* Warren Foster; *anim:* Manny Gould, John Carey, Charles McKimson, Pete Burness, Phil de Lara; *lay:* Cornett Wood; *back:* Richard H. Thomas; *ed:* Treg Brown; *voices:* Mel Blanc; *mus:* Carl Stalling; *prod mgr:* John W. Burton; *prod:* Edward Selzer; *col:* Tech. *sd:* Vit. 7 min. • Henery Hawk is sent on a wild goose chase by Foghorn Leghorn when he sets out to catch a chicken.

2860. Henpecked (*Oswald*) 25 Aug. 1930; *p.c.:* Univ; *dir:* Walter Lantz; *anim:* "Bill" Nolan, Ray Abrams, Manuel Moreno, Clyde Geronimi, "Pinto" Colvig; *mus:* James Dietrich; b&w. *sd:* WE. 6½ min. • Putrid Pete doesn't like neighbor Oswald's music and when Ozzie's nephews arrive to play, he likes it even less.

2861. The Henpecked Duck (*Looney Tunes*) 30 Aug. 1941; *p.c.:* Leon Schlesinger prods for WB; *dir:* Robert Clampett; *story:* Warren Foster; *anim:* John Carey; *ed:* Treg Brown; *voices:* Mel Blanc, Sara Berner; *mus:* Carl W. Stalling; *ph:* John W. Burton; *prod sup:* Henry Binder, Raymond G. Katz; b&w. *sd:* Vit. 7 min. • While Daffy is left in charge of his wife's egg, he does some conjuring tricks, making it disappear and then he can't bring it back.

2862. Henpecked Hoboes 26 Oct. 1946; *p.c.:* MGM; *dir:* Tex Avery; *story:* Heck Allen; *anim:* Ed Love, Ray Abrams, Preston Blair, Walter Clinton; *character des:* Irven Spence; *sets:* John Didrik Johnsen; *ed:* Fred MacAlpin; *voices:* Dick Nelson; *mus:* Scott Bradley; *prod:* Fred Quimby; *col:* Tech. *sd:* WE. 7 min. • Two hungry bears attempt to catch a chicken.

2863. The Hep Cat (*Looney Tunes*) 3 Oct. 1942; *p.c.:* Leon Schlesinger prods for WB; *dir/lay:* Robert Clampett; *story:* Warren Foster; *anim:* Robert McKimson, Vive Risto; *back:* Michael Sasanoff; *ed:* Treg Brown; *voices:* Mel Blanc, Kent Rogers, Sara Berner; *mus:* Carl W. Stalling; *ph:* John W. Burton; *prod sup:* Henry Binder, Raymond G. Katz; *col:* Tech. *sd:* Vit. 7

min. • An alley cat tries to impress a young female feline, but it's all the handywork of an artful dog! First *Looney Tune* to go into color.

2864. Hep Cat Symphony (*Noveltoon*) 4 Feb. 1949; *p.c.*: Famous for Para; *dir*: Seymour Kneitel; *story*: Carl Meyer, Jack Mercer; *anim*: Dave Tendlar, Marty Taras; *sets*: Tom Ford; *voices*: Jack Mercer, Jackson Beck; *mus*: Winston Sharples; *prod mgr*: Sam Buchwald; *col*: Tech. *sd*: RCA. 6 min. • Katnip finds the mouse orchestra next door disturbs his jazz and decides to put a stop to it.

2865. Hep Mother Hubbard (*Terry-Toon*) Mar. 1956; *p.c.*: TT for Fox; *dir*: Connie Rasinski; *story*: Tom Morrison; *anim*: Jim Tyer; *mus*: Philip A. Scheib; *ph*: Douglas Moye; *col*: Tech. *sd*: RCA. 6 min. • Mother Hubbard's dog proceeds to eat her out of house and home to a modern jazz score.

2866. Her Ben (*Aesop's Film Fable*) 25 July 1926; *p.c.*: Fables Pictures Inc for Pathé; *dir*: Paul Terry; b&w. *sil*. 10 min. • Featuring a burlesque on the "Ben-Hur" chariot race.

2867. Her First Egg (*Paul Terry-Toon*) 26 July 1931; *p.c.*: Terry, Moser & Coffman for Educational/Fox; *dir*: Frank Moser, Paul Terry; *mus*: Philip A. Scheib; b&w. *sd*: WE. 6 min. • A festival is given for a hen's first egg. Hawks descend, capture the chick and the hero comes to the rescue in his airplane.

2868. Her Honor the Mare (*Popeye*) 5 Nov. 1943; *p.c.*: Famous for Para; *dir*: I. Sparber; *story*: Jack Mercer, Jack Ward; *anim*: Jim Tyer, Ben Solomon; *sets*: Shane Miller; *voice*: Jack Mercer; *mus*: Sammy Timberg; *prod mgr*: Sam Buchwald; b&w. *sd*: WE. 8 min. Tech reissue: 6 Oct. 1950. • Popeye's nephews try to sneak an old nag into the house.

2869. Herb Alpert and the Tijuana Brass Double Feature 1966; *p.c*: Hubley Studio for Para; *prod/dir/des*: John and Faith Hubley; *anim*: Gerald Baldwin, Phil Duncan, Emery Hawkins, Barry Nelson, Rod Scribner, Ed Smith; *mus*: "Tijuana Taxi" and "Spanish Flea" by Herb Alpert; *col*. *snd*. 5 min. • A bagatelle of satiric visualizations of two songs recorded by Herb Alpert.

2870. Hercules 27 June 1997; *p.c.*: Walt Disney Enterprises, Inc. for BV; *dir*: John Musker, Ron Clements; *prod*: Alice Dewey, John Musker, Ron Clements; *scr*: Ron Clements & John Musker, Donald McEnery & Bob Shaw, Irene Mecchi; *story*: Kelly Wightman, Randy Cartwright, Kaan Kaylon, John Ramirez, Jeff Snow, Vance Gerry, Kirk Hanson, Tamara Lusher-Stocker, Francis Glebas, Mark Kennedy, Bruce M. Morris, Don Dougherty, Thom. Enriquez; *asso prod*: Kendra Haaland; *art dir*: Andy Gaskill; *prod des*: Gerald Scarfe; *artistic sup*: *story*: Barry Johnson; *prod stylist*: Sue C. Nichols; *lay*: Rasoul Azadani; *back*: Thomas Cardone; *visual fx*: Mauro Maressa; *cgi*: Roger L. Gould; *clean-up*: Nancy Kniep; *artistic co-ord*: Dan Hansen; *prod mgr*: Peter del Vecho; *technical co-ord*: Ann Tucker; *character anim*: "Adult Hercules": *anim sup*: Andreas Deja; *anim*: Georges Abolin, Patrick Delage, Sahin Ersoz, Tom Gately, Gilda Palinginis Kouros, Doug Krohn, Jean Morel, Marc Smith, Bill Waldman, Andreas Wessel-Therhorn; "Baby & Young Hercules": *anim sup*: Randy R. Haycock; *anim*: Michael Cadeno, Danny Galieote, Michael Stocker, Eric Walls, Anthony Ho Wong; *asst*: Robb Pratt; "Phil": *anim sup*: Eric Goldberg; *anim*: Caroline Cruikshank, Raul Garcia, Teddy Hall, Richard Hoppe, Bert Klein, Teresa Martin, Tom Roth, Theresa Wiseman; "Hades": *anim sup*: Nik Ranieri; *anim*: James Baker, Bolhem Bouchiba, Roger Chiasson, Eric Delbecq, Juanjo Guarnido, Dave Kuhn, Jamie Duff, Sergio Pablos, Mike Polvani; "Meg": *anim sup*: Ken Duncan; *anim*: Jared Beckstrand, Bob Bryan, Joe Oh, Catherine Poulain, Mark Pudleiner, William Recinos, Stéphane Sainte-Foi, Yoshimichi Tamura; "Pegasus": *anim sup*: Ellen Woodbury; *anim*: David Block, Steven P. Gordon, Kent Hammerstrom, David Hancock, Jeffrey Johnson, Mike Kunkel, Enis Tahsin Özgür; "Zeus & Hera": *anim sup*: Anthony de Rosa; *anim*: Robert Espanto Domingo, Borja Montoro; *asst*: Michael Genz; "The Muses": *anim sup*: Michael Show; *anim*: Adam Dykstra, T. Daniel Hofstedt, Jay Jackson, Dan O'Sullivan; "Pain & Panic": *anim sup* "Pain": James Lopez; *anim sup* "Panic": Brian Ferguson; *anim*: Marc Eoche Duval; "Titans & Cyclops": *anim sup*: Dominique Monfery; *anim*: David Berthier, Thierry Goulard, Ron Husband; "the Fates/Thebans": *anim sup*: Nancy Beiman, Oskar Urretabizkaia; *anim*: Howard E. Baker, Raffaella Filipponi, Bill Fletcher, Steve Hunter, Mike "Moe" Merell; *asst*: Chris Hurtt, William E. Miller; *cgi technical dir*: Shyh-Chyuan Huang, Peter Farson, Timothy Tompkins, Lisa Suzuki, Sergi Sagas-Rica, Mark

Empey, Kee-Suk "Kent" Mahn; *cgi look development & lighting*: Marcus Warren Hobbs, Jeffrey Babcock Wolverton; *cgi modeler*: Erica Cassetti; *Misc*: "Nessus": *anim*: Chris Bailey; "Hermes": *anim*: Michael Swofford; *Gods & Misc*: *anim*: Jean-Luc Ballester, Dave Kupczyk, David Alan Zaboski; *rough inbet*: Pierre Alary, Noreen Beasley, Wendie Lynn Fischer, Benjamin Gonzalez, Clay Kaytis, Mario Menjivar, Gary D. Payne, David Moses Pimentel, Christopher Sonnenburg, Kevin M. Smith, Aliki Theofilopoulos, John Webber, Jean-Claude Tran-Quang-Thieu, George Benavides, James Hull, Joseph C. Moshier, Bobby Alcid Rubio, Wes Sullivan, Michael Wu; *Paris unit artistic sup*: *lay*: Jean Christophe Poulain; *clean-up*: Lieve Miessen, Christophe Charbonnel; *visual fx*: Peter de Mund; *back*: Lisa Keene Robledo; *prod mgrs*: Coralie Cudot, Jean Luc Florinda; *lay*: *lay stylist*: Rasoul Azadani; *journeyman*: Daniel Hu, Doug Walker, Karen A. Keller, Rick Moore, Antonio Navarro, Olivier Adam, Allen C. Tam, Kevin R. Adams, Billy George, Simon O'Leary, Zoltán Maros, Bill Frake, Vincent Massy de la Chesneraye; *lay asst*: Michael B. O'Mara, Denise Louise Klitsie, Mark E. Koerner, Trish Coveney-Rees, Chung Sup Yoon, Robert Cardone, Lissa Ainley, Yong-Hong Zhong, Loic Rastout, Marec Fritzinger, Craig Elliott, Ray Chen, Max Braslavsky, Thomas Debitus; *blue sketch*: Madlyn O'Neill, Valerie Braun, Cyndee Larae Novitch, Eithne Ersöz, Noel C. Johnson; *based on an idea by* Joe Haidar; *character design & visual development*: *key visual development*: Bruce Zick, Hans Bacher, Rowland B. Wilson, Audrey Brandl, Marek Buchwald, Rick Maici, Jean Gillmore, Tina Price, Jeff Ranjo, Joe Grant, Gay Lawrence, Valerio Ventura; *character sculptures*: Kent Melton; *back*: Natalie Franscioni-Karp, Colin Stimpson, Gregory Alexander Drolette, Sunny Apinchapong, Pierre Pavloff, Don Moore, Olivier Besson, Joaquim Royo Morales, George Taylor, Thierry Fournier, Ian S. Gooding, Mi Kyung Juung Raynis, James J. Martin, Leonard Robledo, John Lee, William Lorencz, Brad Hicks, Philip Phillipson, Jean-Paul Fernandez, Jerry Loveland, Patricia Palmer-Phillipson, Tom Woodington, Susan Hackett Dalipagic, Justin Brandstater, Kelly McGraw, Scott Fassett, Serge Michaels, Jason Horley, Brooks Campbell, Michael Kurinsky, Carl Jones, Patricia Millereau, Daniel Read, Maryann Thomas, Christophe Vacher; *digital paint*: David McCamley, Christine Laubach, Elissa Bello, Greg Miller; *CAPS sup*: *scene plan*: Tom Baker; *anim check*: Janet Bruce; *col models*: Karen Comella; *paint/check*: Hortensia M. Casagran; *2d anim process*: Robyn L. Roberts; *digital film print*: Brandy Hill; *admin mgr*: Loni Beckner Black; *asst art co-ord*: Tom Mazzocco; *clean-up anim*: "Hercules": *key*: Dan Tanaka, Marco Allrd, Judith Barnes, Jamie Kezlarian Bolio, Akemi Horiuchi-Gutierrez, Emily Juliano, Wendy J. Muir, Dana M. Reemes, Jacqueline M. Sanchez; *asst*: Gerard Brady, Cynthia Jill French, Chan Woo Jung, Christine Landes, Jean-Christophe Lie, Daniel Yoontaek Lim, Marty Schwartz; *break*: Mike Disa, Carolyn Froblom Gliona; *inbet*: Oliver Acker, Cyndy Bohonovsky, Jill Friemark, Nikolas Frangos, Dietz Toshio Ichishita, Stephanie Olivieri, Flora Sung Park, Jong Won Park, Nicolas Ruedy; "Meg": *key*: Marianne Tucker, Renee Holt, Myung Kang Teague, Florence Montceau, Elizabeth S. Watasin; *asst*: Scott Claus, Teresa Eidenbock, Jeroen Dejonckheere, Sean Gallimore, Pierre Girault, Cyril Pedrosa; *break*: Aidan Flynn, Benoit Meurzec, Nicole Stranz, Cathie Karas Wilke; *inbet*: Kimberly Dwinell, Louis C. Callegos, Jeff W. Hong, Jim Marquez, Nicholas Quere; "Phil": *key*: Edward R. Gutierrez; *asst*: Marcia Kimura Dougherty, Lee Dunkman, Susan McKinsey Goldberg, Celinda S. Kennedy, Brian Mainolfi, Yoon Sook Nam; *break*: Munir A. Bhatti, Jody Kooistra, Jim Snider; *inbet*: Chrissenson M. Casuco, Casey Coffey, Jane Misek, Fara Rose; "Hades": *key*: Bill Berg; *asst*: Carl Philip Hall, Javier Espinosa Banuelos, Eric Pigors, Maria Angela Iturriza Freire, Gizella Gregan, Doug Post, David Recinos; *break*: Dan Bond, Nicole de Bellefroid, Neal Stanley Goldstein, Denise Meehan, Anne Fellerin; *inbet*: Erik Kuska, Luän Vu-Ba; "Zeus/Hera/Muses": *key*: Merry Kanawyer Clingen; *asst*: Debbie Armstrong Holmes, Jane Tucker Bennett, Christophe Charbonnel, Inna Chon, Ray Harris, Vera Lanpher, Rich Wilkie, Eunice (Eun Ok) Yu, Laurence Adam Bessiere, Farouk Cherfi, Annette Morel, Bernadette Moley, Marc Tosolini; *break*: Brian D. Kennon, Ludovic Letrun, Jan Naylor; *inbet*: Kim Dunning, Bernard Dourdent, Eun Sang Jang, Michael Ludy, Kathleen Thorson, Justin (Dusty) Wakefield; "Theban Townspeople": *key*: Terry Naughton; *asst*: Jesus Cortes, Leticia Lichtwardt, Marsha W.J. Park-Yum, Carl A. Bell; *break*: Jim Brummett, Steve Lenze, Cheryl Polakow-Knight; *inbet*: Gary Myers; "Young Hercules/ Baby Hercules": *key*: Juliet Duncan; *asst*: Sue Adnofoz Wesley Chun, Richard Drocha, Bruce Strock, Susan Sugita, Mark Alan Mitchell; *break*: Cliff Freitas, Kevin Grow; *inbet:* Matthew Haber, Bruce B. Heller, Sean Anthony Jimenez; *"Nessus/Agorans/Goddesses": key:* Natasha Dukelski Selfridge; *asst:* Peggy Tonkonogy; *asst:* Rick Kohlschmidt; *inbet:* Sam Levine; *"Pain & Panic":* Stephan Zupkas; *asst:* Karen A. Hardenbergh, Dave Suding, George Sukara; *break:* Steven Thompson, Allison Renna; *inbet:* Donna Marie Dubuc, Jeff Harter; *"The Fates/Gods/Penelope/Baby Pegasus": key:* Gail Frank; *asst:* Mike Hazy, Mary Measures; *break:* Ron Westlund, Chang Yei Cho; *inbet:* Frank Dietz, Patrick McClintock; *"Pegasus": key:* Kathleen M. Bailey; *asst:* Michael G. McKinney, Serge Bussone, Calvin le Duc, Janet Heerhan Kwon; *break:* Whitney Martin; *inbet:* Ramya Kuruppu Black, Ely Lester, Jennifer Phillips, Chun Yin Joey So; *"Amphitryon/Alcmene": key:* Kaaren Lundeen; *asst:* Yung Soo Kim; *break:* Edward B. Goral; *inbet:* Cynthia Landeros, Bob Persichetti; *"Titans/Cyclops": key:* Philippe Briones, Xavier Villez; *asst:* Nicholas Keramidas, Gontran Hoarau, Philippe Hooghe, Pierre Seurin, Sylvaine Terriou; *break:* Philippe Malka-Phirum Sou; *inbet:* Christine Chatal; *addit.clean-up anim: sup key asst:* Marshall L. Toomey, Alex Topete, Tony Anselmo, Philip S. Boyd, Margie Daniels, June M. Fujimoto, Kris Heller, Allison Hollen, Tracy M. Lee, Susan Lantz, Steve Lubin, Miriam McDonnell, Brian B. McKim, Lori Noda, Dorothea B. Paul, Maria Rosetti, Randy Sanchez, Vincent Siracusano, Terry Wozniak; *asst:* Ron Cohee, Mike Lester, Donnie Long, Mary-Jean Repchuk, Trevor Tamboline, Bill Thinnes, Kim Torpey; *break:* Todd H. Ammons, Mary Jo Ayers, Dan Bowman, Diana Coco, Regina Conroy, Larry R. Flores, Brigitte Franzca-Fritz, Arturo A. Hernández, Christopher Hubbard, Al Salgado, Hugo Soriano, Michael Wiesmeier; *inbet:* Raul Aguirre Jr., Kevin A. Barber, Patricia Billings, Jason Feltz; *visual fx: visual fx anim sup:* Dorse A. Lanpher, James DeValera Mansfield; *fx anim:* Chris Jenkins, Dan Lund, Ed Coffey, Allen Blyth, Kathleen Quaife-Hodge, Tom Hush, Joey Mildenberger, Thierry Chaffoin, Phillip D. Vigil, Dan Chaika, Colbert Fennelly, John A. Armstrong, Mike Duhatschek, Kevin O'Neil, Amanda J. Talbot, Allen Stovall, Mark Cumberton, Ko Hashiguchi, Jon William Lopez, Marlon West, Michael Cadwallader Jones, Susan Oslin, James Menehune Goss; *fx technical dir:* Aliza Gesner, Craig L. Hoffman, Chris Hummel; *fx asst:* Mabel Gesner, Elizabeth Holmes, John Tucker, Steve Starr, Joseph Christopher Pepe, Karel Zilliacus, Nate Pacheco, Michael A. Toth, Graham Woods, Geoffrey C. Everts, Dave Lyons, Kristine Brown, Mouloud Oussid, Gregory Regeste, Ivan Kassabov, Thomas Walsh, David M. Kcenich, Peter Francis Pepe Jr., Van Shirvanian; *ex break:* Faris Al-Saffar, Monica Sena, Ida C. Voskanian, Etienne Aubert; *fx inbet:* Dennis Spicer, Steven Filatro, Tatiana Kellert, D. Jay Baker, Melinda Wang, Nicole A. Zamora, Alexis Venet, Gary Gallegos, Thierry Beltrami, Virginie Augustin, J. Joseph Mahoney; *scene set-up asst:* Faye Tipton; *addit visual fx sup:* David A. Bossert, Mark Myer; *addit.visual fx anim:* Margaret Craig-Chang, Joseph Gilland, Brice Mallier, Steve Moore, Masa Oshiro; *fx key asst:* Sean Applegate, Marko Barrows, Angela Anastasia Diamos, Joan Doyle, Ty Elliott, John Fargnoli, Ray Hofstedt, Cynthia Neill Knizek; *fx asst:* Kim Burk, Tom Pope, Lisa Reinert, Mary Mullen; *fx technical dir:* Craig Thayer; *fx break:* Eduardo Brieno. Jeffrey Lawrence van Tuyl; *fx inbet:* John Aquino, Kevin A. Barber, Robert Allen Blalock, Verell (Skip) Bowers, Ernesto Brieño, Paul Briggs, Carl Canga, Paul R. Kashuk Jr., Michael T. Montgomery, Derrick L. McKenzie, Christopher Page, Jeffrey C. Plamenig, Mark Delaine Rath, Jay Shindell, Lora M. Spran, Sean Strain, Dawn Wells; *ed:* Tom Finan, Jeff Jones, John K. Carr, James Melton, Ivan Bilancio, Julie Rogers, Paul Chandler Carrera, Eric C. Daroca, Hermann H. Schmidt; *voices: Adult Hercules:* Tate Donovan; *Young Hercules:* Joshua Keaton; *Young Hercules (singing):* Roger Bart; *Phil:* Danny DeVito; *Hades:* James Woods; *Meg:* Susan Egan; *Zeus:* Rip Torn; *Hera:* Samantha Eggar; *Muses:* Lillias White, Cheryl Freeman, LaChanze, Roz Ryan, Vaneese Thomas; *Pain:* Bobcat Goldthwait; *Panic:* Matt Frewer; *Cyclops:* Patrick Pinney; *The Fates:* Amanda Plummer, Carole Shelley, Paddi Edwards; *Hermes:* Paul Shaffer; *Nessus:* Jim Cummings; *Narrative:* Charlton Heston; *Alcmene:* Barbara Barrie; *Earthquake Lady:* Mary Kay Bergman; *Burnt Man:* Corey Burton; *Apollo:* Keith David; *Heavy-set Woman:* Kathleen Freeman; *Little Boys:* Bug Hall, Kellen Hathaway; *Amphitryon:* Hal Holbrook; *Demetrius:* Wayne Knight; *Ithicles:* Aaron Michael Metchic; *also:* Tawatha Agee, Jack Angel, Bob Bergen, Rodger Bumpass, Debi Derryberry, Bill Farmer, Sherry Lynn, Mickie McGowan, Phil Proctor, Jan Rabson, Fonzi Thornton, Erik von Detten, Shelton Becton, Jennifer Darling, Milt Grayson, Denise Pickering, Riley Steiner, Ken Williams; *songs:* Alan Menken, David Zippel; *ex mus prod:* Chris Montan; *orch/arrangements:* Danny Troob, Michael Starobin; *con-*

ductor/vocal arrangements:* Michael Kosarin; *mus prod sup:* Tod Cooper; *score rec/mix:* John Richards; *song rec/mix:* Frank Wolf, John Richards; *mus ed:* Earl Ghaffari, Kathleen Fogarty-Bennett, Daniel Gaber; *orch contractors:* Sandy de Crescent, John Miller; *vocal contractors:* Fonzi Thornton, Bobbi Page; *mus copyist:* Dominic Fidelibus; *addit.song rec:* Josh Abbey, Malcolm Pollack; *mus co-ord:* Deniece La Rocca, Tom Coyne MacDougall; *"Go the Distance" prod/arrangement:* Walter Afanasieff, Michael Bolton; *performed by* Michael Bolton; *casting:* Ruth Lambert, Meredith Layne; *prod dir:* David J. Steinberg; *snr mgr prod:* Gretchen Maschmeyer Albrecht; *snr mgr scene planning:* Joe Juliano; *asst prod mgrs: story/3d fx:* Kevin Susman; *editorial:* Stacey Ernst; *lay:* Tod Marsden; *anim:* Rebecca Pahr Huntley; *sweatbox:* Brian Behling; *clean-up:* Liane E. Dietz; *cgi:* Cathy Leahy; *visual fx:* Kim Gray; *col models:* Holly E. Bratton; *back:* Lindsey K. Collins; *anim check:* Doeri Welch Greiner; *CAPS & retakes:* Shawne Zarubica; *Paris: lay:* Wendy Plump-Martini; *back & fx:* Michael de la Cruz; *clean-up:* Etienne Longa; *prod co-ords: video ref:* Lorry Ann Shea; *cgi:* Maryann McLeod; *co-ord for the prod:* Patrick Golier; *clean-up co-ord:* Sylvie Bennett-Fauqué; *scene plan:* Katherine A. Kettering; *CAPS:* Kirsten Bulmer; *CAPS & retakes:* Brenda McGill; *scene plan:* Sara Bleick, Cindy Goode, Mark Henley, Ron Jackson, Raphael Vincente, John Cunningham, Mary Lescher; *scene plan & fx data entry:* Samantha Bowers Nicholson, Jamal M. Davis, Gary Stubblefield; *reuse librarian:* Vicki L. Casper; *anim check: asst sup:* Barbara Wiles, Karen S. Paat, Mavis Shafer, M. Janette Adams, Janette Hulett, Willis Middleton, Denise M. Mitchell, Helen O'Flynn, Michael O'Mara, Gary Shafer, Pierre Sucaud, Nicolette Bonnell, Daniel Cohen, Karen Hepburn; *col stylist:* Penny Coulter, Barbara Lynn Hamane, Debbie Jorgensborg, Maria Gonzalez, Sylvia Sanchez, Judith Tolley; *2d anim process: asst sup:* Karen N. China; *digital mark-up:* Lynnette E. Cullen; *2d anim processors:* David Braden, Jo Ann Breuer, Val D'arcy, Gareth Fishbaugh, Corey Fredrickson, Robert Lizardo, Michael McFerren, Richard McFerren, Stacie K. Reece, David J. Rowe, Sarah J. Cole, Jan Gutowski, Barbara J. Poirier, Andrew Simmons, Gary W. Smith; *painting: asst sup painting:* Irma Velez, Russell Blandino, Phyllis Estelle Fields; *asst sup col model mark-up:* David J. Zywicki; *asst mgr:* Chris Hecox; *col model mark-up:* Sherrie Cuzzort, Grace H. Shirado, Beth Ann McCoy-Gee, Gina Evans-Howard, Bill Andres, Cindy Finn, Karrie Keuling; *registration:* Karan Lee-Storr, Leyla C. Amaro-Pelaez; *paint mark-up:* Myrian Tello, Roberta Borchardt, Bonnie A. Ramsey, Barbara Newby, Sally-Anne King, Carmen R. Alvarez, Cathy Wainess Walters; *paint:* Joyce Alexander, Carmen S. Anderson, Phyllis Bird, Kirk Axtell II, Joey Calderon, Ofra Afuta Calderon, Sybil Cuzzort, Janice M. Caston, Florida Dámbrosio, Robert Dettloff, Nika Dunne, Sylvia Filcak, Christina Frazier, Dawn Gates, Patricia L. Gold, Debbie Green, Vernette K. Griffee, Stevie Hirsch, David Karp, Angelika Katz, Kukhee Lee, Jacquewyn Chambers Martin, Harlene Mears, Deborah Mooneyham, Karen Lynne Nugent, Ken O'Malley, Paulino, Bruce G. Phillipson, Rosalinde Praamsma, Matthew J. Schiavone, Patrick Sekino, Heidi Woodward Shellhorn, Don Shump, Fumiko R. Sommer, S. Ann Sullivan, Roxanne M. Taylor, Tami Terusa, Britt van der Nagel, Christine Ng Wong; *final check:* Teri N. McDonald, Monica Albracht Marroquin, Lea Dahlen, Cathy Mirkovich-Peterson, Misoon Kim, Saskia Raevouri; *compositing:* James "JR" Russell, Dolores Pope, Tim Gales, Joseph Pfening, Michelle Sammartino, Shannon Fallis-Kane; *digital film printing & opticals:* Tony Poriazis; *ph/film rec:* John Aardal, John Derderian, Chris Gee, Bill Fadness, Michael Lehman, David J. Link, Jennie Mouzis; *quality control:* Chuck Warren; *ph co-ord:* Jeanne Leone, Jennifer L. Booth; *Render I/O: technical lead:* Mark M. Tokunaga; *admin:* Jason S. MacDonald, Elkeer Zaldumbide; *Richard Purdom Studio: anim sup:* Richard Purdom; *prod mgr:* Jill Thomas, Sue Robertson; *prod secretary:* Carol Ashen; *anim:* Steve Small, Barry Baker, Craig Baxter, Kevin Spruce, Tanya Fenton, Odile Comon; *clean-up:* Sue Baker, Karen Narramore, Glenn Whiting, Sue Woodward, Nicola Ibbotson, Alison Wells, Isabel Radage, Julianna Franchetti; *inbet:* Theresa Whatley, Gideon Rigal, Richard Jeffery, Stuart Ellis, Manu Roig; *rendering:* Dee Morgan; *check:* Paul Gooding, Amanda Plummer; *prod asst:* Rudy Cardenas, Bill Davis, Evariste Ferreira, Bêrangère Fresard, Alexandra Gellad, Autumn Rain Glading, Joyce Ike Miyashiro, Philip B. Isaacs, Wendell L. Harvey, Tanja Knoblich, Monica Lago-Greenberg, Renato Lattanzi, Frederick Lissau, Allyson Mitchell, Jeffrey Moznett, Frederika Pepping, Michele Silverstein, Alexandra Skinazi, Nora Quinn-Souffir, Robert Stemwell, Krista Storm, Carrie A. Wilksen; *rec asst:* Angela Lepito; *prod support:* Lesley Addario, Jennifer Brown, Fred Berning Jr., Joe Crowley, Rose Edmonds, Silvia Gallardo, Michelle A. Hargrett, David Biello, Francois Desnus, Matthew Garbera, Jill Johnson, Catherine A. Jones, Keith Alin Lesser, Tony Matthews, Karenna Mazur, Michael J. Miller, Serge Riou, Tony Rocco, Sethann Schulke, Todd Wilson; *choreog:* Frank Gatson Jr.; *ph:* Al Vasquez, Chris Ullrich; *technology mgrs:* Edward Kummer, Enrique Santos, Dean Schiller, Kirk Bodyfelt, Ben Croy, Michael R. Fodor, Kevin J. Hussey, Michael Jedlicka, Thomas Moore Jr., Edwin R. Leonard, James J. Sepe; *prod support:* Graham S. Allen, Richard M. Barnes, Frank N. Bassi, Michael S. Blum, Brad Brooks, Letha L. Burchard, Mark R. Carlson, Nhi H. Casey, Bernard O. Ceguerra, Loren Chun, Peter Chun, Ray C. Coleman, Ludovic Delmond, Jerry A. Eisenberg, Norbert Faerstain, Robert Falco, Todd Friedline, Mark W. Gilicinski, Maria de Jesus Gomez, Kent Gordon, John D. Hoffman, Le Hua, Dave Kagels, Kevin E. Keech, Michael R. King, Hans Ku, Christine C. Lau, U-Ming "Lawrence" Lee, Jean Mandonnet, Robert A. Mortensen, Jack Mulready, Jeff Nash, Lyle S. Nojima, Troy R. Norin, Alan A. Patel, Todd Scopio, Kevin P. Shauger, Jeffrey Sickler, John Stimson, Sandy Sunseri, Joe Suzow, Warren Lee Theriot, Laurie Tracy, David Troude, Raul Anaya, Michael C. Bolds, Brent Burley, Lawrence Chai, Gina Chen, Carol J. Choy, Charlie Collins, Michael Deerkoski, Scott Doum, Elena Driskill, Dale Drummond, Scott Garrett, Steven L. Groom, Don Gworek, Gregory S. Heflin, Jason Hilkey, Bill James, Mark Jankins, Mark R. Kimball, R. Todd King, Andy C. King, Stanley B. Lippman, Brad Lowman, Michael Neville, Neil Okamoto, John Outten, Carlos Quinonez, Charles Stoner, Michael Sullivan, Dave Tonnesen, Jon Y. Wada, Mark R. Wilkins, Derek E. Wilson; *post prod:* Berenice le Maitre, Sara F. Duran, Eleanor Leah, Heather McDonald-Smith, Robert H. Bagley; *sd:* Gary Rydstrom, Shawn Murphy, Tom Johnson, Lora Hirschberg, Doc Kane, Tim Holland; *ADR supl/dial ed:* Marilyn McCoppen; *sd fx:* Pat Jackson; *foley ed:* Marian Wilde, Mary Helen Leasman, J.R. Grubbs, Ben Gold, Susan Popovic; *foley:* Skywalker Sound; *foley art:* Dennie Thorpe, Jana Vance; *addit dial rec:* Vince Caro, Howard London, Grant Maxwell, Tony Pepper, Brian Riordan; *b&w processing:* John White; *col timing:* Terry Claborn; *neg cutters:* Mary Beth Smith, Rick MacKay, Brenda Monroe; *titles:* Susan Bradley, Mark Dornfeld, Buena Vista Imaging; *col:* Tech. *sd:* Dolby Digital. 92 min. • Empowered with exceptional strength, Hercules, a young man in ancient Greece, attempts to prove himself in the eyes of his father, the great god, Zeus. He is tricked by the villainous Hades, who is plotting to take over Mount Olympus, forcing Hercules to choose between his phenomenal strength or Meg, his only true love. Pegasus, his winged horse, and Phil, his personal trainer, help him overcome obstacles and choose the right path to take.

2871. Here Kiddie, Kiddie *(Loopy de Loop)* 8 Dec. 1960; *p.c.:* Hanna-Barbera for Colum; *prod/dir:* William Hanna, Joseph Barbera; *story sketch:* Dan Gordon; *story:* Warren Foster; *anim dir:* Charles A. Nichols; *anim:* Ken Muse; *lay:* Walter Clinton; *back:* Montealegre; *ed:* Joseph Ruby; *voices:* Daws Butler, Don Messick, Jean van der Pyl; *mus:* Hoyt Curtin; *titles:* Lawrence Gobel; *col:* East. *sd:* RCA. 6 min. • Loopy tries to prevent a baby from wandering through the zoo.

2872. Here Today, Gone Tamale *(Looney Tunes)* 29 Aug. 1959; *p.c.:* WB; *dir:* Friz Freleng; *story:* Michael Maltese; *anim:* Gerry Chiniquy, Art Davis, Virgil Ross; *lay:* Hawley Pratt; *back:* Tom O'Loughlin; *ed:* Treg Brown; *voices:* Mel Blanc, Tom Holland; *mus:* Milt Franklyn; *prod mgr:* William Orcutt; *prod:* David H. DePatie; *col:* Tech. *sd:* Vit. 7 min. • Speedy Gonzales wins the hearts of all the girls. The male mice decide to let Sylvester keep him occupied.

2873. Here's Nudnik Aug. 1965; *p.c.:* Rembrant for Para; *prod:* William L. Snyder; *dir:* Gene Deitch; *mus:* SHQuintet; *col. sd.* 6 min. • The accident-prone Nudnik tries to bake a loaf while dealing with an overflowing sink. • See: *Nudnik*

2874. Here's to Good Old Jail *(Terry-Toon)* 10 June 1938; *p.c.:* TT for Educational/Fox; *dir:* Ed Donnelly; *mus:* Philip A. Scheib; b&w. *sd:* RCA. 6 min. • Dogs break out of jail.

2875. Herman the Catoonist *(Herman & Katnip)* 15 May 1953; *p.c.:* Famous for Para; *dir:* I. Sparber; *story:* I. Klein; *anim:* Myron Waldman, Larry Silverman; *sets:* Joseph Dommerque; *voice:* Arnold Stang; *mus:* Winston Sharples; *title song:* Hal David, Leon Carr; *prod mgr:* Seymour Shultz; *col:* Tech. *sd:* RCA. rt: 6 min. • Herman exploits being a cartoon character!

2876. Herman the Great Mouse *(Aesop's Film Fable)* 2 Mar. 1924; *p.c.:* Fables Pictures Inc for Pathé; *dir:* Paul Terry; b&w. *sil.* 5 min. • Dealing with a magician mouse, a trained fish and escaping from his pursuers.

2877. The Hermit and the Bear *(Aesop's Film Fable)* 18 Sept. 1921; *p.c.:* Fables Pictures Inc for Pathe; *dir:* Paul Terry; b&w. *sil.* 5 min. • The moral is, "Overzealousness often brings harmful results."

2878. Hero for a Day *(Mighty Mouse)* Mar. 1953; *p.c.:* TT for Fox; *dir:* Mannie Davis; *story/voice:* Tom Morrison; *anim:* Jim Tyer; *mus:* Philip A. Scheib; *ph:* Douglas Moye; *col:* Tech. *sd:* RCA. 6 min. • Mighty Mouse helps a weakling mouse whose girl prefers he-men mice.

2879. The Hero Wins *(Aesop's Film Fable)* 10 Oct. 1925; *p.c.:* Fables Pictures Inc for Pathé; *dir:* Paul Terry; b&w. *sil.* 10 min. • Henry Cat uses Mr. Mouse for a fishing lure. A fish frees the rodent who, in turn, sets free a female mouse from the clutches of the cat.

2880. Hero's Reward *(Comic King)* May 1962; *p.c.:* Para Cartoons; *dir:* Seymour Kneitel; *story:* Bill Angelos, Alan Kohan; *anim:* Wm. B. Pattengill; *sets:* Anton Loeb; *voices:* Howard Morris, Allen Melvin; *mus:* Winston Sharples; *col:* Tech. *sd:* RCA. 5 min. • During the war games, General Halftrack entrusts a vital message to Pvt. Beetle Bailey.

2881. Herr Meets Hare *(Merrie Melodies)* 13 Jan. 1945; *p.c.:* WB; *dir:* I. Freleng; *story:* Michael Maltese; *anim:* Gerry Chiniquy, Virgil Ross; *lay:* Hawley Pratt; *back:* Paul Julian; *ed:* Treg Brown; *voices:* Mel Blanc; *mus:* Carl W. Stalling; *prod mgr:* John W. Burton; *prod:* Edward Selzer; *col:* Tech. *sd:* Vit. 7 min. • Bugs locks horns with Hermann Goering in the Black Forest. Caricatures of Goering and Hitler.

2882. The Herring Murder Case *(Talkartoon)* 26 June 1931; *p.c.:* The Fleischer Studio for Para; *prod:* Max Fleischer; *dir:* Dave Fleischer; *dir/story/anim:* James H. Culhane, Al Eugster; *voice:* William A. Costello; *mus:* Art Turkisher; b&w. *sd:* WE. 6 min. • Ruby the herring is shot and Bimbo solves the crime.

2883. The Herring Murder Mystery *(Color Rhapsody)* 20 Jan. 1944; *p.c.:* Col; *prod:* Dave Fleischer; *dir/story:* Dun Roman; *anim:* Volus Jones, Chic Otterstrom; *sets:* Clark Watson; *ed:* Edward Moore; *voices:* John McLeish, Harry E. Lang; *mus:* Eddie Kilfeather; *ph:* Frank Fisher; *prod mgr:* Albert Spar; *col:* Tech. *sd:* RCA. 7 min. • A fish-canner is brought to justice before Judge Shark and a jury of denizens of the deep.

2884. Hesanut *p.c.:* Kalem Co; b&w. *sil.* • *1914:* **Hesanut Hunts Wild Game** 25 Sept. **Hesanut Buys an Auto** 10 Oct. **Hesanut Builds a Skyscraper** Nov. **Hesanut at a Vaudeville Show** Dec. • *1915:* **A Night in New Jersey** 16 Jan. • No further information traced.

2885. Hey Diddle Diddle *(Paul Terry-Toons)* 20 Sept. 1935; *p.c.:* Moser & Terry for Educational/Fox; *dir:* Frank Moser, Paul Terry; *mus:* Philip A. Scheib; b&w. *sd:* WE. 5 min. • A host of nursery rhyme characters attend school and a shocked PTA reform them.

2886. Hey Good Lookin' 1 Oct. 1982; *p.c.:* Bakshi Prods., Inc. for WB; *dir/prod/story:* Ralph Bakshi; *ex prod:* Ronald Kauffman; *asst prod:* Lynne Betner; *anim:* Brenda Banks, Carl Bell, Bob Carlson, John Gentilella, Steve Gordon, Manny Perez, Virgil Ross, John Sparey, Irven Spence, Tom Tataranowicz, Robert Taylor, John E. Walker Snr.; *lay:* Ira Turek, John Sparey, David Jonas, Don Morgan, John Dorman, Joan Drake, Judy Drake, Mabel Gesner, Stod Herbert, Larry Huber, Charlotte Huffine, Sammie Lanham, Larry Leichliter, Fred McManus, Rae McSpadden, Barney Posner, Tom Roth, Ron Scholefield, Ben Shenkman, Emily Steele, James T. Walker, Gwen Wetzler; *Back:* Johnny Vita, Rene Garcia, Matthew Golden; *ed:* Donald W. Ernst; *i&p:* Janet Cummings, Susan Carey Jonas, Diane Dunning, Laurel Harper, Stacey Maniskas, Tasia Williams; *check:* Dotti Foell, Mary J. Adams, Patricia Capozzi, Nelda Ridley, Beverly Robbins, Valentine Vreeland; *cel reproductions:* Edgar Gutierrez, Paul Strickland; *chor:* Toni Basil; *voices: Vinnie:* Richard Romanus; *Crazy Shapiro:* David Proval; *Eva:* Jesse Welles; *Rozzie:* Tina Bowman; *Stompers:* Danny Wells, Bennie Massa, Gelsa Palao, Paul Roman, Larry Bishop, Tabi Cooper; *Waitress:* Juno Dawson; *Chaplin:* Shirley Jo Finney; *Yonkel:* Martin Garner; *Alice:* Terri Haven; *Max:* Allen Joseph; *Chaplin:* Philip M. Thomas; *Old Vinnie:* Frank de Kova; *Solly:* Angelo Grisanti; *Sal:* Candy Candido; *Italian man:* Ed Peck; *Italian women:* Lillian Adams, Mary Dean Lauria; *Gelsa:* Donna Ponteretto; *vocals:* Ric Sandler, Ichshe Sandler; *mus:* John Madara,

Ric Sandler; *mus prod:* John Madara; *mus engineer:* Steve Sykes, Steve Thume; *mus ed:* Eugene Marks; *asst to the prod:* Leah Bernstein; *prod asst:* Steve Sykes; *prod co-ord:* Mark Bakshi; *ph:* Ted C. Bemiller, R&B EFX; *neg cutter:* Jack Hooper; *sd fx:* Echo Film Services; *col:* Tech. *sd:* Mono. 86 min. • Vinnie is the leader of a gang who has everything ... except nerve. His friend, Crazy Shapiro, makes up for his inadequacies and the two of them face an inevitable showdown when confronted with a rival gang, "The Black Chaplains."

2887. Hey-Hey Fever (*Happy Harmonies*) 16 Feb. 1935; *p.c.:* MGM; *prod/dir:* Hugh Harman, Rudolf Ising; *voices:* The Rhythmettes, Billy Bletcher, John T. Murray; *mus:* Scott Bradley; *col:* Tech-2. *sd:* RCA. 9 min. • Bosko and Bruno supply food to a starving Nursery Rhyme Land.

2888. Hey There! It's Yogi Bear 1964; *p.c.:* Hanna-Barbera for Colum; *prod/dir:* William Hanna, Joseph Barbera; *seq dir:* Friz Freleng; *story:* Joseph Barbera, Warren Foster, William Hanna; *story sup:* Dan Gordon; *anim dir:* Charles A. Nichols; *anim:* Don Lusk, Irv Spence, George Kreisl, Ray Patterson, Jerry Hathcock, Grant Simmons, Fred Wolf, Gerry Chiniquy, Don Patterson, Ken Harris, George Goepper, Edwin Aardal, Ed Parks, Kenneth Muse, Harry Holt; *lay:* Richard Bickenbach, Iwao Takamoto, William Perez, Jacques V. Rupp, Willie Ito, Tony Sordi, Ernest Nordli, Jerry Eisenberg, Zigamond Jableski, Bruce Bushman; *back:* F. Montealegre, Art Lozzi, Robert Gentle, Ron Dias, Richard H. Thomas, Dick Kelsey, Fernando Arce, Don Peters, Bob Abrams, Dick Ung, Tom O'Loughlin, Bob Givens, Curtiss D. Perkins; *ed:* Greg Watson, Tony Milch, Larry Cowan, Warner Leighton, Donald A. Douglas, Ken Spears; *voices:* Yogi Bear/Dopey Bear/Ranger/TV Announcer: Daws Butler; *Boo Boo/Ranger Smith/Yogi's Inner Self/Sheriff:* Don Messick; *Cindy:* Julie Bennett; *Grifter:* Mel Blanc; *Cornpone:* Hal Smith; *Snively:* J. Pat O'Malley; *Mugger:* Mel Blanc, Don Messick; *also:* Jean van der Pyl, Howard Morris, Allen Melvin; "Ven-e Ven-e Ven-a" sung by James Darren; *Yogi's singing voice:* Bill Lee; *Boo Boo's singing voice:* Ernie Newton; *mus:* Marty Paich; *songs:* Ray Gilbert, Doug Goodwin; "Hey There! It's Yogi Bear" by David Gates; *i&p:* Roberta Greutert; *continuity:* Evelyn Sherwood; *ph:* Frank Paiker, Roy Wade, Norman Stainback, Charles Flekal; *sd:* Bud Warner; *titles:* Pacific Title; *prod sup:* Alex Lovy, Howard Hanson; *col:* East. *sd:* RCA. 89 min. • Yogi and Boo Boo trek across the country in search of Cindy, who has been captured by a circus.

2889. Hi Diddle Diddle 2 Aug. 1943; *p.c.:* Leon Schlesinger Prods. for UA; *dir:* I. Freleng; b&w. *sd:* WE. 2 min. • Live-action comedy about a young couple and their con-artist in-laws. Animated opening with tropical birds flying down from the treetops. Ending in a restaurant where the cast starts singing and the motifs on the walls become animated and scramble for an exit to escape the racket.

2890. Hi-Fi Jinx (*Modern Madcap*) Mar. 1962; *p.c.:* Para Cartoons; *dir:* Seymour Kneitel; *story:* Burton Goodman, Jack Mercer; *anim:* Martin Taras, Jack Ehret, Wm. B. Pattengill; *sets:* Robert Owen; *voices:* Eddie Lawrence; *mus:* Winston Sharples; *ph:* Leonard McCormick; *prod mgr:* Abe Goodman; *col:* Tech. *sd:* RCA. 6 min. • Percy buys some hi-fi equipment which his neighbor, Ralph, insists on installing for him. • Featuring the prototype for Swifty & Shorty.

2891. Hi-Rise Wise Guys (*Woody Woodpecker*) 1 Aug. 1970; *p.c.:* Walter Lantz prods for Univ; *dir:* Paul J. Smith; *story:* Dale Hale; *anim:* Les Kline, Al Coe; *sets:* Nino Carbe; *voices:* Dal McKennon, Grace Stafford; *mus:* Walter Greene; *prod mgr:* William E. Garity; *col:* Tech. *sd:* RCA. 5 min. • Woody's peace is disturbed by a construction worker. He retaliates by jeapordizing the builder's clean "No Accidents" record.

2892. Hi-Seas Hi-Jacker (*Inspector Willoughby*) 16 Oct. 1963; *p.c.:* Walter Lantz prods for Univ; *dir:* Paul J. Smith; *story:* Dave DeTiege; *anim:* Les Kline, Al Coe; *sets:* Art Landy, Ray Huffine; *voices:* Dal McKennon; *mus:* Darrell Calker; *prod mgr:* William E. Garity; *col:* Tech. *sd:* RCA. 6 min. • Inspector Willoughby is called upon to stop a modern-day pirate from hijacking ships.

2893. Hiawatha's Rabbit Hunt (*Merrie Melodies*) 7 June 1941; *p.c.:* Leon Schlesinger prods for WB; *dir:* I. Freleng; *story:* Michael Maltese; *anim:* Gil Turner; *character models/lay:* Robert Givens; *back:* Lenard Kester; *ed:* Treg Brown; *voices:* Mel Blanc; *mus:* Carl W. Stalling; *prod sup:* Henry Binder, Raymond G. Katz; *col:* Tech. *sd:* Vit. 7 min. • Hiawatha meets his match when he sets out to get a rabbit for supper and encounters Bugs.

2894. Hic-Cup Pup (*Tom & Jerry*) 17 Apr. 1954; *p.c.:* MGM; *dir:* William Hanna, Joseph Barbera; *anim:* Ed Barge, Kenneth Muse, Ray Patterson, Irven Spence; *sets:* Robert Gentle; *ed:* Jim Faris; *voice:* Daws Butler; *mus:* Scott Bradley; *ph:* Jack Stevens; *prod:* Fred Quimby; *col:* Tech. *sd:* WE. 6 min. • Spike warns Tom of the dire consequences if he ever causes his son to get the hiccups again.

2895. Hic-Cups the Champ (*Krazy Kat*) 28 May 1932; *p.c.:* Winkler for Colum; *anim:* Manny Gould; *voice:* Jack Carr; *mus:* Joe de Nat; *prod:* George Winkler; b&w. *sd:* WE. 6 min. • Krazy's incurable hiccups are so fierce, he dreams he's hiccupping for the championship.

2896. Hiccup Hound (*Noveltoon*) Nov. 1963; *p.c.:* Para Cartoons; *dir:* Seymour Kneitel; *story:* Irv Dressler, Jack Mercer; *anim:* Wm. B. Pattengill; *sets:* Robert Little; *voices:* Jack Mercer, Cecil Roy; *mus:* Winston Sharples; *ph:* Leonard McCormick; *prod mgr:* Abe Goodman; *col:* Tech. *sd:* RCA. 6 min. • Goodie the Gremlin helps cure a Pointer of the hiccups.

2897. A Hick, a Slick and a Chick (*Merrie Melodies*) 13 Mar. 1948; *p.c.:* WB; *dir:* Arthur Davis; *story:* Lloyd Vaughan, William Scott; *anim:* J.C. Melendez, Don Williams, Emery Hawkins, Basil Davidovich; *lay:* Don Smith; *back:* Philip de Guard; *ed:* Treg Brown; *voices:* Mel Blanc, Bea Benaderet, Stan Freberg; *mus:* Carl Stalling; *prod mgr:* John W. Burton; *prod:* Edward Selzer; *col:* Ciné. *sd:* Vit. 7 min. • A country mouse's girl wants an ermine coat. He mistakes a cat called Herman for what is needed to make a coat.

2898. The Hick Chick 15 June 1946; *p.c.:* MGM; *dir:* Tex Avery; *story:* Heck Allen; *anim:* Preston Blair, Walt Clinton, Ed Love, Ray Abrams; *character des:* Claude Smith; *sets:* John Didrik Johnsen; *ed:* Fred MacAlpin; *voices:* Stan Freberg, Frank Graham, Sara Berner, The Pickard Family; *mus:* Scott Bradley; *prod:* Fred Quimby; *col:* Tech. *sd:* WE. 7 min. • A slick city chicken steals away a country bumpkin's girl with the promise of a life of luxury. The hick follows them to the big city.

2899. Hide and Go Sidney (*Terry-Toon*) Jan. 1960; *p.c.:* TT for Fox; *ex prod:* Bill Weiss; *dir:* Art Bartsch; *story sup:* Tom Morrison; *lay:* John Zago; *back:* Bill Focht; *voice:* Dayton Allen; *mus:* Phil Scheib; *col:* Tech. *sd:* RCA. 6 min. CS. • Sidney has nobody to play with until he finds playmates in a couple of hungry buzzards.

2900. Hide and Peak (*Herman & Katnip*) 7 Dec. 1956; *p.c.:* Para Cartoons; *dir:* Seymour Kneitel; *story:* Carl Meyer; *anim:* Dave Tendlar, Morey Reden; *sets:* Joe Dommerque; *voices:* Norma MacMillan, Arnold Stang, Sid Raymond, Jack Mercer, Gwen Davies; *mus:* Winston Sharples; *ph:* Leonard McCormick; *prod mgr:* Seymour Shultz; *col:* Tech. *sd:* RCA. 6 min. • The mice are mountain climbing, unaware that the cat is but a few feet below them.

2901. Hide and Seek (*Talkartoons*) 26 May 1932; *p.c.:* The Fleischer Studio for Para; *prod:* Max Fleischer; *dir:* Dave Fleischer; *anim:* Roland Crandall; *mus:* Art Turkisher; b&w. *sd:* WE. 6 min. • Policeman Bimbo saves Betty after a chase.

2902. Hide and Shriek (*Casper*) 28 Jan. 1955; *p.c.:* Famous for Para; *dir:* Seymour Kneitel; *story:* Carl Meyer; *anim:* Myron Waldman, Nick Tafuri; *sets:* Anton Loeb; *voices:* Norma MacMillan, Gwen Davies; *mus:* Winston Sharples; *title song:* Mack David, Jerry Livingston; *ph:* Leonard McCormick; *prod mgr:* Seymour Shultz; *col:* Tech. *sd:* RCA. 7 min. • Casper's naughty cousin, Spooky, pays a visit and the friendly ghost has to cure him of scaring folk.

2903. The High and the Flighty (*Merrie Melodies*) 18 Feb. 1956; *p.c.:* WB; *dir:* Robert McKimson; *story:* Tedd Pierce; *anim:* Ted Bonnicksen, Russ Dyson, Keith Darling; *lay:* Robert Gribbroek; *back:* Richard H. Thomas; *ed:* Treg Brown; *voices:* Mel Blanc; *mus:* Carl Stalling; *prod mgr:* John W. Burton; *prod:* Edward Selzer; *col:* Tech. *sd:* Vit. 7 min. • Daffy puts Foggy and the dog at each other's throats when he sells them jokes and novelties.

2904. High but Not Dry (*Honey Halfwitch*) June 1967; *p.c.:* Para Cartoon; *ex prod:* Shamus Culhane;; *dir:* Chuck Harriton; *story:* Howard Post; *anim:* Irv Dressler; *sets:* Howard Beckerman, Dave Ubinas; *mus:* Winston Sharples; *prod sup:* Harold Robins, Burt Hanft; *col:* Tech. *sd:* RCA. 5 min. • Honey conjures a cloudburst for her garden during a drought. When the weatherman gets her to make one for the whole city she can't turn it off.

2905. High-Diving Hare (*Looney Tunes*) 30 Apr. 1949; *p.c.*: WB; *dir*: I. Freleng; *story*: Tedd Pierce; *anim*: Gerry Chiniquy, Manuel Perez, Ken Champin, Virgil Ross, Pete Burness; *lay*: Hawley Pratt; *back*: Paul Julian; *ed*: Treg Brown; *voices*: Mel Blanc; *mus*: Carl Stalling; *prod mgr*: John W. Burton; *prod*: Edward Selzer; *col*: Tech. *sd*: Vit. 7 min. • Yosemite Sam craves the high-diving act of "Fearless Freep" that Bugs has promised. When he doesn't show up, Sam forces Bugs to take Freep's place.

2906. The High Flyers (*Aesop's Film Fable*) 29 Sept. 1923; *p.c.*: Fables Pictures Inc for Pathé; *dir*: Paul Terry; b&w. *sil*. 5 min. • The farm animals invent various flying devices to enter a cross-country race.

2907. High Note (*Looney Tunes*) 3 Dec. 1960; *p.c.*: WB; *dir*: Chuck Jones; *story*: Michael Maltese; *anim*: Richard Thompson, Ken Harris; *lay*: Maurice Noble; *back*: Philip de Guard, William Butler; *ed*: Treg Brown; *hiccups*: Mel Blanc; *mus*: Milt Franklyn; *prod mgr*: William Orcutt; *prod*: David H. DePatie; *col*: Tech. *sd*: Vit. 7 min; *Academy Award nomination*. • One of the notes on the sheet music for *The Blue Danube* has been dipping into "Little Brown Jug" and is in no fit state to play.

2908. High Seas (*Aesop's Film Fable*) 10 Sept. 1928; *p.c.*: Fables Pictures Inc for Pathé; *dir*: Paul Terry, Mannie Davis; b&w. *sil*. 10 min. • No story available.

2909. High Stakes (*Aesop's Film Fable*) 15 Jan. 1928; *p.c.*: Fables Pictures Inc for Pathé; *dir*: Paul Terry, Hugh Shields; b&w. *sil*. 10 min. • Farmer Al Falfa gets involved in a poker game with a cheating ostrich. A mechanical elephant is spooked by a mechanical mouse. The elephant lodges a complaint with Al who goes after the mouse. He trips over a lion who chases him up a palm tree where he shares a drink with a vulture. Moral: "No one cares how bad your English is, if your Scotch is good."

2910. High Steaks (*Tom & Jerry*) Jan. 1962; *p.c.*: Rembrandt for MGM; *prod*: William L. Snyder; *dir*: Gene Deitch; *story*: Larz Bourne; *anim dir*: Vaclav Bedrich; *voice*: Allen Swift; *mus*: Stepan Konícek; *col*: Metro. *sd*: WE. 6 min. • Tom ruins his master's barbecue in pursuit of Jerry. • See: *Tom and Jerry (Rembrandt Studio)*

2911. High Up (*Oswald the lucky rabbit*) 23 July 1928; *p.c.*: Winkler for Univ; *anim*: Rudolf Ising, R.C. Hamilton; *prod mgr*: Nat L. Mintz; *prod*: George Winkler; b&w. *sil*. 5 min. • Oswald is assisting at the fairground when the barker makes off with his girl and a chase ensues over the high wire.

2912. Highway Hecklers (*Chilly Willy*) Apr. 1968; *p.c.*: Walter Lantz prods for Univ; *dir*: Paul J. Smith; *story*: Homer Brightman; *anim*: Les Kline, Al Coe; *sets*: Ray Huffine; *voices*: Daws Butler, Grace Stafford; *mus*: Walter Greene; *prod mgr*: William E. Garity; *col*: Tech. *sd*: RCA. 6 min. • A reward is offered for Chilly and Maxie, who have escaped from a zoo, and Colonel Potshot tries to recapture them.

2913. Highway Runnery (*Looney Tunes*) 11 Dec. 1965; *p.c.*: DFE for WB; *dir*: Rudy Larriva; *story*: Al Bertino; *anim*: Virgil Ross, Bob Bransford, Hank Smith; *lay*: Ernie Nordli, Don Sheppard; *back*: Anthony Rizzo; *ed*: Joe Siracusa; *mus*: Bill Lava; *prod mgr*: William Orcutt; *col*: Tech. *sd*: Vit. 6 min. • The Coyote continues his quest for the Road-Runner by using an explosive egg, a giant rubber band and a clapped-out car.

2914. Highway Slobbery (*Swifty & Shorty*) July 1964; *p.c.*: Para Cartoons; *dir*: Seymour Kneitel; *story/voices*: Eddie Lawrence; *anim*: Wm. B. Pattengill; *sets*: Robert Little; *mus*: Winston Sharples; *ph*: Leonard McCormick; *prod mgr*: Abe Goodman; *col*: Tech. *sd*: RCA. 6 min. • No story available.

2915. Highway Snobbery (*Krazy Kat*) 9 Aug. 1936; *p.c.*: Charles Mintz prods for Colum; *story*: Allen Rose; *anim*: Harry Love; *mus*: Joe de Nat; *prod mgr*: James Bronis; b&w. *sd*: RCA. 6 min. • Krazy takes his girl for a spin in his super speed auto. Other drivers gang up and even his girl finally deserts him.

2916. Hill-Billing and Cooing (*Popeye*) 13 Jan. 1956; *p.c.*: Famous for Para; *dir*: Seymour Kneitel; *story*: Jack Mercer; *anim*: Tom Johnson, John Gentilella; *sets*: Robert Connavale; *voices*: Jack Mercer, Dorothy Shay, Mae Questel; *mus*: Winston Sharples; *ph*: Leonard McCormick; *prod mgr*: Seymour Shultz; *col*: Tech. *sd*: RCA. 6 min. • While motoring through the Ozarks, Popeye falls victim to a man-hungry mountain girl.

2917. The Hillbilly (*Oswald*) 1 Feb. 1935; *p.c.*: Univ; *prod/dir*: Walter Lantz; *story*: Victor McLeod; *anim*: Fred Avery, Jack Carr, Ray Abrams,

Joe d'Igalo, Ernest Smythe , Virgil Ross; *mus*: James Dietrich; b&w. *sd*: WE. 8 min. • Oswald solves the problems of two backwoods feuding families.

2918. Hillbilly Hare (*Merrie Melodies*) 12 Aug. 1950; *p.c.*: WB; *dir*: Robert McKimson; *story*: Tedd Pierce; *anim*: Rod Scribner, Phil de Lara, John Carey, Emery Hawkins, Charles McKimson; *lay*: Cornett Wood; *back*: Richard H. Thomas; *ed*: Treg Brown; *voices*: Mel Blanc, John T. Smith; *mus*: Carl Stalling; *prod mgr*: John W. Burton; *prod*: Edward Selzer; *col*: Tech. *sd*: Vit. 7 min. • Bugs finds himself in the center of a hillbilly feud.

2919. Hill's Angels • See: *The North Avenue Regulars*

2920. The Hills of Old Wyomin' (*Screen Songs*) 31 July 1936; *p.c.*: The Fleischer Studio for Para; *prod*: Max Fleischer; *dir*: Dave Fleischer; *anim*: Thomas Johnson, Harold Walker; *l/a*: Louise Massey & The Westerners; b&w. *sd*: WE. 10 min. • A newsreel shows showing ideas for the future: Rotating sheep to help you get to sleep, dress lengths, a baby carriage, television and an automated marriage/divorce.

2921. Hip-Hip Hurry (*Merrie Melodies*) 6 Dec. 1958; *p.c.*: WB; *dir*: Chuck Jones; *co-dir*: Ken Harris; *story*: Michael Maltese; *anim*: Ken Harris, Ben Washam, Abe Levitow, Richard Thompson, Keith Darling; *fx*: Harry Love; *lay*: Maurice Noble; *back*: Philip de Guard; *ed*: Treg Brown; *voice*: Paul Julian; *mus*: John Seeley; *prod*: John W. Burton; *col*: Tech. *sd*: Vit. 7 min. • The Coyote fails so dismally in catching the Road-Runner that he drinks a "High Speed Tonic" to make him run as fast as the feathered speed demon.

2922. Hip Hip Olè (*Swifty & Shorty*) Sept. 1964; *p.c.*: Para Cartoons; *dir*: Seymour Kneitel; *story/voices*: Eddie Lawrence; *anim*: Morey Reden; *sets*: Robert Little; *mus*: Winston Sharples; *prod mgr*: Abe Goodman; *col*: Tech. *sd*: RCA. 6 min. • Shorty wants to return a matador's cape to Swifty's novelty shop and Swifty does his best not to give any refund.

2923. Hippety Hopper (*Merrie Melodies*) 19 Nov. 1949; *p.c.*: WB; *dir*: Robert McKimson; *story*: Warren Foster; *anim*: Pete Burness, John Carey, Charles McKimson, Phil de Lara; *lay*: Cornett Wood; *back*: Richard H. Thomas; *ed*: Treg Brown; *voices*: Mel Blanc; *mus*: Carl Stalling; *prod mgr*: John W. Burton; *prod*: Edward Selzer; *col*: Tech. *sd*: Vit. 7 min. • A persecuted mouse gets his revenge on Sylvester in the shape of a baby kangaroo.

2924. Hippydrome Tiger (*Looney Tunes*) 30 Mar. 1968; *p.c.*: W/7A; *dir*: Alex Lovy; *story*: Tony Benedict; *anim*: Ted Bonnicksen, La Verne Harding, Volus Jones, Ed Solomon; *lay*: Jaime R. Diaz; *back*: Bob Abrams; *ed*: Hal Geer; *voices*: Larry Storch; *mus*: William Lava; *prod*: William L. Hendricks; *col*: Tech. *sd*: Vit. 6 min. • Colonel Rimfire and Cool Cat enter the Le Mans road race.

2925. His Better Elf (*Woody Woodpecker*) 14 July 1958; *p.c.*: Walter Lantz prods for Univ; *dir*: Paul J. Smith; *story*: Homer Brightman; *anim*: Les Kline, Don Patterson, Robert Bentley; *lay*: Art Landy; *back*: Irv Wyner; *voices*: Dal McKennon, Grace Stafford; *mus*: Clarence Wheeler; *prod mgr*: William E. Garity; *col*: Tech. *sd*: RCA. 6 min. • A leprechaun grants Woody three wishes ... all of which get him into trouble.

2926. His Bitter Half (*Merrie Melodies*) 20 May 1950; *p.c.*: WB; *dir*: I. Freleng; *story*: Tedd Pierce; *anim*: Ken Champin, Virgil Ross, Arthur Davis, Gerry Chiniquy; *lay*: Hawley Pratt; *back*: Paul Julian; *ed*: Treg Brown; *voices*: Mel Blanc, Nancy Wible; *mus*: Carl Stalling; *prod mgr*: John W. Burton; *prod*: Edward Selzer; *col*: Tech. *sd*: Vit. 7 min. • Daffy marries a wealthy widow but also inherits her brat of a kid in the bargain.

2927. His Hare Raising Tale (*Looney Tunes*) 11 Aug. 1951; *p.c.*: WB; *dir*: I. Freleng; *story*: Warren Foster; *anim*: Virgil Ross, Manuel Perez, Ken Champin, Arthur Davis; *lay*: Hawley Pratt; *back*: Paul Julian; *ed*: Treg Brown; *voices*: Mel Blanc; *mus*: Carl Stalling; *prod mgr*: John W. Burton; *prod*: Edward Selzer; *col*: Tech. *sd*: Vit. 6 min. *Seq: Baseball Bugs; Rabbit Punch; Falling Hare; Hare Devil Hare; Stage Door Cartoon.* • Bugs spins a yarn to his little nephew about his exciting career.

2928. His Mouse Friday (*Tom & Jerry*) 7 July 1951; *p.c.*: MGM; *dir*: William Hanna, Joseph Barbera; *anim*: Kenneth Muse, Irven Spence, Ray Patterson, Ed Barge; *lay*: Dick Bickenbach; *back*: Robert Gentle; *ed*: Jim Faris; *voices*: Paul Frees; *mus*: Scott Bradley; *ph*: Jack Stevens; *prod*: Fred Quimby; *col*: Tech. *sd*: WE. 7 min. • Shipwrecked on a desert isle, Tom soon finds sustenance in the shape of a small native mouse.

2929. His Off Day (*Terry-Toon*) 4 Feb. 1938; *p.c.:* TT for Educational/Fox; *dir:* Connie Rasinski; *mus:* Philip A. Scheib; b&w. *sd:* RCA. 6 min. • Puddy the pup tries to befriend an organ grinder and his monkey but nobody will play with him.

2930. His Trial (*Terry Cartoon Burlesque*) July 1917; *p.c.:* Cartoon Film Service for A. Kay Co.; *anim:* Paul H. Terry; b&w. *sil.* • No story available.

2931. Hiss and Hers (*Blue Racer*) 3 July 1972; *p.c.:* Mirisch/DFE for UA; *dir:* Gerry Chiniquy; *story:* John W. Dunn; *anim:* Bob Taylor, Don Williams, Bob Richardson; *lay:* Dick Ung; *back:* Richard H. Thomas; *ed:* Rick Steward; *voices:* Larry D. Mann, Tom Holland; *mus:* Doug Goodwin; *ph:* John Burton Jr.; *prod sup:* Stan Paperny, Harry Love; *col:* DeLuxe. *sd:* RCA. 6 min. • The racer meets a Karate-trained Japanese beetle.

2932. Hiss and Make Up (*Merrie Melodies*) 31 July 1943; *p.c.:* Leon Schlesinger prods for WB; *dir:* I. Freleng; *story:* Michael Maltese; *anim:* Gerry Chiniquy; *character des:* James Culhane; *lay:* Owen Fitzgerald; *back:* Paul Julian; *ed:* Treg Brown; *voices:* Mel Blanc, Bea Benaderet; *mus:* Carl W. Stalling; *prod sup:* Henry Binder, Raymond G. Katz; *col:* Tech. *sd:* Vit. 7 min. • The old lady gives her cat and dog an ultimatum of the first to start fighting goes out.

2933. Historiets May 1924; *p.c.:* Reel Colors Inc.; col. *sil.* • **The Teapot Dome, Famous Sayings of Famous Americans, Witty Sayings of Witty Frenchmen, Witty Naughty Thoughts,** • No stories or further information traced.

2934. The Hitch Hiker (*Terry-Toon*) 1 Dec. 1939; *p.c.:* TT for Fox; *dir:* Eddie Donnelly; *story:* John Foster; *anim:* Jim Tyer; *mus:* Philip A. Scheib; b&w. *sd:* RCA. • A duck with a trailer unites with a dog who has a car, then mosquitoes tear them apart.

2935. The Hitch Hikers (*Heckle & Jeckle*) 12 Dec. 1947; *p.c.:* TT for Fox; *dir:* Connie Rasinski; *story:* John Foster; *voices:* Tom Morrison, Douglas Moye; *mus:* Philip A. Scheib; *ph:* Douglas Moye; *col:* Tech. *sd:* RCA. 6 min. • The magpies hail a taxi and find themselves in the getaway car of two bandits.

2936. Hittin' the Trail for Hallelujah Land (*Merrie Melodies*) 11 Dec. 1931; *p.c.:* Hugh Harman–Rudolf Ising prods for WB; *prod:* Leon Schlesinger; *anim:* Isadore Freleng, Paul Smith, Robert Clampett; *ed:* Dale Pickett; *voices:* The Kingsmen, Mary Moder; *mus:* Frank Marsales; b&w. *sd:* Vit. 7 min. • An old fashioned riverboat melodrama.

2937. Hitting the Rails (*Aesop's Film Fable*) 5 Dec. 1926; *p.c.:* Fables Pictures Inc for Pathé; *dir:* Paul Terry, John Foster; b&w. *sil.* 10 min. • When a hen lays an egg on the tender of a locomotive, it hatches into a miniature engine with a train of carriages.

2938. Hitting the Trail (*Life Cartoon Comedy*) 27 Feb. 1927; *p.c.:* Sherwood Wadsworth Pictures Inc for Educational; *prod/dir:* John R. McCrory; b&w. *sil.* 5 min. • Little Nibbins and his dog ride a freight car, then chase an elusive rolling pancake stolen from a wayside vendor.

2939. Hobby Horse-Laffs (*Looney Tunes*) 6 June 1942; *p.c.:* Leon Schlesinger prods for WB; *dir:* Norman McCabe; *story:* Melvin Millar; *anim:* John Carey, Cal Dalton, Arthur Davis, David Hoffman, Vive Risto; *back:* Richard H. Thomas; *ed:* Treg Brown; *voices:* Robert C. Bruce, Mel Blanc, Kent Rogers; *mus:* Carl W. Stalling; *prod sup:* Henry Binder, Raymond G. Katz; b&w. *sd:* Vit. 7 min. • Parody of radio's *Hobby Lobby*, offering unique hobbies of the populace.

2940. Hobo Bobo (*Merrie Melodies*) 10 June. 1947; *p.c.:* WB; *dir:* Robert McKimson; *story:* Warren Foster, Robert Clampett; *lay:* Cornett Wood; *back:* Richard H. Thomas; *ed:* Treg Brown; *voices:* Robert C. Bruce, Dick Nelson; *mus:* Carl Stalling; *prod mgr:* John W. Burton; *prod:* Edward Selzer; *col:* Tech. *sd:* Vit. 7 min. • Bobo, a little elephant, decides to go to the big city and is advised to paint himself pink because nobody will admit to seeing a pink elephant.

2941. Hobo Gadget Band (*Merrie Melodies*) 17 June 1939; *p.c.:* Leon Schlesinger prods for WB; *dir:* Ben Hardaway, Cal Dalton; *story:* Jack Miller; *anim:* Richard Bickenbach; *lay:* Griff Jay; *back:* Arthur Loomer; *ed:* Tregoweth E. Brown; *voices:* Pinto Colvig, Mel Blanc, The Foursome (with Delmar Porter); *mus:* Carl W. Stalling; *prod sup:* Henry Binder, Raymond G. Katz; *col:* Tech. *sd:* Vit. 7 min. • A group of hoboes make a hit by singing on the radio but forsake their contract to hop a railroad car.

2942. Hobo Hero (*Simon the Monk*) 1930; *p.c.:* Animated Pictures Corp; *prod:* Jacques Kopfstein; *dir/anim:* Les Elton; b&w. *snd.* 6 min. • No story available.

2943. The Hoboken Nightingale (*Pen & Ink Vaudeville*) 27 Oct. 1924; *p.c.:* Earl Hurd prods for Educational; *dir:* Earl Hurd; b&w. *sil.* 5 min. • The show consists of cats performing jazz music; A tramp bicycle rider with his dog and a burlesque of an opera singer who ends the show.

2944. Hobo's Holiday (*Noveltoon*) Oct. 1963; *p.c.:* Para Cartoons; *dir:* Seymour Kneitel; *story/anim:* Morey Reden; *sets:* Robert Little; *mus:* Winston Sharples; *ph:* Leonard McCormick; *prod mgr:* Abe Goodman; *col:* Tech. *sd:* RCA. 6 min. • A tramp journeys to Utopia, steals a pie and settles down to dream of "The Big Rock Candy Mountain."

2945. The Hockey Champ (*Donald Duck*) 28 Apr. 1939; *p.c.:* Walt Disney prods for RKO; *dir:* Jack King; *asst dir:* Lloyd L. Richardson, Harry Tytle; *story:* Carl Barks, Jack Hannah; *anim:* Paul Allen, Larry Clemmons, James H. Culhane, Max Gray, Eric Larson, John McManus, Lee Morehouse, Don Towsley, Berny Wolf; *fx:* Al Amatuzio, Edwin Aardal, Joseph Gayek, George Rowley; *lay:* Bill Herwig; *voices:* Clarence Nash; *mus:* Oliver Wallace; *col:* Tech. *sd:* RCA. 7 min. • Donald displays his professional ability for playing ice hockey to his sceptical nephews.

2946. Hockey Homicide (*Goofy*) 21 Sept. 1945; *p.c.:* Walt Disney prods for RKO; *dir:* Jack Kinney; *asst dir:* Bee Selck; *story:* Bill Berg, Dick Kinney; *anim:* Hal King, John Sibley, Milt Kahl, Al Bertino, Les Clark, Ward Kimball, Cliff Nordberg; *fx:* Jack Boyd, Andy Engman; *lay:* Don da Gradi; *back:* Art Riley; *voice:* Doodles Weaver; *mus:* Paul J. Smith; *col:* Tech. *sd:* RCA. 8 min. • A frantic ice hockey game demonstrates just what good, clean, wholesome fun can be.

2947. Hocus Pocus 16 July 1993; *p.c.:* Walt Disney for BV; *anim ph:* Brandy Hill; *Pixar:* Tom Hahn, Peter Nye, Michael Shantzis; *anim:* "*Cat*" *sup:* Chris Bailey; "*Talking Cat*": Rhythm & Hues Inc., Bert Terreri, John Hughes, Larry Weinberg, Dani Colajacomo, Colin Brady, Suponwich Somsaman, Nancy Kato, Rodian Paul, Les Major, Joe Yanuzzi, Meg Freeman, Keith Hunter, David Keller, Will McCown; *sup:* Michael Lessa; *fx anim:* James Mansfield, Allen Gonzales, Elissa Bello; *Rotoscope art:* Marsha Gray Carrington; *Binx's voice:* Jason Marsden; *i&p:* Byron Werner, Judith Bell; *col:* Tech. *sd:* Dolby Stereo. 96 min. *l/a.* • Three witches from Salem extract the life force from children to keep themselves young. They turn a little girl's brother into an immortal black cat before the witches are captured and executed by the villagers. Three hundred years later they are accidentally brought back to life and the witches fly off in search of their book of spells so that they can steal children's life forces in order to live forever.

2948. Hocus Pocus Powwow (*Looney Tunes*) 13 Jan. 1968; *p.c.:* W/7A; *dir:* Alex Lovy; *story:* Cal Howard; *anim:* Ted Bonnicksen, La Verne Harding, Volus Jones, Ed Solomon; *lay:* Bob Givens; *back:* Bob Abrams; *ed:* Hal Geer; *voices:* Larry Storch; *mus:* William Lava; *prod:* William L. Hendricks; *col:* Tech. *sd:* Vit. 6 min. • An Indian tries to steal Merlin's magic hat when he produces a full course dinner from it.

2949. Hodge Podge (*Pathe Newsreel*) 1913; *p.c.:* Cartoon Film Service for Pathé; *prod/dir:* Paul Felton, John C. Terry, Hugh M. Shields; *asst:* Lyman H. Howe; *p.c.:* Lyman H. Howe Films Co Inc for Educational/Fox; *prod/dir:* Lyman H. Howe; *super/ed:* Robert E. Gillaum; *narrative:* James F. Clemenger; *anim:* Archie N. Griffith; b&w. *sil./sd.(disc only)* 2 min. *l/a/anim.*

2950. Hokum Hotel (*Aesop's Sound Fable*) 12 Nov. 1932; *p.c.:* Van Beuren for RKO; *dir:* John Foster, Harry Bailey; *voice:* Marjorie Hines; *mus:* Gene Rodemich; b&w. *sd:* RCA. 8 min. • Among the many goings-on at Hokum Hotel, including a cat trying to steal a string of pearls.

2951. Hold Anything (*Looney Tunes*) Sept. 1930; *p.c.:* Hugh Harman–Rudolf Ising Prods for WB; *prod:* Leon Schlesinger; *anim:* Isadore Freleng, Norm Blackburn; *ed:* Dale Pickett; *voices:* Rochelle Hudson; Carmen Maxwell; *mus:* Frank Marsales; b&w. *sd:* Vit. 7 min. • Bosko has fun as a riveter on a skyscraper, serenading Honey with a goat filled with helium.

2952. Hold 'Em, Ozzie (*Oswald*) 8 Jan. 1929; *p.c.:* Winkler for Univ; *anim:* R.C. Hamilton; b&w. *sil.* 6 min. • Oswald provides ingenious merriment on the football field.

2953. Hold It (*Color Classic*) 29 Apr. 1938; *p.c.:* The Fleischer Studio for Para; *prod:* Max Fleischer; *dir:* Dave Fleischer; *anim:* David Tendlar,

Nicholas Tafuri; *ed:* Kitty Pfister; *mus:* Sammy Timberg; *prod sup:* Sam Buchwald, Isidore Sparber; *col:* Tech. *sd:* WE. 7 min. • Cats go out for a night on the town and sing a song called "Hold It."

2954. Hold That Pose *(Goofy)* 13 Nov. 1950; *p.c.:* Walt Disney prods for RKO; *dir:* Jack Kinney; *story:* Dick Kinney, Milt Schaffer; *anim:* John Sibley, Ed Aardal, Hugh Fraser, Charles Nichols; *fx:* Jack Boyd; *lay:* Al Zinnen; *back:* Ed Levitt; *voices:* Bob Jackman, Pinto Colvig, James MacDonald; *mus:* Paul Smith; *col:* Tech. *sd:* RCA. 7 min. • Geef tries to photograph wild life in a zoo.

2955. Hold That Rock *(Chilly Willy)* 2 July 1956; *p.c.:* Walter Lantz prods for Univ; *dir:* Alex Lovy; *story:* Homer Brightman; *anim:* Ray Abrams, La Verne Harding; *sets:* Raymond Jacobs, Art Landy; *voices:* Daws Butler, Grace Stafford; *mus:* Clarence Wheeler; *title song* sung by "Wee" Bonnie Baker; *prod mgr:* William E. Garity; *col:* Tech. *sd:* RCA. 6 min. • Smedley is responsible for keeping the rocks balanced in Balancing Rock Canyon. Chilly arrives with an assortment of noisemakers that upsets the rocks' balance.

2956. Hold That Thought *(Aesop's Film Fable)* 11 Dec. 1924; *p.c.:* Fables Pictures Inc for Pathé; *dir:* Paul Terry; b&w. sil. 5 min • An animal vaudeville show has a hypnotist who makes a hen lay an ostrich egg, a cat walk on air and the Farmer face a lion.

2957. Hold the Lion, Please *(Merrie Melodies)* 6 Jun.1942; *p.c.:* Leon Schlesinger prods for WB; *dir:* Charles M. Jones; *story:* Ted Pierce; *anim:* Ken Harris; *character des/lay:* Robert Givens; *back:* Eugene Fleury; *ed:* Treg Brown; *voices:* Mel Blanc, Ted Pierce, Fred Avery; *mus:* Carl W. Stalling; *prod sup:* Henry Binder, Raymond G. Katz; *col:* Tech. *sd:* Vit. 7 min. • Bugs gives the runaround to an incompetent lion who is trying to catch him.

2958. Hold the Lion, Please *(Noveltoon)* 27 Apr. 1951; *p.c.:* Famous for Para; *dir:* I. Sparber; *story:* I. Klein; *anim:* Steve Muffatti, George Germanetti; *sets:* Robert Owen; *voices:* Mae Questel, Jack Mercer, Cecil Roy; *mus:* Winston Sharples; *prod mgr:* Seymour Shultz; *col:* Tech. *sd:* RCA. 6 min. • Audrey wants a pet and takes a lion home from the zoo in mistake for a dog.

2959. Hold the Wire *(Popeye)* 23 Oct. 1936; *p.c.:* The Fleischer Studio for Para; *prod:* Max Fleischer; *dir:* Dave Fleischer; *anim:* Willard Bowsky, Orestes Calpini; *voices:* Jack Mercer, Mae Questel, Gus Wickie; *mus:* Sammy Timberg; b&w. *sd:* WE. 7 min. • Bluto overhears Popeye quoting poetry to Olive over the phone. He scales the telephone pole and cuts into the conversation.

2960. The Hole 1962; *p.c.:* Story-board prods for Concord/Hunter/Brandon Films Inc.; *prod/story:* Faith & John Hubley; *dir:* John Hubley; *anim:* William Littlejohn, Gary Mooney; *des/prod sup:* Pat Byron, Faith Elliot Hubley; *voices:* Dizzy Gillespie, George Matthews; *ph:* Anicam; *prod mgr:* Jim di Gangi; col. *sd.* 14 min. *Academy Award.* • Two excavators in a deep hole discuss the possibilities of a thermonuclear war, unaware that one is actually happening as they speak.

2961. The Hole Idea *(Looney Tunes)* 16 Apr. 1955; *p.c.:* WB; *dir/anim:* Robert McKimson; *story:* Sid Marcus; *sets:* Richard H. Thomas; *ed:* Treg Brown; *voices:* Mel Blanc, Robert C. Bruce, Bea Benaderet; *mus:* Milt Franklyn; *prod mgr:* John W. Burton; *prod:* Edward Selzer; *col:* Tech. *sd:* Vit. 7 min. • A professor invents a portable hole that gets into the wrong hands.

2962. A Hole in One *(Aesop's Film Fable)* 8 July 1927; *p.c.:* Fables Pictures Inc for Pathé; *dir:* Paul Terry; b&w. sil. 10 min. • Farmer Al and the animals enjoy a game of golf. Al Falfa fails to steer a goat who butts him across the landscape into the 18th hole.

2963. Holiday for Drumsticks *(Merrie Melodies)* 22 Jan. 1949; *p.c.:* WB; *dir:* Arthur Davis; *story:* Lloyd Turner; *anim:* Emery Hawkins, Basil Davidovich, J.C. Melendez, Don Williams; *lay:* Don Smith; *back:* Philip de Guard; *ed:* Treg Brown; *voices:* Mel Blanc; *mus:* Carl Stalling; *prod mgr:* John W. Burton; *prod:* Edward Selzer; *col:* Ciné. *sd:* Vit. 7 min. • Daffy is bothered that Tom Turkey is better fed than he is, so he convinces Tom that he's being fattened for Thanksgiving (which he is) and needs to diet.

2964. Holiday for Shoestrings *(Merrie Melodies)* 23 Feb. 1946; *p.c.:* WB; *dir:* I. Freleng; *story:* Michael Maltese, Tedd Pierce; *anim:* Gerry Chiniquy, Virgil Ross, Ken Champin, Manuel Perez; *lay:* Hawley Pratt;

back: Paul Julian; *ed:* Treg Brown; *mus:* Carl W. Stalling; *prod mgr:* John W. Burton; *prod:* Edward Selzer; *col:* Tech. *sd:* Vit. 7 min. • A cobbler can't cope with the amount of shoes he has to make, so a group of elves come to his assistance. Set to classical music.

2965. Holiday Highlights *(Merrie Melodies)* 12 Oct. 1940; *p.c.:* Leon Schlesinger prods for WB; *dir:* Fred Avery; *story:* Dave Monahan; *anim:* Charles McKimson; *sets:* John Didrik Johnsen; *ed:* Treg Brown; *voices:* Gil Warren, Mel Blanc, Sara Berner, Fred Avery; *mus:* Carl W. Stalling; *prod sup:* Henry Binder, Raymond G. Katz; *col:* Tech. *sd:* Vit. 7 min. • Spot-gags on various holidays of the calendar year from New Year's Day to Christmas.

2966. Holiday in Mexico 1946; *p.c.:* MGM; *dir:* William Hanna, Joseph Barbera; *col:* Tech. *sd:* WE. 1½ min (cartoon seq) • Live-action feature with animated opening scene: A telephone message reaches the Mexican border but can't get through as the animated telephone poles explain to each other.

2967. Holiday Land *(Color Rhapsody)* 30 Nov. 1934; *p.c.:* Charles Mintz prods for Colum; *story:* Sid Marcus; *anim:* Art Davis; *sets:* Phil Davis; *voice:* Frank Luther, The Rhythmettes; *mus:* Joe de Nat; *prod mgr:* James Bronis; *col:* Tech-2. *sd:* RCA. 8 min. *Academy Award nomination.* • "Sleepyhead" Scrappy dreams he's in a land where every day is a holiday.

2968. Holland Days *(Paul Terry-Toon)* 12 Jan. 1934; *p.c.:* Moser & Terry for Educational/Fox; *dir:* Frank Moser, Paul Terry; *mus:* Philip A. Scheib; b&w. *sd:* WE. 5 min. • The chief occupation in Holland is making cheese, and when are loaded on board ship, that's when the mice move in.

2969. Hollywood Babies *(Scrappy)* 11 Nov. 1933; *p.c.:* Winkler for Colum; *prod:* Charles Mintz; *story:* Sid Marcus; *anim:* Art Davis; *mus:* Joe de Nat; *prod mgr:* James Bronis; b&w. *sd:* RCA. 7 min. • Scrappy and Oopy recruit children of the stars to make a movie. Those seen are junior versions of Joe E. Brown, Eddie Cantor, Charlie Chaplin, Marie Dressler, Jimmy Durante, Greta Garbo, Stan Laurel and Oliver Hardy, The Four Marx Brothers, Will Rogers and Ben Turpin.

2970. Hollywood Bowl *(Cartune Comedy)* 5 Oct. 1938; *p.c.:* Walter Lantz prods for Univ; *dir:* Elmer Perkins; *story:* Victor McLeod, Alex Lovy; *anim:* Frank Tipper, Merle Gilson; *mus:* Frank Churchill; b&w. *sd:* WE. 7 min. • Caricatures: Henry Armetta, Fred Astaire, Jack Benny, Ben Bernie, Joe E. Brown, Bob Burns, Clark Gable, Cab Calloway, Bing Crosby, W.C. Fields, Greta Garbo, Benny Goodman, Katharine Hepburn, Hugh Herbert, Charles Laughton, Myrna Loy, Charlie McCarthy, Groucho Marx, Edna May Oliver, Joe Penner, William Powell, Martha Raye, Edward G. Robinson, Leopold Stokowski and Rudy Vallee; b&w. *sd:* WE. 7 min. • Stokowski conducts Liszt's "Unfinished Symphony" to a host of stars. • Many pre–*Fantasia* images are used.

2971. Hollywood Canine Canteen *(Merrie Melodies)* 20 Apr. 1945; *p.c.:* WB; *dir:* Robert McKimson; *story:* Warren Foster; *anim:* Cal Dalton, Don Williams, Richard Bickenbach; *lay:* Cornett Wood; *back:* Richard H. Thomas; *ed:* Treg Brown; *voices:* Robert Lyons, Paul Corley, Paul Regan, Sara Berner, Mel Blanc; *mus:* Carl W. Stalling; *prod mgr:* John W. Burton; *prod:* Edward Selzer; *col:* Tech. *sd:* Vit. 7 min. • The Hollywood dogs form their own canteen for the K-9 Corps. Featuring doggy equivalents of Abbott & Costello, Joe Besser, Blondie & Dagwood, Jerry Colonna, Bing Crosby, Tommy Dorsey, Jimmy Durante, Benny Goodman, Lionel Hampton, Laurel and Hardy, Charlie McCarthy, Carmen Miranda, Edward G. Robinson, Frank Sinatra, Leopold Stokowski and Monty Wooley.

2972. Hollywood Capers *(Looney Tunes)* 19 Oct. 1935; *p.c.:* Leon Schlesinger prods for WB; *dir:* Jack King; *anim:* Rollin Hamilton, Charles Jones, Robert Clampett; *voices:* Tommy Bond, Bernice Hansel; *mus:* Norman Spencer; *prod sup:* Henry Binder, Raymond G. Katz; b&w. *sd:* Vit. 7 min. • Beans gatecrashes a movie studio and has an encounter with Frankenstein's monster.

2973. Hollywood Daffy *(Merrie Melodies)* 22 June 1946; *p.c.:* WB; *dir:* I. Freleng; *story:* Michael Maltese; *anim:* Ken Champin, Virgil Ross, Gerry Chiniquy, Manuel Perez; *lay:* Hawley Pratt; *back:* Paul Julian; *ed:* Treg Brown; *voices:* Mel Blanc, Sara Berner, Dick Bickenbach; *mus:* Carl Stalling; *prod mgr:* John W. Burton; *prod:* Edward Selzer; *col:* Tech. *sd:* Vit. 7 min. • Daffy tries to sneak into a movie studio past a watchful Studio Cop. Caricatures: Jack Benny, Bette Davis, Jimmy Durante and Johnny Weissmuller.

2974. A Hollywood Detour (*Color Rhapsody*) 23 Jan. 1942; *p.c.:* Colum; *prod/dir/story:* Frank Tashlin; *anim:* Emery Hawkins; *sets:* Clark Watson; *ed:* Edward Moore; *voice:* Frank Graham; *mus:* Paul Worth; *ph:* Frank Fisher; *prod mgr:* Ben Schwalb; *col:* Tech. *sd:* RCA. 8 min. • A burlesque tour of Hollywood and it's surroundings. Caricatures of Fred Astaire, John Barrymore, Bing Crosby, W.C. Fields, Clark Gable, Rita Hayworth, Katharine Hepburn and The Three Stooges. Half-finished and completed by Frank Tashlin.

2975. Hollywood Diet (*Paul Terry-Toon*) 11 Dec. 1932; *p.c.:* Moser & Terry for Educational/Fox; *dir:* Frank Moser, Paul Terry; *mus:* Philip A. Scheib; b&w. *sd:* WE. 7 min. • Overweight women are treated at Dr. Fathead the painless fat remover's clinic.

2976. Hollywood Goes Krazy (*Krazy Kat*) 13 Feb. 1932; *p.c.:* Winkler for Colum; *story:* Manny Gould; *anim/voice:* Jack Carr; *mus:* Joe de Nat; *prod:* George Winkler; b&w. *sd:* WE. 6 min. • Krazy and Kitty audition at "Super Flop Productions" where a sleazy casting director tries to seduce Kitty. Caricatures of Joe E. Brown, Eddie Cantor, Charlie Chaplin, Laurel and Hardy, Groucho Marx and Ben Turpin.

2977. Hollywood Graduation (*Color Rhapsody*) 26 Aug. 1938; *p.c.:* Charles Mintz prods for Colum; *dir:* Art Davis; *anim:* Sid Marcus; *sets:* Phil Davis; *voices:* Cliff Nazarro; *mus:* Joe de Nat; *prod mgr:* James Bronis; *col:* Tech. *sd:* RCA. 7 min. • Junior versions of Hollywood stars graduate. Caricatures of John Barrymore, Wallace Beery, Marlene Dietrich, Clark Gable, Charles Laughton, Herbert Marshall and The Three Stooges.

2978. The Hollywood Matador (*Woody Woodpecker*) 9 Feb. 1942; *p.c.:* Walter Lantz prods for Univ; *dir:* Walter Lantz; *story:* Ben Hardaway, Lowell Elliot; *anim:* Alex Lovy, George Dane; *sets:* Fred Brunish; *voice:* Kent Rogers; *mus:* Darrell Calker; *prod mgr:* George Hall; *col:* Tech. *sd:* WE. 7 min. • Woody fights a bull with astonishing results.

2979. Hollywood Party 14 May 1934; *p.c.:* Walt Disney prods for MGM; *Mickey Mouse: dir/anim:* Fred Moore; *The Hot Choc-Late Soldiers: dir:* Ben Sharpsteen; *anim:* Jack Kinney, Frank Oreb, Louis Schmitt, Cy Young, Ugo D'Orsi; *character des:* Ferdinand Huszti Horvath; *back:* Emil Flohri, Carlos Manriquez; *voices: Mickey Mouse:* Walt Disney; "The Hot Choc-Late Soldiers" *tenor:* Kenneth Baker; *mus:* Frank E. Churchill; *song:* Nacio Herb Brown, Arthur Freed; b&w/Tech. *sd:* WE. (seq) 6 min. *l/a/anim.* • Live-action feature (in b&w); Jimmy Durante's party is interrupted by the arrival of Mickey Mouse. The Technicolor *Hot Choc-Late Soldiers* sequence shows the chocolate soldiers at war with the gingerbread men.

2980. Hollywood Picnic (*Color Rhapsody*) 18 Dec. 1937; *p.c.:* Charles Mintz prods for Colum; *story:* Sid Marcus; *anim:* Art Davis; *character des:* Ben Shenkman; *sets:* Phil Davis; *ed:* George Winkler; *voices:* Leo Cleary; *mus:* Joe de Nat; *song* "Truckin'": Ted Koehler, Rube Bloom; *ph:* Otto Reimer; *prod mgr:* James Bronis; *col:* Tech. *sd:* RCA. 7 min. • The Hollywood stars have a picnic. Caricatures of George Arliss, John Barrymore, Wallace Beery, Herman Bing, Fanny Brice, Joe E. Brown, Eddie Cantor, Irvin S. Cobb, Jimmy Durante, Step'n Fetchit, W.C. Fields, Clark Gable, Greta Garbo, Katharine Hepburn, Hugh Herbert, Boris Karloff, Charles Laughton, Laurel and Hardy, The Marx Brothers, Edna May Oliver, George Raft, Martha Raye, Edward G. Robinson, Shirley Temple, Ned Sparks, The Three Stooges and Mae West.

2981. Hollywood Steps Out (*Merrie Melodies*) 24 May 1941; *p.c.:* Leon Schlesinger prods for WB; *dir:* Fred Avery; *character des:* Ben Shenkman; *sets:* John Didrik Johnsen; *ed:* Treg Brown; *voices:* Kent Rogers, Sara Berner; *mus:* Carl W. Stalling; *prod sup:* Henry Binder, Raymond G. Katz; *col:* Tech. *sd:* Vit. 7 min. • The stars relax at Ciro's night club. Among those present are Mischa Auer, Wallace Beery, Henry Binder, Humphrey Bogart, James Cagney, Jerry Colonna, Claudette Colbert, Bing Crosby, Errol Flynn, Henry Fonda, Clark Gable, Greta Garbo, Judy Garland, Cary Grant, Oliver Hardy, Sonja Henie, J. Edgar Hoover, Boris Karloff, Kay Kyser, Buster Keaton, Dorothy Lamour, Peter Lorre, Groucho and Harpo Marx, Adolphe Menjou, David Niven, William Powell, Tyrone Power, George Raft, Sally Rand, Edward G. Robinson, Cesar Romero, Mickey Rooney, Ann Sheridan, Leon Schlesinger, C. Aubrey Smith, Ned Sparks, James Stewart, The Three Stooges, Leopold Stokowski, Lewis Stone, Spencer Tracy, Arthur Treacher, Jane Wyman, Johnny Weissmuller.

2982. Hollywood Sweepstakes (*Color Rhapsody*) 28 July 1939; *p.c.:* Charles Mintz prods for Colum; *dir:* Ben Harrison; *anim:* Manny Gould; *sets:* Phil Davis; *voice:* Dave Weber; *mus:* Joe de Nat; *prod mgr:* James Bronis; *col:* Tech. *sd:* RCA. 8 min. • A pony is substituted at the last minute when the favorite catches a cold and is unable to race. Hollywood personalities caricatured.

2983. Holy Smoke Oct. 1921. *p.c.:* Rialto Prod., for State Rights; b&w. *sil.* 5 min. • Two little dolls come alive and cause mischief with the long clay pipe an old man is smoking. Stop-motion animation.

2984. The Home Agent (*Aesop's Film Fable*) Dec. 1927; *p.c.:* Fables Pictures Inc for Pathé; *dir:* Paul Terry; b&w. *sil.* 10 min. • No story available.

2985. Home Defense (*Donald Duck*) 26 Nov. 1943; *p.c.:* Walt Disney prods for RKO; *dir:* Jack King; *asst dir:* Esther Newell; *story:* Carl Barks; *anim:* Paul Allen, Hal King, Charles A. Nichols, Don Patterson, Judge Whitaker, Marvin Woodward; *lay:* Bill Herwig; *voices:* Clarence Nash; *mus:* Paul J. Smith; *col:* Tech. *sd:* RCA. 8 min. • Air Raid Warden Donald falls asleep at his listening post and gets a rude awakening with a toy airplane and a bee.

2986. The Home Guard (*Terry-Toon*) 7 Mar. 1941; *p.c.:* TT for Fox; *dir:* Mannie Davis; *story:* John Foster; *voices:* Arthur Kay, Thomas Morrison; *mus:* Philip A. Scheib; *col:* Tech. *sd:* RCA. 6 min. • Pvt. Gandy Goose becomes a hero when he routs two sinister Fifth-Column vultures intent on wrecking his H.Q.

2987. Home Life (*Terry-Toon*) Nov. 1962; *p.c.:* TT for Fox; *ex prod:* William M. Weiss; *dir:* Connie Rasinski; *story sup:* Tom Morrison; *story:* Kin Platt; *anim:* Connie Rasinski, Mannie Davis; *sets:* John Zago, Bill Focht; *ed:* George McAvoy; *voices:* Dayton Allen, Lionel Wilson; *mus:* Phil Scheib; *ph:* Charles Schettler *col:* DeLuxe. *sd:* RCA. 6 min. • No story available.

2988. Home Made Home (*Goofy*) 23 Mar. 1951; *p.c.:* Walt Disney prods for RKO; *dir:* Jack Kinney; *story:* Milt Schaffer, Dick Kinney; *anim:* Ed Aardal, John Sibley, Charles Nichols, George Kreisl; *fx:* Dan MacManus, Jack Boyd; *lay:* Al Zinnen; *back:* Dick Anthony; *voices:* John Ployardt, Pinto Colvig, Virginia Beck, Dick Kinney, Milt Schaffer; *mus:* Joseph S. Dubin; *col:* Tech. *sd:* RCA. 7 min. • Goofy attempts to construct his own house.

2989. Home on the Range (*MGM Cartoon*) 23 Mar. 1940; *p.c.:* MGM; *prod/dir:* Rudolf Ising; *chorus:* The King's Men; *mus:* Scott Bradley; *prod mgr:* Fred Quimby; *col:* Tech. *sd:* WE. 7 min. • A calf leaves his mother and is cornered by a hungry wolf. The prairie animals keep the wolf occupied until the calf's mother arrives.

2990. Home, Sweet Home (*Aesop's Film Fable*) 26 Oct. 1926; *p.c.:* Fables Pictures Inc for Pathé; *dir:* Paul Terry; b&w. *sil.* 10 min. • Farmer Al can't escape from the mice overrunning his house and his heckling animals. Even when his flivver explodes, it returns him to home base. Moral: "There is no room for complaint in a modern flat."

2991. Home, Sweet Homewrecker (*Woody Woodpecker*) 30 Jan. 1962; *p.c.:* Walter Lantz prods for Univ; *dir:* Paul J. Smith; *story:* Dalton Sandifer; *anim:* Les Kline, Al Coe, Ray Abrams; *sets:* Art Landy, Ray Huffine; *voices:* Grace Stafford; *mus:* Clarence Wheeler; *prod mgr:* William E. Garity; *col:* Tech. *sd:* RCA. 6 min. • Woody and Buck Beaver destroy each other's homes.

2992. Home, Sweet Nudnik (*Nudnik*) Dec. 1965; *p.c.:* Rembrandt Films for Para; *prod:* William L. Snyder; *dir:* Gene Deitch; *col. sd.* 8 min. • The hapless Nudnik awakens on Friday the 13th to discover his apartment building is being demolished around him. • See: *Nudnik*

2993. Home, Sweet Swampy (*Comic King*) May 1962; *p.c.:* Para Cartoons; *dir:* Seymour Kneitel; *story:* Les Colodny, Al Brodax; *anim:* Martin Taras, John Gentilella, I. Klein, Larry Silverman; *sets:* Anton Loeb; *voices:* Howard Morris, Allen Melvin; *mus:* Winston Sharples; *ex prod:* Al Brodax; *col:* Tech. *sd:* RCA. 5 min. • Beetle Bailey and Sarge win ten days leave but Sgt. Snorkle can't bear being away from Camp Swampy.

2994. Home Talent (*Aesop's Film Fable*) 29 June 1924; *p.c.:* Fables Pictures Inc for Pathé; *dir:* Paul Terry; b&w. *sil.* 5 min. • The gang of animals attends a circus and are deluged when a water main bursts.

2995. Home Town Olympics (*Paul Terry-Toons*) 7 Feb. 1936; *p.c.:*

Moser & Terry for Educational/Fox; *dir:* Frank Moser, Paul Terry; *mus:* Philip A. Scheib; b&w. *sd:* WE. 6 min. • The slow tortoise comes into the race when the hare picks up speed. He wins and is made a hero.

2996. Home, Tweet Home *(Merrie Melodies)* 14 Jan. 1950; *p.c.:* WB; *dir:* I. Freleng; *story:* Tedd Pierce; *anim:* Virgil Ross, Arthur Davis, Gerry Chiniquy, Ken Champin; *lay:* Hawley Pratt; *back:* Phil de Guard; *ed:* Treg Brown; *voices:* Mel Blanc, Bea Benaderet; *mus:* Carl Stalling; *prod mgr:* John W. Burton; *prod:* Edward Selzer; *col:* Tech. *sd:* Vit. 7 min. • Sylvester pursues Tweety in a park.

2997. Homeless Cats *(Aesop's Film Fable)* 26 Apr. 1929; *p.c.:* Fables Pictures Inc for Pathé; *dir:* Paul Terry; *mus:* Josiah Zuro; *sd fx:* Maurice Manne; b&w. *sd:* RCA. 10 min. • No story available.

2998. The Homeless Flea *(MGM Cartoon)* 12 Oct. 1940; *p.c.:* MGM; *prod/dir:* Rudolf Ising; *story:* Henry Allen; *anim:* Robert Allen, Irven Spence; *mus:* Scott Bradley; *prod mgr:* Fred Quimby; *col:* Tech. *sd:* WE. 7 min. • A hobo flea attempts to make a home on a reluctant dog.

2999. Homeless Hare *(Merrie Melodies)* 11 Mar. 1950; *p.c.:* WB; *dir:* Charles M. Jones; *story:* Michael Maltese; *anim:* Ken Harris, Phil Monroe, Ben Washam, Lloyd Vaughan; *lay:* Robert Gribbroek; *back:* Peter Alvarado; *ed:* Treg Brown; *voices:* Mel Blanc, John T. Smith; *mus:* Carl W. Stalling; *prod mgr:* John W. Burton; *prod:* Edward Selzer; *col:* Tech. *sd:* Vit. 7 min. • Bugs locks horns with a construction worker who wants to build over his home.

3000. Homeless Homer *(Oswald)* 12 Nov. 1928; *p.c.:* Winkler for Univ; *anim:* Isadore Freleng, Rudolf Ising; tinted. *sil.* 5 min. • Oswald takes in an orphan and feeds him milk, which Homer doesn't want, starting a food fight. The kid then ties a length of rope to Ozzie and drags him through the house.

3001. The Homeless Pup *(Barker Bill)* 23 July 1937; *p.c.:* TT for Educational/Fox; *dir:* George Gordon; *mus:* Philip A. Scheib; b&w. *sd:* RCA. 6 min. • Barker Bill arrives and is bathed and shaved to look like a French Poodle amid the parrot's chiding. The pup has his revenge by shaving both the parrot and his new master.

3002. Homeless Pups *(Aesop's Film Fable)* 4 May 1924; *p.c.:* Fables Pictures Inc for Pathé; *dir:* Paul Terry; b&w. *sil.* 5 min. • The Dogcatcher breaks up the pups' romance by capturing the girl pup and locking her in a dungeon. She is rescued by her lover who summons hundreds of mutts to storm the jail, rescue her and tie the Dogcatcher to his own wagon. Moral: "In union there is strength."

3003. Homer on the Range *(Noveltoon)* Dec. 1964; *p.c.:* Para Cartoons; *dir/story:* Howard Post; *anim:* Wm. B. Pattengill; *sets:* Robert Little; *voices:* Bob MacFadden, Corinne Orr; *mus:* Winston Sharples; *ph:* Leonard McCormick; *prod mgr:* Abe Goodman; *col:* Tech. *sd:* RCA. 6 min. • A Texas Ranger sets out with his Indian companion to capture a notorious cattle rustler.

3004. Homesteader Droopy *(Droopy)* 10 July 1954; *p.c.:* MGM; *dir:* Tex Avery; *story:* Heck Allen; *anim:* Robert Bentley, Walter Clinton, Grant Simmons, Michael Lah; *sets:* John Didrik Johnsen; *ed:* Jim Faris; *voices:* Bill Thompson, Paul Frees, Marian Richman, Tex Avery; *mus:* Winston Sharples; *ph:* Jack Stevens; *prod:* Fred Quimby; *col:* Tech. *sd:* WE. 8 min. • The homesteaders set up home on the cattle baron's property, causing a traditional western shoot-out.

3005. The Honduras Hurricane *(Captain & the Kids)* 15 Oct. 1938; *p.c.:* MGM; *dir:* Isadore Freleng; *anim:* Jack Zander; *sets:* Bob Kuwahara; *ed:* Fred MacAlpin; *voices:* Billy Bletcher, Mel Blanc; *mus:* Scott Bradley; *prod mgr:* Fred Quimby; *col:* sep. *sd:* WE. 7 min. • Pirate John challenges the Captain's fighting bantam to a match with his robot rooster.

3006. Honest Love and True *(Betty Boop)* 25 Mar. 1938; *p.c.:* The Fleischer Studio for Para; *prod:* Max Fleischer; *dir:* Dave Fleischer; *anim:* Myron Waldman, Lillian Friedman; *ed:* Kitty Pfister; *voice:* Margie Hines; *mus:* Sammy Timberg; b&w. *sd:* WE. 7 min. • Melodrama with Betty being saved in the nick of time by a Mountie.

3007. Honey Harvester *(Donald Duck)* 5 Aug. 1949; *p.c.:* Walt Disney prods for RKO; *dir:* Jack Hannah; *story:* Nick George, Bill Berg; *anim:* Bob Carlson, Volus Jones, Judge Whitaker, Bill Justice; *fx:* Dan MacManus, Jack Boyd; *lay:* Yale Gracey; *back:* Thelma Witmer, Claude Coats; *voices:* Clarence Nash, James MacDonald; *mus:* Oliver Wallace; *col:* Tech. *sd:* RCA.

7 min. • A bee hides a secret hoarde of honey in a car radiator which Donald finds and tries to steal.

3008. Honey, I Blew up the Kid 17 July 1992; *p.c.:* Walt Disney Pictures/Touchwood Pacific Partners 1 for BV; *title anim:* Kurtz and Friends; *opening seq:* Bob Kurtz, Robert Peluce; *fx anim:* Marsha Gray, Carrington, Elissa Bello, Victor Jimenez, Byron Werner, Judith Bell, Robin Penny, Allen Gonzales; *anim fx ph:* Brandy Hill; *visual fx anim sup:* Michael Lessa; *col:* Tech. *sd:* Dolby Stereo. 3 min. • Live-action comedy about a scientist who enlarges his baby son to gigantic proportions. The comic title animation shows the father dealing with the problems of coping with a giant child.

3009. Honey, I Shrunk the Kids 23 June 1989; *p.c.:* Walt Disney Pictures/Silver Screen Partners III/Doric Prods. for BV; *title credits:* Kroyer Films, Inc.; *mus:* James Horner; *col:* Metrocolor. *sd:* Dolby Stereo. 2¹/₂ min. • Live-action comedy featuring an inventor who develops a machine that accidentally shrinks his offspring to ¹/₄ inch high. Humorous animated credits feature two miniature kids on a tabletop menaced by household appliances.

3010. The Honey-Mousers *(Looney Tunes)* 8 Dec. 1956; *p.c.:* WB; *dir:* Robert McKimson; *story:* Tedd Pierce; *anim:* Ted Bonnicksen, George Grandpré, Keith Darling, Russ Dyson; *lay:* Robert Gribbroek; *back:* Richard H. Thomas; *ed:* Irvin Jay; *voices:* Daws Butler, June Foray; *mus:* Milt Franklyn; *prod mgr:* John W. Burton; *prod:* Edward Selzer; *col:* Tech. *sd:* Vit. 6 min. • Satire on TV's *The Honeymooners*. Alice and Ralph Crumbden are two starving mice in an empty house until a new family moves in. Together with neighbor Ned Morton, Ralph sets out to relieve the fridge of it's contents but doesn't count on a hidden element ... a cat!

3011. Honeyland *(Happy Harmonies)* 19 Oct. 1935; *p.c.:* MGM; *prod/dir:* Hugh Harman, Rudolf Ising; *voices:* The Three Harmonettes, Rudolf Ising; *mus:* Scott Bradley; *col:* Tech. *sd:* RCA. 8 min. • The busy bees are preparing honey when they are besieged by a large, ferocious spider.

3012. Honeymoon Hotel *(Merrie Melodies)* 17 Feb. 1934; *p.c.:* Leon Schlesinger prods for WB; *dir:* Earl Duval; *anim:* Jack King, Frank Tipper, Robert Clampett; *mus:* Bernard Brown; *song:* Bert Kalmar, Harry Ruby; *col:* Ciné. *sd:* Vit. 7 min. • Mr. and Mrs. Bug spend their honeymoon in an all-insect hotel. Their love-making gets so hot that it burns the hotel down.

3013. Honeymoon in Vegas 28 Aug. 1992; *p.c.:* Castle Rock Entertainment/New Line Cinema for First Independent; *title des:* Wayne Fitzgerald; *col:* CFI/Tech. *sd:* Dolby Stereo. 4 min. • Live-action comedy about a man who promises his dying mother he will never marry: The amusing animated credits show a little man's struggle to reach a bride atop a wedding cake.

3014. Honey's Money *(Merrie Melodies)* 1 Sept. 1962; *p.c.:* WB; *dir:* Friz Freleng; *story:* John Dunn; *anim:* Gerry Chiniquy, Virgil Ross, Bob Matz, Lee Halpern, Art Leonardi; *lay:* Hawley Pratt; *back:* Tom O'Loughlin; *ed:* Treg Brown; *voices:* Mel Blanc, June Foray, Billy Booth; *mus:* Milt Franklyn; *prod mgr:* William Orcutt; *prod:* David H. DePatie; *col:* Tech. *sd:* Vit. 7 min. • Sam marries a rich widow in order to gain access to her money but also inherits her oversize child in the bargain.

3015. Honolulu Wiles *(Krazy Kat)* 17 July 1930; *p.c.:* Winkler for Colum; *anim:* Ben Harrison, Manny Gould; *mus:* Joe de Nat; *prod:* George Winkler; b&w. *sd:* WE. 6 min. • Krazy utilizes various objects on a tropical island to serenade his girl.

3016. The Honor Man *(Aesop's Film Fable)* 10 Apr. 1927; *p.c.:* Fables Pictures Inc for Pathé; *dir:* Paul Terry; b&w. *sil.* 10 min. • Thomas Cat escapes from prison, eluding the police by hiding in a coal truck. The coal is deposited back in the prison yard.

3017. The Honor System *(Aesop's Film Fable)* 7 Nov. 1925; *p.c.:* Fables Pictures Inc for Pathé; *dir:* Paul Terry; b&w. *sil.* 10 min. • Dealing with the escape of animal convicts from prison and their subsequent return when chased by thousands of guards.

3018. Honorable Cat Story *(Hashimoto)* June 1961; *p.c.:* TT for Fox; *ex prod:* Bill Weiss; *dir:* Connie Rasinski; *story sup:* Tom Morrison; *story:* Bob Kuwahara; *anim:* Juan Guidi, Ed Donnelly; *sets:* John Zago; *voices:* John Myhers; *mus:* Philip Scheib; *prod mgr:* Frank Schudde; *col:* Deluxe. *sd:* RCA. 6 min. CS. • Ichiro, a house cat, narrates the story of why Japanese cats are subservient to the mice. As he tells it, the cats in olden days dominated the mice, being superior at Sumo wrestling until Hashimoto, a mouse expert at Ju-Jitsu, beats their champion. When the cats learn Ju-Jitsu, Hashimoto has now learned a new art of "Mean-Jitsu" whereupon he can vanish and reappear in multiple locations, thus defeating the cats again.

3019. Honorable Family Problem *(Hashimoto)* Mar. 1962; *p.c.*: TT for Fox; *ex prod*: Bill Weiss; *dir/story*: Bob Kuwahara; *story sup*: Tom Morrison; *anim*: Bob Kuwahara, Mannie Davis, Cosmo Anzilotti, Bill Hutten; *sets*: Bill Focht, John Zago; *ed*: George McAvoy; *voices*: John Myhers; *mus*: Philip Scheib; *ph*: Ted Moskowitz; *prod mgr*: Frank Schudde; *col*: DeLuxe. *sd*: RCA. 6 min. • Tired of his family's "Westernized" habits, Hashimoto takes them to see a typical oriental dancer who, in turn, does a westernized dance.

3020. Honorable House Cat *(Hashimoto)* Mar. 1962; *p.c.*: TT for Fox; *ex prod*: Bill Weiss; *dir*: Mannie Davis; *story sup*: Tom Morrison; *story*: Dick Kinney, Al Bertino; *voices*: John Myhers; *mus*: Philip Scheib; *prod mgr*: Frank Schudde; *col*: DeLuxe. *sd*: RCA. 6 min. • Hashimoto's son learns of the exalted position ancient Japanese cats were once held and attempts to show reverence for the local feline who prefers eating to homage.

3021. Honorable Paint in the Neck *(Hashimoto)* Sept. 1962; *p.c.*: TT for Fox; *ex prod*: Bill Weiss; *dir*: Bob Kuwahara; *story sup*: Tom Morrison; *sets*: Bill Focht; *voices*: John Myhers; *mus*: Philip Scheib; *prod mgr*: Frank Schudde; *col*: DeLuxe. *sd*: RCA. 6 min. • Hashimoto's parasol business is visited by a cat demanding protection money. Not wishing to pay, Hashimoto gets into a paint-throwing fight that brightens up the look of his parasols.

3022. Hook 8 Dec. 1991; *p.c.*: Amblin Entertainment for Colum-TriStar; *special visual fx: anim sup*: Wes Ford Takahashi; *anim*: Gordon Baker, Andrew Haldeman, David Cutler, Anthony Stacchi, Victor Jimenez, Paul Johnson; *col*: DeLuxe/Tech. *sd*: Dolby Stereo. 141 min./*l/a.* • Live-action fantasy based on Sir J.M. Barrie's play *Peter Pan*. A grown-up, middle-aged Peter discovers his own children have been spirited away to Neverland and Captain Hook has left a challenge for him to reclaim them. The magic is enhanced by animation, computer generated imagery and puppetry.

3023. Hook and Ladder Hokum *(Tom & Jerry)* 28 Apr. 1933; *p.c.*: Van Beuren for RKO; *dir*: George Stallings, Tish-Tash (Frank Tashlin); *mus*: Gene Rodemich; b&w. *sd*: RCA. 7 min. • Firemen Tom and Jerry attempt to rescue an old geezer from a burning building.

3024. Hook and Ladder No.1 *(Paul Terry-Toon)* 30 Oct. 1932; *p.c.*: Moser & Terry for Educational/Fox; *dir*: Frank Moser, Paul Terry; *mus*: Philip A. Scheib; b&w. *sd*: WE. 6 min. • An operatic fire department attempt to douse a fire to the theme of *Ginsburg's House Burning Down*.

3025. Hook, Line and Sinker *(Aesop's Film Fable)* 22 July 1927; *p.c.*: Fables Pictures Inc for Pathé; *dir*: Paul Terry; b&w. sil. 10 min. • Farmer Al hooks a fish so large that it takes him to the ocean bed.

3026. Hook, Line and Sinker *(Terry-Toon)* 8 Sept. 1939; *p.c.*: TT for Fox; *dir*: Eddie Donnelly; *story*: John Foster; *voices*: Arthur Kay, Thomas Morrison; *mus*: Philip A. Scheib; *col*: Tech. *sd*: RCA. 6 min. • Gandy Goose nets all the fish while Sourpuss catches nothing, so the cat filches Gandy's catch and our hero lands a whale.

3027. Hook, Line and Stinker *(Looney Tunes)* 11 Oct. 1958; *p.c.*: WB; *dir*: Chuck Jones; *story*: Michael Maltese; *anim*: Richard Thompson, Ken Harris, Ben Washam; *sets*: Philip de Guard; *ed*: Treg Brown; *voice*: Paul Julian; *mus*: John Seeley; *prod*: John W. Burton; *col*: Tech. *sd*: Vit. 7 min. • The Coyote enlists a piano, lightning rod and railroad tracks along with an elaborate cannon-firing episode to snare the elusive Road-Runner.

3028. Hook, Line and Stinker *(Woody Woodpecker)* Jan. 1969; *p.c.*: Walter Lantz prods for Univ; *dir*: Paul J. Smith; *story*: Cal Howard; *anim*: Les Kline, Al Coe; *sets*: Nino Carbe; *voices*: Daws Butler, Grace Stafford; *mus*: Walter Greene; *col*: Tech. *sd*: RCA. 6 min. • Woody disrupts a man's fishing and gets booted out for his trouble. He soon wreaks revenge on the unfortunate angler.

3029. Hook, Lion and Sinker *(Donald Duck)* 1 Sept. 1950; *p.c.*: Walt Disney prods for RKO; *dir*: Jack Hannah; *story*: Bill Berg, Nick George; *anim*: John Sibley, Volus Jones, Bob Carlson, Bill Justice; *fx*: Jack Boyd; *lay*: Yale Gracey; *back*: Thelma Witmer; *voices*: Clarence Nash, James MacDonald; *mus*: Paul Smith; *col*: Tech. *sd*: RCA. 7 min. • Donald's catch of fish arouses the interest of two hungry mountain lions.

3030. Hooked Bear 27 Apr. 1956; *p.c.*: Walt Disney prods for BV; *dir*: Jack Hannah; *story*: Al Bertino, Dave DeTiege; *anim*: Bill Justice, Al Coe, Bob Carlson, John Sibley, Jack Parr; *fx*: Dan MacManus; *lay*: Yale Gracey; *back*: Claude Coats; *voices*: Bill Thompson, James MacDonald, Jack Hannah; *mus*: Oliver Wallace; *col*: Tech. *sd*: RCA. 6 min. • Humphrey the bear tries many ploys to steal the fishermen's catch without much luck.

3031. Hooky Spooky *(Casper)* 1 Mar. 1957; *p.c.*: Para Cartoons; *dir*: I. Sparber; *story*: Carl Meyer; *anim*: Myron Waldman, Nick Tafuri; *sets*: Robert Little; *voices*: Norma MacMillan, Jack Mercer; *mus*: Winston Sharples; *ph*: Leonard McCormick; *prod mgr*: Seymour Shultz; *col*: Tech. *sd*: RCA. 6 min. • Casper's cousin Spooky would rather scare the animals in the zoo than go to school.

3032. Hoola Boola *(Madcap Models)* 27 July 1941; *p.c.*: George Pal prods for Para; *prod/dir*: George Pal; *story*: Jack Miller; *anim*: George Pal, Ray Harryhausen; *voices*: Pat McGeehan, Mel Blanc; *mus*: Thurston Knudson; *mus rec*: Augie Goupil; *col*: Tech. *sd*: WE. 9 min. • Jim Dandy is marooned on a desert isle. There he meets a South Sea beauty, Sarong-Sarong. Cannibals capture him but are frightened off by Sarong-Sarong in a Witch Doctor's disguise.

3033. Hootchy Kootchy Parlais Vous *(Felix the Cat)* 1930; *p.c.*: Bijou Films Inc for Copley Pictures Corp; *prod*: Jacques Kopfstein, Pat Sullivan; *anim*: Otto Messmer; *mus*: Bernard Altshuler; *sd fx*: Harry Edison; b&w. *sd*. 6 min. • Felix joins-up when mice declare war on cats. He ends up in the trenches and in the heat of battle. His homecoming to wifey discovers a new stock of kittens have arrived since he's been away.

3034. Hop and Chop *(Tijuana Toads)* 17 June 1970; *p.c.*: Mirisch-DFE for UA; *dir*: Grant Simmons; *story*: Dale Hale; *anim*: Ken Muse, Bob Richardson, Art Leonardi; *lay*: Dick Ung; *back*: Richard Thomas; *ed*: Lee Gunther; *voices*: Don Diamond, Tom Holland; *mus*: Doug Goodwin; *ph*: John Burton Jr.; *prod sup*: Jim Foss, Harry Love; *col*: DeLuxe. *sd*: RCA. 6 min • The Toads do battle with a Japanese Beetle.

3035. Hop and Go *(Looney Tunes)* 6 Feb. 1943; *p.c.*: Leon Schlesinger prods for WB; *dir/lay*: Norman McCabe; *story*: Melvin Millar; *anim*: John Carey, Cal Dalton, Arthur Davis, David Hoffman, Vive Risto; *sets*: Dave Hilberman; *ed*: Treg Brown; *voices*: Pinto Colvig, Mel Blanc; *mus*: Carl W. Stalling; *ph*: John W. Burton; *prod sup*: Henry Binder, Raymond G. Katz; b&w. *sd*: Vit. 6 min. • Two rabbits decide to teach a boastful kangaroo a lesson in hopping.

3036. Hop, Look and Listen *(Looney Tunes)* 17 Apr. 1948; *p.c.*: WB; *dir*: Robert McKimson; *story*: Warren Foster; *anim*: Charles McKimson, Manny Gould, I. Ellis; *lay*: Cornett Wood; *back*: Richard H. Thomas; *ed*: Treg Brown; *voices*: Mel Blanc; *mus*: Carl Stalling; *prod mgr*: John W. Burton; *prod*: Edward Selzer; *col*: Tech. *sd*: Vit. 6 min. • Sylvester is put to shame when he tries to evict a mouse who turns out to be a baby kangaroo.

3037. Hop Off 16 June 1928; *(Educational-Bowers Comedy) p.c.*: Bowers Comedy Corp. for Educational; *prod/story*: Charles R. Bowers; *dir*: H.L. Muller; *l/a*: Charley Bowers, Yvonne Howell, Dan Mason, Robert Graves; b&w. sil. 2 reels. *l/a/anim.* • Charley owns a Flea Circus. A scientist gives him a serum for returning things back to their origins. While he's busy experimenting, two of his fleas go on vacation and Charley has a frantic search before finding them skating on a bald man's head. Live-action/stop-motion animation.

3038. Hop, Skip and a Chump *(Merrie Melodies)* 3 Jan. 1942; *p.c.*: Leon Schlesinger prods for WB; *dir*: I. Freleng; *story*: Michael Maltese; *anim*: Cal Dalton; *character des/lay*: Robert Givens; *back*: Lenard Kester; *ed*: Treg Brown; *voices*: Mel Blanc; *mus*: Carl W. Stalling; *ph*: John W. Burton; *prod sup*: Henry Binder, Raymond G. Katz; *col*: Tech. *sd*: Vit. 7 min. • A grasshopper is the center of attraction for two crows resembling Laurel and Hardy.

3039. Hopalong Casualty *(Looney Tunes)* 8 Oct. 1960; *p.c.*: WB; *dir/story*: Chuck Jones; *anim*: Ken Harris, Tom Ray, Richard Thompson,

Bob Bransford; *lay:* Maurice Noble; *back:* Philip de Guard; *ed:* Treg Brown; *voice:* Paul Julian; *mus:* Milt Franklyn; *prod mgr:* William Orcutt; *prod:* David H. DeTiege; *col:* Tech. *sd:* Vit. 7 min. • The Coyote, in his never ending pursuit of food attempts to feed the elusive bird "Earthquake Pills" but ends up taking them all himself.

3040. The Hopeful Donkey *(Terry-Toon)* 17 Dec. 1943; *p.c.:* TT for Fox; *dir:* Mannie Davis; *story:* John Foster; *voice:* Thomas Morrison; *mus:* Philip A. Scheib; *col:* Tech. *sd:* RCA. 7 min. • Rejected animals form a jazz band and rescue a golden egg-laying goose from bandits.

3041. Hoppy Daze *(Looney Tunes)* Feb. 1961; *p.c.:* WB; *dir:* Robert McKimson; *story:* Tedd Pierce; *anim:* Ted Bonnicksen, Warren Batchelder, Tom Ray, George Grandpre; *fx:* Harry Love; *lay:* Robert Gribbroek; *back:* Bob Singer; *ed:* Treg Brown; *voices:* Mel Blanc; *mus:* Milt Franklyn; *prod mgr:* William Orcutt; *prod:* David H. DePatie; *col:* Tech. *sd:* Vit. 7 min. • A hungry wharf cat convinces Sylvester that he's a champion mouser who can easily catch some warehouse mice. Soon they encounter a baby kangaroo who is taken for a giant mouse.

3042. Hoppy-Go-Lucky *(Looney Tunes)* 9 Aug. 1952; *p.c.:* WB; *dir:* Robert McKimson; *story:* Tedd Pierce; *anim:* Charles McKimson, Herman Cohen, Rod Scribner, Phil de Lara; *lay:* Robert Givens; *back:* Richard H. Thomas; *ed:* Treg Brown; *voices:* Mel Blanc, Stan Freberg; *mus:* Carl Stalling; *prod mgr:* John W. Burton; *prod:* Edward Selzer; *col:* Tech. *sd:* Vit. 7 min. • Sylvester and a dumb cat named Benny go mouse-catching in a warehouse. Benny sends Sylvester to find a giant mouse but it turns out to be an escaped baby kangaroo.

3043. Horning In *(Noveltoon)* Jan. 1965; *p.c.:* Para Cartoons; *dir/story:* Howard Post; *anim:* Morey Reden; *sets:* Robert Little; *voices:* Bob MacFadden; *mus:* Winston Sharples; *ph:* Leonard McCormick; *prod mgr:* Abe Goodman; *col:* Tech. *sd:* RCA. 6 min. • King Artie sets out to recover the stolen Horn of Plenty from Sir Cedric Sorehead who wants to be ruler of Magic Land.

3044. Horse Cops *(Aesop's Fable)* 12 Oct. 1931; *p.c.:* Van Beuren for RKO/Pathé; *dir:* John Foster, J.J. McManus; *mus:* Gene Rodemich; *b&w. sd:* RCA. 10 min. • No story available.

3045. Horse Hare *(Looney Tunes)* 3 Feb. 1960; *p.c.:* WB; *dir:* Friz Freleng; *story:* Michael Maltese; *anim:* Gerry Chiniquy, Virgil Ross, Art Davis; *lay:* Hawley Pratt; *back:* Tom O'Loughlin; *ed:* Treg Brown; *voices:* Mel Blanc; *mus:* Milt Franklyn; *prod mgr:* William Orcutt; *prod:* David H. DePatie; *col:* Tech. *sd:* Vit. 7 min. • Pvt. Bugs is left to guard the fort against Renegade Sam and a band of Indians.

3046. The Horse On the Merry-Go-Round *(Color Rhapsody)* 17 Feb. 1938; *p.c.:* Cartoon Films Ltd/Charles Mintz prods for Colum; *prod/dir:* Ub Iwerks; *voices:* Dave Weber, Bobbie Winkler; *mus:* Eddie Kilfeather, Joe de Nat; *prod mgr:* James Bronis; *col:* Tech. *sd:* RCA 6½ min. • Tired of his boring routine, a Merry-Go-Round horse forsakes his stand and wanders around the fairground.

3047. Horse Play *(Woody Woodpecker)* Apr. 1967; *p.c.:* Walter Lantz prods for Univ; *dir:* Paul J. Smith; *story:* Cal Howard; *anim:* Les Kline, Al Coe; *sets:* Ray Huffine; *voices:* Daws Butler, Grace Stafford; *mus:* Walter Greene; *prod mgr:* William E. Garity; *col:* Tech. *sd:* RCA 6 min. • An Indian brave wants to eat Woody's horse.

3048. Horse Shoo *(Loopy de Loop)* Jan. 1965; *p.c.:* Hanna-Barbera for Colum; *prod/dir:* William Hanna, Joseph Barbera; *story dir:* Paul Sommer; *story:* Michael Maltese; *anim dir:* Charles A. Nichols; *anim:* Don Patterson; *lay:* Bill Perez; *back:* Robert Gentle; *ed:* Warner Leighton; *voices:* Daws Butler, Hal Smith, Doug Young; *mus:* Hoyt Curtin; *titles:* Lawrence Gobel; *prod mgr:* Howard Hanson; *col:* East. *sd:* RCA. 5 min. • Loopy helps hide a horse from a farmer who wants to send him to the glue factory.

3049. A Horse Tale *(Oswald)* 19 Nov. 1928; *p.c.:* Winkler for Univ; *prod:* Charles B. Mintz; *anim:* R.C. Hamilton, Tom Palmer; *b&w. sil.* 6 min. • No story available.

3050. A Horsefly Fleas *(Looney Tunes)* 13 Dec. 1947; *p.c.:* WB; *dir:* Robert McKimson; *story:* Warren Foster; *anim:* Charles McKimson, Phil de Lara, Manny Gould, John Carey; *lay:* Cornett Wood; *back:* Richard H. Thomas; *ed:* Treg Brown; *voices:* Mel Blanc; *mus:* Carl Stalling; *prod mgr:* John W. Burton; *prod:* Edward Selzer; *col:* Ciné. *sd:* Vit. 7 min. • New settler fleas move onto a dog and are instantly involved in a western shoot-out.

3051. Horsefly Opera *(Terry-Toon)* 13 June 1941; *p.c.:* TT for Fox; *dir:* Eddie Donnelly; *story:* John Foster; *mus:* Philip A. Scheib; *col:* Tech. *sd:* RCA. 7 min. • Flies feature in a western drama. A spider holds up the apple stagecoach then gets his comeuppance.

3052. Horses, Horses, Horses *(Aesop's Film Fable)* 22 May 1927; *p.c.:* Fables Pictures Inc for Pathé; *dir:* Paul Terry; *b&w. sil.* 10 min. • A western theme with Milton Mouse engaged in a one-man round-up.

3053. The Horse's Tale *(Aesop's Film Fable)* Dec. 1927; *p.c.:* Fables Pictures Inc for Pathé; *dir:* Paul Terry; *b&w. sil.* 10 min. • No story available.

3054. A Horse's Tale *(Sugarfoot)* 15 Feb. 1954; *p.c.:* Walter Lantz prods for Univ; *dir:* Paul J. Smith; *story:* Michael Maltese; *anim:* Gil Turner, La Verne Harding, Robert Bentley; *sets:* Raymond Jacobs, Art Landy; *voices:* Dal McKennon, Grace Stafford; *mus:* Clarence Wheeler; *prod mgr:* William E. Garity; *col:* Tech. *sd:* RCA. 6 min. • Sugarfoot the plough horse destroys the farmer's new tractor and gets a job as a movie stand-in to pay for a new one.

3055. Horton Hatches the Egg *(Merrie Melodies)* 11 Apr. 1942; *p.c.:* Leon Schlesinger prods for WB; *dir:* Robert Clampett; *story:* Dr. Seuss, Michael Maltese; *anim:* Robert McKimson; *lay:* Thomas McKimson; *back:* Michael Sasanoff; *ed:* Treg Brown; *voice:* Frank Graham, Kent Rogers, Sara Berner, Mel Blanc, Robert Clampett; *mus:* Carl W. Stalling; *ph:* John W. Burton; *prod sup:* Henry Binder, Raymond G. Katz; *col:* Tech. *sd:* Vit. 9 min. • Maisie the lazy bird asks Horton the elephant to babysit with her egg. He faithfully stays with it even when he's captured by hunters and removed from the jungle.

3056. Hospitaliky *(Popeye)* 16 Apr. 1937; *p.c.:* The Fleischer Studio for Para; *prod:* Max Fleischer; *dir:* Dave Fleischer; *anim:* Seymour Kneitel, William Henning; *voices:* Jack Mercer, Gus Wickie; *mus:* Sammy Timberg; *b&w. sd:* WE. 7 min. • Popeye and Bluto try to land in the hospital.

3057. Hot-Air Aces *(Popeye)* 24 June 1949; *p.c.:* Famous for Para; *dir:* I. Sparber; *story:* I. Klein; *anim:* Al Eugster, Bill Hudson; *sets:* Robert Connavale; *voices:* Jack Mercer, Mae Questel, Jackson Beck; *mus:* Winston Sharples; *ph:* Leonard McCormick; *prod mgr:* Sam Buchwald; *col:* Pola. *sd:* RCA. 6 min. • Popeye pits his single-engine airplane against Bluto's jet in an around-the-world race.

3058. The Hot Air Salesman *(Betty Boop)* 12 Mar. 1937; *p.c.:* The Fleischer Studio for Para; *prod:* Max Fleischer; *dir:* Dave Fleischer; *anim:* Thomas Johnson, Dave Hoffman; *voices:* Mae Questel; *mus:* Sammy Timberg; *b&w. sd:* WE. 6 min. • Door-to-door salesman, Wiffle Piffle tries to sell some modern inventions to Betty.

3059. Hot and Cold *(Pooch the Pup)* 14 Aug. 1933; *p.c.:* Univ; *dir:* Walter Lantz; *anim:* Manuel Moreno, Les Kline, Fred Kopietz, Charles Hastings; *mus:* James Dietrich; *b&w. sd:* WE. 6 min. • The Weather King of the North Pole controls the atmosphere.

3060. Hot and Cold Penguin *(Chilly Willy)* 24 Oct. 1955; *p.c.:* Walter Lantz prods for Univ; *dir/story:* Alex Lovy; *anim:* Ray Abrams, La Verne Harding, Don Patterson; *sets:* Raymond Jacobs; *voice:* Daws Butler; *mus:* Clarence Wheeler; *title song sung by* Wee Bonnie Baker; *prod mgr:* William E. Garity; *col:* Tech. *sd:* RCA. 6 min. • Chilly tries to warm himself on a stove in an Army shack but is ejected by the watchdog.

3061. Hot Cross Bunny *(Merrie Melodies)* 21 Aug. 1948; *p.c.:* WB; *dir:* Robert McKimson; *story:* Warren Foster; *anim:* Manny Gould, Charles McKimson, Phil de Lara; *character des:* Jean Blanchard; *lay:* Cornett Wood; *back:* Richard H. Thomas; *ed:* Treg Brown; *voices:* Mel Blanc; *mus:* Carl Stalling; *prod mgr:* John W. Burton; *prod:* Edward Selzer; *col:* Tech. *sd:* Vit. 7 min. • Dr. Cyclops, a scientist, wants to perform a brain transplant on Bugs with a chicken.

3062. Hot Diggety Dog *(Woody Woodpecker)* Apr. 1967; *p.c.:* Walter Lantz prods for Univ; *dir:* Paul J. Smith; *story:* Cal Howard; *anim:* Les Kline, Al Coe; *sets:* Ray Huffine; *voices:* Dal McKennon, Grace Stafford; *mus:* Walter Greene; *prod mgr:* William E. Garity; *col:* Tech. *sd:* RCA. 6 min. • Woody is befriended by a stray dog who keeps stealing meat from a café proprietor.

3063. Hot Dog *(Oswald the Lucky Rabbit)* 20 Aug. 1928; *p.c.:* Winkler for Univ; *dir:* Walt Disney; *ph:* Mike Marcus; *b&w. sil.* 5 min. • Oswald goes to a sideshow and steals a hot dog. He is chased by a policeman until he hides in the Paddy Wagon.

3064. Hot Dog *(Talkartoons)* 29 Mar. 1930; *p.c.:* The Fleischer Studio for Para; *prod:* Max Fleischer; *dir:* Dave Fleischer; *mus:* Lou Fleischer; b&w. *sd:* WE. 7 min. • Bimbo pursues a roller-skating girl in his car. Once he catches her they are chased by a traffic cop. He wins over the court with skat song.

3065. Hot Dogs on Ice *(Krazy Kat)* 21 Oct. 1938; *p.c.:* Charles Mintz prods for Colum; *story:* Allen Rose; *anim:* Harry Love, Louie Lilly; *voice:* Dave Weber; *mus:* Joe de Nat; *prod mgr:* James Bronis; b&w. *sd:* RCA. 6 min. • A bully bulldog breaks up the animals' skating. He is finally lured onto thin ice.

3066. Hot Feet *(Oswald)* 14 Sept. 1931; *p.c.:* Univ; *dir:* Walter Lantz, "Bill" Nolan; *anim:* Clyde Geronimi, Manuel Moreno, Ray Abrams, Fred Avery, Lester Kline, Chet Karrberg, Pinto Colvig; *mus:* James Dietrich; b&w. *sd:* WE. 6 min. • Lemonade vendor Oswald has an encounter with racketeers.

3067. Hot Foot Lights *(Color Rhapsody)* 2 Aug. 1945; *p.c.:* Colum; *dir:* Howard Swift; *story:* Sid Marcus; *anim:* Grant Simmons, Volus Jones; *sets:* Clark Watson; *ed:* Richard S. Jensen; *voices:* Dave Barry; *mus:* Eddie Kilfeather; *i&p:* Elizabeth F. McDowell; *ph:* Frank Fisher; *prod mgr:* Hugh McCollum; *col:* Tech. *sd:* WE. 6 min. • W.C. Fields introduces a nursery rhyme show. Jimmy Durante, Martha Raye, Red Skelton and others are heckled by a boy with a pea shooter.

3068. Hot for Hollywood *(Oswald)* 19 May 1930; *p.c.:* Univ; *dir:* Walter Lantz; *anim:* "Bill" Nolan, Ray Abrams, Manuel Moreno, Clyde Geronimi; *mus:* David Broekman; b&w. *sd:* WE. 6 min. • Oswald arrives in Hollywood for a screen test. He plays the piano and is laughed out of town. Caricatures of Charlie Chaplin and Al Jolson.

3069. Hot Noon *(Woody Woodpecker)* 12 Oct. 1953; *p.c.:* Walter Lantz prods for Univ; *dir:* Paul J. Smith; *story:* Homer Brightman; *anim:* Gil Turner, La Verne Harding, Robert Bentley; *sets:* Raymond Jacobs, Art Landy; *voices:* Dallas McKennon, Grace Stafford; *mus:* Clarence Wheeler; *prod mgr:* William E. Garity; *col:* Tech. *sd:* RCA. 6 min. • Western town piano player Woody gets inundated with sheriffs' badges when western bandit Buzz Buzzard steps off the noon train.

3070. Hot-Rod and Reel *(Looney Tunes)* 9 Apr. 1959; *p.c.:* WB; *dir:* Chuck Jones; *story:* Michael Maltese; *anim:* Richard Thompson, Ben Washam, Keith Darling; *sets:* Philip de Guard; *ed:* Treg Brown; *voice:* Paul Julian; *mus:* Milt Franklyn; *prod:* John W. Burton; *col:* Tech. *sd:* Vit. 7 min. • Roller skates, an explosive camera, a trampoline, a bomb chute and a jet-propelled unicycle are all employed by the coyote to help ensnare his prey.

3071. Hot Rod Huckster *(Woody Woodpecker)* 5 July 1954; *p.c.:* Walter Lantz prods for Univ; *dir:* Don Patterson; *story:* Homer Brightman; *anim:* Ray Abrams, Herman Cohen, Ken Southworth; *sets:* Art Landy; *voices:* Dallas McKennon, Grace Stafford; *mus:* Clarence Wheeler; *prod mgr:* William E. Garity; *col:* Tech. *sd:* RCA. 6 min. • Used car dealer Buzz Buzzard wrecks Woody's car in order to sell him one of his own rejuvenated wrecks.

3072. Hot Rods *(Mighty Mouse)* June 1953; *p.c.:* TT for Fox; *dir:* Eddie Donnelly; *story/voice:* Tom Morrison; *anim:* Jim Tyer; *mus:* Philip A. Scheib; *ph:* Douglas Moye; *col:* Tech. *sd:* RCA. 6 min. • The teenage mice are lured out of mouseville by a cat driving a slicked-up hot rod.

3073. Hot Sands *(Paul Terry-Toon)* 2 Nov. 1934; *p.c.:* Moser & Terry for Educational/Fox; *dir:* Frank Moser, Paul Terry; *mus:* Philip A. Scheib; b&w. *sd:* WE. 5 min. • No story available.

3074. Hot Tamale *(Aesop's Sound Fable)* 3 Aug. 1930; *p.c.:* Van Beuren for Pathé; *dir:* John Foster; *anim:* Arthur Babbitt, Ferdinand Huszti Horvath, Frank Moser, Sarka; *mus:* Gene Rodemich; b&w. *sd:* RCA. 9 min. • Alphonse Mouse serenades his lady love and is challenged by a rival.

3075. A Hot Time in Iceland 2 Feb. 1916; *p.c.:* Univ: *prod:* P.A. Powers; b&w. *sil.* 5 min. • Sheeza Bear chases a fisherman away and makes short work of his box of candy.

3076. A Hot Time in the Old Town Tonight *(Screen Songs)* 2 Aug. 1930; *p.c.:* The Fleischer Studio for Para; *prod:* Max Fleischer; *dir:* Dave Fleischer; *anim:* Seymour Kneitel; *mus:* Art Turkisher; *song:* Joe Hayden, Theodore Metz; b&w. *sd:* WE. (disc) 7 min. • The mice go to a dance. A dancing spider adds to the fun.

3077. Hot Time on Ice *(Chilly Willy)* Mar. 1967; *p.c.:* Walter Lantz prods for Univ; *dir:* Paul J. Smith; *story:* Sid Marcus; *anim:* Al Coe, Les Kline; *sets:* Ray Huffine; *voices:* Daws Butler; *mus:* Walter Greene; *prod mgr:* William E. Garity; *col:* Tech. *sd:* RCA. 6 min. • Smedley discovers that Chilly has drilled fishing holes all over the ice runway he is scheduled to fly supply planes from.

3078. Hot Times in Iceland *(Aesop's Film Fable)* 31 May 1925; *p.c.:* Fables Pictures Inc for Pathé; *dir:* Paul Terry; b&w. *sil.* 5 min. • Noah's Ark goes on a North Pole expedition.

3079. Hot Turkey *(Paul Terry-Toons)* 10 Mar. 1930; *p.c.:* A-C for Educational/Fox; *dir:* Frank Moser, Paul Terry; *anim:* Frank Moser, Sarka, John Terry, Paul Terry, Cy Young; *mus:* Philip A. Scheib; b&w. *sd:* WE. 6 min. • A mouse dashes to the rescue when his sweetie is kidnapped for the Sultan's harem.

3080. The Hotcha Melody *(Krazy Kat)* 15 Mar. 1935; *p.c.:* Winkler for Colum; *prod:* Charles Mintz; *story:* Ben Harrison; *anim:* Manny Gould, Preston Blair; *mus:* Joe de Nat; *prod mgr:* James Bronis; b&w. *sd:* RCA. 6 min. • No story available.

3081. The Hotel Mystery 1934; created by Phil Cook; b&w. *sd:* 8 min. *l/a/anim.* • A blend of human and puppets: Dolls act out a drama in which the hotel is raided by a bear.

3082. Hotlips Jasper *(Madcap Models)* 5 Jan. 1945; *p.c.:* George Pal prods for Para; *prod/dir:* George Pal; *voices:* Roy Glenn, Glenn Leedy; *mus:* Rafael Mendez; *col:* Tech. *sd:* WE. 7 min. • Jasper and the Scarecrow find a lost trumpet and debate whether to return or play it.

3083. Hotsy Footsy *(Mr. Magoo)* 18 Sept. 1952; *p.c.:* UPA for Colum; *ex prod:* Stephen Bosustow; *dir:* William T. Hurtz; *story:* James Raymond; *anim:* Pat Matthews, Phil Monroe; *lay:* Paul Julian; *back:* Paul Julian, Robert Dranko; *voices:* Jim Backus, Jerry Hausner, Isabel Randolph; *mus:* Milton "Shorty" Rogers; *prod mgr:* Herbert Klynn; *col:* Tech. *sd:* RCA. 6 min. • Magoo wanders away from the "Old Grad" Ball into the boxing ring next door and tries dancing with a pugilist.

3084. Hound About That *(Noveltoon)* Apr. 1961; *p.c.:* Para Cartoons: *dir:* Seymour Kneitel; *story:* Irving Dressler; *anim:* Martin Taras, Al Pross; *sets:* Robert Little; *voices:* Bob MacFadden; *mus:* Winston Sharples; *ph:* Leonard McCormick; *prod mgr:* Abe Goodman; *col:* Tech. *sd:* RCA. 6 min. • A nearsighted hunting dog is sent to track a fox. Spotting his disability, the fox steals his glasses.

3085. The Hound and the Rabbit *(Happy Harmonies)* 29 May 1937; *p.c.:* MGM; *prod/dir:* Hugh Harman, Rudolf Ising; *mus:* Scott Bradley; *col:* Tech. *sd:* WE. 7 min. • Sniffy the beagle joins the bunnies' football team and later saves them from a hungry fox.

3086. Hound for Pound *(Noveltoon)* Oct. 1963; *p.c.:* Para Cartoons; *dir:* Seymour Kneitel; *story:* Jack Mercer; *anim:* Nick Tafuri, Jim Logan, Larry Silverman; *sets:* Robert Owen; *voices:* Bob MacFadden, Shari Lewis; *mus:* Winston Sharples; *ph:* Leonard McCormick; *prod mgr:* Abe Goodman; *col:* Tech. *sd:* RCA. 6 min. • A dog makes a deal with the dogcatcher that he will either find a home or turn himself in.

3087. A Hound for Trouble *(Looney Tunes)* 28 Apr. 1951; *p.c.:* WB; *dir:* Charles M. Jones; *story:* Michael Maltese; *anim:* Lloyd Vaughan, Ken Harris, Phil Monroe, Ben Washam, John Carey; *lay:* Robert Gribbroek; *back:* Philip de Guard; *ed:* Treg Brown; *voices:* Mel Blanc, Michael Maltese; *mus:* Carl Stalling; *prod mgr:* John W. Burton; *prod:* Edward Selzer; *col:* Tech. *sd:* Vit. 7 min. • Charlie Dog tries to get himself adopted by an Italian restaurant owner.

3088. Hound Hunters 12 Apr. 1947; *p.c.:* MGM; *dir:* Tex Avery; *story:* Heck Allen; *anim:* Ray Abrams, Walter Clinton, Preston Blair, Ed Love; *character des:* Irven Spence; *sets:* John Didrik Johnsen; *ed:* Fred MacAlpin; *voices:* Dick Nelson; *mus:* Scott Bradley; *prod:* Fred Quimby; *col:* Tech. *sd:* WE. 7 min. • George and Junior try their hands at dog catching.

3089. Houndabout *(Noveltoon)* 10 Apr. 1959; *p.c.:* Para Cartoons; *dir:* Seymour Kneitel; *story:* Carl Meyer, Jack Mercer; *anim:* Tom Johnson, Frank Endres; *sets:* Robert Owen; *voices:* Jackson Beck, Jack Mercer, Sid Raymond; *mus:* Winston Sharples; *ph:* Leonard McCormick; *prod mgr:* Abe Goodman; *col:* Tech. *sd:* RCA. 6 min. • A dog decides to become "human" but soon realizes that that can be a dog's life, too.

3090. Hounding the Hares (*Terry-Toon*) 9 June 1948; *p.c.*: TT for Fox; *dir*: Eddie Donnelly; *story*: John Foster; *voice*: Tom Morrison; *mus*: Philip A. Scheib; *col*: Tech. *sd*: RCA. 6 min. • Three rabbits have fun when the farmer and his dog go hunting.

3091. The House Builder-Upper (*Popeye*) 18 Mar. 1938; *p.c.*: The Fleischer Studio for Para; *prod*: Max Fleischer; *dir*: Dave Fleischer; *anim*: Seymour Kneitel, Abner Matthews; *voices*: Jack Mercer, Margie Hines; *mus*: Sammy Timberg; *prod sup*: Sam Buchwald, Isidore Sparber; b&w. *sd*: WE. 7 min. • Firemen Popeye and Wimpy arrive in time to see the glowing remnants of Olive's house and proceed to rebuild it.

3092. House Busters (*Heckle & Jeckle*) Aug. 1952; *p.c.*: TT for Fox; *dir*: Connie Rasinski; *story*: Tom Morrison; *anim*: Jim Tyer; *voices*: Tom Morrison, Douglas Moye; *mus*: Philip A. Scheib; *col*: Tech. *sd*: RCA. 7 min. • The magpies run afoul of an escaped convict hiding in a house they are demolishing.

3093. House Cleaning (*Aesop's Film Fable*) 17 Aug. 1924; *p.c.*: Fables Pictures Inc for Pathé; *dir*: Paul Terry; b&w. *sil*. 5 min. • Farmer Al Falfa catches all the mice by means of a vacuum cleaner. The bag becomes overloaded and mice explode all over the farmyard.

3094. House Cleaning (*Aesop's Film Fable*) 4 May 1925; *p.c.*: Fables Pictures Inc for Pathé; *dir*: Paul Terry; b&w. *sil*. 10 min. • No story available.

3095. House Cleaning (*Krazy Kat*) 1 June 1933; *p.c.*: Winkler for Colum; *story*: Rudy Zamora; *anim*: Al Rose, Harry Love, Al Eugster; *mus*: Joe de Nat; *prod*: George Winkler; b&w. *sd*: WE. 6 min. • While Krazy helps clean Kitty's house, his dog gets in the way and disrupts everything.

3096. House Cleaning Blues (*Betty Boop*) 15 Jan. 1937; *p.c.*: The Fleischer Studio for Para; *prod*: Max Fleischer; *dir*: Dave Fleischer; *anim*: David Tendlar, Eli Brucker; *voices*: Mae Questel, Everett Clark; *mus*: Sammy Timberg; *ph*: Johnny Burks; b&w. *sd*: WE. 7 min. • Grampy inventively helps Betty clean up her house after a party.

3097. House Cleaning Time (*Aesop's Sound Fable*) 23 July 1929; *p.c.*: Van Beuren for Pathé; *dir*: John Foster; *mus*: Carl Edouarde; b&w. *sd*: RCA. 6 min. • The mice hamper the proceedings while Farmer Al and Thomas Cat clean up the house.

3098. House Hunting Mice (*Looney Tunes*) 6 Sept. 1947; *p.c.*: WB; *dir*: Charles M. Jones; *story*: Michael Maltese; *anim*: Phil Monroe, Ben Washam, Lloyd Vaughan, Ken Harris; *lay*: Robert Gribbroek; *back*: Peter Alvarado; *ed*: Treg Brown; *voices*: Mel Blanc, Stan Freberg; *mus*: Carl Stalling; *prod mgr*: John W. Burton; *prod*: Edward Selzer; *col*: Ciné. *sd*: Vit. 7 min. • Hubie and Bertie the mice move into an automized house of the future.

3099. House of Hashimoto (*Hashimoto*) Nov. 1960; *p.c.*: TT for Fox; *ex prod*: Bill Weiss; *dir*: Connie Rasinski; *story sup*: Tom Morrison; *story*: Bob Kuwahara; *anim*: Ed Donnelly, Ralph Bakshi, Larry Silverman, Cosmo Anzilotti; *sets*: Bill Hilliker; *voices*: John Myhers; *mus*: Phil Scheib; *prod mgr*: Frank Schudde; *col*: DeLuxe. *sd*: RCA. 6 min. • Hashimoto tells a story about an invisible mouse who was born in the community.

3100. House of Magic (*Meany Miny Mo*) 8 Feb. 1937; *p.c.*: Walter Lantz prods for Univ; *dir*: Manuel Moreno; *story*: Walter Lantz, Victor McLeod; *anim*: Manuel Moreno, George Dane, Louis Zukor; *mus*: James Dietrich; b&w. *sd*: WE. 8 min. • The three monkeys take shelter in a house of magic. One has an experience with a magician's hat and dismembered gloves play a piano.

3101. The House of Tomorrow 11 June 1949; *p.c.*: MGM; *dir*: Tex Avery; *story*: Jack Cosgriff, Rich Hogan; *anim*: Walter Clinton, Michael Lah, Grant Simmons; *sets*: John Didrik Johnsen; *ed*: Fred MacAlpin; *voices*: Frank Graham, Don Messick, Colleen Collins; *mus*: Scott Bradley; *prod*: Fred Quimby; *col*: Tech. *sd*: WE. 6 min. *l/a/anim.* • A futuristic house deals with problems of humidifying and pressure cookers, etc.

3102. House on Haunted Hill 29 Oct. 1999; *p.c.*: J&M Enterprises; *digital/visual fx: 3d anim*: Joe Conti, Steward Burris; *vision art dir & anim visual fx sup*: Marc Kolbe; *digital fx prod*: Richard J. Cook; *anim sup*: Daniel Kramer; *snr anim*: Rocco Passionino, Christina Drahos; *col*: Tech. *sd*: Dolby digital/Digital dts sound/SDDS. 93 min. *l/a.* • Live-action horror. An amusement park tycoon arranges a birthday party for his wife in a property that was once a psychiatric institute where abused patients had burned to death. The spirits of the inmates rise to vent their wrath. Animated ghosts, severed heads, etc.

3103. The House That Dinky Built (*Dinky Doodle*) 1 Feb. 1925; *p.c.*: Bray prods for FBO; *dir/story*: Walter Lantz; *anim*: Clyde Geronimi; b&w. *sil*. 6 min. *l/a/anim.* • "The House That Jack Built" is renovated by Walter, Dinky Doodle and company. They are interrupted by the mouse that ate the malt and a cow. Dinky finally gets married and moves into the house.

3104. The House That Jack Built (*Color Rhapsody*) 14 Apr. 1939; *p.c.*: Charles Mintz prods for Colum; *dir*: Sid Marcus; *anim*: Art Davis, Herb Rothwill; *sets*: Phil Davis; *ed*: George Winkler; *voices*: Pinto Colvig, Danny Webb; *mus*: Joe de Nat; *ph*: Otto Reimer; *prod mgr*: James Bronis; *col*: Tech. *sd*: RCA. 6 min. • A bear sends termites to ruin Jack Beaver's house building but Jack turns the tables, forcing the bear to build a new house for him.

3105. House Tricks (*Popeye*) 2 Nov. 1945; *p.c.*: Famous for Para; *dir*: Seymour Kneitel; *story*: Jack Ward, Carl Meyer; *anim*: Graham Place, Martin Taras, Al Eugster; *voices*: Mae Questel, Jackson Beck; *mus*: Sammy Timberg; *prod mgr*: Sam Buchwald; b&w. *sd*: WE. 8 min. • Popeye and Bluto vie for Olive's attentions as they both attempt to build her a house.

3106. Housewife Herman (*Terry-Toon*) 18 Nov. 1938; *p.c.*: TT for Fox; *dir*: Ed Donnelly; *story*: John Foster; *voices*: Thomas Morrison, Arthur Kay, Arthur Boran; *mus*: Philip A. Scheib; *col*: Tech. *sd*: RCA. 7 min. • Herman, a Germanic pig, is left to do the household chores.

3107. The Housing Problem (*Terry-Toon*) 25 Oct. 1946; *p.c.*: TT for Fox; *dir*: Mannie Davis; *story*: John Foster; *mus*: Philip A. Scheib; *col*: Tech. *sd*: RCA. 6 min. • Herman Pig and family build their own pre-fabricated house.

3108. Housing Shortage (*Aesop's Film Fable*) 4 Apr. 1925; *p.c.*: Fables Pictures Inc for Pathé; *dir*: Paul Terry; b&w. *sil*. 10 min. • Finding the Hen Hotel full, a hen tries the farmer's whiskers then settles for his hat.

3109. How Do I Know It's Sunday (*Merrie Melodies*) 19 May 1934; *p.c.*: Leon Schlesinger prods for WB; *dir*: Isadore Freleng; *anim*: Frank Tipper, Don Williams; *mus*: Bernard Brown; *song*: Irving Kahal, Sammy Fain; b&w. *sd*: Vit. 7 min. • Grocery items spring into song.

3110. How Green Is My Spinach? (*Popeye*) 27 Jan. 1950; *p.c.*: Famous for Para; *dir*: Seymour Kneitel; *story*: I. Klein; *anim*: Tom Johnson, William Henning; *sets*: Lloyd Hallock Jr.; *voices*: Jack Mercer, Jackson Beck, Cecil Roy; *mus*: Winston Sharples; *ph*: Leonard McCormick; *prod mgr*: Sam Buchwald; *col*: Tech/b&w. *sd*: RCA. 6 min. *l/a/anim.* • Bluto destroys the world's supply of spinach, leaving Popeye at a loss for muscular stimulant.

3111. How Now Boing Boing 9 Sept. 1954; *p.c.*: UPA for Colum; *ex prod*: Stephen Bosustow; *dir*: Robert Cannon; *story*: T. Hee, R. Cannon; *anim*: Frank Smith, Alan Zaslove, Gerald Ray; *lay*: T. Hee; *back*: Jules Engel; *voices*: Marvin Miller, Marian Richman; *mus*: George Bruns; *prod mgr*: Herbert Klynn; *col*: Tech. *sd*: RCA. 7 min. • Gerald's parents take him for elocution lessons so he can enunciate instead of going "Boing Boing" when he speaks.

3112. How the Bear Got His Short Tail (*Unnatural History*) 18 Oct. 1925; *p.c.*: Bray prods for FBO; *dir*: Walter Lantz; *anim*: Clyde Geronimi; b&w. *sil*. 10 min. *l/a/anim.* • No story available.

3113. How the Elephant Got His Trunk (*Unnatural History*) 17 Oct. 1925; *p.c.*: Bray prods for FBO; *dir*: Walter Lantz; *anim*: Clyde Geronimi; b&w. *sil*. 10 min. *l/a/anim.* • Walter babysits and tells the baby a story of how the elephant got stuck in the river. His hippo nurse, a monkey and mouse extricate him by tugging his nose.

3114. How the Giraffe Got His Long Neck (*Unnatural History*) 7 Feb. 1926; *p.c.*: Bray prods for FBO; *dir*: Walter Lantz; *anim*: Clyde Geronimi; *l/a ph*: Joe Rock; b&w. *sil*. 10 min. *l/a/anim.* • No story available.

3115. How to Be a Detective (*Goofy*) 12 Dec. 1952; *p.c.*: Walt Disney prods for RKO; *dir*: Jack Kinney; *story*: Dick Kinney, Brice Mack; *anim*: Hugh Fraser, John Sibley, Ed Aardal, George Nicholas, Harvey Toombs; *fx*: Dan MacManus, George Rowley; *lay*: Al Zinnen; *back*: Dick Anthony; *voices*: Jack Rourke, Pinto Colvig, June Foray, Billy Bletcher, James Mac-

Donald; *mus:* Joseph S. Dubin; *col:* Tech. *sd:* RCA. 7 min. • Geef sets up as a gumshoe. His first case is to find a character named Al that turns out to be the same policeman who is trailing Geef.

3116. How to Be a Sailor *(Goofy)* 28 Jan. 1943; *p.c.:* Walt Disney prods for RKO; *dir:* Jack Kinney; *asst dir:* Ted Sebern; *anim:* Hugh Fraser, John Sibley; *fx:* Ed Aardal, Andrew Engman; *lay:* Don da Gradi; *voices:* John McLeish, Pinto Colvig; *mus:* Paul J. Smith; *col:* Tech. *sd:* RCA. 7 min. • Goofy demonstrates methods of navigation from early days to modern times when he successfully sinks the enemy fleet.

3117. How to Dance *(Goofy)* 11 July 1953; *p.c.:* Walt Disney prods for RKO; *dir:* Jack Kinney; *story:* Milt Schaffer, Dick Kinney; *anim:* George Nicholas, John Sibley, Ed Aardal; *fx:* Blaine Gibson, Dan MacManus; *lay:* Bruce Bushman; *back:* Claude Coats; *voices:* Art Gilmore, Pinto Colvig; *mus:* Joseph S. Dubin, Firehouse Five Plus Two; *col:* Tech. *sd:* RCA. 6 min. • Geef attends dancing classes in order not to be a wallflower at parties.

3118. How to Fish *(Goofy)* 4 Dec. 1942; *p.c.:* Walt Disney prods for RKO; *dir:* Jack Kinney; *asst dir:* Lou Debney; *anim:* Chester Cobb, Merle Cox, Don Lusk, Frank Oreb, Wolfgang Reitherman, John Sibley, John Sewall, Louis Terri; *fx:* Ed Aardal, Jack Boyd, Joseph Gayek, Harry Hamsel, Jack Huber, Frank Onaitis, Dan MacManus, Ed Parks; *lay:* Don da Gradi; *voice:* John McLeish; *mus:* Paul J. Smith; *col:* Tech. *sd:* RCA. 7 min. • Goofy demonstrates various methods of fishing.

3119. How to Have an Accident at Work 1 June 1959; *p.c.:* Walt Disney prods for BV; *dir:* Charles A. Nichols; *asst dir:* Paul Carlson; *story:* Bill Berg, Jack Kinney; *anim:* Jerry Hathcock, Fred Kopietz, Harvey Toombs, George Nicholas; *fx:* Jack Buckley; *lay:* Erni Nordli; *back:* Al Dempster; *voices:* Bill Thompson, Clarence Nash; *mus:* Oliver Wallace; *col:* Tech. *sd:* RCA. 7 min. • J.J. Fate demonstrates how accidents are caused in the factory using Donald Duck as a bad example.

3120. How to Have an Accident in the Home *(Donald Duck)* 8 June 1956; *p.c.:* Walt Disney prods for BV; *dir:* C. August Nichols; *asst dir:* Bill Gunderson; *story:* Jack Kinney, Bill Berg; *anim:* Jerry Hathcock, George Nicholas, Volus Jones, Bob Bemiller, Earl Combs, Ed Solomon; *fx:* Jack Buckley, Dan MacManus; *lay:* Lance Nolley, Erni Nordli; *back:* Anthony Rizzo; *voices:* Bill Thompson, Clarence Nash; *mus:* Franklyn Marks; *col:* Tech. *sd:* RCA. 7 min. CS. • J.J. Fate demonstrates, with the help of Donald, how accidents are caused in the home.

3121. How to Keep Cool *(Terry-Toon)* Oct. 1953; *p.c.:* TT for Fox; *dir:* Connie Rasinski; *story:* Tom Morrison; *anim:* Jim Tyer; *mus:* Philip A. Scheib; *ph:* Douglas Moye; *col:* Tech. *sd:* RCA. 6 min. • Dimwit battles with a heat wave, finding the only cool place is in the refrigerator.

3122. How to Play Baseball *(Goofy)* 4 Sept. 1942; *p.c.:* Walt Disney prods for RKO; *dir:* Jack Kinney; *asst dir:* Lou Debney; *anim:* Les Clark, Marc Davis, Hugh Fraser, Oliver Johnston, Ward Kimball, Milt Neil, John Sibley, Vladimir Tytla; *fx:* Ed Aardal, Andrew Engman; *lay:* Al Zinnen; *voice:* Fred Shields; *mus:* Paul J. Smith; *col:* Tech. *sd:* RCA. 7 min. • The rules of baseball are explained and the Goof takes part in an actual game.

3123. How to Play Football *(Goofy)* 15 Sept. 1944; *p.c.:* Walt Disney prods for RKO; *dir:* Jack Kinney; *asst dir:* Ted Sebern; *story sup:* Ralph Wright, Dick Shaw, Roy Williams; *story:* Bill Peed; *anim:* Art Babbitt, Milt Kahl, Eric Larson, John Sibley; *fx:* Jack Boyd, Andrew Engman; *lay:* Karl Karpé; *voices:* Frank Bull, Jack Kinney, John Sibley; *mus:* Paul J. Smith; *col:* Tech. *sd:* RCA. 7 min. *Academy Award nomination.* • The game of football is demonstrated with Goofy in the center of a no-holds-barred match.

3124. How to Play Golf *(Goofy)* 10 Mar. 1944; *p.c.:* Walt Disney prods for RKO; *dir:* Jack Kinney; *asst dir:* Bee Selck; *story sup:* Ralph Wright, Jack Kinney; *anim:* Hugh Fraser, Bill Justice, John Sibley; *lay:* Karl Karpé; *voices:* Fred Shields, Pinto Colvig, James MacDonald; *mus:* Oliver Wallace; *col:* Tech. *sd:* RCA. 8 min. • Goofy plays a round of golf that ends with his being chased by an angry bull.

3125. How to Relax *(Dimwit)* Jan. 1954; *p.c.:* TT for Fox; *dir:* Connie Rasinski; *story/voice:* Tom Morrison; *anim:* Jim Tyer; *sets:* Art Bartsch; *mus:* Philip A. Scheib; *ph:* Douglas Moye; *col:* Tech. *sd:* RCA. 6 min. • The Doctor advises Dimwit to try relaxing hobbies ... all of which jangle his nerves even more so.

3126. How to Ride a Horse *(Goofy)* 24 Feb. 1950; *p.c.:* Walt Disney prods for RKO; *dir:* Jack Kinney; *asst dir:* Lou Debney; *story:* Ralph Wright,

Jack Kinney; *anim:* Stephen Bosustow, Chester Cobb, Merle Cox, George de Beeson, Edwin T. Fourcher, Richard McDermott, Frank Oreb, Wolfgang Reitherman, John Sibley, Louis Terri, James Will, Cornett Wood; *fx:* Edwin Aardal, Jerome Brown, Russ Dyson, Andy Engman, Joe Harbaugh, Jack Huber, Frank Onaitis, John F. Reed, George Rowley, Reuben Timmens; *lay:* James Carmichael; *voices:* John McLeish, Clarence Nash; *mus:* Charles Wolcott; *col:* Tech. *sd:* RCA. 8 min. • Goofy tries to mount a reluctant horse. Sequence from *The Reluctant Dragon* reissued as a short. • See: *The Reluctant Dragon*

3127. How to Sleep *(Goofy)* 25 Dec. 1953; *p.c.:* Walt Disney prods for RKO; *dir:* Jack Kinney; *story:* Milt Schaffer, Nick George; *anim:* George Nicholas, Ed Aardal, Jerry Hathcock; *fx:* Dan MacManus; *lay:* Bruce Bushman; *back:* Claude Coats; *voices:* Art Gilmore, Pinto Colvig; *mus:* Edward Plumb; *col:* Tech. *sd:* RCA. 7 min. • Geef demonstrates various methods for getting a decent night's sleep.

3128. How to Stuff a Woodpecker *(Woody Woodpecker)* 18 May 1960; *p.c.:* Walter Lantz prods for Univ; *dir:* Paul J. Smith; *story:* Dalton Sandifer; *anim:* La Verne Harding, Les Kline, Ray Abrams; *sets:* Art Landy; *voices:* Dal McKennon, Grace Stafford; *mus:* Clarence Wheeler; *prod mgr:* William E. Garity; *col:* Tech. *sd:* RCA. 6 min. • A taxidermist tells the story of how he managed to stuff Woody.

3129. How to Swim *(Goofy)* 23 Oct. 1942; *p.c.:* Walt Disney prods for RKO; *dir:* Jack Kinney; *asst dir:* Lou Debney; *story sup:* Webb Smith, Ralph Wright; *anim:* James Armstrong, Al Bertino, George de Beeson, Ken Peterson, Wolfgang Reitherman, John Sibley, Joseph Starbuck; *fx:* Andy Engman, Joseph Gayek; *voice:* John McLeish; *mus:* Paul J. Smith; *col:* Tech. *sd:* RCA. 7 min. • Goofy demonstrates the art of swimming, diving and undressing in a beach locker.

3130. How to Trap a Woodpecker *(Woody Woodpecker)* 1971; *p.c.:* Walter Lantz prods for Univ; *dir:* Paul J. Smith; *story:* Dale Hale; *anim:* Les Kline, Al Coe, Tom Byrne, Joe Voght; *sets:* Nino Carbe; *voices:* Daws Butler, Grace Stafford; *mus:* Walter Greene; *prod mgr:* William E. Garity; *col:* Tech. *sd:* RCA. 5 min. • A woodsman is sent to get Woody's feathers for his wife's hat.

3131. How War Came *(This Changing World)* 7 Nov. 1941; *p.c.:* Cartoon Films Ltd for Colum; *dir:* Paul Fennell; *ed:* Almond Teeter; *mus:* Clarence Wheeler; *prod:* Dave Biedermann; *col:* Dunning. *sd:* RCA. 9 min. *l/a/anim. Academy Award nomination.* • Raymond Gram Swing informs of the activities of Hitler and Stalin through the medium of the animated cartoon as America prepares to go to war.

3132. How Wet Was My Ocean *(Terry-Toon)* 4 Oct. 1940; *p.c.:* TT for Fox; *dir:* Eddie Donnelly; *story:* John Foster; *voice:* Thomas Morrison; *mus:* Philip A. Scheib; *col:* Tech. *sd:* RCA. 6 min. • Herman the pig encounters many pitfalls when he goes swimming at the beach.

3133. Howard 1965; *p.c.:* Ernest Pintoff prods for Colum; *prod:* Ernest Pintoff; *dir/anim:* Leonard Glasser; *col. sd.* 10 min. • The story of three survivors left in the world, each called Howard.

3134. Howard the Duck 1 Aug. 1986; *p.c.:* Lucasfilm for Univ; *dir:* Willard Huyck; based on the Marvel Comics character created by Steve Gerber; *scr:* Willard Huyck, Gloria Katz; *art dir:* Peter Jamison; *special visual fx:* ILM; *visual fx sup:* Michael J. McAlister; *stop motion sup:* Phil Tippett, Harry Walton; *stop motion anim:* Tom St. Amand; *stop motion construction:* Randy Dutra, Tamia Marg, Sheila Duignan; *matte painting sup:* Frank Ordaz; *voice of the Cosmos:* Richard Kiley; *mus:* John Barry; *stop motion ph:* Terry Chostner, Patrick McArdle; *anim ph fx:* Rob Burton, John Alexander; *ph:* Richard H. Kline; *col. sd.* 110 min. *l/a/anim.* • Live-action depiction of the comic character Howard T. Duck who is jettisoned from the tranquility of Duck World to Earth. He soon finds himself involved in a laboratory experiment.

3135. A Howling Success *(Terry Bears)* May 1954; *p.c.:* TT for Fox; *dir:* Connie Rasinski; *story:* Tom Morrison; *anim:* Jim Tyer; *sets:* Art Bartsch; *voices:* Douglas Moye, Tom Morrison, Philip A. Scheib; *mus:* Philip A. Scheib; *ph:* Douglas Moye; *col:* Tech. *sd:* RCA. 6 min. • The kids say that their dog, Pago, will protect Papa against an escaped killer who's loose in the neighborhood. A mouse frightens Pago into capturing Killer Schlabotka.

3136. How's Crops? *(Aesop's Fable)* 23 Mar. 1934; *p.c.:* Van Beuren for RKO; *dir:* George Stallings; *anim:* Steve Muffatti; *mus:* Gene Rodemich; b&w. *sd:* RCA. 8 min. • After a drought clears the land clear of crops, Cubby Bear and Cuddles go underground to force the crops up through the earth.

3137. Huey's Ducky Daddy *(Noveltoon)* 20 Nov. 1953; *p.c.:* Famous for Para: *dir:* I. Sparber; *story:* I. Klein; *anim:* Dave Tendlar, Tom Golden, I. Klein; *sets:* Anton Loeb; *voices:* Sid Raymond, Frank Matalone, Cecil Roy; *mus:* Winston Sharples; *ph:* Leonard McCormick; *prod mgr:* Seymour Shultz; *col:* Tech. *sd:* RCA. 6 min. • Baby Huey's Daddy reluctantly takes him on a fishing trip.

3138. Huey's Father's Day *(Noveltoon)* 8 May 1959; *p.c.:* Para Cartoons; *dir:* Seymour Kneitel; *story:* Carl Meyer, Jack Mercer; *anim:* Tom Johnson, Wm. B. Pattengill; *sets:* Robert Owen; *voices:* Sid Raymond, Frank Matalone; *mus:* Winston Sharples; *ph:* Leonard McCormick; *prod mgr:* Abe Goodman; *col:* Tech. *sd:* RCA. 6 min. • Baby Huey does all the work on Father's Day while Daddy attempts to rest.

3139. Hula-Hula Land *(Heckle & Jeckle)* July 1949; *p.c.:* TT for Fox; *dir:* Mannie Davis; *story:* John Foster; *anim:* Jim Tyer; *voices:* Tom Morrison; *mus:* Philip A. Scheib; *ph:* Douglas Moye; *col:* Tech. *sd:* RCA. 6 min. • When Dimwit comes to buy a hot-dog from the Magpies, he gets the full brunt of their japes.

3140. A Hull of a Mess *(Popeye)* 16 Oct. 1942; *p.c.:* Famous for Para: *dir:* I. Sparber; *story:* Jack Ward, Jack Mercer; *anim:* Al Eugster, Joe Oriolo; *voices:* Jack Mercer; *mus:* Sammy Timberg; *prod mgr:* Sam Buchwald; b&w. *sd:* RCA. 6 min. • Popeye and Bluto compete in building a battleship.

3141. Hullaba-Lulu *(Little Lulu)* 25 Feb. 1944; *p.c.:* Famous for Para: *dir:* Seymour Kneitel; *story:* Joe Stultz; *anim:* Graham Place, Abner Kneitel, Gordon Sheehan, Paul Busch; *sets:* Shane Miller; *voice:* Cecil Roy; *mus:* Sammy Timberg; *prod mgr:* Sam Buchwald; *col:* Tech. *sd:* RCA. 9 min. • Lulu sneaks into the circus and gives the acts a hard time.

3142. The Human Fly *(Aesop's Film Fable)* 16 Aug. 1927; *p.c.:* Fables Pictures Inc for Pathé; *dir:* Paul Terry; b&w. *sil.* 10 min. • Farmer Al tries his hand at flying by using an electric fan. A goat butts him onto a mule who kicks him through the farmhouse roof.

3143. Humorous Phases of Funny Faces 16 Apr. 1906; *p.c.:* Vit; *anim:* James Stuart Blackton; b&w. *sil.* 2 min. • Drawn faces come alive. A city gent blows cigar smoke into a lady's face, which caused a great deal of controversy in 1906.

3144. Humpty Dumpty *(ComiColor)* 17 Dec. 1935; *p.c.:* Celebrity prods; *prod/dir:* Ub Iwerks; *mus:* Carl Stalling; *col:* Ciné. *sd:* PCP. 6 min. • A villainous "Bad Egg" kidnaps Humpty's girl, Easter Egg. Humpty races to the rescue and the villain ends up hard-boiled!

3145. The Hunchback of Notre Dame 21 June 1996; *p.c.:* Walt Disney Enterprises, Inc. for BV; *dir:* Gary Trousdale, Kirk Wise; *prod:* Don Hahn; *story* adapted from the Victor Hugo novel *Notre Dame de Paris*; *adapt:* Tab Murphy; *scr:* Tab Murphy, Irene Mecchi, Bob Zudiker & Noni White, Jonathan Roberts; *art dir:* David Goetz; *artistic co-ord:* Randy Fullmer; *artistic sup: story:* Will Finn; *lay:* Ed Ghertner; *clean-up:* Vera Lanpher-Pacheco; *ed:* Ellen Keneshea, John K. Carr, James Melton, Jessica Ambinder Rojas, Jacqueline Kinney, Bill Shaffer, James D. Kirkpatrick, Hermann H. Schmidt, (*Paris*): Sophie Devillier, (*Florida*): Beth A. Stegmaier; *i&p:* Gretchen Maschmeyer Albrecht, Hortensia M. Casagran; *ph:* Robyn L. Roberts, Joe Jiuliano; *prod mgr:* Patricia Hicks; *artistic sup: lay:* Daniel St. Peters; *back:* Doug Ball; *clean-up:* Lieve Miessen; *fx:* Mike Smith; *prod mgr:* Jean-Luc Florinda; *ex mus prod:* Chris Montan; *character des/visual development:* James Baxter, Anne Marie Bardwell, Marek Buchwald, Peter de Sève, Tony Fucile, Gee Fwee Boedoe, Thom Enriquez, Vance Gerry, Ed Ghertner, Jean Gillmore, Joe Grant, Darek Gogol, Lisa Keene, Shawn E. Keller, Rick Maki, Joseph Moshier, Sue C. Nichols, Rowland B. Wilson; *story:* Kevin Harkey, Gaëtan Brizzi, Paul Brizzi, Edward Gombert, Brenda Chapman, Jeff Snow, Jim Capobianco, Dennis Rich, Burny Mattinson, John Sanford, Kelly Wrightman, James Fujii, Gee Fwee Boedoe, Floyd Norman, Francis Glebas, Kirk Hanson, Christine Blum, Sue C. Nichols; *addit scr:* Will Finn; *lay/workbook:* Fred Craig, Tom Shannon, Scott Caple, Lorenzo Martinez, Samuel Michlap; *lay:* Jean-Christophe Poulain, Tanya T. Wilson, Olivier Adam, Zoltán Maros, Gary Mouri, Peter J. de Luca, Kenneth Spirduso, James P. Alles, Peter Bielicki, Juanjo Guarnido, Jennifer Yuan, David Gardner, Tom Humber, Sherilan Weinhart,

William (Mac) George, Vincent Massy de la Chesneraye, Mark E. Koerner, Marec Fritzinger, Lam Hoang, Denise Blakely Fuller, Cynthia Quimpo Ignacio, Mark Kalesniko, Loïc Rastout, David Martin, John Puglisi, Johan Klingler; *blue sketch:* Madlyn O'Neill, Cyndee Larae Heinbuch, Valerie Braun; *character anim:* "*Quasimodo*": *sup dir:* James Baxter; *anim:* Christopher Bradley, Trey Finney, Doug Frankel, Tom Gately, Shawn E. Keller, Ralf Palmer, John Ripa, Stephane Sainte Foi, Christopher Sauve, Yoshimichi Tamura, Eric Walls, Anthony Ho Wong, Phil Young; *clean-up: lead key:* Marshall L. Toomey; *key asst:* Christophe Charbonnel, Kris Heller, Susan Goldberg, Brian B. McKim, Marsha W.J. Park-Yum, Susan Sugita, Vincent Siracusano, Terry Wozniak, Javier Espinosa, Nicholas Keramidas, Miriam McDonnell, George Sukara, Marc Tosolini, Xavier Villez; *break:* Nicole de Bellefroid, Daniel Bowman, Ron Cohee, Larry R. Flores, Brigitte Franzka-Fritz, Michael Lester, Donnie Long, Nicole Stranz, Ron Westlund, Regina Conroy, Kendra Lammas, Hugo Soriano, Michael Wiesmeier; "*Esmeralda*": *sup dir:* Tony Fucile; *anim:* Anne-Marie Bardwell, Jared Beckstrand, Bolhem Bouchiba, Mark Koetsier, Robert Espanto Domingo, Mark Koetsier, Gilda Kouros, Doug Krohn, Dave Kupczye, Mark Pudleiner, Bill Waldman; *clean-up: key:* Virginia Parmele, Inna Sung Chon, Wesley Chun, Susan Lantz, Marcia Kimura Dougherty, Steve Lubin, Myung Kang-Teague, Kristoff Vergne, Franck Bonay, Serge Bussone, Teresa Eidenbock, Sean Gallimore, Chan Woo Jung, Eunice (Eun Ok) Yu; *break:* Cynthia Jill French, Annette Byrne-Morel, Rich Wilkie; *inbet:* Cyndy Bohonovsky, Philippe Malka; "*Frollo*": *sup dir:* Kathy Zielinski; *anim:* Travis Blaise, Roger Chiasson, Patrick Pablos, William Recinos, Chris Wahl; *clean-up: key:* June M. Fujimoto, Marco Allard, Lee Dunkman, Michael McKinney, Brett Newton, Jamie Kezlarian Bolio, Scott Claus, Maria Angela Iturrize, Veronique Langdon, Gizella Gregan Maros, David Recinos; *break:* Kenneth M. Kinoshita, Mary Measures, Cheryl Polakow-Knight, Pierre Seurin, Jim Snider; *inbet:* Steve Lenze; "*Phoebus*": *sup dir:* Russ Edmonds; *anim:* Robert Bryan, Michael Cedeno, Marc Eoche-Duval, Bradley Kuha, David A. Zaboski; *clean-up: key:* Brian Clift, Allison Hollen, Dorothea Baker Paul, Bill Thinnes; *break:* Mike d'Isa, Doug Post, Trevor Tamboline, Brian Mainolfi, Denise Meehan; *Inbet:* Raul Aguirre Jr.; "*Clopin*": *sup dir:* Michael Surrey; *anim:* Danny Galieote; *clean-up: key:* Margie Daniels, Pierre Girault, Leticia Lichtwardt; *break:* Clay Kaytis; *inbet:* Cathie Karas Wilke; "*Gargoyles*": *sup dir* "*Hugo & Victor*": David Pruiksma; *sup dir* "*LaVerne*": Will Finn; *anim:* Rejean Bourdages, David Hancock, T. Daniel Hofstedt, Jamie Oliff, Larry White; *clean-up: key:* Debra Armstrong Holmes, Maria Wilhelmina Rosetti, Philip S. Boyd, Jesus Cortes, Eric Delbecq, Bruce Strock, Claire Bourdin, Andrew Edward Harkness, James A. Harris, Janet Heerhan Bae, Calvin Le Duc, Mary-Jean Repchuk, Marty Schwartz; *break:* Jonathan Annand, Antony de Fato, Christine Landes, Jan Naylor, Thomas Thorspecken, Cliff Freitas, Phil Ford; *inbet:* Katherine Blackmore, Saul Andrew Blinkoff, Tom de Rosier, Amy Drobeck, John Hurst, Sean Anthony Jimenez, Keith A. Sintay, Ginger Wolf, David W. Zach, Scott A. Burroughs, Will Huneycutt, Sean Luo, Rebecca Wrigley; "*Djali*": *sup dir:* Ron Husband; *anim:* Kent Hammerstrom; *clean-up: key:* Scott Anderson, Lillian Amanda Chapman; *break:* Chang Yei Cho, Diana Coco; *inbet:* Todd H. Ammons; "*Arch Deacon*": *sup dir:* Dave Burgess; *clean-up: key:* Randy Sanchez, Rick Kohlschmidt; "*Gypsies, Guards & others*": *anim:* Sylvain de Boissy, Sasha Dorogov, Raul Garcia, Teresa Martin, Jean Morel, Daniel O'Sullivan, Catherine Poulain; *clean-up: key:* Tracy Mark Lee, Tony Anselmo, Dana M. Reemes, Ray Harris, Florence Montceau, Dave Suding, Laurence Adam-Bessiere, Carl A. Bell, Philippe Ferin, Kent Holaday, Yung Soo Kim, Sylvaine Terriou; *break:* Edward B. Goral, Mark Alan Mitchell, Steven Thompson; *inbet:* Mary Jo Ayers, Gregg Azzoparoi, Daniel Bond, Frank R. Cordero, Tom Dow, James W. Elston, Perry Farinola, Louis C. Gallegos, Neal Stanley Goldsmith, Chris Greco, Kevin Grow, Lisa Lanyon, Whitney Martin, Benoit Meurzec, Jane Misek, Frank Montagna Jr., John Pierro, Ron Zeitler; "*Computer Generated Crowd Character*"; *anim:* Gregory Griffith, Mike "Moe" Merell; *asst anim:* Jay M. Davis, Brian Wesley Green; *visual fx:* Christopher Jenkins; *cgi:* Kiran Bhakta Joshi; *cgi technical dir:* George Katanics, Mira Nikolic; *3d fx technical dir:* Kevin Paul Sheedy; *cgi modeler:* Erica Cassetti; *addit anim:* Ruben A. Aquino, Georges Abolin, Tony Bancroft, Charlie Bonifacio, Roberto Casale, Alain Costa, Ken Hettig, James Young Jackson, Duncan Marjoribanks, Roy Meurin, Gary Perkovac, Carol Seidl, Pres Antonio Romanillos, Ellen Woodbury; *rough inbet:* Pierre Alary, Paulo R. Alvarado, James Baker, Jean-Luc Ballester, Noreen Beasley, Dominic M. Carola, Jerry Yu Ching, Tony Cipriano, Adam Dykstra, Ed

Gabriel, Tim George, Ben Gonzalez, Thierry Goulard, Grant Hiestand, James Hull, Joseph Mateo, Paul McDonald, Mario J. Menjivar, Joseph Moshier, Gary D. Payne, David Pimental, Ross Pratt, Bobby Alcid Rubio, Jacqueline M. Sanchez, Kevin M. Smith, Marc Smith, Tony Stanley; *back:* Lisa Keene, Gregory Alexander Drolette, Don Moore, Colin Stimpson, Mi Kyung Joung-Raynis, Michael Humphries, Pierre Pavloff, Joaquim Royo Morales, Allison Belliveau-Proulx, Dominick R. Domingo, Christophe Vacher, Olivier Besson, William Lorencz, Maryann Thomas, David McCawley, Debbie du Bois, Brooks Campbell, Patricia Palmer-Phillipson, Justin Brandstater, George Taylor, Patricia Millereau, Jean-Paul Fernandez, Tom Woodington, Brad Hicks, Serge Michaels, Jennifer Ando, Carl Jones, Michael Kurinsky, Tia Kratter, Mannix Bennett, Daniel Read, Andy Phillipson, Kathy Altieri, John Emerson, Mel Sommer, Thierry Fournier, Susan Hackett, Dali Pagic, James J. Martin, Jonathan Salt; *voices:* Quasimodo: Tom Hulce; *Esmaralda:* Demi Moore; *Frollo:* Tony Jay; *Phoebus:* Kevin Kline; *Clopin:* Paul Kandel; *Hugo:* Jason Alexander; *Victor:* Charles Kimbrough; *LaVerne:* Mary Wickes, Jane Withers; *Arch Deacon:* David Ogden Stiers; *Oafish Guard:* Bill Fagerbakke; *Brutish Guard/Miller/Crowd:* Corey Burton; *Guards & Gypsies:* Jim Cummings, Patrick Pinney; *Quasimodo's mother:* Mary Kay Bergman; *Esmeralda's singing voice:* Heidi Mollenhauer; *the Old Heraldic:* Gary Trousdale; *Baby Bird:* Frank Welker; *also:* Jack Angel, Bob Bergen, Maureen Brennan, Joan Barber, Scott Barnes, Susan Blu, Rodger Bumpass, Victoria Clark, Philip Clarke, Jennifer Darling, Debi Derryberry, Jonathan Dokuchitz. Bill Farmer, Laurie Faso, Merwin Foard, Dana Hill, Alix Korey, Judy Kaye, Eddie Korbich, Michael Lindsay, Sherry Lynn, Mona Marshall, Howard McGillin, Mickie McGowan, Anna McNeedy, Bruce Moore, Denise Pickering, Peter Samuel, Phil Proctor, Jan Rabson, Mary Scott, Kath Soucie, Gordon Stanley, Marcelo Tubert; "Someday" performed by Eternal; *songs:* Alan Menken, Stephen Schwartz; "Cyclone"by Herbert Stothart, George Bassman, George Stoll; *arrangements:* Alan Menken, Michael Starobin; *score:* Alan Menken; *orch:* Michael Starobin, Danny Troob; *vocal arrangements:* David Friedman; *mus prod sup:* Tod Cooper; *mix:* Bruce Botnick; *songs conducted by* Jack Everly; *orch conductors:* Sandy de Crescent, Seymour Red Press, "Someday" *prod:* Simon Climie; *string arrangement/conducted by:* Mick Kingman; Ken Watson; *mus preparation:* Dominic Fidelibus; *mus ed:* Kathleen Fogarty-Bennett; Mark Green, Gina Spiro Kessler; *scene plan sup:* Ann Tucker; *anim check:* Janet Bruce; *color models sup:* Karen Comella; *addit.clean-up anim: key:* Ruben Procopio, Alex Topete, Kathleen W. Bailey, Bill Berg, Jane Bonnet, Merry Kanawyer Clingen, Dan Daly, Gail Frank, Edward R. Gutierrez, Karen Hardenbergh, Eric Pigors, Kaaren Lundeen, Lori Noda, Natasha Dukelski Selfridge, Bryan M. Sommer, Dan Tanaka, Marianne Tucker, Elizabeth Watasin, Stephan Zupkas, Sue Adnopoz, Judy Barnes, Caroline Clifford, Michael Hazy, Akemi Horiuchi, Wendy Muir, Teresita Quezada, Jean-Christophe Lie, Cyril Pedrosa, Chris Sonnenburg; *break:* Jim Brummett, Cindy Schiefelbein-Kennedy, Daniel Lim, Richard D. Rocha; *inbet:* Stephen N. Austin, Todd Bright, Kevin Chen, Cindy Ge, Carolyn F. Gliona, Krista Heij, Alexander B. McDaniel, Yoon Sook Nam, Daniel Riebold, Elsa Sesto-Vidal, Ronnie Williford; *visual fx:* Tom Hush, Dorse Lanpher, Brice Mallier, Allen Blyth, Ed Coffey, Thierry Chaffoin, Mark Cumberton, Peter de Mund, Joseph Gilland, Troy A. Gustafson, Dan Lund, David (Joey) Mildenberger, Paul Smith, Marlon West, Cynthia Neill Knizek, Mark Barrows, Mabel L. Gesner, Steven Starr, John Tucker, Volker Pajatsch, Karel Zilliacus, Geoffrey C. Everts, James Goss, John E. Hailey, Elizabeth Holmes, Michael Cadwallader Jones, Thomas Walsh, Graham Woods; *fx inbet:* Ida C. Voskanian, Michael Milligan, Monica Sena, Tatiana Allen-Kellert, Phil D. Stapleton, Christine Chatal, Mouloud Oussid; *addit visual fx anim:* David A. Bossert, Mauro Maressa, David Tidgwell, Dan Chaika, Colbert Fennelly, Jazno Francoeur, Bruce Heller, Jeff Howard, Ted Kierscey, Debbie Kupczyk, Rosanna Lyons, James Dev. Mansfield, Steve Moore, Kevin O'Neil, Kathleen Quaife-Hodge, Jeff Topping, Phillip Vigil, Garrett Wren; *asst:* Sean Applegate, Philippe Balmossiere, Bob Bennett, Kristine Brown, Angela Anastasia Diamos, Jack Doyle, Ty Elliott, Ray Hofstedt, Kristine Humber, Michael L. Olive, Paitoon Ratanasirintrawoot, John David Thornton, Michael Toth, Tony West; *fx break:* Stella P. Anbelaez Tascon, Kimberly Burk, John Fargnoli, Lisa Ann Reinert; *fx inbet:* Adeboye Adegbenro, Faris Al-Saffar, Kevin Barber, Eduardo G. Brieño, Jason Peltz, Bob Spang, Tim Massa, Rocky Smith, Jay Shindell, Jeffrey Lawrence van Tuyl; *character sculptress:* Kent Melton; *Paris Unit: Seq dir:* Paul Brizzi, Gaëtan Brizzi; *lay/back:* Coralie Cudot; *clean-*

up/fx: Etienne Longa, Christian Schmidt; *scene plan:* Thomas J. Baker, Sara Bleik, Anna Marie Costa, John R. Cunningham, Cynthia Goode, Mark Henley, Ronald Jackson, Mary Lescher, Raphaël Vincente, Samantha Bowers-Nicholson; *scene plan data entry:* Jamal M. Davis, Karan N. Austin, Kim Gray, Gary Stubblefield; *anim check:* Barbara Wiles, Karen S. Paat, Mavis Shafer, Karen Hepburn, Denise M. Mitchell, Gary Shafer, Laurie Sacks, Albert Francis Moore, Victoria Winner Novak, Pierre Sucaud; *col stylists:* Penny Coulter, Ann Sorensen, Debray Siegel, Barbara Lynn Hamane, Debbie Jorgensborg; *digital ph:* Karen N. China, Lynnette E. Cullen, Jo Ann Breuer, Gina Wootten, David Braden, Val d'Arcy, Gareth Fishbaugh, Corey D. Fredrickson, Robert Lizardo, Michael A. McFerren, Rick McFerren, David J. Rowe, Jason R. Biske, Jan Gutowski, Barbara J. Polkier, Andrew Simmons, Gary W. Smith; *paint:* Irma Velez, Grace H. Shirado; *col model mark-up:* David J. Zywicki, Beth Ann McCoy-Gee, Cindy Finn, Sherrie Cuzzort, Karrie Kruling, Phyllis Estelle Fields; *registration:* Karan Lee-Storr; *paint mark-up:* Leyla C. Amaro Pelazz, Leslie Hinton, Myrian Tello, Wilma Baker, Cathy Mirkovich-Peterson, Roberta Borchardt, Carmen R. Alvarez; *paint:* Joyce Alexander, Russell Blandino, Sybil E. Cuzzort, Gina Evans-Howard, Paulino de Mingo Palero, Stevie Hirsch, Harlene Mears, Ken O'Malley, Patrick Sekino, Don Shump, Roxanne M. Taylor, Carmen Sanderson, Kirk Axtell II, Joey Calderon, Florida d'Ambrosio, Christina E. Frazier, Debbie Green, David Karp, Deborah Mooneyham, Bruce G. Phillipson, Heidi Shellhorn, Fumiko R. Sommer, Tami Terusa, Phyllis Bird, Ofra Afouta Calderon, Robert Dettloff, Etsuko T. Funoka, Vernette K. Griffee, Angelika Katz, Karen Nugent, Rosalinde Praamsma, Eyde Sheppherd, S. Ann Sullivan, Britt van der Nagel; *check:* Monica Marroquin, Michael D. Lusby, Teri N. McDonald, Saskia Raevouri, Lea Dahlen; *compositing:* James "J.R" Russell, Shannon Fallis-Kane, Dolores Pope, Joseph Pfening, Tim Gales; *digital film printing & opticals:* Christopher W. Gee, Brandy Hill; *ph:* John Aardal, Francois Desnus, Michael F. Lehman, David J. Link, Chuck Warren, Jennifer Booth; *admin mgr:* Vicki Case; *prod mgr:* Dana Axelrod; *asst prod mgr: ed/story:* Tone Thyne; *lay:* Diana Blazer; *anim/ed:* Loni Beckner Black; *sweatbox:* Willis Middleton; *clean-up:* Paul S.D. Lanum; *fx:* Lesley Addario; *back/anim check:* Karenna Mazur Alderton, Doerinda Welch Greiner; *color models:* Holly E. Bratton; *cgi:* Tony Matthews; *CAPS & retakes:* Shawne N. Zarubica; *communications mgr:* Dorothy McKim; *i&p:* Chris Hecox; *prod co-ord: video refl dial rec:* Kara Lord; *cgi:* Mary Ann McLeod; *sd:* Terry Porter, Mel Metcalfe, Dean A. Zupancic, Doc Kane; *sd fx:* Soundelux; *sd ed:* Larry Kemp, Lon Bender; *ADR:* Curt Schulkey, Vince Caro, Tony Pepper, Grant Maxwell; *sd fx ed:* Chris Hogan, Alan Rankin, Scott Gershin; *dial ed:* Dan Rich, Richard Dwan; *foley ed:* Frederick H. Stanley, Patrick N. Sellers, Neal Anderson, Victor Rennis, David Stanke, Leslee Grizzell, Kim Waugh, Todd Turner, Nigel Holland; *foley artists:* John Roesch, Hilda Hodges, Jeanette Browning; *PDL:* Judy Nord; *b&w processing:* John White; *col timers:* Dale Grahn, Terry Claborn; *neg cutters:* Mary Beth Smith, Rick MacKay; *title des:* Susan Bradley, Mark Dornfeld, Mark Dornfeld; *co-ord for the producer:* Catherine Alexander; *communications:* Onil Alfredo Chibas; *co-prod:* Roy Conli; *asso prod:* Phil Lofaro; *prod asst:* Patti Conklin, Sylvie Bennett-Fauque, Kirsten Bulmer, Lindsey Collins, Michael de la Cruz, Kristin Fong-Lukavsky, Silvia Gallardo, Jennifer L. Hughes, Joyce Ikemiyashiro, Brenda McGirl, Laurent Lavollay-Porter, Stacie K. Reece, Frederika Pepping, Carrie Wilkensen, Kathy Cavaiola-Hill, Evariste Ferreira, Heather Elisa Hill, Christine Laubach, Heather Moriarty, Robert Stemwell; *post prod:* Sara Duran, Patsy Bougé, Heather Jane MacDonald-Smith; *col:* Tech. *sd:* Dolby Digital. 87 min. • Hunchback, Quasimodo, is kept well away from the public in the bell tower of Paris' Notre Dame Cathedral. He rescues a gypsy girl from the outside world and secretly falls in love with her. Although heartbroken to discover she loves the Captain of the Guards, he places his own life at risk to bring the two together.

3146. Hungarian Goulash *(Paul Terry-Toon)* 29 June 1930; *p.c.:* A-C for Educational; *dir:* Frank Moser, Paul Terry; *mus:* Philip A. Scheib; b&w. *sd:* WE. 6 min. • A mouse girl visits a gypsy fortune teller. Gypsies capture the girl and the hero rescues her.

3147. Hunger Strife *(Cartune)* 5 Oct. 1960; *p.c.:* Walter Lantz prods for Univ; *dir:* Jack Hannah; *story:* Dalton Sandifer; *anim:* Ray Abrams, Al Coe; *sets:* Ray Huffine, Art Landy; *voices:* Daws Butler; *mus:* Clarence Wheeler; *prod mgr:* William E. Garity; *col:* Tech. *sd:* Vit. 6 min. • The park ranger makes Fatso the bear go on a strict diet.

3148. The Hungry Goat *(Popeye)* 25 June 1943; *p.c.:* Famous for Para: *dir:* Dan Gordon; *story:* Carl Meyer; *anim:* Joe Oriolo, John Walworth, Al Eugster; *voices:* Jack Mercer, Arnold Stang; *mus:* Sammy Timberg; *prod mgr:* Sam Buchwald; b&w. *sd:* WE. 7 min. • A goat tries to eat Popeye's battleship.

3149. Hungry Hoboes *(Oswald the Lucky Rabbit)* 14 May 1928; *p.c.:* Winkler for Univ; *dir:* Walter Disney; *anim:* Hugh Harman; *ph:* Mike Marcus; b&w. sil. 5 min. • After Oswald and Putrid Pete are chased from a boxcar, they pretend to be an organ grinder and monkey.

3150. Hungry Hounds *(Aesop's Film Fable)* 26 Sept. 1925; *p.c.:* Fables Pictures Inc for Pathé; *dir:* Paul Terry; b&w. sil. 10 min. • One of a pack of hounds distracts the butcher while the others walk off with his meat.

3151. The Hungry Wolf *(MGM Cartoon)* 21 Feb. 1942; *p.c.:* MGM; *prod:* Rudolf Ising; *dir:* Robert Allen; *voices:* Mel Blanc; *mus:* Scott Bradley; *prod mgr:* Fred Quimby; *col:* Tech. *sd:* WE. 9 min. • A starving wolf doesn't have the heart to eat a lost bunny who finds his way into the wolf's house.

3152. Hunky and Spunky *(Color Classic)* 24 June 1938; *p.c.:* The Fleischer Studio for Para: *prod:* Max Fleischer; *dir:* Dave Fleischer; *anim:* Myron Waldman, Graham Place, Lillian Friedman; *character des:* Myron Waldman; *sets:* Shane Miller; *ed:* Kitty Pfister; *voices:* The Westerners, Pinto Colvig, Jack Mercer; *mus:* Sammy Timberg; *prod sup:* Sam Buchwald, Isidore Sparber; *col:* Tech. *sd:* WE. 7 min. *Academy Award nomination.* • While mother donkey takes a nap, Spunky is captured by a prospector who loads him with a heavy pack. Mother soon comes to the rescue.

3153. The Hunter *(Oswald)* 30 Sept. 1931; *p.c.:* Univ; *dir:* Walter Lantz, "Bill" Nolan; *anim:* Clyde Geronimi, Manuel Moreno, Ray Abrams, Fred Avery, Lester Kline, Vet Anderson, "Pinto"Colvig; *voices:* Mickey Rooney, Pinto Colvig; *mus:* James Dietrich; b&w. *sd:* WE. 7 min. • Oswald goes fox hunting to get a fur coat for Kitty.

3154. The Hunter and His Dog *(Aesop's Film Fable)* 27 Apr. 1922; *p.c.:* Fables Pictures Inc for Pathé; *dir:* Paul Terry; b&w. sil. 5 min. • An ungrateful hunter ill-treats his dog after he has helped capture a bear. The dog disguises a wasps' nest and induces the hunter to kick it. Wasps chase the hunter away as the dog tucks into his dinner. Moral: "Heaven helps those who help themselves."

3155. Hunting in 1950 *(Aesop's Film Fable)* 14 Feb. 1926; *p.c.:* Fables Pictures Inc for Pathé; *dir:* Paul Terry; b&w. sil. 5 min. • Farmer Al hunts rabbits who escape on bicycles, a bear in a suit of armor and a lion and monkey who outwit him.

3156. Hunting in Crazy Land 25 Dec. 1914; *prod:* P.A. Powers; b&w. sil. 5 min. • Picturing the adventures of a hunter with a bear and a goat.

3157. The Hunting Season *(Rainbow Parade)* 9 Aug. 1935; *p.c.:* Van Beuren for RKO; *dir:* Burt Gillett, Tom Palmer; *sets:* Art Bartsch, Eddi Bowlds; *mus:* Winston Sharples; *col:* Ciné. *sd:* RCA. 7½ min. • Molly Moo Cow protects the ducks from the hunter's buckshot.

3158. The Huntsman *(Aesop's Film Fable)* 26 June 1928; *p.c.:* Fables Pictures Inc for Pathé; *dir:* Paul Terry, Frank Moser; b&w. sil. 10 min. • Hunter Al Falfa removes a thorn from a lion's paw. The lion later repays his kindness when Al is menaced by a wild razorback.

3159. Hurdy Gurdy *(Oswald)* 3 Jan. 1930; *p.c.:* Univ; *dir:* Walter Lantz; *anim:* R.C. Hamilton, "Bill" Nolan, Tom Palmer, *mus:* David Broekman; b&w. *sd:* WE. 5 min. • Oswald has to replace the organ grinder's monkey after coating him in bubble gum.

3160. Hurdy-Gurdy Hare *(Merrie Melodies)* 21 Jan. 1950; *p.c.:* WB; *dir:* Robert McKimson; *story:* Warren Foster; *anim:* J.C. Melendez, Emery Hawkins, Charles McKimson, Phil de Lara, John Carey; *lay:* Cornett Wood; *back:* Phil de Guard; *ed:* Treg Brown; *character des:* Jean Blanchard; *voices:* Mel Blanc; *mus:* Carl W. Stalling; *prod mgr:* John W. Burton; *prod:* Edward Selzer; *col:* Tech. *sd:* Vit. 7 min. • Bugs becomes an organ grinder and fires his monkey for keeping the takings. The ape tells a gorilla in the local zoo, who comes after Bugs.

3161. Hurry Doctor 14 Mar. 1931; *p.c.:* The Fleischer Studio for Texaco; *prod:* Max Fleischer; *dir:* Dave Fleischer; *mus:* Art Turkisher; b&w. *sd:* WE. • Commercial for Texaco.

3162. Hurts and Flowers *(Roland & Rattfink)* 11 Feb. 1969; *p.c.:* Mirisch/DFE for UA; *dir:* Hawley Pratt; *story:* John W. Dunn; *anim:* Manny Gould, Manny Perez, Warren Batchelder, Don Williams; *lay:* Dick Ung; *back:* Tom O'Loughlin; *ed:* Lee Gunther; *mus:* Doug Goodwin; *ph:* John Burton Jr.; *prod sup:* Jim Foss, Harry Love; *col:* DeLuxe. *sd:* RCA. 5 min. • Rattfink tries to stem Roland's irritating "Flower Power" habits.

3163. Hush My Mouse *(Looney Tunes)* 4 May 1946; *p.c.:* WB; *dir:* Charles M. Jones; *story:* Tedd Pierce; *anim:* Ken Harris, Basil Davidovich, Lloyd Vaughan, Ben Washam; *sets:* Robert Gribbroek; *ed:* Treg Brown; *voices:* Mel Blanc, Marjorie Tarlton, Dick Nelson; *mus:* Carl Stalling; *prod mgr:* John W. Burton; *prod:* Edward Selzer; *col:* Tech. *sd:* Vit. 7 min. • Down at Tuffy's Tavern, Edward G. Robincat wants "Mouse Knuckles." Artie sends his dumb assistant to find a mouse but Sniffles talks him out of it.

3164. Hy Mayer Cartoons *p.c.:* Univ/Imp Films; *dir:* Henry "Hy" Mayer; *anim:* Hy Mayer, Otto Messmer; b&w. sil. • *1913:* A Study in Crayon Mar. **Hy Mayer: His Magic Hand** 3 May. **Hy Mayer: His Magic Hand** 31 May. **Pen Talks by Hy Mayer** 7 June. **Hy Mayer's Cartoons** 14 June. **Filmograph Cartoons** 21 June. **Fun in Film by Hy Mayer** 28 June. **Sketches from Life by Hy Mayer** 5 July. **Lightning Sketches by Hy Mayer** 12 July. **In Cartoonland with Hy Mayer** 19 July. **Summer Caricatures** 26 July. **Funny Fancies by Hy Mayer** 2 Aug. **The Adventures of Mr. Phiffles** 9 Aug. **In Laughland with Hy Mayer** 16 Aug. **Pen Talks by Hy Mayer** 23 Aug. **Hy Mayer: His Merry Pen** 30 Aug. **Humors of Summer** 6 Sept. **Hy Mayer Cartoons** 13 Sept. **Antics in Ink by Hy Mayer** 20 Sept. **Jolly Jottings by Hy Mayer** 27 Sept. **Whimsicalities by Hy Mayer** 4 Oct. **Hilarities by Hy Mayer** 11 Oct. **Leaves From Hy Mayer's Sketchbook** 18 Oct. • *1914:* Pen Laughs. Topical Topics. Topical War Cartoons Sept. **Topical War Cartoons #2** Oct. **War Cartoons by Hy Mayer** Nov. • *1923:* A Movie Fantasy 8 Dec. A Son of Ananias 10 Dec. • See: *Pathé Review; Travelaughs*

3165. Hy Mayer's Skits 'n' Sketches 14 Feb. 1936; *p.c.:* Univ; *dir/anim:* Hy Mayer; b&w. *sd.* • Sound reissue of a selection of Hy Mayers *Travelaughs.*

3166. Hyde and Go Tweet *(Merrie Melodies)* 14 May 1960; *p.c.:* WB; *dir:* Friz Freleng; *anim:* Art Davis, Gerry Chiniquy, Virgil Ross; *lay:* Hawley Pratt; *back:* Tom O'Loughlin; *ed:* Treg Brown; *voices:* Mel Blanc; *mus:* Milt Franklyn; *prod mgr:* William Orcutt; *prod:* David H. DePatie; *col:* Tech. *sd:* Vit. 7 min. • Tweety is chased into Dr. Jekyll's laboratory and drinks a potion that turns him into a monster.

3167. Hyde and Hare *(Looney Tunes)* 27 Aug. 1955; *p.c.:* WB; *dir:* I. Freleng; *story:* Warren Foster; *anim:* Gerry Chiniquy, Virgil Ross, Arthur Davis, Ted Bonnicksen; *lay:* Hawley Pratt; *back:* Irv Wyner; *ed:* Treg Brown; *voices:* Mel Blanc; *mus:* Carl Stalling: *prod mgr:* John W. Burton; *prod:* Edward Selzer; *col:* Tech. *sd:* RCA. 7 min. • Bugs is taken home by Dr. Jekyll, who is prone to becoming a psychopathic killer when he drinks a certain concoction.

3168. Hyde and Sneak *(Inspector Willoughby)* 24 July 1962; *p.c.:* Walter Lantz prods for Univ; *dir:* Paul J. Smith; *story:* Bill Danch; *anim:* Les Kline, Ray Abrams; *sets:* Art Landy, Ray Huffine; *voices:* Dal McKennon, Grace Stafford; *mus:* Darrell Calker; *prod mgr:* William E. Garity; *col:* Tech. *sd:* RCA. 6 min. • Inspector Willoughby has to apprehend a female Jekyll and Hyde.

3169. The Hyena's Laugh *(Unnatural History)* 18 Jan. 1927; *p.c.:* Bray prods for FBO; *dir:* Walter Lantz, Clyde Geronimi; *l/al ph:* Joe Rock; b&w. sil. 5 min. • The grouchy hyena has his aching tooth removed by a hippo dentist who gives him laughing gas and he's been laughing ever since.

3170. The Hyp-Nut-Tist *(Popeye)* 26 Apr. 1935; *p.c.:* The Fleischer Studio for Para: *prod:* Max Fleischer; *dir:* Dave Fleischer; *anim:* Seymour Kneitel, Roland Crandall; *voices:* Jack Mercer, Gus Wickie, Mae Questel; *mus:* Sammy Timberg; b&w. *sd:* WE. 7 min. • Bluto appears as a theatrical hypnotist who hypnotizes Olive into thinking she's a chicken. Not able to tolerate this, Popeye takes to the stage.

3171. Hypnotic Eyes *(Paul Terry-Toon)* 1 Aug. 1933; *p.c.:* Moser & Terry for Educational/Fox; *dir:* Frank Moser, Paul Terry; *mus:* Philip A. Scheib; b&w. *sd:* WE. 6 min. • Melodrama featuring Fanny Zilch and Oil Can Harry.

3172. Hypnotic Hick *(Woody Woodpecker)* 28 Aug. 1953; *p.c.:* Walter Lantz prods for Univ; *dir:* Don Patterson; *story:* Homer Brightman; *anim:*

Ray Abrams, La Verne Harding, Ken Southworth, Gil Turner, Herman Cohen, Robert Bentley; *sets:* Raymond Jacobs, Art Landy; *voices:* Dal McKennon, Grace Stafford; *mus:* Clarence Wheeler; *technical dir:* William E. Garity; *col:* Tech. *sd:* RCA. 6 min. • Made in 3-D. Woody has to serve a writ on Buzz Buzzard and the only way he can do this is to hypnotize the bully first.

3173. The Hypnotist *(Out of the Inkwell)* 26 July 1922; *p.c.:* Inkwell Films for Winkler; *prod/l/a:* Max Fleischer; *dir:* Dave Fleischer; *b&w. sil. l/a/anim.* • Max buys a book on hypnotism and hypnotises Ko-Ko but the little clown turns the tables.

3174. Hypnotized *(Little Roquefort)* May 1952; *p.c.:* TT for Fox; *dir:* Mannie Davis; *story/voice:* Tom Morrison; *anim:* Jim Tyer; *mus:* Philip Scheib; *ph:* Douglas Moye; *col:* Tech. *sd:* RCA. 6 min. • Percy the Puss tries to hypnotize Roquefort to make him believe he's a bird.

3175. The Hypo-Chondri-Cat *(Merrie Melodies)* 15 Apr. 1950; *p.c.:* WB; *dir:* Charles M. Jones; *story:* Michael Maltese; *anim:* Ben Washam, Lloyd Vaughan, Ken Harris, Phil Monroe; *lay:* Robert Gribbroek; *back:* Phil de Guard; *ed:* Treg Brown; *voices:* Mel Blanc, Stan Freberg; *mus:* Carl Stalling; *prod mgr:* John W. Burton; *prod:* Edward Selzer; *col:* Tech. *sd:* Vit. 7 min. • Hubie and Bert, the two mice, convince a hypochondriac cat that he's sicker than he is.

3176. Hysterical High Spots in American History *(Cartune)* 31 Mar. 1941; *p.c.:* Walter Lantz prods for Univ; *dir:* Walter Lantz; *story:* Ben Hardaway; *anim:* Alex Lovy, (La) Verne Harding; *sets:* Fred Brunish; *voices:* Mel Blanc, Sara Berner; *mus:* Darrell Calker; *prod mgr:* George Hall; *col:* Tech. *sd:* WE. 6 min. • Spot-gags on important moments in U.S. history from Columbus discovering America to Paul Revere's ride, etc.

3177. Hysterical History *(Kartune)* 23 Jan. 1953; *p.c.:* Famous for Para; *dir:* I. Sparber; *story:* Irving Spector; *anim:* Al Eugster, George Germanetti; *sets:* Robert Owen; *voices:* Jackson Beck, Jack Mercer, Gwen Davies; *mus:* Winston Sharples; *song:* George M. Cohan; *ph:* Leonard McCormick; *prod mgr:* Seymour Shultz; *col:* Tech. *sd:* RCA. 6 min. • An insight into historical happenings from Columbus through John Smith and Pocahontas and others.

3178. I Ain't Got Nobody *(Screen Songs)* 17 June 1932; *p.c.:* The Fleischer Studio for Para; *prod:* Max Fleischer; *dir:* Dave Fleischer; *anim:* Willard Bowsky, Thomas Bonfiglio; *mus:* Art Turkisher; *song:* Spencer Williams, Roger Graham; *l/a:* The Mills Brothers (Herbert, Harry, Donald and John); *b&w. sd:* WE. 9 min. *l/a/anim.* • A lion operates a television broadcast then he magicks inanimate objects to come alive. The Mills Brothers' first screen appearance.

3179. I Can't Escape from You *(Screen Songs)* 25 Sept. 1936; *p.c.:* The Fleischer Studio for Para; *prod:* Max Fleischer; *dir:* Dave Fleischer; *anim:* Thomas Johnson, David Hoffman; *mus recorded by* Joe Reichman & His Orchestra; *b&w. sd:* WE. 8 min. *l/a/anim.* • Newsreel parody with a seal watching a man do tricks while the stock market expects elevator stocks to rise but they plummet.

3180. I Don't Scare *(Popeye)* 16 Nov. 1956; *p.c.:* Famous for Para; *dir:* I. Sparber; *story:* Jack Mercer; *anim:* Tom Johnson, Frank Endres; *sets:* Robert Owen; *voices:* Jack Mercer, Jackson Beck, Mae Questel; *mus:* Winston Sharples; *ph:* Leonard McCormick; *prod mgr:* Seymour Shultz; *col:* Tech. *sd:* RCA. 6 min. • Bluto takes advantage of Olive's superstitious beliefs on Hallowe'en to get rid of Popeye.

3181. I Don't Want to Make History *(Screen Songs)* 22 May 1936; *p.c.:* The Fleischer Studio for Para; *prod:* Max Fleischer; *dir:* Dave Fleischer; *anim:* Thomas Johnson, Dave Hoffman; *mus:* Vincent Lopez & His Orchestra; *b&w. sd:* WE. 7½ min. • Features in a newsreel: A Transatlantic express, a method of ending all wars by blowing up the world. Wiffle Piffle displays a new alarm clock and a new "Easy Parker" car is demonstrated.

3182. I Eats My Spinach *(Popeye)* 17 Nov. 1933; *p.c.:* The Fleischer Studio for Para; *prod:* Max Fleischer; *dir:* Dave Fleischer; *anim:* Seymour Kneitel, Roland Crandall; *voices:* William A. Costello, Charles Carver; *mus:* Sammy Timberg; *b&w. sd:* WE. 6 min. • Popeye takes over from Bluto as a rodeo star.

3183. I Feel Like a Feather in the Breeze *(Screen Songs)* 27 Mar. 1936; *p.c.:* The Fleischer Studio for Para; *prod:* Max Fleischer; *dir:* Dave Fleischer; *anim:* Thomas Johnson, Harold Walker; *mus:* Jack Denny &

His Orchestra; *song:* Harry Revel, Mack Gordon; *b&w. sd:* WE. 7 min. • A trick door gets the customers onto a roof garden café. Wiffle Piffle is a waiter being defeated by spaghetti.

3184. I Gopher You *(Merrie Melodies)* 3 Feb. 1954; *p.c.:* WB; *dir:* I. Freleng; *story:* Warren Foster; *anim:* Ken Champin, Virgil Ross, Arthur Davis, Manuel Perez; *lay:* Hawley Pratt; *back:* Irv Wyner; *ed:* Treg Brown; *voices:* Mel Blanc, Stan Freberg; *mus:* Carl Stalling; *prod mgr:* John W. Burton; *prod:* Edward Selzer; *col:* Tech. *sd:* Vit. 7 min. • The gophers raid a food processing plant.

3185. I Got Plenty of Mutton *(Merrie Melodies)* 11 Mar. 1944; *p.c.:* WB; *dir:* Frank Tashlin; *story:* Melvin Millar; *anim:* I. Ellis; *back:* Richard H. Thomas; *ed:* Treg Brown; *voices:* Mel Blanc; *mus:* Carl W. Stalling; *prod mgr:* John W. Burton; *prod:* Edward Selzer; *col:* Tech. *sd:* Vit. 7 min. • A starving wolf disguises himself as a sheep to avoid "Killer Diller" ram when pilfering lambs.

3186. I Haven't Got a Hat *(Merrie Melodies)* 1 July 1935; *p.c.:* Leon Schlesinger prods for WB; *dir:* Isadore Freleng; *story:* Robert Clampett; *anim:* Rollin Hamilton, Jack King; *voices:* Bernice Hansel, Joe Dougherty; *mus:* Bernard Brown; *song:* Bert Kalmar, Harry Ruby; *prod sup:* Henry Binder, Raymond G. Katz; *col:* Tech-2. *sd:* Vit. 7 min. • The initial appearance of Porky Pig involves the kids doing their pieces for the school show. Beans sabotages Oliver Owl's piano solo.

3187. I Like Mountain Music *(Merrie Melodies)* 3 Aug. 1933; *p.c.:* Hugh Harman–Rudolf Ising prods for WB; *story:* Robert Clampett; *anim:* Isadore Freleng, Larry Martin; *ed:* Dale Pickett; *mus:* Frank Marsales; *asso prod:* Leon Schlesinger; *b&w. sd:* Vit. 6 min. • Will Rogers, Eddie Cantor, King Kong and others come alive from book covers and sing the *title* song until a gang of crooks make off with some money.

3188. I Like Mountain Music *(Screen Songs)* 10 Nov. 1933; *p.c.:* The Fleischer Studio for Para; *prod:* Max Fleischer; *dir:* Dave Fleischer; *anim:* Willard Bowsky, Myron Waldman; *mus:* Art Turkisher; *song:* Weldon, Cavanaugh; *l/a:* The Eton Boys; *b&w. sd:* WE. 10 min. *l/a/anim.* • Rip van Winkle rescues a dwarf who takes him to his community of dwarfs. He drinks too much and sleeps for twenty years, awaking in "the age of steam."

3189. I Likes Babies and Infinks *(Popeye)* 17 Sept. 1937; *p.c.:* The Fleischer Studio for Para; *prod:* Max Fleischer; *dir:* Dave Fleischer; *anim:* Seymour Kneitel, Graham Place; *voices:* Jack Mercer, Mae Questel, Gus Wickie; *mus:* Sammy Timberg; *b&w. sd:* WE. 6 min. • Popeye and Bluto try to entertain Swee'Pea but their chore soon turns to competition.

3190. I Love a Lassie *(Song Car-Tune)* 21 Aug. 1926; *p.c.:* Inkwell Studio for Red Seal; *prod:* Max Fleischer; *dir:* Dave Fleischer; *b&w. sil.* 5 min. • No story available.

3191. I Love a Parade *(Merrie Melodies)* Aug. 1932; *p.c.:* Hugh Harman–Rudolf Ising prods for WB; *prod:* Leon Schlesinger; *anim:* Rollin Hamilton, Thomas McKimson, Robert Clampett; *ed:* Dale Pickett; *voices:* John T. Murray, Mary Moder, The Kingsmen; *mus:* Frank Marsales; *song:* Harold Arlen, Ted Koehler; *b&w. sd:* Vit. 6 min. • The circus comes to town showing the various attractions: The India Rubber Man, The Indian Skinny Man (Mahatma Ghandi), Siamese twins and a lion tamer.

3192. I Love to Singa *(Merrie Melodies)* 18 July 1936; *p.c.:* Leon Schlesinger prods for WB; *dir:* Fred Avery; *story:* Robert Clampett; *anim:* Charles Jones, Virgil Ross, Robert Clampett; *sets:* John Didrik Johnsen; *ed:* Tregoweth E. Brown; *voices:* Tommy Bond, Jackie Morrow, Billy Bletcher, Martha Wentworth, Lou Fulton, Bernice Hansel, Ted Pierce; *mus:* Norman Spencer; *song:* Harold Arlen, E.Y. Harburg; *prod sup:* Henry Binder, Raymond G. Katz; *col:* Tech. *sd:* Vit. 8 min. • Professor Owl's jazz-singing offspring proves a musical disappointment and he throws the youngster out. Young Owl Jolson promptly goes and wins Jack Bunny's amateur contest.

3193. I Never Changes My Altitude *(Popeye)* 20 Aug. 1937; *p.c.:* The Fleischer Studio for Para; *prod:* Max Fleischer; *dir:* Dave Fleischer; *anim:* Willard Bowsky, Orestes Calpini; *voices:* Jack Mercer, Mae Questel, Gus Wickie; *mus:* Sammy Timberg; *b&w. sd:* WE. 7 min. • Olive takes off with a sadistic pilot and Popeye takes to the air to bring her down to earth.

3194. I Never Should Have Told You *(Screen Songs)* 29 Jan. 1937;

p.c.: The Fleischer Studio for Para; *prod:* Max Fleischer; *dir:* Dave Fleischer; *mus:* Nat Brandwynne & His Orchestra; b&w. *sd:* WE. 8 min. • A crazy inventor displays his gadgets.

3195. I Only Have Eyes for You *(Merrie Melodies)* 6 Mar. 1937; *p.c.:* Leon Schlesinger prods for WB; *dir:* Fred Avery; *story:* Bob Clampett; *anim:* Bob Clampett, Virgil Ross; *lay:* Griff Jay; *back:* Arthur Loomer; *ed:* Tregoweth E. Brown; *voices:* Elvia Allman, Joe Twerp, The Rhythmettes; *mus:* Carl W. Stalling; *song:* Harry Warren, Al Dubin; *prod sup:* Henry Binder, Raymond G. Katz; *col:* Tech. *sd:* Vit. 8 min. • The Ice-Man's ideal, Katie Canary, only cares for crooners! He gets Prof. Mockingbird to croon so he can mime to it and impress Katie.

3196. I Remember Nudnik *(Nudnik)* July 1967; *p.c.:* Rembrandt for Para; *prod:* William L. Snyder; *dir/voice:* Gene Deitch; *col. sd.* 6 min. • Sequences from earlier productions. Nudnik attempts to paint his apartment, comes into posession of a car, gets involved in a bag-snatch and returns home to find his apartment building is being demolished. • *seq: Drive on, Nudnik; Welcome, Nudnik; Home, Sweet, Nudnik.* • See: *Nudnik*

3197. I-Ski Love-Ski You-Ski *(Popeye)* 3 Apr. 1936; *p.c.:* The Fleischer Studio for Para; *prod:* Max Fleischer; *dir:* Dave Fleischer; *anim:* Willard Bowsky, George Germanetti; *voices:* Jack Mercer, Mae Questel, Gus Wickie; *mus:* Sammy Timberg; b&w. *sd:* WE. 7 min. • Olive chooses to go mountain climbing with Popeye instead of Bluto, who takes umbrage and decides to sabotage the excursion.

3198. I Taw a Putty Tat *(Merrie Melodies)* 3 Apr. 1948; *p.c.:* WB; *dir:* I. Freleng; *story:* Tedd Pierce; *anim:* Virgil Ross, Gerry Chiniquy, Manuel Perez, Ken Champin; *lay:* Hawley Pratt; *back:* Paul Julian; *ed:* Treg Brown; *voices:* Mel Blanc, Bea Benaderet; *mus:* Carl Stalling; *prod mgr:* John W. Burton; *prod:* Edward Selzer; *col:* Ciné. *sd:* Vit. 7 min. • Tweety is brought into the house to replace the last canary who has mysteriously disappeared. Sylvester already has the bird's future planned.

3199. I Wanna Be a Lifeguard *(Popeye)*; rel; 26 June 1936; *p.c.:* The Fleischer Studio for Para; *prod:* Max Fleischer; *dir:* Dave Fleischer; *anim:* David Tendlar, William Sturm. Joseph Oriolo; *voices:* Jack Mercer, Mae Questel, Gus Wickie, Louis Fleischer; *mus:* Sammy Timberg; b&w. *sd:* WE. 7 min. • Popeye and Bluto both apply for the job of lifeguard at the local pool. Bluto plays dirty.

3200. I Wanna Be a Sailor *(Merrie Melodies)* 16 Oct. 1937; *p.c.:* Leon Schlesinger prods for WB; *dir:* Fred Avery; *story/anim:* Robert Clampett; *lay:* Griff Jay; *back:* Arthur Loomer; *ed:* Tregoweth E. Brown; *voices:* Elvia Allman, Tommy Bond, Billy Bletcher, Bernice Hansel; *mus:* Carl W. Stalling; *prod sup:* Henry Binder, Raymond G. Katz; *col:* Tech. *sd:* Vit. 7 min. • Against Ma's wishes, Petey Parrot runs off to sea with Gabby Goose. When a storm sweeps Petey overboard he is saved by his friend.

3201. I Wanna Play House *(Merrie Melodies)* 18 Jan. 1936; *p.c.:* Leon Schlesinger prods for WB; *dir:* I. Freleng; *anim:* Cal Dalton, Sandy Walker; *voice:* Bernice Hansel; *mus:* Bernard Brown; *prod sup:* Henry Binder, Raymond G. Katz; *col:* Tech. *sd:* Vit. 7 min. • Two bear cubs play in a gypsy wagon until it rolls downhill.

3202. I Want My Mummy *(Modern Madcap)* Mar. 1966; *p.c.:* Para Cartoons; *dir:* Shamus Culhane; *story:* Bill Dana, Howard Post; *anim:* Charles Harriton, Nick Tafuri, Al Eugster, Martin Taras; *sets:* Jerry Lieberman; *voices:* Bill Dana, Bob MacFadden; *mus:* Winston Sharples; *prod sup:* Harold Robins, Burt Hanft; *col:* Tech. *sd:* RCA. 6 min. • Jose Jimanez helps an archeologist in his search to retrieve a sacred crown from the lost mummy of Mazuoma.

3203. I Want to Be an Actress *(Scrappy)* 18 July 1937; *p.c.:* Charles Mintz prods for Colum; *story:* Allen Rose; *anim:* Harry Love; *sets:* Phil Davis; *voice:* Elvia Allman, Dave Weber, Leone Le Doux; *mus:* Joe de Nat; *prod mgr:* James Bronis; b&w. *sd:* RCA. 6 min. • Scrappy's girl, Heidi, tries to convince him she has star material for his movie. Then she joins him in the musical numbers "The Balboa Song" and "Sing, Baby Sing."

3204. I Was a Teenage Thumb *(Merrie Melodies)* Jan. 1963; *p.c.:* WB; *dir:* Chuck Jones Esq; *asst dir:* Maurice Noble; *story:* John Dunn, Chuck Jones; *anim:* Bob Bransford, Tom Ray, Ken Harris, Richard Thompson; *lay:* Bob Givens; *back:* Philip de Guard; *ed:* Treg Brown; *voices:* Mel Blanc, Richard Peel, Ben Frommer, Julie Bennett; *mus:* Bill Lava *prod mgr:* William Orcutt; *prod:* David H. DePatie; *col:* Tech. *sd:* Vit. 6 min. • The

story of "Tom Thumb" who one night is stolen by a bird, then eaten by a fish, finally coming to rest in a castle where he is made a prince.

3205. I Wish I Had Wings *(Merrie Melodies)* 16 Jan. 1933; *p.c.:* Hugh Harman–Rudolf Ising prods for WB; *anim:* Rollin Hamilton, Paul Smith, Robert Clampett; *ed:* Dale Pickett; *mus:* Frank Marsales; *asso prod:* Leon Schlesinger; b&w. *sd:* Vit. 7 min. • A chick improvises wings to fly to the food outside the coop but is chased away by the scarecrow. He retaliates by burning the coop.

3206. I Wished on the Moon *(Screen Songs)* 20 Sept. 1935; *p.c.:* The Fleischer Studio for Para; *prod:* Max Fleischer; *dir:* Dave Fleischer; *anim:* Thomas Johnson; *mus:* Abe Lyman & His Californians; *song:* Ralph Rainger, Dorothy Parker; b&w. *sd:* WE. 8 min. *l/a/anim.* • A portable theater is erected in a topsy-turvy fashion and the patrons (Wiffle Piffle included) have a difficult time in seeing the acts.

3207. I Wonder Who's Kissing Her Now? *(Screen Songs)* 14 Feb. 1931; *p.c.:* The Fleischer Studio for Para; *prod:* Max Fleischer; *dir:* Dave Fleischer; *anim:* Al Eugster, George Cannata; *mus:* Art Turkisher; *song:* Will M. Hough, Frank R. Adams, Joseph E. Howard; b&w. *sd:* WE. 6½ min. • A frustrated cat entices his girl away from her "Daddy" with catnip.

3208. I Yam Love Sick *(Popeye)* 20 May 1938; *p.c.:* The Fleischer Studio for Para; *prod:* Max Fleischer; *dir:* Dave Fleischer; *anim:* Seymour Kneitel, William Henning; *ed:* Kitty Pfister; *voices:* Jack Mercer, Mae Questel, Gus Wickie; *mus:* Sammy Timberg; *prod sup:* Sam Buchwald, Isidore Sparber; b&w. *sd:* WE. 7 min. • Popeye feigns illness to win Olive's sympathy.

3209. I Yam What I Yam *(Popeye)* 29 Sept. 1933; *p.c.:* The Fleischer Studio for Para; *prod:* Max Fleischer; *dir:* Dave Fleischer; *anim:* Seymour Kneitel, William Henning; *voices:* William A. Costello, Mae Questel, Charles Carver, Louis Fleischer; *mus:* Sammy Timberg; b&w. *sd:* WE. 7 min. • Popeye, Olive and Wimpy build a log cabin in the woods and are beset by Indians.

3210. Icarus-Montgolfier-Wright 1961; *p.c.:* Format Films for UA; *prod/dir:* Jules Engel; *col. sd. Academy Award nomination.* • The history of flight is shown through photos.

3211. The Ice Carnival *(Terry-Toon)* 22 Aug. 1941; *p.c.:* TT for Fox; *dir:* Eddie Donnelly; *story:* John Foster; *mus:* Philip A. Scheib; b&w. *sd:* RCA. 6 min. • No story available.

3212. Ice Cream for Help *(Hector Heathcote)* Oct. 1971 (© 1963); *p.c.:* TT for Fox; *ex prod:* Bill Weiss; *dir:* Art Bartsch; *story sup:* Tom Morrison; *story:* Larz Bourne; *anim:* Ralph Bakshi, Art Bartsch; *sets:* Bill Focht, John Zago; *ed:* George McAvoy; *voices:* John Myhers; *mus:* Phil Scheib; *ph:* Joe Rasinski *col:* DeLuxe. *sd:* RCA. 5 min. • Iceman Heathcote is fired but soon finds another job with Benedict discovering the North Pole.

3213. The Ice Pond *(Terry-Toon)* 15 Dec. 1939; *p.c.:* TT for Fox; *dir:* Mannie Davis; *story:* John Foster; *mus:* Philip A. Scheib; b&w. *sd:* RCA. 6 min. • A fox lures the bunnies into an ice hockey game and they are saved by an ice skating pig.

3214. Ice Scream *(Casper)* 30 Aug. 1957; *p.c.:* Para Cartoons; *dir:* Seymour Kneitel; *story:* Jack Mercer; *anim:* Myron Waldman, Nick Tafuri; *sets:* Robert Little; *voices:* Norma MacMillan, Gwen Davies; *mus:* Winston Sharples; *ph:* Leonard McCormick; *prod mgr:* Seymour Shultz; *col:* Tech. *sd:* RCA. 6 min. • Casper helps little Billy win a skating contest.

3215. The Iceman Ducketh *(Looney Tunes)* 16 May 1964; *p.c.:* WB; *dir:* Phil Monroe; *asst dir:* Maurice Noble; *story:* John Dunn; *anim:* Bob Bransford, Tom Ray, Ken Harris, Richard Thompson, Bob Matz, Alex Ignatiev; *fx:* Harry Love; *lay:* Bob Givens; *back:* William Butler; *ed:* Treg Brown; *voices:* Mel Blanc; *mus:* Bill Lava; *prod mgr:* William Orcutt; *prod:* David H. DePatie; *col:* Tech. *sd:* Vit. 6 min. • Daffy sets out to trap some furs in the shape of Bugs Bunny.

3216. Iceman's Luck *(Oswald)* 22 June 1929; *p.c.:* Winkler for Univ; *anim:* R.C. Hamilton; *prod mgr:* James Bronis; b&w. *sil.* 5 min. • No story available.

3217. I'd Climb the Highest Mountain *(Screen Songs)* 6 Mar. 1931; *p.c.:* The Fleischer Studio for Para; *prod:* Max Fleischer; *dir:* Dave Fleischer; *anim:* Seymour Kneitel, Reuben Timmens; *mus:* Art Turkisher; *song:* Lew

Brown, Sidney Clare; b&w. *sd:* WE. 6 min. • A dog takes his overweight girlfriend mountain climbing.

3218. I'd Love to Take Orders from You (*Merrie Melodies*) 30 May 1936; *p.c.:* Leon Schlesinger prods for WB; *dir:* Fred Avery; *story:* Bob Clampett; *anim:* Bob Clampett, Cecil Surry; *ed:* Tregoweth E. Brown; *voices:* Elmore Vincent, Tommy Bond, Bernice Hansel; *mus:* Norman Spencer; *prod sup:* Henry Binder, Raymond G. Katz; *col:* Tech. *sd:* Vit. 7 min. • A young scarecrow attempts to emulate his father in crow scaring.

3219. An Ideal Farm (*Aesop's Fable*) 27 Apr. 1924; *p.c.:* Fables Pictures Inc for Pathé; *dir:* Paul Terry; b&w. *sil.* 5 min. • The cat makes a unionized one-egg-a-day hen produce more by making the calendar jump a day each time the light goes out, making her think it's another day.

3220. If Cats Could Sing (*Terry-Toons*) Sept. 1950; *p.c.:* TT for Fox; *dir:* Eddie Donnelly; *story:* John Foster; *anim:* Jim Tyer; *sets:* Art Bartsch; *voices:* Roy Halee; *mus:* Philip A. Scheib; *ph:* Douglas Moye; *col:* Tech. *sd:* RCA. 6 min. • Nocturnal cats stage an improvised opera using ash cans, radiators, etc.

3221. If Noah Had Lived Today (*Aesop's Film Fable*) 13 Apr. 1924; *p.c.:* Fables Pictures Inc for Pathé; *dir:* Paul Terry; b&w. *sil.* 5 min. • Noah's barometer points to "Flood," so he sets up his broadcasting apparatus and signals for his animals to come aboard his airship.

3222. An Igloo for Two (*Willie the Walrus*) May 1955; *p.c.:* TT for Fox; *dir:* Connie Rasinski; *story:* Tom Morrison; *anim:* Jim Tyer; *mus:* Philip A. Scheib; *ph:* Douglas Moye; *col:* Tech. *sd:* RCA. 6 min. CS. • In true Cyrano de Bergerac fashion, Walter Walrus gets Willie to dub a singing voice for him to woo a cute girl. She soon discovers who she prefers.

3223. I'll Be Glad When You're Dead, You Rascal You (*Betty Boop*) 25 Nov. 1932; *p.c.:* The Fleischer Studio for Para; *prod:* Max Fleischer; *dir:* Dave Fleischer; *anim:* Willard Bowsky, Ralph Somerville; *mus/l/a:* Louis Armstrong & His Orchestra; *song:* Sam Theard; b&w. *sd:* WE. 7 min. • Bimbo and Ko-Ko go searching for Betty, who has been captured by cannibals while on safari.

3224. I'll Be Skiing Ya (*Popeye*) 13 June 1947; *p.c.:* Famous for Para; *dir:* I. Sparber; *story:* Bill Turner, Larry Riley; *anim:* Tom Johnson, George Germanetti; *sets:* Robert Connavale; *voices:* Jack Mercer, Jackson Beck, Mae Questel; *mus:* Winston Sharples; *ph:* Leonard McCormick; *prod mgr:* Sam Buchwald; *col:* Ciné. *sd:* RCA. 8 min. • Ski instructor Bluto resents Popeye teaching Olive to ski and wreaks his revenge.

3225. I'll Never Crow Again (*Popeye*) 19 Sept. 1941; *p.c.:* The Fleischer Studio for Para; *prod:* Max Fleischer; *dir:* Dave Fleischer; *story:* Cal Howard; *anim:* Orestes Calpini, Reuben Grossman; *ed:* Kitty Pfister; *voices:* Jack Mercer, Margie Hines; *mus:* Sammy Timberg; *prod sup:* Sam Buchwald, Isidore Sparber; b&w. *sd:* WE. 6 min. • Olive gets Popeye to rid her garden of crows.

3226. I'm a Big Shot Now (*Merrie Melodies*) 11 Apr. 1936; *p.c.:* Leon Schlesinger prods for WB; *dir:* I. Freleng; *anim:* Jack Carr, Riley Thomson, Robert Clampett; *ed:* Tregoweth E. Brown; *voice:* Dave Weber; *mus:* Bernard Brown; *song:* Mort Dixon, Allie Wrubel; *prod sup:* Henry Binder, Raymond G. Katz; *col:* Tech. *sd:* Vit. 7 min. • Birdland's leading gangster and his gang hold up a bank. After a shoot-out he realizes he's not as tough as he thought.

3227. I'm Afraid to Come Home in the Dark (*Screen Songs*) 1 Feb. 1930; *p.c.:* The Fleischer prods for Para; *prod:* Max Fleischer; *dir:* Dave Fleischer; *mus:* Art Turkisher; *song:* Egbert Van Altyne; b&w. *sd:* WE. (disc) 7 min. • Featuring Bimbo as an inebriate who is afraid to return home at three A.M. for fear of his wife's rolling pin.

3228. I'm Cold (*Chilly Willy*) 20 Dec. 1954; *p.c.:* Walter Lantz prods for Univ; *dir:* Tex Avery; *story:* Homer Brightman; *anim:* Ray Abrams, Don Patterson, La Verne Harding; *sets:* Raymond Jacobs; *voice:* Daws Butler; *mus:* Clarence Wheeler; *prod mgr:* William E. Garity; *col:* Tech. *sd:* RCA. 6 min. • Chilly tries to keep warm by stealing furs from a warehouse guarded by a dumb watchdog.

3229. I'm Forever Blowing Bubbles (*Screen Songs*) 15 Mar. 1930; *p.c.:* The Fleischer Studio for Para; *prod:* Max Fleischer; *dir:* Dave Fleischer; *mus:* Art Turkisher; *song:* John Kellette, Jan Kenbrovin (James Kendis, James Brokman, Nat Vincent); b&w. *sd:* WE. (disc) 8 min. • Mice give the jungle animals a bubble bath.

3230. I'm in the Army Now (*Popeye*) 25 Dec. 1936; *p.c.:* The Fleischer Studio for Para; *prod:* Max Fleischer; *dir:* Dave Fleischer; *voices:* Jack Mercer, Mae Questel, Gus Wickie; *mus:* Sammy Timberg; b&w. *sd:* WE. 6 min. Seq: *Blow Me Down; Choose Your Weppins; Shoein' Horses; King of the Mardi Gras.* • Popeye and Bluto both try to enlist in the Army by showing feats of strength in their past films.

3231. I'm Just a Jitterbug (*Car-Tune Comedy*) 23 Jan. 1939; *p.c.:* Walter Lantz prods for Univ; *dir:* Alex Lovy; *story:* Victor McLeod; *anim:* Merle Gilson, Hicks Lokey; *sets:* Edgar Keichle; *voices:* Dick Nelson, Chuck Lowry, The Pied Pipers; *mus:* Frank Marsales, Chuck Lowry; *prod mgr:* George Hall; *col:* Tech-2. *sd:* WE. 7 min. *l/a/anim.* • When the artists finish drawing for the night, the cartoons hold a jam session.

3232. I'm Just Curious (*Little Lulu*) 8 Sept. 1944; *p.c.:* Famous for Para; *dir:* Seymour Kneitel; *story:* William Turner, Jack Ward; *anim:* Graham Place, George Cannata, Lou Zukor, Sidney Pillet; *sets:* Robert Connavale; *voices:* Cecil Roy, Arnold Stang; *mus:* Sammy Timberg; *title song:* Buddy Kaye, Fred Wise, Sammy Timberg; *ph:* Leonard McCormick; *prod mgr:* Sam Buchwald; *col:* Tech. *sd:* RCA. 7 min. • Lulu believes that a hawk raiding the henhouse is really a stork delivering a baby.

3233. I'm Just Wild About Jerry (*Tom & Jerry*) 1965; *p.c.:* MGM; *prod/dir:* Chuck Jones; *asst dir:* Maurice Noble; *story:* Michael Maltese, Chuck Jones; *anim:* Dick Thompson, Ben Washam, Ken Harris, Don Towsley; *back:* Philip de Guard; *mus:* Eugene Poddany; *prod mgr:* Les Goldman; *col:* Metro. *sd:* WE. 6 min. • Tom chases Jerry into a department store.

3234. Imagination (*Color Rhapsody*) 19 Nov. 1943; *p.c.:* Colum; *prod:* Dave Fleischer; *dir:* Bob Wickersham; *story:* Dun Roman; *anim:* Ben Lloyd, Basil Davidovich; *sets:* Clark Watson; *ed:* Edward Moore; *voices:* Harry Stanton; *mus:* Paul Worth; *ph:* Frank Fisher; *prod mgr:* Albert Spar; *col:* Tech. *sd:* RCA. 8 min. *Academy Award nomination.* • A small girl dreams that her dolls are lovers separated by a villain who seduces the girl away from the sailor doll hero.

3235. The Impatient Patient (*Looney Tunes*) 5 Sept. 1942; *p.c.:* Leon Schlesinger prods for WB; *dir:* Norman McCabe. *asst dir:* Robert Clampett; *story:* Don Christiansen; *anim:* John Carey, Cal Dalton, Arthur Davis, David Hoffman, Vive Risto; *back:* Richard H. Thomas; *ed:* Treg Brown; *voices:* Mel Blanc; *mus:* Carl W. Stalling; *prod sup:* Henry Binder, Raymond G. Katz; b&w. *sd:* Vit. 7 min. • Daffy is delivering a telegram when he is afflicted by the hiccups. He consults the nearest doctor ... who happens to be Dr. Jekyll.

3236. The Impossible Possum (*Barney Bear*) 20 Mar. 1954; *p.c.:* MGM; *dir:* Dick Lundy; *story:* Heck Allen, Jack Cosgriff; *anim:* Grant Simmons, Robert Bentley, Michael Lah, Walter Clinton; *sets:* John Didrik Johnsen; *ed:* Jim Faris; *voice:* Paul Frees; *mus:* Scott Bradley; *ph:* Jack Stevens; *prod:* Fred Quimby; *col:* Tech. *sd:* WE. 7 min. • Barney sets out to catch a possum for dinner.

3237. The Impractical Joker (*Betty Boop*) 18 June 1937; *p.c.:* The Fleischer Studio for Para; *prod:* Max Fleischer; *dir:* Dave Fleischer; *anim:* Thomas Johnson, Frank Endres; *voices:* Mae Questel, Everett Clark; *mus:* Sammy Timberg; b&w. *sd:* WE. 6 min. • Irving plays practical jokes on Betty, and Grampy plays him at his own game.

3238. In Again, Out Again (*Aesop's Film Fable*) 16 Aug. 1927; *p.c.:* Fables Pictures Inc for Pathé; *dir:* Paul Terry; b&w. *sil.* 10 min. • The dog and cat escape from prison through a river and are sucked back into jail via the water supply pipe.

3239. In Dutch (*Aesop's Fable*) 9 Nov. 1931; *p.c.:* Van Beuren for Pathé; *dir:* John Foster, Harry Bailey; *mus:* Gene Rodemich; b&w. *sd:* RCA. 6 min. • No story available.

3240. In Dutch (*Aesop's Film Fable*) 13 Feb. 1925; *p.c.:* Fables Pictures Inc for Pathé; *dir:* Paul Terry; b&w. *sil.* 5 min. • The animals demonstrate their own version of making cheese in Holland.

3241. In Dutch (*Pluto*) 9 Oct. 1945; *p.c.:* Walt Disney prods for RKO; *dir:* Charles Nichols; *asst dir:* Bob North; *story:* Harry Reeves, Jesse Marsh; *anim:* George Nicholas, Jerry Hathcock, Marvin Woodward, George Kreisl, James Moore, Frank Thomas, Bob Youngquist; *fx:* Jack Boyd, Brad Case, Andy Engman; *lay:* Karl Karpé; *back:* Ray Huffine, Thelma Witmer; *voices:* Charles Judels, James MacDonald; *mus:* Oliver Wallace; *col:* Tech. *sd:* RCA.

7 min. • Pluto and Dinah are banished by the Dutch villagers when they set off a false flood alarm. They discover a genuine leak in the dike and nobody will believe them.

3242. In His Cups (*Aesop's Film Fable*) 25 June 1929; *p.c.:* Fables Pictures Inc for Pathé; *dir:* Paul Terry; b&w. sil. 10 min. • Farmer Al Falfa's imbibing makes him dream he's in a prehistoric jungle riding an elephant. He meets and romances the Ape Girl. An ape kidnaps the girl, and is pursued by Al into a cave. She clubs the ape and tenderly strokes Al's face. He awakes to find a cow licking his face. Moral: "Give us life, liberty and the pursuit of Flappers."

3243. In My Gondola (*Color Rhapsody*) 6 July 1936; *p.c.:* Charles Mintz prods for Colum; *story:* Sid Marcus; *anim:* Art Davis; *mus:* Joe de Nat; *prod mgr:* James Bronis; *col:* Tech. *sd:* RCA. 8 min. • Scrappy, Margie and Yippy drift down the Venetian canals on a gondola. Scrappy's serenading is upstaged by a violinist lobster and Yippy is chased by a swordfish.

3244. In My Merry Oldsmobile 21 Mar. 1931; *p.c.* The Fleischer Studio for Olds Motor Works; *prod:* Max Fleischer; *dir:* Dave Fleischer; *story/anim:* Jimmie Culhane, Rudy Zamora; *mus:* Art Turkisher; *song:* Vincent Bryan, Gus Edwards; b&w. *sd:* WE. 6½ min. • The villain abducts a lady but the hero saves her and they go for a ride in his merry Oldsmobile. Live-action footage of a couple driving in a vintage car.

3245. In the Bag 1928. (*Aesop's Film Fable*) *p.c.:* Fables Pictures Inc for Pathé; *dir:* Paul Terry; b&w. sil. 5 min. • Farmer Al takes the gang to the Farm Hands' Picnic. He comes off second best in his experiences with the Roller Coaster, the chutes, the "greased pig" and the sack race.

3246. In the Bag 27 July 1956; *p.c.:* Walt Disney prods for BV; *dir:* Jack Hannah; *story:* Dave DeTiege, Al Bertino; *anim:* John Sibley, Bob Carlson, Al Coe, George Kreisl, Jerry Hathcock, Ken O'Brien; *fx:* Dan MacManus; *lay:* Yale Gracey; *back:* Ray Huffine; *voices:* Bill Thompson, Paul Frees, James MacDonald; *mus:* George Bruns; *col:* Tech. *sd:* RCA. 7 min. CS. • The Ranger tricks the bears into cleaning up the park by offering a sumptuous meal as a reward. Humphrey is left to clear everything while the others eat their fill.

3247. In the Bag (*Tom & Jerry*) 26 Mar. 1932; *p.c.:* Van Beuren for RKO; *dir:* John Foster, George Rufle; *mus:* Gene Rodemich; b&w. *sd:* RCA. 7 min. • Tom and Jerry pit their wits against a clever bandit.

3248. In the Dumbwaiter 1926; *p.c.:* Univ; *dir:* Milt Gross; b&w. sil. • No story available.

3249. In the Good Old Summer Time (*Aesop's Film Fable*) 14 Sept. 1924; *p.c.:* Fables Pictures Inc for Pathé; *dir:* Paul Terry; b&w. sil. 5 min. • The barnyard creatures build a swimming pool. Just as the Farmer is about to take a dip, an elephant comes along and drains it.

3250. In the Good Old Summer Time (*Screen Songs*) 7 June 1930; *p.c.:* The Fleischer Studio for Para; *prod:* Max Fleischer; *sup:* Dave Fleischer; *dir/story/anim:* Jimmie Culhane, Rudy Zamora; *mus:* Art Turkisher; *song:* Ren Shields; b&w. *sd:* WE. (disc) 6 min. • The animals have a summer outing to the fairground and ride the switchback.

3251. In the Good Old Summer-Time (*Song Car-Tune*) 1927; *p.c.:* Inkwell Studio for Red Seal; *prod:* Max Fleischer; *dir:* Dave Fleischer; *song:* Ren Shields; b&w. *sd.* (disc) 5 min. • The Ko-Ko Kommunity Chorus sings while Ko-Ko conducts and his pup dances over the lyrics, dodging the rain and lightning.

3252. In the Nicotine (*Modern Madcap*) June 1961; *p.c.:* Para Cartoons; *dir:* Seymour Kneitel; *story:* Carl Meyer, Jack Mercer; *anim:* Irving Spector, Sam Stimson; *sets:* Robert Little; *voices:* Eddie Lawrence, Corrinne Orr; *mus:* Winston Sharples; *ph:* Leonard McCormick; *prod mgr:* Abe Goodman; *col:* Tech. *sd:* RCA. 6 min. • A disgruntled wife sends Charlie Butts, her chain-smoking husband, to a sanitarium to cure him of his smoking habit.

3253. In the Park (*Tom & Jerry*) 26 May 1933; *p.c.:* Van Beuren for RKO; *dir:* Frank Sherman, George Rufle; *mus:* Gene Rodemich; b&w. *sd:* RCA. 8 min. • No story available.

3254. In the Pink (*Pink Panther*) 18 May 1967; *p.c.:* Mirisch/Geoffrey/DFE for UA; *dir:* Hawley Pratt; *story:* John W. Dunn; *anim:* Manny Perez, Norm McCabe, Don Williams, Manny Gould, Warren Batchelder, Art Leonardi; *lay:* Dick Ung; *back:* Peter Alvarado; *ed:* Lee Gunther; *mus:* Walter Greene; *theme tune:* Henry Mancini; *prod sup:* Harry Love, Bill Or-

cutt; *col:* DeLuxe. *sd:* RCA. 6 min. • The Panther thinks he'll get in trim by visiting a gym.

3255. In the Pink of the Night (*Pink Panther*) 18 May 1969; *p.c.:* Mirisch/Geoffrey/DFE for UA; *dir:* Art Davis; *story:* Lee Mishkin; *anim:* Warren Batchelder, Don Williams, Manny Gould, Herman Cohen; *lay:* Dick Ung; *back:* Tom O'Loughlin; *ed:* Lee Gunther; *mus:* Walter Greene; *theme tune:* Henry Mancini; *ph:* John Burton Jr.; *prod sup:* Jim Foss, Harry Love; *col:* DeLuxe. *sd:* RCA. 6 min. • A stubborn cuckoo clock keeps the Panther from his sleep.

3256. In the Rough (*Aesop's Film Fable*) 6 Feb. 1927; *p.c.:* Fables Pictures Inc for Pathé; *dir:* Paul Terry; b&w. sil. 10 min. • The mice disrupt Al Falfa's golf game so that he buys an explosive golf ball with which he accidentally destroys his own house.

3257. In the Shade of the Old Apple Sauce (*Talkartoon*) 16 Oct. 1931; *p.c.:* The Fleischer Studio for Para; *prod:* Max Fleischer; *dir:* Dave Fleischer; *mus:* Art Turkisher; b&w. *sd:* WE. 7 min. • No story available.

3258. In the Shade of the Old Apple Tree (*Screen Songs*) 18 Jan. 1930; *p.c.:* the Fleischer Studio for Para; *prod:* Max Fleischer; *dir:* Dave Fleischer; *mus:* Art Turkisher; *song:* Egbert Van Altyne, Harry H. Williams; b&w. *sd:* WE (disc). 8 min. • During the factory lunch-break, a bear serenades his lady love. A falling apple provides the bouncing ball for the sing-along.

3259. In Vaudeville (*Aesop's Film Fable*) 14 Nov. 1926; *p.c.:* Fables Pictures Inc for Pathé; *dir:* Paul Terry; b&w. sil. 5 min. • A romance blossoms between the animal performers on stage.

3260. In Venice (*Paul Terry-Toon*) 15 Dec 1933; *p.c.:* Moser & Terry for Educational/Fox; *dir:* Frank Moser, Paul Terry; *mus:* Philip A. Scheib; b&w. *sd:* WE. 5 min. • Will Rogers welcomes the arrival of Balboa and a girl is dragged underwater by a fish. Her boyfriend races to save her.

3261. The Incredible Mr. Limpet Mar. 1964; *p.c.:* WB; *prod:* John C. Rose; *anim sup:* Vladimir Tytla; *asso dir:* Gerry Chiniquy, Hawley Pratt; *seq dir:* Robert McKimson; story by Joe de Mineo; *cartoon story:* John Dunn; *des:* Hawley Pratt, Maurice Noble; *back:* Don Peters; *voices:* Henry Limpet: Don Knotts; Crusty: Paul Frees; Lady Fish: Elizabeth MacRae; *mus:* Frank Perkins, Carl Brandt; *songs:* Sammy Fain, Harold Adamson; l/a dir: Arthur Lubin; *col:* Tech. *sd:* RCA. 99 min. l/a/anim. • Live-action feature film starring Don Knotts. Henry Limpet gets his wish to become a fish when he accidentally falls in the ocean.

3262. Independence Day 3 July 1996; *p.c.:* Fox; *cg unit: anim sup:* Hartmut Engel; *anim art:* Kirk Cadrette, Steffan Hermann, Benedikt Niemann, Jurgen "J.R" Schopper, Stephane Couture, Arthur Jeppe, Carolin Quis, Steffen M. Wild; *cg anim:* Daniel Kramer, Carl Hooper, Toan-Vinh Le, Pete Shinners, Todd Boyce; *Alien attacker sup:* Frank Bollinger; *Alien vocal fx:* Gary Hecker, Frank Welker; *col:* DeLuxe. *sd:* Dolby Stereo. 145 min. l/a. *Academy Award*. • Live-action science fiction: Aliens attack Earth. The Earthmen soon realise they can't compete with the invaders' fighting technology and have to rely on luck being on their side. Spectacular special effects of floods, ruination, etc.

3263. Indian Corn (*Woody Woodpecker*) 1972; *p.c.:* Walter Lantz prods for Univ; *dir:* Paul J. Smith; *story:* Tony Benedict; *anim:* Volus Jones, Al Coe, Tom Byrne, Joe Voght; *sets:* Nino Carbe; *voices:* Dal McKennon, Grace Stafford, Daws Butler; *mus:* Walter Greene; *prod mgr:* William E. Garity; *col:* Tech. *sd:* RCA. 5 min. • Buzz Buzzard teams up with a papoose who has been sent to capture Woody's red feathers.

3264. Indian Pudding (*Paul Terry-Toons*) 4 Apr. 1930; *p.c.:* A-C for Educational; *dir:* Frank Moser, Paul Terry; *anim:* Frank Moser, Sarka, Hugh Shields, John Terry, Paul Terry, Cy Young; *mus:* Philip A. Scheib; b&w. *sd:* WE. 6 min. • An Indian attack on the cowboys. Project was initiated at Van Beuren Studios.

3265. Indian Serenade (*Color Rhapsody*) 16 July 1937; *p.c.:* Charles Mintz prods for Colum; *story:* Sid Marcus; *anim:* Art Davis; *sets:* Phil Davis; *mus:* Joe de Nat; *prod mgr:* James Bronis; *col:* Tech. *sd:* RCA. 8 min. • A young Indian brave and a maiden have a romance while his dog gets into a scrape with a snake.

3266. Indian Whoopee (*Aesop's Sound Fables*) 7 July 1933; *p.c.:* Van Beuren for RKO; *dir:* Mannie Davis; *mus:* Gene Rodemich; b&w. *sd:* RCA. 8 min. • Cubby Bear experiences alarming adventures with a war-like gang of Indians.

3267. Indiana Jones and the Last Crusade 24 May 1989; *p.c.:* Lucasfilm for Para; *anim sup:* Wes Takahashi; *anim ph:* Charlie Clavadetscher, Eric Swenson, Bruce Walters; *anim:* Sean Turner, Chris Green; *col:* Eastman Color. *sd:* Dolby Stereo. 127 min. *l/a.* • Live-action adventure: Jones embarks on a quest to find his missing father. Animation enhances the special effects.

3268. Indiana Jones and the Temple of Doom 23 May 1984; *p.c.:* Lucasfilm for Para; *stop-motion anim:* Tom St. Amand, David Sosalla, Randy Ottenberg, Sean Casey; *anim sup:* Charles Mullen; *anim fx:* Bruce Walters, Barbara Brennan, Jack Mongovan, Ellen Lichtwardt, Rebecca Petrulli, Sean Turner, Suki Stern; *col:* DeLuxe. *sd. l/a.* • Live-action adventure: Jones (Harrison Ford) finds himself stranded in an Indian village and is asked to find the Sacred Stone whose theft has doomed the community to starvation and despair. Animation helps improve the special effects.

3269. Indoor Sports 1918; *p.c.:* Bray prods for IFS; *anim:* William Nolan, Walter Lantz; b&w. *sil.* • Based on "Tad" Dorgan's newspaper cartoons

3270. Inferior Decorator *(Donald Duck)* 27 Aug. 1947; *p.c.:* Walt Disney prods for RKO; *dir:* Jack Hannah; *asst dir:* Bee Selck; *story:* Lee Morehouse, Bob Moore; *anim:* Bill Justice, Volus Jones, Ray Patin, Paul Allen, Ted Bonnicksen, Ted Berman; *fx:* Jack Boyd, Dan MacManus; *lay:* Yale Gracey; *back:* Thelma Witmer; *voices:* Clarence Nash, James MacDonald; *mus:* Oliver Wallace; *col:* Tech. *sd:* RCA. 6 min. • Donald's flowered wallpaper attracts a bee. Don torments the creature until he is in a predicament the bee can take advantage of.

3271. Inferior Decorator *(Swifty & Shorty)* Mar. 1965; *p.c.:* Para Cartoons; *dir/story:* Howard Post; *anim:* Wm. B. Pattengill; *sets:* Robert Little; *voices:* Eddie Lawrence; *mus:* Winston Sharples; *ph:* Leonard McCormick; *prod mgr:* Abe Goodman; *col:* Tech. *sd:* RCA. 6 min. • Swifty tricks Shorty into buying him a castle.

3272. Injun Trouble *(Looney Tunes)* 21 May 1938; *p.c.:* Leon Schlesinger prods for WB; *dir:* Robert Clampett; *anim:* Charles Jones, I. Ellis; *sets:* Elmer Plummer; *ed:* Tregoweth E. Brown; *voices:* Mel Blanc, Billy Bletcher; *mus:* Carl W. Stalling; *prod sup:* Henry Binder, Raymond G. Katz; b&w. *sd:* Vit. 7 min. Remade in Tech as *Wagon Heels.* • A wagon train invades Injun Joe's territory and Indian Scout Porky soon discovers his weakness.

3273. Injun Trouble *(Merrie Melodies)* 1969; *p.c.:* W/7A; *dir:* Bob McKimson; *story:* Cal Howard; *anim:* Ted Bonnicksen, La Verne Harding, Jim Davis, Ed Solomon; *lay:* Bob Givens, Jaime Diaz; *back:* Bob McIntosh; *ed:* Hal Geer, Don Douglas; *voices:* Larry Storch; *mus:* William Lava; *prod:* Bill L. Hendricks; *col:* Tech. *sd:* Vit. 5 min. • Cool Cat is involved with spot-gags featuring Indians and a few cowboys.

3274. Injun Trouble *(Mighty Mouse)* June 1951; *p.c.:* TT for Fox; *dir:* Eddie Donnelly; *story/voice:* Tom Morrison; *anim:* Jim Tyer; *mus:* Philip A. Scheib; *ph:* Douglas Moye; *col:* Tech. *sd:* RCA. 6 min. • Mighty Mouse saves an old prospector from an Indian attack.

3275. Inki and the Lion *(Merrie Melodies)* 19 July 1941; *p.c.:* Leon Schlesinger prods for WB; *dir:* Charles M. Jones; *story:* Rich Hogan; *anim:* Philip Monroe; *ed:* Treg Brown; *character des:* Charles Thorson; *lay:* Robert Givens; *back:* Eugene Fleury; *mus:* Carl W. Stalling; *ph:* John W. Burton; *prod sup:* Henry Binder, Raymond G. Katz; *col:* Tech. *sd:* Vit. 7 min. • Inki joins forces with the minah bird against a lion that's stalking him.

3276. Inki and the Minah Bird *(Merrie Melodies)* 13 Nov. 1943; *p.c.:* Leon Schlesinger prods for WB; *dir:* Charles M. Jones; *story:* Ted Pierce; *anim:* Robert Cannon, James Culhane; *character des:* James Culhane; *lay:* Art Heinemann; *back:* Eugene Fleury; *ed:* Tregoweth E. Brown; *voice:* Ted Pierce; *mus:* Carl W. Stalling; *ph:* John W. Burton; *prod sup:* Henry Binder, Raymond G. Katz; *col:* Tech. *sd:* Vit. 7 min. • Inki is hunting food when he encounters a lion with a similar mission. He soon joins forces with the minah bird to rid themselves of the troublesome lion.

3277. Inki at the Circus *(Merrie Melodies)* 21 June 1947; *p.c.:* WB; *dir:* Charles M. Jones; *story:* Michael Maltese; *anim:* Ken Harris, Phil Monroe, Lloyd Vaughan, Ben Washam; *sets:* Robert Gribbroek; *ed:* Treg Brown; *mus:* Carl Stalling; *prod mgr:* John W. Burton; *prod:* Edward Selzer; *col:* Tech. *sd:* Vit. 7 min. • While in the captivity of a circus, a dog fancies the bone through Inki's hair and tries to bury it.

3278. Inklings Nov. 1927/1928; *p.c.:* Inkwell Studio for Red Seal; *anim:* Max Fleischer; b&w. *sil.* • Untitled series of eighteen featuring all types of animation. The artist draws a homely man and woman. He performs a "face to face uplift" by removing superfluous bits from the man's face and applies them to the female, resulting in two good-looking people. Then "The Farmer in the Dell," a representation of the famous song done in silhouette. Made in 1924/1925 but not released until two years later.

3279. Innerspace 1 July 1987; *p.c.:* Amblin Entertainment for WB; *Bugs Bunny anim:* Chuck Jones; *ILM: fx anim:* Gordon Baker, Chuck Eyler, Gordon Clark; *anim ph:* John Knoll; *col:* Tech. *sd:* Dolby Stereo. 120 min. *l/a.* • Live-action comedy about a test pilot who is miniaturized and injected into the bloodstream of a hypochondriac supermarket clerk. Bugs Bunny makes a cameo appearance.

3280. Innertube Antics *(MGM Cartoon)* 22 Jan. 1944; *p.c.:* MGM; *dir:* George Gordon; *anim:* Ed Barge, Arnold Gillespie, Michael Lah; *ed:* Fred MacAlpin; *mus:* Scott Bradley; *ph:* Gene Moore; *prod:* Fred Quimby. *col:* Tech. *sd:* WE. 7 min. • Doc Donkey is collecting rubber for the war effort and comes across a buried innertube that won't relinquish itself.

3281. The Inquisit Visit *(Modern Madcap)* July 1961; *p.c.:* Para Cartoons; *dir:* Seymour Kneitel; *story:* Irving Spector; *anim:* Irving Spector, Jerry Dvorak; *sets:* Robert Little; *mus:* Winston Sharples; *ph:* Leonard McCormick; *prod mgr:* Abe Goodman; *col:* Tech. *sd:* RCA. 6 min. • TV interviewer Charles Huntington interviews socialite Gaby Lament in her sixteen-room bungalow. Her present husband becomes jealous and throws Huntington and the crew out. They continue filming through exterior windows. Gaby is showing them her trophy room with replicas of her sixteen ex-husbands mounted on the wall when her present husband sees the camera crew off with a shotgun.

3282. Insect to Injury *(Popeye)* 10 Aug. 1956; *p.c.:* Famous for Para; *dir:* Dave Tendlar; *story:* I. Klein; *anim:* Morey Reden, Thomas Moore; *sets:* Anton Loeb; *voice:* Jack Mercer; *mus:* Winston Sharples; *ph:* Leonard McCormick; *prod mgr:* Seymour Shultz; *col:* Tech. *sd:* RCA. 6 min. • Popeye's newly-built house is invaded by termites.

3283. Inside Cackle Corners *(Fun & Facts About America)* 10 Nov. 1951; *p.c.:* John Sutherland prods for Harding College/MGM; *prod/dir:* John Sutherland; *voices:* Herburt Vigran, Frank Nelson; *col. sd.* 9 min. • Pop Webfoot, a struggling feathered cobbler, finds out how to produce more and better goods at a lower cost.

3284. Inspector Gadget 23 July 1999; *p.c.:* Walt Disney Pictures/Caravan Pictures for BVI; *anim sup:* Chris Bailey; *anim sup:* Rob Dressel; *lead anim:* Steven F. Yamamoto; *anim TD:* Caleb Owens; *anim:* Kevin K. Lee, David Wainstain; *"Gadgetmobile" anim sup:* Matthew O'Callaghan; *facial anim set-up:* Patrick Taylor; *facial anim:* Megan McBurney, Teresa Williams, Bill Campbell, Lino Di Salvo, Jason McDade; *fx anim:* Brian Lutge, Bruce Wright; *col:* Tech. *sd:* Dolby digital/SDDS/Digital dts Sound. 78 min. *l/a.* • Live-action comedy: When a laboratory guard is critically injured, an advanced robotic scientist fuses his broken limbs with technology to create "Inspector Gadget" ... a robot equipped with various crimefighting gizmos and a "Gadgetmobile," a talking self-driving car.

3285. Insultin' the Sultan *(Willie Whopper)* 24 Feb. 1934; *p.c.:* Celebrity prods for MGM; *prod/dir:* Ub Iwerks; *anim:* Grim Natwick, Berny Wolf; *voice:* Jane Withers; *mus:* Art Turkisher; b&w. *sd:* PCP. 6 min. • While in Arabia, Willie's girl, Mary, is sold to a Sheik's harem. Willie rushes to the rescue and a fight ensues! Caricature of Gandhi.

3286. Intermission 1967; *p.c.:* Pelican Films; *dir/des:* Jo Anne Mitchell; *anim:* Jerry Dvorak; *back:* Linda Shalack; *ed:* Norman Goldstein; *col:* East. *sd.* 5 min. • Filigree designs with rainbow backgrounds made for cinema intermissions.

3287. International News 1919/1920; *p.c.:* IFS; b&w. *sil.* • Untraced series of animated comics attached to newsreel. Featuring the works of Hal Coffman, "Tad" Dorgan, Winsor McCay, Harry Murphy, F. Opper and T.E. Powers.

3288. International Newsreel 1921/1922; *p.c.:* IFS for Univ; b&w. *sil.* • Follow-on from *International News.* Featuring the work of Hearst Newspapers artists: Hal Coffman, "Tad" Dorgan, George Herriman, Harry Hershfield, Walter Hoban, H.H. Knerr, Jean Knott, Winsor McCay,

George McManus, Tom McNamara, Harry Murphy, F. Opper, Tom Powers, James Swinnerton.

3289. International Woodpecker (*Woody Woodpecker*) 1 July 1957; *p.c.:* Walter Lantz prods for Univ; *dir:* Paul J. Smith; *story:* Dick Kinney; *anim:* Robert Bentley, Les Kline; *sets:* Art Landy, Raymond Jacobs; *voices:* Daws Butler, June Foray, Grace Stafford; *mus:* Clarence Wheeler; *prod mgr:* William E. Garity; *col:* Tech. *sd:* RCA. 6 min. • Woody tells Splinter and Knothead some tall tales about their ancestors.

3290. The Interview 1961; *p.c.:* Ernest Pintoff prods for Colum; *prod/dir:* Ernest Pintoff; *anim:* Vinnie Bell, Al Chiarito; *voices:* Henry Jacobs, Woodrow Leafer (Ralph J. Gleason, Lenny Bruce); *mus:* The Stan Getz Quintet; *ph:* Robert Heath; *prod mgr:* Arnold Stone; *col:* East. *sd.* 5 min. • "Shorty" Petterson, a jazz horn player, is interviewed by a "square" interviewer during a recording session.

3291. Into Your Dance (*Merrie Melodies*) 6 Sept. 1935; *p.c.:* Leon Schlesinger prods for WB; *dir:* Isadore Freleng; *anim:* Cal Dalton, Ben Clopton, Robert Clampett; *voices:* Joe Dougherty, Ted Pierce; *mus:* Norman Spencer; *song:* Harry Warren, Al Dubin; *prod sup:* Henry Binder, Raymond G. Katz; *col:* Tech-2. *sd:* Vit. 7 min. • Captain Benny's Showboat has an amateur contest.

3292. Introducing Charlie Chaplin (*Canimated Nooz Pictorial*) 3 Mar. 1915; *p.c.:* Wallace A. Carlson Cartoons for Essanay; *dir:* Wallace A. Carlson; b&w. sil. • Animated item in newsreel. No further information.

3293. The Intruders (*Heckle & Jeckle*) 9 May 1947; *p.c.:* TT for Fox; *dir:* Eddie Donnelly; *story:* John Foster; *sets:* Art Bartsch; *voices:* Tom Morrison, Douglas Moye; *mus:* Philip A. Scheib; *ph:* Douglas Moye; *col:* Tech. *sd:* RCA. 7 min. • The magpies invade a private mansion.

3294. Invasion of Norway (*War Graphs*) June 1940; *p.c.:* Cartoon Films Ltd; *prod:* Lawson Haris; *dir:* Paul Fennell; *ed:* Almon Teeter; *voice:* Thomas Freebain-Smith; *ph:* Richard M. Ising; *sd.* 9½ min. • Propaganda cartoon using limited animation to show the German conquest of Norway in April 1940.

3295. Invention Convention (*Kartune*) 19 June 1953; *p.c.:* Famous for Para; *dir:* I. Sparber; *story:* I. Klein; *anim:* Al Eugster, Wm. B. Pattengill; *sets:* Anton Loeb; *voices:* Michael Fitzmaurice, Jack Mercer; *mus:* Winston Sharples; *song:* Leo Friedman; *ph:* Leonard McCormick; *prod mgr:* Seymour Shultz; *col:* Tech. *sd:* RCA. 7 min. • All the latest inventions are displayed.

3296. Invisible Ink (*Out of the Inkwell*) 3 Dec. 1921; *p.c.:* Inkwell Studios for Winkler; *prod/l/a:* Max Fleischer; *dir:* Dave Fleischer; b&w. sil. 7 min. *l/a/anim.* • Max has fun with Ko-Ko by drawing things that disappear with invisible ink.

3297. The Invisible Mouse (*Tom & Jerry*) 27 Sept. 1947; *p.c.:* MGM; *dir:* William Hanna, Joseph Barbera; *anim:* Ed Barge, Richard Bickenbach, Don Patterson, Irven Spence; *ed:* Fred MacAlpin; *mus:* Scott Bradley; *ph:* Jack Stevens; *prod:* Fred Quimby; *col:* Tech. *sd:* WE. 7 min. • Jerry is immersed in invisible ink and disappears, then has fun with Tom.

3298. Invitation to the Dance 1956; *p.c.:* MGM; *Sinbad the Sailor: seq dir:* William Hanna, Joseph Barbera; *anim:* Irven Spence, Michael Lah; *character des:* Gene Hazelton; *mus:* based on music by Nikolai Rimsky-Korsakov; *adapt:* Roger Edens; *conducted by* Johnny Green; *orch:* Conrad Salinger; *col:* Tech. *sd:* WE. 17 min. *l/a/anim.* • Live-action segmented feature directed by and starring Gene Kelly. Kelly as "Sinbad" buys a magic lamp and is transported by a genie to a harem where his efforts to pursue Scheherazade (Carol Haney) are prevented by two guards.

3299. Ireland or Bust (*Paul Terry-Toons*) 25 Dec. 1932; *p.c.:* Moser & Terry for Educational/Fox; *dir:* Frank Moser, Paul Terry; *mus:* Philip A. Scheib; b&w. *sd:* WE. 6 min. • A cat and mouse parachute into the Arctic regions to rescue a girl tied to a sawmill.

3300. Irish Stew (*Paul Terry-Toons*) 5 Oct. 1930; *p.c.:* A-C for Educational/Fox; *dir:* Frank Moser, Paul Terry; *mus:* Philip A. Scheib; b&w. *sd:* WE. 6 min. • No story available.

3301. Irish Sweepstakes (*Paul Terry-Toons*) 27 July 1934; *p.c.:* Moser & Terry for Educational/Fox; *dir:* Frank Moser, Paul Terry; *mus:* Philip A. Scheib. b&w. *sd:* WE. 6 min. • No story available.

3302. The Iron Giant 17 Dec. 1999; *p.c.:* WB; *dir:* Brad Bird; *prod:* Allison Abbate, Des McAnuff; *asso prod:* John Walker; *scr:* Tim McCanlies; *adapt:* Brad Bird; based on the book *The Iron Man* by Ted Hughes; *storyboard:* Dean Wellins, Mark Andrews, Kevin O'Brien, Viki Anderson, Steven Markowski, Piet Kroon, Fergal Reilly, Teddy Newton, Stephen G. Lumley, Harry A. Sabin Jr., Moroni, Ron Hughart, Brian Kindregan; *anim:* Tony Fucile, Richard Bazley, Bob Davies, Stephan Franck, Gregory S.E. Manwaring, Steven Markowski, Mike Nguyen, Christopher Sauvé, Wendy Perdue, Dean Wellins, Richard Baneham, Adam Burke, Jennifer Cardon, Mike Chavez, Ricardo Curtis, Ruth Daly, Marcelo Fernandes de Moura, Jeff Etter, Lauren Faust, Ralph Fernan, Steve Garcia, Lennie K. Graves, Russell Hall, Adam Henry, Ken Hettig, Kevin Johnson, Ben Jones, Ernest Keen, Jae H. Kim, Holger Leihe, Lane Lueras, Craig R. Maras, Scott T. Petersen, Andrew Schmidt, Sean Springer, Mike Swofford, Derek Thompson, Craig Valde, Jim van der Keyl, Roger Vizard, Alex Williams, Mark A. Williams, John D. Williamson, Joanne Coughlin, Devin Crane, Jean Cullen de Moura, Phil Langone, Brian Larsen, Boowon Lee, Helen HeeSeung Lee, Michael Mullen, Shane Prigmore, Eddie Ross, Andy Schuhler, Michael Shannon, Kyung S. Shin, Peter Sohn, Stephen Steinbach, Michael Venturmi; *cgi anim:* Richard Baneham, Grace Blanco, Brad Booker, Andrew D. Brownlow, Yarrow Cheney, Minhee Choe, Stéphane Cros, Adam Dotson, Bruce Edwards, Mark R.R. Farquhar, Ron Hughart, Yair Kantor, Les Major, Mike Murphy, Susan L. Oslin, Glenn Storm, Vincent Truitner; *fx anim:* John Bermudes, Jesse M. Cosio, John Dillon, Rick Echevarria, Marc Ellis, Michael Gagné, Earl A. Hibbert, Brett Hisey, John MacFarlane, Kevin M. O'Neil, Volker Pajatsch, David Pritchard, Gary Sole, Ryan Woodward; *visual development/character des:* Tony Fucile, Ray Aragon, Victor J. Haboush, Lou Romano, Laura L. Corsiglia, Dominique R. Louis, Teddy Newton; *clean-up:* Eric J. Abjornson, Nathalie Gavet, Karenia Kaminski, Marty Korth, June Myung Nam, Don Parmele, Doris A. Plough, Robert Tyler, Paul Bauman, Andrew Beall, James Burks, Yelena Geodakyan, Wantana Martinelli, Domingo C. Rivera Jr., Karen Rosenfield, Kyung S. Shin, Calvin Suggs, Hamish MacKinnon, Michael Venturini, Tran Vu; *digital fx art:* Miae Kim Ausbrooks, Rick Echevarria, Kevin Oakley, Ryan Woodward, Andrew Jimenez; *anim check:* Susan Burke, Daryl Carstensen, Charlotte Clark-Pitts, Katie Gray, Gillian Higgins, Louie C. Jhocson, Pam Kleyman, Madel Flancia Manhit, Penelope G. Sevier, Carol Li-Chuan Yao, Nick Yates; *workbook des:* Mark Andrews, Stephen G. Lumley, Conor Kavanagh, Francis Lang, Emil Mitev, Felipe Morell, Ronald M. Roesch, Lisa Souza, Audrey Stedman, Bill Thyen, Michael Tracy, Craig Voigt, Jennifer Yuan; *bluesketch art:* Mercedes J. Sichon, Irina Goosby; *lay:* James P. Alles, Teresa Coffey-Wellins, Frederick J. Gardner III, Louis Gonzales, Karen Hamrock; *back:* Christopher Brock, Ruben Chavez, William Dely, Dennis Durrell, James Finn, Greg Gibbons, Annie Guenther, Joel Parod, Craig Robertson, Jonathan Salt, Nadia Vurbenova, Wei M. Zhao; *digital back:* Craig Kelly; *technical dir:* Brett Achorn, Daniel Bunn, Steven Burch, Koija Erman, Babak Forutanpour, Brian Gardner, Corey Hall, Roger Huynh, Hiroki Itokazu, Darren D. Kiner, Andy King, Michael Leung, Sébastien Linage, Mike Meckler, Lyle S. Nojima, Brian Schindler, Teddy T. Yang; *Iron Giant des:* Joe Johnson; Mark Whiting, Hiroki Itoki Itokazu, Teddy T. Yang, Steven Markowski, Michael Bay; *ed:* Darren T. Holmes; *prod des:* Mark Whiting; *artistic co-ord:* Scott F. Johnson; *art dir:* Alan Bodner; *character sculptor:* Carla Larissa Fallberg; *dpt. heads: story:* Jeffrey Lynch; *cg:* Tad Gielow; *lay/workbook:* William H. Frake III; *back:* Dennis Venizelos; *clean-up:* Lureline Kohler; *fx:* Allen Foster; *scene plan:* Steven Wilzback; *anim check: 2d/3d:* Myoung Smith; *ACME:* Rhonda L. Hicks; *ACME sup: col models:* Tania Mitman Burton; *scan:* Irene M. Gringeri; *i&p:* Sarah-Jane King; *final check:* Dennis Bonnell; *scene plan:* Kim Patterson; *post-prod sup:* Jeannine Berger; *ACME Digital specialists:* Will Bilton, James Hathcock, Freddie Vaziri; *animatic prod specialists:* Andrew Jimenez, Dale A. Smith; *voices: Annie Hughes:* Jennifer Aniston; *Dean McCoppin:* Harry Connick Jr.; *the Iron Giant:* Vin Diesel; *Foreman Marv Loach/Floyd Turbeaux:* James Gammon; *Mrs. Tensedge:* Cloris Leachman; *Kent Mansley:* Christopher McDonald; *General Rogard:* John Mahoney; *Hogarth Hughes:* Eli Marienthal; *Earl Stutz:* M. Emmet Walsh; *also:* Jack Angel, Robert Bergen, Mary Kay Bergen, Michael Bird, Devon Borisoff, Rodger Bumpass, Robert Clotworthy, Jennifer Darling, Zack Eginton, Paul Eiding, Bill Farmer, Charles Howerton, Ollie Johnston, Sherry Lynn, Mickie T. McGowan, Ryan O'Donohue, Phil Proctor, Frank Thomas, Patti Tippo, Brian Tochi; *mus:* Michael Kamen; *performed by* the Czech Philharmonic Orchestra; *electronic mus score programmers:* James Brett, Michael Price; *orch:* Michael Kamen, Robert Elhai, Blake Neely; *mus score* *prod:* Gohl/McLaughlin, Michael Kamen, Christopher Brooks; *mus ed:* Christopher Brooks; *mus score recl mix:* Steve McLaughlin; *mus consultants:* James Austin, John "Juke" Logan; *scene plan:* Gina Bradley, George (Bingo) Ferguson, James Keefer, Dan C. Larsen, Karen Hansen; *col stylists:* Constance R. Allen, Anthony C. Clanciolo Jr., Sylvia Marika Filcak, Tanya Moreau-Smith, Catherine O'Leary, Devon P. Oddone, Cathy Wainess-Walters; *color modellists:* Olga Tarin Duff, Dawn Knight, Helga Beatrix, Vanden Berge; *technology: sup:* Steve Y. Chen, Lem Davis, Emmanuel C. Francisco, Bill Perkins, Arjun Ramamurthy, David F. Wolf; *engineers:* George Aluzzi, Cathy E. Blanco, Keith Kobata, José F. Lopez, Darryl McIntosh, Brian Peterson, Leonard J. Reder, Alan L. Stephenson, Aaron L. Thompson, Arnold M. Yee, Cheng-Jui, Zizi Zhao; *operations:* Lori A. Arntzen, Kevin D. Howard, Rusty Howes, Hector A. Martinez, Alexis Pierre, Usha Ramcharitar, Paul Skidmore, Gene Takahashi; *ph:* Christine Beck, Mark Dinicola; *sd des:* Randy Thom, Troy Porter, Doc Kane; *prod sd:* Gregory M. Gerlich, Gregory H. Watkins, Kevin E. Carpenter, Chad Algarin, Mark La Pointe, Dennis Leonard; *dial ed:* Curt Schulkey; *sd fx:* Beau Borders; *foley art:* Dennie Thorpe, Jana Vance, Frank "Pepé" Merel, Tony Eckert, Mary Helen Leasman; *consultant:* Ted Hughes; *titles:* Pacific Title/Mirage; *prod asso:* Sandro Maria Corsaro, Ralph Garcia, Bryan Kulik, Barry O'Donoghue; *prod mgr:* Amy Richards; *col:* Tech. *sd:* Dolby stereo/ Digital SR/dts/SDDS. 86½ min. • Nine-year-old Hogarth Hughes befriends a massive iron robot who crash-lands on earth and needs to consume metal in order to stay alive. The boy tries to get what metal the robot requires while trying to hide it from his parents.

3303. The Iron Man (*Aesop's Sound Fable*) 4 Jan. 1930; *p.c.:* Van Beuren for Pathé; *dir:* John Foster; *mus:* Gene Rodemich; b&w. *sd:* RCA. 6 min. • After a stubborn cockfight, a gnome does some tree-felling and confronts a robot.

3304. Is It Always Right to Be Right? 1970; *p.c.:* Stephen Bosustow prods/Lester A. Schoenfeld Films for Colum; *prod:* Nick Bosustow; *dir:* Lee Mishkin; *story:* Warren H. Schmidt Ph.D; *anim:* Lee Mishkin, Dave Brain; *des:* Corny Cole; *fx:* Lin Dunn, Film Effects of Hollywood; *ed:* Tee Bosustow; *voice:* Orson Welles; *mus:* Ken Heller; *col:* Tech. *sd.* 10 min. *l/a/anim. Academy Award.* • The world's population grows further apart when they can't agree on anything.

3305. Is My Palm Read? (*Betty Boop*) 17 Feb. 1933; *p.c.:* The Fleischer Studio for Para; *prod:* Max Fleischer; *dir:* Dave Fleischer; *anim:* David Tendlar, William Henning; *voice:* Mae Questel; *mus:* Art Turkisher; b&w. *sd:* WE. 7 min. • A fortune-teller sees Betty first as a naked baby in a bath then going on a sea voyage, being shipwrecked and chased by ghosts on a desert island.

3306. Is There a Doctor in the Mouse? (*Tom & Jerry*) 1964; *p.c.:* SIB Tower 12 for MGM; *prod/dir:* Chuck Jones; *asst dir:* Maurice Noble; *story:* Michael Maltese, Chuck Jones; *anim:* Ben Washam, Ken Harris, Don Towsley, Tom Ray, Dick Thompson; *back:* Robert Gribbroek; *voices:* Mel Blanc; *mus:* Eugene Poddany; *prod mgr:* Les Goldman; *col:* Metro. *sd:* WE. 7 min. • Jerry mixes a potion that makes him run faster than the speed of light.

3307. The Island Fling (*Popeye*) 27 Dec. 1946; *p.c.:* Famous for Para; *dir:* Bill Tytla; *story:* Woody Gelman, Larry Riley; *anim:* John Gentilella, George Germanetti; *sets:* Robert Connavale; *voices:* Jackson Beck, Mae Questel, Harry F. Welch, Sid Raymond; *mus:* Winston Sharples; ph; Leonard McCormick; *prod mgr:* Sam Buchwald; *col:* Tech. *sd:* RCA. 7 min. • Castaways Popeye and Olive arrive on Robinson Crusoe's island. Crusoe wants Olive for himself but first has to get rid of Popeye.

3308. Isle of Caprice (*Ant & Aardvark*) 18 Dec. 1969; *p.c.:* Mirisch/ DFE for UA; *dir:* Gerry Chiniquy; *story:* David DeTiege; *anim:* Manny Perez, Don Williams, Bob Bentley, Bob Taylor, Manny Gould; *lay:* Dick Ung; *back:* Richard Thomas; *ed:* Lee Gunther; *voices:* John Byner; *mus:* Doug Goodwin, Pete Candoli, Billy Byers, Jimmy Rowles, Tommy Tedesco, Ray Brown, Shelly Manne; *prod sup:* Jim Foss, Harry Love; *col:* DeLuxe. *sd:* RCA. 6 min. • The Aardvark is marooned on an island and tries to reach an ant-infested island without becoming shark bait.

3309. Isle of Jazz (*Gross Exagerations*) Sept. 1931; *p.c.:* Ideal Pictures; *dir:* Milt Gross; *story:* Tom Johnson; *dialogue:* Frank Dollan; b&w. *sd.* 6 min. • A satire on travelogues.

3310. The Isle of Pingo Pongo (*Merrie Melodies*) 28 May 1938; *p.c.:* Leon Schlesinger prods for WB; *dir:* Fred Avery; *story:* George Manuell, Robert Clampett; *anim:* Irven Spence; *ed:* Tregoweth E. Brown; *voices:* Gil Warren, The Basin Street Boys, Sons of the Pioneers, Mel Blanc, Fred Avery; *mus:* Carl W. Stalling; *prod sup:* Henry Binder, Raymond G. Katz; *col:* Tech. *sd:* Vit. 7 min. • A burlesque on travelogues with Egghead wandering through the movie wanting to know when he can terminate the film by shooting the sun.

3311. It Happened to Crusoe (*Fable*) 14 Mar. 1941; *p.c.:* Colum: *story:* Allen Rose; *anim:* Louie H. Lilly; *sets:* Clark Watson; *ed:* Edward Moore; *voices:* Jack Lescoulie, Danny Webb, Mel Blanc; *mus:* Joe de Nat; *ph:* Otto Reimer; *prod mgr:* George Winkler; b&w. *sd:* RCA. 6 min. • A Jack Benny prototype lives in the jungle with his vegetarian manservant, Winchester, whose cannibal chief father sends them off on a tiger hunt.

3312. It Must Be Love (*Terry-Toon*) 5 Apr. 1940; *p.c.:* TT for Fox; *dir:* Connie Rasinski; *story:* John Foster; *mus:* Philip A. Scheib; b&w. *sd:* RCA. 6 min. • No story available.

3313. The Itch (*Modern Madcap*) May 1965; *p.c.:* Para Cartoons; *dir:* Howard Post; *story:* Tony Peters; *anim:* Martin Taras; *sets:* Robert Little; *voices:* Hermione Gingold, Bob MacFadden; *mus:* Winston Sharples; *ph:* Leonard McCormick; *prod mgr:* Abe Goodman; *col:* Tech. *sd:* RCA. 6 min. • An ordinary Englishman suddenly grows wings and flys around London before he is shot down. Totally alien in style to any other Paramount cartoon.

3314. An Itch in Time (*Merrie Melodies*) 4 Dec. 1943; *p.c.:* Leon Schlesinger prods for WB; *dir:* Robert Clampett; *story/back:* Michael Sasanoff; *anim:* Rod Scribner; *lay:* Thomas McKimson; *ed:* Treg Brown; *voices:* Arthur Q. Bryan, Sara Berner, Mel Blanc, Ted Pierce; *mus:* Carl W. Stalling; *prod sup:* Henry Binder, Raymond G. Katz; *col:* Tech. *sd:* Vit. 7 min. • Elmer threatens his dog with a bath when a flea takes up residence on him.

3315. It's a Bird (*Lowell Thomas Tall Story*) 1 Feb. 1936; *p.c.:* Bowers for J.H. Hoffberg; *prod/dir/ anim:* Charles R. Bowers; *ph:* Harold L. Muller; *sd.* Clarence Wall; *l/a:* Lowell Thomas, Charles R. Bowers, b&w. *sd.* 17 min. *l/a/anim.* aka: *The Metal Eating Bird.* • A strange bird brought from Africa that eats metal. Live-action comedy with stop-frame animation.

3316. It's a Grand Old Nag (*Charlie Horse*) 20 Dec. 1947; *p.c.:* Bob Clampett prods for Republic; *prod/dir:* "Kilroy" (Bob Clampett); *anim sup:* Don Towsley; *anim:* Paul J. Smith, Edward Love; *sets:* Curt Perkins; *voices:* Stan Freberg, Dave Barry; *mus:* Jeff Alexander; *song:* James Palmer; *ph:* Sid Glenar; *col:* Tru. *sd:* RCA. 8 min. • A plough horse is picked by a film director to appear opposite Hay-de la Mare in a movie. He soon finds out he's to be the hero's stand-in. Intended as a series but never materialized as such.

3317. It's a Greek Life (*Rainbow Parade*) 2 Aug. 1936; *p.c.:* Van Beuren for RKO; *dir:* Burt Gillett, Dan Gordon; *mus:* Winston Sharples; *col:* Tech. *sd:* RCA. 7 min. • A Grecian centaur cobbler flies away in Mercury's winged shoes.

3318. It's a Hap-Hap-Happy Day (*Gabby*) 15 Aug. 1941; *p.c.:* The Fleischer Studio for Para; *prod:* Max Fleischer; *dir:* Dave Fleischer; *story:* Bob Wickersham; *anim:* Orestes Calpini, Irving Spector; *ed:* Kitty Pfister; *voices:* Pinto Colvig, Jack Mercer; *mus:* Sammy Timberg; *prod sup:* Sam Buchwald, Isidore Sparber; *col:* Tech. *sd:* WE. 8 min. • Gabby disrupts the mayor's camping holiday by insisting on accompanying him.

3319. It's a Living (*Dinky*) Feb. 1958; *p.c.:* TT for Fox; *ex prod:* Bill Weiss; *dir sup:* Gene Deitch; *dir:* Win Hoskins; *story/sd dir:* Tommy Morrison, Larz Bourne, Bob Kuwahara; *anim:* Ed Donnelly, Mannie Davis, Jim Tyer, Al Chiarito, Johnny Gent, Larry Silverman; *lay:* Art Bartsch; *back:* Bill Hilliker; *voices:* Allen Swift; *mus:* Philip A. Scheib; *prod mgr:* Frank Schudde; *col:* Tech. *sd:* RCA. 7 min. CS. • Dinky forsakes his life as a cartoon duck for that of a TV commercial star.

3320. It's a Mad, Mad, Mad, Mad World 1963; *p.c.:* Saul Bass for UA; *titles: dir:* Saul Bass; *artists:* Bob Carlson, Hugh Childs, Bob Goe, Art Goodman, Bernie Gruver, Bror Lansing, Mary Mate, Bill Melendez, Carl Pederson, Danny Smith, Francis A. Smith, Ade Woolery; *model anim:* Willis O'Brien, Marcel Delgado; *mus:* Ernest Gold; *col:* Tech. *sd:* RCA. Cinerama live-action comedy with animated titles featuring "The World."

Veteran animator Willis O'Brien was working on model animation of characters on a fire ladder when he died during production.

3321. It's All in the Stars (*Gandy Goose*) 12 Apr. 1946; *p.c.:* TT for Fox; *dir:* Connie Rasinski; *story:* John Foster; *voices:* Arthur Kay, Thomas Morrison; *mus:* Philip A. Scheib; *col:* Tech. *sd:* RCA. 7 min. • Sourpuss dreams he frees a canary from its cage and all the animals set on him.

3322. It's an Ill Wind (*Looney Tunes*) 28 Jan. 1939; *p.c.:* Leon Schlesinger prods for WB; *dir:* Ben Hardaway, Cal Dalton; *story:* Melvin Millar; *anim:* Herman Cohen; *lay:* Griff Jay; *back:* Arthur Loomer; *ed:* Tregoweth E. Brown; *voices:* Mel Blanc, Danny Webb; *mus:* Carl W. Stalling; *ph:* John W. Burton; *prod sup:* Henry Binder, Raymond G. Katz; b&w. *sd:* Vit. 7 min. • Porky and Dizzy Duck take shelter from a storm in a warehouse where they are spooked by various things that appear in half-light.

3323. It's Easy to Remember (*Screen Songs*) 29 Nov. 1935; *p.c.:* The Fleischer Studio for Para; *prod:* Max Fleischer; *dir:* Dave Fleischer; *anim:* Thomas Johnson; *mus:* Richard Himber & His Orchestra; b&w. *sd:* WE. 6 min. • No story available.

3324. It's for the Birdies (*Noveltoon*) Nov. 1962; *p.c.:* Para Cartoons; *dir:* Seymour Kneitel; *story:* Irving Dressler; *anim:* Nick Tafuri, Danté Barbetta; *sets:* Robert Owen; *mus:* Winston Sharples; *ph:* Leonard McCormick; *prod mgr:* Abe Goodman; *col:* Tech. *sd:* RCA. 6 min. • A gopher collects golf balls when a golfer creates many difficulties, causing the gopher to shoot himself to the moon.

3325. It's for the Birds (*James Hound*) Mar. 1967; *p.c.:* TT for Fox; *dir/anim:* Ralph Bakshi; *col:* DeLuxe. *sd:* RCA. 6 min. • Diamond Jill uses ducks to smuggle watches across the border. • See: *James Hound*

3326. It's Got Me Again! (*Merrie Melodies*) 11 June 1932; *p.c.:* Hugh Harman–Rudolf Ising prods for WB; *prod:* Leon Schlesinger; *dir:* Isadore Freleng, Robert McKimson, Robert Clampett; *mus:* Frank Marsales; b&w. *sd:* Vit. 6 min. *Academy Award nomination.* • After breaking up a mouse music session, a cat corners a little mouse and the others join forces to put the feline to rout.

3327. It's Greek to Me-Ow (*Tom & Jerry*) 7 Dec. 1961; *p.c.:* Rembrandt for MGM; *prod:* William L. Snyder; *dir:* Gene Deitch; *story:* Eli Bauer; *voices:* Allen Swift; *sd fx:* Tod Dockstader; *col:* Metro. *sd:* WE. 5 min. • A Greek Tom chases a Grecian Jerry against a setting of ancient Greece. • See: *Tom and Jerry (Rembrandt Studio)*

3328. It's Hummer Time (*Looney Tunes*) 22 July 1950; *p.c.:* WB; *dir:* Robert McKimson; *story:* Warren Foster; *anim:* Rod Scribner, J.C. Melendez, Charles McKimson, Phil de Lara, John Carey; *lay:* Cornett Wood; *back:* Richard H. Thomas; *ed:* Treg Brown; *voices:* Mel Blanc; *mus:* Carl Stalling; *prod mgr:* John W. Burton; *prod:* Edward Selzer; *col:* Tech. *sd:* Vit. 7 min. • While on the trail of a hummingbird, the cat keeps running afoul of a bulldog who makes him pay dearly for his mistakes.

3329. It's Nice to Have a Mouse About the House (*Looney Tunes*) 16 Jan. 1965; *p.c.:* DFE for WB; *dir:* Friz Freleng; *asst dir:* Hawley Pratt; *story:* John Dunn; *anim:* Don Williams, Bob Matz, Norm McCabe; *lay:* Dick Ung; *back:* Tom O'Loughlin; *ed:* Lee Gunther; *voices:* Mel Blanc, Gee Gee Pearson; *mus:* Bill Lava; *col:* Tech. *sd:* Vit. 6 min. • Granny employs mouse exterminator, Daffy Duck, to get rid of Speedy Gonzales.

3330. It's Nifty to Be Thrifty (*Little Lulu*) 18 Aug. 1944; *p.c.:* Famous for Para; *dir:* Seymour Kneitel; *story:* Carl Meyer; *anim:* Orestes Calpini, Reuben Grossman, Otto Feuer, Frank Little; *sets:* Robert Little; *voices:* Cecil Roy, Carl Meyer; *mus:* Sammy Timberg; *ph:* Leonard McCormick; *prod mgr:* Sam Buchwald; *col:* Tech. *sd:* RCA. 8 min. • Lulu asks Daddy for money for candy and he encourages her to earn it by relating the story of "The Grasshopper and the Ants."

3331. It's Pink but Is It Mink? (*Pink Panther*) 30 Dec. 1975; *p.c.:* Mirisch/Geoffrey/DFE for UA; *dir:* Robert McKimson; *story:* Tom Yakutis; *anim:* Don Williams, Bob Richardson, John Gibbs, Nelson Shin; *lay:* Tony Rivera; *back:* Richard H. Thomas; *ed:* Rick Steward; *mus:* Walter Greene; *theme tune:* Henry Mancini; *ph:* Hogan-Lee Images; *prod mgr:* Lee Gunther; *col:* DeLuxe. *sd:* RCA. 5 min. • Tarzan attempts to remove Jungle Panther's pelt for a coat for Jane.

3332. It's the Cats (*Out of the Inkwell*) 1 May 1926; *p.c.:* Inkwell Studio for Red Seal; *prod:* Max Fleischer; *dir:* Dave Fleischer; b&w. *sil.* 8 min.

l/a/anim. • Ko-Ko and his dog stage a vaudeville show to an audience of (real-life) kittens. A troop of mice break up the show.

3333. It's the Natural Thing to Do (*Popeye*) 28 July 1939; *p.c.:* The Fleischer Studio for Para; *prod:* Max Fleischer; *dir:* Dave Fleischer; *anim:* Thomas Johnson, Lod Rossner; *ed:* Kitty Pfister; *voices:* Jack Mercer, Pinto Colvig, Margie Hines; *mus:* Sammy Timberg; *prod sup:* Sam Buchwald, Isidore Sparber; b&w. *sd:* WE. 6 min. • The Popeye Fan Club tell the boys to cut out the rough stuff. They do for a while but things are soon back to normal.

3334. It's Tough to Be a Bird 10 Dec. 1969; *p.c.:* Walt Disney prods for BV; *dir:* Ward Kimball; *story:* Ted Berman, Ward Kimball; *anim:* Art Stevens, Eric Larson; *lay:* Joe Hale; *ed:* Lloyd L. Richardson; *voices:* Richard Bakalyan, Ruth Buzzi; *mus:* George Bruns; *songs:* Mel Leven; *l/a:* John Emerson, Ward Kimball, Hank Schloss, Jim Swain, Walter Perkins, Anna Lord, Rolf Darbo; *col:* Tech. *sd:* RCA. 22 min. *l/a/anim. Academy Award.* • A bird relates the hardships of being feathered.

3335. I've Got Ants in My Plans (*Ant & Aardvark*) 14 May 1969; *p.c.:* Mirisch/DFE for UA; *dir:* Gerry Chiniquy; *story:* John W. Dunn; *anim:* Warren Batchelder, Don Williams, Manny Gould, Manny Perez; *lay:* Dick Ung; *back:* Tom O'Loughlin; *ed:* Lee Gunther; *voices:* John Byner; *mus:* Doug Goodwin, Pete Candoli, Billy Byers, Jimmy Rowles, Tommy Tedesco, Ray Brown, Shelly Manne; *ph:* John Burton Jr.; *prod sup:* Jim Foss, Harry Love; *col:* DeLuxe. *sd:* RCA. 6 min. • The Aardvark contends with another anteater after the same ant.

3336. I've Got Rings on My Fingers (*Screen Songs*) 17 Dec. 1929; *p.c.:* The Fleischer Studio for Para; *prod:* Max Fleischer; *dir:* Dave Fleischer; *song:* Weston, Scott, Barnes; b&w. *sd. (disc)* 6 min. • An Irish cop is dragged to a tropic island by an airplane.

3337. I've Got to Sing a Torch Song (*Merrie Melodies*) 23 Sept. 1933; *p.c.:* Leon Schlesinger prods for WB; *dir:* Tom Palmer; *anim:* Jack King; *voices:* Elmore Vincent, Ted Pierce; *mus:* Bernard B. Brown, Norman Spencer; *song:* Harry Warren, Al Dubin; b&w. *sd:* Vit. 7 min. • The radio is listened to world-wide. Caricatures of: Ben Bernie, The Boswell Sisters, James Cagney, Mae Clark, Bing Crosby, Greta Garbo, Benito Mussolini, Zasu Pitts, George Bernard Shaw, Mae West, Wheeler & Woolsey and Ed Wynn.

3338. Ja, Ja, Mein General! But Which Way to the Front? 1970; *p.c.:* WB; *titles:* Don Record; *col:* Tech. *sd:* Vit. • Titles for a Jerry Lewis vehicle about a millionaire who trains his own army to fight the Nazis.

3339. Jack and Old Mack 18 July 1956; *p.c.:* Walt Disney prods for BV; *dir:* Bill Justice; *asst dir:* George Probert; *story:* Dick Kinney, Roy Williams; *anim:* Xavier Atencio, Al Coe, Jack Parr, Bob Carlson, Bill Justice; *character des/lay:* Xavier Atencio; *back:* Eyvind Earle; *voices:* The Jud Conlon Chorus; *mus:* George Bruns; *col:* Tech. *sd:* RCA. 7 min. • Old MacDonald's jazz rendition inspires even the farm animals to play musical instruments.

3340. Jack and the Beanstalk (*ComiColor*) 23 Dec. 1933; *p.c.:* Celebrity prods; *prod:* Ub Iwerks; *dir/lay:* Jimmy Culhane, Al Eugster; *story/song:* Otto Englander; *anim:* Jimmie Culhane, Al Eugster, Grim Natwick; *mus:* Gene Denny; *col:* Ciné. *sd:* PCP. 8 min. • The first ComiColor in the series tells the story of Jack who climbs a magic beanstalk to a giant's castle in the clouds, vanquishes the villain and returns to earth with a fortune.

3341. Jack and the Beanstalk (*Talkartoon*) 21 Nov. 1931; *p.c.:* The Fleischer Studio for Para; *prod:* Max Fleischer; *dir:* Dave Fleischer; *voice:* Mae Questel, Charles Carver; *mus:* Art Turkisher; b&w. *sd:* WE. 6 min. • Bimbo climbs a giant beanstalk to rescue Betty who has been imprisoned by an ogre.

3342. Jack Frost (*ComiColor*) 30 Nov. 1934; *p.c.:* Celebrity prods; *prod/dir:* Ub Iwerks; *anim:* Grim Natwick, Al Eugster; *sets:* Grim Natwick; *mus:* Carl Stalling; *col:* Ciné. *sd:* PCP. 9 min. • When a small bear refuses to hibernate, Jack Frost shows him the folly of his ways.

3343. Jack Frost 11 Dec. 1988; *p.c.:* Azoff Entertainment/Canton Co. for WB; *special fx/anim:* ILM Visual fx; *prod:* Camille Geier; *anim sup:* Paul Griffin; *cg sup:* Gregor Lakner, Robert Marinic, Tom Rosseter; *lead anim:* Chris Armstrong; *lead matchmover:* Lanny Cermak; *modelling sup:* Stewart

Lew; *anim:* Philip Alexy, Alain Costa, David Gosman, Shawn Kelly, David Latour, Steve Lee, Martin L'Heureux, Mark Powers, Dave Sidley, Si Tran, Michaela Zabranska; *col:* Tech. *sd:* Dolby digital/dts digital/SDDS. 101 min. *l/a.* • Live-action fantasy: Young Charlie builds a snowman in the tradition of when his father was alive. The snowman then becomes a reincarnation of his late father.

3344. Jack the Giant Killer 1962; *p.c.:* Zenith Pictures for UA; *prod:* Edward Small; *anim fx:* Wah Chang, Gene Warren, Tim Barr, Jim Danforth, Tom Holland, Dave Pal, Don Sahlin; *Armatures:* Marcel Delgado, Victor Delgado; *col:* Tech. *sd.* 94 min. Fantascope. *l/a/anim.* • Costume romp hightened by a stop-motion animated sea monster.

3345. Jack-Wabbit and the Beanstalk *(Merrie Melodies)* 12 June 1943; *p.c.:* Leon Schlesinger prods for WB; *dir:* I. Freleng; *story:* Michael Maltese; *anim:* Jack Bradbury; *lay:* Owen Fitzgerald; *back:* Lenard Kester; *ed:* Treg Brown; *voices:* Mel Blanc; *mus:* Carl W. Stalling; *prod sup:* Henry Binder, Raymond G. Katz; *col:* Tech. *sd:* Vit. 7 min. • Bugs stumbles across a giant's victory garden and gives the giant a terrible time trying to catch him.

3346. Jack's Shack *(Paul Terry-Toons)* 30 Nov. 1934; *p.c.:* Moser & Terry for Educational/Fox; *dir:* Frank Moser, Paul Terry; *mus:* Philip A. Scheib; b&w. *sd:* WE. 6 min. • The romance between a country girl and a scarecrow is opposed by the grouchy farmer but encouraged by the farm animals.

3347. Jail Birds *(Flip the Frog)* 26 Sept. 1931; *p.c.:* Celebrity prods for MGM; *prod/dir:* Ub Iwerks; *mus:* Carl W. Stalling; b&w. *sd:* PCP. 9 min. • Jail guard Flip has to recapture an escaped giant.

3348. Jail Birds *(Paul Terry Toons)* 21 Sept. 1934; *p.c.:* Moser & Terry for Educational/Fox; *dir:* Frank Moser, Paul Terry; *mus:* Philip A. Scheib; b&w. *sd:* WE. 6 min. • A cat and mouse escape from prison but two persistent skunks force them to return.

3349. Jail Break *(Mighty Mouse)* 20 Sept. 1946; *p.c.:* TT for Fox; *dir:* Eddie Donnelly; *story:* John Foster; *voice:* Thomas Morrison; *mus:* Philip A. Scheib; *ph:* Douglas Moye; *col:* Tech. *sd:* RCA. 6 min. • When Alcatraz Prison can't hold Bad Bill Bunion, Mighty Mouse is called upon to help.

3350. The Jail Breakers *(Aesop's Sound Fable)* 7 June 1929; *p.c.:* Van Beuren for Pathé; *dir:* Paul Terry; *mus:* Josiah Zuro; *sd fx:* Maurice Manne; b&w. *sd:* RCA. 5 min. • Two convicts escape from prison but are soon back where they started.

3351. James and the Giant Peach 12 Apr. 1996; *p.c.:* Allied Filmmakers/Walt Disney Enterprises, Inc., for Guild Entertainment; *dir:* Henry Selick; *prod:* Brian Rosen, Henry Selick, Denise Di Novi, Tim Burton; *ex prod:* Jake Eberts; based on the book by Roald Dahl; *scr:* Karey Kirkpatrick, Jonathan Roberts, Steve Bloom; *storyboard sup:* Kelly Asbury, Joe Ranft; *anim sup:* Paul Berry; *anim:* Anthony Scott, Michael Belzer, Timothy Hittle, Trey Thomas, Justin Kohn, Christopher Gilligan, Richard C. Zimmerman, Steven A. Buckley, Guionne Leroy, Michael B. Johnson, Josephine T. Huang, Daniel K. Mason, Paul Berry, Kent Burton, Tom St. Amand, Webster Colcord, Chuck Duke, Owen Klatte, Sue Pugh, Paul W. Jessel, Tom Gibbons, D. Sean Burns, Jerold Howard; *cut-out anim:* Tim Myers, Owen Klatte; *character des:* James Stimson; *ed:* Stan Webb, Marypat Plottner, Adrianne Sutner, Mildred Iatrou, Aura Gilge, Sean P. Mathieson, Robert Graham Jones; *Avid ed:* Steve Bloom, W. Hamilton Hall, Thayer Syme; *voices: Grasshopper:* Simon Callow; *Centipede:* Richard Dreyfuss; *Ladybug:* Jane Leeves; *Glowworm:* Miriam Margolyes; *Spider:* Susan Sarandon; *James:* Paul Terry; *Earthworm:* David Thewlis; *Centipede's singing voice:* Jeff Bennett; *addit vocals:* Drew Harrah, Sally Stevens; *mus/songs:* Randy Newman; "Heroes Return" by Arnold Steck; "Sail Away" by and sung by Noël Coward; *mus prod:* Chris Montan, Andy Hill, Michael Skloff; *orch:* Steve Bramson, Don Davis, Chris Boardman, Randy Newman; *song arrangements:* Don Davis; "Good News" *horn arrangement:* Jerry Hey; *mus recl/mix:* Frank Wolf, Paul Hume, John Vigran, Geoff Foster; *mus ed:* Bob Badami, Shannon Erbe; *orchestra contractor:* Sandy de Crescent; *violin solos:* Stuart Canin, Arnold Belnick, Maria Newman; *mus preparation:* Dominic Fidelibus; *prod art:* Chance Lane; *prod des:* Harley Jessup; *conceptual des:* Lane Smith; *art dpt: set des:* Dawn Swiderski, Don Weinger; *sculptors:* Jerome E. Ranft, Damon Bard, Kamela B. Portuges; *armature engineers:* Daniel Campbell, Merrick Cheney, David Eugene Meslch, Rodney Morgan, Marc Ribaud, Tony Preciado; *mould makers:* Leigh Barbier,

Michael J. Cummings, Michael Grivett, Matthew McKenna, Dick Hill; *pattern makers:* Mark Buck, Mark "Rhode-Steve" Fiorenza, Isabella Kirkland, Martin Jacques Meunier, John Daniel, Beth Ozarow, Barry Toya; *foam runner:* Erick Jensen; *asst sup:* Lauren Vogt; *fabricators:* Graham G. Maiden, Melanie Walas, Eileen Ridgeway, Jessica Ritts Cadkin, Christine Lashaw, Michael Arbios, Curt Chiarelli, Donelle Estey, Jeni Ryan, Sandy Clifford, Lisa Smith, Cate Cannon, Linda Stone, Miss Amy Adamy; *character co-ordination:* Gisela Hermeling, Catherine Dingman; *puppet wrangler:* Lee Cruikshank; *set construction:* Tom Proost, Phil Brotherton, Junior Lookinland, Fon Davis, Benjamin Nichols, Loren Gitthens; *Peach fabrication:* Steve Gawley, Vilija Kontrimas; *scenic art:* Robert Cook, Robin Cooper, Judith Moman, Peggy Hrastar, Loren Hillman-Morgan, Elizabeth Jennings, Steven J. Walton, Diane M. Godfrey-Weinkauf; *rigging:* Christopher Rand, Erio S. Brown, Reason Bradley; *models:* Susan Alegria, Pamela Kibbee, Jeff Brewer, Natalie O. Roth, Facundo Rabaudi, Gretchen Scharfenberg; *set dressers:* Nancy Noblett, Jeni Ryan; *set/prop/scenic co-ord:* Gregg Olsson; *visual fx:* Pete Kozachik, Nancy St. John, Scott E. Anderson, Dorne Huebler, Sony Pictures Imageworks; *visual fx prod:* Mickey McGovern; *visual fx ed:* Audrey Chang, Juliette Yager; *visual fx co-ord:* Jeanette Volturno; *cg sup:* Jerome Chen; *lighting:* Louis Cetorelli; *anim sup:* Harry Walton, Ron Brinkmann; *art dirs:* Michael Scheffe, Jamie Rama; *anim:* Allen Edwards, David Vallone, Alex Sokoloff, Peter Warner; *compositors:* Heather Davis, M. Scott McKee, Lisa Foster, Steve Kennedy; *3d fx anim:* Arnaud Hervas; *particle anim:* Mike Perry, Tim Teramoto; *technical sup:* Michael Tigar; *software engineers:* Dev Mannemela, Robert Minsk; *modeller:* Kevin Hudson; *roto art:* Kiki Candela, Suzy Brown; *technical asst:* Stephen Kowalski, David Takayama, Janel Alexander, John Decker, Bill Ball; *prod asst:* Nikki Bell, Jason Hanel; *runner:* Guy Wiedman; *I/O sup:* Dennis Webb; *film rec:* John Strauss, Chris Leone, Chris Tsongas; *ed sup:* Michael Moore; *software sup:* Caroline Allen; *systems engineer:* Alberto Velez, Dean Miya; *system admin/resource mgr:* Ted Alexandre; *system technician:* Jesse Carlisle; *digital prod mgr:* Bill Schultz, Gayle Reznik, Katya Culberg; *ex prod:* George Merkert; *gen mgr:* Bill Birrell; *digital sup:* Craig Newman; *digital compositors:* Tim Alexander, Beth Block, Allen Gonzales, Tim Guyer, Kevin Koneval, Terry Moews, January Nordman, Eric Peterson, Winston Quitasol; *digital col timing sup:* Bruce Tauscher; *cg art:* Aaron Campbell, Lee Lanier; *digital art:* Elissa Bello, Lisa Fisher, Eric McLean, Marsha Carrington; *scan/film rec:* William Aylsworth; *visual fx prod sup:* Denise Davis, Lydia Bottegoni; *digital co-ord:* Kathryn Liotta; *ed co-ord:* Brian Keeney; *software engineering:* Scott Miller; *systems admin:* Michael Messina; *technical admin:* Jason Dennis; *prod asst:* Joshua Arsenault; *fx prod:* Reid Burns; *fx sup:* Jeff Matakovich; *compositors:* Tony Noel, John Bermudes, Pacific Ocean Post; *JEX Fx Rhino Unit: fx sup:* Gary Platek; *animatronic des:* Kelly Lepkowsky; *technician:* Bill Maley; *machinist:* Brian Dewe; *puppeteer:* John Stevenson; *costumes:* Victoria Drake; *CEL fx anim dpt: sup/lead fx anim:* Sari Gennis; *fx anim:* Anthony Stacchi, Mike Smith, Joseph Gilland, Billy Burger, Nathan Stanton; *inbet:* Andrew Haldeman; *ph:* Pete Kozachik, Hiro Narita; *prod dpt: visual fx prod:* Lynda Lemon; *visual fx co-ord:* Amy Hollywood Wixson; *asst dir:* Lisa Davidson; *prod co-ord:* Amy Hollywood Wixson, Alexis Engle; *story dpt co-ord:* Andrew Birch; *art dpt co-ord:* Kristen Ross, Mark Nelson; *anim co-ord:* Laura Schulz; *prod asst:* Jennifer C. Hayman, Lance J. Martin, Brent Kirkpatrick, Brian Turner Moran, Peter Lasell, Jessica Samuelson, Amy Lund, Greg Tutton, Zach Passero, J.D. Ryan; *col:* Monaco/Tech. *sd:* Dolby Digital. 79 min. *l/a/anim.* • James (Paul Terry), an orphan boy who is badly treated by his two aunts, one day meets an old man who gives him a magic bag that is responsible for growing a colossal peach. With help from his insect friends, James sets sail inside the peach for New York. Live-action with computer animation.

3352. James Hound *(series)* 1966/1967; *p.c.:* TT for Fox; *ex prod:* Bill Weiss; *dir sup:* Ralph Bakshi; *story sup:* Tom Morrison; *story:* Eli Bauer, Al Kouzel; *anim dir/anim/lay:* Cosmo Anzilotti, Artie Bartsch, Jack Schnerk, Bob Taylor, Dave Tendlar; *sets:* Martin Strudler, Johnny Vita; *ed:* Jack MacConnell; *voices:* Dayton Allen; *mus:* Jim Timmens; *ph:* Bill Fox, Joe Rasinski; *sd:* Elliot Grey; *col:* DeLuxe. *sd:* RCA. 6 min. • An incompetent canine version of James Bond.

3353. Janie Get Your Gun *(Woody Woodpecker)* May 1965; *p.c.:* Walter Lantz prods for Univ; *dir:* Paul J. Smith; *story:* Cal Howard; *anim:* Les Kline, Al Coe; *sets:* Art Landy, Ray Huffine; *voices:* Dal McKennon, Grace Stafford; *mus:* Walter Greene; *prod mgr:* William E. Garity; *col:* Tech. *sd:*

RCA. 6 min. • A bandit puts Woody's photo over one of his own on a "Wanted" poster and gives Woody the problem of Calamity Jane trying to capture him.

3354. Japanese Lanterns (*Rainbow Parade*) 8 Mar. 1935; *p.c.:* Van Beuren for RKO; *dir:* Burt Gillett, Ted Eshbaugh; *mus:* Winston Sharples; *col:* Ciné. *sd:* RCA. 6 min. • Oscar the ostrich becomes a hero by saving his oriental pals.

3355. Jasper and The Beanstalk (*Madcap Models*) 19 Oct. 1945; *p.c.:* George Pal prods for Para; *prod/dir:* George Pal; *voices:* Roy Glenn, Glenn Leedy; *col:* Tech. *sd:* WE. 8 min. *Academy Award nomination.* • The Scarecrow trades Jasper's mouth organ for some beans which grow into a huge beanstalk. Jasper climbs it and rescues a girl being held prisoner in a cage.

3356. Jasper and the Choo-Choo (*Madcap Models*) 1 Jan. 1943; *p.c.:* George Pal prods for Para; *prod/dir:* George Pal; *story:* George Pal, Jack Miller; *anim:* Ray Harryhausen; *voices:* Roy Glenn, Glenn Leedy; *mus:* William Eddison; *col:* Tech. *sd:* WE. 7¹/₂ min. • The Scarecrow tries to con Jasper out of his nickel but dice turn the tables on him.

3357. Jasper and the Haunted House (*Madcap Models*) 23 Oct. 1942; *p.c.:* George Pal prods for Para; *prod/dir:* George Pal; *story:* George Pal, Jack Miller; *anim:* Ray Harryhausen; *voices:* Roy Glenn, Glenn Leedy, The Carlyle Scott Chorus; *mus:* William Eddison; *col:* Tech. *sd:* WE. 7 min. • The Scarecrow and Crow lure Jasper into a haunted house to steal his gooseberry pie.

3358. Jasper and the Watermelons (*Madcap Models*) 27 Feb. 1942; *p.c.:* George Pal prods for Para; *prod/dir:* George Pal; *story:* Jack Miller, Cecil Beard; *anim:* Ray Harryhausen; *voices:* The Carlyle Scott Chorus, Roy Glenn, Glenn Leedy; *mus:* William Eddison; *col:* Tech. *sd:* WE. 9 min. • Jasper falls asleep and dreams he's gone to Watermelon Land.

3359. Jasper Goes Fishing (*Madcap Models*) 8 Oct. 1943; *p.c.:* George Pal prods for Para; *prod/dir:* George Pal; *voices:* Glenn Leedy; *col:* Tech. *sd:* WE. 8 min. • Jasper forsakes church to go fishing. He has adventures with the underwater life and wakes to find it was only a dream.

3360. Jasper Goes Hunting (*Madcap Models*) 10 Mar. 1944; *p.c.:* George Pal prods for Para; *prod/dir:* George Pal; *Bugs Bunny* animated by Robert McKimson; *voices:* Glenn Leedy, Mel Blanc; *col:* Tech. *sd:* WE. 7 min. • Jasper encounters Bugs Bunny on his hunt.

3361. Jasper in a Jam (*Puppetoon*) 18 Oct. 1946; *p.c.:* George Pal prods for Para; *dir:* Duke Goldstone; *story:* Bob Larson; *anim:* Gene Warren; *sets:* Reginald Massie; *voices:* Peggy Lee, Roy Glenn, Sara Berner; *mus:* Charlie Barnet & His Orchestra; *songs:* "Redskin Rhumba": by Dale Barnet; "Old Man Mose": by Louis Armstrong, Zilner Trenton Randolph; "Pumptown Turnpike": by Dick Rogers, Will Osborne; *col:* Tech. *sd:* WE. 7 min. • Jasper is locked in a pawn shop and is menaced by musical instruments coming to life.

3362. Jasper Tell (*Madcap Models*) 23 Mar. 1945; *p.c.:* George Pal prods for Para; *prod/dir:* George Pal; *voices:* Roy Glenn, Glenn Leedy; "The William Tell Overture" by Rossini; *orch:* Clarence Wheeler; *col:* Tech. *sd:* WE. 8 min. • The Scarecrow relates the story of William Tell to Jasper while he eats his apple for the teacher.

3363. Jasper's Booby Traps (*Madcap Models*) 5 Aug. 1945; *p.c.:* George Pal prods for Para; *prod/dir:* George Pal; *voices:* Roy Glenn, Glenn Leedy; *mus:* Clarence Wheeler; *col:* Tech. *sd:* WE. 8 min. • Jasper plays a trick on the Scarecrow by booby-trapping a sumptuous steak meal.

3364. Jasper's Close Shave (*Madcap Models*) 28 Sept. 1945; *p.c.:* George Pal prods for Para; *prod/dir:* George Pal; *voices:* Allan Watson, Roy Glenn, Glenn Leedy; *mus:* Clarence Wheeler; *col:* Tech. *sd:* WE. 7 min. • Jasper feels in need of a shave and asks the Scarecrow to do the honors. He awakes to find his hair has been shaved off.

3365. Jasper's Derby (*Madcap Models*) 9 Aug. 1946; *p.c.:* George Pal prods for Para; *dir:* Duke Goldstone; *story:* Webb Smith; *anim:* Herbert Johnson; *voices:* Elmore Vincent, Sara Berner; *mus:* Clarence Wheeler; *ph:* John S. Abbott; *col:* Tech. *sd:* WE. 8 min. • Jasper befriends an old racehorse and provides a violin solo causing the horse to win the derby.

3366. Jasper's Minstrels (*Madcap Models*) 25 May 1945; *p.c.:* George Pal prods for Para; *prod/dir:* George Pal; *voices:* Roy Glenn, Glenn Leedy; *col:* Tech. *sd:* WE. 9 min. • The Scarecrow recreates a minstrel show.

3367. Jasper's Music Lesson (*Madcap Models*) 21 May 1943; *p.c.:* George Pal prods for Para; *prod/dir:* George Pal; *story:* George Pal, Jack Miller; *voices:* Roy Glenn, Glenn Leedy; *mus:* Arling Martyn; *col:* Tech. *sd:* WE. 8 min. • Jasper's piano practice is interrupted by the Scarecrow and Crow's "Boogie Woogie" music.

3368. Jasper's Paradise (*Madcap Models*) 13 Oct. 1944; *p.c.:* George Pal prods for Para; *prod/dir:* George Pal; *story:* George Pal, Jack Miller; *voices:* Roy Glenn, Glenn Leedy; *mus:* Maurice dePackh; *col:* Tech. *sd:* WE. 7¹/₂ min. • Jasper's reward for not eating a gingerbread man is to go to "Cake Heaven."

3369. The Jaywalker 31 May 1956; *p.c.:* UPA for Colum; *ex prod:* Stephen Bosustow; *dir:* Robert Cannon; *story:* Edwin D. Hicks; *story adapt:* T. Hee, Robt Cannon; *anim:* Frank Smith, Alan Zaslove, Barney Posner; *lay:* Jules Engel; *back:* T. Hee; *voice:* Eugene Bollay; *mus:* Billy May; *vibes:* Red Norvo; *clarinet, alto sax:* Heinie Beau; *prod mgr:* Herbert Klynn; *col:* Tech. *sd:* RCA. 6 min. *Academy Award nomination.* • Milton Muffet displays the art of jaywalking.

3370. The Jazz Fool (*Mickey Mouse*) 20 Nov. 1929; *p.c.:* Walter E. Disney for Colum; *dir:* Walt Disney; *anim:* Ub Iwerks; *mus:* Carl W. Stalling; b&w. *sd:* PCP. 6 min. • Mickey entertains the animals by playing the calliope and the piano.

3371. Jazz Mad (*Paul Terry-Toons*) 9 Aug. 1931; *p.c.:* Terry, Moser & Coffman for Educational/Fox; *dir:* Frank Moser, Paul Terry; *mus:* Philip A. Scheib; b&w. *sd:* WE. 5 min. • A wandering band of street musicians' music affects even the meat in a butcher's shop.

3372. Jazz Rhythm (*Krazy Kat*) 19 June 1930; *p.c.:* Winkler for Colum; *prod:* Charles B. Mintz; *anim:* Ben Harrison, Manny Gould; *mus:* Joe de Nat; *prod mgr:* Nat L. Mintz; b&w. *sd:* RCA. 5 min. • Krazy and a lion slog it out on pianos in a boxing ring.

3373. The Jealous Fisherman (*Aesop's Film Fable*) 18 May 1924; *p.c.:* Fables Pictures Inc for Pathé; *dir:* Paul Terry; b&w. *sil.* 5 min. • Thomas Cat and Isaac Dog fish in the Farmer's pond. Isaac cheats by holding the bait over the water and clubbing the fish as they jump for it.

3374. The Jealous Lover (*Paul Terry-Toon*) 8 Jan. 1933; *p.c.:* Moser & Terry for Educational/Fox; *dir:* Frank Moser, Paul Terry; *mus:* Philip A. Scheib; b&w. *sd:* WE. 6 min. • A mouse waiter serenades a girl in a café. Her jealous boyfriend starts a fight and gangsters pursue them.

3375. The Jeep (*Popeye*) 15 July 1938; *p.c.:* The Fleischer Studio for Para; *prod:* Max Fleischer; *dir:* Dave Fleischer; *anim:* Seymour Kneitel, Graham Place; *ed:* Kitty Pfister; *voices:* Jack Mercer, Margie Hines; *mus:* Sammy Timberg; *prod sup:* Sam Buchwald, Isidore Sparber; b&w. *sd:* WE. 7 min. • Popeye uses Eugene the Jeep to help track down Swee'Pea who has disappeared.

3376. Jeepers Creepers (*Looney Tunes*) 23 Sept. 1939; *p.c.:* Leon Schlesinger prods for WB; *dir:* Robert Clampett; *story:* Ernest Gee; *anim:* Vive Risto; *ed:* Tregoweth E. Brown; *voices:* Mel Blanc; *mus:* Carl W. Stalling; *song:* Harry Warren, Johnny Mercer; *prod sup:* Henry Binder, Raymond G. Katz; b&w. *sd:* Vit. 6 min. • Officer Porky Pig goes after a goofy ghost in a haunted house.

3377. Jefferson Film Corporation (1921/1922) *prod/dir:* Richard McShay Friel; *artists:* Leighton Budd, Louis Glackens, George Gregory, Carl Meyer, Clarence Rigby; *prod mgr:* Eddie Welch.

3378. Jerky Turkey 7 Apr. 1945; *p.c.:* MGM; *dir:* Tex Avery; *story:* Heck Allen; *anim:* Preston Blair, Ed Love, Ray Abrams; *character des:* Claude Smith; *sets:* John Didrik Johnsen; *ed:* Fred MacAlpine; *voices:* Harry E. Lang, Leone Le Doux; *mus:* Scott Bradley; *prod:* Fred Quimby; *col:* Tech. *sd:* WE. 7 min. • A Pilgrim goes hunting a reluctant turkey for Thanksgiving dinner.

3379. Jerky Turkey (*Beary Family*) Jan. 1968; *p.c.:* Walter Lantz prods for Univ; *dir:* Paul J. Smith; *story:* Cal Howard; *anim:* Les Kline, Al Coe; *sets:* Ray Huffine; *voices:* Paul Frees, Grace Stafford; *mus:* Walter Greene; *prod mgr:* William E. Garity; *col:* Tech. *sd:* RCA. 5 min. • Junior returns home with a pet turkey but Charlie wants to eat it for Sunday lunch.

3380. Jerry and Jumbo (*Tom & Jerry*) 21 Feb. 1953; *p.c.:* MGM; *dir:* William Hanna, Joseph Barbera; *anim:* Kenneth Muse, Irven Spence, Ed Barge; *lay:* Richard Bickenbach; *back:* Robert Gentle; *ed:* Jim Faris; *mus:*

Scott Bradley; *ph:* Jack Stevenson; *prod:* Fred Quimby; *col:* Tech. *sd:* WE. 7 min. • A baby elephant falls from a train and rolls into Jerry's home. He paints the pachyderm as a giant mouse to confuse Tom.

3381. Jerry and the Goldfish (*Tom & Jerry*) 3 Mar. 1951; *p.c.:* MGM; *dir:* William Hanna, Joseph Barbera; *anim:* Irven Spence, Ray Patterson, Ed Barge, Kenneth Muse; *lay:* Dick Bickenbach; *back:* Robert Gentle; *ed:* Jim Faris; *voice:* Daws Butler; *mus:* Scott Bradley; *ph:* Jack Stevenson; *prod:* Fred Quimby; *col:* Tech. *sd:* WE. 7 min. • Jerry comes to the rescue of a small goldfish that Tom decides to cook for dinner.

3382. Jerry and the Lion (*Tom & Jerry*) 8 Apr. 1950; *p.c.:* MGM; *dir:* William Hanna, Joseph Barbera; *anim:* Irven Spence, Ed Barge, Kenneth Muse, Ray Patterson; *lay:* Dick Bickenbach; *back:* Robert Gentle; *ed:* Jim Faris; *voice:* Frank Graham; *mus:* Scott Bradley; *ph:* Jack Stevenson; *prod:* Fred Quimby; *col:* Tech. *sd:* WE. 6½ min. • Jerry conceals an escaped lion from Tom who wants to turn him in for a cash reward.

3383. Jerry-Go-Round (*Tom & Jerry*) 1965; *p.c.:* MGM; *prod:* Chuck Jones; *dir:* Abe Levitow; *story:* John Dunn; *anim:* Dick Thompson, Ben Washam, Ken Harris, Don Towsley, Tom Ray; *des:* Maurice Noble; *lay:* Don Morgan; *back:* Philip de Guard; *voice:* Mel Blanc; *mus:* Eugene Poddany; *prod mgr:* Les Goldman; *col:* Metro. *sd:* WE. 6 min. • Jerry befriends a circus elephant.

3384. Jerry, Jerry, Quite Contrary (*Tom & Jerry*) 1966; *p.c.:* MGM; *prod/dir/story:* Chuck Jones; *asst dir:* Maurice Noble; *anim:* Ken Harris, Don Towsley, Tom Ray, Dick Thompson, Ben Washam, Al Pabian; *sets:* Philip de Guard; *voice:* Mel Blanc; *mus:* Dean Elliott; *prod sup:* Earl Jonas, Les Goldman; *col:* Metro. *sd:* WE. 7 min. • Tom's life is put on the firingline when Jerry takes to sleepwalking.

3385. Jerry's Cousin (*Tom & Jerry*) Apr. 1951; *p.c.:* MGM; *dir:* William Hanna, Joseph Barbera; *anim:* Ray Patterson, Ed Barge, Kenneth Muse, Irven Spence; *lay:* Dick Bickenbach; *back:* Robert Gentle; *ed:* Jim Faris; *voices:* Paul Frees; *mus:* Scott Bradley; *ph:* Jack Stevenson; *prod:* Fred Quimby; *col:* Tech. *sd:* WE. 7 min. • Jerry is forced to call upon his muscular cousin "Muscles" to deal with Tom.

3386. Jerry's Diary (*Tom & Jerry*) 22 Oct. 1949; *p.c.:* MGM; *dir:* William Hanna, Joseph Barbera; *anim:* Kenneth Muse, Ed Barge; *lay:* Dick Bickenbach; *back:* Robert Gentle; *ed:* Fred MacAlpin; *voice:* Joe Forte; *mus:* Scott Bradley; *ph:* Jack Stevenson; *prod:* Fred Quimby; *col:* Tech. *sd:* WE. 6 min. • Seq: *Tee for Two; Mouse Trouble; Yankee Doodle Mouse.* • Tom discovers Jerry's diary and reads of the mouse's conquests over him.

3387. Jesse and James (*Paul Terry-Toon*) 6 Sept. 1931; *p.c.:* Terry, Moser & Coffman for Educational/Fox; *dir:* Frank Moser, Paul Terry; *anim:* Arthur Babbitt, George Gordon, Frank Moser, Connie Rasinski, Hugh Shields, Vladimir Tytla; *mus:* Philip A. Scheib; b&w. *sd:* WE. 5 min. • Two cat bandits capture an Indian maiden. Her sweetie chases them and they have a shoot-out in a log cabin.

3388. Jest of Honor (*Little King*) 19 Jan. 1934; *p.c.:* Van Beuren for RKO; *dir:* George Stallings; *anim:* Jim Tyer; *mus:* Gene Rodemich; b&w. *sd:* RCA. 8 min. • The King surfboards in the wake of the Royal Yacht and has a rendezvous with a mermaid.

3389. The Jet Cage (*Looney Tunes*) Sept. 1962; *p.c.:* WB; *dir/story:* Friz Freleng; *anim:* Gerry Chiniquy, Art Leonardi, Virgil Ross, Lee Halpern, Bob Matz; *lay:* Hawley Pratt; *back:* Tom O'Loughlin; *ed:* Treg Brown; *voices:* Mel Blanc, June Foray; *mus:* Milt Franklyn, William Lava; *prod mgr:* William Orcutt; *prod:* David H. DePatie; *col:* Tech. *sd:* Vit. 7 min. • Tweety takes to the skies in a power-driven bird cage.

3390. Jet Pink (*Pink Panther*) 13 June 1967; *p.c.:* Mirisch/Geoffrey/DFE for UA; *dir:* Gerry Chiniquy; *story:* Tony Benedict; *anim:* Don Williams, Bob Matz, Warren Batchelder, Manny Perez, Art Leonardi; *lay:* Lin Larsen; *back:* Tom O'Loughlin; *ed:* Lee Gunther; *mus:* Walter Greene; *theme tune:* Henry Mancini; *prod sup:* Harry Love, Bill Orcutt; *col:* DeLuxe. *sd:* RCA. 6 min. • The Panther causes chaos while piloting a jet plane.

3391. Jetsons: The Movie 6 July 1990; *p.c.:* Hanna-Barbera for Univ; *dir/prod:* William Hanna, Joseph Barbera; *sup prod:* Bruce David Johnson; *sup dir:* Iwao Takamoto; *sup anim dir:* David Michener; *story:* Dennis Marks, Carl Bautter; *Wang Film Prods., Co., Inc.:* *asso prod:* James Wang; *prod sup:* Bob Marples; *sup dir:* Chris Hauge, Dan Hunn, Paul Stibal; *prod des:* Al Gmuer; *post prod des:* Judith Holmes Clarke, Ric Estrada; *storyboard:*

Don Sheppard, Alex Lovy, Chris Otsuki, Kay Wright, Jim Willoughby, Don Jurwich, Scott Jeralds; *anim dir:* Ray Patterson; *asst anim dir:* Joanna Romersa; *anim:* Frank Andrina, Oliver "Lefty" Callahan, David Feiss, Don MacKinnon, Irv Spence, Robert Alvarez, Brad Case, David Concepcion, Jesse Cosio, Charlie Downs, Robert Goe, Dan Hunn, Glen Kennedy, Ernesto Lopez, Istvan Majoros, Ed Love, Jon McGlenahan, Marc Christiansen, Mike Bennett, Barry Anderson, Brenda Banks, Andre Knutson, Bob Tyler, Zeon Davush, Bill Nunes, Simon O'Leary, Joanna Romersa, Carl Urbano, Allen Wilzback, Berny Wolf, Chris Hauge, Paul Stibal, Kevin Petrilak, Gabi Payne, Phil Cummings, Lee Mishkin, Kathi Castillo, Barbara Krueger, Leonard Johnson, Jesus Rodriguez, Beverly Adams, Mitchell Walker, Bill Mims, Doris Plough, Ilona Kaba, Lucinda Sanderson, Sandy Henkin, Ruth Elliot, Dick Williams, Phil Cummings, Mary Robertson, Lloyd Rees, Mac Torres, Jonathan Lyons, Bronwen Barry, Don Judge, Vicki Banks, Sue Houghton, Jeff La Femme, Melissa Freeman, Bill Knoll, Darrell McNeil, Sam Cornell, Cheryl Abood; *character des:* Jack White, Scott Jeralds, Chris Otsuki, Alfred Gimeno, Donna Zeller, Lance Falk, Tony Sgroi, Bwana Takamoto, Mark Christensen, Bob Onorato, Eric Clark, Scott Hill; *lay dir:* Deane Taylor; *lay sup:* John Ahern; *lay:* Andrew Gentle, Peter Alvarado, Lew Ott, Tony Sgroi, Owen Fitzgerald, Bill Proctor, Art Leonardi; *back sup:* Al Gmuer; *back des:* Lorraine Marue, Jim Hickey, Bill Proctor, Ron Roesch, Floro Dery, Melvin Keefer, Frank Brunner; *back:* Joe Binggeli, Lorraine Marue, Melvin Keefer, Frank Brunner, Ruben Chavez, Patti Palmer, Jim Hickey, Eric Herschong, Andy Phillipson, Mike Humphries, Bob Schaeffer, Bonnie Callahan, Dennis Venizelos, Craig Robertson, Jerry Loveland, John Rice, Gloria Wood, Jonathan Goley; *visual des:* Jean-Maxime Perramon, Bob Simmons; *ed:* Pat Foley, Terry W. Moore, Larry C. Cowan, Gregory V. Watson, Jr., Gilbert Iverson, Tim Iverson, Karen Doulac; *optical fx:* Perpetual Motion Pictures, Howard Anderson Company; *voices:* George Jetson: George O'Hanlon; *Mr. Spacely:* Mel Blanc; *Jane Jetson:* Penny Singleton; *Judy Jetson:* Tiffany; *Elroy Jetson:* Patrick Zimmerman; *Astro:* Don Messick; *Rosie the Robot:* Jean van der Pyl; *Rudy 2:* Ronnie Schell; *Lucy 2:* Patti Deutsch, *Teddy 2:* Dana Hill; *Fergie Furbelow:* Russi Taylor; *Apollo Blue:* Paul Kreppel; *Rocket Rick:* Rick Dees; *also:* Michael Bell, Jeff Bergman, Brian Cummings, Brad Garrett, Rob Paulsen, Susan Silo, Janet Waldo, B.J. Ward, Jim Ward, Frank Welker; "You and Me" performed by Tiffany; "Jetsons' Rap" performed by XXL; *mus:* John Dabney; *mus sup:* George Tobin; *orch:* Brad Dechter, Ira Hearshen; *mus ed:* Tom Gleason; *scoring:* Bodie Chandler, Tim James; *songs:* "Jetson main title" by William Hanna, Joseph Barbera, Hoyt Curtin; "Gotcha" by Tim James, Steve McGlintock; performed by Steve McGlintock, Garm Bell; "Maybe Love, Maybe Not" by Tim James, Steve McGlintock, Steve Kempster; performed by Smog; "Staying Together" by Mike Piggirillo; performed by Shane Sutton; "I Always Thought I'd See You Again" by Tim James, Steve McGlintock, Phil Coleman, George Tobin; performed by Tiffany; "With You All the Way" by Carl Wurtz; performed by Shane Sutton; "We're the Jetsons" (Jetsons' Rap) by Mike Piggirillo; *song programming:* John Duarte, Rob Russell; *graphics:* Iraj Paran, Tom Wogatzke, Parviz Parandough; *color timing:* Bud Broughton, Roy Sanders; *check:* Gina Bradley, Bob Revell, Vicki White, Beth Goodwin, Eleanor Dahlen, Jan Adams, Sue Burke, Nelda Ridley, Howard Schwartz, Sandy Wogatzke; *computer anim:* computer fx: Brad de Graf, Michael Wahrman (de Graf/Wahrman, Inc.); *seq prods:* Anne M. Adams, Michelle Porter; *technical dir:* Jim Hillin; *seq dir:* Craig Newman; *technical dirs:* Brian Jennings, Mark Pompian, Brian Schindler; *vehicle anim:* Kroyer Films, Inc.; *computer anim:* Bill Kroyer; *seq mgr:* Leslie Hinton; "You and Me" *seq:* Kurtz and Friends; *seq des:* Robert Peluce; *seq dir:* Bob Kurtz; *Xerox:* Star Wirth, Martin Crossley, Richard Wilson, Jeffrey Eckert; *i&p:* Alison Leopold, FIL Cartoon Studios, Jerry Smith, Joyce Alexander, Kristine Brown, Christine Conklin, Peggy Gregory, Kathy Hardin, Robin Kane, Chris Stocks; *technical:* Gerald Mills, Ken Brain, Liza Keith, Larry Malone, Jay Sloat, Phil Zucco, Brad de Graf, Wendy Elwell, Kim Conte, Audrey Covello, Sybil Cuzzort, Betsy Ergenbright, Mary Fallis, Etsuko Fujioka, Shelly Gillespie, Maria Gonzalez, Lori Jo Hanson, Rhoda Hicks, Christine Kingsland, Delores Mills, Carmen Noriega, Meling Pabian, Jo Anne Plein, Ramona Randa, Nellie Rodriguez, Rose Ann Stire, Lydia Swayne, Pattie Torocsik, Helene Vives; *title seq dir:* Brian Jennings; *title des:* Dale Herigstad; *ph:* Daniel Bunn, Aaron Caughran, Ron Jackson, Robert Jacobs, David J. Link, Steve Mills, Neil Owen Viker, Paul Wainess, Steve Wilzback; *sd:* Gordon Hunt, Andrea Romano, Jamie Thomason, Gregory Ercoland, Joshua Pines; *rec:* Alvy Dorman, Stan Wetzel, Edwin

Collins, Chuck Britz; *mix:* Bill Nicholson, Tony Meldeny, Peter S. Reale, Tim Grace; *sd ed:* Robert R. Rutledge, David A. Arnold, Dave Kulczyxki, Alan Bromberg, Steve Bushelman, Simon Coke, Mark Ormandy, Jerry Sanford, Robert Waxman, Sherman Waze, Michael Murphy; *foley:* Craig Jaeger, Paige Pollack, Ed Steidele; *neg cutter:* William E. De Boer; *ex in charge of prod:* Jayne Barbera; *prod mgr:* Yvonne Palmer; *post prod mgr:* Joed Eaton; *col:* CFI. *sd:* Dolby Stereo. 83 min. • Big screen feature of television's space age family: George Jetson's boss, Mr. Spacely, promotes George to vice-president in the hopes he will deal with the repeated sabotage in his sprocket company. The problem is solved when an underground land of creatures known as "Grungies" is discovered under the Ore Borer which, in turn, is destroying their city. George defies his boss and closes down the factory, later to have it staffed by the Grungies recycling worn sprockets rather than manufacturing new ones.

3392. Jimmy the C 1977; *p.c.:* Jimmy the C prods; *prod/dir/anim:* Jimmy Picker; *des:* Robert Grossman; *coordinator:* Craig Whitaker; "Georgia on My Mind" by Hoagy Carmichael, Stuart Gorrelle; performed by Ray Charles; col. *sd:* 3 min. *Academy Award nomination.* • President Jimmy Carter sings "Georgia" with a chorus of peanuts to accompany him.

3393. Jingle Bells (*Paul Terry-Toon*) 18 Oct. 1931; *p.c.:* Terry, Moser & Coffman for Educational/Fox; *dir:* Frank Moser, Paul Terry; *anim:* Jack King, Vladimir Tytla; *mus:* Philip A. Scheib; b&w. *sd:* WE. 5 min. • While performing their operatics, the hero goes through the motions of rescuing an imprisoned girl from the villainous spider.

3394. Jingle Jangle Jungle (*Screen Song*) 19 May 1950; *p.c.:* Famous for Para; *dir:* Seymour Kneitel; *story:* Joe Stultz, Larry Riley; *anim:* Myron Waldman, Larry Silverman; *sets:* Tom Ford; *voices:* Jackson Beck, Jack Mercer; *mus:* Winston Sharples; *song:* Bob Hilliard, Carl Sigman; *ph:* Leonard McCormick; *prod mgr:* Sam Buchwald; *col:* Tech. *sd:* RCA. 7 min. • A tour through darkest Africa ends with a singalong of the popular song "Civilization."

3395. Jitterbug Follies (*MGM Cartoon*) 25 Feb. 1939; *p.c.:* MGM; *dir/story:* Milt Gross; *anim:* Ray Abrams, George Gordon, Emery Hawkins, Irven Spence; *sets:* Bob Kuwahara; *ed:* Fred MacAlpine; *voices:* Mel Blanc, Georgia Stark, Dave Weber; *mus:* Scott Bradley; *prod mgr:* Fred Quimby; *col:* sep. *sd:* WE. 9 min. • Two thugs from The Citizens' Fair Play Committee arrive to see that Screwloose's amateur talent show is run on the level.

3396. Jitterbug Jive (*Popeye*) 23 June 1950; *p.c.:* Famous for Para; *dir:* Bill Tytla; *story;* Carl Meyer, Jack Mercer; *anim:* George Germanetti, Harvey Patterson; *sets:* Lloyd Hallock Jr.; *voices:* Jack Mercer, Jackson Beck, Mae Questel; *mus:* Winston Sharples; *ph:* Leonard McCormick; *prod mgr:* Sam Buchwald; *col:* Tech. *sd:* RCA. 6 min. • Popeye appears dated to Olive when he invites a "Hep Cat" to visit.

3397. Jitterbug Knights (*Color Rhapsody*) 11 Aug. 1939; *p.c.:* Charles Mintz prods for Colum; *dir:* Sid Marcus; *anim:* Art Davis, Herb Rothwill; *sets:* Phil Davis; *ed:* George Winkler; *voices:* The Rhythmettes, Danny Webb; *mus:* Joe de Nat, King Oliver (pre-recorded); *ph:* Otto Reimer; *prod mgr:* James Bronis; *col:* Tech. *sd:* RCA. 7½ min. • The newly born Prince is granted his every wish by three fairies but all he wants is jitterbug music.

3398. Jittery Jester (*Woody Woodpecker*) 3 Nov. 1958; *p.c.:* Walter Lantz prods for Univ; *dir:* Paul J. Smith; *story:* Homer Brightman; *anim:* Robert Bentley, Les Kline, Don Patterson; *sets:* Art Landy, Raymond Jacobs; *voices:* Dal McKennon, Grace Stafford; *mus:* Clarence Wheeler; *prod mgr:* William E. Garity; *col:* Tech. *sd:* RCA. 6 min. • The King wants Woody to replace his jester, Dooley, who is sent to bring him in. The idea doesn't please Dooley, who tries to dispose of our hero.

3399. A Job for a Gob (*Popeye*) 9 Dec. 1955; *p.c.:* Famous for Para; *dir:* Seymour Kneitel; *story:* Larz Bourne; *anim:* Al Eugster, George Germanetti; *sets:* Robert Connavale; *voices:* Jack Mercer, Jackson Beck, Mae Questel; *mus:* Winston Sharples; *ph:* Leonard McCormick; *prod mgr:* Seymour Shultz; *col:* Tech. *sd:* RCA. 6 min. • Popeye and Bluto vie for the position of handyman on Olive's ranch.

3400. Joe Boko (*Canimated Nooz Pictorial #8*) 4 Apr. 1916; *p.c.:* Wallace Carlson Studio for Essanay; *dir:* Wallace A. Carlson; b&w. sil. • No story available.

3401. Joe Boko Breaking Into the Big League (*Joe Boko*) 10 Oct. 1914; *p.c.:* Wallace Carlson Studio for Historic Feature Film Co; *dir:* Wallace A. Carlson; b&w. sil. 5 min. • No story available.

3402. Joe Boko in a Close Shave (*Canimated Nooz Pictorial*) 1 June 1915; *p.c.:* Wallace Carlson Studio for Essanay; *dir:* Wallace A. Carlson; b&w. sil. • No story available.

3403. Joe Boko in Saved by Gasolene (*Canimated Nooz Pictorial*) 27 Aug. 1915; *p.c.:* Wallace Carlson Studio for Essanay; *dir:* Wallace A. Carlson; b&w. sil. • No story available.

3404. Joe Boko's Adventures (*Joe Boko*) 9 Feb. 1916; *p.c.:* Wallace Carlson Studio for Univ; *prod:* P.A. Powers; *dir:* Wallace A. Carlson; b&w. sil. 5 min. • Cartoonist Joe animates the name "Woodrow" then draws a lion, a donkey and a goat that come to life and make short work of the artist who resigns on the spot.

3405. Joe Glow the Firefly (*Looney Tunes*) 8 Mar. 1941; *p.c.:* Leon Schlesinger prods for WB; *dir:* Charles M. Jones; *story:* Rich Hogan; *anim:* Philip Monroe; *mus:* Carl W. Stalling; *lay:* Robert Givens; *back:* Eugene Fleury; *ed:* Treg Brown; *voice:* Mel Blanc; *mus:* Carl W. Stalling; *prod sup:* Henry Binder, Raymond G. Katz; b&w. *sd:* Vit. 7 min. • A firefly explores the inner sanctum of a tent pitched in the forest and goes on a hiking tour over a sleeping camper.

3406. Joe's Lunch Wagon (*Paul Terry-Toon*) 6 Apr. 1934; *p.c.:* Moser & Terry for Educational/Fox; *dir:* Frank Moser, Paul Terry; *mus:* Philip A. Scheib; b&w. *sd:* WE. 6 min. • No story available.

3407. Johann Mouse (*Tom & Jerry*) 21 Mar. 1953; *p.c.:* MGM; *dir:* William Hanna, Joseph Barbera; *anim:* Kenneth Muse, Ray Patterson, Ed Barge, Irven Spence; *lay:* Dick Bickenbach; *back:* Robert Gentle; *ed:* Jim Faris; *voice:* Hans Conried; *mus:* Scott Bradley; *piano:* Jakob Gimpel; *ph:* Jack Stevens; *prod:* Fred Quimby; *col:* Tech. *sd:* WE. 7 min. *Academy Award.* • Tom takes advantage of Jerry's waltzing to Johann Strauss' music when the master goes away and takes a crash course in piano playing.

3408. John Henry and the Inky-Poo (*Puppetoon*) 6 Sept. 1946; *p.c.:* George Pal prods for Para; *prod/dir:* George Pal; *sup:* George E. Jordan; *story:* Latham Ovens, Robert Monroe; *anim:* Erwin Broner, Gene Warren; *sets:* Reginald Massie; *voices:* Rex Ingram, The Luvenia Nash Singers, Lillian Randolph; *mus:* Clarence Wheeler; *ph:* John S. Abbott; *col:* Tech. *sd:* WE. 7 min. *Academy Award nomination.* • John Henry has a contest with an automated steel driving engine to see which can lay tracks the fastest.

3409. Johnnie Fedora and Alice Bluebonnet (*Marquee Musical*) 21 May 1954; *p.c.:* Walt Disney prods for BV; *dir:* Jack Kinney; *col:* Tech. *sd:* RCA. 7½ min. • A romance between two hats is broken up when one is sold. The boy fedora searches the city for his lady love and eventually finds her. • See: *Make Mine Music*

3410. Johnny Appleseed 22 Dec. 1955; *p.c.:* Walt Disney prods for BV; *dir:* Wilfred Jackson; *col:* Tech. *sd:* RCA. 19 min. • Instead of going to war, Johnny covers the country in apple trees, spurred on by his Angel. • See: *Make Mine Music*

3411. Johnny Out of the Inkwell 1921; *p.c.;* Bray prods; *dir;* Earl Hurd; b&w. sil. *l/a/anim.* • No story available.

3412. Johnny Smith and Poker-Huntas (*Merrie Melodies*) 22 Oct. 1938; *p.c.:* Leon Schlesinger prods for WB; *dir:* Fred Avery; *story:* Richard Hogan, Robert Clampett; *anim:* Paul Smith; *sets:* John Didrik Johnsen; *ed:* Tregoweth E. Brown; *voices:* Mel Blanc, Bernice Hansel; *mus:* Carl W. Stalling; *prod sup:* Henry Binder, Raymond G. Katz; *col:* tech. *sd:* Vit. 7 min. • Johnny Smith (Egghead) sights America in the form of Coney Island. He takes a beautiful Indian maiden back to his ship with the other savages in hot pursuit.

3413. The Johnstown Flood (*Mighty Mouse*) 28 June 1946; *p.c.:* TT for Fox; *dir:* Connie Rasinski; *story:* John Foster; *mus:* Philip A. Scheib; *col:* Tech. *sd:* RCA. 6 min. • A mouse Ranger sees an approaching flood. He drinks "Atomic Energy," becomes Mighty Mouse and flies off to everyone's salvation.

3414. Joint Wipers (*Tom & Jerry*) 23 Apr. 1932; *p.c.:* Van Beuren for RKO; *dir:* John Foster, George Stallings; *mus:* Gene Rodemich; b&w. *sd:* RCA. 7 min. • The boys are plumbers whose handiwork causes a flood that washes away the whole apartment block, just leaving the pipes standing.

3415. The Jolly Fish (*Tom & Jerry*) 19 Aug. 1932; *p.c.:* Van Beuren for RKO; *dir:* John Foster, George Stallings; *mus:* Gene Rodemich; b&w. *sd:*

RCA. 6 min. • The boys are fishing in a row-boat and hear the fish having a party. The fish have fun with the luckless fishermen who end up with catching nothing.

3416. Jolly Good Felons *(Little King)* 16 Feb. 1934; *p.c.:* Van Beuren for RKO; *dir:* George Stallings; *anim:* Jim Tyer; *mus:* Gene Rodemich; b&w. *sd:* RCA. 7 min. • The King visits a prison and causes a jail break.

3417. A Jolly Good Ferlough *(Popeye)* 23 Apr. 1943; *p.c.:* Famous for Para; *dir:* Dan Gordon; *story:* Joseph Stultz; *anim:* Joe Oriolo, John Walworth, Al Eugster; *voices:* Jack Mercer, Margie Hines, Carl Meyer; *mus:* Sammy Timberg; *ph:* Leonard McCormick; *prod mgr:* Sam Buchwald; b&w. *sd:* RCA. 7 min. • Popeye is granted leave but his nephews' shenanigans prove too much for the mighty mariner and he is pleased to return to the relative quiet of the war.

3418. The Jolly Jail Bird *(Aesop's Film Fable)* 25 May 1924; *p.c.:* Fables Pictures Inc for Pathé; *dir:* Paul Terry; b&w. *sil.* 5 min. • A dog escapes from prison to lead the life of a vagabond, travelling by freight train and stealing food. A dog cop chases him, firing an explosive cannonball at him which projects him right back into the prison yard and the rock pile.

3419. Jolly Little Elves *(Cartune Classic)* 1 Oct. 1934; *p.c.:* Univ; *prod:* Walter Lantz; *dir:* Manuel Moreno; *story/lyrics:* Walter Lantz, Victor McLeod; *anim:* Manuel Moreno, Lester Kline, Fred Kopietz; *voice:* Bernice Hansel; *mus:* James Dietrich; *col:* Tech-2. *sd:* WE. 8 min. • A poor cobbler offers an elf his last doughnut for which he repays him by making his shoes.

3420. Jolly the Clown *(Noveltoon)* 25 Oct. 1957; *p.c.:* Para Cartoons; *dir:* Seymour Kneitel; *story:* Carl Meyer; *anim:* Al Eugster, Wm. B. Pattengill; *sets:* Robert Little; *voice:* Jackson Beck; *mus:* Winston Sharples; *ph:* Leonard McCormick; *prod mgr:* Seymour Shultz; *col:* Tech. *sd:* RCA. 6 min. • Elsworth the elephant is fired from the circus and Jolly the clown tries to save his job.

3421. A Jolt for General Germ 21 May 1931; *p.c.:* The Fleischer Studio for Lyson; *prod:* Max Fleischer; *dir:* Dave Fleischer; b&w. *sd:* WE. 6 min. • An army of germs descend upon a country. After a courier is dispatched to the drugstore for a bottle of Lyson, the army is wiped out.

3422. Journey Back to Oz 1974 (made in 1964); *p.c.:* Filmation Associates for Col/WB; *prod:* Norm Prescott, Lou Schiemer; *dir:* Hal Sutherland; *seq dir:* Rudy Larriva, Don Towsley; *dir sup:* Amby Paliwoda; *story:* Fred Ladd, Norman Prescott, Bernard Evslin; *storyboard:* Sherman Labby; *anim:* Bob Bransford, Bob Carlson, Jim Davis, Ed Friedman, Otto Feuer, Fred Grable, La Verne Harding, Lou Kachavis, Les Kaluza, Anatole Kirsanoff, George Kreisl, Paul Krukowski, Bill Nunes, Jack Ozark, Manny Perez, Virgil Raddatz, Bill Reed, Virgil Ross, George Rowley, Ed Solomon, Ralph Somerville, Reuben Timmens, Lou Zukor; *art dir:* Don Christensen; *lay:* Alberto de Mello, Don Bluth, C.L. Hartman, Kay Wright, Herb Hazelton, Dale Baer; *key asst:* Mike Hazy; *des:* Ervin L. Kaplan; *back:* Paul Xander, Maurice Harvey, Don Peters, Phil Lewis, Bill Loudenslager; *ed:* Joseph Simon; *voices: The Cowardly Lion:* Milton Berle; *Woodenhead:* Herschel Bernardi; *Uncle Henry:* Paul Ford; *Aunt Em:* Margaret Hamilton; *The Signpost:* Jack E. Leonard; *Pumpkinhead:* Paul Lynde; *Mombi:* Ethel Merman; *Dorothy:* Lisa Minelli; *Glinda:* Rise Stevens; *The Tin Man:* Danny Thomas; *also:* Mel Blanc, Dallas McKennon, Larry Storch; *songs:* Sammy Cahn, James van Heusen; arranged & conducted by Walter Scharf; *ph:* Sergio Antonio Alcazar, Ray Bloss, R.W. Pope, John Aardal; *checking:* Marion Turk, Jane Philippi, Marjorie Roach, Dottie Poell, Richie Craig; *Xerography:* John Remmel; *i&p:* Betty Brooks; *coord:* June Gilham; *sd.* Horta-Mahana; *prod mgr:* Rock Benedetto; *asso prod:* Fred Ladd, Preston Blair; *col:* Tech. *sd.* 90 min. • Animated sequel to Frank L. Baum's *The Wizard of Oz* with Dorothy returning to see her old friends.

3423. Judge for a Day *(Betty Boop)* 20 Sept. 1935; *p.c.:* The Fleischer Studio for Para; *prod:* Max Fleischer; *dir:* Dave Fleischer; *anim:* Myron Waldman, Hicks Lokey, Lillian Friedman; *lay:* Myron Waldman; *voice:* Mae Questel; *mus:* Sammy Timberg; b&w. *sd:* WE. 6 min. • Betty passes her own sentences on all pests.

3424. Judge's Crossword Puzzles *p.c.:* Pioneer Films for Educational; *dir:* John C. Terry; *prod:* Harry Segal, Jack Segal; *ed:* Isador Schwartz; b&w. st • 1925 • (1) 31 Jan; (2) 8 Mar; (3) 15 Mar; (4) 22 Mar; (5) 29 Mar; (6) 5 Apr; (7) 12 Apr; (8) 19 Apr; (9) 29 Apr; (10) 3 May • The current craze of crosswords is brought to the screen. Definitions are given in a comic vein and are followed by amusing comments. The patron is given a few seconds in which to guess the synonyms before a hand crosses the screen and fills them into the grid.

3425. Judo Kudos *(Sad Cat)* 31 Dec. 1968; *p.c.:* TT for Fox; *col:* DeLuxe. *sd:* RCA. 5 min. • Sad Cat's Super Ego turns him into a judo expert by means of a magic pink belt. • See: *Sad Cat*

3426. The Juggler of Our Lady Apr. 1958; *p.c.:* TT for Fox; *ex prod:* Bill Weiss; *dir sup:* Gene Deitch; *dir/anim:* Al Kouzel; *story/des/consultant:* R.O. Blechman; *voice:* Boris Karloff; *mus:* Phil Scheib; *prod mgr:* Frank Schudde; *col:* Tech. *sd:* RCA. 6 min. CS. • Based on the book by Bob Blechman, a medieval juggler is unhappy because his juggling is not changing the world ... so he joins an order of monks.

3427. Juke Box Jamboree *(Swing Symphony)* 27 July 1942; *p.c.:* Walter Lantz prods for Univ; *dir:* Alex Lovy; *story:* Ben Hardaway, Chuck Couch; *anim:* (La)Verne Harding; *sets:* Fred Brunish; *voices:* Mel Blanc; "Chi Qui Chiquita" sung by Zedra de la Condé; *mus:* Darrell Calker; *col:* Tech. *sd:* WE. 7 min. *Academy Award nomination.* • Muzie Mouse's slumber is disturbed by a jukebox. His efforts to quieten it deposits him into a glass of "Zowie," causing hallucinations.

3428. Jumanji 16 Dec. 1995; *p.c.:* Interscope Communications/Teitler Film Prod. for Colum TriStar; *special visual fx/anim:* ILM: *snr staff:* Jeff Mann, Thomas A. Williams, Patricia Blau Price, Jim Morris; *anim sup:* Kyle Balda; *digital model sup:* Geoff Campbell; *cg sup:* Carl Frederick, Jim Mitchell, Ellen Poon, Doug Smythe; *cg seq sup:* Habib Zargarpour; *cg anim:* Philip Edward Alexy, Eric Armstrong, Peter Daulton, Jenn Emberly, Daniel Jeannette, David Kelly-Andrews, Julija Learie, Dale McBeath, Marjolaine Tremblay, Steve Williams; *cg art:* Joel Aron, Christopher Henry, David Horsley, Ed Kramer, Tim McLaughlin, Steve Molin, Barbara L. Nellis, Damian Steel, Robert Weaver; *visual fx co-ord:* Jill Brooks, Elizabeth Brown; *post prod sup anim:* James Satorustraus; *col:* Tech. *sd:* Dolby stereo/SDDS. 104 min. *l/a.* • Live-action fantasy: A young boy unearths a box that contains "Jumanji," a board game. He plays it with a friend who is chased away by bats when the boy gets sucked right into the board. Twenty-six years later a couple of children discover the board and continue the game, which conjours up various wild beasts that spring from the board, also releasing the original boy from his confinement.

3429. Jumpin' Jupiter *(Merrie Melodies)* 6 Aug. 1955; *p.c.:* WB; *dir:* Charles M. Jones; *story:* Michael Maltese; *anim:* Ken Harris, Keith Darling, Abe Levitow, Richard Thompson; *fx:* Harry Love; *lay:* Robert Givens; *back:* Philip de Guard; *ed:* Treg Brown; *voices:* Mel Blanc; *mus:* Carl Stalling; *prod mgr:* John W. Burton; *prod:* Edward Selzer; *col:* Tech. *sd:* Vit. 7 min. • Porky and Sylvester's camping trip is marred by visiting Martians collecting earth specimens.

3430. Jumping Beans *(Out of the Inkwell)* 15 Dec. 1922; *p.c.:* Inkwell Studio for Winkler; *prod:* Max Fleischer; *dir:* Dave Fleischer; b&w. *sil.* 10½ min. • Max produces a box of Mexican jumping beans which grow into a massive beanstalk when planted. Koko is encouraged to climb to the top where he is chased by a giant "head." He wreaks his revenge by creating hundreds of his own image and instructs them to tie-up Max.

3431. Jumping Beans *(Paul Terry-Toon)* 2 Nov. 1930; *p.c.:* A-C for Educational; *prod/dir:* Frank Moser, Paul Terry; *mus:* Philip A. Scheib; b&w. *sd:* WE. 9 min. • The cowboy hero feeds a Mexican cat bandit with jumping beans in his beer.

3432. Jumping with Toy *(Noveltoon)* 4 Oct. 1957; *p.c.:* Famous for Para; *dir:* Seymour Kneitel; *story:* Jack Mercer; *anim:* Wm. B. Pattengill; *sets:* Robert Owen; *voices:* Sid Raymond, Jackson Beck, Cecil Roy; *mus:* Winston Sharples; *ph:* Leonard McCormick; *prod mgr:* Abe Goodman; *col:* Tech. *sd:* RCA. 6 min. • The fox disguises as Santa on Christmas Eve to fool Baby Huey into the cooking pot.

3433. The June Bride *(Aesop's Film Fable)* 31 Jan. 1926; *p.c.:* Fables Pictures Inc for Pathé; *dir:* Paul Terry; b&w. *sil.* 5 min. • Farmer Al interrupts the matchmaking of two cats. Their love triumphs with the aid of a minister while Al attempts to break down the door.

3434. A June Bride *(Paul Terry-Toon)* 1 Nov. 1935; *p.c.:* Moser & Terry for Educational/Fox; *dir:* Frank Moser, Paul Terry; *mus:* Philip A. Scheib; b&w. *sd:* WE. 5 min. • A couple of cats become embroiled with the Farmer and a wedding ensues.

3435. Jungle Bells (*Hot Dog*) 26 Apr. 1927; *p.c.:* Bray prods for FBO; *dir:* Walt Lantz, Clyde Geronimi; b&w. *sil.* 5 min. *l/a/anim.* • Walt is painting in the jungle when Pete emerges from the paint tube. He encounters a tiger, a rattlesnake and a skunk.

3436. Jungle Bike Riders (*Aesop's Film Fable*) 14 Mar. 1925; *p.c.:* Fables Pictures Inc for Pathé; *dir:* Paul Terry; b&w. *sil.* 10 min. • A ten-day bicycle race in Jungleland.

3437. The Jungle Book 18 Oct. 1967 *p.c.:* Walt Disney prods for BV; *dir:* Wolfgang Reitherman; story inspired by Rudyard Kipling; *story adapt:* Larry Clemmons, Ralph Wright, Ken Anderson, Vance Gerry; *anim dir:* Milt Kahl, Ollie Johnston, Frank Thomas, John Lounsbery; *anim:* Hal King, Eric Cleworth, Eric Larson, Fred Hellmich, Walt Stanchfield, John Ewing, Dick Lucas; *fx:* Dan MacManus; *lay:* Don Griffiths, Basil Davidovich, Tom Codrick, Dale Barnhart, Sylvia Roemer; *back styling:* Al Dempster; *back:* Bill Layne, Ralph Hulett, Art Riley, Thelma Witmer, Frank Armitage; *ed:* Tom Acosta, Norman Carlisle; *voices: Baloo:* Phil Harris; *Bagheera:* Sebastian Cabot; *Shere Kahn:* George Sanders; *King Louie:* Louis Prima; *Kaa:* Sterling Holloway; *Col. Hathi/Buzzie:* J. Pat O'Malley; *Mowgli:* Bruce Reitherman; *Winifred:* Verna Felton; *Hathi's son:* Clint Howard; *Akela:* John Abbott; *Rama:* Ben Wright; *Dizzie:* Lord Tim Hudson; *Flaps:* Chad Stuart; *The Girl:* Darleen Carr; *Ziggy:* Digby Wolfe; *Monkeys:* Leo de Lyon, Bill Skiles, Pete Henderson, Hal Smith; *Monkey singing group:* Sam Butera & The Witnesses; *Vulture singing group:* The Jack Halloran Group; *Shere Kahn's singing voice:* Thurl Ravenscroft; *mus:* George Bruns; *orch:* Walter Sheets; *songs:* Richard M. Sherman, Robert B. Sherman; *The Bare Necessities* by Terry Gilkyson; *mus ed:* Evelyn Kennedy; *sd:* Robert O. Cook; *prod mgr:* Don Duckwall; *col:* Tech. *sd:* RCA. 78 min. • Bagheera the Panther transports Mowgli, a human boy who has been raised by the wolves, to the "Man Village" where he will be safe from the tiger, Shere Kahn. Along the way, Mowgli is side-tracked by Baloo, a fun-loving bear who gets him into many scrapes.

3438. Jungle Days (*Aesop's Film Fable*) 19 Mar. 1928; *p.c.:* Fables Pictures Inc for Pathé; *dir:* John Foster, Paul Terry; b&w. *sil.* 10 min. • A Stone Age cave man sets out to get himself a mate. After a long pursuit, she is finally in his arms but changes her mind and knocks him out cold.

3439. A Jungle Flirtation 6 Sept. 1913; *p.c.* Bray prods for Pathé-Eclectic; *dir/anim:* John R. Bray; b&w. *sil.* • No story available. Reissued as *Jocko the Lovesick Monk*.

3440. The Jungle Fool (*Aesop's Sound Fable*) 15 Sept. 1929; *p.c.:* Van Beuren for Pathé; *dir:* John Foster, Mannie Davis; *mus:* Carl Edouarde; b&w. *sd:* RCA. 6 min. • The fool in question is Al Falfa who appears as an African explorer who is chased by the entire jungle population.

3441. Jungle Jam (*Tom & Jerry*) 14 Nov. 1931; *p.c.:* Van Beuren for RKO; *dir:* John Foster, George Rufle; *mus:* Gene Rodemich; b&w. *sd:* RCA. 7½ min. • No story available.

3442. Jungle Jazz (*Aesop's Sound Fable*) 6 July 1930; *p.c.:* Van Beuren for Pathé; *dir:* John Foster, Harry Bailey; *mus:* Gene Rodemich; b&w. *sd:* RCA. 6 min. • Two cats entertain the jungle inhabitants by performing the jazz hit "Dardanella," then narrowly escape being captured by cannibals.

3443. Jungle Jingles (*Oswald*) 6 July 1929; *p.c.:* Winkler for Univ; *anim:* Ben Clopton; b&w. *sd:*WE. 5 min. • Oswald's adventures on an African safari. He rides an ostrich, tries to capture an elephant and is menaced by a lion until he steals the creature's molars.

3444. Jungle Jitters (*Merrie Melodies*) 19 Feb. 1938; *p.c.:* Leon Schlesinger prods for WB; *dir:* I. Freleng; *story:* George Manuell; *anim:* Phil Monroe; *lay:* Griff Jay; *back:* Arthur Loomer; *ed:* Tregoweth E. Brown; *voices:* Mel Blanc, Ted Pierce; *mus:* Carl W. Stalling; *prod sup:* Henry Binder, Raymond G. Katz; *col:* Tech. *sd:* Vit. 7 min. • A goofy salesman tries to sell some home appliances to a tribe of cannibals.

3445. Jungle Jitters (*Willie Whopper*) 24 July 1934; *p.c.:* Celebrity prods for MGM; *prod/dir:* Ub Iwerks; *anim:* Robert G. Stokes, Norm Blackburn; *mus:* Carl Stalling; b&w. *sd:* PCP. 6 min. • Willie spins a yarn about being shipwrecked on a desert isle and saving a native girl from cannibals.

3446. Jungle Jive (*Swing Symphony*) 4 May 1944; *p.c.:* Walter Lantz prods for Univ; *dir:* James Culhane; *story:* Ben Hardaway, Milt Schaffer; *anim:* Paul Smith, Emery Hawkins, (La)Verne Harding, Les Kline, Pat Matthews, Don Williams; *lay:* Art Heinemann; *back:* Philip de Guard; *mus:* Darrell Calker; *pianist:* Bob Zurkè; *col:* Tech. *sd:* WE. 7 min. • The Sandwich Islanders have a jam session when a whole orchestra of instruments gets washed ashore. Jazz pianist Bob Zurkè recorded this one month before he died.

3447. A Jungle Jumble (*Oswald*) 29 June 1932; *p.c.:* Univ; *dir:* Walter Lantz, "Bill" Nolan; *anim:* Manuel Moreno, Ray Abrams, Fred Avery, "Bill"Weber, Vet Anderson, Lester Kline, Bunny Ellison; *mus:* James Dietrich; b&w. *sd:* WE. 6½ min. • Oswald chases a mouse into a palm tree that dislodges many coconuts which are swallowed by an ostrich. The ostrich becomes a coconut cannon by spitting nuts at the mouse.

3448. Jungle Rhythm (*Mickey Mouse*) 15 Nov. 1929; *p.c.:* Walter E. Disney for Colum; *dir:* Walt Disney; *anim:* Ub Iwerks; *mus:* Carl W. Stalling; b&w. *sd:* PCP. 5 min. • Mickey dances with the elephants, monkeys and other jungle animals.

3449. Jungle Sports (*Aesop's Film Fable*) 4 July 1926; *p.c.:* Fables Pictures Inc for Pathé; *dir:* Paul Terry; b&w. *sil.* 10 min. • Farmer Al Falfa is judge on the jungle field day. He imbibes "hooch" and gives an unfavorable decision resulting in being chased by the whole Noah's ark menagerie.

3450. A Jungle Triangle (*Aesop's Film Fable*) 14 Apr. 1928; *p.c.:* Fables Pictures Inc for Pathé; *dir:* Paul Terry, Mannie Davis; b&w. *sil.* 10 min. • Martin Monk's girl is kidnapped by Jumbo when he follows them to a nightclub and slips a sleeping drug into Martin's drink to reclaim his sweetie.

3451. The Junk Man (*Aesop's Film Fable*) 25 Dec. 1927; *p.c.:* Fables Pictures Inc for Pathé; *dir:* Paul Terry, Mannie Davis; b&w. *sil.* 10 min. • A mouse and cat's warbling is rewarded with junk being thrown at them. They sell it to a junk man (Farmer Al Falfa) then, with the aid of a magnet, go fishing and aggravate a swordfish who chases them up a telegraph pole. Moral: "Some men are as helpless as a blind man with a plate of spaghetti."

3452. Jurassic Park 9 June 1993; *p.c.:* Amblin Entertainment/Univ; *Special visual fx/full motion dinosaurs:* ILM; *sup:* Mark A.Z. Dippé; *prod:* Janet Healy; *exec in charge of prod:* Patricia Blau; *Lead cgi sup:* Stefen M. Frangmeier; *cgi sup:* Alex Seiden, George Murphy; *cgi anim:* Eric Armstrong, Steve Williams, Steve Price, James Satoru Straus, Geoff Campbell, Don Waller; *cgi artist:* Jean M. Cunningham, Carl N. Frederick, Thomas L. Hutchinson, Joe Letteri, Jeffrey B. Light, James D. Mitchell, Joseph Pasquale, Ellen Poon, Stephen Rosenbaum, John Schlag, Tien Truong, Wade Howie; *cg software developer:* Michael J. Natkin, Zoran Kacic-Alesic, Brian Knep, Eric Enderton, John Horn, Paul Ashdown; *cg ph matchmoves:* Patrick T. Myers, Charles Clavadetscher; *cg dpt prod mgr:* Gail Currey; *cg dpt operations mgr:* John Berton; *snr cg dpt mgr:* Douglas Scott Key; *software sup/digital technology:* Thomas A. Williams; *co-ord:* Judith Weaver; *art dir:* TyRuben Ellingson; *ed:* Michael Gleason; *scanning sup:* Joshua Pines; *optical sup:* John Ellis; *plate prod:* Mark S. Miller; *digital art:* Carolyn Ensle-Rendu, Dave Carson, Sandy Houston, Barbara Brennan, Lisa Drostova, Bart Giovanetti, Rita E. Zimmerman, Kathleen Beeler, Greg Maloney; *scanning operator:* Randall K. Bean, Mike Ellis, George Gambetta; *video engineer:* Fred Meyers, Gary Meyer; *cg co-ord:* Ginger Thiesen, Nancy Jill Luckoff; *ph:* Pat Turner, Terry Chostner; *addit plate ph:* Scott Farrar; *Matte art:* Chris Evans, Yusei Uesugi; *editorial co-ord:* David Tanaka; *chief model maker:* Barbara Affonso, Steve Cawley, Chris Reed, Lorne Peterson, Ira Keeler; *optical ph:* Keith L. Johnson, James C. Lim; *optical line-up:* ;John D. Whisnant, Kristen Trattner; *optical/scanning co-ord:* Lisa Vaughn; *"Mr. D.N.A.":* Kurtz & Friends; *movement des:* Bob Kurtz; *lay:* Robert Peluce; *cgi anim:* Eric Armstrong, James Satoru, Steve Spaz Williams, Geoff Campbell, Steve Price, Don Waller; *Mr. D.N.A. voice:* Greg Burson; *mus:* John Williams; *col:* DeLuxe. *sd:* Dolby Stereo. Panavision. 126½ min. *l/a/ cgi.* • Live-action adventure fantasy: A group of experts are brought in to survey a tycoon's latest project, a dinosaur theme park. A storm makes the dinosaurs react in an aggressive way and they run riot, putting the humans' lives in danger.

3453. Just a Clown (*Paul Terry-Toon*) 20 Apr. 1934; *p.c.:* Moser & Terry for Educational/Fox; *dir:* Frank Moser, Paul Terry; *mus:* Philip A. Scheib; b&w. *sd:* WE. 5 min. • A little circus clown is spurned by the pretty bareback rider. She is later captured by a lion and the clown comes to her rescue.

3454. Just a Gigolo (*Screen Songs*) 9 Sept. 1932; *p.c.:* The Fleischer Studio for Para; *prod:* Max Fleischer; *sup:* Dave Fleischer; *dir/story/anim:* James H. Culhane, Rudy Zamora, Reuben Timinsky; *mus:* Art Turkisher; *song:* Irving Caésar, Leo Naello Casucci; *l/a:* Irene Bordoni; b&w. *sd:* WE. 6 min. • Betty is a cigarette girl in a nightclub setting.

3455. Just a Little Bull (*Terry-Toon*) 19 Apr. 1940; *p.c.:* TT for Fox; *dir:* Eddie Donnelly; *story:* John Foster; *mus:* Philip A. Scheib; *col:* Tech. *sd:* RCA. 6 min. • Cattle rustlers steal Mother and Junior bull comes to her rescue.

3456. Just a Wolf at Heart (*Loopy de Loop*) Feb. 1963; *p.c.:* Hanna-Barbera for Colum; *prod/dir:* Joseph Barbera, William Hanna; *story dir:* Paul Sommer; *story:* Dalton Sandifer; *anim dir:* Charles A. Nichols; *anim:* Jack Ozark; *lay:* Dan Noonan; *back:* Neenah Maxwell; *ed:* Donald A. Douglas; *voices:* Daws Butler, Don Messick, Jean van der Pyl; *mus:* Hoyt Curtin; *titles:* Lawrence Gobel; *prod mgr:* Howard Hanson; *col:* East. *sd:* RCA. 6 min. • The arrival of Mlle GaGa affects Loopy enough to make him start stealing lambs to provide her with a lamb's wool stole.

3457. Just Ask Jupiter (*Terry-Toon*) 18 Feb. 1938; *p.c.:* TT for Educational/Fox; *dir:* Mannie Davis; *mus:* Philip A. Scheib; b&w. *sd:* RCA. 6 min. • A mouse dreams he is sent to Jupiter and asks to be made a cat. When he is, he's branded a sissy by the other cats and shunned by the mice.

3458. Just Dogs (*Silly Symphony*) 30 July 1932; *p.c.:* Walt Disney prods for UA; *dir:* Burton F. Gillett; *anim:* Johnny Cannon, Les Clark, Gilles de Tremaudan; Clyde Geronimi, David D. Hand, Albert Hurter, Jack King, Richard Lundy, Tom Palmer, Ben Sharpsteen; *mus:* Bert Lewis; b&w. *sd:* PCP. 7 min. • A little pup in the city pound releases all the other dogs and a free-for-all ensues.

3459. Just Ducky (*Tom & Jerry*) 5 Sept. 1953; *p.c.:* MGM; *dir:* William Hanna, Joseph Barbera; *anim:* Irven Spence, Ray Patterson, Ed Barge, Kenneth Muse, Al Grandmain; *lay:* Dick Bickenbach; *back:* Robert Gentle; *ed:* Jim Faris; *voice:* Red Coffee; *mus:* Scott Bradley; *ph:* Jack Stevens; *prod:* Fred Quimby; *col:* Tech. *sd:* WE. 6 min. • Jerry teaches a duckling who can't swim. Tom takes advantage of the creature's defect.

3460. Just Mickey (*Mickey Mouse*) 6 Mar. 1930; *p.c.:* Walter E. Disney for Colum; *dir/voice:* Walt Disney; *mus:* Bert Lewis; *ph:* William Cottrell; b&w. *sd:* PCP. 6 min. • Violinist Mickey talks to the cinema audience.

3461. Just One More Chance (*Screen Songs*) 1 Apr. 1932; *p.c.:* The Fleischer Studio for Para; *prod:* Max Fleischer; *sup:* Dave Fleischer; *dir/story/anim:* James H. Culhane, Rudy Zamora; *add anim:* David Tendlar; *mus:* Art Turkisher; *song:* Sam Coslow, Arthur Johnston; *l/a:* Arthur Jarrett; b&w. *sd:* WE. 8 min. *l/a/anim.* • Bimbo enters the world of gambling but when the paddy wagon is called, he is left holding five aces.

3462. Just Plane Beep (*Merrie Melodies*) 30 Oct. 1965; *p.c.:* DFE for WB; *dir:* Rudy Larriva; *story:* Don Jurwich; *anim:* Bob Bransford, Hank Smith, Virgil Ross; *lay:* Erni Nordli; *back:* Anthony Rizzo; *ed:* Lee Gunther; *mus:* Bill Lava; *col:* Tech. *sd:* Vit. 5 min. • The Coyote engages the use of a First World War biplane in his pursuit of the elusive bird.

3463. Just Spooks (*Dinky Doodle*) 15 Sept. 1925; *p.c.:* Bray prods for FBO; *dir/story:* Walt Lantz; *anim:* Clyde Geronimi; b&w. sil. 6 min. *l/a/anim.* • Dinky and his pup Weakheart masquerade as ghosts to scare Walter, causing him to go through a number of thrilling adventures to escape the clutching hand.

3464. K-9000: A Space Oddity 1970; *p.c.:* The Haboush Co; *dir/anim:* Robert Mitchell, Robert Swarthe; *also:* John Kimball, Dale Case, Selby Daley, Emeline Seutter, Harry Morrow, Marsha Woodford, Robert Mertz, Roger Chouinard, James Haboush; *ph:* Dickson/Vasu; *col. sd:* Bell Sound System. 5 min. • Canine send-up of Stanley Kubrick's *2001: A Space Odyssey.*

3465. Kangaroo 1917/1920; *p.c.:* Inkwell Studio; *prod:* Max Fleischer; *dir:* Dave Fleischer; b&w. sil. • No story available.

3466. Kangaroo Courting (*Mr. Magoo*) 22 July 1954; *p.c.:* UPA for Colum; *ex prod:* Stephen Bosustow; *dir:* Pete Burness; *story:* Paul Schneider, Jack Fleischman, Tedd Pierce; *anim:* Cecil Surry, Tom McDonald, Rudy Larriva; *lay:* Sterling Sturtevant; *back:* Bob McIntosh; *voices:* Jim Backus, Jerry Hausner; *mus:* George Bruns; *prod mgr:* Herbert Klynn; *col:* Tech. *sd:* RCA. 7 min. • Magoo mistakes a boxing kangaroo for Waldo's girl and tries to reunite the two.

3467. The Kangaroo Kid (*Color Rhapsody*) 28 Dec. 1938; *p.c.:* Charles Mintz prods for Colum; *dir:* Ben Harrison; *anim:* Manny Gould; *voices:* Dave Weber, Robert Winkler, Marha Wentworth; *mus:* Joe de Nat; *col:* Tech. *sd:* RCA. 7½ min. • A young violinist finds himself set to fight the fearsome "Kangaroo Killer." He has no heart for fighting until Killer wrecks his violin.

3468. Kangaroo Steak (*Paul Terry-Toon*) 27 July 1930; *p.c.:* A-C for Educational/Fox; *dir:* Frank Moser, Paul Terry; *anim:* Frank Little; *mus:* Philip A. Scheib; b&w. *sd:* WE. 6 min. • No story available.

3469. Kannibal Kapers (*Krazy Kat*) 27 Dec. 1935; *p.c.:* Winkler for Colum; *story:* Ben Harrison; *anim:* Manny Gould; *mus:* Joe de Nat; *prod mgr:* James Bronis; b&w. *sd:* RCA. 6 min. • Krazy is castaway on a cannibal isle and visits their night club, "The Coconut Grove."

3470. The Karnival Kid (*Mickey Mouse*) 31 July 1929; *p.c.:* Walter E. Disney for Colum; *dir:* Walt Disney; *anim:* Ub Iwerks; *mus:* Carl W. Stalling; b&w/tinted. *sd:* PCP. 6 min. • Hot-Dog vendor Mickey enjoys an amusement park.

3471. Katnip Kollege (*Merrie Melodies*) 11 June 1938; *p.c.:* Leon Schlesinger prods for WB; *dir:* Ben Hardaway, Cal Dalton; *story:* Dave Monahan; *anim:* Joe d'Igalo; *lay:* Griff Jay; *back:* Arthur Loomer; *ed:* Tregoweth E. Brown; *voices:* Cliff Nazarro, Dave Weber, The Pied Pipers, Mel Blanc; *mus:* Carl W. Stalling; *song:* Johnny Mercer, Richard A. Whiting; pre-recorded from *Over the Goal:* Johnny "Scat" Davis, Mabel Todd, Poley McClintock, the Fred Waring Glee Club; *prod sup:* Henry Binder, Raymond G. Katz; *col:* Tech. *sd:* Vit. 7 min. • A Swing College student is no good at "Swingology" and his professor makes him stay after class where he soon picks up the rhythm.

3472. Katnip's Big Day (*Herman & Katnip*) 30 Oct. 1959; *p.c.:* Para Cartoons; *dir:* Seymour Kneitel; *anim:* Wm. B. Pattengill, Jack Ehret; *sets:* Robert Owen; *voices:* Sid Raymond, Arnold Stang, Jackson Beck, Jack Mercer; *mus:* Winston Sharples; *ph:* Leonard McCormick; *prod mgr:* Abe Goodman; *col:* Tech. *sd:* RCA. 6 min. Seq: *A Bicep Built for Two; Drinks on the Mouse; Cat-Choo; Mousetro Herman.* • Katnip is the subject of "This Is Your Life."

3473. The Katnips of 1940 (*Krazy Kat*) 12 Oct. 1934; *p.c.:* Winkler for Colum; *prod:* Charles B. Mintz; *story:* Ben Harrison; *anim:* Manny Gould, Al Rose, Preston Blair; *mus:* Joe de Nat; *prod mgr:* James Bronis; b&w. *sd:* RCA. 6 min. • Krazy picks a new leading lady for his musical after the Prima Donna flops at rehearsal.

3474. The Kat's Meow (*Krazy Kat*) 2 Jan. 1930; *p.c.:* Winkler for Colum; *prod:* Charles B. Mintz; *anim:* Ben Harrison, Manny Gould; *mus:* Joe de Nat; *prod mgr:* James Bronis; b&w. *sd:* RCA. 6 min. • No story available.

3475. The Katzenjammer Kids *p.c.:* IFS for Educational; *prod/dir:* Gregory la Cava; *story:* H.E. Hancock, Louis de Lorme; b&w. sil. • Rudolph Dirks' popular comic strip about a German Captain who is often the recipient of his kids' pranks. • *1918:* **Vanity and Vengeance** 22 Apr. **The Two Twins** 6 May. **His Last Will** 13 May. **Der Black Mitt** 20 May. **Fisherman's Luck** 27 May. **Up in the Air** 3 June. **Swat the Fly** 10 June. **The Best Man Loses** 24 June. **Crabs Iss Crabs** 1 July. **A Picnic for Two** 8 July. **A Heathern Benefit** 15 July. **Pep** 19 July. **War Gardens** Aug. aka: *The Shenanigan Kids* and *The Captain and the Kids.* • See: *Hearst-Vitagraph News Pictorial*

3476. Keen Cartoon Corporation *p.c.:* Keen Cartoon Corp for Univ; *prod:* P.A. Powers, R.F. Taylor, W.W. Wheatley; b&w. sil. • *1916:* **A Romance of Toyland** 9 Mar. *dir:* Horace Taylor. **A Toyland Mystery** 15 Mar. *dir:* Horace Taylor. **The Toyland Villain** 12 Apr. *dir:* Horace Taylor. **A Toyland Robbery** 10 May. *dir:* Horace Taylor. **Henry W. Zippy Buys a Motor Car** Oct. *dir:* Charles E. Howell. **Slinky the Yegg** Oct. *dir:* Lee Connor. **Jerry McDub Collects Some Accident Insurance** Oct. *dir:* H.M. Freck. **Superstitious Ceylon** 29 Nov. *dir:* Hy Mayer. **Henry W. Zippy Buys a Pet Pup** Dec. *dir:* Charles E. Howell. **Dr. Zippy in a Sanatorium** Dec. *dir:* Charles E. Howell. • *1917:* **Mose Is Cured** 1 Jan. **The Old Forty-Niner** 8 Jan. **Jeb Jenkins the Village Genius** 15 Jan. **Zoo-Illogical Studies** 5 Feb. **A Dangerous Girl** 12 Feb. **The Fighting Blood of Jerry McDub** 28 Feb. *dir:* H.M. Freck. **Mr. Coon** Mar. **When Does a Hen Lay an Egg?** 9 May. *dir:* Charles E. Howell. **Superstitious China** 26 May. *dir:* Hy Mayer.

3477. Keep Cool 1971; *p.c.:* Barrie Nelson Studio; *dir/story/anim:* Barrie Nelson; *mus:* Oscar Brown Jr.; *i&p:* Celine Miles; *ph:* Anicam; *col:* DeLuxe. *sd.* 3 min. • The song tells the story of a man who goes nuts after his girl leaves him.

3478. Keep 'Em Growing (*Terry-Toon*) 28 May 1943; *p.c.:* TT for Fox; *dir:* Mannie Davis; *story:* John Foster; *mus:* Philip A. Scheib; *col:* Tech. *sd:* RCA. 6½ min. • To relieve the situation facing the Farmer, the farm animals contribute to the war effort by helping with the ploughing and sowing.

3479. Keep in Style (*Betty Boop*) 16 Nov. 1934; *p.c.:* The Fleischer Studio for Para; *prod:* Max Fleischer; *dir:* Dave Fleischer; *anim:* Myron Waldman, Edward Nolan, Lillian Friedman; *voice:* Mae Questel; *mus:* Sammy Timberg; b&w. *sd:* WE. 7 min. • Betty stages a show to display her new reversable fashions.

3480. Keep Off the Grass (*Aesop's Film Fable*) 27 Mar. 1927; *p.c.:* Fables Pictures Inc for Pathé; *dir:* Paul Terry; b&w. *sil.* 10 min. • Al Falfa joins the Park Police. He later has to explain how he lost his uniform in a crap game with two monkeys.

3481. Keep Our Forests Pink (*Pink Panther*) 20 Nov. 1975; *p.c.:* Mirisch/Geoffrey/DFE for UA; *dir:* Gerry Chiniquy; *story:* John W. Dunn; *anim:* Bob Richardson, Nelson Shin, Norm McCabe, Bob Matz; *lay:* Dick Ung; *back:* Richard H. Thomas; *ed:* Rick Steward; *mus:* Walter Greene; *theme tune:* Henry Mancini; *ph:* John Burton Jr.; *prod mgr:* Lee Gunther; *col:* DeLuxe. *sd:* RCA. 6 min. • Ranger Panther has a task in trying to prevent a tourist from messing up the forest.

3482. Keep the Cool Baby (*Go Go Toon*) Aug. 1967; *p.c.:* Para Cartoons; *ex prod:* Shamus Culhane; *dir:* Chuck Harriton; *story:* Ruth Kneitel, Shamus Culhane; *anim:* Nick Tafuri, Doug Crane; *sets:* Gil Miret, Danté Barbetta; *voices:* Joe Silver; *mus:* Winston Sharples; *prod sup:* Harold Robins, Burt Hanft; *col:* Tech. *sd:* RCA. 6 min. • A hungry spider awaits his breakfast, losing all insects that enter his web, finally becoming captured himself for a grub's breakfast.

3483. Keep Your Grin Up (*Casper*) 27 May 1955; *p.c.:* Famous for Para; *dir:* I. Sparber; *story:* Larz Bourne; *anim:* Myron Waldman, Nick Tafuri; *sets:* Robert Connavale; *voices:* Norma MacMillan, Jack Mercer, Frank Matalone; *mus:* Winston Sharples; *ph:* Leonard McCormick; *prod mgr:* Seymour Shultz; *col:* Tech. *sd:* RCA. 6 min. • Casper attempts to cheer up a glum hyena.

3484. Keeper of the Lions (*Oswald*) 18 Oct. 1937; *p.c.:* Univ; *prod/dir:* Walter Lantz; *story:* Charles Bowers; *mus:* Nathaniel Shilkret, George Lessner; b&w. *sd:* WE. 6 min. • Zookeeper Oswald is chased by lions when Dumb Cluck sets them free.

3485. Keeping Up with Krazy (*Comic King*) Oct. 1962; *p.c.:* Para Cartoons; *dir:* Seymour Kneitel; *story:* Burton Goodman; *anim:* Nick Tafuri, Wm. B. Pattengill, Larry Silverman; *sets:* Anton Loeb; *voices:* Paul Frees, Penny Phillips; *mus:* Winston Sharples; *col:* Tech. *sd:* RCA. 5½ min. • No matter what improvement Kolin Kelly puts on his new Pre-fab, Krazy goes one better.

3486. Keeping Up with the Joneses (*Gaumont Cartoon Comedy*); *p.c.:* INS/King Features for Gaumont/Mutual; *anim:* Harry S. Palmer. b&w. *sil. s/r.* • Arthur "Pop" Momand's comic strip featuring Ma and Pa McGinnis. On same reel: *See America First.* • *1915:* **Dancing Lesson** 14 Sept. **title unknown** 21 Sept. **title unknown** 28 Sept. **The Reelem Moving Picture Co.** 5 Oct. **The Family Adopt a Camel** 12 Oct. **Pa Feigns Sickness** 19 Oct. **The Family's Tastes in Modern Furniture** 26 Oct. **Moving Day** 2 Nov. **The Family in Mexico** 9 Nov. **Pa Takes a Flier in Stocks** 16 Nov. **Pa Buys a Flivver** 23 Nov. **Pa Lectures on the War** 30 Nov. **The Skating Craze** 7 Dec. **Pa Sees Some New Styles** 14 Dec. **Ma Tries to Reduce** 21 Dec. **Pa Dreams He Wins the War** 28 Dec. • *1916:* **The Pet Parrot** 4 Jan. **Ma Drives a Car** 11 Jan. **title unknown** 18 Jan. **The Family Visits Florida** 23 Jan. **Pa Fishes in an Alligator Pond** 30 Jan. **Pa Tries to Write** 6 Feb. **Pa Dreams He Is Lost** 13 Feb. **Pa & Ma Have Their Fortunes Told** 20 Feb. **Pa Rides a Goat** 27 Feb. • Some typical examples of this series: **Pa Dreams He Wins the War** Pa dreams he's "at the Front," ousting all and their weapons from the trenches. He is awarded medals by the Kaiser and other representatives. **Ma Drives a Car** Ma McGinnis takes a joy ride, knocking down everything in her path.

3487. Keeps Rainin' All the Time (*Screen Songs*) 12 Jan. 1934; *p.c.:* The Fleischer Studio for Para; *prod:* Max Fleischer; *dir:* Dave Fleischer; *anim:* Seymour Kneitel, William Henning; *voice:* Mae Questel; *mus:* Sammy Timberg; *song:* Ted Koehler, Harold Arlen; *l/a:* Gertrude Niessen; b&w. *sd:* WE. 10 min. *l/a/anim.* • The little bear teaches the birds to fly. They later rescue him from being blown away by a storm.

3488. Kentucky Belles (*Oswald*) 2 Sept. 1931; *p.c.:* Univ; *dir:* Walter Lantz, "Bill" Nolan; *anim:* Clyde Geronimi, Manuel Moreno, Ray Abrams, Fred Avery, Lester Kline, Chet Karrberg, "Pinto" Colvig; *voices:* Mickey Rooney, Pinto Colvig; *mus:* James Dietrich; b&w. *sd:* WE. 6 min. • Oswald takes part in the Kentucky Derby. The winner gets a kiss from the pretty local belle.

3489. A Kick in Time (*Color Classic*) 17 May 1940; *p.c.:* The Fleischer Studio for Para; *prod:* Max Fleischer; *sup:* Dave Fleischer; *dir:* James Culhane; *story:* George Manuell; *anim:* James Culhane, Alfred Eugster, Nick Tafuri, Bob Wickersham; *sets:* Shane Miller; *ed:* Kitty Pfister; *voices:* Jack Mercer; *mus:* Sammy Timberg; *ph:* Charles Schettler; *prod sup:* Sam Buchwald, Isidore Sparber; *col:* Tech. *sd:* WE. 8 min. • Spunky is sold to a Junk Dealer who mistreats him. Hunky comes to the rescue in time to save him from the wheels of a trolley car.

3490. Kick Me 1975; *p.c.:* Robert Swarthe prods; *dir:* Robert Swarthe; *col. sd.* Academy Award nomination. • No story available.

3491. Kickapoo Juice (*Li'l Abner*) 12 Jan. 1945; *p.c.:* Colum; *prod:* Dave Fleischer; *dir:* Howard Swift; *story:* Sid Marcus; *anim:* Volus Jones, Grant Simmons; *sets:* Clark Watson; *voice:* Lurene Tuttle; *mus:* Eddie Kilfeather; *ph:* Frank Fisher; *col:* Tech. *sd:* RCA. 7 min. • Mammy Yokum tries to marry off Abner's two batchelor "heroes," Lonesome Polecat and Hairless Joe ... if only they could get their attention off Kickapoo Juice.

3492. Kickin' the Conga 'Round (*Popeye*) 16 Jan. 1942; *p.c.:* The Fleischer Studio for Para; *prod:* Max Fleischer; *dir:* Dave Fleischer; *story:* Bill Turner, Ted Pierce; *anim:* Tom Johnson, George Germanetti; *sets:* Anton Loeb; *voices:* Jack Mercer, Margie Hines, Ted Pierce; *mus:* Sammy Timberg; *prod sup:* Sam Buchwald, Isidore Sparber; b&w. *sd:* WE. 7 min. • While on leave in a South American port, Popeye and Bluto are vying for the affections of Olivia Oyla, a Latin songstress who is impressed by Bluto's mastery of the Conga.

3493. Kid from Mars (*Modern Madcap*) Feb. 1960; *p.c.:* Para Cartoons; *dir:* Seymour Kneitel; *story:* Jack Mercer, Carl Meyer; *anim:* Nick Tafuri, William Henning; *sets:* Robert Little; *voices:* Cecil Roy, Eddie Lawrence; *mus:* Winston Sharples; *ph;* Leonard McCormick; *prod mgr:* Abe Goodman; *col:* Tech. *sd:* RCA. 6 min. • A mother mistakes a genuine invader from outer space for her son dressed as a spaceman.

3494. Kid Noah 1925; *p.c.:* Sering D. Wilson; *dir:* Sering D. Wilson. • **The Old Family Toothbrush** 27 Jun., **The Cat's Shimmy** 1 Aug., **The Goldfish's Pajamas** 1 Sept., **Pot Luck** 1 Oct., • b&w. *sil.* 5 min. • No stories available.

3495. Kiddie Koncert (*Musical Miniature*) 23 Apr. 1948; *p.c.:* Walter Lantz prods for UA; *dir:* Dick Lundy; *story:* Ben Hardaway, Jack Cosgriff; *anim:* Ed Love, Sidney Pillet, Les Kline, Pat Matthews; *sets:* Fred Brunish; *voices:* Harry E. Lang, Nina Bara; *mus:* Darrell Calker; *prod mgr:* William E. Garity; *col:* Tech. *sd:* RCA. 6 min. • Wally Walrus is the school orchestra leader who gets stuck with a glob of bubble gum.

3496. Kiddie League (*Woody Woodpecker*) 3 Nov. 1959; *p.c.:* Walter Lantz prods for Univ; *dir:* Paul J. Smith; *story:* Dalton Sandifer; *anim:* Robert Bentley, Les Kline, Don Patterson; *sets:* Art Landy, Raymond Jacobs; *voices:* Dal McKennon, Grace Stafford; *mus:* Eugene Poddany; *prod mgr:* William E. Garity; *col:* Tech. *sd:* RCA. 6 min. • Unorthodox baseball game between the Woody Woodpeckers and The BubbleGummers.

3497. Kiddie Revue (*Oswald*) 21 Sept. 1936; *p.c.:* Univ; *dir:* Walter Lantz; *story:* Walter Lantz, Victor McLeod; *anim:* Manuel Moreno, Bill Mason; *mus:* James Dietrich; b&w. *sd:* RCA. 6 min. • Oswald puts on a show starring Lily Swans. A jealous poodle puts ants in Lily's pants which spread to the audience.

3498. A Kiddie's Kitty (*Merrie Melodies*) 20 Aug. 1955; *p.c.:* WB; *dir:* I. Freleng; *story:* Warren Foster; *anim:* Arthur Davis, Gerry Chiniquy, Ted Bonnicksen; *lay:* Hawley Pratt; *back:* Irv Wyner; *ed:* Treg Brown; *voices:* June Foray, Mel Blanc; *mus:* Milt Franklyn; *prod mgr:* John W. Burton;

prod: Edward Selzer; *col:* Tech. *sd:* Vit. 7 min. • Suzanne, a small girl adopts Sylvester and puts him through the mill, making him anxious to make his escape.

3499. Kiddin' the Kitten (*Merrie Melodies*) 5 Apr. 1952; *p.c.:* WB; *dir:* Robert McKimson; *story:* Tedd Pierce; *anim:* Phil de Lara, Charles McKimson, Rod Scribner; *lay:* Peter Alvarado; *back:* Richard H. Thomas; *ed:* Treg Brown; *voices:* Sheldon Leonard, Bea Benaderet, Mel Blanc; *prod mgr:* John W. Burton; *prod:* Edward Selzer; *col:* Tech; *sd:* Vit. 7 min. • Lazy Dodsworth the cat trains a kitten to do his mouse-catching for him.

3500. Kidnapped (*Aesop's Film Fable*) 2 June 1929; *p.c.:* Fables Pictures Inc for Pathé; *dir:* Paul Terry; b&w. *sil.* 10 min. • No story available.

3501. The Kids in the Shoe (*Color Classic*) 19 May 1935; *p.c.:* The Fleischer Studio for Para; *prod:* Max Fleischer; *dir:* Dave Fleischer; *anim:* Seymour Kneitel, Roland Crandall; *voices:* Elsa Janssen, Smiley Burnett; *mus:* Sammy Timberg; *song:* "Cow Cow" Charles Davenport; *col:* Tech-2. *sd:* WE. 6 min. • The old lady who lives in the shoe's kids are sent to bed without any supper and proceed to have a jam session singing "Mama Don't Allow No Music Playing Here."

3502. Kiko and the Honey Bears (*Terry-Toon*) 21 Aug. 1936; *p.c.:* TT for Educational/Fox; *dir:* George Gordon, Mannie Davis; *mus:* Philip A. Scheib; b&w. *sd:* WE. 6 min. • Kiko babysits the cubs and has to save them from a pack of hunting dogs.

3503. Kiko Foils the Fox (*Terry-Toon*) 2 Oct. 1936; *p.c.:* TT for Educational/Fox; *dir:* George Gordon, Mannie Davis; *mus:* Philip A. Scheib; b&w. *sd:* WE. 6 min. • Kiko saves a little bird from a fox.

3504. Kiko the Kangaroo in a Battle Royal (*Terry-Toon*) 30 Oct. 1936; *p.c.:* TT for Educational/Fox; *dir:* George Gordon, Mannie Davis; *mus:* Philip A. Scheib; b&w. *sd:* WE. 6 min. • Farmer Al tries to win prize money by going a round with a prize fighter but Kiko has to take his place.

3505. Kiko the Kangaroo in Red Hot Music (*Terry-Toon*) 5 May 1937; *p.c.:* TT for Educational/Fox; *dir:* George Gordon, Mannie Davis; *mus:* Philip A. Scheib; b&w. *sd:* WE. 6 min. • Fireman Kiko goes to the rescue when a "red hot" band catches fire.

3506. Kiko the Kangaroo in Skunked Again (*Terry-Toon*) 25 Dec. 1936; *p.c.:* TT for Educational/Fox; *dir:* George Gordon, Mannie Davis; *mus:* Philip A. Scheib; b&w. *sd:* WE. 6 min. • Kiko and Farmer Al head north in an airship ... closely followed by skunks.

3507. Kiko the Kangaroo in the Hay Ride (*Terry-Toon*) 2 Apr. 1937; *p.c.:* TT for Educational/Fox. *dir:* George Gordon, Mannie Davis; *mus:* Philip A. Scheib; b&w. *sd:* WE. 6 min. • Kiko takes five bear cubs ice skating.

3508. Kiko's Cleaning Day (*Terry-Toon*) 17 Sept. 1937; *p.c.:* TT for Educational/Fox; *dir:* George Gordon, Mannie Davis; *mus:* Philip A. Scheib; b&w. *sd:* WE. 6 min. • Kiko's spring cleaning is gerally balked by Ozzie Ostrich plus a runaway vacuum cleaner.

3509. Killarney Blarney (*Blue Racer*) Feb. 1973; *p.c.:* Mirisch/DFE for UA; *dir:* Gerry Chiniquy; *story:* John W. Dunn; *anim:* John Gibbs, Norm McCabe, Manny Gould; *lay:* Dick Ung; *back:* Richard H. Thomas; *ed:* Allan R. Potter; *voices:* Larry D. Mann, Paul Winchell; *mus:* Doug Goodwin; *ph:* John Burton Jr.; *prod sup:* Stan Paperny, Harry Love; *col:* DeLuxe. *sd:* RCA. 5 min. • The Racer finds himself at the mercy of two scheming Leprechauns and a giant shillelagh.

3510. Kindly Scram (*Phantasy*) 5 Mar. 1943; *p.c.:* Colum; *prod:* Dave Fleischer; *dir:* Alec Geiss; *anim:* Ray Patterson; *voices:* Harry E. Lang; *mus:* Paul Worth; *ph:* Frank Fisher; *prod mgr:* Albert Spar; b&w. *sd:* RCA. 6 min. • A billposter has to contend with an unfriendly bull when posting a "Beware of the Bull" sign.

3511. The King and I 19 Mar. 1999; *p.c.:* Morgan Creek Prods., Inc./Rankin-Bass/Nest Entertainment for WB; *dir:* Richard Rich; *prod:* James G. Robinson, Arthur Rankin, Peter Bakalian; *ex prod:* Robert Mandell; *co-prod:* Terry L. Noss, Thomas J. Tobin; *conceived and adapted:* Arthur Rankin; *based on the musical by* Richard Rodgers and Oscar Hammerstein II; *storyboard:* Steven E. Gordon, Floro Dery, Larry Scholl, Larry Leker, Dale L. Baer, Gerald Forton, Robert Souza; *scene plan:* Geoffrey Schroeder, Robert J. Richards II; *addit dial:* Brian Nissen; *anim:* Patrick Gleeson, Colm Duggan, Steven P. Gordon, Athanassios Vakalis, Chrystal S. Klabunde, John Celestri, Chris Derochie, Craig R. Maras, Steven Burke, Michael Coppieters, Elena Kravets, Mark Bykov, Jesse M. Cosio, James A. Davis, Tom Decker, Jeff Etter, Mark Fisher, Heidi Guedel, Leon Joosen, Juliana Korsborn, Larry Leker, Lim Boohwan, Lim Kyunghee, Lee McCaulla, Ken McDonald, Sean P. Mullen, Cynthia Overman, Greg Ramsey, Todd Shaffer, Shin Kyung, Song Kamoon, Susan M. Zytka, Joe D. Suggs, Todd Waterman, Larry Whitaker Jr., Frank Gabriel, Kez Wilson, Deborah Abbott, Dan Abraham, Konrad Winterlich, Siddhartha B. Ahearne, Alan T. Pickett, Gabriel Valles, Manuel Carrasco, Celine Kiernan, Noel Kiernan, Jacques Muller, Sam Fleming, Warren Liang, Marcelo F. De Moura, Nilo Santillan, John D. Williamson, Robert K. Shedlowich, Bradley M. Forbush, G. Sem, Richard Baneham; *cgi anim sup:* Brian McSweeney, Brian Sebern; *cgi prod:* P.M. Anonana, T. Anohana, Christina de Silva, Elektra Shock Inc.; *cgi technical sup:* Aimee Campbell, Usha Ganesarajah; *cgi anim:* Rich Animation Studios, Robert Bardy, Eduardo Silva, Pentafour Software, P. Delle Kumar, J. Pramod Dhaval, P. Ajay Kumar, T.K. Ajish, K. Arun, Anuradha Jayaram, Kumar Chandrasekaran, R. Pio Vaiz, A. Prasanth Kumar, Sreenives Reddy, Srinivas Kannan, Sukumar Subramanian, Vidys Sampath, Vijay Kumar, Ziauddin; *cgi prod co-ord:* Patro Navin Kumar, S. Parasuraman; *cgi prod sup:* Subheesh Raamanathan, Srikanth Pottekula; *cgi modellers:* Rubeesh Ajith, Sukumar Srinivas; *prod ex:* Sriam Sundar Rajan; *fx: des/ sup:* Brian McSweeney; *co-ord:* Rebecca Groombridge; *anim:* Actarus Aksas, John Dillon, Noel Kiernan, Kevin M. O'Neil, Bob Simmons, Ricardo Echevarria, Jeff Howard, Juan Son Montuno, Brett Hisey, John Huey, Lee Crowe, Nate Pacheco, Paul Lewis, Randy Weeks, Harry Moreau, Ryan Woodward, Eusebio Torres, Young Kyu Rhim, Conor Thunder; *digital compositing sup:* Timothy Yoo; *digital compositors:* Robert J. Richards II, Geoffrey Schroeder, Sung Song, Reymundo T. Reynoso, Jayson W. Tom, Youngjune Cho, Hwang Eun Young, Hee Yun; *digital compositing:* Rich Animation Studios, Hanho Heung-up Co. Ltd., Pentafour Software, K. Suresh, Ratheesh Kumar, Gerard Sudhakar, Colorland, Xue Fei, Chai Yi-Tao; *anim check:* Patricia Blackburn; *anim clean-up:* Hanho Heung-up Co. Ltd., Denis Deegan, Mark Sonntag, Raymond Iacovacci, Phillipe Angeles; *snr prod dir:* Choi Young Chul; *prod mgr:* Chae Young Ki; *prod co-ord:* Kim Jung Gon; *digital col mgr:* Helena Collins-Liuag; *lay:* Mike Hodgson, Floro Dery, Andrew Gentle, Dennis Richards, Robert Orona; *col styling:* Jeanette Nouribekian; *model paint:* Karen Noss-Rodgers; *character des:* Bronwen Barry, Elena Kravets, Michael Coppieters; *back:* Donald Towns, Courtney Dane, Colene Riffo, Junn Roca, Annette Alholm, Jeff Richards, Eric Reese, Brian Sebern, J. Riche, Kim Spink, Marilyn Montgomery, Shahan Jordan, Fiona Stokes Gilbert, Eugene Fedorov; *digital i&p:* Rich Animation Studios, Colorland; *ed:* James F. Koford, Paul Murphy, Joseph Campana; *voices: Anna Leonowens:* Miranda Richardson; *Anna (singing voice):* Christine Noll; *The King of Siam:* Martin Vidnovic; *The Kralahome:* Ian Richardson; *Master Little:* Darrell Hammond; *Prince Chululongkorn:* Allen D. Hong; *Prince Chululongkorn (singing voice):* David Burnham; *Tuptim:* Armi Arabe; *Tuptim (singing voice):* Tracy Venner Warren; *Louis Leonowens:* Adam Wylie; *Sir Edward Ramsay:* Sean Smith; *First wife:* J.A. Fujii; *Captain Orton:* Ken Baker; *Sir Edward's Captain:* Ed Trotta; *Burmese Emissary:* Anthony Mozdy; *Princess Ying:* Alexandra Lai; *Princess Naomi:* Katherine Lai; *Steward:* Mark Hunt; *Soldier:* B.K. Tochi; *chorus:* Charles Clark, Earl Grizzell, Jeff Gunn, David Joyce, Larry Kenton, Emma Stevenson-Blythe, Benjamin Fox, Andrew Harper, Beau Bruder, Cailiegh Harper, Tamara Rusque; *mus performed by* The Philharmonic Orchestra; *orch:* William Ashford, John Bell, Louis Forestieri, Benoit Grey, Ron Hess, Larry Kenton, Susan Sommer, Ken Thorne, Steve Zuckerman; *conductor:* William Kidd; *score:* Audrey Deroche; *mus ed:* Douglas Lackey; *mix:* John Richards; *orch rec:* Mike Ross; *vocal/synth rec:* Michael Hutchinson, Gary Grey; *rec:* Paul Talkington; *choreog:* Lee Martino, Lisa Clyde; *rec:* Charlie Ajar Jr., Michael Casper, Dan Leahy, Rick Hart; *ADR:* Greg Lowe, Alan Holly; *foley art:* Paul Holzborn, Dominique Decaudain, Albert Romero; *prod controller:* Edna Wilkerson-Fuentes; *prod co-ord:* Jim Haas, David A. Reiss; *prod mgrs: anim:* Brett Hayden; *digital:* Paul Cowell; *post prod for Morgan Creek:* Alejandro Mendoza; *col. sd:* Dolby stereo/SDDS/dts. 88½ min. • Animated version of the Rodgers and Hammerstein musical: Anna, a widowed English woman, arrives in Siam to take up her post as schoolteacher to the King of Siam's children. The Crown Prince falls for a servant girl but laws and the King forbid him from marrying a commoner. Kralahome, the king's aide, schemes to overthrow the king and sabotages the prince's elopement, making them plunge into a river. The king rescues the two lovers and Kralahome is caught and punished.

3512. King for a Day *(Gabby)* 18 Oct. 1940; *p.c.:* The Fleischer Studio for Para; *prod:* Max Fleischer; *dir:* Dave Fleischer; *story:* Joseph E. Stultz; *anim:* Willard Bowsky, James Davis; *ed:* Kitty Pfister; *voices:* Pinto Colvig, Jack Mercer; *mus:* Sammy Timberg; *ph:* Charles Schettler; *prod sup:* Sam Buchwald, Isidore Sparber; *col:* Tech. *sd:* WE. 7 min. • Gabby stands in for the King unaware the King has received an assassination notice.

3513. King Kelly of the U.S.A. 15 Sept.1934; *p.c.:* A-C for Monogram; *anim prod:* W.P. Bach; *anim dir:* F. Lyle Goldman; b&w. *sd.* 2 min. • Live-action comedy. A showman explains about a show he wants to put on by drawing a stage with a man serenading a girl. The drawings come alive and start singing.

3514. King Klunk *(Pooch the Pup)* 4 Sept. 1933; *p.c.:* Univ; *dir:* Walter Lantz; *anim:* Manuel Moreno, Lester Kline, Fred Kopietz, Charles Hastings, Ernest Smythe; *mus:* James Dietrich; b&w. *sd:* WE. 7 min. • Spoof on *King Kong.* The giant ape is captured and put on exhibition in New York. He escapes and climbs a skyscraper, taking the heroine with him.

3515. King Kong 1933; *p.c.:* RKO; *anim fx:* Willis H. O'Brien; *model maker:* Marcel Delgado; *l/a dir:* Merian C. Cooper, Ernest B. Schoedsack; b&w. *sd:* RCA. 100 min. *l/a/anim.* • Classic live-action film involving a giant ape animated by Willis O'Brien.

3516. King Looney XIV *(Paul Terry-Toons)* 7 June 1935; *p.c.:* Moser & Terry for Educational/Fox; *dir:* Frank Moser, Paul Terry; *mus:* Philip A. Scheib; b&w. *sd:* WE. 6 min. • No story available.

3517. King Midas Jr. *(Color Rhapsody)* 18 Dec. 1942; *p.c.:* Colum; *prod:* Dave Fleischer; *dir:* Paul Sommer, John Hubley; *story:* Jack Cosgriff, Paul Sommer; *anim:* Volus Jones; *sets:* Clark Watson; *ed:* Edward Moore; *voices:* Frank Graham; *mus:* Paul Worth; *prod mgr:* Albert Spar; *col:* Tech. *sd:* RCA. 6 min. • King Midas XIII receives a gift where everything he touches turns to rubber.

3518. King Neptune *(Silly Symphony)* 10 Sept. 1932; *p.c.:* Walt Disney prods for UA; *dir:* Burton F. Gillett; *anim:* Johnny Cannon, Les Clark, Ed Donnelly, Norman Ferguson, Hardie Gramatky, David D. Hand, Jack King, Richard Lundy, Ben Sharpsteen; *lay:* Albert Hurter; *voice:* J. Delos Jewkes; *mus:* Bert Lewis; *col:* Tech. *sd:* PCP. 8 min. • When a pirate crew captures a mermaid, King Neptune conjures up a great tempest and a whirlpool to sink their vessel.

3519. The King of Beasts *(Unnatural History)* 4 Apr. 1926; *p.c.:* Bray prods for FBO; *dir:* Walter Lantz; *anim:* Clyde Geronimi; *l/a ph:* Joe Rock; b&w. *sil.* 5 min *l/a/anim.* • No story available.

3520. The King of Bugs *(Aesop's Sound Fable)* 21 Dec. 1930; *p.c.:* Van Beuren for Pathé; *dir:* John Foster, Harry Bailey; *anim:* George Rufle, J.J. McManus; *mus:* Jack Ward, Gene Rodemich; b&w. *sd:* RCA. 9 min. • The King of Bugs arrives for the "Bugville Race." The spider wins, kidnaps the Princess and a Jester fly rescues her.

3521. The King of Jazz 17 May 1930; *p.c.:* Univ; *dir:* Walter Lantz, Bill Nolan; *anim:* Ted Eshbaugh, Manuel Moreno; *vocal:* The Rhythm Boys (Bing Crosby, Al Rinker, Harry Barris); *mus:* James Dietrich; *col:* Tech-2. *sd:* WE. (seq) 2¹⁄₂ min. *l/a/anim.* • A live-action musical featuring bandleader Paul Whiteman who explains (via animation) how he was made "The King of Jazz": While out hunting in the jungle he was chased by a lion and "crowned" by a monkey throwing coconuts. The first Technicolor cartoon.

3522. King of the Mardi Gras *(Popeye)* 27 Sept. 1935; *p.c.:* The Fleischer Studio for Para; *prod:* Max Fleischer; *dir:* Dave Fleischer; *anim:* David Tendlar, William Sturm; *voices:* Jack Mercer, Mae Questel, Gus Wickie; *mus:* Sammy Timberg; b&w. *sd:* WE. 6 min. • Popeye and Bluto are rivals at the Mardi Gras. The competition develops when Bluto kidnaps Olive and seeks refuge on the roller coaster.

3523. King Rounder *(Luno)* Apr. 1964; *p.c.:* TT for Fox; *ex prod:* Bill Weiss; *dir/anim:* Connie Rasinski; *story sup:* Tom Morrison; *story:* Larz Bourne; *sets:* Bill Focht, John Zago; *ed:* Jack MacConnell; *voices:* Bob MacFadden, Norma MacMillan; *mus:* Phil Scheib; *ph:* Ted Moskowitz, Joe Rasinski; *sd:* Elliot Grey; *col:* DeLuxe. *sd:* RCA. 5 min. • Luno and Tim solve the mystery surrounding the disappearence of King Rounder's crowns.

3524. King-Size Canary 6 Dec. 1947; *p.c.:* MGM; *dir:* Tex Avery; *story:* Heck Allen; *anim:* Robert Bentley, Walter Clinton, Ray Abrams; *character des:* Irven Spence; *sets:* John Didrik Johnsen; *voices:* Frank Graham, Sara Berner; *mus:* Scott Bradley; *prod:* Fred Quimby; *col:* Tech. 7 min. • A starving alley cat makes a puny canary bite-sized by feeding it "Jumbo-Gro," causing monumental results.

3525. King Tut's Tomb *(Heckle & Jeckle)* Aug. 1950; *p.c.:* TT for Fox; *dir:* Mannie Davis; *story/voices:* Tom Morrison; *anim:* Jim Tyer; *mus:* Philip A. Scheib; *ph:* Douglas Moye; *col:* Tech. *sd:* RCA. 6 min. • The magpies disrupt ghosts and mummies while excavating the tomb for treasure.

3526. King Zilch *(Paul Terry-Toon)* 11 June 1933; *p.c.:* Moser & Terry for Educational/Fox; *dir:* Frank Moser, Paul Terry; *mus:* Philip A. Scheib; b&w. *sd:* WE. 6 min. • His Royal Highness is caught flirting with the maid by the Queen. He quickly departs and returns with a bunch of flowers.

3527. The King's Daughter *(Paul Terry-Toon)* 4 May 1934; *p.c.:* Moser & Terry for Educational/Fox; *dir:* Frank Moser, Paul Terry; *mus:* Philip A. Scheib; b&w. *sd:* WE. 5¹⁄₂ min. • No story available.

3528. The King's Jester *(Krazy Kat)* 20 May 1935; *p.c.:* Winkler for Colum; *prod:* Charles Mintz; *story:* Ben Harrison; *anim:* Manny Gould, Al Rose, Harry Love; *mus:* Joe de Nat; *prod mgr:* George Winkler; b&w. *sd:* WE. 6 min. • To win the hand of the Princess, Krazy attempts to make the miserable King laugh.

3529. Kings Up *(Oswald)* 8 Mar. 1934; *p.c.:* Univ; *dir:* Walter Lantz, "Bill" Nolan; *anim:* Ray Abrams, Fred Avery, Cecil Surry, Jack Carr, Ernest Smythe, Merle Gilson; *mus:* James Dietrich; b&w. *sd:* WE. 7 min. • Troubadour Oswald seeks to sing for the Queen. He vanquishes the villainous Black Duke and marries her.

3530. Kiss Me Cat *(Looney Tunes)* 21 Feb. 1953; *p.c.:* WB; *dir:* Charles M. Jones; *story:* Michael Maltese; *anim:* Lloyd Vaughan, Ken Harris, Ben Washam; *lay:* Maurice Noble; *back:* Philip de Guard; *ed:* Treg Brown; *voices:* Mel Blanc, Bea Benaderet; *mus:* Carl Stalling; *prod mgr:* John W. Burton; *prod:* Edward Selzer; *col:* Tech. *sd:* Vit. 6¹⁄₂ min. • Marc Anthony the bulldog tries to keep Pussyfoot gainfully employed as the residential mousecatcher.

3531. The Kisser Plant *(Terry-Toon)* June 1964; *p.c.:* TT for Fox; *ex prod:* Bill Weiss; *dir/anim:* Connie Rasinski; *story sup:* Tom Morrison; *story:* Larz Bourne; *sets:* Bill Focht, John Zago; *ed:* Jack MacConnell; *voices:* Dayton Allen; *mus:* Jim Timmens; *ph:* Ted Moskowitz; *sd:* Elliot Grey; *col:* DeLuxe. *sd:* RCA. 5 min. • Astro presents Oscar Mild with a friendly space plant that grows to outsize proportions.

3532. Kisses and Curses *(Oswald)* 3 Feb. 1930; *p.c.:* Univ; *anim:* Walter Lantz, "Bill" Nolan, Manuel Moreno; *mus:* David Broekman; b&w. *sd:* WE. 6 min. • The Show Boat melodrama concerns an unwilling elopement and a gallant rescuer.

3533. Kit for Cat *(Looney Tunes)* 6 Nov. 1948; *p.c.:* WB; *dir:* I. Freleng; *story:* Michael Maltese, Tedd Pierce; *anim:* Virgil Ross, Gerry Chiniquy, Manuel Perez, Ken Champin; *lay:* Hawley Pratt; *back:* Paul Julian; *ed:* Treg Brown; *voices:* Arthur Q. Bryan, Mel Blanc, Bea Benaderet; *mus:* Carl Stalling; *prod mgr:* John W. Burton; *prod:* Edward Selzer; *col:* Tech. *sd:* Vit. 7 min. • Sylvester and a kitten battle for Elmer's favor for which of them he will keep.

3534. The Kitten Sitter *(Terry-Toon)* May 1949; *p.c.:* TT for Fox; *dir:* Eddie Donnelly; *story:* John Foster; *anim:* Jim Tyer; *mus:* Philip A. Scheib; *ph:* Douglas Moye; *col:* Tech. *sd:* RCA. 6 min. • A dumb dog babysits with a couple of capricious kittens whose pranks land him in the pound.

3535. Kittens' Mittens *(Car-Tune)* 12 Feb. 1940; *p.c.:* Walter Lantz prods for Univ; *dir:* Alex Lovy; *story:* Vic McLeod; *anim:* George Dane, La Verne Harding; *sets:* Willy Pogány; *voices:* Margaret McKay, Bernice Hansel, Danny Webb, The Rhythmettes; *mus:* Frank Marsales; *prod mgr:* George Hall; *col:* Tech. *sd:* WE. 7 min. • The kittens lose their mittens and blame an orphan kitten for stealing them. They are finally overcome with guilt and admit to losing them.

3536. Kitty Caddy *(Phantasy)* 6 Nov. 1947; *p.c.:* Colum; *prod:* Raymond Katz, Henry Binder; *dir:* Sid Marcus; *story:* Cal Howard; *anim:* Ben Lloyd, Chic Otterstrom, Roy Jenkins; *lay:* Clark Watson; *back:* Al Boggs; *ed:* Richard S. Jensen; *voices:* Harry E. Lang, Dave Barry; *mus:* Darrell Calker; *col:* Tech. *sd:* WE. 6 min. • Cat versus Dog in a golf match with interruptions from Bob Hope and Bing Crosby.

3537. Kitty Cornered (*Noveltoon*) 30 Dec. 1955; *p.c.:* Famous for Para; *dir:* Dave Tendlar; *story:* Larz Bourne; *anim:* Martin Taras, Thomas Moore; *sets:* Robert Connavale; *voices:* Jackson Beck, Gwen Davies; *mus:* Winston Sharples; *ph:* Leonard McCormick; *prod mgr:* Seymour Shultz; *col:* Tech. *sd:* RCA. 6 min. • Kitty Kuddles III's fortune will all go to the butler, Snardley, should anything happen to Kitty. This puts ideas in Snardley's head.

3538. Kitty Foiled (*Tom & Jerry*) 1 May 1948; *p.c.:* MGM; *dir:* William Hanna, Joseph Barbera; *anim:* Irven Spence, Kenneth Muse, Irving Levine, Ed Barge; *sets:* Robert Gentle; *ed:* Fred MacAlpin; *whistling:* Georgia Stark; *mus:* Scott Bradley; *prod:* Fred Quimby; *col:* Tech. *sd:* WE. 7 min. • A resourceful canary joins forces with Jerry in his fight against Tom.

3539. Kitty from Kansas City (*Screen Songs*) 31 Oct. 1931; *p.c.:* The Fleischer Studio for Para; *prod:* Max Fleischer; *dir:* Dave Fleischer; *mus:* Art Turkisher; *song:* Edgar Leslie, Walter Donaldson; *l/a:* Rudy Vallee; *b&w. sd:* WE. 8 min. *l/a/anim.* • Rudy Vallee appears as an old-timer waiting for his sweetie at the railway station. Betty Boop helps illustrate the song by appearing as his overweight girlfriend and has some fun under the sea.

3540. Kitty from the City (*Woody Woodpecker*) 1971; *p.c.:* Walter Lantz prods for Univ; *dir:* Paul J. Smith; *story:* Dalton Sandifer; *anim:* Virgil Ross, Al Coe, Tom Byrne, Joe Voght; *sets:* Nino Carbe; *voices:* Grace Stafford, Daws Butler; *mus:* Walter Greene; *col:* Tech. *sd:* RCA. 5½ min. • Woody takes advantage of a very nervous cat.

3541. Kitty Gets the Bird (*Fable*) 13 June 1941; *p.c.:* Colum; *story:* Allen Rose; *anim:* Louie H. Lilly; *sets:* Clark Watson; *ed:* Ed Moore; *voices:* Mel Blanc, Sara Berner; *mus:* Eddie Kilfeather; *ph:* Otto Reimer; *prod mgr:* George Winkler; *b&w. sd:* RCA. 6 min. • Kitty is warned to keep away from the Thanksgiving turkey by the old lady. When she's out a mouse has his sights on it and kitty tries to prevent him from eating the bird.

3542. Kitty Kornered (*Looney Tunes*) 8 June 1946; *p.c.:* WB; *dir/story:* Robert Clampett; *anim:* Manny Gould, Rod Scribner, J.C. Melendez, Robert McKimson; *lay:* Thomas McKimson; *back:* Dorcy Howard; *ed:* Treg Brown; *voices:* Mel Blanc; *mus:* Carl W. Stalling; *prod mgr:* John W. Burton; *prod:* Edward Selzer; *col:* Tech. *sd:* Vit. 7 min. • Porky attempts to put his four reluctant cats out for the night. Inspired by Orson Welles' radio production of *The War of the Worlds*.

3543. Klondike Casanova (*Popeye*) 31 May 1946; *p.c.:* Famous for Para; *dir:* I. Sparber; *story:* I. Klein, George Hill; *anim:* Dave Tendlar, John Gentilella; *sets:* Lloyd Hallock Jr.; *voices:* Mae Questel, Jackson Beck; *mus:* Winston Sharples; *col:* Tech. *sd:* RCA. 8 min. • Popeye and Olive are running a Klondike saloon when Dangerous Dan McBluto enters and centers his attentions on Olive Oyl.

3544. The Klondike Kid (*Mickey Mouse*) 12 Nov. 1932; *p.c.:* Walt Disney prods for UA; *dir:* Wilfred Jackson; *anim:* Johnny Cannon, Les Clark, Gilles de Tremaudan, Norman Ferguson, Clyde Geronimi, Tom Palmer, Ben Sharpsteen, Marvin Woodward; *asst anim:* Arthur Babbitt, Charles Byrne, Chuck Couch, George Drake, Hardie Gramatky, Edward Love, Fred Moore, Harry Reeves, Louis Schmitt, Fred Spencer, Frank Tipper, Roy Williams; *voices:* Marcellite Garner, Pinto Colvig, Walt Disney; *mus:* Frank E. Churchill; *b&w. sd:* PCP. 7 min. • Piano player Mickey rescues Minnie from the cold then Trapper Pierre abducts her and it's Mickey to the rescue. Veteran animator Ben Sharpsteen's first animation work.

3545. Klondike Strike-Out (*Hector Heathcote*) Jan. 1962; *p.c.:* TT for Fox; *ex prod:* Bill Weiss; *dir:* Dave Tendlar; *story sup:* Tom Morrison; *story:* Kin Platt; *anim:* Dave Tendlar, Juan Guidi; *sets:* John Zago; *ed:* George McAvoy; *voice:* John Myhers; *mus:* Phil Scheib; *ph:* Carlos Sanchez; *prod mgr:* Frank Schudde; *col:* DeLuxe. *sd:* RCA. 6 min. • A crook sells Heathcote gold mining equipment and when he discovers gold, a bandit tries to stop him making a claim.

3546. Knick Knack 1989; *p.c.:* PIXAR; *film by:* John Lasseter, Eben Ostby, William Reeves, Ralph Guggenheim, Craig Good, Don Conway, Flip Phillips, Yael Miló, Tony Apodaca, Deirdre Warin; *with help from:* Ed'Nalvy & Chuck, Steve Jobs, David Slusser, Bob Edwards, JLM Sprocket Systems, David Haddick & Associates, Agfa/Matrix, Tektronix, everybody at PIXAR; *mus:* Bobby McFerrin; *sd:* Gary Rydstrom; *col:* Renderman; *sd:* Dolby Stereo. 4 min. • A snowman in a paperweight longs to join the girls

on a Hawaiian trinket and attempts to break out of his glass prison. Computer animation.

3547. A Knight for a Day (*Goofy*) 8 Mar. 1946; *p.c.:* Walt Disney prods for RKO; *dir:* Jack Hannah; *asst dir:* Toby Tobelman; *story:* Bill Peed; *anim:* Hugh Fraser, Eric Larson, Judge Whitaker, Bob Carlson, Al Coe, Jim Moore, Don Patterson; *fx:* John Reed; *lay:* Yale Gracey; *back:* Thelma Witmer; *voices:* John H. Brown, Jack Mather, Arch Dennison; *mus:* Oliver Wallace; *col:* Tech. *sd:* RCA. 7 min. • A knight's squire accidentally knocks his master out and has to replace him in the tournament.

3548. Knight-Mare Hare (*Merrie Melodies*) 1 Oct. 1955; *p.c.:* WB; *dir:* Chuck Jones; *story:* Tedd Pierce; *anim:* Ken Harris, Ben Washam, Abe Levitow, Richard Thompson; *lay:* Ernie Nordli; *back:* Philip de Guard; *ed:* Treg Brown; *voices:* Mel Blanc; *mus:* Milt Franklyn; *prod mgr:* John W. Burton; *prod:* Edward Selzer; *col:* Tech. *sd:* Vit. 7 min. • Bugs is transported back to the Middle Ages where he competes with knights and dragons.

3549. A Knight Out (*Aesop's Film Fable*) 28 Aug. 1926; *p.c.:* Fables Pictures Inc for Pathé; *dir:* Paul Terry; *b&w. sil.* 10 min. • In medieval times, a knight captures a lady cat and imprisons her in his castle tower. The hero cat arrives to rescue her, resulting in a sword fight with the villain knight.

3550. Knights for a Day (*Meany Miny Mo*) 28 Dec. 1936; *p.c.:* Univ; *prod/dir:* Walter Lantz; *story:* Walter Lantz, Victor McLeod; *anim:* Manuel Moreno, Fred Kopietz, Lester Kline; *mus:* James Dietrich; *b&w. sd:* WE. 6 min. • The monks rob rich Henrietta Hen to help poor Mme Duck and her five ducklets on Christmas Eve.

3551. Knights Must Fall (*Merrie Melodies*) 16 July 1949; *p.c.:* WB; *dir:* I. Freleng; *story:* Tedd Pierce; *anim:* Ken Champin, Virgil Ross, Manuel Perez, Gerry Chiniquy; *lay:* Hawley Pratt; *back:* Paul Julian; *ed:* Treg Brown; *voices:* Mel Blanc; *mus:* Carl Stalling; *prod mgr:* John W. Burton; *prod:* Edward Selzer; *col:* Tech. *sd:* Vit. 7 min. • Bugs fights a jousting duel with a champion knight.

3552. Knighty Knight Bugs (*Looney Tunes*) 23 Aug. 1958; *p.c.:* WB; *dir:* Friz Freleng; *story:* Warren Foster; *anim:* Virgil Ross, Gerry Chiniquy, Art Davis; *lay:* Hawley Pratt; *back:* Tom O'Loughlin; *ed:* Treg Brown; *voices:* Mel Blanc; *mus:* Milt Franklyn; *prod:* John W. Burton; *col:* Tech. *sd:* Vit. 7 min. *Academy Award.* • The Court Jester (Bugs) is assigned the task of retrieving the King's Singing Sword from the clutches of The Black Knight (Sam).

3553. Knock! Knock! (*Andy Panda*) 25 Nov. 1940; *p.c.:* Walter Lantz prods for Univ; *dir:* Walter Lantz; *story:* Ben Hardaway, Lowell Elliot; *anim:* Alex Lovy, Frank Tipper; *sets:* Fred Brunish; *voices:* Mel Blanc, Sara Berner; *mus:* Frank Marsales; *col:* Tech. *sd:* WE. 6 min. • Andy and Pop are bothered by a woodpecker destroying their wooden house. • Featuring the initial appearance of Woody Woodpecker.

3554. Ko-Ko Back Tracks (*Out of the Inkwell*) 1 Jan. 1927; *p.c.:* Inkwell Studios for Red Seal; *prod/l/a:* Max Fleischer; *dir:* Dave Fleischer; *b&w. sil.* 5 min. *l/a/anim.* • Max's attempts to return Ko-Ko to the inkwell makes all his actions happen in reverse.

3555. Ko-Ko Baffles the Bulls (*Out of the Inkwell*) 6 Mar. 1926; *p.c.:* Inkwell Studio for Red Seal; *prod/l/a:* Max Fleischer; *dir:* Dave Fleischer; *b&w. sil.* 5 min. *l/a/anim.* • Max draws two detectives to help find Ko-Ko. The clown outwits them by disguising as a rooster then, by dressing in one detective's clothes, obliterates the other.

3556. Ko-Ko Beats Time (*Inkwell Imps*) 8 Feb. 1929; *p.c.:* Inkwell Studio for Para; *prod/l/a:* Max Fleischer; *dir:* Dave Fleischer; *b&w. sil.* 6 min. *l/a/anim.* • Ko-Ko arrives in the year 2000.

3557. Ko-Ko Celebrates the Fourth (*Out of the Inkwell*) 4 July 1925; *p.c.:* Inkwell Studio for Red Seal; *prod/l/a:* Max Fleischer; *dir:* Dave Fleischer; *paint:* Gustave Brock; *col. sil.* 10 min. • While Max is away Ko-Ko finds a box of fireworks and ignites them. One rocket carries him and Fitz to a cannibal isle. Hand-colored expressly for the first-run houses of July 4th week.

3558. Ko-Ko Chops Suey (*Inkwell Imps*) 29 Oct. 1927; *p.c.:* Inkwell Studio for Para; *prod/l/a:* Max Fleischer; *dir:* Dave Fleischer; *b&w. sil.* 10 min. *l/a/anim.* • Ko-Ko visits a Chop Suey factory and mixes explosive ingredients into the dish.

3559. Ko-Ko Cleans Up *(Inkwell Imps)* 21 Sept. 1928; *p.c.:* Inkwell Studio for Para; *prod/l/a:* Max Fleischer; *dir:* Dave Fleischer; b&w. *sil.* 10 min. *l/a/anim.* • No story available.

3560. Ko-Ko Eats *(Out of the Inkwell)* 15 Nov. 1925; *p.c.:* Inkwell Studio for Red Seal; *prod/l/a:* Max Fleischer; *dir:* Dave Fleischer; b&w. *sil.* 10 min. *l/a/anim.* • No story available.

3561. Ko-Ko Explores *(Inkwell Imps)* 15 Oct. 1927; *p.c.:* Inkwell Studio for Para; *prod/l/a:* Max Fleischer; *dir:* Dave Fleischer; b&w. *sil.* 10 min. *l/a/anim.* • Ko-Ko discovers Max's head at the Palace of the South Sea King.

3562. Ko-Ko Gets Egg-Cited *(Out of the Inkwell)* 1 Dec. 1926; *p.c.:* Inkwell Studio for Red Seal; *prod/l/a:* Max Fleischer; *dir:* Dave Fleischer; b&w. *sil.* 7 min. *l/a/anim.* • Ko-Ko trails a chicken to the hen house to gather eggs and, before he knows it, hatches out a brood of chicks.

3563. Ko-Ko Goes Over *(Inkwell Imps)* 23 June 1928; *p.c.:* Inkwell Studio for Para; *prod/l/a:* Max Fleischer; *dir:* Dave Fleischer; b&w. *sil.* 10 min. *l/a/anim.* • No story available.

3564. Ko-Ko Heaves Ho *(Inkwell Imps)* 25 Aug. 1928; *p.c.:* Inkwell Studio for Para; *prod/l/a:* Max Fleischer; *dir:* Dave Fleischer; b&w. *sil.* 5 min. *l/a/anim.* • Ko-Ko and Fitz are lost at sea. A storm springs forth and deposits them on a pirate ship.

3565. Ko-Ko Hops Off *(Inkwell Imps)* 17 Sept. 1927; *p.c.:* Inkwell Studio for Para; *prod/l/a:* Max Fleischer; *dir:* Dave Fleischer; b&w. *sil.* 5 min. • Ko-Ko and Fitz take part in an "Around the World" race.

3566. Ko-Ko Hot After It *(Out of the Inkwell)* 12 June 1926; *p.c.:* Inkwell Studio for Red Seal; *prod/l/a:* Max Fleischer; *dir:* Dave Fleischer; b&w. *sil.* 10 min. *l/a/anim.* • The little clown goes on a treasure hunt.

3567. Ko-Ko in 1999 *(Out of the Inkwell)* 10 Mar. 1927; *p.c.:* Inkwell Studio for Red Seal; *prod/l/a:* Max Fleischer; *dir:* Dave Fleischer; b&w. *sil.* 7 min. *l/a/anim.* • Ko-Ko is transported to the future where everything is automated. Push-buttons supply him with a wife and twins.

3568. Ko-Ko in the Rough *(Inkwell Imps)* 3 Nov. 1928; *p.c.:* Inkwell Studio for Para; *prod/l/a:* Max Fleischer; *dir:* Dave Fleischer; b&w. *sil.* 5 min. *l/a/anim.* • Ko-Ko's golf game is suspended by his Amazonian wife who lands him in hospital.

3569. Ko-Ko in Toyland *(Out of the Inkwell)* 12 Dec. 1925; *p.c.:* Inkwell Studio for Red Seal; *prod/l/a:* Max Fleischer; *dir:* Dave Fleischer; b&w. *sil.* 10 min. *l/a/anim.* • Max draws a doll as a Christmas present for Ko-Ko. The doll gets tied to the railroad tracks by a villain and Ko-Ko comes to the rescue.

3570. Ko-Ko Kicks *(Inkwell Imps)* 12 Nov. 1927; *p.c.:* Inkwell Studio for Para; *prod/l/a:* Max Fleischer; *dir:* Dave Fleischer; b&w. *sil.* 10 min. *l/a/anim.* • No story available.

3571. Ko-Ko Kidnapped *(Out of the Inkwell)* 11 Sept. 1926; *p.c.:* Inkwell Studio for Red Seal; *prod/l/a:* Max Fleischer; *dir:* Dave Fleischer; b&w. *sil.* 10 min. *l/a/anim.* • Fitz meets his live-action counterpart.

3572. Ko-Ko Lamps Aladdin *(Inkwell Imps)* 12 May 1928; *p.c.:* Inkwell Studio for Para; *prod/l/a:* Max Fleischer; *dir:* Dave Fleischer; b&w. *sil.* 10 min. *l/a/anim.* • Ko-Ko discovers a book *Aladdin and His Lamp* and becomes involved with the story.

3573. Ko-Ko Makes 'Em Laugh *(Out of the Inkwell)* 10 Feb. 1927; *p.c.:* Inkwell Studio for Red Seal; *prod/l/a:* Max Fleischer; *dir:* Dave Fleischer; b&w. *sil.* 5 min. *l/a/anim.* • No story available.

3574. Ko-Ko Needles the Boss *(Out of the Inkwell)* 10 May 1927; *p.c.:* Inkwell Studio for Red Seal; *prod/l/a:* Max Fleischer; *dir:* Dave Fleischer; b&w. *sil.* 5 min. *l/a/anim.* • Ko-Ko has some fun with a needle and thread. After filling Max's house with twine, he unintentionally sews himself back into the inkwwell.

3575. Ko-Ko-Nuts *(Out of the Inkwell)* 5 Sept. 1925; *p.c.:* Inkwell Studio for Red Seal; *prod/l/a:* Max Fleischer; *dir:* Dave Fleischer; b&w. *sil.* 10 min. *l/a/anim.* • Max discovers the wheels in Ko-Ko's head are not functioning properly and situates him and Fitz outside the "Nut House." When the Keeper arrives, the little clown is wearing a guard's outfit and sends him on a fool's errand. The Keeper departs, leaving Ko-Ko in charge. Having turned the inmates loose, Max hauls Ko-Ko back but the clown binds Max's hands and paints his face like a clown. A real-life Keeper arrives and drags Max away.

3576. Ko-Ko on the Run *(Out of the Inkwell)* 15 Sept. 1925; *p.c.:* Inkwell Studio for Red Seal; *prod/l/a:* Max Fleischer; *dir:* Dave Fleischer; b&w. *sil.* 10 min. *l/a/anim.* • Ko-Ko and a heftier clown have a race from different points on the compass until they collide. They sail away in a balloon, returning via Max's field glasses.

3577. Ko-Ko on the Track *(Inkwell Imps)* 4 Dec. 1928; *p.c.:* Inkwell Studio for Para; *prod/l/a:* Max Fleischer; *dir:* Dave Fleischer; b&w. *sil.* 10 min. *l/a/anim.* • Jockey Ko-Ko provides his horse with roller-skates for more speed to help win the race.

3578. Ko-Ko Packs 'Em *(Out of the Inkwell)* 17 Oct. 1925; *p.c.:* Inkwell Studio for Red Seal; *prod/l/a:* Max Fleischer; *dir:* Dave Fleischer; b&w. *sil.* 10 min. *l/a/anim.* • Max has to move his studio and Ko-Ko packs everything in sight. He then starts a vacuum which sucks in everything else.

3579. Ko-Ko Plays Pool *(Inkwell Imps)* 6 Aug. 1927; *p.c.:* Inkwell Studio for Para; *prod/l/a:* Max Fleischer; *dir:* Dave Fleischer; b&w. *sil.* 8 min. *l/a/anim.* • Tired of playing with a "drawn" pool table, Ko-Ko and Fitz proceed to disrupt Max's game.

3580. Ko-Ko Sees Spooks *(Out of the Inkwell)* 13 June 1925; *p.c.:* Inkwell Studio for Red Seal; *prod/l/a:* Max Fleischer; *dir:* Dave Fleischer; b&w. *sil.* 10 min. *l/a/anim.* • Max draws Ko-Ko from the number "thirteen," today being Friday the thirteenth. He leaves the little clown to investigate a haunted house when he loses his hat inside it. Ghosts chase him back into the inkwell.

3581. Ko-Ko Smokes *(Inkwell Imps)* 3 Mar. 1928; *p.c.:* Inkwell Studio for Para; *prod/l/a:* Max Fleischer; *dir/l/a:* Dave Fleischer; b&w. *sil.* 10 min. *l/a/anim.* • Ko-Ko and Fitz try to pick up cigar butts and when Fitz gets ill from smoking, he hallucinates being hunted by a giant cigar.

3582. Ko-Ko Song Car-Tunes *(Out of the Inkwell)* (AA): 1 Dec. 1924; (AB): 27 Dec. 1924; (AC): 15 Jan. 1925; (AD): 1 Feb. 1925; *p.c.:* Inkwell Studio for Red Seal; *prod:* Max Fleischer; *dir:* Dave Fleischer; b&w. *sil.* 5 min. • No stories available.

3583. Ko-Ko Song Car-Tunes 15 June 1924; *p.c.:* Out of the Inkwell Films for Red Seal Pictures; *dir:* Dave Fleischer; *prod:* Max Fleischer; b&w. *sil.* 5 min. • Sing-along with a visual interpretation of Charles K. Harris' songs, "Mother, Mother, Mother Pin a Rose on Me" (reissue: 1 Mar. 1925), "Come Take a Trip in my Airship" and "Goodbye my Lady Love" (reissue: 22 May 1926).

3584. Ko-Ko Squeals *(Inkwell Imps)* 26 May 1928; *p.c.:* Inkwell Imps for Para; *prod/l/a:* Max Fleischer; *dir:* Dave Fleischer; b&w. *sil.* 10 min. *l/a/anim.* • A rival artist takes Max's girl on a roller coaster ride at Coney Island. Ko-Ko is dispatched to put a lump of ice down his neck.

3585. Ko-Ko Steps Out *(Out of the Inkwell)* 21 Nov. 1925; *p.c.:* Inkwell Studio for Red Seal; *prod/l/a:* Max Fleischer; *dir:* Dave Fleischer; b&w. *sil.* 10 min. *l/a/anim.* • Ko-Ko and Fitz learn "The Charleston" when the little clown draws his own dance instructress. A real-life dancing girl appears and gets Max, Ko-Ko, Fitz and a real cat and dog all doing the current dance craze.

3586. Ko-Ko the Barber *(Out of the Inkwell)* 25 Feb. 1925; *p.c.:* Inkwell Studio for Red Seal; *prod/l/a:* Max Fleischer; *dir:* Dave Fleischer; b&w. *sil.* 10 min. *l/a/anim.* • Ko-Ko goes mad with a pair of scissors and trims everything in sight then pours hair grower over furniture, clocks, a cat, a horse and even over Max's face.

3587. Ko-Ko the Convict *(Out of the Inkwell)* 1 Nov. 1926; *p.c.:* Inkwell Studio for Red Seal; *prod/l/a:* Max Fleischer; *dir:* Dave Fleischer; b&w. *sil.* 6 min. *l/a/anim.* • To restrain Ko-Ko and Fitz, Max draws them both in prison, from which they try to escape.

3588. Ko-Ko the Hot-Shot *(Out of the Inkwell)* Jan. 1925; *p.c.:* Inkwell Studio for Red Seal; *prod/l/a:* Max Fleischer; *dir:* Dave Fleischer; b&w. *sil.* 5 min. *l/a/anim.* • Ko-Ko falls to Hades where the Devil (Max) torments him on the drawing board.

3589. Ko-Ko the Kid *(Inkwell Imps)* 24 Dec. 1927; *p.c.:* Inkwell Studio for Para; *prod/l/a:* Max Fleischer; *dir:* Dave Fleischer; b&w. *sil.* 10 min. *l/a/anim.* • A beard is drawn on Ko-Ko and he tries to rid himself of it by jumping into the Fountain of Youth, turning him into a baby.

3590. Ko-Ko the Knight *(Inkwell Imps)* 3 Sept. 1927; *p.c.:* Inkwell

Studio for Para; *prod/ll/a:* Max Fleischer; *dir:* Dave Fleischer; b&w. *sil.* 6 min. *ll/alanim.* • Armored in a stove, Ko-Ko sets off to rescue the fair princess from the villain.

3591. Ko-Ko the Kop *(Inkwell Imps)* 1 Oct. 1927; *p.c.:* Inkwell Studio for Para; *prod/ll/a:* Max Fleischer; *dir:* Dave Fleischer; b&w. *sil.* 7 min. *ll/anim.* • Max draws Ko-Ko as a policeman who chases his pup, Fitz, for stealing bones.

3592. Ko-Ko Trains 'Em *(Out of the Inkwell)* 9 May 1925; *p.c.:* Inkwell Studio for Red Seal; *prod/ll/a:* Max Fleischer; *dir:* Dave Fleischer; b&w. *sil.* 10 min. *ll/alanim.* • Ko-Ko insists on showing Max how to train his pup, Fitz, finally unleashing fleas that rout the theater audience.

3593. Ko-Ko's Act *(Inkwell Imps)* 17 Dec. 1928; *p.c.:* Inkwell Studio for Para; *prod/ll/a:* Max Fleischer; *dir:* Dave Fleischer; b&w. *sil.* 10 min. *ll/alanim.* • The little clown displays his versatility as a magician, acrobat and all-round performer on stage.

3594. Ko-Ko's Bawth *((Inkwell Imps)* 18 Feb. 1928; *p.c.:* Inkwell Studio for Para; *prod/ll/a:* Max Fleischer; *dir:* Dave Fleischer; b&w. *sil.* 5 min. *ll/alanim.* • Ko-Ko and Fitz have fun in Max's bath. Dave takes a bath and Ko-Ko removes the stopper, running the water out.

3595. Ko-Ko's Big Pull *(Inkwell Imps)* 7 Sept. 1928; *p.c.:* Inkwell Studio for Para; *prod/ll/a:* Max Fleischer; *dir:* Dave Fleischer; b&w. *sil.* 5 min. *ll/alanim.* • Max pulls Ko-Ko's tooth.

3596. Ko-Ko's Big Sale *(Inkwell Imps)* 28 June 1929; *p.c.:* Inkwell Studio for Para; *prod/ll/a:* Max Fleischer; *dir:* Dave Fleischer; b&w. *sil.* 10 min. *ll/alanim.* • Ko-Ko and Fitz become salesmen who sell one pair of shoes to two one-legged Scotsmen and a genuine bottle of "Hot Stuff" to Max.

3597. Ko-Ko's Catch *((Inkwell Imps)* 7 June 1928; *p.c.:* Inkwell Studio for Para; *prod/ll/a:* Max Fleischer; *dir:* Dave Fleischer; b&w. *sil.* 5 min. *ll/alanim.* • Ko-Ko scuppers Max's affections for his new secretary.

3598. Ko-Ko's Chase *(Inkwell Imps)* 11 Aug. 1928; *p.c.:* Inkwell Studio for Para; *prod/ll/a:* Max Fleischer; *dir:* Dave Fleischer; b&w. *sil.* 5 min. *ll/alanim.* • Ko-Ko is presented with a remarkable automobile and distinguishes himself as an acrobatic driver.

3599. Ko-Ko's Conquest *(Inkwell Imps)* 31 May 1929; *p.c.:* Inkwell Studio for Para; *prod/ll/a:* Max Fleischer; *dir:* Dave Fleischer; b&w. *sil.* 10 min. *ll/alanim.* • Max draws a drowning girl whom Ko-Ko rescues. When a villain kidnaps her, Ko-Ko and Fitz rush to her rescue.

3600. Ko-Ko's Courtship *((Inkwell Imps)* 28 Dec. 1928; *p.c.:* Inkwell Studio for Para; *prod/ll/a:* Max Fleischer; *dir:* Dave Fleischer; b&w. *sil.* 10 min. *ll/alanim.* • Ko-Ko attempts to demonstrate the art of seduction to Max's overweight messenger boy, "Skinny."

3601. Ko-Ko's Crib *(Inkwell Imps)* 23 Mar. 1929; *p.c.:* Inkwell Studio for Para; *prod/ll/a:* Max Fleischer; *dir:* Dave Fleischer; b&w. *sil.* 10 min. *ll/alanim.* • Ko-Ko and his pal tend to a baby in a crib.

3602. Ko-Ko's Dog Gone *(Inkwell Imps)* 22 Oct. 1928; *p.c.:* Inkwell Studio for Para; *prod/ll/a:* Max Fleischer; *dir:* Dave Fleischer; b&w. *sil.* 10 min. *ll/alanim.* • Fitz is missing and Ko-Ko is reproduced one thousand times to scour the city looking for him.

3603. Ko-Ko's Earth Control *(Inkwell Imps)* 31 Mar. 1928; *p.c.:* Inkwell Studio for Para; *prod/ll/a:* Max Fleischer; *dir:* Dave Fleischer; b&w. *sil.* 10 min. • Ko-Ko and Fitz find a lever that disrupts the world. They jump from the crumbling planet to the relative safety of Max's inkwell.

3604. Ko-Ko's Field Daze *(Inkwell Imps)* 9 June 1928; *p.c.:* Inkwell Studio for Para; *prod/ll/a:* Max Fleischer; *dir:* Dave Fleischer; b&w. *sil.* 10 min. *ll/alanim.* • Max and Ko-Ko enter various events at a Field Day.

3605. Ko-Ko's Focus *(Inkwell Imps)* 17 May 1929; *p.c.:* Inkwell Studio for Para; *prod/ll/a:* Max Fleischer; *dir:* Dave Fleischer; b&w. *sil.* 10 min. *ll/alanim.* • Ko-Ko has adventures with a camera that squirts water.

3606. Ko-Ko's Germ Jam *(Inkwell Imps)* 4 Feb. 1928; *p.c.:* Inkwell Studio for Para; *prod/ll/a:* Max Fleischer; *dir:* Dave Fleischer; b&w. *sil.* 10 min. *ll/alanim.* • Ko-Ko unleashes "Love" and "Hate" germs.

3607. Ko-Ko's Harem Scarem *(Inkwell Imps)* 14 June 1929; *p.c.:* Inkwell Studio for Para; *prod/ll/a:* Max Fleischer; *dir:* Dave Fleischer; b&w. *sil.* 10 min. *ll/alanim.* • A (live-action) Sultan is presented with a box con-

taining an inkwell harboring Ko-Ko and Fitz. The Sultan chops their heads off which both grow legs and return to their bodies.

3608. Ko-Ko's Haunted House *(Inkwell Imps)* 28 Apr. 1928; *p.c.:* Inkwell Studio for Para; *prod/ll/a:* Max Fleischer; *dir:* Dave Fleischer; b&w. *sil.* 5 min. *ll/alanim.* • The inkwell forms a haunted house and Ko-Ko and Fitz investigate.

3609. Ko-Ko's Hot Dog *(Inkwell Imps)* 14 Apr. 1928; *p.c.:* Inkwell Studio for Para; *prod/ll/a:* Max Fleischer; *dir:* Dave Fleischer; b&w. *sil.* 5 min. *ll/alanim.* • Ko-Ko overindulges on hot dogs, ending up in the Dog Pound.

3610. Ko-Ko's Hot Ink *(Inkwell Imps)* 8 Mar. 1929; *p.c.:* Inkwell Studio for Para; *prod/ll/a:* Max Fleischer; *dir:* Dave Fleischer; b&w. *sil.* 10 min. *ll/alanim.* • Ko-Ko and Fitz find it too hot so they go to the local pool and make it hot for the other bathers.

3611. Ko-Ko's Hypnotism *(Inkwell Imps)* 12 July 1929; *p.c.:* Inkwell Studio for Para; *prod/ll/a:* Max Fleischer; *dir:* Dave Fleischer; b&w. *sil.* 6 min. *ll/alanim.* • Max hypnotizes Ko-Ko and Fitz. They discover how to do it and hypnotize Max.

3612. Ko-Ko's Kane *(Inkwell Imps)* 20 Aug. 1927; *p.c.:* Inkwell Studio for Para; *prod/ll/a:* Max Fleischer; *dir:* Dave Fleischer; b&w. *sil.* 5 min. *ll/alanim.* • Max invents a mechanical umbrella.

3613. Ko-Ko's Kink *(Inkwell Imps)* 7 Jan. 1928; *p.c.:* Inkwell Studio for Para; *prod/ll/a:* Max Fleischer; *dir:* Dave Fleischer; b&w. *sil.* 5 min. *ll/alanim.* • Ko-Ko sets up as a chiropractor.

3614. Ko-Ko's Klock *(Inkwell Imps)* 12 Nov. 1927; *p.c.:* Inkwell Studio for Para; *prod/ll/a:* Max Fleischer; *dir:* Dave Fleischer; b&w. *sil.* 5 min. *ll/alanim.* • Ko-Ko substitutes for a broken alarm clock.

3615. Ko-Ko's Knock Down *(Inkwell Imps)* 19 Apr. 1929; *p.c.:* Inkwell Studio for Para; *prod/ll/a:* Max Fleischer; *dir:* Dave Fleischer; b&w. *sil.* 10 min. *ll/alanim.* • Ko-Ko is dispatched to escort Max's pretty secretary across town.

3616. Ko-Ko's Kozy Korner *(Inkwell Imps)* 21 Jan. 1928; *p.c.:* Inkwell Studio for Para; *prod/ll/a:* Max Fleischer; *dir:* Dave Fleischer; b&w. *sil.* 5 min. *ll/alanim.* • Max, Ko-Ko and Fitz are evicted.

3617. Ko-Ko's Magic *(Inkwell Imps)* 16 Dec. 1928; *p.c.:* Inkwell Studio for Para; *prod/ll/a:* Max Fleischer; *dir:* Dave Fleischer; b&w. *sil.* 10 min. *ll/alanim.* • A magician has fun with the little clown.

3618. Ko-Ko's Parade *(Inkwell Imps)* 8 Oct. 1928; *p.c.:* Inkwell Studio for Para; *prod/ll/a:* Max Fleischer; *dir:* Dave Fleischer; b&w. *sil.* 10 min. *ll/alanim.* • Ko-Ko exploits a band of animal musicians in his own inimitable fashion.

3619. Ko-Ko's Paradise *(Out of the Inkwell)* 27 Feb. 1926; *p.c.:* Inkwell Studio for Red Seal; *prod/ll/a:* Max Fleischer; *dir:* Dave Fleischer; b&w. *sil.* 10 min. *ll/alanim.* • Max's target practice almost hits Ko-Ko and Fitz. They expire and their spirits lift to Paradise. The clown loses his wings and rides a waterway on a duck's back down to terra firma.

3620. Ko-Ko's Quest *(Inkwell Imps)* 10 Dec. 1927; *p.c.:* Inkwell Studio for Para; *prod/ll/a:* Max Fleischer; *dir:* Dave Fleischer; b&w. *sil.* 10 min. *ll/alanim.* • Max gazes into a crystal ball, sending Ko-Ko and Fitz off on an impossible quest.

3621. Ko-Ko's Reward *(Inkwell Imps)* 23 Feb. 1929; *p.c.:* Inkwell Studio for Para; *prod/ll/a:* Max Fleischer; *dir:* Dave Fleischer; b&w. *sil.* 6 min. *ll/alanim.* • The artist's daughter has an adventure with Ko-Ko and Fitz in an amusement park.

3622. Ko-Ko's Saxaphonies *(Inkwell Imps)* 5 Apr. 1929; *p.c.:* Inkwell Studio for Para; *prod/ll/a:* Max Fleischer; *dir:* Dave Fleischer; b&w. *sil.* 6 min. *ll/alanim.* • No story available.

3623. Ko-Ko's Signals *(Inkwell Imps)* 3 May 1929; *p.c.:* Inkwell Studio for Para; *prod/ll/a:* Max Fleischer; *dir:* Dave Fleischer; b&w. *sil.* 6 min. *ll/alanim.* • Ko-Ko and Fitz enjoy a football game.

3624. Ko-Ko's Tattoo *(Inkwell Imps)* 17 Mar. 1928; *p.c.:* Inkwell Studio for Para; *prod/ll/a:* Max Fleischer; *dir:* Dave Fleischer; b&w. *sil.* 7 min. *ll/alanim.* • Ko-Ko tattoos a cat onto Fitz.

3625. Ko-Ko's Thanksgiving *(Out of the Inkwell)* 21 Nov. 1925; *p.c.:* Inkwell Studio for Red Seal; *prod/ll/a:* Max Fleischer; *dir:* Dave Fleischer;

paint: Gustave Brock; col. *sil.* 10 min. *l/a/anim.* • Ko-Ko humiliates Max by showing home movies at his Thanksgiving party.

3626. Ko-Ko's War Dogs (Inkwell Imps) 21 July 1928; *p.c.:* Inkwell Studio for Para; *prod/l/a:* Max Fleischer; *dir:* Dave Fleischer; b&w. *sil.* 7 min. *l/a/anim.* • No story available.

3627. Kolortone Kartoons 1929 • *p.c.:* Kolortone Prods., Inc.; *prod:* Leo F. Britton, George S. Jeffrey; *mus/dial/sd fx:* David Broekman. *col:* Brewster Color. *sd.* 1 reel each. • (1) **An Egyptian Gyp** (2) **Boney's Boner** (3) **Hectic Hector** (4) **Wanderin's** (5) **A Pikin' Pirate** (6) **Kriss Krosses** • Distinctive synchronized color comedy cartoons. No stories available.

3628. Kongo-Roo (Phantasy) 18 Apr. 1946; *p.c.:* Colum; *dir:* Howard Swift; *story:* Cal Howard; *anim:* Grant Simmons; *sets:* Clark Watson; *ed:* Richard S. Jensen; *voices:* Stan Freberg, Jack Mather; *mus:* Eddie Kilfeather; *ph:* Frank Fisher; *prod mgr:* Hugh McCollum; b&w. *sd:* WE. 6 min. • Fuzzy-Wuzzy goes hunting for a kangaroo astride an ostrich. The situation changes drastically when he meets one face-to-face.

3629. Kooky Cucumbers (Possible Possum) Nov. 1971; *p.c.:* TT for Fox; *col:* DeLuxe. *sd:* RCA. 6 min. • No story available. • See: *Possible Possum*

3630. Kooky Loopy (Loopy de Loop) Nov. 1961; *p.c.:* Hanna-Barbera for Colum; *prod/dir:* William Hanna, Joseph Barbera; *story dir:* Alex Lovy; *story:* Warren Foster; *anim dir:* Charles A. Nichols; *anim:* Jack Ozark; *lay:* Dan Noonan; *back:* F. Montealegre; *ed:* Greg Watson; *voices:* Daws Butler, Arnold Stang, Jean van der Pyl; *mus:* Hoyt Curtin; *titles:* Lawrence Gobel; *prod mgr:* Howard Hanson; *col:* East. *sd:* RCA. 6 min. • Loopy tries to persuade the "Red Riding Hood" wolf to reform.

3631. Kools 1935. *p.c.:* Audio-Cinema for Brown & Williamson; b&w. *sd:* WE. 3 min. • Animated commercial showing penguins leaving the Arctic for Kentucky where they witness how Kools cigarettes are manufactured and then distribute them worldwide.

3632. Korn Plastered in Africa (Trader Korn's Laffalong) circa 1930s; *p.c.:* Featurettes for Screen Classics; *prod:* George Weiss; *dir:* John R. McCrory; *voice:* Uncle Don Carney (Howard Rice); b&w. *sd.* 7 min. • Trader Korn's account of how he went hunting in Africa and ended in the New York subway to escape the cannibal pot.

3633. Kosmo Goes to School (Noveltoon) Nov. 1961; *p.c.:* Para Cartoons: *dir:* Seymour Kneitel; *story:* Carl Meyer, Jack Mercer; *anim:* Nick Tafuri, Jack Ehret, Sam Stimson; *sets:* Robert Little; *voices:* Jack Mercer, Cecil Roy; *mus:* Winston Sharples; *ph:* Leonard Mc Cormick; *prod mgr:* Abe Goodman; *col:* Tech. *sd:* RCA. 6 min. • An outer-space visitor is mistaken for a schoolboy playing truant and taken to school.

3634. Kounty Fair (Oswald) 17 Dec. 1929; *p.c.:* Univ; *dir:* Walter Lantz; *anim:* R.C. Hamilton, "Bill" Nolan, Tom Palmer; *mus:* David Broekman; b&w. *sd:* WE. 7 min. • Oswald is selling hot dogs when he decides to enter a dance contest. Putrid Pete muscles in with his girl but he is soon dispensed with.

3635. Krazy Kat (1925–1929); *p.c.:* Winkler for R-C Pictures Corp; *anim:* William C. Nolan, until Paramount distribution, then Ben Harrison Manny Gould; b&w. *sil.* 5 min. • *1925:* **Hot Dogs** 1 Oct. **The Smoke Eater** 15 Oct. **A Uke-Calamity** 1 Nov. **The Flight That Failed** 1 Nov. **Bokays and Brickbatz** 15 Nov. **Hair Raiser** 15 Nov. **The New Champ** 30 Nov. **James and Gems** 1 Dec. **Monkey Business** 15 Dec. • *1926: p.c.—*Winkler for FBO. **Battling for Barleycorn** 1 Jan. **A Picked Romance** 15 Jan. **The Ghost Fakir** 1 Feb. **Sucker Game** 15 Feb. **Back to Backing** 1 Mar. **Double Crossed** 15 Mar. **Scents and Nonsense** 1 Apr. **Feather Pushers** 15 Apr. **Krazy Chops Suey** 1 May. **The Chicken Chaser** 2 Sept. **East Is Best** 22 Sept. **Shore Enough** 11 Oct. **Watery Gravey** 25 Oct. **Cheese It** 8 Nov. **Dots and Dashes** 22 Nov. **The Wrong Queue** 6 Dec. **Gold Struck** 10 Dec. • *1927:* **Horse Play** 3 Jan. **Busy Birds** 17 Jan. **Sharps and Flats** 31 Jan. **Kiss Crossed** 14 Feb. **A Fool's Errand** 28 Feb. **Stomach Trouble** 14 Mar. **The Rug Fiend** 28 Mar. **Hire a Hall** 11 Apr. **Don't Go On** 25 Apr. **Burnt Up** 9 May. **Krazy Kat: Night Owl** 23 May. **On the Trail** 6 June. **Passing the Hat** 20 June. **Best Wishes** 4 July. **Black and White** 10 July. **Wild Rivals** 18 July. *p.c.—*Winkler for Para. **Sealing Whacks** 1 Aug. **Tired Wheels** 13 Aug. **Bee Cause** 15 Aug. **Web Feet** 27 Aug. **Skinny** 29 Aug. **School Daze** 10 Sept. **Rail Rode** 24 Sept. **Aero Nuts** 8 Oct. **Topsy Turvy** 27 Oct. **Pie Curs** 5 Nov. **For Crime's Sake** 19 Nov. **Milk Made** 3

Dec. **The Stork Exchange** 17 Dec. **Grid Ironed** 31 Dec. • *1928:* **Pig Styles** 14 Jan. **Shadow Theory** 28 Jan. **Ice Boxed** 11 Feb. **A Hunger Stroke** 25 Feb. **Wired and Fired** 10 Mar. **Love Sunk** 24 Mar. **Tong Tied** 7 Apr. **A Bum Steer** 21 Apr. **Gold Bricks** 5 May. **The Long Count** 19 May. **The Patent Medicine Kid** 2 June. **Stage Coached** 12 June. **The Rain Dropper** 30 June. **A Companionate Mirage** 14 July. **News Reeling** 4 Aug. **Baby Feud** 16 Aug. **Sea Sword** 5 Sept. **The Show Vote** 15 Sept. **The Phantom Trail** 29 Sept. **Come Easy, Go Slow** 15 Oct. **Beaches and Scream** 29 Oct. **Nicked Nags** 9 Nov. **The Liar Bird** 23 Nov. **Still Waters** 7 Dec. **Night Howls** 22 Dec. • *1929:* **Cow Belles** 5 Jan. **Hospitalities** 18 Jan. **Reduced Weights** 1 Feb. **Flying Yeast** 15 Feb. **Vanishing Screams** 1 Mar. **A Joint Affair** 15 Mar. **Sheep Skinned** 29 Mar. **The Lone Shark** 12 Apr. **Golf Socks** 10 May. **Petting Larceny** 24 May. **Hat Aches** 7 June. **A Fur Piece** 22 June. **Auto Suggestion** 6 July. **Sleepy Holler** 19 July. • Adaptation of George Herriman's comic strip characters, the following of which are noted: **Aero Nuts** Krazy enters a New York–Paris airplane race. **Baby Feud** Krazy wins First Prize in a Baby Show. **Beaches and Scream** Krazy takes his morning tub prior to finding a place on a crowded train and journeying to Coney Island. **Come Easy, Go Slow** Krazy stands to inherit $10 million if he can prove himself penniless within 24 hours. **Cow Belles** Krazy's attempts to shine as a musician. **Flying Yeast** Krazy's baking with yeast makes his house take to the skies. **For Crime's Sake** Krazy emits melodious notes from a flute that follows him around. **A Fur Piece** Krazy's efforts to acquire a fur for his girl. **Golf Socks** Krazy on the golf links. **Grid Ironed** Concerning Krazy's efforts to achieve a touchdown in a football game. **Hat Aches** Regarding the adventures of a hat with fantastic interludes. **Hospitalities** Krazy's peaceful life in the hospital is disturbed by being dismissed. He successfully manages to return but his stay this time is less idyllic. **Hot Dogs** Upon escaping from a sausage manufacturer, Krazy encounters a savage lion. **A Joint Affair** Krazy's flirtation with a cabaret girl is squashed by the villain. **The Liar Bird** Krazy stands in for a lyre bird which he has allowed to escape. **The Lone Shark** Krazy serenades his girl beneath the shimmering palms but the affair brings tribulations. **Love Sunk** Krazy gets a love potion from a Medicine Man. **News Reeling** Krazy flies to Mars to secure some novel newsreel footage. **Nicked Nags** Krazy wins a horse race but foolishly lets his competitor walk off with the prize money. **Night Howls** Krazy makes the acquaintance of some eccentrics who sing "The More We Are Together." **Petting Larceny** Krazy gets tempted away from his lady love by Nina, the india-rubber girl. **The Phantom Trail** Krazy follows the terrible Black Phantom to secure a reward. **Pig Styles** Krazy introduces the pig family into society when they inherit a fortune. **Reduced Weights** Krazy reduces Mrs. Elephant's weight, turning her into a svelte and graceful dancer. **Sea Sword** Krazy's adventures with some rat pirates. **Sheep Skinned** A "Red Riding Hood" theme. **Shore Enough** Krazy is a hot dog vendor at Coney Island who is menaced by a huge monkey. **The Show Vote** Krazy wins an exciting election. **Sleepy Holler** Krazy's nap is constantly disturbed. **The Stork Exchange** Krazy babysits during the stork's lunch break. **Topsy Turvy** Krazy follows a Southern Belle to heaven. St. Peter directs him to go below. **Vanishing Screams** Krazy's girl's dad frowns upon his advances, so our hero coats himself with vanishing cream. **Web Feet** Krazy's joy ride is sidetracked when he rescues a girl from an army of spiders.

3636. Krazy Kat Studio (Winkler Pictures) *dir/anim:* William C. Nolan, Ben Harrison, Manny Gould; *anim:* Sid Marcus, Allen Rose; *asst anim:* James Culhane, Art Davis, Harry Love, Sid Marcus, Al Rose, David Tendlar; *inbetweeners:* Jack Carr, Ben Shenkman; *i&p:* Mike Balukis, James Culhane, Art Davis, Al Gould, Ira Gould, Harry Love, Dave Tendlar, Berny Wolf; *ph:* Albert Windley; *prod mgr:* Nat L. Mintz; *prod:* George Winkler.

3637. Krazy Kid Kartoons 1932; *p.c.:* McCrory Studios for Harper Producing & Distributing Co; *prod/dir;* John R. McCrory; b&w. *sil.* • Series titles untraced.

3638. Krazy Spooks (Krazy Kat) 13 Oct. 1933; *p.c.:* Winkler for Colum; *prod:* Charles Mintz; *story:* Rudy Zamora, Harry Love; *anim:* Allen Rose, Preston Blair; *mus:* Joe de Nat; b&w. *sd:* RCA. 6 min. • Krazy, Kitty and their dog Happy are menaced by a gorilla in a haunted house. Happy's fleas attack and send the ape packing.

3639. Krazy's Bear Tale (Krazy Kat) 27 Jan. 1939; *p.c.:* Charles Mintz prods for Colum; *story:* Allen Rose; *anim:* Harry Love, Louie Lilly; *lay:*

Clark Watson; *back:* Phil Davis; *voices:* Dave Weber, Billy Bletcher, Leone Le Doux; *mus:* Joe de Nat; *prod mgr:* James Bronis; b&w. *sd:* RCA. 7 min. • Krazy narrates the story "The Three Bears."

3640. Krazy's Magic (*Krazy Kat*) 20 May 1938; *p.c.:* Charles Mintz prods for Colum; *story:* Allen Rose; *anim:* Harry Love; *lay:* Clark Watson; *back:* Phil Davis; *voices:* Mel Blanc, Dave Weber; *mus:* Joe de Nat; *prod mgr:* James Bronis; b&w. *sd:* RCA. 6 min. • While sheltering in an old house, Krazy and Kitty encounter a mad magician.

3641. Krazy's News Reel (*Krazy Kat*) 24 Oct. 1936; *p.c.:* Charles Mintz prods for Colum; *story:* Allen Rose; *anim:* Harry Love; *lay:* Clark Watson; *back:* Phil Davis; *voice:* Dave Weber; *mus:* Joe de Nat; *prod mgr:* James Bronis; b&w. *sd:* RCA. 6 min. • Krazy in a newsreel take-off with wrestling bouts, etc.

3642. Krazy's Race of Time (*Krazy Kat*) 6 May 1937; *p.c.:* Charles Mintz prods for Colum; *story:* Allen Rose; *anim:* Harry Love; *lay:* Clark Watson; *back:* Phil Davis; *voice:* Billy Bletcher; *mus:* Joe de Nat; *prod mgr:* James Bronis; b&w. *sd:* RCA. 6½ min. • Krazy takes a trip to Mars and experiences a War God.

3643. Krazy's Shoe Shop (*Krazy Kat*) 12 May 1939; *p.c.:* Charles Mintz prods for Colum; *story:* Harry Love; *anim:* Allen Rose; *lay:* Clark Watson; *back:* Phil Davis; *voice:* Leone Le Doux; *mus:* Joe de Nat; *prod mgr:* James Bronis; b&w. *sd:* RCA. 6 min. • Krazy is knocked unconcious and dreams all the shoes in his shop come to life.

3644. Krazy's Waterloo (*Krazy Kat*) 16 Nov. 1934; *p.c.:* Winkler for Colum; *prod:* Charles Mintz; *story:* Ben Harrison; *anim:* Manny Gould, Al Rose, Harry Love; *mus:* Joe de Nat; b&w. *sd:* RCA. 7 min. • Krazy assumes the role of Napoleon, recruits an army of four and starts to storm Russia.

3645. Kristopher Kolumbus Jr. (*Looney Tunes*) 13 May 1939; *p.c.:* Leon Schlesinger prods for WB; *dir:* Robert Clampett; *anim:* Norman McCabe, I. Ellis; *ed:* Tregoweth E. Brown; *voices:* John Deering, Mel Blanc; *mus:* Carl W. Stalling. *prod sup:* Henry Binder, Raymond G. Katz; b&w. *sd:* Vit. 7 min. • Kristopher Kolumbus (Porky) discovers a new world and returns with a hoarde of Indians to show Queen Isabella their tribal Jitterbug dance.

3646. Kriterion Komic Kartoons *p.c.:* Kriterion-Pyramid Film Co; *anim:* Harry S. Palmer; b&w. sil. • **1915: Taft Playing Golf** 12 Feb. **Professor Dabbler** 15 Feb. **Hotel de Gink** 26 Feb. **Industrial Investigation** 5 Mar. *(title unknown)* 19 Mar. *(title unknown)* 26 Mar.

3647. Ku-Ku Nuts (*Fox & Crow*) 25 Mar. 1945; *p.c.:* Colum; *dir/story:* Bob Wickersham; *anim:* Paul Sommer, Chic Otterstrom; *sets:* Clark Watson; *ed:* Richard S. Jensen; *voices:* Frank Graham; *mus:* Eddie Kilfeather; *ph:* Frank Fisher; *i&p:* Elizabeth F. McDowell; *prod mgr:* Hugh McCollum. *col:* Tech. *sd:* WE. 7 min. • The Fox and Crow are marooned on a desert island and try to devour each other.

3648. A Lad and His Lamp (*Aesop's Film Fable*) 10 Mar. 1929; *p.c.:* Fables Pictures Inc for Pathé; *dir:* Paul Terry; b&w. sil. 5 min. • An Arabian Nights theme with Milton Mouse trailing an oriental potentate who's guards have kidnapped little Rita. A giant mailed fist breaks through the wall and transports him to the palace. After dealing with some monsters and ghosts, Milton rubs a lamp and a flying carpet takes him for a ride. The mouse goes after the Sultan with a sword and makes his getaway with Rita on a carpet that tranforms into a camel.

3649. A-Lad-in Bagdad (*Merrie Melodies*) 27 Aug. 1938; *p.c.:* Leon Schlesinger prods for WB; *dir:* Cal Howard, Cal Dalton; *story:* Dave Monahan; *anim:* Volney White; *lay:* Griff Jay; *back:* Arthur Loomer; *ed:* Tregoweth E. Brown; *voices:* Dave Weber, Bernice Hansel, Mel Blanc; *mus:* Carl W. Stalling; *prod sup:* Henry Binder, Raymond G. Katz; *col:* Tech. *sd:* Vit. 7 min. • Egghead obtains a magic lamp and proceeds to entertain the Sultan in order to win the hand of his beautiful daughter.

3650. A Lad in Bagdad (*Woody Woodpecker*) Apr. 1968; *p.c.:* Walter Lantz prods for Univ; *dir:* Paul J. Smith; *story:* Cal Howard; *anim:* Les Kline, Al Coe; *sets:* Nino Carbe; *voices:* Daws Butler, Grace Stafford; *mus:* Walter Greene; *prod mgr:* William E. Garity; *col:* Tech. *sd:* RCA. 6 min. • While in Bagdad, Woody buys an old lamp that contains a crazy genie. The lamp seller tries to regain the lamp but lives to rue the day.

3651. A-Lad-in His Lamp (*Looney Tunes*) 23 Oct. 1948; *p.c.:* WB; *dir:* Robert McKimson; *story:* Warren Foster; *anim:* Phil de Guard, Manny Gould, John Carey, Charles McKimson; *fx:* A.C. Gamer; *character des:* Jean Blanchard; *lay:* Cornett Wood; *back:* Richard H. Thomas; *ed:* Treg Brown; *voices:* Mel Blanc, Jim Backus; *mus:* Carl W. Stalling; *prod mgr:* John W. Burton; *prod:* Edward Selzer; *col:* Tech. *sd:* Vit. 7 min. • Bugs discovers Aladdin's lamp complete with a contrary genie.

3652. Laddy and His Lamp Sept. 1964; *p.c.:* Para Cartoons; *dir:* Seymour Kneitel; *story:* Tony Peters; *anim:* Martin Taras; *sets:* Robert Little; *voices:* Bob MacFadden, Cecil Roy; *mus:* Winston Sharples; *ph:* Leonard McCormick; *prod mgr:* Abe Goodman; *col:* Tech. *sd:* RCA. 6 min. • Laddy's personal genie, Ali Presto, makes him the pilot of a jet plane. The Air Force takes it to be an enemy plane and shoots it down.

3653. Lady and the Tramp 22 June 1955; *p.c.:* Walt Disney prods for BV; *dir:* Hamilton Luske, Clyde Geronimi, Wilfred Jackson; *story:* Ward Greene; *story adapt:* Erdman Penner, Joe Rinaldi, Ralph Wright, Don da Gradi, Joe Grant, Frank Tashlin, Sam Cobean; *anim dir:* Milt Kahl, Frank Thomas, Ollie Johnston, John Lounsbery, Wolfgang Reitherman, Eric Larson, Hal King, Les Clark; *anim:* Ed Aardal, Hal Ambro, Jack Campbell, Bob Carlson, Eric Cleworth, Hugh Fraser, John Freeman, Jerry Hathcock, George Kreisl, Don Lusk, George Nicholas, Cliff Nordberg, Ken O'Brien, Leo Salkin, John Sibley, Harvey Toombs, Marvin Woodward; *inbetweener:* Willie Ito; *fx:* Dan MacManus, George Rowley; *lay:* Ken Anderson, Bill Bosché, Colin Campbell, Tom Codrick, Don Griffiths, Victor Haboush, Hugh Hennesy, Lance Nolley, A. Kendall O'Connor, Thor Putnam, Jacques Rupp, McLaren Stewart, Al Zinnen; *back:* Dick Anthony, Claude Coats, Al Dempster, Eyvind Earle, Ray Huffine, Ralph Hulett, Brice Mack, Jimi Trout, Thelma Witmer; *ed:* Don Halliday; *voices: Peg/Darling:* Peggy Lee; *The Tramp:* Larry Roberts; *Trusty:* Bill Baucom; *Aunt Sarah:* Verna Felton; *Tony:* George Givot; *Jim Dear:* Lee Millar; *Lady:* Barbara Luddy; *Jock/Joe/Bull/Daschie/Cop:* Bill Thompson; *The Beaver/Dog Catcher:* Stan Freberg; *Boris:* Alan Reed; *Toughy/Pedro/Professor/Hyena/Misc. Dog Barks:* Dallas McKennon; *Pet Shop Assistant:* Jerry Mann; *Alligator:* Thurl Ravenscroft; *The Pound Hounds/Chorus:* The MelloMen; *Baby Cries:* Tommy Luske; "He's a Tramp"/"Siamese Cat Song"/"La La Lu"/"What Is a Baby" sung by Peggy Lee; "Bella Notte" sung by Bob Hamlin; *mus:* Oliver Wallace; *orch:* Edward Plumb, Sidney Fine; *songs:* Peggy Lee, Sonny Burke; *vocal arr:* John Rarig; *mus ed:* Evelyn Kennedy; *sd:* C.O. Slyfield, Harold J. Steck, Robert O. Cook; *special processes:* Ub Iwerks; *asso prod:* Erdman Penner; *col:* Tech. *sd:* RCA. 76 min. CS. • Ward Green's timeless story of a cocker spaniel from a respectable home who is shown the seamier side of life by a mongrel from the wrong side of the tracks.

3654. The Lady in Red (*Merrie Melodies*) 29 Sept. 1935; *p.c.:* Leon Schlesinger prods for WB; *dir:* Isadore Freleng; *anim:* Bob McKimson, Ben Clopton, Robert Clampett; *mus:* Bernard Brown; *song:* Allie Wrubel; *prod sup:* Henry Binder, Raymong G. Katz; *col:* Tech-2. *sd:* Vit. 7 min. • Dancing and singing cockroaches come to the aid of their lady love when she is captured by a parrot.

3655. Lady Play Your Mandolin (*Merrie Melodies*) 25 Apr. 1931; *p.c.:* Harman–Ising prods for WB; *prod:* Leon Schlesinger; *anim:* Rollin Hamilton, Norm Blackburn, Robert Clampett; *voices:* Johnny Murray, The King's Men; *mus:* Frank Marsales, Abe Lyman & His Brunswick Recording Orchestra; *song:* Irving Caésar, Oscar Levant; b&w. *sd:* Vit. 6 min. • Foxy and his pals get drunk in a Mexican cantina and start hallucinating.

3656. The Lady Says No (*Daffy Ditty*) 26 Apr. 1946; *p.c.:* Plastic prods for UA; *prod:* Larry Morey, John Sutherland; *dir/story:* Frank Tashlin; *anim:* George Grandpré; *character des:* Duke Russell; *models:* Wah Chang, Burton Freud, Frank Irwin, Carl Ryan; *art dir:* Bernice Polifka; *sets:* Miles Pike, Gene Warren, Robert Matey, Charles Mattox; *mus:* Paul J. Smith; *ph:* Robert Newman; *prod mgr:* Tim Barr; *col:* Tech. *sd:* RCA. 7½ min. • Pepito's persistent advances toward a young senorita permits him to take her to a restaurant where he finds he can't pay the bill.

3657. Lafflets 1922/1923; *p.c.:* Laugh-O-Gram Films Inc.; *prod/dir:* Walt Disney; *anim:* Ub Iwerks, Rudolf Ising; *ed:* Aletha Reynolds; b&w. sil. 3 min. • **Golf in Slow Motion, Descha's Tryst with the Moon, Aesthetic Camping, Reuben's Big Day, Rescued, A Star Pitcher, The Woodland Potter, A Pirate for a Day** • Mixture of drawn and stop-motion animation.

3658. Lake Titicaca 18 Feb. 1955; *p.c.:* Walt Disney prods for BV; *dir:* William O. Roberts; *col:* Tech. *sd:* RCA. 7 min. • Donald visits Bolivia, samples the pleasures of a native boat and copes with a stubborn llama. • See: *Saludos Amigos*

3659. A Lamb in a Jam *(Noveltoon)* 4 May 1945; *p.c.:* Famous for Para; *dir:* I. Sparber; *story:* Joe Stultz, Carl Meyer; *mus:* Winston Sharples; *ph:* Leonard McCormick; *prod mgr:* Sam Buchwald; *col:* Tech. *sd:* RCA. 6 min. • The black lamb is skating on ice and Wolfie attempts to snag him for his supper.

3660. Lambert the Sheepish Lion 4 Apr. 1952; *p.c.:* Walt Disney prods for RKO; *dir:* Jack Hannah; *story:* Bill Peet, Ralph Wright, Milt Banta; *anim:* Eric Larson, John Lounsbery, Don Lusk, Judge Whitaker, Hal Ambro, Bob Carlson, Milt Kahl, George Kreisl; *fx:* Dan MacManus; *lay:* Yale Gracey; *back:* Ray Huffine; *voices:* Sterling Holloway, The Jud Conlon Singers, Clarence Nash, James MacDonald; *mus:* Joseph S. Dubin; *song:* Eddy Pola, George Wyle; *col:* Tech. *sd:* RCA. 8 min. *Academy Award nomination.* • A lion cub is mistakenly delivered by the stork to a mother ewe and she rears him as her own. The other lambs rag him for his cowardice but when his mother is cornered by a hungry wolf, he saves the whole flock and becomes a hero.

3661. Lambs Will Gamble *(Krazy Kat)* 1 Nov. 1930; *p.c.:* Winkler for Colum; *prod:* Charles Mintz; *story:* Ben Harrison; *anim:* Manny Gould; *mus:* Joe de Nat; *prod mgr:* James Bronis; b&w. *sd:* WE. 6 min. • After losing everything in the the Wall Street crash, Krazy makes a fortune with birds who lay gold coins.

3662. L'Amour the Merrier *(Noveltoon)* 5 July 1957; *p.c.:* Para Cartoons: *dir:* Seymour Kneitel; *story:* Irving Spector; *anim:* Al Eugster, Danté Barbetta, Nick Tafuri, Wm. B. Pattengill; *sets:* Robert Little; *voices:* Allen Swift; *mus:* Winston Sharples; *ph:* Leonard McCormick; *prod mgr:* Seymour Shultz; *col:* Tech. *sd:* RCA. 6 min. • The French Matchmaker has a problem when trying to make a Princess marry a peasant oaf.

3663. The Lamp Lighter *(Oswald)* 10 Jan 1938; *p.c.:* Univ; *prod/dir:* Walter Lantz; *story:* Victor McLeod, James Miele; *anim:* Ray Fahringer, Ted Dubois; *voice:* Shirley Reed; *mus:* Nathaniel Shilkret; b&w. *sd:* WE. 7 min. • While Oswald lays ill, two cats take his lamplighting equipment.

3664. The Land Before Time 18 Nov. 1988; *p.c.:* Sullivan Bluth Studios (Ireland), Ltd. for Univ.; *dir:* Don Bluth; *prod:* Don Bluth, Gary Goldman, John Pomeroy; *ex prod:* Steven Spielberg, George Lucas; *co-ex prod:* Frank Marshall, Kathleen Kennedy; *scr:* Stu Krieger; *story:* Judy Freudberg, Tony Geiss; *story consultants:* Brent Maddock, Steve Wilson; *prod des:* Don Bluth; *storyboard:* Don Bluth, Larry Leker, Dan Kuenster; *asst dir:* G. Sue Shakespeare, David Steinberg, Russell Boland, Moya Mackle, Nuala O'Toole; *anim dir:* John Pomeroy, Dan Kuenster, Linda Miller, Lorna Pomeroy, Ralph Zondag, Dick Zondag; *anim:* Anne Marie Bardwell, Victoria Brewster, Colm Duggan, Ken Duncan, Jeff Etter, Mark Fisher, Michael Gagne, Raul Garcia, Patrick Gleeson, Kent Hammerstrom, T. Daniel Hofstedt, Jon Hooper, Skip Jones, Jean Morel, Paul Newberry, Ralf Palmer, Gary Perkovac, John Power, Charlie Bonifacio, Jesse Cosio, John Hill, Sylvia Hoefnagels, Fernando Moro, Wendy Perdue, Mark Pudleiner, David Simmons, Konrad Winterlich, Kevin Wurzer; *fx anim:* Dorse A. Lanpher, David Bossert, Joey Mildenberger, Kathleen Quaife-Hodge, Tom Hush, Diann Landau, Steve Moore, Don Paul, Bob Simmons, David Tidgwell; *fx inbet:* Orla Madden, James Mansfield Jr., Janette Owens, Peter Matheson, John O'Neill, Conor Thunder, Garrett Wren; *character key:* Vera Lanpher, Ben Burgess, Nollaig Crombie, Edward Goral, Anne Heeney, Sylvia Hoefnagels, Helen Lawlor, Marion Mathieu, Ashley McGovern, Mark Pudleiner, Terry Shakespeare, Rusty Stoll, Jeff Topping, Wendo van Essen, Sally Voorheis; *rough anim asst sup:* Cathy Jones, *rough break:* Donnachada Daly, Hope Devlin, John Eddings, Edward Gribbin, Tom Higgins, Noel P. Kiernan, Sandra Ryan, Greg Tiernan, Jane Anderson, Peter Anderson, Leslie Aust, Paul Bolger, David Cribbin, Stephen Cullen, Frank Doyle, Robert Fox, David Groome, Martin Hanley, Roisin Hunt, Jerr O'Carroll; *scene plan:* Russell Boland, Aran O'Reilly, David Steinberg, Sean Dempsey, Kip Goldman; *anim check:* Carla Washburn, Lisa Joko, Pam Kleyman, Mary Walsh, Michele McKenna, Saskia Raevouri, Robin Police; *clean-up:* Annette Byrne, Michael Carey, Michael Cassidy, Eileen Conway, Paul Daly, Denis Deegan, Mary Delaney, Peter Donnelly, Sylvia Fitzpatrick, Alan Fleming, Connor Flynn, Michael Garry, Paul M. Kelly,

Michael Kiely, Giorgio Mardegan, Ann McCormick, Margaret McKenna, Brian McSweeney, Anne-Marie Mockler, Julie Molina, Dympna O'Halloran, Tara O'Reilly, Terry Pike, John A. Power, Miriam Reid, Julia Ryan, Paul Shanahan, Hugh Tattan; *col stylists:* Carmen Oliver, Susan Vanderhorst, Laurie Curran, Donal Freeney, Violet McKenna, Suzanne O'Reilly; *lay:* David Goetz, Rick Bentham, Mark Swanson, Mark Swan, Richard Fawdry; *back stylist:* Don Moore; *back:* Barry Atkinson, Sunny Apinchapong, Carl Jones, Mannix Bennett, David McCamley; *fx painting:* Shirley (Sam) Mapes; *ed:* Dan Molina, John K. Carr, Thomas V. Moss, Fiona N. Trayler, Elizabeth Byrne, Fred Reilly, Thomas Daly; *voices: Ducky:* Judith Barsi; *Daddy Topps:* Burke Byrns; *Littlefoot:* Gabriel Damon; *Grandfather:* Bill Erwin; *Narrator/Rooter:* Pat Hingle; *Cera:* Candy Hutson; *Petrie:* Will Ryan; *Littlefoot's Mother:* Helen Shaver; *chorus:* King's College School Choir, the choristers of St. Paul's Cathedral and Ladies' Chorus; *mus:* James Horner; *song:* James Horner, Will Jennings; *mus prod:* Peter Asher; *performed by* Diana Ross; *music performed by* The London Symphony Orchestra, England; *chief dir:* Nick Curtis; *orch:* Greig McRitchie; *mus copyist:* Vic Fraser; *mus ed:* Jim Henrikson; *mus rec:* Shawn Murphy, Andrew Glen; *ADR rec:* Charles Richards, Tom O'Connell, Bill Rowe, Ray Merrin, John Falcini; *sup ex prod for Sullivan Bluth Studios:* Morris F. Sullivan; *prod mgr:* Thad Weinlein; *prod sup:* Cathy J. Carr; *ph:* Jim Mann, David R. Ankney, Aidan Farrell, John Fitzgerald, Gary Hall, Gary Jones, Eimear Joyce, Scott McCartor, Fiona Mackle, Emma Miller, Ciavàn Morris, John O'Flaherty, Eithne Quinn, Eric Ryan, Rocky Solotoff, Graham Tiernan; *Xerox:* Terri Eddings, Daryl Carstensen, Michael Murray, Robert Byrne, Gerard Gogan, Gene Dauer, Mary Boylan, Gerard Duffy, Wayne Farrar, Yvonne McSweeney, Dympna Murray, Collette O'Brien, Siobhan O'Brien, Peadar O'Reilly, Kieron White; *Xerox check:* John Finnegan, Brendan Harris, Gillian Hunt, Stuart Johnstone, Caroline Lynch, Paul Roy, Paul Walsh; *mark-up:* Sarah-Jane King, Maria Farrell; *paint lab:* Deborah Rykoff, Olga Tarin-Craig, Nancy Levey-Bossert, Brenda McGuirk, Damian Murphy, Melanie Strickland, Andrew Molloy, Christine Fluskey, Noirin Dunne, Tracy Arundel; *inking sup:* Jacqueline Hooks; *i&p:* Anne Hazard, Karin Stover, Kerri Swanson, Madeleine Downes, Karen Dwyer, Martine Finucane, Mary Gavin, Sorcha ni Chuimin, Kenneth Slevin, Niamh McClean, Adrienne Bell, Brian Boylan, Ann Brennan, John Brennan, Maureen Buggy, Melanie Burke, Mark Byrne, Michael Carroll, Yvonne Carthy, Vincent Clarke, Orla Coughlan, Bryan Doyle, Gloria Dunne, Franka Elston, Tom English, Cinda Fitzpatrick, Jim Fleming, Claire Gallagher, Philip Garry, Fiona Gavin, Fiona Ginnell, Patricia Gordan, Catherine Gurry, Liam Hannan, Karl Hayes, Liam Hoban, Gary Keleghan, Sheila Kelly, Siobhan Larkin, Pearse Love, Maria Malone, Joseph Manifold Jr., Petula Masterson, Ann May, Colin McGrath, Geraldine McGuinness, Ian McLoughlin, Kate Meredith, Josephine Mulraney, Mary B. Mulvihill, Moira Murphy, John Murray, David Nolan, Philip O'Connor, Brid O'Donnell, Paul O'Rourke, John Phelan, Julie Phelan, Gerard J.D. Phillips, Eileen Ridgeway, Carrie Rumgay, Colum Slevin, Karen Sommerville, Jan Stokes, Iseult Travers; *paint check:* Michael Casey, Gerard Coleman, Sinead Murray, Helen O'Flynn; *optical technicians:* Caroline Gaynor, Liam Halpin; *engineering:* Neil Keaveney, John Henry; *sd ed:* Dan Molina, Kevin Brazier, Ian Fuller, Joe Gallagher, Andy Stears; *foley art:* TAJ Soundtracks, Dan O'Connell, Alicia Stevenson, Jim Ashwill, Mary Jolang; *col timer:* John Stanborough; *neg cutter:* Donah Bassett, Cathy Carr; *studio operations:* Fred Craig; *asso prod:* Deborah Jelin Newmyer; *col:* Tech. *sd:* Dolby Stereo. 69 min. • Set in prehistoric times, a group of lost young dinosaurs start an epic journey in search of their elders who are journeying to the Great Valley in search of greener pastures.

3665. The Land Boom *(Aesop's Film Fable)* 20 June 1926; *p.c.:* Fables Pictures Inc for Pathé; *dir:* Paul Terry; b&w. sil. 10 min. • Farmer Al Falfa learns of a land boom in Florida. Dave Dog sells a beautiful looking semitropical island 25 feet wide by 150 feet deep. As Dave rows away with Al's money and the shirt off his back, Al discovers the island to be the back of a whale.

3666. Land Grab *(Hector Heathcote)* Feb. 1970 (© 1963); *p.c.:* TT for Fox; *ex prod:* Bill Weiss; *dir/anim:* Dave Tendlar; *story sup;* Tom Morrison; *story:* Larz Bourne; *sets:* Bill Focht, John Zago; *ed:* George McAvoy; *voices:* John Myhers; *mus:* Phil Scheib; *ph:* Joe Rasinski; *col:* DeLuxe. *sd:* RCA. 5 min. • The government offers free land in Oklahoma. Benedict and Heathcote fight over the best plot.

3667. Land O' Cotton (*Aesop's Film Fable*) 6 Jan. 1929; *p.c.:* Fables Pictures Inc for Pathé; *dir:* Frank Moser, Paul Terry; b&w. *sil.* 10 min. • A "Simon LeGree" type mouse sells a girl mouse at a slave auction to a mean dog overseer who keeps his slaves in pens and whips them. The boy and girl mouse escape over the ice floes, pursued by bloodhounds. A donkey comes to their rescue by kicking the hounds away and knocking the evil dog cold with his horseshoes. Moral: "The Flapper of today is as good as the one of 30 years ago, unless it's the same one."

3668. The Land of Fun (*Color Rhapsody*) 18 Apr. 1941; *p.c.:* Colum; *dir:* Sid Marcus; *anim:* Art Davis; *sets:* Phil Davis; *ed:* Ed Moore; *voices:* John Wald, Mel Blanc; *mus:* Joe de Nat; *ph:* Otto Reimer; *prod mgr:* George Winkler; *col:* Tech. *sd:* RCA. 6 min. • Spot-gags on holidays with a running gag involving a small car trying to pass a huge truck on a narrow mountain pass.

3669. Land of Lost Watches (*Noveltoon*) 4 May 1951; *p.c.:* Famous for Para; *dir:* Seymour Kneitel; *story:* Isabel Manning Hewson; *story adapt:* I. Klein, Larry Riley; *anim:* Steve Muffatti, George Germanetti, Howard Beckerman; *sets:* Tom Ford; *voices:* Mae Questel, Jackson Beck, Arnold Stang, Jack Mercer, Cecil Roy; *mus:* Winston Sharples; *ph:* Leonard McCormick; *prod mgr:* Sam Buchwald; *col:* Tech. *sd:* RCA. 9 min. • Red Lantern, the magic fish, takes Billy and Isabel to an undersea world of lost watches where they hope to find their father's timepiece.

3670. The Land of the Lost (*Noveltoon*) 7 May 1948; *p.c.:* Famous for Para; *dir:* I. Sparber; *story:* Isabel Manning Hewson; *story adapt:* Larz Bourne, Bill Turner; *anim:* Myron Waldman, Nick Tafuri; *sets:* Anton Loeb; *voices:* Jackson Beck, Gwen Davies, Jack Mercer, Cecil Roy; *mus:* Winston Sharples; *ph:* Leonard McCormick; *prod mgr:* Sam Buchwald; *col:* Tech. *sd:* RCA. 8 min. • Based on the radio program *Billy and Isabel*, the children meet an enchanted fish who takes them to an undersea world. Billy's lost jack-knife rescues lady butter-knife from the clutches of Dirty Dirk.

3671. Land of the Lost Jewels (*Noveltoon*) 6 Jan. 1950; *p.c.:* Famous for Para; *dir:* I. Sparber; *story:* Isabel Manning Hewson; *story adapt:* Bill Turner, Larry Riley; *anim:* Myron Waldman, Gordon Whittier; *sets:* Anton Loeb; *voices:* Jackson Beck, Arnold Stang, Cecil Roy, Gwen Davies; *mus:* Winston Sharples; *ph:* Leonard McCormick; *prod mgr:* Sam Buchwald; *col:* Tech. *sd:* RCA. 9 min. • While fishing, Billy and Isabel lose a grasshopper brooch in the water. Red Lantern, the educated fish, takes them to the sea bed where they help "Hoppy" find a home.

3672. Land of the Midnight Fun (*Merrie Melodies*) 23 Sept. 1939; *p.c.:* Leon Schlesinger prods for WB; *dir:* Fred Avery; *story:* Melvin Millar, Robert Clampett; *anim:* Charles McKimson; *sets:* John Didrik Johnsen; *ed:* Tregoweth E. Brown; *voices:* Robert C. Bruce, Mel Blanc, Sara Berner, Fred Avery; *mus:* Carl W. Stalling; *prod sup:* Henry Binder, Raymond G. Katz; *col:* Tech. *sd:* Vit. 7 min. • An ocean liner journeys to the South Pole.

3673. Landing of the Pilgrims (*Terry-Toon*) 1 Nov. 1940; *p.c.:* TT for Fox; *dir:* Connie Rasinski; *story:* John Foster; *mus:* Philip A. Scheib; *col:* Tech. *sd:* RCA. 6½ min. • The story of how the Pilgrims landed, hunted, set up home and gave the Indians modern gifts.

3674. Landing Stripling (*Tom & Jerry*) Apr. 1962; *p.c.:* MGM; *prod:* William L. Snyder; *dir:* Gene Deitch; *story:* Eli Bauer; *anim dir:* Vaclav Bedrich; *col:* Metro. *sd:* WE. 8 min. • Jerry stems Tom's attempts to catch a small flying bird. • See: *Tom and Jerry (Rembrandt Studio)*

3675. A Language All My Own (*Betty Boop*) 19 July 1935; *p.c.:* The Fleischer Studio for Para; *prod:* Max Fleischer; *dir:* Dave Fleischer; *anim:* Myron Waldman, Hicks Lokey, Lillian Friedman; *voice:* Mae Questel; *mus:* Sammy Timberg; b&w. *sd:* WE. 6 min. • Betty flies all over the world to the Orient to entertain a Japanese audience.

3676. Lantz, Walter, Productions (*Titles and Sequences*) • Sioux City Sue (Rep) 1946, The Egg and I (Univ) 1947, Abbott and Costello Meet Frankenstein (Univ) 1948, Abbott and Costello Meet the Killer (Univ) 1949, Destination Moon (Eagle/Lion) 1950

3677. The Last Action Hero 18 June 1993; *p.c.:* Colum TriStar; *The Baer Animation Company: anim des:* David Baer; *anim sup:* Jane Baer; *prod mgr:* Craig Sost; *col:* Tech. *sd:* Dolby Stereo. 110 min. *l/a.* • Live-action fantasy: A young boy is transported into an action movie he is watching. He helps a cop to track down a criminal and they both pursue the villain who leaves the confines of the film, escaping into the real world.

3678. The Last Dance (*Aesop's Sound Fable*) 23 Nov. 1931; *p.c.:* Van Beuren for RKO/Pathé; *dir:* John Foster; *mus:* Gene Rodemich; b&w. *sd:* RCA. 6 min. • Five compete for the love of a lady. Waffles the cat wins her over with his singing.

3679. The Last Days of Pompeii 1935; *p.c.:* RKO; *prod:* Merian C. Cooper; *anim fx:* Willis O'Brien, Vernon Walker, Harry Redmond, Carroll Shepphird, Marcel Delgado, Gus White; b&w. *sd:* RCA; 90 min. *l/a/anim.* • Earthquake affected by Willis O'Brien in a live-action feature.

3680. The Last Ha Ha (*Aesop's Film Fable*) 15 Aug. 1926; *p.c.:* Fables Pictures Inc for Pathé; *dir:* Paul Terry; b&w. *sil.* 10 min. • As Tom the Cat and Milton Mouse wash the Farmer's porch, Milton relieves the watchdog of his muzzle and the dog bites Tom's tail. A salesman arrives on his motorbike and attaches ropes to the dog and cat, driving off with them in tow. The creatures respond, bringing the salesman and bike in collision with Farmer Al, the dog and cat. Moral: "He who laughs last didn't see the joke in the first place."

3681. The Last Hungry Cat (*Merrie Melodies*) Dec. 1961; *p.c.:* WB; *dir:* Friz Freleng; *asst dir:* Hawley Pratt; *story:* John Dunn, Dave DeTiege; *anim:* Gerry Chiniquy, Virgil Ross, Art Leonardi, Lee Halpern; *back:* Tom O'Loughlin; *ed:* Treg Brown; *voices:* Mel Blanc, June Foray, Ben Frommer; *mus:* Milt Franklyn; *prod mgr:* William Orcutt; *prod:* David H. DePatie; *col:* Tech. *sd:* Vit. 7 min. • Sylvester wrestles with his conscience after being convinced he has finally eaten Tweety.

3682. The Last Indian (*Terry-Toon*) 24 June 1938; *p.c.:* TT for Educational/Fox; *dir:* Connie Rasinski; *mus:* Philip A. Scheib; b&w. *sd:* WE. 6 min. • The Indians were happy until the settlers intruded with oil wells, real estate, etc., leaving all but one Indian who is finally driven to becoming a Cigar Store Indian.

3683. The Last Mail (*Aesop's Sound Fable*) 24 Mar. 1933; *p.c.:* Van Beuren for RKO; *dir:* Mannie Davis; *voice:* Marjorie Hines; *mus:* Gene Rodemich; b&w. *sd:* RCA. 6 min. • Cubby Bear is a mailman in the frozen North. He gets his girl and the mail stolen by a hungry wolf. A helpful eagle carries him to the wolf's lair where he retrieves them both.

3684. The Last Mouse of Hamelin (*Terry-Toon*) Aug. 1955; *p.c.:* TT for Fox; *dir:* Connie Rasinski; *story/voices:* Tom Morrison; *anim:* Jim Tyer; *sets:* Art Bartsch; *mus:* Philip A. Scheib; *ph:* Douglas Moye; *col:* Tech. *sd:* RCA. 6 min. • The story of one mouse who didn't follow the Pied Piper because he is tone deaf.

3685. The Last Round-Up (*Gandy Goose*) 14 May 1943; *p.c.:* TT for Fox; *dir:* Mannie Davis; *story:* John Foster; *voices:* Arthur Kay, Tom Morrison; *mus:* Philip A. Scheib; *col:* Tech. *sd:* RCA. 6½ min. • Pvt. Gandy and Sgt. Sourpuss are blasted into Germany to put a stop to Herr Hitler (a hog) and Mussolini (an ape).

3686. The Last Straw (*Paul Terry-Toon*) 23 Feb. 1934; *p.c.:* Moser & Terry for Educational/Fox; *dir:* Frank Moser, Paul Terry; *mus:* Philip A. Scheib; b&w. *sd:* WE. 5 min. • No story available.

3687. The Last Unicorn 19 Nov. 1982; *p.c.:* Rankin/Bass for ITC Films and Sunn Classic; *dir/prod:* Arthur Rankin Jr., Jules Bass; *ex prod:* Martin Starger; *story:* Peter S. Beagle; *based on the novel by* Peter S. Beagle; *storyboard:* Katsukisa Yamada, Don Duga; *asso prod:* Michael Chase Walker; *des:* Arthur Rankin Jr.; *character des:* Lester Abrams; *continuity/anim dir:* Katsukisa Yamada; *anim co-ord:* Toru Hara, Kiyoshi Sakai; *continuity anim:* Guy Kubo; *key anim:* Kazuyuki Kobayaski, Hidemi Kubo, Tadakatsu Yoshida; *anim:* Yoshiko Sasaki, Masahiro Yoshida, Kayoko Sakano, Fukuo Suzuki; *back:* Minoru Nishida, Kazusuke Yoshihara, Mitsuo Iwasaki; *tapestry des:* Irra Duga; *ed:* Tomoko Kida; *in charge of prod:* Masaki Iizuka; *voices: Schmendrick the Magician:* Alan Arkin; *Prince Lin:* Jeff Bridges; *The Last Unicorn/Lady Amalthea:* Mia Farrow; *Molly Grue:* Tammy Grimes; *The Butterfly:* Robert Klein; *Mommy Fortune:* Angela Lansbury; *King Haggard:* Christopher Lee; *Captain Cully:* Keenan Wynn; *The Talking Cat:* Paul Frees; *The Speaking Skull:* Rene Auberjenois; *also:* Brother Theodore, Don Messick, Jack Lester, Nellie Bellflower, Edward Peck, Kenneth Jennings; *mus/songs:* Jimmy Webb; *orch:* William McCauley, Matthew McCauley, Jimmy Webb, Elton Moser; songs performed by America; *ph:* Hiroyasu Omoto; *sd fx:* Noriyoski Ohira, Tom Clack; *sd:* John Curcio, John Richards, Dave Iveland; *sd re-rec:* Donald O. Mitchell; *prod co-ord:* Lee Dannacher; *col. sd:* Dolby Stereo. 85 min. • A unicorn learns that she is the last of her species and leaves the wood to discover the truth, accompanied by a hopeful magician named Schmendrick. In time they arrive at the realm of King Haggard who is said to have driven the unicorns into the sea. In order to save her, Schmendrick uses magic to turn the unicorn into the Lady Amalthea but is unable to return her to her original form. Amalthea falls for King Haggard's adopted son, Prince Lir, forgetting that she is really a unicorn.

3688. Laughing Gas (*Flip the Frog*) 14 Mar. 1931; *p.c.:* Celebrity for MGM; *prod/dir:* Ub Iwerks; b&w. *sd:* PCP. 6 min. • Dentist Flip demonstrates unorthodox methods for pulling teeth.

3689. The Laundry (*Out of the Inkwell*) 1 Jan. 1924; *p.c.:* Inkwell Studio for Red Seal; *prod:* Max Fleischer; *dir:* Dave Fleischer; b&w. *sil.* 5 min. • No story available.

3690. Laundry Blues (*Aesop's Sound Fable*) 17 Aug. 1930; *p.c.:* Van Beuren for Pathé; *dir:* John Foster, Mannie Davis; *mus:* Gene Rodemich; b&w. *sd:* RCA. 9 min. • Highjinks in a Chinese laundry.

3691. The Laundry Man (*Aesop's Film Fable*) 26 Oct. 1928; *p.c.:* Fables Pictures Inc for Pathé; *dir:* Paul Terry; b&w. *sil.* 10 min. • The feline boss of a laundry abducts the delivery boy's girlfriend and takes her to a Chinatown dive. A Tong war develops, finishing off the boss. The delivery boy rescues his girl and now the laundry is under new management.

3692. Law and Audrey (*Noveltoon*) 23 May 1952; *p.c.:* Famous for Para; *dir:* I. Sparber; *story:* I. Klein; *anim:* Steve Muffatti, Morey Reden; *sets:* Tom Ford; *voices:* Mae Questel, Sid Raymond; *mus:* Winston Sharples; *ph:* Leonard McCormick; *prod mgr:* Seymour Shultz; *col:* Tech. *sd:* RCA. 6 min. • Audrey upsets a policeman while playing with her dog in the park.

3693. Law and Order (*Mighty Mouse*) June 1950; *p.c.:* TT for Fox; *dir:* Eddie Donnelly; *story:* Tom Morrison; *anim:* Jim Tyer; *mus:* Philip A. Scheib; *ph:* Douglas Moye; *col:* Tech. *sd:* RCA. 6 min. • The Catnip Gang escape from jail and proceed to catch mice. Mighty Mouse soon comes out of the heavens to rescue them.

3694. Lazy Little Beaver (*Mighty Mouse*) 26 Dec. 1947; *p.c.:* TT for Fox; *dir:* Eddie Donnelly; *story:* John Foster; *anim:* Jim Tyer; *voices:* Tom Morrison, Cecil Roy; *mus:* Philip A. Scheib; *ph:* Douglas Moye; *col:* Tech. *sd:* RCA. 6 min. • The lazy beaver runs away from home and is rescued from a wolf by Mighty Mouse.

3695. Lazybones (*Screen Songs*) 13 Apr. 1934; *p.c.:* The Fleischer Studio for Para; *prod:* Max Fleischer; *dir:* Dave Fleischer; *anim:* Willard Bowsky, Dave Tendlar; *l/a:* Borrah Minevitch & His Harmonica Rascals; *sung by* Les Reis & Artie Dunn; *song:* Hoagy Carmichael, Johnny Mercer; b&w. *sd:* WE. 10 min. • The cartoon segment deals with a lazy racehorse who wins the race when his owner puts the horse's bed at the end of the track.

3696. The League of Nations (*Out of the Inkwell*) 17 Sept. 1924; *p.c.:* Inkwell Studio for Red Seal; *prod:* Max Fleischer; *dir:* Dave Fleischer; b&w. *sil.* 6 min. • Max draws planets and heavenly bodies so that when the little clown peeps through a powerful telescope to see a Martian army gathering to attack the Earth he summons up clowns from every nation and prepares to repel the enemy.

3697. A Leak in the Dike (*Noveltoon/Jacky's Whacky World*) Feb. 1965; *p.c.:* Para Cartoons; *dir/story:* Jack Mendelsohn; *creative sup:* Howard Post; *anim:* Martin Taras; *voices:* Bob MacFadden; *sets:* Robert Little; *mus:* Winston Sharples; *ph:* Leonard McCormick; *prod mgr:* Abe Goodman; *col:* Tech. *sd:* RCA. 6 min. • A child's eye view of the Dutch boy who put his fist in the dike to stop a leak.

3698. The Leaky Faucet (*Terry-Toon*) Dec. 1959; *p.c.:* TT for Fox; *ex prod:* Bill Weiss; *dir:* Martin Taras; *story sup:* Tom Morrison; *story:* Larz Bourne; *anim:* Ed Donnelly, Mannie Davis; *sets:* John Zago; *mus:* Phil Scheib; *prod mgr:* Frank Schudde; *col:* Tech. *sd:* RCA. 6 min. CS. • Dimwit has problems with the plumbing.

3699. A Leap in the Deep (*Tijuana Toads*) 20 June 1971; *p.c.:* Mirisch/DFE for UA; *dir:* Hawley Pratt; *story:* John W. Dunn; *anim:* Don Williams, Manny Gould, Manny Perez, Robert Taylor, Warren Batchelder; *lay:* Dick Ung; *back:* Richard H. Thomas; *ed:* Lee Gunther; *voices:* Don Diamond, Tom Holland, Larry D. Mann; *mus:* Doug Goodwin; *ph:* John Burton Jr.; *prod sup:* Jim Foss, Harry Love; *col:* DeLuxe. *sd:* RCA. 6 min. • The Toads go in search of another pond. They find the ocean but run afoul of a crane.

3700. Leap Year (*The Boob Weekly*) 22 May 1916; *p.c.:* Barré Cartoons for Pathé; *dir:* R.L. Goldberg; *anim:* George Stallings, Raoul Barré, William C. Nolan, Gregory la Cava; b&w. *sil.* 5 min. • Miss Ophelia Fadeout, whose face frightens the neighborhood populace, still hopes to secure a husband ... by using chloroform.

3701. Learn Polikeness (*Popeye*) 18 Feb. 1938; *p.c.:* The Fleischer Studio for Para; *prod:* Max Fleischer; *dir:* Dave Fleischer; *anim:* David Tendlar, Nicholas Tafuri; *voices:* Jack Mercer, Mae Questel, Gus Wickie; *mus:* Sammy Timberg; *ph:* Johnny Burks; b&w. *sd:* WE. 7 min. • Olive takes Popeye to Professor Bluteau's School of Etiquette in hopes of his learning some manners.

3702. Leave Us Chase It (*Phantasy*) 24 Apr. 1947; *p.c.:* Colum; *prod:* Raymond Katz, Henry Binder; *dir:* Howard Swift; *story:* Cal Howard; *anim:* Grant Simmons, Paul Sommer, Jay Sarbry; *lay:* Bill Weaver; *back:* Ed Starr; *ed:* Richard S. Jensen; *voices:* Stan Freberg, Dick Nelson; *mus:* Darrell Calker; *ph:* Frank Fisher; *col:* Tech. *sd:* WE. 6½ min. • Impressed by a comic he is reading, a cat disguises himself as "Superkat" to try and get the best of a cocky mouse.

3703. Leave Well Enough Alone (*Popeye*) 24 Mar. 1939; *p.c.:* The Fleischer Studio for Para; *prod:* Max Fleischer; *dir:* Dave Fleischer; *anim:* Seymour Kneitel, Abner Matthews; *voices:* Jack Mercer, Margie Hines; *mus:* Sammy Timberg; *ph:* Charles Schettler; *prod sup:* Sam Buchwald, Isidore Sparber; b&w. *sd:* WE. 7 min. • Hating to see caged animals, Popeye buys up all the pets in Olive's Pet Shop and sets them free, soon realizing they were safer in cages.

3704. Leaves from Life (*Reel Life*); *p.c.:* Gaumont Co for Ess; b&w. *sil.* • Animated cartoons from *Life* magazine inserted in live-action interest reel. • **1917:** (*title unknown*) 5 July. **A Hasty Pudding** 12 July. (*title unknown*) 19 July. (*title unknown*) 26 July. (*title unknown*) 2 Aug. **Not a Shadow of a Doubt** 9 Aug. **The Absent Minded Dentist** 16 Aug. (*title unknown*) 23 Aug. **The March of Science** 30 Aug. **Fresh Advances** 6 Sept. **When a Big Car Goes By** 13 Sept. **So Easy** 20 Sept. (*title unknown*) 27 Sept. **Japanese Dwarf Plants** 4 Oct. (*title unknown*) 11 Oct. (*title unknown*) 18 Oct. **How the American Traveller Is Fed** 25 Oct. **Had Your Mining Stock Panned Out** 31 Oct. **It Was Not the Colic** 8 Nov.

3705. The Legend of Coyote Rock (*Pluto*) 24 Aug. 1945; *p.c.:* Walt Disney prods for RKO; *dir:* Charles Nichols; *asst dir:* Esther Newell; *story:* Eric Gurney; *anim:* John Lounsbery, Norman Tate, George Nicholas, Jerry Hathcock, Marvin Woodward, Robert Youngquist; *fx:* Edwin Aardal, Andy Engman; *lay:* Karl Karpé, Bruce Bushman; *back:* Ray Huffine, Al Dempster; *voices:* Cactus Mack McPeters, James MacDonald; *mus:* Oliver Wallace; *col:* Tech. *sd:* RCA. 7 min. • Sheepdog Pluto protects the flock against a coyote.

3706. The Legend of John Henry 1974; *p.c.:* Stephen Bosustow prods for Pyramid; *prod:* Nick Bosustow, David Adams; *dir:* Sam Weiss; *story:* Joe Cavella; *des:* Gary Lund; *voice:* Roberta Flack; *mus:* Tom McIntosh; *backing:* Herbie Hancock, Max Bennett, John Guerin, Victor Feldman, Tommy Tedesco; *col:* Tech. *sd.* 10½ min. • The story of man against machinery.

3707. The Legend of Rockaby Point (*Chilly Willy*) 11 Apr. 1955; *p.c.:* Walter Lantz prods for Univ; *dir:* Tex Avery; *story:* Michael Maltese; *anim:* Ray Abrams, Don Williams; La Verne Harding; *sets:* Raymond Jacobs; *voice:* Dal McKennon; *mus:* Clarence Wheeler; *prod mgr:* William E. Garity; *col:* Tech. *sd:* RCA. 6 min. *Academy Award nomination.* • Chilly and a polar bear attempt to rob a trawler of it's catch, guarded by a fierce watchdog. Chilly uses every opportunity to awaken the sleeping dog when the bear is aboard.

3708. The Legend of Sleepy Hollow 26 Nov. 1958; *p.c.:* Walt Disney prods for BV; *prod sup:* Ben Sharpsteen; *dir:* Clyde Geronimi, James Algar; *col:* Tech. *sd:* RCA. 33 min. • Washington Irving's story of a schoolmaster who moves in on the local beauty, much to the dismay of the village showoff. • See: *The Adventures of Ichabod and Mr. Toad*.

3709. The Leghorn Blows at Midnight (*Looney Tunes*) 6 May 1950; *p.c.:* WB; *dir:* Robert McKimson; *story:* Warren Foster; *anim:* Charles McKimson, Phil de Lara, Rod Scribner, J.C. Melendez, Emery Hawkins; *lay:* Cornett Wood; *back:* Richard H. Thomas; *ed:* Treg Brown; *voices:* Mel Blanc; *mus:* Carl Stalling; *prod mgr:* John W. Burton; *prod:* Edward Selzer;

col: Tech. *sd:* Vit. 7 min. • Foghorn Leghorn convinces Henery Hawk that he is a "Pheasant Hawk" and sends him off to look for a pheasant.

3710. Leghorn Swoggled (*Merrie Melodies*) 28 July 1951; *p.c.:* WB; *dir:* Robert McKimson; *story:* Warren Foster; *anim:* Charles McKimson, Rod Scribner, Phil de Lara, Emery Hawkins; *lay:* Cornett Wood; *back:* Richard H. Thomas; *ed:* Treg Brown; *voices:* Mel Blanc; *mus:* Eugene Poddany, Milt Franklyn; *prod mgr:* John W. Burton; *prod:* Edward Selzer; *col:* Tech. *sd:* Vit. 7 min. • In order to get himself a chicken, Henry Hawk first has to obtain a bone, a fish and some cheese to satisfy a dog, a cat and a mouse.

3711. Lend a Paw (*Mickey Mouse*) 3 Oct. 1941; *p.c.:* Walt Disney prods for RKO; *dir:* Clyde Geronimi; *asst dir:* Donald A. Duckwall; *anim:* Eric Gurney, Emery Hawkins, Kenneth Muse, Charles Nichols, George Nicholas, Chic F. Otterstrom, Morey Reden, William Sturm, Norman Tate; *lay:* Bruce Bushman; *voices:* Dehner Forkum, John McLeish, Marcellite Wall, Walt Disney, Edward J. Marr; *mus:* Leigh Harline; *col:* Tech. *sd:* RCA. 8 min. *Academy Award.* • Jealous of Mickey's attentions to a stray kitten, Pluto does battle with his good/evil egos determining whether he should dispose of the cat or not.

3712. The Leopard's Spots (*Unnatural History*) 13 Dec. 1925; *p.c.:* Bray prods for FBO; *dir:* Walter Lantz; *anim:* Clyde Geronimi; *b&w. sil.* 5 min. *l/a/anim.* • A suitor spins a yarn to his sweetheart's little brother: A monkey splashes the jungle animals with mud, then directs them to the laundry.

3713. Leprechaun's Gold (*Noveltoon*) 14 Oct. 1949; *p.c.:* Famous for Para; *dir:* Bill Tytla; *story:* I. Klein; *anim:* George Germanetti, Steve Muffatti; *sets:* Robert Little; *voices:* Ed Begley, Cecil Roy; *mus:* Winston Sharples; *ph:* Leonard McCormick; *prod mgr:* Sam Buchwald; *col:* Tech. *sd.* 9½ min. • A Leprechaun named Paddy overhears a miserly Landlord threatening to evict a widow for not paying the rent. Paddy lets himself be caught so she can claim a "Crock of Gold."

3714. Let Charlie Do It (*Beary Family*) 1972; *p.c.:* Walter Lantz prods for Univ; *dir:* Paul J. Smith; *story:* Cal Howard; *anim:* Volus Jones, Al Coe, Tom Byrne, Joe Voght; *sets:* Nino Carbe; *voices:* Paul Frees, Grace Stafford; *mus:* Walter Greene; *prod mgr:* William E. Garity; *col:* Tech. *sd:* RCA. 6 min. • No story available.

3715. Let It Be Me (*Merrie Melodies*) 2 May 1936; *p.c.:* Leon Schlesinger prods for WB; *dir:* I. Freleng; *story:* Robert Clampett; *anim:* Bob McKimson, Don Williams, Robert Clampett; *ed:* Tregoweth E. Brown; *voices:* Bernice Hansel, Jessamine See, Jack Carr; *mus:* Bernard Brown; *prod sup:* Henry Binder, Raymond G. Katz; *col:* Tech. *sd:* Vit. 8 min. • A cute country chick forsakes her hick boyfriend for the crooning Mr. Bingo who in turn ditches her for a singing French hen.

3716. Let Me Call You Sweetheart (*Screen Songs*) 20 May 1932; *p.c.:* The Fleischer Studio for Para; *prod:* Max Fleischer; *sup:* Dave Fleischer; *dir/story:* James H. Culhane, Rudy Zamora; *anim:* James H. Culhane, Rudy Zamora, David Tendlar; *mus:* Art Turkisher; *song:* Leo Friedman, Beth Slater Whitson; *l/a:* Ethel Merman; *b&w. sd:* WE. 7 min. • While Policeman Bimbo is philandering with Nurse Betty in the park, the baby's carriage rolls downhill into a pond.

3717. Let's All Sing Like the Birdies Sing (*Screen Songs*) 9 Feb. 1934; *p.c.:* The Fleischer Studio for Para; *prod:* Max Fleischer; *dir:* Dave Fleischer; *anim:* Myron Waldman, Thomas Johnson; *mus:* Art Turkisher; *song:* Robert Hargreaves; *l/a:* Les Reis, Artie Dunn; *b&w. sd:* WE. 7 min. • A trio of kittens go out on the prowl with disastrous results.

3718. Let's Celebrake (*Popeye*) 21 Jan. 1938; *p.c.:* The Fleischer Studioo for Para; *prod:* Max Fleischer; *dir:* Dave Fleischer; *anim:* Seymour Kneitel, William Henning; *voices:* Jack Mercer, Mae Questel, Gus Wickie, Lou Fleischer; *mus:* Sammy Timberg; *prod sup:* Sam Buchwald, Isidore Sparber; *b&w. sd:* WE. 7 min. • Popeye feels pity for Olive's grandma being left at home on New Year's Eve. So he takes Granny along with Olive and Bluto to a party and she ends up winning the dancing contest.

3719. Let's Eat (*Oswald*) 21 Apr. 1932; *p.c.:* Univ; *dir:* Walter Lantz, "Bill" Nolan; *anim:* Manuel Moreno, Ray Abrams, Fred Avery, "Bill"Weber, Vet Anderson; *mus:* James Dietrich; *b&w. sd:* WE. 7 min. • Oswald and his dog go fishing through the ice and catch a fish. The fish is eaten by a seal who, in turn, is eaten by a polar bear.

3720. Let's Get Movin' (*Popeye*) 24 July 1936; *p.c.:* The Fleischer Studio for Para; *prod:* Max Fleischer; *dir:* Dave Fleischer; *anim:* Willard Bowsky, Orestes Calpini; *voices:* Jack Mercer, Mae Questel, Gus Wickie; *mus:* Sammy Timberg; *b&w. sd:* WE. 7 min. • Popeye and Bluto help Olive move from her apartment.

3721. Let's Go (*Color Rhapsody*) 16 Apr. 1937; *p.c.:* Charles Mintz prods for Colum; *story:* Ben Harrison; *anim:* Manny Gould; *voices:* The Rhythmettes; *mus:* Joe de Nat; *col:* Tech. RCA. 8 min. • Morale-boosting cartoon for the depression. A village of bees come to the aid of a starving grasshopper.

3722. Let's Ring Doorbells (*Scrappy*) 7 Dec. 1935; *p.c.:* Charles Mintz prods for Colum; *story:* Art Davis, I. Klein; *anim:* Sid Marcus; *mus:* Joe de Nat; *prod mgr:* James Bronis; *b&w. sd:* RCA. 6 min. • A mad fiend locks Scrappy and Oopy in a mansion full of doorbells and refuses to let them go until they ring every one.

3723. Let's Sing with Popeye (*Popeye*) 1935; *p.c.:* The Fleischer Studio for Para; *prod:* Max Fleischer; *dir:* Dave Fleischer; *voice:* William A. Costello, Jack Mercer; *song:* Sammy Timberg, Sammy Lerner; *b&w. sd:* WE. 3 min. seq: *Popeye the Sailor.* • Popeye introduces a bouncing ball sing-along version of "I'm Popeye the Sailor Man."

3724. Let's Stalk Spinach (*Popeye*) 19 Oct. 1951; *p.c.:* Famous for Para; *dir:* Seymour Kneitel; *story:* I. Klein; *anim:* Steve Muffatti, George Germanetti; *sets:* Anton Loeb; *voices:* Jack Mercer, Jackson Beck; *mus:* Winston Sharples; *ph:* Leonard McCormick; *prod mgr:* Seymour Shultz; *col:* Tech. *sd:* WE. 6 min. • Popeye tells his nephews about the merits of spinach via the story of *Jack and the Beanstalk.*

3725. Let's Stick Together (*Donald Duck*) 25 Apr. 1952; *p.c.:* Walt Disney prods for RKO; *dir:* Jack Hannah; *story:* Nick George, Al Bertino; *anim:* Volus Jones, George Kreisl, Bill Justice, Marvin Woodward; *fx:* Blaine Gibson, Dan MacManus; *lay:* Yale Gracey; *back:* Thelma Witmer; *voices:* Bill Thompson, June Foray, Clarence Nash; *mus:* Oliver Wallace; *col:* Tech. *sd:* RCA. 7 min. • An old bee tells of how he once went into partnership with Donald Duck by using his stinger as a sewing machine.

3726. Let's You and Him Fight (*Popeye*) 16 Feb. 1934; *p.c.:* The Fleischer Studio for Para; *prod:* Max Fleischer; *dir:* Dave Fleischer; *anim:* Willard Bowsky, William Sturm; *voices:* William A. Costello, CharlesCarver, Louis Fleischer; *mus:* Sammy Timberg; *b&w. sd:* WE. 6 min. • Popeye fights "The Champ" in the ring and gets pummelled until Olive comes to his rescue with the inevitable can of spinach.

3727. Liberty Bonds 1917; *p.c.:* Bray prods for Para; *anim:* C.T. Anderson; *b&w. sil.* • The American Bald Eagle flies to Germany to give what-for to the Kaiser's imperial parrot who can do nothing other than repeat his master's predictions of victory.

3728. Lickety-Splat (*Looney Tunes*) June 1961; *p.c.:* WB; *dir/story:* Chuck Jones; *asst dir:* Abe Levitow; *anim:* Richard Thompson, Bob Bransford, Tom Ray, Ken Harris; *fx:* Harry Love; *lay:* Maurice Noble, Philip de Guard; *back:* Corny Cole, Bob Singer; *ed:* treg Brown; *voice:* Paul Julian; *mus:* Milt Franklyn; *prod mgr:* William Orcutt; *prod:* David H. DePatie; *col:* Tech. *sd:* Vit. 7 min. • In order to catch the Road-Runner, the Coyote uses "roller-skis." His *coup de grâce* is a supply of dynamite-darts all of which backfire on him.

3729. Life Begins for Andy Panda (*Cartune*) 9 Oct. 1939; *p.c.:* Walter Lantz prods for Univ; *dir:* Alex Lovy; *story:* Victor McLeod; *sets:* Edgar Keichle; *voices:* Sara Berner, Danny Webb; *mus:* Frank Marsales; *prod mgr:* George Hall; *col:* Tech. *sd:* WE 8½ min. • Andy's Pop is trapped by pygmy panda hunters. Andy is pursued with his turtle friend but manages to turn the tables on them.

3730. Life with Feathers (*Merrie Melodies*) 24 Mar. 1945; *p.c.:* WB; *dir:* I. Freleng; *story:* Tedd Pierce, Robert Clampett; *anim:* Virgil Ross; *lay:* Hawley Pratt; *back:* Paul Julian; *ed:* Treg Brown; *voices:* Mel Blanc, Sara Berner, Dave Barry; *mus:* Carl W. Stalling; *prod mgr:* John W. Burton; *prod:* Edward Selzer; *col:* Tech. *sd:* Vit. 7 min. *Academy Award nomination.* • Rejected, a male lovebird wants to end his life via the cat, who is a little more than suspicious.

3731. Life with Fido (*Lucky Duck*) 21 Aug. 1942; *p.c.:* TT for Fox; *dir:* Connie Rasinski; *story:* John Foster; *mus:* Philip A. Scheib; *col:* Tech.

sd: RCA. 6 min. • The Lucky Duck befriends Fido and follows him home after a hunt.

3732. Life with Loopy *(Loopy de Loop)* 7 Apr. 1960; *p.c.:* Hanna-Barbera for Colum; *prod/dir:* Joseph Barbera, William Hanna; *story dir:* Alex Lovy; *story:* Warren Foster; *anim dir:* Charles A. Nichols; *anim:* Lewis Marshall; *lay:* Walter Clinton; *back:* Robert Gentle; *ed:* Donald A. Douglas; *voices:* Daws Butler, Don Messick; *mus:* Hoyt Curtin; *titles:* Lawrence Gobel; *prod mgr:* Howard Hanson; *col:* East. *sd:* RCA. 6½ min. • Loopy tells a psychiatrist of how he was adopted by a man who thought he was a dog.

3733. Life with Tom *(Tom & Jerry)* 21 Nov. 1953; *p.c.:* MGM; *dir:* William Hanna, Joseph Barbera; *anim:* Kenneth Muse, Irven Spence, Ed Barge; *lay:* Dick Bickenbach; *back:* Robert Gentle; *ed:* Jim Faris; *mus:* Scott Bradley; *ph:* Jack Stevens; *prod:* Fred Quimby; *col:* Tech. *sd:* RCA. 7 min. • Seq: *Cat Fishin'*; *Little Orphan*; *Kitty Foiled*. • Jerry writes a best seller on the art of outwitting Tom.

3734. Lighter Than Air *(Aesop's Film Fable)* 17 Jan. 1926; *p.c.:* Fables Pictures Inf for Pathé; *dir:* Paul Terry; *b&w. sil.* 5 min. • Farmer Al and the animals ride high in the air on soap bubbles. The envious mice bring them down to earth by bursting the bubbles.

3735. Lighter Than Hare *(Merrie Melodies)* Dec. 1960; *p.c.:* WB; *dir/story:* Friz Freleng; *anim:* Virgil Ross, Art Davis, Gerry Chiniquy; *lay:* Hawley Pratt; *back:* Tom O'Loughlin; *ed:* treg Brown; *voices:* Mel Blanc; *mus:* Milt Franklyn; *prod mgr:* William Orcutt; *prod:* David H. DePatie; *col:* Tech. *sd:* Vit. 6 min. • Yosemite Sam from outer space arrives to invade the Earth, sending his robot henchmen to capture an Earth specimen ... Bugs Bunny!

3736. A Lighthouse by the Sea *(Aesop's Film Fable)* 12 Oct. 1924; *p.c.:* Fables Pictures Inc for Pathé; *dir:* Paul Terry; *b&w. sil.* 5 min. • No story available.

3737. Lighthouse Keeping *(Donald Duck)* 20 Sept. 1946; *p.c.:* Walt Disney prods for RKO; *dir:* Jack Hannah; *asst dir:* Toby Tobelman; *story:* Harry Reeves, Jesse Marsh; *anim:* Hal King, Bob Carlson, Judge Whitaker, Fred Jones, Al Coe; *fx:* John F. Reed; *lay:* Yale Gracey; *back:* Howard Dunn; *voice:* Clarence Nash; *mus:* Oliver Wallace; *col:* Tech. *sd:* RCA. 7 min. • Marblehead, a pelican, keeps trying to extinguish the light in Donald's lighthouse.

3738. Lighthouse Keeping *(Krazy Kat)* 15 Aug. 1932; *p.c.:* Winkler for Colum: *prod:* Charles Mintz; *story:* Ben Harrison; *anim:* Al Eugster, Preston Blair; *voice:* Jack Carr; *mus:* Joe de Nat; *prod mgr:* James Bronis; *b&w. sd:* RCA. 6 min. • Lighthouse keeper Krazy rescues his girl who is caught in a storm when she comes to visit in a boat.

3739. Lighthouse Keeping Blues *(Chilly Willy)* Aug. 1964; *p.c.:* Walter Lantz prods for Univ; *dir:* Sid Marcus; *story:* Homer Brightman; *anim:* Ray Abrams, Art Davis; *sets:* Ray Huffine, Art Landy; *voice:* Daws Butler; *mus:* Walter Greene; *prod mgr:* William E. Garity; *col:* Tech. *sd:* RCA. 6 min. • The light in Smedley's lighthouse keeps Chilly awake, so he has to extinguish it.

3740. Lighthouse Mouse *(Merrie Melodies)* 12 Mar. 1955; *p.c.:* WB; *dir:* Robert McKimson; *story:* Sid Marcus; *anim:* Phil de Lara, Charles McKimson, Herman Cohen, Rod Scribner; *lay:* Robert Givens; *back:* Richard H. Thomas; *ed:* Treg Brown; *voice:* Mel Blanc; *mus:* Milt Franklyn; *prod mgr:* John W. Burton; *prod:* Edward Selzer; *col:* Tech. *sd:* Vit. 7 min. • Sylvester has to stop a mouse from switching off the lighthouse light. A ship runs aground, tossing a baby kangaroo into the lighthouse, throwing the luckless cat into a state of confusion, believing it to be a giant mouse.

3741. Lightning Sketches 15 July 1907; *p.c.:* Vit Co; *anim:* J. Stuart Blackton; *b&w. sil.* 6 min. *l/a/anim.* • J. Stuart Blackton sketches Mr. Smith's profile, then turns to caricatures of a Jew and a Negro, followed by a collection of animated drawings.

3742. Lights Fantastic *(Merrie Melodies)* 23 May 1942; *p.c.:* Leon Schlesinger prods for WB; *dir:* I. Freleng; *story:* Sgt Dave Monahan; *anim:* Gil Turner; *lay:* Owen Fitzgerald; *back:* Lenard Kester; *ed:* Treg Brown; *voices:* The Mello Men, Mel Blanc; *mus:* Carl W. Stalling; *prod sup:* Henry Binder, Raymond G. Katz; *col:* Tech. *sd:* Vit. 7 min. • Lights over New York's Great White Way come alive. Gags revolve around electric signs.

3743. Lights Out *(Gandy Goose)* 17 Apr. 1942; *p.c.:* TT for Fox; *dir:* Eddie Donnelly; *story:* John Foster; *voices:* Arthur Kay, Thomas Morrison; *mus:* Philip A. Scheib; *col:* Tech. *sd:* RCA. 6 min. • Gandy and Sourpuss have joint nightmares about a party in a haunted house.

3744. Li'l Anjil *(Krazy Kat)* 19 Mar. 1936; *p.c.:* Charles Mintz prods for Colum; *story:* Ben Harrison; *anim:* Manny Gould; *voices:* William A. Costello, Shirley Reed; *prod mgr:* James Bronis; *b&w. sd:* RCA. 5½ min. • Ignatz invents various methods for hurling bricks at Krazy who takes this as a term of affection. • The only entry of the series to be modeled after George Herriman's originals.

3745. Lindy's Cat *(Aesop's Film Fable)* 2 Sept. 1927; *p.c.:* Fables Pictures Inc for Pathé; *dir:* Paul Terry; *b&w. sil.* 10 min. • Thomas Cat imitates Col. Charles E. Lindbergh's non-stop flight from New York to Paris.

3746. Line of Screammage *(Casper)* 17 Aug. 1956; *p.c.:* Famous for Para; *dir:* Seymour Kneitel; *story:* Jack Mercer; *anim:* Myron Waldman, Nick Tafuri; *sets:* Joseph Dommerque; *voices:* Norma MacMillan, Gwen Davies, Sid Raymond; *mus:* Winston Sharples; *ph:* Leonard McCormick; *prod mgr:* Seymour Shultz; *col:* Tech. *sd:* RCA. 6 min. • Casper helps little Billy win a football game.

3747. The Lion and the Monkey *(Aesop's Film Fable)* 3 Oct. 1925; *p.c.:* Fables Pictures Inc for Pathé; *dir:* Paul Terry; *b&w. sil.* 10 min. • Farmer Al Falfa goes hunting and the animals rib him mercilessly.

3748. The Lion and the Mouse *(Terry-Toon)* 12 Nov. 1943; *p.c.:* TT for Fox; *dir:* Mannie Davis; *story:* John Foster; *voice:* Frank Gallop; *mus:* Philip A. Scheib; *col:* Tech. *sd:* RCA. 7 min. • A puny rodent makes a deal with the King of Beasts to spare him so that he may save the lion one day. The mouse becomes a "Super Mouse" once the lion's life is in danger and saves him.

3749. Lion Around *(Donald Duck)* 20 Jan. 1950; *p.c.:* Walt Disney prods for RKO; *dir:* Jack Hannah; *story:* Bill Berg, Nick George; *anim:* Bob Carlson, Bill Justice, Judge Whitaker, Volus Jones, John Sibley; *fx:* George Rowley; *lay:* Yale Gracey; *back:* Thelma Witmer; *voices:* Clarence Nash, James MacDonald; *mus:* Oliver Wallace; *col:* Tech. *sd:* RCA. 6½ min. • The nephews disguise themselves as a mountain lion in order to steal a pie from Donald. He uncovers their trick but a real lion appears on the scene which Don still believes to be his nephews, acting accordingly.

3750. Lion Down *(Goofy)* 5 Jan. 1951; *p.c.:* Walt Disney prods for RKO; *dir:* Jack Kinney; *story:* Milt Schaffer, Dick Kinney; *anim:* George Nicholas, John Sibley, Charles Nichols, Ed Aardal, Hugh Fraser, George Kreisl; *fx:* Jack Boyd; *lay:* Al Zinnen; *back:* Merle Cox; *voice:* James MacDonald; *mus:* Paul J. Smith; *col:* Tech. *sd:* RCA. 6 min. • The Goof uproots a tree containing a mountain lion to plant in his rooftop garden.

3751. The Lion Hunt *(Heckle & Jeckle)* Mar. 1949; *p.c.:* TT for Fox; *dir:* Eddie Donnelly; *story:* John Foster; *anim:* Jim Tyer; *voices:* Tom Morrison; *mus:* Philip A. Scheib; *ph:* Douglas Moye; *col:* Tech. *sd:* RCA. 6 min. • The Magpies are hunting in Africa. One nearly meets his end as lion-bait but manages to talk the lion into accepting a movie contract.

3752. Lion Hunt *(Terry-Toon)* 7 Jan. 1938; *p.c.:* TT for Educational/Fox; *dir:* Mannie Davis; *mus:* Philip A. Scheib; *b&w. sd:* RCA. 6 min. • A mouse saves a lion's life.

3753. Lion in the Roar *(Noveltoon)* 21 Dec. 1956; *p.c.:* Famous for Para; *dir:* Seymour Kneitel; *story:* Larz Bourne; *anim:* Al Eugster, Wm. B. Pattengill; *sets:* Robert Little; *voices:* Jack Mercer, Cecil Roy; *mus:* Winston Sharples; *ph:* Leonard McCormick; *prod mgr:* Seymour Shultz; *col:* Tech. *sd:* RCA. 6 min. • Little Louie the lion fails at being King of the Jungle until a ferocious gorilla attacks his father, the present King.

3754. The Lion King 24 June 1994; *p.c.:* The Walt Disney Company for BV International; *dir:* Roger Allers, Rob Minkoff; *prod:* Don Hahn; *scr:* Irene Mecchi, Jonathan Roberts, Linda Woolverton; *story:* Burny Mattinson, Barry Johnson, Lorna Cook, Thom Enriquez, Andy Gaskill, Gary Trousdale, Jim Capobianco, Kevin Harkey, Jorgen Klubien, Chris Sanders, Tom Sito, Larry Leker, Joe Ranft, Rick Maki, Ed Gombert, Francis Glebas, Mark Kausler; *art dir:* Andy Gaskill; *art co-ord:* Randy Fullmer; *visual fx:* Scott Santoro; *cgi:* Scott F. Johnston; *character anim:* "Young Simba": *sup anim:* Mark Henn; *anim:* Tom Bancroft, Broose Johnson, T. Daniel Hofstedt, Danny Wawrzaszek; "*Adult Simba*": *sup anim:* Ruben Aquino; *anim:*

Randy Haycock, Joe Ekers, Michael Cedeno, Dale Baer, Lorna Cook; *"Mufasa": sup anim:* Tony Fucile; *anim:* Phil Young, Chris Wahl, Brad Kuha; *"Scar": sup anim:* Andreas Deja; *anim:* Doug Frankel, Jean Morel, Mark Koetsier, Alex Williams; *"Adult Nala": sup anim:* Anthony DeRosa; *anim:* Bob Bryan, Gilda Palinginis; *"Young Nala": sup anim:* Aaron Blaise; *"Pumbaa": sup anim:* Tony Bancroft; *anim:* Ron Husband, Tim Allen, Dave Pruiksma; *"Timon": sup anim:* Michael Surrey; *anim:* Brian Ferguson, James Lopez, Mike Snow; *"Rafiki": sup anim:* James Baxter; *"Zasu": sup anim:* Ellen Woodbury; *anim:* Randy Cartwright, Barry Temple, Michael Swofford; *"Sarabi": sup anim:* Russ Edmonds; *"Hyenas": sup anim:* David Burgess, Alex Kupershmidt; *anim:* Rejean Bourdages, Greg S. Manwaring, Ken Boyer, Lou Dellarosa, Larry White; *"Wildebeest Stampede": computer anim:* Gregory Griffith, Linda Bel; *computer anim software:* Kiran Bhakta Joshi, Mary Jane "MJ" Turner; *addit anim:* Chris Bailey, Ken Duncan Raul Garcia, Dave Stephan; *anim asst:* Trey Finney, Troy A. Gustafson, James Young Jackson, John Ripa, Eric Walls; *rough inbet:* Elliot M. Bour, Rob Corley, Tom Gately, Michael Genz, Grant Hiestand, Craig R. Maras, Paul McDonald, John Ramirez, Jacqueline M. Sanchez, Henry Sato Jr.; *fx anim:* Dorse Lanpher, Ted C. Kierscey, Ed Coffey, Christine Blum, Mauro Maressa, Tom Hush, Allen Blyth, Joey Mildenberger, Eusebio Torres, Steve Moore, Marlon West, Garrett Wren, Chris Jankins, Dave Bossert; *clean-up anim: "Young Simba": sup character lead:* Daniel A. Gracey; *asst:* Christine Lawrence, Kellie D. Lewis, Bryan M. Sommer; *break/inbet:* Dan Daly, Chadd Ferron, Tim Hodge, Pamela Mathues, Maurilio Morales, James Parris, Sherrie H. Sinclair, Theodore Anthony Lee Ty; *"Adult Simba": sup character lead:* Bill Berg; *asst:* Wesley Chun, Janice Inouye, Emily Jiuliano, Susan Lantz, Kaaren Lundeen, Dorothea Baker, Paul Randy Sanchez, Helene Vives-Tennesen; *anim asst:* David Hancock, Caroline K. HU, Leonard F. Johnson, Steve Lubin, Sean Muller; *break:* Wendy Muir, Kevin Smith; *inbet:* Daniel Bond, Sean Gallimore, Daniel Yoontaek Lim, Daniel O'Sullivan; *"Mufasa & Sarabi": sup character lead:* Brian Clift; *asst:* Ginny Parmele, Elizabeth Watasin; *break:* Laurey Foulkes, Norma Rivera, Wendie Fischer; *inbet:* Annette Byrne-Morel; *"Scar": sup character lead:* Nancy Kniep; *character co-lead:* Kathleen M. Bailey, Marianne Tucker; *asst:* Natasha Dukelski-Selfridge; *asst anim:* Mike Hazy, Johan Klinger, Boowon Lee, Marsha W.J. Park-Yum; *break:* Jamie Kezlarian Bolio, Diana Coco, Martin Schwartz; *inbet:* Jody Kooistra, Jung Chan Woo; *"Adult Nala": sup character lead:* Scott Anderson; *asst:* Merry Kanawyer Clingen, Mike McKinney; *asst anim:* Sue Adnopoz, Lillian Amanda Chapman, Peggy Tonkonogy; *break:* Carl Philip Hall, Andrew Ramos; *inbet:* Chang Yei Kim; *"Young Nala": sup character lead:* Tracy Mark Lee; *inbet:* Tom Fish, Mario J. Menjivar; *"Timon & Pumbaa": sup character lead:* Debra Armstrong; *asst:* Margie Daniels, Gail Frank, David Nethery, Juliet Stroud Duncan, Dave Suding, Stephan Zupkas; *asst anim:* Edward R. Guiterrez, Karen Hardenbergh, Brian B. McKim, Maria Rosetti; *inbet:* Moon Hwan Choi, Judy Grabenstatter, Eduardo Oliveras; *"Rafiki": sup character lead:* Marshall Toomey; *asst:* Terry Wozniak, Kris Heller, Susan Y. Sugita; *break:* Miriam McDonnell, Mary-Jean Repchuk; *"Zasu": sup character lead:* Dan Tanaka; *asst:* Marcia Kimura Dougherty, Terry Naughton, Bruce Strock; *asst anim:* Travis Blaise, Lee Dunkman, Rick Kohlschmidt; *break:* Bill Thinnes; *inbet:* Brian Beauchamp, James A. Harris, Richard D. Rocha; *"Hyenas": sup character lead:* Alex Topete; *asst:* Philip S. Boyd, Jesus Cortes, Ray Harris, Tamara Lusher, Monica Murdock, Eric Pigors, Vincent Siracusano, Yung Soo Kim; *break:* Will Huneycutt, Dave Recinos; *inbet:* Paulo R. Alvarado, Rachel R. Bibb, Ernest Keen, Tom Labaff, Samantha Lair, Phil Noto, Lon Smart; *"addit Young Simba/misc characters": sup character lead:* Vera Lanpher; *asst:* Tony Anselmo, Allison Prout-Hollen, Inna Chon, Kent Holaday, Dana M. Reemes, Karen Rosenfield; *break/inbet:* Beverly Adams, Robert Espanto Domingo, Daniel James Galieote, Kenneth Kinoshita, Mary Measures, Jane Misek, Cheryl Polakow; *layl/workbook:* Mitchell Bernal, Jennifer Chiao-Lin Yuan, Fred Craig, Guy Deel, Jeff Dickson, Ed Ghertner, Tom Humber, Lorenzo Martinez, Tom Shannon, Allen Tam, Tanya Wilson; *back:* Gregory Alexander Drolette, Don Moore, Kathy Altieri, Serge Michaels, Debbie Du Bois, Sunny Apinchapong, Michael Humphries, Natalie Franscioni-Karp, Philip Phillipson, Barry Atkinson, Dan Cooper, Kevin Turcotte, Thomas Woodington, David McCamley, Dominick R. Domingo, Charles Vollmer, Barry R. Kooser, Patricia Palmer-Phillipson, Brooks Campbell, Richard Sluiter; *ed:* Tom Finan, John Carnochan, Ivan Bilancio, Jim Melton, Patsy Bouge, Jacqueline Kinney, Deborah Beville, (Florida) Beth Stegmaier, Kat Connolly; *post prod mgr:*

Sara Duran; *voices: Zasu:* Rowan Atkinson; *Simba:* Matthew Broderick; *Young Nala:* Niketa Calame; *Ed:* Jim Cummings; *Shenzi:* Whoopi Goldberg; *Rafiki:* Robert Guillaume; *Scar:* Jeremy Irons; *Mufasa:* James Earl Jones; *Nala:* Moira Kelly; *Timon:* Nathan Lane; *Banzai:* Cheech Marin; *Pumbaa:* Ernie Sabella; *Sarabi:* Madge Sinclair; *Young Simba:* Jonathan Taylor Thomas; *also:* Frank Welker, Cathy Cavadini, Judi Durand, Daamen Krall, David McCharen, Linda Phillips, Phil Proctor, David Randolph; "Can You Feel the Love Tonight" performed by Elton John; "Circle of Life" performed by Carmen Twillie; "I Just Can't Wait to be King" performed by Jason Weaver; *African vocals* performed by Lebo M., Laura Williams, Rowan Atkinson; *misc vocals:* Sally Dworsky, Joseph Edwards, Kristle Edwards; "Circle of Life" *chorus:* Maxi Anderson, Terry Bradford, Johnnie Britt, Baby Cele, Lucky Cele, Rick Charles, Gugwana Dlamini, Kevin Dorsey, Wendy Fraser, Linda Gcwensa, Clydene Jackson, Matoab'sane Jali, Kuyanda Jezile, Bob Joyce, Faith Kekana, Sphiwe Khanyile, FaceKhulu, Stella Khumalo, Skhumbuzo Kubheka, Thembi Kubheka, Ron Kunene, James Langa, Edie Lehmann, Rick Logan, Tsidi Manye, Khanyo Maphumulo, Abner A. Mariri, Myrna Matthews, Batho Mhlongo, Vusi Mhlongo, Nonhlanhla Mkhize, Thembi Mtshali, Bheki Ndlovu, Nandi Ndlovu, Bongani Ngcobo, Nini Nkosi, Bobbi Page, Phindile, Rick Riso, Philile Seme, Alfie Silas, Happy Skhakhane, Kipizane Skweyiya, Sindisiwe Sokhel, Susan D. Stevens, Khuluiwe S'thole, Thandazile, Carmen Twillie, Sam Vamplew, Julia Waters, Luther N. Waters, Maxine Waters, Oren Waters, John West, Yvonne Williams, Terry Young, Zolile Zulu; *mus:* Hans Zimmer; *songs:* Tim Rice, Elton John; *song prod:* Chris Thomas, Alice Dewey, Hans Zimmer, Mark Mancina; *mus rec & mix:* Jay Rifkin; *mus ed:* Adam Milo Smalley; *addit song arrangement:* Bruce Fowler, Danny Troob, Paul Bogave; *addit vocal arrangement:* Bruce Fowler, Bobbi Page, Mark Mancina; *score conductor:* Nick Glennie-Smith; *orch:* Bruce Fowler, Ladd McIntosh, Yvonne Moriarty; *choral arrangement:* Lebo M., Andrea Crouch, Mbongeni Ngema, Nick Glennie-Smith; *choir masters:* Mbongeni Ngema, Andrae Crouch; *vocal contractors:* Tonia Duvall, Mbongeni Ngema, Bobbi Page, Alfie Silas; *mus prod asst:* Nico Golfar (USA), Maggie Rodford (UK), Eric Stark (SA); *asst to Hans Zimmer:* Christopher Ward, Mitchell Lamm, Antonia Bogdanovich; *orch contractor:* Reggie Wilson; *orch copyist:* Dominic Fidelibus; *prod mgr:* Dana Axelrod; *scene plan sup:* Ann Tucker; *anim check sup:* Janet Bruce; *col models sup:* Karen Comella; *i&p mgr:* Gretchen Maschmeyer Albrecht; *paint/final check sup:* Hortensia M. Casagran; *digitizing camera sup:* Robyn L. Roberts; *ph mgr:* Joe Jiuliano; *artistic sup: Florida unit: lay:* Robert Walker; *back:* Robert E. Stanton; *clean-up:* Ruben Procopio; *visual fx:* Jeff Dutton; *Florida prod mgr:* Don Walter; *character des/visual development:* Hans Bacher, Jean Gillmore, Joe Grant, Michael Hodgson, Lisa Keene, Sue C. Nichols, Bruce Zick, Mel Shaw, Bob Smith; *character sculptures:* Kent Melton; *key asst layl des:* Mac George; *key asst lay:* Michael O'Mara; *lay asst:* Tim Callahan, Cynthia Ignacio, Mark Kalesniko, Samuel Joseph Michlap, David Martin, Rick Moore, John Puglisi, Kenneth Spirduso, Doug Walker, Sherilan Weinhart; *blue sketch:* Madlyn O'Neill, Laurie Sacks, Jo Ann Tzuanos; *asst fx anim:* Cynthia Neill-Knizek, Mabel Gesner, John Tucker, Steve Starr, Dan Lund, Jazno Francoeur, Daniel E. Wanket, Joseph Christopher Pepé, Mark Barrows, Tony West, Graham Woods, Michael G. Duhatschek, Colbert Fennelly, Kristine Brown; *fx break/inbet:* Geoffrey C. Everts, Kristine Humber, Elizabeth Holmes, John E. Hailey, Michael Cadwallader-Jones, Paitoon Ratanasirintrawoot, James Goss, John David Thorton, Phil Vigil, Stella P. Arbelaez, Kang Tae Kim; *inbet trainees:* Dominic M. Carols, Leland J. Helper, Lisa G. Lanyon, Russell Lingo, Michael D. Mattesi, Kevin Proctor, Teresita Quezada, Marc Smith, Tony Stanley, Michael Stocker, Darren R. Webb, Jane Zhao; *addit story:* J.T. Allen, George Scribner, Miguel Tejada-Flores, Jenny Tripp, Bob Tzudiker, Chris Vogler, Kirk Wise, Noni White; *casting:* Brian Chavanne; *asst prod mgrs: story/sweatbox:* Holly E. Bratton; *ed:* Lisa M. Smith; *lay:* Patricia Hicks; *anim/pre-prod mgr:* Dorothy L. McKim; *clean-up:* Loni Beckner Black; *fx/cgi:* Kirk Bodyfelt; *col models:* Cathy Lawrence; *back/anim check:* Karenna Mazur; *CAPS & retakes:* Michael "Tony" Meagher; *Florida lay/back:* Paul Steele; *i&p asst mgr:* Chris Hecox; *prod co-ord: anim/fx:* Matt Garbera; *clean-up:* Jeanie Lynd Sorenson; *scene plan:* Annamarie Costa, John Cunningham, Tom Baker, Mary Lescher, Donna Weir; *anim check:* Cynthia Goode, Karen Hepburn, Karen S. Paat, Gary Shafer, Mavis Shafer, Barbara Wiles, Albert F. Moore, Victoria Winner Novak; *digitizing mark-up:* Gina Wootten; *digitizing ph:* Kent Gordon, Tina Baldwin, Jo Ann Breuer, Karen N. China, Lynnette Cullen, Gareth Fishbaugh, Michael

McFerren, David J. Rowe; *asst paint sup:* Barbara Lynn Hamane, Karen L. Hudson, Grace H. Shirado; *col model mark-up:* Rhonda L. Hicks, Cindy Finn, Debra Y. Siegel, David J. Zywicki; *paint mark-up:* Irma Velez, Beth Ann McCoy-Gee, Karan J. Lee-Storr; *paint:* Carmen Sanderson, Kirk Axtell II, Phyllis Bird, Russell Blandino, Joey Calderon, Ofra Calderon, Sherrie Cuzzort, Florida D'Ambrosio, Robert Dettloff, Phyllis Estelle Fields, Paulino, Leslie Hinton, Stevie Hirsch, David Karp, Angelika Katz, Randy McFerren, Harlene Mears, Karen Lynne Nugent, Bill Ohanesian, Leyla Amaro Pelaez, Bruce Phillipson, Fumiko R. Sommer, S. Ann Sullivan, Roxanne M. Taylor, Britt Van der Nagel, Susan Wileman; *final check:* Janette Hulett, Monica Marroquin, Teri N. McDonald, Saskia Raevouri; *composing:* James "JR" Russell, Shannon Fallis-Kane, Dolores Pope; *digital film printing & opticals sup:* Christopher Gee, Chuck Warren, Christine Beck, Ron Jackson, Brandy Hill; *anim ph:* John Aardal, Andrew Simmons, Gary W. Smith; *technology mgrs: computer anim prod software:* Paul Yanover; *computer prod systems:* Dean Schiller; *cg systems:* Edward Kummer; *technical facilities & hardware:* Dave Inglish; *software engineering:* David F. Wolf; *technology-Florida:* Enrique Santos; *technology development & support:* Jeff Alden, Raul Anaya, Michael Bolds, Lawrence Chai, Carol J. Choy, Earl Coffman, David Coons, Ben Croy, Michael R. Fodor, Randy Fukuda, Tad Gielow, Mark W. Gilicinski, Scot Greenidge, Don Gworek, Bruce Hatakeyama, Shyh-Chyuan Huang, Bill James, Kevin E. Keech, Mark R. Kimball, Edwin R. Leonard, Brad Lowman, Tony Matthews, Thomas Moore Jr., Jack Muleady, Alan A. Patel, Marty Prager, Mike Purvis, Carlos Quinonez, John Stimson, Michael Sullivan, Scott S. Terek, Warren Lee Theriot, Mark M. Tokunaga, Phillip Wangenheim; *addit cgi anim:* Steve Goldberg, Rob Bekuhrs, Sandra M. Groeneveld, James Tooley, Marcus Hobbs; *PIXAR:* Thomas Hahn, Peter Nye, Michael A. Shantzis; *sd:* Terry Porter, Mel Metcalfe, David J. Hudson, Richard L. Anderson, Mark Mangini; *sd fx:* John Pospisil, Michael Chock, James Christopher, Paul J. Berolzheimer; *dial ed:* R.J. Kizer; *foley ed:* Don Lee Jorgensen; *ADR ed:* Andrew Patterson, Ralph Stuart; *foley art:* John Roesch, Hilda Hodges; *dubbing rec:* Jeanette Browning, Judy Nord; *dial rec:* Doc Kane, Vince Caro, Weldon Brown, Andrew Morris, Steve Hellaby; *b&w processing:* Joe Parra, John White; *col timer:* Dale Grahn; *neg cutters:* Mary Beth Smith, Rick MacKay; *post prod sup:* Jeannine Berger; *title des:* Burke Mattsson, Susan Bradley, Buena Vista Imaging; *wild life consultant:* Jim Fowler; *col:* Tech. *sd:* Dolby Stereo Digital. 84 min. *Academy Award.* • Simba, a lion cub, does his best to follow in his father's tracks as King of Beasts. His jealous uncle Scar kills the King and convinces Simba that *he* is responsible for the death and should run away, never to return. While in exile, his childhood friend Nala arrives and convinces him to return to the Pride Lands, which have capitulated under Scar's rule, and accept his rightful place as King.

3755. The Lion Tamer *(Amos 'n Andy)* 2 Feb. 1934; *p.c.:* Van Beuren for RKO; *anim:* George Stallings; *voices:* Freeman F. Gosden, Charles Correll; *mus:* Gene Rodemich; b&w. *sd:* RCA. 10 min. • Kingfish uses Andy as a lion tamer to Crawford and Lightnin' in a lion's skin.

3756. Lionel Lion *(Phantasy)* 3 Mar. 1944; *p.c.:* Colum; *prod:* Dave Fleischer; *dir:* Paul Sommer; *story:* John McLeish; *mus:* Eddie Kilfeather; *i&p:* Elizabeth F. McDowell; *ph:* Frank Fisher; b&w. *sd:* RCA. 6 min. • Returning home in the early hours, Lionel enlists the aid of his son to get into the locked house.

3757. The Lioness and the Bugs *(Aesop's Film Fable)* 24 July 1921; *p.c.:* Fables Pictures Inc for Pathé; *dir:* Paul Terry; b&w. sil. 5 min. • The Lioness offers a prize for the best children in a bug village. When the prize goes to a rather small family, the disgruntled losers appeal to the lioness who tells them "I have one child but that one is a lion." Moral: "It's quality, not quantity that counts."

3758. The Lion's Busy *(Merrie Melodies)* 18 Feb. 1950; *p.c.:* WB; *dir:* I. Freleng; *story:* Tedd Pierce; *anim:* Arthur Davis, Gerry Chiniquy, Ken Champin, Virgil Ross; *lay:* Hawley Pratt; *back:* Paul Julian; *ed:* Treg Brown; *voices:* Mel Blanc; *mus:* Carl Stalling; *prod mgr:* John W. Burton; *prod:* Edward Selzer; *col:* Tech. *sd:* Vit. 7 min. • Beaky Buzzard presents the lion with the knowledge that lions rarely live beyond the age of ten. He starts eyeing him as a sizeable meal.

3759. The Lion's Busy *(Noveltoon)* Feb. 1961; *p.c.:* Para Cartoons; *dir:* Seymour Kneitel; *story:* Carl Meyer, Jack Mercer; *anim:* Martin Taras, Al Pross; *sets:* Robert Owen; *voices:* Jack Mercer; *mus:* Winston Sharples; *ph:* Leonard McCormick; *prod mgr:* Abe Goodman; *col:* Tech. *sd:* RCA. 6 min. • Lord Tweedledum's playboy son is sent to Africa to catch a lion trophy. The lion, however, has other ideas.

3760. The Lion's Friend *(Paul Terry-Toon)* 18 May 1934; *p.c.:* Moser & Terry for Educational/Fox; *dir:* Frank Moser, Paul Terry; *mus:* Philip A. Scheib; b&w. *sd:* WE. 6 min. • The German-accented jungle schoolteacher tells his students of how a mouse saved a lion from the hunter.

3761. Liquid Dynamite *(Aesop's Film Fable)* 13 May 1926; *p.c.:* Fables Pictures Inc for Pathé; *dir:* Paul Terry; b&w. sil. 10 min. • Farmer Al Falfa feeds wood alcohol to his auto, drinks some himself and has a nightmare.

3762. The Litterbug 21 June 1961; *p.c.:* Walt Disney prods for BV; *dir:* Hamilton S. Luske; *asst dir:* Jim Swain; *story:* Bill Berg, Lance Nolley; *anim:* John Sibley, Ted Berman, Hal King, Hamilton S. Luske; *fx:* Jack Boyd, Dan MacManus; *des:* McLaren Stewart; *lay:* Joe Hale, Al Zinnen; *back:* Al Dempster; *voices:* John Dehner, Ben Wright; *mus:* Buddy Baker; *songs:* Mel Leven; *col:* Tech. *sd:* RCA. 7 min. • Dr. D.D. Tee demonstrates how litter can destroy public places with help from Donald Duck as the chief offender.

3763. Little Anglers *(Terry Bears)* July 1952; *p.c.:* TT for Fox: *dir:* Eddie Donnelly; *story:* Tom Morrison; *anim:* Jim Tyer; *voices:* Douglas Moye, Tom Morrison, Philip A. Scheib; *mus:* Philip A. Scheib; *ph:* Douglas Moye; *col:* Tech. *sd:* RCA. 6 min. • Papa wants a lazy day's fishing but the cubs disrupt his peace by catching more fish than him and get him dunked in the river.

3764. Little Annie Rooney *(Screen Songs)* 10 Oct. 1931; *p.c.:* The Fleischer Studio for Para; *prod:* Max Fleischer; *dir:* Dave Fleischer; *anim:* Seymour Kneitel, Berny Wolf; *mus:* Art Turkisher; *song:* Michael Nolan; b&w. *sd:* WE. 6 min. • A surprise party is given for Annie. Her sweetheart escapes when he witnesses the amount of candles on the birthday cake.

3765. Little Audrey Riding Hood *(Noveltoon)* 14 Oct. 1955; *p.c.:* Famous for Para; *dir:* Seymour Kneitel; *story:* Larz Bourne; *anim:* Tom Golden, Morey Reden; *sets:* Robert Connavale; *voices:* Mae Questel, Jackson Beck, Gwen Davies; *mus:* Winston Sharples; *ph:* Leonard McCormick; *prod mgr:* Seymour Shultz; *col:* Tech. *sd:* RCA. 6 min. • Audrey takes a cake to her grandmother's house and discovers a burglar there. • First time use of the opening "Noveltoon Tune."

3766. The Little Bantam Weight 12 Mar. 1938; *p.c:* MGM; *prod/dir:* Hugh Harman, Rudolf Ising; *mus:* Scott Bradley; *col:* Tech. *sd:* WE. 8 min. • The weakest of the recently-hatched chicks proves a failure to his boxing champ father ... until he wins a boxing match by accident.

3767. Little Beau Pepé *(Merrie Melodies)* 9 Feb. 1952; *p.c.:* WB; *dir:* Charles M. Jones; *story:* Michael Maltese; *anim:* Lloyd Vaughan, Ben Washam, Ken Harris, Phil Monroe; *lay:* Robert Gribbroek; *back:* Philip de Guard; *ed:* Treg Brown; *voices:* Mel Blanc, Stan Freberg; *mus:* Carl Stalling; *prod mgr:* John W. Burton; *prod:* Edward Selzer; *col:* Tech. *sd:* Vit. 7 min. • Pepé le Pew joins the Foreign Legion and makes a play for the mascot cat.

3768. Little Beau Porky *(Looney Tunes)* 24 Oct. 1936; *p.c.:* Leon Schlesinger prods for WB; *dir:* Frank Tash(lin); *anim:* Robert Bentley, Nelson Demorest; *voices:* Billy Bletcher, Joe Dougherty; *mus:* Carl W. Stalling; *prod sup:* Henry Binder, Raymond G. Katz; b&w. *sd:* Vit. 7 min. • Legionaire Porky is left to guard the fort against an attack from Ali Mode and his gang of cut-throats.

3769. Little Beaux Pink *(Pink Panther)* 20 Oct. 1968; *p.c.:* Mirisch/Geoffrey/DFE for UA; *dir:* Hawley Pratt; *story:* John W. Dunn; *anim:* Warren Batchelder, Manny Gould, Don Williams; *lay:* Dick Ung; *back:* Tom O'Loughlin; *ed:* Lee Gunther; *mus:* Walter Greene; *theme tune:* Henry Mancini; *ph:* John Burton Jr.; *prod sup:* Harry Love, Jim Foss; *col:* DeLuxe. *sd:* RCA. 6 min. • The Panther flaunts trouble when he brings his lamb into Cattle County, Texas.

3770. A Little Bird Told Me *(Burt Gillett's Toddle Tales)* 7 Sept. 1934; *p.c.:* Van Beuren for RKO; *dir:* Burt Gillett, Jim Tyer; *anim:* Frank Little; *mus:* Winston Sharples; *l/a ph:* Harry E. Squires; b&w. *sd:* RCA. 9 min. l/a/anim. • Little Bixie Sawyer steals some jam. His sister finds out by a smear on his face and says "a little bird told her...." The scene shifts to the treetop offices of *The Bugle* where a feathered editor dispatches Walter Finchell and a cameraman to get the lowdown on Bixie's jam pilfering.

3771. **Little Blabber Mouse** (*Merrie Melodies*) 6 July 1940; *p.c.:* Leon Schlesinger prods for WB; *dir:* I. Freleng; *story:* J.B. Hardaway; *anim:* Richard Bickenbach; *sets:* Robert L. Holdeman; *ed:* Treg Brown; *voices:* Bill Thompson, Mel Blanc, The Sportsmen Quartet; *mus:* Carl W. Stalling; *ph:* John W. Burton; *prod sup:* Henry Binder, Raymond G. Katz; *col:* Tech. *sd:* Vit. 7 min. • When the Drug Store closes at night, a W.C. Fieldsian mouse conducts a guided tour of the shop but is interrupted by the arrival of a cat.

3772. **Little Black Sambo** (*ComiColor*) 21 Jan. 1935; *p.c.:* Celebrity prods; *prod/dir:* Ub Iwerks; *anim:* Al Eugster; *mus:* Art Turkisher; *col:* Ciné. *sd:* PCP. 7½ min. • Sambo's dog disguises himself as a tiger to scare the lad. When a real tiger arrives, Sambo deals with him, thinking it's the dog.

3773. **Little Blue Blackbird** (*Cartune*) 26 Dec. 1938; *p.c.:* Walter Lantz prods for Univ; *dir:* Patrick Lenihan; *story:* Victor McLeod; *anim:* Merle Gilson, (La) Verne Harding; *mus:* Frank Marsales; *col:* Tech-2. *sd:* WE. 7 min. • Baby blackbird is a misfit in the bluebird's nest until he proves his worth by saving the family from an attacking eagle.

3774. **Little Bo Bopped** (*Loopy de Loop*) 3 Dec. 1959; *p.c.:* Hanna-Barbera prods for Colum; *prod/dir:* Joseph Barbera, William Hanna; *story dir:* Dan Gordon; *story:* Warren Foster; *anim dir:* Charles A. Nichols; *anim:* Kenneth Muse; *lay:* Dick Bickenbach; *back:* F. Montealegre; *ed:* Warner Leighton; *voices:* Daws Butler, Jean van der Pyl; *mus:* Hoyt Curtin; *titles:* Lawrence Gobel; *prod mgr:* Howard Hanson; *col:* East. *sd:* RCA. 6 min. • Loopy helps Bo Peep look for her sheep.

3775. **Little Boa Peep** (*Blue Racer*) 16 Jan. 1974; *p.c.:* Mirisch/DFE for UA; *dir:* Bob Balsar; *story:* John W. Dunn; *anim:* Dick Nicksen, Harry Paper, Phil Herup, Shad Case; *lay:* Mickey Matz; *back:* Fred Fitz; *ed:* Joe Siracusa; *voices:* Larry D. Mann; *mus:* Doug Goodwin; *ph:* John Burton Jr.; *prod mgr:* Lee Gunther; *col:* DeLuxe. *sd:* RCA. 6 min. • The Racer is told by a psychiatrist that "you are what you believe yourself to be." He believes himself to be a sheepdog and goes in search of sheep. The animators credited are fictitious.

3776. **Little Boo Peep** (*Casper*) 28 Aug. 1953; *p.c.:* Famous for Para; *dir:* Seymour Kneitel; *story:* Larz Bourne; *anim:* Myron Waldman, Larry Silverman; *sets:* Anton Loeb; *voices:* Alan Shay, Sid Raymond, Cecil Roy, Jack Mercer; *mus:* Winston Sharples; *ph:* Leonard McCormick; *prod mgr:* Seymour Kneitel; *col:* Tech. *sd:* RCA. 6 min. • Casper visits Mother Goose Land to help Bo Peep find her lost sheep. Wolfie is about to prepare lamb stew when Casper arrives.

3777. **Little Boy and His Dog** 1947; *p.c.:* John Sutherland prods for Procter & Gamble Co; *prod/dir:* John Sutherland. *col. sd.* • Commercial.

3778. **Little Boy Blue** (*ComiColor*) 30 July 1936; *p.c.:* Celebrity prods; *prod/dir:* Ub Iwerks; *mus:* Carl Stalling; *col:* Ciné. *sd:* PCP. 7 min. • Bo Peep's black sheep disguises himself as the wolf for a joke. The real wolf arrives and steals the black sheep and it's Boy Blue and Bo Peep to the rescue.

3779. **Little Boy Blue** (*Paul Terry-Toon*) 30 Nov. 1933; *p.c.:* Moser & Terry for Educational/Fox; *dir:* Frank Moser, Paul Terry; *mus:* Philip A. Scheib; *b&w. sd:* WE. 5½ min. • No story available.

3780. **Little Boy Boo** (*Looney Tunes*) 26 June 1954; *p.c.:* WB; *dir:* Robert McKimson; *story:* Tedd Pierce; *anim:* Herman Cohen, Rod Scribner, Phil de Lara, Charles McKimson; *lay:* Robert Givens; *back:* Richard H. Thomas; *ed:* Treg Brown; *voices:* Mel Blanc, Bea Benaderet; *mus:* Carl Stalling; *prod mgr:* John W. Burton; *prod:* Edward Selzer; *col:* Tech. *sd:* Vit. 7 min. • In order to gain warmth and security, Foggy proposes to Widow Hen and unwittingly takes on the task of entertaining her bookworm son.

3781. **Little Boy with a Big Horn** 26 Mar. 1953; *p.c.:* UPA for Colum; *ex prod:* Stephen Bosustow; *dir:* Robert Cannon; *story:* Jack Becholdt, T. Hee, Robert Cannon; *anim:* Bill Melendez, Frank Smith, Tom McDonald; *lay:* T. Hee; *back:* Jules Engel; *voices:* John T. Smith, Marian Richman; *mus:* George Bruns; *prod mgr:* Herbert Klynn; *col:* Tech. *sd:* RCA. 6 min. • Nobody likes the noise of Ollie's euphonium playing, so he goes elsewhere to play it and prevents a boat from going on the rocks.

3782. **Little Broadcast** (*Madcap Model*) 25 Sept. 1942; *p.c.:* George Pal prods for Para; *prod/dir:* George Pal; *anim:* Ray Harryhausen; *voices:* Billy Bletcher, Patrick J. McGeehan, Mel Blanc; *mus:* David Raksin; *jazz violin:* Joe Venuti; *col:* Tech. *sd:* WE. 7½ min. • Jim Dandy conducts a musical that gets broken up by witches and devils.

3783. **Little Brother Rat** (*Merrie Melodies*) 2 Sept. 1939; *p.c.:* Leon Schlesinger prods for WB; *dir:* Charles M. Jones; *story:* Rich Hogan; *anim:* Robert McKimson; *lay:* Griff Jay; *back:* Arthur Loomer; *ed:* Tregoweth E. Brown; *voice:* Margaret Hill; *mus:* Carl W. Stalling; *prod sup:* Henry Binder, Raymond G. Katz; *col:* Tech. *sd:* Vit. 7 min. • Sniffles goes on a quest for an owl's egg and encounters the vexing reality of an irate cat.

3784. **The Little Brown Jug** (*Aesop's Film Fable*) 24 Jan. 1926; *p.c.:* Fables Pictures Inc for Pathé; *dir:* Paul Terry; *b&w. sil.* 5 min. • Farmer Al Falfa imbibes too frequently while fishing and has a nightmare of revenge by the fish world.

3785. **Little Brown Jug** (*Screen Song*) 20 Feb. 1948; *p.c.:* Famous for Para; *dir:* Seymour Kneitel; *story:* Bill Turner, Larry Riley; *anim:* Orestes Calpini, Morey Reden, Bill Hudson; *sets:* Tom Ford; *voices:* Jack Mercer, Sid Raymond; *mus:* Winston Sharples; *prod mgr:* Sam Buchwald; *song:* Buddy Kaye; *col:* Tech. *sd:* RCA. 8 min. • During the sing-along, the apples blow from the trees, causing a cider stream which the cows drink to render 100 percent proof milk.

3786. **Little Buck Cheeser** 18 Dec. 1937; *p.c.:* MGM; *prod/dir:* Hugh Harman, Rudolf Ising; *voices:* Bernice Hansel; *mus:* Scott Bradley; *col:* Tech. *sd:* WE. 7½ min. • Cheeser helps the other mice build a rocket ship to get to the moon, which they believe to be made of cheese.

3787. **The Little Buckaroo** (*Krazy Kat*) 11 Apr. 1938; *p.c.:* Charles Mintz prods for Colum; *story:* Allen Rose; *anim:* Harry Love; *sets:* Phil Davis; *ed:* George Winkler; *mus:* Joe de Nat; *prod mgr:* James Bronis; *b&w. sd:* RCA. 6 min. • Krazy Kat in a western burlesque.

3788. **Little Cesario** (*MGM Cartoon*) 30 Aug. 1941; *p.c.:* MGM; *prod:* Rudolf Ising; *dir:* Robert Allen; *mus:* Scott Bradley; *prod mgr:* Fred Quimby; *col:* Tech. *sd:* WE. 9 min. • A monestary in the Alpes houses a group of St. Bernard rescue dogs. The youngest one tries to prove his worth to Big Alexander, the leader.

3789. **Little Cheeser** (*Happy Harmonies*) 11 July 1936; *p.c.:* MGM; *prod/dir:* Hugh Harman, Rudolf Ising; *voice:* Bernice Hansel; *mus:* Scott Bradley; *col:* Tech. *sd:* WE. 8½ min. • Cheeser has a moral battle with his inner "Devil" self when trying to sample the seamier side of life.

3790. **The Little Cut-Up** (*Noveltoon*) 21 Jan. 1949; *p.c.:* Famous for Para; *dir:* I. Sparber; *story:* I. Klein, Mickey Klar Marks; *anim:* Myron Waldman, Gordon Whittier; *sets:* Anton Loeb; *mus:* Winston Sharples; *prod mgr:* Sam Buchwald; *col:* Tech. *sd:* RCA. 6 min. • A small boy fells a tree in the forest, leaving the wildlife homeless. He gives them a new home in his garden and turns out to be the young George Washington.

3791. **Little Dutch Mill** (*Color Classic*) 26 Oct. 1934; *p.c.:* The Fleischer Studio for Para; *prod:* Max Fleischer; *dir:* Dave Fleischer; Willard Bowsky, David Tendlar; *voice:* Mae Questel; *mus:* Sammy Timberg; *song:* Ralph Freed, Harry Barris; *ph:* Johnny Burks; *col:* Ciné. *sd:* WE. 8 min. • Two Dutch children spy on a miser who captures them. The townsfolk discover him and he is sentenced to a bath and a haircut.

3792. **The Little Dutch Plate** (*Merrie Melodies*) 21 Sept. 1935; *p.c.:* Leon Schlesinger prods for WB; *dir:* Isadore Freleng; *story:* Bob Clampett; *anim:* Paul Smith, Bob Clampett; *voices:* Billy Bletcher, Bernice Hansel, Tommy Bond; *mus:* Norman Spencer; *prod sup:* Henry Binder, Raymond G. Katz; *col:* Tech-2. *sd:* Vit. 7 min. • A salt-shaker boy loves a girl in a toy windmill but the villainous vinegar bottle landlord forces the girl to succumb to his evil will.

3793. **Little Ebony** *p.c.:* L.B. Cornwell Inc. • *1925:* **Ebony Cleans Up** 15 Oct. **The Stowaway** 1 Nov. **A Drop in the Bucket** 30 Dec. • *1926:* **High Noon** 15 Jan. **Foam, Sweet Foam** 30 Jan. • A further twenty-one films were released on a one-a-month basis and which have been untraced. b&w. st. 650 ft. each.

3794. **The Little Game Hunter** (*Aesop's Film Fable*) 29 Apr. 1929; *p.c.:* Fables Pictures Inc for Pathé; *dir:* Paul Terry; *b&w. sil.* 10 min. • No story available.

3795. **The Little Goldfish** (*MGM Cartoon*) 15 Apr. 1939; *p.c.:* MGM; *prod/dir:* Rudolf Ising; *chorus:* Jeanne Dunn, The Rhythmettes; *mus:* Scott Bradley; *prod mgr:* Fred Quimby; *col:* Tech. *sd:* WE. 8 min. • In a dream, a goldfish forsakes his bowl and mixes with the denizens of the deep.

3796. **Little Gravel Voice** (*MGM Cartoon*) 16 May 1942; *p.c.:* MGM;

prod/dir: Rudolf Ising; *anim:* Robert Allen; *mus:* Scott Bradley; *prod mgr:* Fred Quimby; *col:* Tech. *sd:* WE. 8 min. • A burro wants to make friends with the prairie animals but his awful bray frightens them away. It later saves them from a hungry wolf.

3797. Little Herman 19 June 1915; *p.c.:* Paul H. Terry for Thanhauser Film Corp; *anim:* Paul H. Terry; b&w. *sil. l/a/anim.* • Herman the magician puts a dog in a sack. It emerges as a string of sausages and develops into a daschund waving the American flag attached to his tail. While employed at Raoul Barré's studio, Terry drew and filmed this on "Double Exposures" on his own.

3798. Little Hiawatha (*Silly Symphony*) 15 May 1937; *p.c.:* Walt Disney prods for UA; *dir:* David D. Hand; *anim:* Ugo d'Orsi, Dick Huemer, Milton Kahl, Louis Schmitt, Eddie Strickland, Franklin Thomas, Bob Wickersham; *character des:* Charles Thorson; *sets:* Gustaf Tenggren; *voice:* Gayne Whitman; *trio:* Millie Walters, Sally Noble, Mary Rosetti; *mus:* Albert Hay Malotte; *col:* Tech. *sd:* RCA. 8 min. • A little Indian is unsuccessful as a mighty hunter but, when confronted by an angry bear, the woodland creatures help his escape.

3799. The Little House 8 Aug. 1952; *p.c.:* Walt Disney prods for RKO; *dir:* Wilfred Jackson; *asst dir:* Mike Holoboff; *story adapt;* Bill Peet, Bill Cottrell; *anim:* Marc Davis, Les Clark, Clair Weeks, Hal Ambro, Judge Whitaker; *fx:* George Rowley; *des:* Mary Blair; *lay:* McLaren Stewart, Thor Putnam; *back:* Ray Huffine, Claude Coats, Eyvind Earle; *voices:* Sterling Holloway, June Foray, Stan Freberg, Bob Jackman, James MacDonald; *mus:* Paul J. Smith; *col:* Tech. *sd:* RCA. 8 min. • Virginia Lee Burton's story about a cottage who, having lived through several generations, is finally saved from demolition and renovated to begin life anew.

3800. Little Johnny Jet 18 Apr. 1953; *p.c.:* MGM; *dir:* Tex Avery; *story:* Heck Allen; *anim:* Walter Clinton, Grant Simmons, Michael Lah, Ray Patterson, Robert Bentley; *sets:* John Didrik Johnsen; *ed:* Jim Faris; *voices:* Daws Butler, Marian Richman; *mus:* Scott Bradley; *ph:* Jack Stevens; *prod:* Fred Quimby; *col:* Tech. *sd:* WE. 7 min. *Academy Award nomination.* • A domesticated B-29 airplane simply can't get work in the "Jet Age." Matters come to a head when his newly delivered offspring turns out to be a jet plane.

3801. Little Lambkins (*Color Classic*) 2 Feb. 1940; *p.c.:* The Fleischer Studio for Para; *prod:* Max Fleischer; *dir:* Dave Fleischer; *story:* Joseph E. Stultz; *anim:* David Tendlar, Nelson Demorest; *ed:* Kitty Pfister; *voice:* Margie Hines; *mus:* Sammy Timberg; *ph:* Charles Schettler; *prod sup:* Sam Buchwald, Isidore Sparber; *col:* Tech. *sd:* WE. 6½ min. • A small boy moves from the country to a fully automated house in the city. He sabotages the electrical connections, forcing his parents to return to the country and his animal friends.

3802. Little Lamby (*Color Classic*) 31 Dec. 1937; *p.c.:* The Fleischer Studio for Para; *prod:* Max Fleischer; *dir:* Dave Fleischer; *anim:* David Tendlar, William Sturm; *mus:* Sammy Timberg; *col:* Tech. *sd:* WE. 7 min. • The Wolf comes to get hold of a lamb through a baby contest.

3803. The Little Lion Hunter (*Merrie Melodies*) 7 Oct. 1939; *p.c.:* Leon Schlesinger prods for WB; *dir:* Charles M. Jones; *story lay:* Robert Givens; *anim:* Philip Monroe; *character des:* Charles Thorson; *back:* Paul Julian; *ed:* Tregoweth E. Brown; *mus:* Carl W. Stalling; *prod sup:* Henry Binder, Raymond G. Katz; *col:* Tech. *sd:* Vit. 7 min. • Inki, the little pigmy, goes lion hunting but soon changes his mind when confronted by one.

3804. The Little Lost Sheep (*Krazy Kat*) 22 Dec. 1939; *p.c.:* Colum; *story:* Allen Rose; *anim:* Harry Love, Louie Lilly; *sets:* Phil Davis; *ed:* George Winkler; *voices:* Dave Weber, Leone Le Doux; *mus:* Joe de Nat; b&w. *sd:* RCA. 6½ min. • Bo Peep gets Krazy to track down a lost lamb.

3805. The Little Match Girl (*Color Rhapsody*) 5 Nov. 1937; *p.c.:* Charles Mintz prods for Colum; *story:* Sid Marcus; *anim:* Art Davis, Emery Hawkins; *i&p:* Christine Phiederman; *sets:* Phil Davis; *ed:* George Winkler; *voices:* The Rhythmettes; *mus:* Joe de Nat; *prod mgr:* James Bronis; *col:* Tech. *sd:* RCA. 8½ min. *Academy Award nomination.* • A little match seller's dream of Christmas becomes a reality when she perishes in the snow and goes to Heaven.

3806. The Little Mermaid 17 Nov.1989; *p.c.:* The Walt Disney Company, Ltd. for BV; *dir/story:* John Musker, Ron Clements; *prod:* Howard Ashman, John Musker; based on the fairy tale by Hans Christian Anderson;

storyboards: Roger Allers, Thom Enriquez, Gary Trousdale, Joe Ranft, Matthew O'Callaghan, Brenda Chapman, Ed Gombert; *anim dir:* Mark Henn, Ruben Aquino, Glen Keane, Andreas Deja, Duncan Marjoribanks, Matthew O'Callaghan; *anim:* Michael Cedeno, Chris Bailey, Rick Familoe, Tony Fucile, Shawn E. Keller, Chris Wahl, David Pruiksma, Chuck Harvey, Dan Jeup, Tom Sito, Phil Young, Will Finn, Anthony DeRosa, Doug Krohn, David Cutler, Leon Joosen, Nik Ranieri, Russ Edmonds, Dave Spafford, David P. Stephan, Jay Jackson, Ellen Woodbury, Barry Temple, Ron Husband, James Baxter, David A. Pacheco, Kathy Zielinski, Tony Anselmo, Jorgen Klubien, Rob Minkoff; *character keys:* Martin Korth, Gilda Palinginis, Richard Hoppe, Lori M. Noda, Dave Suding, Dori Littell Herrick, Renee Holt, Vera Lanpher, Tom Ferriter, June M. Fujimoto, Stephan Zupkas, Lureline Weatherly, Wesley Chun, Philo Barnhart, Bette Isis Baker, Jesus Cortes, Bill Berg, Gail Frank, Brian Clift, Dolores Baker, Chuck Williams, Cyndee Whitney, Emily Juliano, Margaret Flores Nichols, Lou Dellarosa; *anim asst:* Humberto De La Fuentes, Carole Holliday, GeeFwee Boedoe, Arland Barron; *visual fx sup:* Mark Dindal; *fx anim:* Dorse A. Lanpher, Don Paul, Randall Fullmer, Kelvin Yasuda, Mark Myer, Glenn Chaika, Dave Bossert, Barry Cook, Jeff Howard, Chris Jenkins, Christine Harding, Eusebio Torres, Ted C. Kierscey, Dan Chaika, Margaret Craig-Chang, Allen Blyth, Tom Hush, Mabel Gesner, Mike Nguyen, Craig Littell-Herrick, Allen Stovall, Steve Starr, John Tucker, Mark Barrows; *art dir:* Michael A. Peraza Jr., Donald A. Towns; *lay:* David A. Dunnet, Rasoul Azadani, Daniel St. Pierre, Fred Cline, Bill Perkins, Lorenzo E. Martinez, James Beihold, Mark Kalesniko, Mac George, Fred Craig, Rene Garcia, Marc S. Christenson, Dan McHugh, Jennifer Chiao-Lin Yuan, Roxy Steven; *back:* Donald A. Towns, Jim Coleman, Lisa L. Keene, Brian Sebern, Andrew Richard Phillipson, Robert Edward Stanton, Philip Phillipson, Cristy Maltese, Dean Gordon, Doug Ball, Craig Robertson, Greg Drolette, Kathy Altieri, Dennis Durrell; *ed:* John Carnochan, Mark Hester, Bill Wilner, Barbara Gerety, H. Lee Peterson, Scot Scalise; *col models sup:* Elrene Cowan; *computer anim:* Tina Price, Andrew Schmidt; *computer anim engineer:* Mary Jane Turner; *airbrush:* John Emerson, Bill Arance; *fx graphics:* Bernie Gagliano, Sue Adnopoz, David Nethery, Judith Barnes, Maria Rosetti, Kent Culotta, Alan Smart, Teresa Eidenbock, Broose Johnson, Kaaren Lundeen, Terry Naughton, Dana M. Reemes, Michael Show, Peggy Tonkonogy, Debra Armstrong, Carl A. Bell, Margie Daniels, Michael A. Genz, Nancy Kniep, Brian McKim, Alex Topete, Kathleen M. Bailey, Christopher Chu, Lee Dunkman, Ray Harris, Steve Lubin, Mike McKinney, Brett Newton, Natasha Selfridge, Dan Tanaka, Jane Tucker, Marcia Kimura Dougherty, Terrey Hamada Legrady; *break/inbet:* Francesca Allen, Jerry Lee Brice, James A. Davis, Mark Fisher, Peter A. Gullerud, Patrick Joens, Tom Mazzocco, Ginny Parmele, Mike Polvani, Bruce Strock, Marianne Tucker, Dave Woodman, Scott Anderson, Sheila Brown, Eileen Dunn, James Fujii, Karen Hardenbergh, Jason Lethcoe, Cynthia Overman, Eric Pigors, William Recinos, Juliet Stroud, Tuck Tucker, Merry Kanawyer Clingen, Dorris Bergstrom, Lee Crowe, Tom Ellery Jr., Daniel A. Gracey, Tim Ingersoll, Teresa Martin, Don Parmele, Brian Pimental, Stan Somers, Michael Swofford, Jim van der Keyl, Susan M. Zytka; *col modelists:* Cindy Finn, Christina Stocks, Brigitte Strother, Linda Webber; *col model paint:* Betsy Ergenbright, Linda McCall, Carolyn Guske; *col model development:* Barbara McCormack, Jill Stirdivant; *anim check:* Karen S. Paat, Lisa Poitevint, Bob Revell, Mavis E. Shafer, Barbara Wiles; *prod mgr:* Maureen Donley; *prod admin:* Jim Ballantine; *asst prod mgr:* Stephen Hickner; *clean-up:* Sutherland C. Ellwood; *asst prod mgr/post prod:* Dennis Edwards; *asst prod mgr/back:* Dorothy Aronica-McKim; *camera mgr:* Joe Jiuliano; *prod co-ord:* Brett Hayden; *fx co-ord:* Jonathan (Yona) Levit; *script sup:* Nancy Parent; *video shooter:* Gregory Hinds; *prod asst:* Ron D. Allen, Donovan R. Cook III, Bonnie Buckner, Stacy R. Meyer; *asst dir:* Michael Serrian; *scene plan:* Dave Thomson, Ann Tucker; *character des:* Dan Haskett, Glen Keane, Chris Buck, Andreas Deja, Kevin Lima, Philo Barnhart, Ed Gombert; *character sculptures:* Ruben Procopio; *visual development:* Bruce Morris, Rowland B. Wilson, Andy Gaskill, A. Kendall O'Connor, Chris van Allsburg, Doug Lefler, Gary Eggleston, Kay Nielsen, Kelly A. Asbury; *voices: Louis the Chef:* Rene Auberjenois; *Prince Eric:* Christopher Daniel Barnes; *Ariel:* Jodi Benson; *Ursula the Sea Witch:* Pat Carroll; *Flotsam & Jetsam:* Paddi Edwards; *Scuttle:* Buddy Hackett; *Flounder:* Jason Marin; *King Triton:* Kenneth Mars; *Carlotta:* Edie McClurg; *Seahorse:* Will Ryan; *Grimsby:* Ben Wright; *Sebastian:* Samuel E. Wright; *also:* Charlie Adler, Jack Angel, Susan Boyd, Steve Bulen, Hamilton Camp, Nancy Cartwright,

Philip Clarke, Jennifer Darling, Allen Davies, Gail Farrell, Donny Gerrard, Ed Gilbert, Mitch Gordon, Willie Greene Jr., Walter S. Hannah, Linda Harmon, Phillip Ingram, Luana Jackman, William A. Kennedy, Edie Lehmann, Anne Lockhart, Sherry Lynn, Mickie T. McGowan, Guy Maeda, Melissa MacKay, Lynn Dolin Mann, Arne B. Markussen, Gene J. Merlino, Lewis Moreford, Kathleen O'Connor, Patrick Pinney, Marilyn Powell, Gloria G. Prosper, Michael Redman Jr., Debbie Shapiro, Sally Stevens, Robert Tebow, Rob Trow, Joe Turano, Jackie Ward, Bobbi White, Robert S. Zwirn, Robert Weil; *songs:* Howard Ashman, Alan Menken; *song prod:* Howard Ashman, Alan Menkin, Robert Kraft; *song arrangement:* Robby Merkin, Alan Menken; *mus ed:* Kathleen Bennett, Segue Music; *scoring:* John Richards; *orch:* Thomas Pasatieri; *conductor:* J.A.C. Redford; *anim check:* Janet Bruce; *scene plan:* Rick Sullivan; *i&p:* Gretchen Maschmeyer Albrecht; *Xerox ph:* Bill Brazner; *Xerox check/ink:* Carmen Sanderson, Kris Brown, Maria Fenyvesi, Eleanor Dahlen, Peggy Gregory, Eve Fletcher, Darlene Kanagy, Anne Hazard, Karan Lee-Storr, Robin D. Kane, Kitty Schoentag, Charlene Miller, Tatsuko Watanabe, Laura Craig; *final check sup:* Hortensia Casagran; *asso prod:* Maureen Donley; *main & end titles des:* Saxon/Ross Film Design; *i&p asst mgr:* Chris Hecox; *i&p secretary:* Cherie McGowan; *Xerox:* Bert Wilson, Dean Stanley, Robyn Roberts, Jo Ann Breuer, Sherri Vandoli, Tina Baldwin, Janet Rea, Lynnette Cullen, Gareth Fishbaugh, Cindy Garcia, Leyla C. Amaro-Pelaez, Karen China, Douglas E. Casper, Bob Cohen, Warren Coffman, Kathy Gilmore, Diana Dixon, Cynthia Neill Knizek, Suzanne Inglis, Catherine F. Parotino, Marlene Burkhart; *mark-up:* Gina Wootten; *paint:* Ginni Mack, Penny Coulter, Barbara Hamane, James "JR" Russell, Janette Hulett, Beth Ann McCoy; *addit dial:* Howard Ashman, Gerrit Graham, Samuel Graham, Chris Hubbell; *sd ed:* Richard C. Franklin, Louis Edemann, Charles L. Campbell, Leonard T. Geschke, P. Bruce Richardson, G.C. "Chuck" Neely, Nils C. Jensen, J. Chris Jargo; *ADR:* Larry Singer, Pamela G. Kimber, Alan Howarth, Melvin D. Neiman, Jack Nietzsche Jr.; *foley:* John Roesch, Ellen Heuer, Joe Sabella, Greg Orloff; *rec:* Carolyn Tapp, Terry Porter, Mel Metcalfe, David Hudson; *col:* Tech. *sd:* Dolby Stereo. 82 min. • Ariel is the mermaid daughter of King Triton, ruler of the Undersea Kingdom. She is more interested in the human world above the water and, during a storm, she rescues and falls in love with Prince Eric who has been washed overboard from his ship. Ursula the sea witch, anxious to gain control of King Triton's empire, gives Ariel a deal whereupon she can become human in exchange for her voice, to which the mermaid agrees. When in a human form, Ariel seeks out Eric and the two fall in love but Ursula has further designs on gaining power. Ariel and Eric manage to defeat the Sea Witch's scheme and the undersea world is finally returned to normal.

3807. The Little Mole (MGM Cartoon) 5 Apr. 1941; *p.c.:* MGM; *prod/dir:* Hugh Harman; *story:* Hugh Harman, Jack Cosgriff, Charles McGirl; *character des/anim:* Robert Allen; *lay:* John Meandor; *back:* Joe Smith; *voice:* Mel Blanc; *mus:* Scott Bradley; *prod mgr:* Fred Quimby; *col:* Tech. *sd:* WE. 9 min. • Dr. Primrose Skunk sells the little mole some glasses and the mole sets off to see the world a little more clearly. All goes well until he loses them.

3808. Little Moth's Big Flame (Color Rhapsody) 25 Oct. 1938; *p.c.:* Charles Mintz prods for Colum; *dir:* Sid Marcus; *anim:* Art Davis, Herb Rothwill; *i&p:* Christine Phiederman; *sets:* Phil Davis; *ed:* George Winkler; *voices:* Billy Bletcher, Leone LeDoux; *mus:* Joe de Nat; *prod mgr:* James Bronis; *col:* Tech. *sd:* RCA. 8 min. • A girl moth is attracted to a seductive lamp flame. She resists his advances and returns home with singed wings.

3809. Little Nemo 8 Apr. 1911; *p.c.:* Vit Corp; *dir/anim:* Winsor McCay; *l/a dir:* J. Stuart Blackton; *l/a ph:* Walter Arthur; *l/a players:* Winsor McCay, John Bunny, George McManus; *col:* Hand tinted. sil. • Nemo, Flip and Impie visit Dreamland where they squash and stretch, meet the Princess and a friendly dragon before returning. • See: *Winsor McCay Makes His Cartoons Move*

3810. Little Nemo in Slumber Land 21 Aug. 1992; *p.c.:* Hemdale Pictures Corp./The Rest of the World-Tokyo Movie Shinsha; *dir:* Masami Hata, William Hurtz; *prod:* Yutaka Fujioka; *story:* Jean Moebius Giraud, Yutaka Fujioka; based on the comic strip by Winsor McCay; *concept for screen:* Ray Bradbury; *scr:* Chris Columbus, Richard Outten; *story consultants:* Frank Thomas, Oliver Johnston, David Hilberman, Koji Shimizu, Robert Towne; *story sketch:* Ken Anderson, Boyd Kirkland, Nobuo Tomizawa, Bob Taylor, Yasuo Otsuka, Marty Murphy, Lee Mishkin, Roy

Wilson, Leo Salkin, Kazukide Tomonaga, Milt Schaffer; *storyboard:* Masami Hata, Nobuo Tomizawa, Kazukide Tomonaga, Yasuo Otsuka; *anim dir:* Kazukide Tomonaga, Nobuo Tomizawa; *conceptual des:* Jean Moebius Giraud; *des development:* Brian Froud, Paul Julian, Kazukide Tomonaga, Ken Mundie, Corny Cole, Nobuo Tomizawa; *visual image development:* John Canemaker; *dir anim:* Yoshinobu Michihata, Kenji Hachizaki, Toshihiko Masuda; *anim:* Hiroyuki Aoyama, Hiroaki Noguchi, Atsuko Tanaka, Masaaki Kudo, Kuniyuki Ishii, Fumio Lida, Yuji Yanase, Kazuyoshi Takeuchi, Hiroshi Shimizu, Masahiro Neriki, Kitaro Kosaka, Yutaka Oka, Makoto Tanaka, Sadahiko Sakamaki, Teichi Takiguchi, Yuichiro Yano, Masanori Ono, Tomomi Mizuta, Osamu Okubo, Keiko Tomizawa, Noboru Takano, Hiroyuki Horiuchi, Osamu Nabeshima, Shunji Saida, Toshio Kaneko, Satoshi Sasaki, Toshio Mori, Hiroko Takatani, Masayoshi Shimura, Takeshi Konakawa, Yoko Nagashima, Hisao Yokobori, Takashi Kawaguchi, Takuo Tominaga, Takayuki Ishizuka, Setsuya Tanabe, Yuji Yanase, Takuro Shinbo, Junko Isaka, Masami Takebuchi, Keiko Tozawa, Yasuhiro Saiki, Noriko Kiyohara, Tomoko Nemai, Akemi Seki, Shizuko Minami, Yuriko Nagaya, Mayumi Oomura, Yutaka Nakamura, Yasuhiro Buma, Hiroko Yoshizawa, Junko Uenoyama, Natsuko Takahashi, Emiko Hirama, Masayuki Oosawa, Rie Nakagome, Kazuyuki Iizuka, Tatsuya Uetsu, Shusaku Chiba, Yoshitake Iwakami, Midori Nagaoka, Kenji Yamamoto, Issei Okumura, Keiko Yozawa, Mari Yajima, Kumiko Hirama, Koji Usui, Akihiro Yuki, Tomoko Okuno, Noriko Sugiyama, Tomomi Yakou, Kayoho Nakafuji, Yumi Yanagawa, Norio Saito, Koichi Suenaga, Shojiro Nishimi, Maseto Mukai, Noboru Sasaki, Hirokazu Taguchi, Shinichi Sasaki, Koichi Hatsumi, Masami Koiwa, Takayuki Shimura, Satoshi Kazato, Etsuko Uemoto, Yuki Tezuka, Shiho Nakamura, Masako Terada, Keiko Horiuchi, Yurie Sudo, Yoshiko Fujita, Akemi Muramatsu; *col des:* Hiroko Kondo; *art dir:* Nizo Yamamoto, Seiji Sugawara; *lay:* Toshiya Washida; *back sketch:* Ray Aragon, Dan Gordon, Carol Police, Fred Water; *back:* Shuichi Hirata, Norihiro Hiraki, Hiromasa Ogura, Toshio Nosaki, Miyuki Kudo, Yoji Nakaza, Mutsuo Koseki, Kazuo Ebisawa, Masaki Yoshizaki, Yutaka Ito, Toshiharu Mizutani, Kenji Kamiyama, Sachiko Shirakaba, Yukihiro Yokoyama, Tooruhishiyama, Noriko Takaya, Asako Kodaira, Akira Yamakawa, Fukiko Tamura, Katsu Hisamure; *co-prod:* Barry Glasser, Shunzo Kato, Eiji Katayama; *asso prod:* Koji Takeuchi, Kaoru Nishiyama; *addit.dial:* Bruce Reid Schaefer; *slugging:* Sam Weiss, Gwen Wetzler, Sam Nicholson, Ruth Kissane; *exposure sheets:* Robert Alvarez, Steven Clark, Alfred Kouzel, Karen Peterson, Robert Shellhorn, Richard Trueblood; *mouth code:* Eric Peterson; *track reading:* Laurie Wetzler, George Graig, Mark McNally, Mike Truba, Cecil Broughton; *asst dir:* Hiroaki Sato, Keiko Oyamada, Hiro Yuki Ishido, Hiroshi Adachi; *ed:* Takeshi Seyama; *voices: Nemo:* Gabriel Damon; *Flip:* Mickey Rooney; *Professor Genius:* Rene Auberjenois; *Icarus:* Danny Mann; *Princess Camille:* Laura Mooney; *King Morpheus:* Bernard Erhard; *Nightmare King:* William E. Martin; *Oomp:* Alan Oppenheimer; *Oompy:* Michael Bell; *Oompo:* Sidney Miller; *Oompa:* Neil Ross; *Oomp/Dirigible Captain:* John Stephenson; *Nemo's Mother:* Jennifer Darling; *Nemo's Father/Flap:* Greg Burson; *Bon Bon:* Sherry Lynn; *himself:* Larry King; *also:* Shelley Thompson, Dick Vosburgh, Jessica Waite, James Watt, Jessica Wray, Eliza Yoder, Sarah Zilinski, Desiree Zondag, Shannon Zondag; *mus:* Thomas Chase, Steve Rucker; *performed by:* London Symphony Orchestra; *songs:* Richard M. Sherman, Robert B. Sherman; *title song sung by* Melissa Manchester; *anim check:* Yuji Kakamura, Shunsuke Harada, Akiko Kawachi, Junko Saito, Masako Hayashi, Yayoi Toki; *i&p:* Tomoko Yamamoto, Tachiko Kimura, Masajo Sugimori, Yoko Hatta, Kenji Adachi, Mihoko Koda, Naoko Seki, Keiko Nemoto, Hironori Taketomi, Shihoko Ivakayama, Junichi Uehara, Koyuki Keneda, Yasuhiro Hayashi, Yoko Takahashi, Akiko Iizuka, Haremi Miyagawa, Chieko Omachi, Emiko Honda, Kazumi Yamamoto, Hifumi Kamel, Rika Tanaka, Michiko Furikawa, Minoru Ueno, Hiroe Jonai, Junko Igarashi, Yoshihiro Tanaka, Yoko Takahata, Kayo Okubo, Naeko Suganuma, Masahiro Tomiyama, Minako Hayashi, Hiromi Takaya, Yoko Sudo, Toshiko Suzuki, Hideko Onodera, Tomoka Mitsui, Tetsuro Kumase, Akiko Hamanaka, Yasutomo Ouchi; *air bruch art:* Tomoji Hashizume; *Matte art:* Masahito Aoki; *ph:* Hajime Hasegawa, Kenichi Kobayashi, Moriyuki Terashita, Takahisa Ogawa, Kazushige Ichinozuka, Atsuko Ito, Koji Asai, Takashi Nomura, Jin Nishiyama, Kiyoshi Kobayashi, Atsushi Yoshino, Kyoko Dosaki, Ahio Saitch, Hiroshi Kanai, Hitoshi Shirao, Hironori Yoshino, Mika Sakai, Rie Takeuchi, Kazushi Torigoe; *sd mix:* Kunio Ando; *dial rec:* Larry Miller; *dial track ed:* Jeffrey Patch; *ADR:* Vic Radulich, *mus rec:* Gareth Cousins, Dave Forth; *mus ed:* Roy Prendergast; *music mix:* Akihiko Ono; *sd fx ed:* Shizuo Kurahashi; *sd ed:* Masafumi Mima, Nobuyoshi Kanbayashi; *post prod:* Susumu Aketagawe, Heather Probert, Gregory Hicks; *exutives in charge of prod:* Katsuro Tanaka, Sander Schwartz; *prod ex:* Robert Eatman; *prod mgrs:* Tat Ikeuchi, Sachiko Tsuneda, Chuck Shiota; *prod staff:* Masaaki Nanbu, Teruhisa Yamaji, Ryuji Asami, Takeshi Takano, Ryotaro Ishigame, Toshiyuki Hiruma, Kazumi Sawaguchi, Sutherland Ellwood, Zahra Dowlatabadi, James Thornton, Steve Walker, Maria Arnold; *translator:* Miyoko Miura; *col. sd:* Dolby Stereo. 83 min. • Nemo is selected to be heir to the throne of Slumberland and entrusted with the key to a mysterious door. Led astray by a character named Flip, Nemo unknowingly releases the Nightmare King who kidnaps King Morpheus, imprisoning him in Nightmare Castle. Realizing the trouble he has caused, Nemo sets out to rescue the King and restore Slumberland to normality.

3811. Little Nobody (*Betty Boop*) 27 Dec. 1935; *p.c.:* The Fleischer Studio for Para; *prod:* Max Fleischer; *dir:* Dave Fleischer; *anim:* Myron Waldman, Hicks Lokey, Lillian Friedman; *voice:* Mae Questel; *mus:* Sammy Timberg; b&w. *sd:* WE. 7 min. • Pudgy falls for the Pekinese next door but she rejects him. He later saves her from drowning and they become the best of friends.

3812. Little Ol' Bosko and the Cannibals (*Happy Harmonies*) 28 Aug. 1937; *p.c.:* MGM; *prod/dir:* Hugh Harman, Rudolf Ising; *voices:* Ruby Dandridge, Eugene Jackson, The Four Blackbirds; *mus:* Scott Bradley; *col:* Tech. *sd:* WE. 9 min. • Bosko is taking a bag of cookies to his grandma when he's confronted by a band of cannibal frogs. Caricatures of Louis Armstrong, Cab Calloway, Bill Robinson and Fats Waller.

3813. Little Ol' Bosko and the Pirates (*Happy Harmonies*) 1 May 1937; *p.c.:* MGM; *prod/dir:* Hugh Harman, Rudolf Ising; *voices:* Lillian Randolph, The Four Blackbirds, Eugene Jackson; *mus:* Scott Bradley; *col:* Tech. *sd:* WE. 7½ min. • Bosko finds himself aboard a pirate ship with a gang of jazz-loving frogs. Caricatures of Bill Robinson and Fats Waller.

3814. Little Ol' Bosko in Bagdad (*Happy Harmonies*) 1 Jan. 1938; *p.c.:* MGM; *prod/dir:* Hugh Harman, Rudolf Ising; *voices:* Lillian Randolph, The Four Blackbirds, Eugene Jackson, Norm Blackburn; *mus:* Scott Bradley; *col:* Tech. *sd:* WE. 9 min. • Bosko invades a harem and encounters De Sultan and his frog cohorts, all who have their eyes on Bosko's bag of cookies. Caricatures of Louis Armstrong, Step'n Fetchit, Bill Robinson and Fats Waller.

3815. Little Orphan (*Tom & Jerry*) 30 Apr. 1949; *p.c.:* MGM; *dir:* William Hanna, Joseph Barbera; *anim:* Irven Spence, Kenneth Muse, Ed Barge, Ray Patterson; *ed:* Fred MacAlpin; *mus:* Scott Bradley; *prod:* Fred Quimby; *col:* Tech. *sd:* WE. 7 min. *Academy Award.* • Jerry is left an orphan mouse to feed on Thanksgiving night.

3816. Little Orphan Airedale (*Looney Tunes*) 4 Oct. 1947; *p.c.:* WB; *dir:* Charles M. Jones; *story:* Michael Maltese; *anim:* Lloyd Vaughan, Ken Harris, Phil Monroe, Ben Washam; *lay:* Robert Gribbroek; *back:* Peter Alvarado; *ed:* Treg Brown; *voices:* Mel Blanc; *mus:* Carl Stalling; *prod mgr:* John W. Burton; *prod:* Edward Selzer; *col:* Tech. *sd:* Vit. 7 min. • A dog pound escapee runs into a mutt who tells of how he endeared himself into Porky's home.

3817. Little Orphan Willie (*Flip the Frog*) 1930; *p.c.:* Celebrity prods for MGM; *prod/dir:* Ub Iwerks; b&w. *sd:* PCP. 6 min. • The stork's recent visit is chased away by Mrs. Mouse. He leaves the bundle of joy on Flip's doorstep and he has to feed the child's insatiable appetite.

3818. Little Pancho Vanilla (*Merrie Melodies*) 8 Oct. 1938; *p.c.:* Leon Schlesinger prods for WB; *dir:* Frank Tashlin; *story:* Ted Pierce; *anim:* Bob McKimson; *ed:* Tregoweth E. Brown; *voices:* Mel Blanc, the Rhythmettes; *mus:* Carl W. Stalling; *prod sup:* Henry Binder, Raymond G. Katz; *col:* Tech. *sd:* Vit. 7 min. • Little Pancho dreams of being a great bullfighter and disobeys Mama's wishes by entering a bullfight. He wins the contest and buys Mama a new washing machine.

3819. The Little Parade (*Aesop's Film Fable*) 13 June 1926; *p.c.:* Fables Pictures Inc for Pathé; *dir:* Paul Terry; b&w. *sil.* 10 min. • No story available.

3820. The Little Pest (*Scrappy*) 15 Aug. 1931; *p.c.:* Winkler for Colum; *prod:* Charles Mintz; *story:* Dick Huemor; *anim:* Sid Marcus; *mus:* Joe de Nat; *prod mgr:* James Bronis; b&w. *sd:* WE. 6 min. • Despite many attempts to keep him at home, Scrappy's kid brother follows him on a fishing trip. The only thing he catches is the little pest who falls in the lake.

3821. Little Problems (*Terry Bears*) Sept. 1951; *p.c.:* TT for Fox; *dir:* Eddie Donnelly; *story:* Tom Morrison; *anim:* Jim Tyer; *sets:* Art Bartsch; *voices:* Douglas Moye, Tom Morrison, Philip A. Scheib; *mus:* Philip A. Scheib; *ph:* Douglas Moye; *col:* Tech. *sd:* RCA. 6 min. • Papa's book on how to deal with unruly children does him little good.

3822. Little Quacker (*Tom & Jerry*); 7 Jan. 1950; *p.c.:* MGM; *dir:* William Hanna, Joseph Barbera; *anim:* Irven Spence, Ray Patterson, Ed Barge, Kenneth Muse; *lay:* Dick Bickenbach; *back:* Robert Gentle; *ed:* Jim Faris; *voices:* Red Coffee; *mus:* Scott Bradley; *ph:* Jack Stevens; *prod:* Fred Quimby; *col:* Tech. *sd:* WE. 6½ min. • Tom steals a mother duck's egg to eat but the duckling hatches. He then decides to roast the duck but is constantly thwarted by Jerry.

3823. The Little Red Hen (*ComiColor*) 16 Feb. 1934; *p.c.:* Celebrity prods; *prod/dir:* Ub Iwerks; *anim:* Jimmie Culhane, Al Eugster; *mus:* Carl Stalling; *col:* Ciné. *sd:* PCP. 7 min. • The pig, duck, mouse and can won't help the hen sow her wheat but when it's made into bread, they all want to help eat it.

3824. Little Red Hen (*Terry-Toon*) Aug. 1955; *p.c.:* TT for Fox; *dir:* Connie Rasinski; *story:* Tom Morrison; *anim:* Jim Tyer; *mus:* Philip A. Scheib; *ph:* Douglas Moye; *col:* Tech. *sd:* RCA. 7 min. CS. • In this jazzed-up version of the old story, the hen asks the animals to help sow the wheat but they are only interested when it's made into bread.

3825. Little Red Riding Hood (*Dinky Doodle*) 4 Jan. 1925; *p.c.:* Bray prods for FBO; *dir/story:* Walt Lantz; *anim:* Clyde Geronimi; b&w. *sil.* 5 min. *l/a/anim.* • Walter reads a Mother Goose book which contains "Little Red Riding Hood." Dinky Doodle steps in to help her on her visit to Grandma. Dinky's dog is aware of the Wolf pursuing them and follows, thwarting the Wolf's plans.

3826. Little Red Riding Hood (*Laugh-o-Gram*) 29 July 1922; *p.c.:* Laugh-o-Gram Films Inc for Newman Theater, Kansas City; *dir:* Walt Disney; *anim:* Walt Disney, Hugh Harman, Rudolf Ising, Ub Iwerks, Lorey Tague, Carmen Maxwell, Otto Walliman; *ph:* Red Lyon; b&w. *sil.* • Julius forfeits all nine lives by eating one of Granny's doughnuts. While Grandma is away, the hero arrives by plane to rescue Red from the wolf. Reissued with sound in 1929 and retitled *Grandma Steps Out.* • See: *Whoopee Sketches*

3827. Little Red Riding Rabbit (*Merrie Melodies*) 18 Dec. 1943; *p.c.:* Leon Schlesinger prods for WB; *dir:* I. Freleng; *story:* Michael Maltese; *anim:* Manuel Perez; *lay:* Owen Fitzgerald; *back:* Lenard Kester; *ed:* Treg Brown; *voices:* Mel Blanc, Billy Bletcher, Bea Benaderet; *mus:* Carl W. Stalling; *ph:* John W. Burton; *prod sup:* Henry Binder, Raymond G. Katz; *col:* Tech. *sd:* Vit. 7 min. • Red brings Grandma a pet rabbit for dinner but the wolf takes Granny's place while she's working a swing shift at Lockheed.

3828. Little Red Rodent Hood (*Merrie Melodies*) 3 May 1952; *p.c.:* WB; *dir:* I. Freleng; *story:* Warren Foster; *anim:* Ken Champin, Virgil Ross, Arthur Davis, Manuel Perez; *lay:* Hawley Pratt; *back:* Irv Wyner; *ed:* Treg Brown; *voices:* Mel Blanc, Bea Benaderet; *mus:* Carl Stalling; *prod mgr:* John W. Burton; *prod:* Edward Selzer; *col:* Tech. *sd:* Vit. 7 min. • Grandma mouse tells the story of how a mouse Red Riding Hood dealt with the Big Bad Cat.

3829. Little Red School Mouse (*Noveltoon*) 15 Apr. 1949; *p.c.:* Famous for Para; *dir:* I. Sparber; *story:* Carl Meyer, Jack Mercer; *anim:* Tom Johnson, John Gentilella; *sets:* Robert Connavale; *mus:* Winston Sharples; *ph:* Leonard McCormick; *prod mgr:* Sam Buchwald; *col:* Tech. *sd:* RCA. 6 min. • A mouse misses "Cat Identification" classes and doesn't recognize a cat when he meets one, so he brings it back to the classroom.

3830. Little Red Walking Hood (*Merrie Melodies*) 6 Nov. 1937; *p.c.:* Leon Schlesinger prods for WB; *dir:* Fred Avery; *story:* Cal Howard, Robert Clampett; *anim:* Irven Spence; *ed:* Tregoweth E. Brown; *voices:* Mel Blanc, Elvia Allman, Ted Pierce; *mus:* Carl W. Stalling; *prod sup:* Henry Binder, Raymond G. Katz; *col:* Tech. *sd:* Vit. 7 min. • A pool-hall wolf pursues Little Red Riding Hood but gets the cold shoulder. Egghead emerges the hero of the day.

3831. Little Rover *(Color Rhapsody)* 28 June 1935; *p.c.:* Charles Mintz prods for Colum; *story:* Sid Marcus; *anim:* Art Davis; *mus:* Joe de Nat; *prod mgr:* James Bronis; *col:* Tech-2. *sd:* RCA. 7 min. • Little Rover is an outcast pup who is left to roam the streets, escaping many dangers.

3832. Little Runaway *(Tom & Jerry)* 14 June 1952; *p.c.:* MGM; *dir:* William Hanna, Joseph Barbera; *anim:* Ed Barge, Kenneth Muse, Irven Spence, Ray Patterson; *lay:* Dick Bickenbach; *back:* Robert Gentle; *ed:* Jim Faris; *voice:* Paul Frees; *mus:* Scott Bradley; *ph:* Jack Stevens; *prod:* Fred Quimby; *col:* Tech. *sd:* WE. 7 min. • Jerry tries to help an escaped circus seal.

3833. Little Rural Riding Hood 17 Sept. 1949; *p.c.:* MGM; *dir:* Tex Avery; *story:* Rich Hogan, Jack Cosgriff; *anim:* Grant Simmons, Walter Clinton, Bob Cannon, Michael Lah; *character des/lay:* Louis Schmitt; *sets:* John Didrik Johnsen; *ed:* Fred MacAlpin; *voices:* Pinto Colvig, Daws Butler, Imogene Lynn, Coleen Collins; *mus:* Scott Bradley; *ph:* Jack Stevens; *prod:* Fred Quimby; *col:* Tech. *sd:* WE. 6 min. • A country hick wolf visits his suave city cousin who promises rich picking in women at the local night club.

3834. Little School Mouse *(Tom & Jerry)* 29 May 1954; *p.c.:* MGM; *dir:* William Hanna, Joseph Barbera; *anim:* Irven Spence, Ed Barge; *lay:* Dick Bickenbach; *back:* Robert Gentle; *ed:* Jim Faris; *mus:* Scott Bradley; *ph:* Jack Stevens; *prod:* Fred Quimby; *col:* Tech. *sd:* WE. 7 min. • Jerry tries to teach a young student the fundamentals of being a mouse in a cat's world

3835. Little Skeeter *(Woody Woodpecker)* 1969; *p.c.:* Walter Lantz prods for Univ; *dir:* Paul J. Smith; *story:* Homer Brightman; *anim:* Les Kline, Al Coe; *sets:* Nino Carbe; *voices:* Daws Butler, Grace Stafford; *mus:* Walter Greene; *prod mgr:* William E. Garity; *col:* Tech. *sd:* RCA. 6 min. • Woody employs Happy Harry to rid his house of a mosquito but Harry proves to be more of a hindrance than a help.

3836. A Little Soap and Water *(Betty Boop)* 21 June 1935; *p.c.:* The Fleischer Studio for Para; *prod:* Max Fleischer; *dir:* Dave Fleischer; *anim:* Myron Waldman, Edward Nolan, Lillian Friedman; *voice:* Mae Questel; *mus:* Sammy Timberg; *b&w. sd:* WE. 6 min. • When Betty's attempts to bathe Pudgy are accomplished, it's not too long before the pup needs another dousing.

3837. Little Star of Bethlehem Nov. 1963; *p.c.:* MKR Films for Colum; *dir:* Paul Tripp; *mus:* George Kleinsinger; *col. sd.* 10 min. • A film of childrens' Christmas paintings.

3838. The Little Stranger *(Color Classic)* 13 Mar. 1936; *p.c.:* The Fleischer Studio for Para; *prod:* Max Fleischer; *dir:* Dave Fleischer; *anim:* Dave Tendlar, Eli Brucker; *voices:* Everett Clark, Jack Mercer; *mus:* Sammy Timberg; *col:* Tech. *sd:* WE. 8 min. • Mother duck hatches a chicken egg. The chick is shunned by the others until he rescues them from a hungry hawk.

3839. Little Swee' Pea *(Popeye)* 25 Sept. 1936; *p.c.:* The Fleischer Studio for Para; *prod:* Max Fleischer; *dir:* Dave Fleischer; *anim:* Seymour Kneitel, William Henning; *voices:* Jack Mercer, Mae Questel; *mus:* Sammy Timberg; *ph:* Johnny Burks; *b&w. sd:* WE. 6½ min. • Popeye takes Swee'Pea to the zoo where he has to rescue the kid from the jaws of various animals.

3840. Little Televillain *(Chilly Willy)* 8 Dec. 1958; *p.c.:* Walter Lantz prods for Univ; *dir:* Alex Lovy; *story:* Homer Brightman; *anim:* La Verne Harding, Ray Abrams, Don Patterson; *sets:* Raymond Jacobs, Art Landy; *voices:* Daws Butler, Grace Stafford; *mus:* Clarence Wheeler; *prod mgr:* William E. Garity; *col:* Tech. *sd:* RCA. 6 min. • A TV producer puts Smedley on guard to stop intruders while he thinks up a new show idea.

3841. The Little Theatre *(Phantasy)* 7 Feb. 1941; *p.c.:* Colum; *story:* Harry Love; *anim:* Allen Rose; *ed:* George Winkler; *voice:* Sara Berner, Leone Le Doux; *mus:* Joe de Nat; *ph:* Otto Reimer; *prod mgr:* James Bronis; *b&w. sd:* RCA. 6 min. • Oopy ruins Scrappy's performance by throwing pies at his balancing act, cutting the strings on his "Dancing Long Johns" and finally doing his own act on stage.

3842. Little 'Tinker 15 May 1948; *p.c.:* MGM; *dir:* Tex Avery; *anim:* William Shull, Grant Simmons, Walter Clinton, Robert Bentley; *sets:* John Didrik Johnsen; *ed:* Fred MacAlpin; *voices:* Dick Nelson, Tom Clarke, Harry William Roberts, Sara Berner; *mus:* Scott Bradley; *prod:* Fred Quimby; *col:* Tech. *sd:* WE. 6 min. • B.O. Skunk is a failure with the women until he decides to imitate Frank Sinatra.

3843. Little Toot *(Marquee Musical)* 13 Aug. 1954; *p.c.:* Walt Disney prods for BV; *dir:* Clyde Geronimi; *col:* Tech. *sd:* RCA. 9 min. • Former Disney animator, Hardie Gramatky's story about a fun-loving New York harbor tugboat who comes into his own when he rescues an ocean liner in a storm. • See: *Melody Time*

3844. Little Tough Mice *(Car-Tune Comedy)* 13 Mar. 1939; *p.c.:* Walter Lantz prods for Univ; *dir:* Alex Lovy; *story:* Vic McLeod; *anim:* Dick Marion, Ralph Somerville; *sets:* Edgar Keichle; *voices:* Danny Webb, Margaret Hill; *mus:* Frank Marsales; *prod mgr:* George Hall; *b&w. sd:* WE. 7 min. • Three tough mice waylay a genteel one who is on his way home from market with a basket of food.

3845. The Little Trail *(Krazy Kat)* 3 Dec. 1930; *p.c.:* Winkler for Colum; *prod:* Charles Mintz; *story:* Ben Harrison; *anim:* Manny Gould; *mus:* Joe de Nat; *prod mgr:* James Bronis; *b&w. sd:* WE. 6 min. • Krazy in a covered wagon drama where some menacing Indians join in the campfire hoedown.

3846. The Little Whirlwind *(Mickey Mouse)* 14 Feb. 1941; *p.c.:* Walt Disney prods for RKO; *dir:* Riley Thomson; *asst dir:* Ray de Vally; *anim:* James Armstrong, Richard Brown, Les Clark, George de Beeson, Phil Duncan, John Elliotte, Frank Follmer, Volus Jones, Walt Kelly, Ward Kimball, Fred Moore, Kenneth Muse, Bard Wiggenhorn, James Will, Marvin Woodward; *fx:* Jack Boyd, Andy Engman, Art Fitzpatrick, Joe Harbaugh, Jack Huber, Paul B. Kossoff, Ed Parks, Reuben Timmens, Noel Tucker, Cornett Wood; *lay:* Charles Philippi, Charles Connor; *voices:* Marcellite Garner, Walt Disney; *mus:* Oliver Wallace; *col:* Tech. *sd:* RCA. 7 min. • A baby whirlwind has fun at Mickey's expense while he tidies Minnie's back yard.

3847. The Little Wise Quacker *(Barney Bear)* 8 Nov. 1952; *p.c.:* MGM; *dir:* Dick Lundy; *story:* Heck Allen, Jack Cosgriff; *anim:* Grant Simmons, Michael Lah, Ray Patterson, Walter Clinton; *sets:* John Didrik Johnsen; *ed:* Jim Faris; *voice:* Paul Frees; *mus:* Scott Bradley; *ph:* Jack Stevens; *prod:* Fred Quimby; *col:* Tech. *sd:* WE. 7 min. • Barney tries to awaken a sleeping duck in order to shoot him.

3848. Little Woody Riding Hood *(Woody Woodpecker)* 16 Oct. 1962; *p.c.:* Walter Lantz prods for Univ; *dir:* Paul J. Smith; *story:* Dalton Sandifer; *anim:* Ray Abrams, Les Kline, Art Davis; *sets:* Art Landy, Ray Huffine; *voices:* Daws Butler, Grace Stafford; *mus:* Clarence Wheeler; *prod mgr:* William E. Garity; *col:* Tech. *sd:* RCA. 6 min. • Gabby Gator reads *Little Red Riding Hood* and invites Woody to visit his "Granny." The arrival of a wolf complicates matters.

3849. The Littlest Bully *(Sidney)* Aug. 1960; *p.c.:* TT for Fox; *ex prod:* Bill Weiss; *dir:* Martin Taras; *story sup:* Tom Morrison; *story:* Larz Bourne; *anim:* Ed Donnelly, Mannie Davis; *sets:* John Zago, Bill Focht; *voices:* Lionel Wilson; *mus:* Philip Scheib; *prod mgr:* Frank Schudde; *col:* Tech. *sd:* RCA. 6 min. CS. • Melvin the mouse has fun scaring Sidney the elephant until he gets knocked unconcious and imagines Sidney as a cat.

3850. The Littlest Giant 1956; *p.c.:* John Sutherland prods for National Consumer Finance Asso; *prod/dir:* John Sutherland; *col:* Tech. *sd.* 13½ min. • Edgar Q. Smith is an average consumer whose mass makes up the most important giant in the land. When he needs cash, he goes to one of the many small loans offices and pays a sizeable interest.

3851. The Living Circle 1955; *p.c.:* John Sutherland prods; *prod:* John Sutherland, Earl Jonas; *dir:* Carl Urbano; *col. sd.* 13½ min. *l/a/anim.* • Agricultural economy of Central America in terms of coffee, bananas, Abaca, cocoa and African palm oil.

3852. Lo, the Poor Buffal *(Color Rhapsody)* 4 Nov. 1948; *p.c.:* Colum; *prod:* Raymond Katz, Henry Binder; *dir:* Alex Lovy; *story:* Cal Howard, Dave Monahan; *anim:* Grant Simmons, Paul Sommer, Chic Otterstrom, Jay Sarbry; *lay:* Jim Carmichael; *back:* Al Boggs; *ed:* Richard S. Jensen; *voices:* Jack Mather, Dave Barry; *mus:* Darrell Calker; *col:* Tech. *sd:* WE. 6 min. • A buffalo outwits the famous hunter, "Buffalo Billingsley."

3853. The Loan Stranger *(Woody Woodpecker)* 19 Oct. 1942; *p.c.:* Walter Lantz prods for Univ; *dir:* Alex Lovy; *story:* Ben Hardaway, Milt Schaffer; *anim:* Frank Tipper; *sets:* Fred Brunish; *voices:* Kent Rogers, Mel Blanc; *mus:* Darrell Calker; *prod mgr:* George Hall; *col:* Tech. *sd:* WE. 6 min. • Woody gets a $1.00 loan on his car from a loan-shark wolf who unsuccessfully tries to prize the interest from him after three months.

3854. Local Talent *(Life Cartoon Comedy)* 13 Mar. 1927; *p.c.:* Sherwood

Wadsworth Pictures for Educational; *prod/dir:* John R. McCrory; b&w. *sil.* 5 min. • A wide variety of animals are shown participating in sports events at the county fair, ranging from ducks and skunks to elephants.

3855. Loco Lobo (*Color Rhapsody*) 31 Oct. 1946; *p.c.:* Colum; *prod:* Raymond Katz, Henry Binder; *dir:* Howard Swift; *story:* Cal Howard; *anim:* Grant Simmons, Jay Sarbry; *lay:* Bill Weaver; *back:* Ed Starr; *ed:* Richard S. Jensen; *voices:* Dick Nelson; *mus:* Eddie Kilfeather; *ph:* Frank Fisher; *col:* Tech. *sd:* WE. 6 min. • A wolf chases a rabbit, ending in their both fighting a duel. The rabbit cheats, shooting the wolf in self preservation.

3856. Log Jammed (*Woody Woodpecker*) Apr. 1959; *p.c.:* Walter Lantz prods for Univ; *dir:* Paul J. Smith; *story:* Homer Brightman; *anim:* Robert Bentley, Les Kline, Don Patterson; *sets:* Art Landy, Raymond Jacobs; *voices:* Daws Butler, Grace Stafford; *mus:* Clarence Wheeler; *prod mgr:* William E. Garity; *col:* Tech. *sd:* RCA. 6 min. • Woody vents his wrath on a lumberjack who has chopped down his tree-home.

3857. Log Rollers (*Heckle & Jeckle*) Nov. 1954; *p.c.:* TT for Fox; *dir:* Mannie Davis; *story/voices:* Tom Morrison; *anim:* Jim Tyer; *sets:* Art Bartsch; *mus:* Philip A. Scheib; *col:* Tech. *sd:* RCA. 6 min. • The magpies are intent on building a log cabin on private property.

3858. London Derriere (*Inspector*) 7 Feb. 1968; *p.c.:* Mirisch/Geoffrey/DFE for UA; *dir:* Gerry Chiniquy; *story:* Jim Ryan; *anim:* Don Williams, Manny Gould, Chuck Downs, Bob Matz, Manny Perez; *lay:* Dick Ung; *back:* Tom O'Loughlin; *ed:* Lee Gunther; *voices:* Pat Harrington Jr., Lennie Weinrib; *mus:* Walter Greene; *theme tune:* Henry Mancini; *ph:* John Burton Jr.; *prod sup:* Harry Love, Basil Cox; *col:* DeLuxe. *sd:* RCA. 6 min. • The Inspector trails a notorious criminal to London where he is forced to respect the "No Guns" rule.

3859. The Lone Chipmunks (*Chip'n'Dale*) 26 Feb. 1954; *p.c.:* Walt Disney prods for RKO; *dir:* Jack Kinney; *story:* Dick Kinney, Milt Banta; *anim:* Ed Aardal, George Nicholas, Eric Cleworth, Harry Holt, Ken O'Brien; *fx:* Dan MacManus; *lay:* Thor Putnam, Bruce Bushman; *back:* Dick Anthony; *voices:* Billy Bletcher, Dessie Miller, Norma Swank; *mus:* Oliver Wallace; *col:* Tech. *sd:* RCA. 6 min. • The chipmunks capture a dangerous western bank robber for a rich reward.

3860. The Lone Mountie (*Krazy Kat*) 10 Dec. 1938; *p.c.:* Charles Mintz prods for Colum; *story:* Allen Rose; *anim:* Harry Love, Louie Lilly; *voices:* Mel Blanc, Leone Le Doux; *mus:* Joe de Nat; *prod mgr:* James Bronis; b&w. *sd:* RCA. 6 min. • Krazy enlists in the Mounties to impress his girl and finally catches Yukon Jake, the outlaw.

3861. The Lone Star State (*Screen Song*) 20 Aug. 1948; *p.c.:* Famous for Para; *dir:* I. Sparber; *story:* Larz Bourne; *anim:* Dave Tendlar, Morey Reden; *sets:* Robert Connavale; *voice:* Cal Tinney; *mus:* Winston Sharples; *song:* Don Swandon, June Hershey, Jack Cecil; *prod mgr:* Sam Buchwald; *col:* Tech. *sd:* RCA. 9 min. • The history of the West is explored from the early settlers to the advent of peace with the Texas Rangers.

3862. The Lone Stranger and Porky (*Looney Tunes*) 7 Jan. 1939; *p.c.:* Leon Schlesinger prods for WB; *dir:* Robert Clampett; *anim:* I. Ellis, Robert Cannon; *sets:* Elmer Plummer; *ed:* Tregoweth E. Brown; *voices:* Billy Bletcher, Dave Weber; *mus:* Carl W. Stalling; *prod sup:* Henry Binder, Raymond G. Katz; b&w. *sd:* Vit. 6 min. • The Lone Stranger comes to the rescue when Porky and his stagecoach are held up.

3863. Lonesome Ghosts (*Mickey Mouse*) 29 Nov. 1937; *p.c.:* Walt Disney prods for RKO; *dir:* Burton F. Gillett; *story:* Richard M. Friel, Ted Sears; *anim:* Arthur Babbitt, Clyde Geronimi, Jack Hannah, Dick Huemer, Milton Kahl, I. Klein, Edward Love, Ray Patterson, Robert Wickersham, Dick Williams, Marvin Woodward; *lay:* T. Hee; *voices:* Clarence Nash, Pinto Colvig, Billy Bletcher, Jack Bergman, Don Brodie, Harry Stanton, Walt Disney; *mus:* Albert Hay Malotte; *col:* Tech. *sd:* RCA. 9 min • Some bored ghosts call Mickey's ghost-exterminating service for a bit of excitement. • Reportedly Disney's most expensive short.

3864. Lonesome Lenny (*Screwy Squirrel*) 9 May 1946; *p.c.:* MGM; *dir:* Tex Avery; *story:* Heck Allen; *anim:* Ray Abrams, Preston Blair, Walt Clinton, Ed Love; *character des:* Claude Smith; *sets:* John Didrik Johnsen; *voices:* Wally Maher, Sara Berner; *mus:* Scott Bradley; *prod:* Fred Quimby; *col:* Tech. *sd:* WE. 8 min. • A rich dowager buys a playmate for her dog, Lennie, that turns out to be Screwy Squirrel.

3865. The Lonesome Mouse (*Tom & Jerry*) 22 May 1943; *p.c.:* MGM; *dir:* William Hanna, Joseph Barbera; *anim:* Peter Burness, George Gordon, Kenneth Muse, Jack Zander; *lay:* Harvey Eisenberg; *ed:* Fred MacAlpin; *voices:* Lillian Randolph, Frank Graham; *ph:* Gene Moore; *prod:* Fred Quimby; *col:* Tech. *sd:* WE. 7½ min. • Tom gets thrown out of the house, making Jerry lonesome, so they combine forces to get him reingratiated.

3866. Lonesome Ranger (*Woody Woodpecker*) Feb. 1966; *p.c.:* Walter Lantz prods for Univ; *dir:* Paul J. Smith; *story:* Cal Howard; *anim:* Les Kline, Al Coe; *sets:* Ray Huffine, Art Landy; *voices:* Dal McKennon, Grace Stafford; *mus:* Walter Greene; *prod mgr:* William E. Garity; *col:* Tech. *sd:* RCA. 5½ min. • Woody gives a Forest Ranger the runaround.

3867. The Lonesome Stranger (*MGM Cartoon*) 23 Nov. 1940; *p.c.:* MGM; *prod/dir:* Hugh Harman; *story:* Henry Allen; *character des:* Gus Arriola; *lay:* John Meandor; *back:* Joe Smith; *ed:* Fred MacAlpin; *voices:* Mel Blanc; *mus:* Scott Bradley; *prod mgr:* Fred Quimby; *col:* Tech. *sd:* WE. 9 min. • The Lonesome Stranger is called upon to rid a western town of bandits.

3868. The Long Arm of Law and Order (*Paramount-Bray Pictograph*) 9 Apr. 1916; *p.c.:* Bray prods for Para; *dir:* J.R. Bray; b&w. *sil.* 3 min. • The cartoon segment in this newsreel shows Uncle Sam behind a stone barrier (representing the Mexican border), watching the Mexicans rebelling until he stretches out an arm(y) to grab Pancho Villa and drop him in the garbage can alongside Filipino leader Aguinaldo. This represents General Pershing's march into Mexico following Villa's raid on Columbus in March 1916.

3869. Long-Haired Hare (*Looney Tunes*) 25 June 1949; *p.c.:* WB; *dir:* Charles M. Jones; *story:* Michael Maltese; *anim:* Phil Monroe, Ben Washam, Lloyd Vaughan, Ken Harris; *lay:* Robert Gribbroek; *back:* Peter Alvarado; *ed:* Treg Brown; *voices:* Mel Blanc, Nicolay Shutorev; *mus:* Carl Stalling; *prod mgr:* John W. Burton; *prod:* Edward Selzer; *col:* Tech. *sd:* Vit. 7 min. • Bugs' musical pleasures annoy a fat opera singer who puts an end to it. Bugs retaliates by disrupting his concert at the Hollywood Bowl.

3870. Look Who's Talking Now 5 Nov. 1993; *p.c.:* TriStar Pictures for Colum; *special visual fxl titles anim:* Ron Brinkmann, Adrian Iler, Jerome Chen, Mark Sorell, Andrea Losch, David Douglas, Mike Takayama; *previsualization:* David Worman; *voices: Rocks:* Danny DeVito; *Daphne:* Diane Keaton; *Dog & wolf voices:* Bob Bergen, Peter Iacangelo, Nick Jameson, Patricia Parris, Pat Pinney, Rodney Saulsberry, Jeff Winkless; *col:* Tech. *sd:* Dolby Stereo. 95 min. *l/a.* • Live-action comedy: Glib remarks put into the mouths of youngsters and animals via the medium of animation.

3871. Looney Balloonists (*Scrappy*) 24 Sept. 1936; *p.c.:* Charles Mintz prods for Colum; *story:* Allen Rose; *anim:* Harry Love; *mus:* Joe de Nat; *prod mgr:* James Bronis; b&w. *sd:* RCA. 6 min. • Oopy sabotages Scrappy's hot-air balloon ascension but he wins anyway and Oliver Hardy presents the prize.

3872. Loops and Swoops (*Sad Cat*) 31 Dec. 1968; *p.c.:* TT for Fox; *dir/anim:* Art Bartsch; *col:* DeLuxe. *sd:* RCA. 6 min. • Sad Cat takes to the air in a flying contest. • See: *Sad Cat*

3873. Loopy's Hare Do (*Loopy de Loop*) Dec. 1961; *p.c.:* Hanna-Barbera for Colum; *prod/dir:* Joseph Barbera, William Hanna; *story dir:* Alex Lovy; *story:* Warren Foster; *anim dir:* Charles A. Nichols; *anim:* Bob Carr; *lay:* Walter Clinton; *back:* Art Lozzi; *ed:* Greg Watson; *voices:* Daws Butler, Don Messick; *mus:* Hoyt Curtin; *titles:* Lawrence Gobel; *prod mgr:* Howard Hanson; *col:* East. *sd:* RCA. 6½ min. • Loopy substitutes for a hunting dog who has a cold.

3874. Loose in a Caboose (*Little Lulu*) 23 May 1947; *p.c.:* Famous for Para; *dir:* Seymour Kneitel; *story:* Bill Turner, Larry Riley; *anim:* Myron Waldman, Gordon Whittier, Nick Tafuri, Irving Dressler, Wm. B. Pattengill; *sets:* Robert Connavale; *voices:* Cecil Roy, Jackson Beck, Jack Mercer; *mus:* Winston Sharples; *prod mgr:* Sam Buchwald; *col:* Tech. *sd:* RCA. 7 min. • Lulu loses her train ticket en route and the conductor tries to put her off.

3875. The Loose Nut (*Woody Woodpecker*) 17 Dec. 1945; *p.c.:* Walter Lantz prods for Univ; *dir:* James Culhane; *story:* Ben Hardaway, Milt Schaffer; *anim:* La Verne Harding, Emery Hawkins; *sets:* Terry Lind; *voices:* Nestor Paiva, Lee Sweetland, Ben Hardaway; *mus:* Darrell Calker; *col:*

Tech. *sd:* WE. 6 min. • Woody's frantic golf game disrupts a workman laying fresh cement.

3876. The Lord of the Rings 1978; *p.c.:* Fantasy Films for UA; *prod:* Saul Zaentz; *dir:* Ralph Bakshi; *asst dir:* John Sparey; *story adapt:* Chris Conkling, Peter S. Beagle; *key anim:* Craig Armstrong, Dale Baer, Brenda Banks, Carl Bell, Jesus Cortes, Lillian Evans, Frank Gonzales, Steven Gordon, Sean Joyce, Leonard Robinson, Chrystal Russell, Paul Smith, Irven Spence, Hank Tucker, Edward Wexler, Bruce Woodside, James A. Davis; *anim:* Sam Jaimes, Manny Perez, Joe Roman, Phil Roman, Martin Taras; *asst anim:* Retta Davidson, Charlotte Huffine, Rob la Duca, Terrence Lennon, Edward Newman, Barry Temple; *fx:* Stan Green, Nino Carbe, Christopher Andrew; *lay:* Dale Baer, Louise Zingarelli, Mentor Huebner, David Jonas, Mike Ploog, Kevin Hanna; *back:* Barry Jackson, Johnnie Vita, Marcia Adams, Edwin B. Hirth III, Carol Kieffer; *back asst:* Lou Police, J. Michael Spooner, Ira Turek; *ed:* Donald W. Ernst; *voices: Frodo:* Christopher Guard; *Gandalf:* William Squire; *Samwise:* Michael Scholes; *Aragon "Strider":* John Hurt; *Merry:* Simon Chandler; *Pippin:* Dominic Guard; *Bilbo:* Norman Bird; *Boromir:* Michael Graham-Cox; *Legolas:* Anthony Daniels; *Gimli:* David Buck; *Sméagol "Gollum":* Peter Woodthorpe; *Saruman:* Fraser Kerr; *Theoden;* Philip Stone; *Wormtongue:* Michael Deacon; *Elrond:* André Morell; *Innkeeper:* Alan Tilven; *Galadriel:* Annette Crosbie; *Treebeard:* John Westbrook; *mus:* Leonard Roseman; *orch:* Ralph Ferraro; *song:* "Mirthrandir" by Leonard Roseman and Mark Fleischer; *ink & special fx:* Mary Jane Cole, Ann Hamilton, Linda Pearce, Emaline Seutter, Karin Stover; *i&p:* Janet Cummings, Vince Gutierrez, Lee Guttman, Lisa Kshatriya, Sally Reymond, Nelda Ridley, Ruth Thompson, Micki Zurcher; *col models:* Janet Cummings; *cel reproductions:* Edgar Gutierrez; *titles:* Wayne Fitzgerald; *sd ed:* Peter Kirby; *sd fx:* Sam Shaw Enterprises; *Kaleidoscope fx:* Symmetricon; *re-recording:* Bill Varney, Bob Minkler, Bill Mumford; *ph:* Timothy Galfas, Nick Vasu Inc., R&BEFX & Animation, Hogan-Lee Images; *optical fx:* Optical House; *prod sup:* Jacqueline Roettcher, Daniel Pia, Mark Bakshi, Martin Cohen, Christine L. Danzo, Jacquelyn Herst, Cathy Rose, Michael Takamoto; *col:* DeLuxe. *sd.* Dolby Stereo. 133 min. • One and one-half of J.R.R. Tolkien's trilogy of books brought to the animated screen telling the saga of the different Middle Earth races competing for the posession of the power of the Rings. A promised sequel never materialized.

3877. The Lorelei *(Paul Terry-Toon)* 29 Nov. 1931; *p.c.:* Terry, Moser & Coffman for Educational/Fox; *dir:* Frank Moser, Paul Terry; *anim:* Arthur Babbitt, Ferdinand Huszti Horvath, Frank Moser, Connie Rasinski, Jerry Shields, Vladimir Tytla *mus:* Philip A. Scheib; b&w. *sd:* WE. 5½ min. • A mouse in a rowboat is vamped by a sea siren and goes through a hectic adventure in a storm while a German quartet sing "Lorelei."

3878. Lost and Foundling *(Merrie Melodies)* 30 Sept. 1944; *p.c.:* Leon Schlesinger prods for WB; *dir:* Charles M. Jones; *story:* Tedd Pierce; *anim:* Ben Washam; *lay:* Art Heinemann; *ed:* Treg Brown; *voices:* Marjorie Tarlton, Mel Blanc; *mus:* Carl W. Stalling; *prod sup:* Henry Binder, Raymond G. Katz; *col:* Tech. *sd:* Vit. 7 min. • Sniffles accidentally hatches an egg and rears what turns out to be a hawk that eats rodents.

3879. Lost and Foundry *(Popeye)* 16 July 1937; *p.c.:* The Fleischer Studio for Para; *prod:* Max Fleischer; *dir:* Dave Fleischer; *anim:* Seymour Kneitel, Abner Matthews; *voices:* Jack Mercer, Mae Questel; *mus:* Sammy Timberg; b&w. *sd:* WE. 7 min. • Popeye has to rescue little Swee'Pea, who has crawled into a factory and started the mechanism working.

3880. The Lost Chick *(Happy Harmonies)* 8 Mar. 1935; *p.c.:* MGM; *prod/dir:* Hugh Harman, Rudolf Ising; *voices:* Elmore Vincent; *mus:* Scott Bradley; *col:* Tech-2. *sd:* RCA. 10 min. • An unhatched egg rolls away from mother hen and is collected by two squirrels in mistake for a large acorn.

3881. The Lost Dream *(Noveltoon)* 18 Mar. 1949; *p.c.:* Famous for Para; *dir:* Bill Tytla; *story:* Steve Muffatti, Bill Turner, Larz Bourne; *anim:* George Germanetti, Harvey Patterson; *sets:* Shane Miller; *voices:* Mae Questel, Cecil Roy; *mus:* Winston Sharples; *prod mgr:* Sam Buchwald; *col:* Tech. *sd:* RCA. 7 min. • Audrey is addicted to moonlight reading and is warned that she will have bad dreams. She soon finds herself in a dreamland nightmare.

3882. Lost in Space 3 Apr. 1998; *p.c.:* Prelude Pictures/Irwin Allen Prods for New Line Prods., Inc.; *special visual fx anim:* Passion Pictures: *prod:* Hugo Sands; *anim sup:* Dan Sumich, Kevin Spruce; *co-ord:* Marilyn Collis, Felix Joyce; *anim:* Jonathan Webber, Darren Vandenburg, Mark Broecking, Clark Irving, Simon Tofield; *Uli Meyer Studios: anim sup:* Uli Meyer; *prod:* Julie Pye; *character anim:* Dean Roberts, Michael Schlingmann, Andreas von Andrian, Vladimir Todorov, Stuart Evans; *fx sup:* Simon Leech; *fx anim:* Barry Goff; *AMGFX: anim:* Simon Percy, Nick Webber, Andrew Morgan; *col:* DeLuxe. *sd:* Dolby digital. Panavision. 129 min. *l/a.* • Live-action interpretation of the 1960s television show: A space family find themselves marooned on an unknown planet. Animation heightens a spaceship battle, spiders, alien creatures, etc.

3883. The Lost World 1925; *p.c.:* First National for Edison; *anim dir:* Willis O'Brien; *model maker:* Marcel Delgado; *prod:* Earl Hudson; *l/a dir:* Harry Hoyt; b&w. sil. 110 min. *l/a/anim.* • Sir Arthur Conan Doyle's tale about a party who discover a prehistoric world of dinosaurs and Neanderthals.

3884. The Lost World 1960; *p.c.:* Saratoga for Fox; *anim dir:* Willis O'Brien; *l/a prod/dir:* Irwin Allen; *col:* DeLuxe. *sd.* 97 min. CS. • Adaptation of Conan Doyle's story about the discovery of a prehistoric world.

3885. The Lost World: Jurassic Park 19 May 1997; *p.c.:* Amblin Entertainment for Univ; *based on The Lost World* by Michael Crichton; *full-motion dinosaurs:* Dennis Muren; *special dinosaur fx:* Michael Lantieri; *Dinosaur motion sup:* Randal M. Dutra; *visual fx prod:* Ned Gorman; *display graphics sup:* Todd Aron Marks; *cg des:* Alex Mann; *special visual fx:* Industrial Light & Magic; *cg sup:* Kevin Rafferty; *cg sequence sup:* Erik Mattson, Ben Snow; *cg development sup:* Euan MacDonald; *lead digital character anim:* Danny Gordon Taylor, Doug E. Smith, Miguel A. Fuertes, Daniel Jeannette; *asso fx sup:* Rick Schulze; *digital character anim:* George Aleco-Sima, Chris Armstrong, Linda M. Bel, Patrick Bonneau, David Byers Brown, Ken Bryan, Sue Campbell, Bruce Dahl, Peter Daulton, Lou Dellarosa, Michael Eames, Hal T, Hickel, Jason Ivimey, Paul Kavanagh, Heather Knight, Victoria Livingstone, Julie Nelson, Dana O'Connor, Mark Powers, Magali Rigaudias, Chi Chung Tse, Tim Waddy, Brad Woods, William R. Wright; *digital fx art:* Kevin Barnhill, Michael Bauer, Michael di Como, Christina Hill, Samir Hoon, Ed Kramer, Tom Martinek, Curt I. Miyashiro, Min, Kenneth J. Nielsen, Patrick Neary, Khatsho John Orfali, David Parrish, Bruce Powell, Amanda Ronai-Dahle, Corey Rosen, Frederic Schmidt, Durant B. Schoon, Jeff Shank, Doug Sutton, Christopher Townsend, John Walker, Andy Wang, Howie Weed, R. Christopher White; *special model sup:* Paul Giacoppo; *compositing sups:* Pablo Helman, Jon Alexander; *visual art dir:* George Hull; *lead view painter:* Susan Ross; *lead matchmover:* Terry Chostner; *lead roto art:* Jack Monogovan; *location matchmover:* Jack "Edsel" Haye; *sabre art:* Caitlin Content, Grant McGlasham; *digital compositors:* Tim Alexander, Jeff Doran, Mary McCulloch; *view paint:* Donna Ashley Beard, Catherine Craig; *visual fx ed:* Michael Gleason; *fx co-ord:* Vicki L. Engel, Megan I. Carlson; *matchmove art:* Selwyn Body III, David Hanks, Randy Jonsson, Jodie Maier, David Manos Morris; *rotoscope art:* Christine Cram, Kate Elsen, Debbie le Fought, Susan Goldsmith, Scott Charles Stewart, Michael van Eps, Susan McWeeks; *digital timing sup:* Kenneth Smith; *digital Matte art:* Paul Huston; *scan operator:* Randall K. Dean, Michael Ellis; *cg resource asst:* Kimberly Lashbrook; *neg line-up:* Andrea Biklian; *digital plate restoration:* Melissa Monterrosa; *visual fx ed:* Greg Hyman; *projectionist:* Kenn Moynihan; *software development:* Carey Phillips, Jim Hourihan, Rod G. Bogart; *video engineer:* Dana Barks; *computer system engineering:* Ken Byer, Greg Dunn; *mechanical fx:* Geoff Heron; *visual fx ph:* Vance Piper; *cg technical asst:* Paul Vega, Jennifer Maryam Nona, Michael Corcoran; *cg staff:* Barry Armour, Cliff Plumer, Ken Maruyama; *mus:* John Williams; *col:* DeLuxe. *sd:* Skywalker Sound/dts. Panavision. *l/a.* • Live-action adventure sequel: A group of scientists return to the dinosaur island to prevent poachers from killing the dinosaurs. First of two follow-ups to the original *Jurassic Park.*

3886. Lotsa Luck *(Woody Woodpecker);* rel; Jan. 1968; *p.c.:* Walter Lantz prods for Univ; *dir:* Paul J. Smith; *story:* Cal Howard; *anim:* Al Coe, Les Kline; *sets:* Ray Huffine; *voices:* Dal McKennon, Grace Stafford; *mus:* Walter Greene; *prod mgr:* William E. Garity; *col:* Tech. *sd:* RCA. 5½ min. • Woody finds a good luck omen in a three-leaf clover. He foils Dirty McNasty's bank robbery and when McNasty steals the clover, Woody tries to retrieve it from him.

3887. Louvre Come Back to Me! *(Looney Tunes)* 18 Aug. 1962; *p.c.:* WB; *dir:* Chuck Jones; *asst dir:* Maurice Noble; *story:* John Dunn; *anim:*

Richard Thompson, Bob Bransford, Tom Ray, Ken Harris; *back:* Tom O'Loughlin, Philip de Guard; *ed:* Treg Brown; *voices:* Mel Blanc, Julie Bennett; *mus:* Milt Franklyn; *prod mgr:* William Orcutt; *prod:* David H. DePatie; *col:* Tech. *sd:* Vit. 7 min. • Pepé le Pew searches for his girl against a setting of Paris' Louvre Museum.

3888. Love and Curses *(Merrie Melodies)* 9 July 1938; *p.c.:* Leon Schlesinger prods for WB; *dir:* Ben Hardaway, Cal Dalton; *story:* Melvin Millar; *anim:* Herman Cohen; *lay:* Griff Jay; *back:* Arthur Loomer; *ed:* Tregoweth E. Brown; *voices:* Elmore Vincent, Mel Blanc, The Sportsmen Quartet; *mus:* Carl W. Stalling; *prod sup:* Henry Binder, Raymond G. Katz; *col:* Tech. *sd:* Vit. 7 min. • A melodrama featuring Roger St.Claire, a cloaked villain, kidnapping Emily and the hero dashing to her rescue.

3889. Love and Hisses *(Blue Racer)* 3 Aug. 1972; *p.c.:* Mirisch/DFE for UA; *dir:* Gerry Chiniquy; *story:* John W. Dunn; *anim:* Robert Taylor, Manny Gould, Warren Batchelder, Don Williams; *lay:* Dick Ung; *back:* Richard H. Thomas; *ed:* Joe Siracusa; *voices:* Larry D. Mann, Tom Holland; *mus:* Doug Goodwin; *ph:* John Burton Jr.; *prod sup:* Stan Paperny, Harry Love; *col:* DeLuxe. *sd:* RCA. 6 min. • The Japanese Beetle befriends an elephant who comes to his aid when attacked by The Racer.

3890. Love at First Sight *(Aesop's Film Fable)* 11 Apr. 1922; *p.c.:* Fables Pictures Inc for Pathé; *dir:* Paul Terry; *b&w. sil.* 5 min. • Thomas Cat, a Spanish troubadour, serenades Fannie Kitten whose mother objects and calls a cop. That evening an elopement takes place resulting in the happy couple living happily ever after. Moral: "Love will find a way."

3891. Love Comes to Magoo *(Mr. Magoo)* 2 Oct. 1958; *p.c.:* UPA for Colum; *ex prod:* Stephen Bosustow; *dir:* Tom McDonald; *story:* Dick Kinney, Dick Shaw, Pete Burness; *anim:* Ed Friedman, Barney Posner, Stan Wilkins; *lay:* Robert Dranko; *back:* Bob McIntosh; *voices:* Jim Backus, Daws Butler, Nancy Wible; *col:* Tech. *sd:* RCA. 6 min. • A confidence trickster gets his moll to pose as Magoo's high school girlfriend in order to obtain money from him. Magoo takes her to where he believes to be Coney Island for a fun time.

3892. Love in a Cottage *(Aesop's Film Fable)* 1 Sept. 1923; *p.c.:* Fables Studio Inc for Pathé; *dir:* Paul Terry; *b&w. sil.* 5 min. • The marital affairs of a couple of cats. Wifey's biscuits upset the household and when hubby returns, he discovers he has been presented with a new family.

3893. Love in a Cottage *(Terry-Toon)* 28 July 1940; *p.c.:* TT for Fox; *dir:* Volney White; *story:* John Foster; *mus:* Philip A. Scheib; *col:* Tech. *sd:* RCA. 6 min. • The bittersweet story of two newlywed birds.

3894. Love in a Pond *(Aesop's Sound Fable)* 17 Aug. 1931; *p.c.:* Van Beuren for RKO/Pathé; *dir:* John Foster, Mannie Davis; *mus:* Gene Rodemich; *b&w. sd:* RCA. 8 min. • A frog pursues his lady love, eventually marrying her with the pond inhabitants joining in the festivities.

3895. Love Is Blind *(Terry-Toon)* May 1957; *p.c.:* TT for Fox; *dir:* Mannie Davis; *story:* Tom Morrison; *anim:* Jim Tyer; *mus:* Philip A. Scheib; *ph:* Douglas Moye; *col:* Tech. *sd:* RCA. 6 min. • A friendless hippo befriends a near-sighted mole, eventually saving his newfound friend from a pack of hungry weasels.

3896. Love Krazy *(Krazy Kat)* 30 Jan. 1932; *p.c.:* Winkler for Colum; *prod:* Charles B. Mintz; *story:* Manny Gould; *anim:* Allen Rose, Jack Carr; *voice:* Jack Carr; *mus:* Joe de Nat; *prod mgr:* James Bronis; *b&w. sd:* WE. 6 min. • A hippo falls for Krazy and reduces weight to attract him. Krazy refuses to respond.

3897. Love Me, Love My Mouse *(Tom & Jerry)* 1966; *p.c.:* MGM; *prod:* Chuck Jones; *dir:* Chuck Jones, Ben Washam; *story:* Michael Maltese; *anim:* Ben Washam, Philip Roman, Don Towsley, Dick Thompson; *des:* Maurice Noble; *lay:* Robert Givens; *back:* Robert Inman; *voices:* June Foray, Mel Blanc; *mus:* Eugene Poddany; *prod mgr:* Les Goldman; *col:* Metro. *sd:* WE. 6 min. • Tom presents Jerry to his girl who proceeds to protect the rodent from Tom's bullying.

3898. The Love Nest *(Aesop's Film Fable)* 17 July 1927; *p.c.:* Fables Pictures Inc for Pathé; *dir:* Paul Terry; *b&w. sil.* 10 min. • A boastful dog decides to return home after a long absence and sends the cat to pacify his irate spouse. They both are ousted and have to sleep in the park.

3899. Love That Pup *(Tom & Jerry)* 1 Oct. 1949; *p.c.:* MGM; *dir:* William Hanna, Joseph Barbera; *anim:* Ed Barge, Irven Spence, Kenneth Muse; *lay:* Dick Bickenbach; *back:* Robert Gentle; *ed:* FredMacAlpin; *voice:*

Daws Butler; *mus:* Scott Brasdley; *prod:* Fred Quimby; *col:* Tech. *sd:* WE. 7 min. • Tom disrupts Spike and Tyke's slumber.

3900. Love Thy Neighbor *(Screen Songs)* 29 July 1934; *p.c.:* The Fleischer Studio for Para; *prod:* Max Fleischer; *dir:* Dave Fleischer; *anim:* Myron Waldman, Edward Nolan, Lillian Friedman; *mus:* Art Turkisher; *song:* Mack Gordon, Harry Revel; *l/a:* Mary Small; *b&w. sd:* WE. 7½ min. *l/a/anim.* • Nosey Newsreel depicts "the hottest day" and some wrestling before Mary Small sings.

3901. Lovelorn Leghorn *(Looney Tunes)* 8 Sept. 1951; *p.c.:* WB; *dir:* Robert McKimson; *story:* Tedd Pierce; *anim:* Phil de Lara, Charles McKimson, Rod Scribner, Emery Hawkins; *lay:* Cornett Wood; *back:* Richard H. Thomas; *ed:* Treg Brown; *voices:* Mel Blanc, Bea Benaderet; *mus:* Eugene Poddany, Milt Franklyn; *prod mgr:* John W. Burton; *prod:* Edward Selzer; *col:* Tech. *sd:* Vit. 7 min. • Miss Prissy, the "old maid" hen, sets out to snag a husband and Foggy points her in the general direction of the dog. A musician's strike forced Carl Stalling to bow out of this one.

3902. Love's Labor Won *(Aesop's Sound Fable)* 10 Mar. 1933; *p.c.:* Van Beuren for RKO; *dir:* John Foster, Mannie Davis; *mus:* Gene Rodemich; *b&w. sd:* RCA. 6½ min. • Cubby Bear and his girl meet with many obstacles when trying to be on their own.

3903. Love's Labor Won *(Mighty Mouse)* Aug. 1948; *p.c.:* TT for Fox; *dir:* Mannie Davis; *story:* John Foster; *anim:* Jim Tyer; *voices:* Roy Halee, Tom Morrison; *mus:* Philip A. Scheib; *ph:* Douglas Moye; *col:* Tech. *sd:* RCA. 6 min. • Oil Can Harry abducts Pearl Pureheart in the old West and Mighty Mouse corrects matters.

3904. Lovesick *(Oswald)* 4 Oct. 1937; *p.c.:* Univ; *prod/dir:* Walter Lantz; *story:* Victor McLeod, Win Smith; *sets:* Edgar Keichle; *mus:* George Lessner; *orch:* Nathaniel Shilkret; *b&w. sd:* WE. 7 min. • An X-Ray reveals Doxie the dachshund is suffering from a pierced heart for Fifi the French poodle. He is cured upon finding Fifi is espoused to a massive bulldog.

3905. Loyal Royalty *(Hashimoto)* May 1962; *p.c.:* TT for Fox; *ex prod:* Bill Weiss; *dir/story:* Bob Kuwahara; *story sup:* Tom Morrison; *sets:* Bill Focht, John Zago; *voices:* John Myhers; *mus:* Philip Scheib; *prod mgr:* Frank Schudde; *col:* DeLuxe. *sd:* RCA. 6 min. CS. • No story available.

3906. Lucky Dog *(Terry-Toon)* May 1956; *p.c.:* TT for Fox; *dir:* Connie Rasinski; *story/voice:* Tom Morrison; *anim:* Mannie Davis, Jim Tyer, Carlo Vinci; *sets:* Art Bartsch; *mus:* Philip A. Scheib; *ph:* Doug Moye; *col:* Tech. *sd:* RCA. 6 min. CS. • Jealous of the star treatment his wife's dog receives, a man mixes a concoction that turns him into a dog.

3907. The Lucky Duck *(Dinky Duck)* 6 Sept. 1940; *p.c.:* TT for Fox; *dir:* Connie Rasinski; *story:* John Foster; *mus:* Philip A. Scheib; *col:* Tech. *sd:* RCA. 6 min. • No story available.

3908. Lucky Ducky 9 Oct. 1948; *p.c.:* MGM; *dir:* Tex Avery; *story:* Rich Hogan; *anim:* Walter Clinton, Preston Blair, Louis Schmitt, Grant Simmons; *character des:* Louis Schmitt; *sets:* John Didrik Johnsen; *mus:* Scott Bradley; *prod:* Fred Quimby; *col:* Tech. *sd:* WE. 7 min. • Two duck hunting hounds have trouble with an obnoxious duck who refuses to be shot.

3909. Lucky Lulu *(Little Lulu)* 30 June 1944; *p.c.:* Famous for Para; *dir:* Seymour Kneitel; *story:* Carl Meyer; *anim:* Graham Place, Abner Kneitel, Gordon Sheehan; *sets:* Robert Connavale; *voices:* Cecil Roy; *mus:* Winston Sharples; *title song:* Buddy Kaye, Fred Wise, Sammy Timberg; *ph:* Leonard McCormick; *prod mgr:* Sam Buchwald; *col:* Tech. *sd:* RCA. 6 min. • Lulu tries to change her luck with a magnetized horseshoe on Friday the 13th.

3910. Lucky Number *(Donald Duck)* 20 July 1951; *p.c.:* Walt Disney prods for RKO; *dir:* Jack Hannah; *story:* Nick George, Bill Berg; *anim:* Bill Justice, Bob Carlson, Volus Jones, George Kreisl; *fx:* Blaine Gibson, Jack Boyd; *lay:* Yale Gracey; *back:* Thelma Witmer; *voices:* Clarence Nash, Ted Meyers, Bob Jackman; *mus:* Paul Smith; *col:* Tech. *sd:* RCA. 7 min. • Don's nephews leave their job at his garage to collect a surprise sports car he has won. When they return with the car he thinks it's just another of their tricks and deals accordingly.

3911. Lucky Pigs *(Color Rhapsody)* 26 May 1939; *p.c.:* Charles Mintz prods for Colum; *dir:* Ben Harrison; *anim:* Manny Gould; *sets:* Phil Davis; *ed:* George Winkler; *i&p:* Christine Phiederman; *voices:* Alvia Allman, Dave Weber, Mel Blanc; *mus:* Joe de Nat; *prod mgr:* James Bronis; *col:*

Tech. *sd:* RCA. 7 min. • The Pig family win the sweepstake and try to improve their lifestyle. After tax, all that's left is their piggy-bank.

3912. Lucky Pink (*Pink Panther*) 7 May 1968; *p.c.:* Mirisch/Geoffrey/ DFE for UA; *dir:* Hawley Pratt; *story:* Bob Ogle; *anim:* Tom Ray, Manny Gould, Manny Perez, Warren Batchelder, Don Williams; *lay:* Dick Ung; *back:* Tom O'Loughlin; *ed:* Allan Potter; *mus:* Walter Greene; *theme tune:* Henry Mancini; *ph:* John Burton Jr.; *prod sup:* Harry Love, David DeTiege; *col:* Deluxe. *sd:* RCA. 6 min. • A burglar tries to rid himself of an unlucky horseshoe but the Panther keeps returning it.

3913. Lullaby Land (*Silly Symphony*) 18 Aug. 1933; *p.c.:* Walt Disney prods for UA; *dir:* Wilfred Jackson; *anim:* Arthur Babbitt, Dick Huemor, Bob Karp, Hamilton S. Luske, Richard Lundy, Leonard Sebring, Ben Sharpsteen, Roy Williams; *mus:* Frank E. Churchill, Leigh Harline; *col:* Tech. *sd:* RCA. 7 min. • A toddler's adventures in Dreamland with his toy dog.

3914. Lulu at the Zoo (*Little Lulu*) 17 Nov. 1944; *p.c.:* Famous for Para; *dir:* I. Sparber; *story:* Seymour Kneitel; *anim:* Nick Tafuri, Tom Golden, Gordon Whittier, John Walworth; *sets:* Robert Connavale; *voices:* Cecil Roy, Jackson Beck; *mus:* Sammy Timberg; *title song:* Buddy Kaye, Fred Wise, Sammy Timberg; *ph:* Leonard McCormick; *prod mgr:* Sam Buchwald; *col:* Tech. *sd:* RCA. 9 min. • Lulu tries to feed the animals against the Zoo-keeper's wishes.

3915. Lulu Gets the Birdie (*Little Lulu*) 31 Mar. 1944; *p.c.:* Famous for Para; *dir:* I. Sparber; *story:* Carl Meyer; *anim:* Dave Tendlar, John Walworth, Morey Reden, John Gentilella; *voices:* Cecil Roy; *mus:* Sammy Timberg; *song:* Fred Wise, Sidney Lippman, Buddy Kaye; *title song:* Buddy Kaye, Fred Wise, Sammy Timberg; *ph:* Leonard McCormick; *prod mgr:* Sam Buchwald; *col:* Tech. *sd:* RCA. 8 min. • Lulu sets out to find the "Little Bird" that informed Mandy of her mischief making.

3916. Lulu in Hollywood (*Little Lulu*) 19 May 1944; *p.c.:* Famous for Para; *dir:* I. Sparber; *story:* Joe Stultz, Dana Coty; *anim:* Nick Tafuri, Tom Golden, Joe Oriolo, John Walworth; *sets:* Anton Loeb; *voice:* Cecil Roy; *mus:* Sammy Timberg; *title song:* Buddy Kaye, Fred Wise, Sammy Timberg; *ph:* Leonard McCormick; *prod mgr:* Sam Buchwald; *col:* Tech. *sd:* RCA. 7 min. • Lulu is groomed for stardom to appear in her own movie.

3917. Lulu's Birthday Party (*Little Lulu*) 29 Dec. 1944; *p.c.:* Famous for Para; *dir:* I. Sparber; *story:* Bill Turner, Otto Messmer; *anim:* Dave Tendlar, Morey Reden, Joe Oriolo, John Gentilella; *sets:* Robert Little; *voices:* Cecil Roy; *mus:* Sammy Timberg; *title song:* Buddy Kaye, Fred Wise, Sammy Timberg; *ph:* Leonard McCormick; *prod mgr:* Sam Buchwald; *col:* Tech. *sd:* RCA. 7½ min. • Lulu aggravates Mandy with her pet frog then has an elaborate dream about her birthday party.

3918. Lulu's Indoor Outing (*Little Lulu*) 29 Sept. 1944; *p.c.:* Famous for Para; *dir:* I. Sparber; *story:* Carl Meyer, Joe Stultz; *anim:* Nick Tafuri, Tom Golden, John Walworth, Gordon Whittier; *sets:* Anton Loeb; *voices:* Cecil Roy, Sid Raymond, Carl Meyer; *mus:* Winston Sharples; *title song:* Buddy Kaye, Fred Wise, Sammy Timberg; *ph:* Leonard McCormick; *prod mgr:* Sam Buchwald; *col:* Tech. *sd:* RCA. 7 min. • Lulu and Mandy's picnic is ruined by rain and they have to move into a deserted house where hungry ghosts are lurking.

3919. The Lumber Camp (*Meany Miny Mo*) 15 Mar. 1937; *p.c.:* Univ; *prod:* Walter Lantz; *dir:* Manuel Moreno; *story:* Walter Lantz, Victor McLeod; *anim:* Manuel Moreno, Lester Kline, Fred Kopietz; *mus:* James Dietrich; b&w. *sd:* WE. 7 min. • The three monkeys are in the Northwoods where Mo, the cook, tangles with a big bird.

3920. The Lumber Champ (*Pooch the Pup*) 13 Mar. 1933; *p.c.:* Univ; *dir:* Walter Lantz; *anim:* Manuel Moreno, Lester Kline, Fred Kopietz, Charles Hastings; *mus:* James Dietrich; b&w. *sd:* WE. 7 min. • A slave-driving lumberjack whips his crew into action and Pooch, assisted by the trees, comes to the rescue of a girl tied to the railroad tracks.

3921. Lumber Jack-Rabbit (*Looney Tunes*) 13 Nov. 1954; *p.c.:* WB; *dir:* Charles M. Jones; *story:* Michael Maltese; *anim:* Ben Washam, Lloyd Vaughan, Richard Thompson, Abe Levitow, Ken Harris; *lay:* Maurice Noble; *back:* Philip de Guard; *ed:* Treg Brown; *voices:* Mel Blanc, Norman Nesbitt; *mus:* Carl Stalling; *prod mgr:* John W. Burton; *prod:* Edward Selzer; *col:* Tech. *sd:* Vit. 7 min. • Bugs pits his wits against Paul Bunyan's giant-sized dog when he tries to raid a monumental carrot patch. Originally made for 3-D.

3922. Lumber Jacks (*Aesop's Film Fable*) 3 Dec. 1924; *p.c.:* Fables Pictures Inc for Pathé; *dir:* Paul Terry; b&w. sil. 5 min. • The mice and cats are engaged in felling trees and transporting them via the chute to the river.

3923. Lumber Jerks (*Looney Tunes*) 25 June 1955; *p.c.:* WB; *dir:* I. Freleng; *story:* Warren Foster; *anim:* Arthur Davis, Virgil Ross, Manuel Perez; *fx:* Harry Love; *lay:* Hawley Pratt; *back:* Richard H. Thomas; *ed:* Treg Brown; *voices:* Mel Blanc, Stan Freberg; *mus:* Milt Franklyn; *prod mgr:* John W. Burton; *prod:* Edward Selzer; *col:* Tech. *sd:* Vit. 7 min. • The Goofy Gophers find a tree to live in but before they can take posession, it's taken to the sawmill and made into furniture.

3924. The Lumberjack (*Oswald*) 25 Feb. 1929; *p.c.:* Winkler for Univ; *anim:* Ben Clopton; b&w. sil. 6 min. • Lumberjack Oswald chops a tree and discovers a bag of gold hidden inside. A villainous bear grabs it and a chase over water ensues.

3925. Lumberjacks and Jill (*Popeye*) 27 Mar. 1949; *p.c.:* Famous for Para; *dir:* Seymour Kneitel; *story:* Carl Meyer, Jack Mercer; *anim:* Tom Johnson, George Rufle; *sets:* Tom Ford; *voices:* Jack Mercer, Jackson Beck, Mae Questel; *mus:* Winston Sharples; *ph:* Leonard McCormick; *prod mgr:* Sam Buchwald; *col:* Tech. *sd:* RCA. 6 min. • Lumberjacks, Popeye and Bluto are enraptured by the arrival of their new camp cook, Olive Oyl.

3926. The Lunch Hound (*Hot Dog*) 8 Apr. 1927; *p.c.:* Bray prods for FBO; *dir/anim:* Walt Lantz, Clyde Geronimi; *l/a ph:* Harry Squires; b&w. sil. 6 min. *l/a/anim.* • The cook has quit, so Walter and Pete have to cook their own dinner.

3927. Lunch with a Punch (*Popeye*) 14 Apr. 1952; *p.c.:* Famous for Para; *dir:* I. Sparber; *story:* Carl Meyer, Jack Mercer; *anim:* Al Eugster, George Germanetti; *sets:* Tom Ford; *voices:* Jack Mercer, Jackson Beck, Mae Questel; *mus:* Winston Sharples; *ph:* Leonard McCormick; *prod mgr:* Seymour Shultz; *col:* Tech. *sd:* RCA. 6 min. • Popeye explains the values of spinach to his nephews by telling of his childhood with Bluto, still the antagonist.

3928. Lunyland Pictures 1914; *p.c.:* Bray prods for Univ; *dir/anim:* Leighton Budd; b&w. sil. 3 min. • Newspaper cartoonist, Leighton's Budd's first animated film. No story available.

3929. Luxo Jr. 1986; *p.c.:* PIXAR; *story/des/models/anim:* John Lasseter; *anim software/models/rendering:* Eben Ostby; *models/rendering:* Bill Reeves; *rendering:* Sam Leffler; *laser scanning:* Don Conway; *addit modelling:* Paul Heckbert; *sd:* Gary Rydstrom, Sprocket Systems; *post prod co-ord:* Craig Gojo; *computing:* PIXAR, CSRG (*UC Berkeley*), Okeefe (*Manet*); *col. sd.* 2 min. *Academy Award nomination.* • A boisterous table lamp's playing gets too rough with a ball and bursts it. He soon returns with a larger ball to play with. The first fully computer-animated film.

3930. The Lyin' Hunter (*Krazy Kat*) 12 Feb. 1937; *p.c.:* Charles Mintz prods for Colum; *story:* Allen Rose; *anim:* Harry Love; *mus:* Joe de Nat; *prod mgr:* James Bronis; b&w. *sd:* RCA. 6 min. • Krazy takes the kids to the zoo, regaling them with a yarn about being a lion tamer. Then a real lion escapes!

3931. The Lyin' Lion (*Terry-Toon*) 30 May 1949; *p.c.:* TT for Fox; *dir:* Connie Rasinski; *story:* John Foster; *anim:* Jim Tyer; *sets:* Art Bartsch; *voices:* Sid Raymond, Thomas Morrison; *mus:* Philip A. Scheib; *ph:* Douglas Moye; *col:* Tech. *sd:* RCA. 6 min. • Looey the Great, a circus lion, is fired from his balancing act. He almost succeeds with a high-wire act but this time the ringmaster really does "fire" him.

3932. The Lyin' Mouse (*Merrie Melodies*) 16 Oct. 1937; *p.c.:* Leon Schlesinger prods for WB; *dir:* I. Freleng; *story:* Ted Pierce; *anim:* K.R. (Ken) Harris; *lay:* Griff Jay; *back:* Arthur Loomer; *ed:* Tregoweth E. Brown; *voices:* Bernice Hansel, Mel Blanc, Billy Bletcher; *mus:* Carl W. Stalling; *ph:* John W. Burton; *prod sup:* Henry Binder, Raymond G. Katz; *col:* Tech. *sd:* Vit. 7 min. • A mouse, caught in a trap, convinces the cat to let him go by spinning a tall yarn about how he once rescued a lion from captivity.

3933. M-in-A Cartoons *p.c.:* M-in-A Films; *prod:* David S. Horsley; *anim:* Harry Palmer. • *1915:* The Siege of Liege 9 Jan. **Great Americans** 6 Feb. **The Dove of Peace** 6 Mar. **Doctor Monko** 29 May. • No stories available.

3934. Macabre 1957; *p.c.:* Allied Artists; *prod/dir:* William Castle; *ph fx/title des:* Jack Rabin, Louie de Witt, Irving Block; b&w. *sd.* • Thriller with jokey end credits caricaturing cast members in a funeral procession.

3935. MacDono Cartoons Inc *p.c.:* Mastodon Films, Inc. (President: C.C. Burr) for Affiliated; *prod/dir:* J.J. McManus, R.E. Donahue; b&w. sil. • *1921:* Mr. Ima Jonah's Home Brew 4 June. **Skipping the Pen** 4 June. • *1922:* **Burr's Novelty Review #1** 1 Mar. **Burr's Novelty Review #2** 1 Apr. **Burr's Novelty Review #3** 1 May. **Burr's Novelty Review #4** 1 June. **Burr's Novelty Review #5** 1 July. **Burr's Novelty Review #6** 1 Aug.

3936. Mackeral Moocher *(Chilly Willy)* 10 Apr. 1962; *p.c.:* Walter Lantz prods for Univ; *dir:* Jack Hannah; *story:* Bill Danch; *anim:* Don Lusk, Roy Jenkins; *sets:* Ray Huffine, Art Landy; *mus:* Eugene Poddany; *prod mgr:* William E. Garity; *col:* Tech. *sd:* RCA. 6 min. *l/a/anim.* • Chilly gets even when a pelican filches all the fish he catches.

3937. Mad About Music 11 Mar. 1938; *p.c.:* Univ; *fx:* Len Lye; b&w. *sd:* WE 78 min. *l/a/anim.* • Live-action musical about two movie producers who buy up options on a new color process. Effects by Lye include a rocket trip to Saturn and the trial of a modern composer by ghosts of past musicians.

3938. Mad as a Mars Hare *(Merrie Melodies)* Oct. 1963; *p.c.:* WB; *dir:* Chuck Jones; *asst dir:* Maurice Noble; *story:* John Dunn; *anim:* Ken Harris, Richard Thompson, Bob Bransford, Tom Ray; *fx:* Harry Love; *back:* Bob Singer; *ed:* Treg Brown; *voices:* Mel Blanc; *mus:* Bill Lava; *prod mgr:* William Orcutt; *prod:* David H. DePatie; *col:* Tech. *sd:* Vit. 7 min. • The Martian is observing the flora and fauna of Earth when a rocket ship containing Bugs lands. The natural course is to get rid of the intergalactic intruder.

3939. The Mad Doctor *(Mickey Mouse)* 4 Jan. 1933; *p.c.:* Walt Disney prods for UA; *dir:* David D. Hand; *story:* Webb Smith; *anim:* Johnny Cannon, Les Clark, Jack King, Tom Palmer, Ben Sharpsteen; *asst anim:* Arthur Babbitt, Hardie Gramatky; *voices:* Walt Disney, Pinto Colvig; *mus:* Bert Lewis; b&w. *sd:* RCA. 7 min. • Mickey comes to the rescue of Pluto who has been kidnapped by a mad doctor for experimental purposes in a haunted house.

3940. The Mad Dog *(Mickey Mouse)* 27 Feb. 1932; *p.c.:* Walter E. Disney for Colum; *dir:* Burton F. Gillett; *anim:* Johnny Cannon, Les Clark, Joe d'Igalo, Gilles de Tremaudan, Norman Ferguson, Clyde Geronimi, David D. Hand, Albert Hurter, Jack King, Richard Lundy, Fred Moore, Tom Palmer, Ben Sharpsteen, Frank Tipper, Marvin Woodward; *asst anim:* Chuck Couch, Nick George, Harry Reeves, Hardie Gramatky, Andrew Hutchinson; Roy Williams; *voices:* Walt Disney, Lee Millar; *mus:* Bert Lewis; b&w. *sd:* PCP. 7 min. • Pluto accidentally swallows a cake of soap and his foamy chops get him mistaken him for a mad dog.

3941. The Mad Hatter *(Color Rhapsody)* 3 Nov. 1940; *p.c.:* Colum; *dir:* Sid Marcus; *anim:* Art Davis, Herb Rothwill; *sets:* Phil Davis; *ed:* George Winkler; *voices:* John Wald, Mel Blanc; *mus:* Joe de Nat; *ph:* Otto Reimer; *col:* Tech. *sd:* RCA. 6 min. • An insight is shown into those who create women's hats.

3942. The Mad Hatter *(Woody Woodpecker)* Feb. 1948; *p.c.:* Walter Lantz prods for UA; *dir:* Dick Lundy; *story:* Ben Hardaway, Webb Smith; *anim:* Ken O'Brien, Fred Moore; *character des:* Fred Moore; *sets:* Fred Brunish; *ed:* Dave Lurie; *voices:* Jack Mather, Ben Hardaway; *mus:* Darrell Calker; *prod mgr:* William E. Garity; *col:* Tech. *sd:* RCA. 6½ min. • Woody has to appear at the film set with a top hat. En route his hat blows away and lands on a goose.

3943. A Mad House *(Paul Terry-Toon)* 23 Mar. 1934; *p.c.:* Moser & Terry for Educational/Fox; *dir:* Frank Moser, Paul Terry; *mus:* Philip A. Scheib; b&w. *sd:* WE. 5½ min. • A mad scientist mixes a potion that turns him invisible, then he kidnaps a cute little miss who is saved by her boyfriend.

3944. The Mad King *(Paul Terry-Toon)* 26 June 1932; *p.c.:* Moser & Terry for Educational/Fox; *dir:* Frank Moser, Paul Terry; *mus:* Philip A. Scheib; b&w. *sd:* WE. 6 min. • The Mad King is a tyrant cat who keeps the mouse heroine locked in a dungeon. The mouse hero storms the castle with an angry mob.

3945. Mad Maestro *(MGM Cartoon)* 30 Dec. 1939; *p.c.:* MGM; *prod:* Hugh Harman; *dir/anim/lay:* William Littlejohn, Jack Zander; *sets:* Joe Smith; *mus:* Scott Bradley; *prod mgr:* Fred Quimby; *col:* Tech. *sd:* WE. 8 min. • An orchestra leader conducting *Morning, Noon and Night in Vienna* is irritated by some mysterious sour notes.

3946. Mad Melody *(Aesop's Sound Fable)* 26 Apr. 1931; *p.c.:* Van Beuren for RKO/Pathé; *dir:* John Foster, Mannie Davis; *mus:* Gene Rodemich; b&w. *sd:* RCA. 8 min. • An orchestra leading lion conducts a new opera, "Lazaza" which ends in a sword fight.

3947. Mad Monster Party? 1966; *p.c.:* Embassy Pictures Corp/ Videocraft International; *ex prod:* Joseph E. Levine; *prod:* Arthur Rankin Jr.; *dir:* Jules Bass; *story:* Arthur Rankin Jr., Len Korobkin, Harvey Kurtzman; *anim dir:* Kizo Nagashima; *des:* Don Duga; *character des:* Jack Davis; *voices: Dr. Frankenstein:* Boris Karloff; *The Monster's Mate:* Phyllis Diller; *also:* Allen Swift, Gale Garnett; "Mad Monster Party?" sung by Ethel Ennis; *mus:* Maury Laws; *songs:* Maury Laws, Jules Bass; *choreography:* "Killer Joe" Piro; *asso prod:* Larry Roemer; *col:* East/Pathé. *sd:* RCA. 94 min. • Dr. Frankenstein assembles the famous movie monsters to announce his retirement.

3948. Madcap Magoo *(Mr. Magoo)* 23 June 1955; *p.c.:* UPA for Colum; *ex prod:* Stephen Bosustow; *dir:* Pete Burness; *story:* Dick Shaw, Barbara Hammer; *anim:* Rudy Larriva, Cecil Surry, Tom McDonald; *lay:* Robert Dranko; *back:* Bob McIntosh; *voices:* Jim Backus, Jerry Hausner; *mus:* Del Castillo; *prod mgr:* Herbert Klynn; *col:* Tech. *sd:* RCA. 5½ min. • Magoo mistakes an escaped lunatic for his practical joke-playing friend, Smiley.

3949. Madeline *(Jolly Frolics)* 27 Nov. 1952; *p.c.:* UPA for Colum; *ex prod:* Stephen Bosustow; *dir:* Robert Cannon; *story:* Ludwig Bemelmans; *anim:* Bill Melendez, Frank Smith; *lay:* Art Heinemann; *back:* Jules Engel; *voice:* Gladys Holland; *mus:* David Raksin; *prod mgr:* Herb Klynn; *col:* Tech. *sd:* RCA. 6 min. *Academy Award nomination.* • One of twelve little girls at a Paris boarding school is different from her classmates. When she has her appendix out, the others are envious.

3950. Madhattan Island *(Noveltoon)* 27 June 1947; *p.c.:* Famous for Para; *dir:* Seymour Kneitel; *story:* I. Klein; *sets:* Robert Little; *voice:* Kenneth Roberts; *mus:* Winston Sharples; *ph:* Leonard McCormick; *prod mgr:* Sam Buchwald; *col:* Tech. *sd:* RCA. 9 min. • A mixture of animation over live-action settings of New York landmarks.

3951. Madhouse 16 Feb. 1990; *p.c.:* Orion Pictures Corp. *anim title seq:* Sally Cruikshank & Playhouse Pictures; *col:* DeLuxe. *sd:* Dolby Stereo. • Live-action comedy about a new suburban home being besieged by relatives. Animated credits.

3952. Magic Art *(Aesop's Sound Fable)* 25 Apr. 1932; *p.c.:* Van Beuren for RKO; *dir:* John Foster, Harry Bailey; *mus:* Gene Rodemich; b&w. *sd:* RCA. 7 min. • A magician brings all kinds of drawings to life.

3953. The Magic Beans *(Nertzery Rhyme)* 13 Feb. 1939; *p.c.:* Walter Lantz prods for Univ; *dir:* Lester Kline; *story:* Vic McLeod; *anim:* George Dane, Fred Kopietz; *sets:* Edgar Keichle; *voice:* Mel Blanc, Sara Berner; *mus:* Frank Marsales; b&w. *sd:* WE. 7½ min. • Baby Face mouse plants the beans and grows a beanstalk, which he climbs and encounters a giant mouse. The cartoon ends in the motion picture studio where the story is being shot.

3954. The Magic Carpet *(Dinky Doodle)* 24 May 1925; *p.c.:* Bray prods for FBO; *dir/story:* Walt Lantz; *anim:* Clyde Geronimi; b&w. sil. 5 min. • Walter purchases a magic carpet and, after falling victim to it's charms, hands it over to Dinky.

3955. Magic Embroidery 4 Dec. 1916; *p.c.:* H&B Films; b&w. sil. 3 min. • Animated needle and cotton assuming embroidery designs of every description.

3956. The Magic Fish *(Paul Terry-Toon)* 19 Oct. 1934; *p.c.:* Moser & Terry for Educational/Fox; *dir:* Frank Moser, Paul Terry; *mus:* Philip A. Scheib; b&w. *sd:* WE. 5½ min. • A fisherman tells a tall tale about how he once returned a swordfish to the sea who promised to return the favour for him one day.

3957. The Magic Fluke *(Fox & Crow)* 24 Mar. 1949; *p.c.:* UPA for Colum; *dir:* John Hubley; *story:* Sol Barzman; *anim:* Bob Cannon, Rudy Larriva, Willis Pyle, Pat Matthews; *sets:* Herb Klynn, Jules Engel, Bill Hurtz; *voices:* Jack Mather; *mus:* Del Castillo; *ph:* Max Morgan, Mary Cain; *prod sup:* Ade Woolery, Ed Gershman; *col:* Tech. *sd:* RCA. 6½ min. • Fox deserts his musical partner, The Crow, to become a famous conductor. Crow mixes his baton with a magic wand.

3958. The Magic Fountain Pen 17 July 1909; *p.c.:* Vit Corp; *anim:*

J. Stuart Blackton; b&w. *sil.* 3½ min. *l/a/anim.* • J. Stuart Blackton draws Napoleon, evolving into Kaiser Wilhelm then George Washington.

3959. The Magic Garden of Stanley Sweetheart • See: *A Troll in Central Park*

3960. The Magic Hand *(Novel Imp Film)* 22 Sept. 1913; *anim:* Hy Mayer; b&w. *sil.* • The magic hand draws some fishes and a crab. He develops this picture and queries why women wear such things in their hats since the tariff practically prohibits feathers and such.

3961. The Magic Lamp *(Dinky Doodle)* 15 Sept. 1924; *p.c.:* Bray prods for FBO; *dir/story:* Walt Lantz; *anim:* Clyde Geronimi; b&w. *sil.* 5 min. *l/a/anim.* • Dinky Doodle and his dog go through the same adventures that befell Aladdin.

3962. The Magic Mummy *(Tom & Jerry)* 7 Feb. 1933; *p.c.:* Van Beuren for RKO; *dir:* John Foster, George Stallings; *voice:* Margie Hines; *mus:* Gene Rodemich; b&w. *sd:* RCA. 6 min. • Tom and Jerry are cops who investigate a "Phantom of the Opera" type who displays a mummy that sings for a crowd of skeletons.

3963. Magic on Broadway *(Screen Songs)* 26 Nov. 1937; *p.c.:* The Fleischer Studio for Para; *prod:* Max Fleischer; *dir:* Dave Fleischer; *anim:* Roland Crandall; *mus:* Jay Freeman & His Orchestra with Johnny Russell; b&w. *sd:* WE. 7 min. *l/a/anim.* • Wiffle Piffle has some experiences in a Penny Arcade.

3964. The Magic Peartree *(The Amorous Adventures of Juan Novarro)* 1967; *p.c.:* Murakami/Wolf for Bing Crosby prods; *prod:* Jimmy Murakami; *dir:* Charles Swenson; *voices: Juan Novarro:* Paul Frees; *The Queen:* Agnes Moorehead; *The King:* Keenan Wynn; *col. sd.* 10 min. *Academy Award nomination* • Juan has a liason with the Queen and hides in a pear tree from the King.

3965. The Magic Pencil *(Terry-Toon)* 15 Nov. 1940; *p.c.:* TT for Fox; *dir:* Volney White; *story:* John Foster; *voices:* Arthur Kay, Thomas Morrison; *mus:* Philip A. Scheib; b&w. *sd:* RCA. 6 min. • Gandy and Sourpuss create drawings that come alive with a magic pencil obtained from box tops and rescue a damsel from a sawmill.

3966. The Magic Shell *(Terry-Toon)* 16 May 1941; *p.c.:* TT for Fox; *dir:* Mannie Davis; *story:* John Foster; *mus:* Philip A. Scheib; b&w. *sd:* RCA. 7 min. • A starving family of rabbits sends Jack out to forage for food. He comes across a huge shell which he enters and has an adventure with frogs and is rewarded with gold coins.

3967. The Magic Slipper *(Mighty Mouse)* Dec. 1948; *p.c.:* TT for Fox; *dir:* Mannie Davis; *story:* John Foster; *anim:* Jim Tyer; *voice:* Thomas Morrison; *mus:* Philip A. Scheib; *ph:* Douglas Moye; *col:* Tech. *sd:* RCA. 6 min. • Mighty Mouse saves Cinderella from a wolf disguised as Prince Charming.

3968. Magic Strength *(Phantasy)* 4 Feb. 1944; *p.c.:* Colum; *dir:* Bob Wickersham; *story:* Dun Roman; *sets:* Zack Schwartz; *ed:* Ed Moore; *i&p:* Elizabeth F. McDowell; *voices:* John McLeish, Dick Nelson, Sara Berner; *mus:* Eddie Kilfeather; *prod mgr:* Albert Spar; b&w. *sd:* WE. 6 min. • Willoughby Wren posesses a magic hat that gives him untold strength when worn. He is fearless in rescuing a damsel from Dangerous Dan McGrew until he loses it during a hectic ski chase.

3969. The Magic Sword: The Quest for Camelot 15 May 1998; *p.c.:* WB; *dir:* Frederik DuChau; *prod:* Dalisa Cooper Cohen; *prod des:* Steve Pilcher; *asso prod:* Zahra Dowlatabadi, Andre Clavel; *sup anim (UK):* Russell Hall; *anim consultant:* Stan Green; *lead anim:* Lennie K. Graves, Alyson Hamilton; *art dir:* Carol Kieffer Police, J. Michael Spooner; *creative consultant:* Mike Ockrent; based on the novel *The King's Damosel* by Vera Charman; *scr:* Kirk de Mico & William Schifrin, Jacqueline Feather & David Seider; *story dpt.: head of story:* Bruce M. Morris; *story:* Viki Anderson, Mark Andrews, Ken W. Bruce, Fred Cline, Jun Falkenstein, Stephan A. Franck, Daan J. Jippes, Brian T. Kindregan, Piet Kroon, Stephen G. Lumley, Wilbert Plynaar, Fergal Reilly, Harry A. Sabin, David S. Smith, Moroni Taylor, Christine F. Blum, Louis S. Scarborough, Cynthia Wells; *lead anim:* "*Kayley*": Nasson Vakalis; "*Garrett*": Chrystal S. Klabunde; "*Ruber*": Alexander Williams; "*Devon & Cornwall*": Dan Wagner; "*Juliana*": Cynthia L. Overman; "*Bladebeak*" & minions: Stephan A. Franck; "*Ayden*": Mike Nguyen; *anim (U.S.):* Claire D. Armstrong, Dale Baer, Richard Baneham, David B. Boudreau, Adam Burke, Jennifer Cardon, Michael A.

Chavez, Yarrow T. Cheney, Jesse M. Cosio, Alain Costa, Ricardo Curtis, Bob Davies, James A. Davis, Jeffrey P. Etter, Lauren J. Faust, Ralph L. Ferman, Steve Garcia, Heidi Guedel Garofald, Kent Hammerstrom, Adam Henry, Ben Jones, Leon G. Joosen, Ernest Keen, Ken Keys, Julian A. Korsborn, Jacques Muller, Randal I. Myers, Melina Sydney Padua, Scott T. Petersen, Anna Saunders, Sean Springer, Derek L. Thompson, Jim W. van der Keyl, Roger L. Vizard, Mark A. Williams, John D. Williamson, Dan N. Boulos, Larry D. Whitaker; *(UK):* Cinzia Angelini, Laurene Benhamo, Alberto Campos, Luc Chamberland, Murray Debus, Sean Leaning, Paul Lee, Quentin Miles, Stephen Perry, Thierry Schiel, Michael Schlingmann, Sharon Smith, Gerben Steenks, Paul Stone, Mike Swindall, Vladimir Todorov, Jan van Buyten, Duncan Varley, Pete Western, Gabriele Zucchelli; *rough inbet:* Joanne Coughlin, Ruth E. Daly, Phil E. Langone, Boowon Lee, Lane Lueras, George E. Ramsey; *(UK):* Claire Bramwell-Pearson, Dave Coogan, Paul McKeown, Joe Mulligan; *visual development: key stylist:* Tony Pulham; *lighting des:* Anthony B. Christov, Laura L. Corsiglia, Joseph Ekers, Peter A. Gullerud, August N. Hall, Caroline Hu, Alan Kerswell, Dominique R. Louis, Uli Meyer, Philip Mondez, Frank Pé, Louis M. Police, Christopher J. Ure, Simon V. Varelá, Claire Wenduing; *sculptor:* Carla Fallberg; *maquette casting & sculpting:* Mackinnon & Saunders; *lay: head of lay & workbook:* William H. Frake III; *head of lay:* Jeff Purves; *lay/sup (UK):* Brendan Houghton; *blue sketch sup:* Mercedes J. Sichon; *lay art (U.S.):* Karen Hamrock, Arlan Jewell, Conor W. Kavanagh, Davy C. Liu, Emil Mitev, Gary Mouri, Robert J. St. Pierre, Audrey Stedman, Pamela B. Stefan, Greg Voigt, Todd Winter, Brian Woods, Jennifer C. L. Yuan; *lay asst:* Bryan D. Andrews, Norman R. Cabral, Louis E. Gonzales, Kory S. Heinzen, Rolando B. Mercado, Ben Metcalf, Simon Rodgers, Lisa Souza, Bill Thyen; *blue sketch:* Irina Goosby; *lay (UK):* Andrea Blasich, Sven Hoffer, Herve Leblan, Chris Scully; *back: head of back:* Brian Sebern; *back sup (UK):* Ray Rankine; *back sup (U.S.):* Jeff Richards; *back (U.S.):* Mannix Bennett, Ruben Chavez, Hye Con, William J. Dely Jr., Dennis Durrell, James D. Finn, Greg Gibbons, Annie Guenther, Andrew R. Phillipson, Craig D. Robertson, Jonathan C. Salt, Kim Spink, Nadia H. Vurbenova, Scott Wills; *digital back paint:* Craig R. Kelly, Briar Lee Mitchell; *back asst:* Christopher E. Brock, Eugene Fedorov, Wendy Lymm, Joel Parod, Wei M. Zhao; *back painters (UK):* John Gosler, Natasha Gross, Rachael Stedman, Gary Sycamore, Sue Tong; *ed:* Stanford C. Allen, Richard L. McCullough, Darren T. Holmes, John Currin, Rich Dieti, Sheri Galloway, Gregory Plotts, Jennifer Dolce, Evan Fisher, Barbara Gerety, Ken Solomon; *clean-up anim (UK): head of clean-up:* Marty Korth, Sheldon Borenstein; *clean-up sup (UK):* Julia Bracegirdle; *clean-up consultant:* Dori Littell Herrick; *clean-up leads:* "*Kayley*": Lureline Kohler; "*Garrett*": Eric J. Abjornson; "*Rober*": Don Parmele; "*Devon & Cornwall*": Scott R. Bern; "*Juliana*" & "*Arthur*": Doris A. Plough; "*Griffin*": Robert Tyler; "*Bladebeak*" & minions: Karen S. Kaminski; "*Myden*": June Myung Nam; "*Kayley*" (UK): Nathalie Gavet; "*Garrett*" (UK): José Antonio Cerro; *U.S. key anim asst:* Paul A. Bauman, David Bombardier, Sheila Rae Brown, Kimmie Calvere, John Eddings, Ruth Elliott, Anne Heeney, Ilona M. Kaba, Wantana Martinelli, Soonjin Mooney, Celeste Moreno, Sung Noh, Bob Quinn, Domingo C. Rivera Jr., Joe Roman, Kyung S. Shin, Maureen Trueblood, Michael A. Venturmi, Tran M. Vu, Mitchell Walker, Robin White; *asst anim:* Beverly J. Adams, Andrew M. Beall, Gordon R. Bellamy, Wanda L. Brown, Yebbi Cho, Jeffrey D. Clark, Heidi D. Daven, Greg Fleming, Trine Frank, Ken H. Kim, Karen Marjoribanks, Vanessa J. Martin, James McArdle, Viviane (Kamye) K. Miessen, William Mims, Tao Nguyen, Doug E. Ninneman, Nicole Pascal, Andrew J. Ramos, Ivan Camilli Rivera, Jason S. Sallin, Matthew Schofield, Jennifer M. Stillwell, Yevgeniya Suzdaltsey, Helen T. Tse, Terry Walsh, Miri Yoon; *back arts:* Steve Aguilar, Peter Paul R. Bautista, James A. Burks, Patrick T. Dailey, Miriam L. Goodman, Cathlin G. Hidalgo, Jennifer L. Jarmel, Diane Kim, Henry Kim, Patrice Leech, Christine T. Mallouf, Robert G. Nigoghossian, Francisco Rosales, Rudy Rosales, John Rosen, Allison E. Sgroi, Stephen R. Steinbach; *inbet:* Brian Boylan, Greg Checketts, Catherine M. Choi, Cesar S. DeVara, Guy Donovan, Yelena Geodakyan, Barrett Glenn Jr., Danny Raul Gonzalez, Janeane K. Harwell-Camp, Guadalupe Hernandez, Suzanne F. Hirota, Joon Y. Kang, Kevin W. Koch, Kari Pearson Lancaster, Daisy Lee, Ho Young Lee, Rudi S. Liden, Shannon C. O'Connor, Chrissie Schweiger, Angela M. Sigurdson, Jennifer Sigurdson, Viorel Voronca, Elyse M. Whittaker-Paek, Gina Russell Williams, Helen H. Yoon; *U.K. asst anim:* Marcus Arnull, Alexandra Boiger, Franck Bonay, Chris Clarke, Tony Cope, Chris Drew, Deborah

Dryland, Helga Egilson, Gerry Gallego, Bernard Georges, Victoria Goldner, Fiona Gomez, Hilary Gough, Helena Grant, Andrew Griffiths, Nick Hellmas, Natalie Higgs, Stathis Karabateas, Helen Kincaid, Darren Kordich, Nick Large, Sophie Law, Cath Lowdell, Simon Loxton, Peter Mays, Hae Sook Park, Eugenios Plakias, Antonella Russo, Christian Ryitenius, Steve Smith, Claudia Sturli, Dave Webster, Una Woods; *inbet:* Rasmus Andreasen, Simon W.E. Clarke, Camilla G. Fougner, Carla Hamer, Marianne Raismussen Jensen, Dirk Keters, Richard Lowdell, Steve Martin, James Dean O'Shea, John Pickup, Maiken Rix, Bryan Rogers, Alex Stewart, Leona Nordstrom Valentin; *asst clean-up anim:* Monica Brufton, Michael Cole, Carol Davies, Nigel Davies, Angeline de Silva, Annie Elvin, Peter Gambier, Joanne Gooding, Nicholas Harrop, Janette Hynes, Dominic Kynaston, Michael A. Lerman, Brian Malone-West, Samantha Malone-West, Nicola Mariborough, Lala Maredith-Vula, Karen Narramore, Tom Newman, Brent Odell, Theresa Smythe, Debbie Spafford, Ronan Spelman, Theresa J. Whatley, Deborah Womack, Sue Woodward; *fx anim: head of fx:* Michael Gagne; *fx sup (UK):* Mike Smith; *(U.S.):* Ahmed (Agtarus) Aksas, Michael Camarillo, John M. Dillon, Rick Echevarria, Marc Ellis, Earl A. Hibbere, John M. Huey, deBora Kupczyk, John J. MacFarlane, Bob Simmons, Gary Sole, Ryan Woodward, Lynette C. Charters, Jane M. Smethurst; *asst fx anim:* Esmeralda C. Acosta, Mark Ash, Susan B. Keane, Young Kyurhim, Bob Miller, Richard E. Olsen, Robert Rios, Mary J. Sheridan, Ryan L. Simmons; *fx break:* Von J. Williams; *fx inbet:* Kennard F. Betts, Yan Budeen, Greg N. Bumatay, Chris G. Darroca, Robert Ism deToscano, Noe Garcia, Daniel Killien, Matthew L. Maners, Rodd D. Miller, Jorge Hiram Ramos, Jaclyn S. Seymour, Laurie D. Sigueido, Norland M. Tellez, Jeffrey C. Tse; *fx anim (UK):* Jon Brooks, Volker Pajatsch, Antonio Palermo, David Pritchard, Paul Smith, Tim Walton, Martin Wansborough; *asst fx anim:* Tracey Agate, Janet Cable, Michelle L. S. Dabbs, Carl Keeler, Terence R. Kester, Lilas Leblan, Roger Lougher, Giulia Mazz, Jemshaid Mirza, Rhian Wyn Rushton, David Tuffnell, David Demosthenous, Shaun McGlinchey, Ron McMinn, Albert Price, James Pyott, Barnaby Russel, Lorraine Ward; *digital fx anim: head of digital fx:* Allen C. Foster; *digital fx art:* Miae Kim Ausbrooks, James Bentley, Andrew D. Brownlow, Steve Burch, Lee Crowe, Craig Littell-Herrick, Kevin Oakley, Miryam Sharifi; *heads of cgi:* Tad Gielow, Katherine S. Percy; *cgi anim:* Grace Blanco, Brad Booker, Adam Dotson, Bruce Edwards, Corey Hels, Tim Keon, Darren D. Kiner, Sebastian Tinage, Susas L. Oslin, Brian Schindler, Teddy T. Yang; *voices: Kayley:* Jessalyn Gilsig; *singing voice:* Andrea Corr; *Garrett:* Cary Elwes; *singing voice:* Bryan White; *Ruber:* Gary Oldman; *Devon:* Eric Idle; *Cornwall:* Don Rickles; *Lady Juliana:* Jane Seymour; *singing voice:* Celine Dion; *King Arthur:* Pierce Brosnan; *singing voice:* Steve Perry; *Griffin voice:* Bronson Pinchot; *Bladebeak:* Jaleel White; *Sir Lionel:* Gabriel Byrne; *Merlin:* Sir John Gielgud; *Ayden:* Frank Welker; *Young Kayley:* Sarah Rayne; *also:* Jack Angel, Joe Baker, Robert Bergen, Rodger Bumpass, Phillip Clarke, Sheelagh Cullen, Ken Danziger, Jennifer Darling, Fiona Dwyer, Paul Eiding, Fionnula Flanagan, Jean Gilpin, Jess Harnell, Sherry Lynn, Danny Mann, Mickie T. McGowan, Al Roker; *mus:* Patrick Doyle; *mus prod sup:* Daniel Carim; *songs:* David Foster, Carole Bayer Sayer; *song arranger:* David Foster; *additional song orchestral arrangements:* Patrick Doyle, William Ross; *sup mus ed:* Caoimhín Ó Críochám; *song orchestration:* William Ross, James Shearman, Lawrence Ashmore, John Bell; *song rec:* Felipe Elgueta, John Richards, Al Schmitt, Humberto Gatica, David Reitzas; *song mix:* Joseph Magee; *mus consult:* Glen Kelly; *score prod:* Maggie Rodford, Patrick Doyle; *score mus ed:* Roy Prendergast; *score orch:* Lawrence Ashmore, James Shearman; *score engineered/mix:* John Richards, John Rodd, Jimmy Hoyson; *conductor:* Mark Watters; *asst mus ed:* Kim Strand; *asst synthesizer programming:* Simon Frangle; *asst to Mr. Foster:* Lynne Malone, Lily Pollard; *asst to Ms. Bayer Sayer:* Laurie Gonlag; *instrumental soloists: penny whistle:* Jon Clarke, Andrea Corr; *Irish fiddle:* Eileen Ivers, Sharon Corr; *accordian:* Eilish Egan; *E.V.I:* Judd Miller; *Lulleann pipe:* Eric Rigler; *choir leaders:* Edie Lehmann Boddicker, Paul Salamunovich; *concert master:* Bruce Dukov; *choreog:* Kenny Ortega, Peggy Holmes; *casting:* Julie Hughes, Barry Moss; *prod mgrs:* Igor Khait, Patrick J. Love; *prod mgr (UK):* Ian Cook; *asst prod mgrs: (U.S.) prod:* Mary Alice Drumm; *dir:* Cary Biren; *sweatbox:* Michelle O'Hara; *anim:* Lizbeth A. Velasco, Jackie Blaisdell; *story/editorial:* Marcia Gwendolyn Jones; *lay:* J.C. Alverez; *back:* Leonard Vasquez; *clean-up anim:* Michelle Perslow, Virginie Foucault, Susan K. Lee; *fx:* Richmond Horne; *digital fx:*Gregory L. deCamp; *cgi:* Timothy E. Jones; *scene plan & scanning:* Maria R. Guerra;

anim check: April M. Henry; *Acme:* Aaron Parry; *satellite studies:* Laura leGanza Reynolds; *art dir:* Jill Ruzicka Leighton; *prod tracking:* Joan Peter; *(UK): anim & clean-up:* Steve Hollowell; *fx scene plan & check:* John Phelan; *scene plan: head of scene plan:* Steven Wilzback; *scene plan (UK):* Koija Erman, Silvia Barbier, Gina Bradley, George (Bingo) Ferguson, Karen L. Hansen, James Keefer, Katja Schumann; *anim check: head of anim check:* Myoung Smith; *anim check sup (UK):* Corona Maher-Esterhazy, Kathy Barrows-Fullmer, Susan Burke, Daryl Carstensen, Charlotte Clarke-Pitts, Katherine Gray, Brendan Harris, Frances Jacob, Louie C. Jhocson, Pam Kleyman, Madel F. Mannit, Helen P. O'Brien, Penelope Sevier, Debbie Skinner, Carol Li-Chuan Yao, Nick Yates; *Acme sups: mgr of Acme:* Rhonda L. Hicks; *col styling:* Tania M. Burton; *scanning:* Irene M. Gringeri; *i&p:* Sarah-Jane King; *final check:* Kim Patterson; *final scene plan:* James Williams; *col styling:* Marianne C. Cheng, Anthony C. Cianciolo Jr., Sylvia M. Filcak, Leslie C. Hinton, Eric Jon Kurland, Annette L. Leavitt, Catherine P. O'Leary, Cathy Wainess-Walters; *scanning:* David E. Bonnell, Craig Colligan, Geoff Darwin, Darrin M. Drew, Karl Dunne, Terri Eddings, Simon Edwards, Stephen Parkinson, Eric D. Schneider, Edwin S. Shortess, Dean T. Stanley; *col model mark-up:* Constance R. Allen, Helga Beatrix Vanden Berge, Melody J. Hughes, Dawn Knight, Stevan A. King, Devon P. Oddone, Tanya Moreau Smith, Regis Tratton, Janet M. Zoll; *paint mark-up:* Renee L. Alcazar, Staci Gleed, Gina Evans Howard, Gale A. Raleigh; *digital cel painters: i&p asst sup:* Olga Tarin Duff; *paint:* Diane R. Albracht, Amy Azzara, Tina Bastien-Antenorcruz, Katky A. Bauer, Nancy Bihary-Fiske, Martine Clavel, Elena Marie Cox, Damon R. Crowe, Dayle Dodge, Nika Dunne, Nance Finley, Ivis Freeman, Dawn A. Gates, Patricia L. Gold, Leonor Gonzales-Wood, Steve Kindernay, Diana D. McIntosh, David M. Nimitz, Fabio Novais, Kristian Roberts, Sheryl Ann Smith, Susan Lee So, Alice M. Solis, Dirk von Besser, Susan Wileman; *final check:* Dennis M. Bonnell, Thomas J. Jackson, Marisha Noroski, Randy O. Roberg, Freddie Vaziri; *final scene plan:* Daniel Bunn, Dan C. Larsen; *tech dirs:* Brett Achorn, Stephane Cros, Babak Forutanpour, Brian R. Gardner; *track readers:* Armetta Jackson-Hamlett, Brian Masterson; *technology: technology management:* Lem Davis, Emmanuel C. Francisco, William Charles Perkins, David F. Wolf; *technical engineers:* George Aluzzi, Stewart Anderson, Steve Chen, Bruce Hatakeyama, Keith Kobata, José F. Lopez, Margaret Myers, Stephen Myers, Arjun Ramamurthy, Leonard J. Reder, Alan L. Stephenson, Aaron L. Thompson, Cheng-Jui Yu, Zizi Zhao; *Acme Digital specialists:* Mark Aldridge, Will Bilton, Chris Gavin, James B. Hathcock, Dave Hogan; *technical operations:* Lori A. Arntzen, Paul Hernando, Kevin D. Howard, Alexis C. Pierre, Usha Ramcharitar, Paul Skidmore, Gene Takahashi, Alvin S. Tenpo; *prod asst (U.S.):* Leslie Barker, David A. Bemis, Andrea Bivins, E. Tavares Black, Keith Brennan, Jode Craig, Laura M. Diaz, Monte Gagnier, Cirilo R. Gonzales Jr., Scott Grieder, Jean M. Klanecky, Dao Le, Michael Leach, Sam Mendlestein, Louis Moulinet, Roubina Mousessian, Corrine Mulder, Loanne Hizo Ostlie, Ria Rueda, Thomas Shalin, Elaine Siders, Greg T. Smith, Staci Stonerook, Kathy Tajbakhsh, Charlene Tinsley, Sunny Ye, Kathleen Zuelck; *(UK):* Craig Colligan, Tim Denin, David Klein, Catrin Lloyd, Anna Lord, Tiffany Maberley, Jason Palmer, Nic Roberts, Hughes Sarin Townrow; *asst to Mr. Duchau:* Jennifer van der Bliek; *asst to Mr.Cooper Cohen:* Cynthia Garcia; *prod management asst:* Glenda V. Winfield; *prod support:* Patrick Pitch, Madeline Fry, Joe Hernandez; *casting asso:* Jessica Gilburne; *post prod: post prod sup:* Jeannine Bergen; *ph sup:* Mark Dinicola; *sup sd ed:* Alan Robert Murray, Dave Horton Sr.; *sd des:* Chris Boyes, Tom Myers; *sd fx ed:* Bob Asman, Adam Johnston, Andy Kopetzky, Bill Manger; *back fx ed:* Stu Bernstein, Gregory M. Gerlich, Bruce Richardson; *re-rec mix:* David Campbell, John Reitz, Gregg Rudloff; *asst eds:* Stodd Harris, J. Katz, Darrin Martin, Michael Ruiz, David Werniz, Rob Wilson; *asst sd des:* David Hughes; *ADR mix:* Doc Kane; *foley sup:* Dave Horton Jr.; *foley walkers:* John Roesch, David Lee Fein; *foley mix:* Mary Jo Lange; *foley eds:* Scott Jackson, Neil Burrow, Scott Burrow, Scott Tinsley; *neg cutter:* Mo Henry; *ph:* Christine Beck, Richard Wolff; *projectionist:* Preston Oliver; *col timer:* Terry Claborn; *principal dial:* Troy Porter, Bill Higley, Bob Baron, Steve Hellaby, Vince Caro; *A-Film: head of prod:* Anders Mastrup; *anim sup:* Jesper Moller; *prod mgrs:* Helle Hansen, Kristel Toldsepo; *lay/back sup:* Matthias Lechner; *clean-up sup:* Bjorn Pedersen; *clean-up sup (Estonia):* Tine Karrebaek; *tech support:* Hans Perk; *line-test:* Susanne Gloerfeit-Tarp; *asst prod mgr:* Irene Sparre; *anim:* Meelis Arulepp, Svetlana Bezdomnikova, Padraig Collins, Luca Fattore, Stefan Fjeldmark, Michael Helmuth Hansen,

Silvia Hoefnagels, Anne Holmer, Christian Kuntz, Jorgen Lerdam, Anders Madsen, Martin Madsen, Fernando Moro, Janus Sorgenfrey Pedersen, Ando Tammik; *lay art:* Marcus Hoogvelt, John Koch, Jens Moller; *back paint:* Thomas Dryer, Bjarne Hansen, Peter Kielland; *blue sketch:* Steen Dyryed, Kristiina Martinson, Charlotte Worsaae; *clean-up key asst/anim:* Uffe Danielsen, Thomas Fenger, Hope Devlin Kristiansen, Rigmoor Tokured; *clean-up asst anim:* Ahto Aaremae, Morten Bramsen, Margo Busch, Elisabeth Damkjaer, Kristiina Didrik, Mette Fenger, Henrik Hansen, Jorgen Hansen, Karin Hjorth, Soren Jakobsen, Tinna Jespersen, Herle Kühl, Riina Kütt, Marlene Laugeset, Aavi Levin, Tom Lock, Malle Maenurm, Lars Nielsen, Merike Peil, Gunhild Rod, Lils Roden, Chai Sayul, Jesper Ezme Sorensen, Evelin Tennin, Raivo Tihanov, Krista Vanamòlder; *Yowza:* head of prod: Claude Chiasson; *prod mgr:* Pierre Chiasson; *clean-up asst anim:* Vittoria Bologna, Denise Bradshaw, Ron Chevarie, Mike Demur, James McCrimmon, Ron Migilore, Paul Mota, Royston Robinson; *inbet:* Elsie Chen, Dave Cortesi, Rowena Cruz, Gloria Hsu, Karen Kewell, Olen Prys; *The Heart of Texas Prods., Inc.:* head of prod.: R. Don Smith; *prod mgrs:* Susan E. Clark, Michele Vitale; *clean-up sup:* Jeff Foucare; *asst clean-up sup:* Bonnie Brantley, Manuel Carrasco; *anim:* Frank Gabriel, Tom King, Alan T. Pickett, Kez Wilson; *clean-up asst anim:* Richard Bartholomew, Lisa Bozzetto, Eddy Carrasco, Cynthia Crowell, Walt Holcombe, Inez Hunicken, Aaron Long, John Overmyer, Erik Zumalt; *additional animation technology services:* Artscan, Cambridge Animation Systems, Inc.; *col:* Tech. *sd:* Dolby digital/Digital DTS/SDDS. 86 min. • Young Kayley's father, one of King Arthur's knights, is killed by an evil knight named Ruber. She sets out to avenge her father's death teamed with Garrett, a blind knight, and a two-headed dragon, who help her rescue the kingdom from Ruber's malicious grasp.

3970. Magical Maestro 9 Feb. 1952; *p.c.:* MGM; *dir:* Tex Avery; *story:* Rich Hogan; *anim:* Grant Simmons, Michael Lah, Walter Clinton; *ed:* Jim Faris; *voices:* Jack Mather, Carlos Ramirez, The Mary Kaye Trio (Mary & Norman Kaye, Frank Ross); *mus:* Scott Bradley; *prod:* Fred Quimby; *col:* Tech. *sd:* WE. 6 min. • Mysto the Magician gets his revenge on a fat, canine opera singer by conducting his concert with a magic wand.

3971. Magicalulu (*Little Lulu*) 2 Mar. 1945; *p.c.:* Famous for Para; *dir:* Seymour Kneitel; *story:* Jack Ward; *anim:* Graham Place, Lou Zukor, George Cannata, Gordon Whittier; *sets:* Anton Loeb; *voice:* Cecil Roy; *mus:* Winston Sharples; *ph:* Leonard McCormick; *prod mgr:* Sam Buchwald; *col:* Tech. *sd:* RCA. 7 min. • Lulu rues the day she ever pushed her way into a magic act.

3972. The Magician (*Aesop's Film Fable*) 20 Mar. 1927; *p.c.:* Fables Pictures Inc for Pathé; *dir:* Paul Terry; b&w. *sil.* 10 min. • A magician cat takes his girl to Chinatown where he upsets the Tong gangs. His magic produces a mule that kicks the warring gangsters away.

3973. The Magician (*Dinky Doodle*) 24 July 1926; *p.c.:* Bray prods for FBO; *dir/story:* Walt Lantz; *anim:* Clyde Geronimi; b&w. *sil.* 5 min. *l/a/anim.* • Walter recieves his magician's diploma and impresses his overweight girlfriend with tricks. Dinky and Weakheart doubt his ability in magic tricks and steal his magic book, turning the artist into all manner of animals. When they change him into a mouse, it frightens his girl who beats him up.

3974. Magician Mickey (*Mickey Mouse*) 6 Feb. 1937; *p.c.:* Walt Disney prods for UA; *dir:* David D. Hand; *anim:* Johnny Cannon, Les Clark, I. Klein, Edward Love, William O. Roberts; *voices:* Clarence Nash, Pinto Colvig, Lee Millar, Walt Disney, Ralph Scott; *mus:* Albert Hay Malotte; *col:* Tech. *sd:* RCA. 7 min. • Donald heckles Mickey's magic act by going on stage, grabbing his magic pistol and creating havoc during the finale.

3975. The Magnetic Bat (*Aesop's Film Fable*) 17 Sept. 1928; *p.c.:* Fables Pictures Inc for Pathé; *dir:* Paul Terry; b&w. *sil.* 10 min. • A baseball game with the Cheese Eaters (mice) vs. the Yanks (Farmer Al Falfa). The mice are sold a special bat that helps them win the game.

3976. Magoo Beats the Heat (*Mr. Magoo*) 21 June 1956; *p.c.:* UPA for Colum; *ex prod:* Stephen Bosustow; *dir:* Pete Burness; *story:* Dick Shaw, Ed Nofziger; *anim:* Cecil Surry, Gil Turner, Barney Posner; *lay:* Robert Dranko; *back:* Bob McIntosh; *voices:* Jim Backus, Earl Bennett; *mus:* Dennis Farnon; *prod mgr:* Herbert Klynn; *col:* Tech. *sd:* RCA. 5½ min. CS. • Magoo believes the desert to be the seashore and a prospector with his mule to be a couple relaxing on the beach.

3977. Magoo Breaks Par (*Mr. Magoo*) 27 June 1957; *p.c.:* UPA for Colum; *ex prod:* Stephen Bosustow; *dir:* Pete Burness; *story:* Dick Shaw, Bill Berman; *anim:* Cecil Surry, Barney Posner, Gil Turner, Tom McDonald; *lay:* Robert Dranko; *back:* Bob McIntosh; *voices:* Jim Backus, Jerry Hausner; *mus:* Thomas Cutkomb; *col:* Tech. *sd:* RCA. 6½ min. CS. • Magoo is taken to prison in the belief it's a ritzy golf club.

3978. Magoo Express (*Mr. Magoo*) 19 June 1955; *p.c.:* UPA for Colum; *ex prod:* Stephen Bosustow; *dir:* Pete Burness; *story:* Dick Shaw, Barbara Hammer; *anim:* Rudy Larriva, Cecil Surry, Tom McDonald; *lay:* Sterling Sturtevant; *back:* Bob McIntosh; *voices:* Jim Backus, Jerry Hausner, Marian Richman; *mus:* Frank Comstock; *prod mgr:* Herbert Klynn; *col:* Tech. *sd:* RCA. 7 min. • Magoo, travelling on the Orient Express, unwittingly gets mistaken for a secret agent.

3979. Magoo Goes Overboard (*Mr. Magoo*) 21 Feb. 1957; *p.c.:* UPA for Colum; *ex prod:* Stephen Bosustow; *dir:* Pete Burness; *story:* Dick Shaw; *anim:* Cecil Surry, Gil Turner, Barney Posner, Tom McDonald; *lay:* Robert Dranko; *back:* Bob McIntosh; *voices:* Jim Backus, Daws Butler; *mus:* Dennis Farnon; *prod mgr:* Herbert Klynn; *col:* Tech. *sd:* RCA. 6 min. CS. • During an ocean cruise, Magoo falls into the swimming pool and is under the impression he's adrift in the open sea.

3980. Magoo Goes Skiing (*Mr. Magoo*) 23 Nov. 1953; *p.c.:* UPA for Colum; *ex prod:* Stephen Bosustow; *dir:* Pete Burness; *story:* Bill Scott, T. Hee; *anim:* Rudy Larriva, Cecil Surry, Tom McDonald; *lay:* Sterling Sturtevant; *back:* Bob McIntosh; *voices:* Jim Backus, Jerry Hausner; *mus:* Lou Maury; *prod mgr:* Herbert Klynn; *col:* Tech. *sd:* RCA. 6 min. • Magoo decides to climb the most dangerous ski-slope in the Alps.

3981. Magoo Goes West (*Mr. Magoo*) 19 Apr. 1956; *p.c.:* UPA for Colum; *ex prod:* Stephen Bosustow; *dir:* Pete Burness; *story:* Dick Shaw; *anim:* Rudy Larriva, Cecil Surry, Gil Turner, Barney Posner; *lay:* Robert Dranko; *back:* Jules Engel; *voices:* Jim Backus, Jerry Hausner; *mus:* Frank Comstock; *prod mgr:* Herbert Klynn; *col:* Tech. *sd:* RCA. 6 min. CS. • Tired of continuous rain (his lawn sprinkler), Magoo loads his car for a trek towards the California sun but gets no farther than an automatic car wash.

3982. Magoo Makes News (*Mr. Magoo*) 5 Dec. 1955; *p.c.:* UPA for Colum; *ex prod:* Stephen Bosustow; *dir:* Pete Burness; *story:* Dick Shaw; *anim:* Rudy Larriva, Cecil Surry, Tom McDonald, Barney Posner; *lay:* Robert Dranko; *back:* Bob McIntosh; *voices:* Jim Backus, Jerry Hausner; *mus:* Dennis Farnon; *prod mgr:* Herbert Klynn; *col:* Tech. *sd:* RCA. 5½ min. CS. • Outraged by what he thinks to be a shut-off notice from the electric company, Magoo sets out to give the power company a piece of his mind.

3983. Magoo Saves the Bank (*Mr. Magoo*) 29 Sept. 1957; *p.c.:* UPA for Colum; *ex prod:* Stephen Bosustow; *prod/dir:* Pete Burness; *story:* Dick Shaw, Dick Kinney; *anim:* Gil Turner, Barney Posner, Ed Friedman; *lay:* Robert Dranko; *back:* Bob McIntosh; *voices:* Jim Backus, Daws Butler; *mus:* Dennis Farnon; *col:* Tech. *sd:* RCA. 6½ min. CS. • Magoo takes the race track for his local bank, creating a panic with the punters.

3984. Magoo Slept Here (*Mr. Magoo*) 19 Nov. 1953; *p.c.:* UPA for Colum; *ex prod:* Stephen Bosustow; *dir:* Pete Burness; *story:* Tedd Pierce; *anim:* Cecil Surry, Tom McDonald, Rudy Larriva; *lay:* Sterling Sturtevant; *back:* Bob McIntosh, Michi Kataoka *voices:* Jim Backus, Jerry Hausner; *mus:* Ernest Gold; *prod mgr:* Herbert Klynn; *col:* Tech. *sd:* RCA. 6 min. • Magoo attempts to sell his furniture to someone who, in reality, is a tax assessor.

3985. Magoo's Canine Mutiny (*Mr. Magoo*) 8 Mar. 1956; *p.c.:* UPA for Colum; *ex prod:* Stephen Bosustow; *dir:* Pete Burness; *story:* Dick Shaw, Walter Newman; *anim:* Rudy Larriva, Cecil Surry, Barney Posner, Osmond Evans; *lay:* Robert Dranko; *back:* Bob McIntosh; *voices:* Jim Backus, Jerry Hausner; *mus:* Hoyt Curtin; *prod mgr:* Herbert Klynn; *col:* Tech. *sd:* RCA. 6½ min. CS. • The puppy Magoo thinks he's bought turns out to be a criminal on the run from the law.

3986. Magoo's Check Up (*Mr. Magoo*) 24 Feb. 1955; *p.c.:* UPA for Colum; *ex prod:* Stephen Bosustow; *dir:* Pete Burness; *story:* Dick Shaw, Barbara Hammer; *anim:* Rudy Larriva, Cecil Surry, Tom McDonald; *lay:* Sterling Sturtevant; *back:* Bob McIntosh; *voices:* Jim Backus, Jerry Hausner, Colleen Collins; *mus:* Dennis Farnon; *col:* Tech. *sd:* RCA. 6½ min. • When

Magoo mistakes a TV shop for the doctor's surgery, he wanders into the ladies' shop next door in a half-clothed state and is branded an escaped madman.

3987. Magoo's Cruise (*Mr. Magoo*) 11 Sept. 1958; *p.c.*: UPA for Colum; *ex prod*: Stephen Bosustow; *prod*: Pete Burness; *dir*: Rudy Larriva; *story*: Dick Kinney, Dick Shaw; *anim*: Casey Onaitis, Phil Duncan; *sets*: Sam Clayberger; *voices*: Jim Backus, Jerry Hausner; *mus*: Dennis Farnon; *col*: Tech. *sd*: RCA. 5¹⁄₂ min. • Magoo is mistaken for a top Russian spy when he arrives at the dockside, ready to embark on his friend's yacht.

3988. Magoo's Glorious Fourth (*Mr. Magoo*) 25 July 1957; *p.c.*: UPA for Colum; *ex prod*: Stephen Bosustow; *prod/dir*: Pete Burness; *story*: Dick Shaw, Ed Nofziger; *anim*: Tom McDonald, Gil Turner, Barney Posner, Ed Friedman; *lay*: Bob Dranko; *back*: Bob McIntosh; *voices*: Jim Backus, Daws Butler; *mus*: Dean Elliott; *col*: Tech. *sd*: RCA. 6 min. CS. • Magoo wants a colorful flower display for July 4th instead of fireworks. He buys what he imagines to be flowers but in reality are fireworks.

3989. Magoo's Homecoming (*Mr. Magoo*) 6 Mar. 1959; *p.c.*: UPA for Colum; *ex prod*: Stephen Bosustow; *dir*: Gil Turner; *story*: Bill Scott, Dick Kinney; *anim*: Barney Posner, Ed Friedman, Tom McDonald, Maurie Fagin; *lay*: Robert Dranko; *back*: Bob McIntosh; *voices*: Jim Backus, Daws Butler; *mus*: Dean Elliott; *col*: Tech. *sd*: RCA. 6 min. • Magoo takes the local zoo for his college reunion and a jewel thief for a fellow classmate.

3990. Magoo's Lodge Brother (*Mr. Magoo*) 7 May 1959; *p.c.*: UPA for Colum; *ex prod*: Stephen Bosustow; *dir*: Rudy Larriva; *story*: Dick Kinney, Dick Shaw; *anim*: Casey Onaitis, Ed Friedman, Barney Posner; *lay*: Art Heinemann; *back*: Bob McIntosh; *voices*: Jim Backus, Jerry Hausner; *mus*: Jack Meakin; *col*: Tech. *sd*: RCA. 6 min. • Magoo believes he's attending a lodge convention but, in actual fact, is aboard a ship, sharing a cabin with an escaping criminal.

3991. Magoo's Masquerade (*Mr. Magoo*) 15 Aug. 1957; *p.c.*: UPA for Colum; *ex prod*: Stephen Bosustow; *prod*: Pete Burness; *dir*: Rudy Larriva; *story*: Dick Shaw, Ed Nofziger; *anim*: Frank Smith, Allen Zaslove, Casey Onaitis; *lay*: Sam Clayberger; *back*: Jules Engel; *voices*: Jim Backus, Daws Butler; *mus*: Lyn Murray; *col*: Tech. *sd*: RCA. 6 min. CS. • A masquerade party that Magoo believes he's attending turns out to be a cocktail party and arrives escorting an ostrich.

3992. Magoo's Masterpiece (*Mr. Magoo*) 30 July 1953; *p.c.*: UPA for Colum; *ex prod*: Stephen Bosustow; *dir*: Pete Burness; *story*: Don Freeman, Tedd Pierce; *anim*: Rudy Larriva, Cecil Surry, Tom McDonald; *lay*: Sterling Sturtevant; *back*: Bob McIntosh; *voices*: Jim Backus, Jerry Hausner; *mus*: George Bruns; *prod mgr*: Herbert Klynn; *col*: Tech. *sd*: RCA. 6 min. • When Magoo takes up sculpture as a hobby he also manages to capture a notorious jewel thief known as "The Spirit."

3993. Magoo's Moosehunt (*Mr. Magoo*) 28 Nov. 1957; *p.c.*: UPA for Colum; *ex prod*: Stephen Bosustow; *prod/dir*: Robert Cannon; *story*: Bill Scott, Ed Nofziger; *anim*: Alan Zaslove, C.L. Hartman; *lay*: Lew Keller; *back*: Jules Engel; *voices*: Jim Backus, Jerry Hausner; *mus*: Dennis Farnon; *col*: Tech. *sd*: RCA. 6 min. • Magoo wagers Bottomley that he can catch a moose quicker with his old fashioned "Moose Call" than his companion can with his mechanized equipment.

3994. Magoo's Private War (*Mr. Magoo*) 19 Dec. 1957; *p.c.*: UPA for Colum; *ex prod*: Stephen Bosustow; *prod*: Pete Burness; *dir*: Rudy Larriva; *story*: Dick Shaw, Jack Gross Jr., Fred de Gorter; *anim*: Frank Smith, Casey Onaitis, Phil Duncan; *lay*: Sam Clayberger; *back*: Sam Clayberger, Ervin L. Kaplan; *voices*: Jim Backus, Daws Butler, Mary Jane Croft; *mus*: Dennis Farnon; *col*: Tech. *sd*: RCA. 6 min. *l/a/anim*. • "Disaster Warden" Magoo thinks an invasion is on hand when he stumbles into a cinema and witnesses a newsreel.

3995. Magoo's Problem Child (*Mr. Magoo*) 18 Oct. 1956; *p.c.*: UPA for Colum; *ex prod*: Stephen Bosustow; *dir*: Pete Burness; *story*: Dick Shaw; *anim*: Rudy Larriva, Cecil Surry, Gil Turner, Barney Posner, Tom McDonald; *lay*: Robert Dranko; *back*: Bob McIntosh; *voices*: Jim Backus, Daws Butler; *mus*: Dennis Farnon; *prod mgr*: Herbert Klynn; *col*: Tech. *sd*: RCA. 5¹⁄₂ min. CS. • Magoo mistakes a counterfeiter's hideout for his own home and Waldo for having turned to a life of crime.

3996. Magoo's Puddle Jumper (*Mr. Magoo*) 26 July 1956; *p.c.*: UPA for Colum; *ex prod*: Stephen Bosustow; *dir*: Pete Burness; *story*: Dick Shaw;

anim: Rudy Larriva, Gil Turner, Cecil Surry, Barney Posner; *lay*: Robert Dranko; *back*: Bob McIntosh; *voices*: Jim Backus, Daws Butler; *mus*: Dean Elliott; *prod mgr*: Herbert Klynn; *col*: Tech. *sd*: RCA. 6 min. CS. *Academy Award*. • When Magoo buys an electric car, he ends up travelling along the ocean bed when taking it for a trial run.

3997. Magoo's Three Point Landing (*Mr. Magoo*) 5 June 1958; *p.c.*: UPA for Colum; *ex prod*: Stephen Bosustow; *prod/dir*: Pete Burness; *story*: Dick Shaw; *anim*: Gil Turner, Barney Posner, Ed Friedman, Maurie Fagin; *lay*: Robert Dranko; *back*: Bob McIntosh; *voices*: Jim Backus, Daws Butler; *mus*: Dennis Farnon; *col*: Tech. *sd*: RCA. 6¹⁄₂ min. • Magoo's car stalls on a airport runway and inadvertently has an airliner land on his roof.

3998. Magoo's Young Manhood (*Mr. Magoo*) 13 Mar. 1958; *p.c.*: UPA for Colum; *ex prod*: Stephen Bosustow; *prod/dir*: Pete Burness; *story*: Dun Roman; *anim*: Gil Turner, Barney Posner, Ed Friedman, Fred Grable; *lay*: Robert Dranko; *back*: Bob McIntosh; *voices*: Jim Backus, Daws Butler, Mary Jane Croft; *mus*: Dean Elliott; *col*: Tech. *sd*: RCA. 6 min. • Magoo runs into an old schoolfriend, causing him to relate a story about a bet they once made to date a famous actress.

3999. Magpie Madness (*Heckle & Jeckle*) 2 Nov. 1948; *p.c.*: TT for Fox; *dir*: Eddie Donnelly; *story*: John Foster; *anim*: Jim Tyer; *voices*: Thomas Morrison; *mus*: Philip A. Scheib; *ph*: Douglas Moye; *col*: Tech. *sd*: RCA. 6 min. • The Magpies steal a bowl of bones from a hound named "Soupbone."

4000. The Maid and the Millionaire (*Aesop's Film Fable*) 27 Apr. 1922; *p.c.*: Fables Pictures Inc for Pathé; *dir*: Paul Terry; b&w. sil. 5 min. • No story available.

4001. Maid in China (*Terry-Toon*) 29 Apr 1938; *p.c.*: TT for Educational/Fox; *dir*: Connie Rasinski; *mus*: Philip A. Scheib; b&w. sil. 6 min. • Aladdin rescues the Princess from a villain with assistance from a drawling black genie.

4002. The Mail Coach (*Aesop's Film Fable*) 28 Feb. 1926; *p.c.*: Fables Pictures Inc for Pathé; *dir*: Paul Terry; b&w. sil. 5 min. • The mouse stagecoach driver is ill and his grandson takes the reins. Indians attack and capture the girl riding with the young driver but with help from his faithful horse, he pursues and rescues his lady love.

4003. Mail Dog (*Pluto*) 14 Nov. 1947; *p.c.*: Walt Disney prods for RKO; *dir*: Charles Nichols; *asst dir*: Jack Bruner; *story*: Eric Gurney, Bill de la Torre; *anim*: George Nicholas, George Kreisl, Jerry Hathcock, George Goepper, Art Stevens, Robert Youngquist; *fx*: Jack Boyd; *lay*: Karl Karpé; *back*: Ray Huffine; *voices*: Erdman Penner, James MacDonald; *mus*: Oliver Wallace; *col*: Tech. *sd*: RCA. 6¹⁄₂ min. • Mail dog, Pluto is instructed to drop the mail at Outpost 5. Along the way he is hampered by a rabbit trying to get warm.

4004. The Mail Man (*Aesop's Film Fable*) 17 Dec. 1928; *p.c.*: Fables Pictures Inc for Pathé; *dir*: Paul Terry, Mannie Davis; b&w. sil. 10 min. • No story available.

4005. The Mail Pilot (*Aesop's Film Fable*) 20 Feb. 1927; *p.c.*: Fables Pictures Inc. for Pathé; *dir*: Paul Terry; b&w. sil. 10 min. • A mouse mail pilot is attacked by two airway robbers and is saved by his sweetie who rushes to the rescue, riding in a pelican's bill.

4006. The Mail Pilot (*Mickey Mouse*) 28 Apr. 1933; *p.c.*: Walt Disney prods for UA; *dir*: David D. Hand; *anim*: Johnny Cannon, Les Clark, Joseph d'Igalo, Gilles de Tremaudan, Kevin Donnelly, Clyde Geronimi, Leonard Sebring, Ben Sharpsteen, Marvin Woodward; *asst anim*: Thomas Bonfiglio, Chuck Couch, Nick George, Hardie Gramatky, Jack Kinney, Edward Love, Roy Williams; *voice*: Walt Disney; *mus*: Bert Lewis; b&w. sd. 7 min. • Mail Pilot Mickey eludes bandit Pete. After a chase he captures Pete and saves the mail.

4007. Major Google (*Barney Google*) 24 May 1936; *p.c.*: Charles Mintz prods for Colum; *story*: Sid Marcus; *anim*: Art Davis; *sets*: Phil Davis; *voice*: Smiley Burnett; *mus*: Joe de Nat; *prod mgr*: James Bronis; *col*: Tech. *sd*: RCA. 8 min. • Barney stages an "Amateur Hour" with Snuffy, Bunkie Hill and others performing in a melodrama.

4008. The Major Lied 'Til Dawn (*Merrie Melodies*) 13 Aug. 1938; *p.c.*: Leon Schlesinger prods for WB; *dir*: Frank Tashlin; *story*: Richard Hogan; *anim*: Philip Monroe; *lay*: Griff Jay; *back*: Arthur Loomer; *ed*: Tregoweth E. Brown; *voices*: Ted Pierce, Mel Blanc, Tommy Bond; *mus*: Carl

W. Stalling; *prod sup:* Henry Binder, Raymond G. Katz; *col:* Tech. *sd:* Vit. 7 min. • A big-game hunter tells Freddie Bartholemew a far-fetched yarn of how he shot all the animals in his trophy room.

4009. Make Believe Revue *(Color Rhapsody)* 22 Mar. 1935; *p.c.:* Charles Mintz prods for Colum; *story:* Ben Harrison; *anim:* Manny Gould, Harry Love; *mus:* Joe de Nat; *prod mgr:* James Bronis; *col:* Tech. *sd:* RCA. 7¹⁄₂ min. • A small boy is transported by Mother Goose to Fairyland where he witnesses the local musical show.

4010. Make Mine Freedom *(Fun and Facts About America)* 24 Apr. 1948; *p.c.:* John Sutherland prods for Harding College/MGM; *prod/dir:* John Sutherland; *mus:* Scott Bradley, Paul J. Smith; *col:* Tech. *sd:* 10 min. • The basic freedoms enjoyed by Americans and citizens are warned against adoptions of utopian schemes that may cost the nation its liberty.

4011. Make Mine Music 20 Apr. 1946; *p.c.:* Walt Disney prods for RKO; *prod sup:* Joe Grant, Ben Sharpsteen; *story:* Homer Brightman, T. Hee, Dick Huemer, Dick Kelsey, Dick Shaw, Roy Williams, John Walbridge, Jesse Marsh, Charles Palmer, James Bodrero, Ed Penner, Eric Gurney, Sylvia Holland, Erwin Graham, Tom Oreb, Dick Kinney; *lay:* Al Dempster, John Neindorf; *des:* Mary Blair, John Hench, Elmer Plummer; *mus dir:* Charles Wolcott, Ken Darby, Edward H. Plumb; *title song:* Ken Darby, Eliot Daniel; *process fx:* Ub Iwerks; *col consultant:* Mique Nelson; *sd dir:* C.O. Slyfield, Robert O. Cook. • "The Martins and the Coys" *dir:* Jack Kinney; *anim:* Al Bertino, Les Clark, Milt Kahl, Hal King, Cliff Nordberg, John Sibley; *fx:* Jack Boyd, Andy Engman; *voices:* The King's Men, Frankie Marvin; *song:* Al Cameron, Ted Weems; arranged by Oliver Wallace. • The respective boy and girl from two feuding hillbilly families fall in love. • "Blue Bayou" *dir/lay:* Bob Cormack; *asst dir:* Lloyd L. Richardson; *story:* Sylvia Holland; *anim:* Harry Hamsel, Karl van Leuven, Noel Tucker; *fx:* Cy Young; *voices:* The Ken Darby Chorus; *song:* Bobby Worth, Ray Gilbert. • Originally made by Samuel Armstrong for a segment in *Fantasia* picturing the happenings centering around a bayou. • "All the Cats Join In" *dir:* Jack Kinney; *anim:* Al Bertino, Milt Kahl, Hal King, Bill Justice, Fred Moore, Cliff Nordberg, John Sibley; *fx:* Andy Engman; *lay:* Lance Nolley; *back:* Claude Coats; *voices:* The Pied Pipers; *mus:* Benny Goodman and his orchestra; *song:* Eddie Sauter, Ray Gilbert, Alex Wilder; *arrangement:* Charles Wolcott, Benny Goodman. • Teenagers dance to Benny Goodman's music at the Malt Shop. • "Without You" *dir:* Bob Cormack; *fx:* George Rowley; *voice:* Andy Russell; *song:* Osvaldo Farres; *English lyrics:* Ray Gilbert. • Atmospheric piece. • "Casey at the Bat" *dir:* Clyde Geronimi; *story:* Homer Brightman, Eric Gurney; *anim:* Les Clark, Hugh Fraser, Ward Kimball, Eric Larson, Oliver Johnston, Cliff Nordberg, John Sibley; *fx:* George Rowley; *des:* Mary Blair; *lay:* Hugh Hennesy; *back:* Merle Cox, Ralph Hulett; *voices:* Jerry Colonna, John H. Brown; *mus:* Ken Darby; *song:* Ray Gilbert, Ken Darby, Eliot Daniel. • A musical recitation by Jerry Colonna about Casey, the famous baseball player. • "Two Silhouettes" *dir:* Bob Cormack; *story:* Elmer Plummer; *anim:* Les Clark; *fx:* George Rowley; *lay:* John Hench; *back:* Bill Layne; *voice:* Dinah Shore; *song:* Charles Wolcott, Ray Gilbert; *l/a:* Tatiana Riabouchinska, David Lichine. • Two cherubs play while the ballet dancers, Riabouchinska and Lichine, dance. • "Peter and the Wolf" *dir:* Clyde Geronimi; *story:* Dick Huemer, Eric Gurney, Sam Cobean, Frank Tashlin; *anim:* Ollie Johnston, Ward Kimball, Eric Larson, John Lounsbery, Milt Neil, Don Patterson, Judge Whitaker; *fx:* Josh Meador, George Rowley; *lay:* Charles Philippi, Hugh Hennesy; *back:* Claude Coats; *voice:* Sterling Holloway; *mus:* Edward Plumb. • Sergey Prokofiev's musical tale of a Russian boy who, with his animal friends, captures a hungry wolf. • "After You've Gone" *dir:* Jack Kinney; *anim:* Josh Meador; *lay:* Don da Gradi; *mus:* The Goodman Quartet: Cozy Cole, Sid Weiss, Teddy Wilson, Benny Goodman; *song:* Henry Creamer, Turner Layton. • Musical instruments come alive in this musical fantasy. • "Johnnie Fedora and Alice Bluebonnet" *dir:* Jack Kinney; *story:* Joe Grant, Dick Huemer; *anim:* Al Bertino, Jack Campbell, Les Clark, Al Coe, Phil Duncan, Andy Engman, Tom Massey, Cliff Nordberg, Ken O'Brien, John Sibley, Harvey Toombs, Judge Whitaker; *des:* Albert Hurter, Jack Miller, Sylvia Holland; *voice:* The Andrews Sisters (Patty, Maxene, LaVerne); *mus:* Eliot Daniel, Ken Darby; *song:* Allie Wrubel, Ray Gilbert. • A love story between two hats. • "The Whale Who Wanted to Sing at the Met" *dir:* Hamilton Luske, Clyde Geronimi, Bob Cormack; *story:* Irvin Graham; *story adapt:* T. Hee, Richmond Kelsey; *anim:* Hal Ambro, Al Bertino, Les Clark, Hugh Fraser, Jerry Hathcock, Ward Kimball, Hal King, John Lounsbery, Tom

Massey, Fred Moore, Cliff Nordberg, Ken O'Brien, Harvey Toombs; *fx:* Joshua Meador, George Rowley, Dan MacManus; *lay:* A. Kendall O'Connor, Hugh Hennesy, Al Zinnen, John Hench, Ed Benedict, Arthur Byram, Don Griffiths, Robert Cormack, Charles Payzant; *back:* Ralph Hulett, Ray Huffine, Thelma Witmer, Art Riley, Nino Carbe, Claude Coats, John Hench, Bill Layne, Jimi Trout; *voices:* Nelson Eddy; *mus:* Ken Darby. • A musical impresario travels the seven seas to find an operatic whale. • *col:* Tech. *sd:* RCA. 72 min. • Segmented feature, each piece dealing with a different type of contemporary music.

4012. Makin' 'Em Move 5 July 1931; *p.c.:* Van Beuren for RKO; *dir:* John Foster, Harry Bailey; *mus:* Gene Rodemich; *b&w. sd:* RCA. 7 min. • The animals take over the cartoon studio and show us how animated cartoons are made.

4013. Making Friends *(Betty Boop)* 18 Dec. 1936; *p.c.:* The Fleischer Studio for Para; *prod:* Max Fleischer; *dir:* Dave Fleischer; *anim:* Myron Waldman, Hicks Lokey, Lillian Friedman; *voice:* Mae Questel; *mus:* Sammy Timberg; *b&w. sd:* WE. 6 min. • When Pudgy is told to go out and make friends, he befriends beavers, frogs, rabbits, turtles and a porcupine, bringing them all home

4014. Making Good *(Oswald)* 6 Apr. 1932; *p.c.:* Univ; *dir:* Walter Lantz, "Bill" Nolan; *anim:* Manuel Moreno, Ray Abrams, Fred Avery, "Bill" Weber, Vet Anderson; *mus:* James Dietrich; *b&w. sd:* WE. 8 min. • Oswald helps the old woman who lives in a shoe find more shoes for the children when a dog destroys their home.

4015. Making Stars *(Betty Boop)* 18 Oct. 1935; *p.c.:* The Fleischer Studio for Para; *prod:* Max Fleischer; *dir:* Dave Fleischer; *anim:* Edward Nolan, Herman Cohen, Lillian Friedman; *voice:* Mae Questel; *mus:* Sammy Timberg; *b&w. sd:* WE. 6 min. • Betty introduces some tiny tots who will be the stars of the future.

4016. The Male Man *(Talkartoon)* 25 Apr. 1931; *p.c.:* The Fleischer Studio for Para; *prod:* Max Fleischer; *dir:* Dave Fleischer; *anim:* Ted Sears, Seymour Kneitel; *mus:* Art Turkisher; *b&w. sd:* WE. 6 min. • Mailman Bimbo travels to the depths of Davy Jones' Locker to deliver a letter.

4017. Malibu Beach Party *(Merrie Melodies)* 14 Sept. 1940; *p.c.:* Leon Schlesinger prods for WB; *dir:* I. Freleng; *story:* Jack Miller; *anim:* Gil Turner; *character des:* Ben Shenkman; *back:* Robert L. Holdeman; *ed:* Treg Brown; *voices:* Jack Lescoulie, Mel Blanc, Sara Berner, Danny Webb, Marie Greene; *mus:* Carl W. Stalling; *prod sup:* Henry Binder, Raymond G. Katz; *col:* Tech. *sd:* Vit. 7 min. • Jack Benny invites the local celebrities to a party. Caricatures: Don Ameche, Fred Astaire, John Barrymore, Ben Bernie, Fanny Brice, James Cagney, Claudette Colbert, Joan Crawford, Bette Davis, Andy Devine, Robert Donat, Deanna Durbin, Alice Faye, Clark Gable, Greta Garbo, Cary Grant, Phil Harris, Bob Hope, Kay Kyser, Mary Livingstone, Carole Lombard, Fred MacMurray, Robert Montgomery, Adolphe Menjou, George Raft, "Rochester," Ginger Rogers, Cesar Romero; Mickey Rooney, Ned Sparks, Spencer Tracy, Loretta Young; *col:* Tech. *sd:* Vit. 7 min.

4018. Malice in Slumberland *(Phantasy)* 23 Oct. 1942; *p.c.:* Colum; *prod:* Dave Fleischer; *dir:* Alec Geiss; *anim:* Ray Patterson; *sets:* Clark Watson; *ed:* Edward Moore; *i&p:* Elizabeth F. McDowell; *voice:* Harry E. Lang; *mus:* Eddie Kilfeather; *ph:* Frank Fisher; *prod mgr:* Albert Spar; *b&w. sd:* RCA. 6¹⁄₂ min. • An Air Raid Warden's sleep is disturbed by a dripping faucet.

4019. Mama's New Hat *(Captain & the Kids)* 11 Feb. 1939; *p.c.:* MGM; *dir:* Isadore Freleng; *anim:* Jack Zander; *sets:* Bob Kuwahara; *ed:* Fred MacAlpin; *voices:* Billy Bletcher, Martha Wentworth; *mus:* Scott Bradley; *prod mgr:* Fred Quimby; *col:* sep. *sd:* WE. 6 min. • Hans and Fritz buy Mama a hat for Mother's Day and promptly drop it in the mud. They swap hats with a horse who follows them home to retrieve it.

4020. The Man Called Flintstone 7 Aug. 1966; *p.c.:* Hanna-Barbera prods for Colum; *prod/dir:* William Hanna, Joseph Barbera; *story:* Harvey Bullock, Ray Allen; *add story:* William Hanna, Joseph Barbera, Warren Foster, Alex Lovy; *anim dir:* Charles A. Nichols; *anim:* Irv Spence, George Goepper, George Nicholas, Edward Barge, Edwin Aardal, Jerry Hathcock, Don Lusk, Kenneth Muse, Richard Lundy, Bill Keil, Ed Parks, John Sparey, Allen Wilzback, George Kreisl, George Germanetti, Carlo Vinci, Hugh Fraser, Hicks Lokey; *asst anim:* Sam Jaimes, Charlotte Huffine, Frank Carr,

Tom Ferriter, Richard Gonzalez, Jack Carr, Bill Nunes, Joe Roman, Grace Stanzell, Jack Kerns, John Boersema, Joan Orbison, Jack Parr, William Pratt, Jim Brummett, Rae McSpadden, Tony Love, Pat Combs, Vive Risto, Dennis Silas; *fx:* Brooke Linden; *art dir:* Bill Perez; *lay:* Richard Bickenbach, Lance Nolley, Homer Jonas, Jerry Eisenberg, Jack Huber, Bob Singer, Bruce Bushman, Jack Huber, Brad Case, Walter Clinton, Steve Nakagawa; *back:* F. Montealegre, Paul Julian, Robert Gentle, Art Lozzi, Ron Dias, Janet Brown, Tom Knowles, Fernando Arce, René García, Richard Khim, Don Watson; *ed sup:* Warner Leighton; *ed:* Milton Krear, Pat Foley, Larry Cowan, Dave Horton; *i&p:* Roberta Greutert; *anim checkers:* Janet Gusdavison, Marcel Ferguson, Joyce Gard, Maggie Raymond, Evelyn Sherwood, Grace McCurdy, Annie Lee Holm, Betty MacGowan, Woody Chatwood, Florence Hammontre; *voices: Fred Flintstone:* Alan Reed; *Barney Rubble/Helicopter Pilot/Mayor/Turtle/Scales:* Mel Blanc; *Wilma/Pebbles/Nurse/Baby/Old Lady/Girl#1:* Jean van der Pyl; *Betty Rubble:* Gerry Johnson; *Dr. Moonstone/Camera/Announcers/Recorder/Lift Attendant/Doctor:* Don Messick; *Miss Soapstone/Nurse/Stewardess/Girl#2:* Janet Waldo; *Rock Slag/Bo-Bo/Triple X/Mario/Shady Character:* Paul Frees; *Chief Boulder/Ali/Doctor:* Harvey Korman; *Airport Supervisor/Vet/Doctor/Ali:* John Stephenson; *Tania:* June Foray; *Fred's singing voice:* Henry Corden; "Think Love" sung by Louis Prima; *songs:* Ray Gilbert, Doug Goodwin; *mus ed:* Tony Milch; *ph:* Charles Flekal, Roy Wade, Gene Borghi, Bill Kotler, Norm Stainback, Dick Blundell, Frank Parrish, Hal Shiffman, John Pratt; *technical:* Frank Paiker; *sd sup:* Richard Olsen, Bill Getty; *titles:* Robert Schaefer; *prod sup:* Howard Hanson, Bill Schipek, Harvard C. Pennington; *col:* East. *sd:* RCA. 88 min. • TV's favorite Stone Age family, the Flintstones, get mixed up in the world of espionage and secret agents.

4021. The Man from Button Willow 1964; *p.c.:* Eagle Films Ltd for United Screen Arts; *prod:* Phyllis Bounds DeTiege; *dir/story:* David DeTiege; *story:* Dale Robertson; *anim:* Morris Gollub, Ken Hultgren, Don Towsley, Don Lusk, John Sparey, Ed Friedman, Amby Paliwoda, Harry Holt, Stan Green, John Dunn, Walt Clinton, Gil Turner, Benny Washam, George Rowley; *prod des:* Erni Nordli, Lee Mishkin, Bob Singer, Richard Ung, Corny Cole, Sam Weiss; *lay:* Tony Rivera, Bruce Bushman, Don Morgan; *back:* Dick Kelsey, Thelma Witmer, Ron Dias; *seq continuity:* Steve Clark, Gerald Baldwin, Duane Crowther; *i&p:* Avril Thompson; *ed:* Ted Baker, Sam Horta, Ralph Ives; *voices: Justin Eagle:* Dale Robertson; *Sorry:* Edgar Buchanan; *Stormy:* Barbara Jean Wong; *also:* Herschel Bernardi, Ross Martin, Shepard Menken, Verna Felton, John Hiestand; *title song sung by* Howard Keel; *mus:* George Stoll; *songs: lyrics:* Phil Bounds; *mus:* Dale Robertson, George Bruns, Mel Henke; *original themes:* George Stoll, *new arr Eps:* orch: Leo Arnaud, Albert Sendrey; *scene planning:* Buf Nerbovig, Jane Philippi, Katherine Victor, Robert Brown; *Xerox:* Tom Ramsey, Mindy Bagdon, Ron Honthaner, Jim Goodnow; *ph:* Max Morgan; *prod mgr:* Bill Redlin; *col:* East. *sd.* 84 min. • Justin Eagle, the west's first undercover agent, deals with "The Whip," a villain who forces settlers to dispose of their land.

4022. Man Higher Up 8 Oct. 1914; b&w. *sil.* 6 min. • Cartoon satirizing tipplers.

4023. Man Hunt (Oswald) 7 Feb. 1938; *p.c.:* Walter Lantz prods for Univ; *prod/dir:* Walter Lantz; *story:* Victor McLeod, James Miele; *anim:* Lester Kline, Ralph Somerville; *voice:* Mel Blanc, Shirley Reed; *mus:* Frank Marsales; b&w. *sd:* WE. 10 min. • Oswald protects the animals from hunters.

4024. Man in Space 18 Jul. 1956; *p.c.:* Walt Disney prods for BV; *prod/dir:* Ward Kimball; *story:* Ward Kimball, William Bosché, Julius Svendsen; *anim:* Julius Svendsen, Arthur Stevens, John Sibley, Eric Cleworth, Harvey Toombs, John Dunn; *fx:* Jack Boyd; *art dir:* Feild Grey; *lay:* A. Kendall O'Connor, Donald Griffith, Jacques Rupp; *back:* Claude Coats, Donald Peters, Anthony Rizzo, George de Lado, Art Riley; *l/a:* Willy Ley, Dr. Heinz Haber, Dr. Wernher von Braun; *ed:* Archie Dattlebaum, Lloyd L. Richardson; *voice:* Dick Tufeld; *mus:* George Bruns; *ph:* William Skall ASC; *sd:* C.O. Slyfield, Robert O. Cook; *special processes:* Ub Iwerks, Robert Ferguson; *col:* Tech. *sd:* RCA. 33 min. *l/a/anim.* • Space exploration is explained including the problems met during weightlessness.

4025. Man Made Miracles 23 Sept. 1954; *p.c.:* John Sutherland prods for UA; *dir/story:* True Boardman; *anim:* Bill Melendez; *col:* Tech. *sd.* 11 min. • No story available.

4026. Man of Action 1 Jan. 1956; *p.c.:* Transfilm Inc for ACTION; *dir/anim:* David Hilberman; underwritten by The Continental Can Co; col/b&w. *sd.* 13½ min. • The Devil's Emissary tries to pursuade John Q. Citizen against helping fight slums but he is finally beaten. A film showing how citizens can effectively fight slums. Free loan to churches, clubs, etc.

4027. Man of Tin (Phantasy) 23 Feb. 1940; *p.c.:* Colum: *story:* Allen Rose; *anim:* Harry Love; *ed:* George Winkler; *voices:* Danny Webb, Robert Winkler; *mus:* Joe de Nat; *ph:* Otto Reimer; *prod mgr:* James Bronis; b&w. *sd:* RCA. 6 min. • Scrappy brings a robot to life by working it from the inside and gets involved in a wrestling bout.

4028. The Man on the Flying Trapeze (Popeye) 30 Mar. 1934; *p.c.:* The Fleischer Studio for Para; *prod:* Max Fleischer; *dir:* Dave Fleischer; *anim:* Willard Bowsky, David Tendlar; *voices:* William A. Costello, Charles Carver, Louis Fleischer; *mus:* Sammy Timberg; *song:* George Leybourne, Alfred Lee; b&w. *sd:* WE. 6 min. • Popeye goes in search of Olive, who has been taken away by a circus performer.

4029. The Man on the Flying Trapeze 3 Apr. 1954; *p.c.:* UPA for Colum; *ex prod:* Stephen Bosustow; *dir:* Ted Parmelee; *asst dir:* Ray Thursby; *story:* Bill Scott, Fred Grable; *anim:* Pat Matthews, Casey Onaitis; *sets:* Paul Julian; *voices:* Jack Mather, Colleen Collins; *mus:* Lou Maury; *song:* George Leybourne, Alfred Lee; *prod mgr:* Herbert Klynn; *col:* Tech. *sd:* RCA. 6 min. • Fifi leaves her beau for Alonzo, the trapeze artist, then forsakes him for the Circus boss ... where the real money lies.

4030. Mannequin on the Move 17 May 1991; *p.c.:* Gladden Entertainment for Rank; *anim:* Chris Casady; *mannequin sculpture:* Tanya Wolf Ragir; *col. sd.* 95 min. *l/a.* • Live-action comedy: The centerpiece of an exhibition based on the national treasure of Hauptmann-Koenig comes to life.

4031. Man's Best Friend (Cartune) 20 Oct. 1941; *p.c.:* Walter Lantz prods for Univ; *dir:* Walter Lantz; *story:* Ben Hardaway, Jack Cosgriff; *anim:* Alex Lovy, Harold Mason; *sets:* Fred Brunish; *voice:* Pinto Colvig; *mus:* Darrell Calker; *prod mgr:* George E. Morris; *col:* Tech *sd:* WE. 7 min. • A hunting dog is kept awake by his quarry so that he should be too tired for the morning's hunt.

4032. Man's Best Friend (Goofy) 21 Mar. 1952; *p.c.:* Walt Disney prods for RKO; *dir:* Jack Kinney; *story:* Milt Banta, Al Bertino; *anim:* George Nicholas, John Sibley, Charles Nichols, Hugh Fraser, Ed Aardal, Hal King; *fx:* George Rowley, Dan MacManus; *lay:* Al Zinnen; *back:* Dick Anthony; *voices:* Jack Rourke, Pinto Colvig, James MacDonald, Virginia Beck, Al Bertino, Dick Kinney, Brice Mack, Milt Schaffer, John Sibley, Lucille Williams; *mus:* Joseph S. Dubin; *col:* Tech. *sd:* RCA. 6 min. • Geef buys a puppy that develops into an oversized nuisance.

4033. Man's Pest Friend (Little Lulu) 30 Nov. 1945; *p.c.:* Famous for Para; *dir:* Seymour Kneitel; *story:* I. Klein, George Hill; *anim:* Graham Place, Gordon Whittier, Lou Zukor, Martin Taras; *sets:* Shane Miller; *voices:* Cecil Roy, Jackson Beck; *mus:* Winston Sharples; *prod mgr:* Sam Buchwald; *col:* Tech. *sd:* RCA. 8 min. • Lulu has a tough time keeping her dog from the Dogcatcher's clutches.

4034. Many a Slip (Whirlwind Comedy) Jan. 1927; *p.c.:* FBO; *dir/l/a:* Charles R. Bowers; *story:* Charles R. Bowers, H.L. Muller, Ted Sears; *ph:* H.L. Muller; *asst dir:* Eddie James; b&w. *sil.* 20 min. *l/a.* • Live-action comedy: Charley is the inventor of non-skid banana skins. An animated mouse party has two mice staging a poker game over a piece of cheese. Live-action/model animation.

4035. The Many Adventures of Winnie the Pooh 11 Mar. 1977; *p.c.:* Walt Disney prods for BV; *prod:* Wolfgang Reitherman; *dir:* Wolfgang Reitherman, John Lounsbery; based on the books by A.A. Milne, illustrated by E.H. Shepard; *linking animation:* Dale Baer, Don Bluth, Andrew Gaskill, Gary Goldsmith, Burny Mattinson, John Pomeroy, Cliff Nordberg, Richard Sebast, Chuck Williams; *col:* Tech. *sd:* RCA. 74 min. • Compilation trilogy of Winnie the Pooh films with new linking material. • See: *Winnie the Pooh and the Blustery Day; Winnie the Pooh and the Honey Tree; Winnie the Pooh and Tigger Too*

4036. Many Tanks (Popeye) 15 June 1942; *p.c.:* The Fleischer Studio for Para; *prod:* Max Fleischer; *dir:* Dave Fleischer; *story:* Bill Turner, Carl Meyer; *anim:* Tom Johnson, Frank Endres; *ed:* Kitty Pfister; *voices:* Jack Mercer, Ted Pierce, Margie Hines; *mus:* Sammy Timberg; *prod sup:* Sam

Buchwald, Isidore Sparber; b&w. *sd:* WE. 7 min. • Bluto goes AWOL from the Army by switching uniforms with Popeye. Our hero is made to drive a tank, where he lets loose his wonted power.

4037. The Marathon Dancers *(Aesop's Film Fable)* 19 July 1923; *p.c.:* Fables Pictures Inc for Pathé; *dir:* Paul Terry; b&w. *sil.* 5 min. • Everything on the farm, including the inanimate objects, joins in the current dancing craze. Even Farmer Al joins in when the cat puts jumping beans in his boots.

4038. The March of Time 1944/1951; *dir:* Len Lye; b&w. *sd.* • Series of seven films made as inserts for "The March of Time" newsreels.

4039. Marching Along *(Sentinel Louey)* 27 Oct. 1933; *p.c.:* Van Beuren for RKO; *dir:* George Stallings; *anim:* Jim Tyer; *mus:* Gene Rodemich; b&w. *sd:* RCA. 6 min. • Sentinel Louey's day at the pillbox. Intended as a boost for President Roosevelt's NRA.

4040. Marco: "Peace Berry" 1973; *p.c.:* Rankin/Bass prods & Tomorrow Enterprises Inc.; *prod/dir:* Arthur Rankin Jr., Jules Bass; *story/lyrics:* Romeo Muller; *anim:* Akikani Konu; *mus:* Maury Laws; *col. sd.* 109 min. *l/a/anim.* • Animated sequence in live-action film starring Desi Arnaz, Jr. as young Marco Polo and Zero Mostel as Kublai Khan.

4041. Mariutch *(Screen Songs)* 15 Nov. 1930; *p.c.:* The Fleischer Studio for Para; *prod:* Max Fleischer; *dir:* Dave Fleischer; *anim:* Grim Natwick; *mus:* Art Turkisher; b&w. *sd:* WE. 6 min. • "Mariutch" sails away and leaves her lover.

4042. Mark Twain 17 Jan. 1986; *p.c.:* Will Vinton Prods./Harbour Town Films II, III for Entertainment; *dir/prod:* Will Vinton; *ex prod:* Hugh Kennedy Tirrell; *asso prod./scr:* Susan Shadburne; *prod. sup/general mgr.:* David Altschul; *prod. co-ord:* Patricia von Hinckeldey; *post-prod. sup:* Andy Wiskes; *addit. writing/research:* Dan Yost, Mary Yost; *optical fx:* Pat O'Neill, George Lockwood, Lookout Mountain Films; *character des:* Barry Bruce; *set des./claypainting fx:* Joan C. Gratz, Don Merkt; *principal claymation character: (Becky Thatcher):* William L. Fiesterman; *(Tom Sawyer/Dan'l Webster):* Tom Gasek; *(Huck Finn):* Mark Gustafson; *(Mark Twain):* Barry Bruce; *(Stormfield/aliens):* Craig Bartlett; *(airship):* Bruce McKean; *addit. claymation:* Don Merkt, Will Vinton, Matt Wuerker, Douglas Aberle, James McAllister, Joanne Radmilovich; *motion control development:* Sam Longoria; *ed:* Kelley Baker, Michael Gall, Will Vinton, Ed Geis, Skeets McGrew; *computer fx:* Gary McRobert; *voices: Mark Twain:* James Whitmore; *Becky Thatcher/Mysterious Stranger/Girl in Crowd:* Michele Mariana; *Huck Finn:* Gary Krug; *Tom Sawyer:* Chris Ritchie; *Adam:* John Morrison; *Eve:* Carol Edelman; *Jim Smiley/Newspaper Boy:* Dallas McKennon; *Stranger:* Herb Smith; *Aunt Polly:* Marley Stone; *Mysterious Stranger:* Wilbur Vincent; *Captain Stormfield:* Wally Newman; *Three-headed Alien:* Tim Conner; *Saint Peter:* Todd Tolces; *Index-O-Vator:* Billy Scream; *Dan'l Webster:* Wilf Innton; *Homer/Calaveras Miner:* Tom Gasek; *Injun Joe:* Compton Downs; *God:* Billy Victor; *1st Heckler:* Bob Griggs; *2nd Heckler:* Coward Wholesale; *Man in Crowd:* Peter Tomashek; *Woman in Crowd:* Sally Sopwith; *1st Miner:* Andrew Edwards; *2nd Miner:* Harvey Brown; *Calaveras Miners:* Craig Bartlett, Mark Gustafson, Bruce McKean; *Animals:* Neil Suza, Tim Kahn, Stashu Beencof, Billy Scream; *Mud People:* Neil Suza, Kesag Mot, Kim Tonner; *Baby Cain:* Gary Thompson; *mus:* Billy Scream; *mus ed:* Skeets McGrew, Will Vinton; *song:* "Heroes" by Billy Scream, Paul Jamison, Susan Shadburne, performed by The Billy Scream Band; *main title des:* Michael Duffield, Dennis Tabor; *title lay:* Marilyn Zornado; *sd ed:* Jan Baross, Andy Wiskes, Luther Greene, Will Harvey; *sd fx ed:* Kelley Baker, Paul Diener; *sd fx rec:* Gary McRobert, Kelley Baker; *synthesizer fx:* Jim Fischer, Billy Scream; *creative consultant:* Walter Murch; *prod asst:* Carol Hart; *col. sd.* 83 min. • The celebrated writer, Mark Twain, boards his flying machine to take a journey to Halley's Comet. Huck Finn, Tom Sawyer and Becky Thatcher all stow away to meet their author. Twain revisits some of his stories: "The Celebrated Jumping Frog of Calaveras County," "The Diary of Adam and Eve," "The Mysterious Stranger" and "Captain Stormfield's Trip to Heaven." The children realize that Twain is traveling to the comet to be reunited with his deceased wife, Livy, and they try to divert the journey. Claymation.

4043. Marriage Wows *(Screen Song)* 16 Sept. 1949; *p.c.:* Famous for Para; *dir:* I. Sparber; *story:* Bill Turner, Larry Riley; *anim:* Myron Waldman, Gordon Whittier; *sets:* Tom Ford *mus:* Winston Sharples; *song:* Edgar Leslie, E. Ray Goetz, George W. Meyer; *ph:* Leonard McCormick; *prod mgr:* Sam Buchwald; *col:* Tech. *sd:* RCA. 7 min. • An elephant marries a mouse.

4044. Marriage Wows *(Talkartoons)* 8 Jan. 1930; *p.c.:* The Fleischer Studio for Para; *prod:* Max Fleischer; *dir:* Dave Fleischer; *anim:* Al Eugster; *mus:* Art Turkisher; b&w. *sd:* WE. 6 min. • Antics of guests on Hippo's wedding day.

4045. The Marry-Go-Round *(Popeye)* 31 Dec. 1943; *p.c.:* Famous for Para; *dir:* Seymour Kneitel; *story:* Joe Stultz; *anim:* Graham Place, Abner Kneitel; *voices:* Jack Mercer, Margie Hines; *mus:* Sammy Timberg; *prod mgr:* Sam Buchwald; b&w. *sd:* WE. 7½ min. • Shorty the sailor helps Popeye propose to Olive, ending up being engaged to her himself.

4046. Mars *(Oswald)* 29 Dec. 1930; *p.c.:* Univ; *dir:* Walter Lantz, "Bill" Nolan; *anim:* Clyde Geronimi, Manuel Moreno, Ray Abrams, Fred Avery, Lester Kline, "Pinto" Colvig; *mus:* James Dietrich; b&w. *sd:* WE 6 min. • Oswald and Peg-Leg compete for a girl in the park. His rival kicks Oswald to Mars where he sings "The Lucky Rabbit" number.

4047. Mars and Beyond 26 Dec. 1957; *p.c.:* Walt Disney prods for BV; *prod/dir:* Ward Kimball; *story:* William Bosché, Ward Kimball; *cartoon story:* John Dunn, Charles Downs, Con Pederson; *anim:* Julius Svendsen, Art Stevens, Jack Boyd, Charles Downs, John Dunn; *lay:* A. Kendall O'Connor, John Brandt, Tom Yakutis; *backs:* William Layne, J. Gordon Legg; *fx:* Eustace Lycett; *ed:* Lloyd L. Richardson ACE, Lionel A. Ephraim; *models:* Wathel Rogers; *voice:* Paul Frees; *mus:* George Bruns; *l/a:* Dr. Ernst Stuhlinger, Dr. Wernher von Braun, Dr. E.C. Slipher; *sd:* Robert O. Cook; *col:* Tech. *sd:* RCA. 49 min. *l/a/anim.* • An entertaining view on what might be found on Mars when space exploration finally reaches a reality.

4048. Mars Attacks 12 Dec. 1996; *p.c.:* WB; *Martian visual fx anim:* Industrial Light & Magic: *asso fx sup:* Ellen Poon; *visual fx art dir:* Mark Moore; *cg sups:* Roger Guyett, Andy White; *cg seq, sups.:* Joel Aron, David S. Horsley, Barbara L. Nellis, Ben Snow; *lead character anim:* Chris Armstrong, Kyle Balda, Linda M. Del, Lou Dellarosa, Jenn Emberly; *miniature dir. of ph:* Patrick Sweeney; *char anim:* Patrick Bonneau, Sue Campbell, Bruce Dahl, Peter Daulton, Tim Harrington, Jason Ivimey, Heather Knight, Julija Learie, Victoria Livingstone, Neil Michka, Julie Nelson, David Parsons, Magali Pouet Rigaudias, Trish Schutz, Scott Huck Wirtz, William R. Wright, Brad Woods; *digital fx arts:* Jeffrey Benedict, Amelia Chendweth, Natasha Devaud, Russell William Earl, Gerald Gutschimdt d.IV, Mary Beth Haggerty, Christina Hills, David Yukio Hisanaga, Greg Killmaster, Tim McLaughlin, Robert Marinic, David Meny; *miniatures:* Curt I. Miyashiro, Kenneth J. Nielsen, Henry Preston, Amanda Ronai-Dahle, Sean Schur, B. Durant Schoon, John Stillman, R. Christopher White, Robert Weaver; *digital armature des:* Tim Waddy; *snr. visual fx co-ord:* Jill Brooks; *digital character modelers:* Tony Hudson, Frank Gravatt; *software research & development:* Christian Rouet; *software engineers:* David Benson, Jim Hourihan, Gary Phillips; *digital texting paint:* Jean-Claude Langer; *digital timing sup:* Bruce Vegghitto; *scanning sup:* Joshua Pines; *digital paint & roto:* Jack Mongovan, Tami Carter, Susan Goldsmith, Elsa Rodriguez, Jarmila Seflova, Scott Stewart; *location matchmove technician:* Jack Edsel Haye; *3d ph matchmove:* David Washburn, Alia Agha, Randy Jonsson, David Manos Morris, Patrice Saenz, John Whisnant; *sabre art:* Grant Guenin, Ilm Gaffer, Michael Olague; *visual fx ph asst:* Kate O'Neill; *model makers:* Charlie Bailey, Eben Stromquist, Chuck Wiley, Steve Gawley; *ed sup:* Dan McNamara; *visual fx ed:* Bill Kimberlin, Greg Hyman; *voices:* Frank Welker; *Warner Digital Studios: prod sup:* Ellen Somers; *VIX prod.:* Lauren Alexandra Ritchie; *digital fx sup:* Guy Williams; *art dpt sup/matte art:* Jesse Silver; *cgi lead—Robot:* Brian Steiner; *cgi lead—Saucer:* Chris Waegner; *technical sup/cg landing seq:* Bill Konersman; *cg art:* Rhett Bennett, Jeffrey Bendit, Heather Bushman, Vince DeQuaitro, Adam Dotson, Jamie Engel, Mark Farquhar, Vincent M. Giordano, Kelly Hartigan, Christian Hatfield, Matthew Head, Roger Huynh, Todd Jahnke, Arthur Jeppe, Carolyn Ippisch, Hiroki Hokazu, Alice V. Kaiserian, James Kuo, David G. Lawson, Janice Lew, Shanna Lim, Aaron Linton, Mary E. Manning, Rob Ostir, Robert Shrider, David E. Smith, Evelyn Spencer, Kathi Spencer, Kenji Sweeney, Marc Toscano, Kelly Wilcox, Lindy Wilson, Genevieve Yee, Ingrid Yegros; *inferno sup:* Victor Jimenez; *inferno arts:* Fortunato Frattasio, John Kohn; *2d Arts:* Jillian Backus, Katie A. Tucker, Bonjin Byun; *2d Roto arts:* Michael Adkisson, Michael Hemschoot; *2d texture art:* Darren Bedwell, Phil Carlig, Linda Shepard; *Matte paint:* Tim Clark, Michelle Moen; *VFX prod mgr:* Mimi Medel; *2d VFX prod mgr:* Lynn M. Gephart; *VFX asst co-ord:* Lindsay Burnett; *model prod co-ord:* Casey Steele; *oh-set plate mgr:* Bill Maher; *asstfilm assembly technician:* Heather J. Morrison; *col* *imaging sup:* Dave Gregory; *digital ph sup:* Megan Bryant; *digital col. lead:* Christopher Savides, Robert White; *tape operations lead:* Michael Wilhelm; *software lead/systems admin:* Kevin Smith; *hardware lead/systems admin:* Andy Ghua; *software project mgr:* Hiroyuki Miyoshi; *software engineer:* Cesar Velazquez; *Acme Model Shop sup:* Michael Joyce; *model makers:* Mark Ross-Sullivan, Ken Swenson; Martian character/spacesuit design by MacKinnon & Saunders Ltd.; *des sups.:* Peter Saunders, Ian MacKinnon; *des sculptors:* Colin Batty, Noel Baker, Darren Marshall; *prod. sup:* Barry Jones, Christine Walker; *shop co-ords:* Graham Maiden, Simon White; *model des.:* Bridget Smith; *lead paint:* Astrig Akserilian; *costume sup:* Geraldine Corrigan; *mechanics des:* Stuart Sutcliffe, Georgina Hayns; *prototype fabrication:* Lucy Gell, Mark Thompson, Christine Keogh; *col:* Tech. *sd:* Dolby Digital/dts/SDDS. Panavision. 105 min. *l/a.* • Live-action comedy: Washington, D.C., prepares for a visit from Martians who have been observing the Earth. They prove to be vehemently aggressive and start attacking all in their path including Las Vegas, the White House and the President. Computer animation.

4049. Martha *(Song-o-Reel)* 1923; *p.c.:* Laugh-o-Gram Films Inc for Jenkins Music Co; *dir:* Walt Disney; *ph:* Red Lyon; *song:* Joe L. Sanders; b&w. *sil.* 2 min. *l/a/anim.* • Sing-along made specifically for screening at the Isis Theatre, Kansas City.

4050. Martian Moochers *(Astronut)* May 1970 (© 1965); *p.c.:* TT for Fox; *ex prod:* Bill Weiss; *dir/anim:* Bob Kuwahara; *story sup:* Tom Morrison; *story:* Larz Bourne; *sets:* Bill Focht, John Zago; *ed:* Jack MacConnell; *voices:* Dayton Allen; *mus:* Jim Timmens; *ph:* Joe Rasinski; *sd:* Elliot Grey; *col:* DeLuxe. *sd:* RCA. 5½ min. • Two destructive Martians stow away in Astro's spaceship, causing Oscar a headache when trying to have a barbecue.

4051. Martian Through Georgia *(Looney Tunes)* Dec. 1962; *p.c.:* WB; *dir:* Chuck Jones, Abe Levitow; *asst dir:* Maurice Noble; *story:* Carl Kohler, Chuck Jones; *anim:* Tom Ray, Ken Harris, Richard Thompson, Bob Bransford; *back:* Philip de Guard; *voices:* Ed Prentiss, Mel Blanc; *mus:* Bill Lava; *prod mgr:* William Orcutt; *prod:* David H. DePatie; *col:* Tech. *sd:* Vit. 6 min. • A bored Martian comes to Earth, is mistaken for a monster and returns to his own planet where he finds life a lot more tolerable.

4052. The Martins and the Coys *(Marquee Musical)* 18 June 1956; *p.c.:* Walt Disney prods for BV; *dir:* Jack Kinney; *col:* Tech. *sd:* RCA. 6 min. • See: *Make Mine Music*

4053. Marty the Monk 1934; *p.c.:* Boyd la Vero Studios for Associated Films; *prod/dir:* Boyd la Vero; b&w. *sd.* 6 min. • Marty rides the trolley bus to the Parade Grounds where he provides the music and judges the Jungle Town bathing beauties.

4054. Marvin Digs *(Go-Go Toon)* Dec. 1967; *p.c.:* Para Cartoons; *ex prod/dir:* Ralph Bakshi; *story:* Eli Bauer; *anim:* Doug Crane, Al Eugster, Nick Tafuri; *asst anim:* Danté Barbetta, Margaret Breese, Jack Ehret, Ruth Platt; *lay:* Cosmo Anzilotti; *des:* Ralph Bakshi, Cosmo Anzilotti, John Zago, James Simon; *voices:* Dayton Allen, "The Life Cycle" *mus:* Winston Sharples; *song:* "The Life Cycle," Vicki Gailzaid; *col:* Tech. *sd:* RCA. 6 min. • A Hippie and his pals redecorate dad's apartment in psychedelic colors.

4055. Mary and Gretel *(Motoy comedies)* 1917; *p.c.:* Peter Pan Film Corp; *anim:* Howard Moss; b&w. *sil.* 10 min. • Adapted from the "Motoys in Life" books. Mary and Gretel are brought to life by a fairy and follow a white rabbit to meet Rip Van Winkle and some gnomes ten-pin bowling.

4056. Mary Poppins 29 Aug. 1964; *p.c.:* Walt Disney prods for BV; *co-prod:* Bill Walsh; *anim dir:* Hamilton S. Luske; *story:* Bill Walsh, Donald da Gradi; *anim art dir:* McLaren Stewart; *Nursery seq des:* Bill Justice, Xavier Atencio; *anim: opening fx:* Dan MacManus; *animals & jockeys:* Eric Larson; *animals before song:* Cliff Nordberg; *farmyard animals during song:* John Lounsbery; *turtles:* Hal Ambro; *swans:* Julius Svendsen; *penguin dance:* Ollie Johnston, Frank Thomas; *Carousel Guard:* Art Stevens; *Fox & Hounds:* John Lounsbery, Fred Hellmich, Milt Kahl; *Pearlies:* Ward Kimball, Jack Boyd; *sets:* Al Dempster, Art Riley, Don Griffiths, Bill Layne; *voices: Fox/ Horse/Reporter #1/Merry-go-Round Attendant/Penguin/Hound:* Dallas McKennon; *Master of the Hounds/Hound/Horse/Penguin/Reporter #2/Pearly/Photographer:* J. Pat O'Malley; *Huntsman/Reporter#3/Hound:* Alan Napier; *Hound/Reporter #4:* Sean McClory; *Steward/Jockey/Penguin:* David Tomlinson; *Hound/Reporter #5:* George Pelling; *Ram:* Bill Lee; *Lambs:* Mary Virginia Tyler; *Horse:* Paul Frees; *Cow:* Marc Breaux; *Geese:* Marni Nixon; *Turtle/Penguin:* Daws Butler; *Penguin/Pearly:* Dick Sherman; *mus:* Irwin

Kostal; *songs:* Richard M. Sherman, Robert B. Sherman; *col:* Tech. *sd:* RCA. anim. 17 min. *l/a/anim.* • P.L. Travers' stories brought together in a marvellous cocktail of songs, live-action and cartoon. Mary Poppins (Julie Andrews) and Bert (Dick van Dyke) take the children through a pavement chalk drawing into a cartoon world where they join in a dance with penguin waiters and compete in a horse race.

4057. Mary's Little Lamb *(ComiColor)* 14 Apr. 1935; *p.c.:* Celebrity prods; *prod/dir:* Ub Iwerks; *mus:* Carl Stalling; *col:* Ciné. *sd:* PCP. 6 min. • Mary's persistent lamb gate-crashes school and shows considerable talent.

4058. The Mask 29 July 1994; *p.c.:* New Line Prods. for Dark Horse Entertainment; *anim ph:* Brian Adams; *visual fx/computer anim:* ILM; *addit. visual fx:* Dream Quest Images; *visual fx consultants:* Ken Ralston, Scott Squires, Steve "Spaz" Williams; *visual fx ex prod:* Mark Galvin; *visual fx ex in charge of prod:* Patricia Blau; *visual fx sups (anim):* Steve "Spaz" Williams; *anim/visual fx prod:* Clint Goldman; *cgi seq sups:* Ellen Poon, Sandra Ford Karpman, Jim Mitchell; *anim sups:* Jeff Burke, *Milo:* Tom "Noodles" Bertino; *cgi anim:* Chris Armstrong, Kyle Balda, Rob Coleman, Bill Fletcher, Wade Howie, Paul Hunt, Stewart W. Lew, Les Major, Dale McBeath, Kyle Odermatt, Shawna Olwen, Wes Ford Takahashi, Dan Taylor; *title des:* Phill Norman; *titles/opticals:* Pacific Title, Howard Anderson Co.; *col:* Foto-Kem. *sd:* Dolby Stereo. 101 min. *l/a* • Live-action comedy: Underwater workers in the harbor unearth an antique chest containing an ancient wooden mask. A timid bank clerk finds the mask and tries it on, instantly becoming a green-faced cartoon character with super-human powers.

4059. Mask-A-Raid *(Talkartoon)* 7 Nov. 1931; *p.c.:* The Fleischer Studio for Para; *prod:* Max Fleischer; *dir:* Dave Fleischer; *anim:* Bernard Wolf, William Henning, Al Eugster; *mus:* Art Turkisher; *song:* Mortimer Weinberg, Charley Marks, Harry Warren; b&w. *sd:* WE. 6 min. • Bimbo fights a duel for Betty, the Masquerade Queen.

4060. The Masque Raid *(Krazy Kat)* 25 June 1937; *p.c.:* Charles Mintz prods for Colum; *story:* Allen Rose; *anim:* Harry Love; *voices:* Martha Wentworth, Dave Weber; *mus:* Joe de Nat; *prod mgr:* James Bronis; b&w. *sd:* RCA. 6½ min. • Nightwatchman, Krazy, falls asleep while guarding a costume shop and dreams the wax figures come to life.

4061. The Masquerade *(Out of the Inkwell)* 1 Feb. 1924; *p.c.:* Inkwell Studio for Winkler; *dir:* Dave Fleischer; *anim:* Max Fleischer; b&w. *sil.* 5 min. • Max dresses as the Inkwell Clown to go to a masquerade party. The little clown steals his hat and Max chases him into Cartoonland where he is attacked by a band of pen and ink clowns.

4062. The Masquerade Party *(Krazy Kat)* 9 May 1934; *p.c.:* Charles Mintz prods for Colum; *story:* Harry Love; *anim:* Allen Rose, Preston Blair; *mus:* Joe de Nat; *prod mgr:* James Bronis; b&w. *sd:* RCA. 6 min. • Krazy and Kitty throw a masquerade party where characters in strange costumes arrive.

4063. Mass Mouse Meeting *(Phantasy)* 25 June 1943; *p.c.:* Colum; *prod:* Dave Fleischer; *dir:* Alec Geiss; *story:* Dun Roman; *anim:* Chic Otterstrom; *voices:* John McLeish, Sara Berner; *mus:* Paul Worth; *ph:* Frank Fisher; *prod mgr:* Albert Spar; b&w. *sd:* RCA. 6 min. • A rebellious little mouse is chosen against his will to put a bell around the cat's neck.

4064. Matador Magoo *(Mr. Magoo)* 28 Mar. 1957; *p.c.:* UPA for Colum; *dir:* Pete Burness; *story:* Dick Shaw; *anim:* Cecil Surry, Tom McDonald, Gil Turner, Barney Posner; *lay:* Robert Dranko; *back:* Bob McIntosh; *voices:* Jim Backus, Jerry Hausner; *mus:* Dennis Farnon; *solo guitar:* Jeronimo Villarino; *prod mgr:* Herbert Klynn; *col:* Tech. *sd:* RCA. 5½ min. CS. • While motoring through Mexico, Magoo finds himself way off course in the center of a bull ring, unwittingly dealing with an outraged bull.

4065. The Match Kid *(Scrappy)* 9 May 1933; *p.c.:* Winkler for Colum; *prod:* Charles Mintz; *story:* Sid Marcus; *anim:* Art Davis; *mus:* Joe de Nat; *prod mgr:* James Bronis; b&w. *sd:* RCA. 6 min. • The little match boy starves in a shanty while his mean master feeds his face. As the villain prepares to attack him, Scrappy appears and they join forces in overpowering him.

4066. Matinee Mouse *(Tom & Jerry)* 1966; *p.c.:* MGM; *prod:* Chuck Jones; *dir/story/anim:* Tom Ray; *sets:* Philip de Guard; *ed:* Lowell Norman; *voices:* Mel Blanc; *mus:* Dean Elliot; *classic footage: dir:* William Hanna,

Joseph Barbera; *anim:* Ken *Muse*, Ed Barge, Irven Spence, Ray Patterson, Lewis Marshall; *col:* Metro. *sd:* WE. 6 min. Seq: *Love That Pup*; *The Flying Cat*; *Jerry's Diary*; *The Flying Sorceress*; *The Truce Hurts.* • Tom and Jerry form a truce and visit the movies where they view "Tom and Jerry" cartoons.

4067. Maw and Paw 10 Aug. 1953; *p.c.:* Walter Lantz rods for Univ; *dir:* Paul J. Smith; *story:* Homer Brightman; *anim:* Ken Southworth, Gil Turner, Robert Bentley; *sets:* Raymond Jacobs, Art Landy; *voices:* Dal McKennon, Grace Stafford; *mus:* Clarence Wheeler; *prod mgr:* William E. Garity; *col:* Tech. *sd:* RCA. 6 min. • Milford the pig wins a large, modern car. It's too big for the farm but is reduced to the size of a Model-T when it runs into a tree.

4068. The Mayflower (*Paul Terry-Toon*) 27 Dec. 1935; *p.c.:* Moser & Terry for Educational/Fox; *dir:* Frank Moser, Paul Terry; *mus:* Philip A. Scheib; b&w. *sd:* WE. 5¹/₂ min. • When the *Mayflower* runs aground in America, the Indians take advantage of the situation by selling the intruders land and hot-dogs, etc.

4069. McDougal's Rest Farm (*Heckle & Jeckle*) 31 Jan. 1947; *p.c.:* TT for Fox; *dir:* Mannie Davis; *story:* John Foster; *sets:* Art Bartsch; *voices:* Dayton Allen; *mus:* Philip A. Scheib; *ph:* Douglas Moye; *col:* Tech. *sd:* RCA. 6 min. • The rest farm for animals is tranquil until the arrival of the magpies, who make their home in a tree, disrupting the proceedings.

4070. Me Feelins Is Hurt (*Popeye*) 12 Apr. 1940; *p.c.:* The Fleischer Studio for Para; *prod:* Max Fleischer; *dir:* Dave Fleischer; *story:* William Turner, Jack Knight; *anim:* Orestes Calpini, Bob Leffingwell; *ed:* Kitty Pfister; *voices:* Jack Mercer, Pinto Colvig, Margie Hines; *mus:* Sammy Timberg; *prod sup:* Sam Buchwald, Isidore Sparber; b&w. *sd:* WE. 7 min. • Olive falls for Bluto, a cowboy at the Bar None Ranch ... but Popeye soon wins her back.

4071. Me Musical Nephews (*Popeye*) 25 Dec. 1942; *p.c.:* Famous for Para; *dir:* Seymour Kneitel; *story:* Jack Mercer, Jack Ward; *anim:* Tom Johnson, George Germanetti; *voices:* Jack Mercer; *mus:* Sammy Timberg; *ph:* Leonard McCormick; *prod mgr:* Sam Buchwald; b&w. *sd:* WE. 6¹/₂ min. • Popeye's nephews prefer to play jazz while their uncle tries to get some shut-eye.

4072. Meatless Flyday (*Merrie Melodies*) 29 Jan. 1944; *p.c.:* Leon Schlesinger prods for WB; *dir:* I. Freleng; *story:* Michael Maltese; *anim:* Jack Bradbury; *lay:* Owen Fitzgerald; *back:* Lenard Kester; *ed:* Treg Brown; *voices:* Cy Kendall, Ted Pierce; *mus:* Carl W. Stalling; *prod mgr:* Henry Binder, Raymond G. Katz; *col:* Tech. *sd:* Vit. 7 min. • A battle of wits between a spider and fly until the spider finds out today is "Meatless Tuesday."

4073. Meatless Tuesday (*Andy Panda*) 20 Dec. 1943; *p.c.:* Walter Lantz prods for Univ; *dir:* James Culhane; *story:* Ben Hardaway, Milt Schaffer; *anim:* Paul Smith, Pat Matthews; *sets:* Fred Brunish; *mus:* Darrell Calker; *prod mgr:* George Hall; *col:* Tech. *sd:* WE. 6 min. • Andy tries to capture a rooster for dinner.

4074. The Mechanical Bird (*Terry-Toon*) Feb. 1952; *p.c.:* TT for Fox; *dir:* Eddie Donnelly; *story:* Tom Morrison; *anim:* Jim Tyer; *mus:* Philip A. Scheib; *ph:* Douglas Moye; *col:* Tech. *sd:* RCA. 6 min. • The King foresakes his devoted nightingale for a toy bird. When the toy breaks, he realizes the true value of his nightingale friend.

4075. The Mechanical Cow (*Oswald the Lucky Rabbit*) 3 Oct. 1927; *p.c.:* Winkler for Univ; *dir:* Walt Disney; *anim:* Ub Iwerks, Rollin C. Hamilton, Hugh Harman, Isadore Freleng, Paul J. Smith, Norman Blackburn, Ben Clopton; *i&p:* Les Clark; *ph:* Mike Marcus; b&w. sil. 6 min. sd reissue: 4 Jan. 1932. • Oswald's robot cow not only gives milk but helps our hero in escaping from a gang intent on stealing it.

4076. The Mechanical Cow (*Terry-Toon*) 25 June 1937; *p.c.:* TT for Educational/Fox; *dir:* Jack Zander; *mus:* Philip A. Scheib; b&w. *sd:* WE. 6 min. • Farmer Al Falfa creates a mechanical cow to compensate for his cow who has gone on a sit-down strike.

4077. The Mechanical Handy Man (*Oswald*) 20 Oct. 1937; *p.c.:* Walter Lantz prods for Univ; *dir:* Walter Lantz; *story:* Charles Bowers; *anim:* Ray Fahringer, Ted Dubois, Ed Benedict; *mus:* George Lessner; b&w. *sd:* WE. 7 min • The Dumb Cluck is demonstrating his invention to Henry Hippo when it runs amok, landing both him and Oswald in court.

4078. The Mechanical Man (*Oswald*) 2 Feb. 1932; *p.c.:* Univ; *dir:* Walter Lantz, "Bill" Nolan; *anim:* Ray Abrams, Fred Avery, Lester Kline, Vet Anderson; *voice:* Mickey Rooney; *mus:* James Dietrich; b&w. *sd:* WE. 6 min. • A peg-legged villain creates a robot, then kidnaps Oswald's girl. Oswald follows and is chased by Peg-leg with an axe.

4079. The Medicine Man (*Aesop's Film Fable*) 3 Apr. 1927; *p.c.:* Famous Pictures Inc for Pathé; *dir:* Paul Terry; b&w. sil. 10 min. • Al Falfa accidentally invades a bear's cave. A mouse pours hair tonic over a tiger that makes him look like a lion and, out of gratitude, the tiger saves Al from being devoured by the bear.

4080. The Medicine Show (*Krazy Kat*) 7 Feb. 1933; *p.c.:* Winkler for Colum; *story:* Ben Harrison, Manny Gould; *anim:* Al Rose, Harry Love; *mus:* Joe de Nat; *prod mgr:* James Bronis; b&w. *sd:* WE. 6 min. • No story available.

4081. Medicur (*The Dogfather*) 30 Apr. 1976; *p.c.:* Mirisch/DFE for UA; *dir:* Gerry Chiniquy; *story:* John Dunn; *anim:* Bob Richardson, Warren Batchelder, Norm McCabe, Don Williams; *ed:* Rick Steward; *lay:* Roy Morita; *back:* Richard H. Thomas; *voices:* Bob Holt; *mus:* Dean Elliott; *col:* DeLuxe. *sd:* RCA. 6 min. • When his adversary escapes from jail, The Dogfather hides in hospital as a patient, unaware that his mortal enemy is there disguised as a nurse.

4082. Meet John Doughboy (*Looney Tunes*) 5 July 1941; *p.c.:* Leon Schlesinger prods for WB; *dir:* Robert Clampett; *story:* Warren Foster; *anim:* Vive Risto; *ed:* Treg Brown; *voices:* Robert C. Bruce, Mel Blanc, Billy Bletcher, Jack Lescoulie; *mus:* Carl W. Stalling; *prod mgr:* Henry Binder, Raymond G. Katz; b&w. *sd:* Vit. 6 min. • Pvt. Porky Pig introduces an Army newsreel parody on topical events. Made a few months before America's entering the Second World War.

4083. Meet King Joe (*Fun & Facts About America*) 28 May 1949; *p.c.:* John Sutherland prods for Harding College/MGM; *prod/dir:* John Sutherland; *col:* Tech. *sd:* RCA. 9 min. • Demonstrating that the American working man has a higher standard of living, more desirable working conditions and more leisure time than anywhere else in the world.

4084. Meet Mother Magoo (*Mr. Magoo*) 27 Dec. 1956; *p.c.:* UPA for Colum; *dir:* Pete Burness; *story:* Ed Nofziger, Dick Shaw; *anim:* Cecil Surry, Barney Posner, Tom McDonald, Gil Turner; *lay:* Robert Dranko; *back:* Bob McIntosh; *voices:* Jim Backus, Pat Carroll; *mus:* Del Castillo; *prod mgr:* Herbert Klynn; *col:* tech. *sd:* RCA. 6 min. • Magoo believes it to be his mother's birthday and pays her a visit she could well do without.

4085. The Mellow Quartette (*Pen & Ink Vaudeville*) 27 Apr. 1925; *p.c.:* Hurd prods for Educational; *prod/dir:* Earl Hurd; b&w. sil. 5 min. • One of "The Mellow Quartette" is ill and Props has to replace him. He has the foresight to sing behind a door and escapes the barrage of vegetables, then gives a banquet consisting of the produce hurled from the audience.

4086. Melody (*Adventures in Music*) 12 June 1953; *p.c.:* Walt Disney prods for RKO; *dir:* C. August Nichols, Ward Kimball; *story:* Dick Huemer; *anim:* Harvey Toombs, Ward Kimball, Julius Svendsen, Marc Davis, Hal Ambro, Marvin Woodward, Les Clark, Blaine Gibson, Henry Tanous; *lay:* Eyvind Earl; *back:* Ken O'Connor, Victor Haboush; *voices:* Bill Thompson, The Jud Conlon Chorus: (Gloria Wood, Harry Stanton, Charles Parlotto, Loulie-Jean Norman, Mac MacLean, Sue Allen); *mus:* Joseph S. Dubin; *songs:* Sonny Burke, Paul Francis Webster; *col:* Tech. *sd:* RCA. 9¹/₂ min. 3-D/2-D • Professor Owl explains the origins of music via "the bird, the cricket and the willow tree."

4087. Melody Time 27 May 1948 *p.c.:* Walt Disney prods for RKO; *prod sup:* Ben Sharpsteen; *seq dir:* Clyde Geronimi, Wilfred Jackson, Hamilton S. Luske, Jack Kinney, William Cottrell; *anim dir:* Ward Kimball, Milt Kahl, John Lounsbery, Eric Larson; *story:* Harry Reeves, Ken Anderson, Homer Brightman, Ted Sears, John Walbridge; *col/des:* Dick Kelsey, Claude Coats, Mary Blair; *back:* Jimi Trout; *voice:* Buddy Clark; *Tech col dir:* Natalie Kalmus, Morgan Padelford; *l/a ph:* Winton C. Hoch ASC; *special processes:* Ub Iwerks; *ed:* Thomas Scott, Donald Halliday; *sd:* C.O. Slyfield, Robert O. Cook, Harold J. Steck; *mus arr:* Vic Schoen, Al Sack; *Folklore consultant:* Carl Carmer. • "Once Upon a Wintertime" *dir:* Hamilton S. Luske; *story:* Art Scott, Mary Blair, Bob Moore; *anim:* Eric Larson, John Lounsbery, Harvey Toombs, Hal King, Rudy Larriva, Don Lusk, Judge Whitaker; *fx:* George Rowley; *des:* Mary Blair; *lay:* Ken O'Connor, Don

Griffiths, Al Zinnen; *back:* Art Riley, Dick Anthony; *voice:* Frances Langford; *mus:* Eliot Daniel, Ken Darby; *song:* Bobby Worth, Ray Gilbert. • A romance between a boy and girl against a picturesque winter setting. • "Bumble Boogie" *dir:* Jack Kinney; *story:* John Hench; *anim:* Les Clark, Harvey Toombs, Marvin Woodward; *fx:* Jack Boyd; *lay:* Al Zinnen; *back:* John Hench, Ray Huffine; *mus: The Flight of the Bumble Bee* by Nikolai Rimsky-Korsakov; played by Freddy Martin & His Orchestra; adapted by Jack Fina. • A bee gets entangled in jazz instruments. • "Johnny Appleseed" *dir:* Wilfred Jackson; *story:* Winston Hibler, Joe Rinaldi, Erdman Penner, Jesse Marsh; *anim:* Milt Kahl, Ollie Johnston, Eric Larson, Hal Ambro, Don Lusk, Harvey Toombs; *fx:* George Rowley; *des:* Mary Blair; *lay:* McLaren Stewart, Don da Gradi, Thor Putnam; *back:* Claude Coats, Brice Mack; *voice:* Dennis Day; *mus:* Paul Smith; *songs:* Kim Gannon, Walter Kent. • Encouraged by his "Angel," Johnny plants seeds to grow apple trees across the nation. • "Little Toot" *dir:* Clyde Geronimi; *asst dir:* Lou Debney; *story:* Hardie Gramatky; *story adapt:* Bill Cottrell, Jesse Marsh, Elmer Plummer, Dick Kelsey; *anim:* Eric Larson, Ollie Johnston, Bob Cannon, Rudy Larriva, Brad Case, Don Lusk, John McManus, Cliff Nordberg, Jack Parr, Ray Patin; *fx:* Dan MacManus, George Rowley; *lay:* Hugh Hennesy; *back:* Brice Mack, Claude Coats; *voice:* The Andrews Sisters (Patty, Maxene, LaVerne); *mus:* Eliot Daniel, Ken Darby; *song:* Allie Wrubel. • A fun-loving harbor tugboat comes into his own when he rescues an ocean liner in a storm. • "Trees" *dir:* Hamilton S. Luske; *story:* Richmond Kelsey; *anim:* Ed Aardal, Les Clark, Don Lusk; *fx:* Josh Meador, George Rowley; *lay:* A. Kendall O'Connor; *back:* Art Riley, Dick Anthony, Ralph Hulett; *voices:* Fred Waring & His Pennsylvanians; *mus:* Oscar Rasbach. • Joyce Kilmer's famous poem is given a musical interpretation. • "Blame It on the Samba" *dir:* Clyde Geronimi; *anim:* Hal King, John Lounsbery, Les Clark, Harvey Toombs, Ward Kimball; *fx:* Josh Meador, George Rowley; *lay:* Hugh Hennesy, Bob Cormack, Lance Nolley; *back:* Berk Anthony, Ralph Hulett; *voices:* The Dinning Sisters (Lou, Jean, Ginger); *mus:* Ethel Smith; *song:* Ernesto Nazareth, Ray Gilbert. • Donald and José Carioca's blues are dispelled by a cheery song and dance. • "Pecos Bill" *dir:* Clyde Geronimi; *story:* Erdman Penner, Joe Rinaldi; *anim:* Ward Kimball, Milt Kahl, John Sibley, Marvin Woodward, Cliff Nordberg, Ken O'Brien, Les Clark, John Lounsbery, Harvey Toombs; *fx:* Josh Meador, Ed Aardal, George Rowley; *lay:* Hugh Hennesy, Lance Nolley, John Hench; *back:* Claude Coats, Merle Cox, Brice Mack; *voices/l/a:* Roy Rogers, The Sons of the Pioneers; *mus:* Paul Smith; *songs:* Eliot Daniel, Johnny Lange; *l/a:* Bobby Driscoll, Luana Patten. • Roy Rogers narrates the tale of Pecos Bill who, raised by wolves, became the toughest cowboy in the West and whose downfall was due to a woman. • *col:* Tech. *sd:* RCA. 75 min.

4088. Men in Black 2 June 1997; *p.c.:* Amblin Entertainment for Colum TriStar; *special visual fx/anim: special anim consultant:* Oscar Grillo; *anim:* Patrick Bonneau, Sue Campbell, Marc Chu, Tim Harrington, Chris Mitchell, Steve Nichols, Glenn Sylvester, Kim Thompson, Marjolaine Tremblay, Andy Wong; *sup character modeler/anim:* Simon Cheung; *anim sup:* Rob Coleman; *voice of Frank the Pug:* Tim Blaney; *col:* Tech. *sd:* Dolby/dts/SDDS. Panavision. 98 min. *l/a.* • Live-action comedy science-fiction: Two undercover Government agents, "K" and "J," set out to round up invading aliens. Inventive computer animation helps create various alien creatures including a talking dog and a giant cockroach.

4089. Mendelssohn's Spring Song (*Jingles*) 1932; *p.c.:* Bray prods; *dir/anim:* Sy (Cy) Young; *mus dir:* Carlo Peroni; *ph:* Herman Roessle; Brewster color. *sd.* • Butterflies, frogs and insects celebrate the joys of Spring.

4090. Merbabies 9 Dec. 1938; *p.c.:* Walt Disney prods/Harman–Ising Studio for RKO; *sup:* Walt Disney, Ben Sharpsteen, David D. Hand, Otto Englander; *dir:* George Stallings, Rudolf Ising; *story:* Jerry Brewer; *anim:* Carl Urbano, Michael Lah, Lee Blair, Thomas McKimson, James Pabian, Mel Schwartzman, Manuel Moreno, Rollin Hamilton, Peter Burness; *lay:* Maurice Day; *back:* Don Schaffer, Art Riley; *mus:* Scott Bradley; *col:* Tech. *sd:* RCA. 9 min. • The Merbabies hold a circus on the ocean's floor. • At the time, this special was the only Disney product to be farmed out to another company (*Harman–Ising*) due to an excessive workload.

4091. Merkel, Arno (*cartoons*) *p.c.:* Merkel Film Co; *prod:* Arno Merkel; *dir:* Kenneth M. Anderson; b&w. sil. • **1918: Me and Gott** Feb. **Power Pro and Con** Feb. **The Girth of a Nation** Apr. **Truths on the War in Slang** Apr. **Oh What a Beautiful Dream** Apr. **Hocking the Kaiser** Apr. • Animated items in magazine film.

4092. Merlin the Magic Mouse (*Merrie Melodies*) Nov. 1967; *p.c.:* WB/7A; *dir:* Alex Lovy; *story:* Cal Howard; *anim:* Ed Solomon, Ted Bonnicksen, Volus Jones, La Verne Harding; *lay:* Bob Givens; *back:* Bob Abrams; *ed:* Hal Geer; *voice:* Daws Butler; *mus:* William Lava; *prod:* William L. Hendricks; *col:* Tech. *sd:* Vit. 6 min. • Merlin resorts to disguise when he discovers a cat to be his only audience.

4093. The Merry Blacksmith (*Aesop's Film Fable*) 12 Mar. 1926; *p.c.:* Fables Pictures Inc for Pathé; *dir:* Paul Terry; b&w. sil. 5 min. • Henry Cat tantalizes a blacksmith who chases him. He tries to escape on a kite but the smithy drags him back.

4094. The Merry Café (*Krazy Kat*) 26 Dec. 1936; *p.c.:* Charles Mintz prods for Colum; *story:* Allen Rose; *anim:* Harry Love; *voices:* Billy Bletcher, The Rhythmettes; *mus:* Joe de Nat; *prod mgr:* James Bronis; b&w. *sd:* RCA. 6 min. • Krazy is knocked unconcious at the "Eat-o-Mat" and dreams he's about to eat a pile of food. When he awakes, he knocks himself out again and continues his dream.

4095. A Merry Chase (*Heckle & Jeckle*) May 1950; *p.c.:* TT for Fox; *dir:* Mannie Davis; *story/voices:* Tom Morrison; *anim:* Jim Tyer; *mus:* Philip A. Scheib; *ph:* Douglas Moye; *col:* Tech. *sd:* RCA. 6 min. • The magpies are fishing when a policeman discovers their faces on a "Wanted" poster.

4096. The Merry Dog (*Pooch the Pup*) 2 Jan. 1933; *p.c.:* Univ; *dir:* Walter Lantz; *anim:* Manuel Moreno, Lester Kline, George Cannata, "Bill" Weber, Fred Kopietz, Charles Hastings; *mus:* James Dietrich; b&w. *sd.* 6 min. • A wolf poses as Santa on Christmas Eve but all is saved when the toys come to life and, with help from the real Santa, boot him in the city dump.

4097. The Merry Dwarfs (*Silly Symphony*) 1 Dec. 1929; *p.c.:* Walter E. Disney for Colum; *dir:* Walt Disney; *anim:* Ub Iwerks; *mus:* Carl W. Stalling; b&w. *sd:* PCP. 5 min. • The dwarfs do a dance in their village.

4098. The Merry Kittens (*Rainbow Parade*) 31 May 1935; *p.c.:* Van Beuren for RKO; *dir:* Burt Gillett, Jim Culhane; *story:* Ray Kelly, Jim Culhane; *sets:* Art Bartsch, Eddi Bowlds; *mus:* Winston Sharples; *col:* Tech. *sd:* RCA. 7 min. • Three kittens try to arouse the sleeping hound by first tempting him with steak, then dousing him with seltzer water. A chase ensues!

4099. Merry Mannequins (*Color Rhapsody*) 19 Mar. 1937; *p.c.:* Cartoon Films Ltd/Charles Mintz prods for Colum; *prod/dir:* Ub Iwerks; *ed:* George Winkler; *voices:* The Rhythmettes; *mus:* Joe de Nat, Eddie Kilfeather; *ph:* Otto Reimer; *prod mgr:* James Bronis; *col:* Tech. *sd:* RCA. 8 min. • Cupid causes two department store dummies to fall in love and the other dummies to stage a wedding for them.

4100. Merry Minstrel Magoo (*Mr. Magoo*) 9 Apr. 1959; *p.c.:* UPA for Colum; *ex prod:* Stephen Bosustow; *dir:* Rudy Larriva; *story:* Dick Shaw; *anim:* Casey Onaitis, Alan Zaslove; *sets:* Sam Clayberger; *voices:* Jim Backus, Daws Butler, Mary Jane Croft; *mus:* Maury Ellenhorn; *col:* Tech. *sd:* RCA. 6 min. • Magoo arrives at a dentist's surgery in mistake for a TV talent contest.

4101. The Merry Mouse Café (*Phantasy*) 11 Sept. 1941; *p.c.:* Colum; *story:* Allen Rose; *anim:* Lou Lilly; *ed:* George Winkler; *voices:* Danny Webb, Sara Berner; *mus:* Joe de Nat; *ph:* Otto Reimer; *prod mgr:* James Bronis; b&w. *sd:* RCA. 6 min. • When the Squawk Club closes for the night, the mice stage their own entertainment.

4102. The Merry Mutineers (*Color Rhapsody*) 3 Sept. 1936; *p.c.:* Charles Mintz prods for Colum; *story:* Ben Harrison; *anim:* Manny Gould; *voice:* J. Delos Jewkes; *mus:* Joe de Nat; *prod mgr:* James Bronis; *col:* Tech. *sd:* RCA. 8 min. • Scrappy and Oopy sail their boats on the pond and see a battle take place between a bevy of caricatured personalities: George Arliss, Fred Astaire, Wallace Beery, Major Bowes, Joe E. Brown, Bing Crosby, Jimmy Durante, W.C. Fields, Al Jolson, Charles Laughton, Laurel & Hardy and the Marx Brothers.

4103. The Merry Old Soul (*Merrie Melodies*) 17 Aug. 1935; *p.c.:* Leon Schlesinger prods for WB; *dir:* Isadore Freleng; *anim:* Rollin Hamilton, Riley Thomson, Robert Clampett; *voices:* Bernice Hansel, Billy Bletcher; *mus:* Norman Spencer; *prod sup:* Henry Binder, Raymond G. Katz; *col:* Tech-2. *sd:* Vit. 7 min. • Old King Cole marries the woman in the shoe and inherits her unruly brood of kids.

4104. The Merry Old Soul (*Oswald*) 27 Nov. 1933; *p.c.*: Univ; *dir*: Walter Lantz, "Bill" Nolan; *anim*: Manuel Moreno, Lester Kline, Fred Kopietz, George Grandpré, Ernest Smythe; *mus*: James Dietrich; b&w. *sd*: WE. 6 min. • Movie stars caricatured.

4105. Mesa Trouble (*Hoot Kloot*) 16 May 1974; *p.c.*: Mirisch/DFE for UA; *dir*: Sid Marcus; *story*: John W. Dunn; *anim*: John Freeman, Don Williams, Bob Bransford, Ken Muse; *lay*: Pete Alvarado; *back*: Richard Thomas; *ed*: Rick Steward; *voices*: Bob Holt, Larry Mann, Allan Melvin; *mus*: Doug Goodwin; *titles*: Arthur Leonardi; *ph*: John Burton Jr.; *prod mgr*: Lee Gunther; *col*: DeLuxe. *sd*: RCA. 6 min. • Kloot needs help when Big Red comes to town … but the townsfolk don't want to know! He finally captures the villain with help from an alien from outer space.

4106. Mess Production (*Popeye*) 24 Aug. 1945; *p.c.*: Famous for Para; *dir*: Seymour Kneitel; *story*: Bill Turner, Otto Messmer; *anim*: Graham Place, Lou Zukor; *voices*: Jack Mercer, Mae Questel, Jackson Beck; *mus*: Sammy Timberg; *ph*: Leonard McCormick; *prod mgr*: Sam Buchwald; b&w. *sd*: RCA. 7½ min. Tech reissue: 3 Oct. 1952. • Popeye and Bluto are contributing to the war effort with factory work when along comes a welder in the shape of Olive Oyl. They both try to impress her in a dangerous fashion.

4107. A Message from the Sea (*Aesop's Film Fable*) 31 Aug. 1924; *p.c.*: Fables Pictures Inc for Pathé; *dir*: Paul Terry; b&w. *sil*. 5 min. • The feline rumrunners land their load and thwart the dog agents who take up in pursuit. They stash their hooch at the bottom of the sea where the fish discover the haul.

4108. The Message of Emile Coué (*Earl Hurd Comedy*) 18 Feb. 1923; *p.c.*: Earl Hurd prods for Motion Picture Arts Inc.; *dir*: Earl Hurd; b&w. *sil*. 2 reels. • No story available.

4109. A Message to Gracias (*Looney Tunes*) 8 Feb. 1964; *p.c.*: WB; *dir*: Robert McKimson; *story*: John Dunn; *anim*: George Grandpré, Ted Bonnicksen, Warren Batchelder, David R. Green; *fx*: Harry Love; *sets*: Robert Gribbroek; *ed*: Treg Brown; *voices*: Mel Blanc, (David) Roger Green; *mus*: Bill Lava; *prod mgr*: William Orcutt; *prod*: David H. DePatie; *col*: Tech. *sd*: Vit. 6 min. • Speedy Gonzales is dispatched to deliver an important message to General Gracias but is intercepted along the way by Sylvester.

4110. Messed Up Movie Makers (*Heckle & Jeckle*) 1 June 1966; *p.c.*: TT for Fox; *ex prod*: Bill Weiss; *dir/anim*: George Bakes, Al Chiarito; *story sup*: Tom Morrison; *story*: Larz Bourne; *sets*: Bill Focht; *ed*: Elliott Grey; *voices*: Dayton Allen; *mus*: Jim Timmens; *ph*: Ted Moskowitz, Joe Rasinski; *col*: Tech. *sd*: RCA. 6 min. • The Magpies lease their motel to a film company but have to evict them when they start destroying the hotel property.

4111. The Meteor Man 6 Aug. 1993. *p.c.*: MGM for Electric Triangle; *anim*: Thomas L. Hutchinson, Joe Letteri, Joseph Pasquale, Doug Smythe; *anim sup*: Wes Ford Takahashi; *fx anim*: Tim Berglund, Anthony F. Stacchi; *stop-motion anim*: Harry Walton; *col*: DeLuxe. *sd*: Dolby Stereo. 100 min. *l/a*. • Live-action science-fiction: A mild-mannered teacher transforms into the crime-fighting "Meteor Man" when he is struck by an emerald green meteor.

4112. The Method and Maw (*Comic King*) Oct. 1962; *p.c.*: Para Cartoons; *dir*: Seymour Kneitel; *anim*: Irving Dressler; *sets*: Robert Owen; *voices*: Paul Frees, Penny Phillips; *mus*: Winston Sharples; *ph*: Leonard McCormick; *prod mgr*: Abe Goodman; *col*: Tech. *sd*: RCA. 5½ min. • An actress uses Loweezy as a model for her next play. She copies Maw so closely that Snuffy can't tell them apart.

4113. Mexicali Schmoes (*Looney Tunes*) 4 July 1959; *p.c.*: WB; *dir*: Friz Freleng; *story*: Warren Foster; *anim*: Virgil Ross, Gerry Chiniquy, Art Davis; *lay*: Hawley Pratt; *back*: Tom O'Loughlin; *ed*: Treg Brown; *voices*: Mel Blanc, Tom Holland; *mus*: Milt Franklyn; *prod*: John W. Burton; *col*: Tech. *sd*: Vit. 7 min. *Academy Award nomination*. • A couple of Mexican cats do their best to capture "the Fastest Mouse in Mexico," finally settling on the lethargic Slowpoke Rodriquez.

4114. Mexican Baseball (*Gandy Goose*) 14 Mar. 1947; *p.c.*: TT for Fox; *dir*: Mannie Davis; *story*: John Foster; *voices*: Sid Raymond, Arthur Kay, Tom Morrison; *mus*: Philip A. Scheib; *ph*: Douglas Moye; *col*: Tech. *sd*: RCA. 6 min. • Gandy and Sourpuss engage the Mexican League Bulls in a baseball game.

4115. Mexican Boarders (*Looney Tunes*) 22 May 1962; *p.c.*: WB; *dir*: Friz Freleng; *asst dir*: Hawley Pratt; *story*: John Dunn; *anim*: Gerry Chiniquy, Virgil Ross, Bob Matz, Art Leonardi, Lee Halpern; *back*: Tom O'Loughlin; *ed*: Treg Brown; *voices*: Mel Blanc, Tom Holland; *mus*: Milt Franklyn; *prod mgr*: William Orcutt; *prod*: David H. DePatie; *col*: Tech. *sd*: Vit. 7 min. • Speedy Gonzales' cousin Slowpoke arrives to stay and keeps Speedy busy in rescuing him from the grasp of the cat.

4116. The Mexican Cat Dance (*Looney Tunes*) 20 Apr. 1963; *p.c.*: WB; *dir*: Friz Freleng; *story*: John Dunn; *anim*: Gerry Chiniquy, Virgil Ross, Bob Matz, Lee Halpern, Art Leonardi; *lay*: Hawley Pratt; *back*: Tom O'Loughlin; *ed*: Treg Brown; *voice*: Mel Blanc; *mus*: Bill Lava; *prod mgr*: William Orcutt; *prod*: David H. DePatie; *col*: Tech. *sd*: Vit. 6 min. • Speedy stages a bullfight with Sylvester.

4117. Mexican Joyride (*Looney Tunes*) 29 Nov. 1947; *p.c.*: WB; *dir*: Arthur Davis; *story*: Dave Monahan; *anim*: Don Williams, Basil Davidovich, J.C. Melendez, Herman Cohen, Robert McKimson; *lay*: Thomas McKimson; *back*: Philip de Guard; *ed*: Treg Brown; *voices*: Mel Blanc; *mus*: Carl Stalling; *prod mgr*: John W. Burton; *prod*: Edward Selzer; *col*: Tech. *sd*: Vit. 7 min. • Daffy causes so much of a stir in the bullfight arena that he has to fight the bull himself.

4118. Mexican Mousepiece (*Merrie Melodies*) 26 Feb. 1966; *p.c.*: DFE for WB; *dir*: Robert McKimson; *story*: David DeTiege; *anim*: George Grandpré, Bob Matz, Manny Perez; *lay*: Dick Ung; *back*: Tom O'Loughlin; *ed*: Al Wahrman; *voices*: Mel Blanc, Ralph James; *mus*: Bill Lava; *col*: Tech. *sd*: Vit. 6 min. • Daffy tricks the mice into a crate in order to ship them abroad to starving cats. Speedy arrives to help them escape.

4119. Mexico (*Oswald*) 17 Nov. 1930; *p.c.*: Univ; *dir*: Walter Lantz, "Bill" Nolan; *anim*: Clyde Geronimi, Manuel Moreno, Ray Abrams, Fred Avery, Lester Kline, "Pinto" Colvig; *mus*: James Dietrich; b&w. *sd*: WE. 5½ min. • A fighting rooster bout between Oswald's "Jumping Bean" and Putrid Pete's "Hot Tamale."

4120. M.G.M. Cartoon Studio (1937–1942) *prod/dir*: Hugh Harman, Rudolf Ising; *prod sup*: Carmen G. Maxwell, Harry Hershfield, Milt Gross; *dir*: Robert Allen, Joseph Barbera, Jerry Brewer, Isadore Freleng, Milt Gross, William Hanna; *story*: Henry Allen, Joseph Barbera, Jerry Brewer, Moe Caldwell, Pinto Colvig, Jack Cosgriff, Otto Englander, Allen Freleng, Dan Gordon, George Gordon, Walker Harman, Cal Howard, Ray Kelly, Charles McGirl, Carl Meyer, Mel Shaw, Mel Schwartzman, Webb Smith; *anim*: Robert Allen, Preston Blair, Wilson D. (Pete) Burness, Jack Carr, George Gordon, Bert Green, Rollin C. Hamiton, William Hanna, Emery Hawkins, Tex Henson, Michael Lah, John Frank Liggre, William Littlejohn, Manuel Moreno, Kenneth Muse, Lovell Norman, Tony Pabian, Paul Sommer, Carl Urbano, Robert Youngquist, Jack Zander; *prod des*: Gus Arriola, Mary Blair, Bob Kuwahara, Martin Provensen; *lay*: Robert Allen, Maurice "Jake" Day, Harvey Eisenberg, George Gordon, John Meandor, Don Schaffer; *back*: Art Riley, Don Schaffer, Joe Smith; *i&p*: Inez Boswell, Marcellite Garner, Joan Higgins, Brooke Mitchell; *ed*: Fred MacAlpin, Jim Faris; *mus*: Scott Bradley; *ph*: Gene Moore, Jack Stevens; *research*: Ruth Ellen Moore; *cue sheets*: Midge Sturges; *lab head*: J.M. Nickolaus; *prod sup*: Jack Chertok; *prod mgr*: Fred Quimby.

4121. M.G.M. News 16 July 1927; *p.c.*: Bray prods for MGM; *title anim*: David D. Hand; b&w. *sil*. • David D. Hand, Bray Industrial Films animator, shows a great searchlight in the sky picking out the letters "M.G.M. News" with a beam and throwing to bright relief the words "The World's Spotlight."

4122. Miami Maniacs (*Heckle & Jeckle*) Feb. 1956; *p.c.*: TT for Fox; *dir*: Connie Rasinski; *story/voices*: Tom Morrison; *anim*: Jim Tyer; *mus*: Philip A. Scheib; *ph*: Douglas Moye; *col*: Tech. *sd*: RCA 7 min. • The magpies cause havoc for a hotel manager and bellboy when they camp on the lawn of a swanky hotel.

4123. Mice at War (*Aesop's Film Fable*) 4 Sept. 1921; *p.c.*: Fables Pictures Inc for Pathé; *dir*: Paul Terry; b&w. *sil*. 5 min. • Mice wage war in the kitchen on the cat. The leader, when trying to retreat through the mousehole, is restricted by his huge bearskin helmet and is captured by the cat. Moral: "Leaders pay the price of prominence."

4124. Mice Capades (*Herman & Katnip*) 3 Oct. 1952; *p.c.*: Famous for Para; *dir*: Seymour Kneitel; *story*: Irving Spector; *anim*: Al Eugster,

Wm. B. Pattengill; *sets:* Robert Owen; *voices:* Arnold Stang, Sid Raymond, Jack Mercer; *mus:* Winston Sharples; *title song:* Hal David, Leon Carr; *ph:* Leonard McCormick; *prod mgr:* Seymour Shultz; *col:* Tech. *sd:* RCA. 7 min. • While Katnip lies unconcious, the mice convince him he's died and gone to heaven.

4125. Mice Follies *(Looney Tunes)* 20 Aug 1960; *p.c.:* WB; *dir:* Robert McKimson; *story:* Tedd Pierce; *anim:* George Grandpré, Ted Bonnicksen, Warren Batchelder, Tom Ray; *lay:* Robert Gribbroek; *back:* Bob Singer; *voices:* Daws Butler, Merrie Virginia; *mus:* Milt Franklyn; *prod mgr:* William Orcutt; *prod:* David H. DePatie; *col:* Tech. *sd:* Vit. 7 min. • Ralph and Ned Morton have a night on the tiles and can't face returning home late to their irate wives.

4126. Mice Follies *(Tom & Jerry)* 4 Sept. 1954; *p.c.:* MGM; *dir:* William Hanna, Joseph Barbera; *anim:* Kenneth Muse, Ed Barge, Irven Spence, Ray Patterson; *lay:* Dick Bickenbach; *back:* Robert Gentle; *ed:* Jim Faris; *mus:* Scott Bradley; *ph:* Jack Stevenson; *prod:* Fred Quimby; *col:* Tech. *sd:* WE. 7 min. • Jerry and Nibbles have ice skating fun in the kitchen until Tom arrives on the scene.

4127. Mice in Council *(Aesop's Film Fable)* 26 July 1921; *p.c.:* Fables Pictures Inc for Pathé; *dir:* Paul Terry; b&w. *sil.* 5 min. • The mice suggest a bell tied around the cat's neck ... but which one shall tie it there?

4128. Mice in Council *(Paul Terry-Toon)* 29 Aug. 1934; *p.c.:* Moser & Terry for Educational/Fox; *dir:* Frank Moser, Paul Terry; *mus:* Philip A. Scheib; b&w. *sd:* WE. 5½ min. • Grandfather mouse tells a group of youngsters how he came to win a medal for putting a bell on the cat.

4129. Mice Meeting You *(Noveltoon)* 10 Nov. 1950; *p.c.:* Famous for Para; *dir:* Seymour Kneitel; *voices:* Arnold Stang, Sid Raymond, Jack Mercer; *mus:* Winston Sharples; *ph:* Leonard McCormick; *prod mgr:* Sam Buchwald; *col:* Tech. *sd:* RCA. 7 min. • The arrival of the cat spoils the rodents' preperation for Christmas. Herman soon puts matters right.

4130. Mice Paradise *(Noveltoon)* 9 Mar. 1951; *p.c.:* Famous for Para; *dir:* I. Sparber; *story:* Carl Meyer, Jack Mercer; *anim:* Dave Tendlar, Tom Golden; *sets:* Tom Ford; *voices:* Arnold Stang, Sid Raymond, Jack Mercer; *mus:* Winston Sharples; *ph:* Leonard McCormick; *prod mgr:* Seymour Shultz; *col:* Tech. *sd:* RCA. 7 min. • Herman takes his friends to a Hawaiian isle. Katnip follows, intent on destroying their tranquility.

4131. The Mice Will Play *(Merrie Melodies)* 31 Dec. 1938; *p.c.:* Leon Schlesinger prods for WB; *dir:* Fred Avery; *story:* Jack Miller; *anim:* Sid Sutherland; *sets:* John Didrik Johnsen; *ed:* Tregoweth E. Brown; *voices:* Bernice Hansel, Mel Blanc, The Sportsmen Quartet; *mus:* Carl W. Stalling; *prod sup:* Henry Binder, Raymond G. Katz; *col:* Tech. *sd:* Vit. 7 min. • Johnny Mouse rescues a girl mouse from an experimental laboratory and they are married until "Judgment Day."

4132. Miceniks *(Noveltoon)* Dec. 1960; *p.c.:* Para Cartoons; *dir:* Seymour Kneitel; *story:* Carl Meyer, Jack Mercer; *anim:* Tom Johnson, William Henning; *sets:* Robert Owen; *voices:* Dayton Allen, Bob MacFadden; *mus:* Winston Sharples; *ph:* Leonard McCormick; *prod mgr:* Abe Goodman; *col:* Tech. *sd:* RCA. 6 min. • A "Square" cat tries to snare some beatnik mice.

4133. Mickey and the Beanstalk *p.c.:* Walt Disney prods for RKO; *dir:* William O. Roberts, Hamilton S. Luske; *col:* Tech. *sd:* RCA. 20 min. • Mickey swaps his cow for some magic beans that grow into a huge beanstalk. He climbs it to the top with Donald and Goofy where they find a singing harp held prisoner by a giant. • See: *Fun and Fancy Free*

4134. Mickey and the Seal *(Mickey Mouse)* 3 Dec. 1948; *p.c.:* Walt Disney prods for RKO; *dir:* Charles Nichols; *story:* Nick George, Milt Schaffer; *anim:* Phil Duncan, Hugh Fraser, George Nicholas, George Kreisl; *fx:* Dan MacManus; *lay:* Karl Karpé; *back:* Ralph Hulett; *voices:* Ford Banes, James MacDonald; *mus:* Oliver Wallace; *col:* Tech. *sd:* RCA. 6 min. *Academy Award nomination.* • Mickey returns from a trip to the zoo, unaware that a baby seal has stowed away in his picnic basket, giving Pluto many problems.

4135. Mickey Cuts Up *(Mickey Mouse)* 25 Nov. 1931; *p.c.:* Walter E. Disney for Colum; *dir:* Burton F. Gillett; *anim:* Johnny Cannon, Les Clark, Norman Ferguson, Clyde Geronimi, David D. Hand, Jack King, Richard Lundy, Tom Palmer, Ben Sharpsteen; *voices:* Marcellite Garner, Lee Millar, Walt Disney, A. Purvis Pullen; *mus:* Bert Lewis; b&w. *sd:* PCP. 7 min. •

Mickey spring cleans in Minnie's back yard while Pluto creates havoc with a lawnmower.

4136. Mickey Down Under *(Mickey Mouse)* 19 Mar. 1948; *p.c.:* Walt Disney prods for RKO; *dir:* Charles Nichols; *asst dir:* Jack Bruner; *story:* MacDonald MacPherson, Jack Huber; *anim:* Marvin Woodward, Jerry Hathcock, George Kreisl, Sandy Strother, George Goepper, George Nicholas, Robert Youngquist; *lay:* Karl Karpé; *back:* Art Landy; *voice:* James MacDonald; *mus:* Oliver Wallace; *col:* Tech. *sd:* RCA. 7 min. • While visiting the Australian outback, Mickey encounters an irate ostrich while Pluto has problems with a boomerang.

4137. Mickey in Arabia *(Mickey Mouse)* 29 Sept. 1932; *p.c.:* Walter E. Disney for Colum; *dir:* Wilfred Jackson; *anim:* Johnny Cannon, Les Clark, Gilles de Tremaudan, Kevin Donnelly, Clyde Geronimi, David D. Hand, Jack King, Richard Lundy, Tom Palmer, Ben Sharpsteen; *mus:* Frank E. Churchill; b&w. *sd:* PCP. 7 min. • Mickey and Minnie are journeying in Arabia when Pete the Shiek abducts Minnie.

4138. The Mickey Mouse March of Dimes 13 Oct. 1954; *p.c.:* Walt Disney prods for The March of Dimes; *dir:* C. August Nichols; *anim:* Art Stevens, Julius Svendsen, Jerry Hathcock, Henry Tanous; *lay:* A. Kendall O'Connor; *mus:* Oliver Wallace, Clarence Nash; b&w. *sd:* RCA. 10 min. • Mickey heads the parade with Pluto marking time and Donald on a huge drum that rolls away with him attached. The patronage is encouraged to donate while all sing "Hi Ho."

4139. Mickey Plays Papa *(Mickey Mouse)* 29 Sept. 1934; *p.c.:* Walt Disney prods for UA; *dir:* Burton F. Gillett; *anim:* Johnny Cannon, Hardie Gramatky, William Justice, Richard Lundy, Fred Moore, Tom Palmer, William O. Roberts, Roy Williams, Marvin Woodward, Cy Young; *voices:* Walt Disney; *mus:* Bert Lewis, Frank E. Churchill; b&w. *sd:* RCA. 7 min. • A waif is abandoned on Mickey's doorstep. Mickey goes through the process of trying to amuse the child only succeeding when Pluto swallows a toy rabbit.

4140. Mickey Steps Out *(Mickey Mouse)* 10 July 1931; *p.c.:* Walter E. Disney for Colum; *dir:* Burton F. Gillett; *anim:* Johnny Cannon, Les Clark, Gilles de Tremaudan, Norman Ferguson, David D. Hand, Jack King, Richard Lundy, Tom Palmer, Ben Sharpsteen, Marvin Woodward, Rudy Zamora; *asst anim:* Charles Byrne, Jack Cutting, Hardie Gramatky, Harry Reeves; *voices:* Marcellite Garner, Walt Disney; *mus:* Bert Lewis; b&w. *sd:* PCP. 7 min. • Minnie rescues Mickey from the windowsill when Pluto causes havoc by chasing a cat.

4141. Mickey's Amateurs *(Mickey Mouse)* 17 Apr. 1937; *p.c.:* Walt Disney prods for UA; *dir:* Pinto Colvig, Walt Pfeiffer, Erdman Penner; *story:* Erdman Penner, Pinto Colvig; *anim:* Arthur Babbitt, Les Clark, Alfred Eugster, Edward Love, Arthur W. Palmer, Stan Quackenbush, Ralph Somerville, Marvin Woodward; *voices:* Pinto Colvig, Clarence Nash, Florence Gill, Walt Disney; *mus:* Leigh Harline, Oliver Wallace; *col:* Tech. *sd:* RCA. 7 min. • Mickey hosts an Amateur Hour: Clarabelle Cow give a musical recital, Clara Cluck sings an operatic aria, Goofy plays a one-man band and the audience show their usual contempt for Donald's recitation.

4142. Mickey's Birthday Party *(Mickey Mouse)* 7 Feb. 1942; *p.c.:* Walt Disney prods for RKO; *dir:* Riley Thomson; *asst dir:* Ray de Vally; *anim:* Les Clark, Ward Kimball, James Moore, Kenneth Muse, Frank Onaitis, Armin Shafer, Riley Thomson, Bernard Wolf, Marvin Woodward; *lay:* Harold Miles; *voices:* Thelma Boardman, Clarence Nash, George A. Johnson, Walt Disney; *mus:* Charles Wolcott; *col:* Tech. *sd:* RCA. 7½ min. • Minnie and the gang stage a surprise party for Mickey while Goofy attempts to bake a cake.

4143. Mickey's Choo Choo *(Mickey Mouse)* 24 Oct. 1929; *p.c.:* Walter E. Disney for Colum; *dir:* Walt Disney; *anim:* Ub Iwerks; *asst anim:* Ben Sharpsteen, Norman Ferguson; *mus:* Carl W. Stalling; b&w. *sd:* PCP. 6 min. • Mickey as a locomotive engineer. • Veteran Norman Ferguson's first animation and completed in a record eighteen days.

4144. Mickey's Christmas Carol 16 Dec.1983; *p.c.:* Walt Disney; *dir/prod:* Burny Mattinson; *story adapt:* Burny Mattinson, Tony L. Marino, Ed Gombert, Don Griffith, Alan Young, Alan Dinehart; *based on the novella* A Christmas Carol *by Charles Dickens; *anim consult:* Eric Larson; *anim:* Glen Keane, Mark Henn, Ed Gombert, Dale Baer, David Block, Randy Cartwright; *fx anim:* Ted Kierscey, Jeff Howard, Mark Dindal, Jack

Boyd; *lay:* Michael Peraza Jr., Sylvia Roemer, Gary M. Eggleston; *back:* Jim Coleman, Brian Sebern, Kathleen Swain, Tia W. Kratter, Donald A. Towns; *ed:* James Melton, Armetta Jackson; *art dir:* Don Griffith; *voices: Scrooge McDuck:* Alan Young; *Mickey Mouse (Bob Cratchitt)/The Big Bad Wolf (Street Santa)/Moley (2nd Solicitor)/Beggar:* Wayne Allwine; *Goofy (Jacob Marley)/Ratty (1st Solicitor):* Hal Smith; *Jiminy (the Ghost of Christmas Past):* Eddy Carroll; *Daisy Duck (Isabelle):* Patricia Parris; *Willie (The Ghost of Christmas Present)/Pete (The Ghost of Christmas Yet to Come):* Will Ryan; *Donald Duck (Fred):* Clarence Nash; *Tiny Tim:* Susan Sheridan; *Weasels:* Burny Mattinson, Wayne Allwine, Dick Billingsley; *mus:* Irwin Kostal; *mus ed:* Jack Wadsworth, Dennis Ricotta; *song:* "Oh What a Merry Christmas Day" by Irwin Kostal, Frederick Searles; *creative collaborators:* Richard Hoppe, Barry Temple, Dave Suding, John Lasseter, Retta Davidson, Tom Ferriter, Walt Stanchfield, Jane Baer, Sylvia Mattinson, Douglas I. Craig, Jay Jackson, Terry Hamada, Fujiko Miller, Toby Shelton; *prod asst:* Don Hahn; *asst dir:* Timothy O'Donnell; *prod mgr:* Edward Hansen; *col:* Tech. *sd.* 26 min. • Mickey and the gang re-enact Charles Dickens' well loved Christmas story starring Mickey as the poorly paid Bob Cratchett slaving away for the miserly Scrooge McDuck. On Christmas Eve, Scrooge encounters the ghost of his former partner who warns him of the coming of three ghosts who will show him the folly of his ways. Scrooge eventually learns his lesson and becomes a reformed character.

4145. Mickey's Circus *(Mickey Mouse)* 1 Aug. 1936; *p.c.:* Walt Disney prods for UA; *dir:* Ben Sharpsteen; *story:* Jack Kinney; *anim:* James Algar, Larry Clemmons, Chuck Couch, James H. Culhane, Alfred Eugster, Jack Hannah, Milton Kahl, Frank Kelling, John McManus, Ray Patterson, Wolfgang Reitherman, Milt Schaffer, Fred Spencer, Eddie Strickland, Franklin Thomas, Dick Williams, Bernard Wolf, Marvin Woodward, Cy Young; *character des:* Ferdinand Huszti Horvath; *voices:* Clarence Nash, Walt Disney; *mus:* Paul J. Smith; *col:* Tech. *sd.* RCA. 8 min. • Mickey stages a circus for the orphans, who sabotage all the acts and Donald's trained seals steal the show.

4146. Mickey's Delayed Date *(Mickey Mouse)* 3 Oct. 1947; *p.c.:* Walt Disney prods for RKO; *dir:* Charles Nichols; *asst dir:* Jack Bruner; *story:* Art Scott; *anim:* Jerry Hathcock, George Kreisl, George Nicholas, Harry Holt, Marvin Woodward, Robert Youngquist; *fx:* Jack Boyd, Andy Engman; *lay:* Karl Karpé; *back:* Art Landy; *voices:* Leone Le Doux, James MacDonald; *mus:* Oliver Wallace; *col:* Tech. *sd.* RCA. 7 min. • Pluto assists Mickey in getting ready for a date with Minnie.

4147. Mickey's Elephant *(Mickey Mouse)* 10 Oct. 1936; *p.c.:* Walt Disney prods for UA; *dir:* Hamilton S. Luske; *story:* Earl Hurd; *anim:* Johnny Cannon, Norman Ferguson, Nick George, Jack Hannah, Dick Huemer, Leonard Sebring, Franklin Thomas; *voices:* Don Brodie, Walt Disney, Lee Millar; *mus:* Albert Hay Malotte; *col:* Tech. *sd.* RCA. 9 min. • While Mickey sets about building a house for Bobo the elephant, Pluto gets jealous and puts red pepper in the baby pachyderm's trunk.

4148. Mickey's Fire Brigade *(Mickey Mouse)* 14 Aug. 1935; *p.c.:* Walt Disney prods for UA; *dir:* Ben Sharpsteen; *anim:* Paul Allen, Johnny Cannon, Nick George, Milton Kahl, Jack Kinney, Eric Larson, Charles A. Nichols, Grim Natwick, Wolfgang Reitherman, Leonard Sebring, Fred Spencer, Don Towsley, Vladimir Tytla, Roy Williams, Marvin Woodward; *fx:* John McManus, Cy Young; *voices:* Clarence Nash, Pinto Colvig, Elvia Allman, Walt Disney; *mus:* Bert Lewis; *col:* Tech. *sd.* RCA. 8½ min. • Firemen Mickey, Donald and Goofy attempt to extinguish Clarabelle Cow's burning house.

4149. Mickey's Follies *(Mickey Mouse)* 28 Aug. 1929; *p.c.:* Walter E. Disney for Colum; *dir:* Wilfred Jackson; *anim:* Ub Iwerks; *mus/song/voice:* Carl W. Stalling; b&w. *sd:* PCP. 6 min. • A farmyard concert involving a duck revue, an operatic pig and Mickey singing "Minnie's Yoo Hoo" song atop a piano.

4150. Mickey's Gala Premiere *(Mickey Mouse)* 30 June 1933; *p.c.:* Walt Disney prods for UA; *dir:* Burton F. Gillett; *anim:* Arthur Babbitt, Jack King, Richard Lundy, Hamilton Luske, Fred Moore, Ben Sharpsteen; *fx:* Cy Young; *character des:* Joe Grant; *voices:* Marcellite Garner, Walt Disney; *mus:* Frank E. Churchill, Bert Lewis; b&w. *sd:* RCA. 7 min. • Mickey's latest film "Galloping Romeo" is premiered at Grauman's Chinese Theatre. Among the stars in the audience are: Lionel Barrymore, George Arliss, Wallace Beery, Ben Bernie, Joe E. Brown, The Boswell Sisters, Eddie

Cantor, Charlie Chaplin, Maurice Chevalier, Chester Conklin, Marie Dressler, Jimmy Durante, Douglas Fairbanks, Clark Gable, Sid Grauman, Will H. Hays, Boris Karloff, Harry Langdon, Laurel & Hardy, Harold Lloyd, Bela Lugosi, Frederic March, the Four Marx Brothers, Adolphe Menjou, Edward G. Robinson, William Powell, Will Rogers, Ford Sterling, Mack Swain, Ben Turpin, Mae West, Wheeler & Woolsey and Ed Wynn.

4151. Mickey's Garden *(Mickey Mouse)* 24 July 1935; *p.c.:* Walt Disney prods for UA; *dir:* Wilfred Jackson; *anim:* Arthur Babbitt, Les Clark, Ugo d'Orsi, Gilles de Tremaudan, Ferdinand Huszti Horvath, Dick Huemer, Archie Robin, Louis Schmitt, Cy Young; *inbetweener:* Oliver M. Johnston Jr.; *character des:* Ferdinand Huszti Horvath; *voices:* Walt Disney, Pinto Colvig, William E. Sheets; *mus:* Leigh Harline; *col:* Tech. *sd:* RCA. 8 min. • Mickey gets a whiff of the bug killer he's spraying the plants with and dreams that he and Pluto are the size of ants, battling with giant insects.

4152. Mickey's Good Deed *(Mickey Mouse)* 5 Dec. 1932; *p.c.:* Walt Disney prods for UA; *dir:* Burton F. Gillett; *anim:* Johnny Cannon, Les Clark, Gilles de Tremaudan, Norman Ferguson, Clyde Geronimi, Hardie Gramatky, Richard Lundy, Tom Palmer, Ben Sharpsteen; *voices:* Walt Disney, Lee Millar; *mus:* Bert Lewis; b&w. *sd:* PCP. 7 min. • To get enough money to give a poor family a happy Christmas, Mickey has to sell Pluto.

4153. Mickey's Grand Opera *(Mickey Mouse)* 23 Mar. 1936; *p.c.:* Walt Disney prods for UA; *dir:* Wilfred Jackson; *anim:* Les Clark, Gilles de Tremaudan, Norman Ferguson, Paul Hopkins, Richard Lundy; *fx:* Cy Young; *voices:* Florence Gill, Clarence Nash, Walt Disney; *mus:* Leigh Harline; *col:* Tech. *sd:* RCA. 9 min. • With Mickey as conductor, Donald and Clara Cluck join forces in an operatic duet. Pluto finds a magician's hat, causing chaos by unleashing its contents of rabbits and birds.

4154. Mickey's Kangaroo *(Mickey Mouse)* 15 Apr. 1935; *p.c.:* Walt Disney prods for UA; *dir:* David D. Hand; *anim:* Les Clark, Hardie Gramatky, Clyde Geronimi, Jack Hannah, Richard Lundy, Fred Moore; *voices:* Walt Disney, Lee Millar, Don Brodie; *mus:* Bert Lewis; b&w. *sd:* RCA. 8½ min. • Pluto is jealous of Mickey's new pet kangaroo when Mickey and the 'roo have a boxing match.

4155. Mickey's Man Friday *(Mickey Mouse)* 10 Jan. 1935; *p.c.:* Walt Disney prods for UA; *dir:* David D. Hand; *anim:* Johnny Cannon, Clyde Geronimi, Hardie Gramatky, Jack Hannah, Ferdinand Huszti Horvath, Jack Kinney, William O. Roberts, Leonard Sebring, Ben Sharpsteen, Ed Smith, Bob Wickersham, Roy Williams, Marvin Woodward; *fx:* Cy Young; *back:* Carlos Manriquez; *voices:* Billy Bletcher, Pinto Colvig, Walt Disney; *mus:* Bert Lewis, Frank E. Churchill; b&w. *sd:* RCA. 7 min. • When shipwrecked on a desert isle, Mickey rescues a native from cannibals. The native becomes his Man Friday and they both prepare for a second onslaught by the savages.

4156. Mickey's Mechanical Man *(Mickey Mouse)* 17 June 1933; *p.c.:* Walt Disney prods for UA; *dir:* Wilfred Jackson; *anim:* Charles Byrne, Johnny Cannon, Gilles de Trenmaudan, Clyde Geronimi, Richard Lundy, Louis Schmitt, Leonard Sebring, Ben Sharpsteen, Marvin Woodward; *asst anim:* Thomas Bonfiglio, Chuck Couch, Paul Fennell, Nick George, Hardie Gramatky, Jack Kinney, Edward Love, Roy Williams; *sets:* Carlos Manriquez; *voices:* Marcellite Garner, Walt Disney, Lee Millar; *mus:* Leigh Harline; b&w. *sd:* RCA. 7 min. • Mickey's robot has a boxing match with "The Kongo Killer" a gorilla!

4157. Mickey's Mellerdrammer *(Mickey Mouse)* 18 Mar. 1933; *p.c.:* Walt Disney for UA; *dir:* Wilfred Jackson; *anim:* Johnny Cannon, Les Clark, Gilles de Tremaudan, Kevin Donnelly, Clyde Geronimi, Hamilton S. Luske, Tom Palmer, William O. Roberts, Ben Sharpsteen, Marvin Woodward; *asst anim:* Chuck Couch, Paul Fennell, Edward Love, Fred Smith, Harry Reeves, Roy Williams; *mus:* Frank E. Churchill; b&w. *sd:* RCA. 7 min. • The gang stage "Uncle Tom's Cabin" with Horace Horsecollar as Simon Legree and Mickey as Uncle Tom.

4158. Mickey's Nightmare *(Mickey Mouse)* 13 Aug. 1932; *p.c.:* Walt Disney prods for UA; *dir:* Burton F. Gillett; *anim:* Johnny Cannon, Les Clark, Gilles de Tremaudan, Norman Ferguson, Hardie Gramatky, David D. Hand, Tom Palmer, Ben Sharpsteen; *voices:* Walt Disney; *mus:* Bert Lewis; b&w. *sd:* PCP. 7 min. • Mickey dreams he is married to Minnie and heckled by hoards of kids.

4159. Mickey's Orphans (*Mickey Mouse*) 5 Dec. 1931; *p.c.:* Walter E. Disney for Colum; *dir:* Burton F. Gillett; *anim:* Johnny Cannon, Joseph d'Igalo, Norman Ferguson, Hardie Gramatky, David D. Hand, Jack King, Richard Lundy, Tom Palmer, Ben Sharpsteen; *voices:* Marcellite Garner, Walt Disney; *mus:* Bert Lewis; b&w. *sd:* PCP. 7 min. *Academy Award nomination.* • Christmastime sees a basket of kittens on Mickey's doorstep. They are brought in and proceed to wreck the house, strip the tree of the gifts.

4160. Mickey's Pal Pluto (*Mickey Mouse*) 18 Feb. 1933; *p.c.:* Walt Disney prods for UA; *dir:* Burton F. Gillett; *anim:* Johnny Cannon, Les Clark, Gilles de Tremaudan, Norman Ferguson, Tom Palmer, Ben Sharpsteen; *voices:* Pinto Colvig, Marcellite Garner, Walt Disney; *mus:* Frank E. Churchill; b&w. *sd:* RCA. 6 min. • Jealous over Mickey's attentions to a kitten, Pluto's evil self argues with his better self. Remade in Technicolor as *Lend a Paw*.

4161. Mickey's Parrot (*Mickey Mouse*) 9 Sept. 1938; *p.c.:* Walt Disney prods for RKO; *dir:* William O. Roberts; *asst dir:* Mike Holoboff; *story:* Jack Kinney; *anim:* Les Clark, James H. Culhane, Richard Lundy, Arthur W. Palmer, Fred Spencer, Bob Wickersham, Cornett Wood; *fx:* Joshua Meador; *lay:* Hal Doughty; *back:* Emil Flohri; *voices:* Ernie Stanton, Leon M. Leon, Lee Millar, Walt Disney; *mus:* Oliver Wallace; *col:* Tech. *sd:* RCA. 8 min. • A parrot, loose in Mickey's cellar, is mistaken for an escaped killer.

4162. Mickey's Polo Team (*Mickey Mouse*) 22 Jan. 1936; *p.c.:* Walt Disney prods for UA; *dir:* David D. Hand; *anim:* Arthur Babbitt, Johnny Cannon, Jack Hannah, Paul Hopkins, Dick Huemer, Grim Natwick, William O. Roberts; *character des:* Arthur Babbitt; *back:* Emil Flohri; *voices:* Clarence Nash; *mus:* Frank E. Churchill, Paul J. Smith; *col:* Tech. *sd:* RCA. 9 min. • Frantic polo match between Mickey, Donald, The Goof and the Big Bad Wolf with a celebrity team. Caricatures of Charlie Chaplin, W.C. Fields, Clark Gable, Jack Holt, Laurel & Hardy, Harold Lloyd, Harpo Marx, Edna May Oliver, Shirley Temple and Mae West.

4163. Mickey's Revue (*Mickey Mouse*) 12 May 1932; *p.c.:* Walter E. Disney for Colum; *dir:* Wilfred Jackson; *anim:* Johnny Cannon, Les Clark, Gilles de Tremaudan, Kevin Donnelly, Clyde Geronimi, Jack King, Tom Palmer, Ben Sharpsteen; *Character des:* Charles Philippi; *voices:* Marcellite Garner, Pinto Colvig, Walt Disney; *mus:* Bert Lewis; b&w. *sd:* PCP. 6 min. • The gang stage a musical ballet which is marred by Pluto chasing kittens on stage and the curtain being dropped too early on Mickey and Minnie.

4164. Mickey's Rival (*Mickey Mouse*) 20 June 1936; *p.c.:* Walt Disney prods for UA; *dir:* Wilfred Jackson; *anim:* Les Clark, Gilles de Tremaudan, Clyde Geronimi, Jack Hannah, Dick Huemer, Richard Lundy, Leonard Sebring; *voices:* Leone Le Doux, Sonny Dawson, Walt Disney; *mus:* Leigh Harline; *col:* Tech. *sd:* RCA. 9 min. • Minnie's old flame, Mortimer, spoils Mickey's picnic by showing off. All is returned to normal when Mortimer departs at the sight of a ferocious bull.

4165. Mickey's Service Station (*Mickey Mouse*) 16 Mar. 1935; *p.c.:* Walt Disney prods for UA; *dir:* Ben Sharpsteen; *anim:* Paul Allen, Arthur Babbitt, Nick George, Ferdinand Huszti Horvath, Milton Kahl, Jack Hannah, Jack Kinney, Eric Larson, Richard Lundy, Charles A. Nichols, Wolfgang Reitherman, Archie Robin, Leonard Sebring, Fred Spencer, Eddie Strickland, Don Towsley, Harry Tytle; *voices:* Billy Bletcher, Clarence Nash, Pinto Colvig, Walt Disney; *mus:* Leigh Harline, Bert Lewis; b&w. *sd:* RCA. 8 min. • Peg-leg Pete demands Mickey removes a squeak in his car. Donald and the Goof completely dismantle it before discovering the noise is being caused by a cricket.

4166. Mickey's Steam Roller (*Mickey Mouse*) 16 June 1934; *p.c.:* Walt Disney prods for UA; *dir:* David D. Hand; *anim:* Johnny Cannon, Gilles de Tremaudan, Hardie Gramatky, Jack Hannah, Jack Kinney, Edward Love, William O. Roberts, Ben Sharpsteen, Bob Wickersham, Roy Williams, Marvin Woodward; *voices:* Marcellite Garner, Walt Disney; *mus:* Bert Lewis; b&w. *sd:* RCA. 7 min. • Mickey leaves the kids in his steamroller while he has lunch with Minnie. The runaway roller smashes into a hotel.

4167. Mickey's Surprise Party 18 Feb. 1939; *p.c.:* Walt Disney prods for National Biscuit Co; *dir:* Hamilton S. Luske; *anim:* Oliver M. Johnston Jr., Lynn Karp, Walt Kelly, Charles A. Nichols, Ken Peterson, Claude Smith, Riley Thomson, Harvey Toombs; *fx:* Andy Engman, George Rowley; *voices:* Leone Le Doux, Walt Disney; *mus:* Paul J. Smith; *col:* Tech. *sd:* RCA. 4 min. • Minnie's pomeranian spills popcorn into her cooking

dough. Catastrophe follows but Mickey saves the day with a box of Nabisco cookies. • Specifically made for the 1939 World's Fair.

4168. Mickey's Trailer (*Mickey Mouse*) 6 May 1938; *p.c.:* Walt Disney prods for RKO; *dir:* Ben Sharpsteen; *story:* Jack Kinney; *anim:* Johnny Cannon, Clyde Geronimi, Gilles de Tremaudan, Jack Hannah, I. Klein, Edward Love, Arthur W. Palmer, Ray Patterson, Archie Robin, Paul Satterfield, Louis Schmitt; *fx:* Cy Young; *back:* Don Peterson; *voices:* Clarence Nash, Pinto Colvig, Walt Disney; *mus:* Leigh Harline, Oliver Wallace; *col:* Tech. *sd:* RCA. 8 min. • Goofy drives Mickey and Donald in their mechanical trailer. Soon the Goof comes in for breakfast, leaving the car and trailer to run amok.

4169. Midnight (*Aesop's Sound Fable*) 12 Oct. 1930; *p.c.:* Van Beuren for Pathé; *dir:* John Foster, Harry Bailey; *mus:* Gene Rodemich; b&w. *sd:* RCA. 6 min. • Kept awake by warbling cats, a farmer employs the local pound to dispose of them, which they do and start a song of their own.

4170. Midnight Frolics (*Color Rhapsody*) 23 Dec. 1938; *p.c.:* Cartoon Films Ltd/Charles Mintz prods for Colum; *prod/dir:* Ub Iwerks; *voices:* Mel Blanc, Harry Stanton; *mus:* Joe de Nat, Eddie Kilfeather; *prod mgr:* James Bronis; *col:* Tech. *sd:* RCA. 7 min. • A skeptical mouse discusses the existence of ghosts with a cuckoo bird. They are startled when a sextet of spooks arrive, performing a song and dance.

4171. Midnight in a Toyshop (*Silly Symphony*) 28 July 1930; *p.c.:* Walter E. Disney for Colum; *dir:* Wilfred Jackson; *anim:* Johnny Cannon, Les Clark, Norman Ferguson, David D. Hand, Wilfred Jackson, Jack King, Richard Lundy, Tom Palmer, Ben Sharpsteen; *mus:* Bert Lewis; *ph:* William Cottrell; b&w. *sd:* PCP. 7 min. • A spider enters a toyshop and witnesses the toys coming to life.

4172. The Midnight Snack (*Tom & Jerry*) 19 July 1941; *p.c.:* MGM; *dir:* William Hanna, Joseph Barbera; *anim:* Pete Burness, Kenneth Muse, Jack Zander; *back:* Joe Smith; *ed:* Fred MacAlpin; *voice:* Lillian Randolph; *mus:* Scott Bradley; *prod mgr:* Fred Quimby; *col:* Tech. *sd:* WE. 9 min. • Jerry has a midnight raid on the refrigerator but his feast is abruptly halted by Tom.

4173. Midsummer's Day (*Aesop's Sound Fable*) 28 July 1929; *p.c.:* Fables Pictures Inc for Pathé; *dir:* John Foster; *mus:* Josiah Zuro; sd *fx:* Maurice Manne; b&w. *sd:* RCA. 6 min. • No story available.

4174. Mighty Hunters (*Merrie Melodies*) 27 Jan. 1940; *p.c.:* Leon Schlesinger prods for WB; *dir:* Charles M. Jones; *story:* Dave Monahan; *anim:* Ken Harris; *character des/sets:* James Swinnerton, Robert Givens; *ed:* Treg Brown; *voice:* John Deering; *mus:* Carl W. Stalling; *prod sup:* Henry Binder, Raymond G. Katz; *col:* Tech. *sd:* Vit. 7 min. • Based on James Swinnerton's *Canyon Kiddies*. The kids set out: one group tries to shoot wild animals while others have problems with a bear and another with a stubborn mule.

4175. Mighty Joe Young 1949; *p.c.:* RKO *prod:* Merian C. Cooper, John Ford; *l/a dir:* Ernest B. Schoedsack; *fx:* Willis O'Brien, Ray Harryhausen, Peter Peterson, Marcel Delgado, George Lofgren, Fitch Fulton, Harold Stine, Bert Willis, Linwood Dunn; b&w. *sd:* RCA. 94 min. *l/a/anim.* • Similar plot to *King Kong* about a large ape transported from Africa to the big city.

4176. Mighty Joe Young 25 Dec. 1998; *p.c.:* Disney Enterprises, Inc. for BV; *l/a dir:* Ron Underwood; *story:* Merian C. Cooper from RKO Pictures' *Mighty Joe Young* (1949); *"Mighty Joe Young" creature des/prod:* Rick Baker; *visual fx:* Hoyt Yeatman; *anim sup:* Chris Bailey; *visual fx/cg gorilla:* Dreamquist Images; *visual fx prod:* Anjelica Casillas; *cgi ex prod:* Dennis Hoffman; *digital: asso visual fx sup:* Dan Del Dilleuw; *sup character anim:* Rob Dressel; *digital compositing sup:* Blaine Kennison; *digital prod:* Kristina Reed; *2nd Prod co-ord:* Julie Fischer; *lead compositors:* Saki Mitchell, David Laur, Amy Pfaffinger; *compositors:* Brian Adams, Jeffrey Arnold, Tony Noel, Marc Scott, Michael F. Miller, Jeff Olm, Daniel Miller, Cynthia Hyland; *Rotoscope art:* Dan Walker, Daryl Klein, Paul Kulkowski; *anim:* Steven F. Yamamoto, Stephen Baker, Jason McDade, Steward D. Burris, Robert Skiena, Dave Mullins, Michael Polvani, Aaron Campbell, Kevin Culhane, Bill Miller; *facial anim. system: modelers:* Patrick Taylor, Hal Lewis, Chris Keene, Teunis Deraat; *technical sup:* Danny Speck, Bruce Wright, Paul Jordan; *3d paint:* Mark Siegel; *cg fx anim:* Chris Biggs; *match movers:* Matt Mueller, Mike Ramirez; *digital prod mgr:* Kathryn Lioita-

Couture; *3d prod co-ord.:* Elizabeth Kitt; *hair rendering software development:* Bev LeBaredian; *software development:* Mark Rubin, Sean Jenkins, Jacob Sisk, Bruce Tartagua, Chu Tang; *digital col timer:* Jay Cox; *information services:* Hank Barrio, Doug Sherman, Craig Davis, Mark Dawson; *technical asst:* Eric Muenker, John Giffoni, Michael G. Miller, James Blevins, David Bush, Rob White; *scanning/rec technicians:* Rick Lopez, Doug Dilaney, Marc Canas, James Parris; *digital systems admin.:* Paul Takahashi, James Healy, Rob Jones, John Kennedy, Kyle Kirkland, Roy Erickson; *digital operations mgr:* Mike Gunning, Jamie Toscas; *digital technician:* Kyle Healy; *head of digital technology:* Rob Burton; *digital dpt sup:* Mitch Dobrowner; special visual fx & anim by Industrial Light & Magic; *visual fx sup:* Jim Mitchell; *anim sup:* Daniel Jeannette; *anim & visual fx prod:* Mark S. Miller; *visual fx asso sup:* Carl Frederick; *creative sup:* Paul Glacoppo; *lead cg art:* Robert Weaver; *character anim:* Julie Nilson, Steve Nichols, Mark Powers, Doug Edward Smith, Tom St. Amand, Glenn Sylvester, Dan Taylor; *cg art:* Vince deQuaitro, Russell Koonce, Jeroin Lapre, Ken Neilsen, Hiromi Ono, Linda Siegel, Eric Texler, Michael Corcoran; *digital texturing paint art:* Rebecca Petrulli-Heskes; *digital timing sup:* Bruce Vecchito; *visual fx co-ord:* Theresa Corrao; *research & development sup:* Christian Rouet; *software research & development:* John Anderson, Jim Houseman, Florian Kaine, Vishwaranjan; *3d ph:* Keith Johnson, Larry Cleman; *mark-up:* Michael Gleason; digital fx by Computer Film Company: Janek Sires, Janet Yale, Travis Raumann, David Fuhrer, Bob Chapin, Mattdessero; digital matte painting by Matte World Digital; *scanning sup:* ;Joshua Pines; *digital paint/Rotoscope art:* Cathy Burrow, Patrick Jarvis, Terry Molatore; *film scanning:* Earl Beyer, Mike Ellis; *cg asst art:* David Weitzberg, Tom Fejes; *visual fx prod asst:* Julie M. Diantoni; *prod engineers:* Ken Beyer, Suzanne Augusta, Ken Corvino, Jason Uckie, Brian Wong; *systems development:* Russell Darling, Jik Natarajan; *neg cutter:* Doug Jones; *neg line-up:* Tim Glideman, James Lim; *cg technical support:* Marc Wilhite, Kristen Millette, Grace Lan, Masayori Oka; *mus:* James Horner; *col:* Tech. *sd:* SDDS/Dolby digital/Digital dts sound. Panavision. 114 min. *l/a* • Live-action adaptation of the 1949 feature: Jill Young carries on the anthropologist work of her late mother, studying African gorillas. One gorilla, named "Joe," she has grown up with grows to enormous proportions and it is suggested that he be shipped to a Los Angeles wildlife center. A poacher poses as protector of rare species in order to vent his revenge for Joe having once bitten off his fingers.

4177. Mighty Mouse and the Hep Cat *(Mighty Mouse)* 6 Dec. 1946; *p.c.:* TT for Fox; *dir:* Mannie Davis; *story:* John Foster; *mus:* Philip A. Scheib; *ph:* Douglas Moye; *col:* Tech. *sd:* RCA. 6 min. • The cats lure the mice into their clutches by means of playing "hot" music.

4178. Mighty Mouse and the Kilkenny Cats *(Mighty Mouse)* 13 Apr. 1945; *p.c.:* TT for Fox; *dir:* Mannie Davis; *story:* John Foster; *voice:* Thomas Morrison; *mus:* Philip A. Scheib; *col:* Tech. *sd:* RCA. 6½ min. • The mice band together to beat the tough Kilkenny cats but finally have to resort to calling for Mighty Mouse when the going gets tough.

4179. Mighty Mouse and the Magician *(Mighty Mouse)* Mar. 1948; *p.c.:* TT for Fox; *dir:* Eddie Donnelly; *story:* John Foster; *mus:* Philip A. Scheib; *ph:* Douglas Moye; *col:* Tech. *sd:* RCA. 6½ min. • The cats steal a magician's magic wand to use in the process of catching mice.

4180. Mighty Mouse and the Pirates *(Mighty Mouse)* 12 Jan. 1945; *p.c.:* TT for Fox; *dir:* Connie Rasinski; *story:* John Foster; *voice:* Roy Halee; *mus:* Philip A. Scheib; *ph:* Douglas Moye; *col:* Tech. *sd:* RCA. 6 min. • The pirates capture a sarong-clad lovely but it isn't too long before Mighty Mouse is on his way to the rescue.

4181. Mighty Mouse and the Two Barbers *(Mighty Mouse)* 1 Sept. 1944; *p.c.:* TT for Fox; *dir:* Eddie Donnelly; *story:* John Foster; *sets:* Art Bartsch; *mus:* Philip A. Scheib; *col:* Tech. *sd:* RCA. 6 min. • The local mouse barber is invaded and bound-up by a group of cats. Mighty Mouse is summonsed in the nick of time.

4182. Mighty Mouse and the Wolf *(Mighty Mouse)* 20 July 1945; *p.c.:* TT for Fox; *dir:* Eddie Donnelly; *story:* John Foster; *mus:* Philip A. Scheib; *col:* Tech. *sd:* RCA. 7 min. • When Mighty Mouse prevents the wolf from recreating the story of Little Red Riding Hood, he pursues the Three Little Pigs instead.

4183. Mighty Mouse at the Circus *(Mighty Mouse)* 17 Nov. 1944; *p.c.:* TT for Fox; *dir:* Eddie Donnelly; *story:* John Foster; *mus:* Philip A. Scheib; *col:* Tech. *sd:* RCA. 6 min. • Mlle Fifi, an acrobat mouse, falls from her trapeze into the lion's cage. The lions escape and Mighty Mouse is called upon to help the townsfolk.

4184. Mighty Mouse in Krakatoa *(Mighty Mouse)* 14 Dec. 1945; *p.c.:* TT for Fox; *dir:* Connie Rasinski; *story:* John Foster; *anim:* Carlo Vinci; *sets:* Art Bartsch; *mus:* Philip A. Scheib; *ph:* Douglas Moye; *col:* Tech. *sd:* RCA. 7 min. • Mighty Mouse rescues the natives from the errupting volcano on Krakatoa Island.

4185. Mighty Mouse in the Great Space Chase 10 Dec. 1982; *p.c.:* Filmation/Viacom International for Miracle; *dir:* Ed Friedman, Lou Kachivas, Marsh Lamore, Gwen Wetzler, Kay Wright, Lou Zukor; *prod:* Lou Scheimer, Norm Prescott, Don Christensen; *storyboard:* Bob Kline, Kurt Connor, John Dorman, Paul Fennell, Eddie Fitzgerald, Rich Fogel, Karl Geurs, Mike Joens, John Kricfalusi, Lonnie Lloyd, Tom Minton, Mitch Schauer, Wendell Washer; *anim:* Robert Arkwright, John Armstrong, Thomas Baron, James Brummett, Kent Butterworth, William Carney, John Conning, Franco Cristofani, James Davis, Zeon Davush, Jaime Diaz, Chuck Eyler, Francesca Freeman, Kenneth Gaebler, John Garling, Milton Gray, Karen Haus, Barry Helmer, Edward de Mattia, Lawrence Miller, Ron Myrick, Greg Nocon, William Nunes, Frank Onaitis, Jack Ozark, Anthony Pabian, Karen Peterson, Thomas Ray, William Recinos, Virgil Ross, Donald Ruch, Sonja Ruta, Ernie Schmidt, Larry Silverman, Nicholas Stern, Leo Sullivan, Reuben Timmens, Linn Trochim, Robert Trochim, Richard Trueblood, Robert Tyler, Dardo Velez, James Walker, Larry White, Barry Whitebook, Woody Yocum; *key asst:* Mike Hazy; *asst anim sup:* Marlene Robinson; *art dir:* Alberto de Mello, James Fletcher; *lay:* Larry Eikleberry, Sergio Garcia, Ed Haney, Wes Herschensohn, David Hoover, Richard Hoover, Mary Jorgensen, Les Kaluza, John Koch, Lorenzo Martinez, Mike Mitchell, Philip Norwood, John Perry, Sharon Rolnik, Lewis Saw, Gary Terry, Cliff Voorhees, Curt Walstead, David West, Sherry Wheeler, William Wray; *col dir:* Ervin L. Kaplan; *back:* Barbara Benedetto, Alan Bodner, Sheila Brown, Ellen Caster, Dianne Erenberg, Vern Jorgensen, Pat Keppler, Tom O'Loughlin, Norley Paat, Curt Perkins, Don Schweikert, Don Watson, Don Peters; *paint sup:* Val Vreeland, Alla Marshall; *ed:* James Blodgett, Ann Hagerman, Earl Biddle; *voices:* Alan Oppenheimer, Diane Pershing; *mus:* Yvette Blais, Jeff Michael; *mus sup:* George Mahana; *mus ed:* Robert Waxman; *main title song:* Jeff Michael, Dean Andre; *check:* Marion Turk; *Xerography:* John Remmel; *film co-ord:* June Gilham, Toni Christiansen; *ph:* R.W. Pope, Frederick T. Ziegler, Dean Teves, David Link, Don Dinehart, David Valentine, Patricia Burns, Roncie Hantke, Dan Larsen; *sd rec:* Glen Glenn Sound; *sd fx:* George Mahana; *prod controller:* Bob Wilson; *prod mgr:* Joseph Simon; *col:* Tech. *sd.* 87 min. • Harry the Heartless, a malicious cat bent on universal domination, will stop at nothing to find out the location of the Doomsday Device. Mighty Mouse tries to prevent him by flying to Humongo where the Device is held. All it needs to be activated is a few ounces of Hitparadium which can be acquired from a chemestry set kept at the universe's largest toy shop. Mighty Mouse manages to reverse the process and send Harry to another dimension. Compiled from sixteen television episodes.

4186. Mighty Mouse in the Gypsy Life *(Mighty Mouse)* 3 Aug. 1945; *p.c.:* TT for Fox; *dir:* Connie Rasinski; *story:* John Foster; *voice:* Roy Halee; *mus:* Philip A. Scheib; *ph:* Douglas Moye; *col:* Tech. *sd:* RCA. 6 min. *Academy Award nomination.* • The gypsy mice are dancing in their encampment when a group of flying cats attack ... can Mighty Mouse be too far away?

4187. Mighty Mouse Meets Bad Bill Bunion *(Mighty Mouse)* 9 Nov. 1945; *p.c.:* TT for Fox; *dir:* Mannie Davis; *story:* John Foster; *voices:* Thomas Morrison; *mus:* Philip A. Scheib; *ph:* Douglas Moye; *col:* Tech. *sd:* RCA. 7 min. • A cattle thief robs a train and kidnaps a pretty girl. Mighty Mouse soon flies to the rescue.

4188. Mighty Mouse Meets Deadeye Dick *(Mighty Mouse)* 30 May 1947; *p.c.:* TT for Fox; *dir:* Connie Rasinski; *story:* John Foster; *mus:* Philip A. Scheib; *ph:* Douglas Moye; *col:* Tech. *sd:* RCA. 7 min. • The local posse can't tame Dead-Eye Dick, so it's up to Mighty Mouse to save the Western town.

4189. Mighty Mouse Meets Jekyll and Hyde Cat *(Mighty Mouse)* 28 Apr. 1944; *p.c.:* TT for Fox; *dir:* Mannie Davis; *story:* John Foster; *anim:* Vladimir Tytla; *sets:* Art Bartsch; *mus:* Philip A. Scheib; *ph:* Douglas Moye; *col:* Tech. *sd:* RCA. 6 min. • A cat concocts a potion that turns him into a demon, posing a serious threat to Mighty Mouse.

4190. The Mighty Navy (*Popeye*) 14 Nov. 1941; *p.c.:* The Fleischer Studio for Para; *prod:* Max Fleischer; *dir:* Dave Fleischer; *story:* William Turner, Ted Pierce; *anim:* Seymour Kneitel, Abner Matthews; *voices:* Jack Mercer, Ted Pierce; *mus:* Sammy Timberg; *prod sup:* Sam Buchwald, Isidore Sparber; b&w. *sd:* WE. 7 min. • Popeye is put on K.P. duty, peeling potatoes. He hears the ship under attack and single-handedly wipes out the enemy fleet.

4191. The Mighty Smithy (*Life Cartoon Comedy*) 19 Nov. 1926; *p.c.:* Sherwood Wadsworth Pictures for Educational; *prod/dir:* John R. McCrory; b&w. sil. 10 min. • Mike Monkey appears as the village blacksmith. High Hat Harold kidnaps his sweetie and makes off with her on a remarkable steed made from a barrel and folding hat racks.

4192. The Mighty Termite (*Modern Madcap*) Nov. 1961; *p.c.:* Para Cartoons; *dir:* Seymour Kneitel; *story:* Irving Dressler; *anim:* Nick Tafuri, Danté Barbetta; *sets:* Robert Owen; *voices:* Jack Mercer; *mus:* Winston Sharples; *ph:* Leonard McCormick; *prod mgr:* Abe Goodman; *col:* Tech. *sd:* RCA. 6 min. • Prof. Schmaltz needs to find out how a termite operates by capturing one that eats all in sight ... including the Professor.

4193. Mike the Masquerader (*Modern Madcap*) 1 Jan. 1960; *p.c.:* Para Cartoons; *dir:* Seymour Kneitel; *story:* Carl Meyer, Jack Mercer; *anim:* Wm. B. Pattengill, Nick Tafuri; *sets:* Robert Owen; *voices:* Sid Raymond, Bob MacFadden; *mus:* Winston Sharples; *ph:* Leonard McCormick; *prod mgr:* Abe Goodman; *col:* Tech. *sd:* RCA. 6 min. • The police guard an elephant who thinks he can identify a bank robber, so the crook tries various methods to silence him.

4194. Mike Wins a Medal (*Life Cartoon Comedy*) 18 Jan. 1927; *p.c.:* Sherwood Wadsworth Pictures for Educational; *prod/dir:* John R. McCrory; b&w. sil. 6 min. • Little Nibbins accidentally sets a skyscraper alight and Mike Monkey has a tough time putting it out and then rescuing Nibbins by scaling a jet of water.

4195. The Mild West (*Noveltoon*) 22 Aug 1947; *p.c.:* Famous for Para; *dir:* Seymour Kneitel; *story:* Bill Turner, Larry Riley; *anim:* Tom Johnson, George Germanetti; *sets:* Anton Loeb; *mus:* Winston Sharples; *song:* Leo Feist Inc.; *ph:* Leonard McCormick; *prod mgr:* Sam Buchwald; *col:* Tech. *sd:* RCA. 7 min. • A community sing-along in the Old West.

4196. Mile-A-Minute Monty (*Canimated Nooz Pictorial*) 23 Aug. 1915/5 Jan. 1916; *p.c.:* Essanay; *anim:* Leon A. Searl; b&w. sil. s/r. 5 min. • Monty takes his flying machine to meet his wife at the station but is sidetracked by pretty bathers. His wife catches him peeking at the belles and tosses him in the pool.

4197. Milk and Money (*Looney Tunes*) 3 Oct. 1936; *p.c.:* Leon Schlesinger prods for WB; *dir:* Fred Avery; *story:* Robert Clampett; *anim:* Charles Jones, Virgil Ross, Robert Clampett; *voices:* Billy Bletcher, Joe Dougherty; *mus:* Carl W. Stalling; *prod sup:* Henry Binder, Raymond G. Katz; b&w. *sd:* Vit. 7 min. • Poppa Pig's farm will be repossessed unless the mortgage is paid off. Porky goes on a milk round but the horse is bitten by a horsefly, causing them to win a $10 handicap race.

4198. Milk for Baby (*Terry-Toon*) 8 July 1938; *p.c.:* TT for Educational/Fox: *dir:* Mannie Davis; *mus:* Philip A. Scheib; b&w. *sd:* RCA. 6½ min. • A nursemaid (Edna May Oliver) explains how a cow has to be contented to give milk.

4199. The Milkman (*Flip the Frog*) 20 Apr. 1932; *p.c.:* Celebrity prods for MGM; *prod/dir:* Ub Iwerks; *mus:* Gene Denny; b&w. *sd:* PCP. 6 min. • While Flip delivers milk from his dairy his horse is tormented by a brat. They make up and sing "Hail! Hail! The Gang's All Here"!

4200. The Milky Waif (*Tom & Jerry*) 18 May 1946; *p.c.:* MGM; *dir:* William Hanna, Joseph Barbera; *anim:* Michael Lah, Kenneth Muse, Ed Barge; *ed:* Fred MacAlpin; *voice:* Lillian Randolph; *mus:* Scott Bradley; *prod:* Fred Quimby; *col:* Tech. *sd:* WE. 7 min. • An abandoned waif named Nibbles is discovered by Jerry, who has his work cut out for him trying to stop the kid from drinking from Tom's milk bowl.

4201. The Milky Way (*MGM Cartoon*) 22 June 1940; *p.c.:* MGM; *prod:* Rudolf Ising; *dir/lay:* Robert Allen; *sets:* Joe Smith; *ed:* Fred MacAlpin; *voices:* Bernice Hansel; *mus:* Scott Bradley; *prod mgr:* Fred Quimby; *col:* Tech. *sd:* WE. 8 min. *Academy Award.* • Three kittens are sent to bed without any supper and dream of going to The Milky Way and drinking their fill of milk and cream.

4202. The Mill Pond (*Aesop's Sound Fable*) 18 Oct. 1929; *p.c.:* Van Beuren for Pathé; *dir:* John Foster, Mannie Davis; b&w. *sd:* RCA. 10 min. • Farmer Al chases the animals from his pond while the mice glue his feet to the diving board.

4203. The Miller and His Donkey (*Aesop's Film Fable*) 26 Jan. 1922; *p.c.:* Fables Pictures Inc for Pathé; *dir:* Paul Terry; b&w. sil. 5 min. • No story available.

4204. The Miller's Daughter (*Merrie Melodies*) 13 Oct. 1934; *p.c.:* Leon Schlesinger prods for WB; *dir:* Isadore Freleng; *anim:* Rollin Hamilton, Charles M. Jones, Robert Clampett; *voice:* Mary Moder; *mus:* Norman Spencer; b&w. *sd:* Vit. 6 min. • A cat breaks a shepherdess statue and her shepherd boyfriend repairs her while singing.

4205. The Million Dollar Cat (*Tom & Jerry*) 6 May 1944; *p.c.:* MGM; *dir:* William Hanna, Joseph Barbera; *anim:* Irven Spence, Kenneth Muse, Pete Burness, Ray Patterson; *lay:* Harvey Eisenberg; *ed:* Fred MacAlpin; *voices:* Harry E. Lang; *mus:* Scott Bradley; *prod:* Fred Quimby; *col:* Tech. *sd:* WE. 7 min. • Tom inherits one million dollars providing he doesn't harm any living creature. Jerry is quick to see the possibilities of the situation.

4206. Million Dollar Duck 30 June 1971; *p.c.:* Walt Disney prods for BV; *prod:* Bill Anderson; *titles:* Ward Kimball, Ted Berman; *mus:* Buddy Baker; *orch:* Walter Sheets; *col:* Tech. *sd:* RCA. (*titles*) 2 min. • The live-action story involves a duck that lays golden eggs. The title animation has a duck wandering on and off screen, placing eggs to form the zeros in the title word "Million."

4207. The Million Hare (*Looney Tunes*) Apr. 1963; *p.c.:* WB; *dir:* Robert McKimson; *story:* Dave DeTiege; *anim:* Ted Bonnicksen, Warren Batchelder, George Grandpré, Keith Darling; *fx:* Harry Love; *sets:* Robert Gribbroek; *ed:* Treg Brown; *voices:* Mel Blanc; *mus:* Bill Lava; *prod mgr:* William Orcutt; *prod:* David H. DePatie; *col:* Tech. *sd:* Vit. 7 min. • Daffy and Bugs are competitors in a game show and have to reach the TV studio in order to claim a prize of one million bucks.

4208. Millionaire Droopy (*Droopy*) 21 Sept. 1956; *p.c.:* MGM; *prod:* William Hanna, Joseph Barbera; *dir:* Tex Avery; *sets:* Don Driscoll; *ed:* Jim Faris; *ph:* Jack Stevens; *prod mgr:* Hal Elias; *col:* Tech. *sd:* WE. 7 min. CS. • Spike stands to inherit the whole estate ... only Droopy stands in his way. • CS reissue of *Wags to Riches*.

4209. The Millionaire Hobo (*Phantasy*) 24 Nov. 1939; *p.c.:* Colum; *story:* Art Davis; *anim:* Sid Marcus; *lay:* Clark Watson; *back:* Phil Davis; *ed:* George Winkler; *voice:* Mel Blanc, Dave Weber; *mus:* Joe de Nat; *ph:* Otto Reimer; *prod mgr:* James Bronis; b&w. *sd:* RCA. 6½ min. • A tramp believes he's inherited a million dollars and goes about spending accordingly. He turns out to have inherited one million cats.

4210. Minding the Baby (*Scrappy*) 1 Dec 1931; *p.c.:* Winkler for Colum; *prod:* Charles B. Mintz; *story:* Dick Huemor; *anim:* Sid Marcus, Art Davis; *mus:* Joe de Nat; *prod mgr:* James Bronis; b&w. *sd:* WE. 6 min. • Scrappy is left to babysit with Vontzy, his kid brother, who puts him through the mill.

4211. Minding the Baby (*Talkartoons*) 26 Sept. 1931; *p.c.:* The Fleischer Studio for Para; *prod:* Max Fleischer; *sup:* Dave Fleischer; *dir/story:* Jimmie Culhane, Rudy Zamora; *anim:* Jimmie Culhane, Rudy Zamora, Berny Wolf, Al Eugster; *mus:* Art Turkisher; b&w. *sd:* WE. 6 min. • Bimbo leaves the baby to flirt with Betty. The brat returns them with a vacuum cleaner.

4212. The Miner's Daughter (*Jolly Frolic*) 25 May 1950; *p.c.:* UPA for Colum; *ex prod:* Stephen Bosustow; *dir sup:* John Hubley; *dir:* Robert Cannon; *story:* Bob Russell, Phil Eastman, Bill Scott; *anim:* Bill Melendez, Willis Pyle, Paul Smith, Pat Matthews, Pete Burness; *lay:* Bill Hurtz; *back:* Herb Klynn, Jules Engel; *i&p:* Mary Cain; *voice:* Gloria Wood, Jerry Hausner, Thurl Ravenscroft; *mus:* Gail Kubik; *ph:* Jack Eckes; *prod sup:* Ade Woolery, Max Morgan; *col:* Tech. *sd:* RCA. 6 min. • An old prospector's daughter falls for a rugged Harvard type who has no interest in women. Not until the intruder discovers gold is her father anxious to pair the two off.

4213. Miners Forty Niners (*Screen Song*) 18 May 1951; *p.c.:* Famous for Para; *dir:* I. Sparber; *story:* I. Klein; *anim:* Myron Waldman, Larry Silverman; *sets:* Anton Loeb; *voices:* Michael Fitzmaurice, Sid Raymond, Cecil

Roy; *mus:* Winston Sharples; *ph:* Leonard Mc Cormick; *prod mgr:* Sam Buchwald; *col:* Tech. *sd:* RCA. 7 min. • A history of gold mining leads to a sing-along of "Oh My Darling Clementine." • Caricature of Jerry Colonna.

4214. The Mini-Squirts *(Fractured Fable)* Dec. 1967; *p.c.:* Para Cartoons; *ex prod/dir/character des:* Ralph Bakshi; *story:* Eli Bauer; *anim:* Doug Crane, Al Eugster, Nick Tafuri; *lay:* Cosmo Anzilotti; *back:* John Zago, James Simon; *mus:* Winston Sharples; *col:* Tech. *sd:* RCA. 6 min. • Children perform a too-close-to-reality game of "Mothers and Fathers."

4215. Minnie the Moocher *(Talkartoons)* 6 Feb. 1932; *p.c.:* The Fleischer Studio for Para; *prod:* Max Fleischer; *dir:* Dave Fleischer; *anim:* Willard Bowsky, Ralph Somerville; *voice:* Mae Questel; *mus:* Art Turkisher; *l/a:* Cab Calloway and His Orchestra; *song:* Cab Calloway, Clarence L. Gaskill, Irving Mills; b&w. *sd:* WE 8 min. *l/a/anim.* • Betty runs away from home, meets Bimbo and has a scary time in a cave where they see ghosts. Scared stiff, Betty returns home.

4216. Minnie's Yoo Hoo 1929; *p.c.:* Walter E. Disney; *song:* Carl W. Stalling; *addit lyrics:* Walter E. Disney. • Promotional for song used for the Mickey Mouse Clubs (not the later television show of the 1950s), using stock animation from *Mickey's Follies* (1929). Mickey and all the farm animals sing Minnie's praises. b&w. *sd:* PCP.

4217. The Minstrel Show *(Krazy Kat)* 21 Nov. 1932; *p.c.:* Winkler for Colum; *prod:* Charles B. Mintz; *dir:* Ben Harrison, Manny Gould; *anim:* Al Eugster, Preston Blair; *mus:* Joe de Nat; *prod mgr:* James Bronis; b&w. *sd:* RCA. 6 min. • Krazy puts on a show at the opera house, does "The Cake Walk," presents Bing Crosby and gets pelted with fruit for his trouble.

4218. Mint Men *(Heckle & Jeckle)* May 1960; *p.c.:* TT for Fox; *ex prod:* Bill Weiss; *dir:* Connie Rasinski; *story sup:* Tom Morrison; *story:* George Hill; *anim:* Eddie Donnelly; *sets:* John Zago, Bill Focht; *voices:* Roy Halee; *mus:* Phil Scheib; *prod mgr:* Frank Schudde; *col:* DeLuxe. *sd:* RCA. 6 min. • The magpies are government agents posing as janitors in order to find any flaws in a new robot used in the Mint.

4219. Mintz, Charles, Studio (1930–1939); *prod:* Charles B. Mintz; *dir/anim/story:* Art Davis, Manny Gould, Ben Harrison, Harry Love, Sidney Marcus, Allen Rose; *anim:* Felix Alegre, Ed Benedict, Preston Blair, Jack Carr, Chuck Couch, Irv Ellis, Al Eugster, Ray Fahringer, Emery Hawkins, Bill Higgins, Dick Huemor, Fred Jones, Isadore Klein, George Lane, Harry Lieblich, Louie Lilly, Dick Marion, Ray Patin, Don Patterson, Ray Patterson, Frank Powers, Eddie Rehberg, Allen Rose, George Rose, Claude Smith, Irving Spector, Irven Spence, Reuben Timmens, Joe Voght, Robert Wickersham, Rudy Zamora; *inbetween:* Ben Shenkman, Louis Zukowski; *character des:* Ferdinand Huszti Horvath; *sets:* Al Boggs, Phil Davis, Jules Engel, Ray Huffine, Clark Watson; *i&p:* Mike Balukas, Christine Phiederman; *ed:* Edward Moore, George Winkler; *mus:* Joe de Nat, Eddie Kilfeather; *ph:* Sid Glenar, Mike Marcus, Otto Reimer; *misc:* Gladys Ash, Gertrude Bowman, Frankie Brinker, Teddie Carson, Rae Cartner, J. Chatfield, Oneta Coffey, Bub Crabbe, Esther Culbertson, Barbara & Virginia Danielson, Clayre Feinstein, Alma Forshay, Lucille Fuller, Marion Gates, Doris Guilford, Al Jackson, Harriet & Ike Kellet, Hazel Lathrop, Ruth Love, Jack Maxwell, Moishe McDermott, Lucille Miller, Gladys Milligan, Paul Novak, Hal Petersen, Mac Rae, Alice Rehberg, Johnny Roth, Louise Schultz, Abe Sogolwich, Lee Tutson, Carol Wagner, Virginia & Helen Wilson.

4220. The Minute and a ¹/₂ Man *(Hector Heathcote)* July 1959; *p.c.:* TT for Fox; *ex prod:* Bill Weiss; *dir:* Dave Tendlar; *story sup:* Tom Morrison; *story:* Eli Bauer; *anim:* Eddie Donnelly, Mannie Davis, Dave Tendlar; *sets:* Bill Hilliker; *voices:* John Myhers; *mus:* Philip Scheib; *prod mgr:* Frank Schudde; *col:* DeLuxe. *sd:* RCA. 6 min. CS. • No matter how hard Heathcote practices to arrive on parade on time ... somehow he always arrives late. Initial episode.

4221. Mirth Cartoons 1938. • Sound reissues of *Aesop's Fables.*

4222. Les Miserobots *(Inspector)* 21 Mar. 1968; *p.c.:* Mirisch/Geoffrey/DFE for UA; *dir:* Gerry Chiniquy; *story:* Jim Ryan; *anim:* Warren Batchelder, Tom Ray, Manny Perez, Don Williams, Manny Gould; *lay:* Dick Ung; *back:* Tom O'Loughlin; *ed:* Allan Potter; *voices:* Pat Harrington Jr., Marvin Miller; *mus:* Walter Greene; *theme tune:* Henry Mancini; *ph:* John Burton Jr.; *prod*

sup: Harry Love, David DeTiege; *col:* DeLuxe. *sd:* RCA. 6 min. • The Inspector is replaced by a robot and proceeds to dispose of it.

4223. Misguided Missile *(Woody Woodpecker)* 27 Jan. 1958; *p.c.:* Walter Lantz prods for Univ; *dir:* Paul J. Smith; *story:* Homer Brightman; *anim:* Robert Bentley, Les Kline; *sets:* Art Landy, Raymond Jacobs; *voices:* Dal McKennon, Grace Stafford; *mus:* Clarence Wheeler; *prod mgr:* William E. Garity; *col:* Tech. *sd:* RCA. 6 min. • Woody sells Dooley an insurance policy that does not fully cover him from being hit by a guided missile.

4224. The Missing Genie *(Luno)* Apr. 1963; *p.c.:* TT for Fox; *ex prod:* Bill Weiss; *dir/anim:* Connie Rasinski; *story sup:* Tom Morrison; *story:* Larz Bourne; *sets:* Bill Focht, John Zago; *ed:* Jack MacConnell; *voices:* Bob MacFadden, Norma MacMillan; *mus:* Phil Scheib; *ph:* Ted Moskowitz, Joe Rasinski; *sd:* Elliot Grey; *col:* DeLuxe. *sd:* RCA. 5 min. • Luno and Tim investigate the kidnapping of Aladdin's genie.

4225. Missing Links *(Life Cartoon Comedy)* 22 Sept. 1926; *p.c.:* Sherwood Wadsworth Pictures for Educational; *prod/dir:* John R. McCrory; b&w. *sil.* 5 min. • Butcher's boy, Mike Monkey, serenades Myrtle by playing tunes on his stock of meat. High Hat Harold substitutes a trained eel for a string of frankfurters and kidnaps Myrtle.

4226. The Missing Mouse *(Tom & Jerry)* 10 Jan. 1953; *p.c.:* MGM; *dir:* William Hanna, Joseph Barbera; *anim:* Ray Patterson, Ed Barge, Kenneth Muse, Irven Spence; *lay:* Dick Bickenbach; *back:* Robert Gentle; *ed:* Jim Faris; *voice:* Paul Frees; *mus:* Edward Plumb; *ph:* Jack Stevens; *prod:* Fred Quimby; *col:* Tech. *sd:* WE. 6 min. • Jerry takes advantage of the news that a white mouse has escaped from an experimental laboratory after having consumed a quantity of high explosives. He paints himself white and throws a scare into Tom. Ed Plumb takes over for Scott Bradley during a musicians' strike.

4227. Mississippi Hare *(Looney Tunes)* 26 Feb. 1949; *p.c.:* WB; *dir:* Charles M. Jones; *story:* Michael Maltese; *anim:* Ben Washam, Lloyd Vaughan, Ken Harris, Phil Monroe, Virgil Ross; *fx:* Harry Love; *lay:* Robert Gribbroek; *back:* Peter Alvarado; *ed:* Treg Brown; *voices:* Mel Blanc, Billy Bletcher; *mus:* Carl Stalling; *prod mgr:* John W. Burton; *prod:* Edward Selzer; *col:* Tech. *sd:* Vit. 7 min. • While on a Mississippi paddle steamer, Bugs falls afoul of an unscrupulous riverboat gambler.

4228. Mississippi Mud *(Oswald)* 30 Aug. 1928; *p.c.:* Univ; *anim:* Walter Lantz; b&w. *sil.* 6 min. • A riverboat setting with Oswald rescuing the fair one from the clutches of the villain.

4229. Mississippi Slow Boat *(Inspector Willoughby)* 15 Aug. 1961; *p.c.:* Walter Lantz prods for Univ; *dir:* Paul J. Smith; *story:* Homer Brightman; *anim:* Ray Abrams, Les Kline; *sets:* Art Landy, Ray Huffine; *voices:* Dal McKennon; *mus:* Eugene Poddany; *prod mgr:* William E. Garity; *col:* Tech. *sd:* RCA. 6 min. • Inspector Willoughby pits his wits against a riverboat gambler trying to relieve him of a bag of gold.

4230. Mississippi Swing *(Terry-Toon)* 7 Feb. 1941; *p.c.:* TT for Fox; *dir:* Connie Rasinski; *story:* John Foster; *mus:* Philip A. Scheib; *col:* Tech. *sd:* RCA. 6 min. • The folk sing Stephen Foster's songs in the cotton fields until the showboat arrives then they join in the fun of the show.

4231. Mister and Misletoe *(Popeye)* 30 Sept. 1955; *p.c.:* Famous for Para; *dir:* I. Sparber; *story:* Jack Mercer, Carl Meyer; *anim:* Al Eugster, Wm. B. Pattengill; *sets:* Joseph Dommerque; *voices:* Jack Mercer, Jackson Beck, Mae Questel; *mus:* Winston Sharples; *ph:* Leonard McCormick; *prod mgr:* Seymour Shultz; *col:* Tech. *sd:* RCA. 6 min. • Popeye arrives to help Olive prepare for Christmas and Bluto disguises as Santa to gain access.

4232. Mr. and Mrs. Is the Name *(Merrie Melodies)* 3 June 1935; *p.c.:* Leon Schlesinger prods for WB; *dir:* Isadore Freleng; *anim:* Ben Clopton, Cal Dalton, Robert Clampett; *voice:* Tommy Bond; *mus:* Bernard Brown; *prod sup:* Henry Binder, Raymond G. Katz; *col:* Tech-2. *sd:* Vit. 7 min. • A boy and girl mermaid play until an octopus breaks up their fun by capturing the girl.

4233. Mr. Bug Goes to Town 4 Dec. 1941; *p.c.:* The Fleischer Studio for Para; *prod:* Max Fleischer; *dir:* Dave Fleischer; *story:* Dave Fleischer, Dan Gordon, Ted Pierce, Isidore Sparber; *story adapt:* Dan Gordon, Ted Pierce, Isidore Sparber, William Turner, Carl Meyer, Graham Place, Bob Wickersham, Cal Howard; *anim dir:* Willard Bowsky, Myron Waldman, Thomas Johnson, David Tendlar, James Culhane, H.C. Ellison, Stan Quackenbush, Graham Place; *anim:* Els Barthen, Orestes Calpini, James

Davis, Nicholas Tafuri, Carl Meyer, Otto Feuer, Thomas Moore, Bob Wickersham, Irving Spector, Nelson Demorest, Joseph d'Igalo, Thomas Golden, Lod Rossner, Dick Williams, Winfield Hoskins, Anthony di Paola, Alfred Eugster, Vince Fago, Arnold Gillespie, George Germanetti, Frank Endres, William Henning, Joseph Oriolo, Abner Kneitel, Louis Zukor, Harold Whitaker, Sam Stimson, Reuben Grossman, Gordon Sheehan, George Waiss, John Walworth; *sets:* Robert Little, Shane Miller, Hemia Calpini, Eddi Bowlds, Anton Loeb, Robert Connavale, Marjorie Young; *voices: Dick:* Kenny Gardner; *Mary:* Gwen Williams; *Mr. Bumble/Swat:* Jack Mercer; *C. Bagley Beetle:* Ted Pierce; *Smack:* Carl Meyer; *Hoppity:* Stan Freed; *Honey:* Pauline Loth; *Mr. Creepers:* Pinto Colvig; *Mrs. Ladybug/Buzz:* Margie Hines; *miscellaneous insects:* Jack Mercer, Pinto Colvig; *chorus:* The Four Marshalls, The Royal Guards; *atmospheric mus:* Leigh Harline; *songs:* Hoagy Carmichael, Frank Loesser, "Be My Little Baby Bumblebee" by Stanley Murphy; *sd fx:* Maurice Manne; *ph:* Charles Schettler; *col:* Tech. *sd:* WE. 78 min. • The Fleischer brothers' second feature concerns insect life: The insects' idyll is to live in a roof garden away from "the human ones" who treat their present home as a dump. Hoppity the grasshopper tries to fix this but is opposed by the villainous C. Bagley Beetle who wants to gain control.

4234. Mr. Duck Steps Out (*Donald Duck*) 7 June 1940; *p.c.:* Walt Disney prods for RKO; *dir:* Jack King; *asst dir:* Bob Newman; *story dir:* Harry Reeves, Carl Barks; *story:* Chuck Couch, Jack Hannah, Milt Schaffer, Frank Tashlin; *anim:* Paul Allen, James Armstrong, Les Clark, Larry Clemmons, Rex Cox, Phil Duncan, Emery Hawkins, Volus Jones, Richard Lundy, Lee Morehouse, Kenneth Muse, Ray Patin, Ken Peterson, Eddie Strickland, Don Towsley, Judge Whitaker; *lay:* Bill Herwig; *voices:* Clarence Nash; *mus:* Charles Wolcott; *col:* Tech. *sd:* RCA. 7¹/2 min • Don's nephews gatecrash his date with Daisy and perform an improvized jam session.

4235. Mr. Elephant Goes to Town (*Color Rhapsody*) 4 Oct. 1940; *p.c.:* Colum; *dir:* Arthur Davis; *anim:* Sid Marcus; *lay:* Clark Watson; *back:* Phil Davis; *ed:* Edward Moore; *voices:* Mel Blanc, Danny Webb; *mus:* Joe de Nat; *prod mgr:* George Winkler; *col:* Tech. *sd:* RCA. 7¹/2 min. • A circus elephant gets drunk on "cold elixir" and is in no fit state when the ringmaster finds him.

4236. Mr. Fore by Fore (*Phantasy*) 7 July 1944; *p.c.:* Colum; *dir:* Howard Swift; *story:* John McLeish; *anim:* Jim Armstrong, Grant Simmons; *voices:* Harry E. Lang; *mus:* Eddie Kilfeather; *prod mgr:* Paul Worth; b&w. *sd:* WE. 6 min. • A golfer's game disrupts a bull's tranquility.

4237. Mr. Fuller Pep: An Old Bird Pays Him a Visit 4 Mar. 1917; *p.c.:* Powers for Univ; *dir/anim:* F.M. Follett; b&w. *sil.* 6 min. • The stork deposits Fuller Pep's bundle of joy at several houses by mistake before he finds the right one. Pep won't accept two babies and, after a while, he has to escape their constant crying.

4238. Mr. Fuller Pep: He Breaks for the Beach 31 May 1916; *p.c.:* Powers for Univ; *dir/anim:* F.M. Follett; b&w. *sil.* 5¹/2 min. • Fuller Pep foresakes the office for a day at the beach. He takes a swim and seeks refuge from a shark aboard The Good Ship Piffle which turns out to be a target ship. He is then blasted out of the boat, rescued by a fisherman and has his comments censored by the artist.

4239. Mr. Fuller Pep: He Celebrates His Wedding Anniversary 30 Dec. 1916; *p.c.:* Powers for Univ; *dir/anim:* F.M. Follett; b&w. *sil.* 6 min. • Fuller Pep celebrates in a soda fountain. After staggering home he has vivid nightmares and on awakening vows never to indulge in strawberry concoctions in the future.

4240. Mr. Fuller Pep: He Dabbles in the Pond Fuller Pep: He Dabbles in the Pond 17 May 1916; *p.c.:* Powers for Univ; *dir/anim:* F.M. Follett; b&w. *sil.* 6 min. • Pep reprimands a boy for bathing in a "No Swimming" pond, then goes in for a dip himself. While swimming, the boy steals his clothes and a woman calls the police, so he slips out to locate his clothes. Arriving in a cemetary, he finally finds covering in a dog's kennel and is shot at by an irate farmer.

4241. Mr. Fuller Pep: He Does Some Quick Moving 5 Feb. 1917; *p.c.:* Powers for Univ; *dir/anim:* F.M. Follett; b&w. *sil.* 6¹/2 min. • When Mrs. Pep discovers a Ladies' Seminary is to be built next door, they hastily move to another house. Fuller spies a pretty neighbor in distress and hauls himself over via the washing line ... which Mrs. P. cuts and takes him to live in the desert.

4242. Mr. Fuller Pep: He Goes to the Country 9 Jan. 1917; *p.c.:* Powers for Univ; *dir/anim:* F.M. Follett; b&w. *sil.* 4¹/2 min. • On doctor's advice, Pep heads for a more rural atmosphere. In trying to retrieve a lost elephant for a reward, he falls over a cliff, is caught by a balloon and deposited in a fountain.

4243. Mr. Fuller Pep: He Tries Mesmerism 3 May 1916; *p.c.:* Powers for Univ; *dir/anim:* F.M. Follett; b&w. *sil.* 4¹/2 min. • Pep tries out mesmerism first on the cat, then an elephant at the zoo. Confidently he returns home to try it on the missus but suffers a sad awakening.

4244. Mr. Fuller Pep: His Day of Rest 1 Mar. 1917; *p.c.:* Powers for Univ; *dir/anim:* F.M. Follett; b&w. *sil.* 5¹/2 min. • Pep takes Mother-in-law for an airing in her bath chair. He accidentally lets it roll downhill where he finds her next to a beehive. She gets stung and chases him home.

4245. Mr. Fuller Pep: His Wife Goes for a Rest 4 Feb. 1917; *p.c.:* Powers for Univ; *dir/anim:* F.M. Follett; b&w. *sil.* 5 min. • While Mrs. Pep is away, hubby is put in charge of feeding the cat but decides upon a flivver ride instead. His car breaks down and he buys a "Nut Chaser," collides with a box of dynamite and spends two weeks in hospital, returning in time to feed the cat.

4246. Mr. Gallagher and Mr. Shean (*Screen Songs*) 29 Aug. 1931; *p.c.:* The Fleischer Studio for Para; *prod:* Max Fleischer; *dir:* Dave Fleischer; *anim:* Alfred Eugster; *mus:* Art Turkisher; *l/a:* Ed Gallagher, Al Shean; b&w. *sd:* WE. 7 min. *l/a/anim.* • Gallagher and Shean are looking for food and find themselves atop a skyscraper scaffold. The cartoon segment shows two tramps who steal a couple of pies and are made to chop wood. They hop a railroad car to the next town.

4247. Mr. Ickle Meets Mr. Pickle (*Terry-Toon*) 13 Nov. 1942; *p.c.:* TT for Fox; *dir:* Connie Rasinski; *story:* John Foster; *mus:* Philip A. Scheib; b&w. *sd:* RCA. 7 min. • Ickle is a camera fiend and his "double" is a wild game hunter. Together they cause a great deal of confusion.

4248. Mr. Ima Jonah's Home Brew 4 June 1921; *p.c.:* Affiliated Distributors; *prod/dir:* J.J. McManus, R.E. Donahue; b&w. *sil.* • No story available.

4249. Mr. Magoo 25 Dec. 1997; *p.c.:* BV; *opening titles/ending anim: Creative Capers prod:* Sue Shakespeare; *sup:* Greg Tiernan; *storyboards:* Greg Tiernan, Rich Draper, Adam van Wyk; *character des:* Ernie Gilbert; *anim:* Rodney Bills, Larry Cariou, Rich Draper, Connor Flynn, Brad Forbush, Ron Friedman, Ernie Gilbert, Michael Kiely, Mark Koetsier, Victor Marchetti, Gavin Moran, John Pearson, Silvia Pompei, C.J. Sarchene, Natasha Sasic, Martin Scully, Roger Chiasson, Deke Wightman; *fx anim:* Brett Hisey, Shane Hood; *lead 3d art:* Ron Zorman; *3d anim:* Leon Gor, Duane Loose, Caragh O'Connor, Dave Otte; *Colorado Animation: prod co-ord:* Brat Ratcliffe; *studio co-ord:* Patrick Blattner; *addit anim:* Yowza Animation Studios, Inc.; *opticals/end titles:* Buena Vista Imaging; *prod mgr:* Rick Sullivan, Monica Zorman, Cindy Banks; *col:* Dolby digital. 87 min. *l/a.* • Live-action interpretation of the animated cartoon character involving Magoo unwittingly coming into possession of a stolen ruby.

4250. Mr. Money Gags (*Noveltoon*) 7 June 1957; *p.c.:* Para Cartoons; *dir:* I. Sparber; *story:* Carl Meyer; *anim:* Al Eugster, Wm. B. Pattengill; *sets:* Robert Owen; *voices:* Phil Kramer, Sid Raymond, Carl Meyer; *mus:* Winston Sharples; *ph:* Leonard McCor mack; *prod mgr:* Seymour Shultz; *col:* Tech. *sd:* RCA. 6 min. • A slick city hustler tries to take a hayseed hick for all he's got but comes off worse in the end.

4251. Mr. Moocher (*Fox & Crow*) 28 July 1944; *p.c.:* Colum; *dir:* Bob Wickersham; *story:* Sid Marcus; *anim:* Chic Otterstrom, Ben Lloyd; *lay:* Clark Watson; *ed:* Edward Moore; *voices:* Frank Graham; *mus:* Eddie Kilfeather; *prod mgr:* Paul Worth; *col:* Tech. *sd:* WE. 7 min. • "Love Your Neighbor Week" inspires Fox to be lenient with his Crow neighbor. The Crow takes advantage and drives the poor Fox to moving house.

4252. Mr. Mouse Takes a Trip (*Mickey Mouse*) 1 Nov. 1940; *p.c.:* Walt Disney prods for RKO; *dir:* Clyde Geronimi; *asst dir:* Donald A. Duckwall; *story:* Nick George, Milt Schaffer, Frank Tashlin; *anim:* Edward Love, Richard Lundy, Kenneth Muse, Charles A. Nichols, Chic F. Otterstrom, Claude Smith, Marvin Woodward; *fx:* Andy Engman; *lay:* James Carmichael; *voices:* Billy Bletcher, Elvia Allman, Walt Disney; *mus:* Leigh Harline, Oliver Wallace; *col:* Tech. *sd:* RCA. 8 min. • Conductor Pete attempts to throw Mickey off his train for concealing Pluto when a strict "No Dogs Allowed" policy is in effect.

4253. Mr. Strauss Takes a Walk *(Puppetoon)* 8 May 1942; *p.c.:* George Pal prods for Para; *prod/dir:* George Pal; *story:* Jack Miller, Cecil Beard; *voice:* Robert C. Bruce; *mus:* William Eddison; *col:* Tech. *sd:* WE. 8½ min. • Mr. Strauss assembles an orchestra from the forest animals and leads them in *Tales of the Vienna Woods.*

4254. Mr. Winlucky *(James Hound)* Feb. 1967; *p.c.:* TT for Fox; *dir/anim:* Ralph Bakshi; *col:* DeLuxe. *sd:* RCA. 6 min. • James Hound dabbles with gambling. • See: *James Hound*

4255. The Misunderstood Giant *(Terry-Toon)* Feb. 1960; *p.c.:* TT for Fox; *ex prod:* Bill Weiss; *dir:* Connie Rasinski; *story sup:* Tom Morrison; *story:* Larz Bourne; *anim:* Ed Donnelly, Mannie Davis; *lay:* John Zago; *back:* Bill Focht; *voices:* John Myhers; *mus:* Phil Scheib; *prod mgr:* Frank Schudde; *col:* DeLuxe. *sd.* RCA. 6 min. CS. • The Giant appears in court to present his side of the "Jack and the Beanstalk" story.

4256. The Mite Makes Right *(Noveltoon)* 15 Oct. 1948; *p.c.:* Famous for Para; *dir:* Bill Tytla; *story:* I. Klein; *anim:* George Germanetti, Steve Muffatti; *sets:* Anton Loeb; *voices:* Cecil Roy, Jackson Beck, Jack Mercer; *mus:* Winston Sharples; *prod mgr:* Sam Buchwald; *col:* Tech. *sd:* RCA. 8 min. • Tom Thumb runs away from home to join a circus with a troupe of wild mice.

4257. Mixed Master *(Looney Tunes)* 14 Apr. 1956; *p.c.:* WB; *dir:* Robert McKimson; *story:* Tedd Pierce; *anim:* Russ Dyson, Keith Darling, Ted Bonnicksen, George Grandpré; *lay:* Robert Gribbroek; *back:* Richard H. Thomas; *ed:* Treg Brown; *voices:* Mel Blanc, June Foray; *mus:* Milt Franklyn; *prod mgr:* John W. Burton; *prod:* Edward Selzer; *col:* Tech. *sd:* Vit. 7 min. • A pedigree Pekinese doesn't take to kindly to the arrival in his home of Robert, a nondescript mutt, who goes about trying to prove that he is a pedigree dog.

4258. Moans and Groans *(Paul Terry-Toon)* 28 June 1935; *p.c.:* Moser & Terry for Educational/Fox; *dir:* Frank Moser, Paul Terry; *mus:* Philip A. Scheib; *b&w. sd:* WE. 6 min. • No story available.

4259. Mobilizing the Frankfurters *(Universal Current Events)* 1918; *p.c.:* United States Food Administration; *b&w. sil.* • Pied Piper, Uncle Sam, summons a food supply from houses and shops. Coal, sugar lumps, hams and even frankfurters join the merry throng.

4260. Moby Duck *(Looney Tunes)* 27 Mar 1965; *p.c.:* DFE for WB; *dir:* Robert McKimson; *anim:* Don Williams, Manny Perez, Warren Batchelder, Bob Matz, La Verne Harding, Norm McCabe; *lay:* Dick Ung; *back:* Tom O'Loughlin; *ed:* Lee Gunther, Treg Brown; *voices:* Mel Blanc; *mus:* Bill Lava; *col:* Tech. *sd:* Vit. 6 min. • Daffy and Speedy are marooned on a desert island when a box of canned food floats ashore. Daffy claims it for himself ... until he discovers Speedy has the only can opener.

4261. The Model Dairy *(Aesop's Film Fable)* 11 Apr. 1922; *p.c.:* Fables Pictures Inc for Pathé; *dir:* Paul Terry; *b&w. sil.* 5½ min. • Farmer Al Falfa believes contented cows yield more milk so he provides them with golf and billiards.

4262. Modelling *(Out of the Inkwell)* 1 Feb. 1923; *p.c.:* Inkwell Studio for Rodner; *dir:* Dave Fleischer; *anim/l/a:* Max Fleischer, Roland Crandall; *b&w. sil.* 9 min. *l/a/anim.* • Ko-Ko ridicules an ugly man being sculpted by Roland Crandall. Max ends his antics by pinning him to the board with a lump of clay but he escapes and fools around inside the bust.

4263. Modern Inventions *(Mickey Mouse)* 29 May 1937; *p.c.:* Walt Disney prods for RKO; *dir:* Jack King; *story:* Carl Barks; *anim:* Paul Allen, Johnny Cannon, Jack Hannah, John McManus, Milt Schaffer, Roy Williams, Berny Wolf; *voices:* Billy Bletcher, Don Brodie, Sarah Selby, Clarence Nash; *mus:* Oliver Wallace; *col:* Tech. *sd:* RCA. 7 min. • Donald visits a museum of modern inventions and encounters many problems with a baby carriage, a barber's chair and an over-helpful robot. Although released in the *Mickey Mouse* series, this features Donald Duck alone.

4264. A Modern Red Riding Hood *(Paul Terry-Toon)* 3 May 1935; *p.c.:* Moser & Terry for Educational/Fox; *dir:* Frank Moser, Paul Terry; *mus:* Philip A. Scheib; *b&w. sd:* WE. 5½ min. • No story available.

4265. Molecular Mixup *(Astronut)* Dec. 1964; *p.c.:* TT for Fox; *ex prod:* Bill Weiss; *dir/anim:* Dave Tendlar; *story sup:* Tom Morrison; *story:*

Larz Bourne; *sets:* Robert Owen, John Zago; *ed:* Jack MacConnell; *voices:* Dayton Allen; *mus:* Jim Timmens; *ph:* Ted Moskowitz; *sd:* Elliot Grey; *col:* DeLuxe. *sd:* RCA. 5½ min. • Astro dons the guise of a dog when a small boy takes him home as a pet.

4266. Molly Moo-Cow and Rip Van Winkle *(Rainbow Parade)* 27 Dec. 1935; *p.c.:* Van Beuren for RKO; *dir:* Burt Gillett, Tom Palmer; *sets:* Art Bartsch, Eddi Bowlds; *mus:* Winston Sharples; *col:* Tech. *sd:* RCA. 7 min. • Molly watches some dwarfs play ten-pin bowls and toast the slumbering Rip van Winkle. When they leave, she gets drunk on their ale and proceeds to play bowls on her own.

4267. Molly Moo-Cow and Robinson Crusoe *(Rainbow Parade)* 28 Feb. 1936; *p.c.:* Van Beuren for RKO; *dir:* Burt Gillett, Tom Palmer; *sets:* Art Bartsch, Eddi Bowlds; *mus:* Winston Sharples; *col:* Tech. *sd:* RCA. 7 min. • Molly bothers Crusoe on his desert isle but she later saves him from cannibals.

4268. Molly Moo-Cow and the Butterflies *(Burt Gillett's Rainbow Parade)* 15 Nov. 1934; *p.c.:* Van Beuren for RKO; *dir:* Burt Gillett, Tom Palmer; *sets:* Art Bartsch, Eddi Bowlds; *mus:* Winston Sharples; *col:* Ciné. *sd:* RCA. 7 min. • Molly defends her butterfly friends from a collector by disguising herself as a huge butterfly.

4269. Molly Moo-Cow and the Indians *(Burt Gillett's Rainbow Parade)* 15 Nov. 1935; *p.c.:* Van Beuren for RKO; *dir:* Burt Gillett, Tom Palmer; *sets:* Art Bartsch, Eddi Bowlds; *mus:* Winston Sharples; *col:* Tech. *sd:* RCA. 7½ min. • Molly leaves the wagon train when she is captured by Indians, escapes, saves a papoose from drowning and is made a hero.

4270. Mommy Loves Puppy *(Animated Antics)* 29 Nov. 1940; *p.c.:* The Fleischer Studio for Para; *prod:* Max Fleischer; *dir:* Dave Fleischer; *story:* William Turner; *anim:* Willard Bowsky, Jim Davis; *mus:* Sammy Timberg; *col:* Tech. *sd:* WE. 8 min. • A small St. Bernard becomes involved with a sleepy walrus he thinks is drowned and tries to resuscitate with brandy.

4271. M.O.N.E.Y. Spells Love *(The Dogfather)* 23 Apr. 1975; *p.c.:* Mirisch/DFE for UA; *dir:* Art Leonardi; *story:* Dave DeTiege; *anim:* Nelson Shin, Bob Bransford, Warren Batchelder; *ed:* Rick Steward; *lay:* Dick Ung; *back:* Richard H. Thomas; *voices:* Bob Holt, Joan Gerber; *mus:* Dean Elliott; *col:* DeLuxe. *sd:* RCA. 6 min. • The Dogfather competes with another mobster to marry a wealthy widow.

4272. Monkey Business *(Aesop's Film Fable)* 29 Oct.24; *p.c.:* Fables Pictures Inc for Pathé; *dir:* Paul Terry; *b&w. sil.* 5 min. • The mice, elephants, monkeys, cows and other animals contort themselves to make up the equipment of a first class gymnasium.

4273. Monkey Business *(Pen & Ink Vaudeville)* 28 May 1928; *p.c.:* Hurd prods for Educational; *prod/dir:* Earl Hurd; *b&w. sil.* 5 min. • Props helps the zookeeper pull a gorilla's aching tooth. The ape turns the tables and chases Props until he drinks a bottle of monkey gland extract, turning into an ape, himself.

4274. Monkey Doodles *(Noveltoon)* Apr. 1960; *p.c.:* Para Cartoons; *dir:* Seymour Kneitel; *story:* Irving Dressler; *anim:* Nick Tafuri; *sets:* Robert Owen; *voices:* Jack Mercer; *mus:* Winston Sharples; *ph:* Leonard McCormick; *prod mgr:* Abe Goodman; *col:* Tech. *sd:* RCA. 6 min. • A baby monkey is delivered to George Newleywed and his wife by mistake. He takes the chimp for a walk, causing untold problems.

4275. Monkey Love *(Aesop's Film Fable)* 24 Sept. 1928; *p.c.:* Fables Pictures Inc for Pathé; *dir:* Paul Terry; *b&w. sil.* 10 min. • No story available.

4276. Monkey Love *(Color Rhapsody)* 12 Mar. 1935; *p.c.:* Charls Mintz prods for Colum; *story:* Art Davis; *anim:* Sid Marcus; *mus:* Joe de Nat; *prod mgr:* James Bronis; *col:* Tech-2. *sd:* RCA. 7 min. • A boy monkey takes his girl home but runs into a troublesome gorilla on the way. The girl soon dispatches him in no uncertain fashion.

4277. Monkey Love *(Sullivan Cartoon Comedy)* 9 July 1917; *p.c.:* Powers for Univ; *prod/dir:* Pat Sullivan; *anim:* Ernest Smythe; *b&w. sil.* 5½ min. • A flirty girl monkey falls for a big ape. When they marry, all her previous lovers are sad but have reason to rejoice later when they see them both out with a huge family.

4278. Monkey Meat *(Paul Terry-Toon)* 10 Aug. 1930; *p.c.:* A-C for

Educational/Fox; *dir:* Frank Moser, Paul Terry; *anim:* Arthur Babbitt, Ralph Tiller; *mus:* Philip A. Scheib; b&w. *sd:* WE. 5 min. • Monkeys stage a musical extravaganza, eventually drifting away on bubbles.

4279. Monkey Melodies *(Silly Symphony)* 26 Sept. 1930; *p.c.:* Walter E. Disney for Colum; *dir:* Burton F. Gillett; *anim:* Johnny Cannon, Les Clark, Norman Ferguson, David D. Hand, Wilfred Jackson, Jack King, Richard Lundy, Tom Palmer, Ben Sharpsteen; *mus:* Bert Lewis; b&w. *sd:* PCP. 6 min. • A romance blossoms between a boy and girl monkey.

4280. Monkey Wretches *(Oswald)* 11 Nov 1935; *p.c.:* Univ; *prod:* Walter Lantz; *dir:* Manuel Moreno; *story:* Walter Lantz, Victor McLeod; *anim:* Manuel Moreno, Lester Kline, Fred Kopietz, Bill Mason; *voice:* Shirley Reed; *mus:* James Dietrich; b&w. *sd:* WE. 6 min. • An organ grinder deposits three monkeys in Oswald's Pawn Shop who run amok and Ozzie has to pay the organ grinder to retrieve them.

4281. Monkeydoodle *(Simon the Monk)* 1930; *prod:* Jacques Kopfstein; *dir/anim:* Les Elton; b&w. *sd.* 6 min. • Simon and his hound friend are chased by a tiger.

4282. The Monkey's Paw 13 Jan. 1932; *p.c.:* RKO; *anim:* Orville Goldner; b&w. *sd:* RCA. 56 min./*l/a.* • Live-action horror from W.W. Jacob's story about a mother who wishes for the return of her dead son. A severed monkey's paw comes alive via stop-motion animation.

4283. Monster Master *(James Hound)* July 1966; *p.c.:* TT for Fox; *dir/anim:* Ralph Bakshi; *col:* DeLuxe. *sd:* RCA. 6 min. • Secret Agent Hound battles with a mad scientist and his evil monsters. • See: *James Hound*

4284. Monster of Ceremonies *(Woody Woodpecker)* May 1966; *p.c.:* Walter Lantz prods for Univ; *dir:* Paul J. Smith; *story:* Cal Howard; *anim:* Les Kline, Al Coe; *sets:* Ray Huffine; *voices:* Dal McKennon, Grace Stafford; *mus:* Clarence Wheeler; *prod mgr:* William E. Garity; *col:* Tech. *sd:* RCA. 5 min. • A mad scientist experiments on Woody, turning him into a Frankensteinesque monster who turns on the Professor.

4285. Monty the Missionary *(Mile-a-Minute Monty)* 14 Sept. 1915; *p.c.:* Lubin Mfg Co; *anim:* Leon A. Searl; b&w. *sil. s/r.* • No story available.

4286. Moochin' Pooch *(Beary Family)* 1971; *p.c.:* Walter Lantz prods for Univ; *dir:* Paul J. Smith; *story:* Cal Howard; *anim:* Virgil Ross, Al Coe, Tom Byrne, Joe Voght; *sets:* Nino Carbe; *voices:* Paul Frees, Grace Stafford; *mus:* Walter Greene; *prod mgr:* William E. Garity; *col:* Tech. *sd:* RCA. 5½ min. • The boss gets Charlie to look after his pet Great Dane which destroys Charlie's house in the process.

4287. Moonbird 1959; *p.c.:* Storyboard prods for Colum; *dir/des:* John Hubley; *anim:* Robert Cannon, Ed Smith; *voices:* Mark Hubley, Hampy Hubley; *prod:* Edward Harrison, John Hubley, Faith Elliott; *col. sd.* 10 min. *Academy Award.* • Two small boys hunt an imaginary, magical bird at midnight.

4288. Moonlight for Two *(Merrie Melodies)* 2 July 1932; *p.c.:* Hugh Harman, Rudolf Ising prods for WB; *anim:* Isadore Freleng, Larry Martin, Robert Clampett; *voices:* Mary Moder; *mus:* Frank Marsales; *prod:* Leon Schlesinger; b&w. *sd:* Vit. 6½ min. • A couple caper over a wintery landscape, ending at a barn dance. The girl's father arrives ready for a shotgun wedding but a red hot stove burns him up.

4289. The Moose Hunt *(Mickey Mouse)* 31 Apr. 1931; *p.c.:* Walt Disney prods for Colum; *dir:* Burton F. Gillett; *anim:* Les Clark, Norman Ferguson, David D. Hand, Jack King, Richard Lundy, Tom Palmer, Ben Sharpsteen; *mus:* Bert Lewis; b&w. *sd:* PCP. 7 min. • Mickey takes Pluto on a moose hunt. The moose chases them over a cliff where Mickey makes a getaway by using Pluto as an airplane. First appearance of Mickey's faithful hound, Pluto.

4290. Moose Hunters *(Mickey Mouse)* 20 Feb. 1937; *p.c.:* Walt Disney prods for UA; *dir:* Ben Sharpsteen; *story:* Jack Kinney; *anim:* Arthur Babbitt, Gilles de Tremaudan, Norman Ferguson, Clyde Geronimi, Jack Hannah, John Lounsbery, Wolfgang Reitherman; *voices:* Clarence Nash, Pinto Colvig, Walt Disney; *mus:* Paul J. Smith; *col:* Tech. *sd:* RCA. 7 min. • Mickey disguises as a "tree"while Donald and Goofy dress as a vamp moose to lure a moose into the open.

4291. Moose on the Loose *(Heckle & Jeckle)* Nov. 1952; *p.c.:* TT for Fox; *dir:* Mannie Davis; *story/voices:* Tom Morrison; *mus:* Philip A. Scheib;

ph: Douglas Moye; *col:* Tech. *sd:* RCA. 6 min. • The magpies go moose hunting and disguise themselves as a female to attract a male moose.

4292. Mopping Up *(Gandy Goose)* 26 June 1943; *p.c.:* TT for Fox; *dir:* Eddie Donnelly; *story:* John Foster; *voices:* Arthur Kay, Thomas Morrison; *mus:* Philip A. Scheib; *col:* Tech. *sd:* RCA. 6 min. • Pvt. Gandy and Sgt. Cat phone Hitler to warn him they're on their way. They bomb Berlin, chase Hitler and Mussolini to Egypt and wipe out a Japanese plane by using a termite bomb.

4293. More Kittens *(Silly Symphony)* 19 Dec. 1936; *p.c.:* Walt Disney prods for UA; *dir:* Wilfred Jackson; *asst dir:* Jack Cutting; *story dir:* Bill Cottrell, Joe Grant, Bob Kuwahara; *anim:* Gilles de Tremaudan, Ward Kimball, Leonard Sebring, Robert Stokes, Franklin Thomas, Bob Wickersham; *sets:* Bob Kuwahara; *voices:* Lillian Randolph, Esther Campbell; *mus:* Frank E. Churchill; *col:* Tech. *sd:* RCA. 7 min. • The kittens get into various scrapes, seeking refuge with a St. Bernard who shelters them.

4294. More Mice Than Brains *(Aesop's Film Fable)* 21 Nov. 1925; *p.c.:* Fables Pictures Inc for Pathé; *dir:* Paul Terry; b&w. *sil.* 5 min. • The activities of the mice and the difficulties of Farmer Al Falfa in getting rid of them.

4295. The Morning After *(Aesop's Film Fable)* 16 Nov. 1923; *p.c.:* Fables Pictures Inc for Pathé; *dir:* Paul Terry; b&w. *sil.* 5 min. • A canine motor cop has other interests besides catching speeders.

4296. Morning, Noon and Night *(Betty Boop)* 6 Oct. 1933; *p.c.:* The Fleischer Studio for Para; *prod:* Max Fleischer; *dir:* Dave Fleischer; *anim:* Thomas Johnson, David Tendlar; *voice:* Mae Questel; *mus:* (Dave)Rubinoff & His Orchestra; b&w. *sd:* WE. 7 min. • Betty's serene life amongst the birds is disturbed by an invasion of The Tom Kats' Social Club. The birds join forces and oust them.

4297. Morning, Noon and Nightclub *(Popeye)* 18 June 1937; *p.c.:* The Fleischer Studio for Para; *prod:* Max Fleischer; *dir:* Dave Fleischer; *anim:* Willard Bowsky, George Germanetti; *voices:* Jack Mercer, Mae Questel, Gus Wickie, Lou Fleischer; *mus:* Sammy Timberg; b&w. *sd:* WE. 7 min. • Dancing stars, Popeye and Olivita, reject Bluto's amorous advances and so he wreaks his revenge on their act.

4298. Morris the Midget Moose 24 Nov. 1950; *p.c.:* Walt Disney prods for RKO; *dir:* Jack Hannah; *story:* Nick George, Bill Berg; *anim:* Bob Carlson, Bill Justice, George Kreisl, Volus Jones; *fx:* Jack Boyd; *lay:* Yale Gracey; *back:* Brice Mack; *voices:* Francis "Dink" Trout, James MacDonald; *mus:* Paul J. Smith; *col:* Tech. *sd:* RCA. 8 min. • Frank Owen's story about a tiny moose with large antlers who teams with a full-size moose with small antlers to defeat "Thunderclap," the scourge of the forest.

4299. Mortal Kombat 18 Aug. 1995; *p.c.:* Threshold Entertainment/First Independent for New Line Cinema; *addit anim visual fx:* Available Light Ltd.: *anim: des/sup:* John T. van Vliet; *fx prod:* Katherine Kean; *digital sup:* Laurel Klick; *anim:* Bill Arance, Conann Fitzpatrick, January Nordman, Cynthia Hyland, Michael Gagne, Tanya Wilson, P. Andrew Gauvreau; *optical printing:* Beverly Bernacki, Mona B. Howell; *fx ed:* Dana Desselle; *addit digital anim:* R&B Films; *col. sd:* Dolby stereo. 101 min. *l/a.* • Live-action science fiction: In China, martial arts fighters are summoned to a contest to decide whether an alternative universe and its inhabitants should be allowed to cross into our world.

4300. Mortal Kombat 2: Annihilation 21 Nov. 1997; *p.c.:* New Line Cinema; *Motard & Dragon/Hydra seq: character realization:* The Production Plant: *lead sup anim:* Andy Tucker; *Dragon anim:* Tim "Professional Slave" Horne, Jason Barlow; *Dragon motion capture:* House of Moves; *Dragon motion capture choreog:* Nick Lozado; *Hydra lead anim:* Laurent Lavigne; *Hydra anim:* Steve Harwood, Todd Jahnke; *Morphs:* Shawna Olwen; *compositing:* T.J. Morgan; *2d modelling:* Jean Christopher "Toto" Debord; *col:* Fotokem/DeLuxe. *sd:* Dolby stereo/SDDS. 94½ min. *l/a.* • Live-action science fiction: The Emperor of the Outworld creates a "Hell on Earth" by allowing Outworld to merge with the human world.

4301. Mose and Funny Face Make Angel Cake *(Funny Face Comedy)* 29 May1924; *p.c.:* Red Seal; *prod:* Edwin Miles Fadman; b&w. *sil.* 5½ min. • Mose, a Negro puppet, and Funny Face attempt to make a cake which finally explodes, elevating them both off into the air.

4302. The Mosquito *(Aesop's Fable)* 29 June 1945; *p.c.:* TT for Fox; *dir:* Mannie Davis; *story:* John Foster; *mus:* Philip A. Scheib; *col:* Tech. *sd:*

RCA. 7 min. • Gandy Goose and Sourpuss take arms against an onslaught of mosquitoes but the insects win in the end.

4303. Mosquito (*Out of the Inkwell*) 6 Mar. 1922; *p.c.*: Inkwell Studio for WB; *dir:* Dave Fleischer; *anim/l/a:* Max Fleischer; b&w. *sil.* 6 min. *l/a/anim.* • While Max takes a nap, a tremendous mosquito alights on his nose. Ko-Ko engages in a duel with the insect.

4304. The Moth and the Flame (*Silly Symphony*) 1 Apr. 1938; *p.c.*: Walt Disney prods for RKO; *dir:* Burt Gillett; *anim:* Paul Hopkins, I. Klein, Edward Love, John McManus, Archie Robin, Milt Schaffer, Louis Schmidt, Roy Williams; *asst anim:* Jack Kinney; *fx:* Andrew Engman; *character des:* Ferdinand Huszti Horvath; *lay:* Dick Kelsey; *mus:* Albert Hay Malotte; *col:* Tech. *sd:* RCA. 8 min. • A boy and girl moth eat their fill in a clothes shop until the girl is lured away by a Svengali-like candle flame.

4305. The Moth and the Spider (*Paul Terry-Toon*) 8 Mar. 1935; *p.c.*: Moser & Terry for Educational/Fox; *dir:* Frank Moser, Paul Terry; *mus:* Philip A. Scheib; b&w. *sd:* WE. 5 1/2 min. • A spider dresses as a moth to attract a fly but as this doesn't work, he uses a candle to attract a girl moth. A horsefly squadron soon burn him up.

4306. Mother Dogfather (*The Dogfather*) 31 Oct. 1974; *p.c.*: Mirisch/DFE for UA; *dir:* Arthur Leonardi; *story:* Dave Detiege; *anim:* Bob Richardson, Nelson Shin, Bob Bransford, Norm McCabe; *ed:* Rick Steward; *lay:* Dick Ung; *back:* Richard H. Thomas; *voices:* Bob Holt, Larry D. Mann; *mus:* Dean Elliott; *lyrics:* John Bradford; *col:* DeLuxe. *sd:* RCA. 6 min. • A stork tries to deliver a bundle to the Dogfather. The gang tries to prevent this until they discover the bundle to be some missing spoils.

4307. Mother Goose Goes Hollywood (*Silly Symphony*) 23 Dec. 1938; *p.c.*: Walt Disney prods for RKO; *dir:* Wilfred Jackson; *asst dir:* Graham Heid; *story dir:* George Stallings; *story:* Erdman Penner, I. Klein, T. Hee; *anim:* Johnny Campbell, Ward Kimball, I. Klein, Richard Lundy, Grim Natwick, Ray Patterson, Robert Stokes; *character des:* T. Hee; *lay:* Terrell Stapp; *voices:* Elizabeth Talbot-Martin, Dave Weber, Ann Lee, Al Bernie, Thelma Boardman, Lee Murray, Clarence Nash, Cliff Nazarro, Forest "War" Perkins, Scott Whitaker, Steve White, The Four Blackbirds; *mus:* Edward H. Plumb; *col:* Tech. *sd:* RCA. 7 1/2 min. *Academy Award nomination.* • Hollywood celebrities as nursery rhyme characters. Caricatures: George Arliss, Fred Astaire, Wallace Beery, Joe E. Brown, Freddie Bartholomew, Cab Calloway, Eddie Cantor, Donald Duck, Step'n Fetchit, W.C. Fields, Greta Garbo, Katharine Hepburn, Hugh Herbert, Charles Laughton, Laurel & Hardy, The Marx Brothers, Edna May Oliver, Charlie McCarthy, Joe Penner, ZaSu Pitts, Martha Raye, Edward G. Robinson, Ned Sparks, Spencer Tracy, Fats Waller, Mae West and Ed Wynn.

4308. Mother Goose in Swingtime (*Color Rhapsody*) 19 Dec. 1939; *p.c.*: Colum; *dir:* Manny Gould; *anim:* Ben Harrison; *character des:* Ben Shenkman; *voices:* Sara Berner, Mel Blanc, Dave Weber, Kent Rogers; *mus:* Joe de Nat; *prod mgr:* James Bronis; *col:* Tech. *sd:* RCA. 7 min. • Daddy Higgins pacifies Baby Snooks with a bedtime story involving Hollywood personalities as nursery rhyme characters. Caricatures of Henry Armetta, Fred Astaire, John Barrymore, Wallace Beery, Jack Benny, Herman Bing, Joe E. Brown, James Cagney, Claudette Colbert, Joan Crawford, Bing Crosby, Marie Dressler, Nelson Eddy, W.C. Fields, Clark Gable, Cary Grant, Benny Goodman, Katharine Hepburn, Hugh Herbert, Edward Everett Horton, Laurel & Hardy, Jeanette MacDonald, The Three Marx Brothers, Edna May Oliver, William Powell, Martha Raye, George Raft, Ginger Rogers, Edward G. Robinson, Mickey Rooney, Ned Sparks, Leopold Stokowski, Spencer Tracy, Shirley Temple.

4309. Mother Goose Land (*Betty Boop*) 23 June 1933; *p.c.*: The Fleischer Studio for Para; *prod:* Max Fleischer; *dir:* Dave Fleischer; *anim:* Roland Crandall, Seymour Kneitel; *voice:* Bonnie Poe; *mus:* Sammy Timberg; b&w. *sd:* WE. 6 min. • Betty sleeps while reading "Mother Goose" and dreams the characters take her to a land where nursery rhyme characters live.

4310. Mother Goose Land (*Out of the Inkwell*) 21 March 1925; *p.c.*: Inkwell Studio for Red Seal; *prod/l/a:* Max Fleischer; *dir:* Dave Fleischer; b&w. *sil.* 10 min. *l/a/anim.* • The Inkwell clown meets various Mother Goose characters courtesy of Max's nursery rhyme transfers.

4311. Mother Goose Melodies (*Silly Symphony*) 11 Apr. 1931; *p.c.*: Walt Disney prods for Colum; *dir:* Burton F. Gillett; *anim:* Johnny Cannon, Les Clark, Norman Ferguson, David D. Hand, Jack King, Richard Lundy, Tom Palmer, Ben Sharpsteen, Rudy Zamora; *mus:* Bert Lewis; b&w. *sd:* PCP. 8 min. • Mother Goose storybook characters come to life and dance for Old King Cole.

4312. Mother Goose Nightmare (*Terry-Toon*) 4 May 1945; *p.c.*: TT for Fox; *dir:* Connie Rasinski; *story:* John Foster; *voices:* Arthur Kay, Thomas Morrison; *mus:* Philip A. Scheib; *ph:* Douglas Moye; *col:* Tech. *sd:* RCA. 6 min. • Gandy has a nightmare involving Sourpuss and the nursery rhyme characters, culminating in an encounter with a giant.

4313. Mother Goose on the Loose (*Cartune*) 13 Apr. 1942; *p.c.*: Walter Lantz prods for Univ; *dir:* Walter Lantz; story thunk up by "Buggsy" (Ben) Hardaway, "Baby-Face" (Lowell) Elliot; pictures drawed by "Mugsy" (Frank) Tipper, "Stinkey" (Les) Kline; *sets:* Fred Brunish; *voices:* Kent Rogers, Mel Blanc, Sara Berner; music patter written by "Boogie Woogie" (Darrell) Calker; *prod mgr:* George Hall; *col:* Tech. *sd:* WE. 7 min. • Spot-gags on nursery rhymes.

4314. Mother Goose's Birthday Party (*Mighty Mouse*) Dec. 1950; *p.c.*: TT for Fox; *dir:* Connie Rasinski; *story:* Tom Morrison; *anim:* Jim Tyer; *mus:* Philip A. Scheib; *col:* Tech. *sd:* RCA. 6 min. • The wolf is not invited to the birthday gathering and wreaks his revenge on the party.

4315. Mother Hen's Holiday (*Color Rhapsody*) 7 May 1937; *p.c.*: Charles Mintz prods for Colum; *story:* Sid Marcus; *anim:* Art Davis; *lay:* Clark Watson; *back:* Phil Davis; *ed:* George Winkler; *voices:* Mary Lennon, A. Purvis Pullen, Dave Weber, The Rhythmettes; *mus:* Joe de Nat; *prod mgr:* James Bronis; *col:* Tech. *sd:* RCA. 6 1/2 min. • Mother hen's brood of chicks play her up so much, then take pity and send her on a holiday.

4316. Mother Hubba Hubba Hubbard (*Color Rhapsody*) 29 May 1947; *p.c.*: Colum; *prods:* Raymond Katz, Henry Binder; *dir:* Bob Wickersham; *story:* Cal Howard; *anim:* Roy Jenkins, Chic Otterstrom; *lay:* Clark Watson; *back:* Al Boggs; *ed:* Richard S. Jensen; *voices:* Dick Nelson; *mus:* Eddie Kilfeather; *ph:* Frank Fisher; *col:* Tech. *sd:* WE. 5 1/2 min. • A dog accuses a mouse of stealing his bone but discovers he has been sleepwalking.

4317. Mother Pin a Rose on Me (*Screen Song*) 6 July 1929; *p.c.*: The Fleischer Studio for Para; *prod:* Max Fleischer; *dir:* Dave Fleischer; b&w. *sd:* WE. 6 min. • The verse of the old song is presented, then a parody with reference to a modern flapper's hose.

4318. Mother Pluto (*Silly Symphony*) 27 Nov. 1936; *p.c.* Walt Disney prods for UA; *dir:* David D. Hand; *story:* Earl Hurd; *anim:* Johnny Cannon, James Culhane, Norman Ferguson, Clyde Geronimi, I. Klein, William O. Roberts; *voices:* Lee Millar, Florence Gill; *mus:* Leigh Harline; *col:* Tech. *sd:* RCA. 8 1/2 min. • Pluto acts as mother hen to a group of chicks that hatch out in his dog house.

4319. Mother Was a Rooster (*Merrie Melodies*) Oct. 1962; *p.c.*: WB; *dir:* Robert McKimson; *story:* Dave DeTiege; *anim:* George Grandpré, Keith Darling, Ted Bonnicksen, Warren Batchelder; *sets:* Robert Gribbroek; *ed:* Treg Brown; *voices:* Mel Blanc; *mus:* Milt Franklyn; *prod mgr:* William Orcutt; *prod:* David H. DePatie; *col:* Tech. *sd:* Vit. 6 min. • The dog slips an ostrich egg under Foggy while he sleeps. The rooster wakes to think he's hatched a son and proceeds to educate the baby ostrich.

4320. Mother's Little Helper (*Beary Family*) 12 June 1962; *p.c.*: Walter Lantz prods for Univ; *dir:* Jack Hannah; *story:* Al Bertino, Dick Kinney; *anim:* Roy Jenkins, Al Coe, Don Lusk; *sets:* Ray Huffine, Art Landy; *voices:* Paul Frees, Grace Stafford; *mus:* Darrell Calker; *prod mgr:* William E. Garity; *col:* Tech. *sd:* RCA. 6 min. • Goose Beary turns "Stool Pigeon" when Charlie does the housework.

4321. Motion-Painting 1946/1947; *dir/art/ph:* Oskar Fischinger; *mus:* "The Brandenburg Concerto #3" by Johann Sebastian Bach; *col. sd.* 10 min. • Oil color painted on glass (18 × 24").

4322. Motor Mania (*Goofy*) 30 June 1950; *p.c.*: Walt Disney prods for RKO; *dir:* Jack Kinney; *story:* Dick Kinney, Milt Schaffer; *anim:* John Sibley, Charles Nichols, Ed Aardal; *fx:* Jack Boyd; *lay:* Al Zinnen; *back:* Claude Coats; *voices:* John Ployardt, Bob Jackman, James MacDonald; *mus:* Paul J. Smith; *col:* Tech. *sd:* RCA. 7 min. • Brilliant satire on motorists showing the average man (Geef) being transformed into a raging monster once behind the wheel of a car.

4323. Motor Mat and His Fliv (*Sullivan Cartoon Comedy*) 8 Nov. 1916; *p.c.*: Powers for Univ; *prod/dir:* Pat Sullivan; *anim:* Otz Messmer; b&w. *sil.* 6 min. • No story available. Messmer's first solo animation.

4324. Motoy Comedies *p.c.:* Peter Pan Film Corp; *anim:* Howard Moss; b&w. *sil.* 10 min. • *1917:* Cracked Ice. Midnight Frolic. Jimmy Wins the Pennant. Out in the Rain. In the Jungle Land. A Kitchen Romance. Mary and Gretel. Dinkling of the Circus. A Trip to the Moon. Golden Locks and the Three Bears. Dolly Doings. School Days. Little Red Riding Hood. Puss in Boots. Jimmie the Soldier Boy. Jimmie and Jam. In Japoland • Animation using dolls.

4325. Mount Piney *(Possible Possum)* June 1968 (made in 1966); *p.c.:* TT for Fox; *dir/anim:* Artie Bartsch; *col:* DeLuxe. *sd:* RCA. 6 min. • No story available. • See: *Possible Possum*

4326. Mountain Ears *(Color Rhapsody)* 20 Oct. 1939; *p.c.:* Colum; *dir:* Manny Gould; *anim:* Ben Harrison; *lay:* Clark Watson; *back:* Phil Davis; *ed:* George Winkler; *voices:* Jack Lescoulie, Robert Winkler, Sara Berner; *mus:* Joe de Nat; *prod mgr:* James Bronis; *col:* Tech. *sd:* RCA. 7¹/₂ min. • Satire on hillbilly life.

4327. A Mountain Romance *(Terry-Toon)* 1 Apr. 1938; *p.c.:* TT for Educational/Fox; *dir:* Mannie Davis; *mus:* Philip A. Scheib; b&w. *sd:* RCA. 6 min. • A "Romeo and Juliet" romance blossoms between two feuding hillbilly families.

4328. Mouse and Garden *(Little Roquefort)* Oct. 1950; *p.c.:* TT for Fox; *dir:* Mannie Davis; *story:* Tom Morrison; *anim:* Jim Tyer; *sets:* Art Bartsch; *mus:* Philip A. Scheib; *col:* Tech. *sd:* RCA. 6 min. • Percy Puss prevents Roquefort from building himself a new house.

4329. Mouse and Garden *(Looney Tunes)* 16 July 1960; *p.c.:* WB; *dir:* Friz Freleng; *anim:* Gerry Chiniquy, Virgil Ross, Art Davis; *lay:* Hawley Pratt; *back:* Tom O'Loughlin; *ed:* Treg Brown; *voices:* Mel Blanc, Daws Butler; *mus:* Milt Franklyn; *prod mgr:* William Orcutt; *prod:* David H. DePatie; *col:* Tech. *sd:* Vit. 7 min. *Academy Award nomination.* • Sylvester and Sam, the alley cat, have difficulty in trusting one another when it comes to sharing a mouse that comes their way.

4330. The Mouse and the Lion *(Foolish Fable)* 11 May 1953; *p.c.:* Walter Lantz prods for Univ; *dir:* Paul J. Smith; *anim:* Gil Turner, Cecil Surry, Robert Bentley; *sets:* Raymond Jacobs; *mus:* Clarence Wheeler; *prod mgr:* William E. Garity; *col:* Tech. *sd:* RCA. 6 min. • Circus talent scout, Buck Mouse, traps a lion for the high-wire act in his circus.

4331. Mouse Blanche *(Comic King)* Nov. 1962; *p.c.:* Rembrandt for Para; *ex prod:* Al Brodax; *prod:* William L. Snyder; *sup:* Gene Deitch; *anim:* Zdeněk Smetana, Milan Klikar, Antonín Bureš, Věra Marešová, Mirko Kačena, Bohumil Šejda, Věra Kudrnová, Jindřich Barta, Zdenka Skřípková, Olga Šišková; *lay:* Zdeněk Smetana; *back:* Bohumil Šiška; *voices:* Paul Frees, Penny Phillips; *mus:* Štěpán Koníček; *prod mgr:* Zdenka Deitchová; *col. sd:* RCA. 5¹/₂ min. • When Ignatz attempts to get instant friends on a credit card, he learns the limitations of the system.

4332. Mouse Cleaning *(Tom & Jerry)*; rel 11 Dec. 1948; *p.c.:* MGM; *dir:* William Hanna, Joseph Barbera; *anim:* Irven Spence, Kenneth Muse, Ed Barge, Ray Patterson; *ed:* Fred MacAlpin; *voice:* Lillian Randolph; *mus:* Scott Bradley; *ph:* Jack Stevens; *prod:* Fred Quimby; *col:* Tech. *sd:* WE. 7 min. • Tom is ordered to keep the house clean before Mammy Two-Shoes returns from shopping but is constantly heckled by Jerry.

4333. The Mouse Comes to Dinner *(Tom & Jerry)* 5 May 1945; *p.c.:* MGM; *dir:* William Hanna, Joseph Barbera; *anim:* Irven Spence, Kenneth Muse, Pete Burness, Ray Patterson; *lay:* Harvey Eisenberg; *ed:* Fred MacAlpin; *voices:* Anita Brown, Sara Berner, Harry E. Lang; *mus:* Scott Bradley; *prod:* Fred Quimby; *col:* Tech. *sd:* WE. 7 min. • When Tom invites his girl over for dinner, Jerry rebels against being used as a servant.

4334. A Mouse Divided *(Merrie Melodies)* 31 Jan. 1953; *p.c.:* WB; *dir:* I. Freleng; *story:* Warren Foster; *anim:* Arthur Davis, Manuel Perez, Ken Champin, Virgil Ross; *lay:* Hawley Pratt; *back:* Irv Wyner; *ed:* Treg Brown; *voices:* Mel Blanc, Bea Benaderet; *mus:* Carl Stalling; *prod mgr:* John W. Burton; *prod:* Edward Selzer; *col:* Tech. *sd:* Vit. 6¹/₂ min. • An inebriated stork delivers a baby mouse to Mr. and Mrs. Sylvester cat. Sylvester eventually overcomes his compulsion to devour the rodent but the neighborhood cats get wind of it and try to storm his house.

4335. The Mouse Exterminator *(Phantasy)* 26 Jan. 1940; *p.c.:* Colum; *story:* Allen Rose; *anim:* Harry Love; *lay:* Clark Watson; *back:* Phil Davis; *ed:* George Winkler; *voice:* Danny Webb; *mus:* Joe de Nat; *prod mgr:* James Bronis; b&w. *sd:* RCA. 6¹/₂ min. • Allie Kat is a mouse exterminator who gets outwitted by a clever mouse.

4336. Mouse for Sale *(Tom & Jerry)* 21 May 1955 (made in 1953); *p.c.:* MGM; *dir:* William Hanna, Joseph Barbera; *anim:* Kenneth Muse, Ed Barge, Irven Spence, Ray Patterson; *lay:* Dick Bickenbach; *back:* Robert Gentle; *ed:* Jim Faris; *voice:* June Foray; *mus:* Scott Bradley; *ph:* Jack Stevens; *prod:* Fred Quimby; *col:* Tech. *sd:* WE. 7 min. • Tom sells Jerry as a dancing white mouse but is shocked when his mistress buys him back as a pet.

4337. The Mouse from H.U.N.G.E.R. *(Tom & Jerry)* 1967; *p.c.:* MGM; *prod:* Chuck Jones; *dir:* Abe Levitow; *story:* Bob Ogle; *anim:* Phil Roman, Ben Washam, Ken Harris, Don Towsley, Tom Ray, Dick Thompson; *des:* Maurice Noble; *graphics:* Don Foster; *lay:* Don Morgan; *back:* Robert Inman; *mus:* Dean Elliott; *prod sup:* Les Goldman, Earl Jonas; *col:* Metro. *sd:* WE. 6 min. • Spoof on TV spy show, *The Man from U.N.C.L.E.* Agent Jerry sets out to deprive Tom Thrush of his cheese supply.

4338. Mouse in Manhattan *(Tom & Jerry)* 7 July 1945; *p.c.:* MGM; *dir:* William Hanna, Joseph Barbera; *anim:* Kenneth Muse, Ray Patterson, Irven Spence, Ed Barge; *lay:* Harvey Eisenberg; *back:* Robert Gentle; *ed:* Fred MacAlpin; *mus:* Scott Bradley; *prod:* Fred Quimby; *col:* Tech. *sd:* WE. 8 min. • Jerry leaves the country life for the big city. He soon decides that city life is not for him and returns.

4339. Mouse in the House *(Beary Family)* Apr. 1967; *p.c.:* Walter Lantz prods for Univ; *dir:* Paul J. Smith; *story:* Cal Howard; *anim:* Les Kilne, Al Coe; *sets:* Ray Huffine; *voices:* Paul Frees, Grace Stafford; *mus:* Walter Greene; *prod mgr:* William E. Garity; *col:* Tech. *sd:* RCA. 6 min. • Charlie saves the cost of hiring an exterminator by trying to catch the mouse himself.

4340. A Mouse in the House *(Tom & Jerry)* 30 Aug. 1947; *p.c.:* MGM; *dir:* William Hanna, Joseph Barbera; *anim:* Kenneth Muse, Ed Barge, Richard Bickenbach, Don Patterson; *back:* Robert Gentle; *ed:* Fred MacAlpin; *voice:* Lillian Randolph; *mus:* Scott Bradley; *prod:* Fred Quimby; *col:* Tech. *sd:* WE. 8 min. • The two cats are given an ultimatum ... the one who catches a mouse can stay.

4341. Mouse into Space *(Tom & Jerry)* Mar. 1962; *p.c.:* Rembrandt for MGM; *prod:* William L. Snyder; *dir:* Gene Deitch; *story:* Tod Dockstader; *anim:* Vaclav Bedrich; *col:* Metro. *sd:* WE. 5 min. • Tom finds himself shot into orbit when he tries to catch space mouse Jerry. • See: *Tom and Jerry (Rembrandt Studio)*

4342. Mouse Mazurka *(Merrie Melodies)* 11 June 1949; *p.c.:* WB; *dir:* I. Freleng; *story:* Tedd Pierce; *anim:* Gerry Chiniquy, Ken Champin, Virgil Ross, Manuel Perez; *lay:* Hawley Pratt; *back:* Paul Julian; *ed:* Treg Brown; *voices:* Mel Blanc; *mus:* Carl Stalling; *prod mgr:* John W. Burton; *prod:* Edward Selzer; *col:* Tech. *sd:* Vit. 7 min. • Sylvester tries to catch a dancing Russian mouse who tricks the cat into believing he's swallowed some nitroglycerine.

4343. Mouse Meets Bird *(Little Roquefort)* Mar. 1953; *p.c.:* TT for Fox; *dir:* Connie Rasinski; *story/voice:* Tom Morrison; *anim:* Jim Tyer; *sets:* Art Bartsch; *mus:* Philip A. Scheib; *col:* Tech. *sd:* RCA. 6 min. • Roquefort helps a canary in his fight against Percy Puss.

4344. Mouse Meets Lion *(Fable)* 25 Oct. 1940; *p.c.:* Colum; *story:* Allen Rose; *anim:* Harry Love, Louie Lilly; *lay:* Clark Watson; *back:* Phil Davis; *ed:* George Winkler; *voices:* Billy Bletcher, Marjorie Tarlton; *mus:* Joe de Nat; *prod mgr:* James Bronis; b&w. *sd:* RCA. 6 min. • A lion spares a mouse's life and the rodent returns the favor when he is caught in a trap.

4345. Mouse Menace *(Little Roquefort)* Sept. 1953; *p.c.:* TT for Fox; *dir:* Eddie Donnelly; *story:* Tom Morrison; *anim:* Jim Tyer; *sets:* Art Bartsch; *mus:* Philip A. Scheib; *ph:* Douglas Moye; *col:* Tech. *sd:* RCA. 6 min. • Percy Puss traps Roquefort in a toy store but changes his intentions when he discovers an anniversary gift to him from the mouse.

4346. Mouse Menace *(Looney Tunes)* 2 Nov. 1946; *p.c.:* WB; *dir:* Arthur Davis; *story:* George Hill; *anim:* Basil Davidovich, J.C. Melendez, Don Williams; *lay:* Don Smith; *back:* Philip de Guard; *ed:* Treg Brown; *voices:* Mel Blanc; *mus:* Carl Stalling; *prod mgr:* John W. Burton; *prod:* Edward Selzer; *col:* Tech. *sd:* Vit 7 min. • Porky uses a robot cat to rid his house of a pesty rodent.

4347. The Mouse-Merized Cat *(Merrie Melodies)* 9 Oct. 1946; *p.c.:* WB; *dir:* Robert McKimson; *story:* Warren Foster; *anim:* Arthur Davis,

Don Williams, Richard Bickenbach, Cal Dalton; *fx:* A.C. Gamer; *sets:* Richard H. Thomas; *ed:* Treg Brown; *voices:* Mel Blanc, Tedd Pierce; *mus:* Carl Stalling; *prod mgr:* John W. Burton; *prod:* Edward Selzer; *col:* Tech. *sd:* Vit. 7 min. • Babbit sends his fellow rat, Costello, to get some cheese but he has to be hypnotized first to get past the cat.

4348. The Mouse of Tomorrow (*Terry-Toon*) 16 Oct. 1942; *p.c.:* TT for Fox; *dir:* Eddie Donnelly; *story:* John Foster, I. Klein; *mus:* Philip A. Scheib; *col:* Tech. *sd:* RCA. 6 min. • A puny mouse escapes from the cat and flees into a supermarket where he bathes in super soap, eats super celery, super cheese and super soup, thus becoming (for the first time) ... Super Mouse!

4349. The Mouse on 57th Street (*Merrie Melodies*) Feb. 1961; *p.c.:* WB; *dir:* Chuck Jones; *story:* Michael Maltese; *anim:* Ken Harris, Richard Thompson, Bob Bransford; *lay:* Maurice Noble, Owen Fitzgerald; *back:* Philip de Guard; *ed:* Treg Brown; *voices:* Mel Blanc, Julie Bennett; *mus:* Milt Franklyn; *prod mgr:* William Orcutt; *prod:* David H. DePatie; *col:* Tech. *sd:* Vit. 6 min. • For a hangover cure, a mouse steals a diamond to soothe his throbbing head. Two inept cops are assigned to retrieve it. • Animator Jerry Eisenberg caricatured as a dumb cop.

4350. Mouse-Placed Kitten (*Merrie Melodies*) 24 Jan. 1959; *p.c.:* WB; *dir:* Robert McKimson; *story:* Tedd Pierce; *anim:* Ted Bonnicksen, Warren Batchelder, Tom Ray, George Grandpré; *lay:* Robert Gribbroek; *back:* William Butler; *ed:* Treg Brown; *voices:* Mel Blanc, June Foray; *mus:* Milt Franklyn; *prod:* John W. Burton; *col:* Tech. *sd:* Vit. 7 min. • Mr. and Mrs. mouse adopt a stray kitten. They send him to a proper home and the trouble starts when the mice arrive to see their son who has to keep them out of his owner's sight.

4351. Mouse-Taken Identity (*Merrie Melodies*) 16 Nov. 1957; *p.c.:* WB; *dir:* Robert McKimson; *story:* Tedd Pierce; *anim:* George Grandpré, Ted Bonnicksen; *lay:* Robert Gribbroek; *back:* Bill Butler; *ed:* Treg Brown; *voices:* Mel Blanc; *mus:* Carl Stalling, Milt Franklyn; *prod mgr:* John W. Burton; *prod:* Edward Selzer; *col:* Tech. *sd:* Vit. 7 min. • Sylvester takes Junior on his mouse catching job in a local museum. An escaped kangaroo hides in the cellar and junior insists it's a giant mouse that father has to catch.

4352. The Mouse That Jack Built (*Merrie Melodies*) 4 Apr. 1959; *p.c.:* WB; *dir:* Robert McKimson; *story:* Tedd Pierce; *anim:* Tom Ray, George Grandpré, Ted Bonnicksen, Warren Batchelder; *lay:* Robert Gribbroek; *back:* Robert Singer; *ed:* Treg Brown; *voices: Jack:* Jack Benny; *Mary:* Mary Livingstone; *Rochester:* Eddie Anderson; *Don:* Don Wilson; *The Maxwell:* Mel Blanc; *mus:* Milt Franklyn; *col:* Tech. *sd:* Vit. 6 min. *l/a/anim.* • Jack Benny and his associates are depicted as mice. Mary suggests Jack takes her out for a birthday supper. The cat hears this and disguises himself as a free restaurant.

4353. The Mouse That Turned (*Aesop's Film Fable*) 21 Sept. 1924; *p.c.:* Fables Pictures Inc for Pathé; *dir:* Paul Terry; b&w. sil. 5 min. • The cat catches mice and attaches them to a wagon. One harnessed mouse liberates his brothers and dumps the whole show over a cliff. Moral: "Revenge is sweet."

4354. Mouse Trapeze (*Herman & Katnip*) 5 Aug. 1955; *p.c.:* Famous for Para; *dir:* I. Sparber; *story:* Carl Meyer; *anim:* Tom Golden, Bill Hudson; *sets:* Robert Owen; *voices:* Arnold Stang, Sid Raymond, Gwen Davies; *mus:* Winston Sharples; *ph:* Leonard McCormick; *prod mgr:* Seymour Shultz; *col:* Tech. *sd:* RCA. 6 min. • Herman entertains his nephews with circus tricks but is soon interrupted by the arrival of the cat.

4355. Mouse Trapped (*Hickory, Dickory & Doc*) 8 Dec. 1959; *p.c.:* Walter Lantz prods for Univ; *dir:* Alex Lovy; *story:* Homer Brightman; *anim:* La Verne Harding, Don Patterson. Ray Abrams; *sets:* Raymond Jacobs, Art Landy; *voices:* Paul Frees, Dal McKennon, Grace Stafford; *mus:* Eugene Poddany; *prod mgr:* William E. Garity; *col:* Tech. *sd:* RCA. 6 min. • The police are told to arrest all black cats on Friday the 13th. The mice try to help Doc avoid capture.

4356. Mouse Trappers (*Andy Panda*) 7 Jan. 1941; *p.c.:* Walter Lantz prods for Univ; *dir:* Alex Lovy; *story:* Ben Hardaway; *anim:* Alex Lovy, George Dane; *sets:* Fred Brunish; *voices:* Kent Rogers, Sara Berner, Mel Blanc; *mus:* Darrell Calker; *prod mgr:* George Hall; *col:* Tech. *sd:* WE. 6 min. • Mama Panda tells Pop to catch a mouse that's been sighted on the premises.

4357. Mouse Trek (*Fractured Fable*) 31 Dec. 1967; *ex prod/dir:* Ralph Bakshi; *story:* Eli Bauer; *anim:* Doug Crane, Al Eugster, Nick Tafuri; *lay:* Cosmo Anzilotti; *sets:* John Zago, James Simon; *voices:* Bob MacFadden; *mus:* Winston Sharples; *col:* Tech. *sd:* RCA. 6 min. • An Earth cat is captured by Space cats in the hopes of him ridding their planet of a giant mouse who has been terrorizing them.

4358. Mouse Trouble (*Tom & Jerry*) 23 Dec. 1944; *p.c.:* MGM; *dir:* William Hanna, Joseph Barbera; *anim:* Ray Patterson, Irven Spence, Kenneth Muse, Pete Burness; *lay:* Harvey Eisenberg; *ed:* Fred MacAlpin; *voices:* Harry E. Lang; *mus:* Scott Bradley; *prod:* Fred Quimby; *col:* Tech. *sd:* WE. 7 min. *Academy Award.* • Tom takes his mouse-catching methods from a manual.

4359. Mouse-Warming (*Looney Tunes*) 8 Sept. 1952; *p.c.:* WB; *dir:* Charles M. Jones; *story:* Michael Maltese; *anim:* Ben Washam, Lloyd Vaughan, Ken Harris; *lay:* Robert Gribbroek; *back:* Philip de Guard; *ed:* Treg Brown; *mus:* Carl Stalling; *orch:* Milt Franklyn; *prod mgr:* John W. Burton; *prod:* Edward Selzer; *col:* Tech. *sd:* Vit. 7 min. • A boy mouse falls for the girl next door. Claude Cat takes advantage of the situation and tries to lure them out to a lover's tryst.

4360. Mouse Wreckers (*Looney Tunes*) 23 Apr. 1949; *p.c.:* WB; *dir:* Charles M. Jones; *story:* Michael Maltese; *anim:* Lloyd Vaughan, Ken Harris, Phil Monroe, Ben Washam; *lay:* Robert Gribbroek; *back:* Peter Alvarado; *ed:* Treg Brown; *voices:* Mel Blanc, Stan Freberg; *mus:* Carl Stalling; *prod mgr:* John W. Burton; *prod:* Edward Selzer; *col:* Tech. *sd:* Vit. 6 min. *Academy Award nomination.* • Hubie and Bertie, the mice, use psychology to rid the house of a champion mousecatching cat.

4361. The Mouse's Bride (*Aesop's Film Fable*) 14 June 1928; *p.c.:* Fables Pictures Inc for Pathé; *dir:* Paul Terry; b&w. sil. 10 min. • Farmer Al is run ragged by the mice and pays the cat to get rid of them but the rodents throw the cat and Al in the lake. Two mice, trying to romance in the parlor, are constantly annoyed by the arrival of Danny Duck, the pesty butler. Moral: "Many girls are single today because their front porches are too near street corner lamps."

4362. Mousetro Herman (*Herman & Katnip*) 10 Aug. 1956; *p.c.:* Famous for Para; *dir:* I. Sparber; *story:* Jack Mercer; *anim:* Al Eugster, Wm. B. Pattengill; *sets:* John Zago; *voices:* Arnold Stang, Sid Raymond, Jack Mercer; *mus:* Winston Sharples; *ph:* Leonard McCormick; *prod sup:* Seymour Shultz; *col:* Tech. *sd:* RCA. 6 min. • Katnip breaks up the mouse jam session in the music shop ... Herman arrives to sort things out.

4363. Mouseum (*Herman & Katnip*) 24 Feb. 1956; *p.c.:* Famous for Para; *dir:* Seymour Kneitel; *story:* Jack Mercer; *anim:* Al Eugster, Wm. B. Pattengill; *sets:* Robert Owen; *voices:* Arnold Stang, Gwen Davies, Sid Raymond; *mus:* Winston Sharples; *ph:* Leonard McCormick; *prod mgr:* Seymour Shultz; *col:* Tech. *sd:* RCA. 6 min. • Herman takes his nephews to a museum but, once again, Katnip spoils their enjoyment.

4364. Mousie Come Home (*Swing Symphony*) 15 Aug. 1946; *p.c.:* Walter Lantz prods for Univ; *dir:* James Culhane; *story:* Ben Hardaway, Milt Schaffer; *anim:* Pat Matthews, Paul Smith; *sets:* Fred Brunish; *voices:* Walter Tetley, Bill Shaw; *mus:* Darrell Calker; *col:* Tech. *sd:* WE. 6½ min. • A mouse proves a constant source of annoyance to Andy and his dog. In desperation they move away.

4365. Mousieur Herman (*Herman & Katnip*) 25 Nov. 1955; *p.c.:* Famous for Para; *dir:* Dave Tendlar; *story:* Carl Meyer; *anim:* Bill Hudson, Allen Rose; *sets:* Joseph Dommerque; *voices:* Arnold Stang, Sid Raymond, Gwen Davies, Jack Mercer; *mus:* Winston Sharples; *prod mgr:* Seymour Shultz; *col:* Tech. *sd:* RCA. 6 min. • The Parisian mice are trying to paint Katnip's portrait when he awakens and chases them. The arrival of Herman seals Katnip's fate.

4366. The Movie Daredevil (*Mastodon Cartoon*) 1 Apr. 1923; *p.c.:* Earl Hurd prods for Motion Picture Arts Inc.; *prod/dir:* Earl Hurd; b&w. sil. 5 min. • Bobby Bumps is a movie stuntman who wins the Steeplechase with a horse on skis.

4367. Movie Mad (*Flip the Frog*) 29 Aug. 1931; *p.c.:* Celebrity for MGM; *prod/dir:* Ub Iwerks; *mus:* Carl Stalling; b&w. *sd:* PCP. 9 min. • Flip invades a Hollywood movie studio, getting involved in a Laurel and Hardy pie fight, a western and a love scene before being ejected from the studio.

4368. Movie Madness (*Heckle & Jeckle*) 7 Nov. 1951; *p.c.:* TT for Fox; *dir:* Connie Rasinski; *story/voices:* Tom Morrison; *anim:* Jim Tyer; *sets:* Art Bartsch; *mus:* Philip A. Scheib; *ph:* Douglas Moye; *col:* Tech. 7 min. • The magpies gatecrash a movie studio, evading the guard and disguising themselves as knights, penguins and Romeo and Juliet.

4369. Movie Phoney News (*New Universal Cartoon*) 30 May 1938; *p.c.:* Univ; *prod:* Walter Lantz; *dir:* Alex Lovy; *story:* Victor McLeod, Win Smith; *anim:* La Verne Harding, George Dane; *voices:* Billy Bletcher, Danny Webb; *mus:* Frank Marsales; *b&w. sd:* WE. 6min. seq: *Alaska Sweepstakes, House of Magic, The Softball Game, The Hill Billy, The Beauty Shoppe.* • Newsreel satire. Items included are fashion, sport, and the birth of the Quinducklets.

4370. Movie Struck (*Scrappy*) 8 Sept. 1933; *p.c.:* Winkler for Colum; *story:* Sid Marcus; *anim:* Art Davis; *mus:* Joe de Nat; *prod mgr:* James Bronis; *b&w. sd:* RCA. 6 min. • Scrappy and Vontzy operate a movie studio commisary. The stars stage an impromptu party: Joe E. Brown indulges in unrestrained gluttony while George Arliss dances and devours pancakes and Laurel and Hardy dance wearing tutus. As more celebrities arrive, the boys can't cope with the frenzy.

4371. Moving Aweigh (*Popeye*) 22 Sept. 1944; *p.c.:* Famous for Para; *dir/anim:* Jim Tyer, Ben Solomon; *story:* Carl Meyer; *voices:* Jack Mercer, Arnold Stang; *mus:* Sammy Timberg; *ph:* Leonard McCormick; *prod mgr:* Sam Buchwald; *b&w. sd:* WE. 6 min. reissued in Tech. • Shorty helps Popeye move Olive's furniture with disastrous results.

4372. Moving Day (*Mickey Mouse*) 20 June 1936; *p.c.:* Walt Disney prods for UA; *dir:* Ben Sharpsteen; *story:* Jack Kinney; *anim:* Paul Allen, Arthur Babbitt, Alfred Eugster, Jack Hannah, Wolfgang Reitherman, Fred Spencer, Don Towsley, Marvin Woodward; *fx:* Cy Young; *voices:* Billy Bletcher, Pinto Colvig, Clarence Nash, Walt Disney; *mus:* Albert Hay Malotte, Leigh Harline; *col:* Tech. *sd:* RCA. 9 min. • Mickey, Donald and Goofy try to move home before Sheriff Pete can evict them.

4373. Mrs. Doubtfire 24 Nov. 1993; *p.c.:* Blue Wolf for Fox; *anim dir:* Chuck Jones; *anim prod:* Linda Jones Clough; *asso:* Stephen A. Fossati; *anim:* Bill Littlejohn, Barry Nelson, Tom Ray, Tom Roth, Dwayne Gressky, Ralph Newmann, Claude Raynes; *check:* Deborah Rykoff, Charlotte Clark; *ed:* Raja Gosnell; *title des:* Nina Saxon; *cartoon mus:* Fred Steiner; *col:* DeLuxe. *sd:* Dolby Stereo. 2 min. *l/a.* • Live-action comedy with Robin Williams as an out-of-work actor who poses as a nanny in order to gain access to his children and estranged wife. The film opens with Williams as a voice-over artist supplying voices for an animated cat and canary cartoon.

4374. Mrs. Jones' Rest Farm (*Terry-Toon*) Aug. 1949; *p.c.:* TT for Fox; *dir:* Eddie Donnelly; *story:* John Foster; *anim:* Jim Tyer; *sets:* Art Bartsch; *voices:* Sid Raymond; *mus:* Philip A. Scheib; *ph:* Douglas Moye; *col:* Tech. *sd:* RCA. 6 min. • When a lion arrives at the rest farm, he gets drunk and hallucinates pink elephants who chase him. Color remake of *Pink Elephants.*

4375. Mrs. Ladybug (*MGM Cartoon*) 21 Dec. 1940; *p.c.:* MGM; *prod/dir:* Rudolf Ising; *voices:* Mel Blanc, Sara Berner, The Rhythmettes; *mus:* Scott Bradley; *prod mgr:* Fred Quimby; *col:* Tech. *sd:* WE. 9 min. • A hungry spider poses as a maid in order to devour Mrs. Ladybug's offsprings.

4376. Mrs. O'Leary's Cow (*Terry-Toon*) 22 July 1938; *p.c.:* TT for Educational/Fox; *dir:* Ed Donnelly; *mus:* Philip A. Scheib; *b&w. sd:* RCA. 6½ min. • The cow is in court, accused of starting the Great Chicago Fire and relates, in flashback, how it was caused by a bee. When the firemen battle the blaze, the insect turns the hoses on them.

4377. Mrs. Pollifax — Spy Sept. 1972; *p.c.:* UA; *title design:* Don Record; *mus:* Lalo Schifrin; *col:* DeLuxe. *sd.* 1½ min. • Live-action feature about a female fashion guru who is hired as a spy for the CIA. The animated credits show a caped woman dodging assassination.

4378. Much Ado About Mousing (*Tom & Jerry*) 1964; *p.c.:* MGM; *ex prod:* Walter Bien; *prod/dir:* Chuck Jones; *asst dir:* Maurice Noble; *story:* Michael Maltese; *anim:* Ben Washam, Ken Harris, Don Towsley, Tom Ray, Dick Thompson; *back:* Philip de Guard; *voice:* Mel Blanc; *mus:* Eugene Poddany; *prod mgr:* Les Goldman; *col:* Metro. *sd:* WE. 7 min. • Down at Fisherman's Wharf, a bulldog puts a temporary halt to Tom's activities by giving Jerry a whistle to blow whenever help is needed.

4379. Much Ado About Mutton (*Noveltoon*) 25 July 1947; *p.c.:* Famous for Para; *dir:* I. Sparber; *story:* Joe Stultz, Carl Meyer; *anim:* Dave Tendlar, Tom Golden, Al Eugster; *sets:* Anton Loeb; *mus:* Winston Sharples; *ph:* Leonard McCormick; *prod mgr:* Sam Buchwald; *col:* Tech. *sd:* RCA. 8 min. • Wolfie wants lamb for supper but is, once more, outwitted by Blackie the lamb.

4380. Much Ado About Nothing (*Dinky Duck*) 22 Mar. 1940; *p.c.:* TT for Fox; *dir:* Connie Rasinski; *story:* John Foster; *mus:* Philip A. Scheib; *col:* Tech. *sd:* RCA. 6 min. • Love blossoms between Dinky and a chick but when the chick falls in the river it creates a feud between the duck and hen families.

4381. Much Ado About Nutting (*Merrie Melodies*) 23 May 1953; *p.c.:* WB; *dir:* Charles M. Jones; *story:* Michael Maltese; *anim:* Lloyd Vaughan, Ken Harris, Ben Washam; *lay:* Maurice Noble; *back:* Philip de Guard; *ed:* Treg Brown; *mus:* Carl Stalling; *orch:* Milt Franklyn; *prod mgr:* John W. Burton; *prod:* Edward Selzer; *col:* Tech. *sd:* Vit. 7 min. • A squirrel's endeavors to crack a coconut.

4382. Mucho Locos (*Merrie Melodies*) 5 Jan. 1966; *p.c.:* DFE for WB; *dir:* Robert McKimson; *story:* David DeTiege; *anim:* Manny Perez, George Grandpré, Bob Matz; *lay:* Dick Ung; *back:* Tom O'Loughlin; *ed:* Lee Gunther; *voices:* Mel Blanc; *mus:* Herman Stein; *col:* Tech. *sd:* Vit. 6 min. seq: *China Jones, Deduce You Say, Mexicali Schmoes, Robin Hood Daffy, Tortilla Flaps.* • Speedy conjurs up some pictures for a young mouse to envision on an empty television set.

4383. Mucho Mouse (*Tom & Jerry*) 6 Sept 1957; *p.c.:* MGM; *prod/dir:* William Hanna, Joseph Barbera; *anim:* Lewis Marshall, Kenneth Muse, Bill Schipek, Jack Carr, Ken Southworth, Herman Cohen; *lay:* Ed Benedict, Dick Bickenbach; *back:* Robert Gentle; *character des:* Gene Hazelton; *ed:* Jim Faris; *voices:* Julie Bennett, Charlie Lung, Daws Butler; *mus:* Scott Bradley; *ph:* Jack Stevens; *prod mgr:* Hal Elias; *col:* Tech. *sd:* WE. 6½ min. CS. • Tom is engaged to rid a hacienda of "El Magnifico" an uncatchable mouse.

4384. Mud Squad (*Tijuana Toads*) 28 Apr 1971; *p.c.:* Mirisch/DFE for UA; *dir:* Art Davis; *story:* John W. Dunn; *anim:* Warren Batchelder, Ken Muse, Don Williams, Art Leonardi; *sets:* Richard H. Thomas; *ed:* Lee Gunther; *voices:* Don Diamond, Tom Holland, Anthea Lorde; *mus:* Doug Goodwin; *ph:* John Burton Jr.; *prod sup:* Jim Foss, Harry Love; *col:* DeLuxe. *sd:* RCA. 6 min. • Pancho goes to get some food and returns with an egg that hatches into a baby alligator.

4385. Mulan 19 June 1998; *p.c.:* Disney Enterprises Inc. for BV; *dir:* Barry Cook, Tony Bancroft; *prod:* Pam Coats; *based on a story by* Robert D. San Solici; *scr:* Rita Hsiao, Christopher Sanders, Philip LaZebnik, Raymond Singer, Eugenia Bostwick-Singer; *development ed:* Victor Livingston; *addit story:* Linda Woolverton, Jodi Ann Johnson, Alan Ormsby, David Reynolds, Don Dougherty, Joseph Ekers, Daan Jippes, Jorgen Klubien, Theodore Newton, Frank Nissen, Dennis Rich, Larry Scholl, Jeff Snow; *asso prod:* Kendra Haaland, Robert S. Garber; *prod des:* Hans Bacher; *art dir:* Ric Sluiter; *artistic sups: character des:* Chen-Yi Chang; *lay:* Robert Walker; *back:* Robert E. Stanton; *clean-up:* Ruben Procopio; *visual fx:* David Tidgwell; *artistic co-ord:* Jeff Dutton; *story co-head:* Dean DeBlois; *story:* John Sanford, Chris Williams, Tim Hodges, Julius L. Aguimatang, Burny Mattinson, Lorna Cook, Barry Johnson, Thom Enriquez, Ed Gombert, Joe Grant, Floyd Norman; *character des visual development:* Sai Ping Lok, Robh Ruppel, Paul Felix, Alex Nino, Marcelo Vignali, Richard P. Chavez, John Puglisi, Jean Gillmore, Caroline K. Hu, Sue Nichols, Peter de Séve; *Los Angeles unit artistic sup: lay:* Tom Shannon, Scott Caple; *back:* Sunny Apinchapong; *clean-up:* Vera Lanpher-Pacheco; *visual fx:* David "Joey" Mildenberger; *prod mgr:* Rebecca Pahr Huntley; *lay: journeymen:* Arden Chan, Jeff Dickson, Craig Anthony Grasso, Andrew Hickson, Tom Humber, Richard Carl Livingston, Peter Bielicki, Edward L. Chertner, Gary Mouri, Jeff Purves, Doug Walker, Sherilan Weinhart; *lay asst:* Peter J. De Luca, Andrew Edward Harkness, Armand Serrano, Kenneth Spirduso, Ray Chan, Craig Elliott, Yong-Hong Zhong, Tom Dow, Bill Hodman, Norbert Maier, Kevyn Proctor, Franc Reyes, Dermot Walshe, Mark Gaston Kalesniko, Kevyn Wallace; *blue sketch:* Jo Ann Tzuanos, Noel C. Johnson, Madlyn Zusmer O'Neill; *anim: "Mulan & Fa Zhou": sup anim:* Mark Henn; *anim:* Anthony Wayne Michaels, James Young Jackson, Rune Brandt Bennicke, Elliot M. Bour, Carol Sedl, Tom Gately, Robert Espanto Domingo,

Mark Pudleiner; "*Shang & Fa Li*": *sup anim:* Ruben A. Aquino; *anim:* Joe Hadar, Philip Morris, Marcelo Fernandes De Moura, Theodore Anthony Lee Ty, Craig R. Maras, Bill Waldman; "*Mushu*": *sup anim:* Tom Bancroft; *anim:* Charles Bonifacio, Robert O. Corley, Dominic M. Carola, James Baker, Jamie Oliff, John Webber; "*Yao & the Ancestors*": *sup anim:* Aaron Blaise; *anim:* Byron Howard, Christopher Bradley, Ian White; "*Chien-Po & Ling*": *sup anim:* Broose Johnson; *anim:* Michael Benet, Bert Klein, D.M. Wawrzaszek, Dave Kopczyk; "*Shan-Yu & Falcon & Elite Huns*": *sup anim:* Pres Antonio Romanillos; *anim:* Travis Blaise, Trey Finney, Tony Stanley, Anthony Ho Wong; "*Khan & General Li*": *sup anim:* Alex Kupershmidt; *anim:* Sasha Dorogov, Branko Mihanovic; "*Chi Fu & Grandmother Fa*": *sup anim:* Jeffrey J. Varab; *anim:* Darko Cesar, Todd Waterman, Jerry Yuching; "*Cri-Kee*": *sup anim:* Barry Temple; "*The Emperor*": *sup anim:* T. Daniel Hofstedt; "*miscellaneous*": "*The Matchmaker*": *lead anim:* Brian Ferguson; "*Little Brother*": *lead anim:* Shawn Keller; *rough inbet:* Paulo R. Alvarado, Jonathan Annand, Gregg E. Azzopardi, Brad Condie, Krista Heij, John Hurst, Steve Mason, David W. Zach, Paul N. McDonald, Karen Tremblay, Edmund Gabriel, Clay Kaytis, Mark Alan Mitchell, Chris Sonnenburg, Michael Wu, George Benavides, Michael D'isa, Benjamin Gonzalez, Grant Hiestand, Joseph Mateo, Mario J. Menjivar, Gary D. Payne, Bobby Alcid Rubio, Wes Sullivan, Aliki Theofilopoulos; *addit anim:* Caroline Cruikshank, Phil Young, William Recinos, Michael Genz; *cgi: : sup anim:* Rob Bekuhrs; *anim:* Sandra Maria Groeneveld, Chadd Ferron; *asst:* James Michael Crossley, Patricia A. Hannaway, Jason W. Wolbert; *software development: sups:* Hanns-Oskar Porr, Marty Altman, Joel Davis, Tad Gielow; *model dpt: sup:* Mary Ann Pigora, Sean Locke, Thomas C. Meyer; *look development: sup:* Tony Platt; Kathy Kershaw Barshatzky, Michael McNeill, Chalermpon "Yo" Poungpeth, Heather Pritchett; *back:* Charles R. Vollmer, Barry R. Kooser, David Wang (Ying Guang), Peter Moehrle, Sean Sullivan, Xiangyuan Jie, William T. Silvers Jr., Xin-Lin Fan, Barbara Massey, George Taylor, Kevin McNamara, Ron Defelice, David Murray, Marisa Fidanza, Christopher F. Greco, John Lee, Geraldine Kovats, Brad Hick, Kelly McGraw, David Yorke, Ian S. Gooding, Maryann Thomas, Michael Kurinsky, David Wesley Jarvis, Keith Newton; *digital paint:* Kathy Schoeppner, Christine Laubach; *CAPS sup: scene planl/ph:* John R. Cunningham; *anim check:* Laurie A. Sacks; *2d anim processing:* Jan Barley Gutowski; *col models:* Irma Cartaya; *final check:* Hortensia M. Casagran, Michael D. Lusby; *digital film print:* Brandy Hill; *clean-up anim:* "*Mulan*": *lead key:* Daniel A. Gracey; *asst:* Rachel Ribb, Pamela Mathues, Renee Holt, Merritt F. Andrews, Marcia Kimura Dougherty, Lee Duncan, Akemi Gutierrez, Myung Kang-Teague, Marianne Tucker, Elizabeth S. Watson, Eunice (Eun Ok) Yu, Todd Bright, Seung Beom Kim, Rosana Urbes, Ron Zeitler; *break:* Benjamin William Adams, Kevin A. Barber, Phillip A. Jones, Richard C. Trebus Jr., Rebecca Wrigley, Cyndy Bohonovsky, Kimberly Dwinell, Steve Lenze; *inbet:* Russell Braun, David Mar, Sarah Marcey-Boose, Clarence "Boola" Robello, Jacqueline Shepherd, Matt Whitlock, Jeffrey B. Harter, Jeff W. Hong, Dietz Toshio Ichishita, Jim Marquez, Jong Won Park; "*Shang*": *lead key:* Bryan M. Sommer; *asst:* Dan Daly, Caroline Clifford, Teresita Quezada, Yung Soo Kim, Scott A. Burroughs, Chan Woo Jung; *break:* Saul Andrew Bunkoff, Sean Luo, James W. Elston, Cindy Ge, Chang Yei Cho; "*Mushi*": *lead key:* David T. Nethery; *asst:* Sherrie H. Sinclair, Lon Smart, Edward Gutierrez, Calvin Le Duc, Wendy J. Muir, Jason Peltz, Daniel Bond, Yoon Sook Nam, Jan Naylor; *break:* Nathan Greno, Eun Sang Jang, Stephanie Olivieri, Cheryl Polakow-Knight, Jim Robert Snider; *inbet:* Janice Armiger, Dominic A'vant, Antoine Cunningham, Jill Friemark; "*Fa Zhou & Fa Li*": *lead key:* Monica Murdock; *asst:* Kim Torpey, Mi Yul Lee, Wes Chun, Ginger Wolf; *break:* Philip J. Allora, Alex McDaniel, Frank Montagna Jr.; "*Yao & the Ancestors*": *lead key:* Phil Bond; *asst:* Phil Noto; *break:* Will Huneycutt; *inbet:* Tim Massa, Keith A. Sintay, T.C. Starnes Jr., Robert Lee Williams Jr.; "*Chien-Po & Ling*": *lead key:* Tom Fish; *asst:* Vincent Siracusano, John R. Walsh, Ron Cohes, John O'Hailey; *break:* Don Crum, Ilan Wexio Hatukah, Peter Raymundo; *inbet:* Carlos R. Arancibia, Jason Boose, Danny R. Santos, Woody Woodman; "*Shan-Yu & Falcon & Elite Huns*": *lead key:* Christine Lawrence Finney; *asst:* James A. Harris, Yer (Za) Vue, Dan Tanaka, Tracy M. Lee, Augusto Borges Bastos, Richard Scott Morgan; *break:* Frank R. Cordero, Tom de Rosier; *inbet:* Chad Thompson, Michael Ludy; "*Khan & General Li*": *lead key:* Sam Ewing; *asst:* Samantha Lair, Darren R. Webb, Stephan Zupkas, Judith Barnes, Karen Hardenbergh, Terry Naughton, Katherine Blackmore, John J. Pierro, George Sukara; "*Chi Fu*": *lead key:* Scott Anderson; *asst:*

Jane Zhao, Kevin Deters, Mary-Jean Repchuk; *break:* Lisa G. Lanyon, Patrick Tuorto; "*Cri-Kee & Little Brother*": *lead key:* Kellie D. Lewis; *asst:* Antony de Fato, Amy Drobeck; "*Grandmother Fa*": *lead key:* James Parris; "*The Emperor*": *lead key:* Rusty Stoll; *asst:* Roland Mechael B. Ilagan; *inbet:* Janelle C. Bell-Martin, Eddie Pittman; "*The Matchmaker*": *lead key:* Kathleen B. Baily; *asst:* Inna Chon; *break:* Ely Lester, Whitney B. Martin, Chun Yin Joey So; "*Misc Characters*": *lead key:* Ruben Procopio; *asst:* Tom LaBaff, Jang Woo Lee, Maurilio Morales, Thomas Thorspecken, Carl Philip Hall, Leticia Lichtwardt, Michael G. McKinney, Marsha W.J. Park-Yum, Dana M. Reeves, Dave Suding, Brian Orlando Beauchamp, Carl Angus Bell, Brigitte Franzca-Fritz, Doug Post; *break:* Stephen Nelson Austin, Tammy Daniel-Biske, Perry Farinola, Daniel Lawrence Riebold, Elsa Sesto-Vidal, Ronnie Williford, Jim Brummett, Larry Flores, Cliff Freitas, Brian D. Kennon, Denise Meehan, Justin "Dusty" Wakefield; *inbet:* Jean Cullen De Moura, Tony Santo, Casey E. Coffey; *addit.clean-up anim: key asst:* Susan Adnopoz, Tony Anselmo, Debra Armstrong, Bill Berg, Jamie Kezlarian Bolio, Jane Tucker Bonnet, Gail M. Frank, Raymond A. Harris, Michael Hazy, Kris Heller, Allison Hollen, Celinda S. Kennedy, Kaaren E. Lundeen, Miriam C. McDonnell, Brian B. McKim, Lieve Miessen, Dorothea Baker Paul, David Recinos, Richard D. Rocha, Maria W. Rosetti, Randy Sanchez, Susan Sugita, Peggy Tonkonogy, Marshall L. Toomey, Terry Wozniak; *asst:* Lillian A. Chapman, Diana Coco, Kent Holaday, Rick D. Kohlschmidt, Janet Heerhan-Kwon, Daniel Y. Lim, Annette Morel, Martin D. Schwartz; *break:* Munir A. Bhatti, Aidan Flynn, Carolyn F. Gliona, Jocelyn M. Kooistra, Allison Renna, Steven K. Thompson; *inbet:* Frank Dietz, Nikolas M. Frangos, Matthew R. Haber, Cynthia Landers, Kimberly Moriki, Robert Persichetti Jr., Kathleen Thorson; *visual fx anim:* Garrett Wren, Troy A. Gustafson, Bob Bennett, Jazno Francoeur, Joseph F. Giland, Stephen McDermott, John David Thornton, Tony West, Allen Blyth, Colbert Fennelly, Michael Cadwallader Jones, Dorse A. Lanpher, Dan Lund, James de Valera Mansfield, Kevin O'Neil; *fx anim asst:* John Fargnoli; *3d visual fx anim:* Guner Behich, Darlene E. Hadrika; *fx key asst:* Kristine Humber, Paul R. Kashuk Jr., Michael L. Oliva, Paitoon Ratanasirintrawoot, Mabel Gesner, Jon William Lopez, Joseph Christopher Pope, Steve Starr, John Tucker; *fx asst:* Paul Briggs, Derrick L. McKenzie, Gary Schumer, Lora M. Spran, Kristine Brown, Dennis Spicer; *fx break:* Adeboye Saburi Adegberno, Stella P. Arbelaez, Christine Page, Robert Blalock, Michael Montgomery, Rochelle Smith, Faris Al-Saffar, Jay Baker, Melinda Wang, Nicole Alene Zamora; *fx inbet:* Verell "Skip" Bowers, John Cashman, Mark Delaine Rath, Heather M. Shepherd, Gary Louis Gallegos, Tatiana Erika Kellert IV, Ron Pence, Jeffrey C. Tse; *addit.visual fx: anim:* Mauro Maressa, Phillip D. Vigil, Marlon West; *key asst:* Nate Pacheco, Amanda J. Talbot, Michael A. Toth, Graham Woods; *inbet:* Kristin Fong-Lukavsky, Jay Shindell; *fx data entry:* Kip Lanai Stone, Gary Stubblefield; *ed:* Michael Kelly, William J. Caparella, James Melton, Danny Retz, Patsy Bougé, Dave Teller, James Dewey Kirkpatrick, Gary Blair, Bill Shaffer, Beth Collins-Stegmaier, Hermann H. Schmidt; *voices:* Fa Mulan: Ming-Na Wen; Shan-Yu: Miguel Ferrer; Fau: Freda Foh Shen; Yao: Harvey Fierstein; Grandmother Fa: June Foray; Chi Fu: James Hong; The Matchmaker: Miriam Margolyes; The Emperor: Pat Morita; Mushu: Eddie Murphy; *the singing voice of Grandmother Fa:* Marni Nixon; Fa Zhou: Soon-Tek Oh; *the singing voice of Shang:* Donny Osmond; *the singing voice of Mulan:* Lea Salonga; General Li: James Shigeta; First Ancestor: George Takei; Chein-Po: Jerry S. Tondo; Ling: Gedde Watanabe; *Khan the horse/Little Brother the dog/Cri-Kee the cricket:* Frank Welker; *the singing voice of Ling:* Matthew Wilder; Shang: B.D. Wong; *female ancestor:* Mary Kay Bergman; *also:* Tom Amundsen, Arminae Austen, Susan Boyd, Jullanne Buescher, Steve Bullen, Corey Burton, Mitch Carter, Robert Clotworthy, David Cowgill, Sally Dworsky, Beth Fowler, Dan Fullilove, Elisa Gabrielli, Jack Gilpin, Sandie Hall, Richard S. Horvitz, Linda Kerns, Matthew Labyorteaux, Conan Lee, Dana Lee, Edie Lehmann-Boddicker, Luisa Leschin, Christina Ma, Susan McBride, Huanani Minn, Edie Mirman, Mark Moseley, Patrick Pinney, Peter Renaday, Maurta Thornburg-Phillips, John Walcutt, Claudette Wells; *mus:* Jerry Goldsmith; *song:* "True to Your Heart": *mus:* Matthew Wilder; *lyrics:* David Zippel; *performed by* 98° and Stevie Wonder; *song prod:* Matthew Wilder; *song recl/mix:* Frank Wolf; *score recl/mix:* Bruce Besterman; *songs conducted by* Paul Bogaev; *orch:* Alexander Courage, Paul Buckmaster; *song mus ed:* Tom Kramer, Kathleen Fogarty-Bennett, Ken Hall, Robert Bayless; *mus prod:* Tod Cooper, Andrew Page; *mus co-ords:* Deniece LaRocca, Tom Coyne MacDougall; *orch conductors:* Sandy de Crescent, John Miller; *vocal conductors:* Bobbi Page, Jess

Harnell, David Friedman; *addit. mus contractor:* Reggie Wilson; *mus preperation:* Jo Ann Kane Music Service; *mus copyists:* Dominic Fidelibus, Booker White; "Reflection" performed by Vanessa Mae; *mus:* Matthew Wilder (arranged by Vanessa Mae); *ex mus prod:* Chris Montan; *prod:* Jaz Coleman, Pamela Nicholson; *ph dir:* Don Winton, David J. Steinberg; *snr mgr prod:* Gretchen Maschmeyer Albrecht; *snr mgr scene plan/ph:* Joe Juliano; *CAPS mgr:* Fran Kirsten; *digital prod mgr:* Randy Parker; *asst mgr:* Maggie Walsh; *asst artistic co-ord:* Pam Manes Darley; *asst prod mgr: story:* Bruce Seifert; *visual development:* Cathy Lawrence; *ed & rec:* Theresa Bentz; *lay:* Ingrid M. Sander; *character anim:* Sheri Croft; *sweatbox:* Kevin Wade; *clean-up:* Alex Chatfield; *computer anim:* Stephen R. Craig, Aimee Scribner; *visual fx:* Matthew Garbera; *col models:* Diana Blazer; *back & anim check:* Jackie L. Shadrake; *CAPS & retakes:* Fred Berning Jr.; *prod:* Bruce Anderson; *California: lay & back:* Jennifer Magee-Cook; *clean-up:* Wendy L. McNeny; *visual fx:* Kim Gray; *CAPS disk space & retakes:* Shawne Zarubica; *prod co-ords: prod:* Kristine M. Wentz; *CAPS disk space & retakes:* Brenda McGirl; *scene plan:* Katherine A. Kettering; *CAPS:* Kirsten Ann Bulmer; *scene plan:* Mary Lescher, Cynthia Goode, Paul Steele; *asst scene plan/ph:* Karen N. Sickles; *asst scene plan:* Tom Baker, S.J. Bleick, Mark Allen Henley, Ronald Jackson, David Link; *scene plan prod:* Christopher Holland; *anim. check: snr check:* Daniel Cohen; *anim check:* Victoria Winner Novak, Albert Francis Moore, Jacqueline Hooks-Winterlich, Willis Middleton, Denise M. Mitchell, Helen O'Flynn, Gary G. Shafer; *2d anim processing:* Barbara J. Poirier, Sarah J. Cole, Todd LaPlante, David Braden, Michael A. McFerren, Val D'Arcy, Robyn L. Roberts, Karen N. China, Jo Ann Bruer, Robert Lizardo, Lynnette Cullen, David J. Rowe, Richard J. McFerren, Stacie K. Reece; *col stylists:* Debra Y. Siegel, Kenneth C. Landrum, Barbara Lynn Hamane, Pamela L.V. Henn, Sylvia I. Sanchez, Sarah Fancher, Cheryl Davis; *paint: col model mark-up/registration:* Karrie Keuling Nichaels, Laura Lynn Rippberger, Sally Nolan-Smith, Cynthia Kay Sager, Sherrie Cuzzort, Karan Lee-Storr, David J. Zywicki; *paint asst sup:* Irma Valez, Russell Blandino, Phyllis Estelle Fields; *registration/paint:* Suzie Ewing, Debra A. Ptaskiewicz; *paint mark-up:* Leyla Amaro-Pelaez, Roberta Lee-Borchardt, Sally-Anne King, Barbara Newby, Bonnie A. Ramsey, Myrian Ferron Tello; *paint:* Carmen Sanderson, Joyce Alexander, Bill Andres, Kirk Axtell II, Phyllis Bird, Joey Calderon, Ofra Afuta Calderon, Janice M. Caston, Sybil Cuzzort, Florida D'Ambrisio, Robert Edward Dettloff, Nika Dunne, Christina Frazier, Paulino Garcia Ingo, Dawn Gates, Patricia L. Gold, Debbie Green, Steve Hirsch, David Karp, Angelika R. Katz, Kukhee Lee, Beth Ann McCoy-Gee, Deborah Mooneyham-Hughes, Karen Lynne Nugent, Ken O'Malley, Bruce G. Phillipson, Rosalinde Praamsma, Heidi Woodward Shellhorn, Eyde Sheppherd, Grace H. Shirado, Don Shump, Fumiko R. Sommer, S. Ann Sullivan, Roxanne M. Taylor, Tami Terusa, Britt van der Nagel; *i&p:* Chris Hecox; *final check:* Teri N. McDonald, Andrew Simmons, Monty C. Maldovan, Monica Albracht Marroquin, Lea Dahlen, Catherine Markovich-Peterson, Misoon Kim; *compositing:* Jason Leonard, Robert Buske, Earl Scott Coffman, Tim Acton-Gales, Michelle Sammartino, Dolores Pope, Jim "JR" Russell; *digital film printing & opticals:* Tony Poriazis, John Aardal, John Derderian, Jeanne E. Leone-Sterwerf; *Florida prod asst:* Ron Betta, Tony Cosanella, Eric Dapkewicz, Andrew Davenport, Nanette K. Drumtra, Tom Gately, Michelle Arlene Hargrett, Jeff Hermann, Greg Hill, John Richard Hughes, Ilyssa Katz, Tom Kennedy, Chad F. Rogers, Kristin Rovno, Angela Tomlinson, Shellie West, Judy Wolf; *California prod asst:* Rodolfo Cardenas, Stephanie Clifford, Deborah G. Dalton, Flynn Falcone, Philip B. Isaacs, Renato Lattanzi, Michael Nuckols, John Damien Ryan, Michele Silverstein, Jef B. Yowell, Sabrina Waterman; *admin asst:* Stephanie Green Spahn, Christine Ng Wong; *character sculptures:* Tony Cipriano, Kent Melton; *Florida technology:* Enrique Santos, Raul Anaya, Matt Balosuknia, Carol J. Choy, Charles Collins, Jefferson Crutchfield, Larry Edminster, Christine E. George, Don Gworek, Dwayne Harris, Dana Haukoos, R. Todd King, Jerry Lynn Lake, Barbara Le Bruno, Tina O'Hailey, John Outten, Carmen Perreault, James Pirzyk, Deborah L. Snead, Tom Talbot, John W. Wheeler; *California technology:* Kirk Bodyfelt, Michael R. Fodor, Kevin J. Hussey, Edwin R. Leonard, Thomas Moore Jr., James J. Sepe, Graham S. Allen, Richard M. Barnes, Glenn Bell, Michael S. Blum, Michael C. Bolos, Brad Brooks, Letha L. Burchard, Mark R. Carison, Nhi H. Casey, Loren Chun, Peter Chun, Michael Clay, Ray C. Coleman, Scott Dolim, Elena Driskill, Norbert Faerstain, Robert Falco, Kevin G.J. Freels, Mark W. Gilicinski, Maria Gomez De Lizardo, John D. Hoffman, Le Hua, Shyh-Chyuan Huang, James P. Hurrell, Kevin E. Keech,

Daniel C. Kim, Michael R. King, Hans Ku, Mike Larkin, Li-Ming "Lawrence" Lee, Sally Lee, Stanley B. Lippman, James MacBurney, Michael McClure, Kevin A. McGuire, Jim Meyer, Christopher D. Mihaly, Thaddeus P. Miller, Robert A. Mortensen, Jack Mulready, Jeff Nash, Michael Neville, Lyle S. Nohma, Troy R. Norin, David Oguri, Keith Otis, Ron L. Purdy, Carlos Quinonez, Lisette Ranga, Dave Remba, Jeff Rochlin, Ruan Kai-Zhen, Michael Saitta, Nasser B. Salomon, Fe Samala, James A. Sandweiss, Todd Scopio, Jeffrey Sickler, John Stimson, Charles Stoner, Sandy Sunseri, Joe Suzow, Mark M. Tokunaga, Laurie Tracy, Mary Jane "Jill" Turner, Jon Y. Wada, Doug White, Derek E. Wilson, Thomas A. Wong, Fran R. Zandonella, Michael Zarembski; *re-rec mix:* Terry Porter, Mel Metcalfe, Dean A. Zupancic, Doc Kane, Lon E. Bender, Curt Schulkey; *foley:* Kelly Oxford, Jim Moriana, Katherine Harper; *sd ed:* Bryan Bowen, Hector Gika, Peter Lehman, Martin Lopez, Dan Rich, Michael Tempo, Gayle Wesley, David Stanke; *dubbing:* Jeanette Browning; *PDL:* Judy Nord; *neg cutters:* Mary Beth Smith, Rick MacKay; *title des:* Susan Bradley; *titles:* Buena Vista Imaging; *title optics sup.:* Mark Dornfeld; *prod mgr:* Lisa M. Smith; *col:* Tech. *sd:* Sony Dynamic Digital. 84 min. • Based on an ancient Chinese legend: A feisty young oriental girl named Mulan takes the place of her aging father, who has been called upon to join the Imperial Army in fighting invading Huns. Masquerading as a boy, she joins the warriors, blossoming into a skilled soldier and helps to bring victory to her nation and honor to her family.

4386. The Mule's Disposition (*Unnatural History*) 18 July 1926; *p.c.:* Bray prods for FBO; *dir:* Walter Lantz; *anim:* Clyde Geronimi; *l/a ph:* Joe Rock; b&w. sil. 6 min. *l/a/anim.* • When the kids tease their black nurse, she tells them of the mule who had a sweet disposition until Noah kept changing him to poorer quarters to please the other animals. Finally the mule rebelled and wrecked the place.

4387. Mumbo Jumbo (*Ant & Aardvark*) 27 Sept. 1970; *p.c.:* Mirisch/DFE for UA; *dir:* Art Davis; *story:* John W. Dunn; *anim:* Phil Roman, Bob Bentley, Don Williams, Manny Gould, Irv Spence, Ken Muse, Warren Batchelder; *lay:* Lin Larsen; *back:* Richard H. Thomas; *ed:* Lee Gunther; *voices:* John Byner; *mus:* Doug Goodwin, Pete Candoli, Billy Byers, Jimmy Rowles, Tommy Tedesco, Ray Brown, Shelly Manne; *prod sup:* Jim Foss, Harry Love; *col:* DeLuxe. *sd:* RCA. 6 min. • The Ant joins an animal fraternity who help one another. When the Aardvark attacks, a helpful elephant comes to his rescue.

4388. The Mummy 7 May 1999; *p.c.:* Univ; *visual fx:* ILM *character des sup:* Jeff Mann; *anim sup:* Daniel Jeannette; *visual fx prod:* Tom Kennedy; *cg sup:* Ben Snow, Michael Bauer, Scott Frankel; *cg anim sup:* Dennis Turner; *lead seq anim:* Jenn Emberly; *anim:* Rudi Bloss, Alain Costa, Lesley Headrick, Greg Kyle, David Latour, Julija Learie, Aubry Mintz, Mark Powers, David Sidley, Sharonne Sock, Glenn Sylvester, Si Tran; *addit visual fx: cg anim:* John Hewitt, John B. Wallace III, James Peterson, Scott Ballard; *col:* Deluxe. *sd:* Digital dts sound/SDDS/Dolby digital. Vistavision. 125 min. *l/a.* • Live-action adventure: An expedition goes to Egypt to find Hamunaptra, the Lost City of the Dead. Upon opening a casket, an ancient curse brings the High Priest Imhotep, who had been buried alive seven centuries earlier, back to life.

4389. Munro Sept. 1961; *p.c.:* Rembrandt for Para; *dir:* Gene Deitch; *story:* Jules Feiffer from his book *Passionella and Other Stories*; *prod des/lay:* Al Kouzel; *anim:* Zdeněk Smetana, Milan Klikar, Antonín Bureš, Věra Marešová, Mirko Kačena, Bohumil Šejda, Věra Kudrnová, Jindřich Barta, Zdenka Skřípková, Olga Šišková; *back:* Bohumil Šišká; *voices:* Howard Morris, Seth Deitch, Marie Deitch; *prod:* William L. Snyder, Zdenka Deitchová; *col:* Tech. *sd:* 9 min. *Academy Award.* • A four-year-old is inducted into the Army.

4390. Murakami-Wolf Titles & Sequences • *1966:* Never Steal Anything Wet *dir:* Jim Murakami. What's Up Tiger Lily? *dir:* Phill Norman • *1969:* Hello Down There (Para) • *1970:* Gas-s-s-s! (American International) • *1973:* The Naked Ape *dir:* Charles Swenson (Playboy)

4391. Muscle Beach Tom (*Tom & Jerry*) 7 Sept. 1956; *p.c.:* MGM; *prod/dir:* William Hanna, Joseph Barbera; *anim:* Lewis Marshall, Kenneth Muse, Ed Barge, Irven Spence; *lay:* Dick Bickenbach; *back:* Robert Gentle; *ed:* Jim Faris; *mus:* Scott Bradley; *ph:* Jack Stevens; *prod mgr:* Hal Elias; *col:* Tech. *sd:* WE. 6 min. CS. • Tom's efforts to impress a girl at the beach are thwarted by the intervention of a rival cat and then Jerry puts in his two cents worth.

4392. Muscle Tussle (*Merrie Melodies*) 18 Apr. 1953; *p.c.:* WB; *dir:* Robert McKimson; *story:* Tedd Pierce; *anim:* Rod Scribner, Phil de Lara, Charles McKimson, Herman Cohen; *lay:* Robert Givens; *back:* Carlos Manriquez; *ed:* Treg Brown; *voices:* Mel Blanc, Gladys Holland; *mus:* Carl Stalling; *prod mgr:* John W. Burton; *prod:* Edward Selzer; *col:* Tech. *sd:* Vit. 7 min. • Daffy tries to impress his girl with feats of strength until she becomes infatuated by a muscular bully who appears on the scene.

4393. Music Hath Charms (*Oswald*) 7 Sept. 1936; *p.c.:* Univ; *dir:* Walter Lantz; *story:* Walter Lantz, Victor McLeod; *anim:* Ray Abrams, Bill Mason; *mus:* James Dietrich; b&w. *sd:* WE. 6 min. • No story available.

4394. Music Land (*Silly Symphony*) 5 Oct. 1935; *p.c.:* Walt Disney prods for UA; *dir:* Wilfred Jackson; *asst dir:* Graham Heid; *story:* Earl Hurd; *anim:* Les Clark, Ugo d'Orsi, Gilles de Tremaudan, Clyde Geronimi, Dick Huemer, Richard Lundy, Grim Natwick, Wolfgang Reitherman, Archie Robin, Louis Schmitt, Leonard Sebring; *fx:* Cy Young; *story/character des/lay:* Albert Hurter; *mus:* Leigh Harline; *col:* Tech. *sd:* RCA. 8½ min. • A Romeo and Juliet situation between two instruments from the Isles of Symphony and Jazz! A bridge of Harmony is finally established.

4395. The Music Lesson (*Flip the Frog*) 29 Oct. 1932; *p.c.:* Celebrity for MGM; *prod/dir:* Ub Iwerks; *anim:* Jimmie Culhane; *mus:* Carl Stalling; b&w. *sd:* PCP. 6 min. • Flip has to practice while the piano teacher is away but his pals entice him to go swimming where he has a nasty brush with the law.

4396. The Music Mice-Tro (*Merrie Melodies*) 27 May 1967; *p.c.:* Format Films for WB; *dir:* Rudy Larriva; *story:* Tom Dagenais, Cal Howard; *anim:* Bob Bransford, Ed Friedman, Virgil Ross; *lay:* Don Sheppard; *back:* Walter Peregoy; *ed:* Joe Siracusa; *voices:* Mel Blanc; *mus:* William Lava; *prod:* William L. Hendricks, Herbert Klynn; *col:* Tech. *sd:* Vit. 7 min. • Hollywood star, Daffy, retires to Balmy Springs for a rest ... only to find Speedy and his musical combo trying to audition for him.

4397. The Musical Farmer (*Mickey Mouse*) 14 July 1932; *p.c.:* Walter E. Disney for Colum; *dir:* Wilfred Jackson; *anim:* Johnny Cannon, Les Clark, Gilles de Tremaudan, Clyde Geronimi, Jack King, Richard Lundy, Ben Sharpsteen; *mus:* Frank E. Churchill; b&w. *sd:* PCP. 6½ min. • A barnyard musical. Mickey photographs with a flashlight, causing an explosion.

4398. Musical Madness (*Little Roquefort*) May 1951; *p.c.:* TT for Fox; *dir:* Eddie Donnelly; *story:* Tom Morrison; *anim:* Mannie Davis; *mus:* Philip A. Scheib; *col:* Tech. *sd:* RCA. 6 min • Roquefort's slumber in a music shop is disturbed by the cat's jam session.

4399. Musical Memories (*Color Classic*) 8 Nov. 1935; *p.c.:* The Fleischer Studio for Para; *prod:* Max Fleischer; *dir:* Dave Fleischer; *anim:* Seymour Kneitel, Roland Crandall; *voice:* Frank Gallop; *mus:* Sammy Timberg; *ph:* Johnny Burks; *col:* Tech-2. *sd:* WE. 7 min. • An old couple recall via some old songs: *Just a Song at Twilight, Maggie, The Sidewalks of New York, Little Annie Rooney, The Bowery, In the Good Old Summertime, Daisy Daisy, After the Ball, Put on Your Old Grey Bonnet* and *Silver Threads*.

4400. Musical Moments from Chopin (*Musical Miniatures*) 24 Feb. 1947; *p.c.:* Walter Lantz prods for Univ; *dir:* Dick Lundy; *story:* Ben Hardaway, Milt Schaffer; *anim:* La Verne Harding, Les Kline; *sets:* Fred Brunish; *mus:* Darrell Calker; *pianists:* Ted Saidenberg, Ed Rebner; *prod mgr:* William E. Garity; *col:* Tech. *sd:* RCA. 8 min. • Andy gives a piano recital of Chopin's *Polonaise* and Woody joins in. A drunk sets fire to the concert hall but they manage to finish the piece on time.

4401. Musical Mountaineers (*Betty Boop*) 12 Mar. 1939; *p.c.:* The Fleischer Studio for Para; *prod:* Max Fleischer; *dir:* Dave Fleischer; *anim:* Thomas Johnson, Harold Walker; *voices:* Margie Hines, Pinto Colvig, Jack Mercer; *mus:* Sammy Timberg; *ph:* Charles Schettler; *prod mgr:* Sam Buchwald; b&w. *sd:* WE. 7 min. • Betty is stranded in the Ozarks. The mountain folk rally 'round to put moonshine in her auto engine to send her on her way.

4402. The Musical Parrot (*Aesop's Film Fable*) 2 Jan. 1927; *p.c.:* Fables Pictures Inc for Pathé; *dir:* Paul Terry; b&w. *sil.* 10 min. • A parrot interferes with Al Falfa's game of pool with the cat. They toss the bird out of the window where he lands at the feet of an organ grinder's monkey, resulting in a chase.

4403. Musicalulu (*Little Lulu*) 15 Nov. 1946; *p.c.:* Famous Studio for Para; *dir:* I. Sparber; *story:* Bill Turner, Otto Messmer; *anim:* Myron Waldman, Gordon Whittier, Nick Tafuri, Irving Dressler; *sets:* Anton Loeb; *voices:* Cecil Roy, Jackson Beck, Jack Mercer, Arnold Stang; *mus:* Winston Sharples; *ph:* Leonard McCormick; *prod mgr:* Sam Buchwald; *col:* Tech. *sd:* RCA. 7 min. • Lulu deserts her violin practice for a ball game. She is knocked unconcious and dreams that she is on trial before a musical court.

4404. Mutiny Ain't Nice (*Popeye*) 16 Sept. 1938; *p.c.:* The Fleischer Studio for Para; *prod:* Max Fleischer; *dir:* Dave Fleischer; *anim:* David Tendlar, William Sturm; *voices:* Jack Mercer, Mae Questel; *mus:* Sammy Timberg; *ph:* Charles Schettler; b&w. *sd:* WE. 7 min. • Popeye sets sail with a crew who believe that women on board are bad luck. Olive accidentally is brought aboard, causing a mutiny.

4405. Mutiny on the Bunny (*Looney Tunes*) 18 Feb. 1950; *p.c.:* WB; *dir:* I. Freleng; *story:* Tedd Pierce; *anim:* Gerry Chiniquy, Ken Champin, Virgil Ross, Arthur Davis; *lay:* Hawley Pratt; *back:* Paul Julian; *ed:* Treg Brown; *voices:* Mel Blanc; *mus:* Carl Stalling; *prod mgr:* John W. Burton; *prod:* Edward Selzer; *col:* Tech. *sd:* Vit. 7 min. • Bugs is shanghaied into being a one-man crew aboard Sam's galleon.

4406. Mutt and Jeff • Created by Harry "Bud" Fisher; *distributor:* Celebrated Players; *prod/dir:* Charles Bowers. • *1916:* Jeff's Toothache 1 Apr. Mutt and Jeff in the Submarine 8 Apr. The Indestructible Hats 12 Apr. Cramps. The Promoters. Two for Five. The Dog Pound. The Hock Shop. Wall Street. Mutt and Jeff in the Trenches. *p.c.*—Bud Fisher Film Corp. for Mutt and Jeff Film Exchange; b&w. *sil.* • *1917:* The Submarine Chasers 9 July. The Cheese Tamers. Cows and Caws. The Janitors. A Chemical Calamity. The Prospectors. The Bell Hops. In the Theatrical Business. The Boarding House. The Chamber of Horrors. A Day in Camp. A Dog's Life. The Interpreters. Preparedness. Revenge Is Sweet. *p.c.*—Mutt and Jeff Films Inc for the Fox Film Corp.; b&w. *sil.* • *1918:* The Decoy 24 Mar. Back to the Balkans 31 Mar. The Leak 7 Apr. Freight Investigation 14 Apr. On Ice 21 Apr. Helping McAdoo 28 Apr. A Fisherless Cartoon 5 May. Occultism 12 May. Superintendents 19 May. Tonsorial Artists 26 May. The Tale of a Pig 2 June. Hospital Orderlies 9 June. Life Savers 16 June. Meeting Theda Bara 23 June. The Seventy-Five Mile Gun 30 June. The Burglar Alarm 7 July. The Extra Quick Lunch 14 July. Hunting the U-Boats 21 July. Hotel de Mutt 28 July. Joining the Tanks 4 Aug. An Ace and a Joker 11 Aug. Landing a Spy 18 Aug. Efficiency at the Front 25 Aug. The Accident Attorney 1 Sept. Saving Russia 8 Sept. To the Rescue 15 Sept. The Kaiser's New Dentist 22 Sept. Bulling the Bolshevik 29 Sept. Our Four Days in Germany 6 Oct. The Side Show 13 Oct. Mutt and Jeff 20 Oct. Mutt and Jeff 27 Oct. Mutt and Jeff 3 Nov. A Lot of Bull 10 Nov. The Doughboy 17 Nov. Around the World in Nine Minutes 24 Nov. Pot Luck in the Army 1 Dec. The New Champion 8 Dec. Hitting the High Spots 15 Dec. The Draft Board 22 Dec. Throwing the Bull 29 Dec. • *1919:* The Lion Tamers 5 Jan. Here and There 12 Jan. The Hula Hula Cabaret 19 Jan. Dog-Gone Tough Luck 26 Jan. Landing an Heiress 2 Feb. The Bearded Lady 9 Feb. 5000 Miles on a Gallon of Gas 16 Feb. The Pousse Café 23 Feb. Fireman Save My Child 2 Mar. Wild Waves and Angry Women 9 Mar. William Hohenzollern, Sausage Maker 16 Mar. Out An' in Again 23 Mar. The Cow's Husband 30 Mar. Mutt the Mutt Trainer 6 Apr. Subbing for Tom Mix 13 Apr. Pigtails and Peaches 20 Apr. Seeing Things 27 Apr. The Cave Man's Bride 4 May. Sir Sidney 11 May. Left at the Post 18 May. The Shell Game 25 May. Oh Teacher 1 June. Hands Up 8 June. Sweet Papa 15 June. Pets and Pearls 22 June. A Prize Fight 29 June. Look Pleasant Please 6 July. Downstairs and Up 13 July. Tropical Eggs-pedition 20 July. West Is East 27 July. The Jazz Instructors 3 Aug. Oil's Well That Ends Well 10 Aug. The Frozen North 17 Aug. Sound Your "A" 24 Aug. Hard Lions 31 Aug. Mutt and Jeff in Switzerland 7 Sept. All That Glitters Is Not Goldfish 14 Sept. Everybody's Doing It 21 Sept. Mutt and Jeff in Spain 28 Sept. The Honest Book Agent 5 Oct. New York Night Life 12 Oct. Bound in Spaghetti 19 Oct. In the Money 26 Oct. The Window Cleaners 2 Nov. Confessions of a Telephone Girl 9 Nov. The Plumbers 16 Nov. The Chambermaid's Revenge 23 Nov. Why Mutt Left the Village 30 Nov. Cutting Out His Nonsense 7 Dec. For Bitter or Verse 14 Dec. He Ain't Done Right by Our Nell 21 Dec. Another Man's Wife 28 Dec. • *1920:* A Glutton for Punishment Jan. His Musical Soup Jan. A Rose by Any Other Name Jan. Mutt and Jeff in Iceland Jan. Fisherman's Luck Jan. The Latest in

Underwear Jan. On Strike Jan. Shaking the Shimmy Jan. The Rum Runners Jan. The Berth of a Nation Jan. Mutt and Jeff's Nooze Weekly Jan. Pretzel Farming Jan. I'm Ringing Your Party Feb. Fishing Feb. Dead Eye Jeff Feb. The Sour Violin Feb. The Mint Spy Feb. The Pawnbrokers Feb. The Chemists Feb. Putting on the Dog Feb. The Plumbers Feb. The Great Pickle Robbery Mar. The Price of a Good Sneeze Mar. The Chewing Gum Industry Mar. Hula Hula Town Mar. The Beautiful Model Mar. The Honest Jockey Mar. The Bicycle Race Apr. The Bowling Alley Apr. Nothing but Girls Apr. The Private Detectives Apr. The Wrestlers Apr. The Paper Hangers Apr. The Toy Makers May. The Tango Dancers May. One-Round Jeff May. A Trip to Mars May. Three Raisins and a Cake of Yeast June. Departed Spirits June. The Mystery of the Galvanized Iron Ash Can June. The Breakfast Food Industry June. The Bare Idea July. The Merry Café July. In Wrong Aug. Hot Dogs Aug. The Politicians Aug. The Yacht Race Aug. The Cowpunchers Sept. Home, Sweet Home Sept. Napoleon Sept. The Song Birds Sept. The Tailor Shop Oct. The Brave Toreador Oct. The High Cost of Living Oct. Flapjacks Oct. The League of Nations Oct. A Tightrope Romance Oct. Farm Efficiency Nov. The Medicine Man Nov. Home Brew Nov. Gum Shoe Work Nov. A Hard Luck Santa Claus Nov. All Stuck Up Nov. Sherlock Hawkshaw & Co. Dec. The North Woods Dec. On the Hop Dec. The Papoose Dec. The Hypnotist Dec. Cleopatra Dec. The Parlor Bolshevist Dec. • *1921:* The Lion Hunters 26 Feb. The Ventriloquist 27 Feb. Dr. Killjoy 18 Mar. Factory to Consumer 20 Mar. A Crazy Idea Apr. The Naturalists 17 Apr. Mademoiselle Fifi 7 May. Gathering Coconuts 7 May. It's a Bear 7 May. The Far North 7 May. A Hard Shill Game 14 May. The Vacuum Cleaner 7 May. A Rare Bird 21 May. Flivvering 21 May. The Glue Factory 11 June. Cold Tea 11 June. The Gusher 12 June. Watering the Elephants 26 June. The Far East July. Training Woodpeckers Aug. A Shocking Idea Aug. Touring Aug. Darkest Africa 17 Sept. Not Wedded but a Wife 17 Sept. Crows and Scarecrows 17 Sept. The Painter's Frolic 17 Sept. The Stampede 17 Sept. The Tong Sandwich 17 Sept. Shadowed 18 Oct. The Turkish Bath 18 Oct. The Village Cutups 26 Nov. A Messy Christmas 26 Nov. Fast Freight 26 Nov. • *1922:* The Stolen Snooze Jan. Getting Ahead Jan. Bony Parts Jan. A Ghostly Wallop Jan. Beside the Cider Jan. Long Live the King Jan. The Last Laugh Jan. The Hole Cheese Feb. The Phoney Focus Feb. The Crystal Gazer Feb. Stuck in the Mud Feb. The Last Shot 27 Feb. The Cashier Mar. Any Ice Today Mar. Too Much Soap 12 Mar. Hoot Mon Apr. Golfing Apr. Tin Foiled Apr. Around the Pyramids Apr. Getting Even Apr. Hop, Skip and Jump 15 May. Modern Fishing May. Hither and Thither May. Court Plastered Aug. Falls Ahead Aug. Riding the Goat 17 Sept. The Fallen Archers 1 Oct. Cold Turkey 8 Oct. The Wishing Duck 12 Nov. Bumps and Things 26 Nov. Nearing the End 10 Dec. Gym Jams 30 Dec. • *1923:* Down in Dixie 4 Feb. • *1925: p.c.*—Associated Animators for Short Film Syndicate; b&w. sil. The Magician. The Honest Jockey. Accidents Won't Happen Aug. Soda. Where Am I? Sept. The Bear Facts Oct. Mixing in Mexico 17 Oct. All at Sea 14 Nov. Oceans of Trouble Nov. Thou Shalt Not Pass 5 Dec. A Link Missing 12 Dec. • *1926:* Bombs and Bums Jan. On Thin Ice 20 Feb. When Hell Froze Over 6 Mar. Westward Whoa Apr. Slick Sleuths 1 Aug. Ups and Downs 15 Aug. Playing with Fire 1 Sept. Dog Gone 15 Sept. The Big Swim 1 Oct. Mummy O' Mine 15 Oct. A Roman Scandal 1 Nov. Alona of the South Seas 15 Nov. The Globe Trotters 1 Dec. • See: *Associated Animators*

4407. Mutt and Jeff Studio: aka: Bud Fisher Film Corp. (1917–1923); created by Harry "Bud"Fisher; *distributor:* Mutt & Jeff Film Exchange; *prod/dir:* Raoul Barré, Charles Bowers; *artists:* C.T. "Vet" Anderson, Grace Ashton, Leighton Budd, Dick Boyle, Mannie Davis, F.M. Follett, Richard McShay Friel, Burton F. Gillett, Louis Glackens, George Gregory, Milt Gross, Dick Huemor, Albert Hurter, I. Klein, Helen Kroll, Carl Lederer, Lubotsky, Carl Meyer, Frank & Edith Nankerville, John Renza, Clarence Rigby, Ted Sears, Ben Sharpsteen, Frank Sherman, George Stallings, Paul H. Terry, Vladimir Tytla, Edward J. White.

4408. A Mutt in a Rut (*Looney Tunes*) 23 May 1959; *p.c.:* WB; *dir:* Robert McKimson; *story:* Tedd Pierce; *anim:* George Grandpré, Ted Bonnicksen, Warren Batchelder, Tom Ray; *lay:* Robert Gribbroek; *back:* William Butler; *ed:* Treg Brown; *voices:* Mel Blanc, Arthur Q. Bryan, Daws Butler; *mus:* Milt Franklyn; *prod:* John W. Burton; *col:* Tech. *sd:* Vit. 6

min. • Elmer's dog is shocked by a TV broadcast telling how, when a dog gets too old to serve, his master will take him on a one-way hunting trip. When Elmer suggests they go hunting, Rover believes the worst.

4409. Mutt in a Rut (*Noveltoon*) 27 May 1949; *p.c.:* Famous for Para; *dir:* I. Sparber; *story:* Carl Meyer, Jack Mercer; *anim:* Dave Tendlar, Tom Golden; *sets:* Robert Little; *mus:* Winston Sharples; *ph:* Leonard McCormick; *prod mgr:* Sam Buchwald; *col:* Tech. *sd:* RCA. 8 min. • Dogface's tranquil life is disturbed when a stray kitten is brought into his house. The cat makes him wish he were dead ... but dog heaven isn't all it's cracked-up to be, either!

4410. Mutt n' Bones (*Phantasy*) 25 Aug. 1944; *p.c.:* Colum; *prod:* Dave Fleischer; *dir:* Paul Sommer; *story:* Eddie Seward; *anim:* Chic Otterstrom, Grant Simmons; *mus:* Eddie Kilfeather; *prod mgr:* Albert Spar; b&w. *sd:* RCA. 6 min. • A dog is reluctant to give his only bone for the War Bone Drive.

4411. Mutts About Racing (*Droopy*) 4 Apr. 1958; *p.c.:* MGM; *prod:* Joseph Barbera, William Hanna; *dir:* Michael Lah; *story:* Homer Brightman; *anim:* Irven Spence, Herman Cohen, Bill Schipek, Dick Bickenbach, Carlo Vinci, Ken Southworth; *character des/lay:* Ed Benedict; *back:* F. Montealegre; *ed:* Jim Faris; *voices:* Bill Thompson, Vic Perrin; *mus:* Scott Bradley; *ph:* Jack Stevens; *prod mgr:* Hal Elias; *col:* Tech. *sd:* WE. 6 min. CS. • Daredevil Butch and Buzz Droopy compete for a $100,000 prize in a cross-country sports car race.

4412. Muzzle Tough (*Merrie Melodies*) 26 June 1954; *p.c.:* WB; *dir:* I. Freleng; *story:* Warren Foster; *anim:* Ken Champin, Virgil Ross, Arthur Davis, Manuel Perez; *lay:* Hawley Pratt; *back:* Irv Wyner; *ed:* Treg Brown; *voices:* Mel Blanc, Bea Benaderet; *mus:* Carl Stalling; *prod mgr:* John W. Burton; *prod:* Edward Selzer; *col:* Tech. *sd:* Vit. 7 min. • Granny moves into a new house, much to neighbor Sylvester's delight when he spies a Tweety bird!

4413. My Artistical Temperature (*Popeye*) 19 Mar. 1937; *p.c.:* The Fleischer Studio for Para; *prod:* Max Fleischer; *dir:* Dave Fleischer; *anim:* Seymour Kneitel, Abner Matthews; *voices:* Jack Mercer, Mae Questel, Gus Wickie; *mus:* Sammy Timberg; b&w. *sd:* WE. 7 min. • Olive visits Popeye and Bluto's "Sweet Art Studio" where the boys vie for making a reasonable likeness of her.

4414. My Baby Just Cares for Me (*Screen Songs*) 5 Dec. 1931; *p.c.:* The Fleischer Studio for Para; *prod:* Max Fleischer; *dir:* Dave Fleischer; *mus:* Art Turkisher; *song:* Walter Donaldson, Gus Kahn; b&w. *sd:* WE 6½ min. • A jockey spruces up a dilapidated horse to ride on a merry-go-round and then on to the big race.

4415. My Bonnie (*Ko-Ko Song Car-Tune*) 12 Sept. 1925; *p.c.:* Inkwell Studio for Red Seal; *prod:* Max Fleischer; *dir:* Dave Fleischer; b&w. sil. 5½ min. • The Ko-Ko Quartette are brought from the inkwell to start singing "My Bonnie Lies Over the Ocean." The audience is then encouraged to join in.

4416. My Boy Johnny (*Terry-Toon*) 12 May 1944; *p.c.:* TT for Fox; *dir:* Eddie Donnelly; *story:* John Foster; *mus:* Philip A. Scheib; *col:* Tech. *sd:* RCA. 6 min. *Academy Award nomination.* • The Armed Forces come home from the war and are anxious to resume peace-time living.

4417. My Bunny Lies Over the Sea (*Merrie Melodies*) 4 Dec. 1948; *p.c.:* WB; *dir:* Charles M. Jones; *story:* Michael Maltese; *anim:* Ken Harris, Phil Monroe, Ben Washam, Lloyd Vaughan; *lay:* Robert Gribbroek; *back:* Peter Alvarado; *ed:* Treg Brown; *voices:* Mel Blanc; *mus:* Carl Stalling; *prod mgr:* John W. Burton; *prod:* Edward Selzer; *col:* Tech. *sd:* Vit. 7 min. • Bugs finds himself in Scotland, playing in a golf tournament with a canny Scotsman.

4418. My Daddy the Astronaut (*Fractured Fable*) Mar. 1967; *p.c.:* Para Cartoons; *dir:* Shamus Culhane; *story:* Shamus Culhane, Joseph Szabo; *anim:* Al Eugster; *sets:* Gil Miret; *mus:* Winston Sharples; *prod sup:* Harold Robins, Burt Hanft; *col:* Tech. *sd:* RCA. 6 min. • Drawn as a child's drawings, a small boy relates how his Daddy is able to withstand all the rigors of flying to the moon but unable to cope with a Merry-go-Round at the carnival.

4419. My Darling Nellie Gray (*Ko-Ko Song Car-Tune*) 6 Feb. 1926; *p.c.:* Inkwell Studio for Red Seal; *prod:* Max Fleischer; *dir:* Dave Fleischer; *vocals:* Metropolitan Quartet with Jimmy Flora at the Recording Organ

Console; *song:* B.R. Hanby; *b&w. sd:* DPC. 10 min. • Ko-Ko conducts the Ko-Ko Kwartet and the bouncing ball leads the audience into the Negro lament for a girl who was sold into slavery. Ko-Ko's pup helps illustrate the lyrics until he is chased away by fish.

4420. My Dream Is Yours 1949; *p.c.:* WB; *seq dir:* I. Freleng; *col:* Tech. *sd:* Vit. *l/a/anim.* • Michael Curtiz's live-action comedy about Jack Carson making Doris Day a radio star. Bugs Bunny and Tweety try to arouse a sleeping child while Jack and Doris (dressed as rabbits) sing to the "Hungarian Rhapsody."

4421. My Favorite Duck (*Looney Tunes*) 21 Nov. 1942; *p.c.:* Leon Schlesinger prods for WB; *dir:* Charles M. Jones; *story:* Michael Maltese; *anim:* Rudolph Larriva; *lay:* John McGrew; *back:* Eugene Fleury; *ed:* Treg Brown; *voices:* Mel Blanc; *mus:* Carl W. Stalling; *prod sup:* Henry Binder, Raymond G. Katz; *col:* Tech. *sd:* Vit. 7 min. • Porky tries to set up his tent in the woods but is constantly heckled by Daffy Duck.

4422. My Favorite Martian 12 Feb. 1999; *p.c.:* Disney Enterprises, Inc. for BV; *Zoot/Lizzie monster character anim: Tippett Studio Visual fx: sup:* Phil Tippett, Craig Hayes; *visual fx prod:* Jules Roman; *anim sup:* Trey Stokes, Thomas Schelesny; *compositing sup:* Brennan Doyle; *cg sup:* Doug Epps; *digital lighting sup:* Greg Butler; *anim dpt head:* Jeremy Canton; *snr character anim:* Blair Clark, Petey König; *character anim:* Bobby Beck, Tom Gibbons, Bart Goldman, Eric Levin, Randy Link, Joseph Littlejohn, Mark Schreiber, Tanya Spence, Jesse Sugarman, Robin Watts; *art dpt. sup:* Paula Lucchesi; *lead digital paint:* Belinda van Valkenburg; *anim:* Darby Johnston; *digital fx anim:* Al Arthur; *special visual fx/anim: Available Light Ltd.; visual fx des/sup:* John T. van Vliet; *3d modelling/anim:* W.L. Arnace; *3d anim:* Ajoy Mani, Scott Coulter, Kevin van Hook, Chadd Cole, Marco Mire; *2d anim:* Martin Hilke, Laurel Klick, Martine Tomczyk, Tony Vanezia, Donna Tracy, Warren Fuller; *paper anim:* Jeff Howard; *voice of Zoot:* Wayne Knight; *col:* Tech. *sd:* SDDS/Dolby digital/Digital dts sound. 93 min. *l/a.* • Live-action comedy: A television news announcer discovers a spaceship that has crash-landed along with a Martian who assumes human form. The Martian enlists his help in repairing the spaceship. Animated effects and space suit with a life of its own.

4423. My Friend the Monkey (*Betty Boop*) 27 Jan. 1939; *p.c.:* The Fleischer Studio for Para; *prod:* Max Fleischer; *dir:* Dave Fleischer; *anim:* Thomas Johnson, Frank Endres; *ed:* Kitty Pfister; *voice:* Margie Hines, Joe Oriolo; *mus:* Sammy Timberg; *ph:* Charles Schettler; *prod sup:* Sam Buchwald, Isidore Sparber; *b&w. sd:* WE. 6 min. • An organ-grinder's monkey gives Pudgy the runaround while Betty is away.

4424. My Gal Sal (*Screen Songs*) 18 Oct. 1930; *p.c.:* The Fleischer Studio for Para; *dir:* Dave Fleischer; *anim:* Willard Bowsky, Rudy Eggeman; *mus:* Art Turkisher; *b&w. sd:* WE. 8 min. • A street singer's serenadings annoy the tenants of a tenament. They chuck furniture at him, which he uses to his advantage

4425. My Green Fedora (*Merrie Melodies*) 6 Sept. 1935; *p.c.:* Leon Schlesinger prods for WB; *dir:* Isadore Freleng; *story:* Bob Clampett; *anim:* Charles Jones, Bob Clampett; *voices:* Bernice Hansel, Jackie Morrow; *mus:* Bernard Brown; *prod mgr:* Henry Binder, Raymond G. Katz; *col:* Tech-2. *sd:* Vit. 7 min. • Peter Rabbit goes out, leaving baby Elmer unattended. A hungry weasel appears, captures the bunny and it's up to Peter to rescue him.

4426. My Lady's Garden (*Paul Terry-Toon*) 13 July 1934; *p.c.:* Moser & Terry for Educational; *dir:* Frank Moser, Paul Terry; *mus:* Philip A. Scheib; *b&w. sd:* WE. 6 min. • No story available.

4427. My Little Buckaroo (*Merrie Melodies*) 29 Jan. 1938; *p.c.:* Leon Schlesinger prods for WB; *dir:* I. Freleng; *story:* Ted Pierce; *anim:* Bob McKimson; *lay:* Griff Jay; *back:* Arthur Loomer; *ed:* Tregoweth E. Brown; *voices:* Frederich Lindsley, Mel Blanc, Charlie Lung, Fred Avery; *mus:* Carl W. Stalling; *prod sup:* Henry Binder, Raymond G. Katz; *col:* Tech. *sd:* Vit. 7 min. • A western town is plagued by a notorious bandit until the arrival of a heroic cowboy in the shape of Porky Pig.

4428. My Little Duckaroo (*Merrie Melodies*) 27 Nov. 1954; *p.c.:* WB; *dir:* Charles M. Jones; *story:* Michael Maltese; *anim:* Ken Harris, Ben Washam, Abe Levitow, Richard Thompson, Lloyd Vaughan; *lay:* Maurice Noble; *back:* Philip de Guard; *ed:* Treg Brown; *voices:* Mel Blanc; *mus:* Milt Franklyn; *prod mgr:* John W. Burton; *prod:* Edward Selzer; *col:* Tech. *sd:*

Vit. 7 min. • The Masked Avenger (Daffy Duck) arrives to rid a western town of the local villain.

4429. My Little Pony 14 April 1986; *p.c.:* Sunbow Prods for Miracle; *dir:* Michael Jones; *ex prod:* Margaret Loesch, Lee Gunther; *sup prod:* Jay Bacal; *prod:* Joe Bacal, Tom Griffin; *co-prod:* Michael Jones; *prod ex:* Jim Graziano; *prod sup:* Kwang Son; *prod rep:* Gene Margoulis; *prod co-ord:* Gene Pelc, Terri Gruskin, Jeongkuk, Mary Lou Phipps-Winfrey; *prod mgr:* Carole Weitzman, Beth Gunn-Osborn, Kilwoong Kim; *post prod co-ord:* Jimmy Griffin, Larry Whelan; *scr:* George Arthur Bloom; *story consultant:* Roger Slifer, Buzz Dixon; *graphics:* Pamela Easter; *anim: AKOM Prods: in charge of prod:* Nelson Shin, *TOEI Animation: in charge of prod:* Tomoh Fukumoto; *storyboard dir:* Peter J. Alverado Jr., Barny Cladwell, Cornelius Cole, Kurt W. Conners, Holly Forsyth, Adrian P. Gonzales, Glenn W. Hill, Boyd Kirkland, Debra L. Pugh, Lenord Robinson, Glenn V. Vilppu, Frans Vischer, Wendell O. Washer; *sup anim dir:* Pierre DeCelles, Michael Gallows, Ray Lee; *anim dir:* Brad Case, Joan Case, Gerry Chiniquy, Charlie Downs, Bill Exter, Milton Gray, Bob Krik, Songpil Kim, Heungsun Oh, Inyoung Kim, Akimori Matsubara, Margaret Nichols, Karen Peterson, Tom Ray, Bob Shellhorn, Bob Treat, Gregg Vanzo, Gwen Wetzler, Jaeho Hong, Nakjong Kim, Michihiro Kanayama, Yunsik Kim, Aeeryong Cha; *arts:* Seongsoo Bang, Giyong Bae, Choonyoung Lee, Hankil Oh, Changyul Jung, Osung Kwon, Wongok Li, Dongkwan Park, Jeonggoon Kim, Youngkil Lee, Sangmol Park, Huysub Jang, Seewoo Lee, Songhwan Kim, Yungi Lee, Hyuno Shim, Guidon Chei, Jeensong Hong, Yoansoo Lee, Daisung Im, Jiehyun Hwang, Yisoo Yun, Hangduk Jo, Sangbong Bak, Sooyong Jyung, Gunsel Lee, Jyungyul Song, Daesik Moon, Youngsang Yun, Jyoungsik Shu, Donghyun Lee, Eunk Yen Kim, Bonghi Han, Sooyoung Kwon, Dongchun Jung, Hyunsik Lee, Sengil Hong, Hijyng Yoo, Taeik Kim, Kangmoon Byun, Sunggi Kim, Kwangsin Kan, Ulsung Kim, Eunkuk Kim, Junbox Kim, Sangyong Jung, Jae Jun Kim, Jun Kim, Mengkuk Han, Kenji Yukoyama, Takashi Abe, Kazuhida Fujiwara, Masahiro Sasaki, Tatsuhiro Nagaki, Koji Nashizawa, Koichi Arai, Hideki Hamasu; *asst arts:* Hadsoo Mok, Sookyung Choi, Eunja Park, Jungkeun Jang, Namsoo Chang, Haisung Lee, Yojgbok Kim, Junsik Yoo, Seonghee Kim, Mija Jo, Hyecyoung Hong, Jeeun Yun, Soyun Lee, Jongmo You, Gunhi Hong, Sunyoung Kim; *fx anim:* Yusung Lee, Yunsheop; *lay:* Heungsun Oh, Inyoung Kim, Donghun Shin; *back:* Dennis Venizelos, Youngku Kim, Sun Keun Han, Jaiho Lee, Younggwan Ahn, Seungchui Yang, Junga Park, Hounjoo Park, Heagyoung Lee, Yungsik Chung, Sungki Lee, Youngsoon Lee, Goanseo Goo, Heekyung Lee, Chiseek Song, Eunseo Park, Tomoko Eridate; *des:* Alvero Arce, Mike Hodgson, Walt Peregoy, Carol K. Police, Glenn V. Vilppu; *keys:* Dennis Durrell, Paro Hozumi, Michael Humphries, Paul Julian; *col keys:* Harriette Rossall, Robin Draper, Britt Greko, Younghee Park; *promotional art dir:* Bill Dubay, Gary Hoffman; *model des:* Grigor Boyadjiev, Kurt Conners, Mark Christiansen, Lou Dellarosa, Raymond Johnson, Lynette Nuding, Debra L. Pugh, Stephanie Pyren, Gregg Vanzo, Frans Vischer, Bill Wolf; *ed:* Steven C. Brown, Mike DePatie; *voices: Grundle King:* Danny DeVito; *Draggle:* Madeline Kahn; *Hydia:* Cloris Leachman; *Reeka:* Rhea Perlman; *The Moochik:* Tony Randall; *Megan:* Tammy Amerson; *The Smooze:* Jon Bauman; *Baby Lickety Split/1st Bushwoolie:* Alice Playton; *Spike/Woodland Creature:* Charlie Adler; *Grundle:* Michael Bell; *Buttons/Woodland Creature/Bushwoolie:* Sheryl Bernstein; *Loftie/Grundle/Bushwoolie:* Susan Blu; *North Star:* Cathy Cavadini; *Gusty/4th Bushwoolie:* Nancy Cartwright; *Grundle/Ahgg:* Peter Cullen; *Sundance/2ndBushwoolie:* Laura Dean; *Magic Star:* Ellen Gerstell; *Molly:* Keri Houlihan; *Fizzy/Baby Sundance:* Katie Leigh; *Danny:* Scott Menville; *Sweet Stuff:* Laurel Page; *Wind Whistler:* Sarah Partridge; *Morning Glory/Rosedust/Bushwoolie/Skunk:* Russi Taylor; *Shady/Baby Lofty:* Jill Wayne; *3rd Bushwoolie/Grundle:* Frank Welker; *mus:* Rob Walsh; *orch:* Don McGinnis, William Ashford; *mus prod:* Tony Studd; *mus ed:* Mark Shiney, Peter Collier, Ron Fedele; *songs:* Tommy Goodman, Barry Harman; "My Little Pony" by Spencer Michlin, Ford Kinder; *i&p:* Mary Ann Steward, Insook Sunwoo, Chris Brown, Liane Douglas, Debbie Jorgensborg, Celeste McDonald, Hannah Powell; Heidi Shellhorn, Marta Skwara, Heeson Park, Soonkuk Kim, Ockja Song, Sinsook Lee, Hyounjung Hur, Hyunil Lee, Kyungsoon Jang, Chiaki Hirao, Johnsuk Kim, Mekyoung Shin, Yang Kim, Yeonmi Park, Jungman Park, Sunghee Kim, Bockhee Lee, Youngsoon Young, Sangheun Kim, Hoonhee Lee, Jisoon Lee, Insouk You, Hyangram Lee, Yeasoon An, Yoko Yasunaga, Myrna Gibbs, Britt van der Nagel, Kyeyoung Cho, Myongae Huh, Jehang You, Soonhawn Moon, Hyonsug Choi, Youngran Lee, Sunkyoung Son; *Xerox:* Virginia Creamer, Bill Hudson, Sandy Kennedy, Eunbea Park, Jounghe Kwon, Hyunhe Kil, Eunju Choi, Sungman Kim, Eujin Lee, Moongue Han, Jangwon Choi; *sd:* (Los Angeles) Randy Honaken, Gerry Russell, B&B Sound Studios, Jeff Haboush, Greg Russell, (New York) Jimmy Regan, Mastermind Studios; (mus, Los Angeles) Terry Jennings, Dave Cohen, Wilder Brothers Recording Studios, Saturday Morning Studios, (New York) Mega Music; *re-rec:* Jacquie Freeman; *sd fx ed:* Alison Cobb, Karen Doulac, Dave Hankins, Warren Taylor, Mike Tomack, Peter Tomaszewicz; *ph:* Jongsuk Kim, Jaebog Jung, Sanghoa Lee, Eunill Haw, Changbum Kim, Junho An, Johnhyn Lee, Hisao Shirai; *video ph:* Eunmin Jo; *technical advisers:* Maurene Souza, Roger Avery, Deborah Baker, Jane Bennett, David Bilyeu, Michael Brochstein, Beth Buvarsky, Leah Carr, Al Carosi, Robert Collins, Dorland Crosman, William Culbertson, Regis Dalton, Fred Eddins, Janice Figueroa, Robin Fish, Viktor Guyetsky, Douglas Hart, Deborah Heineman, Arthur Heller, Theodore Herbert, Kirk Hindman, Andrea Hollis, Norman Jacques, Barbara Jenkins, Heide Kahme, Deborah Kaplan, Bob Kelley, Liz Knight, Leonid Kronfeld, Paul Kurnit, Susan Lutehr, Steve Schwartz, Frank Manganiello, Thomas Mangiaratti, Jonathan Maynard, Georgina Melone, Susanne Merrigan, Myrtis Moody, Cheryl Moriarty, Charlie Muenchinger, Khipra Nichols, Marty Obsatz, David O'Connell, Orlando Ortiz-Vaccaro, Robert Pagano, Maureen Patterson, Marvin Porter, Roseann Radosevich, Jack Ratier, Mary Sue Robinson, Rich Rossi, Shari Stokols, James Toatley, James Tout, Hildy Travis, Laura Van Etten, Susan Wakeen, Becky Williams, William Walker, Jo Wood, Cathy Yazujian, Bonnie Zacherie; *prod asst:* Tricia Walsh; *col:* Tech. *sd:* Dolby stereo. 100 min. • As the residents of Ponyland prepare for their annual Spring Festival, the wicked witch Hydia orders her daughters to terminate the citizens' enjoyment. A mammoth sludge creature is conjured up to engulf the land and the ponies call in Megan, a human child, to help them. Megan employs the help of the troll-like Grundles, who all go in search of the Flutter Ponies. Together they all beat Hydia and have an enjoyable festival.

4430. My Man Jasper (*Puppetoon*) 19 Oct. 1945; *p.c.:* George Pal prods for Para; *prod/dir:* George Pal; *voices:* Roy Glenn Jr., Glenn Leedy; *mus:* Clarence Wheeler; *col:* Tech. *sd:* WE. 8 min. • After having tricked Jasper out of his possessions, The Crow and Scarecrow dream they are on trial for theft.

4431. My Old Kentucky Home (*Ko-Ko Song Car-Tune*) 13 Mar. 1926; *p.c.:* Inkwell Studio for Red Seal; *prod:* Max Fleischer; *dir:* Dave Fleischer; *mus score:* Carl Edouarde; *vocals:* The Metropolitan Quartet with Jimmy Flora at the Recording Organ Console; b&w. *sd:* DPC. 4 min. • Pinkie the Pup has trouble with eating a ham until he sharpens his teeth. He then plays a trombone and requests the audience to sing along as a brass band emerges from the inkwell ... all in perfect synchronization.

4432. My Old Kentucky Home (*Mighty Mouse*) 29 Mar. 1946; *p.c.:* TT for Fox; *dir:* Eddie Donnelly; *story:* John Foster; *voice:* Roy Halee; *mus:* Philip A. Scheib; *ph:* Douglas Moye; *col:* Tech. *sd:* RCA. 7 min. • When a wolf landlord finds the Colonel can't pay the mortgage on his homestead, he demands his daughter's hand in payment.

4433. My Pal Paul (*Oswald*) 16 June 1930; *p.c.:* Univ; *dir:* Walter Lantz; *anim:* "Bill" Nolan, Ray Abrams, Manuel Moreno, Clyde Geronimi; *mus:* James Dietrich; b&w. *sd:* WE. 7 min. • Paul Whiteman stops Oswald's attempted suicide and Ozzie tries to fix his car.

4434. My Pony Boy (*Screen Songs*) 13 Sept. 1929; *p.c.:* The Fleischer Studio for Para; *prod:* Max Fleischer; *dir:* Dave Fleischer; *song:* J. Hugh O'Donnell, Hy Heath; b&w. *sd:* WE. 6 min. • No story available.

4435. My Pop, My Pop (*Popeye*) 18 Oct. 1940; *p.c.:* The Fleischer Studio for Para; *prod:* Max Fleischer; *dir:* Dave Fleischer; *story:* William Turner; *anim:* Arnold Gillespie, Abner Kneitel; *sets:* Anton Loeb; *ed:* Kitty Pfister; *voices:* Jack Mercer; *mus:* Sammy Timberg; *ph:* Charles Schettler; *prod sup:* Sam Buchwald, Isidore Sparber; b&w. *sd:* WE. 6 min. • Popeye and Pappy respectively each build one side of a boat.

4436. My Son the King 1970; *p.c.:* Bob Kurtz prods/AFI; *prod/dir:* Bob Kurtz; *anim:* Duane Crowther, Gary Mooney, Bob Kurtz; *des:* Jack Heiter; *ed:* Paul Wittenberg, Dick Einfield; *voices:* Howard Morris, Muriel Landers, Rori Gwynn; *ph:* Film Fair: Tom Barnes; col. *sd.* 10 min. • A Jewish mama extols the virtues of her son who happens to be a king.

4437. My Wife's Gone to the Country (*Screen Songs*) 13 June 1931; *p.c.:* The Fleischer Studio for Para; *prod:* Max Fleischer; *dir:* Dave Fleischer; *mus:* Art Turkisher; *song:* Irving Berlin; b&w. *sd:* WE. 6 min. • A man sings of the joys of his wife going away, unaware she is listening to him on the radio. She reaches through the speaker and socks him.

4438. Mysteries of Old Chinatown (*Aesop's Film Fable*) 3 Dec. 1924; *p.c.:* Fables Pictures Inc for Pathé; *dir:* Paul Terry; b&w. *sil.* 5 min. • A mouse pursues his kidnapped sweetie through Chinatown. He overtakes the kidnapper's flying rickshaw by means of climbing the stars seen by a dazed Chinaman.

4439. Mysteries of the Sea (*Aesop's Film Fable*) 19 July 1923; *p.c.:* Fables Pictures Inc for Pathé; *dir:* Paul Terry; b&w. *sil.* 5 min. • By means of an ingenious apparatus, the cat goes to the bottom of the sea and witnesses a procession of strange fish and buried treasure.

4440. The Mysterious Cowboy (*Terry-Toon*) Aug. 1952; *p.c.:* TT for Fox; *dir:* Mannie Davis; *story/voice:* Tom Morrison; *sets:* Art Bartsch; *mus:* Philip A. Scheib; *ph:* Douglas Moye; *col:* Tech. *sd:* RCA. 6 min. • A masked cowboy and his Indian friend, Pronto, are on the trail of Bad Bill Bunion after learning he plans to rob the stagecoach.

4441. The Mysterious Jug (*Oswald*) 29 Nov. 1937; *p.c.:* Univ; *prod/dir:* Walter Lantz; *story:* Walter Lantz, James Miele; *anim:* Lester Kline, Fred Kopietz, George Nicholas; *voices:* Bernice Hansel, Billy Bletcher, Shirley Reed; *mus:* Nathaniel Shilkret; b&w. *sd:* WE. 6 min. • Oswald finds a magician's trunk. When he opens it, a genie materializes and makes the junkyard objects animate. A Devil appears and traps him but Oswald rescues the genie and encases the Devil.

4442. Mysterious Mose (*Talkartoons*) 27 Dec. 1930; *p.c.:* The Fleischer Studio for Para; *prod:* Max Fleischer; *dir:* Dave Fleischer; *story:* Ted Sears; *anim:* Willard Bowsky, Ted Sears; *mus:* Art Turkisher; *song:* Doyle; b&w. *sd:* WE. 6 min. • Betty Boop has a visitor on a dark and stormy night who turns out to be Bimbo.

4443. The Mysterious Package (*Terry-Toon*) Jan. 1961; *p.c.:* TT for Fox; *ex prod:* Bill Weiss; *dir:* Mannie Davis; *story supl/voices:* Tom Morrison; *story:* Bob Kuwahara; *anim:* Ed Donnelly, Ralph Bakshi, Larry Silverman; *lay:* John Zago, *des/back:* Martin Strudler; *mus:* Phil Scheib; *prod mgr:* Frank Schudde; *col:* DeLuxe. *sd:* RCA. 6 min. • Mighty Mouse is called upon to find out why the mice children disappear after recieving a mysterious gift of a space helmet.

4444. The Mysterious Stranger (*Mighty Mouse*) 21 Dec. 1948; *p.c.:* TT for Fox; *dir:* Eddie Donnelly; *story:* John Foster; *anim:* Jim Tyer; *voices:* Tom Morrison; *mus:* Philip A. Scheib; *ph:* Douglas Moye; *col:* Tech. *sd:* RCA. 6 min. • In a big top setting. Oil-Can Harry chases Pearl Pureheart until "The Lone Stranger" reveals his true identity as Mighty Mouse.

4445. The Mystery Box (*Technical Romances*) 28 Nov. 1922; *p.c.:* Bray prods for W.W.Hodkinson Corp; *dir/story:* J.A. Norling; b&w. *sil.* 5 min. • Dealing with how radio works.

4446. Mystery in the Moonlight (*Terry-Toon*) Apr. 1948; *p.c.:* TT for Fox; *dir:* Eddie Donnelly; *story:* John Foster; *voice:* Thomas Morrison; *mus:* Philip A. Scheib; *ph:* Douglas Moye; *col:* Tech. *sd:* RCA. 6 min. • A mouse watches a mystery TV show centering around a black cat who arrives in his house and proceeds to torment him and his bulldog friend.

4447. Mystic Pink (*Pink Panther*) 6 Jan. 1976; *p.c.:* Mirisch/Geoffrey/DFE for UA; *dir:* Robert McKimson; *story:* John W. Dunn; *anim:* John Gibbs, Bob Richardson, Don Williams, Norm McCabe; *lay:* Dick Ung; *back:* Richard H. Thomas; *ed:* Rick Steward; *mus:* Walter Greene; *theme tune:* Henry Mancini; *ph:* John Burton Jr.; *prod mgr:* Lee Gunther; *col:* DeLuxe. *sd:* RCA. 6 min. • The Panther finds a magician's hat and an enormous white rabbit that emerges from it.

4448. Mysto Fox (*Fox & Crow*) 29 Aug. 1946; *p.c.:* Colum; *dir:* Bob Wickersham; *story:* Sid Marcus; *anim:* Chic Otterstrom, Ben Lloyd; *sets:* Clark Watson; *ed:* Richard S. Jensen; *voices:* Frank Graham, Harry E. Lang; *mus:* Eddie Kilfeather; *ph:* Frank Fisher; *prod mgr:* Hugh McCollum; *col:* Tech. *sd:* WE. 7 min. • The Crow, disguised as a rabbit, assists Mysto Fox's magic act and it's not long before he is sawing the magician in half.

4449. Napoleon Blown-Aparte (*Inspector*) 2 Feb. 1966; *p.c.:* Mirisch/DFE for UA; *dir:* Gerry Chiniquy; *story:* John W. Dunn; *anim:* Manny Perez, Don Williams, Bob Matz, Warren Batchelder, Norm McCabe,

George Grandpré; *sets:* T.M. Yakutis; *ed:* Lee Gunther; *voices:* Pat Harrington Jr., Larry Storch; *mus:* William Lava; *theme tune:* Henry Mancini; *prod mgr:* William Orcutt; *col:* DeLuxe. *sd:* RCA. 6 min. • The Inspector guards the Commissioner from "The Mad Bomber" who has sworn to get even for being put in jail.

4450. Napoleon Bunny-Part (*Merrie Melodies*) 16 June 1956; *p.c.:* WB; *dir:* Friz Freleng; *story:* Warren Foster; *anim:* Gerry Chiniquy, Virgil Ross, Arthur Davis; *lay:* Hawley Pratt; *back:* Irv Wyner; *ed:* Treg Brown; *voices:* Mel Blanc; *mus:* Carl Stalling; *prod mgr:* John W. Burton; *prod:* Edward Selzer; *col:* Tech. *sd:* Vit. 7 min. • Bugs has a run-in with "The Little General" and is pursued as being a spy, barely escaping with his head!

4451. Nasty Quacks (*Merrie Melodies*) 27 Oct. 1945; *p.c.:* WB; *dir:* Frank Tashlin; *story:* Warren Foster; *anim:* Art Davis, I. Ellis, Richard Bickenbach; *sets:* Richard H. Thomas; *ed:* Treg Brown; *voices:* Mel Blanc, Robert C. Bruce, Sara Berner; *mus:* Carl Stalling; *prod mgr:* John W. Burton; *prod:* Edward Selzer; *col:* Tech. *sd:* Vit. 7 min. • A little girl's father gives her a pet duckling that grows up to be the thorn in the father's side. Sick of the pest, he tries to dispose of it.

4452. Nature's Work Shop (*Pooch the Pup*) 5 June 1933; *p.c.:* Univ; *dir:* Walter Lantz; *anim:* Manuel Moreno, Lester Kline, Fred Kopietz, Charles Hastings, Ernest Smythe; *mus:* James Dietrich; *b&w. sd:* WE. 8 min. • With the aid of a magnifying glass, Pooch spies on Mother Nature. He sees bees getting honey from a flower filling station and helps rescue the Queen Bee.

4453. Naughty but Mice (*Merrie Melodies*) 10 May 1939; *p.c.:* Leon Schlesinger prods for WB; *dir:* Charles M. Jones; *story:* Rich Hogan, Robert Clampett; *anim:* Phil Monroe; *lay:* Robert Givens; *back:* Paul Julian; *character des:* Charles Thorson; *ed:* Tregoweth E. Brown; *voices:* Margaret Hill, Mel Blanc; *mus:* Carl W. Stalling; *prod sup:* Henry Binder, Raymond G. Katz; *col:* Tech. *sd:* RCA. 6½ min. • Sniffles seeks a cold remedy in a drugstore and finds it in alcoholic rub. The tipsy mouse then befriends an electric shaver who saves him from the grasp of the cat.

4454. Naughty but Mice (*Noveltoon*) 10 Oct. 1947; *p.c.:* Famous for Para; *dir:* Seymour Kneitel; *story:* Bill Turner, Larry Riley; *anim:* Dave Tendlar, Al Eugster; *sets:* Robert Owen; *voices:* Arnold Stang, Sid Raymond; *mus:* Winston Sharples; *ph:* Leonard McCormick; *prod mgr:* Sam Buchwald; *col:* Tech. *sd:* RCA. 6½ min. • The country mice call in Herman to rid the farm of Sam the cat, who ends up down the well, leaving the rest of his nine lives to deal with the mice.

4455. Naughty Neighbors (*Looney Tunes*) 4 Nov. 1939; *p.c.:* Leon Schlesinger prods for WB; *dir:* Robert Clampett; *story:* Warren Foster; *anim:* I. Ellis; *ed:* Tregoweth E. Brown; *voices:* Mel Blanc, Shirley Reed, The Sons of the Pioneers, Danny Webb; *mus:* Carl W. Stalling; *prod sup:* Henry Binder, Raymond G. Katz; *b&w. sd:* Vit. 7 min. • Petunia Pig, the official head of the Martin clan and Porky (a McCoy) try to put an end to the age-long feud between their families.

4456. The Nautical Nut (*Woody Woodpecker*) Mar. 1967; *p.c.:* Walter Lantz prods for Univ; *dir:* Paul J. Smith; *story:* Sid Marcus; *anim:* Les Kline, Al Coe; *sets:* Ray Huffine; *voices:* Daws Butler, Grace Stafford; *mus:* Clarence Wheeler; *prod mgr:* William E. Garity; *col:* Tech. *sd:* RCA. 6 min. • A pirate loses the ship's lucky rabbit mascot but returns with Woody. Since woodpeckers are deemed unlucky by the Captain he tries to get rid of him ... which is easier said than done!

4457. The Navy (*Oswald*) 3 Nov. 1930; *p.c.:* Univ; *dir:* Walter Lantz, "Bill" Nolan; *anim:* Clyde Geronimi, Manuel Moreno, Ray Abrams, Fred Avery, Lester Kline, "Pinto" Colvig; *mus:* James Dietrich; *b&w. sd:* WE. 6 min. • Oswald is ordered to clean up a Man-of-War by the bullying Admiral.

4458. Neapolitan Mouse (*Tom & Jerry*) 2 Oct. 1954; *p.c.:* MGM; *dir:* William Hanna, Joseph Barbera; *anim:* Ed Barge, Irven Spence, Ray Patterson, Kenneth Muse; *lay:* Dick Bickenbach; *back:* John Didrik Johnsen; *ed:* Jim Faris; *mus:* Scott Bradley; *song:* E. di Capua; *ph:* Jack Stevens; *prod:* Fred Quimby; *col:* Tech. *sd:* WE. 7 min. • Tom and Jerry visit Naples where they befriend an Italian mouse who shows them the sights of Napoli.

4459. Nearlyweds (*Popeye*) 8 Feb. 1957; *p.c.:* Famous for Para; *dir:* Seymour Kneitel; *story:* I. Klein; *anim:* Tom Johnson, Frank Endres; *sets:* John Zago; *voices:* Jack Mercer, Jackson Beck, Mae Questel; *mus:* Winston Sharples; *ph:* Leonard McCormick; *prod mgr:* Seymour Shultz; *col:* Tech. *sd:* RCA. 6 min. • Bluto stops at nothing to sabotage Popeye's forthcoming marriage to Olive.

4460. Nearsighted and Far Out (*Modern Madcap*) Nov. 1964; *p.c.:* Para Cartoons; *dir:* Seymour Kneitel; *story:* Joe Cal Cagno; *anim:* I. Klein; *sets:* Robert Little; *voices:* Bob MacFadden, Shari Lewis; *mus:* Winston Sharples; *ph:* Leonard McCormick; *prod mgr:* Abe Goodman; *col:* Tech. *sd:* RCA. 6 min. • Squeegee tries to convert a nearsighted aardvark who has fallen in love with a vacuum cleaner.

4461. Neath the Bababa Tree (*Dr. Seuss Cartoon*) 1 June 1931; *p.c.:* Audio-Cinema/WB for Stanco, Co.; *adapt:* Irving A. Jacoby; *anim:* Dr. Seuss, Frank Little; *mus:* Philip A. Scheib; *b&w. sd:* WE. 5 min. • Commercial for Flit fly spray.

4462. Neck and Neck (*Terry-Toon*) 15 May 1942; *p.c.:* TT for Fox; *dir:* Mannie Davis; *story:* John Foster; *mus:* Philip A. Scheib; *col:* Tech. *sd:* RCA. 7 min. • Dogbiscuit, the champion racehorse falls in love just before his most important race.

4463. Neck 'n' Neck (*Oswald the Lucky Rabbit*) 23 Jan. 1928; *p.c.:* Winkler for Univ; *dir:* Walt Disney; *anim:* Hugh Harman, Rollin C. Hamilton; *ph:* Mike Marcus; *b&w. sil.* 5 min. • Oswald takes his sweetie for a hectic drive that culminates in a crash.

4464. Neighbors (*Color Rhapsody*) 15 Aug. 1935; *p.c.:* Charles Mintz prods for Colum; *story:* Sid Marcus; *anim:* Art Davis; *mus:* Joe de Nat; *col:* Tech-2. *sd:* RCA. 7 min. • A mercenary vulture sells a rooster a gun, then tells his neighbor to arm himself against the rooster. They both eventually arm themselves with an arsenal of weapons and kill each other while the vulture profits.

4465. Nellie of the Circus (*Mello-Drama*) 8 May 1939; *p.c.:* Walter Lantz prods for Univ; *dir:* Alex Lovy; *story:* Victor McLeod, James Miele; *anim:* Merle Gilson, Ray Fahringer; *sets:* Edgar Keichle; *voice:* Mel Blanc, Dave Weber; *mus:* Frank Marsales; *b&w. sd:* WE. 7 min. • Nellie is captured by Rascally Ratbone, a circus talent scout who makes her a trapeze artist. Dan rescues her and puts Ratbone in his rightful place.

4466. Nellie the Indian Chief's Daughter (*New Universal Cartoon*) 6 June 1938; *p.c.:* Univ; *prod:* Walter Lantz; *dir:* Alex Lovy; *story:* Victor McLeod, Win Smith; *anim:* La Verne Harding, George Dane; *sets:* Edgar Keichle; *voices:* Billy Bletcher, Shirley Reed, Dave Weber; *mus:* Frank Churchill; *b&w. sd:* WE. 7 min. • Nellie is rescued from Rudolph Ratbone by Bennie Bigwind Gooseskin, the swing band man.

4467. Nellie the Sewing Machine Girl (or) Honest Hearts and Willing Hands (*New Universal Cartoon*) 11 Apr. 1938; *p.c.:* Univ; *dir:* Alex Lovy; *story:* Victor McLeod, James Miele; *anim:* Ray Fahringer, George Grandpré; *sets:* Edgar Keichle; *voices:* Billy Bletcher, Shirley Reed, Mel Blanc; *mus:* Frank Marsales; *b&w. sd:* WE. 6 min. • In this melodrama we find Nellie tied to a sawmill with Harold reduced to eating a can of spinach to gain enough strength to rescue her.

4468. Nell's Yells (*Color Rhapsody*) 30 June 1939; *p.c.:* Cartoon Films Ltd/Charles Mintz prods for Colum; *prod/dir:* Ub Iwerks; *ed:* George Winkler; *voices:* Mel Blanc; *mus:* Eddie Kilfeather, Joe de Nat; *prod mgr:* James Bronis; *col:* Tech. *sd:* RCA. 7 min. • Old fashioned melodrama: The villain kidnaps little Nell and it's up to the inept hero, Horatio, to rescue her.

4469. Nelly's Folly (*Merrie Melodies*) Dec. 1961; *p.c.:* WB; *dir:* Chuck Jones; *asst dir:* Maurice Noble, Abe Levitow; *story:* Dave DeTiege, Chuck Jones; *anim:* Richard Thompson, Ben Washam, Tom Ray, Ken Harris; *back:* Philip de Guard; *ed:* Treg Brown; *voices:* Ed Prentiss, Gloria Wood, John A. Ford, Mel Blanc; *mus:* Milt Franklyn; *prod:* David H. DePatie; *col:* Tech. *sd:* Vit. 7 min. *Academy Award nomination.* • A singing giraffe is taken from the jungle and made a big star in the USA.

4470. Neptune Nonsense (*Rainbow Parade*) 20 Mar. 1936; *p.c.:* Van Beuren for RKO; *dir:* Burt Gillett, Tom Palmer; *sets:* Art Bartsch, Eddi Bowlds; *voice:* Jimmy Donnelly; *mus:* Winston Sharples; *col:* Tech. *sd:* RCA. 7 min. • Felix the Cat goes beneath the ocean to find a playmate for his pet goldfish.

4471. Nero and His Jazz Band (*Red Head Comedy*) 1925; *dir/story:* Richard M. Friel; *anim:* Frank Nankerville; *b&w. sil.* 8 min. *l/a/anim.* • A small boy is reprimanded for reading Westerns instead of practicing the violin. He falls asleep and dreams he's a fiddler in Nero's court.

4472. Nervy Nat Has His Fortune Told (*Sullivan Cartoon Comedy*) 13 Dec. 1916; *p.c.:* Powers for Univ; *prod/dir:* Pat Sullivan; b&w. *sil.* 4 min. • No story available.

4473. Never Bug an Ant (*Ant & Aardvark*) 2 Feb. 1969; *p.c.:* Mirisch/DFE for UA; *dir:* Gerry Chiniquy; *story:* David DeTiege; *anim:* Warren Batchelder, Don Williams, Manny Gould, Manny Perez; *lay:* Dick Ung; *back:* Tom O'Loughlin; *ed:* Lee Gunther; *voices:* John Byner; *mus:* Doug Goodwin, Ray Brown, Billy Byers, Jimmy Rowles, Tommy Tedesco, Shelly Manne; *ph:* John Burton Jr.; *prod sup:* Jim Foss, Harry Love; *col:* DeLuxe. *sd:* RCA. 6 min. • A typical day in the life of the Aardvark who tries anything from sugar to an iron ball to snare his prey.

4474. Never Kick a Woman (*Popeye*) 28 Aug. 1936; *p.c.:* The Fleischer Studio for Para; *prod:* Max Fleischer; *dir:* Dave Fleischer; *anim:* Seymour Kneitel, Roland Crandall; *voices:* Jack Mercer, Mae Questel; *mus:* Sammy Timberg; b&w. *sd:* WE. 7 min. • Popeye drags Olive into a Sports shop. Olive takes umbrage to the pretty assistant's flirtations and a fight breaks out.

4475. Never on Thirsty (*Tijuana Toads*) 5 Aug. 1970; *p.c.:* Mirisch/DFE for UA; *dir:* Hawley Pratt; *story:* John W. Dunn; *anim:* Manny Gould, Don Williams, Robert Taylor, Manny Perez, Ken Muse; *lay:* Dick Ung; *back:* Richard Thomas; *ed:* Allan Potter; *voices:* Tom Holland, Don Diamond; *mus:* Doug Goodwin; *ph:* John Burton Jr.; *prod sup:* Jim Foss, Harry Love; *col:* DeLuxe. *sd:* RCA. 6 min. • The thirsty toads have to first get by a fierce watchdog to get to a swimming pool.

4476. Never Sock a Baby (*Popeye*) 3 Nov. 1939; *p.c.:* The Fleischer Studio for Para; *prod:* Max Fleischer; *dir:* Dave Fleischer; *anim:* William Henning, Abner Matthews; *sets:* Shane Miller; *voice:* Jack Mercer; *mus:* Sammy Timberg; b&w. *sd:* WE. 5½ min. • Popeye gives Swee'Pea a good hiding, forcing the babe to run away from home and our hero has to retrieve him.

4477. The New Car (*Flip the Frog*) 25 July 1931; *p.c.:* Celebrity prods for MGM; *prod/dir:* Ub Iwerks; *mus:* Gene Denny; b&w. *sd:* PCP. 8 min. • When taking his girl for a spin in his new flivver, Flip runs out of gas and gets a passing drunk to top up the tank with some of his booze. This shoots the car into action and they end up on the railway tracks.

4478. The New Deal Show (*Betty Boop*) 22 Oct. 1937; *p.c.:* The Fleischer Studio for Para; *prod:* Max Fleischer; *dir:* Dave Fleischer; *anim:* Hicks Lokey, Lillian Friedman; *voice:* Mae Questel; *mus:* Sammy Timberg; b&w. *sd:* WE. 6 min. • Betty campaigns for a new deal for pets in alliance with the current "New Deal Policy."

4479. The New Homestead (*Scrappy*) 7 Jan. 1938; *p.c.:* Charles Mintz prods for Colum; *story:* Art Davis; *anim:* Sid Marcus; *voices:* Robert Winkler, Dave Weber; *mus:* Joe de Nat; *prod mgr:* James Bronis; *sd:* RCA. 6 min. • Scrappy and Petey Parrot try to construct a house. Caricature of Ned Sparks.

4480. The New Neighbor (*Donald Duck*) 1 Aug. 1953; *p.c.:* Walt Disney prods for RKO; *dir:* Jack Hannah; *story:* Nick George, Milt Schaffer; *anim:* Al Coe, George Kreisl, Volus Jones, Ed Aardal; *fx:* Dan MacManus; *lay:* Yale Gracey; *back:* Thelma Witmer; *voices:* Billy Bletcher, Bill Walsh, Art Gilmore, Clarence Nash; *mus:* Edward Plumb; *col:* Tech. *sd:* RCA. 7 min. • Donald's war with his next-door neighbor reaches marathon proportions.

4481. The New Spirit (*Donald Duck*) 23 Jan. 1942; *p.c.:* Walt Disney prods for U.S. Treasury Dpt/The War Activities Committee/National Screen; *dir:* Ben Sharpsteen, Wilfred Jackson; *asst dir:* Lou Debney; *story:* Joe Grant, Dick Huemer; *anim:* Edwin Aardal, Andrew Engman, Dan MacManus, Josh Meador, Don Patterson; *lay:* A. Kendall O'Connor; *voices:* Fred Shields, Cliff Edwards, Eddie Holden, Clarence Nash, The Sportsmen; *mus/song:* Oliver Wallace; *col:* Tech. *sd:* RCA. 8 min. *Academy Award nomination.* • Donald is inspired by "The New Spirit" to willingly pay his income tax, realizing it will help the War Effort.

4482. The Newcomer (*Terry-Toon*) 21 Oct. 1938; *p.c.:* TT for Fox; *dir:* Mannie Davis; *mus:* Philip A. Scheib; b&w. *sd:* RCA. 7 min. • No story available.

4483. The Newlyweds (1913–1914); created by George E. McManus; *p.c.:* Eclair Film Co. Inc.; *dir/anim:* Emile Cohl (aka: Emile Courtet); b&w. *sil.* • *1913:* When He Wants a Dog He Wants a Dog 18 Jan.

Business Must Not Interfere 15 Mar. He Wants What He Wants When He Wants It 29 Mar. Poor Little Chap, He Was Only Dreaming 20 Apr. He Loves to Watch the Flight of Time 18 May. He Ruins His Family's Reputation 1 June. He Slept Well 15 June. He Was Not Ill, Only Unhappy 19 June. It Is Hard to Please Him but It Is Worth It 13 July. He Poses for His Portrait 27 July. He Loves to Be Amused 19 Oct. He Likes Things Upside-Down 14 Dec. • *1914:* He Does Not Care to Be Photographed 17 Jan. He Never Objects to Noise Feb. He Only Wanted to Play with Dodo Feb. • Celebrated French animator, Emile Cohl brought George McManus' comic strip to life, centering around a newly married couple's difficult child, Snookums.

4484. News 24 Feb. 1931; *prod:* Maurice Eugene Kains; b&w. *sd.* • Animated letters of a compass.

4485. News Hound (*Noveltoon*) 10 June 1955; *p.c.:* Famous for Para; *dir:* I. Sparber; *story:* Jack Mercer; *anim:* Al Eugster, Gerorge Germanetti; *sets:* Robert Owen; *voices:* Sid Raymond, Jackson Beck; *mus:* Winston Sharples; *ph:* Leonard McCormick; *prod mgr:* Seymour Shultz; *col:* Tech. *sd:* RCA. 6 min. • When Snapper, a news reporter, photographs Public Enemy #1, it leads to a lot of trouble.

4486. News Oddities (*Phantasy*) 19 July 1940; *p.c.:* Colum; *story:* Harry Love; *anim:* Allen Rose; *lay:* Clark Watson; *back:* Phil Davis; *ed:* George Winkler; *voices:* Mel Blanc, Danny Webb; *mus:* Joe de Nat; *prod mgr:* James Bronis; b&w. *sd:* RCA. 6 min. • No story available.

4487. Newslaffs *p.c.:* FBO; *prod/anim:* William C. Nolan; b&w. *sil.* • *1927:* (1) 4 Sept.; (2) 18 Sept.; (3) 2 Oct.; (4) 16 Oct.; (5) 30 Oct.; (6) 13 Nov.; (7) 27 Nov.; (8) 11 Dec.; (9) 25 Dec.; (11) 22 Dec. • *1928:* (10) 8 Jan.; (12) 5 Feb.; (13) 19 Feb.; (14) 2 Mar.; (15) 2 Mar.; (16) 5 Mar.; (17) 16 Apr.; (18) 30 Apr.; (19) 14 May; (20) 28 May; (21) 11 June; (22) 25 June; (23) 9 July; (24) 23 July.

4488. Niagara Fools (*Woody Woodpecker*) 22 Oct. 1956; *p.c.:* Walter Lantz prods for Univ; *dir:* Paul J. Smith; *story:* Milt Schaffer, Dick Kinney; *anim:* Les Kline, Robert Bentley; *sets:* Art Landy, Raymond Jacobs; *voices:* Bob Johnson, Grace Stafford; *mus:* Clarence Wheeler; *prod mgr:* William E. Garity; *col:* Tech. *sd:* RCA. 6 min. • The Niagara Falls Ranger is determined to stop Woody from going over the falls in a barrel.

4489. Nice Doggy (*Terry Bears*) Oct. 1952; *p.c.:* TT for Fox; *dir:* Connie Rasinski; *story:* Tom Morrison; *anim:* Jim Tyer; *sets:* Art Bartsch; *voices:* Douglas Moye, Tom Morrison, Philip A. Scheib; *mus:* Philip A. Scheib; *ph:* Douglas Moye; *col:* Tech. *sd:* RCA. 6 min. • Papa Bear is set against the cubs bringing a large St. Bernard dog in the house as a pet.

4490. Nick's Coffee Pot (*Terry-Toon*) 19 May 1938; *p.c.:* TT for Fox; *dir:* Connie Rasinski; *story:* John Foster; *mus:* Philip A. Scheib; b&w. *sd:* RCA. 7 min. • The bugs all come to Nick's Coffee Pot. A spider kidnaps the girl and is vanquished by the hero.

4491. The Nifty Nineties (*Mickey Mouse*) 20 June 1941; *p.c.:* Walt Disney prods for RKO; *dir:* Riley Thomson; *asst dir:* Ray de Vally; *anim:* Richard Brown, Les Clark, George de Beeson, John Elliotte, Walt Kelly, Ward Kimball, Fred Moore, Claude Smith, David "Bud" Swift, Don Tobin, Marvin Woodward; *fx:* Art Fitzpatrick, Jack Huber, Paul B. Kossoff, Frank Onaitis, Reuben Timmens, Cornett Wood; *lay:* Charles Connor; *voices:* Marcellite Wall, Walt Disney, The Sportsmen, Ward Kimball, Fred Moore; *mus:* Charles Wolcott; "Father, Dear Father": Henry C. Work; illustrated by Virgil Partch; *col:* Tech. *sd:* RCA. 8 min. • Mickey takes Minnie to see an old-time vaudeville show and then have a precarious automobile ride. Caricatures of Ward Kimball and Fred Moore as a couple of corny comics.

4492. Night (*Silly Symphony*) 18 Apr. 1930; *p.c.:* Walter E. Disney for Colum; *dir:* Walt Disney; *anim:* Johnny Cannon, Les Clark, David D. Hand, Norm Ferguson, Wilfred Jackson, Jack King, Tom Palmer,; *back:* Emil Flohri, Carlos Manriquez; *mus:* Bert Lewis; *ph:* William Cottrell; b&w. *sd:* PCP. 6 min. • A musical fantasy with owls, frogs and fireflies, set in an old mill that catches fire.

4493. The Night Before Christmas (*MGM Cartoon*) 6 Dec. 1941; *p.c.:* MGM; *prod:* Rudolf Ising; *dir:* William Hanna, Joseph Barbera; *anim:* Wilson D. (Pete) Burness, Kenneth Muse, Jack Zander; *asst:* Joe Smith; *Chorus:* The King's Men (Ken Darby, Bud Linn, Rad Robinson, Jon Dodson), The Debutantes (Betty Noyes, Marge Briggs, Dorothy Compton); *mus:* Scott Bradley; *prod mgr:* Fred Quimby; *col:* Tech. *sd:* WE. 9 min.

Academy Award nomination. • Christmas Eve sees Tom chasing Jerry into the cold outdoors. He feels remorse and invites him back inside to spend Christmas together.

4494. The Night Before Christmas (*Silly Symphony*) 9 Dec. 1933; *p.c.*: Walt Disney prods for UA; *dir*: Wilfred Jackson; *anim*: Les Clark, Joseph d'Igalo, Ugo d'Orsi, George Drake, Hardie Gramatky, Dick Huemer, Edward Love, Hamilton S. Luske, Tom Palmer, Archie Robin, Louis Schmitt, Leonard Sebring, Ben Sharpsteen, Ed Smith, Bob Wickersham, Roy Williams; *voice*: Kenneth Baker; *mus/song*: Leigh Harline; *col*: Tech. *sd*: RCA. 8 min. • Inspired by Clement Moore's poem, the toys assist Santa in preparing for Christmas in an orphanage. The noise brings the children down in time to see him departing into the heavens.

4495. The Night Club (*Aesop's Sound Fable*) 24 Nov. 1929; *p.c.*: Fables Pictures Inc for Pathé; *dir*: John Foster, Mannie Davis; *mus*: Carl Edouarde; b&w. *sd*. 5 min. • Ballerina pigs, cats dancing an Apache dance and a barbershop quartet go on in the All Night Club until the cops round them all up.

4496. Night Life in the Army (*Terry-Toon*) 2 Oct. 1942; *p.c.*: TT for Fox; *dir*: Mannie Davis; *story*: John Foster; *voices*: Arthur Kay, Thomas Morrison; *mus*: Philip A. Scheib; *col*: Tech. *sd*: RCA. 7 min. • Pvt. Gandy Goose has a nightmare in which he barks out orders and Sgt. Sourpuss obeys them in his sleep.

4497. Night Life in Tokyo (*Hashimoto*) Feb. 1961; *p.c.*: TT for Fox; *ex prod*: Bill Weiss; *dir*: Mannie Davis; *story sup*: Tom Morrison; *story*: Al Bertino, Dick Kinney; *anim*: Ed Donnelly, Juan Guidi, Armand Guidi; *sets*: John Zago; *back*: Bill Hilliker; *voices*: John Myhers; *mus*: Phil Scheib; *prod mgr*: Frank Schudde; *col*: DeLuxe. *sd*: RCA. 6 min. CS. • Hashimoto takes his pal, G.I. Joe, for a night out on the town. They visit a suki-yaki parlor where they have a meal of sushi, inadvertently awakening Oneckosan the cat. The cat catches Joe, but Hashimoto beans him with a rice bowl, causing some fireworks to accidentally go off. The mice escape, leaving Hashimoto's wife to have the last word: "Moral is: Night out with boys, not so hot!"

4498. Night Life of the Bugs (*Oswald*) 9 Oct. 1936; *p.c.*: Univ; *prod/dir*: Walter Lantz; *story*: Walter Lantz, Victor McLeod; *anim*: Dick Bickenbach, Jack Dunham; *mus*: James Dietrich; b&w. *sd*: RCA. 6 min. • As a reward for rescuing a fairy, Oswald is made small enough to enter the Bugs' Nightclub and join in with the frolicking.

4499. The Night Watchman (*Merrie Melodies*) 19 Nov. 1938; *p.c.*: Leon Schlesinger prods for WB; *dir*: Charles M. Jones; *story*: Ted Pierce; *anim*: Ken Harris; *lay*: Griff Jay; *back*: Arthur Loomer; *ed*: Tregoweth E. Brown; *voices*: Margaret Hill, Mel Blanc, The Sportsmen; *mus*: Carl W. Stalling; *prod sup*: Henry Binder, Raymond G. Katz; *col*: Tech. *sd*: Vit. 7 min. • Thomas Cat, the kitchen guardian, leaves his post in the paws of Sonny and the mice quickly take advantage of the situation. Animator Chuck Jones first directorial.

4500. The Nightmare Before Christmas 22 Oct. 1993; *p.c.*: Touchstone for BV; *dir*: Henry Selick; *prod*: Tim Burton, Denise di Novi; *co-prod*: Kathleen Gavin; *scr*: Caroline Thompson; *storyboard*: Joseph Ranft, Mike Cachuela, Jorgen Klubien, Robert Pauley, Steve Moore; *anim sup*: Eric Leighton; *anim*: Mike Belzer, Paul Berry, Kim Blanchette, Steve Buckley, Joel Fletcher, Angie Glocka, Tim Hittle, Owen Klatte, Justin Kohn, Loyd Price, Anthony Scott, Trey Thomas, Harry Walton, Richard Zimmerman; *fx anim*: Gordon Baker, Scott Bonnenfant, Chris Green, Nathan Stanton; *rigging*: Michael Johnson, George Wong; *art dir*: Seane Taylor, Kelly Asbury, Bill Boes, Kendal Cronkhite; *visual consultant*: Rick Heinrichs; *character des*: Mike Cachuela, David Cutler, Barbara Jackson, Jorgen Klubien; *armature sup*: Thomas St.Amand; *armature engineers*: Blair Clark, Merrick Cheney, Chris Rand, Lionel Orozco, Eben Stromquist, Bart Trickel; *character fabricators*: Bonita De Carlo, Jeff Brewer, David Chong, Glenn Clifford, Chrystene Ellis, Margot Hale, Liz Jennings, Barbara Kossy, Grace Murphy, T. Reid Norton, Facundo Rabaudi, Elise Robertson, Edytha Ryan, Valerie Sofranko-Banks, Lauren Voght, Michael Wick; *mold-makers*: John Reed III, Jon Berg, Mike Grivett, Erick Jensen, Michael Jobe, Victoria Lewis, Tony Preciado, Rob Ronning, William Van Thillo; *character sculptors*: Shelley Daniels, Norm De Carlo, Randal Dutra, Greg Dykstra; *set construction sup*: Bo Henry; *set des*: Gregg Olsson; *set foreman*: Tom Proost; *set builders*: Phil Brotherton, Phil Cusick, Fon Davis, Rebecca

House, Todd Lookinland, Ben Nichols, Alessandro Palladini; *set technicians*: J.D. Durst, Aaron Kohr; *lead back painter*: B.J. Fredrickson; *set painters*: Jennifer Clinard, Loren Hillman, Peggy Hrastar, Linda Overbey; *model shop sup*: Mitch Romanauski; *prop/model makers*: Nick Bogle, Joel Friesch, Pam Kibbee, Paula Lucchesi, Jerome Ranft, Marc Ribaud; *set dresser*: Gretchen Scharfenberg; *cel painter*: Loretta Asbury; *ed*: Stan Webb, Edie Ichioka, Andrea Biklian, Patti Tauscher; *track reader*: Dan Mason; *voices*: *Jack Skellington*: Chris Sarandon; *Jack Skellington (singing voice)/Barrel*: Danny Elfman; *Sally/Shock*: Catherine O'Hara; *Oogie Boogie*: Ken Page; *Mayor*: Glenn Shadix; *Evil Scientist*: William Hickey; *Lock*: Paul Reubens; *mus*: Danny Elfman; *mus ed*: Bob Badami; *ph*: Peter Kozachik, Jim Aupperle, Jo Carson, Selwyn Eddy III, Ray Gilberti, Dave Hanks, Rich Lehmann, Pat Sweeney, Eric Swenson, Michael Bienstock, Mark Kohr, Sara Mast, James Matlosz, Carl Miller, Cameron Noble, Chris Peterson, Brian Van't Hul, Matt White; *prod mgr*: Phil Lofaro; *prod co-ords*: Jill Ruzicka, George Young, Kat Miller; *artistic co-ord*: Allison Abbate, Shane Francis; *stage co-ord*: Alia Agha; *stage mgr*: Robert Anderson; *prod asst*: Susan Alegria, John Angle, Thomas Buchanan, David Burke, Daniel Campbell, Anne Etheridge, David Janssen, Denise Rottina, Beth Schneider, Kirk Scott, Adrianne Sutner, David Teller; *col*: Tech. *sd*: Dolby stereo. 76 min. • Jack Skellington, the Pumpkin King of Halloween, discovers Christmastown. Feeling his life to be empty, he tries to bring Christmas back home by kidnapping Santa Claus. The scheme goes badly wrong, leaving Jack having to return things to how they were in time for the Christmas holiday. Stop-motion animation.

4501. A Nightmare on Elm Street: The Dream Child 11 Aug. 1989; *p.c.*: New Line Cinema/Heron Communications/Smart Egg Pictures; *Visual Concept Engineering*: *anim*: Jammie Friday, Kevin Kutchaver, Marsha Carrington; *Doug Beswick Prods*: *sup*: Doug Beswick; *stop-motion anim*: Yancy Calzada; *Mark cut-out anim*: Larry Nikolai; *col*: Metrocolor. *sd*: Dolby stereo. 89 min. *l/a*. • Live-action horror involving ghosts, wild dreams and one character being turned to paper and killed by being cut up.

4502. A Nightmare on Elm Street 3: Dream Warriors 23 Feb. 1987; *p.c.*: New Line Cinema/Heron Communications, Inc./Smart Egg Pictures for Palace Pictures; *anim fx*: Jeff Burks; *stop-motion*: Doug Beswick, *(Skeleton/marionette fx)* Doug Beswick Prods; *stop-motion puppet construction*: Yancy Calzada; *col*: DeLuxe. *sd*. 96 min. *l/a*. • Live-action horror involving stop-motion animated living skeletons and marionettes, etc.

4503. A Nightmare on Elm Street 4: The Dream Master 19 Aug. 1988; *p.c.*: New Line Cinema/Heron Communications, Inc./Smart Egg Pictures for Palace Pictures; *Dream Quest Images*: *sup*: Jeff Burks; *anim*: Jim Shaw; *anim (physics test)*: Motion Opticals, Lynda Obilil; *(Castles/Sandmation)*: Todd van der Pluym; *col*. *sd*: Dolby stereo. 92 min. *l/a*. • Live-action horror: Freddy Krueger once again haunts the dreams of the remaining Dream Warriors and a woman who possesses the knowledge of how to defeat him for good.

4504. The Nine Lives of Fritz the Cat July 1974; *p.c.*: Steve Krantz Animation Inc./Two Gees/American International for Black Ink Films/Fox/Rank; *ex prod*: Samuel Z. Arkoff; *prod*: Steve Krantz; *dir*: Robert Taylor; *story*: Fred Halliday, Eric Monte, Robert Taylor; *anim*: Robert Taylor, Jim Davis, Don Williams, Herb Johnson, Paul Sommer, Jack Foster, Manny Perez, Volus Jones, Manny Gould, Bob Maxfield, Bob Bachman, Cosmo Anzilotti, Art Vitello, John Gentilella, Milt Gray, Marty Taras, Fred Hellmich, Frank Andrina, Bob Bransford, Bob Bemiller, John Bruno; *asst anim*: Greg Nocon, Bob Tyler, Barney Posner, Mike Baez, Jean Blanchard, James Logan, Rae McSpadden, Judith Drake, Nelson Shin, Lewis Irwin, Lloyd Rees, Joe Grey, Tom Ferriter, Mark Karen, Sonja Ruta, John Dorman, Dean Thompson, Francesca Freeman, Richard Trueblood; *new character des*: Robert Taylor; *lay*: Peter Alvarado, Tony Rivera, Ric Gonzalez, Alex Ignatiev, Martin Strudler, Marty Murphy, Sam Kirson, Chris Jenkyns; *back des*: Matt Golden, Eric Semones; *back*: Al Gmuer, Bob Schaefer, Al Budnick; *ed*: Marshall M. Borden; *visual fx*: Modern Film Effects; *checking*: Marcel Ferguson, Joyce Gard, Jeanne Thorpe, Nikki Zelenka; *i&p*: *supervisor*: Eirene Birnkrant; *asst supervisor*: Lisa Kshatriya; Colene Gonzales, Debbie Halberg, Louise Cuarto, Cookie Link, Karan Storr, Kathy Erskine, Myrian Ferron, Mary Jane Cole, Gerry Farkas, Vera McKinney, Christine Kingsland, Hetta van Elk, Darlene Kenagy, Valerie Reed, Diane Dunning, Kathy Mortensen, Diane Proud; *final checkers*: Fran McCracken, Alice Cowing, Jane Gonzales, Bernie Bonnicksen; *fx*: Bernice Bissett, Shurl

Lupin, Judy Mendel; *col models:* Grace Godiva, Eirene Birnkrant, Irene Sandberg; *voices: Fritz:* Skip Hinnant; *Fritz's old lady:* Reva Rose; *many voices:* Bob Holt; "Bowery Buddies": Robert Ridgley, Fred Smoot, Sweet Dick Whittington, Luke Walker; "Sis": Peter Leeds, Louise Moritz; "Hitler": Larry Moss, Joan Gerber, Jim Johnson, Jay Lawrence, Stanley Adams, Pat Harrington Jr., Carol Androsky; "Astrolady": Lynn Roman, Peter Leeds, Ralph James; "Black New Jersey": Eric Monte, Ron Knight, Benny Baker, Buddy Aret, John Hancock, Felton Perry, Serena Grant, Glynn Turman, Gloria Jones, Peter Hobbs, Robert Ridgley, Chris Graham, Anthony Mason; *mus:* Tom Scott & The L.A. Express; "Jumpback," "In My Beat Life" lyrics by Dave Palmer; *mus ed:* James D. Young, Bobbie Shapiro; *re-recording:* Richard Portman, Edward Thirlwell, Don MacDougall; *sd fx:* Edit International Ltd; *ph:* Ted C. Bemiller, Gregg Heschong, Cinecamera; *ph des:* Gregg Heschong; *research:* Craig Henderson; *neg cutter:* Jack Hooper; *administration:* Robert Evans; *prod sup:* Harry Love, Bill Orcutt; *prod services:* Nine Lives Service Co; *col:* DeLuxe. *sd.* 76 min. • Sequential happenings when Friz's spirit is nagged out of his home onto the streets of New Jersey.

4505. The Nine of Spades *(Aesop's Film Fable)* 2 Aug. 1923; *p.c.:* Fables Pictures Inc for Pathé; *dir:* Paul Terry; b&w. *sil.* 5 min. • No story available.

4506. Nine to Five 19 Dec. 1980; *p.c.:* IPC Films for Fox; *anim sup:* Nicholas Eliopoulos; *anim character:* Fred Lucky; *anim:* (Lee) Mishkin, (Fred) Hellmich, Virgien & Friends; *col:* DeLuxe. *sd.* Panavision. *l/a/anim.* • Live-action comedy about three mistreated office employees. One secretary's fantasy involves her being in a "Snow White" situation, surrounded by cartoon animals as she dispenses poisoned coffee to her boss.

4507. The 19th Hole Club *(Paul Terry-Toon)* 24 Jan. 1936; *p.c.:* Moser & Terry for Educational/Fox; *dir:* Frank Moser, Paul Terry; *mus:* Philip A. Scheib; b&w. *sd:* WE. 6 min. • The farm animals take up golfing.

4508. Nippon Tuck *(Blue Racer)* July 1972; *p.c.:* Mirisch/DFE for UA; *dir:* Gerry Chiniquy; *story:* John W. Dunn; *anim:* Don Williams, Warren Batchelder, Bob Richardson, Robert Taylor; *lay:* Dick Ung; *back:* Richard H. Thomas; *ed:* Lee Gunther; *voices:* Larry D. Mann, Tom Holland; *mus:* Doug Goodwin; *ph:* John Burton Jr.; *prod sup:* Stan Paperney, Harry Love; *col:* DeLuxe. *sd:* RCA. 6 min. • The Japanese Beetle is pursued by the Racer against a Latin American setting.

4509. Nit-Witty Kitty *(Tom & Jerry)* 6 Oct. 1951; *p.c.:* MGM; *dir:* William Hanna, Joseph Barbera; *anim:* Ray Patterson, Ed Barge, Kenneth Muse, Irven Spence; *lay:* Dick Bickenbach; *back:* Robert Gentle; *ed:* Jim Faris; *voice:* Lillian Randolph; *mus:* Scott Bradley; *ph:* Jack Stevens; *prod:* Fred Quimby; *col:* Tech. *sd:* WE. 7 min. • Tom is knocked unconcious and imagines that he is a mouse.

4510. Nix on Hypnotricks *(Popeye)* 19 Dec. 1941; *p.c.:* The Fleischer Studio for Para; *prod:* Max Fleischer; *dir:* Dave Fleischer; *story:* Bill Turner, Cal Howard *anim:* Dave Tendlar, John Walworth; *ed:* Kitty Pfister; *voices:* Jack Mercer, Margie Hines; *mus:* Sammy Timberg; *ph:* Charles Schettler; *prod sup:* Sam Buchwald, Isidore Sparber; b&w. *sd:* WE. 7 min. • Professor I Stare ("10¢ a Trance") needs a subject to hypnotize and summons Olive Oyl over the telephone to come to him.

4511. No Barking *(Merrie Melodies)* 27 Feb. 1954; *p.c.:* WB; *dir:* Charles M. Jones; *story:* Michael Maltese; *anim:* Ken Harris; *lay:* Maurice Noble; *back:* Phil de Guard; *ed:* Treg Brown; *voice:* Mel Blanc; *mus:* Milt Franklyn; *prod mgr:* John W. Burton; *prod:* Edward Selzer; *col:* Tech. *sd:* Vit. 7 min. • Claude Cat's attempts to catch a bird for breakfast are constantly marred by a barking puppy.

4512. No Biz Like Shoe Biz *(Loopy de Loop)* 8 Sept. 1960; *p.c.:* Hanna-Barbera for Colum; *prod/dir:* William Hanna, Joseph Barbera; *story dir:* Alex Lovy; *story:* Warren Foster; *anim dir:* Charles A. Nichols; *anim:* Carlo Vinci; *lay:* Ed Benedict; *back:* Robert Gentle; *ed:* Donald A. Douglas; *voices:* Daws Butler, Don Messick, Jean van der Pyl; *mus:* Hoyt Curtin; *titles:* Lawrence Gobel; *prod mgr:* Howard Hanson; *col:* East. *sd:* RCA. 6½ min. • Loopy invades the Cinderella story.

4513. No Deposit No Return 11 Feb. 1976; *p.c.:* Walt Disney Prods for BV; *anim titles:* Art Stevens, Terry Walsh; *mus:* Buddy Baker; *orch:* Walter Sheets; *col:* Tech. *sd:* RCA. 2¾ min. • Live-action comedy about two children affecting a kidnapping to gain attention from their mother.

The animated credits follow the antics of a skunk who travels about with the children.

4514. No Eyes Today *(Inkwell Imps)* 11 Jan. 1929; *p.c.:* Inkwell Studio for Para; *dir:* Dave Fleischer; *anim/l/a:* Max Fleischer; b&w. *sil.* 6 min. *l/a/anim.* • Ko-Ko ogles a bathing beauty so Max erases his eyes.

4515. No Hunting *(Donald Duck)* 14 Jan. 1955; *p.c.:* Walt Disney prods for BV; *dir:* Jack Hannah; *story:* Dick Shaw, Bill Berg, Milt Schaffer; *anim:* John Sibley, Al Coe, Volus Jones, Bill Justice; *fx:* Dan MacManus; *lay:* Yale Gracey; *back:* Ray Huffine; *voices:* Art Gilmore, Bill Thompson, Clarence Nash, James MacDonald, Peggy Connell, Milt Schaffer, Jack Hannah; *mus:* Oliver Wallace; *col:* Tech. *sd:* RCA. 6 min. CS. *Academy Award nomination.* • Donald's "Hunting Spirit" takes him on a hunting trip ... unfortunately everybody else has the same idea.

4516. No Ifs, Ands or Butts *(Noveltoon)* 17 Dec. 1954; *p.c.:* Famous for Para; *dir:* I. Sparber; *story:* Irving Spector; *anim:* Dave Tendlar, Tom Moore; *sets:* Robert Connavale; *voices:* Jackson Beck, Sid Raymond; *mus:* Winston Sharples; *ph:* Leonard McCormick; *prod mgr:* Seymour Shultz; *col:* Tech. *sd:* RCA. 6 min. • The cat reads that a "Crow Salad" might help him give up his chain smoking. He sets out to capture Buzzy but the wiley crow has other ideas.

4517. No Mutton Fer Nuttin' *(Noveltoon)* 26 Nov. 1943; *p.c.:* Famous for Para; *story:* Carl Meyer; *anim:* Dave Tendlar, John Walworth; *voice:* Carl Meyer; *mus:* Winston Sharples; *ph:* Leonard McCormick; *prod mgr:* Sam Buchwald; *col:* Tech. *sd:* RCA. 8 min. • Wolfie tries to catch a smart black sheep. A number of good gags used including Wolfie being disarmed by the iris-out.

4518. No! No! A Thousand Times No!! *(Betty Boop)* 24 May 1935; *p.c.:* The Fleischer Studio for Para; *prod:* Max Fleischer; *dir:* Dave Fleischer; *anim:* Myron Waldman, Edward Nolan, Lillian Friedman; *voices:* Mae Questel, Everett Clark; *mus:* Sammy Timberg; b&w. *sd:* WE. 6 min. • Betty and Fred stage a melodrama. Philip the Fiend offers Betty riches to lure her into his clutches and then kidnaps her.

4519. No Other One *(Screen Songs)* 24 Jan. 1936; *p.c.:* The Fleischer Studio for Para; *prod:* Max Fleischer; *dir:* Dave Fleischer; *anim:* Thomas Johnson; *mus:* Hal Kemp and his orchestra; b&w. *sd:* WE. 8 min. • Wiffle Piffle and another are bill posters.

4520. No Parking Hare *(Looney Tunes)* 1 May 1954; *p.c.:* WB; *dir:* Robert McKimson; *story:* Sid Marcus; *anim:* Herman Cohen, Rod Scribner, Phil de Lara, Charles McKimson; *lay:* Robert Givens; *back:* Richard H. Thomas; *ed:* Treg Brown; *voices:* Mel Blanc, John T. Smith; *mus:* Carl Stalling; *prod mgr:* John W. Burton; *prod:* Edward Selzer; *col:* Tech. *sd:* Vit. 7 min. • Bugs defends his home when a tough construction worker tries to build a freeway through it.

4521. No Place Like Rome *(Kartune)* 31 July 1953; *p.c.:* Famous for Para; *dir:* I. Sparber; *anim:* Al Eugster; *voice:* Michael Fitzmaurice; *mus:* Winston Sharples; *ph:* Leonard McCormick; *prod mgr:* Sam Buchwald; *col:* Tech. *sd:* RCA. 6 min. • Sightseeing tour of Italy: Mount Etna, The Leaning Tower of Pisa, Venice and Milan where a tenor sings "Oh! Ma-Ma."

4522. No Sail *(Donald & Goofy)* 7 Sept. 1945; *p.c.:* Walt Disney prods for RKO; *dir:* Jack Hannah; *asst dir:* Toby Tobelman; *story:* Dick Kinney, Ralph Wright; *anim:* Bob Carlson, Hugh Fraser, Judge Whitaker, Al Coe, Lee Morehouse, Don Patterson, John Sibley; *fx:* John Reed; *lay:* Yale Gracey; *back:* Thelma Witmer; *voices:* Clarence Nash, George Johnson; *mus:* Oliver Wallace; *col:* Tech. *sd:* RCA. 7 min. • Don and the Goof set out in a rented boat and discover they have to deposit 5¢ for the sail. They soon run out of cash and find themselves adrift at sea without a sail.

4523. No Sleep for Percy *(Little Roquefort)* Apr. 1955; *p.c.:* TT for Fox; *dir:* Connie Rasinski; *story/voice:* Tom Morrison; *anim:* Jim Tyer; *sets:* Art Bartsch; *mus:* Philip A. Scheib; *ph:* Douglas Moye; *col:* Tech. *sd:* RCA. 6 min. • Roquefort's radio playing disturbs the cat's slumber.

4524. No Smoking *(Goofy)* 23 Nov. 1951 *p.c.:* Walt Disney prods for RKO; *dir:* Jack Kinney; *story:* George Nicholas, Dick Kinney; *anim:* George Nicholas, John Sibley, Hugh Fraser, Ed Aardal, Charles Nichols; *fx:* Blaine Gibson, Jack Boyd; *lay:* Al Zinnen; *back:* Ralph Hulett; *voices:* Jack Rourke, Bob Jackman, John Sibley, Lance Nolley, Pinto Colvig; *mus:* Paul Smith; *col:* Tech. *sd:* RCA. 6 min. • Geef tries to kick the smoking habit.

4525. No Space Like Home *(Terry-Toon)* Oct. 1971 (© 1965); *p.c.:* TT for Fox; *ex prod:* Bill Weiss; *dir/anim:* Art Bartsch; *story sup:* Tom Morrison; *story:* Larz Bourne; *sets:* Bill Focht, John Zago, Bob Owen; *ed:* Jack MacConnell; *voices:* Dayton Allen; *mus:* Jim Timmens; *col:* DeLuxe. *sd:* RCA. 5 min. • Astronut changes Oscar's house into a modern space home at the same time his boss brings a valid client for dinner.

4526. Noah Had His Troubles *(Aesop's Film Fable)* 27 Dec. 1925; *p.c.:* Fables Pictures Inc for Pathé; *dir:* Paul Terry; b&w. *sil.* 5 min. • Noah's stock of animals is multiplying. The crisis comes to a head when a procession of storks delivers a herd of baby elephants.

4527. Noah Knew His Ark *(Aesop's Sound Fable)* 25 May 1930; *p.c.:* Van Beuren for Pathé; *dir:* John Foster, Mannie Davis; *mus:* Gene Rodemich; b&w. *sd:* RCA. 6 min. • Noah leads his flock in a rousing chorus of "It Ain't Gonna Rain No More."

4528. Noah's Ark 10 Nov. 1959; *p.c.:* Walt Disney prods for BV; *dir:* Bill Justice; *anim:* Bill Justice, Xavier Atencio; *des:* T. Hee, Xavier Atencio; *back:* Ralph Hulett; *voices:* Jerome Courtland, Jeanne Gayle, Paul Frees, The MelloMen, James MacDonald; *mus:* George Bruns; *songs:* Mel Leven; *technical:* Jim Love, E.J. Sekac; *col:* Tech. *sd:* RCA. 21 min. *Academy Award nomination.* • The story of Noah, building his ark, loading it with animals and setting sail. Stop-motion animation made with an assortment of household goods such as pipecleaners, corks and cotton wool, etc.

4529. Noah's Athletic Club *(Aesop's Film Fable)* 3 Dec. 1924; *p.c.:* Fables Pictures Inc for Pathé; *dir:* Paul Terry; b&w. *sil.* 5 min. • A prize fight between Noah and an ape knocks Noah into dreamland where he is attended by fair and affectionate damsels. Upon recovery, he requests to be knocked out again.

4530. Noah's Lark *(Talkartoon)* 26 Oct. 1929; *p.c.:* The Fleischer Studio for Para; *prod:* Max Fleischer; *dir:* Dave Fleischer; *anim:* Al Eugster; *mus:* Art Turkisher; b&w. *sd:* WE. 6 min. • In this, the first *Talkartoon,* Noah's animals desert the ark to enjoy the rides at Lunar Park. When they return, their weight sinks the craft and Noah swims off with some mermaids.

4531. Noah's Outing *(Aesop's Film Fable)* 5 Oct. 1924; *p.c.:* Fables Pictures Inc for Pathé; *dir:* Paul Terry; b&w. *sil.* 5 min. • Noah assembles and takes his brood of animals for a picnic but the arrival of two skunks drives everyone up in the crow's nest.

4532. Noah's Outing *(Paul Terry-Toon)* 24 Jan. 1932; *p.c.:* Terry, Moser & Coffman for Educational/Fox; *dir:* Frank Moser, Paul Terry; *mus:* Philip A. Scheib; b&w. *sd:* WE. 6 min. • Noah has troubles gathering his animals in before the big flood.

4533. Nobody's Ghoul *(Deputy Dawg)* Apr. 1962; *p.c.:* TT for Fox; *ex prod:* Bill Weiss; *dir/anim:* Dave Tendlar; *story sup:* Tom Morrison; *story:* Larz Bourne; *sets:* Bill Focht, John Zago; *voices:* Dayton Allen; *mus:* Phil Scheib; *prod mgr:* Frank Schudde; *col:* DeLuxe. *sd:* RCA. 5 min. • D.D. has to evict a ghost from a house.

4534. Noise Annoys Ko-Ko *(Inkwell Imps)* 25 Jan. 1929; *p.c.:* Inkwell Studio for Para; *dir:* Dave Fleischer; *prod/l/a:* Max Fleischer; b&w. *sil.* 6 min. *l/al aim.* • Ko-Ko leaves for the country to avoid city noises.

4535. Nonsense Newsreel *(Terry-Toon)* Feb. 1954; *p.c.:* TT for Fox; *dir:* Mannie Davis; *story/voice:* Tom Morrison; *anim:* Jim Tyer; *mus:* Philip A. Scheib; *ph:* Douglas Moye; *col:* Tech. *sd:* RCA. 6 min. • A newsreel shows a politician who claims "No Crime" in his town but is always ready to accept a bribe. A hypnotist's patient floats out of the window and the traffic problem is solved.

4536. Norman Normal 3 Feb. 1968; *p.c.:* WB/7A; *dir:* Alex Lovy; *story/voices:* N. Paul Stookey, Paul Dixon; *anim:* Ted Bonnicksen, La Verne Harding, Volus Jones, Ed Solomon; *lay:* John Freeman; *back:* Bob Abrams, Ralph Penn; *ed:* Hal Geer; *mus:* William Lave; *theme:* N. Paul Stookey; *prod:* William L. Hendricks, N. Paul Stookey; *col:* Tech. *sd:* Vit. 6 min. • Norman is considered an outsider because he doesn't comply with everybody else's rules.

4537. The North Avenue Regulars 9 Feb. 1979; *p.c.:* Walt Disney Prods for BV; *titles:* Art Stevens, Joe Hale; *mus:* Robert F. Brunner; *orch:* Walter Sheets; *col:* Tech. *sd:* RCA. 3¹/₂ min. • Live-action comedy concerning a priest and group of church-going old ladies set out to put a stop to organized crime in their community. The animated credits show the progress of a bank robber being pursued by a group of old ladies. Aka *Hill's Angels.*

4538. North of Nowhere *(Life Cartoon Comedy)* 16 May 1927; *p.c.:* Sherwood Wadsworth Pictures for Educational; *prod/dir:* John R. McCrory; b&w. *sil.* 5 min. • Mike and Nibbins arrive at the North Pole where they encounter a couple of angry Polar Bears and escape, thanks to some clever tricks.

4539. North Pal *(Casper)* 29 May 1953; *p.c.:* Famous for Para; *dir:* I. Sparber; *story:* I. Klein; *anim:* Steve Muffatti, Bill Hudson; *sets:* Robert Connavale; *voices:* Alan Shay, Jack Mercer; *mus:* Winston Sharples; *title song:* Mack David, Jerry Livingston; *ph:* Leonard McCormick; *prod mgr:* Seymour Shultz; *col:* Tech. *sd:* RCA. 7 min. • Casper visits the North Pole where he befriends a seal.

4540. North Woods *(Oswald)* 20 June 1931; *p.c.:* Univ; *dir:* Walter Lantz, "Bill" Nolan; *anim:* Clyde Geronimi, Manuel Moreno, Ray Abrams, Fred Avery, Lester Kline, Chet Karrberg, "Pinto" Colvig; *mus:* James Dietrich; b&w. *sd:* WE. 6 min. • Mountie Oswald sets out to capture a desperado ... which he does after covering a fair piece of ground.

4541. Northern Mites *(Noveltoon)* Nov. 1960; *p.c.:* Para Cartoons; *dir:* Seymour Kneitel; *story:* Carl Meyer, Jack Mercer; *anim:* Nick Tafuri, Wm. B. Pattengill; *sets:* Anton Loeb; *voices:* Jack Mercer; *mus:* Winston Sharples; *ph:* Leonard McCormick; *prod mgr:* Abe Goodman; *col:* Tech. *sd:* RCA. 6 min. • The watchdog is told to guard the Artic provisions and two mischievous penguins cause havoc.

4542. Northwest Hounded Police 3 Aug. 1946; *p.c.:* MGM; *dir:* Tex Avery; *story:* Heck Allen; *anim:* Walter Clinton, Ed Love, Ray Abrams; *character des/lay:* Claude Smith; *back:* John Didrik Johnsen; *ed:* Fred MacAlpin; *voices:* Frank Graham, Tex Avery; *mus:* Scott Bradley; *prod:* Fred Quimby; *col:* Tech. *sd:* WE. 8 min. • Sgt. McPoodle of the Mounted Police sets out to capture a dangerous escaped convict.

4543. Northwest Mousie *(Herman & Katnip)* 18 Dec. 1953; *p.c.:* Famous for Para; *dir:* Seymour Kneitel; *story:* Carl Meyer, Jack Mercer; *anim:* Al Eugster, Wm. B. Pattengill; *sets:* Robert Connavale; *voices:* Arnold Stang, Sid Raymond, Jack Mercer; *mus:* Winston Sharples; *title song:* Hal David, Leon Carr; *ph:* Leonard McCormick; *prod mgr:* Seymour Shultz; *col:* Tech. *sd:* RCA. 7 min. • Up in the frozen wilds of Canada, Pierre, a notorious cat, prevents the mice from getting any food. Mountie Herman arrives and captures the cat.

4544. Not Ghoulty *(Casper)* 5 June 1959; *p.c.:* Para Cartoons; *dir:* Seymour Kneitel; *story:* Carl Meyer, Jack Mercer; *anim:* Frank Endres, Nick Tafuri; *sets:* Robert Little; *voices:* Cecil Roy, Jack Mercer, Jackson Beck; *mus:* Winston Sharples; *ph:* Leonard McCormick; *prod mgr:* Abe Goodman; *col:* Tech. *sd:* RCA. 6 min. • Casper's ghostly powers are taken away until he is able to scare somebody. He succeeds in terrifying the other ghosts by posing as a "Ghost Exterminator."

4545. Not in Nottingham *(Loopy de Loop)* Sept. 1963; *p.c.:* Hanna-Barbera for Colum; *prod/dir:* William Hanna, Joseph Barbera; *story dir:* Gerry Ray; *story:* Dalton Sandifer; *anim:* Charles A. Nichols; *anim:* Alex Ignatiev; *lay:* Jack Ozark; *back:* Curtiss D. Perkins; *ed:* Hank Gotzenberg; *voices:* Daws Butler, Don Messick, Jean van der Pyl; *mus:* Hoyt Curtin; *titles:* Lawrence Gobel; *col:* East. *sd:* RCA. 6 min. • Loopy helps Robin Hood rescue Maid Marian from the Sheriff of Nottingham.

4546. Not Now *(Betty Boop)* 28 Feb. 1936; *p.c.:* The Fleischer Studio for Para; *prod:* Max Fleischer; *dir:* Dave Fleischer; *anim:* Myron Waldman, Hicks Lokey, Lillian Friedman; *voices:* Mae Questel; *mus:* Sammy Timberg; b&w. *sd:* WE. 6 min. • Pudgy's slumber is disturbed by the nocturnal howlings of cats.

4547. Not So Quiet *(Oswald)* 30 June 1930; *p.c.:* Univ; *dir:* Walter Lantz; *anim:* "Bill"Nolan, Ray Abrams, Manuel Moreno, Clyde Geronimi, "Pinto" Colvig; *mus:* James Dietrich; b&w. *sd:* WE. 6¹/₂ min. • Parody of "All Quiet on the Western Front." Oswald billeted in France, he befriends a girl whom he marries after Armistice.

4548. Notes to You *(Looney Tunes)* 20 Sept. 1941; *p.c.:* Leon Schlesinger prods for WB; *dir:* I. Freleng; *story:* Michael Maltese; *anim:* Manuel Perez; *lay:* Owen Fitzgerald; *back:* Lenard Kester; *ed:* Treg Brown; *voices:* Mel Blanc; *mus:* Carl W. Stalling; *prod sup:* Henry Binder, Raymond G. Katz; b&w. *sd:* Vit. 7 min. • Porky attempts to silence a singing cat on the backyard fence. Remade as *Back Alley Oproar.*

4549. Nothing but the Tooth *(Merrie Melodies)* 1 May 1948; *p.c.:*

WB; *dir:* Arthur Davis; *story:* Dave Monahan; *anim:* J.C. Melendez, Don Williams, John Carey, Basil Davidovich; *lay:* Don Smith; *back:* Philip de Guard; *ed:* Treg Brown; *voices:* Mel Blanc; *mus:* Carl Stalling; *prod mgr:* John W. Burton; *prod:* Edward Selzer; *col:* Tech. *sd:* Vit. 7 min. • A small Indian wants to scalp Porky.

4550. Novelty Cartoons 1932; *p.c.:* Harper Producing & Distributing Co; b&w. sd. • Series of twelve. Titles and credits untraced.

4551. The Novelty Shop (*Color Rhapsody*) 11 Feb. 1936; *p.c.:* Charles Mintz prods for Colum; *story:* Sid Marcus; *anim:* Art Davis; *lay:* Clark Watson; *ed:* George Winkler; *voices:* The Rhythmettes; *mus:* Joe de Nat; *prod mgr:* James Bronis; *col:* Tech. *sd:* RCA. 6¹⁄₂ min. • When the Novelty Shop closes, the dolls, toy soldiers, clocks and birds all sing and dance then return to their natural state at daybreak. Caricatures of Joe E. Brown, Laurel & Hardy and the Three Stooges.

4552. Now, Hare This (*Looney Tunes*) 31 May 1958; *p.c.:* WB; *dir:* Robert McKimson; *story:* Tedd Pierce; *anim:* Tom Ray, George Grandpré, Ted Bonnicksen, Warren Batchelder; *lay:* Robert Gribbroek; *back:* Bill Butler; *ed:* Treg Brown; *voices:* Mel Blanc; *mus:* Milt Franklyn; *col:* Tech. *sd:* Vit. 7 min. • B.B. Wolf finally realizes that the only way he is going to have a rabbit for dinner is to invite Bugs to dine with him and his nephew.

4553. Now Hear This (*Looney Tunes*) Apr. 1963; *p.c.:* WB; *dir:* Chuck Jones; *asst dir:* Maurice Noble; *story:* John Dunn; *anim:* Ben Washam, Bob Bransford; *back:* Philip de Guard; *ed/sd fx:* Treg Brown; *mus:* Bill Lava; *col:* Tech. *sd:* Vit. 6 min. • A series of events centering around a collection of sound effects.

4554. Now That Summer Has Gone (*Merrie Melodies*) 14 May 1938; *p.c.:* Leon Schlesinger prods for WB; *dir:* Frank Tashlin; *story:* Fred Niemann; *anim:* Bob McKimson; *ed:* Tregoweth E. Brown; *voices:* Mel Blanc, Billy Bletcher; *mus:* Carl W. Stalling; *prod sup:* Henry Binder, Raymond G. Katz; *col:* Tech. *sd:* Vit. 7 min. • Against his grandfather's wishes, little Johnny squirrel gambles away his cache of acorns during the summer and regrets doing so when winter comes.

4555. Now You Tell One (*Whirlwind Comedy*) 14 Dec. 1926; *p.c.:* FBO; *dir/l/a:* Charles R. Bowers; *story:* Charles R. Bowers, H.L. Muller, Ted Sears; *ph:* H.L. Muller; b&w. sil. 20 min. *l/a/anim.* • Bowers spins a yarn about inventing a liquid that grows scores of cats from a sprig of catkin in order to help rid a house of mice. Live-action comedy with stop-motion animation.

4556. Now You're Talking 1927; *p.c.:* Inkwell Studios; *dir:* Dave Fleischer; *prod/scr:* Max Fleischer; *ph:* Sol Luby; b&w st 8³⁄₄ min. *l/a/anim.* • Commercial for the telephone. A (live-action) man is having problems with phoning. The cartoon sequence shows a telephone being rushed to hospital, complaining that his boss has been "abusing the phone." Various methods of misuse of the telephone are shown until matters are put right.

4557. Nudnik (1966–1967); *p.c.:* Rembrandt Films for Para; *prod:* William L. Snyder; *dir/lay:* Gene Deitch; *stories:* Gene Deitch, Eli Bauer, Lars Bourne, Tod Dockstader; *anim:* Věra Marešová, Věra Kudrnová, Mirko Kačena; *back:* Miluse Hluchaníčová; *mus:* Ferdinand Havlík; *prod mgr:* Zdenka Deitchová • **1965:** Here's Nudnik. Drive On, Nudnik. • **1966:** Home, Sweet Nudnik. Welcome Nudnik! Nudnik on the Roof. From Nudnik with Love. • **1967:** Who Needs Nudnik? Nudnik on the Beach. Good Neighbor Nudnik. Nudnik's Nudnickel. I Remember Nudnik. Nudnik on a Shoestring • The misadventures of an all-time "Loser."

4558. Nudnik on a Shoestring (*Nudnik*) Jan. 1967; *p.c.:* Rembrandt for Para; *prod:* William L. Snyder; *dir:* Gene Deitch; *col. sd.* 6 min. • Nudnik visits a huge department store to replace his broken shoelaces. • See: *Nudnik*

4559. Nudnik on the Beach (*Nudnik*) Sept. 1966; *p.c.:* Rembrandt for Para; *prod:* William L. Snyder; *dir:* Gene Deitch; *story:* Eli Bauer; *col. sd.* 6 min. • The ill-fated Nudnik spends a day on the beach. He has trouble with a hot dog and a water fountain and, unintentionally, wins a surfing race. • See: *Nudnik*

4560. Nudnik on the Roof *p.c.:* Rembrandt Films for Para; *prod:* William L. Snyder; *dir:* Gene Deitch; *col. sd.* 6 min. • After having a battle with a coffee machine, Nudnik attempts to erect a television aerial on an ungrateful man's roof. • See: *Nudnik*

4561. Nudnik's Nudnickel (*Nudnik*) July 1967; *p.c.:* Rembrandt for Para; *prod:* William L. Snyder; *dir:* Gene Deitch; *story:* Eli Bauer, Al Kouzel; *col. sd.* 6 min. • The luckless Nudnik finds a quarter down a drain and inadvertently gets involved in a bank robbery. • See: *Nudnik*

4562. Nurse Maid (*Flip the Frog*) 26 Nov. 1932; *p.c.:* Celebrity prods for MGM; *prod/dir:* Ub Iwerks; b&w. sd. PCP. 6 min. • Flip gets a job baby sitting with a brat who drinks muscle-building tonic and takes Flip for a ride in his baby buggy.

4563. Nurse-Mates (*Popeye*) 21 June 1940; *p.c.:* The Fleischer Studio for Para; *prod:* Max Fleischer; *dir:* Dave Fleischer; *story:* George Manuell; *anim:* Orestes Calpini, Louis Zukor; *voices:* Jack Mercer, Pinto Colvig, Margie Hines; *mus:* Sammy Timberg; *ph:* Charles Schettler; *prod sup:* Sam Buchwald, Isidore Sparber; b&w. sd: WE. 7 min. • Popeye and Bluto play nursemaid to Swee'Pea, each hoping to win Olive's affection.

4564. Nurse to Meet Ya (*Popeye*) 11 Feb 1955; *p.c.:* Famous for Para; *dir:* I. Sparber; *story:* Jack Mercer; *anim:* Al Eugster, Wm. B. Pattengill; *sets:* Robert Connavale; *voices:* Jack Mercer, Jackson Beck, Mae Questel; *mus:* Winston Sharples; *ph:* Leonard McCormick; *prod mgr:* Seymour Shultz; *col:* Tech. *sd:* RCA. 6 min. • The boys attempt to get into nurse Olive's favor by entertaining baby Swee'Pea.

4565. Nursery Crimes (*Phantasy*) 8 Oct. 1943; *p.c.:* Colum; *prod:* Dave Fleischer; *dir/story:* Alec Geiss; *voices:* Patrick J. McGeehan, The Betty Allen Trio; *mus:* Eddie Kilfeather; *prod mgr:* Albert Spar; b&w. sd: RCA. 7 min. • A selection of Mother Goose stories are updated. Mussolini is pictured as "Humpty Dumpty."

4566. A Nursery Scandal (*Aesop's Sound Fable*) 2 Sept. 1932; *p.c.:* Van Beuren for RKO; *dir:* John Foster, Harry Bailey; *mus:* Gene Rodemich; b&w. sd: RCA. 6 min. • Mother Goose and other nursery rhyme characters emerge from a fairy tale book. She has a romance with a scarecrow which is dampened by the other characters and chases them all back into the book.

4567. The Nut Factory (*Cubby Bear*) 4 Aug. 1933; *p.c.:* Van Beuren for RKO; *dir:* Mannie Davis; *mus:* Gene Rodemich; b&w. sd: RCA. 6 min. • No story available.

4568. Nuts and Jolts (*Oswald*) 8 Sept. 1929; *p.c.:* Winkler for Univ; *anim:* Hugh Harman; b&w. sil. 6 min. • No story available.

4569. Nuts and Squirrels (*Aesop's Film Fable*) 26 Sept. 1925; *p.c.:* Fables Pictures Inc for Pathé; *dir:* Paul Terry; b&w. sil. 10 min. • A troublesome squirrel and some crows make Farmer Al's photography attempts intolerable.

4570. Nuts and Volts (*Looney Tunes*) 25 Apr. 1964; *p.c.:* WB; *dir:* Friz Freleng; *story:* John Dunn; *anim:* Gerry Chiniquy, Virgil Ross, Bob Matz, Art Leonardi; *lay:* Hawley Pratt; *back:* Tom O'Loughlin; *ed:* Treg Brown; *voices:* Mel Blanc; *mus:* Bill Lava; *prod mgr:* William Orcutt; *prod:* David H. DePatie; *col:* Tech. *sd:* Vit. 6 min. • Sylvester puts the electronic age to good use in his pursuit of Speedy by using a robot.

4571. The Nutty Network (*Terry-Toon*) 24 Mar. 1939; *p.c.:* TT for Fox; *dir:* Mannie Davis; *story:* John Foster; *mus:* Philip A. Scheib; *col:* Tech. *sd:* RCA. 6 min. • The animals working in a radio station are disturbed by a broadcast of an invasion from Mars.

4572. Nutty News (*Looney Tunes*) 23 May 1942; *p.c.:* Leon Schlesinger prods for WB; *dir:* Robert Clampett; *story:* Warren Foster; *anim:* Virgil Ross; *ed:* Treg Brown; *voices:* Arthur Q. Bryan, Mel Blanc; *mus:* Carl W. Stalling; *prod sup:* Henry Binder, Raymond G. Katz; b&w. sd: Vit. 6 min. • A newsreel includes Hunting Season, a Jack-in-the-Box Hitler to get kids to sit still, fireflies that have a blackout and proof that a dollar doesn't go far these days. Caricatures of Leon Schlesinger, Henry Binder and Ray Katz.

4573. Nutty Notes (*Oswald*) 9 Dec. 1929; *p.c.:* Univ; *anim:* Walter Lantz, "Bill" Nolan, Tom Palmer; *mus:* David Broekman; b&w. sd: WE. 6 min. • Oswald serenades his girl against strong opposition.

4574. Nutty Pine Cabin (*Cartune*) 1 June 1942; *p.c.:* Walter Lantz prods for Univ; *dir:* Alex Lovy; *story:* Ben Hardaway, Chuck Couch; *anim:* Harold Mason, Robert Bentley; *sets:* Fred Brunish; *voices:* Margaret Hill, Mel Blanc; *mus:* Darrell Calker; *prod mgr:* George Hall; *col:* Tech. *sd:* WE. 6 min. • Andy builds a cabin in the woods and a community of beavers attempts to use the wood in building a dam.

4575. O-Solar-Meow (*Tom & Jerry*) 1966; *p.c.:* MGM; *prod:* Chuck Jones; *dir:* Abe Levitow; *story:* John Dunn; *anim:* Ken Harris, Don Towsley, Tom Ray, Dick Thompson, Ben Washam; *des:* Maurice Noble; *lay:* Don Morgan; *back:* Philip de Guard; *voice:* Mel Blanc; *mus:* Eugene Poddany; *prod mgr:* Les Goldman; *col:* Metro. *sd:* WE. 6 min. • Tom and Jerry continue their feud aboard a Space Rest Station. Jerry is after some cheese from the supply satellite and Tom uses scientific means to prevent him from getting it.

4576. Ocean Bruise (*Swifty & Shorty*) Apr. 1965; *p.c.:* Para Cartoons; *dir:* Howard Post; *story:* Eli Bauer; *anim:* Wm. B. Pattengill; *sets:* Robert Little; *voices:* Bob MacFadden; *mus:* Winston Sharples; *ph:* Leonard McCormick; *prod mgr:* Abe Goodman; *col:* Tech. *sd:* RCA. 6 min. • Swifty and Shorty go on a "World Cruise" but instead they get shanghaied aboard a schooner with a captain in search of Moby Dick.

4577. The Ocean Hop (*Oswald the Lucky Rabbit*) 14 Nov. 1927; *p.c.:* Winkler for Univ; *dir:* Walt Disney; *anim:* Hugh Harman, Rollin C. Hamilton; *ph:* Mike Marcus; b&w. sil. 5 min. sound reissue in 1932 • Oswald participates in a $25,000 transatlantic flight. When his machine is wrecked by his rival, he enlists the help of a dachshund.

4578. Oceans of Love (*Terry-Toon*) May 1956; *p.c.:* TT for Fox; *dir:* Connie Rasinski; *story:* Tom Morrison; *anim:* Jim Tyer; *voices:* Tom Morrison, Roy Halee; *mus:* Philip A. Scheib; *col:* Tech. *sd:* RCA. 6 min. CS. • A boy goes fishing and gets pulled in by a big fish. He dreams he goes to the ocean's floor and meets a mermaid.

4579. Odd Ant Out (*Ant & Aardvark*) 29 Sept. 1970; *p.c.:* Mirisch/DFE for UA; *dir:* Gerry Chiniquy; *story:* Sid Marcus; *anim:* Warren Batchelder, Don Williams, Bob Taylor, Manny Perez; *lay:* Dick Ung; *back:* Richard H. Thomas; *ed:* Lee Gunther; *voices:* John Byner; *mus:* Doug Goodwin, Pete Candoli, Billy Byers, Jimmy Rowles, Tommy Tedesco, Ray Brown, Shelly Manne; *prod sup:* Jim Foss, Harry Love; *col:* Deluxe. *sd:* RCA. 6 min. • The Aardvark and a rival anteater try to open a can of chocolate coverd ants.

4580. The Odor-Able Kitty (*Looney Tunes*) 6 Jan. 1945; *p.c.:* WB; *dir:* Charles M. Jones; *story:* Tedd Pierce; *anim:* Robert Cannon; *lay:* Robert Gribbroek; *ed:* Treg Brown; *voices:* Mel Blanc, Bea Benaderet; *mus:* Carl W. Stalling; *prod mgr:* John W. Burton; *prod:* Edward Selzer; *col:* Tech. *sd:* Vit. 7 min. • Tired of being mistreated by humanity, an alley cat disguises herself as a skunk with the odor of limburger which also attracts the attentions of an amorous continental skunk.

4581. Odor of the Day (*Looney Tunes*) 2 Oct. 1948; *p.c.:* WB; *dir:* Art Davis; *story:* Lloyd Turner; *anim:* J.C. Melendez, Don Williams, Emery Hawkins, Basil Davidovich; *lay:* Don Smith; *back:* Philip de Guard; *ed:* Treg Brown; *voices:* Mel Blanc; *mus:* Carl Stalling; *prod mgr:* John W. Burton; *prod:* Edward Selzer; *col:* Ciné. *sd:* Vit. 7 min. • A dog and a skunk vie for the same warm bed.

4582. Of All Things (*Cartoon Exhibitors*) 23 Mar. 1935; *p.c.:* State Right Releases; b&w. sd. • No story or credits available.

4583. Of Feline Bondage (*Tom & Jerry*) 1965; *p.c.:* MGM; *prod/dir:* Chuck Jones; *asst dir:* Maurice Noble; *story:* Don Towsley, Chuck Jones; *anim:* Ben Washam, Ken Harris, Don Towsley, Tom Ray, Dick Thompson; *back:* Robert Gribbroek; *voices:* June Foray, Mel Blanc; *mus:* Eugene Poddany; *col:* Metro. *sd:* WE. 6 min. • Jerry's fairy godmother comes to his help when she gives him a potion that turns him invisible.

4584. Of Fox and Hounds (*Merrie Melodies*) 7 Dec. 1940; *p.c.:* Leon Schlesinger prods for WB; *dir:* Draft #412 (Fred Avery); *story:* Draft #1312 (Rich Hogan); *anim:* Draft #6102 (Virgil Ross); *sets:* John Didrik Johnsen; *ed:* Treg Brown; *voices:* Mel Blanc, Fred Avery; *mus:* Draft #158 (Carl W. Stalling); *prod sup:* Henry Binder, Raymond G. Katz; *col:* Tech. *sd:* Vit. 7 min. • Willoughby the hunting dog is fooled by the dog disguise of Charlie Fox.

4585. Of Men and Demons 1969; *p.c.:* the Hubley Studio for IBM/Expo '70/Para; *prod/dir/story/sets:* John Hubley, Faith Hubley; *anim:* Art Babbitt, Vinnie Bell, Shamus Culhane, Tissa David, Nina di Gangi; *col. sd.* 10 min. *Academy Award nomination.* • A farmer and his wife battle three demons, symbolizing wind, rain and fire. He builds a stronger world of brick and steel, then has to cope with modern devils: Pollution, Speed and Overproduction. The indomitable man foils the demons with an age of electronic technology.

4586. Of Mice and Magic (*Herman & Katnip*) 20 Feb. 1953; *p.c.:* Famous for Para; *dir:* I. Sparber; *story:* I. Klein; *anim:* Dave Tendlar, Martin Taras; *sets:* Robert Little; *voices:* Arnold Stang, Sid Raymond, Mae Questel, Jack Mercer; *mus:* Winston Sharples; *title song:* Hal David, Leon Carr; "Personality": Johnny Burke, James van Heusen; *ph:* Leonard McCormick; *prod mgr:* Seymour Shultz; *col:* Tech. *sd:* RCA. 6 min. • Katnip kidnaps Louise, the star of the mouse vaudeville show and it's up to Herman to rescue her.

4587. Of Mice and Menace (*Herman & Katnip*) 25 June 1954; *p.c.:* Famous for Para; *dir:* Seymour Kneitel; *story:* Carl Meyer; *anim:* Tom Golden, Allen Rose; *sets:* Robert Connavale; *voices:* Arnold Stang, Sid Raymond, Gwen Davies; *mus:* Winston Sharples; *title song:* Hal David, Leon Carr; *ph:* Leonard McCormick; *prod mgr:* Seymour Shultz; *col:* Tech. *sd:* RCA. 6 min. • Herman and his nephews' visit to the Penny Arcade is marred by the appearance of Katnip.

4588. Of Rice and Hen (*Looney Tunes*) 14 Nov. 1953; *p.c.:* WB; *dir:* Robert McKimson; *story:* Warren Foster; *anim:* Herman Cohen, Rod Scribner, Phil de Lara, Charles McKimson; *lay:* Robert Givens; *back:* Richard H. Thomas; *ed:* Treg Brown; *voices:* Mel Blanc, Bea Benaderet; *mus:* Carl Stalling; *prod mgr:* John W. Burton; *prod:* Edward Selzer *col:* Tech. *sd:* Vit. 7 min. • Miss Prissy, a spinster hen, tries to trap Foggy into marriage but he doesn't show interest until the dog disguises himself as another suitor.

4589. Of Stars and Men 1961; *p.c.:* Storyboard for Brandon; *prod:* John & Faith Hubley; *dir/des:* John Hubley; *story:* Harlow Shapley, John & Faith Hubley; *key anim:* William Littlejohn, Gary Mooney; *sets/anim:* John Hubley, Patricia Byron, Faith Hubley, Nina di Gangi; *ed:* Faith Hubley; *voices:* Harlow Shapley, Mark & Hampy Hubley; *mus dir:* Walter Trampler; *col:* East. *sd.* 53 min. • Based on Harlow Shapley's book, the story tells of man's place in the universe.

4590. Of Thee I Sting (*Looney Tunes*) 17 Aug. 1946; *p.c.:* WB; *dir:* I. Freleng; *story:* Michael Maltese; *anim:* Gerry Chiniquy, Manuel Perez, Ken Champin, Virgil Ross; *lay:* Hawley Pratt; *back:* Paul Julian; *ed:* Treg Brown; *voices:* Robert C. Bruce, Mel Blanc; *mus:* Carl Stalling; *prod mgr:* John W. Burton; *prod:* Edward Selzer; *col:* Tech. *sd:* Vit. 7 min. • Mosquitoes are seen training for an attack on a fat, succulent farmer. After the battle they receive their decorations.

4591. Off His Rockers 17 July 1992; *p.c.:* Walt Disney; *dir:* Barry Cook; *story/development:* Barry Cook, Paul Steele, Pete Cook, Alex Kupershmidt; *prod:* Tad A. Gielow; *anim sup:* Rob Bekuhrs, Alex Kupershmidt, James R. Tooley; *anim:* Tom Bancroft, Linda Bel, Paul McDonald; *fx anim:* Jeff Dutton, Lisa Reinert, Tony West, Jennifer Oliver; *inbet:* James Young Jackson, Kellie D. Lewis, Tamara Lusher, Anthony Wayne Michaels; *key clean-up:* Tracy M. Lee; *clean-up:* Philip S. Boyd, Robert O. Corley, Sam Ewing, Christine Lawrence Finney, Daniel A. Gracey, Matt Novak, Bryan M. Sommer; *art dir:* Ric Sluiter; *visual development:* Tony Bancroft, Rob Bekuhrs, Lou Dellarosa, Trey Finney, Steve Goldberg, Levi Louis; *lay:* Davy Liu; *back:* Robert E. Stanton, Kevin Turcotte; *compositor:* David J. Rowe; *ed:* Chuck Williams; *mus:* Bruce Broughton; *score mix/rec:* Robert Fernandez; *anim check:* Laurie Sacks; *editorial dpt.: post-prod co-ord:* Jeannine Berger; *asst ed:* Beth Collins-Stegmaier; *col timer:* Dale E. Grahn; *neg cutter:* Mary Beth Smith; *i&p:* Pam Darley, Suzie Ewing, Fran Kirsten, Michael D. Lusby, Monica Murdock, Lynn Rippberger, Jo Ann Tzuanos; *film rec operator:* Christine Beck, Christopher W. Gee, Chuck Warren; *digitizing ph:* Jo Ann Breuer, Karen China, Bob Cohen, Lynnette Cullen, Gareth Fishbaugh, Cindy Garcia, Kent Gordon, Robyn Roberts, Gina Wooten; *ph:* Mary Lescher, Gary W. Smith; *sd re-rec mix:* Nick Alphin, Rick Ash; *foley:* Dorrie Batten, Rob Hill; *asst sd fx ed:* Jean-Pierre Bedoyan; *sd des:* Drew Neumann; *intern:* Travis Blaise, Sandra Groeneveld, Tom LaBaff, Pamela Mathues, Juan Morales, Drew Robinson; *digital systems admin:* Michael C. Bolds, Brad Lowman, Carlos Quinonez, Grace Shirado, Michael T. Sullivan, Mark M. Tokunaga; *digital prod system co-ord:* Don Gworek; *prod management: post-prod sup:* Judith Blume; *prod mgr:* Tim O'Donnell, Suzi Vissitzky Tooley, David F. Wolf; *special thanks:* Wendy Aylsworth, Paul Curasi, Maureen Donley, Joe Jiuliano, Dan Philips; *col. sd.* 5 min. • A young boy forsakes his rocking horse in favor of the latest video game. The horse tries various methods of winning back the child's attention.

4592. Off to China (*Paul Terry-Toon*) 20 Mar. 1936; *p.c.:* Moser &

Terry for Educational/Fox; *dir:* Frank Moser, Paul Terry; *mus:* Philip A. Scheib; b&w. *sd:* WE. 5¹/₂ min. • The animals take off on the *China Clipper.*

4593. Off to the Opera *(Heckle & Jeckle)* Apr. 1952; *p.c.:* TT for Fox; *dir:* Connie Rasinski; *story/voices:* Tom Morrison; *sets:* Art Bartsch; *mus:* Philip A. Scheib; *col:* Tech. *sd:* RCA. 6 min. • The magpies gatecrash the opera. The manager tries to evict them and a chase ensues.

4594. Off We Glow *(Kartune)* 29 Feb. 1952; *p.c.:* Famous for Para; *dir:* I. Sparber; *story:* Larz Bourne, Tex Henson; *anim:* Dave Tendlar, Tom Golden; *sets:* Robert Little; *voices:* Michael Fitzmaurice, Sid Raymond, Cecil Roy, Jack Mercer; *mus:* Winston Sharples *song:* Lilla Cayley Robinson, Paul Lincke; *ph:* Leonard McCormick; *prod mgr:* Seymour Shultz; *col:* Tech. *sd:* RCA. 7 min. • An insight into insect life with emphasis on fireflies.

4595. The Office Boy *(Aesop's Sound Fable)* 23 Nov. 1930; *p.c.:* Van Beuren for RKO/Pathé; *dir:* John Foster, Harry Bailey; *mus:* Gene Rodemich; b&w. *sd:* RCA. 6 min. • Mickey and Minnie clones in the EXY Railroad office. The office boy admits the President's wife in while her husband philanders with his secretary.

4596. The Office Boy *(Flip the Frog)* 16 July 1932; *p.c.:* Celebrity for MGM; *prod/dir:* Ub Iwerks; b&w. *sd:* PCP. 6 min. • Flip falls for the office secretary.

4597. Office Help *(Aesop's Film Fable)* 28 June 1925; *p.c.:* Fables Pictures Inc for Pathé; *dir:* Paul Terry; b&w. *sil.* 10 min. • No story available.

4598. Officer Duck *(Donald Duck)* 10 Oct. 1939; *p.c.:* Walt Disney prods for RKO; *dir:* Clyde Geronimi; *asst dir:* Jack Cutting, Bill McIntyre; *anim:* Ed Dunn, Alfred Eugster, Norman Ferguson, Jack Hannah, John Lounsbery, Edward Love, Lee Morehouse, Ken Peterson, Grant Simmons, Riley Thomson, Judge Whitaker; *fx:* George Rowley; *lay:* David Hilberman; *voices:* Billy Bletcher, Clarence Nash; *mus:* Oliver Wallace; *col:* Tech. *sd:* RCA. 7 min. • Officer Duck is forced to disguise himself as a baby to arrest Tiny Tom, who turns out to be considerably larger than his name indicates.

4599. Officer Pooch *(MGM Cartoon)* 6 Sept. 1941; *p.c.:* MGM; *dir:* William Hanna, Joseph Barbera; *character des:* Gus Arriola; *sets:* Joe Smith; *mus:* Scott Bradley; *prod:* Fred Quimby; *col:* Tech. *sd:* WE. 7¹/₂ min. • Officer Pooch is called upon to retrieve a kitten from atop a tree.

4600. Often an Orphan *(Looney Tunes)* 13 Aug. 1949; *p.c.:* WB; *dir:* Charles M. Jones; *story:* Michael Maltese; *anim:* Lloyd Vaughan, Ken Harris, Phil Monroe, Ben Washam; *lay:* Robert Gribbroek; *back:* Peter Alvarado; *ed:* Treg Brown; *voices:* Mel Blanc; *mus:* Carl Stalling; *prod mgr:* John W. Burton; *prod:* Edward Selzer; *col:* Tech. *sd:* Vit. 7 min. • Charlie Dog adopts himself a new master in the reluctant form of farmer Porky Pig.

4601. Oh Gentle Spring *(Terry-Toon)* 2 Apr. 1942; *p.c.:* TT for Fox; *dir:* Connie Rasinski; *story:* John Foster; *mus:* Philip A. Scheib; *col:* Tech. *sd:* RCA. 7 min. • The coming of Spring heralds new birds, insects and a romance for Br'er Rabbit.

4602. Oh How I Hate to Get Up in the Morning *(Screen Songs)* 22 Apr. 1932; *p.c.:* The Fleischer Studio for Para; *prod:* Max Fleischer; *dir:* Dave Fleischer; *anim:* Seymour Kneitel, Bernard Wolf; *mus:* Art Turkisher; *song:* Irving Berlin; *l/a:* Les Reis, Artie Dunn; b&w. *sd:* WE. 7 min. *l/a/anim.* • Radio stars, Reis and Dunn sing in uniform while the cartoon deals with Army life.

4603. Oh Mable *(Screen Car-Tune)* 15 Sept. 1924; *p.c.:* Inkwell Studio for Red Seal; *prod:* Max Fleischer; *dir:* Dave Fleischer; *anim:* Dick Huemor; *song:* Gus Kahn, Ted Fiorito; b&w. *sd:* DPC. 5 min. • No story available.

4604. Oh Susanna *(Paul Terry-Toon)* 2 Apr. 1933; *p.c.:* Moser & Terry for Educational/Fox; *dir:* Frank Moser, Paul Terry; *mus:* Philip A. Scheib; b&w. *sd:* WE. 6 min. • A wagon train heading West is the victim of an Indian attack. A pup saves the day.

4605. Oh Teacher *(Oswald the Lucky Rabbit)* 19 July 1927; *p.c.:* Winkler for Univ; *dir:* Walt Disney; *anim:* Ub Iwerks, Rollin C. Hamilton, Hugh Harman, Isadore Freleng, Ben Clopton, Norman Blackburn; *i&p:* Les Clark; *ph:* Mike Marcus; b&w. *sil.* 6 min. sd reissue: 1 Feb. 1932. • Oswald is a schoolboy who's sweetie is stolen by a rival cat.

4606. Oh What a Knight! *(Oswald the Lucky Rabbit)* 28 May 1928;

p.c.: Winkler for Univ; *dir:* Walt Disney; *ph:* Mike Marcus; b&w. *sil.* 6 min. • Oswald rescues his lady love from an ogre with all the expertise of Douglas Fairbanks.

4607. Oh, You Beautiful Doll *(Screen Songs)* 14 Oct. 1929; *p.c.:* The Fleischer Studio for Para; *dir/arranger:* Max Fleischer; *anim:* Dave Fleischer; *song:* A. Seymour Brown, Nat D. Ayer; b&w. *sd:* WE. 5 min. • A cat is annoyed by a mouse in a music shop. The mouse intervenes when he tries to romance a female customer.

4608. Oh, You Beautiful Doll *(Song Car-Tune)* Sept. 1926; *p.c.:* Inkwell Studio for Red Seal; *dir/arr:* Max Fleischer; b&w. *sil.* 5 min. • A cat has a fight with a mouse.

4609. The Oil Can Mystery *(Paul Terry-Toons)* 9 July 1933; *p.c.:* Moser & Terry for Educational/Fox; *dir:* Frank Moser, Paul Terry; *mus:* Philip A. Scheib; b&w. *sd:* WE. 6 min. • Operatic melodrama with Oil Can Harry kidnapping Fanny Zilch and tying her to the railroad tracks. T. Leffingwell Strongheart's horse saves the day.

4610. Oil Thru the Day *(Duckwood)* Aug. 1964; *p.c.:* TT for Fox; *ex prod:* Bill Weiss; *dir/anim:* Dave Tendlar; *story sup:* Tom Morrison; *story:* Larz Bourne; *sets:* Bill Focht, John Zago; *ed:* Jack McConnell; *voices:* Dayton Allen; *mus:* Jim Timmens; *ph:* Joseph Rasinski; *sd:* Elliot Grey; *col:* DeLuxe. *sd:* RCA. 6 min. • Duckwood and Donkey Ote try gatecrashing an oil constructor's company picnic.

4611. Oil's Well *(Oswald)* 9 Aug. 1929; *p.c.:* Univ; *story/anim:* Walter Lantz, "Bill" Nolan, Tom Palmer; *mus:* Bert Fiske; b&w. *sd:* WE. 6 min. • Oswald's girl's father dislikes him so much that he orders him to dig his own grave. While doing so, Ozzie strikes oil, which cheers him.

4612. The Oily American *(Merrie Melodies)* 10 July 1954; *p.c.:* WB; *dir:* Robert McKimson; *story:* Sid Marcus; *anim:* Phil de Lara, Charles McKimson, Herman Cohen, Rod Scribner; *lay:* Robert Givens; *back:* Richard H. Thomas; *ed:* Treg Brown; *voices:* Mel Blanc; *mus:* Carl Stalling; *prod mgr:* John W. Burton; *prod:* Edward Selzer; *col:* Tech. *sd:* Vit. 7 min. • A midget moose arrives for the last wealthy Mohican to hunt on his private estate.

4613. The Oily Bird *(Noveltoon)* 30 July 1954; *p.c.:* Famous for Para; *dir:* I. Sparber; *story:* Larz Bourne; *anim:* Myron Waldman, Gordon Whittier; *sets:* John Zago; *voices:* Jack Mercer, Gwen Davies; *mus:* Winston Sharples; *ph:* Leonard McCormick; *prod mgr:* Seymour Shultz; *col:* Tech. *sd:* RCA. 6 min. • A hungry hawk attempts to snare Inchy the worm for his breakfast.

4614. Oily Hare *(Merrie Melodies)* 26 July 1952; *p.c.:* WB; *dir:* Robert McKimson; *story:* Tedd Pierce; *anim:* Rod Scribner, Phil de Lara, Charles McKimson, Herman Cohen; *lay:* Peter Alvarado; *back:* Richard H. Thomas; *ed:* Treg Brown; *voices:* Mel Blanc, Bea Benaderet; *mus:* Carl Stalling; *prod mgr:* John W. Burton; *prod:* Edward Selzer; *col:* Tech. *sd:* Vit. 7 min • A Texan millionaire wants to drill for oil in Bugs' home ... but the rabbit has other ideas.

4615. Okey-Dokey Donkey *(Noveltoon)* 16 May 1958; *p.c.:* Para Cartoons; *dir:* I. Sparber; *story:* Jack Mercer; *anim:* Al Eugster, Danté Barbetta; *sets:* John Zago; *voices:* Gwen Davies; *mus:* Winston Sharples; *ph:* Leonard McCormick; *prod mgr:* Abe Goodman; *col:* Tech. *sd:* RCA. 6 min. • A lonely donkey finds companionship with a Merry-go-Round horse named Marilyn.

4616. The Ol' Swimmin' 'Ole *(Oswald the Lucky Rabbit)* 6 Feb. 1928; *p.c.:* Winkler for Univ; *dir:* Walt Disney; *anim:* Hugh Harman, Rollin C. Hamilton; *ph:* Mike Marcus; b&w. *sil.* 5 min. • Oswald and friends have fun around the local swimming hole.

4617. The Old Army Game *(Donald Duck)* 5 Nov. 1943; *p.c.:* Walt Disney prods for RKO; *dir:* Jack King; *asst dir:* Esther Newell; *story:* Carl Barks, Jack Hannah; *anim:* Paul Allen, Bob Carlson, Hal King, Charles A. Nichols; *lay:* Bill Herwig; *voices:* Billy Bletcher, Clarence Nash; *mus:* Paul J. Smith; *col:* Tech. *sd:* RCA. 7 min. • Pvt. Donald fools Sgt. Pete while he is AWOL. Pete discovers the ruse and a chase ensues culminating in the Sergeant believing Donald has been cut in half.

4618. Old Black Joe *(Screen Songs)* 5 Apr. 1929; *p.c.:* The Fleischer Studio for Para; *dir/arranger:* Max Fleischer; *anim:* Dave Fleischer; *song:* Stephen Foster; b&w. *sd.* 6 min. • No story available.

4619. Old Black Joe (*Song Car-Tune*) Oct. 1926; *p.c.:* Inkwell Studio for Red Seal; *prod:* Max Fleischer; *dir:* Dave Fleischer; *song:* Stephen Foster; b&w. *sil.* 5 min. • A modern parody about a wife being after the dough, ending with Joe being chased by his better half with a rolling pin.

4620. Old Blackout Joe (*Phantasy*) 27 Aug. 1942; *p.c.:* Colum; *dir:* Paul Sommer; *story:* Ford Banes; *anim:* Jim Armstrong; *lay:* Clark Watson; *ed:* Edward Moore; *voices:* Danny Webb; *mus:* Paul Worth; *prod mgr:* Ben Schwalb; b&w. *sd:* RCA. 5¹/₂ min. • A Harlem Air Raid Warden's struggle with a flame that refuses to extinguish. Initiated by Frank Tashlin before he left the studio.

4621. Old Doc Yak *p.c.:* Selig Polyscope Co; created by Sidney Smith; b&w. *sil.* • *1913:* Old Doc Yak 11 July. Old Doc Yak (and) **The Artist's Dream** 29 Oct. Old Doc Yak's Christmas 30 Oct. • *1914:* Old Doc Yak, Moving Picture Artist 22 Jan. Doc Yak, Cartoonist 14 Mar. Doc Yak the Poultryman 11 Apr. Over the Fence and Out 11 Apr. Doc Yak's Temperance Lecture 2 May. Doc Yak the Marksman 9 May. Doc Yak Bowling 23 May. Doc Yak's Zoo 30 May. Doc Yak and the Limited Train 6 June. Doc Yak's Wishes 11 June. Doc Yak's Bottle 16 Sept. Doc Yak's Cats 15 Oct. Doc Yak Plays Golf 24 Oct. Doc Yak and Santa Claus 8 Dec. *p.c.*—Chicago Tribune Animated Weekly • *1915:* Doc in the Ring 18 Sept. Doc the Ham Actor 16 Oct. • Sidney Smith's goat character brought to life from the comic pages.

4622. Old Dog Tray (*Paul Terry-Toons*) 21 Mar. 1935; *p.c.:* Moser & Terry for Educational/Fox; *dir:* Frank Moser, Paul Terry; *mus:* Philip A. Scheib; b&w. *sd:* WE. 5¹/₂ min. • When the dog is tossed out by the Farmer, the mice take over the house. They float about on bubbles and when the dog invites his master to join in, they both land in the mud.

4623. The Old Fire Horse (*Terry-Toon*) 28 July 1939; *p.c.:* TT for Fox; *dir:* Eddie Donnelly; *story:* John Foster; *mus:* Philip A. Scheib; b&w. *sd:* RCA. 7 min. • Old Ned is replaced by a new fire engine.

4624. An Old Flame (*Krazy Kat*) 24 Apr. 1930; *p.c.:* Winkler for Colum; *anim:* Ben Harrison, Manny Gould; *mus:* Joe de Nat; *prod mgr:* James Bronis; b&w. *sd:* RCA. 6 min. • Krazy rescues a girl from a fire.

4625. The Old Folks at Home (*Ko-Ko Song Car-Tune*) 1 Feb. 1925; *p.c.:* Inkwell Studio for Red Seal; *prod:* Max Fleischer; *dir:* Dave Fleischer; b&w. *sil.* 5 min. • Ko-Ko appears and conjures-up a quartet of singers who render "Way Down Upon the Swanee River." The theater audience is encouraged to sing along, while a cartoon character fits his actions to the words.

4626. Old Glory 1964; *p.c.:* Para Cartoons; *dir/sets:* Robert Little; *col:* Tech. *sd:* RCA. • No story available.

4627. Old Glory (*Merrie Melodies*) 1 June 1939; *p.c.:* Leon Schlesinger prods for WB; *dir:* Charles M. Jones; *anim:* Bob McKimson; *lay:* Robert Givens; *back:* Paul Julian; *ed:* Tregoweth E. Brown; *voices:* John Shepperd, Mel Blanc, John Litel, Ted Pierce, Paul Taylor's Sportsmen; *mus:* Carl W. Stalling; *ph:* John W. Burton; *prod sup:* Henry Binder, Raymond G. Katz; *col:* Tech. *sd:* Vit. 10 min. • Porky dozes while trying to learn the Pledge of Allegiance and dreams of Uncle Sam showing him the undefeatable spirit of American pioneers. Produced within months of the outbreak of war in Europe, this "straight" cartoon was commissioned to accompany a Warner Bros. live-action patriotic film series to help boost morale.

4628. The Old Grey Hare (*Merrie Melodies*) 28 Oct. 1944; *p.c.:* WB; *dir:* Robert Clampett; *story/back:* Michael Sasanoff; *anim:* Robert McKimson, Manny Gould; *character des/lay:* Thomas McKimson; *ed:* Treg Brown; *voices:* Mel Blanc, Arthur Q. Bryan; *mus:* Carl W. Stalling; *prod mgr:* John W. Burton; *prod:* Edward Selzer; *col:* Tech. *sd:* Vit. 7 min. • Elmer has a vision into the future and discovers he is still hunting Bugs Bunny!

4629. Old Hokum Bucket (*Aesop's Sound Fables*) 1 Apr. 1931; *p.c.:* Van Beuren for RKO/Pathé; *dir:* John Foster; *mus:* Gene Rodemich; *song:* Samuel Woodsworth; b&w. *sd:* RCA. 6 min. • A salesman sells Farmer Al "Peppo" pills, which he feeds to his animals to pep them up.

4630. The Old House (*Happy Harmonies*) 2 May 1936; *p.c.:* MGM; *prod/dir:* Hugh Harman, Rudolf Ising; *voices:* Martha Wentworth; *mus:* Scott Bradley; *col:* Tech. *sd:* RCA. 7 min. • Honey shelters from the rain in an old house. Frightened by the scary goings-on, she enlists the help of Bosko but they are both rescued by Bosko's hound, Bruno.

4631. Old King Cole 1926; *prod:* Herbert M. Dawley; b&w. *sil.* • Silhouette film made to promote Christmas Seals.

4632. Old King Cole (*Silly Symphony*); rel 9 July 1933; *p.c.:* Walt Disney prods for UA; *dir:* David D. Hand; *anim:* Johnny Cannon, Les Clark, Joseph d'Igalo, Norman Ferguson, Nick George, Clyde Geronimi, Hardie Gramatky, Ferdinand Huszti Horvath, Edward Love, Richard Lundy, William O. Roberts, Louis Schmitt, Ben Sharpsteen, Dick Williams, Roy Williams; *fx:* Cy Young; *character des:* Ferdinand Huszti Horvath; *voice:* The Rhythmettes, Marcellite Garner; *mus:* Frank E. Churchill, Bert Lewis; *col:* Tech. *sd:* RCA. 8 min. • King Cole throws a party attended by all the Mother Goose characters.

4633. Old Mac Donald Duck (*Donald Duck*) 12 Sept. 1941; *p.c.:* Walt Disney prods for RKO; *dir:* Jack King; *asst dir:* Ralph Chadwick, Bob Newman; *story:* Harry Reeves, Carl Barks, Jack Hannah; *anim:* Paul Allen, James Armstrong, Joe Harbaugh, Hal King, Edward Love, Lee Morehouse, Ray Patin, Judge Whitaker; *fx:* Andrew Engman; *lay:* Bill Herwig; *voices:* Clarence Nash, James MacDonald; *mus:* Leigh Harline; *col:* Tech. *sd:* RCA. 7 min. • Farmer Donald has problems in milking a cow when a troublesome fly starts to bother him. Sequence used in *The Reluctant Dragon* illustrating how to animate a "walk" cycle.

4634. Old MacDonald Had a Farm (*Noveltoon*) 31 May 1945; *p.c.:* Famous for Para; *dir:* Seymour Kneitel; *story:* William Turner, Otto Messmer; *anim:* Orestes Calpini, Otto Feuer; *sets:* Robert Little; *mus:* Winston Sharples; *ph:* Leonard McCormick; *prod mgr:* Sam Buchwald; *col:* Tech. *sd:* RCA. 7 min. • The Farmer and the animals stage a jam session in the barn.

4635. The Old Man and the Flower 1962; *p.c.:* Ernest Pintoff prods for Colum; *prod/dir/story/mus:* Ernest Pintoff; *anim:* Vincent Bell, John Renza; *sets:* Leonard Glasser; *ed:* Harry Chame; *i&p:* Tina Paratore; *voices:* Dayton Allen; *mus arranged/conducted:* Norman Paris; *ph:* Robert Heath; *track analyzer:* Richard Stone; *asso prod:* Arnold Stone; *col:* East. *sd:* 8 min. • An old man is befriended by a talking flower.

4636. The Old Man of the Mountain (*Betty Boop*) 4 Aug. 1933; *p.c.:* The Fleischer Studio for Para; *prod:* Max Fleischer; *dir:* Dave Fleischer; *anim:* Bernard Wolf, Thomas Johnson; *voice:* Mae Questel; *mus:* Cab Calloway and his orchestra; b&w. *sd:* WE. 7 min. • The townsfolk are leaving on account of the old man of the mountain. Betty tames him and the villagers return.

4637. The Old Mill (*Silly Symphony*); rel 5 Nov. 1937; *p.c.:* Walt Disney prods for RKO; *dir:* Wilfred Jackson; *story:* Dick Rickard; *anim:* Ugo d'Orsi, Jack Hannah, Robert Martsch, Arthur W. Palmer, Stan Quackenbush, Ralph Somerville, Robert Stokes, Bob Wickersham, Cornett Wood; *fx:* Daniel MacManus, Joshua Meador, George Rowley, Cy Young; *atmospheric sketches:* Maurice Noble, Gustaf Tenggren; *lay:* Terrell Stapp; *back:* Claude Coats; *voices: quartet:* Jerry Phillips, Marie Arbuckle, Marta Nielsen, Barbara Whitson; Jean MacMurray, Louise Myers; *mus:* Leigh Harline; *col:* Tech. *sd:* RCA. 9 min. *Academy Award.* • A storm presents problems for a mother bird when an abandoned mill starts operating. Photographed in Multiplane, this was used as an excercise for the special effects department in preperation for Disney's feature animation.

4638. The Old Mill Pond (*Happy Harmonies*) 7 Mar. 1936; *p.c.:* MGM; *prod/dir:* Hugh Harman, Rudolf Ising; *story:* Jack Caldwell, Norm Blackburn; *anim:* Norm Blackburn; *voices:* The Four Blackbirds, Norm Blackburn; *mus:* Scott Bradley; "Tiger Rag": Harry De Costa, Edwin B. Edwards, D. James La Rocca, Anthony Sbarbaro, Larry Shields; *col:* Tech. *sd:* WE. 8 min. *Academy Award nomination.* • The bullfrogs perform their own jam session. Caricatures: Louis Armstrong, Cab Calloway, Step'n Fetchit, The Mills Brothers, Bill Robinson and Fats Waller.

4639. Old Mother Clobber (*Clint Clobber*) Sept. 1958; *p.c.:* TT for Fox; *ex prod:* Bill Weiss; *dir sup:* Gene Deitch; *dir:* Connie Rasinski; *story dir:* Tom Morrison; *story:* Larz Bourne, Eli Bauer; *anim:* Bob Kuwahara, Johnny Gent, Mannie Davis, Vinnie Bell, Al Chiarito, Jim Tyer, Larry Silverman, Ed Donnelly; *lay:* Eli Bauer; *back:* Bill Hilliker; *voices:* Allen Swift, Norma MacMillan; *mus:* Phil Scheib; *prod mgr:* Sparky Schudde; *col:* Tech. *sd:* RCA. 6 min. • Clobber babysits with a talkative little girl.

4640. Old Mother Hubbard (*ComiColor*) 17 Mar. 1935; *p.c.:* Celebrity prods; *prod/dir:* Ub Iwerks; *mus:* Carl Stalling; *col:* Ciné. *sd:* PCP. 8 min. • Old Mother Hubbard's dog eludes the Dogcatcher by hiding in the King's laundry. His antics cheer up the King who rewards Mother Hubbard with a fully automated laundry.

4641. The Old Oaken Bucket (*Terry-Toon*) 8 Aug. 1941; *p.c.:* TT for Fox; *dir:* Connie Rasinski; *story:* John Foster; *voice:* Thomas Morrison; *mus:* Philip A. Scheib; *song:* Samuel Woodsworth; *col:* Tech. *sd:* RCA. 7 min. • A frog comes calling for his girl at the bottom of a well and he takes her to the fair.

4642. The Old Pioneer (*Happy Harmonies*) 29 Sept. 1934; *p.c.:* MGM; *prod/dir:* Hugh Harman, Rudolf Ising; *voices:* Elmore Vincent, Carmen Maxwell; *mus:* Scott Bradley; *col:* Tech-2. *sd:* RCA. 7½ min. • The old Pioneer tells the tale of how he would have been scalped by savages if he hadn't have saved the Chief's son.

4643. The Old Plantation (*Happy Harmonies*) 21 Sept. 1935; *p.c.:* MGM; *prod/dir:* Hugh Harman, Rudolf Ising; *voices:* The Rhythmettes; *mus:* Scott Bradley; *col:* Tech. *sd:* RCA. 7 min. • The toys help rescue the plantation from the grasp of Simon Legree with a frantic horse race.

4644. Old Rockin' Chair Tom (*Tom & Jerry*) 18 Sept. 1948; *p.c.:* MGM; *dir:* William Hanna, Joseph Barbera; *anim:* Ed Barge, Ray Patterson, Irven Spence, Kenneth Muse; *sets:* Robert Gentle; *ed:* Fred MacAlpin; *voice:* Lillian Randolph; *mus:* Scott Bradley; *prod:* Fred Quimby; *col:* Tech. *sd:* WE. 7 min. • Tom is replaced by a younger, faster cat named "Lightning."

4645. Old Sequoia (*Donald Duck*) 21 Dec. 1945; *p.c.:* Walt Disney prods for RKO; *dir:* Jack King; *asst dir:* Joel Greenhalgh; *story:* Homer Brightman; *anim:* Bill Justice, Don Towsley, Paul Allen, Ed Aardal, Fred Kopietz, Sandy Strother, Tom Massey, Lee Morehouse; *fx:* Josh Meador; *lay:* Ernie Nordli; *back:* Merle Cox; *voices:* Billy Bletcher, Clarence Nash, Perry Norman; *mus:* Oliver Wallace; *col:* Tech. *sd:* RCA. 6½ min. • Park Ranger Donald is ordered to stop the beavers from destroying the largest tree in the national park, "Old Sequoia."

4646. The Old Shell Game (*Noveltoon*) 18 Dec. 1948; *p.c.:* Famous for Para; *dir:* Seymour Kneitel; *story:* Joe Stultz, Larry Riley; *anim:* Dave Tendlar, Tom Golden; *sets:* Robert Connavale; *voice:* Sid Raymond; *mus:* Winston Sharples; *ph:* Leonard McCormick; *prod mgr:* Sam Buchwald; *col:* Tech. *sd:* RCA. 6½ min. • A hungry wolf attempts to eat a tortoise.

4647. Old Smokey (*Captain & Kids*) 3 Sept. 1938; *p.c.:* MGM; *dir:* Isadore Freleng; *voice:* Billy Bletcher, Martha Wentworth; *mus:* Scott Bradley; *prod:* Fred Quimby; *col:* sep. *sd:* WE. 6 min. • Fire Chief Captain retires his old fire horse in favor of a streamlined engine. He then has to extinguish his own house when it catches fire.

4648. Olio for Jasper (*Madcap Models*) 19 Apr. 1946; *p.c.:* George Pal prods for Para; *prod/dir:* George Pal; *voices:* Roy Glenn, Sara Berner; *mus:* Clarence Wheeler; *col:* Tech. *sd:* WE. 7 min. • Scarecrow tries to get Jasper's snow-scene paperweight by telling a sad story of a poverty-stricken youth.

4649. Olive Oyl and Water Don't Mix (*Popeye*) 8 May 1942; *p.c.:* The Fleischer Studio for Para; *prod:* Max Fleischer; *dir:* Dave Fleischer; *story:* Jack Mercer, Jack Ward; *anim:* Dave Tendlar, Abner Kneitel; *voices:* Jack Mercer, Margie Hines, Ted Pierce; *mus:* Sammy Timberg; *prod mgr:* Sam Buchwald, Isidore Sparber; *b&w. sd:* WE. 7 min. • Popeye and Bluto agree women shouldn't be allowed on board ship but both fight for the privilege of showing Olive around their vessel.

4650. Olive Oyl for President (*Popeye*) 30 Jan. 1948; *p.c.:* Famous for Para; *dir:* I. Sparber; *story:* Joe Stultz, Larry Riley; *anim:* Tom Johnson, John Gentilella, Els Barthen; *sets:* Tom Ford; *voices:* Mae Questel, Jack Mercer, Sid Raymond; *mus:* Winston Sharples; *ph:* Leonard McCormick; *prod mgr:* Sam Buchwald; *col:* Ciné. *sd:* RCA. 6 min. • Olive states her personal reasons for being elected President.

4651. Oliver & Company 18 Nov. 1988; *p.c.:* The Walt Disney Company; *dir:* George Scribner; inspired by Charles Dickens' *"Oliver Twist"*; *scr:* Jim Cox, Timothy J. Disney, James Mangold; *story:* Vance Gerry, Mike Gabriel, Joe Ranft, Jim Mitchell, Chris Bailey, Kirk Wise, Dave Michener, Roger Allers, Gary Trousdale, Kevin Lima, Michael Cedeno, Pete Young, Leon Joosen, Samuel Graham, Gerrit Graham, Chris Hubbell, Steve Hullet, Danny Mann; *anim sup:* Mike Gabriel, Hendel Butoy, Mark Henn, Glen Keane, Ruben A. Aquino, Doug Krohn; *anim:* Phil Young, Leon Joosen, Russ Edmonds, Will Finn, Barry Temple, Ron Husband, Rick Farmiloe, Dave Pruiksma, Chris Bailey, Viki Anderson, Kevin Lima, Shawn Keller, Tony Fucile, Anthony Derosa, Jay Jackson, Kathy Zielinski, Kevin Wurzer, Jorgen Klubien, David P. Stephan, Dan Jeup, David Cutler, Jeffrey Lynch; *anim co-ord:* Bill Berg, June M. Fujimoto, Dave Suding, Tom Ferriter, Marty Korth, Chuck Williams; *character keys:* Wesley Chun, Gail Frank, Lureline Weatherly, Brian Clift, Richard Hoppe, Cyndee Whitney; *fx anim:* Barry Cook, Ted Kierscey, Kelvin Yasuda, Randy Fullmer, Dave Bossert, Dorse A. Lanpher, Jeff Howard, Glenn Chaika, Mark Myers, Mark Dindal, Eusebio Torres; *anim asst:* Carole Holiday, Steve Markowski, Ellen Woodbury, Broose Johnson, Kirk Wise, Tony Anselmo, Debra Armstrong, Dorothea Baker, Judy Barnes, Sheila Brown, Jesus Cortes, Kent Culotta, Humberto de la Fuentes, Haroldo Guimaraes, Ray Harris, Kent Holaday, Renee Holt, Emily Jiuliano, Terrey le Grady, Steve Lubin, Kaaren Lundeen, Mike McKinney, Edward Murrieta, Dave Nethery, M. Flores Nichols, Lori Noda, Dave Pacheco, Gilda Palinginis, Dana Reemes, Maria Rosetti, Natasha Selfridge, Margie Wright-Stansbery, George Sukara, Dan Tanaka, Bette Thomson, Peggy Tonkonogy, Alex Topete, Mac Torres, Jane Tucker, Stephan Zupkas; *break/inbet:* Sue Adnopoz, Scott Anderson, Matthew Bates, Carl Bell, Jerry Brice, Lee Dunkman, James Fujii, Mike Genz, Peter Gullerud, Karen Hardenbergh, Kevin Harkey, Marcia Kimura, Nancy Kniep, Teresa Martin, Brian McKim, Terry Naughton, Eric Pigors, Brian Pimental, Mike Polvani, Michael Show, Alan Smart, Juliet Stroud, Chris Wahl, Cathy Zar; *computer anim:* Tina Price, Michael Cedeno; *cgi:* Tad Gielow; *art dir:* Dan Hansen; *character des:* Mike Gabriel, Andreas Deja, Glen Keane; *prod stylist:* Guy Deel; *lay:* Rasoul Azadani, Fred Cline, Dan McHugh, Phil Phillipson, Fred Craig, Bob Smith, Bill Perkins, James Beihold, Alex Mann, Marc Christiansen, Karen Keller; *back:* Jim Coleman, Lisa Keene, Steve Butz, Tia Kratter, Phil Phillipson, Brian Sebern, John Emerson, Andy Phillipson, Bob Stanton; *ed:* Jim Melton, Mark Hester; *scene plan:* Rick Sullivan, Dave Thomson, Joe Jiuliano; *anim check:* Janet Bruce, Annamarie Costa, Karen Paat, Mavis Shafer, Kathy Barrows-Fullmer, Lisa Poitevint; *prod consultant:* Walt Stanchfield; *i&p:* Gretchen Albrecht, Chris Hecox, Cherie McGowan; *voices: Oliver:* Joey Lawrence; *Dodger:* Billy Joel; *Tito:* Cheech Marin; *Einstein:* Richard Mulligan; *Francis:* Roscoe Lee Browne; *Rita:* Sheryl Lee Ralph; *Fagin:* Dom DeLuise; *Roscoe:* Taurean Blacque; *Desoto:* Carl Weintraub; *Sykes:* Robert Loggia; *Jenny:* Natalie Gregory; *Winston:* William Glover; *Georgette:* Bette Midler; *also:* Charles Bartlett, Jonathan Brandis, Kal David, Marcia Delmar, Victor Dimattia, Judi Durand, Greg Finley, Gary Schwartz, Debbie Gates, Javier Grajeda, J.D. Hall, Robert S. Halligan Jr., Jo Ann Harris, Rosanna Huffman, Barbara Iley, Harvey Jason, Karen Kamon, Kaleena Kiff, Carol King, Marylee Kortes, Rocky Krakoff, David Lasley, Christine MacGregor, David McCharen, John McCurry, Arlin L. Miller, Nancy Parent, Whitney Rybeck, Vernon Scott, Pamela Segall, Tom Righter Snow, Eugene F. Van Beren, Frank Welker; "Once Upon a Time in New York City" sung by Huey Lewis; "Streets of Gold" sung by Ruth Pointer; "Good Company" sung by Myhanh Tran; "Buscando Guayaba" sung by Ruben Blades; *mus:* J.A.C. Redford; *orch:* Thomas Pasatieri; *mus sup:* Carole Childs; *mus ed:* Kathleen Bennett, Scot Scalise, Theresa Gilroy, David Marvit; *prod mgr:* Kathleen Gavin, Sherry Argaman, Dennis Edwards, Ron Rocha; *asst dir:* Tim O'Donnell; *prod asst:* Brett Hayden, Gregory Hinde; *post prod sup:* Dianne Ryder-Rennolds; *sd:* Brad Gunther, Sandy Berman, Randle Akerson, Marvin Walowitz, Beth Sterner, Mark Pappas; *ADR ed:* Beth Bergeron, Jessica Gallavan, Becky Sullivan; *sd asst:* Meredith Gold, Gillian Hutshing, Maggie Ostroff, Kim Nolan, Ron Meredith; *foley arts:* Sarah Jacobs, Ed Staidale; *ph:* Ed Austin, John Aardal, Errol Aubry, John Cunningham, Roncie Hantke, Brandy Hill, Ron Jackson, Dan Larsen, Dave Link, Jim Pickel, Lindsay Rogers, Dean Teves, Chuck Warren; *fx graphics:* Bernie Gagliano; *re-rec:* Gary Bourgeois, Chris Carpenter, Marc Smith; *score rec:* Joel Moss, Ethan Chase, Nick "Beemer" Basich, William Talbott, Mark Poniatoski; *opticals:* Chris B. Bushman; *col:* DeLuxe. *sd:* Dolby Surround. 71 min. • An orphan kitten named Oliver wanders the streets of New York and falls in with a pack of petty criminal canines and their human master, Fagin. When a lonely little rich girl adopts Oliver, she is kidnapped by Fagin's evil boss and the dogs come to the rescue.

4652. Olive's Boithday Presink (*Popeye*) 13 June 1941; *p.c.:* The Fleischer Studio for Para; *prod:* Max Fleischer; *dir:* Dave Fleischer; *story:* Ted Pierce; *anim:* Dave Tendlar, Thomas Golden; *ed:* Kitty Pfister; *voices:* Jack Mercer, Margie Hines; *mus:* Sammy Timberg; *prod mgr:* Sam Buchwald, Isidore Sparber; *b&w. sd:* WE. 7 min. • Popeye sets out to capture a fur coat to give Olive for her birthday.

4653. Olive's $weep$take Ticket *(Popeye)* 7 Mar. 1941; *p.c.:* The Fleischer Studio; *prod:* Max Fleischer; *dir:* Dave Fleischer; *story:* Joseph E. Stultz; *anim:* Arnold Gillespie, Abner Kneitel; *ed:* Kitty Pfister; *voices:* Jack Mercer, Margie Hines; *mus:* Sammy Timberg; *ph:* Charles Schettler; *prod mgr:* Sam Buchwald, Isidore Sparber; b&w. *sd:* WE. 6½ min. • Olive has the winning ticket but fate blows it out the window and Popeye has to retrieve it.

4654. Ollie the Owl *(Nooltoon)* Jan. 1963; *p.c.:* Para Cartoons; *dir:* Seymour Kneitel; *sets:* Robert Little; *mus:* Winston Sharples; *ph:* Leonard McCormick; *prod mgr:* Abe Goodman; *col:* Tech. *sd:* RCA. 6 min. • No story available.

4655. Olympic Champ *(Goofy)* 9 Oct. 1942; *p.c.:* Walt Disney prods for RKO; *dir:* Jack Kinney; *asst dir:* Lou Debney; *anim:* James Moore, Ken Peterson, Archie Robin, William, Bernard Wolf; *fx:* Ed Aardal, Andrew Engman, Dan MacManus, Joshua Meador, Frank Onaitis, Ed Parks, Reuben Timmens, Don Tobin; *lay:* Don da Gradi; *voice:* John McLeish; *mus:* Paul J. Smith; *col:* Tech. *sd:* RCA. 7 min. • Goofy demonstrates various aspects of the Olympic Games.

4656. On a Sunday Afternoon *(Screen Songs)* 29 Nov. 1930; *p.c.:* The Fleischer Studio for Para; *prod:* Max Fleischer; *dir:* Dave Fleischer; *anim:* Jimmie Culhane, Rudy Zamora; *mus:* Art Turkisher; b&w. *sd:* WE. 6 min. • The family goes for a Sunday drive to play golf.

4657. On Ice *(Mickey Mouse)* 28 Sept. 1935; *p.c.:* Walt Disney prods for UA; *dir:* Ben Sharpsteen; *story:* Webb Smith; *anim:* Paul Allen, Arthur Babbitt, Johnny Cannon, Norman Ferguson, Milton Kahl, Eric Larson, John McManus, Fred Spencer, Don Towsley, Marvin Woodward; *voices:* Clarence Nash, Pinto Colvig, Marcellite Garner, Walt Disney; *mus:* Bert Lewis, Frank E. Churchill; *col:* Tech. *sd:* RCA. 8 min. • Mickey and the gang go ice skating. Donald ties a kite to Pluto and Goofy uses unorthodox methods to catch fish.

4658. On the Ice *(Aesop's Film Fable)* 3 Dec. 1924; *p.c.:* Fables Pictures Inc for Pathé; *dir:* Paul Terry; b&w. *sil.* 5 min. • Shoes and bathtubs are used as a means of conveyance for the mice over the ice and snow.

4659. On the Ice *(Aesop's Film Fable)* 8 Feb. 1928; *p.c.:* Fables Pictures Inc for Pathé; *dir:* Paul Terry, Frank Moser; b&w. *sil.* 5 min. • Milton Mouse enters a sleigh race and the villainous cat steals his girl while the race is in progress. When he wins the race, he has another chase to rescue his girl.

4660. On the Links *(Aesop's Film Fable)* 10 Nov. 1928; *p.c.:* Fables Pictures Inc for Pathé *dir:* Paul Terry; b&w. *sil.* 5 min. • The mice disrupt Farmer Al and Waffles Cat's game of golf. One mouse drinks from a wishing well and wishes Al would use his nose to push the golf ball around the course, through a water hazard and into a beehive. The angry bees chase him over the horizon.

4661. On the Pan *(Little King)* 24 Nov. 1933; *p.c.:* Van Beuren for RKO; *dir:* George Stallings; *anim:* Jim Tyer; *mus:* Gene Rodemich; b&w. *sd:* RCA. 6 min. • The Little King is on Safari in Africa, only just escaping the cannibal cooking pot.

4662. On with the New *(Betty Boop)* 2 Dec. 1938; *p.c.:* The Fleischer Studio for Para; *prod:* Max Fleischer; *dir:* Dave Fleischer; *voices:* Margie Hines, Jack Mercer; *mus:* Sammy Timberg; *prod sup:* Sam Buchwald, Isidore Sparber; b&w. *sd:* WE. 7 min. • Betty leaves her job in a diner to look after babies in an orphanage.

4663. The Once Over *(Swifty & Shorty)* June 1964; *p.c.:* Para Cartoons; *dir:* Seymour Kneitel; *story/voices:* Eddie Lawrence; *anim:* Morey Reden; *sets:* Robert Little; *mus:* Winston Sharples; *ph:* Leonard McCormick; *prod mgr:* Abe Goodman; *col:* Tech. *sd:* RCA. 6 min. • Shorty makes the cardinal error of entering Swifty's barber shop for a mere haircut.

4664. Once Upon a Forest 18 June 1993; *p.c.:* Hanna-Barbera/HTV Cymru/Wales for Fox; *dir:* Charles Grosvenor; *ex prod:* William Hanna, Paul Gertz; *prod:* David Kirschner, Jerry Mills; based on the Welsh story created by Rae Lambert; *scr:* Mark Young, Kelly Ward; *visual fx sup:* Glenn Chaika; *character des:* Judith Holmes Clarke, Joseph Ekers; *anim dir:* Dave Michener; *key anim:* Joseph Ekers, Cynthia Wells; *anim:* Barry Anderson, Frank Andrina, Brenda Banks, Roger Chiasson, Marc Christiansen, Zeon Davush, David Feiss, Ralph Fernan, Brad Forbush, Kent Hammerstrom, Joe Hawkins, Dan Hunn, Andre Knutson, Ernesto Lopez, Sean Newton,

Mike Nguyen, William Nunes, Dana O'Connor, Kevin Petrilak, Kunio Shimamura, I-Sin "Cyndi" Tang, Robert Tyler, Kevin Wurzer, John Walker; *Lapiz Azul Animacion: key anim:* Javier Gutierrez, Ventura Rodriguez, Manuel Galiana, Paco Alaminos, Sergio Pablos; *anim:* Miguel Alminos, Ma Carmen Gonzalez, Alberto Conejo, Roberto Garcia, Pedro Mohedana, Luis Varela, Antonio Tena, Mariano Rueda; *inbet:* Marisol Garcia, Luis Amor, Ana Carmona, Miguel Canoza, Angel Mafcano, Sabina Suarez, Ma Jesus Gigoso, Raquel Serrano, José Luis Fozo, Ignacio Meneu; *Jaime Diaz Studio: anim sup:* Jaime Diaz; *anim:* Carlos Aguero, Nestor Cordoba, Silvia Nanni, Miguel Nanni, Rudolfo Mutuverria, Alberto Grisolia, Roberto Barrios, Natalio Zirulnik, Omar Hetchenkoff, Franco Bittolo; *asst anim:* Gloria Saavedra, Gaston Oliva, Raul Barbero, Luis Luque, Adriana Cerrotti, Herman Canellas, Tino Cordora; *lay:* Carlos Quartieri, José Sanchez; *ph:* Osvaldo Garcia; *prod sup:* Bill Diaz; *A-Film: key anim:* Jorgen Lerdam; *anim:* Michael Helmuth, Stefan Fjeldmark, Meelis Arulepp, Jesper Moller, Anna Gellert Nielsen, Karsten Kiilerich, Kim Hagen Jensen; *asst anim:* Hope Devlin, Thomas Ferger, Ando Tammik, Tinna Jespersen, Rigmor Tokerod, Ilan Hatukah; *prod sup:* Anders Mastrup; *prod asst:* Helle Hansen; *The Hollywood Cartoon Company: prod sup:* Rocky Solotoff; *studio ex:* G. Sue Shakespeare; *anim sup:* Skip Jones; *anim:* Linda Miller, Jan Hooper, Mark Koetsier, Matthew Bates, Mark Pudleiner, Chad Stewart; *Phoenix Animation Ltd.: anim sup:* Chris Sauve; *prod sup:* Michael Hefferon; *anim:* Charlie Bonafacio, John Collins, Jens Pindal, Greg Court, Doug Bennett, Ron Zorman, Jamie Oliff, Rob Shedlowich, Hanna Kukal, Doug Smith, Chris Shouten, Marc Sevier; *asst anim:* Shannon Murphy, Rich Draper, Denise Bradshaw, James McCrimmon, Monica Luciana, Dave Demorest, June Scannell; *prod co-ord:* Peter Denomme; *lay:* Stephen Wood, Andre Krystoforski, Sean Sullivan, Peter Bielicki; *Matias Marcos Animation: anim:* Matias Marcos, Alberto Conejo; *asst anim:* Julio Santos Rosado, Yolanda Jaraquemada; *inbet:* Lola Gonzalo Rodriguez, Eduardo Varlero Garcia, Pedro Alvarez Moreno; *addit anim:* Wang Films: *fx anim:* Alfred Holter, Frog Shy, Victor Lu, Adam Wu, Harold Tzeng, Richard Tsay, Mars Lu, Jackie Lu; *anim check:* Perng Yuh Tzy, Jong I. Fang, Tsaur Shu Ping, Osvaldo Garcia; *final check:* Jang Yuh Tsyr; *asso prod:* James Wang; *prod mgr:* Catherine Winder, Steve Ho, Bob Marples; *prod sup:* Judy Chang; *Lapiz Azul Animation: prod sup:* Manuel J. Garcia; *visual fx anim:* Margaret Craig-Chang, Kathleen Quaife-Hodge, Kim Knowlton, John Armstrong, Jeff Howard; *computer anim:* Mark Swanson Prods: *anim check sup:* Gina Bradley; *anim check:* Diane Matranga, Bob Revell, Susan Burke, Beverly Randles, Laura Craig, Bonnie Blough, Cindy Goode; *sup film ed:* Pat A. Foley; *prod des:* Carol Holman Grosvenor, Bill Proctor; *art dir:* Carol Holman Grosvenor; *character des:* Joseph Ekers; *storyboard:* Charles Grosvenor, Dave Michener, Robert Onorato, Chris Otsuki; *lay:* James Beihold, Simon Varela Cristales, Bill Proctor, Scott Uehara, Arlan Jewell, Grigor Boyadjiev, James C. Breckenridge, Franklyn F. Brunner, Spencer G. Davis, Shelly Dreman, David Womersley, Enrique May, Owen Fitzgerald, David P. Martin, Darrell Rooney, Dave Hilberman, Lew Ott, Herb Hazelton, Carol Lundberg; *back sup:* Dennis Durrell, (Wang Films) David Womersley, Liou Biing Hwang; *back key:* George Taylor, Donna Prince, Mia Raynis, Craig Armstrong, Bonnie Callahan; *back* (Wang Films): Lin Mei Chun, Liu Jin Chiueh, Yeh Ching Liang, Shen Kai Chen, Fu Pei Kai, Lin Wen An, Yiin Gwo Chi, Chang Chien Shyong, Jou Pen Kai; *back lay* (Jaime Diaz Studio): Carlos Quartieri, José Sanchez, (Phoenix Animation Ltd.) Stephen Wood, Sean Sullivan, Andre J. Krystorforski, Peter Bielicki; *i&p:* Kimberly Conte, Audrey Covello, Etsuko Fijioka, Lori Hanson, Christine Kingsland, JoAnne Plein; *blue sketch:* Roxanne Steven, Mercedes J. Sichon; *color key:* Rose Ann Stire; *anim sup:* Karen Greslie; *mark up/model paint:* Pattie Torocsik, (Wang Films) Yan Fran Yi; *ink:* Alison Leopold; *final check:* Nelda Ridley; *i&p sup* (Wang Films): Saskia Raevouri, Sheih Tai Hua, Sheu Yuh, Liu Feng Jiau, Jaw Yuek Wu; *clean-up* (Wang Films): Chen Shu Li, Huang Shyh An, Hour Chiou Yuan, Li Herng Yu, Jong Jiunn Hui, Wu Jia Shin, Chiang Sheaau Chuan, Chen Shing Dyi, Wu Gwo Chen, Liu Fang Li, Perng Tzu Jung, Juan Shu Ling, Lu Shodu I, Wang Yung Fu, Ku Chih Chieh, Chen Woei Yeh, Chang Wen Jing, Wen Yunn Hua, Shyu Shuang Mei; *voices: Cornelius:* Michael Crawford; *Phineas:* Ben Vereen; *Abigail:* Ellen Blain; *Edgar:* Ben Gregory; *Russell:* Paige Gosney; *Michelle:* Elizabeth Moss; *Abigail's Father:* Paul Eiding; *Edgar's Mother:* Janet Waldo; *Russell's Mother:* Susan Silo; *Willy:* Will Nipper; *Waggs:* Charlie Adler; *Bosworth:* Rickey Collins; *Bosworth's Mother:* Angel Harper; *Marshbird:* Don Reed; *Truck Driver:* Robert David Hall; *Russell's Brother:* Benjamin Smith; *Russell's*

Sister: Haven Hartman; *mus:* James Horner; *orch:* John Neufeld, Conrad Pope, Joel Rosenbaum, Brad Dechter; *mus ed:* Jim Henrikson; *mus rec:* Shawn Murphy; music recorded by the London Symphony Orchestra; *vocal back:* The Andrea Crouch Singers, The New London Children's Choir; *mus co-ord:* Bodie Chandler; *songs:* James Horner, Will Jennings, Michael Tavera, Kelly Ward, Mark Young, Andrea Crouch, Sandra Crouch; *titles & opticals:* Perpetual Motion Pictures; *timing:* Ray Patterson; *ph sup:* Daniel Bunn, Steven A. Mills, (Wang Films) Ling Jinn Yih; *ph:* Roncie Hantke, Robert Jacobs, James Keefer, Neil Owen Viker, Frederick T. Ziegler, (Wang Films) Jin Guey Fuh, Tarng Shiang I; *sd ed:* David Lewis Yewdall, Barbara J. Boguski, Stacey A. Foiles, Paul Jyrala; *sound co-ord:* Lisa A. Yewdall; *sd rec:* Larry Hoki, Ed Collins; *mus:* Shawn Murphy; *ADR rec:* Preston Oliver, Ezra Dweck; *sd rec:* Jeffrey Perkins, Kurt Kassulke, Shawn Murphy; *foley:* Joan Rowe, Ellen Heuer, Robert Girard, Pirjo Jyrala; *prod co-ord:* Yvonne Palmer; *prod mgr:* Zahra Dowlatabadi; *post prod mgr:* Terry W. Moore; *HTV Cymru Prod consultants:* John Watkin, Mike Young; *col:* CFI. *sd:* Dolby stereo. 71 min. • The creatures of Dapplewood Forest witness the crash of a truck transporting chemicals, spilling its toxic cargo. Cornelius the badger's niece, Michelle, is affected by the fumes and the only cure is a herbal remedy. But all vegetation has been destroyed by the spillage. Three young "furlings" have to travel to a meadow within forty-eight hours to find the herbs to save her life.

4665. Once Upon a Mouse 10 July 1981; *p.c.:* Kramer/Rocklen Studios in association with Walt Disney Prods; *dir:* Jerry Kramer, Gary Rocklen; *prod:* Jerry Kramer, Gary Rocklen, Howard E. Green, Cardon Walker; *prod co-ord:* Arthur Pierson; *scr:* Jack Weinstein, Robert Resnikoff; *title anim:* Chris Buchinsky, David Brain; *graphics:* Ken Rudolf, Oscar Pitman, Bill Morgan; *ed:* Arthur Pierson, Richard Bock; *voices:* Aurora Miranda, Betty Lou Gerson, Hans Conried; *songs:* "Brazzle Dazzle Day" by Al Kasha, Joel Hirschhorn, arranged and conducted by Irwin Kostal; "The Rescuers" by and conducted by Artie Butler; "You Can Fly! You Can Fly!" by Sammy Fain; *anim ph:* Dion Hatch, Richard Cohen; *sd fx ed:* James Stanley; *prod asst:* Steven Rodgers; *col:* Tech. *sd.* 27 min. • A tribute to the animated films of Walt Disney, promoting the studio's twentieth feature-length cartoon, *The Fox and the Hound.* To illustrate the music are excerpts from *The Band Concert, Fantasia, Make Mine Music, Melody Time* and *Dumbo.*

4666. Once Upon a Rhyme (*Casper*) 20 Dec. 1950; *p.c.:* Famous for Para; *dir:* I. Sparber; *story:* I. Klein; *anim:* Myron Waldman, Larry Silverman; *sets:* Robert Little; *voices:* Alan Shay, Jackson Beck, Sid Raymond, Cecil Roy; *mus:* Winston Sharples; *title song:* Mack David, Jerry Livingston; *ph:* Leonard McCormick; *prod mgr:* Sam Buchwald; *col:* Tech. *sd:* RCA. 8 min. • Casper journeys to Mother Goose Land where he saves Red Riding Hood from the clutches of Wolfie.

4667. Once Upon a Time Dec. 1934; *p.c.:* A-C for the Massachussetts Dpt of Public Safety and other state groups; *prod:* W.P. Bach; *dir:* F. Lyle Goldman; *col:* Tech. *sd.* 7 min. • Characters "Discourtesy" and "Carelessness," teach road safety. Contributed by Metropolitan Life Insurance and distributed free to cinemas.

4668. Once Upon a Wintertime (*Marquee Musical*) 17 Sept. 1954; *p.c.:* Walt Disney prods for RKO; *dir:* Hamilton Luske; *col:* Tech. *sd:* RCA. • A romance blossoms between a boy and girl against a snow setting. • See: *Melody Time*

4669. The One-Armed Bandit (*Cartune*) 27 Mar. 1939; *p.c.:* Walter Lantz prods for Univ; *dir:* Alex Lovy; *story:* Victor McLeod, James Miele; *anim:* George Grandpré, Hicks Lokey; *sets:* Edgar Keichle; *voices:* Billy Bletcher, Mel Blanc; *mus:* Frank Marsales; *prod mgr:* George Hall; *b&w. sd:* WE. 7 min. • An old fashioned melodrama showing Grandpop losing the mortgage money on a fruit machine until his daughter senses danger and comes to his rescue.

4670. One Cab's Family 15 May 1952; *p.c.:* MGM; *dir:* Tex Avery; *story:* Rich Hogan, Roy Williams; *anim:* Grant Simmons, Michael Lah, Walter Clinton; *character des/lay:* Ed Benedict; *back:* John Didrik Johnsen; *ed:* Jim Faris; *voices:* Daws Butler, June Foray; *mus:* Scott Bradley; *ph:* Jack Stevens; *prod:* Fred Quimby; *col:* Tech. *sd:* WE. 8 min. • Mama and Papa Taxicab have problems with their rebellious son who wants to be a hot-rod.

4671. One Droopy Knight (*Droopy*) 6 Dec. 1957; *p.c.:* MGM; *prod:* William Hanna, Joseph Barbera; *dir:* Michael Lah; *story:* Homer Brightman;

anim: Bill Schipek, Ken Southworth, Irven Spence, Herman Cohen; *character des/lay:* Ed Benedict; *back:* F. Montealegre; *ed:* Jim Faris; *voice:* Bill Thompson; *mus:* Scott Bradley; *ph:* Jack Stevens; *prod mgr:* Hal Elias; *col:* Tech. *sd:* WE. 7 min. CS. • Sir Droop-a-Lot and Sir Butch-a-Lot do battle with a dragon for the hand of the fair princess.

4672. One Froggy Evening (*Merrie Melodies*) 31 Dec. 1955; *p.c.:* WB; *dir:* Charles M. Jones; *story:* Michael Maltese; *anim:* Abe Levitow, Richard Thompson, Ken Harris, Ben Washam; *lay:* Robert Gribbroek; *back:* Philip de Guard; *voice:* Harry Wiliam Roberts; *ed:* Treg Brown; *mus:* Milt Franklyn; *prod mgr:* John W. Burton; *prod:* Edward Selzer; *col:* Tech. *sd:* Vit. 7 min. • A man finds a box containing a singing frog. He tries to exploit his good fortune but the frog won't sing in public.

4673. One Funny Knight (*Herman & Katnip*) 22 Nov. 1957; *p.c.:* Para Cartoons; *dir:* Dave Tendlar; *story:* Jack Mercer; *anim:* Wm. B. Pattengill, Charles Harriton; *sets:* John Zago; *voices:* Arnold Stang, Sid Raymond, Jack Mercer, Gwen Davies; *mus:* Winston Sharples; *ph:* Leonard McCormick; *prod mgr:* Seymour Shultz; *col:* Tech. *sd:* RCA. 6 min. • Sir Katnip captures the mouse Princess for a ransome but Herman is on hand to rescue her.

4674. One Game Pup (*Aesop's Film Fable*) 11 Dec. 1924; *p.c.:* Fables Pictures Inc for Pathé; *dir:* Paul Terry; *b&w. sil.* 5 min. • A black pup is accepted by the Farmer's pack of white pups only after he rescues a duck from the clutches of a ravenous wolf.

4675. One Good Turn (*Aesop's Film Fable*) 25 May 1924; *p.c.:* Fables Pictures Inc for Pathé; *dir:* Paul Terry; *b&w. sil.* 5 min. • A mouse removes a tin can from a pup's tail. The pup returns the favor by saving the mouse from a swarm of bees. Moral: "One good turn deserves another."

4676. One Gun Gary in the Nick of Time (*Terry-Toon*) 27 Jan. 1939; *p.c.:* TT for Fox; *dir:* Ed Donnelly; *story:* John Foster; *mus:* Philip A. Scheib; *b&w. sd:* RCA. 6 min. • No story available.

4677. One Ham's Family 14 Aug. 1943; *p.c.:* MGM; *dir:* Tex Avery; *story:* Rich Hogan; *anim:* Preston Blair, Ed Love, Ray Abrams; *character des:* Claude Smith; *sets:* John Didrik Johnsen; *ed:* Fred MacAlpin; *voices:* Dave Barry, Pinto Colvig, Sara Berner; *mus:* Scott Bradley; *prod:* Fred Quimby; *col:* Tech. *sd:* WE. 7 min. • Junior Pig deals with the Wolf when he arrives on Christmas Eve dressed as Santa.

4678. One Horse Town (*Woody Woodpecker*) May 1968; *p.c.:* Walter Lantz prods for Univ; *dir:* Paul J. Smith; *story:* Cal Howard; *anim:* Les Kline, Al Coe; *sets:* Nino Carbe; *voices:* Daws Butler, Grace Stafford; *mus:* Walter Greene; *prod mgr:* William E. Garity; *col:* Tech. *sd:* RCA. 6 min. • When Dirty Dan takes over a western town, he takes an instant dislike to Woody and Sugarfoot so he challenges them to a race where the loser leaves town.

4679. One Hundred and One Dalmatians 25 Jan. 1961; *p.c.:* Walt Disney prods for BV; *dir:* Wolfgang Reitherman, Hamilton S. Luske, Clyde Geronimi; *prod des:* Ken Anderson; *story adapt:* Bill Peet; *anim dir:* Milt Kahl, Frank Thomas, Marc Davis, John Lounsbery, Oliver Johnston, Eric Larson; *anim:* Hal King, Les Clark, Cliff Nordberg, Blaine Gibson, Eric Cleworth, John Sibley, Art Stevens, Julius Svendsen, Hal Ambro, Ted Berman, Bill Keil, Don Lusk, Dick Lucas, Amby Paliwoda; *fx:* Jack Boyd, Jack Buckley, Dan MacManus, Ed Parks; *character des:* Bill Peet, Tom Oreb; *styling:* Colin Campbell, Don Griffith, Erni Nordli, Walt Peregoy; *lay:* Basil Davidovich, Joe Hale, Vance Gerry, McLaren Stewart, Dale Barnhart, Ray Aragon, Dick Ung, Sammy June Lanham, Homer Jonas, Victor Haboush, Al Zinnen; *back:* Al Dempster, Ralph Hulett, Bill Layne, Anthony Rizzo; *ed:* Donald Halliday, Roy M. Brewer Jr.; *voices: Pongo:* Rod Taylor; *Jasper/The Colonel/Mechanic/Simpkins:* J. Pat O'Malley; *Cruella de Ville/Miss Birdwell:* Betty Lou Gerson; *Nanny–Cook/Lucy/Queen:* Martha Wentworth; *Roger Radcliff:* Ben Wright; *Perdita:* Cate Bauer, Lisa Daniels; *Sgt Tibbs/Skye Terrier:* Dave Frankham; *Horace/Inspector Craven:* Frederick Worlock; *Collie/Quizmaster:* Tom Conway; *Towser/Truck Driver:* Tudor Owen; *Danny:* George Pelling; *TV Announcer:* Ramsay Hill; *Cow:* Sylvia Marriott; *Princess:* Queenie Leonard; *Duchess:* Marjorie Bennett; *Patch:* Micky Maga; *Rover:* Barbara Luddy; *Lucky:* Mimi Gibson, *Penny:* Sandra Abbott; *Captain:* Thurl Ravenscroft; *Rolly:* Barbara Beaird; *Anita:* Lisa Davis; *Puppy:* Rickie Sorenson; *Setter:* Basil Ruysdael; *Sheepdog & Hound barks:* Dal McKennon; *Misc dog barks:* Max Smith, Bob Stevens, Clarence Nash; *Dirty Dawson:* Paul Frees; "*Cruella de Ville* " sung by: Bill Lee, Jeanne Bruns;

"Dalmatian Plantation" *sung by* Bill Lee, Jeanne Bruns, The Mello Men; "Kanine Krunchies" *sung by* Lucille Bliss; *mus:* George Bruns; *orch:* Franklyn Marks; *songs:* Mel Leven; *mus ed:* Evelyn Kennedy; *special processes:* Ub Iwerks ASC, Eustace Lycett; *sd sup:* Robert O. Cook; *prod mgr:* Ken Peterson; *col:* Tech. *sd:* RCA. 79 min. • Adaptation of Dodie Smith's story concerning two dalmatians who go in search of their fifteen pups who have been stolen by the villainess to make dogskin coats. More have been added, totaling ninety-nine and the heroes have the task of rescuing them all.

4680. 101 Dalmatians 27 Nov. 1996; *p.c.:* Disney Enterprises/Great Oaks for BV; *special visual fx/anim:* ILM; *asso visual fx sup:* Doug Smythe; *character anim sup:* Tom Bertino, Daniel Jeannette; *sup digital sculptor:* Geoff Campbell; *character anim:* Philip Edward Alexy, David Byers Brown, John Campanard, Mike Eames, Steve Nichols, Marjolaine Tremblay; *video game seq: Disney Interactive prod:* Scott Pettit; *snr prod:* Noah Dudley; *project mgr:* David A. Lucca; *story sketch:* Ed Olson; *character sketch:* Shelli Droe; *anim mgr:* Bob Rademacher; *Creative Capers Entertainment prod:* Sue Shakespeare; *creative prod:* Terry Shakespeare, David Molina; *3d prod:* Duane Loose; *prod co-ord:* Monica Zorman; *cgi anim:* Ron Zorman, Caragh O'Connor, Rich Draper; *cgi art:* Robert Rose, Dave Otte, Candice Goldfarb, Leon Gor; *storyboard:* Adam van Wyk; *anim:* Shane Zalvin, Adam van Wyk, Michael Kiely, Dermot O'Connor, John Dillon; *col:* Tech. *sd:* DDS. 102 min. *l/a.* • Live-action version of the 1961 animated feature: A struggling computer game designer and his wife have their fifteen dalmatian puppies stolen and the dogs' parents set out to track them down.

4681. 100 Pygmies and Andy Panda *(Andy Panda)* 22 Apr. 1940; *p.c.:* Walter Lantz prods for Univ; *dir:* Alex Lovy; *voices:* Dave Weber, Sara Berner; *mus:* Frank Marsales; *prod mgr:* George Hall; *col:* Tech. *sd:* WE. 7 min. • Andy upsets the Witch Doctor with a magic wand and is chased by pygmies.

4682. The One-Man Dog *(Aesop's Film Fable)* 26 June 1927; *p.c.:* Fables Pictures Inc for Pathé; *dir:* Paul Terry; b&w. sil. 10 min. • A mischievous pup is kicked out but returns evil for good by saving his playmate from kidnappers. Moral: "A stitch in time saves embarrassment."

4683. The One Man Navy *(Terry-Toon)* 5 Sept. 1941; *p.c.:* TT for Fox; *dir:* Mannie Davis; *story:* John Foster; *voices:* Arthur Kay, Thomas Morrison; *mus:* Philip A. Scheib; *col:* Tech. *sd:* RCA. 6 min. • Rejected by the Army, Gandy Goose joins the Navy and goes to war with farm recruitments. He induces the chickens to supply "Hen Grenades" to bomb an enemy submarine.

4684. One Meat Brawl *(Merrie Melodies)* 18 Jan. 1947; *p.c.:* WB; *dir:* Robert McKimson; *story:* Warren Foster; *lay:* Cornett Wood; *back:* Richard H. Thomas; *ed:* Treg Brown; *voices:* Mel Blanc, Stan Freberg, Bill Roy; *mus:* Carl Stalling; *prod mgr:* John W. Burton; *prod:* Edward Selzer; *col:* Tech. *sd:* Vit. 7 min. • Porky wants to add a groundhog to his miniature zoo and sends his dog out to get one.

4685. One More Time *(Merrie Melodies)* June 1931; *p.c.:* Hugh Harman–Rudolf Ising for WB; *prod:* Leon Schlesinger: *anim:* Paul Smith, Isadore Freleng, Robert Clampett; *mus:* Frank Marsales; played by Abe Lyman and his Brunswick Recording Orchestra; b&w. *sd:* Vit. 9 min. • Foxy and Honey in an underworld setting.

4686. One Mother's Family *(MGM Cartoon)* 30 Sept. 1939; *p.c.:* MGM; *prod/dir:* Rudolf Ising; *mus:* Scott Bradley; *prod mgr:* Fred Quimby; *col:* Tech. *sd:* WE. 9 min. • A mother hen takes her brood for an outing and, among other hazards, they encounter a hungry hawk.

4687. One Mouse in a Million *(Terry-Toon)* 3 Nov. 1939; *p.c.:* TT for Fox; *dir:* Connie Rasinski; *story:* John Foster; *mus:* Philip A. Scheib; *col:* Tech. *sd:* RCA. 7 min. • No story available.

4688. One Note Tony *(Terry-Toon)* 22 Oct. 1947; *p.c.:* TT for Fox; *dir:* Connie Rasinski; *story:* John Foster; *mus:* Philip A. Scheib; *ph:* Douglas Moye; *col:* Tech. *sd:* RCA. 6 min. • Little Tony, the jungle band drummer, turns the symphony orchestra into a jam session.

4689. One of the Family *(Modern Madcap)* Dec. 1962; *p.c.:* Para Cartoons; *dir:* Seymour Kneitel; *story:* Jack Mercer, Burton Goodman; *anim:* Wm. B. Pattengill, Larry Silverman, Nick Tafuri; *sets:* Robert Little; *voices:* Bob MacFadden; *mus:* Winston Sharples; *ph:* Leonard McCormick; *prod mgr:* Abe Goodman; *col:* Tech. *sd:* RCA. 6 min. • A persistant mutt tries to get himself adopted.

4690. One Ol' Cat *(Mastodon Cartoon)* 5 Aug. 1922; *p.c.:* Earl Hurd prods for Educational; *dir:* Earl Hurd; b&w. sil. 4 min. *l/a/anim.* • Bobby Bumps plays baseball with the artist. A boxing match is staged in which a black cat takes part.

4691. One Quack Mind *(Noveltoon)* 12 Jan. 1951; *p.c.:* Famous for Para; *dir:* I. Sparber; *story:* Carl Meyer, Jack Mercer; *anim:* George Germanetti, Steve Muffatti; *sets:* Robert Little; *voices:* Sid Raymond, Jackson Beck, Cecil Roy; *mus:* Winston Sharples; *ph:* Leonard McCormick; *prod mgr:* Sam Buchwald; *col:* Tech. *sd:* RCA. 6 min. • When Mama is called away, the hungry fox appears, posing as a baby sitter to mind Baby Huey ... and lives to regret it.

4692. One Step Ahead of My Shadow *(Merrie Melodies)* 12 Apr. 1933; *p.c.:* Hugh Harman, Rudolf Ising prods for WB; *anim:* Isadore Freleng, Max Maxwell, Robert Clampett; *song:* Saul Chaplin; *mus:* Frank Marsales; *asso prod:* Leon Schlesinger; b&w. *sd:* Vit. 7 min. • A romance blossoms between a Chinese boy and girl until a dragon interrupts. The beast is stopped when his flame-breathing ignites some firecrackers.

4693. 1001 Arabian Nights 1959; *p.c.:* UPA for Colum; *prod:* Stephen Bosustow; *dir:* Jack Kinney, Pete Burness; *seq dir:* Rudy Larriva, Gil Turner, Osmond Evans, Tom McDonald, Alan Zaslove; *screenplay:* Czenzi Ormonde; *story:* Dick Shaw, Dick Kinney, Leo Salkin, Pete Burness, Lew Keller, Ed Nofziger, Ted Allen, Margaret Schneider, Paul Schneider; *anim dir:* Abe Levitow; *anim:* Clarke Mallory, Bob Carlson, Harvey Toombs, Phil Duncan, Hank Smith, Ken Hultgren, Jim Davis, Casey Onaitis, Sandy Strother, Ed Friedman, Rudy Zamora, Stan Wilkins, Jack Campbell, Herman Cohen; *prod des:* Robert Dranko; *col des:* Jules Engel, Bob McIntosh; *lay:* Shirley Silvey, Gene Miller, Jimi T. Murakami; *back:* Boris Gorelick, Barbara Begg, Rosemary O'Connor; *ed:* Joe Siracusa, Skip Craig, Earl Bennett; *i&p:* Marion O'Callahan; *dialogue dir:* Bill Scott; *voices: Uncle Abdul Azziz Magoo:* Jim Backus; *Princess Yasminda:* Kathryn Grant; *Aladdin:* Dwayne Hickman; *The Wicked Wazir/The Magic Flame:* Hans Conried; *The Jinni of the Lamp:* Herschel Bernardi; *The Sultan/Chop-Chop:* Alan Reed; *Omar/The Royal Book-Keeper/Barman:* Daws Butler; *Three Maids from Damascus:* The Clark Sisters; *Misc:* Bill Scott, Earl Bennett; *chorus:* The Jud Conlon Singers; *mus:* George Duning; *score:* Morris Stoloff; *orch:* Arthur Morton; *songs:* Ned Washington, George Duning; *ph:* Jack Eckes, J. Dan Miller, Bill Kotler; *sd:* John Livadary, Marne Fallis; *prod mgr:* Bud Getzler; *unit sup:* Paul Marron, Robert C. Brown; *col:* Tech. *sd:* RCA. 76 min. CS. • The nearsighted Mister Magoo gets involved in the story of Aladdin and his Magic Lamp.

4694. One Weak Vacation *(Modern Madcap)* Mar. 1963; *p.c.:* Para Cartoons; *dir:* Seymour Kneitel; *story:* Jack Mercer; *anim:* Martin Taras, John Gentilella, I. Klein; *sets:* Robert Owen; *voices:* Dayton Allen, Valerie Harper; *mus:* Winston Sharples; *ph:* Leonard Cormick; *prod mgr:* Abe Goodman; *col:* Tech. *sd:* RCA. 5½ min. • Morty feels overworked and his wife suggests they take an around-the-world tour ... after which Morty feels more exhausted than ever.

4695. Onion Pacific *(Popeye)* 24 May 1940; *p.c.:* The Fleischer Studio for Para; *prod:* Max Fleischer; *dir:* Dave Fleischer; *story:* Joseph E. Stultz; *anim:* Willard Bowsky, James Davis; *voices:* Jack Mercer, Pinto Colvig, Margie Hines, Louis Fleischer; *mus:* Sammy Timberg; *ph:* Charles Schettler; *prod sup:* Sam Buchwald, Isidore Sparber; b&w. *sd:* WE. 7 min. • Popeye and Bluto run a rail race to see who gets the state franchise for their respective railroads.

4696. Oom Pah Pah *(Aesop's Sound Fable)* 11 May 1930; *p.c.:* Van Beuren for Pathé; *dir:* John Foster, Harry Bailey; *mus:* Gene Rodemich; b&w. *sd:* RCA. 6 min. • A street band is arrested for disturbing the peace, then continue their playing in court.

4697. The Oompahs *(Jolly Frolics)* 24 Jan. 1952; *p.c.:* UPA for Colum; *ex prod:* Stephen Bosustow; *prod/dir:* Robert Cannon; *story/lay:* T. Hee; *anim:* Bill Melendez, Frank Smith, Roger Daley; *back:* Jules Engel; *voice:* Marvin Miller; *mus:* Ray Sherman; *technical:* Mary Cain; *prod mgr:* Herb Klynn; *col:* Tech. *sd:* RCA. 7½ min. • Orville, a trumpet, has a nervous breakdown when his Oompa-pa, a tuba, refuses to let him play with the jazz kids on Downbeat Avenue.

4698. Op, Pop, Wham and Bop *(Noveltoon)* Jan. 1966; *p.c.:* Para Cartoons; *dir:* Howard Post; *story:* Eli Bauer; *anim:* Martin Taras; *sets:* Robert Little; *mus:* Winston Sharples; *ph:* Leonard McCormick; *prod mgr:*

Abe Goodman; *col:* Tech. *sd:* RCA. 6 min. • Ffat Kat and Rat Ffink star in a cat and mouse chase around a museum of way-out art.

4699. Open House *(Terry Bears)* Aug. 1953; *p.c.:* TT for Fox; *dir:* Eddie Donnelly; *story:* Tom Morrison; *anim:* Jim Tyer; *sets:* Art Bartsch; *voices:* Douglas Moye, Tom Morrison, Philip A. Scheib; *mus:* Philip A. Scheib; *ph:* Douglas Moye; *col:* Tech. *sd:* RCA. 6 min. • Papa observes "Be Kind to Animals Week" until the cubs take it literally and bring home a batch of animals.

4700. Opening Night *(Cubby Bear)* 10 Feb. 1933; *p.c.:* Van Beuren for RKO; *mus:* Gene Rodemich; b&w. *sd:* RCA. 7 min. • Cubby gatecrashes the New Roxy Theatre's opening night and ends up conducting the orchestra.

4701. Opens Wednesday 1980; *p.c.:* Barrie Nelson Prods; *dir/story/des/anim:* Barrie Nelson; *mus:* Benny Carter; *played by:* Bud Shank, Shelly Manne, Ray Brown, Kenny Burrell, Jerome Richardson, Andy Simpkins; *sets:* Utit Chumuang; *voice:* June Foray; *sd:* Joe Siracusa; *ph:* Nick Vasu; *neg cutter:* Alice Keillor; *col:* DeLuxe. *sd.* 4¹/₂ min. • A cleaning lady passes her own views about a modern play a director is taking through dress rehearsal.

4702. The Opera Caper *(GoGo Toon)* Nov. 1967; *p.c.:* Para Cartoons; *ex prod/dir:* Shamus Culhane; *story:* Izzy Klein, Shamus Culhane; *anim:* Doug Crane, Al Eugster, Chuck Harriton, Nick Tafuri; *sets:* Gil Miret, John Zago; *voices:* Dayton Allen; *mus:* Winston Sharples; *prod sup:* Harold Robins, Burt Hanft; *col:* Tech. *sd:* RCA. 6 min. • Two bungling Parisian crooks try to kidnap a famous diva but only succeed in capturing her agent. Film completed by Ralph Bakshi.

4703. Opera Night *(Paul Terry-Toon)* 31 May 1935; *p.c.:* Moser & Terry for Educational/Fox; *dir:* Frank Moser, Paul Terry; *mus:* Philip A. Scheib; b&w. *sd:* WE. 5¹/₂ min. • The animals stage "Romeo and Juliet." A villain kidnaps Juliet and the whole audience follows in pursuit.

4704. Operation Cold Feet *(Chilly Willy)* 6 May 1957; *p.c.:* Walter Lantz prods for Univ; *dir:* Alex Lovy; *story:* Homer Brightman; *anim:* Ray Abrams, La Verne Harding; *sets:* Raymond Jacobs, Art Landy; *voices:* Daws Butler; *mus:* Clarence Wheeler; *title song* by Irving Bibo, Jay Carroll, Clarence Wheeler; *sung by* "Wee" Bonnie Baker; *prod mgr:* William E. Garity; *col:* Tech. *sd:* RCA. 6 min. • Chilly invades Admiral Bird's Polar headquarters for food guarded by Smedley the watchdog.

4705. Operation: Rabbit *(Looney Tunes)* 9 Jan. 1952; *p.c.:* WB; *dir:* Charles M. Jones; *story:* Michael Maltese; *anim:* Lloyd Vaughan, Ben Washam, Ken Harris, Phil Monroe; *lay:* Robert Gribbroek; *back:* Philip de Guard; *ed:* Treg Brown; *voices:* Mel Blanc; *mus:* Carl Stalling; *prod mgr:* John W. Burton; *prod:* Edward Selzer; *col:* Tech. *sd:* Vit. 7 min. • Bugs comes into contact with Wile E. Coyote, a genius who uses many inventions to assist his capture of the rabbit.

4706. Operation Sawdust *(Woody Woodpecker)* 15 June 1953; *p.c.:* Walter Lantz prods for Univ; *dir:* Don Patterson; *story:* Homer Brightman; *anim:* La Verne Harding, Ray Abrams; *sets:* Art Landy; *voices:* Dallas McKennon, Grace Stafford; *mus:* Clarence Wheeler; *prod mgr:* William E. Garity; *col:* Tech. *sd:* RCA. 6 min. • Lumberjacks Woody and Buzz Buzzard fight over the food supplies.

4707. Operation Shanghai *(Chilly Willy)* Jan. 1967; *p.c.:* Walter Lantz prods for Univ; *dir:* Sid Marcus; *story:* Homer Brightman; *anim:* Les Kline; *sets:* Ray Huffine; *voices:* Daws Butler; *mus:* Walter Greene; *prod mgr:* William E. Garity; *col:* Tech. *sd:* RCA. 6 min. • Smedley shanghais Chilly to do his chores aboard "The Old Eyesore."

4708. The Op'ry House *(Mickey Mouse)* 20 Mar. 1929; *p.c.:* Walter E. Disney for Colum; *dir:* Walt Disney; *anim:* Ub Iwerks; *mus:* Carl W. Stalling; b&w. *sd:* PCP. 6 min. • Mickey as proprietor of a small-town show.

4709. The Organ Grinder *(Merrie Melodies)* 19 June 1933; *p.c.:* Hugh Harman, Rudolf Ising prods for WB; *prod:* Leon Schlesinger; *anim:* Rollin Hamilton, Thomas McKimson, Robert Clampett; *voices:* John T. Murray, The Rhythmettes; *mus:* Frank Marsales; b&w. *sd:* Vit. 6 min. • An organ grinder goes along singing and playing while Tony, his monkey, imitates Laurel and Hardy and Harpo Marx.

4710. The Organ Grinders *(Aesop's Film Fable)* 22 June 1924; *p.c.:* Fables Pictures Inc for Pathé; *dir:* Paul Terry; b&w. *sil.* 5 min. • Mr. Dago

Cat and Isadore Mouse try their skill with a barrel organ causing disastrous results from the populace of the city, ending in a rabbit chase.

4711. The Organ Grinder's Swing *(Popeye)* 19 Feb. 1937; *p.c.:* The Fleischer Studio for Para; *prod:* Max Fleischer; *dir:* Dave Fleischer; *anim:* David Tendlar, William Sturm; *voices:* Jack Mercer, Gus Wickie, Mae Questel, Donald Bain; *mus:* Sammy Timberg; *song:* Will Hudson, Mitchell Parish, Irving Mills; b&w. *sd:* WE. 6 min. • Bluto wants Wimpy and his barrel-organ music to go but Popeye wants him to stay.

4712. The Orphan Duck *(Terry-Toon)* 6 Oct. 1939; *p.c.:* TT for Fox; *dir:* Connie Rasinski; *story:* John Foster; *mus:* Philip A. Scheib; *col:* Tech. *sd:* RCA. 7 min. • Dinky Duck tries to get adopted by the chickens by hiding in an empty eggshell but is evicted by the rooster. He later engratiates himself into the fold by saving a chick from drowning.

4713. The Orphan Egg *(Dinky)* June 1953; *p.c.:* TT for Fox; *dir:* Eddie Donnelly; *story:* Tom Morrison; *anim:* Jim Tyer; *mus:* Philip A. Scheib; *col:* Tech. *sd:* RCA. 6 min. • Dinky hatches out an egg that contains a baby eagle who eventually saves the barnyard from the clutches of a hungry fox.

4714. Orphans' Benefit *(Mickey Mouse)* 11 Aug. 1934; *p.c.:* Walt Disney prods for UA; *dir:* Burton F. Gillett; *anim:* Johnny Cannon, Les Clark, Norman Ferguson, Richard Lundy, Ben Sharpsteen; *voices:* Florence Gill, Clarence Nash, Walt Disney; *mus:* Frank E. Churchill; b&w. *sd:* RCA. 9 min. • Mickey hosts a show for the orphans: Donald recites, the Goof and Clarabelle Cow perform an adagio act and Dame Clara Cluck sings the sextette from "Lucia."

4715. Orphan's Benefit *(Mickey Mouse)* 22 Aug. 1941; *p.c.:* Walt Disney prods for RKO; *dir:* Riley Thomson; *asst dir:* Ray de Vally; *anim:* James Armstrong, Johnny Cannon, Walter Clinton, Sam Cobean, Merle Cox, Bill Dunham, Art Elliott, Norman Ferguson, Max Gray, Hal King, Edward Love, Richard Lundy, Bob McCrea; *lay:* Bill Tracy; *voices:* Clarence Nash, Florence Gill, Walt Disney; *mus:* Frank E. Churchill; *col:* Tech. *sd:* RCA. 9 min. • Mickey hosts a stage show for the kids. They heckle the acts and Donald gets full brunt of what they have to offer. Tech remake of the 1934 cartoon.

4716. Orphans' Picnic *(Mickey Mouse)* 15 Feb. 1936; *p.c.:* Walt Disney prods for UA; *dir:* Ben Sharpsteen; *story:* Jack Kinney; *anim:* Paul Allen, James H. Culhane, George Drake, Alfred Eugster, Hardie Gramatky, Paul Hopkins, Milton Kahl, Frank Kelling, Hamilton S. Luske, Eddie Strickland, Franklin Thomas, Don Towsley, Roy Williams, Bernard Wolf, Marvin Woodward; *voices:* Clarence Nash, Bernice Hansel, Leone le Doux, Shirley Reed, Gay Seabrook, Walt Disney; *mus:* Albert Hay Malotte; *col:* Tech. *sd:* RCA. 7 min. • Mickey and Donald take the orphans on a picnic. The kids steal the food, causing Donald to swallow an angry bee.

4717. Oscar 26 April 1991; *p.c.:* Touchstone Pictures/Screen Partners IV for WB; *main title anim:* David Allen Prods; *title des:* Penelope Gottlieb; *col:* Tech. *sd:* Dolby stereo. • Live-action comedy about a 1930s bootlegger who tries to become an honest man. Animated titles.

4718. Oscar's Birthday Present *(Astronut)* Jan. 1971 (© 1965); *p.c.:* TT for Fox; *ex prod:* Bill Weiss; *dir/anim:* Dave Tendlar; *story sup:* Tom Morrison; *story:* Larz Bourne; *sets:* Bill Focht, John Zago; *ed:* Jack MacConnell; *voices:* Dayton Allen; *mus:* Jim Timmens; *ph:* Joe Rasinski; *sd:* Elliot Grey; *col:* DeLuxe. *sd:* RCA. 5 min. • Astro gives Oscar Mild a Nuclear Jet-Rod for his birthday and a foreign spy tries to steal it.

4719. Oscar's Thinking Cap *(Astronut)* May 1971 (© 1965); *p.c.:* TT for Fox; *ex prod:* Bill Weiss; *dir/anim:* Art Bartsch; *story sup:* Tom Morrison; *story:* Larz Bourne; *sets:* Bill Focht, John Zago; *ed:* Jack MacConnell; *voices:* Dayton Allen; *mus:* Jim Timmens; *ph:* Joe Rasinski; *sd:* Elliot Grey; *col:* DeLuxe. *sd:* RCA. 5 min. • Oscar Mild poses as a mind reader with Astro's help and causes much distress.

4720. The Ostrich Egg and I *(Maggie & Sam)* 9 Apr. 1956; *p.c.:* Walter Lantz prods for Univ; *dir:* Alex Lovy; *story:* Homer Brightman; *anim:* Ray Abrams, Don Patterson, La Verne Harding; *sets:* Raymond Jacobs, Art Landy; *voices:* Grace Stafford, Daws Butler; *mus:* Eugene Poddany; *prod mgr:* William E. Garity; *col:* Tech. *sd:* RCA. 6 min. • Sam is given an ostrich egg that hatches into a creature that eats everything within range.

4721. Ostrich Feathers *(Meany Miny Mo)* 6 Sept. 1937; *p.c.:* Univ *dir:* Walt Lantz; *story:* Walter Lantz, Victor McLeod; *anim:* Ray Abrams, Ted Dubois, Ralph Somerville; *voice:* Dave Weber; *mus:* George Lessner; b&w. *sd:* WE. 6 min. • The monks are in "Two Shades Darker"Africa in search of ostrich feathers.

4722. The Ostrich's Plumes (*Unnatural History*) 15 Apr. 1926; *p.c.:* Bray prods for FBO; *dir:* Walter Lantz; *anim:* Clyde Geronimi; *l/a ph:* Joe Rock; b&w. *sil.* 5 min. *l/a/anim.* • The teacher asks Tommy to speak about the ostrich. He launches into a fanciful tale of the ostrich being ditched by her mate for the peacock. She consults a monkey beauty specialist who dolls her up with a "Marcel Wave" on a beautiful set of plumes. She strolls past her partner who immediately deserts the peacock for her.

4723. Ouch! 17 Dec. 1925; *p.c.:* Bray prods for Pathé; *dir:* J.D. Leventhal; b&w. *sil.* 5 min. • No story available.

4724. Ouija Board (*Out of the Inkwell*) 4 June 1920; *p.c.:* Bray prods for Goldwyn; *story/dir/l/a:* Max Fleischer; *anim:* Dave Fleischer, Roland C. Crandall; b&w. *sil.* 5 min. *l/a/anim.* • Roland Crandall and a black janitor play with an ouija board, conjuring up ghosts that Ko-Ko fights with. • See: *Goldwyn-Bray Pictographs*

4725. An Ounce of Pink (*Pink Panther*) 20 Oct. 1965; *p.c.:* Mirisch/Geoffrey/DFE for UA; *dir:* Hawley Pratt; *story:* Bob Kurtz; *anim:* La Verne Harding, Don Williams, Norm McCabe; *lay:* Dick Ung; *back:* Tom O'Loughlin; *ed:* Lee Gunther; *voices:* Larry Storch, Laura Olsher; *mus:* William Lava; *theme tune:* Henry Mancini; *prod mgr:* William Orcutt; *col:* DeLuxe. *sd:* RCA. 6 min. • The Panther purchases a friendly "Speak Your Weight" machine that turns out to be more trouble than it's worth.

4726. Our Funny Finny Friends (*Screen Song*) 29 Aug. 1949; *p.c.:* Famous for Para; *dir:* Seymour Kneitel; *story:* Larz Bourne, Larry Riley; *anim:* Al Eugster, Bill Hudson; *sets:* Tom Ford; *voices:* Jackson Beck, Sid Raymond, Gwen Davies, Jack Mercer; *mus:* Winston Sharples; *song:* Saxie Dowell; *ph:* Leonard McCormick; *prod mgr:* Sam Buchwald; *col:* Tech. *sd:* RCA. 6 min. • An underwater travelogue ending with "Three Little Fishes" sing-along.

4727. Our Little Nell (*Aesop's Film Fable*) 2 July 1928; *p.c.:* Fables Pictures Inc for Pathé; *dir:* Paul Terry, Frank Moser; b&w. *sil.* 10 min. • Milton Mouse takes Rita, his sweetie, for a ride in his flivver. When his rig breaks down, Tom Cat arrives in his sports car and drives off with Rita. Our hero follows and finds the villain forcing unwelcome attentions on his girl, resulting in a rooftop chase over the skyscrapers.

4728. Out Again in Again (*Heckle & Jeckle*) Nov. 1948; *p.c.:* TT for Fox; *dir:* Connie Rasinski; *story:* John Foster; *anim:* Jim Tyer; *sets:* Art Bartsch; *voices:* Dayton Allen, Thomas Morrison; *mus:* Philip A. Scheib; *ph:* Douglas Moye; *col:* Tech. *sd:* RCA. 6 min. • The magpies burrow out from prison and board a train. The conductor evicts them but they keep returning in a multitude of disguises.

4729. Out and Out Rout (*Merrie Melodies*) 29 Jan. 1966; *p.c.:* DFE for WB; *dir:* Rudy Larriva; *story:* Dale Hale; *anim:* Virgil Ross, Bob Bransford, Hank Smith; *lay:* Don Sheppard; *back:* Anthony Rizzo; *ed:* Roger Donley; *mus:* Bill Lava; *col:* Tech. *sd:* Vit. 6 min. • The Coyote uses a falcon, pigeons strapped to his feet, a hot-rod, land boat and super glue in his pursuit of the Road-Runner ... all to no avail!

4730. Out of Scale (*Donald Duck*) 2 Nov. 1951; *p.c.:* Walt Disney prods for RKO; *dir:* Jack Hannah; *story:* Bill Berg, Nick George; *anim:* Bill Justice, Volus Jones, George Kreisl, Bob Carlson, Jack Boyd; *fx:* Dan MacManus, Jack Boyd; *lay:* Yale Gracey; *back:* Art Riley; *voices:* Clarence Nash, James MacDonald, Dessie Miller; *mus:* Paul Smith; *col:* Tech. *sd:* RCA. 7 min. • The chipmunks invade Donald's model railway and village.

4731. Out of the Ether (*Krazy Kat*) 5 Sept. 1933; *p.c.:* Charles Mintz prods for Colum; *story:* Ben Harrison, Manny Gould; *anim:* Harry Love, Al Rose; *mus:* Joe de Nat; *prod mgr:* James Bronis; b&w. *sd:* WE. 6 min • Krazy performs an operation on a busted radio and has a strange dream under the ether. Caricatures of The Boswell Sisters, Eddie Cantor, Bing Crosby, Ted Lewis, John McCormack, The Mills Bros, Martha Richmond, Dave Rubinoff, Kate Smith, Arthur Tracy, Rudy Vallee, Paul Whiteman and Ed Wynn.

4732. Out of the Frying Pan Into the Firing Line 30 July 1942; *p.c.:* Walt Disney prods for U.S. War Prod Board; *dir:* Jack King; *asst dir:* Jack Atwood; *anim dir:* Jack Hannah; *anim:* Les Clark, John Lounsbery,

George Nicholas, Charles A. Nichols, Norman Tate, Marvin Woodward; *fx:* Andrew Engman, Joshua Meador, George Rowley; *lay:* Bill Herwig; *voices:* Art Gilmore, Thelma Boardman; *mus:* Leigh Harline; *col:* Tech. *sd:* RCA. • Minnie Mouse is pursuaded to give her waste fats to the country's defense instead of to Pluto. • Governmental film showing the importance of housewives turning over waste fats to make ammunition.

4733. Out of the Inkwell (*Betty Boop*) 22 Apr. 1938; *p.c.:* The Fleischer Studio for Para; *prod:* Max Fleischer; *dir:* Dave Fleischer; *anim:* Thomas Johnson, Otto Feuer; *voice:* Mae Questel; *mus:* Sammy Timberg; b&w. *sd:* WE. 7 min. *l/a/anim.* • While a (live-action) colored porter reads about hypnotism, Betty emerges from an inkwell and makes her own magic ... finally causing the porter to work. The last "Betty Boop" in the series.

4734. Out of This Whirl (*Noveltoon*) 13 Nov. 1959; *p.c.:* Para Cartoons; *dir:* Seymour Kneitel; *story:* Carl Meyer, Jack Mercer; *anim:* Tom Johnson, Wm. B. Pattengill; *sets:* Robert Owen; *mus:* Winston Sharples; *ph:* Leonard McCormick; *prod mgr:* Abe Goodman; *col:* Tech. *sd:* RCA. 6 min. • A woman mistakes an alien for her small son and takes him shopping. The spaceman amuses himself by vanishing people with a ray gun.

4735. Out On a Limb (*Donald Duck*) 15 Dec. 1950; *p.c.:* Walt Disney prods for RKO; *dir:* Jack Hannah; *story:* Bill Berg, Nick George; *anim:* Bill Justice, Bob Carlson, Volus Jones, George Kreisl; *lay:* Yale Gracey; *back:* Thelma Witmer; *voices:* Clarence Nash, Dessie Miller, James MacDonald; *mus:* Joseph S. Dubin; *col:* Tech. *sd:* RCA. 7 min. • Donald teases the chipmunks while he prunes his trees. The chips have their revenge.

4736. Out to Punch (*Popeye*) 8 June 1956; *p.c.:* Famous for Para; *dir:* Seymour Kneitel; *story:* Carl Meyer; *anim:* Tom Johnson, John Gentilella; *sets:* John Zago; *voices:* Jack Mercer, Mae Questel, Jackson Beck; *mus:* Winston Sharples; *ph:* Leonard McCormick; *prod mgr:* Seymour Shultz; *col:* Tech. *sd:* RCA. 6 min. • Bluto decides to slow-down Popeye's training for the big fight tonight.

4737. Outer Galaxy Gazette (*Astronut*) Sept. 1964; *p.c.:* TT for Fox; *ex prod:* Bill Weiss; *dir/anim:* Connie Rasinski; *story sup:* Tom Morrison; *story:* Eli Bauer; *sets:* Bill Focht, John Zago; *ed:* Jack MacConnell; *voices:* Dayton Allen; *mus:* Jim Timmens; *ph:* Ted Moskowitz; *sd:* Elliot Grey; *col:* DeLuxe. *sd:* RCA. 5½ min. • Astro's newspaper predicts various earth disasters and Oscar has a brush with the law.

4738. Outer Space Visitor (*Mighty Mouse*) Nov. 1959; *p.c.:* TT for Fox; *ex prod:* Bill Weiss; *dir:* Dave Tendlar; *story sup:* Tom Morrison; *story:* Jim Tyler; *anim:* Eddie Donnelly, Mannie Davis; *voices:* Dayton Allen; *mus:* Phil Scheib; *prod mgr:* Frank Schudde; *col:* Tech. *sd:* RCA. 5 min. CS. • A baby alien causes Mighty Mouse to do battle with his father, a twenty-foot galactic robot from outer space.

4739. Out-Foxed (*Droopy*) 5 Nov. 1949; *p.c.:* MGM; *dir:* Tex Avery; *story:* Rich Hogan; *anim:* Walter Clinton, Bob Cannon, Michael Lah, Grant Simmons; *character des:* Louis Schmitt; *sets:* John Didrik Johnsen; *ed:* Fred MacAlpin; *voices:* Bill Thompson, Daws Butler; *mus:* Scott Bradley; *prod:* Fred Quimby; *ph:* Jack Stevens; *col:* Tech. *sd:* WE. 8 min. • The fox hounds are promised a steak for each fox they catch. Droopy encounters a reluctant quarry who concedes when he hears of the prize.

4740. Out-Numbered (*Aesop's Film Fable*) 9 July 1928; *p.c.:* Fables Pictures Inc for Pathé; *dir:* Paul Terry, Hugh Shields; b&w. *sil.* 10 min. • A swarm of mice run riot around the Farmer and Henry Cat. Al finally loses his temper and chases them out into the open spaces.

4741. The Outpost (*Gandy Goose*) 10 July 1942; *p.c.:* TT for Fox; *dir:* Mannie Davis; *story:* John Foster; *mus:* Philip A. Scheib; b&w. *sd:* RCA. 6 min. • Pvt. Gandy and Sgt. Sourpuss alone and faced with a Japanese invasion, brilliantly defeat the enemy.

4742. The Outside Dope (*Modern Madcap*) Nov. 1965; *p.c.:* Para Cartoons; *dir:* Howard Post; *story:* Jack Mendelsohn; *anim:* Nick Tafuri; *sets:* Robert Little; *voices:* Bob MacFadden; *mus:* Winston Sharples; *ph:* Leonard McCormick; *prod mgr:* Abe Goodman; *col:* Tech. *sd:* RCA. 6 min. • Newspaper reporter Boobie Baboon is assigned to a "Life Behind Prison Bars" story and has to get himself into jail to write it.

4743. Over the Plate (*Aesop's Film Fable*) 29 Aug. 1925; *p.c.:* Fables Pictures Inc for Pathé; *dir:* Paul Terry; b&w. *sil.* 10 min. • No story available.

4744. The Overture to William Tell *(Musical Miniature)* 16 June 1947; *p.c.:* Walter Lantz prods for Univ; *dir:* Dick Lundy; *story:* Ben Hardaway, Milt Schaffer; *anim:* (La) Verne Harding, S.C. (Casey) Onaitus; *sets:* Fred Brunish; *mus:* Darrell Calker; *prod mgr:* William E. Garity; *col:* Tech. *sd:* WE. 7 min. • Wally conducts an orchestra that gets out of hand when the electrician stages storm effects for the overture to "William Tell."

4745. The Owl and the Grasshopper *(Aesop's Film Fable)* 13 Nov. 1921; *p.c.:* Fables Pictures Inc for Pathé; *dir:* Paul Terry; b&w. sil. 5 min. • An owl imbibes too freely of pre–Volstead beverages then, disturbed by a grasshopper, invites him in for a drink.

4746. The Owl and the Pussycat *(Paul Terry-Toon)* 9 Mar. 1934; *p.c.:* Moser & Terry for Educational/Fox; *dir:* Frank Moser, Paul Terry; *mus:* Philip A. Scheib; b&w. *sd:* WE 6 min. • Al Falfa's cat leaves home to go off with a roustabout tomcat. The mice descend and run riot over the farm.

4747. The Owl and the Pussycat *(Terry-Toon)* 31 Jan. 1939; *p.c.:* TT for Fox; *dir:* Eddie Donnelly; *story:* John Foster; *voice:* Thomas Morrison; *mus:* Philip A. Scheib; *col:* Tech. *sd:* RCA. 7 min. • Sourpuss comes to pay suit to a female owl but has to vie with her boyfriend first. The two owls wed, leaving Sourpuss out in the cold.

4748. Owly to Bed *(Herman & Katnip)* 2 Jan. 1959; *p.c.:* Para Cartoons; *dir:* Seymour Kneitel; *story:* Carl Meyer; *anim:* Tom Johnson, Wm. B. Pattengill; *sets:* John Zago; *voices:* Arnold Stang, Gwen Davies; *mus:* Winston Sharples; *ph:* Leonard McCormick; *prod mgr:* Abe Goodman; *col:* Tech. *sd:* RCA. 6 min. • Herman tries to save a sleepwalking owl from the clutches of the cat.

4749. Ozark Lark *(Woody Woodpecker)* 13 July 1960; *p.c.:* Walter Lantz prods for Univ; *dir:* Paul J. Smith; *story:* Homer Brightman; *anim:* Les Kline, Ray Abrams; *sets:* Art Landy, Ray Huffine; *voices:* Dal McKennon, Grace Stafford; *mus:* Clarence Wheeler; *prod mgr:* William E. Garity; *col:* Tech. *sd:* RCA. 6 min. • Woody's visit to the Ozark mountains rekindles the old feud between the Martins and the Coys.

4750. Ozzie of the Circus *(Oswald)* 5 Jan. 1929; *p.c.:* Univ; *dir:* Walter Lantz, Bill Nolan; b&w. *sd:* 6 min. • No story available.

4751. Ozzie of the Mounted *(Oswald the Lucky Rabbit)* 30 Apr. 1928; *p.c.:* Winkler for Univ; *dir:* Walter Disney; *anim:* Ub Iwerks, Hugh Harman, Rollin C. Hamilton, Ben Clopton, Les Clark; *ph:* Mike Marcus; b&w. sil. 5 min. • Mountie Oswald pursues villainous Foxy Wolf on a mechanical horse throughout the wastelands of Canada.

4752. Ozzie Ostrich Comes to Town *(Terry-Toon)* 28 May 1937; *p.c.:* TT for Educational/Fox; *dir:* George Gordon, Mannie Davis; *mus:* Philip A. Scheib; b&w. *sd:* RCA. 6 min. • Kiko is delivered an ostrich in a crate who creates havoc.

4753. The Pace That Kills *(Aesop's Film Fable)* 7 June 1923; *p.c.:* Fables Pictures Inc for Pathé; *dir:* Paul Terry; b&w. sil. 5 min. • Dealing with the weird experiences of the cat and mouse after sampling a bottle of hooch.

4754. Pack Up Your Troubles *(Song Car-Tune)* 17 July 1926; *p.c.:* Inkwell Studio for Red Seal; *dir:* Dave Fleischer; *anim/l/a:* Max Fleischer; b&w. sil. 6 min. • No story available.

4755. A Package for Jasper *(Puppetoon)* 21 Jan. 1944; *p.c.:* George Pal prods for Para; *prod/dir:* George Pal; *mus:* Leo Diamond; *voices:* Roy Glenn, Glenn Leedy; *col:* Tech. *sd:* WE. 7½ min. • The Scarecrow wants Jasper's new harmonica and tells a tale of how he once played to a packed house at Kornegie Hall.

4756. Pagan Moon *(Merrie Melodies)* Feb. 1932; *p.c.:* Hugh Harman, Rudolf Ising prods for WB; *prod:* Leon Schlesinger; *anim:* Rollin Hamilton, Norm Blackburn, Robert Clampett; *voice:* Johnny Murray; *mus:* Frank Marsales; b&w. *sd:* Vit. 7 min. • The hero woos his girl with a jazz ukelele which he loses in the sea and goes to retrieve it, encountering fish and octopus along the way.

4757. Page Miss Glory *(Merrie Melodies)* 7 Mar. 1936; *p.c.:* Leon Schlesinger prods for WB; *dir:* Fred Avery; *story/anim:* Robert Clampett; *des:* Leadora Congdon; *voices:* Jackie Morrow, Bernice Hansel, Fred Avery, the Varsity Three; *mus:* Norman Spencer; *song:* Harry Warren, Al Dubin; *prod sup:* Henry Binder, Raymond G. Katz; *col:* Tech. *sd:* Vit. 7 min. • A

hick-town page boy dreams he's working in a ritzy New York hotel, anticipating the arrival of Miss Glory, a glamorous movie star. Caricatures of Tex Avery, Chuck Jones and Bob Clampett.

4758. The Pagemaster 9 Dec. 1994; *p.c.:* Fox/Turner Pictures, Inc.; *dir:* Maurice Hunt; *l/a dir:* Joe Johnston; *prod:* David Kirschner, Paul Gertz; *story:* David Kirschner, David Casci; *scr:* David Casci, David Kirschner, Ernie Contreras; *anim co-prod:* David J. Steinberg, Barry Weiss; *l/a scenes prod:* Michael K. Joyce; *asso prod:* Claire Glidden, Roxy Novotny Steven; *anim sup:* Bruce Smith; *art dir:* Pixote; *prod des:* Gay Lawrence, Valerio Ventura; *visual fx sup:* Richard T. Sullivan; *anim seq dir:* Glenn Chaika; *anim sup: story:* Robert Lence; *lay:* Don Morgan; *back:* Jim Hickey; *asst character anim:* Donald Parmele; *fx anim:* Mark Myer; *anim check:* Gina Bradley; *col key:* Clayton Stang; *i&p:* Laura Craig, Bonnie Blough, Deborah Rykoff Bennett; *final check:* Pat Sito; *ed sup:* Jeffrey Patch; *technical sup:* Jerry Mills; *anim asst dir:* Michael Paxton; *prod sup:* Melissa Kurtz; *sup prod co-ord:* Bill Bloom; *character anim:* Anne Marie Bardwell, Ralph Fernan, Kevin Johnson, Dave Kupczyk, Jason Lethcoe, Mike Nguyen, Matt O'Callaghan, Bob Scott, Mike Kunkel, Kevin O'Hara; *fx anim:* John Allen Armstrong, Kathleen Quaife-Hodge, Margaret Craig-Chang, Al Holter, Jeffrey Howard, Brice Mallier, Peter Matheson, Brian McSweeney, Allen Stovall; *fx asst anim:* Stephanie Bolger, Lee Crowe, Peter Demund, Paul W. Lewis, Jon William Lopez, Masa Oshiro, Sean Applegate, Dan Chaika, Angela A. Diamos, Ray Hofstedt, John Huey, Craig Littell-Herrick, John Lyons, George Chialtas, Ty Elliott, Jay Lender, Randy Weeks; *fx break:* Chris Kirshbaum, Mary Mullen, Nate Pacheco, Lou Romano; *character asst anim:* Christopher Chu, Kent Culotta, John Eddings, Millet Henson, Tim Ingersoll, Patrick Joens, Helen Lawlor, Mi Yul Lee, Leticia Lichtwardt, James McArdle, Irene Couloufis Parkins, Doris Plough, Donald Selders, George Sukara, Robert F. Tyler, Tran Vu, Mitchell Walker, Dougg Williams, Paul Bauman, Ron Brown, Dave Courtland, William Exter, Sandra Henkin, William Mims, Celeste Moreno, Bob Quinn, John Ripa, Joe Roman, Pil Yong Song, Terry Walsh, Dave Woodman; *character break:* Wanda L. Brown, Todd Frederiksen, Damien Gilligan, Todd Jacobsen, Michael Lerman, Eric Molina, Andrew Molloy, Sharon Murray, Randal Myers, Yoon Sook Nam, Nicole Pascal, Theresa Pettengill, Edward Rivera, Ivan Camilli Rivera, Dean Wellins; *character clean-up:* Joe Elliott, John Sullivan; *addit character clean-up:* Franci Allen, Carl Bell, Jerry Yu Ching, Sean Gallimore, Judy Grabenstatter, Derek L'Estrange, Levi Louis, Frank Molieri, Craig Maras, Richard Rocha, Rusty Stoll, Betty Tang; *title seq anim:* John Allan Armstrong; *storyboard:* Tom Ellery Jr., Gay Lawrence, Don Morgan, Mike Nguyen, Sue Nichols, Darrell Rooney, Rick Schneider, Valerio Ventura; *workbook art:* Tony Christon, Tom Ellery Jr., Glenn Vippu; *rough lay:* Arlan Jewell, Dan Mills, Simon Varela, David Womersley; *clean-up lay:* Gay Lawrence, Valerio Ventura; *back:* Bill Dely, Jonathan Goley, Jim Hickey, Mi Kyung Joung-Raynis, Jane Nussbaum, George Taylor; *ed:* Dan Molina, Denis Dutton, Sue Odjakjian, Paul Douglas, Gil Iverson; *voices: Richard Tyler:* Macaulay Calkin; *The Pagemaster:* Christopher Lloyd; *Adventure:* Patrick Stewart; *Fantasy:* Whoopi Goldberg; *Horror/Dragon:* Frank Welker; *Dr. Jekyll & Mr. Hyde:* Leonard Nimoy; *Jamaican Pirates:* Dorian Harewood; *George Merry:* Ed Gilbert; *Pirates:* Dick Erdman, Fernando Escandon, Robert Piccardo; *Tom Morgan:* Phil Hartman; *Long John Silver:* Jim Cummings; *Queen of Hearts:* B.J. Ward; *live-action: Richard Tyler:* Macaulay Calkin; *Mr. Dewey:* Christopher Lloyd; *Alan Tyler:* Ed Begley Jr.; *Claire Tyler:* Mel Harris; "Dream Away" performed by Babyface & Lisa Stansfield; "Whatever You Imagine" performed by Wendy Moten; *chorus:* Universal Voices of London; *choral dir:* Nick Curtis; *mus:* James Horner; *score:* The London Symphony Orchestra; *songs:* "Dream Away" by Diane Warren; "Whatever You Imagine" by Cynthia Weil, Barry Mann, James Horner; *prod:* Keith Thomas, Jay Landers; *orch:* Don Davis, Thomas Pasatieri; *mus engineers:* Shawn Murphy, Ashley Alexander, Jonathan Allen, Joanne Kane Music Service; *re-rec:* Steve Maslow, Gregg Landaker; *The Hollywood Cartoon Company: Unit prod ex:* G. Sue Shakespeare; *unit anim sup:* Skip Jones; *studio general mgr:* Rocky Solotoff; *anim;* Matthew Bates, Jon Hooper, Mark Koetsier, Linda Miller, Mark Pudleiner, Chad Stewart; *anim check:* Pamela Kleyman, Diane Jacobs Matranga, Kim Patterson; *fx i&p:* Annette Leavitt; *col model paint:* Lea Dahlen, Don Shump; *scene plan:* Richard T. Sullivan, Dave Thomson; *final check:* Chuck Gefre, Tanya Moreau-Smith, Brian Forsythe, Julia Elizabeth, MacKenzie Orr, Melanie Pava, Penelope Sevier, Muriel Vernon, Jungja

Wolf, Maureen Wray-McCann, Janet M. Zoll; *paint corrections:* Elena Marie Cox, Melody Hughes, Sarah King, Tina Marie Marcaccio, Deborah Jane Mooneyham, Catherine Pauline O'Leary, Sparkie Parker, Denise Wogatzke; *cel service:* Dorma Hughes, Donna Narhuminti, Jessie Palubeski, Nellie B. Rodriguez, Teresita Proctor; *ph:* James Keefer, Steve Mills, Robert Jacobs, Dan Larson, Robert Maine, Neil Viker; *character marquettes:* Cindy Ramstead, Robin Linn; *anim reposition:* Richard Wilson; *i&p:* Peter Gentle, Saskia Raevouri, Jungia Wolf, Tina Marie Marcaccio; *Xerox:* Pepito Manlangit, Star Wirth, Cipriano O. Collantes, Ding de Leon, Martin Crossley, Austin Gallano, Cyrille A. Ebarle, Ronnie P. Ocampo, Girard Miller, Jun A. Rodina, Catherine R. Sabug, Dean Stanley, Kevin Stanley, Richard Wilson; *mark-up:* Mary Grace A. Arguelles, Gale A. Raleigh, Babes S. Consolacion, Lhen-Lhen R. Madlangbayan, Cindy Surage; *i&p:* Dada R. Ortega; *Xerox check:* Ching L. Baylon, Daryl Carstensen, Judi Cassell, Gil B. Ceroriales, Lyndon V. Darrum, Nonilon S.D. de la Torre, Gerry Boy de los Santos, Mars P. Doria, Juvy C. Esmalla, Alexander T. Ferrarez, Vernette Griffee, Brendan Harris, Randall McFerren, José Company Nazareno, Benjamin A. Novila, Sparkie Parker, Vines U. Pedrano, Karin Stover, Nestor R. Velasco, Arnel S. Vivo, Janet M. Zoll; *paint:* Lhen-Lhen R. Madlangbayan, Peter Albito, Argen Geraldine Arela, Allen L. Arucan, Lada Babicka, Ana R. Bacani, Nathan Balboa, Catherine Bazzano, Celina N. Borac, Lyn P. Buenaventura, Judi Cassell, Sybil Cuzzort, Shigeko Doyle, Delia Dumapias, Donn S. Durmiendo III, Yoyong R. Edillo, Arthur D. Evidenté, Ma Teresa D. Frenandez, Lillian (Joni) Fitts, Michael Foley, Linda A. Fuentes, Gemma R. Gabaldon, La Donna Hanover, Cookie Hiatt, Marilyn L. Hinojosa, Steve Hirsch, Gina Howard, Susima Iglesias, Evelyn T. Laguador, Ronnie Lazo, Renato P. Layosa, Arnel Mendones, Terry Mendones, Debbie Mihara, Sola S. Monot, Estella V. Oliva, Marivic R. Natividad, Vic P. Orcullo, Joan Orloff, Prince Paluay, Dada Diaz Pecson, Catherine Peterson, Louie C. Policarpio, Teresita Proctor, Arnold P. Pura, Bonnie Ramsey, Sheryl Ann Smith, Karin Stover, S. Ann Sullivan, Roxie Taylor, Ramon D. Tingzon, Cora M. Tiu, Socorro S. Tolentino, Michelle Urbano, Angga Valenzuela, Helga van den Berge, Romeo M. Villanueva, Benny Vivo, Ronel Vivo, Manon Washburn, Michele Zurcher; *paint check:* Cacay E. Cabuhat, Gemma F. Cabrella, Rod C. Concepcion, Rosemarie S. Cruz, Marlo R. Molina; *i&p:* Processo Rocky Balboa, Eddie Buitizon, Louie de Vera, Felino Domingo, Marjorie Escarda, Rey Gamara, Remy Orsillino, Glen Plaruman, Bebot Sisineros; *computer anim/special fx:* Xerox Inc.: *computer anim sup:* Tony Lupidi; *prod:* Helene Plotkin; *anim:* Henry Preston, Roberta Brando, Chitra Shriram, Agata Bolska, Maggie Hallam, Amelia Chenoweth, Todd Gantzler; *prod co-ord:* Susanna Richards; *software:* Cassidy Curtis, Mark Watt, Eric Texler, Dariusz Bolski; *visual fx sup: l/a:* Scott E. Anderson; *ex support:* Mark Malmberg; computer anim rendered using Kubota Workstations; *Mark Swanson Prods:* Mark Swanson, Kerri Swanson, Don Pierce, Mason Deming; *Sidney Wright Motionworks:* digital fx anim: Steve Wright; *digital compositing by Cinesite:* Brad Kuehn, Michele Vallillo, Tom Smith, Pat Repola; *visual fx:* 4-Ward Prods, Robert Skotak & Elaine Edford; *fx prod:* Jenny Fulle; *ed:* Amy L.C. Pawlowski; *ph:* James Belkin, Chris Duddy, John Paszkiewicz; *miniatures:* Jim Towler, Joel Steiner, Jorge Fuentes; *model maker:* David Mansley; *prod asst:* Kathy Draper; *dpt. co-ords: asst anim:* Fabio Novais; *fx anim:* Shelly Amoroso; *anim check:* Zac Moncrief; *visual fx:* Tiffany L. Kurtz; *lay/back:* Charles Desrochers; *i&p:* William Leavitt; *final check:* Sean Dempsey, Mike Pettengill; *addit character anim:* Brenda Banks, Dan Haskett; *addit back art:* Mannix Bennett, Ruben Chavez; *sd ed:* Dan Rich, Clayton Collins, Randy Kelley, Peter Michael Sullivan, Scott Martin Gershin, Christopher Assells, Robert Garrett, Karen M. Baker, David Stanke, Judson Leach; *foley:* John B. Roesch, Hilda Hodges, Mary Jo Lang, Carolyn Tapp; *ADR mix:* Thomas J. O'Connell, Rich Canelli, Bradley Biggart; *neg cutter:* Steve New; *col timer:* Dale Grahn; *Mercer Title & Optical fx: visual fx:* Philip Meador, Al Magliochetti, Kyle Patterson; *optical operator:* Roger Duerrstein; *fx ph:* Bob Hill; *line-up:* William Koshowany; *ink:* Robin Jespersen; *ed/post prod:* original dial rec: Edwin Collins, Chuck Britz, Preston Oliver; *¼' ed:* Kerry Iverson; *track reading:* Jim Hearn; *pre-dub mix:* Jim Aicholtz, Rex Slinkard; *sd des:* Lon E. Bender, Per Hallberg; *l/a ph:* Alexander Gruszynski, Ted Chu, Brian Hardin; *col:* DeLuxe. *sd:* Dolby Digital Stereo. VistaVision. 75 min. *anim/l/a.* • Young Richard Tyler is on an errand when a storm starts and, sheltering in a library, is knocked unconscious when he slips. Books come alive under the guidance of "The Pagemaster" and accompany Richard on his quest to find the Exit to the library. Along the way, they all experience

great works of literature, including *Dr. Jekyll and Mr. Hyde*, *Moby Dick* and *Treasure Island*.

4759. Paint Pot Symphony (*Terry-Toon*) Dec. 1949; *p.c.:* TT for Fox; *dir:* Connie Rasinski; *story:* John Foster; *anim:* Jim Tyer; *mus:* Philip A. Scheib; *col:* Tech. *sd:* RCA. 6 min. • A cat, dog and bird attempt to paint a skyscraper to music.

4760. The Painter and the Pointer (*Andy Panda*) 18 Dec. 1944; *p.c.:* Walter Lantz prods for Univ; *dir:* James Culhane; *story:* Ben Hardaway, Milt Schaffer; *anim:* Les Kline, Emery Hawkins; *lay:* Art Heinemann; *back:* Philip de Guard; *ed:* Dave Lurie; *voices:* Walter Tetley, Phil Kramer, Sara Berner; *mus:* Darrell Calker; *ph:* Fred Weaver, Eugene Borghi; *prod mgr:* George E. Morris; *col:* Tech. *sd:* WE. 7 min. • Andy's dog refuses to keep still while having his portrait painted so Andy rigs a gun to go off if he moves. He resists temptation until a couple of spiders carry him away.

4761. A Pair of Greenbacks (*Tijuana Toads*) 16 Dec. 1969; *p.c.:* Mirisch/DFE for UA; *dir:* Art Davis; *story:* John W. Dunn; *anim:* Manny Gould, Warren Batchelder, Don Williams, Bob Taylor, Manny Perez; *lay:* Dick Ung; *back:* Richard Thomas; *ed:* Lee Gunther; *voices:* Tom Holland, Don Diamond; *mus:* Doug Goodwin; *prod sup:* Jim Foss, Harry Love; *col:* DeLuxe. *sd:* RCA. 6 min. • The Toads pursue a Mexican cockroach in a reworking of "Two Crows from Tacos."

4762. A Pair of Sneakers (*Roland & Rattfink*) 1969; *p.c.:* Mirisch/DFE for UA; *dir:* Art Davis; *story:* John W. Dunn; *anim:* Manny Perez, Manny Gould, Bob Richardson, Warren Batchelder; *lay:* Dick Ung; *back:* Tom O'Loughlin; *ed:* Lee Gunther; *voices:* Leonard Weinrib; *mus:* Doug Goodwin; *prod sup:* Jim Foss, Harry Love; *col:* DeLuxe. *sd:* RCA. 6 min. • Rattfink, an evil spy, tries to get secret orders away from "good" spy, Roland.

4763. Pal, George, Productions (1940–1948) *prod/dir:* George Pal; *sup:* Duke Goldstone; *stories:* Cecil Beard, Norman Blackburn, Bob Larsen, Victor McLeod, Bill Martin, Jack Miller, Ted Robinson, Edmund Seward Jr., Webb Smith, Norman Vizents; *puppet maker/des:* Wah Ming Chang, Ferdinand Huszti Horvath; *anim sup:* George E. Jordan; *anim:* John S. Abbott, Bob Baker, Norman Blackburn, Erwin S. Broner, Lester Bryan, Jim Danforth, Jack Denton, Bernard Garbutt, Ray Harryhausen, Herb Johnson, Bill King, Fred Madison, Fred Moore, Willis O'Brien, David Pal, Miles E. Pike, Gene Warren, sets: Tim Barr, Reginald Massie, Blanding Sloane; *ed:* Richard Connors, Duke Goldstone, Don Tait; *mus:* William Eddison, Clarence Wheeler; *ph:* John S. Abbott, Robert Bruce Sr, Paul Sprunk, Robert R. Hoag; *prod sup:* David A. Bader, Harry Hinkle; *Misc:* Betty Lou Allen, Siska Ayala, Leo Barklime, Dave Bater, Lloyd Bockhaus, Dick Bosworth, Carmelite Chapman, Chris Christadoro, Jack Denton, Nick Eckert, Dave Epstine, Eleanor Fallberg, Jane Fetzer, Pierre Ganine, Al Hamm, Larry Hollings, Maury Howard, Phil Kellison, Dorothy King-Novak, Roberta Lange, Dick le Grande, Fred Malatesa, Kiva Marcus, Bernard Massie, Al Molinaro, Connie Pinard Morgan, Richard Morley, Johnny Napolitano; Willard Oberlin, Stuart O'Brien, Herb Price, Roy Reynertson, Don Sahlin, Lillian Seaquist, Vern Sion, Isadore (Jimmy) Stone, Boris Tameroff, Dale Tholen, Irma Card Tonat, Zoli Vidor, Eleanor Gale Warren, Evelyn Willy, Felix Zelenka

4764. The Pale-Face (*Flip the Frog*) 12 Aug. 1933; *p.c.:* Celebrity for MGM; *prod/dir:* Ub Iwerks; *anim:* Jimmie Culhane; b&w. *sd:* PCP. 6 min. • When Flip and his girl collect wood they are chased by Indians who tie them to a stake.

4765. Paleface Pup (*Aesop's Sound Fable*) 22 June 1931; *p.c.:* Van Beuren for RKO/Pathé; *dir:* John Foster, Mannie Davis; *mus:* Gene Rodemich; b&w. *sd:* RCA. 6 min. • A pup elopes with an Indian princess.

4766. La Paloma (*Screen Songs*) 12 Apr. 1930; *p.c.:* The Fleischer Studio for Para; *dir:* Dave Fleischer; *anim:* Max Fleischer; *mus:* Art Turkisher; *song:* S. Yradier; b&w. *sd:* WE. 7 min. • A Spanish lover serenades a pretty señorita.

4767. Pals (*Little King*) 22 Dec. 1933; *p.c.:* Van Beuren for RKO; *dir:* George Stallings; *anim:* Jim Tyer; *mus:* Gene Rodemich; b&w. *sd:* RCA. 6 min. • The King befriends a couple of hoboes and brings them back to the palace for Christmas.

4768. Pancho's Hideaway (*Looney Tunes*) 24 Oct. 1964; *p.c.:* DFE for WB; *dir:* Friz Freleng; *asst dir:* Hawley Pratt; *story:* John Dunn; *anim:* Bob Matz, Norm McCabe, Don Williams; *sets:* Tom O'Loughlin; *ed:* Lee

Gunther; *voices:* Mel Blanc, Ralph James; *mus:* Bill Lava; *col:* Tech. *sd:* Vit. 6 min. • Speedy Gonzales returns all the money stolen from the bank by Pancho.

4769. Pandora *(Paul Terry-Toon)* 1 Jan. 1934; *p.c.:* Moser & Terry for Educational/Fox; *dir:* Frank Moser, Paul Terry; *mus:* Philip A. Scheib; b&w. *sd:* WE. 6 min. • No story available.

4770. Pandora's Box *(Super Mouse)* 11 June 1943; *p.c.:* TT for Fox; *dir:* Connie Rasinski; *story:* John Foster; *voice:* Thomas Morrison; *mus:* Philip A. Scheib; *col:* Tech. *sd:* RCA. 6½ min. • Pandora, a little girl mouse opens a mysterious box left by Witch Hazel and releases little devils who wreak havoc. Super Mouse sees this, eats "Super Cheese" and comes to the rescue. Reissued as a "Mighty Mouse"cartoon.

4771. The Paneless Window Washer *(Popeye)* 22 Jan. 1937; *p.c.:* The Fleischer Studio for Para; *prod:* Max Fleischer; *dir:* Dave Fleischer; *anim:* Willard Bowsky, Orestes Calpini; *sets:* Anton Loeb; *voices:* Jack Mercer, Gus Wickie, Mae Questel; *mus:* Sammy Timberg; b&w. *sd:* WE. 7 min. • Popeye outshines Bluto at window cleaning.

4772. Panhandle Scandal *(Woody Woodpecker)* May 1959; *p.c.:* Walter Lantz prods for Univ; *dir:* Alex Lovy; *story:* Dalton Sandifer; *anim:* Don Patterson, Ray Abrams, La Verne Harding; *sets:* Ray Jacobs, Art Landy; *voices:* Dal McKennon, Grace Stafford; *mus:* Clarence Wheeler; *prod mgr:* William E. Garity; *col:* Tech. *sd:* RCA. 6 min. • Marshall Woody tells Dooley to "get out of town by sunset" but Dooley insists on a showdown.

4773. Panhandling on Madison Avenue *(Swifty & Shorty)* Apr. 1964; *p.c.:* Para Cartoons; *dir:* Seymour Kneitel; *story/voices:* Eddie Lawrence; *anim:* Martin Taras; *sets:* Robert Little; *mus:* Winston Sharples; *ph:* Leonard McCormick; *prod mgr:* Abe Goodman; *col:* Tech. *sd:* RCA. 5½ min. • While begging on Madison Avenue, Shorty is confronted by an advertising executive who wants him to star in a commercial for an air mattress.

4774. Panicky Pancakes *(Oswald)* 17 Aug 1928; *p.c.:* Univ; *anim:* Hugh Harman, Ben Clopton; b&w. *sil.* 5 min. • Oswald succumbs to thrilling adventures through his passion for cooking pancakes.

4775. Panicky Pup *(Tom & Jerry)* 24 Feb. 1933; *p.c.:* Van Beuren for RKO; *dir:* John Foster, Harry Bailey; *mus:* Gene Rodemich; b&w. *sd:* RCA. 6 min. • No story available.

4776. Pantry Panic *(Woody Woodpecker)* 24 Nov. 1941; *p.c.:* Walter Lantz prods for Univ; *dir:* Walter Lantz; *story:* Ben Hardaway, L.E. (Lowell) Elliot; *anim:* Alex Lovy, Lester Kline; *sets:* Fred Brunish; *voices:* Kent Rogers, Danny Webb, Margaret Hill; *mus:* Darrell Calker; *prod mgr:* George Hall; *col:* Tech. *sd:* WE. 7 min. • Ignoring Professor Groundhog's warning, Woody finds himself trapped without food with a hungry cat, both trying to devour each other.

4777. Pantry Pirate *(Pluto)* 27 Dec. 1940; *p.c.:* Walt Disney prods for RKO; *dir:* Clyde Geronimi; *asst dir:* Donald Duckwall; *story:* Earl Hurd; *anim:* Nick de Tolly, Eric Gurney, Edward Love, George Nicholas, Charles A. Nichols, Claude Smith, Norman Tate; *fx:* Andrew Engman; *lay:* James Carmichael; *voice:* Lillian Randolph; *mus:* Leigh Harline, Oliver Wallace; *col:* Tech. *sd:* RCA. 7 min. • Pluto's futile attempts to pilfer a roast joint of ham.

4778. Papa Gets the Bird *(Bear Family)* 7 Sept. 1940; *p.c.:* MGM; *prod/dir:* Hugh Harman; *story:* Hugh Harman, Jack Cosgriff, Charles Mc-Girl; *lay:* John Meandor; *back:* Joe Smith; *voices:* Martha Wentworth, Rudolf Ising; *mus:* Scott Bradley; *prod mgr:* Fred Quimby; *col:* Tech. *sd:* WE. 8 min. • Barney tries to give the family canary a bath.

4779. Papa's Day of Rest *(Terry Bears)* Mar. 1952; *p.c.:* TT for Fox; *dir:* Mannie Davis; *story:* Tom Morrison; *voices:* Douglas Moye, Tom Morrison, Philip A. Scheib; *sets:* Art Bartsch; *mus:* Philip A. Scheib; *ph:* Douglas Moye; *col:* Tech. *sd:* RCA. 5 min. • The cubs make Papa flapjacks for Sunday breakfast but gunpowder gets knocked into the mixture and things start exploding.

4780. Papa's Little Helpers *(Terry Bears)* Jan. 1952; *p.c.:* TT for Fox; *dir:* Mannie Davis; *story:* Tom Morrison; *anim:* Jim Tyer; *sets:* Art Bartsch; *voices:* Douglas Moye, Tom Morrison, Philip A. Scheib; *mus:* Philip A. Scheib; *ph:* Douglas Moye; *col:* Tech. *sd:* RCA. 5 min. • The twins help Papa Bear erect a TV antenna.

4781. The Paper Hanger *(Krazy Kat)* 21 June 1932; *p.c.:* Winkler for Colum; *prod:* Charles Mintz; *story:* Ben Harrison; *anim:* Harry Love, Jack Carr; *voice:* Jack Carr; *mus:* Joe de Nat; *prod mgr:* James Bronis; b&w. *sd:* RCA. 6 min. • Krazy is knocked unconcious while redecorating Kitty's parlor so his dog gets some pals to finish it off.

4782. The Paper Hangers *(Terry-Toon)* 30 July 1937; *p.c.:* TT for Educational/Fox; *dir:* Mannie Davis; *mus:* Philip A. Scheib; b&w. *sd:* RCA. 6 min. • While Herman Pig and his assistant paper the walls of a house, two kids mess up their work.

4783. Papoose on the Loose *(Cartune)* 11 Apr. 1961; *p.c.:* Walter Lantz prods for Univ; *dir:* Paul J. Smith; *story:* Homer Brightman; *anim:* La Verne Harding, Les Kline, Ray Abrams; *sets:* Art Landy, Ray Huffine; *voice:* Daws Butler; *mus:* Clarence Wheeler; *prod mgr:* William E. Garity; *col:* Tech. *sd:* RCA. 6 min. • An Indian Chief dons a bearskin to teach his son a lesson in hunting bears.

4784. Pappy's Puppy *(Merrie Melodies)* 17 Dec. 1955; *p.c.:* WB; *dir:* Friz Freleng; *story:* Warren Foster; *anim:* Gerry Chiniquy; *lay:* Hawley Pratt; *back:* Irv Wyner; *ed:* Treg Brown; *voice:* Mel Blanc; *mus:* Carl Stalling; *prod mgr:* John W. Burton; *prod:* Edward Selzer; *col:* Tech. *sd:* Vit. 7 min. • The cross Sylvester has to bear is the bulldog next door's new pup who keeps attacking him.

4785. Parade of the Award Nominees *(Mickey Mouse)* 18 Nov. 1932; *p.c.:* Walt Disney prods for Academy Award; *anim:* Rudy Zamora; *caricatures:* Joe Grant; *col:* Tech. *sd:* PCP. 2½ min. • Mickey, Minnie, Pluto, Horace Horsecollar and Clarabelle Cow head the parade featuring: Wallace Beery, Jackie Cooper ("The Champ"), Lynn Fontanne, Alfred Lunt ("The Guardsman"), Helen Hayes ("The Sin of Madelon Claudet"), Frederic March ("Dr. Jekyll and Mr. Hyde") and Marie Dressler ("Emma"). Made for the 1932 Academy Awards Ceremony and pre-dating Mickey's first Technicolor vehicle, *The Band Concert*, by three years. Mickey finalizes by handing over to the real life Walt Disney, waiting on the podium.

4786. Parade of the Wooden Soldiers *(Betty Boop)* 1 Dec. 1933; *p.c.:* The Fleischer Studio for Para; *prod:* Max Fleischer; *dir:* Dave Fleischer; *anim:* Seymour Kneitel, William Henning; *voice:* Mae Questel; *mus:* (Dave) Rubinoff and his orchestra; b&w. *sd:* WE. 9 min. • A toy Betty arrives in the Toy Shop. The revelry soon awakens a gorilla who seeks revenge.

4787. Paramount-Bray Cartoons *p.c.:* Bray prods for Para; *prod:* John R. Bray; b&w. *sil.* • *1915: The Troubles of Mr. Monk* 21 Aug. *anim:* Earl Hurd • *1916: Colonel Heeza Liar's Waterloo* 6 Jan. *anim:* J.R. Bray. **Haddem Baad's Elopement** 13 Jan. *anim:* L.M. Glackens. **Inbad the Sailor** 20 Jan. *anim:* C. Allen Gilbert. **The Police Dog on the Wire** 27 Jan. *anim:* C.T. Anderson. **Farmer Al Falfa's Catastrophe** 3 Feb. *anim:* Paul H. Terry. **Haunts for Rent** 10 Feb. *anim:* C. Allen Gilbert. **Miss Nanny Goat Becomes an Aviator** 17 Feb. *anim:* Clarence Rigby. **Bobby Bumps and His Pointer Pup** 24 Feb. *anim:* Earl Hurd. **How Dizzy Joe Got to Heaven** 3 Mar. *anim:* L.M. Glackens. **Colonel Heeza Liar and the Pirates** 5 Mar. *anim:* J.R. Bray. **Farmer Al Falfa Invents a New Kite** 12 Mar. *anim:* Paul H. Terry. **Percy the Mechanical Man/The Chess Queen** 19 Mar. *anim:* H.C. Greening/C. Allen Gilbert. **Bobby Bumps Gets a Substitute/Inbad the Sailor Gets Into Deep Water** 26 Mar. *anim:* Earl Hurd/C. Allen Gilbert. **The Police Dog Turns Nurse** 2 Apr. *anim:* C.T. Anderson. **The Stone Age Roost Robber** 9 Apr. *anim:* L.M. Glackens. **Farmer Al Falfa's Scientific Dairy** 16 Apr. *anim:* Paul H. Terry. **Col. Heeza Liar Wins the Pennant** 23 Apr. *anim:* J.R. Bray. **Bobby Bumps and His Goat-Mobile** 30 Apr. *anim:* Earl Hurd. **The Police Dog in the Park** 6 May. *anim:* C.T. Anderson. **Miss Nanny Goat on the Rampage** 14 May. *anim:* Clarence Rigby. **Col. Heeza Liar Captures Villa** 20 May. *anim:* J.R. Bray. **Bobby Bumps Goes Fishing** 26 May. *anim:* Earl Hurd. **Farmer Al Falfa's Tentless Circus** 3 June. *anim:* Paul H. Terry. **Kid Casey the Champion** 10 June. *anim:* Frank Moser. **Col. Heeza Liar and the Bandits** 17 June. *anim:* J.R. Bray. **Bobby Bumps' Fly Swatter** 26 June. *anim:* Earl Hurd. **Farmer Al Falfa's Watermelon Patch** 29 June. *anim:* Paul H. Terry. **The Wild and Woolly West** 7 July. *anim:* A.D. Reed. **Col. Heeza Liar's Courtship** 17 July. *anim:* J.R. Bray. **Bobby Bumps' Detective Story** 22 July. *anim:* Earl Hurd. **In Lunyland** 28 July. *anim:* Leighton Budd. **Farmer Al Falfa's Egg-citement** 4 Aug. *anim:* Paul H. Terry. **Bobby Bumps Loses His Pup** 11 Aug. *anim:* Earl Hurd. **Col. Heeza Liar Plays Hamlet** 18 Aug. *anim:* J.R. Bray. **Farmer Al Falfa's Revenge** 25 Aug. *anim:*

Paul H. Terry. **Bobby Bumps and the Stork** 1 Sept. *anim:* Earl Hurd. **Col. Heeza Liar's Bachelor Quarters** 9 Sept. *anim:* J.R. Bray. **Farmer Al Falfa's Wolfhound** 16 Sept. *anim:* Paul H. Terry. **Bobby Bumps Starts a Lodge** 21 Sept. *anim:* Earl Hurd. **O.U. Rooster** 27 Sept. *anim:* J.R. Bray. **Farmer Al Falfa Sees New York** 9 Oct. *anim:* Paul H. Terry. **Col. Heeza Liar Gets Married** 17 Oct. *anim:* J.R. Bray. **Bobby Bumps Queers the Choir** 23 Oct. *anim:* Earl Hurd. **Greenland's Icy Mountains** 27 Oct. *anim:* L.M. Glackens. **Farmer Al Falfa's Prune Plantation** 3 Nov. *anim:* Paul H. Terry. **Bobby Bumps at the Circus** 11 Nov. *anim:* Earl Hurd. **Col. Heeza Liar, Hobo** 17 Nov. *anim:* J.R. Bray. **What Happened to Willie?** 25 Nov. *anim:* L.M. Glackens. **Farmer Al Falfa's Blind Pig** 1 Dec. *anim:* Paul H. Terry. **Bobby Bumps Helps Out a Book Agent** 11 Dec. *anim:* Earl Hurd. **Percy, Brains He Has Nix** 18 Dec. *anim:* H.C. Greening. **Jack the Giant Killer** 23 Dec. *anim:* L.M. Glackens • Magazine with animated inserts. Series continued as *Paramount-Bray Pictographs*.

4788. Paramount-Bray Pictographs *p.c.:* Bray prods for Para; *prod:* John R. Bray; b&w. *sil.* • *1917:* **Col. Heeza Liar on the Jump** 4 Feb. *anim:* J.R. Bray. **Bobby Bumps in the Great Divide** 11 Feb. *anim:* Earl Hurd. **Quacky Doodles' Picnic** 18 Feb. *anim:* F.M. Follett. **Col. Heeza Liar, Detective** 25 Feb. *anim:* J.R. Bray. **Bobby Bumps Adopts a Turtle** 5 Mar. *anim:* Earl Hurd. **Quacky Doodles' Food Crisis** 12 Mar. *anim:* F.M. Follett. **Col. Heeza Liar, Spy Dodger/Picto Puzzle #1** 19 Mar. *anim:* J.R. Bray/Sam Lloyd. **Bobby Bumps, Office Boy** 26 Mar. *anim:* Earl Hurd. **Quacky Doodles as the Early Bird/Picto Puzzle #2** 2 Apr. *anim:* F.M. Follett/Sam Lloyd. **Miss Nanny Goat at the Circus** 9 Apr. *anim:* Clarence Rigby. **Bobby Bumps Outwits the Dog Catcher/Picto Puzzle #3** 16 Apr. *anim:* Earl Hurd/Sam Lloyd. **Quacky Doodles Soldiering for Fair** 23 Apr. *anim:* F.M. Follett. **Stung** 30 Apr. *anim:* Leighton Budd. **Bobby Bumps Volunteers** 7 May. *anim:* Earl Hurd. **The Submarine Mine-Layer/Picto Puzzle #4** 14 May. *anim:* J.D. Leventhal/Sam Lloyd. **The Awakening of America/Picto Puzzles #5** 21 May. *anim:* Sam Lloyd. **Bobby Bumps Daylight Camper** 28 May. **Otto Luck in the Movies** 4 June. *anim:* Wallace A. Carlson. **Travelling Forts/Evolution of the Dachshund** 11 June. *anim:* J.D. Leventhal/Leighton Budd. **Bobby Bumps: Submarine Chaser** 18 June. *anim:* Earl Hurd. **Otto Luck to the Rescue** 25 June. *anim:* Wallace A. Carlson. **Mechanical Operations of British Tanks/Picto Puzzle #6** 2 July. *anim:* J.D. Leventhal/Sam Lloyd. **Bobby Bumps' Fourth** 9 July. *anim:* Earl Hurd. **Otto Luck and Rudy Razmataz** 16 July. *anim:* Wallace A. Carlson. **Sic 'em Cat** 23 July. *anim:* Leighton Budd. **Fiske Torpedo Plane/Picto Puzzle #7** 30 July. *anim:* J.D. Leventhal/Sam Lloyd. **Bobby Bumps' Amusement Park** 6 Aug. *anim:* Earl Hurd. **Otto Luck's Flivvered Romance** 13 Aug. *anim:* Wallace A. Carlson. **Uncle Sam's Dinner Party** 20 Aug. *anim:* Leighton Budd. **Bobby Bumps, Surf Rider** 27 Aug. *anim:* Earl Hurd. **Goodrich Dirt Among the Beach Nuts** 3 Sept. *anim:* Wallace A. Carlson. **Quack Doodles Signs the Pledge** 10 Sept. *anim:* F.M. Follett. **Bobby Bumps Starts for School** 17 Sept. *anim:* Earl Hurd. **A Submarine Destroyer** 24 Sept. *anim:* J.D. Leventhal. **Goodrich Dirt, Lunch Detective** 1 Oct. *anim:* Wallace A. Carlson. **Bobby Bumps' World Serious** 8 Oct. *anim:* Earl Hurd. **Quacky Doodles the Cheater** 15 Oct. *anim:* F.M. Follett. **The Aeroplane Machine Gun** 22 Oct. *anim:* J.D. Leventhal. **Bobby Bumps, Chef** 29 Oct. *anim:* Earl Hurd. **Goodrich Dirt at the Training Camp** 5 Nov. *anim:* Wallace A. Carlson. **Putting Volcanoes to Work** 12 Nov. *anim:* J.D. Leventhal. **Bobby Bumps and Fido's Birthday Party** 19 Nov. *anim:* Earl Hurd. **The Gasolene Engine** 26 Nov. *anim:* J.D. Leventhal. **Goodrich Dirt's Amateur Show** 3 Dec. *anim:* Wallace A. Carlson. **Bobby Bumps, Early Shopper** 10 Dec. *anim:* Earl Hurd. **Freak Patents: The Balloon R.R.** 17 Dec. *anim:* J.D. Leventhal. **Goodrich Dirt and the $1000 Reward** 24 Dec. *anim:* Wallace A. Carlson • *1918:* **Goodrich Dirt and the Duke de Whatanob** 7 Jan. *anim:* Wallace A. Carlson. **The Panama Canal** 14 Jan. *anim:* J.D. Leventhal. **Bobby Bumps' Disappearing Gun** 21 Jan. *anim:* Earl Hurd. **The Peril of the Prussianism** 28 Jan. *anim:* Leighton Budd. **Putting Fritz on the Water Wagon** 4 Feb. *anim:* Leighton Budd. **Goodrich Dirt's Bear Facts** 11 Feb. *anim:* Wallace A. Carlson. **The Rudiments of Flying** 18 Feb. *anim:* J.D. Leventhal. **Bobby Bumps at the Dentist** 25 Feb. *anim:* Earl Hurd. **The Pinkerton Pup's Portrait** 4 Mar. *anim:* C.T. Anderson. **The Torpedo, Hornet of the Sea** 11 Mar. *anim:* J.D. Leventhal. **Goodrich Dirt in the Barber Business** 18 Mar. *anim:* Wallace A. Carlson. **Bobby Bumps' Fight** 25 Mar. *anim:* Earl Hurd. **Me Und Gott** 1 Apr. *anim:* L.M. Glackens.

Goodrich Dirt, Mat Artist 8 Apr. *anim:* Wallace A. Carlson. **Bobby Bumps on the Road** 15 Apr. *anim:* Earl Hurd. **A Tonsorial Slot Machine** 22 Apr. *anim:* Leighton Budd. **The Third Liberty Loan Bomb** 29 Apr. *anim:* Leighton Budd. **Goodrich Dirt, Bad Man Tamer** 6 May. *anim:* Wallace A. Carlson. **Bobby Bumps Caught in the Jamb** 13 May. *anim:* Earl Hurd. **The Depth Bomb** 20 May. *anim:* E. Dean Parmelee. **Goodrich Dirt in Darkest Africa** 27 May. *anim:* Wallace A. Carlson. **Bobby Bumps Out West** 3 June. *anim:* Earl Hurd **Out of the Inkwell** 10 June. *anim:* Max Fleischer. **Goodrich Dirt, King of Spades** 17 June. *anim:* Wallace A. Carlson. **Bobby Bumps Films a Fire** 24 June. *anim:* Earl Hurd. **The First Flyer/Animated Technical Drawings** 1 July. *anim:* L.M. Glackens/E. Dean Parmelee. **Goodrich Dirt the Cop** 8 July. *anim:* Wallace A. Carlson. **Bobby Bumps Becomes an Ace** 15 July. *anim:* Earl Hurd. **Von Loon's 25,000 Mile Gun** 22 July. *anim:* L.M. Glackens. **Animated Technical Drawings** 29 July. *anim:* E. Dean Parmelee. **Goodrich Dirt the Dark and Stormy Knight** 5 Aug. *anim:* Wallace A. Carlson. **The Kaiser's Surprise Party** 12 Aug. *anim:* Leighton Budd. **Bobby Bumps on the Doughnut Trail** 19 Aug. *anim:* Earl Hurd. **Goodrich Dirt, Coin Collector** 26 Aug. *anim:* Wallace A. Carlson. **Aerial Warfare** 2 Sept. *anim:* E. Dean Parmelee. **A Watched Pot** 9 Sept. *cartoon* 16 Sept. **Bobby Bumps and the Speckled Death** 23 Sept. *anim:* Earl Hurd. **Goodrich Dirt, Millionaire** 30 Sept. *anim:* Wallace A. Carlson. **Von Loon's Non-Capturable Aeroplane** 1 Oct. *anim:* L.M. Glackens. **Bobby Bumps' Incubator** 8 Oct. *anim:* Earl Hurd. *cartoon* 15 Oct. **The Greased Pole** 22 Oct. *anim:* Leighton Budd. **Goodrich Dirt: When Wishes Come True** 29 Oct. *anim:* Wallace A. Carlson. **A German Trick That Failed** 6 Nov. *anim:* Leighton Budd. *cartoon* 13 Nov. **Bobby Bumps in Before and After** 20 Nov. *anim:* Earl Hurd. **Uncle Sam's Coming Problem** 27 Nov. *anim:* Leighton Budd. **Bobby Bumps Puts a Beanery on the Bum** 4 Dec. *anim:* Earl Hurd. **Goodrich Dirt, Cowpuncher** 11 Dec. *anim:* Wallace A. Carlson. **Pictures in the Fire** 18 Dec. *anim:* "Santry." **Goodrich Dirt in Spot Goes Romeoing** 25 Dec. *anim:* Wallace A. Carlson • *1919:* *cartoon* 1 Jan. **Bobby Bumps' Last Smoke** 8 Jan. *anim:* Earl Hurd. **Private Bass: His Pass** 15 Jan. *anim:* L.M. Glackens. **Goodrich Dirt in a Difficult Delivery** 22 Jan. *anim:* Wallace A. Carlson. **The Adventures of Hardrock Dome** 29 Jan. *anim:* Pat Sullivan. **The Adventures of Hardrock Dome #2** 5 Feb. *anim:* Pat Sullivan. **The Further Adventures of Hardrock Dome** 12 Feb. *anim:* Pat Sullivan. **Theory of the Long Range Shell** 19 Feb. *anim:* E. Dean Parmelee. **Goodrich Dirt, Hypnotist** 26 Feb. *anim:* Wallace A. Carlson. **Out of the Inkwell** 5 Mar. *anim:* Max Fleischer. **Shadowgraphs/Theory of the Hand Grenade** 12 Mar. *anim:* E. Dean Parmelee. **Bobby Bumps' Lucky Day** 19 Mar. *anim:* Earl Hurd. **Dud Perkins Gets Mortified** 26 Mar. *anim:* Wallace A. Carlson. **Out of the Inkwell** 2 Apr. *anim:* Max Fleischer. **The Parson** 9 Apr. *anim:* Wallace A. Carlson. **Bobby Bumps' Night Out with Some Night Owls** 16 Apr. *anim:* Earl Hurd. **Bobby Bumps' Pup Gets the Flea-enza** 23 Apr. *anim:* Earl Hurd. **Bobby Bumps' Eel-lectric Launch** 30 Apr. *anim:* Earl Hurd. **Wounded by the Beauty** 7 May. *anim:* Wallace A. Carlson. **Dud the Circus Performer** 14 May. *anim:* Wallace A. Carlson. **Bobby Bumps and the Sand Lizard** 21 May. *anim:* Earl Hurd. **In 1998 A.D.: The Automatic Reducing Machine** 28 May. *anim:* Leighton Budd. **Dud's Greatest Cirkus on Earth** 4 June. *anim:* Wallace A. Carlson. **The Biography of Madame Fashion** 11 June. *anim:* L.M. Glackens. *cartoon* 18 June. **Bobby Bumps and His Hypnotic Eye** 25 June. *anim:* Earl Hurd. *cartoon* 2 July. **At the Ol' Swimmin' Hole** 9 July. *anim:* Wallace A. Carlson. **Bobby Bumps Throwing the Bull** 16 July. *anim:* Earl Hurd. *cartoon* 23 July. **Tying the Nuptial Knot** 30 July. *anim:* L.M. Glackens. • Continued as *Goldwyn-Bray Pictographs*.

4789. Paramount Cartoons *p.c.:* Powers for Para; *prod:* P.A. Powers; *ph:* Harry E. Squires; b&w. *sil.* • Magazine incorporating comic characters: *Bobby Bumps*; *Bud & Susie*; *Felix the Cat*; *Peanut Comedies*; and *The Silly Hoots.* • *1921:* **Bobby Bumps Working on an Idea** 8 May. *anim:* Earl Hurd. **Spaghetti for Two/Felix Goes on Strike** 15 May. *anim:* Harry Leonard/Pat Sullivan. **Padding the Bill** 22 May. *anim:* Harry Bailey. **By the Sea** 29 May. *anim:* Frank Moser. **In Old Madrid/Felix in the Love Punch** 5 June. *anim:* Harry Leonard/Pat Sullivan. **Shootin' Fish** 12 June. *anim:* Earl Hurd. **The Chicken Fancier** 19 June. *anim:* Harry Bailey. **$10,000 Under a Pillow** 26 June. *anim:* Frank Moser. **Felix Out of Luck** 3 July. *anim:* Pat Sullivan. **Bobby Bumps in Shadow Boxing** 9 July. *anim:* Earl Hurd. **Felix Left at Home** 17 July. *anim:* Pat Sullivan. **No Tickee,**

No Shirtee 24 July. *anim:* Harry Bailey. **Dashing North** 31 July. *anim:* Frank Moser. **School Days** 8 Aug. *anim:* Harry Leonard. **Black Magic** 14 Aug. *anim:* Harry Bailey **Bobby Bumps in Hunting and Fishing** 21 Aug. *anim:* Earl Hurd. **Kitchen, Bedroom and Bath** 28 Aug. *anim:* Frank Moser. **The Wars of Mice and Men** Sept. *anim:* Frank Moser. **Felix the Gay Dog** 30 Oct. *anim:* Pat Sullivan

4790. Paramount Magazine *p.c.:* Powers for Para; *prod:* P.A. Powers; b&w. *sil.* • Magazine incorporating comic characters: *Bobby Bumps*; *Bud & Susie*; *Felix the Cat*; *Peanut Comedies* and *The Silly Hoots*. • *1920:* The **Bone of Contention** 14 Mar. *anim:* Paul H. Terry. **Handy Mandy's Goat** 21 Mar. *anim:* Frank Moser. **Feline Follies** 28 Mar. *anim:* Pat Sullivan. **Bobby Bumps** 4 Apr. *anim:* Earl Hurd. **The Kids Find Candy's Catching** 11 Apr. *anim:* Frank Moser. **Felix the Cat** 18 Apr. *anim:* Pat Sullivan. **Bobby Bumps** 25 Apr. *anim:* Earl Hurd. **Bud Takes the Cake** 2 May. *anim:* Frank Moser. **Felix the Cat** 9 May. *anim:* Pat Sullivan. **Bobby Bumps** 15 May. *anim:* Earl Hurd. **The New Cook's Debut** 23 May. *anim:* Frank Moser. **Felix the Cat** 30 May. *anim:* Pat Sullivan. **Bobby Bumps** 6 June. *anim:* Earl Hurd. **Mice and Money** 13 June. *anim:* Frank Moser. **Felix the Cat** 20 June. *anim:* Pat Sullivan. **Silly Hoots** 27 June. *anim:* Henry D. Bailey. **The Translantic Night Express** 4 July. *anim:* Harry Leonard. **Bobby Bumps** 11 July. *anim:* Earl Hurd. **Felix the Cat** 18 July. *anim:* Pat Sullivan. **Down the Mississippi** 25 July. *anim:* Frank Moser. **Silly Hoots** 1 Aug. *anim:* Henry D. Bailey. **Bobby Bumps: The Cave Man** 8 Aug. *anim:* Earl Hurd. **Play Ball** 15 Aug. *anim:* Frank Moser. **Romance and Rheumatism** 22 Aug. *anim:* Frank Moser. **Felix the Cat** 29 Aug. *anim:* Pat Sullivan**Bud and Tommy Take a Day Off** 5 Sept.*anim:* Frank Moser**Silly Hoots** 12 Sept..*anim:* Henry D. Bailey. **Bobby Bumps** 19 Sept. *anim:* Earl Hurd. **Felix the Cat in My Hero** 26 Sept. *anim:* Pat Sullivan. **The North Pole** 3 Oct. *anim:* Frank Moser. **Silly Hoots** 10 Oct. *anim:* Henry D. Bailey. **Bobby Bumps** 27 Oct. *anim:* Earl Hurd. **Felix the Landlord** 24 Oct. *anim:* Pat Sullivan. **The Great Clean-Up** 31 Oct. *anim:* Frank Moser. **A Double Life** 7 Nov. *anim:* Henry D. Bailey. **Bobby Bumps** 14 Nov. *anim:* Earl Hurd. **Felix the Cat/One Hundred Percent Proof** 21 Nov. *anim:* Pat Sullivan/Harry Leonard. **Bud and Susie Join the Tecs** 28 Nov. *anim:* Frank Moser. **Fifty-Fifty** 5 Dec. *anim:* Frank Moser. **Are You Married?** 12 Dec. *anim:* Henry D. Bailey. **Bobby Bumps' Orchestra** 19 Dec. *anim:* Earl Hurd. **Felix the Cat** 26 Dec. *anim:* Pat Sullivan. • *1921:* **Getting Theirs/Some Sayings of Benjamin Franklin** 2 Jan. *anim:* Frank Moser/Harry Leonard. **Bobby Bumps Joins the Band** 16 Jan. *anim:* Earl Hurd. **Felix the Cat** 23 Jan. *anim:* Pat Sullivan. **Bud and Susie** 30 Jan. *anim:* Frank Moser. **Hootch and Mootch in a Steak at Stake/Shimmy Geography** 6 Feb. *anim:* Earl Hurd. **Felix the Cat** 13 Feb. *anim:* Pat Sullivan. **Bobby Bumps: Check-Mated** 20 Feb. *anim:* Earl Hurd. **For Art's Sake/Ma's Wipe Your Feet Campaign** 27 Feb. *anim:* Frank Moser. **Cabaret Courtesy** 6 Mar. *anim:* Henry D. Bailey. **Bobby Bumps** 13 Mar. *anim:* Earl Hurd. **Felix the Hypnotist/The Sheriff** 20 Mar. *anim:* Pat Sullivan/Harry Leonard. **Silly Hoots** 27 Mar. *anim:* Henry D. Bailey. **Circumstancial Evidence** 3 Apr. *anim:* Frank Moser. **Bobby Bumps** 10 Apr. *anim:* Earl Hurd. **Felix the Cat: Free Lunch/In Greenwich Village** 17 Apr. *anim:* Pat Sullivan. **Silly Hoots** 24 Apr. *anim:* Henry D. Bailey. **Bud and Susie** 1 May. *anim:* Frank Moser • Series continued as *Paramount Cartoons*.

4791. Paramount Newsreel 1945; *p.c.:* Famous Studio for Para; *dir/anim/sets:* Gordon Sheehan, Robert Little; b&w. *sd:* RCA. • Animated depiction of how the proposed action, later referred to as "D-Day" could be fought.

4792. Paramount Pictographs *p.c.:* Bray prods for Para; *prod:* John R. Bray; b&w. *sil.* • *1916:* **Our Watch Dog** 20 Feb. *anim:* J.R. Bray. **Priscilla and the Pesky Fly** Feb. *anim:* Ashley Miller. **The Law of Gravitation** Feb. *anim:* Ashley Miller. **The Bronco Buster** 27 Feb. *anim:* J.R. Bray. **Fifty-Fifty** Mar. *anim:* Ashley Miller. **The Struggle/In His Shadows** 12 Mar. *anim:* J.R. Bray/C. Allen Gilbert. **The House in Which They Live** 19 Mar. *anim:* J.R. Bray. **Watchful Waiting/Found a Big Stick** 26 Mar. *anim:* J.R. Bray. **Why?** 2 Apr. *anim:* J.R. Bray. **The Long Arm of Law and Order** 9 Apr. *anim:* J.R. Bray. **The High Cost of Living** Apr. *anim:* Ashley Miller. **Did Sherman Say Law or War?** 7 May. *anim:* Ashley Miller. **Mass Nomination** 30 Apr. *anim:* J.R. Bray. **Fisherman's Luck** 14 May. *anim:* J.R. Bray. **Why the Sphinx Laughed** 9 July. *anim:* Ashley Miller • Magazine film with animated inserts including Ashley Miller's

Plastiques: Clay animation. The series evolves into Paramount-Bray Pictographs.

4793. The Parent Trap 21 June 1961; *p.c.:* Walt Disney prods for BV; *title anim:* T. Hee, Bill Justice, Xavier Atencio; *mus:* Paul Smith; *title song:* Richard M. Sherman, Robert B. Sherman; *voices:* Tommy Sands, Annette Funicello; *col:* Tech. *sd:* RCA. (*titles*) 3¹/₂ min. • The live-action feature concerns twins trying to reunite their divorced parents. The animation involves two cupids trying to unite the parents.

4794. Park Avenue Pussycat (*Terry-Toon*) Jan. 1956; *p.c.:* TT for Fox; *dir:* Connie Rasinski; *story:* Tom Morrison; *anim:* Jim Tyer; *sets:* Art Bartsch; *voice:* Frank Gallop; *mus:* Philip A. Scheib; *ph:* Douglas Moye; *col:* Tech. *sd:* RCA. 6 min. CS. • A pampered cat sees the birth of three birds from his penthouse. His basic instincts get the better of him and he escapes the apartment only to get beaten-up by the fledgelings.

4795. Park Your Baby (*Fable*) 6 Dec. 1939; *p.c.:* Colum; *story:* Allen Rose; *anim:* Harry Love, Louie Lilly; *ed:* George Winkler; *voice:* Robert Winkler, Dave Weber; *mus:* Joe de Nat; b&w. *sd:* RCA. 6 min. • Scrappy looks after two brats in the nursery section of a department store. They destroy everything until he is forced to put them in "The Bad Boy Pacifier."

4796. Parking Space (*Oswald*) 18 Dec. 1933; *p.c.:* Univ; *dir:* Walter Lantz "Bill" Nolan; *anim:* Ray Abrams, Fred Avery, Cecil Surry, Jack Carr, Ernest Smythe; *mus:* James Dietrich; b&w. *sd.* 8 min. • No story available.

4797. Parlez Vous Woo (*Popeye*) 12 Oct. 1956; *p.c.:* Famous for Para; *dir:* I. Sparber; *story:* I. Klein; *anim:* Al Eugster, Wm. B. Pattengill; *sets:* Anton Loeb; *voices:* Jack Mercer, Mae Questel, Jackson Beck; *mus:* Winston Sharples; *ph:* Leonard McCormick; *prod mgr:* Seymour Shultz; *col:* Tech. *sd:* RCA. 6 min. • Olive breaks a date with Popeye to sustain a visit from the suave radio personality "The International," who turns out to be Bluto.

4798. The Parrotville Fire Department (*Rainbow Parade*) 14 Sept. 1934; *p.c.:* Van Beuren for RKO; *dir:* Burt Gillett, Steve Muffatti; *anim:* I. Klein; *mus:* Winston Sharples; *col:* Ciné. *sd:* RCA. 7 min. • No story available.

4799. Parrotville Old Folks (*Rainbow Parade*) 25 Jan. 1935; *p.c.:* Van Beuren for RKO; *dir:* Burt Gillett, Tom Palmer; *mus:* Winston Sharples; *col:* Ciné. *sd:* RCA. 7 min. • Captain and Homer entertain by singing and playing the accordian for the Old Folks' Home.

4800. Parrotville Post Office (*Rainbow Parade*) 28 June 1935; *p.c.:* Van Beuren for RKO; *dir:* Burt Gillett, Tom Palmer; *mus:* Winston Sharples; *col:* Ciné. *sd:* RCA. 7 min. • Postmaster Pete catches a mail robber with help from the kids.

4801. Part-Time Pal (*Tom & Jerry*) 15 Mar. 1947; *p.c.:* MGM; *dir:* William Hanna, Joseph Barbera; *anim:* Michael Lah, Kenneth Muse, Ed Barge; *sets:* Robert Gentle; *ed:* Fred MacAlpin; *voices:* Lillian Randolph, Harry E. Lang; *mus:* Scott Bradley; *prod:* Fred Quimby; *col:* Tech. *sd:* WE. 8 min. • While guarding the kitchen, Tom accidentally gets inebriated in a barrel of cider and befriends Jerry. The friendship only lasts until Tom sobers up.

4802. Party Smarty (*Noveltoon*) 3 Aug. 1951; *p.c.:* Famous for Para; *dir:* Seymour Kneitel; *story:* Carl Meyer, Jack Mercer; *anim:* Dave Tendlar, Morey Reden; *sets:* Robert Connavale; *voices:* Sid Raymond, Jackson Beck; *mus:* Winston Sharples; *ph:* Leonard McCormick; *prod mgr:* Seymour Shultz; *col:* Tech. *sd:* RCA. 6 min. • The Fox invades Oscar the duck's birthday party in hopes of devouring Baby Huey.

4803. Pass the Biscuits Mirandy! (*Swing Symphony*) 25 Aug. 1943; *p.c.:* Walter Lantz prods for Univ; *dir:* James Culhane; *story:* Ben Hardaway, Milt Schaffer; *anim:* Paul Smith; *sets:* Fred Brunish; *voices:* Pinto Colvig, Del Porter, Sara Berner; *mus:* Darrell Calker; *song:* Del Porter, Carl Hoefle; *prod mgr:* George Hall; *col:* Tech. *sd:* RCA. 6 min. • A hillbilly wife's biscuits are too hard to eat and thus play an integral part in a backwoods feud, also helping the war effort in blowing up Hitler, Mussolini and Hirohito.

4804. Passing 1975; *p.c.:* Murakami-Wolf prods; *dir/anim:* Jimmy Murakami; col. sd. • No story available.

4805. Past Perfumance (*Merrie Melodies*) 21 May 1955; *p.c.:* WB; *dir:* Charles M. Jones; *story:* Michael Maltese; *anim:* Ken Harris, Richard Thompson, Lloyd Vaughan; *lay:* Robert Givens; *back:* Philip de Guard;

ed: Treg Brown; *voices:* Mel Blanc, Arthur Q. Bryan, Michael Maltese; *mus:* Milt Franklyn; *prod mgr:* John W. Burton; *prod:* Edward Selzer; *col:* Tech. *sd:* Vit. 7 min. • A 1913 movie studio needs a defumigated skunk for an animal picture. The director's assistant paints a black cat with a white stripe but the arrival of Pepé le Pew empties the studio, leaving him to pursue the cat as his lady love.

4806. Paste Makes Waste *(Beary Family)* Mar. 1968; *p.c.:* Walter Lantz prods for Univ; *dir:* Paul J. Smith; *story:* Cal Howard; *anim:* Les Kline, Al Coe; *sets:* Ray Huffine; *voices:* Paul Frees, Grace Stafford; *mus:* Walter Greene; *prod mgr:* William E. Garity; *col:* Tech. *sd:* RCA. 6 min. • It's raining too hard for Charlie to play golf so he tries his hand at paper-hanging.

4807. Pastry Panic *(Little Roquefort)* Oct. 1951; *p.c.:* TT for Fox; *dir:* Mannie Davis; *story:* Tom Morrison; *anim:* Jim Tyer; *mus:* Philip A. Scheib; *ph:* Douglas Moye; *col:* Tech. *sd:* RCA. 6 min. • Roquefort upsets Percy while he's making a cake. A chase ensues, resulting in the cat believing he's killed the mouse.

4808. The Pastrytown Wedding *(Rainbow Parade)* 14 Sept. 1934; *p.c.:* Van Beuren for RKO; *dir:* Burt Gillett, Ted Eshbaugh; *anim:* I. Klein, William Littlejohn, Jack Zander; *sets:* Art Bartsch, Eddi Bowlds; *mus:* Winston Sharples; *col:* Ciné. *sd:* RCA. 8 min. • One tiny inhabitant of Pastry Town saves a damsel from an angry bee. She concents to marry him and the others bake an enormous wedding cake.

4809. Patch Mah Britches *(Barney Google)* 19 Dec. 1935; *p.c.:* Charles Mintz prods for Colum; *story:* Sid Marcus; *anim:* Art Davis, I. Klein; *lay:* Clark Watson; *back:* Phil Davis; *ed:* George Winkler; *voice:* Smiley Burnett; *mus:* Joe de Nat; *prod mgr:* James Bronis; *col:* Tech. *sd:* RCA. 6 min. • When Barney invites the whole hillbilly troupe to dinner and acts politely ... they don't!

4810. Pathé Daily News *(#90)* 30 Dec. 1914; *p.c.:* Bray prods for Pathé; *prod:* J.R. Bray; *anim:* J.D. Leventhal; b&w. sil. • Animated map of German retreat.

4811. Pathé News *p.c.:* Bray prods for Pathé; *prod:* John R. Bray; b&w. sil. • Animated spots in weekly newsreel. • *1915:* **Col. Heeza Liar, Ghostbreaker** 6 Feb. *anim:* J.R. Bray. **The Boomerang** 17 Feb. **Col. Heeza Liar in the Haunted Castle** 20 Feb. *anim:* J.R. Bray. **Our Defenses** 24 Feb. **Hands Across the Sea** 3 Mar. **The Presidential Chair** 10 Mar. **Patriotism** 17 Mar. *anim:* Robert Flohri. **Col. Heeza Liar Runs the Blockade** 20 Mar. *anim:* J.R. Bray. **A New Method of Fighting Submarines** 31 Mar. **Col. Heeza Liar and the Torpedo** 3 Apr. *anim:* J.R. Bray. **Some Feathers Fly in Turkey** 7 Apr. **Col. Heeza Liar and the Zeppelin** 10 Apr. *anim:* J.R. Bray. **The Wily Jap** 14 Apr. *anim:* Robert Flohri. **The Resourceful Dachshund** 24 Apr. **Col. Heeza Liar Signs the Pledge/The Reward of Patience** 8 May. *anim:* J.R. Bray. **Col. Heeza Liar in the Trenches** 13 May. *anim:* J.R. Bray. **Col. Heeza Liar at the Front** 20 May. *anim:* J.R. Bray. **Col. Heeza Liar, War Aviator** 23 May. *anim:* J.R. Bray. **Another Fallen Idol** 28 May. *anim:* L.M. Glackens. **Col. Heeza Liar Invents a New Kind of Shell** 5 June. *anim:* J.R. Bray. **When Kitty Spilled the Ink** 26 June. **Col. Heeza Liar, Dog Fancier** 10 July. *anim:* J.R. Bray. **Col. Heeza Liar Foils the Enemy/The Dove of Peace** 31 July. *anim:* J.R. Bray/W.C. Morris. **Uncle Sam Gets Wise at Last** 7 Aug. **The Pilot of Peace** 14 Aug. *anim:* W.C. Morris. **Col. Heeza Liar, War Dog** 21 Aug. *anim:* J.R. Bray. **Col. Heeza Liar at the Bat/Grandmothers of Yesterday, Today and Tomorrow** 4 Sept. *anim:* J.R. Bray. **Some Presidential Possibilities** 11 Sept. *anim:* W.C. Morris. **Dr. Worsen Plummer** 2 Oct. **Dumba's Departure** 23 Oct. **Dr. Worsen Plummer Starts a Drug Store** 30 Oct. **I Should Worry** 6 Nov. *anim:* Vincent Colby. **Wilson Surrenders** 13 Nov. *anim:* W.C. Morris. **Bubbling Bill** 18 Dec. **Troubles of a Pacifist** 22 Dec. **Col. Heeza Liar, Nature Faker** 28 Dec. • *1916:* **At It Again** 8 Mar. *anim:* Charles Wilhelm. **Patience Is a Virtue** 13 May **The Black List** 2 Sept. *anim:* W.C. Morris. **An Engineering Problem** 20 Sept. *anim:* J.D. Leventhal. **Responsibility for the War** 23 Sept. *anim:* W.C. Morris. **What Next?** 30 Sept. *anim:* L.M. Glackens. **Misadventures of the Bull Moose** 7 Oct. *anim:* John C. Terry. **Hands Across the Sea** 14 Oct. *anim:* John C. Terry. **Are We Prepared for the International Trade Hunt?** 21 Oct. *anim:* A.D. Reed. **The Courtship of Miss Vote** 28 Oct. *anim:* Leighton Budd. **The Pen Is Mightier Than the Sword** 4 Nov. *anim:* L.M. Glackens. **Somewhere in America** 11 Nov. *anim:* John C. Terry. **Now You See It, Now You Don't** 25 Nov. *anim:* John C. Terry. **Our Merchant Marine** 2 Dec. *anim:* John C. Terry. **The Mexican Border** 9 Dec. *anim:* Leighton Budd. **Uncle Sam's Christmas** 16 Dec. *anim:* Leighton Budd. **Independent Poland** 23 Dec. *anim:* L.M. Glackens. **In Verdun Forests** 30 Dec. *anim:* Hugh M. Shields • Series continued as *Hearst-Pathé News.*

4812. Pathé Review *p.c.:* Pathé Exchange; *anim:* Hy (Henry) Mayer; b&w. sil. • *1920:* **Such Is Life Among the Dogs** 2 Oct. **Such Is Life at the Zoo** 16 Oct. **Such Is Life at Coney Island** 6 Nov. **Such Is Sporting Life: Baseball** 13 Nov. **Such Is Life in Greenwich Village** 20 Nov. **Such Is Life in Mid-Winter: Winter Sports** 4 Dec. **Such Is Life in East Side, New York** 18 Dec. • *1921:* **Behind the Scenes of the Circus** 15 Jan. **Such Is Life in the Land of Fancy** 30 Jan. **Travelaugh** 5 Feb. **Such Is Life at the County Fair** 19 Feb. **Such Is Life in Summer/Water Stuff** 12 Mar. **Such Is Life in Ramblerville/Spring Hats** 9 Apr. **All to the Merry Bow-Wows** 30 Apr. **Travelaugh: In the Silly Summertime** 29 May. **The Door That Has No Lock** 26 June. **Such Is Life at the Race Track** 3 July. **Scenes in the Zoo** 17 July. **A Ramble Through Provincetown** Aug. **Travelaugh: The Little City of Dreams** 4 Sept. **Travelaugh: Day Dreams** 18 Sept. **Jiggin' the Old Sod** *(Sketchograf)* 18 Sept. *anim:* Julian Ollendorff. **Travelaugh: Down to the Fair** 2 Oct. **Travelaugh** Nov. **Such Is Life in New York** 20 Nov. **Travelaugh: Puppies** Dec. • *1922:* **In the Dear Old Summertime** 14 Oct. **Sporting Scenes** 25 Nov. • *1923:* *anim:* Herbert M. Dawley unless stated otherwise. **Faces** 6 Jan. **Silliettes** 24 Mar. **The Lobster Nightmare** 7 Apr. **The Absent Minded Poet** 9 June. **The Classic Centaur** 7 July • *1924:* **Pan the Piper** 9 Feb. **Fable of the Future: The Proxy Lover** 9 Aug. *anim:* Max Fleischer. **The Makin's of An Artist** 13 Sept. *anim:* Hy Mayer. **Thumbelina** 27 Sept. **Jack and the Beanstalk. Cinderella. The Sleeping Beauty. Beauty and the Beast. Tattercoats. Aladdin and His Wonderful Lamp** • *1925:* *cartoon* 28 Mar. **Jack the Giant Killer** 9 May. **The Making of a Man** 16 May. *anim:* Hy Mayer • *1926:* **Around the World in 28 Days** 13 Nov. *anim:* Bert Green • Animated items in magazine film. • As an example of Hy Mayer's contributions; *Day Dreams* shows photographs of cloud formations with Mr. Mayer outlining them with a pen, likening them to various natural objects. • Herbert Dawley's contributions were silhouette animation. • Max Fleischer's *The Proxy Lover* tells the tale of a bashful lover resorting to a mechanical man for the true "Cave Man" effect. • Bert Green's final entry is a jazzed-up version of Evans and Wells' recent record breaking trip around the world.

4813. Patient Porky *(Looney Tunes)* 24 Aug. 1939; *p.c.:* Leon Schlesinger prods for WB; *dir:* Robert Clampett; *story:* Warren Foster; *anim:* Norman McCabe; *ed:* Tregoweth E. Brown; *voices:* Mel Blanc, Ben Frommer, Sara Berner; *mus:* Carl W. Stalling; *prod sup:* Henry Binder, Raymond G. Katz; b&w. *sd:* Vit. 7 min. • Porky makes a pig of himself and ends up in hospital with a mental patient cat deciding to operate on him.

4814. Patriotic Pooches *(Terry-Toon)* 9 Apr. 1943; *p.c.:* TT for Fox; *dir:* Connie Rasinski; *story:* John Foster; *mus:* Philip A. Scheib; *col:* Tech. *sd:* RCA. 6 min. • A small dog is rejected from the Armed Forces until he rounds-up three Nazi pigs who arrive in a submarine.

4815. Patriotic Popeye *(Popeye)* 10 May 1957; *p.c.:* Para Cartoons: *dir:* I. Sparber; *story:* Carl Meyer; *anim:* Tom Johnson, Frank Endres; *sets:* Robert Owen; *voices:* Jack Mercer; *mus:* Winston Sharples; *ph:* Leonard McCormick; *prod mgr:* Seymour Shultz; *col:* Tech. *sd:* RCA. 6 min. • Popeye wants a "Safe and Sane" fourth of July celebration by locking his nephews' fireworks away.

4816. Paul Bunyan 1 Aug. 1958; *p.c.:* Walt Disney prods for BV; *dir:* Les Clark; *asst dir:* Jim Swain; *story:* Lance Nolley, Ted Bermen; *anim:* Jack Bailey, Al Coe, Earl Combs, Xenia De Mattia, George Goepper, Jerry Hathcock, Ken Hultgren, Fred Kopietz, George Nicholas, John Parr, John Reed, John Sibley, Ed Solomon, Bob Youngquist; *fx:* Jack Boyd, Dorse Lanpher; *des:* Eyvind Earle, Tom Oreb; *lay:* Homer Jonas, Jack Huber, Lance Nolley; *back:* Walt Peregoy; *voices:* Shot Gunderson: Ken Christy; *Chris Crosshaul:* Parley Baer; *Cal McNab:* Dallas McKennon; *Joe Muffaw:* Bob Amsberry; *Paul Bunyan:* Thurl Ravenscroft; *chorus:* The MelloMen, The Mitchell Choirboys; *mus:* George Bruns; *songs:* Tom Adair; *col:* Tech. *sd:* RCA. 17 min. *Academy Award nomination.* • The folklore story of a giant lumberjack and his ox who eventually gets beaten by modern day technology. Jack Kinney originally initiated the story.

4817. Paulie 17 Apr. 1998; *p.c.:* Dreamworks LLC for Univ; *special visual fx/anim:* The Computer Film Co., London: *cg lead anim:* Donald Parker; *lead compositor:* Paddy Eason; *compositing art:* John Hardwick, Rudi Holzapfel; *cg anim:* Richard Clarke; *character anim sup:* Martyn Jones; *2d character anim:* Gavin Toomey, Sarah Soulsby; *after fx:* Joe Pavlo; *visual fx prod:* Rachel Penfold; *sup:* Dennis Michelson; *visual fx co-ord:* Tim Wellspring, Laurel Schneider; *visual fx ed:* Mark Gravil; *studio mgr:* Pete Hanson; *addit visual fx: anim sup:* James Satoru Straus; *Santa Barbara Studios: anim:* Michael Parks, Kelly Wilcox, Darren Lurie, Julie Jaros; *Hammerhead Prods, Inc.: lead anim:* Barb Meier, Jamie Dixon; *anim:* Constance Bracewell, Sean Dever; *Light Matters/Pixel Envy: anim:* Michael Z. Huber; *voice of Pauly:* Jay Mohr; *col:* Tech. *sd:* Dolby digital/Digital dts/SDDS. 91½ min. *l/a.* • Live-action comedy about a Russian immigrant who sets out to find the best home for Paulie, a talking parrot.

4818. Paunch 'n' Judy *(Fable)* 13 Dec. 1940; *p.c.:* Colum; *story:* Manny Gould; *anim:* Ben Harrison; *lay:* Clark Watson; *back:* Phil Davis; *ed:* George Winkler; *voices:* Mel Blanc, Sara Berner, Cliff Nazarro; *mus:* Joe de Nat; *prod mgr:* James Bronis; *ph:* Otto Reimer; b&w. *sd:* RCA. 6 min. • Daddy tries his hand at photography with help from Snooks.

4819. Paw's Night Out *(Cartune)* 1 Aug. 1955; *p.c.:* Walter Lantz prods for Univ; *dir:* Paul J. Smith; *story:* Michael Maltese; *anim:* Robert Bentley, Gil Turner, La Verne Harding; *sets:* Art Landy, Raymond Jacobs; *voices:* Dal McKennon, Grace Stafford; *mus:* Clarence Wheeler; *prod mgr:* William E. Garity; *col:* Tech. *sd:* RCA. 6 min. • Paw finds himself locked out and, with help from Milford the pig, he has various attempts to get into the house without waking Maw.

4820. Pay Day *(Out of the Inkwell)* 8 July 1922; *p.c.:* Inkwell Studio for Winkler; *dir:* Dave Fleischer; *anim/l/a:* Max Fleischer; b&w. sil. 5 min. *l/a/anim.* • Max and his clown have a controversy in which he refuses to be disciplined. Ko-Ko finally does Max a good turn by exposing a thief who is robbing the safe.

4821. Pay Your Buffalo Bill *(Hoot Kloot)* 9 Oct. 1973; *p.c.:* Mirisch/DFE for UA; *dir:* Gerry Chiniquy; *story:* John W. Dunn; *anim:* John Gibbs, Ken Muse, Bob Richardson, Don Williams, Norm McCabe; *lay:* Dick Ung; *back:* Richard Thomas; *ed:* Rick Steward; *voices:* Bob Holt, Larry Mann; *mus:* Doug Goodwin; *ph:* John Burton Jr.; *titles:* Arthur Leonardi; *prod mgr:* Lee Gunther; *col:* DeLuxe. *sd:* RCA. 5 min. • Kloot uses Dr. Crazywolf's tonic to make him strong enough to apprehend law breakers.

4822. Paying the Piper *(Looney Tunes)* 12 Mar. 1949; *p.c.:* WB; *dir:* Robert McKimson; *story:* Warren Foster; *anim:* Manny Gould, John Carey, Charles McKimson, Phil de Lara; *lay:* Cornett Wood; *back:* Richard H. Thomas; *ed:* Treg Brown; *voices:* Mel Blanc; *mus:* Carl Stalling *prod mgr:* John W. Burton; *prod:* Edward Selzer; *col:* Tech. *sd:* Vit. 7 min. • Much to the cats' annoyance, Pied Piper Porky is hired to rid the town of rats. The chief cat dresses as a rat to give Porky the runaround.

4823. Peace Conference *(Krazy Kat)* 10 Apr. 1935; *p.c.:* Charles Mintz prods for Colum; *story:* Ben Harrison; *anim:* Manny Gould, Harry Love, Preston Blair; *mus:* Joe de Nat; *prod mgr:* George Winkler; b&w. *sd:* RCA. 6 min. • Three world-power representatives argue over their slice of the globe. Krazy pacifies them by firing a shell that contains Bing Crosby, Rudy Valee and a big band.

4824. Peace on Earth *(MGM Cartoon)* 9 Dec. 1939; *p.c.:* MGM; *prod/dir:* Hugh Harman; *story:* Hugh Harman, Jack Cosgriff, Charles McGirl; *anim:* Irven Spence, Carl Urbano, Arnold Gillespie, Jerry Brewer; *lay:* John Meandor; *back:* Joe Smith; *ed:* Fred MacAlpin; *voices:* Mel Blanc, The Hollywood Choirboys; *mus:* Scott Bradley; *prod mgr:* Fred Quimby; *col:* Tech. *sd:* WE. 10 min. *Academy Award nomination.* • Grandpa squirrel tells the youngsters of how man once destroyed himself through warfare. A parable of present times, with war in Europe having just been declared.

4825. Peace Time Football *(Gandy Goose)* 19 July 1946; *p.c.:* TT for Fox; *dir:* Mannie Davis; *story:* John Foster; *voices:* Thomas Morrison; *mus:* Philip A. Scheib; *ph:* Douglas Moye; *col:* Tech. *sd:* RCA. 6 min. • Gandy is captain of an all-mouse football team playing against the Cats.

4826. The Peaceful City *(Life Cartoon Comedy)* 2 Jan. 1927; *p.c.:* Sherwood Wadsworth Pictures for Educational; *prod/dir:* John McCrory; b&w. sil. 6 min. • Mike Monkey is a New York policeman who eventually rounds up a gang of crooks with help from Little Nibbins.

4827. Peaceful Neighbors *(Color Rhapsody)* 26 Jan. 1939; *p.c.:* Charles Mintz prods for Colum; *dir:* Sid Marcus; *story:* Art Davis, Herb Rothwill; *lay:* Clark Watson; *back:* Phil Davis; *mus:* Joe de Nat; *prod mgr:* James Bronis; *col:* Tech. *sd:* RCA. 8½ min. • Two rival families of hens battle over the division line between two coops. Two doves finally bring a peaceful settlement.

4828. Peachy Cobbler 9 Dec. 1950; *p.c.:* MGM; *dir:* Tex Avery; *story:* Rich Hogan; *anim:* Walter Clinton, Michael Lah, Grant Simmons; *character des/lay:* Ed Benedict; *back:* John Didrik Johnsen; *ed:* Jim Faris; *voice:* Daws Butler; *mus:* Scott Bradley; *ph:* Jack Stevens; *prod:* Fred Quimby; *col:* Tech. *sd:* WE. 6 min. • A starving shoemaker shares his last crumb with some hungry birds. They turn out to be elves who repay his kindness by making shoes for him.

4829. Peanut Battle *(Terry-Toon)* Apr. 1962; *p.c.:* TT for Fox; *ex prod:* Bill Weiss; *dir:* Connie Rasinski; *story sup:* Tom Morrison; *story:* Larz Bourne; *anim:* Cosmo Anzilotti, Doug Crane; *lay:* Martin Strudler; *back:* Bill Focht; *voices:* Lionel Wilson; *mus:* Phil Scheib; *ph:* Ted Moskowitz; *prod mgr:* Frank Schudde; *col:* DeLuxe. *sd:* RCA. 6 min. • No story available.

4830. The Peanut Vendor *(Screen Songs)* 28 Apr. 1933; *p.c.:* The Fleischer Studio for Para; *prod:* Max Fleischer; *dir:* Dave Fleischer; *anim:* Seymour Kneitel, Thomas Johnson; *mus:* Art Turkisher; *l/a:* Armida; b&w. *sd:* WE. 8 min. *l/a/anim.* • The animals in the zoo turn the tables on the visitors. The elephant pinches all the vendor's peanuts to feed the other animals. Armida sings in English and Spanish.

4831. Pearl Crazy *(Hashimoto)* May 1963; *p.c.:* TT for Fox; *ex prod:* Bill Weiss; *dir:* Bob Kuwahara; *story sup:* Tom Morrison; *story:* Larz Bourne; *anim:* Cosmo Anzilotti, Ralph Bakshi; *sets:* Bill Focht, John Zago; *ed:* George McAvoy; *voices:* John Myhers; *mus:* Phil Scheib; *ph:* Ted Moskowitz; *col:* DeLuxe. *sd:* RCA. 6 min. • No story available.

4832. The Pearl Divers *(Aesop's film Fable)* 19 July 1923; *p.c.:* Fables Pictures Inc for Pathé; *dir:* Paul Terry; b&w. sil. 5 min. • Tommy Cat sends Milton Mouse to the ocean bed to find oysters. Finding them all asleep, and not wanting to wake them, Mr. Mouse takes them, beds and all, to the upper regions. Moral: "You can't keep a good man down."

4833. The Pebble and the Penguin 16 Feb. 1996; *p.c.:* Don Bluth for WB; *dir:* Don Bluth; *ex prod:* James Butterworth; *prod:* Russell Boland; *prod mgr:* Gerry Shirren; *post prod: asso prod:* Helene Blitz; *scr:* Rachel Koretsky, Steve Whitestone; *storyboard:* Scott Caple, Kevin Gollaher, Guy Deel; *anim dir:* John Pomeroy, Len Simon, Richard Bazley, Silvia Hoefnagels, Ralf Palmer, John Hill, John Power; *anim;* Sandro Cleuzo, Marcelo de Moura, Alain Costa, Edison Goncalves, Gabor Steisinger, Fernando Moro, Paul Newberry, Rogerio de Godoy, Robert Fox, Celine Cahill, Glen McIntosh, Robert Sprathoff, Stuart Holgate, Konrad Winterlich, Hugo Takashi; *prod des:* David Goetz; *creative consultants:* Jonathan Dern, Paul Sabella, Kelly Ward, Mark Young; *fx anim:* Joe Gilland, Noel P. Kiernan, Julian Hynes, Dainn Landau, Conor Thunder, Leslie Aust, Martine Finucane, John Costello, Conann Fitzpatrick, Bob Cowan, Paul Morris, Mark Cumberton, Janette Owens, Joan Doyle, Deirdre Reynolds, Declan Walsh; *computer anim:* John Byrne, David Moran, Gerry Carty, Olun Riley, Mary Clarke-Miller, David Satchwell; *3d computer anim sup:* Tom Miller; *Snr computer anim:* Gregory Maguire; *lay sup:* Edward Gribbin; *post prod lay:* Mark T. Byrne, Martin Hanley, Gary O'Neill; *lay:* Amy Louise Berenz, Christopher Scully, Robert McCauley, Richard Simmons, Fred Reilly, Sinead Somers, Jonathan Ridge, Peter Wang; *back :* Paul Michael Kelly, Phaedra Craig Finnegan, Inge Daveloose, David Rabbitte, Henry McGrane, Owen Rohu, Kevin McNamara, Norman Teeling, Robyn Christian Nason, Miguel Gil, John Devilin; *ed:* Thomas V. Moore, Fiona Trayler, Aran O'Reilly; *voices: Narrator:* Shani Wallis; *Chubby/Gentoo:* Scott Bullock; *Hubie:* Martin Short; *Marina:* Annie Golden; *Priscilla:* Louise Vallance; *Pola:* Pat Musick; *Gwynne:* Angeline Ball; *Timmy:* Kendall Cunningham; *Petra:* Alissa King; *Beany:* Michael Nunes; *Drake:* Tim Curry; *Scrawny:* Neil Ross; *King:* Philip Clarke; *Megellenics:* B.J. Ward, Hamilton Camp; *Royall/Tika:* Will Ryan; *Chinstraps:* Pat Musick, Louise Vallance, Angeline Ball; *McCallister:* Stanley Jones; *Rocko:* James Belushi; *vocals:* Barry Manilow, Sheena Easton, Stephen Amerson, Kevin Bassinson, Susan Boyd, Randy Crenshaw, Kevin Dorsey, Bob Joyce, Jon Joyce, Tampa Lann, Steve Lively, Joe Pizzulo, Andrea Robinson, Maggie Roswell, Sally Stevens,

Maxine Waters, Yvonne Williams; *choral:* Irish Chamber Choir; *mus:* Mark Watters; *songs:* Barry Manilow, Bruce Sussman; *orch:* Mark Watters, Jeff Atmajian, Ira Hearshen, Chris Klatman, Lesa O'Donovan, Charles Fernandez, Thom Sharp, John Given, Brad Warnaar; *mus arrangements/mus prod/sup:* Barry Manilow; *mus ed:* Dominick Certo; *clean-up:* Eileen Conway; *col stylist:* Violet Margaret McKenna, Carmen Oliver, Donal Freeney; *pre-prod col key:* Rick Bentham, Carl Jones, Kenneth Slevin; *anim check:* Michele McKenna-Mahon, Hughie Shevlin, Mary Walsh, Sandra Breslin; *Xerox:* Michael Murray; *print lab:* Janet O'Carroll; *ink:* Jacqueline Hooks; *special fx sup:* David Tidgwell; *title des:* Johnson & Murphy Design; *choreog:* Kevin Carlisle; *dial ed:* Jim Fleming; *foley mix:* David Jobe, Greg Steele, Ellen Heuer, Zane Bruce; *sd re-rec:* Steve Maslow, Gregg Landaker; *ph:* Ciavàn Morris, Peadar O'Reilly, Emmet Doyle, Brian Kelly, Patrick Duffy, Jeanette Maher, Paul Gallagher, Keith Murray, Gary Hall, John O'Flaherty, Matthew Ferris, Stephen Sinfield, Wayne Alexander, Richard Wolff; *optical fx:* Don Bluth Ireland Ltd., Howell Optical; *col:* Tech. *sd:* Dolby dts stereo. 74 min. • When a meteor crashes to earth leaving a small gem-like rock in its crater, Hubie, a shy penguin, proposes to present it as a betrothal pebble to his lady love. Hubie's rival, Drake, assaults him, leaving him to be swept away on an iceberg. Hubie has many adventures on his long trek home, including being captured by hunters and an escape to the South Seas.

4834. A Peck O' Trouble *(Looney Tunes)* 28 Mar. 1953; *p.c.:* WB; *dir:* Robert McKimson; *story:* Tedd Pierce; *anim:* Herman Cohen, Rod Scribner, Phil de Lara, Charles McKimson; *lay:* Robert Givens; *back:* Richard H. Thomas; *ed:* Treg Brown; *voices:* Sheldon Leonard, Mel Blanc; *mus:* Carl Stalling; *prod mgr:* John W. Burton; *prod:* Edward Selzer; *col:* Tech. *sd:* Vit. 7 min. • Dodsworth tricks a kitten into getting him a woodpecker for breakfast.

4835. Peck of Trouble *(Woody Woodpecker)* Mar. 1968; *p.c.:* Walter Lantz prods for Univ; *dir:* Paul J. Smith; *story:* Cal Howard; *anim:* Al Coe, Les Kline; *sets:* Ray Huffine; *voices:* Dal McKennon, Grace Stafford; *mus:* Walter Greene; *prod mgr:* William E. Garity; *col:* Tech. *sd:* RCA. 5¹⁄₂ min. • A couple of forest rangers try to prevent Woody from destroying the trees.

4836. Peck Up Your Troubles *(Merrie Melodies)* 22 Sept. 1945; *p.c.:* WB; *dir:* I. Freleng; *story:* Michael Maltese; *anim:* Ken Champin; *lay:* Hawley Pratt; *back:* Paul Julian; *ed:* Treg Brown; *mus:* Carl W. Stalling; *prod mgr:* John W. Burton; *prod:* Edward Selzer; *col:* Tech. *sd:* Vit. 7 min. • A cat tries to eat a woodpecker.

4837. Peck Your Own Home *(Noveltoon)* May 1960; *p.c.:* Para Cartoons; *dir:* Seymour Kneitel; *story:* Irving Dressler; *anim:* Tom Johnson, Jack Ehret, Els Barthen; *sets:* Robert Owen; *voice:* Jack Mercer; *mus:* Winston Sharples; *ph:* Leonard McCormick; *prod mgr:* Abe Goodman; *col:* Tech. *sd:* RCA. 6 min. • A man is kept awake by a woodpecker loose in his house.

4838. Pecking Holes in Poles *(Woody Woodpecker)* 1972; *p.c.:* Walter Lantz prods for Univ; *dir:* Paul J. Smith; *story:* Cal Howard; *anim:* Volus Jones, Al Coe, Tom Byrne, Joe Voght; *sets:* Nino Carbe; *voices:* Daws Butler, Grace Stafford; *mus:* Walter Greene; *prod mgr:* William E. Garity; *col:* Tech. *sd:* RCA. 5¹⁄₂ min. • Linesman, Floyd Farkle, is sent to stop Woody from pecking the telephone poles.

4839. Pecos Bill 1955; *p.c.:* Walt Disney prods for BV; *dir:* Clyde Geronimi; *col:* Tech. *sd:* RCA. 23 min. • The toughest cowboy in the west is nearly tamed by the intervention of a woman. • See: *Melody Time*

4840. Pecos Pest *(Tom & Jerry)* 11 Nov. 1955; *p.c.:* MGM; *dir:* William Hanna, Joseph Barbera; *anim:* Ed Barge, Irven Spence, Ray Patterson, Kenneth Muse; *lay:* Dick Bickenbach; *back:* Robert Gentle; *ed:* Jim Faris; *voices:* George "Shug" Fisher, Daws Butler; *mus:* Scott Bradley; *ph:* Jack Stevens; *prod:* Fred Quimby; *col:* Tech. *sd:* WE. 7 min. • Jerry's Uncle Pecos arrives to sing on a talent show. As his guitar strings break, he replaces them with each of Tom's whiskers.

4841. Peculiar Penguins *(Silly Symphony)* 1 Sept. 1934; *p.c.:* Walt Disney prods for UA; *dir:* Wilfred Jackson; *story:* Ted Sears, Bill Cottrell, Dick Huemer; *anim:* Arthur Babbitt, Gilles de Tremaudan, Nick George, Clyde Geronimi, Dick Huemer, Hamilton S. Luske, Charles A. Nichols, Archie Robin, Louis Schmitt, Ben Sharpsteen; *character des:* Albert Hurter; *lay:* Albert Hurter, Hugh Hennesy; *mus:* Leigh Harline; *song:* J.H. Wood, Leigh Harline; *col:* Tech. *sd:* RCA. 8 min. • Life in a penguin community.

Polly Penguin is chased by a shark and finally rescued by her sweetheart, Peter.

4842. Pedagogical Institution (college to you) *(Stoneage)* 13 Sept. 1940; *p.c.:* The Fleischer Studio for Para; *prod:* Max Fleischer; *dir:* Dave Fleischer; *story:* Joseph Stultz; *anim:* Abner Kneitel, Arnold Gillespie; *character des:* Charles Thorson; *mus:* Sammy Timberg; b&w. *sd:* WE. 7 min. • Joe Goof tries for a degree so he can get a job.

4843. Pedro 13 May 1955; *p.c.:* Walt Disney prods for BV; *dir:* Hamilton S. Luske; *col:* Tech. *sd:* RCA 8 min. • A young mail plane has to deliver the mail across the Andes in treacherous weather. • See: *Saludos Amigos*

4844. Pedro and Lorenzo *(Noveltoon)* 13 July 1956; *p.c.:* Para Cartoons; *dir:* David Tendlar; *story:* I. Klein; *anim:* Morey Reden, Martin Taras; *sets:* Robert Little; *voices:* Jackson Beck, Gwen Davies; *mus:* Winston Sharples; *ph:* Leonard McCormick; *prod mgr:* Seymour Shultz; *col:* Tech. *sd:* RCA. 6 min. • A Mexican boy's pet calf has to be sold but the two are reunited as opponents in the Bull Arena.

4845. A Pee-Kool-Yar Sit-Chee-Ay-Shun *(Li'l Abner)* 30 June 1944; *p.c.:* Colum; *prod:* Dave Fleischer; *dir/story:* Sid Marcus; *anim:* Jim Armstrong, Grant Simmons; *lay:* Clark Watson; *voice:* Lurene Tuttle; *i&p:* Elizabeth F. McDowell; *mus:* Eddie Kilfeather; *ph:* Frank Fisher; *prod mgr:* Albert Spar; *col:* Tech. *sd:* RCA. 6¹⁄₂ min. • Daisy Mae courts Disgustin' Jones in an attempt to make Abner jealous.

4846. Pee-Wee's Big Adventure 9 Aug. 1985; *p.c.:* WB; *dir:* Tim Burton; *anim fx sup:* Rick Heinrichs; *anim fx consultants:* John Scheele, Stephen Chicco; *cel anim:* Jorgen Klubien; *col:* Tech. *sd:* Dolby stereo. 91 min. *l/a.* • Live-action comedy featuring television's Pee-Wee Herman (Paul Reubens): Pee-Wee scours the country looking for his stolen bicycle. He has a nightmare where his beloved bicycle is devoured by a dinosaur.

4847. Peekaboo *(Casper)* 24 May 1957; *p.c.:* Para Cartoons; *dir:* Seymour Kneitel; *story:* Larz Bourne; *anim:* Myron Waldman, Nick Tafuri; *sets:* Joe Dommerque; *voices:* Norma MacMillan, Gwen Davies, Jack Mercer; *mus:* Winston Sharples; *ph:* Leonard McCormick; *prod mgr:* Seymour Shultz; *col:* Tech. *sd:* RCA. 6 min. • A kitten abuses Casper's ghostly powers to scare and torment a dog.

4848. A Peep in the Deep *(Fable)* 23 Aug. 1940; *p.c.:* Colum; *story:* Allen Rose; *anim:* Harry Love, Louie Lilly; *lay:* Clark Watson; *back:* Phil Davis; *ed:* George Winkler; *voice:* Robert Winkler, Billy Bletcher; *mus:* Joe de Nat; *ph:* Otto Reimer; *prod mgr:* James Bronis; b&w. *sd:* RCA. 6¹⁄₂ min. • Scrappy and Oopy follow a treasure map to the ocean bed. They battle with the denizens of the deep only to discover more fish inside the treasure chest.

4849. Peep in the Deep *(Popeye)* 15 Mar. 1946; *p.c.:* Famous for Para; *dir:* Seymour Kneitel; *story:* Bill Turner, Otto Messmer; *anim:* Jim Tyer, William Henning; *voices:* Mae Questel, Jackson Beck; *mus:* Winston Sharples; *ph:* Leonard McCormick; *prod mgr:* Sam Buchwald; *col:* Ciné. *sd:* RCA. 7 min. • Popeye and Bluto race to recover some sunken treasure.

4850. Peeping Penguins *(Color Classic)* 27 Aug. 1937; *p.c.:* The Fleischer Studio for Para; *prod:* Max Fleischer; *dir:* Dave Fleischer; *anim:* Myron Waldman, Hicks Lokey, Lillian Friedman; *sets:* Robert Little; *song:* Sammy Timberg, Bob Rothberg; *col:* Tech. *sd:* WE. 7 min. • Against Mama's wishes, the two young penguins explore an abandoned cabin and get chased by a Polar bear.

4851. Peg-Leg Pedro 30 Nov. 1938; *p.c.:* Jam Handy Organization for General Motors; *prod/dir:* Jamison Handy; *col:* Tech. *sd:* WE. • Nicky Nome helps a boy and girl thwart the pirates and discovers their hidden treasure. They drive away in a new Chevrolet.

4852. Peg-Leg Pete *(Paul Terry-Toon)* 21 Feb. 1932; *p.c.:* Moser & Terry for Educational/Fox; *dir:* Frank Moser, Paul Terry; *mus:* Philip A. Scheib; b&w. *sd:* WE. 6 min. • Performed as a "Gilbert and Sullivan" opera, Peg-Leg Pete, a pirate hippo, kidnaps a girl mouse. The hero rescues her from an entire crew of peg-legged cut-throats.

4853. Peg-Leg Pete the Pirate *(Paul Terry-Toon)* 19 Apr. 1935; *p.c.:* Moser & Terry for Educational/Fox; *dir:* Frank Moser, Paul Terry; *mus:* Philip A. Scheib; b&w. *sd:* WE. 6 min. • Pirate cats chase the mice.

4854. The Pelican and the Snipe 7 Jan. 1944; *p.c.:* Walt Disney prods for RKO; *dir:* Hamilton S. Luske; *asst dir:* Riley Thomson; *story:*

Del G. Connell; *anim:* Oliver M. Johnston Jr., Ward Kimball, Hamilton S. Luske; *lay:* Ken Anderson; *voice:* Sterling Holloway; *mus:* Oliver Wallace; *col:* Tech. *sd:* RCA. 9 min. • A Snipe tries to prevent his pelican friend from flying in his sleep. • Made as part of the Good Neighbor Policy and originally intended for inclusion in *The Three Caballeros*.

4855. The Pelican's Bill *(Unnatural History)* 30 May 1926; *p.c.:* Bray prods for FBO; *dir* Walt Lantz; *anim:* Clyde Geronimi; *l/a ph:* Joe Rock; b&w. *sil.* 5 min. *l/a/anim.* • A pickpocketing monkey makes good use of a pelican's bill.

4856. Pencil Mania *(Tom & Jerry)* 9 Dec. 1932; *p.c.:* Van Beuren for RKO; *dir:* John Foster, George Stallings; *mus:* Gene Rodemich; b&w. *sd:* RCA. 7¹/₂ min. • Everything Jerry draws comes to life. He and Tom act out a melodrama having the characters returning into the pencil when it's all over.

4857. Penguin for Your Thoughts *(Casper)* 15 June 1956; *p.c.:* Famous for Para; *dir:* Seymour Kneitel; *story:* Larz Bourne; *anim:* Tom Golden, Bill Hudson; *sets:* Robert Owen; *voices:* Norma MacMillan, Sid Raymond, Jack Mercer; *mus:* Winston Sharples; *ph:* Leonard McCormick; *prod mgr:* Seymour Shultz; *col:* Tech. *sd:* RCA. 6 min. • Casper has the task of returning a baby penguin to the North Pole and anxiously awaiting parents.

4858. The Penguin Parade *(Merrie Melodies)* 23 Apr. 1938; *p.c.:* Leon Schlesinger prods for WB; *dir:* Fred Avery; *story:* J.B. Hardaway, Robert Clampett; *anim:* Paul Smith; *sets:* John Didrik Johnsen; *ed:* Tregoweth E. Brown; *voices:* Cliff Nazarro, Mel Blanc, The Sportsmen Quartet, Fred Avery; *mus:* Carl W. Stalling; *song:* Byron Gay; *prod sup:* Henry Binder, Raymond G. Katz; *col:* Tech. *sd:* Vit. 7 min. • Penguins in a Polar nightclub are entertained by Bob Crispy, Fats Walrus and the penguins' answer to the Ritz Brothers.

4859. Penny Antics *(Popeye)* 11 Mar. 1955; *p.c.:* Famous for Para; *dir:* Seymour Kneitel; *story:* I. Klein; *anim:* Tom Johnson, Frank Endres, Els Barthen; *sets:* Robert Connavale; *voices:* Jack Mercer, Jackson Beck, Frank Matalone; *mus:* Winston Sharples; *ph:* Leonard McCormick; *prod mgr:* Seymour Shultz; *col:* Tech. *sd:* RCA. 8 min. • In this color remake of *Customers Wanted*, Popeye and Bluto run rival Penny Arcades and vie for Wimpy's custom. Seq: *Silly Hillbilly; Wotta Knight; The Fistic Mystic.*

4860. Penny Pals *(Modern Madcap)* Oct. 1962; *p.c.:* Para Cartoons; *dir:* Seymour Kneitel; *story/voices:* Eddie Lawrence; *anim:* Morey Reden, Jim Logan, Sam Stimson; *sets:* Robert Owen; *mus:* Winston Sharples; *ph:* Leonard McCormick; *prod mgr:* Abe Goodman; *col:* Tech. *sd:* RCA. 6 min. • Percy and Ralph visit a penny arcade where Ralph converts Percy's last dime into pennies. Ralph cons Percy into hurting himself on the grip-tester, punching bag and electric-shock machine. The worm turns when Percy picks up a mallet from a strength-testing machine and wallops Ralph with it, saying: "The moral is, for two cents I'd break your head!"

4861. Pent-House Mouse *(Tom & Jerry)* 1963; *p.c.:* MGM; *prod/dir:* Chuck Jones; *asst dir:* Maurice Noble; *story:* Chuck Jones, Michael Maltese; *anim:* Ken Harris, Tom Ray, Richard Thompson, Ben Washam; *back:* Philip de Guard; *voices:* Mel Blanc; *mus:* Eugene Poddany; *prod sup:* Walter Bien, Les Goldman; *col:* Metro. *sd:* WE. 7 min. • Jerry is unwittingly transported to a penthouse suite where he infringes on Tom's privacy.

4862. People Are Bunny *(Merrie Melodies)* 19 Dec. 1959; *p.c.:* WB; *dir:* Robert McKimson; *story:* Tedd Pierce; *anim:* Ted Bonnicksen, Warren Batchelder, Tom Ray, George Grandpré, David R. Green; *lay:* Robert Gribbroek; *back:* William Butler; *ed:* Treg Brown; *voices:* Mel Blanc, Daws Butler; *mus:* Milt Franklyn; *prod mgr:* William Orcutt; *prod:* John W. Burton; *col:* Tech. *sd:* Vit. 6 min. • A TV station offers a cash reward for the first rabbit to be brought to them and Daffy takes full advantage of the situation.

4863. Pepito's Serenade *(Daffy Ditty)* 16 Aug. 1946; *p.c.:* Plastic prods/John Sutherland prods for UA; *prod:* Larry Morey, John Sutherland; *dir:* Robert Newman; *story:* Frank Tashlin; *mus:* Larry Morey; *col:* Tech. *sd:* 6 min. • A young troubador attempts to win favour with a Senorita by crooning under her balcony.

4864. The Perils of Pearl Pureheart *(Mighty Mouse)* Oct. 1949; *p.c.:* TT for Fox; *dir:* Eddie Donnelly; *story:* John Foster; *sets:* Art Bartsch; *voices:* Roy Halee, Thomas Morrison; *mus:* Philip A. Scheib; *ph:* Douglas Moye;

col: Tech. *sd:* RCA. 6 min. • Oil Can Harry kidnaps Pearl Pureheart but can Mighty Mouse be far away?

4865. Permanent Pests *(Aesop's Film Fable)* 17 Sept. 1926; *p.c.:* Fables Pictures Inc for Pathé; *dir:* Paul Terry; b&w. *sil.* 5 min. • No story available.

4866. Permanent Wave *(Oswald)* 30 Sept. 1929; *p.c.:* Univ; *anim/story:* Walter Lantz, "Bill" Nolan, Tom Palmer; *mus:* Bert Fiske; b&w. *sd:* WE. 6¹/₂ min. • Oswald and Captain Pete are shipwrecked on an Hawaiian island where Ozzie meets a mermaid.

4867. Permanent Waves *(Aesop's Film Fable)* 2 May 1925; *p.c.:* Fables Pictures Inc for Pathé; *dir:* Paul Terry; b&w. *sil.* 10 min. • Farmer Al Falfa, the cat and mice have a high old time jazzing around to the radio.

4868. Perpetual Motion *(Out of the Inkwell)* 2 Oct. 1920; *p.c.:* Bray prods for Goldwyn; *dir/story/l/a:* Max Fleischer; b&w. *sil.* 5 min. *l/a/anim.* • Max and Roland Crandall ridicule an inventor who has created a "Perpetual Motion" machine. Ko-Ko falls into the machine, making Max believe it works ... so he buys it. • See: *Goldwyn-Bray Pictographs*

4869. Perry Popgun *(Noveltoon)* Jan. 1962; *p.c.:* Para Cartoons; *dir:* Seymour Kneitel; *story:* Carl Meyer, Jack Mercer; *anim:* Morey Reden, George Germanetti, Wm. B. Pattengill; *sets:* Robert Owen; *mus:* Winston Sharples; *ph:* Leonard McCormick; *prod mgr:* Abe Goodman; *col:* Tech. *sd:* RCA. 6 min. • Private Eye, Perry Popgun, is right on the ball when rounding up a gang of bears.

4870. Person to Bunny *(Merrie Melodies)* 2 Apr. 1960; *p.c.:* WB; *dir:* Friz Freleng; *story:* Michael Maltese; *anim:* Art Davis, Gerry Chiniquy, Virgil Ross; *lay:* Hawley Pratt; *back:* Tom O'Loughlin; *ed:* Treg Brown; *voices:* Mel Blanc, Daws Butler, Arthur Q. Bryan; *mus:* Milt Franklyn; *prod mgr:* William Orcutt; *prod:* David H. DePatie; *col:* Tech. *sd:* Vit. 7 min. • The "Person to Person" cameras do an exclusive on Bugs when he is interrupted by, respectively, Daffy and an irate Elmer Fudd.

4871. Pesky Pelican *(Chilly Willy)* Sept. 1963; *p.c.:* Walter Lantz prods for Univ; *dir:* Sid Marcus; *story:* Al Bertino, Dick Kinney; *anim:* Ray Abrams, Les Kline, Art Davis; *sets:* Ray Huffine, Art Landy; *voices:* Grace Stafford, Dal McKennon; *mus:* Walter Greene; *prod mgr:* William E. Garity; *col:* Tech. *sd:* RCA. 6 min. • A pelican makes a nuisance of himself by stealing Chilly's fish and taking over his home.

4872. A Pest in the House *(Looney Tunes)* 2 Aug. 1947; *p.c.:* WB; *dir:* Charles M. Jones; *story:* Tedd Pierce, Michael Maltese; *anim:* Ben Washam, Ken Harris, Basil Davidovich, Lloyd Vaughan; *sets:* Richard Morley; *ed:* Treg Brown; *voices:* Mel Blanc, Arthur Q. Bryan, Tedd Pierce; *mus:* Carl Stalling; *prod mgr:* John W. Burton; *prod:* Edward Selzer; *col:* Tech. *sd:* Vit. 7 min. • Bellboy Daffy prevents a tired hotel guest from sleeping.

4873. Pest of Show *(Cartune)* 13 Feb. 1962; *p.c.:* Walter Lantz prods for Univ; *dir:* Jack Hannah; *story:* Frank Priest; *anim:* Al Coe, Roy Jenkins; *sets:* Ray Huffine, Art Landy; *voices:* Dal McKennon, Paul Frees, Grace Stafford; *prod mgr:* William E. Garity; *col:* Tech. *sd:* RCA. 6 min. • Doc grooms Champ for a Dog Show but taunting cats revert him back to his old self.

4874. Pest Pilot *(Popeye)* 8 Aug. 1941; *p.c.:* The Fleischer Studio for Para; *prod:* Max Fleischer; *dir:* Dave Fleischer; *story:* George Manuell; *anim:* Dave Tendlar, Tom Baron; *ed:* Kitty Pfister; *voices:* Jack Mercer, Margie Hines; *mus:* Sammy Timberg; *ph:* Charles Schettler; *prod sup:* Sam Buchwald, Isidore Sparber; b&w. *sd:* WE. 6¹/₂ min. • Poopdeck Pappy begs Popeye to let him fly an airplane but Popeye won't, so the old salt takes matters into his own hands.

4875. Pest Pupil *(Noveltoon)* 25 Jan. 1957; *p.c.:* Famous for Para; *dir:* Dave Tendlar; *story:* Carl Meyer; *anim:* Morey Reden, George Germanetti; *sets:* Robert Owen; *voices:* Sid Raymond, Jack Mercer, Cecil Roy; *mus:* Winston Sharples; *ph:* Leonard McCormick; *prod mgr:* Seymour Shultz; *col:* Tech. *sd:* RCA. 6¹/₂ min. • Baby Huey is expelled from Kindergarten so his Mama gets him a private tutor.

4876. The Pest That Came to Dinner *(Looney Tunes)* 11 Sept. 1948; *p.c.:* WB; *dir:* Arthur Davis; *story:* George Hill; *anim:* John Carey, Basil Davidovich, J.C. Melendez, Don Williams; *lay:* Don Smith; *back:* Philip de Guard; *ed:* Treg Brown; *voices:* Mel Blanc; *mus:* Carl Stalling; *prod mgr:* John W. Burton; *prod:* Edward Selzer; *col:* Tech. *sd:* Vit. 7 min. • Porky's house is besieged by a hungry termite.

4877. Pests (*Aesop's Film Fable*) 5 Sept. 1926; *p.c.:* Fables Pictures Inc for Pathé; *dir:* Paul Terry; b&w. *sil.* 10 min. • Thomas Cat arranges for the Farmer to fight "The Great Unknown" ... a gorilla. When the ape is knocked out by a bottle, Thomas collects enough money to "pay off" his sweetie's kid brother to make himself scarce.

4878. Pests for Guests (*Merrie Melodies*) 29 Jan. 1955; *p.c.:* WB; *dir:* I. Freleng; *story:* Warren Foster; *anim:* Virgil Ross, Arthur Davis, Manuel Perez, Ken Champin; *lay:* Hawley Pratt; *back:* Irv Wyner; *ed:* Treg Brown; *voices:* Arthur Q. Bryan, Mel Blanc, Stan Freberg; *mus:* Milt Franklyn; *prod mgr:* John W. Burton; *prod:* Edward Selzer; *col:* Tech. *sd:* Vit. 7 min. • Elmer buys a chest of drawers in which the Goofy Gophers have stored a cache of nuts.

4879. Pests of the West (*Pluto*) 21 July 1950; *p.c.:* Walt Disney prods for RKO; *dir:* Charles Nichols; *story:* Dick Kinney, Milt Schaffer; *anim:* Phil Duncan, George Nicholas, George Kreisl, Jerry Hathcock; *fx:* Josh Meador, Jack Boyd; *lay:* Karl Karpé; *back:* Ralph Hulett; *voices:* James Mac-Donald; *mus:* Paul Smith; *col:* Tech. *sd:* RCA. 7 min. • A mangy wolverine and his son try to raid the chicken house guarded by watchdog, Pluto.

4880. Pesty Guest (*Chilly Willy*) June 1965; *p.c.:* Walter Lantz prods for Univ; *dir:* Sid Marcus; *story:* Homer Brightman; *anim:* Ray Abrams, Art Davis; *sets:* Ray Huffine, Art Landy; *voices:* Daws Butler; *mus:* Walter Greene; *prod mgr:* William E. Garity; *col:* Tech. *sd:* RCA. 6 min. • Bellboy Smedley has a problem with Chilly trying to keep cool by switching on the hotel air conditioning and stealing the ice.

4881. The Pet (*Dreams of the Rarebit Fiend*) 26 Sept. 1921; *p.c.:* Winsor McCay for Vit; *dir/anim:* Winsor McCay; b&w. *sil.* • A dog grows to gargantuan proportions. McCay's eighth film. Drawn of celuloid.

4882. Pet Peeve (*Tom & Jerry*) 20 Nov. 1954; *p.c.:* MGM; *dir:* William Hanna, Joseph Barbera; *anim:* Ed Barge, Irven Spence, Kenneth Muse; *lay:* Dick Bickenbach; *back:* Robert Gentle; *ed:* Jim Faris; *voices:* Daws Butler, June Foray; *mus:* Scott Bradley; *ph:* Jack Stevens; *prod:* Fred Quimby; *col:* Tech. *sd:* WE. 7 min. • Tom and Spike engage in a contest to see which pet the master should rid himself of.

4883. Pet Problems (*Terry Bears*) Mar. 1954; *p.c.:* TT for Fox; *dir:* Eddie Donnelly; *story:* Tom Morrison; *anim:* Jim Tyer; *sets:* Art Bartsch; *voices:* Douglas Moye, Tom Morrison, Philip A. Scheib; *mus:* Philip A. Scheib; *ph:* Douglas Moye; *col:* Tech. *sd:* RCA. 6 min. • The cubs, playing with their St. Bernard dog, Pago, disturb Papa and wreck the entire plumbing system in the house.

4884. The Pet Shop (*Scrappy*) 28 May 1932; *p.c.:* Winkler for Colum; *prod:* Charles Mintz; *story:* Dick Huemor; *anim:* Sid Marcus, Art Davis; *mus:* Joe de Nat; *prod mgr:* James Bronis; b&w. *sd:* RCA. 6 min. • Scrappy and Vontzy are in charge of a pet store. While playing, Scrappy crashes through the front window, setting all the animals free.

4885. The Pet Store (*Mickey Mouse*) 28 Oct. 1933; *p.c.:* Walt Disney prods for UA; *dir:* Wilfred Jackson; *anim:* Arthur Babbitt, Norman Ferguson, Richard Lundy, Hamilton S. Luske, Ben Sharpsteen; *voices:* Marcellite Garner, Walt Disney; *mus:* Leigh Harline; b&w. *sd:* RCA. 8 min. • A gorilla breaks out of Mickey's Pet Store and captures Minnie. Mickey joins forces with the other pets in rescuing her in a "King Kong" fashion.

4886. Petal to Metal 7 Aug. 1992; *p.c.:* Walt Disney Television Animation; *dir/prod:* David Block; *asst prod:* Larry Smith; *asst dir:* Raphaël Vincente; *scr:* David Block, Ralph Sanchez, Len Smith, Len Uhley, Duane Capizzi, Bob Hathcock; *storyboard:* Jill Colbert, Bob Kline, David Schwartz, Wendell Washer; *anim:* Sylvain Deboissy, Patrick Delage, Marc Eoche-Duval, Pierre Fassel, Bruno Gaumétou, Arnold Gransac, Dominique Monfery, Catherine Poulain, Pascal Ropers, Stéphane Sainte-Foi; *fx anim:* Thierry Chaffoin; *character des:* Len Smith, Kenny Thompkins; *col key stylist:* Britt Teegarden; *lay:* Carol Kieffer Police, Jean Duval, Vincent Massy, Richard Poulain; *back:* Pierre Pavloff, James Gallego, Olivier Adam, Jean-Paul Fernandez, Hélène Godefroy, Patricia Millereau-Guilmard, Vincent Massey, Nathalie Nicolas; *prop des:* Terry Hudson; *mus:* Mark Waters; *timing dir:* Dale Case, Woody Yocum; *track reader:* Skip Craig; *sd ed:* Ronald Eng, Rick Hinson; *sd:* Nick Alphin, Rick Ash, Christopher Keith, Dean A. Zupancic; *prod mgr:* Jean-Luc Florinda. *col. sd.* 8 min. • Every hazard possible is thrown in his path to prevent Bonkers D. Bobcat from delivering flowers in a five-minute time scale.

4887. Pete Hothead (*Jolly Frolics*) 25 Sept. 1952; *p.c.:* UPA for Colum; *ex prod:* Stephen Bosustow; *dir:* Pete Burness; *story:* Bill Scott, Phil Eastman; *anim:* Cecil Surry, Rudy Larriva, Phil Monroe, Pat Matthews; *lay:* Ted Parmelee; *back:* Bob McIntosh, Bob Dranko; *voices:* Jerry Hausner, Marian Richman, Jim Backus, Bill Scott; *mus:* Hoyt S. Curtin; *prod mgr:* Herbert Klynn; *col:* Tech. *sd:* RCA. 6 min. • Pete has ordered a radio from the local department store and when a parrot arrives, he storms back to the store to give them a piece of his mind.

4888. Pete Roleum and His Cousin 27 July 1938; *p.c.:* Loucks & Norling Studios Inc/Polaroid Corp/Technicolor Motion Pictures Corp for the Petroleum Industry; *ex prod:* John A. Norling; *prod/dir:* Joseph Losey; *script:* Kenneth White, Joseph Losey; *anim:* Charles R. Bowers; *sets/puppet des:* Howard Bay, Lou Bunin; *ed:* Helen van Dongen; *voice:* Hiram Sherman; *mus:* Hans Eisler, Oscar Levant; *song:* Hans Eisler, Joseph Losey; *ph:* Harold L. Muller; *asso prod:* Hans Tiesler; *col:* Tech. *sd:* WE. 20 min. *l/a/anim.* • The history of the development of oil, using oil droplet characters: Stinky Lube, Grease Boy, Gassy, Miss Polish and Hi Test. Puppet animation made for the petroleum exhibition at the World's Fair.

4889. Peter and the Wolf 14 Sept. 1955; *p.c.:* Walt Disney prods for BV; *dir:* Clyde Geronimi; *col:* Tech. *sd:* RCA. 15½ min. • A Russian boy goes in search of a hungry wolf with his cat and bird friends. • See: *Make Mine Music*

4890. Peter Pan 5 Feb. 1953; *p.c.:* Walt Disney prods for RKO; *dir:* Hamilton S. Luske, Clyde Geronimi, Wilfred Jackson; adapted from the play *Peter Pan* by Sir James M. Barrie; *story:* Bill Cottrell, Ralph Wright, Milt Banta, Joe Rinaldi, Winston Hibler, Bill Peet, Ted Sears, Erdman Penner; story initiated by Jack Kinney, Al Geiss; *anim dir:* Milt Kahl, Frank Thomas, Ward Kimball, Oliver Johnston Jr., Marc Davis, Eric Larson, John Lounsbery, Les Clark, Norm Ferguson, Wolfgang Reitherman; *anim:* Eric Cleworth, Hugh Fraser, Marvin Woodward, Hal Ambro, Bill Justice, Ken O'Brien, Fred Moore, Hal King, Cliff Nordberg, Bob Carlson, Harvey Toombs, Don Lusk, Judge Whitaker, Clair Weeks, Art Stevens, Jerry Hathcock; *fx:* George Rowley, Joshua Meador, Blaine Gibson, Dan MacManus; *des:* Claude Coats, Mary Blair, Don da Gradi, John Hench; *lay:* Charles Philippi, McLaren Stewart, Tom Codrick, Ken O'Connor, Hugh Hennesy, Ken Anderson, Don Griffith, Al Zinnen, Lance Nolley, Thor Putnam; *back:* Ray Huffine, Art Riley, Albert Dempster, Eyvind Earle, Ralph Hulett, Thelma Witmer, Dick Antony, Brice Mack; *ed:* Donald Halliday; *voices: Captain Hook/Father Darling/Look-out:* Hans Conried; *Peter Pan:* Bobby Driscoll; *Wendy:* Kathryn Beaumont; *Mr. Smee/Pirate crew:* Bill Thompson; *Mother Darling:* Heather Angel; *Indian Chief:* Candy Candido; *John:* Paul Collins; *Michael:* Tommy Luske, Margaret Kerry; *Narration:* Tom Conway; *The Lost Boys:* Simon "Stuffy" Singer, Robert Ellis, Johnny McGovern, Jeffrey Silver; *Mermaids:* Karen Kester, Carol Coombs, Norma Jean Nilsson, Ann Whitfield; *Indian Squaw:* June Foray; *Chorus:* The Jud Conlon Singers; "Following the Leader": The Mitchell Choirboys; *mus:* Oliver Wallace; *orch:* Edward H. Plumb; *songs:* Sammy Fain, Ted Sears, Sammy Cahn, Frank Churchill, Jack Lawrence, Oliver Wallace, Winston Hibler, Erdman Penner; *vocal arr:* Jud Conlon; *mus ed:* Al Teeter; *special processes:* Ub Iwerks; *sd:* C.O. Slyfield, Harold J. Steck, Robert O. Cook; *col:* Tech. *sd:* RCA. 76½ min. • The story of a boy who wouldn't grow up who takes the Darling children on a flight of fancy to Never-Land where they have many adventures. They are captured by Indians and battle with pirates before safely returning home.

4891. Peter Pan Handled (*Dinky Doodle*) 26 Apr. 1925; *p.c.:* Bray prods for FBO; *dir/story:* Walt Lantz; *anim:* Clyde Geronimi; b&w. *sil.* 5 min. *l/a/anim.* • No story available.

4892. Peter the Puss *p.c.:* Bollman & Grant for Sound Film Distributing Corp; b&w. *sd.* 7 min. • *1929:* **Peter the Puss in Cat's Whiskers. Peter the Puss in Eggs-plosion. Peter the Puss in Rural Romeo. Peter the Puss in the Slipper-y Kid** • Bollman and Grant reissued a series of twelve silent films with added synchronized soundtracks provided by Carl Edouarde. The origin of this series is unknown except they were originally produced by Walt Disney. One possibility is that they were part of the *Alice* series with live-action scenes removed. The selling point was that they came from the creator of *Mickey Mouse*.

4893. Petering-Out (*Hot Dog*) 16 Feb. 1927; *p.c.:* Bray prods; *dir/l/a:* Walt Lantz; *anim:* Clyde Geronimi; b&w. *sil.* 5 min. *l/a/anim.* • When

Walter and Pete the Pup decorate their home, Walter gets covered in striped wallpaper and a policeman mistakes him for an escaped convict.

4894. Pete's Dragon 16 Dec. 1977; *p.c.:* Walt Disney prods for BV; *anim dir:* Don Bluth; *story:* Malcolm Marmorstein; based on a story by Seton I. Miller, S.S. Field; *anim art dir/Elliott* created by Ken Anderson; *anim:* John Pomeroy, Ron Clements, Gary Goldman, Bill Hajee, Chuck Harvey, Randy Cartwright, Cliff Nordberg, Glen Keane; *fx:* Dorse A. Lanpher; *asst anim sup:* Chuck Williams; *lay:* Joe Hale; *anim ed:* James Melton; *voice:* Charlie Callas; *mus:* Irwin Kostal; *songs:* Al Kasha, Joel Hirschhorn; *mus ed:* Evelyn Kennedy; *prod:* Ron Miller, Jerome Courtland; *l/a dir:* Don Chaffey; *col:* Tech. *sd:* RCA/Dolby. 106 min. *l/a/anim.* • Young orphan Pete (Sean Marshall) has an imaginary dragon named Elliott for a friend who helps him in moments of need. The evil Dr. Terminus (Jim Dale) wants to get his hands on Elliott and exploit him while Nora (Helen Reddy) tries to get Pete away from his cruel foster parents.

4895. Pete's Haunted House (*Hot Dog*) 5 Oct. 1926; *p.c.:* Bray prods; *dir/l/a:* Walt Lantz; *anim:* Clyde Geronimi; b&w. sil. 5 min. *l/a/anim.* • Walter reads a ghost story to Pete, then drops a skeleton down the chimney to scare him. The pup gets wise and blows the artist up with a giant firecracker.

4896. Pete's Party (*Hot Dog*) 26 Oct. 1926; *p.c.:* Bray prods; *dir/l/a:* Walt Lantz; *anim:* Clyde Geronimi; b&w. sil. 5 min. *l/a/anim.* • Walter throws a birthday party for Pete. A few shots of T.N.T. in the punch gets the party going. Alonzo, a stray alley cat, sneaks in and helps himself to the loaded punch, charging the party and putting it to rout.

4897. Pete's Pow Wow (*Hot Dog*) 8 Apr. 1927; *p.c.:* Bray prods; *dir/l/a:* Walt Lantz; *anim:* Clyde Geronimi; b&w. sil. 5 min. *l/a/anim.* • Walter is a dud prize fighter with Pete the Pup as his manager. Pete has to replace Lantz in the ring, wins and becomes the new champ.

4898. La Petite Parade (*Modern Madcap*) 6 Mar. 1959; *p.c.:* Para Cartoons: *dir:* Seymour Kneitel; *story:* Irving Spector; *anim:* Tom Johnson, Nick Tafuri; *sets:* Robert Little; *voices:* Allen Swift; *mus:* Winston Sharples; *ph:* Leonard McCormick; *prod mgr:* Abe Goodman; *col:* Tech. *sd.* RCA. 6 min. • Each morning the parade's dust cart dumps a load of garbage outside the Matchmaker's front door. He pressurizes the council to reroute the parade.

4899. Pettin' in the Park (*Merrie Melodies*) 27 Jan. 1934; *p.c.:* Leon Schlesinger prods for WB; *dir:* Bernard B. Brown; *story:* Bob Clampett; *anim:* Jack King, Bob Clampett; *mus:* Norman Spencer; *song:* Harry Warren, Al Dubin; b&w. *sd:* Vit. 7 min. • A swimming contest by the water fowl of the colony.

4900. Petting Larceny (*Krazy Kat*) 24 May 1929; *p.c.:* Winkler for Para; *anim:* Ben Harrison, Manny Gould; b&w. sil. 5 min. • No story available.

4901. Petunia Natural Park (*Captain & Kids*) 14 Jan. 1939; *p.c.:* MGM; *dir:* Milt Gross; *voices:* Billy Bletcher, Danny Webb; *mus:* Scott Bradley; *prod mgr:* Fred Quimby; *col:* Tech. *sd:* WE. 7 min. • The gang visit a national park, causing destruction wherever they go. Hans and Fritz put geyser water in der Captain's car, causing it to erupt.

4902. The Phantom Moustacher (*Modern Madcap*) Jan. 1961; *p.c.:* Para Cartoons; *dir:* Seymour Kneitel; *story:* I. Klein; *anim:* Myron Waldman; *sets:* Robert Little; *voices:* Bob MacFadden; *mus:* Winston Sharples; *ph:* Leonard McCormick; *prod mgr:* Abe Goodman; *col:* Tech. *sd:* RCA. 6 min. • The whole of London is at the mercy of someone who draws moustaches on everyone and everything.

4903. Phantom of the Horse Opera (*Woody Woodpecker*) 26 Sept. 1961; *p.c.:* Walter Lantz prods for Univ; *dir:* Paul J. Smith; *story:* Dalton Sandifer; *anim:* Les Kline, Ray Abrams; *sets:* Ray Huffine, Art Landy; *voices:* Dal McKennon, Grace Stafford; *mus:* Clarence Wheeler; *prod mgr:* William E. Garity; *col:* Tech. *sd:* RCA. 6 min. • Woody pursues a bank robber into a ghost town where the bandit tries to frighten him off by posing as a ghost.

4904. The Phantom Rocket (*Tom & Jerry*) 21 July 1933; *p.c.:* Van Beuren for RKO; *dir:* Frank Sherman, George Rufle; *mus:* Gene Rodemich; b&w. *sd:* RCA. 8 min. • No story available.

4905. The Phantom Ship (*Looney Tunes*) 1 Feb. 1936; *p.c.:* Leon Schlesinger prods for WB; *dir:* Jack King; *anim:* Paul Smith, Don Williams, Robert Clampett; *voices:* Bernice Hansel; *mus:* Bernard B. Brown; b&w.

sd: Vit. 7 min. • Beans flies to the frozen north with Ham and Ex as stowaways. They explore an old pirate ship where the crew have been frozen in time. A lit stove thaws them out and a chase ensues.

4906. The Phantom Skyscraper (*James Hound*) Dec. 1966; *p.c.:* TT for Fox; *ex prod:* Bill Weiss; *dir/anim:* Art Bartsch, Dave Tendlar; *col:* DeLuxe. *sd:* RCA. 6 min. • Hound investigates Prof. Mad's offer for free accommodation in his apartment tower. • See: *James Hound*

4907. The Phantom Tollbooth 1969; *p.c.:* Chuck Jones prods for MGM/Educational Film Centre; *prod:* Abe Levitow, Les Goldman; *dir:* Chuck Jones, Abe Levitow; *prod des:* Maurice Noble; *story:* Chuck Jones, Sam Rosen; *anim sup:* Ben Washam, Hal Ambro, George Nicholas; *anim:* Irven Spence, Bill Littlejohn, Richard Thompson, Tom Ray, Philip Roman, Alan Zaslove, Ed Aardal, Ed de Mattia, Xenia de Mattia, Lloyd Vaughan, Carl Bell; *lay:* Tony Rivera, Don Morgan, Oscar Dufau, Rosemary O'Connor, Corny Cole, Phyllis Graham; *back:* Philip de Guard, Irving Wyner, Robert McIntosh; *typographics:* Don Foster; *ed:* Jim Faris; *voices: Milo:* Butch Patrick; *Tock:* Larry Thor; *King Azaz/The Mathmagician:* Hans Conried; *The Humbug:* Les Tremayne; *The Spelling Bee:* Shep Menken; *Kakofonus a Dischord/Tollbooth:* Cliff Norton; *The Whether Man/Chroma/Terrible Trivium/Official Senses-Taker/The Gelatinous Giant:* Daws Butler; *The Awful Dynne:* Candy Candido; *Faintly Macabre:* June Foray; *Princess of Sweet Rhyme:* Patty Gilbert; *Officer Short-Shrift/The Letter-Man/Demon of Insincerity/The Dodecahedron:* Mel Blanc; *Lethargians:* Candy Candido, Mel Blanc, Cliff Norton; *The King's Advisers:* Shep Menken, Mel Blanc; *chorus:* The Jack Halloran Group; *mus:* Dean Elliott; *songs:* Norman Gimbel, Lee Pockriss, Paul Vance; *i&p:* Avril Thompson; *checkers:* Buff Nerbovig, Carole Barnes, Ted Bemiller; *ph:* Jack Stevens; *l/a seq: dir:* David Monahan; *asst dir:* Charles Bonniwell Jr.; *ph dir:* Lester Shorr ASC; *art dir:* George W. Davis, Charles Hagedon; *unit prod head:* Robert Vreeland; *set dir:* Henry Grace, Chuck Pierce; *make-up:* William Tuttle; *recording sup:* Franklin Milton; *prod mgr:* Earl Jonas; *col:* Metro. *sd:* WE. 89 min. *l/a/anim.* • Norton Juster's story about a bored boy, Milo, who is delivered a mysterious gift of a Tollbooth. When he enters it, he finds himself in another land where he has to live on his wits. Animator Ben Washam is caricatured as *The Whether Man*.

4908. Philharmaniacs (*Kartune*) 3 Apr. 1953; *p.c.:* Famous for Para; *dir:* Seymour Kneitel; *story:* I. Klein; *anim:* Tom Johnson, John Gentilella, Els Barthen; *sets:* Jack Henegan; *voice:* Jackson Beck; *mus:* Winston Sharples; *song:* Irving Berlin; *ph:* Leonard McCormick; *prod mgr:* Seymour Shultz; *col:* Tech. *sd:* RCA. 7 min. • A band tries to play serious music but is interrupted by a mouse wanting to play Swing.

4909. Phoney Baloney (*Fox & Crow*) 1 Nov. 1945; *p.c.:* Colum; *dir:* Bob Wickersham; *story:* Sid Marcus; *anim:* Paul Sommer, Ben Lloyd; *lay:* Clark Watson; *ed:* Richard S. Jensen; *voices:* Frank Graham, Harry E. Lang; *mus:* Eddie Kilfeather; *ph:* Frank Fisher; *prod mgr:* Hugh McCollum; *col:* Tech. *sd:* WE. 7 min. • A large reward is offered for an escaped wolf. Both the Fox and Crow believe the reward to be for the capture of each other.

4910. The Phoney Express (*Aesop's Film Fable*) 17 Oct. 1926; *p.c.:* Fables Pictures Inc for Pathé; *dir:* Paul Terry; b&w. sil. 5 min. • The mouse Pony Express rider is pictured galloping at full speed on a wooden hobbyhorse and having exciting encounters with feline Indians.

4911. The Phoney Express (*Flip the Frog*) 27 Oct. 1932; *p.c.:* Celebrity prods for MGM; *prod/dir:* Ub Iwerks; *anim:* Jimmie Culhane; b&w. *sd:* PCP. 6 min. • Flip drives a stagecoach that is held up by a bandit named Bronx Cheerio. Flip chases him and so does an old maid passenger on the coach.

4912. Phoney Express (*Hoot Kloot*) 4 Jan. 1974; *p.c.:* Mirisch/DFE for Univ; *dir:* Gerry Chiniquy; *story:* John W. Dunn; *anim:* Bob Matz, Don Williams, Norm McCabe, Bob Richardson, John Gibbs; *lay:* Dick Ung; *back:* Richard Thomas; *ed:* Joe Siracusa; *voices:* Bob Holt; *mus:* Doug Goodwin; *titles:* Arthur Leonardi; *ph:* John Burton Jr.; *prod mgr:* Lee Gunther; *col:* DeLuxe. *sd:* RCA. 6 min. • Kloot encounters many hazards when taking the mail from San Francisco, only to discover the solitary letter is a tax demand for him.

4913. Phoney Express (*Inspector Willoughby*) 15 May 1962; *p.c.:* Walter Lantz prods for Univ; *dir:* Paul J. Smith; *story:* Tedd Pierce, Bill Danch; *anim:* Ray Abrams, Les Kline, Roy Jenkins; *sets:* Art Landy, Ray Huffine; *voice:* Dal McKennon; *mus:* Darrell Calker; *prod mgr:* William E. Garity;

col: Tech. *sd:* RCA. 6 min. • Inspector Willoughby pits his wits against an international spy aboard the Orient Express.

4914. Phoney News Flashes *(Terry-Toon)* Aug. 1955; *p.c.:* TT for Fox; *dir:* Connie Rasinski; *story:* Tom Morrison; *anim:* Jim Tyer; *sets:* Art Bartsch; *mus:* Philip A. Scheib; *ph:* Douglas Moye; *col:* Tech. *sd:* RCA. 6 min. • Flying Saucers, Mothers-in-Law, Miracle Defences, Anti-Noise campaigns, Baseball et al. are depicted in this newsreel.

4915. Phoney Pony *(Woody Woodpecker)* 1 Nov. 1969; *p.c.:* Walter Lantz prods for Univ; *dir:* Paul J. Smith; *story:* Dalton Sandifer; *anim:* Les Kline, Al Coe; *sets:* Nino Carbe; *voices:* Dal McKennon, Grace Stafford; *mus:* Walter Greene; *prod mgr:* William E. Garity; *col:* Tech. *sd:* RCA. 6 min. • Two convicts escape from prison disguised as a horse whom Woody's horse falls in love with.

4916. Piano Mover *(Krazy Kat)* 4 Jan. 1932; *p.c.:* Winkler for Colum; *story:* Manny Gould; *anim:* Allen Rose, Jack Carr; *voice:* Jack Carr; *mus:* Joe de Nat; *prod mgr:* James Bronis; b&w. *sd:* WE. 6 min. • Krazy and his assistant deliver a piano to Kitty on the top floor of a skyscraper.

4917. Piano Tooners *(Tom & Jerry)* 11 Nov. 1932; *p.c.:* Van Beuren for RKO; *dir:* John Foster, George Rufle; *voice:* Marjorie Hines; *mus:* Gene Rodemich; b&w. *sd:* RCA. 7 min. • Tom and Jerry's piano tuning ruins Mme Pflop's operatic recital.

4918. Picadore Porky *(Looney Tunes)* 27 Feb. 1937; *p.c.:* Leon Schlesinger prods for WB; *dir:* Fred Avery; *story:* Robert Clampett; *anim:* Charles Jones, Sid Sutherland, Robert Clampett; *lay:* Griff Jay; *ed:* Tregoweth E. Brown; *voices:* Joe Dougherty, Billy Bletcher, Mel Blanc; *mus:* Carl W. Stalling; *prod sup:* Henry Binder, Raymond G. Katz; b&w. *sd:* Vit. 7 min. • Porky tries for a bull fighting prize by having his pals dress as a bull while he poses as a matador but ends up fighting a real bull.

4919. Pick-Necking *(Paul Terry-Toons)* 8 Sept. 1933; *p.c.:* Moser & Terry for Educational/Fox; *dir:* Frank Moser, Paul Terry; *mus:* Philip A. Scheib; b&w. *sd:* WE. 6 min. • No story available.

4920. Pickaninny Blues *(Aesop's Sound Fable)* 2 Dec. 1932; *p.c.:* Van Beuren for RKO; *dir:* John Foster, Mannie Davis; *voice:* Marjorie Hines; *mus:* Gene Rodemich; b&w. *sd:* RCA. 7 min. • Waffles Cat is shown as a cotton-picker on a plantation who dreams he's in Egypt where the mummies dance to jazz music.

4921. Pickled Pink *(Pink Panther)* 12 May 1965; *p.c.:* Mirisch/Geoffrey/DFE for UA; *dir:* Friz Freleng; *asst dir:* Hawley Pratt; *story:* Bob Kurtz; *anim:* Manuel Perez, Warren Batchelder, Bob Matz, Norm McCabe, La Verne Harding, Don Williams; *lay:* Dick Ung; *back:* Ron Dias; *ed:* Lee Gunther; *voices:* Mel Blanc; *mus:* Bill Lava; *theme tune:* Henry Mancini; *prod mgr:* Bill Orcutt; *col:* DeLuxe. *sd:* RCA. 6 min. • The Panther is taken home by an inebriate, much to the chagrin of his disgruntled spouse.

4922. Pickled Puss *(Phantasy)* 2 Sept. 1948; *p.c.:* Colum; *prod:* Raymond Katz, Henry Binder; *dir:* Howard Swift; *story:* Cal Howard; *anim:* Grant Simmons, Paul Sommer, Morey Reden; *lay:* Bill Weaver; *back:* Ed Starr; *ed:* Richard S. Jensen; *voice:* Patrick J. McGeehan; *mus:* Darrell Calker; *ph:* Frank Fisher; *creative consultant:* Bob Clampett; b&w. *sd:* WE. 6 min. • A mouse seeks refuge from the cat in a barrel of pickled herrings containing 90 percent alcohol. The cat follows and their joint inebriation soon makes them the best of friends.

4923. The Picnic *(Mickey Mouse)* 9 Oct. 1930; *p.c.:* Walter E. Disney for Colum; *dir:* Burton F. Gillett; *anim:* Charles Byrne, Johnny Cannon, Les Clark, Jack Cutting, Gilles de Tremaudan, Norman Ferguson, David D. Hand, Wilfred Jackson, Jack King, Richard Lundy, Tom Palmer, Ben Sharpsteen; *voices:* Marcellite Garner; *mus:* Bert Lewis; *ph:* William Cottrell; b&w. *sd:* PCP. 6 min. • Minnie's big dog proves a nuisance on the picnic but comes in handy when it starts to rain.

4924. Picnic Panic *(Color Rhapsody)* 20 June 1946; *p.c.:* Colum; *dir/story:* Bob Wickersham; *anim:* Chic Otterstrom, Paul Sommer; *ed:* Richard S. Jensen; *i&p:* Elizabeth F. McDowell; *mus:* Eddie Kilfeather; *ph:* Frank Fisher; *prod mgr:* Hugh McCollum; *col:* Tech. *sd:* WE. 8 min. • A Mexican girl insists Tito exchange his burro for an automobile. When a temperamental volcano threatens, they are both glad to have the mule to take them to safety.

4925. A Picnic Panic *(Rainbow Parade)* 3 May 1935; *p.c.:* Van Beuren for RKO; *dir:* Burt Gillett, Tom Palmer; *mus:* Winston Sharples; *l/a sets:*

Robert Little; *l/a ph:* Harry E. Squires; *col:* Ciné. *sd:* RCA. 7 min. *l/a/anim.* • When rain stops the children from going on a picnic an animated coffee pot tells them of when the kitchen utensils all went on a picnic.

4926. Picnic with Papa *(Terry-Toon)* Dec. 1952; *p.c.:* TT for Fox; *dir:* Mannie Davis; *story:* Tom Morrison; *anim:* Jim Tyer; *sets:* Art Bartsch; *voices:* Douglas Moye, Tom Morrison, Philip A. Scheib; *mus:* Philip A. Scheib; *ph:* Douglas Moye; *col:* Tech. *sd:* RCA. 6 min. • Papa takes the cubs camping, imagining himself to be an experienced camper.

4927. A Picture 27 Jan. 1958; *p.c.:* UPA for Coca-Cola Co; *col:* Tech. *sd:* RCA. 2 min. • Commercial for Coca-Cola.

4928. The Pie-Eyed Piper *(Aesop's Film Fable)* 6 May 1927; *p.c.:* Fables Pictures Inc for Pathé; *dir:* Paul Terry; b&w. sil. 10 min. • Farmer Al Falfa is pursuaded to buy a flute, guaranteed to charm the animals, which he tries out on a bear cub and gets chased by its parents.

4929. The Pie Man *(Aesop's Film Fable)* 21 Mar. 1925; *p.c.:* Fables Pictures Inc for Pathé; *dir:* Paul Terry; b&w. sil. 10 min. • The animals rob a Pie Man's cart, rendering his life a misery.

4930. The Pied Piper *(Dinky Doodle)* 1 Dec. 1924; *p.c.:* Bray prods for FBO; *dir/story:* Walt Lantz; *anim:* Clyde Geronimi; b&w. sil. 5 min. • No story available.

4931. The Pied Piper *(Silly Symphony)* 16 Sept. 1933; *p.c.:* Walt Disney prods for UA; *dir:* Wilfred Jackson; *anim:* Arthur Babbitt, Gilles de Tremaudan, Clyde Geronimi, Dick Huemer, Hamilton S. Luske, Ben Sharpsteen; *lay:* Ferdinand Huszti Horvath; *mus/song:* Leigh Harline; *col:* Tech. *sd:* RCA. 7 min. • Hamelin Town is overrun with vermin when a mysterious Piper arrives offering to rid the town of the rats.

4932. The Pied Piper of Basin Street *(Swing Symphony)* 15 Jan. 1945; *p.c.:* Walter Lantz prods for Univ; *dir:* James Culhane; *story:* Ben Hardaway, Milt Schaffer; *anim:* (La) Verne Harding, Pat Matthews, Emery Hawkins, Les Kline, Dick Lundy, Grim Natwick, Paul J. Smith, Don Williams; *lay:* Art Heinemann; *back:* Philip de Guard; *voices:* Kent Rogers, Ge Ge Pearson, Sara Berner; *mus:* Jack Teagarden, Darrell Calker; *prod mgr:* George Hall; *col:* Tech. *sd:* WE. 6½ min. • To rid the town of rats, the Pied Piper impersonates Frank Sinatra, bringing out the "Bobby Sox" brigade, then luring them onto a Swing-ship.

4933. The Pied Piper of Chiclet Town 1948; *p.c.:* Ted Eshbaugh Studio for Badger, Browning & Hersey, American Chick Co; *ex prod:* Ted Eshbaugh; *prod/dir/story/ed:* Alfred Barrow Jr.; *voice:* Kay Lorraine; *ph:* Harry Hamsel, Jack Eshbaugh, Carol Wollen; *col. sd.* • Commercial for Chiclets.

4934. The Pied Piper of Guadelupe *(Looney Tunes)* 19 Aug. 1961; *p.c.:* WB; *dir:* Friz Freleng; *asst dir:* Hawley Pratt; *story:* John Dunn; *anim:* Gerry Chiniquy, Virgil Ross, Bob Matz; *back:* Tom O'Loughlin; *ed:* Treg Brown; *voices:* Mel Blanc; *mus:* Milt Franklyn; *prod mgr:* William Orcutt; *prod:* David H. DePatie; *col:* Tech. *sd:* Vit. 7 min. • Sylvester gets the idea of luring the mice into his clutches by playing a lilting refrain on a flute but doesn't reckon on Speedy Gonzales.

4935. Pied Piper Porky *(Looney Tunes)* 4 Nov. 1939; *p.c.:* Leon Schlesinger prods for WB; *dir:* Robert Clampett; *anim:* John Carey, David Hoffman; *ed:* Tregoweth E. Brown; *voices:* Mel Blanc, Danny Webb; *mus:* Carl W. Stalling; *prod sup:* Henry Binder, Raymond G. Katz; b&w. *sd:* Vit. 7 min. • Pied Piper Porky tries every method to rid the town of one final rat.

4936. Pierre and Cottage Cheese *(Inspector)* 26 Feb. 1969; *p.c.:* Mirisch/Geoffrey/DFE for UA; *dir:* Gerry Chiniquy; *anim:* Manny Gould, Don Williams, Warren Batchelder, Manny Perez; *lay:* Jack Miller; *back:* Tom O'Loughlin; *ed:* Lee Gunther; *voices:* Pat Harrington Jr., Marvin Miller; *mus:* Walter Greene; *theme tune:* Henry Mancini; *prod sup:* Harry Love, Jim Foss; *col:* DeLuxe. *sd:* RCA. 6 min. • The Inspector is teamed with a robot.

4937. Piffles Tries Hair Tonic *(Imp cartoon)* Mar. 1913; *p.c.:* Imp Co; *anim:* Hy Mayer; b&w. sil. 4½ min. • According to Hy Mayer, a new lotion will produce hair at a tremendous rate.

4938. Pig-a-Boo *(Casper)* 12 Sept. 1952; *p.c.:* Famous for Para; *dir:* I. Sparber; *story:* I. Klein; *anim:* Steve Muffatti, Bill Hudson; *sets:* Anton Loeb; *voices:* Alan Shay, Sid Raymond, Gwen Davies; *mus:* Winston

Sharples; *title song:* Mack David, Jerry Livingston; *ph:* Leonard McCormick; *prod mgr:* Seymour Shultz; *col:* Tech. *sd:* RCA. 7 min. • Casper befriends the smallest member of the Three Pigs, later rescuing him and his family from the evil clutches of Wolfie.

4939. Le Pig Al Patrol *(Inspector)* 24 May 1967; *p.c.:* Mirisch/Geoffrey/DFE for UA; *dir:* Gerry Chiniquy; *story:* Jim Ryan; *anim:* Manny Gould, Bob Matz, Waren Batchelder, Manny Perez, Art Leonardi, Don Williams; *lay:* Dick Ung; *back:* Tom O'Loughlin; *ed:* Lee Gunther; *voices:* Pat Harrington Jr., Marvin Miller; *mus:* Walter Greene; *theme tune:* Henry Mancini; *prod sup:* Harry Love, Bill Orcutt; *col:* DeLuxe. *sd:* RCA. 6 min. • The Inspector tries to round up Pig Al, the notorious motorbiker and his gang.

4940. Pig in a Pickle *(Cartune)* 30 Aug. 1954; *p.c.:* Walter Lantz prods for Universal; *dir:* Paul J. Smith; *story:* Michael Maltese; *anim:* La Verne Harding, Robert Bentley, Gil Turner; *sets:* Art Landy, Raymond Jacobs; *voices:* Dal McKennon, Grace Stafford; *mus:* Clarence Wheeler; *prod mgr:* William E. Garity; *col:* Tech. *sd:* RCA. 6 min. • A hungry neighboring family kidnap Milford the pig for their dinner. Maw and Paw come to retrieve him.

4941. Pigeon Holed *(Cartune)* 16 Jan. 1956; *p.c.:* Walter Lantz prods for Univ; *dir:* Alex Lovy; *story:* Homer Brightman; *anim:* Ray Abrams, Don Patterson; *sets:* Raymond Jacobs; *voices:* Dal McKennon; *mus:* Clarence Wheeler; *prod mgr:* William E. Garity; *col:* Tech. *sd:* RCA. 6 min. • Homer Pigeon's need for glasses lets him stumble into an Army recruitment center for training carrier pigeons.

4942. Pigeon Patrol *(Cartune)* 3 Aug. 1942; *p.c.:* Walter Lantz prods for Univ; *dir:* Alex Lovy; *story:* Ben Hardaway; *anim:* Ralph Somerville; *sets:* Fred Brunish; *voices:* Kent Rogers, Grace Stafford; *mus:* Darrell Calker; *prod mgr:* George Hall; *col:* Tech. *sd:* WE. 6½ min. • Homer Pigeon is rejected from the Carrier Pigeons. He later comes into his own when he takes on vulture saboteurs.

4943. The Pig's Curly Tail *(Unnatural History)* 15 Aug. 1926; *p.c.:* Bray prods for FBO; *dir:* Walt Lantz; *anim:* Clyde Geronimi; *l/a:* Walter Lantz, Nancy Kelly; *l/a ph:* Joe Rock; *b&w. sil.* 5 min. *l/a/anim.* • Walter Lantz throws some light on how the pig got his curly tail.

4944. The Pig's Feat *(Modern Madcap)* Oct. 1963; *p.c.:* Para Cartoons; *dir:* Seymour Kneitel; *story:* Jack Mercer, Irv Dressler; *anim:* Martin Taras; *sets:* Robert Little; *voices:* Bob MacFadden; *mus:* Winston Sharples; *ph:* Leonard McCormick; *prod mgr:* Abe Goodman; *col:* Tech. *sd:* RCA. 6 min. • Mr. Harmonica tells the kids a story of how pigs were once clean and tidy creatures until one day, falling into mud made one beautiful.

4945. Pigs in a Polka *(Merrie Melodies)* 9 Jan. 1943; *p.c.:* Leon Schlesinger prods for WB; *dir:* I. Freleng; *lay:* Owen Fitzgerald; *back:* Lenard Kester; *ed:* Treg Brown; *voices:* Mel Blanc, Sara Berner; *mus:* Carl W. Stalling; *prod sup:* Henry Binder, Raymond G. Katz; *col:* Tech. *sd:* Vit. 7 min. *Academy Award nomination.* • The story of "The Three Little Pigs" is re-enacted to the music of Brahms' *Hungarian Rhapsody.*

4946. Pigs Is Pigs 21 May 1954; *p.c.:* Walt Disney prods for BV; *dir:* Jack Kinney; *story:* Leo Salkin from the book by Ellis Parker Butler; *anim:* John Sibley, Ed Aardal, Eric Cleworth, Harry Holt; *fx:* Dan MacManus; *lay:* Bruce Bushman, John Wilson; *back:* Eyvind Earle, Al Dempster; *voices:* William Woodson, Bill Thompson, Dallas McKennon, The Mello Men; *mus:* Oliver Wallace; *col:* Tech. *sd:* RCA. 10 min. *Academy Award nomination.* • A Scotsman refuses to pay the extra tariff on two guinea pigs. The pigs are left with Station Master Flannery until the matter is resolved. Meanwhile the pigs multiply alarmingly.

4947. Pigs Is Pigs *(Merrie Melodies)* 30 Jan. 1937; *p.c.:* Leon Schlesinger prods for WB; *dir:* I. Freleng; *anim:* Bob McKimson, Paul Smith; *lay:* Griff Jay; *back:* Arthur Loomer; *voices:* Bernice Hansel, Billy Bletcher, Martha Wentworth; *mus:* Carl W. Stalling; *prod sup:* Henry Binder, Raymond G. Katz; *col:* Tech. *sd:* RCA. 7 min. • Junior Pig keeps overeating even though he suffers the most appalling nightmares.

4948. Pigskin Capers *(Paul Terry-Toon)* 28 Dec. 1930; *p.c.:* A-C for Educational/Fox; *dir:* Frank Moser, Paul Terry; *anim:* Frank Little; *mus:* Philip A. Scheib; *b&w. sd:* WE. 6 min. • Mice versus the Cats in a football game.

4949. Piker's Peak *(Looney Tunes)* 25 May 1957; *p.c.:* WB; *dir:* Friz Freleng; *story:* Warren Foster; *anim:* Gerry Chiniquy, Art Davis, Virgil Ross; *lay:* Hawley Pratt; *ed:* Treg Brown; *voices:* Mel Blanc; *mus:* Carl Stalling, Milt Franklyn; *prod mgr:* John W. Burton; *prod:* Edward Selzer; *col:* Tech. *sd:* Vit. 7 min. • Bugs and Sam attempt to climb the Schmatterhorn, the world's highest mountain, for a rich reward.

4950. Pilgrim Popeye *(Popeye)* 13 July 1951; *p.c.:* Famous for Para; *dir:* I. Sparber; *story:* Carl Meyer, Jack Mercer; *anim:* Al Eugster, George Germanetti; *sets:* Anton Loeb; *voices:* Jack Mercer; *mus:* Winston Sharples; *ph:* Leonard McCormick; *prod mgr:* Sam Buchwald; *col:* Tech. *sd:* RCA. 6 min. • At Thanksgiving, Popeye saves a turkey from imminent demise by telling his nephews a story of how his Pilgrim ancestor was once saved by a turkey.

4951. Pilgrim Porky *(Looney Tunes)* 16 Mar. 1940; *p.c.:* Leon Schlesinger prods for WB; *dir:* Robert Clampett; *story:* Warren Foster; *anim:* Norman McCabe; *ed:* Treg Brown; *voices:* Mel Blanc, The Sportsmen Quartet, Robert C. Bruce; *mus:* Carl W. Stalling; *prod sup:* Henry Binder, Raymond G. Katz; *b&w. sd:* Vit. 7 min. • Porky disrupts history as the captain of the *Mayflower,* taking the Pilgrims to Plymouth.

4952. Pill Peddlers *(Heckle & Jeckle)* Apr. 1953; *p.c.:* TT for Fox; *dir:* Connie Rasinski; *story:* Tom Morrison; *anim:* Jim Tyer; *voices:* Tom Morrison, Douglas Moye; *mus:* Philip A. Scheib; *ph:* Douglas Moye; *col:* Tech. *sd:* RCA. 6 min. • The Magpies try to sell vitamin pills to an exercise class. The instructor gives them a work-out in his gym.

4953. Pin Feathers *(Pooch the Pup)* 27 Oct. 1933; *p.c.:* Univ; *dir:* Walter Lantz; *anim:* Manuel Moreno, Lester Kline, Fred Kopietz, Charles Hastings, Ernest Smythe; *mus:* James Dietrich; *b&w. sd:* WE. 6 min. • Pooch helps a small bird to fly.

4954. Pincome Tax *(Pink Panther)* 20 Dec 1968; *p.c.:* Mirisch/Geoffrey/DFE for UA; *dir:* Art Davis; *story:* David DeTiege; *anim:* Warren Batchelder, Ed de Mattia, Don Williams, Manny Perez; *lay:* Dick Ung; *back:* Tom O'Loughlin; *ed:* Lee Gunther; *mus:* Walter Greene; *ph:* John Burton Jr.; *prod sup:* Jim Foss, Harry Love; *col:* DeLuxe. *sd:* RCA. 6 min. • The Panther sets himself up an avenger who will free a wrongly imprisoned peasant, only succeeding in getting locked up himself.

4955. Ping Pong Woo 26 June 1915; *p.c.:* Lubin Mfg. Co. Inc.; *prod/anim:* Carl Francis Lederer. *b&w. sil.* 4 min. • No story available.

4956. Pink-A-Boo *(Pink Panther)* 26 June 1966; *p.c.:* Mirisch/Geoffrey/DFE for UA; *dir:* Hawley Pratt; *story:* John W. Dunn; *anim:* Don Williams, Norm McCabe, Brad Case, La Verne Harding, Warren Batchelder; *lay:* Dick Ung; *back:* Tom O'Loughlin; *ed:* Eugene Marks; *mus:* Walter Greene; *theme tune:* Henry Mancini; *prod mgr:* Bill Orcutt; *col:* DeLuxe. *sd:* RCA. 6 min. • The Panther is kept awake by musical mice.

4957. Pink-A-Rella *(Pink Panther)* 8 Jan. 1969; *p.c.:* Mirisch/Geoffrey/DFE for UA; *dir:* Hawley Pratt; *story:* John W. Dunn; *anim:* Manny Perez, Herman Cohen, Warren Batchelder, Manny Gould, Ed de Mattia; *lay:* Dick Ung; *back:* Tom O'Loughlin; *ed:* Lee Gunther; *mus:* William Lava; *theme tune:* Henry Mancini; *ph:* John Burton Jr.; *prod sup:* Jim Foss, Harry Love; *col:* DeLuxe. *sd:* RCA. 6 min. • The Panther invades the Cinderella story.

4958. Pink and Blue Blues *(Mr. Magoo)* 28 Aug. 1952; *p.c.:* UPA for Colum; *ex prod:* Stephen Bosustow; *dir:* Pete Burness; *story:* Bill Scott; *anim:* Rudy Larriva, Tom McDonald, Phil Monroe; *lay:* Ted Parmelee; *back:* Bob McIntosh; *voices:* Jim Backus, Jerry Hausner, Mary Jane Croft; *mus:* Benjamin Lees; *prod mgr:* Herbert Klynn; *col:* Tech. *sd:* RCA. 6½ min. • Magoo babysits for a neighbor and succeeds in capturing a notorious cat burglar in the bargain!

4959. Pink and Shovel *(Pink Panther)* 1981 (© 1978); *p.c.:* Mirisch/Geoffrey/DFE for UA; *dir:* Gerry Chiniquy; *story:* John W. Dunn; *anim:* Don Williams, Lee Halpern, Bernard Posner, Joan Case; *lay:* Martin Strudler; *back:* Richard H. Thomas; *ed:* Robert Gillis; *theme tune:* Henry Mancini; *ph:* Ray Lee; *prod mgr:* Lee Gunther; *col:* DeLuxe. *sd:* RCA. 6 min. • The Panther buries a secret hoarde that has a building built atop of it. When he goes to dig it up, he gets more than he bargained for.

4960. Pink Arcade *(Pink Panther)* 1978; *p.c.:* Mirisch/Geoffrey/DFE for UA; *dir:* Sid Marcus; *story:* Dave DeTiege; *anim:* Warren Batchelder, Bob Richardson, Bob Kirk, Bill Hutten; *lay:* Martin Strudler; *back:* Richard H. Thomas; *ed:* Robert Gillis; *theme tune:* Henry Mancini; *ph:* Ray Lee;

prod mgr: Lee Gunther; *col:* DeLuxe. *sd:* RCA. 6 min. • The Panther wins some money and blows it all in an amusement arcade.

4961. Pink Aye *(Pink Panther)* 16 Mar. 1974; *p.c.:* Mirisch/Geoffrey/DFE for UA; *dir:* Gerry Chiniquy; *story:* John W. Dunn; *anim:* Reuben Timmens, Norm McCabe, Ken Muse, John Freeman; *lay:* Owen Fitzgerald; *back:* Richard H. Thomas; *ed:* Bob Gillis; *mus:* Walter Greene; *theme tune:* Henry Mancini; *ph:* John Burton Jr.; *Prod mgr:* Lee Gunther; *col:* DeLuxe. *sd:* RCA. 6 min. • The Panther stows away in an opera singer's cabin on a luxury liner.

4962. Pink Bananas *(Pink Panther)* 1978; *p.c.:* Mirisch/Geoffrey/DFE for UA; *dir:* Art Davis; *story:* John W. Dunn; *anim:* Warren Batchelder, Bob Richardson, Bob Kirk, Bill Hutten; *lay:* Martin Strudler; *back:* Richard H. Thomas; *ed:* David H. DePatie Jr.; *theme tune:* Henry Mancini; *ph:* Ray Lee; *prod mgr:* Lee Gunther; *col:* DeLuxe. *sd:* RCA. 6 min. • The Panther plays "Tarzan" and has problems with a musical gorilla.

4963. Pink Blue Plate *(Pink Panther)* 18 July 1971; *p.c.:* Mirisch/Geoffrey/DFE for UA; *dir:* Gerry Chiniquy; *story:* Dale Hale; *anim:* Don Williams, Manny Gould, Manny Perez, Warren Batchelder, Bob Taylor; *lay:* Dick Ung; *back:* Richard H. Thomas; *ed:* Lee Gunther; *mus:* Walter Greene; *theme tune:* Henry Mancini; *ph:* John Burton Jr.; *prod sup:* Jim Foss, Harry Love; *col:* DeLuxe. *sd:* RCA. 6 min. • The Panther's job as a cook has a running battle with a worker on a building site.

4964. The Pink Blueprint *(Pink Panther)* 25 May 1966; *p.c.:* Mirisch/Geoffrey/DFE for UA; *dir:* Hawley Pratt; *story:* John W. Dunn; *anim:* Warren Batchelder, Don Williams, Norm McCabe, Dale Case, La Verne Harding; *lay:* Dick Ung; *back:* Tom O'Loughlin; *ed:* Chuck McCann; *mus:* Bill Lava; *theme tune:* Henry Mancini; *prod mgr:* Bill Orcutt; *col:* DeLuxe. *sd:* RCA. 6 min. • The Panther tries to substitute his own plans for a house while another is being constructed.

4965. Pink Breakfast *(Pink Panther)* 1978; *p.c.:* Mirisch/Geoffrey/DFE for UA; *dir:* Brad Case; *story:* Cliff Roberts; *anim:* Norm McCabe, Bob Bransford, Art Vitello, Malcolm Draper; *lay:* Martin Strudler; *back:* Richard H. Thomas; *ed:* David H. DePatie Jr.; *theme tune:* Henry Mancini; *ph:* Gary Gunther; *prod mgr:* Lee Gunther; *col:* DeLuxe. *sd:* RCA. 6 min. • The Panther tries to cook pancakes.

4966. Pink Campaign *(Pink Panther)* 30 Dec. 1975; *p.c.:* Mirisch/Geoffrey/DFE for UA; *dir:* Art Leonardi; *story:* John W. Dunn; *anim:* Bob Richardson, Don Williams, Norm McCabe, Warren Batchelder; *lay:* Dick Ung; *back:* Richard H. Thomas; *ed:* Robert Gillis; *mus:* Walter Greene; *theme tune:* Henry Mancini; *ph:* Hogan-Lee Images; *prod mgr:* Lee Gunther; *col:* DeLuxe. *sd:* RCA. 6 min. • A lumberjack destroys the Panther's tree home and so he retaliates by removing the man's house, piece by piece.

4967. Pink Da Vinci *(Pink Panther)* 23 July 1975; *p.c.:* Mirisch/Geoffrey/DFE for UA; *dir:* Robert McKimson; *story:* John W. Dunn; *anim:* Warren Batchelder, Virgil Ross, Bob Richardson, Nelson Shin, Bob Bemiller; *lay:* Dick Ung; *back:* Richard H. Thomas; *ed:* Rick Steward; *mus:* Walter Greene; *theme tune:* Henry Mancini; *ph:* John Burton Jr.; *prod mgr:* Lee Gunther; *col:* DeLuxe. *sd:* RCA. 6 min. • The Panther persists in altering the dour face that Leonardo da Vinci has painted on the Mona Lisa to a smile.

4968. Pink Daddy *(Pink Panther)* 1978; *p.c.:* Mirisch/Geoffrey/DFE for UA; *dir:* Gerry Chiniquy; *story:* Dave DeTiege; *anim:* Nelson Shin, Bob Bemiller, Virgil Ross, Walter Kubiak; *lay:* Martin Strudler; *back:* Richard H. Thomas; *ed:* Richard Corwin; *theme tune:* Henry Mancini; *ph:* Bob Mills; *prod mgr:* Lee Gunther; *col:* DeLuxe. *sd:* RCA. 6 min. • The Panther acts as foster father to a baby alligator.

4969. Pink 8-Ball *(Pink Panther)* 6 Feb. 1972; *p.c.:* Mirisch/Geoffrey/DFE for UA; *dir:* Gerry Chiniquy; *story:* John W. Dunn; *anim:* Don Williams, Manny Gould, Art Leonardi, John Gibbs, Bob Matz; *lay:* Dick Ung; *back:* Richard H. Thomas; *ed:* Rick Steward; *mus:* Walter Greene; *theme tune:* Henry Mancini; *prod mgr:* Jim Foss, Harry Love; *col:* DeLuxe. *sd:* RCA. 6 min. • The Panther tries to regain a runaway basketball with a mind of it's own.

4970. Pink Elephant *(Pink Panther)* 20 Oct. 1975; *p.c.:* Mirisch/Geoffrey/DFE for UA; *dir:* Gerry Chiniquy; *story:* John W. Dunn; *anim:* John Gibbs, Nelson Shin, Jim Davis; *lay:* Tony Rivera; *back:* Richard H. Thomas; *ed:* Rick Steward; *mus:* Walter Greene; *theme tune:* Henry Mancini; *ph:*

John Burton Jr.; *prod mgr:* Lee Gunther; *col:* DeLuxe. *sd:* RCA. 6 min. • An elephant follows the Panther home from the zoo and he hides it in his apartment.

4971. Pink Elephants *(Terry-Toon)* 9 July 1937; *p.c.:* TT for Educational/Fox; *dir:* Dan Gordon; *story:* Dan Gordon, Joseph Barbera; *mus:* Philip A. Scheib; b&w. *sd:* RCA. 6 min. • A goat eats the Farmer's auto and suffers the DTs which manifest as pink elephants. Farmer Al Falfa chases them with a vacuum cleaner.

4972. The Pink Flea *(Pink Panther)* 15 Sept. 1971; *p.c.:* Mirisch/Geoffrey/DFE for UA; *dir:* Gerry Chiniquy; *story:* John W. Dunn; *anim:* Robert Taylor, Don Williams, Manny Gould, Warren Batchelder; *lay:* Dick Ung; *back:* Richard H. Thomas; *ed:* Lee Gunther; *mus:* Walter Greene; *theme tune:* Henry Mancini; *ph:* John Burton Jr.; *prod mgr:* Jim Foss, Harry Love; *col:* DeLuxe. *sd:* RCA. 6 min. • The Panther is tormented by a persistant flea.

4973. Pink Ice *(Pink Panther)* 10 June 1965; *p.c.:* Mirisch/Geoffrey/DFE for UA; *dir:* Hawley Pratt; *story:* John Dunn; *anim:* Warren Batchelder, Bob Matz, Norm McCabe, La Verne Harding, Don Williams, Manny Perez; *lay:* Dick Ung; *back:* Tom O'Loughlin; *ed:* Lee Gunther; *voices:* Rich Little; *mus:* William Lava; *theme tune:* Henry Mancini; *prod mgr:* Bill Orcutt; *col:* DeLuxe. *sd:* RCA. 6 min. • The Panther's rivals steal a large diamond from his diamond mine.

4974. Pink-In *(Pink Panther)* 20 Oct. 1971; *p.c.:* Mirisch/Geoffrey/DFE for UA; *dir:* Art Davis; *story:* Art Leonardi; *anim:* Warren Batchelder, Robert Taylor, Don Williams, Manny Gould; *lay:* Dick Ung; *back:* Richard H. Thomas; *ed:* Joe Siracusa; *mus:* Walter Greene; *theme tune:* Henry Mancini; *prod sup:* Jim Foss, Harry Love; *col:* DeLuxe. *sd:* RCA. 6 min. • The Panther reads some old letters from an Army buddy. Seq: *G.I. Pink; Pink Pajamas; Pink Package Plot.*

4975. Pink in the Clink *(Pink Panther)* 18 Sept. 1968; *p.c.:* Mirisch/Geoffrey/DFE for UA; *dir:* Gerry Chiniquy; *story:* John W. Dunn; *anim:* Art Leonardi, Warren Batchelder, Don Williams, Manny Gould, Manny Perez; *lay:* Dick Ung; *back:* Tom O'Loughlin; *ed:* Lee Gunther; *mus:* Walter Greene; *theme tune:* Henry Mancini; *ph:* John Burton Jr.; *prod sup:* Jim Foss, Harry Love; *col:* DeLuxe. *sd:* RCA. 6 min. • A burglar forces the Panther to assist him in a daring robbery.

4976. Pink in the Drink *(Pink Panther)* 1978; *p.c.:* Mirisch/Geoffrey/DFE for UA; *dir:* Sid Marcus; *story:* John W. Dunn; *anim:* Bob Matz, John Gibbs, Tiger West, Tony Love; *lay:* Martin Strudler; *back:* Richard H. Thomas; *ed:* Richard Gannon; *theme tune:* Henry Mancini; *ph:* Steve Wilzback; *prod mgr:* Lee Gunther; *col:* DeLuxe. *sd:* RCA. 6 min. • The Panther is duped into being the soul member of a crew on a pirate ship.

4977. Pink in the Woods *(Pink Panther)* 1978; *p.c.:* Mirisch/Geoffrey/DFE for UA; *dir:* Brad Case; *story:* Cullen Houghtaling; *anim:* Nelson Shin, Bob Bemiller, Virgil Ross, Walter Kubiak; *lay:* Martin Strudler; *back:* Richard H. Thomas; *ed:* Joe Siracusa; *theme tune:* Henry Mancini; *ph:* Bob Mills; *prod mgr:* Lee Gunther; *col:* DeLuxe. *sd:* RCA. 6 min. • The Panther creates havoc when applying for a lumberjack job.

4978. Pink Is a Many Splintered Thing *(Pink Panther)* 20 Nov. 1968; *p.c.:* Mirisch/Geoffrey/DFE for UA; *dir:* Gerry Chiniquy; *story:* Don Jurwich; *anim:* Art Leonardi, Warren Batchelder, Ed de Mattia, Don Williams; *sets:* Corny Cole; *ed:* Lee Gunther; *mus:* Walter Greene; *theme tune:* Henry Mancini; *prod sup:* Jim Foss, Harry Love; *col:* DeLuxe. *sd:* RCA. 6 min. • The Panther applies for a job as a lumberjack but can't cut the mustard.

4979. Pink Lemonade *(Pink Panther)* 1977; *p.c.:* Mirisch/Geoffrey/DFE for UA; *dir:* Gerry Chiniquy; *story:* John W. Dunn; *anim:* Norm McCabe, Bob Bransford, Art Vitello, Malcolm Draper; *lay:* Martin Strudler; *back:* Richard H. Thomas; *ed:* Richard Gannon; *theme tune:* Henry Mancini; *ph:* Gary Gunther; *prod mgr:* Lee Gunther; *col:* DeLuxe. *sd:* RCA. 6 min. • The Panther takes refuge in a house where a small girl treats him as a toy.

4980. Pink Lightning *(Pink Panther)* 1978; *p.c.:* Mirisch/Geoffrey/DFE for UA; *dir:* Brad Case; *story:* John W. Dunn; *anim:* Nelson Shin, Bob Bemiller, Virgil Ross, Walter Kubiak; *lay:* Martin Strudler; *back:* Richard H. Thomas; *ed:* David DePatie Jr.; *theme tune:* Henry Mancini; *ph:* Bob Mills; *prod mgr:* Lee Gunther; *col:* DeLuxe. *sd:* RCA. 6 min. • The

Panther buys Dr. Jekyll's car that turns into a raging monster when he steps on the gas.

4981. Pink of Arabee (*Pink Panther*) 13 Mar. 1976; *p.c.:* Mirisch/Geoffrey/DFE for UA; *dir:* Gerry Chiniquy; *story:* Bob Ogle; *anim:* Don Williams, John Gibbs, Bob Richardson; *lay:* Dick Ung; *back:* Richard H. Thomas; *ed:* Robert Gillis; *mus:* Walter Greene; *theme tune:* Henry Mancini; *ph:* John Burton Jr.; *prod mgr:* Lee Gunther; *col:* DeLuxe. *sd:* RCA. 6 min. • While touring Bagdad, a piece of Indian rope falls in love with the Panther's tail. Reissued in March 1981 as *Pink of Bagdad*.

4982. Pink of the Litter (*Pink Panther*) 17 May 1967; *p.c.:* Mirisch/Geoffrey/DFE for UA; *dir:* Hawley Pratt; *story:* John Dunn; *anim:* Warren Batchelder, Don Williams, Manny Gould, Bob Matz, Manny Perez; *lay:* Dick Ung; *back:* Tom O'Loughlin; *ed:* Lee Gunther; *mus:* Walter Greene; *theme tune:* Henry Mancini; *prod sup:* Harry Love, Bill Orcutt; *col:* DeLuxe. *sd:* RCA. 6 min. • The Panther is condemned to cleaning up the town, seemingly for eternity.

4983. Pink on the Cob (*Pink Panther*) 29 May 1969; *p.c.:* Mirisch/Geoffrey/DFE for UA; *dir:* Hawley Pratt; *story:* Jack Miller; *anim:* Manny Perez, Don Williams, Don Towsley, Manny Gould; *lay:* Dick Ung; *back:* Tom O'Loughlin; *ed:* Lee Gunther; *mus:* Walter Greene; *theme tune:* Henry Mancini; *ph:* John Burton Jr.; *prod sup:* Jim Foss, Harry Love; *col:* DeLuxe. *sd:* RCA. 6 min. • The Panther tries to protect his corn field from thieving crows.

4984. Pink Outs (*Pink Panther*) 1968; *p.c.:* Mirisch/Geoffrey/DFE for UA; *dir:* Gerry Chiniquy; *story:* Art Leonardi; *anim:* Manny Perez, Bob Matz, Warren Batchelder, Don Williams, Manny Gould; *lay:* Dick Ung; *back:* Tom O'Loughlin; *ed:* Lee Gunther; *mus:* Walter Greene; *theme tune:* Henry Mancini; *ph:* John Burton Jr.; *prod sup:* Harry Love, David DeTiege; *col:* DeLuxe. *sd:* RCA. 6 min. • Miscellaneous Pink Panther blackout gags.

4985. The Pink Package Plot (*Pink Panther*) 11 Dec. 1968; *p.c.:* Mirisch/Geoffrey/DFE for UA; *dir:* Art Davis; *story:* Chuck Couch; *anim:* Herman Cohen, Warren Batchelder, Tony Love, Ed De Mattia; *lay:* Jack Miller; *back:* Tom O'Loughlin; *ed:* Lee Gunther; *mus:* Walter Greene; *theme tune:* Henry Mancini; *ph:* John Burton Jr.; *prod sup:* Jim Foss, Harry Love; *col:* DeLuxe. *sd:* RCA. 6 min. • The Panther tries to deliver a package to the Slobovian Embassy past a watchful guard dog.

4986. Pink Pajamas (*Pink Panther*) 25 Dec. 1964; *p.c.:* Mirisch/Geoffrey/DFE for UA; *dir:* Friz Freleng; *asst dir/lay:* Hawley Pratt; *story:* John Dunn; *anim:* Bob Matz, Norm McCabe, La Verne Harding, Don Williams; *back:* Tom O'Loughlin; *ed:* Lee Gunther; *mus:* William Lava; *theme tune:* Henry Mancini; *prod mgr:* Bill Orcutt; *col:* DeLuxe. *sd:* RCA. 6 min. • The Panther tries to sleep in the house of an inebriate who imagines him to be a bad case of the DTs.

4987. Pink Panic (*Pink Panther*) 11 Jan. 1967; *p.c.:* Mirisch/Geoffrey/DFE for UA; *dir:* Hawley Pratt; *story:* John W. Dunn; *anim:* Warren Batchelder, John Gibbs, La Verne Harding, Manny Perez, Manny Gould, Don Williams, Bob Matz; *lay:* Jacques Rupp; *back:* Peter Alvarado; *ed:* Lee Gunther; *mus:* Walter Greene; *theme tune:* Henry Mancini; *ph:* Ray Lee; *prod sup:* Harry Love, Bill Orcutt; *col:* DeLuxe. *sd:* RCA. 6 min. • The Panther spends a night in a haunted house.

4988. Pink Panza (*Pink Panther*) 15 Sept. 1965; *p.c.:* Mirisch/Geoffrey/DFE for UA; *dir:* Hawley Pratt; *story:* David DeTiege; *anim:* Norm McCabe, La Verne Harding, Don Williams; *lay:* Dick Ung; *back:* George de Lado; *ed:* Lee Gunther; *voice:* Paul Frees; *mus:* William Lava; *theme tune:* Henry Mancini; *prod mgr:* Bill Orcutt; *col:* DeLuxe. *sd:* RCA. 6 min. • The Panther and his neighbor stage an all-out war over their property ... encouraged by the Devil!

4989. Pink Paradise (*Pink Panther*) 21 June 1967; *p.c.:* Mirisch/Geoffrey/DFE for UA; *dir:* Gerry Chiniquy; *story:* John W. Dunn; *anim:* Manny Gould, Bob Matz, Warren Batchelder; *lay:* Corny Cole; *back:* Tom O'Loughlin; *ed:* Lee Gunther; *mus:* Walter Greene; *theme tune:* Henry Mancini; *prod sup:* Harry Love, Basil Cox; *col:* DeLuxe. *sd:* RCA. 6 min. • The Panther arrives on a desert island and upsets the lives of Robinson Crusoe and his dog.

4990. Pink Pest Control (*Pink Panther*) 12 Feb. 1969; *p.c.:* Mirisch/Geoffrey/DFE for UA; *dir:* Gerry Chiniquy; *story:* John W. Dunn; *anim:* Ed de Mattia, Don Williams, Manny Perez, Warren Batchelder; *sets:* Corny Cole; *ed:* Lee Gunther; *mus:* Walter Greene; *theme tune:* Henry Mancini; *prod sup:* Harry Love, Jim Foss; *col:* DeLuxe. *sd:* RCA. 6 min. • A termite attacks the Panther's log cabin.

4991. The Pink Phink (*Pink Panther*) 18 Dec. 1964; *p.c.:* Mirisch/Geoffrey/DFE for UA; *dir:* Friz Freleng; *asst dir/lay:* Hawley Pratt; *story:* John Dunn; *anim:* Don Williams, Bob Matz, Norman McCabe, La Verne Harding; *back:* Tom O'Loughlin; *ed:* Lee Gunther; *mus:* William Lava; *theme tune:* Henry Mancini; *prod mgr:* Bill Orcutt; *col:* DeLuxe. *sd:* RCA. 6 min. *Academy Award.* • A painter sets to paint a new house blue but the Panther has other ideas for a color scheme.

4992. Pink Pictures (*Pink Panther*) 1978; *p.c.:* Mirisch/Geoffrey/DFE for UA; *dir:* Gerry Chiniquy; *story:* Cliff Roberts; *anim:* Nelson Shin, Bob Bemiller, Virgil Ross, Walter Kubiak; *lay:* Martin Strudler; *back:* Richard H. Thomas; *ed:* Bob Gillis; *ph:* Steve Wilzback; *theme tune:* Henry Mancini; *prod mgr:* Lee Gunther; *col:* DeLuxe. *sd:* RCA. 6 min. • The Panther photographs some unwilling woodland life.

4993. The Pink Pill (*Pink Panther*) 18 Sept. 1968; *p.c.:* Mirisch/Geoffrey/DFE for UA; *dir:* Gerry Chiniquy; *story:* John W. Dunn; *anim:* Don Williams, Manny Gould, Manny Perez, Warren Batchelder; *lay:* Dick Ung; *back:* Tom O'Loughlin; *ed:* Lee Gunther; *mus:* Walter Greene; *theme tune:* Henry Mancini; *ph:* John Burton Jr.; *prod sup:* Harry Love, Jim Foss; *col:* DeLuxe. *sd:* RCA. 6 min. • The Panther finds himself in hospital with a broken leg.

4994. Pink Piper (*Pink Panther*) 30 Apr. 1976; *p.c.:* Mirisch/Geoffrey/DFE for UA; *dir:* Cullen Houghtaling; *story:* John W. Dunn; *anim:* Warren Batchelder, Virgil Ross, John Gibbs, Bob Matz; *lay:* Tony Rivera; *back:* Richard H. Thomas; *ed:* Rick Steward; *mus:* Walter Greene; *theme tune:* Henry Mancini; *ph:* John Burton Jr.; *prod mgr:* Lee Gunther; *col:* DeLuxe. *sd:* RCA. 6 min. • The Panther takes on the role of The Pied Piper to lure the troublesome mice away from the town.

4995. Pink Piston (*Pink Panther*) 16 Mar. 1966; *p.c.:* Mirisch/Geoffrey/DFE for UA; *dir:* Hawley Pratt; *story:* Michael O'Connor; *anim:* Don Williams, Norman McCabe, La Verne Harding, Warren Batchelder; *lay:* Dick Ung; *back:* Tom O'Loughlin; *ed:* Roger Donley; *mus:* William Lava; *theme tune:* Henry Mancini; *prod mgr:* Bill Orcutt; *col:* DeLuxe. *sd:* RCA. 6 min. • The Panther buys a sports car and finds himself in a race with a little old granny.

4996. Pink Plasma (*Pink Panther*) 28 Aug. 1975; *p.c.:* Mirisch/Geoffrey/DFE for UA; *dir:* Art Leonardi; *story:* John W. Dunn; *anim:* Don Williams, Bob Richardson, Virgil Ross, John Gibbs; *lay:* Dick Ung; *back:* Richard H. Thomas; *ed:* Rick Steward; *mus:* Walter Greene; *theme tune:* Henry Mancini; *ph:* John Burton Jr.; *prod sup:* Lee Gunther; *col:* DeLuxe. *sd:* RCA. 6 min. • The Panther spends a night in a vampire castle.

4997. Pink, Plunk, Plink (*Pink Panther*) 25 May 1966; *p.c.:* Mirisch/Geoffrey/DFE for UA; *dir:* Hawley Pratt; *story:* Michael O'Connor; *anim:* Norman McCabe, Brad Case, La Verne Harding, Warren Batchelder, George Grandpré, Don Williams; *lay:* Dick Ung; *back:* Tom O'Loughlin; *ed:* Lee Gunther; *mus:* Walter Greene; *theme tune:* Henry Mancini; *prod mgr:* Bill Orcutt; *col:* DeLuxe. *sd:* RCA. 6 min. *l/a/anim.* • The Panther disrupts an orchestra by playing his own theme tune. The audience consists of a highly appreciative Henry Mancini.

4998. Pink Posies (*Pink Panther*) 26 Apr. 1967; *p.c.:* Mirisch/Geoffrey/DFE for UA; *dir:* Hawley Pratt; *story:* Jim Ryan; *anim:* Bob Matz, Warren Batchelder, Art Leonardi, Don Williams, Manny Gould; *lay:* Corny Cole; *back:* Tom O'Loughlin; *ed:* Lee Gunther; *mus:* Walter Greene; *theme tune:* Henry Mancini; *prod sup:* Harry Love, Bill Orcutt; *col:* DeLuxe. *sd:* RCA. 6 min. • As the gardener plants yellow flowers, the Panther replaces them with pink posies.

4999. Pink Pranks (*Pink Panther*) 18 Aug 1971; *p.c.:* Mirisch/Geoffrey/DFE for UA; *dir:* Gerry Chiniquy; *story:* John W. Dunn; *anim:* Robert Taylor, Manny Gould, Manny Perez, Warren Batchelder, Don Williams; *lay:* Robert Givens; *back:* Richard H. Thomas; *ed:* Lee Gunther; *theme tune:* Henry Mancini; *ph:* John Burton Jr.; *prod sup:* Jim Foss, Harry Love; *col:* DeLuxe. *sd:* RCA. 6 min. • A seal saves the Panther from a Polar Bear, leaving the Panther feeling obliged to save the seal from a hunter.

5000. Pink Press (*Pink Panther*) 1978; *p.c.:* Mirisch/Geoffrey/DFE for UA; *dir:* Art Davis; *story:* John W. Dunn; *anim:* Nelson Shin, Bob

Bemiller, Virgil Ross, Walter Kubiak; *lay:* Martin Strudler; *back:* Richard H. Thomas; *ed:* Robert Gillis; *theme tune:* Henry Mancini; *ph:* Steve Wilzback; *prod mgr:* Lee Gunther; *col:* DeLuxe. *sd:* RCA. 6 min. • The local paper's ace reporter (the Panther) tries to get in to interview Howard Huge.

5001. The Pink Pro *(Pink Panther)* 12 Apr. 1976; *p.c.:* Mirisch/Geoffrey/DFE for UA; *dir:* Robert McKimson; *story:* Lee Mishkin; *anim:* Bob Richardson, John Gibbs, Don Williams, Norm McCabe; *lay:* Dick Ung; *back:* Richard H. Thomas; *ed:* Robert Gillis; *mus:* Walter Greene; *theme tune:* Henry Mancini; *ph:* John Burton Jr.; *prod mgr:* Lee Gunther; *col:* DeLuxe. *sd:* RCA. 6 min. • The Panther gives erratic lessons in archery, skiing, sky-diving, water skiing and golf.

5002. Pink Pull *(Pink Panther)* 1978; *dir:* Sid Marcus; *story:* Cliff Roberts; *anim:* Bob Matz, John Gibbs, Tiger West, Tony Love; *lay:* Martin Strudler; *back:* Richard H. Thomas; *ed:* Bob Gillis; *theme tune:* Henry Mancini; *ph:* Steve Wilzback; *prod mgr:* Lee Gunther; *col:* DeLuxe. *sd:* RCA. 6 min. • The Panther's problems start when he gets a super magnet to retrieve a quarter he's lost down a drain.

5003. Pink Punch *(Pink Panther)* 21 Feb. 1966; *p.c.:* Mirisch/Geoffrey/DFE for UA; *dir:* Hawley Pratt; *story:* Michael O'Connor; *anim:* Warren Batchelder, Don Williams, Norm McCabe, Bob Matz, La Verne Harding; *lay:* Dick Ung; *back:* Tom O'Loughlin; *ed:* Lee Gunther; *voice:* Mel Blanc; *mus:* William Lava; *theme tune:* Henry Mancini; *prod mgr:* Bill Orcutt; *col:* DeLuxe. *sd:* RCA. 6 min. • The Panther contends with a green asterisk while explaining the values of "Pink Punch."

5004. Pink Quackers *(Pink Panther)* 1978 *dir:* Brad Case; *story:* Dave DeTiege; *anim:* Bob Matz, John Gibbs, Tiger West, Tony Love; *lay:* Martin Strudler; *back:* Richard H. Thomas; *ed:* Joe Siracusa; *theme tune:* Henry Mancini; *ph:* Steve Wilzback; *prod mgr:* Lee Gunther; *col:* DeLuxe. *sd:* RCA. 6 min. • The Panther rescues a mechanical duck from being run over and it befriends him.

5005. The Pink Quarterback *(Pink Panther)* 22 May 1968; *p.c.:* Mirisch/Geoffrey/DFE for UA; *dir:* Hawley Pratt; *story:* John W. Dunn; *anim:* Don Williams, Tom Ray, Manny Gould, Manny Perez, Warren Batchelder; *lay:* Dick Ung; *back:* Tom O'Loughlin; *ed:* Allan Potter; *mus:* Walter Greene; *theme tune:* Henry Mancini; *ph:* John Burton Jr.; *prod mgr:* Harry Love, David DeTiege; *col:* DeLuxe. *sd:* RCA. 6 min. • The Panther pursues a runaway quarter.

5006. Pink Sphinx *(Pink Panther)* 23 Oct. 1968; *p.c.:* Mirisch/Geoffrey/DFE for UA; *dir:* Hawley Pratt; *story:* Jim Ryan; *anim:* Warren Batchelder, Don Williams, Manny Gould, Manny Perez, Art Leonardi; *lay:* Dick Ung; *back:* Tom O'Loughlin; *ed:* Allan Potter; *mus:* Walter Greene; *theme tune:* Henry Mancini; *prod mgr:* Harry Love, Jim Foss; *col:* DeLuxe. *sd:* RCA. 6 min. • The Panther is searching for treasure in Egypt with a diminutive camel.

5007. Pink Streaker *(Pink Panther)* 25 July 1975; *p.c.:* Mirisch/Geoffrey/DFE for UA; *dir:* Gerry Chiniquy; *story:* John W. Dunn; *anim:* Bob Matz, Don Williams, Nelson Shin, Norm McCabe; *lay:* Dick Ung; *back:* Richard H. Thomas; *ed:* Robert Gillis; *mus:* Walter Greene; *theme tune:* Henry Mancini; *ph:* John Burton Jr.; *prod mgr:* Lee Gunther; *col:* DeLuxe. *sd:* RCA. 6 min. • The Panther runs into many pitfalls when skiing.

5008. Pink Suds *(Pink Panther)* 1978; *p.c.:* Mirisch/Geoffrey/DFE for UA; *dir:* Art Davis; *story:* Cullen Houghtaling; *anim:* Don Williams, Lee Halpern, Bernard Posner, Joan Case; *lay:* Martin Strudler; *back:* Richard H. Thomas; *ed:* David H. DePatie Jr.; *theme tune:* Henry Mancini; *ph:* Ray Lee; *prod mgr:* Lee Gunther; *col:* DeLuxe. *sd:* RCA. 6 min. • The Panther takes his weekly wash to the laundrette with dire results.

5009. Pink S.W.A.T. *(Pink Panther)* 1978; *p.c.:* Mirisch/Geoffrey/DFE for UA; *dir:* Sid Marcus; *story:* John W. Dunn; *anim:* Don Williams, Lee Halpern, Bernard Posney, Joan Case; *lay:* Martin Strudler; *back:* Richard H. Thomas; *ed:* Joe Siracusa; *theme tune:* Henry Mancini; *ph:* Ray Lee; *prod mgr:* Lee Gunther; *col:* DeLuxe. *sd:* RCA. 6 min. • The Panther is bothered by a pesty fly.

5010. The Pink Tail Fly *(Pink Panther)* 25 Aug. 1965; *p.c.:* Mirisch/Geoffrey/DFE for UA; *dir:* Friz Freleng; *asst dir:* Hawley Pratt; *story:* Bob Kurtz; *anim:* Don Williams, Norman McCabe, La Verne Harding; *lay:* Dick Ung; *back:* Tom O'Loughlin; *ed:* Lee Gunther; *mus:* William Lava;

theme tune: Henry Mancini; *prod mgr:* William Orcutt; *col:* DeLuxe. *sd:* RCA. 6 min. • The Panther's slumber is disturbed by the constant buzzing of a mosquito.

5011. Pink-Tails for Two *(Pink Panther)* 1978; *p.c.:* Mirisch/Geoffrey/DFE for UA; *dir:* Art Davis; *story:* Tony Benedict; *anim:* Nelson Shin, Bob Bemiller, Virgil Ross, Walter Kubiak; *lay:* Martin Strudler; *back:* Richard H. Thomas; *ed:* Richard Gannon; *theme tune:* Henry Mancini; *ph:* Bob Mills; *prod mgr:* Lee Gunther; *col:* DeLuxe. *sd:* RCA. 6 min. • The Panther has problems with an elongated tail when he spills "Quick Grow" on it.

5012. Pink Trumpet *(Pink Panther)* 1978; *p.c.:* Mirisch/Geoffrey/DFE for UA; *dir:* Art Davis; *story:* Dave DeTiege; *anim:* Norm McCabe, Bob Bransford, Art Vitello, Malcolm Draper; *lay:* Martin Strudler; *back:* Richard H. Thomas; *ed:* Richard Gannon; *theme tune:* Henry Mancini; *ph:* Ray Lee; *prod mgr:* Lee Gunther; *col:* DeLuxe. *sd:* RCA. 6 min. • The Panther's nocturnal trumpet playing annoys the man in the next apartment.

5013. Pink Tuba-Dore *(Pink Panther)* 4 Aug. 1971; *p.c.:* Mirisch/Geoffrey/DFE for UA; *dir:* Art Davis; *story:* John W. Dunn; *anim:* Manny Perez, Warren Batchelder, Don Williams, Manny Gould; *lay:* Robert Givens; *back:* Richard H. Thomas; *ed:* Joe Siracusa; *mus:* Walter Greene; *theme tune:* Henry Mancini; *ph:* John Burton Jr.; *prod mgr:* Jim Foss, Harry Love; *col:* DeLuxe. *sd:* RCA. 6 min. • A tuba player and his dog practice under a tree that the Panther happens to be asleep in.

5014. Pink UFO *(Pink Panther)* 1978; *p.c.:* Mirisch/Geoffrey/DFE for UA; *dir/story:* Dave DeTiege; *anim:* Warren Batchelder, Bob Richardson, Bob Kirk, Bill Hutten; *lay:* Martin Strudler; *back:* Richard H. Thomas; *ed:* Joe Siracusa; *theme tune:* Henry Mancini; *ph:* Ray Lee; *prod mgr:* Lee Gunther; *col:* DeLuxe. *sd:* RCA. 6 min. • The Panther mistakes a tiny visitor from another planet for a butterfly for his collection.

5015. Pink Valiant *(Pink Panther)* 10 July 1968; *p.c.:* Mirisch/Geoffrey/DFE for UA; *dir:* Hawley Pratt; *story:* John W. Dunn; *anim:* Tom Ray, Manny Gould, Manny Perez, Warren Batchelder, Don Williams; *lay:* Dick Ung; *back:* Tom O'Loughlin; *ed:* Lee Gunther; *mus:* Walter Greene; *theme tune:* Henry Mancini; *ph:* John Burton Jr.; *prod mgr:* Harry Love, David DeTiege; *col:* DeLuxe. *sd:* RCA. 6 min. • Knight Errant, Panther, attempts to rescue a maiden held captive by a Knight but soon realizes that it's the Knight that needs rescuing.

5016. Pink Z-z-z *(Pink Panther)* 1978; *p.c.:* Mirisch/Geoffrey/DFE for UA; *dir:* Sid Marcus; *story:* Tony Benedict; *anim:* Bob Matz, John Gibbs, Tiger West, Tony Love; *lay:* Martin Strudler; *back:* Richard H. Thomas; *ed:* Richard Gannon; *theme tune:* Henry Mancini; *ph:* Gary Gunther; *prod mgr:* Lee Gunther; *col:* DeLuxe. *sd:* RCA. 6 min. • A cat's nocturnal howling keeps the Panther awake, so he tries to dispose of the creature.

5017. Pinkadilly Circus *(Pink Panther)* 21 Feb. 1968; *p.c.:* Mirisch/Geoffrey/DFE for UA; *dir:* Hawley Pratt; *story:* John W. Dunn; *anim:* Manny Gould, Manny Perez, Bob Matz, Warren Batchelder, Don Williams; *lay:* Dick Ung; *back:* Tom O'Loughlin; *ed:* Lee Gunther; *mus:* Walter Greene; *theme tune:* Henry Mancini; *ph:* John Burton Jr.; *prod sup:* Harry Love, David DeTiege; *col:* DeLuxe. *sd:* RCA. 6 min. • The Panther explores a department store.

5018. Pinkfinger *(Pink Panther)* 13 May 1965; *p.c.:* Mirisch/Geoffrey/DFE for UA; *dir:* Friz Freleng; *asst dir:* Hawley Pratt; *story:* Bob Kurtz; *anim:* La Verne Harding, Don Williams, Norm McCabe; *lay:* Dick Ung; *back:* George de Lado; *ed:* Lee Gunther; *voices:* Paul Frees, Dave Barry; *mus:* Bill Lava; *theme tune:* Henry Mancini; *prod mgr:* Bill Orcutt; *col:* DeLuxe. *sd:* RCA. 6 min. • The Panther gets mixed up in a world of spies.

5019. Pinknic *(Pink Panther)* 6 Jan. 1967; *p.c.:* Mirisch/Geoffrey/DFE for UA; *dir:* Hawley Pratt; *story:* John W. Dunn; *anim:* Don Williams, Warren Batchelder, John Gibbs, Manny Perez, La Verne Harding; *lay:* Dick Ung; *back:* Tom O'Loughlin; *ed:* Lee Gunther; *mus:* Walter Greene; *theme tune:* Henry Mancini; *prod sup:* Harry Love, Bill Orcutt; *col:* DeLuxe. *sd:* RCA. 6 min. • The Panther is snowbound in a log cabin with a starving mouse who's intent on eating him.

5020. Pinkologist *(Pink Panther)* Apr. 1981 (© 1978); *p.c.:* Mirisch/Geoffrey/DFE for UA; *dir:* Gerry Chiniquy; *story:* John W. Dunn; *anim:* Don Williams, Lee Halpern, Bernard Posner, Joan Case; *lay:* Martin Strudler; *back:* Richard H. Thomas; *ed:* David H. DePatie Jr.; *theme tune:* Henry

Mancini; *ph:* Ray Lee; *prod mgr:* Lee Gunther; *col:* DeLuxe. *sd:* RCA. 6 min. Seq: *Pink Posies; Pink Blueprint.* • The Panther's nemesis visits a psychiatrist and relates how the creature victimizes him.

5021. Pinky Doodle *(Pink Panther)* 28 May 1976; *p.c.:* Mirisch/Geoffrey/DFE for UA; *dir:* Sid Marcus; *story:* John Dunn; *anim:* Bob Richardson, Don Williams, Norm McCabe, John Gibbs; *lay:* Rick Gonzalez, Dick Ung, Gary Hoffman; *back:* Richard H. Thomas; *ed:* Bob Gillis; *mus:* Walter Greene; *theme tune:* Henry Mancini; *ph:* John Burton Jr.; *prod mgr:* Lee Gunther; *col:* DeLuxe. *sd:* RCA. 6 min. • The Panther assumes the role of Paul Revere but first has to find a willing horse. Reissued in Jan. 1981 as *Yankee Doodle Pink.*

5022. Pinocchio 7 Feb. 1940; *p.c.:* Walt Disney prods for RKO; *dir sup:* Ben Sharpsteen, Hamilton Luske; *seq dir:* Bill Roberts, Jack Kinney, Norman Ferguson, Wilfred Jackson, T. Hee; *story adapt:* Ted Sears, Webb Smith, Joseph Sabo, Otto Englander, William Cottrell, Erdman Penner, Aurelius Battaglia; *character des:* Campbell Grant, Albert Hurter, John P. Miller, Martin Provensen, John Walbridge; *anim dir:* Fred Moore, Milt Kahl, Ward Kimball, Eric Larson, Franklin Thomas, Vladimir Tytla, Arthur Babbitt, Woolie Reitherman, James H. Culhane; *anim:* Preston Blair, John Bradbury, Jack Campbell, Les Clark, John Elliotte, Hugh Fraser, Al Geiss, Mo Gollub, Ralph Heimdahl, Oliver M. Johnston, Lynn Karp, Walt Kelly, Hank Ketcham, John Lounsbery, Don Lusk, Robert Martsch, Charles Nichols, Ben Oda, Don Patterson, Norman Tate, Don Tobin, Don Towsley, Joe Wehrle, Berny Wolf, Marvin Woodward; *fx:* John McManus, Joshua Meador, Art Palmer, George Rowley; *lay:* Kenneth Anderson, Hugh Hennesy, John Hubley, Dick Kelsey, Kendall O'Connor, Charles Philippi, Thor Putnam, Terrell Stapp, McLaren Stewart, Al Zinnen; *back:* Claude Coats, Merle Cox, Ray Huffine, Ed Starr; *voices: Honest John:* Walter Catlett; *Stromboli/Coachman:* Charles Judels; *Lampwick:* Frankie Darro; *Jiminy Cricket:* Cliff Edwards; *Geppetto:* Christian Rub; *Pinocchio:* Dickie Jones; *The Blue Fairy:* Evelyn Venable; *Pleasure Island barkers:* Don Brodie, Jack Bailey, Linsay MacHarrie, John McLeish, Stuart Buchanan; *French, Dutch & Russian puppets:* Patricia Page; *Alexander:* Virginia Davis; *Figaro/donkey brays:* Clarence Nash; *hiccups:* Mel Blanc; *chorus:* The King's Men Quartet; *mus/songs:* Leigh Harline, Ned Washington, Paul J. Smith; *special processes;* Herman Schultheis; *col:* Tech. *sd:* RCA. 87 min. • Carlo Collodi's evergreen tale about a puppet who is given life and the adventures he encounters along with his acting "Concience," Jiminy Cricket. An Academy Award was recieved for the best original music score and another for Harline and Washington's song, "When You Wish Upon a Star."

5023. Pinocchio and the Emperor of the Night 25 Dec. 1987; *p.c.:* Filmation Associates for Palace Pictures; *dir:* Hal Sutherland; *prod:* Lou Scheimer; *asso prod:* John Grusd, Robby London, Erika Scheimer; *vice-president in charge of prod:* Joe Mazzuca; *prod controller:* Hal Waite Jr.; *pre-prod co-ord:* Chris Weber; *prod co-ord:* Susan O'Brien; *prod mgr:* Bob Pope, Chuck Mitman; *post prod sup:* George Mahan; *story:* Dennis O'Flaherty; *inspired by The Adventures of Pinocchio by* Carlo Collodi; *scr:* Robby London, Barry O'Brien, Dennis O'Flaherty; *storyboard:* Tom Tataranowicz, Warren Greenwood, Kevin Harkey, Victoria Jenson, Tom Sito; *anim sup:* John Celestri, Chuck Harvey, Ka-Moon Song, Bruce Strock, Doris Plough; *anim:* Robert Alvarez, Carl Bell, Bob Carlson, Yi-Chih Chen, Doug Crane, James Davis, Zeon Davush, Edward DeMattia, Will Finn, James George, Fernando Gonzalez, Steve Gordon, Fred Grable, Lennie K. Graves, Daniel Haskett, John Howley, Ruth Kissane, Clark Lagerstrom, Jang Woo Lee, Ernesto Lopez, Mircea Manta, Mauro Maressa, Costy Mustatea, Emory Myrick, Bill Nunes, Eduardo Olivares, Jack Ozark, Kevin Petrilak, Young Kyu Rhim, Leonard Robinson, Joe Roman, Mike Sanger, Louis Scarborough, Thomas Sito, Bruce W. Smith, Jason So, Ken Southworth, Leo Sullivan, Bob Tyler, Larry White, Allen Wilzback, Bruce Woodside; *fx anim:* Bruce Heller, Esther Barr, Glenn Chaika, Margaret Craig-Chang, Mark Dindal, Randy Fullmer, Brett Hisey, Kim Knowlton, Hope London, Mark Myer, James Stribling, Philip Young, Danny Chaika, Phil Cummings, Mabel Gesner, Hector Isola, Craig Littell-Herrick, Celia Mercer; *prod des:* Gerald Forton, Tenny Henson, Rick Maki, Phil Ortiz, Connie Schurr, Cliff Voorhees, Pat Wong, Ray Aragon, Rex Barron, T. Bird, Frank Frezzo, Tom Shannon; *graphic des:* Victoria A. Brooks; *lay:* Dave West, Wes Herschensohn, Barbara Benedetto, Irma Rosien, Craig Armstrong, Rex Barron, T. Bird, Armando Carrillo, Curtis Cim, Tom Coppola, Alberto De Mello, Frank Frezzo, Dave Hilberman, Karenia Kaminski, Chrystal Klabunde,

John Koch, Leandro Martinez, James McLean, Dan Mills, Gale Morgan, Armando Norte, Michael O'Mara, John Perry, William Recinos, Tom Shannon, J. Michael Spooner, Isis Thompson, Cliff Voorhees, Sherilan Weinhart, Bronwen Barry, Ellen Kashan, Jenifer Costin, Patricia Keppler, Susan Semer, Nancy Ugoretz; *col dir:* Ervin L. Kaplan; *back:* Joseph Binggeli, Al Budnick, Ruben Chavez, Gary Conklin, Glamarion Fereira, Dean G. Fordor, Ann Guenther, Robert Kalafut, Tim Maloney, David McBride, Tom O'Loughlin, Rolando Oliva, Don A. Peters, Craig Robertson, Don Schweikert, Robert Stanton, Don Watson, *ed:* Joe Gall, Jeffrey Patch, Rick Gehr; *voices: Scalawag:* Edward Asner; *Geppetto:* Tom Bosley; *Twinkle:* Lana Beeson; *Pinocchio:* Scott Grimes; *Bee-atrice:* Linda Gary; *Lieutenant Grumblebee:* Jonathan Harris; *Emperor of the Night:* James Earl Jones; *Good Fairy:* Rickie Lee Jones; *Gee Willikers:* Don Knotts; *Igor:* Frank Welker; *Puppetino:* William Windom; *mus:* Anthony Marinelli, Brian Banks; *mus sup:* Erika Scheimer; *songs prod:* Steve Tyrell, Brian Banks; *songs:* "Love is the Light Inside Your Heart" by Barry Mann, Will Jennings, performed by Rickie Lee Jones; "You're a Star" by Will Jennings, performed by Kid Creole and the Coconuts; "Do What Makes You Happy" by Steve Tyrell, Will Jennings, performed by Lana Beeson; "Neon Cabaret" by Anthony Marinelli, Brian Banks; *choreog:* Alfred Desio; *clean-up:* Philo Barnhart, Kathi Castillo, Ken Cope, Susan Craig, Dori Littell-Herrick, Rusty Mills, Brett Newton, Judy Niver, Don Parmele, Ginny Parmele, Nelson Recinos, Dana M. Reemes, Karen Rosenfield, Mark Rouse, Randy Sanchez, Michael Show, George Sukara, Haile Taylor, Isis Thompson, Mac Torres, Ron Westlund, Eugene Ahn, Sung Chul Ahn, Ruben Apodaca, Elizabeth Arons, Rich Arons, Arland Barron, Bronwen Barry, Vincent Bassols, Munir Bhatti, James Bird, Virginia Bogart, Sheldon Borenstein, Richard Bowman, Sheila Brown, Ben Burgess, Conuelo Cataldi, Hyunsook Cho, Chris Chu, Pat Clark, Merry Clingen, Lee Crowe, Eric Daniels, Tom Decker, Chris Dent, Betty Doyle, Eileen Dunn, Teresa Eidenbock, Bill Eigle, Derek Eversfield, Diana Falk, Rick Farmiloe, Melissa Freeman, Mike Genz, Mike Gerard, Ko Hashiguchi, Sandra Henkin, Dick Hoffman, La Vera Hoyes, Leonard Johnson, Chan Woo Jung, Michael Kawesky, Paulette King, Nancy Kniep, Rick Kohlschmidt, Jane Krupka, Boo Won Lee, Jim Logan, Jules Marino, Tom Mazzocco, Larry Miller, William Mims, James McArdle, Sherri Murray, David Nethery, Mike Oliva, Sean Platter, Mike Polvani, Cheryl Polakow, Andrew Ramos, Frank Recinos, Lloyd Rees, Mary Robertson, Bonnie Robinson, Susan Rodgers, Chris Rutkowski, Paul Salaiz, Won Chul Shin, Stan Somers, Alan Sperling, Janice Stocks, Susan Sugita-Ray, Marty Schwartz, Louis Tate, Amanda Thompson, Marshall Toomey, Giselle Van Bark, Tran Vu, Allen Wade, Chris Wahl, Mitchell Walker Jr., Stan Wallace, Terry Walsh, Vance Welty, Dave Woodman, Kevin Wurzer, Won Yoo, Mi Ri Yoon, Eun Ok Yu; *anim break:* Mark Barrows, Paul Bauman, Jerry Lee Brice, Lillian Chapman, Kent Culotta, Lee Dunkman, James Fujii, Karen Hardenbergh, Mike Kazaleh, Michael Lipman, Terri Martin, Gary Payne, Sherie Pollack, Lucinda Ann Sanderson, Duffy Steele, David Teague, William Tucker, Cristi L. Vitello, Eileen Wilson, Margie Wright-Stansbery, Tomihiro Yamaguchi; *inbet:* Earl Rock Benedetto, Mark Chavez, Tom Ellery, John Elliot, Craig Evans, Wendie Fischer, Carolyn Froblom Gliona, Guy Hubbard, Hasook Hwang, Tim Ingersoll, Myung Kang, Chang Yei Kim, Dan Kuemmel, Joe McDonough, Hitomi Nishitani, Jong Won Park, Marsha Park, Terri Ro, Sabrina Silver, Bill Thinnes; *anim check:* Kathy Barrows Fulmer, Annamarie Costa, Bunty Dranko, Katherine Victor, Merle Weston; *Xerox:* John Remmel, William Ziegler, Douglas Casper, Warren Coffman, Robert Erhart, Gareth Fishbaugh, Kathy Gilmore, Dan Mendoza, Rosalina Ortiz, Paul Stephen, James Stocks, Angelo Villani; *check:* Robert Avery, Marlene Burkhart, Sharon Dabek, Heidi Ewing, Catherine Parotino, Dean Stanley, Leyla Suero-Pelaez, Carmi Teves, Joanne Villani, Janet Zoll; *i&p:* Flavia Mitman; *mark-up:* Sara Seaberry, Patti Erhart, Gay Smith, Cindy Surage, Irma Velez; *fx:* Ashley S. Lupin, Casey Clayton, Chris Conklin, Marjorie Elliston, Karen Elston, Lillian Fitts, Rita Giddings, Mi Kyung Kwon, Stephanie Myers, Virginia Stockton, Linda Webber, Lee Wood; *paint:* Ann Sorensen, Karen Comella, Lada Babicka, Russell Blandino, Susan Burke, Tania Burton, Daryl Casper, Mimi Clayton, Patricia Cowling, Elena Cox, Sybil Cuzzort, Kim Dahl, Mari Daugherty, Gene Dubois, Betsy Ergenbright, Phyllis Fields, Joyce Frey, Vicki Gaffney, Alison Gefre, Peter Gentle, Staci Gleed, Mary Grant, Valerie Green, Carolyn Guske, Evelyn Hairpetian, Laurel Harper, Karen Hooper, Odin Hot, Dorma Hughes, Kathleen Irvine, David Karp, Kathlyn Kephart, Monica Kogler, Thomas Kurucz, Kristin Lande, Denise Link, Kim Manley,

Sue Masterson, Jean Miller, Lana Nelson, Diane Nielsen, Patricia Pettinelli, Linda Praamsma, Gale Raleigh, Bonnie Ramsey, Susan Reagan, Jean Remmel, Sally Reymond, Colene Riffo, Lori Rudman, Mary Sime, Sheryl Smith, Fumiko Sommer, Roxanne M. Taylor, Helga Vanden Berge, Helene Vives, Valerie Walker, Helen Whitman; *ink:* Maria Alvarez, Laura Craig, Joanna Lohr, Chris Stock, *(repairers)* Chuck Gefre, Anna Helquist; *airbrush:* David J. Zywicki, Melody Hughes, Robin D. Kane, Corry Kingsbury, Annette Leavitt, Kevin Oakley; *final check:* Howard F. Schwartz, Charlotte Clark, Lorraine Couzzi, Laurel Harper, Rhonda Hicks, Naomi Johnson, Teri McDonald, Marisha Noroski, Yolanda Rearick, Karin Texter, Annette Vandenberg; *film co-ord:* June Gilham, Christie Meyer; *art dir:* John Grusd; *prod sculptor:* Christopher G. Peterson; *sd ed:* Steve Burger, Hector Gika, Bill Kean, Charles Rychwalski; *sd rec:* Louis Montoya, Mark Curry, David Kitay, Pat Somerset, Jeff Habush, Greg Russell; *prod asst:* Sandy Cowan, Mary Bloomquist, Joan O'Brien; *ph:* F.T. Ziegler, Dean Teves, Steve P. Damiani, Veronica Hantke, Ronald Jackson, Robert Jacobs, David J. Link, Lin-Z-Rogers, Richard Taylor, Charles Warren, Jerry Whittington; *motion control ph:* Dan C. Larsen, Steven Wilzbach; *camera computer system:* Cinetron Computer Systems; *video:* Brett Hayden, Doug Pakes, Chuck Powell; *col:* CFI. *sd:* Dolby stereo. 87 min. • To celebrate his first anniversary of being a real boy, the Good Fairy presents Pinocchio with a glowbug called "Gee Willikers" to act as his conscience. After being warned not to take his freedom for granted, Pinocchio offers to deliver a valuable jewel box for Geppetto. Scalawag, a rougish raccoon, cheats him out of the box and Pinocchio vows to recover the jewel box that is now in the possession of the evil Emperor of the Night. Along the way he has an encounter with a monstrous fish and is taken to the Land Where Dreams Come True, where he finds he has agreed to sign away his freedom to the Emperor. Pinocchio decides to take charge of his own destiny, finally defeating the Emperor of the Night.

5024. Pinto Pink *(Pink Panther)* 19 July 1967; *p.c.:* Mirisch/Geoffrey/DFE for UA; *dir:* Hawley Pratt; *story:* John W. Dunn; *anim:* Don Williams, Manny Gould, Bob Matz, Manny Perez, Warren Batchelder, Chuck Downs; *lay:* Corny Cole; *back:* Tom O'Loughlin; *ed:* Lee Gunther; *mus:* Walter Greene; *theme tune:* Henry Mancini; *prod sup:* Harry Love, Basil Cox; *col:* DeLuxe. *sd:* RCA. 6 min. • Rather than walk to Anaheim, The Panther attempts to saddle and ride a reluctant horse.

5025. Pioneer Days *(Mickey Mouse)* 20 Nov. 1930; *p.c.:* Walter E. Disney for Colum; *dir:* Burton F. Gillett; *anim:* Charles Byrne, Johnny Cannon, Les Clark, Jack Cutting, Gilles de Tremaudan, Norman Ferguson, David D. Hand, Wilfred Jackson, Jack King, Richard Lundy, Tom Palmer, Ben Sharpsteen; *voices:* Marcellite Garner, Walt Disney; *mus:* Bert Lewis; *ph:* William Cottrell; *b&w. sd:* PCP. 7 min. • Mickey and Minnie are headed west in a covered wagon when they suffer an Indian attack. Mickey simulates a battalion of soldiers and frightens the savages off.

5026. Pip-Eye, Pup-Eye, Poop-Eye An' Peep-Eye *(Popeye)* 10 Apr. 1942; *p.c.:* The Fleischer Studio for Para; *prod:* Max Fleischer; *dir:* Dave Fleischer; *story:* Seymour Kneitel; *anim:* Seymour Kneitel, George Germanetti; *ed:* Kitty Pfister; *voices:* Jack Mercer; *mus:* Sammy Timberg; *ph:* Charles Schettler; *prod sup:* Sam Buchwald, Isidore Sparber; *b&w. sd:* WE. 7 min. • Popeye demonstrates the benefits of spinach to his vegetable-hating nephews.

5027. Pipe Dreams *(Happy Harmonies)* 5 Feb. 1938; *p.c.:* MGM; *prod/dir:* Hugh Harman, Rudolf Ising; *voices:* Elmore Vincent, The Rhythmettes; *mus:* Scott Bradley; *col:* Tech. *sd:* WE. 8 min. • The Three Wise Monkeys have a dream after smoking a pipe. They imagine all smoking implements anthropomorphizing and menacing the doped smokers.

5028. The Pique Poquette of Paris *(Inspector)* 24 Aug. 1966; *p.c.:* Mirisch/Geoffrey/DFE for UA; *dir:* George Singer; *story:* John W. Dunn; *anim:* Warren Batchelder, George Grandpré, Bob Matz, Norm McCabe, Manny Perez; *sets:* T.M. Yakutis; *ed:* Eugene Marks; *voices:* Pat Harrington Jr., Paul Frees, Joan Gerber; *mus:* Walter Greene; *theme tune:* Henry Mancini; *prod sup:* Bill Orcutt; *col:* DeLuxe. *sd:* RCA. 6 min. • The Inspector has to apprehend a notorious pick-pocket, "Spider Pierre."

5029. The Pirate 1957; *p.c.:* UPA for Coca-Cola Co; *col:* Tech. *sd:* RCA. • Commercial for Coca-Cola.

5030. The Pirate Ship *(Paul Terry-Toons)* 30 Apr. 1933; *p.c.:* Moser & Terry for Educational/Fox; *dir:* Frank Moser, Paul Terry; *mus:* Philip A. Scheib; *b&w. sd:* WE. 6 min. • Singing and dancing pirates capture a girl, resulting in the Air Force coming after the cutthroats in full force. The heroine is scooped up in a plane while the ship's rats escape the sinking vessel on doughnut life preservers. Caricature of Jimmy Durante.

5031. Pirates Bold *(Aesop's Film Fable)* 18 July 1926; *p.c.:* Fables Pictures Inc for Pathé; *dir:* Paul Terry; *b&w. sil.* 10 min. • Milton Mouse is out boating with his sweetie when some feline pirates arrive and kidnap the fair maiden. Our hero pursues the buccaneers on the back of a fish, jumps the corsair, single-handedly defeats the crew and rescues his lady love.

5032. Pirate's Gold *(Heckle & Jeckle)* Jan. 1957 (© 1955); *p.c.:* TT for Fox; *dir:* Eddie Donnelly; *story/voices:* Tom Morrison; *anim:* Jim Tyer; *sets:* Art Bartsch; *mus:* Philip A. Scheib; *ph:* Douglas Moye; *col:* Tech. *sd:* RCA. 6 min. • The magpies find themselves aboard Captain Kidd's galleon where they go in search of treasure but the Tax Man gets the final laugh.

5033. Pistol Packin' Woodpecker *(Woody Woodpecker)* Walter Lantz prods for Univ; *dir:* Paul J. Smith; *story:* Dalton Sandifer; *anim:* Robert Bentley, Les Kline, Don Patterson, La Verne Harding; *sets:* Art Landy, Raymond Jacobs; *voices:* Dal McKennon, Grace Stafford; *mus:* Clarence Wheeler; *prod mgr:* William E. Garity; *col:* Tech. *sd:* RCA. 6 min. • Woody assists the posse in finding a bandit who later escapes the confines of prison to wreak his revenge on the hapless bird.

5034. Pitchin' Woo at the Zoo *(Popeye)* 1 Sept. 1944; *p.c.:* Famous for Para; *dir:* I. Sparber; *story:* Bill Turner, Jack Ward; *anim:* Nick Tafuri, Tom Golden; *voices:* Jack Mercer, Mae Questel, Jackson Beck; *mus:* Sammy Timberg; *ph:* Leonard McCormick; *prod mgr:* Sam Buchwald; *b&w. sd:* RCA. 6 min. Tech reissue: 3 Oct. 1952. • Popeye and Olive's visit to the Zoo is marred by Zookeeper Bluto's amorous advances towards Olive.

5035. Pixie Land *(Oswald)* 12 Sept. 1938; *p.c.:* Walter Lantz prods for Univ; *dir:* Elmer Perkins; *story:* Victor McLeod; *anim:* Merle Gilson; *sets:* Edgar Keichle; *voices:* Margaret McKay, Danny Webb; *mus:* Frank Marsales; *b&w. sd:* WE. 7 min. • Professor Slaphappy experiments by spraying a flea with reducing liquid. The flea grows to gigantic proportions and terrorizes Pixie Land.

5036. Pixie Panic *(Musical Miniatures)* Mar. 1948; *p.c.:* Walter Lantz prods for UA; *dir:* Dick Lundy; *story:* Ben Hardaway, Jack Cosgriff; *anim:* (La)Verne Harding, Fred Moore; *sets:* Fred Brunish; *mus:* Darrell Calker; *prod mgr:* William E. Garity; *col:* Tech. *sd:* RCA. 6¹/₂ min. • Set to Rossini's *The Thieving Magpie*, the pixie's picnic has a bee and a box of pepper causing havoc. An avalanche of pumpkins calls a halt to the proceedings.

5037. A Pizza Tweety-Pie *(Looney Tunes)* 22 Feb. 1958; *p.c.:* WB; *dir:* Friz Freleng; *story:* Warren Foster; *anim:* Virgil Ross, Gerry Chiniquy, Art Davis; *lay:* Hawley Pratt; *back:* Tom O'Loughlin; *ed:* Treg Brown; *voices:* Mel Blanc, June Foray; *mus:* Milt Franklyn; *col:* Tech. *sd:* Vit. 7 min. • Tweety has trouble from an Italian Sylvester while holidaying in Venice.

5038. Pizzicato Pussycat *(Merrie Melodies)* 1 Jan. 1955; *p.c.:* WB; *dir:* I. Freleng; *story:* Warren Foster; *anim:* Virgil Ross, Manuel Perez; *lay:* Hawley Pratt; *back:* Richard H. Thomas; *ed:* Treg Brown; *voices:* Norman Nesbitt, Mel Blanc, Marian Richman; *mus:* Milt Franklyn; *prod mgr:* John W. Burton; *prod:* Edward Selzer; *col:* Tech. *sd:* Vit. 7 min. • A piano playing mouse is captured by a cat who hides him in the piano. His master thinks the cat is playing the piano and arranges for him to play a concert at Carnegie Hall.

5039. Plane Crazy *(Mickey Mouse)* 15 May 1928; *p.c.:* Walter E. Disney for Colum; *dir/anim:* Ub Iwerks; *i&p:* Hazel Sewell, Lillian Disney, Edna Disney; *mus:* Carl W. Stalling; *ph:* Mike Marcus; *b&w. sil.* 7 min. Reissued with sound (PCP): 9 Aug. 1928. • Mickey takes Minnie on a hazardous airplane ride. Animated entirely by Iwerks in three weeks.

5040. Plane Daffy *(Looney Tunes)* 16 Sept. 1944; *p.c.:* WB; *dir:* Frank Tashlin; *story:* Warren Foster; *anim:* Cal Dalton; *back:* Richard H. Thomas; *ed:* Treg Brown; *voices:* Mel Blanc, Sara Berner, Robert C. Bruce; *mus:* Carl W. Stalling; *prod mgr:* John W. Burton; *prod:* Edward Selzer; *col:* Tech. *sd:* Vit. 7 min. • Pigeon #13 falls under the spell of Nazi pigeon seductress, Hatta Mari. The carrier pigeon's only woman-hater, Daffy Duck, is called in to deliver an important message. • Caricatures of Adolf Hitler, Hermann Goering and Joseph Goebbels.

5041. Plane Dippy *(Looney Tunes)* 21 Dec. 1935; *p.c.:* Leon Schlesinger prods for WB; *dir:* Fred Avery; *story:* Robert Clampett; *anim:* Sid Sutherland, Virgil Ross; *voices:* Joe Dougherty, Bernice Hansel; *mus:* Bernard Brown; b&w. *sd:* Vit. 8 min. • Porky has an unscheduled ride in a radio-controlled airplane.

5042. Plane Dumb *(Tom & Jerry)* 25 June 1932; *p.c.:* Van Beuren for RKO; *dir:* John Foster, George Rufle; *mus:* Gene Rodemich; b&w. *sd:* RCA. 7 min. • Tom and Jerry attempt to land their plane in Africa but crash and are left adrift in the sea.

5043. Plane Goofy *(Terry-Toon)* 24 Nov. 1940; *p.c.:* TT for Fox; *dir:* Eddie Donnelly; *story:* John Foster; *voice:* Thomas Morrison; *mus:* Philip A. Scheib; *col:* Tech. *sd:* RCA. 7 min. • A salesman sells Farmer Al Falfa an airplane. He soon has a hectic flight.

5044. Planet Mouseola *(Noveltoon)* Sept. 1960; *p.c.:* Para Cartoons; *dir:* Seymour Kneitel; *story:* Jack Mercer; *voices:* Jack Mercer; *mus:* Winston Sharples; *ph:* Leonard McCormick; *prod mgr:* Abe Goodman; *col:* Tech. *sd:* RCA. 6 min. • A mouse disguises himself as an outer-space rodent to ask the cat to come to Planet Mouseola and rule over its ten million mouse population.

5045. The Plant *(Go-Go Toon)* Aug. 1967; *p.c.:* Para Cartoons; *ex prod:* Shamus Culhane; *mus:* Winston Sharples; *prod sup:* Harold Robins, Burt Hanft; *col:* Tech. *sd:* RCA. 6 min • No story available.

5046. Plastered in Paris *(Inspector)* 5 Apr. 1966; *p.c.:* Mirisch/Geoffrey/DFE; *dir:* Gerry Chiniquy; *story:* John W. Dunn; *anim:* Norm McCabe, Manny Perez, Don Williams, Warren Batchelder, Ted Bonnicksen; *sets:* T.M. Yakutis; *ed:* Lee Gunther; *voices:* Pat Harrington Jr., Paul Frees; *mus:* William Lava; *theme tune:* Henry Mancini; *prod mgr:* Bill Orcutt; *col:* DeLuxe. *sd:* RCA. 6 min. • The Inspector enlists the aid of a lucky rabbit's foot to help him capture "Hassan the Assasin."

5047. The Plastics Inventor *(Donald Duck)* 1 Sept. 1944; *p.c.:* Walt Disney prods for RKO; *dir:* Jack King; *asst dir:* Joel Greenhalgh; *story:* Jack Hannah, Dick Shaw, Carl Barks; *anim:* Don Towsley, Paul Allen, Bill Justice, Ed Aardal, Judge Whitaker, Lee Morehouse, Harvey Toombs; *fx:* Brad Case, Josh Meador; *lay:* Ernest Nordli; *back:* Merle Cox; *voices:* Charles Seel, Dehner Forkum, Clarence Nash; *mus:* Oliver Wallace; *col:* Tech. *sd:* RCA. 7 min. • Donald constructs an airplane out of a home-made plastic that disintegrates when wet.

5048. Play Ball *(Aesop's Sound Fable)* 24 May 1931; *p.c.:* Van Beuren for RKO/Pathé; *dir:* John Foster, Mannie Davis; *mus:* Gene Rodemich; b&w. *sd:* RCA. 10 min. • Monkeys vs The Jungleland All Stars in a frantic baseball game.

5049. Play Ball *(Paul Terry-Toon)* 6 Mar. 1932; *p.c.:* Moser & Terry for Educational/Fox; *dir:* Frank Moser, Paul Terry; *mus:* Philip A. Scheib; b&w. *sd:* WE. 6 min. • No story available.

5050. Play Ball *(Terry-Toon)* 11 June 1937; *p.c.:* TT for Educational/Fox; *dir:* Frank Moser, Paul Terry; *mus:* Philip A. Scheib; b&w. *sd:* WE. 6 min. • Kiko the kangaroo is a pitcher for The Jungle Giants baseball team.

5051. Play Ball *(Willie Whopper)* 14 Oct. 1933; *p.c.:* Celebrity prods for MGM; *prod/dir:* Ub Iwerks; *anim:* Grim Natwick, Berny Wolf; b&w. *sd:* PCP. 7 min. • Willie tells a story of how he played baseball in the World Series with Babe Ruth.

5052. Play Safe *(Color Classic)* 16 Oct. 1936; *p.c.:* The Fleischer Studio for Para; *prod:* Max Fleischer; *dir:* Dave Fleischer; *anim:* David Tendlar, Eli Brucker; *character des:* David Tendlar; *voice:* Mae Questel; *music/songs:* Sammy Timberg, Vee Lawnhurst, Tot Seymour; *col:* Tech-2. *sd:* WE. 7 min. • A small boy falls from a train and dreams he's the railroad driver, taking an express for a spin.

5053. Playful Pan *(Silly Symphony)* 16 Dec. 1930; *p.c.:* Walt Disney prods for Colum; *dir:* Burton F. Gillett; *anim:* Johnny Cannon, Les Clark, Jack Cutting, Gilles de Tremaudan, Norman Ferguson, David D. Hand, Wilfred Jackson, Jack King, Richard Lundy, Tom Palmer, Ben Sharpsteen; *mus:* Bert Lewis; *ph:* William Cottrell; *col:* tinted. *sd:* PCP. 7 min. • Pan plays his magic pipes, bringing all flowers and trees to life. Clouds cause lightning and a forest fire which Pan lures into water.

5054. The Playful Pelican *(Cartune)* 8 Oct. 1948; *p.c.:* Walter Lantz prods for UA; *dir:* Dick Lundy; *story:* Ben Hardaway, Jack Cosgriff; *anim:* Ed Love, Ken O'Brien, (La)Verne Harding, Les Kline, Pat Matthews, Fred Moore, Sid Pillet; *sets:* Fred Brunish; *voice:* Walter Tetley; *prod mgr:* William

E. Garity; *col:* Tech. *sd:* RCA. 6 min. • A baby pelican is hatched aboard Andy Panda's ship and hungrily gulps a frog and things start jumping.

5055. The Playful Pest *(Phantasy)* 3 Dec. 1943; *p.c.:* Colum; *prod:* Dave Fleischer; *dir:* Paul Sommer; *story:* Sam Cobean; *lay:* Clark Watson; *voices:* Dick Nelson; *mus:* Eddie Kilfeather; *prod mgr:* Albert Spar; b&w. *sd:* RCA. 6½ min. • An exterminator rids a house of all but one termite.

5056. Playful Pluto *(Mickey Mouse)* 3 Mar. 1934; *p.c.:* Walt Disney prods for UA; *dir:* Burton F. Gillett; *story:* Webb Smith; *anim:* Arthur Babbitt, Johnny Cannon, Jack Cutting, Norman Ferguson, Clyde Geronimi, Jack Kinney, Richard Lundy, Fred Moore, Ben Sharpsteen, Robert Wickersham; *sets:* Carlos Manriquez; *voices:* Walt Disney, Lee Millar; *mus:* Frank E. Churchill; b&w. *sd:* RCA. 8 min. • Pluto makes a nuisance of himself when helping Mickey spring clean. They battle with a hose, fire hydrant and flypaper.

5057. The Playful Polar Bears *(Color Classic)* 28 Oct. 1938; *p.c.:* The Fleischer Studio for Para; *prod:* Max Fleischer; *dir:* Dave Fleischer; *anim:* Myron Waldman, Graham Place, Lillian Friedman; *sets:* Robert Little; *mus:* Sammy Timberg; *col:* Tech. *sd:* WE. 7 min. • Baby polar bear and Mama are chased by hunters.

5058. The Playful Pup *(Oswald)* 12 July 1937; *p.c.:* Univ; *prod/dir:* Walter Lantz; *story:* Walter Lantz, Victor McLeod; *anim:* Manuel Moreno, Fred Kopietz, Lester Kline; *mus:* James Dietrich; b&w. *sd:* RCA. 7 min. • Dorkin the dachshund wants to play with a ball that Elmer the Great Dane has monopolized all day. When night falls, he goes to get it, waking the entire house in doing so.

5059. Playful Puss *(Little Roquefort)* May 1953; *p.c.:* TT for Fox; *dir:* Mannie Davis; *story:* Tom Morrison; *sets:* Art Bartsch; *mus:* Philip A. Scheib; *ph:* Douglas Moye; *col:* Tech. *sd:* RCA. 6 min. • Percy Puss' protégé takes a liking to Roquefort and they join forces against his luckless feline tutor.

5060. Playing Politics *(Scrappy)* 8 July 1936; *p.c.:* Charles Mintz prods for Colum; *story:* Allen Rose; *anim:* Harry Love; *mus:* Joe de Nat; *prod mgr:* James Bronis; b&w. *sd:* RCA. 6 min. • Scrappy promotes Oopy to becoming a presidential candidate. A rival party sabotages their campaign and dares them to smoke a cigar ... which they do and get sick.

5061. Playing the Pied Piper *(Fable)* 8 Aug. 1941; *p.c.:* Colum; *dir:* Lou Lilly; *lay:* Clark Watson; *ed:* Ed Moore; *voices:* Mel Blanc; *mus:* Eddie Kilfeather; *ph:* Otto Reimer; *prod mgr:* George Winkler; b&w. *sd:* RCA. 6 min. • A dopey cat tries to lure a wise-cracking smart mouse into his clutches with music.

5062. Please Go 'Way and Let Me Sleep *(Screen Songs)* 10 Jan. 1931; *p.c.:* The Fleischer Studio for Para; *prod:* Max Fleischer; *sup:* Dave Fleischer; *dir/story/anim:* Jimmie Culhane, Rudy Zamora, Al Eugster; *mus:* Art Turkisher; b&w. *sd:* WE. 6 min. • Depicting various methods for early morning alarms.

5063. Please Keep Me in Your Dreams *(Screen Songs)* 28 May 1937; *p.c.:* The Fleischer Studio for Para; *prod:* Max Fleischer; *dir:* Dave Fleischer; *anim:* Roland Crandall; *voice:* Gus Wickie; *mus:* Henry King and his orchestra; b&w. *sd:* WE. 8 min. • "Snoop Reel" showing a special car for backseat drivers and other news items.

5064. Pleased to Eat You *(Noveltoon)* 21 July 1950; *p.c.:* Famous for Para; *dir:* I. Sparber; *story:* Larz Bourne; *anim:* Myron Waldman, William B. Pattingill; *sets:* Anton Loeb; *mus:* Winston Sharples; *ph:* Leonard McCormick; *prod mgr:* Sam Buchwald; *col:* Tech. *sd:* RCA. 6 min. • A hungry lion responds to a radio broadcast asking for volunteers for a zoo. Leo rebels when given vitamin pills but finally eats his fill.

5065. Pleased to Meet Char! *(Popeye)* 22 Mar. 1935; *p.c.:* The Fleischer Studio for Para; *prod:* Max Fleischer; *dir:* Dave Fleischer; *anim:* Willard Bowsky, Harold Walker; *voices:* Jack Mercer, Mae Questel, Charles Carver; *mus:* Sammy Timberg; b&w. *sd:* WE. 6 min. • Popeye and Bluto are given the option by Olive that whoever performs the best trick can stay. Their antics soon turn into a free-for-all.

5066. Plenty Below Zero *(Fox & Crow)* 14 May 1943; *p.c.:* Colum; *prod:* Dave Fleischer; *dir:* Bob Wickersham; *story:* Leo Salkin; *anim:* Howard Swift; *lay:* Clark Watson; *ed:* Edward Moore; *voices:* Frank Graham, Dick Nelson; *mus:* Eddie Klifeather; *prod mgr:* Albert Spar; *col:* Tech. *sd:* RCA. 7½ min. • The Fox sets out for a skiing picnic and the Crow tries to relieve him of his lunch basket.

5067. Plenty of Money and You *(Merrie Melodies)* 31 July 1937; *p.c.:* Leon Schlesinger prods for WB; *dir:* I. Freleng; *story:* Robert Clampett; *anim:* Cal Dalton, Phil Monroe; *lay:* Griff Jay; *back:* Arthur Loomer; *ed:* Tregoweth E. Brown; *voices:* Mel Blanc, Dave Weber; *mus:* Carl W. Stalling; *prod sup:* Henry Binder, Raymond G. Katz; *col:* Tech. *sd:* Vit. 7 min. • A Weasel captures a baby ostrich and a previously swallowed firecracker helps save the little fellow.

5068. Plop Goes the Weasel *(Looney Tunes)* 22 Aug. 1953; *p.c.:* WB; *dir:* Robert McKimson; *story:* Tedd Pierce; *anim:* Herman Cohen, Rod Scribner, Phil de Lara, Charles McKimson; *lay:* Robert Givens; *back:* Richard H. Thomas; *ed:* Treg Brown; *voices:* Mel Blanc; *mus:* Carl Stalling; *prod mgr:* John W. Burton; *prod:* Edward Selzer; *col:* Tech. *sd:* Vit. 7 min. • To add some spice to his life, Foggy lets the chicks out of the coop to give the guard dog the run-around. A weasel adds to the confusion.

5069. The Plot Sickens *(Modern Madcap)* Dec. 1961; *p.c.:* Para Cartoons; *dir:* Seymour Kneitel; *story:* Irving Spector; *anim:* Irving Spector, John Gentilella, Larry Silverman; *sets:* Robert Owen; *voices:* Eddie Lawrence, Corinne Orr; *mus:* Winston Sharples; *ph:* Leonard McCormick; *prod mgr:* Abe Goodman; *col:* Tech. *sd:* RCA. 6 min. • A henpecked husband tries to dispose of his awful, TV-watching wife ... with little luck.

5070. The Plow Boy *(Mickey Mouse)* 28 June 1929; *p.c.:* Walter E. Disney for Colum; *dir:* Walt Disney; *anim:* Ub Iwerks, Burton F. Gillett, Jack King, Les Clark, Ben Sharpsteen; *character des:* Albert Hurter; *mus:* Carl W. Stalling; b&w. *sd:* PCP. 7 min. • Mickey shows Minnie how to milk a cow. Horace Horsecollar plays a trick on him and Mickey gets his revenge with the aid of a bee. Production completed in twenty-nine days.

5071. The Plow Boy's Revenge *(Aesop's Film Fable)* 13 Jan. 1927; *p.c.:* Fables Pictures Inc for Pathé; *dir:* Paul Terry; b&w. *sil.* 10 min. • Burlesque on melodramas with Milton Mouse arriving in time to rescue the goldfish that has been strapped to a log by the villainous cat.

5072. The Plumber *(Go-Go Toon)* May 1967; *dir:* Shamus Culhane; *story:* Cliff Roberts; *anim:* Howard Beckerman; *sets:* Cliff Roberts, Gil Miret, Dave Ubinas; *mus:* Winston Sharples; *prod sup:* Harold Robins, Burt Hanft; *col:* Tech. *sd:* RCA. 6 min. • A plumber receives musical accolades when playing the heating system in a building. He soon reaches Carnegie Hall, playing various plumbing items.

5073. The Plumber *(Oswald)* 20 Jan. 1933 *p.c.:* Univ; *dir:* Walter Lantz, "Bill" Nolan; *anim:* Ray Abrams, Fred Avery, "Bill"Weber, Jack Carr, Don Williams; *mus:* James Dietrich; b&w. *sd:* WE. 7 min. • Oswald's nephew floods the place. Sardines go swimming and even a swordfish joins in the fray.

5074. Plumber of Seville *(Hercules)* 11 Mar. 1957; *p.c.:* Walter Lantz prods for Univ; *dir:* Alex Lovy; *story:* Dick Kinney; *anim:* Ray Abrams, La Verne Harding; *sets:* Raymond Jacobs, Art Landy; *voice:* Bob Johnson; *mus:* Eugene Poddany; *prod mgr:* William E. Garity; *col:* Tech. *sd:* RCA. 6 min. • A leak is discovered in Carnegie Hall and a plumber is called, creating havoc throughout the concert.

5075. Plumber's Helpers *(Terry Bears)* May 1953; *p.c.:* TT for Fox; *dir:* Connie Rasinski; *story:* Tom Morrison; *anim:* Jim Tyer; *sets:* Art Bartsch; *voices:* Douglas Moye, Tom Morrison, Philip A. Scheib; *mus:* Philip A. Scheib; *ph:* Douglas Moye; *col:* Tech. *sd:* RCA. 6 min. • The cubs help Papa mend a radiator and cause the house to flood.

5076. A Plumber's Life *(Aesop's Film Fable)* 27 June 1926; *p.c.:* Fables Pictures Inc for Pathé; *dir:* Paul Terry; b&w. *sil.* 10 min. • Farmer Al Falfa calls a plumber to fix his burst water pipe.

5077. Plumbing Is a "Pipe" *(Popeye)* 17 June 1938; *p.c.:* The Fleischer Studio for Para; *prod:* Max Fleischer; *dir:* Dave Fleischer; *anim:* Willard Bowsky, Orestes Calpini; *voices:* Jack Mercer, Margie Hines, Louis Fleischer; *mus:* Sammy Timberg; b&w. *sd:* WE. 7 min. • Popeye arrives to help fix a burst pipe in Olive's house.

5078. Pluto and the Armadillo *(Mickey Mouse)* 19 Feb. 1943; *p.c.:* Walt Disney prods for RKO; *dir:* Clyde Geronimi; *asst dir:* Ralph Chadwick; *story:* Jack Miller, Homer Brightman; *anim:* Les Clark, John Lounsbery, George Nicholas, Charles A. Nichols, Norman Tate, Marvin Woodward; *fx:* George Rowley; *lay:* Charles Philippi; *voices:* Fred Shields, Walt Disney; *mus:* Paul J. Smith; *col:* Tech. *sd:* RCA. 7 min. • While holidaying in Brazil, Pluto mistakes an armadillo for his lost beach ball.

5079. Pluto and the Gopher *(Pluto)* 10 Feb. 1950; *p.c.:* Walt Disney prods for RKO; *dir:* Charles Nichols; *story:* Dick Kinney, Milt Schaffer; *anim:* George Kreisl, George Nicholas, Hugh Fraser, Phil Duncan; *fx:* Josh Meador, Jack Boyd; *lay:* Karl Karpé; *back:* Art Landy; *voices:* Leone Le Doux, James MacDonald; *mus:* Oliver Wallace; *col:* Tech. *sd:* RCA. 6 min. • Pluto tries to rid Minnie's garden of a gopher who has, unwittingly, been transported indoors.

5080. Pluto at the Zoo *(Pluto)* 20 Nov. 1942; *p.c.:* Walt Disney prods for RKO; *dir:* Clyde Geronimi; *asst dir:* Ralph Chadwick; *anim:* Hugh Fraser, John Lounsbery, John Lounsbery, Charles A. Nichols, George Nicholas, Norman Tate; *lay:* Thor Putnam; *voice:* J. Dehner Forkum; *mus:* Oliver Wallace; *col:* Tech. *sd:* RCA. 7 min. • When passing a zoo, Pluto spies a sumptuous bone ... in the lion's cage.

5081. Pluto Junior *(Pluto)* 28 Feb. 1942; *p.c.:* Walt Disney prods for RKO; *dir:* Clyde Geronimi; *asst dir:* Donald A. Duckwall; *storyboard:* Ralph Wright; *anim:* George Goepper, Eric Gurney, Emery Hawkins, George Nicholas, Charles A. Nichols, Morey Reden, Norman Tate, Don Towsley; *fx:* Jack Boyd, Andrew Engman, Harry Hamsel, Joshua Meador, Arthur W. Palmer, Ed Parks, George Rowley, Reuben Timmens, Don Tobin; *lay:* Bruce Bushman; *voices:* Lee Millar; *mus:* Leigh Harline; *col:* Tech. *sd:* RCA. 7 min. • Junior disturbs Pluto's slumber with a ball and a balloon. He tracks a caterpillar and ends up being suspended from a clothesline.

5082. Plutopia *(Pluto)* 20 Apr. 1951; *p.c.:* Walt Disney prods for RKO; *dir:* Charles Nichols; *story:* Ralph Wright, Al Bertino; *anim:* Norman Ferguson, George Nicholas, Fred Moore, Les Clark, John Reed, Marvin Woodward; *fx:* Jack Boyd, Dan MacManus; *lay:* Lance Nolley; *back:* Ray Huffine; *voices:* Jim Backus, James MacDonald; *mus:* Joseph S. Dubin; *col:* Tech. *sd:* RCA. 7 min. • Pluto dreams of a utopian life with Milton the cat as his servant providing bones and steak at the slightest provocation.

5083. Pluto's Blue Note *(Pluto)* 26 Dec. 1947; *p.c.:* Walt Disney prods for RKO; *dir:* Charles Nichols; *story:* Milt Schaffer, Jack Huber; *anim:* Jerry Hathcock, George Kreisl, George Nicholas, Marvin Woodward, Bob Youngquist; *fx:* Dan MacManus, Jack Boyd; *lay:* Karl Karpé; *back:* Art Landy; *voices:* John Woodbury, James MacDonald, Billy Bletcher; *mus:* Oliver Wallace, Charles Wolcott; *col:* Tech. *sd:* RCA. 7 min. • Pluto's singing upsets everybody. He enters a music shop and finds he can sing like Sinatra if he puts the tip of his tail on a revolving record.

5084. Pluto's Christmas Tree *(Pluto)* 21 Nov. 1952; *p.c.:* Walt Disney prods for RKO; *dir:* Jack Hannah; *story:* Bill Berg, Milt Schaffer; *anim:* George Kreisl, Fred Moore, Bill Justice, Volus Jones; *fx:* George Rowley, Blaine Gibson, Dan MacManus; *lay:* Yale Gracey; *back:* Thelma Witmer; *voices:* James MacDonald, Helen Seibert, Norma Swank, Marjorie Wilcox, Clarence Nash; *mus:* Joseph S. Dubin; *col:* Tech. *sd:* RCA. 7 min. • Pluto tries to oust the chipmunks from Mickey's Christmas tree.

5085. Pluto's Dream House *(Mickey Mouse)* 30 Aug. 1940; *p.c.:* Walt Disney prods for RKO; *dir:* Clyde Geronimi; *asst dir:* Donald A. Duckwall; *story:* Samuel Armstrong, Frank Tashlin; *anim:* Rex Cox, Andrew Engman, Volus Jones, Richard Lundy, Kenneth Muse, George Nicholas, Claude Smith, Marvin Woodward; *lay:* James Carmichael; *voices:* Billy Mitchell, Elvia Allman, Sharley Simpson, Hyman Averback, Walt Disney; *mus:* Leigh Harline; *col:* Tech. *sd:* RCA. 7 min. • Mickey and Pluto unearth a magic lamp who helps build Pluto a new dog house.

5086. Pluto's Fledgeling *(Pluto)* 10 Sept. 1948; *p.c.:* Walt Disney prods for RKO; *dir:* Charles A. Nichols; *story:* Phil Duncan, George Kreisl, George Nicholas, Jerry Hathcock, Marvin Woodward; *fx:* Jack Boyd; *lay:* Karl Karpé; *back:* Brice Mack; *voice:* James MacDonald; *mus:* Oliver Wallace; *col:* Tech. *sd:* RCA. 7 min. • Pluto attempts to teach a baby bird to fly.

5087. Pluto's Heart Throb *(Pluto)* 6 Jan. 1950; *p.c.:* Walt Disney prods for RKO; *dir:* Charles Nichols; *story:* Roy Williams; *anim:* Hugh Fraser, George Kreisl, George Nicholas, Phil Duncan; *fx:* Jack Boyd; *lay:* Karl Karpé; *back:* Art Landy; *voices:* James MacDonald; *mus:* Oliver Wallace; *col:* Tech. *sd:* RCA. 6 min. • Pluto's affections for Dinah are spurned until he has the opportunity of rescuing her from a bulldog's unwanted advances.

5088. Pluto's House Warming *(Pluto)* 3 Dec. 1946; *p.c.:* Walt Disney prods for RKO; *dir:* Charles Nichols; *asst dir:* Bob North; *story:* Eric

Gurney, Bill de la Torre; *anim:* George Nicholas, Jerry Hathcock, Marvin Woodward, George Kreisl, Harry Holt, Murray McClelland, Bob Youngquist; *fx:* Blaine Gibson, Jack Boyd, Andy Engman; *lay:* Karl Karpé; *back:* Maurice Greenberg; *voices:* James MacDonald; *mus:* Oliver Wallace; *col:* Tech. *sd:* RCA. 7 min. • Pluto's luxurious new doghouse is inhabited by a turtle. He rids himself of the pest only to discover that a ferocious bulldog has taken over.

5089. Pluto's Judgement Day (*Mickey Mouse*) 31 Aug. 1935; *p.c.:* Walt Disney prods for UA; *dir:* David D. Hand; *story:* William Cottrell, Joe Grant; *anim:* Robert W. Carlson, Clyde Geronimi, Jack Hannah, Hardie Gramatky, Richard Lundy, Hamilton S. Luske, Fred Moore, William O. Roberts, Bob Wickersham; *voices:* Don Brodie, Lee Millar, Pinto Colvig, William E. Sheets, The Rhythmettes, Clarence Nash, Walt Disney; *mus:* Frank E. Churchill, Leigh Harline; *col:* Tech. *sd:* RCA. 9 min. • Pluto has a nightmare where he is on trial by cats for chasing a kitten.

5090. Pluto's Kid Brother (*Pluto*) 12 Apr. 1945; *p.c.:* Walt Disney prods for RKO; *dir:* Charles Nichols; *asst dir:* Bob North; *story:* Harry Reeves, Jesse Marsh; *anim:* George Nicholas, Jerry Hathcock, Robert Youngquist, Ward Kimball, George Kreisl, John Lounsbery, Marvin Woodward; *fx:* Jack Boyd, Andy Engman; *lay:* Karl Karpé; *back:* Nino Carbe; *voice:* James MacDonald; *mus:* Oliver Wallace; *col:* Tech. *sd:* RCA. 7 min. • K.B. has complications with a rooster, a cat and a bulldog when pilfering weiners.

5091. Pluto's Party (*Mickey Mouse*) 19 Sept. 1952; *p.c.:* Walt Disney prods for RKO; *dir:* Milt Schaffer, Charles Nichols; *story:* Bill Berg, Leo Salkin; *anim:* Charles Nichols, Fred Moore, Norm Ferguson, Marvin Woodward, George Kreisl, George Nicholas, Ken Walker; *fx:* Blaine Gibson, Dan MacManus; *lay:* Lance Nolley; *back:* Thelma Witmer; *voice:* James MacDonald; *mus:* Oliver Wallace; *col:* Tech. *sd:* RCA. 6 min. • Pluto's birthday party guests give him a rough time, eat all the cake and rapidly depart ... but Mickey has saved him at least one piece of birthday cake. • Completed by Charles Nichols after production ran way over budget.

5092. Pluto's Playmate (*Pluto*) 24 Jan. 1941; *p.c.:* Walt Disney prods for RKO; *dir* Norman Ferguson; *asst dir:* Larry Lansburgh; *story:* Earl Hurd; *anim:* Basil Davidovich, George de Beeson, Ed Dunn, Norman Ferguson, Jerry Hathcock, Joy, Van Kaufman, John Lounsbery, Don Patterson, Morey Reden, Don Schloat, Grant Simmons, Sandy Strother, Don Tobin, Waltz, Bard Wiggenhorn, James Will, Verne Witt, Cornett Wood; *fx:* Edwin Aardal, Jack Boyd, Jerome Brown, Andrew Engman, Art Fitzpatrick, Jack Huber, Paul B. Kossoff, Frank Onaitis, Ed Parks, George Rowley; *lay:* Ernest Nordli; *mus:* Paul J. Smith; *col:* Tech. *sd:* RCA. 7 min. • While playing by the seashore, a baby seal steals Pluto's beachball. In retrieving it, Pluto is nearly drowned by an octopus but the seal comes to his rescue.

5093. Pluto's Purchase (*Pluto*) 9 July 1947; *p.c.:* Walt Disney prods for RKO; *dir:* Charles Nichols; *asst dir:* Jack Bruner; *story:* Eric Gurney, Bill de la Torre; *anim:* George Nicholas, George Kreisl, Robert Youngquist, Jerry Hathcock; *fx:* Dan MacManus; *lay:* Karl Karpé; *back:* Ralph Hulett; *voice:* James MacDonald; *mus:* Oliver Wallace; *col:* Tech. *sd:* RCA. 6 min. • While transporting a salami home to Mickey, Pluto is accosted by Butch the bulldog.

5094. Pluto's Quinpuplets (*Pluto the Pup*) 26 Nov. 1937; *p.c.:* Walt Disney prods for RKO; *dir:* Ben Sharpsteen; *story:* Earl Hurd; *anim:* James H. Culhane, Gilles de Tremaudan, Norman Ferguson, Nick George, Charles A. Nichols, William O. Roberts, Fred Spencer, Robert Wickersham; *voice:* Pinto Colvig; *mus:* Paul J. Smith; *col:* Tech. *sd:* RCA. 9 min. • Pluto is left in charge of his five pups while Mrs. Pluto pursues some weiners.

5095. Pluto's Surprise Package (*Pluto*) 4 Apr. 1949; *p.c.:* Walt Disney prods for RKO; *dir:* Charles Nichols; *story:* Milt Schaffer, Eric Gurney; *anim:* George Nicholas, Hugh Fraser, George Kreisl, Phil Duncan, Hicks Lokey, Jim MacManus; *fx:* George Rowley; *lay:* Karl Karpé; *back:* Brice Mack; *voice:* James MacDonald; *mus:* Oliver Wallace; *col:* Tech. *sd:* RCA. 7 min. • Pluto tries to deliver a wandering baby turtle.

5096. Pluto's Sweater (*Pluto*) 29 Apr. 1949; *p.c.:* Walt Disney prods for RKO; *dir:* Charles Nichols; *story:* Eric Gurney, Milt Schaffer; *anim:* Phil Duncan, George Nicholas, Hugh Fraser, George Kreisl; *fx:* Dan MacManus; *lay:* Karl Karpé; *back:* Brice Mack; *voice:* Leone Le Doux, James MacDonald; *mus:* Oliver Wallace; *col:* Tech. *sd:* 6½ min. • Much to Figaro's amusement, Pluto resents wearing the sweater that Minnie has knitted him.

5097. Plywood Panic (*Maw & Paw*) 28 Sept. 1953; *p.c.:* Walter Lantz prods for Univ; *dir:* Paul J. Smith; *story:* Homer Brightman; *anim:* La Verne Harding, Gil Turner, Robert Bentley; *sets:* Raymond Jacobs, Art Landy; *voices:* Dallas McKennon, Grace Stafford; *mus:* Clarence Wheeler; *technical:* Albert Clettis Glenn; *prod mgr:* William E. Garity; *col:* Tech. *sd:* RCA. 6 min. • Maw and Paw win a do-it-yourself pre-fabricated house which they have to assemble themselves. • Possibly intended to be in 3-D but the process was abandoned in mid-production.

5098. Pocahontas 23 June 1995; *p.c.:* Walt Disney Prods for BV; *dir:* Mike Gabriel, Eric Goldberg; *prod:* James Pentecost; *asso prod:* Baker Bloodworth; *story:* Carl Binder, Susannah Grant, Philip Lazebnik; *addit story development:* Andrew Chapman, Randy Cartwright, Will Finn, Broose Johnson, T. Daniel Hofstedt, Dave Pruiksma, Nik Ranieri, Vincent De Frances, Tom Mazzocco, Don Dougherty, Jorgen Klubien; *based on an idea by* Mike Gabriel; *anim:* "Pocahontas": *anim sup:* Glen Keane; *anim:* Mark Henn, Pres Antonio Romanillos, Randy Haycock, Michael Show, Tom Bancroft, Bob Bryan, Trey Finney, Aaron Blaise, Doug Krohn, Ken Hettig, Brad Kuha, Tom Gately, Gilda Palinginis, John Ripa, Ralf Palmer, Eric Walls; "John Smith": *anim sup:* John Pomeroy; *anim:* Joe Haidar, Richard Bazley, Ron Husband, Dave Kupczyk, David A. Zaboski, Jean Morel, Gary J. Perkovac, Michael Swofford, William Recinos, Bill Waldman, Philip Morris; "Governor Ratcliffe": *anim sup:* Duncan Marjoribanks; *anim:* Doug Frankel, Teresa Martin, Mark Koetsier, Chris Sauve, Ken Boyer; "Meeko": *anim sup:* Nik Ranieri; *anim:* Brian Ferguson, Raul Garcia, Dave Kuhn, Steven P. Gordon; "Powhatan": *anim sup:* Ruben A. Aquino, James Young Jackson, Gregory S. Manwaring; *anim:* Anthony Wayne Michaels, Craig R. Maras; "Thomas": *anim sup:* Ken Duncan; *anim:* Chris Wahl; "Percy/Grandmother Willow & Wiggins": *anim sup:* Chris Buck; "Percy" *anim:* Broose Johnson, Larry White; "Grandma Willow" *anim:* David Burgess; "Wiggins" *anim:* James Lopez, Rejean Bourdages; "Ben & Lon": *anim sup:* T. Daniel Hofstedt; *anim:* Barry Temple, Kent Hammerstrom; "Flit & forest animals": *anim sup:* Dave Pruiksma; "Nakowia": *anim sup:* Anthony De Roas; *anim:* Tim Allen; "Kocoum": *anim sup:* Michael Cedeno; *anim:* Kekata Geefwee Boedoe; "English Settlers/Native Americans": *anim:* D. Anthony Wawtzasak, Sasha Dorogov, Branko Mihanovic, Travis Blaise; *addit anim:* Ellen Woodbury; *scene plan:* Ann Tucker; *anim check sup:* Janet Bruce; *col models sup:* Karen Comella; *i&p snr mgr:* Gretchen Maschmeyer Albrecht; *paint/final check sup:* Hortensia M. Casagran; *digitizing ph mgr:* Joe Jiuliano; *artistic sup:* Florida unit: *lay:* Jeff Dickson; *back:* Robert E. Stanton; *clean-up:* Ruben Procopio; *visual fx:* Jeff Dutton, David Tidgwell; *Florida prod mgr:* Don Walters; *asst anim:* David Hancock, Robert Domingo, Tim Hodge; *key layl/workbook:* Daniel Hu, Karen Keller, Allen Tam, William H. Frake III, Doug Walker, Tom Humber, Mac George, Peter Jielicki; *back:* Allison Belliveau-Proulx, Justin Brandstater, Thomas Cardone, Sunny Apinchapong, Barry Atkinson, Brooks Campbell, Dominick R. Domingo, Debbie Du Bois, Natalie Franscioni-Karp, Mi Kyung Joung-Raynis, Barry Kooser, David McCamley, Serge Michaels, Don Moore, Patricia Palmer-Phillipson, Philip Phillipson, Sean Sullivan, MaryAnn Thomas, Kevin Turcotte, Chuck Vollmer, Thomas Woodington, David Wang Ying Guang, Keith Newton, Dan Cooper; *fx anim:* Dorse Lanpher, Ted C. Kierscey, Ed Coffey, Tom Hush, Garrett Wren, Stephen B. Moore, Kathleen Quaife Hodge, Marlon West, Allen Blyth, James de V. Mansfield, Troy A. Gustafson, Jazno Francoeur; *rough inbet:* James Baker, Jared Beckstrand, Anthony M. Cipriano, Wendie L. Fischer, Michael Genz, Tim George, Grant Hiestand, Jim Hull, Bert Klein, Paul McDonald, Mario J. Menjivar, Gary D. Payne, Kevin M. Smith, Wes Sullivan, Theodore A. Ty, John Webber, Jacqueline M. Sanchez; *clean-up anim:* "Pocahontas": *sup character lead:* Renee Holt-Bird; *key asst:* Merry Kanawyer Clingen, Emily Jiuliano, Steve Lubin, Daniel A. Gracey, Allison Hollen, Jane Bonnet, Christine Lawrence-Finney, Inna Chon; *asst anim:* Teresa Eidenbock, Peggy Tonkonogy, Wendy J. Muir, Beverly Adams, Bill Thinnes, Rachel R. Bibb, Sherrie H. Sinclair, Mary-Jean Repchuk; *break:* Richard D. Rocha, Kenneth M. Kinoshita, Eunice Yu, Pamela Mathues, Jamie Kezlarian Bolio, Scott Claus; *inbet:* Scott Lenze, Regina Conroy, Chang Yei Kim, Yoon Sook Nam, Cynthia Jill French, Robb Pratt, Cyndy Bohonovsky, Tom de Rosier, Byron Howard, Steve Mason, Akemi Horiuchi, Larry R. Flores, John E. Hurst, Gregg E. Azzopardi, Rebecca Wrigley, Judy Grabenstatter; "John Smith": *sup character lead:* Bill Berg; *asso character lead:* Kaaren Lundeen; *key asst:* Jesus Cortes, Brett Newton, Randy Sanchez, Bryan M. Sommer;

asst anim: Lillian A. Chapman, Sean Gallimore, Carl Philip Hall, Kris Heller, Yung Soo Kim, Elyse Pastel, Myung Kang-Teague, David Recinos; *break:* Paulo R. Alvarado, Lon Smart, Ron Westlund, Mary Measures; *inbet:* Joseph Mateo, Robert G. Nigoghossian, John J. Pierro, David Pimentel, Ivan Camilli Rivera, Michael Wiesmeier, Nicole Stranz, Jane Zhao; *"Governor Ratcliffe":* sup *character lead:* Richard Hoppe; *key asst:* Marcia Kimura Dougherty, Eric Pigors, Monica Murdock, Lee Dunkman, Elizabeth Watasin; *break:* James A. Harris, Annette Byrne-Morel; *inbet:* Leland J. Hepler, Denise Meehan, Doug Post; *"Meeko":* sup *character lead:* David Nethery; *asst anim:* Terry Wozniak, Karen A. Hardenbergh, Karen Rosenfield; *break:* Trevor Tamboline; *inbet:* Hugo Soriano, Sean Jimenez; *"Powhatan":* sup *character lead:* Tracy Mark Lee; *key asst:* James Parris; *asst anim:* Dan Daly; *break:* Merritt F. Andrews, Brian Beauchamp, Caroline Clifford, Dominic M. Carola; *inbet:* Marc Smith, Tom Thorspecken, Yer (Za) Vue, Yong-Hong Zhong, Ron Zeitler; *"Thomas":* sup *character lead:* Juliet Duncan, Brett Newton; *asst anim:* Sue Adnopoz; *break:* Diana Coco; *inbet:* Carolyn Froblom Gliona; *"Ben/ Lon & Roy":* sup *character lead:* Gail Frank; *asst anim:* Maria Rosetti, Michael Hazy; *break:* Jim Brummett; *inbet:* Dan Bowman, Greg Fleming, Michael Lester; *"Flit":* sup *character lead:* Stephan Zupkas; *character lead:* Edward Gutierrez; *asst anim:* Mike McKinney, Tony Anselmo; *break:* Andrew Ramos; *inbet:* Bobby Rubio; *"Grandmother Willow":* sup *character lead:* Nancy Kniep; *asst anim:* Wesley Chun, Marsha W.J. Park-Yum; *inbet:* Jim Snider, Chris Sonnenburg, Stevie Wermers; *cgi asst anim:* Michelle Robinson, Henry Sato; *"Percy/ Wiggins":* sup *character lead:* Lori Benson-Noda; *asst anim:* Susan McKinsey Goldberg, Calvin Le Duc; *inbet:* Brian Mainolfi, Kevin Nelson; *"Kocoum/ Nakoma":* sup *character lead:* Marianne Tucker; *asst anim:* Bruce Strock, Boowon Lee, Rick Kohlschmidt; *break:* Daniel Yoontaek Lim; *inbet:* Cathie Karas Wilke; *"Forest animals":* sup *character lead:* Natasha Dukelski Selfridge; *asst anim:* Brian B. McKim, Janet Heerhan Bae, Chan Woo Juno; *inbet:* Jane Misek; *"English Settlers":* sup *character lead:* Dave Suding; *asst anim:* Ray Harris, Carl A. Bell, Marty Schwartz, Susan Y. Sugita; *break:* James McArdle; *"Native Americans":* sup *character lead:* Kathleen M. Bailey; *asst anim:* Kent Holaday; *break:* Jody Kooistra, Michael D'lsa-Hogan; *inbet:* Donnie Long; *"Native Americans/ English Settlers (Florida)":* key *asst anim:* Philip S. Boyd, Sam Ewing, Kellie Lewis, Tom Fish; *break:* Tom La Baff, Antony de Fato, Samantha Lair, Maurilio Morales; *inbet:* Andrew Edward Harkness, Teresita Quezada, Richard S. Morgan, Lisa Gaya Lanyon, Darren R. Webb, Phil Moto, Brad S. Condie, Jonathan Anhand, Chadd Ferron, Seong Kim; *key asst lay:* Rick Moore, Michael O'Mara, Kenneth Spirduso; *lay asst:* Denise Louise Klitsie, Lissa Ainley, John Puglisi, Denise Blakely Fuller, Tim Callahan, Cynthia Ignacio, Robert Cardone, Billy George, Peter Clarke, Peter J. De Luca; *blue sketch:* Cyndee La Rae Heimbuch, Madlyn O'Neill, Jo Anne Tzuanos; *3d fx:* David A. Bossert, Ed Coffey, Stephen B. Moore, Dan Chaika, Daniele Hanket; *anim fx asst:* Daniel Lund, Dan Chaika, Colbert Fennelly, Cynthia Neill-Knizek, Mabel Gesner, John Tucker, Steve Starr, Michael Cadwallader-Jones, Kristine Brown, Daniel E. Wanket, Graham Woods, Tony West, Joseph Christopher Pepé, John David Thornton, Kristine Humber, Michael G. Duhatschek, Geoffrey C. Everts; *fx break/inbet:* James Goss, Phil Vigil, Elizabeth Holmes, John E. Hailey, Paitoon Ratanasirintrawoot, Adeboye Adegbenro, Stella P. Andelaéz Tascón, Tatiana Kellert, Kang Tae Kim, Michael Milligan; *cgi software engineers:* Marcus Warren Hobbs, Mary Jane "MJ" Turner, Umakanth Thumrugoti, Tasso Lappas, Carolyn Chilton-Wiegley, Tad Gielow; *pre-prod fx development:* David A. Bossert, Chris Jenkins; *visual development/character des:* Vance Gerry, Joe Grant, Mike Gabriel, Michael Giaimo, Bruce Zick, Guy Deel, Darek Gogol, Ian Gooding, Jean Gillmore, Glen Keane, Duncan Marjoribanks, Chris Buck, Will Finn, Kathy Zielinski; *character sculpture:* Kent Melton; *addit cgi anim:* Rob Bekuhrs, Sandra M. Groeneveld, Kevin Sheedy; *addit.ruff inbet:* Elliot M. Bour, Robert O. Corley; *addit clean-up anim:* Scott Anderson, Debra Armstrong-Holmes, Margie Daniels, June Fujimoto, Brian Clift, Alex Topete, Vincent Siracusano; *inbet:* Raoul Aguirre, Ron Cones, Adam Dykstra, Brigitte Franzka-Fritz, Ben Gonzalez, Clay Kaytis, Kendre Lammas, Jan Naylor, Rich Wilkie; *addit anim fx:* Mauro Maressa, Brice Mallier, Jeff Howard, Joey Mildenberger, Peter De Mund, Joseph Gilland, Mark Barrows, Sean Applegate, John Huey, John Doyle, Tyrone Elliott, Ray Hofstedt, David Lyons; *inbet:* Kimberly Burk, John Fargnoli, Ida Voskanian, Jay Shindell, Elsa Sesto-Vidal; *art dir:* Michael Giaimo; *artistic sup: lay:* Rasoul Azadani; *back:* Cristy Maltese; *story:* Tom Sito; *clean-up:* Renee Holt-Bird, Nancy

Kniep; *visual fx:* Don Paul; *cgi:* Steve Goldberg; *artistic co-ord:* Dan Hansen; *prod mgr:* TraciTolman Mars; *asso ed:* Mark Hester; *story:* Glen Keane, Joe Grant, Ralph Zondag, Burny Mattinson, Ed Gombert, Kaan Kaylon, Francis Glebas, Robert Gibbs, Bruce Morris, Todd Kurosawa, Duncan Marjoribanks, Chris Buck; *cgi co-ord:* Maryann McLeod; *ed:* H. Lee Peterson, James Melton, Tim Mertens, Anna Solorio, Hermann Schmidt, Deirdre Hepburn-Mangione, Ellen Keneshea, Sandy Nervig; *post prod mgr:* Sara Duran; *post prod sup:* Deborah Edell Underwood; *Florida ed:* Beth A. Collins-Stegmaier, Kat Connolly; *dial ed:* Dan Rich, Chris Hogan, Bob Baron, Gary Littell, Vince Caro; *voices: Pocahontas:* Irene Bedard; *Pocahontas singing voice:* Judy Kuhn; *John Smith:* Mel Gibson; *Governor Ratcliffe/ Wiggin's voice:* David Ogden Stiers; *Meeko:* John Kassir; *Powhatan:* Russell Means; *Thomas:* Christian Bale; *Grandmother Willow's voice:* Linda Hunt; *Percy's voice:* Danny Mann; *Ben:* Billy Connolly; *Lon:* Joe Baker; *Flit:* Frank Welker; *Nakoma:* Michelle St. John; *Kocum:* James Apaumut Fall; *Kekata:* Gordon Tootoosis; *chorus:* Gerard Alessandrini, Joan Barber, Scott Barnes, Liz Callaway, Al De Ruiter, Jonathan Dokuchitz, George Dvorsky, James Apaumut Fall, Bruce Fifer, Merwin Foard, Larry French, David Friedman, Chris Groerendaal, Larry Hansen, Randy Hansen, Ray Harrell, Joan Henry, Alix Korey, Rob Lorey, Bill McKinley, Bruce Moore, Bobbi Page, Wilbur Pauley, Caroline Peyton, Richard Warren Pugh, Patrick Quinn, Peter Samuel, Gordon Stanley, Annie Sutton, Mark Waldrup, Molly Wasserman, Lee Wilkoff; *Shawnee Nation United Remnant Band: Algonquin Singers/Speakers:* Lesa Wakwashbosha Green, Rebecca (Dasse Manitsa) Hawkins, Gayle Melassa Pope, Stephen Snow Owl Bunch, Ginny Ah'Chantooni Frazier, Richard A. "Bear Coat" Bercot, Jim "Great Elk" Waters; *songs:* Alan Menken, Stephen Schwartz; *score:* Alan Menken; *orch/conducted by:* Danny Troob; *vocal arrangement/songs conducted by:* David Friedman; "Colors of the Wind" (end title) performed by Vanessa Williams; *prod:* Keith Thomas; *arrangement:* Robbie Buchanan, Keith Thomas; "If I Never Knew You" performed by John Secada and Shanice; *prod:* Emilio Estefan, Robbie Buchanan; *arrangement:* Robbie Buchanan, Aaron Zigman; *ex mus prod:* Chris Montan; *songs arranged by* Danny Troob, Martin Erskine; *score orch:* Michael Starobin, Douglas Besterman; "Steady at the Beating Drum" performed by Jim Cummings; "Listen With Your Heart" performed by Linda Hunt, Bobbi Page *mus recl/mix:* John Richards; *rec mix:* Terry Porter, Mel Metcalfe, Dean A. Zupancic, Tom Marquette, Paul Wertheimer; *mus ed:* Kathleen Fogarty-Bennett, Brion McIntosh; *mus prod sup:* Tod Cooper; *dial ed:* Doc Kane; *sd ed:* Larry Kemp, Lon E. Bender, Victor R. Ennis, Elizabeth Tobin Kurtz, David Stanke; *ADR sup:* Curt Schulkey; *sd fx ed:* Scott Martin Gershin, Rick Morris, Alan Rankin, Joseph Phillips, Peter J. Lehman, Brian McPherson, Anthony J. Miceli; *foley ed:* Neal J. Anderson, Patrick N. Sellers; *addit audio:* Kim Waugh; *foley art:* John Roesch, Hilda Hodges; *dubbing rec:* Jeanette Browning; *PDL:* Judy Nord; *b&w processing:* Joe Parra, John White; *col timer:* Dale Grahn; *neg cutters:* Mary Beth Smith, Rick MacKay; *prod asst:* Naila Ajmal, Kirsten A. Bulmer, Lindsey K. Collins, Stacey D. Ernst, Maryann Garger, Jeff Hermann, Fred Herrman, Noel C. Johnson, Monica Lago-Greenberg, Francine Mitrofan, Heather Moriarty, Joe Morris, Rebecca Lyn Russell, Sylvia I. Sanchez, Bethann Schulkelorry, Ann Shea, Rocky Smith, Robert Stemwell, Jeffrey Lawrence, Van Tuyl, Carrie A. Wilksen; *post prod admin:* Margaret L. Yu; *post prod co-ord:* Heather Jane MacDonald-Smith; *title des:* Susan Bradley; *titles & opticals:* Buena Vista Imaging, Mark Dornfeld; *native American consultant:* Shirley "Little Dove" Custalow McGowan of the Mattaponi; *asst prod mgr: storyl clean-up:* Angelique N. Yen; *ed:* Brian Behling; *lay:* Tod Marsden; *anim:* Stephanie L. Parker; *fx:* Shelly Amoroso; *cgil/3d fx:* Kirk Bodyfelt; *backl/anim check:* Karenna Mazur Alderton; *col models:* Holly E. Bratton; *communications:* Dorothy L. McKim; *CAPS & retakes asst mgr:* Jill Johnson; *recl/scoring:* Marcia Gwendolyn Jones; *Florida: layl/back:* Paul Steele; *clean-up:* Sheri Croft, Paul S.D. Lanum; *anim/fx:* Matthew Gardera; *i&p asst mgr:* Chris Hecox; *co-ords.: communications:* Onil Chibas; *post prod CAPS:* Jeanie Lynd Sorenson; *scene plan:* Thomas Baker, Sara Bleik, Annamarie Costa, Cindy Goode, Mark Henley, Ron Jackson, Kim Gray, (Florida) John Cunningham, Mary Lescher, Karen N. Austin; *fx data entry:* Gary Stubblefield; *anim check:* Barbara Wiles, Mavis Shafer, Karen Hepburn, Gary Shafer, Pat Sito, Karen S. Paat, Denise M. Mitchell; *sup CAPS/i&p:* Frances Kirsten; *anim check:* Laurie A. Sacks, Albert F. Moore, Victoria Winner Novak; *col models:* Penny Coulter, Barbara Lynn Hamane, Ann Sorensen, Debra Y. Siegel, Irma Cartaya; *col model asst:* Debra Jorgensborg; *digitizing mark-up:* Gina Wootten (Florida): Michael D. Lusby; *digitizing ph:* Karen N. China, David Braden, Val D'Arcy, Corey Dean Fredrickson, Lynnette E. Cullen, Gareth Fishbaugh, Michael A. McFerren, David J. Rowe (*Florida*): Gary W. Smith, Barbara J. Poirier, Jason L.R. Buske; *asst paint sup:* Irma Velez, Karen L. Hudson, Grace H. Shirado; *col model markup:* David J. Zywicki, Sherrie Cuzzort, Cindy Finn, Beth Ann McCoyGee; *paint mark-up:* Leyla Del C. Amaro-Pelaez, Maria Gonzalez, Leslie Hinton, Karan J. Lee-Storr, Sarah Jane King, Gale Raleigh, Myrian Ferron Tello; *paint:* Reneé Alcazar, Russell Blandino, Elena Marie Cox, Florida D'Ambrosio, Christina Frazier, Brendan Harris, Angelika Katz, Debbie Mooneyham, Bill Dhanesian, Patrick Sekino, S. Ann Sullivan, Britt Van Der Nagel, Carmen Sanderson, Kirk Axtell II, Joey Calderon, Sybil Cuzzort, Robert Dettloff, Paulino, Steve Hirsch, Randy McFerren, Tanya Moreau-Smith, Linda Praamsma, Don Shump, Roxanne M. Taylor, Phyllis Biro, Ofra Afouta Calderon, Lea Dahlen, Phyllis Estelle Fields, Irene LaVelle-Gringeri, David Karp, Harlene Mears, Karen Lynne Nugent, Bruce Phillipson, Fumiko R. Sommer, Britt Tjarno Teegarden, Susan Wileman; *final check:* Janette Hulett, Monica Marroquin, Teri N. McDonald, Saskia Raevouri; *compositing:* James "JR" Russell, Shannon Fallis-Kane, Joseph Pfening, Dolores Pope; *trainees: lay:* Scott Uehara; *fx:* Lisa Reinert; *col models:* Pamela L.V. Henn; *PIXAR:* Thomas Hahn, Peter Nye, Michael A. Shantzis; *col:* Tech. *sd:* Dolby stereo. 78 min. • The legendary story of a shipload of English settlers who arrive in New England, distressing the local Indian tribe. When Captain John Smith and the Indian Chief's beautiful daughter, Pocahontas, fall for each other, their love causes unrest between both the settlers and the Indians.

5099. The Poet and Peasant (*Andy Panda*) 18 Mar. 1946; *p.c.:* Walter Lantz prods for Univ; *dir:* Dick Lundy; *story:* Ben Hardaway, Milt Schaffer; *anim:* Les Kline, Paul Smith; *sets:* Terry Lind; *mus:* Darrell Calker; *col:* Tech. *sd:* WE. 6 min. *Academy Award nomination* • Andy conducts a farmyard symphony orchestra.

5100. Point Rationing of Foods 25 Feb. 1943; *p.c.:* Leon Schlesinger prods for the War Office of Information/Victory Film; *dir:* Charles M. Jones; *story:* Phil Eastman; *anim:* Louis Appet, Robert Cannon, Roger Daley, Phil de Lara, Ace Gamer, Ken Harris, Anatole Kirsanoff, Rudy Larriva, Ray Patin, Lloyd Vaughan, Ben Washam; *sets:* Eugene Fleury, Art Heinemann, David Hilberman, Paul Julian, Earl Klein, Bernyce Polifka Fleury, Richard H. Thomas, Cornett Wood; *ed:* Treg Brown; *i&p:* Florence Finkelhor; *voice:* Robert C. Bruce; *mus:* Eugene Poddany; *other contributors:* Eleanor Ames, Helen Archer, Ray Bell, Sara Ben Hillel, Eleanor Brem, Angie Broda, Maxine Cameron, Nadine Chapman, Elaine Cone, Helen Currie, Edith Edgar, Madeline Ellis, Cecilia Finn, Rae Gartner, Catherine Gleeson, Lillian Goldberg, Frieda Goldhirsch, Martha Goldman, Margo Heister, Esther Honiz, Lee Hudson, Murray Hudson, Alla Ivanhoff, Marjorie Jasper, Helen Lampson, Jackie Langton, Paul Marron, Fern McCabe, Cecelia Meyerhoff, Peggy Morgan, Jane Nurre, Joan Pabian, Louise Peters, Bill Pomerance, Bette Rehbeck, Veotis Rich-Archer, Helen Seibert, Margaret Selby, Dorothy Shirley, Marceil Swanson, Shirley Thomas, Avril Thompson, Donna Urbon; *b&w. sd:* Vit. 6 min. • A woman shopper on her first market tour since the Office of Price Administration's new point rationing system of March 1. Wise buying adds up to a minimum of points.

5101. The Pointer (*Mickey Mouse*) 21 July 1939; *p.c.:* Walt Disney prods for RKO; *dir:* Clyde Geronimi; *story:* George Stallings; *anim:* Preston Blair, James H. Culhane, Norman Ferguson, Oliver M. Johnston Jr., Lynn Karp, John Lounsbery, Fred Moore, Lester Novros, Claude Smith, Franklin Thomas; *fx:* Arthur W. Palmer, Joshua Meador; *lay:* David Hilberman; *voices:* Walt Disney, Pinto Colvig; *mus:* Paul J. Smith; *col:* Tech. *sd:* RCA. 8 min. *Academy Award nomination.* • Mickey teaches Pluto the art of being a pointer when hunting quail. A bear arrives on the scene and they make a hasty retreat.

5102. A Polar Flight (*Aesop's Film Fable*) 8 Nov. 1928; *p.c.:* Fables Pictures Inc for Pathé; *dir:* Paul Terry; *b&w. sil.* 10 min. • In a salute to Admiral Byrd's polar expedition, Al Falfa finds himself in the Arctic. He is chased by a polar bear and hides from it in an igloo, which the bear breaks into. He arrives at the North Pole and the Arctic animals chase him away.

5103. Polar Fright (*Chilly Willy*) Apr. 1966; *p.c.:* Walter Lantz prods for Univ; *dir:* Paul J. Smith; *story:* Cal Howard; *anim:* Al Coe, Les Kline; *sets:* Ray Huffine; *voices:* Daws Butler; *mus:* Walter Greene; *prod mgr:* William E. Garity; *col:* Tech. *sd:* RCA. 5½ min. • Chilly tries to prevent a hunter from getting a $100 reward for his polar bear chum's coat.

5104. Polar Pals (*Looney Tunes*) 3 June 1939; *p.c.:* Leon Schlesinger prods for WB; *dir:* Robert Clampett; *story:* Warren Foster; *anim:* John Carey; *ed:* Tregoweth E. Brown; *voices:* Mel Blanc, Billy Bletcher; *mus:* Carl W. Stalling; *prod sup:* Henry Binder, Raymond G. Katz; *b&w. sd:* Vit. 7 min. • Porky protects the North Pole wildlife from I. Killum, Arctic hunter.

5105. Polar Pals (*Tom & Jerry*) 5 Sept. 1931; *p.c.:* Van Beuren for RKO; *dir:* John Foster, George Rufle; *mus:* Gene Rodemich; *b&w. sd:* RCA. 7½ min. • Tom and Jerry are shipwrecked on an Arctic island where they burst into song at the slightest provocation.

5106. Polar Pest (*Barney Bear*) 30 Dec. 1944; *p.c.:* MGM; *p.c.:* MGM; *dir:* George Gordon; *anim:* Arnold Gillespie, Michael Lah, Ed Barge, Jack Carr; *ed:* Fred MacAlpin; *mus:* Scott Bradley; *ph:* Jack Stevens; *prod:* Fred Quimby; *col:* Tech. *sd:* WE. 6 min. aka: *Barney Bear's "Polar Pest."* • Barney's winter hibernation is interrupted by the arrival of his nephew from the North Pole.

5107. Polar Pests (*Chilly Willy*) 19 May 1958; *p.c.:* Walter Lantz prods for Univ; *dir:* Alex Lovy; *story:* Homer Brightman; *anim:* Ray Abrams, La Verne Harding; *sets:* Art Landy, Raymond Jacobs; *voice:* Daws Butler; *mus:* Clarence Wheeler; *prod mgr:* William E. Garity; *col:* Tech. *sd:* RCA. 6 min. • Zoo Keeper, Clyde, goes to the South Pole to retrieve an escaped penguin from the zoo.

5108. Polar Playmates (*Color Rhapsody*) 25 Apr. 1946; *p.c.:* Colum; *dir:* Howard Swift; *story:* Volus Jones; *anim:* Grant Simmons; *lay:* Clark Watson; *ed:* Richard S. Jensen; *i&p:* Elizabeth F. McDowell; *mus:* Eddie Kilfeather; *ph:* Frank Fisher; *prod mgr:* Hugh McCollum; *col:* Tech. *sd:* WE. 6½ min. • An eskimo hunts a bear and a penguin but comes off the worse for wear.

5109. Polar Trappers (*Donald & Goofy*) 17 June 1938; *p.c.:* Walt Disney prods for RKO; *dir:* Ben Sharpsteen; *story:* Jack Kinney; *anim:* Arthur Babbitt, James H. Culhane, Alfred Eugster, Paul Hopkins, Edward Love, Stan Quackenbush, Wolfgang Reitherman, Bob Wickersham, Cornett Wood; *voices:* Pinto Colvig, Clarence Nash, Richard Edwards (Billy Gilbert pre-recorded sneeze); *mus:* Paul J. Smith; *Parade of the Wooden Soldiers* by Raymond Scott; *col:* Tech. *sd:* RCA. 7 min. • While Goofy unsuccessfully tries to capture a reluctant walrus, Donald attempts to seduce a colony of penguins into the cooking pot.

5110. Police Dogged (*Clancy the Bull*) 29 June 1956; *p.c.:* TT for Fox; *dir:* Connie Rasinski; *story:* Tom Morrison; *anim:* Jim Tyer; *mus:* Philip A. Scheib; *ph:* Douglas Moye; *col:* Tech. *sd:* RCA. 6 min. CS. • "Dragnet" parody. Policeman Clancy chases bank robber Pinhead Schlabotnik.

5111. Polka-Dot Puss (*Tom & Jerry*) Mar. 1949; *p.c.:* MGM; *dir:* William Hanna, Joseph Barbera; *anim:* Kenneth Muse, Ed Barge, Ray Patterson, Irven Spence; *sets:* Robert Gentle; *ed:* Fred MacAlpin; *voice:* Lillian Randolph; *mus:* Scott Bradley; *prod:* Fred Quimby; *col:* Tech. *sd:* WE. 7½ min. • Mammy Two-Shoes is about to put Tom out for the night when he feins a cold. She lets him sleep by the fire then Jerry paints spots on his face, convincing him he has measels.

5112. Polly Wants a Doctor (*Phantasy*) 6 Jan. 1944; *p.c.:* Colum; *prod:* Dave Fleischer; *dir:* Howard Swift; *story:* Dun Roman; *anim:* Jim Armstrong, Grant Simmons; *voices:* Byron Kane, Dick Nelson, Sara Berner; *mus:* Eddie Kilfeather; *ph:* Frank Fisher; *prod mgr:* Albert Spar; *b&w. sd:* RCA. 6 min. • Junk-eating Joe Goat tries out some new recipes on Polly Parrot, ending with the unfortunate bird swallowing a radio.

5113. The Polo Match (*Aesop's Film Fable*) 20 May 1929; *p.c.:* Fables Pictures Inc for Pathé; *dir:* Paul Terry; *b&w. sil.* 10 min. • The mice play a lively game of polo on mechanical horses. When a lothario cat's advances get a rebuff by a girl mouse in the stands, he abducts her. A chase ensues over the countryside with the boy mouse on his mechanical horse When the boy mouse knocks the villain cold with a polo ball, the mice are reunited and kiss as the mechanical horse divides into two halves.

5114. Poltergeist 16 Sept. 1982; *p.c.:* MGM/SLM Entertainment for United International Pictures; *dir:* Tobe Hooper; *prod:* Steven Spielberg, Frank Marshall; *anim sup:* John Bruno; *technical anim sup:* Samuel Comstock; *anim:* Art Vitello, José Abel, Milt Gray; *lay:* Terry Windell; *anim ph sup:* James C. Keefer; *col:* Metrocolor. *sd:* Dolby stereo. 114 min. *l/a.* • Live-action horror: A young girl is drawn to whispering "voices" on the television and is physically sucked into the television. This spiritual upheaval is due to the house being erected over a large cemetery site. A medium is brought in to unleash the spirits. Animated spirits, etc.

5115. Poltergeist II: The Other Side 23 May 1986; *p.c.:* MGM for United International Pictures; *dir:* Brian Gibson; *Boss Film: technical anim:* Annick Therrien, Rebecca Petrulli-Heskes, Samuel Recinos; *anim:* Glenn Chaika, Jeff Howard, Mauro Maressa, Peggy Regan; *col:* Metrocolor. *sd:* Dolby stereo. Panavision. 91 min. *l/a.* • Live-action horror: Following the destruction of their house, the Freeling family move in with mother-in-law when they are, once again, beset by a poltergeist attack. Animated spirits, etc.

5116. The Pooch Parade *(Fable)* 19 July 1940; *p.c.:* Colum; *story:* Allen Rose; *anim:* Harry Love, Louie Lilly; *ed:* George Winkler; *voices:* Mel Blanc, Billy Bletcher; *mus:* Joe de Nat; *ph:* Otto Reimer; *prod mgr:* James Bronis; b&w. *sd:* RCA. 6 min. • Scrappy enters Yippy in a Gala Dog Show. Yippy engages the other contestants in a chase while masquerading as a rabbit.

5117. Poop-Deck Pirate *(Woody Woodpecker)* 10 Jan. 1961; *p.c.:* Walter Lantz prods for Univ; *dir:* Jack Hannah; *story:* Homer Brightman; *anim:* Ray Abrams, Al Coe; *sets:* Ray Huffine, Art Landy; *voices:* Dal McKennon, Grace Stafford; *mus:* Eugene Poddany; *prod mgr:* William E. Garity; *col:* Tech. *sd:* RCA. 6 min. • Woody goes to Tooty Fruiti Island for peace and quiet. There he runs afoul of a pirate who wants to dispose of him.

5118. Poop Goes the Weasel *(Noveltoon)* 8 July 1955; *p.c.:* Famous for Para; *dir:* Dave Tendlar; *story/voices:* Carl Meyer, Jack Mercer; *anim:* Martin Taras, Thomas Moore; *sets:* John Zago; *mus:* Winston Sharples; *ph:* Leonard McCormick; *prod mgr:* Seymour Shultz; *col:* Tech. *sd:* RCA. 6 min. • Waxey Weasel takes on more than he bargains for when he robs the chicken house of a very smart little chick.

5119. Poopdeck Pappy *(Popeye)* 15 Nov. 1940; *p.c.:* The Fleischer Studio for Para; *prod:* Max Fleischer; *dir:* Dave Fleischer; *story:* George Manuell; *anim:* Bill Nolan, Winfield Hoskins; *voices:* Jack Mercer; *mus:* Sammy Timberg; *ph:* Charles Schettler; *prod sup:* Sam Buchwald, Isidore Sparber; b&w. *sd:* WE. 6 min. • Popeye tries to put his Pappy to bed when the old boy wants a night out on the town.

5120. Poor Cinderella *(Color Classic)* 3 Aug. 1934; *p.c.:* The Fleischer Studio for Para; *prod:* Max Fleischer; *dir:* Dave Fleischer; *anim:* Seymour Kneitel, Roland Crandall, William Henning; *song:* Charles Tobias, Murray Mencher, Jack Scholl; *mus:* Phil Spitalny; *col:* Ciné. *sd:* WE. 11 min. • Cinderella's Fairy Godmother arranges for her to go to the ball where she dances with the Prince while being entertained by Rudy Vallee. Betty Boop's only appearance in color.

5121. Poor Elmer *(Color Rhapsody)* 22 July 1938; *p.c.:* Charles Mintz prods for Colum; *dir:* Sid Marcus; *anim:* Art Davis, Herb Rothwill; *lay:* Clark Watson; *back:* Phil Davis; *ed:* George Winkler; *voices:* Dave Weber, Elvia Allman, Leone Le Doux; *mus:* Joe de Nat; *prod mgr:* James Bronis; *col:* Tech. *sd:* RCA. 7½ min. • The hospital staff await the arrival of an important patient. When he finally arrives, they discover he is a goldfish.

5122. Poor Little Butterfly *(Color Rhapsody)* 4 July 1938; *p.c.:* Charles Mintz prods for Colum; *dir:* Ben Harrison; *anim:* Manny Gould; *lay:* Clark Watson; *back:* Phil Davis; *ed:* George Winkler; *voices:* Pinto Colvig, Leone Le Doux; *mus:* Joe de Nat; *prod mgr:* James Bronis; *col:* Tech. *sd:* RCA. 8 min. • Two grasshopper sailors dock in Tokyo and meet two oriental butterflies, court them but soon have to return to their ship.

5123. Poor Little Me *(Happy Harmonies)* 11 May 1935; *p.c.:* MGM; *prod/dir:* Hugh Harman, Rudolf Ising; *mus:* Scott Bradley; *col:* Tech. *sd:* RCA. 9 min. • A little skunk is avoided by all until he meets a girl bunny with a cold in her nose. A hungry bobcat arrives and is repelled by the skunk.

5124. Poor Little Witch Girl *(Modern Madcap)* 1965; *p.c.:* Para Cartoons; *dir/story:* Howard Post; *anim:* Al Eugster; *sets:* Dave Ubinas; *voices:* Shari Lewis, Bob MacFadden; *mus:* Winston Sharples; *prod mgr:* Abe Goodman; *col:* Tech. *sd:* RCA 6 min. • While Cousin Maggie is away, Halfwitch gets soaked in a potion that makes her grow to gargantuan proportions.

5125. Poor Papa *(Oswald the Lucky Rabbit)* 6 Aug. 1928; *p.c.:* Winkler for Univ; *dir:* Walt Disney; *anim:* Ub Iwerks, Isadore Freleng, Hugh Harman, Rudolf Ising, Rollin C. Hamilton, Ben Clopton, Norman Blackburn;

i&p: Les Clark; *ph:* Rudolf Ising; b&w. *sil.* 6 min. • Oswald puts a stop to the stork arriving with countless kids by shooting at it.

5126. Pop-a-Long Popeye *(Popeye)* 29 Aug. 1952; *p.c.:* Famous for Para; *dir:* Seymour Kneitel; *story:* Carl Meyer, Jack Mercer; *anim:* Tom Johnson, John Gentilella, Els Barthen; *sets:* John Zago; *voices:* Jack Mercer, Jackson Beck, Carl Meyer; *mus:* Winston Sharples; *ph:* Leonard McCormick; *prod mgr:* Seymour Shultz; *col:* Tech. *sd:* RCA. 6 min. • In order to get his nephews to eat their spinach, Popeye tells of when he was an eastern dude on a western ranch.

5127. Pop and Mom in Wild Oysters 14 Feb. 1941; *p.c.:* J.H. Hoffberg for Para; *dir/anim:* Charles Bowers; *voice:* The Landt Trio (Dan, Earl, Jack) Joseph M. White; *mus:* Jack Austin; *orch:* King Ross; *ph:* Harold L. Muller; b&w. *sd.* 10 min. • Having tied the cat's tail through a knothole, Junior mouse sets out to get some food from the kitchen but encounters some angry oysters. Model animation.

5128. Pop Goes Your Heart *(Merrie Melodies)* 4 Mar. 1935; *p.c.:* Leon Schlesinger prods for WB; *dir:* Isadore Freleng; *anim:* Frank Tipper, Sandy Walker, Robert Clampett; *mus:* Norman Spencer; *song:* Mort Dixon, Allie Wrubel; *prod sup:* Henry Binder, Raymond G. Katz; *col:* Tech-2. *sd:* Vit. 7 min. • The birds and creatures of the forest put pay to a pillaging bear.

5129. Pop 'Im Pop *(Looney Tunes)* 28 Oct 1950; *p.c.:* WB; *dir:* Robert McKimson; *story:* Warren Foster; *anim:* Charles McKimson, Rod Scribner, Manny Gould, Phil de Lara, J.C. Melendez; *lay:* Cornett Wood; *back:* Richard H. Thomas; *ed:* Treg Brown; *voices:* Mel Blanc; *mus:* Carl Stalling; *prod mgr:* John W. Burton; *prod:* Edward Selzer; *col:* Tech. *sd:* Vit. 7 min. • Sylvester mistakes a baby kangaroo for a giant mouse while trying to teach Junior the art of mouse catching.

5130. Pop Pie A'La Mode *(Popeye)* 26 Jan. 1945; *p.c.:* Famous for Para; *dir:* I. Sparber; *story:* Dave Tendlar; *anim:* Joe Oriolo, Morey Reden; *voices:* Jack Mercer, Jackson Beck; *mus:* Sammy Timberg; *ph:* Leonard McCormick; *prod mgr:* Sam Buchwald; b&w. *sd:* RCA. 6½ min. Tech reissue: 3 Nov. 1950. • Marooned on a desert isle, Popeye has to deal with a tribe of hungry cannibals.

5131. Popcorn *(Paul Terry-Toon)* 11 Jan. 1931; *p.c.:* A-C for Educational/Fox; *dir:* Frank Moser, Paul Terry; *mus:* Philip A. Scheib; b&w. *sd:* WE. 6 min. • A circus setting with a mouse and his friend.

5132. Popcorn and Politics *(Modern Madcap)* Feb. 1962; *p.c.:* Para Cartoons; *dir:* Seymour Kneitel; *story:* Jack Mercer, Carl Meyer; *anim:* Martin Taras, John Gentilella, Larry Silverman; *sets:* Robert Little; *voices:* Cecil Roy, Jack Mercer; *mus:* Winston Sharples; *ph:* Leonard McCormick; *prod mgr:* Abe Goodman; *col:* Tech. *sd:* 6 min. • A boy dreams of what he will do when he is elected President.

5133. The Popcorn Story *(Jolly Frolics)* 30 Nov. 1950; *p.c.:* UPA for Colum; *ex prod:* Stephen Bosustow; *dir sup:* John Hubley; *dir:* Art Babbitt; *story:* Bob Russell, Phil Eastman, Bill Scott; *anim:* Willis Pyle, Cecil Surry, Grim Natwick, Roger Daley; *lay:* Bill Hurtz; *back:* Herb Klynn, Jules Engel; *voice:* Jim Backus; *mus:* Hoyt Curtin; *prod mgr:* Adrian Woolery; *col:* Tech. *sd:* RCA. 6½ min. • A young incompetent inventor unwittingly creates popcorn.

5134. Popeye 12 Dec. 1980; *p.c.:* Para/Walt Disney Prods; *Popeye anim:* Hanna-Barbera; *voice:* Jack Mercer; *col. sd:* Vistasonic. • Live-action version of the cartoon character. An animated Popeye appears at the opening of the film, stating that he must be "in the wrong movie."

5135. Popeye and the Pirates *(Popeye)* 12 Sept. 1947; *p.c.:* Famous for Para; *dir:* Seymour Kneitel; *story:* I. Klein, Jack Ward; *anim:* Dave Tendlar, Martin Taras; *sets:* Robert Connavale; *voices:* Jack Mercer, Mae Questel, Jackson Beck; *mus:* Winston Sharples; *ph:* Leonard McCormick; *prod mgr:* Sam Buchwald; *col:* Tech. *sd:* RCA. 8 min. • Popeye and Olive find themselves at the mercy of Pierre the pirate.

5136. Popeye for President *(Popeye)* 30 Mar. 1956; *p.c.:* Famous for Para; *dir:* Seymour Kneitel; *story:* Jack Mercer; *anim:* Tom Johnson, Frank Endres, Els Barthen; *sets:* Robert Connavale; *voices:* Jack Mercer, Mae Questel, Jackson Beck; *mus:* Winston Sharples; *ph:* Leonard McCormick; *prod mgr:* Seymour Shultz; *col:* Tech. *sd:* RCA. 6 min. • Both Popeye and Bluto are in the running for the presidential election. Olive's vote is the decider but she can't vote until her farm chores are finished.

5137. Popeye Makes a Movie *(Popeye)* 11 Aug. 1950; *p.c.:* Famous for Para; *dir:* Seymour Kneitel; *story:* I. Klein; *anim:* Tom Johnson, George Rufle, Els Barthen; *sets:* Robert Little; *voices:* Jack Mercer, Mae Questel, Jackson Beck, Sid Raymond; *mus:* Winston Sharples; *ph:* Leonard McCormick; *prod mgr:* Sam Buchwald; *col:* Tech. *sd:* RCA. 8 min. seq: *Popeye the Sailor Meets Ali Baba and His Forty Thieves.* • Popeye's nephews disrupt the filming of his latest movie.

5138. Popeye Meets Hercules *(Popeye)* 18 June 1948; *p.c.:* Famous for Para; *dir:* Bill Tytla; *story:* I. Klein; *anim:* George Germanetti, Tom Moore; *sets:* Robert Connavale; *voices:* Jack Mercer, Mae Questel, Jackson Beck; *mus:* Winston Sharples; *ph:* Leonard McCormick; *prod mgr:* Sam Buchwald; *col:* Tech. *sd:* RCA. 6½ min. • In ancient Greece, Popeye pits his wits against the mighty Hercules who forces his attentions on Olive.

5139. Popeye Meets Rip Van Winkle *(Popeye)* 9 May 1941; *p.c.:* The Fleischer Studio for Para; *prod:* Max Fleischer; *dir:* Dave Fleischer; *story:* Dan Gordon; *anim:* Sidney Pillet, Myron Waldman; *lay:* Myron Waldman; *voices:* Jack Mercer; *mus:* Sammy Timberg; *ph:* Charles Schettler; *prod mgr;* Sam Buchwald; b&w. *sd:* WE. 6 min. • Popeye takes pity on Winkle who is evicted from his home. He takes the snoozing old gent home and has to cope with his sleepwalking. Caricature of Chico Marx.

5140. Popeye Meets William Tell *(Popeye)* 20 Sept. 1940; *p.c.:* The Fleischer Studio for Para; *prod:* Max Fleischer; *sup:* Dave Fleischer; *dir:* James Culhane; *story:* Dan Gordon; *anim:* James Culhane, Alfred Eugster, Nick Tafuri, Bob Wickersham; *sets:* Shane Miller; *voices:* Jack Mercer, Pinto Colvig; *mus:* Sammy Timberg; *prod sup:* Sam Buchwald, Isidore Sparber; b&w. *sd:* WE. 7 min. • William Tell won't bow down to the High Governor so is forced to shoot an apple from the head of Popeye, posing as his son.

5141. Popeye Presents Eugene the Jeep *(Popeye)* 13 Dec. 1940; *p.c.:* The Fleischer Studio for Para; *prod:* Max Fleischer; *dir:* Dave Fleischer; *story:* Joseph E. Stultz; *anim:* Grim Natwick, Irving Spector; *voices:* Jack Mercer, Pinto Colvig; *mus:* Sammy Timberg; *ph:* Charles Schettler; *prod sup:* Sam Buchwald, Isidore Sparber; b&w. *sd:* WE. 6 min. • Popeye has trouble in putting Eugene the Jeep, the magical dog, out for the night.

5142. Popeye, the Ace of Space *(Popeye)* 2 Oct. 1953; *p.c.:* Famous for Para; *dir:* Seymour Kneitel; *story:* Carl Meyer, Jack Mercer; *anim:* Al Eugster, George Germanetti, Wm. B. Pattengill; *sets:* Robert Little, Anton Loeb; *voices:* Jack Mercer; *mus:* Winston Sharples; *ph:* Leonard McCormick; *prod mgr:* Seymour Shultz; *col:* Tech. 6½ min. a *Stereo-toon* in 3-D. • Popeye is captured by Martians and taken to their planet for an endurance test.

5143. Popeye the Sailor *(Betty Boop)* 14 July 1933; *p.c.:* The Fleischer Studio for Para; *prod:* Max Fleischer; *dir:* Dave Fleischer; *anim:* Seymour Kneitel, Roland Crandall, Willard Bowsky, William Sturm; *voice:* William A. Costello; *music/song:* Sammy Timberg, Sammy Lerner; b&w. *sd:* WE. 8 min. • Popeye and Olive go to the carnival where Olive is abducted by Bluto who ties her to the railroad tracks. Popeye eats his spinach and the rest is history. First in a long line of immensely popular cartoons based on Elzie Crisler Segar's celebrated comic strip character created in 1929.

5144. Popeye the Sailor Meets Ali Baba's Forty Thieves *(Popeye)* 26 Nov. 1937; *p.c.:* The Fleischer Studio for Para; *prod:* Max Fleischer; *dir:* Dave Fleischer; *anim:* Willard Bowsky, George Germanetti, Orestes Calpini; *sets:* Robert Little; *voices:* Jack Mercer; Mae Questel, Gus Wickie, Louis Fleischer; *mus/songs:* Sammy Timberg, Tot Seymour, Vee Lawnhurst, Sammy Lerner; *ph:* Johnny Burks; *col:* Tech. *sd:* WE. 18 min. • Coast Guard Popeye is called upon to deal with Abu Hassan and his band of thieves. Popeye, Olive and Wimpy all find themselves at the mercy of Hassan but spinach saves the day.

5145. Popeye the Sailor Meets Sindbad the Sailor *(Popeye)* 27 Nov. 1936; *p.c.:* The Fleischer Studio for Para; *prod:* Max Fleischer; *dir:* Dave Fleischer; *anim:* Willard Bowsky, George Germanetti, Edward Nolan; *sets:* Shane Miller, Robert Little; *voices:* Jack Mercer, Mae Questel, Gus Wickie, Arthur Boran, Louis Fleischer, Donald Bain; *mus/songs:* Sammy Timberg, Bob Rothberg, Sammy Lerner; *ph:* Johnny Burks; *col:* Tech. *sd:* WE. 20 min. *Academy Award nomination.* • While sailing the Seven Seas, our hero falls afoul of Sindbad, who lives on an island protected by mighty beasts. Popeye's first venture into Technicolor.

5146. Popeye's Mirthday *(Popeye)* 22 May 1953; *p.c.:* Famous for Para; *dir:* Seymour Kneitel; *story:* Carl Meyer, Jack Mercer; *anim:* Tom Johnson, Frank Endres, Els Barthen; *sets:* Robert Connavale; *voices:* Jack Mercer, Mae Questel; *mus:* Winston Sharples; *ph:* Leonard McCormick; *prod mgr:* Seymour Shultz; *col:* Tech. *sd:* RCA. 6 min. • Popeye's nephews prevent him from entering the house until a surprise party is ready.

5147. Popeye's Pappy *(Popeye)* 25 Jan. 1952; *p.c.:* Famous for Para; *dir:* I. Sparber; *story:* Larz Bourne; *anim:* Tom Johnson, Frank Endres, Els Barthen; *sets:* Robert Little; *voices:* Jack Mercer; *mus:* Winston Sharples; *ph:* Leonard McCormick; *prod mgr:* Seymour Shultz; *col:* Tech. *sd:* RCA. 6 min. • Popeye arrives on a cannibal isle to rescue his Pappy ... only to find him the natives' King.

5148. Popeye's Premiere *(Popeye)* 23 Mar. 1949; *p.c.:* Famous for Para; *story:* Bill Turner, I. Klein; *anim:* Dave Tendlar, John Gentilella; *voices:* Jack Mercer, Jackson Beck, Mae Questel; *mus:* Winston Sharples; *ph:* Leonard McCormick; *prod mgr:* Sam Buchwald; *col:* Tech. *sd:* RCA. 10 min. Seq: *Popeye Meets Aladdin and His Wonderful Lamp.* • Popeye and Olive go to the premiere of their latest movie, "Aladdin." Although no director is credited, the linking material would have been "directed" by the animators.

5149. Popeye's 20th Anniversary *(Popeye)* 2 Apr. 1954; *p.c.:* Famous for Para; *dir:* I. Sparber; *story:* I. Klein; *anim:* Al Eugster, George Germanetti; *sets:* Joseph Dommerque; *voices:* Jack Mercer, Jackson Beck; *mus:* Winston Sharples; *ph:* Leonard McCormick; *prod mgr:* Seymour Shultz; *col:* Tech. *sd:* RCA. 8 min. Seq: *Tops in the Big Top*; *Rodeo Romeo.* • The Paramount celebrities throw a presentation dinner for Popeye's twentieth year in movies. Jealous Bluto tries to spoil the fun. Caricatures of Bing Crosby, Jimmy Durante, Bob Hope, Dean Martin and Jerry Lewis.

5150. Popular Melodies *(Screen Songs)* 6 Apr. 1933; *p.c.:* The Fleischer Studio for Para; *prod:* Max Fleischer; *dir:* Dave Fleischer; *anim:* Willard Bowsky, Myron Waldman; *mus:* Art Turkisher; *l/a:* Arthur Jarrett; b&w. *sd:* WE. 6 min. *l/a/anim.* • An artist is distracted by his kids playing, so he drives them to the country for some peace. After painting some subjects, the paintings all come alive.

5151. Popular Song Parodies *p.c.:* Artclass Pictures for FBO; b&w. *sil.* • *1926:* Alexander's Ragtime Band May. Annie Laurie. The Sheik of Araby. In My Harem. When I Lost You. Margie. When the Midnight Choo Choo Leaves for Alabam. Oh What a Pal Was Mary. Everybody's Doing It. My Wife's Gone to the Country. Oh, How I Hate to Get Up in the Morning. Just Try to Picture Me. I Love to Fall Asleep. For Me and My Gal. Yak-A-Hula-Hick-A-Doola. My Sweetie. Old Pal. Tumbledown Shack in Athlone. The Rocky Road to Dublin. When I Leave This World Behind. Finiculese Finicula. When the Angelus Was Ringing. Beautiful Eyes. Call Me Up Some Rainy Afternoon. Micky. Oh I Wish I Was in Michigan. Oh Suzanna. My Old Kentucky Home. East Side, West Side

5152. Pork Chop Phooey *(Loopy de Loop)* Mar. 1965; *p.c.:* Hanna-Barbera for Colum; *prod/dir:* William Hanna, Joseph Barbera; *story dir:* Paul Sommer; *story:* Dalton Sandifer; *anim dir:* Charles A. Nichols; *anim:* Jack Ozark; *lay:* Dan Noonan; *back:* Art Lozzi; *ed:* Warner Leighton; *voices:* Daws Butler, Don Messick; *mus:* Hoyt Curtin; *titles:* Lawrence Gobel; *prod mgr:* Howard Hanson; *col:* East. *sd:* RCA. 6½ min. • Loopy gets involved with the Three Little Pigs.

5153. Porkuliar Piggy *(Li'l Abner)* 13 Oct 1944; *p.c.:* Colum; *dir:* Bob Wickersham; *story:* Al Geiss; *anim:* Chic Otterstrom, Ben Lloyd; *lay:* Clark Watson; *Voice:* Lurene Tuttle; *mus:* Eddie Kilfeather; *ph:* Frank Fisher; *col:* Tech. *sd:* WE. 8 min. • Daisy Mae's only rival is Salomé, Abner's pig. When Salomé is captured by the butcher, Abner and Mammy Yokum come to her rescue.

5154. Porky & Daffy *(Looney Tunes)* 6 Aug. 1938; *p.c.:* Leon Schlesinger prods for WB; *dir:* Robert Clampett; *anim:* Robert Cannon, John Carey; *sets:* Elmer Plummer; *ed:* Tregoweth E. Brown; *voices:* Mel Blanc; *mus:* Carl W. Stalling; *prod mgr:* Henry Binder, Raymond G. Katz; b&w. *sd:* Vit. 7 min. • Fight promoter Porky fixes up a bout between Daffy and a boxing bantam.

5155. Porky and Gabby *(Looney Tunes)* 15 May 1937; *p.c.:* Leon Schlesinger prods for WB; *dir:* Ub Iwerks; *asst dir:* Robert Clampett; *anim:* Charles Jones, Bob Clampett, Irven Spence; *lay:* Griff Jay; *back:* Arthur Loomer; *ed:* Tregoweth E. Brown; *voices:* Mel Blanc, Cal Howard; *mus:*

Carl W. Stalling; *prod mgr:* Henry Binder, Raymond G. Katz; b&w. *sd:* Vit. 8 min. • Porky and Gabby Goat have problems when trying to get their car moving.

5156. Porky and Teabiscuit (*Looney Tunes*) 1 May 1939; *p.c.:* Leon Schlesinger prods for WB; *dir:* Ben Hardaway, Cal Dalton; *story:* Melvin Millar; *anim:* Herman Cohen; *lay:* Griff Jay; *back:* Arthur Loomer; *ed:* Tregoweth E. Brown; *voices:* Mel Blanc, Earl Hodgins, Joe Twerp; *mus:* Carl W. Stalling; *ph:* John W. Burton; *prod sup:* Henry Binder, Raymond G. Katz; b&w. *sd:* Vit. 7 min. • Porky's Poppa sends his son to town to sell grain but he gets tricked into buying a dilapidated race horse instead.

5157. Porky at the Crocadero (*Looney Tunes*) 5 Feb. 1938; *p.c.:* Leon Schlesinger prods for WB; *dir:* Frank Tashlin; *story:* Lew Landsman; *anim:* Volney White; *ed:* Tregoweth E. Brown; *voices:* Mel Blanc, Dave Weber; *mus:* Carl W. Stalling; *prod sup:* Henry Binder, Raymond G. Katz; b&w. *sd:* Vit. 7 min. • When the cabaret acts fail to turn up, Porky has to imitate Cab Calloway, Benny Goodman, Guy Lombardo and Rudy Vallee.

5158. Porky Chops (*Looney Tunes*) 12 Feb. 1949; *p.c.:* WB; *dir:* Arthur Davis; *story:* William Scott, Lloyd Turner; *anim:* Don Williams, Emery Hawkins, Basil Davidovich, J.C. Melendez; *lay:* Don Smith; *back:* Philip de Guard; *ed:* Treg Brown; *voices:* Mel Blanc; *mus:* Carl Stalling; *prod mgr:* John W. Burton; *prod:* Edward Selzer; *col:* Tech. *sd:* Vit. 7 min • Porky's attempts to chop a tree housing a very "Hip" Zoot-suited squirrel.

5159. Porky in Egypt (*Looney Tunes*) 5 Nov. 1938; *p.c.:* Leon Schlesinger prods for WB; *dir:* Robert Clampett; *story:* Ernest Gee; *anim:* Norman McCabe; *sets:* Elmer Plummer; *ed:* Tregoweth E. Brown; *voices:* Mel Blanc, Dave Weber; *mus:* Carl W. Stalling; *ph:* John W. Burton; *prod sup:* Henry Binder, Raymond G. Katz; b&w. *sd:* Vit. 7 min. • Porky is lost in the desert when his camel starts suffering hallucinations.

5160. Porky in the Northwoods (*Looney Tunes*) 14 Dec. 1936; *p.c.:* Leon Schlesinger prods for WB; *dir:* Frank Tash(lin); *anim:* Norman McCabe, Volney White; *ed:* Tregoweth E. Brown; *voices:* Mel Blanc, Billy Bletcher, Bernice Hansel; *mus:* Carl W. Stalling; *prod sup:* Henry Binder, Raymond Katz; b&w. *sd:* Vit. 7 min. • A villainous fur trapper threatens Porky if he sets the trapper's animals free. The animals come to Porky's aid when he is in trouble.

5161. Porky in Wackyland (*Looney Tunes*) 24 Sept. 1938; *p.c.:* Leon Schlesinger prods for WB; *dir:* Robert Clampett; *anim:* Norman McCabe, I. Ellis; *sets:* Elmer Plummer; *ed:* Tregoweth E. Brown; *voices:* Mel Blanc, Ted Pierce, Robert Clampett; *mus:* Carl W. Stalling; *prod sup:* Henry Binder, Raymond G. Katz; b&w. *sd:* Vit. 7 min. • Porky flies to Wackyland in search of a rare bird called the Do-Do and a rich reward. Remade in Tech as *Dough for the Do-Do*.

5162. Porky Pig's Feat (*Looney Tunes*) 17 July 1943; *p.c.:* Leon Schlesinger prods for WB; *dir:* Frank Tashlin; *story:* Melvin Millar; *anim:* Phil Monroe; *lay:* David Hilberman; *back:* Richard H. Thomas; *ed:* Treg Brown; *voices:* Mel Blanc; *mus:* Carl W. Stalling; *prod sup:* Henry Binder, Raymond G. Katz; b&w. *sd:* Vit. 7 min. • Porky and Daffy are held prisoner in their apartment until they can pay their bill.

5163. Porky the Fireman (*Looney Tunes*) 4 June 1938; *p.c.:* Leon Schlesinger prods for WB; *dir:* Frank Tashlin; *story:* Melvin Millar; *anim:* Robert Bentley; *lay:* Griff Jay; *ed:* Tregoweth E. Brown; *voices:* Mel Blanc, Ted Pierce, Elvia Allman, Fred Avery; *mus:* Carl W. Stalling; *prod sup:* Henry Binder, Raymond G. Katz; b&w. *sd:* Vit. 7 min. • Fire Chief Porky and his crew attempt to douse a burning theatrical boarding house.

5164. Porky the Giant Killer (*Looney Tunes*) 18 Nov. 1939; *p.c.:* Leon Schlesinger prods for WB; *dir:* Ben Hardaway, Cal Dalton; *story:* Melvin Miller; *anim:* Gil Turner; *lay:* Griff Jay; *back:* Art Loomer; *ed:* Tregoweth E. Brown; *voices:* Mel Blanc, Billy Bletcher, Danny Webb; *mus:* Carl W. Stalling; *ph:* John W. Burton; *prod sup:* Henry Binder, Raymond G. Katz; b&w. *sd:* Vit. 7 min. • Porky is tricked into entering the giant's castle where he has to entertain the giant's baby.

5165. Porky the Gob (*Looney Tunes*) 17 Dec. 1938; *p.c.:* Leon Schlesinger prods for WB; *dir:* Ben Hardaway, Cal Dalton; *story:* Melvin Millar; *anim:* Gil Turner; *ed:* Tregoweth E. Brown; *voices:* Mel Blanc, The Sportsmen Quartet, Dave Weber; *mus:* Carl W. Stalling; *prod sup:* Henry Binder, Raymond G. Katz; b&w. *sd:* Vit. 7 min. • Seaman Porky is left to guard the battleship when it gets boarded by pirates.

5166. Porky the Rain-Maker (*Looney Tunes*) 1 Aug. 1936; *p.c.:* Leon Schlesinger prods for WB; *dir:* Fred Avery; *asst dir/story:* Robert Clampett; *anim:* Cecil Surry, Sid Sutherland, Robert Clampett; *voices:* Joe Dougherty, Earl Hodgins; *mus:* Norman Spencer; *prod sup:* Henry Binder, Raymond G. Katz; b&w. *sd:* Vit. 7 min. • Porky is sent to buy feed for the starving animals on his drought-ridden farm. He is conned into buying "Weather Pills" and when the animals swallow these pills it creates havoc.

5167. Porky the Wrestler (*Looney Tunes*) 9 Jan. 1937; *p.c.:* Leon Schlesinger prods for WB; *dir:* Fred Avery; *asst dir/story:* Robert Clampett; *anim:* Charles Jones, Elmer Wait; *voices:* Joe Dougherty, Joe Twerp, Fred Avery; *mus:* Carl W. Stalling; *prod sup:* Henry Binder, Raymond G. Katz; b&w. *sd:* Vit. 7 min. • Porky is mistaken for a prize wrestler, ending in the ring opposite the Champ.

5168. Porky's Ant (*Looney Tunes*) 10 May 1941; *p.c.:* Leon Schlesinger prods for WB; *dir:* Charles M. Jones; *story:* Rich Hogan; *anim:* Rudolph Larriva; *lay:* John McGrew; *back:* Eugene Fleiry; *ed:* Treg Brown; *voice:* Mel Blanc; *mus:* Carl W. Stalling; *prod sup:* Henry Binder, Raymond G. Katz; b&w. *sd:* Vit. 7 min. • Porky and Inki go hunting a rare ant who eventually saves them both from a ferocious lion.

5169. Porky's Badtime Story (*Looney Tunes*) 27 July 1937; *p.c.:* Leon Schlesinger prods for WB; *dir/story:* Robert Clampett; *anim:* Charles Jones; *sets:* Elmer Plummer; *ed:* Tregoweth E. Brown; *voices:* Mel Blanc; *mus:* Carl W. Stalling; *prod sup:* Henry Binder, Raymond G. Katz; b&w. *sd:* Vit. 7 min. • Porky and roommate Gabby Goat have problems in getting to sleep. Remade in Tech as *Tick Tock Tuckered*.

5170. Porky's Baseball Broadcast (*Looney Tunes*) 6 June 1940; *p.c.:* Leon Schlesinger prods for WB; *dir:* Isadore Freleng; *story:* J.B. Hardaway; *anim:* Cal Dalton; *sets:* Robert L. Holdeman; *ed:* Treg Brown; *voices:* Mel Blanc; *mus:* Carl W. Stalling; *prod sup:* Henry Binder, Raymond G. Katz; b&w. *sd:* Vit. 7 min. • Porky commentates on a baseball game at Yankum Stadium. • Caricatures of Mayor La Guardia and Babe Ruth.

5171. Porky's Bear Facts (*Looney Tunes*) 29 Mar. 1941; *p.c.:* Leon Schlesinger prods for WB; *dir:* I. Freleng; *story:* Michael Maltese; *anim:* Manuel Perez; *sets:* Robert L. Holdeman; *ed:* Treg Brown; *voice:* Mel Blanc; *mus:* Carl W. Stalling; *prod sup:* Henry Binder, Raymond G. Katz; b&w. *sd:* Vit. 7 min. • While Porky toils through the summer, his idle bear neighbor loafs. When winter arrives the lazy bear begs food from his neighbor.

5172. Porky's Building (*Looney Tunes*) 19 une 1937; *p.c.:* Leon Schlesinger prods for WB; *dir:* Frank Tash(lin); *anim:* Volney White, Norman McCabe; *ed:* Tregoweth E. Brown; *voices:* Mel Blanc, Billy Bletcher, Bernice Kamiat, Ted Pierce; *mus:* Carl W. Stalling; *prod sup:* Henry Binder, Raymond G. Katz; b&w. *sd:* Vit. 8 min. • Porky is a building contractor competing against Dirty Diggs for a building contract. Diggs puts a bricklaying machine to work but one of Porky's assistants wins the contest.

5173. Porky's Cafe (*Looney Tunes*) 21 Feb. 1942; *p.c.:* Leon Schlesinger prods for WB; *dir:* Charles M. Jones; *anim:* Rudolph Larriva; *lay:* John McGrew; *ed:* Treg Brown; *voice:* Mel Blanc; *mus:* Carl W. Stalling; *prod sup:* Henry Binder, Raymond G. Katz; b&w. *sd:* Vit. 7 min. • A small man with an insatiable appitite keeps Porky and Goofy Cat (the chef) busy until an ant gets into the pancake mix.

5174. Porky's Double Trouble (*Looney Tunes*) 13 Nov. 1937; *p.c.:* Leon Schlesinger prods for WB; *dir:* Frank Tashlin; *story:* George Manuell; *anim:* Joe d'Igalo; *lay:* Griff Jay; *ed:* Tregoweth E. Brown; *voices:* Mel Blanc, Frederich Lindsley, Shirley Reed, Dave Weber; *mus:* Carl W. Stalling; *prod sup:* Henry Binder, Raymond G. Katz; b&w. *sd:* Vit. 7 min. • Porky is mistaken for a notorious criminal.

5175. Porky's Duck Hunt (*Looney Tunes*) 17 Apr. 1937; *p.c.:* Leon Schlesinger prods for WB; *dir:* Fred Avery; *story:* Fred Avery, Robert Clampett; *anim:* Virgil Ross, Robert Cannon; *ed:* Tregoweth E. Brown; *voices:* Mel Blanc, Billy Bletcher, Dave Weber, The Sportsmen Quartet; *mus:* Carl W. Stalling; *prod sup:* Henry Binder, Raymond G. Katz; b&w. *sd:* Vit. 9 min. • Porky goes on a duck hunt and has a run-in with a duck who refuses to be shot. First appearance of Daffy Duck.

5176. Porky's Five & Ten (*Looney Tunes*) 16 Apr. 1938; *p.c.:* Leon Schlesinger prods for WB; *dir:* Robert Clampett; *anim:* Charles Jones, John Carey; *sets:* Elmer Plummer; *ed:* Tregoweth E. Brown; *voices:* Mel Blanc; *mus:* Carl W. Stalling; *prod sup:* Henry Binder, Raymond G. Katz;

b&w. *sd:* Vit. 7 min. • A gang of fish set upon Porky's cargo ship, swallowing clocks and radios, etc. A whirlpool sucks the items back on board again.

5177. Porky's Garden (*Looney Tunes*) 11 Sept. 1937; *p.c.:* Leon Schlesinger prods for WB; *dir:* Fred Avery; *anim:* Sid Sutherland, Elmer Wait; *ed:* Tregoweth E. Brown; *voices:* Mel Blanc, Earl Hodgins; *mus:* Carl W. Stalling; *prod sup:* Henry Binder, Raymond Katz; b&w. *sd:* Vit. 7 min. • Porky's jealous neighbor sabotages his prize vegetables, leaving him with just a pumpkin to enter in the County Fair. The neighbor's prize chickens eat reducing pills and shrink away to eggs, leaving Porky to covet the winnings.

5178. Porky's Hare Hunt (*Looney Tunes*) 30 Apr. 1938; *p.c.:* Leon Schlesinger prods for WB; *dir:* Ben Hardaway; *story:* Howard Baldwin, Robert Clampett; *anim:* Volney White; *lay:* Griff Jay; *back:* Arthur Loomer; *ed:* Treg Brown; *voices:* Mel Blanc; *mus:* Carl W. Stalling; *ph:* John W. Burton; *prod sup:* Henry Binder, Raymond G. Katz; b&w. *sd:* Vit. 7 min. • Porky and his dog, Zero, go hunting hare and encounter a screwy rabbit who refuses to be caught.

5179. Porky's Hero Agency (*Looney Tunes*) 4 Dec. 1937; *p.c.:* Leon Schlesinger prods for WB; *dir/story:* Robert Clampett; *anim:* Charles Jones; *sets:* Elmer Plummer; *ed:* Tregoweth E. Brown; *voices:* Mel Blanc, Bernice Hansel, Ted Pierce; *mus:* Carl W. Stalling; *prod sup:* Henry Binder, Raymond G. Katz; b&w. *sd:* Vit. 7 min. • Porky dreams he's "Porkykarkus" an ancient Grecian hero who is employed by the Emperor to stop the Gorgon from turning the populous into stone statues.

5180. Porky's Hired Hand (*Looney Tunes*) 30 Nov. 1940; *p.c.:* Leon Schlesinger prods for WB; *dir:* I. Freleng; *story:* Dave Monahan; *anim: sets:* Robert L. Holdeman; *ed:* Treg Brown; *voices:* Mel Blanc; *mus:* Carl W. Stalling; *ph:* John W. Burton; *prod sup:* Henry Binder, Raymond G. Katz; b&w. *sd:* Vit. 7 min. • Porky hires Gregory Grunt as a guard for his chickens. The fox arrives and promises a partnership with the watchman.

5181. Porky's Hotel (*Looney Tunes*) 2 Sept. 1939; *p.c.:* Leon Schlesinger prods for WB; *dir:* Robert Clampett; *anim:* Norman McCabe, John Carey; *ed:* Tregoweth E. Brown; *voices:* Mel Blanc, Phil Kramer The Rhythmettes; *mus:* Carl W. Stalling; *ph:* John W. Burton; *prod sup:* Henry Binder, Raymond G. Katz; b&w. *sd:* Vit. 7 min. • Porky's hotel recieves it's first guest in weeks in the shape of a cantankerous old goat who Gabby Goose persists in annoying.

5182. Porky's Last Stand (*Looney Tunes*) 6 Jan. 1940; *p.c.:* Leon Schlesinger prods for WB; *dir:* Robert Clampett; *story:* Warren Foster; *anim:* I. Ellis; *sets:* Elmer Plummer; *ed:* Tregoweth E. Brown; *voices:* Mel Blanc, Danny Webb; *mus:* Carl W. Stalling; *ph:* John W. Burton; *prod sup:* Henry Binder, Raymond G. Katz; b&w. *sd:* Vit. 7 min. • Porky and Daffy run a hamburger stand in the middle of a desert. Daffy goes to get a hamburger and is chased by a mad bull.

5183. Porky's Midnight Matinée (*Looney Tunes*) 22 Nov. 1941; *p.c.:* Leon Schlesinger prods for WB; *dir:* Charles M. Jones; *anim:* Robert Cannon; *lay:* John McGrew; *back:* Eugene Fleury; *ed:* Treg Brown; *voice:* Mel Blanc; *mus:* Carl W. Stalling; *ph:* John W. Burton; *prod sup:* Henry Binder, Raymond G. Katz; b&w. *sd:* Vit. 7 min. • Night Watchman Porky has to retrieve a rare pigmy ant which has escaped from captivity.

5184. Porky's Movie Mystery (*Looney Tunes*) 11 Mar. 1939; *p.c.:* Leon Schlesinger prods for WB; *dir:* Robert Clampett; *story:* Ernest Gee *anim:* John Carey; *ed:* Tregoweth E. Brown; *voices:* Mel Blanc, Billy Bletcher, Sara Berner, Danny Webb; *mus:* Carl W. Stalling; *ph:* John W. Burton; *prod sup:* Henry Binder, Raymond G. Katz; b&w. *sd:* Vit. 7 min. • Mr. Motto (Porky) is called in when "The Invisible Man" wreaks his revenge on the Warmer Bros Studio for only having starred in one movie.

5185. Porky's Moving Day (*Looney Tunes*) 7 Oct. 1936; *p.c.:* Leon Schlesinger prods for WB; *dir:* Jack King; *anim:* Paul Smith, Joe d'Igalo; *voices:* Joe Dougherty, Elvia Allman, Jack King; *mus:* Carl W. Stalling; *prod sup:* Henry Binder, Raymond G. Katz; b&w. *sd:* Vit. 7 min. • Miss Cud's house is about to be washed over a cliff when she summons Porky's Moving Van. He and his helpers try to get the furniture out before the house goes over.

5186. Porky's Naughty Nephew (*Looney Tunes*) 15 Oct. 1938; *p.c.:* Leon Schlesinger prods for WB; *dir:* Robert Clampett; *story:* Warren Foster; *anim:* Robert Cannon; *sets:* Elmer Plummer; *ed:* Tregoweth E. Brown;

voices: Mel Blanc, Bernice Kamiat; *mus:* Carl W. Stalling; *prod sup:* Henry Binder, Raymond G. Katz; b&w. *sd:* Vit. 7 min. • At "The Cartoon Animals' Outing," Porky is persuaded to win a swimming contest by his little nephew ... with the aid of a shark's fin.

5187. Porky's Party (*Looney Tunes*) 25 June 1938; *p.c.:* Leon Schlesinger prods for WB; *dir/story:* Robert Clampett; *anim:* Charles Jones, Norman McCabe; *sets:* Elmer Plummer; *ed:* Tregoweth E. Brown; *voices:* Mel Blanc; *mus:* Carl W. Stalling; *prod sup:* Henry Binder, Raymond G. Katz; b&w. *sd:* Vit. 7 min. • Porky invites a greedy penguin, a silkworm, an intoxicated dog and the truculent Goosey to his birthday party.

5188. Porky's Pastry Pirates (*Looney Tunes*) 17 Jan. 1942; *p.c.:* Leon Schlesinger prods for WB; *dir:* I. Freleng; *story:* Dave Monahan; *anim:* Gerald Chiniquy; *sets:* Robert L. Holdeman; *ed:* Treg Brown; *voices:* Mel Blanc, Kent Rogers; *mus:* Carl W. Stalling; *prod sup:* Henry Binder, Raymond G. Katz; b&w. *sd:* Vit. 7 min. • A tough bee shows a dumb fly how to steal food from Porky's sanitized bakery by disguising himself as a bee.

5189. Porky's Pet (*Looney Tunes*) 11 July 1936; *p.c.:* Leon Schlesinger prods for WB; *dir:* Jack King; *anim:* Cal Dalton, Sandy Walker; *voices:* Joe Dougherty, Elmore Vincent; *mus:* Norman Spencer; *prod sup:* Henry Binder, Raymond G. Katz; b&w. *sd:* Vit. 7 min. • Porky tries to sneak his pet ostrich aboard a train that has a strict "No Pets" policy.

5190. Porky's Phoney Express (*Looney Tunes*) 19 Mar. 1938; *p.c.:* Leon Schlesinger prods for WB; *dir:* Cal Howard, Cal Dalton; *story:* Melvin Millar; *anim:* Herman Cohen; *lay:* Griff Jay; *back:* Arthur Loomer; *ed:* Tregoweth E. Brown; *voices:* Mel Blanc, Billy Bletcher, Fred Avery; *mus:* Carl W. Stalling; *prod sup:* Henry Binder, Raymond G. Katz; b&w. *sd:* Vit. 7 min. • The Pony Express boss sends Porky out as a decoy for the Indians.

5191. Porky's Picnic (*Looney Tunes*) 15 July 1939; *p.c.:* Leon Schlesinger prods for WB; *dir/story:* Robert Clampett; *anim:* Robert Cannon, Vive Risto; *sets:* Elmer Plummer; *ed:* Tregoweth E. Brown; *voices:* Mel Blanc, Shirley Reed; *mus:* Carl W. Stalling; *prod sup:* Henry Binder, Raymond G. Katz; b&w. *sd:* Vit. 7 min. • Porky and Petunia take little Pinkie on a picnic. The brat spends all his time playing sadistic tricks on Porky.

5192. Porky's Pooch (*Looney Tunes*) 27 Dec. 1941; *p.c.:* Leon Schlesinger prods for WB; *dir:* Robert Clampett; *story:* Warren Foster; *anim:* I. Ellis; *ed:* Treg Brown; *voices:* Mel Blanc, Sara Berner; *mus:* Carl W. Stalling; *prod sup:* Henry Binder, Raymond G. Katz; b&w. *sd:* Vit. 7 min. • An ex-hobo dog tells of how he obtained a master by perseverance and is now living in style.

5193. Porky's Poor Fish (*Looney Tunes*) 27 Apr. 1940; *p.c.:* Leon Schlesinger prods for WB; *dir:* Robert Clampett; *story:* Melvin Millar; *anim:* David Hoffman; *ed:* Treg Brown; *voices:* Mel Blanc; *mus:* Carl W. Stalling; *ph:* John W. Burton; *prod sup:* Henry Binder, Raymond G. Katz; b&w. *sd:* Vit. 7 min. • A hungry cat walks into Porky's Pet Fish Shop, expecting to dine out but the other fish give him a rough time.

5194. Porky's Poppa (*Looney Tunes*) 15 Jan. 1938; *p.c.:* Leon Schlesinger prods for WB; *dir/story:* Robert Clampett; *anim:* Charles Jones; *sets:* Elmer Plummer; *ed:* Tregoweth E. Brown; *voices:* Mel Blanc, Russ Powell; *mus:* Carl W. Stalling; *prod sup:* Henry Binder, Raymond G. Katz; b&w. *sd:* Vit. 7 min. • To help farm production, Poppa employs a mechanical cow. Porky prefers faithful old Bessie and they have a contest between the two.

5195. Porky's Poultry Plant (*Looney Tunes*) 22 Aug. 1936; *p.c.:* Leon Schlesinger prods for WB; *dir:* Frank Tash(lin); *anim:* Don Williams, Volney White; *voice:* Joe Dougherty; *mus:* Carl W. Stalling; *prod sup:* Henry Binder, Raymond G. Katz; b&w. *sd:* Vit. 7 min. • Porky engages in an aerial dogfight with a flock of hawks who have been preying on his chickens. Tashlin's first for Schlesinger, also Carl Stalling's initiation of a lengthy association.

5196. Porky's Preview (*Looney Tunes*) 19 Apr. 1941; *p.c.:* Leon Schlesinger prods for WB; *dir:* Fred Avery; *story:* Dave Monahan, Robert Clampett; *anim:* Virgil Ross; *sets:* John Didrik Johnsen; *lay:* John McGrew; *back:* Eugene Fleury; *ed:* Treg Brown; *voices:* Mel Blanc, Sara Berner, Cliff Nazarro; *mus:* Carl W. Stalling; *prod sup:* Henry Binder, Raymond G. Katz; b&w. *sd:* Vit. 7 min. • Porky makes his own animated cartoon.

5197. Porky's Prize Pony (*Looney Tunes*) 21 June 1941; *p.c.:* Leon Schlesinger prods for WB; *dir:* Charles M. Jones; *story:* Rich Hogan; *anim:*

Ken Harris; *lay:* John McGrew, *back:* Eugene Fleury; *ed:* Treg Brown; *voice:* Mel Blanc; *mus:* Carl W. Stalling; *prod sup:* Henry Binder, Raymond G. Katz; b&w. *sd:* Vit. 7 min. • Porky's incompetent horse is substituted in the big race when the favorite is discovered to be drunk and incapable.

5198. Porky's Railroad (*Looney Tunes*) 28 Aug. 1937; *p.c.:* Leon Schlesinger prods for WB; *dir:* Frank Tashlin; *anim:* Joe d'Igalo, Robert Bentley; *lay:* Griff Jay; *ed:* Tregoweth E. Brown; *voices:* Mel Blanc, Billy Bletcher, Dave Weber; *mus:* Carl W. Stalling; *prod sup:* Henry Binder, Raymond G. Katz; b&w. *sd:* Vit. 7 min. • Porky and his antiquated train are made redundant in favour of a new streamlined express. A race between the two is soon in process.

5199. Porky's Road Race (*Looney Tunes*) 6 Feb. 1937; *p.c.:* Leon Schlesinger prods for WB; *dir:* Frank Tash(lin); *anim:* Robert Bentley, Joe d'Igalo; *character des:* T. Hee; *lay:* Griff Jay; *ed:* Tregoweth E. Brown; *voices:* Joe Dougherty, Ted Pierce, Elvia Allman, Billy Bletcher; *mus:* Carl W. Stalling; *prod sup:* Henry Binder, Raymond G. Katz; b&w. *sd:* Vit. 7 min. • Porky has a car race against Hollywood personalities with Borax Karoff as the villain of the piece. *Caricatures:* George Arliss, John Barrymore, Freddie Bartholomew, Charles Chaplin, W.C. Fields, Clark Gable, Greta Garbo Leslie Howard, Charles Laughton, Laurel & Hardy and Edna May Oliver.

5200. Porky's Romance (*Looney Tunes*) 17 Apr. 1937; *p.c.:* Leon Schlesinger prods for WB; *dir:* Frank Tash(lin); *anim:* Bob Bentley, Joe d'Igalo; *lay:* Griff Jay; *ed:* Tregoweth E. Brown; *voices:* Joe Dougherty, Shirley Reed, Mel Blanc; *mus:* Carl W. Stalling; *prod sup:* Henry Binder, Raymond G. Katz; b&w. *sd:* Vit. 8 min. • Porky's proposal to Petunia is snubbed and this, coupled with a terrifying dream of matrimony, keeps our hero from the altar. • The first appearance, albeit short-lived, of Porky's girlfriend, Petunia. Also the first use of Mel Blanc's ubiquitous voice.

5201. Porky's Snooze Reel (*Looney Tunes*) 11 Jan. 1941; *p.c.:* Leon Schlesinger prods for WB; *dir:* Robert Clampett, Norman McCabe; *story:* Warren Foster; *anim:* John Carey, Cal Dalton, Arthur Davis, David Hoffman, Vive Risto; *sets:* Richard H. Thomas; *ed:* Treg Brown; *voices:* Robert C. Bruce, Mel Blanc; *mus:* Carl W. Stalling; *prod sup:* Henry Binder, Raymond G. Katz; b&w. *sd:* Vit. 7 min. • Newsreel consisting of topical events of 1940.

5202. Porky's Spring Planting (*Looney Tunes*) 16 July 1938; *p.c.:* Leon Schlesinger prods for WB; *dir:* Frank Tashlin; *story:* George Manuell; *anim:* Joseph d'Igalo; *ed:* Tregoweth E. Brown; *voices:* Mel Blanc, Elvia Allman; *mus:* Carl W. Stalling; *prod sup:* Henry Binder, Raymond G. Katz; b&w. *sd:* Vit. 7 min. • Porky and his dog are bothered by invading crows and chickens raiding his garden.

5203. Porky's Super Service (*Looney Tunes*) 3 July 1937; *p.c.:* Leon Schlesinger prods for WB; *dir:* Ub Iwerks; *asst dir:* Robert Clampett; *anim:* Charles Jones, Robert Clampett, Irven Spence; *sets:* Elmer Plummer; *ed:* Tregoweth E. Brown; *voices:* Mel Blanc, Elvia Allman, Dave Weber; *mus:* Carl W. Stalling; *prod sup:* Henry Binder, Raymond G. Katz; b&w. *sd:* Vit. 7 min. • Porky has to deal with a bump that travels all over a car in for servicing.

5204. Porky's Tire Trouble (*Looney Tunes*) 18 Feb. 1939; *p.c.:* Leon Schlesinger prods for WB; *dir:* Robert Clampett; *story:* Warren Foster; *anim:* Norman McCabe; *ed:* Tregoweth E. Brown; *voices:* Mel Blanc, Billy Bletcher; *mus:* Carl W. Stalling; *prod sup:* Henry Binder, Raymond G. Katz; b&w. *sd:* Vit. 7 min. • Unbeknownst to him, Porky's dog has followed him to work and falls into rubberizing solution, bouncing all over the factory.

5205. The Port of Missing Mice (*Mighty Mouse*) 2 Feb. 1945; *p.c.:* TT for Fox; *dir:* Eddie Donnelly; *story:* John Foster; *voice:* Thomas Morrison; *mus:* Philip A. Scheib; *col:* Tech. *sd:* RCA. 6½ min. • The mice are shanghaied by cats and put on to ships departing the Barbary Coast.

5206. Port Whines (*Krazy Kat*) 10 Oct. 1929; *p.c.:* Winkler for Colum; *anim:* Ben Harrison, Manny Gould; *mus:* Rosario Bourdon; *prod mgr:* George Winkler; b&w. *sd:* WE. 6 min. • Deck hand Krazy is involved in a mutiny against a cruel captain.

5207. Posse Cat (*Tom & Jerry*) 30 Jan. 1954; *p.c.:* MGM; *dir:* William Hanna, Joseph Barbera; *anim:* Irven Spence, Ed Barge, Kenneth Muse, Ray Patterson; *lay:* Dick Bickenbach; *back:* Robert Gentle; *ed:* Jim Faris;

voice: Stan Freberg; *mus:* Scott Bradley; *ph:* Jack Stevens; *prod:* Fred Quimby; *col:* Tech. *sd:* WE. 6 min. • Tom is threatened with no more food until the food-stealing mouse is caught.

5208. Possible Possum (1965–1966); *p.c.:* TT for Fox; *ex prod:* Bill Weiss; *dir/anim:* Cosmo Anzilotti, Connie Rasinski, Artie Bartsch, Dave Tendlar; *story sup:* Tom Morrison; *story:* Larz Bourne; *sets:* Bill Focht; *ed:* Jack MacConnell; *voices:* Lionel Wilson; *mus:* Jim Timmens; *ph:* Ted Moskowitz, Joe Rasinski; *sd:* Elliott Grey; *col:* DeLuxe. *sd:* RCA. 6 min. • Adventures of the animal inhabitants of the rural Sleepy Hollow community.

5209. Possum Pearl (*Noveltoon*) 20 Sept. 1957; *p.c.:* Para Cartoons; *dir:* Seymour Kneitel; *story:* Jack Mercer; *anim:* Tom Johnson, Frank Endres; *sets:* John Zago; *voices:* Dorothy Shay, Jack Mercer; *mus:* Winston Sharples; *ph:* Leonard McCormick; *prod mgr:* Seymour Shultz; *col:* Tech. *sd:* RCA. 6 min. • Pearl, a man-hungry hillbilly, thinks she has at last found a man when a bank robber hides out in her mountain cabin.

5210. Post War Inventions (*Terry-Toon*) 23 Mar. 1945; *p.c.:* TT for Fox; *dir:* Connie Rasinski; *story:* John Foster; *voices:* Arthur Kay, Thomas Morrison; *mus:* Philip A. Scheib; *ph:* Douglas Moye; *col:* Tech. *sd:* RCA. 6½ min. • Gandy and Sourpuss get entangled in many strange futuristic inventions, such as television.

5211. Potions and Notions (*Honey Halfwitch*) Aug. 1966; *p.c.:* Para Cartoons; *dir:* Shamus Culhane; *story:* Heyward Kling, Tony Peters; *anim:* Al Eugster, Wm. B. Pattengill, Martin Taras; *sets:* Robert Little; *voices:* Shari Lewis, Bob MacFadden; *mus:* Winston Sharples; *prod sup:* Harold Robins, Burt Hanft; *col:* Tech. *sd:* RCA. 6 min. • Honey uses Cousin Maggie's "Love Potion" in icing a cake. Maggie eats some and falls for Stanley the Sorcerer.

5212. Pots and Pans (*Aesop's Sound Fable*) 14 May 1932; *p.c.:* Van Beuren for RKO; *dir:* John Foster, George Rufle; *mus:* Gene Rodemich; b&w. *sd:* RCA. 6 min. • Short-order cooks Tom and Jerry do their best to serve the customers when their diner runs amock and onto a railroad track while their patrons sing "I Want Mean Music."

5213. Poultry Pirates (*Captain & Kids*) 16 Apr. 1938; *p.c.:* MGM; *dir:* Isadore Freleng; *anim:* Emery Hawkins, Jack Zander; *ed:* Fred MacAlpin; *voice:* Billy Bletcher; *mus:* Scott Bradley; *prod mgr:* Fred Quimby; *col:* sep. *sd:* WE. 7 min. • The Captain tries to keep the chickens out of his vegetable garden.

5214. The Power 1968; *p.c.:* MGM/Galaxy; *prod:* George Pal; *fx:* Wah Chang, Gene Warren, J. McMillan Johnson; *l/a dir:* Byron Haskin; *col:* Metro; *sd:* WE. 99 min. Panavision; *l/a/anim:* • Based on Frank M. Robinson's novel, this live-action feature involves a scientist (Michael Rennie) with a superbrain that can kill by willpower.

5215. The Power of Thought (*Heckle & Jeckle*) 31 Dec. 1951; *p.c.:* TT for Fox; *dir:* Eddie Donnelly; *story:* John Foster; *anim:* Jim Tyer; *voices:* Thomas Morrison; *mus:* Philip A. Scheib; *ph:* Douglas Moye; *col:* Tech. *sd:* RCA. 6 min. • The Magpies utilize their being "cartoon characters" at the expense of a confused cop.

5216. Powers Cartoons *p.c.:* Powers for Univ; *prod:* Patrick A. Powers; b&w. sil. 4 min. • *1915:* **Hunting in Crazyland** * 2 Jan. **To Frisco By the Cartoon Route** 9 Aug. *anim:* Hy Mayer • *1916:* **Sammie Johnsin, Hunter** 19 Jan. *anim:* Pat Sullivan. **Joe Boko's Adventures** * 9 Feb. *anim:* Wallace A. Carlson. **Sammie Johnsin, Strong Man** 3 Mar. *anim:* Pat Sullivan. **A Romance of Toyland** 9 Mar. *anim:* Horace F. Taylor, W.W. Wheatley. **A Toyland Mystery** 15 Mar. *anim:* Horace F. Taylor, W.W. Wheatley. **The Toyland Villain** 12 Apr. *anim:* Horace F. Taylor, W.W. Wheatley. **Globe Trotting with Hy Mayer** 14 Apr. *anim:* Hy Mayer. **Mr. Fuller Pep: He Tries Mesmerism** * 3 May. *anim:* F.M. Follett. **A Toyland Robbery** 10 May. *anim:* Horace F. Taylor, W.W. Wheatley. **Mr. Fuller Pep: He Dabbles in the Pond** * 17 May. *anim:* F.M. Follett. **Mr. Fuller Pep Breaks for the Beach** * 31 May. *anim:* F.M. Follett. **Professor Wiseguy's Trip to the Moon** 6 June. *anim:* Joseph Cammer. **Sammie Johnsin, Magician** * 20 June. *anim:* Pat Sullivan. **Such Is Life in China** 22 June. *anim:* Hy Mayer. **Sammie Johnsin Gets a Job** * 3 July. *anim:* Pat Sullivan. **Jitney Jack and Gasolena** 20 July. *anim:* Jay Evans. **Sammie Johnsin in Mexico** * 10 Aug. *anim:* Pat Sullivan. **Pen and Inklings Around Jerusalem** 5 Oct. *anim:* Hy Mayer. **Winsor McCay and His Jersey Skeeters** * 11 Oct. *anim:*

Winsor McCay. **Sammie Johnsin Minds the Baby** * 23 Oct. *anim:* Pat Sullivan. **Motor Mat and His Fliv** 8 Nov. *anim:* Pat Sullivan. **High Life on a Farm** 9 Nov. *anim:* Hy Mayer. **A Pen Trip to Palestine** 9 Nov. *anim:* Hy Mayer. **Sammie Johnsin at the Seaside** * 18 Nov. *anim:* Pat Sullivan. **Sammy Johnsin's Love Affair** * 24 Nov. *anim:* Pat Sullivan. **The Trials of a Movie Cartoonist** 29 Nov. *anim:* Pat Sullivan, Otto Messmer. **Sammie Johnsin and His Wonderful Lamp** * 8 Dec. *anim:* Pat Sullivan. **Such Is Life in Alaska** 19 Dec. *anim:* Hy Mayer. **Sammie Johnsin Slumbers Not** * 21 Dec. *anim:* Pat Sullivan, Rudolph L. Eggeman • *1917:* **Boomer Bill's Awakening** 3 Jan. *anim:* Pat Sullivan, George D. Clardy. **The Trials of Willie Winks** 7 Jan. *anim:* Pat Sullivan. **Mr. Fuller Pep: He Celebrates His Wedding Anniversary** * 14 Jan. *anim:* F.M. Follett. **Fearless Freddie in the Woolly West** 20 Jan. *anim:* Pat Sullivan. **Mr. Fuller Pep: He Goes to the Country** * 21 Jan. *anim:* F.M. Follett. **Mr. Fuller Pep: His Wife Goes for a dRest** * 4 Feb. *anim:* F.M. Follett. **A Day in the Life of a Dog** 14 Feb. *anim:* Pat Sullivan, Will Anderson. **Mr. Fuller Pep: He Does Some Quick Moving** * 18 Feb. *anim:* F.M. Follett. **The Tail of Thomas Kat** 3 Mar. *anim:* Pat Sullivan. **Mr. Fuller Pep: An Old Bird Pays Him a Visit** * 4 Mar. *anim:* F.M. Follett. **The Love Affair of Ima Knut** 9 Mar. *anim:* Pat Sullivan, Otto Messmer. **Mr. Fuller Pep: His Day of Rest** * 11 Mar. *anim:* F.M. Follett. **Inbad the Sailor** 21 Mar. *anim:* Pat Sullivan. **The Ups and Downs of Mr. Phool Phancy** 27 Mar. *anim:* Milt Gross. **Boomer Bill Goes to Sea** 31 Mar. *anim:* Pat Sullivan. **A Good Story About a Bad Egg** 12 Apr. *anim:* Pat Sullivan. **A Barnyard Nightmare** 28 Apr. *anim:* Pat Sullivan. **Such Is Life in Algeria** 28 Apr. *anim:* Hy Mayer. **Cupid Gets Some New Dope** * 14 May. *anim:* Pat Sullivan. **20,000 Laughs Under the Sea** 14 May. *anim:* Pat Sullivan. **When Noah's Ark Embarked** 19 May. *anim:* John Colman Terry. **Them Were the Happy Days** 26 May. *anim:* Pat Sullivan, Otto Messmer. **A Pesky Pup** 6 June. *anim:* Pat Sullivan, Joseph Harwitz. **Young Nick Carter, Detectiff** 9 June. *anim:* Pat Sullivan, Will Anderson. **Duke Dolittle's Jungle Fizzle** 18 June. *anim:* Pat Sullivan, Charles Saxon. **China Awakened** 26 June. *anim:* Hy Mayer. **Monkey Love** 3 July. *anim:* Pat Sullivan, Ernest Smythe. **Seven Cutey Pups** 7 July. *anim:* Vincent Colby. **Box Car Bill Falls in Luck** 10 July. *anim:* Pat Sullivan, Bill Cause. **A Good Liar** 24 July. *anim:* Pat Sullivan, Otto Messmer. **A Barnyard Hamlet** * 24 July. *anim:* Pat Sullivan, W.E. Stark. **Hammon Egg's Reminiscences** 24 July. *anim:* Pat Sullivan. **Seeing Ceylon** 6 Aug. *anim:* Hy Mayer. **Colonel Pepper's Mobilized Farm** * 10 Aug. *anim:* Pat Sullivan. **Doing His Bit** 10 Aug. *anim:* Pat Sullivan. **Seeing New York** 15 Oct. • *1918:* **New York by Heck** 1 May. *anim:* Hy Mayer • See previous individual items marked with *.

5217. The Practical Pig (*Three Little Pigs*) 24 Feb. 1939; *p.c.:* Walt Disney prods for RKO; *dir/story:* Dick Rickard; *asst dir:* Ford Beebe; *addit story:* Harry Reeves; *anim:* Larry Clemmons, Gilles de Tremaudan, Norman Ferguson, Max Gray, Jack Hannah, Oliver M. Johnston, Fred Moore, Claude Smith, Franklin Thomas, Riley Thomson, Roy Williams; *fx:* Arthur W. Palmer, George Rowley; *character des:* Ferdinand Huszti Horvath; *lay:* Ken Anderson, A. Kendall O'Connor, Thor Putnam; *voices:* Billy Bletcher, Betty Bruce, Tom Buchanan, Ralph Hansell, Donald Hearin, Dick Holland, Leone Le Doux, Mary Moder, Tommy Wiggins; *mus:* Paul J. Smith; *col:* Tech. *sd:* RCA. 8 min. • The Big Bad Wolf lures two of the pigs to his lair and returns to get their brother who has invented a lie detector to trap him.

5218. Practical Yolk (*Woody Woodpecker*) May 1966; *p.c.:* Walter Lantz prods for Univ; *dir:* Paul J. Smith; *story:* Cal Howard; *anim:* Les Kline, Al Coe; *sets:* Ray Huffine; *voices:* Grace Stafford, Daws Butler; *mus:* Walter Greene; *prod mgr:* William E. Garity; *col:* Tech. *sd:* RCA. 6 min. • Woody has fun with Mrs. Meanie while she's in the desert looking for a 2000-year-old egg.

5219. Practice Makes Perfect (*Fable*) 5 Apr. 1940; *p.c.:* Col; *story:* Harry Love; *anim:* Allen Rose; *lay:* Clark Watson; *back:* Phil Davis; *ed:* George Winkler; *voice:* Robert Winkler; *mus:* Joe de Nat; *ph:* Otto Reimer; *prod mgr:* James Bronis; *b&w. sd:* RCA. 6 min. • Scrappy trys his piano practice despite Yippie speeding up the tempo and Oopy getting inside.

5220. Pre-Hysterical Hare (*Looney Tunes*) 23 Aug. 1958; *p.c.:* WB; *dir:* Robert McKimson; *story:* Tedd Pierce; *anim:* Ted Bonnicksen, Warren Batchelder, Tom Ray, George Grandpré, David R. Green; *lay:* Robert Gribbroek; *back:* William Butler; *ed:* Treg Brown; *voices:* Mel Blanc, Dave Barry; *mus:* John Seely; *prod:* John W. Burton; *col:* Tech. *sd:* Vit. 7 min. • While

hiding from Elmer's shotgun, Bugs discovers a prehistoric roll of film depicting a Neanderthal Fudd and an equally primitive Bugs.

5221. Pre-Hysterical Man (*Popeye*) 26 Mar. 1948; *p.c.:* Famous for Para; *dir:* Seymour Kneitel; *story:* Carl Meyer, Jack Mercer; *anim:* Dave Tendlar, Morey Reden; *sets:* Anton Loeb; *voices:* Jack Mercer, Mae Questel; *mus:* Winston Sharples; *ph:* Leonard McCormick; *prod mgr:* Sam Buchwald; *col:* Pola. *sd:* RCA. 8 min. • On an archaeological expedition, Popeye and Olive encounter an amorous Neanderthal.

5222. Prefabricated Pink (*Pink Panther*) 22 Nov. 1967; *p.c.:* Mirisch/Geoffrey/DFE for UA; *dir:* Hawley Pratt; *story:* Jim Ryan; *anim:* Warren Batchelder, Chuck Downs, Don Williams, Manny Gould, Manny Perez, Bob Matz; *lay:* Dick Ung; *back:* Tom O'Loughlin; *ed:* Lee Gunther; *mus:* Walter Greene; *theme tune:* Henry Mancini; *prod sup:* Harry Love, Basil Cox; *col:* DeLuxe. *sd:* RCA. 6 min. • The Panther causes chaos on a building site.

5223. Prehistoric Perils (*Mighty Mouse*) Mar. 1952; *p.c.:* TT for Fox; *dir:* Connie Rasinski; *story:* Tom Morrison; *anim:* Jim Tyer; *sets:* Art Bartsch; *voice:* Roy Halee; *mus:* Philip A. Scheib; *ph:* Douglas Moye; *col:* Tech. *sd:* RCA. 6 min. • Oil Can Harry abducts Pearl Pureheart into a time machine, transporting them back to stoneage times.

5224. Prehistoric Pink (*Pink Panther*) 7 Aug. 1968; *p.c.:* Mirisch/Geoffrey/DFE for UA; *dir:* Hawley Pratt; *story:* John W. Dunn; *anim:* Warren Batchelder, Don Williams, Manny Gould, Manny Perez, Art Leonardi; *lay:* Dick Ung; *back:* Tom O'Loughlin; *ed:* Lee Gunther; *mus:* Walter Greene; *theme tune:* Henry Mancini; *ph:* John Burton Jr.; *prod sup:* Harry Love, Jim Foss; *col:* Tech. *sd:* RCA. 6 min. • Prehistoric Panther invents the wheel but thinks better of it and destroys the thing.

5225. Prehistoric Porky (*Looney Tunes*) 12 Oct. 1940; *p.c.:* Leon Schlesinger prods for WB; *dir:* Robert Clampett; *story:* Melvin Millar; *anim:* John Carey; *ed:* Treg Brown; *voices:* Mel Blanc, Sara Berner, The Sportsmen Quartet; *mus:* Carl W. Stalling; *prod sup:* Henry Binder, Raymond G. Katz; *b&w. sd:* Vit. 7 min. • Caveman Porky sets out to get a new suit of clothes from a sabretoothed tiger.

5226. Prehistoric Poultry the Diornis (or) The Great Roaring Whiffenpoof 1917; *p.c.:* Thomas A. Edison; *dir:* Willis Harold O'Brien; *b&w. sil.* 3 min. • A bothersome fowl annoys a caveman, a cave woman and a hunter.

5227. Prehistoric Super Salesman (*Woody Woodpecker*) 1 Sept. 1969; *p.c.:* Walter Lantz prods for Univ; *dir:* Paul J. Smith; *story:* Homer Brightman; *anim:* Les Kline, Al Coe; *sets:* Nino Carbe; *voices:* Daws Butler, Grace Stafford; *mus:* Walter Greene; *prod mgr:* William E. Garity; *col:* Tech. *sd:* RCA. 6 min. • Salesman Woody is tricked into an inventor's "Time Tunnel" and transported back to prehistoric times.

5228. Prescription for Percy (*Little Roquefort*) Apr. 1954; *p.c.:* TT for Fox; *dir:* Mannie Davis; *story:* Tom Morrison; *anim:* Jim Tyer; *story:* Tom Morrison; *mus:* Philip A. Scheib; *ph:* Douglas Moye; *col:* Tech. *sd:* RCA. 6 min. • While in a drugstore, Roquefort gets covered in vanishing cream and torments the cat.

5229. Presto — Chango (*Aesop's Sound Fable*) 14 Apr. 1929; *p.c.:* Fables Pictures Inc for Pathé; *dir:* Paul Terry; *anim:* Frank Moser; *mus:* Josiah Zuro; *sd fx:* Maurice Manne; *b&w. sd:* RCA. 6 min. • A cat takes his girl to China Town for a meal where she is kidnapped by the orientals and a rooftop chase ensues.

5230. Prest-o Change-o (*Merrie Melodies*) 25 Mar. 1939; *p.c.:* Leon Schlesinger prods for WB; *dir:* Charles M. Jones; *story:* Rich Hogan; *anim:* Ken Harris; *lay:* Robert Givens; *back:* Paul Julian; *ed:* Tregoweth E. Brown; *voices:* Mel Blanc; *mus:* Carl W. Stalling; *prod sup:* Henry Binder, Raymond G. Katz; *col:* Tech. *sd:* Vit. 7 min. • Two curious pups seek refuge in a magician's house and have adventures with a selection of magical things.

5231. Pretzels (*Paul Terry-Toon*) 24 Mar. 1930; *p.c.:* A-C for Educational/Fox; *dir:* Frank Moser, Paul Terry; *mus:* Philip A. Scheib; *b&w. sd:* WE. 6 min. • A German mouse in a beer garden has a duel with a cat for his lady love.

5232. Pride of the Yard (*Percival Sleuth-hound*) May 1954; *p.c.:* TT for Fox; *dir:* Eddie Donnelly; *story:* Tom Morrison; *anim:* Jim Tyer; *mus:* Philip A. Scheib; *ph:* Douglas Moye; *col:* Tech. *sd:* RCA. 6 min. • Two canine thugs bust out of a London prison and it's up to Scotland Yard's finest to bring them to justice.

5233. Primitive Pluto (*Pluto*) 19 May 1950; *p.c.:* Walt Disney prods for RKO; *dir:* Charles Nichols; *story:* Milt Schaffer, Dick Kinney; *anim:* George Nicholas, George Kreisl, Hugh Fraser, Phil Duncan; *lay:* Karl Karpé; *back:* Ralph Hulett; *voices:* Paul Frees, James MacDonald; *mus:* Oliver Wallace; *col:* Tech. *sd:* RCA. 6½ min. • Pluto's hunting instinct urges him to forsake his soft life of ease and go out to hunt for food like his ancestors.

5234. The Prince and the Pauper 16 Nov.1990; *p.c.:* The Walt Disney Company for BV; *dir:* George Scribner; *prod:* Dan Rounds; *art dir:* Thom Enriquez; *anim sup:* Andreas Deja, Dale L. Baer; *scr:* Gerrit Graham, Samuel Graham, Chris Hubbell, Jenny Tripp, Charles Fleischer; inspired by Mark Twain's *The Prince and the Pauper*; *storyboard:* Vance Gerry, Daan Jippes, Kirk Wise, Gary Trousdale, Robert Lence, Burny Mattinson, Roger Allers, Kevin Harkey, Mark Dindal, Kent Holaday; *anim:* Mark Henn, Tom Sito, Mark Kausler, Doug Frankel, Lennie K. Graves, Tim Allen, Jay Jackson, Tony Anselmo, Michael Gerard, Jesse Cosio, Michael Polvani, Wayne Carlisi, Doug Krohn, Dan Jeup, Ernesto Lopez, Phil Young, Brigitte Hartley, Mike Cedeno, Arland Barron, Brian Ferguson, Michael Surrey, Sue Adnopoz, Thomas Cook, David Courtland, Geoff Everts, Mark Fisher, Stan Green, Carl Hall, Ko Hashiguchi, Timothy Ingersoll, Rick Kohlschmidt, Susan Lantz, Boowon Lee, Leticia Lichtwardt, William Recinos, Joseph Roman Jr., Paul Salaiz, Glenn Schmitz, Sue Sugita, Michael Toth, Douglas Williams, James Van Der Keyl; *asso dir:* Leon Joosen; *visual development:* Dean Jippes, Alvero Arce, Jean Gillmore; *lay:* Jim Beihold, Dan St. Pierre, Mike Hodgson, Dave Dunnet, Lorenzo E. Martinez, Chris Jenkins, Jennifer Yuan, Allen Tam, Jeff Dickson, Mark Kalesniko, Doug Walker, Tom Shannon, Daniel Hu, Mark Hodgson; *back:* Kathy Altieri, Greg Drolette, Natalie Franscioni-Karp, Ric Slutter, Robert E. Stanton, Lucy Tanashian, Jeffrey Richards, Dick Heichberger; *character key:* Brett Newton, Ruben Procopio, Bruce Strock, Kathleen M. Bailey, Chris Chu, Ken Cope, June Fujimoto, Merry Kanawyer Clingen, Pat Jones, Virginia Parmele, Nelson Recinos, Maria Rosetti, Terry Wozniak, Maureen Trueblood, Dana M. Reemes; *fx anim:* Don Paul, Dorse Lanpher, Chris Jenkins, Esther Barr-Howley, Lisze Bechtold, Mauro Maressa, James De V. Mansfield, Ian Gooding, Paul Lewis, Dan Kuemmel, Kris Brown, Dan Wanket; *technical dir:* Scott Johnson; *computer anim:* Linda Bel, Tina Price, Thomas Cardone; *airbrush:* John Emerson; *col stylist:* Elrene Cowan; *col modelists:* Christina Stocks, Linda Webber; *col model paint:* Maria Gonzalez, Betsy Ergenbright; *prod mgr:* Annamarie Costa; *asst dir:* Michael Serrian; *break/inbet:* Lillian A. Chapman, Anthony Christov, Hye Young Curley, Laurey Foulkes, Kris Heller, Janice Inouye, Barry Johnson, Ken Kinoshita, William Mims, Michael Mitchell, Dennis Neil, Gregorio Nocon, Eun Ok Yu, Marsha Park, Cheryl Polakow, Mary-Jean Repchuk, Norma Rivera, Jacqueline M. Sanchez, David Simmons, Pil Yong Song, Christopher Waugh, Ron Westlund, Dave Woodman; *asst prod mgr:* Sutherland Ellwood, Donovan R. Cook III, Alexander Rannie, Alice Dewey; *scene plan:* Dave Thomson; *anim check:* Eleanor Dehlen, Kathy Barrows-Fullmer, Pat Sito, Kim Patterson, Mea Gorman; *bluesketch:* Pat Sito, Dave Recinos, Beverly Randles; *i&p:* Gretchen Maschmeyer Albrecht, Cherie McGowan; *Xerox:* Bill Brazner, Bert Wilson, Dean Stanley, Chuck Hastings, Janet M. Rea, Tina Baldwin, Gareth P. Fishbaugh, Warren R. Coffman, Diana Dixon, Marlene Burkhart, Angelo Villani, Robin Garrison, Catherine F. Parotino, Leyla Pelaez, Douglas Eugene Casper; *Xerox mark-up:* Sherri Vandoli, Jessie A. Palubeski; *Xerox check/ink:* Darlene Kanagy, Eve Fletcher, Tatsuko Watanabe, Peggy Gregory, Valerie Green, Chris Conklin, Karan Lee Storr; *mark-up/paint check:* Barbara Lynn Hamane, Micki Zurcher, Chuck Gefre, Jean A. Du Bois, Susan R. Burke, Annette Vandenberg; *paint:* Lada Babicka, Elena Marie Cox, Sybil E. Cuzzort, Eadie Hofmann, Gina Howard, Mimi Frances Clayton, Annette Leavitt, Denise Ann Link, Monica Albracht Marroquin, Debbie Mihara, Chris Naylor, Valentine Paul, Linda Redondo, Sharon Rehme, Ania M. Rubisz, Gary G. Shafer, Marcia Sinclair, Sheryl Ann Smith, S. Ann Sullivan, Kathy Wilbur, Denise Wogatzke, David Zywicki, Teri McDonald, Tania Burton, Leonor Gonzales Wood; *Florida: i&p:* Frances Kirsten, Al Kirsten, Jason L. Buske, Irma Cartaya, Greg Chin, Suzie Ewing, Robert (Scot) Kerr, Michael Lusby, Pamela Manes, Monica Mendez, Mark Michael, Al Moore, Lisa A. Reinert, L. Rippberger, Laurie J.A. Sacks, Elsa Sesto-Vidal, Andrew Simmons, Jo Ann Tzuanos, Pam Vastbinder, Sharon K. Vincent, Loretta A. Weeks, Victoria L. Winner; *Florida: prod mgr:* Tim O'Donnell; *addit anim services:* The Bear Animation Com-

pany; *second unit dir:* Dale L. Baer, Jane Baer, Jill Skinner, Hope Parker, Paul Bauman; *i&p:* The Cuckoos Nest; *paint sup:* Beth Ann McCoy; *final check:* Bonnie Blough, Wilma Baker, Janette Hulett, Paul Steele, Rhonda L. Hicks, Jan Browning, Howard F. Schwartz, Madlyn O'Neill; *prod asst:* Dan Lund, Greg Chalekian, David Nolan, Robert Lassers, Gregory Hinde, Eric Van Der Nagel; *prod interns:* Cindy Parker, Tone Thyne, Dana Beard; *ed:* H. Lee Peterson, Barbara Gerety, Jacqueline Kinney, Robert Leader; *voices: Mickey/Prince:* Wayne Allwine; *Goofy/Horace/Pluto/1st Weasel:* Bill Farmer; *Captain Pete:* Arthur Burghardt; *Donald Duck:* Tony Anselmo; *2nd & 3rd Weasels/Pig Driver/Peasant/Man in the Street:* Charlie Adler; *Archbishop/Dying King:* Frank Welker; *Clarabelle:* Elvia Allman; *Kid no. 1:* Tim Eyster; *Kid no. 2:* Rocky Krakoff; *Narrator:* Roy Dotrice; *mus:* Nicholas Pike; *scoring:* Dennis Sands, John Richards; "I'm Henry the VIII, I Am": Fred Murray, R.P. Weston; *orch:* Stuart Balcomb; *mus ed:* Do-Re-Mi Music, Stan Jones; *re-rec mix:* John Reitz, David Campbell, Gregg Rudolff; *sd ed:* Tom McCarthy, Robert Kizer, Don S. Walden, Dave Ice, Steve Born; *sd readers:* Jacqueline Kinney, Theresa Gilroy, Jim Melton, Mark Hester; *ph:* Joe Giuliano, John Cunningham, John Aardal, Charles Warren, Glenn Campbell, Chris Beck, Brandy Hill; *Baer Animation Camera:* Dan Larsen, Lin-z Rogers, Ron Jackson, Steven Wilzback, David Link; *Florida: anim ph:* Gary W. Smith, Mary E. Lescher; *fx graphics:* Bernie Gagliano; *title des:* Burke Mattsson; *optical sup:* Peter Montgomery; *col:* Tech. *sd:* Dolby stereo. 25 min. • Animated version of Mark Twain's immortal story featuring Disney characters. A peasant swaps places with a look-alike Prince who, bored with his palace existence, wants to sample life in the outside world. Both eventually realize that this is not the life for them and revert to normal but not before thwarting the evil Captain of the Guards who schemes to take over the country after the King's death.

5235. The Prince of Egypt 18 Dec. 1998; *p.c.:* Dreamworks; *dir:* Brenda Chapman, Steve Hickner, Simon Wells; *ex prod:* Jeffrey Katzenberg; *prod:* Penney Finkelman Cox, Sandra Rabins; *asso prod:* Ron Rocha; *story:* Phil LaZebnik, Ronnie del Carmen, Tony Leondis, James Fujii, Mike Ploog, Ken Harsha, Scott Santoro, Todd Kurosawa, Tom Sito; *addit story:* Nicholas Meyer, David Bowers, Paul Fisher, Randy Cartwright, Carole Holliday, Rebecca Cassady, Frank Tamura; *art dir:* Kathy Altieri, Richard Chavez; *prod des:* Darek Gogol; *artistic sup: story:* Kelly Asbury, Lorna Cook; *character des: des:* Carter Goodrich, Carlos Grangel, Nicholas Marlet, Pascal Alixe, Peter de Seve, Dan Haskett, Cathy Jones, Emil Simeonov; *sculpting:* Kent Melton, Raffaello Vecchione; *visual development/des:* Barry Atkinson, Luc Desmarchelier, Hani D. El-Masri, Barry Jackson, Sam Michlap, Craig Mullins, Christian Schellewald, Paul Shardlow, Bruce Zick; *character anim: (Moses): sup anim (older):* Kristof Serrand; *sup anim (younger):* William Salazar; *anim:* James Baxter, Arnaud Berthier, Dave B. Boudreau, Emanuela Cozzi, Bruce Ferriz, Lionel Gallat, Maximilian Graenitz, Luis Grane, Steve Horrocks, Jakob Hjort Jensen, Cathy Jones, Fabrice Joubert, Teresa Martin, Simon Otto, Jane Poole, Pedro Ramos, Erik C. Schmidt, Andrea Simonti, Dan Wagner, Eric Walls; *(Rameses) sup anim (older):* David Brewster; *sup anim (younger):* Serguei Kouchnerov; *anim:* Dan Boulos, Paul Jesper, Brad Kuha, Jean-Francois Rey; *(Tzipporah) sup anim:* Rodolphe Guenoden; *anim:* Oliver Coipel, Philippe le Brun, MaryAnn Malcomb, Ken Morrissey, Andy Schmidt; *(Jethro) sup anim:* Gary Perkovac; *(Hotep & Huy) sup anim:* Patrick Mate; *anim:* Manuel Almela; *(Miriam) sup anim:* Bob Scott; *anim:* Cecile Bender, Antony Gray; *(Aaron) sup anim:* Fabio Lignini; *(the Queen) sup anim:* David Brewster; *anim:* Robert Milne; *(Seti) sup anim:* Kristof Serrand; *anim:* Kent Culotta; *(the Camel) sup anim:* Rick Farmiloe; *(Yochered) sup anim:* Rodolphe Guenoden; *(Horses) sup anim:* Jurgen Gross; *cgi crowd anim:* Mark Chavez, Li-Han Chen, Michelle Cowart, Wendy Elwell, Ryan Roberts, Michael Spokas, Mike Ullner; *addit anim:* Claudio Acciari, Cinzia Angelini, Gary Dunn, Jerome Guillaud, Ken Hettig, Duncan Marjoribanks, Claire Morrisey, Sylvia Muller, Scott Petersen, Emil Simeonov, Sean Springer, Derek Thompson, Frans Vischer, Kathy Zielinski, Susan Zytka; *asst anim:* Marc Bascougnano, Catherine Feraday, Richard Kim, Erik Kuniak, Kevin O'Hara, Warren O'Neill, Tom Owens, Mariateresa Scarpone, Herman Sharaf, Dimos Vrysellas, Robert Weaver, Greg Whittaker, Scott Wright; *lay:* Lorenzo E. Martinez; *dpt lead:* Mark Mulgrew; *key lay/workbook:* Clive Hutchings, Douglas Kirk, Armen Melkonian, Marcos Mateu Mestre, Damon O'Beirne, Jean Luc Serrano; *lay:* Guillaume Bonamy, Eric N. Clark, Mick de Falco, Christophe Lautrette, Fedja Jovanovic, Matt Lee, Kate Moo King, Mark Marren, Francisco Mora,

Brad Morris, Benoit Le Pennec, Nol Meyer, Felipe Morell, Julia Woolf, Kenard Pak, Edmund Perryman, Alexander Puvilland, Ritche Sacilioc, Tim Soman; *scene planning:* David Morehead, Stephen Childers, Robert Crawford, Deirdre Creed, Brian Riley, Craig F. Simpson, David Valera, James Williams; *back:* Paul Lasaine, Ron Lukas, Steve Albert, Armand Baltazar, Desmond Downes, Thomas Esmeralda, Nathan Fowkes, Bari Greenberg, Tianyi Han, Tang Kheng Heng, Ruben Hickman, Wade Huntsman, Yoriko Ito, Bill Kaufmann, Joty Lam, Kevin Turcotte, Karl Wehrli, Zhaoping Wei, Donald Yatomi; *cgi/digital back:* Carolyn Guske, Robert Lowden, Carolyn Ensle-Rendu; *final line anim: dpt lead:* Brett Newton; *(Moses) sup anim:* Brian Clift; *character leads:* Millet Henson, Mariateresa Scarpone; *key asst:* Helen Michael, Pat Joens, Maureen Bushman, Siobhan Larkin, Paola Lecler, Jenni McCosker, Philippe Tilikete; *asst:* Alexandra Boiger, Mary M. Dowd, Gerry Gallego, Ken Kim, Diana LeBost, Helen T. Tse, Miri Yoon; *break/inbet:* Cindy Andress, Janine Jeongun Cho, Dindo Donglasan, Randy Dormans, Thomas Estrada, Brian Garvey, Kenny Huynh, Bang Won Lee, Daisy Lee, Russell Lingo, Chad L. Morgan, Johnny Painter, Frank Rosales, Mac Spada; *(Young Rameses) character lead:* Judy Howieson; *key asst:* Craig Hilditch, Richard Smitheman; *break/inbet:* Cory Wilson; *(Rameses & Son) character lead:* Kay Sales; *key asst:* Debbie Forster, Todd Jacobsen, Chloe Mauro; *break/inbet:* Donna Dubuc Curtis, Philip Garcia, Russell S. Lorenzo, Jasen Strong, Adam York; *(Tzipporah) character lead:* Tanja Majerus, Dawn Pearce; *asst:* Scott Bern, Gerhard Brammer, Cristi Lyon, Thomas Matzeit, Jane A. McGowan, Xavier Riffault, Tim Window, Guy Duchet, Aaron Kirby, Song Pil Yong; *break/inbet:* Joe Achorn, Glenn Bachman, Kyle Arther Jefferson, Tao Huu Nguyen; *(Hotep & Huy) character lead:* Sarah Marsden, Jennie Langley; *key asst:* Michael Alcouloumre, Nina Haley, Andy Molloy; *break/inbet:* John F. Hinshelwood, Martin P. Hopkins, Laura Murillo; *(Miriam) character lead:* Caroline Brophy, Mariateresa Scarpone; *key asst:* Mark Cote, Derek L'Estrange, Jerry Verschoor; *break/inbet:* Ramya Kuruppu Black, Steve Schumacher; *(Aaron & Moses) character lead:* Irene Parkins; *key asst:* Scott Claus, Tim Ingersoll, Miyul Lee, Michele Yim; *asst:* Trine frank, Cathlin Hidalgo; *break/inbet:* Cameron Hood, Kevin Koch, Erik Kuska, Matthew Schofield, Akemi Nakamura Tyler, Arthur Valancia; *(Queen & Yochered) character lead:* Aurea Terribili, Julia Woolf; *key asst:* Valentina D'Ambrosio, Alexa Goriup, Betty Tang, Jay Wren; *(Seti) character lead:* Sylviane Burnet; *key asst:* Pascal Ludowissy; *break/inbet:* Perfecto Badillo; *(Horses) character lead:* Jennie Langley; *key asst:* Louise Keating; *(misc character) character lead:* Ronan Spelman, Nicola Courtney; *key asst:* Franci Allen, Tom Higgins, Raffaello Vecchione, Uriel Mimran, Ed Rivera, Rick Richards; *asst:* Stan Sommers, Vicki Woodside Banks; *Fox character lead:* Mickey Cassidy; *fx: 2d dpt. lead:* Al Holter; *(Chariot Race) seq lead:* Sean McLaughlin, Leonard F.W. Green; *anim:* Andrew Brownlow, Oliver Malric, David Navarro; *digital fx:* Robert Naudon, Dennis Recchia, Ed Shurla, Pei Zhu; *asst:* Moon Hwan Choi, Martin Lanzinger, Claudio Pacciarella, Aksel Studsgarth, Ida C. Voskanian; *(Burning Bush) seq lead:* Ed Coffey, Jamie Lloyd; *anim:* Esther M. Barr, Lynette Charters, Conánn Fitzpatrick, David Lyons, Paul Teolis; *digital fx:* Stephen Krauth; *("Playing With the Big Boys") seq lead:* Stephen Wood; *anim:* Michael Duhatschek, Jeff Topping; *asst:* Chris Kirshbaum, Mark Peronto; *("the Plagues") seq lead:* Doug Ikeler, Rosanna Lyons; *anim:* John Huey, Jane Smethurst; *digital fx:* Bob Lyss; *asst:* Mark Asai, Noe Garcia, Halen Javan, Susan B. Keane, Chris Kirshbaum, Chance Lane, John McFarlane, Julie Penman, Chris Trorey; *("Red Sea") seq lead:* Henry LaBounta, Jeff Howard; *anim:* David Allen, Doug Cooper, Hock-Lian Law, Bud Myrick, Moon Seun, Amie Slate; *digital fx:* Joe Alter, Suzanne Berger, Jonah Hall, Raymond Hetu, Dan Kessler, Rodney J. McFall, Bud Myrick, Lisa Suzuki; *asst:* Matthew Freeth, Rolando Mercado, Richard Moser, Samuel Recinos; *fx break/inbet:* Lizzie Bentley, Yan Budeen, Chris Darroca, Joseph J. DiMattia, Darren Donovan, Bryce Erickson, Pin Ho, Daniel Killien, Charlene Logan, Susanna Luck, Dustin Pappas, Melanie Pava, Gisele Recinos, Robert Rios, Michael W. Scott, Jaclyn Seymour, Laurie Siqueido, Robert L.S.M. de Toscano, Kenneth Wong; *Natural Phenomenon/2d cgi:* Patrick Witting, E. Jane Gotts; *addit fx anim:* Brett Hisey, Diann Landau, Raymond Pang, Bob Simmons; *visual fx:* Don Paul, Dan Philips; *voices: Moses:* Val Kilmer; *Rameses:* Ralph Fiennes; *Tzipporah:* Michelle Pfeiffer; *Miriam:* Sandra Bullock; *Aaron:* Jeff Goldblum; *Jethro:* Danny Glover; *Seti:* Patrick Stewart; *The Queen:* Helen Mirren; *Hotep:* Steve Martin; *Huy:* Martin Short; *Young Miriam:* Eden Riegel; *Rameses Son:* Bobby Motown; *Yochered:* Ofra Haza; *also:* James Avery, Aria Noelle Curzon, Stephanie Sawyer, Francesca Smith; *Hebrew*

Children chorus: Shira Roth, Michael Patrician, Christopher Marquette, Justin Timsit; *Boys' Choir:* The Boy Choristers of Salisbury Cathedral Choir; *soloist:* Andrew Johnson — St. Paul's Cathedral Choir; "Queen in Reprise" sung by Linda Dee Shayne; "Through Heaven's Eyes" sung by Brian Stokes Mitchell; "When You Believe" sung by Michelle Pfeiffer, Sally Dworsky; *mus:* Marylata E. Jacob; *songs:* Stephen Schwartz; *score:* Hans Zimmer; *graphics software developers:* Saty Raghavachary, Andy Bruss, Peter Cucka, Oliver Unter Ecker, Gigi Yates; *col models:* David Svend Karoll, Alison Flintham, Li René Harmon, Soo King, Eric Kurland, Susan van der Horst; *col mark-up:* Bridgette Hernandez-Biskobing, Gabriella Lynne Shaw, Doug Tiano; *scanning:* Pat Sito, Shauna Stevens; *back scanner:* Nathan Scott, Kevin Blum, Frank P. Brunetto, David John Duff, Christopher Knights, Roger Phillips; *anim/digital/final check:* Benjamin Berkman, James Bird, Torien Blackwolf, Bonnie Blough, Laura Craig, Chuck Gefre, Brendan Harris, Rachel Lagdao, Denise Link, James Scholte, Justin Schultz, Colin Sittig, Kathy St. Germain, Claire Williams; *digital paint:* Jillian Tudor, Danny Albano Jr., Marco Balderrama, Kathy Baur, James Bentley, Brandon Bloch, David A. Craig, Damon Crowe, Alex DeLeón, Alma L. Glick, Patricia L. Gold, Lance Hayashida, Shelly Henderson, Cheryl C. Hills, Wendy Jacobsmeyer, Angel Jemmott, Stevan King, Marty Luber, Judy Manning, Stephen L. Mitchell, Adria Munnerlyn, Eddie Muñoz, Ernesto Navarre, David Nimitz, Devon Oddone, Catherine O'Leary, Joseph Olivares, Kenneth O'Malley, Howard Rogers, Matthew Schiavone, Alice M. Solis, Kevin Stanley, Christopher M. Staples, Steve Stewart, Bryan Taylor, Helga Vanden Berge, Dirk von Besser, John Voors, Liz Werden, Martina Zbirka Schmidt; *editing: sup ed:* Nick Fletcher; *ed:* John Carnochan, Sim Evans-Jones, Vicki Hiatt, Clare de Chenu, Marcus Taylor, Lois Belluci Hoover; *track reader:* James Ryan; *re-rec mix:* Andy Nelson, Anna Behlmer, Sean Murphy; *post prod exe:* Curt Schulkey, Mike Wilhoit; *foley sup:* Kelly Oxford; *sd ed:* Neal Anderson, Chris Assells, Greg Hainer, Phil Hess, Chris Hogan, Craig Jaeger, Randy Kelly, Tony Lamberti, Pete Lehman, David McMoyler, Brian McPherson, Rick Morris, Gayle Wesley, David Stanke; *foley:* David Alstadter, Jim Moriana, Jeff Wilhoit, J.C. Lucas; *addit audio:* Mark Ormandy, Peter Zinda; *ADR voice casting:* Sandy Holt/Loopease, Leslee Feldman; *ADR mix:* Greg Steele; *titles & optics:* Pacific Title/Mirage; *neg cutter:* Mo Henry; *col timer:* Terry Claborn; *Avid Support:* Alex Drought, Steve Moder; *prod management: digital col prod mgr:* Matthew Teevan; *digital operations mgr:* Barbara McCullough; *prod sup: anim/final line:* Mark Swift, Steve Pegram; *fx/story:* Maryann Garger; *snr co-ord: editorial:* Andrew Birch; *sweatbox:* Bret Babos; *co-ord: story:* Tiffany Powell; *lay:* Linda Jo, Frederick Lissau; *scene plan:* Kristen McKittrick; *anim:* Charlie Kranz, Rick Ziegler; *final line:* Randy Sefcik, Tim Kinnaird; *back:* Mark Tarbox; *fx/cgi:* Kim Mackey, Noel Wolfman; *scanning:* Ross Michael Field, Carrie Wilksen, ArtScans Studio Inc.; *plotting:* Sergio Armendariz; *checking:* Ameake Owens; *col models/visual development:* Lisa Fuerst-Brosnan; *digital paint:* Courtney Barron, Brian Faiola; *film rec:* Kathleen Kelly; *script continuity:* Adrienne Lusby; *research: community liaison:* Tzivia Schwartz-Getzug; *archeologist:* Dr. Daniel Polz; *religious consultants:* Everett Fox, Dr. Burton Visotzky, Rabbi Stephen Robbins, Shoshanna Gershenzon; *research:* Wendy Zeller; *librarian:* Elizabeth Faye; *asst:* Lori Feldman, Karin Levinson, Jewane McBride, Sam Ragsdale, Marisa Rothman, Wendy Hills; *mus: ex in charge of mus:* Todd Homme; *mus ed:* Adam Smalley, Brian Richards; *technical mus advisor:* Marc Streitenfeld, Justin Burnett, Slamm Andrews; *orch:* Bruce L. Fowler, Ladd McIntosh, Yvonne S. Moriarty; *mus conducted by:* Gavin Greenaway, Harry Gregson-Williams, Rupert Gregson-Williams; *costume des:* Kelly Kimball; *sd des/sup:* Lon Bender, Wylie Stateman; *sup prod mgr:* Ken Tsumura; *prod mgr:* Bill Damaschke; *col:* Tech. *sd:* Dolby stereo. 99 min. • Animated version of the biblical story from Exodus of how Moses rebels against his father and leads the slaves to a promised land.

5236. The Prince of Whales (*Life Cartoon Comedy*) 10 Apr. 1927; *p.c.:* Sherwood Wadsworth Pictures for Educational; *prod/dir:* John R. McCrory; b&w. sil. 5 min. • Little Nibbins and his pup are aboard a whaler when they spy a school of whales. They row out to sea and chase the creatures back onto the boat in a neat stack.

5237. Prince Violent (*Looney Tunes*) 2 Sept. 1961; *p.c.:* WB; *dir:* Friz Freleng; *asst dir:* Hawley Pratt; *story:* Dave DeTiege; *anim:* Gerry Chiniquy, Virgil Ross, Art Davis, Bob Matz; *lay:* Willie Ito; *back:* Tom O'Loughlin; *ed:* Treg Brown; *voices:* Mel Blanc; *mus:* Milt Franklyn; *prod mgr:* William

Orcutt; *prod:* David H. DePatie; *col:* Tech. *sd:* Vit. 7 min. • Peasant Bugs deals with a pillaging Viking (Sam) who is trying to gain entrance to a castle.

5238. Princess Nicotine 1909; *p.c.:* Vitagraph Co of America; *anim:* J. Stuart Blackton; b&w. *sil.* 8 min. • Animated cigarettes, cigars, matches, and other assorted smoking implements come alive via stop-motion animation.

5239. The Prison Panic (*Oswald*) 30 Apr. 1930; *p.c.:* Univ; *dir:* Walter Lantz; *anim:* "Bill" Nolan, Ray Abrams, Manuel Moreno, Clyde Geronimi; *mus:* David Broekman; b&w. *sd:* WE. 6 min. • Prison guard Oswald pursues a mouse who has broken out of prison. The mouse robs some characters and is caught in a flood before Oswald brings him to justice.

5240. The Prisoner's Song (*Screen Songs*) 1 Mar. 1930; *p.c.:* The Fleischer Studio for Para; *dir/arr:* Max Fleischer; *mus:* Art Turkisher; *song:* Vernon Dalhart; b&w. *sd:* WE. 8 min. • Prisoners laboring on a rock pile in the prison yard.

5241. Private-Eye Pooch (*Woody Woodpecker*) 9 May 1955; *p.c.:* Walter Lantz prods for Univ; *dir:* Paul J. Smith; *story:* Homer Brightman; *anim:* Robert Bentley, Gil Turner, Herman R. Cohen; *sets:* Art Landy; *voices:* Dal McKennon, Grace Stafford; *mus:* Clarence Wheeler; *prod mgr:* William E. Garity; *col:* Tech. *sd:* RCA. 6 min. • A taxidermist employs the help of Strongnose, a bloodhound with a strong sense of smell, to track down Woody.

5242. Private Eye Popeye (*Popeye*) 12 Nov. 1954; *p.c.:* Famous for Paramount; *dir:* I. Sparber; *story:* I. Klein; *anim:* Tom Johnson, Frank Endres, Els Barthen; *sets:* Anton Loeb; *voices:* Jack Mercer, Mae Questel, Jackson Beck; *mus:* Winston Sharples; *ph:* Leonard McCormick; *prod mgr:* Seymour Shultz; *col:* Tech. *sd:* RCA. 6 min. • Olive employs a detective to retrieve a stolen emerald. The thief leads Popeye all over the world and finally straight into Alcatraz.

5243. Private Pluto (*Pluto*) 2 Apr. 1943; *p.c.:* Walt Disney prods for RKO; *dir:* Clyde Geronimi; *asst dir:* Ralph Chadwick; *anim:* Al Bertino, Les Clark, Phil Duncan, John Lounsbery, Charles A. Nichols; *fx:* Joshua Meador, George Rowley; *lay:* Brush Bushman, Charles Philippi; *voices:* Nora Cocreham; *mus:* Oliver Wallace; *col:* Tech. *sd:* RCA. 7 min. • Pvt. Pluto is guarding a Pill-Box and finds it inhabited by two chipmunks, using the cannon to crack nuts.

5244. The Prize Guest (*Terry-Toon*) 2 June 1939; *p.c.:* TT for Fox; *dir:* Mannie Davis; *story:* John Foster; *mus:* Philip A. Scheib; b&w. *sd:* RCA. 6 min. • A hotel guest performs magic tricks.

5245. The Prize Pest (*Merrie Melodies*) 22 Dec. 1951; *p.c.:* WB; *dir:* Robert McKimson; *story:* Tedd Pierce; *anim:* Rod Scribner, Phil de Lara, Emery Hawkins, Charles McKimson; *lay:* Peter Alvarado; *back:* Richard H. Thomas; *ed:* Treg Brown; *voices:* Mel Blanc, Tedd Pierce; *mus:* Carl Stalling; *prod mgr:* John W. Burton; *prod:* Edward Selzer; *col:* Tech. *sd:* Vit. 7 min • Porky receives the prize of freeloading Daffy Duck. When he tries to eject the pest, Daffy pretends to turn into a monster if anyone mistreats him.

5246. Problem Child (*New Universal cartoon*) 16 May 1938; *p.c.:* Univ; *prod:* Walter Lantz; *dir:* Rudy Zamora; *story:* Victor McLeod, James Miele; *anim:* Merle Gilson, Frank Tipper; *sets:* Edgar Keichle; *mus:* Frank Churchill; b&w. *sd:* WE 7 min. • Wildcat Willie, a spoiled kitten, fools Oswald into taking him into his home. Once there, the brat proceeds to wreck the place.

5247. Problem Pappy (*Popeye*) 10 Jan. 1941; *p.c.:* The Fleischer Studio for Para; *prod:* Max Fleischer; *dir:* Dave Fleischer; *story:* Ted Pierce; *anim:* Myron Waldman, Sidney Pillett; *voices:* Jack Mercer; *mus:* Sammy Timberg; *ph:* Charles Schettler; *prod sup:* Sam Buchwald, Isidore Sparber; b&w. *sd:* WE. 6 min. • Pappy performs dare-devil stunts atop a flagpole and our hero resorts to a can of spinach to get the old boy down.

5248. The Prodigal Pup (*Aesop's Film Fable*) 24 Aug. 1924; *p.c.:* Fables Pictures Inc for Pathé; *dir:* Paul Terry; b&w. *sil.* 5 min. • The pup gets in bad with Farmer Al but redeems himself when he rescues the Farmer's son who has floated away on a balloon tire.

5249. Professor Offkeysky (*Terry-Toon*) 14 June 1940; *p.c.:* TT for Fox; *dir:* Connie Rasinski; *story:* John Foster; *mus:* Philip A. Scheib; b&w. *sd:* RCA. 6 min. • A stuffy Professor of old-fashioned music is converted to jazz by a drum-thumping monkey.

5250. Professor Small and Mr. Tall (*Color Rhapsody*); *p.c.:* Colum; *prod:* Dave Fleischer; *dir:* Paul Sommer, John Hubley; *story:* John McLeish; *anim:* Jim Armstrong, Volus Jones; *lay:* Clark Watson; *ed:* Edward Moore; *voices:* John McLeish, Dick Nelson; *mus:* Eddie Kilfeather; *prod mgr:* Albert Spar; *col:* Tech. *sd:* RCA. 6½ min. • Two candy merchants break a mirror. Bad luck lands them in a ghost town without water. They piece the mirror together with miraculous results.

5251. Professor Tom (*Tom & Jerry*) 30 Oct. 1948; *p.c.:* MGM; *dir:* William Hanna, Joseph Barbera; *anim:* Ray Patterson, Irven Spence, Kenneth Muse, Ed Barge; *sets:* Robert Gentle; *ed:* Fred MacAlpin; *mus:* Scott Bradley; *prod:* Fred Quimby; *col:* Tech. *sd:* WE. 7 min. • Tom teaches his protégé to catch mice but the student turns out to be a pacifist.

5252. Project Reject (*Chilly Willy*) 1 May 1969; *p.c.:* Walter Lantz prods for Univ; *dir:* Paul J. Smith; *story:* Homer Brightman; *anim:* Les Kline, Al Coe; *sets:* Nino Carbe; *voices:* Daws Butler; *mus:* Walter Greene; *prod mgr:* William E. Garity; *col:* Tech. *sd:* RCA. 6 min. • Petty Officer Smedley of the Antarctic Strategic Base is dispatched to investigate enemy planes overhead. The heat from his jet melts Chilly's igloo home and Chilly retaliates.

5253. Project X 1967; *p.c.:* William Castle Enterprises for Para; *special seq:* Hanna-Barbera prods; *col:* Tech. *sd:* WE. 97 min. • In the year 2118, a top agent, suffering from memory loss, delivers a message that the West will be destroyed within fourteen days.

5254. Props and the Spirits (*Pen & Ink Vaudeville*) 5 Sept. 1925; *p.c.:* Hurd prods for Educational; *dir:* Earl Hurd; b&w. *sil.* 10 min. • The vaudeville consists of some fat tumblers and a medium producing some spirits out of a cabinet.

5255. Props' Dash for Cash (*Pen & Ink Vaudeville*) 20 June 1925; *p.c.:* Hurd prods for Educational; *dir:* Earl Hurd; b&w. *sil.* 10 min. • While Props sells tickets, a crook bores a hole in the cash register to relieve it of any money. Another brigand steals the register with Props in hot pursuit by auto, motor boat and submarine.

5256. The Prospecting Bear (*MGM Cartoon*) 8 Mar. 1941; *p.c.:* MGM; *prod/dir/voice:* Rudolf Ising; *mus:* Scott Bradley; *prod mgr:* Fred Quimby; *col:* Tech. *sd:* WE. 9 min. • While prospecting, Barney Bear finds a rich vein of gold but his burro eats all the dynamite.

5257. Prosperity Blues (*Krazy Kat*) 8 Oct. 1932; *p.c.:* Winkler for Colum; *dir:* Ben Harrison, Manny Gould; *anim:* Al Eugster, Preston Blair; *mus:* Joe de Nat; *prod mgr:* George Winkler; b&w. *sd:* RCA. 6 min. • Krazy's apple selling to Depression victims is unlucky, so he sings "Smile, Darn Ya, Smile" and pastes fake smiles on everyone's face.

5258. Protek the Weakerist (*Popeye*) 19 Nov. 1937; *p.c.:* The Fleischer Studio for Para; *prod:* Max Fleischer; *dir:* Dave Fleischer; *anim:* Seymour Kneitel, William Henning; *voices:* Jack Mercer, Mae Questel, Gus Wickie; *mus:* Sammy Timberg; *prod sup:* Sam Buchwald, Isidore Sparber; b&w. *sd:* WE. 7 min. • Popeye is forced to take Olive's little pup for a walk and runs into Bluto with his vicious bulldog.

5259. Psst Pink (*Pink Panther*) 15 Sept. 1971; *p.c.:* Mirisch/Geoffrey/ DFE for UA; *dir:* Art Davis; *story:* Larz Bourne; *anim:* Don Williams, Manny Gould, Warren Batchelder; *lay:* Dick Ung; *back:* Richard H. Thomas; *ed:* Lee Gunther; *mus:* Walter Greene; *theme tune:* Henry Mancini; *ph:* John Burton Jr.; *prod sup:* Jim Foss, Harry Love; *col:* DeLuxe. *sd:* RCA. 6 min. • The Panther copes with a runaway wire.

5260. Psychedelic Pink (*Pink Panther*) 13 Mar. 1938; *p.c.:* Mirisch/Geoffrey/DFE: *dir:* Hawley Pratt; *story:* Jim Ryan; *anim:* Bob Matz, Warren Batchelder, Don Williams, Manny Gould, Manny Perez; *lay:* Dick Ung; *back:* Tom O'Loughlin; *ed:* Lee Gunther; *mus:* Walter Greene; *theme tune:* Henry Mancini; *ph:* John Burton Jr.; *prod sup:* Harry Love, David DeTiege; *col:* DeLuxe. *sd:* RCA. 6 min. • The Panther wanders into a bizarre mind-blowing room.

5261. Psychological Testing (*Comic King*) June 1962; *p.c.:* Para Cartoons; *dir:* Seymour Kneitel; *story:* Les Colodny, Al Brodax; *anim:* Morey Reden, Jack Ehret, I. Klein, Larry Silverman; *sets:* Robert Owen; *voices:* Howard Morris, Allen Melvin; *mus:* Winston Sharples; *prod mgr:* Abe Goodman; *ex prod:* Al Brodax; *col:* Tech. *sd:* RCA. 5½ min. • A psychologist arrives at Camp Swampy to select the best men for a new psychological test. Beetle Bailey and Sgt. Snorkle are picked.

5262. Puddle Pranks (*Flip the Frog*) Nov. 1930; *p.c.:* Celebrity prods for MGM; *prod/dir:* Ub Iwerks; b&w. *sd:* PCP. 8 min. • Flip's joy ride is abruptly brought to a halt when a pelican swallows the bug that's pulling his wagon. He then goes for a swim with his girl and witnesses a fish swallowing a bird in retaliation.

5263. Puddy the Pup and the Gypsies (*Paul Terry-Toon*) 24 June 1936; *p.c.:* TT for Educational/Fox; *dir:* Mannie Davis, George Gordon; *mus:* Philip A. Scheib; b&w. *sd.* 6 min. • Puddy is captured by gypsies who raid the farm house. The pup in a bearskin sees them off.

5264. Puddy the Pup in Cats in a Bag (*Terry-Toon*) 11 Dec. 1936; *p.c.:* TT for Educational/Fox; *dir:* Mannie Davis, George Gordon; *mus:* Philip A. Scheib; b&w. *sd.* 6 min. • Puddy saves some kittens from the rapids.

5265. Puddy the Pup in Sunken Treasure (*Paul Terry Toon*) 16 Oct. 1936; *p.c.:* TT for Educational/Fox; *dir:* Mannie Davis, George Gordon; *mus:* Philip A. Scheib; b&w. *sd.* 6 min. • Puddy works the air pump while Farmer Al goes to the ocean bed to look for treasure.

5266. Puddy the Pup in the Bookshop (*Paul Terry-Toons*) 5 Feb. 1937; *p.c.:* TT for Educational/Fox; *dir:* Mannie Davis, George Gordon; *mus:* Philip A. Scheib; b&w. *sd.* 6 min. • While Puddy sleeps in a bookshop, he dreams of travelling to Bookland where he is menaced by the giant in *Jack and the Beanstalk*.

5267. Puddy's Coronation (*Terry-Toon*) 14 May 1937; *p.c.:* TT for Educational/Fox; *dir:* Mannie Davis, George Gordon; *mus:* Philip A. Scheib; b&w. *sd.* 6 min. • Puddy dreams it's his coronation day.

5268. Pudgy and the Lost Kitten (*Betty Boop*) 24 June 1938; *p.c.:* The Fleischer Studio for Para; *prod:* Max Fleischer; *dir:* Dave Fleischer; *anim:* Myron Waldman, Lillian Friedman; *voice:* Mae Questel, Frances Reynolds; *mus:* Sammy Timberg; *prod sup:* Sam Buchwald, Isidore Sparber; b&w. *sd:* WE. 6 min. • Pudgy brings a hungry kitten home and Betty feeds it. The kitten eventually begins to take over and Pudgy is relieved when the mother cat shows up.

5269. Pudgy in More Pep (*Betty Boop*) 14 June 1936; *p.c.:* The Fleischer Studio for Para; *prod/l/a:* Max Fleischer; *dir:* Dave Fleischer; *anim:* Thomas Johnson, Dave Hoffman; *voice:* Mae Questel; *mus:* Sammy Timberg; b&w. *sd:* WE. 6 min. *l/a/anim.* • Uncle Max encourages Pudgy to do some tricks but he seems sluggish. Betty mixes a potion that give the pup more pep.

5270. Pudgy in Thrills and Chills (*Betty Boop*) 23 Dec. 1938; *p.c.:* The Fleischer Studio for Para; *prod:* Max Fleischer; *dir:* Dave Fleischer; *anim:* Roland Crandall; *voices:* Margie Hines; *mus:* Sammy Timberg; *prod sup:* Sam Buchwald, Isidore Sparber; b&w. *sd:* WE. 6 min. • Betty and Pudgy have some hair-raising experiences when participating in winter sports.

5271. Pudgy Picks a Fight (*Betty Boop*) 14 May 1937; *p.c.:* The Fleischer Studio for Para; *prod:* Max Fleischer; *dir:* Dave Fleischer; *anim:* Myron Waldman, Hicks Lokey, Lillian Friedman; *mus:* Sammy Timberg; b&w. *sd:* WE. 6 min. • Pudgy destroys Betty's fur neckpiece in the belief that it's a rival pet ... then feels remorse.

5272. Pudgy Takes a Bow-Wow (*Betty Boop*) 9 Apr. 1937; *p.c.:* The Fleischer Studio for Para; *prod:* Max Fleischer; *dir:* Dave Fleischer; *anim:* Myron Waldman, Lillian Friedman; *voices:* Mae Questel; *mus:* Sammy Timberg; b&w. *sd:* WE. 6 min. • Pudgy intrudes in the middle of Betty's stage show when he chases a cat on stage.

5273. Pudgy the Watchman (*Betty Boop*) 12 Aug. 1938; *p.c.:* The Fleischer Studio for Para; *prod:* Max Fleischer; *dir:* Dave Fleischer; *anim:* Thomas Johnson, Harold Walker; *voices:* Margie Hines; *mus:* Sammy Timberg; b&w. *sd:* WE. 6 min. • Pudgy loses his watchman job to Al E. Cat the mouse radicator. Betty soon discovers Al's weakness and is overrun with mice.

5274. Pueblo Pluto (*Pluto*) 14 Jan. 1949; *p.c.:* Walt Disney prods for RKO; *dir:* Charles Nichols; *story:* Milt Schaffer, Eric Gurney; *anim:* Phil Duncan, George Kreisl, George Nicholas, Jerry Hathcock; *fx:* Dan MacManus, Jack Boyd; *lay:* Karl Karpé; *back:* Ray Huffine; *voice:* James MacDonald; *mus:* Oliver Wallace; *col:* Tech. *sd:* RCA. 7 min. • While in Mexico, Pluto savors a buffalo bone. A pup arrives and attempts to steal the bone, ensnaring Pluto in cacti.

5275. Punch and Judo (*Blue Racer*) 23 July 1973; *p.c.:* Mirisch/DFE for UA; *dir:* Art Davis; *story:* John W. Dunn; *anim:* Manny Gould, Warren Batchelder, Don Williams; *lay:* Dick Ung; *back:* Richard H. Thomas; *ed:* Joe Siracusa; *voices:* Larry D. Mann, Tom Holland; *mus:* Doug Goodwin; *ph:* John Burton Jr.; *prod sup:* Stan Paperny, Harry Love; *col:* DeLuxe. *sd:* RCA. 5 min. • The Racer tries to eat a Japanese Beetle who turns out to be a Judo expert.

5276. Punch and Judo (*Popeye*) 12 Nov. 1951; *p.c.:* Famous for Para; *dir:* I. Sparber; *story:* Irving Spector; *anim:* Tom Johnson, Frank Endres; *sets:* Robert Connavale; *voices:* Jack Mercer, Jackson Beck, Mae Questel, Cecil Roy; *mus:* Winston Sharples; *ph:* Leonard McCormick; *prod mgr:* Seymour Shultz; *col:* Tech. *sd:* RCA. 7 min. • Popeye delivers a TV set to the orphans so they can watch him win a boxing match.

5277. Punch Trunk (*Looney Tunes*) 19 Dec. 1953; *p.c.:* WB; *dir:* Charles M. Jones; *story:* Michael Maltese; *anim:* Lloyd Vaughan, Ken Harris, Ben Washam; *lay:* Maurice Noble; *back:* Philip de Guard; *ed:* Treg Brown; *voices:* Robert C. Bruce, Mel Blanc, Marian Richman; *mus:* Carl Stalling; *prod mgr:* John W. Burton; *prod:* Edward Selzer; *col:* Tech. *sd:* Vit. 7 min. • A nine-inch elephant creates chaos in the streets of New York.

5278. Punchy de Leon (*Jolly Frolics*) 12 Jan. 1950; *p.c.:* UPA for Colum; *dir:* John Hubley; *story:* Millard Kaufman, Phil Eastman; *anim:* Rudy Larriva, Bill Melendez, Pat Matthews, Willis Pyle; *lay:* William Hurtz; *back:* Herb Klynn, Jules Engel; *voices:* Jack Mather, Daws Butler; *mus:* Del Castillo; *technical:* Max Morgan, Mary Cain; *ph:* Jack Eckes; *prod:* Ed Gershman; *col:* Tech. *sd:* RCA. 6½ min. • The Fox and Crow attempt to secure water from the Fountain of Youth for a king's ransom.

5279. Punchy Pooch (*Cartune*) 4 Sept. 1962; *p.c.:* Walter Lantz prods for Univ; *dir:* Jack Hannah; *story:* Bill Danch; *anim:* Al Coe, Roy Jenkins; *sets:* Ray Huffine, Art Landy; *voices:* Dal McKennon, Paul Frees; *mus:* Darrell Calker; *prod mgr:* William E. Garity; *col:* Tech. *sd:* RCA. 6 min. • Doc enters Champ into a boxing match with a kangaroo for a $500 prize.

5280. Puny Express (*Woody Woodpecker*) 22 Jan. 1951; *p.c.:* Walter Lantz prods for Univ; *dir:* Walter Lantz; *story:* Ben Hardaway, Heck Allen; *anim:* Don Patterson, Ray Abrams, La Verne Harding; *sets:* Fred Brunish; *mus:* Clarence E. Wheeler; *prod mgr:* William E. Garity; *col:* Tech. *sd:* RCA. 6½ min. • Pony Express rider Woody has to get the mail past the notorious bandit, Buzz Buzzard.

5281. Pup on a Picnic (*Tom & Jerry*) 30 Apr. 1955; *p.c.:* MGM; *dir:* William Hanna, Joseph Barbera; *anim:* Ray Patterson, Kenneth Muse, Ed Barge, Irven Spence; *lay:* Dick Bickenbach; *back:* Robert Gentle; *voice:* Daws Butler; *ed:* Jim Faris; *mus:* Scott Bradley; *ph:* Jack Stevens; *prod:* Fred Quimby; *col:* Tech. *sd:* WE. 7 min. • Spike and Tyke's picnic is ruined by Tom's relentless pursuit of Jerry.

5282. Puppet Love (*Popeye*) 11 Aug. 1944; *p.c.:* Famous for Para; *dir:* Seymour Kneitel; *story:* Joe Stultz; *anim:* Jim Tyer, William Henning; *voices:* Mae Questel, Jackson Beck; *mus:* Sammy Timberg; *prod mgr:* Sam Buchwald; b&w. *sd:* RCA. 8 min. Tech reissue: 3 Oct. 1952. • Bluto makes a "Popeye" marionette in order for our hero to fall into disfavor with Olive.

5283. The Puppet Murder Case (*Scrappy*) 21 June 1935; *p.c.:* Charles Mintz prods for Colum; *dir:* Art Davis; *anim:* Sid Marcus; *lay:* Clark Watson; *back:* Phil Davis; *mus:* Joe de Nat; *prod mgr:* James Bronis; b&w. *sd:* RCA. 6 min. • Scrappy sees Oopy snapping his puppets' strings and rigs the brat up as a marionette, putting him on trial with the other puppets as judge and jury.

5284. Puppet Show (*Oswald*) 2 Nov. 1936; *p.c.:* Univ; *dir:* Walter Lantz; *story:* Walter Lantz, Victor McLeod; *anim:* Manuel Moreno; *mus:* James Dietrich; *l/a puppets:* Valerie & O'Rourke; b&w. *sd:* RCA 8 min. *l/a/anim.* • Oswald is shown operating a "Live Action" puppet show. He is knocked out and dreams that his puppets escape to Toyland where he rescues one tied to a sawmill.

5285. The Puppetoon Movie 1986; *p.c.:* Leibovit Prods., Ltd.; *prod sup:* Arnold Leibovit; *new anim seq: ph dir:* Gene Warren Jr.; *ed:* Arnold Leibovit; *script consultant:* Peter Kleinow; *Gumby advisor:* Art Clokey; *ph:* John Huneck, Michael Griffen; *art dir:* Gene Warren Jr., Michael Minor; *set/miniature construction:* Gary Campsie, Mike Joyce, Gary Rhodeback, Richard Smiley, Paul Kassler, Dennis Schultz; *Gumby maker:* Kurt Hanson; *Arnie the Dinosaur art finishing:* Charlie Chiodo, Steve Chiodo; *main title* *des/George Pal book rendering: Walt Disney Graphic Services:* Ed Garbert; *addit graphics:* Ernest D. Farino; *asst ph:* Nick Vasu; *optics:* Betty Bromberg, David Emerson; *optical duping:* Harry Walton; *Rotoscope anim:* Bret Mixon, Tony Alderson; *neg cutter:* Brian Ralph; *still ph:* Kurt Hanson, Tony Alderson; *Fantasy II sup:* Leslie Huntley; *prod asst:* Andy Borses, Gene Warren Jr., Christopher Warren; *voices: Arnie the Dinosaur:* Paul Frees; *Gumby:* Dal McKennon; *Pokey:* Art Clokey; *Speedy Alka-Seltzer:* Dick Beals; *Graunke Symphony Orchestra conducted by* Buddy Baker; *mus/sd fx:* Burton Lee Harry, Dennis Patterson; *sd des:* Lajon Prods.; *asst sd ed:* Joseph Earle; *sd transfers: Scott Sound:* Bruce Scott, Jeff Ehrhart; *sd mix:* John "Doc" Wilkinson; *re-rec:* Ryder Sound Services, Inc.; *Ryder Sound Service sup:* Leo Chaloukian; *ultra stereo sup:* Jack Cashen; *stereo consult:* Robert Weitz; *technical advisor:* Sam Spencer; *sd mix:* Zeke Lund; *digital ed at Tonstudio:* Bernard Mahne; *"Puppetoon signature":* Maurice de Packh; *original productions: Einhoven, Holland:* Jan Bax, Hill Beekman, Jan Coolen, Theo Dorelevers, Wim Comes, Frans Hendrix, Ernst Jeschike, Piet Jongeneel, Kisberry van der Kleij, Karel Loçher, Hank van Manen, Jozef Misik, Leonie Pappers, Peter Sachs, Andre Sipp, Piet Schellekes, Brando Szabo, Henk van Tongeren, Wim Lillings, Menzo Wessels; *U.S.:* John S. Abbott, Betty Lou Allen, Siska Ayala, Bob Baker, Leo Barkume, Dave Bater, Lloyd Bockhaus, Dick Bosworth, Erwin Broner, Wah Ming Chang, Carmelite Chapman, Chris Christadoro, Jack Denton, Nick Eckert, Eleanor Fallberg, Jane Fetzer, Duke Goldstone, Bernard Garbutt, Pierre Genine, Al Hamm, Ray Harryhausen, Harry Hinkle, Larry Hollings, Maury Howard, Herb Johnson, George E. Jordan, Phil Kellison, Bill King, Dorothy King Novak, Roberta Lange, Bob Larsen, Dick LeGrande, Bill Martin, Fred Madison, Fred Malatesa, Reginald Massie, Vera McGuire, Kiva Marcus, Jack Miller, Fred Moore, Al Molinaro, Connie Pinard Morgan, Dick Morley, Johnny Napolitano, Willard Oberlin, Stuart O'Brien, Willis O'Brien, Miles Pike, Herb Price, Roy Reynertson, Lillian Seaquist, Vern Sion, Blanding Sloane, Paul Sprunk, Isadore "Jimmy" Stone, Boris Tameroff, Dale Tholen, Irma-card Tonat, Zoli Vidor, Gene Warren, Eleanor Gale Warren, Evelyn Willy, Felix Zelenka; *col:* United Color Lab. *sd:* Ultra Stereo. 79 min. • Gumby is directing a movie in which a menacing Arnie the Dinosaur approaches a timid deer. The dinosaur refuses to carry on and, instead, tells how the inventive model animator, George Pal, is responsible for all their being. To prove this, he shows a selection of Pal's Puppetoons. *seq: The Little Broadcast, Philips Broadcast of 1938, Hoola Boola, South Sea Sweethearts, the Sleeping Beauty, Tulips Shall Grow, Together in the Weather, Philips Cavalcade, John Henry and the Inky-Poo, Jasper in a Jam, Tubby the Tuba, The Ship of Ether.*

5286. The Puppy Express (*Hot Dog*) 4 Feb. 1926; *p.c.:* Bray prods; *dir:* Walt Lantz, Clyde Geronimi; b&w. sil. 5 min. • No story available.

5287. Puppy Love (*Aesop's Film Fable*) 10 May 1928; *p.c.:* Fables Pictures Inc for Pathé; *dir:* Paul Terry, Mannie Davis; b&w. sil. 10 min. • No story available.

5288. Puppy Love (*Flip the Frog*) 9 Apr. 1932; *p.c.:* Celebrity prods for MGM; *prod/dir:* Ub Iwerks; b&w. sd: PCP. 7 min. • Flip's dog saves a pretty girl dog from a rat and later from the dog catcher.

5289. Puppy Love (*Mickey Mouse*) 2 Sept. 1933; *p.c.:* Walt Disney prods for UA; *dir:* Wilfred Jackson; *anim:* Paul Allen, Johnny Cannon, Les Clark, Gilles de Tremaudan, Dick Huemer; Norman Ferguson, Richard Lundy, Fred Moore, Ben Sharpsteen; *voices:* Marcellite Garner, Walt Disney; *mus:* Frank E. Churchill; b&w. *sd:* RCA. 8 min. • Mickey arrives with a box of bon bons for Minnie which Pluto swaps for a bone and gives to his girl, Fifi.

5290. Puppy Tale (*Tom & Jerry*) 23 Jan. 1954; *p.c.:* MGM; *dir:* William Hanna, Joseph Barbera; *anim:* Ed Barge, Irven Spence, Kenneth Muse; *lay:* Dick Bickenbach; *back:* John Didrik Johnsen; *ed:* Jim Faris; *mus:* Scott Bradley; *ph:* Jack Stevens; *prod:* Fred Quimby; *col:* Tech. *sd:* WE. 6½ min. • Jerry rescues a pup from being drowned and courts disaster when it follows him home.

5291. The Pups' Christmas (*Happy Harmonies*) 12 Dec. 1936; *p.c.:* MGM; *prod/dir:* Hugh Harman, Rudolf Ising; *voice:* Bernice Hansel; *mus:* Scott Bradley; *col:* Tech. *sd:* RCA. 8 min. • The pups play with Christmas toys.

5292. The Pups' Picnic (*Happy Harmonies*) 30 May 1936; *p.c.:* MGM; *prod/dir:* Hugh Harman, Rudolf Ising; *mus:* Scott Bradley; *col:* Tech. *sd:* RCA. 7 min. • The pups wander away from their picnic and become involved in a fox hunt.

5293. A Pup's Tale (*Sketch Book*) 26 June 1926; *p.c.:* Pathé; *anim:* Hy Mayer; b&w. sil. • All sorts of dogs are depicted. There are some clever transformations from humans to dogs.

5294. The Purloined Pup (*Pluto*) 19 July 1946; *p.c.:* Walt Disney prods for RKO; *dir:* Charles Nichols; *asst dir:* Bob North; *story:* Harry Reeves, Jesse Marsh; *anim:* George Nicholas, Gerry Hathcock, Robert Youngquist, Harry Holt, George Kreisl, Marvin Woodward;; *fx:* Brad Case, Andy Engman, Ernie Lynch; *lay:* Karl Karpé; *back:* Nino Carbe; *voice:* James MacDonald; *mus:* Oliver Wallace; *col:* Tech. *sd:* RCA. 7 min. • Police dog Pluto rescues Ronnie, a pup who has been kidnapped by Butch the bulldog.

5295. Purr-Chance to Dream (*Tom & Jerry*) 1967; *p.c.:* MGM; *prod:* Chuck Jones; *dir:* Ben Washam; *story:* Irv Spector; *anim:* Dick Thompson, Ken Harris, Don Towsley, Tom Ray, Philip Roman; *des:* Maurice Noble; *graphics:* Don Foster; *lay:* Don Morgan; *back:* Philip de Guard; *mus:* Carl Brandt; *prod sup:* Les Goldman, Earl Jonas; *col:* Metro. *sd:* WE. 6 min. • Tom is persecuted by a miniature bulldog who protects Jerry's welfare.

5296. Push-Button Kitty (*Tom & Jerry*) 6 Sept. 1952; *p.c.:* MGM; *dir:* William Hanna, Joseph Barbera; *anim:* Irven Spence, Ed Barge, Kenneth Muse; *lay:* Dick Bickenbach; *back:* Robert Gentle; *ed:* Jim Faris; *voice:* Lillian Randolph; *mus:* Scott Bradley; *ph:* Jack Stevens; *prod:* Fred Quimby; *col:* Tech. *sd:* WE. 7 min. • Mammy Two-Shoes engages the services of a robot cat to replace Tom.

5297. Puss Café (*Pluto*) 9 June 1950; *p.c.:* Walt Disney prods for RKO; *dir:* Charles Nichols; *story:* Dick Kinney, Milt Schaffer; *anim:* George Kreisl, George Nicholas, Phil Duncan, Marvin Woodward; *fx:* Jack Boyd; *lay:* Karl Karpé; *back:* Merle Cox; *voice:* James MacDonald; *mus:* Oliver Wallace; *mus:* Paul Smith; *col:* Tech. *sd:* RCA. 7 min. • Two Siamese cats invade a garden guarded by Pluto and try to steal birds, fish and milk bottles.

5298. Puss Gets the Boot (*MGM Cartoon*) 10 Feb. 1940; *p.c.:* MGM; *prod:* Rudolf Ising; *dir:* William Hanna, Joseph Barbera; *story/lay:* Joseph Barbera; *anim:* Robert Allen, Peter Burness, Michael Lah, Lovell Norman, Tony Pabian, Carl Urbano, Jack Zander; *sets:* Joe Smith; *ed:* Fred MacAlpin; *voice:* Lillian Randolph; *mus:* Scott Bradley; *ph:* Jack Stevens; *prod mgr:* Fred Quimby; *col:* Tech. *sd:* WE. 8 min. *Academy Award nomination.* • A mouse succeeds in putting the blame on Jasper the cat for breaking up the house. • First in a series featuring the highly successful team of *Tom and Jerry.*

5299. Puss in Boots (*ComiColor*) 17 May 1934; *p.c.:* Celebrity prods; *prod:* Ub Iwerks; *dir/anim/lay:* Jimmie Culhane, Al Eugster; *story:* Otto Englander; *mus:* Carl Stalling; *col:* Ciné. *sd:* PCP. 7 min. • With the aid of kittens, Puss helps a boy rescue the princess from a frightful ogre.

5300. Puss in Boots (*Laugh-o-Gram*) Sept. 1922; *p.c.:* Laugh-o-Gram Films Inc for Newman Theater, Kansas City/Pictorial Clubs Inc.; *dir:* Walt Disney; *ph:* Red Lyon; b&w. sil. • A boy and his cat disguise as a toreador in order to woo the Princess of Kingville. He wins the bullfight and the heart of the Princess.

5301. Puss 'n' Boats (*Tom & Jerry*) 1966; *p.c.:* MGM; *prod:* Chuck Jones; *dir:* Abe Levitow; *story:* Bob Ogle; *anim:* Ben Washam, Ken Harris, Don Towsley, Tom Ray, Dick Thompson; *des:* Maurice Noble; *lay:* Don Morgan; *back:* Philip de Guard; *mus:* Carl Brandt; *prod mgr:* Les Goldman; *col:* Metro. *sd:* WE. 7 min. • Jerry tries to gain entrance to a shipment of cheese, guarded by Tom.

5302. Puss n' Boos (*Casper*) 16 July 1954; *p.c.:* Famous for Para; *dir:* Seymour Kneitel; *story:* Larz Bourne; *anim:* Myron Waldman, Nick Tafuri; *sets:* Robert Connavale; *voices:* Alan Shay, Sid Raymond, Gwen Davies; *mus:* Winston Sharples; *title song:* Mack David, Jerry Livingston; *ph:* Leonard McCormick; *prod mgr:* Seymour Shultz; *col:* Tech. *sd:* RCA. 6 min. • Casper saves two kittens from drowning and tries to find them a decent home.

5303. Puss n' Booty (*Looney Tunes*) 11 Dec. 1943; *p.c.:* Leon Schlesinger prods for WB *dir:* Frank Tashlin; *story:* Warren Foster; *anim:* Cal Dalton, James Culhane, Arthur Davis, I. Ellis, Don Williams; *sets:* Richard H. Thomas; *ed:* Tregoweth E. Brown; *voices:* Bea Benaderet, Mel Blanc; *mus:*

Carl W. Stalling; *ph:* John W. Burton; *prod sup:* Henry Binder, Raymond G. Katz; b&w. *sd:* Vit. 7 min. • Rudolph the cat eagerly awaits the arrival of the next successor in a long line of canaries to be devoured by him.

5304. Puss n' Toots *(Tom & Jerry)* 30 May 1942; *p.c.:* MGM; *dir:* William Hanna, Joseph Barbera; *anim:* Peter Burness, Kenneth Muse, Jack Zander; *sets:* Joe Smith; *voice:* Lillian Randolph; *mus:* Scott Bradley; *col:* Tech. *sd:* WE. 9 min. • Tom tries to impress a cute girl kitten by putting Jerry through his paces.

5305. Pussy Willie *(Oswald)* 17 Oct. 1929; *p.c.:* Univ; *dir:* Walter Lantz; *anim:* R.C. Hamilton, "Bill" Nolan, Tom Palmer; *mus:* Bert Fiske; b&w. *sil.* 5 min. • Oswald displays skills as an amorous musician.

5306. Put on the Spout *(Dr. Seuss Cartoon)* 1 June 1931; *p.c.:* A-C/WB for Stanco, Co.; *adapt:* Irving A. Jacoby; *anim:* Dr. Seuss; *mus:* Philip A. Scheib; b&w. *sd:* WE. 5 min. • A fish family dashes for cover when the dangerous insect alarm sounds. The insect gives a whale a merry chase until he gives the cue: "Jonah, Quick! The Flit" and the invertebrate is dispensed with.

5307. Put On Your Old Grey Bonnet *(Screen Songs)* 22 Nov. 1929; *p.c.:* The Fleischer Studio for Para; *prod:* Max Fleischer; *dir:* Dave Fleischer; *mus:* Art Turkisher; *song:* Stanley Murphy, Percy Wenrich; b&w. *sd:* WE. 6½ min. • A company of animal grotesques and an amazing jazz band unite to provide a community singalong.

5308. Put-Put Pink *(Pink Panther)* 24 Apr 1968; *p.c.:* Mirisch/Geoffrey/DFE for UA; *dir:* Gerry Chiniquy; *story:* Jim Ryan; *anim:* Warren Batchelder, Don Williams, Tom Ray, Manny Gould, Manny Perez; *lay:* Dick Ung; *back:* Tom O'Loughlin; *ed:* Allan Potter; *mus:* Walter Greene; *theme tune:* Henry Mancini; *ph:* John Burton Jr.; *prod sup:* Harry Love, David DeTiege; *col:* DeLuxe. *sd:* RCA. 6 min. • The Panther has a run-in with the law when he builds his own motor bike.

5309. Put-Put Troubles 19 July 1940; *p.c.:* Walt Disney prods for RKO; *dir:* Riley Thomson; *asst dir:* Ralph Chadwick; *story:* Carl Barks; *anim:* James Armstrong, Johnny Cannon, Larry Clemmons, Nick de Tolly, Frank Follmer, George Goepper; *Griffin,* Joseph Harbaugh, Emery Hawkins, Volus Jones, George Kreisl, Lee Morehouse, Ken Peterson, Grant Simmons, Claude Smith, Al Stetter, Judge Whitaker; *fx:* Jack Boyd, Andrew Engman, Art Fitzpatrick, Joseph Gayek, Jack Huber, Ed Parks, Miles E. Pike, Ruben Timmens; *lay:* Bill Tracy; *voices:* Clarence Nash, Lee Millar; *mus:* Oliver Wallace; *col:* Tech. *sd:* RCA. 7 min. • Donald and Pluto go boating. While Don battles with the boat motor, Pluto gets entangled with some springs.

5310. Puttin' on the Act *(Popeye)* 30 Aug. 1940; *p.c.:* The Fleischer Studio for Para; *prod:* Max Fleischer; *dir:* Dave Fleischer; *story:* William Turner; *anim:* Dave Tendlar, Thomas Golden; *voices:* Jack Mercer, Margie Hines; *mus:* Sammy Timberg; *ph:* Charles Schettler; *prod sup:* Sam Buchwald, Isidore Sparber; b&w. *sd:* WE. 7 min. • Olive and Popeye revive their vaudeville act! Popeye imitates Groucho, Durante and Stan Laurel.

5311. Puttin' on the Dog *(Tom & Jerry)* 28 Oct. 1944; *p.c.:* MGM; *dir:* William Hanna, Joseph Barbera; *anim:* Pete Burness, Ray Patterson, Irven Spence, Kenneth Muse; *lay:* Harvey Eisenberg; *ed:* Fred MacAlpin; *mus:* Scott Bradley; *prod:* Fred Quimby; *col:* Tech. *sd:* WE. 6½ min. • Tom disguises himself as a dog in order to retrieve Jerry from the sanctuary of a dog pound.

5312. Puttin' Out the Kitten *(Scrappy)* 26 Mar. 1937; *p.c.:* Charles Mintz prods for Colum; *story:* Art Davis; *anim:* Sid Marcus; *lay:* Clark Watson; *back:* Phil Davis; *ed:* George Winkler; *mus:* Joe de Nat; *prod mgr:* James Bronis; b&w. *sd:* RCA. 6½ min. • Scrappy puts his kitten out for the night then has a nightmare about the cat cavorting with nursery rhyme characters to the music of Dukas' "The Sorcerer's Apprentice."

5313. Putty Tat Trouble *(Looney Tunes)* 24 Feb. 1951; *p.c.:* WB; *dir:* I. Freleng; *story:* Warren Foster; *anim:* Arthur Davis, Manuel Perez, Ken Champin, Virgil Ross; *lay:* Hawley Pratt; *back:* Paul Julian; *ed:* Treg Brown; *voices:* Mel Blanc, Bea Benaderet; *mus:* Carl Stalling; *prod mgr:* John W. Burton; *prod:* Edward Selzer; *col:* Tech. *sd:* Vit. 7 min. • Sylvester and a rival cat battle over Tweety against a winter setting.

5314. The Puzzle *(Out of the Inkwell)* 15 Apr. 1923; *p.c.:* Out of the Inkwell Films for Rodner; *dir/l/a:* Max Fleischer; b&w. *sil.* 5 min. *l/a/anim.* • Max sends Ko-Ko down a tunnel to Puzzletown. When he doesn't return, Max enters the tunnel looking for him.

5315. Puzzled Pals *(Tom & Jerry)* 31 Mar. 1933; *p.c.:* Van Beuren for RKO; *dir:* George Stallings, Frank Sherman; *mus:* Gene Rodemich; b&w. *sd:* RCA. 8 min. • An infant wrecks the boys' jigsaw and, with the aid of a vacuum cleaner, destroys the whole house.

5316. The Pygmy Hunt *(Captain & Kids)* 6 Aug. 1938; *p.c.:* MGM; *dir:* Isadore Freleng; *story:* Henry Allen; *voices:* Billy Bletcher, Pinto Colvig; *mus:* Scott Bradley; *prod:* Fred Quimby; *col:* sep. *sd:* WE. 7 min. • Der Captain, The Inspector and their dog set out to capture a pygmy. The dog attempts to remove the bone from the native's hair.

5317. Quack-a Doodle-Doo *(Noveltoon)* 3 Mar. 1950; *p.c.:* Famous for Para; *dir:* I. Sparber; *story:* Carl Meyer, Jack Mercer, Martin Taras; *anim:* Dave Tendlar, Tom Golden; *sets:* Robert Connavale; *voices:* Sid Raymond, Jack Mercer, Cecil Roy; *mus:* Winston Sharples; *ph:* Leonard McCormick; *prod mgr:* Sam Buchwald; *col:* Tech. *sd:* 6 min. • Mama Duck swallows a bottle of vitamins and gives birth to Baby Huey, a giant duckling. He is ostracized by the community but wins his colors when he saves them from a hungry fox.

5318. Quack Quack *(Paul Terry-Toon)* 8 Mar. 1931; *p.c.:* Terry, Moser & Coffman for Educational/Fox; *dir:* Frank Moser, Paul Terry; *anim:* Arthur Babbitt, Frank Moser, Sarka, Jerry Shields, Vladimir Tytla; *mus:* Philip A. Scheib; b&w. *sd:* WE. 6 min. • Farmer Al, under gas at the dentist, dreams he is riding a frenzied black mare through a storm and engages in a frantic dance with a harem beauty before he awakens.

5319. Quack Shot *(Merrie Melodies)* 30 Oct. 1954; *p.c.:* WB; *dir:* Robert McKimson; *story:* Phil de Lara; *anim:* Rod Scribner, Phil de Lara, Charles McKimson, Herman Cohen; *lay:* Robert Givens; *back:* Richard H. Thomas; *ed:* Treg Brown; *voices:* Mel Blanc, Arthur Q. Bryan; *mus:* Carl Stalling; *prod mgr:* John W. Burton; *prod:* Edward Selzer; *col:* Tech. *sd:* Vit. 7 min. • Duck hunter Elmer is warned by Daffy that if he shoots one more duck, he's going to be in trouble. He does ... and he is!

5320. Quacker Tracker *(Looney Tunes)* 29 Apr. 1967; *p.c.:* Format Films for WB; *dir:* Rudy Larriva; *story:* Tom Dagenais, Don Jurwich; *anim:* Virgil Ross, Bob Bransford, Ed Friedmann; *lay:* Walter Peregoy; *back:* Don Sheppod; *ed:* Joe Siracusa; *voices:* Mel Blanc; *mus:* Frank Perkins; *orch:* William Lava; *prod:* Herbert Klynn; *col:* Tech. *sd:* Vit. 5 min. • A hunting club sends Daffy to capture the only animal they haven't yet been able to capture ... Speedy Gonzales.

5321. Quackodile Tears *(Merrie Melodies)* Mar. 1962; *p.c.:* WB; *dir:* Art Davis; *story:* John Dunn, Carl Kohler; *anim:* Gerry Chiniquy, Virgil Ross, Bob Matz, Lee Halpern, Art Leonardi; *lay:* Robert Gribbroek; *back:* Tom O'Loughlin; *ed:* Treg Brown; *voices:* Mel Blanc, June Foray; *mus:* Milt Franklyn; *prod mgr:* William Orcutt; *prod:* David H. DePatie; *col:* Tech. *sd:* Vit. 6 min. • Daffy is babysitting an egg when it rolls down hill and mixes with some alligator eggs. On the basis of "An egg is an egg" Daffy takes one and father alligator tries to retrieve it from him.

5322. The Quail Hunt *(Oswald)* 23 Sept. 1935; *p.c.:* Univ; *dir:* Walter Lantz; *story/lyrics:* Walter Lantz, Victor McLeod; *anim:* Fred Kopietz, Bill Mason, Ray Abrams, Ed Benedict; *voice:* Shirley Reed; *mus:* James Dietrich; b&w. *sd:* WE. 7 min. • Oswald and Elmer are teased mercilessly by the quail. Eventually Elmer's life is saved by a quail and they end up the best of friends.

5323. The Queen Bee *(Aesop's Film Fable)* 17 Feb. 1929; *p.c.:* Fables Pictures Inc for Pathé; *dir:* Paul Terry, Hugh Shields; b&w. *sil.* 10 min. • No story available.

5324. The Queen of Hearts *(ComiColor)* 25 June 1934; *p.c.:* Celebrity prods; *prod:* Ub Iwerks; *dir/anim:* Jimmie Culhane, Al Eugster; *lay:* Jimmie Culhane; *mus:* Art Turkisher; *col:* Ciné. *sd:* PCP. 7 min. • While the Queen bakes tarts, the playing cards are stolen by the Knave and a battle ensues. All is restored to normal by midnight.

5325. The Queen Was in the Parlor *(Merrie Melodies)* 23 July 1932; *p.c.:* Hugh Harman–Rudolf Ising prods for WB; *prod:* Leon Schlesinger; *anim:* Isadore Freleng, Paul Smith, Robert Clampett; *voice:* John T. Murray, Mary Moder, The Kingsmen; *mus:* Frank Marsales; b&w. *sd:* Vit. 6½ min. • Based on a popular song, the Royal Jester (Goopy Geer) rescues the Queen from the clutches of the villainous Black Knight.

5326. The Queen's Kittens *(Oswald)* 8 Aug. 1938; *p.c.:* Univ; *dir:* Lester Kline; *story:* Victor McLeod, James Miele; *anim:* George Nicholas,

Fred Kopietz; *sets:* Edgar Keichle; *mus:* Frank Marsales; *prod mgr:* George Hall; b&w. *sd:* WE. 6 min. • The kittens cause havoc in the Queen's kitchen.

5327. Quentin Quail *(Merrie Melodies)* 2 Mar. 1946; *p.c.:* WB; *dir:* Charles M. Jones; *story:* Tedd Pierce; *anim:* Ben Washam, Ken Harris, Basil Davidovich, Lloyd Vaughan; *sets:* Robert Gribbroek; *ed:* Treg Brown; *voices:* Sara Berner, Tedd Pierce, Mel Blanc; *mus:* Carl W. Stalling; *prod mgr:* John W. Burton; *prod:* Edward Selzer; *col:* Tech. *sd:* Vit. 7 min. • In this parody of the "Baby Snooks" radio show, Daddy Quail attempts to ensnare an elusive worm for Baby Toots' supper.

5328. Quick on the Vigor *(Popeye)* 6 Oct. 1950; *p.c.:* Famous for Para; *dir:* Seymour Kneitel; *anim:* Tom Johnson, John Gentilella, Els Barthen; *sets:* Robert Owen; *voices:* Jack Mercer, Jackison Beck, Mae Questel; *mus:* Winston Sharples; *ph:* Leonard McCormick; *prod mgr:* Sam Buchwald; *col:* Tech. *sd:* RCA. 6 min. • Popeye and Olive visit an amusement park where Bluto emerges as a Strong Man who makes off with the fair damsel.

5329. Quiet Please *(Tom & Jerry)* 22 Dec. 1945; *p.c.:* MGM; *dir:* William Hanna, Joseph Barbera; *anim:* Kenneth Muse, Ray Patterson, Irven Spence, Ed Barge; *lay:* Harvey Eisenberg; *back:* Robert Gentle; *ed:* Fred MacAlpin; *voices:* Billy Bletcher, Harry E. Lang; *mus:* Scott Bradley; *ph:* Jack Stevens; *prod:* Fred Quimby; *col:* Tech. *sd:* WE. 7 min. *Academy Award.* • Jerry sees to it that Tom gets the blame for waking up a tired bulldog.

5330. Quiet Pleez *(Popeye)* 7 Feb. 1941; *p.c.:* The Fleischer Studio for Para; *prod:* Max Fleischer; *dir:* Dave Fleischer; *story:* Milford Davis; *anim:* Willard Bowsky, Lod Rossner; *ed:* Kitty Pfister; *voices:* Jack Mercer; *mus:* Sammy Timberg; *ph:* Charles Schettler; *prod sup:* Sam Buchwald, Isidore Sparber; b&w. *sd:* WE. 7 min. • Pappy can't sleep because of the noise, so Popeye sets out to quieten things down.

5331. Le Quiet Squad *(Inspector)* 17 Mar. 1967; *p.c.:* Mirisch/Geoffrey/DFE for UA; *dir:* Robert McKimson; *story:* Jim Ryan; *anim:* Ted Bonnicksen, Manny Perez, Norm McCabe, Don Williams, Manny Gould, Bob Matz; *lay:* Lin Larsen; *back:* Tom O'Loughlin; *ed:* Lee Gunther; *voices:* Pat Harrington Jr., Paul Frees; *mus:* Walter Greene; *theme tune:* Henry Mancini; *prod sup:* Harry Love, Bill Orcutt; *col:* DeLuxe, *sd:* RCA. 6 min. • The Inspector tries to keep things quiet for the Commissioner.

5332. Rabbit Every Monday *(Looney Tunes)* 10 Feb. 1951; *p.c.:* WB; *dir:* I. Freleng; *anim:* Manuel Perez, Ken Champin, Virgil Ross, Arthur Davis; *lay:* Hawley Pratt; *back:* Paul Julian; *ed:* Treg Brown; *voices:* Mel Blanc; *mus:* Carl Stalling; *prod mgr:* John W. Burton; *prod:* Edward Selzer; *col:* Tech. *sd:* Vit. 7 min. • When Sam eventually does catch Bugs, he has a job trying to keep him in the oven.

5333. Rabbit Fire *(Looney Tunes)* 9 May 1951; *p.c.:* WB; *dir:* Charles M. Jones; *story:* Michael Maltese; *anim:* Lloyd Vaughan, Ken Harris, Phil Monroe, Ben Washam; *lay:* Robert Gribbroek; *back:* Philip de Guard; *ed:* Treg Brown; *voices:* Mel Blanc, Arthur Q. Bryan; *mus:* Carl Stalling; *prod mgr:* John W. Burton; *prod:* Edward Selzer; *col:* Tech. *sd:* Vit. 7 min. • Daffy and Bugs cause Elmer Fudd some confusion as to whether it's Rabbit Hunting Season or Duck Hunting Season.

5334. Rabbit Hood *(Merrie Melodies)* 24 Dec. 1949; *p.c.:* WB; *dir:* Charles M. Jones; *story:* Michael Maltese; *anim:* Ken Harris, Phil Monroe, Ben Washam, Lloyd Vaughan; *lay:* Robert Gribbroek; *back:* Peter Alvarado; *ed:* Treg Brown; *voices:* Mel Blanc; *mus:* Carl Stalling; *prod mgr:* John W. Burton; *prod:* Edward Selzer; *col:* Tech. *sd:* Vit. 8 min. *l/a/anim.* • The Sheriff of Nottingham tries to arrest Bugs for stealing The King's Royal Carrots but Bugs manages to talk him out of it. • Seq: *The Adventures of Robin Hood* (live-action: 1938)

5335. The Rabbit Hunt *(Oswald)* 17 Oct. 1938; *p.c.:* Walter Lantz prods for Univ; *dir:* Lester Kilne; *story:* Victor McLeod, James Miele; *anim:* Fred Kopietz, George Nicholas; *sets:* Edgar Keichle; *voice:* Shirley Reed; *mus:* Frank Marsales; *sd:* WE. 7½ min. • A rabbit saves a hound from a trap and when the rabbit is cornered in a hunt, the dog recalls his kindness and lets him go free.

5336. The Rabbit of Seville *(Looney Tunes)* 16 Dec. 1950; *p.c.:* WB; *dir:* Charles M. Jones; *story:* Michael Maltese; *anim:* Phil Monroe, Ben Washam, Lloyd Vaughan, Ken Harris, Emery Hawkins; *lay:* Robert Gribbroek; *back:* Philip de Guard; *ed:* Treg Brown; *voices:* Mel Blanc, Arthur Q. Bryan; *mus:* Carl Stalling; *prod mgr:* John W. Burton; *prod:* Edward Selzer; *col:* Tech. *sd:* Vit. 7 min. • Elmer chases Bugs into an Opera House where Rossini's *Barber of Seville* is being performed. Bugs siezes the opportunity to adapt and involve Elmer in the process.

5337. Rabbit Punch *(Merrie Melodies)* 4 Oct. 1948; *p.c.:* WB; *dir:* Charles M. Jones; *story:* Tedd Pierce, Michael Maltese; *anim:* Phil Monroe, Ken Harris, Lloyd Vaughan, Ben Washam; *lay:* Robert Gribbroek; *back:* Peter Alvarado; *ed:* Treg Brown; *voices:* Mel Blanc, Billy Bletcher; *mus:* Carl Stalling; *prod mgr:* John W. Burton; *prod:* Edward Selzer; *col:* Tech. *sd:* Vit. 7 min. • Bugs matches wits in the boxing ring with a champion fighter.

5338. Rabbit Punch *(Noveltoon)* 30 Sept. 1955; *p.c.:* Famous for Para; *dir:* Dave Tendlar; *story:* Larz Bourne; *anim:* Bill Hudson, Thomas Moore; *sets:* Robert Little; *voice:* Jack Mercer; *mus:* Winston Sharples; *ph:* Leonard McCormick; *prod mgr:* Seymour Shultz; *col:* Tech. *sd:* RCA. 6 min. • The Tortoise gets the worst of a boxing match until he reads the cartoon script and decides to alter the course of events.

5339. Rabbit Rampage *(Looney Tunes)* 11 June 1955; *p.c.:* WB; *dir:* Charles M. Jones; *story:* Michael Maltese; *anim:* Ben Washam; *lay:* Ernest Nordli; *back:* Philip de Guard; *ed:* Treg Brown; *voices:* Mel Blanc, Arthur Q. Bryan; *mus:* Milt Franklyn; *prod mgr:* John W. Burton; *prod:* Edward Selzer; *col:* Tech. *sd:* Vit. 6½ min. • Bugs finds himself at the mercy of a sadistic artist.

5340. Rabbit Romeo *(Merrie Melodies)* 14 Dec. 1957; *p.c.:* WB; *dir:* Robert McKimson; *story:* Michael Maltese; *anim:* Ted Bonnicksen, George Grandpré; *lay:* Robert Gribbroek; *back:* Bill Butler; *ed:* Treg Brown; *voices:* Mel Blanc, Arthur Q. Bryan, June Foray; *mus:* Milt Franklyn; *prod mgr:* John W. Burton; *prod:* Edward Selzer; *col:* Tech. *sd:* Vit. 6 min. • Elmer's wealthy uncle lets him look after a Slobovic female rabbit. The rabbit craves male companionship, so Elmer presents her with a reluctant Bugs Bunny.

5341. Rabbit Seasoning *(Merrie Melodies)* 20 Sept. 1952; *p.c.:* WB; *dir:* Charles M. Jones; *story:* Michael Maltese; *anim:* Ben Washam, Lloyd Vaughan, Ken Harris; *lay:* Maurice Noble; *back:* Philip de Guard; *ed:* Treg Brown; *voices:* Mel Blanc, Arthur Q. Bryan; *mus:* Carl Stalling; *prod mgr:* John W. Burton; *prod:* Edward Selzer; *col:* Tech. *sd:* Vit. 7 min. • Daffy tries to convince Elmer that he should be shooting rabbit instead of duck.

5342. Rabbit Stew and Rabbits Too *(Looney Tunes)* 15 Mar. 1969; *p.c.:* WB/7A; *dir:* Robert McKimson; *story:* Cal Howard; *anim:* Ted Bonnicksen, La Verne Harding, Jim Davis, Ed Solomon, Norm McCabe; *lay:* Bob Givens, Jaime Diaz; *back:* Bob McIntosh; *ed:* Hal Geer; *mus:* William Lava; *prod:* Bill L. Hendricks; *col:* Tech. *sd:* Vit. 6 min. • Quick Brownfox attempts to capture Rapid Rabbit but he proves too fast for the sly fox.

5343. Rabbit Transit *(Looney Tunes)* 10 May 1947; *p.c.:* WB; *dir:* I. Freleng; *story:* Michael Maltese, Tedd Pierce; *anim:* Manuel Perez, Ken Champin, Virgil Ross, Gerry Chiniquy; *fx:* A.C. Gamer; *lay:* Hawley Pratt; *back:* Philip de Guard; *ed:* Treg Brown; *voices:* Mel Blanc; *mus:* Carl Stalling; *prod mgr:* John W. Burton; *prod:* Edward Selzer; *col:* Tech. *sd:* Vit. 7 min. • Bugs challenges Cecil Turtle to a race but the turtle cheats by using a jet-propelled shell.

5344. Rabbit's Feat *(Looney Tunes)* 4 June 1960; *p.c.:* WB; *dir/story:* Chuck Jones; *anim:* Ken Harris, Richard Thompson; *sets:* Philip de Guard; *ed:* Treg Brown; *voices:* Mel Blanc; *mus:* Milt Franklyn; *prod mgr:* William Orcutt; *prod:* David H. DePatie; *col:* Tech. *sd:* Vit. 7 min. • Wile E. Coyote plots all kinds of devious methods to seccure Bugs, ending with Bugs confusing the issue by removing the viewfinder from his rifle.

5345. Rabbit's Kin *(Merrie Melodies)* 15 Nov. 1952; *p.c.:* WB; *dir:* Robert McKimson; *story:* Tedd Pierce; *anim:* Charles McKimson, Herman Cohen, Rod Scribner, Phil de Lara; *lay:* Robert Givens; *back:* Richard H. Thomas; *ed:* Treg Brown; *voices:* Mel Blanc, Stan Freberg; *mus:* Carl Stalling; *prod mgr:* John W. Burton; *prod:* Edward Selzer; *col:* Tech. *sd:* Vit. 7 min. • Bugs protects a young rabbit by fighting a battle of wits with Pete Puma ... only Pete is half-armed.

5346. Rabbitson Crusoe *(Looney Tunes)* 28 Apr. 1956; *p.c.:* WB; *dir:* Friz Freleng; *story:* Warren Foster; *anim:* Gerry Chiniquy, Virgil Ross, Arthur Davis; *lay:* Hawley Pratt; *back:* Irv Wyner; *ed:* Treg Brown; *voices:* Mel Blanc; *mus:* Milt Franklyn; *prod mgr:* John W. Burton; *prod:* Edward

Selzer; *col:* Tech. *sd:* Vit. 7 min. • Sam is castaway on an island guarded by a shark. Bugs sails by and Sam tries for an alternative meal to coconuts.

5347. Rabid Hunters (*Tom & Jerry*) Van Beuren for RKO; *dir:* John Foster, George Stallings; *mus:* Gene Rodemich; b&w. *sd:* RCA. 6 min. • Tom and Jerry hunt a rabbit and when they finally catch him they discover a skunk in a rabbit's skin.

5348. Race for Your Life, Charlie Brown Aug. 1977; *p.c.:* Lee Mendelson/Bill Melendez/Charles M. Schulz Creative Associates for CIC/Para; *prod:* Lee Mendelson, Bill Melendez; *dir:* Bill Melendez; *asst dir:* Phil Roman; *story/character des:* Charles M. Schulz; *anim:* Don Lusk, Sam Jaimes, Bob Matz, Bob Bachman, Hank Smith, George Singer, Rod Scribner, Bill Littlejohn, Ken O'Brien, Bob Carlson, Al Pabian, Patricia Joy, Joe Roman, Terry Lennon, Jeff Hall, Larry Leichliter; *sets:* Evert Brown, Bernard Gruver, Tom Yakutis, Dean Spille, Ellie Bogardus; *checking:* Carole Barnes, Eve Fletcher, Peggy Drumm; *i&p:* Joanne Lansing, Pat Capozzi, Sue Dalton, Mickey Kreyman, Cherie Lucas, Sue Rowan, Valerie Pabian, Robina Sarkissian, Adele Lenart, Sheri Barstad, Chandra Poweris, Lee Hoffman; *ed:* Chuck McCann, Roger Donley; *voices: Charlie Brown:* Duncan Watson; *Schroeder:* Greg Felton; *Peppermint Patty:* Stuart Brotman; *Sally:* Gail Davis; *Linus:* Liam Martin; *Bullies:* Kirkland Jue, Jordan Warren, Tom Muller; *Marcie:* Jimmy Ahrens; *Lucy:* Melanie Kohn; *Snoopy:* Bill Melendez; *Radio Announcer:* Fred van Amburg; *title song sung by:* Larry Finlayson; *singers:* Ed Bogas, Larry Finlayson, Judith Munsen, David Riordan, Roberta van der Vort, Bill Melendez, Fred van Amburg; *mus:* Ed Bogas; "Charmaine" by Erno Rapee and Lew Pollacki; *ph:* Dickson/Vasu; *negative cutting:* Alice Keillor; *sd:* Producers Sound Service/Coast Recorders; *prod sup:* Carole Barnes, Sandy Claxton, Lora Sackett, Charlotte Richardson, Babette Montell, Martha Grace; *col:* Metro. 76 min. • The "Peanuts" gang arrives at summer camp and are challenged by the resident bullies to a competition for the "top tent." Snoopy and Woodstock are on hand to help the gang win.

5349. Race Riot (*Oswald*) 26 July 1929; *p.c.:* Univ; *story/anim:* Walter Lantz; "Bill" Nolan, Tom Palmer; *mus:* Bert Fiske; b&w. *sd:* WE. 6 min. • Oswald, Putrid Pete and Cheesy Mouse all participate in a horse race.

5350. Racing Fever (*Life Cartoon Comedy*) 24 Apr. 1927; *p.c.:* Sherwood Wadsworth Pictures for Educational; *prod/dir:* John R. McCrory; b&w. sil. 5 min. • Little Nibbins creates a "dark horse" with the aid of a wooden horse, a blanket and a couple of dogs on stilts. All goes well until the dogs are distracted by a couple of cats and Nibbins finishes the race with only the horse's neck.

5351. The Racket Buster (*Mighty Mouse*) Feb. 1949; *p.c.:* TT for Fox; *dir:* Mannie Davis; *story:* John Foster; *anim:* Jim Tyer; *sets:* Art Bartsch; *voice:* Thomas Morrison; *mus:* Philip A. Scheib; *ph:* Douglas Moye; *col:* Tech. *sd:* RCA. 6 min. • A tough gang of cats, led by Edward G. Robinson, think they have disposed of Mighty Mouse and go on a rampage but are caught making an intergalactic escape.

5352. Racketeer Rabbit (*Merrie Melodies*) 14 Sept. 1946; *p.c.:* WB; *dir:* I. Freleng; *story:* Michael Maltese; *anim:* Gerry Chiniquy, Manuel Perez, Ken Champin, Virgil Ross; *lay:* Hawley Pratt; *back:* Paul Julian; *ed:* Treg Brown; *voices:* Mel Blanc, Dick Nelson; *mus:* Carl Stalling *prod mgr:* John W. Burton; *prod:* Edward Selzer; *col:* Tech. *sd:* Vit. 7 min. • Bugs is trapped in a deserted house by two desperados resembling Edward G. Robinson and Peter Lorre.

5353. Radio Controlled (*Aesop's Film Fable*) 21 Nov. 1926; *p.c.:* Fables Pictures Inc for Pathé; *dir:* Paul Terry; b&w. sil. 10 min. • The farm cat devises a remote-control that can manipulate baseballs. At the baseball game between the Cheese Chasers and the Radio Rustlers, the cat is able to control the speed of the baseball and the position of the bases with his electro-box. When Al Falfa attempts to catch one of the radio-controlled balls, he is beaten to a pulp by the spectators as the mice score a million runs.

5354. Radio Dynamics 1942; *anim:* Oskar Fischinger; *col. sd.* • Colors set to music.

5355. Radio Girl (*Paul Terry-Toon*) 17 Apr. 1932; *p.c.:* Moser & Terry for Educational; *dir:* Frank Moser, Paul Terry; *mus:* Philip A. Scheib; b&w. *sd:* WE. 6 min. • The hero falls for a girl he hears on the radio, finally winning her affection by rescuing her from a fire ... via the radio airwaves.

5356. Radio Racket (*Aesop's Sound Fable*) 1 Mar. 1931; *p.c.:* Van Beuren for RKO/Pathé; *dir:* John Foster; *mus:* Gene Rodemich; b&w. *sd:* RCA. 6 min. • Jungle creatures delight in song and dance to a radio concert.

5357. Radio Rhythm (*Oswald*); rel: 27 July 1931; *p.c.:* Univ; *dir:* Walter Lantz, "Bill" Nolan; *anim:* Clyde Geronimi, Manuel Moreno, Ray Abrams, Fred Avery, Lester Kline, Chet Karrberg, "Pinto" Colvig; *mus:* James Dietrich; b&w. *sd:* WE. 6 min. • Oswald broadcasts worldwide from Radio Station R-A-Z-Z.

5358. Radio Riot (*Talkartoon*) 15 Feb. 1930; *p.c.:* The Fleischer Studio for Para; *prod:* Max Fleischer; *dir:* Dave Fleischer; *mus:* Art Turkisher; b&w. *sd:* WE. 6 min. • The mice listen to a radio broadcast about a gorilla who gobbles up little children.

5359. The Rag Dog (*Rainbow Parade*) 19 July 1935; *p.c.:* Van Beuren for RKO; *dir:* Burt Gillett; *mus:* Winston Sharples; *col:* Ciné. *sd:* RCA. 7 min. • Three kittens throw a scare into a couple of dogs who want to take their milk.

5360. Raggedy Ann and Andy Mar. 1978; *p.c.:* Lester Osterman prods/Harmony Gold/The Bobbs-Merrill Co.Inc for Fox; *prod:* Richard Horner; *dir:* Richard Williams; characters created by Johnny Gruelle; *asst dir:* Cosmo Anzilotti, Fred Berner; *seq dir:* Gerald Potterton; *story:* Patricia Thackray, Max Wilk; *anim:* Art Babbitt, Tissa David, Emery Hawkins, Hal Ambro, Charlie Downs, John Kimball, Gerry Chiniquy, Chrystal Russell, Spencer Peel, John Bruno, Doug Crane, George Bakes, Art Vitello, Grim Natwick, Corny Cole, Cosmo Anzilotti, Tom Roth, Irv Spence, Warren Batchelder, Willis Pyle, Jack Schnerk; *asst anim sup:* Marlene Robinson, Michael Sporn; *asst dir:* Loren Bowie, David Block, Gian Franco-Celestri, Jerry Dvorak, Jeffrey Gatrall, John Gaug, Eric Goldberg, Daniel Haskett, Helen Kormar, Jim Logan, Mary Carol Millican, Lester Pegues Jr., Karen Peterson, Barney Posner, Michael Rochon, Tom Sito, Duane Ullrich; *prod des:* Corny Cole; *back:* Sue Butterworth, Bill Frake, Michael Guerin, Barbara Samuels; *ed:* Harry Chang, Lee Kent, Kenneth McIlwaine, Maxwell Seligman, Peter Grosart; *voices: Raggedy Ann:* Didi Conn; *Raggedy Andy:* Mark Baker; *The Camel with the Wrinkled Knees:* Fred Stuthman; *Babette:* Niki Flacks; *The Captain:* George S. Irving; *Queasy:* Arnold Stang; *The Greedy:* Joe Silver; *The Looney Knight:* Allan Sues; *King Koo Koo:* Marty Brill; *Gazooks:* Paul Dooley; *Grandpa:* Mason Adams; *Maxi-Fixit:* Allen Swift; *Susie Pincushion:* Hetty Galen; *Beanbag/Socko:* Sheldon Harnick; *Topsy:* Ardyth Kaiser; *The Twin Pennies:* Margery Gray, Lynn Stuart; *mus/songs:* Joe Raposo; *orch:* Joe Raposo, Jim Tyler; *asst conductor:* David Conner; *music copyists:* Jack Hansen, Vic Harrington; *mus coordinator:* Danny Epstein; *recording:* Fred Christie, Media Sound, Dick Vorisek, Trans/Audio; *sd fx:* Pisces Music, Bill Taylor; *i&p:* Ida Greenberg, Cel Specialists, Nancy Lane; *ph:* Al Schirano, Nick Mauroson, Bill Goshgarian, Peter Filancia; *Xerox:* Al Rezek Inc., William Kulhanek, Cosmo Pope; *West Coast consultant:* Carl Bell; *Prod consultant:* Shamus Culhane; *prod stills:* Catherine Bushnell; *prod sup:* H. Michael Sisson, David Bennett, Richard Mauro, Norton Virgien; *l/a seq:* Marcella: Claire Williams; *dir:* Dick Mingilone; *asst dir:* Larry Albucher, Barrie Osborne; *art dir:* William Mickley; *col:* DeLuxe. *sd.* 85 min. Panavision. *l/a/anim.* • Babette, a new doll in the playroom, is kidnapped by the Captain and Raggedy Ann and Andy set out to rescue her.

5361. Raggedy Ann and Raggedy Andy 11 Apr. 1941; *p.c.:* The Fleischer Studio for Para; *prod:* Max Fleischer; *dir:* Dave Fleischer; *story:* William Turner, Worth Gruelle; based on the characters created by Johnny Gruelle; *anim:* Myron Waldman, Joseph Oriolo, William Henning, Arnold Gillespie, James Davis; *voices:* Pinto Colvig, Jack Mercer, Bernie Fleischer; *mus:* Sammy Timberg; *ph:* Charles Schettler; *prod sup:* Sam Buchwald, Isidore Sparber; *col:* Tech. *sd:* WE. 19 min. • A small girl wants to buy the Raggedy Ann doll but is told why Ann and Andy are sold as a pair: When Andy meets a cute Senorita doll, Ann is heartbroken but he soon realizes his mistake and returns to Ann for eternity.

5362. Raggedy Rug (*Loopy de Loop*) Jan. 1964; *p.c.:* Hanna-Barbera for Colum; *prod/dir:* William Hanna, Joseph Barbera; *story dir:* Alex Lovy; *story:* Michael Maltese; *anim dir:* Charles A. Nichols; *anim:* Dick Lundy; *lay:* Jerry Eisenberg; *back:* Art Lozzi; *ed:* Warner Leighton; *voices:* Daws Butler, Don Messick, Jean van der Pyl; *mus:* Hoyt Curtin; *titles:* Lawrence Gobel; *prod mgr:* Howard Hanson; *col:* East. *sd:* RCA. 6 min. • Loopy replaces a bearskin rug.

5363. The Raging Tide (*Life Cartoon Comedy*) 27 Nov. 1926; *p.c.:* Sherwood Wadsworth Pictures for Educational; *prod/dir:* John R. McCrory; b&w. *sil.* 6 min. • While Mike and Myrtle are smooching, High-Hat Harold diverts a waterfall, inundating Myrtle's cottage and, of course, Mike rescues her.

5364. The Ragtime Bear (*Jolly Frolic*) 29 Sept. 1949; *p.c.:* UPA for Colum; *ex prod:* Stephen Bosustow; *dir:* John Hubley; *story:* Millard Kaufman; *anim:* Art Babbitt, Pat Matthews, Rudy Larriva, Willis Pyle; *lay:* William Hurtz; *back:* Herb Klynn, Jules Engel; *voices:* Jim Backus, Jerry Hausner; *mus:* Del Castillo; *technical:* Max Morgan, Mary Cain, Jack Eckes; *prod mgr:* Ed Gershman; *col:* Tech. *sd:* RCA. 7 min. • Magoo and Waldo are on an Alpine holiday when Magoo takes a music-loving bear for his fur-coated nephew. The first entry in the highly successful series featuring the myopic Mister Magoo.

5365. Ragtime Romeo (*Flip the Frog*) 2 May 1931; *p.c.:* Celebrity prods for MGM; *prod/dir:* Ub Iwerks; *mus:* Carl Stalling; b&w. *sd:* PCP. 9 min. • Flip serenades his lady love on a piano outside her apartment. Clarabelle Cow is trying to sleep and calls the police who cart him away.

5366. Rah Rah Ruckus (*Beary Family*) 5 May 1964; *p.c.:* Walter Lantz prods for Univ; *dir:* Paul J. Smith; *story:* Cal Howard; *anim:* Les Kline, Al Coe; *sets:* Art Landy, Ray Huffine; *voices:* Paul Frees, Grace Stafford; *mus:* Darrell Calker; *prod mgr:* William E. Garity; *col:* Tech. *sd:* RCA. 6 min. • Charlie disapproves of Junior practicing his cheerleading in the house.

5367. Raiding the Raiders (*Mighty Mouse*) 9 Mar. 1945; *p.c.:* TT for Fox; *dir:* Connie Rasinski; *story:* John Foster; *anim:* Bill Tytla; *mus:* Philip A. Scheib; *col:* Tech. *sd:* RCA. 7 min. • When the rabbits' happy home is threatened, Mighty Mouse steps in and corrects matters.

5368. Rail-Rodents (*Herman & Katnip*) 26 Nov. 1954; *p.c.:* Famous for Para; *dir:* Dave Tendlar; *story:* Jack Mercer; *anim:* Martin Taras, Thomas Moore; *sets:* Robert Little; *voice:* Sid Raymond; *mus:* Winston Sharples; *title song:* Hal David, Leon Carr; *ph:* Leonard McCormick; *prod mgr:* Seymour Shultz; *col:* Tech. *sd:* RCA. 6 min. • Katnip is travelling under the train when he hears the mice on board ... and the chase is on.

5369. Railroad Rhythm (*Krazy Kat*) 20 Nov. 1937; *p.c.:* Charles Mintz prods for Colum; *story:* Allen Rose; *anim:* Harry Love; *lay:* Clark Watson; *back:* Phil Davis; *voices:* Mel Blanc, Leone Le Doux, Dave Weber; *mus:* Joe de Nat; b&w. *sd:* RCA. 6 min. • Locomotive #77 driver, Krazy rescues Handsome Harry and Winsome Winnie who have been tied to the tracks by a wolf. He is rewarded with a deluxe new engine.

5370. Railroad Wretch (*Scrappy*) 31 Mar 1932; *p.c.:* Winkler for Colum; *prod:* Charles Mintz; *story:* Dick Huemer; *anim:* Sid Marcus, Art Davis; *mus:* Joe de Nat; b&w. *sd:* 7 min. • Scrappy and Vontzy are locomotive engineers who crash into a barn when Vontzy throws the controls away.

5371. Railroaded to Fame (*Hector Heathcote*) May 1961; *p.c.:* TT for Fox; *ex prod:* Bill Weiss; *dir:* Dave Tendlar; *story sup:* Tom Morrison; *story:* Al Bertino, Dick Kinney; *anim:* Bill Hutten, Armando Guidi, Larry Silverman; *lay:* Martin Strudler; *back:* Bill Hilliker; *voices:* John Myhers; *mus:* Phil Scheib; *prod mgr:* Frank Schudde; *col:* DeLuxe. *sd:* RCA. 6 min. • Heathcote helps lay railroad tracks across the prairie, causing nothing but chaos.

5372. Railroading (*Mastodon Cartoon*) 2 Dec. 1922; *p.c.:* Earl Hurd prods for Motion Picture Arts Inc./Educational; *prod:* C.C. Burr; *anim:* Earl Hurd; b&w. *sil.* 5 min. • Bobby Bumps makes a movie which requires him to run a locomotive over a broken bridge. After overcoming a cat on the tracks, he carries out this feat only to discover the camera lacking any film.

5373. Rain Drain (*James Hound*) Sept. 1966; *p.c.:* TT for Fox; *dir/anim:* Art Bartsch, Dave Tendlar; *col:* DeLuxe. *sd:* RCA. 6 min. • Hound investigates the disappearance of rain clouds used by Professor Mad to irrigate his own own oasis in the desert. • See: *James Hound*

5374. The Rain Makers (*Heckle & Jeckle*) June 1951; *p.c.:* TT for Fox; *dir:* Connie Rasinski; *story/voice:* Tom Morrison; *anim:* Jim Tyer; *sets:* Art Bartsch; *mus:* Philip A. Scheib; *ph:* Douglas Moye; *col:* Tech. *sd:* RCA. 6 min. • When a rainstorm ruins their picnic, the magpies wish for a drought. This then forces them to mechanically produce clouds and rain.

5375. Rain, Rain Go Away (*Beary Family*) 1972; *p.c.:* Walter Lantz

prods for Univ; *dir:* Paul J. Smith; *story:* Cal Howard; *anim:* Volus Jones, Al Coe, Tom Byrne, Joe Voght; *sets:* Nino Carbe; *voices:* Paul Frees, Grace Stafford; *mus:* Walter Greene; *prod mgr:* William E. Garity; *col:* Tech. *sd:* RCA. 6 min. • Charlie makes a nuisance of himself around the house when rain disrupts his game of golf.

5376. Rainbow Bear 1970; *p.c.:* Bill Melendez prods; *prod/dir:* Bill Melendez; *poem:* Robert Merz; *anim:* Evert Brown, Ruth Kissane, Bill Melendez; *sets:* Evert Brown, Cathy Julian, Jeremy Stieg; *ed:* Bob Gillis, Chuck McCann, Rudy Zamora Jr.; *voice:* Tony Osibisa; *mus:* Spartacus; *col:* Tech. *sd:* Producers' Sound Service. 5 min. • The Rainbow Bear comes alive after four hundred years of hibernation.

5377. Rainbow Brite and the Star Stealer 15 Nov. 1985; *p.c.:* DiC Enterprises/Hallmark; *dir:* Bernard Deyriès, Kimio Yabuki; *ex prod:* Jean Chalopin, Andy Heyward; *prod:* Jean Chalopin, Andy Heyward, Tetsuo Katayama; *asso prod:* Alan Lee, Victor Villegas; *story:* Jean Chalopin, Howard R. Cohen; *storyboard:* Tetsuo Imazawa, Yoshihisa Matsumoto, Akio Mitani, Kimio Yabuki; *anim art dir:* Isamu Kageyama, Rich Rudish; *art des:* Yasuyuki Chiba, Mayumi Hodozuka, Miyoko Kohama, Emiko Koizumi, Hiromi Morikawa, Takuko Nagashima, Takeshi Waki, Hiroshi Yoshikawa; *key anim:* Mitsuru Aoyama, Atsumi Hashimoto, Kahoru Hirata, Nobuyuki Hoga, Takashi Hyôdô, Michio Ikeda, Shin'ichi Imakuma, Masaki Kajishima, Hitomi Kakubari, Katsuko Kanazawa, Toshio Kaneko, Takenori Mihara, Kazukiko Miyake, Yasunori Miyazawa, Yoshio Mukainakano, Satoe Nishiyama, Hiroshi Oikawa, Junzo Ono, Masami Shimoda, Makoto Shinjo, Kin'ichirô Suzuki, Yasuyuki Tada, Akinobu Takahashi, Katsuo Takasaki, Yasushi Tanizawa, Fukuo Yamamoto, Tadakatsu Yoshida; *Doga-Kobou Studio: anim:* Katsumi Eguchi, Hideaki Furusawa, Takuma Haruka, Ikuko Hashikita, Satoshi Ida, Atsushi Irie, Kunitoshi Ishii, Yoshimi Kanbara, Satoshi Kasai, Yayoi Matsushita, Masanori Ooe, Shigeki Sato, Masato Sugimori, Yasuko Suzuki, Akio Taya, Midori Yamada, Hiroshi Yokobayashi, Asako Yuze; *Cockpit Studio: anim:* Kumiko Ando, Kotaro Kaneko, Atsuko Kawarai, Yumiko Kawashima, Fumiko Kawazoe, Mieko Kesen, Yumiko Kitajima, Keiko Matsumura, Satsuki Matsumura, Noriko Mochizuki, Sonomi Murase, Nobuyasu Omura, Akiro Oshima, Yoko Ozone, Kayo Sakazume, Tsukasa Sekine, Noriko Sugiyama, Takako Ueki, Chinatsu Ueno, Momoko Ueno, Yukie Watanabe,Yuichi Yanagihara; *Zaendou Studio: anim:* Isamu Kageyama, Katsuhiko Suzuki, Takeshi Yamazaki; *ed:* Yutaka Chikura, John Bonecutter, Linda Davies, Lars Floden, Ingrid Goncharoff, Kelly Hall, Jon E. Johnson, John Kelly, Richard Kelly, William R. Kowalchuk Jr., Marcelo Mainzer, Izumi Okada, Brian Ravok, Tim Roberts, Lida Parez Saskova, Clinton A. Solomon; *lay dir:* Hiroshi Wagatsuma; *character des/back des:* Laureen Burger, John Calmette; *character development:* Raul Alvarez, Gayle Bergman, Susie Cozad, Gilles Deyriès, Nate Evans, Mary Lou Faltico, John Hatfield, Paul Hindman, Gerry Oliveira, Kora Oliver, Carl Phelps, Coban Rudish, Paul Rudish, G.G. Saniago, Jeanne Slater, Mary Wineland; *fx:* Masayuki Nakajima, Kou Yamamoto; *voices: Rainbow Brite:* Bettina Bush; *Lucky/On-X/Buddy Blue/Dog/Guard/Spectran/Slurthie/Glitterbot:* Pat Fraley; *Popo:* Charlie Adler; *Twink/Shy Violet/Indigo/La La Orange/Spectran/Sprites:* Robbie Lee; *Starlite/Wizard/Spectran:* Andre Stojka; *Count Blogg:* Jonathan Harris; *Khrys:* David Mendenhall; *The Princess/The Creature:* Rhonda Aldrich; *Red Butler/Witch/Spectran/Castle Creature/Patty O'Green/Canary Yellow:* Mona Marshall; *Orin/Bombo/TV Announcer:* Les Tremayne; *Stormy:* Marissa Mendenhall; *Brian:* Scott Menville; *Sergeant Zombo:* David Workman; *DVD Narrator:* G.K. Bowes; *Murky Dismal/Castle Monster/Glitterbot/Guard/Skydancer/Slurthie:* Peter Cullen; *also:* Alan Lee; *mus:* Shuki Levy, Haim Saban; *mus co-ord:* Laurent Omont; *mus ed sup:* Marty Wereski; *anim check:* Mayumi Fujimoto, Hidehiko Kadota, Hiromi Naganawa, Midori Yamada; *Crocus Studio: i&p:* Chizuko Ohshima, Yuichi Takoh, Ayako Tan; *Kozue Animation: i&p:* Akemi Tamura, Keiko Yoshizawa; *Peacock Studio: i&p:* Kiyomi Arakawa, Makiko Hiraga, Shizuka Ishiguro, Akemi Motohashi, Yuji Sawada, Toshiyuki Takahashi, Machiko Tawara; *Suzuki Animation: i&p:* Hiroko Inoue, Shinobu Nakamura, Keiko Nemoto, Susuki Norikata, Toshiko Suzuki, Mariko Tsukagoshi; *Taka Production: i&p:* Kazuko Fujii, Kazuya Sakurada, Toyoji Sawada, Mayumi Shiba; *Tama Studio: i&p:* Kouichi Okuno, Masako Tochi, Kuniko Tsujimura, Kaoru Uchida, Teiko Yonemura; *paint check:* Yuko Nishikawa; *timing:* Myrna Bushman; *ph:* Hirokata Takahashi; *ex in charge of prod:* Kevin O'Donnell; *prod sup:* JoEllyn Marlow; *post-prod sup:* William R. Kowalchuk Jr., Bonnie

J. Sehenuk; *script sup:* Lori Crawford; *dial ed:* Alan Bromberg, Dan M. Rich; *sd ed:* Terry Lynn Allen, John H. Arrufat, Bruce Elliott, Leonard T. Geschke, Joe Gilbert,, Lisa Gilbert, James J. Isaacs, Armetta Jackson-Hamlett, Elliott L. Koretz, Donald L. Warner Jr., Bob Waxman, Ronnie Leon White; *sd fx:* Barry Gilmore, Jeremy MacLaverty; *track reader:* Theresa Gilroy-Nielsen, Robert Hudson III, Rob Rule; *sd rec:* Greg P. Russell; *sd re-rec mix:* Nick Alphin, Gary C. Bourgeois, Thomas Gerard; *voice rec dir:* Howard R. Cohen; *foley:* Denis Blais, Terry Burke; *ph:* Tomoko Akisaka, Atsuo Fukushima, Mitsue Inoue, Norihisa Ishizuka, Izumi Kasama, Takeo Kobayashi, Harutoshi Miyagawa, Hajime Noguchi, Masaaki Oono, Takaharu Shiagami, Yasuyoshi Toyonaga, Yasuji Watanabe, Isao Yarimitsu; *neg cutter:* Mari Kishi; *ex consult:* Cheryl Cazard, Dan Drake, Lanny Julian, Jim McDowell, Joe Morrison,Cassandra Schafhausen, John Weems; *post prod co-ord:* Karen M. Cockrell, Ted Harrison, Patty Hayes,Greg LaPlante, Melinda Miller; *anim studio prod:* Hajime Watanabe; *anim prod co-ord:* Mitsuya Fujimoto, Masami Furukawa, Yuji Himaki, Junichi Sakata; *col:* Tech. *sd:* Dolby stereo. 85 min. • Rainbow Brite sets out to prevent an evil Princess and her cohorts from conquering the Planet Spectra. USA/Japan.

5378. A Rainy Day *(Bear Family)* 20 Apr. 1940; *p.c.:* MGM; *prod/dir:* Hugh Harman; *story:* Hugh Harman, Jack Cosgriff, Charles McGirl; *anim:* William Littlejohn; *lay:* John Meandor; *back:* Joe Smith; *voice:* Martha Wentworth, Rudolf Ising; *mus:* Scott Bradley; *prod mgr:* Fred Quimby; *col:* Tech. *sd:* WE. 7 min. • Papa Bear tries to mend a leaky roof, only succeeding in making matters worse when a thunderstorm occurs.

5379. Rancid Ransom *(Loopy de Loop)* Nov. 1963; *p.c.:* Hanna-Barbera prods for Colum; *prod/dir:* Joseph Barbera, William Hanna; *story dir:* Paul Sommer; *story:* Dalton Sandifer; *anim dir:* Charles A. Nichols; *anim:* Dick Lundy; *lay:* Iwao Takamoto; *back:* F. Montealegre; *ed:* Joseph Ruby; *voices:* Daws Butler, Don Messick; *mus:* Hoyt Curtin; *titles:* Lawrence Gobel; *prod mgr:* Howard Hanson; *col:* East. *sd:* RCA. 6 min. • Loopy tries to rescue a baby from kidnappers.

5380. The Rasslin' Match *(Amos & Andy)* 5 Jan. 1934; *p.c.:* Van Beuren for RKO; *anim:* George Stallings; *voices:* Freeman F. Gosden, Charles Correll; *mus:* Gene Rodemich; *b&w. sd:* RCA. 10 min. • Andy meets Bullneck Mooseface on the canvas for the championship of "Sumphin." Short-lived series featuring the creators and original scripts of the popular radio show.

5381. Rasslin' Round *(Willie Whopper)* 1 June 1934; *p.c.:* Celebrity prods for MGM; *prod/dir:* Ub Iwerks; *anim:* Robert G. Stokes, Norm Blackburn; *mus:* Carl Stalling; *b&w. sd:* PCP. 6 min. • Shoeshine boy Willie spins a yarn to a customer of how he once beat the wrestling champ.

5382. Rastus' Rabid Rabbit Hunt 26 Dec 1914; *p.c.:* Bray prods for Eclectic; *anim:* John R. Bray; *b&w. sil.* 4 min. • Mrs. Rastus Lazybones compels her shiftless other half to bestir himself, grab his "Ole Muzzle Loader" and shoot something for the cooking pot!

5383. Rastus — in Court! 1916; *p.c.:* Bray prods for Eclectic: *anim:* John R. Bray; *b&w. sil.* 4 min. • No story available.

5384. Ration Bored *(Woody Woodpecker)* 26 July 1943; *p.c.:* Walter Lantz prods for Univ; *dir:* Emery Hawkins, Milt Schaffer; *story:* Ben Hardaway; *anim:* Bob Bentley; *sets:* Fred Brunish; *voices:* Kent Rogers; *mus:* Darrell Calker; *prod mgr:* George Hall; *col:* Tech. *sd:* WE. 6 min. • Woody syphons gas from the first car he finds which unfortunately is an occupied police car.

5385. Ration fer the Duration *(Popeye)* 28 May 1943; *p.c.:* Famous for Para; *dir:* Seymour Kneitel; *story:* Jack Mercer, Jack Ward; *anim:* Dave Tendlar, Tom Golden; *voices:* Jack Mercer; *mus:* Sammy Timberg; *ph:* Leonard McCormick; *prod mgr:* Sam Buchwald; *b&w. sd:* WE. 8 min. • Popeye instills some home-front fighting spirit in his nephews by putting himself in the role of "Jack and the Beanstalk"with a food hoarding (New York) giant.

5386. Rats in His Garret *(Aesop's Film Fable)* 11 Dec. 1927; *p.c.:* Fables Pictures Inc for Pathé; *dir:* Paul Terry, Hugh Shields; *b&w. sil.* 10 min. • When the mice steal the farmer's grain, he employs a canine "rat exterminator" from a salesman. The dog leads the mice a merry chase into the trap, but releases them later. The rodents chase Al, the dog and the salesman away.

5387. The Rat's Revenge *(Aesop's Film Fable)* 3 Feb. 1924; *p.c.:* Fables Pictures Inc for Pathé; *dir:* Paul Terry; *b&w. sil.* 5 min. • The fable of "The Lion and the Mouse" is adapted by a rodent getting the cat to free him.

5388. Ratskin *(Krazy Kat)* 15 Aug. 1929; *p.c.:* Winkler for Colum; *anim:* Ben Harrison, Manny Gould; *mus:* Rosario Bourdon; *prod:* George Winkler; *b&w. sd:* WE. 6 min. • Krazy is attacked by wild Indians while heading West in a covered wagon. First sound Krazy Kat.

5389. The Rattled Rooster *(Looney Tunes)* 26 June 1948; *p.c.:* WB; *dir:* Arthur Davis; *story:* Dave Monahan; *anim:* Don Williams, John Carey, Basil Davidovich, J.C. Melendez; *lay:* Don Smith; *back:* Philip de Guard; *ed:* Treg Brown; *voice:* Mel Blanc; *mus:* Carl Stalling; *prod mgr:* John W. Burton; *prod:* Edward Selzer; *col:* Tech. *sd:* Vit. 7 min. • A hungry rooster selects a shrewd worm to have for his breakfast.

5390. The Raven 3 Apr. 1940; *p.c.:* The Fleischer Studio for Para; *prod:* Max Fleischer; *dir:* Dave Fleischer; *story:* Carl Meyer, Pinto Colvig; *ed:* Kitty Pfister; *voices:* Pinto Colvig; *mus:* Sammy Timberg; *ph:* Charles Schettler; *prod sup:* Sam Buchwald, Isidore Sparber; *col:* Tech. *sd:* WE. 14½ min. • A fast-talking raven teams up with a fox to sell Scottie a vacuum cleaner. While he is demonstrating, the Fox is rifling Scottie's safe.

5391. Raw! Raw! Rooster! *(Merrie Melodies)* 25 Aug. 1956; *p.c.:* WB; *dir:* Robert McKimson; *story:* Tedd Pierce; *anim:* Russ Dyson, Ted Bonnicksen, George Grandpré, Keith Darling; *sets:* Richard H. Thomas; *ed:* Treg Brown; *voices:* Mel Blanc, Daws Butler; *mus:* Carl Stalling; *prod mgr:* John W. Burton; *prod:* Edward Selzer; *col:* Tech. *sd:* Vit. 7 min. • Foggy's serene existence is shattered by the arrival of Rhode Island Red, an old collegian and noted practical joker.

5392. Razz Berries *(Paul Terry-Toon)* 8 Feb. 1931; *p.c.:* A-C for Educational/Fox; *dir:* Frank Moser, Paul Terry; *mus:* Philip A. Scheib; *b&w. sd:* WE. 6 min. • Al Falfa arrives in a mechanical elephant while on a jungle expedition. An ape hides in a hollow tree blowing raspberries at passersby, making them jump out of their skins ... which he sells to Al Falfa at a handsome price.

5393. R'Coon Dawg *(Pluto)* 10 Aug. 1951; *p.c.:* Walt Disney prods for RKO; *dir:* Charles Nichols; *story:* Ralph Wright, Al Bertino; *anim:* Norman Ferguson, Fred Moore, Marvin Woodward, Charles Nichols; *fx:* Jack Boyd; *lay:* Lance Nolley; *back:* Art Riley; *voices:* Cactus Mack McPeters, James MacDonald; *mus:* Paul Smith; *col:* Tech. *sd:* RCA. 6 min. • Mickey takes Pluto raccoon hunting but they are outwitted by the creature at every turn.

5394. Reaching for the Moon *(Screen Songs)* 24 Feb. 1933. *p.c.:* The Fleischer Studio for Para; *prod:* Max Fleischer; *dir:* Dave Fleischer; *anim:* Willard Bowsky, Ugo d'Orsi; *mus:* Art Turkisher; *song:* Irving Berlin; *l/a:* Arthur Tracy; *b&w. sd:* WE. 7 min. *l/a/anim.* • Professor I. Shpy watches life on another planet. He asks the moon if it's made of cheese, giving vent for its inhabitants to stage a war.

5395. Readin', Ritin' and Rhythmetic *(Screen Song)* 22 Oct. 1948; *p.c.:* Famous for Para; *dir:* Seymour Kneitel; *story:* I. Klein; *anim:* Al Eugster, Bill Hudson; *sets:* Tom Ford; *mus:* Winston Sharples; *song:* Gus Edwards; *ph:* Leonard McCormick; *prod mgr:* Sam Buchwald; *col:* Pola. *sd:* RCA. 7 min. • The animals have a music lesson.

5396. Reading, Writhing and 'Rithmetic *(Modern Madcap)* Nov. 1964; *p.c.:* Para Cartoons; *dir:* Seymour Kneitel; *story:* Jack Mendelsohn; *anim:* Morey Reden; *sets:* Robert Little; *mus:* Winston Sharples; *ph:* Leonard McCormick; *prod mgr:* Abe Goodman; *col:* Tech. *sd:* RCA. 6 min. • When Buck Weasel spies Wingy the baby Rooster on his way to school, he quickly lures him to his own house, disguised as a school house with himself posing as Schoolma'm. Buck fails at numerous attempts to cook the rooster and when the oven explodes, the kid decides to go home. Wingy tells his Mother that he's through with school because he's "smarter than teacher." While, back at the "schoolhouse" Buck Weasel writes "I am a Dunce" over and over on the blackboard.

5397. Ready Made Magic 1947; *p.c.:* Ted Eshbaugh Studio for Sure-Fit Products Co; *prod/ dir/story/ ed/ph:* Ted Eshbaugh; *voice:* Tom Shirley; *col. sd.* • Commercial for Sure-Fit Products.

5398. Ready ... Set ... Zoom! *(Looney Tunes)* 30 Apr. 1955; *p.c.:* WB; *dir:* Charles M. Jones; *story:* Michael Maltese; *anim:* Ben Washam, Abe Levitow, Richard Thompson, Lloyd Vaughan, Ken Harris; *lay:* Maurice Noble; *back:* Philip de Guard; *ed:* Treg Brown; *voice:* Paul Julian; *mus:* Carl W. Stalling; *prod mgr:* John W. Burton; *prod:* Edward Selzer; *col:* Tech. *sd:*

Vit. 7 min. • In his attempts to ensnare the elusive bird, the Coyote coats the road with glue, uses a 10,000-lb weight, affixes an outboard motor to himself and finally resorts to disguising himself as a female road-runner ... all to no avail.

5399. Ready, Woolen and Able *(Merrie Melodies)* 30 July 1960; *p.c.:* WB; *dir:* Chuck Jones; *story:* Michael Maltese; *anim:* Ken Harris, Richard Thompson, Ben Washam; *lay:* Maurice Noble; *back:* Philip de Guard; *ed:* Treg Brown; *voices:* Mel Blanc; *mus:* Milt Franklyn; *prod mgr:* William Orcutt; *prod:* David H. DePatie; *col:* Tech. *sd:* Vit. 7 min. • While attempting to steal sheep, Ralph Wolf discovers Sam Sheepdog at every turn he makes.

5400. Real Gone Woody *(Woody Woodpecker)* 20 Sept. 1954; *p.c.:* Walter Lantz prods for Univ; *dir:* Paul J. Smith; *story:* Michael Maltese; *anim:* Gil Turner, La Verne Harding, Robert Bentley; *sets:* Raymond Jacobs, Art Landy; *voices:* Dallas McKennon, Grace Stafford; *mus:* Clarence Wheeler; *prod mgr:* William E. Garity; *col:* Tech. *sd:* RCA. 6 min. • Hipsters, Woody and Buzz Buzzard fight over the privilege of taking Winnie Woodpecker to the high school hop.

5401. Really Scent *(Merrie Melodies)* 24 June 1959; *p.c.:* WB; *dir:* Abe Levitow; *story:* Michael Maltese; *anim:* Ken Harris, Richard Thompson, Ben Washam; *lay:* Samuel Armstrong; *back:* Philip de Guard; *ed:* Treg Brown; *voices:* Mel Blanc, June Foray; *mus:* Milt Franklyn; *prod:* John W. Burton; *col:* Tech. *sd:* Vit. 7 min. • A black cat is born with a white stripe down her back. She goes in search of a mate and falls afoul of Pepè le Pew, the amorous French skunk.

5402. Reason and Emotion 27 Aug. 1943; *p.c.:* Walt Disney prods for RKO; *dir:* William O. Roberts; *asst dir:* Harry Love; *story:* William O. Roberts, Harry Love; *anim:* Oliver M. Johnston Jr., Milt Kahl, Ward Kimball, Norman Tate, Vladimir Tytla; *lay:* Hugh Hennesy; *voices:* Frank Graham, Sarah Selby, Mary Lennon, Harry E. Lang; *mus:* Paul J. Smith; *col:* Tech. *sd:* RCA. 7¹⁄₂ min. *Academy Award nomination.* • Morale booster illustrating how reason and emotion can work together to win the war against the Axis. Excellent example of wartime propaganda.

5403. Reaux, Reaux, Reaux Your Boat *(Inspector)* 1 Feb. 1966; *p.c.:* Mirisch/Geoffrey/DFE for UA; *dir:* dir: Gerry Chiniquy; *story:* John W. Dunn; *anim:* Warren Batchelder, Norm McCabe, Manny Perez, Don Williams, Bob Matz, George Grandpré; *sets:* T.M. Yakutis; *ed:* Roger Donley; *voices:* Pat Harrington Jr., Paul Frees; *mus:* William Lava; *theme tune:* Henry Mancini; *prod mgr:* Bill Orcutt; *col:* DeLuxe. *sd:* RCA. 6 min. • The Inspector and Deux-Deux set out to capture Cpt. Clam and Crab Louie aboard a scow known as *The Coddled Clam.*

5404. Rebel Rabbit *(Merrie Melodies)* 9 Apr. 1949; *p.c.:* WB; *dir:* Robert McKimson; *story:* Warren Foster; *anim:* Charles McKimson, Phil de Lara, Manny Gould, John Carey; *character des:* Jean Blanchard; *lay:* Cornett Wood; *back:* Richard H. Thomas; *ed:* Treg Brown; *voices:* Mel Blanc; *mus:* Carl Stalling; *prod mgr:* John W. Burton; *prod:* Edward Selzer; *col:* Tech. *sd:* Vit. 7 min. • Outraged at a 5¢ bounty for rabbits, Bugs sets out to make his presence known throughout the country, eventually landing himself in Alcatraz.

5405. Rebel Trouble *(Deputy Dawg)* June 1962; *p.c.:* TT for Fox; *ex prod:* Bill Weiss; *dir/anim:* Dave Tendlar; *story sup:* Tom Morrison; *story:* Larz Bourne; *sets:* Bill Focht, John Zago; *ed:* George McAvoy; *voices:* Dayton Allen; *mus:* Phil Scheib; *ph:* George Davis; *prod mgr:* Frank Schudde; *col:* DeLuxe. *sd:* RCA. 5 min. • Deputy Dawg forms a two-man army against an invading movie unit.

5406. Rebel Without Claws *(Looney Tunes)* 15 July 1961; *p.c.:* WB; *dir/story:* Friz Freleng; Virgil Ross, Art Davis, Gerry Chiniquy, David R. Green; *lay:* Hawley Pratt; *back:* Tom O'Loughlin; *ed:* Treg Brown; *voices:* Mel Blanc; *mus:* Milt Franklyn; *prod mgr:* William Orcutt; *prod:* David H. DePatie; *col:* Tech. *sd:* Vit. 7 min. • During the Civil War, Rebel cat, Sylvester, tries to stop dispatch bird Tweety from getting his message through the enemy lines. Assistant animator Dave Green is caricatured as a soldier.

5407. The Reckless Driver *(Woody Woodpecker)* 26 Aug. 1946; *p.c.:* Walter Lantz prods for Univ; *dir:* James Culhane; *story:* Ben Hardaway, Milt Schaffer; *anim:* Grim Natwick, Les Kline; *sets:* Terry Lind; *voices:* Nestor Paiva, Ben Hardaway; *mus:* Darrell Calker; *prod mgr:* George Hall; *col:* Tech. *sd:* WE. 6 min. • Woody tries to renew his driving licence with Officer Wally Walrus giving him the test.

5408. Recruiting Daze *(Cartune)* 28 Oct. 1940; *p.c.:* Walter Lantz prods for Univ; *dir:* Alex Lovy; *story:* Ben Hardaway, Lowell Elliot; *anim:* Alex Lovy, Lester Kline; *sets:* Fred Brunish; *voices:* George Fischer, Walter Lantz; *mus:* Frank Marsales; *prod mgr:* George Hall; *col:* Tech. *sd:* WE. 6¹⁄₂ min. • Army blackouts, including Punchy, an inept doughboy who gets himself shot from a "several mile long"cannon to a distant planet.

5409. Red Head Comedies *p.c.:* Lee-Bradford Corp; *dir/story:* Richard McShay Friel; *prod:* Frank A. Nankievell, W.E. Stark, Andrew "Hutch" Hutchinson; *anim:* Richard McShay Friel, Andrew S. Hutchinson, Frank A. Nankievell, W. (Walter) E. Stark; *col. st.* • *1923:* **Robinson Crusoe Returns on Friday** Sept. **Cleopatra and Her Easy Mark** Sept. **Napoleon the Not So Great** Sept. **Kidding Captain Kidd** Sept. **Rip Without a Wink** Sept. **Columbus Discovers a New Whirl** Sept. **Why Sitting Bull Stood Up** Dec. **What Did William Tell** Dec. **A Whale of a Story** Dec. **How Troy Was Collared** Dec. **The James Boys' Sister** Dec. • *1925:* **Nero and His Jazz Band** 12 May • **Balboa Discovers Hollywood** • No stories available.

5410. Red Headed Baby *(Merrie Melodies)* Jan. 1932; *p.c.:* Hugh Harman, Rudolf Ising prods for WB; *anim:* Rollin Hamilton, Max Maxwell, Robert Clampett; *mus:* Frank Marsales; *prod:* Leon Schlesinger; *b&w. sd:* Vit. 7 min. • The playroom toys come alive. A red headed doll is kidnapped by a villainous spider and rescued by her soldier sweetheart.

5411. Red Headed Monkey *(Terry-Toon)* July 1950; *p.c.:* TT for Fox; *dir:* Mannie Davis; *story:* Tom Morrison; *anim:* Jim Tyer; *mus:* Philip A. Scheib; *col:* Tech. *sd:* RCA. 6 min. • Major Throttlebottom travels far to find the rare red headed monkey. He captures it but the ape has the last laugh by putting the Major in his own pet shop window.

5412. Red Hot Mama *(Betty Boop)* 2 Feb. 1934; *p.c.:* The Fleischer Studio for para; *prod:* Max Fleischer; *dir:* Dave Fleischer; *anim:* Willard Bowsky, David Tendlar; *sets:* Erich Schenk; *voice:* Mae Questel; *mus:* Sammy Timberg; *b&w. sd:* WE. 8 min. • Betty falls asleep by the fire and dreams she is in Hades, singing "Hell's Bells"!

5413. Red Hot Rails *(Life Cartoon Comedy)* 15 Aug. 1926; *p.c.:* Sherwood Wadsworth Pictures for Educational; *prod/dir:* John R. McCrory; *b&w. sil.* 6 min. • Myrtle Monkey, the flapper heroine, is kidnapped by High-Hat Harold and locked in the boxcar of a train. Mike Monkey flies to her rescue.

5414. Red Hot Rangers 3 May 1947 *p.c.:* MGM; *dir:* Tex Avery; *story:* Heck Allen; *anim:* Ray Abrams, Preston Blair, Walter Clinton, Ed Love; *character des:* Irven Spence; *sets:* John Didrik Johnsen; *ed:* Fred MacAlpin; *voices:* Dick Nelson; *mus:* Scott Bradley; *ph:* Jack Stevens; *prod:* Fred Quimby; *col:* Tech. *sd:* WE. 7¹⁄₂ min. • Forest Rangers, George and Junior, try their best to douse a stubborn forest fire.

5415. Red-Hot Riding Hood 8 May 1943; *p.c.:* MGM; *dir:* Tex Avery; *story:* Rich Hogan; *anim:* Ed Love. Preston Blair, Ray Abrams; *character des:* Claude Smith; *sets:* John Didrik Johnsen; *ed:* Fred MacAlpine; *voices:* Frank Graham, Kent Rogers, Connie Russell, Sara Berner; *mus:* Scott Bradley; *ph:* Gene Moore; *prod:* Fred Quimby; *col:* Tech. *sd:* WE. 8 min. • Red Riding Hood works as a Hollywood nightclub singer, constantly dodging the amorous advances of a Hollywood wolf. Grandma, however, welcomes any male!

5416. Red Hot Sands *(Aesop's Film Fable)* 8 July 1927; *p.c.:* Fables Pictures Inc for Pathé; *dir:* Paul Terry, Mannie Davis; *b&w. sil.* 10 min. • A cat and mouse visit Arabia where they rescue Harem Helen from being held captive by a sheik who pursues them with Arab guards.

5417. Red Riding Hood *(Aesop's Sound Fable)* 18 Jan. 1931; *p.c.:* Van Beuren for RKO/Pathé; *dir:* John Foster, Harry Bailey; *mus:* Gene Rodemich; *b&w. sd:* RCA. 8 min. • The wolf arrives and finds Grandma dancing like a deb after taking rejuvenating juice. He elopes with her and Red snitches to Mrs. Wolf.

5418. Red Riding Hood Rides Again *(Color Rhapsody)* 25 Dec. 1941; *p.c.:* Colum; *dir:* Sid Marcus; *anim:* Bob Wickersham, Bill Hamner; *lay:* Clark Watson; *voices:* Billy Bletcher, Marjorie Tarlton; *mus:* Eddie Kilfeather; *ph:* Otto Reimer; *prod mgr:* James Bronis; *col:* Tech. *sd:* RCA. 6¹⁄₂ min. • Red mistakes the wolf for a cute police dog. He races to Grandma's house and is about to devour the old girl when her boyfriend arrives to cut a rug with her. The wolf then gets drafted. Caricatures of Clark Gable, Groucho Marx, William Powell, George Raft.

5419. Red Riding Hoodlum (*Woody Woodpecker*) 11 Feb. 1957; *p.c.:* Walter Lantz prods for Univ; *dir:* Paul J. Smith; *story:* Milt Schaffer, Dick Kinney; *anim:* Les Kline, Robert Bentley; *sets:* Art Landy, Raymond Jacobs; *voices:* Dal McKennon, June Foray, Grace Stafford; *mus:* Clarence Wheeler; *prod mgr:* William E. Garity; *col:* Tech. *sd:* RCA. 6 min. • Woody's nephews are taking a basket of groceries to Grandma when a wolf encounters them en route and tries to get the "Little Red Riding Hood" story going.

5420. Red Riding Hoodwinked (*Looney Tunes*) 29 Oct. 1955; *p.c.:* WB; *dir:* I. Freleng; *story:* Warren Foster; *anim:* Arthur Davis, Gerry Chiniquy, Ted Bonnicksen; *lay:* Hawley Pratt; *back:* Irv Wyner; *ed:* Treg Brown; *voices:* Mel Blanc, June Foray; *mus:* Milt Franklyn; *prod mgr:* John W. Burton; *prod:* Edward Selzer; *col:* Tech. *sd:* Vit. 7 min. • Red Riding hood takes Granny a Tweety bird but Sylvester gets to Granny's house first. A wolf also arrives and the two of them dress as Granny to fool their respective prey.

5421. Red Skin Blues (*Tom & Jerry*) 23 July 1932; *p.c.:* Van Beuren for RKO; *anim:* John Foster, George Stallings; *mus:* Gene Rodemich; b&w. *sd:* RCA. 6 min. • The boys find themselves tied to a stake in an Indian encampment. They are rescued by the Army, Navy, Air Force and Tank Corps.

5422. The Red Swamp Pox (*Possible Possum*) May 1969; *p.c.:* TT for Fox; *col:* DeLuxe. *sd:* RCA. 6 min. • Poss believes Mr. General to have caught the Swamp Pox and sets out to fly him to hospital. As it turns out, he has paint splashed on his face. • See: *Possible Possum*

5423. The Red Tractor (*Duckwood*) Feb. 1964; *p.c.:* TT for Fox; *ex prod:* Bill Weiss; *dir/anim:* Dave Tendlar; *story sup:* Tom Morrison; *story:* Larz Bourne; *sets:* Bill Focht, John Zago; *ed:* Jack MacConnell; *voices:* Dayton Allen; *mus:* Jim Timmens; *ph:* Charles Schettler; *sd:* Elliot Grey; *col:* DeLuxe. *sd:* RCA. 6 min. • Duckwood and Donkey try to sell attachments to a farmer for his tractor.

5424. Red, White and Boo (*Casper*) 23 Dec. 1955; *p.c.:* Famous for Para; *dir:* I. Sparber; *story:* I. Klein; *anim:* Myron Waldman, Nick Tafuri; *sets:* Robert Owen; *voices:* Norma MacMillan, Jackson Beck, Sid Raymond, Jack Mercer; *mus:* Winston Sharples; *title song:* Mack David, Jerry Livingston; *col:* Tech. *sd:* RCA. 6 min. • Casper goes through a time machine and visits the stone age, Robert Fulton, Paul Revere and George Washington, helping history on its way.

5425. Reddy Kilowatt in What's Watt 1934; *p.c.:* Audio prods Co/Ashton B. Collins for Philadelphia Electric Co; *dir:* F. Lyle Goldman; *anim:* John Foster; b&w. sd. • Commercial for Reddy Kilowatt.

5426. Reddy Made Magic 25 Mar. 1946; *p.c.:* Walter Lantz prods for Ashton B. Collins; *dir:* Dick Lundy; *story:* Ben Hardaway, Milt Schaffer; *ed:* Dave Lurie; *voices:* George Barclay, Walter Tetley; *mus:* Darrell Calker; *song:* Mabel Ellis, Del Porter; *arr:* Sigmund Spaeth; *ph:* Fred Weaver; *sd:* Bernard B. Brown; *prod mgr:* William E. Garity; *col:* Tech. *sd:* WE. 11 min. • Featuring electric power trademark, *Reddy Kilowatt*. The discovery, development and modern applications of electricity.

5427. Red's Dream 1987; *p.c.:* PIXAR; *dir/story/anim:* John Lasseter; *technical dir:* Eben Ostby, William Reeves, H.B. Siegel; *modeling/anim software:* Eben Ostby, William Reeves; *models:* John Lasseter, Eben Ostby, William Reeves; *Reyes/miracle tilt:* Robert L. Cook; *ChapReyes:* Tony Apodaca, Charlie Gunn, H.B. Siegel; *laser scan:* Don Conway; *sd:* Gary Rydstrom, Sprocket Systems; *mus:* David Slusser; *mus research:* Forrest Patten, Kaleidosound; *computer support:* Bill Carson, David Fong; *prod co-ord:* Susan Anderson Catmull, Ralph Guggenheim; *post prod co-ord:* Craig Good; *col.* sd. 4¼ min. *Academy Award.* • A lonely unicycle in a bicycle shop fantasizes about being a clown's unicycle in a circus.

5428. Reducing Crème (*Willie Whopper*) 19 May 1934; *p.c.:* Celebrity prods for MGM; *prod/dir:* Ub Iwerks; *anim:* Grim Natwick, Berny Wolf; *mus:* Art Turkisher; b&w. *sd:* PCP. 8 min. • A cat spills reducing creme over Willie and shrinks him down to the size of a mouse.

5429. The Redwood Sap (*Woody Woodpecker*) 1 Oct. 1951; *p.c.:* Walter Lantz prods for Univ; *dir/story:* Walter Lantz; *anim:* Don Patterson, Ray Abrams, La Verne Harding, Paul Smith; *sets:* Fred Brunish; *voices:* Grace Stafford, Clarence E. Wheeler; *mus:* Clarence E. Wheeler; *col:* Tech. *sd:* RCA. 6 min. • Woody steals the other animals' food but when winter comes, he begs sustenance from them. By next spring, he is back stealing from them again.

5430. Reel Pink (*Pink Panther*) Jan. 1966; *p.c.:* Mirisch/Geoffrey/DFE for UA; *dir:* Hawley Pratt; *anim:* Don Williams, Norm McCabe, La Verne Harding, Manny Perez; *lay:* Dick Ung; *back:* Tom O'Loughlin; *ed:* Lee Gunther; *mus:* William Lava; *theme tune:* Henry Mancini; *col:* DeLuxe. *sd:* RCA. 6 min. • The Panther's fishing expedition ends with him fighting a duel with a crab.

5431. The Reformed Wolf (*Mighty Mouse*) Aug. 1954; *p.c.:* TT for Fox; *dir:* Connie Rasinski; *story:* Tom Morrison; *anim:* Jim Tyer; *sets:* Art Bartsch; *mus:* Philip A. Scheib; *ph:* Douglas Moye; *col:* Tech. *sd:* RCA. 7 min. • Wilbur Wolf explains to his cohort how he was reduced to being a vegetarian after prevented from sheep stealing by Mighty Mouse.

5432. The Relic 10 Jan. 1997; *p.c.:* Cloud Nine Entertainment/ PolyGram Filmed Entertainment/Toho-Towa Tele München/BBC in asso with Para/Marubeni; "*Kothoga*" *anim:* Joe Henke, Bill Dietrich, Scott Geiger, Ha Ngan Roda, Dan Kaufman, Gary Abrahamian, Stuart Mintz, Anders Ericson; "*Kothoga*" *textures:* Louis Scaduto, Mike Ampon; "*Kothoga*" *tongue anim:* Bruce Berman, Mike Norville; *col:* DeLuxe. *sd:* dts. 109 min. *l/a.* • Live-action fantasy: Kothoga, a South American brain-eating creature, comes to life in a Chicago museum.

5433. The Reluctant Dragon 20 June 1941; *p.c.:* Walt Disney prods for RKO; *l/a dir:* Alfred L. Werker; *story:* Ted Sears, Al Perkins, Larry Clemmons, Bill Cottrell, Harry Clark; *mus:* Frank Churchill, Leigh Harline; *cartoon seq:* "*Baby Weems*": *dir/storyboards:* Joe Grant, Dick Huemer, John P. Miller; *voices: narrator*/"*March of Time*"/*radio announcer:* Gerald Mohr; *Baby Weems:* Raymond Severn; *Nurse:* Jean Fenwick; *Father:* Ernie Alexander; *Mother:* Linda Marwood; *Mayor:* J. Donald Wilson; *President Roosevelt:* Arthur Gilmore; *Walter Winchell:* Edward J. Marr; *Baby cries:* Leone Le Doux; "*How to Ride a Horse*" (see separate item for credits) *The Reluctant Dragon: dir:* Hamilton Luske; *original story by* Kenneth Grahame; *asst dir:* Ford Beebe, Jim Handley, Erwin Verity; *story:* Erdman Penner, T. Hee; *anim:* Ward Kimball, Fred Moore, Milt Neil, Wolfgang Reitherman, Walt Kelly, Jack Campbell, Claude Smith, Harvey Toombs, Tony Strobl, Bud Swift; *addit anim:* Rex Cox, James S. Escalante, George Goepper, Harry Hamsel, Paul Kossoff, Fred Madison, Paul Murray, S.C. Onaitis, Miles Pike, John Reed, Sandy Strother, Don Tobin, Judge Whitaker, Bernard Wolf, John McManus; *fx:* Joshua Meador, Ub Iwerks, Jerome Brown, Brad Case, Ugo D'Orsi, Paul Fitzpatrick, Arthur W. Palmer, John Tucker, Vernon G. Witt; *lay:* Ken Anderson, Hugh Hennesy, Charles Philippi; *back:* Ray Huffine, Arthur Riley, Ray Lockrem, Robert McIntosh, Mique Nelson; *voices: The Dragon:* Barnett Parker; *Sir Giles:* Claud Allister; *The Boy:* Billy Lee; *Father:* Erdman Penner; *Courier:* Val Stanton; *Narrator:* John McLeish; *Donald Duck:* Clarence Nash; *Casey Jr (Sonovox):* Frances Gifford; *Chorus:* The Rhythmaires; "*Bambi*" *seq:* Ub Iwerks; *songs:* Charles Wolcott, Frank Churchill, Larry Morey, Erdman Penner, T. Hee; *special processes:* Herman Schultheis; *caricatures:* T. Hee; *l/a seq: asst dir:* Jasper Blystone; *ph dir:* Bert Glennon ASC; *ed:* Paul Weatherwax; *art dir:* Gordon Wiles, Jim Carmichael, Yale Gracey, Bill Herwig; *technical planning:* Lyle de Grummond; *sets:* Earl Woodin; *sd:* Frank Mahler; *prod mgr:* Earl Rettig; *Tech seq: ph dir:* Winton C. Hoch ASC; *col dir:* Natalie Kalmus; *l/a cast: Himself:* Robert Benchley; *Mrs. Benchley:* Nana Bryant; *Studio Artist: (Doris):* Frances Gifford; *Studio Guide: (Humphrey):* Buddy Pepper; *Themselves:* Clarence Nash, Florence Gill; *Studio Cop:* Henry Hall; *Slim:* Lester Dorr; *Guard:* Gerald Mohr; *Sd fx dir:* Frank Faylen; *Sd fx men:* Frank Fitzgibbons, Dick Leonard, Al Zeedman, Wayne Douglas; *Art student:* George Offerman Jr.; *Art Instructor:* Hamilton McFadden; *Art class:* Ken Anderson, Viola Anderson, Jack Kinney, Milt Kahl, Ethel Kulsar, Eric Larson, Jack Miller, Milt Neil, Charles Philippi, Wolfgang Reitherman, Tony Rivera, Mildred Rossi, Herbert Ryman, Retta Scott, Riley Thomson; *Storyboard dir:* Alan Ladd; *Storymen:* Berk Anthony, J. Dehner Forkum, Maurice Murphy; *Baby:* Jimmy Luske; *Artists, musicians & storymen in projection room:* Frank Churchill, Larry Clemmons, Bill Cottrell, Walt Disney, J. Dehner Forkum, David D. Hand, Hamilton Luske, Grace Harlow, T. Hee, Lance Nolley, Erdman Penner, Al Perkins, Charles Philippi, Ted Sears, Ben Sharpsteen; *Marie:* Verna Hillie; *Paint shop girls:* Louise Curry, Jeanette Tonner; *Wilbur:* Gaylord Pendleton; *Artists with Moviola:* Ward Kimball, Fred Moore; *Dog artist:* Norman Ferguson; *Multiplane operator:* Tom Collins; *Also:* Truman Woodworth, Jeff Corey; *col:* b&w/Tech. *sd:* RCA. 72 min. *l/a/anim.* • Robert Benchley visits the new Walt Disney Studios with the view of selling Mr. Disney the idea of making a cartoon film of

The Reluctant Dragon. He is shown around the studio by way of escaping the guided tour, witnessing a storyboard session, the Multiplane camera, an art class, etc. When he finally gets to see Walt, it's at a preview of his latest film *The Reluctant Dragon*! • Presented in a storyboard fashion the "Baby Weems" seq: A baby is born who has a super I.Q. "*The Reluctant Dragon*" seq: A medieval knight stages a fight with a rather camp, poetry reading dragon to satisfy the villagers. Released as a separate item in 1956.

5434. The Reluctant Pup *(Terry Bears)* Oct. 1953; *p.c.:* TT for Fox; *dir:* Connie Rasinski; *story:* Tom Morison; *anim:* Jim Tyer; *voices:* Douglas Moye, Tom Morrison, Philip A. Scheib; *mus:* Philip A. Scheib; *ph:* Douglas Moye; *col:* Tech. *sd:* RCA. 6 min. • The cubs groom their huge St Bernard dog, Pago, for a dog show.

5435. The Reluctant Recruit *(Woody Woodpecker)* 1971; *p.c.:* Walter Lantz prods for Univ; *dir:* Paul J. Smith; *story:* Dale Hale; *anim:* Les Kline, Al Coe, Tom Byrne, Joe Voght; *sets:* Nino Carbe; *voices:* Daws Butler, Grace Stafford; *mus:* Walter Greene; *prod mgr:* William E. Garity; *col:* Tech. *sd:* RCA. 5½ min. • Woody craves an "Around the World Cruise" and is tricked into joining the Foreign Legion.

5436. Rescue Dog *(Pluto)* 21 Mar. 1947; *p.c.:* Walt Disney prods for RKO; *dir:* Charles Nichols; *asst dir:* Jack Bruner, Bob North; *story:* Eric Gurney, Bill de la Torre; *anim:* George Nicholas, Jerry Hathcock, George Kreisl, Marvin Woodward, Robert Youngquist; *fx:* Jack Boyd, Harry Holt; *lay:* Karl Karpé; *back:* Howard Dunn; *voice:* James MacDonald; *mus:* Oliver Wallace; *col:* Tech. *sd:* RCA. 7 min. • A seal does a balancing act with Pluto's keg of brandy ensuing a chase which leaves Pluto trapped under the ice and the seal rescuing him.

5437. The Rescuers 22 June 1977; *p.c.:* Walt Disney prods for BV; *ex prod:* Ron Miller; *prod:* Wolfgang Reitherman; *dir:* Wolfgang Reitherman, John Lounsbery, Art Stevens; *asst dir:* Jeff Patch, Richard Rich; *suggested by* The Rescuers *and* Miss Bianca *by* Margery Sharp; *story adapt:* Larry Clemmons, Frank Thomas, Ken Anderson, Dave Michener, Vance Gerry, Fred Lucky, Ted Berman, Dick Sebast, Burny Mattinson; *anim dir:* Ollie Johnston, Milt Kahl, Frank Thomas, Don Bluth; *anim:* Cliff Nordberg, John Pomeroy, Gary Goldman, Andy Gaskill, Dale Baer, Art Stevens, Ron Clements, Chuck Harvey, Bill Hajee, Bob McCrea, Glen Keane; *asst anim:* Stan Green, Dale Oliver, Chuck Williams, Harry Hester, Walt Stanchfield, Dave Suding, Leroy Cross; *fx:* Jack Buckley, Ted Kierscey, Dorse A. Lanpher, James L. George, Dick Lucas; *des:* Al Dempster; *art dir:* Don Griffith; *lay:* Joe Hale, Guy Deel, Tom Lay, Sylvia Roemer; *back:* Jim Coleman, Ann Guenther, Daniela Bielecka; *preliminary sketches:* Ralph Hulett; *ed:* James Melton, Jim Kuford; *voices:* Miss Bianca: Eva Gabor; *Bernard:* Bob Newhart; *Rufus the orphanage cat:* John McIntyre; *Orville:* Jim Jordan; *Penny:* Michelle Stacy; *Mme Medusa:* Geraldine Page; *Mr. Snoops:* Joe Flynn; *Ellie Mae:* Jeanette Nolan; *Luke:* Pat Buttram; *Chairman:* Bernard Fox; *Gramps:* Larry Clemmons; *Evenrude/Nero & Brutus:* Jim MacDonald; *Deadeye:* George Lindsey; *TV Announcer:* Bill McMillan; *Digger:* Dub Taylor; *Russian delegate:* Juri Kauk; *German Delegate:* Siggi Rayners; *American Delegate:* Pete Renoudet; *French/Dutch Delegates/Portly female/German singing:* Earl Kress; *French Announcer:* Lilyan Chauvin; *Miss Bianca's singing voice:* Robie Lester; "Someone's Waiting for You" sung by Shelby Flint; *mus:* Artie Butler; *songs:* Carol Connors, Ayn Robbins, Sammy Fain; *mus ed:* Evelyn Kennedy; *sd:* Herb Taylor; *titles:* Melvin Shaw, Eric Larson, Burny Mattinson; *col:* Tech. *sd:* RCA. 76 min. • Bernard and Bianca, two mice from the Rescue Aid Society, set out to rescue Penny, a little girl who has been kidnapped for the specific object of retrieving a huge diamond hidden in a deep pirate's cave.

5438. The Rescuers Down Under 16 Nov. 1990; *p.c.:* Walt Disney Prods for BV; *dir:* Hendel Butoy, Mike Gabriel; *prod:* Thomas Schumacher; *scr:* Jim Cox, Karey Kirkpatrick, Byron Simpson, Joe Ranft; *suggested by* characters created by Margery Sharp; *asso prod:* Kathleen Gavin; *art dir:* Maurice Hunt; *storyboard:* Ed Gombert, Gary Trousdale, Christopher Sanders, Brenda Chapman, Roger Allers, Will Finn, Glen Keane, Robert Lence, Vance Gerry, Kirk Wise, Kelly Asbury; *anim:* Glen Keane, Mark Henn, Russ Edmonds, David Cutler, Ruben A. Aquino, Nik Ranieri, Ed Gombert, Anthony de Rosa, Kathy Zielinski, Duncan Marjoribanks, James Baxter, Ron Husband, Will Finn, David Burgess, Alexander S. Kupershmidt, Chris Bailey, Mike Cedeno, Rick Farmiloe, Jacques Muller, Dave Pruiksma, Rejean Bourdages, Roger Chiasson, Ken Duncan, Joe Haidar,

Ellen Woodbury, Jorgen Klubien, Gee Fwee Boedoe, Barry Temple, David P. Stephan, Chris Wahl, Larry White, Brigitte Hartley, Doug Krohn, Phil Young, Tom Roth, Leon Joosen; *fx anim:* Randy Fullmer, Ted Kierscey, Dave Bossert, Kelvin Yasuda, Mark Myer, Eusebio Torres, Christine Harding, Barry Cook, Glenn Chaika, Mark Dindal, Dan Chaika, John Tucker, Mabel Gesner, Steve Starr, Allen Blyth, Mark Barrows, Allen Stovall, Jeff Dutton, Kevin Turcotte, Margaret Craig-Chang, Hae Sook Hwang, Lee Crowe, Rob Bekuhrs, James R. Tooley; *fx break/inbet:* Cynthia Neill-Knizek, Masa Oshiro, Peter Demund, Kennard Betts, Tony West; *fx graphics:* Bernie Gagliano; *lay:* Dan Hansen, Rasoul Azadani, Bill Perkins, Karen Keller, Robert Walker, Michael O'Mara, Fred Craig, Mac George, André Clavel, Anthony Christov, Tom Shannon, David Gardner, Bob Smith, Bruce Zick, Daniel Hu, Mitchell Bernal, Mark Wallace; *back:* Lisa Keene, Jim Coleman, Donald Towns, Douglas Ball, Phil Phillipson, Cristy Maltese, Dean Gordon, Tom Woodington, Diana Wakeman, Robert E. Stanton, Michael Humphries, Tia Kratter, Debbie DuBois, Serge Michaels; *ed:* Michael Kelly, Mark Hester, Paul Murphy, Jim Melton, Scot Scalise, Deirdre Hepburn, Karen Wanderman; *voices:* Bernard: Bob Newhart; *Miss Bianca:* Eva Gabor; *Wilbur:* John Candy; *Jake:* Tristan Rogers; *Cody:* Adam Ryan; *McLeach:* George C. Scott; *Frank:* Wayne Robson; *Krebbs:* Douglas Seale; *Joanna/vocal fx:* Frank Welker; *Chairmouse/Doctor:* Bernard Fox; *Red:* Peter Firth; *Baitmouse:* Billy Barty; *François:* Ed Gilbert; *Faloo/Mother:* Carla Meyer; *Nurse Mouse:* Russi Taylor; *also:* Charlie Adler, Jack Angel, Vanna Bonta, Peter Greenwood, Marii Mak, Mickie McGowan, Patrick Pinney, Phil Proctor; *mus:* Bruce Broughton; *orch:* Don Nemitz, Mark McKenzie; *mus ed:* Kathleen Bennett, Segue Music; *music score mix:* Robert Fernandez; *conductor:* Bruce Broughton; "Black Slacks" by Joe Bennett & Jimmy Denton; performed by Joe Bennett and the Sparkletones; *clean-up:* Rick Hoppe, Bill Berg, Brian Clift, Renee Holt, Emily Juliano, Marty Korth, Vera Lanpher, Debra Armstrong, Jesus Cortes, Margie Daniels, Nancy Kniep, Kaaren Lundeen, Dan Tanaka, Stephan Zupkas, Alex Topete, Bette Isis Baker, Dorothea Baker, Tom Bancroft, Philo Barnhart, Wes Chun, Kent Culotta, Lou Dellarosa, Marcia Dougherty, Sam Ewing, Tom Ferriter, Trey Finney, Gail Frank, Daniel A. Gracey, Ray Harris, Tracy M. Lee, Margaret Nichols, Lori M. Noda, Jennifer Oliver, Gilda Palinginis, Natasha Selfridge, Alan Simpson, Dave Suding, Jane Tucker, Lureline Weatherly; *asst:* Scott Anderson, Carl Bell, Susan Craig, James Davis, Lee Dunkman, Teresa Eidenbock, Mike Genz, Karen Hardenbergh, Johan Klingler, Terrey Le Grady, Steve Lubin, Teresa Martin, Brian McKim, Mike McKinney, Terry Naughton, Eric Pigors, Pres Romanillos, Juliet Stroud, Peggy Tonkonogy, Marshall Toomey, Marianne Tucker, Susan Zytka, Kathleen M. Bailey, Judy Barnes; *character des/visual development:* Christopher Sanders, Kevin Lima, Bruce Zick, Kelly Asbury, Glen Keane, Duncan Marjoribanks, Chris Buck, Kevin Donoghue, Gay Lawrence-Venture, Valerio Lawrence-Venture, Gil Hung; *prod mgr:* Sarah McArthur; *col models:* Karen Comella, Penny Coulter; *anim check:* Janet Bruce; *scene plan:* Ann Tucker; *i&p:* Gretchen Maschmeyer Albrecht; *final check/paint sup:* Hortensia Casagran; *digitizing ph sup:* Robyn Roberts; *computer anim:* Tina Price, Andrew Schmidt, Linda Bel, Thomas Cardone, Greg Griffith; *computer anim engineers:* Scott Johnston, Mary Jane Turner; *anim asst:* Aaron Blaise, Bob Bryan, Michael Show, Mike Nguyen, Brad Kuha, Broose Johnson, Tony Bancroft, Cynthia Overman, Dan Boulos; *bluesketch:* Roxy Stevens, Madlyn O'Neill; *airbrush:* John Emerson; *break/inbet:* Beverly Adams, Hee Rhan Bae, Noreen Beasley, Gordon Bellamy, Philip S. Boyd, Inna Chon, Robert O. Corley, Tony Craig, Vincent De Frances, Wendie Fischer, James Fujii, Susan Gal, Richard H. Green, Peter Gullerud, Edward Gutierrez, Michael Hazy, Grant Hiestand, Ken Hettig, Todd Hoff, Allison Hollen, Mark Kennedy, Christine Lawrence, Laura Nichols, Matt Novak, Ed Olson, Gary Payne, Karen Rosenfield, Martin Schwartz, Donald Selders, Kevin Smith, Bryan M. Sommer, Michael Swofford, David Teague, Bill Thinnes, Jane Vytiskova, Elizabeth Watasin, Daniel Wawrzaszek, Wendy Werner; *anim checking:* Susan Burke, Madlyn O'Neill, Karen Paat, Gary Shafer, Mavis Shafer, Barbara Wiles; *prod admin:* Dennis Edwards; *asst prod mgr:* Dorothy McKim; *lay/retakes:* Allison Abbate; *clean-up:* Susan Blanchard; *back/color models/anim check:* Pam Coats; *ed:* Tim Christenson; *prod mgr (Florida unit):* Tim O'Donnell; *ph:* Joe Jiuliano; *film rec co-ord:* Ariel Shaw; *digital prod system development:* Randy Cartwright, David Coons, Lem Davis, Scot Greenidge, Don Gworek, Jim Houston, Mark Kimball, Dylan Kohler, Michael Purvis, Marty Prager, David F. Wolf; *technical dir:* Edward Kummer; *technical support:* Michael Bolds, Randy

Fukuda, Pradeep Hiremath, Carlos Quinonez, Grace Shirado, Michael Sullivan; *PIXAR:* Thomas Hahn, Peter Nye, Michael A. Shantzis, Rick Ace; *scene plan:* Geof Schroeder, Rick Sullivan, Donna Weir; *character sculptures:* Ruben Procopio; *title des:* Dan Perri; *i&p:* Chris Hecox; *digitizing mark-up:* Gina Wootten; *digitizing ph:* Jo Ann Breuer, Karen N. China, Bob Cohen, Lynnette Cullen, Cindy Garcia, Kent Gordon, Sherri Vandoli; *paint:* Leslie Ellery, Rhonda Hicks, Ann Sorensen, Tania Mitman Burton, Tanya Moreau-Smith, Irma Velez, Joyce Alexander, Phyllis Bird, Russell Blandino, Bonnie Blough, Sherrie Cuzzort, Phyllis Fields, Paulino Garcia, Carolyn Guske, Anne Hazard, Karen Hepburn, David Karp, Monica Marroquin, Harlene Mears, Beth Ann McCoy, Teri McDonald, Charlene D. Miller, Deborah Jane Mooneyham, Karen Nugent, Leyla Pelaez, Bruce Phillipson, Nellie Rodriguez, Carmen Sanderson, Heidi W. Shellhorn, Fumiko R. Sommer, Roxanne M. Taylor, Britt Van der Nagel, Susan Wileman; *final check:* Saskia Raevouri; *compositing:* James "JR" Russell, David Rowe; *film rec:* Christopher Gee; *sd ed:* Louis L. Edemann, Paul Timothy Carden, Fred Judkins, Doug Jackson, Leonard Geschke, Nils Jensen, Robert O'Brien, Suhail Kafity, Angela K. Lucky, Robert Morrisey; *sd fx:* Mel Neiman, Alan Howarth; *foley:* Taj Soundworks, Kevin Bartnof, Hilda Hodges, James Ashwill; *Didgeridoo:* Adam Rudolph; *rec:* Mary Jo Lang; *re-rec:* Terry Porter, Mel Metcalfe, David J. Hudson; *ph:* John Cunningham, John Aardal, Chris Buck, Mary E. Lescher, Gary W. Smith, Chuck Warren; *process lab:* Joe Parra, John White, Joe Holmes, Rick Engels; *col:* Tech. *sd:* Dolby stereo. 74 min. • In this sequel to *The Rescuers* (1977), a young Australian boy discovers a poacher is trapping endangered wildlife. The boy, Cody, is captured and imprisoned while setting an eagle free, causing a frantic call for help to the Rescue Aid Society. Once again, the mice, Bernard and Miss Bianca, are on hand and fly (via Albatross Air Lines) to the Outback to rescue Cody and help the situation.

5439. The Rest Resort (*Meany Miny Mo*) 23 Aug. 1937; *p.c.:* Univ; *prod:* Walter Lantz; *story:* Walt Lantz, Victor McLeod; *anim:* Manuel Moreno, George Nicholas, Ben Clopton; *mus:* James Dietrich; b&w. *sd:* WE. 7 min. • Mrs. Elephant and her unmanageable child wreck the monks' rest resort.

5440. The Restless Sax (*Krazy Kat*) 1 Dec. 1931; *p.c.:* Winkler for Colum; *prod:* Charles Mintz; *story:* Manny Gould; *anim:* Harry Love; *mus:* Joe de Nat; b&w. *sd:* WE. 6 min. • Krazy is a dismal failure as a saxophonist.

5441. Return of the Swamp Thing 12 May 1989; *p.c.:* Lightyear Entertainment/J & M Entertainment for Medusa; Based on characters appearing in magazines published by DC Comics, Inc.; *anim:* Lisze Bechtold, Kevin Kutchaver, Michael Lessa; *anim ph:* Linda Obalil; *col:* DeLuxe. *sd:* Ultra Stereo. 85 min. *l/a.* • Live-action horror about an industructable swamp beast.

5442. Return to Oz 21 June 1985; *p.c.:* Will Vinton Prods/Walt Disney Prods/Silver Screen Partners II; *Claymation dir:* Will Vinton; *Claymation prod:* David Altschul; *art dir:* Barry Bruce; *anim:* Joan C. Gratz, Tom Gasek, Craig Bartlett, Bruce McClean, Gary McRobert, William Fiesterman, Mark Gustafson, Douglas Aberle, Joanne Radmi Lovich; *technical sup:* Gary McRobert; *col:* Tech. *sd:* Dolby stereo. 109 min. (full running time) *l/a.* • Live-action feature: Dorothy returns to the Land of Oz to find it in ruins and sets out to restore Oz to its former glory. Animation involves one encounter she has with the evil Nome King who materializes from a mountainside.

5443. The Reunion (*Out of the Inkwell*) 27 Oct. 1922; *p.c.:* Inkwell Studio for Winkler; *dir:* Dave Fleischer; *anim/l/a:* Max Fleischer; b&w. *sil.* 7 min. *l/a/anim.* • Ko-Ko's relatives appear at a reunion party and an attempt is made to take a family portrait.

5444. Revenge of the Pink Panther 19 July 1978; *p.c.:* Jewel Prods, Ltd; *title anim:* DePatie-Freleng; *des/anim:* Arthur Leonardi; *story:* John Dunn; *col:* Tech. *sd.* Panavision. 4¹⁄₂ min. • The cartoon credits contain the Inspector trailing the Panther.

5445. R.F.D. 1,000,000 B.C. 26 Apr. 1917; *p.c.:* Thomas A. Edison Inc.; *prod/fx:* Willis H. O'Brien; b&w. *sil.* 4 min. *l/a/anim.* • A jealous prehistoric mailman's attempts to discredit a maiden's favoured suitor by replacing his granite valentine with one proclaiming her an old maid. • aka: *Rural Delivery, Million B.C.*

5446. Rhapsody in Rivets (*Merrie Melodies*) 6 Dec. 1941; *p.c.:* Leon Schlesinger prods for WB; *dir:* I. Freleng; *story:* Michael Maltese; *anim:* Gil Turner; *lay:* Owen Fitzgerald; *back:* Lenard Kester; *ed:* Treg Brown; *mus:* Carl W. Stalling; *ph:* John W. Burton; *prod sup:* Henry Binder, Raymond G. Katz; *col:* Tech. *sd:* Vit. 7 min. • A building is constructed to the music of Liszt's Second Hungarian Rhapsody.

5447. Rhapsody in Wood (*Puppetoon*) 19 Dec. 1947; *p.c.:* George Pal Studio for Para; *prod/dir:* George Pal; *story:* Jack Miller; *anim:* Erwin Broner, Gene Warren; *models:* John S. Abbott; *l/a:* Woody Herman; *voice:* Robert C. Bruce; *mus:* Ralph Burns, Woody Herman & his orchestra; *ph:* Winton C. Hoch; *col:* Tech. *sd:* WE. 9 min. • Woody Herman explains how his clarinet was discovered by his grandfather, a woodchopper, who got it as a reward for sparing a magic tree.

5448. Rhapsody of Steel 1960; *p.c.:* John Sutherland prods for U.S. Steel Corp/Jam Handy Organization; *prod/story:* John Sutherland; *dir:* Carl Urbano; *des:* Eyvind Earle, Maurice Noble; *voice:* Gary Merrill; *mus:* Dimitri Tiomkin; recorded by The Pittsburgh Symphony Orchestra; *col:* Tech. *sd.* 23¹⁄₂ min. • Meteoric iron from outer space, brought by man the hunter. Centuries later, this precious metal is returned to outer space as exploring rockets soar into space. Award winning all-animated educational film.

5449. Rhapsody Rabbit (*Merie Melodies*) 9 Nov. 1946; *p.c.:* WB; *dir:* I. Freleng; *story:* Tedd Pierce, Michael Maltese; *anim:* Manuel Perez, Ken Champin, Virgil Ross, Gerry Chiniquy; *lay:* Hawley Pratt; *back:* Terry Lind; *ed:* Treg Brown; *voices:* Mel Blanc; *mus:* Carl Stalling; *piano:* Jakob Gimpel; *prod mgr:* John W. Burton; *prod:* Edward Selzer; *col:* Tech. *sd:* Vit. 7 min. • Bugs gives a piano recital when he is bothered by a mouse living in the piano.

5450. Rhyme Reels *p.c.:* Filmcraft Corp; *prod/dir/anim:* Walt Mason; b&w. *sil. l/a/anim.* • *1917:* **Bunked and Paid For** 18 Aug. **The Dipper** 18 Aug. **True Love and Fake Money** Aug. **Hash** Aug.

5451. Rhythm in the Bow (*Merrie Melodies*) 1 Feb. 1935; *p.c.:* Leon Schlesinger prods for WB; *dir:* Ben Hardaway; *anim:* Rollin Hamilton, Ben Clopton, Robert Clampett; *mus:* Norman Spencer; b&w. *sd:* Vit. 7 min. • A fiddle-playing hobo is tossed from a train and finds himself entertaining the masses in a hobo community.

5452. Rhythm in the Ranks (*Madcap Models*) 26 Dec. 1941; *p.c.:* George Pal prods for Para; *prod/dir:* George Pal; *story:* Jack Miller; *anim:* George Pal, Ray Harryhausen; *col:* Tech. *sd:* WE. 10 min. *Academy Award nomination.* • Wooden soldiers come alive and march to a swing version of Raymond Scott's *The Toy Trumpet.* Little Jan loses his cannon and falls into military disgrace but subsequent heroism changes his fate.

5453. Rhythm on the Reservation (*Betty Boop*) 7 July 1939; *p.c.:* The Fleischer Studio for Para; *prod:* Max Fleischer; *dir:* Dave Fleischer; *anim:* Myron Waldman, Graham Place, Lillian Friedman; *voices:* Margie Hines, Jack Mercer; *mus:* Sammy Timberg; b&w. *sd:* WE. 7 min. • Betty has a jam session with the Indians on their reservation.

5454. The Rich Cat and the Poor Cat (*Aesop's Film Fable*) 21 Feb. 1922; *p.c.:* Fables Pictures Inc for Pathé; *dir:* Paul Terry; b&w. *sil.* 5 min. • A fat cat lives the life of luxury while a lean cat struggles to feed her family. The fat cat is ruled to be too lazy to catch mice and is booted out of the house. She goes begging to the poor cat who gives her the cold shoulder. Moral: "We must make friends in prosperity if we would have their help in adversity."

5455. Ri¢hie Ri¢h 21 Dec. 1994; *p.c.:* WB; *cg Bee anim:* Theresa Ellis, Dale Baer; *col:* Tech. *sd:* Dolby stereo. 94 min. *l/a.* • Live-action comedy: When millionaire's son, Richie, learns that his parents' plane has come down in the Atlantic Ocean, a board member starts making drastic changes to his father's company. A flying robot "Robobee" is one of the animated gadgets.

5456. Rickety Gin (*Oswald the Lucky Rabbit*) 26 Dec. 1927; *p.c.:* Winkler for Univ; *dir:* Walt Disney; *anim:* Ubbe Iwerks, Isadore Freleng; *ph:* Mike Marcus; b&w. *sil.* 6 min. • Oswald the cop flirts with a nurse in the park. Bootleg Pete manages to get Oswald drunk and substitutes for him with the pretty nurse.

5457. Ride 'Em Cowboy (*Aesop's Film Fable*) 26 June 1928; *p.c.:* Fables Pictures Inc for Pathé; *dir:* Paul Terry, Frank Moser; b&w. *sil.* 10 min. • On his honeymoon, Milton Mouse comes up against two cats who waylay him and make off with his bride. Milt is soon on their trail on his trusty horse.

5458. Ride 'Em Plowboy *(Oswald the Lucky Rabbit)* 16 Apr. 1928; *p.c.:* Winkler for Univ; *dir:* Walter Disney; *anim:* Ubbe Iwerks, Hugh Harman, Rollin C. Hamilton, Isadore Freleng; *ph:* Mike Marcus; b&w. sil. 6 min. • Farmer Oswald runs a musical farm until all is disrupted by the arrival of an unwarranted cyclone.

5459. Ride Him, Bosko *(Looney Tunes)* 17 Sept. 1932; *p.c.:* Hugh Harman–Rudolf Ising prods for WB; *prod:* Leon Schlesinger; *anim:* Isadore Freleng, Norman Blackburn, Robert Clampett; *ed:* Dale Pickett; *voices:* Mary Moder; *mus:* Frank Marsales; *l/a:* Hugh Harman, Rudolf Ising; b&w. *sd:* Vit. 7 min. • Cowboy Bosko chases some stagecoach bandits. The picture ends with Bosko's fate being left in the hands of the animation staff.

5460. Riding High *(Aesop's Film Fable)* 10 July 1927; *p.c.:* Fables Pictures Inc for Pathé; *dir:* Paul Terry; b&w. *sil.* 10 min. • The mice inflate Lengthy Leonard, a dachshund, to use him as a dirigible. All goes well until the dog sneezes and deflates, then a frisky hippo uses the poor creature as a jumping rope. Moral: "It may be painful to crack your head but it never hurts to crack a smile."

5461. Riding the Rails *(Betty Boop)* 28 Jan. 1938; *p.c.:* The Fleischer Studio for Para*: prod:* Max Fleischer; *dir:* Dave Fleischer; *anim:* Myron Waldman, Hicks Lokey, Lillian Friedman; *voice:* Mae Questel; *mus:* Sammy Timberg; b&w. *sd:* WE. 6½ min. • Pudgy is chased by a subway train when he tries to follow Betty to work.

5462. Riff Raffy Daffy *(Looney Tunes)* 27 Nov. 1948; *p.c.:* WB; *dir:* Arthur Davis; *story:* William Scott, Lloyd Turner; *anim:* Don Williams, Emery Hawkins, Basil Davidovich, J.C. Melendez; *lay:* Don Smith; *back:* Philip de Guard; *ed:* Treg Brown; *voices:* Mel Blanc; *mus:* Carl Stalling; *prod mgr:* John W. Burton; *prod:* Edward Selzer; *col:* Ciné. *sd:* Vit. 7 min. • Police Officer Porky spends all night trying to evict Daffy from sleeping in a department store.

5463. Right Off the Bat *(Modern Madcap)* 7 Nov. 1958; *p.c.:* Para Cartoons; *dir:* Seymour Kneitel; *story:* Carl Meyer, Jack Mercer; *anim:* Tom Johnson, Frank Endres, Els Barthen; *sets:* Robert Little; *voices:* Sid Raymond, Jackson Beck, Jack Mercer; *mus:* Winston Sharples; *ph:* Leonard McCormick; *prod mgr:* Abe Goodman; *col:* Tech. *sd:* RCA. 6 min. • If the local baseball team's manager doesn't come up with a star player ... he's out! His scout arrives with a top striker in the shape of a horse.

5464. Ringading Kid *(Modern Madcap)* Jan. 1963; *p.c.:* Para Cartoons; *dir:* Seymour Kneitel; *sets:* Robert Little; *mus:* Winston Sharples; *ph:* Leonard McCormick; *prod mgr:* Abe Goodman; *col:* Tech. *sd:* RCA. 6 min. • No story available.

5465. Riot in Rhythm *(Popeye)* 10 Nov. 1950; *p.c.:* Famous for Para; *dir/story:* Seymour Kneitel; *anim:* Tom Johnson, William Henning, Els Barthen; *sets:* Tom Ford; *voices:* Jack Mercer; *mus:* Winston Sharples; *ph:* Leonard McCormick; *prod mgr:* Sam Buchwald; *col:* Tech. *sd:* RCA. 6 min. • Popeye's slumber is disturbed by his nephews' jam session in this Technicolor remake of *Me Musical Nephews*.

5466. Rip Van Winkle *(Paul Terry-Toon)* 9 Feb. 1934; *p.c.:* Moser & Terry for Educational/Fox; *dir:* Frank Moser, Paul Terry; *mus:* Philip A. Scheib; b&w. *sd:* WE. 6 min. • Farmer Al is knocked unconcious by his harridan wife's rolling pin. He dreams of a vaudeville show incorporating horses, penguins, elephants and a mule who kicks him back to conciousness and his nagging spouse.

5467. Rippling Rhythm *(Color Rhapsody)* 18 May 1945; *p.c.:* Colum; *dir:* Bob Wickersham; *story/music/prod mgr:* Paul Worth; *anim:* Chic Otterstrom, Volus Jones, Ben Lloyd; *i&p:* Elizabeth F. McDowell; *ph:* Frank Fisher; *col:* Tech. *sd:* WE. 7 min. • A swan is too enamored of herself to pay any attention to gentlemen admirers.

5468. The Rise of a Nation June 1917; *p.c.:* Harry Palmer Inc for Educational; *anim:* Harry Palmer; b&w. sil. • A patriotic war subject showing Americans responding to the President's call to war.

5469. The Rise of Duton Lang 1 Dec. 1955; *p.c.:* UPA for Colum; *ex prod:* Stephen Bosustow; *dir:* Osmond Evans; *story:* Percival Wilde, Dick Shaw, Barbara Hammer, T. Hee; *anim:* Osmond Evans, Ken Hultgren; *lay:* Ted Parmalee, Sam Clayberger; *back:* Jules Engel; *voice:* Marvin Miller; *mus:* Dennis Farnon; *prod mgr:* Herbert Klynn; *col:* Tech. *sd:* RCA. 6½ min. • Adapted from Percival Wilde's story in *Esquire*, a man in a bar relates the tale of an inventor who invents a slimming potion that doesn't make you lose your size, just your weight.

5470. The Ritzy Hotel *(Krazy Kat)*; 9 May 1932; *p.c.:* Winkler for Colum; *prod:* Charles Mintz; *story:* Manny Gould; *anim/voice:* Jack Carr; *mus:* Joe de Nat; b&w. *sd:* WE. 5½ min. • Krazy is a bellboy in a hotel, dealing with a cantankerous old geezer in a bathchair.

5471. Rival Romeos 5 May 1928; *p.c.:* Winkler for Univ; *dir:* Walt Disney; *anim:* Ubbe Iwerks; b&w. sil. 5 min. • Oswald in his jalopy races High Hat Pete in a roadster for the hand of a lady.

5472. The Rival Romeos *(Heckle & Jeckle)* 7 Nov. 1950; *p.c.:* TT for Fox; *dir:* Eddie Donnelly; *story/voices:* Tom Morrison; *anim:* Jim Tyer; *mus:* Philip A. Scheib; *col:* Tech. *sd:* RCA. 6 min. • The magpies vie over the affections of a pretty girl.

5473. The River of Doubt *(Film Fable)* 16 Aug. 1927; *p.c.:* Fables Pictures Inc for Pathé; *dir:* Paul Terry; b&w. sil. 10 min. • Farmer Al and his cat try to photograph the jungle animals. Al is attacked by a wildcat while the other animals look on as spectators.

5474. River Ribbers *(Color Rhapsody)* 5 Apr. 1946; *p.c.:* Colum; *dir:* Paul Sommer; *story/voice:* John McLeish; *anim:* Paul Sommer, Jack Gayek; *lay:* Clark Watson; *ed:* Richard S. Jensen; *mus:* Eddie Kilfeather; *ph:* Frank Fisher; *prod mgr:* Hugh McCollum; *col:* Tech. *sd:* WE. 6 min. • Professor Small and Mr. Tall are sailing down the Mississippi when they get involved with a boatload of ghosts.

5475. Riverboat Mission *(Hector Heathcote)* May 1962; *p.c.:* TT for Fox; *ex prod:* Bill Weiss; *dir:* Dave Tendlar; *story sup:* Tom Morrison; *story:* Kin Platt; *anim:* Dave Tendlar, Doug Crane, John Guidi; *sets:* Bill Focht; *ed:* George McAvoy; *voices:* John Myhers; *mus:* Phil Scheib; *ph:* George Davis; *prod mgr:* Frank Schudde; *col:* DeLuxe. *sd:* RCA. 6 min. • Heathcote is given the job of sailing down the Mississippi, past the enemy, to bring some ammunition back for the troops.

5476. The Riveter *(Donald Duck)* 15 Mar. 1940; *p.c.:* Walt Disney prods for RKO; *dir:* Richard Lundy; *asst dir:* Donald A. Duckwall; *anim:* Paul Allen, James Armstrong, John Bradbury, Jack Campbell, Rex Cox, John Elliotte, Alfred Eugster, Hugh Fraser, Volus Jones, Hal King, Edward Love, Richard Lundy, Lee Morehouse, Kenneth Muse, Charles A. Nichols, Grant Simmons, Claude Smith, Judge Whitaker; *lay:* James Carmichael; *voices:* Billy Bletcher, Clarence Nash; *mus:* Oliver Wallace; *col:* Tech. *sd:* RCA. 7 min. • Donald is hired as a riveter on a skyscraper. His inability gives Pete cause to give him a precarious chase over the girders.

5477. The Road House *(Aesop's Film Fable)* 10 Oct. 1926; *p.c.:* Fables Pictures Inc for Pathé; *dir:* Paul Terry; b&w. sil. 10 min. • The mice make life difficult for Farmer Al in his roadside café. They eat all the food, use the Swiss cheese as a piano-player roll and even abscond with the cash register.

5478. Road to Andalay *(Merrie Melodies)* 26 Dec. 1964; *p.c.:* DFE for WB; *dir:* Friz Freleng; *asst dir:* Hawley Pratt; *story:* John Dunn; *anim:* Norm McCabe, Don Williams, Bob Matz; *lay:* Homer Jonas; *back:* Tom O'Loughlin; *ed:* Lee Gunther; *voices:* Mel Blanc; *mus:* Bill Lava; *prod mgr:* William Orcutt; *col:* Tech. *sd:* Vit. 6 min. • Sylvester employs the assistance of Malcolm, a falcon, to catch Speedy Gonzales.

5479. Roamin' Roman *(Woody Woodpecker)* 17 Nov. 1964; *p.c.:* Walter Lantz prods for Univ; *dir:* Paul J. Smith; *story:* Homer Brightman; *anim:* Les Kline, Al Coe; *sets:* Art Landy, Ray Huffine; *voices:* Daws Butler, Grace Stafford; *mus:* Clarence Wheeler; *prod mgr:* William E. Garity; *col:* Tech. *sd:* RCA. 6 min. • A time machine transports Woody to ancient Rome where he encounters the Emeror Nero.

5480. The Robber Kitten *(Silly Symphony)* 20 Apr. 1935; *p.c.:* Walt Disney prods for UA; *dir:* David D. Hand; *anim:* Robert W. Carlson Jr., Hardie Gramatky, Hamilton S. Luske, Robert Wickersham, Marvin Woodward; *voices:* Billy Bletcher, Alyce Ardell, Marcellite Garner; *mus:* Frank E. Churchill; *col:* Tech. *sd:* RCA. 9 min. • Ambrose Kitten runs away from home to become a bandit and meets Dirty Bill, a robber who frightens him back home, submitting to a bath.

5481. Robin Goodhood *(Roland & Rattfink)* 9 Sept. 1970; *p.c.:* Mirisch/DFE for UA; *dir:* Gerry Chiniquy; *story:* John W. Dunn; *anim:*

Robert Taylor, Manny Gould, Manny Perez, Don Williams, Irv Spence; *sets:* Richard Thomas; *ed:* Lee Gunther; *voices:* Leonard Weinrib, Marvin Miller, Athena Lorde; *mus:* Doug Goodwin; *ph:* John Burton Jr.; *prod sup:* Jim Foss, Harry Love; *col:* DeLuxe. *sd:* RCA. 6 min. • Robin Hood Roland robs from the rich to give to the poor while Rattfink robs for his own gain. When Rattfink is robbed of all his cash, Roland feels compelled to give him the money.

5482. Robin Hood 8 Nov. 1973; *p.c.:* Walt Disney prods for BV; *prod/dir:* Wolfgang Reitherman; *asst dir:* Ed Hansen, Dan Alguire, Jeff Patch; *story:* Larry Clemmons; *story seq:* Ken Anderson, Vance Gerry, Frank Thomas, Eric Cleworth, Julius Svendsen, Dave Michener; *character des:* Ken Anderson; *anim dir:* Milt Kahl, Ollie Johnston, Frank Thomas, John Lounsbery; *anim:* Hal King, Eric Larson, Art Stevens, Don Bluth, Cliff Nordberg, Dale Baer, Burny Mattinson, Fred Hellmich, *asst anim:* Dale Oliver, Bob McCrea, Chuck Williams, Stan Green; *fx:* Dan MacManus, Jack Buckley; *des:* Al Dempster; *art dir:* Don Griffith; *lay:* Basil Davidovich, Joe Hale, Sylvia Roemer, Ed Templer Jr.; *back:* Bill Layne, Ralph Hulett, Ann Guenther; *voices: Alan-a-Dale:* Roger Miller; *Prince John/King Richard:* Peter Ustinov; *Sir Hiss:* Terry-Thomas; *Robin Hood:* Brian Bedford; *Maid Marion:* Monica Evans; *Little John:* Phil Harris; *Friar Tuck:* Andy Devine; *Lady Kluck:* Carole Shelley; *The Sheriff of Nottingham:* Pat Buttram; *Trigger:* George Lindsey; *Nutsy:* Ken Curtis; *Skippy:* Billy Whitaker; *Sissy:* Dana Laurita; *Tagalong:* Dori Whitaker; *Toby Tortoise:* Richie Sanders; *Otto:* J. Pat O'Malley; *Alligator:* Candy Candido; *Widow Rabbit:* Barbara Luddy; *Sexton:* John Fiedler; *"Love" sung by* Nancy Adams; *mus:* George Bruns; *orch:* Walter Sheets; *songs:* Roger Miller, Floyd Huddleston, George Bruns, Johnny Mercer; *mus ed:* Evelyn Kennedy; *sd:* Herb Taylor; *prod mgr:* Don Duckwall; *col:* Tech. *sd:* RCA. 83 min. • An all-animal cast of the Robin Hood story. Robin's fight against the tyrannical Prince John who has taken over while his brother, King Richard, is away on the Crusades.

5483. Robin Hood (*Paul Terry-Toon*) 22 Jan. 1933; *p.c.:* Moser & Terry for Educational/Fox; *dir:* Frank Moser, Paul Terry; *mus:* Philip A. Scheib; *b&w. sd:* WE. 6 min. • The King tries to force Fanny Zilch to marry a rich baron for his money. Robin and his Merry Men come to her rescue. Caricatures of Jimmy Durante and Mahatma Gandhi.

5484. Robin Hood Daffy (*Merrie Melodies*) 8 Mar. 1957; *p.c.:* WB; *dir:* Chuck Jones; *story:* Michael Maltese; *anim:* Abe Levitow, Richard Thompson, Ken Harris; *lay:* Maurice Noble; *back:* Philip de Guard; *ed:* Treg Brown; *voices:* Mel Blanc; *mus:* Milt Franklyn; *col:* Tech. *sd:* Vit. 7 min. • Daffy has a tough time convincing Friar Porky Pig that *he* is Robin Hood.

5485. Robin Hood in an Arrow Escape (*Terry-Toon*) 16 Oct. 1936; *p.c.:* TT for Educational/Fox; *dir:* Mannie Davis, George Gordon; *mus:* Philip A. Scheib; *b&w. sd:* RCA. 6 min. • Robin conquers the knights in jousting, rescues Maid Marian and is saved from the Sheriff's wrath by his Merry Men.

5486. Robin Hood Jr. (*Willie Whopper*) 3 Feb. 1934; *p.c.:* Celebrity prods for MGM; *prod/dir:* Ub Iwerks; *anim:* Grim Natwick, Berny Wolf; *col:* Ciné. *sd:* PCP. 6½ min. • Willie spins a yarn of when he was was the legendary character who rescues Maid Marian from the clutches of the evil Prince John.

5487. Robin Hood Makes Good (*Merrie Melodies*) 11 Feb. 1939; *p.c.:* Leon Schlesinger prods for WB; *dir:* Charles M. Jones; *story:* Dave Monahan; *anim:* Robert McKimson; *lay:* Robert Givens; *back:* Paul Julian; *ed:* Tregoweth E. Brown; *voices:* Margaret Hill, Sara Berner, Mel Blanc; *mus:* Carl W. Stalling; *prod sup:* Henry Binder, Raymond G. Katz; *col:* Tech. *sd:* RCA. 7 min. • Three squirrels play "Robin Hood" and encounter a sly fox posing as "Lady Guinevere."

5488. Robin Hoodlum (*Jolly Frolics*) 23 Dec. 1948; *p.c.:* UPA for Colum; *ex prod:* Stephen Bosustow; *dir:* John Hubley; *asst dir:* Max Morgan; *story:* Sol Barzman, Phil Eastman; *anim:* Robert Cannon, Willis Pyle, Rudy Larriva, Pat Matthews; *sets:* Herb Klynn, Jules Engel, Bill Hurtz; *voices:* Jack Mather; *mus:* Del Castillo; *i&p:* Mary Cain; *ph:* Jack Eckes; *prod:* Ed Gershman; *col:* Tech. *sd:* RCA. 7 min. • The Sheriff of Nottingham (The Crow) is told to capture Robin Hood (The Fox) ... otherwise he will lose his cushy job — and his head!

5489. Robin Hood-Winked (*Noveltoon*) Sept. 1966; *p.c.:* Para Cartoons; *dir:* Shamus Culhane; *story:* Heywood Kling; *anim:* Al Eugster, Nick

Tafuri; *sets:* Danté Barbetta, Robert Little; *voices:* Allen Swift; *mus:* Winston Sharples; *prod sup:* Harold Robins, Burt Hanft; *col:* Tech. *sd:* RCA. 6½ min. • Sir Blur is appointed Sheriff of Nottingham and sets out with the King to capture Robin Hood.

5490. Robin Hood-Winked (*Popeye*) 12 Nov. 1948; *p.c.:* Famous for Para; *dir:* Seymour Kneitel; *story:* Larz Bourne, Tom Golden; *anim:* Tom Johnson, Frank Endres, *sets:* Robert Little; *voices:* Jack Mercer, Mae Questel, Jackson Beck, Phil Kramer; *mus:* Winston Sharples; *ph:* Leonard McCormick; *prod mgr:* Sam Buchwald; *col:* Pola. *sd:* RCA. 6½ min. • Robin Hood Popeye is in Olive's tavern when Tax Inspector Bluto arrives, declaring Olive exempt from all taxes if she'll be his girl.

5491. Robin Hoodwinked (*Tom & Jerry*); 6 June 1958; *p.c.:* MGM; *prod/dir:* William Hanna, Joseph Barbera; *anim:* Kenneth Muse, Carlo Vinci, Lewis Marshall, James Escalante; *lay:* Dick Bickenbach; *back:* Robert Gentle; *ed:* Jim Faris; *voices:* Lucille Bliss, Bill Thompson; *mus:* Scott Bradley; *ph:* Jack Stevens; *prod mgr:* Hal Elias; *col:* Tech. *sd:* WE. 7 min. CS. • Robin Hood is locked in Nottingham Castle and it's up to Jerry and his little protégé to rescue him from his cell, guarded by Tom.

5492. Robin Hoody Woody (*Woody Woodpecker*) 13 Feb. 1963; *p.c.:* Walter Lantz prods for Univ; *dir:* Paul J. Smith; *story:* Al Bertino, Dick Kinney; *anim:* Ray Abrams, Les Kline, Art Davis; *sets:* Art Landy, Ray Huffine; *voices:* Daws Butler, Grace Stafford; *mus:* Clarence Wheeler; *prod mgr:* William E. Garity; *col:* Tech. *sd:* RCA. 6 min. • Disturbed by the noise Woody and his merry men are making, Prince John challenges him to a jousting tournament, ending in an all-out war.

5493. Robin Rodenthood (*Herman & Katnip*) 25 Feb. 1955; *p.c.:* Famous for Para; *dir:* Dave Tendlar; *story:* Carl Meyer; *anim:* Martin Taras, Thomas Moore; *sets:* Robert Little; *voices:* Sid Raymond, Arnold Stang, Jack Mercer; *mus:* Winston Sharples; *ph:* Leonard McCormick; *prod mgr:* Seymour Shultz; *col:* Tech. *sd:* RCA. 6 min. • Sir Katnip takes a "Cheese Tax" from the mouse villagers and it's up to Robin Hood Herman to correct matters.

5494. Robinson Crusoe (*ComiColor*) 14 Apr. 1935; *p.c.:* Celebrity prods; *prod/dir:* Ub Iwerks; *mus:* Art Turkisher; *col:* Ciné. *sd:* RCA. 7 min. • No story available.

5495. Robinson Crusoe (*Dinky Doodle*) 21 Jun. 1925; *p.c.:* Bray prods for FBO; *dir/story:* Walt Lantz; *anim:* Clyde Geronimi; *b&w. sil.* 5 min. • No story available.

5496. Robinson Crusoe Isle (*Oswald*) 7 Jan. 1935; *p.c.:* Univ; *dir:* Walter Lantz; *story:* Victor McLeod; *anim:* Fred Avery, Jack Carr, Ray Abrams, Joe d'Igalo, Ernest Smythe; *mus:* James Dietrich; *b&w. sd:* WE. 8 min. • No story available.

5497. Robinson Crusoe Jr. (*Looney Tunes*) 25 Oct. 1941; *p.c.:* Leon Schlesinger prods for WB; *dir/lay:* Norman McCabe; *story:* Melvin Millar; *anim:* John Carey, Cal Dalton, Arthur Davis, David Hoffman, Vive Risto; *sets:* Richard H. Thomas; *ed:* Treg Brown; *voices:* Mel Blanc, Robert C. Bruce; *mus:* Carl W. Stalling; *prod sup:* Henry Binder, Raymond G. Katz; *b&w. sd:* Vit. 6 min. • Shipwrecked on a desert isle, Porky and Man Friday get chased off the island by cannibals.

5498. Robinson Crusoe's Broadcast (*Terry-Toons*) 15 Apr. 1938; *p.c.:* TT for Educational/Fox; *dir:* John Foster; *mus:* Philip A. Scheib; *b&w. sd:* RCA. 6½ min. • Crusoe gives a literal account over the radio of how he was shipwrecked on an island, built a house and was menaced by cannibals.

5499. Robinson Gruesome (*Chilly Willy*) 2 Feb. 1959; *p.c.:* Walter Lantz prods for Univ; *dir:* Alex Lovy; *story:* Homer Brightman; *anim:* La Verne Harding, Ray Abrams, Don Patterson *sets:* Raymond Jacobs, Art Landy; *voice:* Daws Butler; *mus:* Clarence Wheeler; *prod mgr:* William E. Garity; *col:* Tech. *sd:* RCA. 6 min. • Smedley is shipwrecked on an island and, tired of eating bananas, decides to eat penguin when Chilly appears on the scene.

5500. RoboCop 5 Feb. 1988; *p.c.:* Orion Pictures Corp.; based on the characters created by Edward Neumeier, Michael Miner; *anim fx:* Visual Concept Engineering crew: Kevin Kutchaver, Jo Martin; *stop-motion anim:* Randy Dutra; *col. sd:* Dolby stereo. 102 min. *l/a.* • Science-fiction fantasy about a robotic crime-fighter.

5501. RoboCop 2 12 Oct. 1990; *p.c.:* Orion Pictures Corp.; based on the characters created by Edward Neumeier, Michael Miner; *cgi: (sup)* Paul

Sammon, Mike Ribble; *stop-motion anim:* Tom St. Amand, Eric Leighton, Randal Dutra, Peter Kleinow, Mark Sullivan, Justin Kohn, Don Waller, *(ed)* Kevin Williams, *(art dir)* Craig Davies, *(modelling)* Ken Cope, *(moldmaker)* John Reed III, *(model makers)* M. Spencer Owyang, Paula Lucchesi, Marc Ribaud, Merrick Cheney, Jon Berg, Ernie Fosselius, Robert McAndrews, *(monster movement)* Lisa Amy Sturz; Gregory Ballora; *digital character performance:* deGraf/Wahrman, Inc.; *computer puppeteering:* Trey Stokes; *technical sup:* Gregory Ercoland; *anim ex:* Phil Tippett; *RoboCop des/created by:* Rob Bottin; *anim ph:* Jammie Friday; *col:* DuArt/DeLuxe. *sd:* Dolby stereo. 116 min. *l/a.* • Live-action science-fiction adventure: A futuristic tale of a crime-fighting cyborg intent on stamping out the mastermind behind the world's most powerful narcotic.

5502. RoboCop 3 24 June 1994; *p.c.:* Orion Pictures Corp. for Colum TriStar; based on the characters created by Edward Neumeier, Michael Miner; *anim fx:* Kevin Kutchaver, Pam Vick; *computer anim:* Littleton Brothers; *stop-motion anim seq:* Phil Tippett; *Tippett Company crew; fx ph:* Peter Kozachik, Eric Swenson; *fx prod sup:* Julie Roman Tippett; *model makers:* Paula Lucchesi, Merrick Cheney; *opticals:* Harry Walton; *image fx: cgi:* Craig Hayes, Adam J. Valdez; *mold-maker:* John Reed III; *armatures:* Tom St. Amand, Blair Clark; *Delta City/dream seq:* Pacific Data Images; *art dir:* Rebecca Marie; *digital fx sup:* Jamie Dixon; *anim:* Kevin Rafferty, Ray Giarrantana; *prod:* Michele Ferrone, Julia Gibson; *"Johnny Rehab" commercial: dir:* David Silverman; *prod:* Rough Draft Studios; *anim:* Bret Haaland, Gregg Vanzo; *col:* DeLuxe. *sd:* Dolby stereo. 104 min. *l/a.* • Live-action adventure: The return of Murphy, the cybernetically reconstructed law-enforcer.

5503. The Robot *(Talkartoon)* 5 Feb. 1932; *p.c.:* The Fleischer Studio for Para; *prod:* Max Fleischer; *dir:* Dave Fleischer; *mus:* Art Turkisher; b&w. *sd:* WE. 7 min. • Bimbo wins a prize fight.

5504. Robot Rabbit *(Looney Tunes)* 12 Dec. 1953; *p.c.:* WB; *dir:* I. Freleng; *story:* Warren Foster; *anim:* Virgil Ross, Arthur Davis, Manuel Perez, Ken Champin; *lay:* Hawley Pratt; *back:* Irv Wyner; *ed:* Treg Brown; *voices:* Mel Blanc, Arthur Q. Bryan; *mus:* Carl Stalling; *prod mgr:* John W. Burton; *prod:* Edward Selzer; *col:* Tech. *sd:* Vit. 7 min. • Elmer employs the assistance of a robot to help keep Bugs out of his carrot patch.

5505. The Robot Ringer *(Modern Madcap)* Nov. 1962; *p.c.:* Para Cartoons; *dir:* Seymour Kneitel; *story:* Irving Spector; *anim:* Morey Reden, Wm. B. Pattengill, Larry Silverman; *sets:* Anton Loeb; *voices:* Bob MacFadden; *mus:* Winston Sharples; *ph:* Leonard McCormick; *prod mgr:* Abe Goodman; *col:* Tech. *sd:* RCA. 6 min. • A robot mixes with Madison Avenue advertising men and when his creator tries to find him, he can't tell which is the robot. The robot is then hailed as a creative genius!

5506. Robot Rival *(Modern Madcap)* Sept 1964; *p.c.:* Para Cartoons; *dir:* Seymour Kneitel; *story:* Jack Mendelsohn; *anim:* Morey Reden; *sets:* Anton Loeb; *voices:* Bob MacFadden, Corinne Orr; *mus:* Winston Sharples; *ph:* Leonard McCormick; *prod mgr:* Abe Goodman; *col:* Tech. *sd:* RCA. 6 min. • Zippy Zephyr, an inter-galactic cab driver has his job threatened by a robot.

5507. Robots in Toyland *(Astronut)* Aug. 1965; *p.c.:* TT for Fox; *ex prod:* Bill Weiss; *dir/anim:* Connie Rasinski; *story sup:* Tom Morrison; *story:* Eli Bauer; *sets:* Bill Focht, Robert Owen; *ed:* Jack MacConnell; *voices:* Dayton Allen; *mus:* Jim Timmens; *ph:* Ted Moskowitz; *sd:* Elliot Grey; *col:* DeLuxe. *sd:* RCA. 6 min. • Astro helps Oscar work in the toy department of a department store.

5508. Roc-a-By Sinbad *(Luno)* Jan. 1964; *p.c.:* TT for Fox; *ex prod:* Bill Weiss; *dir/anim:* Connie Rasinski; *story sup:* Tom Morrison; *story:* Larz Bourne; *sets:* Bill Focht, John Zago; *ed:* Jack MacConnell; *voices:* Bob MacFadden, Norma MacMillan; *mus:* Jim Timmens; *ph:* Ted Moskowitz, Joe Rasinski; *sd:* Elliot Grey; *col:* DeLuxe *sd:* RCA. 6 min. • Timmy gets Luno, the magic horse, to take him to Sinbad's castle.

5509. Rock-a-By Bear 12 July 1952; *p.c.:* MGM; *dir:* Tex Avery; *story:* Heck Allen, Rich Hogan; *anim:* Michael Lah, Walter Clinton, Grant Simmons; *sets:* John Didrik Johnsen; *ed:* Jim Faris; *voice:* Patrick J. McGeehan; *mus:* Scott Bradley; *ph:* Jack Stevens; *prod:* Fred Quimby; *col:* Tech. *sd:* WE. 7 min. • A pound mutt is hired as watchdog for a hibernating bear who hates noise. A rival canine tries to get the other dog fired by making noise.

5510. Rock-a-By Maybe *(The Dogfather)* 23 Apr. 1975; *p.c.:* Mirisch/ DFE for UA; *dir:* Gerry Chiniquy; *story:* John Dunn; *anim:* Bob Richardson, Don Williams, Norm McCabe, Nelson Shin; *ed:* Rick Steward; *lay:* Dick Ung; *back:* Richard H. Thomas; *voices:* Bob Holt; *mus:* Dean Elliott; *col:* DeLuxe. *sd:* RCA. 6 min. • The Dogfather's rest in his mountain retreat is interrupted by two squirrels.

5511. Rock a By Pinky *(Pink Panther)* 23 Dec. 1966; *p.c.:* Mirisch/ Geoffrey/DFE for UA; *dir:* Hawley Pratt; *story:* John W. Dunn; *anim:* Bob Matz, Warren Batchelder, John Gibbs, La Verne Harding, Manny Perez, Manny Gould, Ted Bonnicksen; *lay:* Dick Ung; *back:* Tom O'Loughlin; *mus:* Walter Greene; *theme tune:* Henry Mancini; *prod sup:* Lee Gunther, Harry Love; *col:* DeLuxe. *sd:* RCA. 6 min. • The Panther is trying to sleep in a tree when a camper and his dog pitch their tent below.

5512. Rock-a-Bye Gator *(Woody Woodpecker)* 9 Jan. 1962; *p.c.:* Walter Lantz prods for Univ; *dir:* Jack Hannah; *story:* Dalton Sandifer; *anim:* Roy Jenkins, Al Coe; *sets:* Ray Huffine, Art Landy; *voice:* Daws Butler, Grace Stafford; *mus:* Eugene Poddany; *prod mgr:* William E. Garity; *col:* Tech. *sd:* RCA. 6 min. • Gabby Gator awakens from his winter sleep and espys Woody who attempts to put him back to sleep by playing "Rock-a-bye Baby" on a variety of instruments.

5513. Rock-A-Doodle 2 Aug. 1991; *p.c.:* Sullivan Bluth Studios Ireland Ltd., for Goldcrest; *dir:* Don Bluth, Gary Goldman, Dan Kuenster; *l/a dir:* Beau Van Den Ecker, Victor French; *ex prod:* George A. Walker, Morris F. Sullivan; *prod:* Don Bluth, Gary Goldman, John Pomeroy; *l/a prod:* Robert Enrietto; *asso prod:* Thad Weinlein; *l/a asso prod:* Fred Craig; *prod sup:* Russell Boland, Cathy Carr-Goldman, Olga Tarin-Craig; *prod co-ord:* Lorraine Stierle; *l/a prod mgr:* David Murphy; *post prod co-ord:* Helene Blitz; *asst dir:* Martin O'Malley, Konrad Jay, Moya Mackle, Nuala O'Toole; *scr:* David N. Weiss; *story:* Don Bluth, David N. Weiss, John Pomeroy, T.J. Kuenster, David Steinberg, Gary Goldman; *storyboard:* Don Bluth, Dan Kuenster, Ralph Zondag, Dick Zondag; *addit dial:* T.J. Kuenster; *seq dir:* Dick Zondag, Ralph Zondag; *anim dir:* John Pomeroy, Jeffrey J. Varab, Jean Morel, Linda Miller, Daniel Hofstedt, Ken Duncan, Lorna Pomeroy-Cook, Jeff Etter; *fx:* David Tidgwell, Stephen B. Moore, Joey Mildenberger, Diann Landau, Tom Hush; *computer:* Jan Carlee, Mark Swanson; *anim:* John Hill, Ralf Palmer, Anne-Marie Bardwell, John Power, Colm Duggan, Alain Costa, Cathy Jones, Dave Kupczyk, Silvia Hoefnagels, Mark Pudleiner, Gary Perkovac, Doug Bennett, John Hooper, Jesper Moller, David G. Simmons, Jean-Jacques Prunes, Piet De Rycker, Chris Derochie, Kim Hagen-Jensen, Dan Harder, Rob Koo, Donnachada Daly, Mark Koetsier, Bruce Smith, Dave Brewster, Charlie Bonifacio; *computer anim:* Don Pierce, Greg Maguire; *fx anim:* Peter Matheson, Robert B. Cowan, Michael Gagné, Jeff Topping, Garrett Wren, Al Holter, James Mansfield, Peter Yamasaki, Joseph Gilland, Bruce Heller, Kathleen Quaife-Hodge, Brett Hisey, Nike Olive, Janette Owens, Bob Simmons; *anim check:* Michele McKenna-Mahon; *lay:* Mark Swan, Scott Caple, Eddie Gribbin, Amy Berenz, Larry Leker, John Byrne, Giorgio Mardegan, Kevin Gollaher, Fred Reilly; *back:* Barry Atkinson, Rick Bentham, Rungsun Apinchapong, David McCamley, Ken Slevin, Mannix Bennett, Carl Jones, Paul M. Kelly; *ed:* Dan Molina, Bernard Caputo, *(anim)* Fiona Trayler, Lisa Dorney, Joe Gall, *(prod des)* Dave Goetz; *art dir:* Don Moore, *(l/a)* Terry Pritchard, *(set des)* William H. Frake III, *(set dresser)* Bryony Foster; *art sup:* Tom Higgins, Tamara Anderson, Paul Kelly, Jan Naylor; *special fx sup:* David Harris, *(l/a)* Morris Foley; *Cloud Tank fx:* Daryl Carstensen, Mannix Bennett; *voices: Narrator/Patou:* Phil Harris; *Chanticleer:* Glen Campbell; *Snipes:* Eddie Deezen; *Mother:* Kathryn Holcomb; *Edmond:* Toby Scott Ganger; *Dad:* Stan Ivar; *Scott:* Christian Hoff; *Mark:* Jason Marin; *The Duke:* Christopher Plummer; *Peepers:* Sandy Duncan; *Stuey:* Will Ryan; *Hunch:* Charles Nelson-Reilly; *Goldie:* Ellen Greene; *Pinky:* Sorrell Booke; *Mother:* Dee Wallace; *Minnie Rabbit:* Louise Chamis; *Radio Announcer:* Bob Galaco; *Farmyard Bully/Max the Bouncer:* Jake Steinfeld; *also:* the Don Bluth Players; *mus:* Robert Folk, T.J. Kuenster; performed by the Irish Film Orchestra, Nashville Rhythm Section; *mus arrangements:* Robert Folk, Andy Miller; *orch:* Bill Whelan; *mus ed:* Michael Connell, Douglas Lackey; *visual fx:* Fred Craig; *(l/a):* Roy Field, Peter Donen; *optical fx (USA):* Robert Shepherd; *project prod:* Denny Kelly; *sup:* R. William Dorney; *co-sup:* Cosmas Paul Bolger Jr.; *optical fx (UK): printer:* Dick Dimbleby, Philip Dimbleby; *Rotoscope art:* Simon Leech; *rostrum ph sup:* Tim Field; *addit:* Peerless Camera Company, Fotherley Ltd.; *Xerox:* John Finnegan, Anthony O'Brien, Frank D. Richards,

Jackie Anderson, Tommy Brennan, Billy Colgan, Philip Grogan, Joanne McSherry, Keith Murray, John Walsh, Kieron White; *check:* Gari Downey, Andy Fitzgerald, Brendan Harris, Stuart Johnstone, Michael Maher, Siobhan O'Brien, Paul Roy, Pauline Walsh-Byrne; *mark-up:* Patricia Browne, Tom English, Patricia Gordon, Collette O'Brien, Olivia Grogan, David Hogan; *i&p:* Jacqueline Hooks, Sorcha Ni Chuimin, Madeleine Downes, Mary Sheridan, Karen Dwyer, Ailish Mullally, Deborah Rykoff-Bennett, Debbie Gold, Seamus Grogan, Kevin Hand, Niamh McClean; *paint check:* Gerard Coleman, Sinéad Murray, Nicholas Connolly; *special fx: technicians:* Ron Hone, Peter Skehan; *modelers:* Chrissie Overs, Carol de Jong; *computer: technical dir:* Christine Zing Chang; *prod co-ord:* Kerri Swanson; *choreog:* Susan Inouye; *wardrobe:* Maeve Paterson; *make-up:* Rosie Blackmore; *sd des:* Ed Bannon; *sd ed:* Denis Dutton, Alan Schultz; *dial ed:* Thomas V. Moss, Jim Fleming; *ADR ed:* John K. Carr, Dennis Dutton, Sue Odjakjian; *sd rec:* Pat Hayes, *(dial)* Jackson Schwartz, Warren Kleiman, *(mus)* Brian Masterson; *sd re-rec:* Bill Rowe, Ray Merrin, John Falcini; *foley:* Greg Orloff, Taj Soundworks, John Roesch, Ellen Heuer; *foley ed:* Willy Allen, Paul Heslin; *prod asst:* Edel MacGinty, Sharon Morgan, Jonathan Martin, Linda O'Carroll, Tara Sheridan; *ph (l/a):* Robert Paynter; *ph:* Paddy Duffy, Jeanette Maher, Gary Hall, Freddy McGavin, Fiona Mackle, John O'Flaherty, Eric Ryan, Ciaván Morris, Freddie Cooper, Cosmas Paul Bolger Jr., Jerry Pooles; *col:* Tech. *sd:* Dolby stereo. 74 min. *anim/l/a.* • Chanticleer, the Rooster, who raises the sun each morning with his singing, misses his morning call one day. The sun rises anyway and, disillusioned, the rooster leaves the farm, deeming himself useless. The moment he leaves, a torrential rainstorm eclipses the sun and the animals panic. A young farm boy, Edmond, sets out to find Chanticleer and return him to the farm, finally managing to locate him at a nightclub where the rooster has now become a famous rock star.

5514. Rock Hound *(Possible Possum)* Apr. 1968; *p.c.:* TT for Fox; *dir/anim:* Dave Tendlar; *col:* DeLuxe. *sd:* RCA. 5 min. • Poss and his pals are disturbed by a geologist digging up their home to find gold. • See: *Possible Possum*

5515. Rock Hounds *(The Dogfather)* 20 Nov. 1975; *p.c.:* Mirisch/DFE for UA; *dir:* Arthur Leonardi; *story:* John Dunn; *anim:* Bob Richardson, Warren Batchelder, Don Williams, Nelson Shin; *lay:* Dick Ung; *back:* Richard H. Thomas; *voices:* Bob Holt; *mus:* Dean Elliott; *col:* DeLuxe. *sd:* RCA. 6 min. • Pug masquerades as a butler in a mansion in order to steal the Pedigree Diamond.

5516. Rock 'n' Rodent *(Tom & Jerry)* 1967; *p.c.:* MGM; *prod:* Chuck Jones; *dir:* Abe Levitow; *story:* Bob Ogle; *anim:* Ben Washam, Dick Thompson, Tom Ray, Don Towsley, Ken Harris; *des:* Maurice Noble; *lay:* Don Morgan; *back:* Philip de Guard; *voice:* June Foray; *mus:* Carl Brandt; *prod mgr:* Les Goldman; *col:* Metro. *sd:* WE. 7 min. • Jerry's jazz combo keeps Tom awake throughout the night.

5517. Rocket-Bye Baby *(Merrie Melodies)* 4 Aug. 1956; *p.c.:* WB; *dir:* Chuck Jones; *story:* Michael Maltese; *anim:* Ken Harris, Abe Levitow, Ben Washam; *fx:* Harry Love; *lay:* Ernie Nordli; *back:* Philip de Guard; *ed:* Treg Brown; *voices:* Daws Butler, June Foray; *mus:* Milt Franklyn; *prod mgr:* John W. Burton; *prod:* Edward Selzer; *col:* Tech. *sd:* Vit. 7 min. • A Martian baby is delivered to an average Earth couple. The green child soon develops and builds himself a rocket to return home in.

5518. The Rocket Racket *(Honey Halfwitch)* Mar. 1966; *p.c.:* Para Cartoons; *dir:* Howard Post; *sets:* Robert Little; *voices:* Shari Lewis; *mus:* Winston Sharples; *ph:* Leonard McCormick; *prod mgr:* Abe Goodman; *col:* Tech. *sd:* RCA. 6 min. • No story available.

5519. Rocket Racket *(Woody Woodpecker)* 24 Apr. 1962; *p.c.:* Walter Lantz prods for Univ; *dir:* Jack Hannah; *story:* Tedd Pierce, Bill Danch; *anim:* Roy Jenkins, Al Coe; *sets:* Art Landy, Ray Huffine; *voices:* Daws Butler, Grace Stafford; *mus:* Clarence Wheeler; *prod mgr:* William E. Garity; *col:* Tech. *sd:* RCA. 6 min. • Gabby Gator learns that Woody is to be sent into space and builds his own rocket from an oven. He convinces Woody that this is the correct one for the launch.

5520. Rocket Squad *(Merrie Melodies)* 10 Mar. 1956; *p.c.:* WB; *dir:* Chuck Jones; *story:* Tedd Pierce; *anim:* Ken Harris, Ben Washam, Abe Levitow, Richard Thompson; *lay:* Ernie Nordli; *back:* Philip de Guard; *ed:* Treg Brown; *voices:* Mel Blanc; *mus:* Milt Franklyn; *prod mgr:* John W. Burton; *prod:* Edward Selzer; *col:* Tech. *sd:* Vit. 7 min. • Space-age

detectives, Daffy and Porky go on the trail of "The Flying Saucer Bandit."

5521. Rocket to Mars *(Popeye)* 9 Aug. 1946; *p.c.:* Famous for Para; *dir:* Bill Tytla; *story:* Bill Turner, Otto Messmer; *anim:* Jim Tyer, John Gentilella; *sets:* Anton Loeb; *voices:* Jack Mercer, Jackson Beck, Mae Questel, Harry F. Welch; *mus:* Winston Sharples; *ph:* Leonard McCormick; *prod mgr:* Sam Buchwald; *col:* Ciné. *sd:* RCA. 6 min. • Popeye and Olive board a museum rocket ship, inadvertently journeying to a war mongering planet that is intent on destroying the Earth.

5522. The Rocketeer 21 June 1991; *p.c.:* Walt Disney Pictures/Silver Screen Partners IV; *cgi/digital sup:* Sandra F. Ford, Stuart Robertson; *anim sup:* Wes Ford Takahashi; *anim:* Crispy Green, Gordon Baker, Kevin Coffey, Anthony Stacchi, Charlie Canfield, Loring Doyle; *Nazi anim: dir:* Mark Dindal; *lay:* Jim Beihold; *back:* Phil Phillipson; *stop-motion anim:* Tom St. Amand; *Rotoscope:* Tom Bertino, Jack Mongovan, Rebecca Heskes, Ellen Mueller, Sandy Houston, Joanne Hafner, Terry Molatore; *col:* Tech. *sd:* Dolby stereo. Panavision. 108 min. *l/a.* • Live-action feature centered around 1938: An air racing pilot discovers a device that enables man to fly. A selection of villains and Nazi spies zero in to grab the gadget for themselves.

5523. Rocketeers *(Tom & Jerry)* 30 Jan. 1932; *p.c.:* Van Beuren for RKO; *dir:* John Foster, George Rufle; *mus:* Gene Rodemich; *b&w. sd:* RCA. 7 min. • Tom and Jerry are launched into space, coming down in the ocean. There they meet a mermaid.

5524. Rockhound Magoo *(Mr. Magoo)* 24 Oct. 1957; *p.c.:* UPA for Colum; *ex prod:* Stephen Bosustow; *prod/dir:* Pete Burness; *story:* Dick Shaw; *anim:* Tom McDonald, Barney Posner, Ed Friedman, Casey Onaitis; *lay:* Robert Dranko; *back:* Bob McIntosh; *voices:* Jim Backus, Earl Bennett; *mus:* Dean Elliott; *col:* Tech. *sd:* RCA. 6 min. CS. • While prospecting in the desert, Magoo pitches his tent under a balancing rock, mistaking it for a rain cloud. A prospector arrives and accuses him of being a "claim jumper."

5525. Rocks and Socks *(Oswald the Lucky Rabbit)* 24 Oct. 1928; *p.c.:* Winkler for Univ; *anim:* Hugh Harman; *prod:* George Winkler; *b&w. sil.* 6 min. • No story available.

5526. Rocky Pink *(Pink Panther)* 9 July 1976; *p.c.:* Mirisch/Geoffrey/DFE for UA; *dir:* Art Leonardi; *story:* John W. Dunn; *anim:* Nelson Shin, Don Williams, Bob Richardson, John Gibbs; *lay:* Dick Ung; *back:* Richard H. Thomas; *ed:* Rick Steward; *mus:* Walter Greene; *theme tune:* Henry Mancini; *ph:* John Burton Jr.; *prod mgr:* Lee Gunther; *col:* DeLuxe. *sd:* RCA. 6 min. • The Panther obtains a rock as a pet which grows to outlandish proportions. Reissued in Feb. 1981 as *Pet Pink Pebbles*.

5527. Rocky Road to Ruin *(Color Rhapsody)* 16 Sept. 1943; *p.c.:* Colum; *prod:* Dave Fleischer; *dir:* Paul Sommer; *story/voice:* John McLeish; *anim:* Jim Armstrong, Basil Davidovich; *lay:* Clark Watson; *ed:* Edward Moore; *mus:* Edward Paul; *prod mgr:* Albert Spar; *col:* Tech. *sd:* RCA. 7 min. • Waldo, the hard working paper boy is the constant brunt of Phineas' practical jokes when they compete for the hand of the fair Eleanor.

5528. Rodent to Stardom *(Looney Tunes)* Sept. 1967; *p.c.:* WB/7A; *dir:* Alex Lovy; *story:* Cal Howard; *anim:* Volus Jones, La Verne Harding, Ted Bonnicksen, Ed Solomon; *lay:* David Hanan, Lin Larsen; *back:* Bob Abrams; *ed:* Hal Geer; *voices:* Mel Blanc; *mus:* William Lava; *col:* Tech. *sd:* Vit. 6 min. • Daffy assumes he has the star role when he is taken to a Hollywood studio, only to end up as stand-in for Speedy Gonzales.

5529. Rodeo Dough *(Krazy Kat)* 13 Feb. 1931; *p.c.:* Winkler for Colum; *prod:* Charles Mintz; *story:* Ben Harrison; *anim:* Manny Gould; *mus:* Joe de Nat; *b&w. sd:* WE. 6 min. • Egged on by his girl, Krazy enters a rodeo.

5530. Rodeo Romeo *(Popeye)* 16 Aug. 1946; *p.c.:* Famous for Para; *dir:* I. Sparber; *story:* I. Klein, Joe Stultz; *anim:* Dave Tendlar, Martin Taras; *sets:* Shane Miller; *voices:* Jackson Beck, Mae Questel, Harry F. Welch; *mus:* Winston Sharples; *ph:* Leonard McCormick; *prod sup:* Sam Buchwald; *col:* Tech. *sd:* RCA. 6¹⁄2 min. • Badlands Bluto and Popeye compete for the affections of Olive at a rodeo.

5531. Roller Coaster Rabbit 15 June 1990; *p.c.:* Walt Disney Pictures/Amblin for Buena Vista; *anim dir:* Rob Minkoff; *prod:* Donald W. Ernst; *ex prod:* Steven Spielberg, Frank Marshall, Kathleen Kennedy; *based upon characters created by* Gary K. Wolf; *asso prod:* Thom Enriquez; *story:*

Bill Kopp, Kevin Harkey, Rob Minkoff, Lynne Naylor, Patrick A. Ventura; *anim:* Brigitte Hartley, Mark Henn, Mark Kausler, Alex Kopershmidt, David P. Stephan, Barry Temple, Alexander Williams; *asst anim:* Tom Bancroft, Tony Bancroft, Philo Barnhart, Aaron Blaise, Lou Dellarosa, Sam Ewing, Daniel Gracey, Alan Simpson, Jane Tucker; *inbet:* Philip S. Boyd, Trey Finney, Susan Gal, Ken Hettig, Christine Lawrence, Tracy M. Lee, Matt Novak, Jennifer Oliver, Daniel Wawrzaszek; *fx anim:*Barry Cook, Rob Bekuhrs, Jeff Dutton, James R. Tooley, Kevin Turcotte, Dorse A. Lanpher, Dave Bossert, Wm. Allen Blyth, Dan Chaika, Christine Harding, Steve Starr, Eusebio Torres; *art dir:* Kelly A. Asbury; *lay:* James Beihold, Robert Walker, Mark R. Wallace; *back:* Ric Sluiter, Katherine Altieri, Robert E. Stanton; *ed:* Chuck Williams; *voices: Roger Rabbit:* Charles Fleischer; *Jessica Rabbit:* Kathleen Turner; *Mom/Young Baby Herman:* April Winchell; *Adult Baby Herman:* Lou Hirsch; *Droopy Dog:* Corey Burton; *Bull:* Frank Welker; *mus:* Bruce Broughton; *orch:* Don Nemitz; *i&p:* Fran Kirsten, Jason L. Buske, Irma Cartaya, Michael Lusby, Pamela A. Manes, Monica Mandel, Lisa A. Reinert, Laura Lynn Rippberger, Laurie A. Sacks, Elsa V. Sesto, Andrew Simmons, Jo Anne Tzuanos, Pam Vastbinder, Sharon K. Vincent, Loretta A. Weeks, Victoria L. Winner; *anim check:* Paul Steele; *l/a dir:* Frank Marshall; *prod mgr:* Tim O'Donnell; *ph:* Gary W. Smith, Mary E. Lescher; *sd fx ed:* Richard C. Franklin Jr., Louis L. Edemann; *sd des:* Drew Neuman; *foley art:* John Roesch, Ellen Heuer; *col:* Tech. *sd:* Dolby stereo. 7 min. • Roger Rabbit is left in charge of Baby Herman at the fair. Herman crawls after a balloon, narrowly escaping many dangers with Roger in hot pursuit landing the two of them on a precipitous roller coaster.

5532. Rolling Stones *(Paul Terry-Toon)* 1 May 1936; *p.c.:* TT for Educational/Fox; *dir:* Mannie Davis, George Gordon; *mus:* Philip A. Scheib; b&w. *sd:* WE. 6 min. • Two pups disguise themselves as a dachshund to gatecrash a dog show.

5533. Roman Legion-Hare *(Looney Tunes)* 12 Nov. 1955; *p.c.:* WB; *dir:* Friz Freleng; *story:* Warren Foster; *anim:* Virgil Ross, Arthur Davis, Gerry Chiniquy; *lay:* Hawley Pratt; *back:* Irv Wyner; *ed:* Treg Brown; *voices:* Mel Blanc; *mus:* Milt Franklyn; *prod mgr:* John W. Burton; *prod:* Edward Selzer; *col:* Tech. *sd:* Vit. 7 min. • Rome: 54 AD, and the Emperor Nero needs a victim for his lion. He summons Sam, the Captain of the Guards to find a victim and, on this quest, he runs afoul of Bugs Bunny.

5534. Roman Punch *(Paul Terry-Toon)* 20 Apr. 1930; *p.c.:* A-C for Educational/Fox; *dir:* Frank Moser, Paul Terry; *mus:* Philip A. Scheib; b&w. *sd:* WE. 5 min. • The activities of a roaring lion in a Roman amphitheatre.

5535. Romance *(Paul Terry-Toon)* 15 May 1932; *p.c.:* Moser & Terry for Educational/Fox; *dir:* Frank Moser, Paul Terry; *mus:* Philip A. Scheib; b&w. *sd:* WE. 6 min. • A mouse's rival employs gangsters to rub him out.

5536. Romantic Melodies *(Screen Songs)* 21 Oct. 1932; *p.c.:* The Fleischer Studio for Para; *prod:* Max Fleischer; *dir:* Dave Fleischer; *anim:* Seymour Kneitel, Bernard Wolf; *mus:* Art Turkisher; *l/a:* Arthur Tracy; b&w. *sd:* WE. 6 min. *l/a/anim.* • Bimbo's street band annoys the populous so much that they send for the wagon. Betty prefers to listen to "The Street Singer."

5537. Romantic Rumbolia, Seat of the Rhumba *(Jerky Journeys)* 15 June 1949; *p.c.:* Impossible Pictures for Republic; *ex prod:* David Flexer; *prod/dir/story:* Leonard Louis Levinson; *sets:* Paul Julian; *voice:* Frank Nelson; *col:* Tru. *sd.* 8 min. • In this, the first in the series, the audience is taken to an imaginary land depicting the discovery, colonization and occasional uprising.

5538. Romeo and Juliet *(Paul Terry-Toon)* 16 Apr. 1933; *p.c.:* Moser & Terry for Educational/Fox; *dir:* Frank Moser, Paul Terry; *mus:* Philip A. Scheib; b&w. *sd:* WE. 6 min. • A wealthy Romeo visits Juliet. Her father sees him off, causing a battle between the two families.

5539. Romeo in Rhythm *(MGM Cartoon)* 10 Aug. 1940; *p.c.:* MGM; *prod/dir:* Rudolf Ising; *voice:* Billy Mitchell; *mus:* Scott Bradley; *prod mgr:* Fred Quimby; *col:* Tech. *sd:* WE. 8 min. • The "Black Crow Light Opera Company" presents a jazz version of *Romeo and Juliet.*

5540. A Romeo Monk *(Aesop's Sound Fable)* 20 Feb. 1932; *p.c.:* Van Beuren for RKO; *dir:* John Foster, Mannie Davis; *mus:* Gene Rodemich; b&w. *sd:* RCA. 6½ min. • A monkey spruces up to go out on the make. A

female hippo arrives, forcing her attentions on him. Rebuffed, he listens to the jungle animals singing on a makeshift radio.

5541. A Romeo Robin *(Aesop's Sound Fable)* 22 June 1930; *p.c.:* Van Beuren for Pathé; *dir:* John Foster, Mannie Davis; *mus:* Gene Rodemich; b&w. *sd:* RCA. 9 min. • A worm makes his escape from the birds in an aeroplane which is swallowed by a cat who is trying to catch the birds.

5542. Romiet and Julio *(Pathé Cartoon Comedy)* 9 Jan. 1915; *p.c.:* Bray prods for Ecletic/Pathé; *anim:* Raoul Barré; b&w. *sil.* • Two cats on a backyard fence.

5543. Romp in a Swamp *(Woody Woodpecker)*; *p.c.:* Walter Lantz prods for Univ; *dir:* Paul J. Smith; *story:* Homer Brightman; *anim:* Robert Bentley, Les Kline; *sets:* Art Landy, Raymond Jacobs; *voices:* Daws Butler, Grace Stafford; *mus:* Clarence Wheeler; *prod mgr:* William E. Garity; *col:* Tech. *sd:* RCA. 6 min. • When Ali Gator attempts to devour Woody, he kids him the Fountain of Youth has some validity.

5544. Roof Top Razzle-Dazzle *(Beary Family)* 29 Sept. 1964; *p.c.:* Walter Lantz prods for Univ; *dir:* Paul J. Smith; *story:* Cal Howard; *anim:* Les Kline, Al Coe; *sets:* Art Landy, Ray Huffine; *voices:* Paul Frees, Grace Stafford; *mus:* Walter Greene; *prod mgr:* William E. Garity; *col:* Tech. *sd:* RCA. 6 min. • Charlie decides to erect a TV antenna.

5545. The Rookie Bear *(MGM Cartoon)* 17 May 1941; *p.c.:* MGM; *prod/dir:* Rudolf Ising; *voice:* Gayne Whitman; *mus:* Scott Bradley; *prod mgr:* Fred Quimby; *col:* Tech. *sd:* WE. 9 min. *Academy Award nomination.* • Barney Bear is the first draftee into the Army. He finds Army life gruelling and awakes to find he was dreaming ... and has *really* been drafted!

5546. Rookie Revue *(Merrie Melodies)* 25 Oct. 1941; *p.c.:* Leon Schlesinger prods for WB; *dir:* I. Freleng; *story:* Dave Monahan; *anim:* Richard Bickenbach; *lay:* Owen Fitzgerald; *back:* Lenard Kester; *ed:* Treg Brown; *voices:* Jackson Wheeler, Mel Blanc; *mus:* Carl W. Stalling; *ph:* John W. Burton; *prod sup:* Henry Binder, Raymond G. Katz; *col:* Tech. *sd:* Vit. 7 min. • A satirical look at today's modern Army.

5547. Room and Bird *(Merrie Melodies)* 2 June 1951; *p.c.:* WB; *dir:* I. Freleng; *story:* Tedd Pierce, Warren Foster; *anim:* Virgil Ross, Arthur Davis, Manuel Perez, Ken Champin; *lay:* Hawley Pratt; *back:* Paul Julian; *ed:* Treg Brown; *voices:* Mel Blanc, Bea Benaderet; *mus:* Eugene Poddany; *orch:* Milt Franklyn; *prod mgr:* John W. Burton; *prod:* Edward Selzer; *col:* Tech. *sd:* Vit. 7 min. • Granny smuggles Tweety into a "No Animals Allowed" hotel. Sylvester is soon on hand with his stomach set on a Tweety-bird supper.

5548. Room and Bored *(Fox & Crow)* 30 Sept. 1943; *p.c.:* Colum; *prod:* Dave Fleischer; *dir:* Bob Wickersham; *story:* John McLeish; *anim:* Phil Duncan, Ben Lloyd; *lay:* Clark Watson; *ed:* Edward Moore; *voices:* Frank Graham; *mus:* Eddie Kilfeather; *ph:* Frank Fisher; *prod mgr:* Albert Spar; *col:* Tech. *sd:* RCA. 7½ min. • The Fox makes the cardinal error of renting a spare room to the Crow who plays jazz music night and day.

5549. Room and Bored *(Woody Woodpecker)* 6 Mar. 1962; *p.c.:* Walter Lantz prods for Univ; *dir:* Paul J. Smith; *anim:* Ray Abrams, Les Kline; *sets:* Art Landy, Ray Huffine; *voice:* Grace Stafford; *mus:* Clarence Wheeler; *prod mgr:* William E. Garity; *col:* Tech. *sd:* RCA. 6 min. • No story available.

5550. Room and Wrath *(Chilly Willy)* 4 June 1956; *p.c.:* Walter Lantz prods for Univ; *dir:* Alex Lovy, Tex Avery; *story:* Homer Brightman; *anim:* La Verne Harding, Ray Abrams, Don Patterson; *sets:* Raymond Jacobs; *voice:* Daws Butler; *mus:* Clarence Wheeler; *prod mgr:* William E. Garity; *col:* Tech. *sd:* RCA. 6 min. • The Snowtel watchdog, Smedley, tries to evict Chilly from his room for failure to pay his bill. Cartoon initiated by Tex Avery.

5551. Room Runners *(Flip the Frog)* 13 Aug. 1932; *p.c.:* Celebrity prods for MGM; *prod/dir:* Ub Iwerks; b&w. *sd:* PCP. 6 min. • Flip attempts a "Moonlight Flit" from his apartment, landlady and an unpaid bill.

5552. The Rooster's Nightmare 1916; *p.c.:* Movca Film Service for Herald Film Co; *prod:* S.J. Sangretti; *anim:* John Colman Terry, G.A. Bronstrup, Hugh M. Shields; b&w. *sil.* • No story available.

5553. Rooty Toot Toot *(Jolly Frolics)* 27 Mar. 1952; *p.c.:* UPA for Colum; *ex prod:* Stephen Bosustow; *dir:* John Hubley; *story:* John Hubley, Bill Scott; *anim:* Art Babbitt, Pat Matthews, Tom McDonald, Grim Natwick; *sets:* Paul Julian; *voice:* Thurl Ravenscroft, Bill Lee, Annette Warren; *mus:* Phil Moore; *song:* Allen Alch; *choreography:* Olga Lunick; *prod sup:* Sherm Glas, Herb Klynn; *col:* Tech. *sd:* RCA. 7 min. *Academy Award nomination.* • The story of *Frankie and Johnny* involving a girl accused of shooting her philandering lover.

5554. Rough and Ready Romeo *(Aesop's Film Fable)* 20 Apr. 1926; *p.c.:* Fables Pictures Inc for Pathé; *dir:* Paul Terry; b&w. *sil.* 10 min. • Oskulusa Pete, the cowboy mouse, loses his sweetie to Izzard Ike the bandit cat when he abducts Minnie Hee-Haw Mouse. The pioneers ride in flivvers and the Indians attack on bicycles.

5555. Rough and Tumbleweed *(Inspector Willoughby)* 31 Jan. 1961; *p.c.:* Walter Lantz prods for Univ; *dir:* Paul J. Smith; *story:* Homer Brightman; *anim:* La Verne Harding, Les Kline, Ray Abrams; *sets:* Art Landy, Ray Huffine; *voice:* Dal McKennon; *mus:* Eugene Poddany; *prod mgr:* William E. Garity; *col:* Tech. *sd:* RCA. 6 min. • The Inspector sets out for the wild and woolly west to bring in a tough hombré named Pretty Boy McCoy.

5556. Rough Brunch *(Ant & Aardvark)* 3 Jan. 1971; *p.c.:* Mirisch/DFE for UA; *dir:* Art Davis; *story:* Sid Marcus; *anim:* Manny Gould, Ken Muse, Don Williams, Irv Spence, Robert Taylor, Manny Perez; *lay:* Al Wilson; *back:* Richard H. Thomas; *ed:* Lee Gunther; *voices:* John Byner; *mus:* Doug Goodwin, Pete Candoli, Billy Byers, Jimmy Rowles, Tommy Tedesco, Ray Brown, Shelly Manne; *prod sup:* Jim Foss, Harry Love; *col:* DeLuxe. *sd:* RCA. 6 min. • A termite assists the Ant in holding the Aardvark at bay.

5557. Rough on Rats *(Aesop's Fable)* 14 July 1933; *p.c.:* Van Beuren for RKO; *dir:* Harry Bailey; *mus:* Genne Rodemich; b&w. *sd:* RCA. 7 min. • Three kittens are having fun in a grocery store when a large rat kidnaps one, tying him to the bacon slicer. His brothers come to the rescue, pelting the rat with produce.

5558. Rough Riding Hood *(Woody Woodpecker)* Jan. 1966; *p.c.:* Walter Lantz prods for Univ; *dir:* Sid Marcus; *story:* Cal Howard; *anim:* Ray Abrams, Art Davis; *sets:* Ray Huffine, Art Landy; *voices:* Daws Butler, Grace Stafford; *mus:* Clarence Wheeler; *prod mgr:* William E. Garity; *col:* Tech. *sd:* RCA. 6 min. • Woody replaces Little Red Riding Hood, giving the Wolf a rough ride.

5559. Roughly Squeeking *(Looney Tunes)* 23 Nov. 1946; *p.c.:* WB; *dir:* Charles M. Jones; *story:* Michael Maltese, Tedd Pierce; *anim:* Ben Washam, Ken Harris, Basil Davidovich, Lloyd Vaughan; *sets:* Robert Gribbroek; *ed:* Treg Brown; *voices:* Mel Blanc, Dick Nelson; *mus:* Carl Stalling; *prod mgr:* John W. Burton; *prod:* Edward Selzer; *col:* Tech. *sd:* Vit. 7 min. • Hubie and Bertie, the two mice, convince a neurotic cat that he is a lion.

5560. Round Trip to Mars *(Woody Woodpecker)* 23 Sept. 1957; *p.c.:* Walter Lantz prods for Univ; *dir:* Paul J. Smith; *story:* Dalton Sandifer; *anim:* Les Kline, Robert Bentley; *sets:* Art Landy; *voices:* Dal McKennon, Grace Stafford; *mus:* Clarence Wheeler; *prod mgr:* William E. Garity; *col:* Tech. *sd:* RCA. 6 min. • Woody is sent to Mars to retrieve Professor Dingledome who has been stranded there.

5561. Rover's Rescue *(Terry-Toon)* 28 June 1940; *p.c.:* TT for Fox; *dir:* Volney White; *story:* John Foster; *mus:* Philip A. Scheib; b&w. *sd:* RCA. 7 min. • Rover tries to befriend a cat he saves from drowning but the cat doesn't get the idea.

5562. Rover's Rival *(Looney Tunes)* 9 Oct. 1937; *p.c.:* Leon Schlesinger prods for WB; *dir/story:* Robert Clampett; *anim:* Charles Jones; *sets:* Elmer Plummer; *ed:* Tregoweth E. Brown; *voices:* Mel Blanc, Robert C. Bruce; *mus:* Carl W. Stalling; *prod sup:* Henry Binder, Raymond G. Katz; b&w. *sd:* Vit. 7 min. • Porky's decrepit dog, Rover, is confronted by a younger replacement who can do tricks, but Rover proves his mettle when a lighted stick of dynamite is retrieved instead of a stick.

5563. Row, Row, Row *(Screen Songs)* 20 Dec. 1930; *p.c.:* The Fleischer Studio for Para; *prod:* Max Fleischer; *dir:* Dave Fleischer; *anim:* Seymour Kneitel, Rudolph Eggeman; *mus:* Art Turkisher; b&w. *sd:* WE. 7 min. • A tough character visits a bar where he does an Apache-style dance with a girl. The arrival of his kids spoils the atmosphere and he escapes from the girl by jumping in a rowboat and rowing off.

5564. Royal Cat-Nap *(Tom & Jerry)* 7 Mar. 1958; *p.c.:* MGM; *prod/dir:* William Hanna, Joseph Barbera; *anim:* Carlo Vinci, Lewis Marshall, Kenneth Muse; *lay:* Dick Bickenbach; *back:* Robert Gentle; *ed:* Jim Faris; *voice:* Francoise Brun-Cottan; *mus:* Scott Bradley; *ph:* Jack Stevens; *prod mgr:* Hal Elias; *col:* Tech. *sd:* WE. 7 min. CS. • Musketeer Tom has the task of guarding the King while he sleeps. The Mouseketeers appear on the scene and do their best to awaken him.

5565. The Royal Four-Flusher *(Popeye)* 12 Sept. 1947; *p.c.:* Famous for Para; *dir:* Seymour Kneitel; *story:* Joe Stultz, Carl Meyer; *anim:* Frank Endres, Tom Johnson, Els Barthen *sets:* Tom Ford; *voices:* Jack Mercer, Jackson Beck, Mae Questel; *mus:* Winston Sharples; *ph:* Leonard McCormick; *prod mgr:* Sam Buchwald; *col:* Tech. *sd:* RCA. 6½ min. • While feeding squirrels in the park, Popeye falls afoul of Count Marvo the Magic King, who whisks Olive away to his penthouse apartment.

5566. A Royal Good Time *(Little King)* 13 Apr. 1934; *p.c.:* Van Beuren for RKO; *dir:* George Stallings; *anim:* Jim Tyer; *mus:* Gene Rodemich; b&w. *sd:* RCA. 6 min. • The Little King visits the Fun Fair.

5567. Rube Goldberg *(cartoons) p.c.:* Barré Studio for Pathé; *prod/dir:* Raoul Barré; *anim:* Raoul Barré, Gregory la Cava, William C. Nolan, George Stallings; b&w. *sil.* • *1916:* The Boob Weekly 8 May. **Leap Year** 22 May. **The Fatal Pie** 5 June. **From Kitchen Mechanic to Movie Star** 19 June. **Nutty News** 3 July. **Home Sweet Home** 17 July. **Losing Weight** 31 July • Series featuring the works of cartoonist Rube Goldberg whose way-out inventions became a part of the American language.

5568. The Ruby Eye of the Monkey God Jan. 1969; (© 1967); *p.c.:* TT for Fox; *ex prod:* Bill Weiss; *dir:* Fred Calvert; *anim:* Jerry Hathcock; *lay:* Iwao Takamoto; *mus:* Jim Timmens; *col:* DeLuxe. *sd:* RCA. 6 min. • The Ruby Eye of stone god in the depths of the jungle has been stolen and it's up to the young prince and his jungle friends to retrieve it.

5569. The Rude Intruder *(Chilly Willy)* 1971; *p.c.:* Walter Lantz prods for Univ; *dir:* Paul J. Smith; *story:* Sid Marcus; *anim:* Volus Jones, Al Coe, Tom Byrne, Joe Voght; *sets:* Nino Carbe; *voice:* Daws Butler; *mus:* Walter Greene; *prod mgr:* William E. Garity; *col:* Tech. *sd:* RCA. 6 min. • Chilly and his polar bear friend, Maxie, defend their Arctic home against intruders drilling for oil.

5570. Rudolph the Red Nosed Reindeer 1948; *p.c.:* The Jam Handy Organization for Montgomery Ward & Co Inc.; *dir:* Max Fleischer; *story:* Robert L. May; *story adapt:* Joseph Stultz; *anim:* Fletcher Smith, William Sturm, Robinson McKee, Howard Kakudo; *sets:* Shane Miller; *voice:* Paul Wing; *mus:* Samuel Benavie; *arr:* James Higgins; *song:* Johnny Marks; *choral arr:* Harry R. Wilson; *theme:* George Kleinsinger; *ph:* Charles Schettler; *col:* Tech. *sd.* 8 min. • All of Santa's reindeer mock Rudolph's shiny red nose but it comes in handy one foggy Christmas Eve when Santa needs a light to guide his sleigh. A one-off departure from commercials for Jam Handy.

5571. Rudy Vallee Melodies *(Screen Songs)* 5 Aug. 1932; *p.c.:* The Fleischer Studio for Para; *prod:* Max Fleischer; *dir:* Dave Fleischer; *mus:* Art Turkisher; *l/a:* Rudy Vallee; b&w. *sd:* WE. 10 min. *l/a/anim.* • While Rudy sings, Betty stages a party for her animal friends. Bunny plays the piano by ear while the others have a sing-song.

5572. Rugged Bear *(Donald Duck)* 23 Oct. 1953; *p.c.:* Walt Disney prods for RKO; *dir:* Jack Hannah; *story:* Al Bertino, Dave DeTiege; *anim:* Bob Carlson, George Kreisl, Volus Jones, Al Coe; *fx:* Dan MacManus; *lay:* Yale Gracey; *back:* Ray Huffine; *voices:* Art Gilmore, Clarence Nash, Jack Mather, James MacDonald, Jack Hannah; *mus:* Oliver Wallace; *col:* Tech. *sd:* RCA. 6 min. *Academy Award nomination.* • Once hunting season begins, Humphrey the bear seeks refuge in a cabin that turns out to be Donald's hunting lodge. Upon Donald's arrival, Humphrey panics and assumes the place of a bearskin rug ... something he lives to regret.

5573. The Rugrats Movie 20 Nov. 1998; *p.c.:* Klasky/Csupo for Para/Nickelodeon Movies; *dir:* Norton Virgien, Igor Kovalyov; *prod:* Arlene Klasky, Gabor Csupo; "Rugrats" created by Arlene Klasky, Gabor Csupo, Paul Germain; *story:* David N. Weiss, J. David Stem; *ex prod:* Albie Hacht, Debby Beece; *co-prod:* Hal Waite, Eryk Casemiro, Julia Pistor; *ex in charge of prod:* Tracy Kramer, Terry Thoren; *sup prod co-ord:* Ramsey Ann Naito, K. Patrick Stapleton; *prod co-ord:* Krista N. Albitz, Maria Guerra, Andy Haug, Ed Johnson, Robin Kay, Penelope Parr Thornton; *prod mgr:* Sean Lurie, (Digital) Jerry Mills; *seq dir:* Zhenia Delioussine, Paul Demeyer, Raymie Muzquiz, Peter Shin, Andrei Svislotsky, Toni Vian, Vitaly Shafirov; *character des:* Arlene Klasky, Gabor Csupo, Peter Chung, Steve Fellner, Konstantin Valov; *Baby Dill Reptar Wagon des:* Igor Kovalyov; *anim timing:*

Raymie Muzquiz, Debbie Baber, Ray Claffey, Phil Cummings, Jaime Diaz, Neal Warner, Richard Kim; *technical dir:* Steven A. Mills, Celine Parker, Mike Giles, Alexandra Goedrich, Robert King, Dan Larsen, Kurt Reinholtz, Denise Wogatzke; *cgi conceptual des:* Dale Herigstad; *cgi anim:* Dot the i Prods, Alisa L. Klein, Mark Levitz, Jim Ovelman, Joe Tseung; *digital scanners:* Tom Bonzon, Devala Marshall; *overseas anim sup:* Annie Elvin; *anim prod:* Grimsaem Animation Co., Ltd., Seoul, Korea: (ex prod) Kang Han-Young, (sup dir) Park Jong-Chul, (managing dir) Kim Joo-Suk, (dir) Lee Sung-Woo, Lee Choon-Young, Baek Dong-Yuel, (prod mgr) An Jae-Ho, (prod co-ord) Kim Byeung-Gon, (anim) Kim Jae-Woung, Kwon Hyuk-Jae, Lee See-Chang, Chun Young-Hwan, Yang Sun-Jin, Shim Sang-Sul, Im Kyeung-Man, Lee Byeung-Kwan, Min Kyung-Suk, Kim Kyung-Yoen, Lee Gi-Dong, Jung Kyung-Sup, Kang Won-Ghu, Kim Jae-Jung, Yang Jin-Chul, Cho Seung-Ki, (model check) Jo Su-Mi, Song Jung-Hwa, Im Yeo-Hee, Kim Mung-Wha, Han Yeung-Ok, Kim Gi-Ran, (final check) Kim Seug-Kuk, Kim Koung-Ho, Won Dan-Ae, (line test) Kim Jong-Tae; *art dir:* Dima Malanitchev; *Anim/Digital Prod Services: Sunwoo Entertainment, LA:* prod ex: Jay E. Moh; *prod co-ord:* Diane Oh; *addit anim prod in USA: Class-Key Chew-Po Commercials:* ex prod: Elizabeth Seidman, John Andrews; *anim:* Bonita Versh, Rebecca Bristow, Eduardo Olivares, Tom Decker; *fx anim des:* Dexter Reed; *workbook dir:* Mark Marren, Steve Loter, Wes Smith; *check:* Diane Matranga, Sean Dempsey, Karen Hansen, Glenn Higa, Lin-Z Rogers, Carol Yao; *character lay:* Andrei Svislotsky, Erben Detablin, Ernie Elicanal, Gerard "Gerry" T. Galang, Freddie Fernandez, Ray Indolos, Mike Kim, Eric Lara, Lee Young Soo, Juanito "Tom" Madrid Jr., Dan O'Sullivan, Benjie Pabulos, Jessie Romero, Shu Kang Lin; *back lay:* Mark Marren, Panagiotis Rappas, Young Baek, William Roger B. Bon, Marco Cinello, Delmindo Datuin, Bismark "Butch" Datuin, Paul Gil, Fides Gutierrez, Bela Kerek, Lee Ki Suk, Willie Martinez, Larry Miravalles, Renato "Joey" Otacan, Leo Quintua, Ryu Jae Heung, Amado Sangalang, Poe Tan, John Tee; *overseas lay sup:* Simon Ward-Horner; *addit lay:* London Stardust Pictures; *prod mgr:* Gayle Martin; *lay:* Panagiotis Rappas, Brendan Houghton, Alan Kerswell, Neal Petty, Mark Broecking, Lee Taylor; *posing:* Darren Vandenberg, Dave McFall, Katerina Manolessou, Katerina Kremasoti, Hara Cfryi; *computer storyboards:* Martyn Jones, Chris Haralambous; *ex prod:* Alfonso Weinlein, Thad Weinlein; *back des:* ;Alex Diltz, Brian Rich; *addit des:* Louie Del Carmen, Gene Kornyshev, Laslo Nosek, Sergey Shramkovski, Jeffrey Varab, Sharon Ross, Steve Small, Todd Waterman; *digital back paint:* Olga Andreyeva, Gene Kornyshev, Micky Rose; *digital paint:* Sam Ades, Mike Giles, Shawn Ahn Lee, Devala Marshall, Fabio Novias; *ed:* Kimberly Rettberg, (pre-prod) Peter Tomaszewicz; *storyboard art:* Peter Avanzino, Peter Chung, Sam Cornell, Vitaly Shafirov, Gyula Szabo, Robert Taylor, Toni Vian, Zhu Kang Lin, Marco Cinello, Alex Diltz, Charles Klein, Jeff McGrath, Shawn Murphy, Mark Risley, Monika Tomova, Bonita Versh, Rossen Varbanov, Barry Vodos, Dave Williams; *ed:* John Bryant, Scott Curtis, Christopher Flick; *digital paint:* Sunwoo Digital International: (technical dir) Park Sang-Wook, (scanners) Oh Yeon-Suk, Oh Jeong-Hyun, Lee Yong-Jin, Choi Inn-Za, Sin Cha-Ho, (painters) Jang Woo-Sin, Im Ja-Eun, Kim Yeon-Jung, Kim Seoung-Hwan, Park Kyung-Hee, Jung Woo-Sung, Lim Sang-Hyung, Shin Young-Ah, Shon Jung-Young; *voices: Tommy Pickles:* E.G. Daily; *Chuckie Finster:* Christine Cavanaugh; *Philip/Lillian & Betty Deville:* Kath Soucie; *Didi Pickles:* Melanie Chartoff; *Howard Deville/Igor:* Philip Proctor; *Susie Carmichael:* Cree Summer; *Woman Guest:* Mary Gross; *Male Guest:* Kevin McBride; *Aunt Miriam:* Andrea Martin; *Chas Finster, Grandpa Boris/Drew Pickles:* Michael Bell; *Charlotte Pickles:* Tress MacNeille; *Stu Pickles:* Jack Riley; *Reptar Wagon:* Busta Rhymes; *Grandpa Lou Pickles:* Joe Alaskey; *Angelica Pickles:* Cheryl Chase; *Dr. Lipshitz:* Tony Jay; *Nurse:* Edie McClurg; *Dr. Lucy Carmichael:* Hattie Winston; *Newborn babies:* Laurie Anderson, Beck, B. Real, Jakob Dylan, Phife, Gordon Gano, Iggy Pop, Lenny Kravitz, Lisa Loeb, Lou Rawls, Patti Smith, Dawn Robinson, Fred Schneider, Kate Pierson, Cindy Wilson of the B-52's; *Dylan Pickles:* Tara Charendoff; *Circus TV Announcer:* Gregg Berger; *United Express Driver:* Charlie Adler; *Air Crewman:* Roger Clinton; *Lieutenant Klavin:* Margaret Cho; *Serge:* Abe Benrubi; *Reporters:* Steve Zirnkilton, Robin Groth, Angel Harper; *Rex Pester:* Tim Curry; *Ranger Margaret:* Whoopi Goldberg; *Ranger Frank:* David Spade; *Monkey vocals:* Bob Dunn Animals, Mark Watters Animal Rentals; *mus:* Mark Mothersbaugh, Jamshied Sharifi; performed by the London Metropolitan Orchestra; *conductors:* Allan Wilson, Jamshied Sharifi, (leader) Tom Bowes; *orch:* Bruce Fowler, John Bell, Walter Fowler, Christopher Guardino,

Vladimir Horunzhy, Ladd McIntosh, Yvonne Moriarty, Carlos Rodriguez, Miyuki Sakamoto, Steven Scott Smalley; *mus sup:* Karyn Rachtman; *music prod: sup:* Graham Walker; *co-ord:* Liz Schrek; *mus ed:* Michael Baber, Jennifer (Jiffy) Blank, Kim Naves; *mus score rec:* Mike Ross-Trevor; *mus score mix:* Shawn Murphy; "Rugrats Theme": Mark Mothersbaugh; "Raider's March": John Williams; *songs:* "All Day" by and performed by Lisa Loeb; "A Baby is a Gift From Bob"/"This World is Something New to Me"/"Dull-a-by": Mark Mothersbaugh; "Take the Train" by and performed by Danny Saber, Rakim; "On Your Marks, Get Set, Ready, Go!": Trevor Smith; performed by Busta Rhymes; "One Way or Another": Debbie Harry, Nigel Harrison; performed by Blondie; *additional lyric:* Eryk Casemiro; performed by Cheryl Chase; "Wild Ride": Kevin Krakower, Mario Caldato Jr., Lisa Stone; performed by Kevi from 1000 Clowns featuring Lisa Stone; "Yo Ho Ho and a Bottle of Yum!"/"Dil-a-Bye": Mark Mothersbaugh; "Witch Doctor": Ross Bagdasarian; performed by Devo; "Also Sprach Zarathustra": Richard Strauss; "Take me There": Teddy Riley, Tamara Savage, Madeline Nelson, Mason Betha, Michael Foster; performed by Blackstreet and MYA; "I Throw My Toys Around": Elvis Costello, Cait O'Riordan; performed by No Doubt featuring Elvis Costello; *dial rec:* Kurt Vanzo, Peter Carlstedt; *re-rec mix:* Steve Pederson, Gary Alexander, Tom Perry; *sd ed:* Kurt Vanzo, Beth Sterner, David Cohen, Chris Welch; *dial ed:* Jeremy Pitts, Clare Freeman, Jeff Payne, Mike Myles, Michelle Rochester; *sd fx:* David Eccles, Rick Arbuckle, Daniel Ben-Shimon, Daniel Cubert, Robert Duran, Robert Hache Derek Pipert, Derek Vanderhorst; *ADR mix:* Bob Baron; *foley:* Sarah Monat, Robin Harlan, Randy K. Singer; *ex consultant:* Paul Germain; *col:* DeLuxe. *sd:* Dolby stereo/Digital dts sound. 80 min. • The kids have an adventure in the woods when they all pile in to an automated "Reptar Wagon."

5574. Ruling the Rooster (*Life Cartoon Comedy*) 27 Mar. 1927; *p.c.:* Sherwood Wadsworth Pictures for Educational; *prod/dir:* John R. McCrory; b&w. sil. 6 min. • A prize egg-laying contest between Kid Quack and Red Leghorn at the Gardens. The contest ends with the losing hen's husband flirting with the winner and being soundly trounced for his pains by his irate spouse.

5575. Run, Sheep, Run (*Happy Harmonies*) 14 Dec. 1935; *p.c.:* MGM; *prod/dir:* Hugh Harman, Rudolf Ising; *mus:* Scott Bradley; *col:* Tech. *sd:* RCA. 10 min. • Of the five sheep, one is constantly crying "Wolf!" to scare the shepherd and his dog. After many false alarms, the sheep are chased by a bear who turns out to be the sheepdog in disguise.

5576. The Runaway (*Out of the Inkwell*) 25 June 1924; *p.c.:* Inkwell Studio for Red Seal; *anim/l/a:* Max Fleischer; *dir:* Dave Fleischer; b&w. sil. 6 min. l/a/anim. • Rebelling to returning to his inkwell, Ko-Ko jumps through a hole in the floor, finding himself in Hades. He is turned into a devil and chased back into his inkwell by demons. Max demonstrates the art of animation by shuffling a stack of drawings of the little clown.

5577. The Runaway Balloon (*Aesop's Film Fable*) 20 June 1925; *p.c.:* Fables Pictures Inc for Pathé; *dir:* Paul Terry; b&w. sil. 10 min. • A gas bag breaks its mooring. Farmer Al is caught by its anchor and deposited in Iceland, warding off approaching polar bears by tuning his radio in to jazz music.

5578. Runaway Blackie (*Cubby Bear*) 7 Apr. 1933; *p.c.:* Van Beuren for RKO; *dir:* Harry D. Bailey; *mus:* Gene Rodemich; b&w. sd: RCA. 7 min. • Cubby runs away and lands himself on a chain-gang. He breaks away, is chased by hounds but awakes to find it was all a dream.

5579. The Runaway Brain 11 Aug. 1995; *p.c.:* Walt Disney; *dir:* Chris Bailey; *prod:* Ron Tippe; *ex prod:* Pam Coats; *asso prod:* Allison Abbate; *scr:* Tim Hauser; *storyboard:* Todd Kurosawa, Don Dougherty, James Fujii, Kirk Hanson, Barry Johnson, Chris Sanders; *anim:* Andreas Deja, Bolhem Bouchiba, Chris Bradley, Sylvain Deboissy, Patrick Delage, Marc Eoche-Duval, Uli Meyer, Dominique Monfery, Sergio Pablos, Catherine Poulain, Stéphane Sainte-Foi, Yoshimichi Tamura, Gary Dunn, Neil Bushnell, Michael Cedeno, James Lopez; *fx:* David A. Bossert, Ahmed Aksas, Sean Applegate, Claude Bony, Kristine Brown, Kimberly Burk, Thierry Chaffoin, Dan Chaika, James DeValera Mansfield, Ty Elliott, John Fargnoli, Colbert Fennelly, James Goss, Bruce Heller, Ray Hofstedt, Elizabeth Holmes, Jeff Howard, John Huey, Tom Hush, Ted Kierscey, Cynthia Neill-Knizek, Rosanna Lyons, David "Joey" Mildenberger, Stephen B. Moore, Kathleen Quaife-Hodge, Lisa Reinert, Serge Verny, Phillip Vigil, Karel Zilliacus; *fx* *sup (Paris):* Jeff Topping; *fx tech dir:* Kevin Paul Sheedy; *airbrush art:* John Emerson; *computer anim:* Tina Price; *inbet:* Jean-Luc Ballester, Javier Espinosa Bañuelos, Eric Delbecq, Thierry Goulard, Matias Marcos, Wes Sullivan; *clean-up:* Dan Tanaka, Laurence Adam-Bessière, Marco Allard, Kathleen M. Bailey, Franck Bonay, Claire Bourdin, Serge Bussone, Christophe Charbonnel, Inna Chon, Merry Kanawyer Clingen, Margie Daniels, Philippe Ferin, Thierry Ferrachat, Gail Frank, Maria Angela Iturriza Freire, Pierre Girault, Carolyn Froblom Gliona, Gizella Gregán, Carl Hall, Mike Hazy, Emily Jiuliano, Nicholas Keramidas, Jody Kooistra, Christine Landés-Tigano, Veronique Langdon, Ludovic Letrun, Daniel Yoontaek Lim, Philippe Malka, Miriam McDonnell, Benoit Meurzec, Florence Montceau, Wendy Muir, Yoon Sook Nam, Eric Pigors, Richard Rocha, Marivi Rodriguez, Celinda Schiefelbein, Natasha Selfridge, Pierre Seurin, Chris Sonnenburg, Phirum Sou, Juliet Stroud Duncan, Pierre Sucaud, Sylvaine Terriou, Marianne Tucker, Kristoff Vergne, Xavier Villez, Stephan Zupkas; *registration:* Karan J. Lee-Storr; *scanning pre-check:* Karen China, Lynnette E. Cullen, Michael D. Lusby; *art dir:* Ian Gooding; *lay:* James Beihold, Olivier Adam, James P. Alles, Peter J. De Luca, Marec Fritzinger, Juanjo Guarnido, Cynthia Ignacio, Zoltan Maros, Vincent Massy de la Chesneraye, Jean-Luc Serrano, Tanya T. Wilson; *back:* Olivier Besson, Dan Cooper, Jean-Paul Fernandez, David McCamley, Patricia Millereau-Guilmard, Joaquim Royo Morales, Pierre Pavloff, Dan Read, Christophe Vacher, Thomas Woodington, *col models:* Irma Cartaya-Torre, Penny Coulter, Cindy Finn, Barbara Lynn Hamane, Debra Jorgensborg, Beth Ann McCoy-Gee, Debra Y. Siegel, Ann Sorensen, David J. Zywicki; *i&p:* Gretchen Maschmeyer Albrecht, Chris Hecox; *paint:* Phyllis Bird, Russell Blandino, Joey Calderon, Ofra Afouta Calderon, Hortensia Casagran, Florida D'Ambrosio, Phyllis Estelle Fields, Paulino Garcia, David Karp, Angelika Katz, Harlene Mears, Karen Lynne Nugent, Bruce Phillipson, Carmen Sanderson, Grace Shirado, Fumiko R. Sommer, S. Ann Sullivan, Roxanne M. Taylor, Britt Van der Nagel, Irma Velez, Susan Wileman, *paint mark-up:* Leyla del C. Amaro-Pelaez, Sherrie Cuzzort, Maria Gonzalez, Leslie Hinton, Myrian Ferron Tello, *blue sketch:* Valerie Braun, *artistic co-ord:* David A. Bossert; *visual development:* Roger Chiasson, Stephen DeStephano, John Loter; *scene plan:* Annamarie Costa, Sara Bleick, John Cunningham, Cynthia Goode, Mark Henley, Ronald Jackson, Ann Tucker, *compositing:* Shannon Michael Fallis-Kane, Joseph Pfening, Dolores Pope, James "J.R" Russell; *anim check (LA):* Janet Bruce, Karen Hepburn, Janette Hulett, Monica Marroquin, Teri N. McDonald, Denise M. Mitchell, Albert Francis Moore, Victoria Novak, Karen S. Paat, Saskia Raevouri, Gary Shafer, Mavis Shafer, Barbara Wiles; *anim check (Florida):* Laurie Sacks; *ed:* Nancy Frazen; *voices: Mickey Mouse:* Wayne Allwine; *Minnie Mouse:* Russi Taylor; *Dr. Frankenollie:* Kelsey Grammer; *Julius:* Jim Cummings; *Pluto:* Bill Farmer; *mus:* John Debney; *anim ph:* John Aardal, François Desnus, Mary Lescher; *digitizing ph:* Robyn Roberts, David Braden, Jason Buske, Val D'Arcy, Gareth Fishbaugh, Corey Dean Fredrickson, Michael A. McFerren, Barbara J. Poirier, David J. Rowe, Andrew Simmons, Gary W. Smith; *dubbing rec:* Jeanette Browning; *sd ed:* Mark A. Mangini, Steve Lee; *sd re-rec mix:* Mel Metcalfe, Terry Porter, Dean A. Zupancic; *PDL:* Judy Nord; *ADR sup:* Curt Schulkey; *CAPS sup (Florida):* Fran Kirsten; *asst prod mgr/anim check:* Karenna Mazur Alderton; *asst prod mgr (Florida):* Jeanie Lynd Sorenson; *asst prod mgr/ed:* Adrianne Sutner; *prod sup:* Susan Blanchard, Tamara Boutcher; *asst prod mgr/color models:* Holly E. Bratton; *prod mgr:* Dana Axelrod, Aaron Pichel, Chris Chase, Kevin Wade; *asst prod mgr/lay & back:* Christian Schmidt; *post-prod mgr:* Deborah Edell Underwood, Sara Duran; *asst prod mgr/CAPS/retakes:* Shawne Zarubica; *pre-prod mgr:* Loren Smith; *col:* Tech. *sd:* Dolby stereo. 7 min. *Academy Award nomination.* • A mad scientist swaps Mickey's brain with that of a monster. Mickey, with the monster's brain, relentlessly pursues Minnie Mouse while the monster with Mickey's brain attempts to save her.

5580. The Runaway Mouse (*Little Roquefort*) Jan. 1954; *p.c.:* TT for Fox; *dir/anim:* Mannie Davis; *story/voice:* Tom Morrison; *mus:* Philip A. Scheib; *ph:* Douglas Moye; *col:* Tech. *sd:* RCA. 6 min. • After Percy Puss has tormented Roquefort beyond redemption, the rodent leaves home and arrives at a zoo where he befriends a squirrel.

5581. Runnin' Wild (*Aesop's Film Fable*) 6 Apr. 1924; *p.c.:* Fables Pictures Inc for Pathé; *dir:* Paul Terry; b&w. sil. 5 min. • A dog catcher pursues a dog who in turn chases a cat who is after a bird that has his eye on a tasty worm.

5582. The Runt (*Aesop's Film Fable*) 6 June 1925; *p.c.:* Fables Pictures Inc for Pathé; *dir:* Paul Terry; b&w. sil. 10 min. • A little black pig who gets nosed out of his breakfast by his bigger brothers becomes a hero by rescuing them from the slaughter house.

5583. Rupert the Runt (*Terry-Toon*) 12 July 1940; *p.c.:* TT for Fox; *dir:* Mannie Davis; *story:* John Foster; *mus:* Philip A. Scheib; b&w. *sd:* RCA. 7 min. • The farm animals bullied the little pig until he became a football hero.

5584. A Rural Romance (*Aesop's Film Fable*) 17 Feb. 1924; *p.c.:* Fables Pictures Inc for Pathé; *dir:* Paul Terry; b&w. sil. 5 min. • A rube mouse's romance is threatened by the activities of the cat.

5585. Rushing Roulette (*Merrie Melodies*) 31 July 1965; *p.c.:* DFE for WB; *dir:* Robert McKimson; *story:* David DeTiege; *anim:* Bob Matz, Manuel Perez, Warren Batchelder, Norm McCabe, Don Williams; *lay:* Dick Ung; *back:* Tom O'Loughlin; *ed:* Lee Gunther; *mus:* Bill Lava; *col:* Tech. *sd:* Vit. 6 min. • The Coyote's pursuit of the Road-Runner continues with him producing a giant magnifying glass to cook his prey in the sun. He also has a battle with a boulder.

5586. Russian Dressing (*Krazy Kat*) 1 May 1933; *p.c.:* Charles Mintz prods for Colum; *dir:* Ben Harrison, Manny Gould; *anim:* Al Rose, Harry Love, Al Eugster; *mus:* Joe de Nat; *prod mgr:* George Winkler; b&w. *sd:* WE. 6 min. • No story available.

5587. Russian Lullaby (*Screen Songs*) 26 Dec. 1931; *p.c.:* The Fleischer Studio for Para; *prod:* Max Fleischer; *dir:* Dave Fleischer; *anim:* Al Eugster; *voice:* Mae Questel; *mus:* Art Turkisher; *song:* Irving Berlin; *l/a:* Arthur Tracy; b&w. *sd:* WE. 8 min. *l/a/anim.* • A Russian wedding ceremony. Later the Stork delivers a Russian baby.

5588. Russian Rhapsody (*Merrie Melodies*) 20 May 1944; *p.c.:* Leon Schlesinger prods for WB; *dir:* Robert Clampett; *story:* Lou Lilly; *anim:* Rod Scribner, Robert McKimson; *sets:* Michael Sasanoff; *ed:* Treg Brown; *voices:* Mel Blanc, Robert C. Bruce; *singers:* Sherry Allen, Carey W. Burch, Robert Lee Teegarden, Bob Remington; *mus:* Carl W. Stalling; *ph:* John W. Burton; *prod sup:* Henry Binder, Raymond G. Katz; *col:* Tech. *sd:* Vit. 7 min. • Adolf Hitler goes to bomb Russia but his plane gets sabotaged by "The Gremlins from the Kremlin." Excellent wartime propaganda featuring caricatures of the staff as the gremlins: Bob Bentley, Henry Binder, Johnny Burton, Lou Cavette, Bob Clampett, Friz Freleng, Ray Katz, Michael Maltese, Melvin Millar, Mike Sasanoff and Rod Scribner.

5589. Ruthless People 27 June 1986; *p.c.:* Touchstone for Silver Screen Partners II; *title anim:* Sally Cruikshank; *col:* DeLuxe. *sd:* Dolby stereo. 2 min. • Live-action feature comedy about a couple of inept kidnappers. The animated credits illustrate various methods of murder in a humorous fashion.

5590. Sacré Bleu Cross (*Inspector*) 1 Feb. 1967; *p.c.:* Mirisch/Geoffrey/DFE for UA; *dir:* Gerry Chiniquy; *story:* John W. Dunn; *anim:* Bob Matz, Ted Bonnicksen, Manny Perez, Norm McCabe, Art Leonardi, Don Williams; *lay:* Dick Ung; *back:* Tom O'Loughlin; *ed:* Lee Gunther; *voices:* Pat Harrington Jr., Paul Frees; *mus:* Walter Greene; *theme tune:* Henry Mancini; *prod sup:* Harry Love, Bill Orcutt; *col:* DeLuxe. *sd:* RCA. 6 min. • The Mysterious "X" leads the Inspector clear across the world, finally revealing himself as the Force's new PT instructor.

5591. Sad Cat (1965–1968); *p.c.:* TT for Fox; *ex prod:* Bill Weiss; *dir:* Ralph Bakshi, Artie Bartsch; *story sup:* Tom Morrison; *story:* Eli Bauer, Dennis Marks; *anim/lay:* Artie Bartsch, Frank Endres, Joe Grey; *back:* Bob Owen; *ed:* Jack McConnell; *voices:* Bob MacFadden; *mus:* Jim Timmens; *ph:* Joe Rasinski; *sd:* Elliot Grey; *col:* DeLuxe. *sd:* RCA. 6 min. • See: *Abominable Mountaineers; All Teed Off; Don't Spill the Beans; Gadmouse, the Apprentice Good Fairy; Judo Kudos; Loops and Swoops; Scuba Dooba Doo; The Third Musketeer*

5592. The Sad Little Guinea Pigs (*Krazy Kat*) 22 Feb. 1938; *p.c.:* Charles Mintz prods for Colum; *story:* Ben Harrison; *anim:* Manny Gould; *lay:* Clark Watson; *back:* Phil Davis; *mus:* Joe de Nat; *prod mgr:* James Bronis; b&w. *sd:* RCA. 6 min. • A scientist injects three guinea pigs with "Pep," "Swing" and "Jitter" tonic.

5593. Saddle Silly (*Merrie Melodies*) 8 Nov. 1941; *p.c.:* Leon Schlesinger prods for WB; *dir:* Charles M. Jones; *anim:* Philip de Lara; *lay:* John McGrew; *back:* Eugene Fleury; *ed:* Treg Brown; *voices:* Mel Blanc; *mus:* Carl

W. Stalling; *ph:* John W. Burton; *prod sup:* Henry Binder, Raymond G. Katz; *col:* Tech. *sd:* Vit. 7 min. • A Pony Express rider is trying to get the mail through when he runs afoul of Moe Hikan, a lone Indian.

5594. Saddle Soap Opera *(Hoot Kloot)* 16 May 1974; *p.c.:* Mirisch/DFE for UA; *dir:* Gerry Chiniquy; *story:* John W. Dunn; *anim:* Bob Bransford, Norm McCabe, Ken *Mus*e, Bob Matz, Bob Bemiller; *lay:* Dick Ung; *back:* Richard Thomas; *ed:* Bob Gillis; *voices:* Bob Holt, Larry Mann; *mus:* Doug Goodwin; *titles:* Arthur Leonardi; *ph:* John Burton Jr.; *prod mgr:* Lee Gunther; *col:* DeLuxe. *sd:* RCA. 6 min. • Sheriff Kloot is assigned to protect Judge Soy Bean, "The Hanging Judge" against potential assassins.

5595. Saddle-Sore Woody *(Woody Woodpecker)* 7 Apr. 1964; *p.c.:* Walter Lantz prods for Univ; *dir:* Paul J. Smith; *story:* Cal Howard; *anim:* Les Kline, Al Coe; *sets:* Art Landy, Ray Huffine; *voices:* Dal McKennon, Grace Stafford; *mus:* Walter Greene; *prod mgr:* William E. Garity; *col:* Tech. *sd:* RCA. 6 min. • Dirty McNasty steals Woody's horse. When Woody discovers a reward for his capture, he goes about bringing the horse thief in.

5596. Sadie Hawkins Day *(Lil Abner)* 4 May 1944; *p.c.:* Colum; *prod:* Dave Fleischer; *dir:* Bob Wickersham; *story:* Al Geiss; *anim:* Chic Otterstrom, Ben Lloyd; *lay:* Clark Watson; *ed:* Edward Moore; *voice:* Lurene Tuttle; *mus:* Eddie Kilfeather; *ph:* Frank Fisher; *col:* Tech. *sd:* RCA. 8 min. • Daisy Mae is set on making Abner her spouse and it takes Mammy Yokum's wiles to prise him from her clutches.

5597. Safari So Good *(Popeye)* 7 Nov. 1947; *p.c.:* Famous for Para; *dir:* I. Sparber; *story:* Larz Bourne; *anim:* Tom Johnson, Morey Reden; *sets:* Anton Loeb; *voices:* Jack Mercer, Mae Questel; *mus:* Winston Sharples; *ph:* Leonard McCormick; *prod mgr:* Sam Buchwald; *col:* Tech. *sd:* RCA. 7 min. • While journeying through the jungle, Popeye and Olive encounter an Ape-Man who makes off with Olive.

5598. Safety Reels *(We Drivers)* Aug. 1936; *p.c.:* General Motors; *col:* Tech. *sd.* 8 min. *l/a/anim.* • Teaching safety and traffic rules with a cartoon segment at the beginning and end.

5599. Safety Second *(Tom & Jerry)* 1 July 1950; *p.c.:* MGM; *dir:* William Hanna, Joseph Barbera; *anim:* Ray Patterson, Ed Barge, Kenneth *Mus*e, Irven Spence, Al Grandmain; *lay:* Dick Bickenbach; *back:* Robert Gentle; *ed:* Jim Faris; *mus:* Scott Bradley; *ph:* Jack Stevens; *prod:* Fred Quimby; *col:* Tech. *sd:* RCA. 6½ min. • Jerry tries to instill a "Safe and Sane" 4th of July into Nibbles who wants to set off fireworks.

5600. Safety Spin *(Mr. Magoo)* 21 May 1953; *p.c.:* UPA for Colum; *ex prod:* Stephen Bosustow; *dir:* Pete Burness; *story:* Phil Davis, Tedd Pierce; *anim:* Rudy Larriva, Tom McDonald, Phil Monroe; *lay:* Sterling Sturtevant; *back:* Bob McIntosh; *voices:* Jim Backus, Peter Leeds, Colleen Collins; *mus:* Hoyt Curtin; *prod mgr:* Herbert Klynn; *col:* Tech. *sd:* RCA. 6 min. • Magoo takes a hair-raising driving test, culminating in his being rushed to a maternity hospital.

5601. The Saga of Windwagon Smith 16 Mar. 1961; *p.c.:* Walt Disney prods for BV; *dir:* C. August Nichols; *asst dir:* Ed Hansen; *story:* Lance Nolley, C. August Nichols; *anim:* Julius Svendsen, Art Stevens; *fx:* Jack Boyd; *des:* Erni Nordli; *lay:* Homer Jonas, Erni Nordli; *back:* Walt Peregoy; *voices:* Rex Allen, The Sons of the Pioneers, J. Pat O'Malley; *mus:* George Bruns; *song:* C. August Nichols; *col:* Tech. *sd:* RCA. 14 min. • Captain Smith arrives in Kansas town riding a wagon converted into a ship. A wind catches his craft, condemning him to sail the prairie for eternity.

5602. Sagebrush Sadie *(Oswald the Lucky Rabbit)* 2 Apr. 1928; *p.c.:* Winkler for Univ *dir:* Walt Disney; *anim:* Ubbe Iwerks, Hugh Harman, Rollin C. Hamilton; *ph:* Mike Marcus; b&w. sil. 5 min. • Cowboy Oswald rescues Sadie from the villainous advances of Peg Leg Pete.

5603. Sahara Hare *(Looney Tunes)* 26 Mar. 1955; *p.c.:* WB; *dir:* I. Freleng; *story:* Warren Foster; *anim:* Gerry Chiniquy, Ted Bonnicksen, Arthur Davis; *lay:* Hawley Pratt; *back:* Irv Wyner; *ed:* Treg Brown; *voices:* Mel Blanc; *mus:* Milt Franklyn; *prod mgr:* John W. Burton; *prod:* Edward Selzer; *col:* Tech. *sd:* Vit. 7 min. • Misrouted on the way to Palm Beach, Bugs finds himself in the desert where he crosses swords with Riff-Raff Sam, an Arab.

5604. Sailing, Sailing Over the Bounding Main *(Ko-Ko Song Car-tune)* 30 Jan. 1926; *p.c.:* Inkwell Studio for Red Seal; *dir:* Dave Fleischer; *anim/l/a:* Max Fleischer; b&w. sil. 6 min. *l/a/anim.* • While Ko-Ko and his Kwartette sing, a ship is shown sailing over the lyrics. A strong wind blows the ship away and a sailor has a hard time before reaching port.

5605. Sailing Zero *(Swifty & Shorty)* Apr. 1964; *p.c.:* Para Cartoons; *dir:* Seymour Kneitel; *story:* Bill Ballard; *anim:* Martin Taras; *sets:* Anton Loeb; *voices:* Eddie Lawrence; *mus:* Winston Sharples; *ph:* Leonard McCormick; *prod mgr:* Abe Goodman; *col:* Tech. *sd:* RCA. 6 min. • Swifty and Shorty put to sea in a catamaran.

5606. Sailor Mouse *(Car-Tune Comedy)* 7 Nov. 1938; *p.c.:* Walter Lantz prods for Univ; *dir:* Alex Lovy; *story:* Victor McLeod; *anim:* George Grandpré, Frank Tipper; *sets:* Edgar Keichle; *voices:* Margaret Hill, Dave Weber; *mus:* Frank Marsales; *col:* Tech-2. *sd:* WE. 7 min. • Sailor Baby-Face, encouraged by the ship's chief rat, steals the Captain's cheese.

5607. The Sailor's Home *(Paul Terry-Toon)* 12 June 1936; *p.c.:* TT for Educational/Fox; *dir:* Frank Moser, Paul Terry; *mus:* Philip A. Scheib; b&w. *sd:* RCA. 6 min. • A sailor (Farmer Al Falfa) spins a yarn of how he met and married the mermaid tattooed on his chest.

5608. St Moritz Blitz *(Chilly Willy)* 16 May 1961; *p.c.:* Walter Lantz prods for Univ; *dir:* Paul J. Smith; *story:* Homer Brightman; *anim:* Ray Abrams, Les Kline; *sets:* Art Landy, Ray Huffine; *voices:* Daws Butler; *title song sung by* "Wee" Bonnie Baker; *mus:* Clarence Wheeler; *prod mgr:* William E. Garity; *col:* Tech. *sd:* RCA. 6 min. • The manager of an Alpine ski lodge tells Smedley to investigate a number of holes that have appeared on the ice skating rink. They turn out to be the product of Chilly's fishing.

5609. Sally Swing *(Betty Boop)* 14 Oct. 1938; *p.c.:* The Fleischer Studio for Para; *prod:* Max Fleischer; *dir:* Dave Fleischer; *anim:* Willard Bowsky, Gordon Sheehan; *voice:* Margie Hines; *mus:* Sammy Timberg; b&w. *sd:* WE. 7 min. • Betty plays Fairy Godmother to scrub woman Sally, giving her a chance to lead a swing band.

5610. Salmon Loafer *(Chilly Willy)* 28 May 1963; *p.c.:* Walter Lantz prods for Univ; *dir:* Sid Marcus; *story:* Ralph Wright; *anim:* Ray Abrams, Art Davis; *sets:* Ray Huffine, Art Landy; *voices:* Daws Butler; *mus:* Walter Greene; *prod mgr:* William E. Garity; *col:* Tech. *sd:* RCA. 6 min. • Chilly raids a salmon canning factory, guarded by watch dog Smedley.

5611. Salmon Pink *(Pink Panther)* 25 July 1975; *p.c.:* Mirisch/Geoffrey/DFE for UA; *dir:* Gerry Chiniquy; *story:* John W. Dunn; *anim:* Nelson Shinn, Bob Richardson, Bob Matz, John Gibbs; *lay:* Roy Morita; *back:* Richard H. Thomas; *ed:* Rick Steward; *mus:* Walter Greene; *theme tune:* Henry Mancini; *ph:* John Burton Jr.; *prod mgr:* Lee Gunther; *col:* DeLuxe. *sd:* RCA. 6 min. • A friendly fish follows the Panther home from the beach and becomes his pet.

5612. Salmon Yeggs *(Windy & Breezy)* 24 Mar. 1958; *p.c.:* Walter Lantz prods for Univ; *dir:* Paul J. Smith; *story:* Homer Brightman; *anim:* Robert Bentley, Les Kline; *sets:* Art Landy, Raymond Jacobs; *voices:* Daws Butler; *mus:* Clarence Wheeler; *prod mgr:* William E. Garity; *col:* Tech. *sd:* RCA. 6 min. • Windy the bear tries to raid a salmon canning factory guarded by watchman Willoughby.

5613. Salt Water Daffy *(Cartune)* 9 June 1941; *p.c.:* Walter Lantz prods for Univ; *dir:* Alex Lovy; *story:* Ben Hardaway, Lowell Elliot; *anim:* Alex Lovy, Lester Kline; *sets:* Fred Brunish; *voices:* Robert C. Bruce, Mel Blanc; *mus:* Darrell Calker; *prod mgr:* George Hall; *col:* Tech. *sd:* WE. 7 min. • Spot-gags involving the Navy, culminating in some expressive war games.

5614. Salt Water Tabby *(Tom & Jerry)* 12 July 1947; *p.c.:* MGM; *dir:* William Hanna, Joseph Barbera; *anim:* Ed Barge, Michael Lah, Kenneth *Mus*e; *sets:* Robert Gentle; *ed:* Fred MacAlpine; *mus:* Scott Bradley; *ph:* Jack Stevens; *prod:* Fred Quimby; *col:* Tech. *sd:* RCA. 7 min. • Tom's attempts to impress a cute girl kitten at the beach are hampered by Jerry filching their picnic.

5615. Salt Water Taffy *(Paul Terry-Toon)* 30 Nov. 1930; *p.c.:* A-C for Educational/Fox; *dir:* Frank Moser, Paul Terry; *anim:* Arthur Babbitt, Ferdinand Huszti Horvath, Frank Moser, Sarka, Frank Sherman, Hugh Shields, Paul Terry; *mus:* Philip A. Scheib; b&w. *sd:* WE. 6 min. • While the mice bathe at the seashore, a girl mouse is chased by a fish and rescued by Salty McGuire the gob.

5616. Salt Water Tuffy *(The Dogfather)* 20 Mar. 1975; *p.c.:* Mirisch/DFE for UA; *dir:* Art Leonardi; *story:* John Dunn; *anim:* Nelson Shin, Bob Bransford; *ed:* Rick Steward; *lay:* Dick Ung; *back:* Richard H. Thomas; *voices:* Bob Holt; *mus:* Dean Elliott; *col:* DeLuxe. *sd:* RCA. 6 min. • The Dogfather puts out a contract on the cat who won his yacht in a card game.

5617. Salty McGuire *(Terry-Toon)* 8 Jan. 1937; *p.c.:* TT for Educational/Fox; *dir:* Mannie Davis, George Gordon; *mus:* Philip A. Scheib; b&w. *sd:* RCA. 6 min. • Salty's lady love is abducted by pirates. He swims after them and, with help from a whale and a dive-bombing pelican he rescues her.

5618. Saludos Amigos 6 Feb. 1943; *p.c.:* Walt Disney prods for RKO; *prod sup:* Norman Ferguson; *story research:* Ted Sears, William Cottrell, Webb Smith; *story:* Roy Williams, Harry Reeves, Dick Huemer, Joe Grant; *foreign sup:* Jack Cutting; *asso:* Gilberto Souto, Alberto Soria, Edmundo Santos; *des sup:* Mary Blair, Lee Blair, Herb Ryman, Jim Bodrero, Jack Miller; *anim:* Paul Allen, John McManus; *sets:* McLaren Stewart, Al Dempster, Art Riley, Claude Coats, Dick Anthony, Yale Gracey, Merle Cox; *voices:* Fred Shields; *mus dir:* Charles Wolcott; *title song:* lyrics: Ned Washington; *mus:* Charles Wolcott; *sd:* C.O. Slyfield. • *Lake Titicaca dir:* William O. Roberts; *anim:* Bill Justice, Milt Kahl, Milt Neil, Art Palmer; *fx:* Josh Meador; *des:* Lee Blair, Mary Blair, James Bodrero; *lay:* Hugh Hennesy; *back:* Herbert Ryman; *add voice:* Clarence Nash; *mus:* Charles Wolcott. • *Pedro dir:* Hamilton S. Luske; *story* William Cottrell, Ted Sears; *anim:* Vladimir Tytla, Fred Moore, Hamilton S. Luske, Ward Kimball; *fx:* Josh Meador; *lay:* Ken Anderson; *mus:* Paul J. Smith. • *El Gaucho Goofy dir:* Jack Kinney; *story:* Homer Brightman, Ralph Wright; *anim:* Hugh Fraser, Wolfgang Reitherman, John Sibley, Harvey Toombs. *fx:* Andrew Engman; *lay:* Al Zinnen; back inspired by F. Molina Campos; *add voice:* Pinto Colvig, *singer:* Muzzy Marcellino; *mus:* Edward Plumb, Paul J. Smith. • *Aquarela do Brazil; dir:* Wilfred Jackson; *story:* Ted Sears, James Bodrero; *anim:* Fred Moore, Bill Tytla, Les Clark; *fx:* Joshua Meador, Dan MacManus; *des:* Mary Blair; *lay:* McLaren Stewart; *back:* Claude Coats, Al Dempster; *voices:* Aloysio Oliveira, Josè Oliveira, Clarence Nash; *Title song singers:* Henry Kruse, Robert Stevens, Robert Ebright, Richard Davis, Harry Stanton, Allan Watson, Dave Knight, Harry Stafford, Ray Linn; *songs:* Ary Barroso, *Tico Tico No Fubà* by Zequinha de Abreu; *mus dir:* Charles Wolcott; *col:* Tech. *sd:* RCA. 42 min. *l/a/anim.* • A group of artists set out on a good will tour of South America. Their tour is gingered up by segmented cartoon stories to help illustrate traditions and folk lore of each place they visit. • For individual stories, see separate items: *Aquarela do Brazil; El Gaucho Goofy; Lake Titicaca* and *Pedro.*

5619. Sammie Johnsin and His Wonderful Lamp *(Sullivan Cartoon Comedy)* 27 Dec. 1916; *p.c.:* Powers for Univ; *anim:* Pat Sullivan; b&w. *sil.* 5¹/₂ min. • Sammie Johnsin finds a lamp that he rubs and a genie materializes and grants him wishes ... which all lead to trouble! He awakes to find it was all a dream.

5620. Sammie Johnsin at the Seaside *(Sullivan Cartoon Comedy)* 18 Nov. 1916; *p.c.:* Powers for Univ; *anim:* Pat Sullivan; b&w. *sil.* 5¹/₂ min. • No story available.

5621. Sammie Johnsin Gets a Job *(Sullivan Cartoon Comedy)* 3 July 1916; *p.c.:* Powers for Univ; *anim:* Pat Sullivan; b&w. *sil.* 5¹/₂ min. • No story available.

5622. Sammie Johnsin, Hunter *(Sullivan Cartoon Comedy)* 1 June 1916; *p.c.:* Powers for Univ; *anim:* Pat Sullivan; b&w. *sil.* 5¹/₂ min. • Sammie, the little black boy, is sent to chop wood. He promptly falls asleep and dreams that he is a brave hunter on safari.

5623. Sammie Johnsin in Mexico *(Sullivan Cartoon Comedy)* 13 Dec. 1917; *p.c.:* Powers for Univ; *anim:* Pat Sullivan; b&w. *sil.* 5¹/₂ min. • Sammie sees a poster offering a big reward for the capture of a Mexican bandito; He gets blown to Mexico by dynamite and sets out to capture the bandit but catches the President instead.

5624. Sammie Johnsin, Magician *(Sullivan Cartoon Comedy)* 20 June 1916; *p.c.:* Powers for Univ; *anim:* Pat Sullivan; b&w. *sil.* 5¹/₂ min. • No story available.

5625. Sammie Johnsin Minds the Baby *(Sullivan Cartoon Comedy)* 23 Oct. 1916; *p.c.:* Powers for Univ; *anim:* Pat Sullivan; b&w. *sil.* 5¹/₂ min. • No story available.

5626. Sammie Johnsin Slumbers Not *(Sullivan Cartoon Comedy)* 21 Dec. 1916; *p.c.:* Powers for Univ; *anim:* Pat Sullivan, Rudolph Eggeman; b&w. *sil.* 5¹/₂ min. • No story available.

5627. Sammie Johnsin, Strong Man *(Sullivan Cartoon Comedy)* 20 July 1916; *p.c.:* Powers for Univ; *anim:* Pat Sullivan; b&w. *sil.* 5¹/₂ min. • Sammie's chores are sidetracked by a hoarding advertising elixir for strength, which he drinks and becomes strong. All in his dreams, though, and Mammy brings him to his senses.

5628. Sammie Johnsin's Love Affair *(Sullivan Cartoon Comedy)* 24 Nov. 1916; *p.c.:* Powers for Univ; *anim:* Pat Sullivan; b&w. *sil.* 5¹/₂ min. • No story available.

5629. Samson Scrap and Delilah (1959–1962) *p.c.:* Rembrandt Films for Para; *prod:* William L. Snyder; *dir/lay:* Gene Deitch; *story:* Gene Deitch, Allen Swift; *anim:* Zdeněk Smetana, Milan Klikar, Antonín Bureš, Věra Marešová, Mirko Kačena, Bohumil Šejda, Věra Kudrnová, Jindřich Barta, Zdenka Skřípková, Olga Šišková; *back:* Bohumil Šišká; *voices:* Allen Swift; *mus:* Štěpan Koníček; *prod mgr:* Zdenka Deitchová; *col. sd.* • **The Bridge Over Avenue 1, Busted Bus, The X-Bomb** • Samson Scrap is a "Pied Piper" who has a trailer built from scrap and is followed around by hordes of children. Series, one of which was issued as a *Modern Madcap* in March 1962. It is unclear which one but "The Bridge Over Avenue 1" received an Academy Award nomination.

5630. Sandman Tales *(Scrappy)* 6 Oct. 1933; *p.c.:* Charles Mintz prods for Colum; *story:* Sid Marcus; *anim:* Art Davis; *lay:* Clark Watson; *back:* Phil Davis; *mus:* Joe de Nat; *prod mgr:* James Bronis; b&w. *sd:* RCA. 6 min. • Scrappy and Vontzy dream they are flying to Dreamland on a winged horse. The idyllic paradise is spoiled by an ogre who snatches Vontzy and the inhabitants come to his rescue.

5631. Sandy Claws *(Looney Tunes)* 2 Apr. 1955; *p.c.:* WB; *dir:* I. Freleng; *story:* Arthur Davis, Warren Foster; *anim:* Arthur Davis, Manuel Perez, Virgil Ross; *lay:* Hawley Pratt; *back:* Irv Wyner; *ed:* Treg Brown; *voices:* Mel Blanc, Bea Benaderet; *mus:* Milt Franklyn; *prod mgr:* John W. Burton; *prod:* Edward Selzer; *col:* Tech. *sd:* Vit. 7 min. *Academy Award nomination.* • Tweety is stranded on a rock in the sea and Sylvester tries his best to retrieve him.

5632. Santa's Surprise *(Noveltoon)* 5 Dec 1947; *p.c.:* Famous for Para; *dir:* Seymour Kneitel; *story:* Larz Bourne; *anim:* Myron Waldman, Wm. B. Pattengill; *sets:* Robert Little; *voices:* Cecil Roy, Mae Questel, Jack Mercer; *mus:* Winston Sharples; *lyrics:* Buddy Kaye; *ph:* Leonard McCormick; *prod mgr:* Sam Buchwald; *col:* Tech. *sd:* RCA. 9 min. • The world's children stow away with Santa to the North Pole and proceed to clean up his home while he sleeps.

5633. Santa's Workshop *(Silly Symphony)* 10 Dec. 1932; *p.c.:* Walt Disney prods for UA; *dir:* Wilfred Jackson; *anim:* Arthur Babbitt, Les Clark, Chuck Couch, Jack Cutting, Joseph d'Igalo, George Drake, Norman Ferguson, Nick George, Clyde Geronimi, Jack King, Jack Kinney, Edward Love, Richard Lundy, Hamilton S. Luske, Fred Moore, Tom Palmer, Harry Reeves, Louis Schmitt, Ben Sharpsteen, Marvin Woodward; *asst anim:* Paul Fennell; *sets:* Carlos Manriquez; *mus:* Frank E. Churchill; *col:* Tech. *sd:* RCA. 7 min. • Santa and his elves make the toys for Christmas which all march into his sack, ready for delivery.

5634. Saps in Chaps *(Looney Tunes)* 11 Apr. 1942; *p.c.:* Leon Schlesinger prods for WB; *dir:* I. Freleng; *story:* Sgt. Dave Monahan; *anim:* Manuel Perez; *sets:* Don Towsley; *ed:* Treg Brown; *voices:* Robert C. Bruce, Mel Blanc, Billy Bletcher; *mus:* Carl W. Stalling; *ph:* John W. Burton; *prod sup:* Henry Binder, Raymond G. Katz; b&w. *sd:* Vit. 7 min. • Wild Western spot-gags.

5635. Sassy Cats *(Scrappy)* 25 Jan. 1933; *p.c.:* Charles Mintz prods for Colum; *story:* Dick Huemer; *anim:* Sid Marcus, Art Davis; *lay:* Clark Watson; *back:* Phil Davis; *mus:* Joe de Nat; *prod mgr:* George Winkler; b&w. *sd:* RCA. 7 min. • Scrappy goes to deal with nocturnal cat howlings returning to find his house full of felines, forcing him to spend the night sleeping on the backyard fence.

5636. Satan's Waitin' *(Looney Tunes)* 7 Aug. 1954; *p.c.:* WB; *dir:* I. Freleng; *story:* Warren Foster; *anim:* Virgil Ross, Arthur Davis, Manuel Perez, Ken Champin; *lay:* Hawley Pratt; *back:* Irv Wyner; *ed:* Treg Brown; *voices:* Mel Blanc; *mus:* Carl Stalling; *prod mgr:* John W. Burton; *prod:* Edward Selzer; *col:* Tech. *sd:* Vit. 7 min. • After a disastrous accident, Sylvester arrives in Hades, only to discover he has eight lives left. Satan encourages him to continue pursuing Tweety and waits for the rest of his lives to arrive.

5637. Satisfied Customers *(Heckle & Jeckle)* Apr. 1954; *p.c.:* TT for

Fox; *dir:* Connie Rasinski; *story/voices:* Tom Morrison; *anim:* Jim Tyer; *sets:* Art Bartsch; *mus:* Philip A. Scheib; *ph:* Douglas Moye; *col:* Tech. *sd:* RCA. 6 min. • The magpies give a supermarket manager a run for his money when caught shoplifting.

5638. Saturday Evening Puss (*Tom & Jerry*) 12 July 1947; *p.c.:* MGM; *dir:* William Hanna, Joseph Barbera; *anim:* Ed Barge, Kenneth Muse, Irven Spence, Ray Patterson; *lay:* Dick Bickenbach; *back:* Robert Gentle; *ed:* Jim Faris; *voice:* Lillian Randolph; *mus:* Scott Bradley; *ph:* Jack Stevens; *prod:* Fred Quimby; *col:* Tech. *sd:* WE. 6½ min. • Tom and his cronies keep Jerry awake with their nocturnal "jam session."

5639. Saucy Sausages (*Oswald*) 19 Aug. 1929; *p.c.:* Winkler for Univ; *anim:* Ben Clopton; b&w. *sd:* WE. 6 min. • No story available.

5640. Saved by a Keyhole (*Aesop's Film Fable*) 13 Nov. 1927; *p.c.:* Fables Pictures Inc for Pathé; *dir:* Paul Terry; b&w. *sil.* 10 min. • Thomas cat intrudes on the love affair of his stenographer, Stella Mouse, with the janitor Milton Mouse. He kidnaps Stella and Milton comes to her rescue, sending Thomas over the falls to his demise.

5641. Saved by the Bell (*Noveltoon*) 15 Sept. 1950; *p.c.:* Famous for Para; *dir:* Seymour Kneitel; *story:* Larz Bourne; *anim:* Dave Tendlar, Morey Reden; *sets:* Tom Ford; *voices:* Sid Raymond, Arnold Stang; *mus:* Winston Sharples; *ph:* Leonard McCormick; *prod:* Sam Buchwald; *col:* Tech. *sd:* RCA. 7 min. • The mice try to put a bell around Katnip's neck.

5642. The Saw Mill Mystery (*Terry-Toon*) 29 Oct. 1937; *p.c.:* TT for Educational/Fox; *dir:* Connie Rasinski; *mus:* Philip A. Scheib; b&w. *sd:* RCA. 6 min. • Oil Can Harry kidnaps the heroine who is saved in the nick of time by the hero.

5643. The Sawmill Four (*Pen & Ink Vaudeville*) 16 Dec. 1924; *p.c.:* Hurd prods Inc for Educational; *anim:* Earl Hurd; b&w. *sil.* 5½ min. • The show opens with a high-diver, a tomcat juggler and four snoring sleepers being broadcast to entertain suffering humanity.

5644. Say Ah-h! (*Educational-Bowers Comedy*) 19 Feb. 1928. *p.c.:* Bowers Comedy Corp. for Educational; *prod:* Charley Bowers; *dir:* H.L. Muller; *l/a:* Charley Bowers, J. Gordon Russell, Jean Douglas, Eddie Dunn, Buster Brodie, Kewpie Morgan, Raymond Turner; b&w. sil. 2 reels. *l/a/anim.* • Charley is an assistant on an ostrich farm when the ostriches refuse to lay eggs. He feeds them an assortment of clothes and hardware, resulting in the hatching of a mechanical (animated) ostrich.

5645. Say Ah! Jasper (*Madcap Models*) 10 Mar. 1944; *p.c.:* George Pal Studio for Para; *prod/dir:* George Pal; *story:* Siska Ayala; *col:* Tech. *sd:* WE. 8 min. • Jasper dozes off while waiting for his tooth to be pulled by somebody opening the door it is tied to. The scarecrow appears and tells of his former prowess at dentistry.

5646. Say Cheese, Please (*Roland & Rattfink*) 7 June 1970; *p.c.:* Mirisch/Geoffrey/DFE for UA; *dir:* Art Davis; *story:* John W. Dunn; *anim:* Don Williams, Bob Taylor, Ken Muse, Warren Batchelder; *lay:* Dick Ung; *back:* Richard Thomas; *ed:* Lee Gunther; *voices:* Leonard Weinrib; *mus:* Doug Goodwin; *ph:* John Burton Jr.; *prod sup:* Jim Foss, Harry Love; *col:* DeLuxe. *sd:* RCA. 6 min. • Tired with always being cast as "The Villain," Rattfink demands the studio boss give him a nicer role. He is then cast as the hero with Roland as his stand-in.

5647. Scaling the Alps (*Aesop's Film Fable*) 21 Mar. 1928; *p.c.:* Fables Pictures Inc for Pathé; *dir:* Paul Terry, Mannie Davis; b&w. *sil.* 10 min. • No story available.

5648. Scalp Treatment (*Woody Woodpecker*) 18 Sept. 1952; *p.c.:* Walter Lantz prods for Univ; *dir:* Walter Lantz; *anim:* Don Patterson, Ray Abrams, La Verne Harding, Paul Smith; *sets:* Fred Brunish; *voices:* Dick Nelson, Grace Stafford; *mus:* Clarence E. Wheeler; *prod mgr:* William E. Garity; *col:* Tech. *sd:* RCA. 6 min. • Woody and Buzz Buzzard are red Indians vying for the love of Pocahontas, who wants a feathered head-dress.

5649. Scalp Trouble (*Looney Tunes*) 24 June 1939; *p.c.:* Leon Schlesinger prods for WB; *dir:* Robert Clampett; *story:* Ernest Gee; *anim:* Norman McCabe; *sets:* Elmer Plummer; *ed:* Tregoweth E. Brown; *voices:* Mel Blanc; *mus:* Carl W. Stalling; *ph:* John W. Burton; *prod sup:* Henry Binder, Raymond G. Katz; b&w. *sd:* Vit. 7 min. • General Daffy and Pvt Porky defend the fort against an invasion by Indians.

5650. The Scared Crows (*Betty Boop*) 4 June 1939; *p.c.:* The Fleischer Studio for Para; *prod:* Max Fleischer; *dir:* Dave Fleischer; *anim:* David Tendlar, William Sturm; *voices:* Margie Hines; *mus:* Sammy Timberg; b&w. *sd:* Vit. 7 min. • Pudgy protects Betty's crops against pilfering crows. One gets hurt and Pudgy tends to him.

5651. Scaredy Cat (*Merrie Melodies*) 18 Dec. 1948; *p.c.:* WB; *dir:* Charles M. Jones; *story:* Michael Maltese; *anim:* Lloyd Vaughan, Ken Harris, Phil Monroe, Ben Washam; *lay:* Robert Gribbroek; *back:* Peter Alvarado; *ed:* Treg Brown; *voices:* Mel Blanc; *mus:* Carl Stalling; *prod mgr:* John W. Burton; *prod:* Edward Selzer; *col:* Tech. *sd:* Vit. 7 min. • Porky insists on spending the night in an old house with Sylvester. The house is inhabited by mice who are intent on seeing off the intruders.

5652. The Scarlet Pinkernell (*Pink Panther*) 30 Dec. 1975; *p.c.:* Mirisch/Geoffrey/DFE for UA; *dir:* Gerry Chiniquy; *story:* John W. Dunn; *anim:* Nelson Shin, John Gibbs, Bob Richardson, Don Williams; *lay:* Tony Rivera; *back:* Richard H. Thomas; *ed:* Rick Steward; *mus:* Walter Greene; *ph:* John Burton Jr.; *prod mgr:* Lee Gunther; *col:* DeLuxe. *sd:* RCA. 6 min. • The Panther turns avenger to help save dogs from the dog catcher.

5653. The Scarlet Pumpernickel (*Looney Tunes*) 4 Mar. 1950 (© 1948); *p.c.:* WB; *dir:* Charles M. Jones; *story:* Michael Maltese; *anim:* Phil Monroe, Ben Washam, Lloyd Vaughan, Ken Harris; *lay:* Robert Gribbroek; *back:* Peter Alvarado; *ed:* Treg Brown; *voices:* Mel Blanc, Marian Richman; *mus:* Carl Stalling; *prod mgr:* John W. Burton; *prod:* Edward Selzer; *col:* Tech. *sd:* Vit. 7 min. • Daffy tries to sell a screenplay to J.L. Warner of a mysterious avenger (himself) in a period pastiche of every swashbuckling movie ever made.

5654. Scary Crows (*Color Rhapsody*) 20 Aug. 1937; *p.c.:* Charles Mintz prods for Colum; *story:* Sid Marcus; *anim:* Art Davis; *lay:* Clark Watson; *back:* Phil Davis; *voice:* Leone Le Doux; *mus:* Joe de Nat; *prod mgr:* James Bronis; *col:* Tech. *sd:* RCA. 7½ min. • Scrappy has problems with the crows stealing his corn seeds as soon as he plants them.

5655. Scat Cats (*Spike & Tyke*) 26 July 1957; *p.c.:* MGM; *prod/dir:* Joseph Barbera, William Hanna; *story:* Homer Brightman; *anim:* Kenneth Muse, Carlo Vinci, Lewis Marshall; *lay:* Dick Bickenbach; *back:* Robert Gentle; *ed:* Jim Faris; *voices:* Daws Butler; *mus:* Scott Bradley; *ph:* Jack Stevens; *prod mgr:* Hal Elias; *col:* Tech. *sd:* WE. 6½ min. CS. • While Spike and Tyke guard the family home, the house cat tries to sneak his cronies in for a party.

5656. Scenic Sketchographs *p.c.:* Pathé; *anim:* Hy Mayer. • **1926:** **The Family Album** 26 July. **Tripping the Rhine** 26 July. **Nurenberg the Toy City** 26 July. **A Pup's Tale** 26 July • Hy Mayer's pen changes photos into sketches and vice versa.

5657. Scent-Imental Over You (*Merrie Melodies*) 28 Dec. 1946; *p.c.:* WB; *dir:* Charles M. Jones; *story:* Tedd Pierce, Michael Maltese; *anim:* Ben Washam, Ken Harris, Basil Davidovich, Lloyd Vaughan; *lay:* Earl Klein; *back:* Richard Morley; *ed:* Treg Brown; *voices:* Mel Blanc, Bea Benaderet, Tedd Pierce; *mus:* Carl Stalling; *prod mgr:* John W. Burton; *prod:* Edward Selzer; *col:* Tech. *sd:* Vit. 7 min. • A Mexican hairless dons a fur coat to enter a 5th Avenue dog show. Stinky, an amorous continental skunk, pursues her, mistaking her for a female skunk.

5658. Scent-Imental Romeo (*Merrie Melodies*) 24 Mar. 1951; *p.c.:* WB; *dir:* Charles M. Jones; *story:* Michael Maltese; *anim:* Ben Washam, Lloyd Vaughan, Ken Harris, Phil Monroe; *lay:* Robert Gribbroek; *back:* Peter Alvarado; *ed:* Treg Brown; *voices:* Mel Blanc; *mus:* Carl Stalling; *prod mgr:* John W. Burton; *prod:* Edward Selzer; *col:* Tech. *sd:* Vit. 7 min. • A hungry cat disguises herself as a skunk in order to get fed by a zoo but doesn't reckon on the amorous advances of Pepé le Pew.

5659. A Scent of the Matterhorn (*Looney Tunes*) June 1961; *p.c.:* WB; *dir/story:* Chuck Jones; *anim:* Tom Ray, Ken Harris, Richard Thompson, Bob Bransford; *fx:* Harry Love; *lay:* Maurice Noble; *back:* Philip de Guard; *ed:* Treg Brown; *voices:* Mel Blanc; *yodeling:* Adolf "Tony" Hartenstein; *mus:* Milt Franklyn; *prod mgr:* William Orcutt; *prod:* David H. DePatie; *col:* Tech. *sd:* Vit. 7 min. • Pepè le Pew's pursuit of his lady love takes him to the pinnacle of the Matterhorn.

5660. School Birds (*Terry-Toon*) 30 Apr. 1937; *p.c.:* TT for Educational/Fox; *dir:* Mannie Davis, George Gordon; *mus:* Philip A. Scheib; b&w. *sd:* RCA. 6 min. • Birdland's answer to the Marx Brothers torment their owl teacher. Harpo saves them all from a cat.

5661. School Days (*Aesop's Film Fable*) 19 Dec. 1926; *p.c.:* Fables Pictures Inc for Pathé *dir:* Paul Terry; b&w. *sil.* 10 min. • School teacher Al Falfa teaches cats, dogs and pigs. A cop investigates the commotion, ending in a mad chase where one of the animals knocks a hornets' nest down Al's neck. Moral: "Children and soup should be seen and not heard."

5662. School Days (*Flip the Frog*) 14 May 1932; *p.c.:* Celebrity prods for MGM; *prod/dir:* Ub Iwerks; b&w. *sd:* PCP. 6 min. • Flip's dog follows him to school and chases a skunk into the classroom, evacuating all.

5663. School Days (*Screen Songs*) 30 Sept 1932; *p.c.:* The Fleischer Studio for Para; *prod:* Max Fleischer; *dir:* Dave Fleischer; *anim:* William Henning, David Tendlar; *voice:* Mae Questel; *mus:* Art Turkisher; *song:* Gus Edwards, Will V. Cobb; b&w. *sd:* WE. 6 min. *l/a/anim.* • The kids get ready for school and are transported there by various ingenious methods.

5664. School Daze (*Nancy*) 18 Sept. 1942; *p.c.:* TT for Fox; *dir:* Eddie Donnelly; *story:* John Foster; *anim:* I. Klein; *mus:* Philip A. Scheib; *col:* Tech. *sd:* RCA. 7 min. • The school children convince teacher that the "Nancy" comics will help them with their lessons and National Defence better than text books.

5665. Schoolboy Dreams (*Phantasy*) 24 Sept. 1940; *p.c.:* Colum; *story:* Harry Love; *anim:* Allen Rose; *lay:* Clark Watson; *back:* Phil Davis; *ed:* George Winkler; *voice:* Robert Winkler; *mus:* Joe de Nat; *ph:* Otto Reimer; *prod mgr:* James Bronis; b&w. *sd:* RCA. 6 min. • Scrappy dreams dreams his teacher is a beautiful princess whom he rescues from a dragon.

5666. The Schooner the Better (*Phantasy*) 4 July 1946; *p.c.:* Colum; *dir:* Howard Swift; *story:* Cal Howard; *anim:* Grant Simmons, Morey Reden; *lay:* Bill Weaver; *back:* Ed Starr; *ed:* Richard S. Jensen; *voices:* Harry E. Lang; *mus:* Eddie Kilfeather; *ph:* Frank Fisher; *prod mgr:* Hugh McCollum; b&w. *sd:* WE. 6 min. • The Sea Hawk tries to shanghai a duck for a $10.00 fee ... only the tables get turned!

5667. Science Friction (*Ant & Aardvark*) 28 June 1970; *p.c.:* Mirisch/DFE for UA; *dir:* Gerry Chiniquy; *story:* Larz Bourne; *anim:* Warren Batchelder, Robert Taylor, Bob Richardson, John Gibbs, Manny Perez; *lay:* Dick Ung; *back:* Richard H. Thomas; *ed:* Lee Gunther; *voices:* John Byner; *mus:* Doug Goodwin, Pete Candoli, Billy Byers, Jimmy Rowles, Tommy Tedesco, Ray Brown, Shelley Manne; *ph:* John Burton Jr.; *col:* DeLuxe. *sd:* RCA. 6 min. • The Aardvark goes after an ant that is being used in a scientific experiment.

5668. Science Friction (*Woody Woodpecker*) Nov. 1963; *p.c.:* Walter Lantz prods for Univ; *dir:* Sid Marcus; *story:* Cal Howard; *anim:* Ray Abrams, Art Davis; *sets:* Ray Huffine, Art Landy; *voices:* Benny Rubin, Grace Stafford; *mus:* Walter Greene; *prod mgr:* William E. Garity; *col:* Tech. *sd:* RCA. 6 min. • A mad scientist wants to transform Woody's brain with that of an ape's.

5669. Scientific Sideshow (*Mighty Heroes*) June 1969; *p.c.:* TT for Fox; *ex prod:* Bill Weiss; *dir:* Robert Taylor; *col:* DeLuxe. *sd:* RCA. 5 min. • A mad scientist wants to set the heroes up as a sideshow.

5670. Scotch High-Ball (*Paul Terry-Toon*) 16 Nov. 1930; *p.c.:* A-C for Educational/Fox; *dir:* Frank Moser, Paul Terry; *mus:* Philip A. Scheib; b&w. *sd:* WE. 6 min. • Showing horses in training for the big race. A mechanical horse takes part but a nag fitted with springs wins the race.

5671. Scottie Finds a Home (*Rainbow Parade*) 23 Aug. 1935; *p.c.:* Van Beuren for RKO; *dir:* Burt Gillett; *voice:* Arthur Kay; *mus:* Winston Sharples; *col:* Ciné. *sd:* RCA. 7 min. • A kitten befriends a lost pup. Grandma doesn't want the dog but warms to him when he ousts an unwelcome hobo.

5672. Scout Fellow (*Noveltoon*) 21 Dec. 1951; *p.c.:* Famous for Para; *dir:* Seymour Kneitel; *story:* Carl Meyer, Jack Mercer; *anim:* Dave Tendlar, Martin Taras; *sets:* Robert Owen; *voices:* Sid Raymond, Jackson Beck, Cecil Roy, Jack Mercer; *mus:* Winston Sharples; *ph:* Leonard McCormick; *prod mgr:* Seymour Shultz; *col:* Tech. *sd:* RCA. 8 min. • Baby Huey desperately wants to become a boy scout and the fox takes advantage of the situation by posing as a scout master.

5673. A Scout with the Gout (*Little Lulu*) 8 Nov. 1947; *p.c.:* Famous for Para; *dir:* Bill Tytla; *story:* Joe Stultz, Carl Meyer; *anim:* George Germanetti, Tom Golden, Martin Taras, Irving Dressler; *sets:* Anton Loeb; *voices:* Cecil Roy, Jackson Beck; *mus:* Winston Sharples; *title song:* Buddy Kaye, Fred Wise, Sammy Timberg; *ph:* Leonard McCormick; *prod mgr:* Sam Buchwald; *col:* Tech. *sd:* RCA. 7 min. • Daddy takes Lulu camping and rues the day.

5674. Scouting for Trouble (*Jeepers & Creepers*) Sept. 1960; *p.c.:* Para Cartoons; *dir:* Seymour Kneitel; *story:* Carl Meyer, Jack Mercer; *anim:* Nick Tafuri, I. Klein; *sets:* Anton Loeb; *voices:* Jack Mercer; *mus:* Winston Sharples; *ph:* Leonard McCormick; *prod mgr:* Abe Goodman; *col:* Tech. *sd:* RCA. 6 min. • Creepers' nephew, Frisky, wants to go camping but, since he's never been camping before, Creepers has to rely on Jeepers to help him out.

5675. Scoutmaster Magoo (*Mr. Magoo*) 10 Apr. 1958; *p.c.:* UPA for Colum; *ex prod:* Stephen Bosustow; *prod/dir:* Robert Cannon; *story:* Bill Scott; *anim:* C.L. Hartman, Alan Zaslove; *lay:* Lew Keller; *back:* Jules Engel, Ervin L. Kaplan; *voices:* Jim Backus, Daws Butler; *mus:* Dennis Farnon; *col:* Tech. *sd:* RCA. 6½ min. • Magoo agrees to look after a scout troop on a camping exercise. The kids are frightened away by some bear cubs, leaving the myopic old gent to mistake the bears for his scout troop.

5676. Scouts to the Rescue (*Good Deed Daly*) Mar. 1956; *p.c.:* TT for Fox; *dir:* Connie Rasinski; *story:* Tom Morrison; *anim:* Jim Tyer; *voices:* Tom Morrison, Douglas Moye; *mus:* Philip A. Scheib; *ph:* Douglas Moye; *col:* Tech. *sd:* RCA. 6 min. • Chico Pico, the buffalo bandit attempts to steal buffalo from a National Park but is thwarted by a battalion of boy scouts.

5677. Scrambled Aches (*Looney Tunes*) 26 Jan. 1957; *p.c.:* WB; *dir:* Chuck Jones; *story:* Michael Maltese; *anim:* Abe Levitow, Richard Thompson, Ken Harris, Ben Washam; *lay:* Maurice Noble; *back:* Philip de Guard; *ed:* Treg Brown; *voice:* Paul Julian; *mus:* Carl Stalling, Milt Franklyn; *prod mgr:* John W. Burton; *prod:* Edward Selzer; *col:* Tech. *sd:* Vit. 7 min. • The Coyote's persistence to snare the elusive Road-Runner include using roller skates, a giant spring, an Acme Dehydrated Boulder and finally an Acme Junior Size Steam Roller.

5678. Scrambled Eggs (*Aesop's Film Fable*) 22 Aug. 1926; *p.c.* Fables Pictures Inc for Patrhè; *dir:* Paul Terry; b&w. *sil.* 10 min. • Thomas the Cat is the supervisor at an Egg Factory. He deviates to make love, scrambling the works and the Farmer.

5679. Scrambled Eggs (*Peterkin*) 4 Dec. 1939; *p.c.:* Walter Lantz prods for Univ; *dir:* Alex Lovy; *story:* Elaine Pogàny; *anim:* Frank Tipper, Hicks Lokey; *character des/sets:* Willy Pogàny; *voices:* Dave Weber, Sara Berner, Marjorie Tarlton, Victor McLeod; *mus:* Frank Marsales; *prod mgr:* George Hall; *col:* Tech. *sd:* WE. 7 min. • Peterkin, a puckish practical joker, swaps the birds' respective eggs. When hatched, all parents depart, leaving Peterkin to babysit.

5680. Scrambled Events (*Gaumont Kartoon Komic*) 5 July 1916; *p.c.:* Gaumont for Mutual Pictures; *anim:* Harry Palmer; b&w. *sil.* • The subject deals with wartime preparedness in a humorous fashion.

5681. Scrap for Victory (*Gandy Goose*) 8 Jan. 1943; *p.c.:* TT for Fox; *dir:* Connie Rasinski; *story:* John Foster; *voices:* Arthur Kay, Thomas Morrison; *mus:* Philip A. Scheib; *col:* Tech. *sd:* RCA. 6½ min. • Pvt. Gandy and Sgt. Sourpuss are on the battlefield when they run out of ammunition, so they call upon the home folks for scrap.

5682. Scrap Happy Daffy (*Looney Tunes*) 21 Aug. 1943; *p.c.:* Leon Schlesinger prods for WB; *dir:* Frank Tashlin; *story:* Don Christensen; *lay:* David Hilberman; *back:* Richard H. Thomas; *ed:* Treg Brown; *voices:* Mel Blanc, Dorothy Lloyd; *mus:* Carl W. Stalling; *ph:* John W. Burton; *prod sup:* Henry Binder, Raymond G. Katz; b&w. *sd:* Vit. 7 min. • Champion scrap-collector, Daffy, receives a challenge from a Nazi goat sent by Hitler to destroy the American war effort.

5683. Scrap the Japs (*Popeye*) 20 Nov. 1942; *p.c.:* Famous for Para; *dir:* Seymour Kneitel; *story:* Carl Meyer; *anim:* Tom Johnson, Ben Solomon; *voices:* Jack Mercer; *mus:* Sammy Timberg; *prod mgr:* Sam Buchwald; b&w. *sd:* WE. 6 min. • Popeye is swabbing the deck when a suspicious cloud housing a Japanese pilot appears overhead. Our hero soon finds an enemy scrap ship and knocks its inhabitants into a giant bird cage.

5684. Scrappily Married (*Noveltoon*) 30 Mar. 1945; *p.c.:* Famous for Para; *dir:* Seymour Kneitel; *story:* William Turner, Jack Ward; *anim:* Orestes Calpini, Otto Feuer; *voices:* Arnold Stang, Jack Mercer; *mus:* Winston Sharples; *ph:* Leonard McCormick; *prod mgr:* Sam Buchwald; *col:* Tech.

sd: RCA. 8 min. • Henry the hen-pecked rooster bribes Herman the mouse to scare his wife while he slips out for a night on the tiles.

5685. Scrappy Birthday (*Andy Panda*) 11 Feb. 1949; *p.c.:* Walter Lantz prods for UA; *dir:* Dick Lundy; *story:* Ben Hardaway, Heck Allen; *anim:* (La) Verne Harding, Les Kline; *sets:* Fred Brunish; *ed:* Dave Lurie; *voices:* Walter Tetley, Edward J. Marr, Walter Craig, Grace Stafford; *mus:* Darrell Calker; *prod mgr:* William E. Garity; *col:* Tech. *sd:* RCA. 7 min. • Andy goes hunting a fox for a fur to give Miranda Panda for her birthday.

5686. Scrappy's Added Attraction (*Scrappy*) 13 Jan. 1939; *p.c.:* Charles Mintz prods for Colum; *story:* Art Davis; *anim:* Sid Marcus; *lay:* Clark Watson; *back:* Phil Davis; *ed:* George Winkler; *voices:* Mel Blanc, Robert Winkler, Dave Weber; *mus:* Joe de Nat; *prod mgr:* James Bronis; b&w. *sd:* RCA. 6½ min. • Scrappy and Margie run a cinema and do impersonations of John Barrymore and Garbo. When a villain named Titan the Terrible Twerp adds to the confusion when the film breaks, he has to be sewn together.

5687. Scrappy's Art Gallery (*Scrappy*) 12 Jan. 1934; *p.c.:* Winkler for Colum; *prod:* Charles Mintz *story:* Sid Marcus; *anim:* Art Davis; *lay:* Clark Watson; *back:* Phil Davis; *mus:* Joe de Nat; *prod mgr:* James Bronis; b&w. *sd:* RCA. 7 min. • No story available.

5688. Scrappy's Auto Show (*Scrappy*) 8 Dec. 1933; *p.c.:* Winkler for Colum; *prod:* Charles Mintz; *story:* Sid Marcus; *anim:* Art Davis; *lay:* Clark Watson; *back:* Phil Davis; *mus:* Joe de Nat; *prod mgr:* James Bronis; b&w. *sd:* RCA. 6 min. • Scrappy and Oopie demonstrate their homemade automobile at the auto show. Henry Ford awards them the first prize.

5689. Scrappy's Band Concert (*Scrappy*) 29 Apr. 1937; *p.c.:* Charles Mintz prods for Colum; *story:* Allen Rose; *anim:* Harry Love; *lay:* Clark Watson; *back:* Phil Davis; *mus:* Joe de Nat; *prod mgr:* James Bronis; b&w. *sd:* RCA. 7 min. • Scrappy's concert is disrupted by hornets.

5690. Scrappy's Big Moment (*Scrappy*) 28 July 1935; *p.c.:* Charles Mintz prods for Colum; *story:* Ben Harrison; *anim:* Manny Gould, Al Rose; *lay:* Clark Watson; *back:* Phil Davis; *mus:* Joe de Nat; *prod mgr:* James Bronis; b&w. *sd:* RCA. 10 min. • Scrappy and Oopie accidentally knock each other unconscious and dream that Oopie fights Max Baer, the champ at Madison Square Garden ... and wins.

5691. Scrappy's Boy Scouts (*Scrappy*) 2 Jan. 1936; *p.c.:* Charles Mintz prods for Colum; *story:* Art Davis; *anim:* Sid Marcus; *lay:* Clark Watson; *back:* Phil Davis; *ed:* George Winkler; *mus:* Joe de Nat; *prod mgr:* James Bronis; b&w. *sd:* RCA. 7 min. • Shunned by Scrappy's scout troop, Oopie forms his own, consisting of three dachshunds. When Scrappy's troop are stranded on a mountain, Oopie's scouts come to the rescue.

5692. Scrappy's Camera Troubles (*Scrappy*) 5 June 1936; *p.c.:* Charles Mintz prods for Colum; *story:* Ben Harrison; *anim:* Manny Gould; *lay:* Clark Watson; *back:* Phil Davis; *voice:* A. Purvis Pullen; *mus:* Joe de Nat; *prod mgr:* James Bronis; b&w. *sd:* RCA. 6 min. • Scrappy's photos of his dog, Yippie, are constantly ruined by his pesky kid brother trying to get into the picture.

5693. Scrappy's Dog Show (*Scrappy*) 8 May 1934; *p.c.:* Winkler for Colum; *prod:* Charles Mintz; *story:* Sid Marcus; *anim:* Art Davis; *lay:* Clark Watson; *back:* Phil Davis; *ed:* George Winkler; *mus:* Joe de Nat; *prod mgr:* James Bronis; b&w. *sd:* RCA. 7 min. • Scrappy and Oopie try to pass off a cat as an airedale in the dog show, then as a St Bernard. They are ejected a number of times until Oopie absconds with the prize trophy.

5694. Scrappy's Expedition (*Scrappy*) 27 Aug. 1934; *p.c.:* Winkler for Colum; *prod:* Charles Mintz; *story:* Sid Marcus; *anim:* Art Davis; *mus:* Joe de Nat; *prod mgr:* James Bronis; b&w. *sd:* RCA. 8 min. • Scrappy goes on expedition to the South Pole. Eddie Cantor, Kate Smith, Walter Winchell and Ed Wynn arrive on board ship as entertainment. A storm neally sinks the ship but Kate Smith plugs the hole by sitting in it.

5695. Scrappy's Ghost Story (*Scrappy*) 24 May 1935; *p.c.:* Charles Mintz prods for Colum; *story:* Ben Harrison; *anim:* Manny Gould, Harry Love; *lay:* Clark Watson; *back:* Phil Davis; *mus:* Joe de Nat; *prod mgr:* James Bronis; b&w. *sd:* RCA. 6 min. • Scrappy is frightened on a stormy night by a series of ghosts, phantoms, spooks and walking trees. They turn out to be Oopie's shadows.

5696. Scrappy's Music Lesson (*Scrappy*) 4 June 1937; *p.c.:* Charles Mintz prods for Colum; *story:* Art Davis; *anim:* Sid Marcus; *lay:* Clark Watson; *back:* Phil Davis; *ed:* George Winkler; *voice:* Robert Winkler, Dave Weber, Rolfe Sedan; *mus:* Joe de Nat; *prod mgr:* James Bronis; b&w. *sd:* RCA. 6½ min. • Petey Parrot torments Scrappy and his piano teacher by coating the piano keys with gum.

5697. Scrappy's News Flashes (*Scrappy*) 8 Dec. 1937; *p.c.:* Charles Mintz prods for Colum; *story:* Allen Rose; *anim:* Harry Love; *lay:* Clark Watson; *back:* Phil Davis; *ed:* George Winkler; *voices:* Dave Weber, Elvia Allman, Robert Winkler; *mus:* Joe de Nat; *prod mgr:* James Bronis; b&w. *sd:* RCA. 6 min. • Burlesque on newsreels: Scrappy impersonates Lowell Thomas, Lew Lehr, Vyvyan Donner's fashions and Ed Thompson with the sports.

5698. Scrappy's Party (*Scrappy*) 13 Feb. 1933; *p.c.:* Winkler for Colum; *prod:* Charles Mintz; *story:* Dick Huemor; *anim:* Sid Marcus; *mus:* Joe de Nat; *prod mgr:* James Bronis; b&w. *sd:* RCA. 6 min. • Scrappy and Vontzy invite notable personalities to their party: Roscoe Ates, Joe E. Brown, Jimmy Durante and George Bernard Shaw exchange noses and beards, Albert Einstein, Frankenstein's monster, Greta Garbo, Laurel & Hardy, Adolf Hitler, Benito Mussolini, Will Rogers, John D. Rockefeller, Babe Ruth and Ben Turpin. The four Marx Brothers dance with Marie Dressler, Al Capone phones from prison to say he can't make it and Mahatma Gandhi arrives on roller skates.

5699. Scrappy's Playmates (*Scrappy*) 11 Mar. 1938; *p.c.:* Charles Mintz prods for Colum; *story:* Art Davis; *anim:* Sid Marcus; *lay:* Clark Watson; *back:* Phil Davis; *ed:* George Winkler; *voices:* Dave Weber, Leonè Le Deux; *mus:* Joe de Nat; *prod mgr:* James Bronis; b&w. *sd:* RCA. 6 min. • Petey Parrot doesn't take too kindly to Scrappy's new dog, Butch, until Scrappy gives them both an ice cream cone and they are pals.

5700. Scrappy's Pony (*Scrappy*) 16 Mar. 1936; *p.c.:* Charles Mintz prods for Colum; *story:* Ben Harrison; *anim:* Manny Gould; *lay:* Clark Watson; *back:* Phil Davis; *ed:* George Winkler; *voice:* The Rhythmettes; *mus:* Joe de Nat; *prod mgr:* James Bronis; b&w. *sd:* RCA. 6 min. • Scrappy and Oopie receive a pony named "Sugar" and they sing a song about it.

5701. Scrappy's Puppet Theatre 1938; *p.c.:* Charles Mintz prods for Colum; b&w. *sd:* RCA. 2 min. *l/a/anim.* • Scrappy encourages the kids to get the giveaway toy theatre when they leave the theatre. Child actress Edith Fellows demonstrates how it works.

5702. Scrappy's Relay Race (*Scrappy*) 7 July 1934; *p.c.:* Winkler for Columbia; *prod:* Charles Mintz; *story:* Sid Marcus; *anim:* Art Davis; *mus:* Joe de Nat; *prod mgr:* James Bronis; b&w. *sd:* RCA. 6 min. • No story available.

5703. Scrappy's Rodeo (*Scrappy*) 2 Sept. 1939; *p.c.:* Charles Mintz prods for Colum; *story:* Allen Rose; *anim:* Harry Love, Louie Lilly; *lay:* Clark Watson; *back:* Phil Davis; *ed:* George Winkler; *voice:* Walter Tetley, Leone Le Doux; *mus:* Joe de Nat; *prod mgr:* James Bronis; b&w. *sd:* RCA. 6 min. • "Brat" wants to join in Scrappy's cowboy game and is told it's no place for little girls but she proves her riding ability when her St Bernard runs amock.

5704. Scrappy's Side Show (*Scrappy*) 3 Mar. 1939; *p.c.:* Charles Mintz prods for Colum; *story:* Allen Rose; *anim:* Harry Love, Louie Lilly; *lay:* Clark Watson; *back:* Phil Davis; *ed:* George Winkler; *voice:* Robert Winkler; *mus:* Joe de Nat; *prod mgr:* James Bronis; b&w. *sd:* RCA. 6 min. • A little girl known as "Brat" unmasks Scrappy's sideshow acts. She reveals "strongman" Scrappy's barbells as balloons and ends being fired from a cannon into a water tower.

5705. Scrappy's Television (*Scrappy*) 29 Jan. 1934; *p.c.:* Winkler for Colum; *prod:* Charles Mintz; *story:* Sid Marcus; *anim:* Art Davis; *lay:* Clark Watson; *back:* Phil Davis; *mus:* Joe de Nat; *prod mgr:* James Bronis; b&w. *sd:* RCA. 8 min. • Scrappy's television broadcast includes a classical violinist, a jazz band, farm animals and a fight between Primo Carnera and Ed Wynn.

5706. Scrappy's Theme Song (*Scrappy*) 15 June 1934; *p.c.:* Winkler for Colum; *prod:* Charles Mintz; *story:* Sid Marcus; *anim:* Art Davis; *lay:* Clark Watson; *back:* Phil Davis; *mus:* Joe de Nat; *prod mgr:* George Winkler; b&w. *sd:* RCA. 6 min. • Songwriter Scrappy gives a show starring himself, Margie, Oopie and singing cats to feature his new song "I Love You and You Love Me."

5707. Scrappy's Toy Shop (*Scrappy*) 13 Apr. 1934; *p.c.:* Winkler for Colum; *prod:* Charles Mintz; *story:* Sid Marcus; *anim:* Art Davis; *mus:* Joe de Nat; *prod mgr:* George Winkler; b&w. *sd:* RCA. 6¹/₂ min. • Scrappy practices ventriloquism and Oopie masquerades as his dummy, crying for help. His cries are answered by armed toy soldiers who attack Scrappy.

5708. Scrappy's Trailer *(Scrappy)* 29 Aug. 1935; *p.c.:* Charles Mintz prods for Colum; *story:* Ben Harrison; *anim:* Manny Gould, Harry Love; *lay:* Clark Watson; *back:* Phil Davis; *ed:* George Winkler; *mus:* Joe de Nat; *prod mgr:* James Bronis; b&w. *sd:* RCA. 6 min. • Scrappy and Oopie set their caravan in a tranquil setting. Insects steal their food and drive the boys up a tree. A bear drives them down again, so they retreat into their trailer.

5709. Scrappy's Trip to Mars *(Scrappy)* 4 Feb. 1938; *p.c.:* Charles Mintz prods for Colum; *story:* Allen Rose; *anim:* Harry Love; *lay:* Clark Watson; *back:* Phil Davis; *ed:* George Winkler; *voices:* Robert Winkler; *mus:* Joe de Nat; *prod mgr:* James Bronis; b&w. *sd:* RCA. 6 min. • Scrappy and Yippie imagine they fly to the Red Planet where they meet the Martian queen. They are taken to a nightclub and enjoy a performance before returning home.

5710. Scratch a Tiger *(Ant & Aardvark)* 28 Jan. 1970; *p.c.:* Mirisch/DFE for UA; *dir:* Hawley Pratt; *story:* Irv Spector; *anim:* Warren Batchelder, Don Williams, Manny Perez, Manny Gould, Art Leonardi; *lay:* Dick Ung; *back:* Tom O'Loughlin; *ed:* Lee Gunther; *voices:* John Byner, Marvin Miller; *mus:* Doug Goodwin, Pete Candoli, Billy Byers, Jimmy Rowles, Tommy Tedesco, Ray Brown, Shelley Manne; *ph:* John Burton Jr.; *prod sup:* Harry Love, Jim Foss; *col:* DeLuxe. *sd:* RCA. 6 min. • A tiger owes Ant a favor and keeps his word by protecting his colony from the Aardvark.

5711. Screen Follies *p.c.:* Capital Film Co; *anim:* Luis Seel, F.A. Dahme; b&w. *sil.* • (1–2): 4 Jan. 1920 • No stories available.

5712. The Screwball *(Woody Woodpecker)* 15 Feb. 1943; *p.c.:* Walter Lantz prods for Univ; *dir:* Alex Lovy; *story:* Ben Hardaway, Milt Schaffer; *anim:* (La)Verne Harding; *sets:* Fred Burnish; *voices:* Kent Rogers; *mus:* Darrell Calker; *prod mgr:* George Hall; *col:* Tech. *sd:* WE. 7 min. • Woody escapes an irate cop by dodging into a baseball game and inevitably participating in the game.

5713. Screwball Football *(Merrie Melodies)* 16 Dec. 1939; *p.c.:* Leon Schlesinger prods for WB; *dir:* Fred Avery; *story:* Melvin Millar; *anim:* Virgil Ross; *sets:* John Didrik Johnsen; *ed:* Tregoweth E. Brown; *voices:* John Wald, Mel Blanc; *mus:* Carl W. Stalling; *prod sup:* Henry Binder, Raymond G. Katz; *col:* Tech. *sd:* Vit. 7 min. • Football gags at the big game.

5714. The Screwball Squirrel 1 Apr. 1944; *p.c.:* MGM; *dir:* Tex Avery; *story:* Heck Allen; *anim:* Preston Blair, Ed Love, Ray Abrams; *character des:* Claude Smith; *sets:* John Didrik Johnsen; *ed:* Fred MacAlpine; *voices:* Wally Maher, Dick Nelson; *mus:* Scott Bradley; *prod:* Fred Quimby; *col:* Tech. *sd:* WE. 6 min. • Screwy Squirrel phones up Meathead, the hunting dog, for no better reason than to have a "Cartoon Chase."

5715. The Screwdriver *(Woody Woodpecker)* 11 Aug. 1941; *p.c.:* Walter Lantz prods for Univ; *dir:* Walter Lantz; *story:* Ben Hardaway, Jack Cosgriff; *anim:* Alex Lovy, Ralph Somerville; *sets:* Fred Brunish; *voices:* Mel Blanc; *mus:* Darrell Calker; *prod mgr:* George Hall; *col:* Tech. *sd:* WE. 6¹/₂ min. • Woody is stopped for speeding and gives the traffic cop a rough time.

5716. The Screwy Truant *(Screwy Squirrel)* 13 Jan. 1945; *p.c.:* MGM; *dir:* Tex Avery; *story:* Heck Allen; *anim:* Preston Blair, Ed Love, Ray Abrams; *character des:* Claude Smith; *sets:* John Didrik Johnsen; *ed:* Fred MacAlpin; *voices:* Wally Maher, Dave Barry; *mus:* Scott Bradley; *ph:* Jack Stevens; *prod:* Fred Quimby; *col:* Tech. *sd:* WE. 7 min. • The truant officer chases Screwy for playing hookey until discovering he has the measles.

5717. Scrooge McDuck and Money 23 Mar. 1967; *p.c.:* Walt Disney prods for BV; *dir:* Hamilton S. Luske; *asst dir:* Jim Swain; *anim:* Charles Downs, Ward Kimball, Hal King, Art Stevenns, Julius Svendsen; *fx:* Jack Boyd; *lay:* Joe Hale, McLaren Stewart; *voices:* Bill Thompson, Dick Beals, the MelloMen Quartet; *col:* Tech. *sd:* RCA. 17 min. • Rich Uncle Scrooge explains the history of money to Huey, Dewey and Louie.

5718. Scrub Me Mama with a Boogie Beat 28 Apr. 1941; *p.c.:* Walter Lantz prods for Univ; *dir:* Walter Lantz; *story:* Ben Hardaway; *anim:* Alex Lovy, Frank Tipper; *sets:* Fred Brunish; *voices:* Nellie Lutcher, Mel Blanc; *mus:* Darrell Calker; *song:* Don Raye; *prod mgr:* George Hall; *col:*

Tech. *sd:* WE. 6 min. • The shiftless folk of Lazy Town come to life when a lively girl arrives on the scene.

5719. Scuba Dooba Doo *(Sad Cat)* June 1966; *p.c.:* TT for Fox; *col:* DeLuxe. *sd:* RCA. 5 min. • Sad Cat's Fairy Godmouse gives him magic waterwings when his mean brothers dive for sunken treasure. • See: *Sad Cat*

5720. Sea Salts *(Donald Duck)* 8 Apr. 1949; *p.c.:* Walt Disney prods for RKO; *dir:* Jack Hannah; *story:* Bill Berg, Nick George; *anim:* Bill Justice, Bob Carlson, John Sibley, Volus Jones; *fx:* Jack Boyd, Dan MacManus; *lay:* Yale Gracey; *back:* Thelma Witmer; *voices:* Francis "Dink" Trout, Clarence Nash; *mus:* Oliver Wallace; *col:* Tech. *sd:* RCA. 7¹/₂ min. • Donald is shipwrecked on a desert isle with his pal, the Bootle Beetle. They still remain friends even if Don is prone to taking advantage of the beetle.

5721. Sea Scouts *(Donald Duck)* 30 June 1939; *p.c.:* Walt Disney prods for RKO; *dir:* Richard Lundy; *asst dir:* Jim Hess; *story:* Carl Barks; *anim:* Preston Blair, Paul Busch, Johnny Cannon, Larry Clemmons, Walter Clinton, Osmond Evans, Jack Hannah, Volus Jones, Edward Love, Hamilton S. Luske, Murray McClellan, Ray Patin, John Sewall; *lay:* James Carmichael; *voices:* Clarence Nash; *mus:* Oliver Wallace; *col:* Tech. *sd:* RCA. 8 min. • Admiral Donald puts his nephews to work on board his yacht. The finale has Don struggling to escape the jaws of a shark.

5722. The Sea Shower *(Aesop's Film Fable)* Feb. 1928; *p.c.:* Fables Pictures Inc for Pathé; *dir:* Paul Terry; b&w. *sil.* 10 min. • No story available.

5723. Seal on the Loose *(Woody Woodpecker)* 1 May 1970; *p.c.:* Walter Lantz prods for Univ; *dir:* Paul J. Smith; *story:* Cal Howard; *anim:* Les Kline, Al Coe; *sets:* Nino Carbe; *voices:* Daws Butler, Grace Stafford; *mus:* Walter Greene; *prod mgr:* William E. Garity; *col:* Tech. *sd:* RCA. 5¹/₂ min. • A seal follows Woody to Mrs. Meany's boarding house where Meany tries to evict them both.

5724. Seal Skinners *(Captain & the Kids)* 28 Jan. 1939; *dir:* Isadore Freleng; *anim:* Emery Hawkins, Irven Spence; *sets:* Bob Kuwahara; *voice:* Billy Bletcher, Dave Weber, Cliff Nazarro, Jeanne Dunn; *mus:* Scott Bradley; *prod:* Fred Quimby; *col:* sep. *sd:* WE. 7 min. • Der Captain captures an escaped seal for a reward and pirate John tries to steal it.

5725. The Seapreme Court *(Noveltoon)* 29 Jan. 1954; *p.c.:* Famous for Para; *dir:* Seymour Kneitel; *story:* Larz Bourne; *anim:* Tom Golden, Morey Reden; *sets:* Robert Owen; *voices:* Mae Questel, Jackson Beck, Sid Raymond, Jack Mercer; *mus:* Winston Sharples; *ph:* Leonard McCormick; *prod mgr:* Seymour Shultz; *col:* Tech. *sd:* RCA. 6 min. • Little Audrey dozes while fishing and dreams she is on trial by the denizens of the deep.

5726. Search for Misery *(Terry-Toon)* Nov. 1964; *p.c.:* TT for Fox; *ex prod:* Bill Weiss; *dir:* Bob Kuwahara; *story sup:* Tom Morrison; *story:* Larz Bourne; *anim:* Cosmo Anzilotti; *ed:* Jack MacConnell; *back:* Bill Focht, John Zago; *voices:* Dayton Allen, Elvi Allen; *mus:* Ashley Miller; *ph:* Charles Schettler; *sd:* Elliot Grey; *col:* DeLuxe. *sd:* RCA. 6 min. • Pitiful Penelope leads a pathetic "soap opera" life.

5727. Seasick Sailors *(Little Roquefort)* July 1951; *p.c.:* TT for Fox; *dir/anim:* Mannie Davis; *story/voice:* Tom Morrison; *anim:* Jim Tyer; *sets:* Art Bartsch; *mus:* Philip A. Scheib; *ph:* Douglas Moye; *col:* Tech. *sd:* RCA. 6 min. • Percy tries to prevent Roquefort leaving on a cruise to Hawaii.

5728. Seaside Adventure *(Terry-Toon)* Feb. 1952; *p.c.:* TT for Fox; *dir/anim:* Mannie Davis; *story:* Tom Morrison; *sets:* Art Bartsch; *mus:* Philip A. Scheib; *ph:* Douglas Moye; *col:* Tech. *sd:* RCA. 6 min. • A poor widow rabbit sends her youngest out to seek his fortune. He has an adventure beneath the sea and is rewarded with gold.

5729. Seasin's Greetinks *(Popeye)* 8 Dec. 1933; *p.c.:* The Fleischer Studio for Para; *prod:* Max Fleischer; *dir:* Dave Fleischer; *anim:* Seymour Kneitel, Roland Crandall; *voices:* William A. Costello, Charles Carver; *mus:* Sammy Timberg; b&w. *sd:* WE. 5¹/₂ min. • Bluto interrupts Popeye and Olive's ice skating fun, culminating in Olive floating down the river on an ice floe towards a waterfall.

5730. Secrecy of American Prosperity *(Fun & Facts About America)* 1947; *p.c.:* John Sutherland Prods/Harding College for MGM; *prod/dir:* John Sutherland; *col:* Tech. *sd:* WE. • No story available.

5731. Secret Agent Woody Woodpecker *(Woody Woodpecker)* May 1967; *p.c.:* Walter Lantz prods for Univ; *dir:* Paul J. Smith; *story:* Cal

Howard; *anim:* Les Kline, Al Coe; *sets:* Ray Huffine; *voices:* Daws Butler, Grace Stafford; *mus:* Walter Greene; *prod mgr:* William E. Garity; *col:* Tech. *sd:* RCA. 6 min. • Secret Agent Woody is called upon to help clean up the town from Louie the Litter-Lout.

5732. The Secret of NIMH 2 July 1982; *p.c.:* Aurora for United International Pictures; *dir:* Don Bluth; *prod:* Don Bluth, Gary Goldman, John Pomeroy; *ex prod:* Rich Irvine, James L. Stewart; *prod ex:* Mel Griffin; *asst dir:* Dan Molina; based on the novel *Mrs. Frisby and the Rats of NIMH* by Robert C. O'Brien; *story:* Don Bluth, John Pomeroy, Gary Goldman, Will Finn; *creative consultant:* Steve Barnes, Richard A. Gabrio, Martin S. Jacobson; *anim dir:* John Pomeroy, Gary Goldman, Don Bluth; *anim:* Lorna Pomeroy, Skip Jones, Dave Spafford, Will Finn, Linda Miller, Dan Kuenster, Heidi Guedel, Kevin M. Wurzer; *fx anim:* Dorse A. Lanpher, Bruce Heller, Diann Landau, Tom Hush, Kelly Anderson, Art Roman; *key character clean-up:* Emily Jiuliano, Vera Law, Philo Barnhart, Terry Shakespeare, Dave Molina, Gary Perkovac, Cheryl Polakow, Sally Voorheis, Bonnie Robinson, Nancy Kniep, Leonard Johnson, Michael Horowitz, Arland Barron, Ayalen Garcia, Tamara Anderson, Auguste Haboush; *col story sketch:* William Lorencz; *anim col stylists:* Carmen Oliver, Cindy Chilko Finn, Debbie Casillas, Phyllis Barnhart, Merlyn Ching, Linda Praamsma, Patti Cowling; *lay:* Don Bluth, Larry Leker; *back:* Don Moore, Ron Dias, David Goetz; *ed:* Jeffrey Patch; *voices: Nicodemus:* Derek Jacobi; *Mrs. Brisby:* Elizabeth Hartman; *Mr. Ages:* Arthur Malet; *Jeremy:* Dom DeLuise; *Auntie Shrew:* Hermoine Baddeley; *Teresa:* Shannen Doherty; *Martin:* Wil Wheaton; *Cynthia:* Jodi Hicks; *Timmy:* Ian Fried; *The Great Owl:* John Carradine; *Justin:* Peter Strauss; *Jenner:* Paul Shenar; *Farmer Fitzgibbons:* Tom Hatten; *Mrs. Fitzgibbons:* Lucille Bliss; *Sullivan:* Aldo Ray; *Councilmen:* Norbert Auerbach, Dick Kleiner, Charles Champlin; *Miss Right:* Edie McClurg; *Billy Fitzgibbons:* Joshua Lawrence; *mus:* Jerry Goldsmith; *songs:* T.J. Kuenster; "Flying Dreams" by Jerry Goldsmith & Paul Williams; *arranger:* Ian Fraser; *mus ed:* Len Engel (London), Mike Clifford; *orch:* Arthur Morton, the National Philharmonic Orchestra — London; *optical fx:* Westheimer Company; *mark-up:* Cynthia Surage; *paint:* Debra Y. Siegel; *check:* Nikki Zelenka, Kathy Barrows, Annamarie Costa; *final check:* Dave Smith, Jim Stocks; *i&p:* Olga Tarin Craig, Karan L. Storr, Chris Stocks, Diane Dunning, Aletha Bernard, Kristine Brown, Merlyn Ching; *cel paint:* Phyllis Barnhart, Phyllis White, Lynn Spees, Diane Albracht, Cathy Mirkovich, Peter Gentle, Patti Cowling, Tammy Cecil, Linda Praamsma, Sandra Moline, Gayle Kanagy, Marta Skwara, Jody Trout, Jeanette Nouribekian, Paulette Knell, Shirley Thomas, Shirley Ferrante, Coolie Palacid, Manon Washburn, Deborah Mooneyham, Joann Cohn, Evie Hairpetian, Sharon Thomas, Terri-Lynn Swears, Shirley Kim Stevens, Gina Evans, Bonnie Ramsey, Robin Police, Robin Draper, Mildred Luuk Konen, Odin Hor, Judy Champin, Colleen Draper, Alison Sassoon; *Xerox:* Robert Erhart, Eric Daniels, Janet Zoll, David Ankney, John Eddings, Michael Kane, Robert Avery, David Braden; *Xerox check:* Daryl Carstensen, Valerie Green; *ph:* Joe Jiuliano, Charles Warren, Jeff Mellquist; *sd rec: dial:* Gary Ulmer; *sd fx:* James Cavarretta Jr.; *mus:* John Richards, Donald O. Mitchell, Rick Kline, Kevin O'Connell; *synthesizer fx:* Stan Levine; *fx ed:* David M. Horton, Pat Foley, John Roesch; *prod mgr/special processes:* Fred Craig; *prod asst:* Caralyn Warren, Dan Molina, Charles Kurtz, Bob Chevalier, Sarah King, Mike Vest, Victor Solis, Carolyn Morris, Julie Spafford, Edna Hartling, Shirley Spafford, Terri Eddings, David Steinberg; *col:* Tech. *sd:* Dolby stereo. 82 min. • A family of field mice are warned that "moving day" is near and that the farmer's tractor will soon be plowing up the field. Mrs. Brisby is concerned that her son, Timmy, is confined to bed with pneumonia and can't be moved. She goes to seek help from Nicodemus, the King of the rat colony, in Farmer Fitzgibbons' rose bush. Mrs. Brisby's late husband's name is held in respect by the rats as he had once helped them escape from the National Institution of Mental Health (NIMH) experimental laboratory. The rats agree to move her and her family to safer ground.

5733. The Secret of the Sword 22 Mar. 1985; *p.c.:* Filmation Associates/Mattel Toys for Atlantic; *dir:* Ed Friedman, Lou Kachivas, Marsh Lamore, Bill Reed, Gwen Wetzler; *prod:* Arthur H. Nadel; *ex prod:* Lou Scheimer; *scr:* Larry Ditillo, Bob Forward; *storyboard:* Bob Arkwright, Don Manuel, Rich Chidlaw, William Barry, Victoria Jenson, Gary Goldstein, Tom Sito; *asst sup anim:* Doris Plough; *anim:* Barry Anderson, Tom Baron, Carl Bell, Yi-Chih Chen, Won Ki Cho, Moon Hwan Choi, Tom Cook,

Doug Crane, James A. Davis, Zeon Davush, Jeff Etter, Lil Evans, Marcia Fertig, Mike Gerard, Frank Gonzales, Carl Hall, Lee Halpern, Karen Haus, Brett Hisey, Richard Hoffman, Hector Isola, Kyong Ui Kim, Yang Kim, Mircea Manta, Burton Medall, Constantin Mustatea, Dennis Neil, Jane Nordin, Bill Nunes, Mike O'Connor, Eduardo Olivares, Dave Prince, Bill Pratt, Joe Roman Jr., Chrystal Russell, Louise Sandoval, Don Schloat, Kunio Schimumura, Karlis Smiltens, Ka-Moon Song, Mike Toth, Dardo Velez, Virgil Raddatz, Neal Warner, Ellen Woodbury; *fx anim:* Shurl Lupin; *lay sup:* Gary L. Hoffman, Alberto de Mello, Wes Herschensohn, Cliff Voorhees, Sherilan Weinhart, David West; *lay:* Craig Armstrong, Rex Barron, Armando Carrillo, Curtis Cim, Tom Coppola, Kevin Frank, Rene Garcia, Sergio Garcia, James Gomez, Ed Haney, Tenny Henson, David Hilberman, David Hoover, Mary Jorgensen, Karenia Kaminski, Warren Marshall, James McLean, Dan Mills, Marcus Nickerson, Greg Nocon, Phil Ortiz, John Perry, William Recinos, Bart Seitz, Desmond Serratore, Michael Spooner, Maureen Trueblood, Robert Tyler, Curt Walstead, Patricia Wong; *col dir:* Ervin L. Kaplan; *back sup:* Lorenzo E. Martinez, John Howley; *back:* Tim Callahan, Dan St. Pierre, Armando Norte, Thomas Shannon, Don Schweikert, Don Watson, Rolando Oliva, Craig Robertson, Flamarion Ferreier, Tom O'Loughlin, Tim Maloney, Don A. Peters, Gary Conklin, James Hickey; *character des:* Diane Keener, Herb Hazelton, Alice Hamm, Lewis Ott, Gerald Forton, Dale Hendrickson, Harry Sabin, Rick Maki; *graphics:* Connie Schurr; *stock co-ord:* Mike Hazy; *ed:* George Mahana, Joe Gall, Rick Gehr, Robert Crawford; *voices: Adam/He-Man:* John Erwin; *Adora/She-Ra:* Melendy Britt; *Bo:* Alan Oppenheimer; *Hordak:* George Dicenzo; *Cowl:* Erik Gunden; *also:* Linda Gary, Erika Scheimer; *mus:* Shuki Levy, Haim Saban, Erika Lane; *music dir:* Haim Saban; *music prod co-ord:* Andrew Dimitroff; *music ed:* Sam Horta, Mary Beth Smith; *music rec:* Nick Carr; *educational/psychological consultant:* Donald F. Roberts; *film co-ord:* June Gilham, Christie Meyer; *i&p:* Flavia Mitman; *checking:* Joyce Gard, Beverly Randles; *mark-up sup:* Letha Prince; *cel service:* Lou Digerolamo; *ph:* F.T. Ziegler, Dean Teves, Dan C. Larsen, Ronald Jackson, R.D. Jacobs, Roncie Hanke, David J. Link, Lin-Z Rogers, Jerry Whittington; *Xerox:* John Remmel; *sd rec:* Patricia Ryan, Erika Scheimer; *sd ed:* Bill Kean, Charlie Rychwalski, Don Kenny, Jeffrey Patch, Don Kenny, Susan Trieste; *sd:* Glen Glenn Sound; *prod ex:* Joseph A. Mazzuca; *prod asso:* Pamela Vincent; *prod controller:* Robert W. Wilson; *prod co-ord:* Coral A. Tracy; *post-prod sup:* Joe Simon; *col:* CFI. *sd:* Dolby Sound. 91 min. • Champion of good, He-Man joins forces with She-Ra, "Princess of Power," in the fight for justice. Made to promote Mattel toys, He-Man's television show and She-Ra's own up-and-coming television series aired in the fall of 1985.

5734. See the World *(Paul Terry-Toon)* 29 June 1934; *p.c.:* Moser & Terry for Educational/Fox; *dir:* Frank Moser, Paul Terry; *mus:* Philip A. Scheib; b&w. *sd:* WE. 6 min. • No story available.

5735. See Ya Later, Gladiator *(Looney Tunes)* 25 May 1968; *p.c.:* WB/7A; *dir:* Alex Lovy; *story:* Cal Howard; *anim:* Ted Bonnicksen, La Verne Harding, Volus Jones, Ed Solomon; *lay:* Bob Givens; *back:* Bob Abrams; *ed:* Hal Geer; *voices:* Mel Blanc; *mus:* William Lava; *prod:* Bill Hendricks; *col:* Tech. *sd:* Vit. 6 min. • By accident, Daffy and Speedy are both transported back to ancient Rome in a time machine where Daffy has to fight a lion for Emperor Nero.

5736. Seein' Red, White 'n' Blue *(Popeye)* 19 Feb. 1943; *p.c.:* Famous for Para; *dir:* Dan Gordon; *story:* Joe Stultz; *anim:* Jim Tyer, Ben Solomon; *voices:* Jack Mercer, Dave Barry; *mus:* Sammy Timberg; *prod mgr:* Sam Buchwald; b&w. *sd:* WE. 7 min. • Blacksmith Bluto's strength is rapidly sapped upon receiving his call-up papers. Officer Popeye is not fooled by his sick act, so Bluto hits him clear into the orphanage next door, which is secretly harboring a nest of Japs! Caricatures of Hirohito, Hitler and Goering.

5737. Seeing Ghosts *(Terry-Toon)* June 1948; *p.c.:* TT for Fox; *dir:* Mannie Davis; *story:* John Foster; *voice:* Thomas Morrison; *mus:* Philip A. Scheib; *col:* Tech. *sd:* RCA. 6½ min. • Herman Pig is sent to renovate a haunted house. Footage used from *Lights Out* and *Fortune Hunters.*

5738. Seeing Stars *(Krazy Kat)* 12 Sept. 1932; *p.c.:* Winkler for Colum; *dir:* Ben Harrison, Manny Gould; *anim:* Al Rose, Harry Love, Jack Carr; *voice:* Jack Carr; *mus:* Joe de Nat; *prod:* George Winkler; b&w. *sd:* WE. 6 min. • Krazy plays piano in a star-studded restaurant. Caricatures of Joe E. Brown, Charlie Chaplin, Maurice Chevalier, Marie Dressler, Jimmy

Durante, Clark Gable, Roscoe Karns, Buster Keaton, Laurel & Hardy, Harold Lloyd, the four Marx Brothers and Ben Turpin.

5739. Self Control (*Donald Duck*) 11 Feb. 1938; *p.c.:* Walt Disney prods for RKO; *dir:* Jack King; *story:* Carl Barks, Jack Hannah; *anim:* Edwin Aardal, Paul Allen, Johnny Cannon, Chuck Couch, Jack Hannah, Don Towsley, Bernard Wolf; *voices:* Cliff Arquette, Charles Caroll, Clarence Nash; *mus:* Oliver Wallace; *col:* Tech. *sd:* RCA. 8 min. • Donald's radio advocates "self control" which he tries to practice ... but a persistent woodpecker and his temper soon overtake.

5740. A Self-Made Mongrel (*Noveltoon*) 29 June 1945; *p.c.:* Famous for Para; *story:* Carl Meyer; *anim:* Dave Tendlar, John Walworth; *sets:* Shane Miller; *voices:* George Matthews, Jack Mercer, Carl Meyer; *mus:* Winston Sharples; *ph:* Leonard McCormick; *prod mgr:* Sam Buchwald; *col:* Tech. *sd:* RCA. 8 min. • A wealthy eccentric plays "cops and robbers" with his dog but is knocked out by a genuine burglar who confronts the dog.

5741. A Self-Winding Sidewinder (*Hoot Kloot*) 9 Oct. 1973; *p.c.:* Mirisch/DFE for UA; *dir/lay:* Roy Morita; *story:* John W. Dunn; *anim:* Bob Matz, Frank Gonzalez, Bob Bransford, Don Williams; *back:* Richard H. Thomas; *ed:* Rick Steward; *voices:* Bob Holt; *mus:* Doug Goodwin; *ph:* John W. Burton Jr.; *titles:* Arthur Leonardi; *prod mgr:* Stan Paperny; *col:* DeLuxe. *sd:* RCA. 6 min. • Kloot runs against Crazywolf in an election for sheriff.

5742. Send Your Elephant to Camp (*Terry-Toon*) July 1962; *p.c.:* TT for Fox; *ex prod:* Bill Weiss; *dir:* Art Bartsch; *story sup:* Tom Morrison; *story:* Larz Bourne; *sets:* John Zago, Bill Focht; *ed:* George McAvoy; *voices:* Dayton Allen; *mus:* Phil Scheib; *ph:* Joseph Rasinski; *prod mgr:* Frank Schudde; *col:* DeLuxe. *sd:* RCA. 6 min. • Sidney wants to go to summer camp but when he gets there he goes off the whole idea.

5743. Señor Droopy (*Droopy*) 9 Apr 1949; *p.c.:* MGM; *dir:* Tex Avery; *story:* Rich Hogan; *anim:* Grant Simmons, Walter Clinton, Bob Cannon, Michael Lah, Preston Blair; *character des:* Louis Schmitt; *sets:* John Didrik Johnsen; *ed:* Fred McAlpine; *voices:* Bill Thompson, Nestor Paiva, Tex Avery; *mus:* Scott Bradley; *l/a:* Lina Romay; *prod:* Fred Quimby; *col:* Tech. *sd:* WE. 8 min. • Droopy and a wolf fight a bull for the hand of the lovely Lina Romay.

5744. Señorella and the Glass Hurachè (*Looney Tunes*) Aug. 1964; *p.c.:* WB; *dir/lay:* Hawley Pratt; *story:* John Dunn; *anim:* Gerry Chiniquy, Bob Matz, Virgil Ross, Lee Halpern; *fx:* Harry Love; *back:* Tom O'Loughlin; *ed:* Treg Brown; *voices:* Mel Blanc, Tom Holland; *mus:* Bill Lava; *prod mgr:* Bill Orcutt; *prod:* David H. DePatie; *col:* Tech. *sd:* Vit. 6 min. • The Cinderella story against a Mexican setting.

5745. September in the Rain (*Merrie Melodies*) 1 Jan. 1938; *p.c.:* Leon Schlesinger prods for WB; *dir:* I. Freleng; *story:* Ted Pierce, Robert Clampett; *anim:* Cal Dalton; *lay:* Griff Jay; *back:* Arthur Loomer; *ed:* Tregoweth E. Brown; *voices:* The Basin Street Boys; *mus:* Carl W. Stalling; *song:* Harry Warren, Al Dubin; *prod sup:* Henry Binder, Raymond G. Katz; *col:* Tech. *sd:* Vit. 6 min. • Sheet music in a music shop comes to life. Caricatures of Al Jolson, Fred Astaire and Ginger Rogers.

5746. Serapé Happy (*Tijuana Toads*) 26 Dec. 1971; *p.c.:* Mirisch/DFE for UA; *dir:* Gerry Chiniquy; *story:* John W. Dunn; *anim:* Manny Gould, Warren Batchelder, Arthur Leonardi, Don Williams; *lay:* Dick Ung; *back:* Richard H. Thomas; *ed:* Lee Gunther; *voices:* Tom Holland, Don Diamond; *mus:* Doug Goodwin; *ph:* John Burton Jr.; *prod sup:* Jim Foss, Harry Love; *col:* DeLuxe. *sd:* RCA. 6 min. • The Toads chase an elusive grasshopper for their breakfast.

5747. Servants' Entrance 1934; *p.c.:* Walt Disney prods for Fox; *story:* Joe Grant; *anim:* Arthur Babbitt, Milt Kahl, Ward Kimball, Jack Kinney, Wolfgang Reitherman, Milt Schaffer; *lay:* Charles Philippi; *voices:* Billy Bletcher, Pinto Colvig, Sidney Jarvis, Paul Taylor, Allan Watson, Betty Rome, Madeline Green, Jean Schock, Helen Jamison, Henry Schnetz, Austin Grout, Frank Carpenter, Lee Typens; *mus:* Frank E. Churchill; b&w. *sd:* WE. *l/a/anim.* • Live-action film directed by Frank Lloyd and starring Janet Gaynor. Animated nightmare featuring Janet on trial by kitchen utensils.

5748. Service with a Guile (*Popeye*) 19 Apr. 1946; *p.c.:* Famous for Para; *dir:* Bill Tytla; *story:* Jack Ward, Carl Meyer; *anim:* James Tyer, Ben Solomon; *voices:* Mae Questel, Jackson Beck, Carl Meyer; *mus:* Sammy Timberg; *ph:* Leonard McCormick; *prod mgr:* Sam Buchwald; *col:* Tech. *sd:* RCA. 6 min. • Popeye and Bluto help attend to the Admiral's car at Olive's service station. First Famous "Popeye" to be made in Technicolor.

5749. Service with a Smile (*Betty Boop*) 23 Sept. 1937; *p.c.:* The Fleischer Studio for Para; *prod:* Max Fleischer; *dir:* Dave Fleischer; *anim:* David Tendlar, William Sturm; *voices:* Everett Clark, Mae Questel; *mus:* Sammy Timberg; b&w. *sd:* WE. 7 min. • Betty's hotel guests complain about the service until Grampy arrives to put things right.

5750. Service with a Smile (*Swifty & Shorty*) June 1964; *p.c.:* Para Cartoons; *dir:* Seymour Kneitel; *story:* Bill Ballard; *anim:* Nick Tafuri; *sets:* Robert Little; *voices:* Eddie Lawrence; *mus:* Winston Sharples; *ph:* Leonard McCormick; *prod mgr:* Abe Goodman; *col:* Tech. *sd:* RCA. 6 min. • Shorty comes up against a despondent short-order cook who refuses to acknowledge his policy of "The Customer Is Always Right" so, to cheer him up, Shorty serves *him*!

5751. Seven Faces of Dr. Lao 1964; *p.c.:* George Pal prods for MGM; *prod/dir:* George Pal; *fx:* Paul B. Byrd, Wah Chang, Jim Danforth, Ralph Rodies, Robert R. Hoag, Pete Kleinow; *mus:* Leigh Harline; *col:* Metro. *sd:* WE. 100 min. *l/a/anim.* • A mysterious Chinese conjurer disrupts a western town. • Live-action film featuring Tony Randall in a multitude of disguises.

5752. The Seven Wise Dwarfs 12 Dec. 1941; *p.c.:* Walt Disney prods for The Candaian Film Board; *dir:* Ford Beebe, Dick Lyford; *anim:* Les Clark, Ted Bonnicksen, Henry Ketcham, Kenneth Muse; *fx:* Joshua Meador; *voices:* The Kings' Men; *mus:* Oliver Wallace; *col:* Tech. *sd:* RCA. 3½ min. • The Seven Dwarfs use their diamonds to buy Canadian War Bonds. Made to demonstrate the advisability and necessity of purchasing Canadian War Bonds.

5753. Shadows (*Out of the Inkwell*) 1 Nov. 1923; *p.c.:* Inkwell Studio for Winkler; *dir:* Dave Fleischer; *anim/l/a:* Max Fleischer; b&w. sil. 5 min. *l/a/anim.* • Max draws silhouettes of animals who annoy the clown. After being chased and crushed by these shadowy figures, Ko-Ko is finally glad to return to the safety of his inkwell.

5754. The Shaggy D.A. 18 Dec.1976. *p.c.:* Walt Disney Prods for BV; *title anim:* Guy Deal, Stan Green, Ed Garbert; *mus:* Buddy Baker; *orch:* Walter Sheets; *song:* Shane Tatum, Richard McKinley; *sung by:* Dean Jones; *col:* Tech. *sd:* RCA. 3 min. • Sequel to *The Shaggy Dog* (1959) concerning a prospective candidate for District Attourney who can turn into a dog. The animated credits show the dog campaigning from a soap-box.

5755. The Shaggy Dog 19 Mar. 1959; Walt Disney prods for BV; *title anim:* T. Hee, Bill Justice, Xavier Atencio; *mus:* Paul Smith; *orch:* Joseph Mullendore; *song:* Gil George, Paul Smith; b&w. *sd:* RCA. 1½min. • Inventive animated titles featuring an exuberant pup rushing around the credits.

5756. Shake Your Powder Puff (*Merrie Melodies*) 17 Oct. 1934; *p.c.:* Leon Schlesinger prods for WB; *dir:* Isadore Freleng; *anim:* Bob McKimson, Bob Clampett; *mus:* Bernard Brown; b&w. *sd:* Vit. 7 min. • Girl bunnies sing a song of how to attract sailor ducks. Other animals entertain and get heckled by a drunken dog.

5757. Shakespearian Spinach (*Popeye*) 19 Jan. 1940; *p.c.:* The Fleischer Studio for Para; *prod:* Max Fleischer; *dir:* Dave Fleischer; *story:* George Manuell; *anim:* Roland Crandall, Ben Solomon; *ed:* Kitty Pfister; *voices:* Jack Mercer, Margie Hines, Pinto Colvig; *mus:* Sammy Timberg; *ph:* Charles Schettler; *prod sup:* Sam Buchwald, Isidore Sparber; b&w. *sd:* WE. 7 min. • Annoyed over having been dropped from the stage musical of "Romeo and Juliet," Bluto proceeds to wreck the current production.

5758. Sham Battle Sheananigans (*Terry-Toon*) 20 Mar. 1942; *p.c.:* TT for Fox; *dir:* Connie Rasinski; *story:* John Foster; *voices:* Arthur Kay, Thomas Morrison; *mus:* Philip A. Scheib; *col:* Tech. *sd:* RCA. 7 min. • Pvt. Gandy Goose and Sgt. Sourpuss play "War Games" between the Blue and Green Army.

5759. Shamrock and Roll (*Merrie Melodies*) 1969; *p.c.:* WB/7A; *dir:* Bob McKimson; *story:* Cal Howard; *anim:* Ted Bonnicksen, La Verne Harding, Jim Davis, Ed Solomon, Norm McCabe; *lay:* Bob Givens, Jaime Diaz; *back:* Bob Abrams; *ed:* Hal Geer; *voices:* Larry Storch; *mus:* William Lava; *prod:* Bill L. Hendricks; *col:* Tech. *sd:* Vit. 6 min. • Merlin the magic mouse and Second Banana match wits with a tricky leprechaun while in Ireland.

5760. Shanghai Woody (*Woody Woodpecker*) 1971; *p.c.:* Walter Lantz prods for Univ; *dir:* Paul J. Smith; *story:* Cal Howard; *anim:* Virgil Ross, Al Coe, Tom Byrne, Joe Voght; *sets:* Nino Carbe; *voices:* Daws Butler, Grace Stafford; *mus:* Walter Greene; *prod mgr:* William E. Garity; *col:* Tech. *sd:* RCA. 6 min. • The captain of a ship and his rat mate rue the day they ever shanghaied Woody who scuppers their vessel by pecking holes in it.

5761. Shanghaied (*Mickey Mouse*) 13 Jan. 1934; *p.c.:* Walt Disney prods for UA; *dir:* Burton F. Gillett; *anim:* Johnny Cannon, Norman Ferguson, Clyde Geronimi, Hardie Gramatky, Edward Love, Richard Lundy, Ben Sharpsteen, Roy Williams; *fx:* Cy Young; *voices:* Billy Bletcher; *mus:* Frank E. Churchill; b&w. *sd:* RCA. 8 min. • Mickey and Minnie are shanghaied aboard Peg-Leg Pete's pirate ship and make a successful attempt to escape the gang of cut-throats.

5762. Shanghaied Shipmates (*Looney Tunes*) 20 June 1936; *p.c.:* Leon Schlesinger prods for WB; *dir:* Jack King; *anim:* Paul Smith, Joseph d'Igalo; *voices:* Billy Bletcher, Joe Dougherty; *mus:* Norman Spencer; b&w. *sd:* Vit. 7 min. • Porky and his chums are shanghaied and treated cruelly by a mean captain. They eventually mutiny and take over the ship.

5763. The Shanty Where Santa Claus Lives (*Merrie Melodies*) 6 Feb. 1933; *p.c.:* Hugh Harman, Rudolf Ising prods for WB; *prod:* Leon Schlesinger; *anim:* Rollin Hamilton, Max Maxwell, Robert Clampett; *mus:* Frank Marsales; b&w. *sd:* Vit. 7 min. • An orphan, living in a barren cabin, is aroused with the arrival of Santa who whisks him away to his workshop at the North Pole.

5764. Shape Ahoy (*Popeye*) 27 Apr. 1945; *p.c.:* Famous for Para; *dir:* I. Sparber; *anim:* Jack Ward, Irving Dressler; *anim:* James Tyer, Ben Solomon; *voices:* Jackson Beck, Mae Questel; *mus:* Winston Sharples; *ph:* Leonard McCormick; *prod mgr:* Sam Buchwald; b&w. *sd:* RCA. 6½ min. Tech reissue: 17 Nov. 1950. • Shipwrecked mariners, Popeye and Bluto, swear-off women until a third castaway in the shape of Olive Oyl appears on the horizon.

5765. Sharp Shooters (*Aesop's Film Fable*) 3 Dec. 1924; *p.c.:* Fables Pictures Inc for Pathé; *dir:* Paul Terry; b&w. *sil.* 5 min. • No story available.

5766. Shaving Muggs (*Popeye*) 30 Oct. 1953; *p.c.:* Famous for Para; *dir:* Seymour Kneitel; *story:* Larz Bourne; *anim:* Tom Johnson, John Gentilella, Els Barthen; *sets:* Anton Loeb; *voices:* Jack Mercer, Jackson Beck Mae Questel; *mus:* Winston Sharples; *ph:* Leonard McCormick; *prod mgr:* Seymour Shultz; *col:* Tech. *sd:* RCA. 6 min. • Olive will go out with the boys only after they've had a haircut and shave. They then proceed to fix each other up. Tech remake of *A Clean Shaven Man*.

5767. She Done Him Right (*Pooch the Pup*) 25 Sept. 1933; *p.c.:* Univ; *dir:* Walter Lantz, "Bill" Nolan; *anim:* Manuel Moreno, Lester Kline, Fred Kopietz, George Grandpré, Ernest Smythe; *mus:* James Dietrich; b&w. *sd:* WE. 6 min. • Pooch marries a "Mae West" type.

5768. She Knew Her Man (*Aesop's Film Fable*) 29 Oct. 1924; *p.c.:* Fables Pictures Inc for Pathé; *dir:* Paul Terry; b&w. *sil.* 5 min. • The farmer's cat elopes and returns with an army of kittens to outnumber the marauding rodents in the house.

5769. She Reminds Me of You (*Screen Songs*) 22 June 1934; *p.c.:* The Fleischer Studio for Para; *prod:* Max Fleischer; *dir:* Dave Fleischer; *anim:* Willard Bowsky, William Sturm; *mus:* Art Turkisher; *l/a:* The Four Eton Boys; b&w. *sd:* WE. 7 min. *l/a/anim.* • Showing the future comforts of an automated movie theatre.

5770. She-Sick Sailors (*Popeye*) 8 Dec. 1944; *p.c.:* Famous for Para; *dir:* Seymour Kneitel; *story:* Bill Turner, Otto Messmer; *anim:* Jim Tyer, Ben Solomon; *voices:* Jack Mercer, Mae Questel, Jackson Beck; *mus:* Sammy Timberg; *ph:* Leonard McCormick; *prod mgr:* Sam Buchwald; b&w. *sd:* RCA. 8 min. Tech reissue: 5 Oct. 1944. • Olive's infatuation with "Superman" finds Bluto posing as the Man of Steel, forcing Popeye to compete against his strength.

5771. She Was An Acrobat's Daughter (*Merrie Melodies*) 10 Apr. 1937; *p.c.:* Leon Schlesinger prods for WB; *dir:* I. Freleng; *story:* Robert Clampett; *anim:* Bob McKimson, A.C. Gamer; *character des:* T. Hee; *lay:* Griff Jay; *back:* Arthur Loomer; *ed:* Tregoweth E. Brown; *voices:* Mel Blanc, Dave Weber; *mus:* Carl W. Stalling; *song:* Bert Kalmar, Harry Ruby; *prod sup:* Henry Binder, Raymond G. Katz; *col:* Tech. *sd:* Vit. 8 min. • The

Warmer Bros Theatre shows "Goofytone News," a sing-along, then the big feature "The Petrified Florist." Caricatures of Bette Davis, Leslie Howard and Adolf Hitler.

5772. She Wronged Him Right (*Betty Boop*) 5 Jan. 1934; *p.c.:* The Fleischer Studio for Para; *prod:* Max Fleischer; *dir:* Dave Fleischer; *anim:* Roland Crandall, Thomas Johnson; *voice:* Mae Questel; *mus:* Sammy Timberg; b&w. *sd:* WE. 6½ min. • Betty stages a melodrama with Fearless Fred as the hero and Heeza Ratt as the villain.

5773. Sheep Ahoy (*Merrie Melodies*) 11 Dec. 1954; *p.c.:* WB; *dir:* Charles M. Jones; *story:* Michael Maltese; *anim:* Richard Thompson, Abe Levitow; *lay:* Maurice Noble; *back:* Philip de Guard; *ed:* Treg Brown; *voice:* Mel Blanc; *mus:* Milt Franklyn; *prod mgr:* John W. Burton; *prod:* Edward Selzer; *col:* Tech. *sd:* Vit. 7 min. • Ralph Wolf, again tries to relieve the watchdog of his flock, this time by using an Acme Artificial Rock, a smoke screen and pole-vaulting ... all to no avail.

5774. Sheep Dog (*Pluto*) 18 Nov. 1949; *p.c.:* Walt Disney prods for RKO; *dir:* Charles Nichols; *story:* Eric Gurney, Milt Schaffer; *anim:* George Nicholas, George Kreisl, Phil Duncan, Hugh Fraser; *fx:* Jack Boyd; *lay:* Karl Karpé; *back:* Brice Mack; *voices:* James MacDonald; *mus:* Oliver Wallace; *col:* Tech. *sd:* RCA. 6½ min. • Pluto guards a flock of sheep against two conniving coyotes.

5775. A Sheep in the Deep (*Merrie Melodies*) Feb. 1962; *p.c.:* WB; *dir/story:* Chuck Jones; *asst dir/lay:* Maurice Noble; *anim:* Tom Ray, Ken Harris, Richard Thompson, Bob Bransford; *asst lay:* Corny Cole; *back:* Philip de Guard, William Butler; *ed:* Treg Brown; *voices:* Mel Blanc; *mus:* Milt Franklyn; *prod mgr:* William Orcutt; *prod:* David H. DePatie; *col:* Tech. *sd:* Vit. 7 min. • Ralph Wolf clocks-on for a day's sheep-stealing. Sam Sheepdog is on guard and the day is rounded off by the two of them disguising themselves as sheep.

5776. The Sheep in the Meadow (*Terry-Toon*) 22 Sept. 1939; *p.c.:* TT for Fox; *dir:* Mannie Davis; *story:* John Foster; *mus:* Philip A. Scheib; b&w. *sd:* RCA. 6 min. • A wolf lures a sheep away from the flock but is stopped by the shepherd lad.

5777. Sheep Shape (*Noveltoon*) 28 June 1946; *p.c.:* Famous for Para; *dir:* Bill Tytla; *story:* Bunny Gough, Bill Turner, Larry Riley; *anim:* George Germanetti, Steve Muffatti; *sets:* Robert Connavale, Lloyd Hallock Jr.; *voices:* Arnold Stang, Sid Raymond, Gwen Davies; *mus:* Winston Sharples; *ph:* Leonard McCormick; *prod mgr:* Sam Buchwald; *col:* Tech. *sd:* RCA. 7 min. • Blackie the sheep collects $10,000 for the orphans' home which Wolfie attempts to steal from him.

5778. Sheep Stealers Anonymous (*Loopy de Loop*) June 1963; *p.c.:* Hanna-Barbera prods for Colum; *prod/dir:* William Hanna, Joseph Barbera; *story dir:* Alex Lovy; *story:* Dalton Sandifer; *anim dir:* Charles A. Nichols; *anim:* George Goepper, George Nicholas; *lay:* Lance Nolley; *back:* Art Lozzi; *ed:* Greg Watson; *voices:* Daws Butler, Don Messick, Doug Young; *mus:* Hoyt Curtin; *titles:* Lawrence Gobel; *prod mgr:* Howard Hanson; *col:* East. *sd:* RCA. 6 min. • Loopy tries to quench another wolf's penchant for stealing sheep.

5779. Sheep Wrecked (*Droopy*) 7 Feb. 1958; *p.c.:* MGM; *prod:* William Hanna, Joseph Barbera; *dir:* Michael Lah; *story:* Homer Brightman; *anim:* Ken Southworth, Irven Spence, Herman Cohen, Bill Schipek, James Escalante; *character des/lay:* Ed Benedict; *back:* F. Montealegre; *ed:* Jim Faris; *voices:* Daws Butler, Bill Thompson; *mus:* Scott Bradley; *ph:* Jack Stevens; *prod mgr:* Hal Elias; *col:* Tech. *sd:* WE. 6 min. CS. • Sheepherder Droopy protects his flock against the hungry advances of an ingenious wolf.

5780. The Sheepish Wolf (*Merrie Melodies*) 17 Oct. 1942; *p.c.:* Leon Schlesinger prods for WB; *dir:* I. Freleng; *story:* Michael Maltese; *anim:* Gil Turner; *lay:* Owen Fitzgerald; *back:* Lenard Kester; *ed:* Treg Brown; *voices:* Mel Blanc; *mus:* Carl W. Stalling; *prod sup:* Henry Binder, Raymond G. Katz; *col:* Tech, *sd:* Vit. 7 min. • The wolf's sheep disguise does not fool the sheep dog.

5781. Sheepish Wolf (*Noveltoon*) Nov. 1963; *p.c.:* Para Cartoons; *dir:* Seymour Kneitel; *sets:* Robert Little; *voices:* Bob MacFadden; *mus:* Winston Sharples; *ph:* Leonard McCormick; *prod mgr:* Abe Goodman; *col:* Tech. *sd:* RCA. 6 min. • A wolf gets a job as a watchdog when he's too tired and old to chase sheep.

5782. The Shell-Shocked Egg (*Merrie Melodies*) 10 July 1948; *p.c.:*

WB; *dir:* Robert McKimson; *story:* Warren Foster; *anim:* Charles McKimson, Manny Gould, I. Ellis; *lay:* Cornett Wood; *back:* Richard H. Thomas; *ed:* Treg Brown; *voices:* Mel Blanc, Lloyd Turner; *mus:* Carl Stalling; *prod mgr:* John W. Burton; *prod:* Edward Selzer; *col:* Tech. *sd:* Vit. 7 min. • A mother turtle loses a half-hatched egg.

5783. Sherlock Pink *(Pink Panther)* 29 June 1976; *p.c.:* Mirisch/Geoffrey/DFE for UA; *dir:* Robert McKimson; *story:* John W. Dunn; *anim:* Nelson Shin, Jim Davis, Bob Bemiller, Bob Bransford; *lay:* Dick Ung; *back:* Richard H. Thomas; *ed:* Rick Steward; *mus:* Walter Greene; *theme tune:* Henry Mancini; *ph:* John Burton Jr.; *prod mgr:* Lee Gunther; *col:* DeLuxe. *sd:* RCA. 6 min. • The Panther eats a chocolate cake in his sleep and awakes to believe someone stole it. In his detection work he runs across a real desperado.

5784. Sherman Was Right *(Paul Terry-Toon)* 18 Sept. 1932; *p.c.:* Moser & Terry for Educational/Fox; *dir:* Frank Moser, Paul Terry; *mus:* Philip A. Scheib; b&w. *sd:* WE. 6 min. • Mice soldiers are under an enemy attack from the air. Al Falfa runs for cover while the mouse hero brings down the adversaries.

5785. She's in Again *(Aesop's Film Fable)* 3 Dec. 1924; *p.c.:* Fables Pictures Inc for Pathé; *dir:* Paul Terry; b&w. *sil.* 5 min. • After numerous attempts attempts to dispose of an egg-stealing cat, Farmer Al Falfa bribes a dog to chase the cat away. The dog and cat unite to drink beer together until the Farmer breaks up the socializing and puts the cat into a cannon, shooting her to the skies. The cat punctures a cloud and makes it rain cats and dogs on the Farmer.

5786. Sh-h-h-h-h-h *(Cartune)* 6 June 1955; *p.c.:* Walter Lantz prods for Univ; *dir/story:* Tex Avery; *anim:* Ray Abrams, Don Patterson, La Verne Harding; *sets:* Raymond Jacobs, Art Landy; *voices:* Daws Butler, Grace Stafford; *mus:* Clarence Wheeler; *prod mgr:* William E. Garity *col:* Tech. *sd:* RCA. 6 min. • A nervous wreck is advised by his doctor to retire to the solitude of an Alpine retreat. When he books in, he can't sleep from the noise the couple in the next room are making. The original OKEH "Laughing Record" is used on the sound track.

5787. Shinbone Alley 1970; *p.c.:* Fine Arts for Allied Artists; *ex prod/dir:* John David Wilson; *prod:* Emanuel L. Wolf, Preston M. Fleet; *dir sup:* David DeTiege, Joe Darion; based on the musical play *Shinbone Alley* by Joe Darion, Mel Brooks and the "Archy and Mehitabel" stories by Don Marquis; *story:* John David Wilson, David DeTiege, Richard Kinney, Marty Murphy; animation created by John David Wilson; *prod des:* Gary Lund, John David Wilson, Cornelius Cole, James Bernardi, David DeTiege, Jules Engel, Sam Cornell; *anim:* Frank Andrina, Bob Bransford, Fred Grable, Ken Southworth, Frank Gonzales, Rudy Cataldi, Frank Onaitis, Gil Rugg, John Sparey, Brad Case, Jim Hiltz, Russ von Neida, Barrie Nelson, Spencer Peel, Bob Bemiller, George Waiss, Amby Paliwoda, Selby Daley; *asst anim:* Mark Kausler, Bob Zamboni, Jim Rutherford, Carson van Osten, Mike Sanger, Barbara DeTiege, Bob Tyler, Greg Iverson, Lou Zukor, James T. Walker, O.B. Barkley, Deborah Wilson, Tony Pabian, Gerard Kane, Morrie Zukor, John Bruno; *sets:* Rosemary O'Connor, Gary Lund, Tom Baron, James Bernardi, Margaret Nichols, Sam Cornell, Ed Nofziger, Alvero Arce, Marsha Gertenbach; *add back:* Carson van Osten; *ed:* Warner Leighton, Larry de Soto; *voices: Mehitabel:* Carol Channing; *Archy:* Eddie Bracken; *Big Bill:* Alan Reed Snr; *Tyrone T. Tattersall:* John Carradine; *Narrator:* Byron Kane; *The Alley Cats:* The Jackie Ward Singers; *Freddie:* Hal Smith; *also:* Joan Gerber, Ken Sansom, Sal de Lano; *mus:* George Kleinsinger; The Fine Arts Hollywood Orchestra (Shelly Manne on drums); *lyrics:* Joe Darion; *mus ed:* Sam Horta; *i&p:* Constance Crawley; *checking:* Margaret Raymond, Angeve Wilson, Virginia McColley; *technical:* James L. Aicholtz, Pat Ieraci, Hank McGill; *prod sup:* David DeTiege, Christine Decker, Dan Anderson; *col:* East. *sd:* 84 min. • Archy is a poet who has been reincarnated as a cockroach, in love with Mehitabel, an alley cat with a zest for life.

5788. The Shindig *(Mickey Mouse)* 11 July 1930; *p.c.:* Walter E. Disney for Colum; *dir:* Burton F. Gillett; *anim:* Richard Lundy; *mus:* Bert Lewis; *ph:* William Cottrell; b&w. *sd:* PCP. 7 min. • A barnyard musical.

5789. Shine on Harvest Moon *(Screen Songs)* 6 May 1932; *p.c.:* The Fleischer Studio for Para; *prod:* Max Fleischer; *sup:* Dave Fleischer; *dir/story/anim:* James H. Culhane, Rudy Zamora *anim:* Reuben Timinsky; *mus:* Art Turkisher; *song:* Jack Norworth, Nora Bayes; *l/a:* Alice Joy; b&w.

sd: WE. 8½ min. *l/a/anim.* • When the moon announces "Harvest Time," the wind blows up a storm.

5790. Ship A-Hooey *(Herman & Katnip)* 20 Aug. 1954; *p.c.:* Famous for Para; *dir:* I. Sparber; *story:* Larz Bourne; *anim:* Tom Golden, Morey Reden; *sets:* Robert Connavale, Anton Loeb; *voices:* Arnold Stang, Sid Raymond, Jack Mercer; *mus:* Winston Sharples; *title song:* Hal David, Leon Carr; *prod mgr:* Seymour Shultz; *col:* Tech. *sd:* RCA. 7 min. • The mice are sailing smoothly along under the guidance of Cpt. Herman when they unwittingly rescue Katnip who is adrift on a raft.

5791. Ship Ahoy *(Aesop's Sound Fable)* 7 Jan. 1930; *p.c.:* Van Beuren for Pathé; *dir:* John Foster; *mus:* Gene Rodemich; b&w. *sd:* RCA. 7½ min. • Depicting an amazing voyage of the animals on, and under the sea.

5792. Ship A-Hoy Woody *(Woody Woodpecker)* 1969; *p.c.:* Walter Lantz prods for Univ; *dir:* Paul J. Smith; *story:* Homer Brightman; *anim:* Les Kline, Al Coe; *sets:* Nino Carbe; *voices:* Dal McKennon, Grace Stafford; *mus:* Walter Greene; *prod mgr:* William E. Garity; *col:* Tech. *sd:* RCA. 6 min. • Seadog, Woody tries to save the ship's gold.

5793. Shipwreck *(Oswald)* 9 Feb. 1931; *p.c.:* Univ; *dir:* Walter Lantz, "Bill" Nolan; *anim:* Clyde Geronimi, Manuel Moreno, Ray Abrams, Fred Avery, Lester Kline, "Pinto" Colvig; *voice:* Mickey Rooney; *mus:* James Dietrich; b&w. *sd:* WE. 6 min. • Oswald is adrift on a raft when he is pulled to the ocean bed by an oversize fish.

5794. The Shipwrecked Brothers *(Paul Terry-Toons)* 17 Nov. 1933; *p.c.:* Moser & Terry for Educational/Fox; *dir:* Frank Moser, Paul Terry; *mus:* Philip A. Scheib; b&w. *sd:* WE. 5½ min. • A sailor (Farmer Al Falfa) and his parrot are castaways on a desert island. They get caught by the Cannibal King who turns out to be "Friday" and the sailor, Robinson Crusoe.

5795. Shipyard Symphony *(Terry-Toon)* 19 Feb. 1943; *p.c.:* TT for Fox; *dir:* Eddie Donnelly; *story:* John Foster; *mus:* Philip A. Scheib; *col:* Tech. *sd:* RCA. 6 min. • The American bald eagle conducts the building of a warship to music.

5796. Shishkabugs *(Looney Tunes)* Dec. 1962; *p.c.:* WB; *dir:* Friz Freleng; *story:* John Dunn; *anim:* Gerry Chiniquy, Virgil Ross, Bob Matz, Lee Halpern, Art Leonardi; *lay:* Hawley Pratt; *back:* Tom O'Loughlin; *ed:* Treg Brown; *voices:* Mel Blanc; *mus:* Bill Lava; *prod mgr:* William Orcutt; *prod:* David H. DePatie; *col:* Tech. *sd:* Vit. 7 min. • The Royal Chef (Sam) is sent to prepare hassenpfeffer for the King. He is stuck for the prime ingredient, rabbit, until the arrival of Bugs Bunny.

5797. Shiver Me Timbers *(Popeye)* 27 July 1934; *p.c.:* The Fleischer Studio for Para; *prod:* Max Fleischer; *dir:* Dave Fleischer; *anim:* Willard Bowsky, William Sturm; *voices:* William A. Costello, Louis Fleischer; *mus:* Sammy Timberg; b&w. *sd:* WE. 7 min. • Despite warnings, Popeye, Olive and Wimpy board a ghost ship that sets sail and they have some spooky adventures.

5798. The Shocker *(Mighty Heroes)* Dec. 1970; *p.c.:* TT for Fox; *ex prod:* Bill Weiss; *dir:* Robert Taylor; *col:* DeLuxe. *sd:* RCA. 5 min. • "The Shocker" has invaded a power plant in Peacehaven to energize his power-hungry robots.

5799. Shocking Pink *(Pink Panther)* 13 May 1965; *p.c.:* Mirisch/Geoffrey/DFE for UA; *dir:* Friz Freleng; *asst dir:* Hawley Pratt; *story:* Bob Kurtz; *anim:* Norm McCabe, La Verne Harding, Don Williams; *lay:* Dick Ung; *back:* Tom O'Loughlin; *ed:* Lee Gunther; *voice:* Larry Storch; *mus:* William Lava; *theme tune:* Henry Mancini; *prod sup:* Lee Gunther; *col:* DeLuxe. *sd:* RCA. 6 min. • The Panther is encouraged to do repairs around the house with disastrous results.

5800. Shoe Flies *(Honey Halfwitch)* Oct. 1965; *p.c.:* Para Cartoons; *dir/story:* Howard Post; *anim:* Al Eugster; *sets:* Robert Little; *voices:* Shari Lewis, Bob MacFadden; *mus:* Winston Sharples; *prod mgr:* Abe Goodman; *col:* Tech. *sd:* RCA. 6 min. • Teeny Meanie tells Honey to clean her shoes by means of magic. When she does, the shoes go haywire, creating havoc along the way.

5801. The Shoe Must Go On *(Hoot Kloot)* 16 June 1973; *p.c.:* Mirisch/DFE for UA; *dir:* Gerry Chiniquy; *story:* John W. Dunn; *anim:* Bob Matz, Manny Gould, Norm McCabe, Ken Muse, Fred Madison; *lay:* Dick Ung; *back:* Richard H. Thomas; *ed:* Allan R. Potter; *voices:* Bob Holt; *mus:* Doug Goodwin; *titles:* Arthur Leonardi; *ph:* John Burton Jr.; *prod* *mgr:* Stan Paperny; *col:* DeLuxe. *sd:* RCA. 6 min. • Kloot tries to shoe his horse, Fester, in order to capture a bank robber.

5802. The Shoe Must Go On (*Modern Madcap*) June 1960; *p.c.:* Para Cartoons; *dir:* Seymour Kneitel; *story:* Carl Meyer, Jack Mercer; *anim:* Irving Dressler, Morey Reden; *sets:* Robert Owen; *voices:* Jack Mercer; *mus:* Winston Sharples; *ph:* Leonard McCormick; *prod mgr:* Abe Goodman; *col:* Tech. *sd:* RCA. 6 min. • An opera impresario tries to quieten the blacksmith's shop adjacent to the opera house.

5803. Shoein' Hosses (*Popeye*) 1 Jan. 1934; *p.c.:* The Fleischer Studio for Para; *prod:* Max Fleischer; *dir:* Dave Fleischer; *anim:* Willard Bowsky, David Tendlar; *voices:* William A. Costello, Charles Carver, Mae Questel; *mus:* Sammy Timberg; *b&w. sd:* WE. 7 min. • Popeye and Bluto compete for a job in Olive's blacksmith shop with tests of strength.

5804. The Shoemaker and the Elves (*Color Rhapsody*) 26 Oct. 1934; *p.c.:* Charles Mintz prods for Colum; *story:* Art Davis; *anim:* Sid Marcus; *mus:* Joe de Nat; *prod mgr:* James Bronis; *col:* Tech-2. *sd:* RCA. 8 min. • Nobody but the kindly shoemaker will take a waif in from the storm. When asleep at night, the elves repay his kindness by making shoes for him. Caricatures of Charlie Chaplin and Greta Garbo. First *Color Rhapsody* in series.

5805. Shoeshine, Jasper (*Madcap Models*) 15 Nov. 1946; *p.c.:* George Pal prods for Para; *prod/dir:* George Pal; *story:* Jack Miller; *voices:* Roy Glenn, Sara Berner; *mus:* Clarence Wheeler; *col:* Tech. *sd:* WE. 7 min. • Jasper's fairy godmother gives him golden slippers, which he tries on and wins the dancing contest.

5806. The Shootin' Fool (*Aesop's Film Fable*) 9 May 1926; *p.c.:* Fables Pictures Inc for Pathé; *dir:* Paul Terry; *b&w. sil.* 10 min. • A cat is the world's Champion Sharpshooter who is bothered by Professor Quack, a pesty top-hatted duck magician. Quack produces miniature animals from his top hat and when the cat shoots him, he turns into various objects like table lamps and trees.

5807. Shootin' Stars (*Modern Madcap*) Aug. 1960; *p.c.:* Para Cartoons; *dir:* Seymour Kneitel; *story:* Carl Meyer, Jack Mercer; *anim:* Tom Johnson, Morey Reden, Els Barthen; *sets:* Robert Owens; *voices:* Jackson Beck, Gwen Davies; *mus:* Winston Sharples; *ph:* Leonard McCormick; *prod mgr:* Abe Goodman; *col:* Tech. *sd:* RCA. 6 min. • Two western stars fight to redeem their own popularity with a child admirer.

5808. The Shooting of Caribu Lou (*Inspector*) 20 Dec. 1967; *p.c.:* Mirisch/Geoffrey/DFE for UA; *dir:* Gerry Chiniquy; *story:* John W. Dunn; *anim:* Manny Perez, Don Williams, Manny Gould, Bob Matz; *lay:* Dick Ung; *back:* Tom O'Loughlin; *ed:* Lee Gunther; *voices:* Pat Harrington Jr., Mark Skor; *mus:* Walter Greene; *theme tune:* Henry Mancini; *prod sup:* Harry Love, Basil Cox; *col:* DeLuxe. *sd:* RCA. 6 min. • The inspector is taken hostage when Caribu Lou breaks out of prison.

5809. The Shooting of Dan McGoo 3 Mar. 1945; *p.c.:* MGM; *dir:* Tex Avery; *story:* Heck Allen; *anim:* Ed Love, Ray Abrams, Preston Blair; *character des:* Claude Smith; *sets:* John Didrik Johnsen; *ed:* Fred MacAlpin; *voices:* Frank Graham, Imogene Lynn, Sara Berner; *mus:* Scott Bradley; *prod:* Fred Quimby; *col:* Tech. *sd:* WE. 7 min. • Yukon desperado, Dan McGoo, pits his wits against "Happy Hound" in a Klondike saloon.

5810. The Shooting of Dan McGrew 1965; *p.c.:* Ed Graham Prods., for Univ; *dir/prod:* Ed Graham; *poem:* Robert W. Service; *anim dir:* George Gordon; *anim:* Manny Gould, Amby Paliwoda, Gary Hoffman; *des:* George Cannata Jr.; *lay:* Bob Dranko; *back:* Walt Peregoy; *ed:* George Mahana, Armand Shaw; *voices: narrator:* Walter Brennan; *The Stranger:* Ernie Banks; *mus:* George Shearing; *i&p:* Connie Crawley; *checking:* Beverly Ann Ware; *prod sup:* Lew Irwin; *prod asst:* Henry Hof III, Ruth Kennedy; *col:* DeLuxe. *sd.* 7 min. • Interpretation of Robert W. Service's famous poem about life in the Klondike in the days of the gold rush.

5811. Shop, Look & Listen (*Merrie Melodies*) 21 Dec. 1940; *p.c.:* Leon Schlesinger prods for WB; *dir:* I. Freleng; *story:* Dave Monahan; *anim:* Cal Dalton; *lay:* Owen Fitzgerald; *back:* Robert L. Holdeman; *ed:* Treg Brown; *voices:* Bill Thompson, Mel Blanc; *mus:* Carl W. Stalling; *prod mgr:* Henry Binder, Raymond G. Katz; *col:* Tech. *sd:* Vit. 7 min. • A W.C. Fieldsian mouse gives a guided tour of J.T. Gimlet's department store.

5812. A Short Circuit (*Aesop's Film Fable*) 8 Jan. 1928; *p.c.:* Fables Pictures Inc for Pathé; *dir:* Paul Terry, John Foster; *b&w. sil.* 10 min. •

Farmer Al tries operating his farm with electricity. The hens start laying bushels of eggs and milk flows from the cow.

5813. Short in the Saddle (*Woody Woodpecker*) Sept. 1963; *p.c.:* Walter Lantz prods for Univ; *dir:* Paul J. Smith; *story:* Cal Howard; *anim:* Les Kline, Al Coe; *sets:* Ray Huffine, Art Landy; *voices:* Dal McKennon, Grace Stafford; *mus:* Clarence Wheeler; *col:* Tech. *sd:* RCA. 6 min. • Woody goes west to pan for gold. A villain mistakes a sack Woody is carrying for gold, which actually houses our hero's lunch.

5814. Short Snorts on Sports (*Phantasy*) 3 June 1948; *p.c.:* Colum; *prod:* Raymond Katz, Henry Binder; *dir:* Alex Lovy; *story:* Cal Howard, Dave Monahan; *anim:* Paul Sommer, Chic Otterstrom, Jay Sarbry; *lay:* Jim Carmichael; *back:* Al Boggs; *voices:* Ken Carpenter, Jack Mather, Daws Butler; *mus:* Darrell Calker; *col:* Ciné. *sd:* WE. 6½ min. • Burlesque on various sports.

5815. Short Term Sheriff (*Duckwood*) May 1964; *p.c.:* TT for Fox; *ex prod:* Bill Weiss; *dir/anim:* Dave Tendlar; *story sup:* Tom Morrison; *story:* Larz Bourne; *sets:* Bill Focht, John Zago; *ed:* Jack McConnell; *voices:* Dayton Allen; *mus:* Jim Timmens; *ph:* Joseph Rasinski; *sd:* Elliott Grey; *col:* DeLuxe. *sd:* RCA. 5 min. • Duckwood and Donkey rue the day they accepted the post of sheriff in a western town.

5816. Short'nin' Bread (*Screen Song*) 24 Mar. 1950; *p.c.:* Famous for Para; *dir:* I. Sparber; *story:* Larz Bourne, Larry Riley; *anim:* Myron Waldman, Gordon Whittier; *sets:* Anton Loeb; *voices:* Cecil Roy, Jack Mercer; *mus:* Winston Sharples; *ph:* Leonard McCormick; *prod mgr:* Sam Buchwald; *col:* Tech. *sd:* RCA. 7 min. • The bakery cakes and pies cut a rug to the title song. Upside-down cakes dance on the ceiling, Napoleon escorts Mme. Eclaire and the rum cake gets drunk.

5817. Shot and Bothered (*Looney Tunes*) 8 Jan. 1966; *p.c.:* DFE for WB; *dir:* Rudy Larriva; *story:* Nick Bennion; *anim:* Bob Bransford, Hank Smith, Virgil Ross; *lay:* Don Sheppard; *back:* Anthony Rizzo; *ed:* Lee Gunther; *mus:* Bill Lava; *col:* Tech. *sd:* Vit. 6 min. • In order to secure the Road-Runner, the Coyote uses Acme Suction Cups on his feet, a skateboard and finally inflates himself with helium to float aloft and drop a bomb on the speed demon. All his plans go awry.

5818. Shove Thy Neighbor (*Terry-Toon*) July 1957; *p.c.:* TT for Fox; *ex prod:* Bill Weiss; *dir sup:* Gene Deitch; *dir:* Connie Rasinski; *story dir:* Tommy Morrison; *story:* Larz Bourne, Bob Kuwahara; *anim:* Ed Donnelly, Larry Silverman, Mannie Davis, Johnnie Gent, Jim Tyer, Al Chiarito; *des:* Al Kouzel; *lay:* Art Bartsch; *back:* Bill Hilliker; *voices:* Allen Swift, Bern Bennett; *mus:* Phil Scheib; *prod mgr:* Frank Schudde; *col:* Tech. *sd:* RCA. 6 min. • John Doormat has trouble with his neighbor's vicious bulldog.

5819. The Show (*Out of the Inkwell*) 21 Sept. 1922; *p.c.:* Inkwell Studio for Winkler; *dir:* Dave Fleischer; *anim/l/a:* Max Fleischer; *b&w. sil.* 6 min. *l/a/anim.* • Ko-Ko and his three partners are rehearsing their parts for a show as they are rushed to the theatre in Max's car.

5820. Show-Biz Beagle (*Woody Woodpecker*) 1972; *p.c.:* Walter Lantz prods for Univ; *dir:* Paul J. Smith; *story:* Cal Howard; *anim:* Volus Jones, Al Coe, Tom Byrne, Joe Voght; *sets:* Nino Carbe; *voices:* Dal McKennon, Grace Stafford; *mus:* Walter Greene; *prod mgr:* William E. Garity; *col:* Tech. *sd:* RCA. 5½ min. • Buzz Buzzard cons Woody into buying a talking dog. When he gets the dog home, Woody finds the dog really can speak and puts him on the stage.

5821. Show-Biz Bugs (*Looney Tunes*) 2 Nov. 1957; *p.c.:* WB; *dir:* Friz Freleng; *story:* Warren Foster; *anim:* Gerry Chiniquy, Art Davis, Virgil Ross; *lay:* Hawley Pratt; *back:* Boris Gorelick; *ed:* Treg Brown; *voices:* Mel Blanc; *mus:* Milt Franklyn; *prod:* John W. Burton; *col:* Tech. *sd:* Vit. 7 min. • Jealous of Bugs' success in a show, Daffy sets out to sabotage his act.

5822. Show Me the Way to Go Home (*Screen Songs*) 30 Jan. 1932; *p.c.:* The Fleischer Studio for Para; *prod:* Max Fleischer; *sup:* Dave Fleischer; *dir/anim:* Jimmie Culhane; *mus:* Art Turkisher; *b&w. sd:* WE. 6 min. • Featuring bar patrons, beer barrel–stacking and an inebriated dog heading home. Some live-action footage shows a drunk staggering homewards.

5823. Showing Off (*Scrappy*) 16 Nov. 1931; *p.c.:* Winkler for Colum; *prod:* Charles Mintz; *story:* Dick Huemor; *anim:* Sid Marcus; *mus:* Joe de Nat; *prod mgr:* James Bronis; *b&w. sd:* WE. 6 min. • Scrappy impresses little Margie by smoking an El Ropo cigar and accidentally sets light to her undergarments ... then calls for a fireman from the theatre audience.

5824. Showing the Making of Animated Cartoons 1 Oct. 1921; *p.c./anim:* Bert Green; b&w. *sil.* • No story available.

5825. The Shriek *(Oswald)* 24 Feb. 1933; *p.c.:* Univ; *dir:* Walter Lantz, "Bill" Nolan; *anim:* Ray Abrams, Fred Avery, Cecil Surry, Jack Carr, Don Williams; *mus:* James Dietrich; b&w. *sd:* WE. 6 min. • While touring the desert, Oswald's girl is kidnapped by a Sheikh. Oswald pursues them to a pyramid inhabited by skeletons.

5826. The Shrinker *(Mighty Heroes)* 1969; *p.c.:* TT for Fox; *ex prod:* Bill Weiss; *dir:* Robert Taylor; *col:* DeLuxe. *sd:* RCA. 6 min. • The Shrinker shrinks the Peacehaven Bank and the Mighty Heroes are soon on call.

5827. Shuffle Off to Buffalo *(Merrie Melodies)* 3 Aug. 1933; Hugh Harman, Rudolf Ising prods for WB; *story:* Robert Clampett; *anim:* Isadore Freleng, Paul Smith, Robert Clampett; *ed:* Dale Pickett; *mus:* Frank Marsales; *song:* Harry Warren, Al Dubin; *asso prod:* Leon Schlesinger; b&w. *sd:* Vit. 7 min. • An insight as to where babies come from. Caricatures of Eddie Cantor and Ed Wynn.

5828. Shut-Eye Popeye *(Popeye)* 3 Oct. 1952; *p.c.:* Famous for Para; *dir:* I. Sparber; *story:* Irving Spector; *anim:* Al Eugster, George Germanetti; *sets:* Robert Connavale; *voices:* Jack Mercer; *mus:* Winston Sharples; *ph:* Leonard McCormick; *prod mgr:* Seymour Shultz; *col:* Tech. *sd:* RCA. 6 min. • Popeye's snoring keeps a mouse awake who sets about quietening the situation.

5829. Shutter Bug *(Woody Woodpecker)* 7 May 1963; *p.c.:* Walter Lantz prods for Univ; *dir:* Paul J. Smith; *story:* Dave DeTiege; *anim:* Les Kline, Al Coe, Art Davis; *sets:* Art Landy, Ray Huffine; *voices:* Jerry Mann, Grace Stafford; *mus:* Clarence Wheeler; *prod mgr:* William E. Garity; *col:* Tech. *sd:* RCA. 5½ min. • "Scoop" Smith, a news photographer, hounds a vacationing Woody for publicity photographs.

5830. Shutter-Bugged Cat *(Tom & Jerry)* 1967; *p.c.:* MGM; *dir/add anim:* Tom Ray; *story:* Bob Ogle; *add back:* Philip de Guard; *ed:* Lovell Norman; *mus:* Dean Elliott; *Seq dir:* William Hanna, Joseph Barbera; *anim:* Irven Spence, Ed Barge, Ken Muse, Ray Patterson, George Gordon, Pete Burness, Lewis Marshall; *col:* Metro. *sd:* WE. 6 min. Seq: *Part-Time Pal; Yankee Doodle Mouse; Johann Mouse; Heavenly Puss; Nit-Witty Kitty; Designs on Jerry.* • Tom runs through some home movies to determine where he went wrong in previous pursuits of Jerry.

5831. Sick Cylinders *(Oswald)* 26 Dec. 1928; *p.c.:* Winkler for Univ; *anim:* Hugh Harman, Ben Clopton; b&w. *sil.* 5 min. • Oswald takes his girl for a spin and his car breaks down. She finally goes off with another.

5832. Sick, Sick Sidney *(Terry-Toon)* Aug. 1958; *p.c.:* TT for Fox; *ex prod:* Bill Weiss; *dir sup:* Gene Deitch; *dir:* Art Bartsch; *story dir:* Tom Morrison; *story:* Larz Bourne, Eli Bauer; *anim:* Larry Silverman, Jim Tyer, Bob Kuwahara, Mannie Davis, Al Chiarito, Vinnie Bell; *lay:* Eli Bauer; *back:* Bill Hilliker; *voices:* Lionel Wilson; *mus:* Phil Scheib; *prod mgr:* Frank Schudde; *col:* Tech. *sd:* RCA. 7 min. CS. • Sidney the elephant eludes the safari until he realizes they don't want elephants ... then he changes his tactics.

5833. Sick Transit *(Noveltoon)* Jan. 1966; *p.c.:* Para Cartoons; *dir:* Howard Post; *story:* Howard Post, Frank Ridgeway, Bud Sagendorf; *anim:* Wm. B. Pattengill; *sets:* Robert Little; *mus:* Winston Sharples; *ph:* Leonard McCormick; *prod mgr:* Abe Goodman; *col:* Tech. *sd:* RCA. 4½ min. • Rapid Rabbit, in his sports car, tries overtaking a road hot. They both land in a hospital!

5834. Sicque! Sicque! Sicque! *(Inspector)* 23 Sept. 1966; *p.c.:* Mirisch/Geoffrey/DFE for UA; *dir:* George Singer; *story:* John W. Dunn; *anim:* Norm McCabe, Manny Perez, Warren Batchelder, Don Williams, Bob Matz; *sets:* T.M. Yakutis; *ed:* Lee Gunther; *voices:* Pat Harrington Jr.; *mus:* Walter Greene; *theme tune:* Henry Mancini; *prod mgr:* Bill Orcutt; *col:* DeLuxe; *sd:* RCA. 6 min. • While investigating a mad scientist's house, Duex Duex drinks a potion which turns him into a monster.

5835. The Sidewalks of New York *(Screen Songs)* 5 Feb. 1929; *p.c.:* The Fleischer Studio for Para; *dir:* Dave Fleischer; *anim:* Max Fleischer; *mus:* Art Turkisher; *song:* Charles B. Lawlor, James Blake; b&w. *sd:* WE. 7 min. • Ko-Ko introduces the singalong in The Fleischer brothers' first sound "Screen Song."

5836. Sidney's Family Tree *(Terry-Toon)* Dec. 1958; *p.c.:* TT for Fox; *ex prod:* Bill Weiss; *dir sup:* Gene Deitch; *dir:* Art Bartsch; *story sup:* Tom Morrison; *story:* Eli Bauer; *anim:* Johnny Gent, Larry Silverman, Ed Donnelly, Vinnie Bell, Jim Tyer; *sets:* Bill Hiliker; *voices:* Lionel Wilson; *mus:* Philip Scheib; *prod mgr:* Frank Schudde; *col:* Tech. *sd:* RCA. 7 min. CS. • Sidney, the neurotic elephant, adopts himself into a family of monkeys. Father ape isn't too pleased with his surrogate son and tries to dispose of him.

5837. Sidney's White Elephant *(Terry-Toon)* June 1963; *p.c.:* TT for Fox; *ex prod:* Bill Weiss; *dir:* Art Bartsch; *story sup:* Tom Morrison; *sets:* John Zago; *voices:* Dayton Allen, Lionel Wilson; *mus:* Phil Scheib; *col:* DeLuxe. *sd:* RCA. 6 min. • Two thieves kidnap the Sultan's white elephant. Sidney intervenes and returns him.

5838. A Sight for Squaw Eyes *(Noveltoon)* Mar. 1963; *p.c.:* Para Cartoons; *dir:* Seymour Kneitel; *story:* Irving Dressler; *anim:* Morey Reden, George Germanetti, Larry Silverman; *sets:* Anton Loeb; *voices:* Jack Mercer, Corinne Orr; *mus:* Winston Sharples; *ph:* Leonard McCormick; *prod mgr:* Abe Goodman; *col:* Tech. *sd:* RCA. 6 min • A "hip" Indian maid tries her hand at being the wife of a wealthy Indian brave.

5839. Signed, Sealed and Clobbered *(Clint Clobber)* Nov. 1959; *p.c.:* TT for Fox; *ex prod:* Bill Weiss; *dir sup:* Gene Deitch; *dir:* Connie Rasinski; *story dir:* Tom Morrison; *story:* Larz Bourne, Eli Bauer, Tod Dockstader, Mike Meyer; *anim:* Johnny Gent, Vinnie Bell, Mannie Davis, Bob Kuwahara, Ed Donnelly, Larry Silverman, Dave Tendlar; *lay:* Al Kouzel; *back:* Bill Hilliker; *voices:* Allen Swift; *mus:* Phil Scheib; *prod mgr:* Sparky Schudde; *col:* Tech. *sd:* RCA. 7 min. • Alvin, the trained seal, escapes from a circus act tenant, resulting in "Happy Ed" auditioning "Clown" Clobber.

5840. Signs of Spring *(Aesop's Film Fable)* 6 Nov. 1927; *p.c.:* Fables pictures Inc for Pathé; *dir:* Paul Terry; b&w. *sil.* 10 min. • Spring fever hits Farmer Al Falfa. He dreams he's dancing with nymphs and is rudely awakened when mosquitoes attack him.

5841. Silent Tweetment *(Flippy)* 14 Sept. 1946; *p.c.:* Colum; *dir:* Bob Wickersham; *story:* Paul Sommer, Ed Friedman; *anim:* Roy Jenkins; *lay:* Clark Watson; *ed:* Richard S. Jensen; *voices:* Frank Graham, A. Purves Pullen; *mus:* Eddie Kilfeather; *ph:* Frank Fisher; *prod mgr:* Hugh McCollum; *col:* Tech. *sd:* WE. 6½ min. • The cat silences Flippy's singing, then thinks he'll get blamed, so he does his best to make the bird sing again.

5842. Silly Hillbilly *(Popeye)* 9 Sept. 1949; *p.c.:* Famous for Para; *dir:* I. Sparber; *story:* I. Klein; *anim:* Tom Johnson, Frank Endres, Els Barthen; *sets:* Robert Little; *voices:* Jack Mercer, Jackson Beck, Mae Questel; *mus:* Winston Sharples; *ph:* Leonard McCormick; *prod mgr:* Sam Buchwald; *col:* Tech. *sd:* Vit. 6½ min. • Popeye tries to sell modern-day conveniences to hillbillies. When mountain girl, Olive, falls for him, Bluto nips the romance in the bud.

5843. Silly Scandals *(Talkartoon)* 23 May 1931; *p.c.:* The Fleischer Studio for Para; *prod:* Max Fleischer; *dir:* Dave Fleischer; *mus:* Art Turkisher; b&w. *sd:* WE. 6 min. • Bimbo sneaks into the theatre to hear Betty sing and becomes part of a magic act.

5844. Silly Science *(Noveltoon)* May 1960; *p.c.:* Para Cartoons; *dir:* Seymour Kneitel; *story:* Carl Meyer, Jack Mercer; *anim:* I. Klein, Irving Dressler; *sets:* Robert Owen; *voices:* Bob MacFadden, Corinne Orr; *mus:* Winston Sharples; *ph:* Leonard McCormick; *prod mgr:* Abe Goodman; *col:* Tech. *sd:* RCA. 6 min. • Spot-gags on inventions including the latest in cars for the push-button age.

5845. Silly Seals *(New Universal cartoon)* 25 July 1938; *p.c.:* Univ; *dir:* Lester Kline; *story:* Victor McLeod, James Miele; *anim:* George Nicholas, Ralph Somerville; *sets:* Edgar Keichle; *voice:* Dave Weber; *mus:* Frank Marsales; *prod mgr:* George Hall; b&w. *sd:* WE. 7½ min. • A baby seal prefers juggling snowballs to learning how to catch fish. He is sent home from school but comes to the rescue when the classroom is invaded by polar bears.

5846. Silly Superstition *(Li'l Eightball)* 28 Aug. 1939; *p.c.:* Walter Lantz prods for Univ; *dir:* Burt Gillett; *sets:* Edgar Keichle; *voice:* Mel Blanc; *mus:* Frank Marsales; *prod mgr:* George Hall; b&w. *sd:* WE. 7 min. • Li'l Eightball shuns all superstitious warnings given him until the arrival of a lion.

5847. The Silver Streak *(Mighty Mouse)* 8 June 1945; *p.c.:* TT for Fox; *dir:* Eddie Donnelly; *story:* John Foster; *mus:* Philip A. Scheib; *col:*

Tech. *sd:* RCA. 6½ min. • The cats overcome the mice's dog friend and tie him to the railroad tracks ... then Mighty Mouse is called in.

5848. Silvery Moon *(Aesop's Sound Fable)* 13 Jan. 1932; *p.c.:* Van Beuren for RKO; *dir:* John Foster, Mannie Davis; *mus:* Gene Rodemich; b&w. *sd:* RCA. 7 min. • A boy and girl cat arrive in Candy Land where they eat their fill and are chased home by a bottle of castor oil and a spoon.

5849. Simple Simon *(ComiColor)* 15 Nov. 1935; *p.c.:* Celebrity prods; *prod/dir:* Ub Iwerks; *mus:* Carl Stalling; *col:* Ciné. *sd:* PCP. 6 min. • Simon takes his goose to the fair where he meets a Pieman, samples his pies and can't pay! The Pieman gives chase and the goose wins first prize in the show ... so all ends well.

5850. Simple Siren *(Phantasy)* 25 Oct. 1945; *p.c.:* Colum; *dir:* Paul Sommer; *story:* Ed Seward; *anim:* Volus Jones, Don Williams; *lay:* Clark Watson; *ed:* Richard S. Jensen; *voice:* Sara Berner; *mus:* Eddie Kilfeather; *ph:* Frank Fisher; *prod mgr:* Hugh McCollum; b&w. *sd:* WE. 6½ min. • An old-maid mermaid chases a fisherman by using a submarine detector and depth charges, falling into her own traps more often than the intended victim.

5851. The Simple Things *(Mickey Mouse)* 18 Apr. 1953; *p.c.:* Walt Disney prods for RKO; *dir:* Charles Nichols; *story:* Bill Berg; *anim:* Marvin Woodward, Fred Moore, Norman Ferguson, Charles Nichols; *fx:* Dan Mac-Manus; *lay:* Lance Nolley; *back:* Ed Starr; *voices:* The Jud Conlon Chorus, James MacDonald, Clarke Mallory; *mus:* Paul Smith; *song:* Gil George; *col:* Tech. *sd:* RCA. 7 min. • Mickey and Pluto go fishing and are beset by seagulls.

5852. Sinbad the Sailor *(ComiColor)* 26 June 1935; *p.c.:* Celebrity prods; *prod/dir:* Ub Iwerks; *anim:* Al Eugster; *mus:* Carl Stalling; *col:* Ciné. *sd:* PCP. 8 min. • Sinbad is discovered by pirates who are digging for treasure. They tie him accidentally to the leg of a roc who flies off, depositing Sinbad and the treasure aboard the empty pirate ship.

5853. Sing a Song *(Screen Songs)* 2 Dec. 1932; *p.c.:* The Fleischer Studio for Para; *prod:* Max Fleischer; *dir:* Dave Fleischer; *anim:* Seymour Kneitel, Myron Waldman; *mus:* Art Turkisher; *l/a:* James Melton; b&w. *sd:* WE. 7 min. • A bear as "Bing Bang Columbo," Kate Smith as a hippo, Rudy Vallee as a horse and Bimbo sucks the four Pills brothers into a vacuum cleaner.

5854. Sing Again of Michigan *(Screen Song)* 29 June 1951; *p.c.:* Famous for Para; *dir:* I. Sparber; *story:* Larz Bourne; *anim:* Al Eugster, George Rufle; *sets:* Robert Owen; *voices:* Michael Fitzmaurice, Jack Mercer; *mus:* Winston Sharples; *ph:* Leonard McCormick; *prod mgr:* Sam Buchwald; *col:* Tech. *sd:* RCA. 7 min. • A guided tour of Michigan including an insight into baseball, unusual furniture, cherry trees and the customary sing-along.

5855. Sing and Be Happy/Cartoon Melodies *anim sup:* Dave Fleischer; *l/a prod/dir:* Will Cowan; *vocals:* The King's Men; b&w. *sd:* RCA. 10 min. *l/a/anim.* • *1950:* **Dreams of Dust** 20 Feb. **Sing Your Thanks** 3 Apr. **Harmony Hall** 29 May. **Melody Moods** 17 July. **Sing Happy** 28 Aug. **Feast of Songs** 2 Oct. **Brother John** 20 Nov. *Cartoon Melodies* • *1951:* **Peggy, Peg and Polly** 22 Jan. **Lower the Boom** 14 Mar. **Bubbles of Song** 7 May. **Readin', Ritin' and Rithmetic** 28 May. **Hill Billy** 25 June. **McDonald's Farm** 30 July. **Down the River** 10 Sept. **Reuben, Reuben** 12 Nov. **Uncle Sam's Songs** 31 Dec. • *1952:* **Songs That Live** 17 Mar. **Memory Song Book** 19 May. **Song Dreams** 23 June. **Toast of Song** 28 July • The King's Men quartet sing a selection of appropriate songs, illustrated with "limited animation" sequences.

5856. Sing, Babies, Sing! *(Screen Songs)* 15 Dec. 1933; *p.c.:* The Fleischer Studio for Para; *prod:* Max Fleischer; *dir:* Dave Fleischer; *anim:* Seymour Kneitel, David Tendlar; *mus:* Art Turkisher; *l/a:* Baby Rosemarie; b&w. *sd:* WE. 8½ min. *l/a/anim.* • A "baby factory" where infants are prepared for delivery by an army of storks. The songs are provided by a child performer of merit who sings "An Orchid to You" and "Hiawatha's Lullaby."

5857. Sing 'em Back Alive *(Organlogue)* 1932; *p.c.:* Master Arts prods; *anim:* Pud Lane; *l/a:* The Four Eton Boys; b&w. *sd.* 5 min. *l/a/anim.* • *Tiger Rag, Jungle Town, Pargie* and *Mumbo Jumbo Jig-a-Boo J* are sung by the boys and illustrated by stills and animated sequences.

5858. Sing or Swim *(Screen Songs)* 7 June 1948; *p.c.:* Famous for Para; *dir:* Seymour Kneitel; *story:* I. Klein, Larry Riley; *anim:* Al Eugster, Irving

Spector; *sets:* Robert Connavale; *voice:* Jackson Beck; *mus:* Winston Sharples; *song:* Harry Carroll, Harold Atteridge; *ph:* Leonard McCormick; *prod mgr:* Sam Buchwald; *col:* Pola. *sd:* RCA. 7 min. • Animals go for a swim and have fun at Coney Island.

5859. Sing Sing Song *(Paul Terry-Toon)* 19 Apr. 1931; *p.c.:* Terry, Moser & Coffman for Educational/Fox; *dir:* Frank Moser, Paul Terry; *anim:* Jack King, Vladimir Tytla; *mus:* Philip A. Scheib; b&w. *sd:* WE. 6 min. • The animals stage a jailbreak from prison. An explosion lands them all back where they started from.

5860. Sing, Sisters, Sing! *(Screen Songs)* 30 June 1933; *p.c.:* The Fleischer Studio for Para; *prod:* Max Fleischer; *dir:* Dave Fleischer; *anim:* Bernard Wolf, David Tendlar; *mus:* Art Turkisher; *l/a:* The Three X Sisters (Jessie, Pearl & Violet Hamilton); b&w. *sd:* WE. 9 min. *l/a/anim.* • A department store sale is in evidence and a cat chases a mouse through different departments. The XXX Sisters sing "Comin' Through the Rye," "Listen to the German Band" and "Skat Song."

5861. The Singing Sap *(Oswald)* 8 Sept. 1930; *p.c.:* Univ; *dir:* Walter Lantz, "Bill" Nolan; *anim:* Clyde Geronimi, Manuel Moreno, Ray Abrams, Fred Avery, Lester Kline, "Pinto" Colvig; *voice:* Mickey Rooney; *mus:* James Dietrich; b&w. *sd:* WE. 6½ min. • Musical fun on a Hawaiian beach and Oswald rescues a drowning hippo.

5862. The Singing Saps *(Aesop's Sound Fable)* 7 Feb. 1930; *p.c.:* Van Beuren for Pathé; *dir:* John Foster, Mannie Davis; *mus:* Carl Edouarde; b&w. *sd:* RCA. 7 min. • Mr. and Mrs. Mouse's courting is rudely interrupted by dire peril.

5863. Sinister Stuff *(Aesop's Sound Fable)* 26 Jan. 1934; *p.c.:* Van Beuren for RKO; *anim:* Steve Muffatti; *mus:* Gene Rodemich; b&w. *sd:* RCA. 6½ min. • Cubby Bear portrays "True-Blue Harold" in a melodrama, coming to the rescue of a damsel tied to a circular saw.

5864. Sink or Swim *(Aesop's Film Fable)* 9 Jan. 1927; *p.c.:* Fables Pictures Inc for Pathé; *dir:* Paul Terry; b&w. *sil.* 10 min. • Milton Mouse and his sweetie join the other swimmers. When a swordfish punctures his girl's waterwings, Milton tangles with the beast.

5865. Sink or Swim *(Dinky Duck)* Nov. 1952; *p.c.:* TT for Fox; *dir:* Connie Rasinski; *story/voices:* Tom Morrison; *mus:* Philip A. Scheib; *ph:* Douglas Moye; *col:* Tech. *sd:* RCA. 6 min. • Dinky visits the Wise Old Owl who gives him a Sky Hook to assist him in his swimming. The others mock him until he saves them from the jaws of a hungry crocodile.

5866. Sink Pink *(Pink Panther)* 12 Apr. 1965; *p.c.:* Mirisch/Geoffrey/DFE for UA; *dir:* Hawley Pratt; *story:* John Dunn; *anim:* Don Williams, La Verne Harding, Manny Perez, Warren Batchelder, Norm McCabe, Bob Matz; *lay:* Dick Ung; *back:* Tom O'Loughlin; *ed:* Lee Gunther, Treg Brown; *voices:* Paul Frees, Rich Little; *mus:* William Lava; *theme tune:* Henry Mancini; *prod mgr:* Bill Orcutt; *col:* DeLuxe. *sd:* RCA. 6 min. • A hunter needs a rare panther pelt for his wife, Nora. He builds Nora's Ark and succeeds in securing every animal but the panther.

5867. Sinkin' in the Bathtub *(Looney Tunes)* 10 May 1930; *p.c.:* Hugh Harman, Rudolf Ising prods for WB; *anim:* Isadore Freleng; *voice:* Rochelle Hudson; *mus:* Frank Marsales; *song:* Al Dubin, Joe Burke; b&w. *sd:* Vit. 7½ min. • Bosko has a bath and prepares to take Honey for an automobile ride. First *Looney Tunes.*

5868. The Sinking of the "Lusitania" 20 July 1918; *p.c.:* Jewel prods Inc for Univ; *anim:* Winsor McCay; *asst anim:* John A. Fitzsimmons, Apthorp Adams; b&w. *sil.* 4 min. • A dramatic account of how the steamliner *Lusitania* was sunk by German torpedoes costing the lives of two thousand passengers in May 1915. Completed by McCay in 22 months.

5869. Sioux City Sue 1946; *p.c.:* Walter Lantz prods for Republic; b&w. *sd.* 69 min *l/a/anim.* • Gene Autry lends his vocal chords to a cartoon sequence featuring two animated donkeys in this live-action western.

5870. Sioux Me *(Merrie Melodies)* 9 Sept. 1939; *p.c.:* Leon Schlesinger prods for WB; *dir:* Ben Hardaway, Cal Dalton; *story:* Melvin Millar; *anim:* Herman Cohen; *lay:* Griff Jay; *back:* Arthur Loomer; *ed:* Tregoweth E. Brown; *voices:* John Deering, Mel Blanc, The Sportsmen Quartet (Bill Days, Maxwell Smith, John Rarig, Thurl Ravenscroft); *mus:* Carl W. Stalling; *prod sup:* Henry Binder, Raymond G. Katz; *col:* Tech. *sd:* Vit. 7 min. • During a drought, a little papoose brings in some rain-making pills, causing strange effects when the animals swallow them.

5871. Sioux Me *(Woody Woodpecker)* June 1965; *p.c.:* Walter Lantz prods for Univ; *dir:* Sid Marcus; *story:* Homer Brightman; *anim:* Art Davis, Ray Abrams; *sets:* Ray Huffine, Art Landy; *voices:* Daws Butler, Grace Stafford; *mus:* Clarence Wheeler; *prod mgr:* William E. Garity; *col:* Tech. *sd:* RCA. 6 min. • Fink Fox tries to sell Woody as a rain-making sacrifice to an Indian tribe.

5872. Sir Irving and Jeams *(Noveltoon)* 19 Oct. 1956; *p.c.:* Famous for Para: *dir:* Seymour Kneitel; *story:* Irving Spector; *anim:* Al Eugster, Wm. B. Pattengill; *sets:* Robert Little; *voices:* Frank Matalone, Jack Mercer, Cecil Roy; *mus:* Winston Sharples; *ph:* Leonard McCormick; *prod mgr:* Seymour Shultz; *col:* Tech. *sd:* RCA. 6 min. • Sir Irving's butler breaks his spectacles and unwittingly sabotages his master until he is forced to give the servant the pension he wants.

5873. Sissy Sheriff *(Woody Woodpecker)* Jan. 1967; *p.c.:* Walter Lantz prods for Univ; *dir:* Paul J. Smith; *story:* Cal Howard; *anim:* Al Coe, Les Kline; *sets:* Ray Huffine; *voices:* Dal McKennon, Grace Stafford; *mus:* Clarence Wheeler; *prod mgr:* William E. Garity; *col:* Tech. *sd:* RCA. 6 min. • Woody is appointed thirteenth sheriff of Lizzard Gizzard Gulch and has the task of arresting the local villain, Dirty McNasty.

5874. Sittin' on a Backyard Fence *(Merrie Melodies)* 16 Dec. 1933; *p.c.:* Leon Schlesinger prods for WB; *dir:* Earl Duval; *story:* Robert Clampett; *anim:* Jack King, Don Williams, Robert Clampett; *mus:* Norman Spencer; *song:* Sammy Fain, Irving Kahal; *prod sup:* Henry Binder, Raymond G. Katz; b&w. *sd:* Vit. 7 min. • The nocturnal habits of male and female cats.

5875. Skating Hounds *(Aesop's Sound Fable)* 27 May 1929; *p.c.:* Van Beuren for Pathé; *dir:* Paul Terry, Mannie Davis; *mus:* Josiah Zuro; *sd fx:* Maurice Manne; b&w. *sd:* RCA. 9 min. • The farmer and his cat go skating. Al Falfa has trouble with an active hot dog while the mice join in the fun.

5876. The Skeleton Dance *(Silly Symphony)* 11 July 1929; *p.c.:* Walter E. Disney for Colum; *dir:* Walt Disney; *story/mus:* Carl W. Stalling; *anim:* Ub Iwerks, Les Clark; b&w. *sd:* PCP. 7 min. • A graveyard fantasy with skeletons coming out to dance at the stroke of midnight. The first in the highly successful series of *Silly Symphonies*, created to utilize the new medium of sound and music.

5877. Skeleton Frolic *(Color Rhapsody)* 29 Jan. 1937; *p.c.:* Cartoon Films Ltd for Colum; *dir:* Ub Iwerks; *mus:* Joe de Nat, Eddie Kilfeather; *ph:* Otto Reimer; *prod mgr:* James Bronis; *col:* Tech. *sd:* RCA. 7½ min. • The skeletons in a graveyard come alive at midnight and stage a concert in this Technicolor, but weaker, remake of The *Skeleton Dance*.

5878. Sketchografs *p.c.:* Educational Films; *anim:* Julian Ollendorff; b&w. *sil.* • **1921:** *Play Ball* 7 Aug. The artist draws prominent baseball players which are faded out as the real stars appear. **Just for Fun** 16 Sept. **Jiggin' on the Old Sod** *(Pathé Review # 121)* 18 Sept. **Eve's Leaves** Oct. **Seeing Greenwich Village** Nov. **What's the Limit?** 24 Dec. • Lightning artist Julian Ollendorff is shown sketching various items.

5879. Ski for Two *(Woody Woodpecker)* 13 Nov. 1944; *p.c.:* Walter Lantz prods for Univ; *dir:* James Culhane; *story:* Ben Hardaway, Milt Schaffer; *anim:* Don Williams, Grim Natwick, (La)Verne Harding, Emery Hawkins, Les Kline, Dick Lundy, Pat Matthews, Paul J. Smith; *lay:* Art Heinemann; *back:* Phil de Guard; *voices:* Jack Mather, Lee Sweetland, Ben Hardaway; *mus:* Darrell Calker; *col:* Tech. *sd:* WE. 7 min. • Woody tries to gain access to the food in Wally's ski lodge.

5880. Ski-Hi the Cartoon Chinaman 10 July 1915; *p.c.:* Universal-Joker; *anim:* Earl Hurd; b&w. *sil.* 5 min. • No story available.

5881. Ski-Napper *(Chilly Willy)* Nov. 1964; *p.c.:* Walter Lantz prods for Univ; *dir:* Sid Marcus; *story:* Cal Howard; *anim:* Ray Abrams, Art Davis; *sets:* Ray Huffine, Art Landy; *voices:* Daws Butler; *mus:* Walter Greene; *prod mgr:* William E. Garity; *col:* Tech. *sd:* WE. 6 min. • Chilly tries to keep warm by stealing a hotel's skis for firewood, guarded by bellboy Smedley.

5882. Skinfolks *(Woody Woodpecker)* 7 July 1964; *p.c.:* Walter Lantz prods for Univ; *dir:* Sid Marcus; *story:* Homer Brightman; *anim:* Ray Abrams, Art Davis; *sets:* Art Landy, Ray Huffine; *voices:* Dal McKennon, Grace Stafford; *mus:* Walter Greene; *prod mgr:* William E. Garity; *col:* Tech. *sd:* RCA. 6 min. • To keep warm for the winter, Woody imposes on his rich uncle Scrooge but the old skinflint sends his butler to evict the freeloader.

5883. Skipping the Pen 4 June 1921; *p.c.:* Affiliated Distributors; *prod/dir/anim:* J.J. McManus, R.E. Donahue; b&w. *sil.* • No story available.

5884. The Ski's the Limit *(Screen Song)* 24 June 1949; *p.c.:* Famous for Para; *dir:* I. Sparber; *story:* Bill Turner, Larry Riley; *anim:* Dave Tendlar, Tom Golden; *sets:* Robert Connavale; *voice:* Jackson Beck; *mus:* Winston Sharples; *ph:* Leonard McCormick; *prod mgr:* Sam Buchwald; *col:* Pola. *sd:* RCA. 8 min. • A tour of Switzerland accompanied by a sing-along.

5885. Sky Blue Pink *(Pink Panther)* 3 Jan. 1968; *p.c.:* Mirisch/Geoffrey/DFE for UA; *dir:* Hawley Pratt; *story:* John Dunn; *anim:* Don Williams, Manny Gould, Manny Perez, Bob Matz, Warren Batchelder; *lay:* Dick Ung; *back:* Tom O'Loughlin; *ed:* Lee Gunther; *mus:* Walter Greene; *theme tune:* Henry Mancini; *prod sup:* Harry Love, Basil Cox; *col:* DeLuxe. *sd:* RCA. 7 min. • The Panther causes chaos when attempting to fly a kite.

5886. The Sky Is Falling *(Mighty Mouse)* 25 Apr. 1947; *p.c.:* TT for Fox; *dir:* Mannie Davis; *story:* John Foster; *voice:* Cecil Roy; *mus:* Philip A. Scheib; *ph:* Douglas Moye; *col:* Tech. *sd:* RCA. 6 min. • Wolves try to entice a pig, duck and rabbit from a pen by convincing them the sky is about to fall but Mighty Mouse saves the day.

5887. Sky Larks *(Oswald)* 22 Oct. 1934; *p.c.:* Univ; *prod/dir/anim:* Walter Lantz; *story:* Victor McLeod; *anim:* Fred Avery, Jack Carr, Ray Abrams, Joe d'Igalo, Ernest Smythe; *mus:* James Dietrich; b&w. *sd:* WE. 8 min. *l/a/anim.* • Inspired by Piccard's ascent, Oswald and Dopey Dick go on a stratospheric flight where they are transported to Mars.

5888. The Sky Princess *(Madcap Models)* 27 Mar. 1942; *p.c.:* George Pal Studio for Para; *prod/dir:* George Pal; *anim:* Ray Harryhausen, Bob Baker; *col:* Tech. *sd:* WE. 9 min. • Fantasy based on Tschaikovsky's "Sleeping Beauty Waltz." A wicked witch casts a spell on a princess in a glass castle in the sky.

5889. Sky Scraping *(Talkartoons)* 1 Nov. 1930; *p.c.:* The Fleischer Studio for Para; *prod:* Max Fleischer; *dir:* Dave Fleischer; *anim:* Alfred Eugster; *mus:* Art Turkisher; b&w. *sd:* WE. 6 min. • Cats construct a skyscraper.

5890. Sky Scrappers *(Herman & Katnip)* 14 June 1957; *p.c.:* Para Cartoons; *dir:* Dave Tendlar; *story:* Carl Meyer; *anim:* Morey Reden; *sets:* John Zago; *voices:* Arnold Stang, Jack Mercer, Gwen Davies; *mus:* Winston Sharples; *ph:* Leonard McCormick; *prod mgr:* Seymour Shultz; *col:* Tech. *sd:* RCA. 6 min. • The mice find new accommodation behind some pipes but discover Katnip has arrived there first.

5891. Sky Scrappers *(Oswald the Lucky Rabbit)* 11 June 1928; *p.c.:* Winkler for Univ; *dir:* Walt Disney; *ph:* Mike Marcus; b&w. *sil.* 6 min. • Foreman Foxy Wolf hoists construction worker Oswald's girl, Fanny, up to a high girder. Oswald rescues her.

5892. Sky Skippers *(Aesop's Sound Fable)* 14 Feb. 1930; *p.c.:* Van Beuren for Pathé; *dir:* John Foster, Harry Bailey; *mus:* Carl Edouarde; b&w. *sd:* RCA. 6 min. • Farmer Al Falfa and the animals fly in their various makeshift aeroplanes.

5893. Sky Trooper *(Donald Duck)* 6 Nov. 1942; *p.c.:* Walt Disney prods for RKO; *dir:* Jack King; *asst dir:* Jack Atwood; *story:* Carl Barks, Jack Hannah; *anim:* Paul Allen, James Armstrong, Hal King, Edward Love, John McManus, Ray Patin, Charles A. Nichols, Walter Scott, Don Towsley, Judge Whitaker; *fx:* Edwin Aardal, Daniel MacManus, Joshua Meador; *lay:* Bill Herwig; *voices:* Billy Bletcher, Clarence Nash; *mus:* Frank E. Churchill; *col:* Tech. *sd:* RCA. 7 min. • Pvt. Donald begs Sgt. Pete to let him fly in a plane. When the sergeant finally does take him for a spin, Don has to parachute down.

5894. The Sky's the Limit *(Terry-Toon)* Feb. 1965; *p.c.:* TT for Fox; *ex prod:* Bill Weiss; *dir/anim:* Dave Tendlar; *story sup:* Tom Morrison; *story:* Bob Ogle, Glan Heisch; *sets:* Robert Owen, John Zago; *ed:* Jack MacConnell; *voices:* Dayton Allen; *mus:* Jim Timmens; *ph:* Joe Rasinski; *sd:* Elliot Grey; *col:* DeLuxe. *sd:* RCA. 5½ min. • Oscar Mild causes havoc when Astro grants him the power of levitation.

5895. Skyscraper Caper *(Looney Tunes)* 9 Mar. 1968; *p.c.:* WB/7A; *dir:* Alex Lovy; *story:* Cal Howard; *anim:* Ted Bonnicksen, La Verne Harding, Volus Jones, Ed Solomon; *lay:* Bob Givens; *back:* Bob Abrams, Ralph Penn; *ed:* Hal Geer; *voices:* Mel Blanc; *mus:* William Lava; *prod:* Bill L. Hendricks; *col:* Tech. *sd:* Vit. 6 min. • Speedy forsakes his own slumber to prevent Daffy from endangering himself while sleepwalking.

5896. Slap Happy Hunters *(Terry-Toon)* 30 Oct. 1941; *p.c.:* TT for Fox; *dir:* Eddie Donnelly; *story:* John Foster; *voices:* Arthur Kay, Thomas Morrison; *mus:* Philip A. Scheib; *ph:* Douglas Moye; *col:* Tech. *sd:* RCA. 7 min. • Gandy Goose and Sourpuss' camping holiday is ruined by the intrusion of mosquitoes.

5897. Slap Happy Pappy *(Looney Tunes)* 13 Apr. 1940; *p.c.:* Leon Schlesinger prods for WB; *dir:* Robert Clampett; *anim:* John Carey, I. Ellis; *sets:* Elmer Plummer; *ed:* Tregoweth E. Brown; *voices:* Cliff Nazarro, Jack Lescoulie, Mel Blanc, Danny Webb; *mus:* Carl W. Stalling; *prod sup:* Henry Binder, Raymond G. Katz; b&w. *sd:* Vit. 6 min. • Down on Porky's farm, Eddie Cackler's wife is about to give birth, only she produces girls and Eddie wants a boy! A Bing Crosby chicken suggests he croon to his spouse for a family of boys.

5898. The Slap-Hoppy Mouse *(Merrie Melodies)* 1 Sept. 1956; *p.c.:* WB; *dir:* Robert McKimson; *story:* Tedd Pierce; *anim:* Ted Bonnicksen, George Grandpré, Keith Darling, Russ Dyson; *lay:* Robert Gribbroek; *back:* Richard H. Thomas; *ed:* Treg Brown; *voices:* Mel Blanc; *mus:* Carl Stalling; *prod mgr:* John W. Burton; *prod:* Edward Selzer; *col:* Tech. *sd:* Vit. 7 min. • A baby kangaroo, escaped from the circus, comes to rest in a deserted house at the same time as Sylvester arrives to prove to Junior that he's not yet "past it" at mouse catching.

5899. Slaphappy Lion 20 Sept. 1947 *p.c.:* MGM; *dir:* Tex Avery; *story:* Heck Allen; *anim:* Ray Abrams, Robert Bentley, Walter Clinton; *character des/lay:* Irven Spence; *sets:* John Didrik Johnsen; *ed:* Fred MacAlpin; *voices:* Frank Graham, Sara Berner; *mus:* Scott Bradley; *ph:* Jack Stevens; *prod:* Fred Quimby; *col:* Tech. *sd:* WE. 7 min. • The King of the Jungle is afraid of nobody ... until a mouse appears on the scene!

5900. Slaphappy Valley *(Crackpot Cruise)* 21 Aug. 1939; *p.c.:* Walter Lantz prods for Univ; *dir:* Alex Lovy; *story:* Vic McLeod; *anim:* George Dane, La Verne Harding; *sets:* Edgar Kiechle; *voices:* Phil Kramer, Mel Blanc, Danny Webb; *mus:* Frank Marsales; *prod mgr:* George Hall; b&w. *sd:* WE. 7 min. • Punchy takes a train journey to Death Valley and back. Caricatures of Greta Garbo, Edna May Oliver, Ned Sparks.

5901. Slapstick of Another Kind March 1982; *p.c.:* The Steven Paul Co./Serendipity for Virgin; *stop-motion anim:* Ernest D. Farino; *col:* Metrocolor. *sd.* 94 min. *l/a.* • Jerry Lewis live-action comedy about a wealthy man who keeps his hideous twins hidden until they escape and are persued by a posse.

5902. Slay It with Flowers *(Color Rhapsody)* 29 Jan. 1943; *p.c.:* Colum; *prod:* Dave Fleischer; *dir:* Bob Wickersham; *story:* Leo Salkin; *anim:* Phil Duncan; *lay:* Clark Watson; *ed:* Edward Moore; *voices:* Frank Graham; *mus:* Ed Kilfeather; *prod mgr:* Albert Spar; *col:* Tech. *sd:* RCA. 6 min. • The Fox's rooftop garden is pillaged by the seed-stealing crow.

5903. Sleep Happy *(Woody Woodpecker)* 26 Mar. 1951; *p.c.:* Walter Lantz prods for Univ; *dir:* Walter Lantz; *story:* Ben Hardaway, Heck Allen; *anim:* Ray Abrams, Don Patterson, La Verne Harding; *sets:* Fred Brunish; *mus:* Clarence E. Wheeler; *prod mgr:* William E. Garity; *col:* Tech. *sd:* RCA. 6 min. • Woody spends the night in Wally Walrus' bed and board where his snoring keeps the proprietor awake all night.

5904. The Sleep Walker *(Pluto)* 3 July 1942; *p.c.:* Walt Disney prods for RKO; *dir:* Clyde Geronimi; *asst dir:* Donald A. Duckwall; *anim:* Jerry Hathcock, Emery Hawkins, Eric Gurney, George Nicholas, Charles A. Nichols, Morey Reden, Norman Tate; *lay:* Bruce Bushman; *mus:* Leigh Harline; *col:* Tech. *sd:* RCA. 7 min. • When Pluto walks in his sleep, he presents Dinah the daschund with a bone. When he awakes, he retrieves it but feels remorse when he discovers her hungry pups in the kennel.

5905. Sleeping Beauty 29 Jan. 1959; *p.c.:* Walt Disney prods for BV; *dir sup:* Clyde Geronimi; *seq dir:* Eric Larson, Wolfgang Reitherman, Les Clark; *story from original by* Charles Perrault; *story adapt:* Erdman Penner; *add story:* Joe Rinaldi, Bill Peet, Ralph Wright, Winston Hibler, Ted Sears, Milt Banta; *anim dir:* Milt Kahl, Frank Thomas, Marc Davis, Ollie Johnston, John Lounsbery; *anim:* Hal King, Blaine Gibson, Ken Hultgren, George Nicholas, Henry Tanous, Hal Ambro, John Sibley, Harvey Toombs, Bob Youngquist, John Kennedy, Don Lusk, Bob Carlson, Fred Kopietz, Eric Cleworth, Ken O'Brien; *asst anim:* Don Bluth; *inbetweener:* Bill Wright; *fx:* Dan MacManus, Joshua Meador, Jack Boyd, Jack Buckley, John F. Reed; *des:* Eyvind Earle; *character des:* Tom Oreb; *prod des:* Don

da Gradi, Ken Anderson; *lay:* McLaren Stewart, Don Griffith, Basil Davidovich, Joe Hale, Jack Huber, Tom Codrick, Erni Nordli, Victor Haboush, Homer Jonas, Ray Aragon; *back:* Frank Armitage, Al Dempster, Bill Layne, Dick Anthony, Richard H. Thomas, Thelma Witmer, Walt Peregoy, Ralph Hulett, Fil Mottola, Anthony Rizzo; *ed:* Roy M. Brewer Jr., Donald Halliday; *voices: Princess Aurora:* Mary Costa; *Maleficent:* Eleanor Audley; *Merryweather:* Barbara Luddy; *King Stefan:* Taylor Holmes; *Prince Philip:* Bill Shirley; *Flora:* Verna Felton; *Fauna:* Barbara Jo Allen; *King Hubert:* Bill Thompson; *Maleficent's goons:* Candy Candido, Pinto Colvig, Bob Amsberry; *Narration:* Marvin Miller; *Diablo (Raven):* Candy Candido; *Owl:* Dallas McKennon; *Bird/animal sounds:* A. Purvis Pullen; *Chorus:* The Jud Conlon Singers; *mus:* George Bruns from Tchaikovsky's *Sleeping Beauty Ballet; song:* George Bruns, Tom Adair, Winston Hibler, Erdman Penner, Sammy Fain, Jack Lawrence, Ted Sears; *choral arr:* John Rarig; *mus ed:* Evelyn Kennedy; *sd:* Robert O. Cook; *special processes:* Ub Iwerks, Eustace Lycett; *prod mgr:* Ken Peterson; *col:* Tech. *sd:* RCA. (Stereophonic). 75 min. Technirama-70. • Jealous over not having been invited to Princess Aurora's christening, Maleficent, an evil fairy, predicts that before she is sixteen, the Princess shall prick her finger and die. Three good fairies hide and raise her as their own until her sixteenth birthday. Maleficent finds her, fulfilling her curse but Aurora only sleeps to be awakened by the kiss of true love. Sumptuously designed and over a $6m budget to produce, this was not a instant hit but has gained a cult status in later years.

5906. The Sleeping Princess *(Nertsery Rhyme)* 20 Nov. 1939; *p.c.:* Walter Lantz prods for Univ; *dir:* Burt Gillett; *story:* Victor McLeod, Gil Burton; *anim:* George Nicholas, Lester Kline; *sets:* Edgar Keichle; *voices:* Sara Berner, Mel Blanc; *mus:* Frank Marsales; *prod mgr:* George Hall; *col:* Tech. *sd:* WE. 9½ min. • One of the Good Fairies believes she hasn't been invited to the Princess' christening so she casts a spell to have the child sleep for one hundred years on her fifteenth birthday.

5907. A Sleepless Night *(Heckle & Jeckle)* 6 Apr. 1948; *p.c.:* TT for Fox; *dir:* Connie Rasinski; *story:* John Foster; *voices:* Tom Morrison, Douglas Moye; *mus:* Philip A. Scheib; *ph:* Douglas Moye; *col:* Tech. *sd:* RCA. 6½ min. • The magpies seek refuge for the night in a bear's cave, trying to oust the bear.

5908. Sleepy Hollow 19 Nov. 1999; *p.c.:* Par; *special visual fx:* ILM; *cg anim:* Kyle Clark, Peter Daulton, Neil Michka; *digital visual fx/3d anim:* Dominic Parker, Stephen Murphy, Richard Clarke, Chris Monks; *col:* DeLuxe. *sd:* Dolby digital/Digital dts sound. 105½ min. *l/a.* • Live-action thriller: A young eighteenth-century New York constable is sent upstate to the village of Sleepy Hollow to investigate a series of mysterious beheadings. He is informed that this is the work of "The Headless Horseman," a beheaded mercenary who has returned from the grave. The constable discovers that the spectre emerges from the roots of a tree that appears to be the gateway to Hell.

5909. Sleepy Time Bear *(Chilly Willy)* 1 Dec. 1969; *p.c.:* Walter Lantz prods for Univ; *dir:* Paul J. Smith; *story:* Homer Brightman; *anim:* Les Kline, Al Coe; *sets:* Nino Carbe; *voices:* Daws Butler; *mus:* Walter Greene; *prod mgr:* William E. Garity; *col:* Tech. *sd:* RCA. 6 min. • Chilly tries to keep his bear friend out of a hunter's view when he starts walking in his sleep.

5910. Sleepy Time Chimes *(Woody Woodpecker)* 1 Feb. 1971; *p.c.:* Walter Lantz prods for Univ; *dir:* Paul J. Smith; *story:* Dale Hale; *anim:* Les Kline, Al Coe, Tom Byrne, Joe Voght; *sets:* Nino Carbe; *voices:* Daws Butler, Grace Stafford; *mus:* Walter Greene; *prod mgr:* William E. Garity; *col:* Tech. r*sd:* RCA. 6 min. • Woody puts a stop to the chimes in a bell tower when they keep him awake. This brings the clock keeper to see what's the matter.

5911. Sleepy Time Donald *(Donald Duck)* 9 May 1947; *p.c.:* Walt Disney prods for RKO; *dir:* Jack King; *asst dir:* Joel Greenhalgh; *story:* Roy Williams; *anim:* Don Towsley, Fred Kopietz, Paul Allen, Ernie Lynch, Ed Aardal, Bob Carlson, Frank McSavage, Sandy Strother; *sets:* Ernie Nordli; *voices:* Gloria Blondell, Clarence Nash; *mus:* Oliver Wallace; *col:* Tech. *sd:* RCA. 7 min. • Daisy desperately tries to prevent Donald from injuring himself while sleepwalking.

5912. Sleepy-Time Possum *(Merrie Melodies)* 3 Nov. 1951; *p.c.:* WB; *dir:* Robert McKimson; *story:* Tedd Pierce; *anim:* Charles McKimson, Rod Scribner, Phil de Lara, Emery Hawkins, John Carey; *lay:* Cornett Wood;

back: Richard H. Thomas; *ed:* Treg Brown; *voices:* Mel Blanc; *mus:* Carl Stalling; *prod mgr:* John W. Burton; *prod:* Edward Selzer; *col:* Tech. *sd:* Vit. 7 min. • Mr. O'Possum teaches his lazy son a lesson by dressing as a dog with the idea of throwing a scare into him ... but the plan hopelessly misfires.

5913. Sleepy-Time Squirrel (*Barney Bear*) 19 June 1954; *p.c.:* MGM; *dir:* Dick Lundy; *story:* Heck Allen, Jack Cosgriff; *anim:* Robert Bentley, Michael Lah, Walter Clinton, Grant Simmons; *sets:* John Didrik Johnsen; *ed:* Jim Faris; *voices:* Paul Frees; *mus:* Scott Bradley; *ph:* Jack Stevens; *prod:* Fred Quimby; *col:* Tech. *sd:* WE. 7 min. • Barney takes pity on a homeless squirrel and lets him stay the winter with him ... something he lives to regret.

5914. Sleepy-Time Tom (*Tom & Jerry*) 26 May 1951; *p.c.:* MGM; *dir:* William Hanna, Joseph Barbera; *anim:* Ed Barge, Kenneth Muse, Irven Spence, Ray Patterson; *lay:* Dick Bickenbach; *back:* Robert Gentle; *ed:* Jim Faris; *voices:* Lillian Randolph, Paul Frees, The King's Men (Bud Linn, Rad Robinson, Jon Dodson); *mus:* Scott Bradley; *ph:* Jack Stevens; *prod:* Fred Quimby; *col:* Tech. *sd:* WE. 7 min. • Tom is the worse for wear from a night out on the tiles but is ordered to guard the refrigerator from the mouse. While Tom makes an effort to stay awake, Jerry is determined to send him back to sleep.

5915. Sleigh Bells (*Oswald the Lucky Rabbit*) 23 July 1928; *p.c.:* Winkler for Univ; *dir:* Walter Disney; *ph:* Mike Marcus; b&w. sil. 6 min. • Oswald teaches a pretty girl bunny to skate by tying helium-filled balloons to her. She floats away with Ozzie in hot pursuit.

5916. Sleuth But Sure (*Noveltoon*) 23 Mar. 1956; *p.c.:* Famous for Para; *dir:* Dave Tendlar; *story:* I. Klein; *anim:* Morey Reden, Martin Taras; *sets:* Robert Little; *voices:* Phil Kramer, Jackson Beck, Cecil Roy; *mus:* Winston Sharples; *ph:* Leonard McCormick; *prod mgr:* Seymour Shultz; *col:* Tech. *sd:* RCA. 6 min. • Moe Hare escapes from prison to marry his best girl but Detective Tommy Tortoise is hot on his trail.

5917. The Slick Chick (*Looney Tunes*) 21 July 1962; *p.c.:* WB; *dir:* Robert McKimson; *story:* Tedd Pierce; *anim:* Ted Bonnicksen, Warren Batchelder, Keith Darling, George Grandpré; *sets:* Robert Gribbroek; *ed:* Treg Brown; *voices:* Mel Blanc, Julie Bennett; *mus:* Milt Franklyn; *prod mgr:* William Orcutt; *prod:* David H. DePatie; *col:* Tech. *sd:* Vit. 7 min. • Foggy babysits a "Mean Widdle Kid" who almost succeeds in half-killing the redoubtable rooster.

5918. Slick Hare (*Merrie Melodies*); 1 Nov. 1946; *p.c.:* WB; *dir:* I. Freleng; *story:* Tedd Pierce, Michael Maltese; *anim:* Virgil Ross, Gerry Chiniquy, Manuel Perez, Ken Champin; *lay:* Hawley Pratt; *back:* Paul Julian; *ed:* Treg Brown; *voices:* Mel Blanc, Arthur Q. Bryan, Dave Barry; *mus:* Carl Stalling; *prod mgr:* John W. Burton; *prod:* Edward Selzer; *col:* Tech. *sd:* Vit. 7 min. • Humphrey Bogart asks waiter Elmer for an order of rabbit but Elmer first has to catch Bugs. Caricatures of Lauren Bacall, Humphrey Bogart, Warren Foster, Sydney Greenstreet, The Marx Brothers, Ray Milland, Carmen Miranda, Tedd Pierce, Gregory Peck, Frank Sinatra and Leopold Stokowski.

5919. Slicked-Up Pup (*Tom & Jerry*) 8 Sept. 1951; *p.c.:* MGM; *dir:* William Hanna, Joseph Barbera; *anim:* Ed Barge, Kenneth Muse, Irven Spence, Ray Patterson; *lay:* Dick Bickenbach; *back:* Robert Gentle; *ed:* Jim Faris; *voices:* Daws Butler; *mus:* Scott Bradley; *ph:* Jack Stevens; *prod:* Fred Quimby; *col:* Tech. *sd:* WE. 6 min. • Tom has a tough time trying to keep bulldog Spike's son, Tyke, clean.

5920. Slide, Donald Slide (*Donald Duck*) 9 Dec. 1949; *p.c.:* Walt Disney prods for RKO; *dir:* Jack Hannah; *story:* Nick George, Bill Berg; *anim:* Bob Carlson, Volus Jones, Bill Justice, Judge Whitaker; *fx:* Jack Boyd; *lay:* Yale Gracey; *back:* Thelma Witmer; *voices:* Ted Meyers, Clarence Nash; *mus:* Oliver Wallace; *col:* Tech. *sd:* RCA. 6½ min. • Donald wants to hear the ball game on his radio until the intrusion of a bee who wants to listen to a symphony orchestra.

5921. Slides (*Out of the Inkwell*) 3 Dec. 1919; *p.c.:* Bray prods for Goldwyn; *anim:* Max Fleischer; b&w. sil. 5 min. • No story available.

5922. Slightly Daffy (*Merrie Melodies*) 17 June 1944; *p.c.:* Leon Schlesinger prods for WB; *dir:* I. Freleng; *story:* Michael Maltese; *anim:* Virgil Ross; *lay:* Owen Fitzgerald; *back:* Paul Julian; *ed:* Treg Brown; *voices:* Mel Blanc; *mus:* Carl W. Stalling; *ph:* John W. Burton; *prod sup:* Henry

Binder, Raymond G. Katz; *col:* Tech. *sd:* Vit. 7 min. • General Daffy and Pvt. Porky defend the fort against an Indian attack. Tech remake of *Scalp Trouble.*

5923. Slingshot 6⅛ (*Woody Woodpecker*) 23 July 1951; *p.c.:* Walter Lantz prods for Univ; *dir:* Walter Lantz; *anim:* Don Patterson, Ray Abrams, La Verne Harding, Paul Smith; *sets:* Fred Brunish; *mus:* Clarence Wheeler; *prod mgr:* William E. Garity; *col:* Tech. *sd:* RCA. 6 min. • A shooting contest between Woody and redskin Buzz Buzzard. Woody outshoots Buzz's bow and arrow each time with his slingshot.

5924. Slink Pink (*Pink Panther*) 2 Apr. 1969; *p.c.:* Mirisch/Geoffrey/DFE for UA; *dir:* Hawley Pratt; *story:* John W. Dunn; *anim:* Ed de Mattia, Manny Perez, Herman Cohen, Art Leonardi, Warren Batchelder; *lay:* Dick Ung; *back:* Tom O'Loughlin; *ed:* Lee Gunther; *mus:* Walter Greene; *theme tune:* Henry Mancini; *ph:* John Burton Jr.; *prod sup:* Jim Foss, Harry Love; *col:* DeLuxe. *sd:* RCA. 6 min. • The Panther poses as a stuffed mountain lion in a man's house in order to get warm.

5925. Slinky Mink (*Possible Possum*) Nov 1970 (© 1965); *p.c.:* TT for Fox; *col:* DeLuxe. *sd:* RCA. 5 min. • Poss and his friends protect a mink from a fur trapper. • See: *Possible Possum*

5926. Slip Us Some Redskin (*Noveltoon*) 6 July 1951; *p.c.:* Famous for Para; *dir:* Seymour Kneitel; *story:* Irving Spector; *anim:* Dave Tendlar, Martin Taras; *sets:* Tom Ford; *voices:* Jack Mercer, Gwen Davies; *mus:* Winston Sharples; *ph:* Leonard McCormick; *prod mgr:* Sam Buchwald; *col:* Tech. *sd:* RCA. 7 min. • An old Indian, living in a brand new apartment, tells his young nephew of how he hunted the bear who is now a rug by the hearth.

5927. Sliphorn King of Polaroo (*Swing Symphony*) 19 Mar. 1945; *p.c.:* Walter Lantz prods for Univ; *dir:* Dick Lundy; *story:* Ben Hardaway, Milt Schaffer; *anim:* Pat Matthews; *sets:* Fred Brunish; *voices:* Hans Conried, Lee Sweetland, Jack Teagarden; *mus:* Darrell Calker, Jack Teagarden; *col:* Tech. *sd:* WE. 7 min. • Jackson, a musical lion, is marooned on an Arctic island. He entertains the inhabitants by playing a "hot" trombone and is appointed king.

5928. Slippery Slippers (*Loopy de Loop*) Sept. 1962; *p.c.:* Hanna-Barbera for Colum; *prod/dir:* William Hanna, Joseph Barbera; *story dir:* Lewis Marshall; *story:* Warren Foster; *anim dir:* Charles A. Nichols; *anim:* Jack Ozark; *lay:* Jerry Eisenberg; *back:* Art Lozzi; *ed:* Warner Leighton; *voices:* Daws Butler, Arnold Stang, Jean van der Pyl; *mus:* Hoyt Curtin; *titles:* Lawrence Gobel; *prod mgr:* Howard Hansen; *col:* East. *sd:* RCA. 6 min. • Loopy helps the Cinderella story on its way.

5929. Sloppy Jalopy (*Mr. Magoo*) 21 Feb. 1952; *p.c.:* UPA for Colum; *ex prod:* Stephen Bosustow; *prod:* John Hubley; *dir:* Pete Burness; *story:* Phil Eastman, Bill Scott; *anim:* Cecil Surry, Rudy Larriva; *lay:* Abe Liss; *back:* Jules Engel, Bob McIntosh; *voices:* Jim Backus, Jerry Hausner; *mus:* David Raksin; *technical:* Max Morgan; *prod mgr:* Herb Klynn; *col:* Tech. *sd:* RCA. 7 min. • Magoo test-drives a used car on a Coney Island rollercoaster with a motorcycle cop hot on his heels.

5930. Slow Beau (*Krazy Kat*) 27 Mar. 1930; *p.c.:* Winkler for Colum; *prod:* Charles Mintz; *anim:* Ben Harrison, Manny Gould; *prod mgr:* James Bronis; b&w. *sd:* WE. 6 min. • The showboat arrives. Krazy and a rival sabotage each other's act for the sake of a girl.

5931. Slow but Sure (*Paul Terry-Toon*) 18 June 1934; *p.c.:* Moser & Terry for Educational/Fox; *dir:* Frank Moser, Paul Terry; *mus:* Philip A. Scheib; b&w. *sd:* WE. 5½ min. • No story available.

5932. Slumberland Express (*Oswald*) 9 Mar. 1936; *p.c.:* Univ; *prod/dir:* Walter Lantz; *story:* Walter Lantz, Victor McLeod; *anim:* Manuel Moreno, La Verne Harding; *mus:* James Dietrich; b&w. *sd:* RCA. 7 min. • Oswald and Sissie visit Slumberland and meet all kinds of peculiar folk.

5933. Small Fry (*Color Classic*) 21 Apr. 1939; *p.c.:* The Fleischer Studio for Para; *prod:* Max Fleischer; *dir:* Dave Fleischer; *anim:* Willard Bowsky, Orestes Calpini; *sets:* Hermia Calpini; *voices:* Margie Hines, Jack Mercer; *mus:* Sammy Timberg; *song:* Frank Loesser, Hoagy Carmichael; *col:* Tech. *sd:* WE. 7 min. • Junior catfish fancies himself "grown up" enough to join the local pool hall's Big Fry club. In the initiation ceremony he experiences enough frightening things to send him home to Mama.

5934. The Small One 16 Dec. 1978; *p.c.:* Walt Disney prods for BV; *ex prod:* Ron Miller; *prod/dir:* Don Bluth; *asst dir:* Richard Rich; *based on*

the story by Charles Tazewell; *story adapt:* Vance Gerry, Pete Young; *anim dir:* Cliff Nordberg, John Pomeroy, Gary Goldman; *anim:* Chuck Harvey, Jerry Rees, Bill Hajee, Ron Husband, Heidi Guedel, Lorna Pomeroy, Emily Juliano, Linda Miller; *asst anim sup:* Walt Stanchfield; *fx:* Dorse A. Lanpher, Ted Kierscey; *lay:* Dan Hansen, Sylvia Roemer; *back:* Jim Coleman, Daniela Bielecka; *ed:* James Melton; *voices: The boy:* Sean Marshall; *Tanner:* William Woodson; *Father:* Olan Soulè; *Auctioneer:* Hal Smith; *Guard:* Joe Higgins; *Joseph:* Gordon Jump; *mus:* Robert F. Brunner; *songs:* Richard Rich, Don Bluth; *col:* Tech. *sd:* RCA. 25¹/₂ min. • A boy has to sell his aging donkey to a decent home. At the end of the day he is about to return home, disillusioned until he finds a buyer in Joseph and Mary on their way to Bethlehem.

5935. Small Soldiers 10 July 1998; *p.c.:* Dreamworks LLC/Amblin Entertainment, Inc. for Univ; *fx/anim:* ILM; *cg sup:* Gerald Gutschmidt, Erik Mattson; *digital model sup:* Tony Hudson; *compositing sup:* Scott Frankel; *digital col timing sup:* Kenneth Smith; *lead seq anim:* David Byers Brown, Jenn Emberly; *anim:* Scott Benza, Chuck Duke, Jason Ivimey, Heather Knight, Martin L'heureux, David La Tour, Julija Leary, Steve Lee, Neil Michka, Christopher Minos, Jacques Muller, David Parsons, Si Tran, Chi Chung Tse, Tim Waddy, Scott Wirtz, Michaela Zabranska, John Zdankiewicz; *cg seq sup:* Michael Di Como, David Meny, Sean Schur; *lead cg art:* Ken Wesley; *lead compositor:* Marshall Krasser; *cg art:* Joel Aron, Mimi Abers, Felix Balbas, Maurice Bastian, Kathleen Beeler, Patrick Brennan, Patrick Conran, David Deuber, Natasha Devaud, Jeff Doran, Gonzald Escudero, Tom Fejes, Dean Foster, Todd Fulford, Jim Hagedorn, Mary Beth Haggerty, Christina Hills, Polly Ing, Hohen Leo, Terrence Masson, Mary McCulloch, Jennifer McKnew, Michael Min, Bruce Powell, Jason Rosson, Kevin Reuter, Jeffrey Shank, Daniel Shumaker, Christa Starr, John Stillman, Ken Ziegler; *anim sup:* David Andrews; *voices: Archer:* Frank Langella; *Mjr. Chip Hazard:* Tommy Lee Jones; *Kip Killagin:* Ernest Borgnine; *Butch Meathook:* Jim Brown; *Link Static:* Bruce Dern; *Brick Bazooka:* George Kennedy; *Nick Nitro:* Clint Walker; *Slamfist/Scratch-it:* Christopher Guest; *Insaniac/Freakenstein:* Michael McKean; *Punch-it:* Harry Shearer; *Ocula:* Jim Cummings; *Gwendy dolls:* Sarah Michelle Gellar, Christina Ricci; *col:* Tech. *sd:* Dolby digital/Digital dts sound/SDDS. Panavision. 110 min. *l/a.* • Live-action fantasy: Toy action Commando figures come alive and stage a battle with alien toys, then turn on the human world.

5936. The Small Town Sheriff (*Aesop's Film Fable*) 22 July 1927; *p.c.:* Fables Pictures Inc for Pathé; *dir:* Paul Terry; b&w. sil. 10 min. • Al Falfa discovers a "Speakeasy Fountain." He drinks too much and dreams he is among the heavens and dons a badge, becoming a small town Sheriff.

5937. Smarty Cat (*Tom & Jerry*) 14 Oct. 1955; *p.c.:* MGM; *dir:* William Hanna, Joseph Barbera; *anim:* Irven Spence, Kenneth Muse, Ed Barge, Michael Lah; *lay:* Dick Bickenbach; *back:* Vera Ohman; *ed:* Jim Faris; *voice:* Daws Butler; *mus:* Scott Bradley; *ph:* Jack Stevens; *prod:* Fred Quimby; *col:* Tech. *sd:* WE. 6 min. seq: *Cat Fishin'; Solid Serenade; Fit to be Tied.* • Tom gives his cat cronies a home movie show, depicting Spike's vulnerabilities. Jerry awakens said bulldog and all hell is let loose.

5938. S'Matter Pete? (*Hot Dog*) 15 Mar. 1927; *p.c.:* Bray prods; *dir:* Walt Lantz; *anim:* Clyde Geronimi; b&w. sil. 5 min. • Walt is teacher when the kids burn the school house down, then flood it by dousing the flames.

5939. Smellot Bones the Dog Detective (*Racket Cartoon*) 10 Jan. 1930; *p.c./anim:* Alexander D. Cruikshank, Rudolph L. Eggeman; b&w. sd. • No story available.

5940. Smile, Darn Ya, Smile! (*Merrie Melodies*) May 1931; *p.c.:* Hugh Harman, Rudolf Ising prods for WB; *prod:* Leon Schlesinger; *story:* Robert Clampett; *anim:* Isadore Freleng, Max Maxwell, Robert Clampett; *voices:* John T. Murray, Mary Moder; *mus:* Frank Marsales; recorded by Abe Lyman's Brunswick Recording Orchestra; *song:* Jack Meskill, Max Rich, Charles O'Flynn; b&w. *sd:* Vit. 6 min. • Foxy has trouble with a cow obstructing his trolley bus.

5941. Smile Pretty Say Pink (*Pink Panther*) 25 May 1966; *p.c.:* Mirisch/Geoffrey/DFE for UA; *dir:* Hawley Pratt; *story:* John W. Dunn; *anim:* La Verne Harding, Warren Batchelder, Don Williams, Norm McCabe, Bob Matz; *lay:* Dick Ung; *back:* Tom O'Loughlin; *ed:* Chuck McCann; *mus:* William Lava; *theme tune:* Henry Mancini; *prod mgr:* Bill Or-

cutt; *col:* DeLuxe. *sd:* RCA. 6 min. • The Panther wages war on a wild life photographer in Pinkstone National Park.

5942. Smiles (*Screen Songs*) 27 Sept. 1929; *p.c.:* The Fleischer Studio for Para; *dir:* Dave Fleischer; *arr:* Max Fleischer; *song:* J. Will Callahan, Lee S. Roberts; b&w. *sd:* DPS. (disc) 7 min. • A barbershop quartet sing the title song.

5943. Smitten Kitten (*Tom & Jerry*) 12 Apr. 1952; *p.c.:* MGM; *dir:* William Hanna, Joseph Barbera; *anim:* Kenneth Muse; *lay:* Dick Bickenbach; *back:* Robert Gentle; *ed:* Jim Faris; *voice:* Daws Butler; *mus:* Scott Bradley; *ph:* Jack Stevens; *prod:* Fred Quimby; *col:* Tech. *sd:* WE. 8 min. seq: *Salt Water Tabby; Solid Serenade; The Mouse Comes to Dinner; Texas Tom; Solid Serenade.* • The devil in Jerry tries to break up Tom's current romance.

5944. The Smoke Fairy 1909; *p.c.:* Vitagraph Corp; *anim:* James Stuart Blackton; b&w. sil. • No story available.

5945. Smoked Hams (*Woody Woodpecker*) 28 Apr. 1947; *p.c.:* Walter Lantz prods for Univ; *dir:* Dick Lundy; *story:* Ben Hardaway, Milt Schaffer; *anim:* Grim Natwick, Stanley C. Onaitus; *sets:* Fred Brunish; *ed:* Dave Lurie; *voices:* Walker Edmiston, Ben Hardaway; *mus:* Darrell Calker; *prod mgr:* William E. Garity; *col:* Tech. *sd:* WE. 7 min. • Night worker, Wally's daytime slumber is disturbed by Woody's lawn-mowing and the crunch comes when he lights a bonfire.

5946. Smoky Joe (*Terry-Toon*) 25 May 1945; *p.c.:* TT for Fox; *dir:* Connie Rasinski; *story:* John Foster; *mus:* Philip A. Scheib; *col:* Tech. *sd:* RCA. 7 min. • Smoky Joe is an old fire horse who has to make way for automation.

5947. Snake in the Gracias (*Tijuana Toads*) 24 Jan. 1971; *p.c.:* Mirisch/DFE for UA; *dir:* Hawley Pratt; *story:* John W. Dunn; *anim:* Don Williams, George Nicholas, Phil Roman, Warren Batchelder, Ken Muse; *lay:* Dick Ung; *back:* Richard Thomas; *ed:* Lee Gunther; *voices:* Don Diamond, Tom Holland, Larry D. Mann; *mus:* Doug Goodwin; *ph:* John Burton Jr.; *prod sup:* Jim Foss, Harry Love; *col:* DeLuxe. *sd:* RCA. 6 min. • Crazylegs Crane suffers memory loss and the toads take the opportunity to convince him he's a frog.

5948. Snake Preview (*Blue Racer*) 10 Aug. 1973; *p.c.:* Mirisch/DFE for UA; *dir:* Cullen Houghtaling; *story:* John W. Dunn; *anim:* Bob Matz, Bob Bransford, Don Williams, John Gibbs, Ken Muse; *lay:* Cullen Houghtaling, Owen Fitzgerald, Martin Strudler *back:* Richard H. Thomas; *ed:* Rick Steward; *voices:* Larry D. Mann; *mus:* Doug Goodwin; *ph:* John Burton Jr.; *prod mgr:* Lee Gunther; *col:* DeLuxe. *sd:* RCA. 5 min. • The racer runs into a spot of trouble with Crazylegs Crane and a bee while trying to steal an egg for breakfast.

5949. Snap Happy (*Little Lulu*) 22 July 1945; *p.c.:* Famous for Para; *dir:* Bill Tytla; *story:* I. Klein; *anim:* Orestes Calpini, Reuben Grossman, Otto Feuer, Frank Little; *sets:* Robert Connavale; *voices:* Cecil Roy, Sid Raymond, Jackson Beck; *mus:* Winston Sharples; *title song:* Buddy Kaye, Fred Wise, Sammy Timberg; *ph:* Leonard McCormick; *prod mgr:* Sam Buchwald; *col:* Tech. *sd:* RCA. 8 min. • Lulu tries to sneak into a news photographer's photos.

5950. Snap Happy Traps (*Phantasy*) 6 June 1946; *p.c.:* Colum; *dir:* Bob Wickersham; *story:* Cal Howard; *anim:* Chic Otterstrom, Ben Lloyd; *lay:* Clark Watson; *back:* Al Boggs; *ed:* Richard S. Jensen; *voices:* Jack Mather; *mus:* Eddie Kilfeather; *ph:* Frank Fisher; *prod mgr:* Hugh McCollum; b&w. *sd:* WE. 6¹/₂ min. • A bear hires a cat to rid his cave of mice. The cat eventually joins the mice and turns on his employer.

5951. Snapping the Whip (*Aesop's Film Fable*) 20 Jan. 1929; *p.c.:* Fables Pictures Inc for Pathé; *dir:* Paul Terry, Harry Bailey; b&w. sil. 10 min. • The roller-skating craze has hit the farmyard. The animals fit Farmer Al Falfa with skates, forcing him to join on the end of a "Snap the Whip" line.

5952. Snappy New Year (*Heckle & Jeckle*) 10 Nov. 1961; *p.c.:* TT for Fox; *ex prod:* Bill Weiss; *dir:* Dave Tendlar; *story sup:* Tom Morrison; *story:* Bob Kuwahara; *anim:* Dick Hall, Armand Guidi, Larry Silverman; *lay:* John Zago, Martin Strudler; *back:* John Zago; *voices:* Roy Halee; *mus:* Phil Scheib; *prod mgr:* Frank Schudde; *col:* DeLuxe. *sd:* RCA. 6 min. • The magpies' New Year resolution is to play no more practical jokes.

5953. The Snappy Salesman (*Oswald*) 18 Aug. 1930; *p.c.:* Univ; *dir:*

Walter Lantz; *anim:* "Bill" Nolan, Ray Abrams, Manuel Moreno, Clyde Geronimi, "Pinto" Colvig; *mus:* James Dietrich; b&w. *sd:* WE. 6 min. • Oswald sells musical instruments to Putrid Pete and his hordes of kids.

5954. Snappy Snapshots *(Terry Bears)* Mar. 1953; *p.c.:* TT for Fox; *dir:* Eddie Donnelly; *story:* Tom Morrison; *voices:* Douglas Moye, Tom Morrison, Philip A. Scheib; *mus:* Philip A. Scheib; *ph:* Douglas Moye; *col:* Tech. *sd:* RCA. 6 min. • Papa attempts to photograph wild life and gets attacked by a mother buzzard.

5955. Sneak, Snoop and Snitch *(Animated Antics)* 25 Oct. 1941; *p.c.:* The Fleischer Studio for Para; *prod:* Max Fleischer; *dir:* Dave Fleischer; *story:* Cal Howard; *anim:* Willard Bowsky, Gordon Sheehan, Al Eugster; *ed:* Kitty Pfister; *mus:* Sammy Timberg; *ph:* Charles Schettler; *prod sup:* Sam Buchwald, Isidore Sparber; b&w. *sd:* WE. 6 min. • No story available.

5956. Sneak, Snoop and Snitch in Triple Trouble *(Animated Antics)* 9 May 1941; *p.c.:* The Fleischer Studio for Para; *prod:* Max Fleischer; *dir:* Dave Fleischer; *story:* George Hill; *anim:* James Culhane, Nicholas Tafuri; *ed:* Kitty Pfister; *mus:* Sammy Timberg; *ph:* Charles Schettler; *prod sup:* Sam Buchwald, Isidore Sparber; b&w. *sd:* WE. 6 min. • The three spies execute a jail break but come up in the warder's garden.

5957. The Sneezing Weasel *(Merrie Melodies)* 12 Mar. 1938; *p.c.:* Leon Schlesinger prods for WB; *dir:* Fred Avery; *story:* Cal Howard; *anim:* Sid Sutherland; *ed:* Tregoweth E. Brown; *voices:* Fred Avery, Bernice Hansen; *mus:* Carl W. Stalling; *prod sup:* Henry Binder, Raymond G. Katz; *col:* Tech. *sd:* Vit. 7 min. • A mother hen believes her unhatched egg to have a cold and dashes for the doctor. A hungry weasel moves in and when the chick hatches, it takes the weasel to be its mother.

5958. Sniffles and the Bookworm *(Merrie Melodies)* 2 Dec. 1939; *p.c.:* Leon Schlesinger prods for WB; *dir:* Charles M. Jones; *story:* Rich Hogan; *anim:* Bob McKimson; *character des/lay:* Robert Givens; *back:* Paul Julian; *ed:* Tregoweth E. Brown; *voices:* Margaret Hill, Mel Blanc, Cliff Nazarro, The Sportsmen Quartet; *mus:* Carl W. Stalling; *song:* Harry Warren; *prod sup:* Henry Binder, Raymond G. Katz; *col:* Tech. *sd:* Vit. 7 min. • Sniffles the mouse seeks refuge in a book shop and befriends a bookworm who introduces him to a score of literary characters.

5959. Sniffles Bells the Cat *(Merrie Melodies)* 1 Feb. 1941; *p.c.:* Leon Schlesinger prods for WB; *dir:* Charles M. Jones; *story:* Rich Hogan; *anim:* Ken Harris; *lay:* Robert Givens; *back:* Eugene Fleury; *ed:* Treg Brown; *character des:* Charles Thorson; *voice:* Margaret Hill; *mus:* Carl W. Stalling; *prod sup:* Henry Binder, Raymond G. Katz; *col:* Tech. *sd:* Vit. 7 min. • Sniffles is elected to tie a bell around the cat's neck. He succeeds only by accident and invents a fantastic story playing on heroism.

5960. Sniffles Takes a Trip *(Merrie Melodies)* 11 May 1940; *p.c.:* Leon Schlesinger prods for WB; *dir:* Charles M. Jones; *story:* Dave Monahan; *anim:* Philip Monroe; *lay:* Robert Givens; *back:* Eugene Fleury; *ed:* Treg Brown; *character des:* Charles Thorson; *voices:* Margaret Hill; *mus:* Carl W. Stalling; *prod sup:* Henry Binder, Raymond G. Katz; *col:* Tech. *sd:* Vit. 7 min. • Sniffles escapes to the countryside from the city noises but beats a hasty retreat when exposed to the night sounds of the country.

5961. 'Sno Fun *(Heckle & Jeckle)* 22 Aug. 1951; *p.c.:* TT for Fox; *dir:* Eddie Donnelly; *story/voices:* Tom Morrison; *anim:* Jim Tyer; *mus:* Philip A. Scheib; *ph:* Douglas Moye; *col:* Tech. *sd:* RCA. 6 min. • The magpies are Mounties, setting out to capture Powerful Pierre. They pursue him from the snowy north clear through to Hollywood.

5962. Snoopy, Come Home July 1972; *p.c.:* National General/Lee Mendelson — Bill Melendez prods for Cinema Center Films/Fox; *prod:* Lee Mendelson, Bill Melendez; *dir:* Bill Melendez; *story/created by* Charles M. Schulz; *anim:* Bob Carlson, Emery Hawkins, Sam Jaimes, Bill LittleJohn, Don Lusk, Al Pabian, Jim Pabian, Phil Roman, Frank Smith, Hank Smith, Rod Scribner, Rudy Zamora; *des/sets:* Ellie Bogardus, Evert Brown, Bernard Gruver, Ruth Kissane, Ed Levitt, Bob Matz, Al Shean, Dean Spille, Carla Washburn; *ed:* Robert T. Gillis, Charles McCann, Rudy Zamora Jr.; *voices: Charlie Brown:* Chad Webber; *Lucy:* Robin Kohn; *Linus:* Stephen Shea; *Schroeder:* David Carey; *Lila:* Joanna Baer; *Sally:* Hilary Momberger; *Peppermint Patty:* Chris de Faria; *Clara:* Linda Ercoli; *Frieda:* Linda Mendelson; *Snoopy:* Bill Melendez; *singers:* Shelby Flint, Thurl Ravenscroft, Guy Pohlman, Linda Ercoli, Ray Pohlman, Don Ralke; *mus rec:* Stan Ross,

Gold Star Recording; *voice rec:* Sid Nicholas, Radio recorders; *i&p/checking:* Carole Barnes, Gwenn Dotzier, Faith Kovaleski, Joanne Lansing, Adele Lenart, Joice Lee Marshall, Celine Miles, Chandra Poweris, Lou Robards, Beverly Robbins, Dawn Smith, Jacques Vasseur, Eleanor Warren, Manon Washburn, Debbie Zamora; *songs:* Richard M. Sherman, Robert B. Sherman; *mus arr:* Donald Ralke; *sd:* Don Minkler; *ph:* Nick Vasu, Jim Dickson; *neg cutter:* Alice Keillor; *pro mgr:* Robert T. Gillis; *pro assts:* Carolyn Klein, Sandy Claxon, Susan Scheid; *col:* Tech. *sd:* 70 min. • The *Peanuts* gang in a story about Charlie Brown's dog, Snoopy, feeling an outcast due to an excess of "No Dogs Allowed" signs.

5963. Snoopy Loopy *(Loopy de Loop)* 16 June 1960; *p.c.:* Hanna-Barbera for Colum; *prod/dir:* William Hanna, Joseph Barbera; *story dir:* Alex Lovy; *story:* Warren Foster; *anim dir:* Charles A. Nichols; *anim:* Ken Muse; *lay:* Dick Bickenbach; *back:* Richard H. Thomas; *ed:* Greg Watson; *voices:* Daws Butler, Don Messick, Jean van der Pyl; *mus:* Hoyt Curtain; *titles:* Lawrence Gobel; *prod mgr:* Howard Hanson; *col:* East. *sd:* RCA. 6½ min. • Loopy helps out the stork by delivering a baby monkey, who leads him a merry chase before delivering it to mother gorilla.

5964. Snooze Reel *(Kartune)* 28 Dec. 1951 *p.c.:* Famous for Para; *dir:* Seymour Kneitel; *story:* Joe Stultz; *anim:* Al Eugster, Wm. B. Pattengill; *sets:* Robert Owen; *voices:* Jackson Beck, Jack Mercer; *mus:* Winston Sharples; *song:* Frank Loesser, Joseph J. Lilley; *ph:* Leonard McCormick; *prod mgr:* Sam Buchwald; *col:* Tech. *sd:* RCA. 7 min. • A newsreel showing a liner being christened that promptly sinks, a two-hundred foot statue of Longfellow and a new western star encourages the audience to sing *Jingle, Jangle Jingle*.

5965. The Snoozin' Bruin *(Woody Woodpecker)* 1971; *p.c.:* Walter Lantz prods for Univ; *dir:* Paul J. Smith; *story:* Dalton Sandifer; *anim:* Virgil Ross, Al Coe, Tom Byrne, Joe Voght; *sets:* Nino Carbe; *voices:* Grace Stafford, Dal McKennon; *mus:* Walter Greene; *prod mgr:* William E. Garity; *col:* Tech. *sd:* RCA. 5½ min. • Woody tries to evict a hibernating bear from his tree home.

5966. Snow Birds *(Aesop's Film Fable)* 24 May 1929; *p.c.:* Fables Pictures Inc for Pathé; *dir:* Paul Terry; b&w. *sil.* 10 min. • No story available.

5967. Snow Business *(Looney Tunes)* 17 Jan. 1953; *p.c.:* WB; *dir:* I. Freleng; *story:* Warren Foster; *anim:* Virgil Ross, Arthur Davis, Manuel Perez, Ken Champin; *lay:* Hawley Pratt; *back:* Carlos Manriquez; *ed:* Treg Brown; *voices:* Mel Blanc, Bea Benaderet, Stan Freberg; *mus:* Carl Stalling; *prod mgr:* John W. Burton; *prod:* Edward Selzer; *col:* Tech. *sd:* Vit. 7 min. • Sylvester and Tweety are trapped in Granny's mountain cabin during a snowstorm. Being no food except bird seed, Sylvester turns to thoughts of cooked Tweety Bird.

5968. Snow Excuse *(Merrie Melodies)* 21 May 1966; *p.c.:* DFE for WB; *dir:* Robert McKimson; *story:* David DeTiege; *anim:* George Grandpré, Bob Matz, Manny Perez, Don Williams, Norm McCabe; *lay:* Dick Ung; *back:* Tom O'Loughlin; *ed:* Al Wahrman; *voices:* Mel Blanc; *mus:* Bill Lava; *col:* Tech. *sd:* Vit. 6 min. • Speedy tries to steal Daffy's firewood during a cold spell.

5969. Snow Foolin' *(Screen Song)* 16 Dec. 1949; *p.c.:* Famous for Para; *dir:* I. Sparber; *story:* I. Klein; *anim:* Myron Waldman, Gordon Whittier; *sets:* Tom Ford; *voices:* Jack Mercer, Sid Raymond, Cecil Roy; *mus:* Winston Sharples; *ph:* Leonard McCormick; *prod mgr:* Sam Buchwald; *col:* Tech. *sd:* RCA. 7 min. • The animals' winter games.

5970. The Snow Man *(Terry-Toon)* 13 Dec. 1940; *p.c.:* TT for Fox; *dir:* Connie Rasinski; *story:* John Foster; *mus:* Philip A. Scheib; b&w. *sd:* RCA. 7 min. • The bunnies' snowman comes to life. Then a bear arrives on the scene and tries to melt him until the North Wind comes to the rescue.

5971. Snow Place Like Home *(Chilly Willy)* Feb. 1966; *p.c.:* Walter Lantz prods for Univ; *dir:* Paul J. Smith; *story:* Homer Brightman; *anim:* Al Coe, Les Kline; *sets:* Ray Huffine, Art Landy; *voices:* Daws Butler; *mus:* Walter Greene; *prod mgr:* William E. Garity; *col:* Tech. *sd:* RCA. 6 min. • Chilly prevents his friend, Smedley, from departing to sunnier climes.

5972. Snow Place Like Home *(Popeye)* 3 Sept. 1948; *p.c.:* Famous for Para; Seymour Kneitel; *story:* Carl Meyer, Jack Mercer; *anim:* Dave Tendlar, Martin Taras; *sets:* Anton Loeb; *voices:* Jack Mercer, Mae Questel, Jackson Beck; *mus:* Winston Sharples; *ph:* Leonard McCormick; *prod mgr:*

Sam Buchwald; *col:* Pola. *sd:* RCA. 6¹/₂ min. • Popeye and Olive are swept away to the North Pole by a tornado. There they encounter Pierre, a fur trader who has amorous views on Olive.

5973. Snow Time *(Aesop's Sound Fable)* 20 July 1930; *p.c.:* Van Beuren for Pathé; *dir:* John Foster, Mannie Davis; *mus:* Gene Rodemich; b&w. *sd:* RCA. 8 min. • Dogs, cats, birds and hippos have winter fun and when a pup falls exhausted, a St. Bernard revives him with brandy. The others see this and want a piece of the action.

5974. Snow Time *(Krazy Kat)* 30 Nov. 1932; *p.c.:* Winkler for Colum; *prod:* Charles Mintz; *anim:* Al Rose, Harry Love; *mus:* Joe de Nat; *prod mgr:* James Bronis; b&w. *sd:* RCA. 6 min. • A horse brings Krazy and his girl to a frozen pond to skate and indulge in winter sports.

5975. Snow Time for Comedy *(Merrie Melodies)* 30 Aug. 1941; *p.c.:* Leon Schlesinger prods for WB; *dir:* Charles M. Jones; *story:* Rich Hogan; *anim:* Robert Cannon; *lay:* Robert Givens; *back:* Eugene Fleury; *ed:* Treg Brown; *voices:* Mel Blanc; *mus:* Carl W. Stalling; *prod sup:* Henry Binder, Raymond G. Katz; *col:* Tech. *sd:* Vit. 7 min. • The two pups battle for a bone in the snow.

5976. Snow Use *(Oswald)*; 25 Nov. 1929; *p.c.:* Univ; *dir:* Walter Lantz; *anim:* R.C. Hamilton, "Bill" Nolan, Tom Palmer; *mus:* Bert Fiske; b&w. *sd:* WE. 7 min. • Putrid Pete moves in on Oswald's girl in a snowbound dance hall.

5977. Snow-White *(Betty Boop)* 31 Mar. 1933; *p.c.:* The Fleischer Studio for Para; *prod:* Max Fleischer; *dir:* Dave Fleischer; *anim:* Roland C. Crandall; *voices:* Cab Calloway, Mae Questel; *mus:* Sammy Timberg; b&w. *sd:* WE. 7 min. • The wicked Queen tries to dispose of Snow White (Betty) then transforms into a dragon but is rousted by the seven dwarfs.

5978. Snow White and the Seven Dwarfs 21 Dec. 1937; *p.c.:* Walt Disney prods for RKO; *dir sup:* David D. Hand; *seq dir:* Larry Morey, William Cottrell, Ben Sharpsteen, Wilfred Jackson, Hamilton S. Luske, Fred Moore, Perce Pearce, Vladimir Tytla; story adapted from Grimm's fairy tale. *story adapt:* Merrill de Maris, Richard Creedon, Dorothy Ann Blank, Dick Rickard, Earl Hurd, Otto Englander, Webb Smith, Ted Sears; *anim:* Frank Thomas, Les Clark, Dick Lundy, Fred Spencer, Art Babbitt, Grim Natwick, Eric Larson, Robert Martsch, Marvin Woodward, Bernard Garbutt, Robert Stokes, Jack Campbell, James Algar, Norman Ferguson, Al Eugster, Ward Kimball, James Culhane, Ugo d'Orsi, Bill Roberts, Wolfgang Reitherman; *inbetweener:* Bob McCrea; *fx:* Josh Meador, George Rowley, Cy Young; *inspirational sketches:* Ferdinand Huszti Horvath, Gustav Tenggren; *lay:* Ken Anderson, Tom Codrick, Joe Grant, Hugh Hennesy, Albert Hurter, Harold Miles, A. Kendall O'Connor, Charles Philippi, Hazel Sewell, Terrell Stapp, McLaren Stewart, Gustaf Tenggren; *back:* Samuel Armstrong, Claude Coats, Merle Cox, Phil Dike, Arthur Fitzpatrick, Ray Lockrem, Mique Nelson, Maurice Noble; *voices: Snow White:* Adriana Caselotti; *The Queen/Witch:* Lucille la Verne; *Doc:* Roy Atwell; *Sneezy:* Billy Gilbert; *Happy:* Otis Harlan; *Bashful:* Scott Mattraw; *Grumpy/Sleepy:* Pinto Colvig; *The Prince:* Harry Stockwell; *The Magic Mirror:* Moroni Olsen; *The Huntsman:* Stuart Buchanan; *Yodelling chorus:* The Fraunfelder Family (William, Ruth & Betty), James MacDonald; *Bird sounds:* Marion Darlington, Esther Campbell, Clarence Nash; *misc. sounds for Dopey:* Clarence Nash; *mus:* Leigh Harline, Frank Churchill, Paul Smith; *songs:* Larry Morey, Frank Churchill; *col:* Tech. *sd:* RCA. 83 min. • Princess Snow White seeks refuge in a cottage in the woods from the wicked Queen who is jealous of her beauty. The cottage belongs to seven dwarfs who protect her until the Queen arrives disguised as a peddler and gives her a poisoned apple. The dwarfs can't bring themselves to bury her but place her in a glass coffin until she is awakened by the kiss of true love. • Walt Disney's ambitious first full-length feature was three years in the making. Disney received a special "Oscar" in 1939, along with seven smaller ones for being a pioneer in his craft.

5979. Snowbody Loves Me *(Tom & Jerry)* 1964; *p.c.:* SIB Tower 12 for MGM; *prod/dir:* Chuck Jones; *asst dir:* Maurice Noble; *story:* Chuck Jones, Michael Maltese; *anim:* Dick Thompson, Ben Washam, Ken Harris, Don Towsley, Tom Ray; *back:* Philip de Guard; *voice:* Mel Blanc; *mus:* Eugene Poddany; *prod mgr:* Les Goldman; *col:* Metro. *sd:* WE. 8 min. • When a frozen Jerry arrives at Tom's Swiss mountain chalet, he makes straight for the Swiss cheese and a chase ensues.

5980. The Snowman 1933; *p.c.:* Ted Eshbaugh Studio for Invincible/Chesterfield; *prod/dir:* Ted Eshbaugh; *anim:* Frank Tipper, "Vet" Anderson; *col:* Tech-2. *sd:* 10 min. • Seals build a snowman who grows to gargantuan proportions and terrorizes the townsfolk. His antics are halted when he is melted by the Northern Lights.

5981. Snowman's Land *(Merrie Melodies)* 29 June 1939; *p.c.:* Leon Schlesinger prods for WB; *dir:* Charles Jones; *story:* Dave Monahan; *anim:* Ken Harris; *lay:* Robert Givens; *back:* Paul Julian; *ed:* Tregoweth E. Brown; *character des:* Charles Thorson; *voices:* Pinto Colvig, Mel Blanc, The Sportsmen Quartet; *mus:* Carl W. Stalling; *prod sup:* Henry Binder, Raymond G. Katz; *col:* Tech. *sd:* Vit. 7 min. • A Mountie goes off to capture Dirty Pierre, finally getting his man by rolling a giant snowball on top of him.

5982. Snowtime *(Color Rhapsody)* 14 Apr. 1938; *p.c.:* Cartoon Films Ltd for Colum; *dir:* Ub Iwerks; *voices:* Cliff Nazarro, The Paul Taylor Quartet, Dave Weber, Harry Stanton, Russ Powell; *mus:* Eddie Kilfeather, Joe de Nat; *prod mgr:* James Bronis; *col:* Tech. *sd:* RCA. 7 min. • Prof. Owl lectures his students on how the elves make snow at the North Pole.

5983. Snubbed by a Snob *(Color Classic)* 19 July 1940; *p.c.:* The Fleischer Studio for Para; *prod:* Max Fleischer; *dir:* Dave Fleischer; *story:* Joseph E. Stultz; *anim:* Stanley Quackenbush, Arnold Gillespie; *sets:* Gustav Tenggren; *ed:* Kitty Pfister; *voices:* Jack Mercer, Margie Hines, Pinto Colvig; *mus:* Sammy Timberg; *prod sup:* Sam Buchwald, Isidore Sparber; *col:* Tech. *sd:* WE. 7 min. • Spunky, the mule, meets an aristocratic colt who isn't interested in his antics. When the colt is menaced by a bull, Spunky saves the day.

5984. Snuffy's Party *(Cartune)* 7 Aug. 1939; *p.c.:* Walter Lantz prods for Univ; *dir:* Elmer Perkins; *story:* Victor McLeod, Hicks Lokey; *anim:* Al Coe, Frank Tipper; *sets:* Edgar Keichle; *voices:* Mel Blanc, Dave Weber; *mus:* Frank Marsales; *prod mgr:* George Hall; b&w. *sd:* WE. 7 min. • Snuffy Skunk is locked out of his own party. When the dam breaks, he forces the water back with his strong odor.

5985. Snuffy's Song *(Comic King)* June 1962; *p.c.:* Para Cartoons: *dir:* Seymour Kneitel; *story:* Michael Ross, Bruce Howard; *anim:* Wm. B. Pattengill, Irving Dressler; *sets:* Robert Owen; *voices:* Paul Frees; *mus:* Winston Sharples; *ph:* Leonard McCormick; *col:* Tech. *sd:* RCA. 5¹/₂ min. • Barney Google decides to cash in on the current music rage by recording Snuffy's wood-chopping song.

5986. So Dear to My Heart 19 Jan. 1949; *p.c.:* Walt Disney prods for RKO; *asso prod:* Perce Pearce; *anim seq dir:* Hamilton Luske; *anim story:* Marc Davis, Ken Anderson, William Peed; *des:* John Hench, Mary Blair, Dick Kelsey; *anim:* Eric Larson, Milt Kahl, John Lounsbery, Les Clark, Hal King, Don Lusk, Marvin Woodward; *fx:* George Rowley, Josh Meador, Dan MacManus; *lay:* A. Kendall O'Connor, Hugh Hennesy, Don Griffith, Thor Putnam; *back:* Art Riley, Dick Anthony, Ralph Hulett, Brice Mack, Jimi Trout, Ray Huffine; *voices: Narrator:* John Beal; *The Wise Old Owl:* Ken Carson; *singers:* Bob Stanton, Charles Prescott, Bob Ebright, Henry Kruse, Eleanor, Dorothy & Marilyn Gourly, Virginia Rees, Howard A. Davis, Emmett Casey, Raymond Clark, Stewart Bair, John Woodbury, Grafton Linn; *Scottish singers:* Jimmy O'Brien, Thomas Dunn; "*Christopher Columbus*": Thurl Ravenscroft; *whistling:* Marion Darlington, Clarence Nash; *mus:* Paul Smith; *orch:* Ed Plumb; *mus ed:* Al Teeter; *voice dir:* Ken Darby; *songs:* Larry Morey, Eliot Daniel; *col:* Tech. *sd:* RCA. 84 min. • This chiefly live-action feature deals with a small boy who grooms a black lamb to be a champion prize-winner. The boy (Bobby Driscoll) receives (animated) sound advice in song from the Wise Old Owl in his scrapbook.

5987. So Does an Automobile *(Betty Boop)* 31 Mar. 1939; *p.c.:* The Fleischer Studio for Para; *prod:* Max Fleischer; *dir:* Dave Fleischer; *anim:* Roland Crandall, Frank Kelling; *voices:* Everett Clark, Margie Hines; *mus:* Sammy Timberg; *ph:* Charles Schettler; *prod sup:* Sam Buchwald, Isidore Sparber; b&w. *sd:* WE. 6 min. • Betty tends to the cars in her automobile hospital.

5988. So Much For So Little 16 March 1949; *p.c.:* Federal Security Agency, Public Health Service/WB; *dir:* Charles M. Jones; *anim:* Ben Washam, Ken Harris, Phil Monroe, Lloyd Vaughan; *sets:* Robert Gribbroek, Paul Julian, Peter Alvarado; *voice:* Frank Graham; *mus:* Carl W. Stalling; *col:* Tech. *sd:* Vit. 11 min. *Academy Award.* • Following the life of John Jones from birth to old age expressing the importance of an adequate health service.

5989. So Sorry, Pussycat (*Hashimoto*) Mar. 1961; *p.c.:* TT for Fox; *ex prod:* Bill Weiss; *dir:* Art Bartsch; *story sup:* Tom Morrison; *story:* Dick Kinney, Al Bertino; *anim:* Ed Donnelly, Juan Guidi, Armando Guidi; *lay:* Bob Taylor, Martin Strudler; *back:* John Zago; *voices:* John Myhers; *mus:* Phil Scheib; *prod mgr:* Frank Schudde; *col:* DeLuxe. *sd:* RCA. 6 min. • No story available.

5990. Soap (*Aesop's Film Fable*) 16 Aug. 1925; *p.c.:* Fables Pictures Inc for Pathé; *dir:* Paul Terry; b&w. *sil.* 5 min. • While Farmer Al Falfa bathes in the family tub, the cat tries to retrieve an elusive bar of soap and the mice join in the fun.

5991. A Soapy Opera (*Mighty Mouse*) Jan. 1953; *p.c.:* TT for Fox; *dir:* Connie Rasinski; *story:* Tom Morrison; *anim:* Jim Tyer; *voice:* Roy Halee; *mus:* Philip A. Scheib; *ph:* Douglas Moye; *col:* Tech. *sd:* RCA. 7 min. • Oil Can Harry convinces Pearl Pureheart that Mighty Mouse has lost his strength and she concedes to be his slave. Mighty Mouse soon arrives, fighting fit and full of pep.

5992. Social Lion 15 Oct. 1954; *p.c.:* Walt Disney prods for BV; *dir:* Jack Kinney; *story:* Milt Schaffer, Dick Kinney; *anim:* Norman Ferguson; *fx:* Dan MacManus, Ernie Bemiller; *lay:* Bruce Bushman; *back:* Thelma Witmer; *voices:* Alan Mowbray, Paul Frees; *mus:* Oliver Wallace; *col:* Tech. *sd:* RCA. 7 min. • A lion breaks loose of his cage and wanders the streets of New York, accepted as one of its many weird inhabitants.

5993. Society Dog Show (*Mickey Mouse*) 3 Feb. 1939; *p.c.:* Walt Disney prods for RKO; *dir:* William O. Roberts; *story:* Jack Kinney; *anim:* Les Clark, James H. Culhane, Alfred Eugster, Norman Ferguson, Clyde Geronimi, Paul Hopkins, Richard Lundy, John McManus, Fred Moore, Lee Morehouse, Ray Patin, Leo Salkin, Milt Schafer, Cornett Wood, Marvin Woodward; *fx:* George Rowley, Cy Young; *voices:* J. Donald Wilson, Lee Millar, Walt Disney; *mus:* Oliver Wallace; *col:* Tech. *sd:* RCA. 8 min. • Mickey enters Pluto in a society dog show who flirts with a pekinese. The Judge expels Pluto but the resourceful hound later saves all from a fire.

5994. Sock-a-By Baby (*Popeye*) 19 Jan. 1934; *p.c.:* The Fleischer Studio for Para; *prod:* Max Fleischer; *dir:* Dave Fleischer; *anim:* Seymour Kneitel, Roland Crandall; *voices:* William A. Costello; *mus:* Sammy Timberg; b&w. *sd:* WE. 6½ min. • Popeye does his best to prevent the baby being awakened by city noises.

5995. Sock-a-Bye Kitty (*Noveltoon*) 22 Dec. 1950; *p.c.:* Famous for Para; *dir:* Seymour Kneitel; *story:* Carl Meyer, Jack Mercer; *anim:* Dave Tendlar, Tom Golden; *sets:* Tom Ford; *voices:* Jackson Beck, Sid Raymond; *mus:* Winston Sharples; *ph:* Leonard McCormick; *prod mgr:* Sam Buchwald; *col:* Tech. *sd:* RCA. 6 min. • Katnip reads that eating crow will cure his insomnia. Buzzy the Crow has different ideas of how to put the insomnicat to sleep.

5996. Sock-a-Doodle Do (*Looney Tunes*) 10 May 1952; *p.c.:* WB; *dir:* Robert McKimson; *story:* Tedd Pierce; *anim:* Charles McKimson, Rod Scribner, Phil de Lara; *lay:* Peter Alvarado; *back:* Richard H. Thomas; *ed:* Treg Brown; *voices:* Mel Blanc, Sheldon Leonard; *mus:* Carl Stalling; *prod mgr:* John W. Burton; *prod:* Edward Selzer; *col:* Tech. *sd:* Vit. 7 min. • Foggy puts a boxing rooster to good use in his ongoing feud with the dog.

5997. Socko in Morocco (*Woody Woodpecker*) 18 Jan. 1954; *p.c.:* Walter Lantz prods for Univ; *dir:* Don Patterson; *story:* Homer Brightman; *anim:* Ray Abrams, Herman Cohen, Ken Southworth; *sets:* Art Landy; *voices:* Dallas McKennon, Grace Stafford; *mus:* Clarence Wheeler; *prod mgr:* William E. Garity; *col:* Tech. *sd:* RCA. 6 min. • Legionaire Woody is ordered to guard a princess against the marauding hands of Sheik el Rancid.

5998. Soda Poppa (*Krazy Kat*) 29 May 1931; *p.c.:* Winkler for Colum; *prod:* Charles Mintz; *anim:* Ben Harrison, Manny Gould; *mus:* Joe de Nat; *prod mgr:* James Bronis; b&w. *sd:* WE. 6 min. • A lecherous customer in Krazy's Soda Fountain abducts his girl and takes her to the top of a skyscraper with Krazy on their trail.

5999. The Soda Squirt (*Flip the Frog*) 12 Oct. 1933; *p.c.:* Celebrity prods for MGM; *prod/dir:* Ub Iwerks; *mus:* Gene Denny; b&w. *sd:* PCP. 6 min. • Many personalities arrive at Flip's Soda Fountain on opening night, including John Barrymore, Joe E. Brown, Jimmy Durante, Buster Keaton, Laurel and Hardy, the Four Marx Brothers and Mae West. A fey character arrives and drinks a potion Flip has mixed, turning him into a raging "Mr. Hyde"who wrecks the place. Ub Iwerks, himself, is also caricatured.

6000. Soft Soap (*Life Cartoon Comedy*) 30 Jan. 1927; *p.c.:* Sherwood Wadsworth Pictures for Educational; *prod/dir:* John R. McCrory; b&w. *sil.* 6 min. • A safe is bequeathed to Mike Monkey. After much trouble in opening it, he discovers it full of cakes of soap. Meanwhile, Little Nibbins has flooded the place and the soap takes care of the rest.

6001. Softball Game (*Oswald*) 27 Jan. 1936; *p.c.:* Univ; *dir:* Walter Lantz; *story:* Walter Lantz, Victor McLeod; *anim:* Manuel Moreno, Bill Mason; *mus:* James Dietrich; b&w. *sd:* WE. 6 min. • Oswald and the gang take part in a baseball game. Segments were used to illustrate Lowell Thomas' "Universal News" item on how cartoons are made.

6002. Soldier Old Man (*Krazy Kat*) 2 Apr. 1932; *p.c.:* Winkler for Colum; *prod:* Charles Mintz; *story:* Manny Gould; *anim:* Al Rose; *voice:* Jack Carr; *mus:* Joe de Nat; *prod mgr:* James Bronis; b&w. *sd:* WE. 7 min. • Old soldiers in a home revive the Civil War with Krazy representing the enemy, ending in a food fight.

6003. Sole Mates 1933; *p.c.:* A-C; *prod:* W.P. Bach; *anim:* F. Lyle Goldman; *col:* Tech. *sd:* WE. • Squeakie rescues Pekie.

6004. Sole Mates (*Krazy Kat*) 7 Nov. 1929; *p.c.:* Winkler for Colum; *anim:* Ben Harrison, Manny Gould; *mus:* Joe de Nat; *prod mgr:* James Bronis; *prod:* George Winkler; b&w. (synchronized score) *sd:* WE. 6 min. • The coterie of animals put on a singing and dancing feastival with ballroom numbers by a pair of elephants, a hippo and a cat. Krazy does a "Joe Frisco" act.

6005. Solid Ivory (*Woody Woodpecker*) 25 Aug. 1947; *p.c.:* Walter Lantz prods for Univ; *dir:* Dick Lundy; *story:* Ben Hardaway, Milt Schaffer; *anim:* Grim Natwick, Hal Mason; *sets:* Fred Brunish; *ed:* Dave Lurie; *voices:* Walter Craig, Mary Lennon, Ben Hardaway; *mus:* Darrell Calker; *prod mgr:* William E. Garity; *col:* Tech. *sd:* WE. 6 min. • Woody tries to retrieve a snooker ball from a hen who attempts to hatch it.

6006. Solid Serenade (*Tom & Jerry*) 31 Aug. 1946; *p.c.:* MGM; *dir:* William Hanna, Joseph Barbera; *anim:* Ed Barge, Michael Lah, Kenneth Muse; *ed:* Fred MacAlpin; *voice:* Ira "Buck" Woods, Walter Craig; *mus:* Scott Bradley; *prod:* Fred Quimby; *col:* Tech. *sd:* WE. 7 min. • Tom impresses his girl by serenading her on a double bass. Complications set in when Jerry's slumber is disturbed and he arouses a ferocious bulldog.

6007. Solid Tin Coyote (*Looney Tunes*) 19 Feb. 1966; *p.c.:* DFE for WB; *dir:* Rudy Larriva; *story:* Don Jurwich; *anim:* Hank Smith, Virgil Ross, Bob Bransford; *sets:* Anthony Rizzo; *ed:* Joe Siracusa; *mus:* Bill Lava; *col:* Tech. *sd:* Vit. 6 min. • The Coyote builds a giant robot coyote to help him with his pursuit of the Road-Runner.

6008. Solitary Refinement (*Modern Madcap*) Sept. 1966; *p.c.:* Para Cartoons; *dir:* Howard Post; *story:* Tony Peters; *anim:* Morey Reden; *sets:* Robert Little; *voices:* Bob MacFadden; *mus:* Winston Sharples; *ph:* Leonard McCormick; *prod mgr:* Abe Goodman; *col:* Tech. *sd:* RCA. 6 min. • Boobie Baboon spends all his time trying to escape from prison. When his reprieve comes through, he realizes that escaping from prison is the only thing he knows how to do.

6009. Some Barrier (*Terry Cartoon Burlesque*) July 1917; *p.c.:* Cartoon Film Services for A. Kay Co.; *anim:* Paul Terry; b&w. *sil.* 6 min. • No story available.

6010. Some Nightmare (*Clay-Toon*) 1930; *p.c.:* Cinemation Studios Inc for Perfex Pictures b&w. *sd.* • No story or credits available.

6011. Somebody Stole My Gal (*Screen Songs*) 21 Mar. 1931; *p.c.:* The Fleischer Studio for Para; *prod:* Max Fleischer; *sup:* Dave Fleischer; *dir/anim:* Jimmie Culhane, Rudy Zamora; *mus:* Art Turkisher; *song:* Leo Wood; b&w. *sd:* WE. 6 min. • No story available.

6012. Something You Didn't Eat 28 June 1945; *p.c.:* Walt Disney prods for Cereal Institute/OWI War Food Admininistration for WB/War Activities Committee; *dir:* James Algar; *anim:* Bill Justice, Murray McClellan, Fred Moore, Harvey Toombs; *fx:* Ub Iwerks, Dan MacManus, Josh Meador; *lay:* Herbert Klynn; *voices:* Frank Graham, Art Shank; *col:* Tech. *sd:* RCA. 9 min. • Designed to acquaint the public with the need to maintain a varied diet for good health.

6013. Somewhere in Dreamland (*Color Classic*) 17 Jan. 1939; *p.c.:* The Fleischer Studio for Para; *prod:* Max Fleischer; *dir:* Dave Fleischer; *anim:* Seymour Kneitel, Roland Crandall; *voice:* Mae Questel; *song:* Murray Mencher, Charles Newman; *col:* Tech-2. *sd:* WE. 9 min. • Two poverty-stricken children sleep and dream they are in a land where food reigns in abundance. They wake to find the local traders have furnished a meal for them and their mother.

6014. Somewhere in Egypt (*Terry-Toon*) 17 Aug. 1943; *p.c.:* TT for Fox; *dir:* Mannie Davis; *story:* John Foster; *voices:* Thomas Morrison; *mus:* Philip A. Scheib; *col:* Tech. *sd:* RCA. 6 min. • Pvt. Gandy Goose plays a flute and makes Sgt. Cat dream he's inside a sphinx with a beautiful dancing girl.

6015. Somewhere in the Pacific (*Terry-Toon*) 25 Dec. 1942; *p.c.:* TT for Fox; *dir:* Mannie Davis; *story:* John Foster; *voices:* Arthur Kay, Thomas Morrison; *mus:* Philip A. Scheib; *col:* Tech. *sd:* RCA. 6 min. • Pvt. Gandy and Sgt. Sourpuss are billeted on a South Sea island where they are threatened by Japs from air, land and sea.

6016. Son of Hashimoto (*Hashimoto*) Apr 1961; *p.c.:* TT for Fox; *ex prod:* Bill Weiss; *dir:* Connie Rasinski; *story sup:* Tom Morrison; *anim:* Juan Guidi; *sets:* Bill Focht, John Zago; *voices:* John Myhers; *mus:* Phil Scheib; *prod mgr:* Frank Schudde; *col:* DeLuxe. *sd:* RCA. 6 min. CS. • No story available.

6017. Son of Kong 1933; *p.c.:* RKO; *prod:* Merian C. Cooper; *fx:* Willis H. O'Brien, E.B. Gibson, Marcel Delgado, Fred Reefe, Orville Goldner, Carroll Shepphird, Mario Larrinaga; *l/a dir:* Ernest B. Schoedsack; b&w. *sd:* RCA. 69 min. *l/a/anim.* • A voyage back to Kong's island finds a younger, cuter offspring who saves the party from destruction.

6018. Son of the Pink Panther 27 Aug. 1993; *p.c.:* Filmauro SRL for UA; *main title seq:* Desert Music Pictures; *title anim:* Bill Kroyer; *mus/l/a:* Henry Mancini; *Pink Panther theme performed and arranged by* Bobby McFerrin; *col. sd.* 3½ min. *l/a/anim.* • Live-action comedy with animated credits showing the Panther conducting the live-action musicians.

6019. The Son Shower (*Aesop's Film Fable*) 12 Feb. 1928; *p.c.:* Fables Pictures Inc for Pathé; *dir:* Paul Terry, Hugh Shields; b&w. *sil.* 10 min. • No story available.

6020. A Song a Day (*Betty Boop*) 22 May 1936; *p.c.:* The Fleischer Studio for Para; *prod:* Max Fleischer; *dir:* Dave Fleischer; *anim:* David Tendlar, Nicholas Tafuri, Joseph Oriolo; *voices:* Mae Questel, Everett Clark; *mus:* Sammy Timberg; b&w. *sd:* WE. 7 min. • Professor Grampy's musical hijinks soon cheer up the patients in Betty's animal hospital.

6021. Song of Norway 1970; *p.c.:* Kinney-Wolf for Cinerama; *seq dir:* Jack Kinney; based on Theadore Kittleson's drawings; *col. sd.* seq 2½ min. Super Panavision. *l/a/anim.* • Live-action feature about the life of composer Edvard Grieg. The children are menaced by animated trolls.

6022. The Song of the Birds (*Color Classic*) 1 Mar. 1935; *p.c.:* The Fleischer Studio for Para; *prod:* Max Fleischer; *dir:* Dave Fleischer; *anim:* Seymour Kneitel, Roland Crandall; *mus:* Sammy Timberg; *col:* Tech-2. *sd:* WE. 8 min. • A naughty boy shoots a baby bird on its maiden flight. He soon feels remorse when the other birds hold a funeral ceremony but joy prevails when he recovers.

6023. Song of the Birds (*Noveltoon*) 18 Nov. 1949; *p.c.:* Famous for Para; *dir:* Bill Tytla *story:* Bill Turner, Larry Riley; *anim:* George Germanetti, Steve Muffatti; *sets:* Robert Little; *voices:* Mae Questel; *mus:* Winston Sharples; *ph:* Leonard McCormick; *prod mgr:* Sam Buchwald; *col:* Tech. *sd:* RCA. 8 min. • While playing with a rifle, Audrey accidentally shoots a baby bird. The other birds hold a funeral service but the bird returns to life, making Audrey throw her gun away. Remake of the 1935 version.

6024. Song of the South 1 Nov. 1946; *p.c.:* Walt Disney prods for RKO; *asso prod:* Perce Pearce; *anim dir:* Wilfred Jackson; based on the tales of Uncle Remus by Joel Chandler Harris; *anim story:* William Peed, Ralph Wright, George Stallings. • "Zip-a-Dee-Doo-Dah" *fx:* Josh Meador; *lay:* Ken Anderson; *des/back:* Mary Blair; *song:* Allie Wrubel, Ray Gilbert. • "Running Away" combination segment: *anim dir:* Les Clark, Marc Davis; *anim:* Tom Massey, Jack Campbell, Al Coe, Don Lusk, Harvey Toombs; *fx:* Josh Meador; *pure anim: anim dir:* John Lounsbery, Oliver M. Johnston Jr.; *anim:* Kenneth O'Brien, Eric Larson, Murray McClellan, Don Lusk, Harvey Toombs; *fx:* George Rowley. • "The Tar Baby" combination segment: *anim dir:* Milt Kahl; *anim:* Kenneth O'Brien, Hal Ambro, Cliff Nordberg; *fx:* Josh Meador; *pure anim: anim dir:* Oliver M. Johnston Jr., Eric Larson, Marc Davis, Milt Kahl; *anim:* Hal Ambro, Kenneth O'Brien; *fx:* George Rowley; *lay:* Ken Anderson; *back:* Brice Mack; *song:* Robert MacGimsey. • "The Laughing Place" *anim dir:* Marc Davis, Oliver M. Johnston Jr., Milt Kahl, Eric Larson, John Lounsbery; *anim:* Hal Ambro, Rudy Larriva, Don Lusk, Murray McClellan, Cliff Nordberg, Kenneth O'Brien, Harvey Toombs; *fx:* George Rowley; *song:* Jesse Cryer; *art dir:* Kenneth Anderson, Charles Philippi, Hugh Hennesy, Harold Doughty, Philip Barber; *add anim:* Jack Campbell, Hal King, Tom Massey; *add fx:* Brad Case, Blaine Gibson; *des:* Mary Blair, Claude Coats; *back:* Albert Dempster, Ralph Hulett, Ray Huffine, Brice Mack, Edgar Starr; *voices: Br'er Fox:* James Baskett; *Br'er Bear:* Nicodemus Stewart; *Br'er Rabbit:* John D. Lee Jr., James Baskett; *Sis Possum:* Helen Crozier; *Miss Nellie (Butterfly):* Ernestine Smith; *Humming Birds chorus:* the DeCastro Sisters; *Mr. Bluebird:* Clarence Nash; *chorus:* The Ken Darby Chorus; *mus:* Paul J. Smith; *orch:* Edward H. Plumb; *vocal dir:* Ken Darby; *l/a: Uncle Remus:* James Baskett; *col:* Tech. *sd:* RCA. 94 min. *l/a/anim.* • Down in the deep South, local storyteller Uncle Remus stops Johnny (Bobby Driscoll) and Ginny (Luana Patten) from running away from home by relating the adventures of Br'er Rabbit. In "Running Away" Br'er Rabbit manages to talk himself out of the snare that the wiley Br'er Fox has set for him. "The Tar Baby" sees Br'er Fox and Bear creating a man out of tar. Br'er Rabbit gets into a fight with him and is gummed up for a while. "The Laughing Place" has Br'er Rabbit caught by the cunning Fox and Dim Bear and manages to convince them that somewhere in the woods lies his "Laughing Place." They go in search of it and only succeed in unearthing a nest of bees.

6025. Song of Victory (*Color Rhapsody*) 4 Sept. 1942; *p.c.:* Colum; *prod:* Dave Fleischer; *dir:* Bob Wickersham; *story:* Leo Salkin; *anim:* Bernard Garbutt, Phil Duncan, William Schull; *sets:* Clark Watson, Zack Schwartz; *ed:* Edward Moore; *voices:* Harry E. Lang; *mus:* Eddie Kilfeather; *ph:* Frank Fisher; *prod mgr:* Ben Schwalb; *col:* Tech. *sd:* RCA. 8½ min. • Beethoven's Fifth Symphony helps illustrate the threat of totalitarianism in the forest presented by Hitler (as a vulture) and Mussolini (portrayed as an ape). Story initiated Frank Tashlin and John Hubley.

6026. Song Shopping (*Screen Songs*) 19 May 1933; *p.c.:* The Fleischer Studio for Para; *prod:* Max Fleischer; *dir:* Dave Fleischer; *anim:* Willard Bowsky, David Tendlar; *l/a:* Ethel Merman, Johnny Green; b&w. *sd:* WE. 7 min. • Kittens in a music factory.

6027. Songs of Erin (*Gandy Goose*) Mar. 1951; *p.c.:* TT for Fox; *dir:* Connie Rasinski; *story:* Tom Morrison; *sets:* Art Bartsch; *voice:* Arthur Kay; *mus:* Philip A. Scheib; *ph:* Douglas Moye; *col:* Tech. *sd:* RCA. 7 min. • Gandy imagines he is in Ireland pursuing a pretty Colleen then chased by a mountain monster, awakening to find it was all a dream!

6028. The Sorcerer's Apprentice • See: *The Wizard's Apprentice*

6029. Sorry Safari (*Tom & Jerry*) 1962; *p.c.:* Rembrandt for MGM; *prod:* William L. Snyder; *dir:* Gene Deitch; *story:* Larz Bourne; *voice:* Allen Swift; *mus:* Stepan Koníček; *col:* Metro. *sd:* WE. 6 min. • Tom disrupts his master's wild game safari. • See: *Tom and Jerry (Rembrandt Films)*

6030. S.O.S. (*Aesop's Film Fable*) 25 Apr. 1925; *p.c.:* Fables Pictures Inc for Pathé; *dir:* Paul Terry; b&w. *sil.* 10 min. • Mrs. Tom Cat vocalizes from Station W.O.W. and is pelted by vegetable through the speakers.

6031. Soup Song (*Flip the Frog*) 21 Jan. 1931; *p.c.:* Celebrity for MGM; *prod/dir:* Ub Iwerks; *mus:* Carl W. Stalling; b&w. *sd:* PCP. 6 min. • Flip is waiter-in-chief as well as bandleader who conducts a customer's noisy soup eating.

6032. Soup to Mutts (*Cartune*) 9 Jan. 1939; *p.c.:* Walter Lantz prods for Univ; *dir:* Lester Kline; *story:* Victor McLeod; *anim:* George Nicholas, Dick Marion; *sets:* Edgar Keichle; *voice:* Mel Blanc; *mus:* Frank Marsales; *prod mgr:* George Hall; b&w *sd:* WE. 7 min. • The canine world stages an amateur entertainment where an applause machine determines the prize for each performer. A disguised cat walks away with a pile of hot dogs

6033. Soup's On (*Donald Duck*) 15 Oct. 1948; *p.c.:* Walt Disney prods for RKO; *dir:* Jack Hannah; *story:* Bill Berg, Milt Banta; *anim:* Volus Jones, Bob Carlson, Bill Justice, Ray Patin; *fx:* Jack Boyd, Josh Meador; *lay:* Yale Gracey; *back:* Ralph Hulett; *voices:* Clarence Nash; *mus:* Oliver Wallace;

col: Tech. *sd:* RCA. 7 min. • Donald discovers his nephews have tricked him and stolen food. A chase ensues, culminating in the nephews convincing Don he has died and become an angel.

6034. Sour Grapes (*Dingbat*) Nov. 1950; *p.c.:* TT for Fox; *dir:* Mannie Davis; *story/voice:* Tom Morrison; *anim:* Jim Tyer; *mus:* Philip A. Scheib; *ph:* Douglas Moye; *col:* Tech. *sd:* RCA. 6½ min. • Dingbat nails a bunch of grapes to a high branch, sabotaging Foxy's attempts to reach it.

6035. Sour Gripes (*Modern Madcap*) Oct. 1963; *p.c.:* Para Cartoons; *dir:* Seymour Kneitel; *story:* Irving Dressler; *anim:* Morey Reden; *sets:* Robert Little; *voices:* Bob MacFadden; *mus:* Winston Sharples; *ph:* Leonard McCormick; *prod mgr:* Abe Goodman; *col:* Tech. *sd:* RCA. 6 min. • A fox tries to disprove the old fable by stealing grapes from Luigi's vinyard.

6036. The Sour Puss (*Looney Tunes*) 2 Nov. 1940; *p.c.:* Leon Schlesinger prods for WB; *dir:* Robert Clampett; *story:* Warren Foster; *anim:* Vive Risto, Dave Hoffman; *ed:* Treg Brown; *voices:* Mel Blanc; *mus:* Carl W. Stalling; *ph:* John W. Burton; *prod sup:* Henry Binder, Raymond G. Katz; b&w. *sd:* Vit. 7 min. • Porky and puss set out to catch a screwball flying fish for their supper.

6037. South Park — Bigger, Longer and Uncut 30 Sept. 1999; *p.c.:* Comedy Central Films/Para-WB; *dir:* Trey Parker; *story/prod:* Trey Parker, Matt Stone; *ex prod:* Scott Rudin, Adam Schroeder; *co-prod:* Anne Garefino, Deborah Liebling; *anim:* Frank C. Agone III; *scr:* Trey Parker, Matt Stone, Pam Brady; *art dir:* J.C. Wegman; *line prod:* Gina Shay; *asso prod:* Mark Roybal; *systems admin:* Sean Laverty, Tim Avery, Amir Bemanian, Robert Borthwick, J.J. Franzen, Ken Harris, Cheri Soriano; *prod co-ord:* David Yanover, Tok Braun; *prod studio co-ord:* Toddy E. Walters; *retake co-ord:* Adam Lagattuta, Andrew Kemler, Stan Sawicki; *unit prod mgr:* Ramsey Ann Naito; *post-prod sup:* David Dresher; *prod consult:* Monica Schmidt Mitchell; *research co-ord:* Michael D. Queenland; *script co-ord:* Robin Kay, Margaret Falzon; *Heaven and Hell seq:* Blur Studio (Venice, CA): *visual fx sup:* David Stinnett; *prod sup:* Stephanie Taylor; *visual fx co-ord:* Al Shier; *anim:* Steve Blackmon, Tom Dillon, Sam Gebhardt, Keith Jenson, Kirby Miller; *fx programmer:* Scott Kirvan; *systems admin:* Duane Powell; *Lux Laser Film Recording:* Digital Film Works, Inc.: *anim dir:* Eric Stough; *sup anim:* Martin Cendreda, Toni Nugnes; *anim:* Fred Baxter, John Fountain, Neil Ishimine, Charles Keagle, Jason A. Lopez, Scott Oberholtzer, Eric Oliver, Jim Ovelman, Lorelei Pepi, Ryan Quincy, Jack Shih, Michael Trull, August Wartenberg, Holly Wenger, Heather R. Wilbur, Amy Winfrey, Dustin Woehrmann; *addit:* Jennifer M. Allen, Alfonso Alpuerto, Andrew Arett, Chris "Crispy" Brion, Matt Brown, Michelle Burry, Lisa Libuha, Sabrina Mar, Peter M. Merryman, Aglaia Mortcheva, Nate Pacheco, Suzanne Smith; *anim co-ord:* David Weiner; *Animation Systems:* Silicon Graphics, Inc.; *compositing sup:* Christopher Fria; *3d des:* Donna Bates, Rick Thomas, Joe Tseung; *character/back des:* Doug Lee, Albert Lozano, Adam T. Talbott, Keo Thongkham; *ed:* John Vanzon, Giancarlo Ganziano; *addit modelling:* Annie Combs, Drake Goosby, Leticia Lacy, Maureen Whelan; *storyboard/des sup:* Adrien Beard; *storyboard art:* Albert Lozano, Keo Thongkham, Gregg Detrich, Charles Keagle, Roxanne Patruznick, Anthony Postma, Greg Postma, Elaina Scott, Phil Weinstein, Eric Yahnker; *storyboard co-ord:* Joshua C. Hersko; *voices:* Stan Marsh/Eric Cartman/Satan/Mr. Herbert Garrison/Officer Barbrady/Mr. Hat/Phillip Niles Argyle/Randy Marsh/Tom—News Reporter/Midget in a bikini/Ticket Taker/Canadian Ambassador/Bombardiers/Mr. Mackey/Army General/Ned Gerblanski:* Trey Parker; *Kyle Broflovski/Kenny McCormick/Saddam Hussein/Terrance Henry Stoot/Pip/Jesus/Jimbo Kearn/Gerald Broflovski/Bill Gates:* Matt Stone; *Liane Cartman/Sheila Broflovski/Sharon Manson/Mrs. Mc-Cormick/Wendy Testeberger/Principal Victoria/Clitoris:* Mary Kay Bergman; *Chef:* Isaac Hayes; *Ike Broflovski:* Jesse Howell, Anthony Cross-Thomas, Francesca Clifford; *Man in Theatre:* Bruce Howell; *Woman in Theatre:* Deb Adair; *Bebe:* Jennifer Howell; *Dr. Gouache:* George Clooney; *Conan O'Brien:* Brent Spiner; *Brooke Shields:* Minnie Driver; *The Baldwin Brothers:* Dave Foley; *Dr. Vosknocker:* Eric Idle; *Canadian fighter pilot:* Nick Rhodes; *Winona Ryder:* Toddy E. Walters; *American Soldiers:* Stewart Copeland, Stanley G. Sawicki; *Kenny's goodbye:* Mike Judge; *mus:* Trey Parker; *score/addit mus/lyrics:* Marc Shaiman; *orch conductor:* Pete Anthony; *orch:* Jeff Atmajian, Pete Antony, Frank Bennett, Larry Blank, Harvey Cohen, Jon Kull; *mus ed:* Dan DiPrima; *mus programmer:* Nick Vidar; *mus rec/mix:* Tim Boyle, Dennis Sands; *sd co-ord:* Chris Welch; *re-rec mix:* Scott Millan, David Fluhr, Bob Beemer, Adam Jenkins, Tom Perry; *sd ed:* Bruce Howell,

Deb Adair, Michael Jonascu, Cameron Frankley, Randall Guth, Dan Yale, Brian Risner, Lydia Quidilla; *dial ed:* Joe Schiff, Julie Feiner, Evan Chen; *ADR: The Loop Group:* Steve Alterman, Doug Burch, David Coburn, Judi Durand, Greg Finley, Jeff Fischer, Barbara Iley, Daamen Krall, David Allen Kramer, David McGregor, Mary Linda Phillips, Paige Pollack, J. Lamont Pope, David Randolph, Noreen Reardon, Vernon Scott, Ruth Zalduondo; *ed:* Avram D. Gold; *foley:* Robin Harlan, Sarah Monat; *mix:* Randall K. Singer; *ed:* Chris Flick, John Wilde, Nancy MacLeod; *technical dir:* Ana Wolovick, Christopher Fria, Michael Chokran, Melanie Stimmel, Allan Arinduque, Amir Bahadori, Ken Bailey, Donna Bates, Javier Bello, Harold Buchman, Greg Connell, Roger Dickes, Nishira Fitzgerald, Karl Fornander, Roger Huynh, Michael Leung, Kimberley Liptrap, Shannon McGee, Gil Nevo, Mark Perry, Jesse Rory Quinn, Valentin Sinlao, Rick Thomas, Joe Tseng, Rick Ziegler; *addit:* Joseph Gerges, Lori Gilmour, Wonhee Jung, Elaine Meejung Kim, Leticia Lacy, Aglaia Mortcheva, Victor Robert, Jenny Shin, Jennifer Sieck, Jon Singer, Omar Smith, Suzanne Smith, Margie Stubbs, Frank Sudol, Jimbo Valladao; *technical dir co-ord:* Fiona Foster; *film col mgr:* Harold Buchman; *col:* DeLuxe. *sd:* Dolby Digital/Digital dts. 81 min. *Academy Award nomination.* • The kids see an R-rated movie featuring Canadians Terrance & Phillip and are declared "corrupted," compelling their parents to force the United States to wage war against Canada.

6038. South Pole or Bust (*Paul Terry-Toon*) 14 Dec. 1934; *p.c.:* Moser & Terry for Educational/Fox; *dir:* Frank Moser, Paul Terry; *mus:* Philip A. Scheib; b&w. *sd:* WE. 5½ min. • A plane departs from New York (against photographed backgrounds) and reaches the Polar regions where it is greeted by a Durante penguin and a skiing walrus.

6039. South Pole Pals (*Chilly Willy*) Mar. 1966; *p.c.:* Walter Lantz prods for Univ; *dir:* Paul J. Smith; *story:* Homer Brightman; *anim:* Les Kline, Al Coe; *sets:* Ray Huffine; *voices:* Grace Stafford, Daws Butler; *mus:* Walter Greene; *prod mgr:* William E. Garity; *col:* Tech. *sd:* RCA. 6 min. • Chilly tries to prevent his friend Smedley from leaving for sunnier climes.

6040. Southbound Duckling (*Tom & Jerry*) 12 Mar. 1955; *p.c.:* MGM; *dir:* William Hanna, Joseph Barbera; *anim:* Kenneth Muse, Ed Barge, Irven Spence; *lay:* Dick Bickenbach; *back:* Vera Ohman; *ed:* Jim Faris; *voice:* Red Coffee; *mus:* Scott Bradley; *ph:* Jack Stevens; *prod:* Fred Quimby; *col:* Tech. *sd:* WE. 7 min. • Tom attempts to prevent Little Quacker's departure south.

6041. Southern Exposure (*Krazy Kat*) 5 Feb. 1934; *p.c.:* Winkler for Colum; *prod:* Charles Mintz; *anim/story:* Ben Harrison, Manny Gould; *mus:* Joe de Nat, Charles Rosoff; *prod mgr:* James Bronis; b&w. *sd:* RCA. 6½ min. • Krazy overthrows a "Simon le Gree" type who is a harsh taskmaster to his slaves.

6042. Southern Fried Hospitality (*Woody Woodpecker*) 29 Nov. 1960; *p.c.:* Walter Lantz prods for Univ; *dir:* Jack Hannah; *story:* Homer Brightman; *anim:* La Verne Harding, Al Coe; *sets:* Ray Huffine, Art Landy; *voices:* Daws Butler, Grace Stafford; *mus:* Eugene Poddany; *prod mgr:* William E. Garity; *col:* Tech. *sd:* RCA. 6 min. • A starving Gabby Gator invites Woody to come to Florida to entertain "the troops."

6043. Southern Fried Rabbit (*Looney Tunes*) 2 May 1953; *p.c.:* WB; *dir:* I. Freleng; *story:* Warren Foster; *anim:* Arthur Davis, Manuel Perez, Ken Champin, Virgil Ross; *lay:* Hawley Pratt; *back:* Irv Wyner; *ed:* Treg Brown; *voices:* Mel Blanc; *mus:* Carl Stalling; *prod mgr:* John W. Burton; *prod:* Edward Selzer; *col:* Tech. *sd:* Vit. 7 min. • Bugs visits the deep south where he falls foul of a southern rebel who still believes the Civil War to be active.

6044. Southern Horse-Pitality (*Paul Terry-Toon*) 29 Nov. 1935; *p.c.:* Moser & Terry for Educational/Fox; *dir:* Frank Moser, Paul Terry; *mus:* Philip A. Scheib; b&w. *sd:* WE. 6 min. • Melodrama with the "wolf at the door" holding an overdue mortgage and the principal finally winning the Derby.

6045. Southern Rhythm (*Paul Terry-Toon*) 18 Sept. 1932; *p.c.:* Moser & Terry for Educational/Fox; *dir:* Frank Moser, Paul Terry; *mus:* Philip A. Scheib; b&w. *sd:* WE. 6 min. • No story available.

6046. Space Jam 15 Nov. 1996; *p.c.:* WB; *dir:* Joe Pytka; *ex prod:* David Falk, Ken Ross; *prod:* Ivan Reitman, Joe Medjuck, Daniel Goldberg; *asst dir:* Austin McCann, Pamela Cederquist, Elizabeth Herbert; *second unit:* Bob Wilson, Michael Neumann; *scr:* Leo Benvenuti, Steve Rudnick, Timothy Harris, Herschel Weingrod; *storyboard:* Kurt Anderson, Rich Arons, Celia Coppock, Skip Jones, Skip Ward, Alex Mann, Linda Miller, Fergal Reilly, Harry Sabin, David Smith, Keith Sparrow, Joe Suggs, Kirk Tingblad; "*Stan*" *anim:* Dylan Robinson; "*M.J. Ball*" *anim:* Robb Gardener; "*Moron Mountain*" *anim:* Chas Cash; *computer character anim:* Roger Kupelian, Michael Kory; *anim dir:* Bruce W. Smith, Tony Cervone; *anim prod.:* Ron Tippe, Jerry Rees, Steven Paul Leiva; *anim co-prod:* Allison Abbate; *anim sup.:* Neil Boyle, Chuck Gammage, Jim Kammerud, Lili Meyer, Jeff Siergey, Dave Spafford, Rob Stevenhagen, Bruce Woodside; *lead anim:* Dino Athanassiou, Roberto Casale, Paul Chung, Shane Doyle, Gary Dunn, Martin Fuller, Dean Roberts, Dan Root, Brian Smith; *anim:* Margot Allen, Claire Armstrong, Stephen Baker, Richard Baneham, Dave Boudreau, Dan Boulos, Spike Brandt, Mark Broecking, Adam Burke, Alberto Campos, Ronaldo Canfora, Claire Cantlie, Jennifer Cardon, Tod Carter, Luc Chamberland, Michael Chaver, Stan Chiu, Jesse Cosio, Alain Costa, Denis Couchon, Greg Court, James Davis, Murray Debus, Jeff Etter, Stuart Evans, Jerry Forder, Stephan Franck, Morgan Ginsberg, Scott Glynn, Heidi Guedel, Chris Hauge, Magnus Hjerpe, Richard Jack, Leon Joosen, Hon-Sik Kim, Sean Leaning, Paul Lee, Holger Leihe, Tom Lock, Lee McCaulla, Kevin McDonagh, Tom McGrath, Quentin Miles, Ken Morrissey, Jacques Muller, Mike Nguyen, Michael S. Nickelson, Cynthia Overman, Clive Pallant, Wendy Parkin, John Perkins, Scott Peterson, Marco Piersma, Jens Pindal, Tom Riggin, Mitch Rose, Michael Schlingmann, Andrew Shortt, Andrea Simonti, Sharon Smith, Kevin Spruce, Neal Sternecky, Paul A. Stone, Mike Swindall, Vladimir Todorov, Daniela Topham, Tony Tulipano, John Tynan, Jan van Buyten, Jim van der Keyl, Darren Vandenburg, Duncan Varley, Andreas Von Andrian, Daniel Wagner, Simon Ward-Horner, Dave Wasson, J.C. Wegman, Andreas Wessel-Therhorn, Pete Western, Larry D. Whitaker Jr., Mark Williams, John D. Williamson, Vincent Woodcock, Chris York, Shane Zalvin; *anim check:* Myoung Smith; *fx co-ord:* Darrell Pritchett; *lay:* Gary Mouri, Tass Darlington, Dan Fausett, Paul Divian, Davy Liu, Daniel McHugh, Ennis McNulty, Don Reich, Roy Naisbitt, Chris Scully, Lisa Souza, Robert St. Pierre, Mark Swan, Craig Voigt, Todd Winter; *back:* William Dely, Catherine Brockhouse, Gerald Cook, Paul Dilworth, James Finn, Greg Gibbons, Julie Gleeson, Natasha Gross, Annie Guenther, Peter Meorhle, Andy Phillipson, Mansoor Shams, Gary Sycamore, Lucy Tanashian-Gentry, Nadia Vurbenova, Claire Wright, Raymond Zibach; *ed:* Sheldon Kahn; *anim:* Nancy Frazen, Bill Gordean; *anim asso:* John Currin, Richard L. McCullough, Mark Solomon; *prod des:* Geoffrey Kirkland; *art dir.:* David Klassen, (*anim*) Bill Perkins, (*set des*) Marco Rubeo, (*set decorator*) Jennifer Williams; *scene plan:* Dan Bunn; *title seq/des:* Geoffrey Nelson; *voices: Bugs Bunny/Elmer Fudd:* Billy West; *Daffy Duck/Tasmanian Devil/Bull:* Dee Bradley Baker; *Swackhammer:* Danny DeVito; *Hubie & Bert/Martian/Porky Pig/Tweety:* Bob Bergen; *Sylvester/Yosemite Sam/Foghorn Leghorn:* Bill Farmer; *Granny:* June Foray; *Pepé le Pew:* Maurice La Marche; *Lola Bunny:* Kath Soucie; *Nerdluck Pound:* Jocelyn Blue; *Nerdluck Blanko:* Charity James; *Nerdluck Bang:* June Melby; *Nerdluck Bupkus:* Catherine Reitman; *Nerdluck Nawt/Sniffles:* Colleen Wainwright; *Monster Bupkus:* Dorian Harewood; *Monster Bang:* Joey Kamen; *Monster Nawt:* T.K. Carter; *Monster Pound:* ; M. Darnell Suttles; *Monster Blanko/Announcer:* Steve Kehela; *Charles the Dog:* Frank Welker; *mus:* James Newton Howard; *conductor:* Artie Kane; *orch:* Brad Dechter, Jeff Atmajian, James Newton Howard; *mus sup:* Ken Ross; *score:* Michael Mason; *mus ed:* Jim Weidman; *score rec mix:* Shawn Murphy; *songs:* "Fly Like an Eagle" by Steve Miller; performed by Seal; "I Believe I Can Fly" by/performed by R. Kelly; "Hit 'em High (the Monsters' Anthem)" by Louis Freese, Trevor Smith, Artis Ivey Jr., Todd Smith, Clifford Smith, Jean Claude Olivier, Samuel Barnes; performed by B. Real, Busta Rhymes, Coolio, L.L. Cool J., Method Man; "I Turn to You" by Diane Warren; performed by All-4-One; "Space Jam" by J. McGowan, N. Orange, V. Bryant; performed by Quad City D.J's; "Basketball Jones" by Richard ("Cheech") Marin, Thomas Chong; performed by Barry White, Chris Rock; "I Found My Smile Again" by/performed by D'Angelo; "Givin' U All That I've Got" by Robin S., Todd Terry; performed by Robin S.; "That's the Way (I Like it)" by Harry W. Casey, Richard Finch; performed by Spin Doctors featuring Biz Markie; "For You I Will" by Diane Warren; performed by Monica; "Upside Down ('Round-n-'Round)" by Bernard Edwards, Nile Rodgers, Sandra "Pepa" Denton, Cheryl "Salt" James; performed by Salt-n-Pepa; "Gonna Make You Sweat (Everybody Dance Now)" by Robert Clivilles, Frederick ("Freedom") Williams; performed by C+C

Music Factory; "Pump up the Jam" by Manuella Kamosi, Thomas De-Quincey; performed by Technotronic; "Wild" by Ivor Davies, Robert Kretschmer; performed by Icehouse; "Misirlou" by Fred Wise, Milton Leeds, S.K. Russell, Nicholas Roubanis; performed by Dick Dale & His Del-Tones; "Take Me Out to the Ball Game" by Jack Norworth, Albert von Tilzer; "What's up Doc?" by Carl W. Stalling; "Get Ready for This" by Jean Paul DeCoster, Flip DeWilde, Simon Harris; performed by 2 Unlimited; "The Merry-Go-Round Broke Down" by Dave Franklin, Cliff Friend; "Merrily We Roll Along" by Eddie Cantor, Murray Mencher; *line prod.: anim:* Richard T. Sullivan; *digital:* Michael Lander; *co-prod.:* Gordon Webb, Sheldon Kahn, Curtis Polk; *asso prod: anim:* Dennis Edwards; *prod co-ord.: anim:* Brent Kirnbauer; *prod mgr: anim:* Melissa Kurtz, Leslie Hough; *ph:* Michael Chapman, Joe Mentzer, Bill Roe; *Steadicam operator:* David Luckenbach; *l/a/anim visual fx:* Ed Jones; *visual fx: prod sup.:* Helen Ostenberg Elswit; *sup:* James Lima; *ed:* Christer Hokanson; *co-ord:* Steve Dellerson; *miniature fabrications:* Vision Crew Unlimited; *Cinesite digital fx sup:* Carlos Arguello, Doug Tubach; *digital fx prod:* Mitzi Gallagher; *cg speciality compositors:* Kevin Lingenfelser, Sean O'Connor, Greg Liegey, Jay Cooper; *cg stadium des:* Pepé Valencia; *cg gym des:* Jonathan Privett; *lead cg ph matchmover:* Cristin Pescoslido; *digital compositors:* Nelson Sepulveda, John Sasaki, Bill Gilman, Chris Holmes, David Lingenfelser, Mark Nettleton, Abra Grupp, Jerry Sells, Mark Michaels, Lisa Dackermann, Ken Dackermann, Ed Hawkins, Sue Rowe, Bob Lyss, Rich Suchevits; *digital art:* Joe Dubs, Laura Hannigan, Matt Johnson, Valerie McMahon, Lisa Polero, David Rey, Barney Robson, Pat Tubach, Nicki Wakefield, Matt Wilson, Aviv Yaron, Tom Zils, Mike Fevert; *cgi: anim:* Tim Ketzer, Raymond King, Gokhan Kisacikoy, Eduardo Batres, Dave Child, Andrew Paquette, Richard Klein; *ex prod:* Warren Franklin; *post prod sup:* Pat Repola; *prod mgr:* Gil Gagnon; *cg prod:* Jinko Gotoh; *lead prod:* Aaron Dem, Scott Dougherty, Alex Bicknell; *digital asso prod:* Michael S. Pryor; *UK prod mgr:* Courtney Vanderslice; *stadium software engineers:* Juan Buhler, Satoshi Koreki; *digital camera motion:* Michael Orlando, Brian Drucker; *digital matte paint:* Charles Darby, Kerry Nordquist; *Rotoscope:* James Valentine, Karen Klein, Mark Lewis; *stadium crowd replication:* Dan Levitan; *visual fx ed:* Shawn Broes; *digital i&p:* Sarah-Jane King, John Huey, Colin Hughes, Janice Inouye, Debora Kupczyk, Simon Leech, Craig Littell-Herrick, Steve McDermott, Mark Naisbitt, Les Newstead, Khai Nguyen, Constantin Nicov, Volker Pajatsch, Antonio Palermo, Susan Pfeiffer, Alan Pickett, David Prichard, Panagiotis Rappas, Barnaby Russel, Anna Saunders, Paul Smith, Gary Sole, Simon Swales, Heather Tailby, Eusebio Torres, Mac Torres, Dan Turner, Gabriel Valles, Tim Walton, Martin Wansborough, Paul West; *sd mix:* James La Rue, Gene Cantamessa, John Reitz, Gregg Rudolff, David Campbell, Gary Bourgeois, Gary Alexander, Jim Fitzpatrick; *sd ed:* Mark Mangini; *dial ed:* Curt Schulkey; *fx ed:* Howell Gibbens, Michael Geisler, Geoff Rubay; *ADR mix:* Troy Porter, Thomas J. O'Connell, Curt Schulkey; *foley ed:* Bruce Nyznik; *col:* Tech. *sd:* Dolby stereo/dts/SDDS. 87 min. *l/a/anim.* • Aliens want "Looney Tunes" for their space theme park. Bugs Bunny and the gang challenge the aliens to a basketball game, enlisting the expertise of basketball ace Michael Jordan to assist them.

6047. Space Kid (*Modern Madcap*) Mar. 1961; *p.c.:* Para Cartoons; *dir:* Seymour Kneitel; *story:* Irving Dressler; *anim:* Larry Silverman; *sets:* Robert Owen; *mus:* Winston Sharples; *ph:* Leonard McCormick; *prod mgr:* Abe Goodman; *col:* Tech. *sd:* RCA. 6 min. • A Martian kid has fun with his ray-gun in New York City.

6048. Space Mouse (*Cartune*) 7 Sept. 1959; *p.c.:* Walter Lantz prods for Univ; *dir:* Alex Lovy; *story:* Homer Brightman; *anim:* La Verne Harding, Don Patterson, Ray Abrams; *sets:* Art Landy, Raymond Jacobs; *voices:* Paul Frees, Dal McKennon, Grace Stafford; *mus:* Clarence Wheeler; *col:* Tech. *sd:* RCA. 6 min. • Doc tries to sell the mice to a space program.

6049. Space Pet (*Astronut*) Mar. 1969 (© 1965); *p.c.:* TT for Fox; *ex prod:* Bill Weiss; *dir/anim:* Cosmo Anzilotti; *story sup:* Tom Morrison; *story:* Larz Bourne; *sets:* Robert Owen, John Zago; *ed:* Jack MacConnell; *voices:* Dayton Allen; *mus:* Jim Timmens; *ph:* Ted Moskowitz; *sd:* Elliot Grey; *col:* DeLuxe. *sd:* RCA. 5 min. • Astro brings a friendly space monster to Earth who, unfortunately, eats metal.

6050. The Space Squid (*Go-Go Toon*) Oct 1966; *p.c.:* Para Cartoons; *dir:* Shamus Culhane; *mus:* Winston Sharples; *prod sup:* Harold Robins, Burt Henft; *col:* Tech. *sd:* RCA. 6 min. • No story available.

6051. Spanish Love (*Aesop's Film Fable*) 7 Mar. 1926; *p.c.*: Fables Pictures Inc for Pathé; *dir:* Paul Terry; b&w. *sil.* 6 min. • A romantic encounter against a Spanish background with a bullfight and a happy ending when the hero saves the matador.

6052. Spanish Onions (*Paul Terry-Toon*) 23 Mar. 1930; *p.c.*: A-C for Educational/Fox; *dir:* Frank Moser, Paul Terry; *mus:* Philip A. Scheib; b&w. *sd:* WE. 6 min. • Featuring two mice, one of whom poses as "The Matador from Brooklyn" in a bullfight.

6053. A Spanish Twist (*Tom & Jerry*) 7 Oct. 1932; *p.c.*: Van Beuren for RKO; *dir:* John Foster, George Stallings; *mus:* Gene Rodemich; b&w. *sd:* RCA. 8 min. • The lads find themselves in the bull ring and give a herd of toros a licking. When they return to the USA, they are notified that the Volstead Law has been repealed.

6054. Spare the Child (*Family Circus*) 27 Jan. 1955; *p.c.*: UPA for Colum; *ex prod:* Stephen Bosustow; *dir:* Abe Liss; *story/lay:* Robert Dranko; *anim:* Grim Natwick, Fred Grable; *back:* Paul Julian; *voices:* Hal Peary, Danny Richards Jr., Gil Herman, Edith Terry; *mus:* Dennis Farnon; *prod mgr:* Herb Klynn; *col:* Tech. *sd:* RCA. 6½ min. • A small boy gets his birthday wish that he could trade places with his father.

6055. Spare the Rod (*Donald Duck*) 15 Jan. 1954; *p.c.*: Walt Disney prods for RKO; *dir:* Jack Hannah; *story:* Roy Williams, Nick George; *anim:* Volus Jones, Bill Justice, George Kreisl, Bob Carlson, Al Coe; *fx:* Dan MacManus; *lay:* Yale Gracey; *back:* Ray Huffine; *voices:* Bill Thompson, Clarence Nash, Pinto Colvig, James MacDonald, Fred Letuli, Margie Liszt; *mus:* Oliver Wallace; • *col:* Tech. *sd:* RCA. 7 min. • Donald mistakes three runaway circus cannibals for his nephews and deals with them accordingly.

6056. Spare the Rod (*Mighty Mouse*) Dec. 1953; *p.c.*: TT for Fox; Connie Rasinski; *story/voice:* Tom Morrison; *anim:* Jim Tyer; *mus:* Philip A. Scheib; *ph:* Douglas Moye; *col:* Tech. *sd:* RCA. 6½ min. • Mighty Mouse is summonsed to put a stop to juvenile delinquents terrorizing the townsfolk.

6057. Spark Plug (*Color Rhapsody*) 12 Apr. 1936; *p.c.*: Charles Mintz prods for Colum; *story:* Sid Marcus; *anim:* Art Davis; *voice:* Smiley Burnett; *mus:* Joe de Nat; *prod mgr:* James Bronis; *col:* Tech. *sd:* RCA. 7 min. • Featuring Billy de Beck's "Barney Google." Beaten in the first race, Snuffy's horse, Spark Plug, wins the next one for his ostrich stable pal, Rudy.

6058. Sparkplug Pink (*Pink Panther*) 1978; *p.c.*: Mirisch/Geoffrey/DFE for UA; *dir:* Brad Case; *story:* Cullen Houghtaling; *anim:* Don Williams, Lee Halpern, Bernard Posner, Joan Case; *lay:* Martin Strudler; *back:* Richard H. Thomas; *ed:* David H. DePatie Jr.; *theme tune:* Henry Mancini; *ph:* Ray Lee; *prod mgr:* Lee Gunther; *col:* DeLuxe. *sd:* RCA. 6 min. • The Panther loses a vital sparkplug for his lawn mower that materializes in a pile of bones, guarded by a ferocious dog.

6059. Sparky the Firefly (*Terry-Toon*) Sept. 1953; *p.c.*: TT for Fox; *dir:* Connie Rasinski; *story:* Tom Morrison; *anim:* Jim Tyer; *mus:* Philip A. Scheib; *ph:* Douglas Moye; *col:* Tech. *sd:* RCA/7 min. • Sparky the firefly loses his light and a bookworm advises him to replace it with a flashlight.

6060. Sparring Partner (*Inkwell Imps*) Oct. 1924; *p.c.*: Inkwell Studio for Red Seal; *dir:* Dave Fleischer; *anim/l/a:* Max Fleischer; b&w. *sil.* 7 min. *l/a/anim.* • Ko-Ko upsets Max's inkwell while he tries to write a love letter to his sweetie. He draws a sparring partner to see to the little clown who then sees to it that Max gets in bad with his girl.

6061. Speaking of Animals *p.c.*: Apex for Para; *prod:* Jerry Fairbanks, Carlisle; *dir:* Tex Avery, Lew Landers, Lou Lilly; *story:* Walter Anthony, Pinto Colvig, Lou Lilly, Dave Mitchell, William Scott, Charles Shows; *anim:* George Crenshaw, Anna Osborne; *narrator:* Ken Carpenter; *voices:* Louise Arthur, Dave Barry, Sara Berner, Daws Butler, Mel Blanc, Pinto Colvig, June Foray, Stan Freberg, Gloria Grant, Harry E. Lang, Jack Mather, Dick Nelson, Kent Rogers, William Scott, John T. Smith, Danny Webb; *mus:* Edward Paul; b&w. *sd:* WE. 8–10 min. Duotone. *l/a/anim.* • *1941:* **Down on the Farm** (*dir:* Tex Avery) 18 Apr. **In a Pet Shop** (*dir:* Tex Avery) 5 Sept. **In a Zoo** (*dir:* Tex Avery) 31 Oct. • *1942:* **At the County Fair** 6 Jan. **In the Circus** 10 Apr. **At the Dog Show** 28 Aug. **In South America** 25 Sept. **And Their Families** 18 Dec. • *1943:* **At the Bird Farm** 19 Mar. **In Current Events** 7 May. **At the Stage Door Canteen** 25 June. **In the Garden** 20 Aug. **In the Desert** 29 Sept. **Tails of the Border** • *1944:* **In Winter Quarters. In the Newsreels. Your Pet Problems. In a Harem**

14 July. **And Monkey Business** 15 Sept. **As Babies** 24 Nov. • *1945:* **Who's Who in Animal Land** 19 Jan. **In the Public Eye** 16 Mar. **And the Talk of the Town** 18 May. **And a Musical Way** 20 July. **And the Ballet of Ostriches** 21 Sept. **From A to Zoo** 7 Sept. **And Animal-Ology** 2 Nov. **And Hillbillies** 28 Dec. • *1946:* **In the Post-War Era** 8 Feb. **In the Wilds** 10 May. **And the Lonesome Ranger** 14 June. **Be Kind to Animals** 30 Aug. **And Stork Crazy** 18 Oct. **And the Pooch Parade** 27 Dec. • *1947:* **In Country Life** 9 Feb. **They're Not So Dumb** 28 Mar. **In Love** 30 May. **As Our Friends** 27 June. **Dog Crazy** (with Sterling Holloway) 3 Oct. **Ain't Nature Grand** 14 Nov. **Monkey Shines** 12 Dec. • *1948:* **Home, Sweet Home** 6 Feb. **'Tain't So** 16 Apr. **Headlines** 18 June. **The Gnu Look** 29 Oct. • *1949:* **Calling All Animals** 7 Jan. **Meet the Champ** 11 Feb. **Hocus Focus** 22 Apr. **Goin' Hollywood** 10 June. **Video Hounds** 12 Aug. **Fun on the Farm** (with Bob Burns) Oct. • Live-action footage of animals with animated mouths and human voices commenting on the situation. *Down on the Farm* got a nomination and *Who's Who in Animal Land* received an Academy Award. The live-action feature *Road to Morocco* (Para: 1942) also used this process for two camels (voiced by Kent Rogers and Sara Berner) remarking on the antics of Bob Hope and Bing Crosby. A later "Road" film, *Road to Utopia* (1945) had a talking bear (Billy Bletcher) and a fish who also voiced their opinions of the goings-on.

6062. Speaking of the Weather (*Merrie Melodies*) 4 Sept. 1937; *p.c.*: Leon Schlesinger prods for WB; *dir:* Frank Tashlin; *anim:* Joseph d'Igalo, Volney White; *character des:* T. Hee; *lay:* Griff Jay; *back:* Arthur Loomer; *ed:* Tregoweth E. Brown; *voices:* Billy Bletcher, Mel Blanc, Fred Avery, Dave Weber; *mus:* Carl W. Stalling; *ph:* John W. Burton; *prod sup:* Henry Binder, Raymond G. Katz; *col:* Tech. *sd:* Vit. 7 min. • Newsstand magazines come to life: The cops from "Police Gazette" chase heavies from crime stories and the "Judge" sentences them to "Life." Caricatures of Bob Burns, Charlie Chan, Clark Gable, Greta Garbo, Hugh Herbert, Ted Lewis, William Powell, Ned Sparks, Leopold Stokowski, Tarzan and Walter Winchell.

6063. Species 7 July 1995; *p.c.*: MGM; *cgi: anim consultant:* Dale Baer; *anim/motion capture:* Mark Swain; *computer anim:* Clint Colver, Mark Pompian, Steve Cummings, Timothy Tompkins, Bill Dietrich, Chris Roda, Jason Dowdeswell, Mark Rodahl, Shine Fitzner, Alan Rosenfeld, Mike Fleming, Brian Samuels, Todd Fulford, Dave Smith, Kevin Geiger, Alex Sokoloff, Jim Green, Brian Steiner, Joe Henke, Marc Toscano, Walt Hyneman, Wayne Vincenzi, Koichi Noguchi, Chris Waegner, Rob Osher, Dave Witters, Dane Picard, Ken Ziegler; *col:* DeLuxe. *sd:* dts stereo. 108 min. • Science fiction live-action feature with animated mutations, etc.

6064. Speedy Ghost to Town (*Merrie Melodies*) July 1967; *p.c.*: WB; *dir:* Alex Lovy; *story:* Cal Howard; *anim:* Volus Jones, Ed Solomon, Ted Bonnicksen, La Verne Harding; *lay:* David Hanan, Lin Larsen; *back:* Bob Abrams; *ed:* Hal Geer; *voices:* Mel Blanc; *mus:* William Lava; *col:* Tech. *sd:* Vit. 6 min. • Daffy overhears that Speedy has a map to a secret mine and steals it only to discover the mine to be full of cheese.

6065. Speedy Gonzales (*Merrie Melodies*) 17 Sept. 1955; *p.c.*: WB; *dir:* I. Freleng; *story:* Warren Foster; *anim:* Gerry Chiniquy, Ted Bonnicksen, Arthur Davis; *lay:* Hawley Pratt; *back:* Irv Wyner; *ed:* Treg Brown; *voices:* Mel Blanc, Jack Edwards; *mus:* Carl Stalling; *prod mgr:* John W. Burton; *prod:* Edward Selzer; *col:* Tech. *sd:* Vit. 7 min. *Academy Award.* • The mice can't gain entrance to a cheese factory guarded by Sylvester. They send for "the Fastest Mouse in All Mexico" to help.

6066. Spellbound Hound (*Jolly Frolics*) 16 Mar. 1950; *p.c.*: UPA for Colum; *ex prod:* Stephen Bosustow; *dir sup:* John Hubley; *anim dir:* Pete Burness; *asst dir:* Max Morgan; *story:* Bob Russell, Phil Eastman; *anim:* Pat Matthews, Willis Pyle, Rudy Larriva, Bill Melendez; *lay:* Bill Hurtz; *back:* Herb Klynn, Jules Engel; *i&p:* Mary Cain; *voices:* Jim Backus, Jerry Hausner; *mus:* Del Castillo; *ph:* Jack Eckes; *prod:* Edward Gershman; *col:* Tech. *sd:* RCA. 7 min. • Magoo mistakes a bloodhound, pursuing an escaped convict, for his friend, Ralph.

6067. The Spendthrift (*Aesop's Film Fable*) 26 Jan. 1922; *p.c.*: Fables Pictures Inc for Pathé; *dir:* Paul Terry; b&w. *sil.* 6½ min. • A spendthrift dog blows his money on gambling and drink then tells his wife he has been robbed. Upon seeing a bottle in his pocket, his spouse clubs him with it. Moral: "A spendthrift blames everybody but himself for his misfortunes."

6068. The Spider and the Fly (*Silly Symphony*) 13 Oct. 1931; *p.c.*:

Walt Disney prods for Colum; *dir:* Wilfred Jackson; *anim:* Charles Byrne, Johnny Cannon, Les Clarke, Emil Flohri, Albert Hurter, Richard Lundy, Ben Sharpsteen, Rudy Zamora; *mus:* Bert Lewis; b&w. *sd:* PCP. 7 min. • A pretty girl fly is captured by a villainous spider and rescued by her boyfriend with a lighted match.

6069. The Spider Talks *(Paul Terry-Toons)* 7 Feb. 1932; *p.c.:* Terry, Moser & Coffman for Educational/Fox; *dir:* Paul Terry, Frank Moser; *anim:* Arthur Babbitt, Ferdinand Huszti Horvath, Frank Moser, Hugh Shields; *mus:* Philip A. Scheib; b&w. *sd:* WE. 5½ min. • No story available.

6070. The Spider's Lair *(Aesop's Film Fable)* 22 Jan. 1928; *p.c.:* Fables Pictures Inc for Pathé; *dir:* Paul Terry, Mannie Davis; b&w. *sil.* 10 min. • A villainous spider disguises himself as a hot dog vendor and kidnaps the girl from a troupe of Dutch trapeze flies. When the spider accidentally sets fire to his lair, the girl and boy fly "trapeze" themselves out of the situation.

6071. Spinach fer Britain *(Popeye)* 22 Jan. 1943; *p.c.:* Famous for Para; *dir:* I. Sparber; *story:* Carl Meyer; *anim:* Jim Tyer, Abner Kneitel; *voices:* Jack Mercer; *mus:* Sammy Timberg; *ph:* Leonard McCormick; *prod mgr:* Sam Buchwald; b&w. *sd:* WE. 6 min. • Popeye is rowing a shipment of spinach to Britain for the war effort when he has an encounter with some mines and an enemy submarine.

6072. The Spinach Overture *(Popeye)* 29 Nov. 1935; *p.c.:* The Fleischer Studio for Para; *prod:* Max Fleischer; *dir:* Dave Fleischer; *anim:* Seymour Kneitel, Roland Crandall; *voices:* Jack Mercer, Mae Questel, Gus Wickie; *mus:* Sammy Timberg; b&w. *sd:* WE. 7 min. • Popeye's band is put to shame by Bluto's professional orchestra and lured away. Popeye eats some spinach and becomes the answer to Stokowski.

6073. Spinach Packin' Popeye *(Popeye)* 21 July 1944; Famous for Para; *dir:* I. Sparber; *story:* Bill Turner; *anim:* David Tendlar, Joe Oriolo; *voices:* Jack Mercer, Mae Questel, Carl Meyer; *mus:* Sammy Timberg; *ph:* Leonard McCormick; *prod mgr:* Sam Buchwald; b&w. *sd:* RCA. 7 min. Tech reissue: 5 Oct. 1951; *seq: Popeye the Sailor Meets Sindbad the Sailor; Popeye the Sailor Meets Ali Baba and His Forty Thieves.* • Popeye gives blood and suffers a nightmare where he believes he has lost all his strength.

6074. The Spinach Roadster *(Popeye)* 26 Nov. 1936; *p.c.:* The Fleischer Studio for Para; *prod:* Max Fleischer; *dir:* Dave Fleischer; *anim:* Willard Bowsky, George Germanetti; *voices:* Jack Mercer, Mae Questel, Gus Wickie; *mus:* Sammy Timberg; b&w. *sd:* WE. 7 min. • Popeye and his old jalopy compete for Olive's favor when Bluto arrives in a flashy new roadster.

6075. Spinach vs. Hamburgers *(Popeye)* 27 Aug. 1948; *p.c.:* Famous for Para; *dir:* Seymour Kneitel; *story:* Bill Turner, Larz Bourne; *anim:* Al Eugster, Tom Moore; *sets:* Tom Ford; *voices:* Jack Mercer, Mae Questel; *mus:* Winston Sharples; *ph:* Leonard McCormick; *prod mgr:* Sam Buchwald; *col:* Tech. *sd:* RCA. 8 min. *seq: The Anvil Chorus Girl; Popeye à la Mode; She-Sick Sailors.* • Popeye shows his nephews the benefits of eating spinach instead of hamburgers.

6076. Spinning Mice *(Rainbow Parade)* 5 Apr. 1935; *p.c.:* Van Beuren for RKO; *dir:* Burt Gillett, Tom Palmer; *mus:* Winston Sharples; *l/a ph:* Harry E. Squires; *col:* Ciné. *sd:* RCA. 8 min. • A wizard mixes his potions and creates imps from mice.

6077. The Spirit of '43 *(Donald Duck)* 7 Jan. 1943; *p.c.:* Walt Disney prods for U.S. Treasury/War Activities Committee/National Screen; *dir:* Jack King; *asst dir:* Esther Newell; *anim:* Paul Allen, Ward Kimball, Hal King, Charles Nichols, John Sibley, Judge Whitaker, Marvin Woodward; *fx:* Josh Meador; *lay:* Bill Herwig; *voices:* Dehner Forkum, Clarence Nash; *mus:* Paul J. Smith; *col:* Tech. *sd:* RCA. 6 min. • Donald's zoot-suited spendthrift ego urges him to waste his cash in "The Idle Hour Club" while his Scots thrifty-self pleads for him to put it in the bank. He eventually pays his taxes and the coins go to make weapons to help the war effort.

6078. Spite Flight *(Willie Whopper)* 14 Oct. 1933; *p.c.:* Celebrity prods for MGM; *prod/dir:* Ub Iwerks; *character des:* Grim Natwick; *anim:* Grim Natwick, Al Eugster; *voice:* Jane Withers; b&w. *sd:* PCP. 6½ min. • Willie recovers the mortgage on his mother's house by winning a flying competition. • Incorporating animation from the completed but unreleased *The Air Race.*

6079. Split Level Tree House *(Sidney)* Nov. 1963; *p.c.:* TT for Fox; *ex prod:* Bill Weiss; *dir/anim:* Art Bartsch; *story sup:* Tom Morrison; *story:* Larz Bourne; *sets:* Bill Focht, Jahn Zago; *ed:* George McAvoy; *voices:* Dayton Allen; *mus:* Phil Scheib; *ph:* Ted Moskowitz, Joe Rasinski; *col:* DeLuxe. *sd:* RCA. 6 min. • To keep him out of the way, Stanley the lion suggests Sidney the elephant builds himself a tree house. A monkey tries to prevent this from ever happening.

6080. Spook and Span *(Casper)* 28 Feb. 1958; *p.c.:* Para Cartoons; *dir:* Seymour Kneitel; *story:* Larz Bourne; *anim:* Myron Waldman, Wm. B. Pattengill; *sets:* John Zago; *voices:* Cecil Roy, Jack Mercer; *mus:* Winston Sharples; *ph:* Leonard McCormick; *prod mgr:* Seymour Shultz; *col:* Tech. *sd:* RCA. 6 min. • Casper endeavors to keep a pig from getting dirty after grooming it for the County Fair.

6081. Spook No Evil *(Casper)* 13 Mar. 1953; *p.c.:* Famous for Para; *dir:* Seymour Kneitel; *story:* I. Klein; *anim:* Myron Waldman, Nick Tafuri; *sets:* Robert Connavale; *voices:* Alan Shay, Jack Mercer; *mus:* Winston Sharples; *title song:* Mack David, Jerry Livingston; *ph:* Leonard McCormick; *prod mgr:* Seymour Shultz; *col:* Tech. *sd:* RCA. 6 min. • Casper befriends a monkey on a desert isle. When the ape is chased by a lion, our hero comes to his rescue.

6082. Spookeasy *(Krazy Kat)* 30 Jan. 1930; *p.c.:* Winkler for Colum; *prod:* Charles Mintz; *anim:* Ben Harrison, Manny Gould; *mus:* Joe de Nat; *prod mgr:* James Bronis; b&w. *sd:* WE. 6 min. • No story available.

6083. Spooking About Africa *(Casper)* 4 Jan. 1957; *p.c.:* Para Cartoons; *dir:* Seymour Kneitel; *story:* Jack Mercer; *anim:* Myron Waldman, Nick Tafuri; *sets:* Robert Owen; *voices:* Norma MacMillan, Sid Raymond, Jack Mercer; *mus:* Winston Sharples; *ph:* Leonard McCormick; *prod mgr:* Seymour Shultz; *col:* Tech. *sd:* RCA. 6 min. • A sneezing elephant causes annoyance amongst the other jungle folk until Casper uses him to extinguish a fire.

6084. Spooking of Ghosts *(Casper)* 12 June 1959; *p.c.:* Para Cartoons; *dir:* Seymour Kneitel; *story:* Sam Dann, Irving Spector; *anim:* Tom Johnson, Nick Tafuri, Els Barthen; *sets:* Robert Owen; *voices:* Allen Swift, Corinne Orr; *mus:* Winston Sharples; *ph:* Leonard McCormick; *prod mgr:* Abe Goodman; *col:* Tech. *sd:* RCA. 6 min. • A hobo tells the story of how an estate agent managed to accommodate a Scotsman with a "live-in" ghost.

6085. Spooking with a Brogue *(Casper)* 27 May 1955; *p.c.:* Famous for Para; *dir:* Seymour Kneitel; *story:* I. Klein; *anim:* Myron Waldman, Nick Tafuri; *sets:* Robert Owen; *voices:* Norma MacMillan, Frank Matalone, Cecil Roy, Jack Mercer; *mus:* Winston Sharples; *ph:* Leonard McCormick; *prod mgr:* Seymour Shultz; *col:* Tech. *sd:* RCA. 6 min. • Casper goes to Ireland and befriends a youngster who believes him to be a leprechaun.

6086. Spooks *(Flip the Frog)* 21 Dec. 1931; *p.c.:* Celebrity prods for MGM; *prod/dir:* Ub Iwerks; *mus:* Carl W. Stalling; b&w. *sd:* PCP. 9 min. • Flip shelters in a haunted house where skeletons are in abundance.

6087. Spooks *(Oswald)* 14 July 1930; *p.c.:* Univ; *dir:* Walter Lantz; *anim:* "Bill" Nolan, Ray Abrams, Manuel Moreno, Clyde Geronimi, "Pinto" Colvig; *mus:* James Dietrich; b&w. *sd:* WE. 6½ min. • Oswald shelters in a haunted house and becomes a part of "The Phantom of the Opera."

6088. Spooky Swabs *(Popeye)* 9 Aug. 1957; *p.c.:* Para Cartoons: *dir:* I. Sparber; *story:* Larz Bourne; *anim:* Thomas Johnson, Frank Endres, Els Barthen; *sets:* John Zago; *voices:* Jack Mercer, Mae Questel, Jackson Beck, Sid Raymond; *mus:* Winston Sharples; *ph:* Leonard McCormick; *prod mgr:* Seymour Shultz; *col:* Tech. *sd:* RCA. 6 min. • Popeye and Olive are adrift on a raft when they board a ship, inhabited by spirits who don't wish to put into port.

6089. Spooky-Yaki *(Hashimoto)* Oct. 1963 *p.c.:* TT for Fox; *ex prod:* Bill Weiss; *dir/story:* Bob Kuwahara; *story sup:* Tom Morrison; *sets:* Bill Focht, John Zago; *ed:* George McAvoy; *voices:* John Myhers; *mus:* Phil Scheib; *ph:* Ted Moskowitz; *col:* DeLuxe. *sd:* RCA. 6 min. • No story available.

6090. Sport Chumpions *(Merrie Melodies)* 16 Aug. 1941; *p.c.:* Leon Schlesinger prods for WB; *dir:* I. Freleng; *story:* Michael Maltese; *anim:* Gerry Chiniquy; *sets:* Lenard Kester; *ed:* Treg Brown; *voices:* Jim Bannon, Mel Blanc; *mus:* Carl W. Stalling; *ph:* John W. Burton; *prod sup:* Henry Binder, Raymond G. Katz; *col:* Tech. *sd:* Vit. 7 min. • Spot-gags on sports, all played in the Avery Memorium Stadium.

6091. The Sport of Kings (*Aesop's Film Fable*) 27 July 1924; *p.c.:* Fables Pictures Inc for Pathé; *dir:* Paul Terry; b&w. *sil.* 5 min. • The animals' big league baseball game at the Polo Grounds. A mouse takes Babe Ruth's place at the bat and clobbers the elephants.

6092. Sporticles (*Noveltoon*) 14 Feb. 1958; *p.c.:* Para Cartoons; *dir:* Seymour Kneitel; *sets:* Robert Little; *voices:* Jackson Beck, Sid Raymond, Jack Mercer; *mus:* Winston Sharples; *ph:* Leonard McCormick; *prod mgr:* Seymour Shultz; *col:* Tech. *sd:* RCA. 6 min. seq: *Sing Again of Michegan*; *Drippy Mississippi*; *Crazy Town.* • A humorous insight into fishing, big game hunting, duck hunting, baseball, golf, etc.

6093. Spree for All (*Noveltoon*) 23 Aug. 1946; *p.c.:* Famous for Para; *dir:* Seymour Kneitel; *story:* Bill Turner, Otto Messmer; *mus:* Winston Sharples; *ph:* Leonard McCormick; *prod mgr:* Sam Buchwald; *col:* Tech. *sd:* RCA. 7 min. • Billy de Beck's comic strip hero, Snuffy Smith, returns from the wars and decides to build a house right in the firing line of the feuding Mulligans and McCoys.

6094. Spree Lunch (*Popeye*) 21 June 1957; *p.c.:* Para Cartoons; *dir:* Seymour Kneitel; *story:* Jack Mercer; *anim:* Tom Johnson, Frank Endres, Els Barthen; *sets:* Joe Dommerque; *voices:* Jack Mercer, Jackson Beck, Frank Matalone; *mus:* Winston Sharples; *ph:* Leonard McCormick; *prod mgr:* Seymour Shultz; *col:* Tech. *sd:* RCA. 6 min. • Popeye and Bluto vie for Wimpy's custom when they set up rival diners.

6095. Spring Antics (*Aesop's Sound Fable*) 21 May 1932; *p.c.:* Van Beuren for RKO; *dir:* John Foster, Mannie Davis; *mus:* Gene Rodemich; b&w. *sd:* RCA. 8 min. • An optimistic duck encourages his pals to come out and play when the snow stops falling. When it starts again, the angry animals chase the duck.

6096. The Spring Festival (*Color Rhapsody*) 6 Aug. 1937; *p.c.:* Charles Mintz prods for Colum; *story:* Ben Harrison; *anim:* Manny Gould; *lay:* Clark Watson; *back:* Phil Davis; *ed:* George Winkler; *voices:* Mel Blanc; *mus:* Joe de Nat; *prod mgr:* James Bronis; *col:* Tech. *sd:* RCA. 7 min. • Depicting the coming of Spring.

6097. Spring Fever (*Gandy Goose*) Apr. 1951; *p.c.:* TT for Fox; *dir:* Mannie Davis; *story:* Tom Morrison; *voices:* Arthur Kay, Tom Morrison; *mus:* Philip A. Scheib; *ph:* Douglas Moye; *col:* Tech. *sd:* RCA. 6 min. • Gandy comes across a sly fox proprietor of a roadside diner. The fox tries to cook him but he escapes by means of a sneezing fit.

6098. Spring in the Park (*Oswald*) 12 Nov. 1934; *p.c.:* Univ; *dir:* Bill Nolan; *story:* Victor McLeod; *anim:* Cecil Surry, Ed Benedict, Ernest Smythe; *mus:* James Dietrich; b&w. *sd:* WE. 7 min. • Oswald is a cop making a play for a pretty nurse in the park. His sergeant arrives and chases him off in order to make a play for her himself. Oswald then returns in a baby's guise.

6099. Spring Is Here (*Paul Terry-Toon*) 24 July 1932; *p.c.:* Moser & Terry for Educational/Fox; *dir:* Frank Moser, Paul Terry; *mus:* Philip A. Scheib; b&w. *sd:* WE. 6 min. • Farmer Al Falfa and his animals are affected by Spring in different ways.

6100. Spring Song (*Screen Song*) 24 June 1949; *dir:* I. Sparber; *story:* I. Klein; *anim:* Myron Waldman, Larry Silverman; *sets:* Shane Miller; *voices:* Jack Mercer, Cecil Roy; *mus:* Winston Sharples; *lyrics:* Buddy Kaye; *ph:* Leonard McCormick; *prod mgr:* Sam Buchwald; *col:* Tech. *sd:* RCA. 7 min. • Pan spreads the joys of Spring. Caricature of Jerry Colonna.

6101. Spring Time (*Silly Symphony*) 4 Oct 1929; *p.c.:* Walter E. Disney for Colum; *dir:* Ub Iwerks; *anim:* Ub Iwerks, Wilfred Jackson, Les Clark; *mus:* Carl W. Stalling; b&w. *sd:* PCP. 7 min. • A fantasy of Spring.

6102. Springtime (*Aesop's Film Fable*) 12 May 1923; *p.c.:* Fables Pictures Inc for Pathé; *dir:* Paul Terry; b&w. *sil.* 5 min. • Farmer Al Falfa flirts with a beauty on the beach without much response.

6103. Springtime for Clobber (*Clint Clobber*) Jan. 1958; *p.c.:* TT for Fox; *ex prod:* Bill Weiss; *dir sup:* Gene Deitch; *dir:* Connie Rasinski; *story sup:* Tom Morrison; *story:* Gene Deitch, Tom Morrison; *anim:* Al Chiarito, Dave Tendlar, Jim Tyer, Mannie Davis, Bob Kuwahara, Vinnie Bell, Larry Silverman; *lay:* Al Kouzel; *back:* Bill Hilliker; *voices:* Allen Swift, Lionel Wilson; *mus:* Phil Scheib; *prod mgr:* "Sparky" Schudde; *col:* Tech. *sd:* RCA. 7 min. CS. • Clobber falls for a bank robber disguised as a woman, hiding out in the apartment building.

6104. Springtime for Pluto (*Pluto*) 23 June 1944; *p.c.:* Walt Disney prods for RKO; *dir:* Charles Nichols; *story:* T. Hee, Nick George, George Nicholas, Eric Gurney; *anim:* George Nicholas, Norman Tate, Marvin Woodward, John Lounsbery, Milt Neil; *fx:* Sandy Strother; *lay:* Charles Philippi; *back:* Lenard Kester; *voices:* J. Dehner Forkum, Thurl Ravenscroft; *mus:* Oliver Wallace; *col:* Tech. *sd:* RCA. 7 min. • Pluto is awakened by "The Spirit of Spring" who induces him to dance. He gets entangled with a beehive and poison ivy, finally chasing the spirit away.

6105. Springtime for Thomas (*Tom & Jerry*) 30 Mar. 1946; *p.c.:* MGM; *dir:* William Hanna, Joseph Barbera; *anim:* Ed Barge, Michael Lah, Kenneth Muse; *sets:* Robert Gentle; *ed:* Fred MacAlpin; *voices:* Frank Graham, Sara Berner, Raul Martinez; *mus:* Scott Bradley; *prod:* Fred Quimby; *col:* Tech. *sd:* WE. 7 min. • Tom's affections for a pretty kitten disrupts Jerry's lifestyle, so he has to enlist reenforcements to bring the relationship to a grinding halt.

6106. Springtime in the Rock Age (*Stone Age*) 30 Aug. 1940; *p.c.:* The Fleischer Studio for Para; *prod:* Max Fleischer; *dir:* Dave Fleischer; *story:* Dan Gordon; *anim:* Myron Waldman, Dick Williams; *ed:* Kitty Pfister; *character des:* Charles Thorson; *mus:* Sammy Timberg; *ph:* Charles Schettler; *prod sup:* Sam Buchwald, Isidore Sparber; b&w. *sd:* WE. 7 min. • Springtime brings out the bugs and moths, who play havoc with the cavemen.

6107. Springtime Serenade (*Cartune Classic*) 27 May 1935; *p.c.:* Univ; *dir:* Walter Lantz; *story:* Walter Lantz, Victor McLeod; *anim:* Manuel Moreno, Lester Kline, Fred Kopietz; *chorus:* The Rhythmettes; *mus:* James Dietrich; *col:* Tech-2. *sd:* WE. 7½ min. • Mr. and Mrs. Oswald Rabbit spring clean, confident that winter has passed. Everyone disbelieves Professor Groundhog's predictions.

6108. Sprinkle Me Pink (*Pink Panther*) 1978; *p.c.:* Mirisch/Geoffrey/DFE for UA; *dir:* Bob Richardson; *story:* Cliff Roberts; *anim:* Warren Batchelder, Bob Richardson, Bill Hutten, Bob Kirk; *lay:* Martin Strudler; *back:* Richard H. Thomas; *ed:* Joe Siracusa; *theme tune:* Henry Mancini; *ph:* Ray Lee; *prod mgr:* Lee Gunther; *col:* DeLuxe. *sd:* RCA. 6 min. • A raincloud follows the Panther around.

6109. Spunky Skunky (*Casper*) 30 May 1952; *p.c.:* Famous for Para; *dir:* I. Sparber; *story:* Larz Bourne; *anim:* Myron Waldman, Larry Silverman; *sets:* Robert Little; *voices:* Alan Shay, Sid Raymond, Gwen Davies, Jack Mercer; *mus:* Winston Sharples; *ph:* Leonard McCormick; *prod mgr:* Seymour Shultz; *col:* Tech. *sd:* RCA. 7 min. • Casper befriends a skunk when all his baseball playing compatriates spurn him.

6110. The Spy Swatter (*Looney Tunes*) June 1967; *p.c.:* Format Films for WB; *dir:* Rudy Larriva; *story:* Tom Dagenais, Cal Howard; *anim:* Ed Friedman, Virgil Ross, Bob Bransford; *lay:* Don Sheppard; *back:* Walt Peregoy; *ed:* Joe Siracusa; *voices:* Mel Blanc; *mus:* William Lava; *prod:* William L. Hendricks, Herb Klynn; *col:* Tech. *sd:* Vit. 6 min. • Secret Agent Daffy is dispatched to steal a formula that will strengthen mice.

6111. Square Shootin' Square (*Woody Woodpecker*) Sept. 1955; *p.c.:* Walter Lantz prods for Univ; *dir:* Paul J. Smith; *story:* Michael Maltese; *anim:* Herman R. Cohen, Robert Bentley, Gil Turner; *sets:* Art Landy; *voices:* Dal McKennon, Grace Stafford; *mus:* Clarence Wheeler; *prod mgr:* William E. Garity; *col:* Tech. *sd:* RCA. 6 min. • Woody tries to capture a western bandit.

6112. Squatter's Rights (*Mickey Mouse*) 7 June 1946; *p.c.:* Walt Disney prods for RKO; *dir:* Jack Hannah; *asst dir:* Toby Tobelman; *story:* Harry Reeves, Rex Cox; *anim:* Hugh Fraser, Murray McClellan, Bob Carlson, Hal Ambro, Al Coe, Paul Murray, Ken O'Brien, Marvin Woodward; *fx:* Blaine Gibson, John F. Reed; *lay:* Yale Gracey; *back:* Thelma Witmer; *voices:* James MacDonald, Milt Neil; *mus:* Oliver Wallace; *col:* Tech. *sd:* RCA. 7 min. *Academy Award nomination.* • Mickey and Pluto find their mountain cabin retreat inhabited by a couple of chipmunks.

6113. The Squaw Path (*Go-Go Toon*) May 1967; *p.c.:* Para Cartoons; *dir:* Shamus Culhane; *story:* Howard Beckerman; *anim:* Al Eugster, Nick Tafuri; *sets:* Howard Beckerman, Danté Barbetta, Dave Ubinas; *voices:* Bob MacFadden; *mus:* Winston Sharples; *prod sup:* Harold Robins, Burt Hanft; *col:* Tech. *sd:* RCA. 6 min. • Geronimo the Indian has a cold and visits the Medicine Man who also has agreed to find an old maid a husband. She pursues Geronimo intent on matrimony.

6114. The Squawkin' Hawk (*Merrie Melodies*)8 Aug. 1942; *p.c.:* Leon Schlesinger prods for WB; *dir:* Charles M. Jones; *story:* Ted Pierce; *lay:* John McGrew; *back:* Eugene Fleury; *ed:* Treg Brown; *voices:* Sara Berner, Kent Rogers, Ted Pierce; *mus:* Carl W. Stalling; *prod sup:* Henry Binder, Raymond G. Katz; *col:* Tech. *sd:* Vit. 7 min. • Henery Hawk sets out to capture a chicken for supper. He is attacked by an angry rooster and has to be rescued by his mama.

6115. A Squeak in the Deep (*Looney Tunes*) 9 July 1966; *p.c.:* DFE for WB; *dir:* Robert McKimson; *story:* Sid Marcus; *anim:* Bob Matz, Manny Perez, Norm McCabe, George Grandpré, Ted Bonnicksen, Warren Batchelder; *lay:* Dick Ung; *back:* Tom O'Loughlin; *ed:* Eugene Marks; *voices:* Mel Blanc; *mus:* Walter Greene; *col:* Tech. *sd:* Vit. 6 min. • Daffy scuttles Speedy's boat in a sailing race and Speedy suggests they become partners.

6116. Squirrel Crazy (*Terry-Toon*) Jan. 1951; *p.c.:* TT for Fox; *dir:* Mannie Davis; *story:* Tom Morrison; *anim:* Jim Tyer; *mus:* Philip A. Scheib; *ph:* Douglas Moye; *col:* Tech. *sd:* RCA. 6 min. • Nutzy the squirrel's search for winter storage leads him to a house with a cache of food that he takes from under the eye of a guard dog.

6117. Stage Door Cartoon (*Merrie Melodies*) 30 Dec. 1944; *p.c.:* WB; *dir:* I. Freleng; *story:* Michael Maltese; *anim:* John Bradbury, Virgil Ross; *lay:* Hawley Pratt; *back:* Paul Julian; *ed:* Treg Brown; *voices:* Mel Blanc, Arthur Q. Bryan; *mus:* Carl W. Stalling; *prod mgr:* John W. Burton; *prod:* Edward Selzer; *col:* Tech. *sd:* Vit. 7 min. • Elmer traps Bugs in a theatre, forcing them both to participate in the acts.

6118. Stage Fright (*Merrie Melodies*) 28 Sept. 1940; *p.c.:* Leon Schlesinger prods for WB; *dir:* Charles M. Jones; *story:* Rich Hogan; *anim:* Ken Harris; *character des/lay:* Robert Givens; *back:* Eugene Fleury; *ed:* Treg Brown; *voices:* Mel Blanc; *mus:* Carl W. Stalling; *prod sup:* Henry Binder, Raymond G. Katz; *col:* Tech. *sd:* Vit. 7 min. • Two pups find themselves backstage in a theatre becoming involved with a performing seal, a tightrope and a magician's pigeon.

6119. Stage Hoax (*Woody Woodpecker*) 21 Apr. 1952; *p.c.:* Walter Lantz prods for Univ; *dir:* Walter Lantz; *anim:* Don Patterson, Ray Abrams, La Verne Harding, Paul Smith; *sets:* Fred Brunish; *mus:* Clarence E. Wheeler; *prod mgr:* William E. Garity; *col:* Tech. *sd:* RCA. 6 min. • Woody tries for a free ride on the stagecoach by posing as a beautiful woman but doesn't reckon on the amorous advances of stagecoach bandit, Buzz Buzzard.

6120. Stage Krazy (*Krazy Kat*) 13 Nov. 1933; *p.c.:* Winkler for Colum; *prod:* Charles Mintz; *story:* Rudy Zamora, Harry Love; *anim:* Allen Rose, Preston Blair; *mus:* Joe de Nat; *prod mgr:* James Bronis; b&w. *sd:* WE. 6 min. • Krazy stages a vaudeville show.

6121. Stage Struck (*Aesop's Sound Fable*) 23 Dec. 1929; *p.c.:* Fables Pictures Inc for Pathé; *dir:* Paul Terry; *mus:* Carl Edouarde; b&w. *sd:* RCA. 10 min. • Farmer Al acts as M.C. to the farmyard amateur theatricals.

6122. Stage Struck (*Terry-Toon*) Mar. 1951; *p.c.:* TT for Fox; *dir:* Mannie Davis; *story/voices:* Tom Morrison; *anim:* Jim Tyer; *mus:* Philip A. Scheib; *ph:* Douglas Moye; *col:* Tech. *sd:* RCA. 6 min. • Half-Pint, a baby elephant, is forever trying to get into the Big Top show.

6123. Stage Stunts (*Oswald*) 29 Mar. 1929; *p.c.:* Winkler for Univ; *prod:* Charles B. Mintz; *anim:* Hugh Harman; b&w. *sd:* WE. 7 min. • Oswald is a vaudeville performer who tries to escape a bomb lobbed from the gallery.

6124. Stagedoor Magoo (*Mr. Magoo*) 6 Oct. 1955; *p.c.:* UPA for Colum; *ex prod:* Stephen Bosustow; *dir:* Pete Burness; *story:* Dick Shaw, Barbara Hammer; *anim:* Rudy Larriva, Cecil Surry, Tom McDonald; *lay:* Robert Dranko; *back:* Jules Engel; *voices:* Jim Backus, Miriam Wolfe; *mus:* Dennis Farnon; *prod mgr:* Herbert Klynn; *col:* Tech. *sd:* RCA. 6½ min. • Magoo insists on playing the leading role in Mrs. Stignee's charity opera without his glasses.

6125. Standard Parade for 1939 23 Feb. 1939; *p.c.:* Walt Disney prods for Standard Oil Co; *story:* Hugh W. Thomas; *col:* b&w/Tech. *sd:* RCA. 2½ min. • Mickey, Donald and Goofy join forces with the Seven Dwarfs to march in a parade bearing flags that spell out the name of "Standard Oil."

6126. Stanley's Magic Garden • See: *A Troll in Central Park*

6127. A Star Is Bored (*Looney Tunes*) 15 Sept. 1956; *p.c.:* WB; *dir:* Friz Freleng; *story:* Warren Foster; *anim:* Art Davis, Gerry Chiniquy, Virgil Ross; *lay:* Hawley Pratt; *back:* Irv Wyner; *ed:* Treg Brown; *voices:* Mel Blanc, June Foray, Arthur Q. Bryan; *mus:* Carl Stalling; *prod mgr:* John W. Burton; *prod:* Edward Selzer; *col:* Tech. *sd:* Vit. 7 min. • Tired of being the studio's dogsbody, Daffy demands to star in the next production. He gets a job as Bugs' stand-in, intent on sabotaging the rabbit's career.

6128. A Star Is Hatched (*Merrie Melodies*) 12 Mar. 1938; *p.c.:* Leon Schlesinger prods for WB; *dir:* I. Freleng; *story:* Ted Pierce; *anim:* Bob McKimson; *lay:* Griff Jay; *back:* Arthur Loomer; *ed:* Tregoweth E. Brown; *voices:* Ted Pierce, Elvia Allman; *mus:* Carl W. Stalling; *song:* Harry Warren, Al Dubin; *prod sup:* Henry Binder, Raymond G. Katz; *col:* Tech. *sd:* Vit. 7 min. • A Hollywood director invites an aspiring chick to hitch-hike two thousand miles for a screen test but she soon realizes the folly of her ways. Caricatures of: John Barrymore, Freddie Bartholomew, Joan Blondell, Charlie Chaplin, W.C. Fields, Clark Gable, Greta Garbo, Charlie McCarthy, Dick Powell, William Powell, Edward G. Robinson, Johnny Weissmuller and Mae West.

6129. The Star Maker 1939; *p.c.:* The Fleischer Studio for Para; b&w. *sd:* WE. • Live-action film with Bing Crosby and the kids singing "School Days" in the hopes that the audience will sing along to a bouncing ball singalong.

6130. Star Pink (*Pink Panther*) 1978; *p.c.:* Mirisch/Geoffrey/DFE for UA; *dir:* Art Davis; *story:* John W. Dunn; *anim:* Bob Matz, John Gibbs, Tiger West, Tony Love; *lay:* Martin Strudler; *back:* Richard H. Thomas; *ed:* Robert Gillis; *theme tune:* Henry Mancini; *ph:* Ray Lee; *prod mgr:* Lee Gunther; *col:* DeLuxe. *sd:* RCA. 6 min. • The Panther owns an intergalactic service station when he is pestered by a villainous star ship.

6131. Star Wars 25 May 1977; *p.c.:* Lucasfilm Ltd., for Fox; *anim/Rotoscope design:* Adam Beckett; *anim:* Michael Ross, Peter Kuran, Jonathan Seay, Chris Casady, Lyn Gerry, Diana Wilson; *stop-motion anim:* John Berg, Philip Tippett; *computer anim/graphic displays:* Dan O'Bannon, Larry Cuba, John Wash, Jay Teitzell; *Image West; col:* Tech/DeLuxe. *sd:* RCA Victor/Dolby stereo. 121 min. Panavision *l/a.* • Live-action science-fiction adventure re-issued in 1997 with added computer generated extras.

6132. Star Wars: A New Hope 1977/1997; *p.c.:* Lucasfilm Ltd., for Fox; *anim/Rotoscope:* Adam Beckett; *anim:* Michael Ross, Peter Kuran, Jonathan Seay, Chris Casady, Lyn Gerry, Diana Wilson; *stop-motion anim:* Jon Berg, Philip Tippett; *computer anim/graphic displays:* Dan O'Bannon, Larry Cuba, John Wash, Jay Teitzell; *col:* Tech. *sd:* Dolby Stereo. 124 min. *l/a.* • Live-action science-fiction adventure: Princess Leia is captured and Luke Skywalker enlists in a quest to rescue her. Re-working of *The Empire Strikes Back* (1980), re-titled with four minutes of additional computer generated footage including a "Dewback Lizard" and "Jabba the Hutt."

6133. Star Wars Episode 1: The Phantom Menace 19 May 1999; *p.c.:* Lucasfilm Ltd.,/JAK Prods for Fox; *lead anim:* Linda Bel, Peter Daulton, Lou Dellarosa, Miguel Fuertes, Hal Hickel, Paul Kavanagh, Kim Thompson, Marjolaine Tremblay; *anim sup:* Tom Bertino; *technical anim sup:* James Tooley; *character anim:* Philip Alexy, Chris Armstrong, Patrick Bonneau, Susan Campbell, Marc Chu, Chi Chung Tse, Kyle Clark, Bruce Dahl, Andrew Doucette, Andrew Grant, Paul Griffin, Kent Hammerstrom, Tim Harrington, Jason Ivimey, Shawn Kelly, Ken King, Steve Lee, Martin L'Heureux, Victoria Livingstone, Kevin Martel, Glen McIntosh, Neil Michka, Christopher Minos, Christopher Mitchell, Jacques Muller, Julie Nelson, Steve Nichols, Dana O'Connor, Rick O'Connor, David Parsons, Steve Rawlins, Jay Rennie, Magali Rigaudias, Trish Schutz, Tom St. Amand, Glenn Sylvester, Si Tran, Scott Wirtz, Andy Wong, William R. Wright; *anim dir:* Rob Coleman; *voices:* Jar Jar Binks: Ahmed Best; TC-14: Lindsay Duncan; *Darth Maul:* Peter Serafinowicz; *Rune Haako:* James Taylor; *Daultay Dofine:* Chris Sanders; *Lott Dod:* Toby Longworth; *Aks Moe:* Marc Silk; *Tey How:* Tey How; *col:* DeLuxe. *sd:* Dolby stereo. 133 min. *l/a.* reissue: 7 April 2001 • Live-action science-fiction adventure. Two Jedi knights are dispatched to negotiate a dispute between planet leaders. The evil Nute Gunray plans to take over the peaceful world of Naboo and, unable to prevent an attack.the knights help the planet's Queen escape the attack of Gunray's army.

6134. Star Wars V: The Empire Strikes Back 21 May 1980; *p.c.:* Lucasfilm for Fox; *stop-motion anim:* Jon Berg, Phil Tippett; *stop-motion technicians:* Tom St. Amand, Doug Beswick; *anim/Rotoscope sup:* Peter

Kuran; *anim:* Samuel Comstock, Garry Waller, John van Yuet, Rick Taylor, Kim Knowlton, Chris Casady, Nina Saxon, Diana Wilson; *col:* Eastman/ DeLuxe. *sd:* Dolby Stereo/SDDS. 127 min. VistaVision. *l/a.* • Live-action science-fiction adventure: The Rebel Alliance takes shelter on a frozen planet in the Hoth System which is overrun by Darth Vader's stormtroopers. Luke Skywalker confronts Vader in a laser duel.

6135. Star Wars: Return of the Jedi 25 May 1983; *p.c.:* Lucasfilm for Fox; *dir:* Richard Marquand; *cgi:* William Reeves, Tom Duff; *anim sup:* James Keefer; *stop-motion anim:* Tom St. Amand; *fx anim:* Garry Waller, Kimberley Knowlton, Terry Windell, Renee Holt, Mike Lessa, Samuel Comstock, Rob la Duca, Annick Therrien, Suki Stern, Margot Pipkin; *col:* DeLuxe. *sd:* Dolby stereo. 132 min. *l/a.* • Live-action science-fiction: Having rescued Han Solo from the palace of Jabba the Hutt, the Rebels endeavor to destroy the Second Death Star.

6136. Starchaser: The Legend of Orin 22 Nov. 1985; *p.c.:* Coleman-Rosenblatt; *dir/prod:* Steven Hahn; *ex prod:* Thomas Coleman, Michael Rosenblatt; *asso prod:* Daniel Pia, Christine Danzo; *prod sup:* Young Chul Choi, Kim Soon Min; *asso dir:* John Sparey; *story:* Jeffrey Scott; *visual fx:* Michael Wolf; *anim dir:* Mitch Rochon, Jang-Gil Kim; *key anim:* Yoon Young Sang, Jung Yul Song, Bill Kroyer, John J. Norton, Steve E. Gordon, Gary Payne, Thomas Sito, Leonard Robinson, James Stribling, Marlene Robinson May; *asst anim:* Daniel Jeup, Chris Bailey, Fred Water, Craig Clark, Christopher Rutkowski, Brian Etienne Ray, Deborah Ann Hayes, David Teague; *inbet:* Greg Manwaring, Stephen Moore, Eric Pigors, Anthony Zierhut, Carlos Baeza, David Woodman, Alan Wright, James Fujii; *fx anim:* Allen Blyth, John Van Vliet, Robert Laduca, Michael Wolf; *asst fx:* Kim Bae Geun, Geri Rochon; *key anim clean-up:* Renee Holt, Michael Lessa, Darrell Rooney; *storyboard:* Boyd Kirkland, Ronald Harris, Mario Piluso, Paul Hugh Gruwell, Dick Sebast; *character des:* Louise Zingarelli; *ed/sd des:* Donald W. Ernst; *ed asst:* Tony Mizgallski, Douglas Nickel, Jonathan Pink; *voices: Orin:* Joe Colligan; *Dagg:* Carmen Argenziano; *Elan/Aviana:* Noelle North; *Zygon:* Anthony Delongis; *Arthur:* Les Tremayne; *Silica:* Tyke Caravelli; *Magreb:* Ken Sansom; *Auctioneer/Z. Gork:* John Moschitta Jr.; *Minemaster:* Mickey Morton; *Pung/Hopps:* Herb Vigran; *Shooter:* Dennis Alwood; *Kallie:* Mona Marshall; *Aunt Bella:* Tina Romanus; *also:* Ryan MacDonald, John Garwood, Joseph Dellasorte, Philip Clarke, Mike Winslow, Thomas H. Watkins, Daryl T. Bartley; *mus/synthesizer:* Andrew Belling; *mus performed by* The New World Philharmonic; *mus sup:* David Katz; *titles/opticals:* Kaleidoscope Film Effects; *hardware des:* Thomas Warkentin; *scene plan:* John Sparey, Mike Svayko, Robert Revell, Dotti Foell, James Finch, Ron Myrick; *computer anim plan:* John Sparey, Bill Kroyer, Christopher Bailey, Craig Clark; *computer operator:* Patricia Capozzi, Edith Fandrey; *asst:* Dave Woodman, Kane Anderson, Laura Capozzi Kelly, Charles Hefner; *lay sup:* Roy Allen Smith; *lay:* Edward Haney, Neil E. Galloway, Rex Barron, Richard Graham, Mario Piluso, David Hoover, Boyd Kirkland, Gary Graham, Robert B. Dewitt, Frank Paur, John Howley, Robert A. Smith, Russell Heath, James Fletcher, John Koch; *back des:* Timothy Callahan, Roy Allen Smith; *back sup:* Carol Police, Kim Young Ku; *back:* Barry Jackson, Edwin B. Hirth, Patricia Doktor, Ray Roberts, John Calmette, Jim Schlenker; *col key des:* Janet Cummings, No Soon Nyeo, Geri Rochon; *i&p:* Laura Craig, Madlyn O'Neill, Robin L. Police, Mi Kyung Kwon; *anim check:* Kim Mee-Young, Don Lauder, Dotti Foell, Robert Revell, Narelle Nixon; *final check:* Narelle Nixon, Patricia Capozzi, Sandy Kumashiro, James Finch; *anim ph:* Charles Flekal, Young Poo Yim, Thomas Ling Yen, Craig Littell-Herrick, David Corbett, Craig Berkos, Paul Mikolyski, Cho Bok Dong, Yim Chul Kyu, Bemiller Camera, R&B Camera; *sd ed:* Denise Horta, Eileen Horta, Robert Canton, Gary Krivacek, Kevin Spears, Rick Crampton, Dave West; *sd rec:* Gregg Rudloff, John Reitz, David Campbell; *Dona; sd fx:* Stan Levine; *computer hardware consultant:* Harvard; *prod asst:* Thomas Watkins; *3-D, col:* DeLuxe. *sd:* Dolby stereo. 100 min. • Young Orin escapes from the tyranical robots in the crystal mins of the planet Trinia. He discovers a sword hilt that has magical properties and has many adventures in this science-fiction feature cartoon made in three dimensions.

6137. Stars and Stripes 1939; *p.c.:* The Guggenheim Museum for International Film Bureau; *anim:* Norman McLaren; *col. sd.* 3 min. • The American flag performs to Sousa's "Stars and Stripes." Painted directly onto film.

6138. Starship Troopers 7 Nov. 1997; *p.c.:* TriStar/Touchstone;

creature visual fx: the Tippett Studio Design Visual Effects: *sup:* Craig Hayes; *visual fx prod:* Jules Roman; *prod sup:* Alonzo Ruvalcaba; *character anim dpt sup:* Trey Stokes; *lead character anim:* Blair Clark, Peter König, Adam Valdez; *character anim:* Jeremy Cantor, Kirrie Edis, Tom Gibbons, Randall Link, Mark Schreiber, Tom Schelesny, Gary Siela, Tanya Spence, Robin Watts, John Zdankiewicz; *art dpt sup:* Paula Lucchesi; *digital model makers:* Martin Meunier, Merrick Cheney; *digital fx anim:* Darby Johnston, Eric Leven, Al Arthur; *3d fx anim:* Manny Wong; *stop-motion anim:* Paul Jessel, Peter Kleinow; *col:* Tech. *sd:* Dolby/SDDS/dts. 129 min. *l/a.* • Live-action action fantasy: Earth in the future where democracy has been replaced by military rule. Four high school pals prepare for a surprise attack from an alien arachnid race known as the Bugs.

6139. Starting from Hatch *(Noveltoon)* 6 Mar. 1953; *p.c.:* Famous for Para; *dir:* Seymour Kneitel; *story:* Jack Mercer, Carl Meyer; *anim:* Dave Tendlar, Thomas Moore; *sets:* Anton Loeb; *voices:* Sid Raymond, Jackson Beck, Cecil Roy; *mus:* Winston Sharples; *ph:* Leonard McCormick; *prod mgr:* Seymour Shultz; *col:* Tech. *sd:* RCA. 6 min. • A fox steals a huge egg that hatches into the giant baby duckling, Baby Huey. He sees this as a twelve course dinner and proceeds to prepare him for the oven.

6140. Static *(Aesop's Film Fable)* 14 Aug. 1928; *p.c.:* Fables Pictures Inc for Pathé; *dir:* Paul Terry; *b&w. sil.* 10 min. • Mice operate Al Falfa's broadcasting station.

6141. Stay Tuned 12 Feb. 1993; *p.c.:* Morgan Creek for WB; *sup/des:* Chuck Jones; *co-sup/storyboard:* Jeffrey M. DeGrandis; *prod:* Steven Paul Leiva, Linda Jones; *anim:* Ken Bruce, Susan M. Zytka, Brad Forbush, Mark Fisher, Lee McCaulla, Travis T. Cowsill; *fx anim:* David Bossert; *art dir/lay:* Guy Vasilovich; *back:* Tim Maloney; *i&p:* Jungja Wolf, Carmen Brooks, Deborah Rykoff-Bennett, Shigeko Doyle, Maria Gonzalez; *mark-up:* Cynthia Surage; *check:* Charlotte Clark, Karen Hansen; *anim prod co-ord:* Melissa Kurtz; *col:* Tech. *sd.* 6 min. *l/a/anim.* • Live-action fantasy: A couple is sucked into a nightmare existence inside their television, initiated by the Devil himself. One instance transforms them into animated mice up against a robot cat in a television cartoon.

6142. Steal Wool *(Looney Tunes)* 8 June 1957; *p.c.:* WB; *dir:* Chuck Jones; *story:* Michael Maltese; *anim:* Richard Thompson, Ken Harris, Abe Levitow; *lay:* Maurice Noble; *back:* Philip de Guard; *ed:* Treg Brown; *voices:* Mel Blanc; *mus:* Milt Franklyn; *prod mgr:* John W. Burton; *prod:* Edward Selzer; *col:* Tech. *sd:* Vit. 7 min. • Ralph Wolf attempts to filch sheep from Sam Sheepdog by using a firecracker bridge and catapaulting himself past the watchdog's eagle eyes.

6143. Stealin' Ain't Honest *(Popeye)* 29 Mar. 1940; *p.c.:* The Fleischer Studio for Para: *prod:* Max Fleischer; *dir:* Dave Fleischer; *story:* George Manuel; *anim:* Thomas Johnson, Frank Endres, Abner Matthews, Graham Place, Harold Walker; *voices:* Jack Mercer, Margie Hines, William Pennell; *mus:* Sammy Timberg; *ph:* Charles Schettler; *prod sup:* Sam Buchwald, Isidore Sparber; *b&w. sd:* WE. 7 min. • Popeye and Olive go on a treasure hunt for Olive's secret gold mine but don't reckon on Bluto trying to get in first.

6144. Steamboat Willie *(Mickey Mouse)* 29 Nov. 1928; *p.c.:* Walter E. Disney for Harry Reichenbach; *dir:* Ub Iwerks; *anim:* Ub Iwerks, Les Clark; *mus:* Carl Edouarde; *prod sup:* Walt Disney, Wilfred Jackson, Johnny Cannon; *b&w. sd:* PCP. 7 min. • Cabin boy Mickey utilises the livestock aboard the steamboat for a musical entertainment. • Already made as a silent film, Walt Disney later added a synchronized soundtrack, using a fifteen piece orchestra with Walt and the artists providing voices and sound effects. Although *Plane Crazy* was the first Mickey Mouse cartoon to be made, this was the first to be released.

6145. The Steel Workers *(Meany Miny Mo)* 26 Apr. 1937; *p.c.:* Univ; *dir:* Walter Lantz; *story:* Walter Lantz, Victor McLeod; *anim:* Ray Abrams, Leo Salkin, Ed Benedict; *mus:* James Dietrich; *b&w. sd:* WE. 6 min. • The monks are working on a scaffolding and have problems with their peg-legged boss.

6146. The Steeple Chase *(Mickey Mouse)* 30 Sept. 1933; *p.c.:* Walt Disney prods for Colum; *dir:* Burton F. Gillett; *anim:* Arthur Babbitt, Johnny Cannon, Les Clark, Gilles de Tremaudan, Joseph d'Igalo, Ugo d'Orsi, Clyde Geronimi, Dick Huemer, Edward Love, Fred Moore, Archie Robin, Louie Schmitt, Ben Sharpsteen; *voice:* Walt Disney; *mus:* Frank E. Churchill; *b&w. sd:* PCP. 7 min. • Mickey's horse gets drunk just before the big race, so he dresses two stable lads in a horse-skin and they win with help from angry hornets!

6147. The Steeplejacks (*Heckle & Jeckle*) June 1951; *p.c.:* TT for Fox; *dir:* Connie Rasinski; *story/voices:* Tom Morrison; *anim:* Jim Tyer; *mus:* Philip A. Scheib; *ph:* Douglas Moye; *col:* Tech. *sd:* RCA. 6 min. • The magpies are chased by the watchman on a construction site.

6148. The Stein Song (*Screen Songs*) 6 Sept. 1930; *p.c.:* The Fleischer Studio for Para; *prod:* Max Fleischer; *sup:* Dave Fleischer; *dir/story/anim:* Rudy Zamora, Jimmie Culhane; *mus:* Rudy Vallee & his Connecticut Yankees; *song:* Lincoln Colcord, E.A. Fenstad; *l/a:* Rudy Vallee; b&w. *sd:* WE. (disc) 5½ min. *l/a/anim.* • Musical adaptation to a football game.

6149. Step on It 21 May 1931; *p.c.:* The Fleischer Studio for Texas Oil; *prod:* Max Fleischer; *dir:* Dave Fleischer; b&w. *sd:* WE. 10 min. • As the fire chief starts to a fire, he stops and takes a bottle of Texas Oil from a billboard advertisement, bringing a smile to his car's face. He starts off with renewed vigor and rescues a maiden from the fire.

6150. Stepping Stones (*Scrappy*) 17 May 1932; *p.c.:* Winkler for Colum; *prod:* Charles Mintz; *story:* Dick Huemor; *anim:* Sid Marcus, Art Davis; *mus:* Joe de Nat; *prod mgr:* James Bronis; b&w. *sd:* RCA. 5½ min. • No story available.

6151. The Stevedores (*Meany Miny Mo*) 24 May 1937; *p.c.:* Univ; *story:* Walter Lantz, Victor McLeod; *anim:* Manuel Moreno, George Nicholas, Ben Clopton; *sets:* Edgar Keichle; *mus:* James Dietrich; b&w. *sd:* WE. 6 min. • The three monkeys are chased all over the ship by a whip-cracking captain.

6152. Stirrups and Hiccups (*Hoot Kloot*) 15 Oct. 1973; *p.c.:* Mirisch/DFE for UA; *dir:* Gerry Chiniquy; *story:* John W. Dunn; *anim:* Don Williams, Bob Matz, Norm McCabe, Ken Muse, John Gibbs; *lay:* Dick Ung; *back:* Richard H. Thomas; *ed:* Joe Siracusa; *voices:* Bob Holt; *mus:* Doug Goodwin; *titles:* Arthur Leonardi; *ph:* John Burton Jr.; *prod mgr:* Lee Gunther; *col:* DeLuxe. *sd:* RCA. 6 min. • Kloot's deputy, Mild Bill Hiccup, turns into Wild Bill — the western desperado — whenever he has a bout of the hiccups.

6153. A Stitch in Time (*Out of the Inkwell*) 1 May 1924; *p.c.:* Inkwell Studio for Winkler; *dir:* Dave Fleischer; *anim/l/a:* Max Fleischer; b&w. *sil.* 5 min. *l/a/anim.* • Max sews the clown together. Ko-Ko grabs the needle and has a swordfight with Max's pen. Sliding off the page, he begins to tie everything down with thread. Re-issued as *Ko-Ko Needles the Boss* in 1927.

6154. A Stitch in Time Nov. 1929; *p.c.:* Visugraphic. • Cartoon featuring a cat who lost eight of his nine lives in a frantic effort to sew its trousers which had become torn in a mixup. Synchronized score with titles and no dialogue. b&w. *sd.* 1 reel.

6155. The Stone Age (*Oswald*) 15 July 1931; *p.c.:* Univ; *dir:* Walter Lantz, "Bill" Nolan; *anim:* Clyde Geronimi, Manuel Moreno, Ray Abrams, Fred Avery, Lester Kline, Chet Karrberg, Pinto Colvig; *mus:* James Dietrich; b&w. *sd:* WE. 7 min. • A prehistoric Oswald sees Putrid Pete club his girl and drag her off. With renewed vigor, Ozzy sets out to be a devil with the ladies by brandishing a club.

6156. A Stone Age Adventure 29 May 1915; *p.c.:* Bray prods for Eclectic; *story/anim:* L.M. Glackens; b&w. *sil.* • No story available.

6157. A Stone Age Error (*Aesop's Sound Fable*) 9 July 1932; *p.c.:* Van Beuren for RKO; *dir:* John Foster, Mannie Davis; *mus:* Gene Rodemich; b&w. *sd:* RCA. 6½ min. • No story available.

6158. A Stone Age Romance (*Aesop's Sound Fable*) 4 Aug. 1929; *p.c.:* Van Beuren for Pathé; *dir:* Paul Terry; *mus:* Josiah Zuro; *sd fx:* Maurice Manne; b&w. *sd:* RCA. 6 min. • A tough caveman frightens off the animals, then a flapper arrives and makes a fool of him.

6159. Stone Age Stunts (*Aesop's Sound Fable*) 7 Dec. 1930; *p.c.:* Van Beuren for Pathé; *dir:* John Foster; *anim:* Geo. Stallings, Ed Donnelly; *mus:* Jack Ward, Gene Rodemich; b&w. *sd:* RCA. 6 min. • A couple of stoneage mice travel on their dinosaur to a café where a bear makes a play for the girl and the whole place catches fire.

6160. Stone and McDonough 12 Dec. 1942; *l/a/anim.* • A devastating swipe at the platitudes emanating from the White House.

6161. Stooge for a Mouse (*Merrie Melodies*) 21 Oct. 1950; *p.c.:* WB; *dir:* I. Freleng; *story:* Warren Foster; *anim:* Arthur Davis, Emery Hawkins,

Gerry Chiniquy, Ken Champin, Virgil Ross; *lay:* Hawley Pratt; *back:* Paul Julian; *ed:* Treg Brown; *voices:* Mel Blanc; *mus:* Carl Stalling; *prod mgr:* John W. Burton; *prod:* Edward Selzer; *col:* Tech. *sd:* Vit. 7 min. • A mouse breaks up a peaceful relationship by convincing the dog that Sylvester is out to kill him.

6162. Stoopnocracy (*Screen Songs*) 18 Aug 1933; *p.c.:* The Fleischer Studio for Para; *prod:* Max Fleischer; *dir:* Dave Fleischer; *anim:* Seymour Kneitel, William Henning; *voice:* Jimmy Donnelly; *mus:* Art Turkisher; *l/a:* Col Lemuel Q. Stoopnagle (F. Chase Taylor), Budd (Wilbur "Budd" Hulick); b&w. *sd:* WE. 7 min. • While the wagon goes around collecting subjects for the "Nut Hatch," Col. Stoopnagle demonstrates many of his new inventions.

6163. Stop! Look! and Hasten! (*Merrie Melodies*) 14 Aug. 1954; *p.c.:* WB; *dir:* Charles M. Jones; *story:* Michael Maltese; *anim:* Abe Levitow, Richard Thompson; *fx:* Harry Love; *lay:* Maurice Noble; *back:* Phil de Guard; *ed:* Treg Brown; *voice:* Paul Julian; *mus:* Carl Stalling; *prod mgr:* John W. Burton; *prod:* Edward Selzer; *col:* Tech. *sd:* Vit. 7 min. • The starving Coyote abandons eating a tin can in favor of chasing the Road-Runner. He builds a Burmese Tiger Trap, also taking Acme Triple-Strength Fortified Leg Muscle Pills.

6164. Stop, Look and Listen (*Mighty Mouse*) Dec. 1949; *p.c.:* TT for Fox; *dir:* Eddie Donnelly; *story:* John Foster; *voice:* Roy Halee; *mus:* Philip A. Scheib; *ph:* Douglas Moye; *col:* Tech. *sd:* RCA. 6½ min. • The malevolent Oil Can Harry once more kidnaps Pearl Pureheart and ties her to the railroad tracks. Can Mighty Mouse be far behind?

6165. Stop That Noise (*Betty Boop*) 15 Mar. 1935; *p.c.:* The Fleischer Studio for Para; *prod:* Max Fleischer; *dir:* Dave Fleischer; *anim:* Myron Waldman, Edward Nolan, Lillian Friedman; *voice:* Mae Questel; *mus:* Sammy Timberg; b&w. *sd:* WE. 7 min. • Betty escapes from the city noises but finds the country sounds just as aggravating.

6166. Stopping the Show (*Betty Boop*) 12 Aug. 1932; *p.c.:* The Fleischer Studio for Para; *prod:* Max Fleischer; *dir:* Dave Fleischer; *anim:* Roland Crandall, Rudolph Eggeman, Al Eugster; *voices:* Mae Questel, Fanny Brice, Maurice Chevalier; *mus:* Art Turkisher; b&w. *sd:* WE. 6 min. • Betty appears on stage imitating famous stars.

6167. The Stork Brought It (*Unnatural History*) 7 Feb. 1926; *p.c.:* Bray prods for FBO; *dir/story:* Walter Lantz; *anim:* Clyde Geronimi; *l/a ph:* Joe Rock; b&w. *sil.* 6 min. *l/a/anim:* • The stork arrives with a bundle of white babies and one black one.

6168. The Stork Market (*Krazy Kat*) 11 July 1931; *p.c.:* Winkler for Colum; *prod:* Charles Mintz; *anim:* Ben Harrison, Manny Gould; *mus:* Joe de Nat; *prod mgr:* James Bronis; b&w. *sd:* WE. 6 min. • Krazy works at a "Baby Factory" and delivers a reluctant child to a family. The baby doesn't want to be surrendered and pushes Krazy into the household instead where the couple believe him to be theirs.

6169. The Stork Market (*Screen Song*) 8 Apr. 1949; *p.c.:* Famous for Para; *dir:* Seymour Kneitel; *story:* Bill Turner, Larry Riley; *anim:* Al Eugster, *sets:* Shane Miller; *voices:* Jack Mercer; *mus:* Winston Sharples; *ph:* Leonard McCormick; *prod mgr:* Sam Buchwald; *col:* Pola. *sd:* RCA. 7 min. • The stork explains mass production methods at the Baby Factory.

6170. Stork Naked (*Merrie Melodies*) 26 Feb. 1955; *p.c.:* WB; *dir:* I. Freleng; *story:* Warren Foster; *anim:* Arthur Davis, Virgil Ross, Manuel Perez; *lay:* Hawley Pratt; *back:* Irv Wyner; *ed:* Treg Brown; *voices:* Mel Blanc; *mus:* Milt Franklyn; *prod mgr:* John W. Burton; *prod:* Edward Selzer; *col:* Tech. *sd:* Vit. 7 min. • Daffy attempts to prevent the stork from delivering a further bundle of joy to his home.

6171. Stork Raving Mad (*Noveltoon*) 3 Oct. 1958; *p.c.:* Para Cartoons; *dir:* Seymour Kneitel; *story:* Carl Meyer; *anim:* Nick Tafuri, Wm. B. Pattengill; *sets:* Robert Owen; *voices:* Jack Mercer, Gwen Davies, Jackson Beck; *mus:* Winston Sharples; *ph:* Leonard McCormick; *prod mgr:* Abe Goodman; *col:* Tech. *sd:* RCA. 6 min. • Simon Stork is assigned to deliver a baby by seven o'clock but the kid wants to see a bit of life first.

6172. The Stork Takes a Holiday (*Color Rhapsody*) 11 June 1937; *p.c.:* Charles Mintz prods for Colum; *story:* Ben Harrison; *anim:* Manny Gould; *lay:* Clark Watson; *back:* Phil Davis; *mus:* Joe de Nat; *prod mgr:* James Bronis; *col:* Tech. *sd:* RCA. 7½ min. • The storks go on strike and pelicans take over.

6173. The Stork's Holiday 23 Oct. 1943; *p.c.*: MGM; *dir*: George Gordon; *story*: Otto Englander, Webb Smith; *anim*: Michael Lah, Rudy Zamora, Carl Urbano, Don Williams, Al Grandmain; *voices*: Danny Webb; *mus*: Scott Bradley; *prod*: Fred Quimby; *col*: Tech. *sd*: WE. 7¹/₂ min. • The war's dislocation of industry spreads to the baby market and John Stork, after having had a nasty experience with enemy planes, decides to go on strike.

6174. The Stork's Mistake (*Aesop's Film Fable*) 12 May 1923; *p.c.*: Fables Pictures Inc for Pathé; *dir*: Paul Terry; b&w. sil. 5 min. • A puppy is mistakenly deposited in a family of kittens by the stork.

6175. The Stork's Mistake (*Terry-Toon*) 26 May 1942; *p.c.*: TT for Fox; *dir*: Eddie Donnelly; *story*: John Foster; *mus*: Philip A. Scheib; *col*: Tech. *sd*: RCA. 7 min. • The stork delivers a baby skunk to a family of rabbits by mistake. He is considered an outcast until he saves his family from a pack of hounds.

6176. The Storm (*Out of the Inkwell*) 21 Mar. 1925; *p.c.*: Inkwell Studio for Red Seal; *dir*: Dave Fleischer; *anim/l/a*: Max Fleischer; b&w. sil. 7 min. *l/a/anim.* • Ko-Ko decides to exercise the baby during a severe storm that seperates him from the child.

6177. Stormy Seas (*Flip the Frog*) 22 Aug. 1931; *p.c.*: Celebrity for MGM; *prod/dir*: Ub Iwerks; b&w. sd: PCP. 8 min. • Flip rides a storm at sea and rescues a girl from a sinking vessel.

6178. The Story of a Mosquito 1912; *p.c.*: Vit Film Corp; *anim/l/a*: Winsor McCay; b&w. sil. 5¹/₂ min. *l/a/anim.* • A mosquito zeroes in on a sleeping man and sucks enough blood for the insect to inflate and explode. McCay's second film. The live-action segment also features McCay's daughter. aka: *How a Mosquito Operates; Winsor McCay and His Jersey Skeeters.*

6179. The Story of a Rose 1936; *p.c.*: Duworld; col. sd. 9 min. *l/a/anim.* • Grandfather tells a bedtime story of how a shepherd loved a princess. The gnomes give him enough courage to send her a beautiful rose. A concoction of live action players, puppet animation (gnomes) and cell animation.

6180. The Story of Anyburg, U.S.A. 19 June 1957; *p.c.*: Walt Disney prods for BV; *dir*: Clyde Geronimi; *asst dir*: George Probert; *story*: Dick Huemer; *anim*: John Sibley, Bob Carlson, George Kreisl, Henry Tanous; *fx*: Dan MacManus; *lay*: Basil Davidovich, Tom Codrick, Erni Nordli; *back*: Ralph Hulett, Donald Peters; *voices*: Bill Thompson, Hans Conried, Dal McKennon, Thurl Ravenscroft; *mus*: Joseph S. Dubin; *col*: Tech. *sd*: RCA. 10 min. • In the town of Anyburg, the cars are put on trial for reckless driving but, so it turns out, the drivers are responsible and not the automobiles.

6181. The Story of George Washington (*Noveltoon*) Feb. 1965; *p.c.*: Para Cartoons; *sup*: Howard Post; *dir/story*: Jack Mendelsohn; *anim*: Al Eugster; *sets*: Robert Little; *voices*: Bob MacFadden; *mus*: Winston Sharples; *ph*: Leonard McCormick; *prod mgr*: Abe Goodman; *col*: Tech. *sd*: RCA. 6 min. • The story of George Washington as seen through the eyes of a small boy.

6182. Stowaway Woody (*Woody Woodpecker*) 5 Mar. 1963; *p.c.*: Walter Lantz prods for Univ; *dir*: Sid Marcus; *story*: Al Bertino, Dick Kinney; *anim*: Ray Abrams, Roy Jenkins, Art Davis; *sets*: Art Landy, Ray Huffine; *voices*: Paul Frees, Grace Stafford; *mus*: Clarence Wheeler; *prod mgr*: William E. Garity; *col*: Tech. *sd*: RCA. 6 min. • Woody stows away on a luxury liner, spending most of the time avoiding the captain and his tracker dog.

6183. The Stowaways (*Heckle & Jeckle*) Apr. 1949; *p.c.*: TT for Fox; *dir*: Connie Rasinski; *story*: John Foster; *voices*: Thomas Morrison; *mus*: Philip A. Scheib; *ph*: Douglas Moye; *col*: Tech. *sd*: RCA. 6¹/₂ min. • Our intrepid heroes stow away on an air liner bound for Africa and create havoc.

6184. Straight Shooters (*Donald Duck*) 18 Apr. 1947; *p.c.*: Walt Disney prods for RKO; *dir*: Jack Hannah; *asst dir*: Toby Tobelman; *story*: MacDonald MacPherson, Jack Huber, Carl Barks; *anim*: William Justice, Judge Whitaker, Volus Jones, Fred Jones, Al Bertino, Al Coe, Harvey Toombs; *fx*: Andy Engman; *lay*: Yale Gracey; *back*: Thelma Witmer; *voices*: Clarence Nash, Billy Bletcher; *mus*: Oliver Wallace; *col*: Tech. *sd*: RCA. 7 min. • Shooting gallery barker, Donald, awards his nephews a tiny box of candy for their shooting prowess. They get their revenge by dressing as a beautiful girl to con him out of a large box of candy.

6185. Straight Talk 3 April 1992; *p.c.*: Sandollar Prods,/Hollywood

Pictures Co., for BV; *title des*: Wayne Fitzgerald; *opticals*: Buena Vista Opticals; Panavision. col: Tech. sd: Dolby stereo. 91 min. • Live-action comedy about a dance instructor who gets mistaken for a radio psychologist. The titles consist of animated dance class footprints.

6186. Strange Companion (*Hashimoto*) Apr. 1961; *p.c.*: TT for Fox; *ex prod*: Bill Weiss; *dir*: Mannie Davis; *story sup*: Tom Morrison; *story*: Bob Kuwahara; *anim*: Eddie Donnelly, Armando Guidi; *sets*: Bill Focht, John Zago; *voices*: John Myhers; *mus*: Phil Scheib; *prod mgr*: Frank Schudde; *col*: DeLuxe. *sd*: RCA. 6 min. CS. • A mouse befriends what grows into a huge dragon who inadvertently wrecks the village. Banished to the hills, the dragon later saves the townsfolk from an erupting volcano.

6187. Strange on the Range (*Hoot Kloot*) 17 Apr. 1974; *p.c.*: Mirisch/DFE for UA; *dir*: Durward Bonaye; *story*: John W. Dunn; *anim*: Richard Rudler, Tim Miller, John Ward; *lay*: Don Roy; *back*: Richard Reuben; *ed*: Rick Steward; *voices*: Bob Holt; *mus*: Doug Goodwin; *titles*: Arthur Leonardi; *ph*: John Burton Jr.; *prod mgr*: Lee Gunther; *col*: DeLuxe. *sd*: RCA. 6 min. • Billy the Kidder escapes from jail and Kloot sets out to recapture him.

6188. The Stranger Rides Again (*Terry-Toon*) 4 Nov. 1938; *p.c.*: TT for Fox; *dir*: Mannie Davis; *mus*: Philip A. Scheib; b&w. *sd*: RCA. 7 min. • The Lone Stranger and his Indian companion attempt to capture the western bandit, Bad Bill Bunion.

6189. Strangled Eggs (*Merrie Melodies*) Mar. 1961; *p.c.*: WB; *dir*: Robert McKimson; *story*: Tedd Pierce; *anim*: George Grandpré, Ted Bonnicksen, Warren Batchelder, Tom Ray; *lay*: Robert Gribbroek; *back*: Bob Singer; *ed*: Treg Brown; *voices*: Mel Blanc, Merrie Virginia; *mus*: Milt Franklyn; *prod mgr*: William Orcutt; *prod*: David H. DePatie; *col*: Tech. *sd*: Vit. 7 min. • Foggy plights his troth with Miss Prissy at the same time a foundling chick arrives on her doorstep. To prove his worth, he looks after the lad, soon discovering it to be a chicken hawk.

6190. Stratos-Fear (*Willie Whopper*) 13 Dec. 1933; *p.c.*: Celebrity prods for MGM; *prod/dir*: Ub Iwerks; *voice*: Benny Rubin; *mus*: Art Turkisher; b&w. *sd*: PCP. 7 min. • While having a tooth pulled, Willie gets inflated with helium and floats to a distant planet where the inhabitants experiment on him.

6191. The Streamlined Donkey (*Fable*) 17 Jan. 1941; *p.c.*: Colum; *story*: Art Davis; *anim*: Sid Marcus; *lay*: Clark Watson; *ed*: Edward Moore; *voices*: John Wald, Mel Blanc; *mus*: Joe de Nat; *prod mgr*: George Winkler; b&w. *sd*: RCA. 6 min. • Mama donkey warns her exuberant son against letting the people discover he can race.

6192. Streamlined Greta Green (*Merrie Melodies*) 19 June 1937; *p.c.*: Leon Schlesinger prods for WB; *dir*: I. Freleng; *anim*: Cal Dalton, Ken Harris; *lay*: Griff Jay; *back*: Arthur Loomer; *ed*: Tregoweth E. Brown; *voices*: Bernice Hansel, Mel Blanc, The Basin Street Boys; *mus*: Carl W. Stalling; *song*: Fred Rose, T. Berwick; *prod sup*: Henry Binder, Raymond G. Katz; *col*: Tech. *sd*: Vit. 8 min. • Junior car is warned by Mama to keep away from the traffic and the railway. He doesn't heed these wise words and subsequently ends up in the garage undergoing surgery.

6193. A Streetcat Named Sylvester (*Looney Tunes*) 5 Sept. 1953; *p.c.*: WB; *dir*: I. Freleng; *story*: Warren Foster; *anim*: Virgil Ross, Arthur Davis, Manuel Perez, Gerry Chiniquy; *lay*: Hawley Pratt; *back*: Irv Wyner; *ed*: Treg Brown; *voices*: Mel Blanc, Bea Benaderet; *mus*: Carl Stalling; *prod mgr*: John W. Burton; *prod*: Edward Selzer; *col*: Tech. *sd*: Vit. 7 min. • Tweety takes refuge from the snow in a house containing Sylvester the cat. He tries to keep the bird from Granny's sight and also has to contend with a sick bulldog.

6194. The Stretcher (*Mighty Heroes*) Apr. 1969 (made in 1966); *p.c.*: TT for Fox; *ex prod*: Bill Weiss; *dir/anim*: Ralph Bakshi; *voices*: Lionel Wilson, Herschel Bernardi; *mus*: Jim Timmens; *col*: DeLuxe. *sd*: RCA. 5 min. • The Mighty Heroes put a stop to the Stretcher, a villain who collects the world's rubber supplies.

6195. Strife with Father (*Merrie Melodies*) 1 Apr. 1950 (© 1948); *p.c.*: WB; *dir*: Robert McKimson; *story*: Warren Foster; *anim*: Emery Hawkins, Charles McKimson, Phil de Lara, Rod Scribner, J.C. Melendez; *lay*: Cornett Wood; *back*: Richard H. Thomas; *ed*: Treg Brown; *voices*: Mel Blanc, Ben Frommer, Bea Benaderet; *mus*: Carl Stalling; *prod mgr*: John W. Burton; *prod*: Edward Selzer; *col*: Tech. *sd*: Vit. 7 min. • Mr. and Mrs.

English Sparrow find themselves the unfortunate parents of Beaky Buzzard. It's up to Monty Sparrow to teach him the fundaments of being a sparrow.

6196. Strike Up the Band (*Screen Songs*) 27 Sept. 1930; *p.c.:* The Fleischer Studio for Para; *prod:* Max Fleischer; *dir:* Dave Fleischer; *anim:* Al Eugster; *mus:* Art Turkisher; *song:* Charles E. Ward, Harry von Tilzer; b&w. *sd:* WE. 7 min. • Bimbo and another are sailors aboard a ship whose chief worry is the others taking all the food.

6197. String Along in Pink (*Pink Panther*) 1968; *p.c.:* Mirisch/Geoffrey/DFE for UA; *dir:* Gerry Chiniquy; *story:* Tony Benedict; *anim:* Norman McCabe, Bob Bransford, Art Vitello, Malcolm Draper; *lay:* Martin Strudler; *back:* Richard H. Thomas; *ed:* Robert Gillis; *theme tune:* Henry Mancini; *ph:* Gary Gunther; *prod mgr:* Lee Gunther; *col:* DeLuxe. *sd:* RCA. 6 min. • The Panther follows a seemingly endless trail of string.

6198. String Bean Jack (*Terry-Toon*) 26 Aug. 1938; *p.c.:* TT for Fox; *dir:* John Foster; *mus:* Philip A. Scheib; *col:* Tech. *sd:* RCA. 7 min. • Jack climbs a giant beanstalk, does battle with a two-headed ogre and rescues the hen that lays the golden eggs. Caricatures of W.C. Fields and Zasu Pitts. • Paul Terry's first in Technicolor.

6199. Stripes and Stars (*Oswald*) 19 Apr. 1929; *p.c.:* Univ; *anim:* Walt Lantz; *mus:* The Universal Orchestra; b&w. *sd:* WE. 6 min. • Oswald is a porter in a police station when the Police Captain promotes him to Special Officer after Putrid Pete puts all the cops out of action.

6200. Strolling Thru the Park (*Screen Song*) 4 Nov. 1949; *p.c.:* Famous for Para; *dir:* Seymour Kneitel; *story:* I. Klein; *anim:* Myron Waldman, Larry Silverman; *sets:* Robert Little; *voices:* Jack Mercer, Cecil Roy, Sid Raymond; *mus:* Winston Sharples; *ph:* Leonard Mc Cormick; *prod mgr:* Sam Buchwald; *col:* Tech. *sd:* RCA. 8 min. • A Sunday outing in the park in 1890. Caricatures of Abbott and Costello and the four Marx Brothers.

6201. Strong to the Finich (*Popeye*) 29 June 1934; *p.c.:* The Fleischer Studio for Para; *prod:* Max Fleischer; *dir:* Dave Fleischer; *anim:* Seymour Kneitel, Roland Crandall; *voices:* William A. Costello; *mus:* Sammy Timberg; b&w. *sd:* WE 7 min. • Olive Oyl runs a health farm for kids but can't get them to eat spinach. Popeye arrives and demonstrates the benefits of the vegetable.

6202. The Strongest Man in the World 6 Feb. 1975; *p.c.:* Walt Disney prods for BV; *title anim:* Art Stevens, Guy Deel; *prod:* Bill Anderson; *mus:* Robert F. Brunner; *orch:* Walter Sheets; *col:* Tech. *sd:* RCA. 3 min. • Animated titles for a live-action feature involving a super-strong child.

6203. Stuart Little 1999; *p.c.:* Colum TriStar Films; *special visual fx: Sony Pictures Imageworks Inc Visual Effect sup:* Jerome Chen; *snr visual fx prod:* Michelle Murdocca; *visual fx art dir:* Martin A. Kline; *creative/visual development:* Thor Freudenthal; *visual fx ex prod:* Debbie Denise; *visual fx prod:* Lydia Bottegoni; *visual fx asso prod:* Audrea Topps-Harjo; *visual fx digital prod mgr:* Jody Echegaray; *cg anim sup:* Henry F. Anderson III; *cg sup:* Jim Berney; *lead cg character anim:* Eric Armstrong, Bart Giovanetti, Jay K. Redd, Scott Stokdyk, Anthony LaMolinara, John Clark Matthews; *cg character anim:* Stephen Baker, Dominick Cercere, Bill Diaz, Paul W. Jessel, Kelvin Lee, Jeff Lin, Jim Moorhead, Sean P. Mullen, Mike Murphy, Dave Mullins, Todd Pilger, Neil Richmond, David Schaub, Alexander E. Sokoloff, Vladimir Todorov, Delio Tramontozzi, Pepé Valencia, David B. Vallone, Todd Wilderman; *addit cg character anim:* Brad Booker, Jason McDade, Tom Roth, Henry Sato Jr.; *Cat visual fx: Rhythm & Hues, Inc. Visual fx sup:* Bill Westenhofer; *cg anim sup:* Erik de Boer; *cg anim:* Ethan Marak, William R. Wright, Jason Ivimey, Mike Stevens, Julius Yang, Hunter Athey, Kevin Bertazzon, Danny Speck, Spyros Tsiounis, Roberto Smith, Dana O'Connor, Davey Crockett Feiten, Raymond Liu; *Centropolis Effects, LLC Visual fx prod:* Robin Griffin; *lead cg character anim:* Benedikt Niemann; *cg character anim:* Steve Harwood, Jordan Harris, Scott Holmes; *cg sup:* Bret St.Clair; *voices: Stuart Little:* Michael J. Fox; *Snowbell:* Nathan Lane; *Smokey:* Chazz Palimpiteri; *Monty:* Steve Zahn; *Lucky:* Jim Doughan; *Red:* David Alan Grier; *Mr. Stout:* Bruno Kirby; *Mrs. Stout:* Jennifer Tilly; *Race Announcer:* Stan Freberg; *col:* CFI/DeLuxe. *sd:* Dolby digital/dts/SDDS. 86½ min. *l/a/anim. Academy Award nomination.* • Live-action comedy based on the book by E.B. White. When Mr. and Mrs. Little go to an orphanage to adopt a brother for their only child, George, they come away with a talking (animated) mouse named Stuart. Although George bonds with Stuart, Snowbell, the family cat plots to get rid of him.

6204. The Stubborn Cowboy (*Fractured Fable*) Oct. 1967; *p.c.:* Para Cartoons: *ex prod/story:* Shamus Culhane; *dir:* Chuck Harriton; *anim:* Al Eugster; *sets:* Gil Miret; *mus:* Winston Sharples; *prod sup:* Harold Robins, Burt Hanft; *col:* Tech. *sd:* RCA. 6 min. • A TV western is related through the eyes of a child ... complete with commercials.

6205. The Stubborn Mule (*Li'l Eightball*) 3 July 1939; *p.c.:* Walter Lantz prods for Univ; *dir:* Burt Gillett; *sets:* Edgar Keichle; *voices:* Mel Blanc, Danny Webb; *mus:* Frank Marsales; *col:* Tech-2. *sd:* WE. 7 min. • Li'l Eightball attempts to move a stubborn mule by using fire, hypnotism and brute force. The animal remains unmoved until struck by lightning.

6206. Stuck on You! Jan. 1983; *p.c.:* Quest Co.,/Troma, Inc. for Premier; *anim/title des:* John Paratore; *col. sd.* 82 min. *l/a.* • Live-action comedy: A fallen angel becomes a New Jersey judge who sorts out a palimony suit which is brought to a higher court in heaven.

6207. The Stuck-Up Wolf (*Fractured Fable*) Sept. 1967; *p.c.:* Para Cartoons, *ex prod/story:* Shamus Culhane; *dir:* Chuck Harriton; *anim:* Al Eugster; *sets:* Cliff Roberts, Gil Miret; *mus:* Winston Sharples; *prod sup:* Harold Robins, Burt Hanft; *col:* Tech. *sd:* RCA. 6 min. • A little boy relates "Little Red Riding Hood" and how the wolf got captured by means of bubble gum.

6208. Stunt Men (*Heckle & Jeckle*) 23 Nov. 1960; *p.c.:* TT for Fox; *ex prod:* Bill Weiss; *dir:* Martin Taras; *story sup:* Tom Morrison; *story:* George Atkins; *anim:* Johnny Gent, Dick Hall, Cosmo Anzilotti; *lay:* John Zago; *back:* Bill Hilliker; *voices:* Roy Halee; *mus:* Phil Scheib; *prod mgr:* Frank Schudde; *col:* DeLuxe. *sd:* RCA. 6 min. • The magpies get a job as stunt men for western star, Flint Lock. They proceed to sabotage him in front of the cameras.

6209. The Stupid Cupid (*Looney Tunes*) 25 Nov. 1944; *p.c.:* WB; *dir:* Frank Tashlin; *story:* Warren Foster; *anim:* Art Davis; *back:* Richard H. Thomas; *ed:* Treg Brown; *voices:* Mel Blanc, Frank Graham; *mus:* Carl W. Stalling; *prod mgr:* John W. Burton; *prod:* Edward Selzer; *col:* Tech. *sd:* Vit. 7 min. • Cupid (Elmer Fudd) sends Daffy into an affair with a married chicken.

6210. The Stupids 30 Aug. 1995; *p.c.:* Savoy Pictures for New Line Prods, Inc.; *stop-motion anim: Chiodo Brothers Productions: prod:* Charles Chiodo, Stephen Chiodo, Edward Chiodo; *ph:* Jene Omens; *anim:* Kent Burton, Joel Fletcher, Don Waller; *anim: Available Light Design: sup:* John van Vliet; *fx prod:* Katherine Kean; *anim:* January Nordman, Chris Bowers; *col. sd:* Dolby stereo. 94 min. *l/a.* • Live-action comedy: When Stanley Stupid sets out to find his missing garbage, he accidentally witnesses a secret arms deal between U.S. Army officers and terrorists. Digitally animated cats and dogs.

6211. The Stupidstitious Cat (*Noveltoon*) 25 Apr. 1947; *p.c.:* Famous for Para; *dir:* Seymour Kneitel; *story:* Carl Meyer, Jack Ward; *anim:* Graham Place, John Walworth; *sets:* Anton Loeb; *voices:* Jackson Beck; *mus:* Winston Sharples; *ph:* Leonard McCormick; *prod mgr:* Sam buchwald; *col:* Tech. *sd:* RCA. 6 min. • Buzzy the crow is captured by a superstitious cat but gets his revenge by spreading bad luck in the feline's path.

6212. The Stupor Salesman (*Looney Tunes*) 20 Nov. 1948; *p.c.:* WB; *dir:* Arthur Davis; *story:* Lloyd Turner, William Scott; *anim:* J.C. Melendez, Don Williams, Emery Hawkins, Basil Davidovich; *lay:* Don Smith; *back:* Philip de Guard; *ed:* Treg Brown; *voices:* Mel Blanc; *mus:* Carl Stalling; *prod mgr:* John W. Burton; *prod:* Edward Selzer; *col:* Tech. *sd:* Vit. 7 min. • Travelling salesman Daffy attempts to sell his wares to a bank robber on the lam.

6213. Stuporduck (*Looney Tunes*) 7 July 1956; *p.c.:* WB; *dir:* Robert McKimson; *story:* Tedd Pierce; *anim:* Ted Bonnicksen, George Grandpré, Russ Dyson, Keith Darling; *fx:* Harry Love; *lay:* Robert Gribbroek; *back:* Richard H. Thomas; *ed:* Treg Brown; *voices:* Mel Blanc, Daws Butler; *mus:* Carl Stalling; *prod mgr:* John W. Burton; *prod:* Edward Selzer; *col:* Tech. *sd:* Vit. 7 min. • When danger rears its ugly head, mild mannered reporter, Cluck Trent (Daffy Duck) becomes super hero, Stuporduck, who tries to prevent Aardvark Ratnick from destroying the world.

6214. Subway Sally (*Aesop's Film Fable*) 24 July 1927; *p.c.:* Fables Pictures Inc for Pathé; *dir:* Paul Terry; b&w. *sil.* 10 min. • Farmer Al Falfa flirts with a charmer he is later informed to be a notorious gold-digger.

6215. Sudden Fried Chicken (*Noveltoon*) 18 Oct. 1946; *p.c.:* Famous for Para; *dir:* Bill Tytla; *story:* Carl Meyer, Jack Ward; *anim:* Orestes Calpini, Otto Feuer; *character des:* Bill Hudson; *sets:* Anton Loeb; *voices:* Arnold Stang, Jack Mercer; *mus:* Winston Sharples; *ph:* Leonard McCormick; *prod mgr:* Sam Buchwald; *col:* Tech. *sd:* RCA. 7 min. • Herman the mouse teams Henpecked Hector with One-Round Hogan in a boxing match.

6216. Suddenly It's Spring! (*Noveltoon*) 28 Apr. 1944; *p.c.:* Famous for Para; *dir:* Seymour Kneitel; *anim:* Otto Feuer, Orestes Calpini; *voices:* Joy Terry, Cecil Roy, Jack Mercer; *mus:* Winston Sharples; *song:* Mack David; *ph:* Leonard McCormick; *prod mgr:* Sam Buchwald; *col:* Tech. *sd:* RCA. 10 min. • Raggedy Ann tries to get Mr. Sun shining on a cold day to make a little girl well. She visits the sun on the end of a kite and thaws Mr. Zero.

6217. Sufferin' Cats! (*Tom & Jerry*) 16 Jan. 1943; *p.c.:* MGM; *dir:* William Hanna, Joseph Barbera; *anim:* Kenneth Muse, George Gordon, Peter Burness, Jack Zander; *lay:* Harvey Eisenberg; *ed:* Fred MacAlpine; *voices:* Harry E. Lang; *mus:* Scott Bradley; *prod:* Fred Quimby; *col:* Tech. *sd:* WE. 7 min. • Tom has trouble with another alley cat who wants to eat Jerry.

6218. Sufferin' Cats (*Woody Woodpecker*) 30 May 1961; *p.c.:* Walter Lantz prods for Univ; *dir:* Paul J. Smith; *story:* Homer Brightman; *anim:* Les Kline, Ray Abrams; *sets:* Ray Huffine, Art Landy; *voices:* Dal McKennon, Grace Stafford; *mus:* Clarence Wheeler; *col:* Tech. *sd:* RCA. 6 min. • A fast, efficient cat named "the Blue Streak" is brought in to replace an old, slow cat in order to catch the troublesome woodpecker.

6219. Sugar and Spies (*Looney Tunes*) 5 Nov. 1966; *p.c.:* DFE for WB; *dir:* Robert McKimson; *story:* Tom Dagenais; *anim:* Bob Matz, Manny Perez, Warren Batchelder, Dale Case, Ted Bonnicksen; *lay:* Dick Ung; *back:* Tom O'Loughlin; *ed:* Lee Gunther; *prod mgr:* William Orcutt; *col:* Tech. *sd:* Vit. 6 min. • The Coyote finds an abandoned spy outfit and attempts to snare the Road-Runner with various secret agent devices.

6220. The Suicide Sheik (*Oswald*) 13 Feb. 1929; *p.c.:* Winkler for Univ; *prod:* Charles B. Mintz; *anim:* Hugh Harman; b&w. *sd:* WE. 6 min. • The unsuccessful endeavors of Oswald to commit suicide.

6221. Suited to a T 21 Feb. 193i; *p.c.:* The Fleischer Studio for India Tea; *prod:* Max Fleischer; *dir:* Dave Fleischer; b&w. *sd:* WE. • Commercial for India Tea.

6222. Sullivan, Pat, Studio (1925–1929) *dir/anim:* Otto Messmer; *anim:* Raoul Barré, Burton F. Gillett, William C. Nolan, Dana Parker, George Stallings, Hal Walker, Ron Zalme; *i&p:* Charles Byrne, George Cannata, Jack Carr, Bill Donnelly, "Doc"Ellison, Alfred Eugster, Sid Garber, Eddie Salter, Ron Zalme, Rudy Zamora; *ph:* Alfred Thurber; *comic strip:* Otto Messmer, Jack Bogle.

6223. Sultan Pepper (*Little King*) 16 Mar. 1934; *p.c.:* Van Beuren for RKO; *dir:* George Stallings; *anim:* Jim Tyer; b&w. *sd:* RCA. 6 min. • When the Little King finally manages to get to the Sultan's harem, he finds himself in bed with the Sultan by error.

6224. The Sultan's Birthday (*Mighty Moose*) 15 Oct. 1944; *p.c.:* TT for Fox; *dir:* Bill Tytla; *story:* John Foster; *voice:* Thomas Morrison; *mus:* Philip A. Scheib; *ph:* Douglas Moye; *col:* Tech. *sd:* RCA. 6 min. • The Sultan of Bagdad's kingdom is attacked by neighboring cats on flying carpets. Mighty Mouse is soon on hand to sort things out.

6225. The Sultan's Cat (*Paul Terry-Toon*) 17 May 1931; *p.c.:* Terry, Moser & Coffman for Educational/Fox; *dir:* Frank Moser, Paul Terry; *anim:* Sarka, Vladimir Tytla; *mus:* Philip A. Scheib; b&w. *sd:* WE. 6 min. • The Sultan drowns his cat in the well and is haunted by a nightmare with cats, skeletons and dancing mummies.

6226. Summer (*Silly Symphony*) 4 Jan. 1930; *p.c.:* Walt Disney prods for Colum; *dir/anim:* Ub Iwerks; *inbet:* Floyd Gottfredson; *mus:* Carl W. Stalling; *prod mgr:* William Cottrell; b&w. *sd:* PCP. 7 min. • A summer fantasy with insects, flowers and fruits.

6227. Summer Harmonies (*Song Cartoon*) 5 Oct. 1930; *p.c.:* Biophone; *anim:* B.M. Powell; b&w. *sd.* • Sing-along cartoon. No story available.

6228. Summer Time (*Paul Terry-Toon*) 13 Dec. 1931; *p.c.:* Terry, Moser & Coffman for Educational/Fox; *dir:* Frank Moser, Paul Terry; *mus:* Philip

A. Scheib; b&w. *sd:* WE. 5½ min. • Farmer Al Falfa's cooling-off methods in the hot weather are ridiculed by the mice. He chases them with a gun then has a goat turn on him.

6229. Summertime (*Aesop's Sound Fable*) 11 Oct. 1929; *p.c.:* Van Beuren for Pathé; *dir:* John Foster; *mus:* Carl Edouarde; b&w. *sd:* RCA. 6 min. • No story available.

6230. Summertime (*ComiColor*) 29 May 1935; *p.c.:* Celebrity prods; *prod/dir:* Ub Iwerks; *mus:* Carl W. Stalling; *col:* Ciné; *sd:* PCP. 8 min. • Jack Frost is chased away and Pan comes out to play with the animals. The centaurs' game of polo is broken up when Jack Frost returns.

6231. A Sunbonnet Blue (*Merrie Melodies*) 21 Aug. 1937; *p.c.:* Leon Schlesinger prods for WB; *dir:* Fred Avery; *story:* Robert Clampett; *anim:* Sid Sutherland, Virgil Ross, Irven Spence, Robert Clampett; *lay:* Griff Jay; *back:* Arthur Loomer; *ed:* Tregoweth E. Brown; *voices:* Bernice Hansel, Tommy Bond, Mel Blanc, Fred Avery, the Sportsmen Quartet; *mus:* Carl W. Stalling; *song:* Bert Kalmar, Harry Ruby; *prod sup:* Henry Binder, Raymond G. Katz; *col:* Tech. *sd:* Vit. 7 min. • Two mice live in harmony in a hat shop until a rat kidnaps the girl. The boy vanquishes the villain, rescues and marries the girl.

6232. Sunday Clothes (*Scrappy*) 15 Sept. 1931; *p.c.:* Winkler for Colum; *prod:* Charles Mintz; *story:* Dick Huemor; *anim:* Sid Marcus; *mus:* Joe de Nat; *prod mgr:* James Bronis; b&w. *sd:* WE. 6 min. • Scrappy dons his Sunday clothes for church and has a task in keeping clean when rousted by the local bullies.

6233. Sunday Go to Meetin' Time (*Merrie Melodies*) 8 Aug. 1936; *p.c.:* Leon Schlesinger prods for WB; *dir:* I. Freleng; *anim:* Bob McKimson, Paul Smith; *voices:* Kenneth Spencer; *mus:* Norman Spencer; *prod sup:* Henry Binder, Raymond G. Katz; *col:* Tech. *sd:* Vit. 7 min. • Nicodemus sneaks out of church to steal chickens. He is knocked unconscious and finds himself on trial in the Court of Hades.

6234. Sunday on the Farm (*Aesop's Film Fable*) 16 Aug. 1928; *p.c.:* Fables Pictures Inc for Pathé; *dir:* Paul Terry, John Foster; b&w. *sil.* 10 min. • No story available.

6235. Sunny Italy (*Aesop's Film Fable*) 26 July 1928; *p.c.:* Fables Pictures Inc for Pathé; *dir:* Paul Terry, Mannie Davis; b&w. *sil.* 10 min. • Maria Mouse is abducted while cruising in a gondola with Antonio Mouse. He pursues the kidnapper to his lair on a seahorse and rescues his girl.

6236. Sunny Italy (*Mighty Mouse*) Mar. 1951; *p.c.:* TT for Fox; *dir:* Connie Rasinski; *story:* Tom Morrison; *voices:* Roy Halee, Tom Morrison; *anim:* Jim Tyer; *mus:* Philip A. Scheib; *ph:* Douglas Moye; *col:* Tech. *sd:* RCA. 7 min. • Oil Can Harry captures Pearl Pureheart and our hero chases them to Venice.

6237. Sunny South (*Oswald*) 23 Mar. 1931; *p.c.:* Univ; *dir:* Walter Lantz, "Bill" Nolan; *anim:* Clyde Geronimi, Manuel Moreno, Ray Abrams, Fred Avery, Lester Kline, Chet Karrberg, "Pinto" Colvig; *voice:* Mickey Rooney; *mus:* James Dietrich; b&w. *sd:* WE. 7 min. • Oswald is a train driver who arrives in Dixie-Land and performs a "Cake Walk" with Kitty.

6238. The Sunny South (*Paul Terry-Toon*) 29 Dec. 1933; *p.c.:* Moser & Terry for Educational/Fox; *dir:* Frank Moser, Paul Terry; *mus:* Philip A. Scheib; b&w. *sd:* WE. 5½ min. • Southern music, cotton fields and Simon le Gree are the main ingredients here.

6239. The Sunshine Makers (*Rainbow Parade*) 11 Jan. 1935; *p.c.:* Van Beuren for Borden's/RKO; *dir:* Burt Gillett, Ted Eshbaugh; *anim:* I. Klein, Peter Burness, William Littlejohn, Jack Zander; *lay:* Robert Little; *back:* Art Bartsch, Eddi Bowlds; *mus:* Winston Sharples; *col:* Ciné. *sd:* RCA. 8 min. • T.E. Powers' brightly costumed "Joys" engage in battle with the blue "Glooms" using bottled sunshine as weapons.

6240. Super Mouse Rides Again (*Super Mouse*) 6 Aug. 1943; *p.c.:* TT for Fox; *dir:* Mannie Davis; *story:* John Foster; *mus:* Philip A. Scheib; *col:* Tech. *sd:* RCA. 6½ min. • Super Mouse is summonsed to ward off threatening cats. Reissued as *Mighty Mouse Rides Again.*

6241. Super Pink (*Pink Panther*) 12 Oct. 1966; *p.c.:* Mirisch/Geoffrey/DFE for UA; *dir:* Hawley Pratt; *story:* John W. Dunn; *anim:* La Verne Harding, Don Williams, Bob Matz, Warren Batchelder, John Gibbs; *lay:* Dick Ung; *back:* Tom O'Loughlin; *ed:* Lee Gunther; *mus:* Walter Greene; *theme tune:* Henry Mancini; *prod sup:* Harry Love, Bill Orcutt; *col:* DeLuxe.

sd: RCA. 6 min. • The Panther wreaks havoc while trying to be a "Super Hero."

6242. Super-Rabbit *(Merrie Melodies)* 3 Apr. 1943; *p.c.:* Leon Schlesinger prods for WB; *dir:* Charles M. Jones; *story:* Tedd Pierce; *anim:* Ken Harris; *lay:* Art Heinemann; *ed:* Treg Brown; *voices:* Mel Blanc, Kent Rogers, Tedd Pierce; *mus:* Carl W. Stalling; *ph:* John W. Burton; *prod sup:* Henry Binder, Raymond G. Katz; *col:* Tech. *sd:* Vit. 8 min. • A scientist feeds Bugs a specially treated carrot which turns him into a "Super Rabbit." He then goes on the trail of the notorious rabbit hater, Cottontail Smith.

6243. The Super Salesmen *(Heckle & Jeckle)* 24 Oct. 1947; *p.c.:* TT for Fox; *dir:* Eddie Donnelly; *story:* John Foster; *voices:* Thomas Morrison; *mus:* Philip A. Scheib; *ph:* Douglas Moye; *col:* Tech. *sd:* RCA. 6 min. • The magpies are chased by a policeman for selling hair tonic without a license.

6244. The Super Snooper *(Looney Tunes)* 1 Nov. 1952; *p.c.:* WB; *dir:* Robert McKimson; *story:* Tedd Pierce; *anim:* Herman Cohen, Rod Scribner, Phil de Lara, Charles McKimson; *lay:* Robert Givens; *back:* Richard H. Thomas; *ed:* Treg Brown; *voices:* Mel Blanc, Grace Lenard; *mus:* Carl Stalling; *prod mgr:* John W. Burton; *prod:* Edward Selzer; *col:* Tech. *sd:* Vit. 7 min. • Duck Drake, private eye (Daffy), is summonsed to investigate a murder. He encounters a glamorous dame who makes advances towards him.

6245. Superlulu *(Little Lulu)* 21 Nov. 1947 *p.c.:* Famous for Para: *dir:* Bill Tytla; *story:* Joe Stultz, Carl Meyer; *anim:* George Germanetti, Steve Muffatti, Bill Hudson; *sets:* Robert Connavale; *voices:* Cecil Roy, Jackson Beck; *mus:* Winston Sharples; *title song:* Buddy Kaye, Fred Wise, Sammy Timberg; *ph:* Leonard McCormick; *prod sup:* Sam Buchwald; *col:* Tech. *sd:* RCA. 7 min. • Daddy objects to Lulu reading "Superman" comics and gives her "Jack and the Beanstalk" to read. She dreams that she's Superlulu, rescuing Daddy from a giant.

6246. Superman 26 Sept. 1941; *p.c.:* The Fleischer Studio for Para; *prod:* Max Fleischer; *dir:* Dave Fleischer; *story:* Seymour Kneitel, I. Sparber; *anim:* Steve Muffatti, Frank Endres, Graham Place; *voices:* Clayton "Bud" Collyer, Joan Alexander, Jack Mercer, Frank Knight; *mus:* Sammy Timberg; *prod sup:* Sam Buchwald, I. Sparber; *col:* Tech. *sd:* WE. 10 min. *Academy Award nomination.* • A mad scientist threatens to destroy the city with his electrothanasia ray. Lois Lane investigates and is captured but Superman isn't too far away.

6247. Superman 1948. *p.c.:* Colum; *prod:* Sam Katzman; *based on Superman* and *Action* comics and the *Superman* radio program; *characters created by* Jerome Siegel, Joe Shuster; *special anim fx:* Howard Swift. b&w. *sd:* WE. 20 min. each • Live-action fifteen-episode serial with animated flying effects for the Man of Steel.

6248. Superman in Destruction, Inc. 25 Dec. 1942; *p.c.:* Famous for Para; *dir:* I. Sparber; *story:* Jay Morton; *anim:* Dave Tendlar, Tom Moore; *voices:* Michael Fitzmaurice, Ted Pierce, Joan Alexander, Jack Mercer; *mus:* Sammy Timberg; *ph:* Leonard McCormick; *prod mgr:* Sam Buchwald; *col:* Tech. *sd:* WE. 8½ min. • Lois Lane investigates a sabotage report at a munitions plant, is discovered and captured.

6249. Superman in Jungle Drums 5 Mar. 1943; *p.c.:* Famous for Para; *dir:* Dan Gordon; *story:* Robert Little, Jay Morton; *anim:* Orestes Calpini, H.C. Ellison; *sets:* Robert W. Little; *voices:* Michael Fitzmaurice, Joan Alexander, Jack Mercer; *mus:* Sammy Timberg *ph:* Leonard McCormick; *prod mgr:* Sam Buchwald; *col:* Tech. *sd:* WE. 8 min. • Lois Lane investigates a huge jungle idol that is being used to broadcast Nazi information. • Caricature of Adolf Hitler.

6250. Superman in Showdown 16 Oct. 1942; *p.c.:* Famous for Para; *dir:* I. Sparber; *story:* Jay Morton; *anim:* Steve Muffatti, Graham Place; *voices:* Michael Fitzmaurice, Joan Alexander, Jack Mercer, Ted Pierce, Carl Meyer; *mus:* Sammy Timberg; *ph:* Leonard McCormick; *prod mgr:* Sam Buchwald; *col:* Tech. *sd:* WE. 8 min. • A crook's henchman poses as Superman while perpetrating a crime and the real Superman has to correct matters.

6251. Superman in Terror on the Midway 28 Aug. 1942; *p.c.:* The Fleischer Studio for Para; *prod:* Max Fleischer; *dir:* Dave Fleischer; *story:* Jay Morton, Dan Gordon; *anim:* Orestes Calpini, Jim Davis; *sets:* Shane Miller; *voices:* Clayton "Bud" Collyer, Joan Alexander; *mus:* Sammy

Timberg; *prod sup:* Sam Buchwald, Isidore Sparber; *col:* Tech. *sd:* WE. 8 min. • A giant circus gorilla breaks loose and terrorizes the circus people. Superman is soon on hand to restrain the beast.

6252. Superman in the Arctic Giant 27 Feb. 1942; *p.c.:* The Fleischer Studio for Para; *prod:* Max Fleischer; *dir:* Dave Fleischer; *story:* Bill Turner, Ted Pierce; *anim:* Willard Bowsky, Reuben Grossman; *sets:* Shane Miller; *voices:* Clayton "Bud" Collyer, Joan Alexander, Frank Knight, Ted Pierce; *mus:* Sammy Timberg; *ph:* Charles Schettler; *prod sup:* Sam Buchwald, Isidore Sparber; *col:* Tech. *sd:* WE. 9 min. • A scientific expedition in Siberia discovers a frozen prehistoric monster which they bring back to civilization where it returns to life and menaces the city. The Man of Steel is on hand to save the townsfolk.

6253. Superman in the Billion Dollar Limited 9 Jan. 1942; *p.c.:* The Fleischer Studio for Para; *prod:* Max Fleischer; *dir:* Dave Fleischer; *story:* Seymour Kneitel, Isidore Sparber; *anim:* Myron Waldman, Frank Endres; *voices:* Clayton "Bud" Collyer, Joan Alexander; *mus:* Sammy Timberg; *ph:* Charles Schettler; *prod sup:* Sam Buchwald, Isidore Sparber; *col:* Tech. *sd:* WE. 8½ min. • Lois Lane is dispatched to cover a story of the world's largest shipment of gold. Superman is on hand to protect the train from disasters.

6254. Superman in the Bulleteers 27 Mar. 1942; *p.c.:* The Fleischer Studio for Para; *prod:* Max Fleischer; *dir:* Dave Fleischer; *story:* Bill Turner, Carl Meyer; *anim:* Orestes Calpini, Graham Place; *voices:* Clayton "Bud" Collyer, Joan Alexander; *mus:* Sammy Timberg; *ph:* Charles Schettler; *prod sup:* Sam Buchwald, Isidore Sparber; *col:* Tech. *sd:* WE. 9 min. • The city of Metropolis is threatened by an attack from a bullet-car that can fly. Its owners plan to rob the treasury.

6255. Superman in the Electronic Earthquake 5 June 1942; *p.c.:* The Fleischer Studio for Para; *prod:* Max Fleischer; *dir:* Dave Fleischer; *story:* Seymour Kneitel, Isidore Sparber; *anim:* Steve Muffatti, Arnold Gillespie; *voices:* Clayton "Bud" Collyer, Joan Alexander; *mus:* Sammy Timberg; *ph:* Charles Schettler; *prod sup:* Sam Buchwald, Isidore Sparber; *col:* Tech. *sd:* WE. 8 min. • An Indian tries to retrieve Manhattan Island by starting an electronic earthquake that will destroy the city.

6256. Superman in the Eleventh Hour 20 Nov. 1942; *p.c.:* Famous for Para; *dir:* Dan Gordon; *story:* Carl Meyer, William Turner; *anim:* Willard Bowsky, William Henning; *sets:* Robert W. Little; *voices:* Michael Fitzmaurice, Joan Alexander, Jack Mercer, Dan McCulloch; *mus:* Sammy Timberg; *ph:* Leonard McCormick; *prod sup:* Sam Buchwald, Isidore Sparber; *col:* Tech. *sd:* WE. 8 min. • Clark and Lois are held captive in Japan until Superman arrives to rescue Lois and sabotage the entire enemy fleet while he's doing so.

6257. Superman in the Japoteurs 18 Sept. 1942; *p.c.:* Famous for Para; *dir:* I. Sparber; *story:* Jay Morton; *anim:* Myron Waldman, Graham Place; *voices:* Michael Fitzmaurice, Joan Alexander, Jack Mercer; *mus:* Sammy Timberg; *ph:* Leonard McCormick; *prod sup:* Sam Buchwald; *col:* Tech. *sd:* WE. 8 min. • The world's largest bomber is captured by the enemy while on a test flight.

6258. Superman in the Magnetic Telescope 24 Apr. 1942; *p.c.:* The Fleischer Studio for Para; *prod:* Max Fleischer; *dir:* Dave Fleischer; *story:* Dan Gordon, Carl Meyer; *anim:* Myron Waldman, Thomas Moore; *sets:* Robert W. Little; *voices:* Clayton "Bud" Collyer, Joan Alexander; *mus:* Sammy Timberg; *ph:* Charles Schettler; *prod sup:* Sam Buchwald, Isidore Sparber; *col:* Tech. *sd:* WE. 9 min. • A scientist erects a giant telescope to attract planets from the sky. The magnetism runs amock, putting Metropolis in the path of a flaming planet heading towards the city.

6259. Superman in the Mechanical Monster 21 Nov. 1941; *p.c.:* The Fleischer Studio for Para; *prod:* Max Fleischer; *dir:* Dave Fleischer; *story:* Isidore Sparber, Seymour Kneitel; *anim:* Steve Muffatti, George Germanetti; *sets:* Marjorie Young; *voices:* Clayton "Bud" Collyer, Joan Alexander, Ted Pierce; *mus:* Sammy Timberg; *prod sup:* Sam Buchwald, Isidore Sparber; *col:* Tech. *sd:* WE. 8 min. • A jewel thief uses a mechanical bird to steal gems. Lois investigates and gets carried off to his lair with Superman not far behind.

6260. Superman in the Mummy Strikes 29 Jan. 1943; *p.c.:* Famous for Para; *dir:* Seymour Kneitel; *story:* Bill Turner, Carl Meyer; *anim:* Myron Waldman, Nicholas Tafuri; *sets:* Robert W. Little; *voices:* Michael Fitzmaurice, Joan Alexander, Frank Gallop; *mus:* Sammy Timberg; *ph:* Leonard McCormick; *prod sup:* Sam Buchwald; *col:* Tech. *sd:* WE. 7 min. • Jan Hogan, Dr. Jordan's secretary, is accused of murdering the famed archeologist while exploring the Tomb of King Tush. Clark Kent investigates, unearthing a murderous mummy.

6261. Superman in the Secret Agent 30 July 1943; *p.c.:* Famous for Para; *dir:* Seymour Kneitel; *story:* Carl Meyer; *anim:* Steve Muffatti, Otto Feuer; *voices:* Michael Fitzmaurice, Joan Alexander; *mus:* Sammy Timberg; *ph:* Leonard McCormick; *prod mgr:* Sam Buchwald; *col:* Tech. *sd:* WE. 7 min. • Superman aids a U.S. government agent in evading the Nazis while transporting valuable documents to Washington.

6262. Superman in the Underground World 21 May 1943; *p.c.:* Famous for Para; *dir:* Seymour Kneitel; *story:* Jay Morton; *anim:* Nicholas Tafuri, Reuben Grossman; *sets:* Robert W. Little; *voices:* Michael Fitzmaurice, Joan Alexander, Frank Gallop; *mus:* Sammy Timberg; *ph:* Leonard McCormick; *prod mgr:* Sam Buchwald; *col:* Tech. *sd:* WE. 8 min. • An explorer discovers an underground world with Lois and Clark. Lois is captured by bat-like creatures and Superman arrives to save her.

6263. Superman in Volcano 10 July 1942; *p.c.:* The Fleischer Studio for Para; *prod:* Max Fleischer; *dir:* Dave Fleischer; *story:* Bill Turner, Carl Meyer; *anim:* Willard Bowsky, Otto Feuer; *voices:* Clayton "Bud" Collyer, Joan Alexander, George Lowther; *mus:* Sammy Timberg; *ph:* Charles Schettler; *prod sup:* Sam Buchwald, Isidore Sparber; *col:* Tech. *sd:* WE. 8 min. • Clark and Lois investigate Mount Monokoa, a restless volcano, when it suddenly erupts.

6264. Supermarket Pink (*Pink Panther*) 1978; *p.c.:* Mirisch/Geoffrey/DFE for UA; *dir:* Brad Case; *story:* Cliff Roberts; *anim:* Warren Batchelder, Bob Richardson, Bob Kirk, Bill Hutten; *lay:* Martin Strudler; *back:* Richard H. Thomas; *ed:* Joe Siracusa; *theme tune:* Henry Mancini; *ph:* Ray Lee; *prod mgr:* Lee Gunther; *col:* DeLuxe. *sd:* RCA. 6 min. • The Panther causes chaos in the local supermarket while collecting provisions.

6265. Support Your Local Serpent (*Blue Racer*) 9 July 1972; *p.c.:* Mirisch/DFE for UA; *dir:* Art Davis; *story:* John W. Dunn; *anim:* Don Williams, Dick Thompson, Bob Matz, John Gibbs; *lay:* Dick Ung; *back:* Richard H. Thomas; *ed:* Lee Gunther; *voices:* Bob Holt; *mus:* Doug Goodwin; *prod sup:* Stan Paperny, Harry Love; *col:* DeLuxe. *sd:* RCA. 6 min. • The racer hunts the Japanese beetle in a flower garden.

6266. Suppressed Duck (*Looney Tunes*) 26 June 1965; *p.c.:* DFE for WB; *dir:* Robert McKimson; *story:* Dave DeTiege; *anim:* Bob Matz, Manuel Perez, Warren Batchelder; *lay:* Dick Ung; *back:* Ron Dias; *ed:* Lee Gunther; *mel:* Mel Blanc; *mus:* Bill Lava; *col:* Tech. *sd:* Vit. 6 min. • Daffy goes hunting a wily bear.

6267. Surf and Sound (*Herman & Katnip*) 5 Mar. 1954; *p.c.:* Famous for Para; *dir:* Dave Tendlar; *story:* I. Klein; *anim:* Martin Taras, Thomas Moore; *sets:* Jack Henegan; *voices:* Arnold Stang, Sid Raymond, Jack Mercer; *mus:* Winston Sharples; *title song:* Hal David, Leon Carr; *ph:* Leonard McCormick; *prod mgr:* Seymour Shultz; *col:* Tech. *sd:* RCA. 7 min. • Mouse fun at the beach is spoiled by Katnip's presence, so Herman has to dispose of the offending party.

6268. Surf Bored (*Noveltoon*) 17 July 1953; *p.c.:* Famous for Para; *dir:* I. Sparber; *story:* Larz Bourne; *anim:* Steve Muffatti, Morey Reden; *sets:* Robert Connavale; *voices:* Mae Questel, Jackson Beck; *mus:* Winston Sharples; *ph:* Leonard McCormick; *prod mgr:* Seymour Shultz; *col:* Tech. *sd:* RCA. 6½ min. • Audrey tries to smuggle her dog onto a "No Dogs Allowed" beach against the life guard's wishes.

6269. Surf-Bored Cat (*Tom & Jerry*) 1967; *p.c.:* MGM; *prod:* Chuck Jones; *dir:* Abe Levitow; *story:* Bob Ogle; *anim:* Dick Thompson, Philip Roman, Ben Washam, Hal Ambro, Don Towsley, Carl Bell; *des:* Maurice Noble; *lay:* Don Morgan; *back:* Philip de Guard; *mus:* Dean Elliott; *checker:* Carole Barnes; *prod sup:* Les Goldman, Kathy Troxel, Earl Jonas; *col:* Metro. *sd:* WE. 7 min. • Both Jerry and a shark spoil Tom's attempts to ride a surf board.

6270. Surface Surf Aces (*Possible Possum*) Mar. 1970; *p.c.:* TT for Fox; *col:* DeLuxe. *sd:* RCA. 5 min. • No story available. • See: *Possible Possum*

6271. The Surprise (*Out of the Inkwell*) 15 Mar. 1923; *p.c.:* Inkwell Studio for Rodner; *dir:* Dave Flreischer; *anim/l/a:* Max Fleischer; b&w. *sil.* 7 min. *l/a/anim.* • Max's fiancée wants to surprise him and blindfolds

him. In this state, he wanders away while Ko-Ko sprays an artist and Max's girl with ink in time for Max to return and catch them in a compromising situation.

6272. Surprisin' Exercisin' (*Possible Possum*) Jan. 1968; *p.c.:* TT for Fox; *ex prod:* Bill Weiss; *dir/anim:* Cosmo Anzilotti; *col:* DeLuxe. *sd:* RCA. 5½ min. • Poss and the gang help Billy Bear lose some weight. • See: *Possible Possum*

6273. Susie the Little Blue Coupe 16 June 1952; *p.c.:* Walt Disney prods for RKO; *dir:* Clyde Geronimi; *asst dir:* Ted Sebern; *story:* Bill Peet; *story adapt:* Bill Peet, Don da Gradi; *anim:* Ollie Johnston, Cliff Nordberg, Hal King, Bob Carlson; *fx:* George Rowley; *des:* Mary Blair; *lay:* Hugh Hennesy, Don Griffith; *back:* Ralph Hulett; *voices:* Sterling Holloway, Stan Freberg, Bob Jackman, Clarke Lagerstrom; *mus:* Paul Smith; *col:* Tech. *sd:* RCA. 8 min. • The life history of a little blue car: Bought new, tended to, later neglected, traded-in, stolen, crashed, finally ending in a junk yard where a teenager buys her and gives her a new lease of life as a hot rod.

6274. Svengali's Cat (*Mighty Mouse*) 18 Jan. 1946; *p.c.:* TT for Fox; *dir:* Eddie Donnelly; *story:* John Foster; *voice:* Thomas Morrison; *mus:* Philip A. Scheib; *ph:* Douglas Moye; *col:* Tech. *sd:* RCA. 7 min. • Svengali's cat hypnotizes a young mouse into luring the town's mice into his cellar.

6275. Svengarlic (*Krazy Kat*) 3 Aug. 1931; *p.c.:* Winkler for Colum; *prod:* Charles B. Mintz; *anim:* Ben Harrison, Manny Gould; *mus:* Joe de Nat; *prod mgr:* James Bronis; b&w. *sd:* WE. 6 min. • No story available.

6276. Swab the Duck (*Noveltoon*) 11 May 1956; *p.c.:* Famous for Para; *dir:* Dave Tendlar; *story:* Carl Meyer; *anim:* Morey Reden, Martin Taras; *sets:* Anton Loeb; *voices:* Sid Raymond, Jackson Beck, Jack Mercer, Cecil Roy; *mus:* Winston Sharples; *ph:* Leonard McCormick; *prod mgr:* Seymour Shultz; *col:* Tech. *sd:* RCA. 6 min. • The Fox takes advantage of an exhibition Pirate Galleon when he discovers Huey wants to play pirates.

6277. Swallow the Leader (*Looney Tunes*) 14 Oct. 1949; *p.c.:* WB; *dir:* Robert McKimson; *story:* Warren Foster; *anim:* Phil de Lara, Pete Burness, John Carey, Charles McKimson; *fx:* A.C. Gamer; *lay:* Cornett Wood; *back:* Richard H. Thomas; *ed:* Treg Brown; *voices:* Robert Cameron Bruce, Mel Blanc; *mus:* Carl Stalling; *prod mgr:* John W. Burton; *prod:* Edward Selzer; *col:* Tech. *sd:* Vit. 7 min. • A cat comes up with many ruses to lure the first swallow in Capistrano into his gullet.

6278. Swamp Snapper (*Possible Possum*) Nov. 1969; *p.c.:* TT for Fox; *col:* DeLuxe. *sd:* RCA. 5 min. • Poss and his pals rid the pond a snapping turtle who has caused it to run out of fish. • See: *Possible Possum*

6279. Swamp Water Taffy (*Possible Possum*) July 1970; *p.c.:* TT for Fox; *col:* DeLuxe. *sd:* RCA. 5 min. • Poss and his pals inadvertently capture a couple of counterfeiters. • See: *Possible Possum*

6280. The Swan Princess 18 Nov. 1994; *p.c.:* Rich Animation Studios/Colum TriStar Films International/Nest Entertainment for MGM; *dir:* Richard Rich; *prod:* Richard Rich, Jared F. Brown; *ex prod:* Jared F. Brown, Seldon Young; *co-ex prod:* Matt Mazer; *co-prod:* Terry L. Noss, Thomas J. Tobin; *story:* Richard Rich, Brian Nissen; *based on* "Swan Lake"; *scr:* Brian Nissen; *character des:* Steven E. Gordon; *art dir:* Mike Hodgson, James Coleman; *storyboard:* Bruce Woodside, Tom Ellery, Kevin Harkey, Peter Gullerud, Steven E. Gordon, John Dorman, Roy Meurin; *anim dir:* Steven E. Gordon; *anim:* "*Prince Derek*": Chrystal S. Klabunde, Nasos Vakalis, Jesse Cosio, Steven E. Gordon, Juliana Korsborn, Cynthia Overman; "*Princess Odette*": Steven E. Gordon, Leon Joosen, Jesse Cosio: "*Rothbart*": Steven E. Gordon, Todd Waterman, Gary Perkovac; "*Jean-Bob*": Bruce Woodside, Jamie Davis, Kevin Petrilak, Mark Fisher, Cynthia Overman; "*Speed*": Daniel Boulos, David Block, Jeff Etter; "*Puffin*": Rick Farmiloe, Larry Whitaker, Jay Jackson; "*The Swan*": Dan Haskett, Colm Duggan, Erik Schmidt, John Sparey; "*Queen Uberta*": Dan Haskett, Jeff Etter, Colm Duggan; "*Lord Rogers*": Gary Perkovac, Colm Duggan; "*Bromley*": Steven E. Gordon; "*King William & Chamberlain*": Dan Wagner; "*Young Derek & Odette*": Todd Waterman, Doug Gregoire, Steven E. Gordon; "*Young Bromley*": Steven E. Gordon, Todd Waterman; "*Musicians*": Colm Duggan, Jamie Davis, Dan Wagner, Donnachada Daly; "*The Hag*": Chuck Harvey, Colm Duggan, Steven E. Gordon, Dan Wagner; "*Footmen*": Nasos Vakalis, Cynthia Overman; "*Princesses*": Donnachada Daly, Jeff Etter, Jamie Davis, Cynthia Overman, Juliana Korsborn, Todd Waterman, Colm Duggan; "*The Great Animal & Crocodiles*": Nasos Vakalis; "*Horses*": Juliana Korsborn,

Steven E. Gordon, Jeff Etter, Jesse Cosio; *"Townspeople"*: Donnachada Daly, Jesse Cosio, Jeff Etter, David Simmons, Steve Garcia; *addit anim*: Adam Burke, Ken McDonald, Kevin O'Neil, Silvia Pompei, Scott Sackett, Jennifer Marie Stillwell; *rough anim asst*: Kimberly Bowles, Darryl H. Gordon, David Simmons; *fx anim*: Bob Simmons, Brian McSweeney, Ricardo Echevarria, James Mansfield, Conann Fitzpatrick, Young Kyu Rhim, Kevin O'Neil, Ko Hashiguchi, Brett Hisey, Bob Miller; *asst anim*: Rolando B. Mercado, Mike Camarillo, David Kracov, Michael Milligan, Phil Cummings, Tyrone Elliott, David M. Kcenich, Susan B. Keane, Jan Naylor, Mary Mullen, David Teague, John Dillon, Mark Cumberton, Hae Sook Hwang, Chan Jung; *clean-up: "Prince Derek," "Young Derek," "Young Odette" & "Young Bromley"*: Adam Burke; *lead key for the children*: Dori Littell-Herrick; *key asst*: David Bombardier, Reed Cardwell, Wes Chun, Lureline Kohler, Mi Yul Lee, Cal Le Duc, Bob Quinn; *asst*: Ellen Heindel, Tom Higgins, Don Judge, Ross Marshall, Vanessa J. Martin, Soonjin Mooney, Greg Ramsey, Theresa M. Smythe, Derek L'Estrange, Eunice Yu; *break*: Ann Cummings, Kevin S. Davis, Ivan Camilli Rivera, Scott Sackett, Al Salgado; *"Princess Odette" & "the Swan" asst*: Silvia Pompei, D.J. Bernard, Mi Yul Lee, Leticia Lichtwardt, Dori Littell-Herrick, Frank Molieri, Laura Nichols, Myung Kang Teague; *asst*: Richard P. Baneham, Gordon Bellamy, Shana Curley, Armena Israelian, Ilona Kaba, Vanessa J. Martin, Yoon Sook Nam, Mi Ri Yoon; *break*: John Dubiel, Heidi Danielle Daven; *inbet*: Donnie Long; *"Rothbart," "Bromley" & "Chamberlain" key asst*: Bronwen Barry, Scott Claus, Akemi Horiuchi, Ken McDonald; *asst*: Michael Lerman, Pil Yong Song; *break*: Kimberly Dwinell, Cynthia Jill French, Michael Lester, Christopher John Sonnenburg; *inbet*: Ben Metcalf; *"Speed," "Jean-Bob" & "the Crocodiles" key asst*: Eric J. Abjornson, Vicki Woodside, Sylvia Fitzpatrick, Sam Bullock, Sue Houghton, James McArdle, Bonnie Robinson; *asst*: Edie Benjamin, Ron Friedman, Darryl .H. Gordon, Robert Nigoghossian, Greg Ray, Melanie Thomas, Cathy Zar; *break*: Ricardo Barahona, Todd Hoff, Ivan Camilli Rivera, Ken Roskos, Lucinda Sanderson, Celinda S. Schiefelbein, Joe Suggs; *inbet*: Diana Dixon, April Haight, John Pattison; *"Puffin" asst*: Melissa Freeman, Franci Allen, Sheldon Borenstein, Ruth Elliott, Helen Lawlor, George D. Sukara, Wes Chun, Michael Coppieters, Trevor Tamboline; *inbet*: Kimberly Bowles, Judith M. Niver; *"Queen Uberta," "Musicians" & "the Hag" asst*: Betty C. Tang, Jared Beckstrand, Dan Bowman, Cristi Lyon, Cathy Karol-Crowther, Jean Paynter, Jennifer Marie Stillwell; *inbet*: Nicole Hatcher; *"Lord Rogers" asst*: Helen Lawlor, Laura Nichols, Bob Quinn, Stan Somers, Richard P. Baneham, Eduardo Olivares, Richard Smitheman; *"King William, Princesses, the Great Animal & Rothbart" (2nd unit) asst*: Jim van der Keyl, Elena Kravets, June Myung Nam; *break*: Myung Sook Miller; *inbet*: Ben Metcalf; *"Horses, Guard & Animals" asst*: Sue Houghton, Cal le Duc, Darryl H. Gordon, Gordon Bellamy, Eduardo Olivares; *inbet*: Carolyn Gliona, Judith M. Niver; *"Townspeople" asst*: Sheila Brown, Eduardo Olivares, Kimmie Calvert, Eileen Dunn; *break*: Judith Ann Drake; *inbet*: Wantana Martinelli, Angel Pastrana; *addit anim: (Character Builders, Inc.): prod mgr*: Ron Price; *anim dir*: Dan Root; *anim*: Lou Dellarosa, Jim Kammerud, Jennifer Gwynne Oliver, Brian Smith, Martin Fuller, Mark Mitchell, Thomas Riggin, Bob Spang; *asst*: Todd Cronin, Jason Piel, Rafael Rosado; *inbet*: James W. Elston, Stephanie Roberts, Tony Lee, Richard Trebus Jr.; *lay*: Mike Hodgson, Gary Mouri, Jeff Purves, Sherilan Weinhart, Lisa Souza, Ricardo Barahona, Ben Metcalf; *bluesketch*: John Pattison, Irina Blueband; *lay scene co-ord*: Jackie Blaisdell; *back*: Donald A. Towns, Jeff Richards, Marzette Bonar, William Dely, Fred Warter, Kim Spink, Eric Reese, Bill Kaufmann, Mannix Bennett, Donna Prince, Brad Hicks, Andrew Phillipson, Alison Julian, David B. McBride, Phillip Young Kim, Sai Ping Lok; *back co-ord*: Gina Shay; *col models*: Jeanette Nouribekian, Carie Nouribekian; *model/scene co-ord*: Jo Ann Cohn, Karen Rodgers; *col model break*: Robert S. Harand, Bonnie Ramsey; *model paint*: Marie Boughamer, Mary Collins, Stevie Hirsch, Gina Evans Howard, Christine Kingsland, Carol M. McMackin, Christopher Naylor, Blake Nouribekian, Carie Nouribekian, Tracey Oakley, Sparkie Parker, Ramona Randa; *airbrush*: Kevin Oakley; *mark-up*: Sarah-Jane King, Gillian Coughlan, Sylvia Filcak, Stacey King; *ink*: Eleanor Dahlen, Kathleen Irvine Evans, Lee Guttman, Chin Kyung Kwon, Mi Kyung Kwon, Sun Woo Park, Karan Storr, Leonor Gonzales Wood; *i&p fx*: Colene Riffo; *ed*: Joseph L. Campana, Paul Murphy; *voices: Rothbart*: Jack Palance; *Prince Derek*: Howard McGillin; *Princess Odette*: Michelle Nicastro; *Princess Odette's singing voice*: Liz Callaway; *Jean-Bob*: John Cleese; *Speed*: Steven Wright; *Puffin*: Steve Vinovich; *Lord Rogers*: Mark Harelik;

Chamberlain: James Arrington; *Chamberlain's singing voice*: David Gaines; *Bromley*: Joel McKinnon Miller; *King William*: Dakin Matthews; *Queen Uberta*: Sandy Duncan; *Narrator*: Brian Nissen; *Young Derek*: Adam Wylie; *Young Odette*: Adrian Zahiri; *Musician*: Tom Allen Robbins; *Hag*: Bess Hopper; *Dancers*: Cate Coplin, Tom Slater, Jim Pearce; *chorus*: Jon Joyce, Susan Boyd, Catte Adams, Angie Jaree, Bobbi Page, Amick Byram, Beth Anderson, Kerry Katz, Stephen W. Amerson, Gary Stockdale, Susan Stevens Logan, Randy Crenshaw, Carmen Twillie, Susan G. McBride, Rick Logan, Tampa M. Lann, Sally Stevens, Debbie Hall, Bob Joyce, Oren Waters, Michael Dees, Jim Haas; *mus score*: Lex de Azevedo; *songs*: David Zippel, Lex de Azevedo; "Far Longer" produced & arranged by Robbie Buchanan; performed by Regina Belle, Jeffrey Osborne; "Eternity" by Miwa Yoshida, Mike Pela, David Zippel; performed by Dreams Come True; composed by Masato Nakamura; orchestra conducted by Lex de Azevedo, Larry Bastian, Larry Schwartz; "This is my Idea" performed by Sandy Duncan, Dakin Matthews, Howard McGillin, Liz Callaway, Adam Wylie, J.D. Daniels, Wes Brewer, Adrian Zahiri, Larisa Oleynik, Alisa Nordberg, Steven Stewart; "Practice, Practice, Practice" performed by Paul Ainsley, Rick Stoneback, Tom Allen Robbins, Lenny Wolfe, Sandy Duncan; "No Fear" performed by Liz Callaway, Steve Vinovich, Jonathan Hadary, David Zippel; "No More Mr. Nice Guy" performed by Lex de Azevedo, Emilie de Azevedo, Emily Pearson, Julie de Azevedo, Rachel de Azevedo, Melissa Pace; "Princess on Parade" performed by David Gaines, Mark Harelik, Jon Joyce, Randy Crenshaw, Amick Byram, Stephen Amerson; *mus ed*: Douglas Lackey, Richard Stewart, Patricia Peck; *mus rec*: Andy D'Addario, Mark Siddoway, Dennis Sands, Michael Greene; *orch co-ord*: Linda Coltrin, Rachel de Azevedo; *snr prod mgr*: Sutherland C. Ellwood; *prod mgr*: Brett Hayden, Richmond Horine; *technical sup*: Geoffrey Schroeder; *asst dir*: Bret Taylor Babos, Gregory Daven; *i&p: post anim prod sup*: Colene Riffo; *anim check*: Eleanor Dahlen, Denise A. Link, Orla McCamley; *Xerox*: John Remmel, Sue Bologna, José Cruz, Marlo Erazo, Fausto Flores, Mario Flores, Bonnie Giannini; *Xerox check*: Daryl Carstensen, Eleanor Dahlen, Lea Dahlen, Valentine D'Arcy, Valerie Pabian Green, Vernette Griffee, Brendan Harris, Leslie Hinton, Mi Yung Kwon, Catherine F. Parotino, Gerry Ringwald, Karan Storr, Leonor Gonzales Wood; *dial ed*: Randy Paton; *ADR ed*: Armetta Jackson-Hamlett; *re-rec mix*: Rick Alexander, Jim Bolt, Andy D'Addario; *ph*: The Baer Animation Company, Camera Service, Steven Wilzback, Daniel Bunn, David Link, Ralph Migliori, Bingo Ferguson, Mark Henley; *foley art*: Paul Holzborn, Bess Hooper, Joseph Sabella; *digital enhancement*: Angel Studios: Scott Vye, Brad Hunt, Michael Limber, Allen Battino; *Dream Quest*: Brian Adams, Tim Landry, Mark M. Galvin, Anjelica Casillas, Dan Deleeuw, Rob Dressel, Amy Pfaffinger, Corey Hels, Mario Pabon, Frank Soronow; *Angst Animation Post Production*: Dylan Kohler, Lisa Clyde; *col timer*: Dale Grahn; *neg cutter*: Mark Lass; *opticals*: Purelight Inc., Robert Habros; *titles*: Title House, Bloomfilm; *col*: Tech. *sd*: Dolby stereo. 89 min. • Princess Odette, the daughter of King William, is captured by Rothbart the wizard and transformed into a swan. Each night, providing the moon shines on the lake, she returns to her human form. Rothbart will only break the spell if she marries him so they can rule the kingdom together but Odette refuses. The enchantment can only be broken with the kiss of true love.

6281. The Swan Princess II: Escape From Castle Mountain

18 July 1997; *p.c.*: Rich Animation Studios/Nest Entertainment for Colum TriStar; *dir*: Richard Rich; *ex prod*: Jared F. Brown, K. Douglas Martin, Seldon O. Young; *prod*: Jared F. Brown, Richard Rich; *co-prod*: Terry L. Noss, Thomas J. Tobin; *story*: Brian Nissen, Richard Rich; *scr*: Brian Nissen; *storyboard*: Steven E. Gordon, Frank Paur, Bruce Woodside; *scene plan*: Geoffrey Schroeder; *character des*: Steven E. Gordon; *col stylist*: Jeanette Nouribekian; *col models*: Karen Noss-Rodgers; *anim*: Adam Burke, John Celestri, Jesse Cosio, Colm Duggan, Melissa Freeman, Steven E. Gordon, Daniel Haskett, Lim Elena Kravetz, Boo Hwan Lim, Kyoung Hee Lim, Silvia Pompei, Athanassios Vakalis, Dan Wagner, Todd Waterman, Larry Whitaker Jr., Ryan Jeremy Woodward; *des*: Mike Hodgson; *lay*: Mike Hodgson, Jeffrey Gatrall, Greg Martin, Birgitta Pollaneni, Dennis Richards; *back sup*: Donald Towns; *back*: Donald Towns, Colene Riffo, Rustico Roca, Jonathan Salt; *ed*: James F. Koford, Joseph Campana, Paul Murphy; *overseas production*: Hanho Heung-up Co., Ltd. (Seoul): *sup*: Denis Deegan; *anim dir*: Lee Han Won, Hong Sang Man; *prod mgr*: Chae Young Chi; *ph*: Lim Jong Soo; *inbet*: Kyung Sook Chun; *fx anim sup*: Brian McSweeney; *fx*

anim: Colm Duggan, Ricardo Echevarria, T. Elliott, Joe Galbavy, Jeff Howard, John Huey, Brian McSweeney, Pil Yong Song, Ryan Woodward; *fx:* Jung Ki Kim; *anim clean-up:* Bronwen Barry, Kimberly Bowles, Michael Coppieters, Helen Lawlor, Ellen Heindel, Leticia Lichtwardt, Jonathan Lyons, Betty Tang; *clean-up:* Joo Kyung Choi, Mi Hyun Han, Mi Ok Joo, Hyun Ja Kang, Ae Kyung Lee, Hyun Hee Lee, Pil Yong Song; *anim check:* Patricia Blackburn; *final check:* Tae Jung Lee, Young Boo Lim; *back:* Won Chul Park, Colene Riffo, Rustico Roca, Jonathan Salt, Donald Towns; *i&p:* Yoon Sun Choi, Moon Sun Chung, Eun Ae Oh, Mi Sook Park; *voices: Princess Odette:* Michelle Nicastro; *Prince Derek:* Douglas Sills; *Clavius:* Jake Williamson; *Uberta:* Christy Landers; *Jean-Bob:* Donald Sage Mackay; *Speed:* Doug Stone; *Puffin:* Steve Vinovich; *Lord Rogers:* Joseph Medrano; *Chamberlain:* James Arrington; *Knuckles:* Joey Camen; *Bromley:* Owen Muller; *Bridget:* Rosie Mann; *mus:* Lex de Azevedo; *mus co-ord:* Peggy de Azevedo; *mus ed:* Douglas Lackey; *mus rec:* Robert Abeyta; *songs:* Lex de Azevedo, Clive Romney; *rec:* Tim Grace, Bill Nicholson, Thomas Meloeny, Fred Law; *foley:* Paul Holzborn, Dominique Decaudain; *ADR/foley mix:* Dean St. John; *prod mgr:* Brett Hayden; *col:* CFI. *sd:* Dolby stereo. 74 min. • Sequel to *The Swan Princess* (1994): Princess Odette and Prince Derek, now married, are under threat from Clavius, a former partner of the evil wizard Rothbart. Clavius wants to retrieve "the Black Arts," powers enclosed in a magic orb secreted somewhere in Derek's castle and so kidnaps his mother. When Derek leaves to pay the ransom, Clavius sneaks into the castle in search of the orb. Odette's maid discovers the Black Arts orb and transforms her back into a swan so she can fly to warn Derek. Clavius finds the magic orb and returns to his mountain hideout. Helped by his animal friends, Derek manages to vanquish Clavius and destroy the orb.

6282. Swanee River *(Ko-Ko Song Car-Tune)* 25 Apr. 1925; *p.c.*; *dir:* Dave Fleischer; *anim:* Max Fleischer; *song:* Stephen Foster; b&w. sil. 6 min. • Ko-Ko calls his "Kwartet" from the inkwell and they proceed to sing Stephen Foster's title song. The words are enhanced by a cartoon Negro who does funny stunts around them.

6283. Swash Buckled *(Loopy de Loop)* Feb. 1962; *p.c.*: Hanna-Barbera prods for Colum; *prod/dir:* Joseph Barbera, William Hanna; *story dir:* Lewis Marshall; *story:* Michael Maltese; *anim dir:* Charles A. Nichols; *anim:* Jack Ozark; *lay:* Iwao Takamoto; *back:* Art Lozzi; *ed:* Greg Watson; *voices:* Daws Butler, Jean van der Pyl; *mus:* Hoyt Curtin; *titles:* Lawrence Gobel; *prod mgr:* Howard Hanson; *col:* East. *sd:* RCA. 6½ min. • Loopy dons the guise of a *Musketeer.*

6284. Swat the Fly *(Betty Boop)* 14 Apr. 1935; *p.c.*: The Fleischer Studio for Para; *prod:* Max Fleischer; *dir:* Dave Fleischer; *anim:* David Tendlar, Samuel Stimson; *voices:* Mae Questel; *mus:* Sammy Timberg; b&w. *sd:* WE. 6 min. • A fly pesters Pudgy and Betty while she makes a cake.

6285. Swat the Fly *(Miracles in Mud)* 1919; *anim:* Willie Hopkins; b&w. *sil.* • Three clay sculptured heads metamorphose into caricatures of public personalities.

6286. Sweet Adeline *(Aesop's Film Fable)* 3 Feb. 1929; *p.c.*: Fables Pictures Inc for Pathé; *dir:* Paul Terry, Frank Moser; b&w. *sil.* 5 min. • Milton Mouse and Rita appear in the neighborhood playhouse. Rita is kidnapped by a villainous cat and Milt chases them up and down skyscrapers.

6287. Sweet Adeline *(Song Car-Tune)* 5 June 1926; *p.c.*: Inkwell Studio for Red Seal; *prod:* Max Fleischer; *dir:* Dave Fleischer; *song:* Harry Armstrong, Richard H. Gerard; b&w. *sd:* DPC. 5 min. • A chorus of back fence felines sing the song.

6288. Sweet and Sourdough *(Roland & Rattfink)* 25 June 1969; *p.c.*: Mirisch/DFE for UA; *dir:* Art Davis; *story:* John W. Dunn; *anim:* Manny Perez, Warren Batchelder, Don Williams, Art Leonardi; *lay:* Dick Ung; *back:* Tom O'Loughlin; *ed:* Lee Gunther; *voices:* Leonard Weinrib; *mus:* Doug Goodwin; *ph:* John Burton Jr.; *prod sup:* Jim Foss, Harry Love; *col:* DeLuxe. *sd:* RCA. 6 min. • Mountie, Roland sets out to "get his man" who has just robbed the bank.

6289. Sweet Jenny Lee *(Screen Songs)* 9 Jan. 1932; *p.c.*: The Fleischer Studio for Para; *prod:* Max Fleischer; *dir:* Dave Fleischer; b&w. *sd:* WE. 6 min. • The Negro cotton-pickers perform a song and dance.

6290. Sweet Sioux *(Merrie Melodies)* 26 June 1937; *p.c.*: Leon Schlesinger prods for WB; *dir:* I. Freleng; *anim:* Bob McKimson, A.C. Gamer; *lay:* Griff Jay; *ed:* Tregoweth E. Brown; *voices:* Mel Blanc, Billy Bletcher; *mus:* Carl W. Stalling; *prod sup:* Henry Binder, Raymond G. Katz; *col:* Tech. *sd:* Vit. 8 min. • Life in an Indian village is interrupted with an attack on a covered wagon.

6291. Swim or Sink *(Betty Boop)* 11 Mar. 1932; *p.c.*: The Fleischer Studio for Para; *prod:* Max Fleischer; *dir:* Dave Fleischer; *anim:* Seymour Kneitel, Bernard Wolf; *voices:* Mae Questel, Charles Carver; *mus:* Art Turkisher; b&w. *sd:* WE. 6½ min. • Betty and the gang are adrift on a raft when they are picked up by a shipful of pirates.

6292. Swimmer Take All *(Popeye)* 16 May 1952; *p.c.*: Famous for Para; *dir:* Seymour Kneitel; *story:* Carl Meyer, Jack Mercer; *anim:* Tom Johnson, John Gentilella; *sets:* Robert Little; *voices:* Jack Mercer, Jackson Beck, Mae Questel; *mus:* Winston Sharples; *ph:* Leonard McCormick; *prod mgr:* Seymour Shultz; *col:* Tech. *sd:* RCA. 6 min. • Popeye and Bluto enter the English Channel swim.

6293. Swing Ding Amigo *(Looney Tunes)* 17 Sept. 1966; *p.c.*: DFE for WB; *dir:* Robert McKimson; *story:* Sid Marcus; *anim:* George Grandpré, Ted Bonnicksen, Bob Matz, Manny Perez; *lay:* Dick Ung; *back:* Tom O'Loughlin; *ed:* Lee Gunther; *voices:* Mel Blanc; *mus:* Walter Greene; *col:* Tech. *sd:* Vit. 6 min. • Daffy is kept awake by Speedy's noisy nightclub and is determined to put an end to it.

6294. Swing, Monkey, Swing *(Color Rhapsody)* 10 Sept. 1937; *p.c.*: Charles Mintz prods for Colum; *story:* Ben Harrison; *anim:* Manny Gould; *lay:* Clark Watson; *back:* Phil Davis; *ed:* George Winkler; *voices:* The Basin Street Boys; *mus:* Joe de Nat; *ph:* Otto Reimer; *prod mgr:* James Bronis; *col:* Tech. *sd:* RCA. 7½ min. • Swing music invades Monkeyland. Monkeys all play "hot" music and sing "St Louis Blues."

6295. The Swing School *(Betty Boop)* 27 May 1938; *p.c.*: The Fleischer Studio for Para; *prod:* Max Fleischer; *dir:* Dave Fleischer; *anim:* Thomas Johnson, Frank Endres; *voices:* Mae Questel, Everett Clark, Frances Reynolds; *mus:* Sammy Timberg; b&w. *sd:* WE. 7 min. • Betty's music school for animals is doing all right until Pudgy strikes a sour note.

6296. Swing Social *(MGM Cartoon)* 18 May 1940; *p.c.*: MGM; *prod:* Rudolf Ising; *dir:* William Hanna, Joseph Barbera; *voice:* Billy Mitchell; *mus:* Scott Bradley; *prod mgr:* Fred Quimby; *col:* Tech. *sd:* WE. 8 min. • A fisherman is told that the black bass never bite on Sunday because of the "Swing Social."

6297. Swing Wedding 13 Feb. 1937; *p.c.*: MGM; *prod/dir:* Hugh Harman, Rudolf Ising; *story:* Jack Caldwell, Hugh Harman, William Hanna; *anim:* Thomas McKimson, Larry Martin; *voices:* The Four Blackbirds; *mus:* Scott Bradley; *songs:* Jack Caldwell; *prod mgr:* Fred Quimby; *col:* Tech. *sd:* RCA. 7½ min. • The bullfrogs hold a jam session for Minnie the Moocher's wedding day. Caricatures: Louis Armstrong, Cab Calloway, Step'n Fetchit and Fats Waller.

6298. Swing You Sinner! *(Talkartoon)* 20 Sept. 1930; *p.c.*: The Fleischer Studio for Para; *prod:* Max Fleischer; *dir:* Dave Fleischer; *story:* Ted Sears; *anim:* Willard Bowsky, William Henning, Jimmie Culhane, Al Eugster; *character des:* Grim Natwick; *mus:* Art Turkisher; b&w. *sd:* WE. 6 min. • Bimbo journeys through a graveyard and is tormented by ghosts.

6299. Swing Your Partner *(Swing Symphony)* 26 Apr. 1943; *p.c.*: Walter Lantz prods for Univ; *dir:* Alex Lovy; *story:* Ben Hardaway, Milt Schaffer; *anim:* Paul Smith; *sets:* Fred Brunish; *voices:* Kent Rogers, Cactus Mack McPeters; *mus:* Darrell Calker; *prod mgr:* George Hall; *col:* Tech. *sd:* WE. 6 min. • Homer Pigeon and Carrie want to go to the barn dance but Hank Horse isn't so keen to take them.

6300. Swingshift Cinderella 25 Aug. 1945; *p.c.*: MGM; *dir:* Tex Avery; *story:* Heck Allen; *anim:* Ray Abrams, Preston Blair, Ed Love; *character des:* Claude Smith; *sets:* John Didrik Johnsen; *ed:* Fred MacAlpine; *voices:* Frank Graham, Imogene Lynn, Sara Berner; *mus:* Scott Bradley; *prod:* Fred Quimby; *col:* Tech. *sd:* WE. 8 min. • Joe Wolf forsakes Little Red Riding Hood for Cinderella. He follows her to the ball, pursued by a man-hungry Fairy Godmother.

6301. Swiss Cheese *(Paul Terry-Toon)* 1 June 1930; *p.c.*: A-C for Educational/Fox; *dir:* Frank Moser, Paul Terry; *anim:* Arthur Babbitt, Frank Moser; *mus:* Philip A. Scheib; b&w. *sd:* WE. 7 min. • A cat moves in on a rodent Goose Girl and chases her beau across the Alpine mountains.

6302. The Swiss Cheese Family Robinson *(Mighty Mouse)* 19 Dec. 1947; *p.c.*: TT for Fox; *dir:* Mannie Davis; *story:* John Foster; *anim:* Jim

Tyer; *voice:* Thomas Morrison; *mus:* Philip A. Scheib; *ph:* Douglas Moye; *col:* Tech. *sd:* RCA. 6½ min. • A mouse family is shipwrecked on a cannibal isle which causes Mighty Mouse to interrupt his holiday in Miami to fly to their rescue.

6303. Swiss Mis-Fits (*Chilly Willy*) 2 Dec. 1957; *p.c.:* Walter Lantz prods for Univ; *dir:* Alex Lovy; *story:* Homer Brightman; *anim:* Ray Abrams, La Verne Harding; *sets:* Raymond Jacobs, Art Landy; *voices:* Dal McKennon; *mus:* Clarence Wheeler; *prod mgr:* William E. Garity; *col:* Tech. *sd:* RCA. 6 min. • A St. Bernard tries to drum up some victims to rescue.

6304. A Swiss Miss (*Mighty Mouse*) Aug. 1951; *p.c.:* TT for Fox; *dir:* Mannie Davis; *story:* Tom Morrison; *anim:* Jim Tyer; *voices:* Roy Halee, Tom Morrison; *mus:* Philip A. Scheib; *ph:* Douglas Moye; *col:* Tech. *sd:* RCA. 6 min. • Oil Can Harry kidnaps Pearl Pureheart and Mighty Mouse pursues them over the Swiss Alps.

6305. Swiss Movements (*Krazy Kat*) 4 Apr. 1931; *p.c.:* Winkler for Colum; *prod:* Charles Mintz; *story:* Ben Harrison; *anim:* Manny Gould; *mus:* Joe de Nat; *prod mgr:* James Bronis; b&w. *sd:* WE. 6 min. • Clock shop proprietor, Krazy cures his girl's sick cuckoo clock.

6306. Swiss Ski Yodelers (*Terry-Toon*) 17 May 1940; *p.c.:* TT for Fox; *dir:* Eddie Donnelly; *story:* John Foster; *mus:* Philip A. Scheib; b&w. *sd:* RCA. 7 min. • No story available.

6307. Swiss Tease (*Color Rhapsody*) 11 Sept. 1947; *p.c.:* Colum; *prod:* Raymond Katz, Henry Binder; *dir:* Sid Marcus; *story:* Michael Maltese, Tedd Pierce; *anim:* Howard Swift, Roy Jenkins; *lay:* Clark Watson; *back:* Al Boggs; *ed:* Richard S. Jensen; *voices:* Jack Mather, Stan Freberg; *mus:* Darrell Calker; *creative consultant:* Bob Clampett; *col:* Tech. *sd:* WE. 5 min. • A drunken St. Bernard tries to rescue a yodeling skier.

6308. A Swiss Trick (*Tom & Jerry*) 19 Dec. 1931; *p.c.:* Van Beuren for RKO; *dir:* John Foster, George Stallings; *mus:* Gene Rodemich; b&w. *sd:* RCA. 6 min. • Tom and Jerry have adventures in the Swiss Alps.

6309. Switch 10 May 1991; *p.c.:* Odyssey-Regency/HBO in association with Cinema Plus, LP., for Colum Tri-Star; *anim sup:* Wes Ford Takahashi; *anim:* Tony Stacchi; *anim co-ord:* Shari Malyn; *col:* Tech. *sd:* Dolby stereo. 103 min. *l/a.* • Live-action comedy about an advertising exutive who finds himself in purgatory where he is informed that his life will be restored if he can find any female who genuinely likes him. If he fails ... he goes straight to Hell.

6310. Switchin' Kitten (*Tom & Jerry*) 1960; *p.c.:* Rembrandt for MGM; *prod:* William L. Snyder; *dir:* Gene Deitch; *story:* Eli Bauer, Gene Deitch; *anim/lay:* Lu Guarnier, Gary Mooney; *mus:* Stepan Konícek; *col:* Metro. *sd.* 9 min. • A mad professor experiments with Tom by transposing his brain with those of other animals. • See: *Tom and Jerry (Rembrandt Studio)*

6311. Swooner Crooner (*Looney Tunes*) 6 May 1944; *p.c.:* Leon Schlesinger prods for WB; *dir:* Frank Tashlin; *story:* Warren Foster, Robert Clampett; *anim:* George Cannata; *sets:* Richard H. Thomas; *ed:* Treg Brown; *voices:* Mel Blanc, Sam Wolfe Glaser, Richard Bickenbach, Sara Berner, Bea Benaderet; *mus:* Carl W. Stalling; *prod sup:* Henry Binder, Raymond G. Katz; *col:* Tech. *sd:* Vit. 7 min. *Academy Award nomination.* • A singing rooster named Frankie stops Porky's hens from laying, so he auditions other singing poultry to combat this, settling for one named Bing.

6312. Swooning the Swooners (*Terry-Toon*) 14 Sept. 1945; *p.c.:* TT for Fox; *dir:* Connie Rasinski; *story:* John Foster; *mus:* Philip A. Scheib; *col:* Tech. *sd:* RCA. 7 min. • A "Frank Sinatra" cat keeps the farmer awake while serenading a group of "Bobby Soxers."

6313. The Sword in the Stone 25 Dec. 1963; *p.c.:* Walt Disney prods for BV; *dir:* Wolfgang Reitherman; *story:* Bill Peet based on the book by T.H. White; *des:* Ken Anderson; *anim dir:* Frank Thomas, Milt Kahl, Ollie Johnston, John Lounsbery; *anim:* Hal Ambro, Les Clark, Eric Cleworth, John Ewing, Hal King, Eric Larson, Dick Lucas, Cliff Nordberg, John Sibley, Walt Stanchfield, Art Stevens; *fx:* Jack Boyd, Jack Buckley, Dan MacManus; *character des:* Milt Kahl, Bill Peet; *lay:* Dale Barnhart, Sylvia Cobb, Basil Davidovich, Vance Gerry, Don Griffith, Homer Jonas; *back:* Al Dempster, Ralph Hulett, Bill Layne, Fil Mottola, Walt Peregoy, Anthony Rizzo; *ed:* Donald Halliday; *voices: Sir Ector/narration:* Sebastian Cabot;

Merlin: Karl Swenson; *Wart:* Rickie Sorenson/Robert Reitherman; *Girl Squirrel:* Ginny Tyler; *Madam Mim/Granny Squirrel:* Martha Wentworth; *Kay:* Norman Alden; *Sir Pelinore:* Alan Napier; *Archimedes:* Junius C. Matthews; *Scullery Maid:* Barbara Jo Allen/Martha Wentworth; *Title singer:* Fred Darian; *Knight:* Tudor Owen; *Bird:* Barbara Jo Allen; *Wolf:* James MacDonald; *Chorus:* The Mello Men; *mus:* George Bruns; *orch:* Franklyn Marks; *mus ed:* Evelyn Kennedy; *songs:* Richard M. Sherman, Robert B. Sherman; *sd:* Robert O. Cook; *prod mgr:* Ken Peterson; *col:* Tech. *sd:* RCA. 79 min. • In medieval times, a young squire befriends Merlin, a wizard, who trains him for great things to come. "Wart," the squire, eventually turns out to be King Arthur when he pulls a sword from an anvil in a churchyard.

6314. Symphony Hour (*Mickey Mouse*) 20 Mar. 1942; *p.c.:* Walt Disney prods for RKO; *dir:* Riley Thomson; *asst dir:* Ray de Vally; *anim:* George de Beeson, Les Clark, Jack Campbell, John Elliotte, Edward Love, James Moore, Kenneth Muse, Riley Thomson, Bernard Wolf, Marvin Woodward; *fx:* Joseph Gayek, Jack Manning, Ed Parks; *lay:* Harold Miles; *voices:* Billy Bletcher, John McLeish, George A. Johnson, Walt Disney; *col:* Tech. *sd:* RCA. 7 min. • Mickey and the gang are about to broadcast a musical interlude on the radio when Goofy crushes all the instruments. They proceed to play with broken instruments.

6315. Symphony in Slang 6 June 1951; *p.c.:* MGM; *dir:* Tex Avery; *story:* Rich Hogan; *anim:* Michael Lah, Grant Simmons, Walter Clinton; *character des/lay:* Tom Oreb; *back:* John Didrik Johnsen; *ed:* Jim Faris; *voices:* John H. Brown; *mus:* Scott Bradley; *ph:* Jack Stevens; *prod:* Fred Quimby; *col:* Tech. *sd:* WE. 6 min. • A "Hip" hipster arrives in heaven and St. Peter refers him to Noah Webster in the hopes that he can understand his "jive talk."

6316. Symphony in Spinach (*Popeye*) 31 Dec. 1948; *p.c.:* Famous for Para; *dir:* Seymour Kneitel; *story:* Bill Turner, Larry Riley; *anim:* Tom Johnson, John Gentilella; *sets:* Robert Connavale; *voices:* Jack Mercer, Mae Questel, Jackson Beck; *mus:* Winston Sharples; *ph:* Leonard McCormick; *prod mgr:* Sam Buchwald; *col:* Pola. *sd:* RCA. 6 min. • Olive needs a musician for her orchestra, so Popeye and Bluto apply for the position.

6317. A Symposium on Popular Songs 19 Dec. 1962; *p.c.:* Walt Disney prods for BV; *dir/stop-motion anim:* Bill Justice; *story/des:* Xavier Atencio; *anim:* Eric Larson, Les Clark, Cliff Nordberg, Art Stevens, Julius Svendsen, Fred Hellmich, Ward Kimball; *sets:* Dale Barnhart; *voices: Ludwig von Drake:* Paul Frees; *also:* Gloria Wood, Billy Storm, Skip Farrell; *songs:* Richard M. Sherman, Robert B. Sherman; *title scenes:* Ralph Hulett; *col:* Tech. *sd:* RCA. 20 min. *Academy Award nomination.* • Ludwig von Drake offers a look at several types of song, illustrated by figures made from material and kitchen utensils.

6318. Syncopated Sioux (*Cartune*) 30 Dec 1940; *p.c.:* Walter Lantz prods for Univ; *dir:* Walter Lantz; *story:* Ben Hardaway, Lowell Elliot; *anim:* Alex Lovy; Ray Fahringer; *sets:* Fred Brunish; *voices:* Dick Nelson; *mus:* Frank Marsales; *prod mgr:* George Hall; *col:* Tech. *sd:* WE. 7 min. • Punchy travels west on a covered wagon and is attacked by Indians.

6319. T-Bone for Two (*Pluto*) 14 Aug. 1942; *p.c.:* Walt Disney prods for RKO; *dir:* Clyde Geronimi; *asst dir:* Donald A. Duckwall; *anim:* Kenneth Muse, George Nicholas, Charles A. Nichols, Morey Reden, Norman Tate; *lay:* Bruce Bushman; *mus:* Oliver Wallace; *col:* Tech. *sd:* RCA. 7 min. • Pluto uses a bulb-horn to retrieve a bone from a particularly ferocious bulldog.

6320. Ta-Ra-Ra Boom Der E (*Ko-Ko Song Car-Tune*) 16 Jan. 1926; *p.c.:* Inkwell Studio for Red Seal; *dir:* Dave Fleischer; *anim/l/a:* Max Fleischer; *song:* Henry J. Sayers; b&w. sil. 5 min. • Ko-Ko's Kartoon Kwartette sing as the words appear on the screen with a ballerina who flits from word to word.

6321. Tabasco Road (*Looney Tunes*) 20 July 1957; *p.c.:* WB; *dir:* Robert McKimson; *story:* Tedd Pierce; *anim:* Ted Bonnicksen, George Grandpré; *lay:* Robert Gribbroek; *back:* Bill Butler; *ed:* Treg Brown; *voices:* Mel Blanc, Tom Holland; *mus:* Carl Stalling, Milt Franklyn; *prod mgr:* John W. Burton; *prod:* Edward Selzer; *col:* Tech. *sd:* Vit. 7 min. • Speedy has the task of keeping two intoxicated mice from the jaws of a cat.

6322. Tail End (*Oswald*) 25 Apr. 1938; *p.c.:* Walter Lantz prods for Univ; *dir:* Lester Kline; *story:* Victor McLeod, Win Smith; *anim:* Fred

Kopietz, Ralph Somerville; *mus:* Frank Churchill; b&w. *sd:* WE. 6 min. • No story available.

6323. The Tail of a Monkey (*Unnatural History*) 29 Dec. 1926; *p.c.:* Bray prods for FBO; *dir:* Walter Lantz, David D. Hand; *anim:* Clyde Geronimi; *l/a ph:* Joe Rock; b&w. *sil.* 6 min. *l/a/anim.* • Walter Lantz explains how a monkey was once called upon to use his tail to make a huge wedding ring for a hippo.

6324. Take Me to Your Gen'rul (*Comic King*) Oct. 1962; *p.c.:* Para Cartoons; *dir:* Seymour Kneitel; *story:* Marty Roth; *anim:* Martin Taras, Irving Dressler, Thomas Johnson; *sets:* Robert Owen; *voices:* Paul Frees; *mus:* Winston Sharples; *col:* Tech. *sd:* RCA. 5 min. • Snuffy Smith joins the Army.

6325. Taken for a Ride (*Krazy Kat*) Jan. 1931; *p.c.:* Winkler for Colum; *prod:* Charles Mintz; *anim:* Ben Harrison, Manny Gould; *mus:* Joe de Nat; *prod mgr:* James Bronis; b&w. *sd:* WE. 6 min. • Krazy gets involved with some gangsters.

6326. Taking the Air (*Aesop's Film Fable*) 6 Mar. 1927; *p.c.:* Fables Pictures Inc for Pathé; *dir:* Paul Terry; b&w. *sil.* 10 min. • Farmer Al sets out to win a prize for the aviator who can establish a new altitude record.

6327. Taking the Blame (*Betty Boop*) 15 Feb. 1935; *p.c.:* The Fleischer Studio for Para; *prod:* Max Fleischer: *dir:* Dave Fleischer; *anim:* Myron Waldman, Hicks Lokey, Lillian Friedman; *mus:* Sammy Timberg; b&w. *sd:* WE. 6 min. • Betty brings home a kitten who disrupts the happy home and puts the blame on Pudgy.

6328. Tale of a Dog (*Terry-Toon*) Feb. 1959; *p.c.:* TT for Fox; *ex prod:* Bill Weiss; *dir sup:* Gene Deitch; *dir:* Dave Tendlar; *story dir:* Tom Morrison; *story:* Larz Bourne, Eli Bauer; *anim:* Al Chiarito, Dave Tendlar, Jim Tyer, Bob Kuwahara, Mannie Davis, Vinnie Bell, Ed Donnelly, Johnny Gent; *des:* Jules Feiffer; *back:* Bill Hilliker *voice:* Allen Swift; *mus:* Phil Scheib; *prod mgr:* Sparky Schudde; *col:* Tech. *sd:* RCA. 7 min. CS. • A hungry dog escapes from a cop by dressing as a human. He joins the Foofer Frankfurter Co. and is eventually elevated to being a partner.

6329. The Tale of a Shirt (*Paul Terry-Toon*) 19 Feb. 1933; *p.c.:* Moser & Terry for Educational/Fox; *dir:* Frank Moser, Paul Terry; *mus:* Philip A. Scheib; b&w. *sd:* WE. 6 min. • Laundry activities in Chinatown.

6330. Tale of a Wolf (*Loopy de Loop*) 3 Mar. 1960; *p.c.:* Hanna-Barbera prods for Colum; *prod/dir:* William Hanna, Joseph Barbera; *story dir:* Alex Lovy; *story:* Warren Foster; *anim dir:* Charles A. Nichols; *anim:* Carlo Vinci; *lay:* Dick Bickenbach; *back:* Robert Gentle; *ed:* Greg Watson; *voices:* Daws Butler, Don Messick, Paul Frees; *mus:* Hoyt Curtin; *titles:* Lawrence Gobel; *prod mgr:* Howard Hanson; *col:* East. *sd:* RCA. 6½ min. • Loopy's endeavors to teach a young wolf to reform fall on stony ground.

6331. Tale of the Vienna Woods (*Happy Harmonies*) 27 Oct. 1934; *p.c.:* MGM; *prod/dir:* Hugh Harman, Rudolf Ising; *mus:* Scott Bradley; *col:* Tech-2. *sd:* RCA. 8 min. • A little fawn cavorts in the woods with a satyr brought to life from a fountain statue.

6332. A Tale of Two Kitties (*Merrie Melodies*) 14 Nov. 1942; *p.c.:* Leon Schlesinger prods for WB; *dir/lay:* Robert Clampett; *story:* Melvin Millar; *anim:* Rod Scribner, Robert McKimson; *back:* Michael Sasanoff; *ed:* Treg Brown; *voices:* Mel Blanc, Tedd Pierce; *mus:* Carl W. Stalling; *prod sup:* Henry Binder, Raymond G. Katz; *col:* Tech. *sd:* Vit. 7 min. • Two cats resembling Abbott and Costello try to secure an elusive Tweety bird.

6333. A Tale of Two Mice (*Looney Tunes*) 30 June 1945; *p.c.:* WB; *dir:* Frank Tashlin; *story:* Warren Foster; *anim:* Arthur Davis; *sets:* Richard H. Thomas; *ed:* Treg Brown; *voices:* Mel Blanc, Tedd Pierce; *mus:* Carl W. Stalling; *prod mgr:* John W. Burton; *prod:* Edward Selzer; *col:* Tech. *sd:* Vit. 7 min. • Two mice resembling Abbott and Costello create many devices to get the cheese past a vicious cat.

6334. Tales From the Crypt: Demon Knight 13 Jan. 1995; *p.c.:* Univ; *anim:* January Nordman, Laurel Klick, Alan Wolfson, W.L. Arance; *voice of the Crypt Keeper:* John Kassir; *col:* DeLuxe. *sd:* dts Stereo. 92 min. *l/a.* • Big screen version of the popular HBO television series of EC Comics' *Tales From the Crypt.*

6335. Tales From the Dark Side: The Movie 4 May 1990; *p.c.:* Para for Colum Tri-Star; *special visual fx "Lover's Vow":* stop-motion *anim:* Justin Kohn; *col:* Tech. *sd:* Dolby stereo. 93 min. *l/a.* • Live-action horror.

An artist has his life spared by a monster as long as he promises not to tell anyone what he has witnessed.

6336. The Talking Dog (*Maggie & Sam*) 27 Aug. 1956; *p.c.:* Walter Lantz prods for Univ; *dir:* Alex Lovy; *story:* Homer Brightman; *anim:* Ray Abrams, La Verne Harding; *sets:* Raymond Jacobs, Robert Givens; *voices:* Daws Butler, Grace Stafford; *mus:* Clarence Wheeler; *prod mgr:* William E. Garity; *col:* Tech. *sd:* RCA. 6 min. • Sam buys a talking dog and gives him a stage act but when a cat is let loose in the theatre, the dog reverts to form and wrecks the show.

6337. Talking Horse Sense (*Modern Madcap*) 11 Sept. 1959; *p.c.:* Para Cartoons; *dir:* Seymour Kneitel; *story:* Sam Dann, Carl Meyer, Jack Mercer; *anim:* Frank Endres, Wm. B. Pattengill; *sets:* Robert Owen; *mus:* Winston Sharples; *ph:* Leonard McCormick; *prod mgr:* Abe Goodman; *col:* Tech. *sd:* RCA. 6 min. • No story available.

6338. The Talking Magpies (*Terry-Toon*) 14 Jan. 1946; *p.c.:* TT for Fox; *dir:* Mannie Davis; *story:* John Foster; *voice:* Thomas Morrison; *mus:* Philip A. Scheib; *col:* Tech. *sd:* RCA. 7 min. • Mr. and Mrs. Magpie search for a new home due to the housing shortage. When they find one, they have to fight the irascible farmer and his dog to keep it.

6339. Talking Through My Heart (*Screen Songs*) 27 Nov. 1936; *p.c.:* The Fleischer Studio for Para; *prod:* Max Fleischer; *dir:* Dave Fleischer; *anim:* Thomas Johnson, Harold Walker; *mus:* Dick Stabile and his orchestra; b&w. *sd:* WE. 7 min. *l/a/anim.* • A sidewalk salesman introduces his wares.

6340. Tall in the Trap (*Tom & Jerry*) Sept. 1962; *p.c.:* Rembrandt for MGM; *prod:* William L. Snyder; *dir:* Gene Deitch; *story:* Bill Danch, Tedd Pierce; *voices:* Allen Swift; *mus:* Stepan Koníček; *played by* George Jirmal; *col:* Metro. *sd:* WE. 8 min. • A western town sheriff hires Tom to rid the town of Jerry, the cheese-stealing mouse. • See: *Tom and Jerry (Rembrandt Studio)*

6341. Tall Tale Teller (*Phoney Baloney*) May 1954; *p.c.:* TT for Fox; *dir:* Connie Rasinski; *story:* Tom Morrison; *anim:* Jim Tyer; *mus:* Philip A. Scheib; *ph:* Douglas Moye; *col:* Tech. *sd:* RCA. 6 min. • Phoney Baloney is arrested for selling drinks from a public fountain which he claims to be "The Fountain of Youth."

6342. Tall Timber (*Oswald the Lucky Rabbit*) 9 July 1928; *p.c.:* Winkler for Univ; *dir:* Walter Disney; *anim:* Hugh Harman, Rollin C. Hamilton; *ph:* Mike Marcus; b&w. *sil.* 6 min. • Oswald goes hunting in the Northwoods, ending by being chased by a bear.

6343. Tall Timber Tale (*Terry Bears*) July 1951; *p.c.:* TT for Fox; *dir:* Connie Rasinski; *story:* Tom Morrison; *anim:* Jim Tyer; *voices:* Douglas Moye, Tom Morrison; *mus:* Philip A. Scheib; *ph:* Douglas Moye; *col:* Tech. *sd:* RCA. 6 min. • Mama Bear sends Papa out to cut some kindling wood. The cubs try to help, causing no end of trouble.

6344. Tally-Hokum (*Noveltoon*) Oct. 1965; *p.c.:* Para Cartoons; *dir:* Howard Post; *story:* Eli Bauer; *anim:* Martin Taras; *sets:* Robert Little; *mus:* Winston Sharples; *ph:* Leonard McCormick; *prod mgr:* Abe Goodman *col:* Tech. *sd:* RCA. 6 min. • Hangdog, a dim-witted hunting dog goes after the quick-witted Moxie Foxie.

6345. Taming the Cat (*Heckle & Jeckle*) 14 Apr. 1948; *p.c.:* TT for Fox; *dir:* Connie Rasinski; *story:* John Foster; *anim:* Jim Tyer; *voices:* Thomas Morrison; *mus:* Philip A. Scheib; *ph:* Douglas Moye; *col:* Tech. *sd:* RCA. 6 min. • A cat advertizes for a song bird, having eaten the previous one and the magpies apply for the job.

6346. The Tangled Angler (*Fable*) 26 Dec. 1941; *p.c.:* Colum; *dir/story:* Frank Tashlin; *anim:* Chic Otterstrom; *lay:* Clark Watson; *ed:* Edward Moore; *voice:* Pinto Colvig, Harry E. Lang; *mus:* Paul Worth; *ph:* Frank Fisher; *prod mgr:* Ben Schwalb; b&w. *sd:* RCA. 8 min. • A fish pleads with Petey Pelican to let him go. He does and is repaid by having a bee put in his pouch. Tashlin completed this half finished cartoon.

6347. Tangled Television (*Color Rhapsody*) 30 Aug. 1940; *p.c.:* Colum; *dir:* Sid Marcus; *anim:* Art Davis, Herb Rothwell; *lay:* Clark Watson; *back:* Phil Davis; *ed:* George Winkler; *voices:* Mel Blanc, Danny Webb; *mus:* Joe de Nat; *ph:* Otto Reimer; *prod mgr:* James Bronis; *col:* Tech. *sd:* RCA. 7 min. • Three television pioneers are introduced who demonstrate how television works: Madame Dish sings, then a trip to India, Egypt, Africa and Venice.

6348. Tangled Travels (*Phantasy*) 9 June 1944; *p.c.*: Colum; *prod*: Dave Fleischer; *dir*: Al Geiss; *anim*: Volus Jones, George Grandpré; *lay*: Clark Watson; *voice*: Harry E. Lang, John McLeish; *mus*: Eddie Kilfeather; *ph*: Frank Fisher; b&w. *sd*: RCA. 6 min. • A heavy-accented professor delivers a literal translation to a travelogue.

6349. Tantalizing Fly (*Out of the Inkwell*) 4 Oct. 1919; *p.c.*: Bray prods for Goldwyn; *dir/story/l/a*: Max Fleischer; b&w. *sil*. 5 min. *l/a/anim*. • A fly bothers Max and Ko-Ko. The clown tries to swat it with a pen and splatters Max with ink.

6350. Tar with a Star (*Popeye*) 12 Aug. 1949; *p.c.*: Famous for Para; *dir*: Bill Tytla; *story*: Carl Meyer, Jack Mercer; *anim*: George Germanetti, Steve Muffatti; *voices*: Jack Mercer, Mae Questel, Jackson Beck; *mus*: Winston Sharples; *ph*: Leonard McCormick; *prod mgr*: Sam Buchwald; *col*: Tech. *sd*: RCA. 6½ min. • Popeye is made sheriff of a western town.

6351. Tarts and Flowers (*Noveltoon*) 26 May 1950; *p.c.*: Famous for Para; *dir*: Bill Tytla; *story*: Bill Turner, Larry Riley; *anim*: George Germanetti, Steve Muffatti; *sets*: Robert Little; *voices*: Mae Questel, Jackson Beck; *mus*: Winston Sharples; *ph*: Leonard McCormick; *prod mgr*: Sam Buchwald; *col*: Tech. *sd*: RCA. 7 min. • Audrey bakes a gingerbread man who is about to marry Miss Angel Cake when she is abducted by the villainous Devil's Food Cake.

6352. Tarzan 18 June 1999; *p.c.*: Walt Disney Enterprises, Inc. for BV; *dir*: Kevin Lima, Chris Buck; *prod*: Bonnie Arnold; based on the story *Tarzan of the Apes* by Edgar Rice Burroughs; *scr*: Tab Murphy, Bob Tzudiker, Noni White, David Reynolds, Jeffrey Stepakoff; *asso prod*: Christopher Chas; *art dir*: Daniel St. Pierre; *artistic sup*: asso art dir: Dan Cooper; *story*: Brian Pimental, Stephen Anderson, Mark D. Kennedy, Carole Holliday, Gaëtan Brizzi, Paul Brizzi, Don Dougherty, Ed Gombert, Randy Hancock, Don Hall, Kevin L. Harkey, Glen Keane, Burny Mattinson, Frank Nissen, John Norton, Jeff Snow, Michael Surrey, Christopher J. Ure, Mark Walton, Stevie Wermers, Kelly Wightman, John Ramirez; *lay*: Jean Christophe Poulain; *back*: Doug Ball; *clean-up*: Marshall Lee Toomey; *visual fx*: Peter Demund; *cg*: Eric Daniels; *prod mgr*: Jean Luc Florinda; *ex mus prod*: Chris Montan; *artistic co-ord*: Fraser MacLean; *Paris unit sup*: *lay*: Olivier Adam; *back*: Joaquim Royo Morales; *clean-up*: Christophe Charbonnel; *visual fx*: Allen Blyth; *prod mgr*: Coralie Cudot-Lissillour; *CAPS sup*: scene plan: Thomas Baker; *anim check*: Barbara Wiles, Janet Bruce; *2d anim processing*: Robyn L. Roberts; *color models*: Karen Comella; *paint/final check*: Hortensia M. Casagran; *compositing*: James "JR" Russell; *digital film print*: Brandy Hill; *technical co-ord*: Ann Tucker; *visual development & character des*: Chen-Yi Chang, Peter de Séve, Vance Gerry, Jean Gillmore, Joe Grant, Ian S. Gooding, Brian Jowers, H.B. "Buck" Lewis, Rick Maki, Henry Mayo, Sergio Pablos, Tina Price, Jeffrey Resolme Ranjo, Harold Siepermann, John Watkiss, Rowland B. Wilson; *anim*: "*Tarzan*": Glen Keane, Georges Abolin, Pierre Alary, Marco Allard, David Berthier, Bolhem Bouchiba, Patrick Delage, Eric Delbecq, Thierry Goulard, Borja Montoro Cavero, Enis Tahsin Ozgur, Stephane Sainte-Foi, Tran-Quang-Thieu JC, Kristoff Vergne; "*Jane*": Ken Stuart Duncan, Jared Beckstrand, Doug Bennett, Robert Bryan, Caroline Cruikshank, Mark Koetsier, Doug Krohn; "*Kala*": Russ Edmonds, Mario J. Menjivar, Dougg Williams, Andreas Wessel-Therhorn; "*Young & Baby Tarzan*": John Ripa, Steven Pierre Gordon, Jeff Johnson, Yoshimichi Tamura; "*Terk*": Michael Surrey, Adam Dykstra, Danny Galieote, David Moses Pimentel, Chad Stewart; "*Clayton*": Randy Haycock, Tim George, Richard Hoppe, Michael Stocker; "*Porter*": David Burgess, David Block, Theresa Wiseman; "*Kerchak*": Bruce W. Smith, Robb Pratt, Marc Smith; "*Tantor*": Sergio Pablos, James Hull, Mike Kunkel, Jean Morel, Steven Wahl; "*Sabor*": Dominique Monfery, Marc Eoche Duval, Juanjo Guarnido, Zoltan Maros; "*Ape Family*": Jay Jackson, Catherine Poulain; "*Baboons & Baby Baboon*": Bruce W. Smith; "*Captain & Thugs*": T. Daniel Hofstedt; "*Flynt & Mungo*": Chris Wahl; *rough inbet*: Noreen Beasley, George Benavides, Casey Coffey, Neal Stanley Goldstein, Benjamin Gonzalez, Nicholas Keramidas, Gary D. Payne, Bob Persichetti, Chris Sonnenburg, Aliki Theofilopoulos, Michael Wu; *principal location des*: Paul Felix, Loic Rastout, David A. Dunnet; *lay*: *journeymen*: James P. Alles, James Beihold, John Byrne, Fred Craig, Vincent Massy de la Chesneraye, Pierre Fassel, Richard Carl Livingston, Antonio Navarro, Simon O'Leary, John Puglisi, Tom Shannon, Allen C. Tam, Sherilan Weinhart, Tanya T. Wilson; *lay asst*: Cent Alantar, Max Braslavsky, Denise Blakely Fuller, Robert Cardone, Marec Fritzinger, Lam Hoang;

Johan Anton Klingler, Denise Louise Klitsie, Mark E. Koerner, Armand Serrano, Lissa Jane Ainley, Edgar Carlos, Thomas Debitus, James Aaron Finch, Matthieu Gosselin, Brian Kesinger, Julio Leon, Cheng Z. "Diane" Lu, David Martin, Birgitta Erja Pollaneni, Donald Reich, Chung Sup Yoon; *blue sketch*: Madlyn Zusmer O'Neill, Valérie Braun, Monica Albracht Marroquin, Bill Davis, Eithne Ersoz, Noel C. Johnson; *back*: traditional *& deep canvas sup digital back painter*: David McCamley; *journeymen*: Jennifer K. Ando, Dominick R. Domingo, Debbie du Bois, Olivier Besson, Justin Brandstater, Hye Young Coh, Scott Fassett, Jean-Paul Fernandez, Thierry Fournier, Susan Hackett, Jason Horley, David Jarvis, Mi Kyung Joung-Raynis, William Lorencz, Jerry Loveland, Serge Michaels, Gregory C. Miller, Patricia Millereau-Guilmard, Don Moore, Patricia Palmer-Phillipson, Pierre Pavloff, Philip Phillipson, William T. Silvers Jr., Christophe Vacher, Thomas Woodington, David Yorke; *back asst*: Suzanne Kyung Bouhours, Nathan Hughes, George Humphrey; *digital re-touch painters*: Christine Laubach, Nancy Olivet Ramirez, Valapa "Oomp" Saubhayana; *clean-up anim*: "*Tarzan*": lead key: Philippe Briones; *asst*: Serge Bussone, Javier Espinosa Banuelos, Florence Montceau, Farouk Cherfi, Pierre Girault, Laurence Adam-Bessiére, Gerard Brady, Claire Bourdin, Christine Chatal-Poli, Jeroen Dejonckheere, Jerome Guillaud, Philippe Hooghe, Maria Angela Iturriza Freire, Christine Landes-Tigano, Ludovic Letrun, Jean-Christophe Lie, Nguyên Dang Long, Anne Pellerin, Sylvaine Terriou, Pierre Seurin; *break*: Oliver Acker, Nicole de Bellefroid, Philippe Malka, Nicolas Ruedy, Nicolas Quere; *inbet*: Valerie Breand, Bernard Dourdent, Graham Gallagher, David Gilson, Celine Papazian, Alice Picard, Didier Poli, Frederic Vilquin; "*Jane*": lead key: Juliet Duncan; *asst*: Jane Tucker Bonnet, Merry Kanawyer Clingen, Wes Chun, Sean Gallimore, Richard D. Rocha, Jacqueline Sanchez, Teresa Eidenbock, Bernadette Moley; *break*: Christenson M. Casuco, Edward B. Goral, Jeffrey B. Harter, Chun Yin Joey So, Kathleen Thorson; *inbet*: Flora Sungsook Park; "*Kala*": lead key: June M. Fujimoto; *asst*: Karen A. Hardenbergh, Celinda S. Kennedy, Daniel Yoontaek Lim, Mary Measures; *break*: Frank Dietz, Toshio Ichishita, Allison Renna; *inbet*: Kompin Kemgumnird; "*Young & Baby Tarzan*": lead key: Margie Daniels; *asst*: Jamie Kezlarian Bolio, Natasha Dukelski Selfridge, Kevin M. Grow, Rick Kohlschmidt; *break*: Nickolas M. Frangos, Cathie Karas Wilke, Cynthia Landeros; "*Adult & Baby Terk*": lead key: Debra Armstrong; *asst*: Maria Wilhemina Rosetti, Mary-Jean Repchuk, Marty Schwartz; *break*: Cliff Freitas; *inbet*: Jong Won Park; "*Young Terk*": lead key: Brian B. McKim; *asst*: Judith Barnes, Marsha W.J. Park-Yum; *break*: Raul Aguirre Jr.; "*Clayton*": lead key: Randy Sanchez, Dan Tanaka; *asst*: Miriam McDonnell, Dorothea Baker Paul, Carl Philip Hall, David E. Recinos; *break*: Denise Meehan, Jim Snider, Ronald John Westlund; *inbet*: Matthew R. Haber; "*Porter*": lead key: Tony Anselmo; *break*: Aidan Flynn, Steven K. Thompson; "*Kerchak*": lead key: Tracy Mark Lee; *asst*: Eric Pigors; *break*: Brian Mainolfi, Doug Post; *inbet*: Michael Ludy; "*Young & Adult Tantor*": lead key: Terry Wozniak; *asst*: Sue Adnopoz, Brigitte T. Franzka-Fritz, Chan Woo Jung; *break*: Jocelyn Kooistra; *inbet*: James Anthony Marquez; "*Sabor*": lead key: Gontran Hoarau; *asst*: Maros Gregan Gizella, Benoit Maurzec, Phirum Sou, Marc Tosolini, Xavier Villez; "*Flynt & Mungo and Ape Family*": lead key: Susan Lantz, Ginny Parmele; *asst*: Jesus Cortes, Kris Heller, Susan Y. Sugita, Peggy Tonkonogy, Cynthia Jill French, Annette Morel; *break*: Hugo Soriano; *inbet*: Jeff W. Hong, Kimberly Moriki Zamlich; "*Baboons & misc. characters*": lead key: Lieve Miessen; *asst*: Raymond A. Harris, Michael G. McKinney, Diana Coco, Janet Heerhan Kwon, Kent Holaday; *break*: Munir Bhatti, Carolyn F. Gliona; "*Captain & Thugs*": lead key: Gail Frank; *asst*: Michael Hazy, Lillian Amanda Chapman; *break*: Jim Brummett; *clean-up 2nd unit sup*: Vera Lanpher-Pacheco; *digital prod Software development*: sup: Tasso Lappas; *snr development technical dir*: George Katanics; *technical dir*: asst technical dir: Peter H. Palombi, Bernard O. Ceguerra, Mayur Patel, Iva S. Itchevska, Christine C. Lau; *model development*: sup: Gil Zimmerman; *technical dir*: Nick Collier, Ian J. Cooney, Bill Konersman, Andrea Losch, Nicholetta Marcialis, Kevin Paul Sheedy, Christopher Poplin; *asst modelers*: Pamela J. Choy, Joe Whyte; *look development*: sup: Dale Drummond; *lighting*: Sean Eckols, Clunie Holt, Mira Nikolic; *asst technical dir*: William Otsuka, Ruth Ramos; *Render I/0-scene set-up*: Rosana D'Andrea, Aileen Kehe, L. Rhiannon Leffanta, Anna Ta, Faye Tipton, David W. Thompson, Elkeer Zaldumbide; *visual fx anim*: anim sup 3d fx: Dan Chaika; *anim sup*: Mark Myer; *visual fx anim*: Etienne Aubert, Thierry Chaffoin, James Menehune Goss, Craig L. Hoffman, Tom Hush, Michael Cadwallader Jones, Dorse A. Lanpher, Dan Lund, Brice

Mallier, David Joseph Mildenberger, Cynthia Neill Knizek, Masa Oshiro, Mouloud Oussid, Kathleen Quaife, Allen M. Stovall, David Tidgwell, Phillip Vigil, Marlon West; *fx asst:* Sean Applegate, Marko Barrows, Mathilde Danton, Angela Anastasia Diamos, Mabel L. Gesner, Ko Hashiguchi, David M. Kcencih, Jon William Lopez, Mary Mullen, Maria Nemeth, Joseph Christopher Pepé, Michael Anthony Toth, John Tucker, Thomas Walsh, Karel Zilliacus, Virginia Augustin, Thierry Beltrami, Ivan Kassabov, Derrick Lee McKenzie, Graham Woods, Gregory Regeste, Van Shiranian, Dennis Spicer, Lora M. Spran; *fx break:* Jay Baker, Robert Blalock, Eduardo Brieno, Delphine Buratti, Alexis Venet, Melinda Wang, Nicole Alene Zamora; *fx inbet:* Ernesto Brieno, Kristin Fong-Lukavsky, Eric Gosselet, Ron Pence, Philip Pignotti, Jeffrey C. Plamenig, Robert Smyth, Sean Strain, Dawn W. Wells; *asst prod mgr: story/visual development:* Dave Okey; *ed:* Kara Lord; *lay:* Paul S.D. Lanum; *character anim:* Tone Thyne; *sweatbox:* Karenna Mazur Alderton; *clean-up:* Lesley Addario Bentivegna; *visual fx:* Leif Green; *back:* Jennifer L. Hughes; *digital prod:* Jason Hintz; *Paris lay/back:* Michael de la Cruz; *Paris anim:* Alexandra Skinazi; *Paris clean-up:* Etienne Longa; *Paris visual fx:* Frederika Pepping; *scene plan:* Katherine A. Irwin; *anim check:* Cathy McGowan Leahy; *col models:* Holly E. Bratton; *prod:* Bill Bloom; *mgr disk space/retakes:* Shawne Zarubica, Brenda McGirl; *Florida Unit sup: Clean-up:* Philip Boyd; *visual fx:* Joseph F. Gilland, Garrett Wren; *back:* Sean Sullivan; *addit lay:* Scott Caple, Arden Chan, Shawn Colbeck, Trish Coveney-Rees, Tom Dow, Mac George, William Samuel Hodman, Gary Mouri, Franc Reyes, Kenneth Spirduso, Kevyn Wallace, Yong-Hong Zhong; *addit anim:* Ruben A. Aquino, Jean-Luc Ballester, Dale Baer, James Baker, Travis Blaise, Tom Bancroft, Richard Bazley, Roger Chiasson, Wayne Carlisi, Michael Cedeno, Robert Espanto Domingo, Jerry Yu Ching, Sandro Cleuzo, Tom Gately, Brian Ferguson, Raul Garcia, David Hancock, Christopher Hubbard, Bert Klein, James Young Jackson, Sang Jin Kim, Sam Levine, Mark Alan Mitchell, Joe Oh, Jamie Oliff, Ralf Palmer, Mark Pudleiner, William Recinos, Michael Show, Bill Waldman, Anthony Ho Wong, Phil Young, Ellen Woodbury; *addit rough inbet:* Gregg Azzopardi, Mike Disa, Larry R. Flores, Edmund Gabriel, Grant Hiestand, John Hurst, Clay Kaytis, Joseph Mateo, Bobby Alcid Rubio, Kevin M. Smith, Wes Sullivan; *addit back:* Sunny Apinchapong, Ron Defelice, Xin-Lin Fan, Christopher F. Greco, Miguel Gil, Brad Hicks, Xiangyuan Jie, Geraldine Kovats, Michael Kurinsky, James J. Martin, Barbara Massey, Kelly McGraw, Kevin McNamara, Peter Moehrle, David Murray, John Piampiano, Leonard Robledo, Robh Ruppel, George Taylor, David Wang (Ying Guang); *addit anim clean-up:* Philip J. Allora, Todd H. Ammons, Scott Anderson, Merritt F. Andrews, Carlos Arancibia, Stephen Nelson Austin, Dominic A'Vant, Mary Jo Ayers, Kathleen M. Bailey, Kevin A. Barber, Augusto Borges Bastos, Bill Berg, Carl Bell, Janelle Bell-Martin, Rachel Renee Bibb, Patricia Ann Billings, Katherine Blackmore, Saul Andrew Blinkoff, Cyndy Bohonovsky, Jason Boose, Daniel Bond, Daniel Bowman, Philip Boyd, Russell Braun, Todd Bright, Scott A. Burroughs, Chang Yei Cho, Inna Chon, Scott Claus, Caroline Clifford, Ron Cohee, Regina Conroy, Frank R. Cordero, Don Crum, Antoine Cunningham, Tammy Daniel-Biske, Dan Daly, Antony de Fato, Tom de Rosier, Kevin Deters, Marcia Kimura Dougherty, Amy Drobeck, Lee Dunkman, Kimberly Dwinell, James W. Elston, Sam Ewing, Perry Farinola, Tom Fish, Larry R. Flores, Jill Friemark, Cindy Ge, Michael Genz, Daniel A. Gracey, Mike Greenholt, Akemi Gutierrez, Edward Gutierrez, James A. Harris, Ilan Wexio Hatukah, Arturo Alejándro Hernandez, Allison Hollen, Renee Holt, Eun Sang Jang, Emily Jiuliano, Phillip A. Jones, Brian D. Kennon, Seung Beom Kim, Yung Soo Kim, Nancy E. Kniep, Samantha Lair, Lisa G. Lanyon, Calvin le Duc, Jang Woo Lee, Mi Yul Lee, Steve Lenze, Ely Lester, Michael Lester, Kellie D. Lewis, Leticia Lichtwardt, Steve Lubin, Kaaren Lundeen, Sean Luo, David Mar, Whitney B. Martin, Tim Massa, Patrick McClintock, Alex McDaniel, Sarah Mercey-Boose, Jane Misek, Frank Montagna Jr., Maurilio Morales, Richard S. Morgan, Wendy J. Muir, Monica Murdock, Gary Myers, Yoon Sook Nam, Jan Naylor, Terry Naughton, David T. Nethery, Phil Noto, John O'Hailey, Stephanie Olivieri, James Parris, Jason Peltz, John Pierro, Eddie Pittman, Cheryl Polakow-Knight, Ruben Procopio, Teresita Quezada, Peter Raymundo, Dana M. Reemes, Daniel Lawrence Riebold, Boola Robello, Al Salgado, Danny R. Santos, Tony Santo, Elsa Sesto-Vidal, Jacqueline M. Shepherd, Sherrie H. Sinclair, Keith A. Sintay, Vincent Siracusano, Lon Smart, Bryan M. Sommer, Rusty Stoll, George Sukara, Trevor Tamboline, Myung Kang Teague, Richard C. Trebus Jr., Bill Thinnes, Chad Thompson, Thomas Thor-

specken, Alex Topete, Kim Tprpey, Marianne Tucker, Patrick Tuorto, Rosana Urbes, Yer (Za) Vue, Elizabeth S. Watasin, Darren R. Webb, Matt Whitlock, Michael W. Wiesmeier, Robert Lee Williams Jr., Ginger Wolf, Woody Woodman, Rebecca Wrigley, Eunice (Eun Ok) Yu, Ron Zeitler, Jane Zhao, Stephan Zupkas; *addit digital prod:* William T. Carpenter, Erica Cassetti, Sanguan V. Chow, Nika Dunne, Eric Gervais-Despres, Steve Goldberg, Claire Lawrence-Slater, Sean Locke, Jean-Louis Malgoire, Chris Springfield, Charles Stoner, Thomas C. Meyer, Gary Tefler, Susan Thayer, Nathan Detroit Warner, Jeff Wolverton; *addit visual fx:* Gordon Baker, Robert Bennett, Guner Behich, Verell "Skip" Bowers, Paul Briggs, John Cashman, Aliza Corson, John Fargnoli, Jazno Francoeur, William J. Haas, Darlene E. Hadrika, Michael Kaschalk, Paul R. Kashuk Jr., Stephen McDermott, Michael Todd Montgomerg, Michael L. Oliva, Christopher R. Page, Sean Simon Ramirez, Paitoon Ratanasirintrawoot, Gary Schumer, Heather M. Shepherd, Rochelle Doriot Smith, John David Thornton, Tony West; *snr mgr prod: CAPS:* Gretchen Maschmeyer Albrecht; *snr mgr scene plan/ph:* Joe Jiuliano; *mgr Florida: CAPS:* Fran Kirsten; *scene plan:* S.J. Bleick, Ronald J. Jackson, Cynthia Goode, David J. Link, Mark Henley, Raphaël Vincente; *scene plan/fx data entry:* Jamal M. Davis, Laura L. Jaime, Sherri H. Villarete; *anim check: asst sup:* Karen S. Paat, Mavis E. Shafer; *anim check:* Janette Hulett, Denise M. Mitchell, Nicolette Bonnell, Janette Adams, Helen O'Flynn, Kathleen O'Mara-Svetlik, Gary G. Shafer; *2d anim. processing: asst sup:* Karen N. China; *digital mark-up:* Lynnette E. Cullen; *paint sup:* Sylvia Bennett Fauque; *2d anim processors:* David Braden, Jo Ann Breuer, Richard J. McFerren, Michael A. McFerren, Robert Lizardo, Stacie K. Reece, David J. Rowe; *col stylists:* Penny Coulter, Maria Gonzalez, Barbara Lynn Hamane, Debbie Jorgensborg, Heidi Lin Loring, Celine O'Sullivan, Sylvia I. Sanchez, Marie St. Clair, Judith L. Tolley; *paint: col model mark-up:* Bill Andres, Sherrie Cuzzort, Beth Ann McCoy-Gee, Grace H. Shirado, Christine Ng Wong, David J. Zywicki; *registration:* Karan Lee-Storr, Leyla C. Amaro-Pelaez; *asst sup. paint:* Irma Velez, Russell Blandino, Phyllis Estelle Fields; *paint mark-up:* Roberta Lee Borchardt, Patricia L. Gold, Bonnie A. Ramsey, Barbara Newby, Myrian Ferron Tello; *paint:* Carmen Sanderson, Joyce Alexander, Kirk Axtell II, Phyllis Bird, Joey Calderon, Ofra Afuta Calderon, Sybil Elaine Cuzzort, Janice M. Caston, Casey Clayton, Florida d'Ambrosio, Robert Edward Dettloff, Nika Dunne, Michael Foley, Paulino Garcia, Debbie Green, Stevie Hirsch, David Karp, Angelika R. Katz, Kukhee Lee, Deborah Mooneyham Hughes, Karen Lynne Nugent, Kenneth O'Malley, Bruce Gordon Phillipson, Rosalinde Praamsma, Heidi Woodward Shellhorn, Eyde Sheppherd, Don Shump, Fumiko Roche Sommer, S. Ann Sullivan, Roxanne M. Taylor, Tami Terusa, Christine E. Toth, Britt-Marie Van der Nagel; *final check:* Teri N. McDonald, Lea Dahlen, Misoon Kim, Catherine Mirkovich-Peterson, Sally-Anne King; *compositing:* Timothy B. Gales, Michelle A. Sammartino, Jason Leonard, Robert Buske, Earl Scott Coffman, Dolores Pope; *digital film printing/opticals: asst sup:* Tony Poriazis; *ph/film rec operators:* John D. Aardal, John Derderian, Jennie Kepenek Mouzis; *asst mgr:* Jeanne E. Leone-Sterwerf; *quality control:* Chuck Warren; *ph operation co-ord:* Stephanie L. Clifford; *digital fx/reuse librarian:* Vicki L. Casper; *addit anim check: Florida sup:* Laurie Sacks; *check:* Daniel Cohen, Jacqueline Hooks-Winterlich, Willis Middleton, Albert Francis Moore, Victoria Winner Novak, Pierre Sucaud; *addit 2d anim processors: Florida sup:* Jan Barley Gutowski; Sarah J. Cole, Gareth P. Fishbaugh, Evariste Ferreira, Corey D. Fredrickson, Todd La Plante, Barbara J. Poirier; *ed:* Gregory Perler, Tim Mertens, James Melton, Gina Gallo Paris, Stephen L. Meek, Teressa Longo, Mark Alan Deimel, Hermann H. Schmidt, Jeff Jones, Ivan Bilancio; *voices: Clayton:* Brian Blessed; *Kala:* Glenn Close; *Jane:* Minnie Driver; *Tarzan:* Tony Goldwyn; *Professor Porter:* Nigel Hawthorne; *Kerchak:* Lance Hendriksen, *Tantor:* Wayne Knight; *Young Tarzan:* Alex D. Linz; *Terk:* Rosie O'Donnell; *also:* Beth Anderson, Jack Angel, Joseph Ashton, Robert Bergen, Billy Warren Bodine, Hillary Brooks, Rodger Bumpass, Lily Collins, Kat Cressida, Jim Cummings, Aria Curzon, Jennifer Darling, Taylor Dempsey, Debi Derryberry, Patti Deutsch, Paul Eiding, Blake Ewing, Francesca Falcone, Michael Geiger, Scott Gershin, Sam Gifaldi, Amy Gleason, Jackie Gonneau, Debbie Hall, Johnnie Hall, Sandie Hall, Tina Halvorson, Linda Harmon, Karen Harper, Micah Hauptman, Jennifer L. Hughes, Grady Hutt, Luana Jackman, Adam Karpel, Theo Lebow, Brandon Lucas, Ricky Lucchese, James Lively, Sherry Lynn, Melissa MacKay, Danny Mann, Ilana Marks, Jason Marsden, Mickie T. McGowan, Donna Medine, Nils Montan, Bobbi Page, Brandon Pollard, Phil Proctor, Scott Record, Michael

Reagan, Ian Redford, Jessica Rotter, Chris Sanders, Stephanie Sawyer, Laurie Schillinger, Brianne Siddall, Frank Simms, Susan Stevens-Logan, Shane Sweet, Tiffany Takara, Dominic Thiroux, Jamie Torcellini, Erik von Detten, Joe Whyte, Danielle Wiener; *songs:* Phil Collins; *mus score:* Mark Mancina; "You'll Be in My Heart" produced by Rob Cavallo and Phil Collins; performed by Phil Collins; *rec:* Elliot Scheiner; *mix:* Chris Lord-Alge; "Two Worlds"/"You'll Be in My Heart"/"Son of Man"/"Strangers Like Me" produced and arranged by Phil Collins, Mark Mancina; performed by Phil Collins; "Trashin' the Camp" produced, arranged & performed by Phil Collins; *vocals:* Rosie O'Donnell; *addit arrangements:* Paul Bogaev; *orch:* David Metzger; *conducted by:* Don Harper; *song recl mix:* Frank Wolf; *score recl mix:* Steve Kempster; *score co-prod:* Christopher Ward; *mus ed:* Earl Ghaffari, Robbie Boyd, Daniel Gaber; *mus prod:* Andrew Page, Tom MacDougall, Deniece Larocca; *post prod:* Patsy Bougé, Eleanor Lesh, Robert H. Bagley; *re-rec mix:* Chris Jenkins, Marc Smith, Ron Bartlett, Doc Kane; *sd ed:* Per Hallberg, Karen Baker; *ADR sup:* Curt Schulkey; *foley:* Craig S. Jaeger, Lou Kleinman, Philip D. Morrill, Tony Negrete, James M. Moriana, Jeff Wilhoit, Nerses Gezalyan, Greg Zimmerman, Mark Ormandy; *title des:* Robert Dawson, Grady Cofer; *col:* Tech. *sd:* Dolby stereo. 84 min. • When a safari appears in the African jungle, they are confronted by Tarzan, a human orphan who has been raised by gorillas. Jane falls for the ape man but Clayton, a trapper, wants to capture him and take him back to civilization to exploit him.

6353. A Taste of Catnip (*Merrie Melodies*) 3 Dec. 1966; *p.c.:* DFE for WB; *dir:* Robert McKimson; *story:* Michael O'Connor; *anim:* Ted Bonnicksen, Bob Matz, Manny Perez, Norm McCabe, George Grandpré, Warren Batchelder; *lay:* Dick Ung; *back:* Tom O'Loughlin; *ed:* Lee Gunther; *voices:* Mel Blanc, Gonzalez Gonzales; *mus:* Walter Greene; *col:* Tech. *sd:* Vit. 6 min. • Daffy consults a psychiatrist when he believes he is turning into a cat by living next door to a Catnip factory and inhaling the fumes.

6354. A Taste of Money (*Roland & Rattfink*) 24 June 1970; *p.c.:* Mirisch/DFE for UA; *dir:* Art Davis; *anim:* Warren Batchelder, Don Williams, Art Leonardi, Bob Taylor, Manny Perez, John Gibbs; *lay:* Al Wilson; *back:* Richard Thomas; *ed:* Lee Gunther; *voices:* Leonard Weinrib, Athena Lorde, Peter Halton; *mus:* Doug Goodwin; *ph:* John Burton Jr.; *prod sup:* Jim Foss, Harry Love; *col:* DeLuxe. *sd:* RCA. 6 min. • Rattfink marries a rich widow and inherits her oversized son in the bargain.

6355. Taxi-Turvy (*Popeye*) 4 June 1954; *p.c.:* Famous for Para; *dir:* Seymour Kneitel; *story:* Irving Spector; *anim:* Tom Johnson, Frank Endres, Els Barthen; *sets:* Robert Owen; *voices:* Jack Mercer, Jackson Beck, Mae Questel; *mus:* Winston Sharples; *ph:* Leonard McCormick; *prod mgr:* Seymour Shultz; *col:* Tech. *sd:* RCA. 6 min. • Taxi cab drivers, Popeye and Bluto vie for Olive Oyl as a potential customer.

6356. Tea for Two-Hundred (*Donald Duck*) 24 Dec. 1948; *p.c.:* Walt Disney prods for RKO; *dir:* Jack Hannah; *story:* Nick George, Bill Berg; *anim:* Judge Whitaker, Bob Carlson, Volus Jones, Bill Justice; *fx:* Jack Boyd; *lay:* Yale Gracey; *back:* Thelma Witmer; *voices:* Clarence Nash, Pinto Colvig, James MacDonald; *mus:* Oliver Wallace; *col:* Tech. *sd:* RCA. 6¹⁄₂ min. *Academy Award nomination.* • Donald's picnic is marred by an army of food pilfering ants.

6357. Tea House Mouse (*Hashimoto*) Jan. 1963; *p.c.:* TT for Fox; *ex prod:* Bill Weiss: *dir:* Bob Kuwahara; *story dir:* Tom Morrison; *story:* Larz Bourne; *anim:* Bob Kuwahara, Cosmo Anzilotti; *sets:* Alan Shapiro, Dave Ubinas; *ed:* George McAvoy; *voices:* John Myhers; *mus:* Phil Scheib; *ph:* Charles Schettler; *col:* DeLuxe. *sd:* RCA. 5 min. CS. • Hashimoto's daughter, Yuriko, is forced to serve as a geisha for a cat. Under disguise, Hashimoto manages to replace her and serve an unusual tea ceremony.

6358. Tea Party (*Hector Heathcote*) Apr. 1963; *p.c.:* TT for Fox; *ex prod:* Bill Weiss; *dir:* Dave Tendlar; *story dir:* Tom Morrison; *story:* Kin Platt; *anim:* Ralph Bakshi, Mannie Davis; *sets:* Bill Focht, John Zago; *ed:* George McAvoy; *voices:* John Myhers; *mus:* Phil Scheib; *ph:* Ted Moskowitz; *col:* DeLuxe. *sd:* RCA. 6 min. CS. • Heathcote manages to unwittingly foil the Boston Tea Party.

6359. Teachers Are People (*Goofy*) 27 June 1952; *p.c.:* Walt Disney prods for RKO; *dir:* Jack Kinney; *story:* Dick Kinney, Brice Mack; *anim:* George Nicholas, Hugh Fraser, Ed Aardal, Harvey Toombs; *fx:* Blaine Gibson; *lay:* Al Zinnen; *back:* Art Riley; *voices:* Alan Reed, Pinto Colvig, Helen Seibert, Lucille Williams, Norma Swank, John Kinney, Mike Kinney; *mus:*

Oliver Wallace; *col:* Tech. *sd:* RCA. 6 min. • Geef takes on the role of a school teacher coping with a classful of unruly kids.

6360. Teacher's Pest (*Noveltoon*) 31 Mar. 1950; *p.c.:* Famous for Para; *dir:* I. Sparber; *story:* I. Klein; *anim:* Myron Waldman, Gordon Whittier; *sets:* Tom Ford; *voices:* Sid Raymond, Cecil Roy; *mus:* Winston Sharples; *ph:* Leonard McCormick; *prod mgr:* Sam Buchwald; *col:* Tech. *sd:* RCA. 7 min. • Junior Owl's efforts to be wise land him in the wolf's cooking pot when Wolfie disguises himself as a school teacher.

6361. Teacher's Pest (*Talkartoon*) 7 Feb. 1931; *p.c.:* The Fleischer Studio for Para; *prod:* Max Fleischer; *dir:* Dave Fleischer; b&w. *sd:* WE. 8 min. • Bimbo's antics in school.

6362. The Teacher's Pests (*Oswald*) 19 Dec. 1932; *p.c.:* Univ; *dir:* Walter Lantz, "Bill" Nolan; *anim:* Ray Abrams, Fred Avery, "Bill" Weber, Jack Carr, Charles Hastings; *mus:* James Dietrich; b&w. *sd:* WE. 7 min. • Oswald and his pals make life miserable for their teacher and numbers on the blackboard come to life.

6363. Teapot Town Ted Eshbaugh prods for Lipton's Tea; *anim:* Ted Eshbaugh. • Commercial for Lipton's tea.

6364. The Tears of an Onion (*Color Classic*) 25 Feb. 1938; *p.c.:* The Fleischer Studio for Para; *prod:* Max Fleischer; *dir:* Dave Fleischer; *anim:* David Tendlar, Joseph Oriolo; *mus:* Sammy Timberg; *col:* Tech. *sd:* WE. 7 min. • An onion is ostracized by the other fruit and vegetables until he rescues a girl peach from the clasp of an evil purple bug.

6365. Tease for Two (*Looney Tunes*) 28 Aug. 1965; *p.c.:* DFE for WB; *dir:* Robert McKimson; *story:* Dave DeTiege; *anim:* Warren Batchelder, Bob Matz, Manny Perez; *lay:* Dick Ung; *back:* Tom O'Loughlin; *ed:* Lee Gunther; *voices:* Mel Blanc; *mus:* Bill Lava; *col:* Tech. *sd:* Vit. 6 min. • Daffy disturbs the Goofy Gophers while digging for gold and they wreak their revenge.

6366. Technical Romances *p.c.:* Bray prods for Hodkinson; *dir/anim:* Ashley Miller, J.A. Norling, F. Lyle Goldman; *story:* J.A. Norling; b&w. *sil.* • *1922:* The Mysterious Box 25 Nov. The Sky Splitter 9 Dec. • *1923:* Gambling with the Gulf Stream 4 Feb. The Romance of Life 1 Mar. The Immortal Voice 10 June. Black Sunlight 1 Dec. • A typical example of this series is "The Sky Splitter" which concerns the subject of light and speed where the illusion of a trip to the stars by a living action is shown.

6367. Techno-Cracked (*Flip the Frog*) 8 May 1933; *p.c.:* Celebrity prods for MGM; *prod/dir:* Ub Iwerks; *anim:* Jimmie Culhane; b&w. *sd:* PCP. 8 min. • Flip creates a robot to help mow the lawn but it runs amock.

6368. Technology, Phooey (*Ant & the Aardvark*) 25 June 1969; *p.c.:* Mirisch/DFE for UA; *dir:* Gerry Chiniquy; *story:* Irv Spector; *anim:* La Verne Harding, Manny Gould, Manny Perez, Warren Batchelder, Don Williams; *lay:* Dick Ung; *back:* Tom O'Loughlin; *ed:* Lee Gunther; *voices:* John Byner; *mus:* Doug Goodwin, Pete Candoli, Billy Byers, Jimmy Rowles, Tommy Tedesco, Ray Brown, Shelly Manne; *ph:* John Burton Jr.; *prod sup:* Jim Foss, Harry Love; *col:* DeLuxe. *sd:* RCA. 6 min. • The aardvark employs the use of a computer in assisting him in catching the ant.

6369. Technoracket (*Scrappy*) 20 May 1933; *p.c.:* Winkler for Colum; *prod:* Charles Mintz; *story:* Sid Marcus; *anim:* Art Davis; *lay:* Clark Watson; *back:* Phil Davis; *mus:* Joe de Nat; *prod mgr:* James Bronis; b&w. *sd:* RCA. 6 min. • Scrappy mechanizes his farm with the introduction of a robot, forcing the farm animals to revolt by putting a spanner in the robot's works.

6370. Teddy and the Angel Cake 15 Apr. 1916; *p.c.:* Pathé Exchange; *dir/anim:* Earl Hurd; b&w. *sil.* 5 min. • No story available.

6371. The "Teddy" Bears 1907; *p.c.:* Edison; *dir:* Edwin S. Porter; b&w. *sil. l/a/anim.* • No story available.

6372. The Tee Bird (*Woody Woodpecker*) 13 July 1959; *p.c.:* Walter Lantz prods for Univ; *dir:* Paul J. Smith; *story:* Homer Brightman; *anim:* Robert Bentley, Les Kline, Don Patterson; *sets:* Art Landy, Raymond Jacobs; *voices:* Dal McKennon, Grace Stafford; *mus:* Clarence Wheeler; *prod mgr:* William E. Garity; *col:* Tech. *sd:* RCA. 6 min. • Woody enters a golfing tournament against Dapper Dan Dooley, a monumental cheat.

6373. Tee for Two (*Tom & Jerry*) 21 July 1945; *p.c.:* MGM; *dir:* William Hanna, Joseph Barbera; *anim:* Ray Patterson, Irven Spence, Pete Burness, Kenneth Muse; *lay:* Harvey Eisenberg; *back:* Robert Gentle; *ed:* Fred

MacAlpin; *mus:* Scott Bradley; *ph:* Jack Stevens; *prod:* Fred Quimby; *col:* Tech. *sd:* WE. 7 min. • Tom plays a round of golf, using Jerry as caddy ... but Jerry has other ideas.

6374. Tee Time 5 Apr. 1931; *p.c.:* Copley Pictures Corp; *prod:* Jacques Kopfstein; *anim:* B.M. Powell; b&w. *sd.* • No story available.

6375. Teeny Weeny Meany (*Chilly Willy*) May 1966; *p.c.:* Walter Lantz prods for Univ; *dir:* Sid Marcus; *story:* Homer Brightman; *anim:* Al Coe; *sets:* Ray Huffine; *voices:* Daws Butler; *mus:* Walter Greene; *prod mgr:* William E. Garity; *col:* Tech. *sd:* RCA. 6 min. • Tuna trawler guard Smedley is put in charge of guarding the captain's lunch from Chilly's pilfering hands.

6376. Telefilm 19 Apr. 1928; *p.c.:* Out of the Inkwell Studio; *anim:* Max Fleischer; b&w. *sil.* • No story available.

6377. Tell Me a Bad-Time Story (*Noveltoon*) Oct. 1963; *p.c.:* Para Cartoons; *dir:* Seymour Kneitel; *story:* I. Klein, Jack Mercer; *anim:* Morey Reden, Jack Ehret, Larry Silverman; *sets:* Anton Loeb; *voices:* Bob Mac-Fadden, *mus:* Winston Sharples; *ph:* Leonard McCormick; *prod mgr:* Abe Goodman; *col:* Tech. *sd:* RCA. 6 min. • Goodie the Gremlin tells Impy a bedtime story about Poncé de Leon discovering the Fountain of Youth.

6378. The Tell-Tale Heart 27 Dec. 1953; *p.c.:* UPA for Colum; *ex prod:* Stephen Bosustow; *dir:* Ted Parmelee; *story adapt:* Bill Scott, Fred Grable; *anim:* Pat Matthews; *sets:* Paul Julian; *voices:* James Mason, Jack Mather; *mus:* Boris Kremenliev; *ph:* Jack Eckes; *prod mgr:* Herbert Klynn; *col:* Tech. *sd:* RCA. 7 min. 3-D. *Academy Award nomination.* • Excellent adaptation of Edgar Allan Poe's story about a servant who suffers a guilty conscience after killing his elderly employer, imagining he can hear the dead man's heart still beating.

6379. The Temperamental Lion (*Terry-Toon*) 27 Dec. 1940; *p.c.:* TT for Fox; *dir:* Connie Rasinski; *story:* John Foster; *anim:* Carlo Vinci; *voice:* Thomas Morrison; *mus:* Philip A. Scheib; *col:* Tech. *sd:* RCA. 7 min. • Major Doolittle cages a tough lion who breaks free and accuses the Major of "Illegal Detention." They fight and the lion goes free.

6380. Ten Miles to the Gallop (*Hoot Kloot*) 15 Oct. 1973; *p.c.:* Mirisch/DFE for UA; *dir/titles:* Arthur Leonardi; *story:* John W. Dunn; *anim:* Don Williams, Bob Matz, John Freeman, Bob Richardson, Bob Bemiller; *lay:* Dick Ung; *back:* Richard Thomas; *ed:* Joe Siracusa; *voices:* Bob Holt, Larry Mann; *mus:* Doug Goodwin; *ph:* John Burton Jr.; *prod mgr:* Lee Gunther; *col:* DeLuxe. *sd:* RCA. 6 min. • Kloot abandons his horse for a car to pursue Crazywolf on his motorbike.

6381. Ten Pin Terrors (*Heckle & Jeckle*) June 1953; *p.c.:* TT for Fox; *dir:* Connie Rasinski; *story:* Tom Morrison; *anim:* Jim Tyer; *voices:* Tom Morrison, Douglas Moye; *mus:* Philip A. Scheib; *ph:* Douglas Moye; *col:* Tech. *sd:* RCA. 6 min. • The Magpies cause destruction in a bowling alley when their sleep is disturbed.

6382. The Tenant's Racket (*Woody Woodpecker*) Aug. 1963; *p.c.:* Walter Lantz prods for Univ; *dir:* Sid Marcus; *story:* Al Bertino, Dick Kinney; *anim:* Ray Abrams, Art Davis; *sets:* Ray Huffine, Art Landy; *voices:* Daws Butler, Grace Stafford; *mus:* Walter Greene; *prod mgr:* William E. Garity; *col:* Tech. *sd:* RCA. 6 min. • Woody takes over a bird house and the owner tries to evict him without much luck.

6383. Tender Game 1958; *p.c.:* Storyboard prods for Edward Harrison; *prod/story/sets:* Faith and John Hubley; *dir:* John Hubley; *anim:* Ed Smith, Robert Cannon, Jack Schnerk, Emery Hawkins; *ed:* Faith Hubley; *voice:* Ella Fitzgerald; *mus:* The Oscar Peterson Trio (*piano:* Oscar Peterson; *guitar:* Herb Ellis; *bass:* Ray Brown); *song:* Jack Lawrence, Walter Gross; *ph:* Wardell Gayner; *col. sd.* 6 min. • Award winning interpretation of the song "Tenderly" depicting a boy and girl falling in love.

6384. Tennis Chumps (*Tom & Jerry*) 10 Dec. 1949; *p.c.:* MGM; *dir:* William Hanna, Joseph Barbera; *anim:* Ray Patterson, Irven Spence, Ed Barge, Kenneth Muse; *back:* Robert Gentle; *ed:* Fred MacAlpin; *mus:* Scott Bradley; *ph:* Jack Stevens; *prod:* Fred Quimby; *col:* Tech. *sd:* WE. 6½ min. • Tom plays an unorthodox game of tennis with Butch, the alley cat.

6385. Tennis Raquet (*Goofy*) 26 Aug. 1949; *p.c.:* Walt Disney prods for RKO; *dir:* Jack Kinney; *story:* Dick Kinney; *anim:* Wolfgang Reitherman, John Sibley, Ed Aardal, Hicks Lokey; *fx:* Jack Boyd; *lay:* Al Zinnen, Charles Philippi; *back:* Merle Cox; *voices:* Doodles Weaver, Herb Dennison; *mus:* Oliver Wallace; *col:* Tech. *sd:* RCA. 7 min. • A tennis match

between Big Ben and Little Joe with a gardener proceeding to cultivate the lawn while they play.

6386. Tepee for Two (*Woody Woodpecker*) Oct. 1963; *p.c.:* Walter Lantz prods for Univ; *dir:* Sid Marcus; *story:* Bob Ogle; *anim:* Ray Abrams, Art Davis; *sets:* Ray Huffine, Art Landy; *voices:* Daws Butler, Grace Stafford; *mus:* Clarence Wheeler; *prod mgr:* William E. Garity; *col:* Tech. *sd:* RCA. 6 min. • Driven out of town, Woody sets up home on top of an Indian's tepee and drives him mad.

6387. Termites from Mars (*Woody Woodpecker*) 8 Dec. 1952; *p.c.:* Walter Lantz prods for Univ; *dir:* Don Patterson; *anim:* Ray Abrams, La Verne Harding, Paul Smith; *sets:* Raymond Jacobs; *voices:* Dallas McKennon, Grace Stafford; *mus:* Clarence Wheeler; *prod mgr:* William E. Garity; *col:* Tech. *sd:* RCA. 6 min. • Martian termites invade the earth, making a start on Woody's tree home.

6388. The Terrible Troubador (*Pooch the Pup*) 30 Jan. 1933; *p.c.:* Univ; *dir:* Walter Lantz; *anim:* Manuel Moreno, Lester Kline, George Cannata, "Bill" Weber, Fred Kopietz, Charles Hastings; *mus:* James Dietrich; b&w. *sd:* WE. 7 min. • No story available.

6389. Terrier-Stricken (*Merrie Melodies*) 29 Nov. 1952; *p.c.:* WB; *dir:* Charles M. Jones; *story:* Michael Maltese; *anim:* Lloyd Vaughan, Ken Harris, Ben Washam; *fx:* Harry Love; *lay:* Robert Gribbroek; *back:* Philip de Guard; *ed:* Treg Brown; *voices:* Bea Benaderet; *mus:* Carl Stalling; *prod mgr:* John W. Burton; *prod:* Edward Selzer; *col:* Tech. *sd:* Vit. 7 min. • Frisky puppy needs a bath and Claude Cat does his best to make him have one, ending in the water himself, more often than not.

6390. Terror Faces Magoo (*Mr. Magoo*) 9 July 1959; *p.c.:* UPA for Colum; *ex prod:* Stephen Bosustow; *dir:* Chris Ishii, Jack Goodford; *story:* Bill Scott, George Atkins; *anim:* Jack Schnerk, Grim Natwick, Lou Guarnier, Bard Wiggenhorn; *lay:* Mordi Gerstein; *back:* Jules Engel, Bob McIntosh; *voices:* Jim Backus, Daws Butler, Marvin Miller; *mus:* Muzzy Marcellino; *col:* Tech. *sd:* RCA. 6 min. • A television crew comes to film Magoo's home at the same time he is being burgled by a trained gorilla. The final Magoo in the series, made at UPA's East Coast studio.

6391. Terry Cartoon Burlesque *p.c.:* Cartoon Film Service for the A. Kay Co.; *anim:* Paul H. Terry; b&w. *sil.* • **1917: 20,000 Feats Under the Sea** 23 Apr. **Golden Spoon Mary** 30 Apr. **Some Barrier** July. **His Trial** July

6392. Terry Human Interest Reels *p.c.:* Cartoon Film Service for the A. Kay Co.; *anim:* John Colman Terry; *story:* Jessie Allen Fowler; b&w. *sil.* • **1917: Character as Revealed by the Nose** June. **Character as Revealed in the Eye** July. **Character as Revealed by the Mouth** Aug. **Character as Revealed by the Ear** Sept.

6393. Terry the Terror (*Modern Madcap*) Dec. 1960; *p.c.:* Para Cartoons; *dir:* Seymour Kneitel; *story:* Carl Meyer, Jack Mercer; *anim:* Tom Johnson, Tom Golden; *sets:* Robert Owen; *voices:* Cecil Roy, Jack Mercer; *mus:* Winston Sharples; *ph:* Leonard McCormick; *prod mgr:* Abe Goodman; *col:* Tech. *sd:* RCA. 6 min. • A "problem child's" mother employs a child psychologist's help, who soon resorts to time honored methods to sort the brat out.

6394. Test Pilot Donald (*Donald Duck*) 8 June 1951; *p.c.:* Walt Disney prods for RKO; *dir:* Jack Hannah; *story:* Bill Berg, Nick George; *anim:* Bill Justice, Volus Jones, Hal King, Bob Carlson; *fx:* Jack Boyd; *lay:* Yale Gracey; *back:* Ralph Hulett; *voices:* Clarence Nash, James MacDonald, Dessie Miller; *mus:* Paul Smith; *col:* Tech. *sd:* RCA. 7 min. • Donald's remote-control toy plane is hijacked by Chip an' Dale.

6395. Tetched in the Head (*Barney Google*) 24 Oct. 1935; *p.c.:* Charles Mintz prods for Colum; *story:* Sid Marcus; *anim:* Art Davis; *lay:* Clark Watson; *back:* Phil Davis; *voice:* Smiley Burnett; *mus:* Joe de Nat; *prod mgr:* James Bronis; *col:* Tech. *sd:* RCA. 7 min. • Barney wants to educate Loweezy away from doing all the work ... and enjoying it!

6396. Texas in 1999 2 May 1931; *p.c.:* The Fleischer Studio for Texaco Co/Para; *prod:* Max Fleischer; *dir:* Dave Fleischer; b&w. *sd:* WE. • A 1999 filling station sees a young couple arrive to put gas in their car. They are serviced with a marriage license, ceremony, twins and a divorce. Commercial for Texaco.

6397. Texas Tom (*Tom & Jerry*) 11 Mar. 1950; *p.c.:* MGM; *dir:* William Hanna, Joseph Barbera; *anim:* Kenneth Muse, Irven Spence, Ray Patterson,

Ed Barge; *lay:* Dick Bickenbach; *back:* Robert Gentle; *ed:* Jim Faris; *chorus:* The King's Men, Ken Darby; *mus:* Scott Bradley; *song:* Ralph Dunham, Terry Shand; *ph:* Jack Stevens; *prod:* Fred Quimby; *col:* Tech. *sd:* WE. 6 min. • Tom tries to impress a pretty cowgirl kitten and Jerry sabotages his romance.

6398. Thanks for the Memory (*Screen Songs*) 25 Mar. 1938; *p.c.:* The Fleischer Studio for Para; *prod:* Max Fleischer; *dir:* Dave Fleischer; *anim:* Roland Crandall; *l/a:* Bert Block and his orchestra; *song:* Leo Robin, Ralph Rainger; b&w. *sd:* WE. 7 min. *l/a/anim.* • How trailers might be used.

6399. That Little Big Fellow 1926; *p.c.:* Inkwell Studio for American Telephone & Telegraph Co; *dir:* Dave Fleischer; *ph:* Charles Schettler; b&w. *sil.* 9 min. • An explanation of the AT&T system.

6400. That Old Can of Mine (*Aesop's Film Fable*) 22 June 1924; *p.c.:* Fables Pictures Inc for Pathé; *dir:* Paul Terry; b&w. *sil.* 5 min. • The farmer's cat enlightens the audience on the point of automobiles.

6401. That Old Gang of Mine (*Screen Songs*) 11 July 1931; *p.c.:* The Fleischer Studio for Para; *prod:* Max Fleischer; *dir:* Dave Fleischer; *voice:* Mae Questel; *mus:* Art Turkisher; b&w. *sd:* WE. 7 min. • A cat laments for her pals and a mouse tries to cheer her up.

6402. That's Entertainment (Part 2) 1976; *p.c.:* MGM; *main title seq:* Saul Bass; *anim seq:* Hanna-Barbera prods; *col:* Metro. *sd:* WE. *l/a/anim.* • Fred Astaire and Gene Kelly sing while reminiscing over musical acts. Animated caricatures appear on the screen behind them: Kelly, Astaire, Judy Garland and Bobby Van.

6403. That's My Mommy (*Tom & Jerry*) 19 Nov. 1955; *p.c.:* MGM; *prod/dir:* Joseph Barbera, William Hanna; *anim:* Kenneth Muse, Ed Barge, Irven Spence, Lewis Marshall; *lay:* Dick Bickenbach; *back:* Robert Gentle; *ed:* Jim Faris; *voice:* Red Coffee; *mus:* Scott Bradley; *ph:* Jack Stevens; *prod mgr:* Hal Elias; *col:* Tech. *sd:* WE. 6 min. CS. • A newly hatched duckling mistakes Tom for his mother and Jerry has to put him right.

6404. That's My Pup! (*Tom & Jerry*) 25 Apr. 1953; *p.c.:* MGM; *dir:* William Hanna, Joseph Barbera; *anim:* Ed Barge, Ray Patterson, Kenneth Muse, Irven Spence; *lay:* Dick Bickenbach; *back:* Robert Gentle; *ed:* Jim Faris; *voice:* Daws Butler; *mus:* Scott Bradley; *ph:* Jack Stevens; *prod:* Fred Quimby; *col:* Tech. *sd:* WE. 7 min. • Spike teaches his offspring how to chase cats with Tom as the hapless candidate.

6405. That's No Lady — That's Notrè Dame (*Inspector*) 26 Oct. 1966; *p.c.:* Mirisch/Geoffrey/DFE for UA; *dir:* George Singer; *story:* John W. Dunn; *anim:* Warren Batchelder Don Williams, Bob Matz, Ted Bonnicksen, John Gibbs, La Verne Harding; *sets:* T.M. Yakutis; *ed:* Lee Gunther; *voices:* Pat Harrington Jr., Paul Frees, Diana Maddock; *mus:* Walter Greene; *theme tune:* Henry Mancini; *prod sup:* Bill Orcutt, Harry Love; *col:* DeLuxe. *sd:* RCA. 6 min. • Disguised as a woman, the Inspector sets out to catch a purse snatcher ... leading to complications with the commissioner's wife.

6406. Their Last Bean (*Terry-Toon*) 21 Apr. 1939; *p.c.:* TT for Fox; *dir:* Eddie Donnelly *story:* John Foster; *mus:* Philip A. Scheib; b&w. *sd:* RCA. 6 min. • The fox family have no food, so little Willie Fox leads the hunters on a merry chase, also succeeding in capturing their banquet.

6407. Their Love Growed Cold (*Mastodon Cartoon*) 2 June 1923; *p.c.:* Earl Hurd prods for Motion Picture Arts Inc./Educational; *anim:* Earl Hurd; *prod:* C.C. Burr; b&w. *sil.* 5 min. *l/a/anim.* • Bobby Bumps loses his heart to a charming (real life) Miss and fights a duel for her, only to discover she has proved fickle.

6408. Them Were the Happy Days (*Sullivan Cartoon Comedy*) 15 Oct. 1917; *p.c.:* Powers for Univ; *dir:* Pat Sullivan; *anim:* Otz Messmer; b&w. *sil.* 5 min. • Grandpa recalls when he was a lad, being carried up by a balloon while escaping a kidnapper. He falls to earth at the feet of a lion and awakens to find his dog licking his face.

6409. Therapeutic Pink (*Pink Panther*) 1 Apr. 1977; *p.c.:* Mirisch/Geoffrey/DFE for UA; *dir:* Gerry Chiniquy; *story:* Tom Yakutis; *anim:* Warren Batchelder, Bob Matz, Norm McCabe, Don Williams; *lay:* Tony Rivera; *back:* Richard H. Thomas; *ed:* Rick Steward; *mus:* Walter Greene; *theme tune:* Henry Mancini; *ph:* John Burton Jr.; *prod mgr:* Lee Gunther; *col:* DeLuxe. *sd:* RCA. 6 min. • The Panther is admitted to hospital with a small dog attached to his tail.

6410. There Auto Be a Law (*Looney Tunes*) 6 June 1953; *p.c.:* WB; *dir:* Robert McKimson; *story:* Tedd Pierce; *anim:* Phil de Lara, Charles McKimson, Herman Cohen, Rod Scribner; *lay:* Robert Givens; *back:* Richard H. Thomas; *ed:* Treg Brown; *voices:* John T. Smith, Bea Benaderet, Mel Blanc; *mus:* Carl Stalling; *prod mgr:* John W. Burton; *prod:* Edward Selzer; *col:* Tech. *sd:* Vit. 7 min. • The history of the automobile is depicted, including a running gag about a man trying to get off the freeway.

6411. There It Is (*Whirlwind Comedy*) 2 Jan. 1928; *p.c.:* Bowers Comedy Corp. for Educational; *dir:* Charles R. Bowers; *story:* Charles R. Bowers, H.L. Muller, Ted Sears; *l/a cast: Charley MacNeesha:* Charley Bowers; *The Nurse:* Kathryn McGuire; *Frisbie Family Patriarch:* Melbourne MacDowell; *The Fuzz-Faced Phantom:* Buster Brodie; *The Butler:* Edgar Blue; *also:* Mack Davis; *ph:* H.L. Muller; b&w. *sil.* 17½ min. *l/a/anim.* • Live-action comedy: The appearance of a mysterious bewhiskered stranger in a mansion warrants a call to Scotland Yard. Their finest detective arrives on the first ship available and starts to track down the intruder. Live-action with a model animation kilted mouse.

6412. There They Go-Go-Go! (*Looney Tunes*) 10 Nov. 1956; *p.c.:* WB; *dir:* Chuck Jones; *story:* Michael Maltese; *anim:* Richard Thompson, Ken Harris, Abe Levitow, Ben Washam; *fx:* Harry Love; *sets:* Philip de Guard; *ed:* Treg Brown; *voice:* Paul Julian; *mus:* Carl Stalling; *prod mgr:* John W. Burton; *prod:* Edward Selzer; *col:* Tech. *sd:* Vit. 7 min. • The starving Coyote continues his ongoing pursuit of the Road-Runner by using a brace of spinning maces and a stack of boulders supported by a trap door.

6413. There's Good Boos Tonight (*Noveltoon*) 23 Apr. 1948; *p.c.:* Famous for Para; *dir:* I. Sparber; *story:* Bill Turner, Larry Riley; *anim:* Myron Waldman, Morey Reden, Nick Tafuri; *sets:* Anton Loeb; *voices:* Frank Gallop, Sid Raymond; *mus:* Winston Sharples; *ph:* Leonard McCormick; *prod mgr:* Sam Buchwald; *col:* Tech. *sd:* RCA. 9 min. • In his search for friends, Casper befriends Ferdy the Fox who, in turn, is hunted and killed by the hunters and becomes a ghost.

6414. There's Music in Your Hair (*Phantasy*) 28 Mar. 1941; *p.c.:* Colum; *story:* Art Davis; *anim:* Sid Marcus; *lay:* Clark Watson; *back:* Phil Davis; *ed:* George Winkler; *mus:* Joe de Nat; *prod mgr:* James Bronis; b&w. *sd:* RCA. 6 min. • A violinist in an orchestra tries to keep on the podium.

6415. There's Something About a Soldier (*Betty Boop*) 17 Aug. 1934; *p.c.:* The Fleischer Studio for Para; *prod:* Max Fleischer; *dir:* Dave Fleischer; *anim:* Myron Waldman, Hicks Lokey, Lillian Friedman; *voices:* Mae Questel; *mus:* Sammy Timberg; b&w. *sd:* WE. 7 min. • Betty helps recruit soldiers in their fight against a swarm of attacking mosquitoes.

6416. There's Something About a Soldier (*Color Rhapsody*) 26 Feb. 1943; *p.c.:* Colum; *prod:* Dave Fleischer; *dir:* Alec Geiss; *story:* Ed Seward; *anim:* Grant Simmons, Chic Otterstrom; *lay:* Clark Watson; *ed:* Edward Moore; *mus:* Paul Worth; *prod mgr:* Albert Spar; *col:* Tech. *sd:* RCA. 6½ min. • A young lad, eager to join up and fight goes to the recruitment center with his dog. He is considered too young but the dog is accepted.

6417. They're Off (*Goofy*) 23 Jan. 1948; *p.c.:* Walt Disney prods for RKO; *dir:* Jack Hannah; *asst dir:* Bee Selck; *story:* Riley Thomson, Campbell Grant; *anim:* John Sibley, Volus Jones, Al Bertino, Art Babbitt, Bill Justice; *fx:* Jack Boyd, Jack Buckley, Andy Engman, Blaine Gibson; *lay:* Yale Gracey; *back:* Howard Dunn; *voices:* Harlow Wilcox, James MacDonald; *mus:* Oliver Wallace; *col:* Tech. *sd:* RCA. 6 min. • An insight into "The Sport of Kings."

6418. The Thing 25 June 1982; *p.c.:* Univ; *anim fx seq: dimensional anim fx created by* Randall William Cook; *crew:* James Aupperle, James Belohovek, Ernest D. Farino, Carl Surges; *col:* Tech. *sd:* Dolby stereo. Panavision. 109 min. *l/a* • Live-action horror. A remote outpost in Alaska is terrorized by an alien creature that can absorb living beings.

6419. Think Before You Pink (*Pink Panther*) 19 Mar. 1975; *p.c.:* Mirisch/Geoffrey/DFE for UA; *dir:* Gerry Chiniquy; *story:* Sid Marcus; *anim:* Don Williams, Manny Gould, Manny Perez, Herman Cohen, Warren Batchelder; *lay:* Jack Miller; *back:* Tom O'Loughlin; *ed:* Lee Gunther; *mus:* Walter Greene; *theme tune:* Henry Mancini; *ph:* John Burton Jr.; *prod sup:* Jim Foss, Harry Love; *col:* DeLuxe. *sd:* RCA. 6 min. • The Panther tries to cross a busy thoroughfare.

6420. Think or Sink (*Merry-Maker*) Sept 1966; *p.c.:* Para Cartoons; *dir:* Shamus Culhane; *story:* James Tyer; *anim:* Al Eugster; *sets:* Hal Silvermintz, Gil Miret, Danté Barbetta; *mus:* Winston Sharples; *prod sup:* Harold Robins, Burt Hanft; *col:* Tech. *sd:* RCA. 6 min. • Roscoe the elephant is taken to a psychiatrist because he finds he can walk on water. The doctor says it's only because he *thinks* he can that he is able to walk on the water.

6421. The Third Musketeer *(Terry-Toon)* Jan. 1965; *p.c.:* TT for Fox; *ex prod:* Bill Weiss; *dir/anim:* Ralph Bakshi; *story dir:* Tom Morrison; *story:* Eli Bauer; *sets:* Bill Focht; *ed:* Jack McConnell; *voices:* Bob MacFadden; *mus:* Jim Timmens; *ph:* Ted Moskowitz; *sd:* Elliot Grey; *col:* DeLuxe. *sd:* RCA. 6 min. • Gadmouse the apprentice good fairy helps Sad Cat by making him one of the Three Musketeers.

6422. This and That from Here and There 1933; *p.c.:* James H. Harper; *prod:* S.O. Watt b&w. *sd.* 6¹/₂ min. • Collection of unrelated gags.

6423. This Is a Life? *(Merrie Melodies)* 9 July 1955; *p.c.:* WB; *dir:* I. Freleng; *story:* Warren Foster; *anim:* Ted Bonnicksen, Arthur Davis; *lay:* Hawley Pratt; *back:* Irv Wyner; *ed:* Treg Brown; *voices:* Mel Blanc, Arthur Q. Bryan, June Foray; *mus:* Milt Franklyn; *prod mgr:* John W. Burton; *prod:* Edward Selzer; *col:* Tech. *sd:* Vit. 6 min. Seq: *Hare Do; Buccaneer Bunny.* • Elmer Fudd springs a "This Is a Life?" surprise on Bugs ... much to Daffy's chagrin.

6424. This Is My Ducky Day *(Loopy de Loop)* 4 May 1961; *p.c.:* Hanna-Barbera prods for Colum; *prod/dir:* William Hanna, Joseph Barbera; *story dir:* Alex Lovy; *story:* Michael Maltese; *anim dir:* Charles A. Nichols; *anim:* William Keil; *lay:* Walter Clinton; *back:* Art Lozzi; *ed:* Greg Watson; *voices:* Daws Butler, Red Coffee; *mus:* Hoyt Curtin; *titles:* Lawrence Gobel; *prod mgr:* Howard Hanson; *col:* East. *sd:* RCA. 6¹/₂ min. • Loopy helps a friendless duck.

6425. This Little Piggie Went to Market *(Screen Songs)* 23 May 1934; *p.c.:* The Fleischer Studio for Para; *prod:* Max Fleischer; *dir:* Dave Fleischer; *anim:* Hicks Lokey, Paul Fennell; *mus:* Sammy Timberg; *l/a:* Singin' Sam (Harry Frankel); b&w. *sd:* WE. 8 min. • A newsreel shows two boats colliding, some bad weather, a blacksmith training football players, a boxer training his wife and a trailer for a film called "The Beginning."

6426. The Thoroughbred *(Aesop's Film Fable)* 29 Sept. 1923; *p.c.:* Fables Pictures Inc for Pathé; *dir:* Paul Terry; b&w. *sil.* 5 min. • A dog saves a baby robin and, in turn, Mother robin saves the dog from the dog-catcher's net.

6427. Those Beautiful Dames *(Merrie Melodies)* 6 Apr. 1935; *p.c.:* Leon Schlesinger prods for WB; *dir:* Isadore Freleng; *anim:* Paul Smith, Charles Jones, Robert Clampett; *voice:* Rochelle Hudson; *mus:* Bernard Brown; *song:* Harry Warren, Al Dubin; *prod sup:* Henry Binder, Raymond G. Katz; *col:* Tech-2. *sd:* Vit. 7 min. • A poverty-stricken child's dingy shack is transformed into a toyland with the toys entertaining her.

6428. Those Were Wonderful Days *(Merrie Melodies)* 26 Apr. 1934; *p.c.:* Leon Schlesinger prods for WB; *dir:* Bernard B. Brown; *anim:* Paul Smith, Don Williams, Robert Clampett; *mus:* Norman Spencer; *prod sup:* Henry Binder, Raymond G. Katz; b&w. *sd:* Vit. 6¹/₂ min. • Spot gags on the "Gay '90s" followed by a melodrama in which our hero rescues a girl from the clutches of a villain.

6429. Thousand Smile Check Up *(Terry-Toon)* Jan. 1960; *p.c.:* TT for Fox; *ex prod:* Bill Weiss; *dir:* Martin Taras; *story dir:* Tom Morrison; *story:* Larz Bourne; *anim:* Ed Donnelly, Vinnie Bell, Mannie Davis, Johnny Gent, Larry Silverman, Cosmo Anzilotti; *lay:* John Zago; *back:* Bill Hilliker; *voices:* Roy Halee; *mus:* Phil Scheib; *prod mgr:* Frank Schudde; *col:* Tech. *sd:* RCA. 6 min. • The Last Chance Filling Station arrives in opposition to Heckle and Jeckle's station and both competitors try to put the other out of business.

6430. The Three Ages of Man 1923; *p.c.:* Inkwell Studio for Metro; *seq anim:* Max Fleischer; *l/a dir:* Buster Keaton, Eddie Kline; b&w. *sil.* 20 min. *l/a/anim.* • Live-action comedy starring Buster Keaton as a caveman with animated dinosaurs.

6431. The Three Bears *(ComiColor)* 30 Aug. 1935; *p.c.:* Celebrity prods; *prod/dir:* Ub Iwerks; *mus:* Carl Stalling; *col:* Ciné. *sd:* PCP. 7 min. • A girl and her dog play hide and seek in the Three Bears' house until the bears arrive, frightening them away.

6432. The Three Bears *(Dinky Doodle)* 19 July 1925; *p.c.:* Bray prods for FBO; *dir/story:* Walt Lantz; *anim:* Clyde Geronimi; b&w. *sil.* 5 min. • No story available.

6433. The Three Bears *(Paul Terry-Toon)* 26 Jan. 1934; *p.c.:* Moser & Terry for Educational/Fox; *dir:* Frank Moser, Paul Terry; *mus:* Philip A. Scheib; b&w. *sd:* WE. 5¹/₂ min. • While Junior Bear is chased by bees, Goldilocks helps herself to the bears' porridge.

6434. The Three Bears *(Terry-Toon)* 10 Feb. 1939; *p.c.:* TT for Fox; *dir:* Mannie Davis; *story:* John Foster; *voice:* Thomas Morrison; *mus:* Philip A. Scheib; *col:* Tech. *sd:* RCA. 7 min. • Goldilocks starts a jam session when she arrives at the bears' home and a hunting dog relieves them of their pelts.

6435. Three Blind Mice *(Aesop's Film Fable)* 9 Jan. 1926; *p.c.:* Fables Pictures Inc for Pathé; *dir:* Paul Terry; b&w. *sil.* 10 min. • The mice are not so blind when the cat tries to steal their collection. Moral: "Many 'blind' beggars are able to see the cop rounding the corner."

6436. Three Blind Mouseketeers *(Silly Symphony)* 26 Sept. 1936; *p.c.:* Walt Disney prods for UA; *dir:* David D. Hand; *anim:* Gilles de Tremaudan, Clyde Geronimi, Hardie Gramatky, Bob Wickersham; *des:* Ferdinand Huszti Horvath; *voices:* Billy Bletcher, Albert Bryant, Betty Bushman, Ace Goodwin, Dorr Stewart; *mus:* Albert Hay Malotte; *col:* Tech. *sd:* RCA. 7 min. • Captain Katt sets traps for the blind mouseketeers, which they persistently elude.

6437. The Three Caballeros 3 Feb. 1945; *p.c.:* Walt Disney prods for RKO; *prod sup/dir:* Norman Ferguson; *seq dir:* Clyde Geronimi, Jack Kinney, Bill Roberts; *story:* Ernest Terrazzas, Homer Brightman, Ted Sears, Roy Williams, Bill Peed, William Cottrell, Ralph Wright, Elmer Plummer, James Bodrero; *anim:* Ward Kimball, Eric Larson, Les Clark, Fred Moore, John Lounsbery, Milton Kahl, Hal King, Franklyn Thomas, Bob Carlson, John Sibley, Ollie Johnston, Milt Neil, Marvin Woodward, Don Patterson; *fx:* Josh Meador, George Rowley, John McManus; *des:* Mary Blair, Ken Anderson, Robert Cormack; *lay:* Donald da Gradi, McLaren Stewart, Herbert Ryman, Yale Gracey, Charles Philippi, John Hench; *back:* Albert Dempster, Art Riley, Ray Huffine, Don Douglas, Claude Coats; *ed:* Don Halliday; *sd:* C.O. Slyfield; *voices: Donald Duck:* Clarence Nash; *Josè Carioca/The Aracuran Bird:* Josè Oliveira; *Panchito:* Joaquin Garay; *Narrator:* Frank Graham; "The Three Caballeros" sung by Trio Calaveros; "Baia" sung by Nestor Amaral; "Mexico" sung by Carlos Ramirez; *mus:* Charles Wolcott, Paul J. Smith, Edward Plumb; *lyrics:* Ray Gilbert; *l/a seq: dir:* Harold Young; *ph:* Ray Rennahan ASC; *art dir:* Richard F. Irvine; *choreography:* Billy Daniels, Aloysio Oliveira, Carmelita Maracci; *col dir:* Phil Dike; *process fx:* Ub Iwerks, Richard Jones; *technical:* Gail Papineau; *l/a:* Aurora Miranda, Carmen Molina, Dora Luz, Almirante, Ascencion del Rio Trio, Padua Hills Players; *prod sup:* Dan Keefe, Larry Lansburgh, Jack Cutting, Gilberto Souto, Aloysio Oliveira, Sidney Field, Edmundo Santos; *col:* Tech. *sd:* RCA. 70 min. *l/a/anim.* • *The Cold Blooded Penguin dir:* William Roberts; *asst dir:* Mike Holoboff; *story:* Del Connell; *anim:* Bill Justice, Milt Kahl, Harvey Toombs; *fx:* Edwin Aardal, Josh Meador; *lay:* Hugh Hennesy; *narration:* Sterling Holloway. • *The Flying Gauchito dir:* Norman Ferguson, Eric Larson; *anim:* Frank Thomas, Olllie Johnston, Eric Larson, John Sibley, Hal King; *lay:* Herbert Ryman; *narration:* Fred Shields; *mus:* Charles Wolcott, Paul Smith, Edward Plumb. • Donald recieves a 16mm movie projector for his birthday. The films include one featuring "Rare Birds," another about a penguin who strives to keep warm and a flying donkey. He reacquaints himself with Josè Carioca and they go to Baia where they meet Panchito Pistolas, a Mexican rooster. The three of them fly off on a magic serapè to tour Mexico. • A clever mixture of live-action, cartoons, color and song blend together to make a delightful cocktail made specifically for the "Good Neighbor Policy." • See: *The Flying Gauchito*

6438. Three for Breakfast *(Donald Duck)* 5 Nov. 1948; *p.c.:* Walt Disney prods for RKO; *dir:* Jack Hannah; *story:* Nick George; *anim:* Bob Carlson, Bill Justice, Volus Jones, Ray Patin; *fx:* Jack Boyd, Dan MacManus; *lay:* Yale Gracey; *back:* Thelma Witmer; *voices:* Clarence Nash, James MacDonald, Dessie Flynn; *mus:* Oliver Wallace; *col:* Tech. *sd:* RCA. 7 min. • Donald's hot-cake making is interrupted when Chip an' Dale invade and try to steal his pancakes.

6439. Three Game Guys *(Aesop's Film Fable)* 29 July 1929; *p.c.:* Fables Pictures Inc for Pathé; *dir:* John Foster; b&w. *sil.* 10 min. • No story available.

6440. Three Is a Crowd *(Little Roquefort)* Feb. 1951; *p.c.:* TT for Fox;

dir: Connie Rasinski; *story:* Tom Morrison; *anim:* Jim Tyer; *mus:* Philip A. Scheib; *col:* Tech. *sd:* RCA. 6 min. • Percy Puss tries to prevent Roquefort from marrying.

6441. Three Is a Family 31 Aug. 1944; *p.c.:* Walt Disney prods for UA; *seq dir:* James Algar; *anim:* Marc Davis, Milton Kahl, Eric Larson, Fred Moore; *lay:* Karl Karpé; *prod:* Sol Lesser; *l/a dir:* Edward Ludwig; b&w. *sd.* • Adaption of a stage play about wartime living conditions — and babies. Animated titles and a "stork" sequence.

6442. Three Lazy Mice (*Cartune Classic*) 15 July 1935; *p.c.:* Univ; *dir:* Walter Lantz; *story/lyrics:* Walter Lantz, Victor McLeod; *anim:* Manuel Moreno; *voices:* The Rhythmettes; *mus:* James Dietrich; *col:* Tech-2. *sd:* WE. 9 min. • Three mice fein "blindness" to avoid working. Their antics lead to them leaving the safety of Mouse Town and into the clutches of a cat.

6443. Three Little Bops (*Looney Tunes*) 5 Jan. 1957; *p.c.:* WB; *dir:* Friz Freleng; *story:* Warren Foster; *anim:* Gerry Chiniquy, Bob Matz; *lay:* Hawley Pratt; *back:* Irv Wyner; *ed:* Treg Brown; *voice:* Stan Freberg; *mus:* Shorty Rogers; *prod mgr:* John W. Burton; *prod:* Edward Selzer; *col:* Tech. *sd:* Vit. 7 min. • The Big Bad Wolf wants to play trumpet in the pigs' jazz band but his playing is considered to be too square.

6444. The Three Little Pigs (*Silly Symphony*) 27 May 1933; *p.c.:* Walt Disney prods for UA; *dir:* Burton F. Gillett; *story:* Ted Sears, William Cottrell, Joe Grant; *anim:* Arthur Babbitt, Norman Ferguson, Jack Hannah, Jack King, Richard Lundy, Fred Moore; *character des/lay:* Albert Hurter; *voices:* Billy Bletcher, Pinto Colvig, Dorothy Compton, Mary Moder; *mus:* Frank E. Churchill; *piano:* Carl W. Stalling; *song:* Larry Morey, Ted Sears; *col:* Tech. *sd:* RCA. 9 min. *Academy Award.* • Two frivolous pigs build their houses of straw and sticks while the Practical Pig builds his house of bricks and mortar to keep the wolf out.

6445. The Three Little Pups 26 Dec. 1954; *p.c.:* MGM; *dir:* Tex Avery; *story:* Heck Allen; *anim:* Walter Clinton, Grant Simmons, Robert Bentley, Michael Lah, Ray Patterson; *character des/lay:* Ed Benedict; *back:* Vera Ohman; *ed:* Jim Faris; *voices:* Daws Butler, Bill Thompson *(whistler)* Joe Trescari; *mus:* Scott Bradley; *ph:* Jack Stevens; *prod:* Fred Quimby; *col:* Tech. *sd:* WE. 6 min. • Three pups build their respective houses of straw, sticks and bricks. The Big Bad Dog-catcher corners them in the house of bricks.

6446. Three Little Wolves (*Silly Symphony*) 18 Apr. 1936; *p.c.:* Walt Disney prods for UA; *dir:* David D. Hand; *story:* William Cottrell, Joe Grant; *anim:* Norman Ferguson, Eric Larson, Fred Moore, William O. Roberts; *voices:* Alyce Ardell, Pinto Colvig, Billy Bletcher; *mus:* Frank E. Churchill; *col:* Tech. *sd:* RCA. 10 min. • The two frivolous pigs blow the "Wolf Alarm" once too often.

6447. Three Little Woodpeckers (*Woody Woodpecker*) 1 Jan. 1965; *p.c.:* Walter Lantz prods for Univ; *dir:* Sid Marcus; *story:* Cal Howard; *anim:* Ray Abrams, Art Davis; *sets:* Ray Huffine, Art Landy; *voices:* Daws Butler, June Foray, Grace Stafford; *mus:* Walter Greene; *prod mgr:* William E. Garity; *col:* Tech. *sd:* RCA. 6 min. • The "Red Riding Hood" story is drastically altered when the wolf goes after Splinter, Knothead and Woody who live in straw, wood and petrified trees, respectively.

6448. The Three Minnies: Sota, Tonka and Ha Ha! (*Jerky Journeys*) 15 Apr. 1949; *p.c.:* Impossible Pictures for Rep; *ex prod:* David Flexer; *prod/dir/story:* Leonard Louis Levinson; *des:* Art Heinemann; *back:* Peter Alvarado, Robert Gribbroek; *voice:* Frank Nelson; *col:* Tru. *sd.* 8 min. • Three Indian maids all fall for the same brave ... but he falls for their mother.

6449. Three Orphan Kittens (*Silly Symphony*) 26 Oct. 1935; *p.c.:* Walt Disney prods for UA; *dir:* David D. Hand; *story:* William Cottrell, Joe Grant; *anim:* Robert W. Carlson Jr., Hamilton S. Luske, Fred Moore, Robert Wickersham, Cornett Wood; *lay:* Ken Anderson; *voices:* Lillian Randolph, Marcellite Garner; *mus:* Frank E. Churchill; *col:* Tech. *sd:* RCA. 9 min. *Academy Award* • Three orphan kittens seek refuge from a storm in a house.

6450. Three Ring Fling (*Cartune*) 6 Oct. 1958; *p.c.:* Walter Lantz prods for Univ; *dir:* Alex Lovy; *story:* Homer Brightman; *anim:* La Verne Harding, Don Patterson, Ray Abrams; *sets:* Raymond Jacobs, Art Landy; *voices:* Daws Butler; *mus:* Clarence Wheeler; *prod mgr:* William E. Garity;

col: Tech. *sd:* RCA. 6 min. • Windy the bear comes up with the idea of substituting for a performing bear to get into the circus for free.

6451. 3 Ring Wing-Ding (*Looney Tunes*) 13 June 1968; *p.c.:* WB/7A; *dir:* Alex Lovy; *story:* Cal Howard; *anim:* Ted Bonnicksen, La Verne Harding, Volus Jones, Ed Solomon; *lay:* Bob Givens; *back:* Bob Abrams; *ed:* Hal Geer; *voices:* Larry Storch; *mus:* William Lava; *prod:* Bill L. Hendricks; *col:* Tech. *sd:* Vit. 6 min. • Col. Rimfire wants to capture Cool Cat after he sees that the circus is offering $1000 for a live tiger.

6452. The Three Stooges Scrapbook Sept. 1963; *p.c.:* Normandy prods/TV Spots for Colum; *prod:* Norman Maurer; *anim dir:* Sam Nicholson; *story:* Al Bertino, Dick Kinney; *anim:* Fred Madison; *voices:* Moe Howard, Larry Fine, Joe de Rita, Mel Blanc; *l/a dir:* Sidney Miller; *l/a story:* Elwood Ullman; *col. sd:* Glenn Glenn. 9 min. *l/a/anim.* • Part of a 25 minute television pilot featuring the Three Stooges in live-action. The cartoon segment (distributed seperately) has the Stooges and their parrot," Feathers" helping Columbus discover America.

6453. Three Wishes 27 Oct. 1995; *p.c.:* Rysher Entertainment for Entertainment; *anim:* Blair Clark, Darby Johnston, Elias D'elia, Tanya Spence; *special fx:* Deanan Da Silva, Brian LaFrance; *col:* Tech. *sd:* Dolby stereo/ SDD. 115 min. *l/a.* • Live-action fantasy: A family take in a tramp whose dog is actually a genie that can grant wishes.

6454. Three's a Crowd (*Merrie Melodies*) 17 Jan. 1933; *p.c.:* Hugh Harman, Rudolf Ising prods for WB; *anim:* Rollin Hamilton, Larry Martin, Robert Clampett; *mus:* Frank Marsales; *asso prod:* Leon Schlesinger; b&w. *sd:* Vit. 7 min. • Book covers come alive. Alice in Wonderland is captured by Mr. Hyde and others come to her rescue.

6455. The Thrifty Cubs (*Terry Bears*) Jan. 1953; *p.c.:* TT for Fox; *dir:* Mannie Davis; *story:* Tom Morrison; *anim:* Jim Tyer; *sets:* Art Bartsch; *voices:* Douglas Moye, Tom Morrison, Philip A. Scheib; *mus:* Philip A. Scheib; *ph:* Douglas Moye; *col:* Tech. *sd:* RCA. 6 min. • Instead of investing in bonds, Papa buys a robot to do the housework. It gets out of control and Papa awakens to find it was all a dream.

6456. The Thrifty Pig 19 Nov. 1941; *p.c.:* Walt Disney prods for NFB; *dir:* Ford Beebe; *anim:* Ub Iwerks, Kenneth Muse; *voices:* Tommy Wiggins, Billy Bletcher, Dorothy Compton, Mary Moder; *mus:* Frank E. Churchill; *col:* Tech. *sd:* RCA. 4 min. • The Nazi Wolf blows down the pigs' homes but retires defeated when he comes up against Practical Pig's house of sturdy War Bonds. Footage reused from *The Three Little Pigs*.

6457. Thrill of Fair (*Popeye*) 20 Apr. 1951; *p.c.:* Famous for Para; *dir:* Seymour Kneitel; *story:* Carl Meyer, Jack Mercer; *anim:* Tom Johnson, John Gentilella; *sets:* Tom Ford; *voices:* Jack Mercer, Mae Questel; *mus:* Winston Sharples; *ph:* Leonard McCormick; *prod mgr:* Seymour Shultz; *col:* Tech. *sd:* RCA. 7 min. • Swee'Pea wanders off at the County Fair after an elusive balloon with Popeye in hot pursuit.

6458. Throne for a Loss (*Honey Halfwitch*) Dec. 1966; *p.c.:* Para Cartoons; *dir:* Shamus Culhane; *story:* Howard Post; *anim:* Wm. B. Pattengill, Martin Taras; *sets:* Robert Little, Gil Miret; *voices:* Bob MacFadden, Shari Lewis; *mus:* Winston Sharples; *prod sup:* Harold Robins, Bert Hanft; *col:* Tech. *sd:* RCA. 6 min. • An enchanted frog tricks Stanley the Sorcerer into turning him back into a King ... but he turns out to be a lion who tries to eat Stanley.

6459. Throwing the Bull (*Mighty Mouse*) 3 May 1946; *p.c.:* TT for Fox; *dir:* Connie Rasinski; *story:* John Foster; *mus:* Philip A. Scheib; *col:* Tech. *sd:* RCA. 7 min. • During a bullfight, the bull charges the spectators. Mighty Mouse is soon on the scene to save the populace.

6460. Thru the Mirror (*Mickey Mouse*) 30 May 1936; *p.c.:* Walt Disney prods for UA; *dir:* David D. Hand; *story:* William Cottrell, Joe Grant, Bob Kuwahara; *anim:* Johnny Cannon, Ugo d'Orsi, Hardie Gramatky, Richard Lundy, Norman Ferguson, Leonard Sebring, Robert Wickersham; *des:* Ferdinand Huszti Horvath; *sets:* Bob Kuwahara; *voices:* Walt Disney, Pinto Colvig; *mus:* Paul J. Smith, Frank E. Churchill; *col:* Tech. *sd:* RCA. 9 min. • Mickey dreams himself into an "Alice Through the Looking Glass" situation. Caricatures of Greta Garbo and Charles Laughton.

6461. Thru Thick and Thin (*Aesop's Film Fable*) 7 Nov. 1926; *p.c.:* Fables Pictures Inc for Pathé; *dir:* Paul Terry; b&w. *sil.* 5 min. • Al Falfa learns of his little boy's kidnapping by Gypsies for a ransom. He pursues the Gypsy Wolf with his dog over an ice pond, where they have a gun battle and the dog sees the wolf off over a waterfall. The dog returns the boy and all are happy.

6462. Thugs with Dirty Mugs (*Merrie Melodies*)6 May 1939; *p.c.:* Leon Schlesinger prods for WB; *dir:* Fred Avery; *story:* Jack Miller; *anim:* Sid Sutherland; *sets:* John Didrik Johnsen; *ed:* Tregoweth E. Brown; *voices:* John Deering, Mel Blanc, Danny Webb, Ted Pierce; *mus:* Carl W. Stalling; *prod sup:* Henry Binder, Raymond G. Katz; *col:* Tech. *sd:* Vit. 7 min. • "Killer Diller" robs the 1st to 112th National Banks until he is captured and made to write out "I am a bad boy" one hundred times.

6463. Thumb Fun (*Looney Tunes*) 1 Mar. 1952; *p.c.:* WB; *dir:* Robert McKimson; *story:* Tedd Pierce; *anim:* Rod Scribner, Phil de Lara, Charles McKimson, Bob Wickersham; *lay:* Peter Alvarado; *back:* Richard H. Thomas; *ed:* Treg Brown; *voices:* Mel Blanc; *mus:* Carl Stalling; *prod mgr:* John W. Burton; *prod:* Edward Selzer *col:* Tech. *sd:* Vit. 7 min. • Daffy hitch-hikes South for the winter with Porky as the unsuspecting victim.

6464. Thumbelina 29 July 1993; *p.c.:* Don Bluth Ltd./Don Bluth Ireland, Ltd. for WB; *dir:* Don Bluth, Gary Goldman; *prod:* Don Bluth, Gary Goldman, John Pomeroy; *scr:* Don Bluth; *prod des:* Rowland Wilson; *art dir:* Barry Atkinson; *asso prod:* Russell Boland; *prod mgr:* Gerry Shirren; *prod sup:* Cathy Goldman, Olga Tarin-Craig; *storyboard:* Scott Caple, Guy Deel, James Finnegan, Bill Frake, Kevin Gollaher, Keith Ingham, Rob Koo, Brad Raymond, Rick Saliba, Mark Swan; *anim dir (LA):* John Pomeroy, John Hill, Richard Bazley, John Morel, Len Simon, Piet de Rycker, Dave Kupczyk; *seq anim dir:* Cathy Jones, Ralf Palmer; *character anim:* Nasson Vakalis, John Power, Kevin Johnson, Bill Waldman, Marcello Moura, Chris Derochie, Oliver Wade, Tom Steisinger, Frank Gabriel, Robert Fox, Sam Fleming, Paul J. Kelly, Sandro Cleuzo, Sylvia Hoefnagels, Shane Zalvin, Edison Goncalves, Ben Burgess, Paul Newberry, Troy Saliba, Rusty Stoll, Sung Kwon, Jackie Corley, Robert Jurgen Sprathoff, Konrad Winterlich, Bill Giggie, Gary Perkovac, Celine Kiernan, Fernando Moro, Rogerio Marques Degodoy, Alain Costa, Valentin Domenech, Stefan Fjeldmark, Dermot O'Connor, Donnachada Daly, Kevin O'Neill, Joe McDonough, Linda Miller, Mark Fisher, Chad Stewart, Jacques Muller, Matthew Bates, Alan Fleming; *asst anim:* Kevin O'Hare, Jane Anderson, Marie Blanchard, Monica Diaz, Sean Gallimore, David Hancock, Myung Kang, Maria Lopez, Dave McDougall, Frank Molieri, Scott Sackett, Peter Anderson, Adam Burke, John Dillon, Damien Gilligan, Roisin Hunt, Kendra Lammas, Paddy Malone, Neil McNeil, Bob Miller, Franz Suarez; *fx sup anim:* Dave Tidgwell; *fx dir anim (LA):* Tom Hush; *fx anim:* Joseph Gilland, Peter Matheson, Diann Landau, Brian McSweeney, Janette Owens, Joan Doyle, Leslie Aust, Robert B. Cowan, Orla Madden, Declan Walsh, Mark Cumberton, Conor Thunder, Noel P. Kiernan, Conann Fitzpatrick, Martine Finucane; *(LA):* Debra Middleton-Kupczyk, Bruce Heller, Michael Gagne; *fx admin asst sup:* Claire Gallagher; *addit fx anim:* Kim Hagen-Jensen, Frank Doyle, Jane Smethurst, Dierdre Reynolds, Julian Hynes, David Lyons, Rolando Mercado, Raymond Hofstedt, Colbert Zinc Fennelly, John Costello, Paul Morris, Gillian Cunningham, Julie Phelan; *fx inbet:* Tracey Meighan, Richard Beneham, Tyrone Elliott, David Kracov, Conor Clancy, Michael Ho, Eric Alley, Susan Keane, Daniel O'Sullivan; *fx technicians:* Michael Casey, Suzanna Badri, Margaret Comerford; *computer anim/digital imagery:* Jan Carlée, Greg Maguire, Thomas Miller, Christine Zing Chang; *computer prod co-ord:* John Finnegan, David Satchwell; *prod continuity sup:* Carla Washburn; *dial ed:* Jim Fleming, Gerard Phillips, Gary Keleghan; *col stylists:* Carmen Oliver, Violet McKenna, Suzanne O'Reilly, Donal Freeney, Ailish Mullally, Majella Burns, Ann McCormick, Mary Cuthbert, Lyn Mulvany, Berenice Keegan, Noirin Dunne, Gareth McKinney, Kathy Carter, Mark Grant, Suzanne Pegley; *col fx art:* Shirley Mapes; *lay:* Eddie Green, Fred Reilly, Amy Berenz, Dean Deblois, Gary O'Neill, Mark T. Byrne, John Byrne, Martin Hanley, Peter Yamasaki, Ken Spirduso, Jonathan Ridge, Eogham Cahill; *lay admin asst sup:* Caroline Lynch; *lay co-ord:* Cormac Slevin; *blue sketch art:* Gari Downey, Sorcha Ni Chuimin; *paste-up art:* Gillian Bolger; *col keys:* Suzanne Lemieux; *back:* Rick Bentham, Carl Jones, Robyn Christian Nason, Paul M. Kelly, Phaedra Craig Finnegan, Kenneth Slevin; *back:* Greg Gibbons, Sunny Apinchapong, Tia Kratter, Kevin McNamara, Miguel Gil, Michael Hirsh, Rachel Kerr, Sean Sullivan, Bill Dely; *back admin asst:* Janette R. Morgan; *ed:* Thomas V. Moss, Fiona Trayler, Annette Stone, Shannon Scudder, Aran O'Reilly; *voices: Jacqimo:* Gino Conforti; *Mother:* Barbara Cook; *Thumbelina:* Jodi Benson; *Hero:* Will Ryan; *Queen Tabitha:* June Foray; *King Colbert:*

Kenneth Mars; *Prince Cornelius:* Gary Imhoff; *Grundel:* Joe Lynch; *Mrs. (Ma) Toad:* Charo; *Mozo:* Danny Mann; *Gringo:* Loren Michaels; *Baby Bug:* Kendall Cunningham; *Gnatty:* Tawny "Sunshine" Glover; *Li'l Bee:* Michael Nunes; *Mr. Beetle:* Gilbert Gottfried; *Mrs. Rabbit:* Pat Musick; *Mr. Fox/Mr. Bear:* Neil Ross; *Mrs. Fieldmouse:* Carol Channing; *Mr. Mole:* John Hurt; *Hero/Reverend Rat:* Will Ryan; "On the Road" *backup singers:* Domenick Allen, Larry Kenton, Rick Riso; "You're Beautiful Baby" *performed by* Randy Crenshaw; *original underscore:* William Ross, Barry Manilow; *composer:* Barry Manilow; *songs:* Barry Manilow, Jack Feldman, Bruce Sussman; music score performed by Irish Film Orchestra; conducted by William Ross; *choral arrangements:* Earl Brown; performed by The Anuna Choir; *choir dir:* Michael McGlynn; *mus ed:* James Harrison; *rough inbet/ break:* Anne C. Murray, Tom Higgins, Jared Beckstrand, Marie Bonis-Charancle, Gerard Brady, Mark C. Byrne, Michael Carroll, David Coogan, David Corbally, Robert D'Arcy, Claudia Dickerson, Michael Dunn, David Farrell, Martha Furley, Debbie Gold, Eddie Goral, Joseph Haugh, Roger Horgan, Tamara A. Iba, Barry Iremonger, Mike Jones, Sandra Keely, Carl Keenan, Joseph Manifold Jr., Craig Maras, Majella Milne, Andrew Molloy, Sharon Morgan, Joseph Mulligan Jr., Andres L. Nieves, Uli Nitzche, Gabrielle O'Regan, Bob Quinn, Paul Shanahan, Elizabeth Stoll, Melanie S. Thomas, Tom Tobey, Hilary Gough, Karl Hayes; *clean-up:* Olivia O'Mahony, Eileen Conway, Jan Naylor, Fionnuala Balance, Sheila Brown, Michael Carey, Mick Cassidy, Roland Chat, Chris Chu, Wesley Chun, Mary Connors, Nollaig Crombie, Finula Cunningham, Peter Donnelly, Martin Fagan, Des Forde, Gerard Gogan, Jason Halpin, Sue Houghton, Ethan Nate Kanfer, Helen Lawlor, Karen Marjoribanks, Ciara McCabe, Glen McIntosh, Margaret McKenna, Anne-Marie Mockler, Annette Morel, Eileen Ridgeway, Bonnie Robinson, Julie Ryan, Richard Smitheman, Sally Voorheis, Chan Woo Jung, Miri Yoon; *character clean-up:* Jane McLoughlin, Jacqui Boland, Rosie Ahern, Tommy Brennan, Scott Brutz, John Cooley, Shana Curley, Dan Daly, Eileen Dunn, Ricardo Echevarria, Eileen Fleming, Paul Fogarty, Michael Garry, Judy Grabenstatter, Joah Hagen-Jensen, Ellen Heindel, Akemi Horiuchi, Jeff Johnson, Heather Jones, Linda Kellagher, Edward Klein, Patrice Leach, Leticia Lichtwardt, Levi Louis, Maria Malone, James McLoughlin, Mark McLoughlin, Bernadette Moley, Julie Moline, Mary Mulvihill, June Myung Park, Soonjin Mooney, Tracy Nelson, Siobhan O'Donnell, Dympna O'Halloran, Carol O'Mara, Alan O'Regan, Terry O'Toole, Michael Oliva, Rob Porter, Wantana Prajanbarn, Rebecca Roche-Murphy, Neal Ryan, Adam van Wyk, John Walsh, San Wei Chan, Suk Yun; *scene plan:* John Phelan, Gerard Carty, Sean Dempsey, Eimear Clonan, Maureen Buggy, Vincent Clarke, Philip Grogan; *anim check:* Michele McKenna-Mahon, Christine Fluskey, Pam Kleyman, Moira Murphy, Carol Thornbury, Linda Fitzpatrick, Hughie Shevlin, Colum Slevin, Sharon Mongey; *final check:* Mary Walsh, Mary Shevlin, Sandra Breslin, Martina McCarron, Sinead Murray, Fiona Mackle, Pearse Love, Melanie Strickland, Susan O'Loughlin, Brian Forsyth, Dympna Murray; *ph:* Ciavàn Morris, Eric Ryan, Emmet Doyle, Paddy Duffy, Gary Hall, Jeanette Maher, Keith Murray, John O'Flaherty, Peadar O'Reilly, Derek Reid; *Xerox:* Michael Murray, Anthony O'Brien, Pearse Cullinane; *Xerox processors:* Jackie Anderson, John Walsh, Ann May, Paul Mulligan, Alan Cronin, Billy Colgan, Kieron White, Brian Thornton, Philip O'Keefe, Sinead McGlynn; *litho processor:* Ronan Nally; *Xerox check:* Paul Roy, Paul Clifford, Greg Fulton, Michael Maher, Damian E. Murphy, Michael O'Toole, Shane Fitzsimons, Marius Herbert, Alan Mongey, James O'Toole, Stephen K. Ratchford, Damien Walsh; *mark-up:* Maria Farrell, David Hogan, Collette O'Brien, Patricia "Bert" Gordon, Linda Bell, Mary Boylin, Breda Devereux, Sam Pouch, Louise Cleary, Sharon Blake, Alison Marnell-Barrass, Henry McGrane, Suzanne Quinn, Antoinette Rafter; *i&p:* Jacqueline Hooks, Brenda McGuirk, Niamh McClean, Mary Aitken, Mary Gavin, Alan Dalton, Marcia Watanabe, Helen Phelan, Karen Dwyer, Christine Byrne, Ann P. Murray, Madeleine Downes; *sd ed:* John K. Carr, Sue Odjakjian, Gretchen Thoma; *foley:* Skywalker Sound, Dan O'Connell, Hilda Hodges, Randy Singer, Nerses Gezalyan, Steve Maslow, Gregg Landaker; *col timer:* John Stanborough; *neg cutter:* Colin Ives; *col:* Tech. *sd:* Dolby stereo. 86 min. • Interpretation of the Hans Christian Anderson story. Thumbelina, a tiny girl no bigger than a thumb, lives with her "Mother" (a full-sized woman) and is visited one night by an enchanted fairy prince who promises to return in the morning to spend more time with her. Overjoyed, Thumbelina falls asleep dreaming of a blissful future but awakens to find herself in the middle of a pond, the prisoner of some singing toads. She is rescued by a swallow and later encounters a smooth-talking beetle whose advances she, again, has to escape. The Prince sets out to look for her but is delayed by an ice storm which also sees Thumbelina taking refuge with Mrs. Fieldmouse. After a few more adventures, her Prince reappears and defends his true love.

6465. Tick Tock Tuckered *(Looney Tunes)* 8 Apr. 1944; *p.c.:* Leon Schlesinger prods for WB; *dir:* Robert Clampett; *story:* Warren Foster; *anim/lay:* Thomas McKimson; *back:* Michael Sasanoff; *ed:* Treg Brown; *voices:* Mel Blanc; *mus:* Carl W. Stalling; *prod sup:* Henry Binder, Raymond G. Katz; *col:* Tech. *sd:* Vit. 7 min; Remake of *Porky's Badtime Story.* • Porky and Daffy try for a decent night's sleep in order to get to work on time the next day.

6466. Tickled Pink *(Pink Panther)* 6 Oct. 1968; *p.c.:* Mirisch/Geoffrey/DFE for UA; *dir:* Gerry Chiniquy; *story:* John W. Dunn; *anim:* Don Williams, Manny Perez, Art Leonardi, Warren Batchelder; *sets:* Tom O'Loughlin; *ed:* Allan Potter; *mus:* Walter Greene; *theme tune:* Henry Mancini; *prod sup:* Harry Love, Jim Foss; *col:* DeLuxe. *sd:* RCA. 6 min. • The Panther is granted the wish of having roller-skates by a fairy.

6467. The Tiger and the Donkey *(Aesop's Film Fable)* 26 Jan. 1922; *p.c.:* Fables Pictures Inc for Pathé; *dir:* Paul Terry; b&w. *sil.* 5 min. • A corrupt tiger with the aid of a donkey manage to rob a stagecoach. Moral: "Bad company is dangerous for man and beast."

6468. The Tiger King *(Aesop's Fable)* Mar. 1960; *ex prod:* Bill Weiss; *dir/anim:* Connie Rasinski; *story/voice:* Tom Morrison; *anim:* Mannie Davis; *lay:* Bill Hilliker; *back:* Dave Evslim; *mus:* Phil Scheib; *prod mgr:* Frank Schudde; *col:* Tech. *sd:* RCA. 6 min. CS. • The tiger deposes the lion as king of the jungle and sends his son to school who eats all his classmates. Finally the lion has to be reinstated.

6469. Tiger Trouble *(Goofy)* 5 Jan. 1945; *p.c.:* Walt Disney prods for RKO; *dir:* Jack Kinney; *asst dir:* Bee Selck; *story:* Bill Peet; *anim:* Milt Kahl, John Sibley, Eric Larson; *fx:* Jack Boyd; *lay:* Lance Nolley; *back:* Claude Coats; *voices:* Fred Shields, Pinto Colvig, Milt Kahl, James MacDonald; *mus:* Paul J. Smith; *col:* Tech. *sd:* RCA. 8 min. • Goofy goes tiger hunting in the jungle.

6470. A Tiger's Tail *(Noveltoon)* Dec. 1964; *p.c.:* Para Cartoons; *dir:* Seymour Kneitel; *story:* Tony Peters; *anim:* Martin Taras; *sets:* Robert Little; *voices:* Bob MacFadden, Norma MacMillan; *mus:* Winston Sharples; *ph:* Leonard McCormick; *col:* Tech. *sd:* RCA. 6 min. • Laddy wants a tiger skin rug for his room and Ali Presto fixes for him to go on safari.

6471. Tightrope Tricks *(Tom & Jerry)* 6 Jan. 1932; *p.c.:* Van Beuren for RKO; *dir:* John Foster, George Rufle; *voice:* Marjorie Hines; *mus:* Gene Rodemich; b&w. *sd:* RCA. 7 min. • The boys work in a circus and steal the lion's lunch. The creature pursues them on to a high wire and the elephant washes him away.

6472. The Tijuana Toads *(Tijuana Toads)* 6 Aug. 1969; *p.c.:* Mirisch/DFE for UA; *dir:* Hawley Pratt; *story:* John W. Dunn; *anim:* Don Williams, Manny Perez, Manny Gould, Bob Richardson, Warren Batchelder; *lay:* Dick Ung; *back:* Richard H. Thomas; *ed:* Lee Gunther; *voices:* Don Diamond, Tom Holland; *mus:* Doug Goodwin; *ph:* John Burton Jr.; *prod sup:* Jim Foss, Harry Love; *col:* DeLuxe. *sd:* RCA. 6 min. • The Toads attempt to catch a tough Texas grasshopper.

6473. Timber *(Donald Duck)* 10 Jan. 1941; *p.c.:* Walt Disney prods for RKO; *dir:* Jack King; *asst dir:* Bob Newman; *story:* Carl Barks, Jack Hannah; *anim:* Paul Allen, James Armstrong, Ted Bonnicksen, Walter Clinton, Emery Hawkins, Volus Jones, Hal King, Edward Love, Richard Lundy, Lee Morehouse, Ray Patin, Don Patterson, Judge Whitaker; *lay:* Bill Herwig; *voices:* Billy Bletcher, Clarence Nash; *mus:* Oliver Wallace; *col:* Tech. *sd:* RCA. 7 min. • Donald tries to steal lumberjack Pierre's lunch and is forced to chop trees as a penance.

6474. Time for Love *(Color Classic)* 6 Sept. 1935; *p.c.:* The Fleischer Studio for Para; *prod:* Max Fleischer; *dir:* Dave Fleischer; *anim:* Willard Bowsky, Nicholas Tafuri; *mus:* Sammy Timberg; *song:* Leo Robin, Ralph Ranger; *col:* Tech-2. *sd:* WE. 7 min. • A black swan wins over a lady swan's affections with fish. She breaks away and returns to her original suitor.

6475. Time Gallops On *(Terry-Toon)* 1 Feb. 1952; *p.c.:* TT for Fox; *dir:* Mannie Davis; *story/voice:* Tom Morrison; *sets:* Art Bartsch; *mus:* Philip A. Scheib; *ph:* Douglas Moye; *col:* Tech. *sd:* RCA. 7 min. • A village blacksmith builds himself a mechanical horse and enters it in an auto race.

6476. The Time Machine Aug. 1960; *p.c.:* Galaxy prods for MGM; *prod/dir:* George Pal; *fx:* Gene Warren, Wah Chang, Tim Barr; *voice:* Paul Frees; *col:* Metro. *sd:* WE. 103 min. • Live-action adaptation of H.G. Wells' story of a time traveller. Starring Rod Taylor.

6477. Time on My Hands *(Screen Songs)* 23 Dec. 1932; *p.c.:* The Fleischer Studio for Para; *prod:* Max Fleischer; *dir:* Dave Fleischer; *anim:* Willard Bowsky, Thomas Goodson; *mus:* Art Turkisher; *song:* Harold Adamson, Mack Gordon, Vincent Youmans; *l/a:* Ethel Merman; b&w. *sd:* WE. 9 min. *l/a/anim.* • A fisherman cat sends a worm to lure the fish from the river but gets a "Betty Boop" mermaid instead.

6478. The Timid Pup *(Color Rhapsody)* 1 Aug. 1940; *p.c.:* Charles Mintz prods for Colum *dir:* Ben Harrison; *anim:* Manny Gould; *lay:* Clark Watson; *ed:* George Winkler; *voice:* Pinto Colvig; *mus:* Joe de Nat; *prod mgr:* James Bronis; *col:* Tech. *sd:* RCA. 8 min. • A timid pup has a grand time chasing a kitten but ends with a parental spanking.

6479. The Timid Rabbit *(Terry-Toon)* 26 Nov. 1937; *p.c.:* TT for Educational/Fox; *dir:* Mannie Davis; *mus:* Philip A. Scheib; *col:* sep. *sd:* RCA. 6 min. • A rabbit is afraid of other animals but becomes heroic after bullying some bullfrogs.

6480. The Timid Scarecrow *(Dinky Duck)* Nov. 1953; *p.c.:* TT for Fox; *dir:* Eddie Donnelly; *story:* Tom Morrison; *anim:* Jim Tyer; *mus:* Philip A. Scheib; *ph:* Douglas Moye; *col:* Tech. *sd:* RCA. 6½ min. • Dinky and the scarecrow join forces to combat the crows.

6481. Timid Tabby *(Tom & Jerry)* 19 Apr. 1957; *p.c.:* MGM; *prod/dir:* William Hanna Joseph Barbera; *anim:* Lewis Marshall, Kenneth Muse, Irven Spence, Ken Southworth, Bill Schipek; *lay:* Dick Bickenbach; *back:* Roberta Gruetert; *ed:* Jim Faris; *voice:* Bill Thompson; *mus:* Scott Bradley; *ph:* Jack Stevens; *prod mgr:* Hal Elias; *col:* Tech. *sd:* WE. 7 min. CS. • When Tom's cowardly cousin arrives, Jerry thinks it's Tom who has suddenly become afraid of mice.

6482. The Timid Toreador *(Looney Tunes)* 21 Dec. 1940; *p.c.:* Leon Schlesinger prods for WB; *dir/lay:* Robert Clampett, Norman McCabe; *story:* Melvin Millar; *anim:* I. Ellis, John Carey, Cal Dalton, Arthur Davis, David Hoffman, Vive Risto; *sets:* Richard H. Thomas; *ed:* Treg Brown; *voices:* Mel Blanc, The Guadalajara Trio; *mus:* Carl W. Stalling; *prod sup:* Henry Binder, Raymond G. Katz; b&w. *sd:* Vit. 7 min. • Hot tamalè vendor, Porky, finds himself in the bull ring fighting a ferocious bull.

6483. Tin Can Concert *(Cartune)* 31 Oct. 1961; *p.c.:* Walter Lantz prods for Univ; *dir/story:* Jack Hannah; *anim:* Don Lusk, Art Landy, Lance Nolley; *sets:* Ray Huffine, Art Landy, Lance Nolley; *voice:* Paul Frees; *orch:* Eugene Poddany; *prod mgr:* William E. Garity; *col:* Tech. *sd:* Vit. 6 min. • A tired mouse can't sleep because of an all-cat concert going on above his bedroom.

6484. Tin Pan Alley Cat Oct. 1960; *p.c.:* TT for Fox; *ex prod:* Bill Weiss; *dir:* Dave Tendlar; *story sup:* Tom Morrison; *story:* Eli Bauer; *anim:* Dick Hall, Johnny Gent, Ed Donnelly, Mannie Davis; *mus:* Phil Scheib; *prod mgr:* Frank Schudde; *col:* DeLuxe. *sd:* RCA. 6 min. CS. • A cat gives inspiration to an aspiring song writer.

6485. Tin Pan Alley Cats *(Merrie Melodies)* 17 July 1943; *p.c.:* Leon Schlesinger prods for WB; *dir:* Robert Clampett; *story:* Warren Foster; *anim:* Rod Scribner; *lay:* Thomas McKimson; *back:* Michael Sasanoff; *ed:* Treg Brown; *voices:* Mel Blanc; *mus/voices:* Harland C. Evans, Leo "Zoot" Watson, Clifford Holland; *singers:* Eddie Beal, Carl Jones, Audrey Flowers, Eddie Lynn; *musicians:* Eddie Beal (piano), Vernon H. Porter (guitar), Ulysses Livingstone (guitar), John E. Miller (bass), Leo "Zoot" Watson (drums); *song:* Carl Stalling, Milt Franklyn; *prod sup:* Henry Binder, Raymond G. Katz; *col:* Tech. *sd:* Vit. 7 min. • A "Fats Waller" cat is blasted to another planet by "hot" music, then realizes that terra firma is the best place to be.

6486. Tin Toy 1988; *p.c.:* PIXAR; *dir/anim/story:* John Lasseter; *technical dir:* William Reeves, Eben Ostby; *addit anim:* William Reeves, Eben Ostby, Craig Good; *modelling:* William Reeves, Eben Ostby, John Lasseter, Craig Good; *output scanning:* Cosmic Don Conway, Ralph Guggenheim; *Render man:* Jeffrey Mach, Tony Apodaca, Pat Hanrahan, Jeff Milgart, Darwyn Peachey, Jim Lawson, Sam Leffler; *elves:* Ralph Guggenheim, Loren Carpenter, Mark Leather, Flip Phillips, Ed Catmull; *3-Space Digiter:* Pelhamus Navigation Science; *PS350 Display System:* Evans and Sutherland; *mus consultant:* Forrest Patten: *Kaleidosound; film rec:*

Matrix Multicolor, David Haddich; *systems support:* Scott Taylor, Ken Jonathan Huey, Carson L. Silkey, Steven Sequera; *Dynamics:* David Salesin; *sd:* Gary Rydstrom, Sprocket Systems; *prod co-ord:* Ralph Guggenheim, Susan Anderson, Deirdre Warin; *best boy:* Tony Apodaca; *post prod co-ord:* Craig Good; *special thanks:* Naftali "El Magnifico" Alverez, James Wilson, Nancy Kemper, *ILM, Dolby Laboratories,* Ed Catmull, Alvy Ray Smith, Bill Adams, Steve Jobs; *col. sd:* Dolby stereo. 5 min. • A toy soldier sees his impending doom with the arrival of a destructive baby. Beating a hasty retreat under the couch ... he finds all the other toys cowering from the child.

6487. Tire Trouble (*Terry-Toon*) 24 July 1942; *p.c.:* TT for Fox; *dir:* Eddie Donnelly; *story:* John Foster; *sets:* Art Bartsch; *voices:* Arthur Kay, Thomas Morrison; *mus:* Philip A. Scheib; *ph:* Douglas Moye; *col:* Tech. *sd:* RCA. 7 min. • Gandy and Sourpuss have to buy ersatz tires made of baloney for their car, which attracts the dogs ... so they opt for walking!

6488. Tired and Feathered (*Looney Tunes*) 18 Sept. 1965; *p.c.:* DFE for WB; *dir/story:* Rudy Larriva; *anim:* Hank Smith, Virgil Ross, Bob Bransford; *lay:* Erni Nordli; *back:* Anthony Rizzo; *ed:* Lee Gunther; *mus:* Bill Lava; *col:* Tech. *sd:* Vit. 6 min. • The Coyote gets hoisted by his own petard when getting the Road-Runner to use a free phone made out of dynamite.

6489. Tit for Tat (*Aesop's Film Fable*) 22 Jan. 1927; *p.c.:* Fables Pictures Inc for Pathé; *dir:* Paul Terry; *b&w. sil.* 10 min. • An adventurous kitten wanders away and saves a bird from a fox. The bird, in turn, saves him when he is cornered on a waterfall.

6490. Tito's Guitar (*Color Rhapsody*) 9 Oct. 1942; *p.c.:* Colum; *prod:* Dave Fleischer; *dir:* Bob Wickersham; *story:* Tony Rivera; *anim:* Howard Swift; *lay:* Clark Watson; *ed:* Edward Moore; *mus:* Paul Worth; *prod mgr:* Albert Spar; *col:* Tech. *sd:* RCA. 7 min. • A young Mexican serenades his lady love but fails to win the heart of her father. Initiated by Frank Tashlin.

6491. To Be or Not to Be (*Sidney*) Feb. 1963; *p.c.:* TT for Fox; *ex prod:* William M. Weiss; *dir/anim:* Connie Rasinski; *story sup:* Tom Morrison; *story:* Bob Kuwahara; *sets:* John Zago, Bill Focht; *ed:* George McAvoy; *voices:* Dayton Allen, Lionel Wilson; *mus:* Phil Scheib; *ph:* Joseph Rasinski; *col:* DeLuxe. *sd:* RCA. 6 min. • Dissatisfied with his lot, Sidney the elephant encounters a Fairy Godmother who changes him into a rabbit, canary and finally invisible.

6492. To Beep or Not to Beep (*Merrie Melodies*) Dec. 1963; *p.c.:* WB; *dir:* Chuck Jones; *asst dir/lay:* Maurice Noble; *story:* John Dunn, Chuck Jones; *anim:* Richard Thompson, Bob Bransford, Tom Ray, Ken Harris; *fx:* Harry Love; *back:* Philip de Guard; *ed:* Treg Brown; *voices:* Paul Julian, Mel Blanc; *mus:* Bill Lava; *prod mgr:* Bill Orcutt; *prod:* David H. DePatie; *col:* Tech. *sd:* Vit. 7 min. • The Coyote uses an obstinate giant catapult that persists in dumping rocks on him.

6493. To Boo or Not to Boo (*Casper*) 8 June 1951; *p.c.:* Famous for Para; *dir:* I. Sparber; *story:* Larz Bourne; *anim:* Myron Waldman, Larry Silverman; *sets:* Robert Little; *voices:* Alan Shay, Jackson Beck, Cecil Roy, Sid Raymond, Jack Mercer; *mus:* Winston Sharples; *song:* Mack David, Jerry Livingston; *ph:* Leonard McCormick; *col:* Tech. *sd:* RCA. 7 min. • Casper tries to win friends with a young girl he meets at a Hallowe'en party.

6494. To Catch a Woodpecker (*Woody Woodpecker*); 29 July 1957; *p.c.:* Walter Lantz prods for Univ; *dir:* Alex Lovy; *story:* Homer Brightman; *anim:* La Verne Harding, Ray Abrams; *sets:* Raymond Jacobs; *voices:* Daws Butler, Grace Stafford; *mus:* Clarence Wheeler; *prod mgr:* William E. Garity; *col:* Tech. *sd:* RCA. 6 min. • Miracle Telephone Co's telephone poles are being destroyed by Woody. The President calls in O'Hoolihan to put a stop to him.

6495. To Duck ... or Not to Duck (*Looney Tunes*) 23 Jan. 1943; *p.c.:* Leon Schlesinger prods for WB; *dir:* Charles M. Jones; *story:* Tedd Pierce; *anim:* Robert Cannon; *lay:* John McGrew; *back:* Eugene Fleury; *ed:* Treg Brown; *voices:* Mel Blanc, Arthur Q. Bryan; *mus:* Carl W. Stalling; *prod sup:* Henry Binder, Raymond G. Katz; *col:* Tech. *sd:* Vit. 6¹/₂ min. • Daffy challenges Elmer's sportsmanship in the boxing ring.

6496. To Hare Is Human (*Merrie Melodies*) 15 Dec. 1956; *p.c.:* WB; *dir:* Chuck Jones; *story:* Michael Maltese; *anim:* Ken Harris, Abe Levitow, Richard Thompson, Ben Washam; *lay:* Maurice Noble; *back:* Philip de Guard; *ed:* Treg Brown; *voices:* Mel Blanc; *mus:* Milt Franklyn; *prod mgr:* John W. Burton; *prod:* Edward Selzer; *col:* Tech. *sd:* Vit. 6¹/₂ min. • Wile E. Coyote engages the help of a computer to assist him in the capture of Bugs.

6497. To Itch His Own (*Merrie Melodies*) 28 June 1958; *p.c.:* WB; *dir:* Chuck Jones; *story:* Michael Maltese; *anim:* Abe Levitow, R.L. Thompson, Ken Harris, Ben Washam; *lay:* Maurice Noble; *back:* Phil de Guard; *ed:* Treg Brown; *voice:* Mel Blanc; *mus:* Carl Stalling; *col:* Tech. *sd:* Vit. 7 min. • A strong circus flea decides to take a holiday on a peaceful dog who is constantly bullied by the selfish bulldog next door.

6498. To Spring (*Happy Harmonies*) 20 June 1936; *p.c.:* MGM; *prod:* Hugh Harman, Rudolf Ising; *dir/anim:* William Hanna, Paul Fennell; *voice:* J. Delos Jewkes, Elmore Vincent; *mus:* Scott Bradley; *col:* Tech. *sd:* RCA. 9 min. • The Trolls who live underground prepare the Earth for the arrival of Spring.

6499. To the Rescue (*Oswald*) 23 May 1932; *p.c.:* Univ; *dir:* Walter Lantz, "Bill" Nolan; *anim:* Manuel Moreno, Ray Abrams, Fred Avery, "Bill" Weber, Vet Anderson, Lester Kline, Bunny Ellison; *mus:* James Dietrich; *b&w. sd:* WE. 6 min. • No story available.

6500. Toby Down South (*Toby the Pup*) 15 Apr. 1931; *p.c.:* Winkler for RKO; *prod:* Charles B. Mintz; *dir:* Dick Huemor, Sid Marcus; *mus:* Joe de Nat; *prod mgr:* James Bronis; *b&w. sd:* 6 min. • Eccentric paddlesteamers on the Mississippi.

6501. Toby in the Brown Derby (*Toby the Pup*) 22 Mar. 1931; *p.c.:* Winkler for RKO; *prod:* Charles B. Mintz; *dir:* Dick Huemor, Sid Marcus; *mus:* Joe de Nat; *prod mgr:* James Bronis; *b&w. sd:* 6 min. • No story available.

6502. Toby in the Bug House (*Toby the Pup*) 7 Dec. 1930; *p.c.:* Winkler for RKO; *prod:* Charles B. Mintz; *dir:* Dick Huemor, Sid Marcus; *mus:* Joe de Nat; *prod mgr:* James Bronis; *b&w. sd:* 6 min. • Toby gets mixed up with worms, bugs and all sorts of dancing insects.

6503. Toby in the Museum (*Toby the Pup*) 22 Aug. 1930; *p.c.:* Winkler for RKO; *prod:* Charles B. Mintz; *dir:* Dick Huemor, Sid Marcus; *mus:* Joe de Nat; *prod mgr:* James Bronis; *b&w. sd:* 6 min. • Museum janitor Toby gets all the statues and exhibitions dancing until his boss arrives and puts a stop to it.

6504. Toby the Bull Thrower (*Toby the Pup*) 23 May 1931; *p.c.:* Winkler for RKO; *prod:* Charles B. Mintz; *dir:* Dick Huemor, Sid Marcus; *mus:* Joe de Nat; *prod mgr:* James Bronis; *b&w. sd:* 6 min. • Toby does some bull-throwing, ending abruptly when he takes a boat out of the moon.

6505. Toby the Fiddler (*Toby the Pup*) 1 Sept. 1930; *p.c.:* Winkler for RKO; *prod:* Charles B. Mintz; *dir:* Dick Huemor, Sid Marcus; *mus:* Joe de Nat; *prod mgr:* James Bronis; *b&w. sd:* 6 min. • No story available.

6506. Toby the Milkman (*Toby the Pup*) 25 Feb. 1931; *p.c.:* Winkler for RKO; *prod:* Charles B. Mintz; *dir:* Dick Huemor, Sid Marcus; *mus:* Joe de Nat; *prod mgr:* James Bronis; *b&w. sd:* 6 min. • After delivering watered-down milk, Toby takes part in a barn dance.

6507. Toby the Miner (*Toby the Pup*) 1 Oct. 1930; *p.c.:* Winkler for RKO; *prod:* Charles B. Mintz; *dir:* Dick Huemor, Sid Marcus; *mus:* Joe de Nat; *prod mgr:* James Bronis; *b&w. sd:* 6 min. • Miner Toby and his horse are trapped in a mine cave-in and discover a group of underground gnomes.

6508. Toby the Pup (*Toby the Pup*) 1 Apr. 1931; *p.c.:* Winkler for RKO; *prod:* Charles B. Mintz; *dir:* Dick Huemor, Sid Marcus; *mus:* Joe de Nat; *prod mgr:* James Bronis; *b&w. sd:* 6 min. • No story available.

6509. Toby the Showman (*Toby the Pup*) 22 Nov. 1930; *p.c.:* Winkler for RKO; *prod:* Charles B. Mintz; *dir:* Dick Huemor, Sid Marcus; *mus:* Joe de Nat; *prod mgr:* James Bronis; *b&w. sd:* 6 min. • Toby displays his talent for playing musical instruments.

6510. Toby Tortoise Returns (*Silly Symphony*) 22 Aug. 1936; *p.c.:* Walt Disney prods for UA; *dir:* Wilfred Jackson; *asst dir:* Graham Heid; *story dir:* Bill Cottrell, Joe Grant, Bob Kuwahara; *story:* I. Klein; *anim:* Dick Huemer, Jack Hannah, Milton Kahl, Ward Kimball, I. Klein, Richard Lundy, Hamilton S. Luske, Robert Stokes, Marvin Woodward; *sets:* Bob Kuwahara; *lay:* Lee Blair; *voices:* Eddie Holden, Edgar Norton, Martha Wentworth, Alyce Ardell; *mus:* Frank E. Churchill, Leigh Harline; *col:*

Tech. *sd:* RCA. 8 min. • Max Hare challenges Toby Tortoise to a boxing match.

6511. Together in the Weather *(Puppetoon)* 24 May 1946; *p.c.:* George Pal prods for Para; *prod/dir:* George Pal; *voice:* Elmore Vincent; *mus:* Clarence E. Wheeler; *col:* Tech. *sd:* WE. 7 min. • A beautiful weather clock girl sets out to lure the boy over from his side of the clock but it takes an artificial storm to do so.

6512. Tokio Jokio *(Looney Tunes)* 15 May 1943; *p.c.:* Leon Schlesinger prods for WB: *dir/lay:* Norman McCabe; *story:* Don Christensen; *anim:* I. Ellis, John Carey, Cal Dalton, Arthur Davis, David Hoffman, Vive Risto; *sets:* David Hilberman; *ed:* Treg Brown; *voices:* Mel Blanc; *mus:* Carl W. Stalling; *prod sup:* Henry Binder, Raymond G. Katz; b&w. *sd:* Vit. 7 min. • Japanese enemy newsreel purporting to show achievements won in the Pacific. Each trick backfires. Propaganda stuff, this!

6513. Tollbridge Troubles *(Fox & Crow)* 27 Nov. 1942; *p.c.:* Colum; *prod:* Dave Fleischer; *dir:* Bob Wickersham; *story:* Leo Salkin; *anim:* Lou Schmidt; *lay:* Clark Watson; *ed:* Edward Moore; *voices:* Frank Graham; *mus:* Eddie Kilfeather; *prod mgr:* Albert Spar; *col:* Tech. *sd:* RCA. 7¹/₂ min. • The Fox refuses to pay a toll to the Crow and invents many ways to cross the river without paying. • Initiated by Frank Tashlin.

6514. Tom and Chèrie *(Tom & Jerry)* 9 Sept. 1955; *p.c.:* MGM; *prod/dir:* William Hanna, Joseph Barbera; *anim:* Irven Spence, Kenneth Muse, Lewis Marshall, Ed Barge; *lay:* Dick Bickenbach; *back:* Robert Gentle; *ed:* Jim Faris; *voice:* Francoise Brun-Cottan; *mus:* Scott Bradley; *ph:* Jack Stevens; *prod mgr:* Hal Elias; *col:* Tech. *sd:* WE. 7 min. CS. • Mouseketeer Jerry uses his assistant to deliver love letters past the royal cat to his girl.

6515. Tom and Jerry *p.c.:* Arrow Films Corp; • *1923:* **The Gasoline Trail** 1 Aug. **Tom's First Flivver** 1 Sept. • Described as "Movie marionettes featuring little darkie Tom and his mule." No stories available.

6516. Tom and Jerry (Rembrandt Studio) 1961–1962; *prod:* William L. Snyder; *dir:* Gene Deitch; *story:* Larz Bourne, Eli Bauer, Tod Dockstader, Gene Deitch, Bill Danch, Chris Jenkyns, Tedd Pierce; *anim dir:* Vaclav Bedrich; *anim:* Zdeněk Smetana, Milan Klikar, Antonín Bureš, Věra Marešová, Mirko Kačena, Boumil Šejda, Věra Kudrnová, Jindřich Barta, Zdenka Skřípková, Olga Šišková; *lay:* Gene Deitch; *back:* Bohumil Šiška; *sd fx:* Tod Dockstader; *mus:* Václav Lidl, Štěpan Koníček. • Although produced in Czechoslovakia, these were made for the American market. • See: *Buddies Thicker Than Water; Calypso Cat; Carmen Get It; Down and Outing; Dickey Moe; High Steaks; It's Greek to Me-Ow!; Landing Stripling; Mouse Into Space; Sorry Safari; Switchin' Kitten; Tall in the Trap; The Tom and Jerry Cartoon Kit*

6517. The Tom and Jerry Cartoon Kit *(Tom & Jerry)* Aug. 1962; *p.c.:* Rembrandt for MGM; *prod:* William L. Snyder; *dir:* Gene Deitch; *story:* Chris Jenkyns; *anim:* Vaclav Bedrich; *voices:* Allen Swift; *mus:* Stepan Konícek; *col:* Metro. *sd:* WE. 8 min. • Tom and Jerry have fun with cartoon implements.

6518. Tom and Jerry in the Hollywood Bowl *(Tom & Jerry)* 16 Sept. 1950; *p.c.:* MGM; *dir:* William Hanna, Joseph Barbera; *anim:* Kenneth Muse, Irven Spence, Ray Patterson, Ed Barge; *lay:* Dick Bickenbach; *back:* Robert Gentle; *ed:* Jim Faris; *mus:* Scott Bradley; *ph:* Jack Stevens; *prod:* Fred Quimby; *col:* Tech. *sd:* WE. 6¹/₂ min. • Tom is the conductor of an orchestra playing Listz's symphonic poem "Les Preludes" when he is pestered by Jerry who also wants to conduct.

6519. Tom and Jerry: The Movie 6 Aug. 1993; *p.c.:* Turner Entertainment Company/WMG for First Independent; *dir/prod:* Phil Roman; *ex prod:* Roger Mayer, Jack Petrik, Hans Brockmann, Justin Ackerman; *co-prod:* Bill Schultz; *asso prod:* James Wang; *prod exs:* Rocky Solotoff, WMG: Su Lim; *prod sup:* Lee Anne Kaplan: *Taiwan/Thailand:* Lynn Hoag, JoEllen Marlow; *prod co-ord:* Monica Diane Mayall, Craig Sost; *prod mgr:* Michael Wolf, Jill S. Bauman; *post prod sup:* Barbara Beck; *l/a dir:* Robert Fisher Jnr.; *scr:* Dennis Marks; based on characters created by William Hanna and Joseph Barbera; *storyboard:* Andrew Austin, Brad Landreth, Marty Murphy, Keith Tucker, Monte Young, Phil Mendez, Mitch Schauer; *seq dir:* John Sparey, Monte Young, Bob Nesler, Adam Kuhlman, Eric Daniels, Jay Jackson, Skip Jones; *Taiwan sup dir:* James Miko, Andre Knutson; *anim dir:* Dale L. Baer; *anim:* J.K. Kim, Adam Dykstra, Dan Haskett, Adam Kuhlman, Kevin Petriak, Ka-Moon Song, Kevin Wurzer, Eric Thomas, Art Roman, Doug Frankel, Tony Fucile, Steve Gordon, Leslie

Gorin, Brian Robert Hogan, Gabi Payn, Irv Spence, Arnie Wong, David Courtland, Frederic Du Chau, Darin Hilton, Sadao Miyamoto, David Nethery, Michael Polvani, Alejandro Reyes, Michael Toth, Larry Whitaker, Tomihiro Yamaguchi, Matthew Bates, Jon Hooper, Mark Koetsier, Dan Koetsier, Linda Miller, Mark Pudleiner, Chad Stewart, Bonita Versh; *fx anim sup:* Jeff Howard, Sean Applegate, George S. Chialtas, Corny Cole, Mark Dindal, Brett Hisey, John Huey, Craig Littell-Herrick, Gary McCarver, Mary Mullen, January Nordman; *computer anim:* Kroyer Films Inc., Mark M. Pompian, Brian Schindler; *lay:* Ray Aragon, Andrew Austin, Peter J. De Luca, Andy Gaskill, Ed Ghertner, Mike Hodgson, Gary L. Hoffman, Brad Landreth, Ken Mimura, Cliff Voorhees, Dean Thompson; *back:* Michael Humphries, Bari Greenberg; *blue sketch:* Peter J. De Luca; *col des:* Phyllis Craig, Leslie Ellery; *col models:* Phyllis Craig, Debbie Mark, Belle Norman, Libby Reed, Brian Mark, Casey Clayton; *models:* Michael Peraza Jr., Jim Franzen, Leonard F. Johnson, David Nethery; *ed:* Sam Horta, Julie Ann Gustafson, *(video)* Noel Roman, Larry Swerdlove; *creative consultants:* Joe Barbera, David Simone; *mus:* Henry Mancini; performed by the National Philharmonic Orchestra of London; *orch:* Henry Mancini, Jack Hayes; *mus sup:* Sharon Boyle, Kathy Nelson; *mus ed:* Stephen A. Hope; *songs:* Henry Mancini, Leslie Bricusse; "All in How Much We Give" by Jody Davidson; *voices:* Tom: Richard Kind; *Jerry:* Dana Hill; *Robyn:* Anndi McAfee; *Aunt Finn:* Charlotte Rae; *Lickboot:* Tony Jay; *Captain Kiddie:* Rip Taylor; *Applecheek:* Henry Gibson; *Ferdinand/Straycatcher:* Michael Bell; *Puggsy/Daddy Starling:* Ed Gilbert; *Frankie de Flea:* David L. Lander; *Squawk:* Howard Morris; *Straycatcher:* Sydney Lassick; *Alleycat/Bulldog:* Raymond McLeod; *Alleycats:* Mitchell D. Moore, Scott Wojahn; *Patrolman:* Tino Insana; *Droopy:* Don Messick; *Woman's voice:* B.J. Ward; *Man's voice:* Greg Burson; *art dir:* Michael Peraza Jr., Michael Humphries; *anim check:* Merle Welton, Jackie Banks, Lolee Aries; *i&p:* Taiwan/Thailand: Karen Hudson, Maria Gonzalez; *choreog:* Lori Eastside; *dancers:* Bryan Anthony, Frankie de Miranda, Steve Messina, Randi Pareira, Kip Reynolds, Maurice Schwartzman, Myles Thoroughgood; *title des:* Neal Thompson; *ph: Taiwan/Thailand:* David Koenigsberg, Allen Foster; *video operators:* Gregory Hinde, Patrick Buchanan, Peter J. De Luca, Cyndy (Heather) Ingram, Robert Ingram; *sd ed:* Tom Syslo, Thomas Jaeger; *ADR ed:* Eileen Horta; *foley ed:* Ken D. Young, Robert N. Brown; *sd rec:* Gordon Hunt; *mus:* Alan Snelling; *foley rec:* Cecilia Perna; *Dolby Stereo consultant:* Thom Ehle; *sd re-rec:* Joe Citarilla, Don MacDougall, Darryl Linkow; *sd fx ed:* Mark L. Crookston, Michael Gollom, John O. Robinson III, Kevin D. Spears; *foley art:* Eileen Horta, Debra O'Connor; *post prod consultant:* Arthur Klein; *col:* CFI. *sd:* Dolby stereo. 84 min. • Tom and Jerry find themselves homeless when Tom's owners vacate the house and it is demolished. In their travels they meet Robyn, a runaway girl escaping from her cruel aunt who is looking after her while her father is on an expedition in Tibet. They are all returned by the police and while Tom and Jerry try to engratiate themselves with the aunt, they uncover a plot to inherit the father's millions. Tom, Jerry and Robyn manage to escape the clutches of the aunt and her slippery lawyer accomplice with a hectic chase ending at a riverside hideaway and with Robyn's father rescuing them in the nick of time.

6520. Tom Schuler — Cobbler, Statesman 1954; *p.c.:* Sketchbook Film prods for U.S. Information Agency; *dir:* Dick Lundy; *story:* Bill Scott; *anim:* Ray Patterson, Grant Simmons, Michael Lah, Osmond Evans, Stan Walsh; *sets:* Curt Perkins; *mus:* Michel Perrier; *ph:* Anicam; *col. sd.* 27 min. • The story of an immigrant cobbler who learns the importance of individual public service to the success of a good government.

6521. Tom Thumb 1958; *p.c.:* Galaxy Pictures Ltd for MGM; *prod/dir:* George Pal; *anim:* Gene Warren, Wah Chang, Don Sahlin, Tim Barr, Herb Johnson; *voices: Yawning Man:* Stan Freberg; *Con-Fu-Shon:* Dal McKennon; *also:* Thurl Ravenscroft; *mus:* Muir Mathieson; *songs:* Peggy Lee, Fred Spielman, Janice Torre, Kermit Goell; *col:* Metro. *sd:* WE. (seq) 6¹/₂ min. l/a/anim. • Live-action feature starring Russ Tamblyn as the tiny hero who sings and dances with the toys. Another sequence has him being put to sleep by "The Yawning Man."

6522. Tom Thumb *(ComiColor)* 30 Mar. 1936; *p.c.:* Celebrity prods; *prod/dir:* Ub Iwerks *mus:* Carl Stalling; *col:* Ciné. *sd:* PCP. 8 min. • When the stork brings tiny Tom he gets in everybody's way. He then goes fishing and gets involved in an underwater adventure.

6523. Tom Thumb *(Krazy Kat)* 26 Feb. 1934; *p.c.:* Charles Mintz prods for Colum; *story:* Harry Love; *anim:* Allen Rose, Preston Blair; *mus:* Joe de Nat; *prod mgr:* James Bronis; *b&w. sd:* RCA. 6 min. • While Krazy and Kitty stroll in the forest, Kitty is kidnapped by a villain and the bugs help Krazy to rescue her.

6524. Tom Thumb in Trouble (*Merrie Melodies*) 8 June 1940; *p.c.:* Leon Schlesinger prods for WB; *dir:* Charles M. Jones; *story:* Rich Hogan; *anim:* Robert Cannon; *character des/lay:* Robert Givens; *back:* Paul Julian; *ed:* Treg Brown; *voice:* John Shepperd, Margaret Hill; *mus:* Carl W. Stalling; *prod sup:* Henry Binder, Raymond G. Katz; *col:* Tech. *sd:* Vit. 7 min. • When little Tom falls into a pan of water and is rescued by a bird, his father thinks the bird has attacked him and chases it away. Tom weathers a raging blizzard to find his friend.

6525. Tom Thumb's Brother (*Color Rhapsody*) 12 June 1941; *p.c.:* Colum; *dir:* Sid Marcus; *anim:* Art Davis; *voices:* Norman Nesbitt, Sara Berner, Leone Le Doux; *mus:* Joe de Nat; *prod mgr:* George Winkler; *col:* Tech. *sd:* RCA. 7 min. • Peewee, Tom's smaller brother, rescues Tom when a kitten chases him.

6526. Tom, Tom the Piper's Son (*Paul Terry-Toon*) 16 Nov. 1934; *p.c.:* Moser & Terry, Inc for Educational/Fox; *dir:* Frank Moser, Paul Terry; *mus:* Philip A. Scheib; *b&w. sd:* WE. 6 min. • Nursery Rhyme characters emerge from the plants when Tom plays his pipe.

6527. Tom Tom Tomcat (*Merrie Melodies*) 27 June 1953; *p.c.:* WB; *dir:* I. Freleng; *story:* Warren Foster; *anim:* Ken Champin, Virgil Ross, Arthur Davis, Manuel Perez; *lay:* Hawley Pratt; *back:* Irv Wyner; *ed:* Treg Brown; *voices:* Mel Blanc, Bea Benaderet; *mus:* Carl Stalling; *prod mgr:* John W. Burton; *prod:* Edward Selzer; *col:* Tech. *sd:* Vit. 6 min. • Granny and Tweety are heading across the prairie in a covered wagon when they are attacked by a band of native "Putty Tats."

6528. Tom Turk and Daffy (*Looney Tunes*) 12 Feb. 1944; *p.c.:* Leon Schlesinger prods for WB; *dir:* Charles M. Jones; *story:* "The Staff"; *anim:* Ken Harris; *sets:* Arthur Heinemann; *ed:* Treg Brown; *voices:* Mel Blanc, Billy Bletcher; *mus:* Carl W. Stalling; *ph:* John W. Burton; *prod sup:* Henry Binder, Raymond G. Katz; *col:* Tech. *sd:* Vit. 7 min. • Daffy's efforts to hide Tom Turkey from Pilgrim Porky are strenuous until Porky reveals his plans for a Thanksgiving dinner.

6529. Tom Turkey and His Harmonica Humdiggers (*MGM cartoon*) 8 June 1940; *p.c.:* MGM; *prod/dir:* Hugh Harman; *story:* Hugh Harman, Jack Cosgriff, Charles McGirl; *lay:* John Meandor; *back:* Joe Smith; *voices:* Mel Blanc; *mus:* Scott Bradley; *prod mgr:* Fred Quimby; *col:* Tech. *sd:* WE. 7 min. • Tom and his harmonica gang practice their playing in the local store and raise the place to the ground.

6530. Tomcat Combat (*Woody Woodpecker*) Mar. 1959; *p.c.:* Walter Lantz prods for Univ; *dir:* Paul J. Smith; *story:* Homer Brightman; *anim:* Robert Bentley, Les Kline, Don Patterson; *sets:* Art Landy, Raymond Jacobs; *voices:* Daws Butler, Grace Stafford; *mus:* Clarence Wheeler; *prod mgr:* William E. Garity; *col:* Tech. *sd:* RCA. 6 min. • The humane officer informs Clyde Cat that woodpeckers are protected by law.

6531. Tom-ic Energy (*Tom & Jerry*) 1964 *p.c.:* MGM; *prod/dir:* Chuck Jones; *asst dir/lay:* Maurice Noble; *story:* Michael Maltese, Chuck Jones; *anim:* Ken Harris, Don Towsley, Tom Ray, Dick Thompson, Ben Washam; *back:* Philip de Guard; *voices:* Mel Blanc, June Foray; *mus:* Eugene Poddany; *prod mgr:* Les Goldman; *col:* Metro. *sd:* WE. 6 min. • Tom continues his "perpetual motion" pursuit of Jerry.

6532. Tomorrow We Diet (*Goofy*) 29 June 1951; *p.c.:* Walt Disney prods for RKO; *dir:* Jack Kinney; *story:* Milt Schaffer, Dick Kinney; *anim:* John Sibley, Ed Aardal, Harvey Toombs, Hugh Fraser, Cliff Nordberg; *fx:* Dan MacManus, Jack Boyd; *lay:* Al Zinnen; *back:* Dick Anthony; *voices:* Jack Rourke, Bob Jackman, James MacDonald, Milt Schaffer, Al Zinnen; *mus:* Joseph S. Dubin; *col:* Tech. *sd:* RCA. 7 min. • An overweight Geef strives to keep to a diet.

6533. Tom's Photo Finish (*Tom & Jerry*) 1 Nov. 1957; *p.c.:* MGM; *prod/dir:* William Hanna, Joseph Barbera; *anim:* Kenneth Muse, Bill Schipek, Lewis Marshall, Jack Carr, Herman Cohen, Ken Southworth; *lay:* Dick Bickenbach; *back:* Robert Gentle; *character des:* Gene Hazelton; *ed:* Jim Faris; *voices:* Daws Butler, Marian Richman; *mus:* Scott Bradley; *ph:* Jack Stevens; *prod mgr:* Hal Elias; *col:* Tech. *sd:* WE. 6 min. • Jerry photographs Tom in the act of framing Spike and plants the photos everywhere.

6534. Tony Sarg's Almanac *p.c.:* Tony Sarg–H.M. Dawley Inc. for Rialto prods; *anim:* Tony Sarg; *ph:* Herbert M. Dawley; *prod mgr:* George R. Meeker; *b&w. sil. l/a/anim.* • Silhouette animation. • **1921:** "The First Circus" 21 May — Prehistoric men find a bottle containing strong waters, causing them to perform primitive circus feats. "The First Dentist" June — The agonies and antics in which primitive folk underwent to avoid toothache. "Why They Love Cavemen" 7 July — No story available. "When the Whale Was Jonahed" 20 Aug. — No story available. "Fireman Save My Child" 10 Sept. — No story available. "Vamp Number One" Oct. — Live-action actress Myrtle Morse and Leward Meeker are used to demonstrate the modern way in which Vamps vamp their victims. Patterson Dial performs "Delilah's Dance." "Adam Raises Cain" — No story available. • **1922:** "The Original Golfer" 7 Jan. — No story available. "Why Adam Walked the Floor" 5 Feb. — Entertaining the baby is traced back to Adam trying to amuse Cain. "The Original Movie" 9 Apr. — No story available. "The First Earfull" 29 May — No story available. "Noah Put the Cat Out" 9 July — No story available. *p.c.:* Educational. "The First Degree" 29 July — No story available. "Baron Bragg and The Devilish Dragon" 9 Aug. — The actual experiences of a straying husband and the alibi he offers his wife. "The First Barber" 19 Aug. — A tonsorial parlor setting where barber shop odors are removed by the arrival of a skunk. "The First Flivver" 28 Oct. — A caveman outwits rivals for the affections of a fair lady with a goat-powered flivver. "The Ogling Ogre" 19 Nov. — No story available. "Baron Bragg and the Haunted Castle" 30 Dec. — The Baron loses all on a bet and spins his wife a yarn of experiences in a haunted castle. • **1923:** "The Terrible Tree" 6 Jan. — When a husband forgets his mission to buy eggs, he tells his wife of a half-human tree that rendered him powerless.

6535. Too Hop to Handle (*Looney Tunes*) 28 Jan. 1956; *p.c.:* WB; *dir/anim:* Robert McKimson; *story:* Warren Foster; *anim:* Keith Darling; *sets:* Richard H. Thomas; *ed:* Treg Brown; *voices:* Mel Blanc; *mus:* Milt Franklyn; *prod mgr:* John W. Burton; *prod:* Edward Selzer; *col:* Tech. *sd:* Vit. 6 min. • Sylvester Junior tries to attract mice with a "Pied Piper" pipe but it only succeeds in attracting an escaped baby kangaroo.

6536. Too Weak to Work (*Popeye*) 19 Mar. 1943; *p.c.:* Famous for Para; *dir:* I. Sparber; *story:* Joe Stultz; *anim:* Jim Tyer, Abner Kneitel; *voices:* Jack Mercer, Dave Barry; *mus:* Sammy Timberg; *prod mgr:* Sam Buchwald; *b&w. sd:* WE. 7 min. • To escape painting a lifeboat, Bluto feigns illness. Popeye sees him living the "life of Riley" in the hospital and administers a fitting treatment.

6537. Toodle-oo-o (*Pepper the Pup*) 1931; *p.c.:* John W. Burton prods; *dir/anim:* John W. Burton; *story:* Joseph d'Amico; *mus:* Arch B. Fritz; *asso prod:* D.K. McClelland; *b&w. sd.* 6 min. • Farm hand Pepper rescues his milk maid from the hands of a villain. Model animation.

6538. Toonerville Picnic (*Rainbow Parade*) 2 Oct. 1936; *p.c.:* Van Beuren for RKO; *dir:* Burt Gillett; *sets:* Art Bartsch, Eddi Bowlds; *mus:* Winston Sharples; *col:* Tech. *sd:* RCA. 7 min. • Fontaine Fox's characters have an airing at the beach to settle Mr. Bang's jangled nerves.

6539. Toonerville Trolley (*Rainbow Parade*) 17 Jan. 1936; *p.c.:* Van Beuren for RKO; *dir:* Burt Gillett; *sets:* Art Bartsch, Eddi Bowlds; *voice:* Elsa Janssen; *mus:* Winston Sharples; *col:* Tech. *sd:* RCA. 7 min. • First in a brief series of Fontaine Fox's comic characters. The trolley races to meet a train.

6540. Toot! Toot! (*Out of the Inkwell*) 5 June 1926; *p.c.:* Inkwell Studios for Red Seal; *dir:* Dave Fleischer; *anim/l/a:* Max Fleischer; *b&w. sil.* 5 min. *l/a/anim.* • Ko-Ko throws Max's railway ticket away, so Max draws the clown his own train. Ko-Ko takes over as engineer, sending the train on a wild ride, ending in the inkwell. Reissued in 1930 with added soundtrack.

6541. Toot, Whistle, Plunk and Boom (*Adventure in Music*) 10 Nov. 1953; *p.c.:* Walt Disney prods for BV; *dir:* C. August Nichols, Ward Kimball; *story:* Dick Huemer; *anim:* Ward Kimball, Julius Svendsen, Marc Davis, Henry Tanous, Art Stevens, Xavier Atencio; *character des:* Tom Oreb; *lay:* A. Kendall O'Connor, Victor Haboush; *back:* Eyvind Earle; *voices:* Bill Thompson, The Rhythmaires, James MacDonald; *mus:* Joseph S. Dubin; *song:* Sonny Burke, Jack Elliott; *col:* Tech. *sd:* RCA. 10 min. *Academy Award.* • Professor Owl tells his music class the origins of music from primitive man to modern times.

6542. Tooth or Consequences (*Phantasy*) 5 June 1947; *p.c.:* Colum; *prod:* Raymond Katz, Henry Binder; *dir:* Howard Swift; *story:* Cal Howard;

anim: Grant Simmons, Paul Sommer; *lay:* Bill Weaver; *back:* Ed Starr; *ed:* Richard S. Jensen; *voice:* Patrick J. McGeehan; *mus:* Darrell Calker; *ph:* Frank Fisher; *col:* Ciné. *sd:* WE. 6½ min. • The Crow offers to pull the Fox's aching tooth.

6543. The Toothless Beaver *(Possible Possum)* Dec. 1965; *p.c.:* TT for Fox; *dir/anim:* Connie Rasinski; *col:* DeLuxe. *sd:* RCA. 6 min. • Poss and his pals help an ancient beaver to build a dam. • See: *Possible Possum*

6544. The Top *p.c.:* Murakami-Wolf Films for Pathé Contemporary; *dir/anim:* Teru Murakami; *ed:* Rich Harrison; *voices:* Paul Shively, Fred Wolf; *ph:* Cartoon Camera; *col:* DeLuxe. *sd.* 7½ min. • Various men make attempts to reach a higher level immediately above, containing riches.

6545. Top Cat *(The Cat)* Sept. 1960; *p.c.:* Para Cartoons; *dir:* Seymour Kneitel; *story:* Irving Spector; *anim:* I. Klein, Morey Reden, Jack Ehret, George Cannata; *sets:* Robert Owen; *voices:* Bob MacFadden; *ph:* Leonard McCormick; *prod mgr:* Abe Goodman; *col:* Tech. *sd:* RCA. 8 min. • J. Caesar Bandwagon of Blockbuster Pictures' search for a new star is complete when he discovers a singing cat.

6546. Tops in the Big Top *(Popeye)* 16 Mar. 1945; *p.c.:* Famous for Para; *dir:* I. Sparber; *story:* Joe Stultz, Carl Meyer; *anim:* Nick Tafuri, Tom Golden, John Walworth; *sets:* Robert Little; *voices:* Jack Mercer, Mae Questel, Jackson Beck; *mus:* Winston Sharples; *ph:* Leonard McCormick; *prod mgr:* Sam Buchwald; *b&w. sd:* RCA. 8 min. Tech reissue: 1950. • Ringmaster Bluto sabotages Popeye's strong man act so he can team-up with Olive.

6547. Tops with Pops *(Tom & Jerry)* 22 Feb. 1957; *p.c.:* MGM; *prod/dir:* Joseph Barbera, William Hanna; *lay:* Dick Bickenbach; *back:* Don Driscoll; *prod mgr:* Hal Elias; *col:* Tech. *sd:* WE. 8 min. CS. • Tom tries to catch Jerry without waking the sleeping bulldogs. Cinemascope reissue of *Love That Pup.*

6548. Topsy Turkey *(Phantasy)* 5 Feb. 1948; *p.c.:* Colum; *prod:* Raymond Katz, Henry Binder; *dir:* Sid Marcus; *story:* Cal Howard, Dave Monahan; *anim:* Ben Lloyd, Howard Swift, Roy Jenkins; *lay:* Clark Watson; *back:* Al Boggs; *ed:* Richard S. Jensen; *voices:* Jack Mather, Dave Barry; *mus:* Darrell Calker; *ph:* Frank Fisher; *col:* Ciné. *sd:* WE. 6½ min. • A turkey resents being hunted by an Indian, so he takes a gun and hunts the redskin.

6549. Topsy TV *(John Doormat)* Jan. 1957; *p.c.:* TT for Fox; *ex prod:* Bill Weiss; *dir sup:* Gene Deitch; *dir:* Connie Rasinski; *story:* Tommy Morrison, Larz Bourne, Bob Kuwahara *anim:* Jim Tyer, Larry Silverman, John Gentilella, George Bakes, Ed Donnelly, Al Chiarito, Mannie Davis; *lay:* Art Bartsch, Bernie Nagler; *back:* Bill Hilliker; *voices:* Bern Bennett; *mus:* Phil Scheib; *prod mgr:* Frank Schudde; *col:* Tech. *sd:* RCA. 7 min. CS. • John's wife attempts to curtail his nocturnal TV viewing habits.

6550. Toreadorable *(Popeye)* 12 June 1953; *p.c.:* Famous for Para; *dir:* Seymour Kneitel; *story:* Carl Meyer, Jack Mercer; *anim:* Tom Johnson, John Gentilella, Els Barthen; *sets:* Anton Loeb; *voices:* Jack Mercer, Mae Questel, Jackson Beck; *mus:* Winston Sharples; *ph:* Leonard McCormick; *prod mgr:* Seymour Shultz; *col:* Tech. *sd:* RCA. 6 min. • Popeye and Olive visit a bullfight where Olive is smitten by the toreador. Popeye claims he can do as well and joins in the competition.

6551. Toro Pink *(Pink Panther)* 1978; *p.c.:* Mirisch/Geoffrey/DFE for UA; *dir:* Sid Marcus; *story:* Dave DeTiege; *anim:* Warren Batchelder, Bob Richardson, Bob Kirk, Bill Hutten; *lay:* Martin Strudler; *back:* Richard H. Thomas; *ed:* Richard Gannon; *theme tune:* Henry Mancini; *ph:* Ray Lee; *prod mgr:* Lee Gunther; *col:* DeLuxe. *sd:* RCA. 6 min. • The Panther is goaded into fighting a bull.

6552. A Torrid Toreador *(Terry-Toon)* 9 Jan. 1942; *p.c.:* TT for Fox; *dir:* Eddie Donnelly; *story:* John Foster; *sets:* Art Bartsch; *voice:* Thomas Morrison; *mus:* Philip A. Scheib; *col:* Tech. *sd:* RCA. 7 min. • Sourpuss is a suitor for a closely-guarded senorita. Her disapproving Papa encourages him to fight a bull.

6553. Tortilla Flaps *(Looney Tunes)* 18 Jan. 1958; *p.c.:* WB; *dir:* Robert McKimson; *story:* Tedd Pierce; *anim:* George Grandpré, Ted Bonnicksen; *lay:* Robert Gribbroek; *back:* Richard H. Thomas; *ed:* Treg Brown; *voices:* Mel Blanc, Dal McKennon; *mus:* Milt Franklyn *prod:* John W. Burton; *col:* Tech. *sd:* Vit. 7 min. • El Vulturo ruins the mouse's fiesta and Speedy takes on the job of disposing of him.

6554. The Tortoise and the Hare *(Silly Symphony)* 5 Jan. 1935; *p.c.:* Walt Disney prods for UA; *dir:* Wilfred Jackson; *story:* Larry Morey, Earl Hurd, William Cottrell; *anim:* Les Clark, Larry Clemmons, Gilles de Tremaudan, Dick Huemer, Jack Hannah, Eric Larson, Richard Lundy, Hamilton S. Luske, Louis Schmitt, Milt Schaffer; *back:* Emil Flohri; *voices:* Eddie Holden, Marcellite Garner, Pinto Colvig; *mus:* Frank E. Churchill, Leigh Harline; *col:* Tech. *sd:* RCA. 9 min. • Max Hare challenges Toby Tortoise to a race. Max dallies while Toby wins the race! • Max's character was based on the egotistic boxing champ, Max Baer.

6555. Tortoise Beats Hare *(Merrie Melodies)* 15 Mar. 1941; *p.c.:* Leon Schlesinger prods for WB; *dir:* Fred Avery; *story:* Dave Monahan, Robert Clampett; *anim:* Charles McKimson; *character des/lay:* Robert Givens; *back:* John Didrik Johnsen; *ed:* Treg Brown; *voices:* Mel Blanc; *mus:* Carl W. Stalling; *prod sup:* Henry Binder, Raymond G. Katz; *col:* Tech. *sd:* Vit. 7 min. • Bugs bets Cecil Turtle $10.00 that he can beat him in a race but he's up against all Cecil's relatives who rally 'round to help him.

6556. The Tortoise Wins Again *(Terry-Toon)* 30 Aug. 1946; *p.c.:* TT for Fox; *dir:* Connie Rasinski; *story:* John Foster; *sets:* Art Bartsch; *mus:* Philip A. Scheib; *col:* Tech. *sd:* RCA. 7 min. • The hare challenges the tortoise to another contest of speed ... this time on ice.

6557. Tortoise Wins by a Hare *(Merrie Melodies)* 20 Feb. 1943; *p.c.:* Leon Schlesinger prods for WB; *dir:* Robert Clampett; *story:* Warren Foster; *anim:* Bob McKimson, Rod Scribner; *lay:* Thomas McKimson; *back:* Michael Sasanoff; *ed:* Treg Brown; *voices:* Mel Blanc, Kent Rogers; *mus:* Carl W. Stalling; *ph:* John W. Burton; *prod sup:* Henry Binder, Raymond G. Katz; *col:* Tech. *sd:* Vit. 7 min. • Bugs challenges Cecil Turtle to another race with Bugs using a motor-powered tortoise shell.

6558. Tot Watchers *(Tom & Jerry)* 1 Aug. 1958; *p.c.:* MGM; *prod/dir:* William Hanna Joseph Barbera; *story:* Homer Brightman; *anim:* Lewis Marshall, James Escalante, Kenneth Muse; *lay:* Dick Bickenbach; *back:* Robert Gentle; *ed:* Jim Faris; *voices:* Barbara Eiler, Bill Thompson; *mus:* Scott Bradley; *ph:* Jack Stevens; *prod mgr:* Hal Elias; *col:* Tech. *sd:* WE. 7 min. • Tom and Jerry take on the task of keeping a wandering baby away from danger.

6559. Tots of Fun *(Popeye)* 15 Aug. 1952; *p.c.:* Famous for Para; *dir:* Seymour Kneitel; *story:* Larz Bourne; *anim:* Tom Johnson, Frank Endres, Els Barthen; *sets:* Robert Owen; *voices:* Jack Mercer; *mus:* Winston Sharples; *ph:* Leonard McCormick; *prod mgr:* Seymour Shultz; *col:* Tech. *sd:* RCA. 6 min. • Popeye's nephews help build a house to the music of "Poet and Peasant Overture."

6560. Touchdown Demons *(Terry-Toon)* 20 Sept. 1940; *p.c.:* TT for Fox; *dir:* Volney White; *story:* John Foster; *mus:* Philip A. Scheib; *b&w. sd:* RCA. 6 min. • The hero wins a football game when his girl is taken from him by a large player.

6561. Touchdown Mickey *(Mickey Mouse)* 15 Oct. 1932; *p.c.:* Walt Disney prods for UA; *dir:* Wilfred Jackson; *anim:* Johnny Cannon, Gilles de Tremaudan, Kevin Donnelly, Richard Lundy, Tom Palmer, Ben Sharpsteen; *voices:* Pinto Colvig; *mus:* Frank E. Churchill; *b&w. sd:* PCP. 7 min. • Mickey's team vs. Alley Cats in a football game where a goat wins the touchdown.

6562. Touché and Go *(Merrie Melodies)* 12 Oct. 1957; *p.c.:* WB; *dir:* Chuck Jones; *story:* Michael Maltese; *anim:* Richard Thompson, Ken Harris, Abe Levitow; *lay:* Maurice Noble; *back:* Philip de Guard; *ed:* Treg Brown; *voices:* Mel Blanc; *mus:* Milt Franklyn; *prod mgr:* John W. Burton; *prod:* Edward Selzer; *col:* Tech *sd:* Vit. 7 min. • A black cat gets white paint down her back and Pepè le Pew, the amorous skunk, pursues her over land and sea, ending on a desert island

6563. Touché, Pussy Cat *(Tom & Jerry)* 18 Dec. 1954; *p.c.:* MGM; *dir:* William Hanna, Joseph Barbera; *anim:* Kenneth Muse, Ed Barge, Irven Spence; *lay:* Dick Bickenbach; *back:* Robert Gentle; *ed:* Jim Faris; *voice:* Francoise Brun-Cottan; *mus:* Scott Bradley; *ph:* Jack Stevens; *prod:* Fred Quimby; *col:* Tech. *sd:* WE. 8 min. *Academy Award nomination.* • Musketeer Tom is no match for the King's Mouseketeers. After doing battle, he is finally washed away in a sea of wine.

6564. A Tough Egg *(Terry-Toon)* 26 June 1936; *p.c.:* TT for Educational/Fox; *dir:* Mannie Davis, George Gordon; *mus:* Philip A. Scheib; *b&w. sd:* WE. 6 min. • No story available.

6565. Toulouse la Trick *(Inspector)* 30 Dec. 1966; *p.c.:* Mirisch/Geoffrey/DFE for UA; *dir:* Robert McKimson; *story:* John W. Dunn; *anim:* Don Williams, Bob Matz, Ted Bonnicksen, Warren Batchelder, Manny Perez; *lay:* T.M. Yakutis; *back:* Tom O'Loughlin; *ed:* Lee Gunther; *voices:* Pat Harrington Jr.; *mus:* Walter Greene; *theme tune:* Henry Mancini; *prod sup:* Harry Love, Bill Orcutt; *col:* DeLuxe. *sd:* RCA. 6 min. • The Inspector is handcuffed to Toulouse la Moose, escorting him to a Paris prison when he makes a break for it, taking his captor with him.

6566. Tour De Farce *(Inspector)* 25 Oct. 1967; *p.c.:* Mirisch/Geoffrey/DFE for UA; *dir:* Gerry Chiniquy; *story:* Jim Ryan; *anim:* Bob Matz, Warren Batchelder, Manny Perez, Don Williams, Manny Gould; *lay:* Dick Ung; *back:* Tom O'Loughlin; *ed:* Lee Gunther; *voices:* Pat Harrington Jr.; *mus:* Walter Greene; *theme tune:* Henry Mancini; *col:* DeLuxe. *sd:* RCA. 6 min. • The Inspector is marooned on a desert island with a bruiser who wants to kill him.

6567. Towne Hall Follies *(Oswald)* 3 June 1935; *p.c.:* Univ; *prod/dir:* Walter Lantz; *story:* Walter Lantz, Victor McLeod; *anim:* Ray Abrams, Fred Avery, Cecil Surry, Virgil Ross; *voice:* Bernice Hansel; *mus:* James Dietrich; b&w. *sd:* WE. 7 min. • A vaudeville show with the Man on the Flying Trapeze and Bunny Lou who sings and is kidnapped by a rat in the audience.

6568. The Toy Man *(Mighty Heroes)* Dec. 1969 (made in 1966); *p.c.:* TT for Fox; *dir:* Ralph Bakshi; *voices:* Lionel Wilson, Herschel Bernardi; *mus:* Jim Timmens; *col:* DeLuxe. *sd:* RCA. 5 min. • The heroes come up against the Toy Man whose jewel-stealing toys are protected by a giant teddy bear.

6569. The Toy Shoppe *(Oswald)* 19 Feb. 1934; *p.c.:* Univ; *dir:* Walter Lantz, "Bill" Nolan; *anim:* Manuel Moreno, Lester Kline, Fred Kopietz, George Grandpré, Ernest Smythe; *mus:* James Dietrich; b&w. *sd:* WE. 7 min. • After the toy shop is closed, the toys come alive and start singing and dancing.

6570. Toy Story 22 Nov. 1995; *p.c.:* PIXAR/The Walt Disney Company for BV; *dir:* John Lasseter; *ex prod:* Edwin Catmull, Steven Jobs; *sup technical dir:* William Reeves; *prod:* Ralph Guggenheim, Bonnie Arnold; *story:* John Lasseter, Pete Docter, Andrew Stanton, Joe Ranft; *scr:* Joss Whedon, Andrew Stanton, Joel Cohen, Alex Sokoloff; *story sup:* Joe Ranft, Robert Lence; *story co-ord:* Susan Levin; *story art:* Andrew Stanton, Kelly Asbury, Ash Brannon, Mike Cachuela, Jill Culton, Pete Docter, Perry Farinola, Jason Katz, Bud Luckey, Jeff Pidgeon; *anim dir:* Rich Quade, Ash Brannon; *anim mgr:* Triva von Klark, B.Z. Petroff; *anim:* Pete Docter, Michael Berenstein, Kim Blanchette, Colin Brady, Davey Crockett Feiten, Angie Glocka, Rex Grignon, Tom K. Gurney, Jimmy Hayward, Hal T. Hickel, Karen Kiser, Anthony B. Lamolinara, Guionne LeRoy, Bud Luckey, Les Major, Glenn McQueen, Mark Oftedal, Jeff Pidgeon, Jeff Pratt, Steve Rabatich, Roger Rose, Steve Segal, Doug Sheppeck, Alan Sperling, Doug Sweetland, David Tart, Ken Willard, Shawn P. Krause, Matt Luhn, Bob Peterson, Andrew Schmidt; *anim co-ord:* Maureen E. Wylie; *art dir:* Ralph Eggleston; *anim check:* Heather Knight; *asso technical dir:* Eben Fiske Ostby; *technical dpt mgr:* Allison Smith Murphy; *modeling team:* Mark Adams, Ronen Barzel, Kevin Björke, Loren C. Carpenter, Deborah R. Fowler, Damir Frkovic, Shalini Govil-Pai, David R. Haumann, Mark Tiberius Henne, Yael Milo, Darwyn Peachey, Rick Sayre, Eliot Smyrl, Galyn Susman, Graham Walters, Mark Eastwood, Monique Hodgkinson, Grey Holland; *modeling & shading co-ord:* Deirdre Warin; *shader & visual fx sup:* Thomas Porter; *shader team:* Anthony A. Apodaca, Brian M. Rosen, Eliot Smyrl, Graham Walters, Keith B.C. Gordon, Larry Gritz, Loren C. Carpenter, Mitch Prater, Rick Sayre; *visual fx:* Mark T. Henne, Oren Jacob, Darwyn Peachey, Mitch Prater, Brian M. Rosen; *lighting sup:* Sharon Calahan, Galyn Susman; *lighting:* Lisa Forssell, Deborah R. Fowler, Truong Gia Tiên, William A. Wise, Mark Adams, Anthony A. Apodaca, Larry Aupperle, Cynthia Dueltgen, Damir Frkovic, Shalini Govil-Pai, Larry Gritz, David R. Haumann, Oren Jacob, Ewan Johnson, Konishi Sonoko, Les Major, Yael Milo, Desiree Mourad, Kelly O'Connell, Jeff Pratt, Mark T. Vandewettering; *illumination:* Ronen Barzel; *lighting & rendering co-ord:* Barbara T. Labounta; *asst co-ord:* Douglas Todd; *render wranglers:* Keith Olenick, Andrew Cho, Michael Fong, Michael Lorenzen, Vivek Verma; *modeling & anim system development:* William Reeves, John Lasseter, Eben Fiske Ostby, Sam Leffler, Darwyn Peachey, Ronen Barzel, Loren C.

Carpenter, Thomas Hahn, Chris King, Peter Nye, Drew Rogge, Brian M. Rosen, Rick Sayre, Michael Shantzis, Eliot Smyrl, Heidi Stettner; *art mgr:* Terry Herrmann McQueen; *des/illustrator:* Bob Pauley; *cg paint:* Tia W. Kratter, Robin Cooper; *sculptors:* Shelley Daniels Lekven, Norm DeCarlo; *character des:* Bob Pauley, Bud Luckey, Andrew Stanton, William Cone, Steve Johnson, Dan Haskett, Tom Holloway, Jean Gillmore; *concept art:* Steve Johnson, Lou Fancher, Kevin Hawkes, William Joyce, William Cone, David Gordon, Bob Pauley, Nilo Rodis; *lay:* B.Z. Petroff, Craig Good, Ewan Johnson, Kevin Björke, Roman Figun, Desiree Mourad, Shawn P. Krause, Bob Peterson, Andrew Schmidt; *set dressers:* Kelly O'Connell, Konishi Sonoko, Ann M. Rockwell; *ed:* Robert Gordon, Lee Unkrich, Julie M. McDonald, Robin Lee, Tom Freeman, Ada Cochavi, Dana Mulligan, Steven Liu, Torbin Xan Bullock, Deidre Morrison, Phyllis Oyama, Ed Fuller; *digital prod asst:* Jesse William Wallace; *story reel mus wrestler:* Robert Randles, Ling Ling Li; *voices: Woody:* Tom Hanks; *Buzz Lightyear:* Tim Allen; *Mr. Potato Head:* Don Rickles; *Slinky Dog:* Jim Varney; *Rex:* Wallace Shawn; *Hamm:* John Ratzenberger; *Bo Peep:* Annie Potts; *Andy:* John Morris; *Sid:* Erik von Detten; *Mrs. Davis:* Laurie Metcalf; *Sergeant:* R. Lee Ermey; *Hannah:* Sarah Freeman; *TV Announcer:* Penn Jillette; *also:* Jack Angel, Spencer Aste, Greg Berg, Lisa Bradley, Kendall Cunningham, Debi Derryberry, Cody Dorkin, Bill Farmer, Craig Good, Gregory Grudt, Danielle Judovits, Sam Lasseter, Brittany Levenbrown, Sherry Lynn, Scott McAfee, Mickie McGowan, Ryan O'Donohue, Jeff Pidgeon, Patrick Pinney, Phil Proctor, Jan Rabson, Joe Ranft, Andrew Stanton, Shane Sweet; *mus/songs:* Randy Newman; "You've Got a Friend in Me" *(end title)* performed by Randy Newman, Lyle Lovett; *ex mus prod:* Chris Montan; *orch:* Don Davis, Randy Newman; *mus rec/mix:* Frank Wolf; *mus ed:* Jim Flamerg, Helena Lea; *mus prod sup:* Tod Cooper; *orch contractor:* Sandy de Crescent; *mus preperation:* Greg Dennen, Tom Hardistry, Bill Kinsley, Susan McLean, Rail Rogut; *dial rec:* Doc Kane, Bob Baron; *col timer:* Dale Grahn; *neg cutter:* Mary Beth Smith, Rick MacKay; *title des:* Susan Bradley; *sd des:* Gary Rydstrom; *ph:* Julie M. McDonald, Louis Rivera, Matthew Martin, Don Conway; *photoscience consultant:* D. Difrancesco; *monitor calibration software:* Michael Shantzis; *computer systems mgr:* David H. Ching; *hardware engineer:* Neftali "El Magnifico" Alvarez; *software engineers:* Bill Carson, Ken Huey; *logistics programmer:* Heidi Stettner; *Macintosh Systems engineer:* Michael E. Murdock; *hardware technician:* Edgar Quiñones; *systems operators:* Onny P. Carr, Alec Wong; *media systems engineer:* Alex Stahl; *prod sup:* Karen Robert Jackson; *prod asso:* Susan Hamana; *prod controller:* Kevin Reher; *prod co-ord:* Lori Lombardo, Ellen Devine, Victoria Jaschob, Lucas Putnam; *renderman software development:* Anthony A. Apodaca, Rob Cook, Loren C. Carpenter, Ed Catmull, Pat Hanrahan, Steve Johnson, Jim Lawson, Sam Leffler, M.W. Mantle, Dan McCoy, Darwyn Peachey, Thomas Porter, William Reeves, David Salesin, Don Schreiter, Mark Vandewettering; *digital massage therapist:* Narottama Alden; *post prod sup.:* Patsy Bougé; *post prod admin.:* Margaret Yu; *post prod scheduler:* Heather Jane MacDonald Smith; *rec mix:* Gary Summers, Gary Rydstrom; *sd ed:* Tim Holland, J.R. Grubbs, Susan Sanford, Susan Popovic, Dan Engstrom; *ADR ed:* Marilyn McCoppen; *sd fx ed:* Pat Jackson; *foley ed:* Mary Helen Leasman; *foley art:* Dennie Thorpe, Tom Barwick; *foley rec:* Tony Eckert; *sd des:* Tom Myers; *col:* Tech. *sd:* Dolby stereo. 81 min. • An outdated toy cowboy named Woody sees his usefulness at an end with the arrival of a flashy new "Space Ranger" named Buzz Lightyear. Woody realizes that his young owner's affections are now going elsewhere and plots to dispose of the new intruder. Things don't go as planned and the two toys land up in the hands of the neighborhood bully. So the two toys have to unite to get back where they belong.

6571. Toy Story 2 24 Nov. 1999; *p.c.:* PIXAR/Disney Enterprises, Inc. for BV; *dir:* John Lasseter; *co-dir:* Lee Unkrich, Ash Brannon; *prod:* Helene Plotkin, Karen Robert Jackson; *ex prod:* Sarah McArthur; *story:* John Lasseter, Pete Docter, Ash Brannon, Andrew Stanton, Dan Jeup, Jeff Pidgeon, Joe Ranft, Lee Unkrich, Jim Capobianco, Colin Brady, Jimmy Hayward, Steve Boyett, Elias Davis, David Reynolds, David Pollock; *scr:* Andrew Stanton, Rita Hsiao, Doug Chamberlin, Chris Webb; *story sup:* Dan Jeup, Joe Ranft; *story dpt mgr:* Renee Jensen, Susan E. Levin; *story art:* Max Brace, Jim Capobianco, Jill Culton, David Fulp, Rob Gibbs, Jason Katz, Matthew Luhn, Bud Luckey, Ken Mitchroney, Ricky Nierva, Sanjay Patel, Bob Peterson, Jeff Pidgeon, Jan Pinkava, Bobby Podesta, David Skelly, Nathan Stanton, Mark A. Walsh; *addit storyboarding:* Don Dougherty, Davey

Crockett Felton, Stephen Gregory, Rick Hanson, Steven Hunter, Charles Keagle, Jorgen Klubien, Angus MacLane, Max Martinez, Jon Mead, Floyd Norman, Karen Prell, John Ramirez, Tasha Wedeen; *story dpt co-ord:* Lee Cruikshank, Adam Bronstein; *sup technical dir:* Galyn Susman, Oren Jacob, Larry Aupperle; *prod des:* William Cone, Jim Pearson; *anim dir:* Kyle Balda, Dylan Brown; *anim mgr:* Jenny Head, Kori Rae; *anim:* Glenn McQueen, Nicholas Alan Barillaro, Stephen Barnes, Bobby Beck, Michael Berenstein, Ash Brannon, Jennifer Cha, Scott Clark, Brett Coderre, Melanie Cordan, Tim Crawford, David Devan, Mark Farquhar, Ike Feldman, Andrew Gordon, Stephen Gregory, Jimmy Hayward, Tim Hittle, Steven Hunter, Ethan Hurd, John Kahrs, Nancy Kato, Patty Kihm, Karen Kiser, Shawn Krause, Bob Koch, Wendell Lee, Peter Lepeniotis, Angus MacLane, Dan Mason, Jon Mead, Billy Merritt, Karyn Metien, Valerie Mih, James Ford Murphy, Peter Nash, Mark Oftedal, Bret Parker, Michael Parks, Sanjay Patel, Bobby Podesta, Jeff Pratt, Karen Prell, Brett Pullam, Rich Quade, Mike Quinn, Roger Rose, Robert H. Russ, Gini Cruz Santos, Anthony Scott, Doug Sheppeck, Alan Sperling, Ross Stevenson, Doug Sweetland, David Tart, Warren Trezevant, Mark A. Walsh, Tasha Wedeen, Adam Wood, Christina Yim, Kureha Yokoo; *anim dpt co-ord:* David Arecklin; *anim dpt prod asst:* Chris Digiovanni; *fx anim:* Paul Mendoza, Andrea Schultz, Jenni Tsoi; *lay:* Rikki Cleland-Hura, Ewan Johnson, Molly Naughton, Craig Good, Shawn Brennan, Jeremy Lasky, Patrick Lin, Gregg Olsson, Robert Anderson, Wade Childress, Roman Figun, Craig McGillivray, Stephen Moros, Mark Sanford, Adam Schitzer, Derek Williams, Stephanie Andrews, Christine Z. Chang, Kevin Edwards, Ross Stevenson, Matt Uhry; *lay dpt co-ord:* Heather Field; *set dressing:* David Eisemann, Jan Childress Farmer, Graham Moloy, Sophie Vincelette, Derek Williams, Trish Carney, Robert Anderson, Wade Childress, Mark Sanford, Adam Schnitzer; *lay & set dressing td's:* Brad Winemiller, Daniel Campbell, Gina Trbovich; *technical art: modeling & shading co-ord:* Mark Nielsen, Vanessa Ross, Alexandria Devon Zech; *modeling art:* Eben Ostby; Mark Adams, Paul Aichele, Lauren Alpert, Stephanie Andrews, James Bancroft, Lawrence D. Cutler, Ruieta Da Silva, Cynthia Dueltgen, Damir Frkovic, Christine Hoffman, Rob Jensen, Stephen King, Michael Krummhoefener, Kelly O'Connell, Eileen O'Neill, Guido Quarom, Dale Ruffolo, Don Schreiter, Gary Schultz, Skeggi Thormar, Patrick Wilson; *shading:* Brad West, Bryn Imagire, John B. Anderson, David Batte, Kirk Bowers, Kevin Edwards, Mark Fontana, Michael Fu, Larry Gritz, Ben Jordan, Michael R. King, Stephen King, Andrew Kinney, Ana Lacaze, Daniel McCoy, Eileen O'Neill, Keith Olenick, John Singh Pottebaum, Mitch Prater, Guido Quaroni, Brian M. Rosen, Steve Upstill, David Valdez, John Warren, Michael Fong, Patrick James, Steve May, Steve McGrath, Tim Milliron, Cynthia "Kiki" Pettit, James Rose; *lighting:* Jean-Claude Kalache, Terry McQueen, Molly Naughton, Lauren Alpert, Jun Han Cho, Cynthia Dueltgen, Danielle Feinberg, Deborah R. Fowler, Christian Hoffman, Jesse Hollander, Ana Lacaze, Ken Lao, Joyce Powell, Kimberly White, Jason Bickerstaff, Kirk Bowers, Onny Carr, Kevin Edwards, Kurt Fleischer, Reid Gershbein, Michael B. Johnson, Jango, Sonoko Konishi, Craig McGillivray, Janet Lucroy, Eileen O'Neill, Kelly O'Connell, John Singh Pottebaum, Brandon Onstott, Seth Plezas, Cynthia "Kiki" Pettit, Sudeep Rangaswamy, Dale Ruffolo, Bill Sheffler, Allison Torres, Tien Truong, John Warren, Patrick Wilson, Brian Daniel Young, Mark Fontana, Clay Welch; *lighting dpt sup:* Tom Kim; *rendering:* Don Schreiter; *rendering mgr:* Victoria Jaschob; *render td's:* Byron Bashforth, Patrick James, Thomas Jordan, Steve Kani, Andrew Kinney, Jack Paulus, James Rose, Scotty Sharp, Jerome Strach, Christine Waggoner; *rendering dpt co-ord:* Jen Kinavey; *technical dpt prod asst:* Jennifer Kinney; *art dpt:* Matt White, Jen Kinavey, Alice Rosen, Lilah Moscoso; *art dir:* David Skelly; *cg paint:* Randy Berrett, Robin Cooper, Yvonne Herbst, Glenn Kim, Laura Phillips; *sketch art:* Randy Berrett, Mark Holmes, Dan Lee, Nathaniel McLaughlin, Paul Mica, Laura Phillips, Jeff Sangalli, Gary Schultz, Bud Thon; *anim software development dir:* Darwyn Peachey; *anim software:* Tony de Rosa, Kurt Fleischer, Peter Nye, Arun Rao, Wayne Wooten; *software engineers:* John Alex, Brad Andalman, David Baraff, Ronen Barzel, Malcolm Blanchard, Mike Cancilla, Bena Currin, Thomas Hahn, Kitt Hirasaki, Jisup Hong, Michael B. Johnson, Steve Johnson, Michael Kass, Chris King, Eric Lebel, Bruce Perens, Chris Perry, John Singh Pottebaum, Sudeep Rangaswamy, Drew Ttv Rogge, Michael Shantzis, Heidi Stettner, Robert W. Sumner, Dirk van Gelder, Karon Weber, Andy Witkin, Audrey Wong; *documentation/support:* Tom Deering, Nghi "Tin" Nguyen, Kay Seirup; *rendering software development:* Anthony A. Apodaca; *special rendering tech-*

nique/support: Craig Kolb, Tom Lokovic; *software engineers:* Phil Beffrey, Sam "Penguin" Black, Loren Carpenter, Rob Cook, Tom Duff, Larry Gritz, David Laur, Dan Lyke, Shaun Oborn, Matt Pharr, Tien Truong, Mark Vandewettering, Eric Veach; *sculptors:* Norm Decarlo, Jerome Ranft; *new character des:* Randy Berrett, Ash Brannon, Colin Brady, Jill Culton, Dan Lee, Bud Luckey, Nathaniel McLaughlin, Ken Mitchroney, Jim Pearson; *visual development:* Sean Hargreaves, Dave Gordon, Harley Jessup; *human team lead td's:* Lisa Forssell, Mitch Prater; *human modeling & shading team:* Jason Bickerstaff, Lawrence D. Cutler, Mark Fontana, Leo Hourvitz, Ben Jordan, Sonoko Konishi, Michael Krummhoefener, Guido Quaroni, John Warren, Kimberly White, Adam Woodbury; *fx dpt mgr:* Kelly T. Peters; *fx technical art:* John B. Anderson, Lawrence D. Cutler, Lisa Forssell, Michael Fu, Leo Hourvitz, Jeffrey Jay, Ewan Johnson, Stephen King, Bill Polson, Guido Quaroni, Brad Winemiller, David Baraff, Andrew Kinney, Brian M. Rosen, Eliot Smyrl, Andy Witkin; *ed:* Edie Bleiman, David Ian Salter, Lee Unkrich, Robert Graham Jones, Jennifer Taylor, Craig Alpert, Christine Steele, Anna Wolhzky, Ed Fuller, Gus Carpenter, James M. Webb, James Austin Stewart, Ken Schretzman, Richard Halsey, Mildred Latroui, Luis Alvarez Y. Alvarez, Torbin Xan Bullock, Jack Curtis Dubowsky, Tom Freeman, Axel Geddes, Christian Hill, Mike Marsh, Lucas Putnam, Katherine Ringgold, Sarah Schubert, Chris Vallance, Mark Yeager; *ed dpt mgr:* Lindsey Collins; *mus ed:* David Slusser, Barney Jones; *ed co-ord:* Anne Pla; *amf co-ord:* Sue Maafouk-Kalache; *ed prod asst:* Shannon Menendez-Chu; *voices: Woody:* Tom Hanks; *Buzz Lightyear:* Tim Allen; *Jessie:* Joan Cusack; *Prospector:* Kelsey Grammer; *Mr. Potato Head:* Don Rickles; *Slinky Dog:* Jim Varney; *Rex:* Wallace Shawn; *Hamm:* John Ratzenberger; *Bo Peep:* Annie Potts; *Al McWhiggin:* Wayne Knight; *Andy:* John Morris; *Sid:* Erik von Detten; *Andy's Mom:* Laurie Metcalf; *Mrs. Potato Head:* Estelle Harris; *Sergeant:* R. Lee Ermey; *Barbie:* Jodi Benson; *the Cleaner:* Jonathan Harris; *Wheezy:* Joe Ranft; *Emperor Zurg:* Andrew Stanton; *Aliens:* Jeff Pidgeon; *Yodeling voice:* Mary Kay Bergman; *also:* Jack Angel, Bob Bergen, Sheryl Bernstein, Rodger Bumpass, Corey Burton, Rachel Davey, Debi Derryberry, Jessica Evans, Bill Farmer, Pat Fraley, Jess Harnell, John Lasseter, Nicolette Little, Sherry Lynn, Mickie McGowan, Andi Peters, Phil Proctor, Jan Rabson, Carly Schoeder, Madylin Sweeter, Hanna Unkrich, Lee Unkrich; "Woody's Roundup" *theme song performed by* Riders in the Sky; "When She Loves Me" *performed by* Sarah McLachlan; "You've Got a Friend in Me" *Wheezy's version performed by* Robert Goulet; "You've Got a Friend in Me" *instrumental version performed by* Tom Scott; *mus/songs:* Randy Newman; *ex mus prod:* Chris Montan; *mus rec/mix:* Frank Wolf; *mus ed:* Bruno Coon, Lisa Jaime, Brenda Heins; *mus prod dir:* Andrew Page; *mus prod mgr:* Tom MacDougall; *mus prod co-ord:* Deniece La Rocca; *addit rec:* Greg Raely; *addit arrangements:* Bruno Coon; *orch contractor:* Sandy de Crescent; *systems admin/support:* Neftali "El Magnifico" Alvarez, Nathan Ardaiz, Adam Beeman, George Bagtas Jr., Lars R. Damerow, Bryan Bird, Edward Escueta, Michael Donnelly, Jason Hendrix, Patrick Guenette, Ken Jonathan J.J. Huey, Ling Hsu, Peter Kaldis, Jason "Jayfish" Hull, Gregory Yong Paik, Cory Knox, May Pon, Auburn "Aubie" Schmidt, M.T. Silva, Nelson Slu, Edilberto Soriano Jr., Alex Stahl, Gene Takahashi, Andy Thomas, Christopher C. Walker, Jay Welland, Dallas Wisehaupt; *ph:* Sharon Calahan, Perrin Cutting, Louis Rivera; *ph software/engineering:* John Hee Soo Lee, Matthew Martin, Drew Ttv Rogge, Don Conway, Jeff Wan; *photoscience mgr:* James Burgess, David Difrancesco; *dpt admin:* Beth Sullivan; *post prod sup.:* Paul Cichocki, Timothy Sorensen; *sd des:* Gary Rydstrom, Tom Myers, Shannon Mills; *sd ed:* Rona Michete, Marcie Romano; *re-rec mix:* Gary Rydstrom, Gary Summers, Jennifer Barin, Jurgen Scharpf, Juan Petalta; *dial mix:* Doc Kane, Bob Baron, Bill Higley, John McGleenan, Brian Reed; *sd ed:* Michael Silvers; *sd fx ed:* Teresa Eckton, Shannon Mills, Al Nelson; *foley ed:* Mary Helen Leasman, Susan Sanford; *foley rec:* Frank "Pepe" Merel; *col timer:* Dale Grahn; *title des:* Susan Bradley; *prod mgr:* Graham Walters; *col:* Tech. *sd:* Dolby Digital. 88 min. • While his young owner is away at summer camp, Woody, the cowboy doll, is stolen by a "rare toy" collector. Buzz Lightyear and the other toys set out to rescue him and return him back home.

6572. Toy Time (*Aesop's Sound Fable*) 27 Jan. 1931; *p.c.:* Van Beuren for RKO; *dir:* John Foster, Harry Bailey; *mus:* Gene Rodemich; *b&w. sd:* RCA. 7 min. • A mouse and his sweetie enter a toy shop after hours to watch the toys do their stuff.

6573. Toy Tinkers (*Donald Duck*) 16 Dec. 1949; *p.c.:* Walt Disney prods for RKO; *dir:* Jack Hannah; *story:* Harry Reeves, Milt Banta; *anim:* Volus Jones, Bob Carlson, Bill Justice, Judge Whitaker; *fx:* Jack Boyd; *lay:* Yale Gracey; *back:* Thelma Witmer; *voices:* Clarence Nash, Dessie Flynn, James MacDonald; *mus:* Paul Smith; *col:* Tech. *sd:* RCA. 7 min. *Academy Award nomination.* • The Chipmunks invade Donald's house at Christmas and play with all the presents.

6574. Toy Trouble (*Merrie Melodies*) 12 Apr. 1941; *p.c.:* Leon Schlesinger prods for WB; *dir:* Charles M. Jones; *story:* Rich Hogan; *anim:* Robert Cannon; *lay:* John McGrew; *back:* Eugene Fleury; *ed:* Treg Brown; *voice:* Margaret Hill; *mus:* Carl W. Stalling; *prod sup:* Henry Binder, Raymond G. Katz; *col:* Tech. *sd:* Vit. 7 min. • Sniffles and the Bookworm explore the toy section of a department store when the arrival of a cat puts an end to their fun.

6575. Toyland (*Paul Terry-Toons*) 27 Nov. 1932; *p.c.:* Moser & Terry for Educational/Fox; *dir:* Frank Moser, Paul Terry; *mus:* Philip A. Scheib; b&w. *sd:* WE. 6 min. • Santa arrives and some kittens and a pup have a wonderful time with their presents. Nursery Rhyme characters do their stuff.

6576. The Toyland Broadcast (*Happy Harmonies*) 22 Dec. 1934; *p.c.:* MGM; *prod/dir:* Hugh Harman, Rudolf Ising; *voices:* The Four Blackbirds, The Radio Rogues, Carmen Maxwell; *mus:* Scott Bradley; *col:* Tech-2. *sd:* RCA. 8 min. • The toys perform a musical show. Caricatures: Bing Crosby, The Ink Spots, Kate Smith, Rudy Vallee, Paul Whiteman.

6577. Toyland Premiere (*Cartune Classics*) 10 Dec. 1934; *p.c.:* Univ; *prod/dir:* Walter Lantz; *story/lyrics:* Walter Lantz, Victor McLeod; *anim:* Manuel Moreno, Frank Kelling, George Grandpré; *voices:* The Rhythmettes; *mus:* James Dietrich *col:* Tech-2. *sd:* WE. 8 min. • Oswald hosts a Hollywood party for Bing Crosby, Al Jolson, Boris Karloff, Laurel & Hardy, Maureen O'Sullivan, Shirley Temple and Johnny Weissmuller.

6578. Toys 18 Dec. 1992; *p.c.:* Fox; *digital visual fx: anim:* Pacific Data Images; *ex prod:* John Swallow, Carl Rosendahl; *prod:* Julia Gibson, Michele Ferrone; *sup:* Jamie Dixon; *prod mgr:* Barbara McCullough; *technical dir:* Andrew Adamson; *anim: co-ord:* Anjelica Casillas; *performance:* Graham Walters; *mechanical lead:* Erik Stohl; *mechanical:* Roland Loew, Tom Quinn, Eric Heisler, Ray Goode, Robert Kohut, Sanford Kennedy, George Bernota, Brian Ripley; *anim:* Rebecca Marie, Barbara Meier, Kevin Rafferty, George Bruder, Wendy Rogers; *col:* CFI/DeLuxe. *sd:* Dolby stereo. 121 min. *l/a.* • Live-action comedy: An Army general is put in charge of a toy factory and develops a line of war-inspired toys.

6579. Toys Will Be Toys (*Screen Song*) 15 July 1949; *p.c.:* Famous for Para; *dir:* Seymour Kneitel; *story:* I. Klein; *anim:* Myron Waldman, Gordon Whittier; *sets:* Robert Little; *voices:* Jackson Beck, Jack Mercer, Cecil Roy; *mus:* Winston Sharples; *ph:* Leonard McCormick; *prod mgr:* Sam Buchwald; *col:* Tech. *sd:* RCA. 7 min. • A nocturnal parade of toy soldiers is accompanied by a sing-along. Featuring Bob Hope, Harpo Marx, Ko-Ko and Popeye!

6580. Toytown Hall (*Merrie Melodies*) 19 Sept. 1936; *p.c.:* Leon Schlesinger prods for WB; *dir:* I. Freleng; *anim:* Bob McKimson, Sandy Walker; *lay:* Griff Jay; *back:* Arthur Loomer; *ed:* Tregoweth E. Brown; *voices:* Bernice Hansel, Tommy Bond, Cliff Nazarro, Lind Hayes; *mus:* Carl W. Stalling; *prod sup:* Henry Binder, Raymond G. Katz; *col:* Tech. *sd:* Vit. 7 min. • A small boy dreams of radio characters coming to life. Caricatures of Fred Allen and Portland, Ben Bernie, Eddie Cantor, Bing Crosby, Joe Penner and Rudy Vallee.

6581. A Toytown Tale (*Aesop's Sound Fable*) 4 Jan. 1931; *p.c.:* Van Beuren for Pathé; *dir:* John Foster, Mannie Davis; *mus:* Gene Rodemich; *organist:* Emil Velazco; b&w. *sd:* RCA. 8 min. • After the toymaker retires, a doll flirts with the soldier captain and a jack-in-the-box throws the police captain into a pot of glue.

6582. Trade Mice (*Oswald*) 28 Feb. 1938; *p.c.:* Walter Lantz prods for Univ; *prod/dir:* Walter Lantz; *story:* Victor McLeod, Win Smith; *anim:* Rudy Zamora, Frank Amon; *voices:* Shirley Reed, Bernice Hansel; *mus:* Nathaniel Shilkret; b&w. *sd:* WE. 6½ min. • The mice are taught to trade fairly by Mama. When they yank a gold tooth from Oswald's mule, they leave an IOU.

6583. Trader Mickey (*Mickey Mouse*) 20 Aug. 1932; *p.c.:* Walt Disney prods for UA; *dir:* David D. Hand; *anim:* Johnny Cannon, Les Clark, Gilles de Tremaudan, Kevin Donnelly, Norman Ferguson, Clyde Geronimi, Hardie Gramatky, David D. Hand, Jack King, Richard Lundy, Tom Palmer, Ben Sharpsteen; *voice:* Pinto Colvig; *mus:* Bert Lewis; b&w. *sd:* PCP. 7 min. • Mickey and Pluto are saved from the cannibal cooking pot by the natives finding their musical instruments and staging a jam session.

6584. Traffic Trouble (*James Hound*) 24 Nov. 1967; *p.c.:* TT for Fox; *dir:* Ralph Bakshi; *col:* DeLuxe. *sd:* RCA. 5 min. • Professor Mad causes chaos with traffic jams. • See: *James Hound*

6585. Traffic Troubles (*Mickey Mouse*) 7 Mar. 1931; *p.c.:* Walter E. Disney for Colum; *dir:* Burton F. Gillett; *anim:* Johnny Cannon, Les Clark, Gilles de Tremaudan, Norman Ferguson, David D. Hand, Jack King, Richard Lundy, Tom Palmer, Ben Sharpsteen; *voices:* Marcellite Garner, Walt Disney; *mus:* Bert Lewis; b&w. *sd:* PCP. 7 min. • When Mickey's taxi breaks down, he puts patent medicine in the engine and the cab runs riot into a farm, covering them both in feathers.

6586. Tragic Magic (*Woody Woodpecker*) 3 July 1962; *p.c.:* Walter Lantz prods for Univ; *dir:* Paul J. Smith; *story:* Dalton Sandifer; *anim:* Ray Abrams, Les Kline, Roy Jenkins; *sets:* Art Landy, Ray Huffine; *voices:* Dal McKennon, Grace Stafford; *mus:* Clarence Wheeler; *prod mgr:* William E. Garity; *col:* Tech. *sd:* RCA. 6 min. • Woody wrecks a magician's act.

6587. Trail Mix-up 12 Mar. 1993; *p.c.:* Walt Disney Pictures/Amblin for Buena Vista; *anim dir:* Barry Cook; *ex prod:* Steven Spielberg, Frank Marshall, Kathleen Kennedy; *co-ex prod:* Rob Minkoff; *asso prod:* Pam Coats; *based upon characters created by* Gary K. Wolf; *story:* Rob Minkoff, Barry Cook, Mark Kausler, Patrick A. Ventura; *artistic sup.: lay:* Robert Walker; *back:* Robert E. Stanton; *clean-up:* Ruben Procopio; *special fx:* Jeff Dutton; *cgi:* Rob Bekuhrs; *art dir:* Ric Sluiter; *visual development:* Thom Enriquez; *character anim:* Tom Bancroft, Aaron Blaise, Lou Dellarosa, Mark Henn, Mark Kausler, Alex Kupershmidt, Greg Manwaring, Barry Temple, D. Alfred Wawrzaszek; *lay:* Fred Craig, Jeff Dickson, Karen Keller, Davy Liu, Ken Spirduso, Michael Vash; *back:* Kevin Turcotte, Charles R. Vollmer, Thomas Cardone; *rough inbet:* Trey Finney, Paul McDonald; *inbet:* Paulo Alvarado, Brian Beauchamp, Travis Blaise, Anthony Cipriano, Dan Daly, Tim Hodge, Barry Kooser, Tom LaBaff, Samantha Lair, Kellie D. Lewis, Tamara D. Lushermario Menjivar, Maurilio Morales, Monica Murdock, Phil Noto, James G. Parris; *asst anim:* Elliot M. Bour, Philip S. Boyd, Robert O. Corley, Sam Ewing, Daniel A. Gracey, James Y. Jackson, Nancy Kniep, Christine Lawrence, Tracy M. Lee, Anthony Wayne Michaels, Bryan M. Sommer; *fx anim:* Allen Blyth, Ed Coffey, Christine Blum, Chris Jenkins, Dorse Lanpher, Eusebio Torres, Sandra Groeneveld, Dan Kuemmel, Steve Starr, John Tucker, Tony West; *fx anim break/inbet:* Kristine Brown, Michael Duhatschek, Jazno Francoeur, Troy A. Gustafson, Dan Lund, Joseph C. Pepé; *ed:* Victor Livingston; *voices:* Roger Rabbit: Charles Fleischer; *Jessica Rabbit:* Kathleen Turner; *Mom/Young Baby Herman:* April Winchell; *Adult Baby Herman:* Lou Hirsch; *Droopy Dog:* Corey Burton; *Bear/Beaver:* Frank Welker; *mus:* Bruce Broughton; *mus ed:* Robin J. Flynn, Jacqueline Roberts, Patricia Carlin (*Trud Music, Inc.*), Chuck Williams, Beth Collins-Stegmaier, Deirdre Mangione, Kat Moore; *anim check:* Janet Bruce, Karen Hepburn, Madlyn O'Neill, Karen S. Paat, Laurie A. Sacks, Gary G. Shafer, Mavis Shafer, Barbara Wiles; *i&p (Florida):* Fran Kirsten, Jason Buske, Pam Darley, Suzie Ewing, Pam Henn, Al Kirsten, Al Moore, Victoria Novak, Lisa Reinert, Lynn Rippberger, Elsa Sesto, Joanne Tzuanos, Sharon Vincent; *i&p (LA):* Gretchen Maschmeyer, Al Brecht; *paint/final check:* Hortensia M. Casagran, Barbara Lynn Hamane, Rhonda L. Hicks, Carmen Sanderson, Phyllis Bird, Russell Blandino, Sherrie Cuzzort, Phyllis Fields, Anne Hazard, David Karp, Angelika Katz, Harlene Mears, Debbie Mooneyham, Karen Nugent, Leyla del C. Pelaez, Bruce Phillipson, Fumiko Sommer, Roxanne Taylor, Britt Van der Nagel, Susan Wileman; *digital film scanning, printing & opticals:* Joe Jiuliano, Ariel Velasco Shaw, Christopher Gee, Christine Beck, Chuck Warren; *anim ph operator:* Gary W. Smith, Andrew Simmons, John D. Aardal; *digitizing ph: (mgr)* Robyn Roberts, *(mark-up)* Gina Wootten, Kent Gordon, Tina Baldwin, Jo Ann Breuer, Karen N. China, Lynnette Cull, Gary Fishbaugh, Cindy Garcia; *mark-up:* Debra Y. Siegel, Irma Valez, Janette Hulett; *final check:* Monica Marroquin, Teri N. McDonald; *compositing:* James "JR" Russell, Shannon Fallis-Kane, David J. Rowe; *engineering:* Dave Inglish, David F. Wolf, Raul E. Anaya, Michael Bolds, Lawrence Chai, Carol J. Choy, David Coons, Bijan Forutanpour, Randy Fukuda, Tad Gielow, Don

Gworek, Bruce Hatakeyama, Marcus W. Ho, James D. Houston, Shyh-Chyuan Huang, Kevin E. Keech, Mark R. Kimball, Brad Lowman, Marty Prager, Michael K. Purvis, Carlos Quinonez, Dean Schiller, Grace Shirado, Michael Sullivan, Mark H. Tokum, Paul Yanover; *scene plan:* Ann Tucker, Annamarie Costa, John Cunningham, Donna Weir, Mary Lescher; *col models:* Karen Comella, Irma Cartaya, Penny Coulter, Ann Sorensen; *sd des:* Lon Bender; *rec mix:* Rick Ash, David Campbell, Dean A. Zupancic; visual fx by Buena Vista Effects; *visual fx sup:* Michael Lessa; *visual fx prod:* Caroline Sopier; *matte art:* Paul Lasaine; *ph:* Les Bernstein, Stephen Brooks, Eric C. Peterson, Wally Schaab; *line-up:* Winston Quitasol; *fx graphics:* Bernie Gagliano; *still ph:* Denna Bendall; miniatures by Stetson Visual: Robert Spurlock, Mark Stetson; *chief model maker:* Henry Gonzalez; *model crew:* Ray Goode, Ronald Gress, Mike Hosch, Dennis Schultz, David Sawartz; *prod mgr:* Donna F. Saul, Bruce Grant Williams, Karenna Mazur, Paul Steele, Dana Axelrod; *prod co-ord:* Matthew Garbera, Jeanie Lynd Sorenson, Kevin Wade; *post prod sup:* Sara Duran; 7 min. *col:* Tech. *sd:* Dolby stereo. • Roger Rabbit is left in charge of Baby Herman while Mom goes off on a hunting expedition in Yellowstone Park. Herman's wanderings place Roger in many precarious situations including being chased by a swarm of bees and an angry bear.

6588. The Trail of the Lonesome Pine (*Song Car-Tune*) 17 July 1926; *p.c.:* Inkwell Studio for Red Seal; *dir:* Dave Fleischer; *anim:* Max Fleischer; b&w. sil. 5 min. • No story available.

6589. Trail of the Lonesome Pink (*Pink Panther*) 27 June 1974; *p.c.:* Mirisch/Geoffrey/DFE for UA; *dir:* Gerry Chiniquy; *story:* John W. Dunn; *anim:* Ken Walker, John Gibbs, Bob Bemiller, Norm McCabe; *lay:* Dick Ung; *back:* Richard H. Thomas; *ed:* Bob Gillis; *mus:* Walter Greene; *theme tune:* Henry Mancini; *ph:* John Burton Jr.; *prod mgr:* Lee Gunther; *col:* DeLuxe. *sd:* RCA. 6 min. • The Panther puts paid to two animal trappers.

6590. The Trail of the Pink Panther 17 Dec. 1982; *p.c.:* Marvel Prods, Ltd. for UA; *title dir/storyboard/anim:* Arthur Leonardi; *character created by* David H. DePatie, Friz Freleng; *mus:* Henry Mancini. *col:* Tech. *sd:* Dolby stereo. Panavision. • Live-action comedy with animated titles featuring Inspector Clouseau tracking down the elusive Panther.

6591. Trailblazer Magoo (*Mr. Magoo*) 13 Sept. 1956; *p.c.:* UPA for Colum; *ex prod:* Stephen Bosustow; *dir:* Pete Burness; *story:* Dick Shaw; *anim:* Rudy Larriva, Cecil Surry, Gil Turner, Barney Posner; *lay:* Robert Dranko; *back:* Bob McIntosh; *voices:* Jim Backus, Barney Phillips; *mus:* Frank Comstock; *prod mgr:* Herbert Klynn; *col:* Tech. *sd:* RCA. 6 min. • Magoo and his Indian guide go for what he believes to be an expedition into the deepest forest but gets no further than the nearest city.

6592. Trailer Horn (*Donald Duck*) 28 Apr. 1950; *p.c.:* Walt Disney prods for RKO; *dir:* Jack Hannah; *story:* Roy Williams; *anim:* Bob Carlson, Bill Justice, Volus Jones, Al Bertino, Ken O'Brien; *fx:* Jack Boyd, Dan MacManus; *lay:* Yale Gracey; *back:* Thelma Witmer; *voices:* Clarence Nash, James MacDonald, Dessie Flynn; *mus:* Paul Smith; *col:* Tech. *sd:* RCA. 6 min. • Chip an' Dale succeed in wrecking Donald's caravan holiday.

6593. Trailer Life (*Terry-Toon*) 20 Aug. 1937; *p.c.:* TT for Educational/Fox; *dir:* Mannie Davis; *mus:* Philip A. Scheib; b&w. *sd:* WE. 6 min. • Farmer Al's ultra-modern trailer is invaded by an Indian and a chase ensues!

6594. Trailer Thrills (*Oswald*) 3 May 1937; *p.c.:* Univ; *prod/dir:* Walter Lantz; *story:* Walter Lantz, Victor McLeod; *anim:* Ray Abrams, Bill Mason; *mus:* James Dietrich; b&w. *sd:* WE. 7 min. • Oswald travels to "Paradise Valley" over terrible roads in a trailer only to find it to be a dump.

6595. Train Terrain (*Hector Heathcote*) Feb. 1971; *p.c.:* TT for Fox; *dir:* Art Bartsch; *col:* DeLuxe. *sd:* RCA. 5 min. • Heathcote and Winston stand to lose their farm to Benedict, who has inside information about a railroad that's about to go through it.

6596. Training Pigeons (*Betty Boop*) 18 Sept. 1936; *p.c.:* The Fleischer Studio for Para; *prod:* Max Fleischer; *dir:* Dave Fleischer; *anim:* Myron Waldman, Edward Nolan, Lillian Friedman; *voice:* Mae Questel; *mus:* Sammy Timberg; b&w. *sd:* WE. 6 min. • Pudgy goes on the trail of some missing homing pigeons.

6597. Tramp, Tramp, Tramp the Boys Are Marching (*Song Car-Tune*) 8 May 1926; *p.c.:* Inkwell Studio for Red Seal; *dir:* Dave Fleischer;

anim: Max Fleischer; *song:* Victor Herbert, Rida Johnson Young, Gus Kahn; b&w. *sd:* DPS (disc). 6 min. • A convict struts over the lyrics to Victor Herbert's song.

6598. Tramping Tramps (*Oswald*) 31 Mar. 1930; *p.c.:* Univ; *anim:* Walter Lantz, "Bill" Nolan, Manuel Moreno; *voice:* Mickey Rooney; *mus:* David Broekman; b&w. *sd:* WE. 6 min. • Oswald and Putrid Pete are hobos who try to filch a pie that's standing on a window ledge.

6599. A Transatlantic Flight (*Aesop's Film Fable*) 19 Jan. 1925; *p.c.:* Fables Pictures Inc for Pathé; *dir:* Paul Terry; b&w. sil. 5 min. • Farmer Al Falfa journeys in a hot-air balloon while the farm animals all devise different travelling machines to enter a race.

6600. Trans-Atlantic Screen Magazine *p.c.:* Trans-Atlantic Film Co.Ltd; b&w. sil. 7 min. *l/a/anim.* • Magazine with animated inserts. • *1917:* "The Hand That Rocks the Cradle Rocks the World"—Animated sculpture. "Trench Warfare in Sahara"—Animated sculpture. • *1918:* No story available. No story available. No story available. • *1919:* No story available. Cartoon by Hy Mayer. • *1920:* "Burlesque News." Cartoon figures in real moving picture scenery. • The cartoon satirizes the Preying Mantis.

6601. The Transformers — The Movie 8 Aug. 1986; *p.c.:* Sunbow Prods for Marvel Prods; *dir/co-prod:* Nelson Shin; *ex prod:* Margaret Loesch, Lee Gunther; *prod:* Joe Bacal, Tom Griffin; *asso prod (Toei Animation):* Masaharu Etoh, Tomoh Fukumoto; *sup prod:* Jim Graziano; *prod co-ord:* Gene Pelc, Elise Goyette, Terri Gruskin, Hildy Mesnik; *prod mgr:* Carole Weitzman, Gerald L. Moeller, Koh Meguro, Satora Nakamura, Takuya Igarashi; *scr:* Ron Friedman; *story consultants:* Flint Dille, Doug Booth, Roger Slifer; *original concept des:* Floro Dery; *character/back des:* Gabriel Hoyos, Fred Carillo, Rico Rival, Delfin Barras, Romeo Tanghal, Lew Ott, Romeo Francisco, Pat Agnasin, Ernie Guanlao, Eufronio R. Cruz, Mike Sekowsky; *storyboard:* Peter Chung, Jooin Kim, Chung Hwan Oh, Sioak Park, Sangil Shim, David Shin, Soo Young Chung, Delfin Barras, James Gomez, Ernie Guanlao, Doug Lefler, Rico Rival, Romeo Tanghal; *anim sup:* Kozo Morishita; *anim dir:* John Patrick Freeman, Norm McCabe, Gerald L. Moeller, Bob Matz, Margaret Nichols; *asst dir:* Shigeyasu Yamauchi, Masao Ito, Baik Seung Kyun; *Toei Animation: chief:* Koichi Tsunoda; *key anim:* Nobuyoshi Sasakado, Shigemitsu Fujitaka, Koichi Fukuda, Yoshitaka Koyama, Yoshinori Kanamori, Yoshinobu Inano, Baik Nam Yeoul, Kiyomitsu Tsuji, Masanori Shino, Toshio Mori, Shigenobu Nagasaki, Yasuyoshi Uwai, Shigeo Matoba, Satoshi Yamaguchi, Yoichi Mitsui, Shigeru Murakami, Yoshito Miki, Takahiro Kagami; *inbet:* Kiyomi Sugita, Ryuji Ajiri, Hiroaki Daiji, Shizuo Tanaka, Tadashi Yahata, Takako Nakamura, Kei Okazaki, Akira Sugiura, Yoshiharu Azuma, Jun Watanabe, Tomoe Morimoto, Takao Sakano, Mario Ishiyama, Tomoko Fukui, Shigeru Hayashi, Kazuya Komai, Takehiro Iima, Miyo Yamada, Teruo Hattori, Kazunori Nakazawa; *model col key:* Phyllis Craig; *back art dir:* Robert Schaefer, Takao Sawada, Dario Campanile; *back:* Kazuo Ebisawa, Toshikatsu Sanuki; *fx anim:* Masayuki Kawachi, Shoji Sato; *ed:* Steven C. Brown, David Hankins; *voices: Wreck-Gar:* Eric Idle; *Hot Rod/Rodimus Prime:* Judd Nelson; *Galvatron:* Leonard Nimoy; *Ultra Magnus:* Robert Stack; *Kup:* Lionel Stander; *Unicron:* Orson Welles; *Blurr:* John Moschitta; *Kranix:* Norm Alden; *Astrotrain:* Jack Angel; *Grimlock:* Gregg Berger; *Arcee:* Susan Blu; *Devastator:* Arthur Burghardt; *Quintesson Judge:* Rege Cordic; *Jazz:* Scatman Crothers; *Dirge:* Bud Davis; *Inferno:* Walker Edmiston; *Percepton:* Paul Eiding; *Blitzwing:* Ed Gilbert; *Bumblebee:* Dan Gilvezan; *Blaster:* Buster Jones; *Scourge:* Stan Jones; *Cliffjumper:* Casey Kasem; *Starscream:* Chris Latta; *Daniel:* David Mendenhall; *Gears:* Don Messick; *Shrapnel:* Hal Rayle; *Kickback:* Clive Revill; *Prowl/Scrapper/Swoop/Junkion:* Michael Bell; *Spike/Brawn/Shockwave:* Corey Burton; *Cyclonus/Quintesson Leader:* Roger C. Carmel; *Optimus Prime/Ironhide:* Peter Cullen; *Bonecrusher/Hook/Springer/Slag:* Neil Ross; *Soundwave/Megatron/Megatron/Rumble/Frenzy/Wheelie/Junkion:* Frank Welker; *mus:* Vince DiCola; *mus arr:* Vince DiCola, Ed Frugé; *synthesizer programming:* Casey Young; *mus sup:* Soundtracs; *mus ed:* Mark Shiney, Ed Frugé, Peter Collier, Robert Randles, Bob Mayer; *songs:* "Instruments of Destruction" by Ernest Petrangelo, Robin Ward, Steven Serpa, performed by NRG; "Dare" by Vince DiCola, Scott Shelly; "The Touch" by Stan Bush, Lenny Malcuso, performed by Stan Bush; "Nothin's Gonna Stand in Our Way" by Randy Bishop; "Hunger" by Larry Gillstron, Brian Gillstron, Victor Langen, George Christon, Ray Harvey, Spencer Proffer, performed by Spectre General; "Dare to Be Stupid" by and performed by "Weird Al" Yankovic; "The Transformers" by Ford Kinder, Anne Bryant, Norman Swan, Douglas Aldrich, performed by Lion; *main title des:* Bill Millar, Deena Burkett; *i&p:* Mary Ann Steward, Kiniko Murata, Junko Furuya, Masatoyo Ogura, Hiroshi Kosakai, Mihoko Irie, Reiko Igarashi, Myrna Gibbs, Marta Skwara, Robin Draper, Britt Van Der Nagel, Britt Greko, Kris Brown, Harriette Rossall, Heidi Shellhorn, Liane Douglas, Hannah Powell, Debbie Jorgensborg; *check:* Koichi Tsunoda, Akira Sato, Hitoshi Abe, Ryukichi Yoshizawa, Kazuo Kinugasa, Hiroshi Morita; *Xerox:* Virginia Creamer, Bill Hudson, Sandy Kennedy; *sd ed:* Jim Blodgett, Alison Cobb, Mike DePatie, John Detra, Karen Doulac, Ron Fedele, Lenny Geschke, Nicholas James, Warren Taylor, Michael Tomack, Peter Tomaszewicz, John Singleton, Ted Chapman; *dial ed:* Jerry Jacobson; *voice recl processing:* Wally Burr Recording; *sd processing:* Scott Brownlee, Craig Harris; *sd rec:* Tony Papa, B&B Sound Studios, Ken Berger, Dave Van Meter; *sd re-rec:* R. William, A. Thiederman, W. Howard Wilmarth, Peter S. Reale, David Koelher, Bob Harman, Jim Cook, Jacquie Freeman; *sd fx:* Brian Courcier; *anim ph (Toei Animation):* Masatoshi Fukui, Masaru Banzai, Yukio Katayama; *opticals:* F. Stop; *col:* Tech. *sd:* Dolby stereo/dts. 85 min. • Set in the future (2005), the battle for Autobot (the good robots) City sees the Decepticons defeated, but at the loss of Optimus Prime, the Autobot's leader in a duel with the opposition's leader, Megatron. The Matrix of Leadership is passed to Prime's successor, Ultra Magnus. Megatron and his henchmen are left to drift in space until they are consumed by the planet-swallowing Unicron. He gets reconstructed in the guarantee of allegiance and materializes under the new identity of "Galvatron." He then sets out to destroy the Matrix while Unicron continues on its way, consuming all in its path. An attack is directed on Unicron that is intercepted by Galvatron who is now back in control of the Decepticons. A battle ensues, resulting in the Unicron being demolished.

6602. Transylvania Mania *(Inspector)* 26 Mar. 1969; *p.c.:* Mirisch/Geoffrey/DFE for UA; *dir:* Gerry Chiniquy; *story:* John W. Dunn; *anim:* Don Williams, Manny Gould, Warren Batchelder, Tom Ray, Manny Perez; *lay:* Dick Ung; *back:* Tom O'Loughlin; *ed:* Lee Gunther; *voices:* Pat Harrington Jr., Marvin Miller, Hal Smith; *mus:* Walter Greene; *theme tune:* Henry Mancini; *ph:* John Burton Jr.; *prod sup:* Harry Love, David DeTiege; *col:* DeLuxe. *sd:* RCA. 6 min. • The Inspector visits a castle and gets pursued by a Vampire who needs a brain for his monster.

6603. Transylvania 6-5000 *(Merrie Melodies)* 30 Nov. 1963; *p.c.:* WB; *dir:* Chuck Jones; *asst dir:* Maurice Noble; *story:* John Dunn; *anim:* Bob Bransford, Tom Ray, Ken Harris, Richard Thompson; *lay:* Bob Givens; *back:* Philip de Guard; *ed:* Treg Brown; *voices:* Mel Blanc, Ben Frommer, Julie Bennett; *mus:* Bill Lava; *prod mgr:* William Orcutt; *prod:* David H. DePatie; *col:* Tech. *sd:* Vit. 7 min. • Bugs lands in Transylvania where he encounters Count Bloodcount, a vampire.

6604. Trap Happy *(Tom & Jerry)* 29 June 1946; *p.c.:* MGM; *dir:* William Hanna, Joseph Barbera; *anim:* Kenneth Muse, Ed Barge, Michael Lah; *ed:* Fred MacAlpin; *voice:* Dick Nelson; *mus:* Scott Bradley; *ph:* Jack Stevens; *prod:* Fred Quimby; *col:* Tech. *sd:* WE. 7 min. • Tom calls in reinforcement from a mouse exterminator but their combined forces are no match for Jerry's resourcefulness.

6605. Trap Happy Porky *(Looney Tunes)* 24 Feb. 1945; *p.c.:* WB; *dir:* Charles M. Jones; *story:* Tedd Pierce; *anim:* Ken Harris; *lay:* Robert Gribbroek; *ed:* Treg Brown; *voices:* Mel Blanc, The Sportsmen (Maxwell Smith, John Rarig, Gurney Bell, Martin Sperzel); *mus:* Carl W. Stalling; *prod mgr:* John W. Burton; *prod:* Edward Selzer; *col:* Tech. *sd:* Vit. 6½ min. • Kept awake by mice, Porky employs cats to get rid of them and then has problems with the drunken, reveling felines.

6606. The Trapeze Artist *(Krazy Kat)* 1 Sept. 1934; *p.c.:* Charles Mintz prods for Colum; *story:* Sid Marcus; *anim:* Art Davis; *mus:* Joe de Nat; *prod mgr:* James Bronis; b&w. *sd:* WE. 7 min. • Krazy goes to court and pleads his case over his girl being taken by a trapeze artist.

6607. Trapeze Please *(Heckle & Jeckle)* July 1960; *p.c.:* TT for Fox; *ex prod:* Bill Weiss; *dir:* Connie Rasinski; *story sup:* Tom Morrison; *story:* George Atkins; *anim:* Larry Silverman, Eddie Donnelly, Johnny Gent, Cosmo Anzilotti; *lay:* John Zago; *back:* Bill Focht; *voices:* Roy Halee; *mus:* Phil Scheib; *prod mgr:* Frank Schudde; *col:* DeLuxe. *sd:* RCA. 6 min. CS. • The magpies are matrimony agents who try to match Hilda Hippo with a trapeze artist.

6608. Trapped *(Out of the Inkwell)* 15 May 1923; *p.c.:* Inkwell Studio for Rodner; *anim/l/a:* Max Fleischer; b&w. sil. 5 min. *l/a/anim.* • Ko-Ko complicates matters for Max when he gets tangled in a life-size spider web.

6609. Trash Program *(Modern Madcap)* Apr. 1963; *p.c.:* Para Cartoons; *dir:* Seymour Kneitel; *story:* Irving Dressler; *anim:* Morey Reden, Jack Ehret, Larry Silverman; *sets:* Robert Little; *voices:* Dayton Allen, Valerie Harper; *mus:* Winston Sharples; *ph:* Leonard McCormick; *prod mgr:* Abe Goodman; *col:* Tech. *sd:* RCA. 6 min. • A nagging housewife goads her husband to improving his status. He elevates from a sewer worker to captain of a garbage scow.

6610. Travel Squawks *(Krazy Kat)* 4 July 1938; *p.c.:* Charles Mintz prods for Colum; *story:* Allen Rose; *anim:* Harry Love, Louie Lilly; *voices:* Dave Weber, Billy Bletcher; *mus:* Joe de Nat; *prod mgr:* James Bronis; b&w. *sd:* RCA. 6½ min. • Krazy goes on a magic carpet tour of the North Pole, Holland and just manages to escape a cannibal pot in Africa.

6611. Travelaffs *(Noveltoon)* 22 Aug. 1958; *p.c.:* Para Cartoons; *dir:* Seymour Kneitel; *sets:* Robert Little; *voices:* Jackson Beck, Jack Mercer, Sid Raymond; *mus:* Winston Sharples; *ph:* Leonard McCormick; *prod mgr:* Abe Goodman; *col:* Tech. *sd:* RCA. 6 min. Seq: *Gag and Baggage; Aero-Nutics; Drippy Mississippi; Sing Again of Michigan; Fiesta Time.* • A travelogue starting at the railway station and ending in Mexico.

6612. Travelaughs *p.c.:* Univ; *anim:* Hy Mayer; b&w. sil. 4 min. *l/a/anim.* • *1913:* **A Study in Crayon** Mar. **Hy Mayer: His Magic Hand** 3 May. **Hy Mayer: His Magic Hand** 31 May. **Pen Talks by Hy Mayer** 7 June. **Hy Mayer's Cartoons** 14 June. **Filmograph Cartoons** 21 June. **Fun in Film by Hy Mayer** 28 June. **Sketches From Life by Hy Mayer** 5 July. **Lightning Sketches by Hy Mayer** 12 July. **In Cartoonland with Hy Mayer** 19 July. **Summer Caricatures** 26 July. **Funny Fancies by Hy Mayer** 2 Aug. **The Adventures of Mr. Phiffles** 9 Aug. **In Laughland with Hy Mayer** 16 Aug. **Pen Talks by Hy Mayer** 23 Aug. **Hy Mayer: His Merry Pen** 30 Aug. **Humors of Summer** 6 Sept. **Hy Mayer Cartoons** 13 Aug. **Antics in Ink by Hy Mayer** 20 Sept. **Jolly Jottings by Hy Mayer** 27 Sept. **Whimsicalities by Hy Mayer** 4 Oct. **Hilarities by Hy Mayer** 11 Oct. **Leaves from Hy Mayer's Sketchbook** 18 Oct. • *1914:* **Pen Laughs. Topical Topics. Topical War Cartoons** Sept. **Topical War Cartoons #2** Oct. **War Cartoons by Hy Mayer** Nov. • *1915:* **To 'Frisco Via the Cartoon Route** 9 Aug. • *1916:* **A Trip to Honolulu** 12 Apr. **Globe Trotting with Hy Mayer** 14 Apr. **Such Is Life in China** 22 June. **Pen and Inkings in and Around Jerusalem** 5 Oct. **High Life on a Farm** 9 Nov. **A Pen Trip to Palestine** 9 Nov. **Such Is Life in Alaska** 19 Dec. • *1917:* **Such Is Life in South Algeria** 28 Apr. **China Awakened** 26 June. **Seeing Ceylon with Hy Mayer** 6 Aug. **Seeing New York with Hy Mayer** 15 Oct. • *1918:* **New York by Heck** 1 May. **Universal Screen Magazine #77** 29 June. **Universal Screen Magazine #81** 27 July. **Universal Screen Magazine #82** 3 Aug. **Universal Screen Magazine #90** 1 Sept. **Universal Screen Magazine #92** 12 Oct. **Universal Screen Magazine #93** 19 Oct. **Universal Screen Magazine #94** 26 Oct. *p.c.:* R.C. Pictures for FBO. • *1922:* **Such Is Life in London's West End** 15 Apr. **Such Is Life in Vollendam** 7 May. **Such Is Life in Monte Carlo** 31 May. **Such Is Life in Mon Petit Paris** 4 June. **Such Life Among the Children of France** 18 June. **Such Is Life in Munich** 22 July. **Such Is Life in Montmartre** 22 July. **Such Is Life on the Riviera** 12 Aug. **Such Is Life Among the Paris Shoppers** 12 Aug. **Such Is LifeNear London** 19 Aug. **Such Is Life In Amsterdam and Alkmaar** 27 Aug. **Such Is LifeAmong the Idlers of Paris** Oct. **Such Is Life in Busy London** 4. Nov. **Such Is Life at a Dutch County Fair** Nov. **Such Is Life in Italy** Dec. *p.c.:* Univ. • *1923:* **A Movie Fantasy** 8 Dec. **A Son of Ananias** 10 Dec.

6613. The Travels of Teddy 1915 *p.c.:* Hy Mayer Studio for Auerbach Chocolates; *dir:* Hy Mayer; *anim:* Otto Messmer; b&w. sil. • Teddy Roosevelt's arrival in the jungle causes quite a stir amongst the animals.

6614. Treasure Jest *(Fox & Crow)* 30 Aug. 1945; *p.c.:* Colum; *dir:* Howard Swift; *anim:* Volus Jones, Grant Simmons; *lay:* Clark Watson; *ed:* Richard S. Jensen; *voices:* Frank Graham; *mus:* Eddie Kilfeather; *prod mgr:* Hugh McCollum; *col:* Tech. *sd:* WE. 6½ min. • The crow bilks the fox of all his cash when he digs for buried treasure on a desert island.

6615. Treasure of the Lost Lamp • See: *Duck Tales the Movie: Treasure of the Lost Lamp*

6616. The Treasure Runt (*Scrappy*) 25 Feb. 1932; *p.c.:* Winkler for Colum; *prod:* Charles Mintz; *story:* Dick Huemor; *anim:* Sid Marcus, Art Davis; *mus:* Joe de Nat; *prod mgr;* James Bronis; b&w. *sd:* WE. 6 min. • Scrappy and Vontzy hunt for treasure at the bottom of the sea.

6617. Tree Cornered Tweety (*Merrie Melodies*) 19 May 1956; *p.c.:* WB; *dir:* Friz Freleng; *story:* Warren Foster; *anim:* Arthur Davis, Gerry Chiniquy, Virgil Ross; *lay:* Hawley Pratt; *back:* Irv Wyner; *ed:* Treg Brown; *voices:* Mel Blanc, June Foray; *mus:* Milt Franklyn; *prod mgr:* John W. Burton; *prod:* Edward Selzer; *col:* Tech. *sd:* Vit. 6½ min. • Tweety keeps a diary dealing with events concerning his encounters with Sylvester.

6618. Tree for Two (*Color Rhapsody*) 21 June 1943; *p.c.:* Colum; *prod:* Dave Fleischer; *dir:* Bob Wickersham; *story:* Sam Cobean; *anim:* Howard Swift, Phil Duncan; *lay:* Clark Watson; *ed:* Edward Moore; *voices:* Frank Graham; *mus:* Paul Worth; *prod mgr:* Albert Spar; *col:* Tech. *sd:* RCA. 7½ min. • Armed with a bucket of cement, "tree surgeon" fox sets out to block-up the crow's front door.

6619. Tree for Two (*Merrie Melodies*) 18 Oct. 1952; *p.c.:* WB; *dir:* I. Freleng; *story:* Warren Foster; *anim:* Ken Champin, Virgil Ross, Arthur Davis, Manuel Perez; *lay:* Hawley Pratt; *back:* Irv Wyner; *ed:* Treg Brown; *voices:* Mel Blanc, Stan Freberg; *mus:* Carl Stalling; *prod mgr:* John W. Burton; *prod:* Edward Selzer; *col:* Tech. *sd:* Vit. 7 min. • Two dogs try to pick a fight with Sylvester but tangle with an escaped panther instead.

6620. A Tree Is a Tree Is a Tree? (*Comic King*) 1 Aug. 1962; *p.c.:* Para Cartoons; *dir:* Seymour Kneitel; *story:* Les Colodny, Al Brodax; *anim:* Nick Tafuri, George Germanetti, Larry Silverman; *sets:* Robert Owen; *voices:* Howard Morris, Allen Melvin; *mus:* Winston Sharples; *prod mgr:* Abe Goodman; *ex prod:* Al Brodax; col. *sd:* RCA. 5½ min. • Beetle Bailey accidentally destroys Sgt. Snorkle's beloved leechie nut tree and has to "borrow" another from a Chinese restaurant.

6621. The Tree Medic (*Woody Woodpecker*) 9 Dec. 1955; *p.c.:* Walter Lantz prods for Univ; *dir:* Alex Lovy; *story:* Homer Brightman; *anim:* Don Patterson, La Verne Harding, Ray Abrams; *sets:* Raymond Jacobs; *voices:* Dal McKennon, Grace Stafford; *mus:* Clarence Wheeler; *prod mgr:* William E. Garity; *col:* Tech. *sd:* RCA. 6 min. • Woody gives "the business" to a tree surgeon who wants to examine his home.

6622. Tree Saps (*Talkartoon*) 21 Feb. 1931; *p.c.:* The Fleischer Studio for Para; *prod:* Max Fleischer; *dir:* Dave Fleischer; *mus:* Art Turkisher; b&w. *sd:* WE. 7 min. • Woodsman Bimbo has problems when menaced by a bear who will only work when fed fish. He is finally rescued by a hurricane.

6623. The Tree Surgeon (*MGM cartoon*) 3 June 1944; *p.c.:* MGM; *dir:* George Gordon; *anim:* Arnold Gillespie, Michael Lah, Ed Barge; *sets:* John Didrik Johnsen; *ed:* Fred MacAlpin; *voice:* Dick Nelson; *mus:* Scott Bradley; *prod:* Fred Quimby; *col:* Tech. *sd:* WE. 7 min. • Tree surgeon, Doc Donkey, attempts to preserve one of the "Grandfathers" of the forest with Vitamin B-Tree.

6624. Tree's a Crowd (*Woody Woodpecker*) 8 Sept. 1958; *p.c.:* Walter Lantz prods for Univ; *dir:* Paul J. Smith; *story:* Homer Brightman; *anim:* Robert Bentley, Les Kline, Don Patterson; *sets:* Art Landy, Raymond Jacobs; *voices:* Daws Butler, Grace Stafford; *mus:* Clarence Wheeler; *prod mgr:* William E. Garity; *col:* Tech. *sd:* RCA. 6 min. • Colonel Fleabush sends his cat, Philbert, to dispose of Woody, who's been destroying all the trees on the colonel's estate.

6625. The Tree's Knees (*Looney Tunes*) Aug. 1931; *p.c.:* Hugh Harman, Rudolf Ising prods for WB; *prod:* Leon Schlesinger; *anim:* Rollin Hamilton, Isadore Freleng; *mus:* Frank Marsales; b&w. *sd:* Vit. 7 min. • When woodsman Bosko goes to chop some trees, they plead with him to spare them.

6626. The Trial of Donald Duck (*Donald Duck*) 30 July 1948; *p.c.:* Walt Disney prods for RKO; *dir:* Jack King, Charles Nichols; *story:* Dan MacManus; *anim:* Ed Aardal, Fred Kopietz, Paul Allen, Mary Kendall, Frank McSavage, Don Towsley; *fx:* Jack Boyd, Sandy Strother; *lay:* Don Griffith; *back:* Merle Cox; *voices:* Dehner Forkum, Clarence Nash, Dan MacManus; *mus:* Oliver Wallace; *col:* Tech. *sd:* RCA. 6½ min. • Donald appears in court after refusing to pay an exorbitant restaurant bill. • Started by King, Nichols completed after a production halt on all shorts went into effect.

6627. The Trial of Mr. Wolf (*Merrie Melodies*) 26 Apr. 1941; *p.c.:* Leon Schlesinger prods for WB; *dir:* I. Freleng; *story:* Michael Maltese; *anim:* Richard Bickenbach; *sets:* Lenard Kester; *ed:* Treg Brown; *voices:* Mel Blanc, Sara Berner; *mus:* Carl W. Stalling; *ph:* John W. Burton; *prod sup:* Henry Binder, Raymond G. Katz; *col:* Tech. *sd:* Vit. 7 min. • The Wolf stands on trial and presents his version of the Little Red Riding Hood saga, putting the blame squarely on the shoulders of Red and Grandma.

6628. The Trials of a Movie Cartoonist (*Sullivan Cartoon Comedy*) 29 Nov. 1916; *p.c.:* Pat Sullivan Studio for Univ; *dir:* Pat Sullivan; *anim:* Otto Messmer; b&w. *sil.* 5 min. • No story available.

6629. The Trials of Willie Winks (*Sullivan Cartoon Comedy*) 7 Jan. 1917; *p.c.:* Pat Sullivan Studio for Univ; *dir:* Pat Sullivan; *anim:* Otto Messmer; b&w. *sil.* 5 min. • No story available.

6630. Trick or Cheat (*Honey Halfwitch*) Mar. 1966; *p.c.:* Para Cartoons; *dir:* Howard Post; *story:* Heywood Kling; *anim:* Martin Taras; *sets:* Robert Little; *voices:* Shari Lewis, Bob MacFadden; *mus:* Winston Sharples; *ph:* Leonard McCormick; *prod mgr:* Abe Goodman; *col:* Tech. *sd:* RCA. 6 min. • The Grand Wizard arrives to see Stanley the Sorcerer perform one successful spell. Honey and Fraidy Bat help him fool the Wizard.

6631. Trick or Retreat (*Roland & Rattfink*) 3 Mar. 1971; *p.c.:* Mirisch/DFE for UA; *dir:* Art Davis; *story:* Sid Marcus; *anim:* Manny Perez, Robert Taylor, Ken Muse, Don Williams; *lay:* Dick Ung; *back:* Richard Thomas; *ed:* Lee Gunther; *voices:* Leonard Weinrib; *mus:* Doug Goodwin; *prod sup:* Jim Foss, Harry Love; *col:* DeLuxe. *sd:* RCA. 6 min. • Sgt. Roland is left in charge of the fort against an Indian attack led by Rattfink.

6632. Trick or Treat (*Donald Duck*) 10 Oct. 1952; *p.c.:* Walt Disney prods for RKO; *dir:* Jack Hannah; *story:* Ralph Wright; *anim:* Bill Justice, George Kreisl, Don Lusk, Volus Jones, Al Coe, Ken Walker; *fx:* Dan Mac Manus; *sets:* Yale Gracey; *voices:* June Foray, Clarence Nash, The MelloMen; *mus:* Paul Smith; *col:* Tech. *sd:* RCA. 8 min. • Witch Hazel, a sympathetic witch, helps Donald's nephews get some "treats" out of their stingy uncle on Hallowe'en night.

6633. Trick or Tree (*Noveltoon*) July 1961; *p.c.:* Para Cartoons; *dir:* Seymour Kneitel; *story:* Irving Dressler; *anim:* Morey Reden, John Gentilella; *sets:* Anton Loeb; *voices:* Bob MacFadden; *mus:* Winston Sharples; *ph:* Leonard McCormick; *prod mgr:* Abe Goodman; *col:* Tech. *sd:* RCA. 6 min. • A construction worker, building a freeway, comes up against a tree guarded by a park ranger and a woodpecker.

6634. Trick or Tweet (*Merrie Melodies*) 21 Mar. 1959; *p.c.:* WB; *dir:* Friz Freleng; *story:* Warren Foster; *anim:* Art Davis, Gerry Chiniquy, Virgil Ross; *lay:* Hawley Pratt; *back:* Tom O'Loughlin; *ed:* Treg Brown; *voices:* Mel Blanc, Daws Butler; *mus:* Milt Franklyn; *prod mgr;* William Orcutt; *prod:* David H. DePatie; *col:* Tech. *sd:* Vit. 7 min. • Sylvester and Sam, another cat, try to prevent each other from devouring Tweety.

6635. Tricky Business (*Terry-Toon*) 1 May 1942; *p.c.:* TT for Fox; *dir:* Eddie Donnelly *story:* John Foster; *voices:* Arthur Kay, Thomas Morrison; *mus:* Philip A. Scheib; b&w. *sd:* RCA. 7 min. • Gandy Goose and Sourpuss are transported to a magic shop.

6636. Tricky Trout (*Chilly Willy*) 5 Sept. 1961; *p.c.:* Walter Lantz prods for Univ; *dir:* Jack Hannah; *story:* Dalton Sandifer; *anim:* Al Coe, Don Lusk, Roy Jenkins; *sets:* Ray Huffine, Art Landy; *voice:* Paul Frees; *mus:* Clarence Wheeler; *prod mgr:* William E. Garity; *col:* Tech. *sd:* RCA. 6 min. • Chilly attempts to steal the fish from Wally Walrus' fish farm.

6637. Trigger Treat (*Modern Madcap*) Apr. 1960; *p.c.:* Para Cartoons; *dir:* Seymour Kneitel; *story:* Irving Dressler; *anim:* Tom Johnson, William Henning, Els Barthen; *sets:* Robert Owen; *voices:* Jack Mercer, Jackson Beck; *mus:* Winston Sharples; *ph:* Leonard McCormick; *prod mgr:* Abe Goodman; *col:* Tech. *sd:* RCA. 6 min. • The Sheriff of a western town tries to apprehend Dirty Dan, a notorious bandit, without the aid of firearms.

6638. The Trip (*Noveltoon*) Apr. 1967; *p.c.:* Para Cartoons; *dir:* Shamus Culhane; *story/anim:* Howard Beckerman; *sets:* Howard Beckerman, Gil Miret; *mus:* Winston Sharples; *prod sup:* Harold Robins, Burt Hanft; *col:* Tech. *sd:* RCA. 6½ min. • Fred Fallguy takes a cruise and is shipwrecked on an island. He befriends an ape whom he takes home with him when rescued.

6639. Trip for Tat (*Merrie Melodies*) 29 Oct. 1960; *p.c.:* WB; *dir:* Friz Freleng; *story:* Michael Maltese; *anim:* Gerry Chiniquy, Virgil Ross, Tom

Ray; *lay:* Hawley Pratt; *back:* Tom O'Loughlin; *ed:* Treg Brown; *voices:* Mel Blanc, June Foray; *mus:* Milt Franklyn; *prod mgr:* William Orcutt; *prod:* David H. DePatie; *col:* Tech. *sd:* Vit. 7 min. • Granny and Tweety go on a world cruise, followed, doggedly by a ravenous Sylvester.

6640. A Trip to Mars *(Out of the Inkwell)* 1 Apr. 1924; *p.c.:* Out of the Inkwell Studio for Red Seal; *dir:* Dave Fleischer; *anim/l/a:* Max Fleischer; b&w. *sil.* 5 min. *l/a/anim.* • Max sends Ko-Ko to Mars in a rocket ship. Aliens threaten the clown who tries to escape by subway and taxi.

6641. A Trip to the Pole *(Aesop's Film Fable)* 20 Apr. 1924; *p.c.:* Fables Pictures Inc for Pathé; *dir:* Paul Terry; b&w. *sil.* 5 min. • The abandoned trip to the North Pole by the Navy dirigible "Shenandoah" is taken up by the cat and mouse who tow back what they think to be the Pole but what is really a serpent.

6642. Triple Trouble *(Mighty Mouse)* Nov. 1948; *p.c.:* TT for Fox; *dir:* Eddie Donnelly; *story:* John Foster; *anim:* Jim Tyer; *voices:* Roy Halee, Thomas Morrison; *mus:* Philip A. Scheib; *col:* Tech. *sd:* RCA. 6 min. • Oil Can Harry kidnaps Pearl Pureheart from her penthouse home and Mighty Mouse flies to the rescue.

6643. Triplet Trouble *(Tom & Jerry)* 19 Apr. 1952; *p.c.:* MGM; *dir:* William Hanna, Joseph Barbera; *anim:* Ray Patterson, Ed Barge, Kenneth Muse, Irven Spence; *lay:* Dick Bickenbach; *back:* Robert Gentle; *ed:* Jim Faris; *voice:* Lillian Randolph; *mus:* Scott Bradley; *prod:* Fred Quimby; *col:* Tech. *sd:* WE. 7 min. • Tom is put in charge of three kittens who turn out not to be the "angels" they first appear to be.

6644. Trocadero 24 April 1944; *p.c.:* Republic; *anim:* Dave Fleischer; b&w. *sd.* *l/a.* • Live action musical about a couple who inherit a nightclub. Dave Fleischer appears on camera, seated at a table. Cliff Nazarro makes a nuisance of himself, stating what he thinks are wrong with Dave's cartoons while Dave draws a character named "Snippy" who leaves the sketch pad to ascend a seltzer bottle and douse Nazarro.

6645. The Trojan Horse *(Mighty Mouse)* 26 July 1946; *p.c.:* TT for Fox; *dir:* Mannie Davis; *story:* John Foster; *voices:* Thomas Morrison, Roy Halee; *mus:* Philip A. Scheib; *ph:* Douglas Moye; *col:* Tech. *sd:* RCA. 6 min. • The Ancient Grecian mouse city is stormed by cats. Mighty Mouse descends from Mount Olympus.

6646. Troll 17 Jan. 1986; *p.c.:* Altat Prods for Empire Pictures; *special optical fx:* Motion Opticals: *Rotoscopel anim sup:* Linda Obalil, *artists:* Kevin Kutchaver, Len Morganti, R.J. Robertson, Martine Tomczyk, *ink:* McNevin Hayes, *paint:* Jim Stewart; *stop-motion visual fx:* James Aupperle; *miniature sup:* James Belohovek, John Mathews, Mark Wallace; *matte art:* Stephen Burg; *troll creatures des:* John Carl Buechler; *MMI creature construction: des:* John Carl Buechler; *fabricators:* Everitt Burrel, Mitch Devane, Howard Berger, Cleve Hall, Gino Gragnale, Desiree Soto, Chris Biggs, Brent Armstrong, Raffaele Battistelli, Irina Bondareva, Thierry Bouffeteau, Daniel Hoffman, Margherita Regina; *vocal fx:* Frank Welker; *mus:* Richard Band; *col. sd:* Dolby stereo. 82 min. *l/a.* • Live-action fantasy: A family moves into an apartment whose basement is inhabited by a troll. Wendy, the young daughter, discovers this and is spirited away to a magical world while the troll takes on her form, setting out to turn the other residents.

6647. A Troll in Central Park 7 Oct. 1994; *p.c.:* WB. *dir:* Don Bluth, Gary Goldman; *prod:* Don Bluth, Gary Goldman, John Pomeroy; *story:* Don Bluth, Gary Goldman, John Pomeroy, T.J. Kuenster, Stu Krieger; *scr:* Stu Krieger; *storyboard:* Scott Caple, James Finnegan, Bill Frake, Kevin Gollaher, Dan Kuenster, Rick Saliba, Mark Swan, Rowland B. Wilson, Dick Zondag, Garry Zondag; *anim/storyboard asst sup:* Bernie Keogh; *prod des:* Dave Goetz; *art dir:* Don Moore; *pre-prod col stylist:* Carmen Oliver; *anim dir:* John Pomeroy, Piet De Rycker, John Hill, T. Daniel Hofstedt, Cathy Jones, Jean Morel, Ralf Palmer, Len Simon, Jeff Varab; *char anim:* Richard Bazley, Doug Bennett, Ben Burgess, Sandro Cleuzo, Chris Derochie, Colm Duggan, Sam Fleming, Robert Fox, Frank Gabriel, Edison Goncalves, Silvia Hoefnagels, Kevin Johnson, Rob Koo, Dave Kupczyk, Joe McDonough, Brian Mitchell, Paul Newberry, Jens Pindal, John Power, Mark Pudleiner, Troy Saliba, Rusty Stoll, Athanassios Vakalis, Oliver Wade, Bill Waldman, Shane Zalvin; *addit char anim:* Matthew Bates, Ken Boyer, Nancy Carrig, Donnachada Daly, Murray Debus, Valentin Doménech, Stefan Fjeldmark, Bill Giggie, Alberto Grisolia, Michael Helmuth Hansen, Dan Harder, Kim Hagen Jensen, Celine Kieman, Karsten Kiilerich, Jørgen Lerdam, Jesper Møller, Fernando Moro, Hans Perk, Gabor Tom Steisinger, Todd Waterman; *asst anim:* Kevin M. O'Neil, Peter Anderson, Marie Blanchard, Marcelo Fernandes De Moura, Joshua Dodson, Alan Fleming, Tim George, Damien Gilligan, Róisin Hunt, Myung Kang, Paul J. Kelly, Johan Klingler, Paddy Malone, Neil McNeill, Brad Raymond, Randy Sanchez, Melanie Sowell, Jennifer Marie Stillwell, Ando Tammik, David Teague, Konrad Winterlich; *anim check sup:* Christine Fluskey, Michele McKenna-Mahon; *anim check:* Pam Kleyman, Moira Murphy, Hughie Shevlin, Carol Anne Thornbury, Aoife Woodlock; *visual fx: fx anim dir:* Diann Landau, Peter Matheson, Stephen B. Moore; *fx anim sup (LA):* Tom Hush; *fx anim sup:* Dave Tidgwell; *fx anim:* Robert B. Cowan, Martine Finucane, Michael Gagné, Joseph Gilland, Bruce Heller, Noel P. Kieman, Brian McSweeney, Debora Middleton-Kupczyk, Janette Owens, Conor Thunder, Jeff Topping; *fx asst anim:* Leslie Aust, Joan Doyle, Natalie Garceau-Turner, Ray Hofstedt, Gillian Hunt-Cunningham, David Lyons, Rosanna Lyons, Rolando Mercado, Paul Morris, Mike Oliva, Debbie Pugh, Deirdre Reynolds, Tracey Meighan; *addit fx anim:* Mark Cumberton, Conánn Fitzpatrick, Leonard F.W. Green, Orla Madden, Dan Turner, Declan Walsh, Garrett Wren; *fx inbet:* Eric Alley, Conor Clancy, Colbert Fennelly, Bob Quinn, Jonathan Ridge; *col fx art:* Shirley "Sam" Mapes, Petula Masterson-O'Reilly, Joanne McSherry; *fx ph:* Daryl Carstensen; *fx admin asst sup:* Claire Gallagher; *fx technician:* Susan B. Keane; *computer anim dir:* Jan Carlée; *computer anim:* Greg Maguire; *computer technical dir:* Christine Zing Chang; *computer prod co-ord:* John Finnegan; *ed:* Fiona Trayler; *asst ed:* Gary Keleghan, Aran O'Reilly, Shannon Scudder-Pudleiner, Annette Stone; *prod des:* Dave Goetz; *art dir:* Don Moore; *poster artist:* John Alvin; *paste-up art:* Gillian Bolger; *rough break/inbet admin sup:* Anne Murray-O'Craobhach; *rough break/inbet:* Tom Higgins, Jan Naylor, Jane Anderson, David Coogan, David Corbally, Jackie Corley, Robert D'Arcy, Claudia Dickerson, John Dillon, Michael Dunne, Martha Furley, Sean Gallimore, Hilary Gough, David Groome, David Hancock, Ilan Hatukah, Joseph Haugh, Karl Hayes, Barry Iremonger, Sandra Keely, Carl Keenan, Kendra Lammas, Diana LeBost, Joseph Manifold Jr., Bob Miller, Majella Milne, Frank Molieri, Andrew Molloy, Sharon Morgan, Joe Mulligan, Dermot O'Connor, Gabrielle O'Regan, Tara O'Reilly, Scott Sackett, June Scannell, Rough Shanahan, Elizabeth Stoll, Frank Suarez, Sean Sullivan; *char clean-up admin sup:* Anne C. Murray, Jane McLoughlin, Olivia O'Mahony; *char clean-up:* Eileen Conway, Rosie Ahern, Tamara A. Iba, Fionnuala Balance, Jared Beckstrand, Tommy Brennan, Scott Brutz, Adam Burke, Annette Byrne-Morel, Michael Carey, Mick Cassidy, Mary Connors, Nollaig Crombie, Theresa Cullen, Finula Cunningham, Shana Curley, Rogerio DeGodoy, Peter Donnelly, Eileen Dunn, Ricardo Echevarria, Martin Fagan, Des Forde, Kevin Fraser, Michael Garry, Gerard Gogan, Catherine Gurry, Jason Halpin, Akemi Horiuchi, Joah Hagen-Jensen, Michael Cadwallader Jones, Chan Woo Jung, Linda Kellagher, Ed Klein, David Kuhn, Helen Lawlor, Patrice Leech, Lawrence Leichliter, Maria Malone, Craig R. Maras, Ciara McCabe, Margaret McKenna, James McLoughlin, Mark McLoughlin, Anne-Marie Mockler, Bernadette Moley, Mary B. Mulvihill, June Myung Nam (June Myung Park), Yoon Sook Nam (Suk Yun), Tracy Nelson, Siobhan O'Donnell, Dympna O'Halloran, Carol O'Mara, Terry O'Toole, Eileen Ridgeway, Julie Ryan, Neal Ryan, Richard Smitheman, Robert Sprathoff, Hugh Tattan, Tom Tobey, Adam Van Wyk, Sally Voorheis, John R. Walsh, Miri Yoon; *col stylist:* Majella Burns, Mary Cuthbert, Noirin Dunne, Donal Freeney, Berenice Keegan, Ann McCormick, Violet McKenna, Ailish Mullally, Lyn Mulvany, Suzanne O'Reilly; *lay co-ord:* Debbie J. Gold; *lay/back admin asst sup:* Caroline Lynch; *lay:* Eddie Gribbin, Fred Reilly, Amy Berenz, John Byrne, Mark T. Byrne, Dean De-Blois, Martin Hanley, Gary O'Neal, Fred Reilly, Jonathan Ridge, Ken Spirduso, Peter Yamasaki; *back:* Rick Bentham, Barry Atkinson, Phaedra Finnegan (Craig), Greg Gibbons, Miguel Gil, Carl Jones, Paul M. Kelly, Henry McGrane, Kevin McNamara, Rob Nason, Kenneth Slevin, Tom Roche, Kenneth Valentine Slevin, Chris Wren; *voices: Stanley:* Dom de Luise; *Gnorga:* Cloris Leachman; *Llort:* Charles Nelson Reily; *Alan:* Jonathan Pryce; *Hillary:* Hayley Mills; *Gus:* Philip Glasser; *Rosie:* Tawny "Sunshine" Glover; *Geriactric Pansy:* Neil Ross; *Boss:* Will Ryan; *Stuffy:* Pat Musick; *mus:* Robert Folk; *songs:* Barry Mann, Cynthia Weil, Norman Gimbel, Robert Folk; *addit orch:* Chris Boardman; *orch leader:* Audrey Collins; *orchestrator:* Robert Folk, Jon Kull, Peter Tomashek; *mus copyist:* Vic Fraser; *mus mix:* Joel Iwataki, Dennis S. Sands; *mus rec engineer:* Eoghan McCarron, Louise McCormick, Brian Masterson, Mary Kettle; *mus ed:*

Douglas M. Lackey; *scoring:* Bill Whelan; *music room:* Linda O'Carroll; *final check:* Mary Walsh, Mary Shevlin, Sandra Breslin, Anne-Marie Daly, Martina McCarron, Nina Phipps, Melanie Strickland; *paint check:* Nicholas Connolly, Catherine Dillon, Liam Hannan, Karen Hennessy, Carlyn Lawlor, Pearse Love, Sinéad Murray, Hugh O'Connor, Susan O'Loughlin, Eilish Whelan; *i&p:* Mary Gavin, Jacqueline Hooks, Karin Stover, Linda Bell, Sharon Blake, Mary Boylan, Christine Byrne, Mark C. Byrne, Michael Carroll, Yvonne Carthy, Kevin Condron, Alan Dalton, Karen Dwyer, Greg Fulton, Fiona Hogan, Marcia Watanabe; *paint lab mix & match:* Alan Boon, Kevin Hand, Tony Harris, Eric Stover; *paint lab filterization:* Éoin Cullen; *cel paint:* Éimear Clonan, Niamh McClean, Ann May, Shane McCormack, Ian McLoughlin, Yvonne McSweeney, Kate Meredith-Delaney, Dympna Murray, Betty O'Shea, Antoinette Rafter, Cormac Slevin; *paint lab sup:* Brenda McGuirk; *scene plan:* Maureen Buggy, Gerard Carty, Vincent Clarke, Séan Dempsey; *mark-up:* Maria Farrell, Louise Cleary, Tom English, David Hogan, Patricia Gordan; *blue sketch:* Linda Fitzpatrick, Sorcha Ni Chuimin; *line test:* Ty Elliott, Brendan Harris, Karen Heintz, Brian Kelly, David Nimitz, Collette O'Brien, Joanne Sugrue; *Xerox:* Michael Murray, Jackie Anderson, Billy Colgan, Pearse Cullinane, Philip Grogan, Frank D. Richards, Jennifer Scudder Trent, John Walsh, Kieron White; *Xerox check:* Anthony O'Brien, Gari Downey, Andy Fitzgerald, Shane Fitzsimons, Stuart Johnstone, Michael Maher, Alan Mongey, Paul Roy; *ph:* Emmet Doyle, Paddy Duffy, Gary Hall, Fiona Mackle, Jeannette Maher-Manifold, John O'Flaherty, Peadár O'Reilly; *apprentice ph:* Keith Murray, Derek Reid; *neg cutter:* Colin Ives; *col timer:* John Stanborough; *cel service:* Brian Forsythe, Anita Ryan; *overseas quality controller (Hungary):* Lucy Melia; *overseas co-ord (Hungary):* Colum Slevin; *prod ph sup:* Ciavàn Morris, Eric Ryan; *sd:* Brian Masterson; *foley mix:* Bruce Bell, Greg Orloff; *foley art:* Ellen Heuer, Dan O'Connell, Alicia Stevenson; *foley recordist:* Nerses Gezalyan; *Skywalker Sound: stage engineer:* John Brunnick; *recordist:* Brion Paccassi; *machine operators:* Jesse K-D. Dodd, Bob Hile, Robin Johnston, David José, Patricio A. Libenson; *dial ed:* Jim Fleming, Thomas V. "Nicky" Moss, Gerard Phillips; *dial engineer:* Warren Kleiman, Tom Mgrdichian, Jackson Schwartz; *sd ed:* John K. Carr, Dan Molina, Gretchen Thoma; *sd re-rec mix:* Gregg Landaker, Steve Maslow; *sd engineer:* Marco Streccioni; *post-prod sup:* Helene Blitz; *asso prod:* Russell Boland; *prod mgr:* Gerry Shirren; *prod sup:* Cathy Goldman, Olga Tarin-Craig; *asst prod sup:* Susan Vanderhorst; *asst dir:* Moya Mackle, Nuala O'Toole; *exec asst (Ireland):* Fionnuala Carpendale; *studio exec (Ireland):* Andrew Fitzpatrick; *studio exec (USA):* George Carrick; *col:* Metrocolor. *sd:* Dolby stereo. 117 min. • Stanley Sweetheart, a friendly troll with a magic green thumb, grows one flower too many for the Queen whose laws require all Trolls to act meanly. Banished to a Central Park cave, he beautifies it and befriends two neglected children, teaching them to believe in themselves. Also known as *Stanley's Magic Garden/ The Magic Garden of Stanley Sweetheart.*

6648. Trolley Ahoy (*Rainbow Parade*) 3 July 1936; *p.c.:* Van Beuren for RKO; *dir:* Burt Gillett; *sets:* Art Bartsch, Eddi Bowlds; *voice:* Elsa Janssen; *mus:* Winston Sharples; *col:* Tech. *sd:* RCA. 7 min. • Fontaine Fox's "Toonerville Folks" characters; Mr. Bang bets Skipper $10 to get him in the trolley in time to catch the train.

6649. Trolley Troubles (*Oswald the Lucky Rabbit*) 5 Sept. 1927; *p.c.:* Winkler for Univ; *dir:* Walt Disney; *anim:* Ub Iwerks, Hugh Harman, Isadore Freleng, Rollin C. Hamilton, Ben Clopton, Norman Blackburn; *i&p:* Les Clark; *ph:* Mike Marcus; b&w. sil. 5 min. sd reissue: 23 Nov. 1931. • Oswald is skipper of a little trolley on a wild ride over the mountains.

6650. Trombone Trouble (*Donald Duck*) 18 Feb. 1944; *p.c.:* Walt Disney prods for RKO; *dir:* Jack King; *asst dir:* Esther Newell; *story:* Carl Barks, Jack Hannah; *anim:* Paul Allen, Les Clark, Jerry Hathcock, Hal King, Charles A. Nichols, Judge Whitaker, Marvin Woodward; *lay:* Bill Herwig; *voices:* Billy Bletcher, John McLeish, Clarence Nash; *mus:* Paul J. Smith; *col:* Tech. *sd:* RCA. 7 min. • The Gods give Donald the power to put a stop to Pete's trombone playing ... but he abuses the privilege.

6651. Tron 9 July 1982; *p.c.:* Walt Disney/Lisberger-Kushner; *back plate ph:* Dave Iwerks, Bernie Gagliano, Gene Larmon; *anim. compositing ph:* Jim Pickel, Don Baker, Glenn Campbell, Neil Viker, John Aardal, Dana Ross, Brandy Whittington, Annie McEveety, Kieran Mulgrew, Dick Kendall, Douglas Eby, George Epperson, Paul Wainess; *fx anim:* Lee Dyer, John Van Vliet, John Norton, Barry Cook, Michael Wolf, Chris Casady, Gail Finkeldei, Darrell Rooney; *airbrush:* Greg Battes, Andy Atkins,

William Arance, James Walter Shaw; *sample art sup:* Stephanie Burt; *international cel co-ord:* Paulette Woods, Julian Pena, Paul Hernandez, Peter Aries; *i&p:* Ann Marie Sorensen, Cathy Crum, Ronnie Prinz, Alison Dicecio, Lisa Adams, Flavia Mitman, Priscilla Alvarez, Elaine Robinson; *computer fx:* Richard Taylor; *computer image choreo:* Bill Kroyer, Jerry W. Rees; *Magi Synthavision images : technology concepts:* Phillip Mittelman, *technical sup:* Larry Elin Popielinski, *scene programmers:* Nancy Hunter Campi, Christian Wedge, *technologists:* Martin O. Cohen, Herbert Steinberg, Eugene Troubetzkoy, Kenneth Perlin, *prod:* John Beach, Tom Bisogno; *Information International computer images: scene programmers:* Craig W. Reynolds, William Dugan Jr., Larry Malone, Jeremy Schwartz, Mal McMillan, *object digitizing:* Art Durinski, *computer prod co-ord:* Lynn Wilkinson; *transition to electronic world/main title:* Robert Abel & Associates, *des sup:* Kenny Mirman, *systems programmers:* Frank Vitz, Bill Kovacs, Richard Baily, Tim McGovern, *systems sup.:* Robert Abel; *digital fx/computer images for "Tron" formation and the "BIT":* Digital Effects Inc.: *systems sup.:* Judson Rosebush, *computer prod sup:* Jeffrey Kleiser, *computer anim:* Donald Leich, Gene Miller; *ed:* Jeff Gourson; *prod des:* Dean Edward Mitzner; *art dir:* John Mansbridge, Al Roelofs; *electronic conceptual des:* Jean "Moebius" Giraud, Richard Taylor; *conceptual art: electronic world:* Syd Mead, Jean "Moebius" Giraud, Peter Lloyd; *computer systems/software development:* Dave Inglish, Mark Kimball, Dave Barnett, Marty Prager, Bill Tondreau, Cinetron; *mus synthesizer performance & processing:* Wendy Carlos; performed by Los Angeles Orchestra; *col:* Tech. *sd:* Dolby stereo. 92 min. l/a/cgi. • Live-action science fiction: When assembling incriminating evidence on a powerful communications corporation, former employee Kevin Flynn tries to de-program the Master Control Program but is blasted into an electronic world populated by the alter-egos of people he is up against in the real world under the tyrannical rule of a warrior named Sark.

6652. Tropical Fish (*Paul Terry-Toon*) 14 May 1933; *p.c.:* Moser & Terry for Educational/Fox; *dir:* Frank Moser, Paul Terry; *mus:* Philip A. Scheib; b&w. *sd:* WE. 6 min. • No story available.

6653. Trouble (*Tom & Jerry*) 10 Oct. 1931; *p.c.:* Van Beuren for RKO; *dir:* John Foster, George Stallings; *mus:* Gene Rodemich; b&w. *sd:* RCA. 8 min. • Accident attorneys Tom and Jerry rush to the rescue when a man falls from the Empire State Building while trying to secure a dirigible.

6654. Trouble Bruin (*Loopy de Loop*) 17 Sept. 1964; *p.c.:* Hanna-Barbera for Colum; *prod/dir:* William Hanna, Joseph Barbera; *story dir:* Paul Sommer; *story:* Michael Maltese; *anim dir:* Charles A. Nichols; *anim:* Kenneth Muse, Jerry Hathcock; *lay:* Jack Huber; *back:* Robert Gentle; *ed:* Donald A. Douglas; *voices:* Daws Butler, Mel Blanc, Nancy Wible; *mus:* Hoyt Curtin; *titles:* Lawrence Gobel; *prod mgr:* Howard Hanson; *col:* East. *sd:* RCA. 6 min. • Loopy helps Braxton Bear control his insanely jealous temper over Emmy-Lou's succession of beaus.

6655. Trouble Date (*Jeepers & Creepers*) 11 Mar. 1960; *p.c.:* Para Cartoons; *dir:* Seymour Kneitel; *mus:* Winston Sharples; *ph:* Leonard McCormick; *prod mgr:* Abe Goodman; *col:* Tech. *sd:* RCA. 6 min. • Jeepers makes Creepers look like a hero to impress a girl. He joins the Marines only to later discover that she is already married.

6656. Trouble in Baghdad (*Luno*) June 1963; *p.c.:* TT for Fox; *ex prod:* Bill Weiss; *dir/anim:* Connie Rasinski; *story dir:* Tom Morrison; *story:* Larz Bourne; *sets:* Bill Focht, John Zago; *ed:* Jack MacConnell; *voices:* Norma MacMillan, Bob MacFadden; *mus:* Phil Scheib; *ph:* Ted Moskowitz, Joe Rasinski; *col:* DeLuxe. *sd:* RCA. 6 min. • Tim and Luno help out the imprisoned Ali Baba and bring the forty thieves to justice.

6657. Trouble Indemnity (*Mr. Magoo*) 14 Sept. 1950; *p.c.:* UPA for Colum; *ex prod:* Stephen Bosustow; *dir sup:* John Hubley; *dir:* Pete Burness; *story:* Al Smalley, Bill Scott, Phil Eastman; *anim:* Pat Matthews, Rudy Larriva, Willis Pyle, Bill Melendez, Grim Natwick; *lay:* Abe Liss; *back:* Herb Klynn, Jules Engel; *voices:* Jim Backus, Jerry Hausner; *mus:* Hoyt S. Curtin; *prod mgr:* Adrian Woolery; *col:* Tech. *sd:* RCA. 6½ min. • Magoo is conned into buying a large insurance policy. Thinking he's received a dog bite, he goes to collect a $10 claim, mistaking a building site for the Insurance Office.

6658. Truant Officer Donald (*Donald Duck*) 1 Aug. 1943; *p.c.:* Walt Disney prods for RKO; *dir:* Jack King; *asst dir:* Bob Newman; *story:* Harry Reeves, Carl Barks, Jack Hannah; *anim:* Paul Allen, James Armstrong, Theodore Bonnicksen, Walter Clinton, Hal King, Jack King, Edward Love,

Frank McSavage, Ray Patin, William N. Shull, Judge Whitaker; *fx:* Andrew Engman, Art Fitzpatrick, Lee Morehouse; *lay:* Bill Herwig; *voices:* Clarence Nash; *mus:* Leigh Harline, Paul J. Smith; *col:* Tech. *sd:* RCA. 7 min. *Academy Award nomination.* • Donald catches his nephews out of school. He corners them in a hut and smokes them out but they have the last laugh by pretending to have been roasted alive.

6659. Truant Student (*Cartune*) 5 Jan. 1959; *p.c.:* Walter Lantz prods for Univ; *dir:* Paul J. Smith; *story:* Homer Brightman; *anim:* Robert Bentley, Les Kline, Don Patterson; *sets:* Art Landy, Raymond Jacobs; *voices:* Daws Butler; *mus:* Clarence Wheeler; *prod mgr:* William E. Garity; *col:* Tech. *sd:* RCA. 6 min. • When Breezy forgets his school books, Windy chases after him with them and gets pursued by a truant officer, thinking he's playing hookey.

6660. The Truce Hurts (*Tom & Jerry*) 17 July 1948; *p.c.:* MGM; *dir:* William Hanna, Joseph Barbera; *anim:* Kenneth Muse, Ed Barge, Ray Patterson, Irven Spence; *lay:* Dick Bickenbach; *back:* Robert Gentle; *ed:* Fred MacAlpin; *voice:* Billy Bletcher; *mus:* Scott Bradley; *prod:* Fred Quimby; *col:* Tech. *sd:* WE. 7¹/₂ min. • Tom, Jerry and Spike sign a peace treaty which holds complications when they try to share a succulent steak.

6661. The Truck That Flew (*Puppetoon*) 6 Aug. 1943; *p.c.:* George Pal Studio for Para; *prod/dir:* George Pal; *story:* Dudley Morris; *char des:* Wah Chang; *col:* Tech. *sd:* WE. 9 min. • When the Sandman puts a small child to sleep, the boy drives his truck through the clouds.

6662. A Truckload of Trouble (*Terry-Toon*) 25 Oct. 1949; *p.c.:* TT for Fox; *dir:* Connie Rasinski; *story:* John Foster; *mus:* Philip A. Scheib; *col:* Tech. *sd:* RCA. 6 min. • A cat, dog and bird stow away in a moving van. When discovered, the driver makes them unload the furniture.

6663. True Boo (*Casper*) 24 Oct. 1952; *p.c.:* Famous for Para; *dir:* I. Sparber; *story:* Larz Bourne; *anim:* Steve Muffatti, Bill Hudson; *sets:* Robert Connavale; *voices:* Alan Shay, Jack Mercer; *mus:* Winston Sharples; *title song:* Mack David, Jerry Livingston; *ph:* Leonard McCormick; *prod mgr:* Seymour Shultz; *col:* Tech. *sd:* RCA. 7 min. • Casper poses as Santa for a poor boy who will obviously have no Christmas.

6664. The Truth About Mother Goose 28 Aug. 1957; *p.c.:* Walt Disney prods for BV; *dir:* Wolfgang Reitherman, Bill Justice; *story:* Bill Peet; *anim:* Cliff Nordberg, Eric Cleworth, Fred Hellmich, Dick Lucas, Kay Wright, Bill Keil, Ed Parks, Al Stetter; *fx:* Dan MacManus; *lay:* Xavier Atencio, Basil Davidovich, Dick Ung, Vance Gerry; *back:* Al Dempster, Eyvind Earle, Richard H. Thomas, Collin Campbell; *voices:* The Page Cavanaugh Trio, John Dehner, Kevin Corchran; *mus:* George Bruns; *songs:* Tom Adair, Bill Peet, George Bruns; *col:* Tech. *sd:* RCA. 14 min. *Academy Award nomination.* • The true stories behind some nursery rhymes.

6665. The Tuba Tooter (*Tom & Jerry*) 4 June 1932; *p.c.:* Van Beuren for RKO; *dir:* John Foster, George Stallings; *mus:* Gene Rodemich; b&w. *sd:* RCA. 5 min. • The whole town turns out to hear Schultz play the tuba in the German band. They march along and sing "Schultz Is Back Again."

6666. Tubby the Tuba (*Puppetoon*) 11 July 1947; *p.c.:* George Pal Studio for Para; *prod/dir:* George Pal; *sup:* George E. Jordan; *story:* Paul Tripp; *anim:* William King, Gene Warren; *sets:* Reginald Massie; *voice:* Victor Jory; *mus:* George Kleinsinger, Clarence Wheeler; *ph:* John S. Abbott; *col:* tech. *sd:* WE. 10 min. *Academy Award nomination.* • Tubby leaves the orchestra to search for a melody to play on his own.

6667. Tugboat Granny (*Merrie Melodies*) 23 June 1956; *p.c.:* WB; *dir:* Friz Freleng; *story:* Warren Foster; *anim:* Virgil Ross, Arthur Davis, Gerry Chiniquy; *lay:* Hawley Pratt; *back:* Irv Wyner; *ed:* Treg Brown; *voices:* Mel Blanc, June Foray; *mus:* Milt Franklyn; *prod mgr:* John W. Burton; *prod:* Edward Selzer; *col:* Tech. *sd:* Vit. 7 min. • Sylvester attempts to snare Tweety who's aboard a moving tugboat.

6668. Tugboat Mickey (*Mickey Mouse*) 26 Apr. 1940; *p.c.:* Walt Disney prods for RKO; *dir:* Clyde Geronimi; *asst dir:* Errol Gray; *story:* Otto Englander; *anim:* Edwin Aardal, James Armstrong, Johnny Cannon, Larry Clemmons, Rex Cox, Andrew Engman, Volus Jones, Hal King, Edward Love, Kenneth Muse, Ken Peterson, Grant Simmons, Cornett Wood; *lay:* Lloyd Harting; *voices:* John McLeish, George A. Johnson, Clarence Nash, Walt Disney; *mus:* Oliver Wallace; *col:* Tech. *sd:* RCA. 7 min. • Mickey, Donald and Goofy rush to get their tugboat ready to answer an S.O.S. call.

6669. Tulips Shall Grow (*Madcap Models*) 26 June 1942; *p.c.:* George Pal Studio for Para; *prod/dir:* George Pal; *story:* George Pal, Jack Miller, Cecil Beard; *anim:* Ray Harryhausen; *character des:* Wah Ming Chang; *mus:* William Eddison; *col:* Tech. *sd:* WE. 7¹/₂ min. • A little Dutch boy and girl's peace is destroyed by the invasion of Goose-Stepping robots. Anti-war theme.

6670. Tumble Down Town (*Aesop's Sound Fable*) 27 Jan. 1933; *p.c.:* Van Beuren for RKO; *dir:* John Foster, Harry Bailey; *mus:* Gene Rodemich; b&w. *sd:* RCA. 7 min. • No story available.

6671. Tumbleweed Greed (*Woody Woodpecker*) 1 June 1969; *p.c.:* Walter Lantz prods for Univ; *dir:* Paul J. Smith; *story:* Homer Brightman; *anim:* Les Kline, Al Coe; *sets:* Nino Carbe; *voices:* Dal McKennon, Grace Stafford; *mus:* Walter Greene; *prod mgr:* William E. Garity; *col:* Tech. *sd:* RCA. 6 min. • When Woody wins a vast amount of money and a car, he heads west and meets Buzz Buzzard who attempts to deprive him of both.

6672. Tummy Trouble 23 June 1989; *p.c.:* Walt Disney Pictures/Amblin for Buena Vista; *anim dir:* Rob Minkoff; *prod:* Don Hahn; *ex prod:* Steven Spielberg, Frank Marshall, Kathleen Kennedy; *story:* Kevin Harkey, Bill Kopp, Rob Minkoff, Mark Kausler, Patrick A. Ventura; *anim:* Mark Kausler, Tom Sito, Frans Vischer, Bruce W. Smith, Roger Chiasson, Larry White, Jacques Muller, Bob Scott, Carlos Baeza, James Baxter, Dale L. Baer, Joe Haidar, Chrystal Klabunde; *asst anim:* Brett Newton, Don Parmele, Francesca Allen, Jane M. Baer, Bronwen A. Barry, Susan I. Craig, Leticia Lichtwardt, Bruce Strock, George D. Sukara, Marianne Tucker; *fx anim:* Tom Hush, Kathleen Quaife-Hodge, Esther Barr, Mauro Maressa, Dave Bossert; *art dir:* Thom Enriquez; *lay:* Karen Keller, James Beihold, Lorenzo E. Martinez, Mark R. Wallace; *back:* Katherine Altieri, Greg Drolette, James Gallego, Jeff Richards, Richard Vander Wende; *ed:* Donald W. Ernst; *voices:* Roger Rabbit: Charles Fleischer; *Mom/Young Baby Herman:* April Winchell; *Adult Baby Herman:* Lou Hirsch; *Orderly:* Corey Burton; *Droopy Dog:* Richard Williams; *Jessica Rabbit:* Kathleen Turner; *mus:* James Horner; *i&p:* Karen Comella, Ann Sorensen; *anim check:* Annamarie Costa; *final check:* Madlyn Z. O'Neill; *scene plan:* Joe Jiuliano; *blue sketch:* Pat Sito; *visual fx:* Industrial Light & Magic, Scott Squires, Kimberly K. Nelson; *visual fx ed:* Michael Gleason; *prod mgr:* Ron Rocha; *prod co-ord:* Tanya T. Wilson; *l/a dir:* Frank Marshall; *col:* Metrocolor. *sd:* Dolby stereo. 7 min. • Roger Rabbit is put in charge of Baby Herman who promptly swallows a rattle. Roger rushes him to the hospital and is mistaken for the patient.

6673. The Tune 4 Sept. 1992; *p.c.:* Bill Plympton; *dir/anim:* Bill Plympton; *story:* Bill Plympton, P.C. Vey, Maureen McElheron; *art sup:* Jessica Wolk-Stanley; *art:* Jerilyn Mettlin, Lorna Munson, Beth O'Grady, Beatrice Schafroth, Leah Singer, Vincenza Zito; *voices: Del:* Daniel Neiden; *Didi:* Maureen McElheron; *Mayor/Mr. Mega/Mrs. Mega:* Marty Nelson; *Dot:* Emily Bindiger; *Wiseone/Surfer/Tango Dancer/Note:* Chris Hoffman; *Cabbie:* Jimmy Ceribello; *Houndog:* Ned Reynolds; *Bellhop:* Jeff Knight; *Surfer:* Jennifer Senko; *ed:* Merril Stern; *mus:* Maureen McElheron (guitar/bass: Hank Bones, guitar: Larry Campbell, Marc Ribot, saxophone: Tom Malone); *ph:* John Donnelly; *sd:* Phil Lee, John Marshall, Reilly Steele; *col:* *sd:* mono. 69 min. • A songwriter has just forty-seven minutes to come up with a hit for his boss, Mr. Mega, or else he will be fired.

6674. Tune Up and Sing (*Screen Songs*) 9 Mar. 1934; *p.c.:* The Fleischer Studio for Para; *prod:* Max Fleischer; *dir:* Dave Fleischer; *anim:* Myron Waldman, Thomas Johnson; *mus:* Sammy Timberg; *song:* Richard Rodgers, Lorenz Hart; *l/a:* Lanny Ross; b&w. *sd:* WE. 7 min. *l/a/anim.* • A romance between a gypsy girl and boy who are united via a "Magic Crystal." Their future sees hordes of kids wrecking their home ... they swiftly depart. Caricature of Maurice Chevalier.

6675. Tuning In (*Aesop's Film Fable*) 7 Nov. 1929; *p.c.:* Van Beuren for Pathé; *dir:* John Foster, Mannie Davis; *mus:* Carl Edouarde; b&w. *sd:* RCA. 7¹/₂ min. • Farmer Al Falfa's radio inspires him to stage a bullfight with his cow.

6676. Turkey Dinner (*Meany Miny Moe*) 30 Nov. 1936; *p.c.:* Univ; *prod/dir:* Walter Lantz; *story:* Walter Lantz, Victor McLeod; *anim:* Ray Abrams, Bill Mason, Dick Bickenbach; *mus:* Irving Actman, Frank Loesser; b&w. *sd:* WE. 8 min. • The monkey trio attempt to catch a turkey for Thanksgiving.

6677. The Turn-Tale Wolf *(Merrie Melodies)* 28 June 1952; *p.c.:* WB; *dir:* Robert McKimson; *story:* Tedd Pierce; *anim:* Phil de Lara, Charles McKimson, Herman Cohen, Rod Scribner; *lay:* Peter Alvarado; *back:* Richard H. Thomas; *ed:* Treg Brown; *voices:* Mel Blanc, Stan Freberg; *mus:* Carl Stalling; *prod mgr:* John W. Burton; *prod:* Edward Selzer; *col:* Tech. *sd:* Vit. 7 min. • B.B. Wolf puts his offspring right with the story of "The Three Little Pigs." In his version, the pigs victimize *him* for a bounty on his tail.

6678. Turning the Fables *(Noveltoon)* July 1960; *p.c.:* Para Cartoons; *dir:* Seymour Kneitel; *story:* Carl Meyer, Jack Mercer; *anim:* Irving Spector, Wm. B. Pattengill; *sets:* Robert Owen; *voices:* Jack Mercer; *mus:* Winston Sharples; *ph:* Leonard McCormick; *prod mgr:* Abe Goodman; *col:* Tech. *sd:* RCA. 6 min. • Tommy Tortoise sets out to find uranium with a Geiger counter with Moe Hare not far behind.

6679. Turtle Scoop *(Noveltoon)* Oct. 1961; *p.c.:* Para Cartoons; *dir:* Seymour Kneitel; *story:* Carl Meyer, Jack Mercer; *anim:* Nick Tafuri, George Germanetti, Sam Stimson; *sets:* Robert Little; *voices:* Bob MacFadden; *mus:* Winston Sharples; *ph:* Leonard McCormick; *prod mgr:* Abe Goodman; *col:* Tech. *sd:* RCA. 6 min. • The Tortoise and Hare are reporters vying for a scoop photograph of a rocket launch.

6680. Tusk Tusk *(Terry-Toon)* May 1960; *p.c.:* TT for Fox; *ex prod:* Bill Weiss; *dir:* Martin Taras; *story dir:* Tom Morrison; *story:* Bob Kuwahara; *anim:* Ed Donnelly, Mannie Davis, Johnny Gent; *sets:* John Zago; *voices:* Lionel Wilson; *mus:* Phil Schieb; *prod mgr:* Frank Schudde; *col:* Tech. *sd:* RCA. 6 min. • Sidney is worried because he has no tusks. He creates fake ones and is captured by ivory hunters.

6681. TV Fuddlehead *(Modern Madcap)* 16 Oct. 1959; *p.c.:* Para Cartoons; *dir:* Seymour Kneitel; *story:* Carl Meyer, Jack Mercer; *anim:* Tom Johnson, William Henning, Els Barthen; *sets:* Robert Owen; *voices:* Bob MacFadden, Jackson Beck, Corinne Orr; *mus:* Winston Sharples; *ph:* Leonard McCormick; *prod mgr:* Abe Goodman; *col:* Tech. *sd:* RCA. 6 min. • TV Fuddlehead lives, breathes and believes all television commercials.

6682. TV of Tomorrow 6 June 1953; *p.c.:* MGM; *dir:* Tex Avery; *story:* Heck Allen; *anim:* Michael Lah, Ray Patterson, Robert Bentley, Walter Clinton, Grant Simmons; *character des/lay:* Ed Benedict; *back:* John Didrik Johnsen; *ed:* Jim Faris; *voice:* Paul Frees; *mus:* Scott Bradley; *ph:* Jack Stevens; *prod:* Fred Quimby; *col:* Tech. *sd:* WE. 6 min. • A future look at television.

6683. TV or Not TV *(Noveltoon)* Mar. 1962; *p.c.:* Para Cartoons; *dir:* Seymour Kneitel; *mus:* Winston Sharples; *ph:* Leonard McCormick; *prod mgr:* Abe Goodman; *col:* Tech. *sd:* RCA. 6 min. • The TV cameras invade the home of a glamorous movie star until they are chased away by her jealous husband.

6684. Tweet and Lovely *(Merrie Melodies)* 18 July 1959; *p.c.:* WB; *dir:* Friz Freleng; *story:* Warren Foster; *anim:* Gerry Chiniquy, Art Davis, Virgil Ross; *lay:* Hawley Pratt; *back:* Tom O'Loughlin; *ed:* Treg Brown; *voices:* Mel Blanc; *mus:* Milt Franklyn; *prod mgr:* William Orcutt; *prod:* David H. DePatie; *col:* Tech. *sd:* Vit. 7 min. • Sylvester employs an inventor's office in order to get past a watchdog to Tweety.

6685. Tweet and Sour *(Looney Tunes)* 24 Mar. 1956; *p.c.:* WB; *dir:* Friz Freleng; *story:* Warren Foster; *anim:* Virgil Ross, Arthur Davis, Gerry Chiniquy; *lay:* Hawley Pratt; *back:* Irv Wyner; *ed:* Treg Brown; *voices:* Mel Blanc, June Foray; *mus:* Milt Franklyn; *prod mgr:* John W. Burton; *prod:* Edward Selzer; *col:* Tech. *sd:* Vit. 7 min. • Granny warns Sylvester that he'll end up as "violin strings" if anything happens to Tweety. He now has to keep a rival alley cat from getting to the bird.

6686. Tweet Dreams *(Looney Tunes)* 5 Dec. 1959; *p.c.:* WB; *dir:* Friz Freleng; *story:* Friz Freleng, Warren Foster; *anim:* Gerry Chiniquy, Art Davis, Virgil Ross; *lay:* Hawley Pratt; *back:* Tom O'Loughlin; *ed:* Treg Brown; *voices:* Mel Blanc, June Foray; *mus:* Milt Franklyn; *prod mgr:* William Orcutt; *prod:* David H. DePatie; *col:* Tech. *sd:* Vit. 6 min. seq: *Too Hop to Handle; Tweety's Circus; A Streetcat Named Sylvester; Sandy Claws; Gift Wrapped.* • Sylvester is on the psychiatrist's couch, discussing his obsession for the Tweety bird.

6687. Tweet Music *(Screen Song)* 9 Feb. 1951; *p.c.:* Famous for Para; *dir:* I. Sparber; *story:* Joe Stultz; *anim:* Al Eugster, George Rufle; *sets:* Robert Owen; *voice:* Michael Fitzmaurice, Cecil Roy; *mus:* Winston Sharples *ph:* Leonard McCormick; *prod mgr:* Sam Buchwald; *col:* Tech. *sd:* RCA. 7 min. • An insight into bird life as we await the birth of Mr. and Mrs. Cuckoo's offspring.

6688. Tweet, Tweet Tweety *(Looney Tunes)* 15 Dec. 1951; *p.c.:* WB; *dir:* I. Freleng; *story:* Warren Foster; *anim:* Manuel Perez, Ken Champin, Virgil Ross, Arthur Davis; *lay:* Hawley Pratt; *back:* Paul Julian; *ed:* Treg Brown; *voices:* Mel Blanc; *mus:* Carl Stalling; *prod mgr:* John W. Burton; *prod:* Edward Selzer; *col:* Tech. *sd:* Vit. 7 min. • The park ranger stops Sylvester from eating Tweety so the cat has to adopt more scientific methods.

6689. Tweet Zoo *(Merrie Melodies)* 12 Jan. 1957; *p.c.:* WB; *dir:* Friz Freleng; *story:* Warren Foster; *anim:* Art Davis, Virgil Ross, Gerry Chiniquy; *lay:* Hawley Pratt; *back:* Irv Wyner; *ed:* Treg Brown; *voices:* Mel Blanc; *mus:* Milt Franklyn; *prod mgr:* John W. Burton; *prod:* Edward Selzer; *col:* Tech. *sd:* Vit. 7 min. • Tweety and Sylvester are let loose in a zoo.

6690. Tweetie Pie *(Merrie Melodies)* 3 May 1947; *p.c.:* WB; *dir:* I. Freleng; *story:* Tedd Pierce, Michael Maltese, Robert Clampett; *anim:* Manuel Perez, Ken Champin, Virgil Ross, Gerry Chiniquy; *lay:* Hawley Pratt; *back:* Paul Julian; *ed:* Treg Brown; *voices:* Mel Blanc, Bea Benaderet; *mus:* Carl Stalling; *prod mgr:* John W. Burton; *prod:* Edward Selzer; *col:* Tech. *sd:* Vit. 7 min. *Academy Award.* • The lady of the house has a job in keeping Thomas the cat away from the canary.

6691. Tweety and the Beanstalk *(Merrie Melodies)* 23 Feb. 1957; *p.c.:* WB; *dir:* Friz Freleng; *story:* Warren Foster; *anim:* Virgil Ross, Gerry Chiniquy, Art Davis; *lay:* Hawley Pratt; *back:* Irv Wyner; *ed:* Treg Brown; *voices:* Mel Blanc, June Foray; *mus:* Milt Franklyn; *prod mgr:* John W. Burton; *prod:* Edward Selzer; *col:* Tech. *sd:* Vit. 7 min. • Sylvester scales a giant beanstalk to Giant Land where he encounters a giant Tweety bird!

6692. Tweety's Circus *(Merrie Melodies)* 4 June 1955; *p.c.:* WB; *dir:* I. Freleng; *story:* Warren Foster; *anim:* Arthur Davis, Gerry Chiniquy, Ted Bonnicksen; *lay:* Hawley Pratt; *back:* Irv Wyner; *voices:* Mel Blanc; *mus:* Milt Franklyn; *prod mgr:* John W. Burton; *prod:* Edward Selzer; *col:* Tech. *sd:* Vit. 7 min. • Sylvester's pursuit of Tweety in a circus is curtailed only by an elephant and a lion.

6693. Tweety's S.O.S. *(Merrie Melodies)* 22 Sept. 1951; *p.c.:* WB; *dir:* I. Freleng; *story:* Warren Foster; *anim:* Arthur Davis, Ken Champin, Virgil Ross; *lay:* Hawley Pratt; *back:* Paul Julian; *ed:* Treg Brown; *voices:* Mel Blanc, Bea Benaderet; *mus:* Carl Stalling; *prod mgr:* John W. Burton; *prod:* Edward Selzer; *col:* Tech. *sd:* Vit. 7 min. • Sylvester follows Tweety aboard an ocean cruise but his attempts to catch the bird are marred by Granny's protection.

6694. Twelve O'Clock and All Ain't Well *(Terry-Toon)* 25 July 1941; *p.c.:* TT for Fox; *dir:* Eddie Donnelly; *story:* John Foster; *mus:* Philip A. Scheib; b&w. *sd:* RCA. 6 min. • No story available.

6695. Twenty Legs Under the Sea *(Talkartoon)* 6 June 1931; *p.c.:* The Fleischer Studio for Para; *prod:* Max Fleischer; *dir:* Dave Fleischer; *mus:* Art Turkisher; b&w. *sd:* WE. 8 min. • While fishing, Bimbo is taken to the ocean bed where he meets the King of Fish.

6696. $21 a Day (once a month) *(Swing Symphony)* 1 Dec. 1941; *p.c.:* Walter Lantz prods for Univ; *dir:* Walter Lantz; *story:* Ben Hardaway, L. (Lowell) E. Elliot; *anim:* Alex Lovy, Frank Tipper; *sets:* Fred Brunish; *voices:* The Pied Pipers; *mus:* Darrell Calker; *song:* Felix Bernard, Ray Klages; *prod mgr:* George Hall; *col:* Tech. *sd:* WE. 7 min. • Toys in a department store sing a song about joining the Army.

6697. 2010 7 Dec. 1984; *p.c.:* MGM/UA for Univ; *anim sup:* Terry Wend, Garry Waller; *anim:* Annick Therrien, Samuel Recinos, Rebecca Petrulli, Wendie Fischer, Margaret Craig-Chang; *technical:* Peggy Regan, Richard Coleman, Eusebio Torres; *stop-motion:* Randall William Cook; *col:* Metrocolor. *sd:* Dolby stereo. Panavision. 116 min. *l/a.* • Science fiction follow-on from Stanley Kubrick's *2001* concerning an expedition to recover a missing American spacecraft.

6698. 20,000 Laughs Under the Sea *(Sullivan Cartoon Comedy)* 14 May 1917; *p.c.:* P.A. Powers for Univ; *dir:* Pat Sullivan; *anim:* Otto Messmer; b&w. sil. • No story available.

6699. Twilight on the Trail *(Screen Songs)* 25 Mar. 1937; *p.c.:* The Fleischer Studio for Para; *prod:* Max Fleischer; *dir:* Dave Fleischer; *anim:* Roland Crandall; *mus:* Sammy Timberg; *l/a:* The Westerners; b&w. *sd:* WE. 7 min. *l/a/anim.* • A boastful Texan brags about his experiences.

6700. The Twilight Zone — the Movie 24 June 1983; *seq:* "*It's a Good Life*": *dir:* Joe Dante; *cartoons: sup:* Sally Cruikshank; *anim:* Sam Cornell, Mark Kausler; *narrator:* Burgess Meredith; *col:* Tech. *sd.* 101 min. (entire film) *l/a.* • Live-action science-fiction adventure: A young boy uses his psychic powers to reduce the real world to an extension of a two-dimensional television cartoon.

6701. Twinkle, Twinkle Little Pink (*Pink Panther*) 30 June 1968; *p.c.:* Mirisch/Geoffrey/DFE for UA; *dir:* Hawley Pratt; *story:* John W. Dunn; *anim:* Manny Gould, Manny Perez, Warren Batchelder, Don Williams, Tom Ray, John Gibbs; *lay:* Dick Ung; *back:* Tom O'Loughlin; *ed:* Lee Gunther; *mus:* Walter Greene; *theme tune:* Henry Mancini; *ph:* John Burton Jr.; *prod sup:* Harry Love, Dave DeTiege; *col:* DeLuxe. *sd:* RCA. 6 min. • An astronomer thinks he's found a newly inhabited star when his telescope tracks in on the panther in his home.

6702. Twinkle Twinkle Little Telstar (*Astronut*) Nov. 1965; *p.c.:* TT for Fox; *ex prod:* Bill Weiss; *dir/anim:* Art Bartsch; *story dir:* Tom Morrison; *story:* Larz Bourne; *sets:* Bill Focht, John Zago; *ed:* Jack MacConnell; *voices:* Dayton Allen; *mus:* Jim Timmens; *ph:* Ted Moskowitz; *sd:* Elliot Grey; *col:* DeLuxe. *sd:* RCA. 5½ min. • Astro is in posession of a satellite that two villains are trying to steal.

6703. Twinkletoes Gets the Bird (*Animated Antics*) 14 Mar. 1941; *p.c.:* The Fleischer Studio for Para; *prod:* Max Fleischer; *dir:* Dave Fleischer; *story:* Bill Turner; *anim:* David Tendlar, Thomas Golden; *mus:* Sammy Timberg; *ph:* Charles Schettler; *prod sup:* Sam Buchwald, Isidore Sparber; *b&w. sd:* WE. 6 min. • Twinkletoes takes a parrot to the zoo.

6704. Twinkletoes in Hat Stuff (*Animated Antics*) 29 Aug. 1941; *p.c.:* The Fleischer Studio for Para; *prod:* Max Fleischer; *dir:* Dave Fleischer; *story:* Carl Meyer; *anim:* Myron Waldman, Sam Stimson; *mus:* Sammy Timberg; *ph:* Charles Schettler; *prod sup:* Sam Buchwald, Isidore Sparber; *b&w. sd:* WE. 6 min. • The pigeon tries to deliver a magician's case.

6705. Twinkletoes — Where He Goes, Nobody Knows (*Animated Antics*) 27 June 1941; *p.c.:* The Fleischer Studio for Para; *prod:* Max Fleischer; *dir:* Dave Fleischer; *story:* Cal Howard; *anim:* David Tendlar, Steve Muffatti; *voices:* Jack Mercer; *mus:* Sammy Timberg; *ph:* Charles Schettler; *prod sup:* Sam Buchwald, Isidore Sparber; *b&w. sd:* WE. 6 min. • The Coo-Coo pigeon is called upon to deliver a package containing a bomb.

6706. Twins 1975; *dir/anim:* Barrie Nelson; *col: sd.* • No story available.

6707. The Twisker Pitcher (*Popeye*) 21 May 1937; *p.c.:* The Fleischer Studio for Para; *prod:* Max Fleischer; *dir:* Dave Fleischer; *anim:* Seymour Kneitel, Abner Matthews; *voices:* Jack Mercer, Mae Questel, Gus Wickie, Lou Fleischer; *mus:* Sammy Timberg; *b&w. sd:* WE. 7 min. • Popeye's Pirates match Bluto's Bears in a no-holds barred game of baseball.

6708. The Two-Alarm Fire (*Popeye*) 26 Oct. 1934; *p.c.:* The Fleischer Studio for Para; *prod:* Max Fleischer; *dir:* Dave Fleischer; *anim:* Willard Bowsky, Nicholas Tafuri; *voices:* William A. Costello, Mae Questel, Charles Carver; *mus:* Sammy Timberg; *b&w. sd:* WE. 7 min. • Firemen Popeye and Bluto rival for the honor of rescuing Olive from a burning building.

6709. Two by Two (*Modern Madcap*) Dec. 1965; *p.c.:* Para Cartoons; *dir/story:* Howard Post; *anim:* Al Eugster; *sets:* Robert Little; *mus:* Winston Sharples; *ph:* Leonard McCormick; *prod mgr:* Abe Goodman; *col:* Tech. *sd:* RCA. 6 min. • Quacky Whack, a duck, tries to find a mate to get him on Noah's Ark.

6710. Two Cats and a Bird (*Pen & Ink Vaudeville*) 10 Mar. 1925; *p.c.:* Hurd prods for Educational; *anim:* Earl Hurd; *b&w. sil.* 5 min. • "Props" is called upon to feed "Two cats and a bird" which turn out to be lions and an ostrich

6711. Two Chips and a Miss (*Chip 'n' Dale*) 29 Feb. 1952; *p.c.:* Walt Disney prods for RKO; *dir:* Jack Hannah; *story:* Nick George, Bill Berg; *anim:* Bill Justice, George Kreisl, Volus Jones; *fx:* Blaine Gibson; *lay:* Yale Gracey; *back:* Ray Huffine; *voices:* Jud Conlon, Mac MacLean, Helen Seibert, Peggy Clark; *mus:* Joseph S. Dubin; *songs:* Jerry Livingston, Mack David, Madeline Hyde, Francis Henry; *col:* Tech. *sd:* RCA. 7 min. • Both Chips have a secret rendezvous with a night club singer named Clarice.

6712. Two Crows from Tacos (*Merrie Melodies*) 24 Nov. 1956; *p.c.:* WB; *dir:* Friz Freleng; *story:* Tedd Pierce; *anim:* Virgil Ross, Arthur Davis; *lay:* Hawley Pratt; *back:* Irv Wyner; *ed:* Treg Brown; *voices:* Tom Holland, Don Diamond; *mus:* Carl Stalling; *prod mgr:* John W. Burton; *prod:* Edward Selzer; *col:* Tech. *sd:* Vit. 7 min. • Two Mexican crows try to catch an elusive grasshopper. Reworking of *Hop, Skip and a Chump*.

6713. Two Faced Wolf (*Loopy de Loop*) 6 Apr. 1961; *p.c.:* Hanna-Barbera for Colum; *prod/dir:* William Hanna, Joseph Barbera; *story dir:* Dan Gordon; *story:* Warren Foster; *anim dir:* Charles A. Nichols; *anim:* George Nicholas; *lay:* Dick Bickenbach; *back:* Robert Gentle; *ed:* Joseph Ruby; *voices:* Daws Butler, Hal Smith; *mus:* Hoyt Curtin; *titles:* Lawrence Gobel; *prod mgr:* Howard Hanson; *col:* East. *sd:* RCA. 6½ min. • Loopy has an encounter with Dr. Jekyll and Mr. Hyde.

6714. Two for the Record 23 Apr. 1954; *p.c.:* Walt Disney prods for BV; *dir:* Jack Kinney; *col:* Tech. *sd:* RCA. Seq: *All the Cats Join In; After You've Gone.* • See: *Make Mine Music*

6715. Two for the Zoo (*Gabby*) 14 Feb. 1941; *p.c.:* The Fleischer Studio for Para; *prod:* Max Fleischer; *dir:* Dave Fleischer; *story/voices:* Pinto Colvig; *anim:* James Culhane, Alfred Eugster; *mus:* Sammy Timberg; *prod sup:* Sam Buchwald, Isidore Sparber; *col:* Tech. *sd:* WE. 6 min. • Gabby insists on delivering a kangaroo to the zoo.

6716. Two Gophers from Texas (*Merrie Melodies*) 17 Jan. 1948; *p.c.:* WB; *dir:* Arthur Davis; *story:* Lloyd Turner, William Scott; *anim:* Emery Hawkins, Basil Davidovich, J.C. Melendez, Don Williams; *lay:* Don Smith; *back:* Philip de Guard; *ed:* Treg Brown; *voices:* Mel Blanc, Stan Freberg; *mus:* Carl Stalling; *prod mgr:* John W. Burton; *prod:* Edward Selzer *col:* Ciné. *sd:* Vit. 7 min. • A Shakespearean dog, dissatisfied with his diet, craves the nourishment of raw food.

6717. Two-Gun Goofy (*Goofy*) 16 May 1952; *p.c.:* Walt Disney prods for RKO; *dir:* Jack Kinney; *story:* Dick Kinney, Brice Mack; *anim:* John Sibley, Wolfgang Reitherman, Ed Aardal, Hugh Fraser, George Nicholas, Cliff Nordberg, Harvey Toombs; *fx:* Dan MacManus; *lay:* Al Zinnen; *back:* Dick Anthony, Ralph Hulett; *voices:* Pinto Colvig, Billy Bletcher, Lucille Williams, Dick Kinney, Brice Mack, James MacDonald; *mus:* Paul Smith; *col:* Tech. *sd:* RCA. 7 min. • Cowpoke Goofy unwittingly thwarts Pete's stagecoach holdup and is appointed sheriff.

6718. Two-Gun Mickey (*Mickey Mouse*) 25 Dec. 1934; *p.c.:* Walt Disney prods for UA; *dir:* Ben Sharpsteen; *anim:* Paul Allen, Ugo d'Orsi, Earl Hurd, Eric Larson, Frank Oreb, Woolfgang Reitherman, Archie Robin, Leonard Sebring, Ed Smith, Paul J. Smith, Don Towsley, Cy Young; *asst anim:* Arthur Babbitt, George Drake, Nick George, Jack Kinney, Fred Moore, Louis Schmitt, Roy Williams; *voices:* Billy Bletcher, Marcellite Garner, Pinto Colvig, Walt Disney; *mus:* Leigh Harline; *b&w. sd:* RCA. 7 min. • Western bandit Pete and his gang rob Minnie and Cowboy Mickey dashes to the rescue.

6719. Two Gun Rusty (*Madcap Models*) 1 Dec. 1944; *p.c.:* George Pal Studio for Para; *prod/dir:* George Pal; *mus:* Maurice de Packh; *col:* Tech. *sd:* WE. 7½ min. • A small boy dreams he's a western hero.

6720. Two Guys from Texas 1948; *p.c.:* WB; *Seq dir:* I. Freleng; *voice:* Mel Blanc; *col:* Tech. *sd:* Vit. 86 min. (seq) 7 min. • Live-action feature starring Dennis Morgan whose singing takes the girls away from Jack Carson. The cartoon segment has Carson as a shepherd having his sheep lured away by a wolf (Morgan). Bugs Bunny advises Carson to don a similar attire to get them back.

6721. The Two-Headed Giant (*Terry-Toon*) 11 Aug. 1939; *p.c.:* TT for Fox; *dir:* Connie Rasinski; *story:* John Foster; *mus:* Philip A. Scheib; *col:* Tech. *sd:* RCA. 7 min. • The ogre is told by his pet vulture of Jack's quest to kill all giants and goes to do battle.

6722. Two Jumps and a Chump (*Tijuana Toads*) 28 Mar. 1971; *p.c.:* Mirisch/DFE for UA; *dir:* Gerry Chiniquy; *story:* John W. Dunn; *anim:* Ken Muse, Manny Gould, Don Williams, Manny Perez; *lay:* Dick Ung; *back:* Richard H. Thomas; *ed:* Lee Gunther; *voices:* Don Diamond, Tom Holland, Larry D. Mann; *mus:* Doug Goodwin; *ph:* John Burton Jr.; *prod sup:* Jim Foss, Harry Love; *col:* DeLuxe. *sd:* RCA. 6 min. • The toads seek refuge from the crane in the city dump.

6723. Two Lazy Crows (*Color Rhapsody*) 26 Nov. 1936; Cartoon Films Ltd/Charles Mintz prods for Colum; *prod/dir:* Ub Iwerks; *voices:* Billy Bletcher, Dave Weber, Bernice Hansel; *mus:* Joe de Nat; *col:* Tech. *sd:* RCA. 7 min. • Two indolent crows go hungry when Winter arrives and talk a squirrel into letting them stay with him and his wife.

6724. Two Little Indians (*Tom & Jerry*) 17 Oct. 1953; *p.c.*: MGM; *dir*: William Hanna, Joseph Barbera; *anim*: Ray Patterson, Kenneth Muse, Irven Spence, Ed Barge; *lay*: Dick Bickenbach; *back*: Robert Gentle; *ed*: Jim Faris; *mus*: Scott Bradley; *ph*: Jack Stevens; *prod*: Fred Quimby; *col*: Tech. *sd*: WE. 7 min. • Scoutmaster Jerry takes two orphan Indians on a hike which ends in a western-style shootout with Tom.

6725. Two Little Lambs (*Oswald*) 11 Mar 1935; *p.c.*: Univ; *prod/dir*: Walter Lantz; *story*: Victor McLeod; *anim*: Manuel Moreno, George Grand-pré, Lester Kline, (La)Verne Harding, Fred Kopietz; *mus*: James Dietrich; b&w. *sd*: WE. 7½ min. • Oswald enters in an air race. Two lambs run off with his plane but he still wins the trophy.

6726. Two Little Pups (*Happy Harmonies*) 4 Apr. 1936; *p.c.*: MGM; *prod/dir*: Hugh Harman, Rudolf Ising; *mus*: Scott Bradley; *col*: Tech. *sd*: RCA. 7 min. • Ruff and Reddy, two pups, run afoul of a bad-tempered hen while playing in the farmyard.

6727. The Two Mouseketeers (*Tom & Jerry*) 15 Mar. 1952; *p.c.*: MGM; *dir*: William Hanna, Joseph Barbera; *anim*: Ed Barge, Kenneth Muse, Irven Spence; *lay*: Dick Bickenbach; *back*: Robert Gentle; *ed*: Jim Faris; *voice*: Francoise Brun-Cottan; *chorus*: The King's Men; *mus*: Scott Bradley; *prod*: Fred Quimby; *col*: Tech. *sd*: WE. 7 min. *Academy Award*. • Tom has to guard the banquet against the King's Mouseketeers.

6728. Two Poor Fish (*Pen & Ink Vaudeville*) 29 May 1925; *p.c.*: Hurd prods for Educational; *anim*: Earl Hurd; b&w. *sil*. 10 min. • "Props" has to catch a fish for the trained seal act, ending up on a floating target. The seal catches a bomb that explodes, showering them both with fish.

6729. Two Scent's Worth (*Merrie Melodies*) 15 Oct. 1955; *p.c.*: WB; *dir/story*: Charles M. Jones; *anim*: Keith Darling, Abe Levitow, Richard Thompson, Ken Harris; *lay*: Robert Gribbroek; *back*: Philip de Guard; *ed*: Treg Brown; *voices*: Mel Blanc; *mus*: Milt Franklyn; *prod mgr*: John W. Burton; *prod*: Edward Selzer; *col*: Tech. *sd*: Vit. 7 min. • A bank robber disguises a female cat as a skunk in order to evacuate the bank. After the crime, the cat encounters Pepè le Pew, the amorous skunk.

6730. The Two Slick Traders (*Aesop's Film Fable*) 12 Aug. 1922; *p.c.*: Fables Pictures Inc for Pathé; *dir*: Paul Terry; b&w. *sil*. 5 min. • Farmer Al gets trouble from his farm animals and is about to trade them all in for Abie's flivver. Moral: "A fair exchange is no robbery."

6731. 2000 B.C. (*Paul Terry-Toon*) 14 June 1931; *p.c.*: Terry, Moser & Coffman for Educational/Fox; *dir*: Frank Moser, Paul Terry; *anim*: Vladimir Tytla; *mus*: Philip A. Scheib; b&w. *sd*: WE. 6 min. • Life and love in prehistoric times.

6732. The 2000 Year Old Man 1974; *p.c.*: Crossbow-Acre prods for Col/EMI/WB; *prod/dir/lay/character des*: Leo Salkin; *created/voices*: Carl Reiner, Mel Brooks; *anim dir*: Dale Case; *anim*: Bill Littlejohn, Brad Case, Bob Bachman, John Kimball, Frank Andrina, Dale Case; *sets*: Mary Cain, Lorraine Andrina; *ed*: Horta-Mahana; *mus*: Mort Garson; *ph*: Ted Bemiller, Cine Camera, Fred Craig; *prod sup*: Marlene Robinson, Sam Pal; *col*: DeLuxe. *sd*. 24 min. • Brooks and Reiner's improvizations on an aged man being interviewed on how things were when he was young compared to today.

6733. Two Ton Baby Sitter (*Terry-Toon*) 4 Sept. 1960; *p.c.*: TT for Fox; *ex prod*: Bill Weiss; *dir*: Dave Tendlar; *story dir*: Tom Morrison; *story*: Bob Kuwahara; *anim*: Ed Donnelly, Mannie Davis, Larry Silverman, Cosmo Anzilotti; *sets*: Bill Hilliker; *voices*: Lionel Wilson; *mus*: Philip Scheib; *prod mgr*: Frank Schudde; *col*: Tech. *sd*: RCA. 7 min. • Sidney starts a babysitting business and loses a pair of kookaburra birds through sneezing.

6734. The Two Trappers (*Aesop's Film Fable*) 1 Dec. 1922; *p.c.*: Fables Pictures Inc for Pathé; *dir*: Paul Terry; b&w. *sil*. 5 min. • Farmer Al Falfa disdains from making use of the cat's help in charming birds.

6735. Two Weeks' Vacation (*Goofy*) 31 Oct. 1952; *p.c.*: Walt Disney prods for RKO; *dir*: Jack Kinney; *story*: Al Bertino; *anim*: George Nicholas, Ed Aardal, Hugh Fraser, John Sibley; *fx*: Dan MacManus; *lay*: Al Zinnen; *back*: Art Riley; *voices*: Alan Reed, Pinto Colvig; *mus*: Oliver Wallace; *col*: Tech. *sd*: RCA. 6 min. • Geef suffers many trials and tribulations on a motoring holiday.

6736. Two's a Crowd (*Looney Tunes*) 30 Dec. 1950; *p.c.*: WB; *dir*: Charles M. Jones; *story*: Michael Maltese; *anim*: Ken Harris, Phil Monroe, Ben Washam, Lloyd Vaughan, Emery Hawkins; *sets*: Peter Alvarado; *ed*: Treg Brown; *voices*: Mel Blanc, Bea Benaderet; *mus*: Carl Stalling; *prod mgr*: John W. Burton; *prod*: Edward Selzer; *col*: Tech. *sd*: Vit. 7 min. • Claude Cat's happy home is disrupted with the arrival of a noisy puppy dog.

6737. Two's Company 1910; *p.c.*: Biograph for Thomas A. Edison Inc.; *anim*: Raoul Barré, William C. Nolan; b&w. *sil*. • No story available.

6738. The Ugly Dino (*Stoneage*) 24 May 1940; *p.c.*: The Fleischer Studio for Para; *prod*: Max Fleischer; *dir*: Dave Fleischer; *story*: George Manuell; *anim*: Bill Nolan, George Germanetti; *ed*: Kitty Pfister; *mus*: Sammy Timberg; *prod sup*: Sam Buchwald, Isidore Sparber; b&w. *sd*: WE. 7 min. • "The Ugly Duckling" story with a dinosaur.

6739. The Ugly Duckling (*Aesop's Film Fable*) 19 Sept. 1925; *p.c.*: Fables Pictures Inc for Pathé; *dir*: Paul Terry; b&w. *sil*. 10 min. • An outcast black duck from a brood of chicks gains favor after rescuing the others from a cat.

6740. The Ugly Duckling (*Silly Symphony*) 12 Dec. 1931; *p.c.*: Walt Disney prods for Colum; *dir*: Wilfred Jackson; *anim*: Johnny Cannon, Les Clark, Gilles de Tremaudan, Clyde Geronimi, David D. Hand, Albert Hurter, Richard Lundy, Frank Tipper, Rudy Zamora; *asst anim*: Chuck Couch, Jack Cutting, Joseph d'Igalo, Hardie Gramatky, Harry Reeves, Andrew Hutchinson, Cecil Surry; *mus*: Bert Lewis; b&w. *sd*: PCP. 6½ min. • After a mother hen disowns a duckling, a cyclone carries her and her chicks into a river and the duckling saves them.

6741. The Ugly Duckling 7 Apr. 1939; *p.c.*: Walt Disney prods for RKO; *dir*: Jack Cutting; *story*: George Stallings; *anim*: Jack Hannah, Milton Kahl, Lynn Karp, Eric Larson, Hamilton S. Luske, Stan Quackenbush, Archie Robin, Paul Satterfield, Riley Thomson; *lay*: David Hilberman; *back*: Gustaf Tenggren; *chorus*: Jerry Phillips, Marie Arbuckle, Marta Nielsen, Barbara Whitson; *mus*: Albert Hay Malotte; *col*: Tech. *sd*: RCA. 8½ min. *Academy Award*. • Mother Duck's new brood brings forth an ugly white one who becomes an outcast until he later discovers he is a swan and joins his own kind.

6742. The Unbearable Bear (*Merrie Melodies*) 17 Apr. 1943; *p.c.*: Leon Schlesinger prods for WB; *dir*: Charles M. Jones; *story*: Michael Maltese; *anim*: Robert Cannon; *lay*: John McGrew; *back*: Eugene Fleury; *ed*: Treg Brown; *voices*: Mel Blanc, Marjorie Tarlton, June Foray; *mus*: Carl W. Stalling; *ph*: John W. Burton; *prod sup*: Henry Binder, Raymond G. Katz; *col*: Tech. *sd*: Vit. 7 min. • A fox burgles the home of a police officer bear and is hampered by a talkative mouse who believes the fox to be Robin Hood.

6743. The Unbearable Salesman (*Woody Woodpecker*) 3 June 1957; *p.c.*: Walter Lantz prods for Univ; *dir*: Paul J. Smith; *story*: Dick Kinney; *anim*: Robert Bentley, Les Kline; *sets*: Art Landy; *voices*: Daws Butler, June Foray, Grace Stafford; *mus*: Clarence Wheeler; *prod mgr*: William E. Garity; *col*: Tech. *sd*: RCA. 6 min. • Woody tries to sell gadgets to a hibernating bear.

6744. Uncle Donald's Ants (*Donald Duck*) 18 July 1952; *p.c.*: Walt Disney prods for RKO; *dir*: Jack Hannah; *story*: Al Bertino, Nick George; *anim*: Volus Jones, Bill Justice, George Kreisl, George Nicholas, John Sibley; *fx*: Dan MacManus; *lay*: Yale Gracey; *back*: Claude Coats; *voices*: Clarence Nash, Pinto Colvig; *mus*: Joseph S. Dubin; *col*: Tech. *sd*: RCA. 7 min. • Donald's home is overrun with ants intent of stealing a jar of maple syrup.

6745. Uncle Joey (*Terry-Toon*) 13 Apr. 1941; *p.c.*: TT for Fox; *dir*: Mannie Davis; *story*: John Foster; *mus*: Philip A. Scheib; *col*: Tech. *sd*: RCA. 7 min. • A "Joe E. Brown" mouse takes the smaller mice swimming then saves them from a cat.

6746. Uncle Joey Comes to Town (*Terry-Toon*) 19 Sept. 1941; *p.c.*: TT for Fox; *dir*: Mannie Davis; *story*: John Foster; *mus*: Philip A. Scheib; b&w. *sd*: RCA. 7 min. • Uncle Joey and the other mice have a baseball game on the dining table of a mansion.

6747. Uncle Tom's Bungalow (*Merrie Melodies*) 5 June 1937; *p.c.*: Leon Schlesinger prods for WB; *dir*: Fred Avery; *story*: Robert Clampett; *anim*: Virgil Ross, Sid Sutherland, Robert Clampett; *ed*: Tregoweth E. Brown; *voices*: Billy Bletcher, Mel Blanc, Kenneth Spencer, Ted Pierce, Fred Avery; *mus*: Carl W. Stalling; *prod sup*: Henry Binder, Raymond G. Katz; *col*: Tech. *sd*: Vit. 8 min. • Burlesque on "Uncle Tom's Cabin."

6748. Uncle Tom's Cabana 19 July 1947; *p.c.:* MGM; *dir:* Tex Avery; *story:* Heck Allen; *anim:* Walter Clinton, Ray Abrams, Preston Blair, Robert Bentley; *character des:* Walter Clinton; *sets:* John Didrik Johnsen; *ed:* Fred MacAlpin; *voices:* Imogene Lynn, Sara Berner; *mus:* Scott Bradley; *prod:* Fred Quimby; *col:* Tech. *sd:* WE. 7¹/₂ min. • Uncle Tom spins a yarn about Simon le Gree who forced him into turning his cabin into a popular nightclub.

6749. Uncultured Vulture (*Phantasy*) 6 Feb. 1947; *p.c.:* Colum; *prod:* Raymond Katz, Henry Binder; *dir:* Bob Wickersham; *story:* Cal Howard; *anim:* Ben Lloyd, Chic Otterstrom; *lay:* Clark Watson; *back:* Al Boggs; *ed:* Richard S. Jensen; *voices:* Harry E. Lang, Dave Barry; *mus:* Eddie Kilfeather; *ph:* Frank Fisher; *col:* Tech. *sd:* WE. 5¹/₂ min. • A professor is marooned on a desert island with a starving vulture.

6750. The Under Dog (*Pooch the Pup*) 7 Nov. 1932; *p.c.:* Univ; *prod/dir:* Walter Lantz; *anim:* Manuel Moreno, Lester Kline, George Cannata, "Bill" Weber; *mus:* James Dietrich; b&w. *sd:* WE. 6 min. • No story available.

6751. Under Sea Dogs (*Chilly Willy*) Feb. 1968; *p.c.:* Walter Lantz prods for Univ; *dir:* Paul J. Smith; *story:* Homer Brightman; *anim:* Les Kline, Al Coe; *sets:* Ray Huffine; *voice:* Daws Butler; *mus:* Walter Greene; *prod mgr:* William E. Garity; *col:* Tech. *sd:* RCA. 6 min. • Commander Shortsnort arrives by submarine to establish a missile base at the North Pole. His periscope crashes through Chilly's igloo, disturbing his and Maxie's slumber.

6752. Under the Counter Spy (*Woody Woodpecker*) 10 May 1954; *p.c.:* Walter Lantz prods for Univ; *dir:* Don Patterson; *story:* Homer Brightman; *anim:* Ray Abrams, Herman Cohen, Ken Southworth; *sets:* Raymond Jacobs, Art Landy; *voices:* Daws Butler, Grace Stafford; *mus:* Clarence Wheeler; *prod mgr:* William E. Garity; *col:* Tech. *sd:* RCA. 6 min. • Presented in the form of "Dragnet": Woody drinks an undisclosed formula instead of his usual tonic that gives him super human strength.

6753. Under the Shedding Chestnut Tree (*Fable*) 2 Feb. 1942; *p.c.:* Colum; *sup:* Frank Tashlin; *dir:* Bob Wickersham; *anim:* Volus Jones; *lay:* Clark Watson; *ed:* Edward Moore; *voice:* John Wald, Pinto Colvig; *mus:* Eddie Klifeather; *ph:* Frank Fisher; *prod mgr:* Ben Schwalb; b&w. *sd:* RCA. 8 min. • Blacksmith Petey Pelican is daunted by nuts falling on his head while trying to shoe a horse.

6754. Under the Spreading Blacksmith Shop (*Cartune*) 12 Jan. 1942; *p.c.:* Walter Lantz prods for Univ; *prod/dir:* Walter Lantz; *story:* Ben Hardaway, L. (Lowell) E. Elliot; *anim:* Alex Lovy, Robert Bentley; *sets:* Fred Brunish; *voices:* Kent Rogers, Margaret Hill; *mus:* Darrell Calker; *prod mgr:* George Hall; *col:* Tech. *sd:* WE. 7 min. • Andy Panda's Pop dresses as a horse to prove to Andy that he's too young to shoe horses.

6755. The Underdog (*Aesop's Film Fable*) 31 Mar. 1929; *p.c.:* Fables Pictures Inc for Pathé; *dir:* Paul Terry; b&w. *sil.* 10 min. • No story available.

6756. The Unexpected Pest (*Merrie Melodies*) 2 June 1956; *p.c.:* WB; *dir:* Robert McKimson; *story:* Warren Foster; *anim:* Keith Darling, Ted Bonnicksen, George Grandpré, Russ Dyson; *lay:* Robert Gribbroek; *back:* Richard H. Thomas; *ed:* Treg Brown; *voices:* Mel Blanc, June Foray; *mus:* Carl Stalling; *prod mgr:* John W. Burton; *prod:* Edward Selzer; *col:* Tech. *sd:* Vit. 6 min. • Sylvester's cushy existence is threatened when there are no mice left to catch. He discovers a solitary mouse and forces him to make multiple appearances to convince the owners the house is infested with rodents.

6757. The Unhandy Man (*Beary Family*) 1970; *p.c.:* Walter Lantz prods for Univ; *dir:* Paul J. Smith; *story:* Cal Howard; *anim:* Les Kline, Al Coe; *sets:* Nino Carbe; *voices:* Paul Frees, Grace Stafford; *mus:* Walter Greene; *prod mgr:* William E. Garity; *col:* Tech. *sd:* RCA. 5¹/₂ min. • Charlie tries to invent his own methods for an automatic garage door.

6758. The Unicorn in the Garden 24 Sept. 1953; *p.c.:* UPA for Colum; *ex prod:* Stephen Bosustow; *dir:* William T. Hurtz; *story:* James Thurber; *anim:* Phil Monroe, Rudy Larriva, Tom McDonald; *sets:* Robert Dranko; *voice:* John H. Brown, Colleen Collins; *mus:* David Raksin; *prod mgr:* Herbert Klynn; *col:* Tech. *sd:* RCA. 7 min. • A man tells his shrewish wife he has seen a unicorn in their garden. The wife phones the Booby Hatch to have him commited but when they arrive the man denies everything.

6759. The Uninvited Pests (*Heckle & Jeckle*) 29 Nov. 1946; *p.c.:* TT for Fox; *dir:* Connie Rasinski; *story:* John Foster; *voices:* Thomas Morrison; *mus:* Philip A. Scheib; *col:* Tech. *sd:* RCA. 6 min. • The magpies annoy Farmer Al Falfa and his dimwit dog when they picnic in the country.

6760. The United Way 1954; *p.c.:* Trans-film Inc for Community Chest United Fund/Red Feather; *dir:* Abe Liss; *story:* Martin Seifert; *des:* Cliff Roberts; *voice:* Paul Tripp; *mus:* George Kleinsinger; *lyrics:* Joe Darion; *col:* East. *sd:* 1¹/₂ min. • Mr. Generous Giver gets a cheerful charity message across.

6761. Universal Current Events *p.c.:* Univ; b&w. *sil.* • *1917:* **On the Way** by Siebel 13 Oct. **Test of Patriotism** by Brown. **Hoch Der Sedition** by Bert Green • *1918:* **Hoch Der Kaiser** by Leslie Elton. **Liberty on Guard** by Leslie Elton. **Doing Their Bit** by Leslie Elton. *cartoon* by Arthur Lewis 28 Sept.

6762. Universal Screen Magazine *p.c.:* Univ; b&w. *sil.* • *1917:* **Trench Warfare in the Sahara** 20 Apr. *anim:* J.R. Williams. **Cartoon** 27 Apr. *sculpture anim:* Willie Hopkins. **Cartoon** 25 May. *sculpture anim:* Willie Hopkins. **Exemption Pleas** 9 Nov. • *sculpture anim:* Willie Hopkins • *1919:* cartoons by Leslie Elton. **The Preying Mantis** 8 Jan. **War in the Air. Won't You Walk Into My Parlor. Nightmare Experiences After a Heavy Supper. How Many Bars in a Beetle's Beat** 23 Mar. **The Sea Serpent and the Flying Dragon** 18 May. **The Courteous Cries of a Cricket** 25 May. **The Lays of an Ostrich Eggstrawdinary** 8 June. **Aphides the Animated Ant's Avarice** 29 June. **The Heart Bug** 13 July. **The Male Mosquito** 3 Aug. **Oft in the Stilly Night** 24 Aug. **Ginger for Pluck** 4 Oct. **Leading Him a Dance** 11 Oct. **Cinema Luke** 6 Dec. • *1920:* **Cartoon** 28 Feb. **Cinema Luke** 11 May. **It's a Bear** 6 May. **Cinema Luke** 28 May • Burlesque newsreel items in weekly magazine • See: *Travelaughs*

6763. Unlucky Potluck (*Beary Family*) 1972; *p.c.:* Walter Lantz prods for Univ; *dir:* Paul J. Smith; *story:* Cal Howard; *anim:* Volus Jones, Al Coe, Tom Byrne, Joe Voght; *sets:* Nino Carbe; *voices:* Paul Frees, Grace Stafford; *mus:* Walter Greene; *prod mgr:* William E. Garity; *col:* Tech. *sd:* RCA. 6 min. • Charlie brings his boss home unexpectedly for dinner when there's no food in the house.

6764. The Unmentionables (*Merrie Melodies*) 7 Sept. 1963; *p.c.:* WB; *dir:* Friz Freleng; *story:* John Dunn; *anim:* Gerry Chiniquy, Virgil Ross, Bob Matz, Art Leonardi, Lee Halpern; *lay:* Hawley Pratt; *back:* Tom O'Loughlin; *ed:* Treg Brown; *voices:* Mel Blanc, Ralph James, Julie Bennett; *mus:* Bill Lava; *prod mgr:* William Orcutt; *prod:* David H. DePatie; *col:* Tech. *sd:* Vit. 7 min. • In a parody of TV's "The Untouchables": Agent Elegant Mess (Bugs) is assigned to bring '20s racketeer, Rocky and his gang, to justice.

6765. Unnatural History (*Merrie Melodies*) 14 Nov. 1959; *p.c.:* WB; *dir:* Abe Levitow; *story:* Michael Maltese; *anim:* Ben Washam, Richard Thompson, Keith Darling; *sets:* Bob Singer; *ed:* Treg Brown; *voices:* Byron Kane, Mel Blanc, June Foray; *mus:* Milt Franklyn; *prod mgr:* William Orcutt; *prod:* David H. DePatie; *col:* Tech. *sd:* Vit. 6 min. • An insight into animal behavior.

6766. The Unpopular Mechanic (*Oswald*) 6 Nov. 1936; *p.c.:* Univ; *prod/dir:* Walter Lantz; *story:* Walter Lantz, Victor McLeod; *anim:* La Verne Harding, Ed Benedict; *mus:* James Dietrich; b&w. *sd:* RCA. 7 min. • Oswald builds a radio machine which transforms peoples' characters; Fooey the duck turns into a crooner, a swimmer and a wrestler.

6767. The Unruly Hare (*Merrie Melodies*) 10 Feb. 1945; *p.c.:* WB; *dir:* Frank Tashlin; *story:* Melvin Miller, Frank Tashlin; *anim:* Cal Dalton; *sets:* Richard H. Thomas; *ed:* Treg Brown; *voices:* Mel Blanc, Arthur Q. Bryan, The Sportsmen; *mus:* Carl W. Stalling; *prod mgr:* John W. Burton; *prod:* Edward Selzer; *col:* Tech. *sd:* Vit. 7 min. • Elmer surveys the land for a railroad right through the center of Bugs' home.

6768. Unsafe and Seine (*Inspector*) 9 Nov. 1966; *p.c.:* Mirisch/Geoffrey/DFE for UA; *dir:* George Singer; *story:* John W. Dunn; *anim:* Manny Perez, Warren Batchelder, Don Williams, Bob Matz, Dale Case; *sets:* T.M. Yakutis; *ed:* Lee Gunther; *voices:* Pat Harrington Jr., Paul Frees, June Foray; *mus:* Walter Greene; *theme tune:* Henry Mancini; *prod sup:* Harry Love, Bill Orcutt; *col:* DeLuxe. *sd:* RCA. 6 min. • The inspector journeys the world over to meet a secret agent only to discover he's an insurance salesman.

6769. The Unshrinkable Jerry Mouse (*Tom & Jerry*) 1964; *p.c.:* SIB Tower 12 for MGM; *prod/dir:* Chuck Jones; *asst dir/lay:* Maurice Noble; *story:* Michael Maltese; *anim:* Don Towsley, Tom Ray, Dick Thompson, Ben Washam, Ken Harris; *back:* Philip de Guard; *voice:* Mel Blanc; *mus:* Eugene Poddany; *prod mgr:* Les Goldman; *col:* Metro. *sd:* WE. 7 min. • A kitten is brought in to disrupt Tom's happy home life.

6770. The Unsung Hero (*Terry-Toon*) July 1961; *p.c.:* TT for Fox; *ex prod:* Bill Weiss; *dir:* Art Bartsch; *story dir:* Tom Morrison; *story:* Dick Kinney, Al Bertino; *anim:* Ralph Bakshi, Johnny Gent; *sets:* Martin Strudler; *ed:* Jack MacConnell; *voices:* John Myhers; *mus:* Phil Scheib; *ph:* George Davis; *prod mgr:* Frank Schudde; *col:* DeLuxe. *sd:* RCA. 6 min. • Heathcote joins the Navy and inadvertently sinks an enemy vessel.

6771. Unsure Runts (*Fox & Crow*) 16 May 1946; *p.c.:* Colum; *dir:* Howard Swift; *story:* Sid Marcus; *anim:* Grant Simmons, Volus Jones; *lay:* Clark Watson; *ed:* Richard S. Jensen; *voices:* Frank Graham; *mus:* Eddie Kilfeather; *prod mgr:* Hugh McCollum; *col:* Tech. *sd:* WE. 7½ min. • The crow's persistence in selling the fox an insurance policy lands the poor fellow in hospital.

6772. The Untrained Seal (*Color Rhapsody*) 26 July 1936; *p.c.:* Charles Mintz prods for Colum; *story:* Art Davis; *anim:* Sid Marcus; *voices:* Benny Rubin, The Rhythmettes; *mus:* Joe de Nat; *prod mgr:* James Bronis; *col:* Tech. *sd:* RCA. 7½ min. • Papa Seal teaches his kids to fend for themselves but the youngest ends up in a circus.

6773. The Unwelcome Guest 17 Feb. 1945; *p.c.:* MGM; *dir:* George Gordon; *anim:* Michael Lah, Ed Barge, Jack Carr; *ed:* Fred MacAlpin; *mus:* Scott Bradley; *prod:* Fred Quimby; *col:* Tech. *sd:* WE. 7 min. • While berry-picking, Barney Bear attracts a skunk he just can't rid himself of.

6774. Up a Tree (*Donald Duck*) 23 Sept. 1955; *p.c.:* Walt Disney prods for BV; *dir:* Jack Hannah; *story:* Milt Schaffer, Dick Kinney; *anim:* Bob Carlson, Al Coe, Volus Jones, Bill Justice; *fx:* Dan MacManus; *lay:* Yale Gracey; *back:* Claude Coats; *voices:* Clarence Nash, Dessie Miller, Norma Swank; *mus:* Oliver Wallace; *col:* Tech. *sd:* RCA. 7 min. CS. • The chipmunks' tranquil life is interrupted when lumberjack Donald decides to chop down their tree-home.

6775. Up in the Air (*Aesop's Film Fable*) 6 Mar. 1926; *p.c.:* Fables Pictures Inc for Pathé; *dir:* Paul Terry; *b&w. sil.* 5 min. • While Farmer Al mends the roof, the mice interfere with the bricks and paint.

6776. Up 'n' Atom (*Color Rhapsody*) 10 July 1947; *p.c.:* Colum; *prod:* Raymond Katz, Henry Binder; *dir:* Sid Marcus; *anim:* Roy Jenkins, Ben Lloyd; *lay:* Clark Watson; *back:* Al Boggs; *ed:* Richard S. Jensen; *voices:* Harry E. Lang, Walter Craig; *mus:* Eddie Kilfeather; *ph:* Frank Fisher; *col:* Tech. *sd:* WE. 6 min. • A dog asks a wise old dog for some advice on cat-catching. The sage turns out to be a cat in disguise, giving misleading information.

6777. The Up-Standing Sitter (*Looney Tunes*) 3 July 1948; *p.c.:* WB; *dir:* Robert McKimson; *story:* Warren Foster; *anim:* Phil de Lara, Manny Gould, John Carey, Charles McKimson; *lay:* Cornett Wood; *back:* Richard H. Thomas; *ed:* Treg Brown; *voices:* Mel Blanc; *mus:* Carl Stalling; *prod mgr:* John W. Burton; *prod:* Edward Selzer; *col:* Tech. *sd:* Vit. 7 min. • Daffy gets a job babysitting with a chick that's intent on running away.

6778. Up to Mars (*Talkartoon*) 22 Nov. 1930; *p.c.:* The Fleischer Studio for Para; *prod:* Max Fleischer; *dir:* Dave Fleischer; *mus:* Art Turkisher; *b&w. sd:* WE. 6 min. • Bimbo is projected by rocket to Mars and finds life all contrary to Earth.

6779. Ups 'an' Downs Derby (*Noveltoon*) 9 June 1950; *p.c.:* Famous for Para; *dir:* Seymour Kneitel; *story:* Larz Bourne; *anim:* Dave Tendlar, Tom Golden; *sets:* Tom Ford; *mus:* Winston Sharples; *ph:* Leonard McCormick; *prod mgr:* Sam Buchwald; *col:* Tech. *sd:* RCA. 6 min. • An anxious jockey tries all methods to awaken his lazy steed in time for the big race.

6780. Ups 'n' Downs (*Looney Tunes*) 5 Feb. 1931; *p.c.:* Hugh Harman, Rudolf Ising prods for WB; *prod:* Leon Schlesinger; *anim:* Rollin Hamilton, Paul Smith; *mus:* Frank Marsales; *b&w. sd:* Vit. 6 min. • Bosko forsakes his hot dog stand to enter his mechanical horse in the derby.

6781. Upswept Hare (*Merrie Melodies*) 14 Mar. 1953; *p.c.:* WB; *dir:* Robert McKimson; *story:* Tedd Pierce; *anim:* Charles McKimson, Herman Cohen, Rod Scribner, Phil de Lara; *lay:* Robert Givens; *back:* Richard H. Thomas; *ed:* Treg Brown; *voices:* Mel Blanc, Arthur Q. Bryan; *mus:* Carl Stalling; *prod mgr:* John W. Burton; *prod:* Edward Selzer; *col:* Tech. *sd:* Vit. 6½ min. • Elmer transplants a rare plant into his penthouse apartment, little realizing he has transplanted Bugs Bunny in the bargain.

6782. Uranium Blues (*Terry-Toon*) Feb. 1956; *p.c.:* TT for Fox; *dir:* Connie Rasinski; *story:* Tom Morrison; *sets:* Art Bartsch; *mus:* Philip A. Scheib; *ph:* Douglas Moye; *col:* Tech. *sd:* RCA. 6 min. • Farmer Al Falfa forsakes his mule for a jeep when he goes prospecting. The mule eventually rescues him from being devoured by buzzards.

6783. U.S. War Bonds (*Universal Newsreel*) 1915; *p.c.:* Keen Cartoon Corp. for Univ; *dir:* Pat Sullivan; *anim:* Otto Messmer; *b&w. sil.* • Commercial for Defence Bonds.

6784. Vacation (*Out of the Inkwell*) 23 July 1924; *p.c.:* Inkwell Studio for Red Seal; *dir:* Dave Fleischer; *anim/l/a:* Max Fleischer; *b&w. sil.* 10 min. *l/a/anim.* • Max draws a vacation spot for Ko-Ko that's too hot. The clown asks for "something with a kick in it" and gets a mule! Max then draws a pleasure resort where everything is made of rubber. Reissued in 1930 with added soundtrack.

6785. Vacation with Play (*Popeye*) 26 Jan. 1951; *p.c.:* Famous for Para; *dir:* Seymour Kneitel; *story:* Carl Meyer, Jack Mercer; *anim:* Tom Johnson, John Gentilella, Els Barthen; *sets:* Tom Ford; *voices:* Jack Mercer, Mae Questel, Jackson Beck; *mus:* Winston Sharples; *ph:* Leonard McCormick; *prod mgr:* Seymour Shultz; *col:* Tech. *sd:* RCA. 7 min. • Popeye prefers to sleep on his vacation at Lake Narrowhead, leaving Olive at the mercy of the hotel's athletic coach.

6786. The Valiant Tailor (*ComiColor*) 29 Oct. 1934; *p.c.:* Celebrity prods; *prod:* Ub Iwerks; *dir/anim:* Jimmie Culhane, Al Eugster; *lay:* Jimmie Culhane; *mus:* Art Turkisher; *col:* Ciné. *sd:* PCP. 8 min. • An ogre menaces the king and the tailor puts honey on its head, causing bees to see him off. • On-screen credit given to Grim Natwick and Berny Wolf who did not participate in the production.

6787. Vampire in Brooklyn 27 Oct. 1995; *p.c.:* Para for UNIV; *special visual fx anim/compositing: Available Light Design: sup:* John T. van Vliet; *prod:* Katherine Kean; *digital sup:* Laurel Klick; *anim:* Michael Gagne, Conann Fitzpatrick, Bill Arance, January Nordman, Randy Weeks; *optical printing:* Beverly Bernacki, Mona B. Howell; *anim ph/scanning:* Joseph Thomas; *col:* DeLuxe. *sd:* Dolby stereo. 102 min. *l/a.* • Live-action fantasy: Vampire Maximillian arrives in New York on a ship crewed by corpses. Rita, a homicide cop, goes to investigate and Max has thoughts of her being his bride.

6788. The Vanishing Duck (*Tom & Jerry*) 2 May 1958; *p.c.:* MGM; *prod/dir:* William Hanna, Joseph Barbera; *anim:* Lewis Marshall, Kenneth Muse, Carlo Vinci, James Escalante; *lay:* Dick Bickenbach; *back:* Robert Gentle; *ed:* Jim Faris; *voices:* Red Coffee, Vic Perrin, Marian Richman; *mus:* Scott Bradley; *ph:* Jack Stevens; *prod mgr:* Hal Elias; *col:* Tech. *sd:* WE. 7 min. CS. • Little Quacker and Jerry make good use of vanishing cream to vent their revenge on Tom.

6789. The Vanishing Private (*Donald Duck*) 25 Sept. 1942; *p.c.:* Walt Disney prods for RKO; *dir:* Jack King; *asst dir:* Jack Atwood; *story:* Harry Reeves, Carl Barks; *anim:* Paul Allen, Hal King, Ed Love, Charles A. Nichols, Don Patterson, Wolfgang Reitherman, Art Scott, Vladimir Tytla, Judge Whitaker; *lay:* Bill Herwig; *voices:* Billy Bletcher, Don Brodie, Clarence Nash; *mus:* Oliver Wallace; *song:* Leigh Harline; *col:* Tech. *sd:* RCA. 7 min. • Pvt. Donald camouflages a cannon with invisible paint then paints himself to escape the wrath of Sgt. Pete.

6790. Variety Girl 1947; *p.c.:* George Pal Studio for Para; *Seq:* "Romeow and Julicat"; *prod:* George Pal; *dir:* Thornton Hee, William Cottrell; *anim:* Gene Warren; *voices/l/a:* Mary Hatcher, Pinto Colvig; *mus:* Edward Plumb; *col:* b&w/Tech. *sd:* WE. *l/a/anim.* • A live-action film about a girl (Mary Hatcher) trying out for the movies. The colored sequence has Hatcher and Colvig demonstrating how voices are lent to cartoons: The story involves a dog and cat romance that is broken up by feuding families. The sequence is left incomplete to make way for the main-line story.

6791. Vaudeville (*Out of the Inkwell*) 20 Aug. 1924; *p.c.:* Inkwell Studio for Red Seal; *dir:* Dave Fleischer; *anim/l/a:* Max Fleischer; *b&w. sil.* 10 min. *l/a/anim.* • Ko-Ko runs his theater single handed. He takes the tickets, plays the instruments and performs on stage. Reissued in 1930 with added sound-track.

6792. Vegetable Vaudeville (*Kartune*) 9 Nov. 1951; *p.c.:* Famous for Para; *dir:* I. Sparber; *story:* Larz Bourne; *anim:* Myron Waldman, Nick Tafuri, Howard Beckerman; *sets:* Robert Little; *voices:* Gwen Davies, Jack Mercer; *mus:* Winston Sharples; *song:* Frank Silver; *ph:* Leonard McCormick; *prod mgr:* Sam Buchwald; *col:* Tech. *sd:* RCA. 6 min. • The vegetables and fruit put on a cabaret with Carmen Banana leading the sing-along.

6793. Venice Vamp (*Aesop's Sound Fable*) 15 May 1932; *p.c.:* Van Beuren for RKO; *dir:* John Foster, Mannie Davis; *voice:* Marjorie Hines; *mus:* Gene Rodemich; b&w. *sd:* RCA. 7½ min. • Performed as an opera, the hero makes love to a girl in a gondola. Her husband intervenes.

6794. Ventriloquist Cat 27 May 1950; *p.c.:* MGM; *dir:* Tex Avery; *story:* Rich Hogan; *anim:* Walter Clinton, Michael Lah, Grant Simmons; *character des:* Louis Schmitt; *sets:* John Didrik Johnsen; *ed:* Jim Faris; *voice:* Harry E. Lang; *mus:* Scott Bradley; *ph:* Jack Stevens; *col:* Tech. *sd:* WE. 6 min. • A cat uses ventriloquism to get his revenge on a dog.

6795. Venus and the Cat (*Aesop's Film Fable*) 9 Oct. 1921; *p.c.:* Fables Pictures Inc for Pathé; *dir:* Paul Terry; b&w. sil. 5 min. • Mistreated by the Farmer, the cat cries to the heavens where an obliging Venus changes the feline into a woman who entices Farmer Al. This works as planned until she spies a mouse and her basic instincts take over. Moral: "What is bred in the bone will out in the flesh."

6796. Venus of Venice (*Aesop's Film Fable*) 1 Aug. 1926; *p.c.:* Fables Pictures Inc for Pathé; *dir:* Paul Terry; b&w. sil. 10 min. • Set in the canals of Venice, Antonio Mouse loves Marie Mouse but a ham actor named Salvatore kidnaps her in his gondola. Our hero rescues her with help from an octopus.

6797. Vernon Howe Bailey's Sketchbook *p.c.:* Essanay Film Mfg Co; *anim:* Vernon Howe Bailey; b&w. sil. s/r • **1915: Vernon Howe Bailey's Sketchbook** 13 Nov. • **1916: Sketchbook of Chicago** 29 Jan. **Sketchbook of London** 1 Mar. **Sketchbook of Paris** 27 Mar. **Sketchbook of Philadelphia** 14 Mar. **Sketchbook of Boston** 14 Apr. **Sketchbook of Rome** 26 Apr. **Sketchbook of San Francisco** 20 May. **Sketchbook of Berlin** 9 June. **Sketchbook of St Louis** 19 June. **Sketchbook of New Orleans** 10 July. **Sketchbook of Petrograd** 27 July. **Sketchbook of Washington** 26 Aug. • Similar format to Hy Mayer's "Travelaughs."

6798. Vicious Viking (*Chilly Willy*) Feb. 1967; *p.c.:* Walter Lantz prods for Univ; *dir:* Paul J. Smith; *story:* Cal Howard; *anim:* Al Coe, Les Kline; *sets:* Ray Huffine; *voice:* Daws Butler; *mus:* Walter Greene; *prod mgr:* William E. Garity; *col:* Tech. *sd:* RCA. 6 min. • Chilly and Smedley thaw out a Viking who has been preserved in ice. He runs amok in search of food.

6799. Victory Through Air Power 17 July 1943; *p.c.:* Walt Disney prods for UA; *anim dir:* David Hand; *seq dir:* Clyde Geronimi, Jack Kinney, James Algar; *story* adapted from "Victory Through Air Power" by Mjr Alexander P. de Seversky; *story dir:* Perce Pearce; *story adapt:* T. Hee, Erdman Penner, William Cottrell, James Bodrero, George Stallings, Josè Rodriquez; *anim:* Ward Kimball, John Lounsbery, Hugh Fraser, John Sibley, Norm Tate, Vladimir Tytla, Bill Justice, Ed Aardal, John McManus, Harvey Toombs, Oliver M. Johnston Jr., Marvin Woodward; *fx:* Joshua Meador, Carleton Boyd, George Rowley; *atmospheric sketches:* Mary Blair; *lay:* Herbert Ryman, Donald da Gradi, Tom Codrick Charles Philippi, Elmer Plummer, Don Griffith, Cliff Devirian, Glenn Scott, Karl Karpé, Bill Herwig; *back:* Albert Dempster, Dick Anthony, Claude Coats, Ray Huffine, Robert Blanchard, Joe Stahley, Nino Carbe; *ed:* Jack Dennis; *voices: narration:* Art Baker; *Secretary* Jan Clayton; *C.S. Rolls:* Lou Merrill; *French accent:* Jean de Briac; *Newspaper woman:* Gloria Holden; *Newspaper men:* Edward Fielding, Roy Gordon, Damian O'Flynn; *Draftsmen:* Carlyle Blackwell Jr., Babe Sheen; *mus:* Edward H. Plumb, Paul J. Smith, Oliver Wallace; *l/a:* Mjr Alexander de Seversky; *l/a dir* H.C. Potter; *ph:* Ray Rennahan; *des:* Morgan Padelford; *sets:* William Kiernan; *sd:* C.O. Slyfield, Lodge Cunningham; *prod mgr:* Dan Keefe; *col:* Tech. *sd:* RCA. 65 min. • The history of aviation is brought up to date to show how air power can be used to beat the Axis.

6800. Victory Vehicles (*Goofy*) 30 July 1943; *p.c.:* Walt Disney prods for RKO; *dir:* Jack Kinney; *asst dir:* Ted Sebern, Bea Selk, Lou Debney; *story:* Ralph Wright, Webb Smith; *anim:* Les Clark, Hugh Fraser, Bill Justice, Ward Kimball, John Sibley, Frank Thomas, Vladimir Tytla; *fx:* Ed Aardal, Andy Engman; *lay:* Don da Gradi; *voices:* Fred Shields; The Betty Allen Trio: (Betty Allen, Sally Mueller, Dorothy Compton); *mus:* Oliver Wallace; *song:* Ned Washington, Oliver Wallace; *col:* Tech. *sd:* RCA. 7 min. • The Goof demonstrates various wartime devices to replace the automobile.

6801. The Vikings 1958; *p.c.:* UPA for UA; *col:* Tech. *sd:* WE. • Live action feature with animated prologue.

6802. The Village and the School 1954; *p.c.:* Film Graphics Inc for U.S. Information Agency; *dir:* Don Towsley; *story:* Maxine Furland; *anim:* Lucifer Guarnier, Ken Walker; *back:* Gene Gogioka; *mus:* Robert McBride; *col. sd.* 9 min. • Designed especially for village people, showing how education brings benefits to the individual.

6803. The Village Barber (*Flip the Frog*) 27 Sept. 1930; *p.c.:* Celebrity prods for MGM; *prod/dir:* Ub Iwerks; b&w. *sd:* PCP. 6 min. • Barber Flip gives a hairy dog the ultimate trim.

6804. The Village Blacksmith (*Paul Terry-Toon*) 6 Nov. 1933; *p.c.:* Moser & Terry for Educational/Fox; *dir:* Paul Terry, Frank Moser; *mus:* Philip A. Scheib; b&w. *sd:* WE. 5½ min. • Farmer Al Falfa dreams of a Valhalla peopled by celebrities including Jimmy Durante.

6805. The Village Blacksmith (*Terry-Toon*) 2 Dec. 1938; *p.c.:* TT for Fox; *dir:* Mannie Davis; *story:* John Foster; *mus:* Philip A. Scheib; b&w. *sd:* WE. 7 min. • No story available.

6806. The Village Smithy (*Donald Duck*) 16 Jan. 1941; *p.c.:* Walt Disney prods for RKO; *dir:* Richard Lundy; *asst dir:* Ted Baker; *story:* Harry Reeves, Carl Barks; *anim:* Theodore Bonnicksen, Robert W. Carlson Jr., Walter Clinton, John Elliotte, Volus Jones, Fred Kopietz, Frank Marsales, Kenneth Muse, Ray Patterson, William Schull; *fx:* Jack Boyd; *lay:* Thor Putnam; *voice:* Clarence Nash; *mus:* Paul J. Smith; *col:* Tech. *sd:* RCA. 7 min. • Blacksmith Donald tries to shoe a wily donkey.

6807. The Village Smithy (*Looney Tunes*) 14 Nov. 1936; *p.c.:* Leon Schlesinger prods for WB; *dir:* Fred Avery; *story:* Robert Clampett; *anim:* Cecil Surry, Sid Sutherland, Robert Clampett; *ed:* Tregoweth E. Brown; *voices:* Earl Hodgins, Joe Dougherty, Fred Avery; *mus:* Carl W. Stalling; *prod sup:* Henry Binder, Raymond G. Katz; b&w. *sd:* Vit. 7 min. • Porky helps out in the blacksmith's shop, accidentally causing a horse to bolt, carrying the smithy with him.

6808. The Village Smitty (*Flip the Frog*) 31 Jan. 1931; *p.c.:* Celebrity prods for MGM; *prod/dir:* Ub Iwerks; *mus:* Carl W. Stalling; b&w. *sd:* PCP. 6 min. • Flip shoes a horse that runs wild with a passenger when bitten by a horsefly.

6809. The Village Specialist (*Flip the Frog*) 12 Sept. 1931; *p.c.:* Celebrity prods for MGM; *prod/dir:* Ub Iwerks; b&w. *sd:* PCP. 8 min. • Plumber Flip fixes a leaky pipe until the whole house is blown to the skies atop a geyser.

6810. The Villain in Disguise (*Aesop's Film Fable*) 2 Jan. 1922; *p.c.:* Fables Pictures Inc for Pathé; *dir:* Paul Terry; b&w. sil. 5 min. • A cat adopts various disguises to fool a canine cop and a mouse family. He appears as a fire hydrant to fool the cop and sets out traps for the mice but Papa mouse stops his game by burying him under an entire brick chimney.

6811. The Villain Still Pursued Her (*Terry-Toon*) 3 Sept. 1937; *p.c.:* TT for Educational/Fox; *mus dir:* Connie Rasinski; Philip A. Scheib; b&w. sil. 6 min. • The villain takes the heroine to a mineshaft where the hero risks his life to rescue her.

6812. The Villain's Curse (*Paul Terry-Toon*) 10 Jan. 1932; *p.c.:* Terry, Moser & Coffman for Educational/Fox; *dir:* Frank Moser, Paul Terry; *mus:* Philip A. Scheib; b&w. *sd:* WE. 6 min. • No story available.

6813. Vim, Vigor and Vitaliky (*Popeye*) 3 Jan. 1936; *p.c.:* The Fleischer Studio for Para; *prod:* Max Fleischer; *dir:* Dave Fleischer; *anim:* Seymour Kneitel, Roland Crandall; *voices:* Jack Mercer, Gus Wickie, Mae Questel; *mus:* Sammy Timberg; b&w. *sd:* WE. 7 min. • Bluto eyes the women entering Popeye's "Ladies' Day" gymnasium. He disguises himself as a female customer, defying our hero to match his strength.

6814. Vincent 1 Oct. 1982; *p.c.:* Walt Disney Prods; *dir/scr:* Tim Burton; *prod:* Rick Heinrichs; *anim/tech dir:* Stephen Chiodo; *des:* Tim Burton, Rick Heinrichs; *sculptor:* Rick Heinrichs; *voice:* Vincent Price; *mus:* Ken Hilton; *ph:* Victor Abdalov; *with gratitude to:* Dave Allen, Eric Brevig, Julie Hickson, Chris Roth, Chas Smith; b&w. *sd:* Dolby stereo. 6 min. •

Made as an homage to the writings of Dr. Seuss and mixed with horror movies: Seven-year-old Vincent Malloy fantasizes about being Vincent Price. His fantasies turn his life into a series of scenes from a horror film. Stop-motion animation.

6815. The Violinist 1959; *p.c.:* Pintoff prods for Colum; *prod/dir/story/mus:* Ernest Pintoff; *anim:* Jim Murakami, Jim Hiltz, Jack Schnerk; *lay:* Jim Murakami; *back:* Jack Heiter; *voice:* Carl Reiner; *mus arrangement:* George Steiner; *prod mgr:* Arnold Stone; *col:* East. *sd:* RCA. 7¹/₂ min. *Academy Award nomination.* • Harry loves to play the violin but nobody likes to listen. He is informed that first, he *must* "suffer"! Suffering improves his playing but then nobody wishes to associate with him.

6816. Vitamin G Man (*Phantasy*) 22 Jan. 1943; *p.c.:* Colum; *dir:* Paul Sommer, John Hubley; *story:* Jack Cosgriff; *anim:* Jim Armstrong; *lay:* Clark Watson; *ed:* Edward Moore; *voices:* Kent Rogers; *mus:* Edward Kilfeather; *prod mgr:* Albert Spar; b&w. *sd:* WE. 6¹/₂ min. • A candidate for Flatfoot College for Snoopers accepts, too literally, the crime he is given to reconstruct and solve.

6817. Vitamin Hay (*Color Classic*) 22 Aug. 1941; *p.c.:* The Fleischer Studio for Para; *prod:* Max Fleischer; *dir:* Dave Fleischer: *story:* Bob Wickersham; *anim:* Dave Tendlar, Otto Feuer; *ed:* Kitty Pfister; *voice:* Jack Mercer; *mus:* Sammy Timberg; *prod sup:* Sam Buchwald, Isidore Sparber; *col:* Tech. *sd:* WE. 7 min. • Spunky the donkey rejects his portion of "vitamin hay." He is soon off on an adventure with a goat and some geese but is chased back home to Mama and vitamin hay.

6818. Vitamin Pink (*Pink Panther*) 6 Apr. 1966; *p.c.:* Mirisch/Geoffrey/DFE for UA; *dir:* Hawley Pratt; *story:* Michael O'Connor; *anim:* Norm McCabe, La Verne Harding, Warren Batcheller, Don Williams; *lay:* Dick Ung; *back:* Tom O'Loughlin; *ed:* Al Wahrman; *mus:* William Lava; *theme tune:* Henry Mancini; *prod mgr:* Bill Orcutt; *col:* DeLuxe; *sd:* RCA. 6 min. • The panther is made sheriff of a western town when he revitalizes an escaped convict with his patent medicine.

6819. Viva Buddy (*Looney Tunes*) 12 Dec. 1934; *p.c.:* Leon Schlesinger prods for WB; *dir:* Jack King; *anim:* Frank Tipper, Cal Dalton, Robert Clampett; *voices:* Billy Bletcher, Jack Carr; *mus:* Norman Spencer; *prod sup:* Henry Binder, Raymond G. Katz; b&w. *sd:* Vit. 7 min. • A parody on "Viva Villa": Pancho shoots up the cantina and makes a play for Buddy's girl. Buddy retaliates.

6820. Viva Willie (*Willie Whopper*) 30 Sept. 1934; *p.c.:* Celebrity prods for MGM; *prod/dir:* Ub Iwerks; *anim:* Grim Natwick, Berny Wolf; *mus:* Carl Stalling; *voice:* Jane Withers; b&w. *sd:* PCP. 6 min. • Willie's tall tales lead him to a wild west cantina where, with help from an inebriated horse, he captures the bandit who has absconded with his girl. Caricature of Wallace Beery.

6821. Voice of the Turkey (*Noveltoon*) 3 Nov. 1950; *p.c.:* Famous for Para; *dir:* Seymour Kneitel; *story:* Larz Bourne; *anim:* George Germanetti, Steve Muffatti; *sets:* Robert Connavale; *voices:* Arnold Stang, Sid Raymond; *mus:* Winston Sharples; *ph:* Leonard McCormick; *prod mgr:* Sam Buchwald; *col:* Tech. *sd:* RCA. 6 min. • The farmer chases a reluctant turkey on Thanksgiving day to have him for dinner.

6822. The Volunteer Worker 1 Sept. 1940; *p.c.:* Walt Disney prods for Community Chests and Councils Inc.; *dir:* Riley Thomson; *asst dir:* Ray de Valley; *anim:* Johnny Cannon, Larry Clemmons, Walter Clinton, Volus Jones, Richard Lundy, Charles Nichols, Frank Onaitis; *fx:* Jack Boyd, Andrew Engman, Jack Huber, Ed Parks; *lay:* Bill Tracy; *voices:* Clarence Nash; *col:* Tech. *sd:* RCA. 3 min. • Donald's house-to-house charity campaign is fruitless. Finally a ditch-digger contributes and Don pins an "I Gave" button on him.

6823. Voo-Doo Boo-Boo (*Woody Woodpecker*) 14 Aug. 1962; *p.c.:* Walter Lantz prods for Univ; *dir:* Jack Hannah; *story:* Tedd Pierce, Bill Danch; *anim:* Roy Jenkins, Al Coe; *sets:* Ray Huffine, Art Landy; *voices:* Daws Butler, Grace Stafford; *mus:* Darrell Calker; *prod mgr:* William E. Garity; *col:* Tech. *sd:* RCA. 6 min. • Gabby Gator uses voo-doo to capture Woody.

6824. Voodoo in Harlem (*New Universal Cartoon*) 18 July 1938; *p.c.:* Univ; *prod:* Walter Lantz; *dir:* Rudy Zamora; *story:* Victor McLeod, Win Smith; *anim:* Frank Tipper, Merle Gilson; *sets:* Edgar Keichle; *mus:* Frank Churchill; *prod mgr:* George Hall; *col:* tinted. *sd:* WE. 7 min. *l/a/anim.* •

A bottle of indigo ink is upset by the janitor in a cartoon studio and a crew of colored figures emerge and indulge in "trucking."

6825. A Voodoo Spell (*James Hound*) 7 June 1967; *p.c.:* TT for Fox; *dir:* Ralph Bakshi; *col:* DeLuxe. *sd:* RCA. 6 min. • Two villains give James Hound a headache. • See: *James Hound*

6826. Voyage to Next 1974; *p.c.:* Hubley Studio for Institute for World Order; *prod:* Faith Hubley; *dir:* John Hubley; *story:* Faith & John Hubley, Saul H. Mendlovitz; *anim:* Phil Duncan, Bill Littlejohn, Earl James, Michael Sporn; *sets:* John & Faith Hubley; *i&p:* Michael Sporn, Mark Hubley, Ray Hubley, Genevieve Hirsch; *voices:* Maureen Stapleton, Dizzy Gillespie, Dee Dee Bridgewater; *mus:* Dizzy Gillespie; *ph:* Anicam; *col:* CFI. *sd:* Media. 9¹/₂ min. • After viewing life on Planet Earth, Father Time projects twenty years on and he and Mother Earth, conjour up their preferred worlds.

6827. Wabbit Twouble (*Merrie Melodies*) 20 Dec. 1941; *p.c.:* Leon Schlesinger prods for WB; *dir:* Robert Clampett; *story:* Dave Monahan; *anim:* Sid Sutherland; *lay:* Thomas McKimson; *back:* Michael Sasanoff; *ed:* Treg Brown; *voices:* Mel Blanc, Arthur Q. Bryan; *mus:* Carl W. Stalling; *prod sup:* Henry Binder, Raymond G. Katz; *col:* Tech. *sd:* Vit. 7 min. • While vacationing in Jellostone National Park, Elmer's tranquility is disrupted with the appearance of Bugs Bunny.

6828. The Wabbit Who Came to Supper (*Merrie Melodies*) 28 Mar. 1942; *p.c.:* Leon Schlesinger prods for WB; *dir:* I. Freleng; *story:* Michael Maltese; *anim:* Richard Bickenbach; *lay:* Owen Fitzgerald; *back:* Lenard Kester; *ed:* Treg Brown; *voices:* Mel Blanc, Arthur Q. Bryan; *mus:* Carl W. Stalling; *prod sup:* Henry Binder, Raymond G. Katz; *col:* Tech. *sd:* Vit. 7 min. • Elmer is about to inherit $5000 providing he is kind to animals. Bugs is quick to see the possibilities of this situation.

6829. Wackiki Wabbit (*Merrie Melodies*) 26 June 1943; *p.c.:* Leon Schlesinger prods for WB; *dir:* Charles M. Jones; *story:* Tedd Pierce; *anim:* Ken Harris; *lay:* John McGrew; *back:* Eugene Fleury; *ed:* Treg Brown; *voices:* Mel Blanc, Tedd Pierce, Michael Maltese; *singers:* Augie Goupil, Thurston Knudson, Hamilton U. Bunkley; *mus:* Carl W. Stalling; *prod sup:* Henry Binder, Raymond G. Katz; *col:* Tech. *sd:* Vit. 7 min. • Two starving castaways land on a desert isle, envisioning Bugs as their dinner. Storymen Tedd Pierce and Michael Maltese are caricatured as castaways.

6830. Wacky Blackouts (*Looney Tunes*) 11 July 1942; *p.c.:* Leon Schlesinger prods for WB; *dir:* Robert Clampett; *story:* Warren Foster; *anim:* Sid Sutherland; *sets:* Michael Sasanoff; *ed:* Treg Brown; *voices:* Mel Blanc, Kent Rogers, Bea Benaderet, Danny Webb, The Sportsmen Quartet (Maxwell Smith, John Rarig, William Days, Thurl Ravenscroft, Paul Taylor); *mus:* Carl W. Stalling; *prod sup:* Henry Binder, Raymond G. Katz; b&w. *sd:* Vit. 7 min. • The effects of blackouts on the farm animals.

6831. Wacky-Bye Baby (*Woody Woodpecker*) May 1948; *p.c.:* Walter Lantz prods for Univ; *dir:* Dick Lundy; *story:* Ben Hardaway, Jack Cosgriff; *anim:* (La)Verne Harding, Les Kline, Ed Love, Pat Matthews, Sid Pillet; *sets:* Fred Brunish; *ed:* Dave Lurie; *voices:* Jack Mather, Ben Hardaway; *mus:* Darrell Calker; *ph:* Fred Weaver, Eugene Borghi; *prod mgr:* William E. Garity; *col:* Tech. *sd:* RCA. 6¹/₂ min. • Woody disguises himself as a baby to freeload off millionaire Wally Walrus.

6832. Wacky Quacky (*Phantasy*) 20 Mar. 1947; *p.c.:* Colum; *prod:* Raymond Katz, Henry Binder; *dir:* Alex Lovy; *story:* Cal Howard; *anim:* Chic Otterstrom, Paul Sommer, Jay Sarbry; *back:* Al Boggs; *ed:* Richard S. Jensen; *voice:* Harry E. Lang; *mus:* Eddie Kilfeather; *ph:* Frank Fisher; *col:* Ciné. *sd:* WE. 6 min. • A hunter sets out for a day's duck hunting, but the tables are turned.

6833. The Wacky Wabbit (*Merrie Melodies*) 2 May 1942; *p.c.:* Leon Schlesinger prods for WB; *dir:* Robert Clampett; *story:* Warren Foster; *anim:* Sid Sutherland, Rod Scribner, Robert McKimson; *lay:* Thomas McKimson; *back:* Michael Sasanoff; *ed:* Treg Brown; *voices:* Mel Blanc, Arthur Q. Bryan; *mus:* Carl W. Stalling; *prod sup:* Henry Binder, Raymond G. Katz; *col:* Tech. *sd:* Vit. 7 min. • Elmer goes prospecting for gold and gets heckled by Bugs Bunny.

6834. The Wacky Weed (*Cartune*) 16 Dec. 1946; *p.c.:* Walter Lantz prods for Univ; *dir:* Dick Lundy; *story:* Ben Hardaway, Milt Schaffer; *anim:* La Verne Harding, Grim Natwick; *sets:* Fred Brunish; *voices:* Walter Tetley, Jack Mather, Walter Lantz; *mus:* Darrell Calker; *prod mgr:* William E. Garity; *col:* Tech. *sd:* WE. 6 min. • Andy Panda tries to kill a stubborn weed.

6835. Wacky Wigwams (*Color Rhapsody*) 22 Feb. 1942; *p.c.:* Colum; *sup:* Frank Tashlin; *dir:* Alec Geiss; *anim:* Volus Jones; *sets:* Clark Watson; *ed:* Edward Moore; *mus:* Paul Worth; *prod mgr:* Ben Schwalb; *col:* Tech. *sd:* RCA. 6½ min. • Satire on Indian life on and off the reservation with a running gag about a rain dancer.

6836. Wacky Wild Life (*Merrie Melodies*) 9 Nov. 1940; *p.c.:* Leon Schlesinger prods for WB; *dir:* Fred Avery; *story:* Dave Monahan, Robert Clampett; *anim:* Virgil Ross; *sets:* John Didrik Johnsen; *ed:* Treg Brown; *voices:* Robert C. Bruce, Mel Blanc, Bernice Hansel; *mus:* Carl W. Stalling; *prod sup:* Henry Binder, Raymond G. Katz; *col:* Tech. *sd:* Vit. 7 min. • Satire on nature documentary shorts.

6837. The Wacky World of Numbers 1970; *p.c.:* Stephen Bosustow prods for Colum; *dir:* Steven Clark; *story:* from the book by Sheldon Wasserman; *des:* Lynn Mishkin, Maggie Kafata, Susan Heick; *ed:* Don Sykes, Tom Desimone; *mus:* Shorty Rogers; *col:* Tech. *sd.* 10 min. • Cartoon helping to understand numbers.

6838. The Wacky Worm (*Merrie Melodies*) 21 June 1941; *p.c.:* Leon Schlesinger prods for WB; *dir:* I. Freleng; *story:* Dave Monahan; *anim:* Cal Dalton; *sets:* Lenard Kester; *ed:* Treg Brown; *voices:* Mel Blanc; *mus:* Carl W. Stalling; *prod sup:* Henry Bindrer, Raymond G. Katz; *col:* Tech. *sd:* Vit. 7 min. • A crow chases a Jerry Colonna–type worm through a Junk Yard.

6839. A Waggily Tale (*Looney Tunes*) 26 Apr. 1958; *p.c.:* WB; *dir:* Friz Freleng; *story:* Warren Foster; *anim:* Art Davis, Virgil Ross, Gerry Chiniquy; *lay:* Hawley Pratt; *back:* Boris Gorelick; *ed:* Treg Brown; *voices:* Daws Butler, Lucille Bliss; *mus:* Milt Franklyn; *prod:* John W. Burton; *col:* Tech. *sd:* Vit. 6 min. • A small boy mistreats his pup and dreams he has been transposed into the dog's position.

6840. Wagon Heels (*Merrie Melodies*) 28 July 1945; *p.c.:* WB; *dir:* Robert Clampett; *anim:* Manny Gould, I. Ellis, J.C. Melendez; *lay:* Thomas McKimson; *back:* Michael Sasanoff; *ed:* Treg Brown; *voices:* Mel Blanc, Robert C. Bruce; *mus:* Carl W. Stalling; *prod mgr:* John W. Burton; *prod:* Edward Selzer; *col:* Tech. *sd:* Vit. 7 min. • Indian Scout Porky has a run-in with Injun Joe when his wagon train invades Joe's territory. • Tech remake of *Injun Trouble.*

6841. Wags to Riches (*Droopy*) 13 Aug. 1949; *p.c.:* MGM; *dir:* Tex Avery; *story:* Jack Cosgriff, Rich Hogan; *anim:* Michael Lah, Grant Simmons, Walter Clinton, Bob Cannon; *character des:* Louis Schmitt; *sets:* John Didrik Johnsen; *ed:* Fred MacAlpin; *voices:* Patrick J. McGeehan, Don Messick, Tex Avery; *mus:* Scott Bradley; *prod:* Fred Quimby; *col:* Tech. *sd:* WE. 7 min. • Droopy stands to inherit a mansion. In the event of his death, the estate reverts to another dog, Spike. So Spike sets about it to dispose of our hero.

6842. A Waif's Welcome (*Rainbow Parade*) 19 June 1936; *p.c.:* Van Beuren for RKO; *dir:* Tom Palmer; *sets:* Art Bartsch, Eddi Bowlds; *voice:* Jimmy Donnelly; *mus:* Winston Sharples; *col:* Tech. *sd:* RCA. 6½ min. • A family takes in an orphan for Christmas. Their own brat of a son frames the orphan to get him slung out ... but conscience gets the better of him.

6843. Wait Till the Sun Shines, Nellie (*Screen Songs*) 4 Mar. 1932; *p.c.:* The Fleischer Studio for Para; *prod:* Max Fleischer; *dir:* Dave Fleischer; *anim:* Seymour Kneitel, Myron Waldman; *mus:* Art Turkisher; *l/a:* Round the Towners Quartette; b&w. *sd:* WE. 7 min. *l/a/anim.* • Betty and Bimbo go skating in an old-time setting. They get stranded on the ice and have to wait 'til the sun melts it.

6844. Wake Up the Gypsy in Me (*Merrie Melodies*) 19 June 1933; *p.c.:* Hugh Harman–Rudolf Ising prods for WB; *anim:* Isadore Freleng, Larry Silverman, Robert Clampett; *mus:* Frank Marsales; *asso prod:* Leon Schlesinger; b&w. *sd:* Vit. 7 min. • In old Russia, Ricepudding "The Mad Monk" forces his attentions on a gypsy girl and is overthrown by a peasant revolution.

6845. Walky Talky Hawky (*Merrie Melodies*); *p.c.:* WB; *dir:* Robert McKimson; *story:* Warren Foster; *anim:* Cal Dalton, Don Williams, Richard Bickenbach; *lay:* Cornett Wood; *back:* Richard H. Thomas; *ed:* Treg Brown; *voices:* Mel Blanc; *mus:* Carl W. Stalling; *prod mgr:* John W. Burton; *prod:* Edward Selzer; *col:* Tech. *sd:* Vit. 7 min. *Academy Award nomination.* • Henery Hawk sets out to capture a chicken but doesn't know what one looks like. He meets Foghorn Leghorn who deliberately puts him on the wrong track.

6846. A Wall Street Wail 1913; *p.c.:* Pathé-Ecletic; *anim:* John Randolph Bray; b&w. *sil.* • No story available. Reissued as *Exploring Ephraim's Exploit.*

6847. The Wallflower (*Phantasy*) 3 July 1941; *p.c.:* Colum; *story:* Ben Harrison; *anim:* Manny Gould; *voices:* Danny Webb, Mel Blanc; *mus:* Joe de Nat; *prod mgr:* James Bronis; b&w. *sd:* RCA. 6 min. • An old maid hen chases a practical joke playing duck at a barn dance.

6848. The Walrus Hunters (*Aesop's Film Fable*) 11 Aug. 1923; *p.c.:* Famous Pictures Inc for Pathé; *dir:* Paul Terry; b&w. *sil.* 5 min. • No story available.

6849. Wandering Bill 9 Sept. 1915; *p.c.:* Lubin Mfg Co; *anim:* Carl Francis Lederer; b&w. *sil.* • No story available.

6850. The Wandering Minstrel (*Aesop's Film Fable*) 4 Jan. 1928; *p.c.:* Fables Pictures Inc for Pathé; *dir:* Paul Terry, Harry Bailey; b&w. st 10 min. • Set in medieval times, a minstrel rescues the fair maiden when her horse bolts. He saves her once again from a gang of bandits.

6851. Wandering Toy (*Cinémagazine #158*) 1929; b&w. *sil.* 10 min. *l/a/anim.* • A brief journey to Europe and Asia with a cartoon figure acting as courier.

6852. Wanted! No Master (*MGM Cartoon*) 18 Mar. 1939; *p.c.:* MGM; *dir:* Milt Gross; *anim:* William Littlejohn; *voice:* Mel Blanc; *mus:* Elbert C. Lewis; *prod:* Fred Quimby; *col:* sep. *sd:* WE. 8 min. • Count Screwloose's dog, J.R. wants him out of his life, so he tries to marry the Count off to a widow.

6853. War and Pieces (*Looney Tunes*) 6 June 1964; *p.c.:* WB; *dir:* Chuck Jones; *asst dir:* Maurice Noble; *story:* John Dunn; *anim:* Ken Harris, Richard H. Thomas, Bob Bransford, Tom Ray; *lay:* Dave Rose; *back:* Philip de Guard; *ed:* Treg Brown; *voice:* Paul Julian; *mus:* Bill Lava; *prod mgr:* William Orcutt; *prod:* David H. DePatie; *col:* Tech. *sd:* Vit. 7 min. • To catch his prey, the Coyote uses invisible paint, a shotgun rigged as a "Peep Show" and finally a rocket ship that shoots him to China.

6854. War and Pieces (*Roland & Rattfink*) 20 Sept. 1970; *p.c.:* Mirisch/DFE for UA; *dir:* Art Davis; *story:* Sid Marcus; *anim:* Robert Taylor, Ken Muse, Warren Batchelder, Manny Gould, Manny Perez, Don Williams; *lay:* Al Wilson; *back:* Richard Thomas; *ed:* Allan Potter; *voices:* Leonard Weinrib; *mus:* Doug Goodwin; *prod sup:* Jim Foss, Harry Love; *col:* DeLuxe. *sd:* RCA. 6 min. • Roland is assigned to bring justice to Rattfink, "The Scourge of the Spanish Maine."

6855. The War Between Men and Women 1972; *p.c.:* Playhouse Pictures for Jalem prods/Llenroc/Four D prods for Fox; *seq dir/des:* Robert Dranko; *anim:* Dale Case; *mus:* Marvin Hamlish; *col:* Tech. *sd.* 105 min. *l/a/anim.* • Live-action feature based on James Thurber's works. In Peter Wilson's (Jack Lemmon) pursuit of Terry Kozlenco (Barbara Harris), he envisions many animated stories related to men against women. Inspired by the TV series, *My World and Welcome to It* (1969–1970).

6856. A War Bride (*Aesop's Film Fable*) 20 Apr. 1928; *p.c.:* Fables Pictures Inc for Pathé; *dir:* Paul Terry, Harry Bailey; b&w. *sil.* 10 min. • No story available.

6857. War Dogs (*MGM Cartoon*) 9 Oct. 1943; *p.c.:* MGM; *dir:* William Hanna, Joseph Barbera; *anim:* Pete Burness, Kenneth Muse, Irven Spence, Jack Zander; *ed:* Fred MacAlpin; *voice:* Gayne Whitman; *mus:* Scott Bradley; *prod:* Fred Quimby; *col:* Tech. *sd:* WE. 6½ min. • Pvt. Smiley of the K-9 Division is a literal "Dogface." He gets entangled with a tank and sinks the whole barracks, earning himself a place in "The Dog House."

6858. Warlock 11 Jan. 1991; *p.c.:* New World Pictures for Medusa; *visual/optical fx: anim sup:* Mauro Maressa; *Rotoscope art:* Nina Chierichetti; *fx anim:* Esther Barr, Jeff Burks, Kevin Kutchaver, Patty Peraza, Kathleen Quaife-Hodge, Megan Williams; *inbet:* Ed Thompson; *stop-motion anim:* Laine Liska; *addit fx/optical compositing: Dream Quest Images: anim sup:* Jeff Burks; *Rotoscope sup:* James Valentine; *col:* DeLuxe/Tech. *sd:* Dolby stereo. 102 min. *l/a.* • Live-action film involving Devil-worship and witches.

6859. Warner Bros. *Titles* and **Sequences** • Sequences and credits made by the Warner Bros Studio for Warner and other studios. • *1932:* **Haunted Gold** (WB) • *1933:* **Footlight Parade** (WB). **Alice in Wonder-**

land (Para) • *1937:* **When's Your Birthday?** (RKO) • *1938:* **The Big Broadcast of 1938** (Para) • *1939:* **She Married a Cop** (Rep) • *1940:* **Love Thy Neighbor** (Para) • *1941:* **The Lady Eve** (Para) • *1943:* **Hi Diddle Diddle** (UA) • *1948:* **Two Guys from Texas** (WB) • *1949:* **My Dream Is Yours** (WB) • For additional information see separate items.

6860. Wash Day (*Aesop's Sound Fable*) 29 July 1929; *p.c.:* Fables Studio/Van Beuren for Pathé; *dir:* Paul Terry, Mannie Davis; *mus:* Josiah Zuro; *sd:* Maurice Manne; b&w. *sd:* RCA. 7 min. • The mice steal a pair of Farmer Al's long johns from his washing. He pursues them on a yeast-filled pig until a bird punctures it. When he returns home, he discovers the mice have converted his house into a recreation field.

6861. Watch the Birdie (*The Dogfather*) 20 Mar. 1975; *p.c.:* Mirisch/DFE for UA; *dir:* Gerry Chiniquy; *story:* John Dunn; *anim:* Nelson Shin, Bob Bransford, Warren Batchelder; *lay:* Dick Ung; *back:* Richard H. Thomas; *titles:* Art Leonardi; *voices:* Bob Holt, Frank Welker; *mus:* Dean Elliott; *lyrics:* John Bradford; *col:* DeLuxe. *sd:* RCA. 6 min. • The Dogfather and Pug chase Charlie the Singer into Dr. Jekyll's laboratory. Charlie drinks a potion that turns him into a monster.

6862. Watch the Birdie (*Woody Woodpecker*) 24 Feb. 1958; *p.c.:* Walter Lantz prods for Univ; *dir:* Alex Lovy; *story:* Homer Brightman; *anim:* Ray Abrams, La Verne Harding; *sets:* Raymond Jacobs, Art Landy; *voices:* Daws Butler, Grace Stafford; *mus:* Clarence Wheeler; *prod mgr:* William E. Garity; *col:* Tech. *sd:* RCA. 6 min. • Woody gives a birdwatcher a rough time.

6863. Watch the Butterfly (*Possible Possum*) Oct. 1966; *p.c.:* TT for Fox; *dir/anim:* Dave Tendlar; *col:* DeLuxe. *sd:* RCA. 5½ min. • An entomologist disturbs the gang by wanting to view a rare butterfly.

6864. Watcha Watchin'? (*Loopy de Loop*) Apr. 1963; *p.c.:* Hanna-Barbera for Colum; *prod/dir:* Joseph Barbera, William Hanna; *story dir:* Lewis Marshall; *story:* Dalton Sandifer; *anim dir:* Charles A. Nichols; *anim:* Bob Carr; *lay:* Dan Gordon; *back:* F. Montealegre; *ed:* Ken Spears; *voices:* Daws Butler, Don Messick; *mus:* Hoyt Curtin; *titles:* Lawrence Gobel; *prod mgr:* Howard Hanson; *col:* East. *sd:* RCA. 6 min. • Loopy tries to keep a sleepy watchdog alert.

6865. The Watchdog (*Aesop's Fable*) 28 Sept. 1945; *p.c.:* TT for Fox; *dir:* Eddie Donnelly; *story:* John Foster; *mus:* Philip A. Scheib; *col:* Tech. *sd:* RCA. 7 min. • Hector the hunting dog is useless at catching rabbits. • Tech reissue of the 1939 release.

6866. The Watchdog (*Terry-Toon*) 20 Oct 1939; *p.c.:* TT for Fox; *dir:* Eddie Donnelly; *story:* John Foster; *mus:* Philip A. Scheib; b&w. *sd:* RCA. 7 min. • Hector is no good as a hunting dog and when he fails to catch a rabbit, the other rabbits adopt him.

6867. Water Babies (*Silly Symphony*) 11 May 1935; *p.c.:* Walt Disney prods for UA; *dir:* Wilfred Jackson; *story:* Albert Hurter, Joe Grant; *anim:* Arthur Babbitt, Ugo d'Orsi, Gilles de Tremaudan, Nick George, Jack Hannah, Dick Huemer, Wolfgang Reitherman, Archie Robin, Louis Schmitt, Roy Williams, Cy Young; *character des:* Albert Hurter; *lay:* Hugh Hennesy; *mus:* Leigh Harline; *col:* Tech. *sd:* RCA. *sd:* 7 min. • The Water Babies hold an aqua-pageant, finishing with prayers as bell-flowers ring.

6868. The Water Cure (*Aesop's Film Fable*) 16 Apr. 1929; *p.c.:* Fables Studio Inc/Van Beuren for Pathé; *dir:* Paul Terry; *mus:* Carl Edouarde; b&w. *sd:* RCA (disc). 10 min. • When Farmer Al tries to take a bath, a monkey drenches his bathroom, causing water to drip into the apartment below Al Falfa's. The resident calls a plumber who is so inept that when he instigates the flood, he causes Al Falfa to be swept over the falls in his tub.

6869. Water, Water Every Hare (*Looney Tunes*) 19 Apr. 1952; *p.c.:* WB; *dir:* Charles M. Jones; *story:* Michael Maltese; *anim:* Ben Washam, Ken Harris, Phil Monroe, Lloyd Vaughan; *fx:* Harry Love; *lay:* Robert Gribbroek; *back:* Philip de Guard; *ed:* Treg Brown; *voices:* Mel Blanc, John T. Smith; *mus:* Carl Stalling; *prod mgr:* John W. Burton; *prod:* Edward Selzer; *col:* Tech. *sd:* Vit. 7 min. • Bugs is washed away by a flood and finds himself at the mercy of a mad scientist who wants to transplant his brain.

6870. Watercolor of Brazil • See: *Aquarela Do Brazil; The Three Caballeros*

6871. Watered Stock (*Aesop's Film Fable*) 26 Sept. 1926; *p.c.:* Fables Pictures Inc for Pathé; *dir:* Paul Terry; b&w. *sil.* 10 min. • Farmer Al waters the milk before setting out with his milk wagon. A drove of felines rob the farmer of his stock, trounce him and a cop.

6872. The Wax Works (*Oswald*) 25 June 1934; *p.c.:* Univ; *dir:* Walter Lantz; *story:* Victor McLeod; *anim:* Manuel Moreno, George Grandpré, Lester Kline, (La)Verne Harding, Fred Kopietz; *voice:* Bernice Hansel; *mus:* James Dietrich; b&w. *sd:* WE. 9 min. • Wax Works proprietor, Oswald, takes in a foundling from his doorstep. The infant witnesses the statues in the Chamber of Horrors coming to life. Caricatures of Groucho Marx, Bela Lugosi and Boris Karloff.

6873. Way Back When a Nag Was Only a Horse (*Stone Age*) 8 Mar. 1940; *p.c.:* The Fleischer Studio for Para; *prod:* Max Fleischer; *dir:* Dave Fleischer; *story:* Joseph Stultz; *anim:* Myron Waldman, George Moreno; *ed:* Kitty Pfister; *character design:* Charles Thorson; *mus:* Sammy Timberg; *prod sup:* Sam Buchwald, Isidore Sparber; b&w. *sd:* WE. 7 min. • A caveman husband is dragged to a store by his spouse. He finds a diversion at the music counter with a pretty sales assistant.

6874. Way Back When a Night Club Was a Stick (*Stone Age*) 12 Apr. 1940; *p.c.:* The Fleischer Studio for Para; *prod:* Max Fleischer; *dir:* Dave Fleischer; *story:* William Turner; *anim:* David Tendlar, Edwin Rehberg; *ed:* Kitty Pfister; *character design:* Charles Thorson; *voices:* Jack Mercer, Margie Hines; *mus:* Sammy Timberg; *prod sup:* Sam Buchwald, Isidore Sparber; b&w. *sd:* WE. 7 min. • Mr. Stonebroke forsakes babysitting to sneak off to Lucky's Wreck-Reation Club. His wife discovers his absence and busts up the joint.

6875. Way Back When a Razzberry Was a Fruit (*Stone Age*) 26 July 1940; *p.c.:* The Fleischer Studio for Para; *prod:* Max Fleischer; *dir:* Dave Fleischer; *story:* Dan Gordon; *anim:* James Culhane, Alfred Eugster; *character des:* Charles Thorson; *ed:* Kitty Pfister; *voice:* William Pennell; *mus:* Sammy Timberg; *prod sup:* Sam Buchwald, Isidore Sparber; b&w. *sd:* WE. 7 min. • Prehistoric gardening tips.

6876. Way Back When a Triangle Had Its Points (*Stone Age*) 9 Feb. 1940; *p.c.:* The Fleischer Studio for Para; *prod:* Max Fleischer; *dir:* Dave Fleischer; *story:* William Turner; *anim:* David Tendlar, Thomas Golden; *ed:* Kitty Pfister; *character design:* Charles Thorson; *mus:* Sammy Timberg; *ph:* Charles Schettler; *prod sup:* Sam Buchwald, Isidore Sparber; b&w. *sd:* WE. 7 min. • I.M. Stonebroke operates a rock company, replacing his wife's job by hiring a pretty stenographer. He takes her to the "Cave Inn" Night Club ... but wifey soon finds out.

6877. Way Back When Women Had Their Weigh (*Stone Age*) 26 Sept. 1940; *p.c.:* The Fleischer Studio for Para; *prod:* Max Fleischer; *dir:* Dave Fleischer; *story:* Ted Pierce; *anim:* Thomas Johnson, Harold Walker; *ed:* Kitty Pfister; *character design:* Charles Thorson; *mus:* Sammy Timberg; *ph:* Charles Schettler; *prod sup:* Sam Buchwald, Isidore Sparber; b&w. *sd:* WE. 7 min. • A portly caveman sees a girl pursuing thin men, so he goes through a rigorous reducing treatment only to discover she prefers fat men.

6878. Way Down Yonder in the Corn (*Fox & Crow*) 25 Nov. 1943; *p.c.:* Colum; *prod:* Dave Fleischer; *story:* Bob Wickersham; *story:* Sam Cobean; *anim:* Phil Duncan, Basil Davidovich; *lay:* Clark Watson; *ed:* Edward Moore; *voices:* Frank Graham; *mus:* Eddie Kilfeather; *prod mgr:* Albert Spar; *col:* Tech. *sd:* RCA. 7½ min. • The crow disguises himself as a scarecrow in order to get a job guarding the fox's cornfield.

6879. The Way of All Pests (*Color Rhapsody*) 28 Feb. 1941; *p.c.:* Colum; *dir:* Art Davis; *anim:* Sid Marcus; *voices:* Mel Blanc; *mus:* Joe de Nat; *prod mgr:* George Winkler; *col:* Tech. *sd:* RCA. 7½ min. • Tired of being stepped on and swatted by a man, the insects retaliate.

6880. The Wayward Canary (*Mickey Mouse*) 12 Nov. 1932; *p.c.:* Walt Disney prods for UA; *dir:* Burton F. Gillett; *anim:* Les Clark, Gilles de Tremaudan, Norman Ferguson, Clyde Geronimi, Hardie Gramatky, David D. Hand, Jack King, Richard Lundy, Tom Palmer; *voices:* Marcellite Garner, Walt Disney; *mus:* Bert Lewis; b&w. *sd:* PCP. 7 min. • Minnie's canary gets covered in ink and chased by a cat. Pluto saves the day.

6881. The Wayward Dog (*Aesop's Film Fable*) 25 Dec. 1921; *p.c.:* Fables Pictures Inc for Pathé; *dir:* Paul Terry; b&w. *sil.* 5 min. • The hero's sweetie leaves him for a matelot. He then returns, dressed as a sailor to fight his rival but the girl forsakes them both for another.

6882. The Wayward Hat (*Terry-Toon*) July 1960; *p.c.:* TT for Fox; *ex prod:* Bill Weiss; *dir:* Dave Tendlar; *story sup:* Tom Morrison; *story:* Larz

Bourne, Eli Bauer; *anim:* Ed Donnelly, Vinnie Bell, Mannie Davis, Johnny Gent, Larry Silverman, Cosmo Anzilotti; *lay:* John Zago; *back:* Bill Focht; *mus:* Phil Scheib; *prod mgr:* Frank Schudde; *col:* Tech. *sd:* RCA. 6 min. CS. • Foofle buys a new hat that leads him chasing around the town after it's taken by a whirlwind.

6883. The Wayward Pups (*Happy Harmonies*) 10 July 1937; *p.c.:* MGM; *prod/dir:* Hugh Harman, Rudolf Ising; *voice:* Russ Powell; *mus:* Scott Bradley; *col:* Tech; *sd:* RCA. 9 min. • The house cat causes the pups, Ruff and Reddy, to run off and then has to retrieve them.

6884. We Aim to Please (*Popeye*) 28 Dec. 1934; *p.c.:* The Fleischer Studio for Para; *prod:* Max Fleischer; *dir:* Dave Fleischer; *anim:* Willard Bowsky, David Tendlar; *voices:* William A. Costello, Mae Questel, CharlesCarver, Lou Fleischer; *mus:* Sammy Timberg; *b&w. sd:* WE. 6 min. • Wimpy impresses Bluto by mooching a hamburger from Popeye's diner. Bluto tries the same idea and rapidly wears out his welcome.

6885. We Did It (*Betty Boop*) 24 Apr. 1936; *p.c.:* The Fleischer Studio for Para; *prod:* Max Fleischer; *dir:* Dave Fleischer; *anim:* Willard Bowsky, George Germanetti; *voices:* Mae Questel; *mus:* Sammy Timberg; *b&w. sd:* WE. 7 min. • Betty's kittens cause havoc in the kitchen and Pudgy bears the blame.

6886. We Give Pink Stamps (*Pink Panther*) 12 Feb. 1965; *p.c.:* Mirisch/Geoffrey/DFE for UA; *dir:* Friz Freleng; *asst dir:* Hawley Pratt; *story:* John Dunn; *anim:* Norman McCabe, La Verne Harding, Don Williams, Manny Perez, Warren Batchelder, Bob Matz; *lay:* Dick Ung; *back:* Tom O'Loughlin; *ed:* Lee Gunther; *mus:* Bill Lava; *theme tune:* Henry Mancini; *prod mgr:* Bill Orcutt; *col:* DeLuxe. *sd:* RCA. 6 min. • The panther's rest is disturbed by a janitor cleaning up Gamble's department store.

6887. We, the Animals — Squeak! (*Looney Tunes*) 9 Aug. 1941; *p.c.:* Leon Schlesinger prods for WB; *dir:* Robert Clampett; *story:* Melvin Millar; *anim:* I. Ellis, John Carey, Lucifer Guarnier; *lay:* John Carey; *ed:* Treg Brown; *voices:* Sara Berner, Phil Kramer, Mel Blanc, Robert C. Bruce, Billy Bletcher; *mus:* Carl W. Stalling; *prod sup:* Henry Binder, Raymond G. Katz; *b&w. sd:* Vit. 6 min. • Kansas City Kitty tells a radio audience of when her infant progidy was kidnapped by rats.

6888. The Weakly Reporter (*Merrie Melodies*) 25 Mar. 1944; *p.c.:* Leon Schlesinger prods for WB; *dir:* Charles M. Jones; *story:* Michael Maltese; *anim:* Ben Washam; *lay:* Robert Gribbroek; *back:* Earl Klein; *ed:* Treg Brown; *voices:* Frank Graham, Mel Blanc, Bea Benaderet; *mus:* Carl W. Stalling; *prod sup:* Henry Binder, Raymond Katz; *col:* Tech. *sd:* Vit. 7 min. • This gazette pictures many war-time problems: Transportation, women in uniform along with food and gas rationing.

6889. The Wearing of the Grin (*Looney Tunes*) 28 July 1951; *p.c.:* WB; *dir:* Charles M. Jones; *story:* Michael Maltese; *anim:* Ben Washam, Lloyd Vaughan, Ken Harris, Phil Monroe; *lay:* Robert Gribbroek; *back:* Philip de Guard; *ed:* Treg Brown; *voices:* Mel Blanc, John T. Smith; *mus:* Eugene Poddany; *orch:* Milt Franklyn; *prod mgr:* John W. Burton; *prod:* Edward Selzer; *col:* Tech. *sd:* Vit. 7 min. • While visiting Ireland, Porky falls victim to the pranks of two mischievious leprechauns.

6890. Weary Willies (*Oswald*) 5 Aug. 1929; *p.c.:* Winkler for Univ; *anim:* Isadore Freleng; *b&w. sil.* 6 min. • A cop chases hobo Oswald from a railroad car. He meets another tramp and they team up to steal a chicken.

6891. Weasel Stop (*Merrie Melodies*) 11 Feb. 1956; *p.c.:* WB; *dir:* Robert McKimson; *story:* Tedd Pierce; *anim:* Keith Darling, Ted Bonnicksen, Russ Dyson; *sets:* Richard H. Thomas; *ed:* Treg Brown; *voices:* Mel Blanc, Lloyd Perryman; *mus:* Milt Franklyn; *prod mgr:* John W. Burton; *prod:* Edward Selzer; *col:* Tech. *sd:* Vit. 7 min. • Foggy teams with a sneaky weasel to teach the apathetic watchdog a lesson.

6892. Weasel While You Work (*Merrie Melodies*) 6 Sept. 1958; *p.c.:* WB; *dir:* Robert McKimson; *story:* Michael Maltese; *anim:* Warren Batchelder, Tom Ray, George Grandpré, Ted Bonnicksen; *sets:* Robert Gribbroek; *ed:* Treg Brown; *voices:* Mel Blanc; *mus:* John Seeley; *prod:* John W. Burton; *col:* Tech. *sd:* Vit. 7 min. • While Foggy has some winter fun, Weary Weasel arrives and tries to eat him. The wily leghorn convinces him that it's the *dog* he wants to eat.

6893. Weather Magic (*Terry-Toon*) May 1965; *p.c.:* TT for Fox; *ex prod:* Bill Weiss; *dir/anim:* Cosmo Anzilotti; *story sup:* Tom Morrison; *story:* Larz Bourne; *sets:* Bill Focht, John Zago; *ed:* Jack MacConnell; *voices:* Day-

ton Allen; *mus:* Jim Timmens; *ph:* Joe Rasinski; *sd:* Elliot Grey; *col:* DeLuxe. *sd:* RCA. 5½ min. • Astro alters the Earth's weather and becomes a valuable property for the Weather Bureau.

6894. Wedding Bells (*Krazy Kat*) 10 Jan. 1933; *p.c.:* Winkler for Colum; *prod:* Charles Mintz; *dir:* Ben Harrison, Manny Gould; *anim:* Al Eugster, Preston Blair; *mus:* Joe de Nat; *prod mgr:* James Bronis; *b&w. sd:* WE. 6 min. • Krazy and Kitty prepare themselves for their wedding and then tie the knot.

6895. Wedding Belts (*Stone Age*) 5 July 1940; *p.c.:* The Fleischer Studio for Para; *prod:* Max Fleischer; *dir:* Dave Fleischer; *story:* George Manuel; *anim:* David Tendlar, Stephen Muffatti; *character design:* Charles Thorson; *voices:* Pinto Colvig, Jack Mercer; *mus:* Sammy Timberg; *ph:* Charles Schettler; *prod sup:* Sam Buchwald, Isidore Sparber; *b&w. sd:* WE. 7 min. • Two lovesick swains are shown the hazards of married life by their parents.

6896. A Wedding Knight (*Modern Madcap*) Aug. 1966; *p.c.:* Para Cartoons; *dir:* Shamus Culhane; *story:* Heyward Kling; *anim:* Al Eugster, Chuck Harriton, Nick Tafuri; *sets:* Danté Barbetta, Howard Beckerman, Robert Little; *voices:* Allen Swift, Shari Lewis; *mus:* Winston Sharples; *prod sup:* Harold Robins, Burt Hanft; *col:* Tech. *sd:* RCA. 6 min. • The King's ugly daughter disguises herself as "The Black Knight," offering marriage to the conquerer. Nearsighted knight, Sir Blur, tries his hand … and wins … with help.

6897. The Wee Men (*Noveltoon*) 8 Aug. 1947; *p.c.:* Famous for Para; *dir:* Bill Tytla; *story:* Ewald Ludwig, I. Klein, Jack Ward; *anim:* Al Eugster, Steve Muffatti, George Germanetti; *sets:* Robert Little; *voice:* Jackson Beck; *mus:* Winston Sharples; *song:* Buddy Kaye, Dick Manning; *ph:* Leonard McCormick; *prod mgr:* Sam Buchwald; *col:* Tech. *sd:* RCA. 10 min. • While delivering shoes to the needy, Patrick Q. Leprechaun is caught by a miser who demands to be taken to be taken to the leprechauns' "Crock of Gold."

6898. Wee-Willie Wildcat (*Barney Bear*) 20 June 1953; *p.c.:* MGM; *dir:* Dick Lundy; *story:* Jack Cosgriff, Heck Allen; *anim:* Michael Lah, Walter Clinton, Grant Simmons, Ray Patterson, Robert Bentley; *sets:* John Didrik Johnsen; *ed:* Jim Faris; *voices:* Paul Frees; *mus:* Scott Bradley; *ph:* Jack Stevens; *prod:* Fred Quimby; *col:* Tech. *sd:* WE. 7 min. • The policy of "There's no such thing as a bad boy" is put to the test when Barney tries to entertain a neighbor's unmanagable brat.

6899. Weenie Roast (*Krazy Kat*) 14 Sept. 1931; *p.c.:* Winkler for Colum; *prod:* Charles Mintz; *anim:* Ben Harrison, Manny Gould; *mus:* Joe de Nat; *prod mgr:* James Bronis; *b&w. sd:* WE. 6 min. • Krazy and his girl on a runaway roller coaster ride at Coney Island.

6900. Welcome, Little Stranger (*Dinky Duck*) 3 Oct. 1941; *p.c.:* TT for Fox; *dir:* Connie Rasinski; *story:* John Foster; *mus:* Philip A. Scheib; *col:* Tech. *sd:* RCA. 7 min. • When a black duck hatches amongst Mother Hen's brood, she doesn't want to know … forcing Dinky Duck to run away from home.

6901. Welcome, Nudnik! (*Nudnik*) Feb. 1966; *p.c.:* Rembrandt Films for Para; *prod:* William L. Snyder; *dir:* Gene Deitch; *after* Rembrandt for Para. *col. sd.* 6 min. • Nudnik's train pulls in at "Crummy Junction" where he has altercations with an outraged woman, a thief, a cop and in a zoo. • See: *Nudnik*

6902. Well Oiled (*Woody Woodpecker*) 30 June 1947; *p.c.:* Walter Lantz prods for Univ; *dir:* Dick Lundy; *story:* Ben Hardaway, Milt Schaffer; *anim:* (La)Verne Harding, Les Kline, Hal Mason, Pat Matthews, Grim Natwick, S.C. Onaitis; *sets:* Fred Brunish; *ed:* Dave Lurie; *voices:* Jack Mather, Ben Hardaway; *mus:* Darrell Calker; *prod mgr:* William E. Garity; *col:* Tech. *sd:* WE. 6 min. • Woody syphons petrol from Wally's car, resulting in the two having a grease-gun duel.

6903. Well Worn Daffy (*Looney Tunes*) 22 May 1965; *p.c.:* DFE for WB; *dir:* Robert McKimson; *story:* Dave DeTiege; *anim:* Warren Batchelder, Bob Matz, La Verne Harding, Norm McCabe, Don Williams, Manny Perez; *lay:* Dick Ung; *ed:* Lee Gunther; *voices:* Mel Blanc; *mus:* Bill Lava; *col:* Tech. *sd:* Vit. 6 min. • Speedy Gonzales and friends are dying of thirst in the desert when Daffy arrives, refusing them a drink from his well.

6904. We're Back! A Dinosaur's Story 24 Nov. 1993; *p.c.:* Amblin Entertainment for Univ; *dir:* Dick Zondag, Ralph Zondag, Phil Nibbelink, Simon Wells; *ex prod:* Steven Spielberg, Frank Marshall, Kathleen Kennedy; *prod:* Stephen Hickner; *co-prod:* Thad Weinlein; *based on the book by*

Hudson Talbot; *scr:* John Patrick Shanley; *storyboard sup:* Darek Gogol, Tom Humber; *storyboard:* Geoff Clowes, Alex Lawrence, Erik Chr. Schmidt, Laurent Ben-Mimoun; *art dir:* Colin Stimpson; *anim sup:* Bibo Bergeron, Sahin Ersöz, Børge Ring, Thierry Schiel, Kristof Serrand, Rob Stevenhagen, Jeffrey J. Varab; *anim:* Georges Abolin, Arnaud Berthier, Rudi Bloss, Eric Bouillette, David Bowers, Alain Costa, Denis Couchon, Michael Eames, Miguel A. Fuertes, Rodolphe Guenoden, Daniel Jeannette, Fabio Lignini, Nicholas Marlet, Patrick Mate, Quentin Miles, Phil Morris, Jacques Muller, Olivier Pont, Jürgen Richter, William Salazar, Glenn Sylvester, Oskar Urretabizkaia, Jan Van Buyten, Frank Vibert, Andreas von Andrian, Todd Waterman, Johnny Zeuthen; *anim asst:* Isabelle Beaudoin, Shari Cohen, Brenda McKie-Chat, Luba Medekova-Klein, Fernando Pastor, Steve Perry, Silvia Pompei, Emil Sergiev, Emil Simeonov, Julia Woolf Thomas Cook, Tony Cope, Claudia Aaron, Philip Anderson, Cécile Bender, Jamie Kezlarian Bolio, Claire Bramwell-Pearson, Sylviane Burnet, Steve Cavalier, Roland Chat, Odile Comon, Denise Dean, Eric Delbecq, Tony Ealey, Cecilia Esteves, Stuart Evans, Nathalie Gavet, Antony Gray, Louise Haley, Nick Harrop, Adam Heller, Katrin Herjean-Malkiewicz, Gontran Hoarau, Paul Jesper, Veronique Langdon, Sean Leaning, Philippe Le Brun, Carl Linton, Pierre Lyphoudt, Janet McKay, Andrew Moss, Paul Mota, Sylvia Muller, Ivelina Nacheva, David Navarro, Dawn Pearce, Vittorio Pirajno, Jane Poole, Jean-Francois Rey, Rick Richards, Kay Sales, Andrew H. Schmidt, Kieron Seamons, Bruce Simpson, Kevin Spruce, Karen Stephenson, Simon Swift, Richard Tang, Matthew Taylor, Vladimir Todorov, Daniela Topham, Marco Trandafilov, Stephanie Walker, Mark Williams; *addit anim:* David Berthier, Luc Chamberland, Emanuela Cozzi, Maximilian Graenitz, Antony Gray, Gontran Hoarau, Steve Horrocks, Andrea Simonti, Pete Western; *anim inbet:* Patrick Beirne, Shaun Blake, Aleisa Bloom, Julia Bracegirdle, Belem Cerqueira, Cathy Childs, David Clarvis, Pierre Coffin, Bojan Djukic, Paul Hallewell, Debbie Hamed, Louise Keating, Sarah Keogh, Sarah Marsden, Vanessa J. Martin, Jason McDonald, Stephen Morgan, Karen Narramore, Andy Paraskos, Scott Pleydell-Pearce, Mark Smith, Aksel Studsgarth, Francesca Talbot, Sylvaine Terriou, Tim White, Sue Woodward; *blue sketch:* Adam Binham; *post anim sup:* Robert Edward Crawford, Matthew Teevan; *check co-ord:* Steve Pegram; *anim check:* Corona Esterhazy, Nondus Banning-Boddy, Deborah Campbell, Shaun Caton, Janice Eason, Frances Jacob, Corine Marcel, Chantal Marsolais, Cindy Moehrle, Michael Myers, Helen O'Brien, Eithne Quinn, Joan Topley; *character des:* Carlos Grangel; *scene plan:* David Allonby, Tim Francis, Harold Kraut, Jean Maluta, James C.J. Williams; *line test:* Tim Davies, Clive Bolger, Phill Kemp, Chris Knights; *lay:* Peter Moehrle, Marco Cinello, Brendan Houghton, Clive Hutchings, Glenn Jeffs, David Kenyon, Douglas Kirk, Hervé Leblan, Mark Marren, Damon O'Beirne, Das Petrou, Tony Pulham, Panagiotis Rappas, Chris Scully; *lay asst:* Neal Petty, Lee Taylor; *lay/back co-ord:* Victoria Morrison-Glenys; *back sup:* Colin Stimpson; *back:* Steven Albert, Luc Desmarchelier, Natasha Gross, Walter Kössler, Marcos Mateu Mastre, Shelley Page, Mike Rose, Gary Sycamore, Ennio Torresan; *key frame paint:* Sarah Fletcher; *character sculptor:* Phillipe Angeles, Caroline Baxter; *col des:* Daniel Cacouault; *col models:* E. Jane Gotts, Alison Flintham, Julie Gleeson; *col seperation:* Sky Bone, Janet Cable, Karin Adams, James Bird, Tanya Blair, Helen Buckingham, Karen Church, Jane Dillon, Annie Elvin, Lucy Fellowes, Segan Friend, Gerald Gallego, Barry Goff, Brian Holmes, Lorea Hoye, Helen Ingham, Wayne Kennedy, Susan Lamson, Derek L'Estrange, Shaun McGlinchey, Ron McMinn, Deirdre Hazel O'Flaherty, Carmen Parrinello, Leanne Rich, Lee Taylor, David Walker, Lorraine Ward, Martin Wiseman, Jay Wren; *fx sup:* Stephen B. Moore; *fx anim:* Philippe Angeles, Jon Brooks, Andrew Brownlow, Steven Burch, Leonard F.W. Green, Mick Harper, Hock-Lian Law, Stephen McDermott, Michael Rivero, Mike Smith, Alexs Stadermann, Jeff Topping, Dan Turner, Garrett Wren; *fx anim asst:* Guner Behich, David Birkenshaw, Michaela Budde, Francine Chassagnac, James M. Clow, Frank Doyle, Natalie Garceau-Turner, Duncan Henry, Earl A. Hibbert, Rosanna Lyons, Giulia Mazz, Pat C. Morton, Albert Price, Gary Sole, Heather Tailby, Jerry Verschoor, H. Grace Waddington; *fx anim inbet:* Joe Berger, Paul Houlihan, Lilas LeBlan, Lee Townsend; *fx graphics:* Bernie Gagliano; *fx co-ord:* Kristine Humber, Pamela Johnson; *l/a fx:* Martin Gutteridge; *cg fx:* Roger Guyett, Christian Hogue, Bert Terreri; *computer mgr:* Alex Volovsek; *digital compositor:* Richard Addison-Wood; *fx graphics:* Bernie Gagliano; *ed:* Nick Fletcher, Sim Evan-Jones, Clare De Chenu, Kieran Evans, Rob Green, Jennifer Keys, Andrew MacRitchie, Marcus Taylor; *voices: Rex:* John Good-

man; *Buster:* Blaze Berdahl; *Mother Bird:* Rhea Perlman; *Vorb:* Jay Leno; *Woog:* René Le Vant; *Elsa:* Felicity Kendal; *Dweeb:* Charles Fleischer; *Captain Neweyes:* Walter Cronkite; *Louie:* Joey Shea; *Dr. Bleeb:* Julia Child; *Professor Screweyes:* Kenneth Mars; *Cecilia Nuthatch:* Yeardly Smith; *Stubbs the Clown:* Martin Short; *Himself:* Larry King; *also:* Jessica Angesow, Zachary Ball, Barbara Barness, Bendar Bashir, Catherine Battistone, Michael Benz, Jamie Bolio, Cory Bonder, Dan Borek, Bill Capizzi, Jim Carter, David Clark, Gillian Chat, Dixie Crespi, J.D. Daniels, Sandra Dickinson, Peter Elliot, Lou Hirsch, David Holt, Justin Isfeld, Ron Karabatsos, Cristy Kelly, Alexandra Large, Marilyn Leubner, Jonathan McCracken, Nigel Pegram, Jennifer Regan, Rick Richards, Liza Ross, Lindsay Schmidt, Jana Shelden, Aaron Teich, Matthew Teich, Shelley Thompson, Dick Vosburgh, Jessica Waite, James Watt, Jessica Wray, Eliza Yoder, Sarah Zilinski, Desiree Zondag, Shannon Zondag; *mus:* James Horner; *songs:* James Horner, Thomas Dolby; *song:* "Roll Back the Rock" performed by Little Richard; *mus prod:* Thomas Dolby; music performed by London Symphony Orchestra; *orch:* Don Davis, Arthur Kempel, Thomas Pasatieri; *mus ed:* Jim Henrikson; *mus copyist:* Jo Ann Kane; *mus score mix:* Shawn Murphy; *mus preparation:* Steven L. Smith; *art co-ord:* Shauna Stevens, Isabel Graczyk, Barbara Nash; *digital compositor: American Film Technologies:* Ken Anderson, Karen Buskirk, Steve W. Childers, Douglas Cooper, Eric Fuss, Jane Jackoskie, Rachel Lagdao; *digital col:* Douglas Ikeler; *digital composition:* John "Woody" Wodynski, Celine Petker, Brandi Stevens, Rachel Lagdao; *scanning technician:* Karl Dunne; *American Film Technologies: art co-ord:* Isabel Graczyk, Barbara Nash, Shauna M. Stevens; *quality control:* Robert Cuilty, Gabriel Garcia, Clifford Presley; *digital col model/fx:* Stephen Childers, Richard Turner, Tia L. Marshall; *digital archivist:* John Goldkamp, Joel Pederson; *technical co-ord:* Darin Hollings, David Morehead; *post operations:* David "Scott" Murdock, Neil Partyka, David Manos Morris; *i&p/digital fx: Sidley Wright & Assoc: digital fx sup:* Steve Wright; *addit electronic i&p/digital compositing:* Sidley Wright Motionworks, U.S. Animation Inc.; *choreog:* Smith Wordes; *l/a fx:* Effects Associates, Martin Gutteridge; *col timer:* Mike Stanwick; *neg cutter:* Kona Cutting, Gary Burritt; *lab contact:* Ray Adams; *title art:* Hans Bacher, Hudson Talbot; *ex in charge of prod:* Joe Mazzuca; *prod management/sup.:* Sean Lurie, Jay Panek, Alex Johns, Ron Alonzo, Ana Cruz, Claudia Ravelo, Rita Perez; *character builders:* Jim Kammerud, Marty Fuller, Pascal Blais; *light box anim:* Yuri Large, Colin Tannen; *sd ed:* Campbell Askew; *re-rec mix:* Rick Alexander, Gerry Humphreys, Jim Bolt, Tim Cavagin, Andy D'Addario, Dean Humphreys, Robin O'Donoghue; *rec:* Albert Romero; *ADR mix:* Alan Holly; *sd fx ed:* Robert Gavin, Michael Trent, Mark Sale, Geraldene Tuchner; *sd fx:* Dave Lawson; *dial ed:* Bill Trent; *foley arts:* Pauline Griffith, Jennie Lee Wright; *foley rec:* John Bateman; *ph:* Stuart Campbell, Graham Tiernan, Brian Riley, Craig Simpson, Deirdre Creed, Sam James; *ex prod: American Film Technologies:* David Hamby, Art Martel, Joe Mazzuca, Barry Sandrew; *American Film Technologies: prod mgr:* Ron Alonzo, Ana Cruz, Alex Johns, Sean Lurie, Jay Panek, Rita Perez, Claudia Ravelo; *post prod:* Stephen Barker; *Sidley Wright & Asso: prod mgr: digital i&p:* Diane Wright; *prod mgr:* Hal Waite; *prod asst:* Hattie Berger, Edward Bignell Colin Hutton, Sophie Law; *col:* DeLuxe. *sd:* Dolby stereo. 64 min. • Captain New Eyes is able to travel back in time to feed the dinosaurs his Brain Grain cereal which makes them intelligent and docile. They agree to come to the present day to grant children wishes in New York City. The Captain's malicious brother, Professor Screw Eyes, has other plans for the dinosaurs.

6905. We're in the Honey *(Noveltoon)* 19 Mar. 1948; *p.c.:* Famous for Para; *dir:* Bill Tytla; *story:* I. Klein, Jack Mercer; *anim:* George Germanetti, Steve Muffatti; *sets:* Anton Loeb; *voices:* Joy Terry, Jack Mercer; *mus:* Winston Sharples; *lyrics:* Buddy Kaye *ph:* Leonard McCormick; *prod mgr:* Sam Buchwald; *col:* Tech. *sd:* RCA. 8 min. • The Queen Bee supervises honey-making in a modernistic hive. Production is interrupted with the arrival of a bear.

6906. We're in the Money *(Merrie Melodies)* 19 Sept. 1933; *p.c.:* Hugh Harman, Rudolf Ising prods for WB; *prod:* Leon Schlesinger; *anim:* Isadore Freleng, Larry Martin, Robert Clampett; *voice:* Mary Moder; *mus:* Frank Marsales; *song:* Harry Warren, Al Dubin; b&w. *sd:* Vit. 7 min. • After closing time, the merchandise in a shop comes to life. Caricatures of Laurel & Hardy and Mae West.

6907. We're on Our Way to Rio *(Popeye)* 21 Apr. 1944; *p.c.:* Famous for Para; *dir:* I. Sparber; *story:* Jack Mercer, Jack Ward; *anim:* Jim Tyer,

Ben Solomon; *voices:* Jack Mercer; *mus:* Winston Sharples; *ph:* Leonard Mc Cormick; *prod mgr:* Sam Buchwald; b&w. *sd:* RCA. 8 min. Tech reissue: 10 May 1951. • The boys' leave in Rio is spent in a night club where they see Olive perform. Bluto puts Popeye forward as a champion Samba dancer.

6908. West of the Pesos *(Merrie Melodies)* 23 Jan. 1960; *p.c.:* WB; *dir:* Robert McKimson; *story:* Tedd Pierce; *anim:* Tom Ray, George Grand-pré, Ted Bonnicksen, Warren Batchelder, David R. Green; *lay:* Robert Givens; *back:* William Butler; *ed:* Treg Brown; *voices:* Mel Blanc, Tom Holland, Merrie Virginia; *mus:* Milt Franklyn; *prod mgr:* William Orcutt; *prod:* David H. DePatie; *col:* Tech. *sd:* Vit. 7 min. • Speedy rescues some mice who are being held in a research laboratory guarded by Sylvester.

6909. Western Daze *(Masdcap Models)* 17 Jan. 1941; *p.c.:* George Pal prods for Para; *prod/dir:* George Pal; *story:* Vic McLeod, Norm Blackburn; *anim:*George Pal, Ray Harryhausen, Bob Larson, Herb Price; *voices:* Pat McGeehan, Billy Bletcher, Mel Blanc, Eloise Rawitzer; *mus:* David Raksin; *conductor:* Andrè Kostelanetz,; *col:* Tech. *sd:* WE. 9 min. • Tenderfoot Jim Dandy arrives in the Wild West and is tricked into riding a stolen horse. He pursues the horse thieves and gets a reward.

6910. The Western Trail *(Terry-Toon)* 13 Apr. 1937; *p.c.:* TT for Educational; *dir:* George Gordon, Mannie Davis; *mus:* Philip A. Scheib; b&w. *sd:* RCA. 6 min. • No story available.

6911. Western Whoopee *(Aesop's Sound Fable)* 13 Apr. 1930; *p.c.:* Van Beuren for Pathé; *dir:* John Foster, Harry Bailey; *mus:* Gene Rodemich; b&w. *sd:* RCA. 6 min. • Burlesque on cowboy pictures.

6912. Westward Whoa *(Looney Tunes)* 25 Apr. 1936; *p.c.:* Leon Schlesinger prods for WB; *dir:* Jack King; *anim:* Paul Smith, Ben Clopton; *voices:* Bernice Hansel, Tommy Bond, Joe Dougherty; *mus:* Norman Spencer; *prod sup:* Henry Binder, Raymond G. Katz; b&w. *sd:* Vit. 7 min. • Porky, Beans and Little Kitty are pioneers heading west. Ham and Ex dress as Indians to throw a scare into them ... then the real redskins show up.

6913. Wet Blanket Policy *(Woody Woodpecker)* 27 Aug. 1948; *p.c.:* Walter Lantz prods for UA; *dir:* Dick Lundy; *story:* Ben Hardaway, Heck Allen; *anim:* (La)Verne Harding, Les Kline, Ed Love, Pat Matthews, Fred Moore, Ken O'Brien, Sid Pillet; *sets:* Fred Brunish; *ed:* Dave Lurie; *voices:* Lionel Stander, Gloria Wood, Harry Babbitt, Ben Hardaway; *mus:* Darrell Calker; *song:* George Tibbles, Ramey Idriss; *prod mgr:* William E. Garity; *col:* Tech. *sd:* RCA. 6 min. • Unscrupulous Buzz Buzzard sells Woody an insurance policy, naming himself as beneficiary upon Woody's demise.

6914. The Wet Hare *(Looney Tunes)* Jan. 1962; *p.c.:* WB; *dir:* Robert McKimson; *story:* Dave DeTiege; *anim:* George Grandpré, Ted Bonnicksen, Warren Batchelder, Keith Darling; *sets:* Robert Gribbroek; *ed:* Treg Brown; *voices:* Mel Blanc; *mus:* Milt Franklyn; *prod mgr:* William Orcutt; *prod:* David H. DePatie; *col:* Tech. *sd:* Vit. 7 min. • Bugs wages war with Blacq Jacq Shellacq who wants to dam the river Bugs bathes in.

6915. A Wet Knight *(Oswald)* 20 June 1932; *p.c.:* Univ; *dir:* Walter Lantz, "Bill" Nolan; *anim:* Manuel Moreno, Ray Abrams, Fred Avery, "Bill" Weber, Vet Anderson, Lester Kline, Bunny Ellison; *mus:* James Dietrich; b&w. *sd:* WE. 7 min. • Oswald and his girl shelter from a storm in a haunted castle. A peg-legged ghost kidnaps the girl and chases Oswald, so does King Kong.

6916. Wet Paint *(Donald Duck)* 9 Aug. 1946; *p.c.:* Walt Disney prods for RKO; *dir:* Jack King; *asst dir:* Joel Greenhalgh; *story:* Roy Williams; *anim:* Don Towsley, Bill Justice, Hal King, Sandy Strother, Ed Aardal, Paul Allen, Fred Kopietz, Tom Massey, Lee Morehouse, Frank McSavage; *lay:* Ernest Nordli; *back:* Howard Dunn; *voice:* Clarence Nash; *mus:* Oliver Wallace; *col:* Tech. *sd:* RCA. 7 min. • A bird's nest-collecting activities annoy Donald while he's trying to paint his car.

6917. Whacks Museum *(Krazy Kat)* 29 Sept. 1933; *p.c.:* Winkler for Colum; *prod:* Charles Mintz; *story:* Harry Love, Al Eugster; *anim:* Allen Rose, Preston Blair; *mus:* Joe de Nat; *prod mgr:* James Bronis; b&w. *sd:* WE. 6 min. • Krazy sees wax models of Jimmy Durante, Mae West and Joe E. Brown come alive. A fire distorts all the figures.

6918. The Whalers *(Mickey Mouse)* 19 Aug. 1938; *p.c.:* Walt Disney prods for RKO; *dir:* Dick Huemer; *story:* Otto Englander; *anim:* Arthur Babbitt, Preston Blair, Alfred Eugster, Robert Leffingwell, Eric Larson,

Edward Love, Lee Morehouse, Thomas Oreb, Milt Schaffer, Louis Schmitt, Marvin Woodward; *fx:* Joshua Meador; *voices:* Pinto Colvig, Clarence Nash, Richard Edwards, Walt Disney; *mus:* Albert Hay Malotte; *col:* Tech. *sd:* RCA. 8 min. • When Mickey and the gang sight a whale, they fire with Goofy entangled in the harpoon, landing in the whale's mouth.

6919. Wham and Eggs *(Blue Racer)*; rel; 18 Feb. 1972; *p.c.:* Mirisch/DEF for UA; *dir:* Art Davis; *story:* John Dunn; *anim:* Norm McCabe, Manny Gould, John Gibbs, Bob Richardson; *lay:* Dick Ung; *back:* Richard H. Thomas; *ed:* Lee Gunther; *voices:* Larry D. Mann, Bob Holt; *mus:* Doug Goodwin; *ph:* John Burton Jr.; *prod sup:* Stan Paperny, Harry Love; *col:* DeLuxe. *sd:* RCA. 6 min. • The racer finds a one million-year-old Chinese egg that hatches out into a dragon who thinks he is its mother.

6920. What a Knight *(Krazy Kat)* 14 Mar 1932; *p.c.:* Winkler for Colum; *prod:* Charles Mintz; *story:* Manny Gould; *anim:* Harry Love; *mus:* Joe de Nat; *prod mgr:* James Bronis; b&w. *sd:* WE. 6½ min. • The dentist gives Krazy gas to have his tooth pulled and he dreams he's a knight in the court of King Arthur.

6921. What a Life *(Flip the Frog)* 26 Mar 1931; *p.c.:* Celebrity prods for MGM; *prod/dir:* Ub Iwerks; b&w. *sd:* PCP. 7 min. • A cop chases Flip and his friend away from their street musicians act. They find refuge in an apartment that turns out to be occupied by the officer's wife.

6922. What a Lion *(Captain & the Kids)* 16 July 1938; *p.c.:* MGM; *dir:* William Hanna; *voices:* Billy Bletcher, Bobbie Winkler; *mus:* Scott Bradley; *prod mgr:* Fred Quimby; *col:* sep. *sd:* WE. 7 min. • Der Captain and Inspector go lion hunting and the kids dress up as a lion to fool them.

6923. What a Little Sneeze Will Do *(Terry-Toon)* 10 Jan. 1941; *p.c.:* TT for Fox; *dir:* Eddie Donnelly; *story:* John Foster; *mus:* Philip A. Scheib; b&w. *sd:* RCA. 7 min. • Oscar the Pig has a cold and one dose of composite gives him the DTs, where he hallucinates meeting "bottle people."

6924. What a Night *(Paul Terry-Toon)* 25 Jan. 1935; *p.c.:* Moser & Terry for Educational/Fox; *dir:* Frank Moser, Paul Terry; *mus:* Philip A. Scheib; b&w. *sd:* WE. 6 min. • No story available.

6925. What Dreams May Come 2 Oct. 1998; *p.c.:* PolyGram Filmed Entertainment, Inc.; *Painted World visual fx: anim:* John Jakubowski, Grant Neisner, Claire Pegorier; *anim Lunarfish:* Nick Phillip; *anim:* Sarma Vanguri, Dan Klem; *visual fx: POP Film & POP anim visual fx sup:* Stuart Robertson; *POP Film & Animation:* Jeff Ross; *special visual fx/digital anim: Digital Domain Visual Effects sup:* Kevin Mack; *Digital Tree anim:* Matthew Butler, David William Prescott, Darin K. Grant; *Digital Bird anim:* Bernd Angerer, Daniel W. Loeb, Christopher Roda, Vernon R. Wilbert Jr.; *cgi anim: pre-visualization Unit:* Scott Harper; *col:* Monaco Labs. *sd:* Dolby digital/Digital dts sound/SDDS. Panavision. 113 min. *l/a.* • Live-action fantasy: When a doctor is killed in a car crash, he goes straight to Heaven and expresses a wish to see his wife again. Depressed at being alone, his artist wife has taken her own life and gone to Hell, as all suicides do. The doctor goes on a pilgrimage to rescue his wife. When he chooses to stay with her rather than return to Heaven, they both are transported up to Paradise. USA/New Zealand

6926. What Happens at Night *(Terry-Toon)* 30 May 1941; *p.c.:* TT for Fox; *dir:* Connie Rasinski; *story:* John Foster; *mus:* Philip A. Scheib; *col:* Tech. *sd:* RCA. 6 min. • As night falls, the weather vane cock wings his way to the mill, arousing scarecrows and bugs en route. Soon they are all revelling.

6927. What Makes Daffy Duck? *(Looney Tunes)* 14 Feb. 1948; *p.c.:* WB; *dir:* Arthur Davis; *story:* William Scott, Lloyd Turner; *anim:* Basil Davidovich, J.C. Melendez, Don Williams, Emery Hawkins; *lay:* Don Smith; *back:* Philip de Guard; *ed:* Treg Brown; *voices:* Mel Blanc, Arthur Q. Bryan; *mus:* Carl Stalling; *prod mgr:* John W. Burton; *prod:* Edward Selzer; *col:* Ciné. *sd:* Vit. 7 min. • Elmer and a fox both set out to capture Daffy.

6928. What Makes Us Tick 1952; *p.c.:* John Sutherland Prods for the New York Stock Exchange; *asso prod:* George Gordon; *anim dir:* Carl Urbano; *anim:* Arnold Gillespie, Emery Hawkins, Bill Higgins; *art dir:* Gerald Nevius, Edgar Starr; *mus:* Eugene Poddany; *col:* Tech. *sd:* RCA. 12 min. • John Q. Public is given a lesson in what to do with his money. Promoting the stock market as the engine of U.S. prosperity.

6929. What — No Spinach? *(Popeye)* 29 May 1936; *p.c.:* The Fleischer

Studio for Para; *prod:* Max Fleischer; *dir:* Dave Fleischer; *anim:* Seymour Kneitel, Roland Crandall; *voices:* Jack Mercer, Gus Wickie, Lou Fleischer; *mus:* Sammy Timberg; b&w. *sd:* WE. 7 min. • Waiter Wimpy robs Popeye of chicken legs while dining at Bluto's Diner. Refusing to pay, our hero slugs it out with Bluto.

6930. What Price Fleadom 20 Mar. 1948; *p.c.:* MGM; *dir:* Tex Avery; *anim:* Walter Clinton, Robert Bentley, Gil Turner; *character des:* Gil Turner, Walter Clinton; *sets:* John Didrik Johnsen; *ed:* Fred MacAlpin; *voice:* Dick Nelson; *mus:* Scott Bradley; *prod:* Fred Quimby; *col:* Tech. *sd:* WE. 6½ min. • Homer Flea deserts his dog pal and happy home to pursue a pretty girl flea on another dog.

6931. What Price Porky (*Looney Tunes*) 26 Feb. 1938; *p.c.:* Leon Schlesinger prods for WB; *dir/story:* Robert Clampett; *anim:* Charles Jones, Bob Cannon; *sets:* Elmer Plummer; *ed:* Tregoweth E. Brown; *voices:* Mel Blanc; *mus:* Carl W. Stalling; *prod sup:* Henry Binder, Raymond G. Katz; b&w. *sd:* Vit. 7 min. • Corn-stealing ducks declare war on farmer Porky and his chickens.

6932. What's Brewin' Bruin? (*Looney Tunes*) 28 Feb. 1948; *p.c.:* WB; *dir:* Charles M. Jones; *story:* Tedd Pierce, Michael Maltese; *anim:* Phil Monroe, Ken Harris, Lloyd Vaughan, Ben Washam; *fx:* A.C. Gamer; *lay:* Robert Gribbroek; *back:* Peter Alvarado; *ed:* Treg Brown; *voices:* Billy Bletcher, Stan Freberg; *mus:* Carl Stalling; *prod mgr:* John W. Burton; *prod:* Edward Selzer; *col:* Tech. *sd:* Vit. 7 min. • Papa Bear has to contend with many interruptions while trying to hibernate.

6933. What's Buzzin' Buzzard? 27 Nov. 1943; *p.c.:* MGM; *dir:* Tex Avery; *anim:* Ed Love, Ray Abrams, Preston Blair; *character des:* Claude Smith; *sets:* John Didrik Johnsen; *ed:* Fred MacAlpin; *voices:* Harry E. Lang, Kent Rogers, John Wald; *mus:* Scott Bradley; *prod:* Fred Quimby; *col:* Tech. *sd:* WE. 8 min. • Two starving vultures try to devour each other in this notorious Avery classic.

6934. What's Cookin' Doc? (*Merrie Melodies*) 1 Jan. 1944; *p.c.:* Leon Schlesinger prods for WB: *dir:* Robert Clampett; *story/back:* Michael Sasanoff; *anim:* Bob McKimson; *lay:* Thomas McKimson; *ed:* Treg Brown; *voices:* Mel Blanc; *mus:* Carl Stalling; *ph:* John W. Burton; *prod sup:* Henry Binder, Raymond G. Katz; *col:* Tech. *sd:* Vit. 6 min. seq: *Hiawatha's Rabbit Hunt; A Star Is Born* (l/a: 1938) • Bugs is confident he will win the "Oscar" this year and when he doesn't, he goes about proving why he should have.

6935. What's My Lion? (*Looney Tunes*) 21 Oct. 1961; *p.c.:* WB; *dir:* Robert McKimson; *story:* Dave DeTiege; *anim:* Keith Darling, George Grandpré, Ted Bonnicksen, Warren Batchelder; *lay:* Robert Gribbroek; *back:* William Butler; *ed:* Treg Brown; *voices:* Hal Smith, Herburt Vigran, Mel Blanc; *mus:* Milt Franklyn; *prod mgr:* William Orcutt; *prod:* David H. DePatie; *col:* Tech. *sd:* Vit. 6 min. • Rocky, a mountain lion, seeks refuge from hunting season in Elmer's cabin by pretending to be a mounted lion head on his trophy wall.

6936. What's Opera, Doc? (*Merrie Melodies*) 6 July 1957; *p.c.:* WB; *dir:* Chuck Jones; *story/lyrics:* Michael Maltese; *anim:* Ken Harris, Abe Levitow, Richard Thompson; *inbetweener:* Willie Ito; *lay:* Maurice Noble; *back:* Philip de Guard; *ed:* Treg Brown; *voices:* Mel Blanc, Arthur Q. Bryan; *mus:* Milt Franklyn; *prod sup:* John W. Burton; *prod:* Edward Selzer; *col:* Tech. *sd:* Vit. 7 min. • Wagner's *Der Ring des Nibelungen* reenacted by Elmer as the Hunter and Bugs transformed into Brunhilde in this Jones classic.

6937. What's Peckin' (*Woody Woodpecker*) 1 July 1965; *p.c.:* Walter Lantz prods for Univ; *dir:* Paul J. Smith; *story:* Cal Howard; *anim:* Les Kline, Al Coe; *sets:* Art Landy, Ray Huffine; *voices:* Dal McKennon, Grace Stafford; *mus:* Clarence Wheeler; *prod mgr:* William E. Garity; *col:* Tech. *sd:* RCA. 6 min. • Prof Grossenfibber invents many plans to keep Woody from destroying telephone poles.

6938. What's Sweepin' (*Woody Woodpecker*) 5 Jan. 1953; *p.c.:* Walter Lantz prods for Univ; *dir:* Don Patterson; *anim:* Ray Abrams, La Verne Harding, Paul Smith; *sets:* Raymond Jacobs; *voices:* Dal McKennon, Grace Stafford; *mus:* Clarence Wheeler; *prod mgr:* William E. Garity; *col:* Tech. *sd:* RCA. 6 min. • When Woody sees Policeman Wally steal an apple, it gives him an idea to dress as a cop and pilfer as much fruit as possible.

6939. What's Up, Doc? (*Looney Tunes*) 17 June 1950; *p.c.:* WB; *dir:* Robert McKimson; *story:* Warren Foster; *anim:* J.C. Melendez, Charles

McKimson, Phil de Lara, Wilson Burness; *lay:* Cornett Wood; *back:* Richard H. Thomas; *ed:* Treg Brown; *voices:* Mel Blanc, Arthur Q. Bryan, Walker Edmiston; *mus:* Carl Stalling; *prod mgr:* John W. Burton; *prod:* Edward Selzer; *col:* Tech. *sd:* Vit. 7 min. • Bugs relates the story of how he broke into show business as Elmer Fudd's stooge.

6940. When G.I. Johnny Comes Home (*Noveltoon*) 2 Feb. 1945; *p.c.:* Famous for Para; *dir:* Seymour Kneitel; *story:* Jack Ward, Bill Turner; *anim:* Al Eugster, Otto Feuer; *sets:* Robert Little; *mus:* Winston Sharples; *ph:* Leonard McCormick; *prod mgr:* Sam Buchwald; *col:* Tech. *sd:* RCA. 8 min. • The troops arrive home from the war to a "new" America.

6941. When I Yoo Hoo (*Merrie Melodies*) 27 July 1936; *p.c.:* Leon Schlesinger prods for WB; *dir:* I. Freleng; *anim:* Bob McKimson, Don Williams; *voices:* Elmore Vincent, Leonard Slye; *mus:* Norman Spencer; *prod sup:* Henry Binder, Raymond G. Katz; *col:* Tech. *sd:* Vit. 7 min. • A mountain feud is settled with a cock fight.

6942. When It's Sleepy-Time Down South (*Screen Songs*) 11 Nov. 1932; *p.c.:* The Fleischer Studio for Para; *prod:* Max Fleischer; *dir:* Dave Fleischer; *anim:* Seymour Kneitel, Berny Wolf; *voice:* Mae Questel; *mus:* Art Turkisher; *song:* Leon Rene, Otis Rene, Clarence Muse; *l/a:* The Boswell Sisters (Connie, Vet, Martha); b&w. *sd:* WE. 10 min. *l/a/anim.* • The Boswell Sisters' counterparts (three Betty Boops) cope with a burning house and a bizarre fire department to extinguish it.

6943. When Knights Were Bold (*Pathé Cartoon Comedy*) 19 June 1915; *p.c.:* Bray prods for Eclectic; *anim:* J.R. Bray; *story:* L.M. Glackens; b&w. *sil.* • No story available.

6944. When Knights Were Bold (*Terry-Toon*) 21 Mar. 1941; *p.c.:* TT for Fox; *dir:* Volney White; *story:* John Foster; *mus:* Philip A. Scheib; b&w. *sd:* RCA. 7 min. • No story available.

6945. When Magoo Flew (*Mr. Magoo*) 6 Jan. 1955; *p.c.:* UPA for Colum; *ex prod:* Stephen Bosustow; *dir:* Pete Burness; *story:* Barbara Hammer, Tedd Pierce; *anim:* Rudy Larriva, Tom McDonald, Cecil Surry; *lay:* Sterling Sturtevant; *back:* Bob McIntosh; *voices:* Jim Backus, Jerry Hausner, Henny Backus; *mus:* Hoyt Curtin; *prod mgr:* Herbert Klynn; *col:* Tech. *sd:* RCA. 6 min. *Academy Award.* • Magoo sets out to go to the movies but ends up wandering around the outside of an airborne airliner.

6946. When Men Were Men (*Aesop's Film Fable*) 18 July 1925; *p.c.:* Fables Pictures Inc for Pathé; *dir:* Paul Terry; b&w. *sil.* 10 min. • A caveman makes dinosaurs work for him and steals his bride in the approved fashion.

6947. When Mousehood Was in Flower (*Mighty Mouse*) July 1953; *p.c.:* TT for Fox; *dir:* Connie Rasinski; *story:* Tom Morrison; *anim:* Jim Tyer; *voice:* Roy Halee; *mus:* Philip A. Scheib; *ph:* Douglas Moye; *col:* Tech. *sd:* RCA. 7 min. • The villainous landlord will forget the rent on the castle if he can marry an impoverished mouse's pretty daughter. She claims a champion knight will win the tournament for her and Mighty Mouse steps into the breach.

6948. When My Ship Comes in (*Betty Boop*) 12 Dec. 1934; *p.c.:* The Fleischer Studio for Para; *prod:* Max Fleischer; *dir:* Dave Fleischer; *anim:* Myron Waldman, Hicks Lokey, Lillian Friedman; *voice:* Mae Questel; *mus:* Sammy Timberg; b&w. *sd:* WE. 7 min. • Betty wins on a horse race and speculates on what she would do with the winnings.

6949. When Snow Flies (*Aesop's Film Fable*) 15 May 1927; *p.c.:* Fables Pictures Inc for Pathé; *dir:* Paul Terry; b&w. *sil.* 10 min. • Farmer Al's winter fun is tormented by cats, eventually causing him to fall through the ice.

6950. When the Cat's Away (*Happy Harmonies*) 16 Feb. 1935; *p.c.:* MGM; *prod/dir:* Hugh Harman, Rudolf Ising; *voice:* Bernice Hansel; *mus:* Scott Bradley; *col:* Tech-2. *sd:* RCA. 8 min. • A girl kitten is lured away from the kitchen by her boyfriend and the mice have a field day. The whole show is marred by the arrival of a mean rat ... but the cat's return sees him off.

6951. When the Cat's Away (*Mickey Mouse*) 3 May 1929; *p.c.:* Walter E. Disney for Colum; *dir:* Walt Disney; *anim:* Ub Iwerks, Ben Sharpsteen; *mus:* Carl W. Stalling; b&w. *sd:* PCP. 7 min. • Mickey leads a gang of mice who cause havoc in the cat's absence.

6952. When the Red, Red Robin Comes Bob Bob Bobbin' Along (*Screen Songs*) 19 Feb. 1932; *p.c.:* The Fleischer Studio for Para; *dir:*

Dave Fleischer; *story:* Max Fleischer; *voices:* William A. Costello; *mus:* Art Turkisher; *song:* Harry Woods; b&w. *sd:* WE. 6½ min. • A trainee robin battles with a stubborn worm.

6953. When They Were Twenty-One 27 May 1915; *p.c.:* Vitagraph Co; *anim:* Carl Francis Lederer; b&w. *sil.* • No story available.

6954. When Winter Comes (*Aesop's Film Fable*) 11 May 1924; *p.c.:* Fables Pictures Inc for Pathé; *dir:* Paul Terry; b&w. *sil.* 5 min. • Dogs, cats, pigs and hippos are engaged in ice skating, snowshoeing and tobogganing.

6955. When Yuba Plays the Rhumba on the Tuba (*Screen Songs*) 15 Sept. 1933; *p.c.:* The Fleischer Studio for Para; *prod:* Max Fleischer; *dir:* Dave Fleischer; *anim:* Bernard Wolf, Thomas Johnson; *mus:* Art Turkisher; *song:* Herman Hupfield; *l/a:* The Mills Brothers; b&w. *sd:* WE. 10 min. *l/a/anim.* • A train chases cats on a buckboard. Caricature of Stan Laurel.

6956. When's Your Birthday? Mar. 1937; *p.c.:* Leon Schlesinger prods for RKO; *dir:* Robert Clampett; *voice:* Pat C. Flick; *col:* Tech. *sd:* RCA. • Live-action (black & white) feature with Joe E. Brown as a boxer whose prowess is affected by the stars. The colored cartoon segment deals with signs of the zodiac. Taurus the Bull is master of Astrological Heaven until the moon stops shining, then he is beaten by a centaur.

6957. Where Do You Go from Here? 1916; *p.c.:* Associated Art Films for the Democratic party; *prod:* Louis J. Beck; *anim:* Walt MacDougall; b&w. *sil.* 2 min. • Political advert.

6958. Where Friendship Ceases (*Aesop's Film Fable*) 15 Jan. 1927; *p.c.:* Fables Pictures Inc for Pathé; *dir:* Paul Terry; b&w. *sil.* 10 min. • Farmer Al Falfa chases the mice through dresser drawers, water pipes and a sewing basket with sharp needles. The mice attach yarn to Al's leg and drag him through a stair railing, trees, the attic and over the horizon. The mice win!

6959. Where There's Smoke (*Deputy Dawg*) Feb. 1962; *p.c.:* TT for Fox; *ex prod:* Bill Weiss; *dir:* Bob Kuwahara; *story sup:* Tom Morrison; *story:* Larz Bourne; *anim:* Cosmo Anzilotti, Ralph Bakshi, Mannie Davis, Doug Crane; *sets:* Bill Focht, John Zago; *ed:* Jack MacConnell; *voices:* Dayton Allen; *mus:* Philip Scheib; *ph:* Joe Rasinski; *col:* DeLuxe. *sd:* RCA. 5 min. • Deputy Dawg organizes a volunteer fire department when the tool shed burns down.

6960. Which Is Witch (*Casper*) 2 May 1958; *p.c.:* Para Cartoons; *dir:* Seymour Kneitel; *story:* Carl Meyer; *anim:* Tom Johnson, Frank Endres, Els Barthen; *sets:* Robert Little; *voices:* Cecil Roy, Jack Mercer; *mus:* Winston Sharples; *ph:* Leonard McCormick; *prod mgr:* Abe Goodman; *col:* Tech. *sd:* RCA. 6 min. • Casper takes Wendy to the beach and Spooky does his best to spoil their enjoyment.

6961. Which Is Witch (*James Hound*) Sept. 1967; *p.c.:* TT for Fox; *dir:* Ralph Bakshi; *col:* DeLuxe. *sd:* RCA. 6 min. • Hound and Conrad thwart Dr. Mad's plan of using witches to rob the city on Hallowe'en.

6962. Which Is Witch (*Looney Tunes*) 3 Dec. 1949; *p.c.:* WB; *dir:* I. Freleng; *story:* Tedd Pierce; *anim:* Ken Champin, Virgil Ross, Arthur Davis, Gerry Chiniquy; *fx:* A.C. Gamer; *lay:* Hawley Pratt; *back:* Paul Julian; *ed:* Treg Brown; *voices:* Mel Blanc; *mus:* Carl Stalling; *prod mgr:* John W. Burton; *prod:* Edward Selzer; *col:* Tech. *sd:* Vit. 7 min. • Bugs has an encounter with an African witch doctor who wants to eat him.

6963. Whispers in the Dark (*Screen Songs*) 24 Sept. 1937; *p.c.:* The Fleischer Studio for Para; *prod:* Max Fleischer; *dir:* Dave Fleischer; *anim:* Roland Crandall; *mus:* Sammy Timberg; *l/a:* Gus Arnheim and his orchestra; *vocal:* June Robbins; b&w. *sd:* WE. 7 min. *l/a/anim.* • Professor Rip van Nutley presents various odd items in "Believe It or Leave It."

6964. A White Elephant (*Aesop's Film Fable*) 13 Jan. 1929; *p.c.:* Fables Pictures Inc for Pathé; *dir:* Paul Terry, Hugh Shields; b&w. *sil.* 10 min. • No story available.

6965. The White Guard 1947; *p.c.:* Ted Eshbaugh Studios for Whitehall Pharmaceutical Co; *prod/dir/ph:* Harry Hamsel; *story/ed:* Ted Eshbaugh; *voice:* Roger Krupp; *ph:* Jack Eshbaugh; *col. sd.* • Commercial.

6966. Whitman, Vincent (*cartoons*) *p.c.:* Lubin Mfg Co; *prod:* Sigmund Lubin; *anim:* Vincent I. Whitman; b&w. *sil.* 6 min. *s/r.* • **1914: A Trip to the Moon** 14 Mar. **The Bottom of the Sea** 21 Mar. **A Strenuous Ride** 11 Apr. **Another Tale** 25 Apr. **A Hunting Absurdity** 3 Oct. **An In-**terrupted Nap 23 Oct. **The Troublesome Cat** 15 Dec. • **1915: Curses! Jack Dalton** 24 Apr. **A Hot Time in Punkville** 3 May. **His Pipe Dreams** 21 May. **Studies in Clay** 6 July. **A Barnyard Mixup** 12 July. **An African Hunt** 15 July. **A One Reel Feature** 26 July. **Relentless Dalton** 2 Aug. **The Victorious Jockey** 16 Aug.

6967. Whiz Quiz Kid (*Noveltoon*) Dec. 1963; *p.c.:* Para Cartoons; *dir:* Seymour Kneitel; *story:* Jack Mercer, Irv Dressler; *anim:* Martin Taras; *sets:* Robert Little; *mus:* Winston Sharples; *ph:* Leonard McCormick; *prod mgr:* Abe Goodman; *col:* Tech. *sd:* RCA. 6 min. • TV executives rig a Kiddie Quiz show with questions the kids couldn't answer ... except Ollie Owl who wins everything.

6968. Who Framed Roger Rabbit 22 June 1988; *p.c.:* Touchstone Pictures/Amblin Entertainment/Silver Screen Partners III; *dir:* Robert Zemeckis; *anim dir:* Richard Williams; *prod:* Robert Watts, Frank Marshall; *ex prod:* Steven Spielberg, Kathleen Kennedy; based on the book *Who Censored Roger Rabbit?* by Gary K. Wolf; *scr:* Jeffrey Price, Peter Seaman; *storysketch:* Joe Ranft, Mark Kausler, Hans Bacher, Harold Siepermann; *anim sup:* Dale L. Baer, Andreas Deja, Russell Hall, Phil Nibbelink, Simon Wells; *anim:* Tom Sito, Roger Chiasson, David Byers-Brown, Alvaro Gaivoto, Nik Ranieri, Rob Stevenhagen, Alyson Hamilton, James Baxter, Jacques Muller, Joe Haidar, Alan Simpson, Caron Creed, Alain Costa, Raul Garcia, Brigitte Hartley, Greg Manwaring, Colin White, Marc Gordon-Bates, Brent Odell, Mike Swindall, Chuck Gammage, Peter Western, Gary Mudd, Dave Spafford; *asst anim:* Margot Allan, Sue Baker, Rej Bourdages, Neil Boyle, Bella Bremner, Paul Chung, Christopher Clarke, Irene Couloufis, Annie Dubois, Helga Egilson, James Farrington, Gary French-Powell, Martyn Jones, Helen Kincaid, Elaine Koo, Vera Lanpher, Calvin le Duc, John McCartney, Brenda Chat-McKie, Denise Mears-Hahn, Robert Newman, Andrew Painter, Isabel Radage, Philippe Rejaudry, Philip Scarroll, Glenn Sylvester, Nicolette van Gendt, Roger Way, Hugh Workman, Boguslaw Wilk, Alexander Williams; *addit anim:* Mark Kausler, Matthew O'Callaghan, Dave Pacheco, Bruce W. Smith, Barry Temple, Frans Vischer; *anim coord:* Jane M. Baer; *asst anim:* Renee Holt, David Nethery, Brett Newton, M. Flores Nichols, Bette Isis Thomson, Gilda Palinginis, Carl A. Bell; *inbet:* Richard Bazley, Stella Benson, Graham Binding, David Bowers, Clare Bramwell, Malcolm Clarke, Anthony Ealey, Matthew Freeth, Peter Gambier, Manjit Jhita, Siobhán Larkin, Debbie Jane Lilly, Adrian Marler, Roman Ostir, Howard Parkins, Silvia Pompei, Emma Tornero, Simon Turner, Anne Whitford, Dorothea Baker, Edward D. Bell, Brenda Chapman, Kent S. Culotta, Eric Daniels, Humberto de la Fuentes Jr., Michael Genz, William Kent Holaday, Nancy Kniep, Teresa Martin, Edward Murrieta; *anim fx sup:* Don Paul; *anim fx:* Christopher Knott, Dave Bossert, Jon Brooks, Andrew Brownlow, Kevin Davies, Christopher Jenkins, Dorse Lanpher, Les Pace, Graham Burt, Lily Dell, Fraser MacLean, Tim Sanpher, David Sigrist, Michael Patrick Smith, Amanda J. Talbot, Glenn Chaika, Randy Fullmer, Scott Santoro; *fx asst:* Allen Blyth, Christine Harding, Eusebio Torres, Mac Torres; *fx inbet:* Lisette Coates, Marc Ellis, Christopher Kingsley-Smith III, Derek Robert Mason, Mike Pfeil, Barney Russel, Dave Pritchard, Derek Wood; *anim sup:* Wes Takahashi; *lay:* Roy Naisbitt, William H. Frake III, Dave Dunnet, Marc Christenson, Leonard V. Smith; *back/renderings:* Shelley Page, Nick Harris, Jill Tudor; *back:* Ron Dias, Michael Humphries, Kathleen Swain; *anim ed:* Nick Fletcher, Keith Holden, Scot Scalise; *voices: Roger Rabbit, Benny the Cab, Greasy & Psycho:* Charles Fleischer; *Baby Herman:* Lou Hirsch; *Jessica:* Kathleen Turner; *Mrs. Herman:* April Winchell; *Gorilla:* Morgan Deare; *Betty Boop:* Mae Questel; *Daffy Duck, Porky Pig, Bugs Bunny, Tweety Bird, Sylvester:* Mel Blanc; *Donald Duck:* Tony Anselmo; *Hippo:* Mary T. Radford; *Yosemite Sam:* Joe Alaskey; *Smart Ass:* David Lander; *Stupid:* Fred Newman; *Wheezy, Lena Hyena:* June Foray; *Birds, Minnie Mouse:* Russi Taylor; *Toad:* Les Perkins; *Droopy:* Richard Williams; *Mickey Mouse:* Wayne Allwine; *Bullet #1:* Pat Buttram; *Bullet #2:* Jim Cummings; *Bullet #3:* Jim Gallant; *The Singing Sword:* Frank Sinatra; *Goofy, Wolf:* Tony Pope; *Pinocchio:* Peter Westy; *Woody Woodpecker:* Cherry Davis; *Jessica's singing voice:* Amy Irving; *Weasel:* Kerry Shale; *mus:* Alan Silvestri; *anim check:* Paul Steele, Andrew Ryder, Daniel Cohen, Annamarie Costa, Kathy Burrows-Fullmer; *anim check sup:* Mavis Shafer; *i&p:* Karen Comella, Barbara McCormack; *anim ph:* John Leatherbarrow, Stuart Holloway, Graham Chenery, Martin Elvin, Pete Wood, Nic Jayne, Brian Riley, John Aardal, Ted Bemiller, Available Light Ltd.; *optical ph sup:* Edward Jones; *visual fx camera operators:* Scott

Farrar, Bruce Waters, Sandy Ford; *anim:* Sean Turner, Tim Berglund, Nick Stern, Gordon Baker, Chris Green; *modelmaking:* Steve Gawley, Ira Keeler, Jeff Olson, Paul Kraus, Rick Anderson, Tony Hudson; *stop-motion anim:* Tony St. Hudson; *stop-motion camera operator:* Harry V. Walton; *anim admin:* Ron McKelvey; *anim research:* Leroy Anderson; *anim consultants:* Walt Stanchfield, Stan Green, Chuck Jones; *chief ex:* Dale L. Baer; *prod mgr:* Patsy de Lord, Ron Rocha; *prod co-ord:* Ian Cook, Steve Hickner, Lori M. Noda; *col:* Tech. *sd:* Dolby stereo. 100 min. *l/a/anim.* • Live-action/animation comedy: It's 1947 and detective Eddie Valiant (Bob Hoskins) is hired by the Maroon Cartoons entrepreneur to check-out whether his star turn, Roger Rabbit's wife, Jessica, is having an affair with Marvin Acme, the owner of Toontown. When Acme is found murdered, all the evidence points to Roger, who then comes to Valiant pleading his innocence. Eddie investigates and uncovers a plot to dispose of the whole of Toontown by the sinister Judge Doom.

6969. Who Killed Cock Robin? *(Paul Terry-Toon)* 19 Mar. 1933; *p.c.:* Moser & Terry for Educational; *dir:* Frank Moser, Paul Terry; *mus:* Philip A. Scheib; *b&w. sd:* WE. 6 min. • A cat drinks a potion that turns him into a monster who shoots Cock Robin. The police then become involved.

6970. Who Killed Cock Robin *(Silly Symphony)* 29 June 1935; *p.c.:* Walt Disney prods for UA; *dir:* David D. Hand; *story:* William Cottrell, Joe Grant, Bob Kuwahara; *anim:* Norman Ferguson, Clyde Geronimi, Hardie Gramatky, Jack Hannah, Eric Larson, Richard Lundy, Hamilton S. Luske, William O. Roberts, Bob Wickersham; *voices:* Billy Bletcher, Esther Dale, Lou Debney, Charlie Lung, Gary Mix, Clarence Nash, A. Purvis Pullen, John Reed, Bill Roberts, Martha Wentworth, Freeman High Quartet, Town Hall Quartet; *mus:* Frank E. Churchill; *song:* Larry Morey, Frank E. Churchill; *col:* Tech. *sd:* RCA. 10 min. *Academy Award nomination.* • Cock Robin is shot with an arrow and a court case ensues. Robin is fashioned after Bing Crosby and Jenny Wren after Mae West.

6971. Who Killed Who? 5 June 1943; *p.c.:* MGM; *dir:* Tex Avery; *story:* Heck Allen; *anim:* Ed Love, Ray Abrams, Preston Blair; *character des:* Claude Smith; *sets:* John Didrik Johnsen; *ed:* Fred MacAlpin; *voices:* Kent Rogers, Sara Berner; *mus:* Scott Bradley; *l/a:* Robert Emmett O'Connor; *prod:* Fred Quimby; *col:* Tech. *sd:* WE. 7 min. *l/a/anim.* • A live-action announcer takes us into an animated murder mystery at Gruesome Grange.

6972. Who Needs Nudnik? *(Nudnik)* Aug. 1966; *p.c.:* Rembrandt for Para; *prod:* William L. Snyder; *dir:* Gene Deitch; *col. sd.* 6 min. • Nudnik unwittingly makes an enemy of a housewife and her dog. • See: *Nudnik*

6973. Who Scent You? *(Looney Tunes)* 23 Apr. 1960; *p.c.:* WB; *dir:* Chuck Jones; *story:* Michael Maltese; *anim:* Richard Thompson, Ken Harris, Ben Washam, Keith Darling; *lay:* Maurice Noble; *back:* Philip de Guard; *ed:* Treg Brown; *voices:* Mel Blanc; *mus:* Milt Franklyn; *prod mgr:* William Orcutt; *prod:* David H. DePatie; *col:* Tech. *sd:* Vit. 7 min. • Pepè le Pew finds himself aboard a deserted luxury ocean liner in pursuit of what he believes to be a beautiful female skunk.

6974. Whoa Be-Gone *(Merrie Melodies)* 12 Apr. 1958; *p.c.:* WB; *dir:* Chuck Jones; *story:* Michael Maltese; *anim:* Ken Harris, Abe Levitow, Richard Thompson; *fx:* Harry Love; *lay:* Maurice Noble; *back:* Philip de Guard; *ed:* Treg Brown; *voice:* Paul Julian; *mus:* Milt Franklyn; *col:* Tech. *sd:* Vit. 7 min. • The Coyote, once more, wages his private war against the speed demon: this time using an Acme "Do-It-Yourself Tornado Kit."

6975. Wholly Smoke *(Looney Tunes)* 27 Aug. 1938; *p.c.:* Leon Schlesinger prods for WB; *dir:* Frank Tashlin; *story:* George Manuell; *anim:* Robert Bentley, Volney White; *ed:* Tregoweth E. Brown; *voices:* Mel Blanc, Cliff Nazarro; The Basin Street Boys; *mus:* Carl W. Stalling; *prod sup:* Henry Binder, Raymond G. Katz; *b&w. sd:* Vit. 7 min. • Porky is encouraged to smoke then passes out. He envisions Nick O'Teen who helps discourage him from the evil habit. Caricatures of the Three Stooges, Bing Crosby, Rudy Vallee and Cab Calloway.

6976. The Whoopee Party *(Mickey Mouse)* 17 Sept. 1932; *p.c.:* Walt Disney prods for UA; *dir:* Wilfred Jackson; *anim:* Johnny Cannon, Les Clark, Gilles de Tremaudan, Kevin Donnelly, Norman Ferguson, Hardie Gramatky, David D. Hand, Jack King, Richard Lundy, Tom Palmer, Ben Sharpsteen; *voices:* Marcellite Garner, Pinto Colvig; *mus:* Frank E. Churchill; *b&w. sd:* PCP. 7 min. • Mickey and the gang have a party and

as the music gets hotter and wilder, the furniture comes to life and joins in the fun.

6977. Whoopee Sketches 1929; *p.c.:* Sound Film Distributing Corp; *prod:* Bollman and Grant; *b&w. sd.* • **Grandma Steps Out, The K.O. Kid, The Four Jazz Boys, On the Up and Up, The Peroxide Kid** • Sound reissues of Laugh-O-Grams: *Little Red Riding Hood; Puss in Boots; Cinderella; The Four Musicians of Bremen; Jack and the Beanstalk* and *Goldie Locks and the Three Bears.* Synchronized music provided by Carl Edouarde. Laugh-O-Grams were produced by Walt Disney specifically for Newman's Theatre Circuit, Kansas City and never received a general distribution. *Cinderella,* which initially had no release, was issued in the *Peter the Puss* series as *The Slipper-y Kid.*

6978. Whoops! I'm a Cowboy *(Betty Boop)* 12 Feb. 1937; *p.c.:* The Fleischer Studio for Para; *prod:* Max Fleischer; *dir:* Dave Fleischer; *anim:* Thomas Johnson, David Hoffman; *voice:* Mae Questel; *mus:* Sammy Timberg; *b&w. sd:* WE. 7 min. • Wiffle Piffle tries to impress Betty by becoming a cowboy.

6979. Whoozit *(Educational-Bowers Comedy)* 1 Apr. 1928. *p.c.:* Bowers Comedy Corp. for Educational; *prod:* Charles R. Bowers; *dir/ph:* H.L. Muller; *l/a:* Charley Bowers, Emily Gerdes, Theodore Lorch, Ann Brody; *b&w. sil.* 2 reels. *l/a/anim.* • No story available.

6980. Who's Cooking Who? *(Woody Woodpecker)* 24 June 1946; *p.c.:* Walter Lantz prods for Univ; *dir:* James Culhane; *story:* Ben Hardaway, Milt Schaffer; *anim:* Les Kline, Grim Natwick; *sets:* Terry Lind; *ed:* Dave Lurie; *voices:* Will Wright, Ben Hardaway; *mus:* Darrell Calker; *prod mgr:* George Hall; *col:* Tech. *sd:* WE. 6 min. • When Winter arrives, Woody finds himself without food. A starving wolf arrives and Woody sets his sights on eating him.

6981. Who's Kitten Who? *(Looney Tunes)* 5 Jan. 1952; *p.c.:* WB; *dir:* Robert McKimson; *story:* Tedd Pierce; *anim:* Phil de Lara, Emery Hawkins, Charles McKimson, Rod Scribner; *lay:* Peter Alvarado; *back:* Richard H. Thomas; *ed:* Treg Brown; *voices:* Mel Blanc; *mus:* Carl Stalling; *prod mgr:* John W. Burton; *prod:* Edward Selzer; *col:* Tech. *sd:* Vit. 7 min. • While Sylvester teaches Junior how to catch a mouse, a baby kangaroo is loose in the cellar which Sylvester takes to be "A giant mouse!"

6982. Who's That Girl? 7 Aug. 1987; *p.c.:* WB; *title seq:* Broadcast Arts Inc.; *mus:* Stephen Bray; *song:* "Who's that Girl" by Madonna, Patrick Leonard; *performed by* Madonna. *col:* Tech. *sd:* Dolby stereo. Panavision. • Acting as a prologue, the animated title credits show Madonna getting framed for a crime she didn't commit and being put in prison.

6983. Who's Who in the Jungle? *(Gandy Goose)* 19 Oct. 1945; *p.c.:* TT for Fox; *dir:* Mannie Davis; *story:* John Foster; *sets:* Art Bartsch; *voices:* Thomas Morrison; *mus:* Philip A. Scheib; *ph:* Douglas Moye; *col:* Tech. *sd:* RCA. 7 min. • Gandy and Sourpuss go hunting in the jungle, only managing to escape with their lives and carrying a lion as an unwelcome passenger.

6984. Who's Who in the Zoo *(Looney Tunes)* 31 Jan. 1942; *p.c.:* Leon Schlesinger prods for WB; *dir:* Norman McCabe; *story:* Melvin Millar; *anim:* John Carey, Cal Dalton, Arthur Davis, David Hoffman, Vive Risto; *ed:* Treg Brown; *voices:* Robert C. Bruce, Mel Blanc; *singers:* Stella Friend, Betty Noyes, Dorothy Compton; *mus:* Carl W. Stalling; *ph:* John W. Burton; *prod sup:* Henry Binder, Raymond G. Katz; *b&w. sd:* Vit. 8 min. • Zookeeper Porky gives us an insight into Azusa Zoo.

6985. Who's Zoo in Hollywood *(Color Rhapsody)* 17 Oct. 1941; *p.c.:* Colum; *dir:* Art Davis; *anim:* Sid Marcus; *lay:* Clark Watson; *ed:* Edward Moore; *mus:* Eddie Kilfeather; *prod mgr:* George Winkler; *col:* Tech. *sd:* RCA. 7 min. • No story available.

6986. Why Argue *(Aesop's Film Fable)* 3 Oct. 1926; *p.c.:* Fables Pictures Inc for Pathé; *dir:* Paul Terry; *b&w. sil.* 10 min. • Farmer Al Falfa, Henry Cat and some dogs feature, ending with the rodents booting the farmer right in front of a charging bull.

6987. Why Do I Dream These Dreams? *(Merrie Melodies)* 30 June 1934; *p.c.:* WB; *dir:* Isadore Freleng; *anim:* Rollin Hamilton, Bob McKimson; *mus:* Norman Spencer; *song:* Harry Warren, Al Dubin; *b&w. sd:* Vit. 7 min. • Rip van Winkle dreams he's been shrunken to the size of an insect and has to fight a spider.

6988. Why Mice Leave Home (*Aesop's Film Fable*) 16 Mar. 1924; *p.c.:* Fables Pictures Inc for Pathé; *dir:* Paul Terry; b&w. *sil.* 5 min. • The mice discover the moon is cheese, devour it and fall back to earth in the farm house.

6989. Why Mules Leave Home (*Paul Terry-Toon*) 7 Sept. 1934; *p.c.:* Moser & Terry for Educational/Fox; *dir:* Frank Moser, Paul Terry; *mus:* Philip A. Scheib; b&w. *sd:* WE. 6 min. • The farmer's mules stage a strike and leave the farm. When Indians attack, the mules dash to the rescue of the farmer and farm.

6990. Why Play Leapfrog (*Fun & Facts About America*) 4 Feb. 1950; *p.c.:* John Sutherland prods for Harding College/MGM; *asso prod:* George Gordon; *dir:* Carl Urbano; *voice:* Frank Nelson; *col:* Tech. *sd:* RCA. 9½ min. • Illustrating that labor makes up approximately 85 percent in cost of most of the commodities consumed, therefore making it impossible to raise wages without raising prices.

6991. Why We Fight 1942; *p.c.:* Walt Disney prods for the War Dpt/Research Council/Academy of Motion Pictures and Sciences. • **Prelude to War, The Nazis Strike, Divide and Conquer, The Battle of Britain, The Battle of China, War Comes to America** • *prod:* Anatole Litvak; *l/a dir:* Frank Capra; *l/a screenplay:* Eric Knight; *anim story:* Yale Gracey, Campbell Grant, Riley Thomson; *artists:* Jack Boyd, Lou Debney, Andrew Engman, Jack Huber, Ray Jacobs, Dick Kelsey, Lenard Kester, Rea Medby, Bill Reese, Dick Taylor, Thelma Witmer; *voices:* Walter Huston, Cpt Anthony Veiller; b&w. *sd. l/a/anim.* • Series of seven informational films using animated diagrams and maps.

6992. Why Women Pay (*Life Cartoon Comedy*) 16 Dec. 1926; *p.c.:* Sherwood Wadsworth Pictures for Educational; *prod/dir:* John R. McCrory; b&w. *sil.* • High-Hat Harold cheats Mike Monkey out of a map to a mine in a crooked gambling game. He sets a bomb outside Mike's cabin but a bird picks it up and deposits it on the villain.

6993. The Wicked Cat (*Aesop's Film Fable*) 4 Mar. 1922; *p.c.:* Fables Pictures Inc for Pathé; *dir:* Paul Terry; b&w. *sil.* 5 min. • A family of goldfish enjoys jumping from their bowl to play. The cat lies in wait to snatch one of the fish. A chase ensues and the villain is captured. Moral: "The want of a good excuse never kept a villain from crime eternal."

6994. The Wicked City (*Aesop's Film Fable*) 21 Jan. 1926; *p.c.:* Fables Pictures Inc for Pathe; *dir:* Paul Terry; b&w. *sil.* 5 min. • A mouse takes his sweetie to a café and is set upon by a cat who wears a magic cloak that enables him to walk through walls. The mouse tracks him down and gives him a trouncing.

6995. Wicked West (*Oswald*) 27 Apr. 1929; *p.c.:* Winkler for Univ; *anim:* Isadore Freleng; b&w. *sd:* WE. 6 min. • Cowboy Oswald goes into a tough Western saloon and gets in a card game with Putrid Pete. He trims the big lug and gets into a fight.

6996. The Wicked Wolf (*Mighty Mouse*) 8 Mar. 1946; *p.c.:* TT for Fox; *dir:* Mannie Davis; *story:* John Foster; *sets:* Art Bartsch; *voice:* Roy Halee; *mus:* Philip A. Scheib; *ph:* Douglas Moye; *col:* Tech. *sd:* RCA. 7 min. • While a group of mice watch a film of "Goldielocks," Mighty Mouse rescues Goldie who is besieged by a pack of wolves.

6997. Wicket Wacky (*Woody Woodpecker*) 28 May 1951; *p.c.:* Walter Lantz prods for Univ; *dir:* Walter Lantz; *anim:* Don Patterson, Ray Abrams, La Verne Harding, Paul Smith; *sets:* Fred Brunish; *voice:* Grace Stafford; *mus:* Clarence E. Wheeler; *prod mgr:* William E. Garity; *col:* Tech. *sd:* RCA. 6 min. • A gopher puts a stop to Woody's croquet game.

6998. A Wicky Wacky Romance (*Terry-Toon*) 17 Nov. 1939; *p.c.:* TT for Fox; *dir:* Mannie Davis; *story:* John Foster; *mus:* Philip A. Scheib; *col:* Tech. *sd:* RCA. 7 min. • Pirates invade a peaceful Hawaiian island, capturing the native hula girls. Tarzan comes to the rescue.

6999. Wide Open Spaces (*Donald Duck*) 12 Sept. 1947; *p.c.:* Walt Disney prods for RKO; *dir:* Jack King; *asst dir:* Joel Greenhalgh; *story:* MacDonald MacPherson, Jack Huber; *anim:* Don Towsley, Paul Allen, Emery Hawkins, Ed Aardal, Rudy Cataldi, Earl Combs, Fred Kopietz, Frank McSavage; *fx:* Sandy Strother; *lay:* Don Griffith; *back:* Howard Dunn; *voices:* Billy Bletcher, Clarence Nash; *mus:* Oliver Wallace; *col:* Tech. *sd:* RCA. 7 min. • Donald tries to get some sleep on an inflatable air-bed.

7000. Wide Open Spaces (*Terry-Toon*) Nov. 1950; *p.c.:* TT for Fox; *dir:* Eddie Donnelly; *story:* Tom Morrison; *anim:* Jim Tyer; *sets:* Art Bartsch;

voice: Arthur Kay; *mus:* Philip A. Scheib; *ph:* Douglas Moye; *col:* Tech. *sd:* RCA. 6½ min. • Gandy Goose arrives in a western town, is appointed sheriff and told to arrest a tough hombre known as Dead-Eye Dick.

7001. Wideo Wabbit (*Merrie Melodies*) 27 Oct. 1956; *p.c.:* WB; *dir:* Robert McKimson; *story:* Tedd Pierce; *anim:* George Grandpré, Ted Bonnicksen, Keith Darling, Russ Dyson; *lay:* Robert Gribbroek; *back:* Richard H. Thomas; *ed:* Irvin Jay; *voices:* Mel Blanc, Arthur Q. Bryan, Daws Butler; *mus:* Carl Stalling; *prod mgr:* John W. Burton; *prod:* Edward Selzer; *col:* Tech. *sd:* Vit. 6½ min. • Bugs becomes Elmer's quarry on "The Sportsman Hour" TV show.

7002. Wigwam Whoopee (*Popeye*) 27 Feb. 1948; *p.c.:* Famous for Para; *dir:* I. Sparber; *story:* I. Klein, Jack Mercer; *anim:* Tom Johnson, William Henning, Els Barthen; *sets:* Robert Connavale; *voices:* Jack Mercer, Mae Questel, Jackson Beck; *mus:* Winston Sharples; *ph:* Leonard McCormick; *prod mgr:* Sam Buchwald; *col:* Pola. *sd:* RCA. 7 min. • Pilgrim Popeye arrives at Plymouth Rock and falls for Pocahontas. The Indian chief takes umbrage and tries to dispose of our hero.

7003. Wilbur the Lion (*Puppetoon*) 18 Apr. 1947; *p.c.:* George Pal prods for Para; *prod/dir:* George Pal; *story:* William E. Molett, Jack Miller; *voices:* William Foreman, Billy Bletcher; *col:* Tech. *sd:* WE. 10 min. • Wilbur is retired from the circus and sent back to the jungle. Not caring for jungle life, he gets himself captured by hunters and returns to a more civilized life in the circus.

7004. Wild About Hurry (*Merrie Melodies*) 10 Oct. 1959; *p.c.:* WB; *dir:* Chuck Jones; *story:* Michael Maltese; *anim:* Ken Harris, Abe Levitow, Richard Thompson, Ben Washam; *fx:* Harry Love; *sets:* Philip de Guard; *ed:* Treg Brown; *voice:* Paul Julian; *mus:* Milt Franklyn; *prod mgr:* William Orcutt; *prod:* David H. DePatie; *col:* Tech. *sd:* Vit. 7 min. • The coyote's endeavours peak with him passing an endurance test inside a steel ball.

7005. Wild and Woody (*Woody Woodpecker*) 31 Dec. 1948; *p.c.:* Walter Lantz prods for UA; *dir:* Dick Lundy; *story:* Ben Hardaway, Heck Allen; *anim:* (La)Verne Harding, Les Kline, Ed Love, Pat Matthews, Ken O'Brien, Sid Pillet; *sets:* Fred Brunish; *ed:* Dave Lurie; *voices:* Lionel Stander, Jack Mather, Pinto Colvig, Grace Stafford, Ben Hardaway; *mus:* Darrell Calker; *prod mgr:* William E. Garity; *col:* Tech. *sd:* RCA. 6 min. • Sheriff Woody sets out to apprehend the western desperado, Buzz Buzzard.

7006. Wild and Woolfy (*Merrie Melodies*) 13 Oct. 1945; *p.c.:* MGM; *dir:* Tex Avery; *story:* Heck Allen; *anim:* Ed Love, Ray Abrams, Preston Blair; *character des:* Claude Smith; *sets:* John Didrik Johnsen; *ed:* Fred MacAlpin; *voices:* Ann Pickard, Harry E. Lang; *mus:* Scott Bradley; *prod:* Fred Quimby; *col:* Tech. *sd:* WE. 6½ min. • A western bandit kidnaps a songstress and is chased to his hideout by the posse ... but "the Hero" saves the day.

7007. Wild and Woolly (*Oswald*) 21 Nov. 1932; *p.c.:* Univ; *dir:* Walter Lantz, "Bill" Nolan; *anim:* Ray Abrams, Fred Avery, "Bill" Weber, Jack Carr, Charles Hastings; *mus:* James Dietrich; b&w. *sd:* WE. 6 min. • Oswald in a western setting.

7008. Wild and Woolly Hare (*Looney Tunes*) 1 Aug. 1959; *p.c.:* WB; *dir:* Friz Freleng; *story:* Warren Foster; *anim:* Virgil Ross, Gerry Chiniquy, Art Davis; *lay:* Hawley Pratt; *back:* Tom O'Loughlin; *ed:* Treg Brown; *voices:* Mel Blanc; *mus:* Milt Franklyn; *prod mgr:* William Orcutt; *prod:* David H. DePatie; *col:* Tech. *sd:* Vit. 7 min. • Cowboy Bugs tries to stop Yosemite Sam from robbing the mail train.

7009. The Wild and Woozy West (*Phantasy*) 30 Apr. 1942; *p.c.:* Colum; *dir/anim:* Allen Rose, Lou Lilly; *sets:* Clark Watson; *ed:* Edward Moore; *voices:* Billy Bletcher, Pinto Colvig, Sara Berner; *mus:* Paul Worth; *prod mgr:* Ben Schwalb; b&w. *sd:* RCA. 7 min. • A battle between a western wolf bank robber and the sheriff.

7010. Wild Bill Hiccup (*Woody Woodpecker*) 1 June 1970; *p.c.:* Walter Lantz prods for Univ; *dir:* Paul J. Smith; *anim:* Les Kline, Al Coe; *sets:* Nino Carbe; *voices:* Dal McKennon, Grace Stafford; *mus:* Walter Greene; *prod mgr:* William E. Garity; *col:* Tech. *sd:* RCA. 6 min. • No story available.

7011. Wild Cats of Paris (*Aesop's Film Fable*) 31 Oct. 1925; *p.c.:* Fables Pictures Inc for Pathé; *dir:* Paul Terry; b&w. *sil.* 10 min. • Farmer Al visits the Latin quarter of Paris.

7012. The Wild Chase (*Merrie Melodies*) 27 Feb. 1965; *p.c.:* DFE for WB; *dir:* Friz Freleng; *asst dir:* Hawley Pratt; *anim:* Norm McCabe, Don

Williams, Manuel Perez, Warren Batchelder, La Verne Harding; *lay:* Dick Ung; *back:* Tom O'Loughlin; *ed:* Lee Gunther; *voice:* Mel Blanc; *mus:* Bill Lava; *prod mgr:* William Orcutt; *col:* Tech. *sd:* Vit. 6 min. • Speedy Gonzales and the Road-Runner take part in a race with Sylvester and the coyote not far behind.

7013. Wild Elephinks *(Popeye)* 29 Dec. 1933; *p.c.:* The Fleischer Studio for Para; *prod:* Max Fleischer; *dir:* Dave Fleischer; *anim:* Willard Bowsky, William Sturm; *voices:* William A. Costello, Charles Carver; *mus:* Sammy Timberg; b&w. *sd:* WE. 7 min. • Popeye and Olive are on a jungle island, surrounded by hostile animals. An ape abducts Olive and Popeye deals with this.

7014. The Wild Goose Chase *(Aesop's Sound Fable)* 12 Aug. 1932; *p.c.:* Van Beuren for RKO; *dir:* John Foster, Mannie Davis; *mus:* Gene Rodemich; b&w. *sd:* RCA. 6 min. • No story available.

7015. A Wild Hare *(Merrie Melodies)* 27 July 1940; *p.c.:* Leon Schlesinger prods for WB; *dir:* Fred Avery; *story:* Rich Hogan, Robert Clampett; *anim:* Virgil Ross; *character des:* Robert Givens; *sets:* John Didrik Johnsen, Richard H. Thomas; *ed:* Treg Brown; *voices:* Mel Blanc, Arthur Q. Bryan; *mus:* Carl W. Stalling; *prod sup:* Henry Binder, Raymond G. Katz; *col:* Tech. *sd:* Vit. 7 min. • Elmer goes hunting and encounters a rabbit who has no intention of being caught. • Reputed to be the definitive "Bugs Bunny" cartoon.

7016. Wild Honey 7 Nov. 1942; *p.c.:* MGM; *story:* Henry Allen; *anim:* Michael Lah, Rudy Zamora, Don Williams; *sets:* Joe Smith; *ed:* Fred MacAlpin; *mus:* Scott Bradley; *prod:* Fred Quimby; *col:* Tech. *sd:* WE. 7 min. • Barney Bear sets out to scientifically steal some honey from a bee hive but the bees object.

7017. Wild Life *(Heckle & Jeckle)* Sept. 1959; *p.c.:* TT for Fox; *ex prod:* Bill Weiss; *dir:* Martin Taras; *story sup:* Tom Morrison; *story:* Larz Bourne, Eli Bauer; *anim:* Eddie Donnelly, Johnny Gent, Mannie Davis, Vinnie Bell, Larry Silverman; *sets:* John Zago; *voices:* Ray Halee; *mus:* Phil Scheib; *prod mgr:* Frank Schudde; *col:* DeLuxe. *sd:* RCA. 6 min. CS. • While Dimwit attempts to photograph wild life, the magpies set themselves up as guides and movie directors.

7018. Wild Over You *(Looney Tunes)* 11 July 1953; *p.c.:* WB; *dir:* Charles M. Jones; *story:* Michael Maltese; *anim:* Ben Washam, Lloyd Vaughan, Richard Thompson, Abe Levitow, Ken Harris; *lay:* Maurice Noble; *back:* Philip de Guard; *ed:* Treg Brown; *voices:* Mel Blanc; *mus:* Carl Stalling; *prod mgr:* John W. Burton; *prod:* Edward Selzer; *col:* Tech. *sd:* Vit. 7 min. • An escaped wildcat disguises herself as a skunk but is forced back to the zoo by the amorous advances of Pepè le Pew.

7019. A Wild Roomer *(Whirlwind Comedy)* 20 Oct. 1926; *p.c.:* FBO; *dir/l/a:* Charles R. Bowers; *story:* Charles R. Bowers, H.L. Muller, Ted Sears; *ph:* H.L. Muller; b&w. *sil.* l/a/anim. 24 min. • An inventor stands to inherit his grandfather's entire fortune if he can demonstrate a fully-functional model of his latest invention within 48 hours. A jealous uncle tries to sabotage the machine. Live-action short with stop-motion animation.

7020. Wild Waves *(Mickey Mouse)* 21 Dec. 1929; *p.c.:* Walter E. Disney for Colum; *dir:* Burton F. Gillett; *voice/mus:* Carl W. Stalling; *ph:* William Cottrell; b&w. *sd:* PCP. 7 min. • Mickey saves Minnie from drowning.

7021. Wild Wife *(Merrie Melodies)* 20 Feb. 1954; *p.c.:* WB; *dir:* Robert McKimson; *story:* Tedd Pierce; *anim:* Rod Scribner, Phil de Lara, Charles McKimson, Herman Cohen; *lay:* Robert Givens; *back:* Richard H. Thomas; *ed:* Treg Brown; *voices:* Bea Benaderet, Mel Blanc; *mus:* Carl Stalling; *prod mgr:* John W. Burton; *prod:* Edward Selzer; *col:* Tech. *sd:* Vit. 7 min. • A hard-working wife explains to her husband how she spent her day.

7022. Wild Wild West 30 June 1999; *p.c.:* WB; *lead tarantula anim:* Scott Benza, John Zdankiecz; *anim:* Heather Knight, Julie Nelson, Steve Nichols, Tom St. Amand, Scott "Huck" Wirtz; *col:* Tech. *sd:* Dolby digital/dts Digital/SDDS. 105 min. l/a. • Live-action adaptation of the 1960s television Western. It is 1869 and U.S. Army Special Officer James T. West sets out on the trail of a former Confederate General. Animated tarantula.

7023. Wild, Wild World *(Merrie Melodies)* 27 Feb. 1960; *p.c.:* WB; *dir:* Robert McKimson; *story:* Tedd Pierce; *anim:* George Grandpré, Ted Bonnicksen, Warren Batchelder, Tom Ray, David R. Green; *lay:* Robert Gribbroek; *back:* William Butler; *ed:* Treg Brown; *voices:* Daws Butler, Mel

Blanc; *mus:* Milt Franklyn; *prod mgr:* William Orcutt; *prod:* David H. DePatie; *col:* Tech. *sd:* Vit. 7 min. • A parody on TV's "Wide, Wide World" where we are given an insight into how primitive cavemen existed.

7024. Wilful Willie *(Terry-Toon)* 26 June 1942; *p.c.:* TT for Fox; *dir:* Connie Rasinski; *story:* John Foster; *mus:* Philip A. Scheib; *col:* Tech. *sd:* RCA. 6 min. • A little chap refuses to drink his milk before retiring. He then suffers a nightmare where he finds himself thirsting in the desert.

7025. Will Do Mousework *(Herman & Katnip)* 29 June 1956; *p.c.:* Famous for Para; *dir:* Seymour Kneitel; *story:* Larz Bourne; *anim:* Tom Golden, Bill Hudson; *sets:* Joe Dommerque; *voices:* Arnold Stang, Sid Raymond, Cecil Roy, Jack Mercer; *mus:* Winston Sharples; *ph:* Leonard McCormick; *col:* Tech. *sd:* RCA. 6 min. • Herman convinces Katnip to "keep the mice to keep his job."

7026. William Tell *(Oswald)* 28 May 1934; *p.c.:* Univ; *dir:* Walter Lantz, "Bill" Nolan; *story:* Victor McLeod; *anim:* Manuel Moreno, George Grandpré, Lester Kline, Verne Harding, Fred Kopietz; *mus:* James Dietrich; b&w. *sd:* WE. 6 min. • The governor instructs Tell to shoot an apple from his son's head. This he does with the arrow hitting Tell's wife who thinks the governor hit her and gives him "what for."

7027. Willie the Kid 26 June 1952; *p.c.:* UPA for Colum; *ex prod:* Stephen Bosustow; *dir/story:* Robert Cannon; *story/lay:* T. Hee; *anim:* Bill Melendez, Frankie Smith, Roger Daley, Grim Natwick; *back:* Jules Engel; *voices:* Marvin Miller, Marian Richman, Martha Wentworth; *mus:* Ernest Gold; *prod mgr:* Herbert Klynn; *col:* Tech. *sd:* RCA. 6½ min. • Little Willie and his pals play "cowboys," turning the suburbs into the old wild west.

7028. Willie the Operatic Whale 16 Aug. 1954; *p.c.:* Walt Disney prods for BV; *dir:* Hamilton Luske, Clyde Geronimi; *col:* Tech. *sd:* RCA. 20 min. • See: *Make Mine Music*

7029. Willie's Blackboard *p.c.:* Sullivan Studio; *dir:* Pat Sullivan; b&w. *sil.* l/a/anim. • Series of twelve made. Titles untraced.

7030. Willoughby's Magic Hat *(Phantasy)* 2 Apr. 1943; *p.c.:* Colum; *prod:* Dave Fleischer; *dir:* Bob Wickersham; *story:* Sam Cobean; *anim:* Phil Duncan, Howard Swift; *sets:* Zack Schwartz, Clark Watson; *voices:* John McLeish; *mus:* Paul Worth; *prod mgr:* Albert Spar; b&w. *sd:* RCA. 6½ min. • Willoughby Wren owns a cap woven from Samson's hair that gives him strength when he wears it. His adventures bring him into contact with a mechanical monster.

7031. The Wily Weasel *(Oswald)* 7 June 1937; *p.c.:* Univ; *dir:* Walter Lantz; *story:* Victor McLeod, James Miele; *anim:* Manuel Moreno, Fred Kopietz, Lester Kline; *mus:* James Dietrich; b&w. *sd:* WE. 7 min. • The weasel steals eggs from the hen house, so Oswald sets a trap.

7032. Wimmin Hadn't Oughter Drive *(Popeye)* 16 Aug. 1940; *p.c.:* The Fleischer Studio for Para; *prod:* Max Fleischer; *dir:* Dave Fleischer; *story:* George Manuell; *anim:* Orestes Calpini, Reuben Grossman; *voices:* Jack Mercer, Margie Hines; *mus:* Sammy Timberg; *ph:* Charles Schettler; *prod sup:* Sam Buchwald, Isidore Sparber; b&w. *sd:* WE. 7 min. • Popeye places his life in his own hands when teaching Olive how to drive his new car.

7033. Wimmin Is a Myskery *(Popeye)* 7 July 1940; *p.c.:* The Fleischer Studio for Para; *prod:* Max Fleischer; *dir:* Dave Fleischer; *story:* Ted Pierce; *anim:* Willard Bowsky, Joseph d'Igalo; *voices:* Jack Mercer, Margie Hines; *mus:* Sammy Timberg; *prod sup:* Sam Buchwald, Isidore Sparber; b&w. *sd:* WE. 7 min. • When Popeye proposes to Olive, she says she will "sleep on it," then suffers a nightmare about being married with unruly kids.

7034. Win, Place and Showboat *(Screen Songs)* 28 Apr. 1950; *p.c.:* Famous for Para; *dir:* I. Sparber; *story:* Larz Bourne, Larry Riley; *anim:* Al Eugster, Wm. B. Pattengill; *sets:* Robert Connavale; *voices:* Jackson Beck, Jack Mercer; *mus:* Winston Sharples; *song:* Gilbert, Muir; *ph:* Leonard McCormick; *prod mgr:* Sam Buchwald; *col:* Tech. *sd:* RCA. 6 min. • An elephant leads the showboat orchestra, heralding various minstrel acts on the bill.

7035. The Wind Jammers *(Aesop's Film Fable)* 7 Feb. 1926; *p.c.:* Fables Pictures Inc for Pathé; *dir:* Paul Terry; b&w. *sil.* 5 min. • Henry Cat sends a mouse under water to inflate the fish with bellows so that they float to the surface. The mice are then driven from the house by smoke being blown down the chimney.

7036. **The Windblown Hare** (*Looney Tunes*) 27 Aug. 1949; *p.c.:* WB; *dir:* Robert McKimson; *story:* Warren Foster; *anim:* Charles McKimson, Phil de Lara, Manny Gould, John Carey; *character des:* Jean Blanchard; *lay:* Cornett Wood; *back:* Richard H. Thomas; *ed:* Treg Brown; *voices:* Mel Blanc, Bea Benaderet; *mus:* Carl Stalling; *prod mgr:* John W. Burton; *prod:* Edward Selzer; *col:* Tech. *sd:* Vit. 7 min. • Bugs buys the Three Pigs' house and the Wolf blows it down! After a similar incident, Bugs wages war on the Wolf ... and the Pigs.

7037. **Window Cleaners** (*Donald Duck*) 20 Sept. 1940; *p.c.:* Walt Disney prods for RKO; *dir:* Jack King; *asst dir:* Bob Newman; *story:* Carl Barks, Jack Hannah; *anim:* Paul Allen, Rex Cox, Emery Hawkins, Hal King, Richard Lundy, Lee Morehouse, Chic F. Otterstrom, Ray Patin, Ken Peterson, Judge Whitaker; *lay:* Bill Herwig; *voices:* Clarence Nash; *mus:* Paul J. Smith, Oliver Wallace; *col:* Tech. *sd:* RCA. 7 min. • Donald is cleaning a skyscraper's windows assisted by Pluto, when he is pestered by a bee.

7038. **Window Pains** (*Beary Family*) Feb. 1967; *p.c.:* Walter Lantz prods for Univ; *dir:* Paul J. Smith; *story:* Cal Howard; *anim:* Les Kline, Al Coe; *sets:* Ray Huffine; *voices:* Paul Frees, Grace Stafford; *mus:* Walter Greene; *prod mgr:* William E. Garity; *col:* Tech. *sd:* RCA. 6 min. • Charlie attempts to save money by cleaning his own windows.

7039. **Window Shopping** (*Color Rhapsody*) 3 June 1938; *p.c.:* Charles Mintz prods for Colum; *dir:* Sid Marcus; *anim:* Art Davis, Herb Rothwill; *voice:* The Rhythmettes; *mus:* Joe de Nat; *prod mgr:* James Bronis; *col:* Tech. *sd:* RCA. 7½ min. • Three mice cavort about the city, ending at a restaurant for an early morning snack.

7040. **The Window Washers** (*Aesop's Film Fable*) 29 Aug. 1925; *p.c.:* Fables Pictures Inc for Pathé; *dir:* Paul Terry; b&w. sil. 10 min. • Farmer Al has posts a "Window Washers Wanted" sign on the farmhouse. The cat uses a mouse as a window washing implement, causing the mouse to douse him with a bucket of water. A gang of mice hose Al and the cat down with seltzer water. Moral: "Laugh and the world laughs with you, snore and you snore alone."

7041. **Windy Day** 1966; *p.c.:* Hubley Studio for Para; *prod/dir:* John & Faith Hubley; *anim:* Barrie Nelson; *i&p:* Sara Calogero, Faith Hubley, Nina di Gangi; *voices:* Emily & Georgia Hubley; *ph:* Jack Buehre; *sd:* Michael Carton, United Recording Labs Inc.; *col.* *sd.* 9 min. *Academy Award nomination.* • Exploring a child's world of romance, marriage and growing up.

7042. **Wine, Women and Song** (*Aesop's Film Fable*) 4 July 1925; *p.c.:* Fables Pictures Inc for Pathé; *dir:* Paul Terry; b&w. sil. 10 min. • Henry Cat, on a roof, demonstrates a novel method of catching mice: A board lies across a log with some cheese at one end. When the mouse comes to eat the cheese, he drops bricks to catapult the rodents into his sack.

7043. **The Winged Horse** (*Oswald*) 9 May 1932; *p.c.:* Univ; *dir:* Walter Lantz, "Bill" Nolan; *anim:* Manuel Moreno, Ray Abrams, Fred Avery, "Bill" Weber, Vet Anderson, Lester Kline, Bunny Ellison; *mus:* James Dietrich; b&w. *sd:* WE. 7½ min. • Oswald in an Arabian setting.

7044. **Winner by a Hare** (*Noveltoon*) 17 Apr. 1953; *p.c.:* Famous for Para: *dir:* I. Sparber; *story:* Irving Spector; *anim:* Myron Waldman, Tom Golden; *sets:* John Zago; *voices:* Sid Raymond, Jackson Beck; *mus:* Winston Sharples; *ph:* Leonard McCormick; *prod mgr:* Seymour Shultz; *col:* Tech. *sd:* RCA. 6 min. • After losing another race, Moe Hare realizes he'd win if he would bet on the Tortoise.

7045. **Winnie the Pooh and a Day for Eeyore** 11 Mar. 1983; *p.c.:* Walt Disney Productions for BV; *dir/prod:* Rick Reinert; based on the books written by A.A. Milne; illustrated by Ernest H. Shepard; *story:* Peter Young, Steve Hulett, Tony L. Marino; *anim dir:* Ennis McNulty, Dave Bennett; *anim:* Nancy Bieman, Irv Anderson, Tom Ray, Ken O'Brien, Virgil Ross, Lars Hult, Spencer Peel; *asst anim:* Robert Shellborn, Emily Jiuliano, Vera Lanpher, Sharon Murray, Philo Barnhart, Ayalen Garcia; *creative talents:* Bev Chiara, Gretchen Heck, Sammie Lanham, Margaret Craig, Richard Williams, Allen Hohnroth, Kathi Castillo, Owen Gladden, Betty May Doyle, Pauline Weber, Judith Drake, Ted Bemiller; *back:* Rick Reinert, Dale Barnhart, Richard Foes; *voices: Pooh/Owl:* Hal Smith; *Eeyore:* Ralph Wright; *Narrator:* Laurie Main; *Piglet:* John Fiedler; *Rabbit:* Will Ryan; *Christopher Robin:* Kim Christianson; *Roo:* Dick Billingsley; *Tigger:* Paul Winchell; *Kanga:* Julie McWhirter Dees; *mus:* Steve Zuckerman;

"Winnie the Pooh" *music & lyrics:* Richard M. Sherman, Robert B. Sherman; *col:* Tech. *sd.* 24 min. • Pooh and his friends celebrate Eeyore's birthday when it appears that nobody has remembered it.

7046. **Winnie the Pooh and the Blustery Day** 20 Dec. 1968; *p.c.:* Walt Disney prods for BV; *dir:* Wolfgang Reitherman; based on the books by A.A. Milne, illustrated by E.H. Shepard; *story dir:* Winston Hibler; *story:* Larry Clemmons, Ralph Wright, Julius Svendsen, Vance Gerry; *anim:* Hal King, John Lounsbery, Milt Kahl, Ollie Johnston, Frank Thomas, Walt Stanchfield, Art Stevens, Fred Hellmich, Dave Michener, Dan Mac-Manus; *lay:* Basil Davidovich, Don Griffith, Dale Barnhart, Sylvia Roemer; *back:* Al Dempster, Bill Layne; *voices: Narration:* Sebastian Cabot; *Pooh:* Sterling Holloway; *Piglet:* John Fiedler; *Christopher Robin:* Jon Walmsley; *Owl:* Hal Smith; *Eeyore:* Ralph Wright; *Rabbit:* Junius C. Matthews; *Gopher:* Howard Morris; *Kanga:* Barbara Luddy; *Roo:* Clint Howard; *Tigger:* Paul Winchell; *mus:* Buddy Baker; *songs:* Richard M. Sherman, Robert B. Sherman; *col:* Tech. *sd:* RCA. 25 min. *Academy Award.* • In which Pooh suffers a nightmare, a flood and encounters Tigger for the first time.

7047. **Winnie the Pooh and the Honey Tree** 4 Feb. 1966; *p.c.:* Walt Disney prods for BV; *dir:* Wolfgang Reitherman; based on the books by A.A. Milne, illustrated by E.H. Shepard; *story:* Larry Clemmons, Ralph Wright, Xavier Atencio, Ken Anderson, Vance Gerry, Dick Lucas; *anim:* Hal King, Eric Cleworth, John Lounsbery, Eric Larson, John Sibley, Hal Ambro, Walt Stanchfield, Fred Hellmich, John Ewing, Bill Keil, Dan Mac-Manus; *lay:* Basil Davidovich, Don Griffith; *back:* Art Riley, Al Dempster, Bill Layne; *voices: Narration:* Sebastian Cabot; *Pooh:* Sterling Holloway; *Gopher:* Howard Morris; *Rabbit:* Junius Matthews; *Christopher Robin:* Bruce Reitherman; *Eeyore:* Ralph Wright; *Owl:* Hal Smith; *Kanga:* Barbara Luddy; *Roo:* Clint Howard; *Bees:* Dal McKennon, Ginny Tyler; *mus:* Buddy Baker; *songs:* Richard M. Sherman, Robert B. Sherman; *col:* Tech. *sd:* RCA. 26 min. • Pooh tries to extract some honey from a hive without the bees being too aware.

7048. **Winnie the Pooh and Tigger Too** 20 Dec. 1974; *p.c.:* Walt Disney prods for BV; *prod:* Wolfgang Reitherman; *dir:* John Lounsbery; based on the books by A.A. Milne, illustrated by E.H. Shepard; *story:* Larry Clemmons, Ted Berman, Eric Cleworth; *anim dir:* Milt Kahl, Frank Thomas, Ollie Johnston, Eric Larson; *anim:* Art Stevens, Don Bluth, Cliff Nordberg, Burny Mattinson, Dale Baer, John Pomeroy, Gary Goldsmith, Chuck Williams, Richard Sebast, Andrew Gaskill, Jack Buckley; *lay:* Don Griffith, Joe Hale, Sylvia Roemer; *back:* Bill Layne, Ann Guenther; *voices: Narration:* Sebastian Cabot; *Pooh:* Sterling Holloway; *Tigger:* Paul Winchell; *Rabbit:* Junius Matthews; *Piglet:* John Fiedler; *Kanga:* Barbara Luddy; *Roo:* Dori Whitaker; *Christopher Robin:* Timothy Turner; *mus:* Buddy Baker; *songs:* Richard M. Sherman, Robert B. Sherman; *col:* Tech. *sd:* RCA. 26 min. *Academy Award nomination.* • Rabbit enlists the inhabitants of Hundred Acre Wood to curb Tigger's bouncing.

7049. **Winning the West** (*Mighty Mouse*) 16 Aug. 1946; *p.c.:* TT for Fox; *dir:* Eddie Donnelly; *story:* John Foster; *sets:* Art Bartsch; *voice:* Thomas Morrison; *mus:* Philip A. Scheib; *ph:* Douglas Moye; *col:* Tech. *sd:* RCA. 7 min. • The Indian cats attack the mouse pioneers. Mighty Mouse soon arrives to settle matters.

7050. **The Winning Ticket** (*Captain & the Kids*) 1 Oct. 1938; *p.c.:* MGM; *dir:* Isadore Freleng; *anim:* Bill Nolan; *voices:* Billy Bletcher, Mel Blanc, Dave Weber, Jeanne Dunn, Elvia Allman; *mus:* Scott Bradley; *prod mgr:* Fred Quimby; *col:* sep. *sd:* WE. 7 min. • John Silver disguises himself as a woman to get der Captain's winning sweepstakes ticket.

7051. **Wins Out** (*Oswald*) 3 Mar. 1932; *p.c.:* Univ; *dir:* Walter Lantz, "Bill" Nolan; *anim:* Manuel Moreno, Ray Abrams, Fred Avery, Lester Kline, Vet Anderson; *mus:* James Dietrich; b&w. *sd:* WE. 6½ min. • Oswald as a harassed baker ordered to bake "Four-and-Twenty Blackbirds" in the King's pie.

7052. **Winsor McCay Makes His Cartoons Move** 12 Apr. 1911; *p.c.:* Vitagraph Corp of America; *anim:* Winsor McCay; *l/a ph:* Walter Arthur; b&w/hand-colored. sil. 7 min. *l/a/anim.* • Winsor McCay explains to rotund comedian, John Bunny and artist George McManus how he animates his drawings, illustrated by a showing of "Little Nemo."

7053. **Winter** (*Silly Symphony*) 22 Oct. 1930; *p.c.:* Walter E. Disney for Colum; *dir:* Burton F. Gillett; *anim:* Johnny Cannon, Les Clark, Jack Cutting, Gilles de Tremaudan, Norman Ferguson, David D. Hand, Wilfred

Jackson, Jack King, Richard Lundy, Tom Palmer, Ben Sharpsteen; *mus:* Bert Lewis; *ph:* William Cottrell; b&w. *sd:* PCP. 6 min. • The snow arrives and the animals come out to frolic and skate until the clouds cover the sun.

7054. Winter Draws On (*Screen Song*) 19 Mar. 1948; *p.c.:* Famous for Para; *dir:* Seymour Kneitel; *story:* Larz Bourne, Bill Turner; *anim:* Al Eugster, Irving Spector; *sets:* Tom Ford; *voices:* Jackson Beck, Cecil Roy; *mus:* Winston Sharples; *song:* Bud Green, Buddy G. de Sylva, Ray Henderson; *ph:* Leonard McCormick; *prod mgr:* Sam Buchwald; *col:* Pola. *sd:* RCA. 7 min. • Mama bird can't fly south for the winter while one of her eggs still has to be hatched.

7055. Winter Storage (*Donald Duck*) 3 June 1949; *p.c.:* Walt Disney prods for RKO; *dir:* Jack Hannah; *story:* Bill Berg, Nick George *anim:* Bob Carlson, Volus Jones, Bill Justice, Judge Whitaker; *fx:* Jack Boyd; *lay:* Yale Gracey; *back:* Thelma Witmer; *voices:* Clarence Nash, James MacDonald, Dessie Flynn; *mus:* Oliver Wallace; *col:* Tech. *sd:* RCA. 6¹/₂ min. • Chip an' Dale steal the acorns that Forest Ranger Donald is planting.

7056. Wireless Telephone (*Goldwyn-Bray Pictograph*) 1919; *p.c.:* Bray prods for Goldwyn; *anim:* Francis Lyle Goldman; b&w. *sil.* 5¹/₂ min. • Diagrams explain the transmitting and receipt of the message.

7057. Wise Flies (*Talkartoon*) 19 July 1930; *p.c.:* The Fleischer Studio for Para; *prod:* Max Fleischer; *dir:* Dave Fleischer; *anim:* Grim Natwick; *mus:* Art Turkisher; b&w. *sd:* WE. 6 min. • A spider performs a duet with a girl fly and suffers at the hands of his irate spouse.

7058. The Wise Little Hen (*Silly Symphony*) 9 June 1934; *p.c.:* Walt Disney prods for UA; *dir:* Wilfred Jackson; *story/lyrics:* Larry Morey; *anim:* Arthur Babbitt, Ugo d'Orsi, Gilles de Tremaudan, Clyde Geronimi, Jack Hannah, Dick Huemer, Wolfgang Reitherman, Archie Robin, Louis Schmitt, Ben Sharpsteen; *voices:* Florence Gill, Clarence Nash, Pinto Colvig; *mus:* Leigh Harline; *song:* Leigh Harline, J.H. Wood; *col:* Tech. *sd:* RCA. 7 min. • Peter Pig and Donald Duck fein "bellyache" when asked to help with the growing of the Little Hen's corn but are both anxious to eat the end product. • The introduction of Donald Duck.

7059. The Wise Owl (*Color Rhapsody*) 6 Dec. 1940; *p.c.:* Cartoon Films Ltd for Colum; *dir:* Ub Iwerks; *mus:* Eddie Kilfeather, Joe de Nat; *col:* Tech. *sd:* RCA. 7 min. • An owl tries to gain entrance into a bat cave.

7060. Wise Quackers (*Looney Tunes*) 1 Jan. 1949; *p.c.:* WB; *dir:* I. Freleng; *story:* Tedd Pierce; *anim:* Manuel Perez, Pete Burness, Ken Champin, Virgil Ross, Gerry Chiniquy; *lay:* Hawley Pratt; *back:* Paul Julian; *ed:* Treg Brown; *voices:* Mel Blanc, Arthur Q. Bryan, Tedd Pierce; *mus:* Carl Stalling; *prod mgr:* John W. Burton; *prod:* Edward Selzer; *col:* Tech. *sd:* Vit. 7 min. • Elmer spares Daffy's life so that he can be a personal slave.

7061. The Wise Quacking Duck (*Looney Tunes*) 1 May 1943; *p.c.:* Leon Schlesinger prods for WB; *dir:* Robert Clampett; *story:* Warren Foster; *anim:* Phil Monroe; *character des/lay:* Thomas McKimson; *back:* Michael Sasanoff; *ed:* Treg Brown; *voices:* Mel Blanc, Darrell R. Payne; *mus:* Carl W. Stalling; *prod sup:* Henry Binder, Raymond G. Katz; *col:* Tech. *sd:* Vit. 7 min. • Mr. Meek has been instructed to prepare a duck dinner but does not care to kill a duck.

7062. Wise Quacks (*Dinky Duck*) Feb. 1953; *p.c.:* TT for Fox; *dir:* Mannie Davis; *story:* Tom Morrison; *sets:* Art Bartsch; *mus:* Philip A. Scheib; *ph:* Douglas Moye; *col:* Tech. *sd:* RCA. 7 min. • A fairy grants Dinky a beautiful singing voice which only leads to trouble when a fox persuades him to sing in the big city.

7063. Wise Quacks (*Looney Tunes*) 5 Aug 1938; *p.c.:* Leon Schlesinger prods for WB; *dir:* Robert Clampett; *story:* Warren Foster; *anim:* I. Ellis, Robert Cannon; *sets:* Elmer Plummer; *ed:* Tregoweth E. Brown; *voices:* Mel Blanc, Harry E. Lang; *mus:* Carl W. Stalling; *prod sup:* Henry Binder, Raymond G. Katz; b&w. *sd:* Vit. 7 min. • A gang of villainous eagles capture one of Daffy's newly born with Daffy in hot pursuit.

7064. Witch Crafty (*Woody Woodpecker*) 14 Mar. 1955; *p.c.:* Walter Lantz prods for Univ; *dir:* Paul J. Smith; *story:* Homer Brightman, Michael Maltese; *anim:* Herman R. Cohen, Gil Turner, Robert Bentley; *sets:* Art Landy; *voices:* Grace Stafford; *mus:* Clarence Wheeler; *prod mgr:* William E. Garity; *col:* Tech. *sd:* RCA. 6 min. • A witch refuses to pay Woody 50¢ for a new handle for her magic broom.

7065. The Witch's Cat (*Mighty Mouse*) July 1946; *p.c.:* TT for Fox; *dir:* Mannie Davis; *story:* John Foster; *sets:* Art Bartsch; *mus:* Philip A. Scheib; *col:* Tech. *sd:* RCA. 6¹/₂ min. • A witch and her cat disrupt the Hallowe'en festivities of the mice.

7066. A Witch's Tangled Hare (*Looney Tunes*) 31 Oct. 1959; *p.c.:* WB; *dir:* Abe Levitow; *story:* Michael Maltese; *anim:* Richard Thompson, Ken Harris, Ben Washam, Keith Darling; *lay:* Owen Fitzgerald; *back:* Bob Singer; *ed:* Treg Brown; *voices:* Mel Blanc, June Foray; *mus:* Milt Franklyn; *prod mgr:* William Orcutt; *prod:* David H. DePatie; *col:* Tech. *sd:* Vit. 7 min. • Bugs and Witch Hazel find themselves unwittingly supplying material to William Shakespeare.

7067. Without Time or Reason (*Modern Madcap*) Jan. 1962; *p.c.:* Para Cartoons; *dir:* Seymour Kneitel; *story/voices:* Eddie Lawrence; *anim:* Martin Taras, George Germanetti, Jim Logan; *sets:* Robert Owen; *mus:* Winston Sharples; *ph:* Leonard McCormick; *prod mgr:* Abe Goodman; *col:* Tech. *sd:* RCA. 6 min. • Shorty regrets the day he ever bought a cuckoo clock from Swifty.

7068. Witty Kitty (*Hickory, Dickory & Doc*) 2 Feb. 1960; *p.c.:* Walter Lantz prods for Univ; *dir:* Alex Lovy; *story:* Homer Brightman; *anim:* La Verne Harding, Don Patterson, Ray Abrams; *sets:* Raymond Jacobs, Art Landy; *voices:* Paul Frees, Dal McKennon, Grace Stafford; *mus:* Clarence Wheeler; *prod mgr:* William E. Garity; *col:* Tech. *sd:* RCA. 6 min. • Two alley cats trick Doc into stealing a turkey from under the eyes of Cecil, the watchdog.

7069. The Wizard of Arts (*Animated Antics*) 8 Aug. 1941; *p.c.:* The Fleischer Studio for Para; *prod:* Max Fleischer; *dir:* Dave Fleischer; *mus:* Sammy Timberg; *ph:* Charles Schettler; *prod sup:* Sam Buchwald, Isidore Sparber; b&w. *sd:* WE. 6 min. • A comic sculptor and his eventual exhibition.

7070. The Wizard of Oz 1931; *p.c.:* Musicolor Fantasies Co; *prod:* Ted Eshbaugh, J.R. Booth; *dir:* Ted Eshbaugh; *story:* Col Frank L. Baum; *anim:* Frank Tipper, Bill Mason, Cal Dalton, C.T.(Vet) Anderson, "Hutch" (Andrew Hutchinson); *mus:* Carl Stalling; *col:* Tech-2. *sd:* 7 min. • Dorothy, The Straw and Tin Man all go to meet the Wizard who does magical tricks involving hens laying eggs containing strange creatures.

7071. Wizards Mar. 1977; *p.c.:* Bakshi prods for Fox; *prod/dir/story:* Ralph Bakshi; *seq anim:* Irven Spence; *anim:* Brenda Banks, Irven Spence, Martin B. Taras, Robert Taylor, Arthur Vitello; *asst anim:* Stod Herbert, Charlotte Huffine, Ben Shenkman; *fx:* Tasia Williams; *col models:* Janet Cummings; *lay:* John Sparey; *back des:* David Jonas, Ian Miller, Martin Strudler, Ira Turek; *back:* Martin Strudler, Johnny Vita; *ed:* Donald W. Ernst; *illustrated histories:* Mike Ploog; *i&p:* Sandy Benanati, Diane Dunning, Louise Cuarto, Alison A. Victory, Manon Washburn, Michele Zurcher; *checkers:* Dotti Foell, Mary J. Adams, Alice Cowing, Kathrin Leichliter, Nelda Ridley; *voices:* Avatar: Bob Holt; Elinore: Jesse Wells; Weehawk: Richard Romanus; Peace: David Proval; President: James Connell; Black Wolf: Steve Gravers; Fairy: Barbara Sloane; Frog: Angelo Grisanti; Priest: Hyman Wien; Peewhittle: Christopher Tayback; Sean: Mark Hamil; General: Peter Hobbs; *mus/song:* Andrew Belling; *ph:* Ted C. Bemiller; *titles:* Howard Miller; *sd fx:* Horta-Mahana Corp; *prod sup:* William Orcutt, John Kaufman, Josè Kfuni, Jim Starlin, Scott Citron, Christine Wirt; *col:* DeLuxe. *sd.* 69 min. • A futuristic world after the holocaust with warring wizards conjuring up Hitler's armies.

7072. The Wizard's Apprentice 1933; *p.c.:* Feature Productions for Artcinema Associates Inc.; *prod:* Hugo Riesenfeld, William Cameron Menzies; *dir:* Sidney Levee; *ed:* D. Marion Staines; *ph:* Alfred Schmid; b&w. *sd.* • The story of the Wizard's helper who gets the broomsticks to do his work for him ... but things get out of control. Model animation.

7073. The Wolf and the Crane (*Aesop's Film Fable*) 2 Oct. 1921; *p.c.:* Fables Pictures Inc for Pathé; *dir:* Paul Terry; b&w. *sil.* 5 min. • A wolf eats a fish and gets a bone stuck in his gullet. He promises Dr. Crane a reward if he can remove the fishbone. The crane extracts it from the wolf's throat with his long beak. When he asks for his reward, the wolf retorts, "Is it not enough that you had your head in a wolf's jaw and are still alive?" Moral: "Those who are charitable only in the hope of reward deserve but jeers."

7074. The Wolf and the Kid (*Aesop's Film Fable*) 18 Dec. 1921; *p.c.:*

Fables Pictures Inc for Pathé; *dir:* Paul Terry; b&w. *sil.* 5 min. • A cornered goat begs the wolf to play a whistle as a last request. When he does a police dog hears it and comes to the rescue.

7075. The Wolf at the Door (*Scrappy*) 12 Dec. 1932; *p.c.:* Winkler for Colum; *story:* Dick Huemor; *anim:* Sid Marcus, Art Davis; *mus:* Joe de Nat; *prod mgr:* James Bronis; b&w. *sd:* WE. 6 min. • A set-upon goat calls the Mounties (Scrappy and Vontzy) to rid him of a troublesome wolf.

7076. Wolf Chases Pigs (*Fable*) 30 Apr. 1942; *p.c.:* Colum; *prod:* Frank Tashlin; *dir:* Bob Wickersham; *story:* Leo Salkin; *anim:* John Hubley, Paul Sommer; *lay:* Clark Watson; *voices:* Billy Bletcher, Dick Nelson; *mus:* Paul Worth; b&w. *sd:* RCA. 6 min. • The Big Bad Wolf enlists in the Army only to discover the Three Little Pigs are his superiors.

7077. Wolf Hounded (*Loopy de Loop*) 7 Nov. 1959; *p.c.:* Hanna-Barbera for Colum; *prod/dir:* William Hanna, Joseph Barbera; *story dir:* Dan Gordon; *story:* Michael Maltese; *anim dir:* Charles A. Nichols; *anim:* Kenneth Muse; *lay:* Dick Bickenbach; *back:* F. Montealegre; *ed:* Greg Watson; *voices:* Daws Butler, June Foray; *mus:* Hoyt Curtin; *titles:* Lawrence Gobel; *prod mgr:* Howard Hanson; *col:* East. *sd:* RCA. 6½ min. • Loopy, the good wolf, tries to help out in the Red Riding Hood story.

7078. A Wolf in Cheap Clothing (*Paul Terry-Toon*) 17 Apr. 1936; *p.c.:* TT for Educational/Fox; *dir:* Mannie Davis, George Gordon; *mus:* Philip A. Scheib; b&w. *sd:* RCA. 5½ min. • A black lamb eludes capture by the wolf and fakes a police raid.

7079. A Wolf in Sheepdog's Clothing (*Loopy de Loop*) July 1963; *p.c.:* Hanna-Barbera for Colum; *prod/dir:* William Hanna, Joseph Barbera; *story dir:* Alex Lovy; *story:* Tony Benedict; *anim dir:* Charles A. Nichols; *anim:* Bill Keil; *lay:* Dan Noonan; *back:* Robert Gentle; *ed:* Warner Leighton; *voices:* Daws Butler, Don Messick, Doug Young; *mus:* Hoyt Curtin; *titles:* Lawrence Gobel; *prod mgr:* Howard Hanson; *col:* East. *sd:* RCA. 6½ min. • Loopy takes over the sheepdog's job of guarding the sheep.

7080. The Wolf in Sheep's Clothing (*Aesop's Film Fable*) 4 Mar. 1922; *p.c.:* Fables Pictures Inc for Pathé; *dir:* Paul Terry; b&w. *sil.* 5 min. • Jimmy Cat and the Kid go ice skating. A wolf sees the Kid as "lamb" stew and proceeds to dress himself in sheep's clothing and makes off with him. A dog Cop pursues him and knocks him through the ice. Moral: "Beware of a wolf in sheep's clothing."

7081. A Wolf in Sheik's Clothing (*Popeye*) 30 July 1948; *p.c.:* Famous for Para; *dir:* I. Sparber; *story:* Larry Riley, I. Klein; *anim:* Tom Johnson, George Rufle; *sets:* Tom Ford; *voices:* Jack Mercer, Mae Questel, Jackson Beck; *mus:* Winston Sharples; *ph:* Leonard McCormick; *prod mgr:* Sam Buchwald; *col:* Pola. *sd:* RCA. 6½ min. • While in Arabia, Olive is besotted by an Arab Sheik and whisked away to his tent. Popeye isn't too far behind.

7082. Wolf! Wolf! (*Mighty Mouse*) 22 June 1944; *p.c.:* TT for Fox; *dir:* Mannie Davis; *story:* John Foster; *sets:* Art Bartsch; *voice:* Thomas Morrison; *mus:* Philip A. Scheib; *col:* Tech. *sd:* RCA. 6 min. • The wolf dons a "Bo Peep" disguise to fool Mary's little lamb. Mighty Mouse is soon on hand to rescue her.

7083. Wolf! Wolf! (*Oswald*) 2 Apr. 1934; *p.c.:* Univ; *dir:* Walter Lantz; *story:* Victor McLeod; *anim:* Manuel Moreno, George Grandpré, Lester Kline, (La)Verne Harding, Fred Kopietz; *voices:* Bernice Hansel, The Rhythmettes; *mus:* James Dietrich; b&w. *sd:* WE. 7 min. • The two lambs fool shepherd Oswald with their cries of "Wolf!" but when a real wolf arrives, Ozzie ignores their cries for a while.

7084. The Wolf's Pardon (*Terry-Toon*) 5 Dec. 1947; *p.c.:* TT for Fox; *dir:* Eddie Donnelly; *story:* John Foster; *anim:* Jim Tyer; *sets:* Art Bartsch; *mus:* Philip A. Scheib; *col:* Tech. *sd:* RCA. 6½ min. • When the wolf is released from jail, he realizes he can't keep up with modern times.

7085. The Wolf's Side of the Story (*Terry-Toon*) 23 Sept. 1938; *p.c.:* TT for Fox; *dir:* Connie Rasinski; *voice:* Jo Miller; *mus:* Philip A. Scheib; b&w. *sd:* RCA. 6 min. • The wolf explains to the police how he only went swimming and was given a beating by Little Red Riding Hood and her grandma.

7086. A Wolf's Tale (*Terry-Toon*) 27 Oct. 1944; *p.c.:* TT for Fox; *dir* Connie Rasinski; *story:* John Foster; *sets:* Art Bartsch; *voices:* Thomas Morrison; *mus:* Philip A. Scheib; *ph:* Douglas Moye; *col:* Tech. *sd:* RCA. 7 min. • The wolf is arrested and tells the story of how he stood in for Red Riding Hood and was given a beating by Grandma. Tech remake of *The Wolf's Side of the Story.*

7087. The Woman and the Hen (*Aesop's Film Fable*) 20 Nov. 1921; *p.c.:* Fables Pictures Inc for Pathé; *dir:* Paul Terry; b&w. *sil.* 5 min. • A woman kills her hen by overdosing it on "magic oil" to increase its laying capacity. Moral: "Conceit begets disaster."

7088. A Woman's Honor (*Aesop's Film Fable*) 20 July 1924; *p.c.:* Fables Pictures Inc for Pathé; *dir:* Paul Terry; b&w. *sil.* 5 min. • The trials of a mouse when his sweetheart is abducted by a silk-hatted villainous cat. After a chase, the mouse manages to rescue his sweetie and foil the scoundrel.

7089. The Wonder Bakers at the World's Fair 1939; *p.c.:* Eshbaugh/Victor; *dir:* Ted Eshbaugh; *col. sd.* 2 min. • The elves make a Hostess cake. Commercial made for the World's Fair.

7090. The Wonder Dog (*Pluto*) 7 Apr. 1950; *p.c.:* Walt Disney prods for RKO; *dir:* Charles Nichols; *story:* Bill Peed, Milt Banta; *anim:* George Nicholas, Phil Duncan, George Kreisl, Hugh Fraser, Marvin Woodward; *fx:* Dan MacManus; *lay:* Karl Karpé; *back:* Brice Mack; *voice:* James MacDonald; *mus:* Oliver Wallace; *col:* Tech. *sd:* RCA. 6½ min. • Dinah is starry-eyed over a performing circus dog, so Pluto tries circus stunts. • In this production, inking was eliminated by pencilling directly onto "frosted"cel.

7091. The Wonder Gloves (*Jolly Frolics*) 29 Nov. 1951; *p.c.:* UPA for Colum; *ex prod:* Stephen Bosustow; *dir:* Robert Cannon; *story:* Bill Scott, Bill Danch; *anim:* Bill Melendez, Frank Smith, Roger Daley; *lay:* Paul Julian; *back:* Jules Engel; *voices:* Walter Tetley, Jerry Hausner; *mus:* Lou Maury; *prod mgr:* Herb Klynn, Max Morgan; *col:* Tech. *sd:* RCA. 6 min. • A boy's uncle spins a yarn of how he won a prize fight with magic boxing gloves.

7092. The Wonderful World of the Brothers Grimm Aug. 1962; *p.c.:* George Pal prods for MGM; *prod/anim dir:* George Pal; *anim/fx:* Gene Warren, Wah Chang, Tim Barr, Robert R. Hoag, David Pal, Jim Danforth, Don Sahlin; *mus:* Leigh Harline; *song:* Bob Merill; *col:* Metro. *sd:* WE. 135 min. Cinerama. *l/a/anim.* • The Grimm brothers' stories brought to life; *The Singing Bone:* A knight's servant slays a dragon and the knight takes the credit after having disposed of the servant. The servant takes the form of a bone and torments him until he tells the truth, returning the serf to life. • *The Cobbler and the Elves:* In repayment for his kindness, the elves do the cobbler's work.

7093. Wonderland (*Oswald*) 22 Oct. 1931; *p.c.:* Univ; *dir:* Walter Lantz, "Bill" Nolan; *anim:* Clyde Geronimi, Manuel Moreno, Ray Abrams, Fred Avery, Lester Kline, Vet Anderson, "Pinto" Colvig; *mus:* James Dietrich; b&w. *sd:* WE. 7 min. • In order to pay the mortgage, Oswald sells his prize cow for some magic beans which grow into a giant beanstalk. He scales it, beats an ogre and returns with a goose that lays golden eggs.

7094. Wood Choppers (*Aesop's Sound Fable*) 9 May 1929; *p.c.:* Fables Pictures Inc for Pathé; *dir:* Paul Terry; *mus:* Josiah Zuro; *sd fx:* Maurice Manne; b&w. *sd:* RCA. 6 min. • A cat and mouse chase culminates with the two fighting a duel on a floating log.

7095. Wood-Peckin' (*Popeye*) 6 Aug. 1943; *p.c.:* Famous for Para; *dir:* I. Sparber; *story:* Joe Stultz; *anim:* Nicholas Tafuri, Tom Golden; *voices:* Jack Mercer; *mus:* Sammy Timberg; *ph:* Leonard McCormick; *prod mgr:* Sam Buchwald; b&w. *sd:* WE. 7 min. • Popeye sets out to chop a tree for a new mast for his boat and is heckled by a woodpecker.

7096. The Wooden Indian (*Terry-Toon*) Jan. 1949; *p.c.:* TT for Fox; *dir:* Connie Rasinski; *story:* John Foster; *sets:* Art Bartsch; *mus:* Philip A. Scheib; *ph:* Douglas Moye; *col:* Tech. *sd:* RCA. 6 min. • The last redskin is ousted from his territory and goes on the war path, finally ending as a Cigar Store Indian.

7097. Wooden Money (*Aesop's Film Fable*) 10 Feb. 1929; *p.c.:* Fables Pictures Inc for Pathé; *dir:* Paul Terry, John Foster; b&w. *sil.* 10 min. • Farmer Al manages to sell his delapidated farmhouse to a couple of saps. He soon discovers that the bag he thought full of money is full of mice.

7098. Wooden Shoes (*Krazy Kat*) 25 Feb. 1933; *p.c.:* Winkler for Colum; *prod:* Charles Mintz; *story:* Ben Harrison, Manny Gould; *anim:* Al Eugster, Preston Blair; *voices:* Rochelle Hudson, Jack Carr; *mus:* Joe de Nat; *prod mgr:* James Bronis; b&w. *sd:* WE. 6 min. • Krazy saves the Dutch town from flooding by plugging a leak in a dyke with his fist.

7099. Woodland *(Paul Terry-Toon)* 1 May 1932; *p.c.:* Moser & Terry for Educational/Fox; *dir:* Frank Moser, Paul Terry; *mus:* Philip A. Scheib; b&w. *sd:* WE. 6 min. • Hunters and hounds invade the peace of the countryside. Rabbits run rings around the hounds and Al Falfa appears as a hunter.

7100. Woodland Café *(Silly Symphony)* 13 Mar. 1937; *p.c.:* Walt Disney prods for RKO; *dir:* Wilfred Jackson; *story:* Bianca Majolie; *anim:* Paul Allen, Tom Byrne, Johnny Cannon, Jack Hannah, Ward Kimball, I. Klein, Richard Lundy, Robert Stokes; *fx:* Cy Young; *atmospheric sketches:* Maurice Noble; *des:* Ferdinand Huszti Horvath; *lay:* Terrell Stapp, John Walbridge; *voices:* Clarrie Collins, Jimmie Cushman, Marie Dickerson, C.B. Johnson, James Miller, Thelma Porter, Eddie Prinz, Lillian Randolph, Duke Upshaw; *mus:* Leigh Harline; *col:* Tech. *sd:* RCA. 8 min. • Dance night at a popular nightclub for insects.

7101. Woodman Spare That Tree *(Color Rhapsody)* 19 July 1942; *p.c.:* Colum; *sup:* Frank Tashlin; *dir:* Bob Wickersham; *story:* Jack Cosgriff; *anim:* Phil Duncan; *lay:* Clark Watson; *ed:* Edward Moore; *voices:* Frank Graham; *mus:* Eddie Kilfeather; *prod mgr:* Ben Schwalb; *col:* Tech. *sd:* RCA. 7 min. • The crow tries to stop the fox from chopping his tree home down.

7102. Woodman, Spare That Tree *(Terry-Toon)* Feb. 1951; *p.c.:* TT for Fox; *dir:* Eddie Donnelly; *story:* Tom Morrison; *sets:* Art Bartsch; *mus:* Philip A. Scheib; *ph:* Douglas Moye; *col:* Tech. *sd:* RCA. 6 min. • The animals rally around to prevent a wood-chopper from axing a fir tree.

7103. Woodpecker from Mars *(Woody Woodpecker)* 2 July 1956; *p.c.:* Walter Lantz prods for Univ; *dir:* Paul J. Smith; *story:* Homer Brightman; *anim:* Herman Cohen, Robert Bentley, La Verne Harding; *sets:* Raymond Jacobs, Art Landy; *voices:* Dal McKennon, Grace Stafford; *mus:* Clarence Wheeler; *prod mgr:* William E. Garity; *col:* Tech. *sd:* RCA. 6 min. • Dressed as a spaceman, Woody wins a TV competition but once in the street, he is mistaken for a real alien and returned to the planet from which he supposedly came.

7104. Woodpecker in the Moon *(Woody Woodpecker)* July 1959; *p.c.:* Walter Lantz prods for Univ; *dir:* Alex Lovy; *story:* Dalton Sandifer; *anim:* Don Patterson, Ray Abrams, (La)Verne Harding; *sets:* Raymond Jacobs, Art Landy; *voices:* Dal McKennon, Grace Stafford; *mus:* Clarence Wheeler; *prod mgr:* William E. Garity; *col:* Tech. *sd:* RCA. 6 min. • Woody is sent to the Moon. When he lands, he meets Prof. Dingledong who has been stranded on a previous flight and fights for possession of Woody's rocket.

7105. Woodpecker in the Rough *(Woody Woodpecker)* 16 June 1952; *p.c.:* Walter Lantz prods for Univ; *dir:* Walter Lantz; *anim:* Don Patterson, Ray Abrams, La Verne Harding, Paul Smith; *sets:* Fred Brunish; *voices:* Dave Barry, Grace Stafford; *mus:* Clarence E. Wheeler; *prod mgr:* William E. Garity; *col:* Tech. *sd:* RCA. 6 min. • A bruiser challenges Woody to a $10-a-hole game of golf.

7106. Woodpecker Wanted *(Woody Woodpecker)* Feb. 1965; *p.c.:* Walter Lantz prods for Univ; *dir:* Paul J. Smith; *story:* Dalton Sandifer; *anim:* Les Kline, Al Coe; *sets:* Art Landy, Ray Huffine; *voices:* Dal McKennon, Grace Stafford; *mus:* Clarence Wheeler; *prod mgr:* William E. Garity; *col:* Tech. *sd:* RCA. 6 min. • Woody changes a "25¢ reward for woodpeckers" poster to $25,000. Dirty McNasty arrives and tries to capture him for the reward.

7107. The Woods Are Full of Cuckoos *(Merrie Melodies)* 4 Dec. 1937; *p.c.:* Leon Schlesinger prods for WB; *dir:* Frank Tashlin; *story:* Melvin Millar; *anim:* Robert Bentley; *ed:* Tregoweth E. Brown; *voices:* Mel Blanc, Ted Pierce, Fred Avery; *mus:* Carl W. Stalling; *prod sup:* Henry Binder, Raymond G. Katz; *col:* Tech. *sd:* Vit. 7 min. • Radio personalities caricatured as animals: Fred Allen and Portland, Jack Benny, Milton Berle, Ben Bernie, Eddie Cantor, Irvin S. Cobb, Bing Crosby, Andy Devine, Deanna Durbin, W.C. Fields, Wendell Hall, The Happinest Boys, Al Jolson, Ruby Keeler, Tizzie Lish, Fred MacMurray, Haven MacQuarrie, Grace Moore, Louella Parsons, Joe Penner, Lily Pons, Dick Powell, Martha Raye, Lanny Ross, Sophie Tucker, Walter Winchell, Alexander Woolcott.

7108. Woody and the Beanstalk *(Woody Woodpecker)* Mar. 1966; *p.c.:* Walter Lantz prods for Univ; *dir:* Paul J. Smith; *story:* Cal Howard; *anim:* Les Kline, Al Coe; *sets:* Art Landy, Ray Huffine; *voices:* Daws Butler, Grace Stafford; *mus:* Walter Greene; *prod mgr:* William E. Garity; *col:* Tech. *sd:* RCA. 6 min. • Woody replaces Jack and climbs the beanstalk to confront the giant who turns out to be smaller than expected.

7109. Woody Dines Out *(Woody Woodpecker)* 14 May 1945; *p.c.:* Walter Lantz prods for Univ; *dir:* James Culhane; *story:* Ben Hardaway, Milt Schaffer; *anim:* Don Williams; *sets:* Philip de Guard; *ed:* Dave Lurie; *voices:* Hans Conried, Ben Hardaway; *mus:* Darrell Calker; *ph:* Fred Weaver; *prod mgr:* George E. Morris; *col:* Tech. *sd:* WE. 7½ min. • A starving Woody mistakes a taxidermist's for a restaurant and confronts a character who wants to stuff him for a rich reward.

7110. Woody Meets Davy Crewcut *(Woody Woodpecker)* 17 Dec. 1956; *p.c.:* Walter Lantz prods for Univ; *dir:* Alex Lovy; *story:* Homer Brightman; *anim:* Ray Abrams, La Verne Harding; *sets:* Raymond Jacobs, Art Landy; *voices:* Daws Butler, Grace Stafford; *mus:* Clarence Wheeler; *prod mgr:* William E. Garity; *col:* Tech. *sd:* RCA. 6 min. • Davy Crewcut goes hunting woodpecker as an alternative to b'ar.

7111. Woody the Freeloader *(Woody Woodpecker)* Jan. 1968; *p.c.:* Walter Lantz prods for Univ; *dir:* Paul J. Smith; *story:* Homer Brightman; *anim:* Al Coe, Les Kline; *sets:* Ray Huffine; *voices:* Dal McKennon, Grace Stafford; *mus:* Walter Greene; *prod mgr:* William E. Garity; *col:* Tech. *sd:* RCA. 6 min. • Woody cons an old lady so he can stay in her luxurious mansion but has her jealous dog, Brutus, to contend with.

7112. Woody the Giant Killer *(Woody Woodpecker)* 15 Dec. 1947; *p.c.:* Walter Lantz prods for Univ; *dir:* Dick Lundy; *story:* Ben Hardaway, Webb Smith; *anim:* (La)Verne Harding, Ed Love, Pat Matthews, Sid Pillet; *sets:* Fred Brunish; *ed:* Dave Lurie; *voices:* Harry E. Lang, Jack Mather, Ben Hardaway; *mus:* Darrell Calker; *prod mgr:* William E. Garity; *col:* Tech. *sd:* WE. 8 min. • The housing shortage leads Woody to climb a magic beanstalk, encounter a giant and eventually open his castle as apartments.

7113. Woody Woodpecker *(Cartune)* 7 July 1941; *p.c.:* Walter Lantz prods for Univ; *dir:* Walter Lantz; *story:* Ben Hardaway, Jack Cosgriff; *anim:* Alex Lovy, Ray Fahringer; *sets:* Fred Brunish; *voices:* Mel Blanc, Danny Webb, Margaret Hill; *mus:* Darrell Calker; *prod mgr:* George Hall; *col:* Tech. *sd:* RCA. 7 min. • The animals tell Woody he's crazy, so he visits Dr. Horace N. Buggy, a psychiatrist.

7114. The Woody Woodpecker Polka *(Woody Woodpecker)* 29 Oct. 1951; *p.c.:* Walter Lantz prods for Univ; *dir:* Walter Lantz; *anim:* Don Patterson, Ray Abrams, La Verne Harding Paul Smith; *sets:* Fred Brunish; *voices:* The Starlighters; *mus:* Clarence E. Wheeler; *prod mgr:* William E. Garity; *col:* Tech. *sd:* RCA. 6 min. • Woody spies a free feed at a barn dance and disguises as a woman to gain entrance.

7115. Woody's Clip Joint *(Woody Woodpecker)* 3 Aug. 1964; *p.c.:* Walter Lantz prods for Univ; *dir:* Sid Marcus; *story:* Homer Brightman; *anim:* Ray Abrams, Art Davis; *sets:* Art Landy, Ray Huffine; *voices:* Dal McKennon, Grace Stafford; *mus:* Darrell Calker; *prod mgr:* William E. Garity; *col:* Tech. *sd:* RCA. 6 min. • An escaped lion demands sanctuary in Woody's barber shop and Woody proceeds to give him the haircut of a lifetime.

7116. Woody's Knight Mare *(Woody Woodpecker)* 1969; *p.c.:* Walter Lantz prods for Univ; *dir:* Paul J. Smith; *story:* Homer Brightman; *anim:* Les Kline, Al Coe; *sets:* Nino Carbe; *voices:* Daws Butler, Grace Stafford; *mus:* Walter Greene; *prod mgr:* William E. Garity; *col:* Tech. *sd:* RCA. 6 min. • Back in medieval times, Woody and Sugarfoot are thrown in jail and give the guard a tough time while trying to escape.

7117. Woody's Kook-Out *(Woody Woodpecker)* 17 Oct. 1961; *p.c.:* Walter Lantz prods for Univ; *dir:* Jack Hannah; *story:* Tedd Pierce, Bill Danch; *anim:* Roy Jenkins, Al Coe; *sets:* Ray Huffine, Art Landy; *voices:* Daws Butler, Grace Stafford; *mus:* Darrell Calker; *prod mgr:* William E. Garity; *col:* Tech. *sd:* RCA. 6 min. • Gabby Gator invites Woody for some "Real Southern cooking," although Woody doesn't realise that *he* is to be the main course.

7118. Woody's Magic Touch *(Woody Woodpecker)* 1971; *p.c.:* Walter Lantz prods for Univ; *dir:* Paul J. Smith; *story:* Dale Hale; *anim:* Virgil Ross, Al Coe, Tom Byrne, Joe Voght; *sets:* Nino Carbe; *voices:* Dal McKennon, Grace Stafford; *mus:* Walter Greene; *prod mgr;* William E. Garity; *col:* Tech. *sd:* RCA. 6 min. • The king's offspring has been changed into a purple dragon and Sir Woody pilfers a witch's magic wand to change him back.

7119.   Woolen Under Where? *(Merrie Melodies)* May 1963; *p.c.:* WB; *dir:* Phil Monroe, Richard Thompson; *story:* Chuck Jones; *anim:* Richard Thompson, Bob Bransford, Tom Ray, Ken Harris; *des:* Maurice Noble; *lay:* Alex Ignatiev; *back:* Philip de Guard; *ed:* Treg Brown; *voices:* Mel Blanc; *mus:* Bill Lava; *col:* Tech. *sd:* Vit. 7 min. • Ralph Wolf attempts to pilfer sheep from under Sam Sheepdog's watchful eye. He uses a tank, dynamite, a suit of armor and underwater diving gear ... all to no avail!

7120.   A Word About Miss Liberty *(Goldwyn-Bray Pictograph)* 1919; *p.c.:* Bray prods for Goldwyn; *anim:* Max Fleischer; *b&w. sil.* 3½ min. • Cartoon film illustrating the construction and erection of the Statue of Liberty.

7121.   Working Dollars 1955; *p.c.:* John Sutherland prods for Modern Talking Picture Service; *asso prod:* George Gordon; *dir:* Carl Urbano; *story:* John Sutherland, Bill Scott, George Gordon; *anim:* Emery Hawkins, James Pabian; *Layout:* Bernard Gruver; *col:* Tech. *sd:* RCA. 13 min. • Mr. Finchley goes about owning a share of American business after he receives a $60 bonus in his wage packet.

7122.   Working for Peanuts *(Donald Duck)* 13 Nov. 1953; *p.c.:* Walt Disney prods for RKO; *dir:* Jack Hannah; *story:* Nick George, Roy Williams; *anim:* Bill Justice, George Kreisl, Volus Jones, Bob Carlson; *fx:* Dan MacManus; *lay:* Yale Gracey; *back:* Eyvind Earle; *voices:* Clarence Nash, James MacDonald, Dessie Miller; *mus:* Oliver Wallace; *3-D ph:* Art Cruikshank; *col:* Tech. *sd:* RCA. 7 min. 3-D. • Chip an' Dale raid Dolores the elephant's peanut cache and Zookeeper Donald is kept busy trying to catch them.

7123.   The World's Affair *(Scrappy)* 5 June 1933; *p.c.:* Winkler for Colum; *prod:* Charles Mintz; *story:* Sid Marcus; *anim:* Art Davis; *mus:* Joe de Nat; *prod mgr:* James Bronis; *b&w. sd:* WE. 6 min. • Scrappy and Vontzy demonstrate recent advancements in art, science, music, agriculture, etc. They are congratulated by President Roosevelt and Mussolini. Also caricatured are Mahatma Gandhi and Jimmy Durante.

7124.   The Worm Turns *(Mickey Mouse)* 2 Jan. 1937; *p.c.:* Walt Disney prods for UA; *dir:* Ben Sharpsteen; *story:* Jack Kinney; *anim:* Chuck Couch, Alfred Eugster, Jack Hannah, Hamilton S. Luske, John McManus, Stan Quackenbush, Wolfgang Reitherman, Berny Wolf; *voices:* Billy Bletcher, Lee Millar, William E. Sheets; *mus:* Paul J. Smith; *col:* Tech. *sd:* RCA. 7 min. • Mickey concocts a courage-building potion which he uses on a fly to destroy a spider, then a mouse to roust a cat and finally to protect Pluto from the dogcatcher.

7125.   A Worm's Eye View *(Scrappy)* 28 Apr. 1939; *p.c.:* Charles Mintz prods for Colum; *story:* Art Davis; *anim:* Sid Marcus; *voices:* Dave Weber, Mel Blanc; *mus:* Joe de Nat; *prod mgr:* James Bronis; *b&w. sd:* RCA. 7 min. • Scrappy's fishing worm manages to convince the fish not to eat him.

7126.   Wot a Night *(Tom & Jerry)* 1 Aug. 1931; *p.c.:* Van Beuren for RKO; *dir:* John Foster, George Stallings; *mus:* Gene Rodemich; *b&w. sd:* RCA. 9 min. • The boys as taxi drivers take two bearded gentlemen to a haunted castle.

7127.   Wot's All th' Shootin' Fer? *(Terry-Toon)* 3 Mar. 1940; *p.c.:* TT for Fox; *dir:* Volney White; *story:* John Foster; *mus:* Philip A. Scheib; *b&w. sd:* RCA. 6 min. • The Hatfields and McCoys' feud is brought to a conclusion when their cats get married.

7128.   Wotta Knight *(Popeye)* 24 Oct. 1947; *p.c.:* Famous for Para; *dir:* I. Sparber; *story:* Carl Meyer, I. Klein; *anim:* Tom Johnson, John Gentilella; *sets:* Anton Loeb; *voices:* Jack Mercer, Mae Questel, Jackson Beck; *mus:* Winston Sharples; *ph:* Leonard McCormick; *prod mgr:* Sam Buchwald; *col:* Tech. *sd:* RCA. 7 min. • A medieval Popeye jousts with Ye Black Knight of Brooklyn for the privilege of waking the Sleeping Beauty with a kiss.

7129.   Wotta Nitemare *(Popeye)* 24 Mar. 1939; *p.c.:* The Fleischer Studio for Para; *prod:* Max Fleischer; *dir:* Dave Fleischer; *anim:* Willard Bowsky, George Germanetti; *voices:* Jack Mercer, Pinto Colvig, Margie Hines; *mus:* Sammy Timberg; *ph:* Charles Schettler; *prod sup:* Sam Buchwald, Isidore Sparber; *b&w. sd:* WE. 7 min. • Popeye has a nightmare where he's in Heaven with Olive and Bluto arrives in the guise of the Devil to disrupt the proceedings.

7130.   The Wreck of the Hesperus *(Super Mouse)* 11 Feb. 1944; *p.c.:* TT for Fox; *dir:* Mannie Davis; *story:* John Foster; *sets:* Art Bartsch; *voice:* Thomas Morrison; *mus:* Philip A. Scheib; *ph:* Douglas Moye; *col:* Tech. *sd:* RCA. 7 min. • Lighthouse keeper, Super Mouse, sees a schooner approaching the rocks and manages to save it in time.

7131.   Wrestling Wrecks *(Woody Woodpecker)* 20 July 1953; *p.c.:* Walter Lantz prods for Univ; *dir:* Don Patterson; *anim:* La Verne Harding, Ray Abrams, Ken Southworth; *sets:* Raymond Jacobs, Art Landy; *voices:* Dal McKennon, John T. Smith,, Grace Stafford; *mus:* Clarence Wheeler; *prod mgr:* William E. Garity; *col:* Tech. *sd:* RCA. 6 min. • Woody visits a wrestling match and gets involved in the bout.

7132.   The Wrong Bedroom *(A Marionette Classic)*; *b&w. sd.* l/a/anim. • Ma Hazard goes in the wrong bedroom in an inebriated state and meets a very forward young woman. Puppet animation.

7133.   Wynken, Blynken and Nod *(Silly Symphony)* 27 May 1938; *p.c.:* Walt Disney prods for RKO; *dir:* Graham Heid; *story:* William Cottrell, Joe Grant; *anim:* Dick Huemer, I. Klein, Edward Love, Arthur W. Palmer, Stan Quackenbush, Bob Wickersham; *fx:* George Rowley; *atmospheric sketches:* Maurice Noble; *lay:* Zack Schwartz; *back:* J. Gordon Legg; *voice:* DeVona Doxie; *mus:* Leigh Harline; *col:* Tech. *sd:* RCA. 8 min. • Eugene Field's poem about three toddlers who go on a celestial fishing trip in a wooden clog-boat. Wynken and Blynken are two eyes and Nod is a little head, and the wooden shoe is a child's crib.

7134.   Xanadu 8 Aug. 1980; *p.c.:* Don Bluth Prods for Univ; *anim seq dir/anim:* Don Bluth; *asst anim:* Heidi Guedel, Linda Miller, Diann Landau, Milton Gray, Vera Law, Dave Spafford, Emily Jiuliano, Lorna Pomeroy, Bruce Heller, Steve Muller, Dan Kuenster, Skip Jones; *fx:* Dorse Lanpher; *lay:* Lou Goold, Jeffrey Kleiser, Janos O. Pilenyi; *back:* Jim Coleman; *col co-ord:* Carmen Oliver; *special visual fx unit: anim des sup:* Kenneth Stytzer; *anim des:* Randy Baismeyer; *asst anim:* Liz Maihock, Sandra Payne; "Don't Walk Away" played by the Electric Light Orchestra; *anim camera:* John Lindahl, Mark Plastrick; *special ph sup:* Joe Hyneh; *addit optical sup:* Harvey Plastrik; *optical printer operators:* Paul Chervin, Frederick Greene, Bill Roberts; *fx ed sup:* Ruth Smerek; *fx ed:* Larry Plastrik; *model ph:* Jim Szalapski; *model mix:* Brian Williams; *special visual fx prod:* Robert Greenberg; *addit optical fx:* Computer Opticals, Efx Unlimited; *ph plan:* Gary Goldman; *anim ph:* Joe Jiuliano, Charles Warren; *prod asso:* Fred Craig, Olga Craig; *col:* Tech. *sd:* Dolby stereo. Panavision. 2 min. • A billboard painter seeks the girl of his dreams who he sees on a record sleeve he is given to copy. The same girl appears in an animated musical number.

7135.   Yankee Dood It *(Merrie Melodies)* 13 Oct. 1956; *p.c.:* The Sloan Foundation for WB; *dir:* Friz Freleng; *story:* Warren Foster; *anim:* Gerry Chiniquy, Virgil Ross, Arthur Davis; *lay:* Hawley Pratt; *back:* Irv Wyner; *ed:* Treg Brown; *voices:* Arthur Q. Bryan, Daws Butler, Mel Blanc; *mus:* Milt Franklyn; *prod mgr:* John W. Burton; *prod:* Edward Selzer; *col:* Tech. *sd:* Vit. 7 min. • The elves explain to the cobbler how he can expand his business and make profit without having to resort to elves' magic.

7136.   Yankee Doodle Boy *(Screen Songs)* 1 Mar. 1929; *p.c.:* The Fleischer Studio for Para; *prod/arranger:* Max Fleischer; *dir:* Dave Fleischer; *mus:* Art Turkisher; *song:* George M. Cohan; *b&w. sd:* WE. 7 min. • No story available.

7137.   Yankee Doodle Bugs *(Looney Tunes)* 28 Aug. 1954; *p.c.:* WB; *dir:* I. Freleng; *story:* Warren Foster; *anim:* Arthur Davis, Manuel Perez, Virgil Ross; *lay:* Hawley Pratt; *back:* Irv Wyner; *ed:* Treg Brown; *voices:* Mel Blanc, Bea Benaderet; *mus:* Milt Franklyn; *prod mgr:* John W. Burton; *prod:* Edward Selzer; *col:* Tech. *sd:* Vit. 6 min. • Bugs teaches his little nephew, Clyde, his own version of American history.

7138.   Yankee Doodle Daffy *(Looney Tunes)* 5 June 1943; *p.c.:* Leon Schlesinger prods for WB; *dir:* I. Freleng; *story:* Tedd Pierce; *anim:* Richard Bickenbach; *lay:* Owen Fitzgerald; *ed:* Treg Brown; *voices:* Mel Blanc, Ken Bennett; *mus:* Carl W. Stalling; *ph:* John W. Burton; *prod sup:* Henry Binder, Raymond G. Katz; *col:* Tech. *sd:* Vit. 7 min. • Theatrical agent Daffy tries to sell the potential talents of his prodigy to the head of "Smeller Productions," Porky Pig.

7139.   Yankee Doodle Donkey *(Noveltoon)* 27 Oct. 1944; *p.c.:* Famous for Para; *dir:* I. Sparber; *story:* Jack Mercer, Jack Ward; *anim:* Nick Tafuri, Tom Golden; *voices:* George Matthews, Jack Mercer; *mus:* Sammy Timberg; *ph:* Leonard McCormick; *prod mgr:* Sam Buchwald; *col:* Tech. *sd:* RCA. 8 min. • Spunky the donkey wants to join WAGS, the canine

Army and disguises himself as a dog; Uncovered, he redeems himself by offgating a flea army.

7140. The Yankee Doodle Mouse (*Tom & Jerry*) 26 June 1944; *p.c.:* MGM; *dir:* William Hanna, Joseph Barbera; *anim:* Irven Spence, Pete Burness, Kenneth Muse, George Gordon; *lay:* Harvey Eisenberg; *ed:* Fred MacAlpine; *mus:* Scott Bradley; *prod:* Fred Quimby; *col:* Tech. *sd:* WE. 7½ min. *Academy Award.* • Tom and Jerry wage a private war in the basement.

7141. Yankee Doodle Swing Shift (*Swing Symphony*) 21 Sept. 1942; *p.c.:* Walter Lantz prods for Univ; *dir:* Alex Lovy; *story:* Ben Hardaway, Milt Schaffer; *anim:* Harold Mason; sets Fred Brunish; *voice:* Dick Nelson; *mus:* Darrell Calker; *prod mgr:* George Hall; *col:* Tech. *sd:* WE. 6½ min. • The Zoot Suit Swing Cats are called up and bring swing to Uncle Sam's munition factories.

7142. Yanky Clippers (*Oswald*) 26 Dec. 1928; *p.c.:* Univ; *anim:* Walt Lantz, Tom Palmer; *mus:* The Universal Jazz Band; b&w. *sd:* WE. 6 min. • Oswald is a barber who drags up as a manicurist for a difficult wolf customer. The wolf believes Oswald to be a girl and takes him off in his car. On discovering the deception, Ozzie is slung out of the car and has to make his way home on roller skates.

7143. A Yarn About a Yarn (*Aesop's Film Fable*) 1 Aug. 1925; *p.c.:* Fables Pictures Inc for Pathé; *dir:* Paul Terry; b&w. *sil.* 10 min. • No story available.

7144. A Yarn About a Yarn (*Terry-Toon*) 26 Dec. 1941; *p.c.:* TT for Fox; *dir:* Connie Rasinski; *story:* John Foster; *mus:* Philip A. Scheib; *col:* Tech. *sd:* RCA. 7 min. • No story available.

7145. A Yarn of Wool (*Aesop's Sound Fable*) 16 Dec. 1932; *p.c.:* Van Beuren for RKO; *dir:* John Foster, Harry Bailey; *voice:* Marjorie Hines; *mus:* Gene Rodemich; b&w. *sd:* RCA. 7 min. • The black sheep causes enough trouble to have the shepherd chase him away but he later saves the flock from thieves.

7146. Ye Happy Pilgrims (*Oswald*) 20 Aug. 1934; *p.c.:* Univ; *dir:* Walter Lantz; *story:* Victor McLeod; *anim:* Manuel Moreno, George Grandpré, Lester Kline, (La)Verne Harding, Fred Kopietz; *mus:* James Dietrich; b&w. *sd:* WE. 8 min. • Oswald as John Alden takes Miles Standish's love plea to Priscilla and when she wants him to stay, Standish calls in the Indians and they have a food fight.

7147. Ye Olde Melodies (*Screen Songs*) 3 May 1929; *p.c.:* The Fleischer Studio for Para; *prod:* Max Fleischer; *dir:* Dave Fleischer; *mus:* Art Turkisher; b&w. *sd:* WE. 7 min. • No story available.

7148. Ye Olde Songs (*Paul Terry-Toon*) 20 Mar. 1932; *p.c.:* Moser & Terry for Educational/Fox; *dir:* Frank Moser, Paul Terry; *mus:* Philip A. Scheib; b&w. *sd:* WE. 6 min. • A mouse plays *Swanee River* which is illustrated by swans on a river and Jenny Lind sings "The Last Rose of Summer."

7149. Ye Olde Swap Shoppe (*Color Rhapsody*) 28 June 1940; *p.c.:* Cartoon Films Ltd/Charles Mintz prods for Colum; *prod/dir:* Ub Iwerks; *voice:* Sara Berner; *mus:* Eddie Kilfeather, Joe de Nat; *prod mgr:* James Bronis; *col:* Tech. *sd:* RCA. 7½ min. • Mother Mouse has to find various methods to hide her kids from the landlord.

7150. Ye Olde Toy Shop (*Paul Terry-Toon*) 13 Dec. 1935; *p.c.:* Moser & Terry for Educational/Fox; *dir:* Frank Moser, Paul Terry; *mus:* Philip A. Scheib; b&w. *sd:* WE. 6 min. • Toys come alive after midnight. Amidst their revelry, a spider enters to frighten Miss Muffet but the toy soldiers rout him.

7151. Ye Olden Days (*Mickey Mouse*) 8 Apr. 1933; *p.c.:* Walt Disney prods for UA; *dir:* Burton F. Gillett; *anim:* Arthur Babbitt, Johnny Cannon, Les Clark, Norman Ferguson, Richard Lundy, Tom Palmer, Ben Sharpsteen, Marvin Woodward; *voices:* Marcellite Garner, Harry Stanton, Pinto Colvig, Walt Disney; *mus:* Frank E. Churchill; b&w. *sd:* RCA. 7 min. • Maiden Minnie is locked in the turret when she refuses to marry Prince Dippy Dawg. Troubador Mickey rescues her and she marries him.

7152. The Year of the Mouse (*Tom & Jerry*); 1965; *p.c.:* MGM; *prod/dir:* Chuck Jones; *asst dir:* Maurice Noble; *story:* Michael Maltese, Chuck Jones; *anim:* Dick Thompson, Ben Washam, Ken Harris, Don Towsley; *back:* Philip de Guard; *voices:* June Foray, Mel Blanc; *mus:* Eugene

Poddany; *prod mgr:* Les Goldman; *col:* Metro. *sd:* WE. 7 min. • Jerry and a friend convince Tom he's trying to kill himself in his sleep.

7153. The Yellow Pirate (*Life Cartoon Comedy*) 5 Oct. 1926; *p.c.:* Sherwood Wadsworth Pictures for Educational; *prod/dir:* John R. McCrory; b&w. *sil.* 6 min. • Rum runner, High-Hat Harold's boat is scuttled by revenue agent Mike Monkey. When he loses his liquor, Harold absconds with Myrtle the lighthouse keeper.

7154. Yelp Wanted (*Scrappy*) 16 July 1931; *p.c.:* Winkler for Colum; *prod:* Charles Mintz; *story:* Dick Huemor; *anim:* Sid Marcus, Art Davis; *mus:* Joe de Nat; *prod mgr:* James Bronis; b&w. *sd:* WE. 6 min. • Scrappy goes to buy tonic for his ailing dog and runs into a number of problems on the return, only to find she doesn't need it.

7155. Yes! We Have No Bananas (*Screen Songs*) 26 Apr. 1930; *p.c.:* The Fleischer Studio for Para; *prod/story:* Max Fleischer; *dir:* Dave Fleischer; *mus:* Art Turkisher; *song:* Frank Silver, Irving Conn; b&w *sd:* WE. 6 min. • The mice steal the grocer's prized bananas. He gives chase but they manage to filch all of them while all in the shop sing the title song.

7156. Yip-Yip-Yippy (*Betty Boop*) 11 Aug. 1939; *p.c.:* The Fleischer Studio for Para: *prod:* Max Fleischer; *dir:* Dave Fleischer; *anim:* Roland Crandall, Robert Bemiller; *mus:* Sammy Timberg; *ph:* Charles Schettler; *prod sup:* Sam Buchwald, Isidore Sparber; b&w. *sd:* WE. 6 min. • Soda jerk, Wiffle Piffle and his little horse assist in the capture of a western bandit.

7157. Yodeling Yokels (*Looney Tunes*) 26 Mar. 1931; *p.c.:* Hugh Harman, Rudolf Ising prods for WB; *prod:* Leon Schlesinger; *anim:* Rollin Hamilton, Norm Blackburn; *ed:* Dale Pickett; *voice:* Mary Moder; *mus:* Frank Marsales; b&w. *sd:* Vit. 7 min. • Bosko uses his wits and a St. Bernard to rescue Honey who has fallen down a mountain.

7158. Yokel Boy Makes Good (*Oswald*) 21 Feb. 1938; *p.c.:* Univ; *prod/dir:* Walter Lantz; *story:* Victor McLeod, Win Smith; *anim:* Ray Fahringer, (La)Verne Harding; *voice:* Dave Weber; *mus:* Nathaniel Shilkret; b&w. *sd:* WE. 6 min. • A skunk lays low a bully who tries to put a stop to the show in Oswald's Red Barn Theatre. Caricatures of Joe Penner and Martha Raye.

7159. Yokel Duck Makes Good (*Terry-Toon*) 26 Nov. 1943; *p.c.:* TT for Fox; *dir:* Eddie Donnelly; *story:* John Foster; *sets:* Art Bartsch; *mus:* Philip A. Scheib; *col:* Tech. *sd:* RCA. 7 min. • A hick duck tries to ingratiate himself with the farmyard fowl. Only when he rescues a duckling from an attacking vulture is he accepted in the pond.

7160. Yokohama Mama (*Blue Racer*) 24 Dec. 1972; *p.c.:* Mirisch/DFE for UA; *dir:* Gerry Chiniquy; *story:* John W. Dunn; *anim:* Bob Richardson, Jim Davis, Manny Gould, Don Williams; *lay:* Dick Ung; *back:* Richard H. Thomas; *ed:* Allan R. Potter; *voices:* Larry D. Mann, Mako; *mus:* Doug Goodwin; *prod sup:* Stan Paperny, Harry Love; *col:* DeLuxe. *sd:* RCA. 6 min. • The racer finds himself in China and up against an Oriental chicken, trying to protect his eggs from theft.

7161. A Yokohama Yankee (*Terry-Toon*) Jan. 1955; *p.c.:* TT for Fox; *dir:* Connie Rasinski; *story:* Tom Morrison; *anim:* Jim Tyer; *sets:* Art Bartsch; *mus:* Philip A. Scheib; *ph:* Doug Moye; *col:* Tech. *sd:* RCA. 7 min. • A Japanese butterfly loves a sailor bug who saves her from the clutches of a villainous spider.

7162. You Came to My Rescue (*Screen Songs*) 30 July 1937; *p.c.:* The Fleischer Studio for Para; *prod:* Max Fleischer; *dir:* Dave Fleischer; *mus:* Sammy Timberg; *song:* Leo Robin, Ralph Rainger; *l/a:* Shep Fields and his orchestra; *prod sup:* Sam Buchwald, Isidore Sparber; b&w. *sd:* WE. 7 min. *l/a/anim.* • No story available.

7163. You Can't Shoe a Horsefly (*Color Classic*) 23 Aug. 1940; *p.c.:* The Fleischer Studio for Para; *prod:* Max Fleischer; *dir:* Dave Fleischer; *story:* William Turner; *anim:* Myron Waldman, Sam Stimson; *character des:* Myron Waldman; *sets:* Shane Miller; *ed:* Kitty Pfister; *voices:* Pinto Colvig, Jack Mercer; *mus:* Sammy Timberg; *prod sup:* Sam Buchwald, Isidore Sparber; *col:* Tech. *sd:* WE. 7 min. • Hunky and Spunky, the donkeys, have problems with a bothersome horsefly.

7164. You Don't Know What You're Doin' (*Merrie Melodies*) 5 Dec. 1931; *p.c.:* Hugh Harman, Rudolf Ising prods for WB; *prod:* Leon Schlesinger; *anim:* Isadore Freleng, Norm Blackburn, Robert Clampett; *orch:* Frank Marsales; *mus:* Gus Arnheim and his Coconut Grove Orchestra;

b&w. *sd:* Vit. 7 min. • Hecklers disrupt a magic show, get Piggy drunk and take him on an alcoholic joy ride.

7165. You Gotta Be a Football Hero (*Popeye*) 30 Aug. 1935; *p.c.:* The Fleischer Studio for Para; *prod:* Max Fleischer; *dir:* Dave Fleischer; *anim:* Willard Bowsky, George Germanetti; *voices:* Jack Mercer, Mae Questel, Gus Wickie; *mus:* Sammy Timberg; *song:* Al Sherman, Al Lewis, Dorothy Fields; b&w. *sd:* WE. 7 min. • Olive forsakes Popeye for Bluto's football team but once he takes some spinach, our hero outruns them all.

7166. You Leave Me Breathless (*Screen Songs*) 27 May 1938; *p.c.:* The Fleischer Studio for Para; *prod:* Max Fleischer; *dir:* Dave Fleischer; *anim:* Roland Crandall; *mus:* Sammy Timberg; *song:* Ralph Freed, Frederick Hollander; *l/a:* Jimmy Dorsey and his orchestra; *prod sup:* Sam Buchwald, Isidore Sparber; b&w. *sd:* WE. 7 min. *l/a/anim.* • TV show of the future.

7167. You Ought to Be in Pictures (*Looney Tunes*) 27 Apr. 1940; *p.c.:* Leon Schlesinger prods for WB; *dir:* I. Freleng; *story:* Jack Miller, Robert Clampett; *anim:* Herman Cohen; *ed:* Treg Brown; *voices:* Mel Blanc; *mus:* Carl W. Stalling; *l/a:* Leon Schlesinger, Michael Maltese, Gerry Chiniquy, Henry Binder; *prod sup:* Henry Binder, Raymond G. Katz; b&w. *sd:* Vit. 9 min. *l/a/anim.* • Daffy persuades Porky to tear up his contract with Schlesinger and enter feature films. When he does, Daffy proceeds to fill his vacant place.

7168. You Said a Mouseful (*Herman & Katnip*) 27 Aug. 1958; *p.c.:* Para Cartoons; *dir:* Seymour Kneitel; *story:* Jack Mercer; *anim:* Tom Johnson, Frank Endres; *sets:* Robert Owen; *voices:* Arnold Stang, Gwen Davies; *mus:* Winston Sharples; *ph:* Leonard McCormick; *prod mgr:* Abe Goodman; *col:* Tech. *sd:* RCA. 6 min. • Katnip's Pizzaria is a going concern and Herman's task is keeping Chubby, a hungry mouse, out of the kitchen.

7169. You Took the Words Right Out of My Heart (*Screen Songs*) 28 Jan. 1938; *p.c.:* The Fleischer Studio for Para; *prod:* Max Fleischer; *dir:* Dave Fleischer; *anim:* Roland Crandall; *mus:* Sammy Timberg; *song:* Leo Robin, Ralph Rainger; *l/a:* Jerry Blaine and his orchestra; *prod sup:* Sam Buchwald, Isidore Sparber; b&w. *sd:* WE. 6 min. *l/a/anim.* • Examining people with a "candid camera."

7170. You Try Somebody Else (*Screen Songs*) 29 July 1932; *p.c.:* The Fleischer Studio for Para; *prod:* Max Fleischer; *sup:* Dave Fleischer; *dir/story:* James H. Culhane, Rudy Zamora; *anim:* James H. Culhane, David Tendlar, Al Eugster; *voice:* Margie Hines; *mus:* Art Turkisher; *l/a:* Ethel Merman; b&w. *sd:* WE. 7 min. • A tough cat is released from jail and burgles Betty's refrigerator in mistake for a safe. He is returned to prison.

7171. You Were Never Duckier (*Merrie Melodies*) 7 Aug. 1948; *p.c.:* WB; *dir:* Charles M. Jones; *story:* Tedd Pierce; *anim:* Ken Harris, Phil Monroe, Ben Washam, Lloyd Vaughan; *lay:* Robert Gribbroek; *back:* Peter Alvarado; *ed:* Treg Brown; *voices:* Mel Blanc; *mus:* Carl Stalling; *prod mgr:* John W. Burton; *prod:* Edward Selzer; *col:* Tech. *sd:* Vit. 7 min. • Daffy disguises himself as a rooster (for a $5,000 prize) but Henry Hawk mistakes him for the genuine article and brings him home for dinner.

7172. You'll be Sorry 1928. (*Educational-Bowers Comedy*) *p.c.:* Bowers Comedy Corp. for Educational; *prod/l/a:* Charles R. Bowers; *dir/ph:* H.L. Muller; 2 reels. b&w. sil. *l/a/anim* • Charley organizes his own police station and is called to a mysterious house where a princess is being held prisoner by foreign plotters. He hides in a room filled with all kinds of (animated) mechanical contraptions that keep him busy dodging trouble.

7173. Young and Healthy (*Merrie Melodies*) 19 Apr. 1933; *p.c.:* Hugh Harman, Rudolf Ising prods for WB; *prod:* Leon Schlesinger; *anim:* Rollin Hamilton, Larry Martin, Robert Clampett; *ed:* Dale Pickett; *mus:* Frank Marsales; *song:* Harry Warren, Al Dubin; b&w. *sd:* Vit. 9 min. • Broken toys on the city dump rejuvenate themselves.

7174. Young Nick Carter, Detectiff (*Sullivan Cartoon Comedy*) 18 June 1917 *p.c.:* Powers for Univ; *dir:* Pat Sullivan; *anim:* Will Powers; b&w. sil. 5 min. • Young Nick Carter and his dog "Sleuth Hound" trace a desperado to his lair but, failing to capture him, give up the profession.

7175. Young Sherlock Holmes 4 Dec. 1985; *p.c.:* Amblin Entertainment for Para; ILM: *anim sup:* Bruce Walters, Ellen Lichtwardt; *anim "Glass man":* Pixar Computer Animation; "*Pastry sequence":* David Allan; *Go-Motion anim:* "*Harpy Sequence":* Harry Walton; *fx anim:* Jack Monogovan, Barbara Brennan, Gordon Baker; *Rotoscope art:* Donna Baker, Sandy Houston, Terry Sittig; *Computer anim Group:* William Reeves, John Las-

seter, David DeFrancesco, Eben Ostby, David H. Salesin, Robert L. Cook, Don Conway, Craig Good; *illustrator:* Mike Ploog; *col:* Tech. *sd:* Dolby stereo. 109 min. (entire film length) *l/a/cgi.* • Live-action mystery. Various people are struck with hallucinations: A diner imagines his meal has come to life; knight in a stained-glass window comes to life; some figurines in an antique shop come alive and Watson imagines pastries and cakes with arms and legs, stuffing his face with cream cakes. An early example of the untold limits that computer animation can reach.

7176. Your Flag and My Flag 21 July 1917; *p.c.:* Thomas A. Edison for KESE (Kline, Edison, Selig & Essanay); *anim:* John C. Terry; b&w. sil. s/r. • A patriotic poem embellished with animated illustrations.

7177. Your Safety First 1956; *p.c.:* John Sutherland Prods., Inc. for Automobile Manufacturers Association; *prod:* John Sutherland; *dir:* George Gordon; *story:* Norman Wright; *anim:* Ken O'Brien, George Cannata, Fred Madison, Cal Dalton; *lay:* Gerald Nevius, Charles McElmurry; *back:* Joe Montell; *voices:* Marvin Miller, George O'Hanlon; *mus:* Eugene Poddany; *prod mgr:* Earl Jonas; *col:* Tech. *sd:* RCA. 13½ min. • Showing the advances made in safer driving. Set in the future, where cars are like automated rockets with wheels. To show how they arrived at this stage, we return to the days of the horseless carriage.

7178. You're a Sap, Mr. Jap (*Popeye*) 7 Aug. 1942; *p.c.:* Famous for Para; *dir:* Dan Gordon; *story:* Jim Tyer, Carl Meyer; *anim:* Jim Tyer, George Germanetti; *voice:* Jack Mercer; *mus:* Sammy Timberg; *song:* James Cavanaugh, John Redmond, Nat Simon; *prod mgr:* Sam Buchwald; b&w. *sd:* WE. 7 min. • Out in a Navy patrol boat, Popeye spies a Japanese fishing boat that is a camouflaged submarine. He battles with the enemy who, defeated, decides to commit Hari Kari. • Very strong propaganda influence.

7179. You're an Education (*Merrie Melodies*) 5 Nov. 1938; *p.c.:* Leon Schlesinger prods for WB; *dir:* Frank Tashlin; *story:* Dave Monahan; *anim:* A.C. Gamer; *ed:* Tregoweth E. Brown; *voices:* Mel Blanc, Billy Bletcher; *mus:* Carl W. Stalling; *prod sup:* Henry Binder, Raymond G. Katz; *col:* Tech. *sd:* Vit. 7 min. • Travel brochures come alive displaying various world wide attractions.

7180. You're Driving Me Crazy (*Screen Songs*) 19 Sept. 1931; *p.c.:* The Fleischer Studio for Para; *prod:* Max Fleischer; *dir:* Dave Fleischer; *mus:* Art Turkisher; *l/a:* Harriet Lee; b&w. *sd:* WE. 5½ min. • A jungle festival is celebrated. A rainstorm finally scatters the animals.

7181. You're Not Built That Way (*Betty Boop*) 17 July 1936; *p.c.:* The Fleischer Studio for Para; *prod:* Max Fleischer; *dir:* Dave Fleischer; *anim:* Myron Waldman, Hicks Lokey, Lillian Friedman; *voice:* Mae Questel; *mus:* Sammy Timberg; b&w. *sd:* WE. 6 min. • Pudgy, in an attempt to emulate a bulldog, tries to steal meat from a butcher's shop.

7182. You're Too Careless with Your Kisses (*Merrie Melodies*) 10 Sept. 1932; *p.c.:* Hugh Harman, Rudolf Ising prods for WB; *prod:* Leon Schlesinger; *anim:* Rollin Hamilton, Larry Martin; *ed:* Dale Pickett; *voice:* Mary Moder; *mus:* Frank Marsales; b&w. *sd:* Vit. 6 min. • A tipsy bug accidentally becomes a hero when rescuing his wife from a beetle.

7183. Yukon Have It (*Chilly Willy*) Apr. 1959; *p.c.:* Walter Lantz prods for Univ; *dir:* Alex Lovy; *story:* Homer Brightman; *anim:* La Verne Harding, Ray Abrams, Don Patterson; *sets:* Raymond Jacobs, Art Landy; *voices:* Daws Butler; *mus:* Clarence Wheeler; *prod mgr:* William E. Garity; *col:* Tech. *sd:* RCA. 6 min. • Chilly's Mountie enrollment photo gets misplaced, making Mountie Smedley believe him to be the notorious criminal, Caribu Lou.

7184. Yule Laff (*Nooteloon*) Oct. 1962; *p.c.:* Para Cartoons; *dir:* Seymour Kneitel; *story:* I. Klein; *anim:* Martin Taras, George Germanetti, Jim Logan; *sets:* Robert Little; *voices:* Eddie Lawrence; *mus:* Winston Sharples; *ph:* Leonard McCormick; *prod mgr:* Abe Goodman; *col:* Tech. *sd:* RCA. 6 min. • Goodie visits the North Pole and puts right all the evils done to Santa by the other gremlins.

7185. Zeigfeld Follies 1945; *p.c.:* MGM; *puppet seq:* Lou Bunin; *dir:* William Ferrai; *col:* Tech. *sd:* WE. (seq) 4 min. • Vincente Minelli live-action feature about Florenz Zeigfeld (William Powell) remembering his past successes. Puppets enact the atmosphere with a stage show featuring Eddie Cantor, Will Rogers, Marilyn Miller and Fanny Brice.

7186. Zero the Hero (*Casper*) 26 Feb. 1954; *p.c.:* Famous for Para; *dir:* Seymour Kneitel; *story:* Carl Meyer, Jack Mercer; *anim:* Myron Waldman, Larry Silverman; *sets:* Robert Connavale; *voices:* Alan Shay, Sid Raymond,

Jack Mercer; *mus:* Winston Sharples; *title song:* Mack David, Jerry Livingston; *ph:* Leonard McCormick; *prod mgr:* Seymour Shultz; *col:* Tech. *sd:* RCA 6 min. • Casper tries to help a failed watchdog to find another job he is more suited to.

7187. Zero the Hound *(Animated Antics)* 30 May 1941; *p.c.:* The Fleischer Studio for Para; *prod:* Max Fleischer; *dir:* Dave Fleischer; *story:* Carl Meyer; *anim:* Tom Johnson, Frank Endres; *mus:* Sammy Timberg; *ph:* Charles Schettler; *prod sup:* Sam Buchwald, Isidore Sparber; b&w. *sd:* WE. 7 min. • Zero and his master have a bad day duck hunting.

7188. Zip 'n' Snort *(Merrie Melodies)* Jan. 1961; *p.c.:* WB; *dir/story:* Chuck Jones; *anim:* Richard Thompson, Bob Bransford, Tom Ray, Ken Harris; *lay:* Maurice Noble; *back:* Philip de Guard; *ed:* Treg Brown; *voice:* Paul Julian; *mus:* Milt Franklyn; *prod mgr:* William Orcutt; *prod:* David H. DePatie; *col:* Tech. *sd:* Vit. 7 min. • The Coyote tries to snare his victim by using a giant bow, iron pellets (mixed with bird seed) and by putting axle grease on his feet but is thwarted by the non-stop New York Express!

7189. Zipping Along *(Merrie Melodies)* 19 Sept. 1953; *p.c.:* WB; *dir:* Charles M. Jones; *story:* Michael Maltese; *anim:* Ken Harris, Ben Washam, Lloyd Vaughan; *lay:* Maurice Noble; *back:* Philip de Guard; *ed:* Treg Brown; *voice:* Paul Julian; *mus:* Carl Stalling, Milt Franklyn; *prod mgr:* John W. Burton; *prod:* Edward Selzer; *col:* Tech. *sd:* Vit. 7 min. • This time the Coyote tries to catch the elusive bird by using a giant kite, hypnosis, a steel wrecking ball, human cannonball and an explosive door ... all to no avail!

7190. The Zoo *(Oswald)* 31 Oct. 1933; *p.c.:* Univ; *dir:* Walter Lantz, "Bill" Nolan; *anim:* Ray Abrams, Fred Avery, Cecil Surry, Jack Carr, Ernest Smythe; *voice:* Shirley Reed; *mus:* James Dietrich; b&w. *sd:* WE. 6 min. • No story available.

7191. Zoo Is Company *(Loopy de Loop)* Nov. 1961; *p.c.:* Hanna-Barbera for Colum; *prod/dir:* Joseph Barbera, William Hanna; *story dir:* Alex Lovy; *story:* Michael Maltese; *anim dir:* Charles A. Nichols; *anim:* George Nicholas; *lay:* Tony Rivera; *back:* Vera Hanson; *ed:* Warner Leighton; *voices:* Daws Butler, Doug Young; *mus:* Hoyt Curtin; *titles:* Lawrence Gobel; *prod mgr:* Howard Hanson; *col:* East. *sd:* RCA. 6½ min. • Loopy visits the zoo and helps an elephant that is being tormented by a bullying mouse named Biggelow.

7192. Zoom and Bored *(Merrie Melodies)* 14 Sept. 1957; *p.c.:* WB; *dir:* Chuck Jones; *story:* Michael Maltese; *anim:* Abe Levitow, Richard Thompson, Ken Harris; *lay:* Maurice Noble; *back:* Philip de Guard; *ed:* Treg Brown; *voice:* Paul Julian; *mus:* Carl Stalling, Milt Franklyn; *prod:* John W. Burton; *col:* Tech. *sd:* Vit. 7 min. • The Coyote is unsuccessful in snaring the Road-Runner when employing an over zealous pneumatic drill, a brick wall, Acme Bumble Bees and a giant harpoon.

7193. Zoom at the Top *(Merrie Melodies)* 30 June 1962; *p.c.:* WB; *dir/story:* Chuck Jones; *asst dir:* Maurice Noble; *anim:* Ken Harris, Richard Thompson, Bob Bransford, Tom Ray; *back:* Philip de Guard; *ed:* Treg Brown; *voices:* Paul Julian, Mel Blanc; *mus:* Milt Franklyn; *prod mgr:* William Orcutt; *prod:* David H. DePatie; *col:* Tech. *sd:* Vit. 7 min. • The Coyote chiefly has trouble with a glue-coated boomerang which he can't rid himself of.

7194. The "Zoot Cat" *(Tom & Jerry)* 26 Feb. 1944; *p.c.:* MGM; *dir:* Bill Hanna, Joseph Barbera; *anim:* Ray Patterson, Kenneth Muse, Irven Spence, Pete Burness; *lay:* Harvey Eisenberg; *ed:* Fred MacAlpin; *voices:* Dick Nelson; *mus:* Scott Bradley; *prod:* Fred Quimby; *col:* Tech. *sd:* WE. 7 min. • Tom gets "with it" by donning a home-made zoot suit to impress his girl.

7195. Zula Hula *(Betty Boop)* 24 Dec. 1937; *p.c.:* The Fleischer Studio for Para; *prod:* Max Fleischer; *dir:* Dave Fleischer; *anim:* Thomas Johnson, Frank Endres; *voices:* Mae Questel, Everett Clark; *mus:* Sammy Timberg; *ph:* Charles Schettler; *prod sup:* Sam Buchwald, Isidore Sparber; b&w. *sd:* WE. 6 min. • Grampy and Betty are stranded on a desert isle surrounded by hungry savages but Grampy saves the day.

Appendix: Series Lists

Aesop's Film Fables

The Adventures of Adenoid; African Huntsman; Aged in the Wood; Air Cooled; Alaska or Bust; All Bull and a Yard Wide; All for a Bride; The All Star Cast; The Alley Cat; An Alpine Flapper; Amateur Night on the Ark; Amelia Comes Back; The Animals' Fair; Ant Life as It Isn't; Anti-Fat; The Ants and the Grasshopper; April Showers; At the Zoo; The Baby Show; Back to the Soil; The Bad Bandit; The Ball Park; Barnyard Artists; Barnyard Follies; Barnyard Lodge #1; The Barnyard Olympics; Barnyard Politics; A Barnyard Rodeo; Bars and Stripes; A Battling Duet; The Bear and the Bees; The Beauty Parlor; The Best Man Wins; The Big Burg; The Big Flood; The Big Game; The Big-Hearted Fish; The Big Retreat; The Big Reward; The Big Scare; The Big Shot; The Big Tent; Bigger and Better Jails; Biting the Dust; The Black Duck; Black Magic; The Black Sheep; A Blaze of Glory; The Boastful Cat; The Body in the Bag; The Bonehead Age; The Boy and the Bear; The Boy and the Dog; A Brave Heart; Break of Day; Brewing Trouble; Bubbles; Bubbling Over; Buck Fever; A Buggy Ride; Bugville Field Day; The Bully; A Bumper Crop; The Burglar Alarm; By Land and Air; Cabaret; Captain Kidder; Carnival Week; The Cat and the Canary; The Cat and the Magnet; The Cat and the Mice; The Cat and the Monkey; The Cat and the Pig; The Cat and the Swordfish; The Cat Came Back; The Cat That Failed; Cats at Law; The Cat's Revenge; The Cat's Whiskers; The Champion; The Charleston Queen; Chasing Rainbows; Cheating the Cheaters; Chop Suey and Noodles; The Circus; City Slickers; Clean Up Week; Closer Than a Brother; Coast to Coast; Cold Steel; The Conceited Donkey; Concentrate; The Cop's Bride; The Country Mouse and the City Cat; The Country Mouse and the City Mouse; The County Fair; The Covered Pushcart; Cracked Ice; The Crawl Stroke Kid; Crime in a Big City; A Cross Country Run; Custard Pies; Cutting a Melon; A Dark Horse; Darkest Africa; Day by Day in Every Way; A Day Off; A Day's Outing; Deep Stuff; Derby Day; Desert Sheiks; Died in

the Wool; Digging for Gold; Dinner Time; The Dissatisfied Cobbler; Do Women Pay?; The Dog and the Bone; The Dog and the Fish; The Dog and the Flea; The Dog and the Thief; The Dog and the Wolves; A Dog's Day; The Dog's Paradise; Donkey in the Lion's Skin; Dough Boys; Down on the Farm; The Early Bird; Echoes from the Alps; The Elephant's Trunk; The Enchanted Fiddle; The Enchanted Flute; The End of the World; English Channel Swim; The Eternal Triangle; Everybody's Flying; A Fair Exchange; The Faithful Pup; The Farm Hand; Farmer Al Falfa's Bride; Farmer Al Falfa's Pet Cat; The Farmer and His Cat; The Farmer and the Mice; The Farmer and the Ostrich; The Farmer's Goat; The Fashionable Fox; A Fast Worker; Fearless Fido; The Fight Game; The Fire Fighters; The First Flying Fish; Fish Day; A Fisherman's Jinx; Fisherman's Luck; The Fishing Fool; A Fishy Story; The Five Fifteen; Five Orphans of the Storm; The Flight That Failed; The Fly and the Ant; Fly Time; The Flying Age; The Flying Carpet; Flying Fever; Flying Fishers; Flying Hoofs; Foiling the Fox; For the Love of a Gal; The Fortune Hunters; The Fox and the Crow; The Fox and the Goat; The Fox and the Grapes; The Fox Hunt; Friday the Thirteenth; The Frog and the Catfish; The Frog and the Ox; The Frogs That Wanted a King; From Rags to Riches and Back Again; The Fruitful Farm; The Gamblers; The Gliders; The Gold Push; Golden Egg Goosie; Good Old Circus Days; Good Old College Days; The Good Old Days; The Good Ship Nellie; The Goose That Laid the Golden Egg; Grandma's House; The Great Explorers; The Great Open Spaces; Grid Iron Demons; Gun Shy; Happy Days; Happy Go Luckies; Hard Cider; The Hare and the Frogs; The Hare and the Tortoise; The Hated Rivals; The Haunted House; Hawks of the Sea; Henpecked Harry; Henry's Busted Romance; Her Ben; Herman the Great Mouse; The Hermit and the Bear; The Hero Wins; The High Flyers; High Seas; High Stakes; Hitting the Rails; Hold That Thought; A Hole in One; The Home Agent; Home Sweet Home; Home Talent; Homeless Cats; Homeless Pups; The Honor Man; The Honor System; Hook, Line and

Sinker; Horses, Horses, Horses; The Horse's Tale; Hot Times in Iceland; The Housing Problem; House Cleaning; The Housing Shortage; The Human Fly; Hungry Hounds; The Hunter and His Dog; Hunting in 1950; The Huntsman; An Ideal Farm; If Noah Lived Today; In Again, Out Again; In Dutch; In His Cups; In the Bag; In the Good Old Summer Time; In the Rough; In Vaudeville; The Jail Breakers; The Jealous Fisherman; The Jolly Jailbird; The Jolly Rounders; The June Bride; Jungle Bike Riders; Jungle Days; Jungle Sports; A Jungle Triangle; The Junk Man; Keep Off the Grass; Kidnapped; Kill or Cure; A Knight Out; A Lad and His Lamp; The Land Boom; Land o' Cotton; The Last Ha-Ha; The Laundry Man; A Lighthouse by the Sea; Lighter Than Air; Lindy's Cat; The Lion and the Monkey; The Lion and the Mouse; The Lioness and the Bugs; Liquid Dynamite; Little Brown Jug; The Little Game Hunter; The Little Parade; Love at First Sight; Love in a Cottage; The Love Nest; Lumber Jacks; The Magician; The Magnetic Bat; Maid and the Millionaire; The Mail Coach; The Mail Pilot; The Man Who Laughs; The Marathon Dancers; The Mechanical Horse; The Medicine Man; The Merry Blacksmith; A Message from the Sea; Mice at War; Mice in Council; The Miller and His Donkey; The Mischievous Cat; The Model Dairy; Monkey Business; Monkey Love; More Mice Than Brains; The Morning After; The Mosquito; The Mouse Catcher; The Mouse That Turned; The Musical Parrot; Mysteries of Old Chinatown; Mysteries of the Sea; The Mysterious Hat; The Nine of Spades; Noah Had His Troubles; Noah's Athletic Club; Noah's Outing; Nuts and Squirrels; Office Help; On the Ice; On the Links; One Game Pup; One Good Turn Deserves Another; One Hard Pull; A One-Man Dog; The Organ Grinder; Our Little Nell; Outnumbered; Over the Plate; The Owl and the Grasshopper; The Pearl Divers; Permanent Waves; Pests; The Pharaoh's Tomb; The Phoney Express; The Pie-Eyed Piper; The Pie Man; Pirates Bold; The Plowboy's Revenge; A Plumber's Life; The Polo-Match; Presto Change-o; The Prodigal Pup; Puppy Love; The Queen Bee; Radio Controlled;

A Raisin and a Cake of Yeast; Rats in His Garret; The Rat's Revenge; Red Hot Sands; The Rich Cat and the Poor Cat; Riding High; The River of Doubt; The Road House; The Rolling Stone; The Romantic Mouse; The Rooster and the Eagle; Rough and Ready Romeo; The Runaway Balloon; Runnin' Wild; The Runt; A Rural Romance; Scaling the Alps; School Days; Scrambled Eggs; The Sea Shower; Sharp Shooters; She Knew Her Man; The Sheik; She's in Again; The Shootin' Fool; Signs of Spring; Sink or Swim; Skating Hounds; A Small Town Sheriff; Snapping the Whip; Snow Birds; Soap; S.O.S.; Spanish Love; The Spendthrift; The Spider and the Fly; The Spider's Lair; Spooks; The Sport of Kings; Springtime; Static; A Stone Age Romeo; The Stork's Mistake; Subway Sally; Sunday on the Farm; Sunny Italy; Sweet Adeline; Taking the Air; That Old Can of Mine; The Pace That Kills; Three Blind Mice; Thru Thick and Thin; The Tiger and the Donkey; The Tiger King; Tit for Tat; A Transatlantic Flight; The Traveling Salesman; Trip to the Pole; Troubles on the Ark; The Two Explorers; Two of a Trade; The Two Slick Traders; The Two Trappers; The Ugly Duckling; The Under Dog; Up in the Air; Venus and the Cat; Venus of Venice; The Villain in Disguise; The Walrus Hunters; A Wandering Minstrel; The War Bride; Wash Day; Watered Stock; The Wayward Dog; When Men Were Men; When Snow Flies; When Winter Comes; Where Friendship Ceases; A White Elephant; Why Argue; Why Mice Leave Home; The Wicked Cat; The Wicked City; Wild Cats of Paris; The Wind Jammers; Window Washers; Wine, Women and Song; The Wolf and the Crane; The Wolf in Sheep's Clothing; The Woman and the Hen; A Woman's Honor; The Wood Choppers; Wooden Money; The Worm That Turned; A Yarn About a Yarn

Aesop's Sound Fables

The Animal Fair; April Showers; The Barnyard Melody; The Big Cheese; Big Game; The Big Scare; Bring 'em Back Half Shot; Bughouse College Days; Bugs and Books; A Bugville Romance; The Bully's End; By Land and Air; A Cat-Fish Romance; The Cat's Canary; Cinderella Blues; Circus Capers; A Close Call; College Capers; Cowboy Blues; Cowboy Cabaret; Custard Pies; Dinner Time; Dixie Days; A Dizzy Day; Down in Dixie; Fairyland Follies; The Faithful Pup; The Family Shoe; Farm Foolery; Farmerette; Fisherman's Luck; Fly Frolics; The Fly Guy; Fly Hi; The Fly's Bride; Foolish Follies; Fresh Ham; Frozen Frolics; Fun on the Ice; Gypped in Egypt; The Haunted Ship; Hokum Hotel; Horse Cops; Hot Tamale; House Cleaning Time; In Dutch; The Iron Man; The Jail Breakers; The Jungle Fool; Jungle Jazz; The King of Bugs; The Last Dance; Laundry Blues; Love in a Pond; Mad Melody; Magic Art; Makin' 'em Move; Midnight; A Midsummer's Day; The Mill Pond; The Night Club; Noah Knew His Ark; A Nursery Scandal; The Office Boy; The Old Hokum Bucket; Oom Pah Pah; The Pale Face Pup; Panicky Pup; Pickaninny Blues; Play Ball; Presto-Chango; Radio Racket; Red Riding Hood; A Romeo Monk; A Romeo Robin; Rough on Rats; Ship Ahoy; Silvery Moon; The Singing Saps;

Skating Hounds; Sky Skippers; Snow Time; Spring Antics; Stage Struck; Stone Age Error; A Stone Age Romance; Stone Age Stunts; Summertime; Toy Time; Toytown Tales; Tumble Down Town; Tuning In; Wash Day; Western Whoopee; Wood Choppers; A Yarn of Wool

Alice

Alice and the Dog Catcher; Alice and the Three Bears; Alice at the Carnival; Alice Cans the Cannibals; Alice Charms the Fish; Alice Chops the Suey; Alice Cuts the Ice; Alice Foils the Pirates; Alice Gets in Dutch (at School); Alice Gets Stung; Alice Helps the Romance; Alice Hunting in Africa; Alice in the Alps; Alice in the Big League; Alice in the Jungle; Alice in the Klondike; Alice in the Wooly West; Alice Loses Out; Alice on the Farm; Alice Picks the Champ; Alice Plays Cupid; Alice Rattled by Rats; Alice Solves the Puzzle; Alice Stage Struck; Alice the Beach Nut; Alice the Collegiate; Alice the Fire Fighter; Alice the Golf Bug; Alice the Jail Bird; Alice the Lumberjack; Alice the Peacemaker; Alice the Piper; Alice the Toreador; Alice the Whaler; Alice Wins the Derby; Alice's Auto Race; Alice's Balloon Race; Alice's Brown Derby; Alice's Channel Swim; Alice's Circus Daze; Alice's Day at Sea; Alice's Egg Plant; Alice's Fishy Story; Alice's Knaughty Knight; Alice's Little Parade; Alice's Medicine Show; Alice's Monkey Business; Alice's Mysterious Mystery; Alice's Orphan; Alice's Picnic; Alice's Rodeo; Alice's Spanish Guitar; Alice's Spooky Adventure; Alice's Three Bad Eggs; Alice's Tin Pony; Alice's Wild West Show

Amos 'n' Andy

The Lion Tamer; The Rasslin' Match

Andy Panda

Andy Panda: Air Raid Warden; Andy Panda Goes Fishing; Andy Panda's Crazy House; Andy Panda's Pop; Andy Panda's Victory Garden; Apple Andy; The Bandmaster; Canine Commandos; Crow Crazy; Dizzy Kitty; Dog Tax Dodgers; Fish Fry; Goodbye Mr. Moth; Knock Knock; Life Begins for Andy Panda; Meatless Tuesday; Mouse Trappers; Mousie Come Home; Musical Moments from Chopin; Nutty Pine Cabin; 100 Pygmies and Andy Panda; The Painter and the Pointer; Playful Pelican; The Poet and Peasant; Scrappy Birthday; Under the Spreading Blacksmith's Shop; The Wacky Weed

Animated Antics

Bring Himself Back Alive; The Copy Cat; The Dandy Lion; Mommy Loves Puppy; Sneak, Snoop and Snitch; Sneak, Snoop and Snitch in Triple Trouble; Twinkletoes Gets the Bird; Twinkletoes in Hat Stuff; Twinkletoes, Where He Goes Nobody Knows; The Wizard of Arts; Zero the Hound

The Ant and the Aardvark

The Ant and the Aardvark; The Ant from U.N.C.L.E.; Ants in the Pantry; Don't Hustle an Ant with Muscle; Dune Bug; From Bed to Worse; The Froze Nose Knows; Hasty but Tasty; Isle of Caprice; I've Got Ants in My Plans; Mumbo Jumbo; Never Bug an Ant; Odd Ant

Out; Rough Brunch; Science Friction; Scratch a Tiger; Technology, Phooey

Astronut

The Balloon Snatcher; Brother from Outer Space; Gems from Gemini; Going Ape; Haunted Housecleaning; The Kisser Plant; Martian Moochers; Molecular Mix-Up; No Space Like Home; Oscar's Birthday Present; Oscar's Thinking Cap; Outer Galaxy Gazette; Robots in Toyland; Scientific Sideshow; The Sky's the Limit; Space Pet; Twinkle, Twinkle Little Telstar; Weather Magic

Barney Bear

Barney's Hungry Cousin; The Bear and the Bean; The Bear and the Hare; Bird-Brain Bird Dog; Busybody Bear; Cobs and Robbers; Goggle Fishing Bear; Half-Pint Palomino; Heir Bear; Impossible Possum; Little Wise Quacker; Sleepy-Time Squirrel; Wee Willy Wildcat

Barney Google
(created by Billy de Beck)

Major Google; Patch Mah Britches; Spark Plug; Tetched in th' Haid

The Beary Family Album

Bugged in a Rug; The Bungling Builder; Charlie in Hot Water; Charlie the Rainmaker; Charlie's Campout; Charlie's Golf Classic; Charlie's Mother-in-Law; Cool It, Charlie; Davey Cricket; Foot Brawl; Fowled-Up Birthday; Goose in the Rough; The Goose Is Wild; Gopher Broke; Guest Who; Jerky Turkey; Moochin' Pooch; Mother's Little Helper; Mouse in the House; Paste Makes Waste; Rah Rah Ruckus; Roof-Top Razzle Dazzle; The Un-Handy Man; Window Pains

Betty Boop

Baby Be Good; Be Human; Be Up to Date; Betty Boop and Grampy; Betty Boop and Little Jimmy; Betty Boop and the Little King; Betty Boop for President; Betty Boop, M.D.; Betty Boop's Bamboo Isle; Betty Boop's Big Boss; Betty Boop's Birthday Party; Betty Boop's Bizzy Bee; Betty Boop's Crazy Inventions; Betty Boop's Halloween Party; Betty Boop's Ker-Choo; Betty Boop's Lifeguard; Betty Boop's Little Pal; Betty Boop's May Party; Betty Boop's Museum; Betty Boop's Penthouse; Betty Boop's Prize Show; Betty Boop's Rise to Fame; Betty Boop's Trial; Betty Boop's Ups and Downs; Betty in Blunderland; Buzzy Boop; Buzzy Boop at the Concert; Candid Candidate; Ding Dong Doggie; The Foxy Hunter; Grampy's Indoor Outing; Ha! Ha! Ha!; Happy You and Merry Me; Honest Love and True; The Hot Air Salesman; House Cleaning Blues; I Heard; I'll Be Glad When You're Dead You Rascal You; The Impractical Joker; Is My Palm Read; Judge for a Day; Keep in Style; A Language All My Own; Little Nobody; A Little Soap and Water; The Lost Kitten; Making Friends; Making Stars; More Pep; Morning, Noon and Night; Mother Goose Land; Musical Mountaineers; My Friend the Monkey; The New Deal Show; No! No! a Thousand Times No!; Not Now; The Old Man of the Mountain; On with the New; Out of the Ink Well; Parade of the

Wooden Soldiers; Popeye the Sailor; Pudgy in Thrills and Chills; Pudgy Picks a Fight; Pudgy Takes a Bow-Wow; Pudgy the Watchman; Red Hot Mama; Rhythm on the Reservation; Riding the Rails; Sally Swing; The Scared Crows; Service with a Smile; She Wronged Him Right; Snow White; So Does an Automobile; A Song a Day; Stop That Noise; Stopping the Show; Swat That Fly; Swing School; Taking the Blame; There's Something About a Soldier; Training Pigeons; We Did It; When My Ship Comes In; Whoops! I'm a Cowboy; With Henry, the Funniest Living American; Yip Yip Yippy; You're Not Built That Way; Zula Hula

The Blue Racer

Aches and Snakes; Blue Racer Blues; The Boa Friend; Camera Bug; Fowl Play; Freeze a Jolly Good Fellow; Hiss and Hers; Little Boa Peep; Love and Hisses; Punch and Judo; Snake Preview; Support Your Local Serpent; Wham and Eggs; Yokahama Mama

Bowers Comedies

Goofy Birds; Hop Off; Say Ah-h!; Whoozit; You'll be Sorry

Burt Gillett's Toddle Tales

Along Came a Duck; Grandfather's Clock; A Little Bird Told Me

The Captain and the Kids
(created by Rudolph Dirks)

Blue Monday; Buried Treasure; The Captain's Christmas; The Captain's Pup; Cleaning House; A Day at the Beach; The Honduras Hurricane; Mama's New Hat; Old Smokey; Petunia Natural Park; Poultry Pirates; Pygmy Hunt; Seal Skinners; What a Lion!; The Winning Ticket

Cartune Classics

Candyland; The Fox and the Rabbit; Jolly Little Elves; Springtime Serenade; Three Lazy Mice; Toyland Premiere

Cartunes

Arabs with Dirty Fezzes; Baby Kittens; Bear and the Bees; Bee Bopped; Birth of a Toothpick; The Bongo Punch; Boogie Woogie Bugle Boy; Broadway Wow Wows; The Cat and the Bell; Charlie Cuckoo; Chilly Willy; Corny Concerto; Crackpot Cruise; Crazy Mixed-Up Pup; Dig That Dog; The Disobedient Mouse; Doc's Last Stand; The Dog That Cried Wolf; Fair Today; Flea for Two; Flying Turtle; Fowled-Up Party; Freeloading Feline; Ghost Town Frolics; The Hams That Couldn't Be Cured; Hay Rube; A Horse's Tale; Hysterical High Spots in American History; I'm Just a Jitterbug; Juke Box Jamboree; Little Blue Blackbird; Little Tough Mice; The Magic Beans; Man's Best Friend; Mother Goose on the Loose; The Mouse and the Lion; Mouse Trapped; The One-Armed Bandit; The Ostrich Egg and I; Papoose on the Loose; Pest of the Show; Pigeon Holed; Pigeon Patrol; Punchy Pooch; Recruiting Daze; Sailor Mouse; Salmon Yeggs; Salt Water Daffy; Scrambled Eggs; Scrub Me Mama with a Boogie Beat; Sh-h-h-h!; The Sleeping Princess; Snuffy's Party; Soup to Mutts; Space Mouse; Swing Your Partner; Syncopated Sioux; Tail End; The Talking Dog; Three-Ring Fling; Tin Can Concert; Truant Student; $21 a Day Once a Month; Witty Kitty

Casper the Friendly Ghost

Boo Bop; Boo Hoo Baby; Boo Kind to Animals; Boo Moon; Boo Ribbon Winner; Boo Scout; Boos and Arrows; Boos and Saddles; Bull Fright; By the Old Mill Scream; Cage Fright; Casper Comes to Clown; Casper Genie; Casper Takes a Bow-Wow; Casper's Birthday Party; Casper's Spree Under the Sea; Deep Boo Sea; Do or Diet; Doing What's Fright; Down to Mirth; Dutch Treat; Fright from Wrong; Frightday the 13th; Ghost of Honor; Ghost of the Town; Ghost Writers; Good Scream Fun; Ground Hog Play; Heir Restorer; Hide and Shriek; Hooky Spooky; Ice Scream; Keep Your Grin Up; Line of Screammage; Little Boo Peep; North Pal; Not Ghoulty; Once Upon a Rhyme; Peek-a-Boo; Penguin for Your Thoughts; Pig-a-Boo; Puss 'n Boos; Red, White and Boo; Spook and Span; Spook No Evil; Spooking About Africa; Spooking with a Brogue; Spunky Skunky; To Boo or Not to Boo; True Boo; Which Is Witch?; Zero the Hero

The Cat

Bopin' Hood; Cane and Able; Cool Cat Blues; Top Cat

Charlie Horse

It's a Grand Old Nag

Chilly Willy

Airlift à la Carte; The Big Snooze; Chiller Dillers; Chilly and the Looney Gooney; Chilly and the Woodchopper; Chilly Chums; A Chilly Reception; Chilly's Cold War; Chilly's Hideaway; Chilly's Ice Folly; Clash and Carry; Deep Freeze Squeeze; Fish and Chips; Fish Hooked; Fractured Friendship; A Gooney Is Born; Gooney's Goofy Landings; Half-Baked Alaska; Highway Hecklers; Hold That Rock; Hot and Cold Penguin; Hot Time on Ice; I'm Cold; The Legend of Rock-a-Bye Point; Little Televillain; Mackerel Moocher; Operation Cold Feet; Operation Shanghai; Pesky Pelican; Pesty Guest; Polar Fright; Polar Pest; Project Reject; Robinson Gruesome; Room and Wrath; The Rude Intruder; St. Moritz Blitz; Salmon Loafer; Sleepy-Time Bear; Snow Place Like Home; South Pole Pals; Swiss Mis-Fit; Teeny Weeny Meany; Tricky Trout; Under Sea Dogs; Vicious Viking; Yukon Have It

Chip an' Dale

Chicken in the Rough; The Lone Chipmunks; Two Chips and a Miss

Clint Clobber

Camp Clobber; Clint Clobber's Cat; Clobber's Ballet Ache; The Flamboyant Arms; Hearts and Glowers; Old Mother Clobber; Signed, Sealed and Clobbered

Color Classics

A Car-Tune Portrait; All's Fair at the Fair; Always Kickin'; Ants in the Plants; The Barnyard Brat; Bunny Mooning; Chicken à la King; Christmas Comes but Once a Year; The Cobweb Hotel; Dancing on the Moon; Educated Fish; An Elephant Never Forgets; The Fresh Vegetable Mystery; Hawaiian Birds; Hold It; Hunky and Spunky; A Kick in Time; The Kids in the Shoe; Little Dutch Mill; Little Lambkins; Little Lamby; The Little Stranger; Musical Memories; Peeping Penguins; Play Safe; The Playful Polar Bears; Poor Cinderella; Small Fry; Snubbed by a Snob; Somewhere in Dreamland; The Song of the Birds; The Tears of an Onion; Time for Love; You Can't Shoe a Horsefly

Color Rhapsody

A-Hunting We Won't Go; The Air Hostess; The Animal Cracker Circus; Babes at Sea; The Big Birdcast; Big House Blues; Birds in Love; Blackboard Revue; Bluebird's Baby; The Bon Bon Parade; Boston Beanie; A Boy, a Gun and Birds; A Boy and His Dog; Cagey Bird; Carnival Courage; The Carpenters; A Cat, a Mouse and a Bell; Cat-Tastrophy; Cinderella Goes to a Party; Co-Coo Bird Dog; Cockatoos for Two; Concerto in B Flat Minor; Crop Chasers, Jitterbug Knights; The Cuckoo I.Q.; The Disillusioned Bluebird; Doctor Bluebird; Dog, Cat and Canary; Dreams on Ice; The Egg Hunt; Fiesta Time; Flora; The Foolish Bunny; Football Bugs; The Fox and the Grapes; The Foxy Pup; The Frog Pond; Gifts from the Air; The Gorilla Hunt; Grape Nutty; The Greyhound and the Rabbit; The Happy Tots; The Happy Tots' Expedition; He Can't Make It Stick; A Helping Paw; The Herring Murder Mystery; Holiday Land; A Hollywood Detour; Hollywood Graduation; Hollywood Picnic; Hollywood Sweepstakes; The Horse on the Merry-Go-Round; Hot Foot Lights; The House That Jack Built; Imagination; In My Gondola; Indian Serenade; The Kangaroo Kid; King Midas Jr.; Land of Fun; Let's Go; The Little Match Girl; Little Moth's Big Flame; Little Rover; Loco Lobo; Lucky Pigs; The Mad Hatter; Make Believe Revue; Merry Manequins; Merry Mutineers; Midnight Frolics; Mr. Elephant Goes to Town; Monkey Love; Mother Goose in Swingtime; Mother Hen's Holiday; Mother Hubba-Hubba Hubbard; Mountain Ears; Neighbors; Nell's Yells; The Novelty Shop; Peaceful Neighbors; Pickled Puss; Picnic Panic; Plenty Below Zero; Polar Playmates; Poor Elmer; Poor Little Butterfly; Professor Small and Mr. Tall; Red Riding Hood Rides Again; Rippling Romance; River Ribber; The Rocky Road to Ruin; Scary Crows; The Shoemaker and the Elves; Skeleton Frolic; Slay It with Flowers; Snowtime; Song of Victory; Spring Festival; The Stork Takes a Holiday; Swing, Monkey, Swing; Swiss Tease; Tangled Television; There's Something About a Soldier; The Timid Pup; Tito's Guitar; Tollbridge Troubles; Tom Thumb's Brother; Tree for Two; Two Lazy Crows; The Untrained Seal; Up 'n' Atom; Wacky Wigwams; The Way of All Pests; Who's Zoo in Hollywood; Window Shopping; The Wise Owl; Woodman Spare That Tree; Ye Old Swap Shoppe

Comic King

Et Tu Otto; The Frogs Legs; The Hat; Hero's Reward; Home Sweet Swampy; Keeping Up with Krazy; The Method and Maw; Mouse Blanche; Psychological Testing; Snuffy's Song;

Take Me to Your Gen'rul; A Tree Is a Tree Is a Tree

ComiColor

Aladdin and the Wonderful Lamp; Ali Baba; Balloon Land; Brave Tin Soldier; The Bremen Town Musicians; Dick Whittington's Cat; Don Quixote; Happy Days; The Headless Horseman; Humpty Dumpty; Jack and the Beanstalk; Jack Frost; Little Black Sambo; Little Boy Blue; The Little Red Hen; Mary's Little Lamb; Old Mother Hubbard; Puss in Boots; Simple Simon; Sinbad the Sailor; The Three Bears; Tom Thumb; The Valiant Tailor

Cubby Bear

Croon Crazy; Cubby's Picnic; Cubby's Stratosphere Flight; Cubby's World Flight; Feathered Follies; Fiddlin' Fun; Galloping Fanny; The Gay Gaucho; How's Crops?; Indian Whoopee; Last Mail; Love's Labor Won; Mild Cargo; The Nut Factory; Opening Night; Sinister Stuff

Daffy Ditties

The Cross-Eyed Bull; Choo Choo Amigo; The Fatal Kiss; The Flying Jeep; The Lady Said No; Pepito's Serenade

Deputy Dawg

Big Chief No Treaty; Nobody's Ghoul; Rebel Trouble; Where There's Smoke

Dinky Doodle

The Babes in the Woods; The Captain's Kid; Cinderella; Dinky Doodle and the Bad Man; Dinky Doodle in Egypt; Dinky Doodle in Lost and Found; Dinky Doodle in the Arctic; Dinky Doodle in the Army; Dinky Doodle in the Circus; Dinky Doodle in the Hunt; Dinky Doodle in the Restaurant; Dinky Doodle in the Wild West; Dinky Doodle in Uncle Tom's Cabin; Dinky Doodle's Bedtime Story; The Giant Killer; The House That Dinky Built; Jack and the Beanstalk; Just Spooks; Little Red Riding Hood; The Magic Carpet; The Magic Lamp; The Magician; Peter Pan Handled; The Pied Piper; Robinson Crusoe; The Three Bears

Dinky Duck

Dinky Finds a Home; Dinky in the Beauty Shop; Featherweight Champ; Flat Foot Fledgeling; The Foolish Duckling; It's a Living; The Orphan Egg; Sink or Swim; The Timid Scarecrow; Wise Quacks

Disney Specials *see* Walt Disney Specials

The Dogfather

The Big House Ain't a Home; Bows and Errors; Deviled Yeggs; The Dogfather; Eagle's Beagles; From Nags to Riches; Goldilox and the Three Hoods; The Goose That Laid a Golden Egg; Haunting Dog; Heist and Seek; Medicur; M-O-N-E-Y Spells Love; Mother Dogfather; Rock-a-Bye ... Maybe; Rockhounds; Saltwater Tuffy; Watch the Birdie

Donald and Goofy

Billposters; Crazy with the Heat; The Fox Hunt; Frank Duck Brings 'em Back Alive; No Sail

Donald Duck

All in a Nutshell; The Autograph Hound; Beach Picnic; Bearly Asleep; Bee at the Beach; Bee on Guard; Beezy Bear; Bellboy Donald; Bootle Beetle; Canvas Back Duck; Chef Donald; Chip an' Dale; Chips Ahoy; The Clock Watcher; Clown of the Jungle; Commando Duck; Contrary Condor; Corn Chips; Crazy Over Daisy; Cured Duck; Daddy Duck; Der Fuehrer's Face; Donald and the Wheel; Donald Applecore; Donald Duck and the Gorilla; Donald Duck March of Dimes; Donald Gets Drafted; Donald in Mathmagic Land; Donald's Better Self; Donald's Camera; Donald's Cousin Gus; Donald's Crime; Donald's Decision; Donald's Diary; Donald's Dilemma; Donald's Dog Laundry; Donald's Double Trouble; Donald's Dream Voice; Donald's Garden; Donald's Gold Mine; Donald's Golf Game; Donald's Happy Birthday; Donald's Lucky Day; Donald's Nephews; Donald's Off Day; Donald's Ostrich; Donald's Penguin; Donald's Snow Fight; Donald's Tire Trouble; Donald's Vacation; Don's Fountain of Youth; Dragon Around; Drip Dippy Donald; Duck Pimples; Dude Duck; Dumb Bell of the Yukon; Early to Bed; The Eyes Have It; Fall Out — Fall In; Fire Chief; Flying Jalopy; The Flying Squirrel; Golden Eggs; Good Scouts; A Good Time for a Dime; Grand Canyonscope; The Greener Yard; Grin and Bear It; Hockey Champ; Home Defense; Honey Harvester; Hook, Lion and Sinker; How to Have an Accident at Work; How to Have an Accident in the Home; Inferior Decorator; Let's Stick Together; Lighthouse Keeping; Lion Around; The Litterbug; Lucky Number; Mr. Duck Steps Out; The New Neighbor; The New Spirit; No Hunting; Officer Duck; The Old Army Game; Old Mac Donald Duck; Old Sequoia; Out of Scale; Out on a Limb; The Plastics Inventor; Polar Trappers; Put-Put Troubles; The Riveter; Rugged Bear; Sea Salts; Sea Scouts; Self Control; Sky Trooper; Sleepy Time Donald; Slide, Donald, Slide; Soup's On; Spare the Rod; The Spirit of '43; Straight Shooters; Tea for Two Hundred; Test Pilot Donald; Three for Breakfast; Timber; Toy Tinkers; Trailer Horn; Trial of Donald Duck; Trick or Treat; Trombone Trouble; Truant Officer Donald; Uncle Donald's Ants; Up a Tree; The Vanishing Private; The Village Smithy; The Volunteer Worker; Wet Paint; Wide Open Spaces; Window Cleaners; Winter Storage; Working for Peanuts

Doormat, John *see* John Doormat

Droopy

Blackboard Jumble; Caballero Droopy; The Chump Champ; Daredevil Droopy; Deputy Droopy; Dixieland Droopy; Drag-Along Droopy; A Droopy Leprechaun; Droopy's Double Trouble; Droopy's Good Deed; Grin and Share It; Homesteader Droopy; Millionaire Droopy; Mutts About Racing; One Droopy Knight; Out-Foxed; Señor Droopy; Sheep Wrecked; The Three Little Pups; Wags to Riches

Fables

Barnyard Babies; The Bulldog and the Baby; Dumb, Like a Fox; Farmer Tom Thumb; The Great Cheese Mystery; It Happened to Crusoe; Kitty Gets the Bird; Little Lost Sheep; Mouse Meets Lion; Park Your Baby; Paunch 'n' Judy; A Peep in the Deep; Playing the Piper; The Pooch Parade; Practice Makes Perfect; The Streamlined Donkey; The Tangled Angler; Under the Shedding Chestnut Tree; Wolf Chases Pig

Felix the Cat

April Maze; Arabiantics; Daze and Knights; Eskimotive; False Vases; Felix All at Sea; Felix All Puzzled; Felix at the Fair; Felix Baffled by Banjos; Felix Brings Home the Bacon; Felix Comes Back; Felix Crosses the Crooks; Felix Dines and Pines; Felix Doubles for Darwin; Felix Fans the Flames; Felix Fills a Shortage; Felix Finds a Way; Felix Finds 'Em Fickle; Felix Finds Out; Felix Finishes First; Felix Flirts with Fate; Felix Follows the Swallows; Felix Foozled; Felix Full o' Fight; Felix Gets Broadcasted; Felix Gets His Fill; Felix Gets Left; Felix Gets Revenge; Felix Gets the Can; Felix Goes A-Hunting; Felix Goes Hungry; Felix Grabs His Grub; Felix "Hyps" the Hippo; Felix in Blunderland; Felix in Fairyland; Felix in Hollywood; Felix in Love; Felix in the Swim; Felix Laughs It Off; Felix Laughs Last; Felix Lends a Hand; Felix Loses Out; Felix Makes a Movie; Felix Makes Good; Felix Minds the Kid; Felix on the Trail; Felix Out of Luck; Felix Pinches the Pole; Felix Puts It Over; Felix Revolts; Felix Saves the Day; Felix Strikes It Rich; Felix the Cat, a Friend in Need; Felix the Cat as Roameo; Felix the Cat at the Rainbow's End; Felix the Cat Behind in Front; Felix the Cat Braves the Briny; Felix the Cat Busts a Bubble; Felix the Cat Busts Into Business; Felix the Cat Calms His Conscience; Felix the Cat Collars the Button; Felix the Cat Cops the Prize; Felix the Cat Dopes It Out; Felix the Cat Ducks His Duty; Felix the Cat Hits the Deck; Felix the Cat Hunts the Hunter; Felix the Cat in a "Loco" Motive; Felix the Cat in a Tale of Two Kitties; Felix the Cat in April Maze; Felix the Cat in Arabiantics; Felix the Cat in Art for Heart's Sake; Felix the Cat in Astronomeows; Felix the Cat in Balloonatics; Felix the Cat in Barn Yarns; Felix the Cat in Comicalamities; Felix the Cat in Daze and Knights; Felix the Cat in Dough Nutty; Felix the Cat in Draggin' th' Dragon; Felix the Cat in Eats Are West; Felix the Cat in Eskimotive; Felix the Cat in Eye Jinks; Felix the Cat in False Vases; Felix the Cat in Flim Flam Films; Felix the Cat in Forty Winks; Felix the Cat in Futuritzy; Felix the Cat in Germ Mania; Felix the Cat in Gym Gems; Felix the Cat in Icy Eyes; Felix the Cat in In and Out Laws; Felix the Cat in Jack from All Trades; Felix the Cat in Japanicky; Felix the Cat in Jungle Bungles; Felix the Cat in Land O' Fancy; Felix the Cat in No Fuelin'; Felix the Cat in Oceantics; Felix the Cat in Ohm, Sweet Ohm; Felix the Cat in One Good Turn; Felix the Cat in Outdoor Indore; Felix the Cat in Pedigreedy; Felix the Cat in Polly-Tics; Felix the Cat in Reverse English; Felix the Cat in Romeeow; Felix the Cat in Sax Appeal; Felix the Cat in School Daze; Felix the

Cat in Scrambled Yeggs; Felix the Cat in Sculls and Skulls; Felix the Cat in Sure-Locked Homes; Felix the Cat in Tee Time; Felix the Cat in the Bone Age; Felix the Cat in the Cold Rush; Felix the Cat in the Ghost Breaker; Felix the Cat in the Last Life; Felix the Cat in the Non-Stop Fright; Felix the Cat in the Oily Bird; Felix the Cat in the Smoke-Scream; Felix the Cat in the Travel-Hog; Felix the Cat in Two-Lip Time; Felix the Cat in Uncle Tom's Crabbin'; Felix the Cat in Why and Other Whys; Felix the Cat in Wise Guise; Felix the Cat in Zoo Logic; Felix the Cat Kept On Walking; Felix the Cat Misses His Swiss; Felix the Cat Misses the Cue; Felix the Cat Monkeys with Magic; Felix the Cat on the Farm; Felix the Cat on the Job; Felix the Cat Outwits Cupid; Felix the Cat Rests in Peace; Felix the Cat Rings the Ringer; Felix the Cat Scoots Thru Scotland; Felix the Cat Seeks Solitude; Felix the Cat Sees 'Em in Season; Felix the Cat Shatters the Sheik; Felix the Cat Spots the Spook; Felix the Cat Stars in Stripes; Felix the Cat Switches Witches; Felix the Cat Tries for Treasure; Felix the Cat Tries the Trades; Felix the Cat Trifles with Time; Felix the Cat Trips Through Toyland; Felix the Cat Trumps the Ace; Felix the Cat Uses His Head; Felix the Cat Woos Whoopee; Felix the Globe Trotter; Felix the Goat-Getter; Felix Tries to Rest; Felix Turns the Tide; Felix Wakes Up; Felix Weathers the Weather; Felix Wins and Loses; Felix Wins Out; Hootchy Kootchy Parlais Vous

Figaro
Bath Day; Figaro and Cleo; Figaro and Frankie

Flip the Frog
Africa Squeaks; Bulloney; The Bully; A Chinaman's Chance; The Circus; Coo Coo the Magician; The Cuckoo Murder Case; Fiddlesticks; Fire! Fire!; Flip's Lunch Room; Flying Fists; Funny Face; Goal Rush; Jail Birds; Laughing Gas; Little Orphan Willie; The Milkman; Movie Mad; The Music Lesson; The New Car; The Office Boy; The Pale Face; Phoney Express; Puddle Pranks; Puppy Love; Ragtime Romeo; Room Runners; School Days; The Soda Squirt; The Soup Song; Spooks; Stormy Seas; Techno-Cracked; The Village Barber; The Village Smithy; The Village Specialist; What a Life

Flippy
Cagey Bird; Catnipped; Silent Tweetment

The Fox and the Crow
Be Patient, Patient; The Dream Kids; The Egg Yegg; Foxy Flatfoots; Ku Ku Nuts; Mr. Moocher; Mysto Fox; Phoney Baloney; Treasure Jest; Unsure Runts; Way Down Yonder in the Corn

Fractured Fables
The Fuz; Mini Squirts; Mouse Trek; My Daddy the Astronaut; The Stubborn Cowboy; The Stuck-Up Wolf

Gabby
All's Well; The Constable; The Fire Cheese; Gabby Goes Fishing; It's a Hap-Hap-Happy Day; King for a Day; Swing Cleaning; Two for the Zoo

Gandy Goose
The Barnyard Actor; The Chipper Chipmunk; Comic Book Land; The Covered Pushcart; Dingbat Land; Dream Walking; The Exterminator; Fisherman's Luck; Fortune Hunters; Gandy's Dream Girl; Ghost Town; The Golden Hen; It's All in the Stars; Mexican Baseball; Mother Goose Nightmare; Peace-Time Football; Post-War Inventions; Spring Fever; Who's Who in the Jungle

Gaston le Crayon
Gaston Go Home; Gaston Is Here; Gaston's Baby; Gaston's Easel Life; Gaston's Mama Lisa

Go-Go Toon
A Bridge Grows in Brooklyn; Keep the Cool, Baby; Marvin Digs; The Opera Caper; The Plumber; The Space Squid; The Squaw Path

Goofy
African Diary; Aquamania; The Art of Self Defense; The Art of Skiing; Baggage Buster; The Big Wash; Californy 'er Bust; Cold War; Double Dribble; Fathers Are People; Father's Day Off; Father's Lion; Father's Week End; For Whom the Bulls Toil; Foul Hunting; Freewayphobia; Get Rich Quick; Goofy and Wilbur; Goofy Gymnastics; Goofy's Freeway Troubles; Goofy's Glider; Hello, Aloha; Hockey Homicide; Hold That Pose; Home Made Home; How to Be a Detective; How to Be a Sailor; How to Dance; How to Fish; How to Play Baseball; How to Play Football; How to Play Golf; How to Sleep; How to Swim; Knight for a Day; Lion Down; Man's Best Friend; Motor Mania; No Smoking; The Olympic Champ; Teachers Are People; Tennis Racquet; They're Off; Tiger Trouble; Tomorrow We Diet; Two-Gun Goofy; Two Weeks Vacation; Victory Vehicles

Gran'Pop
(created by Lawson Haris)
Baby Checkers; The Beauty Shoppe; A Busy Day

Happy Harmonies
Alias St Nick; Barnyard Babies; Bosko's Easter Eggs; Bottles; The Calico Dragon; The Chinese Nightingale; Circus Daze; The Discontented Canary; The Early Bird and the Worm; Good Little Monkeys; Honeyland; The Hound and the Rabbit; Little Bantamweight; Little Buck Cheeser; Little Cheeser; Little ol' Bosko and the Cannibals; Little ol' Bosko and the Pirates; Little ol' Bosko in Bagdad; The Lost Chick; The Old House; The Old Mill Pond; The Old Pioneer; The Old Plantation; Pipe Dreams; Poor Little Me; The Pups' Christmas; Pups' Picnic; Run, Sheep, Run; Swing Wedding; Tale of the Vienna Wood; To Spring; Two Little Pups; The Wayward Pups; When the Cat's Away

Heckle and Jeckle
Bargain Daze; Blind Date; Blue Plate Symphony; Bulldozing the Bull; Cat Trouble; Dancing Shoes; Deep Sea Doodle; Fishing by the Sea; Flying South; The Fox Hunt; Free Enterprise; Gooney Golfers; Hair Cut-ups; Happy Go

Lucky; Happy Landing; The Hitch Hikers; House Busters; Hula Hula Land; The Intruders; King Tut's Tomb; The Lion Hunt; Log Rollers; Magpie Madness; McDougal's Rest Farm; A Merry Chase; Messed-up Movie Makers; Miami Maniacs; Mint Men; Moose on the Loose; Movie Madness; Off to the Opera; Out Again, in Again; Pill Peddlers; Pirate's Gold; The Power of Thought; The Rainmakers; Rival Romeos; Satisfied Customers; A Sleepless Night; Snappy New Year; Sno' Fun; Steeple Jacks; The Stowaways; Stunt Men; The Super Salesman; Taming the Cat; Ten Pin Terrors; Thousand Smile Check-up; Trapeze Pleeze; The Uninvited Pests; Wild Life

Hector Heathcote
A Bell for Philadelphia; Daniel Boone Jr.; Drum Roll; The Minute and a $1/2$ Man; Riverboat Mission; The Unsung Hero; Valley Forge Hero

Hector the Pup *see* Pepper the Pup

Hercules
Goofy Gardener; Plumber of Seville

Herman and Katnip
A Bicep Built for Two; Cat in the Act; Drinks on the Mouse; Felineous Assault; Frighty Cat; From Mad to Worse; Fun on Furlough; Herman the Catoonist; Hide and Peak; Katnip's Big Day; Mice Capades; Mouse Trapeze; Mousetro Herman; Mouseum; Mousieur Herman; Of Mice and Magic; Of Mice and Menace; One Funny Knight; Owly to Bed; Rail Rodents; Robin Rodenthood; Ship-a-Hooey; Sky Scrappers; Surf and Sound; Will Do Mousework; You Said a Mouseful

Honey Halfwitch
Alter Egotist; Baggin' the Dragon; Brother Bat; Clean Sweep; The Defiant Giant; From Nags to Witches; High but Not Dry; Potions and Notions; Shoe Flies; Throne for a Loss; Trick or Cheat

Hoot Kloot
Apache on the County Seat; As the Tumbleweed Turns; The Badge and the Beautiful; Big Beef at OK Coral; By Hoot or by Crook; Giddy-Up Woe; Gold Struck; Kloot's Kounty; Mesa Trouble; Pay Your Buffalo Bill; Phoney Express; Saddle Soap Opera; A Self-Winding Sidewinder; The Shoe Must Go On; Stirrups and Hiccups; Strange on the Range; Ten Miles to the Gallop

Hot Dog
Along Came Fido; Bone Dry; Dog Gone It; The Farm Hand; For the Love o' Pete; Jingle bells; The Lunch Hound; Petering Out; Pete's Haunted House; Pete's Party; Pete's Pow-Wow; The Puppy Express; S'matter Pete

Inkwell Imps
Chemical Ko-Ko; Ko-Ko Beats Time; Ko-Ko Chops Suey; Ko-Ko Cleans Up; Ko-Ko Explores; Ko-Ko Goes Over; Ko-Ko Heaves Ho; Ko-Ko Hops Off; Ko-Ko in the Rough; Ko-Ko Kicks; Ko-Ko Lamps Aladdin; Ko-Ko on the Track;

Ko-Ko Plays Pool; Ko-Ko Smokes; Ko-Ko Squeals; Ko-Ko the Kid; Ko-Ko the Knight; Ko-Ko the Kop; Ko-Ko's Act; Ko-Ko's Big Pull; Ko-Ko's Big Sale; Ko-Ko's Catch; Ko-Ko's Chase; Ko-Ko's Conquest; Ko-Ko's Courtship; Ko-Ko's Crib; Ko-Ko's Dog Gone; Ko-Ko's Earth Control; Ko-Ko's Field Daze; Ko-Ko's Focus; Ko-Ko's Germ Jam; Ko-Ko's Harem Scarum; Ko-Ko's Haunted House; Ko-Ko's Hot Dog; Ko-Ko's Hot Ink; Ko-Ko's Hypnotism; Ko-Ko's Kane; Ko-Ko's Kink; Ko-Ko's Klock; Ko-Ko's Knock-Down; Ko-Ko's Kozy Korner; Ko-Ko's Magic; Ko-Ko's Parade; Ko-Ko's Quest; Ko-Ko's Reward; Ko-Ko's Saxaphonies; Ko-Ko's Signals; Ko-Ko's Tattoo; Ko-Ko's War Dogs; No Eyes Today; Noise Annoys Ko-Ko

The Inspector

Ape Suzette; Le Ball and Chain Gang; Bear de Guerre; Bomb Voyage; Le Bowser Bagger; Canadian Can-Can; Carte Blanched; Cherché le Phantom; Cirrhosis of the Louvre; Cock-a-Doodle Deux Deux; Le Cop on le Rocks; Crow de Guerre; Le Escape Goat; French Fried; The Great De Gaulle Stone Robbery; La Feet's Defeat; London Derriere; Les Miserobots; Napoleon Blown-Apart; Pierre and Cottage Cheese; The Pique Poquette of Paris; Plastered in Paris; Le Quiet Squad; Reaux, Reaux, Reaux Your Boat; The Shooting of Caribu Lou; Sicque! Sicque! Sicque!; That's No Lady, That's Notre Dame; Toulouse La Trick; Tour de Farce; Transylvania Mania; Unsafe and Seine

Inspector Willoughby

The Case of the Cold Storage Yegg; The Case of the Elephant's Trunk; The Case of the Maltese Chicken; The Case of the Red-Eyed Ruby; Coming Out Party; Hi-Seas Hi-Jacker; Hyde and Sneak; Mississippi Slow Boat; Phoney Express; Rough and Tumbleweed

Jeepers and Creepers

The Boss Is Always Right; Busy Buddies; Scouting for Trouble; Trouble Date

Jerky Journeys

Beyond Civilization to Texas; Bungle in the Jungle; Romantic Rumbolia; The Three Minnies

John Doormat

Another Day, Another Doormat; Dustcap Doormat; Shove Thy Neighbor; Topsy TV

Jolly Frolics

Christopher Crumpet; The Emperor's New Clothes; The Family Circus; Georgie and the Dragon; Gerald McBoing Boing; Gerald McBoing Boing's Symphony; Giddyap; Little Boy with a Big Horn; Madeline; The Magic Fluke; The Miner's Daughter; The Oompahs; Pete Hothead; The Popcorn Story; Punchy de Leon; Ragtime Bear; Robin Hoodlum; Rooty Toot Toot; Spellbound Hound; Willie the Kid; The Wonder Gloves

Kartunes

Aero-Nutics; Dizzy Dinosaurs; Forest Fantasy; Fun at the Fair; Gag and Baggage; Hysterical History; Invention Convention; No Place Like Rome; Off We Glow; Philharmaniacs; Snooze Reel; Vegetable Vaudeville

Krazy Kat
(created by George Herriman)

Alaskan Nights; Antique Antics; Apache Kid; The Auto Clinic; The Autograph Hunter; The Bandmaster; Bars and Stripes; The Bill Poster; The Bird Man; The Bird Stuffer; The Birth of Jazz; Bowery Daze; Broadway Malady; Bunnies and Bonnets; The Busy Bus; Canned Music; Cinder Alley; Cinderella; The Crystal Gazebo; The Curio Shop; Desert Sunk; Disarmament Conference; Farm Relief; Garden Gaities; Golf Chumps; Goofy Gondolas; Gym Jams; A Happy Family; Hash House Blues; Hic-Cups the Champ; Hollywood Goes Krazy; Honolulu Wiles; Hot Dogs on Ice; The Hotcha Melody; House Cleaning; Jazz Rhythm; Kannibal Kapers; Katnips of 1940; The Kat's Meow; The King's Jester; Krazy Spooks; Krazy's Bear Tale; Krazy's Magic; Krazy's Race of Time; Krazy's Shoe Shop; Krazy's Travel Squawks; Krazy's Waterloo; Lambs Will Gamble; Light House Keeping; Little Buckaroo; Little Lost Sheep; Little Trail; The Lone Mountie; Love Krazy; The Masque Raid; Masquerade Party; The Medicine Show; The Minstrel Show; An Old Flame; Out of the Ether; The Paper Hanger; The Peace Conference; Piano Mover; Port Whines; Prosperity Blues; Railroad Rhythm; Ratskin; The Restless Sax; The Ritzy Hotel; Rodeo Dough; Russian Dressing; The Sad Little Guinea Pigs; Seeing Stars; Slow Beau; Snow Time; Soldier Old Man; Sole Mates; Southern Exposure; Spookeasy; Stage Krazy; Stork Market; Svengarlic; Taken for a Ride; Tom Thumb; Trapeze Artist; Wedding Bells; Weenie Roast; Whacks Museum; What a Knight; Wooden Shoes

Li'l Abner
(created by Al Capp)

Amoozin' but Confoozin'; Kickapoo Juice; A Pee-Kool-Yar Sit-Chee-Ay-Shun; Porkyliar Piggy; Sadie Hawkin's Day

Li'l Eightball

A-Haunting We Will Go; Silly Superstition; The Stubborn Mule

The Little King
(created by Otto Soglow)

A Royal Good Time; Art for Art's Sake; The Cactus King; The Fatal Note; Jest of Honor; Jolly Good Felons; Marching Along; On the Pan; Sultan Pepper

Little Lulu
(created by "Marge" [Marjorie Henderson Buell])

The Baby Sitter; Bargain Counter Attack; Beau Ties; Bored of Education; A Bout with a Trout; Cad and Caddy; Chick and Double Chick; Daffydilly Daddy; The Dog Show-Off; Eggs Don't Bounce; Hullaba-Lulu; I'm Just Curious; It's Nifty to Be Thrifty; Loose in the Caboose; Lucky Lulu; Lulu at the Zoo; Lulu Gets the Birdie; Lulu in Hollywood; Lulu's Birthday Party; Lulu's Indoor Outing; Magicalulu; Man's Pest Friend; Musicalulu; Snap Happy; Super Lulu

Little Roquefort

Cat Happy; The Cat's Revenge; City Slicker; Flop Secret; Friday the 13th; Good Mousekeeping; The Haunted Cat; Hypnotized; Mouse and Garden; Mouse Meets Bird; Mouse Menace; Musical Madness; No Sleep for Percy; Pastry Panic; Playful Puss; Prescription for Percy; Runaway Mouse; Seasick Sailors; Three Is a Crowd

Looney Tunes

The Abominable Snow Rabbit; Africa Squeeks; A-Haunting We Will Go; Ain't Nature Grand; Ain't She Tweet; Ain't That Ducky; Ali Baba Bound; All a Bir-r-rd; All Fowled Up; Along Came Daffy; Alpine Antics; Angel Puss; Ant Pasted; The Astroduck; Baby Bottleneck; Barbary Coast Bunny; Baseball Bugs; The Bashful Buzzard; Baton Bunny; Battling Bosko; Bear Feat; Beau Bosko; Behind the Meatball; Bewitched Bunny; Big Hearted Bosko; Big House Bunny; Big Man from the North; The Big Snooze; A Bird in a Guilty Cage; Birds of a Feather; Birth of a Notion; The Blow Out; A Bone for a Bone; Boobs in the Woods; Booby Hatched; Book Revue; Boom Boom; The Booze Hangs High; Bosko and Bruno; Bosko at the Beach; Bosko at the Zoo; Bosko in Dutch; Bosko in Person; Bosko the Doughboy; Bosko the Drawback; Bosko the Lumberjack; Bosko the Musketeer; Bosko the Sheepherder; Bosko the Speed King; Bosko's Dizzy Date; Bosko's Dog Race; Bosko's Fox Hunt; Bosko's Holiday; Bosko's Knightmare; Bosko's Mechanical Man; Bosko's Orphans; Bosko's Party; Bosko's Picture Show; Bosko's Shipwreck; Bosko's Soda Fountain; Bosko's Woodland Daze; Boston Quackie; Box Car Blues; Box-Office Bunny; A Broken Leghorn; Broomstick Bunny; Brother Brat; Buccaneer Bunny; Buckaroo Bugs; Buddy and Towser; Buddy in Africa; Buddy of the Apes; Buddy of the Legion; Buddy Steps Out; Buddy the Dentist; Buddy the Detective; Buddy the G-Man; Buddy the Gob; Buddy the Woodsman; Buddy's Adventures; Buddy's Bearcats; Buddy's Beer Garden; Buddy's Bug Hunt; Buddy's Circus; Buddy's Day Out; Buddy's Garage; Buddy's Lost World; Buddy's Pony Express; Buddy's Showboat; Buddy's Theatre; Buddy's Trolley; Bugged by a Bee; Bugs and Thugs; Bugsy and Mugsy; Bully for Bugs; The Bushy Hare; By Word of Mouse; Calling Dr. Porky; Canary Row; Canned Feud; Cannery Woe; Captain Hareblower; Carrotblanca; A Cartoonist's Nightmare; The Case of the Stuttering Pig; The Cat's Bah; Cat's Paw; Caveman Inki; Chariots of Fur; Cheese It, the Cat; The Chewin' Bruin; Chicken Jitters; Chili Corn Corny; China Jones; Chow Hound; Clippety Clobbered; Confusions of a Nutzi Spy; Congo Jazz; Cool Cat; A Coy Decoy; Crowing Pains; Curtain Razor; The Daffy Doc; Daffy Doodles; Daffy Duck Hunt; The Daffy Duckaroo; Daffy Rents; Daffy — The Commando; Daffy's Inn Trouble; Daffy's Southern Exposure; Deduce You Say; Design for Leaving; Devil May Hare; Dime to Retire; Dr.

Jerkyl's Hide; Dog Pounded; Dog Tales; Don't Give Up the Sheep; Double or Mutton; Draftee Daffy; Duck Soup to Nuts; The Ducksters; The Ducktators; The Dumb Patrol; Easter Yeggs; Easy Peckin's; Eatin' on the Cuff; 8 Ball Bunny; The Fair Haired Hare; False Hare; Fast and Furry-ous; The Fastest with the Mostest; A Feather in His Hare; Feline Frame-up; Fiesta Fiasco; The Film Fan; The Fire Alarm; Fish and Slips; Fish Tales; The Fistic Mystic; Flying Circus; Fool Coverage; For Scent-Imental Reasons; Forward March Hare; 14 Carrot Rabbit; Freudy Cat; From A to Z-z-z-z; From Hand to Mouse; Gee Whizzz; Get Rich Quick Porky; Gift Wrapped; Go Fly a Kit; The Gold Diggers; Goldimouse and the Three Cats; Gone Batty; Good Noose; The Goofy Gophers; Gopher Broke; Gopher Goofy; Gorilla My Dreams; The Great Piggy Bank Robbery; Greedy for Tweety; The Greyhounded Hare; Guided Muscle; Hair-Raising Hare; A Ham in a Role; Hare-Breadth Hurry; Hare Brush; Hare Conditioned; Hare-Devil Hare; Hare Lift; Hare Tonic; Hare Way to the Stars; The Hasty Hare; The Haunted Mouse; Heir Conditioned; Henhouse Henery; The Henpecked Duck; The Hep Cat; Here Today, Gone Tamale; The High and the Flighty; High Diving Hare; High Note; Highway Runnery; Hippydrome Tiger; His Hare Raising Tale; Hobby Horse Laffs; Hocus Pocus Pow Wow; Hold Anything; The Hole Idea; Hollywood Capers; The Honey Mousers; Hook, Line and Stinker; Hop and Go; Hop, Look and Listen; Hoppy Daze; Hoppy Go Lucky; Horse Hare; A Horsefly Fleas; Hot Rod and Reel; A Hound for Trouble; Hush My Mouse; Hyde and Hare; The Iceman Ducketh; The Impatient Patient; Injun Trouble; It's An Ill Wind; It's Hummer Time; It's Nice to Have a Mouse Around the House; I've Got Plenty of Mutton; Jeepers Creepers; The Jet Cage; Joe Glow the Firefly; Kiss Me Cat; Kit for Cat; Kitty Kornered; Knighty Knight Bugs; Kristopher Kolumbus Jr.; A-Lad-in His Lamp; The Leghorn Blows at Midnight; Lickety Splat; The Lion's Busy; Little Beau Porky; Little Boy Boo; Little Orphan Airedale; The Lone Stranger and Porky; Long Haired Hare; Louvre Come Back to Me; Lovelorn Leghorn; Lumber Jack Rabbit; Lumber Jerks; Martian Through Georgia; Meet John Doughboy; A Message to Gracias; Mexicali Schmoes; Mexican Boarders; The Mexican Cat Dance; Mexican Joy Ride; Mice Follies; Milk and Money; The Million Hare; Mississippi Hare; Mixed Master; Moby Duck; Mouse and Garden; Mouse Menace; Mouse-Placed Kitten; Mouse Warming; Mutiny on the Bunny; Mutt in a Rut; My Favorite Duck; Naughty Neighbors; No Parking Hare; Notes to You; Now Hare This; Now Hear This; Nuts and Volts; Nutty News; Odor of the Day; The Odor-Able Kitty; Of Rice and Hen; Of Thee I Sting; Often an Orphan; Operation: Rabbit; Pancho's Hideaway; Patient Porky; Paying the Piper; A Peck o' Trouble; The Pest That Came to Dinner; The Phantom Ship; Picadore Porky; The Pied Piper of Guadelupé; Pied Piper Porky; Piker's Peak; Pilgrim Porky; A Pizza Tweety Pie; Plane Daffy; Plane Dippy; Plop Goes the Weasel; Polar Pals; Pop 'im, Pop!; Porky and Daffy; Porky and Gabby; Porky and Teabiscuit; Porky at the Crocadero; Porky

Chops; Porky in Egypt; Porky in Wackyland; Porky of the Northwoods; Porky Pig's Feat; Porky the Fireman; Porky the Giant Killer; Porky the Gob; Porky the Rainmaker; Porky the Wrestler; Porky's Ant; Porky's Badtime Story; Porky's Baseball Broadcast; Porky's Bear Facts; Porky's Building; Porky's Café; Porky's Double Trouble; Porky's Duck Hunt; Porky's 5 and 10; Porky's Garden; Porky's Hare Hunt; Porky's Hero Agency; Porky's Hired Hand; Porky's Hotel; Porky's Last Stand; Porky's Midnight Matinee; Porky's Movie Mystery; Porky's Moving Day; Porky's Naughty Nephew; Porky's Party; Porky's Pastry Pirates; Porky's Pet; Porky's Phoney Express; Porky's Picnic; Porky's Pooch; Porky's Poor Fish; Porky's Poppa; Porky's Poultry Plant; Porky's Preview; Porky's Prize Pony; Porky's Railroad; Porky's Road Race; Porky's Romance; Porky's Snooze Reel; Porky's Spring Planting; Porky's Super Service; Porky's Tire Trouble; Pre-Hysterical Hare; Prehistoric Porky; Prince Violent; Punch Trunk; Puss 'n' Booty; Putty Tat Trouble; Quacker Tracker; Rabbit Every Monday; Rabbit Fire; The Rabbit of Seville; Rabbit Rampage; Rabbit's Feat; Rabbitson Crusoe; Racketeer Rabbit; The Rattled Rooster; Raw! Raw! Rooster; Ready, Set, Zoom; Rebel Without Claws; Red Riding Hoodwinked; Ride Him, Bosko; Riff-Raffy Daffy; Robinson Crusoe Jr.; Robot Rabbit; Rodent to Stardom; Roman Legion Hare; Roughly Squeeking; Rover's Rival; Sahara Hare; Sandy Claws; Saps in Chaps; Satan's Waitin'; Scalp Trouble; Scarlet Pumpernickel; A Scent of the Matterhorn; Scent-Imental Over You; Scrambled Aches; Scrap Happy Daffy; See Ya Later, Gladiator; Señorella and the Glass Huraché; Shanghied Shipmates; The Shell-Shocked Egg; Shish-ka-Bugs; Shot and Bothered; Show Biz Bugs; Sinkin' in the Bathtub; Slap Happy Pappy; The Slick Chick; Snow Business; Sock-a-Doodle Do; Solid Tin Coyote; The Sour Puss; The Spy Swatter; A Squeak in the Deep; Steal Wool; A Streetcat Named Sylvester; The Stupid Cupid; The Stupor Salesman; Stuporduck; Sugar and Spies; The Super Snooper; Swallow the Leader; Swing-Ding Amigo; The Swooner Crooner; A Tale of Two Mice; Tease for Two; There Auto Be a Law; There They Go! Go! Go!; Three Little Bops; 3-Ring Wing Ding; Thumb Fun; Tick Tock Tuckered; The Timid Toreador; To Duck or Not to Duck; Tokio Jokio; Tom Turk and Daffy; Too Hop to Handle; Tortilla Flaps; Trap Happy Porky; The Tree's Knees; Tweet and Sour; Tweet Tweet Tweety; Two's a Crowd; The Up-Standing Sitter; Ups n' Downs; The Village Smithy; Viva Buddy; Wacky Blackouts; A Waggily Tale; War and Pieces; Water, Water, Every Hare; We the Animals Squeek; Wearing of the Grin; Well Worn Daffy; Westward Whoa; The Wet Hare; What Makes Daffy Duck?; What Price Porky; What's Brewin' Bruin?; What's My Lion?; What's Up Doc?; Which Is Witch?; Who Scent You?; Who's Kitten Who?; Who's Who in the Zoo; Wholly Smoke; Wild and Woolly Hare; The Windblown Hare; Wise Quackers; The Wise-Quacking Duck; Wise Quacks; A Witch's Tangled Hare; Yankee Doodle Bugs; Yankee Doodle Daffy; Yodelling Yokels; You Ought to Be in Pictures; Zoom and Bored

Loopy de Loop

Bear Hug; Bear Knuckles; Bear Up; Bearly Able; Beef for and After; The Big Mouse-Take; Bungle Uncle; Bunnies Abundant; Catch Meow; Chicken Fracas-See; Chicken Hearted Wolf; Child Sock-ology; Common Scents; Count-Down Clown; Creepy-Time Pal; The Crook Who Cried Wolf; Crow's Feat; The Do-Good Wolf; Drumsticked; Elephantastic; A Fallible Fable; Fee Fie Foes; Habit Rabbit; Happy Go Loopy; Here Kiddie, Kiddie; Horse Shoo; Just a Wolf at Heart; Kooky Loopy; Life with Loopy; Little Bo Bopped; Loopy's Hare-Do; No Biz Like Shoe Biz; Not in Nottingham; Pork Chop Phooey; Raggedy Rug; Rancid Ransom; Sheep Stealers Anonymous; Slippery Slippers; Snoopy Loopy; Swash-Buckled; Tale of a Wolf; This Is My Ducky Day; Trouble Bruin; Two-Faced Wolf; Watcha Watchin'; Wolf Hounded; A Wolf in Sheepdog's Clothing; Zoo Is Company

Luno

Adventure by the Sea; The Gold Dust Bandit; King Rounder; The Missing Genie; Roc-A-Bye Sinbad; Trouble in Baghdad

Madcap Models

The Dipsy Gypsy; The Gay Knighties; Hoola Boola; The Little Broadcast; Mr. Strauss Takes a Walk; Rhythm in the Ranks; The Sky Princess; The Tulips Shall Grow; Western Daze

Mastodon Cartoons

Chicken Dressing; Fresh Fish; The Message of Emile Coué; The Movie Daredevil; Railroading; Their Love Growed Cold

Meany Miny Moe

Air Express; The Big Race; Country Store; Firemen's Picnic; The Golfers; Knights for a Day; The Lumber Camp; The Magic Shop; Ostrich Feathers; Rest Resort; Steel Workers; The Stevedores; Turkey Dinner

Merrie Melodies

An Acrobat's Daughter; Acrobatty Bunny; Ain't We Got Fun; Ali Baba Bunny; All This and Rabbit Stew; Aloha Hooey; Along Flirtation Walk; Apes of Wrath; Aqua Duck; Aristo-Cat; Assault and Peppered; At Your Service Madame; Aviation Vacation; The Awful Orphan; Baby Buggy Bugs; Bacall to Arms; Backwoods Bunny; Bad Ol' Putty Tat; Ballot Box Bunny; Banty Raids; Bars and Stripes Forever; Bartholomew Versus the Wheel; Beanstalk Bunny; A Bear for Punishment; The Bear's Tale; Beauty and the Beast; Bedevilled Rabbit; Bedtime for Sniffles; The Bee-Devilled Bruin; Beep! Beep!; Beep Prepared; Believe It Or Else; Bell Hoppy; Big Game Haunt; Big Top Bunny; Bill of Hare; Billboard Frolics; Bingo Crosbiana; The Bird Came C.O.D.; A Bird in a Bonnet; Birds Anonymous; Birdy and the Beast; Bonanza Bunny; Bone Sweet Bone; Boulder Wham; Boulevardier from the Bronx; Bowery Bugs; Boyhood Daze; The Brave Little Bat; The Bug Parade; Bugs' Bonnets; Bugs Bunny and the Three Bears; Bugs Bunny Gets the Boid; Bugs Bunny Nips the Nips; Bugs Bunny Rides Again; Bunker Hill Bunny; Bunny and Claude; Bunny Hugged; The Busy Baker;

Bye Bye Bluebeard; The Cagey Canary; The Case of the Missing Hare; Cat Came Back; Catch as Cats Can; Cat Feud; Cats and Bruises; Cats A-Weigh; The Cat's Tail; Cat-Tails for Two; Catty Cornered; Ceiling Hero; Chaser on the Rocks; Cheese Chasers; Chili Weather; Chimp & Zee; Cinderella Meets Fella; Circus Today; Claws for Alarm; Claws in the Lease; Clean Pastures; Coal Black and De Sebben Dwarfs; Compressed Hare; Confederate Honey; Conrad the Sailor; Coo Coo Nut Grove; Corn on the Cop; Corn Plastered; Corny Concerto; Count Me Out; Country Boy; Country Mouse; Cracked Ice; Cracked Quack; The Crackpot Quail; Crazy Cruise; Crockett Doodle-Do; Crosby, Columbo and Vallee; Cross-Country Detours; Crow's Feat; The Curious Puppy; Daffy and Egghead; Daffy Dilly; Daffy Duck and the Dinosaur; Daffy Duck Slept Here; Daffy in Hollywood; Daffy's Diner; Dangerous Dan McFoo; A Day at the Zoo; Detouring America; Devil's Feud Cake; D'Fightin' Ones; Ding Dog Daddy; The Dish Ran Away with the Spoon; The Dixie Fryer; Dr. Devil and Mr. Hare; Dog Collared; Dog Daze; Dog Gone Modern; Dog-Gone South; Dog Tired; Doggone Cats; Doggone People; Don't Axe Me; Don't Look Now; The Door; Double Chaser; Dough for the Do-Do; Dough Ray Me-ow; The Dover Boys; The Draft Horse; Drip Along Daffy; A Duck Amuck; Duck Dodgers in the 24½ Century; Duck! Rabbit! Duck!; Duck Soup to Nuts; Ducking the Devil; Each Dawn I Crow; The Eager Beaver; Early to Bet; The Early Worm Gets the Bird; The Egg Collector; An Egg Scramble; The Eggcited Rooster; Egghead Rides Again; Elmer's Candid Camera; Elmer's Pet Rabbit; Fagin's Freshmen; Fair and Wormer; Falling Hare; Farm Frolics; Fast-Buck Duck; Feather Bluster; Feather Dusted; Feather-finger; Feed the Kitty; Fella with the Fiddle; A Feud There Was; A Feud with a Dude; Fifth Column Mouse; Fighting 69¹/₂th; Fin n' Catty; Flop Goes the Weasel; Flowers for Madame; The Foghorn Leghorn; Foney Fables; Fowl Weather; A Fox in a Fix; Fox Pop; Fox Terror; Foxy by Proxy; The Foxy Duckling; A Fractured Leghorn; Freddy the Freshman; French Rarebit; Fresh Airedale; Fresh Fish; Fresh Hare; Frigid Hare; From Hare to Heir; Gander at Mother Goose; The Gay Anties; Ghost Wanted; The Girl at the Ironing Board; Go Away Stowaway; Go Go Amigo; Go Into Your Dance; Goin' to Heaven on a Mule; Going! Going! Gosh!; Gold Rush Daze; Golden Yeggs; Goldilocks and the Jivin' Bears; Gonzales Tamales; Goo Goo Goliath; The Good Egg; Good Night Elmer; Goofy Groceries; Goopy Geer; A Great Big Bunch of You; The Great Carrot Train Robbery; Greetings Bait; A Gruesome Twosome; Hairied and Hurried; Hamateur Nite; The Hardship of Miles Standish; Hare Do; Hare Force; A Hare Grows in Manhattan; Hare Remover; Hare Ribbin'; Hare Splitter; Hare Trigger; Hare Trimmed; Hare We Go; Hare-Abian Nights; The Hare-Brained Hypnotist; Hare-Less Wolf; Hare-um Scare-um; Have You Got Any Castles; Hawaiian Aye Aye; He Was Her Man; Heaven Scent; The Heckling Hare; Herr Meets Hare; Hiawatha's Rabbit Hunt; A Hick, a Slick and a Chick; Hillbilly Hare; Hip Hip Hurry; Hippety Hopper; His Bitter Half;

Hiss and Make-up; Hittin' the Trail for Hallelijah Land; Hobo Bobo; Hobo Gadget Band; Hold the Lion, Please!; Holiday for Drumsticks; Holiday for Shoestrings; Holiday Highlights; Hollywood Canine Canteen; Hollywood Daffy; Hollywood Steps Out; Home, Tweet Home; Homeless Hare; Honemoon Hotel; Honey's Money; Hop, Skip and a Chump; Hopalong Casualty; Horton Hatches the Egg; Hot-Cross Bunny; House Hunting Mice; How Do I Know It's Sunday; Hurdy Gurdy Hare; Hyde and Go Tweet; The Hypochondri-Cat; I Gopher You; I Haven't Got a Hat; I Like Mountain Music; I Love a Parade; I Love to Singa; I Only Have Eyes for You; I Taw a Putty Tat; I Wanna Be a Sailor; I Wanna Play House with You; I Was a Teenage Thumb; I Wish I Had Wings; I'd Love to Take Orders from You; I'm a Big Shot Now; Injun Trouble; Inki and the Lion; Inki and the Minah Bird; Inki at the Circus; Isle of Pingo Pongo; An Itch in Time; It's Got Me Again!; I've Got Plenty of Mutton; I've Got to Sing a Torch Song; Jack Wabbit and the Beanstalk; Johnny Smith and Poka Huntas; Jumpin' Jupiter; Jungle Jitters; Just Plane Beep; Katnip Kollege; A Kiddie's Kitty; Kiddin' the Kitten; Knight Mare Hare; Knights Must Fall; A Lad in Bagdad; The Lady in Red; Lady Play Your Mandolin; The Land of the Midnight Fun; The Last Hungry Cat; Leghorn Swoggled; Let It Be Me; Life with Feathers; Lighter Than Hare; Lighthouse Mouse; Lights Fantastic; Little Beau Pepé; Little Blabber Mouse; Little Brother Rat; Little Dutch Plate; The Little Lion Hunter; Little Pancho Vanilla; Little Red Riding Rabbit; Little Red Rodent Hood; Little Red Walking Hood; Lost and Foundling; Love and Curses; The Lyin' Mouse; Mad as a Mars Hare; The Major Lied 'Til Dawn; Malibu Beach Party; Meatless Flyday; Merlin the Magic Mouse; Merry Old Soul; Mexican Mousepiece; The Mice Will Play; Mighty Hunters; The Miller's Daughter; Mr. and Mrs. Is the Name; Moonlight for Two; Mother Was a Rooster; A Mouse Divided; Mouse Mazurka; The Mouse on 57th Street; The Mouse That Jack Built; Mouse Wreckers; The Mouse-Merized Cat; Mouse-Taken Identity; Much Ado About Nutting; Mucho Locos; Muscle Tussle; The Music Mice-Tro; Muzzle Tough; My Bunny Lies Over the Sea; My Green Fedora; My Little Buckaroo; My Little Duckaroo; Napoleon Bunny-Part; Nasty Quacks; Naughty but Mice; Nelly's Folly; The Night Watchman; No Barking; Nothing but the Tooth; Now That Summer Is Gone; Of Fox and Hounds; The Oily American; Oily Hare; Old Glory; The Old Grey Hare; One Froggy Evening; One Meat Brawl; One More Time; One Step Ahead of My Shadow; The Organ Grinder; Out and Out Rout; Pagan Moon; Page Miss Glory; Pappy's Puppy; Past Perfumance; Peck Up Your Troubles; The Penguin Parade; People Are Bunny; Person to Bunny; A Pest in the House; Pests for Guests; Pettin' in the Park; Pigs in a Polka; Pigs Is Pigs; Pizzicato Pussycat; Plenty of Money and You; Pop Goes Your Heart; Presto Change-o; The Prize Pest; Quack Shot; Quackodile Tears; The Queen Was in the Parlor; Quentin Quail; Rabbit Hood; Rabbit Punch; Rabbit Romeo; Rabbit Seasoning; Rabbit Stew and Rabbits, Too;

Rabbit Transit; Rabbit's Kin; Ready, Woolen and Able; Really Scent; Rebel Rabbit; Red Headed Baby; Rhapsody in Rivets; Rhapsody Rabbit; Rhythm in the Bow; The Road to Andalay; Robin Hood Daffy; Robin Hood Makes Good; Rocket Squad; Rocket-Bye Baby; Rookie Revue; Room and Bird; Run Run Sweet Roadrunner; Rushing Roulette; Russian Rhapsody; Saddle Silly; Scaredy Cat; Scent-Imental Romeo; Screwball Football; September in the Rain; Shake Your Powder Puff; Shamrock and Roll; A Shanty Where Old Santa Claus Lives; Sheep Ahoy; A Sheep in the Deep; Shop, Look and Listen; Shuffle Off to Buffalo; Sioux Me; Sittin' on a Backyard Fence; Skyscraper Caper; Slap-Hoppy Mouse; Sleepytime Possum; Slick Hare; Slightly Daffy; Smile, Darn Ya, Smile; The Sneezing Weasel; Sniffles and the Bookworm; Sniffles Bells the Cat; Sniffles Takes a Trip; Snow Excuse; Snow Time for Comedy; Snowman's Land; Speaking of the Weather; Speedy Ghost to Town; Speedy Gonzales; Sport Chumpions; Squawkin' Hawk; Stage Door Cartoon; Stage Fright; A Star Is Hatched; Stooge for a Mouse; Stop! Look and Hasten; Stork Naked; Strangled Eggs; Streamline Greta Green; Strife with Father; Sunbonnet Blue; Sunday Go to Meetin' Time; Super Rabbit; Suppresed Duck; Sweet Sioux; The Swooner Crooner; Tabasco Road; A Tale of Two Kitties; A Taste of Catnip; Terrier Stricken; This Is a Life?; Those Beautiful Dames; Those Were Wonderful Days; Three's a Crowd; Thugs with Dirty Mugs; Tick Tock Tuckered; Tin Pan Alley Cats; Tired and Feathered; To Beep or Not to Beep; To Hare Is Human; To Itch His Own; Tom Thumb in Trouble; Tom Tom Tomcat; Tom Turk and Daffy; Tortoise Beats Hare; Tortoise Wins by a Hare; Touché and Go; Toy Trouble; Toytown Hall; Transylvania 65-000; Tree Cornered Tweety; Tree for Two; The Trial of Mr. Wolf; Trick or Tweet; Trip for Tat; Tugboat Granny; The Turntail Wolf; Tweet and Lovely; Tweet Dreams; Tweet Zoo; Tweetie Pie; Tweety and the Beanstalk; Tweety's Circus; Tweety's S.O.S.; Two Crows from Tacos; Two Gophers from Texas; Two Scents Worth; The Unbearable Bear; Uncle Tom's Bungalow; The Unexpected Pest; The Unmentionables; Unnatural History; The Unruly Hare; Upswept Hare; Wabbit Twouble; The Wabbit Who Came to Supper; Wackiki Wabbit; The Wacky Wabbit; Wacky Wild Life; The Wacky Worm; Wagon Heels; Wake Up the Gypsy in Me; Walky-Talky Hawky; The Weakly Reporter; Weasel Stop; Weasel While You Work; We're in the Money; West of the Pesos; What's Cookin' Doc?; What's Opera Doc?; When I Yoo Hoo; Whoa Be Gone; Why Do I Dream Those Dreams; Wideo Wabbit; Wild About Hurry; The Wild Chase; A Wild Hare; Wild Over You; Wild Wife; Wild, Wild World; Woods Are Full of Cuckoos; Woolen Under Where; Yankee Dood It; You Don't Know What You're Doing; You Were Never Duckier; Young and Healthy; You're an Education; You're Too Careless with Your Kisses; Zip n' Snort; Zipping Along; Zoom at the Top

Merry Makers

Forget Me Nuts; From Orbit to Orbit; Halt! Who Grows There?; Think or Sink

MGM Cartoons

Abdul the Bulbul Ameer; The Alley Cat; The Art Gallery; Bad Luck Blackie; Bah Wilderness; Barney Bear and the Uninvited Pest; Barney Bear's Polar Pest; Barney Bear's Victory Garden; Bats in the Belfry; Batty Baseball; The Bear and the Beavers; Bear Raid Warden; Bear That Couldn't Sleep; Billy Boy; The Blitz Wolf; The Blue Danube; The Bookworm; The Bookworm Turns; The Bowling Alley Cat; Boy and the Wolf; The Car of Tomorrow; The Cat That Hated People; The Cat's Meow; Cellbound; Chips Off the Old Block; Cock-a-Doodle Dog; Counterfeit Cat; The Cuckoo Clock; Dance of the Weed; Dog Trouble; Doggone Tired; Dumb Hounded; Early Bird Dood It; Farm of Tomorrow; The Field Mouse; The First Bad Man; The First Swallow; The Fishing Bear; The Flea Circus; The Flying Bear; Fraidy Cat; Gallopin' Gals; Garden Gopher; Goldilocks and the Three Bears; Good Will to Men; The Goose Goes South; Hick Chick; Home on the Range; The Homeless Flea; The House of Tomorrow; The Hungry Wolf; Innertube Antics; Jerky Turkey; Jitterbug Follies; King-Size Canary; Little Cesario; The Little Goldfish; Little Gravel Voice; Little Johnny Jet; Little Mole; Little Rural Riding Hood; Little 'Tinker; The Lonesome Stranger; Lucky Ducky; The Mad Maestro; The Magical Maestro; Midnight Snack; The Milky Way; Mrs. Ladybug; The Night Before Christmas; Officer Pooch; One Cab's Family; One Ham's Family; One Mother's Family; Papa Gets the Bird; Peace on Earth; The Peachy Cobbler; The Prospecting Bear; Puss Gets the Boot; Puss n' Toots; A Rainy Day; Red Hot Riding Hood; Romeo in Rhythm; The Rookie Bear; The Screwball Squirrel; Slap Happy Lion; The Stork's Holiday; Swing Shift Cinderella; Swing Social; Symphony in Slang; Tom Turkey and His Harmonica Humdiggers; The Tree Surgeon; TV of Tomorrow; Uncle Tom's Cabana; The Unwelcome Guest; The Ventriloquist Cat; Wanted! No Master; War Dogs; What's Buzzin' Buzzard?; Who Killed Who?; Wild Honey

Mickey Mouse

Alpine Climbers; The Band Concert; The Barn Dance; The Barnyard Battle; The Barnyard Broadcast; The Barnyard Concert; Barnyard Olympics; The Beach Party; The Birthday Party; Blue Rhythm; Boat Builders; The Brave Little Tailor; Building a Building; The Cactus Kid; Camping Out; The Castaway; The Chain Gang; Clock Cleaners; The Delivery Boy; The Dognapper; Don Donald; Donald and Pluto; The Duck Hunt; The Fire Fighters; Fishin' Around; Gallopin' Gaucho; Giantland; The Gorilla Mystery; The Grocery Boy; Gulliver Mickey; The Haunted House; Hawaiian Holiday; The Jazz Fool; Jungle Rhythm; Just Mickey; The Karnival Kid; The Klondike Kid; The Little Whirlwind; Lonesome Ghosts; The Mad Doctor; The Mad Dog; Magician Mickey; The Mail Pilot; Mickey and the Seal; Mickey Cuts Up; Mickey Down Under; Mickey in Arabia; Mickey Plays Papa; Mickey Steps Out; Mickey's Amateurs; Mickey's Birthday Party; Mickey's Choo Choo; Mickey's Circus; Mickey's Delayed Date; Mickey's Elephant; Mickey's Follies; Mickey's Gala Premiere;

Mickey's Good Deed; Mickey's Man Friday; Mickey's Mechanical Man; Mickey's Mellerdrammer; Mickey's Nightmare; Mickey's Orphans; Mickey's Pal Pluto; Mickey's Parrot; Mickey's Revue; Mickey's Rival; Mickey's Service Station; Mickey's Steam-Roller; Mickey's Surprise Party; Mickey's Trailer; Mr. Mouse Takes a Trip; Modern Inventions; The Moose Hunt; Moose Hunters; Moving Day; The Musical Farmer; The Nifty Nineties; The Opry House; Orphan's Benefit; Parade of the Award Nominees; The Pet Store; The Picnic; Pioneer Days; Plane Crazy; Playful Pluto; The Plow Boy; Plutopia; Pluto's Christmas Tree; Pluto's Dream House; Pluto's Party; The Pointer; Puppy Love; R'Coon Dawg; Shanghaied; The Shindig; The Simple Things; Society Dog Show; The Standard Parade; Steamboat Willie; The Steeple Chase; Symphony Hour; Thru the Mirror; Touchdown Mickey; Trader Mickey; Traffic Troubles; Tugboat Mickey; Two-Gun Mickey; The Wayward Canary; The Whalers; When the Cat's Away; The Whoopee Party; Wild Waves; The Worm Turns; Ye Olden Days

The Mighty Heroes

The Big Freeze; The Duster; The Enlarger; The Frog; The Ghost Monster; The Shocker; The Stretcher; The Toy Man

Mighty Mouse

Aladdin's Lamp; Anti-Cats; Beauty on the Beach; Cat Alarm; The Catnip Gang; The Cat's Tale; The Champion of Justice; A Cold Romance; Comic Book Land; The Crackpot King; Crying Wolf; A Date for Dinner; The Electronic Mouse Trap; Eliza on the Ice; The Feudin' Hillbillies; A Fight to the Finish; The First Snow; Goons from the Moon; The Green Line; Hansel and Gretel; Happy Holland; The Helpless Hippo; Hero for a Day; Hot Rods; Injun Trouble; The Jail Break; The Johnstown Flood; Lazy Little Beaver; Love's Labor Won; The Magic Slipper; Mighty Mouse and the Dead End Cats; Mighty Mouse and the Hep Cat; Mighty Mouse and the Kilkenny Cats; Mighty Mouse and the Magician; Mighty Mouse and the Pirates; Mighty Mouse and the Two Barbers; Mighty Mouse and the Wicked Wolf; Mighty Mouse and the Wolf; Mighty Mouse at the Circus; Mighty Mouse in Krakatoa; Mighty Mouse in the Gypsy Life; Mighty Mouse Meets Bad Bill Bunion; Mighty Mouse Meets Deadeye Dick; Mighty Mouse Meets Jekyll and Hyde Cat; Mother Goose's Birthday Party; My Old Kentucky Home; The Mysterious Package; Outer Space Visitor; The Perils of Pearl Pureheart; The Port of Missing Mice; Prehistoric Perils; The Racket Buster; Raiding the Raiders; The Reformed Wolf; The Silver Streak; The Sky Is Falling; A Soapy Opera; Spare the Rod; Stop, Look and Listen; The Sultan's Birthday; Sunny Italy; Svengali's Cat; The Swiss Cheese Family Robinson; A Swiss Miss; Throwing the Bull; Triple Trouble; The Trojan Horse; When Mousehood Was in Flower; Winning the West; The Witch's Cat; Wolf! Wolf

Mr. Magoo

Barefaced Flatfoot; Bungled Bungalow; Bwana Magoo; Calling Dr. Magoo; Captains

Outrageous; Destination Magoo; The Dog Snatcher; The Explosive Mr. Magoo; Fuddy Duddy Buddy; Grizzly Golfer; Gumshoe Magoo; Hotsy Footsy; Kangaroo Courting; Love Comes to Magoo; Madcap Magoo; Magoo Beats the Heat; Magoo Breaks Par; Magoo Express; Magoo Goes Overboard; Magoo Goes Skiing; Magoo Goes West; Magoo Makes News; Magoo Saves the Bank; Magoo Slept Here; Magoo's Canine Mutiny; Magoo's Check-up; Magoo's Cruise; Magoo's Glorious Fourth; Magoo's Homecoming; Magoo's Lodge Brother; Magoo's Masquerade; Magoo's Masterpiece; Magoo's Moose Hunt; Magoo's Private War; Magoo's Problem Child; Magoo's Puddle Jumper; Magoo's Three-Point Landing; Magoo's Young Manhood; Matador Magoo; Meet Mother Magoo; Merry Minstrel Magoo; Pink and Blue Blues; Ragtime Bear; Rock Hound Magoo; Safety Spin; Scoutmaster Magoo; Sloppy Jalopy; Spellbound Hound; Stage Door Magoo; Terror Faces Magoo; Trailblazer Magoo; Trouble Indemnity; When Magoo Flew

Modern Madcap

And So Tibet; Baa Baa Blacksmith; A Balmy Knight; Bouncing Benny; Cagey Business; Cane and Able; Crumley Cogwheel; Disguise the Limit; Drum Up a Tenant; Electronica; Fiddle Faddle; Fit to Be Toyed; From Dime to Dime; Funderful Suburbia; Galaxia; Giddy Gadgets; Goodie's Good Deed; Harry Happy; Hi-Fi Jinx; The Itch; The Kid from Mars; La Petite Parade; The Mighty Termite; Mike the Masquerader; Muggy-Doo, Boy Cat; Nearsighted and Far Out; One of the Family; One Weak Vacation; The Outside Dope; Penny Pals; The Phantom Moustacher; The Pig's Feat; The Plot Sickens; Poor Little Witch Girl; Popcorn and Politics; Reading, Writhing and 'Rithmetic; Right Off the Bat; Ringading Kid; Robot Ringer; Robot Rival; Samson Scrap; The Shoe Must Go On; Shootin' Stars; Solitary Refinement; Sour Gripes; Space Kid; Spooking of Ghosts; Talking Horse Sense; Tell Me a Badtime Story; Terry the Terror; Trash Program; Trigger Treat; TV Fuddlehead; Two by Two; A Wedding Knight

New Universal Cartoon

Baby Kittens; A Barnyard Romeo; Big Cat and Little Mousie; The Cat and the Bell; Cheese Nappers; The Disobedient Mouse; Feed the Kitty; Ghost Town Frolics; Happy Scouts; Hollywood Bowl; I'm Just a Jitterbug; Little Blue Blackbird; Movie Phoney News; Nellie the Indian Chief's Daughter; Nellie the Sewing Machine Girl; Problem Child; The Queen's Kittens; Silly Seals; Soup to Mutts; Tail End; Voo Doo in Harlem

Noveltoon

A-Haunting We Will Go; Alvin's Solo Flight; Anatole; The Animal Fair; As the Crow Lies; Audrey the Rainmaker; The Awful Tooth; Be Mice to Cats; Better Bait Than Never; The Bored Cuckoo; Butterscotch and Soda; By Leaps and Hounds; Campus Capers; Candy Cabaret; Cape Kidnaveral; The Case of the Cockeyed Canary; Cat Carson Rides Again; Cat Choo; Cat o' Nine Ails; Cat Tamale; Cheese Burglar; Chew Chew

Baby; Cilly Goose; City Kitty; Clown on the Farm; Cock-a-Doodle Dino; Counter Attack; Crazy Town; Danté Dreamer; Dawg Gawn; Dizzy Dishes; The Enchanted Square; Feast and Furious; Fiddlin' Around; Fido Beta Kappa; Fine Feathered Fiend; Finnegan's Flea; Fishing Tackler; Flip Flap; The Friendly Ghost; Gabriel Church Kitten; Geronimo and Son; Git Along Li'l Duckie; The Goal Rush; Good and Guilty; Good Snooze Tonight; Goodie the Gremlin; Goofy, Goofy Gander; Gramps to the Rescue; Grateful Gus; A Hair-Raising Tale; Hair Today — Gone Tomorrow; Hector's Hectic Life; The Hen-Pecked Rooster; The Hep Cat Symphony; Hiccup Hound; Hobo's Holiday; Hold the Lion Please; Homer on the Range; Horning In; Hound About That; Hound for Pound; Houndabout; Huey's Ducky Daddy; Huey's Father's Day; It's for the Birdies; Jolly the Clown; Jumping with Toy; Kitty Cornered; Kosmo Goes to School; Laddy and His Lamp; A Lamb in a Jam; L'amour the Merrier; Land of Lost Watches; Land of the Lost; Land of the Lost Jewels; Law and Audrey; A Leak in the Dike; The Leprichaun's Gold; Lion in the Roar; The Lion's Busy; Little Audrey Riding Hood; Little Cut-Up; Little Red School Mouse; The Lost Dream; Madhattan Island; Mice Meeting You; Mice Paradise; Micenicks; The Mild West; Mr. Money Gags; The Mite Makes Right; Monkey Doodles; Much Ado About Mutton; Munroe; A Mutt in a Rut; Naughty but Mice; News Hound; No Ifs, Ands or Butts; No Mutton for Nuttin'; Northern Mites; The Oily Bird; Okey Dokey Donkey; Old MacDonald Had a Farm; The Old Shell Game; Ollie the Owl; One Quack Mind; Op, Pop, Wham and Bop; Out of This Whirl; Party Smarty; Peck Your Own Home; Pedro and Lorenzo; Perry Popgun; Pest Pupil; Planet Mouseola; Pleased to Eat You; Poop Goes the Weasel; Possum Pearl; Quack-a-Doodle Do; Rabbit Punch; Santa's Surprise; Saved by the Bell; Scout Fellow; Scrappily Married; The Seapreme Court; A Self-Made Mongrel; Sheep Shape; The Sheepish Wolf; Sick Transit; Sight for Squaw Eyes; Silly Science; Sir Irving and Jeams; Sleuth but Sure; Slip Us Some Red Skin; Sock-a-By Kitty; The Song of the Birds; Sporticles; Spree for All; Starting from Hatch; Stork Raving Mad; The Story of George Washington; The Stupidstitious Cat; Sudden Fried Chicken; Suddenly It's Spring; Surf Bored; Swab the Duck; Tally Hokum; Tarts and Flowers; Teacher's Pest; There's Good Boos Tonite; A Tiger's Tail; Travelaffs; Trick or Tree; The Trip; Turning the Fables; Turtle Scoop; TV or Not TV; Ups 'n' Downs Derby; Voice of the Turkey; The Wee Men; We're in the Honey; When GI Johnny Comes Marching Home; Whiz Quiz Kid; Winner by a Hare; Without Time or Reason; Yankee Doodle Donkey; Yule Laff

Oswald the Lucky Rabbit

Africa; Africa Before Dark; Alaska; Alaska Sweepstakes; All Wet; Alpine Antics; Amateur Broadcast; Amateur Nite; Annie Moved Away; At Your Service; The Bandmaster; The Banker's Daughter; The Barnyard Five; Battle Royal; Beach Combers; Beau and Arrows; Beau Best; The Birthday Party; Bowery Bimbos; Bright Lights; Broadway Folly; Bronco Buster; Bulloney; The Busy Barber; Candy House; Carnival Capers; The Case of the Lost Sheep; Cat Nipped; Chicken Reel; Chilé Con Carmen; China; Christopher Columbus Jr.; Cold Feet; College; Confidence; Country School; The County Fair; Day Nurse; The Detective; The Dizzy Dwarf; Do a Good Deed; Doctor Oswald; The Duck Hunt; The Dumb Cluck; Elmer the Great Dane; Empty Socks; Everybody Sing; The Farmer; Farming Fools; Farmyard Fables; Farmyard Follies; The Fiery Fireman; The Fireman; The Fisherman; The Fishing Fool; Five and Dime; Football Fever; Fowl Ball; The Fox Chase; The Fun House; The Gingerbread Boy; Going to Blazes; Goldielocks and the Three Bears; Grandma's Pet; Great Guns; Ham and Eggs; Hare Mail; Harem Scarem; Hash Shop; Hells Heels; Hen Fruit; Hen Pecked; High Up; Hill Billies; Hold 'em, Ozzie; Homeless Homer; A Horse's Tale; Hot Dog; Hot Feet; Hot for Hollywood; Hungry Hoboes; The Hunter; Hurdy Gurdy; Iceman's Luck; Jungle Jingles; Jungle Jumble; Keeper of the Lions; Kentucky Belles; Kiddie Revue; Kings Up; Kounty Fair; Lamplighters; Let's Eat; Lovesick; The Lumberjack; Making Good; Man Hunt; Mars; The Mechanical Cow; Mechanical Handy Man; The Mechanical Man; Merry Old Soul; Mexico; Mississippi Mud; Monkey Wretches; Music Hath Charms; My Pal Paul; The Mysterious Jug; The Navy; Neck n' Neck; Night Life of the Bugs; The Northwoods; Not So Quiet; Nuts and Jolts; Nutty Notes; The Ocean Hop; Oh Teacher; Oh, What a Knight; Oil's Well; Ol, Swimmin' 'Ole; Ozzie of the Circus; Ozzie of the Mounted; Panicky Pancakes; Parking Space; Permanent Waves; The Playful Pup; The Plumber; Poor Papa; Prison Panic; Puppet Show; Pussy Willie; Quail Hunt; Race Riot; Radio Rhythm; Rickety Gin; Ride 'em Plowboy; Rival Romeos; Robinson Crusoe Isle; Rocks and Socks; Sagebrush Sadie; Saucy Sausages; Ship Wreck; The Shriek; Sick Cylinders; The Singing Sap; Sky Larks; Sky Scrappers; Sleigh Bells; The Slumberland Express; Snappy Salesman; Snow Use; The South Pole Flight; Spooks; Spring in the Park; Stage Stunts; The Stone Age; Stripes and Stars; Sunny South; Tall Timber; Teacher's Pests; To the Rescue; Town Hall Follies; The Toy Shoppe; Trade Mice; Trailer Thrills; Tramping Tramps; Trolley Troubles; Two Little Lambs; The Unpopular Mechanic; The Wax Works; Weary Willies; Wet Knight; The Wicked West; Wild and Woolly; William Tell; The Wily Weasel; The Winged Horse; Wins Out; Wolf! Wolf!; Wonderland; Yanky Clippers; Ye Happy Pilgrims; Yokel Boy Makes Good; The Zoo

Out of the Inkwell

The Automobile Ride; Balloons; The Battle; Bedtime; Big Chief Ko-Ko; Birthday; The Boxing Kangaroo; Bubbles; Cartoon Factory; Cartoonland; The Challenge; The Chinaman; The Circus; The Clown's Little Brother; The Clown's Pup; The Contest; The Cure; Dresden Doll (aka *the Dancing Doll*); The False Alarm; Fishing (aka *the Fish*); Flies; The Fortune Teller; The Hypnotist; Invisible Ink; It's the Cats; Jumping Beans; Ko-Ko Back Tracks; Ko-Ko Baffies the Bulls; Ko-Ko Celebrates the Fourth; Ko-Ko Gets Egg-Cited; Ko-Ko Hot After It; Ko-Ko in 1999; Ko-Ko in the Fade-Away; Ko-Ko in Toyland; Ko-Ko Kidnapped; Ko-Ko Makes 'em Laugh; Ko-Ko Needles the Boss; Ko-Ko Nuts; Ko-Ko on the Run; Ko-Ko Packs Up; Ko-Ko Sees Spooks; Ko-Ko Steps Out; Ko-Ko the Barber; Ko-Ko the Cavalier; Ko-Ko the Convict; Ko-Ko the Hot Shot; Ko-Ko Trains 'em; Ko-Ko's Paradise; Ko-Ko's Queen; Ko-Ko's Thanksgiving; Laundry; The Masquerade; Modeling; Mosquito; Mother Goose Land; The Ouija Board; Pay Day; Perpetual Motion; Poker (aka The Card Game); Puzzle; The Restaurant; Reunion; The Runaway; Shadows; The Show; Slides; The Storm; Surprise; The Tantalizing Fly; Toot! Toot!; Trapped; A Trip to Mars; Vacation; Vaudeville

Paul Terry-Toons

Aladdin's Lamp; An Alpine Yodeler; Amateur Night; Around the World; The Banker's Daughter; Barnyard Amateurs; Beanstalk Jack; Birdland; The Black Spider; Bluebeard's Brother; Blues; The Bull Fight; Bull-ero; Bully Beef; Burlesque; By the Sea; Canadian Capers; Caviar; Chain Letters; The Champ; China; Chop Suey; Cinderella; Circus Days; Clowning; Club Sandwich; Cocky Cockroach; Codfish Balls; College Spirit; A Day to Live; The Dog Show; Down on the Levee; Dutch Treat; The Explorer; Fanny in the Lion's Den; Fanny's Wedding Day; Farmer Al Falfa's Ape Girl; Farmer Al Falfa's Birthday Party; The Feud; Fireman, Save My Child; The Fireman's Bride; The First Snow; Five Puplets; Flying Oil; Foiled Again; Football; The Forty Thieves; The Foxy Fox; French Fried; Fried Chicken; Go West; Golf Nuts; Grand Uproar; A Gypsy Fiddler; Hansel and Gretel; Hawaiian Pineapples; Her First Egg; Hey Diddle Diddle; Holland Days; Hollywood Diet; Home Town Olympics; Hook and Ladder No. 1; Hot Sands; Hot Turkey; Hungarian Goulash; Hypnotic Eyes; In Venice; Indian Pudding; Ireland or Bust; Irish Stew; Irish Sweepstakes; Jack's Shack; Jail Birds; Jazz Mad; The Jealous Lover; Jesse and James; Jingle Bells; Joe's Lunch Wagon; Jumping Beans; A June Bride; Just a Clown; Kangaroo Steak; The King's Daughter; King Looney XIV; King Zilch; The Last Straw; The Lion's Friend; Little Boy Blue; A Mad House; The Mad King; The Magic Fish; The Mayflower; Mice in Council; Moans and Groans; A Modern Red Riding Hood; Monkey Meat; The Moth and the Spider; My Lady's Garden; The 19th Hole Club; Off to China; Oh! Susanna; The Oil Can Mystery; Old Dog Tray; Opera Night; The Owl and the Pussy Cat; Pandora; Peg Leg Pete; Pick-Necking; Pigskin Capers; Pirate Ship; Play Ball; Popcorn; Pretzels; Quack Quack; Radio Girl; Razzberries; Rip Van Winkle; Robin Hood; Robinson Crusoe; Roman Punch; Romance; Romeo and Juliet; Salt Water Tuffy; Scotch High-Ball; See the World; Sherman Was Right; Sing Sing Song; Slow but Sure; South Pole or Bust; Southern Horse-Pitality; Southern Rhythm; Spanish Onions; The Spider Talks; Spring Is Here; The Sultan's Cat; Summertime; Swiss Cheese; The Tale of a Shirt; The Three Bears; Tom, Tom the Piper's Son; Tropical Fish; 2000 B.C.; The Villain's Curse; What a Night; Who Killed Cock

Robin?; Why Mules Leave Home; Woodland; Ye Olde Songs; Ye Olde Toy Shop

Pen and Ink Vaudeville

The Artist's Model; Bobby Bumps & Co; Boneyard Blues; Broadcasting; He Who Gets Socked; The Hoboken Nightingale; The Mellow Quartet; Monkey Business; Props and the Spirits; Props' Dash for Cash; The Sawmill Four; Two Cats and a Bird; Two Poor Fish

Pepper the Pup
(aka: *Hector the Pup*)

Hector the Pup; Toodle-oo-o

Phantasy

As the Fly Flies; A Battle for a Bottle; Booby Socks; Cat-Tastrophy; The Charm Bracelet; Cholly Polly; The Cocky Bantam; Coo Coo Bird Dog; The Crystal Gazer; Cute Recruit; Dizzy Newsreel; Dog Meets Dog; The Dumbconscious Mind; Duty and the Beast; Fish Follies; The Fly in the Ointment; Fowl Brawl; Giddy Yapping; Goofy News Views; Grape Nutty; Gullible Canary; Happy Holidays; Kindly Scram; Kitty Caddy; Kongo Roo; Leave Us Chase It; Lionel Lion; The Little Theatre; Lo, the Poor Buffal; Magic Strength; Malice in Slumberland; Man of Tin; Mass Mouse Meeting; The Merry Mouse Café; The Millionaire Hobo; Mr. Fore by Fore; The Mouse Exterminator; Mutt 'n' Bones; News Oddities; Nursery Crimes; Old Blackout Joe; Pickled Puss; The Playful Pest; Polly Wants a Doctor; Schoolboy Dreams; The Schooner the Better; Short Snorts on Sports; Simple Siren; Snap Happy Traps; Tangled Travels; There's Music in Your Hair; Tooth or Consequences; Topsy Turkey; The Uncultured Vulture; Vitamin G-Man; Wacky Quacky; The Wallflower; The Wild and Woozy West; Willoughby's Magic Hat

The Pink Panther

Bobolink Pink; Bully for Pink; Cat and the Pinkstalk; Come on In! The Water's Pink; Congratulations! It's Pink; Dial P for Pink; Dietetic Pink; Doctor Pink; Extinct Pink; Fly in the Pink; Forty Pink Winks; Genie with the Light Pink Fur; G.I. Pink; Gong with the Pink; Hand Is Pinker Than the Eye; In the Pink; In the Pink of the Night; It's Pink but Is It Mink?; Jet Pink; Keep Our Forests Pink; Little Beaux Pink; Lucky Pink; Mystic Pink; An Ounce of Pink; Pickled Pink; Pincome Tax; Pink 8 Ball; Pink and Shovel; Pink Arcade; Pink Aye; Pink Bananas; Pink Blue Plate; The Pink Blueprint; Pink Breakfast; Pink Campaign; Pink da Vinci; Pink Daddy; Pink Elephants; The Pink Flea; Pink Ice; Pink in the Clink; Pink in the Drink; Pink in the Woods; Pink Is a Many Splintered Thing; Pink Lemonade; Pink Lightning; The Pink of Arabee; Pink of the Litter; Pink on the Cob; Pink Outs; The Pink Package Plot; Pink Pajamas; Pink Panic; Pink Panza; Pink Paradise; Pink Pest Control; The Pink Phink; Pink Pictures; The Pink Pill; The Pink Piper; Pink Piston; Pink Plasma; Pink, Plunk, Plink; Pink Posies; Pink Pranks; Pink Press; The Pink Pro; Pink Pull; Pink Punch; Pink Quackers; The Pink Quarterback; The Pink Sphinx; Pink Streaker; Pink Suds; Pink S.W.A.T.; The Pink Tail Fly; Pink Trumpet; Pink Tuba-Dore; Pink U.F.O.; Pink Valiant; Pink Zzz; Pink-a-Boo; Pinkadilly Circus; Pink-A-Rella; Pinkfinger; Pink-In; Pinknic; Pinkologist; Pinktails for Two; Pinky Doodle; Pinto Pink; Prefabricated Pink; Prehistoric Pink; Psst Pink; Psychedelic Pink; Put-Put Pink; Reel Pink; Rock-a-By Pinky; Rocky Pink; Salmon Pink; The Scarlet Pinkernell; Sherlock Pink; Shocking Pink; Sink Pink; Sky Blue Pink; Slink Pink; Smile Pretty, Say Pink; Spark Plug Pink; Sprinkle Me Pink; Star Pink; String Along in Pink; Super Pink; Supermarket Pink; Therapeutic Pink; Think Before You Pink; Tickled Pink; Toro Pink; Trail of the Lonesome Pink; Twinkle, Twinkle Little Pink; Vitamin Pink; We Give Pink Stamps

Pluto

The Army Mascot; Bone Bandit; Bone Trouble; Bubble Bee; Camp Dog; Canine Casanova; Canine Patrol; Cat Nap Pluto; Cold Storage; Cold Turkey; Dog Watch; A Feather in His Collar; First Aiders; Food for Feudin'; In Dutch; The Legend of Coyote Rock; Mail Dog; Pantry Pirate; Pluto and the Gopher; Pluto at the Zoo; Pluto Junior; Plutopia; Pluto's Blue Note; Pluto's Fledgeling; Pluto's Heart Throb; Pluto's Housewarming; Pluto's Kid Brother; Pluto's Playmate; Pluto's Purchase; Pluto's Quinpuplets; Pluto's Surprise Package; Pluto's Sweater; Primitive Pluto; Private Pluto; Pueblo Pluto; The Purloined Pup; Rescue Dog; Sheep Dog; The Sleepwalker; Springtime for Pluto; T-Bone for Two; Wonder Dog

Pooch the Pup

The Athlete; The Butcher Boy; Cats and Dogs; The Crowd Snores; Hot and Cold; King Klunk; The Lumber Champ; The Merry Dog; Nature's Workshop; Pin Feathers; She Done Him Right; The Terrible Troubadour; The Under Dog

Popeye the Sailor
(created by Elzie Chrisler Segar)

Abusement Park; The Adventures of Popeye; Aladdin and His Wonderful Lamp; All's Fair at the Fair; Alona on the Sarong Seas; Alpine for You; Ancient Fistory; The Anvil Chorus Girl; Assault and Flattery; Axe Me Another; Baby Wants a Battle; Baby Wants a Bottleship; A Balmy Swami; Barking Dogs Don't Fite; Be Kind to Aminals; Beach Peach; Beaus Will Be Beaus; Beware of Barnacle Bill; Big Bad Sindbad; Big Chief Ugh-Amugh-Ugh; Blow Me Down; Blunder Below; Bride and Gloom; Bridge Ahoy; Brotherly Love; Bulldozing the Bull; Can you Take It; Car-Azy Drivers; Cartoons Ain't Human; Child Psykolojiky; Child Sock-ology; Choose Your Weppins; A Clean Shaven Man; Cookin' with Gags; Cops Is Always Right; Cops Is Tops; The Crystal Brawl; Customers Wanted; The Dance Contest; A Date to Skate; Dizzy Divers; Doin' Impossikible Stunts; Double-Cross Country Race; A Dream Walking; The Farmer and the Belle; Females Is Fickle; Fightin' Pals; Fireman's Brawl; The Fistic Mystic; Fleets of Strength; Flies Ain't Human; The Floor Flusher; The Fly's Last Flight; The Football Toucher-Downer; For Better or Nurse; For Better or Worser; Fowl Play; Friend or Phoney; Fright to the Finish; Ghosks Is the Bunk; Gift of Gag; Goonland; Gopher Spinach; Greek Mirthology; Gym Jam; Happy Birthdaze; A Haul in One; Hello! How Am I?; Her Honor, the Mare; Hill-Billing and Cooing; Hold the Wire; Hospitaliky; Hot Air Aces; The House Builder-Upper; House Tricks; How Green Is my Spinach?; A Hull of a Mess; The Hungry Goat; The Hyp-Nut-Tist; I Don't Scare; I Eats My Spinach; I Likes Babies and Infinks; I Never Changes My Altitude; I-Ski-Love-Ski-You-Ski; I Wanna Be a Lifeguard; I Yam Love Sick; I Yam What I Yam; I'll Be Skiing Ya; I'll Never Crow Again; I'm in the Army Now; Insect to Injury; The Island Fling; It's the Natural Thing to Do; The Jeep; Jitterbug Jive; A Job for a Gob; A Jolly Good Furlough; Kickin' the Conga 'Round; King of the Mardi Gras; Klondike Casanova; Learn Polikeness; Leave Well Enough Alone; Let's Celebrake; Let's Get Movin'; Let's Stalk Spinach; Lets You and Him Fight; Little Swee' Pea; Lost and Foundry; Lumberjacks and Jill; Lunch with a Punch; The Man on the Flying Trapeze; Many Tanks; Marry-Go-Round; Me Feelin's Is Hurt; Me Musical Nephews; Mess Production; The Mighty Navy; Mister and Misletoe; Morning, Noon and Night Club; Moving Aweigh; Mutiny Ain't Nice; My Artistical Temperature; My Pop, My Pop; Nearly Weds; Never Kick a Woman; Never Sock a Baby; Nix on Hypnotricks; Nurse Mates; Nurse to Meet Ya; Olive Oyl and Water Don't Mix; Olive Oyl for President; Olive's Boithday Presink; Olive's Sweepstake Ticket; Onion Pacific; Organ Grinder's Swing; Out to Punch; The Paneless Window Washer; Parlez Vous Woo; Patriotic Popeye; A Peep in the Deep; Penny Antics; Pest Pilot; Pilgrim Popeye; Pip-Eye, Pup-Eye, Poop-Eye an' Peep-Eye; Pitchin' Woo at the Zoo; Pleased to Meet Char; Plumbing Is a "Pipe"; Poopdeck Pappy; Pop Pie A'la Mode; Popalong Popeye; Popeye and the Pirates; Popeye for President; Popeye Makes a Movie; Popeye Meets Hercules; Popeye Meets Rip Van Winkle; Popeye Meets William Tell; Popeye Presents Eugene the Jeep; Popeye the Ace of Space; Popeye the Sailor Meets Ali Baba and His Forty Thieves; Popeye the Sailor Meets Sindbad the Sailor; Popeye's Mirthday; Popeye's Pappy; Popeye's Premiere; Popeye's 20th Anniversary; Pre-Hysterical Man; Private-Eye Popeye; Problem Pappy; Protek the Weakerist; Punch and Judo; Puppet Love; Puttin' on the Act; Quick on the Vigor; Quiet Pleez; Ration Fer the Duration; Riot in Rhythm; Robin Hoodwinked; Rocket to Mars; Rodeo Romeo; The Royal Four-Flusher; Safari So Good; Scrap the Japs; Seasin's Greetinks; Seein' Red, White and Blue; Service with a Guile; Shakespearian Spinach; Shape Ahoy; Shaving Muggs; She-Sick Sailors; Shiver Me Timbers; Shoein' Hosses; Shuteye Popeye; Silly Hillbilly; Snow Place Like Home; Sock-A-By Baby; Spinach Fer Britain; Spinach Overture; Spinach Packin' Popeye; The Spinach Roadster; Spinach vs. Hamburgers; Spooky Swabs; Spree Lunch; Stealin' Ain't Honest; Strong to the Finich; Swimmer Take All; Symphony in Spinach; A Tar with a Star; Taxi-Turvy; Thrill of Fair; Too Weak to Work; Tops in the Big Top; Toreadorable; Tots of Fun; The Twisker Pitcher; The Two-Alarm Fire; Vacation with Play; Vim, Vigor and Vitaliky; We Aim to Please; We're on Our Way to Rio; What! No Spinach?; Wigwam Whoopee; Wild Elephinks; Wimmin Hadn't Oughta Drive; Wimmin Is a Myskery; A Wolf in Shiek's Clothing; Wood Peckin'; Wotta Knight; Wotta Nitemare; You Gotta Be a Football Hero; You're a Sap, Mr. Jap

Possible Possum

Berry Funny; Big Bad Bobcat; Big Mo; The Bold Eagle; Darn Barn; Freight Fright; The General's Little Helpers; Mount Piney; Red Swamp Pox; Rock Hounds; Slinky Minky; Surface Surf Aces; Surprisin' Excercisin'; Swamp Snapper; Swamp Water Taffy; The Toothless Beaver; Watch the Butterfly

Puppetoons

And to Think That I Saw It in Mulberry Street; Bravo Mr. Strauss; A Date with Duke; The 500 Hats of Bartholomew Cubbins; Good Night Rusty; A Hatful of Dreams; Hotlips Jasper; Jasper and the Beanstalk; Jasper and the Choo Choo; Jasper and the Haunted House; Jasper Goes Fishing; Jasper Goes Hunting; Jasper in a Jam; Jasper Tell; Jasper's Booby Traps; Jasper's Close Shave; Jasper's Derby; Jasper's Minstrels; Jasper's Music Lesson; Jasper's Paradise; John Henry and the Inky Poo; The Little Broadcast; My Man Jasper; Olio for Jasper; A Package for Jasper; Rhapsody in Wood; Say Ah! Jasper; Shoeshine Jasper; Together in the Weather; The Truck That Flew; Tubby the Tuba; Two-Gun Rusty; Wilbur the Lion

Rainbow Parade

Bird Scouts; Bold King Cole; Cupid Gets His Man; Felix the Cat and the Goose That Laid the Golden Egg; The Hunting Season; It's a Greek Life; Japanese Lanterns; The Merry Kittens; Molly Moo Cow and Rip Van Winkle; Molly Moo Cow and Robinson Crusoe; Molly Moo Cow and the Butterflies; Molly Moo Cow and the Indians; Neptune Nonsense; Parrotville Fire Department; Parrotville Old Folks Home; Parrotville Post Office; Pastrytown Wedding; Picnic Panic; The Rag Dog; Scottie Finds a Home; Spinning Mice; The Sunshine Makers; Toonerville Picnic; Toonerville Trolley; Trolley Ahoy; A Waif's Welcome

Roger Rabbit

Roller Coaster Rabbit; Trail Mix-up; Tummy Trouble

Roland and Rattfink

Bridge Work; Cattle Battle; The Deadwood Thunderball; A Fink in the Rink; Flying Yeast; The Foul-Kin; Gem Dandy; The Great Continental Overland Cross-Country Race; Hawks and Doves; Hurts and Flowers; A Pair of Sneakers; Robin Good Hood; Say Cheese, Please; Sweet and Sourdough; A Taste of Money; Trick or Retreat; War and Pieces

Scrappy

Aw Nurse; Bad Genius; The Battle of the Barn; The Beer Parade; The Black Sheep; Camping Out; Canine Capers; Chinatown Mystery; City Slicker; The Clock Goes Round and Round; The Concert Kid; The Dog Snatcher; The Early Bird; False Alarm; Fare Play; Fire Plug; Flop House; The Gloom Chasers; The Gold Getters; Graduation Exercises; The Great Bird Mystery; The Great Experiment; Happy Birthday; Happy Butterfly; Hollywood Babies; I want to Be an Actress; Let's All Ring Doorbells; The Little Pest; Looney Balloonists; Minding the Baby; Movie Struck; The New Homesteaders; The Pet Shop; Playing Politics; The Puppet Murder Case; Puttin' Out the Kitten; Sandman Tales; Sassy Cats; Scrappy's Added Attraction; Scrappy's Art Gallery; Scrappy's Auto Show; Scrappy's Band Concert; Scrappy's Big Moment; Scrappy's Boy Scouts; Scrappy's Camera Troubles; Scrappy's Dog Show; Scrappy's Ghost Story; Scrappy's Music Lesson; Scrappy's News Flashes; Scrappy's Party; Scrappy's Playmates; Scrappy's Pony; Scrappy's Puppet Theatre; Scrappy's Relay Race; Scrappy's Rodeo; Scrappy's Side Show; Scrappy's Television; Scrappy's Theme Song; Scrappy's Toy Shop; Scrappy's Trailer; Scrappy's Trip to Mars; Showing Off; Stepping Stones; Sunday Clothes; Technocracket; Treasure Runt; The Wolf at the Door; The World's Affair; Worm's Eye View; Yelp Wanted

Screen Songs

Base Brawl; Bedelia; Beside a Moonlit Stream; The Big Drip; The Big Flame Up; Blue Hawaii; Boos in the Night; By the Beautiful Sea; The Camptown Races; The Circus Comes to Clown; Come Take a Trip in My Airship; Comin' Round the Mountain; Detouring Thru Maine; Drippy Mississippi; The Emerald Isle; Farm Foolery; Fiesta Time; Fresh Yeggs; The Funshine State; The Glow Worm; Gobs of Fun; The Golden State; Heap Hep Injuns; Helter Swelter; The Hills of Old Wyomin'; A Hot Time in the Old Town Tonight; I Can't Escape from You; I Don't Want to Make History; I Feel Like a Feather in the The Breeze; I Never Should Have Told You; I Wished on the Moon; I Wonder Who's Kissing Her Now; I'm Afraid to Come Home in the Dark; I'm Forever Blowing Bubbles; In the Good Old Summer Time; In the Shade of the Old Apple Tree; It's Easy to Remember; Jingle Jangle Jungle; La Paloma; Little Brown Jug; The Lone Star State; Magic on Broadway; Mariutch; Marriage Wows; Miner's Forty Niners; My Gal Sal; No Other One; On a Sunday Afternoon; Our Funny, Finny Friends; Please Go 'Way and Let Me Sleep; Please Keep Me in Your Dreams; The Prisoner's Song; Readin', Ritin' and Rhytmetic; Row! Row! Row!; Shortenin' Bread; Sing Again of Michigan; Sing or Swim; The Ski's the Limit; Snow Foolin'; Spring Song; The Stein Song; The Stork Market; Strike Up the Band; Strolling Thru the Park; Talking Through My Heart; Thanks for the Memory; Toys Will Be Toys; Tweet Music; Twilight on the Trail; Whispers in the Dark; Win, Place and Showboat; Winter Draws On; Yes! We Have No Bananas; You Came to My Rescue; You Took the Words Right Out of My Heart

Screwy Squirrel

Big Heel-Watha; Happy Go Nutty; Lonesome Lenny; The Screwy Truant

Silly Sidney

The Clown Jewels; Driven to Extraction; The Fleet's Out; Hide and Go Sidney; Home Life; The Littlest Bully; Meat, Drink and Be Merry; Peanut Battle; Really Big Act; Send Your Elephant to Camp; Sick, Sick Sidney; Sidney's Family Tree; Sidney's White Elephant; Split-Level Tree House; To Be or Not to Be; Tree Spree; Tusk Tusk; Two Ton Baby Sitter

Silly Symphony

Arctic Antics; Autumn; Babes in the Woods; The Bear and the Bees; The Big Bad Wolf; The Bird Store; Birds in the Spring; Birds of a Feather; Broken Toys; Bugs in Love; The Busy Beavers; Cannibal Capers; The Cat's Out; The China Plate; China Shop; The Clock Store; Cock o' the Walk; The Cookie Carnival; The Country Cousin; Egyptian Melodies; Elmer Elephant; The Farmyard Symphony; Father Noah's Ark; Flowers and Trees; The Flying Mouse; The Fox Hunt; Frolicking Fish; Funny Little Bunnies; The Goddess of Spring; The Golden Touch; The Grasshopper and the Ants; Hell's Bells; Just Dogs; King Neptune; Little Hiawatha; Lullaby Land; The Merry Dwarfs; Midnight in a Toy Shop; Monkey Melodies; More Kittens; The Moth and the Flame; Mother Goose Goes Hollywood; Mother Goose Melodies; Mother Pluto; Music Land; Night; The Night Before Christmas; Old King Cole; The Old Mill; Peculiar Penguin; The Pied Piper; Playful Pan; The Robber Kitten; Santa's Workshop; The Skeleton Dance; The Spider and the Fly; Springtime; Summer; Three Blind Mouseketeers; The Three Little Pigs; Three Little Wolves; Three Orphan Kittens; Toby Tortoise Returns; The Tortoise and the Hare; The Ugly Duckling; The Water Babies; Who Killed Cock Robin?; Winter; The Wise Little Hen; The Woodland Café; Wynken, Blynken and Nod

Simon the Monk

Hobo Hero; Monkeydoodle

Spike and Tyke

Give and Tyke; Scat Cats

Stone Age Cartoon

The Foul Ball Player; The Fulla Bluff Man; Granite Hotel; Pedagogical Institute; Springtime in the Rock Age; The Ugly Dino; Way Back When a Nag Was Only a Horse; Way Back When a Night Club Was a Stick; Way Back When a Razzberry Was a Fruit; Way Back When a Triangle Had Its Points; Way Back When Women Had Their Weigh; Wedding Belts

Superman
(created by Jerome Siegel and Joe Shuster)

Superman; Superman in: Destruction, Inc; Superman in: Jungle Drums; Superman in: Showdown; Superman in: Terror on the Midway; Superman in: The Arctic Giant; Superman in: The Billion Dollar Limited; Superman in: The Bulleteers; Superman in: The Eleventh Hour; Superman in: The Japoteurs; Superman in: The Magnetic Telescope; Superman in: The Mechanical

Monster; Superman in: The Mummy Strikes; Superman in: The Secret Agent; Superman in: The Underground World; Superman in: Volcano

Swifty and Shorty

Accidents Will Happen; Les Boys; The Bus Way to Travel; Call Me a Taxi; Fix That Clock; Fizzicle Fizzle; A Friend in Tweed; Getting Ahead; Highway Slobbery; Hip Hip Ole; Inferior Decorator; Ocean Bruise; The Once Over; Panhandling on Madison Avenue; Sailing Zero; Service with a Smile

Swing Symphony

Abu Ben Boogie; The Boogie Woogie Man; Boogie Woogie Sioux; Cow Cow Boogie; The Egg-Cracker Suite; The Greatest Man in Siam; Jungle Jive; Pass the Biscuits Mirandy; The Pied Piper of Basin Street; The Sliphorn King of Polaroo; Yankee Doodle Swing Shift

Talkartoons

Accordian Joe; The Ace of Spades; Admission Free; A-Hunting We Will Go; Any Rags; Barnacle Bill; Betty Boop Limited; Bimbo's Express; Bimbo's Initiation; Boop-Oop-a-Doop; The Bum Bandit; Chess Nuts; The Cow's Husband; Crazy Town; The Dancing Fool; Dizzy Dishes; Dizzy Red Riding Hood; Fire Bugs; Grand Uproar; The Herring Murder Case; Hide and Seek; Hot Dog; In the Shade of the Old Applesauce; Jack and the Beanstalk; The Male Man; Marriage Wows; Mask-A-Raid; Minding the Baby; Minnie the Moocher; Mysterious Mose; Noah's Lark; Radio Riot; The Robot; Silly Scandals; Sky Scraping; Swim or Sink; Swing, You Sinner; Teacher's Pest; Tree Saps; Up to Mars; Wise Flies

The Terry Bears

Baffling Bunnies; Duck Fever; Growing Pains; A Howling Success; Little Anglers; Little Problems; Open House; Papa's Day of Rest; Papa's Little Helpers; Pet Problems; Picnic with Papa; Plumber's Helpers; The Reluctant Pup; Snappy Snapshots; Tall Timber Tale; Thrifty Cubs

Terry-Toons

Africa Jungle Hunt; Africa Squawks; Aladdin's Lamp; All About Dogs; All Out for "V"; All This and Rabbit Stew; All's Well That Ends Well; Ants in Your Pantry; Arctic Rivals; The Baby Seal; Back to the Soil; Baffling Bunnies; Barnyard Baseball; Barnyard Blackout; The Barnyard Boss; Barnyard Egg-Citement; The Barnyard WAAC; Beanstalk Jack; Beaver Trouble; Better Late Than Never; The Big Build-Up; The Big Top; The Billy Goat's Whiskers; Billy Mouse's Akwakade; Bird Symphony; The Bird Tower; The Bone Ranger; The Brave Little Brave; Bringing Home the Bacon; The Bug Carnival; Bugs Beetle and His Orchestra; A Bully Frog; A Bum Steer; The Busy Bee; Butcher of Seville; Camouflage; Carmen's Veranda; The Cat Came Back; Cat Meets Mouse; Catnip Capers; Champion Chump; The Champion of Justice; Chris Columbo; Cloak and Stagger; The Clockmaker's Dog; A Close Shave; Club Life in the Stone Age; Comic Book Land; The Cowardly Watchdog; The Cuckoo Bird; Daddy's Little Darling; The Dancing Bear; Day in June; Dear Old Switzerland; Devil of the

Deep; The Dog and His Bone; A Dog in a Mansion; The Dog Show; A Dog's Dream; Doing Their Bit; Down with Cats; Eat Me Kitty, Eight-to-the-Bar; Edgar Runs Again; The Elephant Mouse; Eliza Runs Again; The Fabulous Firework Family; Farmer Al Falfa and the Runt; Farmer Al Falfa in Bedtime Story; Farmer Al Falfa in Flying South; Farmer Al Falfa in the Big Game Hunt; Farmer Al Falfa in the Health Farm; Farmer Al Falfa in the Hot Spell; Farmer Al Falfa in the Tin Can Tourist; Farmer Al Falfa's Ape Girl; Farmer Al Falfa's Birthday Party; Farmer Al Falfa's Prize Package; Farmer Al Falfa's 20th Anniversary; Felix the Fox; The First Robin; Fishing Made Easy; Flebus; Flipper Frolics; Flying Cups and Saucers; Flying Fever; Foofle's Picnic; Foofle's Train Ride; The Fox and the Duck; Foxed by a Fox; Frankenstein's Cat; The Frog and the Princess; Frozen Feet; The Frozen North; Funny Bunny Business; Gag Buster; Gandy Goose in a Bully Romance; Gandy Goose in Doomsday; Gandy Goose in G-Man Jitters; Gandy Goose in the Frame-Up; Gandy the Goose; The Glass Slipper; The Golden West; Good Deed Daly; Good Old Irish Tunes; The Goose Flies High; Hairless Hector; Happy and Lucky; Happy Circus Days; The Happy Cobblers; Happy Haunting Grounds; The Hard Boiled Egg; The Hare and the Hounds; A Hare-Breadth Finish; Harvest Time; He Dood It Again; The Helicopter; The Helpful Genie; Hep Mother Hubbard; Here's to Good Old Jail; His Day Off; The Hitch Hiker; The Home Guard; The Homeless Pup; Hook, Line and Sinker; The Hopeful Donkey; Horsefly Opera; Hounding the Hares; Housewife Herman; The Housing Problem; How to Keep Cool; How to Relax; How Wet Was My Ocean; The Ice Carnival; The Ice Pond; Ickle Meets Pickle; If Cats Could Sing; An Igloo for Two; It Must Be Love; The Juggler of Our Lady; Just a Little Bull; Just Ask Jupiter; Keep 'em Growing; Kiko Foils the Fox; Kiko in Skunked Again; Kiko the Kangaroo and the Honey Bears; Kiko the Kangaroo in Battle Royal; Kiko the Kangaroo in Red Hot Music; Kiko the Kangaroo in the Hay Ride; Kiko's Cleaning Day; The Landing of the Pilgrims; The Last Indian; The Last Mouse of Hamelin; Last Round-Up; The Leaky Faucet; Life with Fido; Lights Out; The Lion and the Mouse; The Lion Hunt; Little Red Hen; Love in a Cottage; Love Is Blind; The Lucky Duck; The Lyin' Lion; The Magic Pencil; The Magic Shell; Maid in China; Mechanical Bird; The Mechanical Cow; Milk for Baby; Mississippi Swing; The Misunderstood Giant; Mopping Up; The Mosquito; A Mountain Romance; The Mouse of Tomorrow; Mrs. O'Leary's Cow; Much Ado About Nothing; My Boy Johnny; The Mysterious Cowboy; Mystery in the Moonlight; Neck and Neck; The Newcomer; Nick's Coffee Pot; Night Life in the Army; The Nutty Network; Oceans of Love; Oh Gentle Spring; Oil Thru the Day; The Old Fire Horse; The Old Oaken Bucket; One-Gun Gary in the Nick of Time; The One-Man Navy; One Mouse in a Million; The Orphan Duck; The Outpost; The Owl and the Pussycat; Ozzie Ostrich Comes to Town; Paint Pot Symphony; Pandora's Box; The Paper Hangers; Park Avenue Pussycat; Patriotic Pooches; Phoney News Flashes; Pink Elephants;

Plane Goofy; Play Ball; Police Dogged; The Prize Guest; Professor Offkeyski; Puddy the Pup and the Gypsies; Puddy the Pup in Cats in a Bag; Puddy the Pup in Puddy's Coronation; Puddy the Pup in Sunken Treasure; Puddy the Pup in the Bookshop; The Red-Headed Monkey; The Red Tractor; Robin Hood in an Arrow Escape; Robinson Crusoe's Broadcast; Rolling Stones; Rover's Rescue; Ruby Eye of the Monkey God; Rupert the Runt; The Sailor's Home; Salty McGuire; The Saw Mill Mystery; School Birds; School Daze; Scouts to the Rescue; Scrap for Victory; Search for Misery; Seaside Adventure; Seeing Ghosts; Sham-Battle Shenanegans; The Sheep in the Meadow; Shipyard Symphony; Short-Term Sheriff; Slap-Happy Hunters; Smoky Joe; The Snow Man; Somewhere in Egypt; Somewhere in the Pacific; Sour Grapes; Sparky the Firefly; Squirrel Crazy; Stage Struck; The Stork's Mistake; The Stranger Rides Again; Stringbean Jack; Super Mouse Rides Again; Swiss Ski Yodellers; Swooning the Swooners; Tale of a Dog; The Talking Magpies; Tall Tale Teller; The Temperamental Lion; Their Last Bean; The Three Bears; Time Gallops On; The Timid Rabbit; Tin Pan Alley Cat; Tire Trouble; The Torrid Toreador; The Tortoise Wins Again; Touchdown Demons; A Tough Egg; Trailer Life; Tricky Business; A Truckload of Trouble; 12 O'Clock and All Ain't Well; The Two-Headed Giant; Uncle Joey; Uncle Joey Comes to Town; Uranium Blues; The Village Blacksmith; The Villain Still Pursued Her; The Watchdog; The Wayward Hat; Welcome Little Stranger; Western Trail; What a Little Sneeze Will Do; What Happens at Night; When Knights Were Bold; A Wicky Wacky Romance; Wilful Willie; A Wolf in Cheap Clothing; The Wolf's Pardon; The Wolf's Side of the Story; A Wolf's Tale; The Wooden Indian; Woodman Spare That Tree; Wot's All Th' Shootin' Fer; The Wreck of the Hesperus; A Yarn About a Yarn; Yokel Duck Makes Good; A Yokohama Yankee

Tijuana Toads

Croakus Pocus; A Dopey Hacienda; The Egg and Ay-Yi-Yi; The Fastest Tongue in the West; Flight to the Finish; Frog Jog; The Froggy Froggy Duo; Go for Croak; Hop and Chop; A Leap in the Deep; Mud Squad; Never on Thirsty; A Pair of Greenbacks; Serapé Happy; A Snake in the Gracias; The Tijuana Toads; Two Jumps and a Chump

Toby the Pup

Aces Up; Circus Time; The Museum; Toby in the Brown Derby; Toby in the Bug House; Toby the Bull Thrower; Toby Down South; Toby the Fiddler; Toby the Milkman; Toby the Miner; Toby the Showman

Toddle Tales *see* Burt Gillett's Toddle Tales

Tom and Jerry

Advance and Be Mechanized; Ah, Sweet Mouse-Story of Life; A-Tom-Inable Snowman; Baby Butch; Baby Puss; Bad Day at Cat Rock; Barbecue Brawl; Barnyard Bunk; Blue Cat Blues; The Bodyguard; The Bowling Alley Cat; The

Brothers Carry Mouse-Off; Buddies Thicker Than Water; Busy Buddies; Calypso Cat; Cannery Rodent; Carmen Get It; Casanova Cat; The Cat Above — the Mouse Below; Cat and Dupli-Cat; The Cat and the Mermouse; The Cat Concerto; Cat Fishin'; Cat Napping; The Cat's Me-ouch; Catty Cornered; Cruise Cat; Cue Ball Cat; Designs on Jerry; Dickey Moe; Dr. Jekyll and Mr. Mouse; The Dog House; Dog Trouble; Dough Nuts; Down and Outing; Downbeat Bear; Downhearted Duckling; The Duck Doctor; Duel Personality; The Egg and Jerry; Feedin' the Kitty; Filet Meow; Fine Feathered Friend; Fit to Be Tied; Flirty Birdy; The Flying Cat; The Flying Sorceress; Fraidy Cat; Framed Cat; Guided Mouse-Ille; Happy Go Ducky; Happy Hoboes; Hatch Up Your Troubles; The Haunted Mouse; Heavenly Puss; Hic-Cup Pup; High Steaks; His Mouse Friday; Hollywood Bowl; Hook and Ladder Hokum; I'm Just Wild About Jerry; In the Bag; In the Park; The Invisible Mouse; Is There a Doctor in the Mouse?; It's Greek to Meow; Jerry and Jumbo; Jerry and the Goldfish; Jerry and the Lion; Jerry-Go-Round; Jerry, Jerry, Quite Contrary; Jerry's Cousin; Jerry's Diary; Johann Mouse; The Jolly Fish; Jungle Jam; Kitty Foiled; Landing Stripling; Life with Tom; Little Orphan; Little Quacker; Little Runaway; Little School Mouse; The Lonesome Mouse; Love Me, Love My Mouse; Love That Pup; The Magic Mummy; Matinee Mouse; Mice Follies; The Milky Waif; The Million Dollar Cat; The Missing Mouse; Mouse Cleaning; The Mouse Comes to Dinner; Mouse for Sale; The Mouse from H.U.N.G.E.R.; Mouse in Manhattan; A Mouse in the House; Mouse Into Space; Mouse Trouble; Much Ado About Mousing; Mucho Mouse; Muscle Beach Tom; Neapolitan Mouse; Nit-Witty Kitty; O-Solar Meow; Of Feline Bondage; Old Rockin' Chair Tom; Panicky Pup; Part-Time Pal; Pecos Pest; Pencil Mania; Penthouse Mouse; Pet Peeve; The Phantom Rocket; Piano Tooners; Plane Dumb; Polar Pals; Polka-Dot Puss; Posse Cat; Professor Tom; Pup on a Picnic; Puppy Tale; Purr-Chance to Dream; Push-Button Kitty; Puss 'n' Boats; Puttin' on the Dog; Puzzled Pals; Quiet Please!; Rabid Hunters; Redskin Blues; Robin Hoodwinked; Rock 'n' Rodent; The Rocketeers; Royal Cat Nap; Safety Second; Salt Water Tabby; Saturday Evening Puss; Shutter-Bugged Cat; Sleepy-Time Tom; Slicked-Up Pup; Smarty Cat; Smitten Kitten; Snow-Body Loves Me; Solid Serenade; Southbound Duckling; A Spanish Twist; Springtime for Thomas; Sufferin' Cats; Surf-Bored Cat; A Swiss Trick; Switchin' Kitten; Tall in the Trap; Tee for Two; Tennis Chumps; Texas Tom; That's My Mommy!; That's My Pup; Tightrope Tricks; Timid Tabby; Tom and Cherie; The Tom and Jerry Cartoon Kit; Tom-ic Energy; Tom's Photo Finish; Tot Watchers; Touché, Pussy Cat; Trap Happy; Triplet Trouble; Trouble; The Truce Hurts; Tuba Tooters; Two Little Indians; The Two Mouseketeers; The Unshrinkable Jerry Mouse; The Vanishing Duck; Wot a Night; Yankee Doodle Mouse; The Year of the Mouse; The "Zoot" Cat

Trader Korn's Laffalong

Korn Plastered in Africa

Unnatural History

The Cat's Whiskers; Goat's Whiskers; How the Bear Got His Short Tail; How the Camel Got His Hump; How the Elephant Got His Trunk; How the Giraffe Got His Long Neck; The King of the Beasts; The Leopard's Spots; The Mule's Disposition; The Ostrich's Plumes; The Pelican's Bill; The Pig's Curly Tail; The Stork Brought It; The Tail of the Monkey

Walt Disney Specials

Ben and Me; The Brave Engineer; Casey Bats Again; Chicken Little; A Cowboy Needs a Horse; Education for Death; Ferdinand the Bull; Football, Now and Then; Goliath II; Hooked Bear; In the Bag; Jack and Old Mack; Lambert the Sheepish Lion; The Little House; Morris the Midget Moose; Noah's Ark; Paul Bunyan; The Pelican and the Snipe; Pigs Is Pigs; The Practical Pig; Reason and Emotion; The Saga of Windwagon Smith; The Small One; Social Lion; The Story of Anyburg, USA; Susie the Little Blue Coupe; A Symposium on Popular Songs; The Truth About Mother Goose; Ugly Duckling

Whirlwind Comedies

Fatal Footsteps; He Done His Best; Many a Slip; There it is

Willie Whopper

The Cave Man; Davey Jones' Locker; Good Scouts; Hell's Fire; Insultin' the Sultan; Jungle Jitters; Play Ball; Rasslin' Round; Reducing Creme; Robin Hood Jr.; Spite Flight; Stratos-Fear; Viva Willie

Woody Woodpecker

Ace in the Hole; After the Ball; All Hams on Deck; Alley to Bali; Arts and Flowers; Astronut Woody; Ballyhooey; Banquet Busters; The Barber of Seville; Bathing Buddies; Bats in the Belfry; The Beach Nut; Bedtime Bedlam; Belle Boys; The Big Bite; Billion Dollar Boner; The Bird Who Came to Dinner; Birds of a Feather; Born to Peck; Box Car Bandit; Buccaneer Woodpecker; Bunko Busters; Busman's Holiday; Buster's Last Stand; Bye Bye Blackboard; Calling All Cuckoos; Calling Dr. Woodpecker; Canned Dog Feud; Careless Caretaker; Chew Chew Baby; Chief Charley Horse; Chili Con Corny; Convict Concerto; The Coo Coo Bird; Coo Coo Nuts; Coy Decoy; Crowin' Pains; Destination Meatball; The Dippy Diplomat; The Dizzy Acrobat; Dopey Dick the Pink Whale; Drooler's Delight; Dumb Like a Fox; Everglade Raid; Fair Weather Friends; Fat in the Saddle; Feudin', Fightin' 'n' Fussin'; Fine Feathered Frenzy; Flim Flam Fountain; Fodder and Son; For the Love of Pizza; Fowled-up Falcon; Franken-Stymied; Freeway Fracas; Gabby's Diner; The Genie with the Light Touch; Get Lost; Get Lost! Little Doggy; The Great Who Dood It; Greedy Gabby Gator; Half Empty Saddles; Hassle in a Castle; Have Gun Can't Travel; Heap Big Hepcat; Helter Shelter; Hi-Rise Wise Guys; His Better Elf; The Hollywood Matador; Home, Sweet Homewrecker; Hook, Line and Stinker; Horse Play; Hot Diggety Dog; Hot Noon; Hot Rod Huckster; How to Stuff a Woodpecker; How to Trap a Woodpecker; Hypnotic Hick; International Woodpecker; Janie Get Your Gun; Jittery Jester; Kiddie League; Kitty from the City; A Lad in Bagdad; Little Woody Riding Hood; The Loan Stranger; Log Jammed; Lonesome Ranger; The Loose Nut; The Mad Hatter; Misguided Missile; Monster of Ceremonies; Musical Moments from Chopin; The Nautical Nut; Niagara Fools; One Horse Town; Operation Sawdust; Ozark Lark; Panhandle Scandal; Pantry Panic; A Peck of Trouble; Pecking Holes in Poles; Phantom of the Horse Opera; Phoney Pony; Pistol Packin' Woodpecker; Poop-Deck Pirate; Practical Yolk; Prehistoric Super Salesman; Private Eye Pooch; Puny Express; Ration Bored; Real Gone Woody; The Reckless Driver; Red Riding Hoodlum; The Redwood Sap; The Reluctant Recruit; Roamin' Roman; Robin Hoody Woody; Rock-a-bye Gator; Rocket Racket; Romp in a Swamp; Room and Bored; Rough Riding Hood; Round Trip to Mars; Saddle-Sore Woody; Scalp Treatment; Science Friction; The Screwball; The Screwdriver; Seal on the Loose; Secret Agent Woody Woodpecker; Shanghai Woody; Ship Ahoy Woody; Short in the Saddle; Show-Biz Beagle; Shutter Bug; Sioux Me; Sissy Sheriff; Ski for Two; Skin Folks; Sleep Happy; Sleepy-Time Chimes; Slingshot 6$^7/_8$; Smoked Hams; The Snoozin' Bruin; Socko in Morocco; Solid Ivory; Southern Fried Hospitality; Square Shootin' Square; Stage Hoax; Stowaway Woody; Sufferin' Cats; The Tee Bird; The Tenant's Racket; Tepee for Two; Termites from Mars; Three Little Woodpeckers; To Catch a Woodpecker; Tomcat Combat; Tragic Magic; The Tree Medic; Tree's a Crowd; Tumble Weed Greed; The Unbearable Salesman; Under the Counter Spy; Voo-Doo Boo Boo; Wacky Bye Baby; Watch the Birdie; Well Oiled; Wet Blanket Policy; What's Peckin'?; What's Sweepin'; Who's Cooking Who?; Wicket Wacky; Wild and Woody; Wild Bill Hiccup; Witch Crafty; Woodpecker from Mars; Woodpecker in the Moon; Woodpecker in the Rough; Woodpecker Wanted; Woody and the Beanstalk; Woody Dines Out; Woody Meets Davy Crewcut; Woody the Freeloader; Woody the Giant Killer; Woody Woodpecker; The Woody Woodpecker Polka; Woody's Clip Joint; Woody's Knight Mare; Woody's Kook-Out; Woody's Magic Touch; Wrestling Wrecks

Index

Numbers refer to entries.